BaseBall america®
2016 ALMANAC

D1306730

BASEBALL AMERICA INC. · DURHAM, N.C.

EDITOR'S NOTE: Major league statistics are based on final, unofficial 2015 averages. >> The organization statistics, which begin on page 43, include all players who participated in at least one game during the 2015 season. >> Pitchers' batting statistics are not included, nor are the pitching statistics of field players who pitched in less than two games. >> For players who played with more than one team in the same league, the player's cumulative statistics appear on the line immediately after the player's statistics with each team. >> Innings pitched have been rounded off to the nearest full inning.

TABLE OF CONTENTS

CLIFF WELCH

BaseballAmerica.com

BaseBall america
2016 ALMANAC

Editor
JOSH LEVENTHAL

Assistant Editors
BEN BADLER, HUDSON BELINSKY, J.J. COOPER, MATT EDDY, VINCENT LARA-CINISOMO, JOHN MANUEL, JOSH NORRIS, JIM SHONERD

Database and Application Development
BRENT LEWIS

Contributing Writers
JOHN PERROTTO, TOM HAUDRICOURT

Photo Editor
JIM SHONERD

Editorial Assistant
BILL WOODWARD

Design & Production
SARA HIATT MCDANIEL, LINWOOD WEBB

Programming & Technical Development
BRENT LEWIS

Cover Photo
BRYCE HARPER BY ED WOLFSTEIN

DISTRIBUTED BY SIMON & SCHUSTER ISBN-13: 978-1-932391-60-2_52395

STATISTICS PROVIDED BY MAJOR LEAGUE BASEBALL ADVANCED MEDIA AND COMPILED BY BASEBALL AMERICA

MAJOR LEAGUES

Youth was served—and serting notice—in 2015

Youth was served—and served notice—in 2015

BY JOHN PERROTTO

Theo Epstein thought back on the 2015 season—both from the standpoint of his team and the major leagues in general—and the Cubs' president of baseball operations made a short, yet astute, observation.

"It's a good time to be a young player," Epstein said.

It certainly was. Rookies took the sport by storm and a number of other young players continued the beginning of careers that appear to be on a course for the Hall of Fame.

The top two finishers in Wins Above Replacement (Baseball-Reference.com version) were Nationals right fielder—and BA Major League Player of the Year—Bryce Harper with 9.9 and Angels center fielder Mike Trout with 9.4.

Harper played the season at age 22 and Trout turned 24 on Aug. 7.

Harper led the National League with 42 home runs while batting .330 with 99 RBIs in 153 games. He also topped the league with 118 runs scored, a .460 on-base percentage, a .629 slugging percentage and a 1.109 on-base-plus-slugging percentage.

Trout hit .299 with 41 home runs, 90 RBIs and 11 stolen bases in 159 games while leading the American League with a .590 slugging percentage and a .991 OPS. He was selected to his fourth straight All-Star Game and was the Most Valuable Player of the All-Star Game for the second consecutive year.

Trout became the youngest player in major league history with 100 home runs and 100 stolen bases after hitting two homers against the Astros on April 17. At 23 years and 253 days old, Trout was 56 days younger than when Alex Rodriguez reached 100/100 in 1999.

Among the other 25-and-unders who starred were Cubs first baseman Anthony Rizzo, who hit .278 with 31 homers and 101 RBIs while leading the NL with 701 plate appearances and 30 hit by pitches.

Like Rizzo, Astros second baseman Jose Altuve helped get his upstart club to the postseason by leading the AL with 200 hits and 38 stolen bases while batting .313 with 15 home runs.

Rockies third baseman Nolan Arenado was

Kyle Schwarber forced his way to the majors and hit 16 homers in 69 games

another 25-and-under who shined. His 42 homers tied Harper for the NL lead and his 130 RBIs paced the senior circuit. He also hit .287 in 157 games.

Orioles third baseman Manny Machado played in all 162 games and hit 35 homers while driving in 86 runs.

Three 25-and-under pitchers flirted with 20-win seasons. Pirates righthander Gerrit Cole finished with 19 victories, while Giants lefthander Madison Bumgarner collected 18 and Cardinals righthander Michael Wacha finished with 17.

Meanwhile, Cardinals closer Trevor Rosenthal set the franchise record with 48 saves, while Jeurys Familia tied the Mets' record with 43.

Third baseman Kris Bryant was the best of three impressive Cubs rookie hitters. He batted .275 with 26 home runs and 99 RBIs and was named Rookie of the Year by BA.

Catcher/outfielder Kyle Schwarber hit 16 home runs in just 69 games and middle infielder

Addison Russell popped 13 homers in 142 games and, though he hit just .242, his move to shortstop from second base in early August sparked the Cubs as they won 46 of their last 65 regular season games.

In the AL, two rookie shortstops took the league by storm despite playing in 99 games each after starting the season in the minor leagues. The Astros' Carlos Correa hit .279 with 22 home runs and 14 stolen bases, while Francisco Lindor batted .313 with 12 homers and 12 steals for the Indians.

"When you look around and see so many great young players," first-year commissioner Rob Manfred said, "it makes me feel good because all that talent gives the fans hope for the future and makes it clear that our game is going to be healthy for years to come."

New Sherriff In Town

Manfred officially took over for Bud Selig, who had been on the job since 1992, on Jan. 25 and had both a busy and interesting first year.

Most notably, Manfred agreed to meet with all-time hits leader Pete Rose and considered the appeal of the lifetime ban he received in 1989 by then-commissioner Bart Giamatti. The meeting took place on Sept. 25 at Major League Baseball headquarters in New York

Neither Manfred nor Ray Genco, Rose's lawyer, would comment on the meeting, and MLB said in a statement that "Commissioner Manfred informed Mr. Rose that he will make a decision on his application by the end of the calendar year."

Then Cincinnati's manager, Rose agreed in 1989 to the ban from baseball after an investigation for MLB by lawyer John Dowd concluded Rose bet on games involving the Reds while managing and playing.

Rose applied for reinstatement in September 1997 and met with Selig in November 2002. However, Selig never made a ruling. Rose then reapplied right after Manfred took over.

Rose repeatedly denied betting on baseball until in his 2004 autobiography, "Pete Rose: My Prison Without Bars," he reversed his stand and acknowledged he bet on the Reds while managing the team.

The Hall of Fame's board of directors voted in 1991 to ban those on the permanently ineligible list from the Baseball Writers' Association of America ballot. Since Rose's last year of BBWAA ballot eligibility would have been 2006, the impact of (possible) reinstatement on his Hall chances is not clear, though he would likely be considered by a special committee.

Rose did reappear on the baseball scene in 2015, serving as a studio analyst for Fox.

Speeding Up The Game

MLB also adopted speedup rules designed to increase the pace of play in Manfred's first season. The new rules helped to shave six minutes off the average time of nine-inning games, which dropped to 2 hours, 56 minutes from 3:02. In 1981, the average time of a nine-inning game was 2:33.

MLB, the Major League Baseball Players Association and the World Umpires Association agreed to enforce the rule requiring a hitter to keep at least one foot in the batter's box in many cases and to post stadium clocks timing pitching changes and between-inning breaks. Managers were also no longer required to come onto the field to ask umpires for video reviews of calls.

The rule requiring hitters keep a foot in the box contained many exceptions, including swinging at a pitch, getting forced out by a pitch, calling time, faking a bunt and wild pitches and passed balls.

Clocks were installed on outfield scoreboards and on facades behind home plate, near most press boxes. Inning breaks were counted down from 2:25 for locally televised games and 2:45 for nationally televised games. Pitchers were required to throw their last warmup pitches before 30 seconds remaining, with exceptions if the pitcher or catcher was on base when the previous half-inning ended.

The sides limited penalties to warnings and fines, and not automatic balls and strikes. The fines didn't start until May 1 and were capped at $500 per offense. No fines were officially announced by MLB, though, which said prior to the season only repeat flagrant violators would be revealed. Any fine money was to be donated to charity.

Manfred, who has four children in their 20s, said the pace-of-play initiatives were designed with the idea of luring and keeping younger fans.

"I have a passing familiarity with that generation, and one thing I can say for sure is their attention span seems to be shorter than the rest of ours," Manfred said.

Triple-A and Double-A leagues used 20-second pitch clocks and began penalizing violators with balls and strikes. At Triple-A, the International League average dropped 16 minutes to 2:40 and the Pacific Coast League fell 13 minutes to 2:45.

MLBPA executive director Tony Clark, though, said the players have no desire to add pitch clocks at the major league level, an issue that would be required to be collectively bargained between labor and management.

BILL MITCHELL

Josh Hamilton admitted to an offseason drug relapse, but he avoided suspension by MLB when an arbitrator ruled in his favor. The Angels promptly traded him back to the Rangers

Manfred's most sticky situation in his first year on the job involved veteran outfielder Josh Hamilton, who self-reported to MLB and the MLBPA prior to spring training that he had experienced a drug relapse. Hamilton was suspended for three full seasons for his drug use before reaching the major leagues in 2007 with the Reds, and Manfred wanted to put him back on the suspended list.

However, he was not disciplined after a four-person treatment board created by MLB's joint drug program with the MLBPA tied 2-2 on a vote and an arbitrator appointed to break the deadlock ruled in favor of Hamilton. Angels owner Arte Moreno contended that Hamilton's admission of drug use should have allowed the team to void the final three years and $83 million remaining on the five-year, $125 million contract he signed as a free agent following the 2012 season.

But that was not an option after the board voted not to punish. Instead, the Angeles traded Hamilton back to the Rangers, for whom he starred from 2008-12, on April 27 and agreed to include $77 million in the deal. Part of the deal included Hamilton, who was AL MVP in 2010, being tested for drugs and alcohol five days a week.

New Policies

MLB and the MLBPA also created the sport's first domestic violence policy in August.

The 13-page agreement followed a series of high-profile domestic violence cases involving NFL players and allows the commissioner to issue discipline for "just cause," the same standard used under the Collective Bargaining Agreement. Discipline is not dependent on a criminal conviction.

"Major League Baseball and its clubs are proud to adopt a comprehensive policy that reflects the gravity and the sensitivities of these significant societal issues," Manfred said. "We believe that these efforts will foster not only an approach of education and prevention but also a united stance against these matters throughout our sport and our communities."

The commissioner can place a player accused of domestic violence, sexual assault or child abuse on paid administrative leave for up to seven days before a disciplinary decision, which can be appealed to the sport's arbitration panel, chaired by an independent arbitrator. The commissioner also may defer a discipline decision until the resolution of criminal charges.

Suspensions that are upheld are without pay, and there are no maximum or minimum penalties. Players will not receive service time for the period of the suspension.

Players can be suspended with pay in "excep-

CONTINUED ON PAGE 10

PLAYER OF THE YEAR

Harper fulfills his destiny

BY MARK ZUCKERMAN

You will find no shortage of complex metrics by which to evaluate Bryce Harper's 2015 season. Whether you prefer WAR, OPS+, wOBA, wRC+ or any other sabermetric-friendly measure of your choosing, Harper's performance this year is confirmed as nothing short of remarkable.

But you really don't need fancy stats to confirm this. Let's keep this about as basic as it gets, using time-honored measures everybody understands.

Harper hit 42 home runs this season, with a .330 batting average and .460 on-base percentage. In the entire history of baseball, just eight others have ever done that: Babe Ruth, Lou Gehrig, Jimmy Foxx, Ted Williams, Mickey Mantle, Todd Helton, Jason Giambi and Barry Bonds. Harper produced one of the great offensive performances of all time.

"It was awesome," teammate Jayson Werth said on the final day of the season. "I'm really proud of him. He had a great season. An MVP-caliber season."

Indeed, Harper is Baseball America's Major League Player of the Year for the first time. He will win the National League MVP award in a landslide, perhaps even unanimously, once the votes are revealed in November.

Ask anyone who has watched Harper closely since his 2012 major league debut what stood about this season, and you'll likely get two answers: First, he was healthy enough to make it through the full year without dealing with injuries, and second, he displayed remarkable

ED WOLFSTEIN

Bryce Harper's season was nothing short of historic

PREVIOUS POY WINNERS

2005: Albert Pujols, 1b, Cardinals
2006: Johan Santana, lhp, Twins
2007: Alex Rodriguez, ss, Yankees
2008: C.C. Sabathia, lhp, Indians/Brewers
2009: Joe Mauer, c, Twins
2010: Roy Halladay, rhp, Phillies
2011: Matt Kemp, of, Dodgers
2012: Mike Trout, of, Angels
2013: Mike Trout, of, Angels
2014: Clayton Kershaw, lhp, Dodgers
Full list: BaseballAmerica.com/awards

patience at the plate.

Good health kept Harper on the field all year. Tremendous patience allowed him to perform to his full ability. He drew a Nationals club record 124 walks, posting a .460 OBP that was baseball's best since Chipper Jones (.470) and Albert Pujols (.462) in 2008.

And opposing pitchers never gave in to him. Just 38.5 percent of all pitches thrown to Harper this season were in the strike zone, according to Baseball Info Solutions, lowest in the majors. For comparison's sake: In 2004, when he drew a major league-record 234 walks, Bonds still saw 44.4 percent of pitches thrown to him in the strike zone.

Put that all together and Harper posted 9.9 wins above replacement this season, according to Baseball-Reference.com, a number surpassed in the past decade only by Mike Trout (10.8 WAR) in 2012.

"He has the world in the palm of his hand," Nationals lefthander Gio Gonzalez said. "It's just fun to see him play. And the sky's the limit."

CONTINUED FROM PAGE 8

tional cases," while criminal charges are pending or if the commissioner determines that "allowing the player to play during the pendency of the criminal or legal proceeding would result in substantial or irreparable harm to either the club or Major League Baseball." If the discipline becomes an unpaid suspension, the player has the right to offset the time served against the penalty but must repay any salary he received from his team during the paid suspension.

The agreement creates a joint policy board to provide treatment, which could include mandatory counseling and psychological evaluation.

Three experts will serve on the board along with two members appointed by MLB and two by the union, and one of the experts will submit a proposed treatment plan to the full board for approval. Players who fail to comply with their treatment plan may be subject to discipline.

"Players are husbands, fathers, sons and boyfriends," Clark said. "And as such want to set an example that makes clear that there is no place for domestic abuse in our society. We are hopeful that this new comprehensive, collectively-bargained policy will deter future violence, promote victim safety, and serve as a step toward a better understanding of the causes and consequences of domestic violence, sexual assault and child abuse."

Race To The Finish

One aspect of the game that Manfred wasn't eager to change was the postseason format, though some felt it should modified after NL Central teams finished with the three best regular season records—the Cardinals (100-62), the Pirates (98-64) and the Cubs (97-65).

Because they did not win their division, the Pirates and Cubs were forced to meet in the winner-take-all NL Wild Card Game, which the Cubs won. Chicago then played the Cardinals—who they beat in four games—in the best-of-five NL Division Series because the rules stipulate that the division winner with the best record faces the wild card team in LDS. Meanwhile, the teams with the fourth- and fifth-best record—the NL West champion Dodgers (92-70) and NL East champion Mets (90-72)—met in the other NLDS.

"Personally, I think it is a mistake to get caught up in the results," Manfred said. "I understand what you're saying about Pittsburgh and what has happened to them. I get it. But I think it's a mistake to focus on an individual team as opposed to the system."

Manfred, though, said he would consider the idea of reseeding the teams in both leagues after the wild card games. That way, a wild-card winner with a better record than two of the division champions would receive home-field advantage in the LDS round.

"It's something to ponder but I don't think we should be rash in making any decisions," Manfred said.

Cubs manager Joe Maddon and his Yankees counterpart Joe Girardi, whose team lost to the

CONTINUED ON PAGE 12

AMERICAN LEAGUE STANDINGS

East	W	L	PCT	GB	Manager	General Manager	Attendance	Average	Last Penn.
Toronto Blue Jays	93	69	.574	—	John Gibbons	Alex Anthopoulos	2,794,891	34,505	1993
* New York Yankees	87	75	.537	6	Joe Girardi	Brian Cashman	3,193,795	39,922	2009
Baltimore Orioles	81	81	.500	12	Buck Showalter	Dan Duquette	2,320,588	29,751	1983
Tampa Bay Rays	80	82	.494	13	Kevin Cash	Matt Silverman	1,247,668	15,403	2008
Boston Red Sox	78	84	.481	15	J. Farrell/T. Lovullo	Ben Cherington	2,880,694	35,564	2013

Central	W	L	PCT	GB	Manager	General Manager	Attendance	Average	Last Penn.
Kansas City Royals	95	67	.586	—	Ned Yost	Dayton Moore	2,708,549	33,439	2015
Minnesota Twins	83	79	.512	12	Paul Molitor	Terry Ryan	2,220,054	27,408	1991
Cleveland Indians	81	80	.503	13 ½	Terry Francona	Chris Antonetti	1,388,905	17,806	1997
Chicago White Sox	76	86	.469	19	Robin Ventura	Rick Hahn	1,755,810	21,948	2005
Detroit Tigers	74	87	.460	20 ½	Brad Ausmus	Dave Dombrowski/Al Avila	2,726,048	33,655	2012

West	W	L	PCT	GB	Manager	General Manager	Attendance	Average	Last Penn.
Texas Rangers	88	74	.543	—	Jeff Banister	Jon Daniels	2,491,875	30,764	2011
* Houston Astros	86	76	.531	2	A.J. Hinch	Jeff Luhnow	2,153,585	26,587	2005 (NL)
Los Angeles Angels	85	77	.525	3	Mike Scioscia	Jerry Dipoto/Bill Stoneman	3,012,765	37,195	2002
Seattle Mariners	76	86	.469	12	Lloyd McClendon	Jack Zduriencik/Jerry Dipoto	2,193,581	27,081	None
Oakland Athletics	68	94	.420	20	Bob Melvin	Billy Beane	1,768,175	21,829	1990

*Wild card

Wild Card: Astros defeated Yankees, 1-0. **Division Series:** Royals defeated Astros 3-2 and Blue Jays defeated Rangers 3-2 in best-of-five series. **Championship Series:** Royals defeated Blue Jays 4-2 in best-of-seven series.

ROOKIE OF THE YEAR

Bryant pulls off triple play

BY GORDON WITTENMYER

CHICAGO

Just before the Cubs made their final decision on the franchise's highest draft pick in more than a decade—what had the chance to be the most significant pick in Theo Epstein's organizational overhaul—Cubs executives flew to California for another meeting with Kris Bryant.

"We asked him if he ever struggled," Cubs general manager Jed Hoyer said of the San Diego slugger who earned College Player of the Year in 2013. "He said, 'Yeah, I struggled in the Cape (Cod) League.' But he really talked about it like he understood the concept of why we were asking the question. It showed a lot of self-awareness."

Then they drafted him. Then they pushed him. Then they started wondering what "struggling" even means to the 6-foot-5 third baseman, who has been a critical part of the Cubs' sudden success in 2015 since his heralded debut nine games into the season.

The Cubs skipped him to high Class A Daytona by the end of that first pro season in 2013. "He was terrific," Hoyer said. "And we thought we'd push him really hard and put him in the (Arizona) Fall League."

And he won the AFL MVP.

Then Double-A and Triple-A in his second pro season—and all he did was win BA's 2014 Minor League Player of the Year Award.

"We kept on thinking we were pushing him to the point of failure, which was kind of our goal," Hoyer said. "He kept on responding to each one of those challenges."

Now that he's run out of leagues to conquer, Bryant settled for the Cubs' first playoff run since 2008, and Baseball America's Rookie of the Year Award—becoming the first player to earn BA's College Player of the Year, Minor League Player of the Year and rookie awards in successive years.

The most anticipated Cubs rookie since Mark Prior—the franchise's previous No. 2 overall draft pick—Bryant came with far more hype.

And yet, Bryant finished the season with 99

TONY FARLOW

Kris Bryant set a Cubs rookie record with 26 home runs

RBIs, to go along with 77 walks and a franchise rookie-record 26 home runs.

Bryant was upset when he didn't make the team out of spring training, though he never publicly criticized the club.

"I'm just playing with a chip on my shoulder," Bryant said. "All that stuff's in the past. I play hard. I play confidently. And I play because it's fun."

PAST 10 WINNERS

2005: Huston Street, rhp, Athletics
2006: Justin Verlander, rhp, Tigers
2007: Ryan Braun, 3b, Brewers
2008: Geovany Soto, c, Cubs
2009: Andrew McCutchen, of, Pirates
2010: Jason Heyward, of, Braves
2011: Jeremy Hellickson, rhp, Rays
2012: Mike Trout, of, Angels
2013: Jose Fernandez, rhp, Marlins
2014: Jose Abreu, 1b, White Sox
Full list: BaseballAmerica.com/awards

CONTINUED FROM PAGE 10

Astros in the AL Wild Card Game, both suggested that the wild-card round become a best-of-three series. However, Manfred said he was not interested in either shortening the regular season or moving the end of the World Series past the first of November to accommodate more series.

The Cardinals won their third straight division title by holding off the Pirates and Cubs while also qualifying for the postseason for the fifth year in a row. Despite becoming the first major league club to win 100 games since the 2011 Phillies, the Cardinals did not clinch the division title until four days remained in the season.

The Pirates qualified for the playoffs for the third consecutive year after finishing under .500 each of the previous 20 seasons from 1993-2012, which set a major North American professional team sports record. The Cubs earned their first playoff berth since 2008. While the Dodgers captured their third straight division crown, the Mets won their first division title and earned their first postseason berth since 2006.

The most exciting division race transpired in the AL West, where the Rangers (88-74) clinched on the final day of the regular season, finishing two games ahead of the Astros (86-76) and three ahead of the Angels (85-77) after finishing in the basement the previous season.

The Astros won the second wild-card berth for their first postseason appearance since losing the 2005 World Series, while the Angeles missed the playoffs by a game one year after having the best regular-season record in the major leagues.

The Blue Jays (93-69), fueled by the acquisition of all-star shortstop Troy Tulowitzki from the Rockies and ace lefthander David Price from the Tigers, won their first AL East title and gained their first postseason berth since 1993, when they won the second of back-to-back World Series titles. The 22 years without going to the playoff was the longest active drought in the major leagues.

Though the Yankees (87-75) couldn't hold off the Blue Jays, they did manage to win the first wild card to make their first playoff appearance since 2012. Before that skid, the Yankees hadn't gone back-to-back season without making the postseason since 1993.

The Royals (95-67) were the division winners with the largest margin of victory, finishing 12 games ahead of the Twins (83-79) in the AL Central. It was Kansas City's first division crown since 1985 and ended the Tigers' four-year reign atop the division.

A-Rod And Milestones

The Yankees' playoff run was improbably sparked by DH Alex Rodriguez, who returned to the lineup after missing the 2014 season while serving a one-year suspension from MLB for violating its performance-enhancing drug policy.

Despite turning 40 on July 27, Rodriguez hit .250 with 33 home runs in 151 games while reaching two significant milestones during the first week of May. He became the 29th player in major league history with 3,000 hits when he singled off the Tigers' Justin Verlander on May 1. Six days

NATIONAL LEAGUE STANDINGS

EAST	W	L	PCT	GB	Manager	General Manager	Attendance	Average	Last Penn.
New York Mets	90	72	.556	—	Terry Collins	Sandy Alderson	2,569,753	31,725	2015
Washington Nationals	83	79	.512	7	Matt Williams	Mike Rizzo	2,619,843	32,344	None
Miami Marlins	71	91	.438	19	M. Redmond/D. Jennings	D. Jennings/M. Hill	1,752,235	21,633	2003
Atlanta Braves	67	95	.414	23	Fredi Gonzalez	John Hart	2,001,392	25,017	1999
Philadelphia Phillies	63	99	.389	27	R. Sandberg/P. Mackanin	R. Amaro Jr./S. Proefrock	1,831,080	23,475	2009
Central	W	L	PCT	GB	Manager	General Manager	Attendance	Average	Last Penn
St. Louis Cardinals	100	62	.617	—	Mike Matheny	John Mozeliak	3,520,889	43,468	2013
*Pittsburgh Pirates	98	64	.605	2	Clint Hurdle	Neal Huntington	2,498,596	30,847	1979
*Chicago Cubs	97	65	.599	3	Joe Maddon	Jed Hoyer	2,959,812	36,541	1945
Milwaukee Brewers	68	94	.420	32	R. Roenicke/C. Counsell	D. Melvin/D. Stearns	2,542,558	31,390	1982 (AL)
Cincinnati Reds	64	98	.395	36	Bryan Price	Walt Jocketty	2,419,506	29,870	1990
West	W	L	PCT	GB	Manager	General Manager	Attendance	Average	Last Penn
Los Angeles Dodgers	92	70	.568	—	Don Mattingly	Farhan Zaidi	3,764,815	46,479	1988
San Francisco Giants	84	78	.519	8	Bruce Bochy	Bobby Evans	3,375,882	41,678	2014
Arizona Diamondbacks	79	83	.488	13	Chip Hale	Dave Stewart	2,080,145	25,681	2001
San Diego Padres	74	88	.457	18	Bud Black/Pat Murphy	A.J. Preller	2,459,742	30,367	1998
Colorado Rockies	68	94	.420	24	Walt Weiss	Jeff Bridich	2,506,789	31,335	2007

*Wild card

Wild Card: Cubs defeated Pirates 1-0. **Division Series:** Cubs defeated Cardinals 3-1 and Mets defeated Dodgers 3-2 in best-of-five series. **Championship Series:** Mets defeated Cubs 4-0 in best-of-seven series.

later, he connected for his 661st home run off the Orioles' Chris Tillman to move past Willie Mays into third place on the all-time list.

The 21-year veteran also reached 2,000 runs scored and 2,000 RBIs in his career.

Red Sox DH David Ortiz became the 27th member of the 500-home run club when he took the Rays' Matt Moore deep on Sept. 12. Earlier in the season, Ortiz also became the 27th player with 550 doubles.

Angels first baseman Albert Pujols hit his 550th homer July 29 with a blast off the Astros' Luke Gregerson. Rangers third baseman Adrian Beltre and Tigers first baseman Miguel Cabrera reached 400 home runs on consecutive days, Beltre reaching the milestone May 15 with a drive off the Indians' Bruce Chen and Cabrera connecting of the Cardinals' Tyler Lyons.

Beltre also tied the major league record by hitting for his third career cycle on Aug. 3 against the Astros. He became the fourth players to achieve the feat, joining John Reilly, Babe Herman and Bob Meusel.

Others reaching significant home run milestones included Phillies first baseman Ryan Howard and Twins right fielder Torii Hunter hitting No. 350 and Rangers DH Prince Fielder hitting No. 300. A quintet of players passed 250 home runs during the 2015 season: Blue Jays right fielder Jose Bautista, Brewers right fielder Ryan Braun, Blue Jays first baseman Edwin Encarnacion, Mets right fielder Curtis Granderson and White Sox first baseman Adam LaRoche.

Dodgers first baseman Adrian Gonzalez drove in his 1,000th run, becoming the 279th player to do so when he hit a two-run home run off the Braves' Julio Teheran on May 27.

Nationals righthander Max Scherzer tossed two of the seven no-hitters thrown in the major leagues after being signed to a seven-year, $210 million contract as a free agent in the offseason. He became the fifth pitcher in major league history to throw two no-nos in the same season and first since Nolan Ryan in 1973.

Scherzer's first gem came June 20 in a 6-0 win against the Pirates at Nationals Park in Washington. Scherzer was one strike away from a perfect game when he hit pinch-hitter Jose Tabata on the left elbow with a pitch in the bottom in the ninth. He then rebounded to get Josh Harrison to hit a game-ending flyout.

Scherzer's second no-no came Oct. 3, the penultimate day of the regular season, when he stymied the Mets in a 2-0 victory at Citi Field in New York. Scherzer struck out 17 in a 109-pitch outing, and

Alex Rodriguez returned from a year-plus PED ban to hit 33 homers for the Yankees

only a throwing error by third baseman Yunel Escobar that allowed Kevin Plawecki to reach first leading off the sixth prevented a perfect game.

Scherzer became the first pitcher in major league history to throw two no-hitters without allowing a walk.

The Mets were also the victims of the season's first no-hitter on June 9 when Giants righthander Chris Heston tossed a gem at Citi Field. Heston struck out 11 and did not walk a batter while throwing 110 pitches.

Lefthander Cole Hamels made his final start with the Phillies a memorable one by no-hitting the Cubs at Wrigley Field in Chicago on July 25. In a 5-0 victory, Hamels had 13 strikeouts and two walks while throwing 129 pitches. After spending his entire 10-year career with Philadelphia, Hamels was traded to the Rangers six days later.

Mariners righthander Hisashi Iwakuma tossed a no-no against the Orioles on Aug. 12 at Safeco Field in Seattle. He struck out seven and walked three in a 3-0 victory.

The Dodgers were on the wrong end of two no-hitters nine days apart, first when Astros righthander Mike Fiers achieved the feat Aug. 21 at Minute Maid Park in Houston. Cubs righthander Jake Arrieta followed with one of his own Aug. 30 at Dodger Stadium in Los Angeles.

Fiers needed 134 pitches to complete his gem,

ALL-ROOKIE TEAM 2015

POS	PLAYER, TEAM	AGE	AB	AVG	OBP	SLG	2B	HR	RBI	SB	RUNDOWN
C	Kyle Schwarber, Cubs	22	232	.246	.355	.487	6	16	43	3	2014 first-rounder moved quickly
1B	Justin Bour, Marlins	26	409	.262	.321	.479	20	23	73	0	Minor league Rule 5 pick showed big power
2B	Addison Russell, Cubs	21	475	.242	.307	.389	29	13	54	4	Took shortstop job from Starlin Castro
3B	Kris Bryant, Cubs	23	559	.275	.369	.488	31	26	99	13	College POY, Minor League POY and now ROY
SS	Francisco Lindor, Indians	21	390	.313	.353	.482	22	12	51	12	Overshadowed by Carlos Correa, but numbers close
CF	Joc Pederson, Dodgers	23	480	.210	.346	.417	19	26	54	4	Was headed for ROY, but slumped in second half
OF	Randal Grichuk, Cardinals	22	323	.276	.329	.548	23	17	47	4	Ranked second on Cardinals with 17 HR
OF	Odubel Herrera, Phillies	23	495	.297	.344	.418	30	8	41	16	Rule 5 pick from Rangers won job in spring
DH	Carlos Correa, Astros	21	387	.279	.345	.512	22	22	68	14	Led all major league shortstops with 22 homers

POS	PITCHER, TEAM	AGE	W	L	SV	ERA	IP	SO	BB	RUNDOWN
SP	Anthony DeSclafani, Reds	24	9	13	0	4.05	185	151	55	Anchored rotation after July trades of Cueto, Leake
SP	Lance McCullers Jr., Astros	22	6	7	0	3.22	126	129	43	Helped pitch the Astros to an AL-best 3.57 ERA
SP	Carlos Rodon, White Sox	22	9	6	0	3.75	139	139	71	Showed notable improvement in the second half
SP	Eduardo Rodriguez, Red Sox	22	10	6	0	3.85	122	98	37	Throws strikes, keeps the ball in the park
SP	Noah Syndergaard, Mets	22	9	7	0	3.24	150	166	31	Led rookie starters with 10.0 strikeouts per nine innings
RP	Roberto Osuna, Blue Jays	20	1	6	20	2.58	70	75	16	Among rookie-reliever leaders for fastball velocity (95.5 mph)

striking out 10 and walking three in 3-0 win. Acquired from the Brewers on July 30, he became the first pitcher to throw a no-hitter in the same season in which he was traded since Jim Bibby in 1973.

Arrieta struck out 12 and walked one in a 116-pitch effort as the Cubs won 2-0.

Meanwhile, Blue Jays lefthander Mark Buehrle became the 116th pitcher in major league history to record 200 career victories when he beat the Orioles on April 10.

Cubs righthander Dan Haren picked up his 150th win Aug. 11 against the Brewers and then became the 74th pitcher to reach 2,000 strikeouts on Sept. 13 against the Phillies when he fanned Brian Bogusevic. Mariners righthander Felix Hernandez also notched his 2,000th strikeout on May 10 when he fanned the Athletics' Sam Fuld.

Yankees lefthander C.C. Sabathia and Pirates righthander A.J. Burnett increased the number of members of the 2,500-strikeout club to 32. Sabathia hit the milestone by whiffing the Angels' Johnny Giavotella on June 7 and Burnett got there Sept. 27 with a punchout of the Cubs' Jorge Soler.

Brewers righthander Francisco Rodriguez notched his 350th career save April 23 against the Reds to become the 10th pitcher to reach that milestone.

Angels righthander Huston Street became the 27th member of the 300-save club when he closed out a win against the Twins on July 22.

The Padres' Craig Kimbrel and Pirates' Joakim Soria both reached 200 saves. Kimbrel became the youngest to reach that mark. He was 11 days past his 27th birthday June 8 when he wrapped up a win against the Braves, who traded him to San Diego on the eve of the season opener.

The race for the NL batting title proved to be exciting. It came down to the final day of the season, when Marlins second baseman Dee Gordon knocked three hits against the Phillies to pass the Nationals' Bryce Harper.

Harper entered the day with a miniscule edge, .330754 to .330606. However, Gordon led off the game with a double and singled in his next two at-bats. He ended the day 3-for-4 to finish with a .333 average, while Harper ended up at .330 after going 1-for-4 against the Cubs.

"It feels kind of surreal," Gordon said. "I don't think it hit me yet. It was an amazing feeling when I walked up the stairs and my teammates were ready and congratulating me. That felt really good."

Miguel Cabrera easily won his fourth AL batting title in five years with a .338 average, outdistancing Red Sox shortstop Xander Bogaerts (.320).

Orioles first baseman Chris Davis hit 47 home runs, including two in the season finale against the Yankees, to lead the major leagues for the second time in three years.

"I was pretty fired up after I hit the first one," Davis said. "The second one, I felt like I was in shock running around the bases,"

Blue Jays third baseman Josh Donaldson led the AL with 123 RBIs and 122 runs scored.

Harper's 42 homers tied Rockies third baseman Nolan Arenado for the NL lead. Harper also topped the NL with 118 runs scored.

A total of 20 players hit 30 or more homers, up from 11 last year, and the major league batting average of .254 was the highest since 2012.

Gordon's 205 hits and 58 stolen bases were both tops in the league, and he became the first NL player to finish first in both categories since Jackie

Robinson in 1949.

Astros second baseman Jose Altuve led the AL in steals for the second straight year. However, his total of 38 was the lowest for a league leader since Luis Aparacio topped the AL with 31 in 1961.

The major league average of 0.52 steals per team each game was the lowest since 1972.

Indians left fielder Michael Brantley had 45 doubles, the fewest for an AL leader since 1999. Diamondbacks outfielder David Peralta had 10 triples, the fewest for the NL leader since 2003.

Pitching In

Dodgers righthander Zack Greinke won the NL ERA title with a 1.66 mark, the lowest for a qualifying pitcher since Greg Maddux's 1.63 in 1995, and the lowest by a Dodgers pitcher since Rube Marquard's 1.58 in 1916. Greinke, who won the AL ERA title in 2009 with the Royals, ended Dodgers lefthander Clayton Kershaw's run of four straight seasons leading the majors in that category.

Arrieta ranked second at 1.77, and his 0.75 ERA after the all-star break was the lowest in major league history. Kershaw was third at 2.13.

Lefthander David Price, traded from the Tigers to the Blue Jays in July, won his second AL ERA title at 2.45, just ahead of Astros ace Dallas Keuchel (2.48). Price also led in ERA in 2012 with the Rays.

Kershaw had 301 strikeouts to become the first pitcher to reach 300 since Randy Johnson and Curt Schilling did so in 2002 for the Diamondbacks. Lefthander Chris Sale led the AL with 274, breaking the White Sox franchise record set in 1908.

The major league average of 7.76 strikeouts per nine innings set a record for the eighth straight year.

Arrieta, who went 22-6, led the major leagues in wins with, and Keuchel topped the AL at 20-9. Keuchel went 15-0 in 18 starts at Minute Maid Park, the first pitcher in big league history to go undefeated at home with at least 14 wins.

The Pirates' Mark Melancon led the NL with 51 saves, and the Rays' Brad Boxberger topped the AL with 41, the lowest total for an AL leader since 2000.

Four For Fame

Four players were inducted into the Hall of Fame—Craig Biggio, Randy Johnson, Pedro Martinez and John Smoltz.

Martinez went 219-100 in his career and helped the Red Sox break an 86-year World Series drought in 2004. He was also the first pitcher inducted who played primarily for the Red Sox and just the second native of the Dominican Republic to gain induction, joining Juan Marichal.

Martinez provided the most memorable moment of the induction ceremony in Cooperstown, when he had Marichal, who was inducted in 1983, join him at the podium.

"We waited 32 years for another Dominican," said Martinez, who wore a patch honoring his nation's flag on one shoulder and one honoring the United States on the other. "I hope all Dominicans remember this. I don't think the Dominican Republic will have a better image than me and Marichal on Father's Day (in the Dominican) to be up there."

Biggio, who spent his entire 20-year career with the Astros, made the all-star team at catcher and second base. He helped lead Houston to its lone World Series appearance in 2005. Biggio is also the only player in history with at least 3,000 hits, 600 doubles, 400 stolen bases and 250 home runs.

"We changed the culture in Houston by making it a baseball city," Biggio said. "To the Astros fans: You guys are the greatest fans in the world."

At 6-foot-10, Johnson became the tallest player elected to the Hall after a 22-year career that saw him finish with 303 victories. He also won four consecutive NL Cy Young Awards with the Diamondbacks from 1999-2002 and retired with more strikeouts (4,875) than any pitcher but Nolan Ryan.

Smoltz pitched on 14 postseason teams with the Braves, including five pennant winners and one World Series champion. He became the first pitcher in history with 200 wins and 150 saves and also became the first pitcher who had Tommy John surgery to reach the Hall.

"I'm a miracle. I'm a medical miracle," Smoltz said. "I never took one day for granted."

Martinez had his No. 45 retired by the Red Sox, and the Diamondbacks did the same with Johnson's No. 51.

The Yankees retired three numbers—Jorge Posada's No. 20, Andy Pettitte's No. 46 and Bernie Williams' No. 51—while the White Sox retired Paul Konerko's No. 14 and the Rays retired the late Don Zimmer's No. 66, representing the number of years he spent in professional baseball.

The Brewers retired No. 1 in honor of Selig, who was the franchise's founder and owned the team before becoming commissioner.

Meanwhile, a number of players retired either during or at the end of the season, including A.J. Burnett, Dan Haren, Torii Hunter, Tim Hudson, LaTroy Hawkins, Aramis Ramirez, Carlos Quentin, Jeff Karstens, Bruce Chen, Rafael Furcal,

Kevin Slowey, Erik Bedard, Dane de la Rosa, Chris Perez, Carlos Pena, Jeremy Affeldt and Barry Zito.

Front Office Fix

There were several in-season general-manager changes, with veteran executive Dave Dombrowski at the center of two high-profile moves.

Dombrowski was fired as president/GM by the Tigers on Aug. 4 during his 14th season. He was jettisoned just days after trading away such veterans as lefthander David Price, left fielder Yoenis Cespedes and closer Joakim Soria, conceding that Detroit had little chance of making the postseason following four straight AL Central championships.

Assistant GM Al Avila was promoted to GM and received a five-year contract.

Dombrowski was not out of work for very long. He was hired Aug. 19 by the Red Sox to be their president of baseball operations. GM Ben Cherington, stripped of his decision-making power with the addition of Dombrowski, resigned and assistant GM Mike Hazen was promoted to GM on Sept. 24.

Jerry Dipoto resigned as the Angels' GM on July 1 when a rocky relationship with manager Mike Scioscia finally reached an end point. The tipping point came when Scioscia and his coaching staff reportedly refused to apply the advanced statistical data provided by Dipoto and his staff.

Former GM Bill Stoneman came out of retirement to finish the season. Yankees assistant GM Billy Eppler was hired as the permanent replacement in October.

Dipoto found another GM job in the AL West when he was hired by the Mariners to replace Jack Zduriencik, who was fired Aug. 28 during his seventh season on the job.

Brewers GM Doug Melvin announced Aug. 11 that he would step away after 13 years on the job and moved into an advisory capacity. Astros assistant GM David Stearns was hired to fill the vacancy.

The Phillies jettisoned GM Ruben Amaro Jr. on Sept. 10 as he was wrapping up his seventh season. Angels assistant GM Matt Klentak was hired to take over a franchise that had the worst record in the major leagues with a 63-99 mark.

The strangest GM scenario occurred with the Marlins when Dan Jennings was asked to take over as field manager on May 17, replacing the fired Mike Redmond after Miami got off to a 16-22 start. Jennings had never managed during his 32 years in professional baseball.

The Marlins not only decided not to have Jennings return as the manager at the end of the

season but also fired him as GM. President of baseball operations Michael Hill will also handle the GM duties.

AMERICAN LEAGUE BEST TOOLS

A Baseball America survey of American League managers, conducted at midseason 2015, ranked players with the best tools.

BEST HITTER
1. Miguel Cabrera
2. Mike Trout
3. Prince Fielder

BEST POWER
1. Mike Trout
2. Nelson Cruz
3. Miguel Cabrera

BEST BUNTER
1. Brett Gardner
2. Erick Aybar
3. Delino DeShields Jr.

BEST STRIKE-ZONE JUDGMENT
1. Jose Bautista
2. Miguel Cabrera
3. Carlos Santana

BEST HIT-AND-RUN ARTIST
1. Jose Altuve
2. Alcides Escobar
3. Erick Aybar

BEST BASERUNNER
1. Jose Altuve
2. Brett Gardner
3. Mike Trout

FASTEST BASERUNNER
1. Jarrod Dyson
2. Billy Burns
3. Mike Trout

MOST EXCITING PLAYER
1. Mike Trout
2. Manny Machado
3. Jose Altuve

BEST PITCHER
1. Chris Sale
2. Dallas Keuchel
3. Chris Archer

BEST FASTBALL
1. Garrett Richards
2. Jake McGee
3. Yordano Ventura

BEST CURVEBALL
1. Corey Kluber
2. Sonny Gray
3. Dellin Betances

BEST SLIDER
1. Chris Archer
2. Corey Kluber
3. Chris Sale

BEST CHANGEUP
1. Felix Hernandez
2. Chris Sale
3. Marco Estrada

BEST CONTROL
1. Phil Hughes
2 (tie). Mark Buehrle
2 (tie). Dallas Keuchel

BEST PICKOFF MOVE
1. Mark Buehrle
2. Wade Miley
3. Chris Capuano

BEST RELIEVER
1. Wade Davis
2. Zach Britton
3. Dellin Betances

BEST DEFENSIVE CATCHER
1. Salvador Perez
2. Russell Martin
3. Yan Gomes

BEST DEFENSIVE 1B
1. Eric Hosmer
2. Mark Teixeira
3. James Loney

BEST DEFENSIVE 2B
1. Dustin Pedroia
2. Robinson Cano
3. Jose Altuve

BEST DEFENSIVE 3B
1. Manny Machado
2. Josh Donaldson
3. Adrian Beltre

BEST DEFENSIVE SS
1. Alcides Escobar
2. Jose Iglesias
3. J.J. Hardy

BEST INFIELD ARM
1. Manny Machado
2. Adrian Beltre
3. Josh Donaldson

BEST DEFENSIVE OF
1 (tie). Kevin Kiermaier
1 (tie). Lorenzo Cain
3. Adam Jones

BEST OUTFIELD ARM
1. Yoenis Cespedes
2. Leonys Martin
3. Kevin Kiermaier

BEST MANAGER
1. Buck Showalter
2. Terry Francona
3. Paul Molitor

CONTINUED ON PAGE 18

Pirates creativty pays off

BY J.J. COOPER

For the Pittsburgh Pirates, orthodoxy has few opportunities.

A smaller revenue team in a division with teams like the Cubs and Cardinals with more financial resources, Pittsburgh can't build consistent success if it doesn't innovate.

So the Pirates were on the vanguard of defensive shifting, creating opportunities to add to infielders' range by putting them in the right place at the right time.

As team after team struggled to figure out how to handle the flow of analytics information from the front office to the clubhouse, the Pirates had no such problems. Director of baseball systems Dan Fox and quantitative analyst Mike Fitzgerald are a regular part of the Pirates clubhouse and have been well integrated into the team's day-to-day operations. Pittsburgh's manager-front office relationship is a model for organizations to emulate.

Without the ability to outbid other teams for the top free agent pitchers, Pittsburgh figured out how to build pitching staffs through reclamation projects. From Francisco Liriano to Edinson Volquez and Vance Worley to A.J. Burnett, the Pirates have managed to help veteran pitchers get back on track.

And now the Pirates have opened up the free agent pipeline from Korea. Estalished Korean pitchers have been coming to the U.S. for years, but no Korean position player had ever gone through the posting process before shortstop Jung Ho Kang made himself eligible last offseason.

PITTSBURGH PIRATES

General manager Neal Huntington's Pirates won 98 games in 2015

Where many teams worried about how well Kang would adjust to the big leagues, the Pirates were convinced that he could make the transition. They paid $5 million for the rights to negotiate with Kang then signed him to a four-year, $16 million deal. Kang hit .287/.355/.461 this season while playing shortstop and third base to easily outplay his contract.

The clever defensive shifting, bolstered rotation and adept free agent moves have been important, but Pittsburgh has also done an excellent job of developing homegrown talent, especially among position player. The homegrown outfield of Starling Marte, Andrew McCutchen and Gregory Polanco is one of the best in baseball.

A team that didn't post a winning record for 20 years has averaged 93 wins a season over the past three years. Pittsburgh's 98 wins was tied for the third most in franchise history.

It has yet to pay off in the playoffs but with patience, persistence and nnovation, Pittsburgh is now a perennial playoff team and one that appears set to remain a contender for several more years.

PREVIOUS WINNERS

2004: Minnesota Twins
2005: Atlanta Braves
2006: Los Angeles Dodgers
2007: Colorado Rockies
2008: Tampa Bay Rays
2009: Philadelphia Phillies
2010: San Francisco Giants
2011: St. Louis Cardinals
2012: Cincinnati Reds
2013: St. Louis Cardinals
2014: Kansas City Royals

Full list: BaseballAmerica.com/awards

CONTINUED FROM PAGE 16

The Braves promoted assistant GM John Coppolella to GM at the end of the season. President of baseball operations John Hart also performed that role during the 2015 season.

In a surprising move, Blue Jays GM Alex Anthopolous walked away from the organization at the end of the season despite Toronto ending its playing drought. Anthopolous reportedly did not want to cede his decision-making power in the baseball operations department to new club president Mark Shapiro, who was hired away from the same job with the Indians.

Shortly after the season, the Reds promoted longtime GM Walt Jocketty to president of baseball operations and assistant Dick Williams was promoted to GM.

In addition to their front-office changes, the Brewers and Phillies also changed managers during the season. Milwaukee fired Ron Roenicke on May 3 and Philadelphia dismissed Ryne Sandberg on June 26.

Craig Counsell, who was a special assistant to Melvin, replaced Roenicke and received a three-year contract. Roenicke had a 342-331 record in four-plus season, but the Brewers were 7-18 when he was fired.

The Phillies promoted third base coach Pete Mackanin to interim manager then removed that tag on Sept. 22 and gave him a one-year contract for 2016. The Phillies were 26-48 when Sandberg was axed and went 37-51 under Mackanin.

Bud Black's nine-year tenure as Padres manager ended when his team got off to a 32-33 start following an offseason in which GM A.J. Prellar made a number of high-profile acquisitions. Pat Murphy, manager of the San Diego's Triple-A El Paso affiliate, served as interim manager for the remainder of the season but was not asked back following the Padres' 74-88 finish.

Red Sox manager John Farrell was forced to take a leave of absence on Aug. 14 after being diagnosed with Stage 1 lymphoma. Bench coach Torey Lovullo served as interim manager for the remainder of the season, but Farrell and the Red Sox were optimistic that he would be ready for the start of the 2016 season. The Mariners' Lloyd McClendon, the Nationals' Matt Williams and the Dodgers' Don Mattingly were all let go at the end of the season. Mattingly wasn't out of work long after leading Los Angeles to three straight NL West title. The Marlins made him their eighth manager since 2010, giving him a four-year contract

The Mariners hired Angels farm director Scott

NATIONAL LEAGUE BEST TOOLS

A Baseball America survey of National League managers, conducted at midseason 2015, ranked players with the best tools.

BEST HITTER	BEST CONTROL
1. Paul Goldschmidt	1. Zack Greinke
2. Bryce Harper	2. Max Scherzer
3. Buster Posey	3. Clayton Kershaw

BEST POWER	BEST PICKOFF MOVE
1. Giancarlo Stanton	1. Julio Teheran
2. Bryce Harper	2. Madison Bumgarner
3. Todd Frazier	3. Johnny Cueto

BEST BUNTER	BEST RELIEVER
1. Dee Gordon	1. Aroldis Chapman
2. Billy Hamilton	2. Craig Kimbrel
3. Gerardo Parra	3. Trevor Rosenthal

BEST STRIKE-ZONE JUDGMENT	BEST DEFENSIVE CATCHER
1. Joey Votto	1. Yadier Molina
2. Paul Goldschmidt	2. Jonathan Lucroy
3. Matt Carpenter	3. Francisco Cervelli

BEST HIT-AND-RUN ARTIST	BEST DEFENSIVE 1B
1. Yadier Molina	1. Paul Goldschmidt
2. Martin Prado	2. Adrian Gonzalez
3. D.J. LeMahieu	3. Joey Votto

BEST BASERUNNER	BEST DEFENSIVE 2B
1. Dee Gordon	1. D.J. LeMahieu
2. Billy Hamilton	2 (tie). Dee Gordon
3. Paul Goldschmidt	2 (tie). Brandon Phillips

FASTEST BASERUNNER	BEST DEFENSIVE 3B
1. Billy Hamilton	1. Nolan Arenado
2. Dee Gordon	2. Todd Frazier
3. Ben Revere	3. Kris Bryant

MOST EXCITING PLAYER	BEST DEFENSIVE SS
1. Bryce Harper	1. Andrelton Simmons
2. Giancarlo Stanton	2. Adeiny Hechavarria
3. Andrew McCutchen	3. Brandon Crawford

BEST PITCHER	BEST INFIELD ARM
1. Zack Greinke	1. Andrelton Simmons
2. Max Scherzer	2. Troy Tulowitzki
3. Clayton Kershaw	3. Nolan Arenado

BEST FASTBALL	BEST DEFENSIVE OF
1. Aroldis Chapman	1. Andrew McCutchen
2. Jake deGrom	2. Denard Span
3. Craig Kimbrel	3. Billy Hamilton

BEST CURVEBALL	BEST OUTFIELD ARM
1. Clayton Kershaw	1. Yasiel Puig
2 (tie). Gio Gonzalez	2. Gerardo Parra
2 (tie). Jose Fernandez	3. Carlos Gonzalez

BEST SLIDER	BEST MANAGER
1. Max Scherzer	1. Bruce Bochy
2. Jose Fernandez	2. Mike Matheny
3. Clayton Kershaw	3. Joe Maddon

BEST CHANGEUP	
1. Cole Hamels	
2. Zack Greinke	
3. James Shields	

Servais as McClendon's replacement and veteran skipper Dusty Baker was tabbed to replace Williams in Washington.

CONTINUED ON PAGE 20

BILL NICHOLS

Buster Posey struck out just 52 times, a career low for a full season.

DIAMOND IMAGES

Zack Greinke's 1.66 ERA was the second-best in the history of the Dodgers' franchise

FIRST TEAM

Pos.	Player, Team	AVG	OBP	SLG	AB	R	H	2B	3B	HR	RBI	BB	SO	SB	CS
C	Buster Posey, Giants	.318	.379	.470	557	74	177	28	0	19	95	56	52	2	0
1B	Paul Goldschmidt, D-backs	.321	.435	.570	567	103	182	38	2	33	110	118	151	21	5
2B	Jason Kipnis, Indians	.303	.372	.451	565	86	171	43	7	9	52	57	107	12	8
3B	Josh Donaldson, Blue Jays	.297	.371	.568	620	122	184	41	2	41	123	73	133	6	0
SS	Carlos Correa, Astros	.279	.345	.512	387	52	108	22	1	22	68	40	78	14	4
CF	Mike Trout, Angels	.299	.402	.590	575	104	172	32	6	41	90	92	158	11	7
OF	Bryce Harper, Nationals	.330	.460	.649	521	118	172	38	1	42	99	124	131	6	4
OF	Andrew McCutchen, Pirates	.292	.401	.488	566	91	165	36	3	23	96	98	133	11	5
DH	Nelson Cruz, Mariners	.302	.369	.566	590	90	178	22	1	44	93	59	164	3	2

Pos	Pitcher, Team	W	L	ERA	G	GS	SV	IP	H	R	ER	HR	BB	SO	WHIP
SP	Jake Arrieta, Cubs	22	6	1.77	33	33	0	229	150	52	45	10	48	236	0.86
SP	Zack Greinke, Dodgers	19	3	1.66	32	32	0	223	148	43	41	14	40	200	0.84
SP	Clayton Kershaw, Dodgers	16	7	2.13	33	33	0	233	163	62	55	15	42	301	0.88
SP	Dallas Keuchel, Astros	20	8	2.48	33	33	0	232	185	68	64	17	51	216	1.02
SP	Max Scherzer, Nationals	14	12	2.79	33	33	0	229	176	74	71	27	34	276	0.92
RP	Wade Davis, Royals	8	1	0.94	69	0	17	67	33	8	7	3	20	78	0.79

SECOND TEAM

Pos	Player, Team	AVG	OBP	SLG	AB	R	H	2B	3B	HR	RBI	BB	SO	SB	CS
C	Francisco Cervelli, Pirates	.295	.370	.401	451	56	133	17	5	7	43	46	94	1	1
1B	Joey Votto, Reds	.314	.459	.541	545	95	171	33	2	29	80	143	135	11	3
2B	Jose Altuve, Astros	.313	.353	.459	638	86	200	40	4	15	66	33	67	38	13
3B	Manny Machado, Orioles	.286	.359	.502	633	102	181	30	1	35	86	70	111	20	8
SS	Francisco Lindor, Indians	.313	.353	.482	390	50	122	22	4	12	51	27	69	12	2
CF	A.J. Pollock, D-backs	.315	.367	.498	609	111	192	39	6	20	76	53	89	39	7
OF	Jose Bautista, Blue Jays	.250	.377	.536	543	108	136	29	3	40	114	110	106	8	2
OF	Yoenis Cespedes, Tigers/Mets	.291	.328	.542	633	101	184	42	6	35	105	33	141	7	5
DH	J.D. Martinez, Tigers	.282	.344	.535	596	93	168	33	2	38	102	53	178	3	2

Pos	Pitcher, Team	W	L	ERA	G	GS	SV	IP	H	R	ER	HR	BB	SO	WHIP
SP	Madison Bumgarner, Giants	18	9	2.93	32	32	0	218	181	73	71	21	39	234	1.01
SP	Gerrit Cole, Pirates	19	8	2.60	32	32	0	208	183	71	60	11	44	202	1.09
SP	Jacob deGrom, Mets	14	8	2.54	30	30	0	191	149	59	54	16	38	205	0.98
SP	Sonny Gray, Athletics	14	7	2.73	31	31	0	208	166	71	63	17	59	169	1.08
SP	David Price, Tigers/Blue Jays	18	5	2.45	32	32	0	220	190	70	60	17	47	225	1.08
RP	Dellin Betances, Yankees	6	4	1.50	74	0	9	84	45	17	14	6	40	131	1.01

EXECUTIVE OF THE YEAR

Sandy Alderson

A U.S. Marine who served a tour in Vietnam, Sandy Alderson knows tough assignments. But even with his training as Marine and with a law degree from Harvard, Alderson might not have been quite as ready to tackle the job as Mets general manager when he was hired in 2010. But Alderson wasn't one to run from challenges. Alderson spun high-priced veterans such as Carlos Beltran and R.A. Dickey into prospects such as Zack Wheeler, Travis d'Arnaud and Noah Syndergaard and drafted Michael Conforto and this year pushed for the necessary offense to back up the high-powered arms. Shrewd trades, most importantly for Yoenis Cespedes, helped the Mets go 20-8 in August en route to their first World Series appearance in 15 years.

PREVIOUS WINNERS

2003: Brian Sabean, Giants
2004: Terry Ryan, Twins
2005: Mark Shapiro, Indians
2006: Dave Dombrowski, Tigers
2007: Jack Zduriencik, Brewers
2008: Theo Epstein, Red Sox
2009: Dan O'Dowd, Rockies
2010: Jon Daniels, Rangers
2011: Doug Melvin, Brewers
2012: Billy Beane, Athletics
2013: Dan Duquette, Orioles
2014: Dan Duquette, Orioles

Full list: BaseballAmerica.com/awards

MANAGER OF THE YEAR

Joe Maddon

Almost from the moment Joe Maddon became aware of his contractural right to leave the Rays and be a managerial free agent, the Cubs were ready to pounce. The Cubs had young talent and the money to chase free agents, but had underachieved with first-year manager Rick Renteria. Theo Epstein did not hide his affinity for Maddon. The deal was sealed as Epstein and Maddon dined outside Maddon's beloved RV—dubbed Cousin Eddie. Maddon brought his innovation and loose managerial style to Wrigley and quickly defused issues involving the status of Rookie of the Year Kris Bryant, and watched as Jake Arrieta blossomed into a Cy Young Award frontrunner. The result was the Cubs' first trip to the postseason since 2008 and their first postseason series victory since 2003.

PREVIOUS WINNERS

2003: Jack McKeon, Marlins
2004: Bobby Cox, Braves
2005: Ozzie Guillen, White Sox
2006: Jim Leyland, Tigers
2007: Terry Francona, Red Sox
2008: Ron Gardenhire, Twins
2009: Mike Scioscia, Angels
2010: Bobby Cox, Braves
2011: Joe Maddon, Rays
2012: Buck Showalter, Orioles
2013: Clint Hurdles, Pirates
2014: Buck Showalter, Orioles

Full list: BaseballAmerica.com/awards

CONTINUED FROM PAGE 18

Hacking Scandal

Major League Baseball experienced its first reported incident of cybercrime between two teams when the FBI and Justice Department began investigating in June whether the Cardinals illegally accessed a computer database of the Astros called "Ground Control."

Though the investigation was still ongoing at the conclusion of the season, the Cardinals fired scouting director Chris Correa in July, reportedly after he admitted to hacking into the database.

The aim of the hack was to obtain information from a front office headed by Astros GM Jeff Luhnow, who helped transform St. Louis' scouting operation when he worked as Cardinals scouting director.

"Major League Baseball has been aware of and has fully cooperated with the federal investigation into the illegal breach of the Houston Astros' baseball operations database," MLB said in a statement. "Once the investigative process has been completed by federal law enforcement officials, we will evaluate the next steps and will make decisions promptly."

Commissioner Manfred said subpoenas have been issued, but did not provide details.

"There are legal problems associated with federal law enforcement officials seeking cooperation from private individuals," Manfred said. "If the federal government wants information from us, they would subpoena information, and that's what they've done."

The FBI office in Houston released a statement that neither confirmed nor denied the investigation, but added, "The FBI aggressively investigates all potential threats to public and private sector systems.

"Once our investigations are complete, we pursue all appropriate avenues to hold accountable those who pose a threat in cyberspace."

The Astros and Cardinals were rivals in the NL Central until Houston moved to the AL in 2013. Luhnow headed the Cardinals' scouting and player development department before being hired as Astros general manager in December 2011.

It was not clear how many Cardinals employees were under investigation or whether top front office officials were aware of the activities.

"Then there's the question of who did it?" Manfred said. "Who knew about it? Is the organization responsible? Is the individual responsible? There's a whole set of issues that are needed to be sorted through."

Manfred said MLB forensics experts were not involved because it was a federal investigation.

In June 2014, the Astros were the victim of hackers who accessed servers and published months of internal trade talks on the Internet.

Manfred downplayed wider security concerns about MLB's digital systems.

"We have a technology company that quite literally is the envy of companies throughout America —not just sports enterprises," the commissioner said. "We routinely make the resources of MLB Advanced Media available to all of the clubs. We have the type of security arrangements that are necessary."

Fan Safety

Fan safety came to the forefront during a season in which a fan fell to his death at Turner Field in Atlanta and another survived life-threatening injuries while struck by a broken bat at Fenway Park in Boston.

Greg Murrey, 60, of Alpharetta, Ga., was pronounced dead at Grady Memorial Hospital in Atlanta following his fall in the seventh inning of the Braves-Yankees game on Aug. 29. The Fulton County medical examiner ruled the death an accident caused by blunt-force injuries to his head and torso.

Murrey, a season-ticket holder for 23 years, fell from the upper deck into the lower seating bowl, where many of the players' family and friends were seated. Braves second baseman Jace Peterson's girlfriend was close to the spot where Murrey landed.

"It was within 10 feet from her," Peterson said. "So everybody whose families were here definitely experienced some part of it. It's not good for any-

CARL KLINE

Alex Anthopoulos surprisingly walked away as Blue Jays general manager

one to see something like that.

"A lot of player families were right there. I heard some pretty graphic stuff. It's not something I really want to get into. It's just unfortunate."

Tonya Carpenter survived after receiving a concussion and multiple facial fractures June 6 at Fenway Park when struck by the broken bat of Athletics third baseman Brett Lawrie. She was carried from the box seats on a stretcher.

"I've seen bats fly out of guys' hands in the stands and everyone's OK, but when one breaks like that, has jagged edges on it, anything can happen," Lawrie said.

Concerned about a rash of flying broken bats and the danger they posed, MLB studied the issue in 2008 and made changes to the composition of bats that has reduced breakage by nearly 50 percent.

According to baseball researchers, the only death caused by a ball or bat in an MLB game came in 1970 when a 14-year-old boy was killed by a foul ball at Dodger Stadium.

Nonetheless, Manfred said MLB would study the fan safety issue during the offseason

"Fan safety is, and always will be, our primary concern," he said.

CONTINUED ON PAGE 23

Trout puts 'star' in All-Star

ALL-STAR GAME

Mike Trout is the first player to win the All-Star Game MVP two years in a row

BILL NICHOLS

The 2014 All-Star Game was a celebration of the end of Derek Jeter's Hall of Fame career. This year's game had the anticipation of a Hall of Fame career for Mike Trout.

Trout became the first player in 38 years to homer leading off an All-Star Game, then became the first player to take home the Midsummer Classic's MVP award two years in row as the American League beat the NL 6-3, the 21st win in the past 28 contests for the AL.

"It's obviously a humbling honor with the MVPs," Trout told reporters.

Trout started the night at Cincinnati's Great American Ballpark by hitting Zack Greinke's fourth pitch, a 94 mph fastball, over the wall in right next to the visiting bullpen.

A year after Jeter was feted, 2015 was a year of new blood. Trout was among six starting position players under the age of 25—the most since 1965.

"He can do anything that anybody can do on a baseball field," AL manager Ned Yost told reporters. "He can hit with power. He can run. You look at a guy that is one of the best baseball players on this planet."

It was the first All-Star Game not presided over by Bud Selig since 1992. New commissioner Rob Manfred was on hand instead following Selig's retirement in January.

The Rangers' Prince Fielder—in the midst of a bounce-back season—drove in two runs, including an RBI single in the fifth off Clayton Kershaw that put the AL ahead for good.

Since the game was in Cincinnati and celebrated the Reds' great history, Pete Rose—baseball's all-time hits leader who's banned from the sport for gambling—was allowed to be on the field and got an 80-second ovation from fans. Rose joined Reds Hall of Famers Johnny Bench, Joe Morgan and Barry Larkin.

But in the end, Trout—who joined Willie Mays, Steve Garvey, Gary Carter and Cal Ripken Jr. as the only two-time All-Star MVPs—was the main attraction.

"He's going to be standing there, I think, with the guys we saw tonight," NL manager Bruce Bochy said, referring to the Hall of Fame Reds.

JULY 15, 2015

American League 6, National League 3

American	AB	R	H	RBI	National	AB	R	H	RBI
Trout CF	3	2	1	1	McCutchen CF	3	1	1	1
Holt PR-LF	1	1	0	0	Pollock CF	1	0	0	0
Donaldson 3B	0	0	0	0	Frazier 3B	3	0	0	0
a-Machado PH-3B	2	1	1	1	Arenado 3B	1	0	0	0
g-Moustakas PH-3B	1	0	0	0	Harper RF	3	0	0	0
Pujols 1B	2	1	0	0	J. Upton RF	1	0	1	0
Teixeira 1B	2	0	0	0	Goldschmidt 1B	3	1	1	0
Cruz DH	2	0	0	0	Gonzalez 1B	1	0	0	0
b-Fielder PH-DH	1	0	1	2	Posey C	2	0	0	0
Cain RF	3	0	2	1	Molina C	1	0	1	0
J.D. Martinez RF	1	0	0	0	b-Grandal PH-C	1	0	0	0
Jones LF	2	0	0	0	Rizzo DH	2	0	0	0
c-Gardner PH-LF-CF	2	0	0	0	a-Tulowitzki PH-DH	1	0	0	0
Pérez C	2	0	0	0	c-Braun PH	1	1	1	0
Vogt C	1	0	0	0	Peralta SS	1	0	1	1
e-Martin PH-C	1	0	0	0	Crawford PR-SS	1	0	0	1
Altuve 2B	2	0	0	0	Pederson LF	2	0	0	0
Kipnis 2B	1	0	0	0	Bryant LF	1	0	0	0
f-Dozier PH-2B	1	1	1	1	LeMahieu 2B	2	0	0	0
Escobar SS	2	0	1	0	Panik 2B	2	0	0	0
d-Iglesias PH-SS	2	0	0	0					
Totals	**34**	**6**	**7**	**6**	**Totals**	**33**	**3**	**6**	**3**

3B: Braun (1, Perkins). **2B:** Cain (1, Kershaw); Machado (1, Rodríguez) **HR:** McCutchen (1, 6th inning off Archer 0 on, 0 Out). **HR:** Trout (1, 1st inning off Greinke 0 on, 0 Out); Dozier (1, 8th inning off Melancon 0 on, 2 Out) **RBI:** Peralta (1), McCutchen (1), Crawford (1). **RBI:** Trout (1), Fielder 2 (2), Cain (1), Machado (1), Dozier (1) **SF:** Crawford. **SF:** Fielder; **E:** Donaldson (1, throw); Britton (1, throw) **SB:** J. Upton (1, 2nd base off Davis/Martin)

American	IP	H	R	SO	National	IP	H	R	SO
Keuchel	2	2	1	1	Greinke	2	1	1	4
Hernández	1	0	0	1	Cole	1	0	0	1
Price (W)	1	0	0	2	Bumgarner	1	1	0	1
Archer (H)	1.1	1	1	1	Kershaw (L)	1	3	2	1
Britton (H)	0.2	1	0	1	deGrom	1	0	0	3
Betances (H)	1	0	0	1	Rodríguez	1	2	2	0
Davis	1	1	0	2	Melancon	1	1	1	2
Perkins	1	1	1	0	Chapman	1	0	0	3
Totals	**9**	**6**	**3**	**9**	**Totals**	**9**	**7**	**6**	**15**

In a season in which MLB mandated that clubs use metal detectors on fans entering the stadium, a game with no fans in attendance was played April 29 at Oriole Park at Camden Yards in Baltimore. The Orioles beat the White Sox 8-2 but the gates were closed after civil unrest swept the city following the death of Freddy Gray while in police custody.

"It was kind of like instructional league, Gulf Coast League, Arizona League," Orioles manager Buck Showalter said.

MLB decided to play the game behind closed doors rather than to disrupt the schedules further after the riots had caused the first two games of a three-game series to be postponed.

Dearly Departed

Baseball lost a number of notable names in 2015, including Hall of Famers Ernie Banks and Yogi Berra.

Banks died on Jan. 22 of natural causes at age 83. The two-time MVP hit 512 home runs in his 19-year career, all with the Cubs, and was known for his boundless energy and his famous phrase "It's a great day for baseball. Let's play two."

"Words cannot express how important Ernie Banks will always be to the Chicago Cubs, the city of Chicago and Major League Baseball," Cubs chairman Tom Ricketts said. "He was one of the greatest players of all time. He was a pioneer in the major leagues. And more importantly, he was the warmest and most sincere person I've ever known."

Though he was an 11-time all-star from 1953-71, Banks never reached the postseason. The Cubs,

Rob Manfred downplayed wider security concerns about MLB's digital systems

TOMASSO DeROSA

who haven't won the World Series since 1908, finished below .500 in all but six of his seasons and remain without a pennant since 1945.

Still, he was inducted into the Hall of Fame in 1977, the first year he was eligible, and was selected to baseball's All-Century team in 1999.

Banks' infectious smile and non-stop good humor endeared him to Chicago fans, including actor Bill Murray, who named his son Homer Banks Murray.

In 2013, Banks was presented with the Presidential Medal of Freedom—by noted White Sox fan, President Barack Obama. The award is one of the nation's highest civilian honors.

Berra, another of baseball's most-beloved characters, died on Sept. 22 of natural causes at 90.

The catcher was a three-time AL MVP and won an unmatched 10 World Series titles with the Yankees. For many, though, he was even better known for all those amusing phrases, eight of which are included in "Bartlett's Famous Quotations," including "It ain't over 'til it's over."

"When I'm sittin' down to dinner with the family, stuff just pops out. And they'll say, 'Dad, you just said another one.' And I don't even know what the heck I said," Berra once said. Berra helped the Yankees reach 14 World Series during his 18 seasons in the Bronx.

"While we mourn the loss of our father, grandfather and great-grandfather, we know he is at

ACTIVE LEADERS

Career leaders among players who played in a game in 2015. Batters require 3,000 plate appearances and pitchers 1,000 innings to qualify for percentage titles.

BATTERS			PITCHERS		
AVG	Miguel Cabrera	.321	ERA	Clayton Kershaw	2.43
OBP	Joey Votto	.423	SO/9	Max Scherzer	9.79
SLG	Albert Pujols	.581	W	Bartolo Colon	218
OPS	Albert Pujols	.977	SV	Francisco Rodriguez	386
R	Alex Rodriguez	2,002	IP	C.C. Sabathia	2,989
H	Alex Rodriguez	3,070	SO	C.C. Sabathia	2,574
2B	David Ortiz	584	GS	Bartolo Colon	467
3B	Carl Crawford	122	BB/9	Doug Fister	1.77
HR	Alex Rodriguez	687	HR/9	Clayton Kershaw	0.54
RBI	Alex Rodriguez	2,055	L	Bartolo Colon	154
BB	Alex Rodriguez	1,324	G	Francisco Rodriguez	856
SO	Alex Rodriguez	2,220	BB	C.C. Sabathia	894
SB	Ichiro Suzuki	498	HR	Bartolo Colon	355
TB	Alex Rodriguez	5,734	CG	C.C. Sabathia	38

peace with Mom," Berra's family said in a statement. "We celebrate his remarkable life, and are thankful he meant so much to so many. He will truly be missed."

Berra served on a gunboat supporting the D-Day invasion in 1944 and played for the Yankees from 1946-63.

Lawrence Peter Berra, the son of Italian immigrants, got his nickname while growing up in St. Louis. Among his amateur baseball teammates was Joe Garagiola, another future big leaguer.

He was a fan favorite, especially with children, and the cartoon character Yogi Bear was named after him.

Berra, who played in 15 straight All-Star Games, never earned more than $65,000 a season. He died on the same date, Sept. 22, as his big league debut 69 years earlier. Berra was the AL MVP in 1951, 1954 and 1955. He holds World Series records for most hits (71) and games (75).

Other notable deaths among former players include former White Sox stars Minnie Minoso and Billy Pierce, 20-game winner Joaquin Andujar and outfielder and broadcaster Darryl Hamilton.

Win For Orioles

A New York Supreme Court justice tossed out a MLB arbitration decision that the Orioles-controlled television network said would unfairly force it to pay tens of millions of dollars in annual broadcast rights fees to the Nationals. Justice Lawrence K. Marks vacated the decision and strongly suggested that the parties settle the matter through a "neutral dispute resolution process."

Manfred tried to the mediate the dispute between the two teams to no avail. The Nationals were assessing their options as of early November, while the Orioles were "pleased."

Meanwhile, the Dodgers nearly became the first team in baseball history to reach the $300 million luxury-tax payroll after acquiring veteran second baseman Chase Utley from the Phillies in an August trade.

The trade raised the Dodgers' projected payroll for tax purposes to about $298.5 million, according to calculations by MLB.

Luxury tax payrolls are based average annual values of contracts for the 40-man roster and include about $13 million per team in benefits, such as the health and pension plan, and payroll, unemployment and Social Security taxes paid by clubs.

The Dodgers went well above the $189 million tax threshold and were to pay at a 40 percent rate for exceeding the mark for the third straight year.

Yogi Berra was as well known for his accomplishments as his malaprops

Its projected tax bill is about $44 million, which would top the record $34 million paid by the Yankees after the 2005 season.

The Dodgers' luxury tax payroll included about $40 million for players no longer with the organization.

A priceless member of the Dodgers' organization, broadcaster Vin Scully, announced in October that he would retire following the 2016 season. That would mark the end of his record 67 years in the broadcast booth with the same franchise.

Scully, who turned 88 in November, calls all nine innings of home games and road games in California and Arizona for the Dodgers' television home on SportsNet LA, while the first three innings of his games are simulcast on the radio.

Scully says he plans to approach his final season the same way as his first 66.

"Do not go gentle into that good night. Rage, rage against the dying of the light," he said, quoting Welsh poet Dylan Thomas' famous verse. "I'm raging against the dying of my career, which has to be around the corner now, but at least for the God-given time that I have left, I'll be raging."

ARIZONA DIAMONDBACKS
Silvino Bracho	Aug. 30
Archie Bradley	April 11
Socrates Brito	Sept. 8
Enrique Burgos	April 29
Danny Dorn	April 21
Brandon Drury	Sept. 1
Zack Godley	July 23
Oscar Hernandez	July 12
Keith Hessler	Aug. 8
Peter O'Brien	Sept. 11
A.J. Schugel	April 12
Yasmany Tomas	April 15

ATLANTA BRAVES
Manny Banuelos	July 2
Jake Brigham	June 30
Daniel Castro	June 17
John Cornely	April 29
Brandon Cunniff	April 7
Adonis Garcia	May 19
Ryan Kelly	June 30
Sugar Ray Marimon	April 14
Matt Marksberry	July 31
Cody Martin	April 7
Andrew McKirahan	April 12
Hector Olivera	Sept. 1
Williams Perez	May 8
Ryan Weber	Sept. 8
Daniel Winkler	Sept. 21
Matt Wisler	June 19

BALTIMORE ORIOLES
Dariel Alvarez	Aug. 28
Oliver Drake	May 23
Jason Garcia	April 8
Mychal Givens	June 24
Rey Navarro	April 24
Tyler Wilson	May 20
Mike Wright	May 17

BOSTON RED SOX
Jonathan Aro	June 25
Dalier Hinojosa	May 3
Brian Johnson	July 21
Deven Marrero	June 28
Henry Owens	Aug. 4
Noe Ramirez	July 3
Eduardo Rodriguez	May 28
Travis Shaw	May 8
Blake Swihart	May 2

CHICAGO CUBS
Kris Bryant	April 17
Carl Edwards Jr.	Sept. 7
Addison Russell	April 21
Kyle Schwarber	June 16

CHICAGO WHITE SOX
Chris Beck	May 28
Junior Guerra	June 12
Micah Johnson	April 6
Frankie Montas	Sept. 2
Carlos Rodon	April 21
Tyler Saladino	July 10
Trayce Thompson	Aug. 4

CINCINNATI REDS
Ramon Cabrera	Sept. 5
Raisel Iglesias	April 12
Ryan LaMarre	Aug. 22
John Lamb	Aug. 14
Michael Lorenzen	April 29
Jon Moscot	June 5
Keyvius Sampson	July 30
Josh Smith	June 23
Kyle Waldrop	Aug. 2

CLEVELAND INDIANS
Cody Anderson	June 21
Shawn Armstrong	Aug. 8
Francisco Lindor	June 14
Toru Murata	June 28
Giovanni Soto	Sept. 5
Giovanny Urshela	June 9

COLORADO ROCKIES
Dustin Garneau	Aug. 20
Jon Gray	Aug. 4
Jason Gurka	Aug. 29
Tom Murphy	Sept. 12
Scott Oberg	April 14
Ken Roberts	May 3

DETROIT TIGERS
Jeff Ferrell	July 4
Daniel Fields	June 4
Guido Knudson	Aug. 22
Dixon Machado	May 25
Jefry Marte	July 5
Angel Nesbitt	April 8
Jose Valdez	July 31

HOUSTON ASTROS
Carlos Correa	June 8
Matt Duffy	Sept. 16
Michael Feliz	May 31
Lance McCullers	May 18
Preston Tucker	May 7
Vincent Velasquez	June 10
Asher Wojciechowski	April 9

KANSAS CITY ROYALS
Scott Alexander	Sept. 2
Miguel Almonte	Sept. 1
Orlando Calixte	April 19
Dusty Coleman	July 3
Cheslor Cuthbert	July 7
Paulo Orlando	April 9

LOS ANGELES ANGELS
Jett Bandy	Sept. 14
Kaleb Cowart	Aug. 18
Taylor Featherston	April 12
Trevor Gott	June 14
Edgar Ibarra	June 2
Kyle Kubitza	June 10
Carlos Perez	May 5

LOS ANGELES DODGERS
Austin Barnes	May 24
Zach Lee	July 25
Adam Liberatore	April 17
Jose Peraza	Aug. 10
Josh Ravin	June 2
Scott Schebler	June 5
Corey Seager	Sept. 3
Ronald Torreyes	Sept. 13

MIAMI MARLINS
Kyle Barraclough	Aug. 7
Adam Conley	June 10
Brian Ellington	Aug. 3
Kendry Flores	June 6
Raudel Lazo	Sept. 5
Scott McGough	Aug. 20
Justin Nicolino	June 20
Chris Reed	Aug. 1
Jose Urena	April 14

MILWAUKEE BREWERS
Nevin Ashley	Sept. 9
Yhonathan Barrios	Sept. 24
Tyler Cravy	June 2
Zach Davies	Sept. 2
David Goforth	May 26
Adrian Houser	Sept. 26
Taylor Jungmann	June 9
Jorge Lopez	Sept. 29
Ariel Pena	Sept. 5
Michael Reed	Sept. 26
Yadiel Rivera	Sept. 22
Tyler Wagner	May 31

MINNESOTA TWINS
Byron Buxton	June 14
Tyler Duffey	Aug. 5
J.R. Graham	April 6
Max Kepler	Sept. 27
Alex Meyer	June 26
Ryan O'Rourke	July 7
Eddie Rosario	May 6
Miguel Sano	July 2

NEW YORK METS
Darrell Ceciliani	May 19
Michael Conforto	July 24
Sean Gilmartin	April 10
Jack Leathersich	April 29
Steven Matz	June 28
Akeel Morris	June 17
Danny Muno	April 17
Kevin Plawecki	April 21
Hansel Robles	April 24
Noah Syndergaard	May 12

NEW YORK YANKEES
Greg Bird	Aug. 13
Danny Burawa	June 21
Caleb Cotham	July 29
Paula Jose De	June 21
Ramon Flores	May 30
Nick Goody	July 30
Slade Heathcott	May 20
Jacob Lindgren	May 25
Diego Moreno	June 22
Rico Noel	Sept. 2
James Pazos	Sept. 5
Branden Pinder	April 15
Rob Refsnyder	July 11
Nick Rumbelow	June 23
Gary Sanchez	Oct. 3
Luis Severino	Aug. 5
Matt Tracy	April 11
Mason Williams	June 12

OAKLAND ATHLETICS
Carson Blair	Sept. 6
Mark Canha	April 8
Angel Castro	May 9
Ryan Dull	Sept. 1
Tyler Ladendorf	April 8
Arnold Leon	April 22
Max Muncy	April 25
Pat Venditte	June 5

PHILADELPHIA PHILLIES
Alec Asher	Aug. 30
Jerad Eickhoff	Aug. 21
Severino Gonzalez	April 28
Odubel Herrera	April 6
Adam Morgan	June 21
Colton Murray	Sept. 2
Aaron Nola	July 21
Nefi Ogando	Sept. 9
Darnell Sweeney	Aug. 20

PITTSBURGH PIRATES
Keon Broxton	Sept. 21
Elias Diaz	Sept. 12
Deolis Guerra	June 27
Jung Ho Kang	April 8

ST. LOUIS CARDINALS
Tim Cooney	April 30
Ed Easley	May 29
Mitch Harris	April 25
Marcus Hatley	July 1
Stephen Piscotty	July 21
Cody Stanley	April 26
Travis Tartamella	Sept. 23

SAN DIEGO PADRES
Cody Decker	Sept. 14
Alex Dickerson	Aug. 6
Rocky Gale	Sept. 6
Austin Hedges	May 4
Jay Jackson	Sept. 14
Travis Jankowski	Aug. 21
Cory Mazzoni	April 27
Colin Rea	Aug. 11
Chris Rearick	April 12

SAN FRANCISCO GIANTS
Mike Broadway	June 13
Trevor Brown	Sept. 19
Cody Hall	Sept. 3
Ryan Lollis	July 4
Josh Osich	July 3
Jarrett Parker	June 13
Kelby Tomlinson	Aug. 3
Mac Williamson	Sept. 23

SEATTLE MARINERS
Steve Baron	Sept. 9
Mayckol Guaipe	June 1
John Hicks	Aug. 29
Ketel Marte	July 31
Mike Montgomery	June 2
Tyler Olson	April 7
David Rollins	July 4
Tony Zych	Sept. 4

TAMPA BAY RAYS
Matt Andriese	April 10
Andrew Bellatti	May 9
Ryan Brett	April 18
Allan Dykstra	April 8
Mikie Mahtook	April 10
Luke Maile	Sept. 1
Richie Shaffer	Aug. 3

TEXAS RANGERS
Hanser Alberto	May 29
Delino DeShields	April 8
Andrew Faulkner	Aug. 31
Joey Gallo	June 2
Chi Chi Gonzalez	May 30
Luke Jackson	Sept. 4
Keone Kela	April 7
Ryan Strausborger	Aug. 5
Logan Verrett	April 8

TORONTO BLUE JAYS
Matt Boyd	June 27
Miguel Castro	April 6
Scott Copeland	May 2
Roberto Osuna	April 8
Ryan Tepera	May 10
Devon Travis	April 6

WASHINGTON NATIONALS
A.J. Cole	April 28
Abel De Los Santos	July 21
Wilmer Difo	May 19
Matt Grace	April 22
Rafael Martin	April 15
Felipe Rivero	April 17
Joe Ross	June 6
Pedro Severino	Sept. 20
Sammy Solis	April 30
Trea Turner	Aug. 21

MAJOR LEAGUES

CLUB BATTING

	AVG	G	AB	R	H	2B	3B	HR	RBI	BB	SO	SB	OBP	SLG
Detroit	.270	161	5605	689	1515	289	49	151	660	455	1259	83	.328	.420
Kansas City	.269	162	5575	724	1497	300	42	139	689	383	973	104	.322	.412
Toronto	.269	162	5509	891	1480	308	17	232	852	570	1151	88	.340	.457
Boston	.265	162	5640	748	1496	294	33	161	706	478	1148	71	.325	.415
Texas	.257	162	5511	751	1419	279	32	172	707	503	1233	101	.325	.413
Cleveland	.256	161	5439	669	1395	303	29	141	640	533	1157	86	.325	.401
Tampa Bay	.252	162	5485	644	1383	278	32	167	612	436	1310	87	.314	.406
New York	.251	162	5567	764	1397	272	19	212	737	554	1227	63	.323	.421
Oakland	.251	162	5600	694	1405	277	46	146	661	475	1119	78	.312	.395
Baltimore	.250	162	5485	713	1370	246	20	217	686	418	1331	44	.307	.421
Chicago	.250	162	5533	622	1381	260	27	136	595	404	1231	68	.306	.380
Houston	.250	162	5459	729	1363	278	26	230	691	486	1392	121	.315	.437
Seattle	.249	162	5544	656	1379	262	22	198	624	478	1336	69	.311	.411
Minnesota	.247	162	5467	696	1349	277	44	156	661	439	1264	70	.305	.399
Los Angeles	.246	162	5417	661	1331	243	21	176	621	435	1150	52	.307	.396

CLUB PITCHING

	ERA	G	CG	SHO	SV	IP	H	R	ER	HR	BB	SO	AVG
Houston	3.57	162	5	13	39	1441	1308	618	572	148	423	1280	.241
Cleveland	3.67	161	11	10	38	1432	1274	640	584	161	425	1407	.237
Kansas City	3.73	162	2	8	56	1452	1372	641	601	155	489	1160	.249
Tampa	3.74	162	1	12	60	1453	1314	642	604	175	477	1355	.240
Toronto	3.80	162	7	10	34	1441	1353	670	609	173	397	1117	.248
Los Angeles	3.94	162	2	12	46	1440	1355	675	630	166	466	1221	.248
Chicago	3.98	162	7	9	37	1452	1443	701	643	162	474	1359	.260
Baltimore	4.05	162	0	10	43	1434	1406	693	646	174	483	1233	.257
New York	4.05	162	3	4	48	1417	1417	698	656	182	474	1370	.253
Minnesota	4.07	162	2	12	45	1443	1506	700	653	163	413	1046	.269
Oakland	4.14	162	5	15	28	1444	1402	729	664	172	474	1179	.254
Seattle	4.16	162	6	12	45	1463	1430	726	677	181	491	1283	.256
Texas	4.24	162	5	9	45	1442	1459	733	680	171	508	1095	.262
Boston	4.31	162	3	10	40	1448	1486	753	694	178	478	1218	.264
Detroit	4.64	161	7	12	35	1447	1491	803	746	193	489	1100	.268

CLUB FIELDING

	FPCT	PO	A	E	DP		FPCT	PO	A	E	DP
Baltimore	.987	4304	1597	77	373	Toronto	.985	4323	1592	88	387
Cleveland	.987	4298	1528	79	373	Boston	.984	4345	1625	97	403
Detroit	.986	4341	1621	86	450	Los Angeles	.984	4322	1491	93	298
Houston	.986	4323	1617	86	373	Tampa Bay	.984	4360	1408	95	300
Minnesota	.986	4329	1637	86	417	Chicago	.983	4358	1582	101	425
Kansas City	.985	4356	1611	88	375	Texas	.981	4328	1695	119	458
New York	.985	4373	1594	92	361	Oakland	.979	4334	1642	126	421
Seattle	.985	4389	1685	94	421						

INDIVIDUAL BATTING LEADERS

	AVG	G	AB	R	H	2B	3B	HR	RBI	BB	SO	SB
Cabrera, Miguel, Detroit	.338	119	429	64	145	28	1	18	76	77	82	1
Bogaerts, Xander, Boston	.320	156	613	84	196	35	3	7	81	32	101	10
Altuve, Jose, Houston	.313	154	638	86	200	40	4	15	66	33	67	38
Brantley, Michael, Cleveland	.310	137	529	68	164	45	0	15	84	60	51	15
Cain, Lorenzo, Kansas City	.307	140	551	101	169	34	6	16	72	37	98	28
Fielder, Prince, Texas	.305	158	613	78	187	28	0	23	98	64	88	0
Kipnis, Jason, Cleveland	.303	141	565	86	171	43	7	9	52	57	107	12
Cruz, Nelson, Seattle	.302	152	590	90	178	22	1	44	93	59	164	3
Trout, Mike, Los Angeles	.299	159	575	104	172	32	6	41	90	92	158	11
Hosmer, Eric, Kansas City	.297	158	599	98	178	33	5	18	93	61	108	7

INDIVIDUAL PITCHING LEADERS

	W	L	ERA	G	GS	CG	SV	IP	H	R	ER	B	SO
Price, David, Detroit/Toronto	18	5	2.45	32	32	3	0	220	190	70	60	47	225
Keuchel, Dallas, Houston	20	8	2.48	33	33	3	0	232	185	68	64	51	216
Gray, Sonny, Oakland	14	7	2.73	31	31	3	0	208	166	71	63	59	169
Kazmir, Scott, Oakland/Houston	7	11	3.10	31	31	0	0	183	162	77	63	59	155
Estrada, Marco, Toronto	13	8	3.13	34	28	0	0	181	134	67	63	55	131
Archer, Chris, Tampa Bay	12	13	3.23	34	34	1	0	212	175	85	76	66	252
Chen, Wei-Yin, Baltimore	11	8	3.34	31	31	0	0	191	192	78	71	41	153
Odorizzi, Jake, Tampa Bay	9	9	3.35	28	28	0	0	169	149	65	63	46	150
Quintana, Jose, Chicago	9	10	3.36	32	32	1	0	206	218	81	77	44	177
Sale, Chris, Chicago	13	11	3.41	31	31	1	0	209	185	88	79	42	274

AWARD WINNERS

Selected by Baseball Writers Association of America

MOST VALUABLE PLAYER

Player	1st	2nd	3rd	Total
Josh Donaldson, Blue Jays	23	7		385
Mike Trout, Angels	7	22	1	304
Lorenzo Cain, Royals			20	225
Manny Machado, Orioles			4	158
Dallas Keuchel, Astros				107
Nelson Cruz, Mariners		1	1	94
Adrian Beltre, Rangers				83
Jose Bautista, Blue Jays			2	82
David Price, Tigers/Blue Jays			1	62
Jose Altuve, Astros				44
Miguel Cabrera, Tigers			1	40
Edwin Encarnacion, Blue Jays				38
Prince Fielder, Rangers				33
Chris Davis, Orioles				32
J.D. Martinez, Tigers				18
Jason Kipnis, Indians				17
Kevin Kiermaier, Rays				10
Kendrys Morales, Royals				7
Chris Sale, White Sox				4
Mookie Betts, Red Sox				4
Jose Abreu, White Sox				3
Ian Kinsler, Tigers				3
Mike Moustakas, Royals				3
Carlos Correa, Astros				2
Brian McCann, Yankees				2
Eric Hosmer, Royals				2
Russell Martin, Blue Jays				2
Michael Brantley, Indians				1
Wade Davis, Royals				1
Brian Dozier, Twins				1
David Ortiz, Red Sox				1
Alex Rodriguez, Yankees				1
Mark Teixeira, Yankees				1

AL CY YOUNG AWARD

Player	1st	2nd	3rd	Total
Dallas Keuchel, Astros	22	8	0	186
David Price, Tigers/Blue Jays	8	21	1	143
Sonny Gray, Athletics		1	24	82
Chris Sale, White Sox		3	7	30
Chris Archer, Rays				29
Wade Davis, Royals				10
Felix Hernandez, Mariners				9
Collin McHugh, Astros				5
Corey Kluber, Indians				4
Marco Estrada, Blue Jays				3
Andrew Miller, Yankees				3
Shawn Tolleson, Rangers				3
Carlos Carrasco, Indians				2
Dellin Betances, Yankees				1

AL ROOKIE OF THE YEAR

Player	1st	2nd	3rd	Total
Carlos Correa, Astros	17	13		124
Francisco Lindor, Indians	13	14	2	109
Miguel Sano, Twins			20	20
Roberto Osuna, Blue Jays		2	2	8
Billy Burns, Athletics		1	3	6
Eddie Rosario, Twins			2	2
Delino DeShields, Rangers			1	1

AL MANAGER OF THE YEAR

Manager	1st	2nd	3rd	Total
Jeff Banister, Rangers	17	8	3	112
A.J. Hinch, Astros	8	13	3	82
Paul Molitor, Twins	2	3	14	33
John Gibbons, Blue Jays	1	5	2	22
Joe Girardi, Yankees	2		2	12
Ned Yost, Royals		1	5	8
Mike Scioscia, Angels			1	1

GOLD GLOVE WINNERS

Selected by AL managers

P—Dallas Keuchel, Astros
C—Salvador Perez, Royals
1B—Eric Hosmer, Royals
2B—Jose Altuve, Astros
SS—Alcides Escobar, Royals
3B—Manny Machado, Orioles
LF—Yoenis Cespedes, Tigers/Mets
CF—Kevin Kiermaier, Rays
RF—Kole Calhoun, Angels

DEPARTMENT LEADERS

BATTING

GAMES
Manny Machado, Baltimore	162
Kyle Seager, Seattle	161
Elvis Andrus, Texas	160
Chris Davis, Baltimore	160
Evan Longoria, Tampa Bay	160

AT-BATS
Jose Altuve, Houston	638
Manny Machado, Baltimore	633
Kole Calhoun, Los Angeles	630
Melky Cabrera, Chicago	629
Brian Dozier, Minnesota	628

PLATE APPEARANCES
Manny Machado, Baltimore	713
Josh Donaldson, Toronto	711
Brian Dozier, Minnesota	704
Prince Fielder, Texas	693
2 players	689

RUNS
Josh Donaldson, Toronto	122
Jose Bautista, Toronto	108
Mike Trout, Los Angeles	104
Manny Machado, Baltimore	102
2 players	101

HITS
Jose Altuve, Houston	200
Xander Bogaerts, Boston	196
Prince Fielder, Texas	187
Ian Kinsler, Detroit	185
Josh Donaldson, Toronto	184

TOTAL BASES
Josh Donaldson, Toronto	352
Mike Trout, Los Angeles	339
Nelson Cruz, Seattle	334
Chris Davis, Baltimore	322
J.D. Martinez, Detroit	319

DOUBLES
Michael Brantley, Cleveland	45
Jason Kipnis, Cleveland	43
Mookie Betts, Boston	42
Josh Donaldson, Toronto	41
Kendrys Morales, Kansas City	41

TRIPLES
Eddie Rosario, Minnesota	15
Kevin Kiermaier, Tampa Bay	12
Rajai Davis, Detroit	11
Evan Gattis, Houston	11
Delino DeShields, Texas	10

EXTRA-BASE HITS
Josh Donaldson, Toronto	84
Mike Trout, Los Angeles	79
Chris Davis, Baltimore	78
David Ortiz, Boston	74
J.D. Martinez, Detroit	73

HOME RUNS
Chris Davis, Baltimore	47
Nelson Cruz, Seattle	44
Josh Donaldson, Toronto	41
Mike Trout, Los Angeles	41
Jose Bautista, Toronto	40
Albert Pujols, Los Angeles	40

RUNS BATTED IN
Josh Donaldson, Toronto	123
Chris Davis, Baltimore	117
Jose Bautista, Toronto	114
Edwin Encarnacion, Toronto	111
David Ortiz, Boston	108

Manny Machado

SACRIFICES
Francisco Lindor, Cleveland	13
Alcides Escobar, Kansas City	11
Johnny Giavotella, Los Angeles	9
Jesus Sucre, Seattle	9
3 players,	8

SACRIFICE FLIES
Melky Cabrera, Chicago	10
Josh Donaldson, Toronto	10
Edwin Encarnacion, Toronto	10
3 players	9

Josh Donaldson

HIT BY PITCH
Brandon Guyer, Tampa Bay	24
Jose Abreu, Chicago	15
Shin-Soo Choo, Texas	15
4 players	14

WALKS
Jose Bautista, Toronto	110
Carlos Santana, Cleveland	108
Mike Trout, Los Angeles	92
Chris Davis, Baltimore	84
Alex Rodriguez, New York	84

STOLEN BASES
Jose Altuve, Houston	38
Lorenzo Cain, Kansas City	28
Billy Burns, Oakland	26
Jarrod Dyson, Kansas City	26
3 players	25

STOLEN BASE PERCENTAGE
Jarrod Dyson, Kansas City	.900
Kevin Pillar, Toronto	.860
Lorenzo Cain, Kansas City	.820
Brett Gardner, New York	.800
George Springer, Houston	.800

STRIKEOUTS
Chris Davis, Baltimore	208
J.D. Martinez, Detroit	178
Kole Calhoun, Los Angeles	164
Nelson Cruz, Seattle	164
Mike Trout, Los Angeles	158

TOUGHEST TO STRIKEOUT
(AT-BATS PER STRIKEOUT)
Michael Brantley, Cleveland	10.37
Jose Altuve, Houston	9.52
Adrian Beltre, Texas	8.72
Alexei Ramirez, Chicago	8.57
Albert Pujols, Los Angeles	8.36

GROUNDED INTO DOUBLE PLAYS
Trevor Plouffe, Minnesota	28
Billy Butler, Oakland	26
Robinson Cano, Seattle	26
Kendrys Morales, Kansas City	24
Salvador Perez, Kansas City	23

MULTI-HIT GAMES
Ian Kinsler, Detroit	61
Jose Altuve, Houston	58
Josh Donaldson, Toronto	57
Xander Bogaerts, Boston	57
Prince Fielder, Texas	57

ON-BASE PERCENTAGE
Miguel Cabrera, Detroit	.440
Mike Trout, Los Angeles	.402
Michael Brantley, Cleveland	.379
Prince Fielder, Texas	.378
Jose Bautista, Toronto	.377

ON-BASE PLUS SLUGGING
Mike Trout, Los Angeles	.991
Miguel Cabrera, Detroit	.974
Josh Donaldson, Toronto	.939
Nelson Cruz, Seattle	.936
Edwin Encarnacion, Toronto	.929

LOWEST AVERAGE
Logan Morrison, Seattle	.225
Carlos Santana, Cleveland	.231
Brian McCann, New York	.232
Brian Dozier, Minnesota	.236
Torii Hunter, Minnesota	.240

DIAMOND IMAGES

ROB CLIN

PITCHING

WINS
Dallas Keuchel, Houston	20
Collin McHugh, Houston	19
Felix Hernandez, Seattle	18
David Price, Detroit, Toronto	18
Colby Lewis, Texas	17

LOSSES
Corey Kluber, Cleveland	16
Jesse Chavez, Oakland	15
John Danks, Chicago	15
Rick Porcello, Boston	15
2 players	13

GAMES
Kevin Jepsen, TB/Minn	75
Dellin Betances, New York	74
Bryan Shaw, Cleveland	74
Justin Wilson, New York	74
Shawn Tolleson, Texas	73

GAMES STARTED
Chris Archer, Tampa Bay	34
5 players	33

GAMES FINISHED
Cody Allen, Cleveland	58
Zach Britton, Baltimore	58
5 players	53

COMPLETE GAMES
Mark Buehrle, Toronto	4
Corey Kluber, Cleveland	4
4 players	3

SHUTOUTS
Sonny Gray, Oakland	2
Felix Hernandez, Seattle	2
Dallas Keuchel, Houston	2
Mike Montgomery, Seattle	2
Jeff Samardzija, Chicago	2

SAVES
Brad Boxberger, Tampa Bay	41
Huston Street, Los Angeles	40
Zach Britton, Baltimore	36
Andrew Miller, New York	36
Shawn Tolleson, Texas	35

INNINGS PITCHED
Dallas Keuchel, Houston	232
Corey Kluber, Cleveland	222
David Price, Detroit, Toronto	220
R.A. Dickey, Toronto	214
Jeff Samardzija, Chicago	214

HITS ALLOWED
Jeff Samardzija, Chicago	228
Jose Quintana, Chicago	218
Mark Buehrle, Toronto	214
Colby Lewis, Texas	211
Collin McHugh, Houston	207

RUNS ALLOWED
Jeff Samardzija, Chicago	122
Colby Lewis, Texas	114
Alfredo Simon, Detroit	112
John Danks, Chicago	104
2 players	103

HOME RUNS ALLOWED
Jeremy Guthrie, Kansas City	29
Phil Hughes, Minnesota	29
Jeff Samardzija, Chicago	29
Anibal Sanchez, Detroit	29
Hector Santiago, Los Angeles	29

WALKS
Dallas Keuchel, Houston	20
Collin McHugh, Houston	19
Felix Hernandez, Seattle	18
David Price, Detroit, Toronto	18
Colby Lewis, Texas	17

WALKS PER NINE INNINGS
Mark Buehrle, Toronto	1.49
Chris Sale, Chicago	1.81
Corey Kluber, Cleveland	1.82
Colby Lewis, Texas	1.85
Jose Quintana, Chicago	1.92

HIT BATTERS
Nick Martinez, Texas	13
Chris Sale, Chicago	13
Mike Pelfrey, Minnesota	12
Jeff Samardzija, Chicago	12
Jered Weaver, Los Angeles	12

STRIKEOUTS
Chris Sale, Chicago	274
Chris Archer, Tampa Bay	252
Corey Kluber, Cleveland	245
David Price, Detroit, Toronto	225
Carlos Carrasco, Cleveland	216
Dallas Keuchel, Houston	216

STRIKEOUTS PER NINE INNINGS
Chris Sale, Chicago	11.82
Chris Archer, Tampa Bay	10.70
Carlos Carrasco, Cleveland	10.58
Corey Kluber, Cleveland	9.93
Danny Salazar, Cleveland	9.49

STRIKEOUTS PER NINE INNINGS (Relievers)
Andrew Miller, New York	14.59
Dellin Betances, New York	14.04
Cody Allen, Cleveland	12.85
David Robertson, Chicago	12.22
Carson Smith, Seattle	11.83

DOUBLE PLAYS
Mike Pelfrey, Minnesota	29
Mark Buehrle, Toronto	28
Kyle Gibson, Minnesota	27
Dallas Keuchel, Houston	21
Rick Porcello, Boston	21

PICKOFFS
Joe Beimel, Seattle	6
Wade Miley, Boston	5
5 players	4

WILD PITCHES
Garrett Richards, Los Angeles	17
Nathan Karns, Tampa Bay	15
Alfredo Simon, Detroit	14
Chris Archer, Tampa Bay	13
Sonny Gray, Oakland	13

WALKS-PLUS-HITS PER INNING
Dallas Keuchel, Houston	1.02
Marco Estrada, Toronto	1.04
Corey Kluber, Cleveland	1.05
Carlos Carrasco, Cleveland	1.07
David Price, Detroit/Toronto	1.08

OPPONENT AVERAGE
Marco Estrada, Toronto	.203
Dallas Keuchel, Houston	.217
Sonny Gray, Oakland	.217
Chris Archer, Tampa Bay	.220
Danny Salazar, Cleveland	.226

WORST ERA
Alfredo Simon, Detroit	5.05
Chris Tillman, Baltimore	4.99
Jeff Samardzija, Chicago	4.96
Rick Porcello, Boston	4.92
C.C. Sabathia, New York	4.73

Chris Sale

CLIFF WELCH

FIELDING

PITCHER
PCT	10 players	1.000
DP	3 players	4
E	Scott Kazmir, Houston	5
A	Dallas Keuchel, Houston	53
PO	Sonny Gray, Oakland	37

CATCHER
PCT	James McCann, Detroit	1.000
E	Rene Rivera, Tampa Bay	11
PO	Brian McCann, New York	980
CS	Russell Martin, Toronto	32
PB	Russell Martin, Toronto	19
A	Salvador Perez, Kansas City	90
DP	Tyler Flowers, Chicago	10
DP	Salvador Perez, Kansas City	10

FIRST BASE
PCT	3 players	.997
PO	Eric Hosmer, Kansas City	1261
A	Eric Hosmer, Kansas City	1010
DP	Eric Hosmer, Kansas City	121
E	Jose Abreu, Chicago	11

SECOND BASE
PCT	Jose Altuve, Houston	.993
PO	Brian Dozier, Minnesota	303
A	Brian Dozier, Minnesota	456
DP	Brian Dozier, Minnesota	111
E	Rougned Odor, Texas	17

THIRD BASE
PCT	Evan Longoria, Tampa Bay	.976
DP	Manny Machado, Baltimore	38
A	Kyle Seager, Seattle	352
PO	Josh Donaldson, Toronto	137
E	Chase Headley, New York	23

SHORTSTOP
PCT	J.J. Hardy, Baltimore	.993
E	Marcus Semien, Oakland	35
PO	Elvis Andrus, Texas	248
A	Elvis Andrus, Texas	516
DP	Elvis Andrus, Texas	114

OUTFIELD
PCT	Mike Trout, Los Angeles	1.000
PCT	Jacoby Ellsbury, New York	1.000
PO	Kevin Pillar, Toronto	440
DP	4 players	4
A	Avisail Garcia, Chicago	4
E	Lorenzo Cain, Kansas City	10

CLUB BATTING

	AVG	G	AB	R	H	2B	3B	HR	RBI	BB	SO	SB	OBP	SLG
San Francisco	.267	162	5565	696	1486	288	39	136	663	457	1159	93	.326	.406
Colorado	.265	162	5572	737	1479	274	49	186	702	388	1283	97	.315	.432
Arizona	.264	162	5649	720	1494	289	48	154	680	490	1312	132	.324	.414
Miami	.260	162	5463	613	1420	236	40	120	575	375	1150	112	.310	.384
Pittsburgh	.260	162	5631	697	1462	292	27	140	661	461	1322	98	.323	.396
St. Louis	.253	162	5484	647	1386	288	39	137	619	506	1267	69	.321	.394
Atlanta	.251	162	5420	573	1361	251	18	100	548	471	1107	69	.314	.359
Milwaukee	.251	162	5480	655	1378	274	34	145	624	412	1299	84	.307	.393
Washington	.251	162	5428	703	1363	265	13	177	665	539	1344	57	.321	.403
Los Angeles	.250	162	5385	667	1346	263	26	187	638	563	1258	59	.326	.413
Philadelphia	.249	162	5529	626	1374	272	37	130	586	387	1274	68	.303	.382
Cincinnati	.248	162	5571	640	1382	257	27	167	613	496	1255	134	.312	.394
Chicago	.244	162	5491	689	1341	272	30	171	657	567	1518	95	.321	.398
New York	.244	162	5527	683	1351	295	17	177	654	488	1290	51	.312	.400
San Diego	.243	162	5457	650	1324	260	36	148	623	426	1327	82	.300	.385

CLUB PITCHING

	ERA	G	CG	SHO	SV	IP	H	R	ER	HR	BB	SO	AVG
St. Louis	2.94	162	1	15	62	1464	1359	525	478	123	477	1329	.246
Pittsburgh	3.21	162	0	13	54	1489	1392	596	532	110	453	1338	.248
Chicago	3.36	162	6	21	48	1461	1276	608	546	134	407	1431	.233
New York	3.43	162	1	14	50	1462	1341	613	557	152	383	1337	.243
Los Angeles	3.44	162	6	21	47	1445	1317	595	553	145	395	1396	.242
Washington	3.62	162	4	13	41	1434	1366	635	577	145	364	1342	.250
San Francisco	3.72	162	7	18	41	1444	1344	627	597	155	431	1165	.246
Miami	4.02	162	0	12	35	1427	1374	678	638	141	508	1152	.255
Arizona	4.04	162	1	12	44	1446	1450	713	659	182	500	1215	.258
San Diego	4.09	162	1	6	41	1440	1371	731	655	171	516	1393	.252
Milwaukee	4.28	162	1	7	40	1435	1432	737	682	176	517	1260	.261
Cincinnati	4.33	162	2	8	35	1453	1436	754	700	177	544	1252	.258
Atlanta	4.41	162	3	10	44	1425	1462	760	698	170	550	1148	.268
Philadelphia	4.69	162	1	7	35	1436	1592	809	749	191	488	1153	.280
Colorado	5.04	162	4	4	36	1426	1579	844	799	183	579	1112	.283

CLUB FIELDING

	FPCT	PO	A	E	DP		FPCT	PO	A	E	DP
Los Angeles	.988	4337	1727	75	347	San Diego	.985	4321	1566	92	363
Miami	.987	4281	1588	77	445	Washington	.985	4304	1533	90	346
San Francisco	.987	4333	1674	78	401	St. Louis	.984	4394	1617	96	424
Arizona	.986	4400	1697	86	389	Chicago	.982	4384	1669	111	333
New York	.986	4388	1599	88	368	Milwaukee	.981	4305	1678	116	440
Atlanta	.985	4276	1593	90	516	Philadelphia	.981	4309	1585	117	388
Cincinnati	.985	4360	1622	90	359	Pittsburgh	.981	4469	1868	122	479
Colorado	.985	4279	1818	95	478						

INDIVIDUAL BATTING LEADERS

	AVG	G	AB	R	H	2B	3B	HR	RBI	BB	SO	SB
Gordon, Dee, Miami	.333	145	615	88	205	24	8	4	46	25	91	58
Harper, Bryce, Washington	.330	153	521	118	172	38	1	42	99	124	131	6
Goldschmidt, Paul, Arizona	.321	159	567	103	182	38	2	33	110	118	151	21
Posey, Buster, San Francisco	.318	150	557	74	177	28	0	19	95	56	52	2
Pollock, A.J., Arizona	.315	157	609	111	192	39	6	20	76	53	89	39
Escobar, Yunel, Washington	.314	139	535	75	168	25	1	9	56	45	70	2
Votto, Joey, Cincinnati	.314	158	545	95	171	33	2	29	80	143	135	11
Peralta, David, Arizona	.312	149	462	61	144	26	10	17	78	44	107	9
Inciarte, Ender, Arizona	.303	132	524	73	159	27	5	6	45	26	58	21
LeMahieu, DJ, Colorado	.301	150	564	85	170	21	5	6	61	50	107	23

INDIVIDUAL PITCHING LEADERS

	W	L	ERA	G	GS	CG	SV	IP	H	R	ER	B	SO
Greinke, Zack, Los Angeles	19	3	1.66	32	32	1	0	223	148	43	41	40	200
Arrieta, Jake, Chicago	22	6	1.77	33	33	4	0	229	150	52	45	48	236
Kershaw, Clayton, Los Angeles	16	7	2.13	33	33	4	0	233	163	62	55	42	301
deGrom, Jacob, New York	14	8	2.54	30	30	0	0	191	149	59	54	38	205
Cole, Gerrit, Pittsburgh	19	8	2.60	32	32	0	0	208	183	71	60	44	202
Harvey, Matt, New York	13	8	2.71	29	29	0	0	189	156	62	57	37	188
Lackey, John, St. Louis	13	10	2.77	33	33	1	0	218	211	71	67	53	175
Scherzer, Max, Washington	14	12	2.79	33	33	4	0	229	176	74	71	34	276
Bumgarner, Madison, S.F.	18	9	2.93	32	32	4	0	218	181	73	71	39	234
Martinez, Carlos, St. Louis	14	7	3.01	31	29	0	0	180	168	65	60	63	184

AWARD WINNERS

Selected by Baseball Writers Association of America

MOST VALUABLE PLAYER

Player	1st	2nd	3rd	Total
Bryce Harper, Nationals	30			420
Paul Goldschmidt, Diamondbacks	18	3		234
Joey Votto, Reds	1	6		175
Anthony Rizzo, Cubs	3	4		162
Andrew McCutchen, Pirates	1	4		139
Jake Arrieta, Cubs	5	3		134
Zack Greinke, Dodgers	2	5		130
Nolan Arenado, Rockies		4		102
Buster Posey, Giants				84
Clayton Kershaw, Dodgers				49
Kris Bryant, Cubs				34
Matt Carpenter, Cardinals				26
Yoenis Cespedes, Mets				24
A.J. Pollock, Diamondbacks				21
Jason Heyward, Cardinals				15
Dee Gordon, Marlins				6
Trevor Rosenthal, Cardinals				5
Curtis Granderson, Mets				4
Gerrit Cole, Pirates				3
Adrian Gonzalez, Dodgers				3

NL CY YOUNG AWARD

Player	1st	2nd	3rd	Total
Jake Arrieta, Cubs	17	11	2	169
Zack Greinke, Dodgers	10	17	3	147
Clayton Kershaw, Dodgers	3	2	23	101
Gerrit Cole, Pirates				40
Max Scherzer, Nationals				32
Madison Bumgarner, Giants				8
Jacob deGrom, Mets				7
Mark Melancon, Pirates				5
John Lackey, Cardinals				1

ROOKIE OF THE YEAR

Player	1st	2nd	3rd	Totals
Kris Bryant, Cubs	30			150
Matt Duffy, Giants		22	4	70
Jung Ho Kang, Pirates		4	16	28
Noah Syndergaard, Mets		3	7	16
Justin Bour, Marlins		1	1	4
Joc Pederson, Dodgers			1	1
Stephen Piscotty, Cardinals			1	1

NL MANAGER OF THE YEAR

Manager	1st	2nd	3rd	Total
Joe Maddon, Cubs	18	11	1	124
Mike Matheny, Cardinals	9	12	6	87
Terry Collins, Mets	3	7	13	49
Clint Hurdle, Pirates			8	8
Bruce Bochy, Giants			1	1
Don Mattingly, Dodgers			1	1

GOLD GLOVE WINNERS

Selected by NL Managers

P—Zach Greinke, Dodgers
C—Yadier Molina, Cardinals
1B—Paul Goldschmidt, Diamondbacks
2B—Dee Gordon, Marlins
SS—Brandon Crawford, Giants
3B—Nolan Arenado, Rockies
LF—Starling Marte, Pirates
CF—A.J. Pollock, Diamondbacks
RF—Jason Heyward, Cardinals

GAMES
Anthony Rizzo, Chicago	160
Paul Goldschmidt, Arizona	159
Joey Votto, Cincinnati	158
7 players	157

AT-BATS
Todd Frazier, Cincinnati	619
Nolan Arenado, Colorado	616
Dee Gordon, Miami	615
Charlie Blackmon, Colorado	614
Nick Markakis, Atlanta	612

PLATE APPEARANCES
Anthony Rizzo, Chicago	701
Paul Goldschmidt, Arizona	695
Joey Votto, Cincinnati	695
Dexter Fowler, Chicago	690
Nick Markakis, Atlanta	686

RUNS
Bryce Harper, Washington	118
A.J. Pollock, Arizona	111
Paul Goldschmidt, Arizona	103
Dexter Fowler, Chicago	102
Matt Carpenter, St. Louis	101

HITS
Dee Gordon, Miami	205
A.J. Pollock, Arizona	192
Paul Goldschmidt, Arizona	182
Nick Markakis, Atlanta	181
2 players,	177

TOTAL BASES
Nolan Arenado, Colorado	354
Bryce Harper, Washington	338
Paul Goldschmidt, Arizona	323
Todd Frazier, Cincinnati	308
A.J. Pollock, Arizona	303

DOUBLES
Matt Carpenter, St. Louis	44
Nolan Arenado, Colorado	43
Todd Frazier, Cincinnati	43
A.J. Pollock, Arizona	39
5 players	38

TRIPLES
David Peralta, Arizona	10
Charlie Blackmon, Colorado	9
Dexter Fowler, Chicago	8
Dee Gordon, Miami	8
3 players	7

EXTRA-BASE HITS
Nolan Arenado, Colorado	89
Bryce Harper, Washington	81
Todd Frazier, Cincinnati	79
Matt Carpenter, St. Louis	75
Paul Goldschmidt, Arizona	73

HOME RUNS
Nolan Arenado, Colorado	42
Bryce Harper, Washington	42
Carlos Gonzalez, Colorado	40
Todd Frazier, Cincinnati	35
Paul Goldschmidt, Arizona	33

RUNS BATTED IN
Nolan Arenado, Colorado	130
Paul Goldschmidt, Arizona	110
Anthony Rizzo, Chicago	101
Matt Kemp, San Diego	100
2 players	99

SACRIFICES
Julio Teheran, Atlanta	14
Tom Koehler, Miami	12
Shelby Miller, Atlanta	11

Paul Goldschmidt

3 players	10

SACRIFICE FLIES
Nolan Arenado, Colorado	11
Ryan Zimmerman, Washington	10
4 players	9

HIT BY PITCH
Anthony Rizzo, Chicago	30
Starling Marte, Pittsburgh	19

Jung Ho Kang, Pittsburgh	17
Kolten Wong, St. Louis	15
Lucas Duda, New York	14

WALKS
Joey Votto, Cincinnati	143
Bryce Harper, Washington	124
Paul Goldschmidt, Arizona	118
Andrew McCutchen, Pittsburgh	98

Zack Greinke

Joc Pederson, Los Angeles	92

STOLEN BASES
Dee Gordon, Miami	58
Billy Hamilton, Cincinnati	57
Charlie Blackmon, Colorado	43
A.J. Pollock, Arizona	39
Starling Marte, Pittsburgh	30

CAUGHT STEALING
Dee Gordon, Miami	20
Charlie Blackmon, Colorado	13
4 players	10

STOLEN-BASE PERCENTAGE
Billy Hamilton, Cincinnati	.880
Jason Heyward, St. Louis	.880
DJ LeMahieu, Colorado	.880
Brandon Phillips, Cincinnati	.880
Ryan Braun, Milwaukee	.860

STRIKEOUTS
Kris Bryant, Chicago	199
Ian Desmond, Washington	187
Joc Pederson, Los Angeles	170
Justin Upton, San Diego	159
Michael Taylor, Washington	158

TOUGHEST TO STRIKE OUT (AT-BATS PER STRIKEOUT)
Daniel Murphy, New York	13.13
Andrelton Simmons, Atlanta	11.15
Buster Posey, San Francisco	10.71
Yangervis Solarte, San Diego	9.39
Ender Inciarte, Arizona	9.03

GROUNDED INTO DOUBLE PLAYS
Yunel Escobar, Washington	24
Jhonny Peralta, St. Louis	23
Aramis Ramirez, Mil/Pitt.	23
Matt Duffy, San Francisco	22
Adrian Gonzalez, Los Angeles	21

MULTI-HIT GAMES
Dee Gordon, Miami	59
A.J. Pollock, D-backs	55
Joey Votto, Reds	55
Nick Markakis, Braves	52
Paul Goldschmidt, D-backs	51

ON-BASE PERCENTAGE
Bryce Harper, Washington	.460
Joey Votto, Cincinnati	.459
Paul Goldschmidt, Arizona	.435
Andrew McCutchen, Pitt.	.401
Anthony Rizzo, Chicago	.387

SLUGGING PERCENTAGE
Bryce Harper, Washington	.649
Nolan Arenado, Colorado	.575
Paul Goldschmidt, Arizona	.570
Joey Votto, Cincinnati	.541
Carlos Gonzalez, Colorado	.540

ON-BASE PLUS SLUGGING
Bryce Harper, Washington	1.109
Paul Goldschmidt, Arizona	1.005
Joey Votto, Cincinnati	1.000
Anthony Rizzo, Chicago	.899
Nolan Arenado, Colorado	.898

PITCHING

WINS
Jake Arrieta, Chicago	22
Gerrit Cole, Pittsburgh	19
Zack Greinke, Los Angeles	19
Madison Bumgarner, , S.F	18
Michael Wacha, St. Louis	17

DEPARTMENT LEADERS

Andrelton Simmons

CLIFF WELCH

LOSSES

Shelby Miller, Atlanta	17
Andrew Cashner, San Diego	16
Aaron Harang, Philadelphia	15
Ian Kennedy, San Diego	15
2 players	14

GAMES

Kevin Siegrist, St. Louis	81
Mark Melancon, Pittsburgh	78
Javier Lopez, San Francisco	77
Tony Watson, Pittsburgh	77
5 players	76

GAMES STARTED

9 players	33

GAMES FINISHED

Jeurys Familia, New York	65
Mark Melancon, Pittsburgh	63
Trevor Rosenthal, St. Louis	57
Santiago Casilla, San Francisco	55
Francisco Rodriguez, Milwaukee	55

COMPLETE GAMES

Jake Arrieta, Chicago	4
Madison Bumgarner, , S. F	4
Clayton Kershaw, L.A.	4
Max Scherzer, Washington	4
4 players	2

SHUTOUTS

Jake Arrieta, Chicago	3
Clayton Kershaw, L.A.	3
Max Scherzer, Washington	3
Madison Bumgarner, S.F.	2
Shelby Miller, Atlanta	2

SAVES

Mark Melancon, Pittsburgh	51
Trevor Rosenthal, St. Louis	48
Jeurys Familia, New York	43
Craig Kimbrel, San Diego	39

INNINGS PITCHED

Clayton Kershaw, L.A.	233
Jake Arrieta, Chicago	229
Max Scherzer, Washington	229
Zack Greinke, L.A.	223
Madison Bumgarner, S.F.	218

HITS ALLOWED

Bartolo Colon, New York	217
John Lackey, St. Louis	211
Jordan Zimmermann, Wash.	204
Andrew Cashner, San Diego	200
Alex Wood, Atlanta/L.A.	198

RUNS ALLOWED

Andrew Cashner, San Diego	111
La Rosa Rubby De, Arizona	103
Matt Garza, Milwaukee	102
Kyle Kendrick, Colorado	102
Aaron Harang, Philadelphia	100

HOME RUNS ALLOWED

Kyle Kendrick, Colorado	33
James Shields, San Diego	33
Rubby De La Rosa, Arizona	32
Dan Haren, Miami, Chicago	31
Ian Kennedy, San Diego	31

WALKS

Tyson Ross, San Diego	84
James Shields, San Diego	81
Tom Koehler, Miami	77
Shelby Miller, Atlanta	73
Julio Teheran, Atlanta	73

WALKS PER NINE INNINGS

Bartolo Colon, New York	1.11
Max Scherzer, Washington	1.34
Madison Bumgarner, S.F.	1.61
Zack Greinke, L.A.	1.62
Clayton Kershaw, L.A.	1.62

HIT BATTERS

Chris Heston, San Francisco	13
Jimmy Nelson, Milwaukee	13
Charlie Morton, Pittsburgh	12
A.J. Burnett, Pittsburgh	11
Gerrit Cole, Pittsburgh	10

STRIKEOUTS

Clayton Kershaw, L.A.	301
Max Scherzer, Washington	276
Jake Arrieta, Chicago	236
Madison Bumgarner, S.F.	234
James Shields, San Diego	216

STRIKEOUTS PER NINE INNINGS

Clayton Kershaw, L.A.	11.64
Max Scherzer, Washington	10.86
Francisco Liriano, Pittsburgh	9.88
Tyson Ross, San Diego	9.73
Jacob deGrom, New York	9.66

STRIKEOUTS PER NINE INNINGS (RELIEVERS)

Aroldis Chapman, Cincinnati	15.74
Will Smith, Milwaukee	12.93
Ken Giles, Philadelphia	11.19
A.J. Ramos, Miami	11.13
Trevor Rosenthal, St. Louis	10.88

DOUBLE PLAYS

John Lackey, St. Louis	29
Chris Heston, San Francisco	26
Alex Wood, Atlanta/L.A.	25
Tom Koehler, Miami	24
Brett Anderson, Los Angeles	23

PICKOFFS

Clayton Kershaw, L.A.	9
Brett Anderson, Los Angeles	6
Chris Rusin, Colorado	5
Julio Teheran, Atlanta	5
Alex Wood, Atlanta/L.A.	5

WILD PITCHES

Tyson Ross, San Diego	14
David Hale, Colorado	11
Jimmy Nelson, Milwaukee	11
4 players	10

WALKS-PLUS-HITS PER INNING

Zack Greinke, L.A.	0.84
Jake Arrieta, Chicago	0.86
Clayton Kershaw, L.A.	0.88
Max Scherzer, Washington	0.92
Jacob deGrom, New York	0.98

OPPONENT AVERAGE

Jake Arrieta, Chicago	.185
Zack Greinke, Los Angeles	.187
Clayton Kershaw, Los Angeles	.194
Max Scherzer, Washington	.208
Jacob deGrom, New York	.215

WORST ERA

Aaron Harang, Philadelphia	4.86
Rubby De La Rosa, Arizona	4.67
Jeff Locke, Pittsburgh	4.49
Andrew Cashner, San Diego	4.34
Ian Kennedy, San Diego	4.28

FIELDING

PITCHER

PCT	10 players	1.000
PO	Jake Arrieta, Chicago	33
A	Jake Arrieta, Chicago	49
E	Tom Koehler, Miami	5
E	Shelby Miller, Atlanta	5
DP	Bartolo Colon, New York	6

CATCHER

PCT	Brayan Pena, Cincinnati	.999
PO	Yadier Molina, St. Louis	1064
A	Francisco Cervelli, Pittsburgh	82
E	Miguel Montero, Chicago	12
DP	Yadier Molina, St. Louis	9
CS	Derek Norris, San Diego	44
PB	Derek Norris, San Diego	13

FIRST BASE

PCT	Brandon Belt, San Francisco	.997
PO	Paul Goldschmidt, Arizona	1378
A	Joey Votto, Cincinnati	139
E	Pedro Alvarez, Pittsburgh	23
DP	Paul Goldschmidt, Arizona	129

SECOND BASE

PCT	Dee Gordon, Miami	0.992
PO	Kolten Wong, St. Louis	312
A	D.J. LeMahieu, Colorado	452
E	Kolten Wong, St. Louis	17
DP	D.J. LeMahieu, Colorado	120

THIRD BASE

PCT	Martin Prado, Miami	.976
PO	Nolan Arenado, Colorado	105
A	Nolan Arenado, Colorado	385
E	Todd Frazier, Cincinnati	19
DP	Nolan Arenado, Colorado	42

SHORTSTOP

PCT	Andrelton Simmons, Atlanta	.988
PO	Andrelton Simmons, Atlanta	235
A	Andrelton Simmons, Atlanta	444
E	Ian Desmond, Washington	27
DP	Andrelton Simmons, Atlanta	126

OUTFIELD

PCT	Marlon Byrd, Cincinnati, S.F.	1.000
PCT	Chris Coghlan, Chicago	1.000
PCT	Billy Hamilton, Cincinnati	1.000
PCT	Ichiro Suzuki, Miami	1.000
PO	A.J. Pollock, Arizona	347
A	Starling Marte, Pittsburgh	16
E	Gregory Polanco, Pittsburgh	8
E	Matt Kemp, San Diego	8
DP	Gregory Polanco, Pittsburgh	5

2015 POSTSEASON

The Royals celebrate their first World Series championship since 1985 at Citi Field in New York after dispatching the Mets in five games

Playing from behind no impediment for Royals

BY TOM HAUDRICOURT

They just kept coming at you.

"Never say die" is an overused credo in sports but it was an appropriate one for the tenacious Kansas City Royals after they came from behind in all four victories in dispatching the New York Mets in five games in the 2015 World Series.

The Royals' first championship in 30 years was bookended by a pair of extra-inning victories in which they erased deficits in the ninth inning to stun the Mets. New York ace Matt Harvey and closer Jeurys Familia couldn't hold a 2-0 lead in Game Five as Kansas City tied the game on a daring dash home by Eric Hosmer and went on to win, 7-2, in 12 innings.

All told, the Royals came from behind to win eight times in the postseason, showing a resolve born from their disappointing seven-game World Series defeat by San Francisco and Madison Bumgarner the previous fall.

"Never die, never-quit attitude," said center fielder Lorenzo Cain, who doubled in three runs in the decisive 12th inning. "We continue to push, no matter if it's not in our favor, continue to fight as a team."

Harvey, who became the center of an innings-pitched controversy late in the regular season, talked manager Terry Collins into going back out for the ninth inning with a 2-0 lead. But he walked Cain, who then scored on a double by Hosmer that sent Harvey from the game. Later in the inning, Hosmer dashed home from third base on an infield out, scoring the tying run in electrifying fashion as Mets first baseman Lucas Duda threw wildly to the plate.

"We knew we weren't going to go out quietly,"

said Hosmer.

That was evident from the first game, when Alex Gordon stunned the Mets with a game-tying home run in the ninth off the previously indomitable Familia. The Royals went on to win in 14 innings and New York never really recovered.

Had the Mets won Game Five to take the series back to Kansas City, who knows what might have happened? Instead, the Royals celebrated at Citi Field, then took the big trophy back home to party with long-suffering fans who stuck with the club during a long rebuilding program.

Perhaps the Royals were destined to win after barely bowing to Bumgarner's excellence the first time around. Christian Colon, who had no post-season at-bats prior to the 12th inning of Game Five, singled in the go-ahead run, a stunning hit that immediately went into club lore.

Kansas City's starter in that game Edinson Volquez, had just returned from the funeral of his father in the Dominican Republic. He allowed a leadoff homer to Curtis Granderson but otherwise kept his team in the game, positioning the Royals for another of their trademark comebacks.

"To be able to win this is very, very special, with this group of guys," said manager Ned Yost, who patiently guided the Royals from years of despair to the title. "With their character, with their heart, with their passion, with the energy that they bring every single day, I mean, they leave everything on the field."

It was a disappointing end for the surprising Mets, who rode their young-stud pitching rotation into the Fall Classic. They simply couldn't suppress the constant pressure put on them by the Royals, including a couple of costly errors by second baseman Daniel Murphy, who had been the second coming of Babe Ruth in the earlier rounds.

Collins preferred to dwell on the Mets' unexpected run to the final round.

"I've done this for a long, long time and this is the most fun I've ever had in all the years," he said. "Tremendous season, all we had to deal with, tremendous guys to be around, great experience. I'm very proud of them."

Another Murphy Thwarts Cubs

As the NLCS began, the primary narrative was the Chicago Cubs' quest to erase their 107-year-old curse and not only make it to the World Series but win it. But the Mets, and in particular Murphy, had other ideas.

With Murphy homering in all four games to

MORRIS FOSTOFF

Daniel Murphy homered in all four games of the NLCS against the Cubs

set a record by going deep in six consecutive post-season games, the Mets swept the Cubs out of the playoffs in dominating fashion. Young pitching won out over young hitting as New York's hard-throwing staff limited Chicago's homer-happy lineup to eight runs over the four games.

Harvey got the ball rolling for the Mets with a strong Game One start that resulted in a 4-2 victory. That loss set up a crucial Game Two for the Cubs with indomitable ace Jake Arrieta taking the mound. If the Mets beat him, Chicago's 2-0 hole in the series would look even worse.

New York went right to work against Arrieta, scoring three first-inning runs, including a two-run homer by Murphy. It was hard-throwing Noah Syndergaard who played the role of ace on this night, tossing 5 ⅔ solid innings, allowing one run while striking out nine.

Bringing the NLCS back to Wrigley Field and an energized crowd, the Cubs knew they had to win Game Two to have any real chance. But Murphy and righthander Jacob deGrom did not cooperate and the Mets came away with a 5-2 victory that put them within a game of their first World Series appearance in 29 years. Making it more painful for the Cubs, the go-ahead run scored on a strikeout/wild pitch by reliever Trevor Cahill.

Only one team in MLB history had escaped from a 3-0 hole in a seven-game postseason series

– the 2004 Boston Red Sox, who shocked the New York Yankees and went on to snap "The Curse of the Bambino" by winning their first World Series since 1918. The architect of that team was Theo Epstein, now president of the Cubs.

"Rumor is it has been done before," said Epstein. But not this time. Duda snapped out of a postseason drought with a three-run homer in the first inning off Jason Hammel and doubled in two more runs in the second as New York bolted to a 6-0 lead and never looked back in rolling to an 8-3 victory.

The ALCS between defending champion Kansas City and Toronto was far more competitive. The Royals appeared to have a sweep on their minds by taking the first two games at home, 5-0 behind Volquez's six shutout innings and 6-3 with a remarkable rally in Game Two.

The Blue Jays appeared in great shape in the second game with a 3-0 lead in the seventh inning and ace David Price cruising with a one-hitter and 18 hitters in a row retired. But the never-quit Royals put together a five-run rally to snatch away the game, an outburst that began when Ben Zobrist's pop fly to right dropped between second baseman Ryan Goins and right fielder Jose Bautista.

Heading back home to Toronto, the Blue Jays were determined not to fall into a 3-0 hole. A team known for its offense bolted to a 9-2 lead after three innings and held on for an 11-8 victory to get back in the series. Troy Tulowitzki and Josh Donaldson homered during a six-run third inning that made for a short day for Cueto.

It was Kansas City that did all of the slugging in Game Four, sending knuckleballer R.A. Dickey

to an early shower in a 14-2 rout. Things got so ugly in the late innings for the Blue Jays, they used utility man Cliff Pennington to pitch the ninth inning, becoming the first team to send a position player to the mound in a postseason game.

On the brink of elimination, Toronto stayed alive in Game Five as journeyman pitcher Marco Estrada pitched sterling ball into the eighth inning of a 7-1 victory. That outcome sent the series back to Kansas City, where the Royals needed to win just once to make it back to the World Series.

Bautista tried to single-handedly stave off elimination with a pair of home runs but it wasn't enough. The Royals scored the decisive run when Cain channeled Enos Slaughter and scored all the way from first base on a single by Hosmer in the eighth inning.

Never Give Up

Before the postseason began, Yankee legend Yogi Berra passed away at age 90. A few weeks later, his most famous saying, "It ain't over until it's over," became the theme of the Division Series round in the American League.

When the Texas Rangers took the first two games of the best-of-five series in Toronto, folks assumed the Blue Jays were down after waiting 22 years to return to the playoffs. And when Houston took a 6-2 lead into the eighth inning of Game Four with a two-games-to-one lead over defending AL champion Kansas City, the Royals' quest to repeat appeared doomed.

Wrong on both counts. The Blue Jays went to Texas and won two games, bringing them back home to eliminate the Rangers to the delight of a long-suffering fan base. KC staged an improbable

AMERICAN LEAGUE CHAMPIONS, 1997–2015

American League postseason results in Wild Card Era, 1995-present, where (*) denotes wild card playoff entrant.

YEAR	CHAMPIONSHIP SERIES	ALCS MVP	DIVISION SERIES 1	DIVISION SERIES 2
2015	Kansas City 4, Toronto 2	Alcides Escobar, ss, Kansas City	Kansas City 3, *Houston 2	Toronto 3, Texas 2
2014	Kansas City* 4, Baltimore 0	Lorenzo Cain, of, Kansas City	Kansas City 3, Los Angeles 0	Baltimore 3, Detroit 0
2013	Boston 4, Detroit 2	Koji Uehara, rhp, Boston	Boston 3, Tampa Bay* 1	Detroit, 3 Oakland 2
2012	Detroit 4, New York 0	Delmon Young, of, Detroit	New York 3, Baltimore* 2	Detroit 3, Oakland 2
2011	Texas 4, Detroit 2	Nelson Cruz, of, Texas	Detroit 3, New York 2	Texas 3, Tampa Bay* 1
2010	Texas 4, New York 2	Josh Hamilton, of, Texas	Texas 3, Tampa Bay 2	New York* 3, Minnesota 0
2009	New York 4, Los Angeles 2	C.C. Sabathia, lhp, New York	New York 3, Minnesota 0	Los Angeles 3, Boston* 0
2008	Tampa Bay 4, Boston 3	Matt Garza, rhp, Tampa Bay	Boston* 3, Los Angeles 1	Tampa Bay 3, Chicago 1
2007	Boston 4, Cleveland 3	Josh Beckett, rhp, Boston	Boston 3, Los Angeles 0	Cleveland 3, New York* 1
2006	Detroit 4, Oakland 0	Placido Polanco, 2b, Detroit	Detroit* 3, New York 1	Oakland 3, Minnesota 0
2005	Chicago 4, Los Angeles 1	Paul Konerko, 1b, Chicago	Chicago 3, Boston* 0	Los Angeles 3, New York 2
2004	Boston 4, New York 3	David Ortiz, dh, Boston	Boston* 3, Anaheim 0	New York 3, Minnesota 1
2003	New York 4, Boston 3	Mariano Rivera, rhp, New York	New York 3, Minnesota 1	Boston* 3, Oakland 2
2002	Anaheim 4, Minnesota 1	Adam Kennedy, 2b, Anaheim	Anaheim* 3, New York 1	Minnesota 3, Oakland 2
2001	New York 4, Seattle 1	Andy Pettitte, lhp, New York	Seattle 3, Cleveland 2	New York 3, Oakland* 2
2000	New York 4, Seattle 2	David Justice, of, New York	New York 3, Oakland 2	Seattle* 3, Chicago 0
1999	New York 4, Boston 1	Orlando Hernandez, rhp, New York	Boston* 3, Cleveland 2	New York 3, Texas 0
1998	New York 4, Cleveland 2	David Wells, lhp, New York	Cleveland 3, Boston* 1	New York 3, Texas 0
1997	Cleveland 4, Baltimore 2	Marquis Grissom, of, Cleveland	Baltimore 3, New York* 2	Baltimore 3, Seattle 1

rally to pull out Game Four in Houston and also returned home to claim the series in front of their adoring fans.

Both series turned on bizarre innings in which everything that could go wrong did for the Astros and Rangers, ending dreams of a Lone Star State shootout in the ALCS. A previously reliable Houston bullpen caved in the eighth inning of Game Four against the Royals, allowing five runs in what became a 9-6 loss.

The Royals were known for grinding out at-bats and keeping the line moving, and that's exactly what they did against relievers Will Harris, Tony Sipp and Luke Gregerson. A big play during the rally was a two-run error by standout rookie shortstop Carlos Correa, who couldn't handle a high hop on a ball up the middle by Kendrys Morales that was deflected by Sipp.

As so often happens when a team blows a seemingly safe lead, the Astros bowed out meekly in Game Five by a 7-2 score. Houston's resurgence was a big storyline in the AL but that didn't soothe the hurt of letting the chance to advance slip away.

Things got even crazier in the seventh inning of Game Five in the other series. In the top of the inning, Texas scored the go-ahead run when Blue Jays catcher Russell Martin struck the bat of Shin-Soo Choo merely throwing the ball back to the pitcher, allowing Rougned Odor to come home from third base.

Toronto put the game under protest but recovered from that bizarre play when the Rangers self-destructed in the bottom of the inning. Three consecutive infield errors loaded the bases with no outs and set the stage for the decisive four-run rally.

Bautista capped the rally with a three-run home run, punctuating it with a dramatic bat flip toward the Texas dugout that prompted a benches-clearing altercation and made him the talk of baseball.

"It's the most emotionally charged game I've ever played in," Bautista said afterward.

There were no such shenanigans in the NLDS round but that didn't make it any less compelling when the upstart Cubs eliminated division winner St. Louis and the surprising Mets overcame the dynamic duo of Clayton Kershaw and Zack Grienke to oust the Los Angeles Dodgers.

Despite having by far the highest payroll in the game, the Dodgers again failed to make it to the World Series, an outcome that led to manager Don Mattingly's exodus.

Quick Outs

You'll have to excuse the Pittsburgh Pirates if they're not huge fans of the one-and-done wild-card format. For the second year in a row, they were blanked by one of the best pitchers in the game, leading to a quick exit from the playoff scene.

In 2014, it was Madison Bumgarner. This time, it was Cubs No. 1 pitcher Arrieta.

"Sometimes, you draw a tough bull," said Pirates manager Clint Hurdle. "Two years in a row, we've drawn a tough bull."

On the AL side, the New York Yankees, who limped into the No. 1 wild card berth amid a slew of injuries, had no gas left in their tank when the upstart Houston Astros came to town for their one-game showdown.

Houston played its ace card and Astros ace Dallas Keuchel responded with six shutout innings in a 3-0 victory.

NATIONAL LEAGUE CHAMPIONS, 1997–2015

National League postseason results in Wild Card Era, 1995-present, where (*) denotes wild card playoff entrant.

YEAR	CHAMPIONSHIP SERIES	NLCS MVP	DIVISION SERIES	DIVISION SERIES
2015	New York 4, Chicago 0	Daniel Murphy, 2b, New York	New York 3, Los Angeles 2	Chicago 3, St. Louis 1
2014	San Francisco* 4, St. Louis 1	Madison Bumgarner, lhp, San Francisco	San Francisco 3, Washington 1	St. Louis 3, Los Angeles 1
2013	St. Louis 4, Los Angeles 2	Michael Wacha, rhp, St. Louis	St. Louis 3, Pittsburgh* 2	Los Angeles 3, Atlanta 1
2012	San Francisco 4, St. Louis 3	Marco Scutaro, 2b, San Francisco	St. Louis* 3, Washington 2	San Francisco 3, Cincinnati 2
2011	St. Louis 4, Milwaukee 2	David Freese, 3b, St. Louis	St. Louis* 3, Philadelphia 2	Milwaukee 3, Arizona 2
2010	San Francisco 4, Philadelphia 2	Cody Ross, of, San Francisco	Philadelphia 3, Cincinnati 0	San Francisco 3, Atlanta* 1
2009	Philadelphia 4, Los Angeles 1	Ryan Howard, 1b, Philadelphia	Los Angeles 3, St. Louis 0	Philadelphia 3, Colorado* 1
2008	Philadelphia 4, Los Angeles 1	Cole Hamels, lhp, Philadelphia	Los Angeles 3, Chicago 0	Philadelphia 3, Milwaukee* 1
2007	Colorado 4, Arizona 0	Matt Holliday, of, Colorado	Arizona 3, Chicago 0	Colorado* 3, Philadelphia 0
2006	St. Louis 4, New York 3	Jeff Suppan, rhp, St. Louis	New York 3, Los Angeles* 0	St. Louis 3, San Diego 1
2005	Houston 4, St. Louis 2	Roy Oswalt, rhp, Houston	St. Louis 3, San Diego 0	Houston* 3, Atlanta 1
2004	St. Louis 4, Houston 3	Albert Pujols, 1b, St. Louis	St. Louis 3, Los Angeles 1	Houston* 3, Atlanta 2
2003	Florida 4, Chicago 3	Ivan Rodriguez, c, Florida	Florida* 3, San Francisco 1	Chicago 3, Atlanta 2
2002	San Francisco 4, St. Louis 1	Benito Santiago, c, San Francisco	San Francisco* 3, Atlanta 2	St. Louis 3, Arizona 0
2001	Arizona 4, Atlanta 1	Craig Counsell, ss, Arizona	Atlanta 3, Houston 0	Arizona 3, St. Louis* 2
2000	New York 4, St. Louis 1	Mike Hampton, lhp, New York	St. Louis 3, Atlanta 0	New York* 3, San Francisco 1
1999	Atlanta 4, New York 2	Eddie Perez, c, Atlanta	Atlanta 3, Houston 1	New York* 3, Arizona 1
1998	San Diego 4, Atlanta 2	Sterling Hitchcock, lhp, San Diego	Atlanta 3, Chicago* 0	San Diego 3, Houston 1
1997	Florida 4, Atlanta 2	Livan Hernandez, rhp, Florida	Florida* 3, San Francisco 0	Atlanta 3, Houston 0

MAJOR LEAGUES

Year	Winner	Loser	Result
1903	Boston (AL)	Pittsburgh (NL)	5-3
1904	NO SERIES		
1905	New York (NL)	Philadelphia (AL)	4-1
1906	Chicago (AL)	Chicago (NL)	4-2
1907	Chicago (NL)	Detroit (AL)	4-0
1908	Chicago (NL)	Detroit (AL)	4-1
1909	Pittsburgh (NL)	Detroit (AL)	4-3
1910	Philadelphia (AL)	Chicago (NL)	4-1
1911	Philadelphia (AL)	New York (NL)	4-2
1912	Boston (AL)	New York (NL)	4-3-1
1913	Philadelphia (AL)	New York (NL)	4-1
1914	Boston (NL)	Philadelphia (AL)	4-0
1915	Boston (AL)	Philadelphia (NL)	4-1
1916	Boston (AL)	Brooklyn (NL)	4-1
1917	Chicago (AL)	New York (NL)	4-2
1918	Boston (AL)	Chicago (NL)	4-2
1919	Cincinnati (NL)	Chicago (AL)	5-3
1920	Cleveland (AL)	Brooklyn (NL)	5-2
1921	New York (NL)	New York (AL)	5-3
1922	New York (NL)	New York (AL)	4-0
1923	New York (AL)	New York (NL)	4-2
1924	Washington (AL)	New York (NL)	4-3
1925	Pittsburgh (NL)	Washington (AL)	4-3
1926	St. Louis (NL)	New York (AL)	4-3
1927	New York (AL)	Pittsburgh (NL)	4-0
1928	New York (AL)	St. Louis (NL)	4-0
1929	Philadelphia (AL)	Chicago (NL)	4-1
1930	Philadelphia (AL)	St. Louis (NL)	4-2
1931	St. Louis (NL)	Philadelphia (AL)	4-3
1932	New York (AL)	Chicago (NL)	4-0
1933	New York (NL)	Washington (AL)	4-1
1934	St. Louis (NL)	Detroit (AL)	4-3
1935	Detroit (AL)	Chicago (NL)	4-2
1936	New York (AL)	New York (NL)	4-2
1937	New York (AL)	New York (NL)	4-1
1938	New York (AL)	Chicago (NL)	4-0
1939	New York (AL)	Cincinnati (NL)	4-0
1940	Cincinnati (NL)	Detroit (AL)	4-3
1941	New York (AL)	Brooklyn (NL)	4-1
1942	St. Louis (NL)	New York (AL)	4-1
1943	New York (AL)	St. Louis (NL)	4-1
1944	St. Louis (NL)	St. Louis (AL)	4-2
1945	Detroit (AL)	Chicago (NL)	4-3
1946	St. Louis (NL)	Boston (AL)	4-3
1947	New York (AL)	Brooklyn (NL)	4-3
1948	Cleveland (AL)	Boston (NL)	4-2
1949	New York (AL)	Brooklyn (NL)	4-1
1950	New York (AL)	Philadelphia (NL)	4-0
1951	New York (AL)	New York (NL)	4-2
1952	New York (AL)	Brooklyn (NL)	4-3
1953	New York (AL)	Brooklyn (NL)	4-2
1954	New York (NL)	Cleveland (AL)	4-0
1955	Brooklyn (NL)	New York (AL)	4-3
1956	New York (AL)	Brooklyn (NL)	4-3
1957	Milwaukee (NL)	New York (AL)	4-3
1958	New York (AL)	Milwaukee (NL)	4-3
1959	Los Angeles (NL)	Chicago (AL)	4-2
1960	Pittsburgh (NL)	New York (AL)	4-3
1961	New York (AL)	Cincinnati (NL)	4-1
1962	New York (AL)	San Francisco (NL)	4-3
1963	Los Angeles (NL)	New York (AL)	4-0
1964	St. Louis (NL)	New York (AL)	4-3
1965	Los Angeles (NL)	Minnesota (AL)	4-3
1966	Baltimore (AL)	Los Angeles (NL)	4-0
1967	St. Louis (NL)	Boston (AL)	4-3

The Royals won their second World Series

Year	Winner	Loser	Result
1968	Detroit (AL)	St. Louis (NL)	4-3
1969	New York (NL)	Baltimore (AL)	4-1
1970	Baltimore (AL)	Cincinnati (NL)	4-1
1971	Pittsburgh (NL)	Baltimore (AL)	4-3
1972	Oakland (AL)	Cincinnati (NL)	4-3
1973	Oakland (AL)	New York (NL)	4-3
1974	Oakland (AL)	Los Angeles (NL)	4-1
1975	Cincinnati (NL)	Boston (AL)	4-3
1976	Cincinnati (NL)	New York (AL)	4-0
1977	New York (AL)	Los Angeles (NL)	4-2
1978	New York (AL)	Los Angeles (NL)	4-2
1979	Pittsburgh (NL)	Baltimore (AL)	4-3
1980	Philadelphia (NL)	Kansas City (AL)	4-2
1981	Los Angeles (NL)	New York (AL)	4-2
1982	St. Louis (NL)	Milwaukee (AL)	4-3
1983	Baltimore (AL)	Philadelphia (NL)	4-1
1984	Detroit (AL)	San Diego (NL)	4-1
1985	Kansas City (AL)	St. Louis (NL)	4-3
1986	New York (NL)	Boston (AL)	4-3
1987	Minnesota (AL)	St. Louis (NL)	4-3
1988	Los Angeles (NL)	Oakland (AL)	4-1
1989	Oakland (AL)	San Francisco (NL)	4-0
1990	Cincinnati (NL)	Oakland (AL)	4-0
1991	Minnesota (AL)	Atlanta (NL)	4-3
1992	Toronto (AL)	Atlanta (NL)	4-2
1993	Toronto (AL)	Philadelphia (NL)	4-2
1994	NO SERIES		
1995	Atlanta (NL)	Cleveland (AL)	4-2
1996	New York (AL)	Atlanta (NL)	4-2
1997	Florida (NL)	Cleveland (AL)	4-3
1998	New York (AL)	San Diego (NL)	4-0
1999	New York (AL)	Atlanta (NL)	4-0
2000	New York (AL)	New York (NL)	4-1
2001	Arizona (NL)	New York (AL)	4-3
2002	Anaheim (AL)	San Francisco (NL)	4-3
2003	Florida (NL)	New York (AL)	4-2
2004	Boston (AL)	St. Louis (NL)	4-0
2005	Chicago (AL)	Houston (NL)	4-0
2006	St. Louis (NL)	Detroit (AL)	4-1
2007	Boston (AL)	Colorado (NL)	4-0
2008	Philadelphia (NL)	Tampa Bay (AL)	4-1
2009	New York (AL)	Philadelphia (NL)	4-2
2010	San Francisco (NL)	Texas (AL)	4-1
2011	St. Louis (NL)	Texas (AL)	4-3
2012	San Francisco (NL)	Detroit (AL)	4-0
2013	Boston (AL)	St. Louis (NL)	4-2
2014	San Francisco (NL)	Kansas City (AL)	4-3
2015	Kansas City (AL)	New York (NL)	4-1

WORLD SERIES BOX SCORES

GAME ONE October 27, 2015
KANSAS CITY 5, NEW YORK 4

NEW YORK	AB	R	H	RBI	BB	SO	LOB	AVG
Granderson, RF	5	1	1	1	2	0	0	.200
Wright, 3B	7	0	2	0	0	2	4	.286
Murphy, 2B	7	1	2	0	0	2	0	.286
Cespedes, CF-LF	6	1	1	0	0	2	3	.167
Duda, 1B	6	0	2	0	0	3	0	.333
d'Arnaud, C	6	0	1	1	0	2	2	.167
Conforto, LF	2	0	0	1	0	0	2	.000
Lagares, CF	3	1	2	0	0	1	0	.667
Flores, SS	4	0	0	0	1	0	3	.000
Johnson, DH	1	0	0	0	0	0	0	.000
a-Cuddyer, PH-DH	3	0	0	0	0	3	2	.000
b-Nieuwenhuis, PH-DH	1	0	0	0	0	0	1	.000
TOTALS	51	4	11	3	3	15	17	

KANSAS CITY	AB	R	H	RBI	BB	SO	LOB	AVG
Escobar, A, SS	6	2	1	1	0	0	2	.167
Zobrist, 2B	6	1	3	0	1	0	0	.500
Cain, CF	6	1	1	0	1	2	3	.167
Hosmer, 1B	3	0	0	2	2	2	1	.000
Morales, DH	3	0	0	0	1	1	2	.000
1-Dyson, PR-DH	2	0	0	0	0	0	3	.000
Moustakas, 3B	6	0	2	1	0	0	2	.333
Perez, S, C	6	0	2	0	0	0	2	.333
Gordon, LF	5	1	1	1	1	2	2	.200
Rios, RF	3	0	0	0	0	0	2	.000
Orlando, RF	3	0	1	0	0	0	1	.333
TOTALS	49	5	11	5	6	7	20	

New York	000	111	010	000	00—4		
Kansas City	100	002	001	000	01—5		

a-Struck out for Johnson in the 7th. b-Popped out for Cuddyer in the 13th.
1-Ran for Morales in the 8th
2B: Zobrist 2. HR: Granderson, Escobar, Gordon. New York LOB: 11. Kansas City LOB: 13. SB: Lagares, Cain. E: Wright, Hosmer.

NEW YORK	IP	H	R	ER	BB	SO	HR	ERA
Harvey	6	5	3	3	2	2	1	4.50
Reed	1	0	0	0	0	0	0	0.00
Clippard	2/3	1	0	0	1	2	0	0.00
Familia	1 1/3	1	1	1	0	0	1	6.75
Niese	2	1	0	0	0	3	0	0.00
Colon, B (L)	2 1/3	3	1	0	3	0	0	0.00

KANSAS CITY	IP	H	R	ER	BB	SO	HR	ERA
Volquez	6	6	3	3	1	3	1	4.50
Duffy	2/3	0	0	0	0	1	0	0.00
Herrera, K	1 1/3	3	1	0	0	2	0	0.00
Hochevar	1	1	0	0	0	0	0	0.00
Davis, W	1	0	0	0	0	3	0	0.00
Madson	1	1	0	0	0	2	0	0.00
Young (W)	3	0	0	0	1	4	0	0.00

Game Scores: Harvey 50, Volquez 50. IBB: Zobrist (by Colon), Hosmer (by Colon), Cain (by Colon). HBP: Johnson (by Volquez).

GAME TWO Oct. 28, 2015
KANSAS CITY 7, NEW YORK METS 1

NEW YORK	AB	R	H	RBI	BB	SO	LOB	AVG
Granderson, RF	3	0	0	0	1	0	0	.125
Wright, 3B	4	0	0	0	0	0	1	.182
Murphy, 2B	2	1	0	0	2	2	0	.222
Cespedes, LF	4	0	0	0	0	1	3	.100
Duda, 1B	3	0	2	1	0	0	0	.444
d'Arnaud, C	3	0	0	0	0	0	3	.111
Conforto, DH	3	0	0	0	0	1	0	.000
Flores, SS	3	0	0	0	0	0	0	.000
Lagares, CF	3	0	0	0	0	0	0	.333
TOTALS	28	1	2	1	3	4	7	

KANSAS CITY	AB	R	H	RBI	BB	SO	LOB	AVG
Escobar, A, SS	5	1	2	2	0	0	1	.273
Zobrist, 2B	5	0	0	0	0	0	3	.273
Cain, CF	4	0	0	0	1	0	4	.100
Hosmer, 1B	4	1	2	2	0	0	1	.286
Morales, DH	4	0	1	0	0	1	3	.143
Moustakas, 3B	3	1	2	1	1	0	0	.444
Perez, S, C	4	1	1	0	0	0	5	.300
Gordon, LF	2	2	1	1	2	0	0	.286
Rios, RF	3	1	1	0	0	1	1	.167
Orlando, RF	0	0	0	1	0	0	0	.333
TOTALS	34	7	10	7	4	3	18	

New York	000	100	000—1	
Kansas City	000	040	03x—7	

2B: Perez, S (1, Niese), Gordon (1, Niese). 3B: Escobar, A (1, Reed). New York LOB: 3. Kansas City LOB: 8. E: Duda.

NEW YORK	IP	H	R	ER	BB	SO	HR	ERA
deGrom (L)	5	6	4	4	3	2	0	7.20
Robles	1	0	0	0	0	0	0	0.00
Niese	1	3	3	3	1	1	0	9.00
Reed	1/3	1	0	0	0	0	0	0.00
Gilmartin	2/3	0	0	0	0	0	0	0.00

KANSAS CITY	IP	H	R	ER	BB	SO	HR	ERA
Cueto (W, 1-0)	9	2	1	1	3	4	0	1.00

Niese pitched to 3 batters in the 8th. Game Scores: deGrom 38, Cueto 80.

GAME THREE Oct. 30, 2015
NEW YORK 9, KANSAS CITY 3

KANSAS CITY	AB	R	H	RBI	BB	SO	LOB	AVG
Escobar, A, SS	4	0	1	0	0	2	0	.267
Zobrist, 2B	4	1	1	0	0	0	1	.267
Cain, CF	4	0	1	0	0	1	0	.143
Hosmer, 1B	4	0	0	1	0	1	1	.182
Moustakas, 3B	4	0	1	0	0	0	1	.385
Perez, S, C	3	1	1	0	1	0	0	.308
Gordon, LF	3	0	1	0	1	2	0	.300
Rios, RF	3	1	1	1	0	0	3	.222
Herrera, K, P	0	0	0	0	0	0	0	.000
Madson, P	0	0	0	0	0	0	0	.000
Medlen, P	0	0	0	0	0	0	0	.000
b-Morales, PH	1	0	0	0	0	0	0	.125
Ventura, P	0	0	0	0	0	0	0	.000
Duffy, P	0	0	0	0	0	0	0	.000
a-Mondesi, PH	1	0	0	0	0	1	0	.000
Hochevar, P	0	0	0	0	0	0	0	.000
Morales, F, P	0	0	0	0	0	0	0	.000
Orlando, RF	1	0	0	0	0	0	0	.250
TOTALS	32	3	7	2	2	7	6	

NY METS	AB	R	H	RBI	BB	SO	LOB	AVG
Granderson, RF	5	3	2	2	0	0	4	.231
Wright, 3B	5	1	2	4	0	2	0	.250
Murphy, 2B	4	0	0	0	1	1	0	.154
Cespedes, CF-LF	3	0	1	1	0	1	0	.154
Duda, 1B	4	1	1	0	0	2	3	.385
d'Arnaud, C	4	0	2	0	0	0	0	.231
Conforto, LF	2	0	1	1	0	0	0	.143
b-Lagares, PH-CF	2	1	1	0	0	0	1	.375
Flores, SS	3	1	0	0	0	0	0	.000
Syndergaard, P	2	1	1	0	0	1	2	.500
c-Uribe, PH	1	1	1	1	0	0	0	1.000
Reed, P	0	0	0	0	0	0	0	.000
d-Nieuwenhuis, PH	1	0	0	0	0	1	1	.000
Clippard, P	0	0	0	0	0	0	0	.000
Familia, P	0	0	0	0	0	0	0	.000
TOTALS	36	9	12	9	1	8	14	

Kansas City	120	000	000—3
New York	202	104	00x—9

c-Struck out for Reed in the 7th.
2B: Zobrist, d'Arnaud. HR: Wright, Granderson. Kansas City LOB: 5. New York LOB: 6. SB: Escobar.

KANSAS CITY	IP	H	R	ER	BB	SO	HR	ERA
Ventura (L)	3 1/3	7	5	5	0	1	2	13.50
Duffy	2/3	0	0	0	0	1	0	0.00
Hochevar	1	1	0	0	0	2	0	0.00
Morales, F	1/3	2	4	4	0	0	0	108.00
Herrera, K	2/3	1	0	0	1	1	0	0.00
Madson	1	1	0	0	0	1	0	0.00
Medlen	1	0	0	0	2	0	0	0.00
NY METS	IP	H	R	ER	BB	SO	HR	ERA
Syndergaard (W)	6	7	3	3	2	6	0	4.50
Reed	1	0	0	0	0	0	0	0.00
Clippard	1	0	0	0	0	0	0	0.00
Familia	1	0	0	0	0	1	0	3.86

Game Scores: *Ventura 27, Syndergaard 50.* **HBP:** Flores (by Morales).

GAME FOUR *Oct. 31, 2015*
KANSAS CITY 5, NEW YORK 3

KANSAS CITY	AB	R	H	RBI	BB	SO	LOB	AVG
Escobar, A, SS	5	0	1	0	0	0	2	.250
Zobrist, 2B	3	2	1	0	1	2	1	.278
Cain, CF	3	1	1	1	1	1	0	.176
Hosmer, 1B	4	1	0	0	0	1	2	.133
Moustakas, 3B	4	0	1	1	0	0	1	.353
Perez, S, C	4	1	3	1	0	1	1	.412
Gordon, LF	4	0	1	1	0	0	3	.286
Rios, RF	3	0	0	0	0	0	1	.167
Orlando, RF	1	0	0	0	0	1	0	.200
Young, P	1	0	0	0	0	1	0	.000
a-Morales, PH	1	0	1	0	0	0	0	.222
Duffy, P	0	0	0	0	0	0	0	.000
Hochevar, P	0	0	0	0	0	0	0	.000
b-Dyson, PH	1	0	0	0	0	1	0	.000
Madson, P	0	0	0	0	0	0	0	.000
Davis, W, P	1	0	0	0	0	1	0	.000
TOTALS	35	5	9	4	2	9	11	
NY METS	AB	R	H	RBI	BB	SO	LOB	AVG
Granderson, RF	3	0	1	1	0	0	0	.250
Wright, 3B	3	0	0	0	1	1	0	.211
Murphy, 2B	4	0	1	0	0	1	1	.176
Cespedes, CF-LF	4	0	1	0	0	2	0	.176
Duda, 1B	4	0	0	0	0	1	2	.294
d'Arnaud, C	3	0	0	0	0	1	0	.188
Conforto, LF	3	2	2	2	0	1	0	.300
Clippard, P	0	0	0	0	0	0	0	.000
Familia, P	0	0	0	0	0	0	0	.000
Nieuwenhuis, CF	0	0	0	0	0	0	0	.000
Flores, SS	3	1	1	0	0	2	0	.077
Matz, P	1	0	0	0	0	0	0	.000
Niese, P	0	0	0	0	0	0	0	.000
Colon, B, P	0	0	0	0	0	0	0	.000
Reed, P	0	0	0	0	0	0	0	.000
Lagares, CF	0	0	0	0	0	0	0	.375
c-Johnson, PH	1	0	0	0	0	0	0	.000
Robles, P	0	0	0	0	0	0	0	.000
TOTALS	29	3	6	3	1	8	3	
Kansas City				000	011	030—5		
New York				002	010	000—3		

a-Singled for Young in the 5th. **b**-Struck out for Hochevar in the 7th. **c**-Flied out for Lagares in the 8th.

2B: Perez, Zobrist. **HR:** Conforto 2. **SAC:** Matz. **SF:** Granderson. **Kansas City LOB:** 5. **New York LOB:** 2. **SB:** Cain. **CS:** Granderson. **E:** Colon, B; Murphy.

KANSAS CITY	IP	H	R	ER	BB	SO	HR	ERA
Young	4	2	2	2	1	3	1	2.57
Duffy	1	2	1	1	0	1	1	3.86
Hochevar	1	0	0	0	0	0	0	0.00
Madson (W)	1	0	0	0	2	0	0	0.00
Davis, W (S)	2	2	0	0	2	0	0	0.00

NY METS	IP	H	R	ER	BB	SO	HR	ERA
Matz	5	7	2	2	0	5	0	3.60
Niese	2/3	0	0	0	0	1	0	7.36
Colon, B	1/3	0	0	0	0	1	0	0.00
Reed	1	0	0	0	0	1	0	0.00
Clippard (L)	1/3	0	2	2	2	0	0	9.00
Familia	2/3	2	1	0	0	0	0	3.00
Robles	1	0	0	0	0	2	0	0.00

Matz pitched to 2 batters in the 6th.
Game Scores: *Young 52, Matz 50.* **WP:** Young.

GAME FIVE *Nov. 1, 2015*
KANSAS CITY 7, NEW YORK 2

KANSAS CITY	AB	R	H	RBI	BB	SO	LOB	AVG
Escobar, A, SS	6	1	1	1	0	2	1	.231
Zobrist, 2B	5	1	1	0	1	0	0	.261
Cain, CF	5	1	2	3	1	2	1	.227
Hosmer, 1B	6	1	2	1	0	2	3	.190
Moustakas, 3B	6	0	1	0	0	1	3	.304
Perez, S, C	5	0	1	1	0	1	2	.364
1-Dyson, PR	0	1	0	0	0	0	0	.000
Butera, C	0	0	0	0	0	0	0	.000
Gordon, LF	4	0	0	0	1	0	3	.222
Rios, RF	3	0	0	0	0	1	3	.133
Herrera, K, P	0	0	0	0	0	0	0	.000
a-Morales, PH	1	0	0	0	0	1	0	.200
Hochevar, P	0	0	0	0	0	0	0	.000
b-Colon, C, PH	1	1	1	1	0	0	1	1.000
Davis, W, P	0	0	0	0	0	0	0	.000
Volquez, P	2	0	1	0	0	1	1	.500
Orlando, RF	3	1	0	0	0	0	1	.125
TOTALS	47	7	10	7	3	11	18	
NY METS	AB	R	H	RBI	BB	SO	LOB	AVG
Granderson, RF	4	2	1	1	1	2	0	.250
Wright, 3B	5	0	1	0	0	3	0	.208
Murphy, 2B	3	0	0	0	2	2	2	.150
Cespedes, CF	3	0	0	0	0	0	4	.150
Lagares, CF	2	0	0	0	0	0	1	.300
Duda, 1B	2	0	0	1	2	1	0	.263
d'Arnaud, C	5	0	0	0	0	1	4	.143
Conforto, LF	5	0	2	0	0	1	1	.333
Flores, SS	4	0	0	0	1	1	2	.059
Harvey, P	3	0	0	0	0	2	0	.000
Familia, P	0	0	0	0	0	0	0	.000
b-Johnson, PH	1	0	0	0	0	0	0	.000
Niese, P	0	0	0	0	0	0	0	.000
Reed, P	0	0	0	0	0	0	0	.000
Colon, B, P	0	0	0	0	0	0	0	.000
TOTALS	37	2	4	2	6	11	16	
Kansas City				000	000	002	005—7	
New York				100	001	000	000—2	

a-Struck out for Herrera, K in the 10th. **b**-Singled for Hochevar in the 12th. **1**-Ran for Perez, S in the 12th. **b**-Popped out for Familia in the 10th.

2B: Hosmer, Escobar, Cain. **HR:** Granderson. **Team LOB:** 7. **SB:** Cain 2, Hosmer, Dyson. **E:** Hosmer, Wright, Murphy.

KANSAS CITY	IP	H	R	ER	BB	SO	HR	ERA
Volquez	6	2	2	1	5	5	1	3.00
Herrera, K	3	1	0	0	0	3	0	0.00
Hochevar (W)	2	0	0	0	1	0	0	0.00
Davis, W	1	1	0	0	0	3	0	0.00
NEW YORK	IP	H	R	ER	BB	SO	HR	ERA
Harvey	8	5	2	2	2	9	0	3.21
Familia (BS, 3)	2	0	0	0	0	2	0	1.80
Niese	1	1	0	0	0	0	0	5.79
Reed (L, 0-1)	1/3	3	5	4	1	0	0	9.82
Colon, B	2/3	1	0	0	0	0	0	0.00

Harvey pitched to 2 batters in the 9th. **Game Scores:** Volquez 62, Harvey 71. **IBB:** Zobrist (by Reed), Flores (by Volquez).

AMERICAN LEAGUE WILD CARD GAME

HOUSTON VS. NEW YORK YANKEES 0

HOUSTON	AB	R	H	RBI	BB	SO	LOB	AVG
Altuve, 2B	4	0	1	1	0	1	3	.250
Springer, RF	4	0	1	0	0	1	1	.250
Correa, SS	4	0	0	0	0	1	1	.000
Rasmus, LF	3	1	1	1	1	1	1	.333
Gattis, DH	4	0	0	0	0	1	2	.000
Gomez, C, CF	3	1	1	1	0	0	0	.333
a-Lowrie, PH	1	0	0	0	0	0	0	.000
Marisnick, CF	0	0	0	0	0	0	0	.000
Valbuena, 3B	4	0	1	0	0	2	0	.250
Carter, 1B	0	0	0	0	3	0	0	.000
1-Villar, PR	0	1	0	0	0	0	0	.000
Gonzalez, M, 1B	1	0	0	0	0	1	0	.000
Castro, J, C	2	0	0	0	1	1	2	.000
TOTALS	30	3	5	3	5	9	10	

HOUSTON	IP	H	R	ER	BB	SO	HR	ERA
Keuchel (W, 1-0)	6.0	3	0	0	1	7	0	0.00
Sipp (H, 1)	1.0	0	0	0	1	1	0	0.00
Harris (H, 1)	1.0	0	0	0	0	0	0	0.00
Gregerson (S, 1)	1.0	0	0	0	0	2	0	0.00

NEW YORK	AB	R	H	RBI	BB	SO	LOB	AVG
Gardner, CF-LF	4	0	0	0	0	3	1	.000
Young, C, LF	2	0	0	0	1	1	1	.000
b-Ellsbury, PH-CF	1	0	0	0	0	0	0	.000
Beltran, RF	4	0	1	0	0	2	1	.250
Rodriguez, A, DH	4	0	0	0	0	2	3	.000
McCann, C	4	0	0	0	0	0	0	.000
Headley, 3B	2	0	0	0	1	1	0	.000
Bird, 1B	3	0	1	0	0	1	1	.333
Refsnyder, 2B	3	0	0	0	0	0	2	.000
Gregorius, SS	3	0	1	0	0	0	0	.333
TOTALS	30	0	3	0	2	10	9	

Houston			010	100	100:3
New York			000	000	000:0

a-Flied out for Gomez, C, in the 9th. **1-**Ran for Carter in the 7th. **b-**Popped out for Young, C in the 8th.

2B: Springer (1, Tanaka).

HR: Rasmus, Gomez, C. **Houston LOB:** 5. **New York LOB:** 5. **SB:** Villar, Altuve.

HOUSTON	IP	H	R	ER	BB	SO	HR	ERA
Keuchel (W)	6	3	0	0	1	7	0	0.00
Sipp	1	0	0	0	1	1	0	0.00
Harris	1	0	0	0	0	0	0	0.00
Gregerson (S)	1	0	0	0	0	2	0	0.00

NEW YORK	IP	H	R	ER	BB	SO	HR	ERA
Tanaka (L)	5	4	2	2	3	3	2	3.60
Wilson	1 1/3	0	0	0	1	0	0	0.00
Betances	1 2/3	1	1	1	1	4	0	5.40
Miller	1	0	0	0	0	2	0	0.00

Game Scores: Keuchel 72, Tanaka 51.

AMERICAN LEAGUE DIVISION SERIES

KANSAS CITY ROYALS VS. HOUSTON ASTROS

HOUSTON	AVG	G	AB	R	H	2B	3B	HR	RBI	BB	SO	SB
Jose Altuve, 2B	.136	5	22	2	3	0	0	0	1	1	2	0
Chris Carter, 1B	.294	5	17	3	5	1	0	1	1	0	7	0
Jason Castro, C	.071	5	14	1	1	0	0	0	2	1	7	0
Hank Conger, C	—	1	0	0	0	0	0	0	0	0	0	0
Carlos Correa, SS	.350	5	20	2	7	1	0	2	4	0	5	0
Evan Gattis, DH	.211	5	19	1	4	0	0	1	0	1	5	0
Carlos Gomez, CF	.250	5	12	1	3	0	0	1	2	0	4	0
Marwin Gonzalez, 1B	.000	3	2	0	0	0	0	0	0	0	1	0
Jed Lowrie, 3B	.000	3	3	0	0	0	0	0	0	0	1	0
Jake Marisnick, CF	.429	3	7	1	3	1	0	0	0	0	2	0
Colby Rasmus, LF	.429	5	14	3	6	1	0	3	5	6	6	1
George Springer, RF	.211	5	19	5	4	1	0	1	3	3	10	0
Preston Tucker, PH	.000	3	2	0	0	0	0	0	0	1	2	0
Luis Valbuena, 3B	.154	5	13	2	2	0	0	1	2	4	6	0
TOTALS	.232	5	164	21	38	5	0	9	21	16	58	1

HOUSTON	W	L	ERA	G	GS	SV	IP	H	R	ER	BB	SO
Josh Fields	0	0	10.80	2	0	0	1.2	1	2	2	2	4
Mike Fiers	0	0	9.00	1	0	0	1.0	1	1	1	0	0
Luke Gregerson	0	0	3.00	3	0	2	3.0	2	1	1	2	4
Will Harris	0	1	18.00	3	0	0	2.0	8	5	4	0	2
Scott Kazmir	0	0	5.06	1	1	0	5.1	5	3	3	1	4
Dallas Keuchel	1	0	4.50	2	1	0	8.0	7	4	4	4	7
Lance McCullers	0	0	2.84	1	1	0	6.1	2	2	2	2	7
Collin McHugh	1	1	4.50	2	2	0	10.0	9	5	5	2	2
Pat Neshek	0	0	0.00	2	0	0	1.0	2	0	0	0	2
Oliver Perez	0	0	27.00	2	0	0	0.1	2	1	1	1	0
Tony Sipp	0	1	0.00	5	0	0	4.1	1	1	0	1	4
TOTALS	2	3	4.81	5	5	2	43.0	40	25	23	15	36

KANSAS CITY	AVG	G	AB	R	H	2B	3B	HR	RBI	BB	SO	SB
Drew Butera, C	—	1	0	0	0	0	0	0	0	1	0	0
Lorenzo Cain, CF	.250	5	20	5	5	1	0	1	2	2	5	0
Jarrod Dyson, LF	.000	2	1	0	0	0	0	0	0	0	1	2
Alcides Escobar, SS	.286	5	21	3	6	1	1	0	0	0	4	0
Alex Gordon, LF	.235	5	17	2	4	1	0	1	2	2	5	0
Terrance Gore, PR	—	1	0	0	0	0	0	0	0	0	0	1
Eric Hosmer, 1B	.190	5	21	3	4	0	0	1	5	0	4	0
Kendrys Morales, DH	.263	5	19	3	5	0	0	3	6	1	4	0
Mike Moustakas, 3B	.111	5	18	1	2	1	0	0	0	2	2	0
Paulo Orlando, RF	.000	3	1	0	0	0	0	0	0	0	1	0
Salvador Perez, C	.286	5	14	3	4	0	0	2	4	2	3	0
Alex Rios, RF	.286	5	14	3	4	2	0	0	2	3	5	0
Ben Zobrist, 2B	.333	5	18	2	6	1	0	0	2	2	2	1
TOTALS	.244	5	164	25	40	7	1	8	23	15	36	4

KANSAS CITY	W	L	ERA	G	GS	SV	IP	H	R	ER	BB	SO
Johnny Cueto	1	0	3.86	2	2	0	14.0	9	6	6	3	13
Wade Davis	0	0	0.00	3	0	2	4.0	1	0	0	1	5
Danny Duffy	0	0	13.50	1	0	0	0.2	1	1	1	0	0
Kelvin Herrera	1	0	3.00	3	0	0	3.0	2	1	1	2	6
Luke Hochevar	0	0	0.00	2	0	0	2.2	3	0	0	0	2
Ryan Madson	1	0	9.00	3	0	0	3.0	6	3	3	0	7
Yordano Ventura	0	1	7.71	2	2	0	7.0	8	6	6	4	10
Edinson Volquez	0	1	4.76	1	1	0	5.2	5	3	3	4	8
Chris Young	0	0	2.25	1	0	0	4.0	3	1	1	2	7
TOTALS	3	2	4.30	5	5	2	44.0	38	21	21	16	58

E:Valbuena, Correa. **LOB:**Houston 28, Kansas City 32. **DP:**Houston 3, Kansas City 3. **GIDP:**Castro, Correa, Altuve, Zobrist, Cain, Gordon. **SAC:**Zobrist, Escobar. **SF:**Zobrist. **HBP:**Moustakas (by Gregerson), Escobar (by McCullers), Perez 2 (by McCullers, McHugh), Correa (by Ventura). **IBB:**Cain 2 (by Keuchel 2), Rasmus 2 (by Volquez, Ventura). **CS:**Altuve, Gore. **WP:**Keuchel.

SCORE BY INNINGS

Houston	362	041	410:21
Kansas City	041	332	183:25

TEXAS	AVG	G	AB	R	H	2B	3B	HR	RBI	BB	SO	SB
Hanser Alberto, 3B	.200	3	10	0	2	1	0	0	2	0	2	0
Elvis Andrus, SS	.182	5	22	1	4	0	0	0	1	0	4	0
Adrian Beltre, 3B	.444	3	9	4	4	0	0	1	1	1	1	0
Robinson Chirinos, C	.273	3	11	1	3	0	0	1	3	0	2	0
Shin-Soo Choo, RF	.238	5	21	4	5	0	0	1	2	1	6	0
Delino DeShields, CF	.292	5	24	4	7	3	0	0	2	0	2	1
Prince Fielder, DH	.150	5	20	1	3	0	0	0	1	1	4	0
Chris Gimenez, C	.250	2	8	1	2	0	0	0	0	0	1	0
Josh Hamilton, LF	.167	5	18	0	3	1	0	0	0	1	5	0
Mitch Moreland, 1B	.000	5	13	0	0	0	0	0	1	2	3	0
Mike Napoli, 1B	.143	4	7	0	1	0	0	0	1	2	3	0
Rougned Odor, 2B	.278	5	18	7	5	1	0	1	2	1	4	0
Drew Stubbs, CF	.000	4	1	0	0	0	0	0	0	0	1	0
Will Venable, LF	.500	4	2	0	1	0	0	0	0	0	1	0
TOTALS	.217	5	184	19	40	6	0	3	16	9	39	1

TEXAS	W	L	ERA	G	GS	SV	IP	H	R	ER	BB	SO
Jake Diekman	0	0	1.50	4	0	0	6.0	2	1	1	0	5
Sam Dyson	0	0	2.45	4	0	1	3.2	6	1	1	1	2
Yovani Gallardo	1	0	3.60	1	1	0	5.0	4	2	2	1	1
Chi Chi Gonzalez	0	0	5.40	1	0	0	1.2	2	1	1	2	0
Cole Hamels	0	1	2.70	2	2	0	13.1	10	9	4	2	14
Derek Holland	0	1	27.00	1	1	0	2.0	5	6	6	1	0
Keone Kela	1	0	3.00	3	0	0	3.0	1	1	1	2	2
Colby Lewis	0	0	3.00	1	0	0	3.0	3	1	1	3	1
Ross Ohlendorf	0	0	0.00	3	0	1	3.1	2	0	0	0	5
Martin Perez	0	1	7.20	1	1	0	5.0	6	4	4	3	2
Shawn Tolleson	0	0	0.00	2	0	0	3.0	1	0	0	0	3
TOTALS	2	3	3.86	5	5	2	49.0	42	26	21	15	35

TORONTO	AVG	G	AB	R	H	2B	3B	HR	RBI	BB	SO	SB
Jose Bautista, RF	.273	5	22	3	6	2	0	2	5	1	2	0
Ezequiel Carrera, PH	.000	1	1	0	0	0	0	0	0	0	0	0
Chris Colabello, 1B	.375	4	16	3	6	2	0	1	2	1	5	0
Josh Donaldson, 3B	.222	5	18	5	4	1	0	2	4	3	4	0
Edwin Encarnacion, DH	.333	5	18	3	6	1	0	1	3	5	1	0
Ryan Goins, 2B	.000	5	17	1	0	0	0	0	0	1	5	0
Russell Martin, C	.200	4	15	2	3	2	0	0	1	1	3	0
Dioner Navarro, C	.200	2	5	1	1	1	0	0	0	0	0	0
Cliff Pennington, 3B	.000	1	1	0	0	0	0	0	0	0	0	0
Kevin Pillar, CF	.333	5	21	3	7	2	0	1	4	0	5	0
Dalton Pompey, RF	—	3	0	0	0	0	0	0	0	0	0	2
Ben Revere, LF	.304	5	23	3	7	0	0	0	0	1	1	0
Justin Smoak, 1B	.000	5	6	0	0	0	0	0	0	0	3	0
Troy Tulowitzki, SS	.095	5	21	2	2	0	0	1	4	2	7	0
TOTALS	.228	5	184	26	42	11	0	8	24	15	35	4

TORONTO	W	L	ERA	G	GS	SV	IP	H	R	ER	BB	SO
Brett Cecil	0	0	0.00	2	0	0	2.0	1	0	0	1	2
R.A. Dickey	0	0	1.93	1	1	0	4.2	5	1	1	0	3
Marco Estrada	1	0	1.42	1	1	0	6.1	5	1	1	0	4
LaTroy Hawkins	0	1	27.00	1	0	0	0.2	3	2	2	0	0
Liam Hendriks	0	0	0.00	1	0	0	0.1	1	0	0	0	0
Aaron Loup	0	0	0.00	2	0	0	1.0	0	0	0	0	0
Mark Lowe	0	0	0.00	1	0	0	1.0	0	0	0	2	2
Roberto Osuna	0	0	0.00	4	0	1	5.2	0	0	0	0	6
David Price	1	1	7.20	2	1	0	10.0	11	8	8	2	7
Aaron Sanchez	1	0	0.00	5	0	0	5.1	3	1	0	1	6
Marcus Stroman	0	0	3.46	2	2	0	13.0	11	6	5	3	9
TOTALS	3	2	3.06	5	5	5	50.0	40	19	17	9	39

E:Alberto, DeShields, Andrus 2, Moreland, Revere, Martin 2, Bautista. LOB:Texas 29, Toronto 30. DP:Texas 5, Toronto 2. GIDP:Fielder, Napoli, Pillar, Goins, Navarro, Colabello, Martin. SAC:Gimenez, Choo, Goins 2. SF:Alberto. HBP:Odor 2 (by Price 2), Martin 2 (by Ohlendorf, Lewis). IBB:Encarnacion 3 (by Dyson, Perez, Hamels). CS:Napoli, Andrus, Pillar.

SCORE BY INNINGS

Texas	314	020	430	000	02:19
Toronto	435	225	500	000	00:26

AMERICAN LEAGUE CHAMPIONSHIP SERIES

KANSAS CITY ROYALS VS. TORONTO BLUE JAYS

TORONTO	AVG	G	AB	R	H	2B	3B	HR	RBI	BB	SO	SB
Jose Bautista, RF	.316	6	19	4	6	1	0	2	6	7	5	0
Ezequiel Carrera, PH	.000	1	1	0	0	0	0	0	0	0	0	0
Chris Colabello, 1B	.217	6	23	2	5	1	0	1	1	1	4	0
Josh Donaldson, 3B	.261	6	23	4	6	2	0	1	4	3	6	1
Edwin Encarnacion, DH	.227	6	22	2	5	1	0	0	2	2	7	0
Ryan Goins, 2B	.263	6	19	3	5	1	0	1	4	0	7	0
Russell Martin, C	.091	4	11	1	1	0	0	0	0	3	5	0
Dioner Navarro, C	.000	3	8	0	0	0	0	0	0	1	5	0
Kevin Pillar, CF	.238	6	21	3	5	3	0	0	2	3	3	2
Dalton Pompey, PH	1.000	2	1	0	1	0	0	0	0	0	0	2
Ben Revere, LF	.208	6	24	4	5	1	0	0	3	0	7	0
Justin Smoak, 1B	.000	3	2	0	0	0	0	0	0	0	0	0
Troy Tulowitzki, SS	.304	6	23	3	7	2	0	1	7	0	7	0
TOTALS	.234	6	197	26	46	12	0	6	26	24	56	5

TORONTO	W	L	ERA	G	GS	SV	IP	H	R	ER	BB	SO
R.A. Dickey	0	1	21.60	1	1	0	1.2	4	5	4	2	1
Marco Estrada	1	1	2.77	2	2	0	13.0	9	4	4	1	11
LaTroy Hawkins	0	0	45.00	2	0	0	1.0	4	5	5	1	0
Liam Hendriks	0	0	5.79	2	0	0	4.2	4	3	3	0	2
Aaron Loup	0	0	9.00	2	0	0	1.0	1	1	1	2	0
Mark Lowe	0	0	5.40	4	0	0	3.1	1	2	2	0	4
Roberto Osuna	0	1	6.75	3	0	0	2.2	3	2	2	1	0
Cliff Pennington	0	0	0.00	1	0	0	0.1	2	0	0	0	0
David Price	0	1	5.40	2	2	0	13.1	11	8	8	1	16
Aaron Sanchez	0	0	0.00	4	0	0	2.0	4	0	0	1	0
Marcus Stroman	1	0	5.68	1	1	0	6.1	11	4	4	1	1
Ryan Tepera	0	0	21.60	1	0	0	1.2	5	4	4	2	0
TOTALS	2	4	6.53	6	6	0	51.0	59	38	37	12	35

KANSAS CITY	AVG	G	AB	R	H	2B	3B	HR	RBI	BB	SO	SB
Drew Butera, C	.000	1	1	0	0	0	0	0	0	0	0	0
Lorenzo Cain, CF	.300	6	20	3	6	0	0	0	5	5	3	2
Jarrod Dyson, CF	—	1	0	0	0	0	0	0	0	0	0	0
Alcides Escobar, SS	.478	6	23	6	11	2	1	0	5	0	2	0
Alex Gordon, LF	.263	6	19	5	5	2	0	0	1	1	5	0
Terrance Gore, PR	—	1	0	0	0	0	0	0	0	0	0	0
Eric Hosmer, 1B	.250	6	24	4	6	1	0	0	6	1	6	0
Kendrys Morales, DH	.273	6	22	2	6	0	0	1	4	2	5	0
Mike Moustakas, 3B	.208	6	24	3	5	0	0	1	5	0	5	0
Paulo Orlando, RF	1.000	4	2	2	2	0	0	0	0	0	0	0
Salvador Perez, C	.136	6	22	4	3	1	0	2	2	1	4	0
Alex Rios, RF	.368	6	19	1	7	0	0	1	3	0	3	1
Ben Zobrist, 2B	.326	6	25	8	8	3	0	2	4	2	2	0
TOTALS	.294	6	201	38	59	9	1	7	35	12	35	3

KANSAS CITY	W	L	ERA	G	GS	SV	IP	H	R	ER	BB	SO
Johnny Cueto	0	1	36.00	1	1	0	2.0	6	8	8	4	2
Wade Davis	1	0	0.00	2	0	1	2.2	2	0	0	2	5
Danny Duffy	1	0	6.00	2	0	0	3.0	4	2	2	0	6
Kelvin Herrera	0	0	0.00	5	0	0	5.2	3	0	0	0	10
Luke Hochevar	1	0	0.00	3	0	0	3.0	1	0	0	0	0
Ryan Madson	0	0	7.71	3	0	0	2.1	4	2	2	2	3
Kris Medlen	0	0	3.60	1	0	0	5.0	3	2	1	5	0
Franklin Morales	0	0	4.50	2	0	0	2.0	3	1	1	1	2
Yordano Ventura	0	0	3.38	2	2	0	10.2	12	4	4	4	11
Edinson Volquez	1	1	4.09	2	2	0	11.0	5	5	5	8	7
Chris Young	0	0	3.86	1	1	0	4.2	3	2	2	2	4
TOTALS	4	2	4.50	6	6	1	52.0	46	26	26	24	56

E:Donaldson, Moustakas. LOB:Toronto 42, Kansas City 31. DP:Toronto 3, Kansas City 3. GIDP:Colabello 2, Encarnacion, Moustakas, Zobrist, Perez. SAC:Goins. SF:Morales, Cain, Moustakas; Escobar 2; Hosmer. HBP:Martin (by Cueto), Donaldson (by Volquez), Escobar (by Hawkins), Escobar (by Dickey), Gordon (by Lowe). CS:Cain, Rios. WP:Stroman, Tepera, Davis. PB:Martin.

SCORE BY INNINGS

Toronto	049	116	140:26
Kansas City	623	120	(10)86:38

NATIONAL LEAGUE WILD CARD GAME
CHICAGO CUBS VS. PITTSBURGH PIRATES 0

CHICAGO	AB	R	H	RBI	BB	SO	LOB	AVG
Fowler, CF	4	3	3	1	0	0	1	.750
Schwarber, RF	3	1	2	3	0	0	0	.667
Denorfia, RF	0	0	0	0	1	0	0	.000
Bryant, LF-3B	3	0	0	0	1	1	2	.000
Rizzo, 1B	4	0	0	0	0	2	2	.000
La Stella, 3B	2	0	0	0	0	1	1	.000
a-Jackson, A, PH-LF	2	0	0	0	0	2	1	.000
Castro, S, 2B	4	0	0	0	0	0	0	.000
Montero, M, C	4	0	1	0	0	0	0	.250
Russell, SS	4	0	1	0	0	2	1	.250
Arrieta, P	2	0	0	0	0	2	0	.000
TOTALS	32	4	7	4	2	10	8	
PITTSBURGH	AB	R	H	RBI	BB	SO	LOB	AVG
Polanco, RF	4	0	0	0	0	2	2	.000
Harrison, 3B-SS	3	0	0	0	0	1	1	.000
McCutchen, CF	4	0	2	0	0	0	0	.500
Marte, LF	4	0	0	0	0	1	4	.000
Cervelli, C	3	0	1	0	0	0	0	.333
Walker, N, 2B	3	0	0	0	0	2	2	.000
Mercer, SS	2	0	0	0	0	1	1	.000
d-Ramirez, Ar, PH-3B	1	0	0	0	0	0	1	.000
Rodriguez, S, 1B	0	0	0	0	0	0	0	.000
b-Alvarez, PH-1B	3	0	0	0	0	3	1	.000
Cole, P	1	0	0	0	0	1	0	.000
Bastardo, P	0	0	0	0	0	0	0	.000
c-Snider, PH	1	0	1	0	0	0	0	1.000
Watson, P	0	0	0	0	0	0	0	.000
Soria, P	0	0	0	0	0	0	0	.000
e-Morse, PH	1	0	1	0	0	0	0	1.000
Melancon, P	0	0	0	0	0	0	0	.000
TOTALS	30	0	5	0	0	11	12	

Chicago	102	010	000:4
Pittsburgh	000	000	000:0

a-Struck out for La Stella in the 6th. **b**-Struck out for Rodriguez, S in the 3rd. **c**-Singled for Bastardo in the 6th. **d**-Grounded into a double play for Mercer in the 7th. **e**-Singled for Soria in the 8th.

HR: Schwarber, Fowler. **Chicago LOB:** 4. **Pittsburgh LOB:** 5. **SB:** Fowler, Arrieta. **E:** Walker.

CHICAGO	IP	H	R	ER	BB	SO	HR	ERA
Arrieta (W, 1-0)	9.0	5	0	0	0	11	0	0.00
PITTSBURGH	IP	H	R	ER	BB	SO	HR	ERA
Cole (L, 0-1)	5.0	6	4	4	1	4	2	7.20
Bastardo	1.0	0	0	0	0	2	0	0.00
Watson	1.0	0	0	0	0	1	0	0.00
Soria	1.0	0	0	0	1	3	0	0.00
Melancon	1.0	1	0	0	0	0	0	0.00

Game Scores: Arrieta 88, Cole 42.

HBP: Arrieta, Cervelli, Harrison. **Ejections:** Pittsburgh Pirates first baseman Sean Rodriguez ejected by HP umpire Jeff Nelson (7th).

NATIONAL LEAGUE DIVISION SERIES
ST. LOUIS CARDINALS VS. CHICAGO CUBS

CHICAGO	AVG	G	AB	R	H	2B	3B	HR	RBI	BB	SO	SB
Jake Arrieta, P	.000	1	2	0	0	0	0	0	0	0	2	0
Javier Baez, SS	.800	2	5	1	4	0	0	1	3	0	0	1
Kris Bryant, 3B	.176	4	17	1	3	0	1	1	2	0	6	0
Starlin Castro, 2B	.286	4	14	2	4	0	0	1	1	1	0	0
Chris Coghlan, LF	.200	2	5	1	1	0	0	0	0	0	3	0
Chris Denorfia, LF	.000	4	3	0	0	0	0	0	0	0	3	0
Dexter Fowler, CF	.188	4	16	2	3	1	0	1	2	1	3	0
Jason Hammel, P	1.000	1	1	1	1	0	0	0	1	0	0	0
Kyle Hendricks, P	.000	1	1	0	0	0	0	0	1	0	1	0
Austin Jackson, RF	.000	3	5	1	0	0	0	0	0	1	2	1
Tommy La Stella, PH	.000	1	1	0	0	0	0	0	0	0	1	0
Jon Lester, P	.000	1	2	0	0	0	0	0	0	0	0	0
Miguel Montero, C	.000	3	9	1	0	0	0	0	1	3	6	0
Anthony Rizzo, 1B	.214	4	14	3	3	0	0	2	2	1	4	0
David Ross, C	.000	1	2	0	0	0	0	0	0	0	1	0

CHICAGO	AVG	G	AB	R	H	2B	3B	HR	RBI	BB	SO	SB
Addison Russell, SS	.250	3	8	0	2	0	1	0	1	0	1	1
Kyle Schwarber, LF	.500	4	10	3	5	0	0	2	2	2	3	0
Jorge Soler, RF	.571	4	7	3	4	1	0	2	4	6	1	0
Travis Wood, P	.000	3	2	0	0	0	0	0	0	0	2	0
TOTALS	.242	4	124	20	30	2	2	10	20	15	38	3

CHICAGO	W	L	ERA	G	GS	SV	IP	H	R	ER	BB	SO
Jake Arrieta	1	0	6.35	1	1	0	5.2	5	4	4	2	9
Trevor Cahill	1	0	3.38	3	0	0	2.2	4	1	1	0	6
Justin Grimm	0	0	0.00	1	0	0	1.0	0	0	0	0	3
Jason Hammel	0	0	6.00	1	1	0	3.0	3	2	2	3	2
Kyle Hendricks	0	0	5.79	1	1	0	4.2	4	3	3	0	7
Jon Lester	0	1	3.68	1	1	0	7.1	5	3	3	1	9
Clayton Richard	0	0	0.00	1	0	0	0.2	0	0	0	0	1
Fernando Rodney	0	0	0.00	1	0	0	0.2	0	0	0	1	1
Hector Rondon	0	0	6.00	3	0	2	3.0	4	2	2	0	2
Pedro Strop	0	0	3.38	3	0	0	2.2	1	1	1	0	4
Travis Wood	1	0	2.45	3	0	0	3.2	2	1	1	0	4
TOTALS	3	1	4.37	4	4	2	35.0	28	17	17	7	48

ST. LOUIS	AVG	G	AB	R	H	2B	3B	HR	RBI	BB	SO	SB
Matt Carpenter, 3B	.235	4	17	3	4	0	0	1	1	1	5	0
Tony Cruz, C	.200	2	5	0	1	0	0	0	1	0	3	0
Greg Garcia, PH	.000	3	3	0	0	0	0	0	0	0	1	0
Randal Grichuk, CF	.250	4	8	2	2	0	0	1	0	4	0	0
Jason Heyward, CF	.357	4	14	2	5	1	0	1	2	2	2	0
Matt Holliday, LF	.125	4	16	2	2	0	0	0	1	1	3	0
Jon Jay, PH	.000	1	1	0	0	0	0	0	0	0	1	0
John Lackey, P	.333	2	3	0	1	0	0	0	0	0	1	0
Yadier Molina, C	.125	3	8	0	1	0	0	0	0	0	2	0
Brandon Moss, 1B	.333	3	3	0	1	0	0	0	1	0	2	0
Jhonny Peralta, SS	.143	4	14	1	2	1	0	0	1	1	6	0
Tommy Pham, CF	.200	3	5	1	1	0	0	0	1	2	0	2
Stephen Piscotty, 1B	.375	4	16	5	6	1	0	3	6	2	8	0
Mark Reynolds, 1B	.000	3	4	0	0	0	0	0	0	0	1	0
Michael Wacha, P	.000	1	2	0	0	0	0	0	0	0	2	0
Kolten Wong, 2B	.143	4	14	1	2	1	0	1	1	1	5	0
TOTALS	.211	4	133	17	28	5	0	8	17	7	48	0

ST. LOUIS	W	L	ERA	G	GS	SV	IP	H	R	ER	BB	SO
Jonathan Broxton	0	0	3.86	3	0	0	2.1	2	1	1	2	3
Jaime Garcia	0	1	0.00	1	1	0	2.0	4	5	0	1	2
John Lackey	1	0	3.48	2	2	0	10.1	6	4	4	2	10
Lance Lynn	0	0	9.00	1	0	0	1.0	1	1	1	1	2
Seth Maness	0	0	5.40	2	0	0	1.2	2	1	1	1	1
Trevor Rosenthal	0	0	0.00	2	0	0	2.0	2	0	0	3	4
Kevin Siegrist	0	1	9.00	3	0	0	3.0	4	3	3	1	5
Carlos Villanueva	0	0	0.00	1	0	0	2.0	0	0	0	1	0
Michael Wacha	0	1	8.31	1	1	0	4.1	6	4	4	3	5
Adam Wainwright	0	0	1.69	3	0	0	5.1	3	1	1	0	6
TOTALS	1	3	3.97	4	4	0	34.0	30	20	15	15	38

E: Baez, Bryant, Wong, Garcia. **LOB:** Chicago 20, St. Louis 19. **DP:** St. Louis 2. **GIDP:** Bryant 2, Rizzo. **SAC:** Hendricks; Russell, Fowler. **HBP:** Moss (by Arrieta). **IBB:** Montero (by Wacha), Castro (by Rosenthal). **CS:** Jackson. **WP:** Lester 2. **PB:** Ross.

SCORE BY INNINGS

Chicago	0(10)1	133	110:20
St. Louis	400	224	032:17

LOS ANGELES DODGERS VS. NEW YORK METS

NEW YORK	AVG	G	AB	R	H	2B	3B	HR	RBI	BB	SO	SB
Yoenis Cespedes, LF	.250	5	20	4	5	0	0	2	4	0	8	0
Michael Conforto, LF	.143	4	7	1	1	0	0	1	2	0	1	0
Michael Cuddyer, LF	.000	3	4	0	0	0	0	0	0	1	2	0
Travis d'Arnaud, C	.158	5	19	3	3	0	0	1	4	0	8	0
Jacob deGrom, P	.000	2	4	0	0	0	0	0	0	0	1	0
Lucas Duda, 1B	.111	5	18	1	2	0	0	0	2	11	0	0
Jeurys Familia, P	.000	4	1	0	0	0	0	0	0	0	0	0
Wilmer Flores, SS	.300	4	10	2	3	1	0	0	0	2	4	0
Curtis Granderson, RF	.389	5	18	1	7	2	0	0	5	3	1	1
Matt Harvey, P	.000	1	2	0	0	0	0	0	0	0	0	0
Kelly Johnson, 2B	.250	4	4	0	1	0	0	0	0	0	2	0
Juan Lagares, CF	.429	4	7	3	3	2	0	0	0	1	0	0

NEW YORK	AVG	G	AB	R	H	2B	3B	HR	RBI	BB	SO	SB
Steven Matz, P	.000	1	1	0	0	0	0	0	0	0	0	0
Daniel Murphy, 2B	.333	5	21	5	7	1	0	3	5	0	3	1
Noah Syndergaard, P	.000	2	2	0	0	0	0	0	0	0	1	0
Ruben Tejada, SS	.000	2	5	1	0	0	0	0	0	1	5	0
David Wright, 3B	.063	5	16	1	1	0	0	0	2	5	7	0
TOTALS	.208	5	159	22	33	6	0	7	22	15	57	2

NEW YORK	W	L	ERA	G	GS	SV	IP	H	R	ER	BB	SO
Tyler Clippard	0	0	5.40	2	0	0	1.2	2	1	1	0	0
Bartolo Colon	0	0	4.50	3	0	0	4.0	3	2	2	0	5
Jacob deGrom	2	0	1.38	2	2	0	13.0	11	2	2	4	20
Jeurys Familia	0	0	0.00	4	0	2	5.1	0	0	0	0	3
Erik Goeddel	0	0	*.**	1	0	0	0.0	4	3	3	0	0
Matt Harvey	1	0	3.60	1	1	0	5.0	7	3	2	2	7
Steven Matz	0	1	5.40	1	1	0	5.0	6	3	3	2	4
Jon Niese	0	0	0.00	1	0	0	0.1	0	0	0	0	1
Addison Reed	0	0	6.75	2	0	0	1.1	2	1	1	0	1
Hansel Robles	0	0	0.00	1	0	0	1.0	0	0	0	0	2
Noah Syndergaard	0	1	3.68	2	1	0	7.1	5	3	3	5	11
TOTALS	3	2	3.48	5	5	2	44.0	40	18	17	13	54

LOS ANGELES	AVG	G	AB	R	H	2B	3B	HR	RBI	BB	SO	SB
Brett Anderson, P	.000	1	1	0	0	0	0	0	0	0	0	0
Carl Crawford, LF	.083	4	12	1	1	0	0	0	0	0	3	1
A.J. Ellis, C	.250	3	8	0	2	0	0	0	0	0	2	0
Andre Ethier, RF	.250	5	16	1	4	1	0	0	2	2	4	0
Adrian Gonzalez, 1B	.316	5	19	4	6	1	0	1	5	2	9	0
Yasmani Grandal, C	.100	3	10	0	1	0	0	0	2	1	6	0
Zack Greinke, P	.000	2	3	0	0	0	0	0	0	0	1	0
Enrique Hernandez, CF	.308	4	13	3	4	0	0	0	0	2	4	1
Howie Kendrick, 2B	.273	5	22	4	6	1	0	1	4	0	2	0
Clayton Kershaw, P	.200	2	5	0	1	0	0	0	0	0	1	0
Joc Pederson, CF	.000	5	4	0	0	0	0	0	0	4	1	0
Yasiel Puig, RF	.000	3	6	0	0	0	0	0	0	0	3	0
Jimmy Rollins, SS	.143	4	7	0	1	0	0	0	0	0	2	0
Justin Ruggiano, LF	.000	3	4	0	0	0	0	0	0	0	3	0
Corey Seager, SS	.188	5	16	2	3	1	0	0	1	8	0	
Justin Turner, 3B	.526	5	19	2	10	6	0	0	4	1	3	1
Chase Utley, PH	.333	3	3	1	1	0	0	0	0	0	1	0
TOTALS	.238	5	168	18	40	10	0	2	17	13	54	3

LOS ANGELES	W	L	ERA	G	GS	SV	IP	H	R	ER	BB	SO
Brett Anderson	0	1	18.00	1	1	0	3.0	7	6	6	0	3
Luis Avilan	0	0	0.00	2	0	0	1.1	0	0	0	0	2
Pedro Baez	0	0	81.00	2	0	0	0.1	2	3	3	2	1
Yimi Garcia	0	0	0.00	1	0	0	1.0	0	0	0	1	3
Zack Greinke	1	1	3.29	2	2	0	13.2	11	5	5	1	17
Chris Hatcher	0	0	0.00	4	0	0	3.2	0	0	0	1	5
J.P. Howell	0	0	0.00	1	0	0	1.0	1	0	0	0	0
Kenley Jansen	0	0	0.00	3	0	2	3.1	1	0	0	3	4
Clayton Kershaw	1	1	2.63	2	2	0	13.2	7	4	4	5	19
Joel Peralta	0	0	0.00	1	0	0	1.0	0	0	0	1	0
Alex Wood	0	0	18.00	1	0	0	2.0	4	4	4	2	2
TOTALS	2	3	4.50	5	5	2	44.0	33	22	22	15	57

E:Granderson, Flores, Hernandez. LOB:New York 23, Los Angeles 33. DP:New York 4, Los Angeles 2. GIDP:Wright 2, Crawford, Rollins, Kendrick, Hernandez. SAC:deGrom, Greinke. SF:Conforto, d'Arnaud. IBB:Wright (by Wood), Flores (by Jansen), Pederson (by deGrom), Hernandez, (by Syndergaard), Turner (by Matz). CS:Murphy.

SCORE BY INNINGS

New York	162	701	500:22
Los Angeles	233	100	513:18

NATIONAL LEAGUE CHAMPIONSHIP SERIES

NEW YORK METS VS. CHICAGO CUBS

CHICAGO	AVG	G	AB	R	H	2B	3B	HR	RBI	BB	SO	SB
Jake Arrieta, P	.000	1	1	0	0	0	0	0	0	0	1	0
Javier Baez, SS	.100	4	10	0	1	0	0	0	0	0	4	1
Kris Bryant, 3B	.214	4	14	1	3	1	0	1	3	2	5	0
Starlin Castro, 2B	.125	4	16	0	2	1	0	0	1	0	1	0
Chris Coghlan, RF	.000	4	7	0	0	0	0	0	0	0	1	0
Chris Denorfia, PH	.000	2	2	0	0	0	0	0	0	0	1	0
Dexter Fowler, CF	.250	4	16	1	4	1	0	0	0	1	3	0
Kyle Hendricks, P	.000	1	1	0	0	0	0	0	0	0	1	0
Austin Jackson, PH	.000	1	1	0	0	0	0	0	0	0	1	0
Tommy La Stella, 2B	.000	4	7	0	0	0	0	0	0	0	1	0
Jon Lester, P	.000	1	2	0	0	0	0	0	0	0	2	0
Miguel Montero, C	.125	4	8	0	1	0	0	0	0	1	4	0
Anthony Rizzo, 1B	.214	4	14	1	3	0	0	0	0	1	2	0
David Ross, C	.000	2	2	0	0	0	0	0	0	2	1	0
Kyle Schwarber, LF	.143	4	14	2	2	0	0	2	3	2	5	0
Jorge Soler, RF	.417	3	12	3	5	2	0	1	1	0	4	0
Travis Wood, P	.000	3	1	0	0	0	0	0	0	0	0	0
TOTALS	.164	4	128	8	21	5	0	4	8	9	37	1

CHICAGO	W	L	ERA	G	GS	SV	IP	H	R	ER	BB	SO
Jake Arrieta	0	1	7.20	1	1	0	5.0	4	4	4	2	8
Trevor Cahill	0	1	3.38	3	0	0	2.2	3	1	1	0	2
Justin Grimm	0	0	0.00	2	0	0	1.0	1	0	0	0	1
Jason Hammel	0	1	33.75	1	1	0	1.1	4	5	5	2	1
Kyle Hendricks	0	0	4.50	1	1	0	4.0	5	2	2	1	4
Jon Lester	0	1	5.40	1	1	0	6.2	8	4	4	1	5
Clayton Richard	0	0	0.00	4	0	0	4.0	3	0	0	1	2
Fernando Rodney	0	0	18.00	1	0	0	1.0	1	2	2	1	2
Hector Rondon	0	0	0.00	2	0	0	2.0	1	0	0	1	2
Pedro Strop	0	0	0.00	3	0	0	2.1	1	0	0	1	2
Travis Wood	0	0	6.75	3	0	0	4.0	4	3	3	1	8
TOTALS	0	4	5.56	4	4	0	34.0	35	21	21	11	37

NEW YORK	AVG	G	AB	R	H	2B	3B	HR	RBI	BB	SO	SB
Yoenis Cespedes, LF	.286	4	14	2	4	1	0	0	3	1	3	1
Michael Conforto, LF	.000	3	8	0	0	0	0	0	0	1	4	0
Michael Cuddyer, 1B	.250	2	4	0	1	0	0	0	0	0	0	0
Travis d'Arnaud, C	.267	4	15	2	4	0	0	2	2	0	5	0
Jacob deGrom, P	.000	1	3	0	0	0	0	0	0	0	0	0
Lucas Duda, 1B	.400	4	10	1	4	2	0	1	6	1	2	0
Wilmer Flores, SS	.286	4	14	0	4	1	1	0	0	1	2	1
Curtis Granderson, RF	.200	4	15	3	3	0	0	0	2	2	4	3
Matt Harvey, P	.000	1	2	0	0	0	0	0	0	0	0	0
Kelly Johnson, PH	.000	2	2	0	0	0	0	0	0	0	2	0
Juan Lagares, CF	.333	4	6	2	2	0	0	0	0	0	2	1
Steven Matz, P	.000	1	2	0	0	0	0	0	0	0	1	0
Daniel Murphy, 2B	.529	4	17	6	9	1	0	4	6	1	3	0
Kirk Nieuwenhuis, LF	.000	1	2	0	0	0	0	0	0	0	1	0
Noah Syndergaard, P	.000	1	2	0	0	0	0	0	0	0	0	0
David Wright, 3B	.286	4	14	5	4	2	0	0	1	4	5	1
TOTALS	.269	4	130	21	35	7	1	7	20	11	37	7

NEW YORK	W	L	ERA	G	GS	SV	IP	H	R	ER	BB	SO
Tyler Clippard	0	0	6.00	3	0	0	3.0	4	2	2	0	2
Bartolo Colon	1	0	0.00	1	0	0	1.1	0	0	0	1	1
Jacob deGrom	1	0	2.57	1	1	0	7.0	4	2	2	1	7
Jeurys Familia	0	0	0.00	4	0	3	4.1	2	0	0	2	3
Matt Harvey	1	0	2.35	1	1	0	7.2	4	2	2	2	9
Steven Matz	0	0	1.93	1	1	0	4.2	4	1	1	2	4
Jon Niese	0	0	0.00	1	0	0	0.1	0	0	0	0	1
Addison Reed	0	0	0.00	2	0	0	2.0	0	0	0	0	1
Noah Syndergaard	1	0	1.59	1	1	0	5.2	3	1	1	1	9
TOTALS	4	0	2.00	4	4	3	36.0	21	8	8	9	37

E:Baez, d'Arnaud. LOB:Chicago 22, New York 24. DP:Chicago 3. GIDP:Cuddyer, deGrom, Murphy. SAC:Harvey, Duda, Lagares. SF:Granderson. HBP: Rizzo (by Harvey), Conforto (by Hammel), d'Arnaud (by Strop). IBB:Ross (by Harvey), Murphy (by Arrieta). CS:Granderson.

WP:Cahill, Syndergaard.

SCORE BY INNINGS

Chicago	100	211	030:8
New York	922	012	320:21

ORGANIZATION STATISTICS

Arizona Diamondbacks

SEASON IN A SENTENCE: Though the 79-83 Diamondbacks still finished on the wrong side of .500, the first season under manager Chip Hale and general manager Dave Stewart was a step forward, as the team went from a last-place NL West finish in 2014 to third in 2015.

HIGH POINT: Starting with a three-game road sweep of the Giants, the Diamondbacks won eight of 12 games from June 12 to June 24 and moved from the NL West cellar to third place.

LOW POINT: On Aug. 24, the Diamondbacks were a game above .500 and just five games back of first place. But they lost seven of their next eight games to effectively remove themselves from the postseason race.

NOTABLE ROOKIES: The Diamondbacks had 12 players make their major league debuts in 2015, most notably No. 1 prospect Archie Bradley and 24-year-old Cuban signee Yasmany Tomas. Bradley, a righthander and 2011 first-rounder, went 2-3, 5.80. Tomas—signed to a six-year, $68.5 million deal before the season—batted .273/.305/.401 with nine homers in 406 at-bats. In the bullpen, lefty Andrew Chafin was a valuable late-inning reliever, going 5-1, 2.76 in 75 innings. Shortstop Nick Ahmed (.226/.275/.359) and third baseman Jake Lamb (.263/.331/.386) each played their first full season in the bigs.

KEY TRANSACTIONS: Rookie lefthander Robbie Ray, acquired in a three-team deal with the Tigers and Yankees in the offseason, went 5-12, 3.52 in 23 starts. Righthander Rubby De La Rosa led the team with 14 wins and 32 starts after coming from the Red Sox in the Wade Miley deal. Catcher Welington Castillo, acquired from the Mariners for Vidal Nuno and Mark Trumbo, belted 17 home runs and hit .255/.317/.496 in 274 at-bats. During the season, Arizona traded 2014 first-round righthander Touki Toussaint and Bronson Arroyo to the Braves for infielder Philip Gosselin. The Diamondbacks also dealt veteran shortstop Cliff Pennington (Blue Jays) and right-hander Addison Reed (Mets) during the summer.

DOWN ON THE FARM: Top pitching prospects Aaron Blair and Braden Shipley—both 2013 draftees—aren't far behind Bradley. Cuban signee Yoan Lopez also reached Double-A Mobile, though he was limited by a blister problem. Infielder Brandon Drury, outfielder Socrates Brito and catcher-turned-outfielder Peter O'Brien earned September callups.

OPENING DAY PAYROLL: $91,518,833 (24)

PLAYERS OF THE YEAR

MAJOR LEAGUE

Paul Goldschmidt
1b
.321/.435/.570
33 HR, 110 RBI
118 BB, 21 SB

MINOR LEAGUE

Aaron Blair
rhp
(Double-A/Triple-A)
13-5, 2.92
11 quality starts

ORGANIZATION LEADERS

BATTING		*Minimum 250 AB
MAJORS		
* AVG	Paul Goldschmidt	.321
* OPS	Paul Goldschmidt	1.005
HR	Paul Goldschmidt	33
RBI	Paul Goldschmidt	110
MINORS		
* AVG	Ildemaro Vargas, Kane County	.321
* OBP	Danny Worth, Reno	.394
* SLG	Peter O'Brien, Reno	.551
R	Daniel Palka, Visalia	95
H	Nick Evans, Reno	161
TB	Daniel Palka, Visalia	272
2B	Jamie Romak, Reno	42
3B	Socrates Brito, Mobile	15
HR	Daniel Palka, Visalia	29
RBI	Peter O'Brien, Reno	107
BB	Jamie Romak, Reno	60
SO	Daniel Palka, Visalia	164
SB	Matt McPhearson, Missoula	30

PITCHING		#Minimum 75 IP
MAJORS		
W	Rubby De La Rosa	14
# ERA	Rubby De La Rosa	4.67
SO	Rubby De La Rosa	150
SV	Brad Ziegler	30
MINORS		
W	Aaron Blair, Mobile, Reno	13
	John Omahen, Visalia, Mobile	13
L	Braden Shipley, Mobile	11
	Blayne Weller, Visalia, Mobile, Reno	11
# ERA	Brad Keller, Kane County	2.60
G	Joey Krehbiel, Visalia	60
GS	4 players	27
SV	Zac Curtis, Kane County	33
IP	Aaron Blair, Mobile, Reno	160
BB	Jeferson Mejia, Kane County, Hillsboro	62
SO	Anthony Banda, Visalia	152
AVG	Aaron Blair, Mobile, Reno	.233

ARIZONA DIAMONDBACKS

General Manager: Dave Stewart. **Farm Director:** Mike Bell. **Scouting Director:** Deric Ladnier.

Class	Team	League	W	L	PCT	Finish	Manager
Majors	Arizona Diamondbacks	National	79	83	.488	8th (15)	Chip Hale
Triple-A	Reno Aces	Pacific Coast	70	74	.486	10th (16)	Phil Nevin
Double-A	Mobile BayBears	Southern	70	67	.511	5th (10)	Robby Hammock
High A	Visalia Rawhide	California	84	56	.600	1st (10)	J.R. House
Low A	Kane County Cougars	Midwest	84	54	.609	2nd (16)	Mark Grudzielanek
Short season	Hillsboro Hops	Northwest	45	31	.592	1st (8)	Shelley Duncan
Rookie	Missoula Osprey	Pioneer	42	33	.560	2nd (8)	Joe Mather
Rookie	Diamondbacks	Arizona	25	30	.455	9th (14)	Mike Benjamin
Overall 2015 Minor League Record			420	345	.549	2nd (30)	

ORGANIZATION STATISTICS

ARIZONA DIAMONDBACKS

NATIONAL LEAGUE

Batting	B-T	HT	WT	DOB	AVG	vLH	vRH	G	AB	R	H	2B	3B	HR	RBI	BB	HBP	SH	SF	SO	SB	CS	SLG	OBP
Ahmed, Nick	R-R	6-2	195	3-15-90	.226	.296	.201	134	421	49	95	17	6	9	34	29	1	5	3	81	4	5	.359	.275
Brito, Socrates	L-L	6-1	200	9-6-92	.303	.000	.345	18	33	5	10	3	1	0	1	1	0	0	0	7	1	0	.455	.324
Castillo, Welington	R-R	5-10	210	4-24-87	.255	.239	.261	80	274	34	70	13	1	17	50	21	5	0	3	75	0	0	.496	.317
2-team total (24 Chicago)					.243	—	—	104	317	39	77	15	1	19	55	24	6	0	3	87	0	0	.476	.306
Dorn, Danny	L-L	6-2	200	7-20-84	.167	.000	.179	23	30	0	5	1	0	0	3	2	0	0	0	10	0	0	.200	.219
Drury, Brandon	R-R	6-1	215	8-21-92	.214	.304	.152	20	56	3	12	3	0	2	8	2	1	0	0	8	0	0	.375	.254
Goldschmidt, Paul	R-R	6-3	225	9-10-87	.321	.364	.309	159	567	103	182	38	2	33	110	118	2	0	7	151	21	5	.570	.435
Gosewisch, Tuffy	R-R	5-11	200	8-17-83	.211	.160	.223	38	128	9	27	6	0	1	13	8	1	0	1	23	2	1	.281	.261
Gosselin, Phil	R-R	6-1	200	10-3-88	.303	.333	.296	24	66	17	20	5	1	3	13	7	2	0	1	11	0	1	.545	.382
2-team total (20 Atlanta)					.311	—	—	44	106	19	33	9	1	3	15	9	2	0	1	16	2	1	.500	.373
Hernandez, Oscar	R-R	6-1	220	7-9-93	.161	.000	.172	18	31	4	5	1	0	0	1	3	1	1	0	15	0	0	.194	.257
Hill, Aaron	R-R	5-11	200	3-21-82	.230	.236	.227	116	313	32	72	18	0	6	39	31	1	0	8	54	7	2	.345	.295
Inciarte, Ender	L-L	5-10	185	10-29-90	.303	.227	.332	132	524	73	159	27	5	6	45	26	4	2	5	58	21	10	.408	.338
Laird, Gerald	R-R	6-1	230	11-13-79	.000	—	.000	1	2	0	0	0	0	0	0	0	0	0	0	0	0	0	.000	.000
Lamb, Jake	L-R	6-3	205	10-9-90	.263	.200	.272	107	350	38	92	15	5	6	34	36	1	0	3	97	3	2	.386	.331
O'Brien, Peter	R-R	6-4	235	7-15-90	.400	1.000	.143	9	10	1	4	1	0	1	2	2	0	0	0	5	0	0	.800	.500
Owings, Chris	R-R	5-10	190	8-12-91	.227	.171	.244	147	515	59	117	27	5	4	43	26	1	7	3	144	16	4	.322	.264
Pacheco, Jordan	R-R	6-1	200	1-30-86	.242	.267	.235	29	66	8	16	0	0	2	8	9	1	0	2	14	1	0	.333	.333
Pennington, Cliff	B-R	5-10	195	6-15-84	.237	.333	.228	72	135	15	32	3	0	1	10	16	0	4	2	29	3	0	.281	.314
Peralta, David	L-L	6-1	215	8-14-87	.312	.250	.325	149	462	61	144	26	10	17	78	44	4	0	7	107	9	4	.522	.371
Pollock, A.J.	R-R	6-1	195	12-5-87	.315	.326	.312	157	609	111	192	39	6	20	76	53	2	0	9	89	39	7	.498	.367
Romak, Jamie	R-R	6-2	220	9-30-85	.333	.333	.333	12	15	2	5	2	0	0	1	1	0	0	0	6	0	0	.467	.375
Saltalamacchia, Jarrod	B-R	6-4	235	5-2-85	.251	.324	.231	70	171	23	43	14	0	8	23	19	2	1	1	57	0	0	.474	.332
2-team total (9 Miami)					.225	—	—	79	200	26	45	15	0	9	24	23	2	1	1	69	0	0	.435	.310
Tomas, Yasmany	R-R	6-2	255	11-14-90	.273	.279	.271	118	406	40	111	19	3	9	48	17	2	0	1	110	5	2	.401	.305
Trumbo, Mark	R-R	6-4	225	1-16-86	.259	.293	.248	46	174	23	45	10	3	9	23	10	0	0	0	39	0	0	.506	.299

Pitching	B-T	HT	WT	DOB	W	L	ERA	G	GS	CG	SV	IP	H	R	ER	HR	BB	SO	AVG	vLH	vRH	K/9	BB/9
Anderson, Chase	R-R	6-1	194	11-30-87	6	6	4.30	27	27	0	0	153	158	75	73	18	40	111	.272	.262	.280	6.54	2.36
Bracho, Silvino	R-R	5-10	190	7-17-92	0	0	1.46	13	0	0	1	12	9	2	2	4	17	.200	.294	.143	12.41	2.92
Bradley, Archie	R-R	6-4	230	8-10-92	2	3	5.80	8	8	0	0	36	36	23	23	3	22	23	.267	.178	.371	5.80	5.55
Burgos, Enrique	R-R	6-3	250	11-23-90	2	2	4.67	30	0	0	2	27	27	15	14	2	15	39	.257	.293	.234	13.00	5.00
Chacin, Jhoulys	R-R	6-3	215	1-7-88	2	1	3.38	5	4	0	0	27	24	11	10	4	10	21	.240	.319	.170	7.09	3.38
Chafin, Andrew	R-L	6-2	225	6-17-90	5	1	2.76	66	0	0	2	75	56	23	23	3	30	58	.207	.182	.225	6.96	3.60
Collmenter, Josh	R-R	6-4	235	2-7-86	4	6	3.79	44	12	1	1	121	129	53	51	18	24	63	.277	.273	.281	4.69	1.79
Corbin, Pat	L-L	6-3	210	7-19-89	6	5	3.60	16	16	0	0	85	91	34	34	9	17	78	.272	.211	.288	8.26	1.80
De La Rosa, Rubby	R-R	6-1	225	3-4-89	14	9	4.67	32	32	0	0	189	193	103	98	32	63	150	.265	.315	.214	7.16	3.01
Delgado, Randall	R-R	6-4	220	2-9-90	8	4	3.25	64	1	0	1	72	63	28	26	7	33	73	.234	.248	.226	9.13	4.13
Godley, Zack	R-R	6-3	245	4-21-90	5	1	3.19	9	6	0	0	37	29	13	13	4	17	34	.227	.182	.260	8.35	4.17
Hellickson, Jeremy	R-R	6-1	190	4-8-87	9	12	4.62	27	27	0	0	146	151	79	75	22	43	121	.264	.273	.257	7.46	2.65
Hernandez, David	R-R	6-3	245	5-13-85	1	5	4.28	40	0	0	0	34	33	18	16	6	11	33	.256	.260	.253	8.82	2.94
Hessler, Keith	L-L	6-4	215	3-15-89	0	1	8.03	18	0	0	0	12	16	11	11	4	4	12	.302	.160	.429	8.76	2.92
Hudson, Daniel	R-R	6-3	235	3-9-87	4	3	3.86	64	1	0	4	68	64	34	29	7	25	71	.245	.186	.291	9.44	3.33
Leone, Dominic	R-R	5-11	210	10-26-91	0	1	14.73	3	0	0	0	4	8	6	6	1	0	2	.444	.500	.400	4.91	0.00
Marshall, Evan	R-R	6-2	225	4-18-90	0	2	6.08	13	0	0	0	13	20	9	9	3	5	7	.357	.385	.333	4.73	3.38
Nuno, Vidal	L-L	5-11	210	7-26-87	0	1	1.88	3	0	0	0	14	10	3	3	1	5	19	.189	.182	.190	11.93	3.14
Perez, Oliver	L-L	6-3	220	8-15-81	2	1	3.10	48	0	0	0	29	25	12	10	2	11	37	.223	.183	.269	11.48	3.41
Ramirez, J.C.	R-R	6-4	250	8-16-88	1	1	4.11	12	0	0	0	15	15	7	7	1	4	11	.254	.160	.324	6.46	2.35
Ray, Robbie	L-L	6-2	195	10-1-91	5	12	3.52	23	23	0	0	128	121	56	50	9	49	119	.255	.262	.252	8.39	3.45
Reed, Addison	L-R	6-4	230	12-27-88	2	2	4.20	38	0	0	3	41	47	19	19	2	14	34	.283	.242	.310	7.52	3.10
2-team total (17 New York)					3	3	3.38	55	0	0	4	56	58	21	21	3	19	51	—			8.20	3.05
Reynolds, Matt	L-L	6-5	240	10-2-84	0	0	4.61	18	0	0	0	14	13	7	7	6	7	18	.259	.241	.280	11.85	4.61
Schugel, A.J.	R-R	6-0	205	6-27-89	0	0	5.00	5	0	0	0	9	17	13	5	2	5	5	.370	.429	.320	5.00	5.00
Stites, Matt	R-R	5-11	195	5-28-90	0	0	12.46	11	0	0	0	9	14	14	12	1	5	6	.368	.375	.364	6.23	5.19

Pitching	B-T	HT	WT	DOB	W	L	ERA	G	GS	CG	SV	IP	H	R	ER	HR	BB	SO	AVG	vLH	vRH	K/9	BB/9
Webster, Allen	R-R	6-2	190	2-10-90	1	1	5.81	9	5	0	0	31	32	28	20	10	20	17	.271	.340	.225	4.94	5.81
Ziegler, Brad	R-R	6-4	220	10-10-79	0	3	1.85	66	0	0	30	68	48	17	14	3	17	36	.198	.217	.179	4.76	2.25

Fielding

Catcher	PCT	G	PO	A	E	DP	PB
Castillo	.991	74	511	34	5	2	5
Gosewisch	.996	37	256	24	1	0	2
Hernandez	1.000	13	74	11	0	2	2
Laird	1.000	1	3	0	0	0	0
Pacheco	.990	18	95	3	1	1	2
Saltalamacchia	.997	38	272	18	1	0	0

First Base	PCT	G	PO	A	E	DP
Dorn	1.000	2	7	0	0	0
Goldschmidt	.997	157	1378	123	5	129
Lamb	1.000	8	27	2	0	2
Pacheco	1.000	2	5	0	0	0
Romak	.750	1	3	0	1	0
Saltalamacchia	1.000	4	14	0	0	1
Tomas	1.000	4	12	1	0	2
Trumbo	1.000	1	5	1	0	1

Second Base	PCT	G	PO	A	E	DP
Drury	.952	6	11	9	1	3
Gosselin	.978	13	17	28	1	4
Hill	.989	47	57	118	2	21
Owings	.991	115	154	289	4	65
Pennington	.972	11	10	25	1	4

Third Base	PCT	G	PO	A	E	DP
Drury	1.000	11	2	14	0	1
Gosselin	1.000	2	0	2	0	0
Hill	.952	38	23	57	4	8
Lamb	.973	95	47	203	7	14
Pacheco	—	1	0	0	0	0
Pennington	.889	12	2	6	1	0
Tomas	.918	31	22	45	6	5

Shortstop	PCT	G	PO	A	E	DP
Ahmed	.977	129	190	368	13	84

Drury	1.000	1	1	2	0	0
Owings	.990	35	37	62	1	10
Pennington	.951	24	17	60	4	13

Outfield	PCT	G	PO	A	E	DP
Brito	1.000	7	15	2	0	1
Dorn	1.000	3	3	0	0	0
Gosselin	1.000	3	3	0	0	0
Inciarte	.978	122	254	10	6	2
O'Brien	1.000	3	1	0	0	0
Pennington	1.000	5	6	1	0	0
Peralta	.991	131	227	3	2	0
Pollock	.992	151	347	5	3	0
Romak	—	2	0	0	0	0
Tomas	.975	63	113	3	3	0
Trumbo	.986	42	67	2	1	0

RENO ACES   TRIPLE-A

PACIFIC COAST LEAGUE

Batting	B-T	HT	WT	DOB	AVG	vLH	vRH	G	AB	R	H	2B	3B	HR	RBI	BB	HBP	SH	SF	SO	SB	CS	SLG	OBP
Belza, Tom	L-R	6-0	190	7-31-89	.162	.077	.208	16	37	4	6	1	0	1	5	0	0	0	12	0	2	.189	.262
Borenstein, Zach	L-R	6-0	225	7-23-90	.154	.143	.156	18	52	3	8	2	0	0	3	1	0	0	0	14	0	0	.192	.170
Buss, Nick	L-R	6-2	190	12-15-86	.296	.356	.280	92	284	43	84	14	3	4	33	24	4	2	6	35	10	4	.408	.352
Dorn, Danny	L-L	6-2	200	7-20-84	.386	.318	.418	75	267	57	103	26	3	10	53	28	4	1	5	45	1	2	.618	.444
Drury, Brandon	R-R	6-1	215	8-21-92	.331	.365	.316	63	251	43	83	26	0	2	25	21	2	0	2	35	0	2	.458	.384
Evans, Nick	R-R	6-2	220	1-30-86	.310	.333	.298	139	520	79	161	37	0	17	94	59	2	0	2	111	0	1	.479	.381
Frandsen, Kevin	R-R	6-0	190	5-24-82	.309	.389	.244	26	81	8	25	2	0	0	7	6	0	1	1	8	0	1	.333	.352
2-team total (86 Sacramento)					.280	—	—	112	404	46	113	17	1	4	48	24	13	4	3	27	5	3	.356	.338
Freeman, Mike	L-R	6-0	190	8-4-87	.317	.293	.324	113	398	79	126	23	5	3	41	34	1	1	1	51	10	0	.422	.371
Glaesmann, Todd	R-R	6-4	220	10-24-90	.286	.257	.305	94	283	49	81	27	3	14	37	14	3	0	0	57	5	2	.551	.327
Gosselin, Phil	R-R	6-1	200	10-3-88	.333	.167	.400	5	21	4	7	4	0	0	5	1	0	0	0	2	0	0	.524	.364
Hernandez, Oscar	R-R	6-1	220	7-9-93	.240	.200	.250	8	25	2	6	3	0	0	1	0	1	0	0	5	0	0	.360	.269
Laird, Gerald	R-R	6-1	230	11-13-79	.267	.125	.429	6	15	1	4	1	0	0	3	0	0	0	1	2	0	0	.333	.250
Lalli, Blake	L-R	6-1	210	5-12-83	.260	.188	.271	81	246	18	64	10	0	3	30	21	2	2	4	28	0	2	.337	.319
Lamb, Jake	L-R	6-3	205	10-9-90	.364	.600	.167	3	11	0	4	1	0	0	2	4	0	0	0	1	0	0	.455	.533
Marzilli, Evan	L-L	6-0	185	3-13-91	.300	.385	.235	9	30	4	9	1	1	0	2	0	0	0	0	7	1	2	.400	.300
Navarro, Raul	R-R	5-10	170	2-5-92	.294	.091	.391	10	34	5	10	2	0	0	4	0	0	1	0	6	0	1	.353	.294
O'Brien, Peter	R-R	6-4	235	7-15-90	.264	.318	.246	131	490	77	139	35	9	26	107	31	7	1	5	124	1	3	.551	.332
Pacheco, Jordan	R-R	6-1	200	1-30-86	.205	.217	.198	58	161	26	33	11	1	2	15	19	3	0	2	26	0	0	.323	.297
Pagnozzi, Matt	R-R	6-2	215	11-10-82	.256	.275	.236	63	180	17	46	8	1	4	20	18	0	4	3	29	0	1	.378	.318
Ransom, Cody	R-R	6-2	200	2-17-76	.210	.200	.215	63	167	14	35	8	1	6	30	10	0	0	4	44	1	0	.377	.249
Robinson, Trayvon	B-R	5-10	200	9-1-87	.276	.250	.294	37	87	22	24	7	1	2	9	10	1	0	0	13	1	1	.448	.357
Romak, Jamie	R-R	6-2	220	9-30-85	.284	.337	.257	129	486	87	138	42	3	27	100	60	4	0	7	143	6	1	.549	.363
Rondon, Alvaro	B-R	5-10	160	9-6-90	.250	.000	.500	3	4	2	1	0	0	0	1	1	0	0	0	0	0	0	.250	.400
Saltalamacchia, Jarrod	B-R	6-4	235	5-2-85	.188	.273	.143	9	32	2	6	0	0	2	7	2	0	0	2	13	0	0	.375	.222
Tomas, Yasmany	R-R	6-2	255	11-14-90	.190	.250	.111	5	21	2	4	1	0	1	3	2	0	0	0	5	0	0	.381	.261
Weber, Garrett	R-R	5-10	165	3-29-89	.303	.277	.319	77	267	49	81	15	4	9	35	30	2	0	2	49	1	2	.491	.375
Worth, Danny	R-R	6-1	195	9-30-85	.314	.320	.311	106	350	53	110	30	3	6	47	46	1	1	1	99	6	2	.469	.394

Pitching	B-T	HT	WT	DOB	W	L	ERA	G	GS	CG	SV	IP	H	R	ER	HR	BB	SO	AVG	vLH	vRH	K/9	BB/9
Arias, Gabriel	R-R	6-2	185	12-6-89	5	4	6.22	14	13	1	0	64	82	51	44	12	25	40	.318	.358	.283	5.65	3.53
Barrett, Jake	R-R	6-3	220	7-22-91	1	3	5.09	22	0	0	11	23	27	15	13	1	12	21	.303	.275	.327	8.22	4.70
Beavan, Blake	R-R	6-7	245	1-17-89	0	1	6.32	4	4	0	0	16	21	12	11	2	5	9	.333	.378	.269	5.17	2.87
Blair, Aaron	R-R	6-5	230	5-26-92	7	2	3.16	13	12	0	0	77	67	31	27	5	27	56	.236	.262	.220	6.55	3.16
Bradley, Archie	R-R	6-4	230	8-10-92	1	0	2.95	4	4	0	0	21	26	7	7	3	5	20	.302	.360	.279	8.44	2.11
Burgos, Enrique	R-R	6-3	250	11-23-90	0	1	6.00	15	0	0	5	15	19	10	10	3	12	23	.302	.385	.243	13.80	7.20
Chacin, Jhoulys	R-R	6-3	215	1-7-88	6	3	3.22	13	13	0	0	87	79	37	31	3	30	63	.248	.242	.254	6.54	3.12
Chafin, Andrew	R-L	6-2	225	6-17-90	0	0	0.00	1	0	0	0	1	0	0	0	0	0	1	.000	.000	.000	9.00	0.00
Clay, Caleb	R-R	6-2	180	2-15-88	8	7	5.25	22	20	0	0	111	142	72	65	13	34	56	.314	.335	.298	4.53	2.75
Crabbe, Tim	R-R	6-4	200	2-20-88	1	0	5.50	19	0	0	0	34	40	22	21	3	23	33	.301	.245	.333	8.65	6.03
DePaula, Julio	R-R	6-0	180	12-31-82	0	0	12.71	3	0	0	0	6	12	8	8	0	4	5	.462	.500	.444	7.94	6.35
Eitel, Derek	R-R	6-4	200	11-21-87	0	0	5.73	10	0	0	0	11	13	7	7	2	8	11	.302	.389	.240	9.00	6.55
Fleck, Kaleb	R-R	6-2	190	1-24-89	4	1	3.46	42	0	0	7	52	47	23	20	2	24	66	.244	.303	.213	11.42	4.15
Frazier, Parker	R-R	6-5	175	11-11-88	1	0	7.20	3	3	0	0	15	26	12	12	0	6	8	.400	.421	.391	4.80	3.60
2-team total (1 Nashville)					1	0	6.98	4	4	0	0	19	38	16	15	0	6	10	—	—	—	4.66	2.79
Garcia, Edgar	R-R	6-2	190	9-20-87	3	1	4.91	6	6	0	0	33	36	18	18	6	9	19	.277	.255	.293	5.18	2.45
Hellickson, Jeremy	R-R	6-1	190	4-8-87	0	0	4.50	1	1	0	0	6	6	3	3	0	1	4	.273	.273	.273	6.00	1.50
Hernandez, Hector	B-L	6-1	190	2-20-91	0	0	9.00	1	0	0	0	1	1	1	1	0	1	1	.250	—	.250	9.00	0.00
Hessler, Keith	L-L	6-4	215	3-15-89	1	1	5.68	17	0	0	0	19	14	12	12	3	8	13	.212	.222	.205	6.16	3.79

Pitching

Pitching	B-T	HT	WT	DOB	W	L	ERA	G	GS	CG	SV	IP	H	R	ER	HR	BB	SO	AVG	vLH	vRH	K/9	BB/9
Hively, R.J.	R-R	6-2	225	11-27-88	2	1	5.94	8	2	0	1	17	22	12	11	1	10	14	.324	.325	.321	7.56	5.40
Marks, Justin	L-L	6-3	205	1-12-88	5	9	5.63	28	19	0	0	109	121	72	68	12	50	84	.289	.216	.308	6.96	4.14
Marks, Troy	R-R	6-5	210	12-31-89	0	0	3.60	3	1	0	0	5	7	2	2	0	1	1	.318	.429	.125	1.80	1.80
Marshall, Evan	R-R	6-2	225	4-18-90	3	2	6.40	31	0	0	0	32	47	28	23	1	13	25	.326	.282	.343	6.96	3.62
Munson, Kevin	R-R	6-2	215	1-3-89	2	3	4.45	30	0	0	2	32	24	16	16	4	25	30	.211	.257	.190	8.35	6.96
Nuno, Vidal	L-L	5-11	210	7-26-87	3	3	3.38	8	8	0	0	51	51	22	19	7	8	41	.258	.091	.291	7.28	1.42
2-team total (1 Tacoma)					4	3	3.65	9	9	0	0	57	58	26	23	8	9	47	—	—	—	7.46	1.43
Paredes, Willy	R-R	6-2	180	2-2-89	0	0	7.13	9	0	0	0	18	25	14	14	2	15	14	.347	.308	.370	7.13	7.64
Ramirez, J.C.	R-R	6-4	250	8-16-88	0	1	2.88	23	0	0	1	25	22	8	8	0	10	18	.234	.161	.270	6.48	3.60
2-team total (14 Tacoma)					1	2	2.72	37	0	0	1	43	39	14	13	2	17	36	—	—	—	7.53	3.56
Ray, Robbie	L-L	6-2	195	10-1-91	2	3	3.67	9	9	0	0	42	44	21	17	1	27	57	.280	.392	.226	12.31	5.83
Reed, Addison	L-R	6-4	230	12-27-88	1	1	1.74	11	0	0	5	10	8	2	2	1	5	11	.200	.313	.125	9.58	4.35
Reynolds, Matt	L-L	6-5	240	10-24-84	3	6	5.58	45	0	0	0	50	55	34	31	5	18	43	.284	.230	.330	7.74	3.24
Runzler, Dan	L-L	6-4	210	3-30-85	0	1	5.26	39	0	0	0	38	48	25	22	2	28	40	.310	.324	.299	9.56	6.69
Schugel, A.J.	R-R	6-0	205	6-27-89	2	7	10.18	9	9	1	0	38	65	45	43	4	17	27	.385	.378	.391	6.39	4.03
Shankin, Brett	R-R	6-0	200	10-30-89	0	0	16.20	3	1	0	0	7	14	12	12	2	6	6	.452	.364	.500	8.10	8.10
Simmons, Seth	R-R	5-9	170	6-14-88	3	3	3.27	32	0	0	0	44	42	16	16	4	18	46	.247	.143	.298	9.41	3.68
Smith, Myles	R-R	6-1	175	3-23-92	0	0	0.00	1	0	0	0	1	0	0	0	0	1	1	.000	—	.000	9.00	9.00
Stites, Matt	R-R	5-11	195	5-28-90	1	1	3.86	23	0	0	3	26	31	16	11	2	14	14	.301	.306	.299	4.91	4.91
Vance, Kevin	R-R	6-0	208	7-8-90	0	0	4.00	6	0	0	0	9	9	4	4	0	6	6	.265	.333	.211	6.00	6.00
Webster, Allen	R-R	6-2	190	2-10-90	4	6	8.18	15	15	0	0	77	117	70	70	8	26	62	.350	.394	.313	7.25	3.04
Weller, Blayne	R-R	6-5	220	1-30-90	1	3	4.62	6	4	0	0	25	26	15	13	2	9	17	.265	.271	.260	6.04	3.20

Fielding

Catcher

Catcher	PCT	G	PO	A	E	DP	PB
Hernandez	.981	8	47	5	1	0	3
Laird	1.000	4	32	1	0	0	0
Lalli	.998	68	443	41	1	3	3
O'Brien	.989	11	83	5	1	0	1
Pacheco	1.000	8	26	2	0	0	0
Pagnozzi	.997	60	338	33	1	4	0
Saltalamacchia	1.000	5	28	0	0	0	0

First Base

First Base	PCT	G	PO	A	E	DP
Dorn	.998	52	411	43	1	54
Evans	.993	76	684	55	5	78
Frandsen	1.000	1	11	0	0	0
Lalli	1.000	2	8	1	0	2
O'Brien	1.000	4	21	2	0	4
Pacheco	1.000	1	5	0	0	0
Romak	1.000	10	76	4	0	12
Weber	1.000	5	31	4	0	3

Second Base

Second Base	PCT	G	PO	A	E	DP
Drury	.979	27	61	76	3	20
Frandsen	1.000	9	20	19	0	9

	PCT	G	PO	A	E	DP
Freeman	.973	29	54	88	4	31
Gosselin	1.000	3	3	10	0	2
Pacheco	.975	33	65	94	4	23
Romak	.983	25	47	69	2	13
Rondon	1.000	1	1	2	0	0
Weber	.958	20	30	38	3	11
Worth	1.000	14	20	32	0	10

Third Base

Third Base	PCT	G	PO	A	E	DP
Drury	.985	28	21	43	1	6
Evans	1.000	13	8	30	0	4
Frandsen	.944	10	3	14	1	1
Gosselin	1.000	1	0	1	0	0
Lamb	.889	2	0	8	1	1
Pacheco	.938	5	2	13	1	1
Ransom	1.000	3	1	8	0	0
Romak	.950	88	59	149	11	16
Worth	—	1	0	0	0	0

Shortstop

Shortstop	PCT	G	PO	A	E	DP
Drury	1.000	9	7	31	0	6
Freeman	.892	8	4	29	4	5

	PCT	G	PO	A	E	DP
Gosselin	.750	1	1	2	1	1
Navarro	.973	10	9	27	1	4
Ransom	.964	39	46	113	6	25
Worth	.953	88	134	255	19	69

Outfield

Outfield	PCT	G	PO	A	E	DP
Belza	.967	14	28	1	1	0
Borenstein	.941	14	16	0	1	0
Buss	.982	85	162	2	3	1
Dorn	1.000	14	27	1	0	0
Evans	1.000	16	17	2	0	0
Frandsen	1.000	4	4	0	0	0
Freeman	.981	75	99	4	2	1
Glaesmann	.994	88	168	9	1	1
Marzilli	1.000	9	15	0	0	0
O'Brien	.939	101	149	6	10	2
Pacheco	1.000	1	1	0	0	0
Robinson	.965	33	55	0	2	0
Romak	1.000	9	11	0	0	0
Tomas	1.000	5	3	1	0	0
Weber	.974	43	69	5	2	0

MOBILE BAYBEARS   DOUBLE-A

SOUTHERN LEAGUE

Batting	B-T	HT	WT	DOB	AVG	vLH	vRH	G	AB	R	H	2B	3B	HR	RBI	BB	HBP	SH	SF	SO	SB	CS	SLG	OBP
Belza, Tom	L-R	6-0	190	7-31-89	.229	.275	.219	92	279	35	64	13	2	4	17	27	1	5	0	72	5	4	.333	.300
Borenstein, Zach	L-R	6-0	225	7-23-90	.314	.281	.324	85	280	45	88	15	5	10	57	38	3	0	6	55	6	4	.511	.394
Brito, Socrates	L-L	6-1	200	9-6-92	.300	.222	.318	129	490	70	147	17	15	9	57	29	1	0	2	84	20	6	.451	.339
Drury, Brandon	R-R	6-2	215	8-21-92	.278	.302	.273	67	273	22	76	14	1	3	36	11	2	0	5	41	4	5	.370	.306
Fields, Matt	R-R	6-5	235	7-8-85	.200	.500	.105	8	25	5	5	1	0	1	2	0	0	0	0	9	0	0	.360	.200
Flores, Rudy	L-R	6-3	205	12-12-90	.241	.215	.248	121	440	54	106	24	0	14	65	32	13	1	4	138	1	2	.391	.309
Freeman, Ronnie	R-R	6-1	190	1-8-91	.232	.373	.192	73	233	22	54	8	0	1	16	20	1	3	1	37	0	0	.279	.294
Gebhardt, Ryan	R-R	5-11	195	10-5-91	.238	.000	.250	15	42	4	10	1	0	0	5	4	1	0	0	9	0	1	.262	.319
Glaesmann, Todd	R-R	6-4	220	10-24-90	.167	.214	.152	24	60	4	10	0	1	1	6	3	0	1	0	19	0	1	.250	.206
Glenn, Alex	L-L	5-11	180	6-11-91	.238	.158	.248	58	172	22	41	12	5	3	18	13	4	0	0	35	4	4	.419	.307
Guerrero, Gabby	R-R	6-3	190	12-11-93	.226	.261	.210	78	283	29	64	15	5	3	32	11	1	0	2	60	8	2	.367	.256
2-team total (48 Jackson)					.222	—	—	126	460	51	102	25	5	7	47	23	1	0	4	108	11	2	.343	.258
Haniger, Mitch	R-R	6-2	215	12-23-90	.281	.367	.260	55	153	23	43	10	1	1	19	16	2	0	3	32	4	4	.379	.351
Ijames, Stewart	L-R	6-0	220	8-21-88	.274	.250	.281	33	73	8	20	8	1	3	12	5	1	0	1	15	1	1	.534	.325
Inciarte, Ender	L-L	5-10	185	10-29-90	.300	.400	.267	5	20	3	6	1	1	1	1	3	0	0	0	2	0	0	.600	.391
Jamieson, Sean	R-R	6-0	195	3-2-89	.272	.257	.277	92	294	53	80	14	0	6	14	40	9	3	0	79	10	4	.381	.376
Jones, Matt	R-R	6-0	195	4-14-92	.200	.400	.143	4	12	0	3	0	0	0	2	0	0	0	0	2	0	0	.250	.250
Marzilli, Evan	L-L	6-0	185	3-13-91	.246	.194	.264	32	122	17	30	5	2	1	8	20	1	0	1	28	6	4	.344	.354
Medrano, Kevin	L-R	6-1	155	5-21-90	.296	.563	.218	17	71	11	21	4	0	0	10	4	0	0	0	9	3	0	.352	.333
Montilla, Gerson	R-R	5-10	170	11-13-89	.225	.238	.219	67	200	22	45	7	0	8	35	26	4	0	1	37	3	3	.380	.325
Navarro, Raul	R-R	5-10	170	2-5-92	.240	.289	.228	75	229	19	55	8	0	0	8	30	4	2	1	55	5	8	.275	.337
Pagnozzi, Matt	R-R	6-2	215	11-10-82	.208	1.000	.174	10	24	2	5	0	0	0	5	7	1	0	0	11	0	0	.208	.406
Reinheimer, Jack	R-R	6-1	186	7-19-92	.265	.271	.263	76	283	39	75	14	2	4	26	37	4	1	3	54	9	5	.371	.355
2-team total (48 Jackson)					.270	—	—	124	485	64	131	24	3	5	42	51	4	3	4	93	21	6	.363	.342
Tarleton, Dallas	L-R	5-11	200	8-5-87	.333	—	.333	4	12	2	4	0	0	0	1	2	0	0	0	0	0	0	.333	.429

ARIZONA DIAMONDBACKS

Batting	B-T	HT	WT	DOB	AVG	vLH	vRH	G	AB	R	H	2B	3B	HR	RBI	BB	HBP	SH	SF	SO	SB	CS	SLG	OBP
2-team total (4 Birmingham)					.227	—	—	8	22	2	5	0	0	0	1	3	0	0	0	6	0	0	.227	.320
Thomas, Mark	R-R	6-1	225	5-5-88	.174	.175	.174	59	195	17	34	13	1	5	21	19	3	1	1	62	3	2	.328	.257
Weber, Garrett	R-R	5-10	165	3-29-89	.299	.289	.303	37	137	14	41	12	0	0	20	13	1	0	1	32	1	0	.387	.362

Pitching	B-T	HT	WT	DOB	W	L	ERA	G	GS	CG	SV	IP	H	R	ER	HR	BB	SO	AVG	vLH	vRH	K/9	BB/9
Arias, Gabriel	R-R	6-2	185	12-6-89	6	2	2.77	10	10	0	0	65	55	23	20	2	12	45	.229	.192	.255	6.23	1.66
Barbosa, Andrew	R-L	6-8	230	11-18-87	0	1	12.27	3	1	0	0	4	4	5	5	0	5	5	.308	.200	.375	12.27	12.27
2-team total (16 Mississippi)					5	3	3.42	19	6	0	0	47	36	20	18	1	22	56	—	—	—	10.65	4.18
Barrett, Jake	R-R	6-3	220	7-22-91	3	0	4.20	25	0	0	4	30	34	14	14	2	11	30	.293	.191	.362	9.00	3.30
Blair, Aaron	R-R	6-5	230	5-26-92	6	3	2.70	13	13	1	0	83	70	28	25	8	23	64	.231	.233	.230	6.91	2.48
Bracho, Silvino	R-R	5-10	190	7-17-92	1	2	1.81	37	0	0	16	45	34	10	9	3	9	59	.207	.264	.163	11.89	1.81
Bradley, J.R.	R-R	6-3	185	6-9-92	0	0	6.75	7	0	0	0	8	12	6	6	1	5	6	.343	.125	.407	6.75	5.63
Burgos, Enrique	R-R	6-3	220	11-23-90	0	0	0.00	10	0	0	6	9	4	0	0	0	8	15	.121	.200	.056	14.46	7.71
Clay, Caleb	R-R	6-2	180	2-15-88	0	0	6.75	1	1	0	0	4	7	3	3	0	1	0	.368	.400	.333	0.00	2.25
Corbin, Pat	L-L	6-3	210	7-19-89	1	0	2.76	3	3	0	0	16	13	6	5	1	5	11	.220	.250	.209	6.06	2.76
Crabbe, Tim	R-R	6-4	200	2-20-88	0	0	3.00	1	0	0	0	3	3	1	1	0	0	5	.250	.500	.200	15.00	0.00
2-team total (16 Birmingham)					2	2	2.38	17	5	0	1	45	36	13	12	4	12	47	—	—	—	9.33	2.38
Delgado, Randall	R-R	6-4	220	2-9-90	1	0	0.00	1	0	0	0	1	0	0	0	0	0	2	.000	.000	.000	18.00	0.00
Doran, Ryan	R-R	6-1	185	8-5-90	0	0	1.50	1	1	0	0	6	5	1	1	0	3	2	.227	.125	.286	3.00	4.50
Eitel, Derek	R-R	6-4	200	11-21-87	0	1	7.71	4	0	0	0	5	4	5	4	0	6	4	.235	.200	.286	7.71	11.57
2-team total (7 Biloxi)					1	1	5.14	11	0	0	0	14	14	9	8	0	8	14	—	—	—	9.00	5.14
Frazier, Parker	R-R	6-5	175	11-11-88	0	0	0.00	1	0	0	0	1	1	0	0	0	1	1	.333	.000	.500	9.00	9.00
Garcia, Edgar	R-R	6-2	190	9-20-87	4	3	4.29	19	10	0	0	71	64	34	34	8	32	43	.243	.236	.248	5.43	4.04
Gibson, Daniel	R-L	6-2	221	10-16-91	1	0	1.50	26	0	0	2	24	18	5	4	0	14	20	.212	.146	.273	7.50	5.25
Godley, Zack	R-R	6-3	245	4-21-90	2	1	4.07	7	5	0	0	24	21	12	11	2	10	12	.244	.310	.211	4.44	3.70
Hernandez, David	R-R	6-3	245	5-13-85	0	0	0.00	5	1	0	0	4	0	0	0	0	2	6	.000	.000	.000	13.50	4.50
Hessler, Keith	L-L	6-4	215	3-15-89	3	1	0.71	24	0	0	1	25	17	2	2	1	5	32	.193	.178	.209	11.37	1.78
Hively, R.J.	R-R	6-2	225	11-27-88	1	2	4.23	19	4	0	0	38	43	23	18	2	15	33	.281	.266	.292	7.75	3.52
Koch, Matt	L-R	6-3	205	11-2-90	1	0	0.00	1	1	0	0	7	2	0	0	0	4	6	.083	.000	.118	7.36	4.91
Leone, Dominic	R-R	5-11	210	10-26-91	1	2	3.90	19	0	0	0	28	22	12	12	1	12	28	.218	.200	.225	9.11	3.90
Locante, Will	L-L	6-0	200	2-2-91	2	4	5.79	44	0	0	0	42	42	33	27	3	34	38	.261	.247	.273	8.14	7.29
Lopez, Yoan	R-R	6-3	185	1-2-93	1	6	4.69	10	9	0	0	48	46	27	25	4	24	32	.261	.292	.243	6.00	4.50
Marks, Troy	R-R	6-5	210	12-31-89	0	0	4.50	1	1	0	0	4	6	2	2	0	1	0	.400	.400	.400	2.25	0.00
Miller, Adam	R-R	6-0	185	12-28-89	2	7	2.88	50	0	0	7	56	60	24	18	0	28	63	.275	.296	.263	10.07	4.47
Munson, Kevin	R-R	6-2	215	1-3-89	0	0	0.00	3	1	0	0	3	1	0	0	0	0	4	.111	.000	.167	12.00	0.00
Omahen, Johnny	R-R	6-0	190	3-15-89	7	1	2.78	13	12	0	1	78	76	26	24	0	27	47	.267	.295	.249	5.45	3.13
Paredes, Willy	R-R	6-2	180	2-2-89	0	0	3.86	4	0	0	0	2	3	2	1	0	7	2	.273	.143	.500	7.71	27.00
Ramirez, Luis	R-R	6-3	240	7-12-92	0	0	0.00	1	0	0	0	2	0	0	0	0	1	4	.167	1.000	.000	18.00	4.50
Schugel, A.J.	R-R	6-0	205	6-27-89	7	2	2.21	12	12	0	0	77	74	21	19	5	15	52	.256	.258	.255	6.05	1.75
Schuster, Patrick	R-L	6-2	185	10-30-90	0	1	3.24	22	0	0	0	25	23	11	9	0	12	20	.253	.256	.250	7.20	4.32
2-team total (30 Pensacola)					2	2	3.33	52	0	0	0	54	50	22	20	1	26	45	—	—	—	7.50	4.33
Sherfy, Jimmie	R-R	6-0	175	12-27-91	1	6	6.52	44	0	0	2	50	50	37	36	3	28	50	.265	.250	.274	9.06	5.07
Shipley, Braden	R-R	6-2	185	2-22-92	9	11	3.50	28	27	1	0	157	147	68	61	7	56	118	.249	.256	.243	6.78	3.22
Shuttlesworth, Johnny	R-R	6-1	220	9-30-89	0	1	4.91	2	2	0	0	7	9	5	4	2	3	4	.346	.500	.300	4.91	3.68
Simmons, Seth	R-R	5-9	170	6-14-88	3	0	2.59	21	0	0	1	31	15	9	9	0	11	41	.143	.159	.133	11.78	3.16
Sinnery, Brandon	R-R	6-4	170	1-26-90	5	7	4.90	17	17	0	0	90	107	55	49	10	32	54	.298	.327	.278	5.40	3.20
Vance, Kevin	R-R	6-0	208	7-8-90	0	0	13.50	2	0	0	0	1	2	2	2	1	1	2	.333	.000	.400	13.50	6.75
Weller, Blayne	R-R	6-5	220	1-30-90	1	4	6.14	7	7	0	0	37	37	25	25	3	14	24	.262	.295	.238	5.89	3.44

Fielding

Catcher	PCT	G	PO	A	E	DP	PB
Freeman	1.000	71	455	37	0	3	2
Jones	1.000	3	22	3	0	0	1
Pagnozzi	.984	8	56	4	1	0	3
Tarleton	1.000	4	19	4	0	0	0
Thomas	.992	59	434	48	4	3	8

First Base	PCT	G	PO	A	E	DP
Belza	.989	30	172	11	2	21
Borenstein	1.000	1	1	0	0	0
Fields	.980	5	46	3	1	3
Flores	.993	111	879	74	7	94
Ijames	1.000	2	19	1	0	3
Pagnozzi	1.000	1	6	1	0	2
Weber	1.000	1	10	2	0	0

Second Base	PCT	G	PO	A	E	DP
Belza	1.000	1	0	4	0	0
Drury	.983	35	64	106	3	27

	PCT	G	PO	A	E	DP
Gebhardt	1.000	7	11	16	0	6
Jamieson	1.000	11	16	17	0	1
Medrano	.985	16	28	36	1	15
Montilla	.967	34	53	93	5	23
Navarro	1.000	14	21	24	0	6
Reinheimer	1.000	5	6	13	0	4
Weber	.981	29	45	61	2	11

Third Base	PCT	G	PO	A	E	DP
Belza	.921	33	20	38	5	5
Drury	.941	33	28	68	6	8
Jamieson	.938	42	24	67	6	4
Montilla	.844	16	7	20	5	1
Navarro	.962	26	11	39	2	4
Weber	1.000	5	2	8	0	1

Shortstop	PCT	G	PO	A	E	DP
Gebhardt	.900	7	11	16	3	2
Jamieson	.957	33	45	88	6	22

	PCT	G	PO	A	E	DP
Medrano	1.000	2	3	3	0	2
Navarro	.963	31	44	86	5	21
Reinheimer	.982	72	115	205	6	49

Outfield	PCT	G	PO	A	E	DP
Belza	1.000	27	38	0	0	0
Borenstein	.981	61	101	3	2	0
Brito	.981	128	296	9	6	3
Glaesmann	1.000	16	30	2	0	0
Glenn	.972	42	70	0	2	0
Guerrero	.981	76	146	7	3	2
Haniger	.946	50	85	3	5	1
Ijames	.963	18	23	3	1	2
Inciarte	1.000	5	13	0	0	0
Marzilli	1.000	31	91	2	0	0
Montilla	1.000	4	5	1	0	0

VISALIA RAWHIDE — HIGH CLASS A

CALIFORNIA LEAGUE

Batting	B-T	HT	WT	DOB	AVG	vLH	vRH	G	AB	R	H	2B	3B	HR	RBI	BB	HBP	SH	SF	SO	SB	CS	SLG	OBP
Almadova, Breland	R-R	6-1	195	10-18-90	.273	.303	.264	105	381	60	104	21	3	4	43	40	5	6	2	80	25	10	.375	.348
Baker, Tyler	L-R	5-9	179	3-8-93	.188	.208	.182	68	240	22	45	11	0	4	24	13	1	4	1	67	2	0	.283	.231

Batting	B-T	HT	WT	DOB	AVG	vLH	vRH	G	AB	R	H	2B	3B	HR	RBI	BB	HBP	SH	SF	SO	SB	CS	SLG	OBP
Cron, Kevin	R-R	6-5	245	2-17-93	.272	.307	.262	127	518	71	141	34	0	27	97	28	6	0	6	131	0	0	.494	.314
Gebhardt, Ryan	R-R	5-11	195	10-5-91	.200	.000	.229	15	55	5	11	2	0	0	2	2	0	0	0	16	0	0	.236	.228
Glaesmann, Todd	R-R	6-4	220	10-24-90	.419	.250	.526	7	31	10	13	4	1	4	9	1	0	0	1	3	0	0	1.000	.424
Glenn, Alex	L-L	5-11	180	6-11-91	.255	.270	.253	58	231	35	59	10	5	8	39	16	1	0	3	53	2	0	.446	.303
Gosselin, Phil	R-R	6-1	200	10-3-88	.318	.250	.333	5	22	3	7	0	0	0	2	1	0	0	0	5	0	0	.318	.348
Haniger, Mitch	R-R	6-2	215	12-23-90	.332	.229	.353	49	202	40	67	16	3	12	36	17	2	0	5	39	8	2	.619	.381
Hutchison, Ryan	R-R	6-3	210	12-21-89	.282	.400	.241	12	39	3	11	1	0	0	2	3	2	0	0	5	1	0	.308	.364
Ijames, Stewart	L-R	6-0	220	8-21-88	.273	.232	.284	70	260	50	71	18	0	18	44	28	1	1	3	95	5	1	.550	.342
Leyba, Domingo	B-R	5-11	160	9-11-95	.237	.212	.245	124	514	60	122	21	5	2	43	26	6	7	9	90	10	6	.309	.277
McQuail, Steve	R-R	6-2	225	6-10-89	.105	.000	.133	5	19	1	2	1	0	0	1	2	0	0	0	12	0	0	.158	.227
Medrano, Kevin	L-R	6-1	155	5-21-90	.292	.345	.279	79	291	44	85	18	4	1	29	30	3	5	1	49	8	2	.392	.363
Montilla, Gerson	R-R	5-10	170	11-13-89	.311	.297	.315	48	183	29	57	11	0	10	26	11	0	0	2	41	6	2	.536	.347
Navarro, Raul	R-R	5-10	170	2-5-92	.154	.118	.182	10	39	4	6	2	0	0	2	3	0	0	1	12	1	0	.205	.209
Palka, Daniel	L-L	6-2	220	10-28-91	.280	.213	.301	129	511	95	143	36	3	29	90	56	4	—	5	164	24	7	.532	.352
Pena, Fidel	R-R	5-11	165	7-19-91	.275	.287	.271	93	342	49	94	21	7	3	21	23	3	—	2	79	13	6	.404	.324
Perez, Michael	L-R	5-11	180	8-7-92	.188	.160	.196	34	117	15	22	6	0	3	20	9	1	2	2	37	1	0	.316	.254
Queliz, Jose	R-R	6-2	224	8-7-92	.275	.500	.196	20	69	8	19	3	0	4	14	1	0	0	2	25	0	0	.493	.278
Roberts, George	R-R	6-0	206	4-17-90	.253	.296	.235	26	95	12	24	8	0	1	10	7	2	0	0	31	0	0	.368	.317
Taylor, Chuck	B-L	5-9	190	9-21-93	.235	.256	.228	48	179	22	42	7	3	2	9	22	2	0	1	45	4	7	.341	.324
Trahan, Stryker	L-R	6-0	232	4-25-94	.138	.115	.144	35	130	6	18	4	0	5	16	11	1	0	1	62	1	0	.285	.210
Westbrook, Jamie	R-R	5-9	170	6-18-95	.319	.356	.307	123	480	75	153	33	4	17	72	24	10	0	10	69	14	4	.510	.357

Pitching	B-T	HT	WT	DOB	W	L	ERA	G	GS	CG	SV	IP	H	R	ER	HR	BB	SO	AVG	vLH	vRH	K/9	BB/9
Banda, Anthony	L-L	6-2	190	8-10-93	8	8	3.32	28	27	1	0	152	150	67	56	8	39	152	.260	.257	.262	9.02	2.31
Bracho, Silvino	R-R	5-10	190	7-17-92	0	0	0.00	6	0	0	3	6	1	0	0	0	1	14	.053	.000	.077	21.00	1.50
Bradley, Archie	R-R	6-4	230	8-10-92	0	0	4.50	1	1	0	0	4	3	4	2	2	2	6	.200	.286	.125	13.50	4.50
Bradley, J.R.	R-R	6-3	185	6-9-92	1	4	3.38	34	0	0	2	35	28	14	13	3	3	42	.220	.240	.208	10.90	0.78
Corbin, Pat	L-L	6-3	210	7-19-89	0	1	54.00	1	1	0	0	1	4	4	4	0	2	0	.667	.500	1.000	0.00	27.00
Diaz, Miller	R-R	6-1	210	6-22-92	0	1	5.25	2	2	0	0	12	12	7	7	2	3	15	.255	.267	.250	11.25	2.25
Doran, Ryan	R-R	6-1	185	8-5-90	8	3	3.62	28	16	1	0	114	118	52	46	13	17	61	.272	.257	.283	4.80	1.34
Geyer, Cody	R-R	5-10	224	5-4-92	1	0	10.34	11	0	0	0	16	23	19	18	0	11	12	.338	.240	.395	6.89	6.32
Gibson, Daniel	R-L	6-2	221	10-16-91	2	1	1.61	27	0	0	1	28	16	6	5	1	7	38	.172	.156	.188	12.21	2.25
Godley, Zack	R-R	6-3	245	4-21-90	8	3	2.27	14	12	0	0	75	64	26	19	3	19	78	.228	.244	.213	9.32	2.27
Hathaway, Steve	L-L	6-1	185	9-13-90	5	1	2.00	29	0	0	1	27	21	9	6	0	9	29	.198	.217	.183	9.67	3.00
Hernandez, David	R-R	6-3	245	5-13-85	0	0	0.00	2	0	0	0	2	1	0	0	0	0	3	.143	.500	.000	13.50	0.00
Hernandez, Hector	B-L	6-1	190	2-20-91	0	0	13.50	1	0	0	0	2	4	3	3	1	2	4	.444	.500	.400	9.00	9.00
Hessler, Keith	L-L	6-4	215	3-15-89	1	0	0.00	10	0	0	0	11	5	0	0	0	2	20	.208	.238	.188	12.27	1.23
Hively, R.J.	R-R	6-2	225	11-27-88	2	2	4.61	8	8	0	0	41	51	25	21	2	12	58	.304	.415	.252	12.73	2.63
Irvine, Luke	R-R	6-1	200	12-1-88	2	2	2.13	2	2	0	0	13	11	3	3	2	1	13	.229	.222	.233	9.24	0.71
Jameson, Tom	R-R	6-7	245	8-4-91	3	0	0.00	6	0	0	0	11	13	0	0	0	2	7	.295	.500	.179	5.56	1.59
Jeter, Bud	R-R	6-3	205	10-21-91	4	0	3.12	48	0	0	1	49	47	18	17	2	19	50	.260	.217	.281	9.18	3.49
Jose, Jose	L-L	6-2	175	7-21-90	0	1	1.74	9	0	0	0	10	10	2	2	0	2	14	.256	.357	.200	12.19	1.74
Krehbiel, Joe	R-R	6-2	185	12-20-92	0	6	3.71	60	0	0	10	68	54	29	28	6	28	96	.215	.291	.176	12.71	3.71
Marks, Troy	R-R	6-5	210	12-31-89	1	0	1.80	1	1	0	0	5	3	1	1	0	1	1	.176	.250	.111	1.80	1.80
McCullough, Mason	R-R	6-4	245	1-7-93	4	2	4.46	39	0	0	1	36	24	23	18	1	28	38	.185	.311	.118	9.41	6.94
Omahen, Johnny	R-R	6-0	190	3-15-89	6	2	3.35	14	14	0	0	81	69	36	30	4	27	58	.236	.246	.228	6.47	3.01
Perry, Blake	R-R	6-5	190	2-3-92	9	4	5.05	22	22	0	0	119	120	75	67	19	55	131	.264	.297	.245	9.88	4.15
Sarianides, Nick	R-R	6-1	200	8-29-91	1	4	2.11	54	0	0	28	55	37	18	13	5	16	91	.185	.182	.187	14.80	2.60
Shankin, Brett	R-R	6-0	200	10-30-89	0	2	7.04	2	2	0	0	8	13	9	6	4	5	5	.351	.412	.300	5.87	4.70
Shuttlesworth, Johnny	R-R	6-1	220	9-30-89	3	3	5.09	31	1	0	1	46	51	30	26	2	9	47	.285	.264	.299	9.20	1.76
Sinnery, Brandon	R-R	6-4	170	1-26-90	4	0	3.53	10	10	1	0	64	58	25	25	7	8	36	.246	.284	.231	5.09	1.13
Smith, Myles	R-R	6-1	175	3-23-92	0	1	4.82	8	0	0	0	9	7	5	5	0	3	12	.194	.000	.292	11.57	2.89
Solbach, Markus	R-R	6-5	202	8-26-91	2	2	5.59	6	5	0	0	29	31	20	18	5	6	17	.270	.302	.250	5.28	1.86
Stites, Matt	R-R	5-11	195	5-28-90	0	0	13.50	2	0	0	0	1	2	3	2	0	1	5	.286	.250	.333	33.75	6.75
Vance, Kevin	R-R	6-0	208	7-8-90	4	1	4.17	34	0	0	1	50	44	23	23	5	9	55	.233	.247	.223	9.97	1.63
Vargas, Emilio	R-R	6-3	200	8-12-96	0	0	10.13	1	0	0	0	3	5	3	3	0	1	3	.455	.400	.500	10.13	3.38
Weller, Blayne	R-R	6-5	220	1-30-90	5	4	4.55	16	16	0	0	89	101	52	45	7	35	95	.282	.303	.269	9.61	3.54

Fielding

Catcher	PCT	G	PO	A	E	DP	PB
Baker	.986	66	557	70	9	7	6
Perez	.986	34	327	37	5	3	4
Queliz	.973	18	131	15	4	0	0
Trahan	.989	27	252	30	3	0	5

First Base	PCT	G	PO	A	E	DP
Cron	.990	106	860	59	9	75
McQuail	.917	1	11	0	1	0
Palka	.990	37	278	23	3	15

Second Base	PCT	G	PO	A	E	DP
Gebhardt	1.000	2	3	4	0	1
Gosselin	1.000	2	3	5	0	2
Medrano	.958	14	27	42	3	11
Pena	1.000	30	53	74	0	11

	PCT	G	PO	A	E	DP
Westbrook	.970	93	151	231	12	46

Third Base	PCT	G	PO	A	E	DP
Gebhardt	.913	11	4	17	2	0
Gosselin	1.000		0	2	0	0
Medrano	.924	50	21	64	7	1
Montilla	.925	30	15	47	5	6
Navarro	.900	8	9	3	2	0
Pena	.955	20	8	34	2	1
Roberts	1.000	24	15	27	0	4

Shortstop	PCT	G	PO	A	E	DP
Gebhardt	1.000	2	0	2	0	0
Leyba	.962	123	171	333	20	71
Medrano	.958	13	19	27	2	5
Navarro	.889	2	3	5	1	2

	PCT	G	PO	A	E	DP
Pena	.750	1	1	2	1	0

Outfield	PCT	G	PO	A	E	DP
Almadova	.980	105	241	1	5	0
Glaesmann	1.000	6	12	1	0	0
Glenn	1.000	47	105	3	0	0
Haniger	.991	46	101	4	1	0
Hutchison	1.000	8	10	1	0	1
Ijames	.974	40	68	6	2	0
Montilla	1.000	9	15	2	0	1
Palka	.957	88	145	10	7	2
Pena	1.000	36	62	4	0	1
Taylor	1.000	47	84	1	0	0
Trahan	1.000	1	3	1	0	1

ARIZONA DIAMONDBACKS

MIDWEST LEAGUE

ARIZONA DIAMONDBACKS

Batting	B-T	HT	WT	DOB	AVG	vLH	vRH	G	AB	R	H	2B	3B	HR	RBI	BB	HBP	SH	SF	SO	SB	CS	SLG	OBP
Alcantara, Sergio	B-R	5-9	168	7-10-96	.113	.143	.100	20	71	5	8	1	0	0	5	4	1	2	1	17	1	0	.127	.169
Bray, Colin	B-L	6-3	197	6-18-93	.308	.320	.305	130	490	78	151	25	8	3	52	47	5	12	6	109	27	9	.410	.370
Castillo, Henry	B-R	5-11	189	12-8-94	.315	.298	.319	79	289	36	91	16	4	3	32	7	2	4	2	55	5	2	.429	.333
Cribbs, Galli	L-R	6-0	170	10-8-92	.174	.000	.190	9	23	2	4	0	0	0	2	3	0	0	0	10	2	0	.174	.269
Elander, Josh	R-R	6-1	220	3-19-91	.244	.231	.250	14	45	6	11	2	0	0	2	8	2	0	0	7	0	1	.289	.382
Gebhardt, Ryan	R-R	5-11	195	10-5-91	.275	.311	.263	47	182	18	50	7	2	0	13	10	1	1	2	25	1	2	.335	.313
Hernandez, Oscar	R-R	6-1	220	7-9-93	.154	.000	.200	5	13	0	2	0	0	0	2	0	1	0	0	3	0	0	.154	.214
Herum, Marty	R-R	6-3	214	12-16-91	.303	.327	.297	129	511	71	155	23	6	7	79	29	4	1	10	77	5	5	.413	.339
Heyman, Grant	L-R	6-4	222	11-7-93	.273	.107	.315	37	139	21	38	8	2	2	18	10	3	0	1	28	2	3	.403	.333
Hutchison, Ryan	R-R	6-3	210	12-21-89	.226	.056	.273	26	84	4	19	5	0	1	6	3	3	1	0	19	0	1	.321	.278
Kalamar, Scott	L-L	6-0	206	3-24-91	.125	.333	.000	2	8	0	1	0	0	0	0	0	0	0	0	3	0	0	.125	.125
Lugo, Dawel	R-R	6-0	190	12-31-94	.333	.286	.343	22	81	12	27	1	1	0	3	4	1	0	0	13	2	2	.370	.372
2-team total (31 Lansing)					.335	—	—	53	203	27	68	7	2	2	26	9	1	0	5	37	5	3	.419	.358
Mack, Quinnton	R-R	6-0	195	2-11-92	.167	.143	.179	34	84	7	14	3	0	2	8	10	5	0	1	25	1	1	.274	.290
McFarland, Dane	R-R	6-4	210	10-24-94	.045	.200	.000	9	22	1	1	0	0	0	0	0	0	0	0	14	0	0	.045	.045
McQuail, Steve	R-R	6-2	225	6-10-89	.250	.360	.209	27	92	11	23	6	0	1	9	11	4	0	2	22	1	2	.348	.349
Munoz, Joe	R-R	6-3	195	12-28-93	.246	.195	.261	104	349	48	86	14	3	7	38	45	5	2	5	106	7	4	.364	.337
Ozuna, Fernery	B-R	5-8	170	11-9-95	.188	.107	.210	35	133	14	25	6	1	1	12	4	0	2	0	34	4	2	.301	.212
Perez, Michael	L-R	5-11	180	8-7-92	.224	.225	.224	55	183	18	41	9	0	1	26	20	2	0	1	31	4	3	.290	.306
Queliz, Jose	R-R	6-2	224	8-7-92	.261	.214	.281	15	46	7	12	3	0	0	4	2	1	0	0	7	0	0	.326	.306
Regis, Cody	L-R	6-2	235	6-8-91	.290	.225	.303	124	476	67	138	25	3	1	58	41	9	5	4	66	10	7	.361	.355
Reyes, Victor	L-R	6-3	170	10-5-94	.311	.238	.329	121	424	57	132	17	5	2	59	22	1	6	5	58	13	4	.389	.343
Rondon, Alvaro	B-R	5-10	160	9-6-90	.077	.000	.091	8	13	1	1	0	0	0	0	1	0	0	0	3	0	1	.077	.143
Soto, Elvin	B-R	5-10	210	2-12-92	.228	.259	.216	32	101	11	23	5	1	1	5	9	0	3	1	24	1	2	.327	.288
Taylor, Chuck	B-L	5-9	190	9-21-93	.280	.206	.303	73	289	39	81	7	2	0	24	28	7	3	4	48	8	3	.318	.354
Trahan, Stryker	R-R	6-0	232	4-25-94	.236	.184	.247	59	208	31	49	16	1	11	42	15	0	1	2	67	1	0	.481	.284
Vargas, Ildemaro	R-R	6-0	170	7-16-91	.321	.325	.320	86	336	62	108	18	3	5	39	35	3	5	5	16	9	6	.438	.385

Pitching	B-T	HT	WT	DOB	W	L	ERA	G	GS	CG	SV	IP	H	R	ER	HR	BB	SO	AVG	vLH	vRH	K/9	BB/9
Baker, Nick	R-R	6-1	190	8-2-92	10	1	3.14	40	4	0	0	83	78	32	29	8	8	59	.252	.290	.226	6.40	0.87
Burr, Ryan	R-R	6-4	224	5-28-94	1	0	0.46	13	0	0	0	20	12	1	1	0	6	28	.174	.167	.178	12.81	2.75
Curtis, Zac	L-L	5-9	179	7-24-92	4	4	1.33	53	0	0	33	54	33	9	8	2	12	75	.176	.167	.180	12.50	2.00
Doran, Ryan	R-R	6-1	185	8-5-90	1	0	3.48	2	2	0	0	7	4	1		2	6		.184	.313	.091	5.23	1.74
Elias, Ethan	R-R	6-3	180	4-27-93	11	6	3.19	24	20	1	0	118	108	53	42	5	48	85	.245	.257	.234	6.46	3.65
Geyer, Cody	R-R	5-10	224	5-4-92	3	1	1.08	37	0	0	0	42	22	9	5	0	23	35	.162	.141	.181	7.56	4.97
Hathaway, Steve	L-L	6-1	185	9-13-90	0	2	4.32	16	0	0	1	17	14	10	8	0	6	19	.226	.143	.294	10.36	3.24
Hernandez, Hector	B-L	6-1	190	2-20-91	1	0	1.15	4	0	0	0	16	10	2	2	0	2	12	.179	.167	.182	6.89	1.15
Huang, Wei-Chieh	R-R	6-1	170	9-26-93	7	3	2.00	15	12	0	0	77	58	24	17	1	16	68	.208	.189	.224	7.98	1.88
Jameson, Tom	R-R	6-7	245	8-4-91	1	0	3.71	17	0	0	0	27	24	11	11	1	11	21	.267	.243	.283	7.09	3.71
Jeter, Bud	R-R	6-3	205	10-27-91	2	1	3.14	10	0	0	0	14	15	8	5	0	2	11	.268	.217	.303	6.91	1.26
Jones, Brent	R-R	6-3	215	1-10-93	2	5	4.15	11	11	0	0	56	60	27	26	4	24	35	.278	.302	.262	5.59	3.83
Keller, Brad	R-R	6-5	230	7-27-95	8	9	2.60	26	25	0	0	142	128	57	41	3	37	109	.243	.273	.218	6.91	2.35
Marks, Troy	R-R	6-5	210	12-31-89	0	0	2.19	8	1	0	0	12	9	5	3	2	5	8	.205	.211	.200	5.84	3.65
Martinez, Jose	R-R	6-1	160	4-14-94	1	1	3.31	23	0	0	0	33	35	13	12	2	18	27	.271	.188	.321	7.44	4.96
McCullough, Mason	R-R	6-4	245	1-7-93	0	0	4.15	9	0	0	4	9	6	4	4	0	7	10	.188	.154	.211	10.38	7.27
Mejia, Jefferson	R-R	6-7	195	8-24-94	0	0	6.29	10	6	0	0	34	38	29	24	1	31	17	.288	.356	.233	4.46	8.13
Miller, Jared	L-L	6-7	240	8-21-93	4	5	5.88	13	12	0	0	60	69	48	39	5	31	42	.291	.407	.253	6.34	4.68
Oliver, Chris	R-R	6-4	170	7-8-93	2	2	5.67	17	5	0	0	40	49	34	25	2	26	17	.310	.286	.326	3.86	5.90
Ramirez, Luis	R-R	6-4	240	7-12-92	2	1	2.63	48	0	0	10	51	36	17	15	4	29	67	.197	.203	.192	11.75	5.08
Schultz, Scott	R-R	6-2	212	12-15-91	1	0	3.00	2	1	0	0	6	5	2	2	0	2	4	.217	.429	.125	6.00	3.00
Smith, Myles	R-R	6-1	175	3-23-92	2	0	1.27	11	0	0	0	21	10	3	3	0	9	29	.141	.129	.150	12.23	3.80
Solbach, Markus	R-R	6-5	202	8-26-91	9	4	2.88	20	20	0	0	122	112	46	39	4	30	56	.246	.208	.273	4.14	2.22
Solis, Jency	R-R	6-3	235	2-22-93	6	1	2.84	50	0	0	1	57	50	18	18	1	13	54	.242	.314	.190	8.53	2.05
Taylor, Josh	L-L	6-5	225	3-2-93	4	3	3.20	11	11	1	0	59	73	29	21	2	20	53	.311	.316	.309	8.08	3.05
Toussaint, Touki	R-R	6-3	185	6-20-96	2	2	3.69	7	7	0	0	39	31	19	16	4	15	29	.218	.192	.250	6.69	3.46

Fielding

Catcher	PCT	G	PO	A	E	DP	PB
Hernandez	1.000	3	17	1	0	0	0
Perez	.993	52	356	46	3	3	3
Queliz	1.000	15	98	16	0	2	2
Soto	.980	28	180	17	4	1	3
Trahan	.986	49	314	41	5	3	14

First Base	PCT	G	PO	A	E	DP
Herum	.990	122	1073	73	11	120
McQuail	.942	7	47	2	3	6
Regis	.982	12	94	13	2	6
Soto	1.000	2	4	1	0	0

Second Base	PCT	G	PO	A	E	DP
Castillo	.963	31	55	75	5	20
Cribbs	.966	7	8	20	1	7
Gebhardt	.949	10	20	17	2	9
Lugo	1.000	2	2	5	0	1
Ozuna	.987	32	57	92	2	22
Regis	.976	39	55	109	4	28
Rondon	.955	6	9	12	1	0
Vargas	.957	21	39	71	5	20

Third Base	PCT	G	PO	A	E	DP
Castillo	.920	10	6	17	2	2
Gebhardt	1.000	1	0	2	0	1
Herum	.813	7	4	9	3	1
Munoz	.903	84	57	166	24	22
Ozuna	1.000	1	0	1	0	0
Regis	.929	45	25	79	8	12

Shortstop	PCT	G	PO	A	E	DP
Alcantara	.916	20	25	62	8	12
Cribbs	1.000	2	5	3	0	1
Gebhardt	.951	35	47	108	8	26
Lugo	.932	14	20	35	4	5
Munoz	—	1	0	0	0	0
Ozuna	.786	4	4	7	3	2
Rondon	1.000	1	0	1	0	0
Vargas	.978	64	118	193	7	48

Outfield	PCT	G	PO	A	E	DP
Bray	.994	126	305	10	2	4
Castillo	—	2	0	0	0	0
Elander	.917	10	11	0	1	0
Heyman	1.000	32	34	1	0	1

Outfield	PCT	G	PO	A	E	DP					
Hutchison	1.000	16	29	2	0	1					
Kalamar	1.000	2	2	0	0	0					

	PCT	G	PO	A	E	DP
Mack	1.000	23	34	1	0	0
McFarland	.917	8	11	0	1	0
Regis	.944	17	15	2	1	0

	PCT	G	PO	A	E	DP
Reyes	.982	120	263	10	5	2
Taylor	.993	71	148	4	1	0
Trahan	1.000	3	7	0	0	0

HILLSBORO HOPS

SHORT-SEASON

NORTHWEST LEAGUE

Batting	B-T	HT	WT	DOB	AVG	vLH	vRH	G	AB	R	H	2B	3B	HR	RBI	BB	HBP	SH	SF	SO	SB	CS	SLG	OBP
Alcantara, Sergio	B-R	5-9	168	7-10-96	.253	.284	.240	71	257	34	65	12	2	1	23	24	0	4	2	46	6	0	.327	.314
Anderson, Josh	R-R	6-0	220	11-4-92	.270	.295	.259	43	152	14	41	8	0	2	14	9	9	0	1	28	1	1	.362	.345
Armstrong, Joey	R-R	5-11	195	8-20-93	.154	.143	.160	13	39	2	6	1	0	0	1	6	0	2	1	14	2	1	.179	.261
Coffman, Nic	R-B	6-3	180	12-15-92	.182	1.000	.100	4	11	1	2	0	0	0	1	2	0	0	0	1	0	0	.182	.308
Cribbs, Galli	L-R	6-0	170	10-8-92	.135	.100	.145	37	96	11	13	1	0	0	4	9	2	1	0	33	9	1	.167	.224
Dezzi, Stephen	L-R	6-1	190	2-4-93	.208	.095	.227	48	149	25	31	10	1	2	15	24	4	2	1	30	3	1	.329	.331
Flores, Raymel	B-R	5-9	155	9-22-94	.063	.143	.000	5	16	1	1	0	0	0	2	0	0	1	1	6	1	0	.063	.059
Freeman, Mike	L-R	6-0	190	8-4-87	.200	.200	.200	3	10	1	2	1	0	0	1	0	0	0	0	2	0	0	.300	.273
Hernandez, Gerard	L-L	5-10	195	10-16-95	.194	.121	.213	49	155	16	30	5	2	2	18	10	0	2	7	41	2	2	.290	.233
Heyman, Grant	L-R	6-4	222	11-7-93	.280	.222	.298	19	75	8	21	3	0	0	8	5	0	0	0	18	0	0	.320	.325
Hoffpauir, Zach	R-R	6-0	195	9-21-93	.167	.333	.048	10	36	1	6	1	0	1	2	2	1	0	0	11	1	0	.278	.231
Irving, Nate	R-R	6-0	235	10-17-92	.276	.448	.170	24	76	6	21	3	0	0	10	11	2	0	1	10	1	2	.316	.378
Lopez, B.J.	R-R	5-9	185	9-29-94	.182	.000	.188	11	33	1	6	0	0	1	1	1	0	0	5	0	0	.182	.229
Mack, Quinnton	R-R	6-0	195	2-11-92	.222	.286	.182	6	18	5	4	2	0	0	1	5	2	0	0	5	0	0	.333	.440
McFarland, Dane	R-R	6-4	210	10-24-94	.209	.360	.119	17	67	13	14	10	0	1	10	11	0	0	1	27	1	1	.403	.316
Mitsui, Trevor	R-R	6-5	225	10-1-92	.237	.208	.250	69	257	33	61	14	0	10	42	27	6	0	4	49	0	0	.409	.320
Nehrir, Zach	R-R	6-2	205	1-28-93	.297	.286	.303	40	165	31	49	15	1	1	21	13	4	0	0	31	11	2	.418	.363
Olmeda, Alexis	R-R	6-0	225	4-15-92	.265	.324	.242	40	136	15	36	6	1	0	12	18	0	0	1	50	5	1	.324	.348
Ozuna, Fernery	B-R	5-8	170	11-9-95	.239	.234	.241	52	201	23	48	12	4	3	20	12	0	1	4	41	16	2	.383	.276
Peevyhouse, Jake	L-L	5-10	184	9-4-92	.167	.333	.111	5	12	2	2	0	0	0	2	1	0	0	0	4	0	0	.167	.231
Queliz, Jose	R-R	6-2	224	8-7-92	.273	.296	.256	20	66	4	18	3	1	1	3	3	3	0	0	11	0	0	.394	.333
Robertson, Nate	R-R	6-2	200	11-16-92	.196	.176	.205	54	163	19	32	8	1	4	21	13	2	1	1	43	5	1	.331	.263
Smith, Jeff	R-R	6-0	180	10-2-92	.294	.333	.231	11	34	5	10	4	0	0	5	6	0	0	0	13	2	0	.412	.400
Swanson, Dansby	R-R	6-0	175	2-11-94	.289	.263	.297	22	83	19	24	7	3	1	11	14	1	0	1	14	0	0	.482	.394
Trahan, Stryker	L-R	6-0	232	4-25-94	.143	.125	.148	10	35	4	5	3	0	0	1	2	3	0	0	9	0	0	.314	.211
Veras, Luis	R-R	6-1	180	11-4-93	.276	.271	.279	58	232	20	64	14	2	2	24	6	2	1	0	42	1	2	.379	.300

Pitching	B-T	HT	WT	DOB	W	L	ERA	G	GS	CG	SV	IP	H	R	ER	HR	BB	SO	AVG	vLH	vRH	K/9	BB/9
Bellow, Kirby	L-L	6-1	190	11-14-91	0	0	7.62	9	0	0	0	13	19	12	11	0	9	12	.345	.200	.400	8.31	6.23
Bolton, Tyler	R-R	6-4	205	1-27-93	2	4	3.89	16	15	0	0	83	94	45	36	4	21	56	.284	.226	.315	6.05	2.27
Burr, Ryan	R-R	6-4	224	5-28-94	3	0	1.88	13	0	0	3	14	7	3	3	1	5	21	.140	.100	.167	13.19	3.14
Cetta, Mike	R-R	5-11	198	12-30-92	1	1	7.20	5	0	0	0	5	2	4	4	0	4	3	.118	.000	.167	5.40	7.20
Clarke, Taylor	R-R	6-4	200	5-13-93	0	0	0.00	13	0	0	3	21	8	0	0	0	4	27	.114	.150	.100	11.57	1.71
Donatella, Justin	R-R	6-6	225	9-16-94	1	0	3.24	3	1	0	0	8	6	4	3	0	1	5	.188	.167	.200	5.40	1.08
Donino, Joey	R-R	6-4	220	10-26-91	0	0	2.79	5	1	0	1	10	8	3	3	0	4	11	.235	.364	.174	10.24	3.72
Gann, Cameron	R-R	6-0	195	10-8-92	0	1	2.76	18	0	0	3	29	22	9	9	0	10	33	.206	.225	.194	10.13	3.07
Greer, Brody	R-R	6-1	190	5-15-91	1	1	0.83	24	0	0	5	33	14	8	3	1	14	51	.126	.130	.123	14.05	3.86
Hernandez, Ariel	R-R	6-3	180	3-2-92	1	1	6.04	22	0	0	2	22	18	15	15	1	21	32	.222	.200	.224	12.90	8.46
Hernandez, Carlos	R-R	5-11	170	4-26-94	6	3	2.32	15	15	0	0	85	58	24	22	4	27	93	.193	.145	.224	9.81	2.85
Jones, Brent	R-R	6-3	215	1-10-93	0	0	5.40	1	1	0	0	5	6	3	3	1	0	3	.286	.273	.300	5.40	0.00
Landsheft, Will	R-R	6-1	205	7-27-92	3	2	4.74	23	0	0	1	25	31	17	13	3	15	27	.304	.281	.314	9.85	5.47
Mark, Tyler	R-R	6-1	195	10-18-94	2	2	5.25	9	8	0	0	36	43	23	21	4	9	24	.291	.327	.269	6.00	2.25
Marks, Troy	R-R	6-5	210	12-31-89	1	1	3.38	13	3	0	1	35	27	13	13	0	5	23	.213	.125	.266	5.97	1.30
Martinez, Jose	R-R	6-1	160	4-14-94	0	0	18.00	1	0	0	0	1	1	2	2	0	2	1	.333	.000	.500	9.00	18.00
Mejia, Jefferson	R-R	6-7	195	8-2-94	6	4	4.47	15	6	0	0	48	42	28	24	2	31	52	.235	.200	.257	9.68	5.77
Miller, Jared	L-L	6-7	240	8-21-93	7	2	1.81	9	9	1	0	60	42	18	12	2	12	57	.194	.167	.208	8.60	1.81
Pardo, Lawrence	L-L	6-0	180	10-22-91	1	1	4.50	11	0	0	0	12	11	7	6	0	8	5	.262	.125	.294	3.75	6.00
Reed, Cody	L-L	6-3	245	4-7-96	5	4	3.27	15	14	0	0	63	51	29	23	5	21	72	.219	.163	.232	10.23	2.98
Shankin, Brett	R-R	6-0	200	10-30-89	1	0	0.60	3	2	0	0	15	6	1	1	0	4	10	.122	.077	.139	10.20	2.40
Simmons, Kevin	R-R	6-1	185	9-1-93	1	2	4.45	22	0	0	1	28	32	15	14	1	17	23	.291	.265	.303	7.31	5.40
Smith, Myles	R-R	6-1	175	3-23-92	0	1	2.57	6	0	0	3	7	3	3	2	2	3	12	.111	.000	.158	15.43	3.86
Ward, Tucker	R-R	6-5	230	5-10-92	0	1	1.59	4	0	0	0	6	3	1	1	0	1	3	.150	.100	.200	4.76	1.59
Williams, Breckin	R-R	6-0	200	9-5-93	2	0	2.92	12	0	0	0	12	11	4	4	0	4	12	.234	.200	.259	8.76	2.92
Young, Alex	L-L	6-2	205	9-9-93	0	0	1.50	6	1	0	1	6	5	1	1	0	1	5	.238	.429	.143	7.50	1.50

Fielding

Catcher	PCT	G	PO	A	E	DP	PB
Irving	.967	12	109	8	4	1	0
Lopez	1.000	11	91	8	0	0	2
Olmeda	.990	31	273	25	3	0	6
Queliz	.995	20	165	21	1	1	4
Trahan	.978	6	35	10	1	1	2

First Base	PCT	G	PO	A	E	DP
Anderson	.961	16	139	7	6	6
Cribbs	1.000	1	2	0	0	0
Mitsui	.998	56	447	23	1	33
Robertson	1.000	10	54	4	0	2

Second Base	PCT	G	PO	A	E	DP
Alcantara	.978	20	33	57	2	10
Cribbs	.906	7	11	18	3	5
Flores	.929	3	4	9	1	0
Freeman	—	1	0	0	0	0
Ozuna	.989	45	78	104	2	19
Smith	.917	4	6	5	1	0

Third Base	PCT	G	PO	A	E	DP
Anderson	1.000	18	13	26	0	1
Armstrong	—	1	0	0	0	0
Coffman	.556	4	1	4	4	0

	PCT	G	PO	A	E	DP
Cribbs	.923	13	1	11	1	1
Ozuna	.941	6	5	11	1	0
Robertson	.939	44	16	77	6	3
Smith	.900	7	3	6	1	0

Shortstop	PCT	G	PO	A	E	DP
Alcantara	.917	52	70	150	20	24
Cribbs	1.000	1	1	0	0	0
Flores	.900	2	1	8	1	0
Freeman	1.000	1	0	1	0	0
Ozuna	.750	1	0	6	2	0
Swanson	.970	22	36	62	3	10

ARIZONA DIAMONDBACKS

Outfield	PCT	G	PO	A	E	DP
Armstrong	1.000	12	22	0	0	0
Cribbs	1.000	17	28	1	0	0
Dezzi	1.000	37	53	1	0	0
Freeman	1.000	1	4	0	0	0
Hernandez	.943	45	61	5	4	2
Heyman	.900	11	8	1	1	0
Hoffpauir	1.000	5	3	0	0	0
Mack	1.000	6	7	0	0	0
McFarland	.956	17	42	1	2	1
Nehrir	.978	39	84	4	2	1
Peevyhouse	1.000	5	7	0	0	0
Robertson		1	0	0	0	0
Smith	.667	2	2	0	1	0
Veras	.972	46	101	2	3	0

AZL DIAMONDBACKS

ARIZONA LEAGUE

ROOKIE

Batting	B-T	HT	WT	DOB	AVG	vLH	vRH	G	AB	R	H	2B	3B	HR	RBI	BB	HBP	SH	SF	SO	SB	CS	SLG	OBP
Bracho, Didimo	R-R	5-11	170	9-2-96	.125	.000	.167	6	16	0	2	1	0	0	1	0	0	0	0	6	0	1	.188	.125
Branigan, Michael	R-R	5-10	175	1-9-96	.268	.313	.255	24	71	6	19	2	1	0	8	5	3	0	1	12	0	1	.324	.338
Brown, Max	R-R	6-4	195	4-30-93	.265	.214	.278	38	136	13	36	4	5	0	11	13	1	1	0	37	6	1	.368	.333
Cave, Jacy	R-R	6-2	190	1-21-95	.240	.040	.304	31	104	12	25	4	3	1	10	10	5	0	0	25	7	1	.365	.336
Coffman, Nic	R-R	6-3	180	12-15-92	.302	.375	.286	12	43	4	13	0	0	0	1	2	0	0	0	10	0	1	.302	.333
Comstock, Daniel	R-R	5-11	210	9-24-93	.247	.111	.284	30	85	13	21	1	1	0	14	21	4	0	1	26	2	0	.282	.414
Cordero, Jacob	R-R	5-10	174	11-14-94	.179	.227	.164	32	95	15	17	2	0	0	12	14	1	0	1	16	5	1	.200	.288
Ehmcke, Maik	L-L	6-2	200	7-14-94	.210	.095	.238	34	105	12	22	6	1	0	8	10	0	2	2	29	2	1	.286	.274
Gosselin, Phil	R-R	6-1	200	10-3-88	.286	—	.286	4	14	3	4	1	0	2	4	0	0	0	0	0	0	0	.786	.286
Hernandez, Ramon	R-R	6-4	195	3-2-96	.278	.250	.284	26	90	12	25	6	1	0	11	3	4	0	1	22	1	0	.367	.327
Herrera, Jose	B-R	5-10	185	2-24-97	.304	.385	.288	24	79	7	24	3	0	1	9	13	2	0	1	10	0	0	.380	.415
Heyman, Grant	L-R	6-4	222	11-7-93	.235	.000	.250	5	17	4	4	2	0	0	2	3	0	0	0	4	0	0	.353	.350
Inciarte, Ender	L-L	5-10	185	10-29-90	.400	1.000	.250	2	5	1	2	0	0	0	1	0	0	0	0	0	0	0	.400	.500
Kelly, Dylan	L-R	5-11	200	6-5-91	.067	.000	.077	6	15	0	1	0	0	0	1	0	0	0	0	8	0	0	.067	.125
Laird, Gerald	R-R	6-1	230	11-13-79	.364	—	.364	4	11	0	4	0	0	0	1	2	0	0	0	1	0	0	.364	.462
Lopez, B.J.	R-R	5-9	185	9-29-94	.200	.000	.273	6	15	0	3	0	0	0	2	1	0	0	0	4	0	0	.200	.250
Martinez, Francis	B-R	6-4	187	6-28-97	.198	.300	.171	27	96	13	19	7	1	0	9	6	1	0	0	37	0	0	.292	.252
Marzilli, Evan	L-L	6-0	185	3-13-91	.409	.714	.267	8	22	5	9	0	1	0	1	7	0	0	0	3	0	0	.500	.552
Mezquita, Melvin	B-R	6-3	175	6-2-95	.286	.100	.333	16	49	9	14	4	1	0	2	2	0	4	0	10	1	0	.408	.314
Olmeda, Alexis	R-R	6-0	225	4-5-94	.500	—	.500	1	4	0	2	0	0	0	0	0	0	0	0	0	0	0	.500	.500
Pena, Ismael	L-L	6-3	175	12-15-95	.238	.222	.242	45	164	13	39	1	2	3	19	9	2	0	2	23	1	1	.323	.282
Ramos, Eudy	R-R	6-1	195	2-19-96	.194	.200	.192	28	98	15	19	4	2	1	8	3	1	0	1	38	0	2	.306	.223
Ransom, Cody	R-R	6-2	200	2-17-76	.357	.500	.333	5	14	2	5	1	0	0	2	1	0	0	0	2	0	0	.429	.400
Rondon, Alvaro	B-R	5-10	160	9-6-90	.313	.289	.319	47	176	36	55	6	4	0	20	16	1	3	4	27	20	1	.392	.365
Saltalamacchia, Jarrod	B-R	6-4	235	5-2-85	.250	.000	.333	2	4	1	1	0	0	0	1	0	0	1	0	0	0	0	.250	.333
Silverio, Luis	R-R	6-3	180	6-27-95	.266	.118	.306	28	79	14	21	2	4	1	12	7	2	3	2	27	5	3	.430	.333
Smith, Jeff	R-R	6-0	180	10-2-92	.174	.150	.212	24	86	8	15	1	0	0	9	7	1	1	0	27	3	0	.186	.245
Soole, Logan	L-L	6-0	185	5-28-96	.261	.115	.295	37	138	12	36	4	2	0	10	3	1	0	0	22	7	4	.319	.282

Pitching	B-T	HT	WT	DOB	W	L	ERA	G	GS	CG	SV	IP	H	R	ER	HR	BB	SO	AVG	vLH	vRH	K/9	BB/9
Anderson, Chase	R-R	6-1	194	11-30-87	0	0	0.00	1	1	0	0	4	4	0	0	0	0	3	.250	.667	.154	6.75	0.00
Bellow, Kirby	L-L	6-1	190	11-14-91	0	0	0.00	9	0	0	2	9	8	0	0	0	2	12	.250	.444	.174	11.57	1.93
Bradley, Archie	R-R	6-4	230	8-10-92	0	0	0.00	1	1	0	0	4	2	0	0	0	3	6	.143	.250	.000	13.50	6.75
Cancio, Roberto	L-L	6-1	180	8-8-95	0	0	10.29	7	2	0	0	7	11	9	8	0	7	7	.344	.250	.357	9.00	9.00
Castillo, Luis	R-R	6-2	180	3-10-95	2	0	1.93	11	0	0	1	33	25	8	7	1	6	23	.214	.359	.141	6.34	1.65
Cetta, Mike	R-R	5-11	198	12-30-92	0	0	4.50	7	0	0	1	12	13	6	6	0	4	7	.260	.333	.229	5.25	3.00
Delgado, Randall	R-R	6-4	220	2-9-90	0	0	18.00	1	1	0	0	1	2	2	2	1	0	0	.400	1.000	.250	0.00	0.00
Donatella, Justin	R-R	6-6	225	9-16-94	1	0	0.98	9	5	0	0	18	9	2	2	0	2	15	.150	.238	.103	7.36	0.98
Donino, Joey	R-R	6-4	220	10-26-91	0	0	4.50	1	0	0	0	2	2	2	1	0	0	2	.222	.000	.286	9.00	0.00
Gonzalez, Erbert	R-R	5-10	170	10-21-95	1	1	0.95	15	0	0	2	19	9	3	2	0	12	24	.138	.143	.135	11.37	5.68
Helmink, Holden	R-R	6-4	180	11-10-93	0	1	4.63	12	1	0	0	12	14	8	6	1	9	13	.311	.500	.242	10.03	6.94
Hernandez, Hector	B-L	6-1	190	2-20-91	0	2	3.86	6	6	0	0	16	16	9	7	1	3	15	.232	.250	.226	8.27	1.65
Jones, Brent	R-R	6-3	215	1-10-93	1	2	6.17	4	2	0	0	12	16	10	8	0	1	14	.314	.300	.323	10.80	0.77
Jose, Jose	L-L	6-2	175	7-21-90	0	2	2.25	6	0	0	0	8	8	4	2	1	2	11	.258	.375	.217	12.38	2.25
Lopez, Yoan	R-R	6-3	185	1-2-93	1	0	0.00	1	1	0	0	6	3	0	0	0	0	6	.158	.000	.200	9.00	0.00
Lowman, Will	R-L	6-0	185	7-27-94	0	0	2.25	4	0	0	0	4	6	3	1	0	2	3	.400	.250	.455	6.75	4.50
Madero, Luis	R-R	6-3	175	4-15-97	5	5	2.30	13	2	0	0	55	40	21	14	0	14	46	.204	.212	.200	7.57	2.30
Mark, Tyler	R-R	6-1	195	10-18-94	1	0	4.50	3	1	0	0	4	5	3	2	0	2	5	.294	.000	.417	11.25	4.50
Montero, Merkis	R-R	6-2	155	12-1-95	0	1	3.14	14	0	0	3	29	27	10	10	2	5	19	.245	.295	.162	5.97	1.57
Munson, Kevin	R-R	6-2	215	1-3-89	0	0	0.00	4	4	0	0	6	4	0	0	1	0	8	.182	.375	.071	6.00	1.50
Pimentel, Chester	R-R	6-5	210	11-12-95	1	4	7.28	14	10	0	1	38	55	36	31	3	16	32	.333	.333	.333	7.51	3.76
Polanco, Oliver	R-R	6-3	210	5-13-97	5	3	5.98	14	4	0	0	41	36	31	27	3	24	33	.234	.254	.220	7.30	5.31
Price, Scooter	R-R	6-1	195	9-23-91	1	3	3.57	13	0	0	0	18	21	11	7	1	4	20	.288	.240	.313	10.19	2.04
Pujols, Rafael	R-R	6-6	175	8-21-95	1	3	4.57	14	0	0	2	22	24	13	11	0	5	14	.316	.304	.321	5.82	2.08
Romero, Pierce	R-R	6-3	200	5-12-94	0	0	1.54	7	6	0	0	12	15	8	2	0	6	5	.313	.353	.290	3.86	4.63
Smith, Josh	R-R	6-3	185	7-8-96	0	1	9.22	13	0	0	0	14	18	15	14	0	12	9	.327	.368	.306	5.93	7.90
Vargas, Emilio	R-R	6-3	200	8-12-96	5	1	2.53	13	7	0	0	53	46	17	15	0	13	49	.228	.351	.152	8.27	2.19
Ward, Tucker	R-R	6-3	230	5-10-92	0	1	5.06	12	0	0	0	16	19	11	9	1	5	16	.297	.190	.349	9.00	2.81
Young, Alex	L-L	6-2	205	9-9-93	0	0	0.00	1	1	0	0	1	0	0	0	0	0	0	.000	.000	.000	9.00	0.00

Fielding

Catcher	PCT	G	PO	A	E	DP	PB
Branigan	.975	23	170	27	5	3	8
Comstock	.982	9	46	9	1	1	2
Herrera	.987	21	138	19	2	0	5
Kelly	1.000	3	11	1	0	0	0
Laird	1.000	2	5	0	0	0	
Lopez	.971	6	31	3	1	0	1
Olmeda	1.000	1	11	1	0	0	0
Saltalamacchia	1.000	1	6	0	0	0	0

First Base	PCT	G	PO	A	E	DP
Comstock	.959	9	69	2	3	5
Hernandez	.989	10	83	6	1	7
Pena	.977	40	324	17	8	34
Ramos	1.000	2	7	0	0	0

Second Base	PCT	G	PO	A	E	DP
Bracho	1.000	1	1	1	0	0
Cordero	.918	24	43	69	10	18
Gosselin	1.000	2	2	5	0	0
Rondon	1.000	8	16	25	0	5
Smith	.965	24	37	74	4	16

Third Base	PCT	G	PO	A	E	DP
Coffman	.800	10	5	15	5	0
Cordero	.900	5	3	15	2	1
Gosselin	—	1	0	0	0	0

Hernandez	.944	14	7	27	2	1
Ramos	.867	27	19	33	8	3
Ransom	1.000	1	0	1	0	0
Rondon	1.000	3	2	6	0	1

Shortstop	PCT	G	PO	A	E	DP
Bracho	.833	3	1	4	1	1
Cordero	1.000	4	4	12	0	1
Mezquita	.843	16	23	47	13	13
Ransom	.833	2	1	4	1	1
Rondon	.942	36	56	106	10	24

Outfield	PCT	G	PO	A	E	DP
Brown	.984	31	60	1	1	1
Cave	.977	24	40	2	1	0
Ehmcke	.983	33	54	3	1	1
Heyman	1.000	5	3	0	0	0
Inciarte	1.000	2	2	0	0	0
Martinez	.970	21	29	3	1	0
Marzilli	1.000	8	16	0	0	0
Pena	1.000	3	0	1	0	0
Silverio	.971	19	31	2	1	0
Soole	1.000	33	44	1	0	0

MISSOULA OSPREY
PIONEER LEAGUE
ROOKIE

Batting

Batting	B-T	HT	WT	DOB	AVG	vLH	vRH	G	AB	R	H	2B	3B	HR	RBI	BB	HBP	SH	SF	SO	SB	CS	SLG	OBP
Abreu, Mike	R-R	5-11	185	9-29-93	.240	.071	.306	19	50	8	12	2	0	1	3	5	0	1	0	16	2	0	.340	.309
Armstrong, Joey	R-R	5-11	195	8-20-93	.217	.175	.240	48	161	22	35	6	0	2	20	23	0	2	3	37	2	2	.292	.310
Bracho, Didimo	R-R	5-11	170	9-2-96	.077	.200	.000	4	13	1	1	1	0	0	2	2	0	0	0	4	0	0	.154	.200
Byler, Austin	L-R	6-3	225	10-15-92	.298	.324	.286	66	228	59	68	22	5	15	57	50	4	0	7	67	9	1	.636	.422
Christy, Francis	L-R	6-2	220	9-1-95	.200	.205	.198	44	145	20	29	7	4	4	23	17	5	0	2	40	3	2	.386	.302
Coffman, Nic	R-R	6-3	180	12-15-92	.045	.083	.000	7	22	1	1	0	0	1	4	0	0	0	0	4	0	0	.182	.045
Diaz, Isan	L-R	5-10	185	5-27-96	.360	.325	.375	68	272	58	98	25	6	13	51	34	4	0	2	65	12	7	.640	.436
Flores, Raymel	B-R	5-9	155	9-22-94	.301	.323	.289	52	183	33	55	8	2	6	18	19	1	4	0	45	8	6	.464	.369
Hoffpauir, Zach	R-R	6-0	195	9-21-93	.385	.417	.357	7	26	4	10	2	0	2	5	3	0	0	0	8	0	1	.692	.448
Humphreys, Tyler	R-R	6-2	215	9-23-93	.203	.225	.194	42	143	20	29	8	1	1	19	19	2	0	1	45	2	3	.294	.303
Jones, Matt	R-R	6-0	195	4-14-92	.255	.240	.260	29	98	11	25	7	1	1	12	10	1	1	0	20	0	0	.378	.330
Lowery, Luke	R-R	6-2	230	12-8-93	.289	.286	.290	67	239	43	69	12	5	9	43	30	4	0	1	65	8	2	.494	.376
McPhearson, Matt	L-L	5-8	175	4-18-95	.237	.296	.210	56	173	29	41	1	1	0	14	18	3	1	1	53	30	7	.254	.318
Morozowski, Jason	R-R	6-1	175	6-10-94	.292	.381	.260	63	240	37	70	15	6	6	41	28	2	1	1	48	8	4	.479	.369
Peevyhouse, Jake	L-L	5-10	184	9-4-92	.268	.444	.219	14	41	6	11	1	0	0	6	5	0	1	1	5	1	1	.293	.340
Railey, Matt	L-L	5-11	190	3-16-95	.222	.100	.250	19	54	7	12	2	1	1	6	13	4	0	0	15	3	2	.352	.408
Simmons, Kal	B-R	6-1	180	12-10-93	.222	.146	.246	50	171	23	38	3	3	2	18	14	0	1	2	43	3	3	.310	.278
Smith, Jeff	R-R	6-0	180	10-2-92	.292	.333	.278	7	24	5	7	2	0	0	3	3	0	0	1	0	12	0	0	.375	.370
Wilson, Marcus	R-R	6-3	175	8-15-96	.258	.306	.238	57	213	42	55	12	1	1	22	33	1	0	2	61	7	4	.338	.357

Pitching

Pitching	B-T	HT	WT	DOB	W	L	ERA	G	GS	CG	SV	IP	H	R	ER	HR	BB	SO	AVG	vLH	vRH	K/9	BB/9
Benitez, Anfernee	L-L	6-1	180	7-24-95	3	6	4.75	14	14	0	0	66	77	49	35	7	25	78	.293	.348	.274	10.58	3.39
Clark, Cody	R-R	6-2	215	7-22-93	0	3	2.43	25	0	0	0	30	18	13	8	0	9	48	.165	.143	14.56	2.73
Garcia, Junior	L-L	6-1	180	10-1-95	2	2	3.74	5	5	0	0	22	29	13	9	2	6	19	.315	.303	.322	7.89	2.49
Holtmann, Bryant	R-L	6-5	200	2-5-93	2	2	4.89	15	8	0	0	53	62	29	29	2	26	43	.291	.327	.280	7.26	4.39
Lees, Matt	L-L	6-0	170	2-7-93	0	0	3.38	22	0	0	0	21	20	8	8	0	6	22	.247	.174	.276	9.28	2.53
Long, Keegan	R-R	6-2	190	8-27-93	2	0	0.68	23	0	0	2	27	13	2	2	0	8	36	.148	.174	.138	12.15	2.70
Lowman, Will	R-L	6-0	185	7-27-94	0	2	14.54	11	0	0	0	9	9	14	14	0	18	6	.257	.429	.214	6.23	18.69
Mason, Austin	R-R	6-2	200	12-10-93	2	0	3.21	26	1	0	0	28	24	12	10	2	11	30	.231	.229	.232	9.64	3.54
Moya, Gabriel	L-L	6-0	175	1-9-95	2	1	1.93	25	0	0	0	23	15	6	5	2	8	36	.185	.188	.184	13.89	3.09
Newton, Dallas	L-R	6-5	215	9-3-94	2	3	6.85	18	7	0	0	45	55	42	34	1	21	30	.302	.281	.312	6.04	4.23
Paredes, Willy	R-R	6-2	180	2-2-89	0	0	11.57	2	0	0	1	2	4	3	3	0	2	5	.364	1.000	.300	19.29	7.71
Potter, Andrew	R-R	6-0	208	2-9-94	0	1	7.15	22	0	0	0	23	31	29	18	4	15	22	.320	.400	.284	8.74	5.96
Ramirez, Yefrey	R-R	6-2	165	11-28-93	5	5	5.35	14	13	0	0	69	68	46	41	11	21	61	.259	.327	.218	7.96	2.74
Savas, Dan	R-R	6-5	241	7-11-92	1	2	2.49	26	0	0	14	25	29	9	7	0	5	24	.293	.286	.297	8.53	1.78
Schultz, Scott	R-R	6-2	212	12-15-91	3	2	4.70	14	8	0	0	46	52	28	24	5	10	55	.294	.246	.317	10.76	1.96
Smith, Cameron	L-R	6-0	165	12-12-92	7	1	1.68	13	4	0	1	54	36	12	10	4	7	62	.190	.183	.194	10.40	1.17
Sookee, Aaron	R-R	6-3	175	6-5-91	2	2	3.94	24	0	0	0	30	35	15	13	3	9	37	.285	.326	.263	11.22	2.73
Takahashi, Bo	R-R	5-11	180	1-23-97	8	1	4.66	15	15	0	0	77	77	42	40	8	30	54	.266	.278	.259	6.28	3.49
Vargas, Emilio	R-R	6-3	200	8-12-96	1	0	0.00	2	0	0	0	4	3	0	0	0	1	3	.200	.200	.200	6.75	2.25

Fielding

Catcher	PCT	G	PO	A	E	DP	PB
Christy	.990	36	261	46	3	3	6
Jones	.984	26	219	33	4	2	3
Lowery	.965	19	151	14	6	0	7

First Base	PCT	G	PO	A	E	DP
Byler	.996	55	474	33	2	39
Humphreys	1.000	4	15	4	0	1
Lowery	.981	20	146	13	3	12

Second Base	PCT	G	PO	A	E	DP
Abreu	.951	16	30	28	3	7
Bracho	1.000	3	7	7	0	2
Diaz	.966	5	16	12	1	5

Flores	.975	43	68	124	5	21
Simmons	.980	13	19	30	1	4
Smith	1.000	1	2	3	0	1

Third Base	PCT	G	PO	A	E	DP
Bracho	1.000	1	0	2	0	0
Coffman	.929	5	3	10	1	1
Humphreys	.879	38	25	55	11	0
Simmons	.938	33	23	52	5	2
Smith	.600	5	0	6	4	0

Shortstop	PCT	G	PO	A	E	DP
Diaz	.945	64	102	172	16	36
Flores	.821	8	6	17	5	2

Simmons	1.000	6	9	14	0	5

Outfield	PCT	G	PO	A	E	DP
Abreu	1.000	3	3	0	0	0
Armstrong	.970	44	61	4	2	2
Hoffpauir	.944	6	17	0	1	0
McPhearson	.976	47	74	6	2	0
Morozowski	.989	53	85	5	1	1
Peevyhouse	1.000	11	21	1	0	1
Railey	.842	19	16	0	3	0
Wilson	.963	52	73	5	3	1

DSL D-BACKS — ROOKIE

DOMINICAN SUMMER LEAGUE

Batting	B-T	HT	WT	DOB	AVG	vLH	vRH	G	AB	R	H	2B	3B	HR	RBI	BB	HBP	SH	SF	SO	SB	CS	SLG	OBP
Araujo, Juan	R-R	6-2	195	6-24-98	.269	.273	.268	70	275	39	74	23	3	2	47	21	9	0	3	65	5	7	.396	.338
Arroyo, Mailon	B-R	6-0	200	1-2-98	.201	.189	.204	67	264	29	53	8	1	5	26	18	3	0	3	80	1	1	.295	.257
Benjamin, Jose	R-R	6-2	180	8-22-97	.118	.167	.107	30	102	9	12	3	1	1	6	14	4	1	1	50	1	2	.196	.248
Cabral, Carlos	R-R	6-1	185	9-5-92	.232	.143	.247	34	99	13	23	8	0	0	10	9	4	1	0	25	2	0	.313	.321
Cordero, Remy	L-L	6-2	170	12-18-97	.196	.206	.193	46	148	17	29	4	1	1	13	10	3	0	0	57	2	1	.257	.261
Garcia, Oswaldo	R-R	6-3	210	11-28-95	.273	.400	.240	57	216	28	59	10	3	0	36	14	4	0	4	26	9	3	.347	.324
Graciano, Vicson	R-R	6-1	155	11-23-95	.250	.000	.292	20	76	10	19	6	1	1	5	6	0	0	0	10	0	0	.395	.305
Herrera, Kendry	R-R	5-11	180	6-23-96	.222	.167	.233	12	36	6	8	2	1	0	4	4	0	0	0	12	0	0	.333	.300
Jimenez, Gerson	R-R	6-1	200	12-2-94	.285	.213	.302	71	246	38	70	11	3	2	34	39	8	0	6	30	10	5	.378	.391
Moreno, Oscar	R-R	6-0	180	12-10-97	.243	.182	.258	39	111	23	27	1	2	0	10	23	6	0	3	24	4	6	.288	.392
Novas, Joel	R-R	6-1	185	12-31-94	.391	—	.391	7	23	7	9	0	0	0	3	2	1	1	0	3	0	0	.391	.462
Polanco, Frank	R-R	6-0	190	8-1-94	.271	.229	.280	56	192	38	52	7	6	0	20	34	4	0	2	37	15	3	.370	.388
Ramirez, Waldy	R-R	6-4	175	6-16-97	.218	.227	.215	26	87	11	19	0	1	0	7	13	3	0	0	28	5	2	.241	.340
Rodriguez, Victor	L-L	5-9	157	1-31-97	.267	.364	.245	64	236	32	63	2	5	1	25	19	0	5	2	45	20	7	.331	.319
Sanchez, Yan	R-R	6-2	170	8-31-96	.290	.245	.301	70	272	56	79	17	3	0	22	30	9	4	0	51	29	9	.375	.379
Santana, Rafael	R-R	6-0	186	10-24-95	.379	.353	.388	18	66	18	25	4	3	0	8	11	2	1	1	9	7	2	.530	.475

Pitching	B-T	HT	WT	DOB	W	L	ERA	G	GS	CG	SV	IP	H	R	ER	HR	BB	SO	AVG	vLH	vRH	K/9	BB/9
Abreu, Oscar	L-L	6-4	185	12-19-94	1	2	3.45	19	0	0	4	31	18	16	12	0	20	23	.173	.235	.161	6.61	5.74
Angel, Ricardo	R-R	6-2	175	2-18-98	0	0	4.50	9	0	0	0	12	10	8	6	0	11	16	.222	.133	.267	12.00	8.25
Beato, Anyel	R-R	6-3	175	3-3-96	0	1	4.15	3	0	0	0	4	5	2	2	0	2	2	.313	.000	.385	4.15	4.15
Berroa, Silvestre	L-L	6-0	175	5-13-97	4	3	2.87	20	0	0	4	47	38	19	15	1	13	54	.220	.257	.210	10.34	2.49
De Leon, Robert	R-R	6-5	200	12-18-97	2	4	7.36	17	1	0	1	29	28	26	24	1	21	32	.246	.238	.250	9.82	6.44
Duran, Jhoan	R-R	6-5	175	1-8-98	4	1	3.25	12	12	0	0	64	62	29	23	1	22	44	.263	.278	.253	6.22	3.11
Felix, Wellinton	R-R	6-1	185	11-25-94	0	1	7.27	4	0	0	0	9	6	7	7	0	4	6	.200	.143	.217	6.23	4.15
Ferrand, Javier	L-L	6-0	185	4-26-96	3	5	5.12	13	12	0	0	51	50	41	29	0	39	43	.250	.324	.233	7.59	6.88
Hiciano, Argeny	R-R	6-3	160	10-19-96	6	4	2.67	17	7	0	0	64	64	36	19	5	23	52	.267	.281	.261	7.31	3.23
Ovalles, Melvin	R-R	6-2	180	11-21-96	3	2	2.86	11	11	0	0	50	48	25	16	0	19	38	.238	.225	.244	6.79	3.40
Ramirez, Delvi	R-R	6-1	200	12-23-91	1	1	6.75	12	0	0	1	23	17	23	17	0	30	29	.205	.150	.222	11.51	11.91
Ramirez, Nestor	R-R	6-4	195	9-4-95	1	2	2.06	23	0	0	10	39	29	10	9	0	6	33	.209	.184	.222	7.55	1.37
Rodriguez, Diony	R-R	6-4	210	5-14-97	1	0	4.12	12	0	0	0	20	15	11	9	1	14	15	.217	.200	.224	6.86	6.41
Salas, Alber	R-R	6-2	180	11-1-95	0	0	16.88	6	0	0	0	3	2	5	5	0	15	2	.222	.000	.286	6.75	50.63
Santana, Yeison	R-R	6-0	160	10-25-96	2	5	5.65	16	9	0	1	51	63	47	32	5	17	50	.301	.265	.313	8.82	3.00
Soriano, Franklyn	L-L	6-2	173	7-21-95	3	2	2.02	13	12	0	0	62	50	25	14	1	18	76	.208	.216	.206	10.97	2.60
Trejo, Yeferson	R-R	6-2	219	2-3-96	0	2	5.32	11	0	0	1	24	25	17	14	0	6	15	.275	.250	.286	5.70	2.28

Fielding

Catcher	PCT	G	PO	A	E	DP	PB
Arroyo	.976	7	33	7	1	0	5
Cabral	.967	25	177	26	7	1	10
Garcia	.987	38	274	35	4	2	6
Herrera	.958	11	86	6	4	0	9

First Base	PCT	G	PO	A	E	DP
Garcia	.973	11	65	6	2	12
Graciano	.984	7	57	3	1	3
Jimenez	.992	56	475	19	4	41
Novas	1.000	1	9	0	0	1
Ramirez	1.000	1	8	0	0	0

Second Base	PCT	G	PO	A	E	DP
Arroyo	.857	3	3	9	2	1
Benjamin	.897	22	54	51	12	9
Cabral	1.000	8	9	9	0	1
Graciano	.961	10	20	29	2	5
Novas	.882	3	7	8	2	0
Ramirez	.950	12	21	36	3	3
Sanchez	.962	21	48	54	4	12

Third Base	PCT	G	PO	A	E	DP
Arroyo	.913	58	53	136	18	12
Cabral	1.000	3	1	3	0	0
Garcia	.964	10	10	17	1	0
Graciano	1.000	3	4	8	0	1
Novas	1.000	1	0	2	0	0

Shortstop	PCT	G	PO	A	E	DP
Benjamin	.872	11	18	16	5	2
Novas	1.000	1	5	1	0	0
Ramirez	.949	13	23	52	4	9
Sanchez	.931	51	81	150	17	22

Outfield	PCT	G	PO	A	E	DP
Araujo	1.000	59	96	8	0	3
Cordero	.941	41	46	2	3	0
Jimenez	1.000	5	2	0	0	0
Moreno	.979	29	45	1	1	0
Polanco	1.000	30	43	5	0	1
Rodriguez	.968	63	114	7	4	3
Santana	1.000	3	4	0	0	0

Atlanta Braves

SEASON IN A SENTENCE: The Braves nearly became the first team to lose 100 games after being at .500 (42-42 on July 7) so far into a season, going 22-47 in the second half.

HIGH POINT: The Braves won five in a row from April 6-11, and had their biggest lead—two games. It was all downhill from there.

LOW POINT: Two accidents involving Braves' farmhands punctuated the worst season for the major league team in 25 years. High Class A Carolina saw several players hurt in a bus crash in May, while several DSL players were injured in a car crash in the Dominican Republic in August. None of the injuries were career-threatening. On the field, the Braves suffered through a 12-game losing streak from Aug. 25 to Sept. 6.

NOTABLE ROOKIES: This was one category in which the Braves had some success. Thanks to a multitude of trades in the offseason designed to bring in high-impact but high-risk arms, the Braves saw the debuts of righthanders Matt Wisler and Mike Foltyniewicz, and lefthanders Manny Banuelos and Williams Perez. Also making his debut was Cuban utility man Adonis Garcia, who was surprisingly effective in the second half. But the most notable debut was that of a midseason addition. Hector Olivera, the 30-year-old big-money Cuban signee, was acquired from the Dodgers in a three-team deal. Olivera battled injuries, but finally made his debut in September.

KEY TRANSACTIONS: John Hart made several deals in the winter to prop up a deflated farm system and acquired several intriguing arms, including Wisler, Banuelos and righthander Tyrell Jenkins. But the biggest move—with an eye toward 2016—was the three-team deal to acquire Olivera. It cost the Braves young lefthander Alex Wood and top prospect Jose Peraza, but the Braves feel their young pitching could come together next season and that Olivera can step in at third and provide some immediate offense.

DOWN ON THE FARM: The acquiring Olivera meant parting ways with Peraza, Atlanta feels Ozzie Albies can be a more useful player than Peraza and one who can stick at shortstop. Jenkins is among the higher-profile arms in the system, along with the rehabbing Max Fried and Touki Toussaint, stolen from the Diamondbacks in a much-derided deal. Among position players to watch are speedy outfielder Mallex Smith and 2014 first-rounder Braxton Davidson.

OPENING DAY PAYROLL: $97,578,565 (23rd)

PLAYERS OF THE YEAR

MAJOR LEAGUE	MINOR LEAGUE
Freddie Freeman	**Mallex Smith**
1b	cf
.276/.370/.471	(Double-A/Triple-A)
18 HR, 66 RBIs	.310/.371/.392
Led club in HR, RBIs	Led org in SB (53)

ORGANIZATION LEADERS

BATTING		*Minimum 250 AB
MAJORS		
* AVG	Nick Markakis	.296
* OPS	Nick Markakis	.746
HR	Freddie Freeman	18
RBI	Freddie Freeman	66
MINORS		
* AVG	Ozhaino Albies, Rome	.310
* OBP	Braxton Davidson, Rome	.381
* SLG	Jacob Schrader, Carolina, Gwinnett	.470
R	Mallex Smith, Mississippi	84
H	Mallex Smith, Mississippi	148
TB	Cedric Hunter, Gwinnett	199
2B	Carlos Franco, Carolina	30
3B	Joseph Daris, Rome	12
HR	Jacob Schrader, Carolina, Gwinnett	15
RBI	Cedric Hunter, Gwinnett	77
BB	Braxton Davidson, Rome	84
SO	Braxton Davidson, Rome	135
SB	Mallex Smith, Mississippi	57

PITCHING		#Minimum 75 IP
MAJORS		
W	Julio Teheran	11
# ERA	Shelby Miller	3.02
SO	Shelby Miller	171
	Julio Teheran	171
SV	Jason Grilli	24
MINORS		
W	Brandon Barker, Rome, Carolina, Gwinnett	12
L	Yean Carlos Gil, Rome, Carolina	15
# ERA	Greg Smith, Gwinnett	2.71
G	Tyler Jones, Carolina, Mississippi	49
GS	Brandon Barker, Rome, Carolina, Gwinnett	27
	Yean Carlos Gil, Rome, Carolina	27
SV	Ryan Kelly, Mississippi	23
IP	Yean Carlos Gil, Rome, Carolina	155
BB	Alec Grosser, Rome, Danville	65
SO	Brandon Barker, Rome, Carolina, Gwinnett	109
AVG	Tyrell Jenkins, Mississippi, Gwinnett	.246

2015 PERFORMANCE

General Manager: John Hart/John Coppolella. **Farm Director:** Dave Trembley. **Scouting Director:** Brian Bridges.

Class	Team	League	W	L	PCT	Finish	Manager
Majors	Atlanta Braves	National	67	95	.414	13th (15)	Fredi Gonzalez
Triple-A	Gwinnett Braves	Interntional	69	67	.507	6th (10)	Brian Snitker
Double-A	Mississippi Braves	Southern	69	67	.507	6th (10)	Aaron Holbert
High A	Carolina Mudcats	Carolina	71	68	.511	4th (8)	Luis Salazar
Low A	Rome Braves	South Atlantic	58	82	.414	13th (14)	Randy Ingle
Rookie	Danville Braves	Appalachian	34	34	.500	t-5th (10)	Rocket Wheeler
Rookie	Braves	Gulf Coast	27	33	.450	11th (16)	Robinson Cancel
Overall 2015 Minor League Record			336	351	.489	19th (30)	

ORGANIZATION STATISTICS

ATLANTA BRAVES

NATIONAL LEAGUE

Batting	B-T	HT	WT	DOB	AVG	vLH	vRH	G	AB	R	H	2B	3B	HR	RBI	BB	HBP	SH	SF	SO	SB	CS	SLG	OBP
Bethancourt, Christian	R-R	6-2	205	9-2-91	.200	.170	.213	48	155	16	31	8	0	2	12	5	0	0	0	33	1	1	.290	.225
Bourn, Michael	L-R	5-10	180	12-27-82	.221	.217	.221	46	136	10	30	3	1	0	11	17	0	1	2	31	4	2	.257	.303
Callaspo, Alberto	B-R	5-9	225	4-19-83	.206	.056	.236	37	107	12	22	2	0	1	8	14	0	0	2	10	0	0	.252	.293
2-team total (60 Los Angeles)					.235	—	—	97	230	20	54	7	0	1	15	28	0	1	2	34	0	0	.278	.315
Castro, Daniel	R-R	5-11	175	11-14-92	.240	.268	.218	33	96	14	23	2	1	2	5	3	0	1	0	15	0	0	.344	.263
Ciriaco, Pedro	R-R	6-0	180	9-27-85	.261	.209	.283	84	142	14	37	8	1	1	15	2	2	2	3	38	4	2	.352	.275
Cunningham, Todd	B-R	6-0	205	3-20-89	.221	.200	.224	39	86	13	19	4	0	0	4	5	2	0	0	17	2	1	.267	.280
Freeman, Freddie	L-R	6-5	225	9-12-89	.276	.219	.298	118	416	62	115	27	0	18	66	56	7	0	2	98	3	1	.471	.370
Garcia, Adonis	R-R	5-9	190	4-12-85	.277	.328	.256	58	191	20	53	12	0	10	26	5	0	0	2	35	0	0	.497	.293
Gomes, Jonny	R-R	6-1	230	11-22-80	.221	.240	.208	83	195	27	43	7	0	7	22	28	3	0	2	67	1	1	.364	.325
Gosselin, Phil	R-R	6-1	200	10-3-88	.325	.250	.375	20	40	2	13	4	0	0	2	2	0	0	0	5	2	0	.425	.357
2-team total (24 Arizona)					.311	—	—	44	106	19	33	9	1	3	15	9	2	0	1	16	2	1	.500	.373
Johnson, Chris	R-R	6-3	225	10-1-84	.235	.323	.176	56	153	12	36	7	0	2	11	7	1	0	1	49	2	1	.320	.272
Johnson, Kelly	R-R	6-1	195	2-22-82	.275	.292	.272	62	182	20	50	5	0	9	34	13	0	0	1	43	1	1	.451	.321
2-team total (49 New York)					.265	—	—	111	310	38	82	11	0	14	47	23	0	0	1	81	2	1	.435	.314
Lavarnway, Ryan	R-R	6-4	240	8-7-87	.227	.222	.231	27	66	5	15	5	0	2	6	8	0	0	0	21	0	0	.394	.311
Markakis, Nick	L-L	6-1	190	11-17-83	.296	.273	.306	156	612	73	181	38	1	3	53	70	3	0	1	83	2	1	.376	.370
Maybin, Cameron	R-R	6-3	215	4-4-87	.267	.237	.276	141	505	65	135	18	2	10	59	45	1	1	3	102	23	6	.370	.327
Olivera, Hector	R-R	6-2	220	4-5-85	.253	.067	.297	24	79	4	20	4	1	2	11	5	2	0	1	12	0	0	.405	.310
Perez, Eury	R-R	6-0	190	5-30-90	.269	.278	.267	47	119	10	32	4	0	0	5	7	4	3	0	23	3	1	.303	.331
Peterson, Jace	L-R	6-0	200	5-9-90	.239	.190	.251	152	528	55	126	23	5	6	52	56	3	7	3	120	12	10	.335	.314
Pierzynski, A.J.	L-R	6-3	235	12-30-76	.300	.265	.309	113	407	38	122	24	1	9	49	19	7	0	3	37	0	2	.430	.339
Simmons, Andrelton	R-R	6-2	195	9-4-89	.265	.224	.276	147	535	60	142	23	2	4	44	39	6	1	2	48	5	3	.338	.321
Swisher, Nick	B-L	6-0	195	11-25-80	.195	.243	.173	46	118	8	23	5	0	4	17	27	2	0	2	30	0	0	.339	.349
Terdoslavich, Joey	B-R	6-2	200	9-9-88	.214	.111	.234	28	56	5	12	4	1	1	4	3	0	0	0	14	0	0	.375	.254
Uribe, Juan	R-R	6-0	245	3-22-79	.285	.306	.278	46	151	17	43	6	0	7	17	15	1	0	0	37	1	0	.464	.353
3-team total (29 Los Angeles, 44 New York)					.253	—	—	119	360	40	91	17	0	14	43	34	2	0	1	80	2	0	.417	.320
Young Jr., Eric	B-R	5-10	195	5-25-85	.169	.125	.174	35	77	7	13	4	2	0	5	6	0	2	0	17	3	0	.273	.229
2-team total (18 New York)					.153	—	—	53	85	16	13	4	2	0	5	6	1	2	0	18	6	2	.247	.217

Pitching	B-T	HT	WT	DOB	W	L	ERA	G	GS	CG	SV	IP	H	R	ER	HR	BB	SO	AVG	vLH	vRH	K/9	BB/9
Aardsma, David	R-R	6-3	220	12-27-81	1	1	4.70	33	0	0	0	31	25	17	16	6	14	35	.223	.353	.167	10.27	4.11
Avilan, Luis	L-L	6-2	220	7-19-89	2	4	3.58	50	0	0	0	38	35	15	15	4	10	31	.245	.294	.200	7.41	2.39
2-team total (23 Los Angeles)					2	5	4.05	73	0	0	0	53	48	24	24	6	15	49	—	—	—	8.27	2.53
Banuelos, Manny	L-L	5-10	205	3-13-91	1	2	5.13	7	6	0	0	26	30	17	15	4	12	19	.283	.286	.282	6.49	4.10
Brigham, Jake	R-R	6-3	210	2-10-88	0	1	8.64	12	0	0	0	17	28	16	16	1	8	12	.384	.517	.295	6.48	4.32
Burawa, Danny	R-R	6-2	210	12-30-88	0	0	3.65	12	0	0	0	12	8	5	5	1	4	10	.195	.167	.217	7.30	2.92
Cahill, Trevor	R-R	6-4	240	3-1-88	0	3	7.52	15	3	0	0	26	36	23	22	2	11	14	.330	.298	.355	4.78	3.76
2-team total (11 Chicago)					1	5	5.40	26	3	0	0	43	44	27	26	4	16	36	—	—	—	7.48	3.32
Carpenter, David	R-R	6-3	180	9-1-87	0	0	7.36	4	0	0	0	6	6	3	3	2	0	5	.353	.250	.385	12.27	0.00
Cornely, John	R-R	6-1	205	5-17-89	0	0	36.00	1	0	0	0	1	3	4	4	1	1	1	.500	.667	.333	9.00	9.00
Cunniff, Brandon	R-R	6-0	185	10-7-88	2	2	4.63	39	0	0	0	35	27	20	18	4	22	37	.213	.341	.151	9.51	5.66
Detwiler, Ross	R-L	6-3	215	3-6-86	1	0	7.63	24	0	0	0	15	20	14	13	1	16	13	.333	.250	.458	7.63	9.39
Eveland, Dana	L-L	6-1	235	10-29-83	0	1	5.40	10	0	0	0	3	5	2	2	1	3	4	.357	.333	.400	10.80	8.10
Foltynewicz, Mike	R-R	6-4	220	10-7-91	4	6	5.71	18	15	0	0	87	112	63	55	17	29	77	.313	.328	.298	8.00	3.01
Frasor, Jason	R-R	5-9	180	8-9-77	0	0	0.00	6	0	0	0	5	3	0	0	3	4	.176	.333	.091	7.71	5.79
Grilli, Jason	R-R	6-4	230	11-11-76	3	4	2.94	36	0	0	24	34	28	13	11	2	10	45	.217	.222	.213	12.03	2.67
Jackson, Edwin	R-R	6-3	210	9-9-83	2	2	2.92	24	0	0	1	25	14	11	8	4	9	17	.167	.139	.188	6.20	3.28
2-team total (23 Chicago)					4	3	3.07	47	0	0	1	56	44	25	19	4	21	40	—	—	—	6.47	3.40
Jaime, Juan	R-R	6-2	250	8-2-87	0	1	6.75	2	0	0	0	1	0	1	1	0	4	1	.000	.000	.000	6.75	27.00
Johnson, Jim	R-R	6-6	240	6-27-83	2	3	2.25	49	0	0	9	48	45	14	12	2	14	33	.256	.250	.260	6.19	2.63
2-team total (23 Los Angeles)					2	6	4.46	72	0	0	10	67	73	36	33	5	20	50	—	—	—	6.75	2.70
Kelly, Ryan	R-R	6-2	180	10-30-87	0	0	7.02	17	0	0	0	17	21	14	13	5	6	10	.313	.261	.341	5.40	3.24
Kohn, Michael	R-R	6-2	200	6-26-86	0	0	0.00	9	0	0	0	5	0	0	0	0	6	4	.000	.000	.000	7.71	11.57
Marimon, Sugar Ray	R-R	6-1	195	9-30-88	0	1	7.36	16	0	0	0	26	30	21	21	3	14	14	.300	.317	.288	4.91	4.91

Pitching	B-T	HT	WT	DOB	W	L	ERA	G	GS	CG	SV	IP	H	R	ER	HR	BB	SO	AVG	vLH	vRH	K/9	BB/9
Marksberry, Matt	L-L	6-1	200	8-25-90	0	3	5.01	31	0	0	0	23	22	16	13	2	16	21	.247	.170	.361	8.10	6.17
Martin, Cody	R-R	6-3	230	9-4-89	2	3	5.40	21	0	0	0	22	24	13	13	4	7	24	.296	.182	.339	9.97	2.91
Masset, Nick	R-R	6-5	235	5-17-82	2	2	6.46	20	0	0	0	15	18	12	11	3	8	12	.286	.333	.267	7.04	4.70
2-team total (8 Miami)					2	2	4.68	28	0	0	0	25	30	15	13	3	9	18	—	—	—	6.48	3.24
McKirahan, Andrew	R-L	6-2	195	2-8-90	1	0	5.93	27	0	0	0	27	40	18	18	2	10	22	.345	.300	.393	7.24	3.29
Miller, Shelby	R-R	6-3	215	10-10-90	6	17	3.02	33	33	2	0	205	183	82	69	13	73	171	.238	.262	.214	7.50	3.20
Moylan, Peter	R-R	6-2	225	12-2-78	1	0	3.48	22	0	0	0	10	12	5	4	1	0	8	.273	.750	.225	6.97	0.00
Perez, Williams	R-R	6-1	230	5-21-91	7	6	4.78	23	20	1	1	117	130	66	62	13	51	73	.291	.303	.278	5.63	3.93
Stults, Eric	L-L	6-2	220	12-9-79	1	5	5.85	9	8	0	0	48	48	31	31	10	13	31	.268	.255	.273	5.85	2.45
Teheran, Julio	R-R	6-2	200	1-27-91	11	8	4.04	33	33	0	0	201	189	99	90	27	73	171	.253	.300	.207	7.67	3.27
Thomas, Ian	L-L	6-4	215	4-20-87	0	0	3.38	5	0	0	0	5	4	3	2	1	5	5	.222	.000	.364	8.44	8.44
2-team total (9 Los Angeles)					1	1	3.86	14	1	0	0	23	20	11	10	2	11	23	—	—	—	8.87	4.24
Veal, Donnie	L-L	6-4	235	9-18-84	0	0	14.54	5	0	0	0	4	8	7	7	3	2	3	.400	.500	.333	6.23	4.15
Vizcaino, Arodys	R-R	6-0	190	11-13-90	3	1	1.60	36	0	0	9	34	27	7	6	1	13	37	.218	.196	.235	9.89	3.48
Weber, Ryan	R-R	6-0	180	8-12-90	0	3	4.76	5	5	0	0	28	25	15	15	3	6	19	.248	.255	.239	6.04	1.91
Winkler, Dan	R-R	6-3	200	2-2-90	0	0	10.80	2	0	0	0	2	2	2	2	1	2	2	.286	.200	.500	10.80	5.40
Wisler, Matt	R-R	6-3	195	9-12-92	8	8	4.71	20	19	0	0	109	119	59	57	16	40	72	.280	.327	.238	5.94	3.30
Wood, Alex	L-L	6-4	215	1-12-91	7	6	3.54	20	20	0	0	119	132	50	47	8	36	90	.288	.255	.297	6.79	2.72
2-team total (12 Los Angeles)					12	12	3.84	32	32	0	0	190	198	86	81	15	59	139	—	—	—	6.60	2.80

Fielding

Catcher	PCT	G	PO	A	E	DP	PB
Bethancourt	.988	42	305	22	4	4	8
Lavarnway	.993	21	134	5	1	0	0
Pierzynski	.997	107	729	44	2	7	5

First Base	PCT	G	PO	A	E	DP
Ciriaco	1.000	2	14	1	0	4
Freeman	.996	117	893	63	4	103
Johnson	.992	20	108	11	1	18
Johnson	.977	20	111	18	3	22
Lavarnway	1.000	1	2	0	0	0
Swisher	1.000	12	85	4	0	12
Terdoslavich	1.000	12	87	10	0	12

Second Base	PCT	G	PO	A	E	DP
Callaspo	1.000	4	11	12	0	4
Castro	1.000	12	23	39	0	13
Ciriaco	1.000	7	13	15	0	7
Gosselin	.900	3	4	5	1	3
Johnson	1.000	1	2	0	0	0
Peterson	.987	144	287	395	9	109
Uribe	1.000	1	2	2	0	0

Third Base	PCT	G	PO	A	E	DP
Callaspo	.946	28	9	44	3	4
Castro	.857	5	3	3	1	3
Ciriaco	.964	24	11	16	1	1
Garcia	.896	42	23	63	10	6
Gosselin	.917	5	2	9	1	1
Johnson	.923	23	9	27	3	4
Johnson	.867	11	4	9	2	0
Olivera	.905	21	15	23	4	2
Uribe	.942	42	18	79	6	14

Shortstop	PCT	G	PO	A	E	DP
Castro	1.000	10	12	23	0	10
Ciriaco	1.000	9	12	21	0	5
Simmons	.988	147	235	444	8	126

Outfield	PCT	G	PO	A	E	DP
Bourn	.989	42	91	3	1	1
Ciriaco	1.000	1	1	0	0	0
Cunningham	1.000	27	47	1	0	1
Garcia	1.000	10	9	1	0	0
Gomes	1.000	59	64	4	0	0
Johnson	.959	31	45	2	2	0
Markakis	.997	153	295	4	1	0
Maybin	.991	139	331	7	3	2
Perez	.985	36	61	3	1	0
Swisher	.980	26	48	1	1	0
Terdoslavich	—	2	0	0	0	0
Young Jr.	1.000	22	45	0	0	0

ATLANTA BRAVES

GWINNETT BRAVES

TRIPLE-A

INTERNATIONAL LEAGUE

Batting	B-T	HT	WT	DOB	AVG	vLH	vRH	G	AB	R	H	2B	3B	HR	RBI	BB	HBP	SH	SF	SO	SB	CS	SLG	OBP
Benson, Joe	R-R	6-1	215	3-5-88	.246	.188	.267	41	118	18	29	8	1	0	9	15	3	1	0	27	4	0	.331	.346
Bethancourt, Christian	R-R	6-2	205	9-2-91	.327	.297	.341	52	202	25	66	19	0	4	31	12	0	1	3	31	5	0	.480	.359
Castro, Daniel	R-R	5-11	175	11-14-92	.268	.264	.269	89	310	19	83	9	0	0	36	22	1	7	5	32	1	1	.297	.314
Ciriaco, Pedro	R-R	6-0	180	9-27-85	.234	.273	.218	20	77	8	18	1	0	1	7	1	1	1	0	15	1	0	.286	.253
Cunningham, Todd	B-R	6-0	205	3-20-89	.261	.253	.265	97	329	42	86	13	3	2	31	23	10	9	4	34	9	4	.337	.325
Freeman, Freddie	L-R	6-5	225	9-12-89	.375	.500	.333	2	8	0	3	1	0	0	2	2	0	0	0	3	0	0	.500	.500
Garcia, Adonis	R-R	5-9	190	4-12-85	.284	.294	.280	87	331	43	94	17	1	3	47	15	1	0	3	41	5	1	.369	.314
Hunter, Cedric	L-L	5-11	200	3-10-88	.283	.252	.291	138	474	52	134	21	4	12	77	34	2	1	4	67	11	6	.420	.331
Johnson, Chris	R-R	6-3	225	10-1-84	.000	.000	—	1	1	0	0	0	0	0	0	0	0	0	0	0	0	0	.000	.000
Johnson, Kelly	L-R	6-1	195	2-22-82	.143	—	.143	2	7	0	1	0	1	0	2	0	0	0	0	1	0	0	.429	.143
Jones, Mycal	R-R	5-10	190	5-30-87	.262	.429	.191	62	164	23	43	7	1	4	26	20	1	1	1	42	4	2	.390	.344
Kazmar, Sean	R-R	5-9	190	8-5-84	.280	.297	.273	106	397	53	111	25	6	3	38	17	5	0	5	39	3	0	.395	.314
Kennelly, Matt	R-R	6-1	200	3-21-89	.204	.083	.243	18	49	6	10	3	0	0	7	7	0	0	1	12	0	0	.265	.304
Kleinknecht, Barrett	R-R	6-0	200	7-30-88	.195	.159	.205	87	282	39	55	9	0	4	22	14	2	6	2	44	0	2	.270	.237
Lavarnway, Ryan	R-R	6-4	240	8-7-87	.268	.333	.257	13	41	5	11	2	0	2	8	8	0	0	0	7	0	0	.463	.388
Lennerton, Jordan	L-L	6-2	230	2-16-86	.202	.132	.242	33	104	9	21	2	0	1	10	11	1	0	2	27	0	0	.250	.280
2-team total (54 Toledo)					.227	—	—	87	286	31	65	15	1	5	34	36	1	1	3	68	0	1	.339	.313
Mateo, Luis	R-R	6-0	175	5-23-90	.194	.200	.192	32	108	8	21	2	1	2	9	1	3	1	0	15	4	0	.287	.223
Nieves, Wil	R-R	5-11	190	9-25-77	.238	.278	.222	22	63	5	15	3	0	0	8	8	0	0	0	14	0	0	.286	.324
Olivera, Hector	R-R	6-2	220	4-5-85	.231	.000	.273	10	39	5	9	3	0	0	3	2	1	0	0	4	0	0	.308	.286
Peraza, Jose	R-R	6-0	180	4-30-94	.294	.333	.281	96	391	52	115	10	7	3	37	15	2	12	7	35	26	7	.379	.318
Perez, Ryan	R-R	6-0	190	5-30-86	.297	.352	.280	64	236	35	70	8	2	2	21	22	6	6	1	39	28	8	.373	.370
Reyes, Elmer	R-R	5-11	175	11-26-90	.216	.258	.200	30	111	13	24	4	0	1	13	6	1	0	2	30	1	0	.279	.258
Schlehuber, Braeden	R-R	6-2	210	1-7-88	.158	.238	.140	39	114	3	18	4	0	0	9	9	1	3	1	20	0	1	.193	.224
Schrader, Jake	R-R	6-2	215	3-1-91	.000	.000	.000	4	6	4	0	0	0	0	0	2	0	0	0	1	0	0	.000	.250
Smith, Mallex	L-R	5-9	180	5-6-93	.281	.262	.286	69	278	49	78	12	6	0	13	24	1	3	1	44	34	7	.367	.339
Terdoslavich, Joey	B-R	6-2	200	9-9-88	.281	.326	.262	42	146	23	41	11	1	4	24	29	0	0	4	33	1	1	.452	.391
Yepez, Jose	R-R	6-0	210	6-19-81	.188	.276	.162	46	128	5	24	2	0	1	12	8	1	2	3	23	1	0	.227	.236
Young Jr., Eric	B-R	5-10	195	5-25-85	.248	.338	.209	67	234	36	58	6	3	1	27	33	4	8	1	43	23	3	.312	.349

Pitching	B-T	HT	WT	DOB	W	L	ERA	G	GS	CG	SV	IP	H	R	ER	HR	BB	SO	AVG	vLH	vRH	K/9	BB/9
Aardsma, David	R-R	6-3	220	12-27-81	0	0	0.00	1	0	0	0	1	0	0	0	0	0	2	.000	.000	.000	18.00	0.00

Pitching

Pitching	B-T	HT	WT	DOB	W	L	ERA	G	GS	CG	SV	IP	H	R	ER	HR	BB	SO	AVG	vLH	vRH	K/9	BB/9
Banuelos, Manny	L-L	5-10	205	3-13-91	6	2	2.23	16	16	1	0	85	64	24	21	2	40	69	.215	.198	.222	7.33	4.25
Barker, Brandon	R-R	6-3	200	8-20-92	1	1	4.82	2	2	0	0	9	9	6	5	0	4	10	.257	.278	.235	9.64	3.86
Boggs, Mitchell	R-R	6-4	235	2-15-84	1	1	6.08	13	0	0	0	13	18	9	9	0	10	2	.360	.321	.409	1.35	6.75
Brigham, Jake	R-R	6-3	210	2-10-88	4	1	4.50	8	3	0	0	26	31	14	13	1	7	20	.304	.364	.259	6.92	2.42
Burawa, Danny	R-R	6-2	210	12-30-88	0	0	2.08	4	0	0	0	4	4	1	1	1	2	5	.235	.429	.100	10.38	4.15
2-team total (32 Scranton/W-B)					1	3	2.52	36	1	0	1	54	41	18	15	3	23	44	—		—	7.38	3.86
Carpenter, David	R-R	6-3	180	9-1-87	3	1	1.78	40	0	0	2	51	34	12	10	1	22	49	.195	.284	.130	8.70	3.91
Cervenka, Hunter	L-L	6-1	225	1-3-90	1	0	0.00	14	0	0	0	17	13	1	0	0	8	23	.217	.167	.238	12.42	4.32
Cornely, John	R-R	6-1	205	5-17-89	2	2	4.42	12	0	0	1	18	15	10	9	2	7	24	.217	.154	.256	11.78	3.44
2-team total (4 Pawtucket)					2	3	4.76	23	0	0	2	23	23	13	12	3	10	28	—		—	11.12	3.97
Cunniff, Brandon	R-R	6-0	185	10-7-88	1	0	9.00	6	0	0	0	5	8	5	5	2	8	4	.421	.400	.444	7.20	14.40
Eveland, Dana	L-L	6-1	235	10-29-83	0	0	0.00	1	0	0	0	2	0	0	0	0	0	3	.000	.000	.000	16.20	0.00
3-team total (16 Norfolk, 16 Pawtucket)					4	0	1.95	33	3	0	2	55	42	13	12	0	14	45	—		—	7.32	2.28
Feigl, Brady	R-R	6-4	195	12-27-90	0	0	0.00	1	0	0	0	1	1	2	0	0	2	0	.333	—	.333	0.00	27.00
Fisher, Carlos	R-R	6-4	220	2-22-83	2	4	1.61	43	0	0	6	56	36	12	10	3	28	58	.188	.169	.202	9.32	4.50
Foltynewicz, Mike	R-R	6-4	220	10-7-91	1	6	3.49	10	10	1	0	57	52	28	22	7	26	63	.242	.271	.223	10.01	4.13
Hursh, Jason	R-R	6-3	200	10-2-91	1	0	5.40	10	0	0	0	15	16	9	9	2	5	5	.281	.407	.167	3.00	3.00
Jaime, Juan	R-R	6-2	250	8-2-87	0	0	9.82	4	0	0	0	4	4	4	4	0	6	4	.308	.667	.000	9.82	14.73
Jenkins, Tyrell	R-R	6-4	180	7-20-92	3	4	3.57	9	9	0	0	45	43	20	18	4	20	29	.256	.217	.283	5.76	3.97
Kelly, Ryan	R-R	6-2	180	10-30-87	3	1	0.95	24	0	0	13	28	12	4	3	0	7	30	.132	.103	.154	9.53	2.22
Kohn, Michael	R-R	6-2	200	6-26-86	0	1	4.50	7	0	0	0	10	9	5	5	0	5	11	.250	.333	.190	9.90	4.50
Kurcz, Aaron	R-R	6-0	175	8-8-90	4	3	3.27	31	0	0	7	33	29	13	12	2	21	38	.232	.259	.209	10.36	5.73
Lambson, Mitchell	L-L	6-1	195	9-4-89	0	1	4.50	4	0	0	0	6	4	3	3	2	7	7	.182	.000	.267	10.50	3.00
Marimon, Sugar Ray	R-R	6-1	195	9-30-88	5	4	3.31	17	14	0	0	82	75	34	30	4	26	48	.248	.255	.240	5.29	2.87
Marksberry, Matt	L-L	6-1	200	8-25-90	0	0	2.61	11	0	0	1	10	10	3	3	0	1	8	.256	.188	.304	6.97	0.87
Martin, Cody	R-R	6-3	230	9-4-89	1	3	2.10	7	6	0	1	34	24	11	8	2	9	33	.198	.231	.174	8.65	2.36
Mateo, Victor	R-R	6-5	225	7-27-89	4	3	5.36	8	7	0	0	40	47	25	24	4	15	28	.292	.244	.342	6.25	3.35
Mazzaro, Vin	R-R	6-2	220	9-27-86	1	0	2.36	17	0	0	1	27	22	8	7	0	13	18	.224	.209	.236	6.08	4.39
McKirahan, Andrew	R-L	6-2	195	2-8-90	0	0	3.18	6	0	0	0	6	6	2	2	2	3	8	.273	.143	.333	12.71	4.76
Moylan, Peter	R-R	6-2	215	12-2-78	2	0	3.14	27	0	0	6	29	22	10	10	1	9	24	.218	.356	.107	7.53	2.83
Perez, Williams	R-R	6-1	230	5-21-91	3	1	1.16	8	8	0	0	39	32	8	5	1	10	36	.227	.211	.243	8.38	2.33
Peterson, Dave	R-R	6-5	205	1-4-90	2	0	2.08	16	0	0	2	22	20	6	5	2	4	11	.247	.333	.204	4.57	1.66
Reyes, Jorge	B-R	6-3	200	12-7-87	0	1	14.40	1	1	0	0	5	8	8	8	3	2	3	.348	.273	.417	5.40	3.60
Smith, Greg	L-L	6-1	195	12-22-83	6	7	2.71	31	19	0	0	120	119	47	36	5	25	67	.255	.261	.252	5.04	1.88
Texeira, Kanekoa	R-R	6-2	190	2-6-86	6	4	3.55	26	14	0	1	101	92	43	40	6	49	71	.249	.220	.274	6.31	4.35
Thomas, Ian	L-L	6-4	215	4-20-87	0	0	0.00	7	0	0	0	13	5	0	0	0	1	16	.122	.067	.154	11.37	0.71
Veal, Donnie	L-L	6-4	235	9-18-84	2	0	0.00	17	0	0	0	16	9	3	0	0	2	13	.161	.148	.172	7.31	1.13
Vizcaino, Arodys	R-R	6-0	190	11-13-90	0	0	9.00	2	0	0	0	2	3	2	2	0	1	3	.333	.400	.250	13.50	4.50
Wang, Chien-Ming	R-R	6-4	225	3-31-80	2	6	6.10	11	10	0	0	62	96	46	42	3	21	28	.366	.390	.341	4.06	3.05
Weber, Ryan	R-R	6-0	180	8-12-90	6	3	2.21	27	6	0	3	73	60	18	18	7	9	35	.226	.202	.244	4.30	1.10
White, Alex	R-R	6-3	220	8-29-88	1	3	4.31	8	7	0	0	40	49	20	19	2	26	26	.213	.245	.193	5.90	5.90
Wisler, Matt	R-R	6-3	195	9-12-92	3	4	4.29	12	12	0	0	65	68	34	31	5	13	49	.266	.315	.217	6.78	1.80

Fielding

Catcher	PCT	G	PO	A	E	DP	PB
Bethancourt	.991	48	318	31	3	3	1
Kennelly	1.000	10	68	6	0	1	1
Lavarnway	1.000	5	23	2	0	0	0
Nieves	.982	14	103	6	2	0	0
Schlehuber	1.000	39	260	19	0	2	3
Yepez	.987	36	215	18	3	3	4

First Base	PCT	G	PO	A	E	DP
Freeman	.950	2	18	1	1	0
Kazmar	.994	23	155	12	1	18
Kennelly	1.000	7	46	3	0	3
Kleinknecht	.993	63	498	36	4	50
Lavarnway	.974	5	31	6	1	6
Lennerton	.994	32	292	15	2	39
Terdoslavich	.990	21	186	7	2	19
Yepez	.955	3	20	1	1	2

Second Base	PCT	G	PO	A	E	DP
Castro	1.000	1	3	0	0	—
Kazmar	1.000	30	56	86	0	22
Mateo	.992	22	42	76	1	27
Peraza	.950	81	136	227	19	57
Reyes	1.000	4	8	6	0	2
Young Jr.	.968	11	22	38	2	10

Third Base	PCT	G	PO	A	E	DP
Ciriaco	.938	13	5	25	2	2
Garcia	.949	66	31	117	8	9
Johnson	—	1	0	0	0	0
Kazmar	.955	37	23	62	4	5
Kleinknecht	.914	21	15	38	5	7
Olivera	.957	9	3	19	1	0
Reyes	1.000	3	4	0	0	0

Shortstop	PCT	G	PO	A	E	DP
Castro	.972	88	119	263	11	67
Ciriaco	1.000	5	7	12	0	2
Kazmar	1.000	23	26	62	0	17
Kleinknecht		1	0	0	0	0
Mateo	1.000	9	9	28	0	7
Peraza	1.000	3	0	5	0	0
Reyes	.959	23	33	61	4	18

Outfield	PCT	G	PO	A	E	DP
Benson	.944	32	82	3	5	1
Cunningham	.991	90	200	10	2	2
Garcia	1.000	9	17	1	0	0
Hunter	.975	83	155	2	4	0
Johnson	1.000	2	3	0	0	0
Jones	.973	46	107	3	3	0
Peraza	1.000	13	25	1	0	0
Perez	.982	55	100	7	2	2
Smith	.984	68	178	6	3	0
Terdoslavich	1.000	8	13	0	0	0
Young Jr.	.982	46	102	5	2	0

MISSISSIPPI BRAVES

DOUBLE-A

SOUTHERN LEAGUE

Batting	B-T	HT	WT	DOB	AVG	vLH	vRH	G	AB	R	H	2B	3B	HR	RBI	BB	HBP	SH	SF	SO	SB	CS	SLG	OBP
Ahrens, Kevin	B-R	6-2	210	4-26-89	.238	.235	.239	122	407	51	97	23	0	9	64	47	1	2	6	79	8	0	.361	.315
Castro, Daniel	R-R	5-11	175	11-14-92	.389	.611	.333	23	90	17	35	5	0	0	14	4	0	3	1	8	4	2	.444	.411
Garcia, Eric	L-R	5-11	175	2-18-91	.200	.231	.192	92	250	21	50	11	1	2	23	23	1	0	2	59	3	2	.276	.268
Godfrey, Sean	R-R	6-2	180	1-2-92	.194	.295	.162	58	180	19	35	5	3	1	19	8	1	4	1	36	5	5	.272	.232
Hyams, Levi	L-R	6-2	215	10-6-89	.274	.275	.273	72	223	25	61	9	4	3	19	36	0	3	0	56	3	2	.390	.375
Jones, Mycal	R-R	5-10	190	5-30-87	.259	.375	.211	8	27	8	7	3	0	0	3	10	0	0	0	7	3	0	.370	.459
Joseph, Corban	L-R	6-0	185	10-28-88	.268	.125	.290	40	123	11	33	4	0	0	20	11	1	1	0	12	1	3	.301	.333

Batting

Batting	B-T	HT	WT	DOB	AVG	vLH	vRH	G	AB	R	H	2B	3B	HR	RBI	BB	HBP	SH	SF	SO	SB	CS	SLG	OBP
Kang, K.D.	L-L	6-2	210	2-6-88	.271	.279	.269	119	398	48	108	15	6	6	52	45	3	0	3	111	4	3	.384	.347
Kennelly, Matt	R-R	6-1	200	3-21-89	.220	.227	.217	73	241	25	53	7	0	0	16	30	1	3	2	42	0	4	.249	.307
Kleinknecht, Barrett	R-R	6-0	200	7-30-88	.257	.400	.233	10	35	4	9	3	0	0	3	1	1	0	0	7	0	0	.343	.297
Landoni, Emerson	B-R	5-11	189	2-19-89	.297	.310	.293	118	411	53	122	23	4	1	45	24	3	3	2	43	4	8	.380	.339
Lipka, Matt	R-R	6-1	200	4-15-92	.246	.176	.265	119	402	45	99	14	3	2	26	16	4	6	4	64	16	5	.311	.279
Loman, Seth	L-R	6-4	235	12-16-85	.199	.250	.181	55	171	16	34	6	0	4	22	13	10	0	3	46	1	0	.304	.289
Mateo, Luis	R-R	6-0	175	5-23-90	.231	.000	.250	3	13	1	3	1	0	0	3	0	0	0	0	1	0	0	.308	.231
O'Dowd, Chris	B-R	5-11	190	10-4-90	.304	.167	.344	26	79	13	24	5	1	2	16	18	0	0	1	19	3	1	.468	.429
Rodriguez, Steven	L-R	6-1	200	1-8-90	.205	.184	.211	61	166	16	34	6	0	0	20	21	2	5	3	39	0	1	.241	.297
Rohm, David	R-R	6-4	230	1-22-90	.255	.237	.261	101	321	39	82	12	1	1	30	34	2	3	3	51	5	2	.308	.328
Ruiz, Rio	L-R	6-2	215	5-22-94	.233	.221	.237	127	420	48	98	21	1	5	46	63	1	3	2	94	2	2	.324	.333
Schlehuber, Braeden	R-R	6-2	210	1-7-88	.184	.222	.175	32	98	6	18	4	1	0	4	5	0	1	0	13	1	0	.245	.223
Smith, Mallex	L-R	5-9	170	5-6-93	.340	.326	.344	57	206	35	70	5	2	2	22	27	2	3	2	41	23	6	.413	.418
Terdoslavich, Joey	B-R	6-2	200	9-9-88	.333	.500	.000	1	3	0	1	0	0	0	1	1	0	0	1	2	0	0	.667	.400

Pitching

Pitching	B-T	HT	WT	DOB	W	L	ERA	G	GS	CG	SV	IP	H	R	ER	HR	BB	SO	AVG	vLH	vRH	K/9	BB/9
Barbosa, Andrew	R-L	6-8	230	11-18-87	5	2	2.68	16	5	0	0	44	32	15	13	1	17	51	.206	.200	.210	10.51	3.50
2-team total (3 Mobile)					5	3	3.42	19	6	0	0	47	36	20	18	1	22	56	—	—	—	10.65	4.18
Bird, Zack	R-R	6-4	205	7-14-94	1	1	4.26	3	3	0	0	13	8	6	6	0	12	8	.186	.214	.172	5.68	8.53
Brigham, Jake	R-R	6-3	210	2-10-88	6	3	3.05	12	12	1	0	65	55	30	22	1	14	49	.226	.250	.210	6.78	1.94
Brocker, Cole	R-R	6-2	220	4-17-90	0	0	13.50	4	0	0	0	5	13	10	7	0	2	5	.464	.545	.412	9.64	3.86
Cabrera, Mauricio	R-R	6-3	230	9-22-93	0	1	5.71	13	0	0	0	17	12	12	11	1	18	25	.188	.211	.154	12.98	9.35
Cervenka, Hunter	L-L	6-1	225	1-3-90	0	0	0.00	3	0	0	0	4	3	0	0	0	1	8	.200	.125	.286	18.00	2.25
2-team total (3 Tennessee)					1	0	1.08	6	0	0	1	8	5	1	1	0	4	12	—	—	—	12.96	4.32
Cunniff, Brandon	R-R	6-0	185	10-7-88	0	0	0.00	1	0	0	0	1	1	0	0	0	0	1	.250	.333	.000	13.50	0.00
Gant, John	R-R	6-5	205	8-6-92	4	0	1.99	7	7	0	0	41	28	11	9	1	14	43	.201	.111	.259	9.52	3.10
Harper, Ryne	R-R	6-3	215	3-27-89	0	1	1.87	23	0	0	0	34	22	8	7	1	11	40	.186	.176	.194	10.69	2.94
Hursh, Jason	R-R	6-3	200	10-2-91	3	6	5.14	24	15	0	2	82	111	52	47	3	32	60	.323	.328	.319	6.56	3.50
Jackson, Justin	R-R	6-2	190	12-11-88	1	0	8.10	8	0	0	0	10	14	9	9	2	9	10	.333	.333	.333	9.00	8.10
Jaime, Juan	R-R	6-2	250	8-2-87	0	0	0.00	2	0	0	0	2	2	0	0	0	3	3	.286	.500	.000	16.20	16.20
Janas, Steve	R-R	6-5	200	4-21-92	2	8	4.87	13	13	0	0	68	83	42	37	1	20	33	.309	.355	.277	4.35	2.63
Jenkins, Tyrell	R-R	6-4	180	7-20-92	5	5	3.00	16	16	3	0	93	84	41	31	3	41	59	.241	.257	.229	5.71	3.97
Jones, Tyler	R-R	6-4	250	9-5-89	0	1	3.07	39	0	0	16	44	43	15	15	0	18	49	.270	.297	.253	10.02	3.68
Kelly, Ryan	R-R	6-2	180	10-30-87	1	1	0.48	17	0	0	10	19	13	2	1	0	6	18	.197	.100	.239	8.68	2.89
Kinman, Kyle	L-L	5-11	185	9-25-90	0	0	3.14	15	0	0	6	14	18	5	5	0	7	19	.300	.290	.310	11.93	4.40
Lambson, Mitchell	L-L	6-1	205	7-20-90	1	0	1.08	12	0	0	2	17	12	3	2	0	2	15	.207	.294	.171	8.10	4.86
Lamm, Mark	R-R	6-4	215	3-8-88	2	1	2.93	20	0	0	1	43	41	19	14	1	20	23	.253	.316	.219	4.81	4.19
Mateo, Victor	R-R	6-5	225	7-27-89	6	6	2.68	19	18	0	0	107	95	32	32	4	39	50	.241	.254	.230	4.19	3.27
McKirahan, Andrew	R-L	6-2	195	2-8-90	0	0	0.00	1	0	0	0	2	0	0	0	0	0	0	.000	—	.000	0.00	13.50
Nesseth, Mike	R-R	6-5	210	4-19-88	0	0	4.50	4	0	0	1	4	2	2	2	0	3	2	.143	.125	.167	4.50	6.75
Outman, Josh	L-L	6-1	205	9-14-84	0	1	4.50	2	0	0	0	2	2	3	1	0	1	3	.250	.667	.000	13.50	4.50
Peterson, Dave	R-R	6-5	205	1-4-90	2	0	1.23	7	0	0	3	7	6	6	1	0	4	6	.207	.182	.222	7.36	4.91
Reyes, Jorge	B-R	6-3	200	12-7-87	6	8	3.84	32	7	0	2	80	80	42	34	7	26	66	.263	.309	.226	7.46	2.94
Robinson, Andrew	R-R	6-1	185	2-13-88	4	1	2.91	34	0	0	2	43	35	16	14	4	10	39	.222	.232	.213	8.10	2.08
Rondon, Francisco	L-L	6-0	190	4-18-94	3	2	6.52	30	0	0	1	29	34	26	21	0	21	31	.283	.245	.313	9.62	6.52
Ross, Greg	R-R	6-3	205	9-6-89	7	9	3.99	25	23	0	0	138	146	65	61	6	47	80	.279	.292	.271	5.23	3.07
Sims, Lucas	R-R	6-2	225	5-10-94	3	2	3.21	9	9	0	0	48	29	18	17	1	29	56	.180	.220	.157	10.57	5.48
Thomas, Ian	L-L	6-4	215	4-20-87	0	0	0.00	2	0	0	0	3	0	0	0	0	0	4	.000	.000	.000	12.00	0.00
Thurman, Andrew	R-R	6-3	225	12-10-91	1	4	5.18	5	5	0	0	24	29	15	14	0	16	14	.302	.326	.280	5.18	5.92
Trepagnier, Bryton	R-R	6-6	208	9-18-91	4	2	4.40	42	0	0	0	57	56	29	28	2	44	30	.260	.272	.254	4.71	6.91
Vizcaino, Arodys	R-R	6-0	190	11-13-90	0	0	1.80	4	0	0	0	5	3	1	1	0	0	7	.167	.111	.222	12.60	0.00
Waszak, Andrew	R-R	6-1	205	10-8-90	1	0	3.38	4	0	0	0	5	8	2	2	1	2	5	.364	.500	.333	8.44	3.38
Weber, Ryan	R-R	6-0	180	8-12-90	0	2	2.73	11	3	0	1	26	23	8	8	1	1	24	.232	.286	.193	8.20	0.34

Fielding

Catcher	PCT	G	PO	A	E	DP	PB
Kennelly	.991	45	295	28	3	0	0
O'Dowd	.981	22	138	13	3	2	1
Rodriguez	.997	49	323	19	1	2	4
Schlehuber	.982	28	199	23	4	3	2

First Base	PCT	G	PO	A	E	DP
Ahrens	.989	71	493	38	6	40
Hyams	.990	17	91	5	1	11
Joseph	1.000	5	17	0	0	2
Kennelly	1.000	24	198	12	0	21
Kleinknecht	1.000	1	3	0	0	0
Loman	.994	39	295	19	2	30

Second Base	PCT	G	PO	A	E	DP
Castro	1.000	1	6	5	0	4
Garcia	.982	39	73	94	3	25

(Second Base cont.)	PCT	G	PO	A	E	DP
Hyams	.979	54	99	130	5	25
Joseph	.969	32	56	101	5	12
Kleinknecht	1.000	2	6	4	0	3
Landoni	.955	24	37	48	4	13

Third Base	PCT	G	PO	A	E	DP
Ahrens	1.000	25	17	46	0	8
Garcia	—	2	0	0	0	0
Hyams	—	1	0	0	0	0
Kleinknecht	—	1	0	0	0	0
Landoni	1.000	1	1	2	0	0
Ruiz	.950	120	92	214	16	10

Shortstop	PCT	G	PO	A	E	DP
Castro	.949	22	24	50	4	3
Garcia	.965	35	52	84	5	19
Hyams	.889	1	6	2	1	1

(Shortstop cont.)	PCT	G	PO	A	E	DP
Landoni	.966	84	113	230	12	50
Mateo	.882	3	7	8	2	3

Outfield	PCT	G	PO	A	E	DP
Ahrens	1.000	9	16	0	0	0
Garcia	1.000	7	6	0	0	0
Godfrey	.969	51	93	2	3	0
Hyams	1.000	1	1	0	0	0
Jones	1.000	8	18	0	0	0
Kang	.952	97	176	3	9	0
Kleinknecht	1.000	6	13	0	0	0
Landoni	1.000	1	0	1	0	0
Lipka	.985	112	261	9	4	2
O'Dowd	1.000	4	5	0	0	0
Rohm	.988	85	153	17	2	4
Smith	.979	55	137	4	3	1
Terdoslavich	.750	1	3	0	1	0

ATLANTA BRAVES

CAROLINA LEAGUE

ATLANTA BRAVES

Batting	B-T	HT	WT	DOB	AVG	vLH	vRH	G	AB	R	H	2B	3B	HR	RBI	BB	HBP	SH	SF	SO	SB	CS	SLG	OBP
Briceno, Jose	R-R	6-1	210	9-19-92	.183	.169	.189	88	311	32	57	14	0	4	20	12	1	1	2	52	2	0	.267	.215
Camargo, Johan	B-R	6-0	160	12-13-93	.258	.227	.269	130	391	50	101	15	6	1	32	30	4	20	4	54	4	2	.335	.315
Curcio, Keith	L-R	5-10	170	12-28-92	.241	.277	.229	101	382	43	92	14	5	4	38	29	4	6	4	61	20	10	.335	.298
Franco, Carlos	R-R	6-3	208	12-20-91	.254	.202	.271	134	461	54	117	30	3	11	62	66	1	0	2	108	5	5	.403	.347
Garcia, Eric	L-R	5-11	175	2-18-91	.286	.417	.243	14	49	8	14	4	0	1	9	7	0	0	0	6	0	0	.429	.375
Gebhardt, Ryan	R-R	5-11	195	10-5-91	.083	.333	.000	3	12	0	1	0	0	0	0	0	0	0	0	0	1	0	0	.083	.083
Giardina, Sal	B-R	6-4	215	4-30-92	.185	.214	.182	42	146	8	27	5	0	0	7	5	4	3	0	40	1	1	.219	.232
Godfrey, Sean	R-R	6-2	180	1-2-92	.304	.333	.296	62	240	37	73	12	1	5	22	8	2	2	1	41	10	6	.425	.331
Harper, Reed	R-R	6-2	200	12-21-90	.218	.253	.200	82	234	30	51	9	0	1	21	20	2	10	5	30	1	0	.269	.280
Hyams, Levi	L-R	6-2	205	10-6-89	.221	.211	.224	34	104	12	23	4	1	2	8	11	1	3	1	19	3	0	.337	.299
Krietemeier, Tanner	B-R	6-2	210	5-11-92	.237	.357	.188	29	97	6	23	7	0	0	5	6	2	0	0	17	0	1	.309	.295
Lien, Connor	R-R	6-3	205	3-15-94	.285	.360	.256	128	453	72	129	22	5	9	47	33	11	5	2	129	34	12	.415	.347
Meneses, Joey	R-R	6-3	190	5-6-92	.239	.231	.241	113	394	32	94	18	4	3	41	32	3	0	4	80	2	2	.327	.298
Odom, Joseph	R-R	6-2	205	1-9-92	.222	.304	.194	65	216	29	48	16	1	7	40	20	1	1	5	53	0	0	.403	.285
Oliver, Connor	L-R	6-0	180	10-13-93	.174	.133	.181	33	109	9	19	0	3	1	6	14	0	0	0	22	2	2	.257	.268
Peterson, Dustin	R-R	6-2	180	9-10-94	.251	.205	.266	118	446	58	112	15	2	8	62	44	2	0	6	91	6	3	.348	.317
Schrader, Jake	R-R	6-2	215	3-1-91	.268	.262	.270	103	377	52	101	28	3	15	59	19	7	0	3	103	1	0	.477	.313
Terdoslavich, Joey	B-R	6-2	200	9-9-88	.231	.000	.273	5	13	1	3	2	0	0	2	2	0	0	1	0	0	0	.385	.313

Pitching	B-T	HT	WT	DOB	W	L	ERA	G	GS	CG	SV	IP	H	R	ER	HR	BB	SO	AVG	vLH	vRH	K/9	BB/9
Barker, Brandon	R-R	6-3	200	8-20-92	8	5	3.00	17	17	0	0	96	90	35	32	5	24	64	.254	.225	.280	6.00	2.25
Brocker, Cole	R-R	6-2	220	4-17-90	0	0	0.00	5	0	0	2	7	5	1	0	0	1	9	.179	.077	.267	11.05	1.23
Brosius, Tyler	R-R	6-4	230	1-7-92	2	1	3.33	5	5	0	0	27	26	10	10	1	7	17	.265	.283	.250	5.67	2.33
Bywater, Matt	L-L	6-2	190	6-15-89	2	2	4.74	5	5	0	0	25	37	16	13	2	10	27	.339	.235	.359	9.85	3.65
Cabrera, Mauricio	R-R	6-3	230	9-22-93	2	2	5.52	23	0	0	1	31	30	22	19	1	17	28	.250	.245	.254	8.13	4.94
Cook, Clayton	R-R	6-3	175	7-23-90	1	0	4.50	7	0	0	0	8	8	4	4	0	11	7	.267	.286	.250	7.88	12.38
2-team total (16 Lynchburg)					4	2	5.11	23	3	0	0	44	43	31	25	2	32	31	—	—	—	6.34	6.55
Dirks, Caleb	R-R	6-4	225	6-9-93	0	0	0.00	11	0	0	2	17	8	0	0	0	12	18	.148	.136	.156	9.72	6.48
Emmons, Dustin	R-R	6-2	175	10-29-91	0	0	10.80	1	0	0	0	2	2	2	2	0	3	3	.286	.400	.000	16.20	16.20
Furney, Sean	R-R	6-5	220	6-2-91	0	4	6.67	6	5	0	0	28	46	22	21	2	11	15	.377	.364	.388	4.76	3.49
Gil, Yean Carlos	L-L	6-2	190	12-10-90	4	10	5.16	17	17	1	0	89	107	58	51	3	27	63	.296	.275	.301	6.37	2.73
Jackson, Justin	R-R	6-2	190	12-11-88	3	1	2.05	27	0	0	6	53	30	15	12	1	26	42	.166	.175	.158	7.18	4.44
Janas, Steve	R-R	6-5	200	4-21-92	5	0	0.49	6	6	1	0	37	18	2	2	0	4	24	.146	.175	.121	5.84	0.97
Jones, Tyler	R-R	6-4	250	9-5-89	0	0	0.00	10	0	0	6	10	6	1	0	2	16	.171	.200	.150	14.40	1.80
Kinman, Kyle	L-L	5-11	185	9-25-90	0	0	0.87	6	0	0	1	10	5	1	1	0	3	16	.139	.063	.200	13.94	2.61
Marksberry, Matt	L-L	6-1	200	8-25-90	3	1	2.78	22	0	0	2	36	22	11	11	2	13	35	.175	.087	.225	8.83	3.28
Nesseth, Mike	R-R	6-5	210	4-19-88	0	0	3.86	4	0	0	0	5	5	2	2	1	1	6	.294	.200	.333	11.57	1.93
Otero, Andy	L-L	5-9	165	6-3-92	1	5	2.58	34	2	0	3	59	58	21	17	1	16	53	.256	.301	.234	8.04	2.43
Outman, Josh	L-L	6-1	205	9-14-84	0	0	0.00	3	0	0	0	3	2	0	0	0	2	4	.200	.167	.250	13.50	6.75
Parsons, Wes	R-R	6-5	190	9-6-92	1	0	7.20	1	1	0	0	5	8	4	4	0	1	0	.381	.750	.294	0.00	1.80
Peterson, Dave	R-R	6-5	205	1-4-90	1	0	2.82	15	0	0	6	22	24	8	7	1	4	18	.270	.381	.170	7.25	1.61
Povse, Max	R-R	6-8	185	8-23-93	1	3	9.33	5	5	0	0	18	24	20	19	0	7	10	.316	.258	.356	4.91	3.44
Robertshaw, Britt	R-R	6-4	205	1-15-90	0	0	4.04	22	0	0	2	36	32	19	16	4	12	41	.232	.228	.235	10.35	3.03
Roney, Bradley	R-R	6-2	180	9-5-92	2	1	2.18	15	0	0	6	21	10	7	5	0	11	28	.147	.192	.119	12.19	4.79
Salazar, Carlos	R-R	6-0	200	11-23-94	1	1	4.38	10	0	0	1	12	8	6	6	0	21	14	.190	.364	.129	10.22	15.32
Sims, Lucas	R-R	6-2	225	5-10-94	3	4	5.18	9	9	1	0	40	39	27	23	2	23	37	.260	.316	.197	8.33	5.18
Tate, Richie	R-R	6-6	225	4-11-92	3	1	2.50	28	0	0	4	36	36	12	10	0	24	35	.277	.228	.315	8.75	6.00
Thurman, Andrew	R-R	6-3	225	12-10-91	5	4	3.77	11	11	0	0	57	57	26	24	2	11	43	.256	.258	.254	6.75	1.73
Walters, Blair	L-L	6-0	200	11-8-89	6	8	3.13	29	22	0	0	135	126	52	47	6	40	85	.249	.232	.256	5.67	2.67
Waszak, Andrew	R-R	6-1	205	10-8-90	7	6	3.30	25	12	0	1	85	80	39	31	0	36	54	.244	.223	.259	5.74	3.83
Webster, Seth	R-R	6-5	205	2-8-89	8	7	2.82	20	19	1	0	131	131	43	41	4	8	96	.263	.302	.222	6.61	0.55
Whalen, Rob	R-R	6-2	200	1-31-94	1	2	3.29	3	3	0	0	14	11	6	5	2	4	7	.224	.318	.148	4.61	2.63
Zavala, Jorge	R-R	6-4	200	6-10-94	1	0	2.90	23	0	0	1	31	34	10	10	1	20	38	.274	.298	.254	11.03	5.81

Fielding

Catcher	PCT	G	PO	A	E	DP	PB
Briceno	.983	71	453	78	9	5	8
Giardina	.967	12	79	8	3	0	1
Odom	.996	56	415	34	2	7	4

First Base	PCT	G	PO	A	E	DP
Giardina	.939	5	44	2	3	4
Hyams	1.000	1	9	0	0	0
Krietemeier	.973	15	105	5	3	18
Meneses	.994	85	733	47	5	64
Schrader	.983	39	326	17	6	23

Second Base	PCT	G	PO	A	E	DP
Curcio	.976	36	56	106	4	21

	PCT	G	PO	A	E	DP
Garcia	.977	9	16	26	1	3
Gebhardt	.929	3	6	7	1	2
Harper	.993	68	102	186	2	43
Hyams	.963	31	52	79	5	14

Third Base	PCT	G	PO	A	E	DP
Franco	.961	133	72	225	12	14
Garcia	1.000	1	0	3	0	1
Giardina	1.000	1	0	1	0	0
Harper	.778	3	1	6	2	2
Hyams	1.000	2	1	5	0	2

Shortstop	PCT	G	PO	A	E	DP
Camargo	.959	130	196	365	24	78

	PCT	G	PO	A	E	DP
Garcia	.875	1	4	3	1	1
Harper	.971	11	12	21	1	4

Outfield	PCT	G	PO	A	E	DP
Curcio	.993	71	145	5	1	2
Godfrey	.989	46	87	6	1	1
Krietemeier	.944	15	16	1	1	0
Lien	.973	127	304	21	9	7
Meneses	.978	24	42	3	1	1
Oliver	1.000	32	48	4	0	0
Peterson	.984	114	177	9	3	0
Terdoslavich	1.000	4	6	0	0	0

ROME BRAVES   LOW CLASS A
SOUTH ATLANTIC LEAGUE

Batting	B-T	HT	WT	DOB	AVG	vLH	vRH	G	AB	R	H	2B	3B	HR	RBI	BB	HBP	SH	SF	SO	SB	CS	SLG	OBP
Albies, Ozzie	B-R	5-9	150	1-7-97	.310	.322	.305	98	394	64	122	21	8	0	37	36	2	4	3	56	29	8	.404	.368
Baez, Leudys	B-R	6-0	160	6-26-96	.206	.163	.234	29	107	12	22	5	2	1	6	3	1	0	1	30	1	4	.318	.232
Black, Justin	R-R	6-0	190	5-20-93	.200	.250	.167	11	30	5	6	0	1	1	6	5	0	0	1	15	1	1	.367	.306
Curcio, Keith	L-R	5-10	170	12-28-92	.342	.366	.329	32	117	23	40	6	5	0	19	14	3	0	3	12	4	1	.479	.416
Daris, Joseph	L-R	5-10	170	11-22-91	.272	.259	.277	127	394	57	107	13	12	4	35	33	5	5	0	77	23	7	.396	.336
Davidson, Braxton	L-L	6-2	210	6-18-96	.242	.225	.250	124	401	51	97	23	0	10	45	84	7	0	2	135	1	6	.374	.381
De La Rosa, Bryan	R-R	5-8	193	3-26-94	.205	.178	.218	79	283	31	58	18	0	5	23	24	5	1	2	75	0	1	.322	.277
Dykstra, Luke	R-R	6-1	195	11-7-95	.348	.353	.345	26	92	9	32	10	1	0	10	3	2	2	1	5	1	0	.478	.378
Edgerton, Jordan	R-R	6-1	190	8-30-93	.245	.266	.236	107	416	34	102	17	2	3	57	26	2	2	4	85	7	6	.317	.290
Franco, J.J.	R-R	5-9	180	2-2-92	.100	.000	.125	6	20	3	2	0	0	0	1	1	0	0	0	5	0	2	.100	.143
Gaylor, Stephen	L-R	6-1	180	10-4-91	.285	.288	.284	74	249	44	71	7	4	0	12	28	7	4	0	33	15	11	.345	.373
Gebhardt, Ryan	R-R	5-11	195	10-5-91	.200	.278	.136	10	40	3	8	0	0	0	3	1	0	0	1	6	0	1	.200	.214
Harper, Reed	R-R	6-2	200	12-21-90	.258	.222	.273	11	31	2	8	1	0	0	2	2	0	0	6	0	0	.290	.303
Krietemeier, Tanner	R-R	6-2	210	5-11-92	.243	.267	.234	47	173	18	42	7	2	1	23	12	5	0	4	34	0	2	.324	.304
McElroy, Codey	R-R	6-5	195	12-13-92	.168	.150	.180	32	101	8	17	3	0	0	7	10	0	0	0	31	2	0	.198	.243
Mendez, Erison	R-R	5-11	170	5-4-92	.223	.186	.243	70	206	16	46	8	1	0	9	8	12	4	1	46	1	8	.272	.291
Murphy, Tanner	R-R	6-1	215	2-27-95	.193	.177	.200	98	337	33	65	17	1	7	35	38	3	0	4	91	0	0	.312	.277
Nevarez, Wigberto	R-R	6-3	230	7-17-91	.177	.188	.171	57	175	9	31	6	0	2	21	12	3	1	4	47	1	2	.246	.237
Obregon, Omar	B-R	5-10	150	4-18-94	.274	.243	.291	119	441	52	121	11	4	0	51	38	6	11	6	58	31	19	.317	.336
Oliver, Connor	L-R	6-0	180	10-13-93	.199	.265	.167	53	151	14	30	8	2	0	11	18	0	0	1	43	7	6	.278	.282
Olivera, Hector	R-R	6-2	220	4-5-85	.083	.000	.143	4	12	1	1	0	0	0	0	2	0	0	0	1	0	0	.083	.214
Perez, Angel	R-R	6-0	185	6-14-95	.000	.000	.000	1	3	0	0	0	0	0	0	0	0	0	0	1	0	0	.000	.000
Tellor, Matt	B-R	6-5	210	9-24-91	.235	.207	.250	99	357	34	84	22	0	5	44	23	0	0	2	99	0	2	.339	.280
Terdoslavich, Joey	B-R	6-2	200	9-9-88	.385	.000	.417	3	13	1	5	1	0	0	2	1	0	0	0	2	0	0	.462	.467
Valenzuela, Luis	L-R	5-10	150	8-25-93	.429	.429	.429	6	21	1	9	1	0	1	2	1	0	0	0	2	0	2	.619	.455
2-team total (48 Lexington)					.343	—	—	54	198	31	68	11	3	4	17	9	0	3	0	30	8	3	.490	.372

Pitching	B-T	HT	WT	DOB	W	L	ERA	G	GS	CG	SV	IP	H	R	ER	HR	BB	SO	AVG	vLH	vRH	K/9	BB/9
Bare, Dustin	R-R	6-0	170	12-12-92	0	0	11.57	1	0	0	0	2	3	3	3	0	2	0	.375	.250	.500	0.00	7.71
Barker, Brandon	R-R	6-3	200	8-20-92	3	4	3.48	8	8	0	0	41	43	21	16	2	13	35	.270	.250	.283	7.62	2.83
Beech, Caleb	R-R	6-4	215	4-18-93	5	2	2.87	11	10	0	0	63	56	27	20	2	17	43	.235	.212	.252	6.18	2.44
Belicek, Trevor	L-L	6-3	215	12-10-92	1	0	1.86	4	4	0	0	19	22	5	4	1	6	8	.301	.333	.279	3.72	2.79
Brocker, Cole	R-R	6-2	220	4-17-90	0	0	4.50	1	0	0	0	2	1	1	1	0	0	1	.222	.167	.333	4.50	0.00
Caicedo, Oriel	L-L	5-11	190	1-14-94	5	7	3.55	25	15	0	0	101	118	50	40	8	14	56	.289	.264	.300	4.97	1.24
Cockrell, Taylor	R-R	6-2	170	6-21-94	1	1	12.79	4	0	0	0	6	14	12	9	3	1	7	.424	.526	.286	9.95	1.42
Cordero, Daniel	R-R	6-0	180	6-7-93	1	1	7.88	9	3	0	0	24	35	23	21	1	13	20	.347	.386	.316	7.50	4.88
Dill, Dakota	L-R	6-4	215	5-20-91	0	1	4.26	3	0	0	0	6	5	3	3	1	3	11	.208	.286	.100	15.63	4.26
Dirks, Caleb	R-R	6-4	225	6-9-93	1	2	1.80	6	0	0	1	10	12	2	2	0	2	11	.293	.188	.360	9.90	1.80
Emmons, Dustin	R-R	6-2	175	10-29-91	2	6	3.49	36	0	0	5	57	65	29	22	3	20	39	.289	.268	.301	6.19	3.18
Furney, Sean	R-R	6-5	220	6-21-91	7	8	3.03	21	14	4	0	113	97	41	38	5	41	63	.233	.266	.214	5.02	3.27
Geekie, Dalton	R-R	6-5	200	10-3-94	0	0	4.50	1	0	0	0	2	3	1	1	0	1	1	.429	.000	.500	4.50	0.00
Gil, Yean Carlos	L-L	6-2	190	12-10-90	2	5	4.07	10	10	2	0	66	60	32	30	3	18	38	.244	.236	.247	5.16	2.44
Gonzalez, Francisco	R-R	6-0	170	9-21-94	3	2	7.52	24	0	0	0	41	43	36	34	5	26	29	.274	.333	.237	6.42	5.75
Grosser, Alec	R-R	6-4	205	1-12-95	4	6	7.32	26	15	0	0	82	84	75	67	4	64	46	.272	.290	.259	5.03	7.00
Harper, Ryne	R-R	6-3	215	3-27-89	0	0	5.40	1	0	0	0	2	2	1	1	0	0	3	.286	.400	.000	16.20	0.00
Kinman, Kyle	L-L	5-11	185	9-25-90	1	0	2.00	23	0	0	11	27	21	9	6	0	16	30	.219	.138	.254	10.00	5.33
Lewis, Taylor	R-R	6-1	170	10-4-94	0	2	2.77	9	0	0	2	13	13	4	4	1	4	7	.260	.250	.273	4.85	2.77
Marte, Felix	R-R	6-1	180	11-14-90	1	1	4.34	33	0	0	1	46	41	25	22	1	39	43	.238	.260	.221	8.47	7.69
McLaughlin, Sean	L-R	5-11	175	5-16-94	0	0	1.02	9	1	0	2	18	15	4	2	0	5	20	.221	.216	.226	10.19	2.55
Miranda, Fernando	R-R	5-11	180	9-5-94	1	0	8.44	5	0	0	0	11	16	11	10	0	3	10	.340	.188	.419	8.44	2.53
Osnowitz, Mitchell	R-R	6-5	245	7-2-91	1	2	5.13	22	0	0	0	33	39	24	19	2	20	29	.293	.393	.221	7.83	5.40
Outman, Josh	L-L	6-1	205	9-14-84	0	0	0.00	2	0	0	0	2	0	0	0	0	2	0	.000	.000	.000	0.00	9.00
Parsons, Wes	R-R	6-5	190	9-6-92	1	0	1.80	1	1	0	0	5	2	1	1	0	2	2	.118	.000	.182	3.60	0.00
Phillips, Evan	R-R	6-2	215	9-11-94	1	2	4.41	12	0	0	2	16	13	9	8	1	8	20	.228	.250	.212	11.02	4.41
Povse, Max	R-R	6-8	185	8-23-93	4	2	2.56	12	12	0	0	60	50	23	17	2	16	50	.226	.263	.197	7.54	2.41
Quintana, Zach	R-R	5-11	180	4-15-94	5	6	3.25	32	17	1	3	114	122	47	41	1	36	68	.277	.299	.261	5.38	2.85
Roney, Bradley	R-R	6-2	180	9-1-92	1	0	4.07	16	0	0	4	24	7	11	11	0	23	35	.091	.143	.061	12.95	8.51
Salazar, Carlos	R-R	6-0	200	11-23-94	1	4	2.23	23	0	0	0	44	22	17	11	1	29	46	.146	.118	.160	9.34	5.89
Sanchez, Ricardo	L-L	5-11	170	4-11-97	1	6	5.45	10	10	0	0	40	37	28	24	3	21	31	.250	.318	.238	7.03	4.76
Sobotka, Chad	R-R	6-7	200	7-10-93	1	6	7.31	12	9	0	0	32	45	32	26	5	21	18	.346	.262	.420	5.06	5.91
Toussaint, Touki	R-R	6-3	185	6-20-96	3	5	5.73	10	10	1	0	49	40	33	31	6	33	38	.229	.293	.197	7.03	6.10
Vizcaino, Arodys	R-R	6-0	190	11-13-90	0	0	9.00	2	0	0	0	2	4	3	2	0	2	4	.364	.250	.429	18.00	9.00
Waszak, Andrew	R-R	6-1	205	10-8-90	0	0	9.82	1	0	0	0	4	5	4	4	0	2	1	.333	—	.333	2.45	4.91
Webster, Seth	R-R	6-5	205	6-27-89	0	1	10.80	1	1	0	0	5	7	6	6	1	2	7	.350	.375	.333	12.60	3.60
Zavala, Jorge	R-R	6-4	200	6-10-94	1	0	0.73	10	0	0	4	12	6	2	1	0	6	17	.158	.182	.148	12.41	4.38

Fielding

Catcher	PCT	G	PO	A	E	DP	PB
De La Rosa	.983	50	291	46	6	2	9
Murphy	.992	82	509	90	5	4	7
Nevarez	1.000	18	65	9	0	0	0

First Base	PCT	G	PO	A	E	DP
Krietemeier	.981	35	292	16	6	26
Mendez	1.000	2	20	0	0	1
Nevarez	.984	27	238	10	4	20

	PCT	G	PO	A	E	DP
Obregon	1.000	3	6	0	0	0
Tellor	.989	79	674	33	8	54
Second Base	**PCT**	**G**	**PO**	**A**	**E**	**DP**
Curcio	1.000	2	6	5	0	2

Second Base	PCT	G	PO	A	E	DP
Dykstra	.969	21	40	54	3	10
Franco	1.000	5	13	17	0	2
Gebhardt	1.000	1	1	4	0	0
Harper	.935	7	12	17	2	4
Mendez	.983	22	48	65	2	14
Obregon	.973	85	179	219	11	43

Third Base	PCT	G	PO	A	E	DP
Edgerton	.929	100	76	210	22	18
Gebhardt	.944	8	7	10	1	2
Harper	.917	2	0	11	1	0
McElroy	.917	3	4	7	1	0

Mendez	.935	19	6	37	3	4
Nevarez	.000	3	0	0	1	0
Obregon	.800	5	1	7	2	1
Olivera	.833	3	3	7	2	0

Shortstop	PCT	G	PO	A	E	DP
Albies	.959	93	121	275	17	53
Harper	1.000	1	1	0	0	0
McElroy	1.000	1	1	1	0	0
Mendez	.936	15	15	29	3	0
Obregon	.963	28	48	83	5	11
Perez	1.000	1	0	3	0	0
Valenzuela	1.000	6	13	16	0	4

Outfield	PCT	G	PO	A	E	DP
Baez	.974	20	37	0	1	0
Black	1.000	10	14	0	0	0
Curcio	.986	30	72	0	1	0
Daris	.955	116	186	7	9	2
Davidson	.973	109	206	10	6	1
Gaylor	.987	69	152	4	2	0
Krietemeier	1.000	4	7	1	0	0
McElroy	.970	20	32	0	1	0
Mendez	1.000	7	17	0	0	0
Oliver	.983	47	117	2	2	1
Terdoslavich	1.000	3	3	0	0	0

DANVILLE BRAVES   ROOKIE

APPALACHIAN LEAGUE

Batting	B-T	HT	WT	DOB	AVG	vLH	vRH	G	AB	R	H	2B	3B	HR	RBI	BB	HBP	SH	SF	SO	SB	CS	SLG	OBP
Acuna, Ronald	R-R	6-0	180	12-18-97	.290	.133	.333	18	69	10	20	5	2	1	7	10	1	0	0	19	5	1	.464	.388
Baez, Leudys	B-R	6-0	160	6-26-96	.311	.167	.368	33	148	19	46	8	2	4	13	3	2	1	1	31	5	1	.473	.331
Campbell, Jeff	R-R	6-4	225	7-5-92	.277	.345	.246	25	94	9	26	9	0	0	13	4	0	0	1	30	0	1	.372	.303
Castro, Carlos	R-R	6-1	195	5-24-94	.319	.481	.263	50	204	22	65	10	3	1	31	8	0	0	3	42	2	2	.412	.340
Didder, Ray-Patrick	R-R	6-0	170	10-1-94	.247	.273	.238	61	223	31	55	5	7	0	16	20	14	2	0	51	10	7	.332	.346
Dykstra, Luke	R-R	6-1	195	11-7-95	.298	.394	.265	32	131	18	39	9	1	0	12	5	3	1	1	11	2	1	.382	.336
Ellison, Justin	L-L	6-2	175	2-6-95	.238	.238	.237	23	80	11	19	6	1	3	11	9	0	0	1	15	1	0	.450	.311
Estevez, Kelvin	R-R	6-1	190	11-17-95	.207	.179	.219	28	92	6	19	2	1	1	8	5	0	0	0	40	0	1	.283	.247
Flores, Alejandro	B-R	6-1	180	12-27-95	.125	.200	.102	20	64	1	8	3	0	0	6	11	0	0	1	21	0	1	.172	.250
Gaylor, Stephen	L-R	6-1	180	10-4-91	.333	—	.333	2	6	4	2	0	1	0	0	0	1	2	1	0	0	2	.667	.556
Grullon, Yeudi	B-R	6-1	170	7-18-94	.207	.200	.211	44	140	16	29	1	1	1	8	13	0	11	1	23	1	0	.250	.273
Hagenmiller, Ian	R-R	6-1	215	9-3-94	.108	.000	.148	20	74	7	8	3	0	1	8	3	1	1	0	33	0	0	.189	.154
Hoekstra, Kurt	L-R	6-2	190	6-27-93	.257	.229	.265	48	167	23	43	5	5	2	18	9	4	1	2	36	8	0	.383	.344
Keegan, Trey	R-R	5-10	205	5-11-93	.267	.095	.323	26	86	11	23	4	0	0	6	10	1	2	2	12	1	0	.314	.343
Lanning, Jake	B-R	6-1	205	2-4-93	.273	.375	.228	40	132	14	36	9	0	0	16	13	2	0	1	30	0	1	.341	.345
Manwaring, Dylan	R-R	6-3	210	9-27-94	.121	.190	.081	17	58	6	7	3	0	1	3	6	1	0	0	25	0	1	.224	.215
Martinez, Carlos	R-R	5-11	204	5-2-95	.229	.225	.231	32	105	10	24	4	0	1	7	10	3	1	1	16	0	0	.295	.311
Morel, Jose	B-R	6-1	195	8-2-93	.313	.295	.321	54	195	26	61	10	1	1	19	17	2	1	1	48	3	4	.390	.372
Riley, Austin	R-R	6-2	230	4-2-97	.351	.316	.359	30	111	18	39	9	1	5	19	14	5	0	1	28	0	1	.586	.443
Yepez, Juan	R-R	6-1	200	2-19-98	.291	.409	.259	28	103	12	30	7	1	3	14	6	0	0	2	29	0	1	.466	.324

Pitching	B-T	HT	WT	DOB	W	L	ERA	G	GS	CG	SV	IP	H	R	ER	HR	BB	SO	AVG	vLH	vRH	K/9	BB/9
Belicek, Trevor	L-L	6-3	215	12-10-92	4	0	2.87	10	5	0	0	38	33	17	12	2	6	33	.228	.254	.209	7.88	1.43
Borkowski, Steve	R-R	6-2	215	11-7-92	3	1	9.00	10	0	0	0	20	32	23	20	3	6	14	.352	.370	.333	6.30	2.70
Clark, Ryan	R-R	6-5	220	12-9-93	6	1	3.08	13	7	0	0	53	43	23	18	2	10	40	.221	.263	.191	6.84	1.71
Cordero, Daniel	R-R	6-0	180	6-7-93	1	2	1.80	8	3	0	1	25	20	9	5	1	3	23	.222	.214	.229	8.28	1.08
Custred, Matt	R-R	6-5	205	9-8-93	1	0	1.42	18	0	0	4	32	16	8	5	0	9	45	.148	.154	.143	12.79	2.56
Dill, Dakota	L-R	6-4	215	5-20-91	1	2	3.07	17	0	0	1	29	30	15	10	5	5	22	.263	.268	.259	6.75	1.53
Fulenchek, Garrett	R-R	6-4	205	6-7-96	0	1	7.71	2	2	0	0	5	5	4	4	0	8	4	.278	.600	.154	7.71	15.43
2-team total (10 Princeton)					1	1	6.11	12	4	0	0	18	18	17	12	0	30	19	—	—	—	9.68	15.28
Gamez, Luis	R-R	6-2	175	6-25-96	2	4	5.79	13	5	0	0	28	32	27	18	3	19	21	.276	.261	.286	6.75	6.11
Geekie, Dalton	R-R	6-5	200	10-3-94	1	0	0.00	3	0	0	0	6	1	0	0	0	3		.053	.000	.077	4.50	0.00
Graham, Josh	R-R	6-1	215	10-14-93	1	1	2.60	6	5	0	0	17	17	6	5	0	3	21	.239	.200	.308	10.90	1.56
Grosser, Alec	R-R	6-4	205	1-12-95	0	1	3.00	3	0	0	0	3	2	1	1	0	1	4	.200	.000	.250	12.00	3.00
Johnson-Mullins, Chase	L-L	6-9	280	7-19-94	0	3	2.81	16	0	0	6	26	26	10	8	0	17	21	.268	.250	.279	7.36	5.96
Jones, Grayson	R-R	6-1	205	8-22-94	4	3	3.03	19	0	0	2	33	21	11	11	0	19	27	.189	.234	.156	7.44	5.23
Lawlor, Ryan	R-L	6-0	170	1-8-94	1	0	2.30	8	7	0	0	27	23	9	7	1	12	25	.225	.353	.162	8.23	3.95
Lewis, Taylor	R-R	6-1	170	10-4-93	1	0	0.00	6	0	0	0	7	6	4	0	1	2	8	.214	.333	.158	9.82	2.45
Libuda, Ben	L-L	6-7	185	4-14-93	3	1	5.73	12	0	0	0	22	29	19	14	2	13	17	.315	.258	.344	6.95	5.32
McLaughlin, Sean	L-R	5-11	175	5-16-94	0	1	4.43	11	0	0	3	22	24	11	11	0	8	24	.276	.308	.250	9.67	3.22
Miranda, Fernando	R-R	5-11	180	9-5-94	1	2	2.70	4	0	0	1	7	3	2	2	0	2	8	.125	.182	.077	10.80	2.70
Osnowitz, Mitchell	R-R	6-5	245	7-2-91	0	0	16.20	1	0	0	0	2	4	3	3	0	1	2	.444	.333	.500	10.80	5.40
Phillips, Evan	R-R	6-2	215	9-11-94	1	1	0.68	6	0	0	0	13	8	1	1	1	4	17	.178	.227	.130	11.48	2.70
Roney, Bradley	R-R	6-2	180	9-1-92	0	0	0.00	2	0	0	1	3	0	0	0	0	1	7	.000	.000	.000	18.90	2.70
Sobotka, Chad	R-R	6-7	200	7-10-93	0	0	0.00	1	0	0	0	1	0	0	0	0	0	9	.000	.000	.000	9.00	0.00
Soroka, Mike	R-R	6-4	195	8-4-97	0	2	3.75	6	6	0	0	24	28	12	10	0	4	26	.283	.431	.125	9.75	1.50
Stiffler, Ian	L-R	6-1	175	2-12-95	1	3	6.26	12	1	0	2	23	19	16	16	1	18	14	.238	.237	.238	5.48	7.04
Weigel, Patrick	R-R	6-6	200	7-8-94	0	3	4.53	14	14	0	0	52	53	35	26	2	26	49	.256	.283	.228	8.54	4.53
Withrow, Matt	R-R	6-3	210	9-23-93	0	4	3.56	13	13	0	0	48	48	24	19	2	16	35	.257	.200	.299	6.56	3.00

Fielding

Catcher	PCT	G	PO	A	E	DP	PB
Flores	.983	14	102	12	2	0	2
Keegan	.995	25	200	15	1	2	5
Martinez	.988	32	209	34	3	1	4

First Base	PCT	G	PO	A	E	DP
Campbell	.948	12	85	6	5	8
Castro	.982	16	147	14	3	12

Hagenmiller	.982	19	143	18	3	13
Yepez	.977	22	193	15	5	15

Second Base	PCT	G	PO	A	E	DP
Dykstra	.959	32	48	91	6	13
Grullon	.967	21	43	76	4	13
Lanning	.984	15	21	39	1	7

Third Base	PCT	G	PO	A	E	DP
Grullon	1.000	2	0	4	0	0
Lanning	.857	12	17	19	6	4
Manwaring	.944	17	10	24	2	1
Riley	.897	29	25	53	9	4
Yepez	1.000	1	1	1	0	0

Shortstop	PCT	G	PO	A	E	DP
Grullon	.948	21	30	61	5	11
Hoekstra	.920	47	78	117	17	27

Outfield	PCT	G	PO	A	E	DP
Acuna	1.000	18	30	1	0	0
Baez	.979	29	44	2	1	0
Didder	.979	59	129	9	3	1
Ellison	1.000	22	31	0	0	0
Estevez	.981	25	48	3	1	1
Gaylor	1.000	2	5	0	0	0
Morel	.933	50	80	4	6	1

GCL BRAVES
ROOKIE

GULF COAST LEAGUE

Batting	B-T	HT	WT	DOB	AVG	vLH	vRH	G	AB	R	H	2B	3B	HR	RBI	BB	HBP	SH	SF	SO	SB	CS	SLG	OBP
Acuna, Ronald	R-R	6-0	180	12-18-97	.258	.357	.231	37	132	31	34	9	2	3	11	18	7	0	0	23	11	3	.424	.376
Arias, Elias	L-L	6-1	180	6-30-94	.130	.000	.167	14	46	7	6	2	0	0	5	4	0	0	1	11	1	1	.174	.196
Azuaje, Franklin	R-R	6-1	170	3-31-95	.000	—	.000	2	2	0	0	0	0	0	1	2	0	0	0	0	0	0	.000	.500
Cabrera, Jeyson	R-R	6-0	185	11-21-95	.333	.000	.500	2	6	0	2	0	0	0	0	0	0	0	0	2	0	0	.333	.333
Ellison, Justin	L-L	6-2	175	2-6-95	.255	.211	.266	27	98	11	25	5	1	2	17	9	0	0	1	22	5	0	.388	.315
Estevez, Kelvin	R-R	6-1	190	11-17-95	.375	.250	.400	13	48	5	18	2	0	1	10	3	0	0	0	8	1	1	.479	.412
Freeman, Freddie	L-R	6-5	225	9-12-89	.182	.250	.143	3	11	2	2	0	0	1	3	0	0	0	0	4	0	0	.455	.182
Guillermo, Ronny	R-R	6-1	170	8-2-96	.155	.043	.188	37	103	6	16	2	0	0	5	7	2	2	1	34	4	1	.175	.221
Herbert, Lucas	R-R	6-0	200	11-28-96	.500	1.000	.333	3	4	1	2	0	0	1	2	0	0	1	0	0	1	0	1.250	.600
Josephina, Kevin	B-R	6-0	170	10-2-96	.272	.500	.206	22	81	11	22	1	1	0	3	3	0	1	0	18	2	2	.309	.298
Keller, Brad	R-R	6-1	195	12-15-96	.245	.194	.259	44	143	22	35	6	0	3	17	13	4	0	2	50	7	4	.350	.321
Morales, Jonathan	R-R	5-11	180	1-29-95	.304	.308	.303	46	135	24	41	7	0	7	22	14	2	1	0	14	2	2	.511	.377
Nesovic, Robby	R-R	6-3	220	3-31-94	.242	.200	.253	31	99	17	24	5	0	0	7	19	3	0	1	22	6	2	.293	.377
Olivera, Hector	R-R	6-2	220	4-5-85	.000	—	.000	2	5	0	0	0	0	0	0	0	0	0	0	1	0	0	.000	.000
Perez, Angel	R-R	6-0	185	6-14-95	.224	.154	.241	41	134	13	30	1	0	0	17	10	1	1	0	32	0	1	.231	.283
Perez, Ruben	R-R	6-0	180	9-21-95	.148	.071	.162	37	88	9	13	1	0	1	9	12	3	0	4	43	1	1	.193	.262
Pina, Jose	R-R	6-2	180	4-22-96	.280	.333	.268	32	100	10	28	5	0	1	12	4	0	0	2	19	5	1	.360	.302
Reiher, Kevin	R-R	5-10	190	5-24-94	—	—	—	—	—	—	—	—	—	—	—	—	—	—	—	—	—	—	—	—
Riley, Austin	R-R	6-2	230	4-2-97	.255	.304	.241	30	106	18	27	5	0	7	21	12	1	0	2	37	2	1	.500	.331
Salazar, Alejandro	R-R	6-0	170	10-5-96	.284	.282	.284	51	194	36	55	5	2	2	25	20	1	3	1	32	8	3	.361	.352
Wilson, Israel	L-R	6-3	185	3-6-98	.222	.265	.209	48	144	29	32	5	1	0	22	26	2	1	0	56	3	4	.479	.349
Yelich, Collin	L-R	6-2	180	10-1-93	.242	.357	.208	43	124	13	30	5	1	1	13	23	2	1	0	15	2	2	.306	.369
Yepez, Juan	R-R	6-1	200	2-19-98	.306	.190	.338	31	98	12	30	9	1	1	17	16	1	0	2	26	3	2	.449	.402

Pitching	B-T	HT	WT	DOB	W	L	ERA	G	GS	CG	SV	IP	H	R	ER	HR	BB	SO	AVG	vLH	vRH	K/9	BB/9
Allard, Kolby	L-L	6-1	175	8-13-97	0	0	0.00	3	3	0	0	6	1	0	0	0	0	12	.053	.000	.071	18.00	0.00
Avalos, Gabino	R-R	6-0	185	8-15-94	4	4	3.53	12	8	0	0	43	44	20	17	1	28	38	.277	.194	.297	7.89	5.82
Banuelos, Manny	L-L	5-10	205	3-13-91	0	0	0.00	1	1	0	0	2	2	3	0	0	2	3	.200	.000	.222	13.50	9.00
Barrios, Luis	L-L	6-4	210	3-4-97	1	1	4.26	14	0	0	0	25	24	17	12	1	13	16	.250	.375	.208	5.68	4.62
Cockrell, Taylor	R-R	6-2	170	6-21-94	0	1	7.11	4	0	0	0	6	6	5	5	0	4	9	.250	.143	.294	12.79	5.68
Cunniff, Brandon	R-R	6-0	185	10-7-88	0	0	0.00	1	1	0	0	1	0	0	0	0	0	1	.000	.000	.000	9.00	0.00
Custred, Matt	R-R	6-5	205	9-8-93	0	0	0.00	1	0	0	0	1	1	0	0	0	0	1	.250	—	.250	9.00	0.00
Falcon, Felix	L-L	6-2	190	8-7-95	1	6	4.46	12	7	0	0	34	43	30	17	0	25	35	.319	.282	.333	9.17	6.55
Gamez, Luis	R-R	6-2	175	6-25-96	0	2	1.80	3	3	0	0	10	8	3	2	0	5	9	.222	.105	.353	8.10	4.50
Geekie, Dalton	R-R	6-5	200	10-3-94	3	0	2.25	13	0	0	2	20	18	6	5	1	9	22	.250	.200	.297	9.90	4.05
Guardado, Anthony	R-R	6-1	185	11-14-97	0	0	0.00	1	0	0	0	1	1	0	0	0	2	2	.250	.500	.000	18.00	18.00
Hellinger, Jarret	R-L	6-4	170	11-18-96	2	2	3.15	10	6	0	0	34	34	19	12	1	14	33	.258	.250	.261	8.65	3.67
Javier, Odalvi	R-R	6-0	180	9-4-96	1	1	2.37	10	1	0	0	19	22	5	5	2	9	18	.310	.296	.318	8.53	4.26
Kohn, Michael	R-R	6-2	200	6-26-86	1	0	0.00	2	1	0	0	2	1	0	0	0	1	2	.143	.000	.167	9.00	0.00
Leon, Nelson	L-L	6-0	175	6-29-95	0	0	27.00	2	0	0	0	1	3	3	3	0	2	1	.500	.000	.600	9.00	18.00
Libuda, Ben	L-L	6-7	185	4-14-93	2	1	5.06	4	0	0	0	5	8	4	3	0	2	2	.348	.400	.308	3.38	3.38
Martinez, Jhon	L-L	6-0	165	2-9-95	1	2	2.23	10	7	1	0	40	34	16	10	2	8	31	.228	.211	.234	6.92	1.79
Matos, Bladimir	R-R	6-0	190	1-20-94	1	2	4.58	17	0	0	1	20	20	16	10	1	7	20	.247	.167	.311	9.15	3.20
Mejia, Dilmer	L-L	5-11	160	7-9-97	0	3	5.82	7	2	0	0	22	24	15	14	2	4	19	.279	.304	.270	7.89	1.66
Miranda, Fernando	R-R	5-11	180	9-5-94	0	0	0.00	1	0	0	0	1	0	0	0	0	0	1	.000	.000	.000	9.00	0.00
Orozco, Evertz	R-R	6-5	192	9-16-94	5	1	2.33	15	0	0	3	27	26	7	7	1	5	22	.257	.268	.250	7.33	1.67
Outman, Josh	L-L	6-1	205	9-14-84	0	0	0.00	2	2	0	0	2	2	0	0	0	0	3	.286	1.000	.167	13.50	0.00
Parsons, Wes	R-R	6-5	190	9-6-92	0	0	0.93	3	2	0	0	10	7	1	1	0	0	14	.206	.273	.174	13.03	0.00
Rangel, Alan	R-R	6-2	170	8-21-97	0	2	6.31	14	1	0	0	26	31	22	18	3	9	23	.295	.302	.290	8.06	3.16
Reese, Monte'	R-R	6-1	195	11-6-91	0	0	6.75	2	0	0	0	1	2	3	1	0	2	2	.286	.200	.500	13.50	13.50
Rodriguez, Alberto	L-L	6-5	205	12-13-95	0	3	5.31	13	0	0	0	20	26	13	12	0	14	18	.321	.235	.344	7.97	6.20
Rodriguez, Kelvin	L-L	6-5	195	12-4-95	2	1	2.63	15	0	0	0	24	26	14	7	1	9	18	.274	.154	.319	6.75	3.38
Santana, Jordany	R-R	6-0	190	7-17-95	0	0	11.57	2	0	0	0	2	2	3	3	0	4	0	.250	.250	.250	0.00	15.43
Sepulveda, Jhoniel	R-R	6-2	175	5-15-97	0	1	14.40	13	0	0	0	15	22	26	24	2	14	7	.338	.241	.417	4.20	8.40
Sims, Lucas	R-R	6-2	225	5-10-94	0	0	9.00	2	2	0	0	5	7	5	5	0	2	7	.333	.444	.250	12.60	3.60
Sobotka, Chad	R-R	6-7	200	7-10-93	0	0	0.00	2	0	0	0	3	1	0	0	0	1	3	.111	.000	.143	6.00	3.00
Soroka, Mike	R-R	6-4	195	8-4-97	0	1	1.80	4	3	0	0	10	5	2	2	0	1	11	.143	.188	.105	9.90	0.90
Suarez, Gilbert	R-R	6-2	215	6-19-97	0	1	4.54	10	8	0	0	36	35	19	18	4	15	33	.250	.130	.326	8.33	3.79
Thurman, Andrew	R-R	6-3	225	12-10-91	1	0	3.38	3	2	0	0	8	6	3	3	1	1	9	.207	.200	.211	10.13	1.13

Fielding

Catcher	PCT	G	PO	A	E	DP	PB
Herbert	1.000	3	13	3	0	0	0
Morales	.996	34	203	36	1	2	11
Perez	.963	11	47	5	2	0	2
Yelich	.991	32	190	24	2	5	4

First Base	PCT	G	PO	A	E	DP
Freeman	.941	2	16	0	1	1
Nesovic	.979	21	177	11	4	15
Perez	.986	18	138	6	2	12
Yepez	.994	23	162	9	1	14

Second Base	PCT	G	PO	A	E	DP
Guillermo	.924	23	28	33	5	8
Josephina	.951	21	33	44	4	14
Perez	.978	22	39	49	2	15
Salazar	.667	2	2	0	1	1

ATLANTA BRAVES

Third Base	PCT	G	PO	A	E	DP
Azuaje	1.000	2	1	1	0	0
Guillermo	.792	15	9	33	11	2
Nesovic	.941	11	12	20	2	1
Olivera	.833	2	2	3	1	1
Perez	.870	7	4	16	3	0
Riley	.919	24	27	52	7	6

	PCT	G	PO	A	E	DP
Yepez	1.000	5	2	8	0	0
Shortstop	PCT	G	PO	A	E	DP
Josephina	1.000	1	2	2	0	0
Perez	.927	12	20	31	4	5
Salazar	.936	50	67	139	14	24
Outfield	PCT	G	PO	A	E	DP
Acuna	.964	33	50	3	2	1

	PCT	G	PO	A	E	DP
Arias	1.000	11	17	1	0	0
Cabrera	—	1	0	0	0	0
Ellison	.970	23	30	2	1	1
Estevez	.952	13	18	2	1	0
Keller	.941	38	45	3	3	0
Pina	.958	27	43	3	2	0
Wilson	.900	42	69	3	8	1

DSL BRAVES   ROOKIE

DOMINICAN SUMMER LEAGUE

Batting	B-T	HT	WT	DOB	AVG	vLH	vRH	G	AB	R	H	2B	3B	HR	RBI	BB	HBP	SH	SF	SO	SB	CS	SLG	OBP
Alonso, Luis	R-R	6-0	160	7-1-96	.197	.095	.240	34	71	13	14	4	0	0	5	8	2	2	0	18	0	0	.254	.296
Aquino, Alex	R-R	6-2	165	7-6-96	.266	.245	.273	63	214	30	57	5	3	0	19	10	2	3	1	50	8	4	.318	.304
Boeldak, Sander	L-L	5-10	160	7-17-96	.317	.366	.305	55	205	36	65	5	2	1	37	19	5	1	2	34	9	4	.376	.385
Centeno, Carlos	R-R	5-9	180	11-19-97	.231	.167	.242	14	39	1	9	0	0	0	3	1	3	1	0	12	0	1	.231	.302
Concepcion, Anthony	R-R	6-1	200	3-23-95	.308	.240	.325	68	253	58	78	15	3	5	40	30	15	0	2	51	12	6	.451	.410
Contreras, William	R-R	6-0	180	12-24-97	.314	.324	.312	49	172	21	54	9	4	0	32	15	1	1	1	21	2	2	.413	.370
Estrada, Richard	R-R	5-10	172	4-4-98	.167	.000	.250	4	12	0	2	0	0	0	2	0	0	0	2	2	0	1	.167	.286
Fernandez, Jeremy	R-R	6-1	150	7-11-97	.262	.200	.280	30	107	12	28	3	1	0	10	9	3	0	1	19	3	1	.308	.333
Ferrer, Grendis	R-R	6-3	190	9-29-96	.202	.235	.194	29	84	10	17	5	1	0	10	4	0	0	1	26	1	0	.286	.236
Guerrero, Jan	L-R	6-3	195	7-18-96	.133	.000	.160	9	30	2	4	0	0	0	5	2	0	0	1	6	0	0	.133	.182
2-team total (32 Phillies)					.222	—		41	117	11	26	2	0	2	14	14	1	3	1	24	3	0	.291	.308
Josephina, Terrence	R-R	6-2	185	12-5-94	.267	.158	.292	54	206	23	55	10	0	3	40	9	7	0	2	42	1	1	.359	.317
Martina, Ildion	R-R	5-11	195	5-24-97	.170	.000	.196	17	53	5	9	5	0	0	5	2	0	1	1	11	0	0	.264	.196
Martinez, Yander	R-R	5-11	185	1-29-97	.385	.500	.333	5	13	2	5	2	0	0	1	1	2	0	0	4	0	0	.538	.500
Mejia, Luis	B-R	5-10	160	3-8-97	.282	.156	.317	60	209	41	59	4	3	0	20	29	3	4	1	25	7	5	.330	.376
Michel, Shean	R-R	5-11	170	9-26-97	.272	.318	.260	54	213	33	58	6	5	0	35	15	2	2	3	44	9	7	.347	.322
Oliveros, Yonathan	R-R	5-11	180	9-17-96	.212	.200	.214	10	33	2	7	1	0	0	2	0	3	0	0	9	0	1	.242	.278
Olmos, Luis	R-R	6-0	175	8-28-97	.256	.217	.265	40	125	19	32	7	0	0	10	15	2	2	0	29	0	1	.312	.345
Salazar, Danyer	R-R	6-1	180	2-19-98	.203	.111	.219	40	123	16	25	3	0	1	17	13	17	1	1	33	3	0	.252	.357
Ventura, Randy	B-R	5-9	165	7-11-97	.329	.275	.344	58	231	61	76	11	2	0	25	35	3	3	2	27	55	9	.394	.421
Zorrilla, Felipe	R-R	6-3	171	12-5-96	.172	.250	.157	32	99	12	17	2	1	0	8	8	1	0	0	33	8	2	.212	.241

Pitching	B-T	HT	WT	DOB	W	L	ERA	G	GS	CG	SV	IP	H	R	ER	HR	BB	SO	AVG	vLH	vRH	K/9	BB/9
De La Cruz, Jasseel	R-R	6-1	175	6-26-97	0	1	7.11	7	0	0	0	6	6	8	5	0	8	6	.261	.429	.188	8.53	11.37
Diaz, Jhonny	L-L	6-0	180	6-22-96	0	2	3.63	22	3	0	0	40	36	19	16	3	19	26	.254	.258	.252	5.90	4.31
Gil, Frank	R-R	6-2	165	9-24-96	0	2	6.11	20	4	0	0	35	39	34	24	2	24	32	.275	.263	.279	8.15	6.11
Henry, Gabriel	R-R	6-3	180	11-16-95	0	3	3.07	18	10	0	0	44	34	18	15	2	18	31	.219	.319	.176	6.34	3.68
Iriarte, Roy	R-R	6-2	170	2-13-97	3	3	4.43	23	4	0	1	41	39	26	20	2	24	23	.258	.268	.255	5.09	5.31
Joaquin, Victor	R-R	6-5	220	12-29-93	1	0	7.20	7	0	0	1	10	12	8	8	2	4	9	.308	.167	.370	8.10	3.60
Jones, Jesus	R-R	6-2	165	5-15-96	1	1	8.22	7	0	0	1	8	11	8	7	0	8	3	.355	.250	.370	3.52	9.39
Julian, Deyvis	R-R	6-2	165	4-10-96	2	1	3.54	18	2	0	1	28	35	17	11	0	10	20	.315	.379	.293	6.43	3.21
Laguna, Jason	R-R	5-11	170	1-8-96	4	0	2.73	19	0	0	1	33	35	14	10	1	7	29	.278	.314	.264	7.91	1.91
Lopez, Carlos	R-R	6-4	173	3-20-98	4	1	3.64	17	1	0	0	30	27	13	12	1	8	33	.248	.310	.225	10.01	2.43
Mora, Luis	R-R	6-4	160	6-17-95	0	3	3.80	18	14	0	0	45	32	25	19	1	21	42	.195	.196	.195	8.40	4.20
Moreno, Jean	R-R	6-2	175	5-2-96	0	1	5.40	10	1	0	0	15	14	10	9	0	9	13	.259	.154	.293	7.80	5.40
Pantoja, Ali	R-R	6-4	180	1-31-97	0	2	3.16	23	2	0	3	37	25	20	13	1	33	41	.191	.244	.167	9.97	8.03
Perez, Luis	R-R	6-2	165	4-7-97	0	2	4.32	17	8	0	1	25	26	17	12	0	15	19	.283	.240	.299	6.84	5.40
Sanchez, Alexander	R-R	6-0	175	8-9-96	7	0	3.82	23	0	0	0	35	37	19	15	0	24	29	.272	.333	.245	7.39	6.11
Sanchez, Filyer	L-L	6-1	175	2-8-97	3	0	2.59	23	4	0	1	42	36	17	12	0	10	26	.225	.080	.252	5.62	2.16
Sanchez, Javier	L-R	6-4	210	10-3-96	1	3	4.63	18	10	0	0	45	48	30	23	1	12	29	.276	.258	.258	5.84	2.42
Severino, Luis	R-R	6-1	175	7-6-93	4	2	5.40	23	1	0	0	28	28	21	17	0	20	17	.269	.303	.254	5.40	6.35
Tavers, Ramon	R-R	6-1	200	8-31-95	3	3	3.15	23	1	0	7	34	30	15	12	0	6	20	.238	.324	.202	5.24	1.57
Vega, Bredio	R-R	6-3	185	4-8-96	3	4	6.75	18	1	0	1	28	29	21	21	0	17	30	.287	.267	.296	9.64	5.46

Fielding

Catcher	PCT	G	PO	A	E	DP	PB
Alonso	.979	32	159	24	4	0	6
Centeno	.985	13	59	6	1	2	6
Contreras	.972	28	179	33	6	2	9
Martina	.979	17	126	16	3	0	4

First Base	PCT	G	PO	A	E	DP
Concepcion	.994	22	165	9	1	19
Guerrero	.959	9	68	3	3	6
Josephina	1.000	26	199	11	0	9
Salazar	.983	23	161	8	3	13

Second Base	PCT	G	PO	A	E	DP
Aquino	.963	13	18	34	2	4

	PCT	G	PO	A	E	DP	PB
Fernandez	.887	11	28	27	7	2	
Martinez	1.000	5	12	17	0	3	
Mejia	.989	21	39	49	1	8	
Olmos	.948	31	55	73	7	19	
Third Base	PCT	G	PO	A	E	DP	
Fernandez	.333	1	1	0	2	0	
Josephina	.907	27	36	52	9	4	
Mejia	.916	37	33	76	10	8	
Salazar	.870	15	21	19	6	3	
Shortstop	PCT	G	PO	A	E	DP	
Aquino	.896	46	70	110	21	19	
Fernandez	.848	16	24	32	10	6	

	PCT	G	PO	A	E	DP
Mejia	.917	5	11	11	2	5
Olmos	.932	10	17	24	3	2
Outfield	PCT	G	PO	A	E	DP
Boeldak	.981	35	48	5	1	0
Concepcion	.970	32	62	3	2	0
Ferrer	.966	18	23	5	1	0
Michel	.977	51	79	6	2	1
Oliveros	1.000	9	12	4	0	1
Ventura	.931	57	134	14	11	3
Zorrilla	.945	28	48	4	3	1

ATLANTA BRAVES

Baltimore Orioles

SEASON IN A SENTENCE: The Orioles made few additions to the 2014 roster that won the AL East by 12 games—opting not to re-sign home run champ Nelson Cruz or pursue an impact arm but instead counted on healthy returns from Manny Machado, Matt Wieters and Chris Davis—and paid the price with a punchless rotation and a shortage of corner outfielders during a second-half collapse that left them 12 games out of first.

HIGH POINT: Ubaldo Jimenez and Chris Tillman combined for 15 shutout innings to sweep a doubleheader from the Indians on June 28 and move the Orioles into a share of first with the Yankees, where they would remain for the next four days before fading back to the pack. After a disastrous 2014 campaign, Jimenez took over as Orioles ace in the first half of the season (7-4, 2.81 in 99 innings) before regressing in the second half (5-6, 5.63). Manny Machado (team-high .286 average) and Chris Davis (AL-best 47 homers) bounced back from down years.

LOW POINT: The Orioles stuck in first place for just four days in July before losing 13 of their next 16 games. A late-season sweep of the Nationals gave Baltimore hope in the wild-card race, but that was erased after dropping five in a row—including three straight shutouts against the Red Sox. Baltimore couldn't overcome down seasons from Chris Tillman, Jimenez, and Bud Norris.

KEY TRANSACTIONS: The O's didn't get the return they desired when they shipped slight right-hander Zach Davies to the Brewers at the trade deadline for corner outfielder Gerardo Parra, who hit just .237—100 points below his average in Milwaukee. Dan Duquette's playing of the margins didn't pay off—offseason acquisitions Travis Snider and Everth Cabrera scuffled in Baltimore.

DOWN ON THE FARM: Bowie won its first Eastern League title when light-hitting utilityman Garabez Rosa hit a pair of homers to knock off Reading in Game Five. Meanwhile, injuries sidelined top pitching prospects Dylan Bundy, who has made just 17 appearances since his breakout 2012 campaign, and Hunter Harvey. Sluggers Christian Walker and Dariel Alvarez took steps back after breakout 2014 campaigns and spent the full season in Triple-A. Bright spots included the emergence of 23-year-old first baseman Trey Mancini and the rise of converted shortstop Mychal Givens, who reached Baltimore as a hard-throwing reliever.

OPENING DAY PAYROLL: $110,146,097 (17).

PLAYERS OF THE YEAR

MAJOR LEAGUE	MINOR LEAGUE
Manny Machado	**Trey Mancini**
3b	1b
.286/.359/.502	(High-A, Double-A)
30 2B, 35 HR, 20 SB	.341/.375/.563
Led majors in PA	43 2B, 21 HR, 89 RBIs

ORGANIZATION LEADERS

BATTING		*Minimum 250 AB
MAJORS		
*AVG	Manny Machado	.286
*OPS	Chris Davis	.923
HR	Chris Davis	47
RBI	Chris Davis	117
MINORS		
*AVG	Trey Mancini, Frederick, Bowie	.341
*OBP	Jay Gonzalez, Delmarva, Frederick	.381
*SLG	Trey Mancini, Frederick, Bowie	.563
R	Trey Mancini, Frederick, Bowie	88
H	Trey Mancini, Frederick, Bowie	182
TB	Trey Mancini, Frederick, Bowie	300
2B	Trey Mancini, Frederick, Bowie	43
3B	Jay Gonzalez, Delmarva, Frederick	8
HR	Trey Mancini, Frederick, Bowie	21
RBI	Trey Mancini, Frederick, Bowie	89
BB	Jay Gonzalez, Delmarva, Frederick	87
SO	Christian Walker, Norfolk	136
SB	Jay Gonzalez, Delmarva, Frederick	34

PITCHING		#Minimum 75 IP
MAJORS		
W	Ubaldo Jimenez	12
#ERA	Wei-Yin Chen	3.34
SO	Ubaldo Jimenez	168
SV	Zach Britton	36
MINORS		
W	Terry Doyle, Bowie, Norfolk	16
L	Mitch Horacek, Frederick	17
#ERA	Terry Doyle, Bowie, Norfolk	2.16
G	Pedro Beato, Norfolk	63
GS	Mitch Horacek, Frederick	28
	Elih Villanueva, Bowie, Norfolk	28
SV	Oliver Drake, Norfolk	23
IP	Elih Villanueva, Bowie, Norfolk	168
BB	Eddie Gamboa, Norfolk	84
SO	Mitch Horacek, Frederick	146
AVG	David Hess, Frederick, Bowie	.226

2015 PERFORMANCE

General Manager: Dan Duquette. **Farm Director:** Brian Graham. **Scouting Director:** Gary Rajsich.

Class	Team	League	W	L	PCT	Finish	Manager
Majors	Baltimore Orioles	American	81	81	.500	9th (15)	Buck Showalter
Triple-A	Norfolk Tides	International	78	66	.542	3rd (14)	Ron Johnson
Double-A	Bowie Baysox	Eastern	79	63	.556	2nd (12)	Gary Kendall
High A	Frederick Keys	Carolina	64	76	.457	7th (8)	Orlando Gomez
Low A	Delmarva Shorebirds	South Atlantic	71	67	.514	6th (14)	Ryan Minor
Short season	Aberdeen IronBirds	New York-Penn	40	36	.526	6th (14)	Luis Pujols
Rookie	Orioles	Gulf Coast	34	25	.576	t-5th (16)	Matt Merrullo
Overall 2015 Minor League Record			366	333	.524	9th (30)	

ORGANIZATION STATISTICS

BALTIMORE ORIOLES

AMERICAN LEAGUE

Batting	B-T	HT	WT	DOB	AVG	vLH	vRH	G	AB	R	H	2B	3B	HR	RBI	BB	HBP	SH	SF	SO	SB	CS	SLG	OBP
Alvarez, Dariel	R-R	6-2	180	11-7-88	.241	.261	.167	12	29	3	7	1	0	1	1	2	0	0	0	8	0	0	.379	.290
Cabrera, Everth	B-R	5-10	190	11-17-86	.208	.148	.232	29	96	7	20	2	0	0	4	5	1	1	2	22	2	0	.229	.250
Clevenger, Steve	L-R	5-10	210	4-5-86	.287	.375	.280	30	101	11	29	4	2	2	15	4	0	0	0	13	0	0	.426	.314
Davis, Chris	L-R	6-3	230	3-17-86	.262	.268	.258	160	573	100	150	31	0	47	117	84	8	0	5	208	2	3	.562	.361
De Aza, Alejandro	L-L	6-0	195	4-11-84	.214	.000	.244	30	103	16	22	4	1	3	7	7	2	0	0	34	2	2	.359	.277
2-team total (60 Boston)					.261	—	—	90	264	39	69	13	6	7	32	19	4	2	1	70	5	3	.436	.319
Flaherty, Ryan	L-R	6-3	220	7-27-86	.202	.179	.209	91	267	34	54	8	3	9	31	26	4	2	2	81	0	1	.356	.281
Hardy, J.J.	R-R	6-1	200	8-19-82	.219	.210	.223	114	411	45	90	14	0	8	37	20	0	2	4	88	0	1	.311	.253
Janish, Paul	R-R	6-2	200	10-12-82	.286	.167	.412	14	35	4	10	3	0	0	3	0	0	0	1	3	0	0	.371	.278
Jones, Adam	R-R	6-2	215	8-1-85	.269	.261	.272	137	546	74	147	25	3	27	82	24	4	0	3	102	3	1	.474	.308
Joseph, Caleb	R-R	6-3	180	6-18-86	.234	.250	.226	100	320	38	75	16	1	11	49	27	3	3	1	72	0	0	.394	.299
Lake, Junior	R-R	6-3	215	3-27-90	.136	.200	.000	8	22	2	3	3	0	0	0	0	0	0	0	9	0	0	.273	.136
Lavarnway, Ryan	R-R	6-4	240	8-7-87	.107	.333	.045	10	28	1	3	1	0	0	4	0	0	0	0	7	0	0	.143	.219
Lough, David	L-L	5-10	175	1-20-86	.201	.214	.200	84	134	14	27	1	1	4	12	5	2	3	0	36	2	4	.313	.241
Machado, Manny	R-R	6-3	185	7-6-92	.286	.258	.295	162	633	102	181	30	1	35	86	70	4	2	4	111	20	8	.502	.359
Navarro, Rey	B-R	5-10	185	12-22-89	.276	.375	.238	10	29	5	8	2	0	1	3	0	0	1	0	3	0	0	.448	.276
Paredes, Jimmy	B-R	6-3	200	11-25-88	.275	.263	.278	104	363	46	100	17	2	10	42	19	0	0	2	111	4	4	.416	.310
Parmelee, Chris	L-L	6-1	220	2-24-88	.216	.125	.235	32	97	11	21	7	1	4	9	4	1	0	0	26	0	1	.433	.255
Parra, Gerardo	L-L	5-11	210	5-6-87	.237	.193	.251	55	224	30	53	12	0	5	20	8	2	3	1	35	5	1	.357	.268
Pearce, Steve	R-R	5-11	200	4-13-83	.218	.196	.231	92	294	42	64	13	1	15	40	23	7	0	1	69	1	1	.422	.289
Reimold, Nolan	R-R	6-4	205	10-12-83	.247	.278	.220	61	170	24	42	5	1	6	20	23	2	0	0	47	0	0	.394	.344
Schoop, Jonathan	R-R	6-1	225	10-16-91	.279	.232	.301	86	305	34	85	17	0	15	39	9	4	1	2	79	2	0	.482	.306
Snider, Travis	L-L	6-0	235	2-2-88	.237	.256	.233	69	211	23	50	9	2	3	20	23	2	0	0	56	1	0	.341	.318
Urrutia, Henry	L-R	6-5	200	2-13-87	.265	.000	.290	10	34	3	9	1	0	1	6	2	0	0	0	3	0	0	.382	.306
Walker, Christian	R-R	6-0	220	3-28-91	.111	.125	.000	7	9	0	1	0	0	0	0	3	0	0	0	4	0	0	.111	.333
Wieters, Matt	B-R	6-5	230	5-21-86	.267	.265	.268	75	258	24	69	14	1	8	25	21	0	0	3	67	0	0	.422	.319
Young, Delmon	R-R	6-3	240	9-14-85	.270	.310	.250	52	174	20	47	6	0	2	16	4	1	0	1	29	0	0	.339	.289

Pitching	B-T	HT	WT	DOB	W	L	ERA	G	GS	CG	SV	IP	H	R	ER	HR	BB	SO	AVG	vLH	vRH	K/9	BB/9
Brach, Brad	R-R	6-6	215	4-12-86	5	3	2.72	62	0	0	1	79	57	25	24	7	38	89	.203	.184	.224	10.10	4.31
Britton, Zach	L-L	6-3	195	12-22-87	4	1	1.92	64	0	0	36	66	51	16	14	3	14	79	.214	.145	.243	10.83	1.92
Cabral, Cesar	L-L	6-3	250	2-11-89	0	0	0.00	2	0	0	0	1	0	0	0	1	1	.000	.000	.000	9.00	9.00
Chen, Wei-Yin	L-L	6-0	195	7-21-85	11	8	3.34	31	31	0	0	191	192	78	71	28	41	153	.262	.223	.274	7.20	1.93
Drake, Oliver	R-R	6-4	215	1-13-87	0	0	2.87	13	0	0	0	16	16	7	5	1	9	17	.262	.167	.324	9.77	5.17
Garcia, Jason	R-R	6-0	185	11-21-92	1	0	4.25	21	0	0	0	30	25	19	14	3	17	22	.223	.208	.667	5.16	
Gausman, Kevin	R-R	6-3	190	1-6-91	4	7	4.25	25	17	0	0	112	109	56	53	17	29	103	.251	.227	.278	8.25	2.32
Givens, Mychal	R-R	6-0	210	5-13-90	2	0	1.80	22	0	0	0	30	20	7	6	1	6	38	.185	.205	.174	11.40	1.80
Gonzalez, Miguel	R-R	6-1	170	5-27-84	9	12	4.91	26	26	0	0	145	151	81	79	24	51	109	.270	.278	.262	6.78	3.17
Hunter, Tommy	R-R	6-3	250	7-3-86	2	2	3.63	39	0	0	0	45	41	19	18	3	11	32	.250	.263	.238	6.45	2.22
Jimenez, Ubaldo	R-R	6-5	210	1-22-84	12	10	4.11	32	32	0	0	184	182	89	84	20	68	168	.257	.227	.290	8.22	3.33
Johnson, Steve	R-R	6-1	220	8-31-87	0	0	10.13	6	0	0	0	5	8	6	6	2	5	3	.333	.300	.357	5.06	8.44
Matusz, Brian	L-L	6-5	190	2-11-87	1	4	2.94	58	0	0	0	49	38	18	16	5	20	56	.211	.186	.244	10.29	3.67
McFarland, T.J.	L-L	6-3	219	6-8-89	2	2	4.91	30	0	0	0	40	52	26	22	4	18	26	.306	.232	.375	5.80	4.02
Norris, Bud	R-R	6-0	195	3-2-85	2	9	7.06	18	11	0	0	66	84	57	52	14	25	50	.309	.323	.288	6.78	3.39
O'Day, Darren	R-R	6-4	220	10-22-82	6	2	1.52	68	0	0	6	65	47	13	11	5	14	82	.198	.210	.192	11.30	1.93
Roe, Chaz	R-R	6-5	190	10-9-86	4	2	4.14	36	0	0	0	41	44	19	19	4	17	38	.280	.333	.242	8.27	3.70
Rondon, Jorge	R-R	6-1	215	2-16-88	0	1	7.43	8	0	0	0	13	20	15	11	3	6	8	.333	.280	.371	5.40	4.05
Tillman, Chris	R-R	6-5	200	4-15-88	11	11	4.99	31	31	0	0	173	176	97	96	20	64	120	.267	.262	.271	6.24	3.33
Wilson, Tyler	R-R	6-2	185	9-25-89	2	2	3.50	9	5	0	0	36	39	14	14	1	11	13	.289	.282	.297	3.25	2.75
Wright, Mike	R-R	6-6	215	1-3-90	3	5	6.04	12	9	0	0	45	52	30	30	9	18	26	.291	.322	.258	5.24	3.63
Wright, Wesley	R-L	5-11	185	1-28-85	0	0	5.40	2	0	0	0	2	2	1	1	0	0	0	.333	—	.333	0.00	0.00
2-team total (9 Los Angeles)					0	0	3.68	11	0	0	0	7	6	4	3	1	3	5	—	—	—	6.14	3.68

Fielding

Catcher	PCT	G	PO	A	E	DP	PB				
Clevenger	1.000	9	43	3	0	0	1				
Joseph	.996	94	749	45	3	3	6	Wieters	.989	55	423	23	5	3	2
Lavarnway	.983	9	55	3	1	1	1				

BALTIMORE ORIOLES

First Base	PCT	G	PO	A	E	DP
Clevenger	1.000	1	4	0	0	0
Davis	.997	111	882	53	3	77
Flaherty	1.000	11	92	2	0	8
Joseph	1.000	1	2	0	0	1
Parmelee	1.000	25	176	12	0	17
Pearce	.995	28	184	18	1	15
Walker	1.000	2	7	0	0	1
Wieters	1.000	3	22	1	0	2

Second Base	PCT	G	PO	A	E	DP
Cabrera	1.000	2	4	5	0	0
Flaherty	.995	56	88	132	1	35
Janish	1.000	1	2	5	0	2
Navarro	.972	9	16	19	1	6
Paredes	1.000	6	11	17	0	2

	PCT	G	PO	A	E	DP
Pearce	1.000	18	25	35	0	7
Schoop	.982	84	145	235	7	50

Third Base	PCT	G	PO	A	E	DP
Flaherty	.957	8	3	19	1	3
Machado	.961	156	132	337	19	38
Paredes	.571	8	1	3	3	0

Shortstop	PCT	G	PO	A	E	DP
Cabrera	.966	27	22	62	3	9
Flaherty	1.000	15	17	17	0	6
Hardy	.993	114	141	301	3	57
Janish	1.000	13	16	31	0	7
Machado	.905	7	4	15	2	3

Outfield	PCT	G	PO	A	E	DP
Alvarez	1.000	12	16	1	0	1

	PCT	G	PO	A	E	DP
Davis	1.000	30	39	2	0	0
De Aza	.983	27	56	2	1	0
Flaherty	1.000	6	7	0	0	0
Jones	.991	134	317	13	3	4
Lake	.600	6	3	0	2	0
Lough	1.000	77	78	2	0	0
Paredes	1.000	3	2	0	0	0
Parmelee	.944	8	16	1	1	1
Parra	1.000	55	100	5	0	0
Pearce	.974	49	72	4	2	0
Reimold	.976	51	76	4	2	0
Snider	.991	57	105	5	1	1
Urrutia	1.000	8	14	1	0	0
Young	.972	42	62	8	2	0

NORFOLK TIDES
INTERNATIONAL LEAGUE

TRIPLE-A

Batting	B-T	HT	WT	DOB	AVG	vLH	vRH	G	AB	R	H	2B	3B	HR	RBI	BB	HBP	SH	SF	SO	SB	CS	SLG	OBP
Almanzar, Michael	R-R	6-3	190	12-2-90	.225	.227	.225	138	502	40	113	26	0	4	50	27	6	0	5	93	1	0	.301	.270
Alvarez, Dariel	R-R	6-2	180	11-7-88	.275	.295	.268	130	512	61	141	24	2	16	72	16	8	0	5	63	7	3	.424	.305
Borbon, Julio	L-L	6-0	195	2-20-86	.269	.309	.257	114	346	39	93	9	3	1	28	16	0	8	2	47	23	8	.321	.299
Cabrera, Everth	B-R	5-10	190	11-17-86	.208	.200	.211	6	24	3	5	1	0	0	1	1	0	0	0	7	0	0	.250	.240
Caronia, Anthony	L-R	6-0	170	5-22-91	.125	—	.125	3	8	1	1	0	0	0	0	0	0	0	0	1	0	0	.125	.125
Clevenger, Steve	L-R	5-10	210	4-5-86	.305	.258	.321	75	262	28	80	11	0	4	32	32	1	0	6	37	0	1	.393	.375
Flaherty, Ryan	L-R	6-3	220	7-27-86	.000	.000	.000	2	5	1	0	0	0	0	2	3	0	0	1	0	0	0	.000	.333
Freitas, David	R-R	6-3	225	3-18-89	.231	.000	.250	4	13	1	3	2	0	0	0	0	0	0	0	0	0	0	.385	.231
Gibson, Derrik	R-R	6-1	170	12-5-89	.234	.263	.222	48	128	15	30	2	2	0	5	19	1	2	0	31	3	3	.281	.338
Halton, Sean	R-R	6-4	260	6-7-87	.221	.244	.209	73	258	25	57	11	0	3	30	28	4	0	3	72	3	2	.298	.304
Janish, Paul	R-R	6-2	200	10-12-82	.235	.233	.236	95	302	29	71	7	2	0	21	31	4	5	2	41	2	1	.272	.313
Lake, Junior	R-R	6-3	215	3-27-90	.300	.286	.302	15	50	2	15	3	0	0	5	0	0	0	1	16	3	2	.360	.410
Lough, David	L-L	5-10	175	1-20-86	.259	.154	.289	14	58	7	15	1	0	0	6	3	0	0	1	9	1	1	.310	.290
Navarro, Rey	B-R	5-10	185	12-22-89	.261	.216	.278	89	360	49	94	20	1	6	23	27	0	4	3	48	4	4	.372	.310
Nix, Jayson	R-R	5-11	195	8-26-82	.167	.233	.136	25	96	5	16	3	0	0	8	3	0	0	1	31	1	1	.198	.190
2-team total (29 Lehigh Valley)					.162	—	—	54	185	11	30	5	0	0	12	8	0	1	1	53	1	2	.222	.196
Parmelee, Chris	L-L	6-1	220	2-24-88	.314	.284	.329	63	239	33	75	13	0	6	32	29	1	0	3	52	3	1	.444	.386
Perez, Audry	R-R	5-10	220	12-23-88	.243	.228	.251	78	267	18	65	10	0	2	21	12	1	2	0	31	0	0	.303	.279
Perez, Rossmel	B-R	5-9	200	8-26-89	.196	.200	.184	17	51	3	10	2	0	0	1	6	1	0	0	5	0	0	.235	.293
Reimold, Nolan	R-R	6-4	205	10-12-83	.274	.311	.257	54	197	25	54	13	0	2	15	26	2	0	1	42	5	1	.371	.363
Rosa, Garabez	R-R	6-2	166	10-12-89	.100	.000	.111	4	10	5	1	0	0	0	1	2	2	0	0	1	1	0	.400	.250
Ruettiger, John	L-L	6-1	193	9-21-89	.000	—	.000	1	4	0	0	0	0	0	0	0	0	0	0	0	0	0	.000	.000
Schoop, Sharlon	R-R	6-2	190	4-15-87	.217	.214	.218	53	166	14	36	3	0	1	13	15	0	2	1	34	1	0	.253	.280
Urrutia, Henry	L-R	6-5	200	2-13-87	.291	.259	.305	115	460	58	134	22	1	10	53	40	0	0	5	81	1	3	.409	.345
Walker, Christian	R-R	6-0	220	3-28-91	.257	.306	.238	138	534	68	137	33	1	18	74	49	6	0	3	136	1	3	.423	.324
Wieters, Matt	B-R	6-5	230	5-21-86	.667	.500	.667	2	3	0	2	0	0	0	1	0	0	0	0	0	0	0	1.200	.667

Pitching	B-T	HT	WT	DOB	W	L	ERA	G	GS	CG	SV	IP	H	R	ER	HR	BB	SO	AVG	vLH	vRH	K/9	BB/9
Beato, Pedro	R-R	6-6	230	10-27-86	5	5	2.65	63	0	0	16	75	66	26	22	5	25	61	.240	.179	.272	7.35	3.01
Belfiore, Mike	R-L	6-3	220	10-3-88	0	1	2.31	3	3	0	0	12	10	4	3	1	4	5	.222	.267	.200	3.86	3.09
2-team total (22 Toledo)					5	12	5.32	25	25	0	0	135	153	85	80	15	53	82	—	—	—	5.45	3.52
Bowden, Michael	R-R	6-3	215	9-9-86	7	2	1.91	24	9	0	0	75	60	19	16	4	20	52	.219	.167	.260	6.21	2.39
2-team total (8 Rochester)					11	5	2.63	32	17	0	0	123	110	41	36	6	31	99	—	—	—	7.24	2.27
Buschmann, Matt	R-R	6-3	195	2-13-84	0	0	6.00	1	1	0	0	3	2	2	2	1	0	2	.182	.400	.000	6.00	0.00
3-team total (13 Durham, 9 Louisville)					8	10	4.08	23	23	2	0	135	123	62	61	13	47	109	—	—	—	7.28	3.14
Cabral, Cesar	L-L	6-3	250	2-11-89	2	1	4.95	45	0	0	2	40	42	23	22	0	19	43	.263	.211	.303	9.68	4.28
Davies, Zach	R-R	6-0	160	2-7-93	5	6	2.84	19	18	1	0	101	91	33	32	4	33	81	.241	.290	.201	7.19	2.93
De La Rosa, Dane	R-R	6-7	245	2-1-83	0	0	4.35	8	0	0	0	10	6	5	5	2	8	7	.250	.250	.250	6.10	6.97
Doyle, Terry	R-R	6-4	250	11-2-85	4	1	2.57	7	7	0	0	49	39	15	14	3	10	28	.215	.295	.159	5.14	1.84
Drake, Oliver	R-R	6-4	215	1-13-87	1	2	0.82	42	0	0	23	44	23	4	4	1	16	66	.151	.133	.163	13.50	3.27
Escat, Gene	R-R	6-2	195	9-3-89	0	0	6.00	1	1	0	0	3	3	2	2	0	4	1	.250	.250	.250	3.00	12.00
Eveland, Dana	L-L	6-1	235	10-29-83	2	0	2.37	16	3	0	0	30	25	9	8	0	11	22	.234	.278	.211	6.53	3.26
3-team total (1 Gwinnett, 16 Pawtucket)					4	0	1.95	33	3	0	0	55	42	13	12	0	14	45	—	—	—	7.32	2.28
Gamboa, Eddie	R-R	6-1	215	12-21-84	8	11	4.61	26	19	0	0	113	94	61	58	6	84	79	.230	.225	.233	6.27	6.67
Gausman, Kevin	R-R	6-3	190	1-6-91	0	1	1.29	3	3	0	0	14	10	3	2	2	6	14	.204	.192	.217	9.00	3.86
Johnson, Steve	R-R	6-1	220	8-31-87	4	1	2.30	32	3	0	1	55	43	14	14	2	16	67	.222	.197	.237	11.03	2.63
Jones, Chris	L-L	6-2	205	9-19-88	8	8	2.94	30	22	0	0	150	158	60	49	15	29	105	.273	.305	.262	6.30	1.74
Kasparek, Kenn	R-R	6-10	245	9-23-85	0	1	10.13	2	1	0	0	3	4	3	3	1	2	3	.333	.333	.333	10.13	6.75
McCoy, Pat	L-L	6-3	230	11-8-88	2	3	4.18	27	1	0	1	52	59	24	24	4	15	36	.289	.219	.321	6.27	2.61
McFarland, T.J.	L-L	6-3	219	6-8-89	2	3	2.91	16	9	0	1	53	42	20	17	0	14	31	.216	.170	.234	5.30	2.39
Oliver, Andy	L-L	6-3	215	12-3-87	3	1	3.72	16	0	0	0	29	23	12	12	1	14	34	.221	.135	.269	10.55	4.97
2-team total (25 Durham)					4	2	3.79	41	0	0	1	57	43	25	24	4	40	66	—	—	—	10.42	6.32
Rodriguez, Richard	R-R	6-4	205	3-4-90	1	3	3.54	13	0	0	0	20	19	12	8	2	10	15	.247	.333	.182	6.64	4.43
Roe, Chaz	R-R	6-5	190	10-9-86	3	1	2.19	17	0	0	2	25	17	6	6	0	9	22	.195	.233	.175	8.03	3.28
Rondon, Jorge	R-R	6-1	215	2-16-88	3	1	2.33	30	0	0	1	54	38	14	14	0	17	46	.202	.203	.202	7.67	2.83

Pitching	B-T	HT	WT	DOB	W	L	ERA	G	GS	CG	SV	IP	H	R	ER	HR	BB	SO	AVG	vLH	vRH	K/9	BB/9
Rowen, Ben	R-R	6-3	195	11-15-88	0	0	2.79	6	0	0	0	10	8	3	3	0	3	6	.242	.182	.273	5.59	2.79
2-team total (14 Buffalo)					0	1	2.28	20	0	0	1	28	20	7	7	0	5	17	—	—	—	5.53	1.63
Villanueva, Elih	R-R	6-2	230	7-27-86	4	5	4.71	11	11	0	0	57	67	33	30	6	14	24	.295	.303	.287	3.77	2.20
Wilson, Tyler	R-R	6-2	185	9-25-89	5	5	3.24	17	17	0	0	94	94	35	34	8	18	63	.261	.255	.266	6.01	1.72
Wright, Mike	R-R	6-6	215	1-3-90	9	1	2.22	15	14	0	0	81	59	21	20	4	25	63	.207	.229	.188	7.00	2.78
Wright, Wesley	R-L	5-11	185	1-28-85	0	2	7.71	10	0	0	0	12	15	11	10	1	7	5	.326	.368	.296	3.86	5.40

Fielding

Catcher	PCT	G	PO	A	E	DP	PB
Clevenger	.996	61	430	31	2	7	10
Freitas	1.000	4	20	2	0	0	0
Perez	.996	78	499	42	2	3	9
Perez	.984	9	58	5	1	0	3
Wieters	1.000	1	5	0	0	0	0

First Base	PCT	G	PO	A	E	DP
Halton	1.000	2	16	5	0	1
Parmelee	.991	12	98	14	1	10
Walker	.993	130	1168	71	9	119

Second Base	PCT	G	PO	A	E	DP
Cabrera	1.000	4	4	19	0	3
Caronia	1.000	2	6	7	0	1
Clevenger	—	1	0	0	0	0

	PCT	G	PO	A	E	DP
Flaherty	1.000	1	1	3	0	0
Gibson	.953	21	30	51	4	8
Navarro	.992	49	102	149	2	33
Nix	.972	20	51	52	3	13
Rosa	1.000	4	7	6	0	2
Schoop	.980	47	98	145	5	42

Third Base	PCT	G	PO	A	E	DP
Almanzar	.944	138	98	259	21	18
Flaherty	1.000	1	1	0	0	0
Nix	1.000	1	0	1	0	0
Schoop	1.000	4	3	10	0	1

Shortstop	PCT	G	PO	A	E	DP
Cabrera	1.000	2	2	5	0	0
Gibson	.957	7	5	17	1	5

	PCT	G	PO	A	E	DP
Janish	.990	95	114	289	4	60
Navarro	.974	40	57	130	5	31
Nix	1.000	4	8	8	0	2

Outfield	PCT	G	PO	A	E	DP
Alvarez	.972	126	268	10	8	4
Borbon	.991	110	214	4	2	0
Gibson	1.000	13	18	1	0	0
Halton	.988	41	77	5	1	1
Lake	.960	15	24	0	1	0
Lough	1.000	14	37	0	0	0
Parmelee	.941	31	46	2	3	0
Reimold	1.000	43	71	5	0	0
Ruettiger	.000	1	0	0	1	0
Urrutia	.991	61	109	3	1	0

BOWIE BAYSOX

DOUBLE-A

EASTERN LEAGUE

Batting	B-T	HT	WT	DOB	AVG	vLH	vRH	G	AB	R	H	2B	3B	HR	RBI	BB	HBP	SH	SF	SO	SB	CS	SLG	OBP
Burgess, Michael	L-L	5-11	195	10-20-88	.161	.000	.169	21	62	8	10	3	1	0	5	4	1	0	0	14	0	1	.242	.224
Davis, Glynn	R-R	6-3	170	12-7-91	.268	.340	.244	96	365	45	98	21	1	2	36	34	2	6	1	79	22	11	.348	.333
Dosch, Drew	L-R	6-2	200	6-24-92	.238	.217	.246	68	231	17	55	7	3	1	21	15	1	3	1	45	2	1	.307	.286
Esposito, Jason	R-R	6-2	200	7-19-90	.190	.133	.209	47	174	19	33	5	0	3	16	10	2	0	0	59	1	0	.270	.242
Freitas, David	R-R	6-3	225	3-18-89	.242	.309	.210	71	248	28	60	12	0	8	33	17	6	1	4	37	1	0	.387	.302
Gibson, Derrik	R-R	6-1	170	12-5-89	.245	.286	.222	31	98	14	24	3	0	1	8	17	2	2	1	17	0	0	.306	.364
Halton, Sean	R-R	6-4	260	6-7-87	.240	.205	.252	45	167	15	40	10	0	4	22	15	6	0	5	25	1	0	.371	.316
Joseph, Corban	L-R	6-0	185	10-28-88	.280	.308	.273	63	246	31	69	14	1	6	21	12	1	3	1	24	2	3	.419	.315
Latimore, Quincy	R-R	5-11	175	2-3-89	.274	.291	.267	122	442	74	121	32	6	20	64	38	3	2	1	105	6	4	.509	.335
Ledesma, Ronarsy	R-R	5-11	170	4-19-93	.273	.000	.500	4	11	0	3	0	0	0	1	0	1	0	0	2	0	0	.273	.333
Mancini, Trey	R-R	6-4	215	3-18-92	.359	.370	.355	84	326	60	117	29	3	13	57	22	1	0	5	58	2	1	.586	.395
Martinez, Ozzie	R-R	5-10	200	5-7-88	.252	.271	.245	122	433	48	109	14	1	2	30	36	2	3	3	65	9	4	.303	.310
McDade, Mike	B-R	6-1	250	5-8-89	.186	.125	.209	17	59	5	11	5	0	0	7	9	0	0	2	13	0	0	.271	.286
Nathans, Tucker	L-R	6-0	200	11-6-88	.235	.188	.242	35	115	16	27	4	1	3	11	6	2	3	2	25	0	0	.365	.280
O'Brien, Chris	R-R	5-11	225	7-24-89	.243	.139	.291	44	115	12	28	6	1	5	19	8	0	0	0	17	0	0	.443	.293
Perez, Rossmel	B-R	5-9	200	8-26-89	.276	.318	.267	67	246	21	68	8	1	1	30	19	1	1	5	16	2	1	.329	.325
Rosa, Garabez	R-R	6-2	166	10-12-89	.253	.202	.271	107	368	40	93	16	1	4	35	16	5	5	4	72	3	8	.334	.290
Ruettiger, John	L-L	6-1	193	9-21-89	.269	.286	.250	11	26	3	7	1	0	0	2	1	0	0	0	7	0	0	.308	.296
Schoop, Jonathan	R-R	6-1	225	10-16-91	.240	.111	.313	7	25	3	6	2	0	3	6	1	0	0	0	6	0	0	.680	.269
Schoop, Sharlon	R-R	6-2	190	4-15-87	.224	.231	.220	27	85	6	19	5	0	0	11	7	0	0	1	17	0	0	.282	.280
Sisco, Chance	L-R	6-2	193	2-24-95	.257	.111	.304	20	74	9	19	4	0	2	8	9	0	1	0	14	0	1	.392	.337
Snyder, Brandon	R-R	6-2	225	11-23-86	.278	.289	.275	93	334	59	93	26	2	11	52	37	4	0	1	105	1	0	.467	.356
Wynns, Austin	R-R	6-2	205	12-10-90	.375	.333	.385	4	16	1	6	2	0	0	3	0	0	0	0	4	0	0	.500	.375
Yastrzemski, Mike	L-L	5-11	180	8-23-90	.246	.268	.238	128	476	63	117	30	6	6	59	43	9	1	7	100	8	7	.372	.316

Pitching	B-T	HT	WT	DOB	W	L	ERA	G	GS	CG	SV	IP	H	R	ER	HR	BB	SO	AVG	vLH	vRH	K/9	BB/9
Additon, Nick	L-L	6-5	215	12-16-87	3	2	2.97	6	6	0	0	36	30	13	12	2	8	25	.226	.244	.217	6.19	1.98
Berry, Tim	L-L	6-3	180	3-18-91	2	7	7.32	23	15	0	0	82	107	70	67	8	34	57	.314	.289	.322	6.23	3.72
Bierman, Sean	L-L	6-0	195	10-20-88	0	1	9.00	1	1	0	0	5	6	7	5	3	2	3	.261	—	.261	5.40	3.60
Bridwell, Parker	R-R	6-4	190	8-2-91	4	5	3.99	18	18	1	0	97	96	48	43	7	38	93	.257	.278	.245	8.63	3.53
Bundy, Dylan	R-R	6-1	200	11-15-92	0	3	3.68	8	8	0	0	22	21	10	9	0	5	25	.253	.267	.245	10.23	2.05
Bundy, Bobby	R-R	6-2	215	1-13-90	1	0	4.20	8	0	0	0	15	15	7	7	0	10	14	.263	.211	.289	8.40	6.00
Cabral, Cesar	L-L	6-3	250	2-11-89	1	0	0.00	2	0	0	0	4	0	0	0	0	2	5	.000	—	.000	11.25	4.50
Doyle, Terry	R-R	6-4	250	11-2-85	12	1	1.97	19	14	2	1	110	98	31	24	7	12	82	.238	.222	.250	6.73	0.98
Escat, Gene	R-R	6-2	195	9-3-89	1	6	3.92	32	6	0	2	67	65	36	29	5	42	56	.261	.296	.238	7.56	5.67
Garcia, Jason	R-R	6-0	185	11-21-92	1	2	4.20	9	0	0	0	15	12	8	7	2	9	14	.214	.290	.120	8.40	5.40
Givens, Mychal	R-R	6-0	210	5-13-90	4	2	1.73	35	0	0	15	57	38	14	11	1	16	79	.185	.263	.136	12.40	2.51
Gunkel, Joe	R-R	6-5	225	12-30-91	8	4	2.59	17	17	0	0	104	85	35	30	7	15	69	.222	.215	.228	5.95	1.29
2-team total (4 Portland)					10	5	2.79	21	20	0	0	123	111	43	38	8	23	91	—	—	—	6.68	1.69
Hart, Donnie	L-L	5-11	180	9-6-90	0	0	3.86	3	0	0	0	2	4	1	1	0	2	4	.444	.500	.400	0.00	7.71
Hess, David	R-R	6-2	180	7-10-93	1	1	4.50	2	2	0	0	8	12	6	4	0	1	12	.256	.222	.286	10.80	3.60
Hobgood, Matt	R-R	6-4	245	8-3-90	1	1	6.52	6	0	0	0	10	6	8	7	1	8	7	.176	.000	.261	6.52	7.45
Kasparek, Kenn	R-R	6-10	245	9-23-85	4	1	5.29	36	0	0	2	49	61	32	29	5	12	43	.299	.356	.267	7.84	2.19
Keller, Jon	R-R	6-5	210	8-8-92	0	0	3.55	7	0	0	0	13	6	5	5	0	8	8	.150	.200	.100	5.68	5.68
Kline, Branden	R-R	6-3	210	9-29-91	3	3	3.66	8	8	0	0	39	35	20	16	4	19	27	.243	.267	.232	6.18	4.35
Lee, Chris	L-L	6-4	175	8-17-92	4	2	3.08	7	7	0	0	38	32	13	13	0	20	26	.232	.158	.260	6.16	4.74
McCoy, Pat	L-L	6-3	220	8-3-88	2	1	3.57	14	0	0	0	18	22	8	7	1	8	15	.306	.296	.311	7.64	4.08

Pitching	B-T	HT	WT	DOB	W	L	ERA	G	GS	CG	SV	IP	H	R	ER	HR	BB	SO	AVG	vLH	vRH	K/9	BB/9
Miranda, Ariel	L-L	6-2	190	1-10-89	5	2	3.60	8	8	0	0	45	40	23	18	1	18	41	.241	.245	.239	8.20	3.60
O'Brien, Mikey	R-R	5-11	190	3-3-90	2	1	4.88	6	4	0	0	24	27	17	13	0	8	17	.284	.304	.256	6.38	3.00
Prado, Marcel	R-R	6-4	230	11-22-87	3	1	4.54	29	1	0	1	42	45	25	21	2	28	32	.281	.339	.248	6.91	6.05
Ramos, Jhonatan	L-L	5-10	190	10-7-89	0	0	2.61	2	2	0	0	10	10	4	3	1	2	8	.244	.231	.250	6.97	1.74
Robinson, Andrew	R-R	6-1	185	2-13-88	0	1	3.79	14	0	0	0	19	13	8	8	2	6	14	.203	.333	.125	6.63	2.84
Rodriguez, Richard	R-R	6-4	205	3-4-90	1	1	1.27	10	0	0	0	21	11	3	3	2	2	23	.147	.100	.200	9.70	0.84
Rowen, Ben	R-R	6-3	195	11-15-88	2	0	2.28	20	0	0	1	28	24	7	7	1	3	18	.242	.214	.254	5.86	0.98
Stoffel, Jason	R-R	6-1	230	9-15-88	1	0	1.42	11	0	0	0	13	7	3	2	0	4	10	.167	.111	.208	7.11	2.84
Tolliver, Ashur	L-L	6-0	170	1-24-88	1	2	2.91	39	2	0	1	59	51	19	19	2	29	61	.235	.250	.227	9.36	4.45
Torres, Dennis	R-R	6-3	200	5-17-90	2	1	4.91	7	2	0	0	15	16	11	8	0	7	7	.276	.227	.306	4.30	4.30
Triggs, Andrew	R-R	6-4	210	3-16-89	0	2	1.03	43	0	0	17	61	42	9	7	0	11	70	.196	.218	.184	10.33	1.62
Villanueva, Elih	R-R	6-2	230	7-27-86	8	7	2.93	17	17	3	0	111	92	40	36	6	21	67	.226	.196	.246	5.45	1.71

Fielding

Catcher	PCT	G	PO	A	E	DP	PB
Freitas	.994	47	338	17	2	0	4
O'Brien	.976	19	149	15	4	1	1
Perez	.989	53	416	45	5	3	6
Sisco	.992	17	107	15	1	1	1
Wieters	1.000	3	21	4	0	0	0
Wynns	1.000	4	17	3	0	0	0

First Base	PCT	G	PO	A	E	DP
Halton	.995	20	170	20	1	14
Mancini	.995	75	604	46	3	60
McDade	.992	13	108	9	1	13
Pearce	1.000	4	1	0	1	
Rosa	1.000	1	3	1	0	0
Schoop	1.000	5	53	3	0	1
Snyder	.989	31	256	19	3	22

Second Base	PCT	G	PO	A	E	DP
Flaherty	1.000	3	4	6	0	2

	PCT	G	PO	A	E	DP	PB
Gibson	.990	25	36	68	1	13	
Joseph	.972	59	94	147	7	34	
Ledesma	.909	3	3	7	1	3	
Martinez	1.000	3	7	5	0	3	
Nathans	1.000	1	1	3	0	0	
Rosa	.970	48	85	112	6	21	
Schoop	1.000	7	10	16	0	4	
Schoop	.963	7	12	14	1	3	

Third Base	PCT	G	PO	A	E	DP
Dosch	.951	68	43	112	8	8
Esposito	.922	46	35	83	10	3
Joseph	1.000	2	1	4	0	1
Paredes	1.000	1	0	1	0	0
Rosa	1.000	7	6	10	0	0
Schoop	.906	13	9	20	3	1
Snyder	.920	10	7	16	2	2

Shortstop	PCT	G	PO	A	E	DP
Gibson	1.000	3	3	9	0	1
Hardy	1.000	3	4	10	0	3
Martinez	.973	119	140	328	13	61
Rosa	.974	20	25	49	2	11
Schoop	1.000	4	5	8	0	2

Outfield	PCT	G	PO	A	E	DP
Burgess	.952	8	20	0	1	0
Davis	.988	96	233	6	3	1
Halton	1.000	7	16	3	0	0
Latimore	.980	117	240	5	5	0
Nathans	.981	27	51	0	1	0
Pearce	1.000	1	7	0	0	0
Rosa	.989	35	88	1	1	1
Ruettiger	1.000	7	14	0	0	0
Snyder	.889	16	24	0	3	0
Yastrzemski	.959	125	223	12	10	1

FREDERICK KEYS

CAROLINA LEAGUE

HIGH CLASS A

Batting	B-T	HT	WT	DOB	AVG	vLH	vRH	G	AB	R	H	2B	3B	HR	RBI	BB	HBP	SH	SF	SO	SB	CS	SLG	OBP
Alvarez, Dariel	R-R	6-2	180	11-7-88	.313	.500	.286	5	16	2	5	1	1	0	1	3	0	0	0	3	1	0	.500	.421
Bierfeldt, Conor	R-R	6-2	220	4-2-91	.202	.148	.226	56	178	15	36	14	0	5	29	19	3	1	1	58	1	1	.365	.289
Caronia, Anthony	L-R	6-0	170	5-22-91	.242	.148	.264	104	330	38	80	9	3	1	28	19	0	6	3	68	20	10	.297	.281
Dosch, Drew	L-R	6-2	200	6-24-92	.275	.273	.276	55	207	30	57	8	3	2	34	23	1	0	2	37	4	2	.372	.348
Fajardo, Daniel	R-R	6-1	175	11-14-89	.167	.000	.200	2	6	0	1	0	0	0	0	0	0	0	0	3	0	0	.167	.167
Gold, Tad	L-L	6-1	195	3-1-91	.254	.217	.261	47	134	12	34	4	0	1	10	13	1	1	0	28	4	3	.306	.324
Gonzalez, Jay	L-L	5-9	170	12-11-91	.234	.151	.263	61	205	18	48	2	3	0	21	26	0	3	2	61	10	7	.273	.318
Hart, Josh	L-L	6-1	180	10-2-94	.255	.279	.246	104	424	43	108	15	3	1	28	11	6	1	3	81	30	15	.311	.282
Hewitt, Anthony	R-R	6-1	190	4-27-89	.225	.250	.200	13	40	4	9	2	0	0	4	5	1	0	0	16	3	0	.275	.326
Kemp, Jeff	R-R	6-0	190	3-23-90	.260	.309	.244	107	404	57	105	19	4	6	36	39	7	4	5	92	6	5	.371	.332
Levy, Stuart	R-R	6-2	185	8-21-92	.200	.000	.222	3	10	0	2	0	0	0	1	1	1	0	0	6	1	0	.200	.333
Llewellyn, Phildrick	R-R	6-1	205	9-25-93	.167	.000	.188	5	18	1	3	1	0	0	2	0	1	0	3	1	1	.222	.250
Lorenzo, Gregory	R-R	6-0	160	5-31-91	.174	.178	.173	52	172	12	30	2	0	0	6	5	3	1	4	47	4	6	.186	.223
Mancini, Trey	R-R	6-4	215	3-18-92	.314	.333	.309	52	207	28	65	14	3	8	32	9	0	0	1	35	4	2	.527	.341
Marin, Adrian	R-R	6-0	180	3-8-94	.238	.270	.228	114	416	57	99	22	5	4	41	23	6	6	2	74	25	8	.344	.286
Mederos, Yaisel	R-R	5-5	225	3-20-89	.218	.206	.224	32	119	11	26	4	0	2	9	5	1	0	0	40	4	1	.303	.256
Nathans, Tucker	L-R	6-0	200	11-6-88	.290	.350	.275	61	207	38	60	11	1	7	30	25	4	0	2	30	1	2	.454	.374
Olesczuk, T.J.	R-R	6-1	205	2-5-92	.158	1.000	.111	7	19	3	3	1	0	0	0	1	1	0	0	5	0	0	.211	.238
Peterson, Derek	R-R	6-1	195	1-26-94	.226	.300	.209	15	53	6	12	1	1	0	9	2	0	0	0	13	0	0	.283	.255
Ramirez, Ramon	R-R	5-10	175	2-27-92	.143	.000	.214	7	21	5	3	0	0	0	2	1	0	1	0	6	0	0	.143	.182
Ruettiger, John	L-L	6-1	193	9-21-89	.265	.200	.277	57	196	16	52	6	2	0	13	16	0	6	1	31	10	3	.316	.319
Russell, Steel	L-R	6-0	195	9-5-90	.148	.000	.182	9	27	2	4	2	0	0	4	1	1	1	0	7	0	0	.222	.207
Sawyer, Wynston	R-R	6-3	205	11-14-91	.228	.246	.222	74	254	32	58	14	2	2	33	28	3	1	4	53	9	0	.323	.308
Sisco, Chance	L-R	6-2	193	2-24-95	.308	.286	.318	75	263	30	81	12	3	4	26	33	2	0	2	41	8	1	.422	.387
Uxa, Logan	L-R	6-4	220	1-25-91	.265	.000	.333	13	34	2	9	3	0	1	2	7	0	0	0	6	0	1	.441	.390
Webb, Brenden	L-R	6-1	185	2-24-90	.261	.220	.282	39	71	14	0	7	30	25	3	1	1	80	12	1	.390	.329
2-team total (19 Potomac)					.240	—	—	99	334	48	80	18	0	8	36	31	3	1	3	97	15	2	.365	.307
Witt, Tanner	R-R	6-0	195	1-25-91	.245	.277	.230	49	147	15	36	7	2	1	11	20	2	4	0	24	3	3	.340	.343
Wynns, Austin	R-R	6-2	205	12-10-90	.274	.364	.238	74	230	21	63	16	0	3	28	26	2	0	4	39	2	1	.383	.347

Pitching	B-T	HT	WT	DOB	W	L	ERA	G	GS	CG	SV	IP	H	R	ER	HR	BB	SO	AVG	vLH	vRH	K/9	BB/9
Cortright, Garrett	R-R	6-5	210	10-2-91	0	2	4.91	11	0	0	1	15	17	13	8	0	4	8	.279	.400	.194	4.91	2.45
Crichton, Stefan	R-R	6-3	200	2-29-92	0	0	4.05	7	0	0	2	13	14	6	6	0	1	18	.286	.316	.267	12.15	0.68
Delgado, Dariel	R-R	5-11	185	8-24-93	0	1	12.00	3	1	0	0	9	14	12	12	0	4	4	.359	.316	.400	4.00	4.00
Gonzalez, Luis	L-L	6-2	170	1-17-92	6	11	6.88	26	24	0	0	118	169	104	90	13	59	91	.347	.321	.354	6.96	4.51
Hart, Donnie	L-L	5-11	180	9-6-90	5	1	1.03	27	0	0	3	35	26	6	4	0	10	29	.208	.095	.265	7.46	2.57
Hess, David	R-R	6-2	180	7-10-93	9	4	3.58	26	25	1	0	133	112	53	53	8	53	110	.224	.231	.218	7.43	3.58
Horacek, Mitch	L-L	6-5	185	12-3-91	7	17	4.90	28	28	1	0	154	156	95	84	22	52	146	.263	.222	.278	8.51	3.03

Pitching	B-T	HT	WT	DOB	W	L	ERA	G	GS	CG	SV	IP	H	R	ER	HR	BB	SO	AVG	vLH	vRH	K/9	BB/9
Jones, Devin	R-R	6-2	170	7-4-90	0	0	7.71	3	0	0	0	5	8	4	4	0	2	5	.381	.200	.438	9.64	3.86
Keller, Jon	R-R	6-5	210	8-8-92	3	4	3.82	30	0	0	4	64	65	32	27	1	27	50	.262	.217	.288	7.07	3.82
Lee, Chris	L-L	6-4	175	8-17-92	3	6	3.07	14	14	0	0	76	76	29	26	1	29	48	.266	.158	.305	5.66	3.42
Louico, Williams	R-R	6-0	200	4-10-90	2	2	5.70	22	0	0	0	30	33	23	19	5	22	19	.284	.286	.284	5.70	6.60
Means, John	L-L	6-3	195	4-24-93	0	3	6.41	4	4	0	0	20	22	14	14	2	10	10	.297	.323	.279	4.58	4.58
Miller, Jarrett	R-R	6-1	195	9-28-89	2	3	4.87	11	9	0	0	44	51	29	24	2	33	43	.293	.233	.337	8.73	6.70
Miranda, Ariel	L-L	6-2	190	1-10-89	1	1	4.09	5	5	0	0	22	16	10	10	2	8	24	.200	.188	.203	9.82	3.27
Nowottnick, Nik	R-R	6-4	195	12-5-91	4	2	4.91	37	0	0	0	62	69	49	34	4	35	40	.278	.247	.298	5.78	5.05
O'Brien, Mikey	R-R	5-11	190	3-3-90	3	5	1.94	12	11	1	0	60	50	21	13	3	21	48	.216	.243	.195	7.16	3.13
Pacheco, Ronan	L-L	6-6	195	7-29-88	0	0	8.00	6	0	0	0	9	11	8	8	0	6	7	.297	.083	.400	7.00	6.00
Ramos, Jhonatan	L-L	5-10	190	10-7-89	0	0	2.18	4	4	0	0	21	23	6	5	2	5	9	.303	.292	.308	3.92	2.18
Rheault, Dylan	R-R	6-9	245	3-21-92	3	2	6.39	38	1	0	1	69	75	51	49	7	40	26	.293	.236	.323	3.39	5.22
Taylor, Matt	R-L	6-1	185	4-1-91	2	2	3.21	20	7	0	2	48	32	17	17	0	21	28	.199	.214	.193	5.29	3.97
Torres, Dennis	R-R	6-3	200	5-17-90	3	1	1.88	12	0	0	1	24	18	8	5	0	11	16	.202	.231	.180	6.00	4.13
Urban, Austin	L-R	6-1	185	7-8-92	1	3	3.58	20	0	0	1	38	34	18	15	4	22	28	.239	.167	.270	6.69	5.26
Vader, Sebastian	R-R	6-4	175	6-3-92	0	0	4.91	1	1	0	0	4	3	2	2	0	2	4	.267	.200	.300	9.82	4.91
Walker, Josh	R-R	6-2	175	12-18-91	0	2	5.79	3	2	0	0	14	20	11	9	4	1	6	.333	.343	.320	3.86	0.64
Wheeler, Cody	L-L	5-11	165	8-19-89	5	1	2.79	42	0	0	17	52	35	17	16	2	18	56	.194	.154	.211	9.75	4.88
Yacabonis, Jimmy	R-R	6-3	205	3-21-92	3	3	4.02	43	0	0	2	63	74	41	28	3	33	66	.296	.255	.321	9.48	4.74

Fielding

Catcher	PCT	G	PO	A	E	DP	PB
Fajardo	1.000	2	15	3	0	0	0
Levy	1.000	3	17	4	0	0	0
Llewellyn	.941	4	29	3	2	0	1
Russell	.933	9	37	5	3	0	1
Sawyer	.972	17	94	9	3	1	4
Sisco	.977	57	338	36	9	2	9
Wynns	.986	62	430	48	7	9	7

First Base	PCT	G	PO	A	E	DP
Mancini	.996	51	422	38	2	49
Mederos	.976	15	108	14	3	15
Peterson	.962	4	25	0	1	1
Sawyer	.996	58	461	36	2	56
Uxa	.981	13	96	8	2	10
Webb	1.000	3	9	1	0	1
Wynns	1.000	2	16	1	0	1

Second Base	PCT	G	PO	A	E	DP
Caronia	.969	46	92	95	6	22

	PCT	G	PO	A	E	DP	PB
Kemp	.984	84	165	253	7	65	
Llewellyn	1.000	1	2	0	0	0	
Nathans	1.000	3	4	9	0	3	
Olesczuk	1.000	1	0	2	0	0	
Schoop	1.000	2	4	7	0	4	
Witt	.972	11	14	21	1	6	

Third Base	PCT	G	PO	A	E	DP
Caronia	.926	46	24	76	8	8
Dosch	.926	52	32	93	10	12
Llewellyn	1.000	1	0	1	0	0
Nathans	.813	4	2	11	3	1
Peterson	.947	9	13	23	2	5
Ramirez	1.000	2	0	2	0	0
Witt	.882	35	20	40	8	5

Shortstop	PCT	G	PO	A	E	DP
Dosch	1.000	1	3	5	0	2
Kemp	.944	22	36	65	6	18
Marin	.968	113	185	301	16	70

	PCT	G	PO	A	E	DP
Ramirez	.938	5	4	11	1	2
Witt	1.000	3	5	6	0	1

Outfield	PCT	G	PO	A	E	DP
Alvarez	1.000	3	7	0	0	0
Bierfeldt	.984	31	59	4	1	1
Caronia	—	1	0	0	0	0
Gold	1.000	45	76	6	0	3
Gonzalez	.978	61	135	1	3	0
Hart	.978	103	222	4	5	3
Hewitt	1.000	9	16	0	0	0
Kemp	.667	1	2	0	1	0
Lorenzo	.955	49	101	6	5	3
Lough	1.000	1	2	0	0	0
Nathans	.985	38	62	4	1	0
Olesczuk	1.000	5	10	0	0	0
Peterson	1.000	1	1	0	0	0
Ruettiger	1.000	51	92	5	0	2
Webb	.980	52	89	8	2	2

DELMARVA SHOREBIRDS

LOW CLASS A

SOUTH ATLANTIC LEAGUE

Batting	B-T	HT	WT	DOB	AVG	vLH	vRH	G	AB	R	H	2B	3B	HR	RBI	BB	HBP	SH	SF	SO	SB	CS	SLG	OBP
Bierfeldt, Conor	R-R	6-2	220	4-2-91	.247	.311	.223	62	227	32	56	19	2	7	56	30	3	0	2	47	0	0	.441	.340
Breen, Jared	R-R	5-11	185	5-11-91	.242	.262	.234	62	198	32	48	10	2	1	22	31	2	0	1	53	1	0	.328	.349
Franco, Daniel	R-R	6-0	165	10-31-94	.200	.200	.200	5	15	2	3	0	0	1	0	0	0	0	2	0	0	.200	.200
Gonzalez, Jay	L-L	5-9	170	12-11-91	.294	.182	.341	72	262	54	77	9	5	0	21	61	0	2	1	72	24	7	.366	.426
Heim, Jonah	B-R	6-3	190	6-27-95	.248	.315	.211	43	149	13	37	8	1	1	16	6	1	0	1	26	0	0	.336	.280
Kneeland, Cam	R-R	6-1	195	6-23-90	.267	.252	.273	112	408	65	109	26	5	6	63	47	8	0	6	62	3	0	.400	.350
Lartiguez, Oswill	R-R	6-1	179	8-11-92	.195	.267	.154	11	41	6	8	2	0	0	1	3	0	0	0	13	0	0	.244	.250
Ledesma, Ronarsy	R-R	5-11	170	4-19-93	.234	.291	.208	50	175	26	41	4	0	3	16	13	3	0	0	60	6	1	.309	.298
Leyva, Elier	R-R	6-2	210	9-8-90	.238	.256	.231	118	407	42	97	22	2	3	43	42	3	0	4	116	1	2	.324	.311
Llewellyn, Phildrick	B-R	6-1	205	9-25-93	.167	.000	.220	17	54	10	9	1	0	0	6	6	2	2	0	7	0	0	.185	.274
Mercedes, Yermin	R-R	5-11	175	2-14-93	.272	.290	.265	64	239	33	65	16	2	8	42	11	1	0	4	41	1	0	.456	.302
Moquete, Jamill	R-R	6-3	215	2-19-92	.221	.233	.211	22	68	9	15	4	1	3	13	16	2	0	0	25	0	2	.485	.384
Murphy, Alex	R-R	5-11	210	10-5-94	.258	.286	.244	32	120	17	31	8	2	2	28	11	2	0	1	31	0	0	.408	.328
Murphy, Tanner	L-R	6-1	190	7-4-92	.222	.143	.237	14	45	5	10	3	0	0	4	0	0	0	0	8	1	2	.289	.286
Olesczuk, T.J.	R-R	6-1	205	2-9-92	.251	.224	.259	73	251	33	63	20	5	4	46	22	6	5	3	55	4	1	.418	.323
Palmer, Riley	L-R	6-4	215	11-15-91	.209	.213	.207	80	278	34	58	14	3	4	21	17	8	3	0	96	7	4	.324	.274
Peterson, Derek	R-R	6-3	195	3-6-91	.198	.286	.160	53	187	19	37	9	0	3	19	22	0	0	1	39	1	0	.294	.281
Reyes, Jomar	R-R	6-3	220	2-20-97	.278	.347	.248	84	309	36	86	27	4	5	44	18	8	0	0	73	1	0	.440	.334
Rifaela, Ademar	L-L	5-10	180	11-20-94	.262	.194	.292	59	233	39	61	15	1	5	20	25	3	1	0	59	4	4	.399	.341
Russell, Steel	L-R	6-0	195	9-5-90	.239	.286	.231	14	46	4	11	3	0	0	6	0	0	0	3	10	0	0	.304	.224
Salas, Guillermo	B-R	6-0	175	4-21-94	.202	.286	.158	56	183	11	37	6	2	0	18	2	0	2	1	46	3	3	.268	.210
Uxa, Logan	L-R	6-4	220	1-25-91	.243	.320	.256	72	268	38	65	16	5	7	37	26	4	0	1	59	2	0	.478	.319
Wilkerson, Steve	B-R	6-1	195	1-11-92	.287	.350	.259	92	342	61	98	15	4	2	30	45	7	2	5	84	10	5	.371	.376

Pitching	B-T	HT	WT	DOB	W	L	ERA	G	GS	CG	SV	IP	H	R	ER	HR	BB	SO	AVG	vLH	vRH	K/9	BB/9
Bleeker, Derrick	R-R	6-5	220	3-11-91	1	2	6.53	10	0	0	2	21	26	17	15	2	0	18	.299	.154	.361	7.84	0.00
Burke, Mike	R-R	6-2	200	8-27-92	2	2	3.36	28	1	0	1	67	58	27	25	5	10	53	.238	.275	.216	7.12	1.34
Chleborad, Tanner	R-R	6-6	185	11-4-92	1	2	4.09	9	2	0	1	24	15	10	0	2	18	20	.167	.333	.208	7.36	0.82
Cortright, Garrett	R-R	6-5	210	10-2-91	3	1	0.96	34	0	0	12	47	38	13	5	2	7	34	.218	.288	.176	6.51	1.34
Crichton, Stefan	R-R	6-3	200	2-29-92	4	4	3.27	28	1	0	4	66	64	34	24	1	12	50	.251	.277	.234	6.82	1.64

Pitching	B-T	HT	WT	DOB	W	L	ERA	G	GS	CG	SV	IP	H	R	ER	HR	BB	SO	AVG	vLH	vRH	K/9	BB/9
Cunningham, Nick	R-R	6-2	205	5-21-91	4	3	3.23	20	2	0	1	53	47	22	19	1	17	33	.239	.296	.206	5.60	2.89
Delgado, Dariel	R-R	5-11	185	8-24-93	8	3	3.09	25	11	0	0	93	90	37	32	6	32	63	.252	.245	.257	6.08	3.09
Gonzalez, Brian	R-L	6-3	230	10-25-95	4	9	5.71	23	23	0	0	106	98	76	67	8	59	81	.249	.273	.241	6.90	5.03
Grimes, Matt	R-R	6-5	185	9-4-91	10	7	4.14	24	24	2	0	126	148	72	58	6	35	91	.293	.291	.294	6.50	2.50
Hart, Donnie	L-L	5-11	180	9-6-90	1	1	2.12	19	0	0	10	17	14	4	4	0	4	17	.215	.316	.174	9.00	2.12
Hernandez, Ivan	R-R	6-2	249	7-28-91	3	0	4.00	22	0	0	4	36	31	17	16	0	15	27	.230	.204	.244	6.75	3.75
Jimenez, Francisco	R-R	6-1	160	10-4-94	2	0	2.45	4	4	0	0	22	16	6	6	1	7	11	.208	.250	.171	4.50	2.86
Kellogg, Caleb	R-R	5-11	185	6-3-92	0	1	5.66	12	1	0	0	21	28	13	13	2	11	15	.326	.385	.277	6.53	4.79
Long, Lucas	R-R	6-0	195	10-12-92	2	4	4.91	11	8	0	0	44	44	25	24	5	9	35	.267	.351	.193	7.16	1.84
Louico, Williams	R-R	6-0	200	4-10-90	0	0	6.17	5	0	0	0	12	19	9	8	1	5	9	.380	.348	.407	6.94	3.86
McGranahan, Zeke	R-R	6-4	215	1-3-91	0	3	2.53	12	0	0	1	21	14	13	6	0	20	28	.184	.091	.222	11.81	8.44
Means, John	L-L	6-3	195	4-24-93	9	8	3.50	23	23	1	0	118	136	66	46	10	26	89	.283	.265	.289	6.77	1.98
Nootbaar, Nigel	R-R	6-0	180	3-24-93	4	2	7.33	21	0	0	0	27	33	24	22	1	15	17	.300	.302	.299	5.67	5.00
Nowottnick, Nik	R-R	6-4	195	12-5-91	0	0	0.00	2	0	0	0	2	2	0	0	0	0	1	.250	.500	.167	3.86	3.86
Parry, Bennett	L-L	6-4	225	8-7-91	3	3	2.82	9	9	0	0	45	37	19	14	2	11	35	.223	.154	.236	7.05	2.22
Schuh, Max	L-L	6-4	210	3-13-92	0	1	1.79	24	0	0	3	40	39	14	8	0	15	36	.252	.229	.262	8.03	3.35
Scott, Tanner	R-L	6-2	220	7-22-94	0	3	4.29	9	2	0	2	21	19	12	10	0	10	29	.247	.286	.224	12.43	4.29
Torres, Dennis	R-R	6-3	200	5-17-90	0	1	6.55	3	3	0	0	11	14	9	8	1	4	4	.318	.348	.286	3.27	3.27
Trowbridge, Matt	L-L	5-10	175	3-24-93	0	0	4.22	9	0	0	0	11	11	6	5	0	8	13	.256	.429	.222	10.97	6.75
Vader, Sebastian	R-R	6-4	175	6-3-92	2	3	3.22	8	8	0	0	45	42	19	16	2	6	24	.259	.350	.230	5.04	2.82
Walker, Josh	R-R	6-2	175	12-18-91	8	4	3.20	16	16	0	0	84	83	39	30	5	15	59	.252	.234	.266	6.30	1.60

Fielding

Catcher	PCT	G	PO	A	E	DP	PB
Heim	1.000	35	209	48	0	1	4
Llewellyn	.989	14	78	13	1	1	3
Mercedes	.984	53	321	58	6	3	8
Murphy	.978	13	81	9	2	0	0
Murphy	.976	13	77	6	2	0	0
Russell	.988	13	75	6	1	0	3

First Base	PCT	G	PO	A	E	DP
Kneeland	.987	25	207	16	3	24
Mercedes	1.000	1	2	0	0	0
Palmer	.974	42	382	23	11	36
Peterson	.990	31	288	14	3	27
Uxa	.988	43	370	39	5	28

Second Base	PCT	G	PO	A	E	DP
Kneeland	.971	27	33	66	3	11
Ledesma	.941	39	80	94	11	27
Peterson	1.000	1	2	1	0	0
Salas	.942	8	22	27	3	11
Wilkerson	.971	68	133	196	10	45

Third Base	PCT	G	PO	A	E	DP
Kneeland	.962	49	45	108	6	10
Ledesma	.917	6	4	7	1	0
Peterson	.932	15	26	3	5	
Reyes	.948	74	52	130	10	18
Salas	—	1	0	0	0	0

Shortstop	PCT	G	PO	A	E	DP
Breen	.934	61	84	184	19	37

	PCT	G	PO	A	E	DP
Kneeland	1.000	12	18	42	0	7
Salas	.898	48	65	120	21	21
Wilkerson	.941	22	22	58	5	7

Outfield	PCT	G	PO	A	E	DP
Bierfeldt	.969	51	84	9	3	3
Franco	1.000	5	4	0	0	0
Gonzalez	.976	72	160	5	4	2
Kneeland	.833	2	5	0	1	0
Lartiguez	1.000	10	15	0	0	0
Leyva	.964	115	182	7	7	3
Moquete	1.000	17	20	2	0	0
Olesczuk	.994	73	166	5	1	1
Palmer	.944	11	16	1	1	0
Peterson	.769	6	10	0	3	0
Rifaela	.992	59	122	2	1	1

ABERDEEN IRONBIRDS

NEW YORK-PENN LEAGUE

SHORT-SEASON

Batting	B-T	HT	WT	DOB	AVG	vLH	vRH	G	AB	R	H	2B	3B	HR	RBI	BB	HBP	SH	SF	SO	SB	CS	SLG	OBP
Andujar, Ricardo	B-R	6-0	160	8-6-92	.270	.322	.254	61	244	27	66	7	2	2	23	8	2	1	0	35	1	0	.340	.299
Davis, Glynn	R-R	6-3	170	12-7-91	.241	.000	.304	7	29	3	7	0	0	0	2	1	0	0	0	8	0	0	.241	.267
De La Cruz, Alexander	R-R	6-1	185	8-22-91	.000	.000	.000	4	12	0	0	0	0	0	0	1	0	0	0	6	0	0	.000	.077
Gassaway, Randolph	R-R	6-4	210	5-23-95	.273	.242	.285	60	227	22	62	14	0	0	22	13	3	0	2	48	0	2	.335	.318
Graham, Jack	R-R	5-10	178	9-10-92	.143	.000	.250	7	1	1	1	0	0	0	0	0	0	0	0	3	0	0	.286	.143
Juvier, Alejandro	L-R	6-1	180	1-20-96	.340	.231	.378	17	50	7	17	1	2	0	8	3	0	1	0	7	4	0	.440	.377
Lartiguez, Oswill	R-R	6-1	179	4-8-94	.288	.250	.310	22	66	10	19	4	2	0	9	1	0	0	1	20	0	0	.409	.294
Laurino, Steve	R-R	6-3	230	1-5-93	.244	.306	.222	73	266	34	65	13	1	2	24	23	11	0	2	61	4	2	.323	.328
Ledesma, Ronarsy	R-R	5-11	170	4-19-93	.158	.111	.172	12	38	5	6	0	1	0	2	5	2	0	0	8	2	0	.211	.289
Lee, Alexander	R-R	6-3	205	1-14-91	.237	.000	.290	13	38	3	9	3	0	0	3	6	0	1	0	11	0	0	.316	.341
Levy, Stuart	R-R	6-2	185	8-21-92	.190	.077	.241	12	42	3	8	0	1	0	5	1	3	0	1	7	0	0	.238	.255
McClanahan, Jerry	R-R	6-1	200	6-11-92	.167	.250	.149	27	90	6	15	4	0	0	8	10	3	0	0	26	1	0	.211	.272
Moesquit, Kirvin	B-R	5-8	165	3-10-95	.200	.167	.206	12	40	6	8	0	0	0	2	1	0	0	1	8	2	1	.200	.214
Mountcastle, Ryan	R-R	6-3	185	2-18-97	.212	.167	.222	10	33	2	7	0	0	1	5	0	0	0	1	10	0	1	.303	.206
Mullins, Cedric	B-L	5-8	175	10-1-94	.264	.181	.293	68	277	34	73	15	5	2	32	22	7	3	0	33	17	4	.375	.333
Murphy, Alex	R-R	5-11	210	10-5-94	.291	.333	.279	15	55	8	16	7	0	2	8	7	0	0	0	0			.527	.371
Odenwaelder, Mike	R-R	6-5	225	9-18-92	.214	.122	.238	54	192	21	41	3	1	2	16	14	3	1	2	52	1	3	.271	.275
Pfeiffer, Austin	R-R	6-4	225	5-25-91	.207	.167	.224	48	188	18	39	9	1	3	17	5	1	2	0	59	0	1	.314	.232
Rifaela, Ademar	L-L	5-10	180	11-20-94	.200	.100	.250	7	30	3	6	2	0	0	1	3	0	0	0	4	0	1	.267	.273
Salas, Guillermo	B-R	6-0	175	4-21-94	.182	.111	.208	11	33	1	6	0	0	0	2	0	0	2	0	8	0	0	.182	.182
Shaw, Chris	R-R	6-0	165	4-25-94	.283	.267	.184	29	106	10	22	9	0	1	9	4	4	0	1	31	0	0	.321	.261
Stewart, D.J.	L-R	6-0	230	11-30-93	.218	.258	.203	62	238	25	52	8	2	6	24	23	2	1	4	52	4	1	.345	.288
Turbin, Drew	L-R	6-0	200	4-24-93	.254	.208	.272	70	256	31	65	16	2	2	30	22	7	2	1	54	4	4	.355	.329
Vargas, Yariel	R-R	6-0	180	9-25-94	.238	.000	.333	7	21	2	5	1	0	0	1	2	1	0	0	5	0	0	.286	.333

Pitching	B-T	HT	WT	DOB	W	L	ERA	G	GS	CG	SV	IP	H	R	ER	HR	BB	SO	AVG	vLH	vRH	K/9	BB/9
Albin, Zach	R-R	6-2	195	6-14-93	2	5	4.56	12	9	0	0	49	55	33	25	3	8	14	.282	.308	.260	2.55	1.46
Alvarado, Cristian	R-R	6-3	175	9-20-94	3	2	2.92	7	7	1	0	37	30	13	12	2	11	29	.221	.197	.240	7.05	2.68
Ayers, Danny	L-L	6-3	210	3-24-95	2	1	5.22	16	0	0	0	29	37	24	17	0	20	23	.308	.286	.321	7.06	6.14
Baker, Patrick	R-R	6-3	215	8-15-93	1	1	4.41	16	3	0	1	33	36	16	16	0	10	27	.275	.294	.263	7.44	2.76
Bray, Jake	R-R	6-1	185	12-8-92	0	0	0.87	5	0	0	0	10	3	1	1	1	2	14	.088	.000	.125	12.19	1.74
Cleavinger, Garrett	L-L	6-1	220	4-23-94	6	1	2.16	19	0	0	1	25	14	8	6	2	18	32	.165	.133	.182	11.52	6.48

Pitching

Pitching	B-T	HT	WT	DOB	W	L	ERA	G	GS	CG	SV	IP	H	R	ER	HR	BB	SO	AVG	vLH	vRH	K/9	BB/9
Cosme, Jean	R-R	6-2	155	5-24-96	3	5	4.74	12	12	0	0	57	46	31	30	2	18	53	.217	.256	.194	8.37	2.84
Dennis, Will	L-L	6-2	195	8-9-93	0	0	5.79	3	0	0	0	5	5	3	3	0	2	3	.313	.500	.250	0.00	5.79
Elliot, Andrew	R-R	6-0	200	2-4-92	0	1	3.38	14	0	0	2	24	21	9	9	2	4	24	.228	.371	.140	9.00	1.50
Flaa, Jay	R-R	6-3	225	6-10-92	1	0	1.31	17	0	0	4	21	10	4	3	1	5	23	.133	.194	.091	10.02	2.18
Ghidotti, Keegan	R-R	6-2	210	4-4-92	0	0	5.40	3	0	0	0	5	7	3	3	0	3	6	.318	.571	.200	10.80	5.40
Grendell, Kevin	L-L	6-2	210	8-22-93	4	1	1.64	15	1	0	0	38	35	11	7	0	12	36	.241	.267	.230	8.45	2.82
Groves, Kory	R-R	6-2	205	9-2-92	0	0	1.17	3	0	0	0	8	5	1	1	0	0	11	.179	.111	.211	12.91	0.00
Homick, Max	L-L	6-3	215	6-10-92	0	0	6.75	2	0	0	0	1	2	1	1	1	0	2	.286	.000	.333	13.50	0.00
Jimenez, Francisco	R-R	6-1	160	10-4-94	2	5	4.73	9	8	0	0	40	51	21	21	2	9	19	.325	.357	.299	4.28	2.03
Kellogg, Caleb	R-R	5-11	185	6-3-92	0	0	0.00	3	0	0	1	6	2	0	0	1	3	4	.105	.125	.091	6.00	4.50
Leyva, Lazaro	R-R	6-2	190	8-8-94	0	3	2.90	15	7	0	1	40	31	13	13	0	16	36	.214	.155	.270	8.03	3.57
Lin, Yi-Hsiang	L-L	6-0	175	12-16-92	2	0	3.04	14	0	0	0	24	22	8	8	2	4	19	.256	.219	.278	7.23	1.52
Love, Reid	R-L	5-11	195	5-15-92	3	4	5.06	11	6	0	0	37	42	24	21	4	9	34	.286	.268	.292	8.20	2.17
Meisinger, Ryan	R-R	6-4	240	5-4-94	0	0	1.99	17	0	0	8	23	15	5	5	0	5	33	.188	.194	.182	13.10	1.99
Pinales, Elias	L-L	6-4	155	11-7-92	4	0	4.15	15	0	0	1	35	41	17	16	1	9	23	.301	.265	.322	5.97	2.34
Rennie, Luc	R-R	6-2	200	4-26-94	0	0	5.14	2	2	0	0	7	8	4	4	0	5	7	.333	.250	.375	9.00	6.43
Scott, Tanner	L-L	6-2	220	7-22-94	0	0	3.38	9	1	0	0	21	16	9	8	0	12	31	.211	.192	.220	13.48	5.06
Seabrooke, Travis	R-L	6-6	205	9-16-95	3	7	4.95	14	14	0	0	64	74	35	35	1	15	43	.296	.273	.306	6.08	2.12
Strader, Robert	R-L	6-5	225	3-15-94	0	0	1.80	11	6	0	0	20	16	4	4	0	12	17	.232	.292	.200	7.65	5.40
Turnipseed, Christian	R-R	5-11	220	5-30-92	0	0	0.00	10	0	0	4	18	9	0	0	0	3	17	.148	.250	.081	8.50	1.50

Fielding

Catcher	PCT	G	PO	A	E	DP	PB
De La Cruz	1.000	4	24	4	0	0	0
Levy	1.000	12	82	12	0	1	2
McClanahan	.996	27	200	31	1	0	7
Murphy	.992	12	110	9	1	0	2
Shaw	.994	22	146	14	1	0	8

First Base	PCT	G	PO	A	E	DP
Laurino	.995	66	638	25	3	60
Lee	.970	11	90	8	3	10

Second Base	PCT	G	PO	A	E	DP
Andujar	1.000	2	8	2	0	1
Graham	.750	2	5	1	2	0
Juvier	1.000	1	1	4	0	1

	PCT	G	PO	A	E	DP
Ledesma	1.000	1	2	3	0	0
Sprowl	1.000	1	1	3	0	1
Turbin	.991	70	125	219	3	46

Third Base	PCT	G	PO	A	E	DP
Andujar	.667	2	0	2	1	0
Juvier	.882	11	2	28	4	3
Ledesma	.778	10	3	18	6	0
Moesquit	.769	8	3	7	3	1
Pfeiffer	.958	46	32	82	5	7
Ramirez	1.000	1	0	1	0	0

Shortstop	PCT	G	PO	A	E	DP
Andujar	.950	57	92	155	13	36
Juvier	.929	4	3	10	1	1

	PCT	G	PO	A	E	DP
Moesquit	.800	2	3	5	2	1
Mountcastle	.957	6	4	18	1	4
Salas	1.000	11	13	33	0	12

Outfield	PCT	G	PO	A	E	DP
Davis	1.000	6	14	0	0	0
Gassaway	.920	24	46	0	4	0
Gold	1.000	2	3	0	0	0
Grim	—	2	0	0	0	0
Lartiguez	.900	21	26	1	3	0
Mullins	.992	66	126	1	1	1
Odenwaelder	.991	54	101	8	1	0
Rifaela	1.000	7	15	0	0	0
Stewart	.969	52	89	5	3	0
Vargas	1.000	4	1	1	0	0

GCL ORIOLES

ROOKIE

GULF COAST LEAGUE

Batting	B-T	HT	WT	DOB	AVG	vLH	vRH	G	AB	R	H	2B	3B	HR	RBI	BB	HBP	SH	SF	SO	SB	CS	SLG	OBP
Becker, Branden	L-R	6-1	175	9-13-96	.219	.286	.212	42	151	17	33	3	0	0	12	15	2	1	0	20	1	4	.238	.298
Bencid, Allan	R-R	6-1	190	7-31-92	.267	.000	.286	11	15	4	4	0	0	0	4	4	0	0	0	6	0	0	.267	.421
Blanco, Hernys	R-R	5-10	175	10-7-94	.222	.500	.167	27	36	10	8	3	0	0	2	5	4	1	0	12	3	0	.306	.378
Crinella, Frank	R-R	5-11	188	6-9-94	.260	.294	.255	40	123	24	32	3	5	1	12	19	5	1	2	27	5	6	.390	.376
Curran, Seamus	L-R	6-6	240	9-6-97	.232	.375	.223	40	138	16	32	10	1	1	18	15	1	1	1	29	0	1	.341	.310
Diaz, Carlos	L-L	6-2	220	12-16-96	.180	.063	.197	41	133	9	24	6	0	3	19	19	2	0	0	36	0	1	.293	.292
Fajardo, Daniel	R-R	6-1	170	11-19-94	.403	.300	.421	21	67	7	27	3	0	0	11	3	2	0	0	9	0	1	.448	.444
Ferguson, Jaylen	R-R	6-2	180	7-21-97	.234	.235	.234	48	158	23	37	4	3	1	18	14	1	2	0	43	10	1	.316	.301
Franco, Daniel	R-R	6-0	165	10-31-94	.236	.063	.262	42	123	16	29	3	0	1	10	5	3	5	1	28	8	4	.285	.280
Graham, Jack	R-R	5-10	178	9-10-92	.121	—	.121	11	33	2	4	0	0	0	2	2	0	0	0	10	0	1	.121	.216
Grim, Gerrion	R-R	6-2	190	9-17-93	.241	.182	.250	49	162	25	39	6	1	5	16	15	2	0	2	46	7	3	.383	.309
Heim, Jonah	B-R	6-3	190	6-27-95	.333	—	.333	2	6	2	2	1	0	0	2	1	0	0	0	0	0	0	.500	.429
Heinrich, Jason	R-R	6-1	205	6-7-96	.270	.346	.254	45	152	14	41	7	2	2	33	16	7	0	3	40	0	1	.382	.360
Juvier, Alejandro	L-R	6-1	180	1-20-96	.291	.333	.290	29	103	14	30	4	2	0	10	5	2	1	0	22	4	1	.369	.336
Levy, Stuart	R-R	6-2	185	8-21-92	.255	.222	.261	18	55	10	14	3	0	0	7	4	6	1	1	14	1	1	.309	.364
McKenna, Ryan	R-R	5-9	175	2-14-97	.265	.250	.267	10	34	5	9	0	1	0	3	6	0	0	1	6	1	0	.324	.366
Moesquit, Ruben	B-R	5-8	165	3-10-95	.315	.417	.295	18	73	13	23	4	0	0	10	5	2	0	0	18	4	3	.370	.355
Mountcastle, Ryan	R-R	6-3	185	2-18-97	.313	.320	.312	43	163	21	51	7	0	3	14	9	1	0	2	36	10	4	.411	.349
Murphy, Alex	R-R	5-11	210	10-5-94	.000	.000	.000	2	8	0	0	0	0	0	0	0	0	0	0	1	0	0	.000	.111
Ortega, Irving	R-R	6-2	165	10-30-96	.000	—	.000	4	8	3	0	0	0	0	1	3	2	0	0	5	1	1	.000	.385
Ramirez, Ramon	R-R	5-10	175	2-27-92	.146	.000	.162	15	41	1	6	1	0	0	2	3	0	2	0	6	3	0	.171	.205
Reyes, Jomar	R-R	6-3	220	2-20-97	.250	—	.250	5	16	2	4	2	0	0	4	2	1	0	0	5	0	0	.375	.368
Russell, Steel	L-R	6-0	195	9-5-90	.286	—	.286	5	14	2	4	0	0	0	1	0	0	0	0	3	0	0	.286	.333
Shaw, Chris	R-R	6-0	165	4-25-94	.059	.000	.067	7	17	0	1	0	0	0	1	0	0	0	0	6	1	0	.059	.158
Soto, Ronald	R-R	6-4	220	10-5-94	.221	.000	.241	30	86	6	19	7	0	1	9	7	2	0	2	23	3	0	.337	.289

Pitching	B-T	HT	WT	DOB	W	L	ERA	G	GS	CG	SV	IP	H	R	ER	HR	BB	SO	AVG	vLH	vRH	K/9	BB/9
Alvarado, Cristian	R-R	6-3	175	9-20-94	5	0	0.33	5	3	0	0	27	15	6	1	1	0	20	.152	.136	.164	6.67	0.00
Bautista, Miguel	R-R	5-11	158	12-11-92	1	1	4.34	17	1	0	0	29	24	20	14	2	21	21	.216	.176	.279	6.52	6.52
Borde, Xavier	L-L	6-2	225	4-12-93	1	1	0.63	16	0	0	0	14	16	4	1	0	8	16	.267	.471	.186	10.05	5.02
Bray, Jake	R-R	6-1	185	12-8-92	1	0	0.87	17	0	0	10	21	11	3	2	1	3	25	.155	.162	.147	10.89	1.31
Chleborad, Tanner	R-R	6-6	185	11-4-92	0	0	3.00	4	0	0	0	6	7	2	2	0	1	4	.292	.500	.188	6.00	1.50
Costello, Mike	R-R	6-5	215	7-10-92	1	2	3.19	9	8	0	0	31	33	11	11	0	5	20	.284	.304	.267	5.81	1.45

Pitching	B-T	HT	WT	DOB	W	L	ERA	G	GS	CG	SV	IP	H	R	ER	HR	BB	SO	AVG	vLH	vRH	K/9	BB/9
Dennis, Will	L-L	6-2	195	8-9-93	4	2	3.66	13	0	0	1	20	24	10	8	0	5	10	.312	.250	.340	4.58	2.29
Elliot, Andrew	R-R	6-0	200	2-4-92	0	1	0.00	1	1	0	0	2	2	2	0	0	2	2	.222	.333	.167	9.00	0.00
Fenter, Gray	R-R	6-1	210	1-25-96	0	0	1.66	9	8	0	0	22	15	6	4	0	6	18	.200	.229	.175	7.48	2.49
Flaa, Jay	R-R	6-3	225	6-10-92	0	0	0.00	1	0	0	0	1	1	0	0	0	0	1	.250	.000	.500	9.00	0.00
Floranus, Wendell	R-R	6-0	158	4-16-95	1	2	1.75	17	0	0	0	26	17	6	5	0	8	20	.189	.267	.111	7.01	2.81
Groves, Kory	R-R	6-2	205	9-2-92	3	0	1.09	14	0	0	1	25	13	3	3	0	7	20	.155	.119	.190	7.30	2.55
Herrera, Alvin	R-R	6-1	165	3-15-93	0	1	3.15	10	1	0	2	20	20	8	7	1	4	10	.256	.243	.268	4.50	1.80
Klimek, Steven	L-R	6-3	205	4-4-94	3	0	5.40	13	0	0	0	17	7	11	10	1	12	8	.132	.143	.125	4.32	6.48
Koch, Brandon	R-R	6-4	210	12-7-95	0	0	0.00	2	0	0	0	4	3	0	0	0	2	5	.214	.286	.143	11.25	4.50
2-team total (8 Marlins)					0	0	0.59	10	0	0	3	15	8	4	1	1	4	16	—	—	—	9.39	2.35
Leyva, Lazaro	R-R	6-2	190	8-8-94	0	0	0.00	1	0	0	0	2	1	0	0	0	2	3	.167	.333	.000	13.50	9.00
Love, Reid	R-L	5-11	195	5-15-92	0	0	0.00	1	1	0	0	2	1	0	0	0	1	1	.167	.000	.333	4.50	0.00
McCord, Rocky	R-R	6-1	170	11-16-92	2	2	3.81	14	3	0	0	26	26	17	11	0	19	23	.250	.188	.304	7.96	6.58
McLeod, John	L-L	6-4	220	6-3-92	0	0	3.86	3	0	0	0	7	6	3	3	1	2	7	.261	.091	.417	9.00	2.57
Meisinger, Ryan	R-R	6-4	240	5-4-94	0	0	0.00	1	0	0	0	1	0	0	0	0	0	3	.000	.000	.000	27.00	0.00
Novak, Jan	R-L	6-3	190	1-19-94	1	1	4.21	18	0	0	0	26	25	12	12	0	7	19	.250	.269	.243	6.66	2.45
Peralta, Ofelky	R-R	6-5	195	4-20-97	0	2	5.61	11	10	0	0	26	20	20	16	0	19	31	.202	.235	.167	10.87	6.66
Richardson, David	R-R	5-11	170	1-31-91	2	1	1.23	13	2	0	0	15	10	4	2	0	9	13	.192	.190	.194	7.98	5.52
Shepley, Will	R-L	6-1	190	5-17-93	1	2	2.79	16	0	0	1	19	17	6	6	0	8	19	.246	.294	.231	8.84	3.72
Strader, Robert	R-L	6-5	225	3-15-94	0	0	0.00	1	0	0	0	1	1	0	0	0	2	2	.250	.000	.333	18.00	0.00
Taylor, Matt	R-L	6-1	185	4-1-91	0	1	1.29	2	2	0	0	7	8	1	1	0	3	4	.296	.250	.316	5.14	3.86
Turnipseed, Christian	R-R	5-11	220	5-30-92	0	0	0.00	9	0	0	5	10	2	0	0	0	4	13	.061	.125	.000	11.32	3.48
Valdez, Juan	R-R	6-2	160	2-6-91	4	4	3.33	11	8	0	0	46	39	19	17	1	20	37	.241	.274	.205	7.24	3.91
Vespi, Nick	L-L	6-3	205	10-10-95	3	0	3.00	17	1	0	1	24	21	8	8	1	3	25	.226	.111	.273	9.38	1.13
Yoon, Jeong-Hyeon	L-L	6-2	220	5-17-93	1	2	2.23	12	5	0	0	36	27	12	9	0	10	37	.206	.205	.207	9.17	2.48

Fielding

Catcher	PCT	G	PO	A	E	DP	PB
Bencid	1.000	5	18	3	0	0	3
Fajardo	.980	18	122	24	3	0	0
Heim	1.000	1	5	0	0	0	0
Levy	1.000	12	78	11	0	0	0
Murphy	1.000	2	12	0	0	0	0
Russell	1.000	4	14	2	0	1	0
Shaw	1.000	7	31	4	0	0	4
Soto	.957	23	154	23	8	1	7

First Base	PCT	G	PO	A	E	DP
Curran	.985	29	248	10	4	22
Diaz	.985	31	240	22	4	15

Second Base	PCT	G	PO	A	E	DP
Becker	.964	9	11	16	1	3
Crinella	.968	7	15	15	1	5
Graham	.943	11	16	17	2	5
Juvier	.968	24	39	53	3	12
Moesquit	.981	11	24	29	1	5
Ramirez	1.000	3	4	3	0	0

Third Base	PCT	G	PO	A	E	DP
Becker	.981	18	19	32	1	1
Crinella	.871	26	21	40	9	2
Moesquit	.950	7	3	16	1	1
Mountcastle	.778	3	0	7	2	0
Ramirez	.857	6	2	4	1	0
Reyes	.714	2	1	4	2	0

Shortstop	PCT	G	PO	A	E	DP
Becker	.930	13	20	33	4	10
Juvier	.867	4	4	9	2	1
Mountcastle	.942	33	46	83	8	10
Ortega	.895	4	4	13	2	2
Ramirez	.963	6	10	16	1	4

Outfield	PCT	G	PO	A	E	DP
Blanco	1.000	19	26	1	0	0
Ferguson	.989	44	92	2	1	1
Franco	.976	37	79	1	2	0
Grim	.989	48	86	7	1	0
Heinrich	.957	35	41	4	2	0
McKenna	1.000	10	17	0	0	0
Pearce	1.000	1	4	0	0	0

DSL ORIOLES   ROOKIE

DOMINICAN SUMMER LEAGUE

Batting	B-T	HT	WT	DOB	AVG	vLH	vRH	G	AB	R	H	2B	3B	HR	RBI	BB	HBP	SH	SF	SO	SB	CS	SLG	OBP
Acosta, Rauel	R-R	6-4	210	12-23-95	.292	.333	.275	54	185	23	54	11	1	0	25	30	2	0	1	32	1	1	.362	.394
Adames, Angel	R-R	6-0	179	5-22-96	.186	.148	.198	39	118	12	22	6	1	0	8	14	3	3	1	26	2	0	.254	.287
Alexander, Rochendrick	R-R	6-3	189	11-10-94	.162	.143	.171	43	105	14	17	2	2	0	12	14	3	2	0	34	8	0	.219	.279
Alvarado, Nicanor	R-R	6-3	205	6-22-94	.208	.242	.190	38	96	12	20	9	0	0	6	6	8	0	0	36	0	0	.302	.309
Baez, Carlos	R-R	6-3	175	11-22-97	.167	.125	.176	14	42	3	7	1	0	0	1	4	2	0	0	14	0	0	.190	.271
Barcenas, Richard	R-R	6-1	165	10-22-97	.246	.265	.240	36	130	16	32	3	1	0	7	5	2	2	0	38	1	5	.285	.285
Carrillo, Jean	R-R	6-0	200	6-16-97	.255	.227	.269	46	137	13	35	8	0	0	18	26	4	2	2	14	2	3	.314	.385
Chaves, Luis	R-R	6-2	190	11-26-94	.183	.222	.170	33	115	12	21	5	1	1	12	12	1	0	1	37	5	0	.270	.264
De Los Santos, Manuel	R-R	6-0	180	1-15-96	.228	.189	.242	39	136	13	31	8	0	0	12	5	3	0	1	53	1	3	.287	.269
Dixon, Johnny	R-R	6-1	185	2-15-97	.238	.271	.224	54	206	27	49	11	1	5	38	10	7	0	2	61	0	0	.374	.293
Engelhardt, Rachid	R-R	5-11	190	11-9-95	.212	.361	.156	39	132	21	28	5	1	1	7	12	4	2	1	31	11	3	.288	.295
Estrella, Jean	L-R	5-11	170	4-16-96	.232	.162	.261	41	125	14	29	3	2	0	9	16	4	2	1	24	7	9	.288	.336
Flores, Pedro	B-R	5-10	141	4-18-96	.267	.224	.282	61	232	42	62	10	2	1	23	22	5	2	1	32	11	5	.341	.342
Galastica, Gonzalo	B-R	5-11	160	5-15-96	.265	.361	.219	51	189	32	50	5	2	0	19	13	5	0	4	37	14	1	.312	.322
Garcia, Alejandro	R-R	6-3	185	2-24-97	.179	.188	.176	32	67	8	12	3	0	0	5	10	4	0	1	20	1	3	.224	.317
Gil, Jorge	R-R	6-4	200	4-13-94	.294	.328	.281	55	197	26	58	6	1	0	23	21	5	0	1	21	7	3	.335	.375
Giron, Victor	R-R	6-1	200	10-23-96	.200	.261	.175	33	80	10	16	1	0	0	13	14	2	3	1	13	8	2	.213	.330
Gonzalez, Alfredo	R-R	6-0	165	12-14-95	.273	.238	.289	21	66	10	18	2	1	0	4	5	1	0	0	8	1	0	.333	.333
Grasso, Victor	R-R	6-2	245	8-28-96	.185	.200	.181	34	108	9	20	6	0	0	8	8	4	0	0	33	1	0	.241	.267
Hernandez, Luis	B-R	6-2	175	5-13-98	.194	.145	.215	57	206	15	40	12	1	2	21	23	1	1	1	64	0	3	.291	.277
Jimenez, Hansel	L-L	5-11	170	7-10-96	.236	.221	.244	51	195	25	46	8	3	0	15	26	1	1	1	51	4	1	.308	.327
Laureano, Carlos	R-R	6-3	175	6-27-94	.262	.255	.264	54	191	30	50	4	0	1	14	18	4	2	0	51	23	9	.288	.338
Lizardo, Yeridolfo	R-R	6-3	195	6-29-93	.224	.171	.245	42	143	11	32	9	2	3	16	16	3	2	0	35	0	2	.378	.315
Medina, Robertico	R-R	6-0	170	1-12-94	.221	.258	.203	57	190	32	42	6	5	5	35	35	7	0	2	62	9	2	.384	.359
Montes, Juan	B-R	6-2	185	5-15-95	.188	.067	.242	16	48	9	9	0	2	2	5	4	5	0	0	10	1	0	.396	.316
Mora, Ivan	R-R	6-1	171	7-22-94	.273	.250	.280	51	187	32	51	6	5	1	19	9	4	2	2	37	4	4	.374	.317
Morillo, Antony	L-R	6-1	190	10-9-97	.147	.125	.156	32	109	10	16	3	2	0	11	6	2	0	0	43	1	0	.211	.205
Ortega, Irving	R-R	6-2	165	10-30-96	.280	.250	.294	54	200	27	56	10	5	0	19	22	7	5	1	32	10	4	.380	.370

Batting	B-T	HT	WT	DOB	AVG	vLH	vRH	G	AB	R	H	2B	3B	HR	RBI	BB	HBP	SH	SF	SO	SB	CS	SLG	OBP
Pichardo, Miguel	L-L	6-1	160	10-21-94	.069	—	—	41	87	8	6	0	0	0	2	13	1	0	1	44	3	3	.069	.196
Ramirez, Wagner	R-R	5-11	170	12-11-94	.221	.182	.236	22	77	10	17	2	0	0	5	2	3	0	0	18	1	1	.247	.268
Rivero, Leisxonyer	R-R	6-1	165	2-12-97	.092	—	—	34	76	6	7	0	0	0	1	13	0	1	0	40	4	1	.092	.225
Rodriguez, Carlos	R-R	6-1	160	3-22-95	.226	.333	.189	48	177	19	40	6	1	0	16	6	3	4	0	44	12	4	.271	.263
Sanchez, Richi	L-R	5-10	185	5-6-94	.280	.306	.270	25	125	17	35	7	4	0	17	13	1	0	1	19	3	0	.400	.350
Santa, Adelyn	R-R	6-1	195	6-1-94	.164	.184	.156	38	128	7	21	6	0	2	10	11	4	0	2	60	0	2	.258	.248
Tucen, Adony	R-R	6-0	175	5-10-95	.223	—	—	44	103	18	23	4	1	2	11	8	3	0	1	42	7	1	.340	.296
Vizcaino, Fabian	R-R	5-11	178	5-27-95	.307	.520	.222	33	88	17	27	3	1	0	13	14	3	1	1	11	2	4	.364	.415

Pitching	B-T	HT	WT	DOB	W	L	ERA	G	GS	CG	SV	IP	H	R	ER	HR	BB	SO	AVG	vLH	vRH	K/9	BB/9
Alcantara, Jose	R-R	6-1	190	11-29-92	0	1	2.01	10	1	0	0	22	17	6	5	0	13	34	.215	.125	.255	13.70	5.24
Alcantara, Nichel	R-R	6-2	185	5-8-96	0	1	3.00	6	4	0	0	21	15	7	7	1	5	11	.203	.150	.222	4.71	2.14
Bonilla, Miguel Angel	R-R	6-3	185	9-29-94	1	2	5.18	16	0	0	1	33	36	21	19	3	6	24	.271	.244	.284	6.55	1.64
Cabrera, Oscar	L-L	6-2	215	5-22-94	0	2	6.64	11	0	0	0	20	25	19	15	0	16	19	.287	.192	.328	8.41	7.08
Cuevas, Yanuel	R-R	5-11	180	10-25-93	3	2	2.14	25	0	0	3	42	43	15	10	0	14	38	.270	.354	.234	8.14	3.00
De La Cruz, Andy	L-L	6-1	185	8-29-94	6	1	1.93	21	0	0	4	42	37	14	9	0	21	38	.240	.240	.240	8.14	4.50
Diaz, Jose	R-R	6-3	185	8-1-96	4	5	3.03	14	14	0	0	62	60	31	21	5	13	41	.248	.276	.235	5.92	1.88
Encarnacion, Erick	L-L	6-1	180	4-4-96	0	2	4.50	5	0	0	0	8	9	7	4	0	7	8	.281	.250	.286	9.00	7.88
Encarnacion, Virgilio	R-R	6-2	190	2-8-92	0	1	9.00	3	0	0	1	3	5	3	3	0	0	2	.385	.600	.250	6.00	0.00
Fabian, Edward	R-R	6-3	170	8-23-95	0	2	9.70	16	0	0	0	21	27	28	23	0	17	15	.314	.300	.321	6.33	7.17
Feliz, Henry	R-R	6-0	185	5-23-92	3	2	5.26	7	0	0	0	51	66	37	30	0	24	29	.314	.315	.314	5.08	4.21
Gonzalez, Miguel	R-R	6-3	185	9-29-95	0	5	6.93	13	7	0	0	38	42	38	29	1	30	19	.286	.333	.260	4.54	7.17
Guance, Hector	R-R	6-6	200	7-12-95	1	2	6.37	18	0	0	0	30	32	26	21	1	19	22	.283	.310	.274	6.67	5.76
Hernandez, Juan	R-R	6-3	220	1-24-93	1	2	3.56	21	0	0	4	30	22	13	12	0	12	36	.208	.286	.179	10.68	3.56
Jimenez, Julin	R-R	6-1	200	1-29-93	1	1	2.48	15	0	0	0	36	30	16	10	0	23	15	.227	.200	.239	3.72	5.70
LeFranc, Lu Franc-Cito	R-R	6-4	220	3-3-93	0	1	5.73	16	1	0	0	22	25	21	14	1	25	17	.269	.241	.281	6.95	10.23
Leoncio, Tomas	R-R	6-2	180	3-3-95	3	3	1.91	14	14	0	0	71	60	24	15	2	18	63	.227	.191	.240	8.02	2.29
Liranzo, Jesus	R-R	6-2	175	3-7-95	3	2	2.35	23	0	0	0	38	28	14	10	0	19	46	.200	.150	.220	10.80	4.46
Marrugo, Yeizer	R-R	6-0	170	10-1-94	6	2	2.02	14	14	0	0	71	66	24	16	0	16	63	.243	.235	.245	7.95	2.02
Martinez, Leybi	R-R	6-1	180	1-20-95	0	0	3.07	5	4	0	0	15	13	12	5	0	11	13	.245	.136	.323	7.98	6.75
Medina, Cesar	R-R	6-3	180	6-16-94	5	3	3.32	20	0	0	1	43	38	19	16	2	21	28	.253	.245	.257	5.82	4.36
Negrette, Alirio	L-L	6-0	210	4-5-94	4	5	3.45	14	14	0	0	63	50	29	24	2	29	62	.220	.233	.217	8.90	4.16
Pacheco, Johalis	L-L	6-0	170	3-29-94	2	5	3.71	15	14	0	0	63	69	39	26	0	25	61	—	—	—	8.71	3.57
Palumbo, Angelo	R-R	6-3	180	11-10-95	2	5	3.48	17	12	0	0	52	62	25	20	0	23	45	.297	.320	.284	7.84	4.01
Peluffo, Jhon	R-R	6-3	140	6-16-97	2	4	2.21	14	14	0	0	57	56	28	14	1	20	53	.255	.268	.248	8.37	3.16
Polanco, Miguel	L-L	6-4	200	1-28-94	0	0	5.06	3	0	0	0	5	7	7	3	1	7	3	.292	.000	.318	5.06	11.81
Rodriguez, Ramon	R-R	5-11	169	12-27-91	2	2	4.23	20	0	0	2	45	43	26	21	0	15	38	—	—	—	7.66	3.02
Ramirez, Victor	R-R	6-2	185	5-12-95	3	2	1.38	23	0	0	8	26	18	6	4	0	8	28	.196	.286	.156	9.69	2.77
Rojas, Edwin	R-R	6-6	200	9-26-95	2	1	8.22	14	4	0	0	31	43	34	28	4	19	25	.319	.333	.314	7.34	5.58
Romero, Victor	R-R	6-3	170	2-17-95	2	0	0.61	4	6	2.42	15	15	0	0	74	65	31	20	0	15	57	6.90	1.82
Taveras, Juan	R-R	6-1	170	1-28-95	0	1	10.38	10	0	0	0	9	3	14	10	0	17	9	—	—	—	9.35	17.65
Valdez, Juan	R-R	6-2	160	2-6-91	0	1	2.55	4	4	0	0	18	22	7	5	0	5	17	.293	.400	.240	8.66	2.55
Vizcaino, Dember	R-R	6-4	205	5-12-95	0	1	5.76	17	1	0	0	30	39	30	19	1	21	23	.317	.300	.325	6.98	6.37

Fielding

Catcher	PCT	G	PO	A	E	DP	PB
Alvarado	1.000	6	12	0	0	0	3
Carrillo	.980	46	335	62	8	3	5
Gonzalez	.987	21	122	30	2	2	2
Grasso	.968	34	237	36	9	0	6
Ramirez	.977	22	146	26	4	3	9
Sanchez	.975	7	36	3	1	0	2
Vizcaino	.977	28	187	28	5	1	8

First Base	PCT	G	PO	A	E	DP
Acosta	.986	41	353	12	5	27
Adames	.990	12	100	2	1	6
Alvarado	.963	16	100	4	4	10
De Los Santos	.954	24	193	13	10	15
Engelhardt	1.000	1	2	0	0	0
Estrella	1.000	5	36	4	0	4
Garcia	.875	4	7	0	1	0
Lizardo	.963	4	24	2	1	3
Mora	.926	3	24	1	2	4
Morillo	.857	1	6	0	1	1
Rodriguez	1.000	2	10	1	0	0
Sanchez	.993	17	130	11	1	14
Santa	.986	31	271	13	4	13
Vizcaino	—	1	0	0	0	0

Second Base	PCT	G	PO	A	E	DP
Adames	.929	9	13	26	3	3
Baez	1.000	2	6	3	0	1
Engelhardt	1.000	1	1	1	0	0
Estrella	.966	27	55	60	4	13
Flores	.956	61	132	175	14	31
Galastica	.944	43	86	118	12	24
Lizardo	1.000	1	0	2	0	0
Pichardo	.941	5	7	9	1	1
Rivero	.968	8	14	16	1	4

Third Base	PCT	G	PO	A	E	DP
Baez	.800	7	5	15	5	0
Estrella	—	1	0	0	0	0
Garcia	.842	18	12	20	6	1
Lizardo	.859	37	37	73	18	5
Medina	.882	56	49	115	22	9
Morillo	.803	25	10	39	12	7
Pichardo	.429	4	0	3	4	0
Rivero	.909	15	17	24	5	3
Santa	.846	7	4	7	2	0

Shortstop	PCT	G	PO	A	E	DP
Baez	.818	2	5	4	2	1
Galastica	.955	6	5	16	1	1
Hernandez	.864	46	66	106	27	17
Ortega	.952	53	89	170	13	25
Pichardo	.923	30	24	60	7	8
Rivero	.905	12	13	25	4	7

Outfield	PCT	G	PO	A	E	DP
Adames	—	1	0	0	0	0
Alexander	.985	38	63	3	1	1
Barcenas	.942	34	47	2	3	0
Chaves	.968	18	26	4	1	2
De Los Santos	.952	11	18	2	1	0
Dixon	.947	45	69	2	4	1
Engelhardt	.967	34	49	9	2	0
Gil	.949	40	50	6	3	1
Giron	.960	31	45	3	2	2
Jimenez	.949	50	89	4	5	1
Laureano	.977	53	125	4	3	4
Montes	.947	15	18	0	1	0
Mora	.925	32	59	3	5	1
Rodriguez	.968	40	86	6	3	1
Tucen	1.000	30	47	4	0	2

Boston Red Sox

SEASON IN A SENTENCE: General manager Ben Cherington's high-priced signings of Hanley Ramirez and Pablo Sandoval backfired as both underperformed, and Cherington resigned in the wake of Dave Dombrowski's hiring as the team slid to another second-division finish.

HIGH POINT: A quick start from Ramirez—10 homers in April—led the Red Sox to a two-game lead on April 21 and a winning first month. In the second half—long after the outcome of the season was known—Boston went 27-19 in August and September, led by Mookie Betts and the resurgent Jackie Bradley.

LOW POINT: No matter the team's record, the news about manager John Farrell's lymphoma diagnosis overshadowed everything. Farrell took a leave of absence in August to have chemotherapy treatment but will be back in spring training.

NOTABLE ROOKIES: With injuries and trades, three position players were pressed into more action than expected, with largely positive results. Blake Swihart was made the everyday catcher when Christian Vazquez needed elbow surgery and showed power and a solid handling of the staff; Travis Shaw flexed his muscle as he made a case to be the everyday first baseman in 2016 after the trade of Mike Napoli; and Rusney Castillo flashed intriguing tools as he got a regular run in the outfield. Among the pitchers, Eduardo Rodriguez and Henry Owens look like they can be mainstays for a rebuilt rotation in 2016, with Rodriguez particularly impressive. Brian Johnson got a shot as well, but a sore arm ended his season in August. He is expected to be ready for spring training and have a shot at making the rotation.

KEY TRANSACTIONS: For the second year in a row, Boston was a seller at the trade deadline, but did not trade as many big parts this time around as in 2014. Instead, the Red Sox swapped spare pieces such as Napoli and Shane Victorino to give younger players an opportunity.

DOWN ON THE FARM: The Red Sox have perhaps the top feeder system even after the promotions of Rodriguez, Owens, Johnson, Swihart, Shaw and others. Intriguing pitchers—such as 17-year-old Anderson Espinoza, hard-throwing righthander Michael Kopech and lefthander Trey Ball—highlight the pitchers. Boston is rife with position players such as Yoan Moncada, Rafael Devers, Manuel Margot, Javier Guerra, Michael Chavis, Mauricio Dubon and others.

OPENING DAY PAYROLL: $187,407,202 (3rd)

PLAYERS OF THE YEAR

MAJOR LEAGUE	MINOR LEAGUE
David Ortiz dh	**Yoan Moncada** if
.273/.360/.553	(low Class A)
37 HR, 108 RBI	.278/.380/.438
Led club in HR, RBIs	.915 OPS post ASG

ORGANIZATION LEADERS

BATTING		*Minimum 250 AB
MAJORS		
*AVG	Xander Bogaerts	.320
*OPS	David Ortiz	.913
HR	David Ortiz	37
RBI	David Ortiz	108
MINORS		
*AVG	Sam Travis, Salem, Portland	.307
*OBP	Kevin Heller, Portland, Salem	.393
*SLG	Marco Hernandez, Portland, Pawtucket	.454
R	Manuel Margot, Salem, Portland	73
H	Sam Travis, Salem, Portland	150
TB	Sam Travis, Salem, Portland	221
2B	Rafael Devers, Greenville	38
3B	Manuel Margot, Salem, Portland	9
HR	Michael Chavis, Greenville	16
RBI	Sam Travis, Salem, Portland	78
BB	Sam Travis, Salem, Portland	59
SO	Michael Chavis, Greenville	144
SB	Yoan Moncada, Greenville	49

PITCHING		#Minimum 75 IP
MAJORS		
W	Wade Miley	11
#ERA	Wade Miley	4.46
SO	Rick Porcello	149
SV	Koji Uehara	25
MINORS		
W	William Cuevas, Portland, Pawtucket	11
	Kevin McAvoy, Salem	11
	Aaron Wilkerson, Greenville, Salem, Portland	11
L	Justin Haley, Portland	16
#ERA	Aaron Wilkerson, Greenville, Salem, Portland	3.10
G	Pat Light, Portland, Pawtucket	47
GS	Luis Diaz, Portland	27
	Justin Haley, Portland	27
SV	Austin Maddox, Salem/Bobby Poyner, Lowell	10
IP	Jalen Beeks, Greenville	146
BB	Kevin McAvoy, Salem	71
SO	Aaron Wilkerson, Greenville, Salem, Portland	137
AVG	Henry Owens, Pawtucket	.193

2015 PERFORMANCE

General Manager: Ben Cherington/Mike Hazen. **Farm Director:** Ben Crockett. **Scouting Director:** Mike Rikard.

Class	Team	League	W	L	PCT	Finish	Manager
Majors	Boston Red Sox	American	78	84	.481	11th (15)	John Farrell
Triple-A	Pawtucket Red Sox	International	59	85	.410	14th (14)	Kevin Boles
Double-A	Portland Sea Dogs	Eastern	53	89	.373	12th (12)	Billy McMillon
High A	Salem Red Sox	Carolina	66	73	.475	5th (8)	Carlos Febles
Low A	Greenville Drive	South Atlantic	72	68	.514	7th (14)	Darren Fenster
Short season	Lowell Spinners	New York-Penn	37	39	.487	9th (14)	Joe Oliver
Rookie	Red Sox	Gulf Coast	41	17	.707	1st (16)	Tom Kotchman
Overall 2015 Minor League Record			328	371	.469	24th (30)	

ORGANIZATION STATISTICS

BOSTON RED SOX

AMERICAN LEAGUE

Batting	B-T	HT	WT	DOB	AVG	vLH	vRH	G	AB	R	H	2B	3B	HR	RBI	BB	HBP	SH	SF	SO	SB	CS	SLG	OBP
Betts, Mookie	R-R	5-9	180	10-7-92	.291	.311	.285	145	597	92	174	42	8	18	77	46	2	3	6	82	21	6	.479	.341
Bianchi, Jeff	R-R	5-11	185	10-5-86	.000	.000	.000	3	2	0	0	0	0	0	0	0	0	0	0	0	0	0	.000	.000
Bogaerts, Xander	R-R	6-1	210	10-1-92	.320	.365	.304	156	613	84	196	35	3	7	81	32	3	3	3	101	10	2	.421	.355
Bradley, Jackie	L-R	5-10	200	4-19-90	.249	.306	.221	74	221	43	55	17	4	10	43	27	3	1	3	69	3	0	.498	.335
Castillo, Rusney	R-R	5-9	195	7-9-87	.253	.318	.222	80	273	35	69	10	2	5	29	13	1	1	1	54	4	5	.359	.288
Cecchini, Garin	L-R	6-3	220	4-20-91	.000	—	.000	2	4	0	0	0	0	0	0	0	0	0	0	3	0	0	.000	.000
Craig, Allen	R-R	6-2	215	7-18-84	.152	.222	.115	36	79	6	12	1	0	1	3	7	2	0	0	26	0	0	.203	.239
De Aza, Alejandro	L-L	6-0	195	4-11-84	.292	.208	.307	60	161	23	47	9	5	4	25	12	2	2	1	36	3	1	.484	.347
2-team total (30 Baltimore)					.261	—	—	90	264	39	69	13	6	7	32	19	4	2	1	70	5	3	.436	.319
Hanigan, Ryan	R-R	6-0	215	8-16-80	.247	.364	.208	54	174	28	43	8	0	2	16	20	4	1	1	39	0	0	.328	.337
Holt, Brock	L-R	5-10	180	6-11-88	.280	.312	.270	129	454	56	127	27	6	2	45	46	3	4	2	97	8	1	.379	.349
Jimenez, Luis	R-R	6-1	205	1-18-88	.000	—	.000	1	1	0	0	0	0	0	0	0	0	0	0	0	0	0	.000	.000
Leon, Sandy	B-R	5-10	225	3-13-89	.184	.059	.238	41	114	8	21	2	0	3	7	1	6	0	0	28	0	1	.202	.238
Marrero, Deven	R-R	6-1	195	8-25-90	.226	.150	.273	25	53	8	12	0	0	1	3	3	0	0	0	19	2	1	.283	.268
Napoli, Mike	R-R	6-1	225	10-31-81	.207	.229	.197	98	329	37	68	18	1	13	40	45	3	0	1	99	3	1	.386	.307
2-team total (35 Texas)					.224	—	—	133	407	46	91	20	1	18	50	57	4	0	1	118	3	3	.410	.324
Nava, Daniel	B-L	5-11	200	2-22-83	.152	.125	.155	29	66	6	10	2	0	0	7	8	2	1	1	17	0	0	.182	.260
2-team total (31 Tampa Bay)					.194	—	—	60	139	13	27	4	0	1	10	20	5	1	1	36	1	0	.245	.315
Ortiz, David	L-L	6-3	230	11-18-75	.273	.231	.292	146	528	73	144	37	0	37	108	77	0	0	9	95	0	1	.553	.360
Pedroia, Dustin	R-R	5-9	175	8-17-83	.291	.275	.297	93	381	46	111	19	1	12	42	38	2	1	3	51	2	2	.441	.356
Peguero, Carlos	L-L	6-5	260	2-22-87	.200	.000	.250	4	5	1	1	0	0	0	0	0	0	0	0	1	0	0	.200	.333
2-team total (30 Texas)					.187	—	—	34	75	11	14	4	0	4	9	13	1	0	1	37	2	0	.400	.311
Ramirez, Hanley	R-R	6-2	225	12-23-83	.249	.230	.257	105	401	59	100	12	1	19	53	21	4	0	4	71	6	3	.426	.291
Rutledge, Josh	R-R	6-1	190	4-21-89	.284	.318	.269	39	74	11	21	1	0	1	10	5	2	1	3	26	0	0	.338	.333
Sandoval, Pablo	B-R	5-11	255	8-11-86	.245	.197	.266	126	470	43	115	25	1	10	47	25	7	1	2	73	0	0	.366	.292
Shaw, Travis	L-R	6-4	225	4-16-90	.274	.329	.243	65	226	31	62	10	0	13	36	18	2	0	2	57	0	1	.491	.331
Swihart, Blake	B-R	6-1	205	4-3-92	.274	.225	.293	84	288	47	79	17	1	5	31	18	1	2	0	77	4	2	.392	.319
Victorino, Shane	B-R	5-9	190	11-30-80	.245	.343	.186	33	94	10	23	2	0	1	4	9	2	1	0	14	5	0	.298	.324
2-team total (38 Los Angeles)					.230	—	—	71	178	19	41	4	2	1	7	16	5	3	2	32	7	0	.292	.308
Weeks, Jemile	B-R	5-9	170	1-26-87	.333	.667	.167	3	9	1	3	0	0	0	1	0	0	0	0	2	0	0	.333	.333

Pitching	B-T	HT	WT	DOB	W	L	ERA	G	GS	CG	SV	IP	H	R	ER	HR	BB	SO	AVG	vLH	vRH	K/9	BB/9
Aro, Jonathan	R-R	6-0	175	10-10-90	0	1	6.97	6	0	0	0	10	15	8	8	2	4	8	.341	.316	.360	6.97	3.48
Barnes, Matt	R-R	6-4	210	6-17-90	3	4	5.44	32	2	0	0	43	56	28	26	9	15	39	.311	.284	.333	8.16	3.14
Breslow, Craig	L-L	6-1	185	8-8-80	0	4	4.15	45	2	0	1	65	69	33	30	12	23	46	.279	.295	.270	6.37	3.18
Buchholz, Clay	L-R	6-3	190	8-14-84	7	7	3.26	18	18	1	0	113	114	48	41	6	23	107	.260	.239	.284	8.50	1.83
Cook, Ryan	R-R	6-2	215	6-30-87	0	0	27.00	5	0	0	0	4	13	14	13	4	4	3	.481	.583	.400	6.23	8.31
2-team total (4 Oakland)					0	2	18.69	9	0	0	0	9	20	19	18	4	7	6	—	—	—	6.23	7.27
Hembree, Heath	R-R	6-4	210	1-13-89	2	0	3.55	22	0	0	0	25	25	10	10	5	9	15	.258	.256	.259	5.33	3.20
Hill, Rich	L-L	6-5	220	3-11-80	2	1	1.55	4	4	1	0	29	14	5	5	2	5	36	.141	.158	.138	11.17	1.55
Hinojosa, Dalier	R-R	6-1	230	2-10-86	0	0	0.00	1	0	0	0	2	0	0	0	0	3	2	.000	.000	10.80	16.20	
Johnson, Brian	L-L	6-4	235	12-7-90	0	1	8.31	1	1	0	0	4	3	4	4	0	4	3	.214	.000	.250	6.23	8.31
Kelly, Joe	R-R	6-1	190	6-9-88	10	6	4.82	25	25	0	0	134	145	76	72	15	49	110	.276	.254	.299	7.37	3.28
Layne, Tommy	L-L	6-2	190	11-24-84	2	1	3.97	64	0	0	1	48	41	22	21	3	27	45	.234	.148	.322	8.50	5.10
Machi, Jean	R-R	6-0	255	2-1-82	1	0	5.09	26	0	0	4	23	21	14	13	5	8	20	.236	.200	.282	7.83	3.13
Masterson, Justin	R-R	6-6	260	3-22-85	4	2	5.61	18	9	0	0	59	68	38	37	7	27	49	.289	.310	.266	7.43	4.10
Mendez, Roman	R-R	6-3	235	7-25-90	0	0	4.50	3	0	0	0	2	3	1	1	1	1	1	.375	.000	.500	4.50	4.50
2-team total (12 Texas)					0	1	5.27	15	0	0	0	14	14	8	8	2	8	10	—	—	—	6.59	5.27
Miley, Wade	L-L	6-0	220	11-13-86	11	11	4.46	32	32	1	0	194	201	98	96	17	64	147	.265	.241	.272	6.83	2.97
Mujica, Edward	R-R	6-3	220	5-10-84	1	1	4.61	11	0	0	0	14	15	7	7	3	3	8	.294	.259	.333	5.27	1.98
2-team total (38 Oakland)					3	5	4.75	49	0	0	1	47	52	28	25	10	7	30	—	—	—	5.70	1.33
Ogando, Alexi	R-R	6-4	195	10-5-83	3	1	3.99	64	0	0	0	65	59	29	29	12	28	53	.242	.206	.265	7.30	3.86
Owens, Henry	L-L	6-6	220	7-21-92	4	4	4.57	11	11	0	0	63	62	35	32	7	24	50	.255	.293	.248	7.14	3.43
Porcello, Rick	R-R	6-5	200	12-27-88	9	15	4.92	28	28	0	0	172	196	103	94	25	38	149	.287	.289	.286	7.80	1.99

Pitching	B-T	HT	WT	DOB	W	L	ERA	G	GS	CG	SV	IP	H	R	ER	HR	BB	SO	AVG	vLH	vRH	K/9	BB/9
Ramirez, Noe	R-R	6-3	205	12-22-89	0	1	4.15	17	0	0	0	13	13	12	6	3	7	13	.250	.200	.262	9.00	4.85
Rodriguez, Eduardo	L-L	6-2	210	4-7-93	10	6	3.85	21	21	0	0	122	120	55	52	13	37	98	.255	.272	.249	7.25	2.74
Ross, Robbie	L-L	5-11	215	6-24-89	0	2	3.86	54	0	0	6	61	59	28	26	7	20	53	.254	.224	.272	7.86	2.97
Tazawa, Junichi	R-R	5-11	200	6-6-86	2	7	4.14	61	0	0	3	59	65	28	27	5	13	56	.280	.299	.267	8.59	1.99
Uehara, Koji	R-R	6-2	195	4-3-75	2	4	2.23	43	0	0	25	40	28	14	10	3	9	47	.188	.153	.221	10.49	2.01
Varvaro, Anthony	R-R	6-0	190	10-31-84	0	1	4.09	9	0	0	0	11	14	5	5	0	6	8	.311	.263	.346	6.55	4.91
Wright, Steven	R-R	6-1	215	8-30-84	5	4	4.09	16	9	0	0	73	67	38	33	12	27	52	.239	.232	.246	6.44	3.34

Fielding

Catcher	PCT	G	PO	A	E	DP	PB
Hanigan	.993	53	411	25	3	4	4
Leon	.997	37	258	28	1	4	2
Swihart	.995	83	570	39	3	4	16

First Base	PCT	G	PO	A	E	DP
Cecchini	1.000	1	4	1	0	1
Craig	1.000	6	29	3	0	3
Holt	1.000	8	46	3	0	6
Napoli	.993	96	748	65	6	64
Nava	1.000	6	47	1	0	6
Ortiz	.982	9	51	5	1	2
Shaw	.993	55	419	36	3	50

Second Base	PCT	G	PO	A	E	DP
Holt	.981	58	67	137	4	32
Marrero	1.000	3	1	5	0	2

	PCT	G	PO	A	E	DP
Pedroia	.986	92	165	272	6	61
Rutledge	.966	30	33	53	3	14
Weeks	1.000	3	6	7	0	2

Third Base	PCT	G	PO	A	E	DP
Bianchi	1.000	2	0	2	0	0
Holt	.955	33	16	47	3	2
Leon	—	1	0	0	0	0
Marrero	.955	13	3	18	1	4
Ramirez	—	1	0	0	0	0
Rutledge	.875	5	1	6	1	0
Sandoval	.949	123	78	200	15	19
Shaw	1.000	8	5	14	0	0

Shortstop	PCT	G	PO	A	E	DP
Bianchi	1.000	1	1	1	0	1
Bogaerts	.984	156	236	429	11	95

	PCT	G	PO	A	E	DP
Holt	.950	11	11	27	2	7
Marrero	1.000	6	3	6	0	2

Outfield	PCT	G	PO	A	E	DP
Betts	.987	144	358	10	5	2
Bradley	.994	73	159	4	1	2
Castillo	.969	75	152	6	5	0
Craig	1.000	16	26	0	0	0
De Aza	1.000	52	64	2	0	0
Holt	1.000	35	67	1	0	0
Nava	1.000	21	30	1	0	1
Peguero	1.000	4	5	0	0	0
Ramirez	.969	92	120	3	4	1
Shaw	—	1	0	0	0	0
Victorino	1.000	32	57	1	0	1

PAWTUCKET RED SOX

TRIPLE-A

INTERNATIONAL LEAGUE

Batting	B-T	HT	WT	DOB	AVG	vLH	vRH	G	AB	R	H	2B	3B	HR	RBI	BB	HBP	SH	SF	SO	SB	CS	SLG	OBP
Berry, Quintin	L-L	6-1	190	11-21-84	.228	.234	.226	106	359	44	82	7	1	4	36	51	5	6	5	89	35	6	.287	.329
Bianchi, Jeff	R-R	5-11	185	10-5-86	.262	.256	.264	42	130	13	34	5	1	0	8	13	0	3	0	19	4	2	.315	.329
Bradley, Jackie	L-R	5-10	200	4-19-90	.305	.250	.333	71	282	38	86	18	1	9	29	30	5	1	0	44	4	4	.472	.382
Brentz, Bryce	R-R	6-0	210	12-30-88	.232	.266	.218	59	220	28	51	9	0	8	26	24	2	0	4	74	0	0	.382	.308
Castillo, Rusney	R-R	5-9	195	7-9-87	.282	.298	.275	40	156	17	44	7	0	3	17	14	0	0	2	28	10	2	.385	.337
Cecchini, Garin	L-R	6-3	220	4-20-91	.213	.188	.224	117	422	34	90	14	0	7	28	40	4	1	2	100	9	0	.296	.286
Coyle, Sean	R-R	5-8	175	1-17-92	.159	.138	.165	39	126	21	20	3	0	5	16	20	0	2	0	44	4	1	.302	.274
Craig, Allen	R-R	6-2	215	7-18-84	.274	.330	.253	93	343	29	94	14	0	4	30	49	4	0	3	70	0	0	.350	.368
Gragnani, Reed	B-R	5-11	180	9-5-90	.000	.000	.000	2	6	0	0	0	0	0	0	1	0	0	0	0	0	0	.000	.143
Hanigan, Ryan	R-R	6-0	215	8-16-80	.182	—	.182	4	11	2	2	0	0	0	0	3	0	0	0	1	0	0	.182	.357
Hernandez, Marco	L-R	6-0	170	9-6-92	.271	.315	.252	46	181	27	49	9	2	4	22	8	0	0	1	39	1	0	.409	.300
Jimenez, Luis	R-R	6-1	205	1-18-88	.140	.105	.158	14	57	4	8	0	1	2	6	0	0	0	0	9	0	0	.281	.140
Leon, Sandy	B-R	5-10	225	3-13-89	.263	.346	.233	26	99	8	26	4	0	1	13	10	2	0	0	23	0	1	.333	.342
Marrero, Chris	R-R	6-3	229	7-2-88	.239	.179	.266	22	92	10	22	5	0	3	8	2	0	0	0	19	0	0	.391	.255
2-team total (39 Charlotte)					.262			61	225	28	59	13	1	7	25	17	0	0	2	47	0	0	.422	.311
Marrero, Deven	R-R	6-1	195	8-25-90	.256	.266	.252	102	375	49	96	13	1	6	29	33	2	5	4	87	12	5	.344	.316
Martinez, Luis	R-R	6-0	210	4-3-85	.164	.000	.205	18	55	7	9	0	0	0	6	11	0	1	0	12	0	0	.164	.303
Miller, Mike	R-R	5-9	170	9-27-89	.219	.224	.217	74	247	17	54	10	1	3	19	14	0	4	3	34	6	3	.304	.258
Montz, Luke	R-R	6-1	225	7-7-83	.167	.167	.167	48	162	15	27	12	0	5	21	23	1	1	3	58	1	0	.333	.270
Nava, Daniel	B-L	5-11	200	2-22-83	.250	.200	.269	10	36	4	9	1	0	1	8	4	2	0	0	11	2	0	.361	.357
Peguero, Carlos	L-L	6-5	260	2-22-87	.237	.217	.243	26	97	9	23	4	0	7	21	9	1	0	1	33	0	0	.495	.306
Quintero, Humberto	R-R	5-10	210	8-2-79	.257	.262	.255	81	288	19	74	7	0	7	33	9	3	2	3	53	2	0	.354	.284
Rivero, Carlos	R-R	6-3	200	5-20-88	.248	.278	.235	28	117	12	29	4	0	1	15	10	0	0	0	26	0	0	.308	.307
Roof, Jonathan	R-R	6-1	175	1-23-89	.214	.136	.242	48	168	16	36	7	0	2	12	8	1	1	2	33	2	0	.292	.251
Shaw, Travis	L-R	6-4	225	4-16-90	.249	.232	.258	77	289	29	72	12	2	5	30	26	4	1	2	54	0	1	.356	.318
Spring, Matt	R-R	6-2	225	11-7-84	.191	.125	.212	60	199	17	38	10	0	6	18	22	0	0	1	71	0	0	.332	.270
Swihart, Blake	B-R	6-1	205	4-3-92	.311	.233	.364	20	74	7	23	3	0	0	11	6	0	0	0	14	1	1	.351	.363
Tavarez, Aneury	L-R	5-9	175	4-14-92	.389	.200	.462	6	18	6	7	2	0	1	5	3	2	0	0	4	2	0	.667	.522
Victorino, Shane	B-R	5-9	190	11-30-80	.308	.330	.286	4	13	1	4	1	0	0	0	0	0	0	0	2	0	0	.385	.308
Weeks, Jemile	B-R	5-9	170	1-26-87	.204	.195	.209	70	235	25	48	11	2	1	6	29	2	0	0	53	7	0	.281	.297

Pitching	B-T	HT	WT	DOB	W	L	ERA	G	GS	CG	SV	IP	H	R	ER	HR	BB	SO	AVG	vLH	vRH	K/9	BB/9
Aro, Jonathan	R-R	6-0	175	10-10-90	0	1	3.14	26	0	0	2	52	43	18	18	2	10	53	.225	.247	.212	9.23	1.74
Barnes, Matt	R-R	6-4	210	6-17-90	1	1	4.06	17	5	0	0	38	36	17	17	3	22	41	.252	.258	.247	9.80	5.26
Belisario, Ronald	R-R	6-3	240	12-31-82	0	1	0.00	5	0	0	0	6	4	0	0	0	2		.167	.000	.211	2.84	4.26
2-team total (27 Durham)					0	3	2.70	32	0	0	17	37	32	13	11	2	12	20	—	—	—	4.91	2.95
Celestino, Miguel	R-R	6-6	215	10-10-89	0	4	3.67	17	1	0	0	34	36	17	14	3	16	26	.271	.224	.307	6.82	4.19
2-team total (9 Louisville)					0	5	2.96	26	1	0	1	49	47	19	16	4	21	35	—	—	—	6.47	3.88
Cook, Ryan	R-R	6-2	215	6-30-87	0	0	0.00	7	0	0	1	9	2	0	0	0	2	10	.067	.000	.118	9.64	1.93
Cornely, John	R-R	6-1	205	5-17-89	0	1	6.23	4	0	0	1	4	8	3	3	1	3	4	.400	.556	.273	8.31	6.23
2-team total (12 Gwinnett)					2	3	4.76	16	0	0	2	23	13	13	12	3	10	28	—	—	—	11.12	3.97
Couch, Keith	R-R	6-2	210	11-5-89	4	10	6.14	26	21	0	0	125	152	90	85	11	50	62	.310	.339	.284	4.48	3.61
Cuevas, William	R-R	6-0	160	10-14-90	3	2	2.63	7	7	0	0	41	29	12	12	3	14	37	.195	.208	.181	8.12	3.07
Diaz, Dayan	R-R	5-10	190	2-10-89	2	1	1.89	28	0	0	4	57	47	16	12	3	28	49	.221	.235	.212	7.74	4.42
Escobar, Edwin	L-L	6-2	225	4-22-92	3	3	5.07	19	6	0	0	50	52	29	28	8	25	24	.274	.323	.250	4.35	4.53

Pitching

Pitching	B-T	HT	WT	DOB	W	L	ERA	G	GS	CG	SV	IP	H	R	ER	HR	BB	SO	AVG	vLH	vRH	K/9	BB/9
Eveland, Dana	L-L	6-1	235	10-29-83	2	0	1.54	16	0	0	2	23	17	4	4	0	3	20	.205	.267	.170	7.71	1.16
3-team total (1 Gwinnett, 16 Norfolk)					4	0	1.95	33	3	0	2	55	42	13	12	0	14	45	—	—	—	7.32	2.28
Haviland, Shawn	R-R	6-2	200	11-10-85	1	5	4.17	6	6	0	0	37	41	18	17	1	9	23	.289	.300	.278	5.65	2.21
2-team total (19 Charlotte)					5	10	4.18	25	19	0	0	114	124	63	53	11	28	82	—	—	—	6.47	2.21
Hembree, Heath	R-R	6-4	210	1-13-89	0	5	2.27	29	0	0	8	32	23	10	8	1	10	32	.207	.208	.206	9.09	2.84
Hill, Rich	L-L	6-5	220	3-11-80	3	2	2.78	5	5	0	0	32	27	11	10	3	9	29	.231	.286	.219	8.07	2.51
2-team total (25 Syracuse)					5	4	2.83	30	5	0	0	54	39	20	17	4	30	61	—	—	—	10.17	5.00
Hinojosa, Dalier	R-R	6-1	230	2-10-86	3	1	3.21	19	0	0	0	42	39	21	15	2	17	39	.248	.242	.253	8.36	3.64
2-team total (10 Lehigh Valley)					3	2	3.76	29	0	0	0	55	53	29	23	3	22	52	—	—	—	8.51	3.60
Johnson, Brian	L-L	6-4	235	12-7-90	9	6	2.53	18	18	1	0	96	74	34	27	6	32	90	.211	.173	.221	8.44	3.00
Kelly, Joe	R-R	6-1	190	6-9-88	1	1	2.84	4	4	0	0	19	14	7	6	1	6	18	.206	.154	.238	8.53	2.84
Kraus, Kyle	R-R	5-11	185	1-19-90	0	0	0.00	1	0	0	0	3	3	0	0	0	0	2	.333	.250	.400	6.75	0.00
Layne, Tommy	L-L	6-2	190	11-2-84	0	0	3.52	7	0	0	3	8	8	3	3	0	2	9	.267	.417	.167	10.57	2.35
Light, Pat	R-R	6-5	195	3-29-91	2	4	5.18	26	0	0	2	33	31	19	19	2	26	35	.248	.300	.213	9.55	7.09
Marban, Jorge	R-R	6-1	215	12-5-88	3	0	0.69	6	0	0	0	13	6	1	1	0	4	13	.143	.222	.083	9.00	2.77
Masterson, Justin	R-R	6-6	260	3-22-85	0	2	3.29	3	3	0	0	14	8	6	5	0	7	12	.182	.278	.115	7.90	4.61
McCarthy, Mike	R-R	6-3	185	11-18-87	0	1	9.00	1	1	0	0	6	8	6	6	2	3	3	.348	.333	.353	4.50	4.50
Owens, Henry	L-L	6-6	220	7-21-92	3	8	3.16	21	21	0	0	122	84	47	43	7	56	103	.193	.204	.190	7.58	4.12
Porcello, Rick	R-R	6-5	200	12-27-88	0	0	4.76	1	1	0	0	6	3	3	3	1	0	6	.158	.167	.154	9.53	0.00
Ramirez, Noe	R-R	6-3	205	12-22-89	4	1	2.32	30	1	0	3	43	33	13	11	1	18	38	.217	.250	.188	8.02	3.80
Rodriguez, Eduardo	L-L	6-2	210	4-7-93	4	3	2.98	8	8	1	0	48	46	22	16	2	7	44	.256	.163	.285	8.19	1.30
Ross, Robbie	L-L	5-11	215	6-24-89	0	0	3.86	4	0	0	0	7	5	3	3	0	4	6	.208	.182	.231	7.71	5.14
Scott, Robby	B-L	6-3	220	8-29-89	1	1	7.67	13	1	0	1	32	47	31	27	5	9	27	.341	.250	.378	7.67	2.56
Spruill, Zeke	B-R	6-5	200	9-11-89	5	10	3.94	35	14	0	2	114	132	58	50	8	34	67	.293	.293	.294	5.27	2.68
Todd, Jess	R-R	5-11	210	4-20-86	3	5	5.07	22	13	0	0	82	93	50	46	6	30	45	.290	.355	.239	4.96	3.31
Wright, Steven	R-R	6-1	215	8-30-84	2	5	3.81	8	8	1	0	52	55	31	22	2	15	42	.274	.270	.277	7.27	2.60
Younginer, Madison	R-R	6-4	195	11-3-90	0	0	2.45	2	0	0	0	4	4	1	1	0	0	2	.308	.167	.429	4.91	0.00

Fielding

Catcher	PCT	G	PO	A	E	DP	PB
Hanigan	1.000	2	9	0	0	0	0
Leon	.994	21	153	14	1	2	1
Martinez	.992	18	120	6	1	1	0
Quintero	.990	67	457	51	5	5	8
Spring	.990	29	183	10	2	3	8
Swihart	.992	16	119	11	1	0	5

First Base	PCT	G	PO	A	E	DP
Bianchi	1.000	7	47	5	0	4
Cecchini	.994	23	161	6	1	19
Craig	.993	46	395	29	3	31
Montz	.995	21	177	20	1	13
Nava	1.000	3	16	1	0	2
Shaw	.989	31	266	16	3	36
Spring	.971	22	154	12	5	20

Second Base	PCT	G	PO	A	E	DP
Bianchi	1.000	21	37	51	0	12
Coyle	.964	28	49	85	5	21
Hernandez	.947	15	34	38	4	9
Marrero	.929	8	8	18	2	4

	PCT	G	PO	A	E	DP
Miller	.979	44	74	113	4	27
Roof	1.000	4	2	15	0	3
Weeks	.966	32	62	82	5	20

Third Base	PCT	G	PO	A	E	DP
Bianchi	1.000	2	1	6	0	0
Cecchini	.917	19	8	36	4	3
Coyle	.913	10	7	14	2	0
Gragnani	.800	2	2	2	1	1
Hernandez	.895	5	6	11	2	1
Jimenez	.959	13	8	39	2	8
Marrero	1.000	3	4	7	0	1
Miller	1.000	8	6	20	0	0
Rivero	.972	25	23	46	2	6
Roof	1.000	15	7	33	0	3
Shaw	.968	43	30	92	4	8
Weeks	1.000	4	4	6	0	2

Shortstop	PCT	G	PO	A	E	DP
Bianchi	.923	6	9	15	2	3
Hernandez	.975	22	33	46	2	13
Marrero	.963	90	154	261	16	59

	PCT	G	PO	A	E	DP
Miller	1.000	14	31	34	0	6
Weeks	.941	16	16	48	4	9

Outfield	PCT	G	PO	A	E	DP
Berry	.982	102	205	9	4	2
Bianchi	.923	6	10	2	1	1
Bradley	.982	69	154	6	3	1
Brentz	.978	43	78	11	2	0
Castillo	.985	32	64	2	1	1
Cecchini	.983	65	112	1	2	0
Coyle	1.000	4	7	0	0	0
Craig	1.000	23	46	1	0	0
Marrero	1.000	21	38	0	0	0
Miller	1.000	5	11	0	0	0
Montz	1.000	3	6	0	0	0
Nava	.889	6	7	1	1	0
Peguero	.966	15	27	1	1	0
Roof	1.000	30	81	4	0	0
Shaw	1.000	3	4	2	0	0
Tavarez	1.000	6	13	1	0	1
Victorino	1.000	3	6	0	0	0
Weeks	.977	16	41	1	1	0

PORTLAND SEA DOGS DOUBLE-A

EASTERN LEAGUE

Batting	B-T	HT	WT	DOB	AVG	vLH	vRH	G	AB	R	H	2B	3B	HR	RBI	BB	HBP	SH	SF	SO	SB	CS	SLG	OBP
Allday, Forrestt	R-R	5-11	190	4-24-91	.267	.750	.091	5	15	3	4	0	0	0	3	5	0	1	0	3	0	0	.267	.450
Asuaje, Carlos	R-R	5-9	160	11-2-91	.251	.216	.261	131	495	60	124	23	7	8	61	56	7	10	2	88	9	6	.374	.334
Bethea, Danny	R-R	6-1	210	1-31-90	.318	.400	.276	12	44	7	14	5	0	0	5	0	0	0	0	14	0	0	.432	.318
Betts, Mookie	R-R	5-9	180	10-7-92	.500	.333	1.000	1	4	1	2	0	0	1	0	0	0	0	0	0	0	0	1.250	.500
Blanke, Mike	R-R	6-4	225	10-17-88	.167	.200	.000	2	6	2	1	0	0	0	1	3	0	0	0	0	0	0	.167	.444
Brenly, Mike	R-R	6-3	220	10-14-86	.179	.250	.150	28	28	3	5	0	0	0	3	0	0	0	0	11	1	0	.179	.179
Chester, David	R-R	6-5	230	3-31-89	.181	.127	.201	67	232	21	42	7	0	7	21	17	5	0	3	57	1	1	.302	.249
De La Cruz, Keury	L-L	5-11	170	11-28-91	.240	.255	.234	112	405	39	97	22	3	9	47	23	2	1	2	95	3	6	.375	.282
Gragnani, Reed	B-R	5-11	180	9-5-90	.234	.243	.230	40	137	15	32	3	0	0	7	23	1	4	1	28	1	0	.255	.346
Hanigan, Ryan	R-R	6-0	215	8-16-80	.250	.000	.333	3	8	0	2	1	0	0	3	0	0	0	0	1	0	0	.375	.455
Heller, Kevin	R-R	5-10	195	9-12-89	.132	.000	.161	13	38	4	5	2	0	0	5	4	3	2	1	13	0	0	.184	.261
Hernandez, Marco	L-R	6-0	170	9-6-92	.326	.318	.330	68	282	30	92	21	4	5	31	9	1	2	0	49	4	2	.482	.349
Lawley, Dustin	R-L	6-1	205	4-11-89	.196	.188	.197	26	92	8	18	3	0	2	12	5	2	0	1	24	0	1	.293	.250
2-team total (67 Binghamton)					.208	—	—	93	322	39	67	21	0	8	38	16	5	0	3	82	8	4	.348	.254
Lin, Tzu-Wei	L-R	5-9	155	2-15-94	.202	.282	.179	46	173	21	35	5	3	0	14	16	0	4	1	27	8	3	.266	.268
Margot, Manuel	R-R	5-11	170	9-28-94	.271	.381	.236	64	258	38	70	21	4	3	33	21	1	0	2	36	19	8	.419	.326
Martinez, Luis	R-R	6-0	210	4-3-85	.219	.177	.236	25	219	10	48	13	0	1	23	22	3	1	1	44	1	2	.292	.298
Miller, Mike	R-R	5-9	170	9-28-87	.273	.280	.270	40	165	26	45	9	2	1	12	11	2	2	3	21	6	2	.370	.320
Ramos, Henry	B-R	6-2	190	4-15-92	.244	.278	.232	37	131	8	32	11	2	0	8	14	0	2	0	26	0	0	.359	.317

Batting

Batting	B-T	HT	WT	DOB	AVG	vLH	vRH	G	AB	R	H	2B	3B	HR	RBI	BB	HBP	SH	SF	SO	SB	CS	SLG	OBP
Roberson, Tim	R-R	5-10	190	7-19-89	.300	.458	.254	57	217	27	65	12	1	4	30	13	1	0	0	46	1	1	.419	.342
Romanski, Jake	R-R	5-11	185	12-22-90	.268	.375	.225	16	56	4	15	1	0	1	6	3	0	0	0	6	0	0	.339	.305
Roof, Jonathan	R-R	6-1	175	1-23-89	.234	.243	.231	47	141	24	33	4	2	1	9	20	2	3	2	19	4	2	.312	.333
Sappelt, Dave	R-R	5-9	195	1-2-87	.207	.000	.222	8	29	5	6	1	0	2	2	3	0	0	0	7	0	0	.448	.281
Sturgeon, Cole	L-L	6-0	180	9-17-91	.203	.135	.229	40	133	13	27	8	1	0	7	5	0	5	1	30	3	3	.278	.230
Suarez, Alixon	R-R	6-1	180	7-25-94	.100	—	.100	3	10	1	1	1	0	0	0	0	0	0	0	2	0	0	.200	.100
Swihart, Blake	B-R	6-1	205	4-3-92	.429	1.000	.333	2	7	1	3	1	0	0	0	0	0	0	0	2	0	0	.571	.429
Tavarez, Aneury	L-R	5-9	175	4-14-92	.226	.191	.235	67	234	25	53	13	1	5	14	8	3	3	0	64	4	5	.355	.261
Tejeda, Oscar	R-R	6-1	170	12-26-89	.247	.292	.233	103	392	45	97	20	2	4	38	26	1	0	2	77	4	5	.339	.295
Tekotte, Blake	L-R	5-11	180	5-24-87	.275	.300	.264	49	160	17	44	9	3	3	20	18	5	1	1	29	4	3	.425	.364
Travis, Sam	R-R	6-0	195	8-27-93	.300	.370	.284	65	243	35	73	17	2	4	38	33	2	0	3	34	9	6	.436	.384
Victorino, Shane	B-R	5-9	190	11-30-80	.154	.100	.333	4	13	1	2	1	0	0	1	0	1	0	0	2	0	0	.231	.214
Vinicio, Jose	B-R	5-11	150	7-10-93	.273	.000	.333	3	11	1	3	0	0	0	0	0	0	0	0	1	0	0	.273	.273
Weems, Jordan	L-R	6-3	175	11-7-92	.224	.100	.246	17	67	8	15	5	1	1	8	4	0	0	0	16	1	0	.373	.268
Witte, Jantzen	R-R	6-2	195	1-4-90	.283	.347	.264	85	314	36	89	25	2	4	48	36	6	0	5	47	3	3	.414	.363

Pitching

Pitching	B-T	HT	WT	DOB	W	L	ERA	G	GS	CG	SV	IP	H	R	ER	HR	BB	SO	AVG	vLH	vRH	K/9	BB/9
Aro, Jonathan	R-R	6-0	175	10-10-90	3	2	2.82	8	0	0	0	22	15	12	7	0	8	19	.181	.192	.175	7.66	3.22
Augliera, Mike	R-R	6-0	200	6-8-90	3	15	5.21	28	17	0	0	114	150	79	66	10	34	77	.318	.330	.310	6.08	2.68
Celestino, Miguel	R-R	6-6	215	10-10-89	0	2	7.15	7	0	0	0	11	15	9	9	3	6	8	.326	.379	.235	6.35	4.76
Cornely, John	R-R	6-1	205	5-17-89	0	2	4.38	29	0	0	2	39	25	20	19	3	29	38	.185	.219	.155	8.77	6.69
Cuevas, William	R-R	6-0	160	10-14-90	8	5	3.40	19	19	0	0	95	84	43	36	4	41	91	.233	.279	.201	8.59	3.87
Diaz, Dayan	R-R	5-10	190	2-10-89	0	0	1.15	9	0	0	2	16	7	2	2	0	2	17	.130	.143	.121	9.77	1.15
Diaz, Luis	R-R	6-3	210	4-9-92	2	10	5.47	27	27	0	0	137	156	94	83	11	59	86	.286	.288	.284	5.66	3.89
Gunkel, Joe	R-R	6-5	225	12-30-91	2	1	3.93	4	3	0	0	18	26	8	8	1	8	22	.347	.381	.333	10.80	3.93
2-team total (17 Bowie)					10	5	2.79	21	20	0	0	123	111	43	38	8	23	91	—	—	—	6.68	1.69
Haley, Justin	R-R	6-5	230	6-16-91	5	16	5.15	27	27	0	0	124	142	80	71	7	50	95	.289	.301	.279	6.90	3.63
Jerez, Williams	L-L	6-4	190	5-16-92	1	2	3.65	22	0	0	1	37	34	15	15	2	17	31	.245	.222	.259	7.54	4.14
Kaminska, Kyle	L-R	6-4	180	10-5-88	1	0	2.03	4	0	0	1	8	3	3	3	2	2	8	.167	.107	.250	5.40	1.35
Kraus, Kyle	R-R	5-11	185	1-19-90	0	1	4.59	15	2	0	1	49	51	28	25	7	10	25	.266	.256	.272	4.59	1.84
Light, Pat	R-R	6-5	195	3-29-91	1	1	2.43	21	0	0	3	30	18	11	8	3	11	32	.168	.189	.157	9.71	3.34
Marban, Jorge	R-R	6-1	215	12-5-88	2	1	1.36	24	0	0	5	33	25	9	5	0	22	26	.207	.151	.250	7.09	6.00
Martin, Kyle	R-R	6-7	220	1-18-91	2	1	4.50	27	0	0	5	42	43	22	21	3	16	48	.264	.210	.317	10.29	3.43
Masterson, Justin	R-R	6-6	260	3-22-85	0	0	3.86	1	1	0	0	5	8	2	2	0	1	2	.381	.167	.467	3.86	1.93
McCarthy, Mike	R-R	6-3	185	11-18-87	6	8	4.59	29	18	0	0	116	119	64	59	10	41	58	.267	.263	.270	4.51	3.19
Mercedes, Simon	R-R	6-4	200	2-17-92	3	3	4.88	37	0	0	0	79	85	54	43	8	38	63	.276	.262	.287	7.15	4.31
Quevedo, Heri	R-R	6-2	211	6-7-90	0	5	5.40	19	8	0	1	57	65	38	34	6	36	45	.290	.243	.333	7.15	5.72
Rosenbaum, Danny	R-L	6-2	210	10-10-87	0	7	6.02	11	11	0	0	40	49	37	27	5	28	26	.302	.262	.330	5.80	6.25
Scott, Robby	B-L	6-3	220	8-29-89	1	1	2.06	25	2	0	0	44	32	14	10	3	13	41	.198	.111	.241	8.45	2.68
Wilkerson, Aaron	R-R	6-3	190	5-24-89	4	1	2.66	7	7	0	0	41	28	13	12	0	13	35	.192	.229	.143	7.75	2.88
Younginer, Madison	R-R	6-4	195	11-3-90	8	4	3.05	39	0	0	2	74	62	30	25	4	25	55	.225	.214	.233	6.72	3.05

Fielding

Catcher	PCT	G	PO	A	E	DP	PB
Bethea	1.000	12	67	3	0	0	1
Blanke	.941	2	16	0	1	0	1
Brenly	1.000	6	55	6	0	0	0
Hanigan	1.000	2	17	0	0	0	1
Martinez	.982	64	441	43	9	2	5
Roberson	.985	22	128	7	2	0	3
Romanski	.991	16	95	19	1	1	3
Suarez	1.000	3	20	2	0	0	0
Swihart	1.000	1	5	0	0	0	0
Weems	.958	16	108	5	5	2	1

First Base	PCT	G	PO	A	E	DP
Brenly	.950	2	17	2	1	2
Chester	.995	23	187	10	1	14
Tejeda	1.000	4	29	1	0	5
Travis	.997	63	550	39	2	38
Witte	.993	51	378	26	3	39

Second Base	PCT	G	PO	A	E	DP
Asuaje	.973	106	190	244	12	47
Gragnani	.980	19	37	61	2	18
Miller	.979	7	15	31	1	8
Roof	1.000	3	2	6	0	1
Tejeda	.966	6	10	18	1	4
Vinicio	.941	3	11	5	1	2

Third Base	PCT	G	PO	A	E	DP
Asuaje	.864	9	8	11	3	2
Gragnani	.947	15	14	22	2	0
Lawley	.903	24	12	44	6	0
Miller	.900	12	15	21	4	1
Roof	.923	5	3	9	1	3
Tejeda	.913	52	38	77	11	8
Witte	.962	31	22	53	3	6

Shortstop	PCT	G	PO	A	E	DP
Hernandez	.935	67	89	184	19	33
Lin	.953	46	77	144	11	29

Miller	.962	22	23	52	3	4
Tejeda	.974	8	14	24	1	5

Outfield	PCT	G	PO	A	E	DP
Allday	.909	5	10	0	1	0
Asuaje	1.000	3	4	0	0	0
Betts	1.000	1	4	0	0	0
De La Cruz	.977	87	166	5	4	0
Gragnani	1.000	3	6	0	0	0
Heller	1.000	13	22	1	0	0
Margot	.989	64	176	2	2	0
Ramos	.976	37	78	2	2	0
Roof	.974	36	73	2	2	0
Sappelt	.920	8	22	1	2	1
Sturgeon	.987	39	76	2	1	0
Tavarez	.981	65	146	7	3	1
Tejeda	.977	26	43	0	1	0
Tekotte	1.000	49	121	0	0	0
Victorino	1.000	3	6	0	0	0

SALEM RED SOX
CAROLINA LEAGUE

HIGH CLASS A

Batting	B-T	HT	WT	DOB	AVG	vLH	vRH	G	AB	R	H	2B	3B	HR	RBI	BB	HBP	SH	SF	SO	SB	CS	SLG	OBP
Allday, Forrestt	R-R	5-11	190	4-24-91	.249	.231	.255	79	249	36	62	7	0	2	20	48	8	8	3	52	7	9	.301	.383
Bethea, Danny	R-R	6-1	210	1-31-90	.182	.167	.188	12	44	3	8	3	0	0	2	2	0	1	0	12	0	1	.250	.217
Betts, Jordan	R-R	6-3	220	10-6-91	.212	.221	.208	113	387	40	82	21	1	4	33	33	4	0	3	121	5	1	.302	.279
Cerse, Yoilan	R-R	5-9	175	3-29-87	.243	.242	.244	64	226	26	55	12	3	3	26	25	3	3	1	31	5	5	.363	.325
Coste, Carlos	R-R	6-2	186	5-11-93	.041	.071	.029	16	49	2	2	0	0	0	4	2	0	0	27	0	0	.041	.145
Dubon, Mauricio	R-R	6-0	160	7-19-94	.274	.298	.267	62	237	27	65	9	0	1	18	23	3	4	2	38	12	3	.325	.343
Guzman, Franklin	R-R	5-11	185	2-4-92	.232	.184	.248	49	151	16	35	5	0	8	21	11	0	1	3	44	6	3	.424	.279
Heller, Kevin	R-R	5-10	195	9-12-89	.297	.321	.288	93	313	40	93	18	2	7	52	49	13	0	4	86	13	5	.435	.409

Batting	B-T	HT	WT	DOB	AVG	vLH	vRH	G	AB	R	H	2B	3B	HR	RBI	BB	HBP	SH	SF	SO	SB	CS	SLG	OBP
Kapstein, Zach	R-R	6-2	195	5-28-92	.250	.265	.241	26	88	9	22	5	0	1	13	9	0	0	1	27	3	0	.341	.316
Lawley, Dustin	R-R	6-1	205	4-11-89	.276	.167	.304	8	29	0	8	4	0	0	2	1	0	0	0	8	0	1	.414	.300
Lin, Tzu-Wei	L-R	5-9	155	2-15-94	.281	.257	.289	73	281	37	79	12	3	2	34	22	0	2	2	32	15	3	.367	.331
Lopez, Deiner	B-R	6-0	165	5-30-94	.270	.333	.240	41	141	18	38	8	0	0	12	6	3	0	1	35	4	5	.326	.311
Lorenzana, Hector	R-R	5-11	190	9-29-91	.214	.000	.250	6	14	0	3	1	0	0	3	3	0	0	1	2	0	0	.286	.333
Margot, Manuel	R-R	5-11	170	9-28-94	.282	.391	.244	46	181	35	51	6	5	3	17	11	1	2	3	15	20	5	.420	.321
Martinez, Mario	R-R	6-3	220	11-13-89	.271	.264	.274	93	339	39	92	23	0	6	48	23	3	0	1	80	1	0	.392	.322
Meyers, Mike	R-R	6-1	175	12-28-93	.164	.250	.128	17	67	7	11	2	0	1	3	6	0	0	0	22	2	0	.239	.233
Miller, Derek	R-R	6-2	180	7-18-92	.186	.133	.214	14	43	10	8	1	0	0	2	10	1	0	0	12	2	0	.209	.352
Procyshen, Jordan	L-R	5-10	185	3-11-93	.209	.235	.200	38	129	9	27	5	0	0	11	18	1	2	1	22	1	2	.248	.309
Rijo, Wendell	R-R	5-11	170	9-4-95	.260	.315	.240	108	404	47	105	27	2	6	47	34	6	7	4	94	15	7	.381	.324
Romanski, Jake	R-R	6-0	190	12-22-90	.262	.244	.268	47	164	19	43	9	0	0	21	16	3	1	2	21	4	3	.317	.335
Sturgeon, Cole	L-L	6-0	180	9-17-91	.265	.321	.243	76	287	34	76	14	2	3	26	18	1	4	1	40	10	3	.359	.309
Tavarez, Aneury	L-R	5-9	175	4-14-92	.280	.286	.279	39	132	7	37	8	4	2	18	17	2	1	1	28	8	1	.447	.368
Tejeda, Oscar	R-R	6-1	170	12-26-89	.273	.167	.313	6	22	3	6	3	0	0	5	1	0	0	0	6	0	1	.409	.304
Travis, Sam	R-R	6-0	195	8-27-93	.313	.294	.320	66	246	35	77	15	4	5	40	26	2	0	4	43	10	6	.467	.378
Vinicio, Jose	B-R	5-11	150	7-10-93	.294	.276	.301	57	201	29	59	11	3	0	13	6	2	3	0	24	7	6	.378	.321
Watkins, J.T.	R-R	6-0	190	8-30-89	.000	.000	.000	2	7	0	0	0	0	0	0	0	0	0	0	2	0	0	.000	.000
Weems, Jordan	L-R	6-3	175	11-7-92	.257	.154	.291	31	105	12	27	6	1	0	7	12	0	0	0	26	2	1	.343	.333

Pitching	B-T	HT	WT	DOB	W	L	ERA	G	GS	CG	SV	IP	H	R	ER	HR	BB	SO	AVG	vLH	vRH	K/9	BB/9
Adams, Mike	L-L	6-3	215	10-4-90	1	3	3.47	35	0	0	6	60	66	29	23	5	18	44	.280	.227	.311	6.64	2.72
Ball, Trey	L-L	6-6	185	6-27-94	9	13	4.73	25	25	0	0	129	129	78	68	16	60	77	.263	.272	.259	5.36	4.18
Bautista, Denny	R-R	6-5	190	8-23-80	3	0	4.88	4	4	0	0	24	28	14	13	3	5	10	.292	.297	.288	3.75	1.88
Buttrey, Ty	R-R	6-6	235	3-31-93	8	10	4.20	21	21	0	0	116	117	62	54	5	45	81	.268	.265	.272	6.30	3.50
Dahlstrand, Jacob	R-R	6-5	205	3-26-92	3	0	1.96	4	4	0	0	23	14	5	5	0	10	14	.171	.200	.135	5.48	2.35
Grover, Taylor	R-R	6-3	195	4-22-91	2	2	3.62	34	1	0	4	75	54	36	30	6	35	61	.205	.182	.224	7.35	4.22
Gunkel, Joe	R-R	6-5	225	12-30-91	1	1	2.05	8	2	0	2	22	16	6	5	2	4	22	.203	.227	.171	9.00	1.64
Gunn, Michael	L-L	6-0	205	1-25-93	0	0	0.00	1	0	0	0	1	1	0	0	0	2	0	.250	.000	.500	0.00	18.00
Jerez, Williams	L-L	6-4	190	5-16-92	1	0	0.73	5	0	0	0	12	11	2	1	0	4	12	.234	.182	.250	8.76	2.92
Kaminska, Kyle	L-R	6-4	180	10-5-88	1	2	3.12	12	1	0	3	35	39	12	12	2	3	24	.293	.281	.303	6.23	0.78
Kraus, Kyle	R-R	5-11	185	1-19-90	2	2	1.34	14	1	0	2	47	38	14	7	1	11	33	.218	.208	.225	6.32	2.11
Maddox, Austin	R-R	6-2	220	5-13-91	1	4	3.71	20	0	0	10	27	24	13	11	2	5	22	.238	.222	.255	7.43	1.69
Marban, Jorge	R-R	6-1	215	12-5-88	2	1	1.69	8	0	0	1	16	14	7	3	1	7	13	.226	.194	.269	7.31	3.94
McAvoy, Kevin	R-R	6-4	210	7-21-93	11	9	3.89	26	26	0	0	141	136	72	61	5	71	82	.261	.272	.250	5.23	4.53
McEachern, Kuehl	R-R	6-4	195	5-7-93	0	0	5.87	4	0	0	0	8	12	5	5	1	2	6	.364	.533	.222	7.04	2.35
McGrath, Daniel	R-L	6-3	205	7-7-94	4	6	3.84	17	17	0	0	84	72	43	36	6	37	71	.227	.171	.247	7.58	3.95
Shepherd, Chandler	R-R	6-3	185	8-25-92	0	2	3.61	28	0	0	6	52	48	23	21	3	7	46	.241	.226	.252	7.91	1.20
Show, Brandon	R-R	6-2	180	10-31-92	1	1	2.83	12	0	0	2	35	33	14	11	1	7	13	.252	.293	.233	3.34	1.80
Stankiewicz, Teddy	R-R	6-4	200	11-25-93	5	11	4.01	25	25	1	0	141	149	74	63	11	32	77	.280	.296	.267	4.90	2.04
Taveras, German	R-R	6-2	180	2-15-93	4	4	5.04	30	0	0	2	61	53	41	34	3	35	48	.237	.248	.227	7.12	5.19
Wilkerson, Aaron	R-R	6-3	190	5-24-89	7	2	2.96	17	12	0	0	79	62	28	26	0	21	85	.218	.258	.186	9.68	2.39
Ysla, Luis	L-L	6-1	185	4-27-92	0	0	0.00	2	0	0	0	5	0	0	0	0	2	6	.000	.000	.000	10.80	3.60

Fielding

Catcher	PCT	G	PO	A	E	DP	PB
Bethea	.960	12	65	7	3	0	1
Coste	.960	16	109	10	5	0	2
Procyshen	.992	37	208	37	2	2	4
Romanski	.997	45	275	32	1	4	1
Watkins	1.000	2	12	2	0	0	1
Weems	.985	29	173	20	3	0	2

First Base	PCT	G	PO	A	E	DP
Betts	.979	37	317	17	7	34
Martinez	.996	60	481	34	2	46
Travis	.993	46	397	26	3	41

Second Base	PCT	G	PO	A	E	DP
Cerse	1.000	7	16	15	0	7
Dubon	1.000	5	8	14	0	6
Lin	1.000	3	3	11	0	3
Lopez	1.000	1	1	3	0	2

	PCT	G	PO	A	E	DP
Lorenzana	1.000	5	6	8	0	0
Rijo	.977	97	180	296	11	63
Vinicio	.991	24	43	72	1	14

Third Base	PCT	G	PO	A	E	DP
Betts	.927	77	31	135	13	14
Cerse	.750	4	2	4	2	0
Dubon	1.000	3	1	3	0	0
Lawley	.850	7	3	14	3	0
Lopez	.976	26	24	56	2	6
Martinez	.833	7	8	7	3	1
Tejeda	1.000	1	1	1	0	0
Vinicio	.955	18	11	31	2	4

Shortstop	PCT	G	PO	A	E	DP
Dubon	.975	52	90	147	6	37
Lin	.960	69	107	202	13	47
Lopez	1.000	2	3	7	0	2

	PCT	G	PO	A	E	DP
Lorenzana	1.000	1	0	1	0	0
Rijo	1.000	4	9	13	0	3
Vinicio	.964	12	18	35	2	6

Outfield	PCT	G	PO	A	E	DP
Allday	.981	74	205	6	4	1
Cerse	.980	49	94	3	2	0
Guzman	.973	47	70	3	2	0
Heller	1.000	70	133	9	0	2
Kapstein	1.000	9	14	0	0	0
Lopez	1.000	11	20	0	0	0
Margot	.977	42	125	1	3	1
Meyers	.893	14	24	1	3	0
Miller	1.000	13	27	0	0	0
Sturgeon	.968	65	141	8	5	2
Tavarez	1.000	37	65	3	0	0

GREENVILLE DRIVE   LOW CLASS A

SOUTH ATLANTIC LEAGUE

Batting	B-T	HT	WT	DOB	AVG	vLH	vRH	G	AB	R	H	2B	3B	HR	RBI	BB	HBP	SH	SF	SO	SB	CS	SLG	OBP
Benintendi, Andrew	L-L	5-10	170	7-6-94	.351	.214	.383	19	74	17	26	5	0	4	16	10	1	0	1	9	3	2	.581	.430
Bethea, Danny	R-R	6-1	210	1-31-90	.250	.417	.217	22	72	8	18	4	0	0	10	7	2	0	2	19	0	0	.306	.325
Chavis, Michael	R-R	5-10	190	8-11-95	.223	.209	.229	109	435	56	97	29	1	16	58	29	4	2	1	144	8	5	.405	.277
Devers, Rafael	L-R	6-0	195	10-24-96	.288	.252	.302	115	469	71	135	38	1	11	70	24	8	1	6	84	3	2	.443	.329
Downs, Jerry	L-L	6-2	215	12-22-93	.250	.000	.333	1	4	0	1	0	0	0	0	0	0	0	0	2	0	0	.250	.250
Dubon, Mauricio	R-R	6-0	160	7-19-94	.301	.310	.295	58	236	43	71	12	3	4	29	18	2	4	1	34	18	4	.428	.354
Guerra, Javier	L-R	5-11	155	9-25-95	.279	.244	.292	116	434	64	121	23	3	15	68	30	4	6	3	112	7	9	.449	.329
Hudson, Bryan	L-R	6-1	185	2-10-95	.292	.326	.279	49	168	29	49	7	0	0	11	29	1	1	0	30	18	5	.333	.399

Batting	B-T	HT	WT	DOB	AVG	vLH	vRH	G	AB	R	H	2B	3B	HR	RBI	BB	HBP	SH	SF	SO	SB	CS	SLG	OBP
Longhi, Nick	R-L	6-2	205	8-16-95	.281	.262	.289	115	442	52	124	27	3	7	62	34	6	3	3	88	2	0	.403	.338
Lopez, Deiner	B-R	6-0	165	5-30-94	.282	.273	.288	36	124	14	35	2	3	2	11	7	0	1	0	29	5	3	.395	.321
Lorenzana, Hector	R-R	5-11	190	9-29-91	.240	.200	.257	15	50	8	12	2	0	0	5	5	0	0	0	6	1	0	.280	.309
Mars, Danny	B-R	6-0	195	1-22-94	.283	.282	.283	41	166	23	47	6	1	0	16	13	0	1	0	23	13	3	.331	.335
McKeon, Alex	R-R	6-2	215	5-20-93	.250	—	.250	3	8	0	2	0	0	0	1	1	0	0	0	4	0	0	.250	.333
Mesa, Carlos	R-R	6-2	215	2-10-88	.212	.274	.163	53	165	17	35	9	0	7	25	11	4	2	1	63	1	1	.394	.276
Meyers, Mike	R-R	6-1	175	12-28-93	.296	.248	.320	92	345	57	102	18	6	5	40	36	2	1	2	108	12	2	.426	.364
Miller, Derek	R-R	6-2	180	7-18-92	.283	.276	.288	63	240	34	68	11	0	0	34	32	9	2	2	35	10	5	.329	.385
Moncada, Yoan	B-R	6-2	205	5-27-95	.278	.310	.262	81	306	61	85	19	3	8	38	42	10	2	3	83	49	3	.438	.380
Monge, Joseph	R-R	6-0	170	5-18-95	.241	.257	.235	109	373	46	90	23	3	2	37	21	4	10	3	89	22	4	.335	.287
Moore, Ben	R-R	6-1	195	9-22-92	.319	.333	.304	24	94	16	30	8	1	0	9	5	1	1	1	13	3	0	.426	.356
Procyshen, Jordan	L-R	5-10	185	3-11-93	.285	.304	.276	51	179	22	51	8	0	2	28	16	5	1	2	32	3	2	.363	.356
Sopilka, David	R-R	6-0	170	8-30-93	.240	.188	.264	35	104	10	25	7	1	1	15	5	2	0	0	24	0	0	.356	.288
Tellez, Cisco	L-L	5-11	217	6-5-92	.223	.234	.218	76	251	39	56	20	1	3	26	30	2	1	0	67	3	0	.347	.311
Watkins, J.T.	R-R	6-0	190	8-30-89	.214	.194	.220	37	145	12	31	4	1	1	14	4	0	1	0	27	1	1	.276	.235

Pitching	B-T	HT	WT	DOB	W	L	ERA	G	GS	CG	SV	IP	H	R	ER	HR	BB	SO	AVG	vLH	vRH	K/9	BB/9
Alcantara, Mario	R-R	6-2	225	12-27-92	4	2	3.51	35	0	0	3	74	67	34	29	6	38	71	.245	.236	.250	8.60	4.60
Beeks, Jalen	L-L	5-11	195	7-10-93	9	7	4.32	26	26	0	0	146	156	82	70	17	28	100	.272	.244	.283	6.18	1.73
Buttrey, Ty	L-R	6-6	235	3-31-93	1	0	2.45	4	4	0	0	22	17	8	6	2	3	22	.210	.250	.189	9.00	1.23
Callahan, Jamie	R-R	6-2	230	8-24-94	7	6	4.53	31	6	0	3	89	94	52	45	4	33	94	.263	.331	.215	9.47	3.32
Drehoff, Jake	L-L	6-4	195	6-5-92	3	2	2.89	24	7	0	0	72	76	29	23	6	15	65	.272	.234	.287	8.16	1.88
Escobar, Edwin	L-L	6-2	225	4-22-92	0	0	0.00	1	1	0	0	1	0	0	0	0	0	0	.000	—	.000	0.00	0.00
Espinoza, Anderson	R-R	6-0	160	3-9-98	0	1	8.10	1	1	0	0	3	4	3	3	0	2	4	.267	.333	.167	10.80	5.40
Fernandez, Jeffry	R-R	6-1	220	3-25-93	3	9	5.95	25	23	0	0	115	127	86	76	17	46	64	.280	.280	.280	5.01	3.60
Garcia, Edwar	R-R	6-4	175	11-19-93	0	0	2.08	5	0	0	0	9	8	4	2	1	4	4	.258	.455	.150	4.15	4.15
Gunn, Michael	L-L	6-0	205	1-25-93	0	3	6.08	20	0	0	1	40	44	27	27	3	29	40	.280	.296	.272	9.00	6.53
Harris, Ryan	R-R	6-2	195	1-25-93	4	4	2.72	30	0	0	4	50	40	18	15	3	18	38	.222	.197	.239	6.89	3.26
Jerez, Williams	L-L	6-4	190	5-16-92	3	1	2.06	14	0	0	3	39	43	16	9	3	10	43	.279	.265	.286	9.84	2.29
Jimenez, Dedgar	L-L	6-3	240	3-6-96	9	9	4.43	23	23	1	0	126	160	77	62	6	21	66	.313	.291	.322	4.71	1.50
Kaminska, Kyle	L-R	6-4	180	10-5-88	0	0	0.00	2	0	0	1	4	2	0	0	0	0	4	.154	.250	.000	9.00	0.00
Kopech, Michael	R-R	6-3	205	4-30-96	4	5	2.63	16	15	0	0	65	53	25	19	2	27	70	.228	.242	.220	9.69	3.74
McEachern, Kuehl	R-R	6-4	195	5-7-93	7	4	2.52	34	0	0	9	82	80	25	23	1	21	44	.272	.342	.226	4.83	2.30
Nunez, Taylor	R-R	6-4	185	7-28-92	0	0	0.00	1	0	0	0	3	3	2	0	0	0	3	.214	.167	.250	8.10	0.00
Pinales, Carlos	R-R	6-1	180	4-5-92	5	4	4.14	30	0	0	3	74	81	40	34	7	12	52	.284	.282	.286	6.32	1.46
Ramos, Luis	L-L	6-1	180	6-5-95	3	7	7.12	7	7	0	0	30	45	25	24	3	4	20	.341	.286	.367	5.93	1.19
Reilly, Reed	R-R	6-4	220	1-5-92	4	5	4.01	21	14	0	1	101	117	54	45	12	15	58	.290	.257	.310	5.17	1.34
Shepherd, Chandler	R-R	6-3	185	8-25-92	3	0	1.23	7	0	0	1	15	16	5	2	1	3	16	.267	.263	.268	9.82	1.84
Show, Brandon	R-R	6-2	180	10-31-92	1	0	0.00	1	0	0	0	4	2	0	0	0	2	2	.154	.000	.200	4.50	4.50
Taylor, Ben	R-R	6-3	225	11-12-92	0	2	3.40	10	10	0	0	45	43	23	17	2	15	37	.250	.319	.204	7.40	3.00
Wilkerson, Aaron	R-R	6-3	190	5-24-89	0	0	4.76	5	1	0	0	17	17	10	9	2	5	17	.266	.286	.256	9.00	2.65

Fielding

Catcher	PCT	G	PO	A	E	DP	PB
Bethea	.992	19	119	9	1	1	0
McKeon	1.000	3	18	2	0	0	0
Moore	1.000	19	154	23	0	1	2
Procyshen	.970	47	270	51	10	2	2
Sopilka	.991	33	184	34	2	1	7
Watkins	.980	31	172	24	4	0	5

First Base	PCT	G	PO	A	E	DP
Bethea	1.000	1	1	0	0	0
Downs	1.000	1	14	0	0	2
Longhi	.991	71	596	41	6	58
Mesa	1.000	1	10	0	0	2
Tellez	.989	74	615	37	7	54

	PCT	G	PO	A	E	DP
Watkins	.984	7	61	2	1	7

Second Base	PCT	G	PO	A	E	DP
Dubon	.973	38	60	122	5	28
Guerra	1.000	1	3	5	0	1
Lopez	.975	25	50	68	3	14
Lorenzana	.950	10	20	18	2	6
Moncada	.942	71	165	206	23	62

Third Base	PCT	G	PO	A	E	DP
Chavis	.907	68	41	144	19	11
Devers	.949	72	49	137	10	15
Lopez	1.000	1	1	2	0	0

Shortstop	PCT	G	PO	A	E	DP
Chavis	.857	1	3	3	1	1

	PCT	G	PO	A	E	DP
Dubon	.940	18	23	55	5	8
Guerra	.954	112	192	362	27	78
Lopez	1.000	8	13	19	0	3
Lorenzana	.933	4	3	11	1	2

Outfield	PCT	G	PO	A	E	DP
Benintendi	.974	18	37	1	1	0
Hudson	.953	47	80	2	4	0
Longhi	.976	50	78	4	2	0
Mars	.987	39	73	2	1	0
Mesa	.946	30	35	0	2	0
Meyers	.964	87	155	4	6	1
Miller	.973	63	103	7	3	3
Monge	.971	108	257	15	8	3

LOWELL SPINNERS   SHORT-SEASON

NEW YORK-PENN LEAGUE

Batting	B-T	HT	WT	DOB	AVG	vLH	vRH	G	AB	R	H	2B	3B	HR	RBI	BB	HBP	SH	SF	SO	SB	CS	SLG	OBP
Acosta, Victor	R-R	5-11	160	6-2-96	.251	.274	.239	57	211	28	53	16	1	1	25	12	6	1	2	42	9	3	.351	.307
Austin, Jordon	R-R	5-11	195	3-14-95	.266	.267	.265	23	64	5	17	1	1	0	6	5	1	1	0	33	3	1	.313	.329
Baldwin, Roldani	R-R	5-11	180	3-16-96	.286	—	.286	3	7	0	2	1	0	0	0	0	0	0	0	1	0	0	.429	.286
Basabe, Luis Alexander	B-R	6-0	160	8-26-96	.243	.242	.244	56	222	36	54	8	3	7	23	32	1	0	1	67	15	4	.401	.340
Benintendi, Andrew	L-L	5-10	170	7-6-94	.290	.313	.283	35	124	19	36	2	4	7	15	25	1	1	2	15	7	1	.540	.408
Coyle, Sean	R-R	5-8	175	1-17-92	.250	.000	.300	3	12	2	3	1	0	0	1	1	0	0	0	3	1	0	.333	.308
De La Guerra, Chad	L-R	5-11	190	11-24-92	.265	.291	.256	58	223	28	59	14	3	2	29	21	0	0	5	46	4	3	.381	.321
Gunsolus, Mitchell	L-R	6-0	200	1-23-93	.225	.125	.250	49	160	18	36	6	0	1	21	20	2	1	0	46	3	1	.281	.319
Hill, Tyler	R-R	6-0	195	3-4-96	.400	.500	.333	4	15	4	6	1	0	0	0	0	0	0	0	2	2	0	.467	.400
Hudson, Bryan	L-R	6-1	185	2-10-95	.385	.375	.400	6	26	9	10	0	1	0	5	2	0	0	0	6	3	0	.462	.429
Kemp, Trenton	R-R	6-2	195	9-30-95	.069	.091	.056	10	29	3	2	1	0	1	4	1	0	0	0	8	0	0	.207	.100
Lorenzana, Hector	R-R	5-11	190	9-29-91	.184	.100	.214	21	76	8	14	0	0	2	9	4	2	0	0	16	1	0	.263	.244
Lucena, Isaias	B-R	5-11	180	11-15-94	.455	1.000	.333	4	11	0	5	1	0	0	2	1	0	1	0	2	0	0	.545	.500

Batting	B-T	HT	WT	DOB	AVG	vLH	vRH	G	AB	R	H	2B	3B	HR	RBI	BB	HBP	SH	SF	SO	SB	CS	SLG	OBP
Magee, Brandon	L-R	6-0	225	10-22-90	.231	.100	.262	25	52	10	12	2	1	1	8	7	6	0	0	21	5	0	.365	.385
Matheny, Tate	R-R	6-0	175	2-9-94	.181	.190	.178	52	193	24	35	7	0	0	20	9	5	3	3	52	6	4	.218	.233
McKeon, Alex	R-R	6-2	215	5-20-93	.217	.333	.176	8	23	2	5	1	0	1	1	0	0	0	0	7	0	0	.391	.217
Nunez, Jhon	B-R	5-9	165	12-5-94	.204	.225	.191	35	108	14	22	3	3	0	11	14	2	4	3	24	5	0	.287	.299
Ockimey, Josh	L-R	6-1	215	10-18-95	.266	.196	.288	56	199	30	53	13	3	4	38	25	2	0	3	78	2	2	.422	.349
Peralta, Aneudis	R-R	5-11	195	8-21-93	.184	.267	.140	30	87	10	16	3	0	0	4	3	1	1	0	18	2	0	.218	.220
Ramos, Henry	B-R	6-2	190	4-15-92	.333	—	.333	3	12	1	4	0	0	0	1	0	0	1	1	4	0	0	.333	.308
Rei, Austin	R-R	6-0	180	10-27-93	.179	.333	.136	34	112	14	20	5	1	2	12	11	6	0	1	39	1	0	.295	.285
Rivera, Jeremy	B-R	5-9	150	1-30-95	.256	.359	.212	63	215	22	55	4	1	0	12	24	0	7	2	37	8	6	.284	.328
Spoon, Tyler	R-R	5-11	190	9-28-92	.286	.364	.250	17	70	9	20	5	0	1	11	5	0	0	0	10	3	1	.400	.333
Suarez, Alixon	R-R	6-1	180	7-25-94	.087	.200	.000	8	23	1	2	0	0	0	1	0	0	1	0	5	0	0	.087	.087
Tovar, Carlos	R-R	5-11	180	9-25-94	.222	.500	.143	4	9	3	2	0	0	0	2	1	0	1	1	2	0	0	.222	.273
Tubbs, Tucker	R-R	6-4	205	9-11-92	.216	.136	.266	47	153	24	33	8	2	1	14	17	4	2	4	33	3	1	.314	.303
Washington, Kyri	R-R	5-11	220	7-11-94	.263	.385	.204	24	80	13	21	8	1	0	15	8	1	0	2	29	4	1	.388	.330

Pitching	B-T	HT	WT	DOB	W	L	ERA	G	GS	CG	SV	IP	H	R	ER	HR	BB	SO	AVG	vLH	vRH	K/9	BB/9
Allen, Logan	R-L	6-3	200	5-23-97	0	0	2.08	1	1	0	0	4	6	1	1	0	0	2	.300	.167	.357	4.15	0.00
Almonte, Jose	R-R	6-2	185	9-8-95	3	3	3.43	14	14	0	0	66	38	31	25	1	38	64	.171	.198	.149	8.77	5.21
Boyd, Logan	L-L	6-2	205	11-26-93	4	0	2.85	13	1	0	0	41	41	13	13	3	13	37	.265	.373	.198	8.12	2.85
Cosart, Jake	R-R	6-2	175	2-11-94	2	2	5.45	9	9	0	0	33	26	20	20	3	20	27	.215	.264	.143	7.36	5.45
De Jesus, Enmanuel	L-L	6-3	190	12-10-96	0	0	2.70	1	0	0	0	3	1	2	1	0	1	2	.083	.000	.167	5.40	2.70
Garcia, Edwar	R-R	6-4	175	11-19-93	3	1	1.96	14	0	0	5	23	20	6	5	1	15	26	.235	.194	.259	10.17	5.87
Glorius, Austin	R-R	6-3	205	5-10-93	2	3	2.70	7	5	0	0	27	21	13	8	3	13	36	.206	.220	.192	12.15	4.39
Gonzalez, Daniel	R-R	6-5	180	2-9-96	3	3	3.29	15	1	0	0	63	61	33	23	4	16	51	.252	.248	.255	7.29	2.29
Gunn, Michael	L-L	6-0	205	1-25-93	0	1	6.35	3	0	0	0	6	6	4	4	0	4	4	.286	.333	.267	6.35	6.35
Kelley, Trevor	R-R	6-2	210	10-20-93	1	3	4.50	12	0	0	1	18	20	9	9	1	8	20	.282	.192	.333	10.00	4.00
Kent, Matt	L-L	6-0	180	9-13-92	7	1	1.86	14	0	0	1	48	44	13	10	1	10	35	.239	.183	.274	6.52	1.86
Martinez, Enfember	R-R	5-11	140	8-30-95	3	3	4.07	16	0	0	1	42	46	22	19	4	13	31	.277	.203	.330	6.64	2.79
Nunez, Taylor	R-R	6-4	185	7-28-92	2	3	2.54	15	0	0	1	28	26	15	8	0	8	13	.239	.325	.188	4.13	2.54
Perez, Randy	L-L	5-10	165	4-1-94	0	2	1.62	7	0	0	1	17	12	6	3	0	8	12	.188	.167	.200	6.48	4.32
Poyner, Bobby	L-L	6-0	205	12-1-92	1	2	2.28	17	0	0	10	24	29	7	6	3	2	22	.299	.250	.328	8.37	0.76
Ramos, Luis	R-R	6-1	180	6-5-95	1	1	4.89	8	1	0	0	39	52	23	21	3	9	29	.315	.264	.339	6.75	2.09
Rodriguez, Javier	L-L	6-2	165	5-1-95	0	5	7.68	11	10	0	0	34	32	37	29	1	36	19	.234	.135	.270	5.03	9.53
Romero, Dioscar	R-R	6-3	230	4-17-95	3	3	3.72	14	14	0	0	58	52	29	24	3	28	36	.241	.257	.226	5.59	4.34
Show, Brandon	R-R	6-2	180	10-31-92	1	0	0.93	3	0	0	0	10	6	1	1	0	4	6	.171	.222	.154	5.59	3.72
Steen, Kevin	R-R	6-1	170	7-24-96	0	1	3.38	7	7	0	0	32	29	12	12	1	16	23	.250	.273	.236	6.47	4.50
Taylor, Ben	R-R	6-3	225	11-12-92	0	0	1.80	4	0	0	2	10	8	2	2	0	2	17	.222	.250	.167	15.30	1.80
Zandona, Danny	R-R	6-1	200	2-27-93	1	0	5.46	16	0	0	0	28	32	20	17	4	7	24	.291	.366	.246	7.71	2.25

Fielding

Catcher	PCT	G	PO	A	E	DP	PB
Lucena	1.000	1	2	2	0	0	0
McKeon	1.000	7	33	4	0	1	0
Nunez	.982	35	233	42	5	3	8
Rei	.980	31	223	23	5	1	1
Spoon	1.000	2	7	2	0	0	1
Suarez	.975	8	33	6	1	0	1

First Base	PCT	G	PO	A	E	DP
Gunsolus	1.000	1	1	1	0	0
Ockimey	.968	47	369	22	13	41
Peralta	1.000	1	1	0	0	0
Tubbs	.989	33	255	24	3	21

Second Base	PCT	G	PO	A	E	DP
Acosta	.902	9	16	21	4	6
Coyle	1.000	2	5	4	0	1

	PCT	G	PO	A	E	DP
De La Guerra	.966	51	86	138	8	29
Gunsolus	1.000	2	1	6	0	0
Lorenzana	1.000	6	10	14	0	1
Peralta	.975	11	21	18	1	9

Third Base	PCT	G	PO	A	E	DP
Acosta	.959	36	39	55	4	4
Baldwin	.667	2	1	1	1	0
Gunsolus	.951	34	27	50	4	7
Peralta	.842	9	13	19	6	3

Shortstop	PCT	G	PO	A	E	DP
De La Guerra	1.000	3	4	7	0	2
Lorenzana	.914	15	20	33	5	9
Rivera	.950	60	94	151	13	35
Tovar	.917	4	5	6	1	0
Weeks	1.000	1	0	2	0	0

Outfield	PCT	G	PO	A	E	DP
Acosta	1.000	9	10	0	0	0
Austin	.909	23	28	2	3	1
Basabe	.985	56	125	8	2	4
Benintendi	1.000	31	87	6	0	1
Hill	1.000	4	8	0	0	0
Hudson	1.000	6	6	0	0	0
Kapstein	1.000	2	2	0	0	0
Kemp	1.000	9	19	0	0	0
Magee	.971	21	33	1	1	0
Matheny	.991	48	102	3	1	1
Ramos	1.000	2	8	1	0	0
Spoon	1.000	16	42	1	0	0
Washington	1.000	15	23	0	0	0

GCL RED SOX   ROOKIE

GULF COAST LEAGUE

Batting	B-T	HT	WT	DOB	AVG	vLH	vRH	G	AB	R	H	2B	3B	HR	RBI	BB	HBP	SH	SF	SO	SB	CS	SLG	OBP
Aybar, Yoan	L-L	6-2	165	7-3-97	.268	.150	.285	45	157	19	42	5	3	0	16	7	1	1	3	46	6	6	.338	.298
Baldwin, Roldani	R-R	5-11	180	3-16-96	.288	.211	.299	47	156	18	45	8	0	3	25	14	8	0	7	19	1	1	.397	.362
Basabe, Luis Alejandro	B-R	5-10	160	8-26-96	.260	.400	.244	28	100	22	26	5	0	0	6	21	1	0	2	33	8	4	.310	.387
Coyle, Sean	R-R	5-8	175	1-17-92	.289	.500	.265	10	38	10	11	4	0	1	8	3	1	0	0	9	0	0	.474	.357
Downs, Jerry	L-L	6-2	215	12-22-93	.275	.227	.284	42	131	23	36	8	0	2	24	23	6	0	3	27	5	2	.382	.399
Fisher, Devon	R-R	6-0	215	5-1-96	.192	.333	.179	31	73	9	14	4	0	0	9	22	1	1	3	30	0	0	.247	.374
Hamilton, Nick	R-R	6-0	165	12-4-93	.102	.333	.050	18	49	3	5	1	0	0	2	6	2	0	0	29	7	0	.122	.228
Hill, Tyler	R-R	6-0	195	3-4-96	.250	.105	.274	39	132	16	33	4	0	0	16	16	3	0	0	22	11	2	.280	.344
Kemp, Trenton	R-R	6-2	195	9-30-95	.234	.357	.218	40	124	20	29	6	4	0	14	24	4	1	1	33	8	3	.347	.373
Lameda, Raiwinson	L-R	5-11	175	10-7-95	.393	.429	.381	12	28	3	11	2	1	0	5	8	0	0	0	4	0	2	.536	.528
Lucena, Isaias	R-R	5-11	180	11-15-94	.280	.667	.195	19	50	7	14	3	0	0	2	10	0	0	0	10	0	0	.340	.400
Madera, Chris	R-R	5-10	190	8-23-92	.264	.167	.278	28	91	13	24	2	0	1	13	9	2	0	1	16	6	2	.319	.340
Mars, Danny	B-R	6-0	195	1-22-94	.125	.000	.129	9	32	4	4	1	0	0	3	3	1	0	1	6	2	0	.156	.216
Noviello, Andrew	L-R	6-0	195	10-24-96	.132	.111	.138	18	38	7	5	2	0	0	1	7	0	1	0	15	0	0	.184	.267

Batting	B-T	HT	WT	DOB	AVG	vLH	vRH	G	AB	R	H	2B	3B	HR	RBI	BB	HBP	SH	SF	SO	SB	CS	SLG	OBP
Oliveras, Rafael	R-R	5-10	180	1-4-95	.248	.333	.237	41	153	20	38	2	0	1	11	24	2	1	2	34	2	1	.281	.354
Pena, Darwin	L-L	6-0	180	3-5-93	.210	.286	.203	27	81	7	17	3	1	0	9	11	0	0	0	12	0	0	.272	.304
Perez, Andy	R-R	6-0	175	2-23-93	.355	.429	.342	26	93	14	33	3	1	0	18	12	2	1	2	8	3	3	.409	.431
Ramos, Henry	B-R	6-2	190	4-15-92	.292	.200	.316	8	24	4	7	0	0	0	2	5	1	0	0	3	2	0	.292	.433
Rusconi, Jagger	B-R	5-11	165	7-18-96	.170	.200	.167	16	53	7	9	2	2	0	7	2	2	0	1	11	1	0	.283	.224
Spoon, Tyler	R-R	5-11	190	9-28-92	.143	.333	.103	13	35	5	5	0	0	0	3	3	1	0	0	6	0	0	.143	.231
Tovar, Carlos	R-R	5-11	170	8-20-95	.250	.364	.224	18	60	7	15	3	0	0	5	3	0	1	1	16	5	1	.300	.281
Valentin, Yomar	B-R	5-8	145	12-26-97	.233	.368	.194	24	86	15	20	3	1	0	7	9	1	3	0	12	1	0	.291	.313
Washington, Kyri	R-R	5-11	220	7-11-94	.263	.000	.278	11	38	6	10	1	0	1	7	6	0	0	0	11	0	1	.368	.364

Pitching	B-T	HT	WT	DOB	W	L	ERA	G	GS	CG	SV	IP	H	R	ER	HR	BB	SO	AVG	vLH	vRH	K/9	BB/9
Allen, Logan	R-L	6-3	200	5-23-97	0	0	0.90	7	7	0	0	20	12	2	2	0	1	24	.171	.167	.172	10.80	0.45
Bautista, Gerson	R-R	6-2	168	5-31-95	3	3	2.77	12	11	0	0	52	36	18	16	1	27	41	.196	.215	.176	7.10	4.67
Caceres, Carlos	R-R	6-3	200	9-30-94	1	1	5.26	10	0	0	0	26	25	16	15	2	11	19	.255	.275	.241	6.66	3.86
De Jesus, Enmanuel	L-L	6-3	190	12-10-96	6	2	1.66	10	4	0	0	43	34	11	8	2	9	29	.213	.175	.225	6.02	1.87
Duron, Nick	R-R	6-4	190	1-30-96	2	1	1.71	14	0	0	2	26	20	5	5	1	5	28	.200	.137	.265	9.57	1.71
Espinoza, Anderson	R-R	6-0	160	3-9-98	0	1	0.68	10	10	0	0	40	24	5	3	0	9	40	.170	.234	.138	9.00	2.03
Garcia, Carlos	L-L	6-0	170	12-15-94	2	1	2.22	15	0	0	2	28	25	11	7	1	8	22	.234	.229	.236	6.99	2.54
Goetze, Pat	R-R	6-6	200	3-3-94	5	0	2.37	14	0	0	0	30	30	11	8	3	5	16	.263	.133	.348	4.75	1.48
Kelley, Trevor	R-R	6-2	210	10-20-93	0	0	1.29	6	0	0	3	7	5	1	1	0	2	8	.208	.000	.313	10.29	2.57
Lau, Adam	R-R	6-2	210	7-5-94	0	0	4.09	11	0	0	3	11	14	5	5	1	6	14	.304	.167	.455	11.45	4.91
Martinez, Algenis	R-R	6-1	185	9-12-93	4	1	3.72	16	0	0	4	29	32	15	12	1	6	19	.281	.288	.274	5.90	1.86
McGrath, Daniel	R-L	6-3	205	7-7-94	0	0	0.00	3	3	0	0	6	6	0	0	0	0	7	.286	.000	.375	10.50	0.00
Pennington, Josh	R-R	6-0	175	7-6-95	2	1	0.82	7	6	0	0	22	17	3	2	0	13	22	.218	.200	.226	9.00	5.32
Pimentel, Yankory	R-R	6-2	210	9-29-93	4	0	1.60	16	1	0	6	34	32	9	6	0	7	42	.250	.241	.257	11.23	1.87
Raudes, Roniel	R-R	6-1	160	1-16-98	3	0	0.90	4	4	0	0	20	13	2	2	0	6	16	.191	.207	.179	7.20	2.70
Rodriguez, Javier	L-L	6-2	165	5-1-95	0	0	0.75	3	3	0	0	12	6	1	1	0	8	3	.158	.118	.190	2.25	6.00
Steen, Kevin	R-R	6-1	170	7-24-96	3	1	1.82	6	3	0	0	25	18	8	5	1	4	24	.189	.171	.204	8.76	1.46
Stone, Brad	L-L	6-3	170	6-18-94	1	2	6.89	10	0	0	0	16	23	14	12	0	24	13	.365	.364	.366	7.47	13.79
Watt, Max	R-R	6-8	250	8-9-94	0	0	0.00	2	0	0	0	2	0	0	0	0	0	3	.000	.000	.000	13.50	0.00
Williams, Jalen	R-R	6-4	210	4-21-95	3	1	2.65	12	3	0	2	34	41	20	10	0	13	18	.306	.309	.303	4.76	3.44

Fielding

Catcher	PCT	G	PO	A	E	DP	PB
Baldwin	1.000	4	25	4	0	0	2
Fisher	.971	31	211	24	7	3	3
Lucena	.983	18	96	19	2	3	0
Noviello	.969	15	55	7	2	0	3
Spoon	1.000	8	30	2	0	1	3

First Base	PCT	G	PO	A	E	DP
Downs	.984	36	281	19	5	20
Pena	.991	26	205	24	2	22

Second Base	PCT	G	PO	A	E	DP
Basabe	1.000	12	16	32	0	5
Coyle	1.000	6	9	15	0	1

	PCT	G	PO	A	E	DP
Oliveras	.973	20	24	47	2	11
Perez	1.000	17	31	38	0	12
Rusconi	1.000	8	13	17	0	3

Third Base	PCT	G	PO	A	E	DP
Baldwin	.906	40	31	56	9	7
Madera	.800	4	1	3	1	0
Oliveras	.964	18	17	36	2	5
Perez	.500	2	1	1	2	0
Valentin	.833	1	3	2	1	0

Shortstop	PCT	G	PO	A	E	DP
Basabe	.897	18	26	44	8	8
Oliveras	.882	4	7	8	2	1

Tovar	.914	18	22	42	6	6
Valentin	.891	23	34	56	11	17

Outfield	PCT	G	PO	A	E	DP
Aybar	.990	45	91	7	1	1
Hamilton	1.000	15	19	2	0	0
Hill	.983	36	57	0	1	0
Kemp	.984	39	59	1	1	0
Lameda	1.000	8	13	0	0	0
Madera	1.000	24	41	1	0	1
Mars	.923	5	11	1	1	0
Ramos	1.000	3	1	0	0	0
Washington	1.000	8	11	0	0	0

DSL RED SOX
DOMINICAN SUMMER LEAGUE

ROOKIE

Batting	B-T	HT	WT	DOB	AVG	vLH	vRH	G	AB	R	H	2B	3B	HR	RBI	BB	HBP	SH	SF	SO	SB	CS	SLG	OBP
Aponte, Dawill	L-L	6-0	155	8-19-97	.180	.111	.197	50	183	15	33	4	2	0	10	18	1	2	1	29	3	4	.224	.256
Barriento, Juan	R-R	6-2	201	4-28-96	.268	.255	.271	68	272	41	73	15	4	5	51	15	4	0	2	46	7	6	.408	.314
Benoit, Luis	L-R	5-10	165	11-29-94	.209	.200	.211	56	187	20	39	7	1	1	17	20	3	5	3	50	5	2	.273	.291
Berroa, Ramfis	R-R	6-2	190	11-2-95	.253	.409	.229	49	162	28	41	10	2	3	21	21	7	0	3	32	7	6	.395	.358
Campana, Marino	R-R	6-4	180	11-28-97	.275	.237	.289	72	280	39	77	16	4	2	36	19	8	0	1	66	10	4	.382	.338
Carrizalez, Gerardo	R-R	6-1	175	7-28-95	.216	.140	.234	66	218	33	47	8	1	0	21	25	4	3	4	42	7	5	.261	.303
Cedrola, Lorenzo	R-R	5-11	170	1-12-98	.321	.226	.344	67	265	61	85	8	7	1	31	23	23	0	1	33	27	7	.415	.420
Conde, Eduard	L-R	5-9	155	2-13-98	.211	.314	.173	59	190	13	40	5	2	0	19	20	2	3	2	43	5	4	.258	.290
Diaz, Imeldo	R-R	6-0	155	11-2-97	.217	.226	.214	70	277	40	60	4	2	0	22	24	6	4	4	36	7	3	.245	.289
Espinal, Stanley	R-R	6-2	188	11-15-96	.281	.356	.263	72	295	44	83	14	7	6	59	14	7	0	6	50	5	2	.437	.323
Figueroa, Willis	R-R	5-10	165	12-31-94	.222	.224	.221	61	203	36	45	2	4	0	13	53	7	3	1	48	17	9	.271	.398
Hernandez, Angel	R-R	6-0	180	8-22-97	.074	.000	.111	15	27	2	2	0	0	0	1	1	2	0	0	12	0	0	.074	.167
Hernandez, Juan	L-R	5-10	155	4-9-96	.326	.356	.319	62	230	43	75	9	0	0	14	32	3	1	0	43	22	8	.365	.415
Lozada, Jose	R-R	5-11	165	2-4-97	.216	.200	.220	19	51	8	11	1	2	0	3	3	0	1	1	15	1	0	.314	.255
Marin, Freiberg	B-R	5-11	170	9-5-97	.194	.244	.180	62	206	24	40	3	4	0	29	33	1	3	3	51	2	1	.248	.305
Martinez, Marcos	L-R	5-11	165	1-28-98	.220	.348	.176	30	91	12	20	1	1	0	8	17	4	2	1	18	4	3	.253	.363
Miranda, Samuel	L-R	6-1	175	8-21-97	.262	—	—	50	172	18	45	11	0	0	25	18	4	1	3	17	0	2	.326	.340
Nieva, Fabian	B-R	6-0	175	8-18-95	.059	.100	.042	15	34	5	2	0	0	0	6	1	0	0	17	0	1	.059	.220
Perez, Jesus	L-L	6-3	184	10-23-95	.125	.250	.100	34	96	17	12	3	3	2	13	22	2	0	0	49	4	1	.281	.300
Petit, Keibert	R-R	6-1	175	8-3-98	.201	.242	.188	41	134	18	27	4	1	0	7	5	2	2	0	33	6	2	.246	.241
Pulido, Carlos	B-R	5-10	170	2-7-98	.273	.333	.260	36	121	22	33	3	2	0	21	15	8	1	2	26	5	1	.331	.384
Reynoso, Eddy	R-R	6-0	195	8-7-94	.302	.302	.303	43	162	17	49	10	0	3	17	16	0	0	0	22	1	1	.420	.365
Serven, Hemerson	B-R	5-11	210	11-11-97	.237	.258	.228	57	224	28	53	14	2	0	21	21	5	0	1	40	6	3	.317	.315
Tejeda, Elwin	R-R	6-2	140	9-14-97	.184	.250	.168	57	185	12	34	7	1	0	12	27	1	3	1	59	1	5	.232	.290

BOSTON RED SOX

Batting	B-T	HT	WT	DOB	AVG	vLH	vRH	G	AB	R	H	2B	3B	HR	RBI	BB	HBP	SH	SF	SO	SB	CS	SLG	OBP
Toribio, Rafael	R-R	5-8	160	1-26-96	.299	.310	.296	52	154	25	46	4	4	0	21	14	6	4	0	34	19	2	.377	.379
Ugueto, Reinaldo	R-R	5-11	165	12-9-97	.175	.190	.169	52	166	17	29	3	0	0	17	6	3	0		48	10	1	.193	.275
Urena, Pablo	R-R	6-0	175	10-17-94	.274	—	—	30	73	16	20	4	2	1	8	7	4	0	3	15	2	1	.425	.356
Yovera, Luis	R-R	6-2	170	10-15-95	.267	.234	.278	53	191	14	51	6	4	0	17	10	4	0	2	37	0	2	.340	.314

Pitching	B-T	HT	WT	DOB	W	L	ERA	G	GS	CG	SV	IP	H	R	ER	HR	BB	SO	AVG	vLH	vRH	K/9	BB/9
Acosta, Christopher	R-R	6-4	180	1-15-98	1	4	4.28	9	9	0	0	34	36	20	16	0	5	22	.273	.154	.323	5.88	1.34
Batista, Edilson	L-L	6-2	175	7-7-97	1	2	4.50	13	1	0	0	36	50	35	18	1	9	18	.323	.407	.305	4.50	2.25
Bazardo, Eduard	R-R	6-0	155	9-1-95	3	6	4.37	14	14	0	0	58	60	32	28	2	16	55	.276	.290	.271	8.58	2.50
Caceres, Carlos	R-R	6-3	200	9-30-94	0	1	4.76	3	3	0	0	11	13	7	6	0	7	7	.302	.333	.286	5.56	5.56
Calvo, Gary	R-R	6-3	180	10-4-96	1	2	4.58	15	9	0	1	37	27	29	19	1	29	36	—	—	—	8.68	6.99
Caraballo, William	R-R	6-1	170	7-18-98	1	0	15.75	8	0	0	0	8	15	15	14	1	10	8	.405	.400	.409	9.00	11.25
Clemente, Nicolo	R-R	6-0	176	2-18-98	3	3	2.97	18	0	0	2	39	36	23	13	1	13	24	—	—	—	5.49	2.97
Colmenares, Luis	L-L	6-0	180	4-22-98	0	1	3.06	16	0	0	2	50	33	24	17	3	26	38	.196	.115	.211	6.84	4.68
Cortes, Carlos	R-R	6-1	165	7-26-96	0	0	4.20	7	0	0	0	15	19	9	7	1	4	10	.322	.333	.317	6.00	2.40
Cortez, Jhosmar	R-R	6-0	158	12-21-97	0	1	10.13	3	2	0	0	5	8	6	6	1	3	3	.333	.400	.316	5.06	5.06
Diaz, Victor	R-R	6-3	189	5-24-94	6	1	1.38	21	0	0	7	33	20	7	5	0	16	35	.183	.190	.182	9.64	4.41
Espinoza, Anderson	R-R	6-0	160	3-9-98	0	0	1.20	4	4	0	0	15	13	6	2	0	3	21	.232	.231	.233	12.60	1.80
Espinoza, Junior	R-R	6-4	185	9-16-97	2	4	4.13	13	13	0	0	57	55	29	26	5	20	63	.257	.232	.269	10.01	3.18
Familia, Victor	R-R	6-0	170	4-3-98	0	0	10.45	6	0	0	0	10	21	22	12	3	5	8	.412	.632	.281	6.97	4.35
Guzman, Warlyn	R-R	6-2	196	9-9-95	3	2	1.80	18	1	0	3	40	46	14	8	0	14	28	—	—	—	6.30	3.15
Garcia, Victor	R-R	6-4	204	6-15-97	3	5	2.40	12	12	0	0	45	25	16	12	0	25	50	.161	.200	.148	10.00	5.00
Gonzalez, Jose	R-R	6-0	175	7-27-98	3	2	4.50	12	1	0	1	36	44	22	18	1	9	27	.297	.350	.278	6.75	2.25
Hernandez, Darwinzon	L-L	6-2	180	12-17-96	6	1	1.10	16	13	0	0	65	55	17	8	0	30	66	.227	.389	.199	9.09	4.13
Lacrus, Shair	R-R	6-1	170	12-22-96	2	2	6.81	17	0	0	2	37	46	30	28	1	17	27	.315	.275	.337	6.57	4.14
Lantigua, Marcos	R-R	6-3	200	12-14-95	0	0	6.67	17	0	0	2	27	25	25	20	2	13	24	—	—	—	8.00	4.33
Medina, Roberto	R-R	6-3	160	1-13-95	3	1	2.74	17	0	0	2	23	20	15	7	1	14	18	.225	.290	.190	7.04	5.48
Medrano, Jeison	R-R	6-6	202	9-15-92	0	0	1.86	7	0	0	0	10	2	6	2	1	10	11	.063	.000	.083	10.24	9.31
Mendoza, Ritzi	R-R	6-2	175	1-10-96	2	3	6.37	16	0	0	2	30	37	27	21	1	11	12	.316	.424	.274	3.64	3.34
Oduber, Ryan	L-L	5-11	140	8-16-97	2	1	3.50	14	2	0	1	46	54	23	18	2	8	31	.290	.306	.287	6.02	1.55
Padron, Angel	L-L	5-11	175	9-16-97	2	3	5.21	18	0	0	1	38	39	25	22	2	23	29	.271	.222	.282	6.87	5.45
Pantoja, Yorvin	L-L	5-11	175	9-22-97	4	0	2.35	14	14	0	0	69	53	24	18	1	29	66	.209	.159	.219	8.61	3.78
Perez, Juan	L-L	5-11	180	9-9-96	2	2	9.90	6	0	0	0	10	13	12	11	0	8	7	.310	.222	.333	6.30	7.20
Raudes, Roniel	R-R	6-1	160	1-16-98	4	3	3.52	11	10	0	0	54	46	21	21	3	3	63	.228	.295	.199	10.57	0.50
Requena, Hildemaro	R-R	6-2	170	7-20-97	1	4	2.73	16	0	0	1	53	44	27	16	4	11	35	.218	.194	.229	5.98	1.88
Reyes, Denyi	R-R	6-4	209	11-2-96	7	1	2.88	15	14	0	0	75	73	28	24	0	3	63	.253	.301	.237	7.56	0.36
Rivero, Luis	R-R	6-3	195	1-23-98	1	2	1.61	10	0	0	0	22	15	8	4	0	7	18	.205	.316	.167	7.25	2.82
Rodriguez, Alejandro	L-L	6-1	160	10-30-96	4	6	3.00	14	14	0	0	60	61	25	20	1	23	47	.257	.196	.272	7.05	3.45
Rosario, Ramses	R-R	6-3	180	10-18-95	0	1	1.53	7	0	0	1	18	17	4	3	0	4	12	.270	.444	.200	6.11	2.04
Tena, Francisco	L-L	6-3	160	3-4-95	0	0	3.38	9	0	0	4	11	6	4	4	0	4	12	.158	.286	.129	10.13	3.38
Torrealba, Jervis	L-L	6-0	165	6-9-95	4	1	3.05	14	0	0	3	38	36	14	13	2	19	33	.257	.242	.262	7.75	4.46
Zacarias, Jose	R-R	5-11	160	1-9-97	1	4	2.70	13	8	0	0	50	55	23	15	4	8	50	.284	.233	.298	9.00	1.44

Fielding

Catcher	PCT	G	PO	A	E	DP	PB
Martinez	.978	27	197	26	5	1	8
Miranda	.985	47	321	67	6	0	8
Petit	.978	24	161	13	4	2	7
Pulido	.975	33	236	33	7	3	8
Reynoso	.988	19	143	23	2	1	5
Urena	1.000	4	19	5	0	0	2

First Base	PCT	G	PO	A	E	DP
Barriento	1.000	8	58	1	0	5
Berroa	—	1	0	0	0	0
Carrizalez	.996	55	464	23	2	36
Miranda	.929	2	10	3	1	1
Nieva	.982	10	54	2	1	6
Perez	1.000	1	10	0	0	0
Petit	1.000	1	5	0	0	0
Pulido	1.000	1	11	0	0	0
Reynoso	.991	14	101	10	1	6
Serven	.983	44	311	34	6	24
Urena	.990	16	94	3	1	4

Second Base	PCT	G	PO	A	E	DP
Benoit	.981	13	24	29	1	8
Conde	.967	58	107	124	8	18
Figueroa	.933	7	13	15	2	3
Lozada	.973	8	23	13	1	1
Marin	.967	62	132	163	10	35
Toribio	.833	3	7	3	2	0

Third Base	PCT	G	PO	A	E	DP
Benoit	.868	19	15	31	7	1
Carrizalez	.906	10	9	20	3	0
Espinal	.877	58	72	99	24	12
Figueroa	1.000	1	2	0	1	0
Tejeda	.884	57	50	95	19	6
Toribio	.905	6	10	9	2	1
Ugueto	.500	1	0	1	1	0
Urena	.333	1	1	0	2	0

Shortstop	PCT	G	PO	A	E	DP
Benoit	.879	28	37	50	12	10
Yovera	1.000	8	57	5	0	5
Diaz	.931	70	95	202	22	29
Lozada	.833	5	2	13	3	2
Toribio	.500	1	1	0	1	1
Ugueto	.882	50	71	115	25	17

Outfield	PCT	G	PO	A	E	DP
Aponte	.991	50	101	5	1	
3 Barriento	.978	52	85	6	2	3
Berroa	.984	40	58	3	1	1
Campana	.974	71	143	6	4	0
Carrizalez	1.000	1	1	0	0	0
Cedrola	.993	63	132	11	1	3
Conde	—	1	0	0	0	0
Figueroa	.941	53	92	4	6	0
Hernandez	.991	56	96	13	1	1
Hernandez	1.000	3	1	0	0	0
Serven	.963	16	26	0	1	0
Toribio	.933	12	10	4	1	0
Yovera	.990	35	91	8	1	2

Chicago Cubs

SEASON IN A SENTENCE: The Cubs incorporated their top four prospects into the lineup behind new manager Joe Maddon, matched their highest wins total—97—since their last pennant winner in 1945 and won a Division Series against the rival Cardinals.

HIGH POINT: Chicago won the wild-card game at Pittsburgh behind ace Jake Arrieta, then was shut out by John Lackey and the Cardinals in the opening game of the Division Series. But they pounced on St. Louis in Game Two, won Game Three behind Arrieta and clinched a playoff series at Wrigley Field in Game Four for the first time ever.

LOW POINT: The Mets beat Arrieta and Jon Lester in the first two games of the National League Championship Series, leaving the Cubs to start Kyle Hendricks and Jason Hammel in must-win games at Wrigley. That wasn't good enough on the mound, and Mets pitchers shut down the explosive Cubs lineup, holding Chicago to eight runs in a four-game LCS sweep.

NOTABLE ROOKIES: Rookie of the Year Kris Bryant, shortstop Addison Russell, catcher/left fielder Kyle Schwarber and right fielder Jorge Soler totaled 1,850 plate appearances between them, accounting for 30 percent of the Cubs' total. They combined for 65 home runs in the regular season and nine more in the playoffs. Carl Edwards made his big league debut as a reliever.

KEY TRANSACTIONS: Hiring Maddon last offseason and signing Lester as a free agent for six years and $155 million proved crucial in helping the Cubs change their clubhouse culture and see themselves as contenders rather than merely up-and-coming. The January trade with the Astros, sending Luis Valbuena and Dan Straily to the Astros for center fielder Dexter Fowler, proved beneficial for both clubs as Fowler was installed as the leadoff hitter. Austin Jackson, added in-season from the Mariners as a righthanded bat and defensive replacement, provided little impact.

DOWN ON THE FARM: Domestic affiliates combined to go 371-316 (.540), third-best in the minors, with new high Class A affiliate Myrtle Beach sweeping to the Carolina League championship. Schwarber was dominating the minors before his big league promotion, but his fellow Double-A Tennessee catcher, Willson Contreras, won the Southern League batting championship in a breakout season.

OPENING DAY PAYROLL: $119,006,885 (13th)

PLAYERS OF THE YEAR

MAJOR LEAGUE	MINOR LEAGUE
Jake Arrieta rhp	**Willson Contreras** c
22-6, 1.77	(Double-A)
Led majors in wins,	333/.413/.478
CG and shutouts	8 HR, 75 RBIs

ORGANIZATION LEADERS

BATTING		*Minimum 250 AB
MAJORS		
*AVG	Anthony Rizzo	.278
*OPS	Anthony Rizzo	.899
HR	Anthony Rizzo	31
RBI	Anthony Rizzo	101
MINORS		
*AVG	Willson Contreras, Tennessee	.333
*OBP	Willson Contreras, Tennessee	.413
*SLG	Willson Contreras, Tennessee	.478
R	Chesny Young, South Bend, Myrtle Beach	88
H	Chesny Young, South Bend, Myrtle Beach	163
TB	Willson Contreras, Tennessee	217
2B	Jeimer Candelario, Myrtle Beach, Tennessee	35
3B	Arismendy Alcantara, Iowa	10
HR	Christian Villanueva, Tennessee	20
RBI	Christian Villanueva, Tennessee	95
BB	Mark Zagunis, Myrtle Beach	80
SO	Jacob Rogers, Tennessee	137
SB	Jeffrey Baez, South Bend, Myrtle Beach	36

PITCHING		#Minimum 75 IP
MAJORS		
W	Jake Arrieta	22
#ERA	Jake Arrieta	1.77
SO	Jake Arrieta	236
SV	Hector Rondon	30
MINORS		
W	Ryan Williams, South Bend, Tennessee	14
L	Trevor Clifton, South Bend	10
#ERA	Ryan Williams, South Bend, Tennessee	2.16
G	Blake Cooper, Iowa	50
GS	Carlos Pimentel, Iowa	26
SV	Brian Schlitter, Iowa	23
IP	Carlos Pimentel, Iowa	143
BB	Carlos Pimentel, Iowa	68
SO	Felix Pena, Tennessee	140
AVG	Jonathan Martinez, Myrtle Beach	.199

General Manager: Jed Hoyer. **Farm Director:** Jaron Madison. **Scouting Director:** Matt Dorey.

Class	Team	League	W	L	PCT	Finish	Manager
Majors	Chicago Cubs	National	97	65	.599	3rd (15)	Joe Maddon
Triple-A	Iowa Cubs	Pacific Coast	80	64	.556	3rd (16)	Marty Pevey
Double-A	Tennessee Smokies	Southern	76	63	.547	4th (10)	Buddy Bailey
High A	Myrtle Beach Pelicans	Carolina	81	57	.587	1st (10)	Mark Johnson
Low A	South Bend Cubs	Midwest	65	72	.474	12th (16)	Jimmy Gonzalez
Short season	Eugene Emeralds	Northwest	38	38	.500	5th (8)	Gary Van Tol
Rookie	Cubs	Arizona	31	22	.585	2nd (14)	Carmelo Martinez
Overall 2015 Minor League Record			371	316	.540	5th (30)	

ORGANIZATION STATISTICS

CHICAGO CUBS

CHICAGO CUBS

NATIONAL LEAGUE

Batting	B-T	HT	WT	DOB	AVG	vLH	vRH	G	AB	R	H	2B	3B	HR	RBI	BB	HBP	SH	SF	SO	SB	CS	SLG	OBP
Alcantara, Arismendy	B-R	5-10	170	10-29-91	.077	.000	.091	11	26	5	2	0	0	0	1	5	0	1	0	11	1	0	.077	.226
Baez, Javier	R-R	6-0	190	12-1-92	.289	.421	.246	28	76	4	22	6	0	1	4	4	0	0	0	24	1	2	.408	.325
Baxter, Mike	L-R	6-0	205	12-7-84	.246	1.000	.204	34	57	6	14	1	0	0	2	7	2	0	0	14	0	0	.263	.348
Berry, Quintin	L-L	6-1	190	11-21-84	.000	—	.000	8	1	0	0	0	0	0	0	0	0	0	0	1	2	1	.000	.000
Bryant, Kris	R-R	6-5	215	1-4-92	.275	.246	.284	151	559	87	154	31	5	26	99	77	9	0	5	199	13	4	.488	.369
Castillo, Welington	R-R	5-10	210	4-24-87	.163	.167	.160	24	43	5	7	2	0	2	5	3	1	0	0	12	0	0	.349	.234
2-team total (80 Arizona)					.243	—	—	104	317	39	77	15	1	19	55	24	6	0	3	87	0	0	.476	.306
Castro, Starlin	R-R	6-0	190	3-24-90	.265	.281	.261	151	547	52	145	23	2	11	69	21	5	1	4	91	5	5	.375	.296
Coghlan, Chris	L-R	6-0	195	6-18-85	.250	.116	.264	148	440	64	110	25	6	16	41	58	3	1	1	94	11	2	.443	.341
Denorfia, Chris	R-R	6-0	195	7-15-80	.269	.211	.301	103	212	18	57	11	1	3	18	15	1	2	1	56	0	1	.373	.319
Fowler, Dexter	B-R	6-5	195	3-22-86	.250	.326	.228	156	596	102	149	29	8	17	46	84	5	2	3	154	20	7	.411	.346
Herrera, Jonathan	B-R	5-9	180	11-3-84	.230	.286	.209	73	126	14	29	5	1	2	14	2	0	4	0	23	3	0	.333	.242
Jackson, Austin	R-R	6-1	205	2-1-87	.236	.208	.250	29	72	10	17	7	0	1	10	5	2	0	0	19	2	1	.375	.304
La Stella, Tommy	L-R	5-11	190	1-31-89	.269	.000	.286	33	67	4	18	6	0	1	11	5	1	0	1	7	2	0	.403	.324
Lake, Junior	R-R	6-3	215	3-27-90	.224	.375	.167	21	58	2	13	4	0	1	5	4	0	0	0	20	4	0	.345	.274
Montero, Miguel	L-R	5-11	210	7-9-83	.248	.234	.250	113	347	36	86	11	0	15	53	49	4	0	3	103	1	1	.409	.345
Olt, Mike	R-R	6-2	210	8-27-88	.133	.250	.091	6	15	1	2	0	0	1	1	0	1	0	0	6	0	0	.333	.188
Rizzo, Anthony	L-L	6-3	240	8-8-89	.278	.294	.272	160	586	94	163	38	3	31	101	78	30	0	7	105	17	6	.512	.387
Ross, David	R-R	6-2	230	3-19-77	.176	.156	.184	72	159	6	28	9	0	1	9	20	0	2	1	61	1	0	.252	.267
Russell, Addison	R-R	6-0	200	1-23-94	.242	.156	.268	142	475	60	115	29	1	13	54	42	3	1	2	149	4	3	.389	.307
Schwarber, Kyle	L-R	6-0	235	3-5-93	.246	.143	.278	69	232	52	57	6	1	16	43	36	4	0	1	77	3	3	.487	.355
Soler, Jorge	R-R	6-4	215	2-25-92	.262	.240	.268	101	366	39	96	18	1	10	47	32	3	0	1	121	3	1	.399	.324
Szczur, Matt	R-R	6-0	200	7-20-89	.222	.243	.200	47	72	5	16	5	0	1	8	6	0	1	1	15	2	0	.333	.278
Teagarden, Taylor	R-R	6-0	210	12-21-83	.200	.300	.000	8	15	0	3	0	0	0	2	0	0	0	0	4	0	0	.200	.200

Pitching	B-T	HT	WT	DOB	W	L	ERA	G	GS	CG	SV	IP	H	R	ER	HR	BB	SO	AVG	vLH	vRH	K/9	BB/9
Arrieta, Jake	R-R	6-4	225	3-6-86	22	6	1.77	33	33	4	0	229	150	52	45	10	48	236	.185	.159	.207	9.28	1.89
Beeler, Dallas	R-R	6-5	210	6-12-89	0	1	9.72	3	3	0	0	8	14	11	9	0	7	7	.359	.474	.250	7.56	7.56
Cahill, Trevor	R-R	6-4	240	3-1-88	1	0	2.12	11	0	0	0	17	8	4	4	2	5	22	.143	.105	.162	11.65	2.65
2-team total (15 Atlanta)					1	3	5.40	26	3	0	0	43	44	27	26	4	16	36	—	—	—	7.48	3.32
Coke, Phil	L-L	6-1	210	7-19-82	0	0	6.30	16	0	0	0	10	14	7	7	1	3	9	.341	.304	.389	8.10	2.70
Edwards, Carl	R-R	6-3	170	9-3-91	0	0	3.86	5	0	0	0	5	3	3	2	0	3	4	.188	.333	.100	7.71	5.79
Germen, Gonzalez	R-R	6-1	200	9-23-87	0	0	7.50	6	0	0	0	6	8	5	5	0	5	8	.348	.167	.412	12.00	7.50
2-team total (29 Colorado)					0	0	4.42	35	1	0	1	39	41	19	19	4	26	33	—	—	—	7.68	6.05
Grimm, Justin	R-R	6-3	210	8-16-88	3	5	1.99	62	0	0	3	50	31	18	11	4	26	67	.178	.140	.197	12.14	4.71
Hammel, Jason	R-R	6-6	225	9-2-82	10	7	3.74	31	31	0	0	171	158	79	71	23	40	172	.242	.235	.247	9.07	2.11
Haren, Dan	R-R	6-5	215	9-17-80	4	2	4.01	11	11	0	0	58	58	29	26	10	13	44	.256	.279	.236	6.79	2.01
2-team total (21 Miami)					11	9	3.60	32	32	0	0	187	174	79	75	31	38	132	—	—	—	6.34	1.83
Hendricks, Kyle	R-R	6-3	190	12-7-89	8	7	3.95	32	32	1	0	180	166	82	79	17	43	167	.244	.267	.225	8.35	2.15
Hunter, Tommy	R-R	6-3	250	7-3-86	2	0	5.74	19	0	0	1	16	20	10	10	4	3	15	.303	.320	.293	8.62	1.72
Jackson, Edwin	R-R	6-3	210	9-9-83	2	1	3.19	23	0	0	0	31	30	14	11	0	12	23	.254	.200	.282	6.68	3.48
2-team total (24 Atlanta)					4	3	3.07	47	0	1	0	56	44	25	19	4	21	40	—	—	—	6.47	3.40
Lester, Jon	L-L	6-4	240	1-7-84	11	12	3.34	32	32	1	0	205	183	83	76	16	47	207	.240	.247	.237	9.09	2.06
Medina, Yoervis	R-R	6-3	245	7-27-88	0	0	7.00	5	0	0	0	9	12	7	7	1	4	7	.308	.360	.214	7.00	4.00
Motte, Jason	R-R	6-0	205	6-22-82	8	1	3.91	57	0	0	6	48	48	21	21	6	14	34	.255	.294	.233	6.33	2.05
Ramirez, Neil	R-R	6-4	190	5-25-89	1	0	3.21	19	0	0	0	14	12	5	5	1	6	15	.231	.238	.226	9.64	3.86
Richard, Clayton	L-L	6-5	245	9-12-83	4	2	3.83	23	3	0	0	42	47	18	18	3	7	22	.272	.234	.294	4.68	1.49
Roach, Donn	R-R	6-0	195	12-14-89	0	1	10.80	1	1	0	0	3	8	4	4	0	1	1	.471	.500	.455	2.70	2.70
Rodney, Fernando	R-R	5-11	220	3-18-77	2	0	0.75	14	0	0	0	12	8	4	1	1	4	15	.186	.067	.250	11.25	3.00
Rondon, Hector	R-R	6-3	180	2-26-88	6	4	1.67	72	0	0	30	70	55	19	13	4	15	69	.212	.231	.196	8.87	1.93
Rosscup, Zac	R-L	6-2	220	6-9-88	2	1	4.39	33	0	0	0	27	26	13	13	5	13	29	.252	.158	.308	9.79	4.39
Russell, James	L-L	6-4	205	1-8-86	0	2	5.29	49	0	0	1	34	42	24	20	3	9	20	.307	.273	.338	5.29	2.38
Schlitter, Brian	R-R	6-5	235	12-21-85	1	2	7.36	10	0	0	0	7	12	6	6	2	2	4	.364	.500	.333	4.91	2.45
Soriano, Rafael	R-R	6-4	230	12-19-79	2	0	6.35	6	0	0	0	6	8	4	4	2	1	4	.333	.545	.154	6.35	1.59
Strop, Pedro	R-R	6-1	220	6-13-85	2	6	2.91	76	0	0	3	68	39	24	22	5	29	81	.167	.186	.156	10.72	3.84

Pitching

Pitching	B-T	HT	WT	DOB	W	L	ERA	G	GS	CG	SV	IP	H	R	ER	HR	BB	SO	AVG	vLH	vRH	K/9	BB/9
Wada, Tsuyoshi	L-L	5-11	180	2-21-81	1	1	3.62	8	7	0	0	32	30	14	13	5	11	31	.246	.308	.229	8.63	3.06
Wood, Travis	R-L	5-11	175	2-6-87	5	4	3.84	54	9	0	4	101	86	48	43	11	39	118	.229	.231	.228	10.55	3.49

Fielding

Catcher	PCT	G	PO	A	E	DP	PB
Castillo	.966	9	56	0	2	1	1
Montero	.986	109	820	55	12	3	3
Ross	.998	59	397	36	1	3	4
Schwarber	.967	21	110	7	4	1	2
Teagarden	1.000	6	30	3	0	0	0

First Base	PCT	G	PO	A	E	DP
Baez	—	1	0	0	0	0
Baxter	1.000	2	16	1	0	1
Bryant	1.000	1	2	1	0	0
Coghlan	1.000	5	19	0	0	3
Rizzo	.994	160	1330	126	9	102

Second Base	PCT	G	PO	A	E	DP
Alcantara	.970	8	14	18	1	2
Baez	.967	17	13	16	1	7

	PCT	G	PO	A	E	DP
Castro	.957	38	47	85	6	20
Coghlan	.971	15	14	20	1	1
Herrera	.977	29	39	46	2	11
La Stella	1.000	14	12	33	0	4
Russell	.977	86	151	226	9	47

Third Base	PCT	G	PO	A	E	DP
Alcantara	1.000	2	1	1	0	0
Baez	.960	11	5	19	1	1
Bryant	.951	144	81	249	17	21
Coghlan	1.000	3	1	0	0	0
Herrera	.960	16	6	18	1	0
La Stella	.857	12	3	3	1	0
Olt	1.000	6	2	5	0	0

Shortstop	PCT	G	PO	A	E	DP
Baez	1.000	8	7	14	0	3

	PCT	G	PO	A	E	DP
Castro	.963	109	143	323	18	58
Herrera	—	1	0	0	0	0
Russell	.981	61	67	139	4	29

Outfield	PCT	G	PO	A	E	DP
Baxter	.938	11	15	0	1	0
Berry	—	5	0	0	0	0
Bryant	1.000	19	20	1	0	0
Coghlan	1.000	119	164	9	0	0
Denorfia	1.000	75	88	5	0	0
Fowler	.988	152	337	5	4	2
Jackson	.970	28	31	1	1	1
Lake	.958	15	21	2	1	0
Schwarber	.979	43	45	1	1	0
Soler	.993	95	144	4	1	1
Szczur	1.000	33	24	0	0	0

IOWA CUBS   TRIPLE-A

PACIFIC COAST LEAGUE

Batting	B-T	HT	WT	DOB	AVG	vLH	vRH	G	AB	R	H	2B	3B	HR	RBI	BB	HBP	SH	SF	SO	SB	CS	SLG	OBP
Alcantara, Arismendy	B-R	5-10	170	10-29-91	.231	.217	.239	120	454	72	105	20	10	12	36	35	0	7	3	125	16	6	.399	.285
Amendolare, Angelo	R-R	5-9	170	12-2-92	.200	.750	.000	8	15	1	3	0	0	0	1	0	1	0	0	3	0	0	.200	.294
Andreoli, John	R-R	6-1	215	6-9-90	.277	.279	.276	106	379	72	105	20	6	5	32	55	3	10	1	97	33	8	.401	.372
Baez, Javier	R-R	6-0	190	12-1-92	.324	.333	.320	70	281	49	91	14	2	13	61	21	8	1	2	76	17	3	.527	.385
Baxter, Mike	L-R	6-0	205	12-7-84	.279	.288	.276	74	222	31	62	9	3	1	20	39	2	0	1	45	7	3	.360	.390
Berry, Quintin	L-L	6-1	190	11-21-84	.143	.000	.182	5	14	0	2	0	0	0	2	0	1	0	7	0	0	.143	.250
Bonifacio, Emilio	B-R	5-11	205	4-23-85	.469	.316	.567	13	49	12	23	2	0	0	3	8	0	0	0	6	6	1	.510	.544
Brockmeyer, Cael	R-R	6-5	235	10-8-91	.125	.250	.000	5	8	0	1	0	0	0	0	0	0	0	2	0	0	.125	.125
Brown, Kevin	L-R	6-0	195	10-30-90	.278	.333	.222	11	18	4	5	2	0	0	3	1	0	0	1	3	0	0	.389	.300
Bryant, Kris	R-R	6-5	215	1-4-92	.321	.308	.333	7	28	7	9	1	0	3	10	2	1	0	2	9	2	0	.679	.364
Carlin, Luke	B-R	5-10	190	12-20-80	.182	.250	.163	21	55	8	10	3	1	0	2	9	2	1	0	11	1	0	.273	.318
2-team total (34 Nashville)					.158	—	—	55	158	14	25	10	1	0	13	32	5	2	1	35	1	1	.234	.316
Caro, Roberto	R-R	6-0	185	9-25-93	.000	.000	.000	5	5	1	0	0	0	0	0	0	0	0	0	0	0	0	.000	.000
Chambers, Adron	L-L	5-10	200	10-8-86	.280	.324	.262	88	261	40	73	18	2	1	30	30	3	2	2	53	9	5	.375	.358
Cuevas, Varonex	R-R	6-0	165	7-24-92	.333	1.000	.000	2	3	0	1	0	0	0	0	0	0	0	1	0	0	.333	.333
Davis, Taylor	R-R	5-11	185	11-28-89	.309	.284	.322	83	259	29	80	19	2	4	29	21	0	2	0	37	0	1	.444	.361
Dent, Ryan	R-R	6-0	190	3-15-89	.237	.074	.375	25	59	7	14	4	1	1	8	4	0	2	1	16	0	1	.390	.281
Giansanti, Anthony	R-R	5-10	195	9-28-88	.176	.250	.111	5	17	2	3	2	0	0	2	0	0	0	0	4	0	0	.294	.176
La Stella, Tommy	L-R	5-11	190	1-31-89	.333	.200	.391	9	33	3	11	2	1	1	6	4	0	0	1	3	0	0	.545	.395
Lake, Junior	R-R	6-3	215	3-27-90	.315	.303	.321	58	197	37	62	10	0	7	31	30	1	1	2	53	9	4	.472	.404
Lopez, Rafael	L-R	5-9	200	10-2-87	.276	.229	.289	46	156	14	43	8	1	0	17	14	0	1	1	37	3	1	.340	.333
2-team total (21 Salt Lake)					.266	—	—	67	218	24	58	10	1	1	24	25	0	1	2	50	3	1	.335	.339
Mota, Jonathan	R-R	6-0	200	6-1-87	.252	.323	.200	82	234	26	59	9	2	3	29	14	1	3	0	43	2	1	.346	.297
Olt, Mike	R-R	6-2	210	8-27-88	.265	.236	.281	59	211	30	56	14	0	9	25	20	2	0	1	71	0	1	.460	.333
Russell, Addison	R-R	6-0	200	1-23-94	.318	.500	.167	11	44	7	14	4	0	1	9	1	0	0	1	7	1	0	.477	.326
Schwarber, Kyle	L-R	6-0	235	3-5-93	.333	.379	.290	17	60	7	20	7	1	3	10	7	0	0	0	23	0	0	.633	.403
Silva, Rubi	L-R	5-11	180	6-25-89	.282	.154	.318	98	298	45	84	16	6	11	48	5	1	2	1	83	5	3	.487	.295
Soler, Jorge	R-R	6-4	215	2-25-92	.154	.167	.143	4	13	1	2	0	0	0	1	3	0	0	0	4	0	0	.154	.313
Szczur, Matt	R-R	6-0	200	7-20-89	.292	.250	.310	70	267	40	78	12	2	8	31	22	6	4	5	51	20	5	.442	.355
Teagarden, Taylor	R-R	6-0	210	12-21-83	.305	.337	.279	63	197	26	60	12	1	5	31	23	2	0	2	70	0	0	.452	.379
Valaika, Chris	R-R	5-11	205	8-14-85	.266	.278	.259	106	334	34	89	22	1	8	41	25	6	5	6	76	1	2	.401	.323
Villanueva, Christian	R-R	5-11	210	6-19-91	.259	.294	.244	123	455	56	118	23	2	18	88	35	5	4	9	80	2	3	.437	.313

Pitching	B-T	HT	WT	DOB	W	L	ERA	G	GS	CG	SV	IP	H	R	ER	HR	BB	SO	AVG	vLH	vRH	K/9	BB/9
Antigua, Jeffry	R-L	6-1	205	6-23-90	1	1	2.61	10	6	0	0	41	28	17	12	6	13	19	.192	.190	.192	4.14	2.83
Batista, Frank	R-R	5-10	170	4-26-89	1	5	5.71	13	5	0	0	35	49	26	22	5	15	11	.331	.344	.321	4.41	3.89
Beeler, Dallas	R-R	6-5	210	6-12-89	8	5	4.07	21	21	0	0	111	114	64	50	5	37	83	.264	.308	.225	6.75	3.01
Britton, Drake	L-L	6-2	215	5-22-89	7	8	5.08	28	11	0	1	83	80	51	47	7	33	45	.255	.228	.266	4.86	3.56
Buchter, Ryan	L-L	6-3	250	2-13-87	2	0	2.00	16	0	0	0	18	9	4	4	0	9	23	.148	.148	.147	11.50	4.50
2-team total (27 Oklahoma City)					2	0	1.78	43	0	0	3	51	36	10	10	0	25	62	—	—	—	11.01	4.44
Cahill, Trevor	R-R	6-4	240	3-1-88	0	0	0.00	5	0	0	0	8	5	0	0	0	3	7	.185	.200	.143	8.22	3.52
2-team total (6 Oklahoma City)					1	3	4.95	11	6	0	0	36	37	22	20	3	17	24	—	—	—	5.94	4.21
Cervenka, Hunter	L-L	6-1	225	1-3-90	0	1	11.08	12	0	0	0	13	21	16	16	2	15	20	.333	.280	.368	13.85	10.38
Cooper, Blake	R-R	5-11	190	3-30-88	7	4	2.63	50	0	0	5	68	59	27	20	4	28	63	.236	.287	.201	8.30	3.69
Cruz, Fernando	B-R	6-2	205	3-28-90	0	1	22.50	1	0	0	0	4	10	10	10	0	3	2	.500	.583	.375	4.50	4.50
Edwards, Carl	R-R	6-3	170	9-3-91	3	1	2.84	23	0	0	2	32	15	11	10	0	24	39	.142	.091	.177	11.08	6.82
Francescon, Patrick	R-R	5-11	185	1-4-89	0	0	0.00	3	1	0	0	6	4	0	0	0	4	7	.160	.308	.000	7.88	4.50
Germen, Gonzalez	R-R	6-1	200	9-23-87	5	1	3.78	24	0	0	4	33	29	16	14	3	17	27	.234	.123	.328	7.29	4.59
2-team total (3 Albuquerque)					5	1	3.68	27	0	0	4	37	32	17	15	3	18	31	—	—	—	7.61	4.42
Grimm, Justin	R-R	6-3	210	8-16-88	0	0	0.00	1	0	0	0	1	0	0	0	0	1	2	.000	.000	.000	18.00	9.00

Pitching

Pitching	B-T	HT	WT	DOB	W	L	ERA	G	GS	CG	SV	IP	H	R	ER	HR	BB	SO	AVG	vLH	vRH	K/9	BB/9
Ihrig, Tyler	L-L	6-0	210	9-17-91	0	1	3.60	1	1	0	0	5	5	2	2	0	2	3	.263	.000	.278	5.40	3.60
Jokisch, Eric	R-L	6-2	205	7-29-89	5	4	4.37	14	14	1	0	70	81	41	34	6	23	39	.289	.270	.296	5.01	2.96
Loux, Barret	R-R	6-5	230	4-6-89	0	1	2.38	3	3	0	0	11	12	4	3	0	6	8	.279	.381	.182	6.35	4.76
Medina, Yoervis	R-R	6-3	245	7-27-88	0	2	6.29	28	0	0	1	34	40	25	24	3	21	35	.299	.232	.346	9.17	5.50
2-team total (4 Tacoma)					1	2	5.63	32	0	0	2	40	41	26	25	4	22	39	—	—	—	8.78	4.95
Negrin, Yoanner	R-R	5-11	190	4-29-84	1	0	2.97	13	2	0	0	30	24	11	10	4	8	30	.224	.200	.242	8.90	2.37
Ortiz, Joe	L-L	5-7	175	8-13-90	3	1	5.24	38	0	0	1	55	61	36	32	4	16	25	.281	.214	.323	4.09	2.62
Parker, Blake	R-R	6-3	225	6-19-85	0	0	2.70	3	0	0	0	3	1	1	1	0	1	3	.100	.000	.200	2.70	8.10
Paulino, Felipe	R-R	6-3	260	10-5-83	5	9	4.93	20	20	0	0	104	108	64	57	9	52	83	.275	.292	.263	7.18	4.50
Pimentel, Carlos	R-R	6-3	180	12-1-89	12	6	2.95	27	26	2	0	143	121	59	47	12	68	118	.229	.235	.223	7.41	4.27
Ramirez, Neil	R-R	6-4	190	5-25-89	0	0	0.00	1	0	0	0	1	1	0	0	0	1	1	.333	—	.333	13.50	0.00
Richard, Clayton	L-L	6-5	245	9-12-83	1	0	0.00	1	1	0	0	7	3	0	0	0	4	4	.125	.200	.105	5.14	0.00
Rivero, Armando	R-R	6-4	190	2-1-88	2	2	3.16	48	0	0	0	57	45	26	20	4	32	53	.216	.191	.237	8.37	5.05
Roach, Donn	R-R	6-0	195	12-14-89	7	2	2.33	15	15	1	0	89	83	26	23	6	16	33	.249	.256	.242	3.34	1.62
Rosscup, Zac	R-L	6-2	220	6-9-88	0	0	4.76	11	0	0	0	11	8	7	6	1	4	20	.186	.056	.280	15.88	3.18
Rowen, Ben	R-R	6-3	195	11-15-88	2	0	0.00	8	0	0	0	9	6	0	0	0	1	7	.200	.100	.250	6.75	0.96
Russell, James	L-L	6-4	205	1-8-86	2	0	2.45	9	0	0	3	11	8	5	3	0	4	13	.205	.133	.250	10.64	3.27
Santiago, Andres	R-R	6-1	220	10-26-89	0	0	0.00	2	0	0	0	5	5	0	0	0	5	4	.278	.286	.273	6.75	8.44
Schlereth, Daniel	L-L	6-0	215	5-9-86	0	0	3.00	3	0	0	0	3	2	4	1	0	6	3	.167	.000	.286	9.00	18.00
Schlitter, Brian	R-R	6-5	235	12-21-85	2	3	1.61	45	0	0	23	45	41	11	8	1	26	35	.248	.234	.261	7.05	5.24
Soriano, Rafael	R-R	6-4	230	12-19-79	0	0	1.80	5	0	0	0	5	2	1	1	0	6	.118	.250	.000	10.80	1.80
Wada, Tsuyoshi	L-L	5-11	180	2-21-81	4	5	3.95	16	16	0	0	87	93	44	38	4	26	62	.274	.315	.254	6.44	2.70
Wagner, Michael	R-R	6-3	175	10-3-91	0	1	5.65	7	1	0	0	14	12	10	9	0	9	10	.218	.333	.080	6.28	5.65

Fielding

Catcher	PCT	G	PO	A	E	DP	PB
Brockmeyer	1.000	4	6	1	0	0	0
Carlin	.985	17	115	14	2	3	2
Davis	.996	38	233	16	1	1	4
Lopez	.986	40	248	26	4	2	4
Schwarber	.979	15	90	4	2	1	3
Teagarden	.993	42	257	21	2	4	3

First Base	PCT	G	PO	A	E	DP
Baxter	.989	32	254	16	3	29
Carlin	1.000	1	5	1	0	0
Davis	.996	30	215	13	1	28
Dent	1.000	1	2	0	0	0
Lake	1.000	5	37	4	0	5
Mota	1.000	15	75	2	0	9
Olt	.988	20	156	6	2	18
Teagarden	1.000	8	41	1	0	4
Valaika	.995	23	196	19	1	16
Villanueva	.991	35	318	27	3	23

Second Base	PCT	G	PO	A	E	DP
Alcantara	.964	74	116	232	13	57
Amendolare	.875	3	4	10	2	3

	PCT	G	PO	A	E	DP	PB
Baez	.973	19	37	72	3	13	
Bonifacio	.885	6	13	10	3	2	
Dent	1.000	2	4	4	0	0	
La Stella	.974	5	20	17	1	6	
Mota	1.000	6	4	14	0	0	
Russell	.938	5	6	9	1	3	
Valaika	1.000	34	48	87	0	20	
Villanueva	1.000	1	0	2	0	0	

Third Base	PCT	G	PO	A	E	DP
Alcantara	.857	6	2	4	1	0
Baez	.963	9	9	17	1	3
Bryant	.889	7	7	9	2	0
Davis	1.000	1	0	2	0	1
Dent	—	2	0	0	0	0
Mota	1.000	8	4	6	0	1
Olt	.918	33	14	75	8	7
Valaika	1.000	11	2	12	0	1
Villanueva	.931	85	65	165	17	15

Shortstop	PCT	G	PO	A	E	DP
Alcantara	.846	3	3	8	2	6
Baez	.930	40	82	143	17	36

	PCT	G	PO	A	E	DP
Bonifacio	1.000	1	1	2	0	0
Cuevas	—	1	0	0	0	0
Dent	.950	16	17	40	3	10
Mota	.975	45	60	134	5	24
Russell	.895	6	4	13	2	2
Valaika	.993	38	52	87	1	22

Outfield	PCT	G	PO	A	E	DP
Alcantara	.947	36	67	4	4	0
Andreoli	.987	104	222	3	3	2
Baxter	1.000	35	57	3	0	1
Berry	1.000	5	10	0	0	0
Bonifacio	1.000	5	4	0	0	0
Brown	1.000	5	8	0	0	0
Caro	1.000	1	6	1	0	1
Chambers	.973	62	102	5	3	1
Davis	1.000	1	5	0	0	0
Giansanti	1.000	3	3	2	0	0
Lake	1.000	46	91	4	0	0
Mota	.913	12	20	1	2	0
Silva	.963	84	145	10	6	
2 Soler	1.000	4	5	0	0	0
Szczur	1.000	63	129	6	0	2

TENNESSEE SMOKIES   DOUBLE-A

SOUTHERN LEAGUE

Batting	B-T	HT	WT	DOB	AVG	vLH	vRH	G	AB	R	H	2B	3B	HR	RBI	BB	HBP	SH	SF	SO	SB	CS	SLG	OBP
Almora, Albert	R-R	6-2	180	4-16-94	.272	.322	.257	106	405	69	110	26	4	6	46	32	4	4	6	47	8	4	.400	.327
Brockmeyer, Cael	R-R	6-5	235	10-8-91	.238	.000	.250	7	21	1	5	2	0	1	4	2	0	0	1	4	0	0	.476	.292
Bruno, Stephen	R-R	5-9	165	11-17-90	.263	.209	.276	105	342	44	90	17	1	2	48	26	13	3	4	64	9	3	.336	.335
Candelario, Jeimer	B-R	6-1	210	11-24-93	.291	.302	.287	46	158	21	46	10	1	5	25	22	1	0	1	21	0	0	.462	.379
Castillo, Erick	R-R	5-11	178	2-25-93	.000	—	.000	2	2	0	0	0	0	0	0	0	0	0	0	1	0	0	.000	.000
Chen, Pin-Chieh	L-R	6-1	170	7-23-91	.247	.111	.261	28	97	15	24	5	3	1	12	15	1	1	0	20	1	1	.392	.354
Contreras, Willson	R-R	6-1	175	5-13-92	.333	.371	.323	126	454	71	151	34	4	8	75	57	7	0	3	62	4	4	.478	.413
Cuevas, Varonex	R-R	6-0	165	7-24-92	.240	.333	.227	7	25	0	6	1	0	0	1	0	0	0	0	9	0	0	.280	.240
Darvill, Wes	L-R	6-2	190	9-10-91	.173	.091	.190	69	191	18	33	2	1	2	25	22	0	2	4	41	3	1	.225	.253
Davis, Taylor	R-R	5-11	185	11-28-89	.319	.357	.310	21	72	11	23	7	0	5	14	5	0	1	0	11	0	0	.625	.364
Denorfia, Chris	R-R	6-0	195	7-15-80	.167	.000	.250	2	6	2	1	1	0	0	2	1	0	0	1	2	0	0	.333	.250
Dent, Ryan	R-R	6-0	190	3-15-89	.258	.358	.223	72	302	32	56	11	0	4	24	18	4	10	2	60	2	2	.361	.321
Flete, Bryant	B-R	5-10	146	1-31-93	.195	.250	.187	44	123	13	24	3	1	1	10	18	1	3	0	27	0	1	.260	.303
Geiger, Dustin	R-R	6-2	180	12-2-91	.000	.000	.000	13	16	0	0	0	0	0	0	1	0	0	1	6	0	0	.000	.056
Giansanti, Anthony	R-R	5-10	195	9-28-88	.231	.311	.202	64	169	16	39	4	1	0	22	17	1	3	1	30	3	2	.266	.303
Hannemann, Jacob	L-L	6-1	200	4-29-91	.233	.250	.229	112	434	60	101	20	9	6	41	32	5	10	4	113	17	1	.362	.291
La Stella, Tommy	L-R	5-11	190	1-31-89	.250	.333	.242	10	36	9	9	3	0	0	3	3	1	0	0	1	0	0	.333	.325
McKinney, Billy	L-L	6-1	205	8-23-94	.285	.192	.306	77	274	29	78	26	1	3	39	27	1	2	4	47	0	0	.420	.346
Montero, Miguel	L-R	5-11	210	7-9-83	.188	1.000	.133	4	16	1	3	0	0	1	4	0	0	0	0	3	0	0	.375	.188
Mota, Jonathan	R-R	6-0	200	6-1-87	.250	.235	.255	21	72	7	18	2	0	1	13	5	0	1	2	10	0	0	.319	.291
Olt, Mike	R-R	6-2	210	8-27-88	.444	—	.444	3	9	5	4	2	1	0	3	0	0	0	0	4	0	0	.889	.583
Pearson, Tyler	R-R	6-0	185	4-15-92	.150	.111	.161	16	40	5	6	3	1	0	1	7	1	1	0	19	0	0	.275	.292

Batting	B-T	HT	WT	DOB	AVG	vLH	vRH	G	AB	R	H	2B	3B	HR	RBI	BB	HBP	SH	SF	SO	SB	CS	SLG	OBP
Penalver, Carlos	R-R	6-0	170	5-17-94	.364	.500	.333	3	11	3	4	0	0	1	3	3	0	0	0	3	0	0	.636	.500
Rademacher, Bijan	L-L	6-0	200	6-15-91	.261	.250	.263	113	357	56	93	19	4	4	47	67	2	5	2	60	7	4	.370	.379
Rogers, Jacob	L-R	6-4	220	8-23-89	.247	.125	.262	23	73	9	18	3	0	1	13	16	0	0	2	23	0	1	.329	.374
Schwarber, Kyle	L-R	6-0	235	3-5-93	.320	.256	.338	58	197	39	63	10	1	13	39	42	1	1	2	49	1	0	.579	.438
Soto, Elliot	R-R	5-9	160	8-21-89	.275	.308	.266	88	306	47	84	10	1	0	18	55	2	9	0	58	5	4	.314	.388
2-team total (32 Jacksonville)					.256	—	—	120	414	59	106	11	2	0	26	69	3	10	1	82	7	5	.292	.366
Villanueva, Christian	R-R	5-11	210	6-19-91	.208	.000	.217	6	24	5	5	0	0	2	7	4	0	0	0	5	0	0	.458	.321
Vogelbach, Dan	L-R	6-0	250	12-17-92	.272	.207	.291	76	254	41	69	16	1	7	39	57	0	0	2	61	1	1	.425	.403
Whiting, Sutton	B-R	5-8	170	5-13-92	.438	.250	.500	8	16	3	7	0	1	0	1	7	0	0	0	4	0	1	.563	.609

Pitching	B-T	HT	WT	DOB	W	L	ERA	G	GS	CG	SV	IP	H	R	ER	HR	BB	SO	AVG	vLH	vRH	K/9	BB/9
Antigua, Jeffry	R-L	6-1	205	6-23-90	5	5	4.40	20	16	0	0	92	99	45	45	6	33	58	.281	.253	.292	5.67	3.23
Batista, Frank	R-R	5-10	170	4-26-89	7	2	1.73	14	14	1	0	83	66	19	16	4	23	56	.217	.222	.213	6.05	2.48
Black, Corey	R-R	5-11	175	8-4-91	3	5	4.92	37	9	0	0	86	74	54	47	7	47	101	.237	.226	.245	10.57	4.92
Brazis, Matt	R-R	6-3	215	9-6-89	1	0	3.29	12	0	0	0	14	10	6	5	0	16	12	.208	.118	.258	7.90	10.54
Cates, Zach	R-R	6-3	195	12-17-89	2	4	5.30	14	0	0	0	19	19	18	11	0	22	15	.244	.306	.190	7.23	10.61
Cervenka, Hunter	L-L	6-1	225	1-3-90	1	0	2.08	3	0	0	1	4	2	1	1	0	3	4	.143	.286	.000	8.31	6.23
2-team total (3 Mississippi)					1	0	1.08	6	0	0	1	8	5	1	1	0	4	12	—	—	—	12.96	4.32
Concepcion, Gerardo	L-L	6-2	200	2-29-92	0	1	8.24	31	0	0	0	32	45	30	29	4	29	25	.333	.286	.360	7.11	8.24
Cruz, Fernando	B-R	6-2	205	3-28-90	2	1	5.46	16	1	0	1	31	31	25	19	4	20	31	.258	.277	.247	8.90	5.74
Edwards, Carl	R-R	6-3	170	9-3-91	2	2	2.66	13	0	0	4	24	11	12	7	1	17	36	.136	.133	.137	13.69	6.46
Francescon, Patrick	R-R	5-11	185	1-4-89	4	2	1.69	42	0	0	22	53	38	11	10	5	17	50	.201	.208	.197	8.44	2.87
Ihrig, Tyler	L-L	6-0	210	9-17-91	0	1	3.38	4	1	0	0	8	11	3	3	0	1	4	.333	.111	.417	4.50	1.13
Jensen, Michael	R-R	6-1	185	12-10-90	2	2	2.23	22	0	0	1	32	29	9	8	0	16	29	.242	.195	.266	8.07	4.45
Johnson, Pierce	R-R	6-3	200	5-10-91	2	2	2.08	16	16	1	0	95	76	24	22	4	32	72	.223	.157	.262	6.82	3.03
Paniagua, Juan Carlos	R-R	6-1	200	4-4-90	0	2	7.32	11	0	0	0	20	23	18	16	3	15	14	.291	.207	.340	6.41	6.86
Pena, Felix	R-R	6-2	190	2-25-90	7	8	3.75	25	23	1	0	130	111	60	54	10	49	140	.231	.218	.241	9.72	3.40
Peraklis, Steve	R-R	6-1	185	1-15-91	2	2	4.22	14	0	0	0	21	18	11	10	2	8	16	.234	.147	.302	6.75	3.38
Peralta, Starling	R-R	6-4	210	11-11-90	3	1	1.99	39	0	0	6	54	40	19	12	5	18	26	.206	.211	.203	4.31	2.98
Pineyro, Ivan	R-R	6-1	200	9-29-91	7	5	3.69	19	19	1	0	107	104	46	44	6	30	92	.254	.259	.250	7.71	2.52
2-team total (1 Jacksonville)					7	6	3.87	20	20	1	0	109	107	49	47	6	33	92	—	—	—	7.57	2.72
Pugliese, James	R-R	6-3	220	8-12-92	0	1	6.75	2	0	0	0	3	4	2	2	0	3	2	.364	.667	.250	6.75	10.13
Ramirez, Neil	R-R	6-4	190	5-25-89	1	1	3.38	6	0	0	0	5	3	2	2	0	3	8	.158	.167	.154	13.50	5.06
Rosscup, Zac	R-L	6-2	220	6-9-88	0	0	3.86	3	0	0	1	2	2	1	1	0	2	7	.222	.000	.250	27.00	7.71
Santiago, Andres	R-R	6-1	220	10-26-89	4	5	4.17	24	7	0	1	73	72	36	34	2	31	51	.259	.282	.238	6.26	3.80
Scott, Tayler	R-R	6-3	185	6-1-92	4	1	5.23	15	0	0	1	31	32	19	18	3	20	21	.278	.190	.329	6.10	5.81
Soriano, Rafael	R-R	6-4	230	12-19-79	0	0	0.00	5	0	0	0	5	3	1	0	0	3	4	.188	.143	.222	7.20	5.40
Turner, Jacob	R-R	6-5	215	5-21-91	1	1	2.00	2	2	0	0	9	7	5	2	2	1	2	7	.161	.235	.071	7.00	2.00
Wada, Tsuyoshi	L-L	5-11	180	2-21-81	0	1	9.00	1	1	0	0	4	8	4	4	2	0	5	.421	.375	.455	11.25	0.00
Wagner, Michael	R-R	6-3	175	10-3-91	0	1	4.22	6	0	0	0	11	8	5	5	1	6	9	.211	.250	.182	7.59	5.06
Williams, Ryan	R-R	6-4	220	11-1-91	10	2	2.76	17	16	0	0	88	73	29	27	2	16	61	.227	.225	.229	6.24	1.64
Zastryzny, Rob	R-L	6-3	205	3-26-92	2	5	6.23	14	14	0	0	61	77	47	42	9	28	48	.310	.344	.299	7.12	4.15

Fielding

Catcher	PCT	G	PO	A	E	DP	PB
Brockmeyer	1.000	3	15	2	0	0	0
Castillo	1.000	1	2	0	0	0	0
Contreras	.987	75	533	59	8	4	7
Davis	.990	11	81	14	1	1	0
Montero	1.000	2	13	0	0	0	0
Pearson	.967	15	79	9	3	0	1
Schwarber	.984	37	265	41	5	3	7

First Base	PCT	G	PO	A	E	DP
Brockmeyer	.875	1	6	1	1	1
Darvill	1.000	39	275	24	0	25
Geiger	.926	6	25	0	2	1
Giansanti	.988	13	73	7	1	11
Rogers	.994	20	145	19	1	12
Vogelbach	.990	75	550	40	6	61

Second Base	PCT	G	PO	A	E	DP
Bruno	.975	97	154	229	10	58

Catcher	PCT	G	PO	A	E	PB
Darvill	1.000	1	3	2	0	1
Dent	1.000	30	43	54	0	20
Flete	.974	18	25	49	2	8
La Stella	1.000	5	6	14	0	1
Soto	.900	3	5	4	1	2
Whiting	.889	3	6	2	1	2

Third Base	PCT	G	PO	A	E	DP
Candelario	.950	44	28	68	5	1
Contreras	1.000	8	2	10	0	2
Cuevas	.857	5	1	11	2	0
Darvill	.982	24	19	36	1	3
Davis	.750	2	1	2	1	0
Dent	.919	24	15	42	5	6
Flete	.929	6	4	9	1	2
Geiger	.500	2	1	1	2	0
Giansanti	.949	23	14	23	2	4
La Stella	1.000	4	1	10	0	3

	PCT	G	PO	A	E	DP
Olt	1.000	3	1	5	0	2
Villanueva	.917	6	4	7	1	1

Shortstop	PCT	G	PO	A	E	DP
Dent	.976	19	26	57	2	12
Flete	.938	18	24	51	5	7
Mota	.933	21	28	42	5	8
Penalver	1.000	3	5	10	0	3
Soto	.983	84	124	233	6	56

Outfield	PCT	G	PO	A	E	DP
Almora	.976	101	240	6	6	1
Chen	.966	26	54	2	2	0
Denorfia	1.000	2	7	1	0	1
Giansanti	.968	22	29	1	1	0
Hannemann	.996	108	255	10	1	2
McKinney	.986	72	135	4	2	1
Rademacher	.981	101	197	5	4	2

MYRTLE BEACH PELICANS   HIGH CLASS A

CAROLINA LEAGUE

Batting	B-T	HT	WT	DOB	AVG	vLH	vRH	G	AB	R	H	2B	3B	HR	RBI	BB	HBP	SH	SF	SO	SB	CS	SLG	OBP
Baez, Jeffrey	R-R	6-0	180	10-30-93	.188	.000	.273	5	16	2	3	0	1	0	1	1	0	1	0	5	2	0	.313	.235
Brockmeyer, Cael	R-R	6-5	235	10-8-91	.217	.244	.200	36	120	15	26	6	0	3	24	17	4	0	4	32	0	1	.342	.324
Brown, Kevin	L-R	6-0	195	10-30-90	.225	.177	.240	75	262	29	59	11	3	4	21	23	1	1	2	35	1	1	.336	.288
Candelario, Jeimer	B-R	6-1	210	11-24-93	.270	.217	.289	82	318	42	86	25	3	5	39	20	3	0	2	62	0	1	.415	.318
Caratini, Victor	B-R	6-1	215	8-17-93	.257	.238	.264	112	393	39	101	31	1	4	53	49	5	0	6	75	0	0	.372	.342
Carhart, Ben	R-R	5-10	200	1-21-90	.255	.254	.255	44	153	25	39	8	0	7	25	14	3	2	3	24	0	1	.444	.324
Chen, Pin-Chieh	L-R	6-1	170	7-23-91	.268	.304	.255	96	366	52	98	17	5	4	34	32	5	6	1	48	20	5	.374	.334
Darvill, Wes	L-R	6-2	190	9-10-91	.220	.222	.220	20	59	9	13	4	1	1	5	8	0	3	0	11	1	1	.373	.313

CHICAGO CUBS

Batting

Batting	B-T	HT	WT	DOB	AVG	vLH	vRH	G	AB	R	H	2B	3B	HR	RBI	BB	HBP	SH	SF	SO	SB	CS	SLG	OBP
Denorfia, Chris	R-R	6-0	195	7-15-80	.333	.333	—	2	3	0	1	1	0	0	0	1	1	0	0	1	0	0	.667	.600
Dunston Jr., Shawon	L-R	6-2	195	2-5-93	.211	.200	.216	17	57	4	12	2	3	0	3	1	1	0	0	12	3	1	.351	.237
Hankins, Jordan	L-R	5-10	215	2-18-92	.227	.111	.246	23	66	8	15	5	0	1	6	9	0	0	1	12	2	1	.348	.316
Hannemann, Jacob	L-L	6-1	200	4-29-91	.328	.261	.368	16	61	12	20	4	0	0	4	6	0	1	0	15	7	1	.393	.388
Lockhart, Danny	L-R	5-11	175	11-4-92	.223	.218	.225	118	408	41	91	18	4	2	34	22	6	3	3	73	9	2	.301	.271
Martin, Trey	R-R	6-2	190	12-11-92	.239	.232	.241	90	306	35	73	13	1	2	31	17	2	5	2	83	14	4	.307	.281
McKinney, Billy	L-L	6-1	205	8-23-94	.340	.242	.386	29	103	19	35	5	2	4	25	17	2	0	3	13	0	2	.544	.432
Mineo, Alberto	L-R	5-10	170	7-23-94	.182	.000	.200	5	11	5	2	0	0	0	3	3	0	0	0	3	0	0	.182	.357
Penalver, Carlos	R-R	6-0	170	5-17-94	.197	.237	.183	114	381	38	75	10	4	2	42	42	3	6	5	80	11	8	.260	.278
Rogers, Jacob	L-R	6-4	220	8-23-89	.249	.217	.262	106	373	43	93	20	0	12	69	54	3	0	2	114	0	0	.399	.347
Torres, Gleyber	R-R	6-1	175	12-13-96	.174	.000	.250	7	23	1	4	0	0	0	2	1	0	0	0	7	0	1	.174	.208
Vosler, Jason	L-R	6-1	190	9-6-93	.244	.194	.264	38	127	19	31	7	0	6	20	26	4	0	0	27	0	0	.441	.389
Whiting, Sutton	B-R	5-8	170	5-13-92	.000	—	.000	3	6	0	0	0	0	0	0	0	0	0	0	4	0	0	.000	.000
Young, Chesny	R-R	6-0	170	10-6-92	.321	.348	.310	102	402	65	129	18	3	1	30	45	4	0	1	44	12	5	.388	.394
Zagunis, Mark	R-R	6-0	205	2-5-93	.271	.322	.252	115	413	78	112	24	5	8	54	80	16	0	3	86	12	10	.412	.406

Pitching

Pitching	B-T	HT	WT	DOB	W	L	ERA	G	GS	CG	SV	IP	H	R	ER	HR	BB	SO	AVG	vLH	vRH	K/9	BB/9
Berg, David	R-R	6-0	195	3-28-93	1	1	1.69	16	0	0	4	16	18	3	3	0	3	14	.286	.318	.268	7.88	1.69
Blackburn, Paul	R-R	6-1	195	12-4-93	7	5	3.11	18	18	0	0	90	89	36	31	3	22	63	.264	.263	.265	6.32	2.21
Brazis, Matt	R-R	6-3	215	9-6-89	0	0	3.86	3	0	0	2	5	3	2	2	0	4	6	.188	.000	.273	11.57	7.71
Cates, Zach	R-R	6-3	195	12-17-89	2	1	1.50	12	0	0	2	18	11	5	3	1	11	20	.175	.172	.176	10.00	5.50
Concepcion, Gerardo	L-L	6-2	200	2-29-92	0	2	3.55	7	0	0	1	13	9	6	5	0	8	14	.205	.273	.182	9.95	5.68
Conway, Josh	R-R	6-1	190	4-12-91	2	2	2.92	34	0	0	3	52	49	21	17	2	31	49	.251	.243	.256	8.43	5.33
Cruz, Fernando	B-R	6-2	205	3-28-90	1	2	3.78	15	3	0	2	33	31	15	14	4	12	25	.252	.245	.257	6.75	3.24
Farris, James	R-R	6-2	210	4-4-92	0	4	4.58	17	0	0	0	18	20	12	9	0	9	17	.282	.333	.244	8.66	4.58
Garner, David	R-R	6-1	180	9-21-92	2	1	2.37	16	0	0	2	30	17	9	8	3	10	36	.162	.128	.190	10.68	2.97
Heesch, Michael	R-L	6-5	265	5-15-90	8	2	2.24	33	2	0	3	64	57	19	16	2	24	49	.238	.160	.278	6.85	3.36
Ihrig, Tyler	L-L	6-0	210	9-17-91	0	1	2.86	14	2	0	0	44	44	15	14	2	12	34	.260	.213	.287	6.95	2.45
Markey, Brad	R-R	5-11	185	3-3-92	7	0	1.15	9	8	0	0	55	35	7	7	1	6	40	.186	.190	.183	6.55	0.98
Martinez, Jonathan	R-R	6-1	200	6-27-94	9	2	2.56	23	21	0	0	116	82	35	33	10	27	66	.199	.244	.169	5.12	2.09
Null, Jeremy	R-R	6-7	200	9-27-93	2	3	4.70	10	9	0	0	52	60	28	27	5	7	34	.300	.274	.319	5.92	1.22
Paniagua, Juan Carlos	R-R	6-1	200	4-4-90	3	2	2.58	20	0	0	0	38	25	11	11	2	11	35	.182	.156	.225	8.22	2.58
Peralta, Starling	R-R	6-4	210	11-11-90	1	0	4.50	3	0	0	1	4	5	2	2	0	2	7	.313	.500	.286	15.75	4.50
Pugliese, James	R-R	6-3	220	8-12-92	4	2	2.62	30	0	0	5	55	52	17	16	0	13	49	.255	.360	.194	8.02	2.13
Rakkar, Jasvir	R-R	6-2	200	4-27-91	3	3	2.96	38	0	0	16	46	44	18	15	0	10	37	.254	.315	.210	7.29	1.97
Scott, Tayler	R-R	6-3	185	6-1-92	2	2	1.96	11	1	0	2	23	18	6	5	1	6	27	.222	.259	.204	10.57	2.35
Skulina, Tyler	R-R	6-5	230	9-18-91	3	6	3.11	16	15	0	0	75	53	33	26	5	31	73	.199	.187	.210	8.72	3.70
Torrez, Daury	R-R	6-3	210	6-11-93	10	6	3.75	24	23	2	0	134	137	60	56	11	21	86	.266	.258	.271	5.76	1.41
Tseng, Jen-Ho	L-R	6-1	195	10-3-94	7	7	3.55	22	22	0	0	119	115	48	47	5	30	87	.256	.259	.254	6.58	2.27
Underwood, Duane	R-R	6-2	215	7-20-94	6	3	2.58	14	14	0	0	73	52	26	21	6	24	48	.202	.210	.195	5.89	2.95
Wells, Ben	R-R	6-3	220	9-10-92	1	0	6.75	5	0	0	0	9	9	7	7	0	5	5	.250	.188	.300	4.82	4.82

Fielding

Catcher	PCT	G	PO	A	E	DP	PB
Brockmeyer	.994	20	148	15	1	2	1
Caratini	.992	86	572	49	5	3	2
Carhart	1.000	21	135	15	0	0	0
Hankins	1.000	10	54	11	0	1	1
Mineo	1.000	3	19	2	0	0	1

First Base	PCT	G	PO	A	E	DP
Brockmeyer	.970	6	57	7	2	11
Caratini	1.000	12	121	6	0	9
Carhart	1.000	4	40	2	0	3
Rogers	.993	105	888	88	7	81
Vosler	1.000	3	29	1	0	3
Young	.986	8	65	4	1	7

Second Base	PCT	G	PO	A	E	DP
Darvill	1.000	9	17	22	0	4
Lockhart	.980	107	201	349	11	71
Whiting	1.000	1	3	2	0	1
Young	1.000	21	38	60	0	17

Third Base	PCT	G	PO	A	E	DP
Candelario	.951	77	45	111	8	9
Carhart	.333	2	0	1	2	0
Darvill	1.000	1	1	1	0	0
Vosler	.943	35	15	68	5	8
Young	.983	23	18	39	1	5

Shortstop	PCT	G	PO	A	E	DP
Lockhart	.909	6	9	11	2	3
Penalver	.963	114	156	336	19	69

	PCT	G	PO	A	E	DP
Torres	.960	7	8	16	1	7
Whiting	1.000	1	2	3	0	1
Young	.967	10	11	18	1	0

Outfield	PCT	G	PO	A	E	DP
Baez	1.000	5	8	0	0	0
Brown	.990	56	101	1	1	0
Chen	.986	95	198	7	3	2
Darvill	1.000	6	6	0	0	0
Denorfia	1.000	2	1	0	0	0
Dunston Jr.	1.000	14	28	1	0	0
Hannemann	1.000	16	28	1	0	0
Martin	1.000	90	224	4	0	2
McKinney	1.000	17	27	2	0	1
Young	1.000	17	23	4	0	0
Zagunis	.982	100	160	5	3	1

SOUTH BEND CUBS — LOW CLASS A

MIDWEST LEAGUE

Batting	B-T	HT	WT	DOB	AVG	vLH	vRH	G	AB	R	H	2B	3B	HR	RBI	BB	HBP	SH	SF	SO	SB	CS	SLG	OBP
Amaya, Gioskar	R-R	5-11	175	12-13-92	.260	.224	.270	110	400	45	104	18	2	4	43	44	6	—	2	73	17	5	.345	.341
Amendolare, Angelo	R-R	5-9	170	12-2-92	.310	.500	.238	8	29	6	9	3	0	0	6	4	0	0	1	4	0	0	.414	.382
Baez, Jeffrey	R-R	6-0	180	10-30-93	.284	.291	.282	101	377	67	107	17	5	9	34	22	1	—	1	67	34	10	.427	.324
Balaguert, Yasiel	R-R	6-2	215	1-9-93	.271	.333	.253	82	317	34	86	18	2	7	40	17	2	0	3	54	3	1	.407	.310
Bote, David	R-R	5-11	185	4-7-93	.251	.308	.228	98	315	46	79	20	2	6	41	29	7	—	0	54	8	3	.384	.328
Brockmeyer, Cael	R-R	6-5	235	10-8-91	.274	.349	.247	63	237	31	65	16	1	5	33	27	3	0	0	60	1	1	.414	.356
Burks, Charcer	R-R	6-0	170	3-9-95	.257	.202	.275	116	435	63	112	22	4	3	44	51	4	—	3	83	28	9	.347	.339
Castillo, Erick	B-R	5-11	178	2-25-93	.222	.192	.229	40	135	9	30	4	0	0	13	4	2	1	3	18	0	0	.252	.250
Crawford, Rashad	B-B	6-3	185	10-15-93	.280	.289	.277	107	361	54	101	15	5	4	50	20	4	—	3	90	20	5	.382	.322
Ely, Andrew	L-R	5-11	180	1-23-93	.196	.261	.185	42	153	12	30	9	0	2	14	7	1	0	1	29	0	1	.294	.235
Encarnacion, Kevin	B-R	6-0	175	11-23-91	.276	.256	.281	63	210	31	58	6	3	3	17	17	5	—	0	43	5	5	.376	.345

Batting	B-T	HT	WT	DOB	AVG	vLH	vRH	G	AB	R	H	2B	3B	HR	RBI	BB	HBP	SH	SF	SO	SB	CS	SLG	OBP
Flete, Bryant	B-R	5-10	146	1-31-93	.075	.091	.069	14	40	2	3	1	0	0	0	2	0	1	0	12	1	0	.100	.119
Hankins, Jordan	L-R	5-10	215	2-18-92	.375	.667	.308	5	16	0	6	0	0	0	5	2	1	0	0	1	0	0	.375	.474
Happ, Ian	B-R	6-0	205	8-12-94	.241	.188	.257	38	145	24	35	9	3	5	22	17	0	0	3	39	1	1	.448	.315
Hodges, Jesse	R-R	6-1	212	3-29-94	.238	.237	.238	90	303	32	72	18	1	6	34	28	7	1	1	86	1	2	.363	.316
Machin, Vimael	L-R	5-10	173	9-25-93	.177	.150	.183	33	113	9	20	4	0	0	7	15	0	—	1	20	1	0	.212	.271
Marra, Justin	L-R	5-10	190	1-18-93	.161	.071	.178	28	87	12	14	3	0	4	9	9	0	0	0	33	0	0	.333	.240
Martin, Trey	R-R	6-2	190	12-11-92	.250	.280	.234	16	72	11	18	5	2	0	8	2	0	0	0	19	6	0	.375	.270
Rose, Matt	R-R	6-4	195	8-2-94	.308	.417	.275	14	52	4	16	1	0	1	10	3	1	—	0	14	0	1	.385	.357
Spingola, Daniel	L-L	6-1	165	5-5-93	.100	.333	.000	4	10	1	1	0	0	0	0	1	0	0	0	2	0	0	.100	.182
Torres, Gleyber	R-R	6-1	175	12-13-96	.293	.291	.294	119	464	53	136	24	5	3	62	43	2	—	4	108	22	13	.386	.353
Vosler, Jason	L-R	6-1	190	9-6-93	.235	.196	.244	69	255	26	60	11	2	4	20	15	3	2	1	34	3	4	.341	.285
Young, Chesny	R-R	6-0	170	10-6-92	.315	.400	.282	28	108	23	34	5	1	0	14	12	1	0	1	7	9	3	.380	.385

Pitching	B-T	HT	WT	DOB	W	L	ERA	G	GS	CG	SV	IP	H	R	ER	HR	BB	SO	AVG	vLH	vRH	K/9	BB/9
Carrillo, Francisco	R-R	6-0	190	3-15-90	0	5	4.40	16	0	0	2	31	32	20	15	1	8	24	.262	.244	.273	7.04	2.35
Clifton, Trevor	R-R	6-4	170	5-11-95	8	10	3.98	23	22	0	0	109	91	55	48	7	47	103	.230	.244	.220	8.53	3.89
Farris, James	R-R	6-2	210	4-4-92	2	4	2.79	21	0	0	9	29	27	12	9	0	9	39	.239	.250	.233	12.10	2.79
Garner, David	R-R	6-1	180	9-21-92	2	0	5.33	16	0	0	1	25	27	15	15	1	10	31	.265	.231	.286	11.01	3.55
Hedges, Zach	R-R	6-4	195	10-21-92	8	8	4.16	23	23	0	0	132	133	74	61	5	36	80	.260	.291	.236	5.45	2.45
Hoffner, Corbin	R-R	6-5	235	7-30-93	1	0	1.32	19	0	0	9	27	22	4	4	0	9	16	.232	.379	.167	5.27	2.96
Ihrig, Tyler	L-L	6-0	210	9-17-91	3	1	2.70	12	1	0	2	33	27	11	10	0	5	26	.223	.139	.259	7.02	1.35
Knighton, John Michael	R-R	6-2	190	4-30-94	0	1	18.00	1	0	0	0	1	3	2	2	0	0	1	.600	.500	1.000	9.00	0.00
Leal, Erick	R-R	6-3	180	3-17-95	10	8	3.85	23	23	0	0	129	138	63	55	11	32	86	.273	.244	.293	6.02	2.24
Lewis, Daniel	R-R	6-0	200	3-26-91	0	2	3.68	24	0	0	0	37	31	16	15	1	30	22	.223	.270	.184	5.40	7.36
Maples, Dillon	R-R	6-2	195	5-9-92	1	1	4.15	15	0	0	1	30	28	16	14	2	12	19	.252	.146	.314	5.64	3.56
Markey, Brad	R-R	5-11	185	3-3-92	0	0	2.48	12	1	0	2	29	24	9	8	0	4	23	.222	.264	.182	7.14	1.24
McNeil, Ryan	R-R	6-3	210	2-1-94	3	3	2.80	32	1	0	2	61	60	27	19	3	24	57	.259	.284	.241	8.41	3.54
Minch, Jordan	L-L	6-3	180	7-16-93	0	4	4.31	36	0	0	3	63	70	41	30	2	32	46	.290	.231	.319	6.61	4.60
Norwood, James	R-R	6-2	205	12-24-93	2	4	4.95	13	7	0	1	40	40	25	22	2	19	30	.267	.222	.292	6.75	4.28
Null, Jeremy	R-R	6-7	200	9-27-93	6	2	2.33	12	12	0	0	66	68	21	17	2	4	48	.265	.268	.263	6.58	0.55
Rakkar, Jasvir	R-R	6-2	200	4-27-91	0	0	2.35	3	0	0	0	8	9	4	2	0	1	8	.273	.333	.222	9.39	1.17
Santana, Alex	R-R	6-1	170	10-23-93	0	2	3.15	13	0	0	0	20	13	10	7	1	9	17	.183	.290	.100	7.65	4.05
Stinnett, Jake	R-R	6-4	202	4-25-92	7	6	4.46	22	22	0	0	117	117	66	58	6	50	91	.267	.295	.247	7.00	3.85
Thorpe, Tommy	L-L	6-0	185	9-20-92	5	7	3.08	27	12	0	1	96	95	42	33	3	41	65	.265	.271	.263	6.07	3.83
Wagner, Michael	R-R	6-3	175	10-3-91	2	2	3.22	15	5	0	1	50	49	19	18	3	19	38	.254	.266	.246	6.79	3.40
Williams, Ryan	R-R	6-4	220	11-1-91	4	1	1.17	9	8	0	0	54	36	12	7	0	2	37	.190	.200	.184	6.20	0.34
Wilson, Sam	L-L	6-2	200	7-30-91	1	1	5.95	11	0	0	2	20	25	18	13	3	7	17	.298	.370	.263	7.78	3.20

Fielding

Catcher	PCT	G	PO	A	E	DP	PB
Amaya	.993	60	363	60	3	3	17
Brockmeyer	.996	35	259	22	1	1	0
Castillo	.996	40	240	37	1	1	3
Hankins	1.000	1	7	1	0	0	0
Hodges	.900	1	7	2	1	0	0
Marra	1.000	7	38	7	0	0	0

First Base	PCT	G	PO	A	E	DP
Amaya	.990	43	359	30	4	34
Balaguert	.991	36	311	16	3	31
Bote	1.000	12	91	6	0	4
Brockmeyer	.991	23	208	10	2	14
Encarnacion	1.000	3	16	1	0	3
Hankins	.950	3	19	0	1	4
Hodges	.988	8	78	6	1	6
Marra	1.000	2	5	0	0	1
Rose	1.000	12	119	8	0	8

	PCT	G	PO	A	E	DP
Vosler	.980	5	47	3	1	3

Second Base	PCT	G	PO	A	E	DP
Amaya	1.000	1	1	0	0	0
Amendolare	.947	8	21	15	2	5
Bote	.992	57	94	155	2	32
Ely	.987	37	50	104	2	22
Flete	.958	7	8	15	1	4
Machin	1.000	5	9	17	0	3
Vosler	.968	7	15	15	1	7
Young	.981	26	38	65	2	10

Third Base	PCT	G	PO	A	E	DP
Bote	.923	10	8	16	2	0
Flete	1.000	1	1	0	0	0
Hodges	.902	76	47	128	19	7
Machin	.949	14	9	28	2	2
Rose	1.000	2	1	6	0	0
Vosler	.925	38	28	70	8	4

Shortstop	PCT	G	PO	A	E	DP
Flete	.875	4	2	12	2	2
Machin	.964	12	13	41	2	10
Torres	.949	119	162	319	26	75
Vosler	1.000	5	7	15	0	2
Young	.917	4	3	8	1	2

Outfield	PCT	G	PO	A	E	DP
Baez	.969	95	168	17	6	3
Balaguert	.968	31	58	2	2	1
Bote	1.000	1	2	0	0	0
Burks	.991	102	215	4	2	0
Crawford	.992	105	244	10	2	1
Ely	—	1	0	0	0	0
Encarnacion	.987	38	73	3	1	3
Happ	.986	32	71	1	1	1
Martin	1.000	15	41	1	0	0
Spingola	.800	3	4	0	1	0

CHICAGO CUBS

EUGENE EMERALDS — SHORT-SEASON

NORTHWEST LEAGUE

Batting	B-T	HT	WT	DOB	AVG	vLH	vRH	G	AB	R	H	2B	3B	HR	RBI	BB	HBP	SH	SF	SO	SB	CS	SLG	OBP
Alamo, Tyler	R-R	6-4	200	5-2-95	.261	.296	.238	41	138	19	36	1	0	0	14	16	1	0	2	24	1	1	.268	.338
Bautista, Alex	R-R	6-0	210	9-6-93	.242	.167	.267	28	99	15	24	6	0	2	13	7	2	0	1	29	1	2	.364	.303
Cuevas, Varonex	B-R	6-0	165	7-24-92	.207	.182	.222	11	29	3	6	1	0	0	3	5	1	0	1	10	0	0	.241	.333
Delarosa, Frandy	B-R	6-1	180	1-24-96	.273	.256	.282	62	256	32	70	20	2	0	30	15	2	2	3	64	11	7	.367	.315
Dewees, Donnie	L-L	5-11	180	9-29-93	.266	.314	.245	66	282	42	75	14	1	5	30	14	3	2	2	54	19	7	.376	.306
Ely, Andrew	L-R	5-11	180	1-23-93	.301	.361	.280	37	143	16	43	13	2	1	15	14	3	0	1	25	3	0	.441	.373
Ha, Jae-Hoon	R-R	6-1	185	10-29-90	—	—	—	1	0	0	0	0	0	0	0	0	0	0	0	0	0	0	—	—
Happ, Ian	B-R	6-0	205	8-12-94	.283	.350	.242	29	106	26	30	8	1	4	11	23	0	0	1	28	9	0	.491	.408
Headley, Blake	L-R	6-2	218	5-7-93	.230	.200	.240	60	191	21	44	10	1	0	19	18	2	1	1	45	2	1	.293	.302
Higgins, P.J.	R-R	5-10	185	5-10-93	.316	.231	.341	15	57	8	18	4	0	0	5	3	1	0	0	11	1	0	.386	.361
Jimenez, Eloy	R-R	6-4	205	11-27-96	.284	.320	.268	57	232	36	66	10	0	7	33	15	1	0	2	43	3	2	.418	.328
Machin, Vimael	L-R	5-10	173	9-25-93	.188	.000	.222	11	32	2	6	2	0	0	3	1	2	0	0	6	1	1	.250	.257
Marcano, Ricardo	L-R	6-2	190	10-18-94	.236	.273	.224	35	89	12	21	3	1	0	14	14	1	2	1	28	2	2	.292	.343

Batting	B-T	HT	WT	DOB	AVG	vLH	vRH	G	AB	R	H	2B	3B	HR	RBI	BB	HBP	SH	SF	SO	SB	CS	SLG	OBP
Marra, Justin	L-R	5-10	190	1-18-93	.194	.154	.204	22	62	5	12	2	1	1	8	11	1	0	0	26	0	0	.306	.324
Martarano, Joe	R-R	6-4	235	7-28-94	.133	.000	.222	4	15	0	2	0	0	0	1	0	0	0	0	5	0	0	.133	.133
Mineo, Alberto	L-R	5-10	170	7-23-94	.202	.174	.211	32	99	9	20	6	2	0	12	16	1	0	4	26	1	0	.303	.308
Mitchell, Kevonte	R-R	6-4	185	8-12-95	.169	.145	.183	49	148	19	25	6	2	0	9	18	0	0	1	47	10	1	.236	.257
Paula, Adonis	R-R	6-1	185	6-21-94	.261	.268	.257	47	157	12	41	9	2	2	19	11	2	0	1	48	1	1	.382	.316
Rice, Ian	R-R	6-0	195	8-19-93	.252	.300	.229	47	159	16	40	8	0	2	19	26	6	1	1	34	2	0	.340	.375
Rose, Matt	R-R	6-4	195	8-2-94	.254	.238	.264	31	114	15	29	7	0	3	27	7	0	0	4	26	0	0	.395	.288
Son, Ho-Young	R-R	5-11	170	3-4-95	.218	.275	.190	39	119	15	26	7	0	0	8	9	4	1	2	17	4	3	.277	.291
Spingola, Daniel	L-L	6-1	165	5-5-93	.125	.000	.143	2	8	0	1	0	0	0	0	0	0	0	0	2	0	0	.125	.125
Whiting, Sutton	B-R	5-8	170	5-13-92	.235	.500	.219	14	34	7	8	2	0	0	1	3	0	3	0	7	3	2	.294	.297

Pitching	B-T	HT	WT	DOB	W	L	ERA	G	GS	CG	SV	IP	H	R	ER	HR	BB	SO	AVG	vLH	vRH	K/9	BB/9
Alzolay, Adbert	R-R	6-0	179	3-1-95	6	2	2.04	12	3	0	0	53	29	13	12	5	15	49	.159	.179	.151	8.32	2.55
Araujo, Pedro	R-R	6-3	214	7-2-93	0	2	2.68	21	0	0	1	50	43	17	15	1	9	70	.224	.262	.206	12.52	1.61
Berg, David	R-R	6-0	195	3-28-93	1	0	0.00	2	0	0	1	3	0	0	0	0	0	4	.000	.000	.000	10.80	0.00
Bloomquist, Casey	R-R	6-3	190	1-25-94	0	2	2.29	8	4	0	0	20	13	5	5	0	2	22	.183	.217	.167	10.07	0.92
Brink, Jordan	L-R	6-0	200	3-18-93	1	0	1.93	2	0	0	0	5	5	3	1	0	1	8	.250	.429	.154	15.43	1.93
Brooks, Craig	R-R	5-10	180	9-23-92	2	0	3.38	10	0	0	2	11	7	6	4	0	3	21	.179	.188	.174	17.72	2.53
Carrillo, Francisco	R-R	6-0	190	3-15-90	1	1	3.55	5	0	0	1	13	11	5	5	0	5	11	.229	.222	.233	7.82	3.55
Cheek, Jared	R-R	5-11	180	10-31-92	0	0	7.84	9	0	0	2	10	13	9	9	1	7	9	.310	.250	.346	7.84	6.10
De La Cruz, Oscar	R-R	6-4	200	3-4-95	6	3	2.84	13	13	0	0	73	56	27	23	4	17	73	.211	.245	.192	9.00	2.10
Diaz, Andin	L-L	6-0	182	9-2-92	0	2	7.36	4	4	0	0	15	13	13	12	1	15	18	.232	.273	.222	11.05	9.20
Dwyer, Heath	L-L	6-3	200	6-4-93	0	0	4.50	4	0	0	0	6	10	3	3	0	2	8	.385	.222	.471	12.00	3.00
Effross, Scott	R-R	6-1	195	12-28-93	0	0	1.26	7	0	0	2	14	9	3	2	0	5	11	.173	.227	.133	6.91	3.14
Eregua, Greyfer	R-R	5-11	160	10-15-93	0	3	2.47	17	0	0	2	44	31	15	12	0	14	45	.197	.170	.212	9.27	2.89
Frazier, Scott	R-R	6-7	215	12-3-91	1	0	7.71	7	0	0	0	7	11	7	6	3	0	8	.333	.250	.381	10.29	0.00
Griggs, Tanner	R-R	6-2	165	6-14-94	0	1	12.91	6	0	0	1	8	11	12	11	0	6	9	.333	.375	.320	10.57	7.04
Hernandez, Luis	R-R	6-5	210	3-13-95	0	0	4.50	4	0	0	0	6	4	3	3	1	5	9	.190	.143	.214	13.50	7.50
Hoffner, Corbin	R-R	6-5	235	7-30-93	0	0	0.00	3	0	0	0	4	4	0	0	0	2	2	.250	.200	.273	4.15	0.00
Kellogg, Ryan	R-L	6-5	225	2-4-94	0	1	4.98	10	9	0	0	22	27	14	12	1	8	14	.307	.391	.277	5.82	3.32
Maples, Dillon	R-R	6-2	195	5-9-92	0	1	7.20	3	0	0	0	5	7	9	4	0	1	8	.292	.500	.222	14.40	1.80
Masek, Trey	R-R	6-0	175	1-9-92	0	0	3.31	14	0	0	2	16	12	6	6	1	7	17	.190	.190	.190	9.37	3.86
Miller, Kyle	R-R	6-3	185	12-2-93	1	1	3.94	8	3	0	0	16	16	8	7	1	7	12	.267	.214	.283	6.75	3.94
Morrison, Preston	R-R	6-2	185	7-19-93	1	1	0.81	9	4	0	0	22	15	2	2	0	3	30	.183	.200	.173	12.09	1.21
Paulino, Jose	L-L	6-1	160	4-9-95	4	6	4.42	12	6	0	0	55	59	33	27	5	21	57	.272	.146	.301	9.33	3.44
Peitzmeier, Tyler	L-L	6-2	210	2-26-93	2	3	5.94	12	0	0	1	17	14	11	11	2	5	16	.230	.263	.214	8.64	2.70
Sands, Carson	L-L	6-3	205	3-28-95	3	4	3.92	14	14	0	0	57	62	40	25	0	21	41	.277	.250	.283	6.44	3.30
Santana, Alex	R-R	6-1	170	10-23-93	2	1	6.52	7	0	0	1	10	11	9	7	2	3	11	.289	.357	.250	10.24	2.79
Steele, Justin	L-L	6-2	195	7-11-95	3	1	2.66	10	10	0	0	41	38	24	12	0	15	38	.245	.324	.220	8.41	3.32
Twomey, Kyle	L-L	6-3	165	12-29-93	1	1	2.35	10	6	0	0	23	17	7	6	1	13	22	.207	.200	.210	8.61	5.09
Williamson, John	L-L	6-1	195	9-27-92	0	1	12.38	7	0	0	0	8	13	13	11	0	6	7	.371	.273	.417	7.88	6.75
Wilson, Sam	L-L	6-2	200	7-30-91	0	0	0.00	3	0	0	1	4	3	2	0	0	0	4	.214	.000	.273	9.82	0.00

Fielding

Catcher	PCT	G	PO	A	E	DP	PB
Alamo	.997	36	309	50	1	1	13
Marra	1.000	3	24	3	0	0	0
Mineo	.990	22	173	23	2	1	3
Rice	.975	18	144	10	4	0	0

First Base	PCT	G	PO	A	E	DP
Alamo	1.000	4	27	3	0	2
Cuevas	.985	7	60	5	4	9
Headley	1.000	35	284	24	0	20
Martarano	1.000	4	29	1	0	1
Mineo	.979	7	46	1	1	3
Rose	.996	27	222	14	1	18

Second Base	PCT	G	PO	A	E	DP
Cuevas	.800	2	1	3	1	0

	PCT	G	PO	A	E	DP
Delarosa	.943	61	103	147	15	30
Ely	1.000	3	3	3	0	1
Higgins	.960	9	9	15	1	1
Whiting	1.000	4	3	12	0	1

Third Base	PCT	G	PO	A	E	DP
Ely	1.000	5	1	9	0	1
Headley	.955	22	19	44	3	5
Higgins	1.000	7	2	14	0	0
Machin	.933	4	2	12	1	1
Paula	.906	42	24	82	11	5
Rose	1.000	4	2	3	0	0

Shortstop	PCT	G	PO	A	E	DP
Ely	.978	32	38	94	3	15
Headley	1.000	2	1	1	0	0

	PCT	G	PO	A	E	DP
Machin	.955	7	7	14	1	3
Paula	.900	3	5	4	1	1
Son	.884	37	41	81	16	13
Whiting	.600	2	0	3	2	0

Outfield	PCT	G	PO	A	E	DP
Bautista	.972	20	35	0	1	0
Dewees	.985	59	130	1	2	0
Happ	1.000	28	43	2	0	0
Jimenez	.976	54	79	3	2	2
Marcano	.952	30	35	5	2	1
Mitchell	.963	44	76	2	3	1
Spingola	—	1	0	0	0	0
Whiting	1.000	1	1	0	0	0

AZL CUBS

ROOKIE

ARIZONA LEAGUE

Batting	B-T	HT	WT	DOB	AVG	vLH	vRH	G	AB	R	H	2B	3B	HR	RBI	BB	HBP	SH	SF	SO	SB	CS	SLG	OBP
Alcala, Roney	B-R	6-1	223	2-15-94	.000	—	.000	1	3	0	0	0	0	0	0	0	0	0	0	1	0	0	.000	.000
Amendolare, Angelo	R-R	5-9	170	12-2-92	.268	.200	.278	14	41	4	11	1	0	0	6	9	2	0	0	3	1	2	.293	.423
Baez, Javier	R-R	6-0	190	12-1-92	.417	.667	.333	4	12	3	5	1	0	0	1	1	2	0	0	1	0	0	.500	.533
Bautista, Alex	R-R	6-0	190	6-9-93	.274	.556	.226	18	62	10	17	1	2	1	8	3	1	0	0	14	0	2	.403	.318
Carhart, Ben	R-R	5-10	200	1-21-90	.333	.400	.300	4	15	2	5	2	0	0	3	0	0	0	0	4	0	0	.467	.333
Caro, Roberto	B-R	6-0	185	9-25-93	.255	.161	.299	31	98	19	25	3	3	0	9	14	1	5	1	22	8	3	.347	.351
Cimino, Donnie	L-L	6-2	205	8-21-93	.217	.286	.196	20	60	7	13	1	0	0	3	4	2	0	1	11	0	1	.233	.284
Cuevas, Varonex	B-R	6-0	165	7-24-92	.344	.375	.333	10	32	2	11	3	1	0	2	5	0	0	0	9	3	0	.500	.432
Dunston Jr., Shawon	L-R	6-2	195	2-5-93	.350	.400	.333	7	20	1	7	2	0	0	2	3	0	0	1	3	1	0	.450	.417
Emeterio, Jenner	R-R	6-1	170	3-19-93	.333	—	.333	1	3	1	1	0	0	0	0	0	0	0	0	0	0	0	.333	.500
Foster, Michael	R-R	6-0	170	11-4-93	.241	.188	.254	25	87	12	21	2	1	0	11	11	3	0	1	19	2	3	.287	.343

Batting

Batting	B-T	HT	WT	DOB	AVG	vLH	vRH	G	AB	R	H	2B	3B	HR	RBI	BB	HBP	SH	SF	SO	SB	CS	SLG	OBP
Galindo, Wladimir	R-R	6-3	210	11-6-96	.358	.438	.333	19	67	15	24	7	2	0	11	4	2	0	2	15	1	1	.522	.400
Garcia, Robert	B-R	5-10	170	12-6-93	.341	.306	.350	47	173	32	59	4	4	2	23	16	4	5	0	31	17	8	.445	.409
Graves, Calvin	R-R	5-9	170	3-18-91	.000	.000	.000	1	3	0	0	0	0	0	0	0	0	0	0	0	0	0	.000	.000
Gutierrez, Danny	R-R	5-7	152	3-1-91	.286	.000	.400	2	7	1	2	1	0	0	0	0	0	0	0	2	0	1	.429	.286
Higgins, P.J.	R-R	5-10	185	5-10-93	.288	.238	.305	21	80	17	23	4	3	2	10	7	0	0	0	15	3	0	.488	.345
Jimenez, Carlos	R-R	5-10	175	7-3-93	.236	.269	.225	30	106	11	25	5	1	1	11	3	1	1	0	15	0	0	.330	.264
Martarano, Joe	R-R	6-4	235	7-28-94	.315	.455	.279	14	54	5	17	4	1	0	12	1	2	0	1	9	1	0	.426	.345
Mastrobuoni, Marcus	R-R	5-11	205	11-28-93	.159	.167	.156	16	44	4	7	1	0	0	2	6	1	1	1	3	0	0	.182	.269
Matos, Yohan	R-R	6-0	175	10-6-96	.156	.235	.133	23	77	7	12	2	0	1	11	5	2	1	0	25	1	1	.221	.226
Mitchell, Kevonte	R-R	6-4	185	8-12-95	.235	.250	.231	5	17	5	4	2	0	0	1	5	1	0	0	4	3	0	.353	.435
Monasterio, Andrews	B-R	6-0	175	5-30-97	.252	.308	.239	42	135	18	34	6	2	1	16	16	4	2	1	20	6	2	.348	.346
Paniagua, Jose	R-R	6-2	180	6-7-94	.255	.237	.261	42	157	23	40	9	1	4	25	8	3	0	0	39	1	4	.401	.304
Payne, Tyler	R-R	5-11	210	10-25-92	.192	.333	.184	16	52	3	10	1	0	3	11	0	0	0	8	0	1	.212	.333
Pereda, Jhonny	R-R	6-1	170	4-18-96	.143	.200	.120	11	35	6	5	3	0	0	1	3	1	0	1	6	0	0	.229	.225
Rico, Miguel	R-R	6-2	204	9-15-93	.500	.500	.500	2	8	1	4	0	0	1	0	0	0	0	0	2	0	0	.500	.500
Sepulveda, Carlos	L-R	5-10	10	8-27-96	.281	.279	.282	47	185	27	52	5	0	0	25	19	2	5	2	30	6	1	.308	.351
Son, Ho-Young	R-R	5-11	170	8-23-94	.667	.667	—	1	3	0	2	0	0	0	0	1	0	0	0	0	0	0	.667	.750
Spingola, Daniel	L-L	6-1	165	5-5-93	.529	.400	.583	6	17	4	9	4	2	0	7	3	0	1	1	2	1	0	1.000	.571
Vogelbach, Dan	L-R	6-0	250	12-17-92	.455	1.000	.333	5	11	4	5	2	0	0	6	0	0	0	1	0	0	0	.636	.647
Whiting, Sutton	B-R	5-8	170	5-13-92	.200	.000	.231	5	15	4	3	1	0	0	1	1	0	0	4	3	0	.267	.294
Wilson, D.J.	R-R	5-9	177	10-8-96	.266	.313	.254	22	79	12	21	3	2	0	6	6	1	2	1	15	5	1	.354	.322

Pitching

Pitching	B-T	HT	WT	DOB	W	L	ERA	G	GS	CG	SV	IP	H	R	ER	HR	BB	SO	AVG	vLH	vRH	K/9	BB/9
Bloomquist, Casey	R-R	6-3	190	1-25-94	0	0	0.00	1	0	0	1	0	0	0	0	0	2		.000	.000	.000	18.00	0.00
Brazis, Matt	R-R	6-3	215	9-6-89	0	0	0.00	4	1	0	0	5	2	0	0	0	3		.125	.143	.111	5.79	0.00
Brink, Jordan	L-R	6-0	200	3-18-93	0	0	0.00	2	0	0	0	2	3	0	0	0	1		.300	.500	.250	4.50	0.00
Brooks, Craig	R-R	5-10	180	9-23-92	0	0	10.80	4	0	0	0	3	5	4	4	0	1	4	.333	.200	.400	10.80	2.70
Camargo, Jesus	R-R	5-11	170	11-23-95	3	1	3.30	11	7	0	0	46	36	18	17	1	12	57	.214	.219	.212	11.07	2.33
Carreno, Marcelo	R-R	6-1	170	6-26-91	—																		
Carrillo, Francisco	R-R	6-0	190	3-15-90	1	0	3.86	2	0	0	0	2	1	1	1	1	0	2	.125	.000	.167	7.71	0.00
Castillo, Jesus	R-R	6-2	165	8-27-95	1	2	4.58	11	0	0	0	20	26	12	10	1	9	17	.306	.379	.268	7.78	4.12
Cease, Dylan	R-R	6-1	175	12-28-95	1	2	2.63	11	8	0	0	24	12	12	7	0	16	25	.145	.172	.130	9.38	6.00
Cheek, Jared	B-R	5-11	180	10-31-92	0	0	0.00	3	0	0	2	5	1	0	0	0	1	6	.063	.143	.000	10.80	1.80
De Los Rios, Enrique	R-R	6-1	175	5-24-95	1	1	3.46	8	4	0	0	26	25	14	10	1	5	18	.245	.341	.180	6.23	1.73
Dwyer, Heath	L-L	6-3	200	6-4-93	0	0	3.00	8	2	0	1	15	15	6	5	0	3	20	.268	.294	.256	12.00	1.80
Effross, Scott	R-R	6-1	195	12-28-93	0	1	4.05	5	0	0	0	7	7	3	3	1	0	6	.292	.364	.231	8.10	0.00
Frazier, Scott	R-R	6-7	215	12-3-91	0	0	3.00	3	0	0	1	3	1	1	1	0	2	3	.100	.250	.000	9.00	6.00
Griggs, Tanner	R-R	6-2	165	6-14-94	1	1	0.00	8	0	0	2	11	5	1	0	0	4	10	.147	.200	.105	8.71	3.48
Hernandez, Luis	R-R	6-5	210	3-13-95	1	1	0.82	7	0	0	0	11	9	2	1	0	3	18	.220	.250	.207	14.73	2.45
Hudson, Bryan	L-L	6-8	220	5-8-97	0	0	2.70	5	0	0	0	7	6	4	2	0	2	5	.222	.167	.238	6.75	2.70
Jokisch, Eric	R-L	6-2	205	7-8-89	1	1	0.79	3	3	0	0	11	3	1	1	0	3	8	.283	.571	.231	6.35	2.38
Knighton, John Michael	R-R	6-2	190	4-30-94	2	0	5.40	12	0	0	0	22	24	13	13	4	4	18	.282	.320	.267	7.48	1.66
Lima, Gabriel	R-R	6-2	180	5-2-96	0	1	6.00	3	1	0	0	6	6	5	4	0	5	3	.300	.400	.267	4.50	7.50
Marte, Junior	R-R	6-0	175	6-6-95	0	0	3.00	2	0	0	0	3	3	1	1	0	2	6	.300	.500	.000	18.00	6.00
Masek, Trey	R-R	6-0	175	1-9-92	0	1	15.75	4	0	0	0	4	8	7	7	0	4	4	.286	.167	.375	9.00	9.00
McNutt, Trey	R-R	6-4	220	8-2-89	2	0	6.75	8	1	0	0	8	9	6	6	1	3	4	.290	.333	.263	4.50	3.38
Miller, Kyle	R-R	6-3	185	12-2-93	0	0	0.00	1	0	0	0	1	2	0	0	0	0	1	.500	1.000	.000	9.00	0.00
Minacci, M.T.	R-R	6-0	170	6-6-95	0	0	7.94	9	0	0	0	11	16	11	10	0	6	7	.327	.333	.323	5.56	4.76
Moreno, Erling	R-R	6-3	200	1-13-97	1	1	1.93	3	0	0	0	5	3	1	1	0	2	2	.176	.000	.273	3.86	3.86
Norwood, James	R-R	6-2	205	12-24-93	0	2	3.60	4	4	0	0	10	9	5	4	0	2	9	.257	.286	.238	8.10	1.80
Peitzmeier, Tyler	L-L	6-2	210	2-26-93	0	0	0.00	1	0	0	0	1	1	0	0	0	0	1	.333	.000	.500	9.00	0.00
Rodriguez, Carlos A.	L-L	5-11	178	7-18-95	4	1	4.21	11	0	0	0	26	23	12	12	3	8	26	.247	.259	.242	9.12	2.81
Rodriguez, Santiago	R-R	6-0	185	6-14-94	1	1	3.55	7	0	0	0	13	14	5	5	1	4	9	.286	.250	.303	6.39	2.84
Rondon, Manuel	L-L	6-1	165	3-7-95	1	2	4.88	8	5	0	0	31	33	21	17	0	11	27	.270	.375	.233	7.76	3.16
2-team total (2 Angels)					2	3	5.67	10	7	0	0	40	46	29	25	0	15	34	—	—	—	7.71	3.40
Rosscup, Zac	R-L	6-2	220	6-9-88	0	0	0.00	1	0	0	0	2	0	0	0	0	0	5	.000	.000	.000	22.50	0.00
Silverio, Pedro	R-R	6-2	210	6-29-94	1	0	3.38	6	0	0	0	24	20	10	9	1	8	15	.227	.118	.296	5.63	3.00
Skulina, Tyler	R-R	6-5	230	9-18-91	0	0	2.70	3	1	0	0	3	5	1	1	0	2	4	.357	.750	.200	10.80	5.40
Underwood, Duane	R-R	6-2	215	7-20-94	0	0	0.00	2	2	0	0	5	3	0	0	0	0	6	.167	.222	.111	10.80	0.00
Williamson, John	L-L	6-1	195	9-27-92	1	0	0.00	4	0	0	0	10	7	1	0	0	2	11	.189	.250	.172	9.58	1.74
Willis, Austyn	R-R	6-6	205	6-13-96	3	3	3.45	11	9	0	1	44	42	18	17	2	16	23	.264	.279	.255	4.67	3.25
Zastryzny, Rob	R-L	6-3	205	3-26-92	0	0	2.25	1	1	0	0	4	3	1	1	0	2	4	.200	1.000	.143	9.00	4.50

Fielding

Catcher	PCT	G	PO	A	E	DP	PB
Carhart	1.000	1	6	0	0	0	0
Mastrobuoni	.986	15	119	19	2	3	3
Matos	.984	17	98	23	2	2	7
Payne	1.000	15	122	18	0	0	3
Pereda	.988	9	68	13	1	0	1

First Base	PCT	G	PO	A	E	DP
Alcala	1.000	1	9	1	0	0
Carhart	1.000	1	6	1	0	0
Cimino	—	1	0	0	0	0
Cuevas	1.000	2	8	1	0	1
Galindo	1.000	1	3	0	0	0
Martarano	.974	7	70	4	2	5
Matos	1.000	2	14	3	0	3
Paniagua	.988	35	301	21	4	33
Pieters	.978	5	41	4	1	5
Vogelbach	1.000	3	26	1	0	1

Second Base	PCT	G	PO	A	E	DP
Amendolare	.909	4	3	7	1	3
Baez	1.000	1	2	2	0	0
Higgins	1.000	2	7	7	0	2
Jimenez	1.000	1	0	3	0	0
Monasterio	1.000	1	0	1	0	1
Sepulveda	.991	44	96	126	2	32
Whiting	.900	3	6	3	1	0

Third Base	PCT	G	PO	A	E	DP
Amendolare	1.000	3	1	3	0	0
Carhart	1.000	1	0	3	0	0
Cuevas	.857	1	2	4	1	0
Galindo	.780	16	8	31	11	4
Higgins	.976	13	8	32	1	4
Jimenez	.833	22	12	33	9	6
Son	.750	1	1	2	1	0

Shortstop	PCT	G	PO	A	E	DP
Baez	1.000	2	2	3	0	1
Higgins	.913	5	8	13	2	4
Jimenez	1.000	6	11	16	0	4
Monastero	.955	40	48	123	8	24
Sepulveda	.941	4	5	11	1	2

Outfield	PCT	G	PO	A	E	DP
Amendolare	1.000	4	5	0	0	0

	PCT	G	PO	A	E	DP
Bautista	.917	15	22	0	2	0
Caro	.952	29	58	2	3	1
Cimino	1.000	16	19	0	0	0
Dunston Jr.	.833	4	5	0	1	0
Emeterio	—	1	0	0	0	0
Foster	1.000	22	25	1	0	1
Garcia	.973	43	69	4	2	3
Graves	1.000	1	3	0	0	0
Gutierrez	—	2	0	0	0	0
Mitchell	1.000	5	4	0	0	0
Paniagua	1.000	4	4	0	0	0
Pieters	—	1	0	0	0	0
Spingola	1.000	3	1	0	0	0
Whiting	.000	1	0	0	1	0
Wilson	1.000	21	34	1	0	0

DSL CUBS   ROOKIE

DOMINICAN SUMMER LEAGUE

Batting	B-T	HT	WT	DOB	AVG	vLH	vRH	G	AB	R	H	2B	3B	HR	RBI	BB	HBP	SH	SF	SO	SB	CS	SLG	OBP
Cuevas, Yovanny	R-R	6-0	170	7-28-98	.259	.286	.253	59	212	35	55	15	3	2	25	27	8	5	0	46	13	6	.387	.364
Diaz, Daniel	R-R	5-11	200	4-5-97	.286	.500	.200	3	7	2	2	1	0	0	1	1	2	0	0	3	0	0	.429	.500
Feliz, Wander	R-R	6-2	185	9-9-97	.235	.185	.244	54	162	15	38	9	2	1	21	28	9	2	1	38	7	3	.333	.375
Gonzalez, Erick	R-R	5-10	175	9-2-96	.278	.136	.314	31	108	12	30	5	1	2	15	9	1	0	2	15	0	0	.398	.333
Jules, Jose	R-R	6-2	170	10-13-97	.218	.325	.187	52	174	22	38	4	1	1	11	17	2	1	1	53	11	3	.270	.294
Lara, Samir	R-R	6-0	165	10-29-96	.272	.240	.282	28	103	18	28	9	1	2	19	10	2	2	0	22	6	1	.437	.348
Mejia, Fidel	R-R	5-11	160	8-30-98	.275	.333	.257	37	142	21	39	4	2	0	13	19	0	1	0	27	6	3	.331	.360
Mejia, Rafael	R-R	6-1	195	12-12-97	.263	.342	.244	54	194	28	51	12	0	4	30	31	7	0	3	45	9	3	.387	.379
Nunez, Richard	R-R	5-10	170	3-14-95	.246	.138	.277	40	130	17	32	6	1	1	23	19	2	0	1	25	4	3	.331	.349
Peguero, Yeiler	B-R	5-10	150	9-20-97	.284	.216	.303	64	236	48	67	8	6	0	18	39	3	4	2	30	15	5	.369	.389
Pena, Raymond	R-R	5-10	160	4-7-97	.109	.000	.150	35	110	12	12	2	0	0	5	16	3	1	1	37	3	0	.127	.238
Rijo, Tony	R-R	6-0	170	11-3-97	.193	.290	.169	47	161	24	31	6	0	1	12	29	7	1	1	50	7	5	.248	.338
Rondon, Edgar	L-R	5-7	170	1-14-95	.322	.386	.300	52	174	36	56	8	7	1	27	29	8	1	2	37	12	6	.466	.437
Ruiz, Miguel	R-R	6-1	170	11-5-96	.182	.167	.188	18	44	4	8	2	0	0	7	7	0	2	1	11	2	0	.227	.288
Tineo, Franklin	R-R	6-1	176	12-30-94	.214	.310	.186	44	131	21	28	6	1	3	19	27	5	1	1	27	3	4	.344	.366
Ubiera, Luis	R-R	6-2	170	9-17-96	.195	.212	.188	41	113	18	22	2	1	0	11	12	4	1	1	23	6	5	.230	.292

Pitching	B-T	HT	WT	DOB	W	L	ERA	G	GS	CG	SV	IP	H	R	ER	HR	BB	SO	AVG	vLH	vRH	K/9	BB/9
Aquino, Assael	R-R	6-3	180	7-16-92	0	0	6.00	2	0	0	0	3	2	2	2	1	6	6	.182	—	.182	18.00	18.00
Aquino, Luis	R-R	6-1	170	6-30-93	3	2	0.82	22	0	0	3	44	32	14	4	0	13	47	.201	.205	.200	9.69	2.68
Aybar, Julian	R-R	6-1	188	2-13-92	8	1	1.82	20	0	0	2	40	26	12	8	1	9	47	.194	.242	.178	10.66	2.04
Cabrera, Wander	L-L	6-1	185	11-7-97	4	3	2.34	14	7	0	0	42	30	18	11	0	23	47	.199	.107	.220	9.99	4.89
Disla, Wagner	R-R	6-4	180		0	0	10.13	9	0	0	0	13	16	15	15	2	11	12	.286	.412	.318	8.10	7.43
Escanio, Luiz	R-R	6-5	190	7-31-92	0	0	0.00	4	0	0	2	3	3	0	0	0	2	5	.250	.333	.222	13.50	5.40
Estevez, Miguel	R-R	6-3	160	10-31-93	0	0	7.82	7	0	0	0	13	14	13	11	0	5	8	.264	.267	.263	5.68	3.55
Garcia, Hector	R-R	6-0	157	5-30-98	3	2	3.98	14	7	0	0	52	55	34	23	1	11	38	.267	.333	.236	6.58	1.90
Gomez, Yapson	L-L	5-10	160	10-2-93	0	0	4.50	3	0	0	0	6	5	5	3	0	3	4	.217	.000	.308	6.00	4.50
Guerrero, Fauris	R-R	5-11	180	10-5-96	4	0	3.28	10	0	0	1	25	21	13	9	1	9	24	.223	.207	.231	8.76	3.28
Leidenz, Jose	R-R	6-1	171	10-16-94	0	0	3.60	3	0	0	0	5	5	2	2	0	3	6	.238	.200	.250	10.80	5.40
Marte, Junior	R-R	6-1	170	6-6-95	4	1	1.29	11	11	0	0	56	33	9	8	0	16	68	.175	.178	.174	10.99	2.59
Morel, Jose	L-R	6-6	204	11-13-94	2	3	7.67	15	0	0	0	32	42	34	27	3	18	26	.323	.226	.354	7.39	5.12
Ochoa, Pablo	L-L	6-0	180	1-11-98	3	6	2.68	14	7	0	0	50	51	27	15	2	19	41	.273	.258	.276	7.33	3.40
Ramos, Eury	R-R	6-3	152	10-10-97	0	1	4.41	14	4	0	1	33	32	23	16	2	13	24	.260	.125	.308	6.61	3.58
Romero, Jhon	R-R	5-10	195	1-17-95	0	1	3.60	3	0	0	0	5	8	3	2	0	1	3	.364	.500	.313	5.40	1.80
Rondon, Andri	R-R	6-2	190	9-16-95	3	2	2.41	14	12	0	0	56	44	20	15	3	15	67	.212	.267	.189	10.77	2.41
Rosario, Aneuris	R-R	6-0	165	3-4-95	2	1	2.01	22	0	0	11	22	23	9	5	1	8	30	.261	.364	.227	12.09	3.22
Silverio, Pedro	R-R	6-2	210	6-29-94	1	0	0.00	3	0	0	0	17	11	2	0	2	17	.186	.222	.171	9.00	1.06
Tejada, Jesus	R-R	6-1	168	10-24-96	2	0	1.60	14	7	0	0	51	38	10	9	1	25	32	.209	.178	.219	5.68	4.44
Torres, Deibi	R-R	6-3	190	12-8-94	2	4	6.17	15	13	0	0	54	64	50	37	3	26	26	.294	.254	.310	4.33	4.33
Valdez, Sucre	R-L	6-2	180	9-1-93	2	2	4.26	12	1	0	1	25	27	15	12	4	10	24	.250	.241	.253	8.53	3.55

Fielding

Catcher	PCT	G	PO	A	E	DP	PB
Diaz	1.000	2	16	1	0	0	1
Gonzalez	.996	30	235	41	1	3	12
Nunez	.981	14	82	19	2	0	1
Pena	.960	35	249	40	12	3	6
Tineo	1.000	1	3	0	0	0	0

First Base	PCT	G	PO	A	E	DP
Feliz	1.000	2	16	1	0	2
Mejia	1.000	4	28	3	0	4
Nunez	.995	20	176	8	1	14
Pieters	.977	37	331	11	8	22
Tineo	.987	19	145	11	2	9

Second Base	PCT	G	PO	A	E	DP
Mejia	.977	9	18	24	1	4
Nunez	1.000	1	0	2	0	0
Peguero	.931	7	13	14	2	5
Rondon	.962	38	80	97	7	19
Ruiz	.944	6	6	11	1	1
Tineo	.954	20	38	45	4	9

Third Base	PCT	G	PO	A	E	DP
Mejia	.776	14	14	24	11	3
Mejia	.839	42	22	93	22	6
Nunez	.955	8	4	17	1	3
Peguero	1.000	2	3	1	0	0
Rondon	.889	7	2	14	2	1
Ruiz	.871	9	7	20	4	0
Tineo	—	1	0	0	0	0

Shortstop	PCT	G	PO	A	E	DP
Mejia	.846	12	13	31	8	4
Peguero	.946	54	94	151	14	27
Rondon	.947	10	15	21	2	3
Ruiz	—	1	0	0	0	0

Outfield	PCT	G	PO	A	E	DP
Cuevas	.989	51	83	5	1	0
Diaz	—	1	0	0	0	0
Feliz	.944	52	45	6	3	2
Jules	.911	41	49	2	5	0
Lara	.944	20	34	0	2	0
Pieters	.946	18	34	1	2	0
Rijo	.960	22	21	3	1	0
Ubiera	1.000	31	30	1	0	0

VSL CUBS   ROOKIE

VENEZUELAN SUMMER LEAGUE

Batting	B-T	HT	WT	DOB	AVG	vLH	vRH	G	AB	R	H	2B	3B	HR	RBI	BB	HBP	SH	SF	SO	SB	CS	SLG	OBP
Ayala, Luis	R-L	6-0	176	12-21-95	.285	.216	.305	68	228	36	65	13	8	0	23	47	4	7	4	60	25	9	.412	.410

Batting	B-T	HT	WT	DOB	AVG	vLH	vRH	G	AB	R	H	2B	3B	HR	RBI	BB	HBP	SH	SF	SO	SB	CS	SLG	OBP
Bethencourt, Jhonny	R-R	5-11	160	2-12-97	.319	.167	.363	61	216	49	69	11	3	0	15	32	4	2	4	29	15	14	.398	.410
Diaz, Daniel	R-R	5-11	200	4-5-97	.160	.037	.186	54	156	22	25	1	0	1	12	28	9	0	3	47	0	1	.186	.316
Garay, Francisco	R-R	6-2	170	3-19-98	.126	.125	.127	61	198	18	25	4	0	0	15	13	3	4	2	96	0	4	.146	.190
Gonzalez, Jose	R-R	6-1	160	1-12-96	.242	.260	.238	70	256	34	62	6	2	3	45	34	12	2	5	36	14	10	.316	.352
Hidalgo, Luis	R-R	6-1	190	2-23-96	.179	.056	.212	30	84	8	15	3	0	0	11	12	2	0	1	12	5	3	.214	.293
Lopez, Ronaldo	R-R	6-1	160	5-22-98	.186	.267	.164	19	70	8	13	0	1	1	6	2	0	1	0	17	0	0	.257	.208
Matos, Fidel	R-R	6-0	190	2-6-95	.247	.258	.245	51	174	18	43	9	2	4	19	19	4	1	0	42	5	2	.391	.335
Narea, Rafael	R-R	5-10	160	4-3-98	.212	.286	.190	63	189	31	40	4	0	1	18	40	3	0	1	36	7	7	.249	.356
Pedra, Henrry	R-R	5-11	175	4-26-94	.209	.216	.207	59	182	30	38	9	0	0	20	20	6	1	0	49	10	8	.258	.308
Polanco, Gustavo	R-R	6-0	190	6-13-97	.282	.333	.268	53	195	23	55	10	0	0	23	10	6	1	3	12	3	3	.333	.332
Rojas, Jose	R-R	5-11	210	4-1-94	.264	.216	.278	66	231	28	61	15	1	3	40	23	6	0	6	34	10	7	.377	.338
Vahlis, Roberto	R-R	5-10	190	11-19-93	.267	.419	.221	39	135	21	36	8	0	1	16	20	5	1	0	16	2	0	.348	.381

Pitching	B-T	HT	WT	DOB	W	L	ERA	G	GS	CG	SV	IP	H	R	ER	HR	BB	SO	AVG	vLH	vRH	K/9	BB/9
Arias, Jesus	R-R	6-1	185	9-29-93	2	3	2.55	14	8	0	0	53	50	18	15	1	16	39	.256	.209	.281	6.62	2.72
Bermudez, Harrinson	R-R	6-6	190	3-6-95	1	2	3.72	19	0	0	0	46	39	29	19	2	19	26	.223	.149	.269	5.09	3.72
Bonalde, Andres	L-L	6-2	198	12-12-97	2	4	4.76	13	9	0	0	40	53	32	21	2	11	27	.306	.304	.307	6.13	2.50
Colorado, Alejandro	R-R	6-1	170	6-22-96	1	0	3.00	3	0	0	0	6	7	4	2	0	1	3	.280	.200	.300	4.50	1.50
Fernandez, Riger	L-L	6-2	190	1-1-98	1	5	6.52	12	12	0	0	39	47	34	28	2	20	14	.311	.273	.318	3.26	4.66
Ferrebus, Emilio	R-R	6-2	165	11-25-97	0	3	9.51	10	10	0	0	29	40	32	31	2	19	18	.351	.306	.372	5.52	5.83
Gomez, Yapson	L-L	5-10	160	10-2-93	1	3	1.40	7	3	0	1	26	30	9	4	1	6	14	.294	.333	.282	4.91	2.10
Leidenz, Jose	R-R	6-1	171	10-16-94	3	0	3.08	15	0	0	2	26	26	15	9	1	4	16	.250	.278	.235	5.47	1.37
Lima, Gabriel	R-R	6-2	180	5-2-96	4	2	1.36	10	9	0	0	46	37	14	7	1	7	29	.214	.133	.257	5.63	1.36
Medina, Ivan	R-R	6-3	162	2-26-96	0	0	0.00	2	0	0	0	8	6	0	0	0	3	4	.240	.214	.273	4.50	3.38
Molina, Bryan	R-R	6-1	187	3-21-95	2	1	7.96	21	0	0	0	32	50	35	28	2	23	32	.357	.316	.386	9.09	6.54
Pacheco, Alex	L-R	6-3	184	9-20-94	1	4	4.86	15	1	0	0	37	36	23	20	1	10	33	.255	.136	.277	8.03	2.43
Palma, Eugenio	L-L	5-11	170	11-26-96	3	2	2.03	25	0	0	2	49	39	15	11	2	8	32	.217	.174	.223	5.92	1.48
Ramirez, Moises	R-R	5-11	170	12-11-95	3	3	2.01	19	0	0	2	49	48	16	11	4	12	34	.250	.284	.229	6.20	2.19
Rengifo, Juan	R-R	6-3	206	6-12-94	4	4	1.77	26	0	0	11	46	29	10	9	1	13	31	.180	.231	.156	6.11	2.56
Rodriguez, Carlos A.	L-L	5-11	178	7-18-95	1	0	2.42	4	4	0	0	22	15	6	6	2	0	23	.190	.261	.161	9.27	0.00
Tineo, Freddy	R-R	6-0	160	11-22-97	0	4	5.70	12	12	0	0	43	49	34	27	4	16	21	.293	.271	.309	4.43	3.38
Ventura, Omar	R-R	6-2	190	9-10-96	0	0	8.31	7	0	0	0	9	10	10	8	2	9	6	.303	.357	.263	6.23	9.35
Vides, Mauro	R-R	6-3	230	10-19-95	1	0	7.91	11	0	0	0	19	24	19	17	0	23	10	.312	.344	.289	4.66	10.71

Fielding

Catcher	PCT	G	PO	A	E	DP	PB
Diaz	.984	44	202	44	4	4	10
Polanco	.969	28	151	37	6	1	8
Rojas	1.000	2	3	1	0	0	2
Vahlis	.984	8	54	7	1	0	5

First Base	PCT	G	PO	A	E	DP
Diaz	.967	7	54	5	2	4
Garay	1.000	2	16	2	0	0
Matos	.980	26	224	15	5	14
Narea	1.000	1	1	0	0	0
Pedra	1.000	11	87	10	0	10
Polanco	1.000	11	92	4	0	7
Rojas	.950	4	37	1	2	1
Vahlis	.970	18	153	8	5	11

Second Base	PCT	G	PO	A	E	DP
Bethencourt	.941	49	91	131	14	29
Garay	.950	5	11	8	1	4
Lopez	.846	5	7	15	4	0
Narea	.944	5	8	9	1	3
Pedra	.986	18	17	51	1	6

Third Base	PCT	G	PO	A	E	DP
Garay	.825	33	26	59	18	4
Lopez	.917	8	12	10	2	0
Narea	.947	7	4	14	1	1
Pedra	.976	27	24	57	2	6
Rojas	.333	2	1	0	2	0

Shortstop	PCT	G	PO	A	E	DP
Garay	.852	21	34	41	13	10

	PCT	G	PO	A	E	DP
Lopez	.838	6	13	18	6	6
Narea	.893	46	75	134	25	21

Outfield	PCT	G	PO	A	E	DP
Ayala	.968	64	139	11	5	4
Bermudez	1.000	1	1	0	0	0
Bethencourt	.905	14	18	1	2	0
Gonzalez	.989	69	155	17	2	3
Hidalgo	.929	17	25	1	2	0
Matos	1.000	8	14	3	0	0
Pedra	1.000	1	1	0	0	0
Rojas	.940	54	75	4	5	1
Vahlis	1.000	3	7	0	0	0

Chicago White Sox

SEASON IN A SENTENCE: The White Sox limped to a 76-86 record and a fourth-place finish in the American League Central after a busy offseason in which they added Melky Cabrera, Zach Duke, Adam LaRoche, David Robertson and Jeff Samardzija to a core that already included Jose Abreu and Chris Sale—two of the top talents in the league.

HIGH POINT: On May 18, Chris Sale outdueled Indians ace Corey Kluber in a 2-1 White Sox victory that pushed their record to 18-17. However, Chicago would never top .500 again during the season.

LOW POINT: The White Sox went just 10-16 in June and lost eight games in a row from June 12-19. Chicago averaged 3.08 runs per game for the month, and on the season, no AL team finished with fewer runs (622) or home runs (136).

NOTABLE ROOKIES: The White Sox turned to 22-year-old lefthander Carlos Rodon on April 21 after just 35 career innings in the minors. The third overall pick in the 2014 draft went 9-6, 3.75 in 26 games (23 starts) and improved in the second half, when he struck out 8.8 and walked 3.7 per nine innings while holding opponents to a .237 average. Chicago turned over two infield positions to rookies and received the worst offensive production in the league at both second base (Carlos Sanchez and Micah Johnson) and third base (Tyler Saladino, with an assist from veterans Conor Gillaspie and Mike Olt). Outfielder Trayce Thompson and righthander Frankie Montas made late-season appearances but retained their prospect eligibility.

KEY TRANSACTIONS: Chicago made no trades involving major league players during the season, and only the September wavier claim of Mike Olt qualifies as an intriguing low-cost maneuver, so the most significant acquisition in 2015 probably was the selection of Vanderbilt righthander Carson Fulmer with the eighth overall pick in June. He ranked as the No. 2 college pitcher on the board and he could join Chris Sale and Carlos Rodon in the big league rotation before long.

DOWN ON THE FARM: White Sox domestic affiliates finished with a middle-of-the-road .504 winning percentage, though the Rookie-level Arizona League club won its league. A couple of the system's pitchers won league pitcher-of-the-year honors: righthanders Erik Johnson (International) and Matt Heidenreich (Carolina).

OPENING DAY PAYROLL: $115,238,678 (15th).

ORGANIZATION LEADERS

BATTING		*Minimum 250 AB
MAJORS		
*AVG	Jose Abreu	.290
*OPS	Jose Abreu	.849
HR	Jose Abreu	30
RBI	Jose Abreu	101
MINORS		
*AVG	Tim Anderson, Birmingham	.312
*OBP	Eddy Alvarez, Kannapolis, Winston-Salem	.409
*SLG	Matt Tuiasosopo, Charlotte	.447
R	Adam Engel, Winston-Salem	90
H	Tim Anderson, Birmingham	160
TB	Jason Coats, Birmingham, Charlotte	239
2B	Jason Coats, Birmingham, Charlotte	38
3B	Tim Anderson, Birmingham	12
HR	Matt Davidson, Charlotte	23
RBI	Jason Coats, Birmingham, Charlotte	83
BB	Danny Hayes, Birmingham	98
SO	Matt Davidson, Charlotte	191
SB	Adam Engel, Winston-Salem	65

PITCHING		#Minimum 75 IP
MAJORS		
W	Chris Sale	13
#ERA	Jose Quintana	3.36
SO	Chris Sale	274
SV	David Robertson	34
MINORS		
W	Jordan Guerrero, Kannapolis, Winston-Salem	13
	Matt Heidenreich, Winston-Salem, Birm.	13
L	Luis Martinez, Kannapolis	14
#ERA	Erik Johnson, Charlotte	2.37
G	Zach Phillips, Charlotte	46
GS	Mark Blackmar, Birmingham	26
	Tyler Danish/Myles Jaye, Birmingham	26
	Thaddius Lowry, Kannapolis	26
SV	Peter Tago, Kannapolis, Winston-Salem, Birm.	15
IP	Matt Heidenreich, Winston-Salem, Birm.	155
BB	Tyler Danish, Birmingham	60
SO	Jordan Guerrero, Kannapolis, Winston-Salem	148
AVG	Frankie Montas, Birmingham	.219

General Manager: Rick Hahn. **Farm Director:** Nick Capra. **Scouting Director:** Doug Laumann.

Class	Team	League	W	L	PCT	Finish	Manager
Majors	Chicago White Sox	American	76	86	.469	t-12 (15)	Robin Ventura
Triple-A	Charlotte Knights	International	74	70	.514	7th (14)	Joel Skinner
Double-A	Birmingham Barons	Southern	69	70	.496	7th (10)	Julio Vinas
High A	Winston-Salem Dash	Carolina	75	63	.543	2nd (8)	Tim Esmay
Low A	Kannapolis Intimidators	South Atlantic	64	74	.464	10th (14)	Tommy Thompson
Rookie	Great Falls Voyagers	Pioneer	35	39	.473	6th (8)	Cole Armstrong
Rookie	White Sox	Arizona	30	25	.545	5th (14)	Mike Gellinger
Overall 2015 Minor League Record			347	341	.504	t-15th (30)	

ORGANIZATION STATISTICS

CHICAGO WHITE SOX

AMERICAN LEAGUE

Batting	B-T	HT	WT	DOB	AVG	vLH	vRH	G	AB	R	H	2B	3B	HR	RBI	BB	HBP	SH	SF	SO	SB	CS	SLG	OBP
Abreu, Jose	R-R	6-3	255	1-29-87	.290	.232	.308	154	613	88	178	34	3	30	101	39	15	0	1	140	0	0	.502	.347
Beckham, Gordon	R-R	6-0	185	9-16-86	.209	.218	.202	100	211	24	44	8	0	6	20	19	2	1	4	43	0	1	.332	.275
Bonifacio, Emilio	B-R	5-11	205	4-23-85	.167	.176	.159	47	78	5	13	2	0	0	4	2	1	1	0	27	1	4	.192	.198
Brantly, Rob	L-R	6-1	195	7-14-89	.121	.000	.167	14	33	3	4	1	0	1	6	2	0	0	1	8	0	0	.242	.167
Cabrera, Melky	B-L	5-10	210	8-11-84	.273	.240	.286	158	629	70	172	36	2	12	77	40	2	2	10	88	3	0	.394	.314
Eaton, Adam	L-L	5-8	185	12-6-88	.287	.268	.294	153	610	98	175	28	9	14	56	58	14	5	2	131	18	8	.431	.361
Flowers, Tyler	R-R	6-4	245	1-24-86	.239	.270	.231	112	331	21	79	12	0	9	39	21	6	2	1	104	0	1	.356	.295
Garcia, Avisail	R-R	6-4	240	6-12-91	.257	.293	.247	148	553	66	142	17	2	13	59	36	8	0	4	141	7	7	.365	.309
Garcia, Leury	B-R	5-8	170	3-18-91	.214	.200	.222	17	14	0	3	0	0	0	1	1	0	0	0	7	1	0	.214	.267
Gillaspie, Conor	L-R	6-1	195	7-18-87	.237	.333	.234	58	173	10	41	11	1	3	15	9	1	0	2	34	0	1	.364	.276
2-team total (17 Los Angeles)					.228	—	—	75	237	14	54	15	2	4	24	13	1	0	2	47	0	1	.359	.269
Johnson, Micah	L-R	6-0	210	12-18-90	.230	.174	.247	36	100	10	23	4	0	0	4	9	2	2	0	30	3	2	.270	.306
LaRoche, Adam	L-L	6-3	205	11-6-79	.207	.157	.221	127	429	41	89	21	0	12	44	49	4	0	2	133	0	0	.340	.293
Olt, Mike	R-R	6-2	210	8-27-88	.203	.174	.214	24	79	6	16	0	0	3	4	7	0	0	0	29	0	1	.316	.267
Ramirez, Alexei	R-R	6-2	180	9-22-81	.249	.283	.239	154	583	54	145	33	0	10	62	31	1	1	6	68	17	7	.357	.285
Saladino, Tyler	R-R	6-0	200	7-20-89	.225	.207	.230	68	236	33	53	6	4	4	20	12	2	3	1	51	8	2	.335	.267
Sanchez, Carlos	B-R	5-11	195	6-29-92	.224	.218	.225	120	389	40	87	23	1	5	31	19	5	6	1	81	2	2	.326	.268
Shuck, J.B.	L-L	5-11	195	6-18-87	.266	.217	.275	79	143	15	38	8	2	0	15	16	1	3	2	16	7	5	.350	.340
Soto, Geovany	R-R	6-1	235	1-20-83	.219	.246	.208	78	187	20	41	8	0	9	21	21	1	1	0	63	0	1	.406	.301
Thompson, Trayce	R-R	6-3	210	3-15-91	.295	.327	.269	44	122	17	36	8	3	5	16	13	0	0	0	26	1	0	.533	.363

Pitching	B-T	HT	WT	DOB	W	L	ERA	G	GS	CG	SV	IP	H	R	ER	HR	BB	SO	AVG	vLH	vRH	K/9	BB/9
Albers, Matt	L-R	6-1	225	1-20-83	2	0	1.21	30	0	0	0	37	31	6	5	3	9	28	.228	.275	.200	6.75	2.17
Beck, Chris	R-R	6-3	225	9-4-90	0	1	6.00	1	1	0	0	6	10	5	4	0	4	3	.385	.438	.300	4.50	6.00
Carroll, Scott	R-R	6-4	215	9-24-84	1	1	3.44	18	0	0	0	37	40	19	14	2	13	27	.280	.254	.303	6.63	3.19
Danks, John	L-L	6-1	210	4-15-85	7	15	4.71	30	30	2	0	178	195	104	93	24	56	124	.281	.240	.294	6.28	2.84
Drabek, Kyle	R-R	6-2	205	12-8-87	0	0	5.06	3	0	0	0	5	9	3	3	1	2	3	.375	.571	.294	5.06	3.38
Duke, Zach	L-L	6-2	210	4-19-83	3	6	3.41	71	0	0	1	61	47	26	23	9	32	66	.218	.181	.241	9.79	4.75
Guerra, Junior	R-R	6-0	205	1-16-85	0	0	6.75	3	0	0	0	4	7	3	3	1	1	3	.412	.500	.385	6.75	2.25
Guerra, Javy	R-R	6-1	190	10-31-85	0	0	0.00	3	0	0	0	2	2	0	0	0	1	0	.333	.000	.667	0.00	5.40
Jennings, Dan	L-L	6-3	210	4-17-87	2	3	3.99	53	0	0	0	56	55	28	25	3	24	46	.256	.274	.242	7.35	3.83
Johnson, Erik	R-R	6-3	230	12-30-89	3	1	3.34	6	6	0	0	35	32	14	13	8	17	30	.248	.262	.234	7.71	4.37
Jones, Nate	R-R	6-5	220	1-28-86	2	2	3.32	19	0	0	0	19	12	7	7	5	6	27	.188	.125	.225	12.79	2.84
Montas, Frankie	R-R	6-2	185	3-21-93	0	2	4.80	7	2	0	0	15	14	8	8	1	9	20	.246	.286	.222	12.00	5.40
Noesi, Hector	R-R	6-3	205	1-26-87	0	4	6.89	10	5	0	0	33	41	26	25	7	17	22	.301	.239	.362	6.06	4.68
Petricka, Jake	R-R	6-5	205	6-5-88	4	3	3.63	62	0	0	2	52	56	21	21	2	18	33	.284	.358	.257	5.71	3.12
Putnam, Zach	R-R	6-3	210	6-25-87	3	3	4.07	49	0	0	4	49	42	24	22	7	24	64	.239	.229	.247	11.84	4.44
Quintana, Jose	L-L	6-1	220	1-24-89	9	10	3.36	32	32	1	0	206	218	81	77	16	44	177	.272	.233	.283	7.72	1.92
Robertson, David	R-R	5-11	195	4-9-85	6	5	3.41	60	0	0	34	63	46	27	24	7	13	86	.196	.175	.210	12.22	1.85
Rodon, Carlos	L-L	6-3	235	12-10-92	9	6	3.75	26	23	1	0	139	130	63	58	11	71	139	.251	.194	.272	8.98	4.59
Sale, Chris	L-L	6-6	180	3-30-89	13	11	3.41	31	31	1	0	209	185	89	79	23	42	274	.233	.250	.230	11.82	1.81
Samardzija, Jeff	R-R	6-5	225	1-23-85	11	13	4.96	32	32	2	0	214	228	122	118	29	49	163	.273	.278	.268	6.86	2.06
Webb, Daniel	R-R	6-3	215	8-18-89	1	0	6.30	27	0	0	0	30	41	26	21	3	22	22	.325	.362	.304	6.60	6.60

Fielding

Catcher	PCT	G	PO	A	E	DP	PB
Brantly	1.000	14	82	3	0	1	2
Flowers	.995	110	877	63	5	10	15
Soto	.988	73	398	24	5	1	5

First Base	PCT	G	PO	A	E	DP
Abreu	.989	115	952	60	11	100
Flowers	1.000	2	3	1	0	0
Gillaspie	1.000	2	4	1	0	0
LaRoche	.997	48	351	27	1	43
Olt	.920	5	21	2	2	1

Saladino	1.000	1	3	0	0	0

Second Base	PCT	G	PO	A	E	DP
Beckham	1.000	11	22	25	0	10
Bonifacio	.955	17	27	37	3	11
Garcia	1.000	2	0	2	0	0
Johnson	.978	33	58	76	3	14
Sanchez	.990	117	229	268	5	83

Third Base	PCT	G	PO	A	E	DP
Beckham	.976	76	24	96	3	7
Bonifacio	—	1	0	0	0	0

Gillaspie	.890	52	23	74	12	4
Olt	.905	20	17	21	4	1
Saladino	.970	60	39	122	5	6

Shortstop	PCT	G	PO	A	E	DP
Beckham	.957	5	9	13	1	6
Garcia	.000	3	0	0	1	0
Ramirez	.977	152	206	462	16	105
Saladino	1.000	11	11	13	0	2

CHICAGO WHITE SOX

Outfield	PCT	G	PO	A	E	DP
Bonifacio	1.000	5	3	0	0	0
Cabrera	.979	150	220	8	5	0
Eaton	.986	145	343	8	5	2
Garcia	.988	130	235	17	3	4
Garcia	1.000	6	4	0	0	0
Shuck	1.000	48	75	4	0	0
Thompson	.986	39	68	0	1	0

CHARLOTTE KNIGHTS   TRIPLE-A

INTERNATIONAL LEAGUE

Batting	B-T	HT	WT	DOB	AVG	vLH	vRH	G	AB	R	H	2B	3B	HR	RBI	BB	HBP	SH	SF	SO	SB	CS	SLG	OBP
Beltre, Engel	L-L	6-2	180	11-1-89	.234	.200	.255	21	77	13	18	3	0	1	7	4	0	2	1	21	2	1	.312	.268
Black, Dan	L-R	6-4	255	7-2-87	.324	.200	.382	34	111	20	36	5	2	6	24	27	1	0	1	24	0	0	.568	.457
Bonifacio, Emilio	B-R	5-11	205	4-23-85	.364	.333	.375	3	11	0	4	2	0	0	1	0	0	0	0	2	0	0	.545	.364
Brantly, Rob	L-R	6-1	195	7-14-89	.291	.250	.306	23	86	11	25	3	0	4	16	5	0	0	3	17	0	0	.465	.319
Coats, Jason	R-R	6-2	200	2-24-90	.270	.301	.256	122	489	56	132	29	1	17	81	29	4	3	5	93	11	2	.438	.313
Colvin, Tyler	L-L	6-3	210	9-5-85	.226	.211	.231	88	305	27	69	15	3	4	25	15	1	1	1	92	0	1	.334	.264
Curley, Chris	R-R	6-0	185	8-25-87	.300	.267	.314	15	50	6	15	1	1	2	5	2	0	2	0	9	0	0	.480	.327
Davidson, Matt	R-R	6-3	230	3-26-91	.203	.217	.196	141	528	63	107	22	0	23	74	62	7	1	4	191	1	0	.375	.293
Dowdy, Jeremy	R-R	6-2	230	7-13-90	.208	.400	.071	8	24	3	5	3	0	0	3	8	0	0	0	3	0	0	.333	.406
Garcia, Drew	B-R	6-1	175	4-22-86	.217	.270	.197	83	272	27	59	13	1	1	16	15	1	3	1	49	4	3	.283	.260
Garcia, Leury	B-R	5-8	170	3-18-91	.298	.333	.276	90	349	57	104	19	3	3	31	20	4	9	3	66	30	12	.395	.340
Jacobs, Chris	R-R	6-5	260	11-25-88	.224	.091	.263	15	49	5	11	1	0	2	5	5	2	0	0	13	0	0	.367	.321
Jirschele, Justin	L-R	5-11	195	4-15-90	.143	.000	.250	2	7	0	1	0	0	0	0	0	0	0	0	1	0	0	.143	.143
Johnson, Micah	L-R	6-0	210	12-18-90	.315	.310	.318	78	311	54	98	17	3	8	36	32	0	4	4	63	28	7	.466	.375
Kottaras, George	L-R	6-0	200	5-10-83	.247	.217	.257	31	97	12	24	4	0	7	19	26	0	1	1	38	0	0	.505	.403
2-team total (16 Buffalo)					.238	—	—	47	147	17	35	4	0	8	25	32	0	1	1	56	0	0	.429	.372
Marrero, Chris	R-R	6-3	229	7-2-88	.278	.344	.257	39	133	18	37	8	1	4	17	15	0	0	2	28	0	0	.444	.347
2-team total (22 Pawtucket)					.262	—	—	61	225	28	59	13	1	7	25	17	0	0	2	47	0	0	.422	.311
Mayberry Jr., John	R-R	6-6	235	12-21-83	.162	.167	.161	13	37	2	6	1	0	0	3	0	0	0	0	7	0	0	.189	.225
Mitchell, Jared	L-L	6-0	205	10-13-88	.050	.154	.000	13	40	4	2	0	1	0	0	6	0	0	0	22	1	0	.100	.174
O'Connell, Sean	L-R	6-4	230	12-12-91	.250	.500	.000	1	4	0	1	0	0	0	0	0	0	0	0	2	0	0	.250	.250
Rondon, Cleuluis	R-R	6-0	155	4-13-94	.000	—	.000	2	6	0	0	0	0	0	0	1	0	0	0	1	0	0	.000	.143
Saladino, Tyler	R-R	6-0	200	7-20-89	.255	.236	.266	52	196	28	50	7	2	4	29	22	4	2	7	33	25	2	.372	.332
Sanchez, Carlos	B-R	5-11	195	6-29-92	.344	.375	.330	29	131	17	45	10	0	2	17	4	1	1	0	28	5	2	.466	.368
Sellers, Justin	R-R	5-10	175	2-1-86	.206	.429	.148	8	34	2	7	2	0	0	2	0	0	0	1	5	0	0	.265	.200
2-team total (4 Indianapolis)					.182	—	—	12	44	2	8	2	0	0	2	2	0	1	1	9	0	0	.227	.213
Shuck, J.B.	L-L	5-11	195	6-18-87	.100	.000	.125	3	10	2	1	0	0	0	0	1	0	0	0	2	0	0	.100	.182
Simon, Alexander	B-R	6-2	185	9-28-92	.143	.000	.200	2	7	0	1	0	0	0	0	0	0	0	0	2	0	0	.143	.143
Smith, Kevan	R-R	6-4	230	6-28-88	.260	.296	.240	97	319	41	83	13	2	6	36	29	5	5	2	66	0	1	.370	.330
Soto, Neftali	R-R	6-1	210	2-28-89	.246	.200	.271	53	199	25	49	6	0	2	24	30	0	1	1	40	0	0	.307	.343
Thompson, Trayce	R-R	6-3	210	3-15-91	.260	.314	.237	104	388	53	101	23	4	13	39	23	2	2	2	79	11	5	.441	.304
Tuiasosopo, Matt	R-R	6-2	225	5-10-86	.230	.289	.200	103	356	50	82	21	1	18	52	51	6	1	3	123	3	0	.447	.344
Vicledo, Dayan	R-R	5-11	240	5-10-87	.341	.278	.363	36	138	17	47	7	0	7	20	13	1	0	0	23	0	0	.543	.401
Wilson, Ethan	R-R	6-0	195	3-9-89	.200	.167	.211	23	50	5	10	2	0	0	3	5	0	0	0	18	0	1	.240	.273

Pitching	B-T	HT	WT	DOB	W	L	ERA	G	GS	CG	SV	IP	H	R	ER	HR	BB	SO	AVG	vLH	vRH	K/9	BB/9
Albers, Matt	L-R	6-1	225	1-20-83	1	0	5.59	7	0	0	0	10	10	6	6	2	1	5	.263	.059	.429	4.66	0.93
Asencio, Jairo	R-R	6-2	180	5-30-83	0	2	5.03	17	0	0	9	20	26	14	11	1	6	28	.310	.313	.308	12.81	2.75
Beck, Chris	R-R	6-3	225	9-4-90	3	2	3.15	10	10	0	0	54	50	20	19	3	14	40	.239	.202	.267	6.63	2.32
Carroll, Scott	R-R	6-4	215	9-24-84	7	4	3.47	16	16	0	0	83	85	41	32	8	29	45	.263	.270	.257	4.88	3.14
Casey, Jarrett	R-L	6-0	185	10-27-87	9	2	4.29	36	0	0	0	57	59	27	27	7	23	44	.271	.284	.265	6.99	3.65
Chalas, Miguel	R-R	5-11	155	6-27-92	1	6	6.39	23	4	0	0	44	53	31	31	5	15	35	.298	.321	.280	7.21	3.09
Cleto, Maikel	R-R	6-3	250	5-1-89	3	2	3.00	31	0	0	5	51	31	17	17	6	24	61	.172	.189	.160	10.76	4.24
Crabbe, Tim	R-R	6-4	200	2-20-88	0	0	0.00	1	0	0	0	2	0	0	0	0	1	2	.000	.000	.000	9.00	4.50
Drabek, Kyle	R-R	6-2	205	12-8-87	7	11	3.47	24	24	0	0	137	125	62	53	8	53	84	.243	.236	.248	5.50	3.47
Garcia, Onelki	L-L	6-3	225	8-2-89	0	1	4.70	25	0	0	3	38	45	23	20	3	22	48	.287	.298	.282	11.27	5.17
Guerra, Junior	R-R	6-0	205	1-16-85	2	4	3.39	26	8	0	7	64	44	24	24	5	29	79	.193	.183	.202	11.17	4.10
Guerra, Javy	R-R	6-1	190	10-31-85	0	0	17.18	4	0	0	0	4	8	7	7	1	4		.421	.500	.364	9.82	2.45
Hagan, Sean	L-L	6-6	215	3-5-91	1	0	0.00	1	0	0	0	3	2	0	0	0	1	2	.200	.000	.400	6.00	3.00
Haviland, Shawn	R-R	6-2	200	11-10-85	4	5	4.19	19	13	0	0	77	83	45	36	10	19	59	.272	.250	.288	6.87	2.21
2-team total (6 Pawtucket)					5	10	4.18	25	19	0	0	114	124	63	53	11	28	82	—	—		6.47	2.21
Isler, Zach	R-R	6-5	230	10-31-90	0	0	18.00	1	0	0	0	1	2	6	4	4	0	0	.500	.500	.500	0.00	0.00
Jennings, Dan	L-L	6-3	210	4-17-87	0	0	3.00	3	0	0	0	6	6	2	2	0	1	5	.250	.222	.267	7.50	1.50
Johnson, Erik	R-R	6-3	230	12-30-89	11	8	2.37	23	22	0	0	133	108	40	35	5	41	136	.224	.234	.215	9.23	2.78
Jones, Nate	R-R	6-5	220	1-28-86	0	0	1.42	6	0	0	0	6	3	1	1	1	2	4	.136	.182	.091	5.68	2.84
Leon, Arcenio	R-R	6-2	230	9-22-86	1	0	11.91	9	0	0	0	11	20	15	15	2	8	12	.400	.421	.387	9.53	6.35
Lindstrom, Matt	R-R	6-3	215	2-11-80	2	1	5.56	18	0	0	2	23	23	16	14	1	5	17	.256	.286	.236	6.75	1.99
Marin, Terance	R-R	6-1	170	8-21-89	3	4	2.93	19	10	0	1	77	73	27	25	4	17	43	.252	.250	.253	5.05	2.00
Noesi, Hector	R-R	6-3	230	1-26-87	4	4	3.32	11	10	0	0	65	46	25	24	9	16	50	.201	.143	.250	7.75	2.22
Penny, Brad	R-R	6-4	230	5-24-78	7	10	4.46	24	24	1	0	135	173	78	67	11	33	81	.315	.352	.279	5.39	2.19
Petricka, Jake	R-R	6-5	205	6-5-88	0	0	0.00	2	0	0	0	2	0	0	0	0	2	3	.000	.000	.000	13.50	9.00
Phillips, Zach	L-L	6-1	200	9-21-86	1	1	3.13	46	0	0	12	55	47	20	19	1	20	64	.232	.213	.242	10.54	3.29
Rodon, Carlos	L-L	6-3	235	12-10-92	1	0	3.60	2	2	0	0	10	8	5	4	1	3	13	.216	.000	.267	11.70	2.70
Smith, Blake	L-R	6-2	225	12-9-87	1	2	3.30	24	0	0	0	30	29	11	11	1	15	42	.244	.240	.246	12.60	4.50
Surkamp, Eric	L-L	6-5	220	7-16-87	3	0	2.81	11	1	0	0	26	19	8	8	2	9	30	.204	.189	.214	10.52	3.16
Webb, Daniel	R-R	6-3	215	8-18-89	2	1	3.81	18	0	0	2	28	25	12	12	3	15	24	.234	.255	.214	7.62	4.76
Wendelken, J.B.	R-R	6-0	190	3-24-93	0	0	4.50	12	0	0	0	12	16	14	11	8	5	13	.246	.179	.265	7.31	2.81

Fielding

Catcher	PCT	G	PO	A	E	DP	PB
Brantly	.990	14	94	8	1	0	1
Dowdy	.974	8	72	4	2	0	0
Kottaras	.996	31	244	16	1	1	3
O'Connell	1.000	1	5	2	0	0	2
Smith	.990	93	652	57	7	7	4

First Base	PCT	G	PO	A	E	DP
Black	.988	19	147	13	2	16
Curley	1.000	8	68	2	0	7
Davidson	1.000	2	2	0	0	0
Jacobs	1.000	2	14	3	0	1
Marrero	.996	27	241	17	1	21
Saladino	1.000	1	7	1	0	2
Simon	1.000	2	18	0	0	3
Soto	.997	36	340	19	1	29
Tuiasosopo	.991	23	201	11	2	15
Viciedo	.997	31	289	19	1	28

Second Base	PCT	G	PO	A	E	DP
Bonifacio	.875	2	3	4	1	2

	PCT	G	PO	A	E	DP
Garcia	.970	20	34	64	3	11
Garcia	.979	11	15	31	1	6
Jirschele	.900	2	2	7	1	2
Johnson	.972	75	121	231	10	45
Saladino	1.000	1	4	2	0	0
Sanchez	.980	26	66	81	3	26
Wilson	.977	11	17	25	1	4

Third Base	PCT	G	PO	A	E	DP
Curley	1.000	1	0	2	0	0
Davidson	.971	130	58	281	10	24
Garcia	1.000	5	1	13	0	3
Garcia	1.000	4	3	6	0	0
Saladino	1.000	2	4	2	0	0
Soto	.778	4	3	4	2	0
Tuiasosopo	1.000	1	0	2	0	0
Wilson	1.000	1	1	1	0	0

Shortstop	PCT	G	PO	A	E	DP
Davidson	1.000	2	2	3	0	1
Garcia	.962	60	73	154	9	28

	PCT	G	PO	A	E	DP
Garcia	.930	43	53	121	13	35
Rondon	.900	2	4	5	1	1
Saladino	.964	34	39	95	5	18
Sanchez	1.000	3	5	13	0	2
Sellers	.909	8	11	29	4	6
Wilson	1.000	1	1	1	0	1

Outfield	PCT	G	PO	A	E	DP
Beltre	1.000	18	26	1	0	0
Bonifacio	1.000	2	7	0	0	0
Coats	.980	121	233	7	5	2
Colvin	1.000	66	96	5	0	0
Curley	1.000	6	9	2	0	0
Garcia	.934	35	80	5	6	2
Marrero	1.000	1	3	0	0	0
Mayberry Jr.	.909	9	10	0	1	0
Mitchell	.957	12	22	0	1	0
Shuck	1.000	2	2	0	0	0
Thompson	.992	103	243	4	2	1
Tuiasosopo	1.000	66	92	2	0	1

BIRMINGHAM BARONS
SOUTHERN LEAGUE

DOUBLE-A

Batting	B-T	HT	WT	DOB	AVG	vLH	vRH	G	AB	R	H	2B	3B	HR	RBI	BB	HBP	SH	SF	SO	SB	CS	SLG	OBP
Anderson, Tim	R-R	6-1	185	6-23-93	.312	.339	.303	125	513	79	160	21	12	5	46	24	7	4	2	114	49	13	.429	.350
Brantly, Rob	L-R	6-1	195	7-14-89	.325	.462	.286	30	117	13	38	6	1	4	22	3	1	0	0	14	0	1	.496	.347
Coats, Jason	R-R	6-2	200	2-24-90	.340	1.000	.311	12	47	6	16	9	0	0	2	1	0	0	0	6	0	2	.532	.354
Curley, Chris	R-R	6-0	185	8-25-87	.145	.158	.140	23	76	5	11	3	0	2	9	4	1	1	1	17	0	0	.263	.195
Delmonico, Nick	L-R	6-2	200	7-12-92	.238	.319	.199	62	223	26	53	24	0	3	26	25	1	1	3	52	2	1	.386	.313
DeMichele, Joey	L-R	5-11	190	2-5-91	.246	.238	.249	135	488	53	120	22	6	2	45	40	4	7	2	119	15	4	.328	.307
Dowdy, Jeremy	R-R	6-2	230	7-13-90	.194	.241	.158	20	67	6	13	2	0	1	10	11	0	0	1	11	0	0	.269	.304
Farrell, Jeremy	R-R	6-3	200	11-11-86	.226	.333	.199	52	190	21	43	10	1	2	18	7	7	3	2	59	1	0	.321	.277
Fletcher, Brian	R-R	6-0	195	10-26-88	.234	.225	.238	75	252	40	59	13	2	7	34	26	3	1	3	72	4	1	.385	.310
Garcia, Drew	B-R	6-1	175	4-22-92	.500	—	.500	5	10	0	5	2	0	0	1	1	1	2	0	2	0	0	.700	.583
Hawkins, Courtney	R-R	6-3	230	11-12-93	.243	.250	.242	78	300	39	73	19	2	9	41	20	5	3	2	100	1	4	.410	.300
Hayes, Danny	L-R	6-4	210	9-21-90	.248	.303	.230	129	431	53	107	21	3	7	58	98	3	2	4	109	0	2	.360	.388
Jacobs, Chris	R-R	6-5	260	11-25-88	.265	.143	.314	15	49	7	13	3	1	0	5	6	1	0	0	17	1	0	.367	.357
Jirschele, Justin	L-R	5-11	195	4-15-90	.400	—	.400	4	5	0	2	0	0	0	2	0	2	1	0	0	0	0	.400	.571
Lemon, Marcus	L-R	5-11	175	6-3-88	.268	.292	.263	95	265	28	71	11	3	3	33	16	5	10	3	60	3	3	.366	.318
Leonards, Ryan	R-R	5-11	195	7-22-91	.190	.000	.235	8	21	2	4	0	0	0	2	1	0	1	1	5	0	0	.190	.250
Marrero, Christian	L-L	6-1	185	7-28-86	.282	.262	.288	129	450	69	127	20	4	13	63	78	6	2	7	77	2	2	.431	.390
Marrero, Chris	R-R	6-3	229	7-2-88	.324	.375	.310	9	37	0	12	3	0	0	4	1	0	0	0	7	0	0	.405	.342
May, Jacob	B-R	5-10	180	1-23-92	.275	.338	.261	98	389	47	107	15	1	2	32	29	3	9	2	73	37	17	.334	.329
Medina, Martin	R-R	6-0	200	3-24-90	.130	.000	.154	15	46	3	6	2	0	0	1	5	2	2	0	19	0	0	.174	.245
Nieto, Adrian	R-R	6-0	200	11-12-89	.207	.164	.221	81	256	27	53	9	2	5	27	52	2	4	1	77	0	0	.316	.344
Tarleton, Dallas	L-R	5-11	200	8-5-87	.100	.000	.111	4	10	0	1	0	0	0	0	1	0	0	0	6	0	0	.100	.182
2-team total (4 Mobile)					.227	—	—	8	22	2	5	0	0	0	1	3	0	0	0	6	0	0	.227	.320
Thomas, Tony	R-R	5-10	180	7-10-86	.255	.241	.262	26	94	9	24	7	2	1	13	10	0	0	0	35	1	1	.404	.327
Walker, Keenyn	B-R	6-3	190	8-12-90	.187	.183	.189	62	203	22	38	2	0	2	20	20	0	2	5	55	12	10	.227	.258

Pitching	B-T	HT	WT	DOB	W	L	ERA	G	GS	CG	SV	IP	H	R	ER	HR	BB	SO	AVG	vLH	vRH	K/9	BB/9
Albers, Matt	L-R	6-1	225	1-20-83	0	0	0.00	1	0	0	0	2	0	0	0	0	0	4	.000	.000	.000	18.00	0.00
Barnette, Tyler	R-R	6-3	190	5-28-92	5	4	2.38	29	6	0	1	76	72	27	20	3	25	51	.249	.257	.244	6.07	2.97
Blackmar, Mark	R-R	6-3	215	4-28-92	6	8	3.63	26	26	1	0	151	142	69	61	7	55	65	.250	.260	.244	3.87	3.27
Bucciferro, Tony	R-R	6-3	205	12-27-89	1	7	4.75	21	10	0	0	83	113	47	44	11	21	31	.333	.336	.332	3.35	2.27
Chalas, Miguel	R-R	5-11	155	6-27-92	3	0	2.03	14	0	0	0	27	15	6	6	0	4	19	.163	.195	.137	6.41	1.35
Crabbe, Tim	R-R	6-4	200	2-20-88	2	2	2.34	16	5	0	1	42	33	12	11	4	12	42	.214	.177	.239	8.93	2.55
2-team total (1 Mobile)					2	2	2.38	17	5	0	1	45	36	13	12	4	12	47	—	—	—	9.33	2.38
Danish, Tyler	R-R	6-0	205	9-12-94	8	12	4.50	26	26	2	0	142	175	82	71	13	60	90	.311	.306	.314	5.70	3.80
Davis, Devon	L-L	6-4	235	8-20-91	2	2	4.71	16	0	0	0	21	29	15	11	2	25	18	.337	.346	.333	7.71	10.71
Fernandez, Raul	R-R	6-2	180	6-22-90	4	7	4.26	36	0	0	5	61	57	32	29	4	22	45	.260	.220		6.60	3.23
Garcia, Onelki	L-L	6-3	225	8-2-89	1	0	5.09	13	0	0	0	18	19	13	10	0	7	24	.260	.207	.295	12.23	3.57
Guerra, Junior	R-R	6-0	205	1-16-85	2	3	2.29	5	3	0	0	20	15	5	5	2	4	26	.221	.267	.184	11.90	1.83
Hagan, Sean	L-L	6-6	215	3-5-91	0	0	3.27	7	0	0	0	11	7	4	4	1	8	3	.194	.222	.185	2.45	6.55
Hansen, Kyle	R-R	6-8	200	4-20-91	1	2	3.74	43	0	0	2	67	62	33	28	3	30	47	.252	.286	.232	6.28	4.01
Heidenreich, Matt	L-R	6-5	185	1-17-91	1	2	3.38	4	4	0	0	24	22	9	9	1	6	23	.242	.293	.200	8.63	2.25
Isler, Zach	R-R	6-5	230	10-31-90	1	1	3.44	24	0	0	7	34	30	14	13	5	7	16	.236	.244	.232	4.24	1.85
Jaye, Myles	B-R	6-3	230	12-28-91	12	9	3.29	26	26	0	0	148	135	64	54	8	47	104	.244	.249	.241	6.34	2.86
Leyer, Robin	R-R	6-2	175	3-13-93	3	1	4.93	12	6	0	0	38	42	26	21	3	17	30	.280	.177	.352	7.04	3.99
Montas, Frankie	R-R	6-2	185	3-21-93	5	5	2.97	23	23	1	0	112	89	49	37	3	48	108	.219	.189	.241	8.68	3.86
Olacio, Jefferson	L-L	6-7	295	1-16-94	0	0	0.00	1	0	0	0	2	1	0	0	0	4	3	.167	.000	.200	13.50	18.00
Recchia, Mike	R-R	6-1	210	4-2-89	0	1	6.60	3	0	0	0	15	15	12	11	3	6	9	.259	.310	.207	5.40	3.60
Sanburn, Nolan	R-R	6-1	205	7-21-91	0	2	6.60	22	1	0	2	30	26	24	22	1	23	30	.224	.220	.227	9.00	6.90

Pitching	B-T	HT	WT	DOB	W	L	ERA	G	GS	CG	SV	IP	H	R	ER	HR	BB	SO	AVG	vLH	vRH	K/9	BB/9
Smith, Blake	L-R	6-2	225	12-9-87	1	0	4.26	4	0	0	0	6	8	4	3	1	3	6	.296	.143	.462	8.53	4.26
Tago, Peter	R-R	6-3	190	7-5-92	1	0	1.89	12	0	0	6	19	6	5	4	0	9	16	.102	.125	.086	7.58	4.26
Wendelken, J.B.	R-R	6-0	190	3-24-93	6	2	2.72	27	0	0	5	43	36	14	13	4	11	56	.220	.227	.214	11.72	2.30
Winiarski, Cody	R-R	6-3	205	8-27-89	1	0	1.54	17	0	0	6	23	16	5	4	1	7	28	.203	.194	.209	10.80	2.70

Fielding

Catcher	PCT	G	PO	A	E	DP	PB
Brantly	.995	29	168	20	1	3	8
Dowdy	.992	18	113	5	1	1	2
Medina	.991	15	108	3	1	0	3
Nieto	.993	77	499	54	4	6	7
Tarleton	1.000	4	23	1	0	0	0

First Base	PCT	G	PO	A	E	DP
Curley	1.000	2	17	3	0	3
Dowdy	1.000	2	2	0	0	0
Farrell	1.000	2	3	0	0	0
Hayes	.995	117	1091	83	6	113
Jacobs	.977	9	74	12	2	11
Marrero	.990	11	98	6	1	6

Second Base	PCT	G	PO	A	E	DP
DeMichele	.985	135	233	422	10	91

	PCT	G	PO	A	E	DP
Garcia	1.000	1	1	1	0	0
Jirschele	1.000	1	1	2	0	1
Lemon	.941	5	8	8	1	3

Third Base	PCT	G	PO	A	E	DP
Curley	.950	13	7	31	2	2
Delmonico	.919	59	34	125	14	8
Farrell	.911	50	33	80	11	8
Garcia	.833	2	0	5	1	0
Jirschele	1.000	1	1	0	0	0
Lemon	1.000	10	2	12	0	1
Leonards	1.000	1	0	4	0	0
Thomas	.920	9	4	19	2	1

Shortstop	PCT	G	PO	A	E	DP
Anderson	.952	110	167	328	25	81
Curley	1.000	1	1	3	0	0

	PCT	G	PO	A	E	DP
Garcia	1.000	1	2	2	0	2
Lemon	.937	25	39	79	8	13
Leonards	.964	6	6	21	1	5
Thomas	.955	3	6	15	1	2

Outfield	PCT	G	PO	A	E	DP
Coats	1.000	12	24	0	0	0
Farrell	1.000	1	1	0	0	0
Fletcher	.880	17	22	0	3	0
Hawkins	.959	62	112	5	5	0
Jirschele	1.000	2	3	0	0	0
Lemon	1.000	54	78	6	0	0
Marrero	.990	105	186	6	2	2
Marrero	1.000	9	15	1	0	0
May	.991	98	223	3	2	1
Thomas	.905	12	19	0	2	0
Walker	.993	62	134	8	1	2

WINSTON-SALEM DASH
CAROLINA LEAGUE

HIGH CLASS A

Batting	B-T	HT	WT	DOB	AVG	vLH	vRH	G	AB	R	H	2B	3B	HR	RBI	BB	HBP	SH	SF	SO	SB	CS	SLG	OBP
Alvarez, Eddy	B-R	5-9	180	1-30-90	.325	.459	.265	34	120	24	39	6	1	3	14	19	0	2	2	17	11	7	.467	.411
Austin, Brett	B-R	6-1	210	11-24-92	.200	.286	.143	9	35	3	7	1	0	0	2	0	0	0	0	6	0	0	.229	.200
Barnum, Keon	L-L	6-5	225	1-16-93	.257	.291	.243	105	382	40	98	24	0	9	67	35	4	2	5	112	0	1	.390	.322
Basto, Nick	R-R	6-2	210	4-1-94	.203	.185	.209	83	300	33	61	18	0	7	33	19	5	1	3	94	1	2	.333	.260
Beatty, C.J.	B-R	5-10	190	9-28-88	.000	—	.000	2	7	0	0	0	0	0	0	0	0	0	0	0	0	0	.000	.000
Danner, Michael	L-R	5-10	186	9-18-91	.319	.207	.400	21	69	6	22	4	0	0	7	6	0	0	0	13	1	0	.377	.373
Dowdy, Jeremy	R-R	6-2	230	7-13-90	.247	.231	.254	27	89	7	22	4	0	0	11	10	0	0	0	11	0	0	.292	.323
Earley, Nolan	L-L	6-0	205	3-27-91	.257	.208	.279	94	315	27	81	19	1	2	34	35	2	0	1	65	1	2	.343	.334
Engel, Adam	R-R	6-1	215	12-9-91	.251	.220	.262	136	529	90	133	23	9	7	43	62	6	8	3	132	65	11	.369	.335
Jacobs, Chris	R-R	6-5	260	11-25-88	.283	.321	.270	59	205	27	58	12	1	3	27	24	3	2	0	47	1	0	.395	.366
Jirschele, Justin	L-R	5-11	195	4-15-90	.000	—	.000	2	5	0	0	0	0	0	0	0	0	0	0	0	0	0	.000	.000
Michalczewski, Trey	B-R	6-3	210	2-27-95	.259	.291	.248	127	474	59	123	35	4	7	75	50	5	0	3	114	4	3	.395	.335
Narvaez, Omar	B-R	5-10	175	2-12-92	.274	.221	.292	98	339	38	93	10	0	1	27	40	2	1	3	31	1	0	.313	.352
O'Connell, Sean	R-R	6-4	230	12-12-91	.138	.000	.154	10	29	3	4	1	0	0	3	2	0	0	1	3	0	0	.172	.188
Peter, Jake	L-R	6-1	185	4-5-93	.260	.217	.274	130	497	76	129	25	5	3	57	53	2	4	6	89	23	3	.348	.330
Plourde, Ryan	R-R	6-0	210	2-26-92	.500	.500	.500	1	4	0	2	1	0	0	0	0	0	0	0	0	0	0	.750	.500
Rondon, Cleuluis	R-R	6-0	155	4-13-94	.168	.189	.160	120	400	35	67	9	0	3	26	32	4	6	3	86	12	6	.213	.235
Suiter, Michael	R-R	6-1	200	4-9-92	.171	.135	.186	41	123	13	21	3	0	1	6	7	4	1	1	27	3	1	.220	.237
Thomas, Toby	R-R	5-11	185	12-9-93	.216	.184	.234	30	102	10	22	7	1	2	10	5	2	3	1	25	0	0	.363	.264
Walker, Keenyn	B-R	6-3	190	8-12-90	.274	.282	.272	51	164	30	45	6	4	0	13	22	2	3	0	38	25	6	.360	.367
Williams, Tyler	R-R	6-2	200	1-5-91	.233	.234	.232	67	215	18	50	6	4	1	21	19	0	2	2	82	0	1	.312	.292
Wilson, Ethan	R-R	6-0	195	3-9-89	.170	.214	.152	17	47	7	8	0	0	1	5	7	1	0	0	18	0	0	.234	.291

Pitching	B-T	HT	WT	DOB	W	L	ERA	G	GS	CG	SV	IP	H	R	ER	HR	BB	SO	AVG	vLH	vRH	K/9	BB/9
Adams, Spencer	R-R	6-3	171	4-13-96	3	0	2.15	5	5	0	0	29	31	9	7	1	7	23	.267	.326	.229	7.06	2.15
Almonte, Yency	B-R	6-3	205	6-4-94	3	3	2.42	7	6	0	0	45	28	14	12	1	12	39	.179	.176	.182	7.86	2.42
Barnette, Tyler	R-R	6-3	190	5-28-92	0	0	0.00	3	0	0	0	4	4	1	0	0	2	2	.308	.333	.250	4.50	4.50
Brennan, Brandon	R-R	6-4	220	7-26-91	3	4	3.55	12	12	0	0	58	55	29	23	2	24	39	.247	.247	.246	6.02	3.70
Brito, Jose	R-R	6-7	210	10-10-90	2	3	4.66	16	0	0	1	29	27	18	15	3	19	18	.252	.298	.217	5.59	5.90
Bucciferro, Tony	R-R	6-3	205	12-27-89	1	2	5.01	4	4	0	0	23	27	15	13	3	6	9	.297	.333	.269	3.47	2.31
Clark, Brian	R-L	6-3	225	4-27-93	10	4	2.33	29	5	0	0	89	78	29	23	0	38	85	.239	.235	.240	8.60	3.84
Cooper, Matt	R-R	6-0	190	9-30-91	1	0	1.42	8	0	0	1	13	11	3	2	0	3	12	.224	.278	.194	8.53	2.13
Cose, Jake	B-R	6-5	195	8-20-94	8	3	2.28	25	7	0	1	71	61	30	18	2	34	56	.234	.271	.208	7.10	4.31
Davis, Devon	L-L	6-4	235	8-20-91	1	0	0.00	3	0	0	0	7	3	0	0	0	0	9	.125	.000	.143	11.57	0.00
Dykstra, James	R-R	6-4	195	11-22-90	7	10	3.51	25	19	1	1	128	133	60	50	3	18	87	.271	.271	.271	6.10	1.26
Fry, Jace	L-L	6-1	190	7-9-93	1	8	3.63	10	10	0	0	52	60	26	21	1	17	39	.287	.273	.294	6.75	2.94
Fulmer, Carson	R-R	6-1	190	12-13-93	0	0	2.05	8	8	0	0	22	16	5	5	2	9	25	.205	.250	.180	10.23	3.68
Goldberg, Brad	R-R	6-4	228	2-21-90	1	4	2.97	39	0	0	11	58	57	25	19	4	25	58	.271	.322	.236	9.05	3.90
Guerrero, Jordan	L-L	6-3	190	5-31-94	7	3	3.56	16	16	0	0	94	82	41	37	6	21	88	.240	.235	.241	8.46	2.02
Hagan, Sean	L-L	6-6	215	3-5-91	1	1	4.22	11	1	0	2	21	20	10	10	1	4	10	.253	.129	.333	4.22	1.69
Heidenreich, Matt	L-R	6-5	185	1-17-91	12	3	2.76	21	21	1	0	131	129	46	40	8	23	103	.254	.233	.270	7.09	1.58
Isler, Zach	R-R	6-5	230	10-31-90	0	2	3.47	14	0	0	3	23	27	13	9		4	15	.297	.340	.250	5.79	1.54
Jones, Nate	R-R	6-5	220	1-28-86	0	0	2.25	4	0	0	0	4	3	1	1	1	0	1	.273	.000	.333	2.25	0.00
Leyer, Euclides	R-R	6-2	175	12-28-90	4	2	1.93	31	0	0	5	47	31	16	10	1	27	46	.193	.302	.139	8.87	5.21
Leyer, Robin	R-R	6-2	175	3-13-93	3	6	4.30	16	16	1	0	84	79	47	40	7	26	64	.239	.272	.212	6.88	2.80
Olacio, Jefferson	L-L	6-7	295	1-16-94	1	1	5.32	20	0	0	1	22	24	18	13	0	20	28	.282	.200	.327	11.45	8.18
Tago, Peter	R-R	6-3	190	7-5-92	2	0	2.80	23	0	0	8	35	33	11	11	1	18	47	.252	.220	.272	11.97	4.58

Pitching	B-T	HT	WT	DOB	W	L	ERA	G	GS	CG	SV	IP	H	R	ER	HR	BB	SO	AVG	vLH	vRH	K/9	BB/9
Wheeler, Andre	L-L	6-1	170	9-27-91	4	2	3.86	32	6	0	1	63	63	37	27	3	28	61	.259	.203	.287	8.71	4.00
Winiarski, Cody	R-R	6-3	205	8-27-89	0	0	0.00	1	0	0	0	2	2	0	0	0	2	1	.250	.500	.167	4.50	9.00
Ynoa, Michael	R-R	6-7	210	9-24-91	0	2	2.61	28	0	0	6	38	37	14	11	2	16	40	.255	.228	.273	9.47	3.79

Fielding

Catcher	PCT	G	PO	A	E	DP	PB
Austin	1.000	9	81	15	0	1	1
Dowdy	.990	25	190	17	2	0	3
Narvaez	.983	96	694	61	13	5	8
O'Connell	1.000	10	43	7	0	1	2
Plourde	1.000	1	4	0	0	0	0

First Base	PCT	G	PO	A	E	DP
Barnum	.988	96	880	61	11	89
Jacobs	1.000	29	240	17	0	21
Williams	.980	15	138	9	3	13

Second Base	PCT	G	PO	A	E	DP
Alvarez	1.000	4	7	10	0	3

Jirschele	1.000	2	1	2	0	0
Peter	.980	107	193	333	11	88
Rondon	.957	18	36	53	4	9
Wilson	1.000	9	12	19	0	5

Third Base	PCT	G	PO	A	E	DP
Basto	.875	3	3	4	1	0
Michalczewski	.934	127	56	253	22	22
Thomas	.913	9	7	14	2	3
Wilson	1.000	2	0	1	0	0

Shortstop	PCT	G	PO	A	E	DP
Alvarez	.963	26	43	86	5	20
Peter	.955	13	18	45	3	7

Rondon	.964	101	151	325	18	71

Outfield	PCT	G	PO	A	E	DP
Basto	.951	76	110	6	6	0
Beatty	1.000	1	3	0	0	0
Danner	1.000	11	16	0	0	0
Earley	.975	86	117	2	3	1
Engel	.986	136	273	9	4	2
Peter	1.000	6	10	0	0	0
Suiter	.985	41	63	2	1	0
Thomas	.941	11	16	0	1	0
Walker	.934	50	96	3	7	0

KANNAPOLIS INTIMIDATORS

LOW CLASS A

SOUTH ATLANTIC LEAGUE

Batting	B-T	HT	WT	DOB	AVG	vLH	vRH	G	AB	R	H	2B	3B	HR	RBI	BB	HBP	SH	SF	SO	SB	CS	SLG	OBP
Alvarez, Eddy	B-R	5-9	180	1-30-90	.285	.242	.302	89	330	64	94	23	6	2	39	69	2	6	3	68	42	8	.409	.408
Austin, Brett	B-R	6-1	210	11-24-92	.201	.081	.263	85	293	29	59	12	5	4	33	35	0	4	3	74	1	1	.317	.284
Baldwin III, James	L-R	6-3	205	10-10-91	.182	.167	.185	34	99	17	18	5	2	2	7	11	1	1	2	45	6	1	.333	.265
Basto, Nick	R-R	6-2	210	4-1-94	.217	.135	.264	42	143	22	31	11	0	3	18	17	5	0	5	35	2	2	.357	.312
Curley, Chris	R-R	6-0	185	8-25-87	.278	.318	.267	25	97	14	27	10	0	5	21	5	2	0	0	19	1	1	.536	.327
Daily, Cody	R-R	6-3	220	7-28-92	.233	.214	.239	35	120	9	28	11	0	1	12	8	1	1	1	22	1	1	.350	.285
Danner, Michael	L-R	5-10	186	9-18-91	.238	.207	.250	31	101	13	24	10	2	0	17	12	2	0	2	25	3	2	.376	.325
Delmonico, Nick	L-R	6-2	200	7-12-92	.400	.667	.353	5	20	4	8	1	1	1	8	1	0	0	1	4	0	0	.700	.409
Earley, Nolan	L-L	6-0	205	3-27-91	.318	.500	.278	7	22	4	7	1	1	0	3	3	1	0	0	3	0	0	.455	.423
Fish, Zach	R-R	6-1	200	11-5-92	.125	.091	.140	20	72	2	9	0	0	1	7	3	0	0	0	27	0	0	.167	.160
Gonzalez, Daniel	R-R	6-1	190	12-6-95	.227	.000	.250	7	22	3	5	0	0	0	5	4	0	0	0	4	0	0	.227	.346
Gross, Ethan	R-R	6-0	193	9-12-91	.187	.258	.159	77	230	25	43	5	1	0	13	29	1	6	0	44	3	3	.217	.281
Jones, Hunter	R-R	6-2	185	8-17-91	.205	.242	.195	46	166	25	34	4	0	0	9	21	5	2	3	42	15	3	.229	.308
Lechich, Louie	L-L	6-4	200	11-19-91	.253	.203	.274	130	494	59	125	19	3	6	71	36	3	5	5	99	19	3	.340	.305
Leonards, Ryan	R-R	5-11	195	7-22-91	.272	.264	.277	83	283	37	77	16	1	2	26	37	4	2	2	49	12	5	.357	.362
O'Connell, Sean	L-R	6-4	230	12-12-91	.138	.000	.148	11	29	1	4	0	0	1	1	1	0	1	9	0	0	.138	.188
Plourde, Ryan	R-R	6-0	210	2-26-92	.200	.235	.183	40	105	19	21	5	0	1	9	27	2	1	0	27	1	3	.276	.373
Robbins, Mason	L-L	6-0	200	2-1-93	.263	.254	.266	124	468	51	123	19	9	3	47	12	2	3	6	76	3	4	.361	.281
Silverio, Louis	R-R	6-2	195	12-15-93	.185	.083	.267	17	54	5	10	2	0	0	3	0	0	2	0	19	1	0	.222	.185
Simon, Alexander	R-R	6-2	200	1-5-92	.252	.243	.257	80	321	39	81	14	3	4	40	10	1	1	3	68	4	4	.352	.275
Stringer, Christian	L-R	5-11	175	6-25-90	.288	.358	.257	57	219	33	63	16	4	1	21	20	5	2	3	27	12	3	.411	.356
Suiter, Michael	R-R	6-1	200	4-9-92	.249	.264	.243	76	301	45	75	14	2	2	34	17	3	1	9	59	12	6	.329	.308
Thomas, Toby	R-R	5-11	185	12-9-93	.252	.208	.269	69	254	29	64	11	3	3	33	13	0	0	2	54	3	3	.354	.286
Williams, Tyler	R-R	6-2	200	1-5-91	.273	.357	.257	25	88	13	24	7	1	0	9	5	0	0	0	25	1	0	.375	.312
Ziznewski, John	R-R	6-2	190	4-28-91	.273	.296	.259	70	216	34	59	12	2	2	39	31	3	3	1	65	10	1	.375	.371

Pitching	B-T	HT	WT	DOB	W	L	ERA	G	GS	CG	SV	IP	H	R	ER	HR	BB	SO	AVG	vLH	vRH	K/9	BB/9
Adams, Spencer	R-R	6-3	171	4-13-96	9	5	3.24	19	19	1	0	100	111	49	36	7	11	73	.275	.308	.259	6.57	0.99
Almonte, Yency	B-R	6-3	205	6-4-94	8	4	3.88	17	16	0	0	93	92	42	40	8	26	71	.256	.303	.233	6.90	2.53
Banks, Tanner	L-L	6-1	205	10-24-91	0	0	4.09	8	0	0	1	11	14	9	5	0	3	5	.304	.286	.313	4.09	2.45
Brito, Jose	R-R	6-7	210	10-10-90	1	2	4.66	17	2	0	3	46	44	34	24	3	17	29	.250	.278	.227	5.63	3.30
Bruening, Brett	R-R	6-8	240	12-30-88	0	0	9.72	5	0	0	0	8	14	9	9	0	5	9	.378	.417	.360	9.72	5.40
Cooper, Matt	R-R	6-0	190	9-30-91	3	0	1.59	30	0	0	11	40	20	8	7	2	9	64	.146	.136	.151	14.52	2.04
Davis, Devon	L-L	6-4	235	8-20-91	2	3	4.40	15	0	0	1	29	22	15	14	0	10	32	.216	.212	.217	10.05	3.14
Erwin, Zack	L-L	6-5	195	1-24-94	0	2	1.89	7	3	0	0	19	15	5	4	0	4	15	.224	.231	.220	7.11	1.89
Frebis, Jonathan	L-L	6-3	220	9-24-92	1	0	10.29	5	0	0	1	7	11	8	8	1	7	6	.355	.333	.368	7.71	9.00
Guerrero, Jordan	L-L	6-3	190	5-31-94	6	2	2.28	9	9	0	0	55	42	15	14	1	10	60	.214	.293	.194	9.76	1.63
Lowry, Thaddius	R-R	6-4	215	10-4-94	12	8	4.48	26	26	1	0	151	158	82	75	8	40	94	.274	.252	.289	5.62	2.39
Martinez, Luis	R-R	6-6	190	1-29-95	4	14	5.38	24	24	0	0	109	102	75	65	8	53	69	.247	.254	.241	5.71	4.39
Olacio, Jefferson	L-L	6-7	295	1-16-94	0	1	10.80	5	0	0	2	5	7	7	6	1	4	3	.318	.333	.313	5.40	7.20
Peralta, Yelmison	R-R	6-1	210	3-3-95	4	8	6.04	21	20	0	0	95	120	79	64	8	52	48	.314	.345	.290	4.53	4.91
Riga, Ryan	L-L	6-0	210	10-22-92	0	1	4.76	8	0	0	2	11	14	7	6	1	3	9	.311	.235	.357	7.15	2.38
Salgado, Brad	R-R	6-2	205	7-15-91	2	5	3.69	35	0	0	5	76	71	41	31	3	24	49	.243	.328	.188	5.83	2.85
Tago, Peter	R-R	6-3	190	7-5-92	0	1	3.75	7	0	0	1	12	10	5	5	1	2	10	.238	.263	.217	7.50	1.50
Thompson, Zach	R-R	6-7	215	10-23-93	3	8	4.44	16	16	0	0	75	77	48	37	2	37	64	.270	.239	.291	7.68	4.44
Trexler, David	R-R	6-3	185	9-4-90	0	3	4.93	36	0	0	7	69	68	42	38	5	37	76	.250	.270	.236	9.87	4.80
Valerio, Kelvis	R-R	6-1	190	9-26-91	2	2	4.23	33	4	0	5	77	83	42	36	5	31	60	.275	.310	.254	7.04	3.64
Walsh, Connor	L-R	6-2	176	10-18-92	2	3	4.92	29	0	0	0	53	39	34	29	3	44	79	.201	.195	.205	13.42	7.47

Fielding

Catcher	PCT	G	PO	A	E	DP	PB
Austin	.994	78	540	85	4	4	8

Fish	.991	14	100	5	1	0	5
Gonzalez	.963	7	41	11	2	0	1

O'Connell	.971	10	49	17	2	1	3
Plourde	.983	39	211	20	4	0	8

First Base	PCT	G	PO	A	E	DP
Basto	.993	14	140	6	1	16
Curley	1.000	7	64	6	0	1
Daily	.992	14	121	9	1	7
Robbins	.970	12	95	2	3	7
Simon	.991	58	522	35	5	29
Thomas	.978	10	88	2	2	4
Williams	.994	19	163	6	1	6
Ziznewski	1.000	9	79	3	0	7

Second Base	PCT	G	PO	A	E	DP
Gross	.969	61	97	149	8	23
Leonards	.937	13	19	40	4	7
Stringer	.959	49	73	137	9	25
Thomas	.983	14	23	36	1	6

Third Base	PCT	G	PO	A	E	DP
Basto	1.000	1	0	2	0	0
Curley	.914	14	7	25	3	0
Daily	.917	15	17	27	4	1
Delmonico	1.000	4	3	10	0	0
Gross	.824	7	4	10	3	2
Leonards	.895	34	26	51	9	7
Thomas	.915	15	8	35	4	2
Williams	—	1	0	0	0	0
Ziznewski	.944	51	30	88	7	4

Shortstop	PCT	G	PO	A	E	DP
Alvarez	.936	85	127	236	25	33
Gross	1.000	2	0	3	0	1

Leonards	.938	29	33	89	8	15
Thomas	.949	24	50	61	6	9

Outfield	PCT	G	PO	A	E	DP
Baldwin III	.987	31	73	3	1	1
Basto	.974	22	36	2	1	2
Danner	1.000	21	40	2	0	1
Earley	1.000	6	10	0	0	0
Jones	.979	44	88	5	2	0
Lechich	.980	117	236	13	5	1
Robbins	1.000	88	144	1	0	0
Silverio	1.000	13	25	1	0	0
Simon	.947	9	17	1	1	0
Suiter	.984	73	123	1	2	0

AZL WHITE SOX   ROOKIE

ARIZONA LEAGUE

Batting	B-T	HT	WT	DOB	AVG	vLH	vRH	G	AB	R	H	2B	3B	HR	RBI	BB	HBP	SH	SF	SO	SB	CS	SLG	OBP
Adolfo, Micker	R-R	6-3	200	9-11-96	.253	.273	.250	22	83	14	21	3	1	0	10	6	3	0	1	25	3	2	.313	.323
Alfaro, Jhoandro	B-R	6-1	180	11-4-97	.182	.231	.173	28	88	7	16	2	0	0	7	4	2	0	1	15	0	0	.205	.232
Cooper, Jacob	R-R	5-10	221	6-1-96	.197	.200	.197	29	71	9	14	3	0	0	7	7	4	1	2	17	1	0	.239	.298
Daily, Cody	R-R	6-3	220	7-28-92	.390	.294	.415	20	82	20	32	10	3	3	15	5	3	0	1	13	0	1	.695	.440
Feliz, Maiker	R-R	6-0	195	8-17-97	.161	.143	.167	9	31	1	5	0	0	0	5	3	0	0	1	10	0	2	.161	.229
Fincher, Jake	R-R	6-1	185	1-26-93	.292	.227	.302	45	161	26	47	8	6	1	12	12	5	1	0	27	17	6	.435	.360
Gonzalez, Daniel	R-R	6-1	190	12-6-95	.273	.438	.230	26	77	8	21	3	0	1	15	4	1	0	1	11	0	1	.351	.313
Johnson, Micah	L-R	6-0	210	12-18-90	.333	—	.333	5	15	4	5	2	0	0	2	0	0	0	0	2	0	0	.467	.412
Jones, Hunter	R-R	6-2	185	8-17-91	.226	.000	.259	7	31	6	7	0	1	0	1	3	0	0	0	6	7	1	.290	.294
May, Jacob	B-R	5-10	180	1-23-92	.250	.200	.273	3	16	4	4	1	0	0	3	1	0	0	0	3	1	0	.313	.294
Mendick, Danny	R-R	5-10	180	9-28-93	.256	.241	.258	49	180	34	46	8	1	5	27	20	4	2	2	28	8	2	.394	.340
Mercedes, Felix	R-R	6-2	185	2-13-97	.209	.250	.198	37	115	15	24	3	2	1	7	20	6	1	0	48	2	1	.296	.352
Nunez, Amado	R-R	6-2	178	10-10-97	.145	.214	.129	21	76	7	11	1	0	0	4	5	1	0	0	20	1	0	.158	.207
Otano, Hanleth	R-R	6-3	195	7-16-96	.105	.000	.118	6	19	3	2	0	0	0	2	0	0	0	0	11	0	0	.105	.190
Silverio, Louis	R-R	6-2	195	12-15-93	.333	.000	1.000	2	3	1	1	1	0	0	1	1	0	0	0	1	0	0	.667	.500
Strong, Bradley	L-R	5-8	175	7-1-92	.326	.423	.310	48	184	35	60	15	4	2	31	20	1	2	3	18	12	6	.484	.389
Sullivan, Tyler	L-L	5-9	175	11-21-92	.287	.517	.239	45	171	26	49	7	1	0	14	20	5	1	3	23	9	2	.339	.372
Walker, David	L-R	5-9	180	3-24-92	.312	.211	.333	32	109	17	34	4	1	0	5	10	3	3	0	19	6	3	.367	.385
Yallen, Jordan	R-R	5-10	170	10-15-90	.143	.250	.108	24	49	8	7	0	0	0	3	11	3	0	0	18	0	1	.143	.333
Zangari, Corey	R-R	6-4	240	5-7-97	.323	.273	.333	48	195	29	63	14	1	6	40	11	0	0	2	49	1	0	.492	.356
Zavala, Seby	R-R	6-0	185	8-28-93	.326	.364	.318	35	129	33	42	17	5	4	35	15	2	0	1	27	2	0	.628	.401

Pitching	B-T	HT	WT	DOB	W	L	ERA	G	GS	CG	SV	IP	H	R	ER	HR	BB	SO	AVG	vLH	vRH	K/9	BB/9
Charleston, Jack	R-R	6-5	170	9-14-92	0	2	5.00	16	0	0	1	18	17	16	10	0	6	18	.236	.250	.229	9.00	3.00
Cherry, Taylore	R-R	6-9	260	6-24-93	1	1	0.42	14	0	0	1	21	10	7	1	0	9	24	.135	.167	.114	10.13	3.80
Comito, Chris	R-R	6-5	220	6-25-96	5	2	3.32	13	11	0	0	57	63	32	21	5	16	33	.285	.301	.275	5.21	2.53
Crain, Jesse	R-R	6-1	215	7-5-81	0	1	6.75	6	5	0	0	5	5	4	4	0	4	10	.217	.300	.154	16.88	6.75
Done, Victor	R-R	6-3	195	9-3-95	0	0	4.38	14	0	0	0	25	24	14	12	1	16	29	.255	.206	.283	10.58	5.84
Escorcia, Kevin	L-L	6-1	170	1-5-95	2	2	6.17	13	4	0	0	35	48	28	24	5	14	34	.331	.406	.310	8.74	3.60
Frebis, Johnathan	L-L	6-3	220	9-24-92	3	0	1.25	11	0	0	0	22	14	3	3	1	6	20	.192	.286	.169	8.31	2.49
Fulmer, Carson	R-R	6-1	190	12-13-93	0	0	0.00	1	1	0	0	1	1	0	0	0	1		.333	—	.333	9.00	0.00
Guerrero, Yeuris	R-R	6-1	180	9-20-95	3	6	9.32	13	10	0	0	47	66	51	49	5	29	39	.351	.407	.304	7.42	5.51
Katz, Alex	L-L	5-10		10-12-94	0	1	4.00	6	0	0	1	9	7	5	4	0	4	9	.206	.125	.231	9.00	4.00
McWilliams, Richard	R-R	6-4	210	4-21-93	0	0	0.56	11	0	0	2	16	6	2	1	0	9	11	.120	.190	.069	6.19	5.06
Peralta, Yelmison	R-R	6-1	210	3-3-95	1	1	5.40	2	2	0	0	10	11	6	6	1	3	10	.306	.444	.259	9.00	2.70
Powers, Ryan	R-R	6-5	215	1-1-93	2	2	4.29	16	1	0	1	36	34	19	17	3	10	31	.246	.283	.218	7.82	2.52
Quintero, Brandon	R-R	6-2	180	2-2-94	3	1	3.50	13	7	0	0	54	48	23	21	1	23	45	.239	.272	.217	7.50	3.83
Riga, Ryan	L-L	6-0	210	10-22-92	2	0	1.80	4	0	0	0	10	5	2	2	0	2	8	.161	.000	.208	7.20	1.80
Rocha, Jaider	R-R	6-1	185	5-23-93	2	1	3.43	14	0	0	2	21	19	12	8	1	9	18	.253	.333	.167	7.71	3.86
Sanchez, Andres	R-R	6-4	180	10-7-96	1	3	3.52	9	2	0	0	15	14	10	6	1	5	13	.233	.333	.167	7.63	2.93
Solorzano, Yosmer	R-R	6-2	181	2-11-97	5	2	3.02	12	11	0	0	63	64	24	21	0	16	43	.260	.324	.233	6.18	2.30
Stephens, Jordan	R-R	6-0	180	9-12-92	0	0	0.61	9	1	0	0	15	7	1	1	0	2	18	.140	.231	.108	11.05	1.23

Fielding

Catcher	PCT	G	PO	A	E	DP	PB
Alfaro	.959	25	143	19	7	2	3
Cooper	.958	13	59	9	3	0	1
Gonzalez	.966	17	98	16	4	2	9
Zavala	.967	17	111	7	4	1	2

First Base	PCT	G	PO	A	E	DP
Daily	.989	8	87	6	1	7
Gonzalez	1.000	2	14	0	0	2
Silverio	1.000	2	14	2	0	1
Zangari	.969	45	442	22	15	46

Second Base	PCT	G	PO	A	E	DP
Johnson	.947	5	5	13	1	4
Mendick	1.000	11	21	37	0	8
Strong	.974	45	80	149	6	30
Yallen	1.000	1	2	1	0	0

Third Base	PCT	G	PO	A	E	DP
Daily	.905	9	6	13	2	1
Feliz	.909	8	7	23	3	3
Mendick	1.000	3	1	10	0	1
Mercedes	.906	37	18	69	9	4

Shortstop	PCT	G	PO	A	E	DP
Mendick	.965	36	54	141	7	33
Nunez	.865	21	18	46	10	9

Outfield	PCT	G	PO	A	E	DP
Adolfo	1.000	21	29	2	0	0
Fincher	.967	42	54	5	2	1
Jones	1.000	7	5	0	0	0
May	1.000	3	7	0	0	0
Otano	.778	6	6	1	2	0
Sullivan	.988	45	75	7	1	0
Walker	.929	32	37	2	3	0
Yallen	1.000	23	17	0	0	0

CHICAGO WHITE SOX

GREAT FALLS VOYAGERS — ROOKIE

PIONEER LEAGUE

Batting	B-T	HT	WT	DOB	AVG	vLH	vRH	G	AB	R	H	2B	3B	HR	RBI	BB	HBP	SH	SF	SO	SB	CS	SLG	OBP
Califano, Frank	L-L	5-11	185	3-31-94	.291	.397	.235	53	182	23	53	5	2	0	19	19	2	3	0	39	7	3	.341	.365
Cruz, Johan	R-R	6-2	170	10-8-95	.312	.302	.318	65	269	40	84	17	0	6	38	12	0	1	3	61	0	0	.442	.338
Fish, Zach	R-R	6-1	200	11-5-92	.291	.309	.282	48	179	30	52	12	0	10	33	19	1	0	1	45	0	0	.525	.360
Flores, Dante	L-R	5-9	160	4-8-93	.276	.277	.276	52	199	32	55	14	2	6	30	18	2	3	2	57	2	0	.457	.339
Garcia, Joxelier	R-R	5-10	185	4-30-94	.245	.250	.242	18	49	8	12	3	0	1	4	6	3	0	0	11	0	0	.367	.362
Glines, Jackson	L-L	6-0	195	4-13-92	.240	.156	.277	45	146	19	35	8	0	2	10	15	10	0	1	14	3	0	.336	.349
Jarvis, Jake	R-R	5-10	175	2-23-95	.234	.203	.252	45	171	18	40	7	2	3	21	6	3	1	1	44	1	0	.351	.271
Jones, Ryan	L-L	6-4	215	6-27-91	.250	.091	.326	22	68	9	17	8	0	0	7	9	2	0	0	21	0	0	.368	.354
Lassiter, Landon	R-R	5-11	172	6-14-93	.312	.286	.327	49	170	34	53	10	2	3	21	30	4	4	3	37	6	1	.447	.420
Massey, Grant	R-R	5-11	185	7-10-92	.256	.222	.273	60	211	26	54	5	0	8	26	18	22	4	4	1	34	11	4	.280	.336
Orvis, Sikes	L-R	6-3	235	11-12-92	.231	.167	.263	42	147	25	34	6	0	4	21	23	1	1	4	40	0	0	.354	.337
Parent, Nick	R-R	6-3	235	7-30-90	.186	.179	.190	19	70	9	13	2	0	3	9	1	0	0	1	27	0	0	.343	.194
Rodriguez, Antonio	R-R	6-0	180	5-7-95	.260	.258	.261	70	296	39	77	16	3	8	39	7	0	0	2	54	6	1	.416	.275
Schroeder, Casey	R-R	6-2	190	7-12-93	.236	.264	.218	40	140	20	33	11	1	2	13	17	2	1	2	36	1	1	.371	.323
Silverio, Louis	R-R	6-2	195	12-15-93	.221	.250	.200	20	68	10	15	3	0	4	15	3	0	0	1	16	0	1	.441	.250
Velasquez, Victor	B-R	5-11	195	2-5-95	.252	.175	.289	36	123	21	31	6	1	3	15	8	1	1	1	30	3	1	.390	.301
Zangari, Corey	R-R	6-4	240	5-7-97	.235	.375	.111	6	17	0	4	2	0	0	1	3	1	1	0	9	0	0	.353	.381

Pitching	B-T	HT	WT	DOB	W	L	ERA	G	GS	CG	SV	IP	H	R	ER	HR	BB	SO	AVG	vLH	vRH	K/9	BB/9
Ball, Matt	R-R	6-5	200	1-23-95	2	9	8.16	15	15	0	0	61	80	61	55	7	34	52	.325	.439	.268	7.71	5.04
Banks, Tanner	L-L	6-1	205	10-24-91	5	5	2.51	14	14	0	0	75	71	31	21	3	6	38	.248	.226	.257	4.54	0.72
Barrow, Dylan	R-R	6-3	205	7-29-93	1	1	6.29	17	0	0	1	24	23	19	17	5	12	24	.250	.250	.250	8.88	4.44
Cherry, Taylore	R-R	6-9	260	6-24-93	0	0	0.00	2	0	0	1	4	1	0	0	0	3	5	.077	.000	.167	11.25	6.75
Dopico, Danny	R-R	6-2	190	12-18-93	2	3	4.37	21	0	0	7	35	29	22	17	3	14	56	.218	.354	.141	14.40	3.60
Easterling, Brannon	R-R	6-4	230	8-1-90	5	4	3.50	15	15	0	0	82	81	38	32	6	18	55	.261	.219	.286	6.01	1.97
Einhardt, Evin	R-R	6-3	191	7-2-91	5	3	4.02	14	14	0	0	63	68	30	28	3	19	41	.283	.292	.278	5.89	2.73
Erwin, Zack	L-L	6-5	195	1-24-94	2	0	0.84	8	4	0	0	21	17	5	2	0	3	15	.210	.240	.196	6.33	1.27
Freudenberg, Chris	L-L	6-3	195	6-19-93	1	1	6.28	18	0	0	0	29	32	24	20	5	16	32	.281	.276	.282	10.05	5.02
Gomez, Mike	L-L	6-1	195	10-17-91	1	1	7.23	18	0	0	1	24	23	21	19	4	24	23	.264	.200	.284	8.75	9.13
Hasler, Drew	R-R	6-6	245	8-14-93	1	1	3.34	18	0	0	0	30	31	14	11	1	9	23	.267	.333	.238	6.98	2.73
Hinchley, Ryan	L-L	6-3	205	1-9-93	3	2	6.15	21	0	0	0	26	34	28	18	0	23	32	.306	.207	.341	10.94	7.86
Katz, Alex	L-L	5-10	185	10-12-94	0	1	1.52	12	1	0	3	24	19	9	4	0	7	31	.216	.167	.241	11.79	2.66
Magallones, Brandon	R-R	6-3	195	1-19-93	3	2	4.35	9	6	0	0	31	29	15	15	2	14	26	.252	.077	.342	7.55	4.06
Mendonca, Tanner	R-R	6-4	215	6-18-92	1	1	2.38	14	0	0	0	23	13	9	6	0	14	31	.169	.167	.170	12.31	5.56
Ortiz, Braulio	R-R	6-5	205	12-20-91	0	1	7.29	17	0	0	1	21	13	19	17	3	13	39	.171	.227	.148	16.71	
5.57 Riga, Ryan	L-L	6-0	210	10-22-92	0	1	1.50	7	0	0	0	12	10	3	2	0	6	15	.238	.167	.267	11.25	4.50
Shearrow, Luke	R-R	6-4	225	2-10-91	3	3	3.17	19	5	0	2	48	35	22	17	2	22	26	.201	.227	.182	4.84	4.10
Stephens, Jordan	R-R	6-0	180	9-12-92	0	0	0.00	2	0	0	0	3	2	0	0	0	1	3	.182	.200	.167	9.00	3.00

Fielding

Catcher	PCT	G	PO	A	E	DP	PB
Fish	.974	32	236	23	7	2	12
Garcia	.985	17	121	14	2	1	1
Schroeder	.966	29	204	21	8	0	3

First Base	PCT	G	PO	A	E	DP
Jones	.983	16	165	11	3	11
Orvis	.994	37	336	22	2	30
Parent	1.000	17	163	15	0	11
Zangari	1.000	5	28	5	0	2

Second Base	PCT	G	PO	A	E	DP
Flores	.965	32	66	98	6	20
Jarvis	.939	26	34	89	8	16
Velasquez	.985	18	30	36	1	8

Third Base	PCT	G	PO	A	E	DP
Cruz	.925	58	26	135	13	5
Jarvis	.889	7	6	10	2	1
Velasquez	.839	10	7	19	5	2

Shortstop	PCT	G	PO	A	E	DP
Cruz	.971	7	10	24	1	4

Massey	.977	60	88	211	7	31
Velasquez	.903	7	9	19	3	5

Outfield	PCT	G	PO	A	E	DP
Califano	.987	50	75	2	1	1
Glines	.976	44	82	1	2	1
Jones	—	2	0	0	0	0
Lassiter	.958	43	43	3	2	0
Rodriguez	.933	69	115	11	9	2
Silverio	.966	20	26	2	1	0

DSL WHITE SOX — ROOKIE

DOMINICAN SUMMER LEAGUE

Batting	B-T	HT	WT	DOB	AVG	vLH	vRH	G	AB	R	H	2B	3B	HR	RBI	BB	HBP	SH	SF	SO	SB	CS	SLG	OBP
Beltre, Ramon	R-R	5-11	160	10-18-96	.301	.300	.301	45	173	33	52	5	5	1	24	19	0	3	1	23	8	5	.405	.368
Castillo, Luis	R-R	6-3	200	7-14-96	.231	.241	.228	40	143	14	33	3	1	0	16	12	2	1	3	38	0	0	.266	.294
Colina, Jose	R-R	6-0	180	3-26-98	.187	.100	.211	29	91	6	17	2	0	1	10	14	1	1	2	24	0	0	.242	.296
Feliz, Maiker	R-R	6-0	195	8-17-97	.349	.419	.326	47	175	27	61	4	5	1	29	31	4	0	1	40	3	3	.446	.455
Gideon, Yolberth	R-R	5-11	155	2-6-96	.222	.150	.243	38	90	18	20	3	0	0	5	26	1	1	0	12	8	2	.256	.402
Gonzalez, Carlos	R-R	6-1	175	8-30-93	.250	.270	.240	38	112	11	28	5	0	0	7	15	1	1	0	23	1	4	.295	.344
Guzman, Anderson	L-L	5-11	155	10-21-83	—																			
Hernandez, Nelson	L-R	6-0	180	2-29-96	.263	.350	.236	50	167	30	44	6	2	0	13	16	3	1	0	34	8	6	.323	.339
Mejia, Carlos	R-R	6-3	190	9-27-95	.154	.286	.111	43	143	5	22	3	0	0	7	17	3	1	0	53	1	2	.175	.258
Mejia, Droherlin	R-R	6-1	180	8-20-94	.333	.263	.365	37	123	21	41	4	1	0	20	17	2	0	1	23	11	5	.382	.420
Mota, Ricky	R-R	5-11	170	2-21-98	.208	.125	.238	60	245	32	51	9	0	0	28	19	3	4	7	77	6	4	.245	.272
Otano, Hanleth	R-R	6-3	195	7-16-96	.264	.214	.281	55	216	25	57	12	2	1	22	16	5	0	2	64	4	0	.352	.326
Perez, Carlos	R-R	5-10	160	9-10-96	.333	.293	.347	47	162	32	54	8	3	1	21	22	5	0	2	5	5	0	.438	.424
Requena, Carlos	R-R	6-0	170	4-8-97	.216	.222	.214	36	74	16	16	0	0	0	5	9	2	1	0	22	3	0	.216	.318
Reyes, Jose	B-R	6-0	155	9-24-96	.259	.333	.243	31	85	14	22	0	0	0	10	16	0	0	0	13	4	1	.259	.376
Rosas, Jorgen	R-R	5-9	160	1-10-98	.242	.217	.252	61	215	26	52	11	2	1	27	12	6	1	2	42	6	2	.326	.298

CHICAGO WHITE SOX

Batting	B-T	HT	WT	DOB	AVG	vLH	vRH	G	AB	R	H	2B	3B	HR	RBI	BB	HBP	SH	SF	SO	SB	CS	SLG	OBP
Tejeda, Anderson	L-R	6-0	165	8-1-96	.200	.063	.232	40	85	15	17	3	1	0	5	12	0	1	1	28	7	1	.259	.296
Valdez, Bradley	L-R	6-0	195	12-11-94	.143	.100	.160	13	35	4	5	2	0	0	4	6	1	0	0	9	1	1	.200	.286
Villarroel, Ylexander	B-R	6-2	190	6-4-97	.247	.194	.262	43	158	25	39	8	1	1	15	13	7	1	1	44	1	1	.329	.330

Pitching	B-T	HT	WT	DOB	W	L	ERA	G	GS	CG	SV	IP	H	R	ER	HR	BB	SO	AVG	vLH	vRH	K/9	BB/9
Acosta, Nelson	R-R	6-3	195	8-22-97	2	2	3.27	14	10	0	0	55	45	26	20	1	23	51	.224	.217	.229	8.35	3.76
Aponte, Luis	R-R	6-2	180	8-27-97	1	0	6.14	9	1	0	0	15	20	12	10	1	4	12	.328	.238	.375	7.36	2.45
Arias, Edinxon	R-R	6-2	155	12-5-97	0	3	5.08	15	15	0	0	44	57	36	25	1	28	34	.311	.333	.298	6.90	5.68
Caro, Fernando	R-R	6-3	192	2-25-97	1	1	2.12	24	0	0	2	47	39	18	11	1	18	30	.228	.300	.189	5.79	3.47
Coroba, Josbel	L-R	6-0	180	5-18-97	6	3	2.40	23	0	0	2	41	38	18	11	0	29	31	.242	.226	.246	6.75	6.31
De La Cruz, Leonardo	L-L	6-4	180	4-29-94	4	2	2.70	22	7	0	0	53	49	26	16	0	21	56	.244	.222	.248	9.45	3.54
Diaz, Carlos	L-L	6-0	186	1-1-94	4	3	1.56	14	0	0	0	58	59	24	10	1	15	50	.268	.189	.293	7.80	2.34
Espinosa, Ramon	R-R	6-2	185	11-30-93	1	1	3.09	26	0	0	2	44	42	25	15	0	35	35	.250	.271	.242	7.21	7.21
Gerardo, Josue	R-R	6-3	180	3-27-93	2	7	5.89	16	10	0	0	47	47	41	31	0	33	33	.266	.333	.240	6.27	6.27
Herrera, Antonio	R-R	6-4	195	9-26-94	0	3	10.36	14	7	0	1	29	40	40	33	0	20	20	.345	.268	.387	6.28	6.28
Ledo, Luis	R-R	6-4	208	5-28-95	2	3	3.57	5	3	0	0	18	20	9	7	0	5	11	.299	.310	.289	5.60	2.55
Mora, Hansel	R-R	6-4	185	8-10-94	2	3	3.83	18	4	0	0	52	59	28	22	2	13	46	.288	.302	.282	8.01	2.26
Percel, Eriberto	R-R	6-5	200	8-2-92	3	1	3.00	13	0	0	2	21	13	10	7	1	8	20	.173	.190	.167	8.57	3.43
Perez, Victor	L-L	6-3	195	8-11-95	1	2	7.52	16	0	0	0	20	18	20	17	0	25	12	.231	.176	.246	5.31	11.07
Quijada, Jhoan	L-L	6-3	210	12-27-94	2	8	3.94	18	15	0	1	78	81	46	34	2	15	75	.267	.344	.247	8.69	1.74
Rodriguez, Juan	L-L	6-0	185	8-2-92	0	1	1.02	12	0	0	4	18	8	3	2	0	14	20	.131	.400	.078	10.19	7.13

Fielding

Catcher	PCT	G	PO	A	E	DP	PB
Colina	.988	25	147	19	2	3	12
Mejia	1.000	1	8	1	0	0	0
Perez	.992	47	326	38	3	1	12
Villarroel	.963	9	75	3	3	3	4

First Base	PCT	G	PO	A	E	DP
Castillo	.947	24	198	17	12	17
Colina	.913	3	19	2	2	5
Gideon	—	1	0	0	0	0
Gonzalez	.981	26	199	13	4	20
Perez	1.000	1	5	1	0	0
Reyes	1.000	1	2	1	0	0
Valdez	1.000	6	43	3	0	5
Villarroel	.994	21	160	6	1	19

Second Base	PCT	G	PO	A	E	DP
Beltre	1.000	3	5	12	0	2
Gideon	1.000	6	9	14	0	5
Hernandez	1.000	1	6	0	0	0
Reyes	.957	17	39	27	3	7
Rosas	.968	56	99	145	8	32

Third Base	PCT	G	PO	A	E	DP
Beltre	.923	18	18	42	5	5
Feliz	.889	44	39	105	18	12
Gideon	.818	4	2	7	2	1
Gonzalez	.919	12	8	26	3	2
Mota	1.000	1	1	5	0	0
Reyes	.500	1	0	1	1	0

Shortstop	PCT	G	PO	A	E	DP
Beltre	1.000	3	4	3	0	0
Gideon	.989	24	41	51	1	9
Mota	.863	52	78	130	33	29
Rosas	1.000	5	6	15	0	1

Outfield	PCT	G	PO	A	E	DP
Beltre	.947	14	17	1	1	0
Castillo	1.000	1	2	0	0	0
Feliz	1.000	1	0	1	0	0
Hernandez	.974	48	72	3	2	2
Mejia	.915	38	52	2	5	1
Mejia	.970	35	58	7	2	3
Otano	.948	52	82	9	5	1
Requena	.944	32	32	2	2	1
Reyes	—	1	0	0	0	0
Rosas	1.000	1	1	0	0	0
Tejeda	.872	31	39	2	6	0

Cincinnati Reds

SEASON IN A SENTENCE: After injuries knocked out Homer Bailey, Devin Mesoraco and Zack Cosart, the Reds traded off veterans and turned to wave after wave of rookie pitchers in a dive to the basement of the NL Central.

HIGH POINT: Johnny Cueto struck out 10 in a dominating Opening Day outing and Cincinnati swept the Pirates in its season-opening series on their way to a 4-0 start. It was the last time all year that the Reds were four games above .500. It wasn't long before the disabled list started filling up with Reds regulars.

LOW POINT: There are many, but a 1-15 finish sent the team limping into the offseason. Cincinnati lost 13 straight at one point and were outscored 94-35 over the final 16 games. Cincinnati also had a nine-game losing streak in May that effectively took them out of the playoff race before summer arrived.

NOTABLE ROOKIES: Righthander Anthony DeSclafini proved to be a reliable back-of-the-rotation starter who showed enough to be penciled into next year's rotation as well. Righthander Raisel Iglesias showed some flashes of greatness, reaching double-digits in strikeouts in three consecutive late-season starts. He also had bouts of wildness, including an eight-walk outing earlier in the year. Righthanders Michael Lorenzen struggled in a lengthy audition in the rotation. Lefthanders John Lamb and Brandon Finnegan and righthanders Keyvius Sampson, Josh Smith and Jon Moscot each contributed to the Reds setting a major league record of 64-consecutive starts by rookies.

KEY TRANSACTIONS: The Reds were very busy at the trade deadline. They sent Johnny Cueto to the Royals, landing three lefthanded pitching prospects (Cody Reed, Finnegan and Lamb) in return. Righthander Mike Leake went to the Giants for righthander Keury Mella and outfielder Adam Duvall. Outfielder Marlon Byrd netted righthander Stephen Johnson.

DOWN ON THE FARM: The Reds' trades added pitching prospects to a system that already was loaded with pitching. Lefthander Amir Garrett was excellent for high Class A Pensacola (9-7, 2.44) while Tyler Mahle (13-8, 2.43) was dominant for low Class A Dayton. First baseman/DH James Vasquez was among the best hitters in the Arizona League (.359/.415/.669), although the 22-year-old was old for the league.

OPENING DAY PAYROLL: $117,197,072 (14th)

PLAYERS OF THE YEAR

MAJOR LEAGUE

Joey Votto
1b
.314/.459/.541
29 HR, 80 RBI,
144 BB

MINOR LEAGUE

Amir Garrett
lhp
(High Class A)
9-7, 2.44
133 SO in 140 IP

ORGANIZATION LEADERS

BATTING		*Minimum 250 AB
MAJORS		
*AVG	Joey Votto	.314
*OPS	Joey Votto	1.000
HR	Todd Frazier	35
RBI	Todd Frazier	89
MINORS		
*AVG	Jesse Winker, Pensacola	.282
*OBP	Jesse Winker, Pensacola	.390
*SLG	Jesse Winker, Pensacola	.433
R	Phillip Ervin, Daytona, Pensacola	75
H	Gavin LaValley, Dayton	125
	Jesse Winker, Pensacola	125
TB	Jesse Winker, Pensacola	192
2B	Gavin LaValley, Dayton	29
3B	Tomas De Los Santos, DSL Reds	12
HR	Phillip Ervin, Daytona, Pensacola	14
RBI	Sebastian Elizalde, Daytona	77
BB	Jesse Winker, Pensacola	74
SO	Taylor Sparks, Daytona	162
SB	Junior Felix Arias, Daytona	37

PITCHING		#Minimum 75 IP
MAJORS		
W	Anthony DeSclafani	9
	Mike Leake	9
#ERA	Anthony DeSclafani	4.05
SO	Anthony DeSclafani	151
SV	Aroldis Chapman	33
MINORS		
W	Tyler Mahle, Dayton	13
L	Robert Stephenson, Pensacola, Louisville	11
	Daniel Wright, Pensacola	11
#ERA	Tyler Mahle, Dayton	2.43
G	Zack Weiss, Daytona, Pensacola	54
GS	Wyatt Strahan, Dayton	28
SV	Zack Weiss, Daytona, Pensacola	30
IP	Wyatt Strahan, Dayton	164
BB	Robert Stephenson, Pensacola, Louisville	70
SO	Robert Stephenson, Pensacola, Louisville	140
AVG	Robert Stephenson, Pensacola, Louisville	.218

2015 PERFORMANCE

General Manager: Walt Jocketty. **Farm Director:** Jeff Graupe. **Scouting Director:** Chris Buckley.

Class	Team	League	W	L	PCT	Finish	Manager
Majors	Cincinnati Reds	National	64	98	.395	14th (15)	Bryan Price
Triple-A	Louisville Bats	International	64	80	.444	11th (14)	Delino DeShields
Double-A	Tennessee Smokies	Southern	76	63	.547	4th (10)	Buddy Bailey
High A	Daytona Tortugas	Florida State	77	58	.570	2nd (12)	Eli Marrero
Low A	Dayton Dragons	Midwest	71	68	.511	9th (16)	Jose Nieves
Rookie	Billings Mustangs	Pioneer	37	38	.493	5th (8)	Dick Schofield
Rookie	Reds	Arizona	27	29	.482	8th (14)	Ray Martinez
Overall 2015 Minor League Record			352	336	.512	t-11th (30)	

ORGANIZATION STATISTICS

CINCINNATI REDS

NATIONAL LEAGUE

Batting	B-T	HT	WT	DOB	AVG	vLH	vRH	G	AB	R	H	2B	3B	HR	RBI	BB	HBP	SH	SF	SO	SB	CS	SLG	OBP
Barnhart, Tucker	B-R	5-11	190	1-7-91	.252	.178	.269	81	242	23	61	9	0	3	18	25	2	2	3	45	0	1	.326	.324
Boesch, Brennan	L-L	6-4	225	4-12-85	.146	.143	.146	51	89	4	13	2	0	1	5	4	1	0	0	30	1	0	.202	.191
Bourgeois, Jason	R-R	5-9	200	1-4-82	.240	.167	.268	68	196	28	47	5	2	3	14	14	1	1	0	33	3	1	.332	.294
Bruce, Jay	L-L	6-3	225	4-3-87	.226	.229	.225	157	580	72	131	35	4	26	87	58	2	0	9	145	9	5	.434	.294
Byrd, Marlon	R-R	6-0	245	8-30-77	.237	.280	.224	96	359	46	85	13	3	19	42	23	3	0	3	101	2	1	.448	.286
2-team total (39 San Francisco)					.247	—	—	135	506	58	125	25	5	23	73	29	4	0	5	145	2	1	.453	.290
Cabrera, Ramon	B-R	5-8	195	11-5-89	.367	.375	.364	13	30	4	11	1	0	1	3	0	0	0	0	5	0	0	.500	.367
Cozart, Zack	R-R	6-0	195	8-12-85	.258	.326	.236	53	194	28	50	10	1	9	28	14	2	1	3	29	3	3	.459	.310
De Jesus Jr., Ivan	R-R	5-11	200	5-1-87	.244	.263	.236	76	201	15	49	10	2	4	20	19	1	0	1	55	0	2	.373	.311
Dominguez, Chris	R-R	6-4	235	11-22-86	.261	.111	.357	14	23	2	6	1	1	3	0	0	0	0	12	0	0	.522	.261
Duvall, Adam	R-R	6-1	205	9-4-88	.219	.176	.234	27	64	6	14	2	0	5	9	6	2	0	0	26	0	0	.484	.306
Frazier, Todd	R-R	6-3	220	2-12-86	.255	.261	.253	157	619	82	158	43	1	35	89	44	7	1	7	137	13	8	.498	.309
Hamilton, Billy	B-R	6-0	160	9-9-90	.226	.241	.220	114	412	56	93	8	3	4	28	28	1	9	4	75	57	8	.289	.274
Holt, Tyler	R-R	5-10	200	3-10-89	.091	.167	.000	5	11	2	1	0	0	0	0	2	0	0	0	2	1	0	.091	.231
LaMarre, Ryan	R-L	6-1	205	11-21-88	.080	.000	.091	21	25	2	2	0	0	0	0	0	0	1	0	9	0	0	.080	.080
Mesoraco, Devin	R-R	6-1	220	6-19-88	.178	.077	.219	23	45	2	8	1	0	2	5	1	0	0	0	9	1	0	.244	.275
Negron, Kris	R-R	6-0	190	2-1-86	.140	.091	.167	43	93	5	13	2	0	2	9	3	2	0	2	23	2	0	.161	.238
Pena, Brayan	B-R	5-9	240	1-7-82	.273	.217	.295	108	333	29	91	17	0	0	18	29	2	2	1	34	2	0	.324	.334
Phillips, Brandon	R-R	6-0	210	6-28-81	.294	.303	.291	148	588	69	173	19	2	12	70	27	4	—	3	68	23	3	.395	.328
Schumaker, Skip	L-R	5-10	190	2-3-80	.242	.273	.239	131	244	23	59	20	0	1	21	23	0	0	1	51	2	2	.336	.306
Suarez, Eugenio	B-R	5-11	180	7-18-91	.280	.289	.277	97	372	42	104	19	2	13	48	17	3	4	2	94	4	1	.446	.315
Votto, Joey	L-R	6-2	220	9-10-83	.314	.331	.306	158	545	95	171	33	2	29	80	143	5	0	2	135	11	3	.541	.459
Waldrop, Kyle	L-L	6-2	215	11-26-91	.000	—	.000	1	1	0	0	0	0	0	0	0	0	0	0	1	0	0	.000	.000

Pitching	B-T	HT	WT	DOB	W	L	ERA	G	GS	CG	SV	IP	H	R	ER	HR	BB	SO	AVG	vLH	vRH	K/9	BB/9
Adcock, Nate	R-R	6-4	235	2-25-88	1	2	6.00	13	0	0	0	18	15	12	12	3	12	13	.221	.259	.195	6.50	6.00
Axelrod, Dylan	R-R	6-0	185	7-30-85	0	1	7.30	6	0	0	0	12	11	13	10	5	8	12	.220	.217	.222	8.76	5.84
Badenhop, Burke	R-R	6-5	210	2-8-83	2	4	3.93	68	0	0	0	66	71	30	29	4	20	36	.273	.265	.280	4.88	2.71
Bailey, Homer	R-R	6-4	225	5-3-86	0	1	5.56	2	2	0	0	11	16	7	7	3	4	3	.340	.500	.222	2.38	3.18
Balester, Collin	R-R	6-4	190	6-6-86	1	1	7.47	15	0	0	0	16	17	13	13	3	13	13	.274	.174	.333	7.47	7.47
Chapman, Aroldis	L-L	6-4	215	2-28-88	4	4	1.63	65	0	0	33	66	43	13	12	3	33	116	.181	.143	.194	15.74	4.48
Cingrani, Tony	L-L	6-4	210	7-5-89	0	3	5.67	35	1	0	0	33	31	21	21	3	25	39	.250	.267	.241	10.53	6.75
Contreras, Carlos	R-R	5-11	215	1-8-91	0	0	4.82	22	0	0	0	28	22	16	15	3	20	19	.214	.167	.246	6.11	6.43
Cueto, Johnny	R-R	5-11	220	2-15-86	7	6	2.62	19	19	1	0	131	93	42	38	11	29	120	.196	.173	.217	8.27	2.00
DeSclafani, Anthony	R-R	6-1	190	4-18-90	9	13	4.05	31	31	0	0	185	194	93	83	17	55	151	.273	.268	.279	7.36	2.68
Diaz, Jumbo	R-R	6-4	280	2-27-84	2	1	4.18	61	0	0	1	60	58	29	28	9	18	70	.253	.248	.258	10.44	2.69
Finnegan, Brandon	L-L	5-11	185	4-14-93	2	2	4.18	6	4	0	0	24	21	11	11	5	8	24	.239	.250	.236	9.13	3.04
Gregg, Kevin	R-R	6-6	245	6-20-78	0	2	10.13	11	0	0	0	11	13	12	12	3	5	14	.289	.174	.409	11.81	4.22
Hand, Donovan	R-R	6-3	235	4-20-86	0	0	0.00	1	0	0	0	3	2	0	0	1	1	3	.182	.000	.250	9.00	3.00
Holmberg, David	R-L	6-3	245	7-19-91	1	4	7.62	6	6	0	0	28	36	24	24	10	16	15	.321	.148	.376	4.76	5.08
Hoover, J.J.	R-R	6-3	245	8-13-87	8	2	2.94	67	0	0	1	64	44	24	21	7	31	52	.196	.217	.174	7.27	4.34
Iglesias, Raisel	R-R	6-2	185	1-4-90	3	7	4.15	18	16	0	0	95	81	45	44	11	28	104	.228	.286	.176	9.82	2.64
Lamb, John	L-L	6-4	205	7-10-90	1	5	5.80	10	10	0	0	50	58	32	32	8	19	58	.296	.341	.284	10.51	3.44
Leake, Mike	R-R	5-10	190	11-12-87	9	5	3.56	21	21	1	0	137	123	55	54	14	34	90	.240	.263	.212	5.93	2.24
2-team total (9 San Francisco)					11	10	3.70	30	30	2	0	192	174	80	79	22	49	119	—	—	—	5.58	2.30
LeCure, Sam	R-R	6-0	210	5-4-84	0	2	3.15	19	0	0	0	20	16	9	7	1	15	16	.216	.138	.267	6.75	3.15
Lorenzen, Michael	R-R	6-3	205	1-4-92	4	9	5.40	27	21	0	0	113	131	70	68	18	57	83	.292	.332	.262	6.59	4.53
Marquis, Jason	L-R	6-1	220	8-21-78	3	4	6.46	9	9	0	0	47	64	37	34	10	14	37	.330	.310	.351	7.04	2.66
Mattheus, Ryan	R-R	6-3	220	11-10-83	2	4	4.09	57	0	0	0	55	67	31	25	3	17	35	.300	.347	.262	5.73	2.78
Moscot, Jon	R-R	6-3	210	8-15-91	1	1	4.63	3	3	0	0	12	11	6	6	2	5	6	.250	.238	.261	4.63	3.86
Parra, Manny	L-L	6-3	215	10-30-82	1	2	3.90	40	0	0	0	32	32	15	14	2	6	23	.264	.271	.258	6.40	1.67
Sampson, Keyvius	R-R	6-2	205	1-6-91	2	6	6.54	13	12	0	0	52	67	43	38	7	26	42	.303	.340	.274	7.22	4.47
Smith, Josh	R-R	6-2	220	8-7-87	0	4	6.89	9	7	0	0	33	42	27	25	5	21	30	.316	.361	.278	8.27	5.79
Villarreal, Pedro	R-R	6-1	235	12-9-87	1	3	3.42	29	0	0	0	50	57	24	19	6	12	29	.294	.321	.276	5.22	2.16

Fielding

Catcher	PCT	G	PO	A	E	DP	PB
Barnhart	.996	73	492	42	2	0	4
Cabrera	1.000	8	41	5	0	0	0
Mesoraco	1.000	6	52	2	0	0	0
Pena	.999	86	683	31	1	4	5

First Base	PCT	G	PO	A	E	DP
De Jesus Jr.	1.000	4	9	2	0	1
Dominguez	1.000	2	8	0	0	0
Duvall	1.000	4	17	0	0	2
Negron	1.000	2	16	2	0	0
Pena	1.000	5	22	1	0	1
Votto	.993	156	1212	139	9	122

Second Base	PCT	G	PO	A	E	DP
De Jesus Jr.	1.000	20	25	50	0	9

	PCT	G	PO	A	E	DP
Negron	1.000	6	3	13	0	4
Phillips	.991	141	261	394	6	79
Schumaker	1.000	12	2	19	0	4

Third Base	PCT	G	PO	A	E	DP
De Jesus Jr.	1.000	13	6	15	0	0
Frazier	.952	155	102	274	19	21
Negron	.000	2	0	0	1	0
Suarez	—	1	0	0	0	0

Shortstop	PCT	G	PO	A	E	DP
Cozart	.986	52	79	132	3	30
De Jesus Jr.	.929	10	15	24	3	6
Negron	.977	10	11	31	1	7
Phillips	—	1	0	0	0	0
Suarez	.956	96	147	265	19	59

Outfield	PCT	G	PO	A	E	DP
Barnhart	—	1	0	0	0	0
Boesch	1.000	23	36	0	0	0
Bourgeois	.978	48	85	2	2	0
Bruce	.990	150	300	11	3	0
Byrd	1.000	92	173	2	0	0
De Jesus Jr.	.938	18	30	0	2	0
Dominguez	1.000	3	5	0	0	0
Duvall	1.000	15	24	0	0	0
Hamilton	1.000	110	273	8	0	1
Holt	1.000	5	13	0	0	0
LaMarre	.944	16	16	1	1	0
Negron	.952	16	20	0	1	0
Schumaker	.944	46	65	3	4	1

LOUISVILLE BATS   TRIPLE-A
INTERNATIONAL LEAGUE

Batting	B-T	HT	WT	DOB	AVG	vLH	vRH	G	AB	R	H	2B	3B	HR	RBI	BB	HBP	SH	SF	SO	SB	CS	SLG	OBP
Barnhart, Tucker	B-R	5-11	190	1-7-91	.313	.000	.333	5	16	0	5	3	0	0	2	1	0	0	1	4	0	0	.500	.333
Benedetti, Nick	R-R	6-0	150	2-27-93	.091	.000	.111	7	11	0	1	0	0	0	0	1	0	0	0	6	0	0	.091	.167
Berset, Chris	B-R	6-0	195	1-27-88	.218	.243	.210	45	142	10	31	7	0	0	14	11	3	5	2	25	0	1	.268	.285
Boesch, Brennan	L-L	6-4	225	4-12-85	.326	.400	.306	51	187	17	61	9	0	4	30	19	0	1	1	41	0	2	.439	.386
Bourgeois, Jason	R-R	5-9	200	1-4-82	.309	.368	.278	14	55	8	17	2	1	0	7	3	1	1	0	5	1	1	.382	.356
Buckley, Sean	R-R	6-3	224	9-3-89	.206	.000	.259	11	34	4	7	1	1	0	1	4	1	0	0	8	0	0	.294	.308
Cabrera, Ramon	B-R	5-8	195	11-5-89	.290	.303	.285	86	317	29	92	14	0	2	35	27	0	4	3	44	1	1	.353	.343
Constanza, Jose	L-L	5-9	185	9-1-83	.256	.185	.276	41	125	16	32	4	2	0	14	12	0	2	0	16	6	4	.320	.321
2-team total (5 Durham)					.253		—	46	146	17	37	6	2	0	17	12	1	2	0	20	9	4	.322	.314
Curtis, Jermaine	R-R	5-11	190	7-10-87	.273	.282	.268	74	227	30	62	10	0	2	20	21	11	0	1	25	5	1	.344	.362
De Jesus Jr., Ivan	R-R	5-11	200	5-1-87	.303	.280	.311	50	185	22	56	9	3	0	16	22	1	0	1	43	2	1	.384	.378
Dominguez, Chris	R-R	6-4	235	11-22-86	.223	.236	.217	96	296	32	66	19	0	9	36	16	6	1	2	92	5	3	.378	.275
Duvall, Adam	R-R	6-1	205	9-4-88	.189	.037	.250	25	95	11	18	4	0	4	7	6	3	0	0	23	1	0	.358	.260
Falu, Irving	B-R	5-9	185	6-6-83	.270	.273	.268	121	460	55	124	16	6	3	43	48	1	9	5	46	19	9	.350	.337
Iribarren, Hernan	L-R	6-1	195	6-29-84	.256	.239	.260	111	407	52	104	13	2	1	28	40	2	8	1	64	6	3	.305	.324
Johnson, Dan	R-L	6-2	210	8-10-79	.069	.143	.045	9	29	3	2	0	0	1	2	10	1	0	0	9	1	0	.069	.325
LaMarre, Ryan	R-L	6-1	205	11-21-88	.257	.264	.254	91	300	33	77	17	1	8	18	18	5	3	3	88	11	4	.400	.307
Lutz, Donald	L-R	6-3	240	2-6-89	.190	.071	.250	13	42	3	8	3	0	0	3	5	1	0	0	10	0	0	.262	.292
Mesoraco, Devin	R-R	6-1	220	6-19-88	.143	.000	.250	3	7	0	1	0	0	0	0	1	0	0	0	3	0	0	.143	.250
Morillo, Julio	R-R	5-10	175	12-27-92	.000	.000	—	1	2	0	0	0	0	0	0	0	0	1	0	0	0	0	.000	.333
Negron, Kris	R-R	6-0	190	2-1-86	.216	.261	.203	59	204	13	44	5	1	4	15	15	4	5	2	47	3	1	.309	.280
Perez, Juan	L-R	5-11	185	11-1-91	.209	.250	.194	25	91	8	19	3	0	2	4	6	0	0	0	23	7	0	.308	.258
Rodriguez, Yorman	R-R	6-2	210	8-15-92	.269	.277	.267	85	308	42	83	13	3	10	41	17	0	1	0	80	4	1	.429	.308
Satin, Josh	R-R	6-2	215	12-23-84	.247	.258	.243	70	235	22	58	12	1	4	31	34	4	3	4	44	1	1	.357	.347
Selsky, Steve	R-R	6-0	203	7-20-89	.317	.284	.336	51	180	23	57	10	2	2	29	19	2	0	1	44	3	1	.428	.386
Silva, Juan	L-L	5-11	204	1-8-91	.244	.361	.202	43	135	20	33	7	0	2	7	23	3	0	2	27	2	1	.341	.354
Skipworth, Kyle	L-R	6-4	230	3-1-90	.160	.333	.136	9	25	3	4	2	0	0	1	3	0	1	1	8	0	0	.240	.241
Smith, Bryson	R-R	6-1	195	12-17-88	.260	.240	.271	26	73	8	19	3	0	0	6	7	1	1	0	18	1	0	.301	.333
Suarez, Eugenio	B-R	5-11	180	7-18-91	.256	.279	.244	57	203	30	52	9	2	8	25	26	3	5	1	40	3	4	.438	.348
Tromp, Chadwick	R-R	5-9	180	3-21-95	.500	.000	.667	1	4	0	2	1	0	0	1	0	0	0	0	0	0	0	.750	.500
Veras, Josciel	R-R	5-8	175	12-7-92	.219	.100	.273	15	32	2	7	0	1	0	4	5	0	0	1	11	0	0	.281	.324
Waldrop, Kyle	L-L	6-2	215	11-26-91	.185	.179	.187	55	205	8	38	6	0	1	13	7	0	0	1	54	0	1	.229	.211

Pitching	B-T	HT	WT	DOB	W	L	ERA	G	GS	CG	SV	IP	H	R	ER	HR	BB	SO	AVG	vLH	vRH	K/9	BB/9
Adcock, Nate	R-R	6-4	235	2-25-88	0	2	2.96	22	0	0	11	24	23	11	8	0	7	20	.240	.293	.200	7.40	2.59
Axelrod, Dylan	R-R	6-0	185	7-30-85	6	8	4.68	22	19	0	0	106	124	65	55	13	28	69	.297	.360	.252	5.88	2.38
Bailey, Homer	R-R	6-4	225	5-3-86	0	1	4.76	1	1	0	0	6	5	4	3	2	3		.250	.231	.286	4.76	3.18
Balester, Collin	R-R	6-4	190	6-6-86	0	0	2.05	21	0	0	7	22	16	5	5	1	3	13	.200	.214	.192	5.32	1.23
2-team total (8 Indianapolis)					0	0	2.45	29	0	0	7	37	28	11	10	2	8	21	—			5.15	1.96
Bender, Joel	R-R	6-4	210	8-3-91	0	0	0.87	4	1	0	0	10	10	1	1	1	1	10	.250	.111	.290	8.71	0.87
Bernardino, Brennan	L-L	6-4	180	1-15-92	0	0	6.75	2	0	0	0	1	3	1	1	0	0	6	.500	.500	.500	0.00	0.00
Brattvet, Scott	R-R	6-1	195	7-21-91	0	0	0.00	2	0	0	2	1	0	0	0	1	1		.167	.500	.000	5.40	5.40
Buschmann, Matt	R-R	6-3	195	2-13-84	2	5	4.25	9	9	2	0	53	52	25	25	3	18	44	.268	.271	.265	7.47	3.06
3-team total (13 Durham, 1 Norfolk)					8	10	4.08	23	23	2	0	135	123	62	61	13	47	109	—			7.28	3.14
Cabrera, Daniel	R-R	6-7	225	5-28-81	0	0	3.00	1	1	0	0	3	2	2	1	0	4	1	.182	.286	.000	3.00	12.00
Carpenter, Chris	R-R	6-4	220	12-26-85	0	0	16.20	6	0	0	0	7	18	12	12	0	7	9	.500	.471	.526	12.15	9.45
Celestino, Miguel	R-R	6-6	215	10-10-89	0	1	1.26	9	0	0	1	14	11	2	2	1	5	9	.216	.235	.206	5.65	3.14
2-team total (17 Pawtucket)					0	5	2.96	26	1	0	1	49	47	19	16	4	21	35	—			6.47	3.88
Christiani, Nick	R-R	6-0	190	7-17-87	0	2	5.74	22	0	0	0	31	46	24	20	1	24	17	.357	.471	.282	4.88	6.89
Cingrani, Tony	L-L	6-4	210	7-5-89	0	1	1.82	9	6	0	0	25	20	6	5	2	23	25	.222		.225	11.68	4.01
Contreras, Carlos	R-R	5-11	215	1-8-91	2	2	2.95	31	0	0	3	40	32	13	13	3	30	55	.222	.230	.217	12.48	6.81
De La Torre, Jose	R-R	5-10	195	10-17-85	6	6	3.32	51	0	0	3	65	54	26	24	4	36	46	.230	.238	.223	6.37	4.98
Dennick, Ryan	L-L	6-0	200	1-10-87	0	0	6.75	2	0	0	0	3	4	3	2	0	0	5	.333	.125	.750	16.88	0.00
Diaz, Jumbo	R-R	6-4	280	2-27-84	0	1	1.13	13	0	0	8	16	11	2	2	0	4	12	.183	.222	.152	6.75	2.25

CINCINNATI REDS

CINCINNATI REDS

Pitching	B-T	HT	WT	DOB	W	L	ERA	G	GS	CG	SV	IP	H	R	ER	HR	BB	SO	AVG	vLH	vRH	K/9	BB/9
Finnegan, Brandon	L-L	5-11	185	4-14-93	0	3	6.23	8	8	0	0	30	31	22	21	3	17	30	.263	.250	.265	8.90	5.04
Hand, Donovan	R-R	6-3	235	4-20-86	1	6	4.92	33	11	0	0	97	113	55	53	11	18	52	.294	.276	.307	4.82	1.67
Hayes, Drew	R-R	6-1	205	9-3-87	4	4	2.95	43	0	0	3	58	58	22	19	2	30	56	.271	.326	.230	8.69	4.66
Holmberg, David	R-L	6-3	245	7-19-91	7	7	4.34	21	19	0	0	120	142	63	58	14	41	71	.299	.308	.296	5.31	3.07
Iglesias, Raisel	R-R	6-2	185	1-4-90	1	3	3.41	6	6	0	0	29	26	12	11	4	8	21	.236	.239	.234	6.52	2.48
Johnson, Jacob	R-R	6-4	215	9-12-90	0	0	22.50	2	0	0	0	2	6	5	5	0	2	2	.500	.400	.571	9.00	9.00
Klimesh, Ben	R-R	6-4	220	5-14-90	2	0	3.65	9	0	0	0	12	11	5	5	0	16	6	.250	.250	.250	4.38	11.68
Lamb, John	L-L	6-4	205	7-10-90	1	1	2.65	3	3	0	0	17	14	5	5	0	7	21	.222	.250	.216	11.12	3.71
LeCure, Sam	R-R	6-0	210	5-4-84	5	4	5.25	41	0	0	1	60	63	39	35	7	24	44	.272	.250	.287	6.60	3.60
Lorenzen, Michael	R-R	6-3	205	1-4-92	4	2	1.88	6	6	1	0	43	34	9	9	3	8	19	.219	.271	.176	3.98	1.67
Magill, Matt	R-R	6-3	210	11-10-89	1	1	7.90	3	3	0	0	14	22	12	12	2	8	13	.379	.400	.357	8.56	5.27
Moran, Jimmy	R-R	6-1	180	6-7-90	1	0	3.38	6	0	0	0	8	11	3	3	1	2	5	.344	.467	.235	5.63	2.25
Moscot, Jon	R-R	6-4	210	8-15-91	7	1	3.15	9	9	0	0	54	50	20	19	5	19	34	.250	.262	.241	5.63	3.15
Parra, Manny	L-L	6-3	215	10-30-82	0	0	0.00	2	2	0	0	3	1	0	0	0	2	6	.111	.333	.000	20.25	6.75
Paterson, Joe	R-L	6-0	190	5-19-86	1	1	4.50	9	0	0	0	8	12	4	4	0	5	5	.324	.133	.455	5.63	5.63
Roach, Donn	R-R	6-0	195	12-14-89	2	4	6.00	7	7	0	0	42	57	32	28	7	7	18	.324	.357	.302	3.86	1.50
2-team total (3 Buffalo)					2	4	5.00	10	8	0	0	54	67	35	30	2	10	20	—	—	—	3.33	1.67
Sampson, Keyvius	R-R	6-2	225	1-6-91	2	4	5.08	8	7	0	0	39	40	22	22	1	22	33	.267	.233	.299	7.62	5.08
Smith, Josh	R-R	6-2	220	8-7-87	3	5	3.75	15	12	0	0	86	84	37	36	2	24	69	.255	.242	.262	7.19	2.50
Somsen, Layne	R-R	6-0	190	6-5-89	0	1	2.73	15	3	0	0	30	24	10	9	2	14	29	.220	.212	.228	8.80	4.25
Stephenson, Robert	R-R	6-2	200	2-24-93	4	4	4.04	11	11	0	0	56	51	25	25	2	27	51	.245	.192	.298	8.25	4.37
Villarreal, Pedro	R-R	6-1	235	12-9-87	1	0	3.81	19	0	0	1	26	26	11	11	0	4	21	.260	.200	.309	7.27	1.38

Fielding

Catcher	PCT	G	PO	A	E	DP	PB
Barnhart	1.000	5	35	5	0	0	1
Berset	.994	45	316	19	2	4	2
Cabrera	.990	84	546	41	6	7	6
Morillo	1.000	1	11	0	0	0	0
Skipworth	.969	8	60	3	2	0	2
Tromp	1.000	1	10	1	0	1	0

First Base	PCT	G	PO	A	E	DP
De Jesus Jr.	1.000	22	175	12	0	21
Dominguez	.986	47	326	28	5	49
Duvall	1.000	8	60	7	0	5
Johnson	1.000	7	60	6	0	5
Satin	.995	42	345	26	2	39
Selsky	.990	11	89	10	1	15
Waldrop	.976	20	152	8	4	20

Second Base	PCT	G	PO	A	E	DP
Curtis	.987	18	31	46	1	15
De Jesus Jr.	1.000	1	2	3	0	0
Falu	.980	98	182	259	9	77

	PCT	G	PO	A	E	DP
Iribarren	.966	24	48	67	4	22
Perez	.964	8	13	14	1	3
Veras	1.000	6	4	10	0	1
Third Base	PCT	G	PO	A	E	DP
Curtis	.958	35	26	65	4	5
De Jesus Jr.	.955	31	13	50	3	9
Dominguez	.987	27	21	53	1	5
Falu	1.000	2	1	6	0	0
Iribarren	.937	39	25	79	7	7
Negron	1.000	4	3	6	0	1
Perez	1.000	2	1	7	0	0
Satin	.953	21	5	36	2	3
Shortstop	PCT	G	PO	A	E	DP
De Jesus Jr.	1.000	1	3	2	0	2
Falu	—	1	0	0	0	0
Iribarren	.957	31	50	82	6	23
Negron	.949	46	69	118	10	26
Perez	.968	16	21	40	2	11
Suarez	.956	55	88	149	11	42

Outfield	PCT	G	PO	A	E	DP
Benedetto	1.000	7	7	0	0	0
Boesch	1.000	31	53	2	0	1
Bourgeois	.950	12	18	1	1	0
Buckley	1.000	9	15	0	0	0
Constanza	.985	33	64	0	1	0
Dominguez	.973	17	34	2	1	0
Duvall	1.000	16	34	1	0	0
Iribarren	1.000	15	25	0	0	0
LaMarre	.983	81	222	5	4	2
Lutz	.905	9	18	1	2	0
Mesoraco	1.000	3	1	1	0	0
Negron	1.000	8	21	0	0	0
Rodriguez	.983	84	169	6	3	0
Satin	1.000	2	4	0	0	0
Selsky	1.000	35	52	2	0	1
Silva	1.000	41	85	1	0	0
Smith	.923	25	36	0	3	0
Veras	.958	6	20	3	1	2
Waldrop	.980	33	47	2	1	0

PENSACOLA BLUE WAHOOS   DOUBLE-A

SOUTHERN LEAGUE

Batting	B-T	HT	WT	DOB	AVG	vLH	vRH	G	AB	R	H	2B	3B	HR	RBI	BB	HBP	SH	SF	SO	SB	CS	SLG	OBP
Amaral, Beau	L-L	5-10	177	2-11-91	.224	.178	.237	112	339	30	76	8	1	4	27	21	6	4	2	77	9	5	.289	.280
Berset, Chris	B-R	6-0	195	1-27-88	.125	.111	.129	14	40	3	5	3	0	0	5	2	2	0	2	12	0	0	.200	.196
Blandino, Alex	R-R	6-0	190	11-6-92	.235	.238	.234	30	115	15	27	7	0	3	18	18	3	1	1	21	2	2	.374	.350
Buckley, Sean	R-R	6-3	224	9-3-89	.261	.125	.287	69	203	21	53	11	0	3	16	17	4	0	1	53	0	0	.360	.329
Byrd, Marlon	R-R	6-0	245	8-30-77	.286	—	.286	2	7	1	2	1	0	1	3	0	0	0	0	2	0	0	.857	.286
Chang, Ray	R-R	6-1	195	8-24-83	.283	.241	.297	87	240	32	68	16	1	1	28	31	2	2	3	37	1	1	.371	.366
Duran, Juan	R-R	6-7	230	9-2-91	.256	.182	.274	59	219	29	56	16	3	6	43	12	1	0	6	88	2	1	.438	.290
Ervin, Phillip	R-R	5-10	205	7-15-92	.235	.143	.270	17	51	7	12	3	0	2	8	13	2	0	0	15	4	3	.412	.409
Gonzalez, Yovan	R-R	5-10	190	11-11-89	.223	.393	.167	38	112	14	25	4	0	5	14	14	0	0	1	16	0	0	.393	.307
Hamilton, Billy	B-R	6-0	160	9-9-90	.273	.000	.300	3	11	3	3	0	0	0	0	3	0	0	0	2	1	0	.273	.429
Maron, Cam	L-R	6-1	195	1-20-91	.230	.217	.234	35	87	13	20	3	0	1	8	15	0	2	1	16	0	0	.299	.340
Marson, Lou	R-R	6-1	205	6-26-86	.263	.333	.250	6	19	2	5	2	0	0	2	2	0	0	0	2	0	0	.368	.333
Mejias-Brean, Seth	R-R	6-2	216	4-5-91	.247	.250	.246	122	405	41	100	18	5	6	53	63	4	0	3	96	9	3	.360	.352
Morillo, Julio	R-R	5-10	175	12-27-92	.143	.500	.000	3	7	1	1	0	0	0	0	0	0	0	0	0	0	0	.143	.143
Perez, Juan	L-R	5-11	195	11-1-87	.236	.302	.222	93	296	30	70	15	6	1	19	26	4	2	3	54	14	5	.338	.304
Silva, Juan	L-L	5-11	204	1-8-91	.176	.231	.162	55	125	12	22	5	3	0	10	18	1	2	0	27	6	2	.264	.285
Skipworth, Kyle	L-R	6-4	230	3-1-90	.204	.138	.214	69	216	25	44	12	1	11	28	21	6	1	2	108	0	1	.421	.290
Smith, Bryson	R-R	6-1	195	12-17-88	.284	.300	.280	25	95	12	27	6	1	3	13	4	3	0	0	17	2	0	.463	.333
Smith, Marquez	R-R	5-10	205	3-20-85	.267	.229	.277	125	408	56	109	23	4	8	46	63	6	0	5	97	7	5	.402	.369
Vincej, Zach	R-R	5-11	177	12-9-91	.241	.220	.247	90	286	39	69	10	0	5	22	44	4	2	3	48	7	7	.329	.347
Waldrop, Kyle	L-L	6-2	215	11-26-91	.277	.213	.292	67	242	33	67	13	2	6	31	12	2	0	3	61	2	2	.430	.313
Winker, Jesse	L-L	6-2	210	8-5-93	.282	.211	.302	123	443	69	125	24	2	13	55	74	6	0	3	83	8	4	.433	.390
Wright, Ryan	R-R	6-1	200	12-3-89	.247	.192	.264	89	304	30	75	15	4	1	27	27	1	3	3	37	2	0	.332	.307

Pitching	B-T	HT	WT	DOB	W	L	ERA	G	GS	CG	SV	IP	H	R	ER	HR	BB	SO	AVG	vLH	vRH	K/9	BB/9
Adleman, Tim	R-R	6-5	200	11-13-87	9	10	2.64	27	26	0	0	150	134	52	44	7	49	113	.243	.256	.232	6.78	2.94

CINCINNATI REDS

Pitching

Pitching	B-T	HT	WT	DOB	W	L	ERA	G	GS	CG	SV	IP	H	R	ER	HR	BB	SO	AVG	vLH	vRH	K/9	BB/9
Astin, Barrett	R-R	6-1	210	10-22-91	4	6	5.63	14	14	0	0	77	85	50	48	9	39	61	.290	.290	.290	7.16	4.58
Bender, Joel	L-L	6-4	210	8-3-91	0	0	4.91	12	0	0	0	18	20	10	10	1	12	16	.303	.435	.233	7.85	5.89
Celestino, Miguel	R-R	6-6	215	10-10-89	1	0	1.69	10	0	0	4	11	10	2	2	0	5	10	.256	.250	.261	8.44	4.22
Christiani, Nick	R-R	6-0	190	7-17-87	0	0	7.71	4	0	0	0	5	8	4	4	0	4	5	.381	.750	.154	9.64	7.71
Cisnero, Jose	R-R	6-3	245	4-11-89	0	0	3.38	4	0	0	0	5	2	2	2	0	4	6	.118	.400	.000	10.13	6.75
Corcino, Daniel	R-R	5-11	210	8-26-90	0	0	0.00	1	0	0	0	1	0	0	0	0	2	2	.000	.000	—	18.00	18.00
Gonzalez, Carlos	R-R	6-1	195	6-12-90	2	3	4.39	21	0	0	0	27	30	17	13	1	13	11	.283	.238	.313	3.71	4.39
Hayes, Drew	R-R	6-1	205	9-3-87	0	0	0.00	4	0	0	0	6	4	0	0	0	1	4	.200	.000	.308	6.35	1.59
Howell, Blaine	L-L	5-11	210	10-2-88	1	2	6.48	12	0	0	0	17	17	13	12	3	7	11	.270	.250	.286	5.94	3.78
Johnson, Jacob	R-R	6-4	215	9-12-90	5	2	4.75	33	3	0	0	78	89	43	41	8	28	47	.285	.288	.284	5.45	3.24
Johnson, Stephen	R-R	6-5	215	2-21-91	0	0	0.00	6	0	0	1	9	4	0	0	0	2	11	.133	.083	.167	11.42	2.08
Klimesh, Ben	R-R	6-4	220	5-14-90	0	1	6.16	19	0	0	5	19	16	14	13	2	15	21	.235	.357	.150	9.95	7.11
McMyne, Kyle	R-R	5-11	220	10-18-89	1	4	2.77	52	0	0	9	62	58	20	19	2	33	30	.260	.271	.254	4.38	4.82
Moran, Jimmy	R-R	6-1	180	6-7-90	0	0	4.20	13	0	0	0	15	16	9	7	1	13	8	.281	.320	.250	4.80	7.80
Peralta, Wandy	L-L	6-0	210	7-27-91	7	7	5.09	29	20	0	0	117	129	74	66	7	60	80	.288	.306	.281	6.17	4.63
Reed, Cody	L-L	6-5	220	4-15-93	6	2	2.17	8	8	0	0	50	39	14	12	1	16	60	.220	.095	.259	10.87	2.90
Rogers, Chad	R-R	5-11	205	8-3-89	0	1	5.25	10	0	0	0	12	18	8	7	2	6	11	.340	.429	.308	8.25	4.50
Romano, Sal	L-R	6-4	250	10-12-93	0	4	10.96	7	7	0	0	23	35	28	28	4	12	9	.354	.333	.367	3.52	4.70
Sampson, Keyvius	R-R	6-2	225	1-6-91	1	2	1.85	8	8	0	0	44	35	11	9	2	24	41	.217	.137	.284	8.45	4.95
Schuster, Patrick	R-L	6-2	185	10-30-90	2	1	3.41	30	0	0	0	29	27	11	11	1	14	25	.255	.214	.300	7.76	4.34
2-team total (22 Mobile)					2	2	3.33	52	0	0	0	54	50	22	20	1	26	45	—		—	7.50	4.33
Shackelford, Kevin	R-R	6-5	210	4-7-89	2	4	3.72	35	0	0	3	39	45	19	16	1	17	25	.294	.254	.329	5.82	3.96
Smith, Josh	R-R	6-2	220	8-7-87	5	4	3.05	9	9	1	0	56	51	23	19	5	9	53	.243	.231	.190	8.52	1.45
Somsen, Layne	R-R	6-0	190	6-5-89	2	0	2.76	12	1	0	0	33	23	11	10	1	16	31	.204	.189	.211	8.54	4.41
Stephenson, Robert	R-R	6-2	200	2-24-93	4	7	3.68	14	14	1	0	78	53	36	32	8	43	89	.197	.200	.195	10.23	4.94
Walden, Marcus	R-R	6-0	195	9-13-88	0	1	12.00	1	1	0	0	3	7	5	4	0	3	2	.538	.600	.500	6.00	9.00
Weiss, Zack	R-R	6-3	210	6-16-92	1	3	2.42	45	0	0	25	52	40	16	14	5	14	68	.214	.161	.260	11.77	2.42
Wright, Daniel	R-R	6-2	205	4-3-91	10	11	4.53	27	27	0	0	155	154	83	78	6	47	130	.264	.255	.271	7.55	2.73

Fielding

Catcher	PCT	G	PO	A	E	DP	PB
Berset	.979	14	84	8	2	1	1
Chang	1.000	1	2	0	0	0	0
Gonzalez	.992	36	226	23	2	2	3
Maron	.989	26	164	13	2	1	3
Marson	1.000	5	36	0	0	0	0
Morillo	1.000	3	8	0	0	0	1
Skipworth	.990	65	466	51	5	9	11

First Base	PCT	G	PO	A	E	DP
Chang	1.000	44	330	22	0	43
Mejias-Brean	1.000	15	109	9	0	14
Skipworth	1.000	2	5	0	0	0
Smith	.997	79	591	40	2	77
Waldrop	.992	15	118	9	1	18
Wright	1.000	2	5	1	0	1

Second Base	PCT	G	PO	A	E	DP
Blandino	.963	6	10	16	1	7
Chang	1.000	22	31	52	0	17
Perez	.992	28	48	76	1	23
Vincej	.989	21	35	53	1	17
Wright	.975	76	144	207	9	56

Third Base	PCT	G	PO	A	E	DP
Chang	.947	8	7	11	1	2
Mejias-Brean	.946	103	83	199	16	28
Perez	1.000	5	5	15	0	4
Smith	.971	30	17	51	2	7

Shortstop	PCT	G	PO	A	E	DP
Blandino	.983	24	36	83	2	17
Chang	1.000	3	1	4	0	3
Perez	.980	51	64	129	4	35
Vincej	.982	68	105	161	5	49

Outfield	PCT	G	PO	A	E	DP
Amaral	.995	108	211	5	1	0
Buckley	.952	27	38	2	2	0
Byrd	1.000	2	2	0	0	0
Chang	—	1	0	0	0	0
Duran	.954	53	97	6	5	2
Ervin	1.000	15	28	2	0	0
Hamilton	1.000	3	5	0	0	0
Perez	1.000	5	10	0	0	0
Silva	.986	36	71	1	1	0
Smith	1.000	24	42	1	0	0
Waldrop	.989	49	85	6	1	3
Winker	.990	119	183	15	2	2
Wright	—	1	0	0	0	0

DAYTONA TORTUGAS

HIGH CLASS A

FLORIDA STATE LEAGUE

Batting	B-T	HT	WT	DOB	AVG	vLH	vRH	G	AB	R	H	2B	3B	HR	RBI	BB	HBP	SH	SF	SO	SB	CS	SLG	OBP
Arias, Junior	R-R	6-1	200	1-9-92	.243	.261	.235	99	383	57	93	11	4	11	40	21	3	0	2	106	37	9	.379	.286
Benedetto, Nick	R-R	6-0	150	2-27-93	.071	.150	.000	15	42	3	3	0	0	0	1	4	1	0	0	19	1	5	.071	.170
Blandino, Alex	R-R	6-0	190	11-6-92	.294	.337	.276	80	299	46	88	18	2	7	35	31	7	1	4	56	7	10	.438	.370
Bueno, Ronald	B-R	5-10	154	10-4-92	.226	.229	.225	32	106	15	24	3	1	0	12	9	1	1	4	24	4	3	.274	.283
Daal, Carlton	R-R	6-2	160	8-1-93	.230	.257	.276	112	381	38	103	6	0	0	30	21	3	6	4	61	21	5	.286	.311
Diaz, Sammy	B-R	5-10	192	2-28-91	.311	.438	.241	13	45	9	14	3	1	1	9	3	0	1	1	8	2	0	.489	.347
Elizalde, Sebastian	L-R	6-0	175	11-20-91	.253	.229	.264	128	474	58	120	28	5	10	77	39	4	0	8	107	9	1	.397	.310
Ervin, Phillip	R-R	5-10	205	7-15-92	.242	.245	.241	109	405	68	98	18	0	12	63	53	9	1	7	83	30	7	.375	.338
Gelalich, Jeff	L-R	6-0	210	3-16-91	.208	.209	.275	85	260	29	67	9	4	1	19	36	6	5	0	97	16	4	.335	.361
Hudson, Joe	R-R	6-0	205	5-21-91	.214	.297	.164	81	266	23	57	13	0	7	31	31	3	5	0	70	1	0	.342	.303
Maron, Cam	L-R	6-1	195	1-20-91	.333	.750	.261	10	27	3	9	0	0	1	3	4	0	0	0	7	1	0	.444	.419
Matthews, Jon	R-R	6-1	190	4-24-93	.124	.139	.113	32	89	6	11	3	0	0	4	15	1	1	0	23	0	2	.157	.257
Morillo, Julio	R-R	5-10	175	12-27-92	.067	.333	.000	4	15	0	1	0	0	0	0	0	0	0	1	0	0	0	.067	.067
O'Grady, Brian	L-R	6-2	215	5-17-92	.210	.237	.200	45	138	15	29	3	0	5	18	18	3	1	1	41	4	1	.341	.313
Pigott, Daniel	R-R	6-2	205	10-4-89	.208	.227	.200	21	77	6	16	3	1	2	12	6	0	0	1	27	0	1	.351	.262
Ramirez, Robert	L-R	6-0	190	7-18-92	.209	.146	.225	65	239	26	50	11	4	5	26	11	1	1	4	78	2	2	.351	.243
Soto, Wendell	B-R	5-9	170	5-11-92	.146	.033	.180	43	130	10	19	0	2	0	8	14	0	1	2	38	6	4	.177	.226
Sparks, Taylor	R-R	6-4	200	4-3-93	.247	.273	.235	125	446	68	110	22	4	13	54	30	8	3	6	162	14	4	.401	.302
Trahan, Blake	R-R	5-9	180	9-5-93	.114	.091	.125	11	35	1	4	0	0	0	0	1	0	0	0	5	0	0	.114	.139
Wallach, Chad	R-R	6-3	215	11-4-91	.246	.242	.248	106	370	41	91	28	1	3	32	39	7	1	3	77	2	3	.351	.327
Washington, Ty	R-R	5-9	160	9-1-93	.197	.241	.156	18	61	10	12	4	0	0	2	9	0	0	0	17	0	1	.262	.300

Pitching	B-T	HT	WT	DOB	W	L	ERA	G	GS	CG	SV	IP	H	R	ER	HR	BB	SO	AVG	vLH	vRH	K/9	BB/9
Astin, Barrett	R-R	6-1	210	10-22-91	4	3	2.29	16	11	1	0	75	62	28	19	0	18	61	.222	.222	.222	7.35	2.17

Pitching	B-T	HT	WT	DOB	W	L	ERA	G	GS	CG	SV	IP	H	R	ER	HR	BB	SO	AVG	vLH	vRH	K/9	BB/9
Becker, Nolan	R-L	6-6	225	6-13-91	3	2	3.15	45	0	0	3	46	35	18	16	0	28	42	.217	.246	.202	8.28	5.52
Bender, Joel	L-L	6-4	210	8-3-91	3	2	3.69	31	0	0	1	54	50	26	22	2	14	46	.245	.266	.236	7.71	2.35
Brattvet, Scott	R-R	6-1	195	7-21-91	2	1	3.03	21	1	0	0	30	35	11	10	2	6	16	.304	.308	.303	4.85	1.82
Chacin, Alejandro	R-R	5-11	205	6-24-93	2	0	2.45	29	0	0	10	37	23	12	10	3	11	56	.177	.205	.165	13.75	2.70
Crawford, Jonathan	R-R	6-2	205	11-1-91	0	1	8.44	2	2	0	0	5	5	5	5	0	3	6	.250	.333	.182	10.13	5.06
Garrett, Amir	L-L	6-5	210	5-3-92	9	7	2.44	26	26	1	0	140	117	50	38	4	55	133	.230	.259	.221	8.53	3.53
Gonzalez, Carlos	R-R	6-1	195	6-12-90	1	2	1.21	20	0	0	0	30	18	4	4	1	7	26	.171	.063	.219	7.89	2.12
Howard, Nick	R-R	6-4	215	4-6-93	3	2	6.63	24	5	0	2	38	34	32	28	0	50	31	.258	.273	.250	7.34	11.84
Howell, Blaine	L-L	5-11	210	12-2-88	1	0	1.65	12	0	0	0	16	14	4	3	0	6	11	.250	.235	.256	6.06	3.31
Mantoni, Joe	R-R	6-0	220	6-4-91	1	2	6.06	13	0	0	0	16	17	12	11	3	4	11	.270	.375	.234	6.06	2.20
Mella, Keury	R-R	6-2	200	8-2-93	3	1	2.95	4	4	0	0	21	11	7	7	2	15	23	.151	.138	.159	9.70	6.33
Mitchell, Evan	R-R	6-2	175	3-18-92	3	2	3.84	46	0	0	0	59	61	29	25	2	33	42	.274	.310	.252	6.44	5.06
Moran, Jimmy	R-R	6-1	180	6-7-90	2	2	3.94	33	0	0	1	32	33	15	14	0	13	31	.277	.367	.247	8.72	3.66
Muhammad, El'Hajj	R-R	6-2	200	7-7-91	6	6	2.96	52	0	0	17	55	43	23	18	1	43	42	.214	.291	.185	6.91	7.08
Romano, Sal	L-R	6-4	250	10-12-93	6	5	3.46	19	18	1	0	104	103	48	40	2	33	79	.261	.270	.255	6.84	2.86
Routt, Nick	L-L	6-4	215	8-28-90	6	3	3.47	24	14	0	0	91	102	44	35	2	22	74	.285	.275	.288	7.35	2.18
Stephens, Jackson	R-R	6-3	205	5-11-94	12	7	2.97	26	26	0	0	145	157	56	48	11	30	97	.276	.286	.271	6.01	1.86
Travieso, Nick	R-R	6-2	225	1-31-94	6	6	2.70	19	19	0	0	93	82	40	28	4	30	76	.231	.246	.224	7.33	2.89
Varner, Seth	L-L	6-3	225	1-27-92	4	4	2.97	13	9	0	0	61	54	25	20	5	6	57	.233	.264	.223	8.46	0.89
Weiss, Zack	R-R	6-3	210	6-16-92	0	0	0.00	9	0	0	5	12	2	0	0	1	22	.056	.000	.083	16.97	0.77

Fielding

Catcher	PCT	G	PO	A	E	DP	PB
Hudson	.983	78	550	79	11	5	13
Maron	1.000	9	53	12	0	0	0
Morillo	.957	4	22	1	1	0	0
Wallach	1.000	46	322	48	0	3	2

First Base	PCT	G	PO	A	E	DP
Diaz	.939	6	44	2	3	7
Elizalde	1.000	5	50	5	0	3
O'Grady	.993	16	138	10	1	20
Pigott	.981	11	100	4	2	5
Ramirez	.987	45	421	22	6	51
Wallach	.984	53	464	26	8	44

Second Base	PCT	G	PO	A	E	DP
Blandino	.905	6	6	13	2	2

	PCT	G	PO	A	E	DP
Bueno	.991	22	44	63	1	14
Daal	.967	59	118	172	10	38
Diaz	1.000	3	3	6	0	2
Ramirez	1.000	1	2	1	0	0
Soto	.990	39	79	115	2	34
Washington	.974	7	17	21	1	5

Third Base	PCT	G	PO	A	E	DP
Bueno	.833	7	3	7	2	1
Diaz	1.000	3	7	4	0	0
Ramirez	.833	5	2	13	3	1
Soto	1.000	1	0	1	0	0
Sparks	.902	119	82	249	36	20

Shortstop	PCT	G	PO	A	E	DP
Blandino	.952	68	114	201	16	46

	PCT	G	PO	A	E	DP
Bueno	.833	2	0	5	1	1
Daal	.954	53	65	182	12	43
Soto	1.000	2	0	6	0	0
Trahan	.955	11	11	31	2	11

Outfield	PCT	G	PO	A	E	DP
Arias	.964	98	183	3	7	1
Benedetto	1.000	15	30	1	0	0
Elizalde	.976	68	115	8	3	0
Ervin	.975	107	184	13	5	4
Gelalich	.979	83	137	4	3	1
Matthews	.964	17	26	1	1	1
O'Grady	1.000	22	30	3	0	0
Pigott	1.000	3	3	0	0	0

DAYTON DRAGONS   LOW CLASS A

MIDWEST LEAGUE

Batting	B-T	HT	WT	DOB	AVG	vLH	vRH	G	AB	R	H	2B	3B	HR	RBI	BB	HBP	SH	SF	SO	SB	CS	SLG	OBP
Aldazoro, Argenis	L-L	6-2	160	9-17-92	.262	.053	.295	38	141	10	37	8	2	0	16	11	0	1	0	31	3	2	.348	.316
Aquino, Aristides	R-R	6-4	190	4-22-94	.234	.250	.230	61	231	25	54	9	3	5	27	11	5	0	2	53	6	1	.364	.281
Benedetto, Nick	R-R	6-0	150	2-27-93	.192	.250	.182	17	52	9	10	4	0	1	5	2	4	0	0	19	0	2	.327	.276
Boulware, Garrett	R-R	6-2	200	9-9-92	.245	.345	.221	80	277	25	68	7	0	4	28	23	12	2	0	44	1	1	.314	.330
Bueno, Ronald	B-R	5-10	154	10-4-92	.270	.136	.301	61	230	34	62	11	6	1	22	28	3	7	3	50	12	2	.383	.352
Chavez, Alberti	R-R	5-10	170	7-21-95	.400	.333	.429	3	10	3	4	2	1	0	1	1	0	0	0	3	0	0	.800	.455
Crook, Narciso	R-R	6-3	220	7-12-95	.236	.213	.243	105	381	42	90	19	5	9	47	15	3	2	1	103	13	3	.383	.270
Gonzalez, Luis	R-R	6-0	175	7-28-94	.245	.296	.233	124	497	55	122	18	3	2	50	14	5	9	7	82	7	4	.306	.270
Kronenfeld, Paul	L-R	6-3	225	9-27-91	.249	.136	.270	74	277	30	69	17	4	6	33	28	1	0	0	66	1	0	.404	.320
LaValley, Gavin	R-R	6-3	235	12-28-94	.267	.253	.270	125	469	52	125	29	1	4	53	50	7	0	4	114	4	1	.358	.343
Long, Shedric	L-R	5-10	180	8-22-95	.283	.333	.275	42	152	22	43	7	2	6	16	18	1	2	0	31	2	3	.474	.363
Lopez, Maikel	B-R	6-2	185	10-31-93	.375	.000	.429	2	8	1	3	0	0	1	0	0	0	0	0	3	0	0	.750	.375
Matthews, Jon	R-R	6-1	195	4-6-91	.306	.333	.300	13	49	4	15	2	0	0	6	6	1	0	0	5	1	3	.347	.393
Morillo, Julio	R-R	5-10	175	12-27-94	.000	—	.000	1	3	0	0	0	0	0	0	0	0	0	0	0	0	0	.000	.000
O'Grady, Brian	R-L	6-2	215	5-17-92	.271	.208	.288	71	251	44	68	15	6	6	36	46	3	1	4	55	21	5	.450	.385
Ortiz, Jose	R-R	5-11	205	6-11-94	.199	.267	.183	43	156	13	31	8	0	3	23	6	1	0	3	35	0	0	.308	.229
Pickens, Jimmy	L-R	6-0	220	3-18-92	.247	.233	.250	95	332	44	82	21	3	5	31	20	4	2		89	9	3	.373	.296
Rachal, Avain	R-R	6-0	195	2-16-94	.239	.284	.229	110	389	47	93	16	4	3	46	43	11	2	4	101	14	6	.332	.332
Reynoso, Jonathan	R-R	6-3	177	1-7-93	.273	.328	.258	89	315	47	86	5	6	3	25	17	3	9	0	54	16	3	.356	.316
Soto, Wendell	B-R	5-9	170	5-11-92	.295	.417	.250	15	44	8	13	2	1	1	8	14	0	2	1	12	4	3	.455	.458
Thompson, Cory	R-R	5-11	180	9-23-94	.196	.161	.202	51	194	23	38	6	1	4	14	9	9	1	2	47	10	1	.299	.262
Tromp, Chadwick	R-R	5-9	180	3-21-95	.293	.188	.318	24	82	7	24	8	0	0	6	5	2	1	0	15	0	0	.390	.348
Washington, Ty	R-R	5-9	160	9-1-93	.267	.250	.271	39	150	15	40	10	2	1	17	17	1	2	0	28	4	4	.380	.345

Pitching	B-T	HT	WT	DOB	W	L	ERA	G	GS	CG	SV	IP	H	R	ER	HR	BB	SO	AVG	vLH	vRH	K/9	BB/9
Antone, Tejay	R-R	6-4	205	12-5-93	6	10	2.91	26	26	1	0	158	174	66	51	2	33	101	.285	.330	.251	5.75	1.88
Armstrong, Mark	R-R	6-2	180	11-26-94	3	3	3.20	13	12	0	0	65	71	27	23	1	14	44	.283	.367	.229	6.12	1.95
Bernardino, Brennan	L-L	6-4	180	1-15-92	2	3	3.64	37	0	0	3	54	64	30	22	0	21	49	.299	.318	.291	8.12	3.48
Boyles, Ty	R-L	6-3	270	9-30-95	0	2	8.62	4	4	0	0	16	15	15	15	2	6	9	.254	.308	.240	5.17	3.45
Brattvet, Scott	R-R	6-1	195	7-21-91	1	2	1.80	17	0	0	0	25	16	13	5	1	10	17	.172	.172	.172	6.12	3.60
Chacin, Alejandro	R-R	5-11	205	6-24-93	3	0	5.52	10	0	0	1	15	16	9	9	0	5	16	.281	.273	.286	9.82	2.45
Ehret, Jake	R-R	6-3	190	3-18-93	3	3	3.71	40	0	0	3	80	80	40	29	1	37	59	.237	.222	.246	7.55	4.73
Hunter, Brian	R-R	6-3	215	11-22-92	5	3	2.20	28	0	0	7	33	26	10	8	1	13	41	.213	.170	.240	11.30	3.58

CINCINNATI REDS

Pitching

Pitching	B-T	HT	WT	DOB	W	L	ERA	G	GS	CG	SV	IP	H	R	ER	HR	BB	SO	AVG	vLH	vRH	K/9	BB/9
Kivel, Jeremy	R-R	6-1	200	10-16-93	0	1	5.40	37	0	0	2	50	51	36	30	5	38	55	.260	.316	.225	9.90	6.84
Krauss, Conor	R-R	6-5	205	6-14-93	3	3	2.97	42	0	0	9	61	57	26	20	0	25	44	.253	.216	.285	6.53	3.71
Mahle, Tyler	R-R	6-4	200	9-29-94	13	8	2.43	27	26	0	0	152	145	54	41	7	25	135	.252	.292	.224	7.99	1.48
Mantoni, Joe	R-R	6-0	220	6-4-91	1	1	2.63	12	0	0	1	14	15	4	4	0	4	14	.283	.333	.241	9.22	2.63
Moody, Jacob	R-L	5-9	185	10-29-92	1	0	9.00	11	0	0	0	14	24	18	14	1	15	15	.369	.211	.435	9.64	9.64
Morillo, Junior	L-L	6-0	175	10-30-91	4	9	6.86	18	14	0	0	79	115	64	60	12	22	45	.343	.253	.375	5.15	2.52
Parmenter, Tyler	R-R	6-2	185	5-4-93	1	0	1.29	2	0	0	0	7	4	2	1	0	4	6	.167	.182	.154	7.71	5.14
Paulson, Jake	R-R	6-6	210	2-17-92	8	5	2.60	33	14	0	1	118	106	45	34	5	18	92	.233	.269	.209	7.04	1.38
Smith, Josh	R-R	6-2	220	8-7-87	0	0	0.00	1	1	0	0	1	0	0	0	0	0	1	.000	.000	.000	9.00	9.00
Sterner, Ty	L-L	6-1	208	12-9-92	1	1	7.45	12	0	0	1	19	19	18	16	1	12	22	.250	.120	.314	10.24	5.59
Strahan, Wyatt	R-R	6-3	190	4-18-93	9	10	2.79	28	28	1	0	164	158	68	51	10	53	132	.253	.214	.285	7.23	2.90
Sullivan, Michael	L-L	6-0	210	1-14-94	2	0	3.38	18	0	0	1	37	28	15	14	3	12	31	.211	.163	.233	7.47	2.89
Varner, Seth	L-L	6-3	225	1-27-92	7	4	2.88	14	14	0	0	78	82	30	25	4	5	77	.269	.204	.283	8.88	0.58

Fielding

Catcher

Catcher	PCT	G	PO	A	E	DP	PB
Boulware	.981	77	529	51	11	3	14
Lopez	1.000	2	13	2	0	0	1
Ortiz	.989	41	313	33	4		6
Tromp	.994	22	150	23	1	1	2
Long	.960	23	51	70	5		14
Rachal	.976	10	13	28	1		5
Soto	1.000	5	13	13	0		6
Thompson	.957	34	63	114	8		27
Washington	.979	30	54	87	3		18
Gonzalez	.935	123	167	435	42		90
Long	.500	1	0	1	1		0
Soto	.800	2	1	7	2		1
Thompson	.923	12	21	39	5		6

First Base

First Base	PCT	G	PO	A	E	DP
Aldazoro	1.000	1	17	1	0	0
Kronenfeld	.983	37	340	13	6	32
LaValley	.977	9	79	7	2	7
O'Grady	1.000	9	63	5	0	3
Rachal	.991	89	874	54	8	76

Second Base

Second Base	PCT	G	PO	A	E	DP
Bueno	.976	39	60	142	5	25
Chavez	1.000	2	6	5	0	1

Third Base

Third Base	PCT	G	PO	A	E	DP
Bueno	1.000	15	4	28	0	2
LaValley	.933	113	60	233	21	14
Rachal	1.000	7	3	19	0	1
Soto	.667	1	1	1	1	0
Washington	1.000	3	1	7	0	2

Shortstop

Shortstop	PCT	G	PO	A	E	DP
Bueno	1.000	2	3	6	0	0
Chavez	1.000	1	2	2	0	0

Outfield

Outfield	PCT	G	PO	A	E	DP
Aldazoro	.953	24	38	3	2	0
Aquino	.966	60	104	8	4	1
Benedetto	1.000	17	33	0	0	0
Bueno	1.000	1	1	0	0	0
Crook	.971	100	193	7	6	1
Matthews	1.000	8	11	0	0	0
O'Grady	.964	59	103	3	4	0
Pickens	.963	73	101	4	4	1
Reynoso	.966	84	131	9	5	0

AZL REDS   ROOKIE

ARIZONA LEAGUE

Batting

Batting	B-T	HT	WT	DOB	AVG	vLH	vRH	G	AB	R	H	2B	3B	HR	RBI	BB	HBP	SH	SF	SO	SB	CS	SLG	OBP
Aldazoro, Argenis	L-L	6-2	160	9-17-92	.400	1.000	.333	3	10	3	4	1	0	0	5	3	0	0	1	2	0	1	.500	.500
Azcona, Francis	B-R	5-10	155	11-20-95	.266	.368	.233	32	79	13	21	5	0	0	4	9	0	1	0	18	4	3	.329	.341
Beltre, Michael	B-R	6-3	180	7-3-95	.220	.222	.219	28	82	6	18	3	0	1	7	5	1	0	0	27	5	1	.293	.273
Benedetto, Nick	R-R	6-0	150	2-27-93	.333	—	.333	4	12	3	4	1	1	0	3	2	1	0	0	2	3	1	.583	.467
Butler, Blake	R-R	6-3	195	10-29-93	.319	.310	.321	45	163	23	52	13	3	2	21	7	3	0	4	31	4	2	.472	.350
Chavez, Alberti	R-R	5-10	170	7-21-95	.265	.158	.286	41	117	8	31	4	2	0	11	8	0	0	1	22	2	1	.333	.310
Diaz, Sammy	B-R	5-10	170	2-28-91	.448	.667	.423	9	29	7	13	3	1	0	6	1	0	0	0	3	0	0	.621	.467
Duran, Juan	R-R	6-7	230	9-2-91	.391	.400	.389	7	23	5	9	2	0	2	9	4	0	0	1	8	0	0	.739	.464
Gordon, Miles	L-R	6-1	185	12-3-97	.220	.316	.202	31	118	15	26	4	3	0	12	7	0	3	1	26	5	3	.305	.262
Guerrero, Francis	R-R	5-11	170	11-11-94	.204	.200	.205	17	49	3	10	2	0	2	6	1	1	0	0	19	0	0	.367	.235
Ljatifi, Nadir	R-R	5-10	170	2-21-98	.313	.000	.357	8	16	2	5	2	0	0	3	2	1	0	0	6	0	1	.438	.421
Lofstrom, Morgan	L-R	6-1	185	8-17-95	.250	.500	.200	6	12	1	3	0	0	0	2	1	0	0	0	3	1	0	.250	.400
Lopez, Alejo	B-R	5-10	170	5-5-96	.419	.400	.423	12	31	3	13	2	0	0	5	5	2	0	0	2	2		.484	.526
Lopez, Maikel	B-R	6-2	185	10-31-93	.167	.300	.140	19	60	5	10	3	0	0	1	6	1	0	0	10	0	1	.217	.254
Marshall, Montrell	R-R	6-5	215	4-2-96	.159	.125	.165	43	145	9	23	5	0	1	12	9	0	0	0	52	0	0	.214	.218
Matthews, Jon	R-R	6-1	195	4-6-91	.280	.000	.304	10	25	5	7	0	0	0	2	1	1	0		6	3	2	.280	.455
McElroy, Satchel	R-R	5-10	170	8-13-96	.255	.333	.238	36	102	16	26	0	1	0	2	6	1	0	0	26	7	5	.275	.303
Pigott, Daniel	R-R	6-2	205	10-4-89	.289	.143	.323	11	38	10	11	3	0	4	9	2	0	0	0	7	3	0	.684	.325
Salmon-Williams, J.D.	R-R	5-9	195	3-21-97	.226	.286	.208	14	31	3	7	1	1	0	6	0	0	0		6	1	0	.323	.351
Santana, Leandro	R-R	6-2	175	2-19-97	.190	.087	.214	39	126	15	24	8	3	0	10	14	1	1	1	40	2	2	.302	.275
Saunders, Dario	R-R	5-9	165	3-8-97	.167	.500	.000	2	6	1	1	0	0	0	0	0	1	1	0	1	1	0	.167	.286
Siri, Jose	R-R	6-2	175	7-22-95	.246	.250	.245	43	171	34	42	7	9	3	19	3	0	1	0	64	9	2	.444	.259
Thompson, Cory	R-R	5-11	180	9-23-94	.323	.286	.333	8	31	7	10	3	0	1	3	1	0	0	1	5	3	0	.516	.333
Turnbull, Jake	R-R	6-0	195	2-28-91	.291	.238	.303	35	110	19	32	6	0	1	17	17	2	0	0	31	1	1	.373	.395
Vasquez, James	L-L	6-0	220	11-8-92	.359	.389	.349	42	142	19	51	11	3	9	36	15	2	0	5	25	0	1	.669	.415
Wallace, Raul	R-R	6-0	180	8-19-95	.285	.379	.255	34	123	13	35	7	2	3	15	3	2	1	0	38	7	4	.447	.313
Washington, Ty	R-R	5-9	160	9-1-93	.324	.571	.259	11	34	7	11	3	0	1	6	3	0	0	2	4	5	1	.500	.359
Wright, Ryan	R-R	6-1	200	12-3-89	.400	.250	.455	4	15	3	6	1	0	0	1	1	0	0	0	0	0	0	.467	.438

Pitching

Pitching	B-T	HT	WT	DOB	W	L	ERA	G	GS	CG	SV	IP	H	R	ER	HR	BB	SO	AVG	vLH	vRH	K/9	BB/9
Aguilar, Miguel	R-R	6-0	180	7-25-95	0	1	2.87	11	0	0	0	16	12	8	5	0	10	15	.200	.200	.200	8.62	5.74
Anesty, Isaac	L-L	6-2	190	6-6-97	0	2	3.68	8	0	0	0	7	11	9	3	0	6	8	.367	.333	.375	9.82	7.36
Aybar, Manuel	R-R	6-3	185	1-6-93	2	1	4.86	13	8	0	0	33	27	19	18	4	19	34	.216	.208	.221	9.18	5.13
Bautista, Wendolyn	R-R	6-0	185	3-27-93	3	1	2.60	13	4	0	0	55	54	23	16	3	12	55	.254	.317	.227	8.95	1.95
Bennett, Connor	R-R	5-9	192	4-10-97	0	1	1.62	11	0	0	3	17	17	7	3	0	8	18	.254	.391	.182	9.72	4.32
Correll, Zac	R-R	6-6	230	1-28-96	3	4	4.46	13	4	0	1	40	36	26	20	3	16	35	.235	.275	.216	7.81	3.57
Crawford, Jonathon	R-R	6-2	205	11-1-91	0	0	4.32	3	3	0	0	8	8	5	4	0	1	8	.250	.286	.222	8.64	1.08
Cuevas, Israel	R-R	6-1	178	9-19-93	2	5	3.90	14	0	0	2	30	28	18	13	2	14	31	.250	.304	.212	9.30	4.20
Damian, Pedro	R-R	6-1	170	11-29-92	2	1	5.19	14	0	0	1	17	16	13	10	0	16	19	.250	.211	.267	9.87	8.31
De Jesus, Yoel	R-R	6-2	180	10-8-94	0	0	5.79	3	0	0	0	5	10	3	3	1	0	4	.435	.400	.462	7.71	0.00

Pitching	B-T	HT	WT	DOB	W	L	ERA	G	GS	CG	SV	IP	H	R	ER	HR	BB	SO	AVG	vLH	vRH	K/9	BB/9
Diaz, Alexis	R-R	6-2	170	9-28-96	0	1	1.38	9	0	0	0	13	8	6	2	1	5	11	.178	.056	.259	7.62	3.46
Felt, Mason	R-L	6-2	195	3-16-94	0	0	0.73	8	8	0	0	12	10	1	1	0	13	10	.238	.357	.179	7.30	9.49
Jordan, Andrew	R-R	6-2	175	8-3-97	0	0	1.65	8	1	0	1	16	9	3	3	0	2	19	.161	.250	.136	10.47	1.10
Kahaloa, Ian	R-R	6-1	185	10-3-97	0	0	2.25	8	6	0	0	24	16	7	6	1	6	31	.184	.156	.200	11.63	2.25
Lara, Jean	R-R	6-3	200	4-15-93	0	1	0.00	4	0	0	2	6	3	3	0	0	0	8	.130	.333	.059	12.71	0.00
Lugo, Sandy	R-R	6-0	170	3-26-94	0	0	2.89	4	0	0	1	9	9	4	3	0	1	13	.265	.357	.200	12.54	0.96
Machorro, Carlos	R-R	6-2	175	9-20-96	1	0	1.50	5	0	0	2	12	7	3	2	0	4	13	.171	.158	.182	9.75	3.00
Mena, Alfredo	R-R	6-3	205	12-6-93	2	1	2.83	12	1	0	4	35	26	16	11	2	14	39	.202	.200	.202	10.03	3.60
Ramirez, Bernardo	R-R	6-2	180	2-2-93	2	0	2.70	5	3	0	0	7	4	2	2	1	1	8	.160	.143	.182	10.80	1.35
Reyes, Jesus	R-R	6-2	180	2-21-93	5	4	3.40	13	5	0	0	50	46	29	19	1	22	43	.251	.288	.227	7.69	3.93
Rodriguez, Adrian	R-R	6-1	185	8-8-96	5	4	3.42	13	6	0	0	50	58	24	19	1	8	48	.289	.368	.240	8.64	1.44
Rucker, Rock	L-L	6-5	220	3-24-93	0	0	6.75	6	0	0	0	5	7	7	4	0	9	7	.304	.571	.188	11.81	15.19
Santillan, Antonio	R-R	6-3	240	4-15-97	0	2	5.03	8	7	0	0	20	15	12	11	1	11	19	.217	.276	.175	8.69	5.03

Fielding

Catcher	PCT	G	PO	A	E	DP	PB
Guerrero	.980	17	124	22	3	0	6
Lofstrom	.978	5	40	5	1	0	1
Lopez	.970	19	135	29	5	1	5
Turnbull	.989	21	150	38	2	3	12

First Base	PCT	G	PO	A	E	DP
Aldazoro	1.000	3	19	1	0	1
Marshall	.980	39	272	22	6	21
Pigott	1.000	6	38	1	0	5
Vasquez	.992	16	115	7	1	11
Wright	1.000	1	10	0	0	1

Second Base	PCT	G	PO	A	E	DP
Azcona	.934	28	36	49	6	11
Butler	.957	12	17	27	2	3
Chavez	1.000	9	8	13	0	5
Diaz	1.000	2	3	2	0	0

Lopez	1.000	4	4	9	0	0
Salmon-Williams	.907	10	20	19	4	1
Washington	1.000	9	10	11	0	4
Wright	1.000	3	8	8	0	3

Third Base	PCT	G	PO	A	E	DP
Butler	.972	15	10	25	1	2
Chavez	1.000	3	0	11	0	0
Diaz	1.000	3	2	5	0	0
Marshall	1.000	3	0	9	0	0
Santana	.826	36	30	46	16	7

Shortstop	PCT	G	PO	A	E	DP
Azcona	1.000	1	0	1	0	0
Butler	.916	17	31	45	7	8
Chavez	.919	28	44	69	10	14
Diaz	1.000	1	1	1	0	1
Ljatifi	.850	5	7	10	3	1

Lopez	.889	5	10	14	3	5
Thompson	.882	8	10	20	4	2

Outfield	PCT	G	PO	A	E	DP
Aldazoro	—	2	0	0	0	0
Beltre	1.000	26	42	0	0	0
Benedetto	1.000	4	7	0	0	0
Chavez	1.000	2	3	1	0	0
Diaz	1.000	2	4	0	0	0
Duran	.909	7	7	3	1	0
Gordon	.962	30	48	3	2	0
Matthews	.900	7	9	0	1	0
McElroy	.966	31	54	2	2	3
Pigott	.857	5	6	0	1	0
Saunders	—	2	0	0	0	0
Siri	.942	41	63	2	4	0
Wallace	1.000	33	44	4	0	2

BILLINGS MUSTANGS   ROOKIE

PIONEER LEAGUE

Batting	B-T	HT	WT	DOB	AVG	vLH	vRH	G	AB	R	H	2B	3B	HR	RBI	BB	HBP	SH	SF	SO	SB	CS	SLG	OBP
Aquino, Aristides	R-R	6-4	190	4-22-94	.308	.267	.324	13	52	7	16	1	3	2	13	2	0	0	0	9	0	1	.558	.333
Bell, Brantley	R-R	6-3	185	11-16-94	.275	.313	.259	62	229	30	63	16	2	0	34	25	3	3	1	58	14	6	.362	.353
Butler, Blake	R-R	6-3	195	10-29-93	.222	.000	.267	5	18	0	4	0	0	0	2	0	1	1	0	9	0	0	.222	.263
Carter, Dalton	L-L	6-2	200	4-3-95	.269	.217	.286	31	93	12	25	10	1	3	22	7	2	1	0	20	0	0	.495	.333
Charlton, Ed	R-R	6-1	190	11-20-92	.267	.212	.296	54	191	30	51	17	2	5	27	21	3	0	0	54	6	2	.455	.349
Duarte, Jose	R-R	6-2	190	4-23-93	.178	.200	.170	22	73	5	13	3	0	0	7	1	0	0	0	19	0	0	.219	.189
Franklin, K.J.	R-R	6-1	220	11-24-94	.267	.259	.272	49	172	15	46	16	1	4	25	12	4	0	0	44	0	1	.442	.330
Garcia, Kevin	R-R	6-1	177	6-19-93	.317	.281	.333	51	183	27	58	12	0	1	19	26	1	2	1	24	6	2	.399	.403
Jocketty, Joe	R-R	5-10	165	10-9-92	.150	.040	.200	15	40	3	6	0	0	1	3	0	0	0	1	8	1	0	.150	.209
Mardirosian, Shane	R-R	5-10	175	10-13-95	.297	.224	.330	44	155	20	46	9	3	2	16	10	3	4	2	35	12	5	.432	.347
Martijn, Jonathan	L-R	6-2	200	2-23-94	.268	.339	.224	45	157	19	42	7	3	2	22	9	3	0	1	32	2	2	.389	.318
Medina, Reydel	L-L	6-0	195	2-14-93	.241	.197	.260	57	216	41	52	10	2	13	32	17	2	0	1	66	14	5	.486	.301
Piatnik, Mitch	B-R	5-11	160	9-12-94	.210	.156	.228	39	124	18	26	3	0	1	7	10	0	3	2	41	10	5	.258	.265
Shields, Zach	L-R	6-2	160	5-12-93	.220	.171	.233	55	168	19	37	4	2	0	9	5	2	5	1	24	8	3	.268	.250
Siri, Jose	R-R	6-2	175	7-22-95	.200	.000	.333	3	5	1	1	0	0	0	1	0	0	0	0	1	2	0	.200	.333
Stephenson, Tyler	R-R	6-4	225	8-16-96	.268	.263	.270	54	194	28	52	15	0	1	16	22	3	0	0	42	0	2	.361	.352
Trahan, Blake	R-R	5-9	180	9-5-93	.312	.362	.295	47	186	32	58	8	3	1	15	25	3	1	1	19	10	3	.403	.400
Trees, Mitch	R-R	6-0	200	7-18-95	.179	.029	.250	34	106	11	19	3	1	2	8	5	3	2	0	53	1	0	.283	.237
Vargas, Hector	R-R	6-2	170	1-27-95	.296	.338	.271	52	186	24	55	9	5	1	23	3	1	3	3	16	5	9	.414	.306

Pitching	B-T	HT	WT	DOB	W	L	ERA	G	GS	CG	SV	IP	H	R	ER	HR	BB	SO	AVG	vLH	vRH	K/9	BB/9
Arias, Junior Joselin	R-R	6-3	170	11-10-93	3	2	5.02	16	3	0	0	38	44	30	21	2	23	24	.289	.329	.256	5.73	5.50
Bautista, Wendolyn	R-R	6-0	185	3-27-93	0	0	3.00	1	1	0	0	6	5	3	2	0	1	4	.208	.250	.188	6.00	1.50
Boyles, Ty	R-L	6-3	270	9-30-95	4	3	2.17	10	10	0	0	58	51	22	14	2	17	48	.243	.290	.223	7.45	2.64
Constante, Jacob	L-L	6-4	215	3-22-94	4	3	3.56	14	13	0	0	68	59	33	27	2	38	58	.241	.269	.230	7.64	5.00
Crouse, Shane	R-R	6-3	195	7-17-93	1	0	10.13	5	0	0	1	5	10	8	6	2	4	6	.385	.125	.500	10.13	6.75
Cuevas, Israel	R-R	6-1	178	9-19-93	1	0	1.80	2	0	0	0	5	3	1	1	0	4	2	.176	.200	.167	3.60	7.20
Herget, Jimmy	R-R	6-3	155	9-9-93	3	0	3.20	24	0	0	15	26	19	9	9	1	11	26	.188	.194	.184	9.24	3.91
Johnson, Jake	R-R	6-2	180	6-5-93	4	1	2.76	25	0	0	4	29	28	16	9	1	14	33	.252	.390	.171	10.13	4.30
Lopez, Jose	R-R	6-1	185	9-1-93	3	2	3.16	15	14	0	0	57	53	23	20	4	19	67	.248	.230	.257	10.58	3.00
Lugo, Sandy	R-R	6-0	170	3-26-94	0	0	5.60	13	0	0	0	18	18	13	11	2	8	23	.250	.172	.302	11.72	4.08
Machorro, Carlos	R-R	6-2	175	9-20-96	1	1	4.76	9	0	0	0	9	9	5	5	1	8	17	.314	.300	.325	9.00	4.24
Marquez, Soid	R-R	6-3	165	1-3-95	3	3	5.80	17	1	0	1	40	42	29	26	2	23	41	.275	.282	.268	9.15	5.13
Martinez, Juan	L-L	6-2	175	7-15-92	1	5	3.51	24	0	0	0	33	36	21	13	1	7	25	.275	.190	.315	6.75	1.89
Moody, Jacob	R-L	5-9	185	10-29-92	1	0	4.05	9	0	0	0	13	13	9	6	0	10	11	.271	.313	.250	7.43	6.75
Ohanian, Sarkis	R-R	5-11	195	8-6-93	2	2	4.10	18	0	0	0	28	21	17	13	3	21	54	.206	.182	.217	13.02	5.06
Orewiler, Austin	R-R	6-2	200	5-18-93	0	1	4.68	19	0	0	1	25	19	18	13	4	15	23	.207	.270	.164	8.28	5.40
Parmenter, Tyler	R-R	6-2	185	5-4-93	1	3	4.68	17	0	0	0	25	28	16	13	2	22	32	.289	.242	.313	11.52	7.92

Pitching

Pitching	B-T	HT	WT	DOB	W	L	ERA	G	GS	CG	SV	IP	H	R	ER	HR	BB	SO	AVG	vLH	vRH	K/9	BB/9
Rainey, Tanner	R-R	6-2	235	12-25-92	2	2	4.27	15	15	0	0	59	58	37	28	2	28	57	.258	.337	.209	8.69	4.27
Ramsey, Jordan	L-R	6-3	185	9-6-92	0	4	7.20	9	8	0	0	20	20	18	16	3	17	21	.253	.324	.200	9.45	7.65
Romero, Franderlyn	R-R	6-1	190	2-21-93	3	4	3.34	15	10	0	0	67	74	37	25	4	21	46	.277	.255	.292	6.15	2.81
Sterner, Ty	L-L	6-1	208	12-9-92	0	2	4.91	8	0	0	0	11	13	11	6	1	6	13	.265	.211	.300	10.64	4.91

Fielding

Catcher	PCT	G	PO	A	E	DP	PB
Duarte	1.000	4	9	3	0	0	1
Stephenson	.981	46	364	53	8	5	13
Trees	.972	33	227	46	8	6	7

First Base	PCT	G	PO	A	E	DP
Duarte	1.000	18	134	7	0	17
Franklin	.987	32	279	20	4	21
Medina	.985	28	250	19	4	24

Second Base	PCT	G	PO	A	E	DP
Bell	.957	5	9	13	1	4
Jocketty	1.000	3	3	12	0	4
Mardirosian	.943	36	54	94	9	22

	PCT	G	PO	A	E	DP
Piatnik	.920	14	28	41	6	11
Vargas	.924	22	29	44	6	8
Third Base	**PCT**	**G**	**PO**	**A**	**E**	**DP**
Bell	.919	53	28	86	10	3
Franklin	.864	10	7	12	3	1
Trahan	1.000	1	1	1	0	0
Vargas	.884	13	11	27	5	0
Shortstop	**PCT**	**G**	**PO**	**A**	**E**	**DP**
Bell	.778	2	3	4	2	2
Butler	1.000	4	5	12	0	4
Piatnik	.900	11	14	31	5	7
Trahan	.964	44	71	142	8	34

	PCT	G	PO	A	E	DP
Vargas	.942	15	21	44	4	14
Outfield	**PCT**	**G**	**PO**	**A**	**E**	**DP**
Aquino	.941	11	14	2	1	1
Carter	.963	20	26	0	1	0
Charlton	.978	52	82	5	2	1
Garcia	.942	43	78	3	5	1
Martijn	.902	31	35	2	4	0
Medina	1.000	26	51	5	0	1
Piatnik	1.000	4	5	1	0	0
Shields	.989	49	90	4	1	3
Siri	1.000	3	7	0	0	0

DSL REDS

ROOKIE

DOMINICAN SUMMER LEAGUE

Batting	B-T	HT	WT	DOB	AVG	vLH	vRH	G	AB	R	H	2B	3B	HR	RBI	BB	HBP	SH	SF	SO	SB	CS	SLG	OBP
Abreu, Hidekel	R-R	5-10	155	10-30-97	.222	.000	.261	27	81	15	18	2	1	0	2	14	1	4	1	19	3	1	.272	.340
Alegria, Benjamin	R-R	5-10	165	8-6-97	.301	.259	.316	27	103	16	31	3	1	0	12	12	0	2	0	17	2	1	.350	.374
Bautista, Mariel	R-R	6-3	170	10-15-97	.259	.282	.252	51	170	33	44	10	3	2	25	20	5	2	2	43	6	2	.388	.350
Berroa, Melbin	R-R	6-4	175	3-10-97	.185	.294	.132	48	157	11	29	7	1	3	11	5	2	0	0	45	2	2	.299	.220
Capitillo, Derik	R-R	5-11	205	4-11-95	.263	.266	.262	49	186	31	49	11	2	1	24	16	4	1	3	23	13	4	.360	.330
De Los Santos, Tomas	L-R	6-3	180	4-16-95	.306	.243	.336	60	222	41	68	4	12	5	38	25	2	2	1	55	18	6	.500	.380
Doval, Sucre	R-R	6-3	175	9-6-96	.217	—		36	115	15	25	5	1	2	13	7	2	2	0	35	3	3	.330	.274
Encarnacion, Johan	R-R	6-0	170	9-21-96	.202	.220	.193	36	124	21	25	7	3	2	13	19	5	3	0	39	3	3	.355	.331
Gabo, Erick	R-R	6-3	190	2-22-95	.332	.269	.363	63	238	44	79	13	9	2	50	24	11	0	3	58	23	5	.487	.413
Garzon, Angel	B-R	6-2	160	8-21-97	.278	.333	.255	23	72	5	20	3	1	0	9	9	1	0	1	33	4	1	.347	.361
Herrera, Edgar	L-R	5-10	180	1-30-96	.309	.321	.305	61	223	69	16	6	2	29	15	7	4	3	48	6	5	.462	.367
Jimenez, Daniel	R-R	5-11	175	4-23-96	.337	.313	.346	67	258	58	87	17	5	5	40	20	9	0	1	26	15	8	.500	.403
Juaquin, Urwin	R-R	6-0	140	12-29-97	.253	.237	.261	45	174	29	44	5	0	0	13	22	3	2	0	40	7	2	.282	.347
Juarez, Raul	R-R	6-1	165	5-21-98	.205	.206	.204	49	166	18	34	8	2	2	18	9	11	3	1	37	5	4	.313	.289
Liberatore, Ernesto	R-R	6-0	180	3-26-96	.233	.237	.231	50	163	15	38	10	0	1	24	8	5	0	2	30	5	4	.313	.287
Manzanero, Pabel	R-R	6-3	170	1-30-96	.301	.256	.318	39	153	17	46	6	1	8	34	3	4	0	3	41	0	0	.510	.325
Martinez, Valentin	R-R	6-0	175	9-21-96	.281	—		21	64	6	18	1	0	0	5	3	0	2	1	13	1	2	.297	.309
Martinez, Victor	R-R	6-1	170	1-29-97	.172	.091	.188	34	134	11	23	1	0	0	6	2	4	8	0	24	1	3	.179	.207
Mateo, Carlos	R-R	6-3	175	5-17-95	.301	.275	.313	41	136	18	41	2	3	1	11	4	3	0	0	24	8	3	.382	.336
Munroe, Reshard	L-L	6-0	170	6-15-96	.249	.212	.264	51	177	33	44	2	6	2	20	29	2	0	0	31	14	3	.362	.361
Ortiz, Leonardo	R-R	6-1	198	3-4-97	.218	.219	.218	33	110	13	24	4	2	0	11	4	2	1	0	23	0	0	.291	.259
Ovalle, Gabriel	B-R	6-2	170	12-10-94	.238	.231	.241	46	164	28	39	3	3	0	8	28	7	2	1	25	24	2	.293	.370
Paulino, Alejandro	R-R	6-0	150	11-23-96	.263	.259	.265	58	224	34	59	8	1	1	20	12	4	3	4	37	8	2	.321	.307
Rivero, Carlos	L-R	6-0	175	4-30-97	.206	.179	.219	63	218	31	45	10	1	1	19	14	5	5	1	46	20	5	.275	.269
Rolle, Quinton	R-R	6-0	200	1-16-98	.111	—		14	45	4	5	1	0	1	3	2	0	0	0	20	0	2	.200	.149
Rubicondo, Anthony	R-R	6-1	175	4-24-96	.249	.239	.252	49	177	26	44	10	1	0	17	20	4	2	2	25	8	1	.316	.335
Saba, Vidauri	R-R	6-2	170	9-17-95	.136	.176	.119	22	59	6	8	2	0	0	2	7	3	1	0	29	1	0	.169	.261
Sanchez, Aristides	R-R	6-2	180	3-22-97	.188	.086	.226	39	128	11	24	5	0	0	10	14	4	1	2	32	2	2	.227	.232
Sims, Johnny	R-R	6-3	192	10-29-96	.200	.310	.168	53	185	24	37	7	3	4	26	27	5	0	1	66	6	3	.335	.317
Sugilio, Andy	B-R	6-2	170	10-26-96	.272	.272	.272	62	228	40	62	10	8	1	29	25	1	3	3	34	8	4	.399	.342
Tello, Jose	R-R	6-0	170	5-21-98	.264	—		39	125	20	33	3	1	2	14	16	4	1	4	33	3	0	.352	.356
Vargas, Franklin	R-R	5-11	170	11-06-94	.257	.200	.280	12	35	5	9	1	0	0	5	5	0	1	0	5	0	1	.286	.350
Yon, Edwin	R-R	6-5	180	7-24-98	.192	.250	.156	34	104	17	20	3	1	0	6	15	1	0	0	42	3	3	.240	.300

Pitching	B-T	HT	WT	DOB	W	L	ERA	G	GS	CG	SV	IP	H	R	ER	HR	BB	SO	AVG	vLH	vRH	K/9	BB/9
Acevedo, Pedro	L-L	6-5	178	1-16-95	0	1	8.54	20	0	0	0	26	25	29	25	1	31	20	.248	.222	.253	6.84	10.59
Alecis, Luis	R-R	6-3	190	6-7-97	1	1	3.23	15	14	0	0	61	52	28	22	1	27	64	.227	.265	.205	9.39	3.96
Azcarate, Geremi	L-L	6-1	210	9-6-97	1	0	6.30	8	0	0	0	10	3	7	7	0	18	12	.107	.333	.100	10.80	16.20
Castillo, Jose	R-R	6-4	190	6-10-96	1	2	5.93	16	0	0	1	27	33	26	18	2	20	16	.308	.273	.324	5.27	6.59
De Jesus, Jhon	R-R	6-4	180	1-9-97	4	5	3.35	13	11	0	0	51	45	23	19	0	23	42	.228	.147	.279	7.41	4.06
De Jesus, Yoel	R-R	6-2	180	10-8-94	0	1	13.50	1	0	0	0	1	1	2	2	1	2	1	.200	.000	.333	6.75	13.50
Encarnacion, Marcos	R-R	6-2	180	11-28-95	3	2	3.34	15	15	0	0	62	54	38	23	0	34	55	.234	.239	.232	7.98	4.94
Escoboza, Edward	R-R	6-5	185	12-5-95	3	8	6.11	18	9	0	0	56	66	49	38	5	25	60	.288	.356	.245	9.64	4.02
Espinal, Jhon	R-R	6-1	175	9-24-96	2	4	4.94	12	0	0	0	24	20	14	13	1	12	16	.238	.250	.233	6.08	4.56
Garcia, Eriberto	R-R	5-11	180	11-7-95	5	1	1.85	21	0	0	4	44	48	17	9	0	14	40	.274	.327	.252	8.24	2.89
Gomez, Ranfi	R-R	6-2	230	8-23-95	2	0	4.60	19	0	0	0	47	60	32	24	1	22	37	.314	.315	.314	7.09	4.21
Guzman, Hernando	R-R	6-2	170	3-12-96	6	2	4.25	23	0	0	8	49	45	25	23	1	21	46	.250	.224	.262	8.51	3.88
Ismail, Ross	R-R	6-0	195	2-19-97	0	6	6.20	15	7	0	0	45	64	42	31	1	27	40	.335	.288	.356	8.00	5.40
Jimenez, Felix	R-R	6-3	170	9-29-95	2	1	4.02	20	0	0	1	40	32	25	18	2	27	27	.205	.203	.207	6.02	6.02
Jimenez, Hector	L-L	6-0	160	4-3-95	2	1	2.08	3	0	0	0	4	5	4	1	0	3	7	.278	.500	.214	14.54	6.23
Mata, Jose	R-R	5-11	170	9-18-97	0	0	11.70	8	0	0	0	10	11	13	13	1	8	8	.268	.182	.300	7.20	7.20

CINCINNATI REDS

Pitching

Pitching	B-T	HT	WT	DOB	W	L	ERA	G	GS	CG	SV	IP	H	R	ER	HR	BB	SO	AVG	vLH	vRH	K/9	BB/9
Moncion, Isaac	R-R	6-5	210	8-11-95	0	1	6.48	3	3	0	0	8	9	10	6	0	9	10	.265	.111	.320	10.80	9.72
Morales, Enyer	R-R	6-2	175	9-14-97	5	0	4.93	18	0	0	0	35	33	25	19	3	18	32	.244	.220	.255	8.31	4.67
Moreta, Dauri	R-R	6-2	185	4-15-96	1	2	1.69	11	0	0	4	21	19	7	4	1	7	30	.226	.214	.232	12.66	2.95
Nayib, David	R-R	6-5	180	8-31-94	0	0	4.40	10	0	0	0	14	9	8	7	0	7	9	.173	.294	.114	5.65	4.40
Nino, Jeffry	R-R	6-4	170	9-26-96	0	3	4.65	16	4	0	0	31	26	20	16	0	15	17	.224	.282	.195	4.94	4.35
Nova, Moises	R-R	6-3	190	8-2-95	2	1	3.25	14	14	0	0	55	41	27	20	0	28	64	.207	.172	.224	10.41	4.55
Paredes, Yean	L-L	6-3	185	8-17-95	0	0	11.81	4	0	0	0	5	7	8	7	2	8	5	.292	—	.292	8.44	13.50
Perez, Geremi	R-R	5-11	180	8-3-97	5	2	3.45	21	0	0	0	47	47	21	18	1	36	50	.269	.353	.234	9.57	6.89
Reinoso, Gregory	L-L	6-1	170	11-17-95	0	3	7.50	12	5	0	1	30	44	31	25	1	17	31	.336	.414	.314	9.30	5.10
Roman, Jesus	R-R	6-2	195	2-2-97	1	3	5.40	14	0	0	2	37	51	34	22	1	11	28	.333	.286	.351	6.87	2.70
Romero, Wennington	L-L	5-11	175	1-29-98	2	3	2.13	14	14	0	0	72	60	26	17	2	9	82	.221	.105	.251	10.30	1.13
Santos, Yerry	R-R	6-4	194	11-30-94	0	10	9.98	17	12	0	1	46	54	59	51	1	52	48	—	—	—	9.39	10.17
Salas, Jose	R-R	6-3	190	2-7-95	3	6	3.99	16	11	0	0	65	80	39	29	1	16	44	.304	.250	.333	6.06	2.20
Segura, Dayrol	R-R	6-3	195	8-19-95	0	1	14.14	5	0	0	0	7	15	13	11	2	2	3	.405	.182	.500	3.86	2.57
Smith, Ricardo	R-R	6-2	175	2-16-96	2	3	3.73	17	10	0	1	70	77	42	29	4	8	56	.282	.276	.284	7.20	1.03
Soleana, Cerilio	L-L	5-11	150	4-22-97	0	0	1.66	11	0	0	1	22	16	7	4	1	9	21	.213	.286	.197	8.72	3.74
Soto, Mario	R-R	6-3	190	7-29-94	0	1	14.73	3	0	0	0	4	6	8	6	1	5	4	.353	1.000	.214	9.82	12.27
Telleria, Adolfi	R-R	6-1	170	4-12-94	5	1	1.66	12	2	0	1	49	49	12	9	2	6	34	.275	.283	.271	6.29	1.11
Veras, Jose	R-R	6-4	180	2-10-94	3	4	1.86	13	13	0	0	68	57	23	14	4	15	46	.230	.214	.236	6.12	2.00

Fielding

Catcher

Catcher	PCT	G	PO	A	E	DP	PB
Capitillo	.972	27	215	30	7	0	5
Liberatore	.976	38	279	45	8	1	15
Manzanero	.979	25	183	45	5	3	8
Martinez	.980	17	130	12	3	0	4
Ortiz	.968	32	186	27	7	0	23
Rolle	.986	10	64	9	1	0	9
Tello	.975	12	69	10	2	0	10

First Base

First Base	PCT	G	PO	A	E	DP
Capitillo	.987	18	150	4	2	13
Gabo	.969	9	61	2	2	5
Juarez	.966	18	129	13	5	15
Liberatore	.978	13	88	3	2	4
Manzanero	.959	9	66	5	3	11
Martinez	1.000	3	15	0	0	1
Rolle	1.000	1	1	0	0	0
Rubicondo	.987	41	372	18	5	18
Sanchez	.993	17	143	5	1	8
Sugilio	1.000	1	7	0	0	0
Tello	.978	27	212	12	5	33

Second Base

Second Base	PCT	G	PO	A	E	DP
Abreu	.918	18	36	54	8	4
Alegria	.925	10	23	26	4	8
Encarnacion	1.000	1	2	4	0	2
Garzon	1.000	4	2	6	0	2
Juaquin	.956	38	89	105	9	21
Herrera	.957	22	28	60	4	8
Ovalle	1.000	3	9	5	0	0
Paulino	.932	28	50	74	9	13
Rivero	.950	33	86	85	9	23

Third Base

Third Base	PCT	G	PO	A	E	DP
Encarnacion	.667	4	3	1	2	0
Garzon	.625	3	2	3	3	1
Herrera	.861	37	29	64	15	4
Juarez	.823	29	12	39	11	5
Ovalle	.826	9	5	14	4	0
Paulino	1.000	4	3	4	0	0
Rubicondo	.958	8	9	14	1	3
Rivero	.945	23	16	53	4	6
Saba	.833	7	1	9	2	0
Sanchez	.843	22	10	33	8	0
Sugilio	.727	7	2	14	6	2
Vargas	.900	6	2	16	2	2

Shortstop

Shortstop	PCT	G	PO	A	E	DP
Alegria	.946	17	28	59	5	10
Encarnacion	.916	29	43	88	12	21
Juaquin	.833	6	12	8	4	1
Martinez	.943	34	53	95	9	13
Ovalle	.940	35	52	88	9	18
Paulino	.907	24	47	70	12	12
Rivero	.923	7	5	19	2	2
Sanchez	—	1	0	0	0	0

Outfield

Outfield	PCT	G	PO	A	E	DP
Bautista	.941	47	107	5	7	2
Berroa	.989	47	80	6	1	2
De Los Santos	.963	57	96	7	4	1
Doval	.889	26	29	3	4	0
Gabo	.938	52	82	8	6	1
Jimenez	.964	58	97	9	4	4
Mateo	.945	32	48	4	3	1
Munroe	.946	41	48	5	3	0
Rivero	1.000	1	1	0	0	0
Sims	.902	32	34	3	4	0
Sugilio	.944	51	79	5	5	1
Yon	1.000	22	30	2	0	0

Cleveland Indians

SEASON IN A SENTENCE: The Indians entered the year with lofty expectations, but despite the fantastic and long-awaited debut of shortstop Francisco Lindor, they were unable to overcome a slow start to the season and finished just a game above .500 in third place in the AL Central.

HIGH POINT: Lindor was promoted on July 14. Though the Indians lost to the Tigers that night, it would be his play that stabilized the Indians' defense and keyed a second half-revival to keep them in the wild-card race deep into September.

LOW POINT: The Indians lost eight of their first 11 games after the all-star break. The stretch included a four-game sweep at the hands of the White Sox, during which the Indians were outscored 26-5. By the end of the skid, they were in last place in the AL Central, 16 games behind the Royals, and all but out of the playoff race.

NOTABLE ROOKIES: Lindor, the team's No. 1 prospect for the past four years, was phenomenal in his debut. He hit .313/.353/.482 with 12 home runs and 12 stolen bases in 99 games, all while playing exemplary defense. Third baseman Giovanny Urshela was promoted a few days before Lindor and also excelled with his glove, though he had a tougher time at the plate. Righthander Cody Anderson ran with his opportunity in the rotation, going 7-3, 3.05 in 15 starts.

KEY TRANSACTIONS: The Indians' biggest move before the trade deadline was to send Brandon Moss, who had arrived in an offseason deal with the Athletics, to the Cardinals in exchange for promising lefthander Rob Kaminsky. Then, in a surprising August deal, the Indians traded outfielder Michael Bourn and first baseman Nick Swisher to the Braves in exchange for third baseman Chris Johnson. The trade allowed the organization to move on from the pair of high-profile, highly paid free agents brought in before the 2013 season, freeing up playing time as well as providing payroll flexibility.

DOWN ON THE FARM: Outfielders Clint Frazier and Bradley Zimmer, the team's top picks in the last two drafts, opened the season as teammates with high Class A Lynchburg and posted solid seasons. Frazier hit .285/.377/.465 with 16 home runs in 133 games. Zimmer made the Futures Game and was promoted to Double-A Akron in his first full professional season. First baseman Bobby Bradley hit 27 home runs to lead the Midwest League as a 19-year-old.

OPENING DAY PAYROLL: $86,091,175 (26th)

PLAYERS OF THE YEAR

MAJOR LEAGUE	MINOR LEAGUE
Jason Kipnis	**Bobby Bradley**
2b	1b
.303/.372/.451,	(low Class A)
9 HR, 52 RBIs,	.264/.357/.518,
42 2Bs, 12 SB	Led MWL with 27 HR

ORGANIZATION LEADERS

BATTING   *Minimum 250 AB

MAJORS

* AVG	Michael Brantley	.310
* OPS	Michael Brantley	.859
HR	Carlos Santana	19
RBI	Carlos Santana	85

MINORS

* AVG	Yandy Diaz, Akron, Columbus	.309
* OBP	Yandy Diaz, Akron, Columbus	.403
* SLG	Bobby Bradley, Lake County, Lynchburg	.518
R	Clint Frazier, Lynchburg	88
H	Yandy Diaz, Akron, Columbus	153
TB	Clint Frazier, Lynchburg	233
2B	Clint Frazier, Lynchburg	36
3B	Ivan Castillo, Lynchburg	12
HR	Bobby Bradley, Lake County, Lynchburg	27
RBI	Nellie Rodriguez, Lynchburg, Akron	98
BB	Mike Papi, Lynchburg	81
SO	Nellie Rodriguez, Lynchburg, Akron	159
SB	Greg Allen, Lake County, Lynchburg	46

PITCHING   #Minimum 75 IP

MAJORS

W	Carlos Carrasco	14
	Danny Salazar	14
# ERA	Danny Salazar	3.45
SO	Corey Kluber	245
SV	Cody Allen	34

MINORS

W	Toru Murata, Columbus	15
L	Sean Brady, Lake County	12
	Mitch Brown, Lynchburg	12
	Shawn Morimando, Akron	12
# ERA	Adam Plutko, Lynchburg, Akron	2.39
G	Zack Weiss, Daytona, Pensacola	54
GS	2 players	28
SV	Zack Weiss, Daytona, Pensacola	30
IP	Ryan Merritt, Akron, Columbus	171
BB	Mitch Brown, Lynchburg	77
SO	Mike Clevinger, Akron	145
AVG	Adam Plutko, Lynchburg, Akron	.208

2015 PERFORMANCE

General Manager: Chris Antonetti/Mike Chernoff. **Farm Director:** Ross Atkins. **Scouting Director:** John Mirabelli.

Class	Team	League	W	L	PCT	Finish	Manager
Majors	Cleveland Indians	American	81	80	.503	8th (15)	Terry Francona
Triple-A	Columbus Clippers	International	83	61	.576	1st (14)	Chris Tremie
Double-A	Akron RubberDucks	Eastern	73	69	.514	7th (12)	Dave Wallace
High A	Lynchburg Hillcats	Carolina	72	68	.514	3rd (8)	Mark Budzinski
Low A	Lake County Captains	Midwest	71	66	.518	8th (16)	Shaun Larkin
Short season	Mahoning Valley Scrappers	New York-Penn	31	44	.413	t-13th (14)	Travis Fryman
Rookie	Indians	Arizona	23	33	.411	t-12th (14)	Anthony Medrano
Overall 2015 Minor League Record			353	341	.509	14th (30)	

ORGANIZATION STATISTICS

CLEVELAND INDIANS

AMERICAN LEAGUE

Batting	B-T	HT	WT	DOB	AVG	vLH	vRH	G	AB	R	H	2B	3B	HR	RBI	BB	HBP	SH	SF	SO	SB	CS	SLG	OBP
Aguilar, Jesus	R-R	6-3	250	6-30-90	.316	.250	.364	7	19	0	6	1	0	0	2	0	1	0	0	7	0	0	.368	.350
Almonte, Abraham	B-R	5-9	210	6-27-89	.264	.250	.269	51	178	30	47	9	5	5	20	16	0	0	2	33	6	0	.455	.321
Aviles, Mike	R-R	5-10	205	3-13-81	.231	.242	.219	98	290	37	67	10	0	5	17	20	1	5	1	38	3	1	.317	.282
Bourn, Michael	L-R	5-10	180	12-27-82	.246	.235	.249	95	289	29	71	12	1	0	19	29	0	7	1	76	13	5	.294	.313
Brantley, Michael	L-L	6-2	200	5-15-87	.310	.294	.321	137	529	68	164	45	0	15	84	60	2	0	5	51	15	1	.480	.379
Chisenhall, Lonnie	L-R	6-2	190	10-4-88	.246	.241	.247	106	333	38	82	19	1	7	44	23	1	2	3	69	4	1	.372	.294
Gomes, Yan	R-R	6-2	215	7-19-87	.231	.208	.240	95	363	38	84	22	0	12	45	13	7	0	6	104	0	0	.391	.267
Hayes, Brett	R-R	6-1	210	2-13-84	.156	.214	.111	14	32	4	5	0	0	3	6	3	0	1	0	7	0	0	.438	.229
Holt, Tyler	R-R	5-10	200	3-10-89	.100	.000	.118	9	20	2	2	0	0	0	1	1	0	0	0	9	0	0	.100	.143
Johnson, Chris	R-R	6-3	225	10-1-84	.289	.333	.267	27	90	6	26	4	0	1	7	3	0	0	0	25	0	0	.367	.312
Kipnis, Jason	L-R	5-11	195	4-3-87	.303	.250	.334	141	565	86	171	43	7	9	52	57	9	4	6	107	12	8	.451	.372
Lindor, Francisco	B-R	5-11	190	11-14-93	.313	.321	.308	99	390	50	122	22	4	12	51	27	1	13	7	69	12	2	.482	.353
Martinez, Michael	B-R	5-9	175	9-16-82	.267	.222	.286	16	30	7	8	2	0	0	2	1	0	1	0	12	0	1	.333	.290
Moore, Adam	R-R	6-3	220	5-8-84	.250	—	.250	1	4	0	1	0	0	0	1	0	0	0	0	2	0	0	.250	.250
Moss, Brandon	L-R	6-0	210	9-16-83	.217	.265	.191	94	337	36	73	17	1	15	50	32	3	0	3	106	0	0	.407	.288
Murphy, David	L-L	6-3	210	10-18-81	.296	.286	.297	84	206	22	61	12	1	5	27	16	1	1	4	29	0	1	.437	.344
2-team total (48 Los Angeles)					.283	—	—	132	361	38	102	18	1	10	50	20	1	1	5	49	0	2	.421	.318
Perez, Roberto	R-R	5-11	225	12-23-88	.228	.265	.215	70	184	30	42	9	1	7	21	33	2	5	2	64	0	0	.402	.348
Raburn, Ryan	R-R	6-0	185	4-17-81	.301	.325	.136	82	173	22	52	16	1	8	29	23	4	0	1	44	0	0	.543	.393
Ramirez, Jose	B-R	5-9	180	9-17-92	.219	.202	.226	97	315	50	69	14	3	6	27	32	1	5	2	39	10	4	.340	.291
Sands, Jerry	R-R	6-4	225	9-28-87	.236	.297	.169	50	123	11	29	5	1	4	19	9	0	0	1	36	0	0	.390	.286
Santana, Carlos	B-R	5-11	210	4-8-86	.231	.268	.211	154	550	72	127	29	2	19	85	108	3	—	5	122	11	3	.395	.357
Swisher, Nick	B-L	6-0	195	11-25-80	.198	.209	.190	30	101	6	20	4	0	2	8	8	1	0	1	24	0	0	.297	.261
Urshela, Giovanny	R-R	6-0	215	10-11-91	.225	.275	.207	81	267	25	60	8	1	6	21	18	2	1	0	58	0	1	.330	.279
Walters, Zach	B-R	6-2	210	9-5-89	.133	.182	.105	12	30	0	4	0	0	0	3	0	0	0	0	15	0	0	.133	.133

Pitching	B-T	HT	WT	DOB	W	L	ERA	G	GS	CG	SV	IP	H	R	ER	HR	BB	SO	AVG	vLH	vRH	K/9	BB/9
Adams, Austin	R-R	5-11	200	8-19-86	2	0	3.78	28	0	0	1	33	37	15	14	2	13	23	.276	.267	.284	6.21	3.51
Allen, Cody	R-R	6-1	210	11-20-88	2	5	2.99	70	0	0	34	69	56	26	23	2	25	99	.219	.176	.260	12.85	3.25
Anderson, Cody	R-R	6-4	235	9-14-90	7	3	3.05	15	15	1	0	91	77	32	31	9	24	44	.231	.238	.225	4.34	2.36
Armstrong, Shawn	R-R	6-2	225	9-11-90	0	0	2.25	8	0	0	0	8	5	2	2	1	2	11	.179	.143	.214	12.38	2.25
Atchison, Scott	R-R	6-2	200	3-29-76	1	1	6.86	23	0	0	0	20	23	15	15	6	4	12	.288	.179	.346	5.49	1.83
Bauer, Trevor	R-R	6-1	200	1-17-91	11	12	4.55	31	30	1	0	176	152	90	89	23	79	170	.232	.225	.239	8.69	4.04
Carrasco, Carlos	R-R	6-4	210	3-21-87	14	12	3.63	30	30	3	0	184	154	75	74	18	43	216	.228	.216	.238	10.58	2.11
Chen, Bruce	L-L	6-2	215	6-19-77	0	1	12.79	2	2	0	0	6	17	9	9	3	1	4	.500	.333	.591	5.68	1.42
Crockett, Kyle	L-L	6-2	175	12-15-91	0	0	4.08	31	0	0	0	18	17	9	8	1	7	15	.266	.256	.286	7.64	3.57
Floyd, Gavin	R-R	6-4	245	1-27-83	0	0	2.70	7	0	0	0	13	11	4	4	0	4	7	.220	.111	.281	4.73	2.70
Hagadone, Nick	L-L	6-5	230	1-1-86	0	1	4.28	36	0	0	0	27	30	16	13	3	12	28	.273	.264	.281	9.22	3.95
House, T.J.	R-L	6-1	205	9-29-89	0	4	13.15	4	4	0	0	13	21	19	19	1	12	7	.362	.412	.392	4.85	8.31
Kluber, Corey	R-R	6-4	215	4-10-86	9	16	3.49	32	32	4	0	222	189	92	86	22	45	245	.231	.261	.197	9.93	1.82
Lee, C.C.	R-R	5-11	190	10-21-86	0	0	5.40	2	0	0	0	2	4	1	1	0	1	3	.444	1.000	.375	16.20	5.40
Manship, Jeff	R-R	6-2	205	1-16-85	1	0	0.92	32	0	0	0	39	20	4	4	1	10	33	.155	.235	.103	7.55	2.29
Marcum, Shaun	R-R	6-0	195	12-14-81	3	2	5.40	7	6	0	0	35	32	21	21	9	11	30	.246	.319	.164	7.71	2.83
McAllister, Zach	R-R	6-4	240	12-8-87	4	4	3.00	61	1	0	1	69	70	28	23	7	23	84	.258	.252	.264	10.96	3.00
Murata, Toru	L-R	6-0	175	5-20-85	0	1	8.10	1	1	0	0	3	4	5	3	2	1	2	.267	.250	.333	5.40	2.70
Rzepczynski, Marc	L-L	6-2	220	8-29-85	2	3	4.43	45	0	0	0	20	23	15	10	1	10	24	.280	.264	.310	10.62	4.43
Salazar, Danny	R-R	6-0	195	1-16-90	14	10	3.45	30	30	0	0	185	156	79	71	23	53	195	.226	.232	.220	9.49	2.58
Shaw, Bryan	B-R	6-1	210	11-8-87	3	3	2.95	74	0	0	2	64	59	24	21	8	19	54	.242	.226	.252	7.59	2.67
Soto, Giovanni	L-L	6-2	190	5-18-91	0	0	0.00	6	0	0	0	3	3	0	0	0	2	3	.231	.222	.250	0.00	0.00
Swarzak, Anthony	R-R	6-4	215	9-10-85	0	0	3.38	10	0	0	0	13	18	9	5	1	4	13	.316	.250	.351	8.78	2.70
Tomlin, Josh	R-R	6-1	190	10-19-84	7	2	3.02	10	10	2	0	66	47	22	22	13	8	57	.195	.156	.235	7.81	1.10
Webb, Ryan	R-R	6-6	245	2-5-86	1	0	3.20	40	0	0	0	51	46	21	18	4	12	31	.245	.224	.262	5.51	2.13

Fielding

Catcher	PCT	G	PO	A	E	DP	PB
Gomes	.996	91	746	58	3	8	6
Hayes	.987	14	74	4	1	0	0
Moore	1.000	1	4	0	0	0	0
Perez	.993	69	568	42	4	2	4

First Base	PCT	G	PO	A	E	DP
Aguilar	1.000	4	26	3	0	1
Johnson	1.000	10	74	3	0	10
Moss	1.000	10	62	9	0	4
Sands	1.000	11	78	4	0	2
Santana	.997	132	1061	77	3	110

Second Base	PCT	G	PO	A	E	DP
Aviles	.980	11	11	39	1	8
Kipnis	.987	124	203	311	7	69
Ramirez	.985	33	34	94	2	17

	PCT	G	PO	A	E	DP
Walters	1.000	2	1	3	0	1

Third Base	PCT	G	PO	A	E	DP
Aviles	.912	28	17	35	5	3
Chisenhall	.963	50	30	101	5	12
Johnson	1.000	4	0	6	0	0
Martinez	1.000	1	0	1	0	0
Ramirez	.969	13	8	23	1	3
Urshela	.969	80	41	145	6	17
Walters	.500	2	1	1	2	0

Shortstop	PCT	G	PO	A	E	DP
Aviles	.959	23	19	52	3	10
Lindor	.974	98	132	247	10	60
Ramirez	.948	46	46	99	8	20
Walters	1.000	2	1	2	0	0

Outfield	PCT	G	PO	A	E	DP
Almonte	1.000	50	123	2	0	1
Aviles	.982	39	54	1	1	0
Bourn	1.000	89	182	4	0	2
Brantley	.991	118	212	8	2	1
Chisenhall	.989	51	87	5	1	2
Holt	1.000	9	13	0	0	0
Martinez	1.000	12	21	0	0	0
Moss	.975	79	149	6	4	1
Murphy	1.000	37	39	0	0	0
Raburn	.978	35	43	1	1	0
Ramirez	1.000	2	3	0	0	0
Sands	1.000	37	46	1	0	0
Swisher	.000	1	0	0	1	0
Walters	1.000	4	3	0	0	0

COLUMBUS CLIPPERS
TRIPLE-A
INTERNATIONAL LEAGUE

Batting	B-T	HT	WT	DOB	AVG	vLH	vRH	G	AB	R	H	2B	3B	HR	RBI	BB	HBP	SH	SF	SO	SB	CS	SLG	OBP
Aguilar, Jesus	R-R	6-3	250	6-30-90	.267	.250	.271	131	510	57	136	29	1	19	93	47	6	0	7	115	0	0	.439	.332
Almonte, Abraham	B-R	5-9	210	6-27-89	.250	.000	.400	2	8	2	2	0	1	0	0	1	0	0	0	2	0	0	.500	.333
Chisenhall, Lonnie	L-R	6-2	190	10-4-88	.280	.217	.306	40	157	18	44	13	0	3	21	11	1	1	1	35	1	0	.420	.329
Choice, Michael	R-R	6-0	230	11-10-89	.204	.231	.195	14	54	5	11	5	0	1	7	5	3	0	0	21	1	0	.352	.306
Ciriaco, Audy	R-R	6-3	225	6-16-87	.236	.238	.235	77	263	33	62	14	2	6	37	22	1	2	7	58	2	1	.373	.290
Diaz, Yandy	R-R	6-2	185	8-8-91	.158	.333	.077	4	19	1	3	2	0	0	1	0	0	0	0	5	0	0	.263	.158
Gallas, Anthony	R-R	6-2	210	12-14-87	.202	.095	.227	30	109	9	22	3	1	5	12	3	0	1	0	33	0	0	.385	.223
Gomes, Yan	R-R	6-2	215	7-19-87	.333	.333	.333	4	12	2	4	0	0	0	1	1	0	1	0	3	0	0	.333	.400
Gonzalez, Erik	R-R	6-3	195	8-31-91	.223	.250	.218	65	238	32	53	6	3	3	23	15	3	5	0	47	8	2	.311	.277
Hayes, Brett	R-R	6-1	210	2-13-84	.189	.175	.194	51	164	11	31	7	0	2	17	6	1	4	1	42	0	1	.268	.221
Holt, Tyler	R-R	5-10	200	3-10-89	.302	.293	.304	101	368	63	111	17	4	0	28	50	2	8	2	62	25	5	.370	.386
Hood, Destin	R-R	6-2	210	4-3-90	.169	.083	.191	17	59	3	10	2	2	0	2	4	0	0	0	21	1	0	.271	.222
Lavisky, Alex	R-R	6-1	209	1-13-91	.116	.125	.111	15	43	5	5	0	0	2	4	3	1	1	0	5	0	0	.256	.191
Lindor, Francisco	B-R	5-11	190	11-14-93	.284	.339	.266	59	229	26	65	11	5	2	22	25	0	5	3	38	9	7	.402	.350
Martinez, Michael	B-R	5-9	175	9-16-82	.289	.221	.310	102	363	53	105	24	5	5	42	32	0	3	3	60	11	3	.424	.344
Moncrief, Carlos	L-R	6-0	220	11-3-88	.187	.216	.174	57	166	21	31	3	0	7	24	32	2	1	2	59	5	0	.331	.322
Moore, Adam	R-R	6-3	220	5-8-84	.282	.143	.319	92	330	30	93	20	0	6	44	23	0	1	1	101	0	0	.397	.328
Naquin, Tyler	L-R	6-2	190	4-24-91	.263	.213	.281	50	186	34	49	13	0	6	17	25	2	3	2	49	6	2	.430	.353
Ramirez, Jose	B-R	5-9	180	9-17-92	.293	.277	.299	44	174	29	51	13	2	1	12	17	0	3	1	9	15	4	.408	.354
Ramsey, James	L-R	6-0	200	12-19-89	.243	.245	.243	126	440	46	107	21	2	12	42	53	3	5	2	128	3	4	.382	.327
Rohlinger, Ryan	R-R	6-0	195	10-7-83	.183	.184	.182	67	208	25	38	4	0	4	15	27	6	7	2	28	0	1	.260	.292
Sands, Jerry	R-R	6-4	225	9-28-87	.287	.309	.280	66	223	41	64	12	1	14	46	45	4	0	4	40	1	2	.538	.409
Swisher, Nick	B-L	6-0	195	11-25-80	.375	.000	.444	8	32	6	12	2	0	1	5	5	0	0	0	8	0	0	.531	.459
Toole, Justin	R-R	6-0	180	9-10-86	.276	.333	.269	9	29	3	8	0	0	0	4	1	0	0	0	6	0	0	.276	.300
Urshela, Giovanny	R-R	6-0	215	10-11-91	.272	.235	.281	22	81	12	22	5	1	3	9	3	0	0	0	12	0	0	.469	.298
Walters, Zach	B-R	6-2	210	9-5-89	.249	.227	.256	91	341	39	85	21	3	10	48	30	2	1	5	79	3	0	.416	.310

Pitching	B-T	HT	WT	DOB	W	L	ERA	G	GS	CG	SV	IP	H	R	ER	HR	BB	SO	AVG	vLH	vRH	K/9	BB/9
Adams, Austin	R-R	5-11	200	8-19-86	2	2	4.50	13	0	0	4	12	13	6	6	1	7	17	.283	.300	.269	12.75	5.25
Anderson, Cody	R-R	6-4	235	9-14-90	1	1	2.33	3	3	0	0	19	17	6	5	0	5	18	.239	.172	.286	8.38	2.33
Armstrong, Shawn	R-R	6-2	225	9-11-90	1	2	2.36	46	0	0	16	50	37	15	13	0	26	80	.206	.179	.221	14.50	4.71
Chacin, Jhoulys	R-R	6-3	215	1-7-88	1	3	3.21	7	7	0	0	42	39	17	15	3	15	25	.245	.163	.282	5.36	3.21
Chen, Bruce	L-L	6-2	215	6-19-77	2	1	1.74	5	5	2	0	31	19	6	6	4	3	23	.178	.250	.157	6.68	0.87
Colon, Joseph	R-R	6-0	167	2-18-90	1	0	3.12	12	0	0	0	17	19	6	6	2	3	24	.275	.273	.278	12.46	1.56
Cooper, Jordan	R-R	6-2	190	5-10-89	4	3	4.18	15	15	0	0	75	90	37	35	7	33	31	.301	.294	.307	3.70	3.94
Crockett, Kyle	L-L	6-2	175	12-15-91	3	1	5.97	29	0	0	0	29	42	19	19	3	11	27	.339	.320	.351	8.48	3.45
Grube, Jarrett	R-R	6-4	220	11-5-81	9	0	2.26	15	13	0	1	80	69	22	20	10	19	68	.238	.222	.255	7.68	2.15
Haley, Trey	R-R	6-4	205	6-21-90	4	2	2.57	18	0	0	1	21	17	9	6	0	21	22	.230	.267	.205	9.43	9.00
House, T.J.	R-L	6-1	205	9-29-89	0	2	3.86	4	4	0	0	21	21	13	9	3	13	13	.273	.235	.283	5.57	5.57
Lee, C.C.	R-R	5-11	190	10-21-86	4	3	3.39	48	0	0	5	58	53	25	22	3	16	65	.248	.286	.220	10.03	2.47
Manship, Jeff	R-R	6-2	205	1-16-85	0	2	1.99	23	0	0	2	32	25	7	7	3	9	31	.219	.256	.197	8.81	2.56
Marcum, Shaun	R-R	6-0	195	12-14-81	7	4	3.26	16	14	0	0	88	.85	36	32	7	21	67	.255	.340	.183	6.83	2.14
Marmol, Carlos	R-R	6-1	215	10-14-82	3	1	2.03	28	0	0	13	31	19	7	7	1	27	48	.176	.138	.220	13.94	7.84
Maronde, Nick	B-L	6-3	210	9-5-89	0	8	4.76	28	11	0	0	85	102	51	45	9	33	79	.301	.287	.307	8.36	3.49
Merritt, Ryan	L-L	6-0	170	2-21-92	2	0	4.20	5	5	0	0	30	38	14	14	1	6	16	.309	.316	.306	4.80	1.80
Molleken, Dustin	R-R	6-4	230	8-21-84	5	3	3.25	40	3	0	1	53	45	21	19	4	27	52	.236	.200	.264	8.89	4.61
Murata, Toru	L-R	6-0	175	5-20-85	15	4	2.90	27	26	1	0	164	148	59	53	16	45	101	.242	.256	.230	5.53	2.46
Price, Bryan	R-R	6-4	215	11-13-86	0	0	0.00	4	0	0	0	5	1	0	0	0	3	3	.071	.000	.111	5.79	5.79
Roberts, Will	L-R	6-5	220	8-17-90	3	4	3.06	12	12	0	0	71	69	26	24	9	12	39	.258	.256	.260	4.97	1.53
Romero, Antonio	R-R	6-0	187	12-22-90	0	0	2.25	1	1	0	0	4	3	1	1	0	1	5	.200	.000	.500	11.25	2.25
Roth, Michael	L-L	6-1	210	2-15-90	9	9	4.85	31	19	2	0	124	142	71	67	20	43	75	.290	.281	.293	5.43	3.11
Salazar, Danny	R-R	6-0	195	1-11-90	1	0	0.00	1	1	0	0	6	4	0	0	0	0	7	.200	.167	.250	10.50	0.00
Soto, Giovanni	L-L	6-2	190	5-18-91	2	1	2.68	46	1	0	2	54	35	22	16	1	29	51	.187	.224	.162	8.55	4.86

Pitching	B-T	HT	WT	DOB	W	L	ERA	G	GS	CG	SV	IP	H	R	ER	HR	BB	SO	AVG	vLH	vRH	K/9	BB/9
Sturdevant, Tyler	R-R	6-0	185	12-20-85	1	1	3.16	26	0	0	3	31	24	11	11	5	10	30	.214	.263	.189	8.62	2.87
Swarzak, Anthony	R-R	6-4	215	9-10-85	0	1	3.60	6	0	0	0	5	6	2	2	0	1	5	.286	.333	.278	9.00	1.80
Tejeda, Enosil	R-R	6-0	175	6-21-89	1	0	1.13	5	0	0	0	8	5	1	1	0	1	8	.185	.167	.200	9.00	1.13
Tomlin, Josh	R-R	6-1	190	10-19-84	1	2	4.22	4	4	0	0	21	25	10	10	3	1	17	.298	.364	.225	7.17	0.42
Webb, Ryan	R-R	6-6	245	2-5-86	1	1	1.13	5	0	0	0	8	4	1	1	0	1	5	.148	.333	.056	5.63	1.13

Fielding

Catcher	PCT	G	PO	A	E	DP	PB
Gomes	1.000	3	10	3	0	0	0
Hayes	.992	48	365	23	3	3	3
Lavisky	.991	15	97	9	1	0	0
Moore	.997	85	598	50	2	5	5

First Base	PCT	G	PO	A	E	DP
Aguilar	.999	98	801	58	1	85
Ciriaco	.977	23	157	15	4	14
Moore	1.000	4	29	4	0	4
Sands	1.000	14	110	9	0	10
Walters	.965	11	79	3	3	8

Second Base	PCT	G	PO	A	E	DP
Ciriaco	.957	12	16	28	2	5
Martinez	.984	66	106	147	4	33
Ramirez	.979	28	60	79	3	20
Rohlinger	.993	35	70	79	1	24

	PCT	G	PO	A	E	DP
Toole	.966	8	9	19	1	6
Walters	1.000	5	7	16	0	5

Third Base	PCT	G	PO	A	E	DP
Chisenhall	.971	32	18	48	2	4
Ciriaco	.960	31	36	60	4	5
Diaz	1.000	4	4	8	0	0
Martinez	1.000	4	3	9	0	3
Ramirez	1.000	3	3	6	0	1
Rohlinger	1.000	33	23	57	0	7
Toole	1.000	2	0	3	0	2
Urshela	.943	17	11	39	3	4
Walters	.898	24	11	33	5	4

Shortstop	PCT	G	PO	A	E	DP
Gonzalez	.978	62	76	187	6	37
Lindor	.967	56	84	147	8	30
Martinez	.942	13	16	49	4	6

	PCT	G	PO	A	E	DP
Ramirez	.958	10	21	25	2	10
Walters	1.000	6	8	9	0	1

Outfield	PCT	G	PO	A	E	DP
Almonte	1.000	2	5	1	0	0
Chisenhall	1.000	4	9	1	0	0
Choice	.960	10	22	1	1	1
Gallas	1.000	23	45	3	0	0
Holt	.982	91	211	7	4	1
Hood	.946	15	32	3	2	0
Martinez	1.000	22	47	2	0	0
Moncrief	.978	52	81	7	2	1
Naquin	.992	47	115	3	1	1
Ramirez	1.000	2	6	0	0	0
Ramsey	.996	112	220	6	1	0
Sands	1.000	25	54	2	0	0
Swisher	.857	6	5	1	1	0
Walters	.988	37	77	7	1	0

AKRON RUBBERDUCKS

DOUBLE-A

EASTERN LEAGUE

Batting	B-T	HT	WT	DOB	AVG	vLH	vRH	G	AB	R	H	2B	3B	HR	RBI	BB	HBP	SH	SF	SO	SB	CS	SLG	OBP
Diaz, Yandy	R-R	6-2	185	8-8-91	.315	.349	.305	132	476	61	150	13	5	7	55	78	3	3	4	65	8	7	.408	.412
Gallas, Anthony	R-R	6-2	210	12-14-87	.266	.289	.258	88	335	37	89	24	2	12	43	28	6	1	2	80	2	1	.457	.332
Gonzalez, Erik	R-R	6-3	195	8-31-91	.280	.358	.258	72	311	38	87	18	4	6	46	11	1	1	3	56	10	5	.421	.304
Hankins, Todd	R-R	5-9	175	11-18-90	.261	.272	.257	109	445	56	116	20	5	6	36	31	4	4	2	105	21	12	.369	.313
Hood, Destin	R-R	6-2	210	4-3-90	.293	.385	.257	40	140	20	41	11	3	3	19	10	2	0	2	36	4	1	.479	.344
2-team total (42 Reading)					.290	—	—	82	307	39	89	24	4	10	56	17	2	1	3	78	5	2	.492	.328
Ison, Bobby	L-L	5-8	170	7-5-93	.000	.000	.000	1	3	0	0	0	0	0	0	0	0	1	0	0	0	0	.000	.000
Johnson, Chris	R-R	6-3	225	10-1-84	.143	.000	.167	2	7	1	1	0	0	0	0	0	0	0	0	2	0	0	.143	.143
Lavisky, Alex	R-R	6-1	209	1-13-91	.167	.208	.152	29	90	13	15	3	0	1	8	11	2	1	1	21	0	0	.233	.269
Linton, Ollie	L-L	5-8	160	4-7-86	.273	.429	.220	16	55	8	15	3	0	0	2	7	3	2	0	18	5	3	.327	.385
Lowery, Jake	L-R	6-0	200	7-21-90	.164	.189	.157	50	177	17	29	9	1	3	19	19	0	1	2	50	1	1	.277	.242
Lucas, Jeremy	R-R	6-2	215	1-10-91	.239	.193	.254	68	238	25	57	11	0	2	22	23	1	4	3	41	0	1	.311	.306
Medina, Yhoxian	R-R	5-10	165	5-11-90	.400	—	.400	4	10	2	4	1	0	0	1	2	0	0	1	0	0	0	.500	.462
Mendoza, Yonathan	B-R	5-11	167	2-10-94	.281	.158	.342	19	57	6	16	1	0	1	6	9	0	2	3	6	0	0	.351	.362
Moncrief, Carlos	L-R	6-0	220	11-3-88	.261	.270	.259	56	199	29	52	9	3	4	27	34	0	2	1	28	6	4	.397	.368
Myles, Bryson	R-R	5-11	230	9-18-89	.268	.183	.289	102	365	53	98	23	5	9	51	46	14	3	5	85	25	10	.433	.367
Naquin, Tyler	L-R	6-2	190	4-24-91	.348	.324	.356	34	141	16	49	12	1	1	10	15	3	0	1	24	7	1	.468	.419
Ortiz, Ryan	R-R	6-3	200	9-29-87	.167	1.000	.000	3	6	1	1	0	0	0	0	1	0	0	0	1	0	0	.167	.286
Rodriguez, Nellie	R-R	6-2	225	6-12-94	.118	.100	.123	25	93	7	11	2	0	4	14	9	1	0	2	37	0	0	.269	.200
Rodriguez, Ronny	R-R	6-0	170	4-17-92	.286	.286	.286	72	269	34	77	14	4	11	29	10	2	3	1	60	4	5	.491	.316
Rohlinger, Ryan	R-R	6-0	195	10-7-83	.194	.214	.189	22	67	6	13	3	0	1	5	17	1	0	1	9	0	1	.284	.360
Sever, Joe	R-R	6-0	205	8-12-90	.219	.360	.175	30	105	8	23	3	0	2	13	7	0	1	1	25	0	0	.305	.265
Smith, Jordan	L-R	6-4	235	7-5-90	.257	.229	.265	126	475	57	122	24	5	5	47	52	4	2	3	94	18	6	.360	.333
Stamets, Eric	R-R	6-0	190	9-25-91	.197	.227	.189	33	117	14	23	1	1	1	12	8	2	3	4	14	2	0	.248	.252
Swisher, Nick	B-L	6-0	195	11-25-80	.067	.000	.111	5	15	1	1	0	0	0	0	0	1	0	0	4	0	0	.067	.176
Toole, Justin	R-R	6-0	190	10-16-86	.236	.261	.227	58	178	22	42	7	1	0	23	10	0	1	2	31	1	1	.287	.274
Wolters, Tony	L-R	5-10	200	6-9-92	.209	.115	.242	65	239	23	50	7	2	2	17	21	7	2	2	63	3	2	.280	.290
Zimmer, Bradley	L-R	6-4	185	11-27-92	.219	.231	.216	49	187	24	41	9	1	6	24	18	8	0	1	54	12	2	.374	.313

Pitching	B-T	HT	WT	DOB	W	L	ERA	G	GS	CG	SV	IP	H	R	ER	HR	BB	SO	AVG	vLH	vRH	K/9	BB/9
Anderson, Cody	R-R	6-4	235	9-14-90	3	2	1.73	10	10	0	0	52	44	12	10	2	9	36	.233	.229	.235	6.23	1.56
Atchison, Scott	R-R	6-2	200	3-29-76	0	0	0.00	1	0	0	0	1	1	0	0	0	0	3	.250	.500	.000	27.00	0.00
Brewer, Charles	R-R	6-3	210	4-7-88	1	1	2.92	3	3	0	0	12	12	5	4	1	4	7	.261	.200	.333	5.11	2.92
Brown, D.J.	R-R	6-6	205	11-28-90	2	3	3.26	5	5	0	0	30	33	13	11	4	4	22	.289	.415	.219	6.53	1.19
Clevinger, Mike	R-R	6-4	220	12-21-90	9	8	2.73	27	26	0	0	158	127	53	48	8	40	145	.219	.225	.214	8.26	2.28
Colon, Joseph	R-R	6-0	167	2-18-90	2	0	3.16	21	1	0	0	31	28	11	11	1	11	23	.233	.213	.247	6.61	3.16
Cook, Clayton	R-R	6-3	175	7-23-90	0	0	3.38	2	0	0	0	3	5	2	1	0	2	0	.500	.500	.500	0.00	6.75
Cooper, Jordan	R-R	6-2	190	5-10-89	0	3	4.75	7	4	0	1	30	32	19	16	4	13	20	.276	.263	.288	5.93	3.86
Floyd, Gavin	R-R	6-4	245	1-27-83	0	1	16.88	1	1	0	0	3	5	5	5	2	1	3	.385	.556	.000	10.13	3.38
Haley, Trey	R-R	6-4	205	6-21-90	0	2	2.38	25	0	0	0	34	30	12	9	0	11	38	.238	.245	.234	10.06	2.91
Head, Louis	R-R	6-1	180	4-23-90	3	3	4.03	47	0	0	0	60	54	27	27	2	33	59	.244	.289	.210	8.80	4.92
Heller, Ben	R-R	6-3	205	8-5-91	0	0	1.50	5	0	0	0	6	5	1	1	0	1	15	.200	.154	.250	22.50	1.50
Johnson, Jeff	R-R	6-0	185	2-9-90	1	2	1.05	51	0	0	27	51	27	9	6	0	19	56	.156	.152	.160	9.82	3.33
Lee, Jacob	R-R	6-1	190	10-25-89	5	3	4.19	37	0	0	0	62	73	33	29	2	19	48	.294	.275	.309	6.93	2.74
Maronde, Nick	B-L	6-3	210	9-5-89	0	1	3.86	7	0	0	0	7	10	3	3	1	0	14	.323	.417	.263	18.00	0.00

Pitching

Pitching	B-T	HT	WT	DOB	W	L	ERA	G	GS	CG	SV	IP	H	R	ER	HR	BB	SO	AVG	vLH	vRH	K/9	BB/9
Martin, Josh	R-R	6-5	230	12-30-89	8	1	2.27	44	0	0	2	67	47	23	17	4	19	80	.192	.157	.212	10.69	2.54
Merritt, Ryan	L-L	6-0	170	2-21-92	10	7	3.51	22	22	2	0	141	145	63	55	8	16	89	.269	.236	.281	5.68	1.02
Morimando, Shawn	L-L	5-11	195	11-20-92	10	12	3.18	28	28	0	0	159	139	62	56	9	65	128	.240	.163	.265	7.26	3.69
Nuding, Zach	R-R	6-4	260	3-29-90	1	2	3.32	24	3	0	1	41	32	17	15	3	17	26	.219	.267	.169	5.75	3.76
Pasquale, Nick	R-R	6-0	190	10-27-90	0	0	0.00	1	0	0	0	0	0	0	0	0	0	2	.000	.000	.000	6.00	0.00
Plutko, Adam	R-R	6-3	195	10-3-91	9	5	2.86	19	19	1	0	116	96	39	37	9	23	90	.222	.261	.180	6.96	1.78
Roberts, Will	L-R	6-5	220	8-17-90	6	2	3.77	14	14	1	0	86	81	37	36	9	11	45	.252	.272	.237	4.71	1.15
Sides, Grant	R-R	6-4	215	6-22-89	0	3	3.91	15	0	0	1	25	21	11	11	1	20	18	.226	.229	.224	6.39	7.11
Suarez, Benny	R-R	6-1	190	9-28-91	0	1	14.54	3	0	0	0	4	6	7	7	0	5	6	.316	.400	.286	12.46	10.38
Tejeda, Enosil	R-R	6-0	175	6-21-89	1	1	1.27	31	0	0	2	35	24	6	5	0	15	29	.197	.229	.176	7.39	3.82
Tomlin, Josh	R-R	6-1	190	10-19-84	0	0	0.00	1	1	0	0	3	3	0	0	0	1	2	.300	.429	.000	6.75	3.38
von Schamann, Duke	R-R	6-5	220	6-3-91	1	3	7.92	5	5	0	0	25	36	22	22	8	9	19	.340	.361	.311	6.84	3.24
Weathers, Casey	R-R	6-1	205	6-10-85	0	3	3.63	22	0	0	0	22	22	11	9	1	11	22	.253	.302	.205	8.87	4.43

Fielding

Catcher	PCT	G	PO	A	E	DP	PB
Lavisky	.988	28	216	21	3	2	1
Lowery	.994	25	153	21	1	2	1
Lucas	.996	34	243	21	1	1	2
Ortiz	1.000	3	19	3	0	0	0
Wolters	.994	56	431	56	3	4	3

First Base	PCT	G	PO	A	E	DP
Johnson	1.000	1	6	0	0	0
Lowery	.984	23	177	6	3	13
Lucas	.988	29	237	17	3	23
Rodriguez	.982	22	157	11	3	14
Rodriguez	.984	34	282	17	5	20
Sever	.989	22	174	9	2	11
Toole	1.000	16	93	10	0	15

Second Base	PCT	G	PO	A	E	DP
Hankins	.984	86	159	217	6	50

	PCT	G	PO	A	E	DP
Medina	1.000	3	3	5	0	1
Mendoza	.966	10	16	12	1	4
Rodriguez	.972	25	36	68	3	20
Sever	1.000	5	4	4	0	0
Toole	.987	20	34	42	1	6

Third Base	PCT	G	PO	A	E	DP
Diaz	.927	122	94	174	21	17
Mendoza	.857	3	2	4	1	0
Sever	1.000	3	2	5	0	1
Toole	.980	19	14	34	1	2

Shortstop	PCT	G	PO	A	E	DP
Gonzalez	.945	71	101	193	17	46
Hankins	.846	8	8	14	4	1
Mendoza	1.000	1	0	2	0	0
Rodriguez	1.000	5	7	18	0	2
Rohlinger	1.000	22	25	39	0	7

	PCT	G	PO	A	E	DP
Stamets	1.000	33	53	88	0	14
Toole	1.000	1	2	5	0	1
Wolters	.941	3	4	12	1	2

Outfield	PCT	G	PO	A	E	DP
Gallas	.990	49	98	2	1	1
Hankins	1.000	16	33	2	0	0
Hood	1.000	30	73	2	0	0
Ison	1.000	1	2	0	0	0
Linton	1.000	15	31	2	0	0
Moncrief	.979	43	91	3	2	0
Myles	.988	83	165	3	2	1
Naquin	.989	33	88	4	1	0
Smith	.997	122	319	6	1	2
Swisher	1.000	3	5	0	0	0
Zimmer	.991	42	105	4	1	0

LYNCHBURG HILLCATS

HIGH CLASS A

CAROLINA LEAGUE

Batting	B-T	HT	WT	DOB	AVG	vLH	vRH	G	AB	R	H	2B	3B	HR	RBI	BB	HBP	SH	SF	SO	SB	CS	SLG	OBP
Allen, Greg	B-R	6-0	175	3-15-93	.154	.167	.143	3	13	2	2	1	0	0	0	2	1	0	0	3	3	0	.231	.313
Bautista, Claudio	R-R	5-11	170	11-29-93	.197	.108	.220	52	178	24	35	10	0	2	12	16	0	—	2	51	3	2	.287	.260
Bradley, Bobby	L-R	6-1	225	5-29-96	.000	.000	.000	2	8	0	0	0	0	0	0	1	0	0	0	2	0	0	.000	.111
Castillo, Ivan	B-R	5-11	150	5-30-95	.249	.266	.241	120	418	53	104	17	12	0	36	27	8	—	3	69	20	4	.347	.305
De La Cruz, Juan	B-R	6-1	195	8-5-93	.100	.200	.067	9	20	0	2	0	0	0	1	0	0	0	3	0	0	.100	.143
Frazier, Clint	R-R	6-1	190	9-6-94	.285	.301	.279	133	501	88	143	36	3	16	72	68	9	5	5	125	15	7	.465	.377
Haase, Eric	R-R	5-10	180	12-18-92	.247	.240	.250	90	320	46	79	26	7	9	55	36	11	1	2	114	3	2	.456	.341
Hendrix, Paul	R-R	6-2	190	11-18-91	.247	.244	.248	121	442	46	109	23	2	6	40	43	7	0	3	122	4	3	.348	.321
Ison, Bobby	L-L	5-8	170	7-5-93	.240	.375	.176	14	50	3	12	2	1	0	4	1	0	2	5	1	1	.320	.250
Loopstok, Sicnarf	R-R	5-11	195	4-26-93	.218	.294	.200	28	87	8	19	7	0	4	12	8	3	—	4	26	2	0	.437	.294
Medina, Yhoxian	R-R	5-10	165	5-11-90	.308	.353	.288	57	214	29	66	11	0	0	27	21	3	—	1	29	9	4	.360	.377
Mendoza, Yonathan	B-R	5-11	167	2-10-94	.167	.333	.000	3	6	0	1	0	0	0	0	0	1	0	0	0	0	0	.167	.286
Monsalve, Alex	R-R	6-2	225	4-22-92	.250	.192	.273	26	92	14	23	7	0	1	15	9	2	0	1	14	0	0	.359	.327
Papi, Mike	L-R	6-2	190	9-19-92	.236	.212	.244	127	416	53	98	34	2	4	45	81	3	—	3	118	6	7	.356	.362
Paulino, Dorssys	R-R	6-0	175	11-21-94	.305	.364	.282	43	154	27	47	10	6	4	30	17	1	2	3	30	5	2	.526	.371
Roberts, James	R-R	6-2	180	12-11-91	.228	.283	.204	43	149	14	34	11	0	0	15	6	1	2	2	24	6	0	.302	.259
Rodriguez, Luigi	B-R	5-11	160	11-13-92	.293	.317	.284	92	372	59	109	22	8	12	49	24	0	—	1	82	24	8	.492	.335
Rodriguez, Nellie	R-R	6-2	225	6-12-94	.275	.298	.268	108	396	65	109	32	2	17	84	51	4	—	8	122	1	0	.495	.357
Salters, Daniel	L-R	6-3	210	2-5-93	.250	.250	—	1	4	1	1	0	0	0	0	0	0	0	0	1	0	0	.250	.250
Sever, Joe	R-R	6-0	205	8-12-90	.264	.308	.240	82	296	41	78	17	2	10	41	17	5	0	2	59	1	0	.436	.313
Washington, LeVon	L-R	5-11	170	7-26-91	.244	.222	.252	48	193	24	47	12	4	3	32	15	3	—	2	40	4	1	.394	.305
Zimmer, Bradley	L-R	6-4	185	11-27-92	.308	.315	.305	78	286	60	88	17	3	10	39	37	10	—	2	77	32	5	.493	.403

Pitching	B-T	HT	WT	DOB	W	L	ERA	G	GS	CG	SV	IP	H	R	ER	HR	BB	SO	AVG	vLH	vRH	K/9	BB/9
Aquino, Jayson	L-L	6-1	180	11-22-92	1	3	2.45	6	6	0	0	33	31	9	9	5	5	20	.250	.355	.215	5.45	1.36
Aviles, Robbie	L-R	6-4	200	12-17-91	7	1	3.49	44	0	0	3	59	66	33	23	2	25	24	.291	.311	.277	3.64	3.79
Baker, Dylan	R-R	6-2	215	4-6-92	1	0	0.00	1	1	0	0	5	0	0	0	0	1	9	.000	.000	.000	16.20	1.80
Brantley, Justin	R-R	5-11	160	3-5-91	5	6	2.84	39	0	0	2	70	53	23	22	2	20	65	.209	.196	.218	8.40	2.58
Brown, D.J.	R-R	6-6	205	11-28-90	11	3	3.95	22	15	0	0	112	120	52	49	8	19	69	.276	.279	.275	5.56	1.53
Brown, Mitch	R-R	6-1	195	4-13-94	9	12	5.15	27	26	0	0	142	147	94	81	15	77	109	.275	.263	.282	6.92	4.89
Cook, Clayton	R-R	6-3	175	7-23-90	3	2	5.25	16	3	0	0	36	35	27	21	2	21	24	.254	.315	.214	6.00	5.25
2-team total (7 Carolina)					4	2	5.11	23	3	0	0	44	43	31	25	2	32	31	—	—	—	6.34	6.55
Feyereisen, J.P.	R-R	6-2	215	2-7-93	0	1	2.61	30	0	0	2	31	23	9	9	1	10	31	.204	.333	.135	9.00	2.90
Francisco, Delvy	R-R	6-1	190	8-24-92	0	0	6.25	27	0	0	1	36	40	28	25	4	25	30	.292	.346	.259	7.50	6.25
Frank, Trevor	R-R	6-0	195	6-23-91	0	1	1.59	17	0	0	1	17	18	3	3	0	5	17	.261	.190	.292	9.00	2.65
Garner, Perci	R-R	6-3	225	12-13-88	3	1	2.93	18	1	0	1	31	27	12	10	3	12	33	.239	.175	.274	9.68	3.52
Heller, Ben	R-R	6-3	205	8-5-91	0	2	4.46	36	0	0	12	34	30	18	17	0	13	43	.229	.286	.195	11.27	3.41
Kaminsky, Rob	R-L	5-11	190	9-2-94	0	1	3.72	2	2	0	0	10	13	6	4	0	5	4	.342	.444	.310	3.72	4.66

Pitching

Pitching	B-T	HT	WT	DOB	W	L	ERA	G	GS	CG	SV	IP	H	R	ER	HR	BB	SO	AVG	vLH	vRH	K/9	BB/9
Kime, Dace	R-R	6-4	200	3-6-92	3	8	4.42	22	22	0	0	112	121	59	55	1	43	83	.282	.310	.263	6.67	3.46
Lugo, Luis	L-L	6-5	200	3-5-94	8	10	4.15	25	25	0	0	126	129	83	58	11	52	119	.266	.262	.268	8.52	3.72
Pasquale, Nick	R-R	6-0	190	10-27-90	0	1	8.00	5	0	0	0	9	10	8	8	1	6	5	.294	.154	.381	5.00	6.00
Peoples, Scott	R-R	6-5	190	9-5-91	11	4	3.42	25	23	0	0	140	133	65	53	9	53	89	.254	.269	.243	5.74	3.42
Plutko, Adam	R-R	6-3	195	10-3-91	4	2	1.27	8	8	1	0	50	30	7	7	3	5	47	.173	.229	.122	8.52	0.91
Radeke, Mason	R-R	6-1	175	6-13-90	0	0	0.00	3	0	0	1	4	1	0	0	1	1	1	.083	.000	.111	2.25	2.25
Rayl, Mike	L-L	6-5	180	11-1-88	0	2	8.36	5	5	0	0	14	23	14	13	0	5	7	.377	.348	.395	4.50	3.21
Romero, Antonio	R-R	6-0	187	12-22-90	1	1	2.47	27	3	0	2	62	49	18	17	1	23	56	.222	.250	.204	8.13	3.34
Sides, Grant	R-R	6-4	215	6-22-89	1	1	2.59	19	0	0	7	24	19	8	7	1	9	30	.213	.229	.204	11.10	3.33
Speer, David	L-L	6-1	185	8-14-92	1	0	0.00	5	0	0	0	5	5	0	0	0	2	5	.263	.500	.200	8.44	3.38
Suarez, Benny	R-R	6-1	190	9-28-91	1	1	1.80	7	0	0	0	10	8	3	2	0	7	2	.229	.200	.250	1.80	6.30
Weathers, Casey	R-R	6-1	205	6-10-85	2	1	2.67	25	0	0	4	27	23	10	8	2	15	33	.230	.317	.169	11.00	5.00

Fielding

Catcher	PCT	G	PO	A	E	DP	PB
De La Cruz	1.000	7	40	7	0	0	1
Haase	.989	88	562	88	7	7	16
Loopstok	.985	25	167	30	3	2	9
Monsalve	.982	22	142	25	3	1	3
Salters	1.000	1	9	4	0	0	0

First Base	PCT	G	PO	A	E	DP
Bradley	1.000	1	9	3	0	1
Loopstok	1.000	1	1	0	0	1
Papi	.985	6	62	4	1	4
Rodriguez	.988	105	887	52	11	94
Sever	.996	30	265	17	1	29

Second Base	PCT	G	PO	A	E	DP
Bautista	.988	51	108	132	3	40

	PCT	G	PO	A	E	DP
Castillo	—	1	0	0	0	0
Hendrix	1.000	1	3	6	0	1
Medina	.981	19	42	60	2	15
Mendoza	1.000	1	1	3	0	0
Roberts	.944	42	80	122	12	34
Sever	.970	28	50	79	4	13

Third Base	PCT	G	PO	A	E	DP
Hendrix	.936	112	77	203	19	19
Medina	1.000	18	11	25	0	3
Mendoza	1.000	1	0	1	0	0
Sever	.939	16	6	25	2	3

Shortstop	PCT	G	PO	A	E	DP
Castillo	.941	119	197	364	35	80
Hendrix	.970	7	6	26	1	7

	PCT	G	PO	A	E	DP
Medina	.957	15	18	49	3	15
Outfield	PCT	G	PO	A	E	DP
Allen	1.000	4	4	0	0	0
Frazier	.978	128	267	3	6	0
Ison	.947	14	18	0	1	0
Loopstok	1.000	1	1	1	0	0
Medina	1.000	2	4	0	0	0
Papi	.955	118	175	15	9	3
Paulino	.951	36	56	2	3	1
Rodriguez	.955	39	83	1	4	1
Washington	1.000	19	29	0	0	0
Zimmer	.982	63	159	4	3	0

LAKE COUNTY CAPTAINS   LOW CLASS A

MIDWEST LEAGUE

Batting

Batting	B-T	HT	WT	DOB	AVG	vLH	vRH	G	AB	R	H	2B	3B	HR	RBI	BB	HBP	SH	SF	SO	SB	CS	SLG	OBP
Allen, Greg	B-R	6-0	175	3-15-93	.273	.248	.280	123	479	83	131	27	2	7	45	53	20	10	2	57	43	16	.382	.368
Armendariz, David	B-R	6-0	190	8-22-91	.204	.246	.189	67	216	24	44	11	0	1	12	18	4	3	1	52	5	4	.269	.276
Bautista, Claudio	R-R	5-11	170	11-29-93	.300	.304	.300	64	253	39	76	19	1	7	39	20	0	2	2	49	5	4	.466	.349
Bradley, Bobby	L-R	6-1	225	5-29-96	.269	.261	.272	108	401	62	108	15	4	27	92	56	4	0	4	148	3	0	.529	.361
Cervenka, Martin	R-R	6-1	175	8-3-92	.184	.200	.180	49	174	12	32	8	0	1	15	12	0	4	3	39	0	0	.247	.233
Chang, Yu-Cheng	R-R	6-1	175	8-18-95	.232	.261	.223	105	393	52	91	16	4	9	52	47	2	9	7	4	103	5	6	.361	.293
Fink, Grant	R-R	6-3	215	12-14-90	.198	.182	.201	62	182	20	36	7	1	2	19	26	1	1	3	71	3	0	.280	.297
Fisher, Austin	L-R	6-1	195	1-8-93	.250	1.000	.000	2	4	0	1	0	0	0	0	0	0	0	0	1	0	0	.250	.250
Gomes, Yan	R-R	6-2	215	7-19-87	.500	.000	.667	2	4	1	2	0	0	0	1	0	0	0	0	0	0	0	.500	.600
Ison, Bobby	L-L	5-8	170	7-5-93	.251	.250	.252	94	342	38	86	10	3	1	32	28	1	9	3	46	9	6	.307	.307
Loopstok, Sicnarf	R-R	5-11	195	4-26-93	.186	.200	.184	14	43	5	8	1	0	1	6	4	1	0	0	13	1	0	.279	.271
Mejia, Francisco	B-R	5-10	175	10-27-95	.243	.298	.228	109	391	45	95	13	0	9	53	38	10	5	2	78	4	1	.345	.324
Mendoza, Yonathan	R-R	5-11	167	2-10-94	.286	.326	.275	60	213	31	61	13	0	1	23	24	2	7	3	22	5	1	.362	.360
Murphy, Taylor	L-R	6-2	200	11-3-92	.258	.287	.250	115	407	76	105	21	0	8	51	66	4	4	4	98	3	4	.369	.364
Patterson, Steven	L-R	5-9	205	8-3-92	.191	.313	.166	51	183	17	35	8	1	2	17	16	1	1	2	33	2	0	.279	.257
Paulino, Dorssys	R-R	6-0	175	11-21-94	.256	.328	.237	83	313	38	80	12	2	6	39	22	8	3	2	61	11	5	.364	.319
Santander, Anthony	B-R	6-2	190	10-19-94	.278	.296	.273	64	248	46	69	16	0	10	42	18	6	0	4	53	4	2	.464	.337
Sayles, Silento	R-R	5-9	185	8-28-95	.283	.308	.275	16	53	6	15	5	0	0	6	4	2	3	2	14	0	1	.377	.344
Swisher, Nick	B-L	6-0	195	11-25-80	.429	.333	.500	5	14	5	6	2	0	0	1	5	1	0	0	2	0	0	.571	.600
Valdez, Ordomar	B-R	5-9	150	4-27-94	.249	.163	.268	79	233	29	58	10	1	1	22	23	0	9	2	41	24	6	.313	.314

Pitching

Pitching	B-T	HT	WT	DOB	W	L	ERA	G	GS	CG	SV	IP	H	R	ER	HR	BB	SO	AVG	vLH	vRH	K/9	BB/9
Brady, Sean	L-L	6-0	175	6-9-94	7	12	3.81	26	26	1	0	146	151	76	62	15	29	118	.264	.233	.273	7.26	1.78
Carter, Jordan	R-R	6-4	195	9-29-91	2	3	5.85	22	0	0	0	48	67	34	31	4	14	27	.338	.269	.374	5.10	2.64
Cox, Cortland	R-R	6-1	185	11-3-94	2	0	3.00	3	0	0	0	6	3	2	2	1	0	6	.150	.250	.125	9.00	0.00
DeMasi, Dominic	R-R	6-3	190	5-18-93	1	0	4.80	8	0	0	1	15	13	10	8	1	8	12	.217	.200	.225	7.20	4.80
Eubank, Luke	R-R	6-0	180	2-24-94	2	3	2.70	41	0	0	5	50	39	18	15	3	11	52	.217	.200	.225	9.36	1.98
Feyereisen, J.P.	R-R	6-2	215	2-7-93	1	0	1.08	16	0	0	10	17	7	2	2	1	6	25	.127	.000	.167	13.50	3.24
Francisco, Delvy	R-R	6-1	190	8-24-92	0	0	4.50	11	0	0	0	14	13	8	7	2	6	16	.250	.143	.323	10.29	3.86
Garcia, Justin	R-R	6-1	180	9-16-92	3	0	1.89	32	0	0	0	52	40	12	11	4	15	40	.207	.212	.205	6.88	2.58
Hamrick, Caleb	R-R	6-2	210	9-25-93	4	2	3.59	29	0	0	3	43	38	20	17	4	17	46	.238	.321	.192	9.70	3.54
Hill, Cameron	R-R	6-1	185	5-24-94	5	4	1.53	42	0	0	10	59	36	14	10	1	20	70	.173	.235	.143	10.68	3.05
House, T.J.	R-L	6-1	205	9-29-89	0	0	0.00	1	1	0	0	3	1	0	0	0	0	5	.100	.000	.143	15.00	0.00
Kime, Dace	R-R	6-4	200	3-6-92	2	3	3.34	6	6	0	0	35	33	19	13	3	6	32	.252	.319	.214	8.23	1.54
Merryweather, Julian	R-R	6-4	200	10-14-91	2	3	4.08	21	4	0	1	71	89	40	32	6	14	69	.299	.318	.288	8.79	1.53
Milbrath, Jordan	R-R	6-6	215	8-1-91	7	11	4.54	27	26	0	0	141	167	79	71	15	46	130	.293	.326	.268	8.32	2.94
Pannone, Thomas	L-L	6-0	195	4-28-94	7	6	4.02	27	20	0	0	116	98	58	52	12	37	120	.231	.223	.234	9.28	2.86
Pasquale, Nick	R-R	6-0	190	10-27-90	4	2	3.10	40	0	0	2	61	68	21	21	1	20	49	.288	.289	.288	7.23	2.95
Polanco, Anderson	L-L	6-4	190	5-18-93	8	8	4.14	26	26	0	0	126	123	67	58	7	58	119	.256	.237	.264	8.50	4.14
Shane, Casey	R-R	6-4	200	8-23-95	0	0	4.35	2	2	0	0	10	11	5	5	1	3	9	.275	.250	.300	7.84	2.61
Sheffield, Justus	L-L	5-10	196	5-13-96	9	4	3.31	26	26	0	0	128	135	60	47	8	38	138	.264	.264	.264	9.73	2.68
Speer, David	L-L	6-1	185	8-14-92	5	5	1.73	38	0	0	2	62	66	26	12	4	14	59	.276	.243	.291	8.52	2.02

Fielding

Catcher	PCT	G	PO	A	E	DP	PB
Cervenka	.985	41	342	42	6	2	7
Gomes	1.000	1	5	0	0	0	0
Loopstok	1.000	2	11	1	0	0	0
Mejia	.984	94	765	93	14	9	16

First Base	PCT	G	PO	A	E	DP
Bradley	.982	101	832	75	17	91
Fink	.989	35	254	17	3	27
Loopstok	1.000	5	40	3	0	4
Mendoza	.952	2	20	0	1	1

Second Base	PCT	G	PO	A	E	DP
Bautista	.984	64	114	137	4	42
Mendoza	.939	8	10	21	2	3
Patterson	.951	36	78	98	9	26
Valdez	.956	35	63	89	7	26

Third Base	PCT	G	PO	A	E	DP
Fink	.959	20	19	52	3	6
Mendoza	1.000	10	3	13	0	1
Murphy	.865	97	57	148	32	10
Patterson	.923	5	6	6	1	0
Valdez	.750	11	2	13	5	0

Shortstop	PCT	G	PO	A	E	DP
Chang	.948	99	139	314	25	71
Fisher	.857	1	1	5	1	1
Mendoza	.920	26	32	72	9	19
Paulino	1.000	1	1	3	0	1
Valdez	.913	12	12	30	4	7

Outfield	PCT	G	PO	A	E	DP
Allen	.986	122	274	9	4	1
Armendariz	.985	44	62	3	1	2
Fink	—	1	0	0	0	0
Ison	.983	92	163	11	3	6
Paulino	.991	80	105	4	1	1
Santander	.975	55	75	4	2	3
Sayles	.974	16	37	0	1	0
Swisher	1.000	3	3	0	0	0
Valdez	1.000	4	1	0	0	0

MAHONING VALLEY SCRAPPERS — SHORT-SEASON

NEW YORK-PENN LEAGUE

Batting	B-T	HT	WT	DOB	AVG	vLH	vRH	G	AB	R	H	2B	3B	HR	RBI	BB	HBP	SH	SF	SO	SB	CS	SLG	OBP
Armendariz, David	R-R	6-0	190	8-22-91	.175	.158	.190	11	40	5	7	2	0	3	5	2	0	1	0	9	0	0	.450	.214
Bautista, Gerald	R-R	6-0	190	7-20-94	.250	.500	.167	3	8	3	2	1	0	0	1	2	0	0	0	3	0	0	.375	.400
Carter, Jodd	R-R	5-10	170	7-20-96	.233	.282	.217	41	159	15	37	8	1	3	17	2	3	1	1	20	2	1	.352	.255
Castro, Willi	R-R	6-1	165	4-24-97	.264	.263	.264	67	273	34	72	9	3	1	25	10	7	8	3	31	20	7	.330	.304
Chu, Li-Jen	R-R	5-11	200	3-13-94	.200	.219	.190	25	95	14	19	4	2	2	17	6	2	0	1	20	1	0	.347	.260
De La Cruz, Juan	B-R	6-1	195	8-5-93	.302	.429	.261	30	116	9	35	7	1	1	9	8	0	0	0	33	0	1	.405	.347
Fisher, Austin	L-R	6-1	195	1-8-93	.251	.300	.241	50	167	23	42	8	1	0	16	17	3	2	2	48	1	1	.311	.328
Goihl, Jack	R-R	6-2	215	3-2-93	.145	.105	.167	17	55	4	8	4	0	0	3	1	0	2	1	17	0	0	.218	.158
Haggerty, Sam	B-R	5-11	175	5-26-94	.283	.313	.270	16	53	8	15	4	1	1	7	7	0	2	1	14	3	0	.453	.361
Loopstok, Sicnarf	R-R	5-11	195	4-26-93	.214	.000	.333	5	14	4	3	1	0	0	1	3	0	0	0	5	0	0	.286	.353
Lukes, Nathan	L-R	5-11	185	7-12-94	.313	.125	.500	5	16	4	5	2	0	0	5	2	0	0	0	4	0	0	.438	.389
Marabell, Connor	L-R	6-1	195	3-28-94	.222	.267	.211	61	230	19	51	5	3	1	18	6	2	7	1	17	0	2	.283	.247
Mathias, Mark	R-R	6-0	200	8-2-94	.282	.319	.267	67	245	38	69	19	3	2	32	35	8	1	5	36	5	4	.408	.382
McClure, D'vone	R-R	6-3	190	1-22-94	.231	.400	.125	8	26	5	6	3	0	0	3	4	0	0	0	8	0	0	.346	.333
Mejia, Gabriel	B-R	5-11	160	7-30-95	.304	.286	.310	16	56	9	17	1	0	0	4	1	0	0	0	8	6	1	.321	.316
Pantoja, Alexis	B-R	5-11	150	1-18-96	.195	.438	.136	25	82	8	16	2	0	0	5	1	1	4	0	15	1	2	.220	.214
Salters, Daniel	L-R	6-3	210	2-5-93	.279	.342	.262	47	179	14	50	8	0	2	26	12	2	0	1	36	0	1	.358	.330
Santander, Anthony	B-R	6-2	190	10-19-94	.419	.500	.381	8	31	6	13	6	0	3	9	4	0	0	0	8	0	0	.903	.486
Sayles, Silento	R-R	5-9	185	8-28-95	.242	.353	.202	38	128	17	31	2	1	1	18	11	3	1	2	31	6	3	.297	.313
Tapia, Emmanuel	L-L	6-3	215	2-26-96	.286	.238	.310	33	126	20	36	10	0	2	17	12	1	0	1	31	0	0	.413	.350
Tom, Ka'ai	L-R	5-9	185	5-24-94	.283	.292	.280	66	258	38	73	18	2	3	29	33	5	2	1	46	14	5	.403	.374
Winfrey, Nate	R-R	6-2	205	9-29-94	.270	.286	.264	58	196	22	53	9	1	1	20	22	6	1	2	55	0	0	.342	.358

Pitching	B-T	HT	WT	DOB	W	L	ERA	G	GS	CG	SV	IP	H	R	ER	HR	BB	SO	AVG	vLH	vRH	K/9	BB/9
Algarin, Erick	R-R	6-1	195	3-31-95	0	0	3.86	6	0	0	0	9	6	4	4	0	4	9	.200	.176	.231	8.68	3.86
Carter, Jordan	R-R	6-4	190	9-29-91	1	2	5.56	11	0	0	0	23	27	17	14	1	4	15	.293	.311	.277	5.96	1.59
Chen, Ping-Hsueh	R-R	6-2	195	7-8-94	0	0	20.25	2	0	0	0	1	3	3	3	0	4	2	.375	.250	.500	13.50	27.00
Chiang, Shao-Ching	R-R	6-0	175	11-10-93	3	2	3.92	9	8	0	0	41	39	24	18	3	7	18	.241	.235	.245	3.92	1.52
Cox, Cortland	R-R	6-1	185	11-3-94	3	1	1.59	10	0	0	0	23	13	5	4	0	8	27	.167	.184	.150	10.72	3.18
DeMasi, Dominic	R-R	6-3	190	5-18-93	2	0	3.12	13	1	0	1	35	28	13	12	0	10	19	.215	.190	.236	4.93	2.60
Esparza, Matt	R-R	6-2	185	8-22-94	4	1	2.30	16	3	0	0	43	40	13	11	1	13	54	.242	.260	.227	11.30	2.72
Hagadone, Nick	L-L	6-5	230	1-1-86	0	0	0.00	1	0	0	0	0	0	0	0	0	0	0	.000	.000	—	0.00	0.00
Hartson, Brock	R-R	6-2	195	8-9-93	4	1	1.66	14	3	0	0	38	27	12	7	1	15	29	.197	.200	.194	6.87	3.55
Hentges, Sam	L-L	6-6	245	7-18-96	0	2	14.21	2	2	0	0	6	13	11	10	0	8	2	.433	.333	.500	2.84	11.37
Linares, Leandro	R-R	6-3	205	1-27-94	0	7	6.55	13	12	0	0	44	40	36	32	3	44	31	.248	.243	.253	6.34	9.00
Lovegrove, Kieran	R-R	6-4	185	7-28-94	1	8	6.08	14	14	0	0	61	66	50	41	3	31	37	.287	.304	.271	5.49	4.60
Marquina, Yoiber	R-R	5-10	190	2-3-96	2	2	2.28	23	0	0	5	24	18	12	6	2	12	23	.200	.239	.159	8.75	4.56
Martinez, Henry	R-R	6-1	175	4-21-94	0	0	1.00	4	0	0	0	9	12	1	1	0	1	5	.353	.476	.154	5.00	1.00
Meister, Christian	R-R	6-3	210	10-29-93	0	0	5.87	2	1	0	0	8	6	6	5	0	5	4	.231	.231	.231	4.70	5.87
Melo, Carlos	R-R	6-3	180	2-27-91	0	0	9.00	2	0	0	0	2	4	2	2	0	5	3	.444	.500	.429	13.50	22.50
Miniard, Micah	R-R	6-7	195	4-12-96	0	1	14.29	2	0	0	0	6	11	9	9	1	3	1	.407	.538	.286	1.59	4.76
Perez, Ryan	B-L	6-0	190	10-27-93	0	1	6.48	22	0	0	0	25	30	19	18	4	22	22	.303	.250	.345	7.92	7.92
Puello, Johan	R-R	5-11	165	1-5-94	1	1	6.00	7	0	0	0	12	14	9	8	0	12	6	.304	.333	.280	4.50	9.00
Robinson, Jared	R-R	6-0	190	11-26-94	2	4	3.25	14	14	0	0	75	76	32	27	4	23	42	.262	.267	.257	5.06	2.77
Shane, Casey	R-R	6-4	200	8-23-95	2	4	3.45	12	12	0	0	60	56	29	23	2	15	41	.248	.269	.236	6.15	2.25
Stewart, Devon	R-R	6-2	205	12-26-92	0	2	3.68	18	0	0	2	22	19	11	9	1	7	19	.232	.229	.234	7.77	2.86
Stokes, Jim	R-R	6-6	225	10-9-90	1	1	2.87	16	0	0	0	31	35	13	10	0	19	23	.289	.340	.250	6.61	5.46
Strode, Billy	L-L	6-1	185	8-10-92	1	0	1.71	20	0	0	0	26	20	5	5	1	6	25	.204	.205	.203	8.54	2.05
Tomlin, Josh	R-R	6-1	190	10-19-84	0	1	7.36	1	1	0	0	4	3	3	3	0	2	3	.250	.429	.000	7.36	4.91
Zapata, Jose	R-R	6-4	200	5-21-93	3	3	4.50	16	2	0	2	26	22	14	13	1	18	28	.224	.116	.309	9.69	6.23

Fielding

Catcher	PCT	G	PO	A	E	DP	PB
Chu	.984	17	113	9	2	0	1
De La Cruz	.982	7	50	5	1	0	1
Fisher	1.000	1	1	1	0	1	0
Goihl	.990	14	93	10	1	0	5
Loopstok	1.000	1	5	1	0	0	0
Salters	.983	39	240	44	5	6	11

First Base	PCT	G	PO	A	E	DP
De La Cruz	.979	14	132	11	3	13
Fisher	.974	16	141	8	4	9
Loopstok	1.000	2	14	2	0	1

CLEVELAND INDIANS

First Base	PCT	G	PO	A	E	DP
Tapia	.973	28	239	12	7	17
Winfrey	.974	18	139	9	4	15

Second Base	PCT	G	PO	A	E	DP
Fisher	.909	4	2	8	1	0
Haggerty	1.000	6	17	18	0	2
Mathias	.980	61	129	216	7	46
Pantoja	1.000	6	6	18	0	1

Third Base	PCT	G	PO	A	E	DP
Bautista	.600	3	2	1	2	0
Fisher	.937	27	25	49	5	5
Pantoja	.944	11	10	24	2	0
Winfrey	.930	39	19	61	6	2

Shortstop	PCT	G	PO	A	E	DP
Castro	.934	66	123	190	22	41
Fisher	.944	4	4	13	1	1
Pantoja	.923	8	11	25	3	8

Outfield	PCT	G	PO	A	E	DP
Armendariz	.846	11	11	0	2	0
Carter	.937	38	67	7	5	1
Lukes	1.000	5	13	2	0	0
Marabell	.976	59	117	3	3	1
McClure	1.000	8	14	1	0	0
Mejia	.939	14	30	1	2	0
Santander	1.000	3	6	0	0	0
Sayles	.958	35	67	1	3	0
Tom	.955	55	80	5	4	0

AZL INDIANS   ROOKIE
ARIZONA LEAGUE

Batting	B-T	HT	WT	DOB	AVG	vLH	vRH	G	AB	R	H	2B	3B	HR	RBI	BB	HBP	SH	SF	SO	SB	CS	SLG	OBP
Caro, Hector	R-R	6-3	195	10-3-95	.266	.412	.226	22	79	8	21	4	0	0	9	2	0	0	0	21	1	0	.316	.284
Carter, Jodd	R-R	5-10	170	7-20-96	.273	.250	.277	16	55	8	15	6	0	1	13	9	3	0	2	14	1	0	.436	.391
Cerda, Erlin	R-R	5-9	170	5-5-94	.223	.333	.200	29	103	14	23	3	2	0	9	4	6	1	1	18	3	4	.291	.289
Cruz, Grofi	R-R	6-2	175	4-3-96	.243	.294	.235	31	115	5	28	4	0	0	9	7	2	0	0	15	1	2	.278	.298
Eladio, Miguel	R-R	6-1	160	5-10-96	.168	.263	.152	37	131	12	22	4	0	1	9	9	0	1	1	41	6	3	.221	.220
Garcia, Juan	R-R	6-3	195	8-17-97	.226	.111	.245	19	62	7	14	3	0	2	8	5	1	0	0	28	0	0	.371	.294
Gomes, Juan	R-R	6-2	180	12-25-91	.179	.500	.154	18	56	6	10	5	0	0	2	5	1	0	1	19	0	0	.268	.254
Gonzalez, Gianpaul	R-R	6-0	185	1-11-96	.274	.556	.240	26	84	9	23	2	0	0	7	9	3	2	1	27	1	0	.298	.361
Isaacs, Todd	R-R	5-11	175	5-22-96	.214	.214	.214	34	117	12	25	1	2	1	6	1	1	3	1	27	5	1	.282	.225
Lucas, Simeon	L-R	6-2	195	2-7-96	.188	.250	.175	28	96	12	18	6	2	2	13	12	0	1	1	43	0	1	.354	.275
McClure, D'vone	R-R	6-3	190	1-22-94	.000	—	.000	1	2	0	0	0	0	0	0	0	0	0	0	2	0	0	.000	.000
Medina, Jose	L-L	6-1	185	2-14-95	.249	.333	.235	47	177	25	44	7	5	2	15	15	3	0	1	36	1	2	.379	.316
Mejia, Gabriel	B-R	5-11	160	7-30-95	.357	.296	.369	43	168	41	60	8	1	0	18	21	4	2	1	20	34	10	.417	.438
Miller, Anthony	L-R	6-4	240	10-4-94	.226	.214	.228	46	177	19	40	12	0	3	19	14	2	0	0	68	1	0	.345	.290
Monsalve, Alex	R-R	6-2	225	4-22-92	1.000	—	1.000	1	1	1	1	0	0	0	0	0	0	2	0	0	0	0	1.000	1.000
Pantoja, Alexis	B-R	5-11	150	1-18-96	.309	.417	.293	24	94	12	29	6	1	0	17	6	0	4	1	11	5	1	.394	.347
Rodriguez, Jason	R-R	5-11	180	1-11-95	.193	.444	.146	21	57	5	11	1	0	0	3	2	0	0	2	15	0	0	.211	.213
Rodriguez, Jorma	R-R	5-10	150	3-25-96	.160	.222	.153	26	81	7	13	2	0	0	8	3	2	1	0	19	3	1	.185	.258
Soto, Junior	R-R	6-3	175	1-21-97	.229	.211	.232	32	118	18	27	9	1	1	8	4	1	1	1	40	4	2	.347	.256
Wakamatsu, Luke	B-R	6-3	180	10-10-96	.267	.313	.258	27	105	8	28	5	3	1	12	11	1	1	1	40	4	2	.400	.339

Pitching	B-T	HT	WT	DOB	W	L	ERA	G	GS	CG	SV	IP	H	R	ER	HR	BB	SO	AVG	vLH	vRH	K/9	BB/9
Algarin, Erick	R-R	6-1	195	3-31-95	3	0	3.60	14	0	0	2	25	18	11	10	1	7	32	.202	.194	.208	11.52	2.52
Angulo, Argenis	R-R	6-3	220	2-26-94	0	0	13.50	3	1	0	0	2	1	3	3	1	5	3	.125	.333	.000	13.50	22.50
Brewer, Charles	R-R	6-3	210	4-7-88	0	0	0.00	2	2	0	0	5	1	0	0	0	0	7	.067	.000	.100	12.60	0.00
Chen, Ping-Hsueh	R-R	6-2	195	7-8-94	0	0	1.56	13	0	0	3	17	13	7	3	2	6	15	.203	.167	.225	7.79	3.12
Colegate, Ryan	R-R	6-5	195	11-12-93	0	1	7.45	14	0	0	0	19	30	17	16	1	8	12	.375	.400	.364	5.59	3.72
Cox, Cortland	R-R	6-1	185	11-3-94	0	1	0.00	5	0	0	1	6	2	3	0	0	2	11	.091	.000	.143	15.63	2.84
Estrella, Edward	R-R	6-1	170	1-28-94	1	0	4.68	15	0	0	0	25	31	14	13	0	10	23	.313	.432	.242	8.28	3.60
Floyd, Gavin	R-R	6-4	245	1-27-83	0	0	8.31	2	2	0	0	4	7	4	4	1	1	8	.368	.500	.273	16.62	2.08
Frank, Trevor	R-R	6-0	195	6-23-91	0	0	0.00	5	0	0	0	5	2	1	0	0	0	5	.111	.143	.091	9.00	0.00
Hentges, Sam	L-L	6-6	245	7-18-96	3	3	3.10	11	9	0	0	49	49	28	17	4	19	59	.254	.271	.246	10.76	3.47
Hillman, Juan	L-L	6-2	183	5-15-97	0	2	4.13	8	6	0	0	24	26	13	11	0	5	20	.286	.333	.269	7.50	1.88
Jimenez, Domingo	R-R	6-3	175	8-29-93	3	5	5.82	12	8	1	0	43	35	32	28	0	34	40	.230	.241	.223	8.31	7.06
Jimenez, Luis	R-R	6-4	170	1-2-95	3	5	5.01	11	11	0	0	47	53	32	26	1	25	41	.290	.270	.300	7.91	4.82
Lopez, Francisco	R-R	5-11	170	2-13-94	0	2	7.90	7	1	0	0	14	16	14	12	1	4	5	.281	.222	.308	3.29	2.63
Martinez, Henry	R-R	6-1	175	4-27-94	1	0	3.34	13	0	0	2	32	35	17	12	0	12	24	.273	.278	.272	6.68	3.34
McKenzie, Triston	R-R	6-5	160	8-2-97	1	1	0.75	4	3	0	0	12	4	1	1	0	3	17	.100	.105	.095	12.75	2.25
Meister, Christian	R-R	6-3	210	10-29-93	2	1	0.98	8	0	0	0	18	15	2	2	0	4	17	.211	.385	.111	8.35	1.96
Miniard, Micah	R-R	6-7	195	4-12-96	3	7	3.29	12	10	0	0	63	62	30	23	3	16	46	.252	.241	.257	6.57	2.29
Puello, Johan	R-R	5-11	165	1-5-94	0	1	5.56	9	0	0	0	11	13	7	7	0	10	7	.325	.273	.345	5.56	7.94
Rodriguez, Jose	R-R	6-0	185	3-18-95	0	2	8.14	15	0	0	0	21	24	21	19	2	11	18	.293	.280	.298	7.71	4.71
Tomlin, Josh	R-R	6-1	190	10-19-84	0	0	9.00	1	1	0	0	2	3	2	2	0	0	3	.333	.333	.333	13.50	0.00
Valladares, Randy	L-L	5-11	155	7-6-94	0	0	3.80	14	0	0	0	21	23	12	9	0	11	19	.274	.286	.270	8.02	4.64
Whitehouse, Matt	L-L	6-1	175	4-13-91	0	1	0.00	2	2	0	0	2	1	3	0	0	0	3	.143	.333	.000	16.20	16.20
Wyatt, Jonas	R-R	6-1	185	9-16-97	3	1	1.62	8	0	0	0	17	8	3	3	0	6	20	.145	.188	.128	10.80	3.24

Fielding

Catcher	PCT	G	PO	A	E	DP	PB
Gomes	.973	9	66	5	2	0	5
Gonzalez	1.000	24	182	30	0	2	5
Lucas	.983	15	102	15	2	1	8
Rodriguez	1.000	17	98	12	0	1	5

First Base	PCT	G	PO	A	E	DP
Medina	.981	12	92	9	2	8
Miller	.978	45	388	18	9	31

Second Base	PCT	G	PO	A	E	DP
Cerda	.930	8	15	25	3	4
Eladio	.964	27	57	75	5	16
Pantoja	1.000	3	4	10	0	1
Rodriguez	.960	18	44	52	4	13

Third Base	PCT	G	PO	A	E	DP
Cerda	.935	21	25	47	5	7
Cruz	.916	30	18	58	7	3
Rodriguez	.750	6	4	5	3	0

Shortstop	PCT	G	PO	A	E	DP
Eladio	.933	9	15	27	3	5
Pantoja	.938	21	28	63	6	8

	PCT	G	PO	A	E	DP
Wakamatsu	.971	26	32	67	3	10

Outfield	PCT	G	PO	A	E	DP
Caro	.929	11	12	1	1	0
Carter	.964	16	26	1	1	0
Garcia	1.000	14	21	3	0	0
Isaacs	.942	30	46	3	3	1
Medina	.980	32	45	4	1	1
Mejia	.985	43	61	3	1	0
Soto	.969	28	55	7	2	0

DSL INDIANS   ROOKIE

DOMINICAN SUMMER LEAGUE

Batting	B-T	HT	WT	DOB	AVG	vLH	vRH	G	AB	R	H	2B	3B	HR	RBI	BB	HBP	SH	SF	SO	SB	CS	SLG	OBP
Beltre, Enmanuel	R-R	6-3	215	4-27-95	.233	.143	.261	12	30	5	7	1	0	1	2	2	0	1	0	8	1	0	.367	.281
Brito, Bryan	R-R	6-0	160	4-4-96	.235	.297	.214	48	149	23	35	2	0	0	7	23	2	2	0	30	18	8	.248	.345
Cabrera, Julio	L-L	6-0	190	11-21-97	.147	.000	.161	44	102	9	15	2	3	0	11	19	2	1	3	28	5	1	.225	.286
Cespedes, Cristopher	R-R	6-3	200	5-18-98	.210	.217	.207	65	210	21	44	11	3	4	28	21	7	1	2	64	1	3	.348	.300
De Jesus, Christopher	R-R	5-11	170	9-24-96	.214	.294	.194	38	84	8	18	0	1	0	3	4	1	1	0	12	3	0	.238	.258
De La Rosa, Luis	R-R	6-4	170	8-31-98	.239	.200	.250	19	71	6	17	4	0	0	3	6	3	0	0	12	2	1	.296	.325
De Oleo, Henderson	R-R	6-4	210	2-11-98	.189	.128	.208	62	169	18	32	5	0	4	21	28	6	2	0	52	0	2	.290	.325
Dominguez, Manuel	R-R	6-0	185	6-10-97	.048	.000	.083	13	21	2	1	0	0	0	2	6	1	0	0	8	0	0	.048	.286
Fernandez, Felix	R-R	6-0	185	12-9-96	.187	.161	.194	59	155	12	29	4	0	0	11	15	1	1	0	18	0	1	.213	.263
Gonzalez, Oscar	R-R	6-0	180	1-10-98	.203	.200	.204	70	256	25	52	17	1	4	38	19	3	0	4	65	1	3	.324	.262
Marcelino, Melvin	L-L	5-11	150	5-23-97	.128	.000	.158	45	47	16	6	0	0	0	1	3	3	2	0	18	6	4	.128	.226
Marte, Francisco	R-R	6-2	180	4-16-97	.222	.280	.184	30	63	9	14	4	1	1	8	2	2	0	0	19	2	0	.365	.269
Ortega, Efrin	R-R	6-0	165	7-20-97	.167	.192	.159	39	108	19	18	2	1	0	6	13	2	0	0	17	7	5	.204	.268
Perez, Elvis	B-R	6-0	165	1-10-96	.300	.292	.302	71	250	41	75	9	6	0	29	33	6	2	3	35	6	9	.384	.390
Santiago, Wilbis	L-R	6-0	180	1-20-96	.274	.353	.264	47	146	22	40	2	3	0	10	16	4	0	2	19	7	0	.329	.357
Torrealba, Hazzent	R-R	6-0	170	10-21-96	.000		.000	1	2	0	0	0	0	0	0	0	0	0	0	0	0	0	.000	.000
Vicente, Jose	R-R	5-11	175	11-13-95	.275	.196	.297	70	233	33	64	15	2	4	35	32	3	0	1	34	1	2	.408	.368

Pitching	B-T	HT	WT	DOB	W	L	ERA	G	GS	CG	SV	IP	H	R	ER	HR	BB	SO	AVG	vLH	vRH	K/9	BB/9
Araujo, Luis	R-R	6-1	155	8-1-96	1	3	4.15	9	5	0	0	26	27	18	12	1	10	27	.267	.293	.250	9.35	3.46
Cedeno, Orlando	R-R	6-2	195	9-16-97	2	2	4.02	8	3	0	0	16	10	7	7	0	13	6	.192	.364	.146	3.45	7.47
Diaz, Darlin	R-R	6-8	220	12-1-95	0	0	9.00	1	0	0	0	1	1	1	1	0	1	1	.250	.500	.000	9.00	9.00
Figueroa, Hector	R-R	6-3	190	11-30-94	4	0	2.93	17	0	0	3	31	31	20	10	1	16	22	.261	.267	.258	6.46	4.70
Izaguirre, Alejandro	R-R	6-0	175	3-5-97	1	3	4.91	9	0	0	2	11	9	6	6	0	7	16	.220	.250	.216	13.09	5.73
Madera, Christopher	L-L	6-4	175	9-16-94	2	0	2.45	10	0	0	0	15	12	4	4	0	18	8	.250	.333	.244	4.91	11.05
Marte, Randy	R-R	6-1	175	12-27-96	0	0	1.48	9	5	0	0	24	24	4	4	1	9	20	.264	.278	.260	7.40	3.33
Mejia, Jean Carlos	R-R	6-4	205	8-26-96	4	3	1.37	19	0	0	1	39	30	17	6	1	12	25	.217	.298	.176	5.72	2.75
Pereda, Leomar	R-R	6-1	160	9-27-97	2	1	3.71	16	1	0	3	27	26	14	11	0	15	19	.260	.379	.211	6.41	5.06
Perez, Francisco	L-L	6-2	195	7-20-97	2	2	2.49	13	12	0	0	51	49	18	14	0	19	48	.254	.214	.257	8.53	3.38
Rodriguez, Robert	R-R	5-11	170	4-27-96	0	0	0.00	1	0	0	0	1	1	0	0	0	0	1	.250	.000	.333	9.00	0.00
Rozon, Willy	R-R	6-0	170	4-19-96	0	0	6.75	4	0	0	0	4	8	6	3	0	3	1	.444	—	.444	2.25	6.75
Salinas, Jhonleider	R-R	6-0	205	9-25-95	2	2	2.66	14	9	0	0	41	13	19	12	0	40	39	.100	.139	.085	8.63	8.85
Santana, Christophers	R-R	6-2	195	2-26-98	1	1	21.00	7	0	0	0	6	8	14	14	0	15	7	.333	.600	.263	10.50	22.50
Santos, Luis	R-R	6-4	180	9-18-94	2	0	3.66	13	11	0	0	52	51	25	21	1	16	33	.254	.241	.259	5.75	2.79
Siri, Dalbert	R-R	6-2	190	7-19-95	2	3	2.72	16	5	0	1	36	27	13	11	1	20	29	.209	.179	.218	7.18	4.95
Tati, Felix	R-R	6-2	190	4-1-97	1	1	1.40	10	6	0	0	39	32	10	6	1	11	28	.230	.139	.262	6.52	2.56
Tineo, Ramon	R-L	6-0	170	1-31-96	6	0	1.32	20	0	0	3	34	24	11	5	0	16	37	.202	.389	.168	9.79	4.24
Valdez, Luis	R-R	6-3	170	10-14-96	0	0	2.70	3	0	0	0	3	4	2	1	0	4	0	.308	.000	.400	0.00	10.80
Vasquez, Gregori	R-R	6-1	185	9-8-97	1	1	2.36	15	3	0	3	42	34	14	11	0	7	50	.218	.200	.226	10.71	1.50
Ventura, Cesar	R-R	6-0	195	3-14-95	3	2	3.13	20	1	0	6	46	36	21	16	0	20	29	.218	.195	.226	5.67	3.91
Ventura, Jhon	R-R	6-5	200	3-12-95	0	2	3.86	7	0	0	0	14	16	9	6	0	9	8	.302	.364	.286	5.14	5.79
Vizcaino, Gabriel	R-R	6-2	190	3-26-94	4	6	2.50	15	11	0	0	68	59	27	19	2	15	30	.247	.338	.206	3.95	1.98

Fielding

Catcher	PCT	G	PO	A	E	DP	PB
De Jesus	.966	36	175	23	7	0	5
Fernandez	.983	50	241	43	5	2	13
Vicente	.964	15	71	10	3	0	1

First Base	PCT	G	PO	A	E	DP
Beltre	.975	11	74	4	2	5
De Jesus	1.000	1	1	0	0	0
De Oleo	1.000	6	31	1	0	1
Dominguez	.963	5	26	0	1	0
Fernandez	1.000	2	6	0	0	1
Vicente	.990	61	466	27	5	44

Second Base	PCT	G	PO	A	E	DP
Brito	.936	13	21	23	3	3

	PCT	G	PO	A	E	DP
Cespedes	1.000	1	0	3	0	0
Medrano	1.000	3	5	7	0	1
Ortega	.955	21	42	43	4	8
Santiago	.986	43	106	109	3	30
Torrealba	1.000	1	0	3	0	0

Third Base	PCT	G	PO	A	E	DP
Brito	.615	4	2	6	5	2
De Jesus	—	1	0	0	0	0
De Oleo	.899	56	57	86	16	8
Medrano	.852	33	21	48	12	3

Shortstop	PCT	G	PO	A	E	DP
Brito	.909	8	2	8	1	2
Perez	.949	71	95	187	15	33

Outfield	PCT	G	PO	A	E	DP
Brito	.000	1	0	0	1	0
Cabrera	.953	30	39	2	2	0
Cespedes	.978	59	84	6	2	0
De La Rosa	.970	19	29	3	1	0
Dominguez	1.000	7	5	0	0	0
Gonzalez	.972	68	132	7	4	2
Marcelino	.922	35	46	1	4	0
Marte	.947	15	17	1	1	0
Medrano	1.000	21	40	4	0	2
Santiago	1.000	1	4	0	0	0

Colorado Rockies

SEASON IN A SENTENCE: As is often the case in the high elevation of Denver, the Rockies led the league in runs scored and runs allowed, unable to pitch their way out of the NL West cellar and finishing 68-94.

HIGH POINT: The Rockies briefly surged out of last place after an 11-5 run from May 23 to June 9 brought them to just three games below .500 and six games back of first.

LOW POINT: In a down season, the lowest of lows came July 28, when the Rockies traded away the face of the franchise, Troy Tulowitzki, to the Blue Jays.

NOTABLE ROOKIES: With Justin Morneau continuing to deal with concussion symptoms, 27-year-old rookie Ben Paulsen filled in admirably, batting .277/.326/.462 with 11 homers in 325 at-bats while also seeing time as an outfielder. Righthander Jon Gray, the third overall pick out of Oklahoma in 2013, made nine starts and went 0-2, 5.53 but remains a top prospect. Top catching prospect Tom Murphy showcased his power in a short September stint, hitting three home runs and batting .257/.333/.543 in 35 at-bats. Outfielder Kyle Parker, a 2010 first-rounder, struggled at the plate, batting .179/.223/.311 in 106 at-bats.

KEY TRANSACTIONS: There had been talk of trading star shortstop Troy Tulowitzki for a couple of seasons, but the Rockies finally pulled the trigger in July, sending him along with veteran reliever LaTroy Hawkins to the Blue Jays. Colorado received shortstop Jose Reyes in the deal as well as high-velocity righthanders Jeff Hoffman, Jesus Tinoco and Miguel Castro. Hoffman, a first-round pick in 2014, is the best prospect of the bunch.

DOWN ON THE FARM: A frightening collision and a splenectomy limited outfielder David Dahl, the organization's top prospect and 2012 first-rounder, but he still finished .278/.304/.417 in 288 at-bats for Double-A New Britain, slugging six home runs. Lefthander Kyle Freelander, taken eighth overall in 2014 out of Evansville, had surgery early in the season to remove bone chips in his elbow and went 3-2, 4.05 in 47 innings between the Rookie-level Pioneer League and high Class A Modesto. Third baseman Ryan McMahon, outfielder Raimel Tapia and second baseman Forrest Wall each had productive offensive seasons but are still far away from helping the major league club. Middle infielder Trevor Story is closest to the bigs, popping 20 homers.

OPENING DAY PAYROLL: $102,006,130 (20)

PLAYERS OF THE YEAR

TONY FARLOW

MAJOR LEAGUE	MINOR LEAGUE
Nolan Arenado, 3b	**Trevor Story, ss/2b**
.287/.323/.575	(Double-A, Triple-A)
42 HR, 130 RBI	279/.350/.514
Tied for NL HR lead	20 HR, 40 2B, 22 SB

ORGANIZATION LEADERS

BATTING		*Minimum 250 AB
MAJORS		
*AVG	DJ LeMahieu	.301
*OPS	Nolan Arenado	.898
HR	Nolan Arenado	42
RBI	Nolan Arenado	130
MINORS		
*AVG	Shane Hoelscher, Modesto, Asheville	.318
*OBP	Shane Hoelscher, Modesto, Asheville	.413
*SLG	Jordan Patterson, Modesto, New Britain	.543
R	Jordan Patterson, Modesto, New Britain	88
H	Raimel Tapia, Modesto	166
TB	Jordan Patterson, Modesto, New Britain	265
2B	Jordan Patterson, Modesto, New Britain	45
3B	Jordan Patterson, Modesto, New Britain	12
HR	Tom Murphy, New Britain, Albuquerque	20
	Trevor Story, New Britain, Albuquerque	20
RBI	Trevor Story, New Britain, Albuquerque	80
BB	Mike Papi, Lynchburg	81
SO	Correlle Prime, Modesto	156
SB	Wes Rogers, Grand Junction, Asheville	53

PITCHING		#Minimum 75 IP
MAJORS		
W	Jorge De La Rosa	9
#ERA	Jorge De La Rosa	4.17
SO	Jorge De La Rosa	134
SV	John Axford	25
MINORS		
W	Shane Carle, Albuquerque, New Britain	14
L	Ryan Carpenter, New Britain	13
#ERA	Antonio Senzatela, Modesto	2.51
G	Josh Michalec, Asheville	55
GS	Ryan Carpenter, New Britain	28
SV	Josh Michalec, Asheville	30
IP	Matt Flemer, New Britain	170
BB	Helmis Rodriguez, Asheville	63
SO	Antonio Senzatela, Modesto	143
AVG	Antonio Senzatela, Modesto	.229

General Manager: Jeff Briddich. **Farm Director:** Zach Wilson. **Scouting Director:** Marc Gustafson.

Class	Team	League	W	L	PCT	Finish	Manager
Majors	Colorado Rockies	National	68	94	.420	t-11th (15)	Walt Weiss
Triple-A	Albuquerque Isotopes	Pacific Coast	62	82	.431	14th (16)	Glenallen Hill
Double-A	New Britain Rock Cats	Eastern	69	71	.493	8th (12)	Darin Everson
High A	Modesto Nuts	California	67	73	.479	7th (10)	Fred Ocasio
Low A	Asheville Tourists	South Atlantic	72	67	.518	5th (14)	Warren Schaeffer
Short season	Boise Hawks	Northwest	30	46	.395	8th (8)	Frank Gonzales
Rookie	Grand Junction Rockies	Pioneer	33	43	.434	7th (8)	Anthony Sanders
Overall 2015 Minor League Record			333	382	.466	26th (30)	

ORGANIZATION STATISTICS

COLORADO ROCKIES

NATIONAL LEAGUE

Batting	B-T	HT	WT	DOB	AVG	vLH	vRH	G	AB	R	H	2B	3B	HR	RBI	BB	HBP	SH	SF	SO	SB	CS	SLG	OBP
Adames, Cristhian	B-R	6-0	185	7-26-91	.245	.286	.219	26	53	4	13	1	1	0	3	3	1	1	0	11	0	1	.302	.298
Arenado, Nolan	R-R	6-2	205	4-16-91	.287	.267	.293	157	616	97	177	43	4	42	130	34	4	0	11	110	2	5	.575	.323
Barnes, Brandon	R-R	6-2	210	5-15-86	.251	.224	.261	106	255	30	64	13	2	2	17	21	3	1	1	67	4	2	.341	.314
Blackmon, Charlie	L-L	6-3	210	7-1-86	.287	.264	.295	157	614	93	176	31	9	17	58	46	13	5	4	112	43	13	.450	.347
Descalso, Daniel	L-R	5-10	190	10-19-86	.205	.167	.211	101	185	22	38	3	2	5	22	20	0	4	0	45	1	2	.324	.283
Dickerson, Corey	L-R	6-1	205	5-22-89	.304	.268	.315	65	224	30	68	18	2	10	31	10	0	0	0	56	0	1	.536	.333
Garneau, Dustin	R-R	6-0	200	8-13-87	.157	.211	.137	22	70	6	11	3	0	2	8	6	0	0	0	14	0	0	.286	.224
Gonzalez, Carlos	L-L	6-1	220	10-17-85	.271	.195	.301	153	554	87	150	25	2	40	97	46	1	1	6	133	2	0	.540	.325
Hundley, Nick	R-R	6-1	205	9-8-83	.301	.292	.303	103	366	45	110	21	5	10	43	21	1	0	1	76	5	6	.467	.339
LeMahieu, D.J.	R-R	6-4	215	7-13-88	.301	.316	.297	150	564	85	170	21	5	6	61	50	1	3	2	107	23	3	.388	.358
McBride, Matt	R-R	6-2	215	5-23-85	.167	.200	.156	20	42	5	7	0	0	0	0	1	0	0	0	4	0	0	.167	.186
McKenry, Michael	R-R	5-10	205	3-4-85	.205	.263	.194	58	127	20	26	7	3	4	17	22	2	0	1	41	2	2	.402	.329
Morneau, Justin	L-R	6-4	220	5-15-81	.310	.342	.300	49	168	19	52	10	3	3	15	13	1	0	0	25	0	0	.458	.363
Murphy, Tom	R-R	6-1	220	4-3-91	.257	.167	.353	11	35	5	9	1	0	3	9	4	0	0	0	10	0	0	.543	.333
Parker, Kyle	R-R	6-0	205	9-30-89	.179	.194	.171	46	106	10	19	3	1	3	11	6	0	0	0	37	1	0	.311	.223
Paulsen, Ben	L-R	6-4	210	10-27-87	.277	.235	.282	116	325	42	90	19	4	11	49	23	2	1	3	92	1	2	.462	.326
Reyes, Jose	B-R	6-0	195	6-11-83	.259	.308	.234	47	193	21	50	8	2	3	19	9	0	5	1	24	8	4	.368	.291
Rosario, Wilin	R-R	5-11	220	2-23-89	.268	.282	.260	87	231	22	62	14	1	6	29	8	1	1	1	56	2	1	.416	.295
Stubbs, Drew	R-R	6-4	205	10-4-84	.216	.196	.232	51	102	14	22	3	2	5	10	9	1	2	0	50	2	1	.431	.286
Tulowitzki, Troy	R-R	6-3	215	10-10-84	.300	.375	.279	87	323	46	97	19	0	12	53	24	1	0	3	72	0	1	.471	.348
Ynoa, Rafael	R-R	6-0	190	8-7-87	.260	.260	.260	72	127	14	33	8	1	0	9	3	0	1	0	28	1	0	.339	.277

Pitching	B-T	HT	WT	DOB	W	L	ERA	G	GS	CG	SV	IP	H	R	ER	HR	BB	SO	AVG	vLH	vRH	K/9	BB/9
Axford, John	R-R	6-5	220	4-1-83	4	5	4.20	60	0	0	25	56	56	27	26	4	32	62	.259	.258	.261	10.02	5.17
Bergman, Christian	R-R	6-1	180	5-4-88	3	1	4.74	30	4	0	0	68	82	36	36	8	15	37	.306	.215	.366	4.87	1.98
Betancourt, Rafael	R-R	6-2	215	4-29-75	2	4	6.18	45	0	0	1	39	43	29	27	4	12	40	.267	.204	.295	9.15	2.75
Bettis, Chad	R-R	6-1	200	4-26-89	8	6	4.23	20	20	0	0	115	120	56	54	11	42	98	.268	.252	.284	7.67	3.29
Brothers, Rex	L-L	6-2	210	12-18-87	1	0	1.74	17	0	0	0	10	9	2	2	0	8	5	.243	.227	.267	4.35	6.97
Brown, Brooks	L-R	6-3	205	6-20-85	1	3	4.91	36	0	0	0	33	32	18	18	2	16	20	.254	.265	.247	5.45	4.36
Butler, Eddie	B-R	6-2	180	3-13-91	3	10	5.90	16	16	1	0	79	102	57	52	13	42	44	.322	.353	.292	4.99	4.76
Castro, Miguel	R-R	6-5	190	12-24-94	0	1	10.13	5	0	0	0	5	6	6	6	2	4	6	.273	.300	.250	10.13	6.75
Castro, Simon	R-R	6-5	230	4-9-88	2	0	6.10	11	0	0	0	10	11	7	7	0	5	9	.282	.333	.250	7.84	4.35
De La Rosa, Jorge	L-L	6-1	215	4-5-81	9	7	4.17	26	26	1	0	149	137	73	69	17	65	134	.247	.240	.249	8.09	3.93
Diaz, Jairo	R-R	6-0	200	5-27-91	0	1	2.37	21	0	0	0	19	16	6	5	2	6	18	.222	.222	.222	8.53	2.84
Flande, Yohan	L-L	6-2	180	1-27-86	3	3	4.74	19	10	0	0	68	73	36	36	14	25	43	.277	.262	.281	5.66	3.29
Friedrich, Christian	R-L	6-4	215	7-8-87	0	4	5.25	68	0	0	0	58	75	37	34	5	25	45	.321	.268	.369	6.94	3.86
Germen, Gonzalez	R-R	6-1	200	9-23-87	0	0	3.86	29	1	0	1	33	33	14	14	4	21	25	.262	.263	.261	6.89	5.79
2-team total (6 Chicago)					0	0	4.42	35	1	0	1	39	41	19	19	4	26	33	—	—	—	7.68	6.05
Gray, Jon	R-R	6-4	235	11-5-91	0	2	5.53	9	9	0	0	41	52	26	25	4	14	40	.319	.295	.341	8.85	3.10
Gurka, Jason	L-L	6-0	180	1-10-88	0	0	9.39	9	0	0	0	8	16	8	8	1	2	7	.432	.500	.381	8.22	2.35
Hale, David	R-R	6-2	210	9-27-87	5	5	6.09	17	12	0	0	78	95	56	53	14	20	61	.298	.297	.298	7.01	2.30
Hawkins, LaTroy	R-R	6-5	220	12-21-72	2	1	3.63	24	0	0	2	22	22	9	9	3	4	20	.259	.206	.294	8.06	1.61
Kahnle, Tommy	R-R	6-1	235	8-7-89	0	1	4.86	36	0	0	2	33	31	22	18	3	28	39	.250	.320	.203	10.53	7.56
Kendrick, Kyle	R-R	6-3	210	8-26-84	7	13	6.32	27	27	0	0	142	172	102	100	33	45	80	.302	.314	.291	5.06	2.85
Laffey, Aaron	L-L	6-0	200	4-15-85	1	0	3.68	3	0	0	0	7	8	3	3	1	3	3	.296	.300	.294	3.68	3.68
Logan, Boone	R-L	6-5	215	8-13-84	0	3	4.33	60	0	0	0	35	40	17	17	3	17	44	.280	.225	.333	11.21	4.33
Lyles, Jordan	R-R	6-4	230	10-19-90	2	5	5.14	10	10	0	0	49	54	32	28	2	19	30	.290	.305	.275	5.51	3.49
Matzek, Tyler	L-L	6-3	230	10-19-90	2	1	4.09	5	5	0	0	22	21	10	10	2	19	15	.269	.214	.281	6.14	7.77
Miller, Justin	R-R	6-3	215	6-13-87	3	3	4.05	34	0	0	1	33	21	15	15	2	11	38	.178	.184	.175	10.26	2.97
Oberg, Scott	R-R	6-2	205	3-13-90	3	4	5.09	64	0	0	1	58	58	35	33	10	31	44	.266	.275	.261	6.79	4.78
Ottavino, Adam	L-R	6-5	220	11-22-85	1	0	0.00	10	0	0	3	10	3	0	0	0	2	13	.094	.133	.059	11.32	1.74
Roberts, Ken	L-L	6-1	200	3-9-88	0	1	5.79	9	0	0	0	9	13	6	6	2	5	.333	.429	.280	4.82	1.93
2-team total (6 Philadelphia)					1	1	7.24	15	0	0	0	14	22	11	11	0	3	6	—	—	—	3.95	1.98
Rondon, Jorge	R-R	6-1	215	2-16-88	0	0	90.00	2	0	0	0	1	8	11	10	0	3	1	.667	1.000	.556	9.00	27.00
Rusin, Chris	L-L	6-2	195	10-22-86	6	10	5.33	24	22	2	0	132	170	88	78	19	41	86	.310	.305	.312	5.88	2.80

Fielding

Catcher

Catcher	PCT	G	PO	A	E	DP	PB
Garneau	.987	22	146	10	2	0	1
Hundley	.993	102	643	51	5	5	5
McKenry	.979	32	226	8	5	0	1
Murphy	.989	11	82	5	1	0	0
Rosario	1.000	2	19	1	0	0	0

First Base

First Base	PCT	G	PO	A	E	DP
Descalso	1.000	7	29	1	0	1
McBride	1.000	4	33	2	0	3
Morneau	.997	44	357	32	1	54
Parker	1.000	2	10	2	0	0
Paulsen	.996	91	660	48	3	63
Rosario	.986	53	389	22	6	38

Second Base

Second Base	PCT	G	PO	A	E	DP
Adames	1.000	2	4	7	0	1
Descalso	.941	15	24	24	3	8
LeMahieu	.988	149	300	452	9	120
Ynoa	1.000	5	1	10	0	2

Third Base

Third Base	PCT	G	PO	A	E	DP
Arenado	.966	157	105	385	17	42
Descalso	1.000	5	3	12	0	1
Ynoa	.857	10	1	5	1	0

Shortstop

Shortstop	PCT	G	PO	A	E	DP
Adames	.957	13	15	30	2	8
Descalso	.959	33	36	80	5	16
Reyes	.987	47	63	161	3	32
Tulowitzki	.978	82	107	241	8	59
Ynoa	1.000	8	3	14	0	3

Outfield

Outfield	PCT	G	PO	A	E	DP
Barnes	.986	97	134	4	2	2
Blackmon	.991	155	327	9	3	2
Descalso	—	1	0	0	0	0
Dickerson	1.000	55	88	1	0	0
Gonzalez	.974	151	253	8	7	1
Gurka	—	1	0	0	0	0
McBride	1.000	5	4	0	0	0
Parker	.972	32	35	0	1	0
Paulsen	1.000	20	19	0	0	0
Stubbs	1.000	40	49	2	0	0
Ynoa	.960	19	22	2	1	0

ALBUQUERQUE ISOTOPES   TRIPLE-A

PACIFIC COAST LEAGUE

Batting	B-T	HT	WT	DOB	AVG	vLH	vRH	G	AB	R	H	2B	3B	HR	RBI	BB	HBP	SH	SF	SO	SB	CS	SLG	OBP
Adames, Cristhian	B-R	6-0	185	7-26-91	.311	.308	.312	116	463	62	144	20	3	11	51	36	2	8	2	56	11	7	.438	.362
Baker, Abel	L-R	6-1	200	10-26-90	.267	.100	.350	9	30	3	8	3	0	0	4	4	0	0	0	11	0	0	.367	.353
Barfield, Jeremy	R-L	6-5	220	7-12-88	.267	.283	.257	42	120	10	32	7	1	3	15	10	0	0	2	25	0	0	.417	.318
Barnes, Brandon	R-R	6-2	210	5-15-86	.205	.264	.165	33	132	19	27	6	0	5	12	10	1	0	0	34	7	3	.364	.266
Bernadina, Roger	L-L	6-2	200	6-12-84	.276	.233	.296	119	373	62	103	18	4	15	62	58	7	8	1	121	20	6	.466	.383
Bond, Brock	R-R	5-11	190	9-11-85	.259	.296	.241	45	81	7	21	1	0	0	5	11	0	3	1	15	3	1	.272	.344
Casteel, Ryan	R-R	5-11	205	6-6-91	.292	.390	.247	34	130	12	38	8	1	2	20	2	0	1	1	33	2	1	.415	.301
Culberson, Charlie	R-R	6-0	200	4-10-89	.200	.286	.154	5	20	3	4	1	0	1	2	0	0	0	0	6	0	0	.400	.200
Dickerson, Corey	L-R	6-1	205	5-22-89	.286	.250	.292	7	28	3	8	1	0	1	3	1	0	0	0	4	0	0	.429	.310
Galvez, Cesar	R-R	5-9	145	7-24-91	.000	.000	.000	1	3	0	0	0	0	0	0	0	0	0	0	0	0	0	.000	.250
Garneau, Dustin	R-R	6-0	200	8-13-87	.274	.323	.252	81	303	44	83	16	0	15	61	28	2	3	4	44	2	1	.475	.335
McBride, Matt	R-R	6-2	215	5-23-85	.328	.295	.347	78	308	59	101	30	1	12	49	23	4	0	2	41	5	1	.549	.380
Murphy, Tom	R-R	6-1	220	4-3-91	.271	.364	.224	33	129	19	35	9	2	7	19	5	1	0	1	40	1	0	.535	.301
Nina, Angelys	R-R	5-11	165	11-16-88	.300	.356	.274	114	420	57	126	21	5	4	50	22	0	2	3	46	18	7	.402	.333
Osborne, Zach	R-R	5-8	175	4-2-90	.000	.000	.000	2	4	0	0	0	0	0	0	0	0	0	0	0	0	0	.000	.000
Parker, Kyle	R-R	6-0	205	9-30-89	.280	.279	.280	93	357	53	100	19	4	9	58	24	2	2	3	102	6	4	.431	.326
Paulsen, Ben	L-R	6-4	210	10-27-87	.256	.163	.305	36	125	19	32	8	2	3	15	15	1	0	0	34	1	0	.424	.340
Ribera, Jordan	L-R	6-0	225	12-22-88	.167	.000	.200	4	6	0	1	0	0	0	0	0	0	0	0	0	0	0	.167	.167
Rivera, Jose	R-R	5-10	170	4-18-90	.258	.132	.309	51	132	15	34	8	0	1	9	6	1	2	0	36	0	1	.341	.295
Rosario, Wilin	R-R	5-11	220	3-23-89	.297	.468	.218	38	148	18	44	12	1	7	23	5	2	0	0	31	1	1	.534	.329
Smalling, Tim	R-R	6-3	207	10-14-87	.256	.260	.254	115	367	44	94	12	1	6	37	26	6	3	2	61	7	3	.343	.314
Story, Trevor	R-R	6-1	180	11-15-92	.277	.197	.308	61	256	37	71	20	4	10	40	16	2	0	1	68	7	1	.504	.324
Stubbs, Drew	R-R	6-5	205	10-4-84	.263	.273	.258	38	122	22	36	4	3	2	20	24	2	0	2	39	6	3	.380	.376
2-team total (7 Round Rock)					.256	—		45	164	28	42	5	3	2	20	27	2	0	2	46	10	3	.360	.364
Wheeler, Tim	L-R	6-4	205	1-21-88	.245	.203	.263	124	384	56	94	15	1	10	45	58	3	7	4	122	16	0	.367	.345
Wong, Joey	L-R	5-10	185	4-12-88	.197	.115	.257	21	61	5	12	3	2	0	8	2	0	1	1	15	1	0	.311	.219
Ynoa, Rafael	R-R	6-0	180	8-7-87	.286	.232	.310	56	224	29	64	12	4	1	11	16	0	3	0	36	5	1	.388	.333

Pitching	B-T	HT	WT	DOB	W	L	ERA	G	GS	CG	SV	IP	H	R	ER	HR	BB	SO	AVG	vLH	vRH	K/9	BB/9
Arrowood, Ryan	R-R	6-3	190	8-24-90	1	1	7.29	18	1	0	0	33	42	27	27	8	15	25	.311	.347	.291	6.75	4.05
Bergman, Christian	R-R	6-1	180	5-4-88	0	0	0.00	2	2	0	0	5	2	0	0	0	2	6	.125	.143	.111	10.80	3.60
Betancourt, Rafael	R-R	6-2	215	4-29-75	0	0	13.50	1	0	0	0	1	2	2	1	1	1	2	.333	.500	.250	13.50	6.75
Bettis, Chad	R-R	6-1	200	4-26-89	3	2	3.46	7	7	0	0	39	41	16	15	5	10	33	.273	.303	.250	7.62	2.31
Brothers, Rex	L-L	6-0	210	12-18-87	5	2	4.46	45	0	0	3	42	27	24	21	1	44	61	.181	.192	.175	12.97	9.35
Brown, Brooks	L-R	6-3	205	6-20-85	0	0	6.00	16	0	0	0	15	20	10	10	1	5	17	.323	.345	.303	10.20	3.00
Broyles, Shane	R-R	6-1	180	8-19-91	0	0	0.00	4	0	0	0	5	1	0	0		3	4	.063	.111	.000	6.75	5.06
Burke, Devin	R-R	6-1	205	2-20-91	0	0	1.23	7	1	1	0	7	2	1	1	0	2	8	.087	.167	.000	9.82	2.45
Butler, Eddie	B-R	6-2	180	3-13-91	2	6	5.40	11	11	0	0	63	71	43	38	6	25	37	.293	.333	.254	5.26	3.55
Carle, Shane	R-R	6-4	185	8-30-91	0	1	9.00	1	1	0	0	6	9	6	6	1	1	3	.333	.385	.286	4.50	1.50
Castro, Miguel	R-R	6-5	190	12-24-94	0	0	1.32	11	0	0	0	14	6	3	2	0	7	10	.136	.120	.158	6.59	4.61
Castro, Simon	R-R	6-5	230	4-9-88	5	5	3.79	36	0	0	0	57	53	27	24	6	20	74	.242	.215	.257	11.68	3.16
De La Rosa, Jorge	L-L	6-1	215	4-5-81	0	0	3.00	2	2	0	0	9	9	4	3	2	3	7	.265	.333	.250	7.00	3.00
Diaz, Jairo	R-R	6-0	200	5-27-91	3	5	4.58	47	0	0	8	55	51	31	28	6	37	50	.245	.227	.258	8.18	6.05
Flande, Yohan	L-L	6-2	180	1-27-86	3	3	7.11	6	6	0	0	32	55	30	25	8	7	11	.379	.429	.371	3.13	1.99
Germen, Gonzalez	R-R	6-1	200	9-23-87	0	0	2.70	3	0	0	0	3	3	1	1	0	1	4	.231	.143	.333	10.80	2.70
2-team total (24 Iowa)					5	1	3.68	27	0	0	4	37	32	17	15	3	18	31	—	—		7.61	4.42
Gomez, Leuris	R-R	6-0	170	10-20-86	0	2	6.75	8	3	0	0	21	26	16	16	2	9	20	.299	.282	.313	8.44	3.80
Gonzalez, Nelson	R-R	6-1	168	2-15-90	4	3	3.53	30	0	0	0	51	46	28	20	5	17	51	.250	.258	.246	9.00	3.00
Gray, Jon	R-R	6-4	235	11-5-91	4	6	4.33	21	20	1	0	114	129	61	55	9	41	110	.281	.287	.278	8.66	3.23
Gurka, Jason	L-L	6-0	180	1-10-88	2	1	3.18	21	1	0	0	40	42	14	14	3	15	30	.280	.220	.333	7.49	2.72
Hale, David	R-R	6-2	210	9-27-87	0	3	6.66	11	11	0	0	50	68	40	37	4	21	37	.333	.361	.308	6.66	3.78
Hawkins, LaTroy	R-R	6-5	220	12-21-72	0	0	7.71	5	0	0	0	5	8	4	4	0	1	4	.348	.300	.385	7.71	1.93
Hernandez, Carlos	L-L	5-11	155	3-4-87	1	1	4.91	3	3	0	0	11	13	6	6	2	1	6	.289	.262	.462	4.91	0.82
Jurrjens, Jair	R-R	6-1	180	1-29-86	2	5	6.88	17	14	0	0	71	105	62	54	9	23	39	.344	.338	.349	4.97	2.93
Kahnle, Tommy	R-R	6-1	235	8-7-89	1	3	4.67	21	0	0	6	27	19	14	14	3	12	28	.196	.182	.208	9.33	4.00

Pitching

Pitching	B-T	HT	WT	DOB	W	L	ERA	G	GS	CG	SV	IP	H	R	ER	HR	BB	SO	AVG	vLH	vRH	K/9	BB/9
Laffey, Aaron	L-L	6-0	200	4-15-85	5	4	3.90	27	12	0	0	90	103	45	39	7	42	63	.289	.329	.276	6.30	4.20
Lannan, John	L-L	6-4	235	9-27-84	6	10	5.39	26	25	1	0	152	209	107	91	11	40	83	.329	.361	.321	4.91	2.37
Matzek, Tyler	L-L	6-3	230	10-19-90	0	1	8.74	10	1	0	1	11	5	12	11	1	17	15	.128	.056	.190	11.91	13.50
Miller, Justin	R-R	6-3	215	6-13-87	0	2	2.30	25	0	0	7	27	20	7	7	2	8	33	.192	.175	.203	10.87	2.63
Oberg, Scott	R-R	6-2	205	3-13-90	1	0	1.13	7	0	0	2	8	14	1	1	0	2	11	.378	.636	.269	12.38	2.25
Owens, Rudy	L-L	6-3	240	12-18-87	2	3	6.17	8	7	0	0	35	44	25	24	2	12	24	.312	.286	.329	6.17	3.09
2-team total (7 Oklahoma City)					2	5	4.84	15	10	0	0	58	70	36	31	3	22	40	—	—		6.24	3.43
Roberts, Ken	L-L	6-1	200	3-9-88	1	3	5.12	23	0	0	0	32	50	24	18	3	4	28	.370	.378	.367	7.96	1.14
Rondon, Jorge	R-R	6-1	215	2-16-88	0	0	1.35	5	0	0	0	7	2	1	1	0	2	4	.095	.000	.125	5.40	2.70
Rusin, Chris	L-L	6-2	195	10-22-86	3	2	6.29	7	6	0	0	34	47	28	24	6	11	18	.313	.167	.350	4.72	2.88
Whiting, Boone	R-R	6-1	175	8-20-89	4	7	6.04	17	11	0	1	73	93	58	49	9	40	45	.312	.295	.325	5.55	4.93
2-team total (7 Memphis)					4	9	6.44	24	14	0	1	95	123	78	68	12	61	59	—	—		5.59	5.78

Fielding

Catcher	PCT	G	PO	A	E	DP	PB
Baker	1.000	9	48	3	0	0	0
Casteel	.979	31	219	17	5	1	0
Garneau	.992	78	561	62	5	10	9
Murphy	.966	27	200	25	8	3	4

First Base	PCT	G	PO	A	E	DP
McBride	.994	34	294	21	2	39
Parker	.993	48	429	29	3	49
Paulsen	.987	18	134	14	2	15
Ribera	1.000	1	4	2	0	1
Rosario	.979	34	299	21	7	34
Smalling	.990	10	95	6	1	2

Second Base	PCT	G	PO	A	E	DP
Adames	.973	20	47	60	3	20
Bond	1.000	11	18	27	0	6
Galvez	1.000	1	2	0	0	0
Nina	.971	47	92	145	7	39

	PCT	G	PO	A	E	DP
Rivera	.987	33	69	87	2	27
Story	.983	12	24	33	1	7
Wong	1.000	3	8	8	0	5
Ynoa	.984	26	46	79	2	17

Third Base	PCT	G	PO	A	E	DP
Adames	1.000	15	8	40	0	4
Nina	.932	22	10	58	5	4
Rivera	.800	4	2	6	2	0
Smalling	.943	68	26	138	10	17
Story	.872	14	8	33	6	2
Wong	.909	10	4	16	2	3
Ynoa	.918	24	10	35	4	3

Shortstop	PCT	G	PO	A	E	DP
Adames	.970	79	111	208	10	52
Culberson	.952	5	7	13	1	9
Nina	.918	16	21	35	5	9
Osborne	1.000	2	2	5	0	1

	PCT	G	PO	A	E	DP
Smalling	.947	3	5	13	1	4
Story	.976	35	51	110	4	24
Wong	.969	9	13	18	1	3
Ynoa	1.000	2	2	10	0	3

Outfield	PCT	G	PO	A	E	DP
Barfield	.982	34	53	1	1	0
Barnes	1.000	29	59	2	0	1
Bernadina	.975	108	223	9	6	3
Dickerson	1.000	5	6	0	0	0
McBride	.965	39	53	2	2	0
Nina	.971	28	30	3	1	1
Parker	.947	40	53	1	3	0
Paulsen	1.000	8	17	0	0	0
Smalling	1.000	19	15	0	0	0
Stubbs	1.000	34	89	2	0	0
Wheeler	.986	107	207	7	3	1
Ynoa	1.000	4	4	0	0	0

NEW BRITAIN ROCK CATS

DOUBLE-A

EASTERN LEAGUE

Batting	B-T	HT	WT	DOB	AVG	vLH	vRH	G	AB	R	H	2B	3B	HR	RBI	BB	HBP	SH	SF	SO	SB	CS	SLG	OBP
Baker, Abel	L-R	6-1	200	10-26-90	.158	.000	.171	12	38	3	6	2	0	0	0	2	0	0	0	16	0	0	.211	.200
Barfield, Jeremy	R-L	6-5	220	7-12-88	.195	.348	.136	26	82	9	16	4	0	2	8	8	1	0	1	18	0	0	.317	.272
Casteel, Ryan	R-R	5-11	205	6-6-91	.467	.333	.500	4	15	2	7	2	0	0	2	0	0	0	0	4	0	0	.600	.467
Ciriaco, Juan	R-R	5-9	165	7-6-90	.266	.273	.264	93	297	28	79	5	5	0	29	5	1	6	1	42	18	10	.316	.280
Cuevas, Noel	R-R	6-2	190	10-2-91	.264	.303	.251	112	406	47	107	21	2	4	51	17	8	10	2	87	31	12	.355	.305
Dahl, David	L-R	6-2	195	4-1-94	.278	.218	.292	73	288	46	80	16	3	6	24	11	0	3	0	72	22	7	.417	.304
Espy, Dean	R-R	6-1	210	10-30-89	.206	.219	.203	79	209	17	43	8	0	5	20	12	4	3	3	45	4	0	.316	.259
Langfels, Jayson	R-R	6-2	205	8-17-88	.185	.173	.188	79	238	34	44	5	5	1	19	35	8	0	2	86	10	8	.261	.307
Massey, Tyler	L-L	6-1	205	7-21-89	.227	.212	.231	72	260	33	59	14	3	1	24	25	2	3	2	46	12	7	.315	.298
Morneau, Justin	L-R	6-4	220	5-15-81	.500	.714	.364	5	18	4	9	2	0	2	9	0	0	0	0	3	0	0	.944	.500
Murphy, Tom	R-R	6-1	220	4-3-91	.249	.220	.257	72	265	36	66	17	1	13	44	23	5	0	1	80	5	2	.468	.320
Osborne, Zach	R-R	5-8	175	4-2-90	.258	.194	.278	41	128	14	33	5	1	0	16	8	2	7	0	11	0	1	.313	.312
Patterson, Jordan	L-L	6-4	215	2-12-92	.286	.268	.292	48	185	26	53	19	0	7	32	11	5	0	1	42	4		.503	.342
Pohl, Phil	R-R	5-11	215	7-22-90	.063	.000	.111	5	16	1	1	0	0	0	0	0	0	0	0	5	0	0	.063	.063
Ribera, Jordan	L-R	6-0	225	12-22-88	.238	.750	.118	7	21	4	5	1	0	0	3	1	1	0	0	2	0	0	.286	.304
Story, Trevor	R-R	6-1	180	11-15-92	.281	.261	.286	69	256	46	72	20	6	10	40	35	5	0	4	73	15	2	.523	.373
Swanner, Will	R-R	6-2	195	9-10-91	.260	.286	.252	115	358	42	93	19	0	17	50	44	2	4	1	126	7	8	.455	.343
Tauchman, Mike	L-L	6-2	200	12-3-90	.294	.260	.303	131	507	62	149	23	6	3	43	47	2	5	2	69	25	13	.381	.355
Thurber, Charley	L-L	6-4	200	12-8-89	.244	.500	.200	18	41	5	10	2	0	0	3	3	0	1	0	13	0	1	.293	.295
Valaika, Pat	R-R	5-11	200	9-9-92	.235	.200	.245	124	468	57	110	25	5	8	57	30	2	6	6	117	19	7	.361	.281
Vazquez, Jan	B-R	5-10	165	4-29-91	.223	.219	.223	65	211	25	47	8	2	3	20	26	7	5	2	61	2	3	.322	.325
Wong, Joey	L-R	5-10	185	4-12-88	.287	.167	.313	51	164	23	47	11	0	0	14	15	3	8	0	24	3	2	.354	.357

Pitching	B-T	HT	WT	DOB	W	L	ERA	G	GS	CG	SV	IP	H	R	ER	HR	BB	SO	AVG	vLH	vRH	K/9	BB/9
Arrowood, Ryan	R-R	6-3	190	8-24-90	1	2	4.15	10	3	0	0	26	27	14	12	1	13	15	.267	.302	.241	5.19	4.50
Bettis, Chad	R-R	6-1	200	4-26-89	0	0	0.00	1	1	0	0	3	2	0	0	0	2	4	.167	.000	.250	10.80	5.40
Broyles, Shane	R-R	6-1	180	8-19-91	0	6	4.35	28	1	0	2	41	37	21	20	4	22	44	.247	.193	.280	9.58	4.79
Burke, Devin	R-R	6-1	180	2-20-91	0	1	6.75	6	3	0	0	16	15	14	12	0	8	10	.250	.138	.563	5.63	4.50
Carle, Shane	R-R	6-4	185	8-30-91	14	7	3.48	26	26	3	0	160	167	71	62	12	31	100	.261	.272	.561	5.61	1.74
Carpenter, Ryan	L-L	6-5	210	8-22-90	9	13	4.04	28	28	2	0	167	165	85	75	19	37	132	.255	.262	.252	7.11	1.99
Estevez, Carlos	R-R	6-4	210	12-28-92	0	3	4.50	34	0	0	13	36	39	19	18	2	9	43	.275	.247	.304	10.75	2.25
Evans, Bryan	R-R	6-2	200	2-25-87	6	5	3.33	12	12	1	0	73	81	30	27	9	17	66	.225	.212	.239	8.14	2.10
Flande, Yohan	L-L	6-2	180	1-27-86	5	0	1.36	6	6	1	0	40	27	7	6	1	4	30	.193	.243	.175	6.81	0.91
Flemer, Matt	R-R	6-2	210	11-22-90	7	11	3.87	28	27	1	0	170	179	81	73	12	39	83	.269	.289	.249	4.40	2.07
Gonzalez, Nelson	R-R	6-1	168	2-15-90	1	1	1.50	12	0	0	0	18	14	6	3	0	3	11	.212	.148	.256	5.50	1.50
Gurka, Jason	L-L	6-0	180	1-10-88	3	0	2.31	14	0	0	0	23	17	6	6	0	6	20	.205	.194	.212	7.71	2.31
Hernandez, Carlos	L-L	5-11	155	3-4-87	2	0	4.25	5	5	0	0	30	39	19	14	6	6	18	.307	.333	.291	5.46	1.82
Hoffman, Jeff	R-R	6-4	185	1-8-93	2	2	3.22	7	7	0	0	36	27	14	13	3	10	29	.209	.222	.200	7.18	2.48

Pitching	B-T	HT	WT	DOB	W	L	ERA	G	GS	CG	SV	IP	H	R	ER	HR	BB	SO	AVG	vLH	vRH	K/9	BB/9
2-team total (2 New Hampshire)					2	2	2.81	9	9	0	0	48	36	16	15	3	12	37	—	—	—	6.94	2.25
House, Austin	R-R	6-4	200	1-24-91	3	4	4.13	52	0	0	20	52	73	28	24	1	18	39	.333	.318	.348	6.71	3.10
Marshall, Brett	R-R	6-1	195	3-22-90	1	4	5.40	7	7	1	0	42	43	26	25	3	14	31	.276	.277	.275	6.70	3.02
Miller, Justin	R-R	6-3	215	6-13-87	1	1	0.84	6	0	0	0	11	7	3	1	0	4	10	.175	.188	.167	8.44	3.38
Moll, Sam	L-L	5-10	185	1-3-92	0	0	1.23	13	0	0	0	15	7	2	2	0	4	17	.140	.222	.094	10.43	2.45
Musgrave, Harrison	L-L	6-1	205	3-3-92	3	4	3.18	11	11	0	0	57	55	27	20	7	13	53	.255	.250	.257	8.42	2.06
Ortega, Jose	R-R	5-11	190	10-12-88	0	1	4.19	45	0	0	1	54	47	28	25	3	31	40	.240	.256	.229	6.71	5.20
Schlosser, Gus	R-R	6-4	225	10-20-88	7	4	4.82	28	3	0	0	47	53	28	25	4	21	31	.280	.313	.257	5.98	4.05
Sitton, Kraig	L-L	6-5	190	7-13-88	3	2	2.97	46	0	0	1	58	64	23	19	0	14	37	.281	.325	.255	5.77	2.18
Ybarra, Tyler	L-L	6-2	210	12-11-89	1	0	4.87	38	0	0	3	44	48	25	24	1	28	44	.282	.310	.268	8.93	5.68
Zurat, Chad	R-R	6-2	215	11-22-91	0	0	6.23	3	0	0	0	4	3	3	3	1	5	0	.188	.286	.111	0.00	10.38

Fielding

Catcher	PCT	G	PO	A	E	DP	PB
Baker	1.000	9	46	4	0	0	1
Casteel	.963	3	25	1	1	0	0
Murphy	.983	58	364	35	7	3	7
Pohl	1.000	4	24	1	0	0	0
Swanner	1.000	13	74	6	0	0	2
Vazquez	.991	56	392	28	4	3	2

First Base	PCT	G	PO	A	E	DP
Casteel	1.000	1	11	0	0	0
Espy	.989	49	349	27	4	34
Morneau	1.000	3	17	1	0	1
Patterson	.989	21	161	14	2	16
Ribera	1.000	6	48	4	0	2
Swanner	.990	72	536	30	6	47
Wong	1.000	1	7	0	0	1

Second Base	PCT	G	PO	A	E	DP
Ciriaco	.942	71	112	179	18	32
Langfels	1.000	1	1	0	0	0
Osborne	.973	19	27	45	2	13
Story	.984	12	26	35	1	9
Valaika	.989	33	80	107	2	26
Wong	.962	12	21	30	2	8

Third Base	PCT	G	PO	A	E	DP
Ciriaco	1.000	4	2	1	0	1
Espy	.928	77	44	162	16	14
Langfels	1.000	4	2	1	0	1
Story	.952	5	8	12	1	1
Valaika	.945	29	25	44	4	7
Wong	.984	30	12	51	1	2

Shortstop	PCT	G	PO	A	E	DP
Ciriaco	.929	3	5	8	1	3
Osborne	.962	21	21	54	3	10
Story	.963	50	86	145	9	29
Valaika	.970	62	93	162	8	34
Wong	1.000	4	9	9	0	2

Outfield	PCT	G	PO	A	E	DP
Barfield	1.000	24	43	4	0	0
Cuevas	.980	103	238	3	5	0
Dahl	.988	65	156	5	2	1
Espy	1.000	9	19	1	0	0
Massey	.973	66	139	4	4	1
Patterson	.973	27	71	0	2	0
Tauchman	.994	126	299	7	2	3
Thurber	.929	12	13	0	1	0

MODESTO NUTS

HIGH CLASS A

CALIFORNIA LEAGUE

Batting	B-T	HT	WT	DOB	AVG	vLH	vRH	G	AB	R	H	2B	3B	HR	RBI	BB	HBP	SH	SF	SO	SB	CS	SLG	OBP
Benjamin Jr., Mike	R-R	6-0	190	3-18-92	.261	.274	.256	81	322	39	84	19	3	12	46	18	6	6	3	85	11	6	.450	.309
Dickerson, Corey	L-R	6-1	205	5-22-89	.375	.250	.500	2	8	2	3	0	0	0	1	0	0	0	0	1	0	0	.375	.375
Galvez, Cesar	B-R	5-9	145	7-24-91	.239	.304	.226	41	138	12	33	1	0	0	6	11	0	1	2	21	7	4	.246	.291
Graeter, Ashley	R-R	6-1	190	10-3-89	.242	.205	.253	82	306	26	74	14	2	1	25	15	4	1	1	64	7	5	.310	.285
Herrera, Rosell	B-R	6-3	195	10-16-92	.260	.291	.249	123	466	55	121	20	6	4	36	37	1	6	2	97	9	8	.354	.314
Hoelscher, Shane	R-R	6-0	195	9-21-91	.118	.400	.000	4	17	3	2	1	0	0	1	1	1	0	0	5	1	0	.176	.211
Jimenez, Emerson	L-R	6-1	160	12-16-94	.216	.179	.228	45	153	18	33	7	2	1	3	2	3	0	1	33	4	1	.307	.241
McMahon, Ryan	L-R	6-2	185	12-14-94	.300	.290	.304	132	496	85	149	43	6	18	75	49	9	0	2	153	6	13	.520	.372
Osborne, Zach	R-R	5-8	175	4-2-90	.242	.194	.256	48	153	23	37	6	2	0	16	13	2	10	2	18	2	0	.307	.306
Parris, Jordan	R-R	6-3	205	7-2-92	.000	.000	.000	4	13	0	0	0	0	0	0	0	0	0	0	8	0	0	.000	.000
Patterson, Jordan	L-L	6-4	215	2-12-92	.304	.342	.291	77	303	62	92	26	12	10	43	19	17	0	0	88	9	6	.568	.378
Prime, Correlle	R-R	6-5	222	2-18-94	.239	.262	.232	132	518	64	124	32	1	12	72	23	3	1	2	156	8	4	.375	.275
Quintanilla, Omar	L-R	5-9	185	10-24-81	.500	—	.500	2	4	0	2	0	0	0	1	0	0	0	0	0	0	0	.500	.500
Rodriguez, Wilfredo	R-R	5-10	200	1-25-94	.224	.263	.211	64	228	22	51	6	1	3	27	8	1	2	3	30	5	5	.298	.250
Soriano, Wilson	R-R	5-9	140	12-31-91	.266	.257	.269	81	278	28	74	4	1	0	21	6	3	8	3	36	17	9	.288	.286
Stein, Troy	R-R	6-1	210	4-17-92	.241	.269	.231	77	266	34	64	17	1	3	19	25	7	1	1	81	7	2	.346	.321
Tapia, Raimel	L-L	6-2	160	2-4-94	.305	.387	.278	131	544	74	166	34	9	12	71	24	5	7	13	105	26	10	.467	.333
Thomas, Dillon	L-L	6-1	195	12-10-92	.245	.160	.269	113	399	44	99	21	7	6	49	22	5	9	2	143	17	8	.381	.294
Weeks, Drew	R-R	6-1	180	6-9-93	.268	.226	.280	41	149	16	40	5	0	1	15	11	2	3	2	26	3	2	.322	.323

Pitching	B-T	HT	WT	DOB	W	L	ERA	G	GS	CG	SV	IP	H	R	ER	HR	BB	SO	AVG	vLH	vRH	K/9	BB/9
Balog, Alex	R-R	6-5	210	7-16-92	3	8	3.71	16	16	0	0	97	93	44	40	5	19	72	.251	.181	.288	6.68	1.76
Broyles, Shane	R-R	6-1	180	8-19-91	0	0	5.60	10	1	0	0	18	21	11	11	1	6	28	.288	.387	.214	14.26	3.06
Burke, Devin	R-R	6-1	205	2-20-91	2	2	2.93	20	0	0	0	46	44	17	15	4	10	29	.251	.141	.327	5.67	1.96
Carasiti, Matt	R-R	6-3	205	7-23-91	3	7	3.02	49	0	0	22	57	54	28	19	3	22	57	.251	.253	.250	9.05	3.49
Chatwood, Tyler	R-R	6-0	185	12-16-89	0	0	2.25	2	2	0	0	4	3	1	1	1	2	5	.200	.250	.182	11.25	4.50
Daniel, Trent	L-L	6-1	190	7-1-90	3	5	3.04	43	0	0	4	50	54	23	17	3	26	41	.277	.264	.285	7.33	4.65
Estevez, Carlos	R-R	6-4	210	12-28-92	5	0	1.37	14	0	0	5	20	12	3	3	0	5	25	.179	.147	.212	11.44	2.29
Freeland, Kyle	L-L	6-3	170	5-14-93	3	2	4.76	7	7	0	0	40	48	22	21	5	8	19	.308	.302	.310	4.31	1.82
Gonzalez, Rayan	R-R	6-3	175	10-18-90	1	3	6.45	22	0	0	1	22	27	19	16	1	13	25	.307	.282	.327	10.07	5.24
Hale, David	R-R	6-2	210	9-27-87	0	1	0.00	1	1	0	0	2	2	0	0	0	3	.182	.222	.000	11.57	3.86
Jemiola, Zach	L-R	6-3	200	4-6-94	5	4	4.08	16	14	0	0	90	90	49	41	13	27	69	.251	.238	.259	6.87	2.69
Jiminian, Johendi	R-R	6-3	170	10-14-92	4	11	4.82	28	21	0	0	133	146	86	71	11	42	101	.281	.265	.295	6.85	2.85
Moll, Sam	L-L	5-10	185	1-3-92	0	1	3.02	25	0	0	2	54	40	20	18	7	12	57	.206	.175	.221	9.56	2.01
Musgrave, Harrison	L-L	6-1	205	3-3-92	10	1	2.88	16	16	0	0	91	81	34	29	7	19	83	.240	.233	.242	8.24	1.89
Neiman, Troy	R-R	6-6	195	11-13-90	3	2	4.76	40	0	0	3	64	65	36	34	5	22	48	.266	.240	.284	6.72	3.08
Newberry, Jacob	R-R	6-2	210	10-10-90	1	1	3.21	28	0	0	0	34	34	16	12	2	8	43	.252	.302	.220	11.50	2.14
Pierpont, Matt	R-R	6-2	215	1-25-91	5	4	4.50	42	0	0	6	56	54	34	28	5	15	56	.250	.255	.246	9.00	2.41
Schlitter, Craig	R-R	6-0	195	5-16-92	0	0	0.00	1	0	0	0	1	1	0	0	0	0	3	.167	1.000	.000	27.00	0.00
Senzatela, Antonio	R-R	6-1	180	1-21-95	9	9	2.51	26	26	1	0	154	131	53	43	10	33	143	.229	.207	.245	8.36	1.93
Sheehan, John	R-R	5-11	190	8-16-90	0	0	0.00	1	0	0	0	1	0	0	0	0	1	.250	—	.250	9.00	0.00

COLORADO ROCKIES

Pitching	B-T	HT	WT	DOB	W	L	ERA	G	GS	CG	SV	IP	H	R	ER	HR	BB	SO	AVG	vLH	vRH	K/9	BB/9
Thompson, Dylan	L-R	6-3	195	9-4-92	0	0	0.00	2	0	0	0	3	1	2	0	0	2	1	.111	.000	.167	3.38	6.75
Wade, Konner	L-R	6-3	190	12-3-91	8	9	3.96	26	26	2	0	168	171	91	74	14	40	95	.265	.259	.269	5.08	2.14
Wiest, Grahamm	R-R	6-3	195	8-9-91	2	3	5.65	10	10	0	0	43	52	28	27	10	14	22	.306	.286	.329	4.60	2.93

Fielding

Catcher	PCT	G	PO	A	E	DP	PB
Graeter	.963	19	142	16	6	0	6
Rodriguez	.987	53	351	34	5	1	10
Stein	.991	69	512	60	5	3	16

First Base	PCT	G	PO	A	E	DP
Graeter	.982	12	106	3	2	8
Patterson	1.000	1	7	2	0	1
Prime	.992	127	1164	75	10	111

Second Base	PCT	G	PO	A	E	DP
Benjamin Jr.	.972	43	82	129	6	30
Galvez	.965	25	44	67	4	11
Graeter	1.000	10	20	22	0	6

	PCT	G	PO	A	E	DP
Hoelscher	1.000	3	9	7	0	2
Rodriguez	—	1	0	0	0	0
Soriano	.969	63	116	165	9	41

Third Base	PCT	G	PO	A	E	DP
Benjamin Jr.	.905	8	5	14	2	1
Graeter	.900	3	2	7	1	0
McMahon	.913	129	106	303	39	29
Soriano	.800	2	0	4	1	0

Shortstop	PCT	G	PO	A	E	DP
Benjamin Jr.	.961	29	51	71	5	18
Galvez	.926	16	25	50	6	7
Herrera	1.000	1	0	2	0	0

	PCT	G	PO	A	E	DP
Jimenez	.924	45	48	123	14	28
Osborne	.978	48	67	111	4	17
Quintanilla	1.000	2	0	1	0	1
Soriano	.917	3	4	7	1	3

Outfield	PCT	G	PO	A	E	DP
Dickerson	1.000	1	5	0	0	0
Herrera	.974	103	184	2	5	0
Patterson	.976	64	119	3	3	0
Soriano	.917	10	10	1	1	0
Tapia	.982	119	265	9	5	1
Thomas	.963	87	155	2	6	0
Weeks	.951	41	73	5	4	2

ASHEVILLE TOURISTS

LOW CLASS A

SOUTH ATLANTIC LEAGUE

Batting	B-T	HT	WT	DOB	AVG	vLH	vRH	G	AB	R	H	2B	3B	HR	RBI	BB	HBP	SH	SF	SO	SB	CS	SLG	OBP
Carrizales, Omar	L-L	6-0	175	1-30-95	.286	.321	.272	96	388	64	111	13	7	7	46	31	0	10	7	74	23	16	.410	.333
Causey, Nate	L-R	6-2	205	3-6-93	.250	.400	.143	3	12	2	3	0	0	1	3	2	0	0	0	6	0	0	.500	.357
Daza, Yonathan	R-R	6-2	190	2-28-94	.301	.282	.309	70	259	27	78	13	4	1	39	6	6	7	1	36	6	11	.394	.331
Derkes, Marcos	B-R	6-0	155	9-12-91	.196	.167	.206	13	46	4	9	2	0	0	2	2	2	1	0	16	2	2	.239	.260
Dwyer, Sean	L-L	6-0	200	12-5-91	.192	.154	.205	49	156	17	30	7	0	1	16	29	1	3	3	58	3	5	.256	.317
Fuentes, Josh	R-R	6-2	215	2-19-93	.252	.235	.260	93	337	45	85	24	1	6	42	29	8	6	5	64	7	6	.383	.322
Galvez, Cesar	B-R	5-9	145	7-24-91	.391	.368	.407	14	46	7	18	3	0	0	5	5	0	2	0	8	1	3	.457	.451
Garcia, Henry	R-R	6-2	195	9-23-91	.220	.143	.259	13	41	4	9	3	0	1	3	4	0	1	0	9	0	1	.366	.289
George, Max	R-R	5-9	180	4-7-96	.158	.189	.143	36	114	18	18	5	1	1	11	20	4	3	1	39	8	0	.246	.302
Hoelscher, Shane	R-R	6-0	195	9-21-91	.328	.347	.320	92	348	64	114	37	0	11	61	53	6	3	3	53	14	9	.529	.422
Jean, Luis	R-R	6-1	150	8-4-94	.267	.266	.268	89	303	32	81	12	2	0	31	25	4	19	6	45	27	11	.320	.325
Jimenez, Emerson	R-R	6-1	160	12-16-94	.185	.254	.160	63	232	33	43	11	1	1	17	5	1	7	2	52	16	5	.254	.204
Nunez, Dom	L-R	6-0	175	1-17-95	.282	.223	.304	104	373	61	105	23	0	13	53	53	4	7	4	55	7	7	.448	.373
Padlo, Kevin	R-R	6-2	200	7-15-96	.145	.167	.136	27	83	11	12	5	0	2	7	14	1	0	0	26	2	1	.277	.273
Perkins, Robbie	R-R	6-0	175	5-29-94	.200	.227	.187	41	135	11	27	9	1	1	14	11	0	5	1	47	3	1	.304	.259
Ramos, Roberto	L-R	6-5	220	12-28-94	.341	.238	.377	46	164	33	56	14	0	10	40	18	4	1	3	39	4	0	.610	.413
Reyes, Randy	R-R	6-0	175	9-4-92	.216	.158	.236	23	74	9	16	5	0	3	11	2	2	1	2	28	5	3	.405	.250
Rogers, Wes	R-R	6-3	180	3-7-94	.273	.263	.278	77	278	43	76	14	5	3	27	29	8	5	1	61	46	4	.392	.358
Rosario, Jairo	R-R	5-10	175	1-21-93	.258	.355	.210	25	93	12	24	11	0	3	13	2	1	2	1	26	0	4	.473	.278
Stephens, Ryan	L-L	5-11	175	7-6-92	.225	.220	.228	42	151	16	34	12	2	3	15	10	1	0	2	41	1	5	.391	.274
Wall, Forrest	L-R	6-0	176	11-20-95	.280	.238	.297	99	361	57	101	16	10	7	46	41	3	7	4	72	23	9	.438	.355
Weeks, Drew	R-L	6-1	180	6-9-93	.290	.280	.293	88	335	46	97	24	5	6	55	34	5	1	6	48	26	6	.445	.358
White, Max	L-L	6-2	175	10-10-93	.306	.290	.312	71	248	58	76	13	7	9	36	47	5	3	1	84	34	15	.524	.425

Pitching	B-T	HT	WT	DOB	W	L	ERA	G	GS	CG	SV	IP	H	R	ER	HR	BB	SO	AVG	vLH	vRH	K/9	BB/9
Bello, Yoely	L-L	6-2	150	12-16-90	5	5	3.33	53	0	0	2	68	57	31	25	5	22	53	.222	.219	.224	7.05	2.93
Castellani, Ryan	R-R	6-3	193	4-1-96	2	7	4.45	27	27	0	0	113	134	71	56	5	29	94	.291	.313	.275	7.46	2.30
Crawford, Alec	R-R	6-2	205	1-10-92	1	0	12.00	5	0	0	0	6	12	8	8	1	0	5	.414	.293	.500	7.50	0.00
Firth, Scott	R-R	6-0	170	1-2-91	0	1	4.01	20	0	0	0	25	22	15	11	3	10	20	.242	.129	.300	7.30	3.65
Glanz, Gavin	R-R	6-2	205	12-13-91	0	2	2.84	9	0	0	0	13	10	7	4	1	9	9	.204	.000	.278	6.39	6.39
Halley, Shane	B-R	6-2	200	9-28-89	0	1	3.55	17	0	0	1	25	26	13	10	1	6	25	.263	.237	.279	8.88	2.13
Howard, Sam	R-L	6-3	170	3-5-93	11	9	3.43	25	25	1	0	134	131	62	51	8	32	122	.252	.285	.242	8.19	2.15
Jemiola, Zach	L-R	6-3	200	4-6-94	6	3	3.16	10	10	1	0	63	58	23	22	6	13	52	.248	.259	.237	7.47	1.87
Lomangino, James	R-R	6-0	205	10-5-91	2	5	4.71	39	1	0	2	71	82	47	37	8	25	58	.295	.306	.287	7.39	3.18
McCrummen, Jerad	R-R	6-1	190	9-11-90	4	3	3.20	38	0	0	4	51	55	21	18	2	15	38	.275	.274	.276	6.75	2.66
Michalec, Josh	R-R	6-2	185	6-20-92	3	4	4.10	55	0	0	30	59	62	33	27	1	20	55	.268	.286	.256	8.34	3.03
Polanco, Carlos	R-R	6-2	175	2-18-94	9	10	3.90	25	25	1	0	141	154	70	61	9	36	115	.274	.253	.291	7.36	2.30
Rodriguez, Helmis	L-L	5-11	155	6-10-94	9	8	3.36	27	27	1	0	147	137	71	55	9	63	101	.250	.285	.237	6.17	3.85
Sawyer, Logan	R-R	6-5	215	12-29-92	5	2	5.79	14	4	0	0	47	58	37	30	3	25	33	.297	.361	.235	6.36	4.82
Sheehan, John	R-R	5-11	190	8-16-90	1	0	3.98	19	0	0	0	20	19	10	9	1	9	27	.250	.152	.326	11.95	3.98
Shouse, Blake	R-R	6-2	185	3-9-93	3	2	4.11	40	2	0	3	70	73	40	32	3	33	45	.274	.224	.313	5.79	4.24
Tinoco, Jesus	R-R	6-4	190	4-30-95	5	0	1.80	7	7	0	0	40	36	9	8	2	8	37	.243	.197	.276	8.33	1.80
Vasto, Jerry	L-L	6-2	195	2-12-92	2	4	2.93	46	0	0	3	58	42	24	19	3	20	68	.199	.211	.193	10.49	3.09
Wiest, Grahamm	R-R	6-3	195	8-9-91	4	1	2.81	17	11	0	0	77	76	30	24	3	20	54	.263	.302	.231	6.31	2.34

Fielding

Catcher	PCT	G	PO	A	E	DP	PB
Nunez	.981	99	742	79	16	6	11
Perkins	.978	40	264	41	7	3	5

First Base	PCT	G	PO	A	E	DP
Causey	1.000	3	21	2	0	4
Dwyer	.986	36	325	27	5	24

	PCT	G	PO	A	E	DP
Fuentes	.992	52	445	30	4	35
Garcia	.990	11	88	8	1	14
Jean	1.000	2	19	0	0	2
Ramos	.984	41	352	20	6	24

Second Base	PCT	G	PO	A	E	DP
Galvez	1.000	4	6	17	0	3

	PCT	G	PO	A	E	DP
George	1.000	13	26	37	0	10
Hoelscher	.977	8	15	27	1	5
Jean	.976	25	49	74	3	16
Wall	.952	92	149	246	20	54

Third Base	PCT	G	PO	A	E	DP
Fuentes	.908	39	32	96	13	7

	PCT	G	PO	A	E	DP
Hoelscher	.896	61	42	122	19	10
Jean	.971	17	12	22	1	1
Padlo	.951	25	19	58	4	6
Rosario	.800	3	2	2	1	1
Shortstop	**PCT**	**G**	**PO**	**A**	**E**	**DP**
Galvez	.944	10	14	20	2	2
George	.919	23	40	62	9	11

	PCT	G	PO	A	E	DP
Jean	.925	49	65	133	16	22
Jimenez	.900	63	89	191	31	36
Outfield	**PCT**	**G**	**PO**	**A**	**E**	**DP**
Carrizales	.974	90	178	12	5	3
Daza	.961	66	134	12	6	3
Derkes	.947	11	15	3	1	1
Dwyer	1.000	2	3	0	0	0

	PCT	G	PO	A	E	DP
Jean	—	1	0	0	0	0
Reyes	.897	15	23	3	3	0
Rogers	.966	63	108	4	4	1
Stephens	.976	40	78	2	2	1
Weeks	.981	77	146	13	3	5
White	.965	60	108	3	4	0

BOISE HAWKS

SHORT-SEASON

NORTHWEST LEAGUE

COLORADO ROCKIES

Batting	B-T	HT	WT	DOB	AVG	vLH	vRH	G	AB	R	H	2B	3B	HR	RBI	BB	HBP	SH	SF	SO	SB	CS	SLG	OBP
Burcham, Scotty	R-R	5-11	185	6-17-93	.235	.265	.218	35	136	20	32	4	1	2	11	10	0	3	0	38	7	2	.324	.288
Carroll, Brian	R-R	5-11	175	12-31-91	.306	.475	.222	38	121	23	37	5	4	0	9	12	5	6	0	19	14	5	.413	.391
Casteel, Ryan	R-R	5-11	205	6-6-91	.267	.333	.250	4	15	2	4	1	0	0	0	0	0	0	0	6	0	0	.333	.267
Castro, Luis	R-R	6-1	187	9-19-95	.219	.286	.179	43	151	18	33	7	1	2	13	10	6	2	2	43	3	3	.318	.290
Causey, Nate	L-R	6-2	205	3-6-93	.225	.185	.245	25	80	8	18	4	2	2	21	19	0	0	1	24	0	1	.400	.370
Dahl, David	L-R	6-2	195	4-1-94	.125	.111	.133	6	24	1	3	1	0	0	1	0	0	0	0	9	0	0	.167	.125
Daza, Yonathan	R-R	6-2	190	2-28-94	.418	.441	.394	16	67	18	28	7	2	2	14	4	1	0	0	11	4	3	.672	.458
Derkes, Marcos	B-R	6-0	155	9-12-91	.240	.226	.246	52	175	23	42	6	3	1	26	36	0	1	1	56	21	7	.326	.368
Ferguson, Collin	L-L	6-2	216	2-9-93	.200	.273	.111	6	20	3	4	0	0	0	1	0	1	0	0	7	0	0	.200	.238
Follis, Tyler	L-R	6-2	200	7-19-93	.282	.379	.214	23	71	10	20	2	1	0	7	7	2	0	0	25	5	1	.338	.363
George, Max	R-R	5-9	180	4-7-96	.200	.125	.263	10	35	6	7	4	0	1	4	2	2	0	0	13	0	1	.400	.317
Herrera, Carlos	L-R	6-0	145	9-23-96	.267	.282	.260	53	221	35	59	6	1	2	21	14	2	6	0	47	28	5	.339	.316
Jimenez, Wilkyns	R-R	6-2	180	7-18-95	.264	.265	.264	33	121	12	32	4	0	1	17	9	1	0	1	28	1	0	.322	.318
Jones, Wesley	R-R	6-2	180	8-12-95	.190	.238	.170	40	142	9	27	3	0	1	5	7	4	1	1	19	4	3	.232	.247
Leonard, Steven	R-R	5-10	185	12-30-92	.250	.222	.262	31	92	10	23	3	0	1	11	8	3	3	0	25	5	3	.315	.330
Marte, Hamlet	R-R	5-10	180	2-3-94	.297	.328	.279	46	172	16	51	17	0	3	19	13	0	2	1	45	3	1	.448	.344
Massey, Tyler	L-L	6-1	205	7-21-89	.136	.167	.125	6	22	3	3	0	1	0	0	3	0	0	0	9	3	2	.227	.240
McClure, Terry	R-R	6-2	190	9-29-95	.261	.245	.269	45	161	23	42	6	0	4	18	17	0	3	2	46	14	8	.373	.328
Mundell, Brian	R-R	6-2	201	2-28-94	.275	.284	.271	69	244	35	67	19	1	4	36	32	4	0	10	45	7	1	.410	.355
Padlo, Kevin	R-R	6-2	200	7-15-96	.294	.222	.328	70	255	44	75	22	2	9	46	45	4	1	3	62	33	5	.502	.404
Park, Jensen	R-R	5-10	168	12-10-92	.268	.269	.267	19	71	6	19	4	1	0	9	2	1	2	2	19	8	1	.352	.289
Prigatano, Richard	R-R	6-3	195	9-24-92	.100	.125	.091	8	30	2	3	1	0	0	3	2	0	0	0	16	0	0	.133	.156
Toole, Eric	L-R	6-0	180	2-8-93	.291	.289	.292	29	103	17	30	5	0	0	7	8	1	3	1	18	9	3	.340	.345
Wall, Forrest	L-R	6-0	176	11-20-95	.500	.667	.429	4	14	4	5	0	0	0	1	6	0	0	1	2	2	5	.500	.647
White, Max	L-L	6-2	175	10-10-93	.375	.000	.500	3	8	4	3	0	2	0	1	3	0	0	1	2	1	0	.875	.545
Wong, Joey	L-R	5-10	185	4-12-88	.059	.000	.111	5	17	2	1	1	0	0	1	0	0	0	0	2	0	0	.118	.059

Pitching	B-T	HT	WT	DOB	W	L	ERA	G	GS	CG	SV	IP	H	R	ER	HR	BB	SO	AVG	vLH	vRH	K/9	BB/9
Black, Taylor	R-R	6-2	190	12-16-91	2	3	3.52	17	0	0	5	23	24	11	9	3	2	28	.255	.192	.279	10.96	0.78
Cozart, Logan	R-R	6-2	215	1-27-93	3	0	3.96	25	0	0	0	36	31	19	16	3	14	30	.226	.231	.222	7.43	3.47
Craig, Dylan	R-L	6-2	210	5-1-93	5	5	3.18	5	5	0	0	17	18	7	6	0	5	16	.265	.217	.289	8.47	2.65
Hill, David	R-R	6-2	180	5-27-94	0	0	3.09	8	7	0	0	23	20	8	8	1	9	23	.233	.188	.259	8.87	3.47
Johnson, Drasen	R-R	6-3	200	12-23-91	2	4	2.37	15	4	0	0	38	39	13	10	1	13	28	.269	.283	.261	6.63	3.08
Jones, Hayden	R-R	6-0	185	1-5-94	0	1	11.00	10	0	0	0	9	14	14	11	1	8	8	.326	.200	.393	8.00	8.00
Justo, Salvador	R-R	6-5	210	10-14-94	2	0	3.22	15	0	0	0	22	21	13	8	1	15	13	.259	.314	.217	5.24	6.04
Kenilvort, Alec	R-R	6-6	230	1-7-93	1	2	5.40	22	0	0	0	38	37	25	23	2	20	31	.257	.200	.287	7.28	4.70
Lawrence, Justin	R-R	6-4	220	11-25-94	0	3	8.05	16	0	0	0	17	21	22	17	3	15	15	.273	.367	.213	7.11	7.11
Lezama, Angel	R-R	6-0	164	3-1-94	1	3	8.10	13	7	0	0	40	66	48	36	4	9	24	.359	.324	.381	5.40	2.03
Matzek, Tyler	L-L	6-3	230	10-19-90	0	1	23.14	3	0	0	0	2	2	6	6	0	8	4	.286	.500	.200	15.43	30.86
McCormick, Ryan	R-R	6-2	205	3-15-94	1	2	4.09	12	7	0	0	44	54	29	20	2	15	25	.316	.306	.323	5.11	3.07
Meier, Matt	R-R	6-1	190	5-6-92	0	0	5.49	17	0	0	0	20	18	15	12	2	11	13	.234	.281	.200	5.95	5.03
Palacios, Javier	R-R	6-1	165	9-29-93	3	3	3.26	12	12	0	0	61	68	28	22	0	12	38	.281	.210	.331	5.64	1.78
Quintin, Cristian	R-R	6-3	165	12-27-93	3	5	3.68	26	0	0	7	37	34	17	15	3	9	31	.248	.192	.282	7.61	2.21
Sawyer, Logan	R-R	6-5	215	12-29-92	4	4	4.11	11	10	0	0	61	61	33	28	2	22	41	.260	.308	.229	6.02	3.23
Schlitter, Craig	R-R	6-0	195	5-16-92	2	0	2.25	9	0	0	1	12	8	3	3	0	2	17	.186	.231	.118	12.75	1.50
Sheehan, John	R-R	5-11	190	8-16-90	0	0	0.00	3	0	0	0	3	0	0	0	1	3	.000	.000	.000	8.10	2.70
Thompson, Dylan	L-R	6-3	195	9-4-92	1	3	4.65	19	3	0	2	41	38	27	21	1	25	30	.241	.243	.239	6.64	5.53
Villarroel, Cesar	R-R	6-3	188	7-27-94	0	3	9.38	14	0	0	0	24	32	27	25	2	11	13	.311	.303	.314	4.88	4.13
Welmon, Colin	L-R	6-2	180	8-7-92	2	5	4.20	12	12	0	0	49	56	31	23	2	15	37	.281	.250	.301	6.75	2.74
Wynkoop, Jack	L-L	6-5	205	11-2-93	2	4	4.25	11	9	0	0	49	52	28	23	6	8	34	.274	.273	.274	6.29	1.48
Zurat, Chad	R-R	6-2	215	11-22-91	1	0	0.00	2	0	0	0	2	0	0	0	0	1	.000	.000	.000	5.40	0.00

Fielding

Catcher	PCT	G	PO	A	E	DP	PB
Casteel	1.000	4	20	2	0	0	0
Causey	1.000	7	50	4	0	0	0
Jimenez	.973	22	129	17	4	0	7
Leonard	1.000	9	56	4	0	0	0
Marte	.989	38	240	30	3	3	12

First Base	PCT	G	PO	A	E	DP
Causey	1.000	6	36	5	0	4
Ferguson	1.000	6	52	1	0	6
Jimenez	.981	11	100	5	2	14

	PCT	G	PO	A	E	DP
Mundell	.980	56	511	35	11	50
Second Base	**PCT**	**G**	**PO**	**A**	**E**	**DP**
Burcham	1.000	12	17	33	0	6
Castro	.911	26	59	74	13	15
Follis	.938	4	6	9	1	2
George	1.000	7	18	32	0	11
Jones	.967	24	38	79	4	19
Wall	.933	4	7	7	1	0
Wong	1.000	3	7	8	0	2

Third Base	PCT	G	PO	A	E	DP
Follis	.860	11	12	25	6	1
Jones	.933	6	5	9	1	1
Padlo	.948	59	34	129	9	8
Wong	1.000	2	0	6	0	0

Shortstop	PCT	G	PO	A	E	DP
Burcham	.943	23	41	74	7	26
Herrera	.918	52	83	175	23	30
Jones	1.000	1	2	4	0	1

Outfield	PCT	G	PO	A	E	DP
Carroll	.985	38	64	1	1	0
Dahl	1.000	6	15	0	0	0
Daza	1.000	16	29	3	0	1
Derkes	.980	52	96	2	2	0

	PCT	G	PO	A	E	DP
Follis	.900	7	9	0	1	0
Jones	1.000	1	1	0	0	0
Leonard	.972	21	31	4	1	1
Massey	1.000	3	6	1	0	1
McClure	.956	45	84	3	4	2

	PCT	G	PO	A	E	DP
Park	1.000	19	35	2	0	1
Prigatano	.833	5	10	2	2	0
Toole	.952	29	58	2	3	0
White	1.000	3	6	0	0	0

GRAND JUNCTION ROCKIES

ROOKIE

PIONEER LEAGUE

Batting	B-T	HT	WT	DOB	AVG	vLH	vRH	G	AB	R	H	2B	3B	HR	RBI	BB	HBP	SH	SF	SO	SB	CS	SLG	OBP
Anderson, Cole	R-R	5-11	190	2-7-97	.248	.255	.245	43	149	27	37	5	2	6	14	11	3	1	0	59	4	3	.430	.313
Benjamin Jr., Mike	R-R	6-0	190	3-18-92	.238	.250	.231	6	21	2	5	2	0	0	1	3	1	0	0	6	3	0	.333	.360
Brito, Antony	R-R	5-11	180	2-15-95	.316	.295	.330	42	155	28	49	6	2	0	23	9	0	0	1	19	5	1	.381	.352
Ferguson, Collin	L-L	6-2	216	2-9-93	.346	.281	.375	51	185	42	64	17	2	9	38	35	2	1	2	32	7	4	.605	.463
Hilliard, Sam	L-L	6-5	225	2-21-94	.306	.253	.336	60	222	45	68	13	8	7	42	36	0	0	4	55	12	4	.532	.397
Jones, Mylz	R-R	6-1	185	4-13-94	.300	.333	.279	52	207	42	62	9	3	2	27	18	2	6	1	34	12	6	.401	.360
Keck, Chris	L-R	6-2	180	9-2-92	.291	.273	.297	35	134	22	39	9	4	6	32	10	6	1	1	29	0	0	.552	.364
Nevin, Tyler	R-R	6-4	200	5-29-97	.265	.226	.283	53	189	29	50	15	1	2	18	29	3	0	2	42	3	7	.386	.368
Park, Jensen	R-R	5-10	168	12-10-92	.341	.381	.321	30	123	22	42	6	4	3	24	3	1	1	0	23	8	2	.528	.362
Paulino, Elvin	R-R	6-1	195	12-3-94	.200	.175	.213	32	120	8	24	9	0	0	12	5	0	0	3	30	0	2	.275	.227
Piron, Jonathan	L-R	6-0	175	11-14-94	.312	.275	.331	56	231	48	72	11	5	11	40	8	0	0	6	56	16	6	.545	.335
Rabago, Chris	R-R	5-11	185	4-22-93	.306	.311	.303	45	170	28	52	10	2	3	28	10	4	1	3	35	6	3	.441	.353
Ramos, Roberto	L-R	6-5	220	12-28-94	.289	.368	.211	9	38	11	11	3	0	3	10	4	2	0	0	12	0	0	.605	.386
Richardson, Denzel	R-R	6-2	174	1-7-94	.222	.200	.250	2	9	2	2	1	0	0	1	1	0	0	0	1	0	1	.333	.300
Rodgers, Brendan	R-R	6-0	180	8-9-96	.273	.256	.279	37	143	22	39	8	2	3	20	15	0	0	1	37	4	3	.420	.340
Rodriguez, Wilfredo	R-R	5-10	200	1-25-94	.167	.222	.111	6	18	2	3	1	0	0	1	3	1	0	0	2	1	0	.222	.318
Rogers, Wes	R-R	6-3	180	3-7-94	.414	.364	.444	10	29	7	12	2	0	0	8	0	0	0	0	4	7	0	.483	.541
Stahel, Bobby	R-R	5-9	200	9-1-92	.293	.254	.312	52	184	32	54	8	6	3	33	14	9	2	5	32	11	7	.451	.363
Stephens, Ryan	L-L	5-11	175	7-6-92	.412	.450	.357	8	34	10	14	3	1	4	11	4	0	0	0	5	2	1	.912	.474
Wear, Campbell	R-R	6-3	205	10-23-93	.256	.320	.230	27	86	11	22	4	0	1	9	8	1	0	1	33	2	2	.337	.323

Pitching	B-T	HT	WT	DOB	W	L	ERA	G	GS	CG	SV	IP	H	R	ER	HR	BB	SO	AVG	vLH	vRH	K/9	BB/9
Behr, Dakota	R-R	6-2	185	12-9-91	3	1	6.31	15	1	0	0	26	32	24	18	7	6	28	.294	.366	.250	9.82	2.10
Brothers, Hunter	L-R	6-1	210	12-20-91	3	3	3.75	25	0	0	6	36	31	16	15	3	16	43	.226	.214	.232	10.75	4.00
Crawford, Alec	R-R	6-2	205	1-10-92	2	0	5.14	21	0	0	0	35	42	24	20	6	11	20	.290	.317	.271	5.14	2.83
Fernandez, Julian	R-R	6-2	160	12-5-95	0	0	3.60	4	0	0	0	5	2	4	2	0	3	6	.118	.000	.154	10.80	5.40
Firth, Scott	R-R	6-0	170	1-2-91	0	0	9.72	9	0	0	0	8	15	11	9	1	4	10	.395	.353	.429	10.80	4.32
Franco, Kelvin	R-R	6-1	165	10-29-94	2	0	4.65	24	0	0	2	31	29	21	16	2	12	33	.230	.302	.178	9.58	3.48
Freeland, Kyle	L-L	6-3	170	5-14-93	0	0	0.00	2	2	0	0	7	2	0	0	0	2	9	.087	.083	.091	11.57	2.57
French, Parker	L-R	6-2	200	3-19-93	2	4	3.72	10	10	0	0	48	50	22	20	4	2	36	.260	.308	.236	6.70	0.37
Glanz, Gavin	R-R	6-2	205	12-13-91	2	3	5.28	16	11	0	0	58	62	48	34	2	28	29	.267	.200	.306	4.50	4.34
Guillen, Adonis	R-R	6-2	175	11-23-95	0	1	17.18	4	0	0	0	4	8	8	7	1	1	7	.444	.500	.429	17.18	2.45
Killian, Trey	R-R	6-3	185	9-8-93	1	4	9.09	9	9	0	0	34	55	38	34	10	11	22	.369	.404	.348	5.88	2.94
Koger, Daniel	R-L	6-6	185	8-12-93	2	2	3.47	23	0	0	4	23	21	13	9	0	10	12	.233	.308	.203	10.41	3.86
Lambert, Peter	R-R	6-2	185	4-18-97	0	4	3.45	8	8	0	0	31	29	18	12	3	11	26	.227	.184	.244	7.47	3.16
Lawrence, Justin	R-R	6-4	220	11-25-94	0	0	9.53	6	0	0	0	6	10	6	6	1	1	3	.370	.500	.316	4.76	1.59
McMahon, James	R-R	6-1	210	9-28-91	2	2	6.44	19	3	0	0	36	50	33	26	7	12	35	.373	.429	.343	8.67	2.97
Medina, Javier	R-R	6-2	190	8-9-96	1	3	6.82	9	9	0	0	34	51	30	26	7	10	30	.342	.281	.388	7.86	2.62
Nikorak, Mike	R-R	6-5	220	9-16-96	0	4	11.72	8	8	0	0	18	26	28	23	1	32	14	.347	.310	.370	7.13	16.30
Ozuna, Lorenz	R-R	6-0	175	9-22-94	3	2	5.73	25	0	0	0	38	47	30	24	5	18	34	.305	.237	.347	8.12	4.30
Pena, Jhon	R-R	6-2	175	8-25-95	1	2	9.00	24	1	0	0	42	64	43	42	6	17	36	.356	.322	.372	7.71	3.64
Stamey, Dylan	R-R	6-2	185	1-7-92	0	0	0.00	1	0	0	0	1	1	0	0	0	0	1	.333	.000	.500	13.50	0.00
Talley, Christian	R-R	6-4	190	9-22-91	2	4	7.00	16	4	0	0	36	49	41	28	7	11	40	.312	.291	.324	10.00	2.75
Thoele, Sam	R-R	6-3	205	10-17-92	0	1	4.64	21	0	0	5	21	17	13	11	1	16	27	.215	.250	.196	11.39	6.75
Villarroel, Hector	L-L	6-3	150	8-12-95	0	0	48.60	3	0	0	0	2	5	9	9	0	7	0	.625	.500	.667	0.00	37.80
Zimmerman, Michael	L-L	6-2	170	8-13-96	2	0	4.85	11	5	0	0	26	35	14	14	1	7	16	.343	.357	.338	5.54	2.42
Zurat, Chad	R-R	6-2	215	11-22-91	3	3	3.92	15	5	0	0	41	50	25	18	3	16	16	.305	.268	.324	3.48	3.48

Fielding

Catcher	PCT	G	PO	A	E	DP	PB
Paulino	.971	13	87	12	3	2	7
Rabago	.989	43	303	44	4	2	9
Rodriguez	1.000	6	32	4	0	0	0
Wear	.963	17	117	14	5	1	2

First Base	PCT	G	PO	A	E	DP
Ferguson	.982	50	438	40	9	36
Keck	1.000	8	62	6	0	3
Paulino	.976	9	76	6	2	3
Ramos	.979	9	84	9	2	7

Second Base	PCT	G	PO	A	E	DP
Benjamin Jr.	1.000	3	4	4	0	0

	PCT	G	PO	A	E	DP
Brito	.923	37	58	97	13	13
Jones	.971	7	15	18	1	4
Piron	.950	36	70	82	8	17

Third Base	PCT	G	PO	A	E	DP
Brito	.889	5	2	6	1	0
Jones	.864	7	8	11	3	1
Keck	.953	19	13	28	2	1
Nevin	.900	47	35	91	14	8

Shortstop	PCT	G	PO	A	E	DP
Benjamin Jr.	.857	1	4	2	1	1
Jones	.937	28	47	71	8	13
Piron	.900	23	23	67	10	10

	PCT	G	PO	A	E	DP
Rodgers	.923	29	35	109	12	16

Outfield	PCT	G	PO	A	E	DP
Anderson	.969	37	60	3	2	0
Hilliard	.962	53	93	7	4	1
Jones	1.000	7	10	1	0	0
Park	.940	26	45	2	3	0
Richardson	1.000	2	4	0	0	0
Rogers	.882	9	15	0	2	0
Stahel	.990	51	91	7	1	0
Stephens	1.000	4	6	0	0	0
Suero	.906	49	93	3	10	0

DOMINICAN SUMMER LEAGUE

Batting	B-T	HT	WT	DOB	AVG	vLH	vRH	G	AB	R	H	2B	3B	HR	RBI	BB	HBP	SH	SF	SO	SB	CS	SLG	OBP
Brito Jr., Luis	L-L	6-0	165	1-28-96	.272	.164	.309	60	217	29	59	15	4	0	28	17	1	1	3	46	10	5	.378	.324
Chal, Welington	L-R	6-1	170	11-18-97	.210	.182	.218	38	100	10	21	2	0	0	4	22	4	0	0	31	1	3	.230	.373
Diaz, Joel	R-R	6-1	175	9-18-95	.290	.375	.265	62	241	38	70	19	0	6	34	14	5	1	5	35	3	4	.444	.336
Garcia, Franklin	R-R	6-0	170	3-3-98	.282	.340	.262	56	188	31	53	9	1	0	22	12	3	6	1	28	7	5	.340	.333
Gomez, Jose	R-R	5-11	173	12-10-96	.300	.327	.291	66	220	35	66	13	1	2	28	16	13	8	1	25	12	7	.395	.380
Gonzalez, Hidekel	R-R	6-0	189	10-7-96	.326	.421	.300	51	178	21	58	8	1	2	27	16	4	1	4	27	6	4	.416	.386
Gonzalez, Pedro	R-R	6-3	160	10-27-97	.251	.292	.237	63	251	46	63	14	2	8	33	19	7	2	3	81	8	12	.418	.318
Guevara, Javier	R-R	5-11	165	9-25-97	.246	.282	.233	41	142	24	35	8	1	2	15	15	3	2	1	40	0	1	.359	.329
Herrera, Carlos	L-R	6-0	145	9-23-96	.340	.357	.333	12	53	12	18	2	0	0	5	2	2	0	0	11	10	2	.377	.386
Jimenez, Anderson	R-R	6-1	180	7-31-97	.203	.270	.178	43	138	16	28	2	1	2	20	13	3	1	2	33	6	5	.275	.282
Marcelino, Ramon	L-R	6-1	175	12-23-96	.290	.276	.295	54	214	30	62	17	0	1	35	11	8	1	5	40	7	5	.383	.340
Melendez, Manuel	L-L	5-11	165	1-10-97	.267	.208	.291	65	266	37	71	12	7	1	31	23	9	4	2	32	15	13	.376	.343
Reyes, Alvaro	L-L	6-1	174	7-10-98	.132	.100	.143	15	38	1	5	1	0	0	2	1	1	0	0	15	0	0	.158	.175
Rodriguez, Jose	L-R	5-10	135	2-23-96	.277	.333	.260	40	101	16	28	3	0	0	9	16	0	2	2	19	3	5	.307	.370
Rosario, Yeremi	R-R	5-11	150	2-4-98	.181	.135	.198	43	138	17	25	6	0	0	12	16	1	2	1	52	9	4	.225	.269

Pitching	B-T	HT	WT	DOB	W	L	ERA	G	GS	CG	SV	IP	H	R	ER	HR	BB	SO	AVG	vLH	vRH	K/9	BB/9
Cespedes, Richard	R-R	6-0	185	8-29-97	0	1	4.91	3	2	0	0	4	3	3	2	0	4	0	.250	1.000	.100	0.00	9.82
Eusebio, Breiling	L-L	6-1	175	10-21-96	4	4	1.88	14	14	0	0	72	59	30	15	1	16	76	.215	.282	.204	9.50	2.00
Fernandez, Julian	R-R	6-2	160	12-5-95	3	2	3.55	24	0	0	4	33	25	15	13	0	12	29	.219	.138	.247	7.91	3.27
Garcia, Evaryn	R-R	6-0	192	6-13-96	1	1	10.05	13	0	0	0	14	29	18	16	0	7	11	.460	.545	.415	6.91	4.40
Garcia, Henry	R-R	6-5	195	3-29-97	3	1	2.13	17	1	0	4	38	34	15	9	1	17	31	.245	.256	.240	7.34	4.03
Guillen, Adonis	R-R	6-2	175	11-23-95	3	5	2.18	18	5	0	3	58	42	25	14	0	22	66	.199	.134	.229	10.30	3.43
Guzman, Luis	L-L	6-1	165	2-27-96	3	3	4.29	14	10	0	0	57	57	31	27	3	28	43	.264	.353	.247	6.83	4.45
Lopez, Carlos	R-R	6-2	175	4-24-96	2	5	4.85	21	2	0	0	43	49	33	23	0	16	36	.287	.293	.283	7.59	3.38
Martinez, Alexander	R-R	6-1	165	12-28-96	1	1	5.09	11	0	0	0	18	27	12	10	1	3	18	.346	.500	.286	9.17	1.53
Moreta, Hector	R-R	6-3	170	12-9-95	0	0	2.70	8	0	0	2	13	15	4	4	0	3	5	.283	.300	.273	3.38	2.03
Olivares, Keinter	L-L	6-0	170	12-1-97	1	0	1.64	5	2	0	0	11	10	6	2	0	1	7	.227	.000	.250	5.73	0.82
Oviedo, Jorge	L-L	6-2	180	10-6-96	3	2	2.59	14	10	1	0	66	59	23	19	2	4	55	.236	.156	.248	7.50	0.55
Perez, Esmerlin	R-R	6-0	165	1-8-96	0	1	7.00	13	0	0	1	18	33	19	14	0	5	15	.407	.379	.423	7.50	2.50
Quintana, Yohander	R-R	6-3	175	4-9-97	4	2	3.38	14	9	0	0	51	45	26	19	4	17	32	.231	.177	.256	5.68	3.02
Requena, Alejandro	R-R	6-2	200	11-29-96	2	4	4.14	15	11	0	0	63	61	34	29	2	12	44	.245	.231	.250	6.29	1.71
Rodriguez, Jose	R-R	6-1	186	12-27-95	1	1	3.31	19	0	0	4	33	29	13	12	1	11	30	.238	.214	.250	8.27	3.03
Santos, Antonio	R-R	6-3	180	10-6-96	1	2	0.75	6	5	0	0	24	23	7	2	0	5	17	.245	.243	.246	6.38	1.88
Valdez, Jefry	R-R	6-1	165	8-20-95	0	1	15.00	2	1	0	0	3	4	5	5	0	4	1	.308	.333	.300	3.00	12.00
Villarroel, Cesar	R-R	6-3	188	7-27-94	0	0	2.25	7	0	0	1	8	7	4	2	0	3	9	.241	.300	.211	10.13	3.38
Viloria, Ismael	R-R	6-1	165	3-31-95	1	3	3.97	18	0	0	0	23	23	15	10	1	7	20	.253	.200	.286	7.94	2.78

Fielding

Catcher	PCT	G	PO	A	E	DP	PB
Diaz	.973	10	60	13	2	0	3
Gonzalez	.965	28	188	31	8	0	4
Guevara	.985	39	274	52	5	0	16

First Base	PCT	G	PO	A	E	DP
Diaz	.996	43	434	21	2	24
Gomez	1.000	11	64	10	0	4
Gonzalez	.991	24	215	16	2	12

Second Base	PCT	G	PO	A	E	DP
Garcia	.945	26	41	63	6	12
Gomez	.941	9	13	19	2	7

Third Base	PCT	G	PO	A	E	DP
Herrera	.667	1	0	2	1	0
Rodriguez	.981	14	24	28	1	3
Rosario	.911	33	54	90	14	10
Diaz	1.000	5	2	5	0	0
Garcia	.857	14	11	31	7	1
Gomez	.915	49	38	102	13	8
Gonzalez	.875	12	8	13	3	0
Guevara	1.000	1	0	1	0	1

Shortstop	PCT	G	PO	A	E	DP
Garcia	.968	17	18	42	2	7

	PCT	G	PO	A	E	DP
Gonzalez	.867	45	53	110	25	12
Herrera	.962	10	18	32	2	6
Rosario	.893	7	9	16	3	2

Outfield	PCT	G	PO	A	E	DP
Brito Jr.	.949	52	91	3	5	1
Chal	.895	14	16	1	2	0
Jimenez	.938	38	59	1	4	0
Marcelino	.977	53	78	6	2	1
Melendez	.970	65	122	9	4	2
Reyes	1.000	7	8	1	0	0
Rodriguez	1.000	3	6	1	0	0

Detroit Tigers

SEASON IN A SENTENCE: After promising a World Series-or-bust mentality, the Tigers started strong, sputtered in May and wound up selling rather than buying at the trade deadline. Dealing the likes of Yoenis Cespedes and David Price helped restock the farm system, but they were the last acts for general manager Dave Dombrowski, who was forced out in early August.

HIGH POINT: Despite scoring four runs in three games, Detroit opened a West Coast road trip by winning two of three at Oakland, moving to 28-20 overall and one game behind the Royals in the American League Central. Price tossed seven innings in the middle game of the series, and Joakim Soria notched his 14th and 15th saves of the early season in the two victories.

LOW POINT: Detroit lost its next eight games, capped by a June 5 walk-off loss in Chicago against the White Sox. A July 10 walk-off loss at Minnesota, as the Twins went on to win three of four, showed Detroit truly wasn't a contender, and by the end of the month Dombrowski had acted. Injuries to Miguel Cabrera and Victor Martinez—neither of whom played more than 120 games—didn't help as the Tigers scored fewer runs than in any season since the 119-loss debacle of 2003.

NOTABLE ROOKIES: James McCann outplayed injury-prone Alex Avila and became the everyday catcher, throwing out 41 percent of opposing basestealers and holding his own offensively until he wore down late. Tyler Collins established himself as a potential option in left field with a solid finish. Buck Farmer failed in his bid to shore up the rotation in the first half, while sot-tossing lefty Kyle Ryan had his moments.

KEY TRANSACTIONS: Trading Price to Toronto netted lefties Daniel Norris, who looks like a future rotation fixture, and vexing lefty Matt Boyd, who dominates the minors but has faltered badly in the majors. Cespedes yielded top prospect righty Michael Fulmer as a key piece from the Mets. Soria was sent to the Pirates for Double-A shortstop JaCoby Jones.

DOWN ON THE FARM: Detroit's domestic affiliates posted a .472 winning percentage, with low Class A West Michigan providing the bright spot by winning the Midwest League championship behind prospects such as outfielder Mike Gerber and Spencer Turnbull and 2015 draft picks such as shortstop A.J. Simcox and outfielder Christin Stewart.

OPENING DAY PAYROLL: $173,813,750 (4th)

PLAYERS OF THE YEAR

MAJOR LEAGUE
J.D. Martinez
of
.282/.344/.535
38 HR, 102 RBI
Led team in HR, RBI

MINOR LEAGUE
Mike Gerber
of
.292/.355/.468
(low Class A)
10 3B, 13 HR, 76 RBI

ORGANIZATION LEADERS

BATTING — *Minimum 250 AB

MAJORS

*AVG	Miguel Cabrera	.338
*OPS	Miguel Cabrera	.974
HR	J.D. Martinez	38
RBI	J.D. Martinez	102

MINORS

*AVG	Curt Powell, Erie, Lakeland	.303
*OBP	Curt Powell, Erie, Lakeland	.384
*SLG	Jefry Marte, Toledo	.487
R	Wynton Bernard, Erie	78
H	Wynton Bernard, Erie	161
TB	Mike Gerber, West Michigan	240
2B	Steven Moya, Lakeland, Toledo	33
3B	Mike Gerber, West Michigan	10
HR	Steven Moya, Lakeland, Toledo	23
RBI	Steven Moya, Lakeland, Toledo	82
BB	Daniel Fields, Toledo	66
SO	Steven Moya, Lakeland, Toledo	175
SB	Wynton Bernard, Erie	43

PITCHING — #Minimum 75 IP

MAJORS

W	Alfredo Simon	13
#ERA	David Price	2.53
SO	Anibal Sanchez	138
	David Price	138
SV	Joakim Soria	23

MINORS

W	Josh Turley, Erie	13
L	Chad Green, Erie	14
#ERA	Spencer Turnbull, West Michigan	3.01
G	Alberto Cabrera, Toledo	47
GS	Chad Green/Austin Kubitza, Erie	27
	Tim Melville, Toledo	27
	Thad Weber, Toledo	27
	Kevin Ziomek, Lakeland	27
SV	Paul Voelker, West Michigan, Lakeland, Erie	18
IP	Thad Weber, Toledo	161
BB	Tim Melville, Toledo	68
SO	Kevin Ziomek, Lakeland	143
AVG	Kevin Ziomek, Lakeland	.242

General Manager: Dave Dombrowski/Al Avila. **Farm Director:** Dan Lunetta. **Scouting Director:** Scott Pleis.

Class	Team	League	W	L	PCT	Finish	Manager
Majors	Detroit Tigers	American	74	87	.460	14th (15)	Brad Ausmus
Triple-A	Toledo Mud Hens	International	61	83	.424	13th (14)	Larry Parrish
Double-A	Erie SeaWolves	Eastern	64	78	.451	11th (12)	Lance Parrish
High A	Lakeland Flying Tigers	Florida State	55	79	.410	11th (12)	Dave Huppert
Low A	West Michigan Whitecaps	Midwest	75	64	.540	6th (16)	Andrew Graham
Short season	Connecticut Tigers	New York-Penn	35	38	.479	10th (14)	Mike Rabelo
Rookie	Tigers	Gulf Coast	36	23	.610	3rd (16)	Basilio Cabrera
Overall 2015 Minor League Record			326	365	.472	23rd (30)	

ORGANIZATION STATISTICS

DETROIT TIGERS

AMERICAN LEAGUE

Batting	B-T	HT	WT	DOB	AVG	vLH	vRH	G	AB	R	H	2B	3B	HR	RBI	BB	HBP	SH	SF	SO	SB	CS	SLG	OBP
Avila, Alex	L-R	5-11	210	1-29-87	.191	.133	.203	67	178	21	34	5	0	4	13	40	0	1	0	66	0	1	.287	.339
Cabrera, Miguel	R-R	6-4	240	4-18-83	.338	.313	.344	119	429	64	145	28	1	18	76	77	3	0	2	82	1	1	.534	.440
Castellanos, Nick	R-R	6-4	210	3-4-92	.255	.351	.230	154	549	42	140	33	6	15	73	39	1	0	6	152	0	3	.419	.303
Cespedes, Yoenis	R-R	5-10	210	10-18-85	.293	.183	.321	102	403	62	118	28	2	18	61	19	1	0	4	87	3	4	.506	.323
Collins, Tyler	L-L	5-11	215	6-6-90	.266	.286	.264	60	192	18	51	11	3	4	25	13	1	1	0	43	2	1	.417	.316
Davis, Rajai	R-R	5-9	195	10-19-80	.258	.245	.267	112	341	55	88	16	11	8	30	22	3	1	3	76	18	8	.440	.306
Fields, Daniel	L-R	6-2	215	1-23-91	.333	—	.333	1	3	1	1	1	0	0	0	0	0	0	0	2	0	0	.667	.333
Gose, Anthony	L-L	6-1	190	8-10-90	.254	.192	.265	140	485	73	123	24	8	5	26	45	3	2	0	145	23	11	.367	.321
Holaday, Bryan	R-R	6-0	205	11-19-87	.281	.316	.267	24	64	3	18	5	0	2	13	1	0	0	0	13	0	0	.453	.292
Iglesias, Jose	R-R	5-11	185	1-5-90	.300	.354	.284	120	416	44	125	17	3	2	23	25	6	4	3	44	11	8	.370	.347
Kinsler, Ian	R-R	6-0	200	6-22-82	.296	.305	.294	154	624	94	185	35	7	11	73	43	3	0	5	80	10	6	.428	.342
Krauss, Marc	L-R	6-2	245	10-5-87	.152	.000	.167	12	33	1	5	0	0	1	2	0	0	0	0	13	0	0	.242	.152
3-team total (11 Los Angeles, 4 Tampa Bay)					.141	—	—	27	78	3	11	3	0	2	8	3	0	0	0	31	0	0	.256	.173
Machado, Dixon	R-R	6-1	170	2-22-92	.235	.250	.231	24	68	6	16	3	0	0	5	7	0	3	0	14	1	0	.279	.307
Marte, Jefry	R-R	6-1	220	6-21-91	.213	.270	.163	33	80	9	17	4	0	4	11	8	0	2	2	22	0	0	.413	.284
Martinez, J.D.	R-R	6-3	220	8-21-87	.282	.265	.286	158	596	93	168	33	2	38	102	53	5	0	3	178	3	2	.535	.344
Martinez, Victor	B-R	6-2	210	12-23-78	.245	.348	.219	120	440	39	108	20	0	11	64	31	7	0	7	52	0	0	.366	.301
McCann, James	R-R	6-2	210	6-13-90	.264	.320	.247	114	401	32	106	18	5	7	41	16	3	4	1	90	0	1	.387	.297
Moya, Steven	L-R	6-7	260	8-9-91	.182	.000	.211	9	22	1	4	0	1	0	3	0	0	0	0	10	0	0	.273	.280
Perez, Hernan	R-R	6-1	185	3-26-91	.061	.071	.053	22	33	1	2	0	0	0	1	0	0	0	0	11	1	0	.061	.088
Romine, Andrew	L-R	6-1	200	12-24-85	.255	.257	.255	109	184	25	47	5	0	2	15	11	3	4	1	46	10	5	.315	.307
Wilson, Josh	R-R	6-0	175	3-26-81	.316	.357	.292	21	38	4	12	2	0	0	5	0	2	1	0	5	0	0	.395	.350

Pitching	B-T	HT	WT	DOB	W	L	ERA	G	GS	CG	SV	IP	H	R	ER	HR	BB	SO	AVG	vLH	vRH	K/9	BB/9
Alburquerque, Al	R-R	6-0	195	6-10-86	4	1	4.21	67	0	0	0	62	63	29	29	4	33	58	.269	.256	.278	8.42	4.79
Boyd, Matt	L-L	6-3	215	2-2-91	1	4	6.57	11	10	0	0	51	56	39	37	12	19	36	.290	.327	.278	6.39	3.38
2-team total (2 Toronto)					1	6	7.53	13	12	0	0	57	71	50	48	17	20	43	—	—	—	6.75	3.14
Chamberlain, Joba	R-R	6-2	250	9-23-85	0	2	4.09	30	0	0	0	22	32	15	10	5	5	15	.340	.419	.275	6.14	2.05
2-team total (6 Kansas City)					0	2	4.88	36	0	0	0	28	38	20	15	6	9	23	—	—	—	7.48	2.93
Farmer, Buck	L-R	6-4	225	2-20-91	0	4	7.36	14	5	0	0	40	53	35	33	10	17	24	.323	.389	.272	5.36	3.79
Feliz, Neftali	R-R	6-3	225	5-2-88	2	2	7.62	30	0	0	4	28	33	24	24	3	9	23	.303	.268	.340	7.31	2.86
2-team total (18 Texas)					3	4	6.38	48	0	0	10	48	57	34	34	5	18	39	—	—	—	7.31	3.38
Ferrell, Jeff	R-R	6-3	185	11-23-90	0	0	6.35	9	0	0	0	11	12	8	8	3	4	6	.267	.222	.296	4.76	3.18
Gorzelanny, Tom	L-L	6-2	210	7-12-82	2	2	5.95	48	0	0	0	39	45	28	26	4	23	36	.292	.222	.354	8.24	5.26
Greene, Shane	R-R	6-4	210	11-17-88	4	8	6.88	18	16	0	0	84	103	67	64	13	27	50	.308	.363	.245	5.38	2.90
Hardy, Blaine	L-L	6-2	230	3-14-87	5	3	3.08	70	0	0	0	61	61	23	21	2	22	55	.260	.241	.276	8.07	3.23
Knudson, Guido	R-R	6-1	185	8-5-89	0	0	18.00	4	0	0	0	5	13	10	10	5	3	6	.464	.778	.316	10.80	5.40
Krol, Ian	L-L	6-1	210	5-9-91	2	3	5.79	33	0	0	0	28	31	19	18	4	17	26	.287	.326	.262	8.36	5.46
Lobstein, Kyle	L-L	6-3	200	8-12-89	3	5	5.94	13	11	0	0	64	78	43	42	7	23	32	.305	.244	.331	4.52	3.25
Nathan, Joe	R-R	6-4	230	11-22-74	0	0	0.00	1	0	0	1	0	0	0	0	0	0	1	.000	—	.000	27.00	0.00
Nesbitt, Angel	R-R	6-1	240	12-4-90	1	1	5.40	24	0	0	0	22	22	14	13	2	8	14	.265	.368	.178	5.82	3.32
Norris, Daniel	L-L	6-2	195	4-25-93	2	1	3.68	8	8	0	0	37	30	20	15	6	11	27	.216	.220	.214	6.63	1.72
2-team total (5 Toronto)					3	2	3.75	13	13	0	0	60	53	31	25	9	19	45	—	—	—	6.75	2.85
Price, David	L-L	6-6	210	8-26-85	9	4	2.53	21	21	3	0	146	133	50	41	13	29	138	.241	.267	.233	8.51	1.79
2-team total (11 Toronto)					18	5	2.45	32	32	3	0	220	190	70	60	17	47	225	—	—	—	9.19	1.92
Rondon, Bruce	R-R	6-3	275	12-9-90	1	0	5.81	35	0	0	5	31	31	22	20	3	19	36	.261	.288	.239	10.45	5.52
Ryan, Kyle	L-L	6-5	210	9-25-91	2	4	4.47	16	6	0	0	56	60	29	28	9	20	30	.282	.333	.263	4.79	3.20
Sanchez, Anibal	R-R	6-0	205	2-27-84	10	10	4.99	25	25	1	0	157	152	89	87	29	49	138	.252	.217	.291	7.91	2.81
Simon, Alfredo	R-R	6-6	265	5-8-81	13	12	5.05	31	31	2	0	187	201	112	105	24	68	117	.276	.289	.257	5.63	3.27
Soria, Joakim	R-R	6-3	200	5-18-84	1	3	2.85	43	0	0	23	41	32	13	13	5	11	36	.212	.227	.197	7.90	2.41
Valdez, Jose	R-R	6-1	200	3-1-90	0	1	4.00	7	0	0	0	9	10	4	4	2	4	4	.286	.308	.273	4.00	4.00
VerHagen, Drew	R-R	6-6	230	10-22-90	2	0	2.05	20	0	0	0	26	18	6	6	1	6	14	.200	.226	.186	4.44	4.78
Verlander, Justin	R-R	6-5	225	2-20-83	5	8	3.38	20	20	1	0	133	113	56	50	13	32	113	.229	.216	.244	7.63	2.16
Wilson, Alex	R-R	6-0	215	11-3-86	3	3	2.19	59	1	0	2	70	61	19	17	5	11	38	.238	.222	.252	4.89	1.41
Wolf, Randy	L-L	6-0	205	8-22-76	0	5	6.23	8	7	0	0	35	46	28	24	5	15	28	.319	.148	.359	7.27	3.89

Fielding

Catcher	PCT	G	PO	A	E	DP	PB
Avila	1.000	44	291	18	0	3	2
Holaday	1.000	18	112	5	0	1	0
McCann	1.000	112	723	54	0	5	3

First Base	PCT	G	PO	A	E	DP
Avila	.992	23	120	9	1	12
Cabrera	.996	107	903	76	4	96
Holaday	1.000	1	1	0	0	1
Krauss	1.000	12	68	7	0	11
Marte	.975	22	106	11	3	9
Martinez	.989	10	81	5	1	13
Perez	1.000	4	9	1	0	0
Romine	.988	17	73	6	1	7

Second Base	PCT	G	PO	A	E	DP
Holaday	—	1	0	0	0	0
Kinsler	.982	153	289	425	13	109
Perez	1.000	5	5	5	0	1
Romine	1.000	13	19	25	0	11
Wilson	1.000	11	6	12	0	3

Third Base	PCT	G	PO	A	E	DP
Castellanos	.966	145	92	249	12	27
Marte	.944	7	2	15	1	3
Perez	1.000	8	3	7	0	0
Romine	.961	59	14	35	2	1
Wilson	.800	10	3	5	2	1

Shortstop	PCT	G	PO	A	E	DP
Iglesias	.977	119	162	315	11	81
Machado	.979	24	37	56	2	14
Perez	1.000	3	1	2	0	0
Romine	.967	27	48	71	4	19
Wilson	1.000	2	1	6	0	1

Outfield	PCT	G	PO	A	E	DP
Cespedes	.977	99	204	9	5	1
Collins	.950	43	73	3	4	1
Davis	.988	91	161	2	2	0
Fields	.667	1	2	0	1	0
Gose	.989	137	352	4	4	1
Martinez	.993	148	265	15	2	3
Moya	1.000	7	12	0	0	1
Romine	1.000	2	2	0	0	0

TOLEDO MUD HENS
INTERNATIONAL LEAGUE

TRIPLE-A

DETROIT TIGERS

Batting	B-T	HT	WT	DOB	AVG	vLH	vRH	G	AB	R	H	2B	3B	HR	RBI	BB	HBP	SH	SF	SO	SB	CS	SLG	OBP
Avery, Xavier	L-L	6-0	190	1-1-90	.305	.367	.273	73	285	42	87	18	2	1	28	30	2	2	4	62	14	10	.393	.371
2-team total (38 Rochester)					.285	—	—	111	431	65	123	21	3	6	51	37	3	2	5	105	19	12	.390	.342
Avila, Alex	L-R	5-11	210	1-29-87	.300	.111	.455	6	20	2	6	0	0	1	5	0	0	0	2	8	0	0	.450	.273
Casilla, Alexi	B-R	5-9	170	7-20-84	.269	.277	.267	57	208	28	56	11	2	1	17	14	1	2	0	29	6	3	.356	.318
2-team total (37 Durham)					.287	—	—	94	335	43	96	19	2	4	31	27	1	4	0	51	10	5	.391	.342
Collins, Tyler	L-L	5-11	215	6-6-90	.247	.188	.278	53	190	21	47	10	0	2	20	22	3	0	3	40	9	2	.332	.330
Fields, Daniel	L-R	6-2	215	1-23-91	.228	.213	.234	122	447	59	102	25	8	7	41	66	7	3	3	146	17	7	.367	.335
Gaynor, Wade	R-R	6-3	225	4-19-88	.188	.235	.161	15	48	4	9	4	1	0	4	3	0	0	1	10	2	1	.313	.231
Gonzalez, Alberto	R-R	5-10	195	4-18-83	.100	—	.100	2	10	0	1	1	0	0	0	0	0	0	0	1	0	0	.200	.100
Gonzalez, Miguel	R-R	5-11	220	12-3-90	.221	.186	.243	38	113	13	25	9	0	0	11	8	2	1	0	21	1	1	.301	.285
Green, Dean	L-R	6-4	255	6-30-89	.253	.217	.268	23	79	7	20	4	0	1	5	8	1	0	0	14	0	0	.342	.330
Harris, Brendan	R-R	6-1	200	8-26-80	.228	.208	.242	18	57	8	13	3	1	0	4	7	1	1	1	7	0	0	.316	.318
Hessman, Mike	R-R	6-5	215	3-5-78	.237	.202	.253	114	405	48	96	25	4	16	57	57	9	0	4	103	0	0	.437	.341
Holaday, Bryan	R-R	6-0	205	11-19-87	.224	.234	.219	49	161	18	36	8	0	2	17	10	4	2	2	35	1	1	.311	.282
Jones, Corey	L-R	6-0	205	9-14-87	.280	.271	.282	82	268	33	75	15	1	2	29	18	2	4	2	50	1	2	.366	.328
Krauss, Marc	L-R	6-2	245	10-5-87	.247	.174	.274	23	85	14	21	4	2	0	9	18	0	0	0	26	2	2	.341	.379
Krizan, Jason	L-R	6-0	185	6-28-89	.169	.143	.175	20	71	7	12	1	0	0	5	7	0	2	2	15	0	1	.183	.238
Lennerton, Jordan	L-L	6-2	230	2-16-86	.242	.265	.233	54	182	22	44	13	1	4	24	25	0	1	1	41	0	1	.390	.332
2-team total (33 Gwinnett)					.227	—	—	87	286	31	65	15	1	5	34	36	1	1	3	68	0	1	.339	.313
Machado, Dixon	R-R	6-1	170	2-22-92	.261	.279	.254	127	509	61	133	22	1	4	48	36	4	15	3	85	15	3	.332	.313
Marte, Jefry	R-R	6-1	220	6-21-91	.275	.384	.224	95	357	49	98	25	3	15	65	31	7	0	4	64	8	5	.487	.341
Martinez, Victor	B-R	6-2	210	12-23-78	.294	.333	.286	4	17	1	5	1	0	0	3	0	0	0	0	2	0	0	.353	.294
McVaney, Jeff	R-R	6-2	210	1-16-90	.186	.204	.178	48	161	19	30	5	1	0	8	10	1	1	3	35	3	4	.230	.260
Moya, Steven	L-R	6-7	260	8-9-91	.240	.213	.253	126	500	53	120	30	4	20	74	27	4	1	3	162	5	4	.420	.283
Pina, Manny	R-R	6-0	215	6-5-87	.305	.292	.309	77	256	28	78	19	0	7	39	24	8	2	2	34	2	0	.461	.379
Robinson, Trayvon	B-R	5-10	200	9-1-87	.211	.225	.205	49	152	11	32	5	0	1	9	24	1	2	0	24	11	1	.263	.322
Wilson, Josh	R-R	6-0	175	3-26-81	.252	.295	.234	79	262	30	66	14	1	3	30	22	4	2	3	70	10	2	.347	.316

Pitching	B-T	HT	WT	DOB	W	L	ERA	G	GS	CG	SV	IP	H	R	ER	HR	BB	SO	AVG	vLH	vRH	K/9	BB/9
Belfiore, Mike	R-L	6-3	220	10-3-88	5	11	5.60	22	22	0	0	124	143	81	77	14	49	77	.294	.321	.286	5.60	3.57
2-team total (3 Norfolk)					5	12	5.32	25	25	0	0	135	153	85	80	15	53	82	—	—	—	5.45	3.52
Boyd, Matt	L-L	6-3	215	2-2-91	0	0	0.00	1	1	0	0	2	0	0	0	0	3	1	.000	.000	.000	4.50	13.50
2-team total (6 Buffalo)					3	1	2.63	7	7	0	0	41	32	13	12	5	9	38	—	—	—	8.34	1.98
Cabrera, Alberto	R-R	6-4	210	10-25-88	3	2	6.59	47	0	0	9	56	64	43	41	10	29	47	.283	.306	.266	7.55	4.66
Cessa, Luis	R-R	6-3	190	4-25-92	1	3	5.97	7	7	0	0	38	46	27	25	2	15	34	.307	.277	.329	8.12	3.58
Dolis, Rafael	R-R	6-4	215	1-10-88	7	5	4.61	43	0	0	1	66	63	40	34	2	42	54	.251	.260	.245	7.33	5.70
Farmer, Buck	L-R	6-4	225	2-20-91	7	3	4.15	16	16	0	0	87	85	45	40	6	25	76	.251	.238	.262	7.89	2.60
Faulk, Kenny	L-L	6-0	235	5-27-87	0	0	7.62	9	0	0	0	13	18	11	11	2	3	13	.316	.143	.372	9.00	2.08
Ferrell, Jeff	R-R	6-3	185	4-16-91	0	1	4.76	11	0	0	4	11	8	6	6	3	5	10	.195	.143	.222	7.94	3.97
Gorzelanny, Tom	L-L	6-2	210	7-12-82	0	0	4.00	9	0	0	0	9	5	4	4	2	9	11	.167	.214	.125	11.00	9.00
Greene, Shane	R-R	6-4	210	11-17-88	1	1	3.86	7	7	0	0	35	37	15	15	2	11	21	.272	.290	.257	5.40	2.83
Hankins, Derek	R-R	6-4	195	7-1-83	1	1	6.75	4	0	0	0	16	18	14	12	2	8	13	.277	.313	.242	7.31	4.50
Knudson, Guido	R-R	6-1	185	8-5-89	1	2	2.34	32	0	0	10	42	28	12	11	1	21	44	.189	.232	.163	9.35	4.46
Krol, Ian	L-L	6-1	210	5-9-91	1	1	2.30	18	0	0	1	31	21	10	8	0	13	34	.186	.179	.189	9.77	3.73
Lobstein, Kyle	L-L	6-3	200	8-12-89	0	2	6.62	4	4	0	0	18	26	16	13	0	9	13	.347	.000	.394	6.62	4.58
Mantiply, Joe	R-L	6-4	215	3-1-91	2	0	0.90	7	0	0	1	10	6	1	1	1	1	7	.162	.187	.185	6.30	0.90
Melville, Tim	R-R	6-4	225	10-9-89	7	10	4.63	27	27	1	0	152	141	89	78	14	68	102	.250	.230	.261	6.05	4.04
Mercedes, Melvin	R-R	6-3	250	11-2-90	0	1	6.68	22	1	0	0	34	47	28	25	3	14	32	.329	.302	.350	8.55	3.74
Nathan, Joe	R-R	6-4	230	11-22-74	0	0	0.00	1	0	0	0	1	0	0	0	0	0	1	.000	—	.000	13.50	0.00
Nesbitt, Angel	R-R	6-1	240	12-4-90	1	5	6.25	27	0	0	0	40	54	30	28	3	21	30	.327	.328	.327	6.69	4.69
Perry, Ryan	R-R	6-5	215	2-13-87	0	0	12.71	5	0	0	0	6	11	8	8	1	4	5	.423	.222	.529	7.94	6.35
Putkonen, Luke	R-R	6-6	215	5-10-86	0	0	32.40	2	0	0	0	2	6	6	6	2	1	2	.545	.250	.714	5.40	10.80
Robowski, Ryan	L-L	6-0	185	2-3-88	0	0	4.15	2	0	0	0	4	4	2	2	1	2	3	.267	.000	.333	6.23	4.15

Pitching

Pitching	B-T	HT	WT	DOB	W	L	ERA	G	GS	CG	SV	IP	H	R	ER	HR	BB	SO	AVG	vLH	vRH	K/9	BB/9
Rondon, Bruce	R-R	6-3	275	12-9-90	2	2	7.11	13	0	0	1	13	16	11	10	1	6	14	.302	.333	.281	9.95	4.26
Ryan, Kyle	L-L	6-5	210	9-25-91	4	9	4.19	17	17	0	0	103	117	53	48	3	33	63	.292	.300	.290	5.50	2.88
Saupold, Warwick	R-R	6-1	195	1-16-90	1	2	4.43	6	3	0	0	20	14	10	10	1	6	23	.203	.214	.195	10.18	2.66
Seaton, Ross	L-R	6-4	200	9-18-89	1	1	5.73	2	2	0	0	11	12	7	7	0	4	9	.293	.294	.292	7.36	3.27
Valdez, Jose	R-R	6-1	200	3-1-90	4	5	3.32	43	0	0	5	57	49	23	21	3	38	43	.239	.280	.241	6.79	6.00
VerHagen, Drew	R-R	6-6	230	10-22-90	1	3	3.58	15	0	0	1	28	26	13	11	0	11	21	.265	.280	.250	6.83	3.58
Verlander, Justin	R-R	6-5	225	2-20-83	0	0	3.24	2	2	0	0	8	10	4	3	0	2	12	.294	.158	.467	12.96	2.16
Weber, Thad	R-R	6-2	205	9-28-84	6	10	4.19	27	27	0	0	161	168	82	75	19	41	105	.271	.275	.267	5.87	2.29
Wilson, Alex	R-R	6-0	215	11-3-86	1	0	0.00	4	0	0	3	5	4	0	0	1	5	.211	.143	.250	8.44	1.69
Zeid, Josh	R-R	6-4	225	3-24-87	4	3	4.46	42	4	0	2	71	68	38	35	4	39	59	.260	.230	.282	7.51	4.97

Fielding

Catcher	PCT	G	PO	A	E	DP	PB
Avila	1.000	4	18	0	0	1	0
Gonzalez	1.000	38	233	18	0	3	2
Holaday	.989	48	326	38	4	5	2
Jones	1.000	1	2	0	0	0	0
Pina	.996	66	424	45	2	4	3

First Base	PCT	G	PO	A	E	DP
Gaynor	1.000	1	13	1	0	2
Green	.970	21	176	18	6	11
Hessman	.990	47	351	29	4	31
Holaday	1.000	1	8	1	0	1
Jones	1.000	5	22	1	0	1
Krauss	.991	23	207	18	2	30
Krizan	1.000	2	24	1	0	1
Lennerton	1.000	50	392	29	0	32
Marte	1.000	4	27	2	0	3

Second Base	PCT	G	PO	A	E	DP
Casilla	.984	52	98	145	4	32
Harris	.984	15	28	33	1	10
Jones	.972	40	69	105	5	25
Krizan	1.000	10	14	26	0	2
Wilson	.982	34	71	96	3	20

Third Base	PCT	G	PO	A	E	DP
Gaynor	.941	8	7	9	1	0
Harris	1.000	1	0	2	0	0
Hessman	.950	18	5	33	2	6
Jones	.833	9	4	16	4	3
Machado	.500	2	0	2	2	0
Marte	.937	91	48	176	15	8
Wilson	.952	24	12	48	3	7

Shortstop	PCT	G	PO	A	E	DP
Casilla	.833	1	2	3	1	1

Gonzalez	.917	2	3	8	1	1
Harris	.800	2	1	3	1	1
Machado	.975	125	197	344	14	72
Marte	—	1	0	0	0	0
Wilson	.986	18	18	50	1	10

Outfield	PCT	G	PO	A	E	DP
Avery	.993	59	138	2	1	1
Collins	.990	49	98	3	1	1
Fields	.990	116	293	3	3	0
Gaynor	1.000	4	4	0	0	0
Jones	1.000	11	19	0	0	0
Krizan	1.000	4	4	1	0	0
McVaney	.960	43	94	3	4	0
Moya	.982	110	223	0	4	0
Robinson	1.000	43	87	6	0	1
Wilson	1.000	2	2	0	0	0

ERIE SEAWOLVES

DOUBLE-A

EASTERN LEAGUE

Batting	B-T	HT	WT	DOB	AVG	vLH	vRH	G	AB	R	H	2B	3B	HR	RBI	BB	HBP	SH	SF	SO	SB	CS	SLG	OBP
Bernard, Wynton	R-R	6-2	195	9-24-90	.301	.317	.297	135	534	78	161	29	8	4	36	38	4	11	0	73	43	16	.408	.352
Castro, Harold	L-R	6-0	165	11-30-93	.256	.190	.265	101	336	41	86	12	2	1	26	14	1	6	6	63	17	9	.313	.283
Ficociello, Dominic	B-R	6-4	205	4-10-92	.284	.302	.277	43	155	24	44	12	2	3	30	6	2	0	2	34	0	0	.445	.315
Gaynor, Wade	R-R	6-3	225	4-19-88	.193	.159	.204	105	363	36	70	14	2	11	38	27	0	1	2	101	10	4	.333	.247
Gonzalez, Alberto	R-R	5-10	195	4-18-83	.283	.349	.262	50	173	19	49	11	1	2	19	9	0	1	0	13	3	1	.393	.319
Gonzalez, Miguel	R-R	5-11	220	12-3-90	.264	.258	.267	31	106	10	28	9	0	2	15	4	0	4	1	21	2	1	.406	.288
Green, Austin	R-R	6-1	200	2-22-90	.259	.357	.235	86	294	25	76	14	2	3	29	20	3	4	2	56	0	1	.350	.310
Green, Dean	L-R	6-4	255	6-30-89	.312	.307	.314	90	324	38	101	11	1	15	60	39	5	0	5	46	0	0	.491	.389
Harrell, Connor	R-R	6-3	215	3-24-91	.222	.243	.216	125	436	49	97	19	3	7	41	29	11	3	3	125	8	6	.328	.286
Harris, Brendan	R-R	6-1	200	8-26-80	.245	.190	.260	32	94	22	23	3	0	2	11	22	3	1	1	18	0	1	.340	.400
Jones, Corey	L-R	6-0	205	9-14-87	.293	.462	.258	21	75	8	22	4	0	0	10	10	3	0	1	7	2	1	.347	.393
Jones, JaCoby	R-R	6-2	205	5-10-92	.250	.130	.274	37	136	26	34	7	2	6	20	17	2	0	5	52	10	3	.463	.331
2-team total (3 Altoona)					.267	—	—	40	146	28	39	7	2	6	22	18	2	0	5	52	11	3	.466	.345
Krizan, Jason	L-R	6-0	185	6-28-89	.266	.174	.292	114	414	53	110	22	2	8	53	51	0	5	5	43	13	5	.386	.343
Longley, Andrew	R-R	6-3	215	10-5-88	.212	.286	.184	32	104	9	22	6	1	4	17	6	1	1	1	42	0	0	.404	.259
McVaney, Jeff	R-R	6-2	210	1-16-90	.301	.314	.297	79	292	44	88	17	3	3	35	35	5	0	3	59	14	3	.411	.382
Powell, Curt	R-R	6-0	180	4-30-91	.241	.200	.258	26	87	12	21	2	1	0	2	10	1	1	0	20	2	1	.287	.327
Prince, Josh	R-R	6-0	180	1-26-88	.205	.308	.154	40	117	13	24	5	0	2	9	15	0	0	0	18	6	4	.299	.295
Reaves, Jared	R-R	5-10	185	7-20-90	.269	.600	.190	9	26	3	7	3	0	0	3	3	0	0	0	5	1	0	.385	.345
Robbins, James	L-L	6-0	225	9-26-90	.236	.186	.245	112	385	33	91	18	3	5	45	15	4	1	1	92	3	1	.338	.272
Thomas, Tony	R-R	5-10	180	7-10-86	.258	.340	.222	43	155	21	40	7	0	7	26	12	1	1	1	43	3	1	.439	.314
2-team total (25 Reading)					.247	—	—	68	235	29	58	13	2	8	34	15	3	2	1	68	5	2	.421	.299
Wells, Casper	R-R	6-2	220	11-23-84	.209	.222	.206	15	43	4	9	2	0	1	6	4	1	0	0	17	0	0	.326	.292

Pitching	B-T	HT	WT	DOB	W	L	ERA	G	GS	CG	SV	IP	H	R	ER	HR	BB	SO	AVG	vLH	vRH	K/9	BB/9
Collier, Tommy	R-R	6-2	205	12-3-89	4	4	4.40	18	18	0	0	108	111	54	53	6	28	76	.269	.294	.245	6.31	2.33
Crouse, Matt	L-L	6-4	185	7-1-90	0	0	2.55	14	0	0	3	25	25	7	7	2	11	13	.278	.194	.333	4.74	4.01
De La Rosa, Edgar	R-R	6-8	235	11-12-90	0	1	7.56	13	0	0	1	17	21	15	14	1	18	12	.323	.409	.279	6.48	9.72
Drummond, Calvin	R-R	6-3	200	9-22-89	1	0	2.89	5	0	0	0	9	10	3	3	0	5	4	.303	.167	.381	3.86	4.82
Duran, Omar	L-L	6-3	220	2-26-90	1	1	8.64	7	0	0	0	8	10	9	8	1	4	10	.303	.286	.308	10.80	4.32
Ferrell, Jeff	R-R	6-3	185	11-23-90	0	0	1.67	17	1	0	12	27	21	5	5	4	4	35	.212	.316	.148	11.67	1.33
Fulmer, Michael	R-R	6-3	200	3-15-93	4	1	2.84	6	6	0	0	32	27	10	10	4	7	33	.231	.293	.169	9.38	1.99
2-team total (15 Binghamton)					10	3	2.14	21	21	0	0	118	100	35	28	7	30	116	—	—	—	8.87	2.29
Green, Chad	R-R	6-3	210	5-24-91	5	14	3.93	27	27	1	0	149	170	84	65	9	43	137	.287	.299	.277	8.29	2.60
Hankins, Derek	R-R	6-4	195	7-1-83	5	7	5.40	16	16	1	0	83	103	55	50	13	24	54	.310	.304	.315	5.83	2.59
Hemmer, Gabe	R-R	6-3	220	6-22-90	1	0	1.13	5	0	0	1	8	4	1	1	0	4	9	.148	.071	.231	10.13	4.50
Knudson, Guido	R-R	6-1	185	8-5-89	0	0	3.12	8	1	0	1	17	16	6	6	2	8	16	.239	.273	.222	8.31	4.15
Kubitza, Austin	R-R	6-5	225	11-16-91	9	13	5.79	27	27	2	0	134	191	108	86	6	48	96	.336	.353	.323	6.46	3.23
Lara, Confesor	R-R	6-2	170	8-7-90	1	2	4.68	26	0	0	0	42	51	31	22	3	11	23	.293	.280	.303	4.89	2.34
Maciel, Jon	R-R	6-2	225	11-17-92	0	1	9.00	1	1	0	0	7	10	7	7	2	1	1	.333	.231	.412	1.29	1.29
Mantiply, Joe	R-L	6-4	215	3-1-91	2	2	2.53	32	0	0	2	53	49	18	15	4	12	44	.240	.233	.244	7.43	2.03

Pitching

Pitching	B-T	HT	WT	DOB	W	L	ERA	G	GS	CG	SV	IP	H	R	ER	HR	BB	SO	AVG	vLH	vRH	K/9	BB/9
Mayberry, Whit	R-R	6-0	190	5-29-90	3	3	2.97	18	0	0	1	36	48	15	12	3	7	31	.316	.259	.351	7.68	1.73
Mercedes, Melvin	R-R	6-3	250	11-2-90	1	1	2.73	16	1	0	1	26	28	9	8	0	9	20	.277	.227	.316	6.84	3.08
Perry, Ryan	R-R	6-5	215	2-13-87	0	0	0.00	2	0	0	1	3	0	0	0	0	2	2	.000	.000	.000	6.00	6.00
Reininger, Zac	R-R	6-3	170	1-28-93	0	2	10.22	9	0	0	0	12	19	16	14	3	7	9	.358	.556	.257	6.57	5.11
Robertson, Montreal	R-R	6-4	205	6-19-90	2	4	3.48	15	1	0	2	31	35	14	12	3	15	30	.285	.234	.339	8.71	4.35
Robowski, Ryan	L-L	6-0	185	2-3-88	2	4	7.31	15	2	0	0	28	48	26	23	4	7	27	.384	.465	.341	8.58	2.22
Rogers, Joe	L-L	6-1	205	2-18-91	2	1	4.76	13	0	0	0	17	13	10	9	0	7	13	.220	.182	.243	6.88	3.71
Saupold, Warwick	R-R	6-1	195	1-16-90	5	6	4.01	23	15	0	1	103	102	49	46	5	36	71	.263	.288	.244	6.18	3.14
Sitz, Scott	R-R	5-10	210	9-10-90	0	0	0.00	1	0	0	0	2	0	0	0	0	1	2	.000	.000	.000	9.00	4.50
Smith, Brennan	R-R	6-3	200	8-4-89	0	0	14.04	7	0	0	0	8	11	13	13	2	9	8	.333	.308	.350	8.64	9.72
Smith, Slade	R-R	6-2	190	9-26-90	0	2	6.86	27	1	0	0	41	50	33	31	5	16	28	.298	.269	.322	6.20	3.54
Turley, Josh	L-L	6-0	185	8-26-90	13	8	3.29	25	25	1	0	153	151	70	56	15	35	103	.256	.238	.262	6.06	2.06
VerHagen, Drew	R-R	6-6	230	10-22-90	2	0	2.70	5	0	0	2	7	6	2	2	1	2	5	.261	.429	.188	6.75	2.70
Voelker, Paul	R-R	5-10	185	8-19-92	1	1	2.60	16	0	0	9	17	14	5	5	1	10	17	.222	.240	.211	8.83	5.19

Fielding

Catcher	PCT	G	PO	A	E	DP	PB
Gonzalez	.986	28	185	27	3	4	1
Green	.986	86	573	50	9	4	9
Longley	1.000	31	176	19	0	3	1

First Base	PCT	G	PO	A	E	DP
Ficociello	1.000	26	206	9	0	25
Gaynor	1.000	3	15	1	0	2
Green	.962	5	45	6	2	3
Krizan	1.000	13	94	3	0	8
Robbins	.994	101	788	53	5	82

Second Base	PCT	G	PO	A	E	DP
Castro	.986	59	128	149	4	38
Gonzalez	.969	14	28	34	2	10

	PCT	G	PO	A	E	DP	PB
Krizan	.909	8	18	22	4	6	
Powell	1.000	9	14	25	0	2	
Prince	.962	16	31	44	3	11	
Thomas	.955	39	68	102	8	20	

Third Base	PCT	G	PO	A	E	DP
Castro	.951	17	15	24	2	4
Gaynor	.922	97	73	152	19	10
Gonzalez	1.000	6	5	11	0	0
Harris	1.000	4	2	9	0	0
Jones	.872	20	8	33	6	4
Powell	.800	2	2	2	1	0

Shortstop	PCT	G	PO	A	E	DP
Castro	.935	22	28	59	6	7

	PCT	G	PO	A	E	DP
Gonzalez	.946	29	47	76	7	21
Harris	.950	27	29	67	5	14
Jones	.979	37	68	118	4	25
Powell	.931	14	16	38	4	5
Prince	.966	7	8	20	1	5
Reaves	.961	9	15	34	2	7

Outfield	PCT	G	PO	A	E	DP
Bernard	.980	131	291	7	6	1
Gaynor	1.000	1	1	1	0	0
Harrell	.980	124	236	7	5	2
Krizan	1.000	85	170	9	0	0
McVaney	.987	74	148	4	2	2
Prince	1.000	9	21	1	0	0
Wells	1.000	8	12	2	0	1

LAKELAND FLYING TIGERS

HIGH CLASS A

FLORIDA STATE LEAGUE

Batting	B-T	HT	WT	DOB	AVG	vLH	vRH	G	AB	R	H	2B	3B	HR	RBI	BB	HBP	SH	SF	SO	SB	CS	SLG	OBP
Allen, Will	R-R	6-3	220	3-25-92	.222	.143	.273	5	18	2	4	0	0	0	2	1	0	0	0	2	0	0	.222	.263
Betancourt, Javier	R-R	6-0	180	5-8-95	.263	.250	.269	122	491	45	129	17	5	3	48	29	2	4	5	44	4	1	.336	.304
Borchering, Bobby	B-R	6-2	205	10-25-90	.203	.164	.218	64	232	14	47	11	0	3	16	18	1	0	1	70	1	1	.289	.262
Ficociello, Dominic	B-R	6-4	210	4-10-92	.297	.333	.277	85	327	41	97	13	3	5	30	31	5	0	2	69	2	0	.401	.364
Gonzalez, David	R-R	5-9	140	12-1-93	.178	.152	.193	27	90	7	16	1	0	0	1	7	0	2	0	19	1	2	.189	.237
Greiner, Grayson	R-R	6-6	220	10-11-92	.183	.213	.170	89	312	24	57	12	0	3	21	27	3	1	0	90	0	0	.250	.254
Hanover, Tyler	R-R	5-7	170	8-25-89	.238	.240	.237	72	227	28	54	12	1	1	16	25	2	3	2	43	0	2	.313	.316
James, Jiwan	B-R	6-4	180	4-11-89	.249	.241	.254	114	477	56	119	10	8	7	31	32	2	8	0	91	22	8	.348	.299
Jones, Keaton	R-R	6-2	195	10-8-92	.065	.000	.077	14	46	1	3	0	0	0	2	5	3	0	0	14	0	1	.065	.204
Longley, Andrew	R-R	6-3	215	10-5-88	.200	.167	.208	19	60	4	12	2	0	2	9	12	1	0	0	27	0	0	.333	.342
Martinez, Francisco	R-R	6-2	210	9-14-90	.270	.242	.282	131	508	56	137	30	4	10	58	22	1	0	2	103	20	8	.404	.300
Moya, Steven	L-R	6-7	260	8-9-91	.275	.200	.300	9	40	3	11	3	0	3	8	1	0	0	1	13	0	0	.575	.286
Pirtle, Brett	B-R	5-9	175	3-23-91	.180	.167	.184	14	50	4	9	1	0	0	4	4	1	0	0	11	0	0	.200	.255
Powell, Curt	B-R	6-0	180	4-30-91	.322	.282	.338	80	289	39	93	14	5	0	23	29	10	2	1	76	2	3	.405	.401
Reaves, Jared	R-R	5-10	185	7-20-90	.253	.237	.260	53	190	16	48	12	2	0	16	13	3	0	1	40	0	2	.337	.309
Remes, Tim	R-R	6-0	205	6-17-92	.232	.207	.245	25	82	6	19	2	0	1	3	9	0	2	0	27	0	0	.293	.308
Rhymes, Raph	R-R	6-0	190	10-22-89	.220	.230	.215	121	460	41	101	19	0	8	39	54	6	3	2	80	1	0	.313	.308
Salgado, Ismael	R-R	6-1	165	1-11-93	.167	.082	.206	57	192	15	32	6	2	0	12	10	5	2	2	50	4	2	.219	.225
Schotts, Austin	R-R	5-11	180	9-16-93	.238	.160	.176	5	21	1	5	1	0	0	2	1	0	0	0	4	0	0	.286	.333
Verlander, Ben	R-R	6-4	200	1-31-92	.213	.239	.202	126	456	38	97	18	2	5	52	41	5	3	8	108	3	0	.294	.280

Pitching	B-T	HT	WT	DOB	W	L	ERA	G	GS	CG	SV	IP	H	R	ER	HR	BB	SO	AVG	vLH	vRH	K/9	BB/9
Briceno, Endrys	R-R	6-5	171	2-7-92	2	3	4.09	8	6	0	0	33	39	20	15	2	14	16	.302	.340	.276	4.36	3.82
Castellanos, Ryan	R-R	6-3	185	4-15-94	0	0	0.00	2	0	0	1	4	0	0	0	0	2	0	.000	.000	.000	4.50	0.00
Clinard, Will	R-R	6-4	225	11-3-89	0	1	1.85	18	0	0	0	39	32	10	8	0	16	32	.221	.246	.200	7.38	3.69
Collier, Tommy	R-R	6-2	205	12-3-89	3	4	2.09	8	8	0	0	47	43	16	11	2	11	38	.243	.255	.229	7.23	2.09
Crouse, Matt	L-L	6-4	185	7-19-90	4	2	2.55	14	6	0	3	49	44	15	14	3	6	33	.233	.294	.210	6.02	1.09
Davenport, Matt	R-R	6-8	200	10-11-89	0	0	7.56	5	1	0	0	8	12	8	7	0	4	5	.324	.308	.333	5.40	4.32
Drummond, Calvin	R-R	6-3	200	9-22-89	4	1	2.44	27	0	0	2	55	56	19	15	2	20	52	.257	.241	.266	8.46	3.25
Felix, Julio	R-R	6-1	210	2-23-92	3	5	5.40	27	0	0	0	57	59	34	34	3	14	37	.269	.279	.266	5.88	2.22
Ford, Tyler	L-L	5-8	175	9-11-91	1	0	1.84	15	0	0	1	29	27	8	6	0	6	31	.245	.234	.254	9.51	1.84
Fury, Nate	R-R	5-11	200	2-6-91	0	0	5.14	4	0	0	0	7	10	4	4	0	3	11	.333	.375	.318	14.14	3.86
Hemmer, Gabe	R-R	6-3	220	6-22-90	0	1	0.47	9	0	0	2	19	18	1	1	0	3	21	.250	.310	.209	9.78	1.40
Kellogg, Micah	R-R	6-4	195	11-29-89	0	0	4.50	3	0	0	0	8	4	4	4	1	2	3	.300	.000	.346	3.38	2.25
Labourt, Jairo	L-L	6-4	205	3-7-94	1	5	6.31	7	7	0	0	36	45	31	25	3	15	34	.319	.229	.349	8.58	3.79
2-team total (18 Dunedin)					3	12	5.12	25	25	0	0	116	128	81	66	9	59	104	—	—	—	8.07	4.58
Lara, Confesor	R-R	6-2	170	8-7-90	1	0	1.10	9	0	0	3	16	10	2	2	1	3	20	.175	.231	.129	11.02	1.65
Lobstein, Kyle	L-L	6-3	200	8-12-89	0	1	3.52	2	2	0	0	8	7	4	3	1	2	4	.269	.250	.278	4.70	2.35
Longstreth, Ryan	L-L	6-1	205	4-16-90	2	4	3.72	10	10	0	0	48	43	25	20	1	23	31	.239	.324	.219	5.77	4.28

Pitching

Pitching	B-T	HT	WT	DOB	W	L	ERA	G	GS	CG	SV	IP	H	R	ER	HR	BB	SO	AVG	vLH	vRH	K/9	BB/9
Longwith, Logan	R-R	6-3	170	3-30-94	0	0	9.00	1	0	0	0	2	4	2	2	0	0	2	.444	.750	.200	9.00	0.00
Maciel, Jon	R-R	6-2	225	11-17-92	5	8	4.68	24	24	0	0	127	155	77	66	10	32	67	.300	.302	.300	4.75	2.27
Mayberry, Whit	R-R	6-0	190	5-29-90	1	3	1.01	15	0	0	5	27	22	6	3	0	7	25	.227	.216	.233	8.44	2.36
Reininger, Zac	B-R	6-3	170	1-28-93	1	0	0.00	7	0	0	3	13	8	0	0	0	5	8	.178	.118	.214	5.40	3.38
Robertson, Montreal	R-R	6-4	205	6-19-90	2	6	3.16	19	0	0	0	37	28	15	13	0	20	28	.203	.283	.153	6.81	4.86
Rogers, Joe	L-L	6-1	205	2-18-91	0	0	0.00	6	0	0	1	10	4	1	0	0	3	8	.121	.000	.200	7.20	2.70
Sitz, Scott	R-R	5-10	210	9-10-90	2	2	3.41	22	1	0	1	37	38	16	14	2	8	27	.284	.326	.264	6.57	1.95
Smith, Brennan	R-R	6-3	200	8-4-89	5	6	3.08	23	15	0	1	102	92	37	35	4	24	84	.241	.211	.264	7.39	2.11
Smith, Gage	R-R	6-2	185	2-13-91	2	0	0.00	4	0	0	1	10	5	1	0	0	2	8	.143	.167	.138	7.20	1.80
Smith, Slade	R-R	6-2	190	9-26-90	1	0	0.53	8	0	0	0	17	17	1	1	0	6	13	.266	.238	.279	6.88	3.18
St. John, Locke	L-L	6-3	180	1-31-93	2	10	5.00	19	19	0	0	94	112	59	52	2	39	47	.311	.336	.299	4.52	3.75
Szkutnik, Trent	R-L	6-0	195	8-21-93	1	4	5.84	11	9	0	0	45	63	30	29	4	17	27	.344	.341	.345	5.44	3.43
Verastegui, Adenson	R-R	5-11	205	2-19-93	0	1	3.24	18	0	0	0	42	40	16	15	2	17	40	.253	.269	.245	8.64	3.67
Voelker, Paul	R-R	5-10	185	8-19-92	3	0	1.64	14	0	0	7	22	17	5	4	1	6	26	.215	.304	.179	10.64	2.45
Ziomek, Kevin	R-L	6-3	200	3-21-92	9	11	3.43	27	27	2	0	155	142	69	59	3	34	143	.242	.233	.245	8.32	1.98

Fielding

Catcher	PCT	G	PO	A	E	DP	PB
Allen	.919	5	33	1	3	0	1
Greiner	.988	88	607	52	8	3	3
Longley	.986	19	126	18	2	1	1
Remes	.994	25	158	17	1	1	7

First Base	PCT	G	PO	A	E	DP
Borchering	.980	12	96	4	2	11
Ficociello	.995	76	715	45	4	70
Martinez	.997	32	295	25	1	30
Powell	.987	16	138	10	2	7
Verlander	1.000	1	6	2	0	0

Second Base	PCT	G	PO	A	E	DP
Betancourt	.982	116	250	347	11	85
Hanover	.944	6	14	20	2	2
Pirtle	.973	6	17	19	1	6
Powell	.979	9	23	24	1	6

Third Base	PCT	G	PO	A	E	DP
Borchering	—	1	0	0	0	0
Hanover	.941	48	20	91	7	7
Martinez	.905	68	47	153	21	15
Powell	.940	21	14	33	3	4

Shortstop	PCT	G	PO	A	E	DP
Gonzalez	.969	27	41	82	4	21

	PCT	G	PO	A	E	DP
Hanover	.930	12	10	30	3	3
Jones	.918	14	24	32	5	6
Powell	.936	31	34	83	8	15
Reaves	.965	53	70	180	9	35

Outfield	PCT	G	PO	A	E	DP
Hanover	1.000	1	2	0	0	0
James	.975	112	233	5	6	1
Moya	1.000	9	24	0	0	0
Rhymes	.995	110	181	5	1	3
Salgado	.986	55	137	7	2	2
Schotts	1.000	5	14	0	0	0
Verlander	.984	117	234	7	4	0

WEST MICHIGAN WHITECAPS   LOW CLASS A

MIDWEST LEAGUE

Batting	B-T	HT	WT	DOB	AVG	vLH	vRH	G	AB	R	H	2B	3B	HR	RBI	BB	HBP	SH	SF	SO	SB	CS	SLG	OBP
Brown, Rashad	L-L	5-11	180	12-17-93	.289	.200	.321	56	225	31	65	6	3	0	22	19	1	5	0	35	11	1	.342	.347
Brugnoni, Giancarlo	R-R	6-3	225	2-25-91	.215	.417	.170	18	65	9	14	2	2	1	4	7	0	0	1	31	0	0	.354	.288
Contreras, Francisco	R-R	6-1	180	12-3-91	.188	.250	.167	59	192	19	36	11	2	0	23	10	1	2	2	44	1	1	.266	.229
Fuentes, Steven	B-R	5-11	180	10-21-94	.163	.111	.175	16	49	6	8	2	0	0	2	5	0	1	1	18	0	0	.204	.236
Gerber, Mike	L-R	6-2	175	7-8-92	.292	.208	.318	135	513	74	150	31	10	13	76	49	7	2	12	97	16	4	.468	.355
Gonzalez, David	R-R	5-9	140	12-1-93	.256	.236	.263	85	289	29	74	9	5	1	23	22	2	10	1	43	7	1	.332	.312
Hill, Derek	R-R	6-2	195	12-30-95	.238	.206	.244	53	210	33	50	6	5	0	16	20	1	2	2	44	25	7	.314	.305
Kengor, Will	L-R	6-3	180	7-24-92	.286	.282	.288	111	391	48	112	19	3	1	38	54	5	5	2	100	4	3	.358	.378
Kivett, Ross	R-R	6-1	195	10-19-91	.267	.243	.274	133	524	75	140	28	2	5	50	44	9	1	7	66	28	5	.357	.330
Lester, Josh	L-L	6-0	189	7-17-94	.158	.000	.188	5	19	3	3	2	0	0	4	2	0	0	0	6	0	0	.263	.238
Maddox, Will	L-R	5-10	180	6-11-92	.395	.364	.406	13	43	5	17	2	0	0	1	1	2	0	0	6	2	2	.442	.422
Mattlage, Garrett	B-R	5-10	175	2-25-93	.194	.209	.189	54	170	16	33	5	1	2	14	14	3	3	1	48	0	2	.271	.266
Navarro, Franklin	B-R	5-10	181	10-17-94	.172	.132	.187	43	145	11	25	5	0	0	11	6	0	4	2	26	1	1	.207	.203
Padron, Victor	L-R	5-8	160	7-5-94	.200	.222	.192	9	35	2	7	2	0	0	1	2	0	1	0	5	0	0	.257	.243
Pankake, Joey	R-R	6-2	185	11-23-92	.268	.284	.264	126	462	64	124	22	4	5	58	52	3	1	7	94	9	3	.366	.342
Perez, Arvicent	R-R	5-10	180	1-14-94	.229	.241	.225	33	118	7	27	4	0	0	5	3	1	2	1	20	1	0	.263	.252
Schotts, Austin	R-R	5-11	180	9-6-94	.237	.340	.207	61	211	16	50	7	1	2	26	10	1	6	0	74	11	3	.308	.275
Scivicque, Kade	R-R	5-11	223	3-22-93	.242	.263	.236	42	165	21	40	4	0	5	17	9	6	0	0	26	2	1	.358	.306
Shepherd, Zac	R-R	6-3	185	9-14-95	.245	.265	.240	114	383	48	94	17	2	5	51	47	3	3	7	117	4	3	.339	.327
Simcox, A.J.	R-R	6-3	185	3-9-94	.400	.350	.415	20	85	11	34	3	0	1	8	5	1	0	0	11	4	2	.471	.440
Stewart, Christin	L-R	6-0	205	12-10-93	.286	.200	.314	51	185	29	53	9	4	7	31	18	10	0	3	45	3	2	.492	.375
Zeile, Shane	R-R	6-1	195	6-14-93	.191	.333	.172	36	131	12	25	5	2	0	14	13	2	2	2	30	0	0	.260	.270

Pitching	B-T	HT	WT	DOB	W	L	ERA	G	GS	CG	SV	IP	H	R	ER	HR	BB	SO	AVG	vLH	vRH	K/9	BB/9
Belisario, Johan	R-R	5-11	165	8-13-93	3	2	1.79	41	0	0	12	55	46	12	11	1	23	54	.227	.275	.188	8.78	3.74
Davenport, Matt	R-R	6-8	200	10-11-89	0	1	16.62	4	0	0	0	4	12	9	8	0	5	5	.480	.500	.455	10.38	10.38
Edwards, Chase	R-R	6-1	180	2-4-94	0	0	18.00	2	0	0	0	2	8	4	4	0	1	1	.667	1.000	.600	4.50	0.00
Ford, Tyler	L-L	5-8	175	9-11-91	0	3	2.41	17	1	0	1	41	28	12	11	3	6	43	.188	.189	.188	9.44	1.32
Fury, Nate	R-R	5-11	200	2-6-91	0	0	3.95	8	0	0	0	11	9	8	6	1	13	12	.309	.333	.286	7.90	8.56
Heddinger, Josh	R-R	6-4	220	1-16-93	0	2	8.46	21	0	0	0	45	68	47	42	5	31	32	.356	.377	.344	6.45	6.25
Hemmer, Gabe	R-R	6-3	220	6-22-90	1	2	1.29	20	0	0	3	35	24	6	5	0	11	37	.190	.256	.157	9.51	2.83
Hicks, Taylor	R-R	6-3	204	2-26-92	0	0	81.00	1	0	0	0	0	3	3	3	0	1	0	.750	.500	1.000	0.00	27.00
Jimenez, Joe	R-R	6-3	220	1-17-95	5	1	1.47	40	0	0	17	43	23	8	7	2	11	61	.153	.172	.140	12.77	2.30
Ladwig, A.J.	R-R	6-5	180	12-24-92	12	9	3.59	22	22	0	0	138	153	63	55	10	18	85	.284	.266	.298	5.54	1.17
Lewicki, Artie	R-R	6-3	195	4-8-92	3	4	3.52	15	15	0	0	79	87	37	31	4	25	77	.280	.296	.271	8.74	2.84
Moreno, Dominic	R-R	5-11	190	3-12-93	1	1	3.22	13	0	0	2	19	10	8	5	0	5	24	.226	.206	.240	9.67	2.01
Moreno, Gerson	R-R	6-0	175	9-10-95	0	0	3.95	5	0	0	1	9	3	0	0	0	3	9	.107	.214	.000	8.68	2.89
Perez, Fernando	R-R	6-3	181	12-17-93	2	12	4.51	21	21	0	0	102	119	60	51	7	32	72	.301	.311	.292	6.37	2.83
Ravenelle, Adam	R-R	6-3	185	10-5-92	2	0	3.93	19	0	0	0	34	31	16	15	2	19	40	.238	.328	.167	10.49	4.98
Seaton, Ross	L-R	6-4	200	9-18-89	11	8	3.73	21	21	0	0	133	126	64	55	5	16	86	.252	.270	.240	5.83	1.09

Pitching

Pitching	B-T	HT	WT	DOB	W	L	ERA	G	GS	CG	SV	IP	H	R	ER	HR	BB	SO	AVG	vLH	vRH	K/9	BB/9
Sitz, Scott	R-R	5-10	210	9-10-90	0	0	0.00	1	0	0	0	2	1	0	0	0	0	2	.143	.000	.167	10.80	0.00
Smith, Drew	R-R	6-2	190	9-24-93	1	0	0.00	1	0	0	0	2	1	0	0	1	2	.167	.250	.000	10.80	5.40
Smith, Gage	R-R	6-2	185	2-13-91	4	1	2.40	24	0	0	2	56	55	16	15	1	9	33	.261	.322	.215	5.27	1.44
Speier, Gabe	L-L	6-0	175	4-12-95	4	2	2.86	33	0	0	0	44	40	16	14	0	12	36	.240	.204	.254	7.36	2.45
Szkutnik, Trent	R-L	6-0	195	8-21-93	3	1	3.88	9	9	0	0	53	48	26	23	6	14	40	.240	.163	.265	6.75	2.36
Teakell, Trey	R-R	6-5	175	2-17-92	3	1	2.06	13	2	0	2	35	33	9	8	0	7	24	.244	.226	.260	6.17	1.80
Thompson, Jeff	R-R	6-6	245	9-23-91	7	11	3.79	23	23	1	0	119	116	60	50	9	47	105	.256	.245	.265	7.96	3.56
Turnbull, Spencer	R-R	6-3	215	9-18-92	11	3	3.01	22	22	1	0	117	106	45	39	0	52	106	.242	.242	.242	8.18	4.01
Voelker, Paul	R-R	5-10	185	8-19-92	2	0	2.25	10	0	0	2	16	9	5	4	0	4	20	.164	.111	.189	11.25	2.25
Watkins, Spenser	R-R	6-1	190	8-27-92	0	0	3.38	4	3	0	0	19	21	7	7	0	6	14	.288	.286	.289	6.75	2.89

Fielding

Catcher	PCT	G	PO	A	E	DP	PB
Navarro	.988	43	302	26	4	0	5
Perez	.958	32	203	23	10	2	4
Scivicque	.988	35	295	26	4	1	6
Zeile	.988	32	224	31	3	1	2

First Base	PCT	G	PO	A	E	DP
Brugnoni	.985	17	131	3	2	12
Contreras	.983	13	107	9	2	7
Kengor	.991	109	904	70	9	69
Maddox	1.000	2	18	0	0	2

Second Base	PCT	G	PO	A	E	DP
Contreras	.978	11	19	25	1	6

	PCT	G	PO	A	E	DP
Gonzalez	.989	21	37	49	1	6
Maddox	1.000	1	0	2	0	
Mattlage	.929	10	9	17	2	2
Pankake	.964	101	176	247	16	52

Third Base	PCT	G	PO	A	E	DP
Contreras	.986	30	23	50	1	6
Fuentes	1.000	3	2	3	0	0
Lester	.875	4	5	9	2	1
Mattlage	—	1	0	0	0	0
Shepherd	.935	105	64	179	17	17

Shortstop	PCT	G	PO	A	E	DP
Fuentes	.963	13	22	30	2	2

	PCT	G	PO	A	E	DP
Gonzalez	.968	64	108	195	10	30
Mattlage	.972	43	59	117	5	18
Simcox	.986	20	29	43	1	7

Outfield	PCT	G	PO	A	E	DP
Brown	.991	54	103	6	1	1
Contreras	1.000	5	2	1	0	0
Gerber	.983	85	168	4	3	1
Hill	.977	51	118	9	3	2
Kivett	.985	121	253	15	4	3
Padron	.933	9	11	3	1	2
Schotts	.969	61	124	3	4	0
Stewart	.950	39	56	1	3	0

CONNECTICUT TIGERS   SHORT-SEASON

NEW YORK-PENN LEAGUE

Batting	B-T	HT	WT	DOB	AVG	vLH	vRH	G	AB	R	H	2B	3B	HR	RBI	BB	HBP	SH	SF	SO	SB	CS	SLG	OBP
Alfaro, Adrian	L-R	5-9	176	9-19-95	.200	.000	.240	8	30	1	6	0	0	0	3	0	0	1	0	11	1	0	.200	.273
Allen, Will	R-R	6-3	220	3-25-92	.324	.391	.293	57	204	28	66	13	0	2	31	20	3	0	3	43	0	1	.417	.387
Azocar, Jose	R-R	5-11	165	5-11-96	.087	.000	.095	7	23	1	2	1	0	0	1	0	0	0	0	7	0	0	.130	.125
Baptist, Corey	R-R	6-4	215	4-19-95	.265	.265	.264	49	189	16	50	7	1	5	18	10	1	0	0	37	0	2	.328	.305
Donnels, Tanner	L-R	6-2	210	8-3-93	.265	.259	.267	55	204	15	54	7	3	0	19	9	0	1	2	44	0	0	.328	.293
Fuentes, Steven	B-R	5-11	180	10-21-94	.150	.143	.154	35	120	14	18	2	4	1	10	13	2	1	1	44	2	1	.258	.243
Gibson, Cam	L-R	6-0	180	2-12-94	.252	.231	.261	33	131	19	33	1	4	6	24	8	2	1	1	24	4	4	.458	.303
Gonzalez, Cesar	R-R	6-2	175	5-31-95	.130	.200	.111	6	23	2	3	0	0	0	1	0	0	0	0	9	1	0	.130	.130
Havrilak, Joey	L-R	6-1	195	11-25-91	.213	.211	.214	52	188	24	40	5	4	4	17	21	0	3	1	36	1	2	.346	.290
Jones, Keaton	R-R	6-2	195	10-8-92	.192	.212	.184	33	120	10	23	5	0	1	9	6	2	0	1	34	2	0	.258	.240
Kapstein, Jacob	R-R	6-2	215	2-24-94	.179	.138	.193	37	117	11	21	3	1	0	8	16	1	2	2	37	1	0	.222	.279
Lester, Josh	L-L	6-0	189	7-17-94	.204	.176	.214	38	137	15	28	6	0	2	17	17	2	0	4	21	0	0	.292	.294
MacKenzie, Pat	L-R	5-8	170	3-5-92	.288	.302	.282	43	156	23	45	2	3	1	14	26	2	0	1	11	7	5	.359	.395
Navarro, Franklin	R-R	5-10	181	10-17-94	.125	.000	.158	8	24	1	3	1	0	0	2	3	2	1	0	3	0	0	.167	.222
Padron, Victor	L-R	5-8	160	7-5-94	.325	.302	.336	43	163	19	53	4	1	0	15	14	2	2	0	20	3	2	.362	.385
Perez, Arvicent	R-R	5-10	180	1-14-94	.263	.500	.235	5	19	3	5	1	0	0	1	0	1	0	0	2	0	1	.316	.263
Pirtle, Brett	R-R	5-9	175	3-23-91	.333	.250	.356	30	114	14	38	3	2	1	8	7	2	0	0	15	1	2	.421	.382
Sayers, Aaron	R-R	5-25-93	.000	.000	.000	2	6	0	0	0	0	0	0	0	0	0	0	0	0	0	.000	.143
Scivicque, Kade	R-R	5-11	223	3-22-93	.406	.455	.381	9	32	5	13	3	0	0	1	3	1	0	0	3	0	0	.500	.472
Servais, Tyler	B-R	6-2	210	11-18-92	.171	.214	.143	12	35	4	6	1	0	0	2	8	0	0	0	7	0	0	.200	.326
Simcox, A.J.	R-R	6-3	185	6-22-94	.270	.448	.197	25	100	14	27	5	1	0	12	5	1	0	2	14	5	2	.340	.306
Stewart, Christin	L-R	6-0	205	12-10-93	.245	.000	.308	14	49	7	12	2	2	2	11	5	2	0	3	18	0	0	.490	.322
Thomas, Michael	R-R	5-11	210	1-27-91	.000	.000	—	1	2	0	0	0	0	0	0	1	0	0	0	0	0	0	.000	.333
Valdez, Ignacio	R-R	6-3	195	7-16-95	.125	.000	.150	6	24	3	3	2	0	1	4	0	0	0	0	10	0	0	.333	.125
Zambrano, Jose	B-R	5-7	155	11-4-93	.256	.239	.264	40	156	14	40	5	0	1	14	9	0	2	3	14	0	1	.308	.292
Zeile, Shane	R-R	6-1	195	6-14-93	.252	.357	.195	35	119	20	30	9	1	6	20	8	0	0	0	30	1	0	.496	.299

Pitching	B-T	HT	WT	DOB	W	L	ERA	G	GS	CG	SV	IP	H	R	ER	HR	BB	SO	AVG	vLH	vRH	K/9	BB/9
Aldridge, Dean	R-R	6-3	190	7-29-94	0	0	11.57	2	0	0	0	2	6	5	3	0	3	1	.500	.800	.286	3.86	11.57
Alexander, Tyler	R-L	6-3	200	7-14-94	0	2	0.97	12	12	0	0	37	17	7	4	3	5	33	.133	.128	.136	8.03	1.22
Baez, Sandy	R-R	6-2	180	11-25-93	3	4	4.13	14	14	0	0	65	73	36	30	4	22	52	.289	.302	.272	7.16	3.03
Boardman, Toller	L-L	6-3	210	11-15-92	0	0	1.50	1	1	0	0	6	4	1	1	1	1	5	.211	—	.211	7.50	1.50
Castellanos, Ryan	R-R	6-2	185	4-15-94	1	2	4.03	8	8	0	0	38	48	21	17	3	5	20	.314	.314	.313	4.74	1.18
Castillo, Oswaldo	R-R	6-3	193	8-18-96	1	3	5.14	12	0	0	0	21	20	17	12	1	17	20	.250	.195	.308	8.57	7.29
Davenport, Matt	R-R	6-8	200	10-11-89	1	0	5.09	15	0	0	0	23	28	16	13	0	8	14	.286	.367	.250	5.48	3.13
Edwards, Chase	R-R	6-1	180	2-4-94	6	6	6.54	15	6	0	0	63	80	47	46	3	17	36	.309	.295	.320	5.12	2.42
Fischer, Jack	R-R	6-1	175	8-28-91	1	1	3.38	17	0	0	2	27	22	15	10	1	10	25	.216	.317	.148	8.44	3.38
Fury, Nate	R-R	5-11	200	2-6-91	0	0	1.78	15	0	0	3	25	16	6	5	0	14	30	.180	.244	1.25	10.66	4.97
Hall, Matt	L-L	6-0	200	7-23-93	0	1	2.90	10	10	0	0	31	29	11	10	3	7	30	.246	.324	.214	8.71	2.03
Heddinger, Josh	R-R	6-4	220	1-16-93	2	1	2.87	8	2	0	0	31	28	18	10	0	12	19	.235	.250	.227	5.46	3.45
Hicks, Taylor	R-R	6-3	204	2-26-94	0	0	3.60	4	0	0	0	5	3	3	2	0	2	7	.167	.100	.250	12.60	3.60
Idrogo, Eudis	L-L	6-1	198	6-6-95	1	1	2.70	2	2	0	0	10	8	4	3	1	1	10	.211	.000	.222	9.00	0.90
Longwith, Logan	R-R	6-3	170	3-30-94	1	0	0.00	1	0	0	0	1	0	0	0	0	0	3	.000	—	.000	27.00	0.00
Lopez, Jose	R-R	5-9	174	6-21-95	0	0	27.00	2	0	0	0	2	5	5	5	0	1	2	.455	.600	.333	10.80	5.40
Milton, Ryan	R-R	6-4	215	12-18-91	2	0	2.45	3	0	0	0	11	10	4	3	0	5	14	.256	.200	.292	11.45	4.09

Pitching	B-T	HT	WT	DOB	W	L	ERA	G	GS	CG	SV	IP	H	R	ER	HR	BB	SO	AVG	vLH	vRH	K/9	BB/9
Moreno, Dominic	R-R	5-11	190	3-12-93	1	0	0.00	4	0	0	1	10	5	0	0	1	10	.147	.200	.071	9.31	0.93
Moreno, Gerson	R-R	6-0	175	9-10-95	2	5	3.86	15	0	0	2	28	28	19	12	0	12	29	.259	.290	.205	9.32	3.86
Shull, Jake	R-R	5-10	190	4-26-94	0	4	3.32	16	0	0	7	22	20	8	8	1	7	17	.244	.289	.205	7.06	2.91
Smith, Drew	R-R	6-2	190	9-24-93	2	0	0.33	11	0	0	2	28	15	1	1	0	4	33	.155	.154	.155	10.73	1.30
Smith, Jordan	R-R	6-1	210	4-23-92	2	1	1.91	17	1	0	3	33	28	7	7	0	8	21	.235	.250	.224	5.73	2.18
Soto, Gregory	L-L	6-1	180	2-11-95	0	1	22.50	2	1	0	0	2	1	6	5	0	6	5	.143	.333	.000	22.50	27.00
St. John, Locke	L-L	6-3	180	1-31-93	0	0	5.63	2	0	0	0	8	11	5	5	1	1	11	.333	.250	.412	12.38	1.13
Szkutnik, Trent	R-L	6-0	195	8-21-93	1	0	0.00	3	0	0	1	10	6	1	0	0	2	10	.171	.118	.222	9.00	1.80
Teakell, Trey	R-R	6-5	175	2-17-92	1	0	1.50	3	3	0	0	12	6	2	2	1	0	6	.146	.045	.263	4.50	0.00
Tejada, Andres	R-R	6-5	190	2-2-95	2	1	4.34	11	0	0	0	19	22	10	9	2	5	11	.289	.250	.325	5.30	2.41
Vinson, Mike	R-R	6-2	185	2-9-94	0	1	1.93	2	1	0	0	5	5	1	1	0	2	6	.263	.286	.250	11.57	3.86
Watkins, Spenser	R-R	6-1	190	8-27-92	5	4	2.23	12	12	0	0	65	45	21	16	1	19	55	.193	.190	.196	7.65	2.64

Fielding

Catcher	PCT	G	PO	A	E	DP	PB
Allen	.961	15	117	5	5	0	3
Navarro	1.000	8	58	9	0	0	1
Perez	.946	5	31	4	2	0	1
Scivicque	1.000	8	50	8	0	0	1
Servais	1.000	10	69	3	0	1	0
Thomas	1.000	1	3	0	0	0	0
Zeile	.987	31	194	27	3	0	2

First Base	PCT	G	PO	A	E	DP
Allen	.988	35	288	32	4	32
Baptist	.997	31	317	24	1	23
Donnels	1.000	7	49	5	0	5
Kapstein	.975	5	36	3	1	3
Lester	1.000	1	1	1	0	0

Second Base	PCT	G	PO	A	E	DP
Fuentes	—	1	0	0	0	0
MacKenzie	.954	40	71	137	10	30
Pirtle	.957	27	50	84	6	22
Zambrano	1.000	6	6	24	0	3

Third Base	PCT	G	PO	A	E	DP
Fuentes	.845	25	13	47	11	3
Lester	.937	34	26	63	6	5
Sayers	.500	1	0	1	1	0
Zambrano	.956	15	13	30	2	6

Shortstop	PCT	G	PO	A	E	DP
Alfaro	.941	8	10	22	2	6
Fuentes	.870	6	6	14	3	4

	PCT	G	PO	A	E	DP
Jones	.935	33	44	85	9	20
Simcox	.986	25	50	90	2	17
Zambrano	.857	2	0	6	1	1

Outfield	PCT	G	PO	A	E	DP
Azocar	1.000	7	19	1	0	0
Donnels	.968	48	86	4	3	0
Gibson	1.000	6	9	0	0	0
Gonzalez	1.000	6	12	1	0	0
Havrilak	.980	52	98	1	2	0
Kapstein	1.000	27	45	2	0	0
Padron	.954	42	60	2	3	0
Stewart	1.000	13	19	1	0	1
Valdez	1.000	6	7	1	0	0
Zambrano	.952	15	17	3	1	0

GCL TIGERS   *ROOKIE*

GULF COAST LEAGUE

Batting	B-T	HT	WT	DOB	AVG	vLH	vRH	G	AB	R	H	2B	3B	HR	RBI	BB	HBP	SH	SF	SO	SB	CS	SLG	OBP
Alfaro, Adrian	L-R	5-9	176	9-19-95	.281	.325	.268	46	178	25	50	10	1	1	12	20	3	2	24	6	4	.365	.356
Azocar, Jose	R-R	5-11	165	5-11-96	.325	.350	.318	51	194	29	63	10	5	0	29	7	2	5	3	31	6	4	.428	.350
Bauml, Cole	R-R	6-2	205	11-2-92	.214	.185	.224	37	103	10	22	2	0	0	7	6	2	0	3	25	2	1	.233	.263
Brugnoni, Giancarlo	R-R	6-3	225	2-25-91	.239	.130	.275	33	92	18	22	4	0	9	21	21	3	0	1	31	0	1	.576	.393
Castano, Adrian	L-L	6-3	180	8-20-95	.343	.667	.231	14	35	7	12	2	0	0	5	5	0	1	0	9	0	0	.400	.425
Donnels, Tanner	L-R	6-2	210	8-3-93	.214	.200	.222	5	14	3	3	0	0	1	3	2	0	0	1	3	0	0	.429	.294
Gibson, Cam	L-R	6-0	180	2-12-94	.200	.000	.250	3	10	2	2	0	1	0	3	1	0	0	2	2	0	.400	.273
Gonzalez, Cesar	R-R	6-2	175	5-31-95	.265	.318	.253	35	117	12	31	4	1	0	12	11	1	4	0	39	2	2	.316	.333
Havrilak, Joey	L-R	6-1	195	11-25-91	.067	.000	.125	5	15	1	1	0	0	0	2	2	0	0	0	4	2	0	.067	.176
Jones, Keaton	R-R	6-2	195	10-8-92	.000	.000	.000	1	4	0	0	0	0	0	0	0	0	0	0	0	0	0	.000	.000
Ledezma, Junnell	B-R	5-9	165	11-9-95	.329	.273	.346	44	140	24	46	10	0	1	13	10	7	2	1	18	2	2	.421	.399
Lester, Josh	L-L	6-0	189	7-17-94	.391	.300	.462	6	23	5	9	4	0	1	7	2	1	0	0	2	0	0	.696	.462
MacKenzie, Pat	L-R	5-8	170	3-5-92	.438	.750	.333	4	16	3	7	1	0	0	1	2	0	0	0	2	0	0	.500	.500
Ordonez Jr., Magglio	R-R	6-1	200	10-14-95	.108	.100	.111	19	37	3	4	0	0	0	3	5	0	0	0	15	0	0	.108	.214
Pereira, Anthony	R-R	6-0	170	11-28-96	.219	.200	.225	48	155	20	34	2	1	4	21	15	3	4	2	29	7	1	.323	.297
Salter, Blaise	R-R	6-5	245	6-25-93	.293	.257	.306	36	133	22	39	8	1	2	21	6	3	0	1	23	0	0	.414	.336
Sanjur, Mario	R-R	5-7	174	12-23-95	.200	.250	.187	31	95	13	19	3	0	1	7	8	2	1	0	13	3	0	.263	.276
Santana, Felix	R-R	5-10	180	8-19-94	.302	.341	.282	37	126	12	38	9	0	2	15	5	3	3	0	23	0	0	.421	.343
Sayers, Aaron	L-R	6-1	175	5-25-94	.263	.105	.300	29	99	12	26	6	0	1	6	10	2	1	0	19	1	3	.354	.342
Servais, Tyler	B-R	6-2	210	11-18-92	.167	.000	.250	3	6	0	1	0	0	0	0	0	0	0	0	2	0	0	.167	.167
Simcox, A.J.	R-R	6-3	185	6-22-94	.333	.500	.273	4	15	4	5	0	0	0	1	1	0	0	0	3	2	0	.333	.375
Stewart, Christin	L-R	6-0	205	12-10-93	.364	.375	.357	6	22	5	8	2	1	1	2	3	1	0	0	5	2	1	.682	.462
Sthormes, Andres	R-R	5-10	171	8-7-96	.240	.227	.244	32	100	9	24	2	1	1	21	8	4	3	1	18	0	1	.310	.319
Taladay, Chris	L-R	6-1	220	5-22-91	.000	—	.000	1	1	0	0	0	0	0	0	0	0	0	0	0	0	0	.000	.000
Thomas, Michael	R-R	5-11	210	1-27-91	.167	.100	.182	22	54	6	9	1	0	1	2	7	0	2	0	12	0	0	.241	.262
Valdez, Ignacio	R-R	6-3	195	7-16-95	.139	.111	.144	33	108	13	15	2	0	2	10	13	2	0	1	44	1	0	.213	.242

Pitching	B-T	HT	WT	DOB	W	L	ERA	G	GS	CG	SV	IP	H	R	ER	HR	BB	SO	AVG	vLH	vRH	K/9	BB/9
Aldridge, Dean	R-R	6-3	190	7-29-94	1	0	2.49	12	1	0	1	22	14	10	6	0	20	29	.179	.200	.170	12.05	8.31
Boardman, Toller	L-L	6-3	210	11-15-92	3	2	2.95	10	8	0	0	40	43	14	13	2	5	28	.291	.220	.318	6.35	1.13
Briceno, Endrys	R-R	6-5	171	2-7-92	0	1	1.98	5	5	0	0	14	12	5	3	0	1	21	.231	.375	.107	13.83	0.66
Burrows, Beau	R-R	6-2	200	9-18-96	1	0	1.61	10	9	0	0	28	18	7	5	0	11	33	.184	.132	.217	10.61	3.54
Castellanos, Ryan	R-R	6-3	185	4-15-94	1	0	0.00	2	0	0	0	8	4	0	0	0	1	10	.143	.364	.000	11.25	0.00
Chavez, Emanuel	R-R	6-3	175	1-19-95	0	0	4.50	3	0	0	0	4	2	2	2	1	2	4	.154	.000	.200	9.00	4.50
Clinard, Will	R-R	6-4	225	11-3-89	1	0	0.00	2	0	0	1	4	1	0	0	0	1	4	.083	.143	.000	9.00	2.25
De La Rosa, Edgar	R-R	6-8	235	11-12-90	1	0	3.00	3	0	0	0	3	2	1	1	0	2	2	.200	.000	.333	6.00	6.00
German, Francisco	R-R	6-2	160	12-26-96	5	0	2.57	10	1	0	0	21	15	8	6	1	6	26	.192	.138	.224	11.14	2.57
Gutierrez, Alfred	R-R	6-0	143	6-12-95	6	4	3.38	11	11	0	0	59	55	25	22	4	15	42	.257	.271	.248	6.44	2.30
Hall, Matt	L-L	6-0	200	7-23-93	0	0	3.00	1	1	0	0	3	4	1	1	0	1	4	.308	.286	.333	12.00	3.00
Hicks, Taylor	R-R	6-3	204	2-26-92	1	0	0.00	1	0	0	0	2	0	0	0	0	1	1	.000	.000	.000	5.40	0.00
Idrogo, Eudis	L-L	6-1	198	6-6-95	5	2	2.03	8	8	2	0	44	28	12	10	2	11	49	.183	.167	.188	9.95	2.23

Pitching	B-T	HT	WT	DOB	W	L	ERA	G	GS	CG	SV	IP	H	R	ER	HR	BB	SO	AVG	vLH	vRH	K/9	BB/9
Jimenez, Eduardo	R-R	6-0	183	4-4-95	1	0	0.00	4	0	0	0	5	4	0	0	0	1	5	.211	.000	.286	8.44	1.69
Kisena, Alec	L-R	6-5	250	10-12-95	1	1	2.25	9	9	0	0	40	35	13	10	2	16	44	.232	.180	.267	9.90	3.60
Lara, Carlos	R-R	6-2	170	3-2-94	0	0	34.71	10	0	0	0	5	3	19	18	0	20	5	.188	.167	.200	9.64	38.57
Longwith, Logan	R-R	6-3	170	3-30-94	2	1	2.42	15	0	0	5	26	22	8	7	1	1	24	.224	.167	.258	8.31	0.35
Lopez, Jose	R-R	5-9	174	6-21-95	1	1	4.09	16	0	0	3	22	21	12	10	0	12	30	.253	.216	.283	12.27	4.91
Milton, Ryan	R-R	6-4	215	12-18-91	1	1	2.61	11	0	0	2	21	15	7	6	0	12	29	.203	.167	.220	12.63	5.23
Moreno, Dominic	R-R	5-11	190	3-12-93	0	0	6.00	2	0	0	1	3	5	2	2	0	2	4	.357	.333	.364	12.00	6.00
Mueses, Victor	R-R	6-1	175	10-13-95	1	2	3.04	14	0	0	1	24	18	11	8	0	18	22	.207	.273	.167	8.37	6.85
Ravenelle, Adam	R-R	6-3	185	10-5-92	0	0	0.00	2	0	0	0	4	0	0	0	0	3	1	.000	.000	.000	2.25	6.75
Shull, Jake	R-R	5-10	190	4-26-94	0	0	0.00	2	0	0	1	3	3	0	0	0	1	2	.250	.000	.429	6.00	3.00
Smith, Drew	R-R	6-2	190	9-24-93	0	0	0.00	1	0	0	0	2	1	0	0	0	0	3	.167	.250	.000	16.20	0.00
Soto, Gregory	L-L	6-1	180	2-11-95	2	4	2.19	9	5	0	0	37	34	20	9	0	25	40	.250	.184	.276	9.73	6.08
St. John, Locke	L-L	6-3	180	1-31-93	1	0	0.69	3	1	0	0	13	7	1	1	1	5	18	.152	.308	.091	12.46	3.46
Tejada, Andres	R-R	6-5	190	2-2-95	0	2	2.16	6	0	0	1	8	7	2	2	0	2	8	.212	.083	.286	8.64	2.16
Vasquez, Angel	R-R	6-5	190	10-8-93	0	0	0.73	8	0	0	0	12	7	2	1	1	7	9	.171	.313	.080	6.57	5.11
Vinson, Mike	R-R	6-2	185	2-9-94	1	2	2.96	14	0	0	1	27	28	12	9	0	10	31	.255	.182	.286	10.21	3.29

Fielding

Catcher	PCT	G	PO	A	E	DP	PB
Sanjur	.980	30	223	22	5	1	4
Servais	1.000	2	5	1	0	0	1
Sthormes	.986	29	253	27	4	2	4
Thomas	1.000	12	44	4	0	0	4

First Base	PCT	G	PO	A	E	DP
Brugnoni	.987	32	212	11	3	16
Donnels	1.000	2	16	1	0	2
Salter	.987	29	226	9	3	16

Second Base	PCT	G	PO	A	E	DP
Alfaro	.960	10	16	32	2	4
Ledezma	.974	43	68	82	4	26

	PCT	G	PO	A	E	DP
MacKenzie	.938	4	5	10	1	3
Pereira	.900	6	7	11	2	4

Third Base	PCT	G	PO	A	E	DP
Ledezma	—	1	0	0	0	0
Lester	1.000	6	4	8	0	1
Pereira	.852	25	11	41	9	2
Sanjur	1.000	1	0	1	0	0
Sayers	.921	29	21	49	6	5

Shortstop	PCT	G	PO	A	E	DP
Alfaro	.964	37	45	90	5	22
Jones	1.000	1	2	4	0	1
Pereira	.931	18	17	50	5	4

	PCT	G	PO	A	E	DP
Simcox	.857	4	3	9	2	1

Outfield	PCT	G	PO	A	E	DP
Azocar	.977	51	117	8	3	0
Bauml	1.000	27	41	1	0	1
Castano	1.000	5	3	0	0	0
Gibson	1.000	3	3	0	0	0
Gonzalez	.962	35	49	2	2	2
Havrilak	1.000	4	5	0	0	0
Ordonez Jr.	.933	12	14	0	1	0
Santana	.955	21	20	1	1	0
Stewart	1.000	6	14	0	0	0
Valdez	.981	32	50	2	1	0

DSL TIGERS

ROOKIE

DOMINICAN SUMMER LEAGUE

Batting	B-T	HT	WT	DOB	AVG	vLH	vRH	G	AB	R	H	2B	3B	HR	RBI	BB	HBP	SH	SF	SO	SB	CS	SLG	OBP
Alcantara, Randel	L-R	6-1	180	5-13-97	.305	.208	.333	60	213	37	65	21	6	2	36	26	14	1	0	42	7	4	.488	.415
De La Cruz, Isrrael	R-R	6-0	150	6-15-97	.253	.239	.258	51	174	36	44	8	3	0	15	20	6	4	0	56	14	7	.333	.350
Garcia, Alexis	R-R	6-2	170	7-1-97	.219	.229	.216	44	137	24	30	9	1	0	9	16	2	2	1	37	7	6	.299	.308
Hidalgo, Gregoris	R-R	5-10	160	12-18-93	.212	.174	.226	56	170	20	36	6	1	3	20	15	3	1	3	33	7	1	.312	.283
Martinez, Hector	R-R	5-11	175	11-1-96	.336	.288	.351	55	223	42	75	11	6	5	34	9	7	0	2	41	5	8	.507	.378
Martinez, Julio	R-R	6-2	195	12-15-97	.274	.294	.268	57	208	29	57	13	7	4	41	15	7	0	3	64	6	5	.462	.339
Mejia, Sauris	L-L	5-9	150	11-28-96	.251	.333	.227	63	167	42	42	5	2	3	19	38	5	4	1	42	12	7	.359	.403
Melo, Jeffrei	R-R	6-4	185	6-24-98	.161	.073	.187	51	180	15	29	3	4	0	15	9	1	1	2	88	3	0	.222	.203
Nunez, Moises	R-R	6-2	190	2-7-97	.225	.118	.254	26	80	7	18	7	1	0	14	11	1	0	1	23	1	3	.338	.323
Rodriguez, Sandy	R-R	6-1	180	10-19-94	.206	.225	.200	54	170	23	35	4	1	1	16	23	6	1	1	39	2	2	.259	.320
Santos, Allan	R-R	6-1	180	6-5-98	.233	.230	.207	63	225	21	48	8	1	1	27	34	3	1	3	70	4	6	.271	.321
Serrano, Ariel	R-R	5-10	174	6-23-96	.244	.269	.236	58	217	37	53	9	0	3	20	17	1	3	2	51	11	7	.327	.300
Tejeda, Bryan	R-R	6-0	190	1-17-96	.309	.386	.278	45	152	23	47	12	0	2	13	10	5	4	1	21	1	1	.428	.369
Ynirio, Jorge	R-R	5-11	170	10-19-97	.230	.188	.241	27	74	12	17	3	0	0	8	11	1	2	1	18	5	3	.270	.333

Pitching	B-T	HT	WT	DOB	W	L	ERA	G	GS	CG	SV	IP	H	R	ER	HR	BB	SO	AVG	vLH	vRH	K/9	BB/9
Almonte, Yei	R-R	6-2	210	10-8-95	5	3	1.89	15	10	0	0	62	73	32	13	1	12	40	.286	.250	.304	5.81	1.74
Appleton, Jose	R-R	6-3	170	7-2-97	0	1	7.94	3	2	0	0	6	6	8	5	0	6	6	.250	.000	.316	9.53	9.53
Baez, Jorge	R-R	6-2	185	5-9-95	2	5	5.26	15	11	0	0	51	62	41	30	0	20	42	.298	.212	.338	7.36	3.51
Batista, Franchi	R-R	6-0	170	5-26-96	2	2	6.35	12	4	0	0	23	30	19	16	2	9	22	.303	.222	.333	8.74	3.57
Cabrera, Rusbell	R-R	6-3	170	9-29-95	0	6	5.29	15	9	0	0	48	56	47	28	0	25	38	.283	.203	.321	7.17	4.72
De la Cruz, Juancito	R-R	6-4	200	1-21-93	0	0	5.40	6	0	0	0	5	7	7	3	1	3	2	.318	.000	.389	3.60	5.40
De La Rosa, Bairon	R-R	6-0	195	7-17-96	0	2	4.96	12	0	0	0	16	13	10	9	0	19	4	.255	.188	.286	2.20	10.47
De Pena, Enrique	R-R	6-0	170	7-25-95	0	1	7.12	21	0	0	1	37	51	37	29	1	23	31	.325	.255	.358	7.61	5.65
Espinal, Derlin	L-L	6-0	160	10-3-94	1	2	4.26	19	0	0	0	25	32	19	12	0	12	9	.296	.278	.300	3.20	4.26
Guante, Julio	R-R	6-3	180	5-29-97	2	0	4.95	17	1	0	3	36	40	22	20	2	16	20	.290	.268	.299	4.95	3.96
Javier, Xavier	R-R	6-4	170	2-9-98	0	4	8.19	13	5	0	1	30	34	40	27	0	28	26	.268	.371	.228	7.89	8.49
Martinez, Malvin	R-R	6-0	170	4-19-95	3	1	1.45	27	0	0	9	37	26	8	6	0	11	43	.190	.265	.148	10.37	2.65
Martinez, Stanley	R-R	6-3	185	11-29-94	4	2	3.81	15	6	0	0	57	66	36	24	2	12	49	.289	.284	.292	7.78	1.91
Morel, Melvin	L-L	6-2	185	12-14-93	3	0	0.42	15	0	0	0	22	5	2	1	0	13	29	.082	.000	.100	12.05	5.40
Munoz, Dionis	R-R	5-11	155	6-5-97	1	1	6.46	15	0	0	0	24	29	18	17	0	13	19	.319	.455	.275	7.23	4.94
Obispo, Janry	R-R	6-3	205	10-30-93	0	1	13.03	10	0	0	2	10	20	18	14	1	4	6	.417	.412	.419	5.59	3.72
Ovalles, Noel	R-R	6-2	180	3-24-97	3	5	2.70	14	14	0	0	53	58	23	16	0	17	57	.274	.409	.212	9.62	2.87
Romero, Diosfer	R-R	5-11	155	4-29-98	2	2	5.40	11	0	0	1	27	18	18	16	0	21	29	.200	.240	.185	9.79	7.09
Viloria, Felix	L-L	6-1	165	12-2-96	2	3	2.47	14	10	0	1	62	50	23	17	1	13	67	.223	.265	.211	9.73	1.89

Fielding

Catcher	PCT	G	PO	A	E	DP	PB
Nunez	.975	9	68	10	2	0	2
Rodriguez	.974	54	350	58	11	1	20
Tejeda	.959	19	105	12	5	0	9

First Base	PCT	G	PO	A	E	DP
Hidalgo	.997	39	292	18	1	22

Nunez	.993	16	127	11	1	8	
Santos	.926	2	23	2	2	1	
Tejeda	.971	23	195	8	6	19	
Second Base	**PCT**	**G**	**PO**	**A**	**E**	**DP**	
De La Cruz	.973	7	15	21	1	6	
Garcia	.957	7	11	11	1	2	
Hidalgo	.889	7	6	10	2	4	
Martinez	.951	50	108	107	11	21	

Ynirio	.946	11	14	21	2	3
Third Base	**PCT**	**G**	**PO**	**A**	**E**	**DP**
Alcantara	.860	56	49	104	25	8
Garcia	.813	14	5	21	6	2
Hidalgo	.929	9	7	19	2	1
Shortstop	**PCT**	**G**	**PO**	**A**	**E**	**DP**
De La Cruz	.902	43	55	119	19	22

Garcia	.857	21	23	55	13	14
Ynirio	.906	13	19	39	6	5
Outfield	**PCT**	**G**	**PO**	**A**	**E**	**DP**
Martinez	.952	48	75	5	4	0
Mejia	.978	38	86	3	2	1
Melo	.909	36	39	1	4	0
Santos	.947	56	85	5	5	1
Serrano	.973	55	103	4	3	0

VSL TIGERS   *ROOKIE*

VENEZUELAN SUMMER LEAGUE

Batting	B-T	HT	WT	DOB	AVG	vLH	vRH	G	AB	R	H	2B	3B	HR	RBI	BB	HBP	SH	SF	SO	SB	CS	SLG	OBP
Arias, Franklin	R-R	6-0	165	1-9-97	.266	.226	.280	59	203	31	54	5	3	2	21	25	3	0	1	30	12	3	.350	.353
Aristigueta, Keyder	R-R	5-11	165	2-2-96	.170	.125	.189	48	106	14	18	3	1	0	15	24	3	2	1	27	3	1	.217	.336
Azuaje, Jheyser	R-R	5-9	165	2-12-97	.293	.262	.305	61	225	30	66	10	0	2	29	12	7	3	3	18	3	1	.364	.344
Bello, Moises	R-R	5-10	160	6-13-97	.211	.222	.208	61	227	43	48	9	3	1	16	20	10	2	2	44	11	4	.291	.301
Castillo, Eliezer	R-R	6-0	169	1-10-95	.292	.405	.254	51	168	29	49	6	2	1	12	16	2	4	1	18	5	5	.369	.358
Chirinos, Irwin	L-R	6-1	170	9-24-97	.245	.083	.293	14	53	5	13	3	0	0	3	2	2	0	0	12	3	1	.302	.298
Cortez, Johandry	R-R	5-10	170	5-24-98	.209	.222	.202	41	129	11	27	10	0	1	18	10	5	0	1	44	3	0	.310	.290
Escobar, Elys	R-R	6-0	190	9-21-96	.280	.264	.287	53	189	27	53	13	1	1	21	25	2	1	4	32	0	0	.376	.364
Gonzalez, Jose	R-R	6-2	165	7-14-98	.234	.275	.216	48	137	24	32	6	1	1	10	23	4	0	2	37	3	4	.314	.355
Guzman, Carlos	R-R	6-1	170	5-16-98	.156	.091	.176	34	90	5	14	3	0	0	5	8	1	0	0	19	1	1	.189	.232
Hernandez, Hector	L-R	6-0	175	2-23-96	.274	.304	.262	68	252	33	69	12	4	1	32	38	8	0	2	46	7	6	.365	.383
Pereira, Anthony	R-R	6-0	170	11-28-96	.298	.474	.246	22	84	17	25	7	1	1	10	10	0	0	0	15	9	4	.440	.372
Rodriguez, Alexander	R-R	5-11	170	3-13-98	.218	.100	.281	38	87	11	19	2	4	1	15	8	4	0	0	21	1	0	.368	.313
Salas, Jose	R-R	6-0	160	4-17-97	.270	.222	.289	49	196	29	53	9	0	2	20	10	3	1	0	27	0	7	.347	.316
Torrealba, Luis	B-R	6-1	175	9-23-96	.228	.190	.241	67	237	33	54	10	2	3	36	28	2	0	3	53	7	3	.325	.311

Pitching	B-T	HT	WT	DOB	W	L	ERA	G	GS	CG	SV	IP	H	R	ER	HR	BB	SO	AVG	vLH	vRH	K/9	BB/9
Del Valle, Esmeiro	R-R	6-6	193	10-9-93	2	3	3.16	20	4	0	1	51	49	22	18	2	22	40	.254	.292	.231	7.01	3.86
Figuera, Adonis	R-R	6-2	165	12-10-97	3	1	1.64	19	0	0	3	38	23	9	7	2	8	26	.173	.133	.184	6.10	1.88
Figueroa, Ken	R-R	6-0	165	5-30-96	5	5	2.19	14	13	0	0	66	45	21	16	3	13	46	.191	.191	.190	6.30	1.78
Fuentes, Jose	R-R	6-1	165	10-6-94	5	2	2.90	13	13	0	0	68	74	27	22	1	12	39	.287	.292	.284	5.14	1.58
Gonzalez, Daniel	R-R	6-3	200	8-15-95	2	3	1.95	15	11	0	1	51	44	18	11	0	15	42	.228	.171	.260	7.46	2.66
Ledezma, Luis	R-R	6-0	150	1-27-97	0	2	14.09	9	0	0	0	8	8	13	12	1	8	3	.296	.125	.368	3.52	9.39
Lopez, Jose	R-R	5-9	174	6-21-95	—																		
Lopez, Ronaldo	R-R	6-2	165	1-7-98	0	1	5.73	14	8	0	1	38	43	28	24	2	26	18	.307	.305	.309	4.30	6.21
Matute, Marlon	L-L	6-1	170	6-10-97	0	1	18.00	8	0	0	0	6	11	15	12	0	16	7	.379	.429	.364	10.50	24.00
Moreno, Willians	R-R	6-0	182	3-30-96	2	0	6.99	15	0	0	1	28	33	22	22	3	14	18	.306	.258	.325	5.72	4.45
Paricaguan, Jesus	R-R	6-0	165	12-3-95	0	0	0.00	1	0	0	0	1	1	0	0	0	0	0	.250	.000	.333	0.00	0.00
Pinto, Wladimir	R-R	5-11	170	2-12-98	2	1	3.90	16	0	0	1	28	16	14	12	0	28	24	.167	.241	.134	7.81	9.11
Rodriguez, Hector	R-R	6-4	210	12-4-96	2	3	3.48	24	0	0	14	31	28	15	12	1	8	34	.228	.293	.195	9.87	2.32
Rodriguez, Jesus	R-R	6-3	170	2-16-98	6	1	2.18	13	8	0	0	54	40	14	13	2	6	30	.215	.224	.210	5.03	1.01
Rodriguez, Perkyn	R-R	6-1	165	5-6-98	1	0	5.40	8	0	0	0	15	17	10	9	0	7	12	.283	.381	.231	7.20	4.20
Vargas, Miguel	R-R	6-4	190	3-5-95	1	0	1.65	8	2	0	0	16	9	5	3	0	4	10	.164	.214	.146	5.51	2.20
Vasquez, Jose	R-R	6-0	175	3-19-96	5	2	2.52	13	10	0	1	54	41	21	15	1	15	36	.218	.183	.239	6.04	2.52
Villarroel, Javier	R-R	6-1	180	10-31-97	1	4	5.97	13	0	0	0	29	32	26	19	0	16	16	.283	.240	.317	5.02	5.02
Yanez, Wildenson	R-R	6-1	165	11-23-96	1	3	4.69	16	1	0	0	40	52	28	21	2	16	30	.331	.358	.317	6.69	3.57

Fielding

Catcher	PCT	G	PO	A	E	DP	PB
Azuaje	.986	39	218	65	4	4	4
Cortez	.974	9	30	8	1	0	0
Escobar	.991	29	170	44	2	5	4

First Base	PCT	G	PO	A	E	DP
Azuaje	.991	22	201	23	2	16
Castillo	.994	24	158	17	1	7
Cortez	1.000	1	1	0	0	0
Escobar	.983	20	156	16	3	11
Torrealba	.993	21	130	10	1	5

Second Base	PCT	G	PO	A	E	DP
Aristigueta	.947	42	69	91	9	14
Bello	.979	13	15	31	1	4

Castillo	.958	16	27	41	3	5
Pereira	.909	3	3	7	1	0
Rodriguez	.976	14	13	27	1	4

Third Base	PCT	G	PO	A	E	DP
Aristigueta	—	2	0	0	0	0
Bello	.916	30	28	70	9	5
Castillo	.864	8	5	14	3	2
Gonzalez	.500	1	0	1	1	0
Guzman	.877	30	20	51	10	4
Pereira	.938	5	3	12	1	1
Rodriguez	.938	8	5	10	1	1
Salas	1.000	4	1	5	0	1

Shortstop	PCT	G	PO	A	E	DP
Bello	.946	20	35	52	5	8
Guzman	.750	1	3	0	1	0
Pereira	.934	15	33	38	5	4
Salas	.921	39	90	97	16	12

Outfield	PCT	G	PO	A	E	DP
Arias	.964	56	96	11	4	2
Chirinos	.857	9	12	0	2	0
Gonzalez	.959	43	87	6	4	2
Hernandez	.978	63	129	7	3	0
Rodriguez	1.000	5	8	0	0	0
Torrealba	.960	50	67	5	3	0

DETROIT TIGERS

Houston Astros

SEASON IN A SENTENCE: After years of enduring plenty of losses as part of a multi-year rebuilding plan, Houston turned the corner by earning the team's first playoff spot in a decade.

HIGH POINT: Houston ran off a 10-game winning streak in late April and early May—the team's longest winning streak in over a decade—to give a clear sign to Houston fans that the rebuilding effort had turned the corner. That fast start opened up a seven-game lead in the division that ensured the club remained on top of the AL West for the next three months.

LOW POINT: With an AL West title within their grasp, Houston faltered down the stretch, going 11-16 in September as the Rangers caught and then ran away with the division crown. The Astros made the postseason as a wild card and appeared on their way to a Division Series win over the Royals before Kansas City rallied to win Game Four with seven runs over the final two innings and breezed to a 7-2 win in Game Five.

NOTABLE ROOKIES: Shortstop Carlos Correa lived up to every possible expectation, hitting .279/.345/.512 with 22 home runs in 99 games. He added two more home runs in the playoffs. Righthander Lance McCullers (6-7, 3.22) erased any memory of a poor 2014 in the minors by becoming a vital part of the Astros' rotation and finished his season with an impressive postseason outing against the Royals. Outfielder Preston Tucker hit 13 home runs in a part-time role.

KEY TRANSACTIONS: The Astros were busy at the trade deadline, acquiring outfielder Carlos Gomez and righthander Mike Fiers from the Brewers (for lefthander Josh Hader, outfielders Domingo Santana and Brett Phillips and righthander Adrian Houser). Lefthander Scott Kazmir was picked up from the Astros for catcher Jacob Nottingham and righthander Daniel Megden.

DOWN ON THE FARM: Houston had success at virtually every level of the minors and sent seven teams to the playoffs. Fresno won the Triple-A national title while Rookie-level Greeneville won the Appalachian League crown. First baseman A.J. Reed was runner-up for Minor League Player of the Year thanks to his .340/.432/.612 season between high Class A Lancaster and Double-A Corpus Christi. First baseman Chase McDonald hit 30 home runs for Lancaster. Third baseman Tyler White hit .325/.442/.496 between Corpus Christi and Fresno.

OPENING DAY PAYROLL: $70,910,100 (29th)

PLAYERS OF THE YEAR

MAJOR LEAGUE	MINOR LEAGUE
Dallas Keuchel	**A.J. Reed**
lhp	**1b**
20-8, 2.48	(High A/Double-A)
Led AL in wins, innings	.340/.432/.612
(232) and WHIP (1.02)	34 HR, 127 RBIs

ORGANIZATION LEADERS

BATTING		*Minimum 250 AB
MAJORS		
* AVG	Jose Altuve	.313
* OPS	Jose Altuve	.812
HR	Evan Gattis	27
RBI	Evan Gattis	88
MINORS		
* AVG	A.J. Reed, Lancaster, Corpus Christi	.340
* OBP	Tyler White, Corpus Christi, Fresno	.442
* SLG	A.J. Reed, Lancaster, Corpus Christi	.612
R	A.J. Reed, Lancaster, Corpus Christi	113
H	A.J. Reed, Lancaster, Corpus Christi	178
TB	A.J. Reed, Lancaster, Corpus Christi	320
2B	Mott Hyde, Quad Cities, Lancaster	40
3B	Ronnie Mitchell, Lancaster	11
HR	A.J. Reed, Lancaster, Corpus Christi	34
RBI	A.J. Reed, Lancaster, Corpus Christi	127
BB	Jamie Ritchie, Quad Cities, Lancaster	95
SO	J.D. Davis, Lancaster	157
SB	Bobby Boyd, Quad Cities	40

PITCHING		#Minimum 75 IP
MAJORS		
W	Dallas Keuchel	20
# ERA	Dallas Keuchel	2.48
SO	Dallas Keuchel	216
SV	Luke Gregerson	31
MINORS		
W	Edison Frias, Lancaster, Corpus Christi	12
	Mike Hauschild, Corpus Christi, Fresno	12
	Joe Musgrove, Quad Cities, Lan., Corpus Christi	12
L	Dan Straily, Fresno	9
# ERA	Joshua James, Quad Cities	2.63
G	Jordan Jankowski, Fresno	55
GS	Mark Appel, Corpus Christi, Fresno	25
SV	Jandel Gustave, Corpus Christi	20
IP	Mike Hauschild, Corpus Christi, Fresno	138
BB	Troy Scribner, Lancaster	57
SO	Dan Straily, Fresno	124
AVG	Joshua James, Quad Cities	.237

General Manager: Jeff Luhnow. **Farm Director:** Quinton McCracken. **Scouting Director:** Mike Elias.

Class	Team	League	W	L	PCT	Finish	Manager
Majors	Houston Astros	American	86	76	.531	5th (15)	A.J. Hinch
Triple-A	Fresno Grizzlies	Pacific Coast	84	59	.587	2nd (16)	Tony DeFrancesco
Double-A	Corpus Christi Hooks	Texas	89	51	.636	1st (8)	Rodney Linares
High A	Lancaster JetHawks	California	75	65	.536	4th (10)	Omar Lopez
Low A	Quad Cities River Bandits	Midwest	88	50	.638	1st (16)	Josh Bonifay
Short season	Tri-City ValleyCats	New York-Penn	42	33	.560	2nd (14)	Ed Romero
Rookie	Greeneville Astros	Appalachian	34	33	.507	4th (10)	Lamarr Rogers
Rookie	Astros	Gulf Coast	19	41	.317	15th (16)	Marty Malloy
Overall 2015 Minor League Record			431	332	.565	1st (30)	

ORGANIZATION STATISTICS

HOUSTON ASTROS

AMERICAN LEAGUE

Batting	B-T	HT	WT	DOB	AVG	vLH	vRH	G	AB	R	H	2B	3B	HR	RBI	BB	HBP	SH	SF	SO	SB	CS	SLG	OBP
Altuve, Jose	R-R	5-6	165	5-6-90	.313	.372	.289	154	638	86	200	40	4	15	66	33	9	3	6	67	38	13	.459	.353
Carter, Chris	R-R	6-4	250	12-18-86	.199	.201	.198	129	391	50	78	17	0	24	64	57	6	0	5	151	1	2	.427	.307
Castro, Jason	L-R	6-3	215	6-18-87	.211	.192	.219	104	337	38	71	19	0	11	31	33	2	0	3	115	0	0	.365	.283
Conger, Hank	B-R	6-2	220	1-29-88	.229	.175	.279	73	201	25	46	11	0	11	33	23	2	1	2	63	0	1	.448	.311
Correa, Carlos	R-R	6-4	210	9-22-94	.279	.274	.281	99	387	52	108	22	1	22	68	40	1	0	4	78	14	4	.512	.345
Duffy, Matt	R-R	6-3	215	2-6-89	.375	.333	.500	8	8	0	3	1	0	0	3	1	0	0	0	2	0	0	.500	.444
Gattis, Evan	R-R	6-4	260	8-18-86	.246	.237	.250	153	566	66	139	20	11	27	88	30	3	0	5	119	0	1	.463	.285
Gomez, Carlos	R-R	6-3	220	12-4-85	.242	.235	.243	41	149	19	36	9	0	4	13	8	2	3	1	31	10	3	.383	.288
Gonzalez, Marwin	B-R	6-1	205	3-14-89	.279	.295	.268	120	344	44	96	18	1	12	34	16	3	7	0	74	4	5	.442	.317
Grossman, Robbie	B-L	6-0	205	9-16-89	.143	.136	.148	24	49	7	7	2	0	1	5	5	0	0	0	17	0	0	.245	.222
Hoes, L.J.	R-R	6-0	200	3-5-90	.267	.333	.167	8	15	1	4	0	0	0	1	1	0	0	0	3	0	0	.267	.313
Lowrie, Jed	B-R	6-0	180	4-17-84	.222	.267	.206	69	230	35	51	14	0	9	30	28	3	0	2	43	1	0	.400	.312
Marisnick, Jake	R-R	6-4	220	3-30-91	.236	.204	.259	133	339	46	80	15	4	9	36	18	5	6	4	105	24	9	.383	.281
Presley, Alex	L-L	5-10	195	7-25-85	.250	1.000	.182	8	12	1	3	0	0	0	1	1	0	0	0	5	0	0	.250	.308
Rasmus, Colby	L-L	6-2	195	8-11-86	.238	.252	.233	137	432	67	103	23	2	25	61	47	2	1	3	154	2	1	.475	.314
Santana, Domingo	R-R	6-5	225	9-22-92	.256	.200	.316	14	39	6	10	2	0	2	8	2	1	0	0	17	2	1	.462	.310
Singleton, Jon	L-L	6-2	225	9-18-91	.191	.333	.158	19	47	6	9	2	0	1	6	10	0	0	1	17	1	0	.298	.328
Springer, George	R-R	6-3	215	9-19-89	.276	.296	.265	102	388	59	107	19	2	16	41	50	8	2	3	109	16	4	.459	.367
Stassi, Max	R-R	5-10	200	3-15-91	.400	.333	.444	11	15	4	6	0	0	1	2	1	0	1	0	5	0	0	.600	.438
Tucker, Preston	L-L	6-0	215	7-6-90	.243	.200	.255	98	300	35	73	19	0	13	33	20	3	0	6	68	0	2	.437	.297
Valbuena, Luis	L-R	5-10	200	11-30-85	.224	.158	.247	132	434	62	97	18	0	25	56	50	6	0	3	106	1	0	.438	.310
Villar, Jonathan	B-R	6-1	215	5-2-91	.284	.279	.291	53	116	18	33	7	1	2	11	10	0	1	1	29	7	2	.414	.339

Pitching	B-T	HT	WT	DOB	W	L	ERA	G	GS	CG	SV	IP	H	R	ER	HR	BB	SO	AVG	vLH	vRH	K/9	BB/9
Buchanan, Jake	R-R	6-0	225	9-24-89	0	0	2.00	5	0	0	0	9	5	2	2	1	4	5	.161	.100	.190	5.00	4.00
Chapman, Kevin	L-L	6-3	225	2-19-88	0	0	3.38	3	0	0	0	5	4	2	2	1	3	8	.211	.154	.333	13.50	5.06
Deduno, Sam	R-R	6-3	210	7-2-83	0	1	6.86	9	2	0	1	21	24	16	16	3	9	17	.293	.279	.308	7.29	3.86
Feldman, Scott	L-R	6-7	220	2-7-83	5	5	3.90	18	18	0	0	108	115	49	47	13	27	61	.275	.258	.294	5.07	2.24
Feliz, Michael	R-R	6-4	225	6-28-93	0	0	7.88	5	0	0	0	8	9	7	7	2	4	7	.273	.250	.294	7.88	4.50
Fields, Josh	R-R	6-0	195	8-19-85	4	1	3.55	54	0	0	0	51	39	20	20	2	19	67	.210	.234	.193	11.90	3.38
Fiers, Mike	R-R	6-2	200	6-15-85	2	1	3.32	10	9	1	0	62	45	26	23	10	21	59	.197	.189	.205	8.52	3.03
Gregerson, Luke	L-R	6-3	200	5-14-84	7	3	3.10	64	0	0	31	61	48	24	21	5	10	59	.213	.235	.189	8.70	1.48
Harris, Will	R-R	6-4	225	8-28-84	5	5	1.90	68	0	0	2	71	42	18	15	8	22	68	.168	.129	.201	8.62	2.79
Hernandez, Roberto	R-R	6-4	230	8-30-80	3	5	4.36	20	11	0	0	85	90	48	41	9	26	42	.275	.268	.282	4.46	2.76
Kazmir, Scott	L-L	6-0	185	1-24-84	2	6	4.17	13	13	0	0	73	78	42	34	13	24	54	.270	.348	.245	6.63	2.95
2-team total (18 Oakland)					7	11	3.10	31	31	0	0	183	162	77	63	20	59	155	—	—	—	7.62	2.90
Keuchel, Dallas	L-R	6-3	210	1-1-88	20	8	2.48	33	33	3	0	232	185	68	64	17	51	216	.217	.177	.227	8.38	1.98
McCullers Jr., Lance	L-R	6-2	205	10-2-93	6	7	3.22	22	22	1	0	126	106	49	45	10	43	129	.226	.209	.243	9.24	3.08
McHugh, Collin	R-R	6-2	190	6-19-87	19	7	3.89	32	32	0	0	204	207	89	88	19	53	171	.263	.235	.288	7.56	2.34
Neshek, Pat	B-R	6-3	210	9-4-80	3	6	3.62	66	0	0	1	55	49	25	22	8	12	51	.240	.276	.219	8.40	1.98
Oberholtzer, Brett	L-L	6-1	225	7-1-89	2	2	4.46	8	8	0	0	38	44	21	19	4	17	27	.293	.357	.269	6.34	3.99
Peacock, Brad	R-R	6-1	210	2-2-88	0	1	5.40	1	1	0	0	5	5	3	3	0	2	3	.278	.444	.111	5.40	3.60
Perez, Oliver	L-L	6-3	220	8-15-81	0	3	6.75	22	0	0	0	12	14	12	9	2	4	14	.275	.188	.421	10.50	3.00
Qualls, Chad	R-R	6-4	235	8-17-78	3	5	4.38	60	0	0	4	49	46	24	24	6	9	46	.247	.230	.256	8.39	1.64
Sipp, Tony	L-L	6-0	190	7-12-83	3	4	1.99	60	0	0	0	54	41	13	12	5	15	62	.208	.227	.190	10.27	2.48
Straily, Dan	R-R	6-2	215	12-1-88	0	1	5.40	4	3	0	0	17	16	11	10	2	8	14	.239	.243	.233	7.56	4.32
Thatcher, Joe	L-L	6-2	230	10-4-81	1	3	3.18	43	0	0	0	23	23	8	8	1	12	26	.274	.245	.323	10.32	4.76
Velasquez, Vincent	B-R	6-3	205	6-7-92	1	1	4.37	19	7	0	0	56	50	28	27	5	21	58	.240	.214	.271	9.38	3.40
Wojciechowski, Asher	R-R	6-4	235	12-21-88	0	1	7.16	5	3	0	0	16	23	13	13	2	7	16	.329	.372	.259	8.82	3.86

Fielding

Catcher	PCT	G	PO	A	E	DP	PB
Castro	.999	103	777	62	1	5	7
Conger	.992	69	472	22	4	5	1
Stassi	1.000	10	39	1	0	1	0

First Base	PCT	G	PO	A	E	DP
Carter	.992	115	911	67	8	85
Duffy	1.000	2	2	0	0	0
Gonzalez	.995	43	203	14	1	14

	PCT	G	PO	A	E	DP
Singleton	.991	14	107		5	1	9
Valbuena	.995	31	205	13	1	12

Second Base	PCT	G	PO	A	E	DP
Altuve	.993	153	247	417	5	81
Gonzalez	.982	15	17	38	1	7
Valbuena	1.000	1	0	2	0	0
Villar	1.000	3	0	1	0	0

Third Base	PCT	G	PO	A	E	DP
Duffy	1.000	2	1	6	0	0
Gonzalez	.935	21	7	22	2	1
Lowrie	.966	47	25	60	3	1
Valbuena	.974	99	54	168	6	20

Villar	.862	12	10	15	4	3

Shortstop	PCT	G	PO	A	E	DP
Correa	.967	99	112	265	13	41
Gonzalez	.975	32	34	81	3	15
Lowrie	1.000	17	21	53	0	6
Villar	.943	22	21	62	5	15

Outfield	PCT	G	PO	A	E	DP
Conger	—	1	0	0	0	0
Gattis	.833	11	5	0	1	0
Gomez	.990	39	97	3	1	2
Gonzalez	.957	15	21	1	1	0
Grossman	1.000	19	18	0	0	0
Hoes	1.000	7	6	0	0	0
Marisnick	.988	126	245	8	3	3
Presley	1.000	6	8	0	0	0
Rasmus	.980	131	235	9	5	3
Santana	1.000	13	18	0	0	0
Springer	.985	102	189	6	3	3
Tucker	.992	90	121	2	1	0
Villar	1.000	7	6	0	0	0

FRESNO GRIZZLIES

TRIPLE-A

PACIFIC COAST LEAGUE

Batting	B-T	HT	WT	DOB	AVG	vLH	vRH	G	AB	R	H	2B	3B	HR	RBI	BB	HBP	SH	SF	SO	SB	CS	SLG	OBP
Aplin, Andrew	L-L	6-0	205	3-21-91	.275	.338	.242	74	233	37	64	7	2	2	28	45	0	7	0	41	20	7	.348	.392
Correa, Carlos	R-R	6-4	210	9-22-94	.276	.333	.242	24	98	19	27	6	1	3	12	12	0	0	3	14	3	1	.449	.345
Dominguez, Matt	R-R	6-1	220	8-28-89	.251	.290	.230	45	175	14	44	9	0	4	26	4	6	1	2	28	0	0	.371	.289
2-team total (72 Colorado Springs)					.269	—	—	117	442	51	119	30	1	10	56	19	9	1	4	65	0	0	.410	.310
Duffy, Matt	R-R	6-3	215	2-6-89	.294	.318	.282	127	490	94	144	29	2	20	104	48	12	0	7	90	4	1	.484	.366
Flores, Luis	R-R	5-9	215	11-2-86	.200	.214	.194	14	45	5	9	3	0	1	5	5	0	1	0	12	0	0	.333	.280
Fontana, Nolan	L-R	5-11	205	6-6-91	.241	.273	.225	117	361	56	87	21	6	3	40	74	3	12	6	99	6	11	.357	.369
Grossman, Robbie	B-L	6-0	205	9-16-89	.254	.303	.220	93	347	54	88	16	1	5	37	55	1	1	4	85	14	8	.349	.354
Heineman, Tyler	B-R	5-11	195	6-19-91	.271	.275	.268	56	192	27	52	10	0	3	25	11	1	4	1	15	2	0	.370	.312
Heras, Leonardo	L-R	5-9	190	5-29-90	.194	.182	.200	9	31	3	6	1	1	0	3	2	1	1	0	11	0	0	.290	.265
Hoes, L.J.	R-R	6-0	200	3-5-90	.295	.375	.248	99	370	69	109	24	3	3	53	52	3	1	3	62	26	8	.400	.383
Kemp, Tony	L-R	5-6	165	10-31-91	.273	.253	.282	71	271	42	74	9	3	3	29	21	5	12	2	37	20	6	.362	.334
Marisnick, Jake	R-R	6-4	220	3-30-91	.167	.250	.125	3	12	3	2	2	0	0	3	2	0	0	0	4	3	0	.333	.286
Moon, Chan	L-R	6-0	185	3-23-91	.000	.000	.000	2	6	0	0	0	0	0	0	0	0	0	1	1	0	0	.000	.000
Presley, Alex	L-L	5-10	195	7-25-85	.292	.333	.274	89	332	48	97	14	1	3	49	27	1	5	2	41	15	4	.367	.345
Santana, Domingo	R-R	6-5	225	8-5-92	.320	.341	.310	75	275	62	88	18	3	16	59	48	3	0	0	91	1	4	.582	.426
2-team total (20 Colorado Springs)					.333	—	—	95	354	75	118	23	4	18	77	54	3	0	0	108	2	5	.573	.426
Sclafani, Joe	B-R	5-11	195	4-22-90	.300	.245	.341	72	220	39	66	4	3	0	25	28	2	4	2	38	4	1	.345	.381
Singleton, Jon	L-L	6-2	225	9-18-91	.254	.172	.312	102	378	72	96	25	2	22	83	64	1	0	5	99	2	1	.505	.359
Stassi, Max	R-R	5-10	200	3-15-91	.211	.196	.220	84	294	37	62	8	2	13	43	26	3	2	3	93	1	1	.384	.279
Torreyes, Ronald	R-R	5-10	150	9-2-92	.200	.095	.245	19	70	7	14	1	0	0	5	1	0	1	0	9	0	1	.214	.211
2-team total (13 Oklahoma City)					.244	—	—	32	119	17	29	3	1	0	8	3	1	1	1	13	0	1	.286	.266
Tucker, Preston	L-L	6-0	215	7-6-90	.295	.333	.274	33	129	20	38	4	0	11	35	12	1	0	1	25	1	0	.581	.357
Villar, Jonathan	B-R	6-1	215	5-2-91	.271	.317	.246	70	280	59	76	13	5	5	32	27	3	3	0	77	35	9	.407	.342
White, Tyler	R-R	5-11	225	10-29-90	.362	.407	.333	57	213	37	77	19	1	7	59	42	2	0	2	38	0	1	.559	.467
Woodward, Trent	B-R	6-2	215	2-4-92	.214	.125	.333	4	14	0	3	0	0	0	0	0	0	0	4	0	0	.214	.214

Pitching	B-T	HT	WT	DOB	W	L	ERA	G	GS	CG	SV	IP	H	R	ER	HR	BB	SO	AVG	vLH	vRH	K/9	BB/9
Appel, Mark	R-R	6-5	220	7-15-91	5	2	4.48	12	12	0	0	68	67	39	34	6	28	61	.255	.266	.247	8.03	3.69
Ballew, Travis	R-R	6-0	160	5-1-91	1	0	3.60	3	0	0	0	5	5	2	2	0	1	4	.294	.222	.375	7.20	1.80
Buchanan, Jake	R-R	6-0	225	9-24-89	5	5	4.76	30	7	0	3	81	101	47	43	5	22	46	.306	.329	.289	5.09	2.43
Chapman, Kevin	L-L	6-3	225	2-19-88	3	2	4.75	49	0	0	8	53	60	35	28	3	26	61	.286	.212	.319	10.36	4.42
Cotton, Chris	R-L	5-10	166	11-21-90	0	0	7.71	2	0	0	0	2	3	2	2	0	0	1	.300	.500	.250	3.86	0.00
Cruz, Luis	L-L	5-9	205	9-10-90	7	5	4.27	28	19	0	0	116	119	60	55	18	52	93	.268	.189	.293	7.22	4.03
Deduno, Sam	R-R	6-3	210	7-2-83	0	0	9.00	1	0	0	0	1	0	1	1	0	4	2	.000	.000	.000	18.00	36.00
Downs, Darin	R-L	6-3	200	12-26-84	0	0	4.96	15	0	0	2	16	19	11	9	2	3	11	.279	.250	.292	6.06	1.65
Dufek, Jonas	R-R	6-5	230	6-30-88	0	1	9.31	7	0	0	0	10	13	10	10	1	7	7	.325	.313	.333	6.52	6.52
Fields, Josh	R-R	6-0	195	8-19-85	0	0	3.00	5	0	0	0	6	5	2	2	0	4	3	.217	.125	.267	4.50	6.00
Gouvea, Murilo	R-R	6-2	200	9-15-88	0	0	2.25	4	0	0	0	4	4	1	1	0	0	3	.250	.167	.500	6.75	0.00
Hauschild, Mike	R-R	6-3	210	1-22-90	7	5	3.49	15	15	0	0	88	86	37	34	6	27	81	.253	.211	.278	8.32	2.77
Hoyt, James	R-R	6-5	220	9-30-86	0	1	3.49	47	0	0	9	49	48	23	19	1	11	66	.246	.257	.240	12.12	2.02
Jankowski, Jordan	R-R	6-1	225	5-17-89	8	3	3.18	55	0	0	5	62	55	24	22	0	34	77	.236	.270	.215	11.12	4.91
Lambson, Mitchell	L-L	6-1	205	7-20-90	0	0	2.60	13	0	0	0	17	15	5	5	0	5	12	.242	.348	.179	6.23	2.60
Minaya, Juan	R-R	6-4	195	9-19-90	0	0	0.87	6	0	0	0	10	6	1	1	0	5	11	.188	.250	.169	9.58	4.35
Oberholtzer, Brett	L-L	6-1	225	7-1-89	7	4	3.86	12	12	0	0	70	71	35	30	9	12	52	.257	.244	.260	6.69	1.54
Peacock, Brad	R-R	6-1	210	2-2-88	0	0	0.00	1	1	0	0	5	0	0	0	0	5	2	.000	.000	.000	3.86	9.64
Perez, Tyson	R-R	6-3	215	12-27-89	1	3	2.62	39	0	0	5	45	33	13	13	3	16	42	.206	.197	.213	6.45	2.22
Rodgers, Brady	R-R	6-2	205	9-17-90	9	7	4.51	21	21	0	0	116	136	61	58	13	25	89	.299	.299	.281	6.93	1.95
Rodriguez, Richard	R-R	6-4	205	3-4-90	5	0	2.57	23	0	0	0	42	32	14	12	4	10	36	.204	.254	.170	7.71	2.14
Sanudo, Gonzalo	L-R	6-3	235	1-10-92	0	0	30.38	2	0	0	0	3	10	9	9	3	1	4	.556	.667	.533	13.50	3.38
Shirley, Tommy	R-L	6-2	220	11-11-88	3	1	3.07	11	7	0	0	41	32	15	14	1	11	37	.212	.244	.200	8.12	2.41
Stoffel, Jason	R-R	6-1	230	9-15-88	4	2	4.91	35	0	0	3	44	35	25	24	4	18	50	.211	.236	.191	10.23	3.68
Straily, Dan	R-R	6-2	215	12-1-88	10	9	4.77	22	22	1	0	123	147	69	65	13	25	124	.289	.276	.301	9.10	1.83
Thatcher, Joe	L-L	6-2	230	10-4-81	0	0	1.04	9	0	0	0	9	4	1	1	0	4	10	.138	.000	.190	10.38	4.15
Veras, Jose	R-R	6-6	240	10-20-80	0	1	5.68	18	0	0	0	19	23	13	12	2	8	16	.291	.355	.250	7.58	3.79
White, Alex	R-R	6-3	220	8-29-88	1	4	5.56	9	7	0	1	44	56	37	27	6	17	18	.306	.326	.289	3.71	3.50
Wojciechowski, Asher	R-R	6-4	235	12-21-88	8	4	4.92	20	20	1	0	115	129	68	63	13	41	87	.285	.299	.274	6.79	3.20

Fielding

Catcher	PCT	G	PO	A	E	DP	PB
Flores	.991	14	99	8	1	0	2
Heineman	.997	50	373	25	1	3	2
Stassi	.997	83	600	47	2	2	4
Woodward	1.000	4	26	2	0	0	0

First Base	PCT	G	PO	A	E	DP
Dominguez	1.000	4	35	1	0	0
Duffy	.991	33	201	17	2	13
Heineman	1.000	1	4	0	0	0
Singleton	.990	84	658	67	7	57
White	1.000	25	224	7	0	15

Second Base	PCT	G	PO	A	E	DP
Fontana	.976	31	41	79	3	10
Heras	1.000	1	1	1	0	0
Kemp	1.000	51	74	111	0	23
Moon	1.000	1	2	8	0	0

	PCT	G	PO	A	E	DP
Sclafani	.970	55	94	132	7	24
Torreyes	.938	13	26	34	4	6
Villar	1.000	1	0	1	0	0

Third Base	PCT	G	PO	A	E	DP
Dominguez	1.000	38	40	77	0	9
Duffy	.945	75	45	145	11	9
Fontana	.973	29	17	55	2	0
Sclafani	.778	2	2	5	2	0
Torreyes	—	1	0	0	0	0
Villar	.889	6	4	4	1	0
White	1.000	3	3	7	0	0

Shortstop	PCT	G	PO	A	E	DP
Correa	.946	24	40	47	5	8
Fontana	.979	57	62	123	4	22
Moon	.667	1	0	4	2	1
Sclafani	.929	3	6	7	1	3

	PCT	G	PO	A	E	DP
Torreyes	.955	5	6	15	1	2
Villar	.934	59	74	140	15	29

Outfield	PCT	G	PO	A	E	DP
Aplin	.983	73	170	3	3	0
Fontana	1.000	1	3	0	0	0
Grossman	1.000	84	165	5	0	1
Heras	1.000	8	16	1	0	0
Hoes	.971	82	163	7	5	1
Kemp	1.000	23	53	1	0	0
Marisnick	1.000	2	1	0	0	0
Presley	.990	79	188	5	2	1
Santana	.969	61	121	2	4	1
Torreyes	1.000	1	2	0	0	0
Tucker	.983	22	55	4	1	0
Villar	.800	3	8	0	2	0

HOUSTON ASTROS

CORPUS CHRISTI HOOKS

DOUBLE-A

TEXAS LEAGUE

Batting	B-T	HT	WT	DOB	AVG	vLH	vRH	G	AB	R	H	2B	3B	HR	RBI	BB	HBP	SH	SF	SO	SB	CS	SLG	OBP
Aplin, Andrew	L-L	6-0	205	3-21-91	.343	.421	.326	31	105	27	36	3	4	0	12	24	0	3	2	13	12	3	.448	.458
Booth, Brett	R-R	5-11	215	10-12-90	.211	.467	.119	18	57	4	12	1	0	3	8	2	1	0	0	11	0	0	.386	.250
Correa, Carlos	R-R	6-4	210	9-22-94	.385	.619	.433	29	117	25	45	15	2	7	32	15	1	0	0	25	15	0	.726	.459
Gonzalez, Alfredo	R-R	6-1	190	7-13-92	.300	.258	.319	32	100	14	30	2	0	0	12	17	0	2	2	21	0	0	.320	.395
Gregor, Conrad	L-R	6-3	225	2-27-92	.239	.280	.227	127	435	57	104	29	2	10	73	65	3	1	6	102	5	1	.384	.338
Heineman, Tyler	B-R	5-11	195	6-19-91	.318	.111	.342	22	85	12	27	7	0	0	5	8	1	1	0	6	0	0	.400	.383
Heras, Leonardo	L-R	5-9	190	5-29-90	.244	.281	.234	77	262	44	64	14	2	5	30	35	1	1	5	32	13	1	.370	.332
Hernandez, Teoscar	R-R	6-2	180	10-15-92	.219	.208	.223	121	470	92	103	12	2	17	48	33	4	5	2	126	33	7	.362	.275
Kemmer, Jon	L-L	6-2	220	11-17-90	.327	.319	.329	104	364	67	119	28	4	18	65	45	12	0	4	89	9	1	.574	.414
Kemp, Tony	L-R	5-6	165	7-31-91	.358	.353	.358	50	193	36	69	10	1	0	19	35	1	0	1	28	15	8	.420	.457
Lowrie, Jed	B-R	6-0	180	4-17-84	.214	.333	.125	5	14	0	3	1	0	0	2	0	1	0	0	2	0	0	.286	.267
Mayfield, Jack	R-R	5-11	190	9-30-90	.260	.196	.291	48	173	34	45	6	0	7	22	19	0	2	2	36	3	1	.416	.330
Meredith, Brandon	R-R	6-2	225	12-19-89	.248	.333	.227	40	149	18	37	4	1	4	23	18	1	0	1	38	2	4	.369	.331
Mier, Jio	R-R	6-2	180	8-26-90	.258	.323	.236	109	376	53	97	18	2	7	56	51	5	6	5	77	10	3	.372	.350
Moon, Chan	L-R	6-0	185	3-23-91	.266	.186	.291	81	248	40	66	9	1	3	18	35	0	5	1	48	17	5	.347	.356
Moran, Colin	L-R	6-4	215	10-1-92	.306	.235	.332	96	366	47	112	25	2	9	67	43	4	0	4	79	1	0	.459	.381
Nash, Telvin	R-R	6-1	248	2-20-91	.228	.222	.230	30	114	17	26	5	0	7	27	13	2	1	0	49	0	0	.456	.318
Pena, Roberto	B-R	6-0	225	6-8-92	.237	.250	.234	74	257	25	61	10	0	1	22	16	1	5	1	37	1	0	.288	.284
Phillips, Brett	L-R	6-0	180	5-30-94	.321	.288	.341	31	134	22	43	8	4	1	18	8	3	0	0	26	7	2	.463	.372
Reed, A.J.	L-L	6-4	240	5-10-93	.332	.238	.373	53	205	38	68	14	1	11	46	27	1	0	4	49	0	0	.571	.405
Sclafani, Joe	B-R	5-11	195	4-22-90	.154	.000	.167	3	13	2	2	1	0	0	0	0	0	1	0	1	0	0	.231	.154
Springer, George	R-R	6-3	215	9-19-89	.278	.250	.286	5	18	4	5	1	0	0	2	0	0	2	0	6	1	0	.333	.350
Vasquez, Danry	L-R	6-3	190	1-8-94	.245	.200	.259	73	277	30	68	13	1	0	19	16	3	0	0	42	3	7	.300	.294
White, Tyler	R-R	5-11	225	10-29-90	.284	.375	.260	59	190	33	54	6	0	7	40	42	2	0	2	35	1	0	.426	.415
Woodward, Trent	R-R	6-2	215	2-4-92	.600	—	.600	2	5	0	3	1	0	0	0	0	0	0	0	0	1	0	.800	.600

Pitching	B-T	HT	WT	DOB	W	L	ERA	G	GS	CG	SV	IP	H	R	ER	HR	BB	SO	AVG	vLH	vRH	K/9	BB/9
Alaniz, R.J.	R-R	6-4	175	6-14-91	6	4	4.55	14	5	0	0	57	69	32	29	2	23	25	.304	.303	.305	3.92	3.61
Appel, Mark	R-R	6-5	220	7-15-91	5	1	4.26	13	13	1	0	63	68	34	30	7	23	49	.279	.319	.242	6.96	3.27
Baez, Angel	R-R	6-3	230	2-14-91	1	0	8.03	8	0	0	1	12	10	11	11	2	10	10	.217	.375	.045	7.30	7.30
Ballew, Travis	R-R	6-0	160	5-1-91	4	5	4.04	47	0	0	3	62	69	30	28	2	23	53	.280	.237	.318	7.65	3.32
Brunnemann, Tyler	R-R	6-2	220	8-9-91	0	0	9.53	7	0	0	0	6	8	7	6	1	3	3	.333	.333	.333	4.76	4.76
Cotton, Chris	R-L	5-10	166	11-21-90	2	1	3.05	33	0	0	5	41	37	15	14	4	12	34	.243	.187	.299	7.40	2.61
Devenski, Chris	R-R	6-3	195	11-13-90	7	4	3.01	24	17	0	2	120	117	43	40	12	33	104	.253	.210	.301	7.82	2.48
Dufek, Jonas	R-R	6-5	215	6-30-88	1	0	4.32	4	0	0	0	8	7	4	4	0	4	6	.226	.250	.200	4.32	6.48
Emanuel, Kent	L-L	6-3	225	6-4-92	1	1	3.68	4	2	0	0	15	21	8	6	1	5	5	.350	.400	.325	3.07	3.07
Feldman, Scott	L-R	6-7	220	2-7-83	1	0	5.40	2	2	0	0	8	10	4	4	0	5	7	.303	.353	.250	7.88	5.63
Feliz, Michael	R-R	6-4	225	6-28-93	6	3	2.17	15	12	0	1	79	52	19	19	5	20	70	.185	.182	.188	8.01	2.29
Fields, Josh	R-R	6-0	195	8-19-85	0	0	0.00	2	0	0	0	2	1	0	0	0	2	1	.200	.250	.000	5.40	10.80
Freeman, Michael	R-L	6-8	235	10-7-91	0	0	4.50	2	0	0	0	2	3	1	1	0	1	1	.429	.000	.500	4.50	4.50
Frias, Edison	R-R	6-1	180	12-18-91	4	1	5.35	8	6	0	0	34	44	22	20	3	10	42	.314	.379	.248	11.23	2.67
Guduan, Reymin	L-L	6-4	205	3-16-92	1	3	11.57	16	0	0	0	16	20	23	21	3	19	19	.294	.286	.300	10.47	10.47
Gustave, Jandel	R-R	6-2	160	10-12-92	5	2	2.15	46	0	0	20	59	51	18	14	2	25	49	.235	.263	.213	7.52	3.84
Hader, Josh	L-R	6-3	160	4-7-94	3	3	3.17	10	10	1	0	65	60	31	23	5	24	69	.237	.219	.248	9.51	3.31
Hauschild, Mike	L-R	6-3	210	1-22-90	5	1	3.20	10	8	1	0	51	53	19	18	2	8	35	.272	.330	.211	6.22	1.42
Holmes, Brian	L-L	6-4	210	1-30-91	6	6	5.07	16	14	0	0	71	82	45	40	11	31	70	.292	.232	.323	8.87	3.93
Houser, Adrian	R-R	6-4	230	2-2-93	1	0	6.21	7	5	0	0	29	36	25	20	5	23	23	.293	.298	.289	6.21	4.05
Lambson, Mitchell	L-L	6-1	205	7-24-90	2	1	2.60	11	0	0	0	17	15	5	5	0	4	18	.242	.240	.243	9.35	2.08
Martes, Francis	R-R	6-1	225	11-24-95	1	0	4.91	3	3	0	0	15	19	9	8	2	7	16	.311	.286	.333	9.82	4.30
McCullers Jr., Lance	L-R	6-2	205	10-2-93	3	1	0.56	7	5	0	0	32	16	4	2	1	14	48	.142	.141	.143	13.50	3.94
Minaya, Juan	R-R	6-4	195	9-18-90	3	3	3.25	29	0	0	1	44	43	19	16	2	16	48	.259	.263	.256	9.74	3.25
Minnis, Albert	R-L	6-0	190	11-5-91	0	0	9.00	2	0	0	0	3	5	3	3	1	4	0	.385	.000	.417	0.00	12.00

Pitching	B-T	HT	WT	DOB	W	L	ERA	G	GS	CG	SV	IP	H	R	ER	HR	BB	SO	AVG	vLH	vRH	K/9	BB/9
Minor, Daniel	R-R	5-11	195	2-9-91	0	1	3.48	7	0	0	0	10	7	4	4	1	7	8	.189	.174	.214	6.97	6.10
Musgrove, Joe	R-R	6-5	255	12-4-92	4	0	2.20	8	7	0	1	45	35	13	11	7	6	33	.210	.214	.203	6.60	1.20
Peacock, Brad	R-R	6-1	210	2-2-88	0	0	0.00	1	1	0	0	2	2	0	0	0	1	2	.250	.200	.333	9.00	4.50
Perez, Tyson	R-R	6-3	215	12-27-89	0	0	0.00	3	0	0	1	3	1	0	0	0	2	2	.111	.000	.333	6.00	6.00
Qualls, Chad	R-R	6-4	235	8-17-78	0	0	5.40	2	2	0	0	2	2	1	1	1	0	1	.286	.400	.000	5.40	0.00
Sanudo, Gonzalo	L-R	6-3	235	1-10-92	1	0	0.00	4	0	0	0	6	2	0	0	0	0	8	.100	.167	.071	11.37	0.00
Velasquez, Vincent	B-R	6-3	205	6-7-92	4	0	1.91	9	5	0	0	33	20	9	7	2	13	45	.175	.205	.157	12.27	3.55
West, Aaron	R-R	6-1	195	6-1-90	3	4	2.77	30	4	0	5	84	84	28	26	5	11	68	.260	.261	.259	7.26	1.17
Westwood, Kyle	R-R	6-3	190	4-13-91	11	7	4.23	26	19	2	3	132	160	70	62	12	26	71	.303	.326	.283	4.84	1.77

Fielding

Catcher	PCT	G	PO	A	E	DP	PB
Booth	.993	18	130	13	1	1	0
Gonzalez	.996	32	231	16	1	1	6
Heineman	.989	22	157	17	2	0	2
Pena	.993	72	540	65	4	9	2
Woodward	1.000	1	5	2	0	0	0

First Base	PCT	G	PO	A	E	DP
Gregor	.992	104	825	64	7	82
Kemmer	.944	3	15	2	1	1
Nash	.952	3	19	1	1	4
Reed	.991	32	215	10	2	18
White	1.000	3	30	1	0	1

Second Base	PCT	G	PO	A	E	DP
Heras	.933	3	3	11	1	2
Kemp	.983	41	81	97	3	28
Mayfield	.995	41	74	124	1	25

	PCT	G	PO	A	E	DP
Mier	.895	10	13	21	4	3
Moon	.972	47	69	102	5	20
Pena	1.000	3	4	7	0	1
Sclafani	.941	3	5	11	1	5

Third Base	PCT	G	PO	A	E	DP
Correa	—	1	0	0	0	0
Gregor	1.000	1	0	1	0	0
Lowrie	.833	5	3	2	1	0
Mayfield	.000	2	0	0	1	0
Mier	.800	2	1	3	1	0
Moon	.941	17	8	24	2	1
Moran	.940	78	33	125	10	12
White	.914	46	23	62	8	7

Shortstop	PCT	G	PO	A	E	DP
Correa	.992	28	41	89	1	20
Mayfield	.944	4	6	11	1	4

	PCT	G	PO	A	E	DP
Mier	.955	96	159	219	18	58
Moon	.942	17	22	43	4	8
Pena	—	1	0	0	0	0

Outfield	PCT	G	PO	A	E	DP
Aplin	.984	31	62	1	1	0
Heras	.960	72	136	8	6	3
Hernandez	.989	120	275	7	3	2
Kemmer	.985	70	128	5	2	1
Kemp	1.000	9	11	0	0	0
Meredith	.986	35	65	4	1	0
Nash	1.000	5	5	0	0	0
Phillips	1.000	31	99	3	0	2
Springer	1.000	3	4	0	0	0
Vasquez	.985	57	126	4	2	0

HOUSTON ASTROS

LANCASTER JETHAWKS

HIGH CLASS A

CALIFORNIA LEAGUE

Batting	B-T	HT	WT	DOB	AVG	vLH	vRH	G	AB	R	H	2B	3B	HR	RBI	BB	HBP	SH	SF	SO	SB	CS	SLG	OBP
Booth, Brett	R-R	5-11	215	10-12-90	.167	.000	.222	7	24	4	4	0	0	1	3	5	0	0	1	8	0	0	.292	.300
Bregman, Alex	R-R	6-0	180	3-30-94	.319	.364	.312	37	160	19	51	8	4	3	21	12	1	2	3	17	8	4	.475	.364
Castro, Ruben	L-R	5-10	182	7-10-96	.184	.429	.143	13	49	4	9	3	0	0	3	2	0	0	0	12	0	0	.245	.216
Davis, J.D.	R-R	6-3	215	4-27-93	.289	.310	.284	120	485	93	140	28	3	26	101	54	10	0	3	157	5	2	.520	.370
Fernandez, Jose	R-R	6-1	190	5-20-93	.208	.333	.175	57	202	35	42	1	2	3	18	28	1	1	1	84	7	7	.277	.306
Fisher, Derek	L-R	6-1	207	8-21-93	.262	.250	.264	84	344	74	90	10	7	16	63	47	4	0	3	95	23	5	.471	.354
Gonzalez, Alfredo	R-R	6-1	190	7-13-92	.340	.250	.378	27	106	20	36	3	0	2	15	9	0	0	1	12	0	0	.425	.388
Holberton, Brian	L-R	5-10	200	6-10-92	.244	.243	.244	58	201	32	49	12	3	4	33	25	2	2	6	25	1	2	.393	.325
Hyde, Mott	R-R	5-10	190	3-12-92	.263		.320	74	282	46	88	24	4	2	49	32	4	4	5	73	4	2	.447	.384
Mayfield, Jack	R-R	5-11	190	9-30-90	.303	.375	.287	66	271	46	82	13	4	7	43	25	5	2	2	46	2	1	.458	.370
McDonald, Chase	R-R	6-4	265	6-2-92	.279	.257	.285	105	390	66	109	30	1	30	80	45	5	0	4	117	2	1	.592	.358
McMullen, Sean	L-L	5-9	186	6-4-92	.293	.091	.321	25	92	23	27	8	3	2	16	5	3	0	1	23	5	0	.511	.394
Medina, Edwin	R-R	5-8	170	2-11-93	.183	.000	.229	19	60	7	11	3	0	1	5	8	0	0	0	21	5	0	.283	.279
Mitchell, Ronnie	L-L	5-11	200	6-21-91	.286	.224	.299	111	405	57	116	27	11	12	72	45	1	5	4	89	3	3	.496	.356
Moon, Chan	L-R	6-0	185	3-23-91	.322	.294	.333	17	59	13	19	4	1	1	10	8	1	2	1	14	5	2	.475	.406
Morales, Jobduan	R-R	5-10	211	4-3-95	.217	.385	.152	13	46	6	10	0	0	0	6	5	0	0	0	9	0	0	.217	.294
Nottingham, Jacob	R-R	6-3	230	4-3-95	.324	.167	.338	17	71	14	23	6	1	4	14	3	2	0	0	10	0	0	.606	.368
2-team total (43 Stockton)					.306	—	—	60	235	39	72	15	1	7	36	15	5	0	3	48	1	0	.468	.357
Phillips, Brett	R-R	6-0	180	5-30-94	.320	.273	.331	66	291	68	93	19	7	15	53	22	6	3	6	62	15	6	.588	.379
Ramsay, James	L-L	5-11	200	3-2-92	.322	.275	.333	127	497	86	160	32	4	10	64	52	2	14	6	86	16	12	.463	.384
Reed, A.J.	L-L	6-4	240	5-10-93	.346	.303	.357	82	318	75	110	16	4	23	81	59	4	0	4	73	0	0	.638	.449
Ritchie, Jamie	R-R	6-2	205	4-9-93	.308	.188	.325	39	133	26	41	11	2	1	8	25	2	3	1	27	3	1	.444	.422
Vasquez, Danry	L-R	6-3	190	1-8-94	.315	.176	.351	40	168	21	53	13	2	3	21	13	0	0	4	46	4	4	.470	.365
Wik, Marc	L-R	5-11	223	7-18-92	.266	.308	.257	90	301	51	80	17	4	8	40	51	2	3	2	98	9	6	.429	.374

Pitching	B-T	HT	WT	DOB	W	L	ERA	G	GS	CG	SV	IP	H	R	ER	HR	BB	SO	AVG	vLH	vRH	K/9	BB/9
Bostick, Akeem	R-R	6-6	215	5-4-95	6	4	5.88	13	12	0	0	64	77	50	42	7	18	48	.291	.306	.281	6.72	2.52
Brunnemann, Tyler	R-R	6-2	220	8-9-91	4	1	3.50	38	0	0	5	62	54	24	24	10	22	70	.241	.294	.209	10.22	3.21
Chavez, Enrique	R-R	5-11	194	4-13-96	0	0	2.70	3	1	0	0	7	8	2	2	0	2	4	.333	.375	.313	5.40	2.70
Chrismon, Austin	R-R	6-2	230	9-16-92	7	4	5.01	15	11	0	0	74	92	44	41	11	19	48	.314	.345	.294	5.86	2.32
Comer, Kevin	R-R	6-3	205	8-1-92	2	4	4.45	19	7	0	1	63	58	36	31	4	25	54	.251	.225	.275	7.76	3.59
Cotton, Chris	R-L	5-10	166	11-21-90	1	2	1.40	13	0	0	4	26	20	6	4	2	7	37	.206	.138	.237	12.97	2.45
De Leon, Ambiorix	L-L	6-3	235	7-8-91	1	0	10.00	3	0	0	0	9	14	10	10	2	11	5	.350	.357	.346	5.00	11.00
Fant, Randall	L-L	6-4	180	1-28-91	0	0	12.27	4	0	0	0	7	14	10	10	4	3	4	.412	.300	.458	4.91	3.68
Feliz, Michael	R-R	6-4	225	6-28-93	1	1	4.41	8	5	0	0	33	30	19	16	3	12	33	.246	.322	.175	9.09	3.31
Freeman, Michael	R-L	6-8	235	10-7-91	0	0	0.49	7	0	0	2	18	5	1	1	1	8	19	.088	.000	.135	9.33	3.93
Frias, Edison	R-R	6-1	180	12-18-90	8	4	4.18	18	14	0	0	80	79	47	37	14	23	73	.248	.241	.256	8.25	2.60
Greenwood, Aaron	R-R	6-2	225	8-18-91	1	0	4.85	7	0	0	0	13	16	7	7	1	2	8	.314	.438	.257	5.54	1.38
Grills, Evan	L-L	6-4	205	6-13-92	3	5	7.20	13	9	0	0	45	59	40	36	7	9	35	.307	.296	.312	7.00	1.80
Guduan, Reymin	L-L	6-4	205	3-16-92	0	3	3.12	13	0	0	4	17	12	9	6	0	11	25	.188	.185	.189	12.98	5.71
Holmes, Brian	L-L	6-4	210	1-30-91	2	1	2.37	7	4	0	1	30	20	11	8	1	8	45	.183	.163	.197	13.35	2.37
Houser, Adrian	R-R	6-4	230	2-2-93	2	2	4.35	12	8	0	0	50	48	30	24	3	20	55	.254	.229	.280	9.97	3.62

HOUSTON ASTROS

Pitching	B-T	HT	WT	DOB	W	L	ERA	G	GS	CG	SV	IP	H	R	ER	HR	BB	SO	AVG	vLH	vRH	K/9	BB/9
Martes, Francis	R-R	6-1	225	11-24-95	4	1	2.31	6	5	0	0	35	31	10	9	1	8	37	.230	.204	.244	9.51	2.06
Mengden, Daniel	R-R	6-2	190	2-19-93	2	1	5.26	10	8	0	1	50	59	30	29	4	18	48	.298	.247	.336	8.70	3.26
2-team total (8 Stockton)					6	3	4.79	18	16	0	1	92	98	53	49	10	28	89	—	—	—	8.71	2.74
Mills, Jordan	L-L	6-5	215	5-11-92	1	2	3.81	17	0	0	2	26	30	12	11	2	16	22	.300	.345	.282	7.62	5.54
Minnis, Albert	R-L	6-0	190	11-5-91	3	4	4.43	27	0	0	1	45	51	26	22	3	17	36	.290	.318	.273	7.25	3.43
Morton, Zach	R-R	6-1	180	7-12-90	0	3	6.42	11	3	0	0	34	42	27	24	3	17	23	.302	.241	.341	6.15	4.54
Musgrove, Joe	R-R	6-5	255	12-4-92	4	0	2.40	6	4	0	0	30	28	9	8	2	1	43	.243	.255	.233	12.90	0.30
Naemark, Steve	L-L	6-3	200	3-23-90	0	0	2.08	2	0	0	0	4	2	1	1	1	2	4	.154	.000	.250	8.31	4.15
Paulino, David	R-R	6-7	215	2-6-94	1	1	4.91	6	5	0	1	29	24	17	16	1	10	30	.220	.200	.234	9.20	3.07
Powell, Christian	L-R	6-4	225	7-3-91	3	3	8.31	6	4	0	0	22	35	25	20	4	6	18	.343	.313	.357	7.48	2.49
Radziewski, Bryan	L-L	6-0	180	2-21-92	4	6	3.86	18	14	0	1	84	78	42	36	7	36	72	.247	.238	.250	7.71	3.86
Sanudo, Gonzalo	L-R	6-3	235	1-10-92	2	0	6.92	8	0	0	0	13	17	11	10	3	2	11	.304	.308	.300	7.62	1.38
Scribner, Troy	R-R	6-3	190	7-2-91	2	6	5.49	29	13	0	1	100	94	69	61	14	57	111	.249	.195	.285	9.99	5.13
Sims, Blaine	L-L	6-0	185	3-10-89	1	4	10.48	5	0	0	0	22	35	30	26	3	16	10	.365	.323	.385	4.03	6.45
Thompson, Ryan	R-R	6-6	221	6-26-92	1	0	5.19	9	0	0	2	9	8	5	5	0	2	5	.250	.200	.273	5.19	2.08
Tiburcio, Frederick	R-R	6-3	192	11-1-90	2	0	4.55	24	0	0	4	32	39	19	16	4	17	30	.305	.222	.365	8.53	4.83
Walter, Andrew	R-R	6-4	200	10-18-90	2	2	6.69	26	0	0	0	39	51	29	29	5	13	51	.309	.386	.269	11.77	3.00
Yuhl, Keegan	R-R	6-2	220	1-23-92	4	1	1.94	24	8	0	3	79	77	20	17	5	18	68	.256	.225	.274	7.75	2.05

Fielding

Catcher	PCT	G	PO	A	E	DP	PB
Booth	1.000	5	48	4	0	0	1
Castro	.973	8	66	7	2	0	2
Gonzalez	.981	27	245	14	5	3	3
Holberton	.991	42	313	25	3	0	7
Morales	.992	13	117	6	1	0	7
Nottingham	.993	16	131	15	1	3	0
Ritchie	.993	33	254	23	2	1	2

First Base	PCT	G	PO	A	E	DP
McDonald	.990	67	583	37	6	63
Nottingham	1.000	1	6	0	0	0
Reed	.989	64	498	49	6	49
Ritchie	1.000	3	23	0	0	3
Wik	1.000	6	46	5	0	5

Second Base	PCT	G	PO	A	E	DP
Castro	.944	4	7	10	1	2
Fernandez	.930	49	99	114	16	32
Hyde	.990	45	70	128	2	30
Mayfield	1.000	13	21	34	0	10
McDonald	1.000	1	3	4	0	0
Wik	.953	32	59	83	7	21

Third Base	PCT	G	PO	A	E	DP
Davis	.932	117	57	202	19	18
Wik	.944	25	16	51	4	7

Shortstop	PCT	G	PO	A	E	DP
Bregman	.953	37	61	102	8	25
Hyde	.992	29	33	87	1	15

	PCT	G	PO	A	E	DP
Mayfield	.972	53	73	136	6	33
Moon	.947	16	19	35	3	12
Wik	1.000	6	7	15	0	1

Outfield	PCT	G	PO	A	E	DP
Fisher	.975	78	153	3	4	2
Holberton	1.000	12	15	1	0	0
McMullen	1.000	17	32	0	0	0
Medina	.968	19	26	4	1	0
Mitchell	.931	60	94	0	7	0
Phillips	.986	62	137	5	2	0
Ramsay	.985	120	260	10	4	5
Vasquez	.986	38	67	3	1	1
Wik	.971	20	30	4	1	2

QUAD CITIES RIVER BANDITS

LOW CLASS A

MIDWEST LEAGUE

Batting	B-T	HT	WT	DOB	AVG	vLH	vRH	G	AB	R	H	2B	3B	HR	RBI	BB	HBP	SH	SF	SO	SB	CS	SLG	OBP
Avea, Marlon	R-R	6-1	218	8-31-93	.136	.200	.118	6	22	2	3	1	0	0	2	0	0	0	0	7	0	0	.182	.136
Bottger, Ryan	B-R	6-1	210	4-14-93	.218	.200	.224	103	363	37	79	11	1	6	46	53	1	0	8	95	0	5	.303	.313
Boyd, Bobby	L-R	5-9	175	1-4-93	.283	.241	.292	117	446	67	126	19	7	1	36	45	2	13	5	103	40	12	.363	.347
Bregman, Alex	R-R	6-0	180	3-30-94	.259	.316	.247	29	112	18	29	5	0	1	13	17	3	0	1	13	5	2	.330	.368
Ferguson, Drew	R-R	5-11	180	8-3-92	.287	.208	.317	44	174	23	50	10	1	1	21	16	0	0	2	32	10	4	.374	.344
Fernandez, Jose	R-R	6-1	190	5-20-93	.198	.194	.200	27	91	19	18	1	2	2	10	17	0	0	2	24	9	1	.319	.318
Fisher, Derek	L-R	6-1	207	8-21-93	.305	.342	.292	39	151	32	46	11	1	6	24	19	1	0	0	37	8	2	.510	.386
Franco, Wander	B-R	6-1	189	10-11-96	.261	.167	.294	7	23	2	6	1	0	1	6	3	0	0	1	4	0	0	.435	.333
Gonzalez, Alfredo	R-R	6-1	190	7-13-92	.326	.231	.367	13	43	7	14	1	0	0	8	11	2	1	0	8	2	0	.395	.482
Hernandez, Alex		5-7	187	2-4-92	.175	.162	.179	46	143	12	25	3	0	1	18	24	1	3	1	29	6	1	.217	.296
Hyde, Mott	R-R	5-10	190	3-10-92	.292	.486	.245	50	178	31	52	16	1	1	18	27	1	5	2	38	1	4	.410	.385
Laureano, Ramon	R-R	5-10	190	7-15-94	.265	.311	.252	76	287	43	76	15	8	4	34	21	4	1	1	83	18	3	.415	.323
Lindauer, Thomas	R-R	6-2	185	12-2-91	.200	.174	.209	32	90	11	18	4	0	2	15	19	1	2	4	36	3	2	.311	.333
Martin, Jason	L-R	5-11	190	9-5-95	.270	.228	.281	105	396	65	107	12	7	8	57	47	1	12	4	74	14	15	.396	.346
Martinez, Jorge	B-R	6-1	183	3-29-93	.171	.133	.192	11	41	4	7	1	0	2	5	5	0	0	0	15	2	1	.341	.261
McMullen, Sean	L-L	5-9	186	6-4-92	.239	.118	.261	66	218	28	52	13	3	3	32	28	2	4	7	70	6	4	.394	.322
Muniz, Bryan	R-R	6-0	210	6-5-93	.286	.310	.277	45	161	24	46	14	0	4	31	28	6	0	1	27	1	1	.447	.408
Nottingham, Jacob	R-R	6-3	230	4-3-95	.326	.318	.328	59	230	34	75	18	1	10	46	18	5	0	0	51	1	2	.543	.387
Reynoso, Luis	R-R	5-9	190	9-2-94	.226	.195	.230	50	155	20	35	2	0	1	16	8	0	0	2	49	1	0	.258	.303
Ritchie, Jamie	R-R	6-2	205	4-9-93	.266	.254	.270	72	259	46	69	10	2	4	27	70	4	0	1	54	7	6	.367	.428
Stubbs, Garrett	L-R	5-10	165	5-26-93	.274	.174	.311	25	84	15	23	5	0	0	5	14	0	3	2	21	1	0	.333	.370
Tanielu, Nick	R-R	5-11	215	9-4-92	.308	.301	.310	110	419	55	129	27	4	6	70	30	5	0	9	65	2	8	.434	.354
Trompiz, Kristian	R-R		184	12-2-95	.251	.283	.241	113	403	48	101	19	5	6	40	20	2	11	7	85	7	4	.367	.285
Woodward, Trent	B-R	6-2	215	2-4-92	.294	.400	.260	31	102	16	30	2	1	0	9	10	1	0	4	24	1	2	.333	.363

Pitching	B-T	HT	WT	DOB	W	L	ERA	G	GS	CG	SV	IP	H	R	ER	HR	BB	SO	AVG	vLH	vRH	K/9	BB/9
Armenteros, Rogelio	R-R	6-1	215	6-30-94	1	0	2.65	3	3	0	0	17	9	5	5	1	7	21	.150	.292	.056	11.12	3.71
Barrios, Agapito	R-R	6-2	201	11-30-93	2	1	1.65	5	5	0	0	27	17	7	5	2	4	23	.172	.135	.194	7.57	1.33
Bostick, Akeem	R-R	6-6	215	5-4-95	3	1	1.50	8	1	1	2	42	29	10	7	3	3	33	.193	.266	.140	7.07	0.64
Chrisman, Austin	R-R	6-2	230	9-16-92	4	1	2.96	11	7	0	2	49	45	20	16	2	5	31	.245	.244	.245	5.73	0.92
Comer, Kevin	R-R	6-3	205	8-1-92	5	1	4.47	11	7	0	1	44	47	28	22	2	13	39	.269	.311	.224	7.92	2.64
Davis, Chase	L-L	6-2	215	12-16-91	0	1	3.10	13	0	0	1	20	17	8	7	1	6	20	.218	.273	.196	8.85	2.64
Deetz, Dean	R-R	6-1	195	11-29-93	5	1	0.76	7	6	0	0	35	17	5	3	0	13	29	.136	.120	.147	7.39	3.31
Dorris, Jacob	R-R	6-2	165	3-24-93	1	0	0.00	4	0	0	1	7	3	0	0	0	1	9	.125	.000	.214	11.57	1.29
Dykxhoorn, Brock	R-R	6-8	250	7-2-94	8	5	3.88	22	18	0	0	109	100	52	47	8	26	94	.241	.231	.251	7.76	2.15

Pitching

Pitching	B-T	HT	WT	DOB	W	L	ERA	G	GS	CG	SV	IP	H	R	ER	HR	BB	SO	AVG	vLH	vRH	K/9	BB/9
Eshelman, Thomas	R-R	6-3	212	6-20-94	0	0	4.26	2	2	0	0	6	9	3	3	0	3	5	.346	.417	.286	7.11	4.26
Ferrell, Justin	R-R	6-7	205	4-21-94	4	3	1.95	12	11	0	0	65	47	22	14	2	28	37	.204	.200	.207	5.15	3.90
Ferrell, Riley	R-R	6-1	230	10-18-93	0	0	1.08	12	0	0	1	17	10	3	2	0	13	17	.175	.250	.103	9.18	7.02
Freeman, Michael	R-L	6-8	235	10-7-91	1	1	1.50	8	0	0	0	18	15	7	3	0	6	14	.224	.083	.302	7.00	3.00
Greenwood, Aaron	R-R	6-3	225	8-18-91	0	0	0.63	9	0	0	1	14	8	1	1	0	6	9	.182	.118	.222	5.65	3.77
Guduan, Reymin	L-L	6-4	205	3-16-92	3	0	0.75	6	0	0	0	12	6	1	1	0	3	15	.146	.176	.125	11.25	2.25
Heredia, Angel	R-R	5-9	170	7-22-92	4	3	2.56	27	0	0	13	46	26	14	13	2	21	47	.165	.217	.124	9.26	4.14
Hernandez, Elieser	R-R	6-0	210	5-3-95	3	3	3.94	10	7	0	1	46	45	23	20	3	11	46	.251	.284	.214	9.07	2.17
James, Josh	R-R	6-3	206	3-8-93	7	4	2.63	24	18	0	1	116	102	43	34	2	41	89	.237	.273	.203	6.89	3.17
Lee, Chris	L-L	6-4	175	8-17-92	3	2	4.11	7	6	0	0	31	36	17	14	1	10	24	.283	.218	.333	7.04	2.93
Madden, Lachlan	R-R	5-11	170	6-3-96	0	2	9.00	2	0	0	0	3	3	5	3	0	2	2	.273	.333	.200	6.00	6.00
Martes, Francis	R-R	6-1	225	11-24-95	3	2	1.04	10	8	1	2	52	33	11	6	1	13	45	.181	.190	.175	7.79	2.25
McNitt, Brandon	R-R	5-11	185	1-9-92	1	3	4.97	14	8	0	0	54	57	31	30	7	21	40	.266	.226	.298	6.63	3.48
Mengden, Daniel	R-R	6-2	190	2-19-93	4	1	1.16	8	6	0	0	39	30	7	5	1	8	36	.216	.210	.221	8.38	1.86
Mills, Jordan	L-L	6-5	215	5-11-92	1	2	2.25	13	0	0	2	16	15	8	4	0	6	13	.246	.263	.238	7.31	3.38
Minnis, Albert	R-L	6-0	190	11-5-91	0	0	0.00	6	0	0	1	8	3	0	0	0	1	10	.120	.250	.059	11.74	1.17
Montero, Jose	R-R	6-4	204	1-22-93	1	0	4.50	12	0	0	4	16	9	11	8	1	16	16	.161	.190	.143	9.00	9.00
Musgrove, Joe	R-R	6-5	255	12-4-92	4	1	0.70	5	3	0	0	26	22	4	2	0	1	23	.232	.234	.229	8.06	0.35
Naemark, Steve	L-L	6-3	200	3-23-90	1	0	1.54	8	0	0	0	12	8	2	2	2	4	6	.195	.200	.194	4.63	3.09
Paulino, David	R-R	6-7	215	2-6-94	3	2	1.57	5	5	0	0	29	21	6	5	0	7	32	.202	.227	.183	10.05	2.20
Perez, Jorge	R-R	6-0	185	7-30-93	1	3	5.40	19	2	0	1	43	58	30	26	1	29	31	.324	.438	.245	6.44	6.02
Peterson, Eric	R-R	6-4	195	3-8-93	6	4	2.59	34	0	0	6	63	62	23	18	2	22	75	.261	.238	.278	10.77	3.16
Powell, Christian	L-R	6-4	225	7-3-91	3	1	2.59	11	8	0	0	49	44	16	14	2	11	41	.235	.279	.198	7.58	2.03
Radziewski, Bryan	L-L	6-0	180	2-21-92	1	0	2.05	5	3	0	1	22	15	5	5	0	5	25	.185	.211	.163	10.23	2.05
Robles, Juan	R-R	6-0	185	11-6-97	0	0	5.40	2	0	0	0	3	2	2	2	0	5	2	.167	.200	.143	5.40	13.50
Thome, Andrew	R-R	6-3	215	1-13-93	0	0	0.00	1	0	0	0	4	3	1	0	0	1	2	.214	.250	.000	4.50	2.25
Thompson, Ryan	R-R	6-6	221	6-26-92	4	2	2.65	38	0	0	5	54	43	18	16	4	15	55	.216	.278	.165	9.11	2.48
Yuhl, Keegan	R-R	6-0	220	1-23-92	1	0	0.93	9	0	0	1	19	10	3	2	0	7	19	.147	.133	.158	8.84	3.26

Fielding

Catcher	PCT	G	PO	A	E	DP	PB
Avea	1.000	6	42	6	0	1	1
Gonzalez	1.000	12	95	16	0	1	2
Nottingham	.994	39	311	30	2	1	7
Ritchie	.996	34	255	14	1	1	5
Stubbs	1.000	25	203	16	0	1	2
Woodward	.989	24	160	18	2	2	3

First Base	PCT	G	PO	A	E	DP
Bottger	.990	56	474	28	5	40
Franco	1.000	2	12	0	0	0
Muniz	.985	34	304	26	5	27
Nottingham	.979	10	84	9	2	10
Ritchie	.996	28	224	18	1	22
Tanielu	1.000	11	76	7	0	12
Woodward	1.000	4	27	3	0	3

Second Base	PCT	G	PO	A	E	DP
Fernandez	.914	26	37	69	10	11
Hernandez	.967	33	49	98	5	23
Hyde	.963	29	49	81	5	20
Lindauer	.969	7	15	16	1	9
Reynoso	.966	14	23	34	2	8
Tanielu	1.000	6	5	19	0	1
Trompiz	.950	28	39	76	6	17

Third Base	PCT	G	PO	A	E	DP
Fernandez	—	1	0	0	0	0
Franco	1.000	5	3	7	0	1
Hernandez	.688	8	3	8	5	2
Martinez	.750	1	2	1	1	0
Reynoso	.938	30	14	62	5	9
Tanielu	.937	91	57	152	14	13
Trompiz	.889	14	11	29	5	4

Shortstop	PCT	G	PO	A	E	DP
Bregman	.948	26	66	80	8	23
Hyde	.905	13	10	28	4	6
Lindauer	.929	25	28	77	8	13
Reynoso	1.000	5	6	10	0	3
Trompiz	.948	75	112	199	17	41

Outfield	PCT	G	PO	A	E	DP
Bottger	1.000	39	52	2	0	0
Boyd	.985	111	262	3	4	0
Ferguson	.966	28	53	3	2	1
Fisher	.971	33	66	0	2	0
Laureano	.972	67	129	9	4	4
Martin	.988	92	160	3	2	2
Martinez	.875	8	6	1	1	0
McMullen	1.000	43	83	1	0	0

TRI-CITY VALLEYCATS

SHORT-SEASON

NEW YORK-PENN LEAGUE

Batting	B-T	HT	WT	DOB	AVG	vLH	vRH	G	AB	R	H	2B	3B	HR	RBI	BB	HBP	SH	SF	SO	SB	CS	SLG	OBP
Avea, Marlon	R-R	6-1	218	8-31-93	.083	.000	.125	6	12	1	1	1	0	0	1	1	2	2	0	4	0	0	.167	.267
Ballard, Keach	L-R	6-0	180	7-16-92	.208	.233	.200	45	125	16	26	2	0	0	13	14	1	3	1	21	3	1	.224	.291
Carpenter, Kolbey	R-R	6-0	190	9-8-93	.255	.267	.250	53	192	16	49	13	1	2	26	12	4	0	1	39	1	1	.365	.311
Carrasco, Cesar	R-R	6-2	185	10-3-93	.258	.370	.212	50	159	21	41	12	0	4	22	16	0	2	1	28	0	1	.409	.324
Ferguson, Drew	R-R	5-11	180	8-3-92	.328	.250	.357	17	58	13	19	6	0	3	6	8	1	1	0	4	1	1	.586	.418
Gonzalez, Richard	R-R	5-9	180	11-18-93	.179	.200	.171	19	56	4	10	4	0	1	4	5	0	0	1	16	0	1	.304	.242
Hermelyn, Anthony	R-R	6-1	200	11-18-93	.241	.309	.213	57	191	25	46	4	0	2	25	26	0	2	2	41	3	1	.293	.329
Marlow, Brooks	L-R	5-9	185	6-24-93	.255	.283	.247	56	204	24	52	15	0	6	31	14	0	2	3	53	0	1	.417	.299
McCall, Dex	R-R	6-1	220	1-29-94	.295	.288	.298	59	200	26	59	9	0	4	37	25	1	0	0	59	0	0	.400	.376
Medina, Edwin	R-R	5-8	170	2-11-93	.269	.350	.219	17	52	12	14	3	1	0	5	10	1	0	1	14	11	1	.365	.391
Melendez, Alexander	R-R	6-1	185	4-21-95	.200	.200	.200	33	85	10	17	1	0	0	3	2	4	3	0	25	5	3	.212	.253
Mizell, Aaron	L-R	6-0	165	10-14-93	.238	.212	.248	49	189	29	45	9	7	4	28	19	2	1	1	31	13	1	.423	.313
Muniz, Bryan	R-R	6-0	210	6-5-93	.292	.341	.262	29	106	13	31	8	1	2	17	16	1	0	1	16	0	1	.443	.387
Nunez, Antonio	R-R	5-9	165	1-10-93	.250	.304	.212	40	112	20	28	4	0	0	4	21	2	4	0	29	4	4	.286	.378
Porter, Pat	L-L	6-0	215	10-12-93	.245	.266	.236	58	204	24	50	15	4	3	20	17	7	0	2	59	0	0	.402	.322
Roa, Hector	R-R	6-0	195	3-1-95	.244	.280	.231	27	90	12	22	3	0	5	13	4	2	0	1	36	1	0	.444	.289
Santos, Jeffy	R-R	6-2	150	1-4-93	.000	.000	.000	2	4	0	0	0	0	0	0	0	0	0	0	3	0	0	.000	.000
Sewald, Johnny	L-R	6-0	160	11-11-93	.289	.316	.277	70	249	57	72	10	0	1	28	46	7	4	1	54	31	5	.341	.413
Stubbs, Garrett	L-R	5-10	165	5-26-93	.235	.222	.240	11	34	5	8	0	0	0	2	7	0	1	0	3	2	0	.235	.366
Wernes, Bobby	R-R	6-3	200	7-4-94	.346	.375	.333	53	188	32	65	8	0	0	29	27	3	3	1	27	3	2	.388	.434
Woodward, Trent	B-R	6-2	215	2-4-92	.222	.500	.143	7	27	5	6	1	0	1	4	7	0	0	0	7	0	0	.370	.382

Pitching

Pitching	B-T	HT	WT	DOB	W	L	ERA	G	GS	CG	SV	IP	H	R	ER	HR	BB	SO	AVG	vLH	vRH	K/9	BB/9
Arauz, Harold	R-R	6-2	185	5-29-95	0	5	5.75	15	10	0	0	52	72	39	33	5	18	52	.329	.381	.287	9.06	3.14
Armenteros, Rogelio	R-R	6-1	215	6-30-94	2	2	4.09	12	9	0	0	44	44	24	20	3	17	40	.262	.280	.244	8.18	3.48
Barrios, Agapito	R-R	6-2	201	11-30-93	0	0	2.50	6	2	0	0	18	22	6	5	0	4	13	.301	.278	.324	6.50	2.00
Bower, Matt	R-L	6-5	190	6-16-94	2	0	3.68	2	0	0	0	7	10	3	3	1	0	5	.323	.400	.308	6.14	0.00
Davis, Zach	L-L	6-3	225	12-16-91	0	0	4.09	11	0	0	0	11	17	5	5	0	4	12	.362	.316	.393	9.82	3.27
Deemes, Ryan	R-R	6-2	205	6-11-93	1	0	3.20	7	3	0	0	25	20	10	9	1	8	24	.220	.244	.196	8.53	2.84
Deetz, Dean	R-R	6-1	195	11-29-93	4	2	2.86	7	5	0	0	28	22	12	9	1	10	21	.208	.170	.245	6.67	3.18
Del Rosario, Yeyfry	R-R	6-2	182	4-27-94	4	4	3.73	21	0	0	2	31	28	15	13	2	12	33	.233	.214	.250	9.48	3.45
Dorris, Jacob	R-R	6-2	165	3-24-93	0	0	1.80	8	0	0	6	10	5	2	2	0	2	15	.143	.200	.100	13.50	1.80
Garcia, Junior	L-L	6-1	180	10-1-95	0	1	0.00	2	1	0	0	8	9	4	0	0	0	7	.281	.273	.286	7.88	0.00
Garza, Ralph	R-R	6-2	195	4-6-94	1	1	3.89	14	3	0	0	37	37	16	16	1	10	47	.264	.354	.187	11.43	2.43
Grotz, Zac	R-R	6-2	195	2-17-93	4	3	4.24	16	0	0	4	17	16	8	8	0	4	11	.250	.290	.212	5.82	2.12
Hernandez, Elieser	R-R	6-0	210	5-3-95	0	1	1.31	5	2	0	0	21	13	5	3	0	2	30	.173	.211	.135	13.06	0.87
Hernandez, Jose	R-R	6-0	180	5-1-95	1	0	4.96	5	2	0	0	16	18	9	9	1	5	17	.290	.257	.333	9.37	2.76
McCanna, Kevin	L-R	6-1	185	2-1-94	3	3	3.72	14	3	0	0	39	38	19	16	3	8	32	.255	.232	.275	7.45	1.86
Murphy, Chris	R-R	6-4	205	9-28-92	2	1	2.25	7	4	0	1	28	26	7	7	1	5	23	.245	.263	.224	7.39	1.61
Naemark, Steve	L-L	6-3	200	3-23-90	1	0	1.54	9	0	0	0	12	7	2	2	3	9	.171	.190	.150	6.94	2.31
Nicely, Austin	B-L	6-1	170	12-13-94	0	1	5.17	6	2	0	0	16	15	10	9	0	9	9	.259	.250	.263	5.17	5.17
Paulino, David	R-R	6-7	215	2-6-94	1	0	0.00	2	2	0	0	9	4	0	0	0	2	10	.125	.167	.071	9.64	1.93
Person, Zac	L-L	6-1	185	10-13-92	1	4	7.33	13	6	0	0	27	32	25	22	2	15	25	.288	.286	.289	8.33	5.00
Pinales, Joselo	R-R	6-1	180	11-16-94	0	1	2.70	5	0	0	0	7	6	2	2	0	6	6	.240	.286	.222	8.10	8.10
Santos, Juan	R-R	6-4	240	8-30-95	0	0	3.16	20	0	0	2	26	14	12	9	2	24	28	.161	.133	.190	9.82	8.42
Schmidt, David	R-R	6-0	175	1-21-93	1	0	7.56	15	0	0	0	17	17	15	14	2	15	12	.266	.300	.235	6.48	8.10
Thornton, Trent	R-R	6-0	175	9-30-93	4	0	3.27	15	12	0	0	55	62	21	20	2	10	48	.286	.325	.240	7.85	1.64
Weathersby, Scott	R-R	6-2	180	12-23-91	3	1	2.48	12	2	0	0	33	31	12	9	4	6	39	.248	.293	.209	10.74	1.65
Whitt, Adam	R-R	6-3	205	3-22-93	2	2	5.33	16	0	0	2	25	32	17	15	2	4	22	.299	.321	.278	7.82	1.42
Winkelman, Alex	L-L	6-2	180	2-8-94	5	1	3.83	11	7	0	0	42	43	20	18	0	8	45	.264	.342	.240	9.57	1.70

Fielding

Catcher	PCT	G	PO	A	E	DP	PB
Avea	1.000	6	47	8	0	0	0
Gonzalez	.987	19	145	8	2	1	5
Hermelyn	.989	44	328	30	4	0	10
Stubbs	1.000	10	63	8	0	0	2
Woodward	1.000	4	49	4	0	1	2

First Base	PCT	G	PO	A	E	DP
Carrasco	.972	19	135	5	4	7
Hermelyn	1.000	5	31	1	0	2
McCall	.976	32	231	11	6	24
Muniz	.994	22	158	14	1	13
Porter	1.000	4	15	4	0	1
Roa	.909	4	18	2	2	1

Second Base	PCT	G	PO	A	E	DP
Carpenter	.969	23	32	61	3	7
Marlow	.983	51	98	137	4	31
Mizell	1.000	2	1	3	0	0
Nunez	1.000	4	4	13	0	1

Third Base	PCT	G	PO	A	E	DP
Ballard	—	4	0	0	0	0
Carpenter	1.000	4	2	6	0	0
Carrasco	.840	25	13	29	8	1
Wernes	.976	53	38	82	3	10

Shortstop	PCT	G	PO	A	E	DP
Ballard	.934	42	59	82	10	14
Carpenter	.833	5	6	9	3	2

Marlow	1.000	5	5	7	0	2
Nunez	.957	33	43	69	5	13
Santos	1.000	1	0	1	0	0
Wernes	1.000	1	0	1	0	1

Outfield	PCT	G	PO	A	E	DP
Carpenter	—	2	0	0	0	0
Ferguson	1.000	16	31	1	0	0
Medina	1.000	15	26	2	0	0
Melendez	.949	30	37	0	2	0
Mizell	.978	47	83	4	2	0
Porter	.987	55	73	3	1	0
Roa	.957	12	22	0	1	0
Sewald	.988	69	153	5	2	1

GREENEVILLE ASTROS

ROOKIE

APPALACHIAN LEAGUE

Batting

Batting	B-T	HT	WT	DOB	AVG	vLH	vRH	G	AB	R	H	2B	3B	HR	RBI	BB	HBP	SH	SF	SO	SB	CS	SLG	OBP
Avea, Marlon	R-R	6-1	218	8-31-93	.184	.125	.200	12	38	5	7	2	0	1	4	2	3	0	0	9	0	1	.316	.279
Ayarza, Rodrigo	B-R	5-8	145	2-20-95	.292	.000	.311	16	48	3	14	1	0	2	13	0	0	4	1	6	0	0	.438	.286
Bracamonte, Gabriel	R-R	5-9	165	5-15-95	.154	.143	.158	18	52	5	8	3	0	0	1	10	2	1	0	13	0	0	.212	.313
Cameron, Daz	R-R	6-2	185	1-15-97	.272	.400	.250	30	103	20	28	2	3	0	11	16	1	3	1	31	11	6	.350	.372
Cesar, Randy	R-R	6-1	180	1-19-95	.236	.167	.250	51	182	22	43	8	0	4	30	23	2	0	1	49	0	0	.346	.322
Correa, Christian	R-R	5-10	210	5-18-93	.167	.000	.174	13	24	1	4	2	0	0	5	1	2	0	0	4	0	0	.250	.333
Duarte, Osvaldo	R-R	5-9	160	1-18-96	.235	.297	.222	61	217	39	51	9	4	4	20	22	1	7	1	74	17	6	.369	.307
Garcia, Justin	L-L	6-0	185	10-28-94	.155	.313	.138	46	161	14	25	10	1	1	14	12	2	0	1	58	0	0	.248	.222
Goedert, Connor	R-R	6-2	190	12-14-93	.286	.351	.274	63	245	37	70	20	1	6	43	20	5	0	2	51	1	0	.449	.349
Martir, Kevin	R-R	5-11	210	2-11-94	.218	.313	.204	37	124	10	27	2	0	0	16	23	4	0	1	21	1	0	.234	.355
Mejia, Brauly	R-R	6-0	185	10-28-94	.283	.316	.278	42	152	20	43	11	1	3	21	11	1	0	0	34	0	2	.428	.335
Michelena, Arturo	R-R	5-11	165	10-15-94	.210	.105	.233	32	105	9	22	2	1	1	5	1	2	2	2	17	1	2	.276	.286
Mizell, Aaron	L-R	6-0	165	10-14-93	.325	.250	.333	20	77	13	25	5	1	0	8	6	0	0	0	18	3	0	.416	.373
Payano, Luis	R-R	6-1	175	5-12-96	.243	.208	.253	36	103	15	25	8	0	2	13	9	1	1	1	36	0	5	.379	.307
Pena, Brian	R-R	6-1	185	6-14-94	.111	—	.111	5	9	0	1	0	0	0	0	0	0	0	0	5	0	0	.111	.200
Roa, Hector	R-R	6-0	195	3-1-95	.315	.389	.300	27	108	15	34	6	2	6	22	3	0	0	0	31	0	0	.574	.333
Stainback, Ford	B-R	5-11	185	1-19-93	.248	.435	.214	45	149	22	37	6	1	0	16	22	1	6	2	29	3	4	.302	.345
Straw, Myles	R-R	5-10	180	10-17-94	.268	.400	.246	58	209	47	56	10	3	0	13	29	1	6	3	52	11	9	.344	.355
Tucker, Kyle	L-R	6-4	190	1-17-97	.286	.188	.302	30	112	15	32	5	4	3	25	12	0	0	1	24	2	1	.393	.322

Pitching

Pitching	B-T	HT	WT	DOB	W	L	ERA	G	GS	CG	SV	IP	H	R	ER	HR	BB	SO	AVG	vLH	vRH	K/9	BB/9
Abreu, Albert	R-R	6-2	175	9-26-95	2	3	2.51	13	7	1	1	47	35	18	13	2	21	51	.206	.218	.196	9.84	4.05
Acosta, Yhoan	L-L	6-1	175	6-17-95	1	4	4.10	13	9	0	0	48	45	26	22	4	21	56	.242	.245	.241	10.43	3.91
Almengo, Diogenes	R-R	6-2	190	6-2-95	3	1	2.31	6	5	0	0	23	18	6	6	0	6	16	.209	.227	.190	6.17	2.31
Bower, Matt	R-L	6-5	190	6-16-94	1	2	2.84	7	2	0	1	19	18	9	6	0	6	24	.243	.261	.235	11.37	0.00
Culbreth, Brandon	R-R	6-4	200	7-27-92	0	0	18.00	3	0	0	0	3	8	6	6	0	6	3	.471	.625	.333	9.00	18.00
De Los Santos, Samil	R-R	6-4	175	1-8-94	1	3	3.72	16	0	0	4	19	19	9	8	3	5	26	.181	.250	.125	12.10	2.33

Pitching	B-T	HT	WT	DOB	W	L	ERA	G	GS	CG	SV	IP	H	R	ER	HR	BB	SO	AVG	vLH	vRH	K/9	BB/9
Deemes, Ryan	R-R	6-2	205	6-11-93	2	0	0.75	7	2	0	1	24	16	2	2	0	1	16	.188	.219	.170	6.00	0.38
Delis, Juan	R-R	6-1	195	5-29-94	0	1	3.60	6	0	0	0	5	8	3	2	0	6	7	.364	.222	.462	12.60	10.80
Dorris, Jacob	R-R	6-2	165	3-24-93	0	0	0.84	6	0	0	0	11	4	1	1	0	6	13	.111	.133	.095	10.97	5.06
Garcia, Junior	L-L	6-1	180	10-1-95	3	0	1.23	7	5	0	0	29	20	7	4	1	7	19	.179	.280	.149	5.83	2.15
German, Devonte	R-R	6-5	240	10-14-94	3	2	4.67	10	4	0	0	27	27	19	14	2	11	14	.262	.227	.288	4.67	3.67
Grotz, Zac	R-R	6-2	195	2-17-93	1	0	0.00	3	0	0	1	5	1	0	0	0	1	4	.063	.143	.000	7.20	1.80
Hernandez, Jose	R-R	6-0	180	5-1-95	1	1	2.11	6	3	0	1	21	16	5	5	0	4	25	.211	.207	.213	10.55	1.69
Hiraldo, Carlos	L-L	5-10	175	7-15-96	1	1	4.50	2	1	0	0	6	7	4	3	1	1	1	.292	.200	.316	1.50	1.50
James, Dylan	R-R	6-2	185	6-27-92	0	0	1.35	6	0	0	0	7	7	2	1	1	1	5	.259	.091	.375	6.75	1.35
Madden, Lachlan	R-R	5-11	170	6-3-96	0	2	2.13	9	0	0	0	13	10	3	3	0	9	15	.217	.227	.208	10.66	6.39
Montano, Salvador	L-L	6-3	150	7-14-94	2	3	5.20	13	7	0	0	45	47	29	26	3	27	36	.261	.286	.250	7.20	5.40
Montero, Jose	R-R	6-4	204	1-22-93	1	0	0.00	3	0	0	0	2	0	0	0	0	0	1	.000	.000	.000	3.86	0.00
Murphy, Chris	R-R	6-2	185	8-28-92	1	0	2.25	7	2	0	0	20	18	6	5	1	2	17	.247	.242	.250	7.65	0.90
Naemark, Steve	L-L	6-3	200	3-23-90	0	0	0.00	2	0	0	1	3	1	0	0	0	0	3	.091	.333	.000	9.00	0.00
Nelson, Makay	R-R	5-11	180	7-27-94	0	2	4.45	12	6	0	0	30	37	19	15	1	11	16	.298	.322	.277	4.75	3.26
Perez, Hector	R-R	6-3	180	6-6-96	0	0	0.00	1	0	0	0	2	0	0	0	0	1	2	.000	.000	.000	9.00	4.50
Pinales, Erasmo	R-R	5-11	180	11-25-94	1	0	1.93	9	5	0	0	33	22	9	7	0	10	33	.188	.196	.180	9.09	2.76
Pinales, Joselo	R-R	6-1	180	11-16-94	1	2	2.29	14	0	0	1	20	19	5	5	1	7	19	.260	.229	.289	8.69	3.20
Polanco, Moreno	R-R	6-3	180	7-29-94	0	0	7.36	4	2	0	0	11	12	10	9	0	5	5	.279	.269	.294	4.09	4.09
Ramirez, Luis	L-L	5-10	160	11-27-95	0	0	0.00	2	0	0	0	2	0	0	0	0	2	0	.000	.000	.000	9.00	9.00
Sanchez, Starlyng	L-L	5-11	170	8-6-94	1	0	4.30	8	0	0	0	15	18	8	7	0	2	12	.286	.276	.294	7.36	1.23
Sandoval, Edgardo	R-R	6-0	170	7-9-96	0	0	1.13	4	2	0	0	16	11	3	2	0	6	14	.200	.240	.167	7.88	3.38
Santamaria, CristhopherL	L-L	5-11	175	6-19-96	3	1	4.63	18	0	0	2	33	34	13	12	3	7	19	.177	.200	.163	7.33	2.70
Solarte, Alejandro	L-L	6-4	180	9-22-94	0	4	8.00	15	0	0	1	18	33	20	16	4	9	8	.393	.444	.368	4.00	4.50
Thome, Andrew	R-R	6-3	215	1-13-93	2	1	0.87	11	4	0	0	31	31	7	3	0	1	19	.256	.250	.262	5.52	0.29
Winkelman, Alex	L-L	6-2	180	2-8-94	2	1	4.35	4	1	0	0	10	12	6	5	0	5	14	.286	.235	.320	12.19	4.35

Fielding

Catcher	PCT	G	PO	A	E	DP	PB
Avea	1.000	9	51	6	0	0	2
Bracamonte	.993	17	136	13	1	0	2
Correa	1.000	13	70	4	0	2	1
Martir	.988	32	233	23	3	0	3
Pena	1.000	5	19	5	0	1	0

First Base	PCT	G	PO	A	E	DP
Garcia	.944	18	129	7	8	6
Goedert	.988	49	404	21	5	37

Second Base	PCT	G	PO	A	E	DP
Ayarza	.926	12	16	34	4	5

	PCT	G	PO	A	E	DP	PB
Duarte	1.000	1	2	2	0	1	
Michelena	.887	12	21	26	6	8	
Mizell	.925	10	19	30	4	7	
Stainback	.966	35	63	80	5	15	

Third Base	PCT	G	PO	A	E	DP
Ayarza	1.000	2	1	3	0	0
Bracamonte	—	1	0	0	0	0
Cesar	.918	50	41	82	11	5
Michelena	.913	17	10	32	4	1

Shortstop	PCT	G	PO	A	E	DP
Duarte	.945	60	111	147	15	33

	PCT	G	PO	A	E	DP
Michelena	1.000	2	1	3	0	0
Mizell	1.000	1	2	4	0	1
Stainback	1.000	7	7	15	0	2

Outfield	PCT	G	PO	A	E	DP
Cameron	.986	28	73	0	1	0
Garcia	1.000	5	5	0	0	0
Mejia	.977	33	42	0	1	0
Mizell	1.000	8	12	0	0	0
Payano	.933	29	55	1	4	0
Roa	.938	24	42	3	3	0
Straw	1.000	53	121	9	0	2
Tucker	.983	27	56	2	1	1

GCL ASTROS
GULF COAST LEAGUE
ROOKIE

Batting	B-T	HT	WT	DOB	AVG	vLH	vRH	G	AB	R	H	2B	3B	HR	RBI	BB	HBP	SH	SF	SO	SB	CS	SLG	OBP
Almonte, Marcos	R-R	5-10	163	3-28-96	.299	.296	.300	19	77	7	23	2	0	1	8	3	0	0	1	13	4	3	.364	.321
Ayarza, Rodrigo	B-R	5-8	145	2-20-95	.196	.118	.241	16	46	4	9	1	0	1	4	1	1	1	0	5	1	0	.283	.229
Beltre, Reiny	R-R	6-0	180	7-16-96	.185	.000	.233	17	54	7	10	1	1	0	5	7	3	2	0	7	0	2	.241	.313
Bernal, Ihan	R-R	6-1	195	10-20-96	.167	.045	.250	29	54	5	9	1	0	0	3	13	1	0	1	16	0	1	.185	.333
Bowey, Jake	L-R	6-0	205	7-16-96	.215	.333	.180	29	79	8	17	5	1	0	7	3	0	2	0	16	0	0	.304	.244
Cameron, Daz	R-R	6-2	185	1-15-97	.222	.348	.163	21	72	14	16	2	0	0	6	9	3	1	2	18	13	4	.250	.326
Castro, Ruben	L-R	5-10	182	7-10-96	.263	.200	.304	19	38	1	10	0	0	0	3	6	0	0	0	3	4	0	.263	.364
Correa, Christian	R-R	5-10	210	5-18-93	.059	.167	.000	11	17	0	1	0	0	0	2	2	2	1	0	3	0	0	.059	.238
Cruz, Jared	R-R	6-1	175	3-29-95	.194	.217	.184	25	72	5	14	3	0	0	8	6	0	1	1	25	1	1	.236	.253
De la Cruz, Bryan	R-R	6-2	175	12-16-96	.242	.175	.266	44	149	16	36	2	1	0	12	14	2	3	1	41	2	6	.268	.313
Fernandez, Frankeny	R-R	6-1	170	12-7-96	.148	.229	.115	43	122	11	18	4	1	1	10	19	0	0	2	44	7	6	.221	.259
Franco, Wander	B-R	6-1	189	10-11-96	.232	.204	.244	50	185	23	43	11	0	3	26	15	1	2	2	38	4	1	.341	.291
Lorenzo, Edgar	R-R	5-11	160	1-15-97	.000	.000	.000	3	12	0	0	0	0	0	1	0	1	0	0	4	0	0	.000	.077
MacDonald, Connor	R-R	6-5	200	2-27-96	.208	.233	.202	48	154	11	32	9	0	1	17	20	5	0	4	65	1	1	.286	.311
Martinez, Jorge	R-R	5-11	184	12-19-96	.129	.182	.100	19	31	2	4	2	0	0	3	5	0	0	0	8	0	0	.194	.250
Matute, Jonathan	R-R	6-0	170	4-28-97	.203	.095	.256	24	64	5	13	2	0	0	1	10	0	3	0	15	1	1	.234	.311
Mauricio, Joan	L-R	5-11	160	10-22-96	.181	.172	.184	34	105	7	19	2	2	0	7	8	1	1	0	32	2	0	.238	.246
Muriel, Nestor	R-R	6-2	170	6-11-98	.127	.095	.138	36	79	9	10	2	0	1	3	11	1	5	0	38	2	1	.190	.242
Pena, Brian	R-R	6-1	185	6-14-94	.200	.000	.250	12	20	1	4	1	0	0	5	3	1	1	1	4	0	0	.250	.320
Sanchez, Vicente	R-R	5-11	170	10-4-96	.217	.167	.242	27	92	19	20	4	0	0	4	18	1	2	1	38	6	3	.261	.348
Sierra, Miguelangel	R-R	5-11	165	12-2-97	.160	.105	.179	24	75	6	12	3	0	0	3	3	2	0	3	4	3	2	.213	.267
Tejada, Nestor	L-L	5-11	175	4-17-97	.176	.250	.163	34	102	11	18	4	1	0	4	10	2	4	1	31	4	2	.235	.261
Tucker, Kyle	L-R	6-4	190	1-17-97	.208	.229	.200	33	120	19	25	3	2	2	13	9	1	2	1	14	4	2	.317	.267

Pitching	B-T	HT	WT	DOB	W	L	ERA	G	GS	CG	SV	IP	H	R	ER	HR	BB	SO	AVG	vLH	vRH	K/9	BB/9
Almengo, Diogenes	R-R	6-2	190	6-2-95	0	0	2.78	7	3	0	0	23	19	8	7	0	6	15	.226	.240	.220	5.96	2.38
Benzant, Gerald	R-R	6-2	185	12-21-94	0	0	40.50	3	0	0	0	1	4	6	6	0	7	1	.667	1.000	.333	6.75	47.25
Chavez, Enrique	R-R	5-11	194	4-13-96	3	5	3.51	14	8	0	0	49	49	22	19	1	17	40	.269	.370	.202	7.40	3.14
Eshelman, Thomas	R-R	6-3	212	6-20-94	0	1	4.50	2	2	0	0	4	3	2	2	0	2	3	.200	.333	.111	6.75	4.50

Pitching

Pitching	B-T	HT	WT	DOB	W	L	ERA	G	GS	CG	SV	IP	H	R	ER	HR	BB	SO	AVG	vLH	vRH	K/9	BB/9
Garcia, Junior	R-R	6-3	175	1-29-96	1	3	2.79	17	0	0	0	19	20	9	6	0	7	15	.256	.225	.289	6.98	3.26
Guzman, Jorge	R-R	6-2	182	1-28-96	1	1	2.00	4	1	0	0	9	8	5	2	0	7	2	.258	.167	.280	2.00	7.00
Hiraldo, Carlos	L-L	5-10	175	7-15-96	3	3	2.04	13	4	0	0	35	33	11	8	0	10	24	.250	.143	.289	6.11	2.55
James, Dylan	R-R	6-2	185	6-27-92	0	0	3.00	5	0	0	1	6	2	2	2	1	1	5	.100	.250	.063	7.50	1.50
Madden, Lachlan	R-R	5-11	170	6-3-96	1	0	2.00	8	0	0	3	9	8	3	2	0	2	7	.276	.333	.250	7.00	2.00
Martinez, Michel	R-R	5-10	220	9-16-93	0	1	4.82	7	2	0	0	19	18	11	10	1	12	15	.243	.355	.163	7.23	5.79
Pena, Adonis	R-R	6-4	195	10-29-93	0	0	3.68	13	0	0	0	15	13	10	6	1	12	7	.236	.190	.265	4.30	7.36
Perez, Franklin	R-R	6-3	197	12-6-97	0	2	4.80	5	1	0	0	15	19	9	8	0	3	17	.292	.348	.262	10.20	1.80
Perez, Hector	R-R	6-3	190	6-6-96	1	0	1.16	9	3	0	1	23	10	5	3	0	16	16	.135	.100	.159	6.17	6.17
Polanco, Moreno	R-R	6-3	180	7-29-94	1	1	0.60	8	5	0	0	30	19	6	2	0	10	24	.181	.163	.196	7.20	3.00
Ramirez, Luis	L-L	5-10	160	11-27-95	1	3	3.82	17	3	0	0	35	43	18	15	2	7	26	.299	.351	.280	6.62	1.78
Robles, Juan	R-R	6-0	185	11-6-97	1	1	1.80	6	2	0	0	15	12	3	3	1	4	15	.214	.263	.189	9.00	2.40
Rosario, Jose	R-R	6-0	180	2-15-95	1	5	5.40	14	6	0	0	40	53	32	24	4	16	31	.314	.305	.318	6.98	3.60
Saldana, Abdiel	R-R	5-11	195	3-13-96	0	4	7.01	16	2	0	1	26	25	21	20	2	20	16	.266	.154	.345	5.61	7.01
Sanabria, Carlos	R-R	6-0	165	1-24-97	2	5	4.71	15	7	0	0	50	51	31	26	3	20	31	.271	.269	.273	5.62	3.62
Sanchez, Starlyng	L-L	5-11	170	6-8-96	0	1	3.60	7	0	0	0	10	8	4	4	1	0	7	.216	.371	.132	6.30	0.00
Sandoval, Edgardo	R-R	6-0	170	7-9-96	1	1	2.45	9	0	0	0	33	25	11	9	0	9	27	.207	.105	.253	7.36	2.45
Sandoval, Patrick	L-L	6-3	190	10-18-96	0	3	6.08	6	6	0	0	13	22	12	9	1	4	11	.349	.250	.383	7.43	2.70
Taveras, Starlyn	R-R	6-3	205	4-21-94	2	1	3.07	15	0	0	0	15	10	9	5	0	14	14	.192	.208	.179	8.59	8.59
Uribe, Josue	R-R	6-0	180	2-6-95	0	0	7.71	3	0	0	0	2	2	2	2	1	2	1	.222	.500	.143	3.86	7.71

Fielding

Catcher	PCT	G	PO	A	E	DP	PB
Bernal	.991	21	90	15	1	0	3
Bowey	.980	19	89	10	2	1	7
Castro	.976	19	69	11	2	0	5
Correa	.951	11	37	2	2	0	0
Martinez	1.000	19	43	11	0	0	7
Pena	1.000	1	1	0	0	0	0
Pena	.980	12	43	6	1	2	2

First Base	PCT	G	PO	A	E	DP
Bernal	1.000	10	45	2	0	3
Bowey	.750	1	2	1	1	1
Franco	.990	10	87	8	1	4
MacDonald	.985	47	371	27	6	34

Second Base	PCT	G	PO	A	E	DP
Almonte	.970	9	19	13	1	2
Ayarza	.958	10	20	26	2	9
Beltre	.979	10	23	23	1	7
Cruz	1.000	10	16	24	0	4
Matute	.920	23	47	45	8	10
Mauricio	1.000	4	11	13	0	5
Sierra	1.000	2	2	2	0	0

Third Base	PCT	G	PO	A	E	DP
Beltre	.900	7	1	17	2	0
Cruz	.936	15	14	30	3	2
Franco	.953	39	33	90	6	12

Shortstop	PCT	G	PO	A	E	DP
Almonte	1.000	2	3	4	0	1

Ayarza	.944	6	8	26	2	3
Matute	1.000	2	5	4	0	0
Mauricio	.965	29	47	92	5	14
Sierra	.867	22	38	63	14	10

Outfield	PCT	G	PO	A	E	DP
Almonte	1.000	4	7	1	0	0
Cameron	1.000	17	40	2	0	0
De La Cruz	1.000	27	49	2	0	0
Fernandez	1.000	33	33	7	0	1
Lorenzo	1.000	2	7	0	0	0
Muriel	1.000	31	61	2	0	0
Sanchez	.955	23	41	1	2	1
Tejada	1.000	31	53	6	0	2
Tucker	1.000	21	36	3	0	0

DSL ASTROS

DOMINICAN SUMMER LEAGUE

ROOKIE

Batting	B-T	HT	WT	DOB	AVG	vLH	vRH	G	AB	R	H	2B	3B	HR	RBI	BB	HBP	SH	SF	SO	SB	CS	SLG	OBP
Almonte, Marcos	R-R	5-10	163	3-28-96	.271	—	—	51	203	32	55	15	0	5	26	21	4	4	0	32	15	5	.419	.351
Amador, Wilson	R-R	6-1	160	12-14-96	.173	.171	.174	54	202	34	35	6	6	0	16	17	8	1	2	52	14	3	.262	.262
Beltre, Reiny	R-R	6-0	180	7-16-96	.282	.233	.293	42	163	35	46	11	1	6	28	18	7	1	1	32	2	1	.472	.376
Benavente, Brandon	B-R	5-10	200	9-3-97	.214	.360	.172	37	112	16	24	7	0	0	10	15	2	0	2	26	2	2	.277	.362
Benjamin, Jose	R-R	6-2	170	12-16-95	.179	.188	.177	30	95	20	17	2	1	1	10	14	7	1	0	21	3	1	.253	.328
Campos, Oscar	R-R	5-10	170	12-8-96	.279	.290	.277	56	197	31	55	9	1	0	24	16	6	3	2	13	2	2	.335	.348
Canelon, Carlos	R-R	5-11	170	12-15-95	.205	—	—	31	73	11	15	4	0	1	11	13	4	1	1	6	3	1	.301	.352
Carrillo, Jose	R-R	6-0	165	1-24-98	.224	—	—	24	49	9	11	2	0	0	3	5	6	1	0	8	0	0	.265	.367
De Leon, Angel	R-R	6-1	170	5-26-96	.245	.216	.250	63	229	36	56	10	4	5	29	35	5	0	0	63	5	2	.389	.357
Figueroa, Darlin	R-L	5-11	170	9-9-95	.204	.200	.205	14	49	6	10	0	1	3	5	1	0	0	0	11	1	4	.429	.220
Fuente, Juan	R-R	6-0	155	11-8-94	.288	—	—	56	198	31	57	11	2	3	24	16	9	10	1	37	21	9	.409	.366
Garcia, Alejandro	R-R	5-10	182	6-21-91	.483	.571	.457	14	60	10	29	4	3	1	9	1	1	1	0	5	3	4	.700	.500
Hernandez, Jose	R-R	6-3	185	3-12-96	.200	.000	.239	23	55	8	11	0	0	1	7	7	1	0	1	32	1	1	.255	.297
Hernandez, Jose	R-R	6-5	201	11-3-96	.091	.000	.125	12	22	1	2	0	0	0	2	4	0	0	1	13	0	0	.091	.222
Jimenez, Ronny	R-R	6-6	185	9-19-94	.201	.258	.191	57	204	26	41	12	0	1	26	19	2	1	3	37	7	6	.275	.272
Lorenzo, Edgar	R-R	5-11	160	1-15-97	.407	.429	.400	17	59	8	24	8	2	0	13	7	2	1	0	11	1	1	.610	.485
Lucas, Felix	R-R	6-3	195	3-27-97	.198	.194	.199	54	187	16	37	6	0	5	25	17	6	0	1	74	0	3	.310	.284
Luciano, Christopher	R-R	6-0	180	10-6-96	.266	.239	.271	72	256	50	68	19	2	4	51	54	11	0	4	51	11	7	.402	.409
Machado, Carlos	R-R	6-2	170	6-5-98	.344	.280	.357	49	154	28	53	2	2	0	20	13	5	3	1	17	10	4	.383	.410
Marquez, Orlando	R-R	5-10	180	3-12-96	.223	.154	.243	55	179	29	40	16	3	3	36	39	6	1	5	47	3	1	.397	.371
Martinez, Hector	R-R	6-1	185	7-6-98	.251	.267	.248	49	167	19	42	5	1	2	13	12	5	1	1	52	8	5	.329	.319
Medina, Fredy	R-R	5-10	160	9-26-97	.143	—	—	16	49	4	7	0	0	0	5	3	0	1	2	14	0	0	.143	.185
Miranda, Nicolas	R-R	5-10	160	6-12-96	.262	.250	.265	47	145	20	38	3	0	0	12	14	0	0	2	31	3	6	.324	.323
Peralta, Anardo	B-R	5-11	170	5-11-96	.182	—	—	54	148	20	27	6	1	1	9	17	11	2	2	41	2	7	.257	.309
Pineda, Andy	L-R	6-1	165	11-19-94	.293	.300	.292	69	249	51	73	10	4	1	29	46	9	13	3	44	30	16	.378	.417
Pineda, Juan	R-R	5-10	145	1-31-98	.293	.250	.304	19	58	12	17	3	0	0	6	9	2	0	0	6	3	1	.345	.406
Rafael, Ronny	R-R	6-2	185	10-14-97	.180	.310	.154	50	178	26	32	11	1	1	10	13	6	1	0	77	3	1	.270	.259
Rodriguez, Anthony	R-R	6-2	195	7-23-96	.218	.222	.217	61	202	29	44	14	0	3	24	18	9	1	2	54	0	3	.332	.307
Sanchez-galan, Ozziel	R-R	5-11	160	10-30-97	.238	.167	.250	56	168	35	40	9	0	0	22	32	5	6	5	34	11	2	.292	.367
Sierra, Miguelangel	R-R	5-11	165	12-2-97	.302	.276	.307	45	169	31	51	17	2	3	19	20	11	0	2	48	8	5	.479	.406
Tejeda, Angel	L-L	6-0	168	1-22-97	.249	—	—	60	193	22	48	7	5	0	18	21	2	6	2	47	11	4	.337	.326
Toribio, Oliver	R-R	5-10	180	6-7-96	.184	.143	.192	45	125	14	23	8	0	0	11	18	4	3	2	32	1	2	.248	.302
Vasquez, Randy	R-R	5-10	190	3-13-96	.309	.211	.330	64	223	34	69	17	1	3	14	35	3	1	4	22	4	4	.448	.405

Pitching	B-T	HT	WT	DOB	W	L	ERA	G	GS	CG	SV	IP	H	R	ER	HR	BB	SO	AVG	vLH	vRH	K/9	BB/9
Abreu, Bryan	R-R	6-1	175	4-22-97	2	2	3.83	14	10	0	0	52	34	29	22	2	36	48	.195	.244	.178	8.36	6.27
Alcala, Jorge	R-R	6-3	180	7-28-95	2	0	3.06	12	2	0	1	32	27	14	11	0	19	20	.227	.209	.237	5.57	5.29
Almengo, Diogenes	R-R	6-2	190	6-2-95	0	0	0.51	4	4	0	0	18	9	5	1	0	10	17	.145	.333	.113	8.66	5.09
Belboder, Joel	R-R	6-0	185	10-5-95	3	0	4.25	8	1	0	0	30	30	17	14	2	9	28	.261	.238	.266	8.49	2.73
Castro, Luis	R-R	6-3	190	5-11-95	1	2	5.48	12	0	0	0	23	22	17	14	0	27	22	—	—	—	8.61	10.57
Castro, Ricardo	R-R	6-3	187	1-12-96	1	0	1.63	7	7	0	0	28	19	13	5	1	7	25	.196	.172	.206	8.13	2.28
Chavez, Enrique	R-R	5-11	194	4-13-96	2	0	2.50	4	3	1	0	18	18	9	5	0	2	12	.250	.143	.294	6.00	1.00
Corniel, Robert	R-R	6-3	190	6-23-95	0	2	5.27	8	1	0	0	14	18	10	8	1	8	13	.333	.471	.270	8.56	5.27
Cuevas, Juan	R-R	6-0	195	5-4-94	3	6	3.94	14	1	0	1	48	60	42	21	4	6	33	—	—	—	6.19	1.13
De La Cruz, Yan	R-R	5-11	165	8-5-93	0	2	8.74	11	0	0	4	11	20	12	11	1	4	6	.385	.389	.382	4.76	3.18
Espinoza, Carlos	L-L	6-1	180	8-16-94	0	1	12.00	1	1	0	0	3	6	4	4	0	2	3	.429	.000	.545	9.00	6.00
Florencio, Harlen	R-R	6-4	210	9-24-95	1	1	7.47	16	0	0	0	16	16	21	13	3	19	7	.258	.200	.286	4.02	10.91
Gonzalez, Dioswardo	R-R	6-0	180	7-7-95	2	0	4.30	9	0	0	0	15	6	10	7	1	16	7	.128	.286	.061	4.30	9.82
Guzman, Jorge	R-R	6-2	182	1-28-96	2	3	5.63	13	11	0	0	46	55	42	29	2	23	27	—	—	—	5.24	4.47
Javier, Cristian	R-R	6-1	170	3-26-97	4	0	2.13	14	4	0	0	42	30	12	10	1	9	50	—	—	—	10.63	1.91
Lopez, Juan	R-R	6-2	175	6-25-97	1	2	3.86	6	5	0	0	16	17	11	7	0	8	15	.283	.273	.286	8.27	4.41
Madera, Ezequiel	R-R	6-2	180	3-22-96	1	1	5.88	18	0	0	1	26	28	31	17	0	33	17	.269	.343	.232	5.88	11.42
Martinez, Michel	R-R	5-10	220	9-16-93	4	1	1.06	10	6	0	0	34	33	16	4	0	11	28	.254	.233	.260	7.41	2.91
Martinez, Saul	R-R	6-2	185	6-21-95	0	0	0.00	2	0	0	0	1	0	0	0	0	2	1	.000	.000	.000	6.75	13.50
Melendez, Cristofer	R-R	6-3	170	9-16-97	2	4	2.78	17	0	0	0	23	20	10	7	1	14	19	.244	.348	.203	7.54	5.56
Navas, Javier	L-L	5-11	165	2-3-98	1	2	2.86	9	5	0	0	28	33	16	9	0	13	24	.297	.357	.289	7.62	4.13
Paulino, Hansel	R-R	6-2	170	1-3-96	1	4	4.93	13	2	0	1	42	57	32	23	1	5	31	.320	.466	.250	6.64	1.07
Perez, Franklin	R-R	6-3	197	12-6-97	1	2	4.37	11	9	0	0	35	34	22	17	1	11	44	.250	.226	.257	11.31	2.83
Perez, Hector	R-R	6-3	190	6-6-96	1	0	2.12	7	7	0	0	30	20	10	7	0	6	32	.185	.103	.215	9.71	1.82
Pirela, Gabriel	R-R	6-1	165	5-1-94	3	5	4.45	17	0	0	1	32	36	17	16	2	16	29	—	—	—	8.07	4.45
Quiala, Yoanys	R-R	6-3	235	1-15-94	2	0	1.54	9	4	0	0	35	26	6	6	1	9	34	.208	.207	.208	8.74	2.31
Quintin, Yonathan	R-R	6-1	170	11-16-96	0	2	3.80	17	0	0	0	21	19	9	9	1	12	17	—	—	—	7.17	5.06
Ramos, Jose	R-R	6-1	160	8-4-96	1	1	1.93	15	11	0	0	65	43	18	14	0	19	56	—	—	—	7.71	2.62
Richez, Michael	R-R	6-1	173	5-15-97	0	0	16.05	1	0	0	0	12	18	26	22	0	25	10	.316	.583	.244	7.30	18.24
Robles, Juan	R-R	6-0	185	11-6-97	1	1	1.49	9	0	0	0	36	29	14	6	0	12	39	.215	.143	.234	9.66	2.97
Rodriguez, Leovanny	R-R	6-0	160	6-13-96	1	3	3.26	10	10	0	0	39	37	21	14	0	11	27	.243	.219	.250	6.28	2.56
Rosado, Cesar	R-R	6-1	172	6-22-96	4	3	2.76	14	4	0	1	46	35	19	14	1	24	46	.217	.250	.200	9.07	4.73
Rosario, Jose	R-R	6-6	180	2-15-95	3	1	2.08	4	2	0	0	17	12	5	4	0	6	20	.200	.188	.205	10.38	3.12
Sambo, Jacques	R-R	6-2	180	7-27-98	0	2	4.40	15	0	0	2	14	10	9	7	0	17	11	.213	.143	.242	6.91	10.67
Sanchez, Starlyng	L-L	5-11	170	8-6-94	1	0	1.13	2	0	0	0	8	8	1	1	0	2	4	.267	.400	.240	4.50	2.25
Sepulveda, Maikel	L-L	6-1	165	12-31-96	2	3	4.95	14	5	0	0	36	43	30	20	1	20	21	.301	.250	.305	5.20	4.95
Serrano, Angelo	R-R	6-3	190	5-18-92	2	0	5.40	6	0	0	0	17	17	13	10	1	10	15	—	—	—	8.10	5.40
Tejada, Felipe	R-R	6-1	190	2-27-98	4	3	5.79	14	6	0	1	51	65	40	33	3	14	45	.297	.306	.293	7.89	2.45
Toribio, Luidin	R-R	6-4	215	2-13-96	3	0	9.95	11	0	0	0	13	18	14	14	1	14	9	.340	.214	.385	6.39	9.95
Uribe, Josue	R-R	6-0	180	2-6-95	2	2	4.23	20	0	0	8	38	38	18	18	2	17	28	—	—	—	6.57	3.99
Valdez, Framber	L-L	5-11	170	11-19-93	4	1	3.68	16	0	0	3	37	36	19	15	1	17	36	.259	.286	.258	8.84	4.17
Valdez, Gabriel	R-R	6-2	185	10-25-95	2	5	4.20	15	12	0	0	60	70	36	28	2	12	38	—	—	—	5.70	1.80
Villarroel, Edwin	L-L	6-3	165	5-18-95	1	3	4.17	17	2	0	0	37	48	26	17	3	7	33	—	—	—	8.10	1.72

Fielding

Catcher	PCT	G	PO	A	E	DP	PB
Benavente	.972	34	204	40	7	3	9
Campos	.996	37	222	46	1	1	8
Canelon	.995	28	159	39	1	2	6
Carrillo	1.000	2	4	0	0	0	0
Carrillo	.958	6	21	2	1	0	0
Marquez	.983	21	143	28	3	1	7
Toribio	1.000	20	101	17	0	0	2
Vasquez	.995	25	183	36	1	0	5

First Base	PCT	G	PO	A	E	DP
Benavente	1.000	1	3	0	0	0
Campos	1.000	7	56	3	0	1
Hernandez	.917	2	9	2	1	1
Hernandez	1.000	1	1	0	0	1
Jimenez	—	1	0	0	0	0
Lucas	.973	36	300	19	9	37
Luciano	.983	54	472	35	9	24
Marquez	.990	12	85	11	1	8
Peralta	1.000	4	10	0	0	1
Pirela	.800	1	3	1	1	0
Toribio	.978	14	84	7	2	7
Vasquez	.983	27	223	11	4	21

Second Base	PCT	G	PO	A	E	DP
Almonte	.945	23	57	63	7	13
Beltre	1.000	1	2	1	0	1
Carrillo	.929	7	11	15	2	2
Fuente	.958	24	49	42	4	15
Jimenez	.980	34	72	77	3	11
Marquez	1.000	1	3	2	0	0
Medina	.950	5	12	7	1	3
Miranda	.978	28	72	60	3	14
Peralta	.982	12	30	24	1	6
Pineda	1.000	13	28	27	0	6
Sanchez-galan	.938	17	41	34	5	5
Vasquez	1.000	1	0	1	0	0

Third Base	PCT	G	PO	A	E	DP
Almonte	.857	7	2	16	3	0
Beltre	.877	40	34	94	18	9
Jimenez	.885	8	7	16	3	2
Luciano	.785	18	27	24	14	3
Miranda	1.000	2	0	2	0	0
Peralta	.905	20	28	39	7	3
Rodriguez	.854	53	50	79	22	8
Sierra	1.000	1	0	1	0	0

Shortstop	PCT	G	PO	A	E	DP
Almonte	.859	15	15	40	9	4
Amador	.805	17	21	41	15	9
Jimenez	.975	9	12	27	1	2
Medina	.852	11	16	30	8	5
Miranda	.942	12	14	35	3	5
Peralta	.846	7	8	14	4	4
Pineda	.955	6	5	16	1	1
Sanchez-galan	.932	36	49	89	10	7
Sierra	.927	41	60	131	15	25

Outfield	PCT	G	PO	A	E	DP
Almonte	1.000	2	1	0	0	0
Amador	.926	30	50	0	4	0
Benjamin	.930	24	37	3	3	2
Campos	1.000	4	5	1	0	0
Canelon	—	1	0	0	0	0
De Leon	.948	55	72	1	4	0
Figueroa	.882	14	14	1	2	0
Fuente	.948	33	51	4	3	0
Garcia	1.000	14	32	0	0	0
Hernandez	—	2	0	0	0	0
Jimenez	1.000	5	3	1	0	0
Lorenzo	.933	16	25	3	2	2
Lucas	1.000	1	1	0	0	0
Machado	.925	43	57	5	5	1
Martinez	.943	44	77	5	5	3
Rafael	.958	49	87	5	4	2
Peralta	.909	7	8	2	1	1
Pineda	.971	66	156	9	5	2
Sanchez-galan	—	1	0	0	0	0
Tejada	.920	58	77	3	7	0
Vasquez	—	1	0	0	0	0

Kansas City Royals

SEASON IN A NUTSHELL: If 2014 was a season-long sugar rush of success for Royals' fans, 2015 was an even more satisfying culmination of a 10-year rebuilding process.

HIGH POINT: The entire season was a long run of high points as the Royals finished the regular season with the best record in the American League, rallied to beat the Astros in the Division Series and then topped the Blue Jays in the Championship Series. But the World Series is what Royals fans will remember. Eric Hosmer made a mad dash home to tie the game, Christian Colon's RBI single spurred a five-run 12th inning and Wade Davis closed out the Royals' first World Series title since 1985. Over the past two seasons, the Royals are 22-9 in the playoffs.

LOW POINT: The lowest point for the Royals' in 2015 was still far beyond the imagination of any Royals fan from the 1990s or 2000s. Kansas City never trailed by more than one game all season and were in first place by themselves from early June until the end of the year. Kansas City did go 11-17 in September, but that was a pre-playoffs pause for a team that had already wrapped up the division.

NOTABLE ROOKIES: Outfielder Paulo Orlando hit .249/.269/.444 with six triples and seven home runs in a part-time role. He filled in as a starter when Alexis Rios missed time, but after graduating a large wave of rookies in recent years, Kansas City filled its holes in 2015 with free-agent signings and veteran pickups in trades.

KEY TRANSACTIONS: The Royals went all-in at the trade deadline, picking up righthander Johnny Cueto from the Reds for three lefthanded pitching prospects (Cody Reed, John Lamb and Brandon Finnegan). Second baseman Ben Zobrist came over from the Athletics for lefthander Sean Manaea and righthander Aaron Brooks. Both moves proved vital to the Royals' championship. Cueto won Game Five of the ALCS with eight strong innings and then topped that with a complete-game, two-hitter to beat the Mets in Game Two of the World Series. Zobrist scored 15 runs in 16 postseason games.

DOWN ON THE FARM: Veteran minor leaguer Jose Martinez jumped from high Class A to Triple-A and responded with a Pacific Coast League and minor league-best .384 batting average. First baseman Brandon O'Hearn hit 27 home runs between low Class A Lexington and high Class A Wilmington.

OPENING DAY PAYROLL: $113,618,650 (16th)

PLAYERS OF THE YEAR

MAJOR LEAGUE	MINOR LEAGUE
Lorenzo Cain, of	**Jose Martinez, of**
.307/.361/.477	.384/.461/.563
101 R, 34 2B, 6 3B, 16 HR, 72 RBIs, 28 SB in 34 Att.	(Rookie, Triple-A) Led minor leagues in batting and OBP

ORGANIZATION LEADERS

BATTING		*Minimum 250 AB
MAJORS		
*AVG	Lorenzo Cain	.307
*OPS	Kendrys Morales	.847
HR	Kendrys Morales	22
	Mike Moustakas	22
RBI	Kendrys Morales	106
MINORS		
*AVG	Jose Martinez, Omaha	.384
*OBP	Jose Martinez, Omaha	.461
*SLG	Balbino Fuenmayor, NW Arkansas, Omaha	.589
R	Whit Merrifield, Omaha	83
H	Whit Merrifield, Omaha	144
TB	Alex Liddi, NW Arkansas	228
2B	Alex Liddi, NW Arkansas	39
3B	Marten Gasparini, Idaho Falls	10
HR	Ryan O'Hearn, Lexington, Wilmington	27
RBI	Brett Eibner, Omaha	81
BB	Ryan O'Hearn, Lexington, Wilmington	55
SO	Hunter Dozier, NW Arkansas	151
SB	Carlos Garcia, Lexington, Wilmington	42

PITCHING		#Minimum 75 IP
MAJORS		
W	Yordano Ventura	13
	Edinson Volquez	13
#ERA	Edinson Volquez	3.55
SO	Yordano Ventura	156
SV	Greg Holland	32
MINORS		
W	Andy Ferguson, NW Arkansas, Omaha	11
L	Jake Junis, NW Arkansas, Wilmington	12
#ERA	Alec Mills, Wilmington	3.02
G	Malcom Culver, NW Arkansas	43
	Aroni Nina, NW Arkansas	43
GS	Jake Junis, NW Arkansas, Wilmington	27
SV	Scott Alexander, Omaha	14
IP	Jake Junis, NW Arkansas, Wilmington	160
BB	Clayton Mortensen, Omaha	59
SO	Jake Junis, NW Arkansas, Wilmington	126
AVG	Luke Farrell, Wilmington, NW Arkansas	.251

2015 PERFORMANCE

General Manager: Dayton Moore. **Farm Director:** Scott Sharp. **Scouting Director:** Lonnie Goldberg.

Class	Team	League	W	L	PCT	Finish	Manager
Majors	Kansas City Royals	American	95	67	.586	1st (15)	Ned Yost
Triple-A	Omaha Storm Chasers	Pacific Coast	80	64	.556	t-3rd (16)	Brian Poldberg
Double-A	Northwest Arkansas Naturals	Texas	69	70	.496	4th (8)	Vance Wilson
High A	Wilmington Blue Rocks	Carolina	62	77	.446	8th (8)	Brian Buchanan
Low A	Lexington Legends	South Atlantic	58	80	.420	12th (14)	Omar Ramirez
Rookie	Burlington Royals	Appalachian	31	37	.456	7th (10)	Scott Thorman
Rookie	Idaho Falls Chukars	Pioneer	38	38	.500	4th (8)	Justin Gemoll
Rookie	Royals	Arizona	40	16	.714	1st (14)	Darryl Kennedy
Overall 2015 Minor League Record			378	382	.497	18th (30)	

ORGANIZATION STATISTICS

KANSAS CITY ROYALS

AMERICAN LEAGUE

Batting	B-T	HT	WT	DOB	AVG	vLH	vRH	G	AB	R	H	2B	3B	HR	RBI	BB	HBP	SH	SF	SO	SB	CS	SLG	OBP
Butera, Drew	R-R	6-1	200	8-9-83	.198	.259	.169	45	86	6	17	3	0	1	5	6	2	5	0	24	0	0	.267	.266
2-team total (10 Los Angeles)					.196	—	—	55	107	9	21	3	0	1	5	6	2	5	0	26	0	1	.252	.252
Cain, Lorenzo	R-R	6-2	205	4-13-86	.307	.335	.292	140	551	101	169	34	6	16	72	37	12	0	4	98	28	6	.477	.361
Calixte, Orlando	R-R	5-11	160	2-3-92	.000	.000	.000	2	3	1	0	0	0	0	0	0	0	0	0	0	0	0	.000	.000
Coleman, Dusty	R-R	6-2	205	4-20-87	.000	.000	.000	4	5	0	0	0	0	0	0	0	0	0	0	3	0	0	.000	.000
Colon, Christian	R-R	5-10	190	5-14-89	.290	.333	.268	43	107	8	31	5	0	0	6	11	0	1	0	17	3	2	.336	.356
Cuthbert, Cheslor	R-R	6-1	190	11-16-92	.217	.250	.192	19	46	6	10	2	1	1	8	4	0	0	0	9	0	0	.370	.280
Dyson, Jarrod	L-R	5-10	160	8-15-84	.250	.222	.256	90	200	31	50	8	6	2	18	14	4	6	1	37	26	3	.380	.311
Escobar, Alcides	R-R	6-1	185	12-16-86	.257	.269	.252	148	612	76	157	20	5	3	47	26	8	11	5	75	17	5	.320	.293
Gomes, Jonny	R-R	6-1	230	11-22-80	.167	.182	.125	12	30	2	5	2	0	0	4	3	0	0	1	14	0	0	.233	.235
Gordon, Alex	L-R	6-1	220	2-10-84	.271	.280	.266	104	354	40	96	18	0	13	48	49	14	—	5	92	2	5	.432	.377
Gore, Terrance	R-R	5-7	165	6-8-91	.000	.000	.000	9	3	1	0	0	0	0	0	0	0	1	0	1	3	0	.000	.250
Hosmer, Eric	L-L	6-4	225	10-24-89	.297	.279	.310	158	599	98	178	33	5	18	93	61	3	1	3	108	7	3	.459	.363
Infante, Omar	R-R	5-11	195	12-26-81	.220	.228	.217	124	440	39	97	23	7	2	44	9	0	2	4	69	2	2	.318	.234
Kratz, Erik	R-R	6-4	240	6-15-80	.000	—	—	4	4	0	0	0	0	1	0	0	0	1	2	0	0	.000	.000
Morales, Kendrys	B-R	6-1	225	6-20-83	.290	.298	.284	158	569	81	165	41	2	22	106	58	8	0	4	103	0	0	.485	.362
Moustakas, Mike	L-R	6-0	215	9-11-88	.284	.282	.286	147	549	73	156	34	1	22	82	43	13	4	5	76	1	2	.470	.348
Orlando, Paulo	R-R	6-2	210	11-1-85	.249	.265	.238	86	241	31	60	14	6	7	27	5	2	2	1	53	3	3	.444	.269
Pena, Francisco	R-R	6-2	230	10-12-89	.143	1.000	.000	8	7	0	1	0	0	0	0	0	0	0	0	3	0	0	.143	.143
Perez, Salvador	R-R	6-3	240	5-10-90	.260	.215	.281	142	531	52	138	25	0	21	70	13	4	0	5	82	1	0	.426	.280
Rios, Alex	R-R	6-5	210	2-18-81	.255	.229	.264	105	385	40	98	22	2	4	32	15	5	0	6	67	9	0	.353	.287
Zobrist, Ben	B-R	6-3	210	5-26-81	.284	.338	.261	59	232	37	66	16	1	7	23	29	1	0	2	30	2	3	.453	.394
2-team total (67 Oakland)					.276	—	—	126	467	76	129	36	3	13	56	62	1	0	5	56	3	4	.450	.359

Pitching	B-T	HT	WT	DOB	W	L	ERA	G	GS	CG	SV	IP	H	R	ER	HR	BB	SO	AVG	vLH	vRH	K/9	BB/9
Alexander, Scott	L-L	6-2	190	7-10-89	0	0	4.50	4	0	0	0	6	5	3	3	0	3	3	.238	.333	.200	4.50	4.50
Almonte, Miguel	R-R	6-2	180	4-4-93	0	2	6.23	9	0	0	0	9	7	6	6	4	7	10	.212	.231	.200	10.38	7.27
Blanton, Joe	R-R	6-3	215	12-11-80	2	2	3.89	15	4	0	2	42	43	19	18	6	7	40	.265	.282	.247	8.64	1.51
Brooks, Aaron	R-R	6-4	220	4-27-90	0	0	6.23	2	0	0	0	4	6	3	3	0	0	3	.333	.222	.444	6.23	0.00
2-team total (11 Oakland)					3	4	6.67	13	9	0	0	55	73	41	41	9	14	38	—	—	—	6.18	2.28
Chamberlain, Joba	R-R	6-2	250	9-23-85	0	0	7.94	6	0	0	0	6	6	5	5	1	4	8	.261	.200	.375	12.71	6.35
2-team total (30 Detroit)					0	2	4.88	36	0	0	0	28	38	20	15	6	9	23	—	—	—	7.48	2.93
Coleman, Louis	R-R	6-4	205	4-4-86	1	0	0.00	4	0	0	0	3	1	0	0	0	2	1	.111	.000	.167	3.00	6.00
Cueto, Johnny	R-R	5-11	220	2-15-86	4	7	4.76	13	13	1	0	81	101	45	43	10	17	56	.307	.278	.331	6.20	1.88
Davis, Wade	R-R	6-5	220	9-7-85	8	1	0.94	69	0	0	17	67	33	8	7	3	20	78	.144	.146	.141	10.43	2.67
Duffy, Danny	L-L	6-3	205	12-21-88	7	8	4.08	30	24	0	1	137	137	64	62	15	53	102	.264	.239	.271	6.72	3.49
Finnegan, Brandon	L-L	5-11	185	4-14-93	3	0	2.96	14	0	0	0	24	16	8	8	3	13	21	.193	.172	.204	7.77	4.81
Frasor, Jason	R-R	5-9	180	8-9-77	1	0	1.54	26	0	0	0	23	24	5	4	1	15	18	.276	.326	.220	6.94	5.79
Guthrie, Jeremy	R-R	6-1	205	4-8-79	8	8	5.95	30	24	0	0	148	186	101	98	29	44	84	.310	.325	.292	5.10	2.67
Herrera, Kelvin	R-R	5-10	200	12-31-89	4	3	2.71	72	0	0	0	70	52	23	21	5	26	64	.206	.151	.256	8.27	3.36
Hochevar, Luke	R-R	6-5	225	9-15-83	1	1	3.73	49	0	0	1	51	49	23	21	7	16	49	.250	.263	.241	8.70	2.84
Holland, Greg	R-R	5-10	205	11-20-85	3	2	3.83	48	0	0	32	45	37	20	19	2	26	49	.239	.250	.230	9.87	5.24
Madson, Ryan	L-R	6-6	210	8-28-80	1	2	2.13	68	0	0	3	63	47	17	15	5	14	58	.205	.205	.205	8.24	1.99
Mariot, Michael	R-R	6-0	190	10-20-88	0	0	3.00	2	0	0	0	3	2	1	1	1	2	1	.200	.333	.000	3.00	6.00
Medlen, Kris	R-R	5-10	190	10-7-85	6	2	4.01	15	8	0	0	58	56	30	26	6	18	40	.252	.239	.266	6.17	2.78
Morales, Franklin	L-L	6-1	210	1-24-86	4	2	3.18	67	0	0	0	62	58	24	22	4	14	41	.246	.192	.285	5.92	2.02
Pino, Yohan	R-R	6-2	190	12-26-83	0	2	3.26	7	1	0	0	19	23	8	7	2	3	13	.291	.238	.351	6.05	1.40
Vargas, Jason	L-L	6-0	215	2-2-83	5	2	3.98	9	9	0	0	43	46	20	19	5	12	27	.271	.286	.264	5.65	2.51
Ventura, Yordano	R-R	6-0	180	6-3-91	13	8	4.08	28	28	0	0	163	154	75	74	14	58	156	.248	.255	.240	8.60	3.20
Volquez, Edinson	R-R	6-0	220	7-3-83	13	9	3.55	34	33	1	0	200	190	89	79	16	72	155	.251	.240	.262	6.96	3.23
Young, Chris	R-R	6-10	255	5-25-79	11	6	3.06	34	18	0	0	123	91	44	42	16	43	83	.202	.242	.159	6.06	3.14

Fielding

Catcher	PCT	G	PO	A	E	DP	PB
Butera	.984	42	171	12	3	1	1
Kratz	1.000	4	12	1	0	0	0
Pena	1.000	8	12	0	0	0	0
Perez	.996	139	974	90	4	10	4

First Base	PCT	G	PO	A	E	DP
Butera	1.000	5	17	4	0	0
Cuthbert	—	1	0	0	0	0
Hosmer	.997	154	1261	101	4	121
Morales	1.000	9	62	3	0	3
Perez	1.000	1	2	0	0	1

Second Base	PCT	G	PO	A	E	DP
Colon	1.000	14	19	25	0	9
Cuthbert	1.000	1	1	0	0	0
Infante	.981	124	193	320	10	67
Zobrist	.979	35	56	82	3	21

Third Base	PCT	G	PO	A	E	DP
Coleman	1.000	2	1	2	0	0
Colon	.920	8	10	13	2	2
Cuthbert	.974	17	7	31	1	3
Moustakas	.969	146	112	257	12	21
Zobrist	1.000	4	2	4	0	0

Shortstop	PCT	G	PO	A	E	DP
Calixte	1.000	1	0	2	0	0

Colon	.957	21	20	47	3	9
Escobar	.980	148	217	417	13	80

Outfield	PCT	G	PO	A	E	DP
Cain	.975	137	391	6	10	2
Dyson	.987	79	145	8	2	4
Gomes	1.000	6	3	0	0	0
Gordon	1.000	101	193	4	0	1
Gore	—	4	0	0	0	0
Hosmer	—	1	0	0	0	0
Orlando	.971	79	129	5	4	1
Rios	.986	105	215	4	3	0
Zobrist	.974	20	36	1	1	0

OMAHA STORM CHASERS

TRIPLE-A

PACIFIC COAST LEAGUE

Batting	B-T	HT	WT	DOB	AVG	vLH	vRH	G	AB	R	H	2B	3B	HR	RBI	BB	HBP	SH	SF	SO	SB	CS	SLG	OBP
Adams, Lane	R-R	6-4	190	11-13-89	.226	.226	.226	37	115	14	26	5	0	4	13	13	1	1	2	21	2	1	.374	.305
Boscan, J.C.	R-R	6-2	215	12-26-79	.216	.229	.210	42	116	13	25	2	0	1	11	7	0	1	0	19	0	1	.259	.260
Calixte, Orlando	R-R	5-11	160	2-3-92	.229	.202	.243	107	354	38	81	11	2	8	27	27	2	11	0	84	22	3	.339	.287
Coleman, Dusty	R-R	6-2	205	4-20-87	.275	.274	.275	73	251	31	69	11	2	7	27	14	4	7	0	69	8	2	.418	.323
Colon, Christian	R-R	5-10	190	5-14-89	.281	.263	.289	51	192	19	54	9	0	1	17	21	1	2	1	18	8	2	.344	.353
Cuthbert, Cheslor	R-R	6-1	190	11-16-92	.277	.258	.287	104	397	55	110	22	1	11	51	37	1	1	2	60	5	2	.421	.339
Diekroeger, Kenny	R-R	6-2	190	11-5-90	.167	—	.167	2	6	1	1	0	0	0	0	0	0	0	0	0	0	0	.333	.167
Eibner, Brett	R-R	6-3	195	12-2-88	.303	.308	.301	103	389	65	118	23	1	19	81	38	0	2	2	79	10	0	.514	.364
Fields, Matt	R-R	6-5	235	7-8-85	.244	.268	.233	53	172	16	42	12	1	4	25	17	2	0	3	69	1	1	.395	.314
Franco, Angel	B-R	5-10	155	5-23-90	.212	.276	.187	32	104	8	22	6	0	0	8	2	0	2	0	13	0	2	.269	.268
Fuenmayor, Balbino	R-R	6-3	230	11-26-89	.377	.438	.358	16	69	12	26	6	1	2	15	0	0	0	1	13	0	0	.580	.371
Fuentes, Reymond	L-L	6-0	160	2-12-91	.308	.342	.293	107	396	70	122	10	4	9	46	30	3	14	2	72	29	6	.422	.360
Gibbs, Micah	B-R	5-11	205	7-27-88	.147	.091	.174	13	34	3	5	1	0	1	4	4	0	0	0	9	0	0	.265	.237
Gordon, Alex	L-R	6-1	220	2-10-84	.429	.667	.364	8	28	6	12	2	0	1	5	8	1	0	0	6	0	0	.607	.568
Jackson, Ryan	R-R	6-3	180	5-10-88	.305	.333	.286	19	59	9	18	3	0	1	2	7	0	2	0	13	0	1	.407	.379
2-team total (85 Salt Lake)					.295	—	—	104	373	42	110	19	3	2	28	47	0	9	2	79	1	4	.378	.372
Kotchman, Casey	L-L	6-3	220	2-22-83	.290	.225	.316	90	317	39	92	20	1	7	44	39	4	0	1	32	1	0	.426	.374
Kratz, Erik	R-R	6-4	240	6-15-80	.214	.053	.297	15	56	7	12	2	0	4	12	5	0	0	1	9	0	0	.464	.274
2-team total (10 Tacoma)					.211	—	—	25	95	10	20	6	0	4	17	8	1	0	1	16	0	0	.400	.276
Martinez, Jose	R-R	6-7	210	7-25-88	.384	.375	.388	98	341	57	131	25	3	10	60	48	3	1	3	55	8	2	.563	.461
Merrifield, Whit	R-R	6-1	175	1-24-89	.265	.270	.262	135	544	83	144	29	5	5	38	39	4	4	3	66	32	9	.364	.317
Noriega, Gabriel	R-R	6-2	180	9-13-90	.204	.211	.200	33	103	6	21	2	0	0	11	1	0	3	0	21	1	2	.223	.212
Orlando, Paulo	R-R	6-2	210	11-1-85	.276	.264	.282	41	170	20	47	11	0	3	17	8	1	1	2	32	9	0	.394	.309
Pena, Francisco	R-R	6-2	230	10-12-89	.251	.274	.240	95	342	42	86	20	1	13	48	23	4	3	2	56	4	1	.430	.305
Rios, Alex	R-R	6-5	210	2-18-81	.176	.333	.143	4	17	2	3	1	0	1	2	0	0	0	0	4	0	0	.412	.176
Sierra, Moises	R-R	6-1	220	9-24-88	.289	.317	.275	65	235	26	68	8	0	3	28	20	2	2	0	51	13	7	.362	.350

Pitching	B-T	HT	WT	DOB	W	L	ERA	G	GS	CG	SV	IP	H	R	ER	HR	BB	SO	AVG	vLH	vRH	K/9	BB/9
Alexander, Scott	L-L	6-2	190	7-10-89	2	3	2.56	41	0	0	14	63	48	21	18	5	17	50	.209	.140	.250	7.11	2.42
Almonte, Miguel	R-R	6-2	180	4-4-93	2	2	5.40	11	6	0	0	37	33	24	22	3	15	41	.244	.284	.197	10.06	3.68
Baumann, Buddy	L-L	5-10	175	12-9-87	3	4	3.04	34	6	0	3	77	65	29	26	5	25	84	.224	.148	.269	9.82	2.92
Binford, Christian	R-R	6-6	220	12-20-92	1	4	5.86	6	6	0	0	28	31	19	18	4	15	9	.284	.280	.288	2.93	4.88
Blanton, Joe	R-R	6-3	215	12-11-80	3	2	3.89	7	6	0	0	39	34	17	17	7	10	30	.227	.250	.203	6.86	2.29
Broderick, Brian	R-R	6-6	205	9-1-86	5	4	2.90	42	0	0	2	62	60	28	20	4	16	38	.254	.299	.217	5.52	2.32
Brooks, Aaron	R-R	6-4	220	4-27-90	6	5	3.71	18	17	1	0	107	118	46	44	9	21	92	.282	.259	.303	7.76	1.77
2-team total (2 Nashville)					7	5	3.56	20	19	1	0	119	127	49	47	10	21	103	—	—	—	7.81	1.59
Chamberlain, Joba	R-R	6-2	250	9-23-85	1	0	6.43	8	0	0	0	7	11	5	5	0	2	9	.355	.500	.263	11.57	2.57
Clemens, Paul	R-R	6-4	200	2-14-88	2	1	2.57	5	0	0	0	7	8	2	2	1	2	4	.320	.385	.250	5.14	2.57
Coleman, Louis	R-R	6-4	205	4-4-86	8	2	1.69	38	0	0	9	64	48	12	12	4	23	63	.212	.152	.260	8.86	3.23
Coleman, Casey	L-R	6-0	185	7-3-87	5	4	4.92	33	6	0	1	82	102	49	45	6	41	54	.311	.331	.292	5.90	4.48
Duffy, Danny	L-L	6-3	205	12-21-88	0	0	2.25	3	3	0	0	8	5	3	2	1	1	10	.172	.200	.167	11.25	1.13
Dwyer, Chris	R-L	6-3	205	4-10-88	3	3	4.01	33	10	0	0	92	99	47	41	4	55	63	.280	.272	.285	6.16	5.38
Dziedzic, Jonathan	R-L	6-0	165	2-4-91	0	1	21.60	1	1	0	0	3	10	8	8	3	2	4	.526	.167	.692	10.80	5.40
Ferguson, Andy	R-R	6-1	195	9-2-88	7	3	3.21	16	14	0	0	73	65	27	26	11	16	71	.237	.239	.235	8.75	1.97
Finnegan, Brandon	L-L	5-11	185	4-14-93	0	2	7.07	6	4	0	0	14	17	12	11	1	7	19	.293	.286	.295	12.21	4.50
Flynn, Brian	L-L	6-7	250	4-19-90	0	0	0.00	1	0	0	0	1	1	0	0	0	1	1	.333	1.000	.000	13.50	0.00
Hochevar, Luke	R-R	6-5	225	9-15-83	0	1	7.84	9	4	0	0	10	16	9	9	2	8	10	.364	.500	.227	8.71	6.97
Lamb, John	L-L	6-4	205	7-10-90	9	1	2.67	17	17	0	0	94	80	35	28	7	29	96	.233	.214	.241	9.16	2.77
Mariot, Michael	R-R	6-0	190	10-20-88	4	2	2.32	42	0	0	8	62	52	23	16	3	16	72	.224	.214	.231	10.45	2.32
Medlen, Kris	B-R	5-10	190	10-7-85	1	0	4.11	3	3	0	0	15	16	7	7	6	1	9	.267	.385	.176	5.28	0.59
Mortensen, Clayton	R-R	6-4	185	4-10-85	7	9	5.40	24	17	0	0	107	104	68	64	9	59	81	.256	.266	.248	6.83	4.98
Murray, Matt	R-R	6-3	240	12-28-89	1	0	3.20	9	0	0	1	20	17	7	7	1	12	10	.236	.188	.275	4.58	5.49
Paterson, Joe	R-L	6-0	190	5-19-86	1	2	5.68	12	0	0	2	13	14	8	8	0	6	12	.275	.179	.391	8.53	4.26
2-team total (2 Nashville)					2	2	6.14	14	0	0	2	15	18	11	10	0	8	13	—	—	—	7.98	4.91
Patton, Troy	B-L	6-1	180	9-3-85	0	1	2.37	20	0	0	0	30	25	10	8	3	9	25	.216	.217	.214	7.42	2.67
Pino, Yohan	R-R	6-2	190	12-26-83	6	3	4.69	16	14	1	0	79	83	41	41	12	20	69	.267	.233	.297	7.89	2.29
Rodriguez, Wandy	R-L	5-10	195	1-18-79	0	0	1.13	5	0	0	0	8	5	1	1	0	4	7	.185	.364	.063	7.88	4.50
2-team total (2 Round Rock)					0	0	1.80	7	2	0	0	15	9	3	3	1	4	17	—	—	—	10.20	2.40

Pitching	B-T	HT	WT	DOB	W	L	ERA	G	GS	CG	SV	IP	H	R	ER	HR	BB	SO	AVG	vLH	vRH	K/9	BB/9
Sulbaran, J.C.	R-R	6-2	220	11-9-89	3	3	6.17	8	8	0	0	42	49	29	29	9	14	33	.290	.269	.316	7.02	2.98
Ventura, Yordano	R-R	6-0	180	6-3-91	0	2	3.86	2	2	0	0	9	6	4	4	1	6	9	.194	.286	.118	8.68	5.79
Yambati, Robinson	R-R	6-3	185	1-15-91	0	0	0.00	1	0	0	0	1	1	0	0	0	0	0	.500	—	.500	0.00	0.00

Fielding

Catcher	PCT	G	PO	A	E	DP	PB
Boscan	.993	38	259	10	2	1	1
Gibbs	.990	12	95	4	1	2	0
Kratz	.992	14	115	9	1	0	1
Pena	.993	89	627	45	5	4	3

First Base	PCT	G	PO	A	E	DP
Boscan	—	1	0	0	0	0
Cuthbert	1.000	25	164	14	0	23
Fields	.994	37	300	11	2	22
Fuenmayor	1.000	14	113	5	0	12
Kotchman	.986	38	262	20	4	26
Martinez	1.000	22	164	11	0	18
Merrifield	1.000	14	82	10	0	11

Second Base	PCT	G	PO	A	E	DP
Calixte	.976	18	30	51	2	10
Coleman	.992	27	51	80	1	17
Colon	.986	16	34	38	1	7

	PCT	G	PO	A	E	DP
Diekroeger	1.000	2	4	2	0	1
Franco	.935	10	13	16	2	3
Jackson	.970	7	16	16	1	5
Martinez	1.000	1	1	2	0	0
Merrifield	.980	57	96	148	5	36
Noriega	.958	12	20	26	2	11

Third Base	PCT	G	PO	A	E	DP
Calixte	.902	21	12	34	5	2
Coleman	.939	10	11	20	2	3
Colon	.957	7	11	11	1	1
Cuthbert	.962	75	50	126	7	12
Franco	.885	15	9	14	3	2
Jackson	1.000	1	1	2	0	0
Merrifield	.917	15	18	15	3	2
Noriega	.875	6	3	4	1	0

Shortstop	PCT	G	PO	A	E	DP
Calixte	.945	55	82	124	12	33

	PCT	G	PO	A	E	DP
Coleman	.962	36	58	95	6	22
Colon	.973	26	42	66	3	15
Franco	1.000	1	1	3	0	0
Jackson	.958	10	14	32	2	4
Merrifield	.923	4	5	7	1	1
Noriega	.953	15	12	29	2	6

Outfield	PCT	G	PO	A	E	DP
Adams	.976	37	79	1	2	0
Calixte	1.000	9	14	0	0	0
Eibner	.986	101	203	8	3	0
Fuentes	.981	103	243	9	5	3
Gordon	1.000	4	6	1	0	0
Martinez	.963	55	101	4	4	0
Merrifield	.981	49	97	5	2	1
Orlando	.978	37	85	2	2	0
Rios	1.000	2	4	0	0	0
Sierra	.954	51	111	13	6	1

NORTHWEST ARKANSAS NATURALS

DOUBLE-A

TEXAS LEAGUE

Batting	B-T	HT	WT	DOB	AVG	vLH	vRH	G	AB	R	H	2B	3B	HR	RBI	BB	HBP	SH	SF	SO	SB	CS	SLG	OBP
Adams, Lane	R-R	6-4	190	11-13-89	.298	.341	.284	97	373	58	111	21	3	12	49	36	2	0	3	98	29	6	.466	.360
Bianucci, Mike	R-R	6-1	215	6-26-86	.278	.273	.279	58	209	31	58	12	0	12	34	13	1	0	2	52	1	0	.507	.320
Bonifacio, Jorge	R-R	6-1	195	6-4-93	.240	.245	.239	125	483	60	116	30	2	17	64	42	5	1	5	126	3	2	.416	.305
Chapman, Ethan	L-R	6-0	180	1-5-90	.203	.143	.222	23	59	7	12	1	0	1	5	7	0	0	1	17	1	0	.271	.284
Coleman, Dusty	R-R	6-2	205	4-20-87	.341	.318	.348	26	91	12	31	9	0	2	18	14	7	1	1	23	4	4	.505	.460
Davis, Logan	L-R	6-2	175	8-23-91	.105	.000	.125	19	19	1	2	0	0	1	2	1	3	0	4	2	0	0	.105	.227
De La Rosa, Anderson	R-R	5-11	190	8-1-84	.147	.300	.083	10	34	2	5	2	0	1	4	2	1	0	0	8	0	0	.294	.216
Diekroeger, Kenny	R-R	6-2	190	5-11-90	.260	.282	.255	68	204	23	53	10	0	2	14	18	5	2	1	35	5	2	.338	.333
Dozier, Hunter	R-R	6-4	220	8-22-91	.213	.177	.222	128	475	65	101	27	1	12	53	45	1	0	2	151	6	2	.349	.281
Evans, Zane	R-R	6-2	210	11-29-91	.252	.315	.234	65	238	21	60	14	0	6	41	8	1	1	6	41	1	0	.387	.278
Franco, Angel	B-R	5-10	155	5-23-90	.309	.200	.338	42	165	27	51	12	2	4	19	15	0	4	4	17	1	1	.479	.359
Fuenmayor, Balbino	R-R	6-3	230	11-26-89	.354	.424	.336	73	291	50	103	22	1	15	51	12	4	0	1	46	1	0	.591	.386
Furcal, Rafael	B-R	5-8	195	10-24-77	.333	.500	.000	3	9	2	3	0	0	0	2	2	0	0	1	2	0	0	.333	.417
Gibbs, Micah	B-R	5-11	205	7-27-88	.291	.167	.326	18	55	6	16	4	1	1	8	8	0	1	0	14	0	0	.455	.381
Gore, Terrance	R-R	5-7	165	6-8-91	.284	.261	.290	85	222	42	63	4	1	0	16	26	3	8	0	50	39	2	.311	.367
Liddi, Alex	R-R	6-4	225	8-14-88	.287	.333	.275	128	481	65	138	39	6	13	56	25	3	1	4	128	8	3	.474	.324
Mondesi, Raul A.	B-R	6-1	185	7-27-95	.243	.271	.237	81	304	36	74	11	5	6	33	17	0	12	5	88	19	6	.372	.279
Morin, Parker	L-R	5-11	195	7-2-91	.309	.231	.322	56	178	23	55	10	5	4	30	11	0	1	1	36	1	1	.489	.347
Nessy, Santiago	R-R	6-2	230	12-8-92	.185	.250	.167	17	54	5	10	1	1	1	6	4	2	1	0	11	0	1	.296	.267
Noriega, Gabriel	R-R	6-2	180	9-13-90	.353	.333	.357	5	17	1	6	1	0	0	3	1	0	1	0	4	0	0	.412	.389
Salcedo, Edward	R-R	6-3	210	7-30-91	.100	.000	.111	6	20	0	2	0	0	0	3	1	0	0	1	5	0	0	.100	.136
Schwindel, Frank	R-R	6-1	205	6-29-92	.212	.108	.241	50	170	14	36	7	0	4	22	2	1	0	1	37	0	1	.324	.224
Starling, Bubba	R-R	6-4	210	8-3-92	.254	.289	.242	91	331	51	84	19	4	10	32	30	2	1	2	91	4	5	.426	.318
Torres, Ramon	B-R	5-10	155	1-22-93	.275	.356	.250	51	189	23	52	10	1	4	13	17	1	7	0	23	4	8	.402	.338

Pitching	B-T	HT	WT	DOB	W	L	ERA	G	GS	CG	SV	IP	H	R	ER	HR	BB	SO	AVG	vLH	vRH	K/9	BB/9
Almonte, Miguel	R-R	6-2	180	4-4-93	4	4	4.03	17	17	0	0	67	65	31	30	4	27	55	.255	.254	.257	7.39	3.63
Binford, Christian	R-R	6-6	220	12-20-92	4	7	5.03	16	16	0	0	91	118	58	51	6	23	60	.319	.327	.312	5.91	2.27
Clemens, Paul	R-R	6-4	200	2-14-88	0	1	7.47	5	3	0	1	16	15	13	13	2	6	9	.254	.257	.250	5.17	3.45
Culver, Malcom	R-R	6-1	205	2-9-90	2	6	4.19	43	0	0	8	58	58	29	27	2	30	59	.253	.259	.248	9.16	4.66
Dziedzic, Jonathan	R-L	6-4	165	12-13-90	10	6	3.12	26	25	1	0	138	138	57	48	9	35	93	.258	.242	.265	6.05	2.28
Farrell, Luke	R-R	6-6	210	6-7-91	5	3	3.09	19	16	0	0	93	89	38	32	7	29	65	.251	.254	.249	6.27	2.80
Ferguson, Andy	R-R	6-1	195	9-2-88	4	0	0.85	4	4	0	0	32	19	4	3	2	8	37	.173	.208	.140	10.52	2.27
Finnegan, Brandon	L-L	5-11	185	4-14-93	0	1	2.77	5	3	0	1	13	10	9	4	1	12	13	.204	.227	.185	9.00	8.31
Junis, Jake	R-R	6-2	225	9-16-92	0	1	9.00	1	1	0	0	4	7	5	4	0	1	3	.412	.417	.400	6.75	2.25
Manaea, Sean	R-L	6-5	235	2-1-92	0	1	5.14	2	2	0	0	7	9	5	4	1	6	11	.310	.385	.250	14.14	7.71
2-team total (7 Midland)					6	1	2.36	9	9	0	0	50	43	16	13	4	21	62	—	—	—	11.23	3.81
McCarthy, Kevin	R-R	6-3	200	2-22-92	1	0	5.71	11	0	0	0	17	24	11	11	1	8	9	.329	.289	.371	4.67	4.15
Medlen, Kris	B-R	5-10	190	10-7-85	0	1	3.00	3	3	0	0	15	13	8	5	2	4	11	.228	.294	.130	6.60	2.40
Murray, Matt	R-R	6-3	240	12-28-89	6	3	4.19	23	7	0	1	73	80	41	34	8	24	54	.278	.314	.243	6.66	2.96
Nina, Aroni	R-R	6-4	180	4-9-90	4	4	5.15	43	0	0	9	51	47	36	29	2	46	50	.244	.226	.260	8.88	8.17
Peterson, Mark	R-R	6-0	190	9-7-90	4	1	2.82	39	1	0	4	73	72	27	23	7	27	44	.258	.271	.247	5.40	3.31
Pounders, Brooks	R-R	6-4	270	9-26-90	3	4	2.19	8	8	0	0	49	39	16	12	3	19	32	.223	.226	.220	5.84	3.47
Pruneda, Benino	R-R	5-9	170	8-8-88	2	0	3.76	31	0	0	2	38	36	18	16	1	19	34	.254	.354	.169	7.98	4.46
Redman, Reid	R-R	6-2	220		0	0	3.63	9	0	0	1	17	18	7	7	4	1	14	.246	.250	.242	7.27	0.52
Reed, Cody	L-L	6-5	220	4-15-93	2	2	3.45	5	5	0	0	29	26	16	11	3	8	19	.239	.243	.236	5.97	2.51
Rico, Luis	L-L	6-1	175	11-29-91	0	0	4.50	1	0	0	0	4	4	2	2	0	1	3	.250	.143	.333	6.75	2.25

Pitching

Pitching	B-T	HT	WT	DOB	W	L	ERA	G	GS	CG	SV	IP	H	R	ER	HR	BB	SO	AVG	vLH	vRH	K/9	BB/9
Selman, Sam	R-L	6-3	195	11-14-90	3	5	5.27	41	0	0	3	56	56	39	33	3	42	69	.262	.211	.287	11.02	6.71
Sparkman, Glenn	B-R	6-2	210	5-11-92	2	2	3.60	4	4	0	0	20	17	9	8	1	9	21	.233	.306	.162	9.45	4.05
Stout, Eric	L-L	6-3	185	3-27-93	0	1	7.71	1	0	0	0	2	5	2	2	0	1	2	.455	.333	.600	7.71	3.86
Stumpf, Daniel	L-L	6-2	200	1-4-91	5	4	3.57	42	1	0	3	71	55	31	28	6	31	76	.212	.167	.245	9.68	3.95
Sulbaran, J.C.	R-R	6-2	220	11-9-89	4	7	4.80	20	15	0	0	90	100	50	48	17	35	66	.282	.322	.241	6.60	3.50
Vargas, Jason	L-L	6-0	215	2-2-83	1	0	3.38	1	1	0	0	5	7	2	2	2	2	2	.318	.400	.250	3.38	3.38
Williams, Ali	R-R	6-2	185	7-8-89	1	1	7.04	19	0	0	0	23	18	18	18	4	20	16	.209	.256	.163	6.26	7.83
Zimmer, Kyle	R-R	6-3	215	9-13-91	2	5	2.81	15	7	0	3	48	42	20	15	4	14	51	.235	.217	.250	9.56	2.63

Fielding

Catcher	PCT	G	PO	A	E	DP	PB
De La Rosa	.971	10	96	5	3	0	0
Evans	.988	55	366	36	5	6	4
Gibbs	1.000	16	113	5	0	0	6
Morin	.997	45	298	24	1	3	8
Nessy	1.000	17	122	12	0	1	1
Schwindel	.500	1	1	0	1	0	0

First Base	PCT	G	PO	A	E	DP
Fuenmayor	.987	65	502	26	7	45
Liddi	.979	39	261	18	6	27
Morin	1.000	1	3	0	0	1
Schwindel	.992	44	370	20	3	40

Second Base	PCT	G	PO	A	E	DP
Coleman	1.000	2	2	5	0	1
Davis	1.000	4	3	9	0	3
Diekroeger	.985	33	46	82	2	13
Franco	.993	32	58	87	1	26

Furcal	1.000	1	2	1	0	0
Liddi	.976	33	53	70	3	17
Mondesi	.974	18	38	37	2	9
Noriega	1.000	1	2	0	0	
Torres	.993	24	51	85	1	23

Third Base	PCT	G	PO	A	E	DP
Davis	—	1	0	0	0	0
Diekroeger	.909	5	2	8	1	0
Dozier	.924	115	87	182	22	17
Liddi	.961	20	11	38	2	6
Torres	1.000	1	0	1	0	0

Shortstop	PCT	G	PO	A	E	DP
Coleman	.959	24	41	77	5	24
Davis	1.000	3	2	4	0	1
Diekroeger	.973	19	25	48	2	6
Franco	.871	10	6	21	4	2
Furcal	.889	2	2	6	1	1

Mondesi	.953	63	93	169	13	39
Noriega	1.000	2	4	11	0	2
Torres	.982	24	39	71	2	12

Outfield	PCT	G	PO	A	E	DP
Adams	.966	91	193	4	7	1
Bianucci	1.000	7	12	0	0	0
Bonifacio	.975	115	186	7	5	2
Chapman	1.000	19	43	1	0	0
Davis	1.000	1	1	0	0	0
Diekroeger	1.000	2	3	0	0	0
Gibbs	1.000	1	1	0	0	0
Gore	.966	71	142	1	5	0
Liddi	.986	38	66	2	1	0
Morin	—	1	0	0	0	0
Salcedo	1.000	4	10	0	0	0
Starling	1.000	84	194	3	0	1

WILMINGTON BLUE ROCKS
HIGH CLASS A
CAROLINA LEAGUE

Batting	B-T	HT	WT	DOB	AVG	vLH	vRH	G	AB	R	H	2B	3B	HR	RBI	BB	HBP	SH	SF	SO	SB	CS	SLG	OBP
Arteaga, Humberto	R-R	6-1	160	1-23-94	.235	.286	.215	48	179	21	42	7	0	1	16	7	3	4	3	31	3	3	.291	.271
Diekroeger, Kenny	R-R	6-2	190	11-5-90	.270	.286	.267	13	37	2	10	1	0	0	3	1	0	0	1	12	2	0	.297	.282
Downes, Brandon	R-R	6-3	195	9-29-92	.000	—	.000	1	1	0	0	0	0	0	0	0	0	0	0	1	0	0	.000	.000
Escalera, Alfredo	R-R	6-1	186	2-17-95	.206	.259	.186	57	199	18	41	7	2	2	14	17	5	—	0	61	7	3	.291	.285
Evans, Zane	R-R	6-2	210	11-29-91	.271	.250	.276	28	107	12	29	8	0	4	15	6	2	0	1	22	0	0	.458	.319
Furcal, Rafael	B-R	5-8	195	10-24-77	.188	—	.188	4	16	2	3	1	0	0	1	0	0	0	0	2	0	0	.250	.235
Gallagher, Cam	R-R	6-3	210	12-6-92	.245	.308	.223	77	253	24	62	15	0	5	23	28	2	—	2	34	0	0	.364	.323
Garcia, Carlos	R-R	5-10	172	3-18-92	.274	.164	.304	78	307	36	84	11	8	1	26	30	5	7	3	56	21	8	.371	.345
Hernandez, Elier	R-R	6-3	197	11-21-94	.232	.236	.230	50	177	15	41	7	2	1	12	10	4	0	5	47	4	2	.311	.281
Hill, Mike	L-R	6-2	195	1-29-92	.000	—	.000	1	1	0	0	0	0	0	0	0	0	0	0	0	0	0	.000	.000
Kjerstad, Dex	R-R	6-1	210	1-19-92	.247	.293	.231	51	158	12	39	3	1	2	15	7	3	0	2	47	6	5	.316	.288
Lopez, Jack	R-R	5-9	165	12-16-92	.238	.342	.199	116	429	52	102	15	1	6	43	32	7	—	3	88	13	10	.319	.299
Moon, Logan	R-R	6-2	195	2-15-92	.254	.253	.254	121	386	39	98	12	4	0	28	35	0	—	3	93	12	7	.306	.314
Morin, Parker	L-R	5-11	195	7-2-91	.000	.000	.000	3	8	0	0	0	0	0	0	1	0	1	0	2	0	0	.000	.100
Nessy, Santiago	R-R	6-2	230	12-8-92	.232	.283	.211	49	155	12	36	10	0	3	19	11	3	1	1	40	0	0	.355	.294
O'Hearn, Ryan	L-L	6-3	200	7-26-93	.236	.158	.260	46	161	14	38	10	0	8	21	19	0	0	1	54	0	0	.447	.315
Pehl, Robert	R-R	6-1	205	9-23-92	.225	.270	.207	81	258	23	58	8	0	4	22	30	9	0	3	61	2	2	.302	.323
Ramos, Mauricio	R-R	6-1	181	2-2-92	.265	.260	.267	123	468	54	124	22	2	8	59	25	9	—	3	89	1	1	.372	.313
Rockett, Daniel	R-R	6-2	200	11-9-90	.141	.154	.139	27	85	8	12	4	1	1	6	11	1	1	1	23	0	2	.247	.245
Schwindel, Frank	R-R	6-1	205	6-29-92	.277	.304	.268	73	274	30	76	28	1	3	32	12	4	—	2	52	0	1	.420	.315
Starling, Bubba	R-R	6-4	210	8-3-92	.386	.333	.400	12	44	6	17	4	0	2	12	7	0	0	0	17	2	1	.614	.471
Stubbs, Cody	L-L	6-4	215	1-14-91	.283	.200	.299	35	127	15	36	8	2	4	17	7	1	—	1	33	0	1	.472	.324
Taylor, Dominique	R-R	6-1	190	8-11-92	.215	.245	.204	110	349	45	75	17	3	1	26	21	9	—	3	83	10	4	.289	.275
Torres, Ramon	B-R	5-10	145	2-2-93	.257	.258	.257	71	288	29	74	10	3	1	18	11	1	—	0	32	14	7	.323	.287
Villegas, Luis	R-R	5-10	170	12-2-92	.278	.333	.250	6	18	0	5	1	0	0	2	2	0	0	0	2	0	0	.333	.350

Pitching	B-T	HT	WT	DOB	W	L	ERA	G	GS	CG	SV	IP	H	R	ER	HR	BB	SO	AVG	vLH	vRH	K/9	BB/9
Alvarez, Matt	R-R	6-2	190	1-11-91	2	2	3.66	32	0	0	2	52	44	23	21	3	27	49	.234	.232	.236	8.54	4.70
Beal, Evan	R-R	6-5	195	8-2-93	0	2	2.77	11	0	0	0	26	30	10	8	1	11	19	.291	.341	.254	6.58	3.81
Caramo, Yender	R-R	6-0	175	8-25-91	6	7	3.68	30	10	0	0	111	125	47	38	1	13	57	.283	.285	.282	4.62	1.05
Cordero, Estarlin	L-L	6-0	145	3-3-93	4	2	2.33	35	0	0	11	54	41	15	14	2	21	42	.211	.247	.188	7.00	3.50
Deshazier, Torey	R-R	6-0	160	9-16-93	0	0	10.80	1	0	0	0	2	2	2	2	0	3	0	.286	.667	.000	0.00	16.20
Edwards, Andrew	R-R	6-6	265	10-7-91	0	2	3.86	29	0	0	2	42	33	19	18	2	19	30	.223	.224	.222	6.43	4.07
Farrell, Luke	R-R	6-6	210	6-7-91	2	0	3.03	7	3	0	2	30	27	12	10	0	6	41	.250	.245	.255	12.44	1.82
Fernandez, Pedro	R-R	6-0	175	5-25-94	0	6	8.82	7	7	0	0	33	56	34	32	2	8	25	.376	.371	.379	6.89	2.20
Goudeau, Ashton	R-R	6-6	205	7-23-92	4	4	3.26	24	5	0	1	69	69	32	25	8	10	61	.260	.250	.270	7.96	1.30
Green, Nick	R-L	6-2	190	9-21-90	2	1	6.66	17	0	0	2	24	34	20	18	3	5	21	.340	.350	.333	7.77	1.85
Junis, Jake	R-R	6-2	225	9-16-92	5	11	3.64	26	26	0	0	156	145	71	63	11	29	123	.251	.273	.229	7.11	1.68
Lovvorn, Zach	R-R	6-0	185	5-26-94	4	5	3.93	12	11	1	0	66	65	31	29	2	19	35	.258	.235	.278	4.75	2.58
Manaea, Sean	R-L	6-1	235	2-1-92	1	0	3.66	4	4	0	0	20	22	12	8	4	5	22	.297	.400	.227	10.07	1.83
McCarthy, Kevin	R-R	6-3	180	2-22-92	3	3	1.64	16	0	0	4	33	24	7	6	2	5	23	.205	.263	.150	6.27	1.36
Mills, Alec	R-R	6-4	185	11-30-91	7	7	3.02	21	21	1	0	113	122	42	38	3	14	111	.271	.270	.272	8.81	1.11

Pitching	B-T	HT	WT	DOB	W	L	ERA	G	GS	CG	SV	IP	H	R	ER	HR	BB	SO	AVG	vLH	vRH	K/9	BB/9
Pounders, Brooks	R-R	6-4	270	9-26-90	0	1	5.40	2	2	0	0	10	12	6	6	1	1	10	.316	.231	.360	9.00	0.90
Pruneda, Benino	R-R	5-9	170	8-8-88	1	0	0.00	5	0	0	0	7	1	0	0	0	4	7	.048	.000	.100	8.59	4.91
Reed, Cody	L-L	6-5	220	4-15-93	5	5	2.14	13	10	1	1	67	62	19	16	3	18	65	.243	.162	.276	8.69	2.41
Rico, Luis	L-L	6-1	175	11-29-93	7	8	3.93	25	14	1	4	94	86	44	41	6	46	91	.248	.288	.227	8.71	4.40
Skoglund, Eric	L-L	6-7	200	10-26-92	6	3	3.52	15	15	1	0	84	83	36	33	2	11	66	.260	.267	.256	7.04	1.17
Strahm, Matt	R-L	6-4	180	11-12-91	1	6	2.78	15	11	0	1	68	48	25	21	7	19	83	.194	.158	.211	10.99	2.51
Yambati, Robinson	R-R	6-3	185	1-15-91	0	2	5.12	31	0	0	6	46	43	29	26	2	20	33	.251	.273	.234	6.50	3.94

Fielding

Catcher	PCT	G	PO	A	E	DP	PB
Evans	.979	15	121	17	3	3	1
Gallagher	.993	71	488	73	4	6	9
Morin	1.000	3	10	3	0	0	0
Nessy	.977	46	306	40	8	4	7
Schwindel	.955	3	19	2	1	0	1
Villegas	.980	6	44	5	1	0	2

First Base	PCT	G	PO	A	E	DP
O'Hearn	.986	42	349	13	5	26
Pehl	.996	25	222	7	1	15
Schwindel	.995	67	553	47	3	51
Stubbs	1.000	8	48	1	0	2

Second Base	PCT	G	PO	A	E	DP
Arteaga	.981	19	39	62	2	14
Diekroeger	1.000	5	7	18	0	4
Furcal	1.000	2	1	4	0	1
Garcia	.966	44	80	91	6	20
Lopez	1.000	19	32	41	0	8
Torres	.968	50	84	126	7	30

Third Base	PCT	G	PO	A	E	DP
Diekroeger	1.000	2	5	3	0	0
Hill	1.000	1	0	2	0	0
Pehl	.913	19	12	30	4	5
Ramos	.966	119	87	222	11	18

Shortstop	PCT	G	PO	A	E	DP
Arteaga	.948	26	40	69	6	11

Furcal	1.000	2	5	3	0	1
Lopez	.948	94	140	228	20	42
Torres	.967	18	31	56	3	15

Outfield	PCT	G	PO	A	E	DP
Downes	1.000	1	2	0	0	0
Escalera	.973	51	106	3	3	0
Hernandez	.974	45	110	2	3	0
Kjerstad	.989	49	92	2	1	1
Moon	.972	119	230	12	7	0
Rockett	1.000	27	44	2	0	2
Starling	1.000	11	26	1	0	0
Stubbs	.944	14	17	0	1	0
Taylor	.987	108	222	4	3	1

LEXINGTON LEGENDS

SOUTH ATLANTIC LEAGUE

LOW CLASS A

Batting	B-T	HT	WT	DOB	AVG	vLH	vRH	G	AB	R	H	2B	3B	HR	RBI	BB	HBP	SH	SF	SB	CS	SLG	OBP
Arteaga, Humberto	R-R	6-1	160	1-23-94	.259	.265	.256	70	286	37	74	12	2	1	28	15	2	9	3	46	15	8	.325	.297
Bailey, Austin	L-R	5-10	160	7-3-92	.318	.455	.260	30	110	19	35	10	2	3	17	10	3	0	1	13	3	2	.527	.387
Bien, Brian	R-R	6-0	175	9-2-92	.421	.750	.333	5	19	4	8	1	0	0	0	1	0	0	0	1	2	0	.474	.450
Castellano, Angelo	R-R	6-0	170	1-13-95	.125	.000	.143	4	16	1	2	0	0	0	1	0	0	1	0	0	0		.125	.176
Clark, DonAndre	B-R	5-10	180	7-31-92	.267	.267	.267	51	165	23	44	5	0	0	7	9	2	0	0	25	10	4	.297	.313
Davis, Logan	L-R	6-2	175	8-23-91	.133	.111	.137	24	60	5	8	1	0	0	2	6	1	2	0	10	2	1	.150	.224
Downes, Brandon	R-R	6-3	195	9-29-92	.251	.269	.244	106	391	52	98	29	3	14	59	31	6	5	4	115	19	7	.448	.313
Duenez, Samir	L-R	6-1	195	6-11-96	.266	.298	.256	101	361	47	96	13	4	1	37	24	2	7	2	33	11	5	.332	.314
Escalera, Alfredo	R-R	6-1	180	2-17-95	.313	.323	.310	64	262	40	82	13	3	8	33	10	9	1	3	58	12	2	.477	.356
Franco, Wander	R-R	6-2	170	12-13-94	.268	.319	.247	123	477	62	128	30	2	10	74	21	9	2	3	83	2	9	.403	.310
Garcia, Carlos	R-R	5-10	172	3-18-92	.254	.200	.275	35	126	18	32	4	0	2	11	17	2	3	1	22	21	5	.333	.349
Hernandez, Elier	R-R	6-3	197	11-21-94	.290	.365	.264	74	290	37	84	19	2	5	42	14	5	3	2	73	6	5	.421	.331
Hill, Mike	L-R	6-2	195	1-29-92	.252	.203	.266	90	302	49	76	18	5	6	37	23	2	1	4	81	11	3	.404	.305
Johnson, Chad	R-R	6-0	190	5-31-94	.284	.224	.301	77	264	36	75	20	1	3	32	50	2	2	1	81	1	0	.402	.401
Miller, Anderson	L-L	6-3	208	5-6-94	.260	.275	.256	43	169	15	44	8	1	2	21	14	1	0	1	28	0	1	.355	.319
O'Hearn, Ryan	L-L	6-3	200	7-26-93	.277	.259	.284	81	314	44	87	11	0	19	56	36	2	0	4	87	7	2	.494	.351
Pollock, Kyle	R-R	6-0	200	8-15-92	.214	.318	.167	22	70	3	15	6	0	0	9	6	1	1	0	22	1	1	.300	.286
Rivera, Alexis	L-L	6-2	225	6-17-94	.219	.182	.235	34	114	12	25	5	2	3	16	8	2	1	0	28	3	2	.377	.282
Toups, Corey	R-R	5-10	170	2-12-93	.291	.256	.306	102	388	75	113	27	5	7	44	44	6	2	4	82	31	5	.441	.369
Valenzuela, Luis	L-R	5-10	150	8-25-93	.333	.196	.389	48	177	30	59	10	3	3	15	8	0	3	0	28	8	1	.475	.362
2-team total (6 Rome)					.343	—	—	54	198	31	68	11	3	4	17	9	0	3	0	30	8	3	.490	.372
Vallot, Chase	R-R	6-0	215	8-21-96	.219	.215	.220	80	279	46	61	13	3	13	40	41	8	1	4	105	1	0	.427	.331
Villegas, Luis	R-R	5-10	170	12-2-92	.267	.321	.241	26	86	10	23	6	1	4	15	10	2	0	1	19	2	0	.500	.354

Pitching	B-T	HT	WT	DOB	W	L	ERA	G	GS	CG	SV	IP	H	R	ER	HR	BB	SO	AVG	vLH	vRH	K/9	BB/9
Beal, Evan	R-R	6-5	195	8-2-93	2	1	2.00	22	0	0	5	36	27	12	8	3	17	30	.206	.217	.197	7.50	4.25
Blewett, Scott	R-R	6-6	210	4-10-96	3	5	5.20	18	18	0	0	81	88	51	47	6	24	60	.272	.261	.281	6.64	2.66
Davis, Tripp	L-L	6-1	200	2-12-91	0	0	0.00	2	0	0	0	4	2	0	0	0	3	2	.167	.400	.000	4.50	6.75
Deshazier, Torey	R-R	6-0	160	9-16-93	4	5	5.92	24	9	0	1	87	98	58	57	11	43	68	.286	.296	.277	7.06	4.47
Fernandez, Pedro	R-R	6-0	175	5-25-94	6	2	3.12	18	13	0	0	78	53	31	27	2	27	89	.191	.190	.192	10.27	3.12
Goudeau, Ashton	R-R	6-6	205	7-23-92	1	0	3.06	7	0	0	1	18	17	7	6	0	2	21	.243	.324	.152	10.70	1.02
Green, Nick	R-L	6-2	190	9-21-90	0	2	7.43	6	0	0	0	13	20	12	11	2	3	10	.351	.263	.395	6.75	2.03
Griffin, Foster	L-L	6-3	200	7-27-95	4	6	5.44	22	22	0	0	103	123	73	62	8	35	71	.296	.269	.307	6.22	3.07
Guevara, Cruz	L-L	6-0	155	5-29-94	0	0	8.10	3	0	0	0	3	7	5	3	0	3	2	.389	.500	.333	5.40	8.10
Henry, Brennan	L-L	6-4	200	10-23-91	2	3	4.00	19	0	0	0	36	35	20	16	5	14	21	.259	.289	.247	5.25	3.50
Lovvorn, Zach	R-R	6-0	185	5-26-94	5	6	4.20	14	13	0	1	71	87	42	33	5	15	50	.302	.322	.283	6.37	1.91
Marte, Yunior	R-R	6-2	165	2-2-95	4	5	6.44	18	11	0	0	66	80	59	47	4	38	60	.302	.248	.347	8.22	5.21
McCarthy, Kevin	R-R	6-3	200	2-22-92	1	1	1.50	6	0	0	2	12	10	3	2	0	1	8	.222	.167	.259	6.00	0.75
Newberry, Jake	R-R	6-2	195	11-20-94	4	2	5.04	35	0	0	8	61	66	38	34	4	18	55	.277	.264	.288	8.16	2.67
Ogando, Emilio	L-L	6-2	180	8-13-93	5	8	4.19	26	4	0	0	92	100	59	43	8	40	78	.278	.245	.291	7.60	3.90
Ray, Corey	R-R	6-4	175	12-15-92	5	7	6.06	25	18	0	0	107	138	85	72	6	42	88	.317	.328	.304	7.40	3.53
Rodgers, Colin	L-L	5-10	181	12-2-93	3	11	5.02	24	8	0	0	95	124	76	53	2	43	57	.312	.290	.322	5.40	4.07
Stephenson, Niklas	R-R	6-2	195	11-6-93	4	9	5.73	29	10	0	2	104	107	76	66	13	51	61	.272	.253	.284	5.30	4.43
Stout, Eric	L-L	6-3	185	3-27-93	0	0	3.26	16	0	0	3	30	24	11	11	2	6	15	.224	.219	.227	4.45	1.78
Strahm, Matt	R-L	6-4	180	11-12-91	2	1	2.08	14	0	0	4	26	12	7	6	1	12	38	.140	.103	.158	13.15	4.15
Tenuta, Matt	L-L	6-4	225	12-16-93	2	6	4.25	13	12	0	0	59	62	30	28	7	22	39	.273	.259	.278	5.92	3.34
Zimmer, Kyle	R-R	6-3	215	9-13-91	1	0	1.13	9	0	0	0	16	11	3	2	1	0	20	.190	.136	.222	11.81	3.38

Fielding

Catcher	PCT	G	PO	A	E	DP	PB
Hill	.981	8	39	12	1	2	4
Johnson	.972	50	297	50	10	3	6
Pollock	.982	19	140	25	3	1	3
Vallot	.975	44	284	24	8	1	12
Villegas	.985	23	169	23	3	2	4

First Base	PCT	G	PO	A	E	DP
Duenez	.961	38	311	12	13	23
Franco	1.000	3	19	0	0	1
Hill	.982	27	258	16	5	16
O'Hearn	.986	64	607	37	9	31
Rivera	.974	8	72	3	2	2

Second Base	PCT	G	PO	A	E	DP
Arteaga	1.000	1	0	2	0	0
Bailey	.968	23	34	56	3	8
Bien	1.000	1	5	3	0	1

	PCT	G	PO	A	E	DP
Castellano	1.000	1	1	4	0	0
Davis	.973	14	18	54	2	7
Garcia	.943	21	30	53	5	7
Toups	.978	66	123	182	7	29
Valenzuela	.986	16	26	42	1	6

Third Base	PCT	G	PO	A	E	DP
Castellano	1.000	1	1	1	0	0
Davis	1.000	3	2	5	0	1
Franco	.933	91	57	180	17	6
Garcia	.828	13	6	18	5	1
Hill	.954	34	25	79	5	5
Valenzuela	1.000	1		4	0	0

Shortstop	PCT	G	PO	A	E	DP
Arteaga	.967	67	100	191	10	26
Bien	1.000	3	10	10	0	2
Castellano	1.000	2	2	5	0	2

	PCT	G	PO	A	E	DP
Davis	—	1	0	0	0	0
Hill	.929	3	6	7	1	2
Toups	.928	36	49	93	11	13
Valenzuela	.953	30	56	86	7	14

Outfield	PCT	G	PO	A	E	DP
Bailey	1.000	5	4	2	0	0
Clark	.966	50	83	3	3	0
Davis	1.000	2	3	0	0	0
Downes	.981	102	250	11	5	2
Duenez	.985	49	60	4	1	0
Escalera	.932	63	116	7	9	2
Hernandez	.942	73	110	3	7	1
Hill	1.000	16	23	1	0	0
Miller	.990	43	96	4	1	2
O'Hearn	1.000	3	9	0	0	0
Rivera	1.000	23	32	1	0	0

BURLINGTON ROYALS   ROOKIE

APPALACHIAN LEAGUE

Batting	B-T	HT	WT	DOB	AVG	vLH	vRH	G	AB	R	H	2B	3B	HR	RBI	BB	HBP	SH	SF	SO	SB	CS	SLG	OBP
Bailey, Austin	L-R	5-10	160	7-3-92	.308	.345	.299	35	146	21	45	8	1	3	19	8	2	1	0	17	4	1	.438	.353
Bien, Brian	R-R	6-0	175	9-2-92	.302	.297	.304	41	162	23	49	4	0	0	26	7	2	3	0	18	6	2	.327	.339
Castellano, Angelo	R-R	6-0	170	1-13-95	.230	.235	.228	58	213	24	49	4	2	0	17	13	3	9	1	26	2	2	.268	.283
Dulin, Brandon	L-R	6-3	225	12-29-92	.280	.265	.284	59	225	41	63	17	3	10	34	22	6	0	0	55	3	1	.516	.360
Fernandez, Xavier	R-R	5-11	197	7-15-95	.329	.432	.291	42	140	21	46	10	1	4	27	10	7	0	2	19	0	0	.500	.396
Frabasilio, Colton	R-R	6-2	205	4-18-93	.293	.370	.275	42	147	24	43	9	0	3	13	13	1	1	0	21	0	0	.415	.354
Johnson, Ben	R-R	6-0	185	5-4-94	.282	.265	.286	53	188	22	53	9	5	6	28	17	7	0	2	36	1	2	.479	.360
King, Riley	R-L	6-4	210	4-23-94	.167	.321	.122	40	126	17	21	3	1	1	15	15	3	2	3	44	4	1	.262	.265
Martinez, Jose	B-R	5-10	150	8-15-96	.243	.244	.243	57	218	27	53	4	1	1	24	20	1	6	3	30	4	6	.284	.306
Miller, Anderson	L-L	6-3	208	5-6-94	.342	.143	.387	10	38	6	13	3	0	2	7	0	1	0	0	7	3	0	.579	.359
Newman, Alex	R-R	6-1	200	12-7-92	.164	.250	.128	22	67	6	11	1	1	0	7	7	0	1	0	22	1	1	.209	.243
Stanley, Tanner	L-L	5-10	180	9-12-93	.214	.231	.211	20	70	8	15	1	0	1	7	5	2	1	1	5	3	0	.271	.282
Stover, Trey	R-R	5-10	175	6-10-93	.195	.240	.177	26	87	9	17	2	0	0	6	9	0	3	1	18	2	0	.218	.268
Thomasson, Brandon	R-R	6-4	220	3-15-92	.246	.174	.273	47	167	31	41	12	2	9	24	17	2	0	2	48	1	2	.503	.319
Villegas, Luis	R-R	5-10	170	12-2-92	.667	—	.667	1	3	1	2	0	0	0	1	1	0	0	0	0	0	0	.667	.750
Viloria, Meibrys	L-R	5-11	175	2-15-97	.260	.267	.258	45	150	20	39	0	0	6	16	11	1	2	2	23	0	0	.260	.335
Willis, Luke	R-R	5-11	190	11-9-92	.260	.188	.284	31	127	16	33	1	2	0	7	6	1	1	0	18	8	1	.299	.299

Pitching	B-T	HT	WT	DOB	W	L	ERA	G	GS	CG	SV	IP	H	R	ER	HR	BB	SO	AVG	vLH	vRH	K/9	BB/9
Bodner, Jacob	R-R	5-10	185	1-31-93	2	0	0.77	16	0	0	5	23	15	2	2	0	3	26	.188	.250	.136	10.03	1.16
Camacho, Enmanuel	L-L	6-0	160	1-9-95	3	3	5.76	12	7	0	0	50	77	39	32	6	13	35	.352	.434	.325	6.30	2.34
Concepcion, Daniel	R-R	6-4	230	9-3-93	2	0	0.90	4	0	0	0	10	8	1	1	0	1	9	.229	.300	.200	8.10	0.90
Cramer, Gabe	R-R	6-2	205	11-1-94	1	2	7.43	12	0	0	0	13	16	11	11	1	4	17	.291	.250	.314	11.48	2.70
Darhower, Chase	R-R	6-4	215	1-12-93	4	3	4.94	12	1	0	0	47	53	39	26	8	19	34	.282	.318	.252	6.46	3.61
Davis, Andre	L-L	6-6	230	9-29-93	3	1	7.16	12	0	0	0	28	37	22	22	4	18	27	.336	.417	.297	8.78	5.86
Ditman, Matt	R-R	6-1	205	8-13-92	2	3	1.50	16	0	0	4	24	22	15	4	2	8	20	.244	.238	.250	7.50	3.00
Feliz, Igol	R-R	6-3	195	5-31-93	4	6	3.32	13	10	0	0	62	53	37	23	3	27	29	.226	.223	.228	4.19	3.90
Flecha, Christian	L-L	6-2	150	5-9-95	0	1	5.88	14	0	0	1	34	35	29	22	5	10	26	.259	.276	.247	6.95	2.67
Kalish, Jake	B-L	6-2	210	7-9-91	3	1	2.20	10	1	0	1	29	20	9	7	1	3	31	.189	.139	.214	9.73	0.94
Luna, Alex	R-R	6-4	200	2-11-93	1	3	4.54	15	4	0	0	42	50	25	21	3	6	24	.296	.257	.326	5.18	1.30
Markus, Joey	R-L	6-7	220	5-29-96	0	4	9.87	12	5	0	0	31	35	35	34	0	29	30	.292	.368	.256	8.71	8.42
McCoy, Mark	L-L	5-11	185	4-30-94	1	1	2.17	13	0	0	1	29	22	8	7	0	11	11	.208	.226	.200	9.00	3.41
Pinto, Julio	R-R	6-3	185	11-18-95	3	2	4.14	10	10	0	0	41	40	23	19	2	17	30	.252	.197	.290	6.53	3.70
Russell, Ashe	R-R	6-4	201	8-28-96	0	3	4.21	11	11	0	0	36	32	18	17	8	13	24	.235	.288	.186	5.94	3.22
Sandness, Eric	R-R	6-6	210	10-14-94	0	0	4.81	14	0	0	0	24	35	17	13	1	19	21	.337	.255	.404	7.77	7.03
Tenuta, Matt	L-L	6-4		2-12-96	1	1	3.33	7	7	1	0	24	24	10	9	2	7	21	.255	.211	.267	7.77	2.59
Watson, Nolan	R-R	6-2	195	1-25-97	0	3	4.91	11	11	0	0	29	39	24	16	2	11	16	.320	.302	.339	4.91	3.38
Way, Cole	L-L	6-11	235	10-23-91	1	0	7.11	3	1	0	0	13	14	10	10	2	6	10	.286	.167	.324	7.11	4.26

Fielding

Catcher	PCT	G	PO	A	E	DP	PB
Fernandez	.982	30	186	32	4	1	5
Frabasilio	.991	16	99	14	1	1	1
Villegas	1.000	1	9	1	0	1	0
Viloria	.978	27	148	27	4	1	3

First Base	PCT	G	PO	A	E	DP
Dulin	.965	53	486	35	19	35
Fernandez	.857	1	6	0	1	0
Thomasson	.976	14	114	10	3	11

Second Base	PCT	G	PO	A	E	DP
Bailey	.913	26	44	72	11	10

	PCT	G	PO	A	E	DP
Bien	.970	34	69	94	5	20
Castellano	1.000	3	5	11	0	4
Stover	.903	5	9	19	3	3

Third Base	PCT	G	PO	A	E	DP
Bien	.500	1	0	1	1	0
Castellano	.934	48	30	84	8	9
Stover	.820	20	16	25	9	3

Shortstop	PCT	G	PO	A	E	DP
Bien	1.000	5	12	12	0	3
Castellano	.955	7	5	16	1	3
Martinez	.962	57	76	175	10	26

Outfield	PCT	G	PO	A	E	DP
Bailey	.750	3	3	0	1	0
Frabasilio	.950	14	18	1	1	0
Johnson	.992	53	121	4	1	1
King	.972	38	67	3	2	0
Miller	1.000	9	23	0	0	0
Newman	.931	21	26	1	2	0
Stanley	1.000	20	51	1	0	0
Thomasson	.978	23	43	2	1	1
Willis	.984	30	63	0	1	0

AZL ROYALS
ARIZONA LEAGUE

ROOKIE

Batting	B-T	HT	WT	DOB	AVG	vLH	vRH	G	AB	R	H	2B	3B	HR	RBI	BB	HBP	SH	SF	SO	SB	CS	SLG	OBP
Aracena, Ricky	B-R	5-8	160	10-2-97	.294	.222	.308	26	109	14	32	2	2	0	9	2	0	6	0	21	8	3	.349	.306
Arroyo, Michael	R-R	6-0	181	12-31-95	.235	.125	.250	26	68	12	16	6	0	0	9	5	8	0	0	20	1	1	.324	.358
Cancel, Gabriel	R-R	6-1	185	12-8-96	.209	.200	.210	34	134	16	28	5	4	2	14	10	3	3	0	44	6	1	.351	.279
Clemmons, Leland	R-R	5-9	170	6-17-93	.312	.308	.313	32	77	19	24	4	3	5	21	15	4	0	1	28	7	2	.636	.443
Close, Alex	R-R	6-3	225	3-19-93	.173	.250	.164	28	75	7	13	2	0	3	9	8	2	1	3	26	2	0	.320	.261
Diaz, Carlos	B-R	5-8	145	11-15-92	.301	.286	.304	39	146	30	44	3	0	0	15	4	3	5	2	13	8	2	.322	.329
Esposito, Nate	R-R	5-11	180	6-25-93	.250	.125	.268	27	64	11	16	4	0	0	5	9	4	0	0	17	3	1	.313	.377
Franco, Angel	B-R	5-10	155	5-23-90	.357	.500	.333	4	14	2	5	0	0	0	1	2	0	0	0	1	0	0	.357	.438
Fuentes, Reymond	L-L	6-0	160	2-12-91	.357	—	.357	4	14	7	5	3	1	0	1	3	0	0	0	5	0	0	.714	.471
Jones, Cody	B-R	5-11	170	5-25-93	.545	—	.545	3	11	4	6	0	1	0	3	2	0	0	0	1	2	0	.727	.615
Lara, Luis	R-R	5-11	170	3-2-95	.278	.333	.267	18	36	3	10	0	0	0	2	5	1	0	0	8	2	2	.278	.381
Martin, Rudy	L-L	5-7	150	1-31-96	.338	.227	.360	40	133	41	45	6	9	1	11	34	3	1	2	28	14	3	.541	.477
Martinez, Jose	R-R	6-7	210	7-25-88	.333	—	.333	4	15	2	5	2	0	0	2	1	0	0	1	0	0	1	.467	.353
McCray, Jonathan	B-R	5-10	180	1-8-95	.267	.143	.285	44	172	26	46	6	3	4	28	14	0	2	2	39	8	2	.407	.319
Melo, Yeison	R-R	6-1	180	7-30-95	.318	.238	.329	43	173	17	55	8	4	1	34	7	1	5	2	23	4	0	.428	.344
Miller, Anderson	L-L	6-3	208	5-6-94	.333	—	.333	1	3	1	1	0	0	0	1	0	0	0	0	0	0	0	.333	.333
Nottebrok, Logan	R-R	6-4	230	3-24-92	.286	.333	.273	3	14	3	4	1	0	0	5	0	1	0	0	5	0	0	.357	.333
Olloque, Manny	R-R	6-2	165	5-11-96	.169	.100	.184	18	59	7	10	2	0	0	3	4	1	2	0	10	0	2	.203	.234
Ostrich, Taylor	L-R	6-3	220	9-16-92	.308	.310	.308	50	185	23	57	13	2	0	27	34	7	0	2	37	2	1	.400	.430
Rivera, Emmanuel	R-R	6-1	193	6-29-96	.174	.143	.178	38	115	13	20	5	0	0	14	23	1	1	0	32	9	4	.217	.317
Sanchez, Jose	L-L	5-10	155	7-21-94	.266	.200	.278	20	64	10	17	2	0	0	12	7	0	1	1	12	2	3	.297	.333
Stanley, Tanner	L-L	5-10	180	1-12-93	.189	.200	.188	10	37	3	7	2	0	0	4	4	1	0	0	3	1	0	.243	.286
Vasquez, Cristhian	L-L	6-0	175	9-11-96	.182	.148	.189	42	154	28	28	4	2	1	10	22	1	4	0	40	9	1	.253	.288
Willis, Luke	R-R	5-11	190	11-9-92	.313	.250	.318	16	48	9	15	3	0	0	9	7	2	0	1	8	3	0	.375	.414

Pitching	B-T	HT	WT	DOB	W	L	ERA	G	GS	CG	SV	IP	H	R	ER	HR	BB	SO	AVG	vLH	vRH	K/9	BB/9
Andros, Nick	L-L	6-4	230	11-21-92	0	0	0.00	11	0	0	3	13	5	0	0	0	2	15	.119	.222	.091	10.38	1.38
Brickhouse, Bryan	R-R	6-0	195	6-6-92	0	0	2.84	4	4	0	0	6	5	2	2	1	6	7	.217	.125	.267	9.95	8.53
Carvalho, Tyler	R-R	5-11	160	12-15-94	3	1	4.02	12	0	0	4	16	22	14	7	0	3	10	.324	.364	.304	5.74	1.72
Cepin, Reinaldo	L-L	6-1	160	1-10-94	1	1	3.57	14	0	0	3	18	25	9	7	2	5	11	.338	.667	.232	5.60	2.55
Cramer, Gabe	R-R	6-2	205	11-1-94	1	1	1.93	4	0	0	1	5	2	1	1	0	2	8	.125	.000	.154	15.43	3.86
Familia, Felix	L-L	6-0	170	11-28-95	5	0	5.22	14	1	0	2	40	47	33	23	4	12	28	.281	.333	.270	6.35	2.72
Freeman, Jason	L-R	6-4	200	10-3-91	3	0	0.44	13	0	0	1	21	13	2	1	0	7	28	.173	.136	.189	12.19	3.05
Garabito, Gerson	R-R	6-0	160	8-19-95	3	2	4.11	14	11	0	0	57	52	32	26	2	19	42	.242	.296	.209	6.63	3.00
Hernandez, Arnaldo	R-R	6-0	175	2-9-96	7	3	2.82	14	10	0	0	67	60	25	21	3	5	68	.235	.183	.260	9.13	0.67
Hope, Carter	L-R	6-3	195	2-5-95	0	0	5.91	3	2	0	1	11	13	7	7	1	1	5	.289	.250	.303	4.22	0.84
Kalish, Jake	B-L	6-2	210	7-9-91	0	2	5.40	4	0	0	0	5	5	3	3	0	2	6	.278	.200	.308	10.80	3.60
Kimber, Eric	R-R	5-10	165	8-25-92	1	0	4.60	11	0	0	1	16	18	10	8	0	3	14	.300	.333	.282	8.04	1.72
Kubat, Kyle	L-L	6-1	195	12-4-92	4	1	0.76	12	0	0	3	35	26	5	3	0	3	26	.202	.156	.216	6.62	0.76
Manaea, Sean	R-L	6-5	235	2-1-92	0	0	1.80	1	1	0	0	5	2	1	1	1	1	6	.118	.000	.143	10.80	1.80
McCoy, Mark	L-L	5-11	185	4-30-94	1	0	0.00	1	0	0	0	2	2	0	0	0	1	3	.250	.000	.286	13.50	4.50
Pena, Yimauri	R-R	6-2	160	10-15-93	5	0	2.43	14	9	0	0	56	61	16	15	3	6	34	.286	.274	.293	5.50	0.97
Pounders, Brooks	R-R	6-4	270	9-26-90	0	0	1.50	4	4	0	0	6	5	4	1	0	0	5	.217	.364	.083	7.50	0.00
Rodriguez, Jorge	L-L	6-0	160	6-30-96	2	4	4.38	12	10	0	0	49	51	32	24	2	19	53	.267	.217	.283	9.67	3.47
Staumont, Josh	R-R	6-2	190	12-21-93	0	0	0.00	4	3	0	0	9	3	0	0	0	8	7	.103	.000	.120	7.27	8.31
Stout, Eric	L-L	6-3	185	3-27-93	0	0	0.00	2	0	0	0	5	4	1	0	0	0	3	.267	.250	.273	5.79	0.00
Tenuta, Matt	L-L	6-4	225	12-16-93	0	0	0.00	1	0	0	0	1	1	0	0	0	0	1	.250	—	.250	9.00	0.00
Terrero, Franco	R-R	6-0	180	5-20-95	4	1	2.74	14	1	0	5	46	42	19	14	1	6	51	.231	.197	.250	9.98	1.17
Veras, Jose	R-R	6-1	170	7-15-94	0	0	3.05	13	0	0	3	21	27	10	7	1	3	21	.310	.419	.250	9.15	1.31

Fielding

Catcher	PCT	G	PO	A	E	DP	PB
Arroyo	.979	26	163	25	4	2	4
Close	.970	10	61	3	2	0	0
Esposito	.994	27	153	27	1	1	3
Lara	.953	18	75	6	4	1	0

First Base	PCT	G	PO	A	E	DP
Close	.944	10	65	3	4	7
Martinez	1.000	1	4	0	0	0
Ostrich	.992	48	437	44	4	24

Second Base	PCT	G	PO	A	E	DP
Cancel	.953	18	35	47	4	7
Diaz	1.000	4	8	10	0	2

Franco	.923	3	6	6	1	1
McCray	.954	33	57	87	7	16

Third Base	PCT	G	PO	A	E	DP
Diaz	.912	13	4	27	3	2
Nottebrok	—	1	0	0	0	0
Olloque	.826	15	11	27	8	2
Rivera	.937	35	19	70	6	3

Shortstop	PCT	G	PO	A	E	DP
Aracena	.886	24	31	70	13	9
Cancel	.824	12	14	28	9	5
Diaz	.937	24	24	65	6	9
Franco	1.000	1	2	4	0	0

Outfield	PCT	G	PO	A	E	DP
Clemmons	.911	25	37	4	4	0
Fuentes	1.000	3	2	0	0	0
Jones	1.000	3	4	2	0	0
Martin	.961	37	71	2	3	1
Martinez	—	2	0	0	0	0
Melo	.906	29	47	1	5	0
Miller	—	1	0	0	0	0
Sanchez	1.000	17	20	3	0	0
Stanley	1.000	10	19	0	0	0
Vasquez	1.000	41	86	4	0	2
Willis	1.000	15	20	0	0	0

IDAHO FALLS CHUKARS
PIONEER LEAGUE

ROOKIE

Batting	B-T	HT	WT	DOB	AVG	vLH	vRH	G	AB	R	H	2B	3B	HR	RBI	BB	HBP	SH	SF	SO	SB	CS	SLG	OBP
Banuelos, Josh	R-R	6-2	215	9-3-91	.357	.304	.374	67	280	46	100	21	2	4	62	29	2	1	1	56	3	2	.489	.420
Burt, D.J.	R-R	5-9	160	10-13-95	.290	.281	.293	65	248	56	72	6	8	1	28	40	3	10	2	58	20	7	.391	.392
Collins, Roman	L-L	6-2	210	6-17-94	.292	.234	.310	68	267	49	78	14	6	4	45	36	1	0	3	34	11	4	.434	.375

Batting	B-T	HT	WT	DOB	AVG	vLH	vRH	G	AB	R	H	2B	3B	HR	RBI	BB	HBP	SH	SF	SO	SB	CS	SLG	OBP
Dale, Ryan	R-R	6-3	180	3-16-96	.203	.275	.177	47	153	18	31	6	1	2	14	16	10	2	0	60	0	0	.294	.318
Diaz, Carlos	B-R	5-8	145	11-15-92	.182	.000	.222	3	11	1	2	0	0	0	1	0	0	0	0	2	0	0	.182	.182
Dini, Nick	R-R	5-8	180	7-27-93	.316	.222	.345	42	155	31	49	11	0	4	29	16	2	2	2	17	2	0	.465	.383
Dulin, Brandon	L-R	6-3	225	12-29-92	.286	.333	.273	7	28	5	8	1	0	0	6	1	0	0	2	6	0	0	.321	.290
Fernandez, Xavier	R-R	5-11	197	7-15-95	.316	.200	.357	5	19	3	6	2	0	0	3	4	0	0	0	4	0	0	.421	.435
Flores, Jecksson	R-R	5-11	145	10-28-93	.305	.273	.315	42	141	29	43	9	1	1	15	15	3	3	0	19	15	5	.404	.384
Fukofuka, Amalani	R-R	6-1	180	9-25-95	.339	.386	.324	67	280	53	95	18	9	3	38	26	4	1	2	70	10	3	.500	.401
Gasparini, Marten	B-R	6-0	165	5-24-97	.259	.255	.260	54	197	36	51	4	10	2	25	25	2	4	5	80	26	9	.411	.341
Gomez, Brawlun	R-R	6-2	185	8-5-92	.231	.283	.209	53	208	27	48	6	3	11	41	16	0	2	5	85	5	5	.447	.279
Gonzalez, Pedro	R-R	6-2	162	1-28-92	.328	.308	.333	16	58	15	19	4	0	3	10	6	2	0	1	10	0	0	.552	.403
Jones, Cody	B-R	5-11	170	5-25-93	.278	.184	.305	53	216	47	60	6	4	0	16	26	2	2	0	48	22	5	.343	.361
King, Riley	R-L	6-4	210	4-23-94	.333	—	.333	1	3	1	1	0	0	0	0	0	0	0	0	2	0	0	.333	.500
Lara, Luis	R-R	5-11	170	3-2-95	.320	.167	.368	7	25	3	8	0	0	0	0	1	2	1	0	5	1	0	.320	.393
Martin, Rudy	L-L	5-7	150	1-31-96	.167	.000	.200	2	6	1	1	0	0	0	1	0	1	0	0	3	2	0	.167	.286
Martinez, Jose	B-R	5-10	180	8-15-96	.273	.333	.263	6	22	2	6	0	0	1	5	1	1	2	0	3	0	0	.409	.333
Noriega, Gabriel	R-R	6-2	180	9-13-90	.389	.500	.375	4	18	5	7	1	0	0	3	2	0	0	1	4	0	0	.444	.429
Nottebrok, Logan	R-R	6-4	230	3-24-92	.252	.345	.221	33	115	18	29	7	3	4	18	16	1	0	3	31	0	0	.470	.341
Pollock, Kyle	R-R	6-0	200	8-15-92	.280	.294	.275	34	125	15	35	9	1	4	15	11	0	0	0	23	0	0	.464	.348
Rivera, Alexis	L-L	6-2	225	6-17-94	.362	.375	.358	17	69	19	25	5	0	7	25	17	1	0	0	14	3	0	.739	.494
Valenzuela, Luis	L-R	5-10	150	8-25-93	.486	.333	.538	8	35	9	17	1	0	1	8	0	0	1	1	3	1	1	.600	.472

Pitching	B-T	HT	WT	DOB	W	L	ERA	G	GS	CG	SV	IP	H	R	ER	HR	BB	SO	AVG	vLH	vRH	K/9	BB/9
Andros, Nick	L-L	6-4	230	11-21-92	0	0	23.14	2	0	0	0	2	3	6	6	0	6		.300	.500	.250	15.43	23.14
Bayliss, Brian	R-R	6-2	200	8-4-94	1	2	6.39	18	0	0	3	25	37	20	18	2	8	21	.293	.357	7.46	2.84	
Bodner, Jacob	R-R	5-10	185	1-31-93	0	0	13.50	2	0	0	0	3	4	4	4	1	5	4	.333	.500	.300	13.50	16.88
Brickhouse, Bryan	R-R	6-0	195	6-6-92	0	0	3.00	3	3	0	0	9	5	3	3	1	5	6	.167	.091	.211	6.00	5.00
Concepcion, Daniel	R-R	6-4	230	9-3-93	2	2	4.83	10	9	0	0	41	53	28	22	2	16	35	.301	.269	.321	7.68	3.51
Davis, Tripp	L-L	6-1	200	2-12-91	6	2	2.81	17	0	0	0	32	24	14	10	1	11	30	.252	.152	.233	8.44	3.09
Ditman, Matt	R-R	6-1	205	8-13-92	0	0	0.00	2	0	0	1	5	2	0	0	0	0	7	.125	.200	.091	13.50	0.00
Eaton, Todd	R-R	6-1	190	5-9-92	4	5	6.46	15	14	0	0	70	103	63	50	10	14	38	.340	.336	.342	4.91	1.81
Gordon, Derek	R-R	6-6	220	6-14-91	2	3	3.47	13	13	0	0	70	73	33	27	8	18	65	.271	.358	.215	8.36	2.31
Green, Nick	R-L	6-2	190	9-21-90	0	1	3.52	9	0	0	0	15	13	8	6	2	7	15	.224	.263	.205	8.80	4.11
Guevara, Cruz	L-L	6-0	155	5-29-94	1	0	5.30	16	0	0	0	37	39	23	22	1	17	37	.260	.241	.272	8.92	4.10
Haynes, Hunter	L-L	6-1	175	2-12-94	4	6	7.04	13	8	0	0	47	72	58	37	7	24	27	.355	.372	.344	5.13	4.56
Henry, Brennan	L-L	6-4	200	10-23-91	1	1	1.69	4	0	0	0	5	4	1	1	0	2	5	.211	.429	.083	8.44	3.38
Hernandez, Arnaldo	R-R	6-0	175	2-9-96	1	1	4.50	1	1	0	0	4	5	6	2	1	3	3	.294	.000	.333	6.75	6.75
Herrera, Carlos	R-R	6-3	180	7-4-93	1	2	9.45	4	3	0	0	20	27	22	21	2	10	8	.325	.226	.385	3.60	4.50
Hope, Carter	L-R	6-3	195	2-5-95	0	3	6.07	11	11	0	0	56	75	41	38	4	12	28	.322	.325	.321	4.47	1.92
Milligan, Drew	L-L	6-6	230	3-14-93	1	1	4.07	17	0	0	2	24	22	11	11	0	13	25	.247	.192	.270	9.25	4.81
Pinto, Julio	R-R	6-3	185	11-18-95	0	0	7.20	2	2	0	0	5	8	7	4	0	4	6	.348	.400	.308	10.80	7.20
Portland, Matt	R-L	6-3	225	2-11-94	0	0	3.10	15	0	0	2	29	21	13	10	0	14	28	.202	.152	.225	8.69	4.34
Pounders, Brooks	R-R	6-4	270	9-26-90	0	0	0.00	1	0	0	0	3	1	0	0	0	3	4	.100	.250	.000	12.00	9.00
Rodriguez, Alberto	R-R	6-1	225	12-24-91	6	1	3.38	16	0	0	0	29	27	14	11	3	13	21	.243	.238	.246	6.44	3.99
Sons, Dylan	L-L	6-3	176	7-15-93	0	4	10.80	7	7	0	0	27	53	43	32	5	14	21	.424	.412	.432	7.09	4.73
Staumont, Josh	R-R	6-2	190	12-21-93	3	1	3.16	14	1	0	1	31	18	11	11	0	24	51	.168	.128	.191	14.65	6.89
Stout, Eric	L-L	6-3	185	3-27-93	0	0	3.38	1	1	0	0	3	4	3	1	0	0	5	.308	.000	.444	16.88	0.00
Thomas, Brandon	L-L	5-11	200	9-16-93	2	2	3.35	16	2	0	3	46	46	23	17	4	25	34	.272	.215	.308	6.70	4.93
Tompkins, Ian	L-L	6-0	195	3-23-93	4	1	4.44	14	0	0	0	24	21	16	12	2	20	25	.236	.143	.279	9.25	7.40

Fielding

Catcher	PCT	G	PO	A	E	DP	PB
Dini	.991	28	201	32	2	1	6
Fernandez	.976	5	39	2	1	0	1
Gonzalez	.986	10	61	8	1	1	0
Lara	.971	7	57	9	2	2	0
Pollock	.995	28	178	36	1	0	3
Flores	.922	12	28	31	5	5	
Nottebrok	—	1	0	0	0	0	
Valenzuela	1.000	1	0	3	0	1	

First Base	PCT	G	PO	A	E	DP
Banuelos	.988	63	513	57	7	40
Nottebrok	.980	12	90	6	2	11
Rivera	1.000	3	22	1	0	5

Second Base	PCT	G	PO	A	E	DP
Burt	.945	62	114	197	18	38
Diaz	1.000	2	4	4	0	1

Third Base	PCT	G	PO	A	E	DP
Dale	.859	37	19	54	12	5
Diaz	.500	1	0	1	1	0
Flores	.846	13	8	25	6	3
Martinez	1.000	2	3	0	0	
Nottebrok	.955	22	17	46	3	6
Valenzuela	.867	6	5	8	2	1

Shortstop	PCT	G	PO	A	E	DP
Burt	—	1	0	0	0	0
Flores	.984	15	31	32	1	9
Gasparini	.871	52	99	138	35	31
Martinez	.900	4	4	14	2	0
Noriega	1.000	4	2	10	0	3
Valenzuela	.900	1	3	6	1	2

Outfield	PCT	G	PO	A	E	DP
Collins	.969	65	118	5	4	1
Fukofuka	.959	63	136	4	6	1
Gomez	.987	40	74	2	1	1
Jones	.981	51	98	5	2	0
King	1.000	1	1	0	0	0
Martin	1.000	2	6	0	0	0
Rivera	1.000	7	16	1	0	0

DSL ROYALS   ROOKIE

DOMINICAN SUMMER LEAGUE

Batting	B-T	HT	WT	DOB	AVG	vLH	vRH	G	AB	R	H	2B	3B	HR	RBI	BB	HBP	SH	SF	SO	SB	CS	SLG	OBP
Arias, Joel	R-R	6-0	160	4-6-97	.178	.316	.157	46	146	16	26	6	3	0	11	17	1	4	2	39	6	4	.260	.265
Atencio, Jesus	R-R	5-10	165	8-22-96	.241	.067	.259	48	162	13	39	7	0	0	18	21	2	2	1	16	0	1	.284	.333
Bejaran, Leonel	B-R	5-9	160	7-23-97	.244	.333	.233	34	82	15	20	3	0	0	3	17	2	2	0	18	6	2	.280	.386
Caraballo, Jose	R-R	6-1	180	1-7-97	.269	.350	.260	56	197	30	53	13	3	0	23	19	5	3	1	48	15	6	.365	.347
Caro, Anderson	R-R	6-4	180	9-23-97	.031	.000	.038	10	32	2	1	0	0	0	1	0	0	0	0	12	0	1	.031	.061
Collado, Offerman	R-L	5-10	140	6-10-96	.286	.231	.295	56	199	28	57	8	3	0	16	31	0	3	0	11	8	7	.357	.383

Batting

Batting	B-T	HT	WT	DOB	AVG	vLH	vRH	G	AB	R	H	2B	3B	HR	RBI	BB	HBP	SH	SF	SO	SB	CS	SLG	OBP
Marquez, Jose	R-R	6-0	175	10-7-97	.278	.200	.290	55	194	22	54	10	3	0	26	16	4	8	4	36	1	7	.361	.339
Martin, Andres	R-R	6-0	190	2-14-97	.253	.292	.247	53	174	24	44	9	1	0	21	19	2	2	1	33	6	4	.316	.332
Martinez, Yorly	R-R	6-0	190	8-23-94	.232	.258	.227	58	194	17	45	11	0	1	23	13	11	1	2	30	5	3	.304	.314
Nunez, Oliver	B-R	5-10	170	2-21-95	.306	.235	.318	66	232	44	71	9	5	1	23	39	0	7	2	27	14	7	.401	.403
Peguero, Juan	R-R	6-2	190	2-9-98	.086	.000	.101	32	81	6	7	3	0	0	3	13	2	2	1	29	0	1	.123	.227
Ramirez, Dagin	B-R	6-0	175	7-4-96	.126	.214	.111	36	95	6	12	2	0	0	6	13	2	0	1	18	2	3	.147	.243
Rodriguez, Ismaldo	B-R	6-0	175	7-3-98	.228	.304	.214	47	149	20	34	9	0	0	17	13	5	0	0	47	4	4	.289	.311
Saez, Alberto	R-R	6-1	155	7-11-96	.143	.000	.200	10	28	3	4	1	0	0	2	4	0	0	0	13	0	1	.179	.250
Torres, Jose	R-R	6-0	175	9-16-95	.239	.235	.239	41	134	16	32	8	0	0	17	7	5	1	1	19	2	3	.299	.299
Tovar, Roberto	B-R	6-1	180	11-16-94	.218	.250	.213	31	101	10	22	2	0	0	9	8	1	3	0	16	1	0	.238	.282
Vital, Jose	R-R	6-2	180	3-25-96	.152	.000	.170	44	105	8	16	2	1	0	3	7	4	2	0	39	6	4	.190	.233

Pitching

Pitching	B-T	HT	WT	DOB	W	L	ERA	G	GS	CG	SV	IP	H	R	ER	HR	BB	SO	AVG	vLH	vRH	K/9	BB/9
Acevedo, Randy	R-R	6-1	155	3-14-97	3	5	3.15	14	11	0	1	60	54	25	21	2	14	28	.247	.220	.256	4.20	2.10
Adames, Samuel	R-R	6-4	190	9-27-94	1	2	6.59	8	0	0	1	14	16	14	10	0	11	9	.286	.167	.318	5.93	7.24
Castillo, Cristian	L-L	6-0	190	9-25-94	0	4	2.67	14	14	0	0	67	52	28	20	4	15	58	.213	.184	.218	7.75	2.00
Cruz, Aronny	L-L	6-2	175	7-23-95	4	2	1.60	18	0	0	3	34	23	10	6	0	19	31	.198	.263	.186	8.29	5.08
De La Cruz, Joel	R-R	6-2	190	11-9-96	2	2	4.15	10	0	0	2	22	24	14	10	0	9	15	.267	.323	.237	6.23	3.74
De Leon, Jose	R-R	5-11	175	4-19-95	0	0	2.53	8	0	0	0	11	5	5	3	0	10	12	.135	.111	.143	10.13	8.44
Diaz, Frandy	L-L	5-10	155	3-25-95	1	3	4.36	18	0	0	1	33	33	25	16	1	16	26	.264	.125	.297	7.09	4.36
Escotto, Jeicol	R-R	6-4	185	12-28-95	2	2	6.18	16	0	0	0	28	21	22	19	0	21	26	.212	.200	.216	8.46	6.83
Estevez, Emmanuel	R-R	6-3	210	8-22-96	0	2	15.75	6	0	0	0	8	11	16	14	1	9	5	.344	.500	.188	5.63	10.13
Feliz, Darwin	R-R	6-1	171	9-19-96	4	5	3.55	13	13	1	0	58	62	31	23	5	10	31	.272	.284	.267	4.78	1.54
Flores, Juan	R-R	6-3	190	6-22-94	0	0	10.29	6	0	0	0	7	6	13	8	0	10	4	.222	.500	.174	5.14	12.86
Gomez, Ofreidy	R-R	6-3	190	7-6-95	0	4	3.04	14	11	0	2	50	44	22	17	1	17	42	.238	.353	.194	7.51	3.04
Hernandez, Arnaldo	R-R	6-0	175	2-9-96	1	0	0.82	2	2	0	0	11	13	1	1	0	0	8	.302	.200	.357	6.55	0.00
Mateo, Yeison	R-R	6-2	185	4-17-93	1	1	4.44	16	0	0	1	26	22	17	13	0	21	17	.220	.318	.192	5.81	7.18
Medrano, Miguel	R-R	6-2	175	6-19-95	1	7	4.30	13	11	0	0	59	65	32	28	5	14	32	.284	.238	.301	4.91	2.15
Pena, Yimauri	R-R	6-2	160	10-15-93	0	0	0.00	2	0	0	1	3	1	0	0	0	2	.083	.200	.000	5.40	0.00
Rodriguez, Jorge	L-L	6-0	160	6-30-96	2	0	0.78	5	5	1	0	23	8	2	2	0	3	28	.104	.111	.103	10.96	1.17
Santiago, Felix	R-R	6-0	170	12-7-93	4	0	2.05	8	4	0	0	31	30	9	7	1	7	33	.270	.279	.265	9.68	2.05
Tapia, Jose	R-R	6-1	178	10-19-96	1	2	5.09	17	0	0	3	35	38	22	20	4	15	29	.275	.294	.269	7.39	3.82

Fielding

Catcher	PCT	G	PO	A	E	DP	PB
Atencio	.983	30	186	40	4	1	5
Torres	.982	27	132	34	3	2	6
Tovar	.976	20	146	18	4	0	4

First Base	PCT	G	PO	A	E	DP
Atencio	.965	17	129	7	5	7
Martinez	.983	38	315	23	6	15
Torres	1.000	10	80	7	0	9
Tovar	1.000	11	90	7	0	5

Second Base	PCT	G	PO	A	E	DP
Bejaran	1.000	7	9	6	0	0
Collado	.960	36	76	68	6	9

	PCT	G	PO	A	E	DP
Marquez	.955	30	52	74	6	12
Nunez	.909	3	6	4	1	0
Ramirez	.950	6	10	9	1	0

Third Base	PCT	G	PO	A	E	DP
Collado	.970	9	9	23	1	1
Marquez	.875	3	2	5	1	0
Martinez	.929	21	18	34	4	2
Nunez	.846	3	3	8	2	2
Ramirez	.750	5	1	8	3	2
Rodriguez	.835	42	30	61	18	2

Shortstop	PCT	G	PO	A	E	DP
Collado	1.000	1	2	2	0	0

Nunez	.933	51	64	159	16	17
Ramirez	.911	27	30	42	7	5

Outfield	PCT	G	PO	A	E	DP
Arias	.972	44	100	3	3	1
Bejaran	1.000	15	23	0	0	0
Caraballo	1.000	52	99	5	0	2
Caro	1.000	9	22	0	0	0
Martin	.976	51	73	10	2	2
Peguero	.964	28	50	3	2	0
Saez	.875	6	7	0	1	0
Vital	.954	35	59	3	3	1

Los Angeles Angels

SEASON IN A SENTENCE: Even front office turmoil could not derail the Angels' contention in 2015 as Mike Trout continued to show why he's the best player in baseball and Albert Pujols hit 40 homers.

HIGH POINT: The Angels ultimately fell short of the playoffs, but not before a spirited run that had its apex on Oct. 3, the penultimate day of the regular season. The Angels, down four runs and facing elimination, scored five times in the ninth to beat the Rangers and move within a game of the Astros for the second wild card. The Angels lost the next day, but that Oct. 3 contest was one of the most exciting games of the regular season.

LOW POINT: A faceoff between the analytics bent of general manager Jerry Dipoto and old-school scouting mentality of manager Mike Scioscia resulted in Dipoto's resignation on July 1. At the time, the team was in second place and scuffling. The Angels hired longtime Yankees executive Billy Eppler as GM following the season, while Dipoto landed in Seattle as GM.

NOTABLE ROOKIES: Andrew Heaney, the lefthander acquired in the three-way deal that sent Dee Gordon to the Marlins and Howie Kendrick to the Dodgers, more than held his own, showing solid control and an ability to keep the ball in the yard. Kyle Kubitza, acquired from the Braves in the offseason, got 36 at-bats as the Angels looked for a larger role for the third baseman in 2016.

KEY TRANSACTIONS: Although they received nothing in return, the trade of Josh Hamilton to the Rangers in April ended a bad marriage for both sides. Hamilton did not perform in Los Angeles and was facing the possibility of a drug suspension, although that ultimately did not happen. At the trade deadline, the Angels beefed up their outfield with the acquisitions of outfielders Shane Victorino, David Murphy and David De Jesus—although the trio contributed little in the Angels' near-playoff berth.

DOWN ON THE FARM: One of the weaker systems was damaged with the graduation of Heaney and the trade of Ricardo Sanchez for Kubitza. Lefthander Sean Newcomb is the organization's best prospect and is on the precipice of helping the big league team, which contemplated calling him up late in the season. Righthander Chris Ellis had a solid season, but needs to improve his command, while 2014 second-round pick Joe Gatto looked impressive.

OPENING DAY PAYROLL: $150,933,083 (7th)

PLAYERS OF THE YEAR

MAJOR LEAGUE

MINOR LEAGUE

Mike Trout, cf	Sean Newcomb, lhp
.299/.402/.590	(low Class A/High
Career high 41 HR,	Class A/Double-A)
Led AL in SLG, OPS	9-3, 2.38

ORGANIZATION LEADERS

BATTING — *Minimum 250 AB

MAJORS

*AVG	Mike Trout	.299
*OPS	Mike Trout	.992
HR	Mike Trout	41
RBI	Albert Pujols	95

MINORS

*AVG	Alfredo Marte, Salt Lake	.318
*OBP	Caleb Adams, Burlington, Inland Empire	.390
*SLG	Eric Aguilera, Inland Empire, Arkansas	.509
R	Eric Aguilera, Inland Empire, Arkansas	80
	Bo Way, Inland Empire	80
H	Eric Aguilera, Inland Empire, Arkansas	155
TB	Eric Aguilera, Inland Empire, Arkansas	252
2B	Kyle Kubitza, Salt Lake	43
3B	Kody Eaves, Inland Empire	11
HR	Eric Aguilera, Inland Empire, Arkansas	17
RBI	Eric Aguilera, Inland Empire, Arkansas	94
BB	Sherman Johnson, Arkansas	89
SO	Kody Eaves, Inland Empire	150
SB	Chad Hinshaw, AZL Angels, Arkansas	30

PITCHING — #Minimum 75 IP

MAJORS

W	Garrett Richards	15
#ERA	Hector Santiago	3.59
SO	Garrett Richards	176
SV	Huston Street	40

MINORS

W	Christopher Ellis, Inland Empire, Arkansas	11
	Albert Suarez, Arkansas	11
L	Harrison Cooney, Arkansas, Inland Empire	16
#ERA	Sean Newcomb, Burl., Inland Empire, Ark.	2.38
G	Jeremy McBryde, Salt Lake	62
GS	Austin Robichaux, Burlington	28
SV	Greg Mahle, Inland Empire, Arkansas	25
IP	Albert Suarez, Arkansas	163
BB	Sean Newcomb, Burl., Inland Empire, Ark.	76
SO	Sean Newcomb, Burl., Inland Empire, Ark.	168
AVG	Sean Newcomb, Burl., Inland Empire, Ark.	.199

General Manager: Billy Eppler. **Farm Director:** Bobby Scales. **Scouting Director:** Ric Wilson.

Class	Team	League	W	L	PCT	Finish	Manager
Majors	Los Angeles Angels	American	85	77	.525	6th (15)	Mike Scioscia
Triple-A	Salt Lake Bees	Pacific Coast	58	86	.403	t-15th (16)	Dave Anderson
Double-A	Arkansas Travelers	Texas	71	68	.511	3rd (8)	Bill Richardson
High A	Inland Empire 66ers	California	61	79	.436	t-8th (10)	Denny Hocking
Low A	Burlington Bees	Midwest	63	76	.453	13th (16)	Chad Tracy
Rookie	Orem Owls	Pioneer	41	35	.539	3rd (8)	Dave Stapleton
Rookie	Angels	Arizona	23	30	.434	10th (14)	Elio Sarmiento
Overall 2015 Minor League Record			**317**	**374**	**.459**	**27th (30)**	

ORGANIZATION STATISTICS

LOS ANGELES ANGELS

AMERICAN LEAGUE

Batting	B-T	HT	WT	DOB	AVG	vLH	vRH	G	AB	R	H	2B	3B	HR	RBI	BB	HBP	SH	SF	SO	SB	CS	SLG	OBP
Aybar, Erick	B-R	5-10	180	1-14-84	.270	.270	.270	156	597	74	161	30	1	3	44	25	4	7	5	73	15	6	.338	.301
Bandy, Jett	R-R	6-4	235	3-26-90	.500		.500	—	2	2	1	0	0	1	1	0	0	0	0	0	0	0	2.000	.500
Butera, Drew	R-R	6-1	200	8-9-83	.190	.000	.200	10	21	3	4	0	0	0	0	0	0	0	0	2	0	1	.190	.190
2-team total (45 Kansas City)					.196	—	—	55	107	9	21	3	0	1	5	6	2	5	0	26	0	1	.252	.252
Calhoun, Kole	L-L	5-10	200	10-14-87	.256	.220	.272	159	630	78	161	23	2	26	83	45	5	2	4	164	4	1	.422	.308
Cowart, Kaleb	B-R	6-3	225	6-2-92	.174	.150	.192	34	46	8	8	2	0	1	4	5	0	1	0	19	1	1	.283	.255
Cowgill, Collin	R-L	5-9	185	5-22-86	.188	.225	.138	55	69	10	13	2	1	1	2	4	0	1	0	19	2	1	.290	.233
Cron Jr., C.J.	R-R	6-4	235	1-5-90	.262	.260	.263	113	378	37	99	17	1	16	51	17	5	0	3	82	3	1	.439	.300
DeJesus, David	L-L	5-11	190	12-20-79	.125	.000	.132	30	56	3	7	1	0	0	4	2	2	0	0	13	0	0	.143	.183
2-team total (82 Tampa Bay)					.233	—	—	112	288	27	67	9	2	5	30	21	6	0	2	52	3	2	.330	.297
Featherston, Taylor	R-R	6-1	185	10-8-89	.162	.217	.139	101	154	23	25	5	1	2	9	7	3	4	1	46	4	2	.247	.212
Freese, David	R-R	6-2	225	4-28-83	.257	.213	.272	121	424	53	109	27	0	14	56	31	12	0	3	107	1	1	.420	.323
Giavotella, Johnny	R-R	5-8	185	7-10-87	.272	.250	.279	129	453	51	123	25	5	4	49	32	2	9	6	59	2	1	.375	.318
Gillaspie, Conor	L-R	6-1	195	7-18-87	.203	.222	.200	17	64	4	13	4	1	1	9	4	0	0	0	13	0	0	.344	.250
2-team total (58 Chicago)					.228	—	—	75	237	14	54	15	2	4	24	13	1	0	2	47	0	1	.359	.269
Green, Grant	R-R	6-3	180	9-27-87	.190	.083	.233	21	42	6	8	0	0	1	3	2	0	0	0	14	0	1	.262	.227
Iannetta, Chris	R-R	6-0	230	4-8-83	.188	.230	.172	92	272	28	51	10	0	10	34	41	1	0	3	83	0	1	.335	.293
Jackson, Ryan	R-R	6-3	180	5-10-88	.000	.000	.000	22	9	0	0	0	0	0	0	1	0	4	0	5	0	0	.000	.100
Joyce, Matt	L-R	6-2	200	8-3-84	.174	.048	.186	93	247	17	43	12	1	5	21	30	4	1	2	67	0	3	.291	.272
Krauss, Marc	L-R	6-2	245	10-5-87	.143	.000	.152	11	35	2	5	2	0	1	5	3	0	0	0	11	0	0	.286	.211
3-team total (12 Detroit, 4 Tampa Bay)					.141	—	—	27	78	3	11	3	0	2	8	3	0	0	0	31	0	0	.256	.173
Kubitza, Kyle	L-R	6-3	210	7-15-90	.194	.250	.188	19	36	6	7	0	0	0	1	3	0	0	0	15	0	0	.194	.256
Marte, Alfredo	R-R	5-11	200	3-31-89	.333	.250	.500	5	6	0	2	0	0	0	0	1	1	0	0	1	0	0	.333	.500
Murphy, David	L-L	6-3	210	10-18-81	.265	.333	.260	48	155	16	41	6	0	5	23	4	0	0	1	20	0	1	.400	.281
2-team total (84 Cleveland)					.283	—	—	132	361	38	102	18	1	10	50	20	1	1	5	49	0	2	.421	.318
Navarro, Efren	L-L	6-0	210	5-14-86	.253	.182	.264	54	83	9	21	4	0	0	5	5	0	0	0	16	0	2	.301	.295
Nieuwenhuis, Kirk	L-R	6-3	225	8-7-87	.136	.000	.158	10	22	4	3	2	0	0	1	2	0	0	0	9	0	1	.227	.208
Perez, Carlos	R-R	6-0	210	10-27-90	.250	.186	.274	86	260	20	65	13	0	4	21	19	0	2	2	49	2	0	.346	.299
Pujols, Albert	R-R	6-3	230	1-16-80	.244	.219	.253	157	602	85	147	22	0	40	95	50	6	0	3	72	5	3	.480	.307
Robertson, Dan	R-R	5-8	205	9-30-85	.280	.225	.343	37	75	10	21	2	0	0	7	2	0	3	0	7	0	0	.307	.299
Trout, Mike	R-R	6-2	235	8-7-91	.299	.313	.295	159	575	104	172	32	6	41	90	92	10	0	5	158	11	7	.590	.402
Victorino, Shane	B-R	5-9	190	11-30-80	.214	.194	.333	38	84	9	18	2	0	3	7	3	2	2	1	18	2	0	.286	.292
2-team total (33 Boston)					.230	—	—	71	178	19	41	4	2	1	7	16	5	3	2	32	7	0	.292	.308

Pitching	B-T	HT	WT	DOB	W	L	ERA	G	GS	CG	SV	IP	H	R	ER	HR	BB	SO	AVG	vLH	vRH	K/9	BB/9
Alvarez, Jose	L-L	5-11	180	5-6-89	4	3	3.49	64	0	0	0	67	58	29	26	5	23	59	.228	.219	.235	7.93	3.09
Bedrosian, Cam	R-R	6-0	230	10-2-91	1	0	5.40	34	0	0	0	33	40	21	20	3	19	34	.303	.391	.256	9.18	5.13
Gott, Trevor	R-R	6-0	190	8-26-92	4	2	3.02	48	0	0	0	48	43	18	16	2	16	27	.242	.275	.214	5.10	3.02
Heaney, Andrew	L-L	6-2	185	6-5-91	6	4	3.49	18	18	0	0	106	99	41	41	9	28	78	.248	.228	.255	6.64	2.38
Ibarra, Edgar	L-L	6-0	190	5-31-89	0	0	2.25	2	0	0	0	4	4	1	1	0	3	3	.250	.000	.308	6.75	6.75
Latos, Mat	R-R	6-6	245	12-9-87	0	0	4.91	2	0	0	0	4	2	2	2	1	3	2	.267	.375	.143	7.36	2.45
Mattheus, Ryan	R-R	6-3	220	11-10-83	0	0	0.00	1	0	0	0	1	0	0	0	0	1	2	.000	.000	.000	18.00	9.00
Morin, Mike	R-R	6-4	220	5-3-91	4	2	6.37	47	0	0	1	35	36	28	25	3	9	41	.265	.269	.262	10.44	2.29
Pestano, Vinnie	R-R	6-0	210	2-20-85	1	0	5.40	19	0	0	0	12	15	9	7	3	8	13	.306	.375	.273	10.03	6.17
Ramos, Cesar	L-L	6-2	200	6-22-84	2	1	2.75	65	0	0	0	52	55	17	16	2	15	43	.279	.274	.284	7.39	2.58
Rasmus, Cory	R-R	6-0	200	11-6-87	0	0	5.23	16	1	0	0	21	15	12	12	3	11	27	.200	.214	.182	11.76	4.79
Reyes, Jo-Jo	L-L	6-2	230	11-20-84	1	0	0.00	5	0	0	0	0	0	0	0	0	0	0	.000	.000	—	0.00	0.00
Richards, Garrett	R-R	6-3	210	5-27-88	15	12	3.65	32	32	1	0	207	181	94	84	20	76	176	.236	.226	.247	7.64	3.30
Rucinski, Drew	R-R	6-2	190	12-30-88	0	2	7.71	4	1	0	0	7	10	6	6	1	6	4	.357	.500	.250	5.14	7.71
Salas, Fernando	R-R	6-2	200	5-30-85	5	2	3.47	72	0	0	0	64	61	34	30	8	12	74	.249	.271	.232	10.46	1.70
Santiago, Hector	R-L	6-0	215	12-16-87	9	9	3.59	33	32	0	0	181	156	80	72	29	71	162	.227	.220	.229	8.07	3.54
Shoemaker, Matt	R-R	6-2	225	9-27-86	7	10	4.46	25	24	0	0	135	135	70	67	24	35	116	.259	.248	.270	7.71	2.33
Smith, Joe	R-R	6-2	205	3-22-84	5	5	3.58	70	0	0	5	66	64	26	26	4	19	57	.259	.288	.233	7.85	2.62
Street, Huston	R-R	6-0	195	8-2-83	3	3	3.18	62	0	0	40	62	57	24	22	7	20	57	.256	.252	.200	8.23	2.89
Tropeano, Nick	R-R	6-4	200	8-27-90	3	2	3.82	8	7	0	0	38	40	18	16	2	10	38	.270	.267	.274	9.08	2.39

Pitching

Pitching	B-T	HT	WT	DOB	W	L	ERA	G	GS	CG	SV	IP	H	R	ER	HR	BB	SO	AVG	vLH	vRH	K/9	BB/9
Weaver, Jered	R-R	6-7	210	10-4-82	7	12	4.64	26	26	1	0	159	163	84	82	24	33	90	.264	.264	.264	5.09	1.87
Wilk, Adam	L-L	6-2	180	12-9-87	0	0	4.50	1	0	0	0	2	2	1	1	1	1	2	.250	.500	.167	9.00	4.50
Wilson, C.J.	L-L	6-1	210	11-18-80	8	8	3.89	21	21	0	0	132	118	59	57	13	46	110	.240	.248	.238	7.50	3.14
Wright, Wesley	R-L	5-11	185	1-28-85	0	0	3.18	9	0	0	0	6	4	3	2	1	3	5	.200	.214	.167	7.94	4.76
2-team total (2 Baltimore)					0	0	3.68	11	0	0	0	7	6	4	3	1	3	5	—	—	—	6.14	3.68

Fielding

Catcher	PCT	G	PO	A	E	DP	PB
Bandy	1.000	1	1	1	0	0	0
Butera	.978	7	40	5	1	0	0
Iannetta	.996	85	624	44	3	3	6
Perez	.992	80	545	71	5	1	7

First Base	PCT	G	PO	A	E	DP
Butera	1.000	3	1	0	0	0
Calhoun	1.000	1	1	0	0	0
Cron Jr.	.986	58	385	31	6	33
Green	1.000	5	22	0	0	1
Iannetta	1.000	2	5	0	0	0
Krauss	1.000	4	21	2	0	1
Navarro	1.000	29	113	5	0	7
Perez	1.000	2	4	1	0	0
Pujols	.994	95	718	55	5	57

Second Base	PCT	G	PO	A	E	DP
Featherston	.981	33	48	55	2	12

(Catcher cont.)	PCT	G	PO	A	E	DP	PB
Giavotella	.978	128	216	307	12	64	
Gillaspie	—	1	0	0	0	0	
Green	.971	11	14	19	1	4	
Jackson	.944	17	5	12	1	1	
Kubitza	—	2	0	0	0	0	

Third Base	PCT	G	PO	A	E	DP
Cowart	.962	33	10	40	2	4
Featherston	1.000	39	9	32	0	3
Freese	.967	113	54	179	8	13
Gillaspie	.946	17	11	24	2	1
Jackson	1.000	2	1	2	0	0
Kubitza	.900	13	4	14	2	1
Pujols	—	1	0	0	0	0

Shortstop	PCT	G	PO	A	E	DP
Aybar	.973	154	244	359	17	71
Featherston	.932	22	21	34	4	4
Giavotella	—	1	0	0	0	0

(cont.)					
Green	1.000	1	1	0	0	0
Jackson	1.000	3	0	1	0	0

Outfield	PCT	G	PO	A	E	DP
Calhoun	.989	157	342	11	4	1
Cowgill	1.000	46	52	2	0	0
DeJesus	1.000	15	12	0	0	0
Green	1.000	1	1	0	0	0
Joyce	.990	65	95	2	1	0
Krauss	1.000	1	1	0	0	0
Kubitza	—	2	0	0	0	0
Marte	1.000	3	2	0	0	0
Murphy	1.000	32	53	0	0	0
Navarro	1.000	17	22	1	0	0
Nieuwenhuis	1.000	10	17	0	0	0
Robertson	1.000	33	51	3	0	0
Trout	1.000	156	428	7	0	1
Victorino	.963	33	47	5	2	1

SALT LAKE BEES   TRIPLE-A

PACIFIC COAST LEAGUE

Batting	B-T	HT	WT	DOB	AVG	vLH	vRH	G	AB	R	H	2B	3B	HR	RBI	BB	HBP	SH	SF	SO	SB	CS	SLG	OBP
Bandy, Jett	R-R	6-4	235	3-26-90	.291	.247	.307	87	309	47	90	21	0	11	60	16	13	1	5	63	0	0	.466	.347
Bayardi, Brandon	R-R	6-2	235	11-27-90	.278	.167	.333	5	18	4	5	0	0	1	5	0	0	0	1	9	0	0	.444	.263
Brown, Gary	R-R	6-1	190	9-28-88	.247	.226	.257	102	372	57	92	16	6	7	47	21	7	7	4	64	14	12	.379	.297
2-team total (9 Memphis)					.242	—	—	111	397	58	96	16	6	7	48	22	7	7	4	68	14	12	.365	.291
Cowart, Kaleb	B-R	6-3	225	6-2-92	.323	.293	.333	62	220	35	71	13	3	6	45	29	0	0	4	64	2	1	.491	.395
Cowgill, Collin	R-L	5-9	185	5-22-86	.364	.500	.324	12	44	5	16	3	0	1	4	2	1	0	0	5	0	0	.500	.404
Cron Jr., C.J.	R-R	6-4	235	1-5-90	.323	.389	.281	23	93	15	30	10	2	6	23	4	0	0	1	14	0	0	.667	.347
Cutler, Charlie	L-R	6-1	215	7-29-86	.380	.567	.244	22	71	7	27	1	1	0	8	6	1	0	1	7	1	0	.423	.430
Featherston, Taylor	R-R	6-1	185	10-8-89	.172	.111	.200	7	29	4	5	1	1	0	1	2	0	0	1	8	0	0	.276	.219
Freese, David	R-R	6-2	225	4-28-83	.286	.400	.250	7	21	2	6	0	0	1	6	3	1	0	0	4	0	0	.429	.400
Gil, Jose	R-R	6-0	205	9-4-86	.077	.200	.000	4	13	2	1	0	0	0	3	0	0	0	0	4	0	0	.077	.250
Gillaspie, Conor	L-R	6-1	195	7-18-87	.000	.000	.000	2	3	0	0	0	0	0	0	0	0	0	0	1	0	0	.000	.000
Green, Grant	R-R	6-3	180	9-27-87	.306	.424	.270	93	385	59	118	26	7	5	43	18	2	4	5	70	2	3	.449	.337
Hernandez, Luis	B-R	5-10	180	6-26-84	.286	.400	.222	4	14	1	4	0	0	0	2	0	0	0	0	0	0	0	.286	.286
Jackson, Ryan	R-R	6-3	180	5-10-88	.293	.265	.303	85	314	33	92	16	3	1	26	40	0	7	2	66	1	3	.373	.371
2-team total (19 Omaha)					.295	—	—	104	373	42	110	19	3	2	28	47	0	9	2	79	1	4	.378	.372
Joyce, Matt	L-R	6-2	200	8-3-84	.393	.222	.370	11	36	3	12	1	0	2	6	5	1	0	1	9	0	0	.528	.419
Kieschnick, Roger	L-R	6-3	225	1-21-87	.263	.295	.251	108	399	51	105	22	3	15	59	31	4	0	3	107	3	2	.446	.320
Krauss, Marc	L-R	6-2	245	10-5-87	.289	.269	.304	47	159	23	46	8	3	4	29	35	0	0	1	38	0	1	.453	.415
Kubitza, Kyle	L-R	6-3	210	7-15-90	.271	.259	.277	117	457	63	124	43	5	7	50	60	4	0	5	125	7	1	.433	.357
Lopez, Rafael	L-R	5-9	200	10-2-87	.242	.294	.222	21	62	10	15	2	0	1	7	11	0	1	1	13	0	0	.323	.351
2-team total (46 Iowa)					.266	—	—	67	218	24	58	10	1	1	24	25	0	1	2	50	3	1	.335	.339
Marte, Alfredo	R-R	5-11	200	3-31-89	.318	.321	.316	97	343	54	109	25	3	7	55	36	2	0	5	81	7	2	.469	.381
McGee, Stephen	R-R	6-3	225	1-21-89	.393	.364	.412	8	28	2	11	2	0	1	8	2	0	1	0	5	0	0	.571	.433
Mitchell, Jared	L-L	6-0	205	10-13-88	.255	.320	.232	29	94	11	24	7	0	2	11	12	0	0	1	28	5	1	.394	.336
Myers, D'Arby	R-R	6-3	185	12-9-88	.300	.333	.286	6	10	1	3	0	0	0	2	1	0	1	0	2	0	1	.300	.364
Navarro, Efren	L-L	6-0	210	5-14-86	.329	.318	.333	72	283	53	93	24	1	2	29	27	0	0	6	55	0	1	.442	.380
Perez, Carlos	R-R	6-0	210	10-27-90	.361	.409	.340	17	72	11	26	8	0	2	12	7	0	0	0	7	1	0	.556	.418
Robertson, Dan	R-R	5-8	205	9-30-85	.265	.282	.256	60	245	27	65	16	0	1	20	24	2	1	3	32	6	6	.343	.332
Rosa, Angel	R-R	6-2	185	9-19-92	.333	.125	.448	13	45	7	15	2	1	0	4	4	0	0	1	9	0	0	.422	.380
Rutledge, Josh	R-R	6-1	190	4-21-89	.274	.289	.268	78	310	45	85	19	3	5	32	19	5	0	3	67	2	1	.403	.323
Salcedo, Erick	B-R	5-10	155	6-28-93	.250	.167	.300	6	8	3	4	1	0	0	2	0	0	0	0	3	0	0	.313	.333
Wheeler, Ryan	L-R	6-3	230	7-10-88	.291	.333	.283	14	55	6	16	2	1	1	10	1	0	0	0	10	0	1	.418	.304
Yarbrough, Alex	B-R	6-0	200	8-3-91	.236	.258	.226	128	500	56	118	29	3	8	48	26	3	9	7	136	1	1	.324	.274

Pitching	B-T	HT	WT	DOB	W	L	ERA	G	GS	CG	SV	IP	H	R	ER	HR	BB	SO	AVG	vLH	vRH	K/9	BB/9
Adams, Austin	R-R	6-2	225	5-5-91	0	0	9.82	2	0	0	0	4	1	4	4	0	9	1	.091	.000	.200	2.45	22.09
Bedrosian, Cam	R-R	6-0	230	10-2-91	1	1	2.78	24	0	0	3	36	32	11	11	0	14	42	.242	.277	.224	10.60	3.53
DeLoach, Tyler	R-L	6-6	240	4-12-91	2	6	6.20	18	18	0	0	94	108	68	65	11	47	91	.300	.200	.329	8.68	4.48
Gott, Trevor	R-R	6-0	190	8-26-92	0	0	0.00	7	0	0	0	8	5	1	0	0	10	5	.161	.083	.353	10.80	5.40
Heaney, Andrew	L-L	6-2	185	6-5-91	2	4	4.71	14	14	0	0	78	95	49	41	2	25	74	.298	.227	.320	8.50	2.87
Hensley, Steven	R-R	6-3	190	12-27-86	2	4	6.85	26	2	0	1	45	64	37	34	9	20	42	.342	.342	.342	8.46	4.03
Herrmann, Frank	L-R	6-4	220	5-30-84	3	1	4.05	37	0	0	1	47	62	23	21	5	5	47	.320	.325	.316	9.06	0.96
Ibarra, Edgar	L-L	6-0	190	5-31-89	3	3	5.43	49	1	0	2	61	70	45	37	5	33	66	.294	.290	.296	9.68	4.84
Mattheus, Ryan	R-R	6-3	220	11-10-83	0	2	2.84	11	0	0	1	13	10	5	4	2	2	12	.208	.222	.200	8.53	1.42

Pitching

Pitching	B-T	HT	WT	DOB	W	L	ERA	G	GS	CG	SV	IP	H	R	ER	HR	BB	SO	AVG	vLH	vRH	K/9	BB/9
McBryde, Jeremy	R-R	6-3	235	5-1-87	5	6	4.66	62	0	0	11	64	70	37	33	3	23	68	.275	.295	.263	9.61	3.25
Morin, Mike	R-R	6-4	220	5-3-91	4	2	6.23	14	0	0	1	17	25	14	12	3	6	19	.342	.346	.340	9.87	3.12
O'Grady, Chris	L-L	6-4	220	4-17-90	0	0	3.12	7	0	0	0	9	5	3	3	1	4	10	.167	.273	.105	10.38	4.15
Pestano, Vinnie	R-R	6-0	210	2-20-85	1	3	2.10	35	0	0	10	34	18	8	8	1	8	42	.154	.211	.127	11.01	2.10
Rasmus, Cory	R-R	6-0	200	11-6-87	0	1	2.35	10	3	0	1	15	9	5	4	0	2	25	.164	.158	.167	14.67	1.17
Reyes, Jo-Jo	L-L	6-2	230	11-20-84	4	5	4.76	15	11	0	1	68	83	41	36	8	23	45	.312	.362	.301	5.96	3.04
Richards, Garrett	R-R	6-3	210	5-27-88	0	1	9.00	1	1	0	0	5	7	5	5	1	4	5	.333	.333	.333	9.00	7.20
Rucinski, Drew	R-R	6-2	190	12-30-88	5	7	5.69	22	22	0	0	112	141	73	71	21	44	87	.311	.304	.316	6.97	3.53
Sanabia, Alex	R-R	6-2	210	9-8-88	3	10	6.80	26	14	0	0	87	127	72	66	9	32	55	.339	.364	.321	5.67	3.30
Severino, Atahualpa	L-L	5-11	220	11-6-84	1	1	8.44	26	0	0	0	27	41	26	25	1	17	20	.363	.408	.328	6.75	5.74
Shoemaker, Matt	R-R	6-2	225	9-27-86	0	1	0.00	1	1	0	0	6	5	3	0	1	2	5	.208	.200	.214	7.50	3.00
Smith, Chad	R-R	6-3	215	10-2-89	0	0	9.72	6	0	0	0	8	18	9	9	1	2	6	.429	.444	.417	6.48	2.16
2-team total (8 Nashville)					1	1	5.40	14	0	0	2	20	31	12	12	1	7	13	—	—	—	5.85	3.15
Smith, Nate	L-L	6-3	205	8-28-91	2	4	7.75	7	7	0	0	36	48	36	31	7	15	23	.308	.194	.336	5.75	3.75
Snodgrass, Scott	L-L	6-6	235	9-20-89	1	1	11.16	24	1	0	0	25	46	31	31	2	10	22	.411	.385	.425	7.92	3.60
Spomer, Kurt	B-R	6-2	215	7-10-89	2	2	3.77	31	0	0	0	45	46	21	19	5	18	23	.272	.268	.273	4.57	3.57
Stewart, Zach	R-R	6-2	205	9-28-86	1	2	3.43	12	8	0	0	39	43	19	15	4	13	27	.289	.250	.329	6.18	2.97
Tropeano, Nick	R-R	6-4	200	8-27-90	3	6	4.81	16	16	1	0	88	97	51	47	9	36	96	.279	.331	.237	9.82	3.68
Verdugo, Ryan	L-L	6-0	200	4-10-87	2	2	5.52	23	0	0	0	29	25	19	18	1	16	33	.231	.167	.256	10.13	4.91
2-team total (19 Nashville)					4	5	4.31	42	4	0	0	71	60	38	34	4	34	68	—	—	—	8.62	4.31
Wilk, Adam	L-L	6-2	180	12-9-87	7	11	5.59	27	25	1	0	145	189	106	90	16	40	105	.313	.302	.317	6.52	2.48
Wright, Wesley	R-L	5-11	185	1-28-85	0	1	1.42	12	0	0	0	13	9	2	2	0	5	13	.209	.222	.200	9.24	3.55

Fielding

Catcher

Catcher	PCT	G	PO	A	E	DP	PB
Bandy	.990	84	654	40	7	5	4
Cutler	.975	19	104	11	3	1	3
Gil	1.000	3	19	3	0	0	1
Lopez	.982	21	155	6	3	0	1
McGee	.949	8	54	2	3	0	0
Perez	.994	16	142	13	1	0	0

First Base

First Base	PCT	G	PO	A	E	DP
Bayardi	1.000	4	26	2	0	5
Cron Jr.	.986	16	130	9	2	19
Cutler	1.000	2	5	0	0	2
Green	.989	23	172	12	2	18
Krauss	1.000	38	306	18	0	24
Kubitza	1.000	3	29	5	0	1
Navarro	.994	60	466	32	3	51
Wheeler	1.000	3	23	2	0	2

Second Base

Second Base	PCT	G	PO	A	E	DP
Brown	.889	2	5	3	1	1
Featherston	1.000	3	5	10	0	3

Green	1.000	8	14	15	0	4
Hernandez	1.000	3	4	10	0	2
Jackson	1.000	1	1	3	0	1
Rutledge	1.000	14	24	48	0	11
Yarbrough	.971	115	206	262	14	78

Third Base

Third Base	PCT	G	PO	A	E	DP
Cowart	.966	49	35	105	5	9
Freese	1.000	3	1	6	0	1
Gillaspie	—	2	0	0	0	0
Green	1.000	1	0	4	0	0
Kubitza	.928	73	56	137	15	16
Rutledge	.885	13	4	19	3	3
Wheeler	1.000	3	4	5	0	0
Yarbrough	1.000	4	2	9	0	0

Shortstop

Shortstop	PCT	G	PO	A	E	DP
Cowart	.727	2	3	5	3	1
Featherston	.867	4	3	10	2	1
Green	.953	11	17	24	2	11
Hernandez	1.000	1	0	3	0	0

Jackson	.970	74	81	179	8	43
Rosa	.979	12	16	30	1	10
Rutledge	.972	38	40	100	4	26
Salcedo	1.000	4	3	13	0	1

Outfield

Outfield	PCT	G	PO	A	E	DP
Brown	.987	98	224	7	3	0
Cowart	.875	5	5	2	1	0
Cowgill	1.000	9	20	0	0	0
Green	.983	40	58	1	1	0
Jackson	1.000	4	1	1	0	0
Joyce	1.000	7	10	0	0	0
Kieschnick	.966	91	157	12	6	1
Krauss	1.000	3	8	0	0	0
Kubitza	.962	18	23	2	1	0
Marte	.959	90	181	5	8	3
Mitchell	.967	24	58	0	2	0
Myers	1.000	4	4	0	0	0
Navarro	1.000	9	13	0	0	0
Robertson	.975	56	152	6	4	1
Salcedo	1.000	1	2	0	0	0

ARKANSAS TRAVELERS

DOUBLE-A

TEXAS LEAGUE

Batting	B-T	HT	WT	DOB	AVG	vLH	vRH	G	AB	R	H	2B	3B	HR	RBI	BB	HBP	SH	SF	SO	SB	CS	SLG	OBP
Aguilera, Eric	L-L	6-2	218	7-3-90	.121	.222	.083	9	33	1	4	2	0	0	1	0	0	0	0	11	0	0	.182	.147
Bemboom, Anthony	L-R	6-2	195	1-18-90	.253	.241	.256	80	257	29	65	7	1	5	35	23	0	7	4	60	2	1	.346	.310
Bond, Brock	B-R	5-11	190	9-11-85	.179	.182	.179	15	39	4	7	0	0	0	1	4	1	1	0	6	0	0	.179	.273
Cutler, Charlie	L-R	6-1	215	7-29-86	.265	.444	.200	8	34	2	9	3	0	0	3	0	0	0	0	6	0	0	.353	.265
Davis, Kentrail	L-R	5-9	200	6-29-88	.205	.194	.208	51	161	18	33	5	1	3	14	16	1	0	0	44	7	1	.304	.281
Fish, Mike	R-R	6-1	205	1-3-91	.100	.143	.077	7	20	1	2	0	0	0	1	0	0	0	0	10	0	1	.100	.143
Gailen, Blake	L-L	5-9	180	3-27-85	.232	.190	.251	76	267	37	62	15	1	10	48	50	1	1	4	47	7	3	.408	.351
Gomez, Raywilly	B-R	5-11	200	1-25-90	.291	.276	.296	73	244	21	71	8	0	1	20	38	0	1	1	28	2	0	.336	.385
Hernandez, Brian	R-R	6-1	205	11-25-88	.250	.279	.239	136	516	59	129	27	0	8	77	41	2	0	10	98	1	1	.349	.302
Hinkle, Wade	L-L	6-0	230	9-5-89	.248	.282	.238	106	347	35	86	18	0	8	45	44	6	1	7	93	2	1	.369	.337
Hinshaw, Chad	R-R	6-1	205	9-10-90	.289	.324	.276	71	263	48	76	17	0	1	26	37	7	6	0	75	27	5	.365	.391
Johnson, Sherman	L-R	5-10	190	7-15-90	.204	.135	.232	135	490	75	100	29	2	7	53	89	2	3	7	102	20	3	.314	.325
Linares, Raul	B-R	5-11	160	10-4-90	.500	—	.500	1	2	0	1	0	0	0	0	0	0	0	0	1	0	0	.500	.500
Maggi, Drew	R-R	6-0	192	5-16-89	.242	.228	.247	125	422	50	102	18	0	3	31	45	6	8	2	82	29	12	.284	.322
McGee, Stephen	R-R	6-3	215	2-7-91	.250	.500	.200	5	12	1	3	1	0	0	3	0	0	0	2	0	0	.333	.400
Mitchell, Jared	L-L	6-0	205	10-13-88	.220	.260	.205	58	177	19	39	4	3	3	11	21	1	0	0	72	9	4	.328	.307
Myers, D'Arby	R-R	6-3	185	12-9-88	.235	.219	.243	56	179	21	42	4	2	1	15	11	3	2	0	25	8	2	.296	.290
Salcedo, Erick	B-R	5-10	155	6-28-93	.213	.050	.273	25	75	10	16	1	0	0	3	5	0	3	1	11	5	1	.227	.259
Shannon, Mark	L-L	6-0	185	4-12-91	.250	.000	.500	1	4	0	1	0	0	0	0	0	0	0	0	2	0	0	.250	.250
Snyder, Mike	R-R	6-4	240	6-17-90	.234	.190	.257	47	167	19	39	8	0	5	23	17	2	0	1	59	2	0	.371	.310
Sosa, Ruben	B-R	5-7	170	9-23-90	.277	.212	.302	32	119	22	33	6	3	1	8	16	0	1	0	22	11	3	.403	.363
Stamets, Eric	R-R	6-0	190	9-25-91	.248	.262	.242	62	214	17	53	13	1	3	23	18	1	6	2	25	5	3	.360	.306
Towey, Cal	L-R	6-1	215	2-6-90	.215	.186	.226	98	316	39	68	16	3	2	49	56	7	0	6	110	11	3	.304	.340
Wright, Zach	R-R	6-1	205	1-10-90	.137	.143	.133	34	102	11	14	3	0	2	5	15	6	0	0	33	2	0	.225	.285

Pitching

Pitching	B-T	HT	WT	DOB	W	L	ERA	G	GS	CG	SV	IP	H	R	ER	HR	BB	SO	AVG	vLH	vRH	K/9	BB/9
Adams, Austin	R-R	6-2	225	5-5-91	1	1	2.95	27	0	0	1	37	22	13	12	0	31	49	.183	.170	.192	12.03	7.61
Antonini, Mike	R-L	6-1	210	8-6-85	1	1	4.95	4	4	0	0	20	21	12	11	3	7	19	.266	.188	.286	8.55	3.15
Brady, Michael	R-R	6-0	195	3-21-87	7	7	3.77	32	19	0	0	119	124	55	50	10	12	113	.267	.310	.242	8.52	0.91
Broussard, Geoff	R-R	6-0	185	9-21-90	0	0	5.79	4	0	0	0	5	7	3	3	0	1	2	.350	.167	.429	3.86	1.93
Busenitz, Alan	R-R	6-1	180	8-22-90	1	5	6.75	16	8	1	0	53	80	43	40	7	16	38	.357	.409	.321	6.41	2.70
Cooney, Harrison	R-R	6-2	175	3-23-92	0	1	9.00	1	1	0	0	4	7	6	4	2	2	0	.350	.429	.308	0.00	4.50
DeLoach, Tyler	R-L	6-6	240	4-12-91	3	2	2.40	7	7	1	0	45	37	14	12	3	10	42	.230	.233	.229	8.40	2.00
Ellis, Chris	R-R	6-4	220	9-22-92	7	4	3.92	15	15	0	0	78	77	42	34	9	43	62	.258	.285	.236	7.15	4.96
Gott, Trevor	R-R	6-0	190	8-26-92	1	0	3.20	18	0	0	8	20	19	9	7	0	7	20	.268	.379	.190	9.15	3.20
Hyatt, Nate	R-R	6-0	200	9-26-90	1	2	5.06	36	0	0	1	43	44	34	24	3	38	42	.270	.304	.245	8.86	8.02
Mahle, Greg	L-L	6-2	225	4-17-93	3	3	3.06	31	0	0	16	35	34	16	12	1	11	36	.258	.257	.258	9.17	2.80
McGowin, Kyle	R-R	6-3	200	11-27-91	9	9	4.38	27	27	0	0	154	148	80	75	16	50	125	.255	.259	.253	7.31	2.92
Newcomb, Sean	L-L	6-5	245	6-12-93	2	2	2.75	7	7	0	0	36	22	12	11	2	24	39	.176	.196	.162	9.75	6.00
O'Grady, Chris	L-L	6-4	220	4-17-90	0	5	3.31	38	0	0	4	49	42	20	18	5	10	47	.233	.232	.234	8.63	1.84
Reynolds, Danny	R-R	6-0	190	5-2-91	3	3	4.57	43	0	0	10	43	34	22	22	1	28	50	.213	.267	.180	10.38	5.82
Santos, Eduard	R-R	6-2	240	10-22-89	4	2	2.31	39	0	0	0	58	33	16	15	3	32	78	.175	.177	.173	12.03	4.94
Smith, Nate	L-L	6-3	205	8-28-91	8	4	2.48	17	17	1	0	102	82	31	28	10	28	81	.216	.179	.229	7.17	2.48
Sneed, Kramer	L-L	6-3	185	10-7-88	0	0	0.00	1	0	0	0	4	2	0	0	0	1	2	.154	.000	.222	4.50	2.25
Snodgress, Scott	L-L	6-6	235	9-20-89	0	0	5.19	9	0	0	0	9	9	7	5	0	8	7	.300	.308	.294	7.27	8.31
Spomer, Kurt	R-R	6-2	215	7-10-89	2	1	4.26	16	0	0	0	19	21	12	9	5	5	13	.273	.258	.283	6.16	2.37
Suarez, Albert	R-R	6-3	205	10-8-89	11	9	2.98	27	27	1	0	163	142	64	54	14	40	121	.234	.208	.255	6.68	2.21
Winkler, Kyle	R-R	5-11	195	6-18-90	0	2	5.10	21	0	0	0	30	28	18	17	1	14	22	.264	.167	.314	6.60	4.20
Wood, Austin	R-R	6-4	230	7-11-90	8	5	3.95	31	7	0	0	80	73	38	35	5	41	51	.246	.239	.250	5.76	4.63

Fielding

Catcher	PCT	G	PO	A	E	DP	PB
Bemboom	.993	75	533	70	4	6	6
Cutler	.957	3	21	1	1	0	0
Gomez	.975	30	221	12	6	2	1
McGee	.956	5	39	4	2	0	0
Wright	.996	31	244	23	1	3	3

First Base	PCT	G	PO	A	E	DP
Aguilera	.963	6	49	3	2	5
Cutler	1.000	2	17	2	0	3
Hernandez	.993	38	279	18	2	22
Hinkle	.991	87	687	50	7	64
Snyder	.990	15	99	4	1	15

Second Base	PCT	G	PO	A	E	DP
Bond	.905	7	8	11	2	3

Hernandez	1.000	1	0	3	0	0
Johnson	.980	120	215	281	10	73
Maggi	.955	14	16	48	3	7
Salcedo	.600	1	1	2	2	1

Third Base	PCT	G	PO	A	E	DP
Bemboom	—					
Hernandez	.942	92	54	156	13	13
Johnson	1.000	3	3	6	0	3
Maggi	.960	51	30	90	5	7

Shortstop	PCT	G	PO	A	E	DP
Johnson	.896	9	14	29	5	3
Maggi	.963	51	73	137	8	30
Salcedo	.989	23	36	57	1	16
Stamets	.981	61	96	169	5	34

Outfield	PCT	G	PO	A	E	DP
Bemboom	1.000	2	1	0	0	0
Davis	.979	44	89	5	2	0
Fish	1.000	6	11	1	0	0
Gailen	.993	68	136	4	1	0
Hinshaw	1.000	70	172	4	0	0
Linares	—	1	0	0	0	0
Maggi	.970	14	29	3	1	0
Mitchell	.973	52	108	1	3	0
Myers	1.000	49	87	1	0	0
Shannon	1.000	1	1	0	0	0
Sosa	.982	29	54	2	1	0
Towey	.962	91	142	10	6	3

INLAND EMPIRE 66ERS

HIGH CLASS A

CALIFORNIA LEAGUE

Batting	B-T	HT	WT	DOB	AVG	vLH	vRH	G	AB	R	H	2B	3B	HR	RBI	BB	HBP	SH	SF	SO	SB	CS	SLG	OBP
Adams, Caleb	R-R	5-10	185	1-26-93	.293	.237	.308	51	181	24	53	11	3	4	26	22	4	0	1	60	3	2	.453	.380
Aguilera, Eric	L-L	6-2	218	7-3-90	.327	.365	.316	119	462	79	151	38	3	17	94	47	6	5	5	110	14	6	.532	.392
Baldoquin, Roberto	R-R	5-11	185	5-14-94	.235	.182	.248	77	289	23	68	12	1	1	27	9	4	4	3	70	4	5	.294	.266
Bayardi, Brandon	R-R	6-2	235	11-27-90	.302	.302	.302	63	225	39	68	12	4	9	36	26	5	0	1	54	2	0	.511	.385
Cowart, Kaleb	R-R	6-3	225	6-2-92	.242	.089	.289	51	194	32	47	14	4	2	23	22	3	0	2	43	10	2	.387	.324
Cowgill, Collin	R-L	5-9	185	5-22-86	.167	.000	.200	2	6	2	1	0	0	0	0	1	0	0	0	1	0	0	.167	.286
Daniel, Andrew	R-R	6-1	195	1-27-93	.265	.275	.263	53	196	27	52	17	4	1	28	18	3	0	2	54	4	3	.408	.333
Davis, Quinten	R-R	6-1	185	8-1-92	.231	.353	.209	34	108	15	25	3	3	2	11	8	3	0	0	42	1	2	.370	.303
Eaves, Kody	L-R	6-0	175	7-8-93	.248	.186	.265	134	520	70	129	17	11	11	71	45	2	3	5	150	21	9	.387	.308
Fish, Mike	R-R	6-1	205	1-3-91	.297	.387	.273	88	350	46	104	15	1	2	34	30	1	1	5	64	5	4	.363	.350
Koch, Matt	R-R	6-0	220	11-21-88	.278	1.000	.235	6	18	1	5	0	0	0	1	1	0	0	0	4	0	1	.278	.316
McGee, Stephen	R-R	6-3	215	2-7-90	.255	.263	.250	55	182	16	46	11	1	5	27	25	3	0	4	48	1	2	.341	.352
Moreno, Juan	R-R	6-1	160	11-17-94	.162	.000	.182	13	37	7	6	0	0	1	4	0	2	0	1	2	0	1	.162	.244
Palmer, Tyler	R-R	5-11	189	9-20-91	.274	.282	.273	60	215	34	59	12	1	2	21	31	2	2	0	50	11	2	.363	.371
Rosa, Angel	R-R	6-2	185	9-19-92	.252	.240	.255	78	270	30	68	15	1	3	42	18	1	1	6	69	5	0	.348	.295
Ruiz, Pedro	B-R	5-9	190	8-30-91	.175	.190	.170	61	183	20	32	4	0	2	18	43	0	4	1	56	1	8	.230	.330
Salcedo, Erick	B-R	5-10	155	6-28-93	.500	.500	.500	2	6	2	3	1	0	0	0	0	0	0	0	2	0	0	.667	.500
Santana, Gabriel	R-R	6-2	180	8-18-95	.227	.000	.263	6	22	3	5	1	1	0	3	1	0	0	0	6	0	0	.364	.261
Shannon, Mark	L-L	6-0	185	4-12-91	.200	.267	.180	37	130	13	26	2	1	0	13	9	1	0	1	24	3	0	.231	.255
Snyder, Mike	R-R	6-4	240	1-17-90	.226	.216	.230	49	190	25	43	11	0	7	26	16	2	0	4	59	0	0	.395	.288
Sosa, Ruben	B-R	5-7	170	9-23-90	.256	.154	.283	31	125	20	32	4	1	2	9	8	1	2	2	28	10	2	.352	.301
Spivey, Eason	R-R	6-1	205	5-16-92	.100	.000	.143	7	20	1	2	0	0	0	3	0	0	0	0	9	0	0	.100	.308
Strentz, Michael	R-R	6-1	215	11-10-91	.262	.300	.254	65	221	37	58	13	2	6	26	20	1	0	0	64	4	1	.421	.326
Wass, Wade	R-R	6-0	215	9-23-91	.289	.375	.267	13	38	8	11	3	0	4	6	2	0	0	0	8	0	0	.684	.325
Way, Bo	L-L	6-0	180	11-17-91	.277	.170	.302	135	520	80	144	25	9	2	52	49	10	10	3	90	27	19	.371	.349
Yacinich, Jake	R-R	6-2	195	3-2-93	.259	.182	.313	10	27	5	7	3	0	0	3	1	0	0	0	6	1	0	.370	.286

Pitching	B-T	HT	WT	DOB	W	L	ERA	G	GS	CG	SV	IP	H	R	ER	HR	BB	SO	AVG	vLH	vRH	K/9	BB/9
Adams, Austin	R-R	6-2	225	5-5-91	2	1	2.45	9	0	0	0	15	10	5	4	0	7	21	.189	.182	.194	12.89	4.30
Alcantara, Victor	R-R	6-2	190	4-3-93	7	12	5.63	27	27	0	0	136	152	98	85	10	58	125	.282	.303	.261	8.27	3.84

Pitching	B-T	HT	WT	DOB	W	L	ERA	G	GS	CG	SV	IP	H	R	ER	HR	BB	SO	AVG	vLH	vRH	K/9	BB/9
Alonzo, Eric	B-R	6-2	210	8-28-91	0	1	4.15	3	0	0	0	9	12	5	4	0	1	6	.333	.273	.429	6.23	1.04
Blackford, Alex	R-R	5-11	200	11-16-90	2	4	5.12	28	1	0	0	51	59	36	29	3	24	73	.282	.247	.313	12.88	4.24
Broussard, Geoff	R-R	6-0	185	9-21-90	2	2	2.42	37	0	0	15	45	30	13	12	4	13	72	.189	.224	.168	14.51	2.62
Busenitz, Alan	R-R	6-1	180	8-22-90	0	2	3.30	21	0	0	2	46	49	17	17	2	16	44	.278	.353	.231	8.55	3.11
Carpenter, Tyler	R-R	6-5	225	2-25-92	0	0	6.91	16	0	0	0	27	36	22	21	4	7	31	.310	.255	.348	10.21	2.30
Cooney, Harrison	R-R	6-2	175	3-23-92	1	15	6.54	28	23	0	0	136	171	109	99	11	57	104	.310	.293	.325	6.87	3.76
Ellis, Chris	R-R	6-4	220	9-22-92	4	5	3.88	11	11	1	0	63	53	27	27	6	20	70	.224	.240	.211	10.05	2.87
Etsell, Ryan	R-R	6-4	180	12-18-91	7	5	4.65	28	16	0	0	110	116	66	57	6	27	89	.272	.276	.268	7.26	2.20
Foss, Trevor	R-R	6-3	175	11-15-89	4	2	3.36	30	2	0	0	78	83	40	29	7	18	63	.268	.294	.246	7.30	2.09
Kipper, Jordan	R-R	6-4	185	10-6-92	6	12	5.63	26	26	0	0	128	148	92	80	13	39	95	.288	.320	.261	6.68	2.74
Kopra, Jacob	R-R	6-4	205	10-25-90	0	0	9.00	3	0	0	0	3	4	4	3	0	2	3	.286	.333	.273	9.00	6.00
Loconsole, Brian	R-R	6-2	215	8-10-90	5	2	4.83	40	0	0	1	60	72	32	32	3	18	45	.308	.323	.297	6.79	2.72
Mahle, Greg	L-L	6-2	225	4-17-93	0	1	3.57	21	0	0	9	23	26	10	9	1	3	31	.299	.313	.291	12.31	1.19
Muck, Ronnie	R-R	6-0	195	8-23-91	3	0	4.66	27	0	0	2	39	41	24	20	3	14	43	.277	.310	.247	10.01	3.26
Newcomb, Sean	L-L	6-5	245	6-12-93	6	1	2.47	13	13	0	0	66	50	22	18	2	33	84	.207	.222	.201	11.51	4.52
Nuss, Garrett	R-R	6-1	180	4-15-91	0	7	9.56	23	9	0	1	54	82	63	57	9	36	45	.358	.358	.358	7.55	6.04
Paredes, Eduardo	R-R	6-1	170	3-6-95	0	0	4.73	11	0	0	1	13	13	7	7	0	2	13	.245	.360	.143	8.78	1.35
Petersen, Jake	L-R	6-4	205	4-12-91	1	0	4.15	6	0	0	0	9	9	4	4	0	6	15	.265	.222	.280	15.58	6.23
Rhoades, Jeremy	R-R	6-4	225	2-12-93	4	5	8.35	10	10	0	0	51	65	49	47	14	18	57	.310	.244	.352	10.13	3.20
Smith, Michael	R-R	6-1	195	1-31-90	6	1	1.98	27	0	0	2	36	25	13	8	0	5	36	.192	.200	.188	8.92	1.24
Swanson, Cole	L-L	6-5	200	4-22-91	1	1	5.06	21	0	0	0	21	27	15	12	1	14	24	.297	.341	.260	10.13	5.91
Weaver, Jered	R-R	6-7	210	10-4-82	0	0	1.93	2	2	0	0	9	7	4	2	2	4	7	.219	.100	.273	6.75	3.86

Fielding

Catcher	PCT	G	PO	A	E	DP	PB
Koch	1.000	6	52	5	0	0	0
McGee	.987	55	499	35	7	0	12
Spivey	1.000	7	40	5	0	0	0
Strentz	.989	65	489	60	6	4	13
Wass	1.000	12	82	8	0	0	1

First Base	PCT	G	PO	A	E	DP
Aguilera	.989	84	695	52	8	74
Bayardi	.900	1	9	0	1	0
Cowart	1.000	2	10	0	0	1
Palmer	1.000	7	63	0	0	4
Rosa	.987	17	144	13	2	10
Santana	.967	6	55	3	2	8
Snyder	.988	27	229	13	3	28

Second Base	PCT	G	PO	A	E	DP
Daniel	.950	26	50	65	6	13
Eaves	.974	108	153	330	13	74

	PCT	G	PO	A	E	DP
Ruiz	1.000	6	10	17	0	1
Yacinich	1.000	2	2	5	0	2

Third Base	PCT	G	PO	A	E	DP
Cowart	.974	42	24	89	3	11
Daniel	.985	25	18	46	1	6
Eaves	.942	20	14	51	4	4
Moreno	1.000	1	0	2	0	0
Palmer	.900	15	14	22	4	3
Rosa	.944	12	9	25	2	2
Ruiz	.884	19	17	44	8	3
Sosa	.500	1	2	0	2	0

Shortstop	PCT	G	PO	A	E	DP
Baldoquin	.956	75	101	162	12	33
Cowart	.909	4	3	7	1	1
Eaves	1.000	2	5	7	0	2
Moreno	.919	12	12	22	3	4
Rosa	.926	29	32	56	7	12

	PCT	G	PO	A	E	DP
Ruiz	.944	19	28	56	5	21
Salcedo	1.000	2	1	8	0	2
Yacinich	1.000	6	8	16	0	6

Outfield	PCT	G	PO	A	E	DP
Adams	.974	47	73	3	2	1
Aguilera	1.000	18	22	0	0	0
Bayardi	.952	18	18	2	1	0
Cowart	1.000	1	2	0	0	0
Cowgill	1.000	1	1	0	0	0
Davis	.946	31	52	1	3	1
Fish	.966	82	139	5	5	1
Palmer	.957	33	43	2	2	0
Rosa	1.000	2	2	0	0	0
Ruiz	.000	2	0	0	1	0
Shannon	.983	37	56	1	1	0
Sosa	.942	30	48	1	3	0
Way	.990	131	285	14	3	4

BURLINGTON BEES
LOW CLASS A

MIDWEST LEAGUE

Batting	B-T	HT	WT	DOB	AVG	vLH	vRH	G	AB	R	H	2B	3B	HR	RBI	BB	HBP	SH	SF	SO	SB	CS	SLG	OBP
Abbott, Alex	L-R	6-1	195	11-2-94	.091	.000	.100	4	11	1	1	0	0	0	0	1	1	0	0	2	0	0	.091	.231
Adams, Caleb	R-R	5-10	185	1-26-93	.302	.395	.281	65	235	32	71	10	5	3	30	32	6	3	1	77	7	5	.426	.398
Allen, Trever	R-R	5-11	196	10-16-91	.226	.224	.227	60	221	21	50	8	2	5	17	8	4	0	0	52	0	0	.348	.266
Arakawa, Tim	L-R	5-8	175	4-18-93	.279	.355	.253	64	240	39	67	15	1	4	30	40	2	0	3	52	2	3	.400	.382
Cayones, Exicardo	L-L	6-0	185	10-9-91	.129	.167	.120	11	31	3	4	1	0	0	4	10	3	0	1	10	0	1	.161	.378
Coffman, Kasey	L-R	6-3	200	9-8-91	.077	.333	.043	9	26	3	2	0	0	0	3	7	0	0	2	5	0	0	.077	.257
Daniel, Andrew	R-R	6-1	195	1-27-93	.263	.314	.251	69	266	33	70	17	2	8	43	24	4	2	6	61	7	4	.432	.327
Delgado, Natanael	L-L	6-1	170	10-23-95	.241	.192	.251	108	411	32	99	19	5	6	46	19	3	0	5	104	2	2	.355	.276
Esser, Mitch	L-L	6-0	190	11-3-92	.211	.500	.133	6	19	5	4	1	0	0	1	3	0	0	1	7	2	1	.263	.304
Flair, Nick	R-R	6-3	200	10-31-92	.218	.227	.214	48	170	13	37	12	1	4	12	18	0	1	1	50	1	2	.371	.291
Fletcher, David	R-R	5-10	175	5-31-94	.283	.333	.264	32	120	18	34	4	1	1	10	12	2	1	0	13	6	1	.358	.358
Gildea, Brandon	R-R	6-0	205	8-7-92	.179	.189	.176	46	162	12	29	3	2	1	9	7	4	5	2	39	0	0	.241	.229
Gretzky, Trevor	L-L	6-4	190	9-14-92	.242	.149	.263	78	264	29	64	10	2	2	21	25	2	3	1	54	5	3	.318	.312
Hermosillo, Michael	R-R	5-11	190	1-17-95	.218	.271	.207	79	261	33	57	7	0	0	23	45	5	4	4	49	19	13	.245	.340
Houchins, Zach	R-R	6-2	210	9-16-92	.253	.300	.241	131	494	69	125	27	2	14	66	39	7	0	6	67	0	0	.401	.313
Koenig, Sam	R-R	6-2	200	3-16-92	.120	.333	.091	9	25	1	3	1	0	0	2	1	0	0	1	11	0	0	.160	.214
Linares, Raul	B-R	5-11	160	10-4-90	.182	.000	.200	11	22	5	4	1	0	0	3	6	0	0	0	5	3	1	.227	.357
Mateo, Steven	R-R	6-2	188	8-19-92	.254	.375	.214	51	193	17	49	6	2	1	22	15	1	1	1	57	1	0	.321	.310
Moreno, Juan	R-R	6-1	160	11-17-94	.280	.333	.273	8	25	3	7	2	0	0	4	1	0	1	0	9	0	0	.360	.308
Perez, Ayendy	L-R	5-9	170	10-9-93	.314	.400	.291	45	169	32	53	8	2	0	12	21	0	3	1	34	19	8	.385	.387
Salcedo, Erick	B-R	5-10	155	6-28-93	.230	.273	.220	62	183	23	42	3	0	0	13	13	0	4	1	31	5	0	.246	.279
Seiz, Ryan	B-R	6-3	227	12-8-91	.221	.186	.229	61	213	24	47	9	0	5	23	25	1	0	3	60	0	0	.333	.302
Ward, Taylor	R-R	6-1	180	12-14-93	.348	.500	.304	24	92	10	32	3	0	1	16	15	1	0	0	15	1	1	.413	.412
Wass, Wade	R-R	6-0	215	9-23-91	.257	.263	.255	79	269	32	69	18	2	7	37	39	8	1	2	82	1	1	.416	.365
Whitten, Fran	L-R	6-4	230	12-1-90	.241	.148	.260	44	158	18	38	7	0	2	18	16	3	1	2	44	0	1	.323	.318
Yacinich, Jake	R-R	6-2	195	3-2-93	.268	.115	.303	82	328	49	88	8	4	2	26	19	2	5	1	55	6	3	.335	.311

Pitching

Pitching	B-T	HT	WT	DOB	W	L	ERA	G	GS	CG	SV	IP	H	R	ER	HR	BB	SO	AVG	vLH	vRH	K/9	BB/9
Alonzo, Eric	B-R	6-2	210	8-28-91	1	2	3.60	17	0	0	0	35	34	14	14	1	4	30	.258	.193	.307	7.71	1.03
Anderson, Justin	L-R	6-3	220	9-28-92	9	9	3.41	28	22	0	0	143	148	68	54	4	51	112	.273	.291	.259	7.07	3.22
Bolaski, Michael	R-R	6-3	210	2-5-92	10	11	3.63	27	23	1	1	144	143	70	58	8	55	73	.269	.330	.223	4.57	3.45
Bumgardner, Gaither	R-R	6-6	210	1-29-91	3	0	2.97	18	0	0	0	30	28	12	10	1	14	32	.252	.220	.271	9.49	4.15
Carpenter, Tyler	R-R	6-5	225	2-25-92	1	1	2.97	20	0	0	0	30	33	13	10	0	11	21	.275	.255	.288	6.23	3.26
Fernandez, Arjenis	R-R	6-4	195	7-29-93	0	0	4.50	2	0	0	0	2	2	1	1	0	1	3	.250	.000	.667	13.50	4.50
Hoppe, Jason	R-R	6-1	170	6-13-92	0	0	5.04	14	0	0	1	25	25	16	14	0	8	24	.258	.378	.154	8.64	2.88
Jewell, Jake	R-R	6-3	200	5-16-93	6	8	4.77	31	15	0	2	111	110	67	59	8	31	110	.263	.262	.263	8.89	2.51
Klonowski, Alex	R-R	6-4	195	4-1-92	2	5	3.98	31	1	0	0	63	59	36	28	6	23	78	.251	.324	.195	11.08	3.27
Kopra, Jacob	R-R	6-2	205	10-25-90	0	3	1.99	21	0	0	0	32	30	11	7	1	13	31	.252	.300	.228	8.81	3.69
Middleton, Keynan	R-R	6-2	185	9-12-93	6	11	5.30	26	26	0	0	126	148	78	74	15	47	88	.306	.306	.306	6.30	3.37
Muck, Ronnie	R-R	6-1	195	4-23-92	2	2	1.93	15	0	0	0	23	12	6	5	0	5	31	.156	.103	.211	11.96	1.93
Newcomb, Sean	L-L	6-5	245	6-12-93	1	0	1.83	7	7	0	0	34	25	9	7	1	19	45	.208	.280	.189	11.80	4.98
Nuss, Garrett	R-R	6-1	180	4-15-93	1	0	1.88	6	2	0	1	29	18	7	6	1	14	27	.186	.195	.179	8.48	4.40
Paredes, Eduardo	R-R	6-1	170	3-6-95	0	2	1.71	37	0	0	19	42	31	10	8	2	8	59	.207	.229	.188	12.64	1.71
Petersen, Jason	L-L	6-4	205	4-12-91	0	1	5.87	5	0	0	0	8	5	5	5	0	5	3	.185	.250	.158	5.32	5.87
Piche, Jordan	R-R	6-1	180	9-3-91	3	5	3.64	43	0	0	9	59	57	28	24	5	16	64	.253	.258	.250	9.71	2.43
Rhoades, Jeremy	R-R	6-4	225	2-12-93	5	5	2.69	16	15	0	0	87	75	27	26	4	19	78	.231	.242	.221	8.07	1.97
Robichaux, Austin	R-R	6-5	170	11-23-92	9	8	3.74	28	28	0	0	142	136	68	59	12	50	90	.253	.222	.275	5.83	3.17
Varela, Zach	R-R	6-2	220	8-19-92	0	1	4.00	5	0	0	0	9	12	4	4	0	2	5	.333	.333	.333	5.00	2.00
Wesely, Jonah	L-L	6-1	215	12-8-94	4	2	2.97	22	0	0	0	30	23	16	10	1	13	43	.205	.125	.266	12.76	3.86
Young, Austin	R-R	6-4	220	4-20-92	0	0	3.52	7	0	0	0	8	9	5	3	1	6	3	.300	.389	.167	3.52	7.04

Fielding

Catcher	PCT	G	PO	A	E	DP	PB
Gildea	.983	46	350	45	7	6	12
Ward	1.000	20	135	16	0	3	4
Wass	.977	73	568	68	15	5	11

First Base	PCT	G	PO	A	E	DP
Flair	.985	28	250	17	4	24
Gretzky	1.000	3	14	1	0	2
Houchins	1.000	2	10	3	0	2
Koenig	1.000	5	51	3	0	4
Mateo	.992	36	336	24	3	35
Seiz	.990	53	487	29	5	38
Whitten	.974	16	146	6	4	15

Second Base	PCT	G	PO	A	E	DP
Arakawa	.983	62	106	184	5	41
Daniel	.972	65	109	202	9	38
Flair	1.000	1	1	0	0	0
Fletcher	1.000	3	1	6	0	3
Moreno	1.000	5	11	19	0	5

	PCT	G	PO	A	E	DP
Salcedo	1.000	5	6	21	0	4
Yacinich	1.000	1	2	5	0	1

Third Base	PCT	G	PO	A	E	DP
Arakawa	1.000	1	1	6	0	1
Daniel	1.000	2	3	3	0	1
Flair	.946	14	11	24	2	5
Houchins	.960	111	80	230	13	24
Linares	1.000	8	3	14	0	0
Mateo	1.000	1	0	1	0	0
Moreno	1.000	1	0	4	0	0
Salcedo	.870	9	5	15	3	3
Seiz	.667	1	0	2	1	1

Shortstop	PCT	G	PO	A	E	DP
Arakawa	—	1	0	0	0	0
Fletcher	.977	29	39	91	3	15
Houchins	.962	13	20	30	2	11
Moreno	.889	2	3	5	1	0
Salcedo	.943	23	29	54	5	11

	PCT	G	PO	A	E	DP
Yacinich	.949	76	101	214	17	49

Outfield	PCT	G	PO	A	E	DP
Abbott	1.000	4	4	0	0	0
Adams	.979	58	91	3	2	0
Allen	.978	55	79	10	2	0
Arakawa	—	1	0	0	0	0
Cayones	.933	9	13	1	1	0
Coffman	1.000	8	9	0	0	0
Delgado	.947	91	117	7	7	3
Esser	1.000	6	11	0	0	0
Gretzky	.977	58	84	2	2	0
Hermosillo	.969	75	148	8	5	2
Koenig	—	1	0	0	0	0
Linares	.500	3	2	0	2	0
Perez	1.000	43	87	7	0	2
Salcedo	.975	20	37	2	1	0
Whitten	—	1	0	0	0	0

AZL ANGELS   ROOKIE

ARIZONA LEAGUE

Batting	B-T	HT	WT	DOB	AVG	vLH	vRH	G	AB	R	H	2B	3B	HR	RBI	BB	HBP	SH	SF	SO	SB	CS	SLG	OBP
Allen, Trevor	R-R	5-11	196	10-16-91	.231	.000	.273	4	13	2	3	1	0	0	1	0	1	0	1	3	1	0	.308	.267
Almao, Angel	R-R	5-10	145	11-5-94	.219	.333	.192	33	96	13	21	1	1	0	9	12	3	5	0	26	2	1	.250	.324
Barnes, Jimmy	R-R	6-4	190	6-16-97	.139	.111	.148	25	79	7	11	1	0	1	7	8	1	0	0	32	2	2	.190	.227
Bayardi, Brandon	R-R	6-2	235	11-27-90	.158	.200	.152	11	38	6	6	3	0	1	5	6	2	0	1	9	1	0	.316	.298
Blumenfeld, Dalton	R-R	6-3	210	11-14-96	.143	.067	.167	20	63	8	9	0	1	1	5	6	1	0	1	29	1	0	.222	.225
Delph, Josh	L-L	6-0	166	11-9-92	.313	.300	.316	20	48	10	15	0	1	0	5	8	3	0	0	8	3	1	.354	.441
Esser, Mitch	L-L	6-0	195	11-10-92	.208	.100	.233	20	53	5	11	2	0	0	6	8	4	1	0	12	8	2	.245	.354
Flair, Nick	R-R	6-3	200	10-31-92	.238	.333	.200	6	21	1	5	1	0	0	3	1	0	1	1	3	0	0	.286	.261
Garcia, Julio	R-R	6-0	175	7-31-97	.224	.333	.204	14	58	5	13	2	0	0	6	2	0	1	0	16	4	0	.259	.250
Genao, Angel	R-R	6-2	175	3-22-93	.220	.111	.240	17	59	6	13	4	1	0	7	5	0	2	0	13	2	3	.322	.281
Hinshaw, Chad	R-R	6-1	205	9-10-90	.308	.000	.320	8	26	7	8	2	1	0	4	6	2	0	0	4	3	0	.462	.471
Jones, Jahmai	R-R	5-11	205	8-4-97	.244	.318	.232	40	160	28	39	6	2	2	20	17	4	1	1	33	16	7	.344	.330
Lynch, Nick	R-R	6-1	205	2-23-92	.222	.273	.209	17	54	5	12	4	0	0	8	3	5	0	0	7	2	4	.296	.323
McDonnell, Sam	L-R	6-0	185	8-10-95	.261	.308	.242	27	92	8	24	3	1	0	12	13	0	0	1	17	5	5	.315	.349
Pina, Keinner	R-R	5-10	165	2-12-97	.108	.143	.100	12	37	4	4	0	0	0	2	3	0	1	1	10	0	1	.108	.171
Robertson, Dan	R-R	5-8	205	9-30-85	.000	—	.000	2	5	0	0	0	0	0	0	2	0	0	0	2	0	0	.000	.286
Rodriguez, Jose	R-R	5-11	163	11-3-95	.159	.059	.192	23	69	7	11	1	0	0	2	10	1	1	0	24	3	2	.174	.275
Rutledge, Josh	R-R	6-1	190	4-21-89	.583	.857	.200	3	12	6	7	2	1	1	2	2	0	0	0	0	1	0	1.167	.643
Sanchez, Jeyson	R-R	5-10	170	7-4-94	.556	1.000	.429	6	9	4	5	3	0	0	3	2	1	0	1	1	0	0	.889	.615
Santana, Gabriel	R-R	6-2	180	8-18-95	.224	.226	.224	42	156	21	35	10	2	1	17	10	6	0	1	34	0	0	.333	.295
Sebra, Ryan	R-R	6-2	190	6-8-93	.346	.182	.371	26	81	8	28	5	1	0	13	10	1	3	0	14	3	1	.432	.436
Serena, Jordan	R-R	6-1	175	8-4-92	.232	.313	.212	24	82	19	19	4	2	0	10	11	8	2	0	26	14	0	.329	.376
Shannon, Mark	L-L	6-0	185	4-12-91	.286	—	.286	3	7	2	2	0	0	0	1	1	0	0	0	0	0	0	.286	.375
Silva, Izaak	R-R	5-10	190	5-4-92	.211	.154	.224	23	71	10	15	5	0	0	9	11	0	0	0	13	3	2	.282	.317
Torres, Franklin	R-R	6-1	170	10-27-96	.272	.182	.296	39	147	24	41	6	2	0	13	13	3	2	1	23	11	1	.340	.348
Towey, Cal	L-R	6-1	215	2-6-90	.222	—	.222	3	9	3	2	1	0	0	0	5	0	0	0	1	0	0	.222	.500
Vega, Ryan	R-R	6-2	180	9-17-96	.188	.188	.188	28	96	11	18	4	0	0	5	7	3	0	1	17	4	0	.229	.262

Batting	B-T	HT	WT	DOB	AVG	vLH	vRH	G	AB	R	H	2B	3B	HR	RBI	BB	HBP	SH	SF	SO	SB	CS	SLG	OBP
Walsh, Jared	L-L	6-0	208	7-30-93	.339	.364	.333	30	109	19	37	12	4	2	28	11	2	1	3	17	0	0	.578	.400
Welz, Zach	R-R	6-1	190	5-7-92	.214	.000	.273	7	28	6	6	2	0	0	10	2	1	1	0	5	1	2	.286	.290

Pitching	B-T	HT	WT	DOB	W	L	ERA	G	GS	CG	SV	IP	H	R	ER	HR	BB	SO	AVG	vLH	vRH	K/9	BB/9
Barria, Jaime	R-R	6-1	180	7-18-96	3	0	2.00	7	6	0	0	36	40	12	8	0	3	31	.280	.186	.320	7.75	0.75
Bertness, Nathan	L-L	6-5	185	8-4-95	0	1	4.13	12	3	0	0	28	38	21	13	2	12	27	.330	.231	.360	8.58	3.81
Cobb, Taylor	R-R	6-4	225	11-20-92	1	2	5.17	8	0	0	1	16	16	11	9	0	7	6	.276	.333	.250	3.45	4.02
Foss, Trevor	R-R	6-3	175	11-15-89	0	0	0.00	1	0	0	0	1	1	0	0	0	0	1	.333	.000	.500	9.00	0.00
Glazer, Brandon	R-R	6-3	190	1-29-92	2	4	3.63	13	6	0	0	45	46	22	18	4	3	25	.261	.230	.278	5.04	0.60
Hartman, Zach	R-R	5-11	190	1-1-92	0	0	0.00	9	0	0	1	9	7	1	0	0	1	14	.212	.182	.227	13.50	0.96
Henson, Alex	L-L	6-4	215	7-2-92	2	1	2.76	13	0	0	0	33	32	13	10	1	9	26	.256	.324	.231	7.16	2.48
Heredia, Andres	R-R	6-3	175	8-15-96	0	2	9.00	5	4	0	0	11	16	14	11	0	9	9	.364	.500	.250	7.36	7.36
Herrin, Travis	R-R	6-3	210	4-29-95	1	1	3.93	9	1	0	0	18	20	10	8	1	4	12	.278	.167	.333	5.89	1.96
Hurtado, Daniel	R-R	6-3	180	7-25-92	0	0	6.00	3	3	0	0	3	3	2	2	0	1	2	.250	.125	.500	6.00	3.00
Lavendier, Winston	L-L	6-2	215	8-7-92	2	1	1.65	17	0	0	2	27	19	12	5	0	4	27	.190	.105	.210	8.89	1.32
Lillis-White, Conor	L-L	6-3	210	7-22-92	0	1	2.93	8	0	0	0	15	14	7	5	0	4	18	.233	.500	.180	10.57	2.35
Loconsole, Brian	R-R	6-2	215	8-10-90	0	0	9.00	1	0	0	0	1	3	1	1	0	0	1	.750	1.000	.667	9.00	0.00
McCreery, Adam	L-L	6-8	195	12-31-92	0	0	2.41	16	0	0	0	19	16	5	5	0	14	28	.159	.125	.170	13.50	6.75
McDavid, Jacob	R-R	6-5	195	2-20-93	3	2	2.84	15	0	0	0	32	27	14	10	1	8	29	.221	.227	.218	8.24	2.27
Mendoza, Jose	R-R	6-2	165	7-29-94	0	2	6.86	10	2	0	0	21	30	19	16	0	14	13	.333	.323	.339	5.57	6.00
Mieses, Crusito	R-R	6-5	190	9-15-96	3	4	7.02	12	10	0	0	41	58	35	32	3	12	36	.337	.466	.272	7.90	2.63
Morin, Mike	R-R	6-4	220	5-3-91	0	0	0.00	1	1	0	0	1	1	0	0	0	0	1	.250	.000	.333	9.00	0.00
Pastrone, Sam	R-R	6-0	175	6-28-97	0	2	3.26	10	10	0	0	30	30	12	11	0	8	22	.265	.292	.246	6.53	2.37
Pena, Luis	R-R	5-11	170	8-24-95	1	0	1.80	7	0	0	2	10	7	2	2	0	1	12	.194	.250	.167	10.80	0.90
Petersen, Jake	L-L	6-4	205	4-12-91	0	0	0.00	2	1	0	0	2	1	0	0	0	1	1	.167	—	.167	4.50	4.50
Rondon, Manuel	L-L	6-1	165	3-7-95	1	1	8.64	2	2	0	0	8	13	8	8	0	4	7	.342	.200	.393	7.56	4.32
2-team total (8 Cubs)					2	3	5.67	10	7	0	0	40	46	29	25	0	15	34	—	—	—	7.71	3.40
Snyder, Brandon	L-L	6-0	195	4-13-92	2	1	2.76	15	0	0	2	16	16	5	5	0	5	19	.258	.250	.260	10.47	2.76
Suarez, Jose	L-L	5-10	170	1-3-98	1	1	5.60	4	2	0	0	18	28	15	11	0	4	12	.364	.412	.350	6.11	2.04
Tindall, Matt	R-R	6-3	230	5-16-92	1	3	6.95	15	0	0	1	22	32	19	17	1	12	30	.337	.371	.317	12.27	4.91
Tropeano, Nick	R-R	6-4	200	8-27-90	0	1	2.57	2	2	0	0	7	6	2	2	1	1	6	.222	.091	.313	7.71	1.29

Fielding

Catcher	PCT	G	PO	A	E	DP	PB
Blumenfeld	1.000	5	10	2	0	0	1
Genao	.976	17	140	24	4	1	5
Pina	.989	12	80	10	1	2	2
Sanchez	1.000	4	21	4	0	0	0
Silva	1.000	23	145	34	0	1	4

First Base	PCT	G	PO	A	E	DP
Flair	1.000	2	19	2	0	2
Lynch	1.000	1	14	0	0	1
Santana	.986	35	321	28	5	35
Walsh	.993	18	147	5	1	6

Second Base	PCT	G	PO	A	E	DP
Almao	1.000	13	21	33	0	8
Rodriguez	1.000	2	3	4	0	2
Sebra	.833	3	2	3	1	0

Torres	.957	39	68	112	8	22

Third Base	PCT	G	PO	A	E	DP
Almao	.846	6	3	8	2	2
Flair	.917	3	3	8	1	1
Lynch	.765	10	7	19	8	1
Rodriguez	—	1	0	0	0	0
Sanchez	—	1	0	0	0	0
Sebra	.917	20	10	34	4	4
Serena	.894	17	10	32	5	1

Shortstop	PCT	G	PO	A	E	DP
Almao	.841	13	11	26	7	2
Garcia	.926	14	17	46	5	12
Rodriguez	.930	21	36	71	8	11
Rutledge	1.000	2	4	6	0	2
Serena	.800	7	8	16	6	3

Outfield	PCT	G	PO	A	E	DP
Allen	1.000	4	5	0	0	0
Barnes	.920	17	22	1	2	0
Bayardi	1.000	7	8	0	0	0
Delph	.972	19	31	4	1	1
Esser	1.000	17	28	2	0	1
Hinshaw	1.000	5	8	0	0	0
Jones	.965	40	79	3	3	0
McDonnell	1.000	26	42	3	0	0
Robertson	1.000	2	4	0	0	0
Shannon	1.000	3	2	2	0	0
Towey	1.000	2	3	0	0	0
Vega	.936	28	43	1	3	0
Welz	1.000	7	8	3	0	0

OREM OWLZ   ROOKIE

PIONEER LEAGUE

Batting	B-T	HT	WT	DOB	AVG	vLH	vRH	G	AB	R	H	2B	3B	HR	RBI	BB	HBP	SH	SF	SO	SB	CS	SLG	OBP
Abbott, Alex	L-R	6-1	195	11-2-94	.247	.208	.263	52	186	27	46	14	2	8	34	24	5	0	0	41	8	6	.473	.349
Alberto, Ranyelmy	R-R	6-2	200	5-27-94	.271	.234	.289	52	192	34	52	13	2	9	34	28	3	1	3	52	14	5	.500	.367
Arakawa, Tim	L-R	5-8	175	4-18-93	.250	.400	.143	4	12	3	3	0	0	0	1	0	0	0	0	4	0	0	.250	.250
Boehm, Jeff	L-L	6-1	195	11-4-92	.306	.319	.299	65	248	34	76	19	2	3	45	27	6	0	2	47	13	7	.435	.385
Fletcher, David	R-R	5-10	175	5-31-94	.331	.304	.346	37	160	28	53	12	4	0	30	16	1	1	2	9	11	4	.456	.391
Foster, Jared	R-R	6-1	200	11-2-92	.259	.288	.243	57	232	36	60	11	1	6	38	16	1	0	2	42	13	5	.392	.307
Genao, Angel	R-R	6-2	175	3-22-93	.256	.167	.290	14	43	5	11	3	1	1	12	2	0	0	0	7	2	1	.488	.289
Hermosillo, Michael	R-R	5-11	190	1-17-95	.294	.235	.324	14	51	9	15	3	0	0	2	6	0	0	0	10	5	3	.353	.368
Koenig, Sam	R-R	6-4	220	3-16-92	.271	.167	.318	28	96	19	26	6	1	1	8	14	0	0	0	33	4	1	.385	.364
Lubach, Tanner	R-R	6-0	185	11-21-92	.265	.345	.232	28	98	21	26	5	1	3	19	10	1	0	2	17	1	0	.429	.333
Martinez, Ricky	R-R	6-3	210	11-30-95	.000	.000	.000	1	3	0	0	0	0	0	1	0	0	0	0	1	0	0	.000	.250
Mateo, Steven	R-R	6-2	188	8-19-92	.300	.385	.259	10	40	7	12	1	1	0	5	5	0	0	0	9	0	0	.375	.378
Moreno, Juan	R-R	6-1	160	11-17-94	.314	.302	.319	43	156	23	49	3	0	0	14	16	0	0	1	22	13	4	.333	.376
Moyer, Hutton	B-R	5-11	175	4-30-93	.241	.289	.217	35	137	27	33	7	4	4	29	9	8	0	1	33	4	2	.438	.323
Perez, Ayendy	L-R	5-9	170	9-10-93	.222	.444	.111	12	27	5	6	1	0	0	2	4	1	3	0	3	4	0	.259	.344
Pierson, Michael	L-R	5-11	190	5-3-92	.395	.425	.374	52	195	51	77	15	1	3	31	22	6	1	2	30	17	10	.528	.467
Rodriguez, Jose	R-R	5-11	163	11-3-95	.000	—	.000	2	7	1	0	0	0	0	0	0	0	0	0	2	0	1	.000	.125
Sanger, Brendon	L-R	6-0	185	9-11-93	.300	.224	.340	60	217	45	65	20	1	4	29	45	3	1	4	39	13	3	.456	.420
Serena, Jordan	R-R	6-1	175	8-4-92	.169	.190	.160	20	71	5	12	0	1	0	3	6	1	2	0	17	4	4	.197	.244
Spivey, Eason	R-R	6-1	205	5-16-92	.222	.231	.217	13	36	4	8	4	0	0	5	8	1	0	1	11	0	0	.333	.370
Survance, Kyle	L-R	6-1	190	12-6-93	.363	.360	.365	29	124	27	45	7	1	2	21	15	2	0	2	23	17	5	.484	.434

LOS ANGELES ANGELS

Batting	B-T	HT	WT	DOB	AVG	vLH	vRH	G	AB	R	H	2B	3B	HR	RBI	BB	HBP	SH	SF	SO	SB	CS	SLG	OBP
Torres, Franklin	R-R	6-1	170	10-27-96	.179	.143	.190	8	28	2	5	0	0	0	3	4	2	0	0	9	2	1	.179	.324
Towns, Kenny	R-R	5-11	180	12-19-92	.245	.324	.221	42	147	26	36	12	0	2	15	9	1	1	0	18	9	2	.367	.293
Walsh, Jared	L-L	6-0	208	7-30-93	.182	.500	.111	3	11	1	2	0	0	0	1	1	0	0	1	0	0	0	.182	.231
Ward, Taylor	R-R	6-1	180	12-14-93	.349	.368	.338	32	109	20	38	4	1	2	19	29	2	0	1	8	5	2	.459	.489

Pitching	B-T	HT	WT	DOB	W	L	ERA	G	GS	CG	SV	IP	H	R	ER	HR	BB	SO	AVG	vLH	vRH	K/9	BB/9
Barria, Jaime	R-R	6-1	180	7-18-96	2	4	6.21	8	8	0	0	33	45	27	23	4	7	30	.324	.359	.293	8.10	1.89
Bates, Nathan	R-R	6-8	205	3-1-94	1	3	5.40	14	2	0	0	27	26	17	16	6	6	16	.252	.314	.221	5.40	2.03
Cobb, Taylor	R-R	6-4	225	11-20-92	0	0	10.61	7	0	0	1	9	16	11	11	2	4	7	.372	.471	.308	6.75	3.86
Cox, Aaron	R-R	6-3	205	8-5-94	4	0	3.08	24	0	0	0	38	32	14	13	5	15	35	.239	.259	.225	8.29	3.55
Fernandez, Arjenis	R-R	6-4	195	7-29-93	3	2	6.00	16	0	0	1	27	38	22	18	5	7	19	.322	.326	.319	6.33	2.33
Gatto, Joe	R-R	6-3	204	6-14-95	2	3	4.31	12	12	0	0	54	73	31	26	4	17	38	.340	.341	.339	6.29	2.82
Glazer, Brandon	R-R	6-3	190	1-29-92	0	0	6.43	2	1	0	0	7	13	9	5	0	3	5	.371	.438	.316	6.43	3.86
Glenn, Ronnie	L-L	6-3	230	7-15-93	6	1	3.73	23	0	0	0	41	37	21	17	2	14	54	.231	.149	.265	11.85	3.07
Hartman, Zach	R-R	5-11	190	1-1-92	2	0	2.61	13	0	0	0	21	25	8	6	1	2	26	.305	.353	.271	11.32	0.87
Herrin, Travis	R-R	6-3	210	4-29-95	1	1	11.57	9	0	0	0	9	16	12	12	5	5	8	.364	.667	.207	7.71	4.82
Hofacket, Adam	R-R	6-1	195	2-18-94	4	0	3.77	26	0	0	8	31	32	14	13	5	3	23	.269	.304	.247	6.68	0.87
Lavendier, Winston	L-L	6-2	215	8-7-92	1	0	5.06	3	0	0	0	5	6	3	3	1	1	3	.300	.400	.267	5.06	1.69
Long, Grayson	R-R	6-5	200	5-27-94	0	0	5.03	13	12	0	0	20	19	12	11	1	10	22	.253	.217	.269	10.07	4.58
Lopez, Eduar	R-R	6-0	180	2-21-95	2	2	4.32	8	8	0	0	33	39	21	16	3	16	33	.295	.180	.366	8.91	4.32
Malm, Jeff	L-L	6-3	225	10-31-90	5	2	5.09	15	6	0	0	53	67	33	30	10	17	42	.315	.415	.270	7.13	2.89
McDavid, Jacob	R-R	6-5	195	2-20-93	1	0	3.38	4	0	0	0	5	7	5	2	0	1	3	.333	.200	.455	5.06	1.69
Pena, Luis	R-R	5-11	170	8-24-95	0	2	5.04	19	0	0	1	25	28	16	14	0	8	25	.280	.216	.317	9.00	2.88
Petersen, Jake	L-L	6-4	205	4-12-91	0	0	3.68	4	0	0	0	7	5	4	3	0	3	6	.192	.333	.118	7.36	3.68
Pope, Cody	R-R	6-4	230	5-13-93	1	2	5.79	21	0	0	0	33	37	21	21	7	11	31	.285	.220	.338	8.54	3.03
Rhodes, Aaron	L-R	6-0	190	9-24-92	0	2	6.86	14	0	0	3	21	23	19	16	2	4	23	.271	.344	.226	9.86	1.71
Rodriguez, Jose	R-R	6-2	155	8-29-95	3	3	4.79	15	0	0	0	62	77	35	33	5	16	58	.312	.356	.281	8.42	2.32
Ruxer, Jared	R-R	6-3	190	7-29-92	0	3	4.85	14	11	0	0	30	30	18	16	2	11	33	.261	.255	.267	10.01	3.34
Varela, Zach	R-R	6-2	220	3-29-92	0	1	1.69	12	0	0	0	16	11	4	3	0	2	8	.193	.190	.194	4.50	1.13
Watson, Tyler	L-L	5-11	175	6-9-93	2	4	4.57	24	1	0	0	45	63	31	23	7	9	44	.332	.345	.326	8.74	1.79
Young, Austin	R-R	6-4	220	4-20-92	1	0	5.68	14	0	0	1	19	16	12	12	1	14	11	.225	.227	.224	5.21	6.63

Fielding

Catcher	PCT	G	PO	A	E	DP	PB
Genao	.963	12	95	10	4	2	1
Lubach	.983	28	203	29	4	1	3
Spivey	.981	13	93	11	2	0	1
Ward	.984	29	206	34	4	7	1

First Base	PCT	G	PO	A	E	DP
Boehm	.987	58	496	31	7	49
Koenig	.990	11	97	5	1	11
Mateo	.988	7	76	5	1	3
Walsh	.889	1	8	0	1	0

Second Base	PCT	G	PO	A	E	DP
Arakawa	1.000	2	7	7	0	0
Moreno	.813	4	4	9	3	3
Moyer	.963	34	70	112	7	33
Pierson	1.000	12	19	32	0	3
Serena	.970	20	36	61	3	13
Torres	.905	8	12	26	4	3

Third Base	PCT	G	PO	A	E	DP
Arakawa	1.000	1	2	0	0	0
Koenig	.500	2	0	1	1	1
Moreno	.923	3	0	12	1	1
Pierson	.945	35	17	69	5	12
Serena	—	1	0	0	0	0
Towns	.883	39	23	68	12	8

Shortstop	PCT	G	PO	A	E	DP
Fletcher	.970	37	74	119	6	27
Moreno	.917	36	60	94	14	18
Moyer	1.000	1	1	3	0	0
Rodriguez	.833	2	2	3	1	1
Torres	1.000	1	0	1	0	0

Outfield	PCT	G	PO	A	E	DP
Abbott	.979	50	87	8	2	2
Alberto	.927	32	46	5	4	1
Foster	.939	57	98	10	7	2
Hermosillo	1.000	13	18	2	0	0
Koenig	—	1	0	0	0	0
Perez	1.000	10	11	2	0	1
Sanger	.963	47	71	7	3	0
Survance	.983	26	54	5	1	3

DSL ANGELS · ROOKIE

DOMINICAN SUMMER LEAGUE

Batting	B-T	HT	WT	DOB	AVG	vLH	vRH	G	AB	R	H	2B	3B	HR	RBI	BB	HBP	SH	SF	SO	SB	CS	SLG	OBP
Arias, Jonathan	R-R	6-2	170	1-31-96	.227	.265	.219	59	203	27	46	5	4	1	19	19	2	0	0	49	8	6	.305	.299
Castillo, Deyvi	R-R	6-1	175	8-13-97	.241	.000	.280	18	58	8	14	2	0	0	7	5	1	0	0	10	4	4	.276	.313
Diaz, Argenis	R-R	6-2	160	9-17-96	.245	.053	.287	51	106	18	26	1	3	0	14	21	2	1	1	27	11	2	.311	.377
Flores, Jeans	R-R	5-11	165	3-20-98	.237	.107	.262	50	169	27	40	3	2	1	13	20	7	0	3	24	11	5	.296	.337
Garcia, Julio	R-R	6-0	175	7-31-97	.214	.381	.177	32	117	14	25	1	2	0	6	4	1	3	2	28	11	2	.256	.242
Garcia, Stevens	R-R	6-2	170	7-30-97	.213	.118	.229	39	122	13	26	4	1	1	4	14	7	0	0	59	1	2	.287	.329
Martinez, Ricky	R-R	6-3	210	11-30-95	.228	.294	.216	36	114	13	26	5	2	2	12	21	1	0	2	39	10	3	.360	.348
Mendoza, Willian	R-R	5-11	175	12-1-97	.231	.250	.229	18	39	3	9	1	0	0	2	5	4	0	0	12	1	2	.256	.375
Mills, Goldny	B-R	5-11	170	12-11-95	.252	.111	.282	38	103	18	26	3	1	0	15	19	4	1	3	19	3	3	.301	.380
Molina, Angel	R-R	6-1	175	8-20-97	.273	.219	.285	51	183	29	50	13	0	4	22	21	11	1	3	41	7	3	.410	.376
Mota, Darlyn	B-R	6-1	165	8-2-96	.286	.444	.259	56	189	24	54	10	4	0	33	22	4	1	1	42	6	6	.381	.370
Pedie, Junior	R-R	6-3	185	6-17-97	.223	.294	.213	43	139	20	31	5	0	2	16	19	3	0	0	51	5	4	.302	.329
Pina, Keinner	R-R	5-10	165	2-12-97	.246	.174	.263	35	122	15	30	2	1	0	13	21	1	0	1	21	7	4	.279	.359
Pineda, Gleylin	L-R	5-11	160	8-19-96	.221	.241	.218	60	208	18	46	5	3	1	17	37	2	0	0	39	8	9	.288	.344
Richiez, Danny	R-R	6-2	175	8-13-96	.276	.571	.182	8	29	6	8	0	1	1	3	1	2	0	0	10	2	0	.448	.344
Rivas, Leonardo	R-S	5-10	150	10-10-97	.258	.366	.233	65	213	38	55	8	7	1	31	37	17	4	5	53	21	12	.376	.401
Sala, Johan	R-R	6-1	175	12-17-97	.233	.189	.229	53	229	23	51	8	1	0	13	19	3	1	1	54	15	11	.266	.290
Santana, Yefry	R-R	6-1	170	11-8-95	.429	.500	.412	7	21	5	9	3	1	1	4	3	0	0	1	4	2	2	.810	.480

Pitching	B-T	HT	WT	DOB	W	L	ERA	G	GS	CG	SV	IP	H	R	ER	HR	BB	SO	AVG	vLH	vRH	K/9	BB/9
Acosta, Geovanny	R-R	6-2	165	8-15-93	1	1	2.21	19	0	0	5	20	18	9	5	1	7	22	.222	.115	.273	9.74	3.10
Castro, Jesus	R-R	6-0	165	2-20-98	3	4	4.28	14	8	0	1	55	64	31	26	3	17	31	.303	.277	.315	5.10	2.80
Galan, Lianmy	R-R	6-3	165	8-23-96	1	4	2.88	14	10	0	1	59	58	25	19	2	22	28	.265	.250	.272	4.25	3.34

Pitching	B-T	HT	WT	DOB	W	L	ERA	G	GS	CG	SV	IP	H	R	ER	HR	BB	SO	AVG	vLH	vRH	K/9	BB/9
Gonzalez, Raymundo	R-R	6-3	190	9-8-95	4	5	4.91	17	4	0	0	33	38	28	18	0	18	29	.273	.286	.268	7.91	4.91
Melendez, Cesar	R-R	6-1	162	3-20-95	3	3	5.75	21	0	0	2	41	57	32	26	1	10	36	.333	.404	.306	7.97	2.21
Molina, Cristopher	R-R	6-3	170	6-10-97	1	3	3.86	15	15	0	0	61	59	38	26	0	32	52	.255	.299	.234	7.71	4.75
Montilla, Anderson	R-R	6-4	180	10-23-95	1	5	7.82	14	5	0	0	36	43	36	31	2	34	22	.309	.381	.297	5.55	8.58
Ortega, Oliver	R-R	6-0	165	10-2-96	1	3	4.33	19	2	0	0	44	43	31	21	0	18	37	.254	.267	.250	7.63	3.71
Peralta, Alexis	R-R	6-3	170	11-3-96	1	4	5.79	17	6	0	0	33	19	34	21	2	41	23	.186	.269	.158	6.34	11.30
Pina, Shakiro	L-L	5-11	170	3-4-97	0	0	4.76	21	0	0	0	23	25	15	12	0	21	17	.284	.143	.296	6.75	8.34
Pineda, Roberto	R-R	6-3	190	6-2-96	2	0	4.06	16	0	0	0	31	31	21	14	2	10	24	.252	.241	.255	6.97	2.90
Rodriguez, Elvin	R-R	6-3	160	3-31-98	0	6	4.59	12	11	0	0	51	48	29	26	4	19	36	.250	.061	.289	6.35	3.35
Salomon, Franklin	L-L	5-11	160	3-17-95	0	0	3.67	25	0	0	1	27	20	17	11	0	17	19	.198	.100	.209	6.33	5.67
Suarez, Jose	L-L	5-10	170	1-3-98	2	2	2.13	11	11	0	0	55	43	18	13	0	8	34	.215	.261	.209	5.56	1.31
Tavarez, Jorge	R-R	5-10	150	8-4-95	3	3	5.93	23	0	0	6	30	38	24	20	1	11	38	.314	.316	.313	11.27	3.26
Yan, Jefry	L-L	6-3	170	8-17-96	4	2	1.56	24	0	0	1	35	23	12	6	1	20	26	.200	.182	.202	6.75	5.19

Fielding

Catcher	PCT	G	PO	A	E	DP	PB
Flores	.971	41	257	41	9	2	12
Mendoza	.987	17	67	7	1	1	7
Molina	1.000	2	9	2	0	0	2
Pina	.965	23	134	33	6	1	1

First Base	PCT	G	PO	A	E	DP
Arias	.984	16	120	7	2	13
Molina	.982	49	424	23	8	48
Pina	1.000	10	76	7	0	6
Richiez	.960	3	24	0	1	3

Second Base	PCT	G	PO	A	E	DP
Arias	1.000	3	2	3	0	1
Mills	.956	37	77	76	7	17
Mota	.920	5	11	12	2	5
Pineda	.932	12	21	34	4	9
Rivas	.967	30	54	65	4	20

Third Base	PCT	G	PO	A	E	DP
Arias	.857	36	39	69	18	12
Mota	.894	27	23	53	9	7
Pineda	.625	4	3	2	3	0
Richiez	.842	5	6	10	3	0
Rivas	.763	11	12	17	9	0

Shortstop	PCT	G	PO	A	E	DP
Garcia	.911	30	47	97	14	18
Pineda	.955	42	79	134	10	24
Rivas	.818	3	1	8	2	2

Outfield	PCT	G	PO	A	E	DP
Arias	1.000	2	1	0	0	0
Castillo	.964	16	27	0	1	0
Diaz	1.000	49	70	5	0	2
Garcia	.833	18	17	3	4	1
Martinez	1.000	34	59	3	0	0
Pedie	.889	36	54	2	7	2
Rivas	.980	25	45	3	1	1
Sala	.963	62	103	2	4	1
Santana	1.000	7	10	1	0	0

Los Angeles Dodgers

SEASON IN A SENTENCE: The Dodgers rode two of the game's elite pitchers to a third consecutive National League West crown, but a 3-2 loss to the Mets in the decisive Game Five of the NL Division Series ended another year without a World Series appearance.

HIGH POINT: Zack Greinke twirled a stretch of 45 ⅔ innings without allowing a run into late July. Greinke's 1.66 ERA led the majors, ending Clayton Kershaw's run of four straight years with the best ERA in baseball. Not that Kershaw was off his game by any means—his 2.13 ERA ranked third in the majors, while his 301 strikeouts marked the first time a pitcher struck out at least 300 in a season since Randy Johnson and Curt Schilling each did it in 2002.

LOW POINT: There weren't many rough patches during the season for the Dodgers, but failling to the Mets in the Championship Series qualifies as a disappointment for an ownership group with high expectations and the game's highest payroll. Regular season wins wasn't enough for Don Mattingly to keep his job. He parted ways with Los Angeles after the season despite three straight postseason berths and 446 wins over five years.

NOTABLE ROOKIES: Center fielder Joc Pederson got off to a torrid start before struggling in the second half. He matched Kris Bryant for most home runs by a rookie with 26 and was second to the Rookie of the Year in strikeouts with 170. Second baseman Enrique Hernandez provided a pleasant surprise with his offensive performance and defensive versatility. Righthanders Pedro Baez and Yimi Garcia played key roles in the bullpen while top prospect Corey Seager excelled as a September callup.

KEY TRANSACTIONS: The Dodgers swung a monster three-team, 13-player deal at the trade deadline to send Hector Olivera, the big-ticket Cuban infielder the Dodgers had just signed before the season, to the Braves in exchange for righthander Alex Wood and shortstop Jose Peraza.

DOWN ON THE FARM: The Dodgers continue to have one of the brightest farm systems in baseball, led by Seager and 19-year-old lefthander Julio Urias. Double-A righthander Jose De Leon isn't too far behind Urias, while the addition of Peraza adds another near big league-ready youngster to the organization. Lower in the system, first baseman/outfielder Cody Bellinger and outfielder Alex Verdugo both had breakout seasons.

OPENING DAY PAYROLL: $272,789,040 (1st)

PLAYERS OF THE YEAR

MAJOR LEAGUE	MINOR LEAGUE
Clayton Kershaw	**Corey Seager**
lhp	ss
16-7, 2.13	(Double-A/Triple-A)
First pitcher with 300	.293/.344/.487
strikeouts since 2002	18 HR, 76 RBI, 37 2B.

ORGANIZATION LEADERS

BATTING   *Minimum 250 AB

MAJORS

* AVG	Adrian Gonzalez	.275
* OPS	Adrian Gonzalez	.830
HR	Adrian Gonzalez	28
RBI	Adrian Gonzalez	90

MINORS

* AVG	Alex Verdugo, Great Lakes, Rancho Cucamonga	.311
* OBP	Lars Anderson, Okla. City, Tulsa	.370
* SLG	Cody Bellinger, Rancho Cucamonga	.538
R	Cody Bellinger, Rancho Cucamonga	97
H	Alex Verdugo, Great Lakes, Rancho Cucamonga	159
TB	Cody Bellinger, Rancho Cucamonga	257
2B	Kyle Farmer, Rancho Cucamonga, Tulsa	40
3B	Scott Schebler, Okla. City	9
HR	Cody Bellinger, Rancho Cucamonga	30
RBI	Cody Bellinger, Rancho Cucamonga	103
BB	Lars Anderson, Okla. City, Tulsa	93
SO	Cody Bellinger, Rancho Cucamonga	150
SB	Darnell Sweeney, Okla. City	32

PITCHING   #Minimum 75 IP

MAJORS

W	Zack Greinke	19
# ERA	Zack Greinke	1.66
SO	Clayton Kershaw	301
SV	Kenley Jansen	36

MINORS

W	Zach Lee, AZL, Rancho Cucamonga, Okla. City	13
L	Chris Anderson, Tulsa, Okla. City	10
# ERA	Trevor Oaks, Great Lakes, Rancho Cucamonga	2.65
G	Ramon Benjamin, Rancho Cucamonga, Tulsa	51
GS	Chris Anderson, Tulsa, Okla. City	24
	Grant Holmes, Great Lakes	24
SV	David Aardsma, Okla. City	15
IP	Deck McGuire, Tulsa, Okla. City	137
BB	Chris Anderson, Tulsa, Okla. City	68
SO	Jose De Leon, Rancho Cucamonga, Tulsa	163
AVG	Jose De Leon, Rancho Cucamonga, Tulsa	.208

2015 PERFORMANCE

General Manager: Farhan Zaidi. **Farm Director:** Gabe Kapler. **Scouting Director:** Billy Gasparino.

Class	Team	League	W	L	PCT	Finish	Manager
Majors	Los Angeles Dodgers	National	92	70	.568	2nd (15)	Don Mattingly
Triple-A	Oklahoma City Dodgers	Pacific Coast	86	58	.597	1st (16)	Damon Berryhill
Double-A	Tulsa Drillers	Texas	62	77	.446	6th (8)	Razor Shines
High A	Rancho Cucamonga Quakes	California	78	62	.557	3rd (10)	Bill Haselman
Low A	Great Lakes Loons	Midwest	68	69	.496	11th (16)	Luis Matos
Rookie	Ogden Raptors	Pioneer	43	33	.566	1st (8)	John Shoemaker
Rookie	Dodgers	Arizona	29	27	.518	6th (14)	Jack McDowell
Overall 2015 Minor League Record			366	326	.529	8th (30)	

ORGANIZATION STATISTICS

LOS ANGELES DODGERS

NATIONAL LEAGUE

Batting	B-T	HT	WT	DOB	AVG	vLH	vRH	G	AB	R	H	2B	3B	HR	RBI	BB	HBP	SH	SF	SO	SB	CS	SLG	OBP
Barnes, Austin	R-R	5-10	185	12-28-89	.207	.167	.235	20	29	4	6	2	0	0	1	6	1	1	0	6	1	0	.276	.361
Barney, Darwin	R-R	5-10	180	11-8-85	.000	.000	.000	2	4	0	0	0	0	0	0	0	0	0	0	0	0	0	.000	.000
Callaspo, Alberto	B-R	5-9	225	4-19-83	.260	.227	.267	60	123	8	32	5	0	0	7	14	0	1	0	24	0	0	.301	.336
2-team total (37 Atlanta)					.235	—	—	97	230	20	54	7	0	1	15	28	0	1	2	34	0	0	.278	.315
Crawford, Carl	L-L	6-2	230	8-5-81	.265	.296	.260	69	181	19	48	9	2	4	16	10	0	0	0	41	10	2	.403	.304
Ellis, A.J.	R-R	6-2	230	4-9-81	.238	.260	.221	63	181	24	43	9	0	7	21	32	1	3	0	38	0	0	.403	.355
Ethier, Andre	L-L	6-2	210	4-10-82	.294	.200	.306	142	395	54	116	20	7	14	53	43	4	0	3	75	2	3	.486	.366
Gonzalez, Adrian	L-L	6-2	220	5-8-82	.275	.294	.267	156	571	76	157	33	0	28	90	62	6	0	3	107	0	1	.480	.350
Grandal, Yasmani	B-R	6-1	225	11-8-88	.234	.308	.221	115	355	43	83	12	0	16	47	65	2	1	3	92	0	1	.403	.353
Guerrero, Alex	R-R	6-0	215	11-20-86	.233	.238	.230	106	219	25	51	9	1	11	36	7	2	0	2	57	1	0	.434	.261
Heisey, Chris	R-R	6-1	215	12-14-84	.182	.146	.286	33	55	8	10	2	0	2	9	15	0	0	2	17	0	1	.327	.347
Hernandez, Enrique	R-R	5-11	200	8-24-91	.307	.423	.234	76	202	24	62	12	2	7	22	11	2	1	2	46	0	2	.490	.346
Kendrick, Howie	R-R	5-11	200	7-12-83	.295	.291	.297	117	464	64	137	22	9	9	54	27	2	1	1	82	6	2	.409	.336
Pederson, Joc	L-L	6-1	215	4-21-92	.210	.216	.209	151	480	67	101	19	1	26	54	92	9	2	2	170	4	7	.417	.346
Peraza, Jose	R-R	6-0	180	4-30-94	.182	.267	.000	7	22	3	4	1	0	0	1	2	0	1	0	2	3	0	.318	.250
Puig, Yasiel	R-R	6-2	255	12-7-90	.255	.279	.248	79	282	30	72	12	3	11	38	26	2	0	1	66	3	3	.436	.322
Rollins, Jimmy	B-R	5-7	175	11-27-78	.224	.292	.204	144	517	71	116	24	3	13	41	44	0	1	1	86	12	8	.358	.285
Ruggiano, Justin	R-R	6-1	210	4-12-82	.291	.333	.100	21	55	12	16	4	1	4	12	3	2	0	0	14	2	0	.618	.350
Schebler, Scott	L-R	6-0	225	10-6-90	.250	.000	.281	19	36	6	9	0	0	3	4	3	1	0	0	13	2	1	.500	.325
Seager, Corey	L-R	6-4	215	4-27-94	.337	.325	.345	27	98	17	33	8	1	4	17	14	1	0	0	19	2	0	.561	.425
Torreyes, Ronald	R-R	5-10	150	9-2-92	.333	.000	.400	8	6	1	2	1	0	0	1	1	0	1	0	1	0	0	.500	.429
Turner, Justin	R-R	5-11	205	11-23-84	.294	.248	.312	126	385	55	113	26	1	16	60	36	13	—	4	71	5	2	.491	.370
Uribe, Juan	R-R	6-0	245	3-22-79	.247	.250	.246	29	81	6	20	2	0	1	6	5	0	0	1	9	1	0	.309	.287
3-team total (46 Atlanta, 44 New York)					.253	—	—	119	360	40	91	17	0	14	43	34	2	0	1	80	2	0	.417	.320
Utley, Chase	L-R	6-1	190	12-17-78	.202	.171	.213	34	124	14	25	9	1	3	9	10	6	0	1	29	1	0	.363	.291
2-team total (73 Philadelphia)					.212	—	—	107	373	37	79	21	2	8	39	32	10	0	8	64	4	0	.343	.286
Van Slyke, Scott	R-R	6-4	220	7-24-86	.239	.258	.225	96	222	19	53	14	0	6	30	23	4	1	3	62	3	1	.383	.317

Pitching	B-T	HT	WT	DOB	W	L	ERA	G	GS	CG	SV	IP	H	R	ER	HR	BB	SO	AVG	vLH	vRH	K/9	BB/9
Anderson, Brett	L-L	6-3	240	2-1-88	10	9	3.69	31	31	1	0	180	194	82	74	18	46	116	.278	.284	.276	5.79	2.30
Avilan, Luis	L-L	6-2	220	7-19-89	0	1	5.17	23	0	0	0	16	13	9	9	2	5	18	.224	.214	.233	10.34	2.87
2-team total (50 Atlanta)					2	5	4.05	73	0	0	0	53	48	24	24	6	15	49	—	—		8.27	2.53
Baez, Pedro	R-R	6-0	230	3-11-88	4	2	3.35	52	0	0	0	51	47	22	19	4	11	60	.247	.255	.245	10.59	1.94
Baker, Scott	R-R	6-4	215	9-19-81	0	1	5.73	2	2	0	0	11	11	7	7	4	3	8	.262	.308	.241	6.55	2.45
Beachy, Brandon	R-R	6-2	215	9-3-86	0	1	7.88	2	2	0	0	8	10	7	7	1	6	5	.313	.200	.412	5.63	6.75
Bolsinger, Mike	R-R	6-1	215	1-29-88	6	6	3.62	21	21	0	0	109	104	49	44	11	45	98	.251	.287	.224	8.07	3.70
Coulombe, Daniel	L-L	5-10	190	10-26-89	0	0	7.56	5	0	0	0	8	9	7	7	0	6	7	.265	.133	.368	7.56	6.48
Frias, Carlos	R-R	6-4	195	11-13-89	5	5	4.06	17	13	0	0	78	88	38	35	7	26	43	.297	.357	.251	4.98	3.01
Garcia, Yimi	R-R	6-1	210	8-18-90	3	5	3.34	59	1	0	1	57	44	23	21	8	10	68	.209	.172	.224	10.80	1.59
Greinke, Zack	R-R	6-0	195	10-21-83	19	3	1.66	32	32	1	0	223	148	43	41	14	40	200	.187	.194	.182	8.08	1.62
Hatcher, Chris	R-R	6-1	200	1-12-85	3	5	3.69	49	0	0	4	39	35	19	16	4	13	45	.238	.180	.268	10.38	3.00
Howell, J.P.	L-L	6-0	180	4-25-83	6	1	1.43	65	0	0	1	44	47	9	7	3	14	39	.272	.224	.318	7.98	2.86
Huff, David	L-L	6-1	210	8-22-84	0	0	9.00	3	0	0	0	6	11	6	6	2	1	4	.407	.333	.444	6.00	1.50
Jansen, Kenley	B-R	6-5	265	9-30-87	2	1	2.41	54	0	0	36	52	33	14	14	6	8	80	.176	.200	.151	13.76	1.38
Johnson, Jim	R-R	6-6	240	6-27-83	0	3	10.13	23	0	0	1	19	32	22	21	3	6	17	.381	.406	.365	8.20	2.89
2-team total (49 Atlanta)					2	6	4.46	72	0	0	10	67	77	36	33	5	20	50	—	—		6.75	2.70
Kershaw, Clayton	L-L	6-4	225	3-19-88	16	7	2.13	33	33	4	0	233	163	62	55	15	42	301	.194	.203	.192	11.64	1.62
Latos, Mat	R-R	6-6	245	12-9-87	0	3	6.66	5	0	0	0	24	31	19	18	3	6	18	.323	.298	.347	6.66	2.22
2-team total (16 Miami)					4	10	4.95	22	21	0	0	113	116	65	62	11	31	97	—	—		7.75	2.48
Lee, Zach	R-R	6-4	210	9-13-91	0	1	13.50	1	1	0	0	5	11	7	7	1	1	3	.478	.563	.286	5.79	1.93
Liberatore, Adam	L-L	6-3	240	5-12-87	2	2	4.25	39	0	0	0	30	26	14	14	3	9	29	.232	.242	.220	8.80	2.73
McCarthy, Brandon	R-R	6-7	225	7-7-83	3	0	5.87	4	4	0	0	23	24	15	15	9	4	29	.267	.234	.302	11.35	1.57
Nicasio, Juan	R-R	6-4	250	8-31-86	1	3	3.86	53	1	0	1	58	59	25	25	1	32	65	.263	.348	.226	10.03	4.94
Peralta, Joel	R-R	5-10	210	3-23-76	3	1	4.34	33	0	0	3	29	28	14	14	6	8	24	.248	.229	.267	7.45	2.48

Pitching	B-T	HT	WT	DOB	W	L	ERA	G	GS	CG	SV	IP	H	R	ER	HR	BB	SO	AVG	vLH	vRH	K/9	BB/9
Ravin, Josh	R-R	6-4	230	1-21-88	2	1	6.75	9	0	0	0	9	13	7	7	3	4	12	.310	.318	.300	11.57	3.86
Rodriguez, Paco	L-L	6-3	220	4-16-91	0	0	2.61	18	0	0	0	10	10	3	3	0	3	8	.263	.292	.214	6.97	2.61
Santos, Sergio	R-R	6-4	215	7-4-83	0	0	4.73	12	0	0	0	13	13	7	7	2	7	15	.245	.400	.152	10.13	4.73
Surkamp, Eric	L-L	6-5	220	7-16-87	0	0	10.80	1	0	0	0	3	4	4	4	2	1	4	.308	.400	.250	10.80	2.70
Thomas, Ian	L-L	6-4	215	4-20-87	1	1	4.00	9	1	0	0	18	16	8	8	1	6	18	.239	.154	.293	9.00	3.00
2-team total (5 Atlanta)					1	1	3.86	14	1	0	0	23	20	11	10	2	11	23	—	—	—	8.87	4.24
Tsao, Chin-Hui	R-R	6-1	210	6-2-81	1	1	10.29	5	0	0	0	7	15	9	8	3	3	7	.441	.571	.350	9.00	3.86
West, Matt	R-R	6-1	200	11-21-88	0	0	0.00	2	0	0	0	3	2	0	0	0	1	2	.200	.167	.250	6.00	3.00
Wieland, Joe	R-R	6-2	205	1-21-90	0	1	8.31	2	2	0	0	9	10	8	8	2	5	4	.294	.400	.250	4.15	5.19
Wood, Alex	L-L	6-4	215	1-12-91	5	6	4.35	12	12	0	0	70	66	36	34	7	23	49	.253	.174	.281	6.27	2.94
2-team total (20 Atlanta)					12	12	3.84	32	32	0	0	190	198	86	81	15	59	139	—	—	—	6.60	2.80

Fielding

Catcher	PCT	G	PO	A	E	DP	PB
Barnes	1.000	11	57	5	0	0	1
Ellis	1.000	62	515	49	0	3	3
Grandal	.997	107	811	60	3	5	8

First Base	PCT	G	PO	A	E	DP
Gonzalez	.996	149	1267	116	6	100
Grandal	1.000	6	26	1	0	6
Turner	.983	10	53	5	1	6
Utley	1.000	2	12	2	0	0
Van Slyke	.990	21	95	6	1	10

Second Base	PCT	G	PO	A	E	DP
Barnes	1.000	1	0	1	0	0
Hernandez	1.000	20	36	47	0	11
Kendrick	.990	113	193	295	5	52
Peraza	.926	6	5	20	2	5
Torreyes	1.000	4	2	4	0	1
Turner	1.000	5	1	10	0	2
Utley	.985	26	54	81	2	21

Third Base	PCT	G	PO	A	E	DP
Barnes	—	1	0	0	0	0
Barney	—	1	0	0	0	0
Callaspo	.970	37	17	48	2	4
Guerrero	.978	22	10	34	1	3
Hernandez	—	1	0	0	0	0
Seager	1.000	6	1	11	0	1
Torreyes	—	3	0	0	0	0
Turner	.960	100	39	175	9	18
Uribe	.981	24	9	44	1	3
Utley	1.000	3	1	8	0	0

Shortstop	PCT	G	PO	A	E	DP
Barney	1.000	1	0	3	0	0
Hernandez	.957	16	11	34	2	2
Rollins	.983	134	166	351	9	65
Seager	.949	21	23	70	5	12
Turner	.800	1	2	2	1	1

Outfield	PCT	G	PO	A	E	DP
Crawford	1.000	51	38	0	0	0
Ethier	.979	127	177	6	4	2
Guerrero	.938	29	29	1	2	0
Heisey	1.000	28	27	1	0	0
Hernandez	.979	34	45	2	1	0
Pederson	.986	147	269	5	4	1
Peraza	1.000	1	2	0	0	0
Puig	.993	78	132	6	1	0
Ruggiano	1.000	16	18	0	0	0
Schebler	1.000	13	18	0	0	0
Van Slyke	.978	74	81	8	2	1

OKLAHOMA CITY DODGERS — *TRIPLE-A*

PACIFIC COAST LEAGUE

Batting	B-T	HT	WT	DOB	AVG	vLH	vRH	G	AB	R	H	2B	3B	HR	RBI	BB	HBP	SH	SF	SO	SB	CS	SLG	OBP
Anderson, Lars	L-L	6-4	215	9-25-87	.000	.000	.000	3	9	1	0	0	0	0	0	2	0	0	0	2	0	0	.000	.182
Barnes, Austin	R-R	5-10	185	12-28-89	.315	.412	.267	81	292	40	92	17	2	9	42	35	3	1	4	36	12	2	.479	.389
Barney, Darwin	R-R	5-10	180	11-8-85	.277	.268	.281	96	347	52	96	15	0	4	31	22	4	4	2	44	7	4	.354	.325
Britton, Buck	L-R	6-0	170	5-16-86	.262	.222	.282	117	385	43	101	14	4	7	49	27	1	0	2	52	11	5	.374	.311
Burgamy, Brian	B-R	5-10	190	6-27-81	.152	.267	.097	24	46	5	7	3	0	0	4	6	0	0	0	13	0	1	.217	.250
Carp, Mike	L-R	6-0	210	6-30-86	.091	.000	.125	7	22	0	2	1	0	0	0	1	0	0	0	7	1	0	.136	.130
Carson, Matt	R-R	6-2	200	7-1-81	.179	.091	.200	24	56	4	10	4	0	0	9	8	1	1	2	15	1	0	.250	.284
2-team total (33 Nashville)					.199	—	—	57	166	23	33	9	0	3	22	18	5	2	3	37	4	1	.307	.292
Chubb, Austin	R-R	6-1	200	4-17-89	.500	.667	.000	1	4	1	2	0	0	0	1	0	0	0	1	0	0	0	.500	.400
Crawford, Carl	L-L	6-2	230	8-5-81	.367	1.000	.321	8	30	8	11	2	1	1	6	1	0	0	1	3	0	0	.600	.375
Dickson, O'Koyea	R-R	5-11	220	2-9-90	.262	.266	.259	117	386	48	101	27	0	13	50	21	6	1	6	63	2	0	.433	.305
Grandal, Yasmani	B-R	6-1	225	11-8-88	.300	.200	.400	3	10	6	3	1	0	0	0	5	0	0	0	3	0	0	.400	.533
Heisey, Chris	R-R	6-1	215	12-14-84	.241	.213	.257	66	216	46	52	8	1	15	41	39	6	0	1	57	3	0	.495	.370
Henriquez, Ralph	B-R	6-1	205	4-7-87	.254	.448	.119	26	71	8	18	4	0	2	7	3	0	0	0	23	0	0	.394	.284
Hernandez, Enrique	R-R	5-11	200	8-24-91	.169	.136	.189	16	59	6	10	2	0	1	9	4	0	0	1	14	1	0	.254	.219
Jensen, Kyle	R-L	6-3	230	5-20-88	.259	.271	.251	128	417	59	108	28	3	20	71	31	4	0	4	110	0	0	.484	.314
Johnson, Elliot	B-R	6-1	190	3-9-84	.244	.311	.200	55	156	28	38	13	0	3	13	20	2	0	0	38	3	2	.385	.337
Lavin, Peter	L-L	5-11	180	12-27-87	.417	.444	.333	3	12	0	5	1	0	0	0	0	0	0	0	1	0	0	.500	.417
Mateo, Luis	R-R	6-0	175	5-23-90	.071	.000	.125	7	14	0	1	0	0	0	1	1	0	1	0	4	0	0	.071	.133
Olivera, Hector	R-R	6-2	220	4-5-85	.387	.375	.391	7	31	5	12	1	1	1	1	0	0	0	0	3	0	0	.581	.387
Peraza, Jose	R-R	6-0	180	4-30-94	.289	.414	.230	22	90	11	26	3	1	1	5	2	0	2	0	10	7	0	.378	.304
Redman, Hunter	R-R	5-10	180	8-25-92	.667	—	.667	1	3	0	2	0	0	0	0	0	0	0	0	1	0	0	.667	.667
Rivas, Webster	R-R	6-2	218	8-8-90	.667	.667	—	1	3	0	2	0	0	0	0	0	0	0	0	0	0	0	.667	.667
Samson, Nate	R-R	6-1	190	8-19-87	.231	.333	.000	7	13	1	3	0	0	0	0	1	0	1	0	1	1	0	.231	.286
Schebler, Scott	L-R	6-0	225	10-6-90	.241	.244	.239	121	432	57	104	16	9	13	50	40	12	0	1	93	15	2	.410	.322
Seager, Corey	L-R	6-4	215	4-27-94	.278	.331	.249	105	421	64	117	30	2	13	61	32	5	0	6	65	3	0	.451	.332
Solis, Ali	R-R	6-0	175	9-29-87	.143	.222	.000	7	14	2	2	1	0	0	0	2	0	0	0	5	0	0	.214	.250
Sweeney, Darnell	B-R	6-1	195	2-1-91	.271	.270	.272	116	472	69	128	30	4	9	49	42	3	1	4	116	32	13	.409	.332
Tabata, Jose	R-R	5-11	210	8-12-88	.225	.161	.259	28	89	6	20	4	0	2	8	8	0	1	1	13	1	0	.337	.286
Torreyes, Ronald	R-R	5-10	150	9-2-92	.306	.438	.242	13	49	10	15	2	1	0	3	2	1	0	1	4	0	0	.388	.340
2-team total (19 Fresno)					.244	—	—	32	119	17	29	3	1	0	8	3	1	1	1	13	0	1	.286	.266
Ward, Brian	R-R	5-11	210	10-17-85	.210	.250	.189	27	81	11	17	2	0	3	13	15	2	1	0	21	1	0	.346	.347
Wilkins, Andy	L-R	6-1	220	9-13-88	.249	.291	.229	105	362	53	90	25	1	18	70	36	0	1	13	81	0	0	.472	.307
Zarraga, Shawn	R-R	6-0	245	1-21-89	.303	.500	.268	18	66	8	20	5	0	1	9	4	0	1	1	11	0	0	.424	.338

Pitching	B-T	HT	WT	DOB	W	L	ERA	G	GS	CG	SV	IP	H	R	ER	HR	BB	SO	AVG	vLH	vRH	K/9	BB/9
Aardsma, David	R-R	6-3	220	12-27-81	0	1	2.41	20	0	0	15	19	12	5	5	0	7	23	.176	.111	.220	11.09	3.38
Anderson, Chris	R-R	6-3	235	7-29-92	0	3	18.47	3	1	0	0	6	14	15	13	2	9	2	.452	.429	.471	2.84	12.79
Baez, Pedro	R-R	6-0	230	3-11-88	0	0	0.00	3	1	0	0	3	2	0	0	0	0	2	.200	.167	.250	6.00	0.00
Baker, Scott	R-R	6-4	215	9-19-81	7	3	3.39	13	13	2	0	77	64	31	29	6	7	51	.228	.205	.247	5.96	0.82

Pitching	B-T	HT	WT	DOB	W	L	ERA	G	GS	CG	SV	IP	H	R	ER	HR	BB	SO	AVG	vLH	vRH	K/9	BB/9
Barlow, Scott	R-R	6-3	170	12-18-92	0	1	14.73	1	1	0	0	4	7	6	6	0	3	3	.438	.400	.500	7.36	7.36
Beachy, Brandon	R-R	6-2	215	9-3-86	1	1	3.64	10	9	0	0	47	40	22	19	4	21	36	.235	.200	.250	6.89	4.02
Bolsinger, Mike	R-R	6-1	215	1-29-88	3	3	2.31	10	8	0	0	47	30	12	12	2	18	61	.186	.135	.211	11.76	3.47
Buchter, Ryan	L-L	6-3	250	2-13-87	0	0	1.65	27	0	0	3	33	27	6	6	0	16	39	.227	.205	.240	10.74	4.41
2-team total (16 Iowa)					2	0	1.78	43	0	0	3	51	36	10	10	0	25	62	—	—	—	11.01	4.44
Cahill, Trevor	R-R	6-4	240	3-1-88	1	3	6.28	6	6	0	0	29	32	22	20	3	14	17	.286	.308	.274	5.34	4.40
2-team total (5 Iowa)					1	3	4.95	11	6	0	0	36	37	22	20	3	17	24	—	—	—	5.94	4.21
Cash, Ralston	R-R	6-3	215	8-20-91	0	0	0.00	1	0	0	0	1	2	0	0	0	1	2	.400	.500	.333	18.00	9.00
Cotton, Jharel	R-R	5-11	195	1-19-92	0	0	4.91	5	0	0	0	7	9	4	4	0	2	9	.321	.364	.294	11.05	2.45
Coulombe, Daniel	L-L	5-10	190	10-26-89	3	1	3.27	38	0	0	1	41	35	16	15	1	24	41	.235	.304	.204	8.93	5.23
Dayton, Grant	L-L	6-2	195	11-25-87	1	1	9.26	9	0	0	0	12	16	12	12	1	3	13	.327	.333	.325	10.03	2.31
2-team total (25 New Orleans)					3	2	4.44	34	0	0	0	47	41	23	23	2	8	48	—	—	—	9.26	1.54
De La Rosa, Eury	L-L	5-9	165	2-24-90	2	0	6.14	6	0	0	0	7	12	5	5	2	4	6	.364	.400	.357	7.36	4.91
3-team total (17 El Paso, 7 Nashville)					2	1	5.17	30	0	0	1	31	44	24	18	5	19	25	—	—	—	7.18	5.46
De Leon, Jorge	R-R	6-0	185	8-15-87	0	1	10.80	5	1	0	0	7	13	8	8	4	6	5	.394	.375	.444	6.75	8.10
2-team total (3 New Orleans)					0	2	8.03	8	1	0	0	12	18	11	11	4	9	9	—	—	—	6.57	6.57
Dennick, Ryan	L-L	6-0	200	1-10-87	0	1	39.00	3	0	0	0	3	14	14	13	1	2	3	.667	.625	.692	9.00	6.00
Fontanez, Randy	R-R	6-1	205	5-18-89	1	4	6.04	9	6	0	0	28	35	20	19	2	13	19	.307	.233	.333	6.04	4.13
Frias, Carlos	R-R	6-4	195	11-13-89	2	0	2.95	8	3	0	0	21	24	9	7	2	5	19	.282	.298	.263	8.02	2.11
Garcia, Freddy	R-R	6-4	250	10-6-76	0	1	7.36	4	1	0	0	7	8	7	6	0	4	7	.286	.238	.429	8.59	4.91
Garcia, Yimi	R-R	6-1	210	8-18-90	0	0	4.22	9	0	0	0	11	9	5	5	1	5	12	.231	.250	.217	10.13	4.22
Gonzalez, Juan	R-R	6-2	200	4-5-90	2	1	2.18	31	0	0	12	33	27	8	8	1	11	33	.233	.316	.192	9.00	3.00
Guilmet, Preston	R-R	6-2	200	7-27-87	0	0	3.00	3	0	0	0	3	2	1	1	0	1	4	.182	.000	.222	12.00	3.00
2-team total (13 Colorado Springs)					2	2	2.57	16	0	0	1	21	13	6	6	0	5	18	—	—	—	7.71	2.14
Hatcher, Chris	R-R	6-1	200	1-12-85	1	0	8.31	5	0	0	0	4	5	4	4	0	2	3	.294	.167	.364	6.23	4.15
Huff, David	L-L	6-1	210	8-22-84	5	2	2.20	23	4	0	0	57	49	18	14	4	8	43	.237	.224	.242	6.75	1.26
Jaime, Juan	R-R	6-2	250	8-2-87	0	0	1.86	7	0	0	0	10	10	2	2	0	3	7	.270	.235	.300	6.52	2.79
League, Brandon	R-R	6-2	200	3-16-83	0	0	1.59	5	0	0	0	6	5	2	1	0	2	4	.238	.100	.364	6.35	3.18
Lee, Zach	R-R	6-4	210	9-13-91	11	6	2.70	19	19	1	0	113	107	40	34	5	19	81	.257	.277	.242	6.43	1.51
Liberatore, Adam	L-L	6-3	240	5-12-87	0	1	3.74	19	0	0	3	22	18	9	9	2	10	18	.237	.048	.309	7.48	4.15
McGuire, Deck	R-R	6-6	220	6-23-89	5	4	3.84	12	9	0	0	66	70	30	28	6	17	53	.287	.296	.279	7.26	2.33
Owens, Rudy	L-L	6-3	240	12-18-87	0	2	2.78	7	3	0	0	23	26	11	7	1	10	16	.295	.174	.338	6.35	3.97
2-team total (8 Albuquerque)					2	5	4.84	15	10	0	0	58	70	36	31	3	22	40	—	—	—	6.24	3.43
Peralta, Joel	R-R	5-10	210	3-23-76	0	0	4.50	2	0	0	0	2	1	1	1	0	0	1	.222	.333	.167	4.50	0.00
Ravin, Josh	R-R	6-4	230	1-21-88	3	1	3.86	22	0	0	3	28	23	12	12	2	16	38	.221	.205	.233	12.21	5.14
Reed, Chris	L-L	6-3	225	5-20-90	0	0	3.27	8	0	0	0	11	11	4	4	0	4	5	.289	.333	.281	4.09	3.27
2-team total (14 New Orleans)					1	0	3.69	22	0	0	0	32	29	13	13	3	17	28	—	—	—	7.96	4.83
Richardson, Dustin	L-L	6-6	220	1-9-84	0	0	1.29	7	0	0	0	7	3	1	1	0	4	4	.125	.000	.167	5.14	5.14
Rodriguez, Paco	L-L	6-3	220	4-16-91	0	0	0.00	2	1	0	0	2	1	0	0	0	1	4	.143	—	.143	18.00	4.50
Santos, Sergio	R-R	6-4	215	7-4-83	0	0	3.86	6	0	0	0	5	5	2	2	0	3	8	.278	.400	.125	15.43	5.79
Shelton, Matt	R-R	6-4	205	11-30-88	0	1	1.80	3	1	0	0	10	6	2	2	1	1	6	.167	.250	.125	5.40	0.90
Smith, Steve	R-R	6-2	215	5-15-86	3	1	5.12	15	1	0	0	39	52	26	22	4	17	28	.335	.386	.306	6.52	3.96
Stults, Eric	L-L	6-2	220	12-9-79	2	1	3.19	6	6	0	0	37	34	15	13	3	6	26	.248	.243	.250	6.38	1.47
Surkamp, Eric	L-L	6-5	220	7-16-87	9	3	3.57	16	15	1	0	88	97	39	35	8	23	70	.280	.346	.251	7.13	2.34
Thomas, Ian	L-L	6-4	215	4-27-87	4	1	5.74	14	6	0	0	42	55	29	27	5	15	38	.314	.352	.298	8.08	3.19
Thomas, Mike	L-L	6-2	185	1-6-89	0	0	2.25	2	0	0	0	4	2	1	1	0	0	4	.167	.333	.111	0.00	0.00
Troncoso, Ramon	R-R	6-2	215	2-16-83	5	1	1.98	29	2	0	0	36	29	9	8	1	11	21	.228	.194	.242	5.20	2.72
Tsao, Chin-Hui	R-R	6-1	210	6-2-81	2	1	2.77	30	0	0	7	39	31	13	12	3	11	42	.217	.228	.209	9.69	2.54
Urias, Julio	L-L	6-2	205	8-12-96	0	1	18.69	2	2	0	0	4	11	9	9	0	6	5	.458	.500	.438	10.38	12.46
Walters, P.J.	R-R	6-4	215	3-12-85	2	1	4.70	4	4	0	0	23	28	12	12	2	7	15	.315	.296	.323	5.87	2.74
West, Matt	R-R	6-1	200	11-21-88	1	1	7.83	14	0	0	0	13	21	24	20	3	9	17	.313	.341	.291	6.65	3.52
Wieland, Joe	R-R	6-2	205	1-21-90	10	5	4.59	22	21	1	0	114	135	64	58	7	25	92	.299	.347	.270	7.28	1.98

Fielding

Catcher	PCT	G	PO	A	E	DP	PB
Barnes	.989	78	589	42	7	4	4
Chubb	1.000	1	9	1	0	0	0
Henriquez	.980	17	90	7	2	1	0
Redman	1.000	1	6	0	0	0	0
Rivas	1.000	1	3	0	0	0	0
Solis	1.000	4	20	1	0	1	1
Ward	.979	27	213	22	5	4	1
Zarraga	1.000	17	137	3	0	1	0

First Base	PCT	G	PO	A	E	DP
Anderson	.889	2	7	1	1	0
Burgamy	1.000	1	1	0	0	1
Carp	1.000	5	38	2	0	2
Dickson	1.000	51	400	32	0	48
Jensen	.995	27	179	12	1	16
Samson	—	1	0	0	0	0
Wilkins	.988	64	533	37	7	77

Second Base	PCT	G	PO	A	E	DP
Barney	.990	58	134	167	3	54
Britton	.929	10	16	23	3	3

Hernandez	1.000	3	3	7	0	0
Johnson	.929	7	8	18	2	7
Mateo	.929	1	3	10	1	0
Olivera	.900	2	3	6	1	2
Peraza	.963	14	38	39	3	15
Sweeney	.971	45	99	101	6	39
Torreyes	.971	7	16	18	1	5

Third Base	PCT	G	PO	A	E	DP
Barney	.969	14	6	25	1	6
Britton	.976	88	54	149	5	17
Burgamy	1.000	4	1	3	0	1
Johnson	.963	15	5	21	1	2
Mateo	1.000	1	1	1	0	0
Olivera	1.000	5	4	9	0	2
Seager	.962	15	9	41	2	9
Sweeney	1.000	4	2	15	0	1
Wilkins	.769	11	4	16	6	2

Shortstop	PCT	G	PO	A	E	DP
Barney	.964	18	15	39	2	3
Britton	1.000	1	2	0	0	0

Hernandez	.969	8	11	20	1	5
Johnson	.965	21	24	58	3	7
Mateo	1.000	1	2	5	0	2
Peraza	1.000	4	3	9	0	1
Samson	—	1	0	0	0	0
Seager	.974	9	121	285	11	77
Torreyes	.958	5	7	16	1	5

Outfield	PCT	G	PO	A	E	DP
Britton	1.000	9	18	0	0	0
Burgamy	.900	7	8	1	1	0
Carson	1.000	17	28	1	0	1
Crawford	1.000	6	12	0	0	0
Dickson	.977	48	84	2	2	1
Heisey	.979	58	138	2	3	0
Hernandez	1.000	4	11	0	0	0
Jensen	.993	79	146	5	1	2
Johnson	1.000	4	7	1	0	0
Lavin	1.000	3	6	1	0	0
Peraza	1.000	4	9	0	0	0
Samson	.750	2	3	0	1	0

Outfield	PCT	G	PO	A	E	DP
Schebler	.981	119	255	3	5	1
Sweeney	.979	62	138	4	3	0
Tabata	1.000	22	34	0	0	0
Wilkins	1.000	9	10	1	0	0

TULSA DRILLERS

DOUBLE-A

TEXAS LEAGUE

LOS ANGELES DODGERS

Batting	B-T	HT	WT	DOB	AVG	vLH	vRH	G	AB	R	H	2B	3B	HR	RBI	BB	HBP	SH	SF	SO	SB	CS	SLG	OBP
Anderson, Lars	L-L	6-4	215	9-25-87	.247	.197	.267	130	449	52	111	34	0	14	65	91	3	0	5	92	3	2	.416	.374
Arruebarrena, Erisbel	R-R	6-1	230	3-25-90	.287	.270	.293	38	136	10	39	6	1	1	9	6	0	0	0	35	1	0	.368	.317
Burgamy, Brian	B-R	5-10	190	6-27-81	.268	.258	.272	67	220	26	59	11	0	9	29	32	2	0	2	52	0	2	.441	.363
Cunningham, Jarek	R-R	6-1	195	12-25-89	.211	.255	.196	69	209	29	44	12	3	7	24	25	2	3	3	76	2	2	.397	.297
Curletta, Joey	R-R	6-4	245	3-8-94	.273	1.000	.200	3	11	3	3	1	0	1	4	2	0	0	0	4	0	0	.636	.385
Dixon, Brandon	R-R	6-2	215	1-29-92	.244	.250	.242	83	336	33	82	16	2	8	38	12	1	0	0	98	16	6	.375	.272
Drake, Yadir	R-R	6-0	200	4-12-90	.269	.330	.244	106	361	36	97	13	1	3	32	28	4	0	6	41	0	2	.335	.323
Farmer, Kyle	R-R	6-0	200	8-17-90	.272	.256	.279	76	283	25	77	26	1	2	39	14	4	0	4	55	0	1	.392	.311
Garcia, Jon	R-R	5-11	175	11-11-91	.189	.357	.128	20	53	5	10	3	1	0	6	6	0	0	2	20	1	0	.283	.262
Garvey, Robbie	L-L	5-8	165	4-26-89	—	—	—	24	0	6	0	0	0	0	0	0	0	0	0	0	11	7	—	—
Hazelbaker, Jeremy	L-R	6-3	200	8-14-87	.245	.286	.239	14	53	5	13	2	2	0	2	3	0	2	0	11	6	0	.358	.286
2-team total (40 Springfield, MO)					.291	—	—	54	196	35	57	15	5	3	22	21	3	5	1	44	16	0	.464	.367
Hoenecke, Paul	L-R	6-2	205	7-8-90	.150	.167	.143	6	20	2	3	0	0	1	4	1	0	0	0	11	0	0	.300	.190
Lavin, Peter	L-L	5-11	180	12-27-87	.248	.217	.260	123	435	51	108	24	6	9	42	40	0	2	5	73	7	5	.393	.308
Law, Adam	R-R	6-0	193	2-5-90	.236	.218	.245	72	229	32	54	10	0	0	15	18	2	5	1	36	10	2	.279	.296
Mateo, Luis	R-R	6-0	175	5-23-90	.258	.313	.239	50	190	19	49	10	1	2	8	6	2	0	0	47	3	3	.353	.288
Mayora, Daniel	R-R	5-11	175	7-27-85	.248	.179	.269	68	242	16	60	15	0	2	24	13	0	4	3	49	1	0	.335	.283
Morales, Delvis	B-R	6-2	175	8-29-90	.333	—	.333	1	3	0	1	0	0	0	0	0	0	0	0	1	0	0	.333	.333
Oguisten, Faustino	R-R	6-2	165	1-17-91	.000	—	.000	2	1	0	0	0	0	0	0	0	0	0	0	1	0	0	.000	.000
Olivera, Hector	R-R	6-2	220	4-5-85	.318	.000	.467	6	22	3	7	0	1	0	6	3	0	0	0	5	0	0	.455	.400
Rathjen, Jeremy	R-R	6-5	195	1-28-90	.197	.123	.226	73	203	19	40	9	1	7	20	15	3	0	0	55	2	1	.355	.262
Redman, Hunter	R-R	5-10	180	8-25-92	.000	—	.000	1	2	0	0	0	0	0	0	0	0	0	0	1	0	0	.000	.000
Rivas, Webster	R-R	6-2	218	8-8-90	.273	.100	.348	13	33	1	9	0	0	0	2	3	0	0	0	6	0	2	.273	.333
Samson, Nate	R-R	6-1	190	8-19-87	.222	.179	.245	29	81	7	18	4	0	0	8	8	0	0	1	11	2	1	.272	.292
Seager, Corey	L-R	6-4	215	4-27-94	.375	.476	.339	20	80	17	30	7	1	5	15	5	0	0	1	11	1	1	.675	.407
Solis, Ali	R-R	6-0	175	9-29-87	.145	.193	.129	69	220	8	32	8	0	1	16	7	1	5	1	61	0	0	.195	.175
Torreyes, Ronald	R-R	5-10	150	9-2-92	.293	.235	.321	62	249	39	73	13	2	4	19	20	2	1	2	23	3	3	.410	.348
Trinkwon, Brandon	L-R	6-1	170	3-30-92	.232	.192	.246	58	190	30	44	3	2	2	14	27	0	2	0	26	5	2	.300	.327
Witherspoon, Travis	R-R	6-2	190	4-16-89	.218	.129	.241	41	147	16	32	5	0	3	11	13	0	1	0	44	4	2	.313	.281
Zarraga, Shawn	R-R	6-0	245	1-21-89	.277	.208	.295	44	119	6	33	6	0	0	9	14	0	0	0	19	0	1	.328	.353

Pitching	B-T	HT	WT	DOB	W	L	ERA	G	GS	CG	SV	IP	H	R	ER	HR	BB	SO	AVG	vLH	vRH	K/9	BB/9
Anderson, Chris	R-R	6-3	235	7-29-92	9	7	4.05	23	23	1	0	127	123	66	57	12	59	98	.256	.234	.273	6.96	4.19
Benjamin, Ramon	R-L	6-1	195	6-14-87	2	2	4.50	24	0	0	1	26	22	15	13	4	16	22	.234	.167	.276	7.62	5.54
Cannon, John	R-R	6-0	180	5-11-90	0	0	9.00	1	0	0	0	1	2	1	1	0	0	0	.400	.500	.333	0.00	0.00
Cash, Ralston	R-R	6-3	215	8-20-91	2	6	3.47	49	0	0	3	57	42	24	22	7	27	56	.207	.170	.235	8.84	4.26
Corcino, Daniel	R-R	5-11	210	8-26-90	0	0	9.53	3	2	0	0	6	4	7	6	0	6	9	.190	.182	.200	14.29	9.53
Cotton, Jharel	R-R	5-11	195	1-19-92	5	2	2.30	11	8	0	0	63	49	18	16	4	21	71	.221	.255	.195	10.20	3.02
Dayton, Grant	L-L	6-2	195	11-25-87	0	2	2.53	8	0	0	1	11	9	3	3	0	7	17	.231	.250	.222	14.34	5.91
De Leon, Jorge	R-R	6-0	185	11-8-87	1	3	3.80	34	0	0	2	43	39	19	18	4	18	27	.250	.323	.198	5.70	3.80
De Leon, Jose	R-R	6-2	185	8-7-92	2	6	3.64	16	16	1	0	77	61	35	31	11	29	105	.216	.240	.195	12.33	3.40
Dennick, Ryan	L-L	6-0	200	1-10-87	4	1	2.94	47	0	0	5	52	45	17	17	2	14	37	.233	.147	.280	6.40	2.42
Dirks, Caleb	R-R	6-4	225	6-9-93	0	0	1.35	14	0	0	0	13	7	3	2	0	6	17	.149	.000	.269	11.48	4.05
Fontanez, Randy	R-R	6-1	205	5-18-89	1	1	4.97	9	5	0	0	29	27	18	16	4	13	23	.255	.243	.261	7.14	4.03
Gonzalez, Juan	R-R	6-2	200	4-5-90	0	0	0.53	13	0	0	0	17	7	1	1	0	5	18	.125	.207	.037	9.53	2.65
Griggs, Scott	R-R	6-4	225	5-13-91	0	0	4.50	1	0	0	0	2	2	1	1	0	0	3	.250	.500	.167	13.50	0.00
Heredia, Jairo	R-R	6-1	190	10-8-89	1	3	3.22	8	3	0	0	22	16	8	8	3	8	13	.198	.135	.250	5.24	3.22
Horst, Jeremy	L-L	6-2	235	10-1-85	0	2	1.64	32	0	0	9	38	38	10	7	4	20	42	.257	.240	.265	9.86	4.70
Jaime, Juan	R-R	6-2	250	8-2-87	0	2	3.86	11	0	0	0	12	8	5	5	0	12	20	.205	.294	.136	15.43	9.26
Kehrt, Jeremy	R-R	6-2	190	12-21-85	7	8	3.46	22	22	1	0	120	119	55	46	7	27	94	.254	.256	.252	7.07	2.03
Martinez, Fabio	R-R	6-3	190	10-29-89	0	0	11.25	5	0	0	0	4	5	5	5	1	14	5	.294	.333	.256	11.25	31.50
McGuire, Deck	R-R	6-6	220	6-23-89	4	2	3.55	18	9	0	1	71	58	28	28	5	19	66	.223	.190	.252	8.37	2.41
Owens, Rudy	L-L	6-3	240	12-18-87	0	1	5.91	2	2	0	0	11	10	8	7	4	1	8	.244	.400	.194	6.75	0.84
Peralta, Joel	R-R	5-10	210	3-23-76	0	0	0.00	3	0	0	0	3	0	0	0	0	0	3	.000	.000	.000	9.00	0.00
Reed, Chris	L-L	6-3	225	5-20-90	2	2	7.23	16	0	0	1	24	22	21	19	2	18	16	.250	.321	.217	6.08	6.85
Rhame, Jacob	R-R	6-1	190	3-16-93	3	3	3.06	39	0	0	2	50	34	17	17	5	19	57	.192	.162	.214	10.26	3.42
Richardson, Dustin	L-L	6-6	220	1-9-84	2	0	2.37	19	0	0	6	19	12	6	5	2	6	21	.179	.190	.174	9.95	2.84
Riekenberg, Drayton	R-R	6-2	205	3-27-94	1	0	2.25	2	0	0	0	4	2	1	1	0	5	2	.167	.143	.200	4.50	11.25
Rogers, Rob	R-R	6-0	205	10-25-90	1	1	1.50	2	0	0	0	6	8	6	1	0	2	1	.308	.364	.267	7.50	3.00
Shelton, Matt	R-R	6-4	205	11-30-88	1	0	3.68	4	3	0	0	15	12	6	6	1	8	12	.226	.208	.241	7.36	4.91
Smith, Blake	L-R	6-2	225	12-9-87	0	3	1.62	16	0	0	3	17	8	4	3	1	9	16	.151	.208	.103	8.64	4.86
Smith, Steve	R-R	6-2	215	5-15-86	0	0	5.59	3	1	0	0	10	15	9	6	2	5	6	.395	.444	.350	5.59	4.66
Storey, Mickey	R-R	6-1	185	3-16-86	1	1	3.47	4	4	1	0	23	21	9	9	5	11	16	.247	.281	.226	6.17	4.24
Stripling, Ross	R-R	6-3	190	11-23-89	3	6	3.88	13	13	1	0	67	61	29	29	7	19	55	.242	.207	.272	7.35	2.54
Stults, Eric	L-L	6-2	220	12-9-79	4	4	3.38	10	8	1	1	53	47	25	20	2	15	43	.232	.162	.267	7.31	2.53
Thomas, Mike	L-L	6-2	185	1-6-89	1	1	4.80	26	0	0	0	30	27	16	16	3	16	32	.243	.175	.282	9.60	4.80
Tillman, Daniel	R-R	6-1	185	3-14-89	0	0	3.48	11	0	0	0	10	8	4	4	1	4	14	.205	.278	.143	12.19	3.48
Troncoso, Ramon	R-R	6-2	215	2-16-83	0	0	6.00	2	0	0	0	3	6	2	2	0	1	1	.400	.500	.364	3.00	3.00

Pitching	B-T	HT	WT	DOB	W	L	ERA	G	GS	CG	SV	IP	H	R	ER	HR	BB	SO	AVG	vLH	vRH	K/9	BB/9
Tsao, Chin-Hui	R-R	6-1	210	6-2-81	0	1	7.20	4	0	0	2	5	2	4	4	1	4	8	.133	.286	.000	14.40	7.20
Urias, Julio	L-L	6-2	205	8-12-96	3	4	2.77	13	13	0	0	68	53	24	21	4	15	74	.213	.095	.253	9.75	1.98
Walters, P.J.	R-R	6-4	215	3-12-85	0	1	5.40	1	1	0	0	5	9	6	3	1	2	5	.375	.308	.455	9.00	3.60
West, Matt	R-R	6-1	200	11-21-88	1	1	0.56	12	0	0	0	16	8	4	1	0	4	17	.145	.263	.083	9.56	2.25

Fielding

Catcher	PCT	G	PO	A	E	DP	PB
Farmer	.997	51	361	28	1	5	7
Rivas	.991	11	102	5	1	1	1
Solis	.991	68	532	49	5	2	6
Zarraga	1.000	27	148	14	0	2	3

First Base	PCT	G	PO	A	E	DP
Anderson	.994	128	1018	107	7	84
Burgamy	1.000	4	32	3	0	2
Hoenecke	1.000	6	46	1	0	7
Law	1.000	1	1	0	0	0
Mayora	1.000	6	32	3	0	5
Zarraga	1.000	2	12	1	0	2

Second Base	PCT	G	PO	A	E	DP
Arruebarrena	1.000	8	14	17	0	4
Cunningham	1.000	3	5	8	0	2
Dixon	.975	69	108	167	7	40
Law	.939	12	17	29	3	9
Mateo	1.000	1	2	2	0	1
Mayora	1.000	2	3	1	0	2

	PCT	G	PO	A	E	DP
Olivera	.714	2	3	2	2	1
Samson	1.000	11	13	25	0	2
Torreyes	1.000	7	14	18	0	5
Trinkwon	.990	35	42	58	1	13

Third Base	PCT	G	PO	A	E	DP
Arruebarrena	.938	7	6	9	1	1
Cunningham	.951	47	29	87	6	7
Farmer	.980	22	10	40	1	3
Mateo	1.000	1	1	0	0	0
Mayora	.902	42	16	67	9	4
Olivera	.917	4	2	9	1	0
Samson	1.000	2	2	3	0	0
Seager	1.000	4	4	3	0	1
Torreyes	1.000	7	1	6	0	1
Trinkwon	.914	14	6	26	3	1

Shortstop	PCT	G	PO	A	E	DP
Arruebarrena	.947	24	25	47	4	11
Law	1.000	4	4	7	0	2
Mateo	.983	42	50	127	3	22

	PCT	G	PO	A	E	DP
Morales	.800	1	0	4	1	0
Samson	1.000	2	6	6	0	2
Seager	.974	15	34	40	2	9
Torreyes	.964	48	62	127	7	24
Trinkwon	.958	8	6	17	1	3

Outfield	PCT	G	PO	A	E	DP
Anderson	1.000	2	3	0	0	0
Burgamy	.988	45	81	2	1	0
Curletta	1.000	3	6	0	0	0
Dixon	1.000	17	39	2	0	0
Drake	.982	96	154	9	3	2
Garcia	1.000	20	24	0	0	0
Hazelbaker	.917	12	19	3	2	0
Lavin	.988	119	235	12	3	2
Law	.985	37	65	1	1	0
Rathjen	.990	59	92	5	1	3
Samson	1.000	6	4	0	0	0
Smith	1.000	1	1	0	0	0
Witherspoon	1.000	40	111	2	0	0

RANCHO CUCAMONGA QUAKES

HIGH CLASS A

CALIFORNIA LEAGUE

Batting	B-T	HT	WT	DOB	AVG	vLH	vRH	G	AB	R	H	2B	3B	HR	RBI	BB	HBP	SH	SF	SO	SB	CS	SLG	OBP
Ahart, Devan	L-R	6-1	175	10-21-92	.288	.233	.301	43	163	32	47	6	4	3	17	23	1	1	2	27	7	6	.429	.376
Arruebarrena, Erisbel	R-R	6-1	230	3-25-90	.306	.250	.317	12	49	10	15	4	0	2	5	2	0	0	0	14	2	0	.510	.333
Bellinger, Cody	L-L	6-4	180	7-13-95	.264	.245	.269	128	478	97	126	33	4	30	103	52	4	2	8	150	10	2	.538	.336
Bereszniewicz, Billy	L-L	5-10	170	9-7-91	.133	.250	.091	6	15	1	2	1	0	0	2	0	0	0	0	3	0	0	.200	.133
Calhoun, Willie	L-R	5-9	177	11-4-94	.329	.429	.305	20	73	11	24	7	0	3	14	7	1	0	1	13	0	0	.548	.390
Celli, Federico	R-R	6-3	215	2-15-95	.286	.000	.333	2	7	1	2	1	0	0	2	0	0	0	0	2	0	0	.429	.286
Chubb, Austin	R-R	6-1	200	4-17-89	.207	.167	.217	10	29	4	6	0	0	2	4	2	0	0	0	8	0	0	.414	.258
Cordero, Josmar	R-R	5-10	175	9-10-91	.271	.235	.279	28	85	5	23	6	0	1	9	3	2	0	0	15	1	0	.376	.311
Crawford, Carl	L-L	6-2	230	8-5-81	.250	—	.250	2	4	1	1	0	1	0	2	1	1	0	0	0	0	0	.750	.500
Cunningham, Jarek	R-R	6-1	195	12-25-89	.313	.526	.246	20	80	12	25	6	3	1	21	9	0	0	0	24	1	2	.500	.382
Curletta, Joey	R-R	6-4	245	3-8-94	.233	.193	.244	119	403	44	94	33	1	10	53	37	4	0	3	130	1	2	.395	.302
Dixon, Brandon	R-R	6-2	215	1-29-92	.299	.355	.287	45	174	37	52	9	3	11	30	16	1	0	2	46	10	0	.575	.358
Drake, Yadir	R-R	6-0	200	4-12-90	.407	.444	.389	7	27	5	11	3	0	0	3	5	0	0	0	3	0	0	.519	.500
Drexler, Edwin	B-R	6-2	185	7-1-92	—	—	—	5	0	1	0	0	0	0	0	0	0	0	0	0	3	2	—	—
Farmer, Kyle	R-R	6-0	200	8-17-90	.337	.353	.333	44	163	33	55	14	6	1	27	12	5	0	2	25	5	2	.515	.396
Garlick, Kyle	R-R	6-1	210	1-26-92	.389	.556	.356	14	54	16	21	4	0	5	14	4	1	0	2	20	0	0	.741	.426
Garvey, Robbie	L-L	5-8	165	4-26-89	.240	.130	.265	45	125	18	30	2	1	0	9	5	0	6	1	30	8	2	.272	.267
Hoenecke, Paul	L-R	6-2	205	7-8-90	.295	.237	.309	107	393	48	116	33	2	9	63	23	2	0	4	76	2	0	.458	.334
Hudson, Kyle	L-L	5-11	175	1-7-87	—	—	—	9	0	4	0	0	0	0	0	0	0	0	0	0	4	3	—	—
Law, Adam	R-R	6-0	193	2-5-90	.394	.500	.353	17	71	15	28	5	1	0	8	8	1	0	1	14	4	2	.493	.457
Locastro, Tim	R-R	6-1	200	7-14-92	.224	.286	.207	41	156	30	35	7	1	1	14	14	11	1	2	30	11	5	.327	.328
Mieses, Johan	R-R	6-2	185	7-13-95	.245	.283	.233	51	196	35	48	18	1	6	19	13	2	3	0	57	3	1	.439	.299
Morales, Delvis	B-R	6-2	175	8-29-90	.246	.192	.259	52	138	15	34	3	0	0	10	12	5	4	0	39	6	3	.268	.329
Moyer, Dillon	R-R	6-0	200	7-18-91	.175	.178	.174	94	314	24	55	13	3	4	30	20	2	5	3	135	4	2	.242	.227
Navin, Spencer	R-R	6-1	185	8-11-92	.133	.190	.120	40	113	13	15	5	0	2	9	18	3	0	3	40	1	1	.230	.263
Ogle, Tyler	R-R	5-10	210	8-9-90	.263	.348	.237	111	384	63	101	20	1	20	75	51	4	0	4	89	0	3	.477	.352
Puig, Yasiel	R-R	6-2	255	12-7-90	.286	.333	.273	4	14	3	4	1	0	2	2	1	0	0	0	4	0	1	.786	.333
Rathjen, Jeremy	R-R	6-5	195	1-28-90	.167	.000	.217	9	30	3	5	2	0	0	4	2	0	0	0	7	1	0	.233	.219
Rivas, Webster	R-R	6-2	218	8-8-90	.258	.325	.239	54	178	15	46	11	1	1	11	9	2	1	3	27	0	2	.348	.297
Samson, Nate	R-R	6-1	190	8-19-87	.230	.154	.250	15	61	7	14	6	0	0	4	0	0	0	0	5	1	2	.328	.277
Scavuzzo, Jacob	R-R	6-4	185	1-15-94	.308	.286	.314	61	227	47	70	18	1	13	49	21	5	0	2	54	3	4	.568	.376
Trinkwon, Brandon	L-R	6-1	190	3-30-92	.312	.340	.305	70	260	43	81	10	0	5	29	38	1	1	4	51	7	5	.408	.396
Van Slyke, Scott	R-R	6-4	220	7-24-86	.364	.000	.400	3	11	4	4	1	0	1	2	1	0	0	0	1	0	0	.727	.417
Verdugo, Alex	L-L	6-0	205	5-15-96	.385	.444	.370	23	91	20	35	9	2	4	19	4	0	0	1	12	1	0	.659	.406
Wampler, Tyler	R-R	6-0	175	9-11-91	.250	.500	.167	4	8	1	2	0	0	0	0	0	0	0	0	0	0	0	.625	.250
Witherspoon, Travis	R-R	6-2	190	4-16-89	.161	.227	.144	31	112	11	18	3	0	1	6	7	0	2	2	19	9	2	.214	.207
Wolfe, Brian	L-L	6-4	210	10-16-90	.219	.111	.236	24	64	3	14	4	0	0	2	6	1	0	0	13	0	0	.281	.286

Pitching	B-T	HT	WT	DOB	W	L	ERA	G	GS	CG	SV	IP	H	R	ER	HR	BB	SO	AVG	vLH	vRH	K/9	BB/9
Araujo, Victor	R-R	5-11	170	11-9-92	3	3	5.40	32	0	0	0	50	50	36	30	6	14	55	.255	.264	.248	9.90	2.52
Barlow, Scott	R-R	6-3	170	12-18-92	8	3	2.52	14	13	0	0	71	61	30	20	4	32	64	.236	.215	.256	8.07	4.04
Beachy, Brandon	R-R	6-2	215	9-3-86	0	0	0.00	1	1	0	0	2	0	0	0	0	1	.000	.000	.000	5.40	5.40
Bedard, Erik	L-L	6-1	195	3-5-79	1	1	5.02	3	3	0	0	14	16	8	8	2	1	7	.286	.353	.256	4.40	0.63
Benjamin, Ramon	R-L	6-1	195	6-14-87	5	2	1.82	27	0	0	5	40	32	13	8	1	11	30	.215	.167	.253	6.81	2.50

Pitching	B-T	HT	WT	DOB	W	L	ERA	G	GS	CG	SV	IP	H	R	ER	HR	BB	SO	AVG	vLH	vRH	K/9	BB/9
Bird, Zack	R-R	6-4	205	7-14-94	5	7	4.75	19	17	0	0	89	74	52	47	6	48	95	.226	.244	.211	9.61	4.85
Brigham, Jeff	R-R	6-0	200	2-16-92	4	5	5.96	17	14	0	0	68	78	51	45	8	36	64	.286	.395	.195	8.47	4.76
Broussard, Joe	R-R	6-1	220	1-28-91	1	2	4.74	23	1	0	0	49	62	35	26	4	11	46	.300	.298	.301	8.39	2.01
Cahill, Trevor	R-R	6-4	240	3-1-88	0	0	0.00	1	1	0	0	4	0	0	0	0	2	8	.000	.000	.000	18.00	4.50
Campbell, James	R-R	6-1	195	9-20-91	0	1	3.60	2	2	0	0	5	6	2	2	0	2	6	.316	.800	.143	10.80	3.60
Cotton, Jharel	R-R	5-11	195	1-19-92	1	0	1.61	4	1	0	0	22	14	4	4	1	7	28	.182	.167	.195	11.28	2.82
De Leon, Jose	R-R	6-2	185	8-7-92	4	1	1.67	7	7	0	0	38	26	9	7	1	8	58	.193	.194	.190	13.86	1.91
De Paula, Luis	L-L	6-1	170	4-23-92	0	1	4.70	17	4	0	0	44	34	26	23	3	23	35	.218	.207	.224	7.16	4.70
DeJong, Chase	L-R	6-4	205	12-29-93	4	3	3.96	11	10	0	0	50	44	27	22	6	15	52	.228	.225	.230	9.36	2.70
Dirks, Caleb	R-R	6-4	225	6-9-93	2	0	0.90	9	0	0	3	10	8	1	1	1	2	18	.211	.300	.111	16.20	1.80
Fernandez, Pablo	R-R	6-1	185	8-5-89	2	1	4.22	4	4	0	0	21	26	11	10	3	4	18	.306	.333	.286	7.59	1.69
Fontanez, Randy	R-R	6-1	205	5-18-89	1	2	0.93	5	0	0	2	10	5	2	1	0	2	12	.143	.176	.111	11.17	1.86
Frias, Carlos	R-R	6-4	195	11-13-89	0	0	7.71	2	2	0	0	5	7	4	4	0	0	9	.318	.333	.313	17.36	0.00
Hatcher, Chris	R-R	6-1	200	1-12-85	0	0	6.00	3	1	0	0	3	4	2	2	0	0	5	.308	.500	.000	15.00	0.00
Hershiser, Jordan	R-R	6-8	245	9-15-88	1	0	0.00	1	0	0	0	1	1	0	0	0	1	1	.250	.500	.000	9.00	9.00
2-team total (11 Lake Elsinore)					1	0	4.02	12	0	0	1	16	16	8	7	1	5	14	—	—		8.04	2.87
Hooper, Kyle	R-R	6-4	195	5-28-91	0	2	3.10	19	1	0	1	29	27	15	10	1	10	34	.241	.205	.260	10.55	3.10
Jaime, Juan	R-R	6-2	250	8-2-87	0	0	0.00	3	0	0	0	3	1	0	0	0	2	5	.100	.200	.000	15.00	6.00
Jansen, Kenley	B-R	6-5	265	9-30-87	0	1	5.06	6	5	0	0	5	6	3	3	1	1	8	.300	.429	.000	13.50	1.69
Johnson, Michael	L-L	6-1	185	1-3-91	7	1	3.07	46	2	0	1	70	51	24	24	5	24	75	.204	.189	.213	9.60	3.07
Kowalczyk, Karch	R-R	6-1	215	3-31-91	1	2	4.26	24	0	0	2	32	30	16	15	1	16	35	.242	.300	.203	9.95	4.55
League, Brandon	R-R	6-2	200	3-16-83	0	1	0.00	5	0	0	0	5	5	1	0	0	0	4	.238	.364	.100	7.20	0.00
Lee, Zach	R-R	6-4	210	9-13-91	1	0	3.60	1	1	0	0	5	4	2	2	0	1	2	.211	.182	.250	3.60	1.80
Mesa, Luis	R-R	6-4	200	7-13-90	0	0	13.26	12	0	0	0	19	38	28	28	2	10	13	.427	.455	.400	6.16	4.74
Molina, Jose	L-L	5-11	160	6-26-91	0	0	3.38	5	0	0	0	8	6	4	3	1	3	6	.214	.143	.238	6.75	3.38
Oaks, Trevor	R-R	6-3	220	3-6-93	3	0	3.04	5	5	0	0	24	28	11	8	2	5	16	.292	.294	.290	6.08	1.90
Owens, Rudy	L-L	6-3	240	12-18-87	0	1	4.32	2	2	0	0	8	4	4	4	1	4	7	.226	.200	.250	7.56	4.32
Peralta, Joel	R-R	5-10	210	3-23-76	0	1	10.13	3	1	0	0	3	4	3	3	0	1	0	.400	.200	.600	0.00	3.38
Reid-Foley, David	L-R	6-3	190	1-2-91	0	1	17.65	5	0	0	0	9	19	17	17	4	5	5	.432	.429	.433	5.19	5.19
Rhame, Jacob	R-R	6-1	190	3-16-93	0	0	0.00	5	0	0	1	7	2	0	0	0	1	5	.091	.000	.154	16.71	1.29
Richy, John	R-R	6-4	215	7-28-92	10	5	4.20	22	18	1	0	124	143	63	58	11	34	105	.288	.292	.285	7.60	2.46
Rodriguez, Paco	L-L	6-3	220	4-16-91	0	0	0.00	2	2	0	0	2	2	0	0	0	0	2	.250	.000	.286	9.00	0.00
Rogers, Rob	R-R	6-0	205	10-25-91	5	5	3.42	46	1	0	4	74	80	35	28	0	30	70	.278	.272	.282	8.55	3.67
Sborz, Josh	R-R	6-2	209	12-17-93	0	0	1.50	9	0	0	2	12	12	2	2	1	3	12	.255	.176	.300	9.00	2.25
Shelton, Matt	R-R	6-4	205	11-30-88	1	2	9.30	4	0	0	0	20	24	21	21	2	15	15	.304	.293	.316	6.64	6.64
Stewart, Brock	L-R	6-3	210	10-3-91	2	4	5.43	18	12	0	0	63	75	39	38	6	18	65	.291	.291	.290	9.29	2.57
Tillman, Daniel	R-R	6-1	185	3-14-89	1	4	2.61	37	0	0	7	48	42	22	14	7	13	54	.231	.147	.290	10.06	2.42
Urias, Julio	L-L	6-2	205	8-12-96	0	0	7.71	1	1	0	0	5	7	4	4	1	0	4	.350	.333	.364	7.71	0.00
Vanegas, A.J.	R-R	6-3	215	8-16-92	3	1	2.59	34	2	0	1	59	40	19	17	3	34	46	.190	.173	.202	7.02	5.19

Fielding

Catcher	PCT	G	PO	A	E	DP	PB
Chubb	.982	8	53	2	1	0	2
Farmer	.996	33	243	27	1	0	5
Hoenecke	.957	4	22	0	1	1	1
Navin	.994	37	291	31	2	3	4
Ogle	.991	36	313	15	3	0	6
Rivas	.997	35	279	29	1	3	7

First Base	PCT	G	PO	A	E	DP
Bellinger	.991	91	683	59	7	67
Chubb	1.000	1	12	1	0	0
Cordero	1.000	12	75	3	0	4
Hoenecke	1.000	9	53	3	0	2
Navin	1.000	2	12	0	0	1
Ogle	.986	30	204	12	3	17
Rivas	.989	11	88	5	1	5
Van Slyke	1.000	1	4	1	0	2
Wolfe	1.000	1	2	0	0	0

Second Base	PCT	G	PO	A	E	DP
Arruebarrena	.964	6	8	19	1	6
Calhoun	.946	20	32	56	5	12
Cunningham	.938	3	9	6	1	3
Dixon	.972	24	28	42	2	9
Law	.933	9	11	17	2	2
Locastro	1.000	4	6	6	0	2
Morales	.921	23	23	47	6	7

	PCT	G	PO	A	E	DP
Moyer	1.000	9	12	22	0	3
Trinkwon	.974	57	88	175	7	32

Third Base	PCT	G	PO	A	E	DP
Arruebarrena	—	1	0	0	0	0
Cordero	1.000	2	1	1	0	0
Cunningham	.929	9	5	8	1	1
Curletta	1.000	1	0	1	0	0
Dixon	.800	4	1	7	2	1
Farmer	1.000	5	2	9	0	0
Hoenecke	.945	86	40	114	9	11
Morales	.862	12	7	18	4	1
Moyer	.902	16	12	25	4	0
Ogle	.828	12	5	19	5	0
Samson	1.000	1	1	1	0	0
Trinkwon	.923	10	4	8	1	1

Shortstop	PCT	G	PO	A	E	DP
Arruebarrena	.929	4	7	6	1	2
Hoenecke	—	1	0	0	0	0
Locastro	.964	37	49	84	5	24
Morales	.946	10	16	19	2	4
Moyer	.962	70	108	197	12	42
Samson	.902	14	13	42	6	7
Trinkwon	1.000	8	6	18	0	3
Wampler	.800	4	3	5	2	0

Outfield	PCT	G	PO	A	E	DP
Ahart	.990	41	90	5	1	0
Bellinger	1.000	27	59	1	0	0
Bereszniewicz	1.000	5	4	0	0	0
Celli	.800	2	4	0	1	0
Cordero	.667	4	4	0	2	0
Cunningham	.875	6	7	0	1	0
Curletta	.989	109	173	6	2	1
Dixon	.960	15	23	1	1	0
Drake	1.000	4	7	0	0	0
Garlick	.929	10	13	0	1	0
Garvey	.967	41	56	2	2	1
Law	1.000	10	12	1	0	0
Mieses	.935	50	110	5	8	0
Morales	1.000	2	1	0	0	0
Moyer	—	1	0	0	0	0
Navin	1.000	1	3	0	0	0
Puig	1.000	3	7	0	0	0
Rathjen	1.000	8	8	0	0	0
Scavuzzo	.932	44	68	1	5	0
Van Slyke	1.000	1	1	0	0	0
Verdugo	1.000	23	56	3	0	1
Witherspoon	1.000	29	62	3	0	1
Wolfe	1.000	21	35	3	0	1

GREAT LAKES LOONS   LOW CLASS A

MIDWEST LEAGUE

Batting	B-T	HT	WT	DOB	AVG	vLH	vRH	G	AB	R	H	2B	3B	HR	RBI	BB	HBP	SH	SF	SO	SB	CS	SLG	OBP
Ahmed, Mike	R-R	6-2	195	1-20-92	.264	.263	.264	118	447	56	118	21	6	4	30	61	6	0	1	111	24	12	.365	.359
Allen, Jimmy	R-R	5-10	190	1-4-92	.272	.318	.259	103	386	43	105	20	1	4	43	21	11	2	4	75	7	1	.360	.325
Beaty, Matt	L-R	6-1	195	4-28-93	.297	.431	.262	62	246	37	73	7	2	4	25	21	2	1	3	28	2	1	.390	.353

Batting	B-T	HT	WT	DOB	AVG	vLH	vRH	G	AB	R	H	2B	3B	HR	RBI	BB	HBP	SH	SF	SO	SB	CS	SLG	OBP
Calhoun, Willie	L-R	5-9	177	11-4-94	.393	.455	.359	15	61	9	24	3	0	1	8	5	0	0	0	7	0	0	.492	.439
Celli, Federico	R-R	6-3	215	2-15-95	.230	.273	.219	58	213	23	49	9	3	2	19	11	2	2	1	71	1	2	.329	.273
Chigbogu, Justin	L-L	6-1	240	7-8-94	.209	.188	.215	94	354	33	74	24	0	13	51	33	2	0	3	136	1	2	.387	.278
Chubb, Austin	R-R	6-1	200	4-17-89	.000	.000	.000	1	2	0	0	0	0	0	0	1	0	0	0	1	0	0	.000	.333
Cordero, Josmar	R-R	5-10	175	9-10-91	.286	.319	.273	47	175	21	50	13	1	4	18	12	5	0	2	38	1	0	.440	.345
De Jong, Scott	R-R	6-4	230	4-26-93	.182	.000	.200	9	33	0	6	1	0	0	0	1	0	0	0	11	0	0	.212	.206
Dean, Nick	R-R	6-1	190	5-11-92	.225	.259	.216	39	129	11	29	6	0	0	9	14	6	0	0	27	5	3	.271	.329
Drake, Yadir	R-R	6-0	200	4-12-90	.310	.200	.368	7	29	3	9	5	0	0	3	4	1	0	0	3	1	0	.483	.412
Garlick, Kyle	R-R	6-1	210	1-26-92	.327	.394	.307	38	147	24	48	12	2	4	24	10	4	0	0	35	2	2	.517	.385
Gomez, Cristian	R-R	5-11	185	1-11-96	.200	.250	.182	24	90	7	18	3	1	0	5	3	1	1	0	22	1	0	.256	.234
Green, Gage	R-R	5-10	190	8-27-92	.154	—	.154	4	13	2	2	1	0	0	0	2	1	0	0	4	1	0	.231	.313
Hennigan, Dan	R-R	5-7	170	4-30-90	.000	.000	.000	1	4	0	0	0	0	0	0	0	0	0	0	1	0	0	.000	.000
Kennedy, Garrett	R-R	6-1	210	12-13-92	.228	.300	.213	16	57	5	13	4	0	1	6	0	0	0	0	11	0	0	.351	.302
Landon, Logan	R-R	6-2	180	2-17-93	.278	.800	.224	15	54	9	15	1	0	2	5	5	2	0	1	10	4	0	.407	.355
Leon, Julian	R-R	5-11	200	1-24-96	.201	.115	.222	83	309	30	62	15	0	5	26	22	7	1	0	107	0	1	.298	.269
Mieses, Johan	R-R	6-2	185	7-13-95	.237	.308	.268	45	166	16	46	10	1	5	20	11	1	0	3	31	7	4	.440	.320
Navin, Spencer	R-R	6-1	185	8-11-92	.279	.316	.271	36	104	14	29	3	0	1	10	14	3	0	1	21	3	1	.337	.377
Oguisten, Faustino	R-R	6-2	165	1-17-91	.233	.167	.244	27	90	10	21	2	1	0	9	9	1	3	0	23	6	1	.278	.310
Ramos, Kelvin	R-R	5-10	170	12-21-93	.241	.284	.225	73	245	29	59	10	0	1	23	13	6	1	1	56	10	3	.294	.294
Rivas, Webster	R-R	6-2	218	8-8-90	.333	.250	.375	3	12	1	4	1	0	1	4	0	0	0	0	1	0	0	.667	.333
Santana, Alex	R-R	6-4	200	8-21-93	.238	.185	.257	64	244	32	58	9	4	4	28	15	1	2	2	84	2	1	.324	.282
Scavuzzo, Jacob	R-R	6-4	185	1-15-94	.263	.191	.283	58	213	30	56	14	3	5	20	7	3	0	3	44	4	1	.427	.292
Scott, Ryan	R-R	6-1	180	2-7-95	.053	.000	.077	7	19	1	1	0	0	0	1	5	0	0	0	7	2	0	.053	.250
Sell, Nick	R-R	6-1	195	2-15-92	.211	.462	.171	24	95	12	20	2	0	2	11	9	1	1	1	23	1	1	.295	.283
Tarsovich, Jordan	R-R	5-10	180	6-20-91	.269	.250	.270	17	67	13	18	2	0	1	8	7	2	0	1	17	2	1	.343	.351
Vela, Osvaldo	L-R	6-3	205	9-15-92	.158	.000	.180	16	57	2	9	0	0	0	3	6	0	0	0	15	0	0	.158	.200
Verdugo, Alex	L-L	6-0	205	5-15-96	.295	.340	.280	101	421	50	124	23	2	5	42	17	3	1	2	53	13	5	.394	.325
Wampler, Tyler	R-R	6-0	175	9-11-91	.163	.000	.212	13	43	4	7	1	0	0	1	3	1	0	0	9	1	0	.186	.234
Whiting, Brant	L-R	5-9	190	2-6-92	.238	.353	.196	21	63	5	15	2	0	2	3	9	1	0	0	13	0	0	.365	.333
Wolfe, Brian	L-L	6-4	210	10-16-90	.328	.154	.348	32	125	9	41	5	2	1	24	3	3	0	2	19	1	0	.424	.353

Pitching	B-T	HT	WT	DOB	W	L	ERA	G	GS	CG	SV	IP	H	R	ER	HR	BB	SO	AVG	vLH	vRH	K/9	BB/9
Anderson, Isaac	R-R	6-2	185	9-4-93	1	3	2.41	9	9	0	0	37	34	15	10	1	7	26	.234	.188	.258	6.27	1.69
Barlow, Scott	R-R	6-3	170	12-18-92	0	1	5.79	1	1	0	0	5	8	8	3	2	1	1	.381	.368	.500	1.93	1.93
Bergjans, Tommy	R-R	6-1	190	12-1-92	1	3	3.60	9	9	0	0	40	43	16	16	2	11	37	.277	.282	.273	8.33	2.48
Boyle, Michael	R-L	6-3	185	4-12-94	1	1	3.00	4	4	0	0	18	16	8	6	0	5	15	.232	.286	.208	7.50	2.50
Brigham, Jeff	R-R	6-0	200	2-16-92	2	0	1.29	2	0	0	0	7	3	1	1	0	2	11	.125	.222	.067	14.14	2.57
Broussard, Joe	R-R	6-1	220	1-28-91	3	2	2.41	15	2	0	3	34	25	10	9	0	4	38	.210	.256	.184	10.16	1.07
Campbell, James	R-R	6-1	195	9-20-91	0	3	4.50	19	0	0	3	32	31	17	16	2	9	19	.254	.273	.239	5.34	2.53
Campbell, Matt	R-R	5-10	195	9-28-91	1	1	2.70	22	0	0	1	37	28	12	11	1	16	35	.214	.190	.233	8.59	3.93
Caughel, Lindsey	R-R	6-3	205	8-13-90	0	0	21.00	1	1	0	0	3	7	7	7	4	0	2	.438	.444	.429	6.00	0.00
Cotton, Jharel	R-R	5-11	195	1-19-92	0	0	5.40	1	1	0	0	3	4	2	2	0	1	6	.286	.500	.200	16.20	2.70
De Paula, Luis	L-L	6-1	190	4-23-92	1	2	2.67	10	5	0	1	34	32	12	10	0	17	29	.252	.222	.264	7.75	4.54
Fernandez, Pablo	R-R	6-1	185	8-5-89	1	1	4.08	4	4	0	0	18	20	11	8	2	2	16	.278	.379	.209	8.15	1.02
Fernandez, Roberth	L-L	6-1	165	3-21-95	1	1	6.75	4	0	0	0	15	18	11	11	2	8	7	.300	.261	.324	4.30	4.91
Gonzalez, Victor	L-L	6-0	180	11-16-95	1	6	5.49	16	11	0	0	57	75	41	35	4	16	45	.316	.297	.324	7.06	2.51
Gonzalez, Yeuri	R-R	6-2	170	12-22-92	1	2	7.50	11	0	0	1	24	29	22	20	1	11	11	.302	.351	.271	4.13	4.13
Griggs, Scott	R-R	6-4	215	5-13-91	3	1	2.08	21	0	0	0	30	22	10	7	0	18	44	.202	.214	.194	13.05	5.34
Guzman, Kevin	R-R	6-3	165	11-6-94	5	7	3.90	17	15	1	0	83	94	45	36	5	29	62	.294	.283	.302	6.72	3.14
Hering, Colin	L-L	6-3	215	2-14-91	1	0	3.00	2	0	0	0	3	1	1	1	1	3	.182	.200	.167	9.00	3.00
Holmes, Grant	L-R	6-1	215	3-22-96	6	4	3.14	24	24	0	0	103	86	46	36	6	54	117	.229	.242	.216	10.19	4.70
Hooper, Kyle	R-R	6-4	195	5-28-91	3	0	1.69	17	0	0	5	27	17	5	5	1	6	34	.173	.059	.234	11.48	2.03
Kowalczyk, Karch	R-R	6-1	215	3-31-91	4	1	2.53	22	0	0	6	32	32	10	9	0	12	19	.282	.280	.284	5.34	3.38
Long, Nolan	R-R	6-10	240	1-19-94	0	0	4.32	2	1	0	0	8	10	5	4	1	0	7	.294	.250	.333	7.56	0.00
Martinez, Brandon	R-R	6-4	162	11-25-90	1	1	4.67	6	6	0	0	27	25	14	14	1	8	20	.248	.333	.170	6.67	2.67
Molina, Jose	L-L	5-11	160	6-26-91	4	2	3.23	37	0	0	2	61	54	23	22	2	29	65	.242	.263	.231	9.54	4.26
Oaks, Trevor	R-R	6-3	220	3-26-93	5	5	2.56	18	16	2	0	102	86	29	29	3	14	58	.221	.217	.223	5.12	1.24
Palmer, Cameron	R-R	6-3	220	12-3-91	5	1	3.68	18	0	0	0	37	26	17	15	3	30	40	.197	.237	.164	9.82	7.36
Reid-Foley, David	L-R	6-3	190	1-2-91	2	2	2.61	33	0	0	0	69	63	26	20	3	21	56	.244	.218	.261	7.30	2.74
Reyes, Bernardo	R-R	6-0	175	7-22-95	1	0	0.00	1	0	0	0	2	0	0	0	1	2	.000	.000	.000	9.00	4.50
Rossman, Bubby	B-R	6-5	220	6-29-92	3	1	2.26	29	0	0	4	52	41	22	13	1	26	54	.218	.256	.186	9.41	4.53
Sborz, Josh	R-R	6-2	209	12-17-93	0	1	2.84	2	2	0	0	6	5	4	2	2	2	9	.185	.267	.083	12.79	2.84
Shelton, Matt	R-R	6-2	205	11-30-88	1	3	7.68	7	7	0	0	36	38	34	31	2	29	21	.277	.295	.263	5.20	7.18
Sopko, Andrew	R-R	6-3	180	8-7-94	3	1	2.74	5	5	0	0	23	18	9	7	2	4	18	.212	.353	.118	7.04	1.57
Stewart, Brock	L-R	6-3	210	10-3-91	2	2	2.84	7	7	0	0	38	38	13	12	4	6	38	.262	.275	.250	9.00	1.42
Stripling, Ross	R-R	6-3	190	11-23-89	0	0	0.00	1	1	0	0	4	1	0	0	0	2	4	.077	.000	.111	9.00	4.50
Sylvester, Derrick	R-R	6-6	220	4-19-91	1	6	5.72	14	5	0	1	39	43	32	25	1	20	37	.272	.239	.297	8.47	4.58
Underwood, J.D.	L-R	6-2	215	9-2-92	4	3	2.63	37	0	0	5	75	62	23	22	4	15	71	.219	.241	.206	8.48	1.79

Fielding

Catcher	PCT	G	PO	A	E	DP	PB									First Base	PCT	G	PO	A	E	DP
Chubb	1.000	1	12	2	0	0	1	Rivas	1.000	3	22	5	0	0	Ahmed	1.000	2	11	1	0	1
Kennedy	1.000	16	123	16	0	0	1	Scott	.981	5	49	3	1	0	Beaty	.972	17	129	10	4	12
Leon	.989	67	485	62	6	3	7	Whiting	1.000	18	130	9	0	1	Celli	1.000	1	8	0	0	1
Navin	.989	34	228	42	3	1	3								Chigbogu	.981	77	630	42	13	63

First Base	PCT	G	PO	A	E	DP
Cordero	.992	29	237	22	2	21
De Jong	1.000	2	13	1	0	2
Navin	—	1	0	0	0	0
Vela	.981	8	51	2	1	1
Wolfe	1.000	7	50	6	0	6

Second Base	PCT	G	PO	A	E	DP
Ahmed	.972	14	29	41	2	11
Allen	.965	38	61	103	6	25
Calhoun	.935	12	13	30	3	5
Leon	1.000	1	0	1	0	0
Oguisten	1.000	2	7	9	0	2
Ramos	.980	61	115	179	6	45
Tarsovich	.962	14	30	45	3	11

Third Base	PCT	G	PO	A	E	DP
Ahmed	.949	51	34	78	6	5
Allen	.949	42	23	52	4	4
Beaty	.945	33	16	53	4	4
Cordero	.900	8	2	7	1	1
Oguisten	.636	2	2	5	4	0
Vela	.952	7	5	15	1	0

Shortstop	PCT	G	PO	A	E	DP
Ahmed	.929	32	40	78	9	16
Dean	.933	37	60	94	11	21
Gomez	.934	24	46	67	8	19
Hennigan	.625	1	2	3	3	1
Oguisten	.924	20	35	62	8	9
Ramos	.950	9	15	23	2	8
Tarsovich	.870	3	12	8	3	4
Wampler	.953	12	22	39	3	17

Outfield	PCT	G	PO	A	E	DP
Ahmed	1.000	6	8	2	0	1
Allen	.929	10	12	1	1	0
Celli	.973	49	107	2	3	2
Cordero	1.000	1	4	0	0	0
De Jong	1.000	2	7	2	0	0
Drake	1.000	7	13	0	0	0
Garlick	.986	34	64	4	1	4
Green	1.000	4	10	0	0	0
Landon	1.000	15	48	0	0	0
Mieses	.990	42	98	2	1	0
Santana	.950	56	93	2	5	0
Scavuzzo	.975	52	76	2	2	0
Sell	.981	23	52	1	1	1
Verdugo	.970	99	240	21	8	6
Wolfe	1.000	21	35	3	0	0

AZL DODGERS

ARIZONA LEAGUE

ROOKIE

LOS ANGELES DODGERS

Batting	B-T	HT	WT	DOB	AVG	vLH	vRH	G	AB	R	H	2B	3B	HR	RBI	BB	HBP	SH	SF	SO	SB	CS	SLG	OBP
Ahart, Devan	L-R	6-1	175	10-21-92	.222	.333	.200	6	18	0	4	0	1	0	1	2	0	0	1	1	1	0	.333	.300
Albert, Shakir	R-R	6-0	185	12-24-96	.223	.350	.202	41	139	17	31	9	2	0	11	8	3	1	1	39	2	3	.317	.278
Aquino, Carlos	R-R	6-0	165	10-20-95	.246	.200	.255	40	118	16	29	5	2	0	12	17	0	1	1	32	4	7	.322	.338
Arruebarrena, Erisbel	R-R	6-1	230	3-25-90	.444	1.000	.286	3	9	4	4	2	0	0	1	2	1	0	0	5	1	0	.667	.583
Capellan, Yensys	R-R	6-2	190	10-4-93	.227	.278	.211	24	75	6	17	6	2	0	9	7	0	0	1	23	1	0	.360	.289
Clementina, Hendrik	R-R	6-0	165	6-17-97	.284	.571	.224	26	81	12	23	5	0	0	10	7	2	0	2	22	1	1	.346	.348
Davis, Brendon	R-R	6-4	163	7-28-97	.278	.333	.264	23	90	14	25	2	1	0	14	4	0	0	0	26	2	0	.322	.309
Drexler, Edwin	B-R	6-2	185	7-1-92	.353	.250	.385	13	17	9	6	0	0	0	2	0	0	0	0	8	9	1	.353	.421
Estrella, Alberto	R-R	6-3	190	5-22-97	.063	.000	.077	10	32	2	2	0	1	0	3	1	0	0	1	20	0	0	.125	.088
Garlick, Kyle	R-R	6-1	210	1-26-92	.375	.333	.385	4	16	6	6	2	2	0	3	1	0	0	1	2	0	0	.750	.389
Garvey, Robbie	L-L	5-8	165	4-26-89	—	—	—	1	0	1	0	0	0	0	0	0	0	0	0	0	0	0	—	—
Giordani, Federico	R-R	5-11	180	11-23-97	.143	.158	.138	32	84	7	12	4	0	1	6	8	3	0	1	46	2	4	.226	.240
Green, Gage	R-R	5-10	190	8-27-92	.262	.200	.270	14	42	8	11	1	1	0	2	6	0	0	0	8	5	0	.333	.354
Hansen, Mitch	L-L	6-2	195	5-1-96	.201	.143	.215	44	149	23	30	6	3	0	17	15	2	0	1	51	6	1	.282	.281
Hope, Garrett	R-R	6-2	245	12-27-93	.203	.111	.217	23	69	7	14	1	1	1	8	2	1	0	0	17	1	0	.290	.236
Hudson, Kyle	L-L	5-11	175	1-7-87	—	—	—	6	0	3	0	0	0	0	0	0	0	0	0	0	7	1	—	—
Isabel, Ibandel	R-R	6-4	185	6-20-95	.295	.310	.292	47	149	29	44	7	4	5	26	13	1	1	1	57	5	1	.497	.354
Landon, Logan	R-R	6-2	180	2-17-93	.350	.400	.333	5	20	5	7	2	1	0	4	0	0	0	0	5	1	0	.550	.350
Mayora, Daniel	R-R	5-11	175	7-27-85	.333	.333	.333	4	15	3	5	0	0	0	1	1	1	0	0	3	0	0	.333	.412
Olivera, Hector	R-R	6-2	220	4-5-85	.313	—	.313	6	16	4	5	1	0	0	0	2	0	0	0	1	0	0	.375	.389
Ortiz, Samuel	B-R	5-11	170	8-4-96	.133	.375	.045	11	30	3	4	0	0	0	2	6	1	0	0	4	2	0	.133	.297
Paroubeck, Jordan	B-R	6-2	190	11-2-94	.245	.364	.211	13	49	11	12	4	1	1	8	6	0	0	0	13	0	0	.429	.327
Perez, Jimy	R-R	6-2	185	2-12-94	.316	.400	.286	5	19	3	6	2	0	0	3	1	0	0	0	6	0	0	.421	.350
Perez, Moises	R-R	5-10	150	7-18-97	.162	.087	.178	40	130	9	21	4	1	0	8	11	1	1	2	43	3	6	.208	.229
Pitre, Gersel	R-R	6-0	180	7-23-96	.392	.333	.407	29	74	14	29	5	2	0	12	10	2	0	0	9	3	4	.514	.477
Rios, Edwin	L-R	6-3	235	4-21-94	.429	—	.429	2	7	1	3	0	0	0	0	0	0	0	0	1	0	1	.429	.429
Sandoval, Ariel	R-R	6-2	180	11-6-95	.325	.242	.341	50	200	30	65	11	2	8	33	3	1	1	1	49	10	4	.520	.337
Scott, Ryan	R-R	6-1	180	2-7-95	.000	.000	.000	2	7	0	0	0	0	0	0	1	0	0	0	2	0	0	.000	.125
Sell, Nick	R-R	6-1	195	2-15-92	.118	.000	.125	6	17	3	2	1	0	1	1	0	1	0	0	4	0	0	.353	.167
Tarsovich, Jordan	R-R	5-10	180	6-20-91	.286	—	.286	4	14	2	4	0	0	0	0	0	0	0	0	2	0	0	.286	.286
Tirado, Lucas	L-R	6-2	180	11-13-96	.139	.000	.167	17	36	3	5	3	0	0	2	2	1	0	0	20	2	1	.222	.205
Walker, Jared	L-R	6-2	195	2-4-96	.240	.308	.225	44	146	22	35	6	2	2	21	15	2	0	3	55	7	2	.349	.313

Pitching	B-T	HT	WT	DOB	W	L	ERA	G	GS	CG	SV	IP	H	R	ER	HR	BB	SO	AVG	vLH	vRH	K/9	BB/9
Abdullah, Imani	B-R	6-5	205	4-20-97	0	1	4.85	6	3	0	0	13	9	9	7	0	5	13	.173	.250	.125	9.00	3.46
Anderson, Isaac	R-R	6-2	185	9-4-93	0	0	0.00	2	0	0	0	2	0	0	0	0	0	2	.000	.000	.000	9.00	0.00
Barlow, Scott	R-R	6-3	170	12-18-92	0	1	4.00	3	3	0	0	9	8	7	4	1	4	11	.216	.083	.280	11.00	4.00
Bass, Brian	R-R	6-4	200	5-11-92	2	0	0.86	11	0	0	2	21	17	2	2	0	8	14	.230	.185	.255	6.00	3.43
Boyle, Michael	R-L	6-3	185	4-12-94	0	0	0.00	2	0	0	0	2	1	0	0	0	0	4	.143	.000	.167	18.00	0.00
Cahill, Trevor	R-R	6-4	240	3-1-88	0	0	0.00	1	0	0	0	2	3	3	0	0	0	4	.300	.250	.333	21.60	0.00
Campbell, James	R-R	6-1	195	9-20-91	0	0	0.00	2	0	0	1	3	1	1	0	0	1	5	.091	.000	.111	15.00	3.00
Chica, Dennys	L-L	6-3	175	8-31-95	1	0	7.71	4	0	0	0	5	6	5	4	0	5	2	.333	—	.333	3.86	9.64
Crouse, Logan	R-R	6-6	225	12-2-96	0	0	5.40	2	0	0	0	2	1	3	1	0	2	0	.143	.000	.200	0.00	10.80
Eadington, Eric	R-L	6-2	220	2-9-88	0	0	0.00	1	0	0	0	1	0	0	0	0	0	0	.000	—	.000	0.00	0.00
Ferguson, Caleb	R-L	6-3	215	7-2-96	0	3	8.59	14	4	0	1	15	17	19	14	0	16	16	.298	.333	.289	9.82	12.89
Fernandez, Pablo	R-R	6-1	185	8-5-89	0	0	1.93	2	2	0	0	5	3	1	1	1	1	7	.176	.333	.091	13.50	1.93
Fernandez, Roberth	L-R	6-1	165	3-21-95	0	1	5.40	6	0	0	0	12	12	7	7	0	1	8	.255	.417	.200	6.17	7.71
German, Angel	R-R	6-4	185	5-25-96	0	3	4.53	12	8	0	0	46	51	28	23	1	24	36	.277	.314	.254	7.09	4.73
Gonzalez, Victor	L-L	6-0	180	11-16-95	0	0	0.00	1	1	0	0	2	1	0	0	1	0	6	.143	.000	.167	27.00	4.50
Harcksen, Misja	R-R	6-2	165	4-19-95	1	0	1.46	10	0	0	2	12	11	4	2	0	2	18	.216	.294	.176	13.14	1.46
Heredia, Jairo	R-R	6-1	190	10-8-89	0	0	0.00	3	2	0	1	9	7	0	0	0	0	9	.212	.083	.286	9.00	0.00
Jaime, Juan	R-R	6-2	250	8-2-87	0	0	0.00	5	0	0	2	4	2	0	0	0	0	9	.133	.000	.182	18.69	4.15
Lee, Zach	R-R	6-4	210	9-13-91	1	0	0.00	1	1	0	0	5	0	0	0	0	0	3	.000	.000	.000	3.60	0.00
Long, Nolan	R-R	6-10	240	1-19-94	5	1	1.11	10	3	0	0	24	14	4	3	0	12	30	.163	.194	.145	11.10	4.44

182 · Baseball America 2016 Almanac

BaseballAmerica.com

Pitching	B-T	HT	WT	DOB	W	L	ERA	G	GS	CG	SV	IP	H	R	ER	HR	BB	SO	AVG	vLH	vRH	K/9	BB/9
Mora, Gregor	R-R	6-2	190	8-28-95	2	1	2.38	12	3	0	0	45	35	20	12	3	14	39	.208	.189	.217	7.74	2.78
Mullholland, Casey	R-R	6-3	180	12-17-91	0	0	0.00	1	0	0	0	1	0	0	0	0	0	1	.400	.000	.500	9.00	0.00
Pittore, Gavin	R-R	6-3	230	9-18-93	1	1	5.19	7	0	0	0	9	8	5	5	0	6	5	.250	.375	.208	5.19	6.23
Powell, Chris	R-R	6-2	170	9-21-92	2	0	1.86	12	0	0	0	19	14	5	4	0	7	27	.197	.158	.212	12.57	3.26
Ramirez, Osiris	R-R	6-3	185	9-14-95	0	4	5.60	14	3	0	1	27	30	30	17	5	15	24	.254	.234	.268	7.90	4.94
Riekenberg, Drayton	R-R	6-2	205	3-27-94	2	3	3.38	13	0	0	0	19	14	10	7	0	8	20	.206	.222	.195	9.64	3.86
Rodriguez, Hector	R-R	6-3	190	10-17-94	1	1	1.47	8	0	0	0	18	12	4	3	1	4	19	.179	.182	.178	9.33	1.96
Rodriguez, Luis	R-R	6-4	190	10-10-96	0	0	2.84	5	0	0	0	6	4	2	2	0	1	4	.174	.000	.235	5.68	1.42
Santos, Jose	R-R	6-0	165	3-8-92	1	0	0.75	9	1	0	0	12	3	3	1	0	7	13	.077	.000	.097	9.75	5.25
Schuller, Sven	R-R	6-3	205	1-17-96	1	3	6.82	13	5	0	0	32	33	29	24	2	30	31	.266	.333	.239	8.81	8.53
Spitzbarth, Shea	R-R	6-1	195	10-4-94	2	1	0.00	8	0	0	2	8	1	1	0	0	7	17	.037	.000	.053	18.36	7.56
Sylvester, Derrick	R-R	6-6	220	4-19-91	0	0	10.13	2	2	0	0	3	6	3	3	0	0	3	.462	1.000	.364	10.13	0.00
Urena, Miguel	R-R	6-8	210	2-27-95	5	2	2.73	13	6	0	1	56	56	25	17	1	15	37	.251	.271	.242	5.95	2.41
Urias, Julio	L-L	6-2	205	8-12-96	0	0	0.00	2	2	0	0	3	2	0	0	0	1	5	.200	.250	.167	15.00	3.00
Uter, Kam	R-R	6-3	200	1-26-96	0	0	7.88	9	0	0	0	8	12	12	7	0	4	13	.293	.545	.200	14.63	4.50
Villegas, M.J.	R-R	6-2	190	9-6-94	0	0	0.00	4	0	0	0	5	2	0	0	0	2	5	.133	.143	.125	8.44	3.38
West, Matt	R-R	6-1	200	11-21-88	0	0	0.00	1	1	0	0	2	1	0	0	0	0	4	.167	.250	.000	18.00	0.00

Fielding

Catcher

Catcher	PCT	G	PO	A	E	DP	PB
Clementina	.984	24	172	16	3	2	4
Green	.969	4	26	5	1	2	1
Hope	.957	12	77	11	4	0	1
Pitre	.961	27	193	26	9	3	9
Scott	1.000	2	19	0	0	0	0
Perez	.905	9	17	21	4		6
Sell	—	2	0	0	0		0
Tarsovich	.889	2	2	6	1		0
Tirado	.894	15	19	23	5		7
Walker	.870	7	9	11	3		2

First Base

First Base	PCT	G	PO	A	E	DP
Clementina	1.000	2	14	1	0	2
Estrella	1.000	4	20	2	0	0
Hope	.954	10	56	6	3	8
Isabel	.962	44	356	25	15	28
Perez	1.000	3	19	0	0	1
Rios	1.000	1	7	1	0	0
Sell	1.000	1	9	0	0	1

Second Base

Second Base	PCT	G	PO	A	E	DP
Aquino	.929	26	30	49	6	7
Capellan	.941	3	4	12	1	3
Ortiz	.969	8	16	15	1	6

Third Base

Third Base	PCT	G	PO	A	E	DP
Capellan	.889	13	8	32	5	3
Estrella	.900	5	1	8	1	0
Mayora	1.000	1	3	2	0	0
Olivera	1.000	4	2	8	0	1
Ortiz	1.000	1	1	2	0	0
Perez	.500	2	0	3	3	0
Sell	.750	1	1	2	1	0
Walker	.831	37	32	66	20	5

Shortstop

Shortstop	PCT	G	PO	A	E	DP
Aquino	.758	7	10	15	8	3
Arruebarrena	1.000	2	0	3	0	0
Davis	.940	15	18	29	3	7
Ortiz	1.000	1	2	1	0	1
Perez	.892	33	28	96	15	16
Tarsovich	1.000	1	1	3	0	1

Outfield

Outfield	PCT	G	PO	A	E	DP
Ahart	1.000	5	6	0	0	0
Albert	.943	37	46	4	3	0
Drexler	1.000	2	3	0	0	0
Garlick	1.000	2	5	0	0	0
Giordani	.973	28	34	2	1	0
Green	.895	8	17	0	2	0
Hansen	.984	39	58	3	1	0
Landon	1.000	4	6	0	0	0
Paroubeck	.938	11	13	2	1	1
Pitre	—	1	0	0	0	0
Sandoval	.978	46	86	1	2	0
Sell	1.000	1	2	1	0	0
Walker	—	1	0	0	0	0

OGDEN RAPTORS   ROOKIE

PIONEER LEAGUE

Batting	B-T	HT	WT	DOB	AVG	vLH	vRH	G	AB	R	H	2B	3B	HR	RBI	BB	HBP	SH	SF	SO	SB	CS	SLG	OBP
Beaty, Matt	L-R	6-0	195	4-28-93	.480	.412	.625	6	25	3	12	1	0	0	3	2	0	1	0	3	2	2	.520	.519
Calhoun, Willie	L-R	5-9	177	11-4-94	.278	.308	.263	38	151	28	42	13	1	7	26	23	0	0	1	18	2	1	.517	.371
Capellan, Yensys	R-R	6-2	190	10-4-93	.266	.360	.205	16	64	9	17	3	1	3	16	3	0	1	0	13	1	1	.484	.299
Castillo, Deivy	L-L	6-3	170	7-21-95	.130	.048	.161	24	77	11	10	2	0	0	6	6	2	1	1	17	2	0	.156	.209
Davis, Brendon	R-R	6-4	163	7-28-97	.167	.000	.200	7	24	5	4	1	0	1	3	2	0	0	1	8	0	0	.333	.222
De Jong, Scott	R-R	6-4	230	4-26-93	.293	.288	.294	60	222	39	65	9	4	10	45	29	2	0	3	69	5	1	.505	.375
Dean, Nick	R-R	6-1	190	5-11-92	.390	.310	.434	23	82	24	32	4	1	3	17	9	1	0	1	10	3	1	.573	.452
Garlick, Kyle	R-R	6-1	210	1-26-92	.400	.250	.571	4	15	2	6	3	0	0	3	1	0	0	1	2	0	0	.600	.412
Garvey, Robbie	L-R	5-8	165	4-26-89	—			6	0	2	0	0	0	0	0	0	0	0	0	0	5	1	—	—
Godinez, Chris	R-R	5-8	185	4-20-93	.226	.250	.219	30	93	23	21	2	1	1	11	20	4	0	0	17	4	2	.301	.385
Gomez, Cristian	R-R	5-11	185	1-11-96	.111	.000	.200	3	9	0	1	0	0	0	0	0	0	0	0	1	0	0	.111	.111
Green, Gage	R-R	5-10	190	8-27-92	.370	.384	.349	47	181	30	67	14	2	4	33	18	5	2	4	31	6	3	.536	.433
Henson, Jake	R-R	5-11	215	8-4-93	.296	.395	.260	39	142	22	42	5	1	3	18	11	2	0	0	29	2	1	.408	.355
Hope, Garrett	R-R	6-2	245	12-27-93	.200	.500	.125	3	10	0	2	0	0	0	0	0	0	0	0	4	0	0	.200	.200
Jones, Matt	L-R	6-7	250	3-9-94	.300	.229	.325	67	267	50	80	18	3	11	47	17	2	0	3	87	0	2	.513	.343
Kennedy, Garrett	L-R	6-1	210	12-13-92	.265	.059	.333	19	68	11	18	7	1	0	12	10	0	0	2	7	1	0	.397	.350
Landon, Logan	R-R	6-2	180	2-17-93	.241	.250	.237	15	54	9	13	4	0	0	6	9	1	0	1	4	0	0	.315	.354
Medina, Michael	R-R	6-2	190	8-24-96	.254	.218	.270	46	181	31	46	14	3	9	38	10	4	0	4	73	2	1	.514	.302
Morales, Delvis	B-R	6-2	175	8-29-90	.500			4	12	4	6	1	0	1	3	2	0	0	0	0	0	0	.833	.571
Oguisten, Faustino	R-R	6-2	165	1-17-91	.281	.333	.265	27	89	16	25	3	1	1	13	8	2	1	0	21	1	2	.371	.354
Paroubeck, Jordan	B-R	6-2	190	11-2-94	.379	.375	.380	22	87	21	33	7	1	4	20	12	0	0	0	27	1	1	.621	.455
Perez, Jimy	R-R	6-2	185	2-12-94	.211	.286	.194	12	38	6	8	0	0	1	4	3	0	0	0	14	0	0	.289	.268
Pitre, Gersel	R-R	6-0	180	7-23-96	.279	.385	.233	11	43	8	12	1	1	1	7	2	0	1	0	10	0	0	.419	.311
Ramos, Kelvin	R-R	5-10	170	12-21-93	.294	.233	.315	33	119	23	35	11	0	1	18	9	2	2	3	22	1	3	.412	.346
Redman, Hunter	R-R	5-10	180	8-25-92	.333	.500	.000	2	6	2	2	0	0	0	0	0	0	0	0	0	0	0	.333	.333
Rios, Edwin	L-R	6-3	185	4-21-94	.235	.143	.259	20	68	9	16	7	0	3	13	7	0	0	0	29	0	0	.471	.307
Santana, Alex	R-R	6-4	200	8-21-93	.282	.238	.293	26	103	19	29	5	3	5	20	10	3	0	1	27	1	1	.534	.359
Scott, Ryan	R-R	6-1	180	2-7-95	.156	.063	.188	20	64	8	10	2	1	0	2	7	1	0	1	23	0	1	.219	.247
Sell, Nick	R-R	6-1	195	2-15-92	.347	.306	.364	31	124	26	43	11	6	4	32	9	3	0	1	21	1	1	.629	.401
Tarsovich, Bryan	R-R	5-10	180	6-20-91	.264	.385	.225	16	53	11	14	3	0	2	10	11	2	1	1	11	0	0	.434	.403
Torres, Reymundo	R-R	5-11	170	1-25-94	.000	.000	.000	2	9	0	0	0	0	0	0	0	1	0	0	3	0	0	.000	.000
Ulmer, Deion	R-R	5-9	170	7-18-94	.255	.191	.277	55	188	34	48	7	2	2	14	22	6	3	0	49	13	1	.346	.352
Vela, Osvaldo	L-R	6-3	205	9-15-92	.129	.000	.148	11	31	4	4	1	0	0	3	0	0	1	0	6	0	0	.161	.229

Pitching	B-T	HT	WT	DOB	W	L	ERA	G	GS	CG	SV	IP	H	R	ER	HR	BB	SO	AVG	vLH	vRH	K/9	BB/9
Anderson, Isaac	R-R	6-2	185	9-4-93	1	0	0.71	6	1	0	1	13	13	1	1	0	3	15	.271	.240	.304	10.66	2.13
Bass, Brian	R-R	6-4	200	5-11-92	0	0	4.15	2	0	0	0	4	5	2	2	0	1	2	.294	.375	.222	4.15	2.08
Bergjans, Tommy	R-R	6-1	190	12-1-92	2	0	2.63	5	3	0	0	14	9	7	4	0	4	16	.180	.172	.190	10.54	2.63
Boyle, Michael	R-L	6-3	185	4-12-94	2	1	1.33	9	6	0	1	27	27	8	4	1	6	27	.252	.233	.260	9.00	2.00
Bray, Adam	R-R	6-2	210	4-14-93	2	2	3.86	11	8	0	0	35	42	22	15	5	4	33	.286	.286	.286	8.49	1.03
Brown, Kevin	R-R	6-3	220	6-9-92	1	1	2.86	15	5	0	0	28	23	14	9	3	7	21	.213	.310	.152	6.67	2.22
Copping, Corey	R-R	6-1	175	1-11-94	0	0	3.38	14	0	0	0	16	14	9	6	0	10	21	.246	.316	.211	11.81	5.63
Crescentini, Marcus	R-R	6-4	225	12-26-92	1	1	7.43	24	0	0	3	27	26	24	22	3	23	42	.243	.278	.225	14.18	7.76
Fernandez, Roberth	L-L	6-1	165	3-21-95	1	3	10.47	6	4	0	0	16	26	20	19	2	10	20	.366	.423	.333	11.02	5.51
Gonzalez, Victor	L-L	6-0	180	11-16-95	0	1	6.43	2	2	0	0	7	10	5	5	1	2	5	.333	.333	.333	6.43	2.57
Harcksen, Misja	R-R	6-2	165	4-19-95	0	0	7.71	8	0	0	0	12	20	12	10	3	2	9	.364	.381	.353	6.94	1.54
Helsabeck, Wes	L-L	6-0	195	7-7-92	2	0	2.32	21	0	0	1	31	22	9	8	1	19	28	.193	.270	.156	8.13	5.52
Hering, Colin	L-L	6-3	215	2-14-91	3	0	3.63	19	0	0	0	35	41	23	14	3	16	44	.287	.311	.276	11.42	4.15
Istler, Andrew	R-R	5-11	180	9-18-92	2	1	8.38	22	1	0	1	29	49	27	27	1	12	25	.377	.431	.342	7.76	3.72
Jaime, Juan	R-R	6-2	250	8-2-87	0	0	2.70	3	0	0	0	3	2	2	1	0	1	6	.167	.250	.125	16.20	2.70
McDonnell, Rob	L-L	6-1	220	4-28-92	3	2	4.76	20	0	0	0	34	43	21	18	3	18	43	.314	.271	.337	11.38	4.76
Mora, Gregor	R-R	6-2	190	8-28-95	1	1	10.50	4	2	0	0	12	21	14	14	0	8	5	.438	.444	.433	3.75	6.00
Mullholland, Casey	R-R	6-3	180	12-17-91	1	0	3.68	7	0	0	0	7	6	4	3	0	9	11	.222	.333	.167	13.50	11.05
Osuna, Lenix	R-R	6-2	220	11-11-95	1	1	6.92	11	0	0	1	13	23	15	10	0	5	15	.377	.433	.323	10.38	3.46
Pacheco, Jairo	L-L	6-0	165	7-6-96	7	4	4.08	15	15	0	0	71	56	37	32	5	31	57	.216	.224	.214	7.26	3.95
Palmer, Cameron	R-R	6-3	220	12-3-91	0	0	0.00	2	0	0	0	2	1	0	0	0	0	3	.143	—	.143	13.50	0.00
Pfeifer, Philip	L-L	6-0	190	7-15-92	0	0	0.00	1	1	0	0	2	1	0	0	0	3	2	.167	.000	.250	10.80	16.20
Powell, Chris	R-R	6-2	170	9-21-92	2	0	3.54	5	5	0	0	20	20	12	8	1	7	19	.260	.138	.333	8.41	3.10
Reyes, Bernardo	R-R	6-0	175	7-22-95	2	3	5.59	20	0	0	4	29	35	24	18	4	16	27	.302	.327	.281	8.38	4.97
Rodriguez, Hector	R-R	6-3	190	10-17-94	2	0	5.79	8	0	0	0	14	18	9	9	1	8	5	.327	.357	.317	3.21	5.14
Santos, Jose	R-R	6-0	165	3-8-92	1	0	6.75	6	1	0	0	13	20	11	10	3	8	11	.351	.190	.444	7.43	5.40
Sborz, Josh	R-R	6-2	209	12-17-93	0	1	4.50	2	1	0	0	4	2	2	2	0	4	4	.167	.000	.250	9.00	9.00
Sopko, Andrew	R-R	6-2	180	8-7-94	0	0	2.57	6	1	0	0	14	14	6	4	1	1	18	.264	.208	.310	11.57	0.64
Soto, William	R-R	6-4	185	2-13-96	1	0	3.38	3	2	0	0	8	7	4	3	1	4	3	.226	.222	.231	3.38	4.50
Spitzbarth, Shea	R-R	6-1	195	10-4-94	0	2	4.76	7	0	0	0	11	9	6	6	1	7	11	.220	.250	.207	8.74	5.56
Vieitez, Ivan	L-R	6-2	170	5-8-93	1	4	6.10	17	11	0	0	52	67	39	35	2	28	37	.328	.304	.341	6.45	4.88
Villegas, M.J.	R-R	6-2	190	9-6-94	2	0	3.09	13	0	0	1	23	18	11	8	0	10	21	.212	.194	.224	8.10	3.86

Fielding

Catcher	PCT	G	PO	A	E	DP	PB
Green	1.000	3	29	1	0	0	1
Henson	.993	31	255	26	2	5	5
Hope	.963	3	25	1	1	0	1
Kennedy	1.000	15	109	10	0	0	4
Pitre	.976	10	69	14	2	1	3
Redman	.929	2	12	1	1	0	0
Scott	.976	18	140	22	4	0	2

First Base	PCT	G	PO	A	E	DP
Beaty	1.000	1	11	0	0	0
De Jong	.986	39	331	16	5	31
Jones	.989	36	249	17	3	18
Perez	—	1	0	0	0	0
Rios	1.000	3	15	1	0	1
Sell	.857	1	6	0	1	0

Second Base	PCT	G	PO	A	E	DP
Calhoun	.919	33	38	75	10	11
Godinez	.940	12	26	21	3	5
Oguisten	.955	11	18	24	2	6
Ramos	.950	9	12	26	2	8

Third Base	PCT	G	PO	A	E	DP
Beaty	.938	5	6	9	1	1
Capellan	.824	14	9	19	6	2
Dean	1.000	4	0	9	0	1
Godinez	.867	8	5	8	2	1
Gomez	—	1	0	0	0	0
Oguisten	.846	7	2	9	2	2
Perez	.870	12	2	18	3	1
Rios	.917	14	13	20	3	2
Sell	.833	5	5	5	2	3
Tarsovich	.958	10	3	20	1	1
Ulmer	1.000	2	1	1	0	0
Vela	.941	10	2	14	1	2

Shortstop	PCT	G	PO	A	E	DP
Davis	.947	6	10	8	1	4
Dean	.950	18	23	34	3	7
Gomez	1.000	3	1	9	0	1
Morales	1.000	4	6	7	0	3

	PCT	G	PO	A	E	DP
Oguisten	.909	6	6	14	2	2
Ramos	.942	23	32	65	6	15
Tarsovich	1.000	1	1	2	0	0
Ulmer	.901	22	26	47	8	4
Vela	1.000	1	1	0	0	0

Outfield	PCT	G	PO	A	E	DP
Castillo	.930	19	37	3	3	0
Garlick	1.000	4	10	0	0	0
Green	.991	42	102	3	1	1
Jones	.967	24	28	1	1	1
Landon	.974	14	37	1	1	0
Medina	.953	44	95	6	5	1
Oguisten	1.000	5	7	0	0	0
Paroubeck	.919	18	33	1	3	0
Pitre	1.000	1	1	0	0	0
Santana	.981	24	51	1	1	0
Scott	1.000	1	1	0	0	0
Sell	.949	27	36	1	2	0
Torres	1.000	2	3	0	0	0
Ulmer	.976	22	40	1	1	0

DSL DODGERS ROOKIE

DOMINICAN SUMMER LEAGUE

Batting	B-T	HT	WT	DOB	AVG	vLH	vRH	G	AB	R	H	2B	3B	HR	RBI	BB	HBP	SH	SF	SO	SB	CS	SLG	OBP
Asencio, Luis	R-R	6-2	160	9-4-97	.221	.214	.222	32	95	11	21	2	1	2	6	8	0	0	0	25	5	6	.326	.282
Calderon, Jhoan	R-R	6-3	200	9-14-97	.145	.118	.155	42	131	5	19	6	0	1	14	12	3	0	0	70	4	2	.214	.233
Cuadrado, Romer	R-R	6-4	185	9-12-97	.222	.173	.237	62	221	26	49	9	2	2	22	23	5	0	0	57	10	9	.308	.309
Dometilia, Jerson	R-R	5-8	165	8-13-98	.192	.045	.250	32	78	7	15	1	1	0	8	8	0	0	1	14	2	0	.231	.264
Estrella, Alberto	R-R	6-3	190	5-22-97	.189	.214	.179	14	53	6	10	0	0	1	6	7	0	0	2	17	0	0	.245	.274
Mosquera, Carlos	B-L	5-9	150	1-9-96	.271	.269	.271	55	170	32	46	7	3	0	18	16	5	5	0	26	20	10	.347	.358
Padilla, Daniel	R-R	6-2	175	2-16-97	.321	.357	.308	48	159	28	51	1	2	2	18	15	3	3	2	33	12	2	.390	.385
Paz, Luis	L-R	6-1	190	5-7-96	.270	.170	.303	57	189	30	51	5	6	1	30	17	1	0	2	41	4	2	.376	.330
Peguero, Alex	L-L	6-7	190	12-23-95	.143	.059	.167	27	77	6	11	4	0	0	2	4	1	0	0	42	0	0	.195	.195
Perez, Jimy	R-R	6-2	185	2-12-94	.262	.246	.268	54	210	36	55	12	2	10	33	12	5	0	0	62	5	3	.481	.317
Reyes, Edwin	R-R	6-2	175	12-14-97	.105	.111	.103	21	57	2	6	1	0	0	3	7	0	0	0	30	0	1	.123	.203
Rubi, Alvaro	R-R	6-2	185	2-16-97	.167	.167	.167	26	78	8	13	2	0	0	4	11	2	0	0	7	1	0	.192	.286
Ruiz, Keibert	B-R	6-0	165	7-20-98	.300	.333	.288	44	150	14	45	8	1	1	19	8	1	0	0	15	4	2	.387	.340
Sanchez, Frank	R-R	6-3	170	8-25-98	.175	.125	.190	32	103	10	18	4	0	1	13	7	2	1	1	32	1	2	.243	.239
Santana, Cristian	R-R	6-2	175	2-24-97	.276	.328	.256	59	217	30	60	13	0	3	18	16	1	1	0	35	3	6	.378	.329

Batting

Batting	B-T	HT	WT	DOB	AVG	vLH	vRH	G	AB	R	H	2B	3B	HR	RBI	BB	HBP	SH	SF	SO	SB	CS	SLG	OBP
Souffront, Jefrey	R-R	6-1	190	5-23-97	.265	.197	.288	60	238	28	63	10	3	3	21	19	1	2	0	60	6	7	.370	.322
Tirado, Lucas	L-R	6-2	180	11-13-96	.096	.375	.045	14	52	3	5	0	1	0	2	5	1	0	0	31	1	2	.135	.190

Pitching	B-T	HT	WT	DOB	W	L	ERA	G	GS	CG	SV	IP	H	R	ER	HR	BB	SO	AVG	vLH	vRH	K/9	BB/9
Ascanio, Raul	R-R	6-3	185	11-18-96	1	1	5.67	16	2	0	1	27	33	21	17	0	18	23	.300	.325	.286	7.67	6.00
Bautista, Angel	R-R	6-3	190	4-25-95	0	3	4.78	24	0	0	3	38	45	30	20	2	13	26	.281	.255	.294	6.21	3.11
Crawford, Leonardo	L-L	6-0	180	2-2-97	5	4	1.41	15	14	0	0	64	55	16	10	0	10	74	.228	.238	.226	10.46	1.41
Diaz, Johan	R-R	6-2	195	11-1-92	1	3	1.38	20	6	0	6	52	37	25	8	1	16	57	.192	.177	.198	9.87	2.77
Flames, Celis	R-R	6-1	175	9-5-97	3	2	2.61	12	3	0	0	41	34	18	12	1	17	30	.224	.205	.231	6.53	3.70
Forbes, Melvyn	R-R	6-3	185	12-2-93	1	4	7.43	18	0	0	0	23	32	27	19	0	16	14	.330	.310	.338	5.48	6.26
Gooding, Max	L-L	5-11	165	3-7-96	3	1	3.44	20	0	0	2	37	33	16	14	2	13	35	.243	.043	.283	8.59	3.19
Lacen, Felix	R-R	6-3	190	4-1-98	0	5	3.61	16	8	0	1	62	54	37	25	1	16	36	.227	.250	.215	5.20	2.31
Martinez, Sebastian	R-R	6-2	175	1-30-96	1	0	5.59	8	0	0	0	10	13	7	6	1	8	5	.342	.429	.292	4.66	7.45
Pena, Adalberto	R-R	6-2	173	3-11-95	3	5	4.26	14	11	0	0	63	62	40	30	2	13	45	.252	.250	.253	6.39	1.85
Peralta, Rawel	R-R	6-4	190	6-3-97	1	3	7.34	14	5	0	1	34	43	35	28	0	26	15	.312	.261	.337	3.93	6.82
Perez, Edward	R-R	6-2	174	11-25-95	1	4	6.23	22	1	0	2	35	39	26	24	0	21	32	.293	.282	.298	8.31	5.45
Santos, Jose	R-R	6-0	165	3-8-92	2	2	3.09	5	4	0	0	23	20	9	8	1	7	19	.235	.450	.169	7.33	2.70
Sequera, Gregorio	R-R	6-1	165	12-9-97	2	2	2.97	12	7	0	0	36	35	15	12	0	10	35	.252	.267	.245	8.67	2.48
Soto, Algenis	R-R	6-4	185	5-24-96	0	3	3.35	13	7	0	0	40	43	26	15	0	8	26	.276	.255	.284	5.80	1.79
Suero, Angel	R-R	6-7	220	10-8-96	0	0	0.00	3	0	0	0	5	1	0	0	0	5	3	.063	.200	.000	5.40	9.00
Vargas, Jesus	R-R	6-2	175	8-18-98	0	1	4.70	5	4	0	0	8	5	4	4	1	5	7	.185	.250	.133	8.22	5.87
Vrolijk, Wally	R-R	6-4	225	11-19-94	1	2	6.04	18	0	0	0	22	27	18	15	1	10	25	.290	.343	.259	10.07	4.03

Fielding

Catcher	PCT	G	PO	A	E	DP	PB
Paz	1.000	13	64	7	0	2	4
Rubi	.972	26	156	18	5	0	7
Ruiz	.977	43	293	49	8	1	7

First Base	PCT	G	PO	A	E	DP
Estrella	.933	2	12	2	1	2
Paz	.988	48	382	21	5	29
Peguero	.979	22	168	15	4	10
Perez	.941	13	101	10	7	9
Souffront	1.000	1	3	0	0	0

Second Base	PCT	G	PO	A	E	DP
Asencio	.902	12	15	22	4	3

	PCT	G	PO	A	E	DP
Dometilia	.967	24	34	54	3	13
Santana	.954	17	31	52	4	7
Souffront	.977	19	34	52	2	7
Tirado	.920	12	28	41	6	6

Third Base	PCT	G	PO	A	E	DP
Estrella	.946	13	11	24	2	2
Perez	.929	42	37	93	10	7
Reyes	.773	10	5	12	5	0
Santana	.818	15	4	32	8	3
Souffront	1.000	2	0	2	0	0

Shortstop	PCT	G	PO	A	E	DP
Asencio	.872	16	16	25	6	5

	PCT	G	PO	A	E	DP
Santana	.881	23	24	50	10	7
Souffront	.903	41	56	111	18	21

Outfield	PCT	G	PO	A	E	DP
Calderon	.889	38	60	4	8	1
Cuadrado	.973	54	103	6	3	4
Dometilia	.000	1	0	0	1	0
Mosquera	.905	38	52	5	6	1
Osorio	.929	38	62	3	5	1
Padilla	.971	41	63	3	2	1
Sanchez	.948	25	50	5	3	1

Miami Marlins

SEASON IN A SENTENCE: A season of promise that was prompted by the $325 million signing of Giancarlo Stanton crumpled quickly with a poor start (16-22) that cost Mike Redmond his job.

HIGH POINT: There were not many, but the return of one of baseball's real aces was a point of exhilaration for not just the Marlins but all of the majors. Jose Fernandez returned from Tommy John surgery in July, and though he missed another five weeks because of a strained biceps, he showed dominant stuff, a beacon of hope for the franchise.

LOW POINT: Mike Redmond, the subject of praise in 2014 for guiding the Fish to 77 wins, was canned just 38 games into the season, with general manager Dan Jennings—who had no professional managerial experience—taking over the team. Giancarlo Stanton's broken hand in June ruined what could have been a 50-homer season.

NOTABLE ROOKIES: The Marlins summoned catcher J.T. Realmuto from Triple-A New Orleans on April 13 when they lost backup Jeff Mathis to a fractured hand, and Realmuto quickly was inserted as the starter, to the point that big-money free agent signing Jarrod Saltalamacchia was designated for assignment and eventually released. The Marlins are enthused with how Realmuto handles pitches and receives the ball and his power (.407 SLG) has been an unexpected bonus. Lefthander Justin Nicolino, a pitchability-over-stuff starter, doesn't strike out many, but had some success and is young and cheap. Righthander Jose Urena showed flashes and projects as a future closer.

KEY TRANSACTIONS: The Marlins' most important acquisition came in the offseason with a three-team deal that cost Miami its top prospect in lefthander Andrew Heaney but netted Dee Gordon, who only went on to compile a 200-hit, 56-steal season.

DOWN ON THE FARM: To say the system is threadbare is polite and the Marlins will toward the bottom in organizational talent. The positives are massive righthander Tyler Kolek, who had a poor season but retains a big fastball, and outfielder Stone Garrett, a 2014 eighth-round pick who had a breakout season and will be among the organization's top prospects. Brett Lilek and Justin Jacome, two college lefthanders drafted in 2015, immediately became two of the team's better prospects with chances to move quickly in a barren organization, and outfielder Isaiah White has tremendous upside.

OPENING DAY PAYROLL: $68,479,000 (30th)

PLAYERS OF THE YEAR

MAJOR LEAGUE	MINOR LEAGUE
Giancarlo Stanton	**Stone Garrett**
rf	cf
.265/.346/.606	(short-season)
27 HR led team in	.297/.352/.581
just 74 games	11 homers

ORGANIZATION LEADERS

BATTING   *Minimum 250 AB

MAJORS

*AVG	Dee Gordon	.333
*OPS	Christian Yelich	.782
HR	Giancarlo Stanton	27
RBI	Justin Bour	73

MINORS

*AVG	Zack Cox, Jacksonville, New Orleans	.304
*OBP	David Adams, Jacksonville	.399
*SLG	K.J. Woods, Greensboro	.496
R	Kenny Wilson, Jacksonville	77
H	Austin Dean, Jupiter	139
TB	Arturo Rodriguez, Greensboro	206
2B	Austin Dean, Jupiter	32
3B	Isaac Galloway, Jacksonville, New Orleans	8
	Ryan Rieger, Jacksonville	8
HR	Arturo Rodriguez, Greensboro	19
RBI	Arturo Rodriguez, Greensboro	69
BB	Viosergy Rosa, Jacksonville	77
SO	K.J. Woods, Greensboro	133
SB	Yefri Perez, Jupiter	71

PITCHING   #Minimum 75 IP

MAJORS

W	Tom Koehler	11
#ERA	Tom Koehler	4.08
SO	Tom Koehler	137
SV	A.J. Ramos	32

MINORS

W	Scott Squier, Greensboro, Batavia	11
L	Michael Mader, Greensboro	12
	Matt Tomshaw, New Orleans, Jacksonville	12
#ERA	Kendry Flores, J-ville, New Orleans, Jupiter	2.29
G	Ramon Benjamin, Rancho Cucamonga, Tulsa	51
GS	Michael Mader, Greensboro	27
SV	Nick Wittgren, Jacksonville, New Orleans	20
IP	Scott Lyman, Jupiter, Jacksonville	146
BB	Austin Brice, Jacksonville	69
SO	Austin Brice, Jacksonville	127
AVG	Kendry Flores, J-ville, New Orleans, Jupiter	.198

2015 PERFORMANCE

General Manager: Dan Jennings/Michael Hill. **Farm Director:** Marc DelPiano. **Scouting Director:** Stan Meek.

Class	Team	League	W	L	PCT	Finish	Manager
Majors	Miami Marlins	National	71	91	.438	10th (15)	M. Redmond/D. Jennings
Triple-A	New Orleans Zephyrs	Pacific Coast	58	86	.403	t-15th (16)	Andy Haines
Double-A	Jacksonville Suns	Southern	57	81	.413	9th (10)	Dave Berg
High A	Jupiter Hammerheads	Florida State	67	73	.479	8th (12)	Brian Schneider
Low A	Greensboro Grasshoppers	South Atlantic	51	88	.367	14th (14)	Kevin Randel
Short season	Batavia Muckdogs	New York-Penn	31	44	.413	t-13th (14)	Angel Espada
Rookie	Marlins	Gulf Coast	33	27	.550	7th (16)	Julio Bruno
Overall 2015 Minor League Record			297	399	.427	30th (30)	

ORGANIZATION STATISTICS

MIAMI MARLINS

NATIONAL LEAGUE

Batting	B-T	HT	WT	DOB	AVG	vLH	vRH	G	AB	R	H	2B	3B	HR	RBI	BB	HBP	SH	SF	SO	SB	CS	SLG	OBP
Baker, Jeff	R-R	6-2	220	6-21-81	.208	.208	.211	41	72	11	15	3	0	3	8	8	0	0	0	25	0	0	.375	.288
Bour, Justin	L-R	6-4	250	5-28-88	.262	.221	.270	129	409	42	107	20	0	23	73	34	2	0	1	101	0	0	.479	.321
Brignac, Reid	L-R	6-3	215	1-16-86	.077	—	.077	17	13	2	1	0	0	0	0	3	0	1	0	5	0	0	.077	.250
Dietrich, Derek	L-R	6-0	210	7-18-89	.256	.178	.273	90	250	38	64	14	3	10	24	23	13	0	3	65	0	2	.456	.346
Gillespie, Cole	R-R	6-2	205	6-20-84	.290	.368	.262	67	145	17	42	10	2	2	16	10	0	1	1	27	4	1	.428	.333
Gordon, Dee	L-R	5-11	170	4-22-88	.333	.350	.327	145	615	88	205	24	8	4	46	25	2	6	5	91	58	20	.418	.359
Hechavarria, Adeiny	R-R	6-2	215	4-15-89	.281	.352	.264	130	470	54	132	17	6	5	48	23	2	0	4	78	7	2	.374	.315
Kelly, Don	L-R	6-4	190	2-15-80	.000	—	.000	2	1	0	0	0	0	0	0	0	0	0	0	0	0	0	.000	.000
Mathis, Jeff	R-R	6-0	205	3-31-83	.161	.231	.150	32	93	9	15	4	1	2	12	7	0	0	3	24	0	0	.290	.214
McGehee, Casey	R-R	6-1	220	10-12-82	.182	.273	.159	60	110	7	20	7	0	0	9	10	0	0	0	22	1	0	.245	.250
2-team total (49 San Francisco)					.198	—	—	109	237	14	47	12	0	2	20	21	0	0	0	50	1	1	.274	.264
Morse, Mike	R-R	6-5	245	3-22-82	.213	.091	.232	53	160	8	34	4	0	4	12	12	2	0	0	50	0	0	.313	.276
2-team total (45 Pittsburgh)					.231	—	—	98	229	14	53	7	1	5	19	23	4	0	0	76	0	0	.336	.313
Ozuna, Marcell	R-R	6-1	225	11-12-90	.259	.341	.241	123	459	47	119	27	0	10	44	30	3	0	2	110	2	3	.383	.308
Prado, Martin	R-R	6-1	190	10-27-83	.288	.325	.277	129	500	52	144	22	2	9	63	37	5	1	8	68	1	0	.394	.338
Realmuto, J.T.	R-R	6-1	205	3-18-91	.259	.281	.253	126	441	49	114	21	7	10	47	19	2	1	4	70	8	4	.406	.290
Rojas, Miguel	R-R	6-0	150	2-24-89	.282	.125	.314	60	142	13	40	7	1	1	17	11	0	2	2	16	0	1	.366	.329
Saltalamacchia, Jarrod	B-R	6-4	235	5-2-85	.069	.000	.080	9	29	3	2	1	0	1	1	4	0	0	0	12	0	0	.207	.182
2-team total (70 Arizona)					.225	—	—	79	200	26	45	15	0	9	24	23	2	1	1	69	0	1	.435	.310
Solano, Donovan	R-R	5-9	205	12-17-87	.189	.077	.234	55	90	6	17	3	1	0	7	1	2	1	0	18	0	0	.244	.215
Solano, Jhonatan	R-R	5-9	212	8-12-85	.050	.000	.056	7	20	1	1	0	0	0	1	1	0	0	0	1	0	0	.100	.095
Stanton, Giancarlo	R-R	6-6	240	11-8-89	.265	.288	.259	74	279	47	74	12	1	27	67	34	2	0	3	95	4	2	.606	.346
Suzuki, Ichiro	L-R	5-11	170	10-22-73	.229	.278	.214	153	398	45	91	5	6	1	21	31	0	5	4	51	11	5	.279	.282
Telis, Tomas	B-R	5-8	215	6-18-91	.148	.000	.160	17	27	1	4	0	0	0	0	1	1	0	0	3	0	0	.148	.207
Valdespin, Jordany	L-R	6-0	190	12-23-87	.000	—	.000	2	4	0	0	0	0	0	0	0	0	0	0	1	0	0	.000	.000
Yelich, Christian	L-R	6-2	195	12-5-91	.300	.288	.305	126	476	63	143	30	2	7	44	47	2	0	0	101	16	5	.416	.366

Pitching	B-T	HT	WT	DOB	W	L	ERA	G	GS	CG	SV	IP	H	R	ER	HR	BB	SO	AVG	vLH	vRH	K/9	BB/9
Alvarez, Henderson	R-R	6-0	205	4-18-90	0	4	6.45	4	4	0	0	22	28	18	16	1	7	9	.311	.360	.250	3.63	2.82
Barraclough, Kyle	R-R	6-3	225	5-23-90	2	1	2.59	25	0	0	0	24	12	8	7	1	18	30	.154	.161	.149	11.10	6.66
Capps, Carter	R-R	6-5	220	8-7-90	1	0	1.16	30	0	0	0	31	18	5	4	2	7	58	.168	.160	.175	16.84	2.03
Cishek, Steve	R-R	6-6	215	6-18-86	2	6	4.50	32	0	0	3	32	37	19	16	2	14	28	.291	.271	.309	7.88	3.94
2-team total (27 St. Louis)					2	6	3.58	59	0	0	4	55	55	26	22	4	27	48	—	—	—	7.81	4.39
Conley, Adam	L-L	6-3	185	5-24-90	4	1	3.76	15	11	0	0	67	65	28	28	7	21	59	.258	.286	.253	7.93	2.82
Cordier, Erik	R-R	6-4	215	2-25-86	0	0	5.84	8	0	0	0	12	13	8	8	1	6	7	.271	.353	.226	5.11	4.38
Cosart, Jarred	R-R	6-3	195	5-25-90	2	5	4.52	14	13	0	0	70	63	35	35	10	33	47	.243	.228	.257	6.07	4.26
Dunn, Mike	L-L	6-0	210	5-23-85	2	5	4.50	72	0	0	0	54	46	27	27	6	29	65	.227	.227	.226	10.83	4.83
Dyson, Sam	R-R	6-1	210	5-7-88	3	3	3.68	44	0	0	0	44	41	21	18	3	17	41	.247	.233	.258	8.39	3.48
Ellington, Brian	R-R	6-4	195	8-4-90	2	1	2.88	23	0	0	0	25	17	10	8	1	13	18	.193	.222	.180	6.48	4.68
Fernandez, Jose	R-R	6-2	215	7-31-92	6	1	2.92	11	11	0	0	65	61	21	21	4	14	79	.249	.333	.176	10.99	1.95
Flores, Kendry	R-R	6-2	175	11-24-91	1	2	4.97	7	1	0	0	13	16	8	7	0	4	9	.314	.333	.286	6.39	2.84
Hand, Brad	L-L	6-3	215	3-20-90	4	7	5.30	38	12	0	0	93	107	55	55	9	32	67	.292	.206	.326	6.46	3.09
Haren, Dan	R-R	6-5	215	9-17-80	7	7	3.42	21	21	0	0	129	116	50	49	21	25	88	.241	.276	.209	6.14	1.74
2-team total (11 Chicago)					11	9	3.60	32	32	0	0	187	174	79	75	31	38	132	—	—	—	6.34	1.83
Koehler, Tom	R-R	6-3	240	6-29-86	11	14	4.08	32	31	0	0	187	180	96	85	22	77	137	.255	.258	.252	6.58	3.70
Latos, Mat	R-R	6-6	245	12-9-87	4	7	4.48	16	16	0	0	88	85	46	44	8	25	79	.251	.278	.227	8.05	2.55
2-team total (6 Los Angeles)					4	10	4.95	22	21	0	0	113	116	65	62	11	31	97	—	—	—	7.75	2.48
Lazo, Raudel	L-L	5-9	165	4-12-89	0	0	3.18	7	0	0	0	6	5	2	2	1	2	5	.238	.429	.143	7.94	3.18
Masset, Nick	R-R	6-5	235	5-17-82	0	0	1.86	8	0	0	0	10	12	3	2	0	1	6	.324	.190	.500	5.59	0.93
2-team total (20 Atlanta)					2	2	4.68	28	0	0	0	25	30	15	13	3	9	18	—	—	—	6.48	3.24
Mazzaro, Vin	R-R	6-2	220	9-27-86	0	0	3.75	10	0	0	0	12	15	6	5	0	6	6	.319	.313	.323	4.50	4.50
McGough, Scott	R-R	6-0	170	10-31-89	0	0	9.45	6	0	0	0	7	7	7	7	0	4	4	.387	.667	.273	5.40	5.40
Morris, Bryan	R-R	6-3	225	3-28-87	5	4	3.14	67	0	0	0	63	67	26	22	3	26	47	.275	.297	.259	6.71	3.71
Narveson, Chris	L-L	6-3	205	12-20-81	3	1	4.45	15	2	0	0	30	24	15	15	7	9	32	.214	.081	.280	9.49	2.67
Nicolino, Justin	L-L	6-3	190	11-22-91	5	4	4.01	12	12	0	0	74	72	33	33	8	20	23	.267	.283	.262	2.80	2.43

MIAMI MARLINS

Pitching	B-T	HT	WT	DOB	W	L	ERA	G	GS	CG	SV	IP	H	R	ER	HR	BB	SO	AVG	vLH	vRH	K/9	BB/9
Phelps, David	R-R	6-2	200	10-9-86	4	8	4.50	23	19	0	0	112	119	59	56	11	33	77	.272	.277	.267	6.19	2.65
Ramos, A.J.	R-R	5-10	205	9-20-86	2	4	2.30	71	0	0	32	70	45	18	18	6	26	87	.184	.202	.169	11.13	3.33
Reed, Chris	L-L	6-3	225	5-20-90	0	0	4.50	2	0	0	0	4	6	2	2	0	1	1	.375	.571	.222	2.25	2.25
Rienzo, Andre	R-R	6-3	190	7-5-88	0	1	5.95	14	0	0	0	20	17	14	13	2	13	15	.230	.217	.235	6.86	5.95
Urena, Jose	R-R	6-3	175	9-12-91	1	5	5.25	20	9	0	0	62	73	37	36	5	25	28	.307	.288	.321	4.09	3.65

Fielding

Catcher	PCT	G	PO	A	E	DP	PB
Mathis	.996	30	210	13	1	1	0
Realmuto	.993	118	836	46	6	6	11
Saltalamacchia	.968	9	54	6	2	1	0
Solano	1.000	6	39	2	0	1	0
Telis	1.000	7	28	1	0	0	0

First Base	PCT	G	PO	A	E	DP
Baker	.983	17	115	2	2	7
Bour	.993	111	836	47	6	106
Dietrich	1.000	2	1	1	0	0
Kelly	—	1	0	0	0	0
McGehee	.991	20	104	5	1	12
Morse	1.000	36	316	14	0	29

Second Base	PCT	G	PO	A	E	DP
Baker	1.000	1	1	2	0	0

Dietrich	1.000	2	2	0	0	0
Gordon	.992	145	293	434	6	111
Prado	1.000	11	13	20	0	4
Rojas	1.000	9	9	7	0	1
Solano	.917	7	8	14	2	1

Third Base	PCT	G	PO	A	E	DP
Baker	—	1	0	0	0	0
Brignac	1.000	2	1	0	0	0
Dietrich	.911	26	6	35	4	4
Kelly	1.000	1	0	2	0	0
McGehee	.917	10	4	7	1	0
Prado	.976	124	72	218	7	28
Rojas	.944	9	3	14	1	0
Solano	1.000	10	1	15	0	0

Shortstop	PCT	G	PO	A	E	DP
Hechavarria	.984	130	173	373	9	93
Rojas	.991	32	33	75	1	19
Solano	.957	10	4	18	1	4

Outfield	PCT	G	PO	A	E	DP
Baker	—	1	0	0	0	0
Dietrich	.974	46	76	0	2	0
Gillespie	.952	52	80	0	4	0
Morse	1.000	6	6	1	0	0
Ozuna	.996	122	273	5	1	0
Stanton	.981	71	149	6	3	3
Suzuki	1.000	109	217	5	0	0
Valdespin	1.000	1	1	0	0	0
Yelich	.992	124	256	6	2	1

NEW ORLEANS ZEPHYRS   TRIPLE-A
PACIFIC COAST LEAGUE

Batting	B-T	HT	WT	DOB	AVG	vLH	vRH	G	AB	R	H	2B	3B	HR	RBI	BB	HBP	SH	SF	SO	SB	CS	SLG	OBP
Bantz, Brandon	R-R	6-1	205	1-7-87	.258	.259	.258	63	178	18	46	10	0	4	25	17	0	2	1	34	0	0	.382	.321
Barber, Blake	R-R	5-10	180	4-4-90	.000	.000	.000	2	2	0	0	0	0	0	0	0	0	0	0	1	0	0	.000	.000
Black, Danny	L-R	6-3	185	8-19-88	.095	.100	.091	13	21	4	2	0	1	0	6	0	1	0	9	1	0	.190	.296
Bour, Justin	L-R	6-4	250	5-28-88	.275	.357	.243	14	51	8	14	1	0	1	5	11	0	0	6	1	0	.353	.403
Brignac, Reid	L-R	6-3	215	1-16-86	.268	.250	.274	93	347	38	93	20	1	5	37	42	2	4	3	62	3	1	.375	.348
Cox, Zack	L-R	5-11	225	5-9-89	.200	.125	.231	16	55	8	11	5	0	1	4	1	0	0	0	17	0	0	.345	.214
Diaz, Juan	B-R	6-4	220	12-12-88	.272	.211	.292	110	367	35	100	18	2	5	35	22	2	2	3	77	0	2	.373	.315
Dietrich, Derek	L-R	6-0	210	7-18-89	.260	.258	.262	56	192	25	50	13	2	7	27	15	15	0	2	45	0	2	.458	.357
Flores, Jesus	R-R	6-1	210	10-26-84	.216	.286	.200	27	74	3	16	7	0	0	5	8	2	1	2	18	0	0	.311	.302
Galloway, Isaac	R-R	6-2	190	10-10-89	.249	.289	.233	123	441	45	110	13	7	7	42	18	1	6	4	105	14	9	.358	.278
Gillespie, Cole	R-R	6-2	205	6-20-84	.291	.243	.312	67	247	30	72	15	1	0	23	27	1	0	6	31	7	2	.360	.356
Ka'aihue, Kila	L-R	6-4	240	3-29-84	.197	.222	.188	66	183	17	36	9	0	3	21	34	2	0	0	33	0	0	.295	.329
Mathis, Jeff	R-R	6-0	205	3-31-83	.000	.000	.000	4	10	0	0	0	0	0	0	0	0	0	0	2	0	0	.000	.000
Morse, Mike	R-R	6-5	245	3-22-82	.235	.000	.267	5	17	2	4	0	0	0	1	0	1	0	1	9	0	0	.235	.263
Nola, Austin	R-R	6-0	190	12-28-89	.280	.217	.306	61	207	18	58	11	1	0	18	22	3	4	2	40	0	1	.343	.355
Ozuna, Marcell	R-R	6-1	225	11-12-90	.317	.333	.312	33	120	21	38	12	1	5	11	11	1	0	0	23	1	0	.558	.379
Realmuto, J.T.	R-R	6-1	205	3-18-91	.385	1.000	.333	3	13	3	5	0	0	0	0	0	0	0	0	1	1	0	.385	.385
Riddle, J.T.	L-R	6-3	175	10-12-91	.667	1.000	.500	1	3	2	2	0	0	0	0	2	0	0	0	0	0	0	.667	.800
Rojas, Miguel	R-R	6-0	150	2-24-89	.301	.298	.303	65	249	32	75	15	4	3	23	13	4	7	2	26	2	5	.430	.343
Rottino, Vinny	R-R	6-1	215	4-7-80	.266	.314	.245	127	451	55	120	24	1	10	51	54	4	0	5	97	2	0	.390	.346
Shoemaker, Brady	R-R	6-0	200	5-10-87	.284	.302	.276	94	324	32	92	14	1	9	50	36	3	0	2	68	4	0	.417	.359
Sizemore, Scott	R-R	6-0	185	1-4-85	.223	.289	.179	63	193	23	43	9	0	2	18	34	3	2	3	36	2	0	.301	.343
Solano, Donovan	R-R	5-9	205	12-17-87	.271	.244	.283	36	140	10	38	3	0	0	4	0	1	2	0	24	0	1	.293	.288
Solano, Jhonatan	R-R	5-9	212	8-12-85	.228	.212	.234	55	193	13	44	7	0	3	22	10	2	1	2	27	0	0	.311	.271
Telis, Tomas	B-R	5-8	215	6-18-91	.333	.235	.387	13	48	3	16	0	0	0	4	5	0	1	1	6	2	0	.333	.389
2-team total (70 Round Rock)					.297	—	—	83	330	46	98	15	1	5	29	19	1	4	1	37	3	2	.394	.336
Valdespin, Jordany	L-R	6-0	190	12-23-87	.293	.331	.320	76	256	34	75	12	3	2	20	18	5	4	3	31	7	3	.387	.348
Wates, Austin	R-R	6-1	209	9-2-88	.236	.222	.242	109	305	36	72	18	0	1	28	21	4	4	2	57	4	3	.305	.292

Pitching	B-T	HT	WT	DOB	W	L	ERA	G	GS	CG	SV	IP	H	R	ER	HR	BB	SO	AVG	vLH	vRH	K/9	BB/9
Batista, Lay	R-R	6-2	200	8-4-89	0	2	5.40	18	0	0	2	25	22	18	15	3	18	23	.232	.293	.185	8.28	6.48
Blackley, Travis	L-L	6-3	205	11-4-82	5	7	5.46	23	12	0	0	87	103	54	53	14	24	66	.299	.269	.311	6.80	2.47
Bremer, Tyler	R-R	6-2	210	12-7-89	0	0	5.00	5	0	0	0	9	8	5	5	5	8	.242	.412	.063	8.00	5.00
Capps, Carter	R-R	6-5	220	8-7-90	0	2	1.80	13	0	0	3	15	10	5	3	0	10	15	.196	.077	.320	9.00	6.00
Chaffee, Ryan	R-R	6-2	195	5-18-88	1	0	2.45	6	0	0	0	7	8	2	2	1	7	5	.308	.000	.320	6.14	8.59
Conley, Adam	L-L	6-3	185	5-24-90	9	3	2.52	19	18	1	0	107	85	34	30	4	40	81	.219	.294	.198	6.81	3.36
Cordier, Erik	R-R	6-4	215	2-25-86	0	0	3.38	4	0	0	0	5	7	3	2	0	1	7	.318	.364	.273	11.81	1.69
2-team total (31 Sacramento)					2	1	1.35	35	0	0	9	40	27	12	6	0	26	50	—	—	—	11.25	5.85
Cosart, Jarred	R-R	6-3	195	5-25-90	0	1	6.06	4	4	0	0	16	21	11	11	2	11	8	.309	.235	.333	6.06	4.41
Dayton, Grant	L-L	6-2	195	11-25-87	2	1	2.83	25	0	0	0	35	25	11	11	1	5	35	.207	.182	.216	9.00	1.29
2-team total (9 Oklahoma City)					3	2	4.44	34	0	0	0	47	41	23	23	2	8	48	—	—	—	9.26	1.54
De Leon, Jorge	R-R	6-0	185	8-15-87	0	1	4.76	3	0	0	0	6	5	3	3	0	3	4	.250	.111	.364	6.35	4.76
2-team total (5 Oklahoma City)					0	2	8.03	8	1	0	0	12	18	11	11	4	9	9	—	—	—	6.57	6.57
Ege, Cody	L-L	6-1	185	5-8-91	0	0	0.75	8	0	0	0	12	6	2	1	1	2	13	.146	.000	.214	9.75	1.50
Ellington, Brian	R-R	6-4	195	8-4-90	0	0	0.00	1	0	0	0	1	1	0	0	0	0	1	.000	.000	.000	6.75	0.00
Esch, Jacob	R-R	6-4	190	3-27-90	1	3	5.40	6	6	0	0	30	34	20	18	3	9	20	.331	.311	.349	6.00	2.70
Flores, Kendry	R-R	6-2	175	11-24-91	3	2	2.61	10	10	0	0	59	49	19	17	3	14	42	.224	.277	.168	6.44	2.15

Pitching

Pitching	B-T	HT	WT	DOB	W	L	ERA	G	GS	CG	SV	IP	H	R	ER	HR	BB	SO	AVG	vLH	vRH	K/9	BB/9
Jose, Jose	L-L	6-2	175	7-21-90	0	0	0.00	1	0	0	0	1	0	0	0	0	0	0	.000	.000	.000	0.00	0.00
Latos, Mat	R-R	6-6	245	12-9-87	0	0	1.93	1	1	0	0	5	3	1	1	0	5	4	.176	.273	.000	7.71	9.64
Link, Jon	R-R	6-0	205	3-23-84	0	0	4.50	6	0	0	0	8	11	4	4	0	4	4	.333	.429	.308	4.50	4.50
Logan, Blake	R-R	6-1	245	1-12-92	1	4	4.76	8	5	0	0	34	34	20	18	4	12	27	.266	.262	.270	7.15	3.18
Masset, Nick	R-R	6-5	235	5-17-82	0	0	1.50	5	0	0	2	6	3	1	1	0	0	3	.150	.167	.143	4.50	0.00
Mazzaro, Vin	R-R	6-2	220	9-27-86	3	1	3.15	11	1	0	1	20	22	7	7	0	4	22	.278	.270	.286	9.90	1.80
McGough, Scott	R-R	6-0	170	10-31-89	0	1	2.12	13	0	0	1	17	9	5	4	1	9	12	.153	.161	.143	6.35	4.76
Misch, Pat	R-L	6-2	195	8-18-81	5	7	3.25	16	11	1	0	72	65	33	26	4	23	40	.246	.268	.238	5.00	2.88
Morey, Robert	R-R	6-1	185	11-27-88	2	7	4.55	22	14	0	1	87	100	46	44	7	32	53	.297	.315	.282	5.48	3.31
Nappo, Greg	L-L	5-10	195	8-25-88	2	3	2.66	33	0	0	0	47	37	14	14	4	12	43	.218	.220	.216	8.18	2.28
Narveson, Chris	L-L	6-3	205	12-20-81	0	3	5.19	10	4	0	0	26	38	16	15	4	10	29	.342	.417	.307	10.04	3.46
Nicolino, Justin	L-L	6-3	190	11-22-91	7	7	3.52	20	20	0	0	115	134	51	45	11	29	63	.300	.294	.302	4.93	2.27
Nygren, James	R-R	6-0	195	3-8-89	1	2	5.18	17	0	0	1	24	26	17	14	2	7	12	.268	.325	.228	4.44	2.59
Pineyro, Ivan	R-R	6-1	200	9-29-91	2	2	2.70	6	6	0	0	37	31	11	11	2	8	26	.237	.279	.200	6.38	1.96
Reed, Chris	L-L	6-3	225	5-20-90	1	0	3.92	14	0	0	0	21	18	9	9	3	13	23	.237	.306	.175	10.02	5.66
2-team total (8 Oklahoma City)					1	0	3.69	22	0	0	0	32	29	13	13	3	17	28	—	—	—	7.96	4.83
Rienzo, Andre	R-R	6-3	190	7-5-88	2	6	3.01	15	14	0	0	78	66	36	26	5	32	56	.232	.250	.217	6.49	3.71
Sanchez, Salvador	R-R	6-6	195	9-13-85	1	2	3.38	13	0	0	0	16	20	11	6	0	7	15	.303	.286	.311	8.44	3.94
Stem, Craig	R-R	6-5	215	1-5-90	0	2	13.80	7	2	0	0	15	31	24	23	4	7	8	.431	.500	.344	4.80	4.20
Tomshaw, Matt	L-L	6-2	200	12-17-88	0	2	17.18	2	2	0	0	7	19	15	14	2	2	9	.475	.500	.462	11.05	2.45
Urckfitz, Pat	L-L	6-4	196	7-21-88	1	5	4.39	37	0	0	0	53	60	30	26	6	23	41	.278	.300	.265	6.92	3.88
Urena, Jose	R-R	6-3	175	9-12-91	6	1	2.66	11	11	1	0	68	65	23	20	4	19	41	.259	.239	.283	5.45	2.53
Williams, Trevor	R-R	6-3	230	4-25-92	0	2	2.57	3	3	0	0	14	15	5	4	0	7	13	.268	.257	.286	8.36	4.50
Williamson, Fabian	R-L	6-2	175	10-20-88	2	1	5.64	18	0	0	0	22	24	16	14	4	14	12	.279	.267	.286	4.84	5.64
Wittgren, Nick	R-R	6-3	210	5-29-91	1	6	3.03	51	0	0	19	62	58	22	21	6	8	64	.245	.183	.293	9.24	1.16

Fielding

Catcher	PCT	G	PO	A	E	DP	PB
Bantz	.985	47	302	27	5	2	1
Flores	1.000	18	91	6	0	1	1
Mathis	1.000	4	21	1	0	0	0
Realmuto	1.000	3	19	3	0	0	1
Rottino	.991	16	107	8	1	1	0
Solano	.992	51	358	29	3	4	5
Telis	.989	12	81	6	1	0	0

First Base	PCT	G	PO	A	E	DP
Bantz	1.000	3	17	0	0	2
Bour	1.000	13	104	6	0	14
Brignac	1.000	5	17	3	0	2
Dietrich	.985	8	63	4	1	9
Ka'aihue	.989	42	345	16	4	30
Morse	.967	4	27	2	1	4
Rottino	.991	53	397	24	4	47
Shoemaker	.996	30	227	14	1	29
Solano	1.000	5	29	4	0	4

Second Base	PCT	G	PO	A	E	DP
Black	1.000	3	6	7	0	2
Brignac	.988	55	96	160	3	36
Diaz	.974	12	18	20	1	8
Dietrich	.994	35	80	88	1	32
Nola	1.000	7	15	16	0	3
Sizemore	1.000	12	25	39	0	14
Solano	1.000	9	17	18	0	4
Valdespin	.987	18	33	41	1	8

Third Base	PCT	G	PO	A	E	DP
Black	1.000	1	1	0	0	0
Cox	.968	13	8	22	1	2
Diaz	.926	77	29	133	13	14
Dietrich	1.000	7	4	15	0	1
Nola	1.000	1	0	1	0	1
Rojas	1.000	1	0	3	0	1
Rottino	.900	4	4	5	1	0
Sizemore	.926	48	23	89	9	8
Solano	1.000	7	5	5	0	3
Valdespin	1.000	2	1	1	0	0

Shortstop	PCT	G	PO	A	E	DP
Black	1.000	3	6	7	0	1
Brignac	1.000	9	8	21	0	4
Diaz	.947	9	13	23	2	7
Nola	.983	51	87	146	4	40
Riddle	1.000	1	1	7	0	1
Rojas	.980	63	98	196	6	47
Solano	.966	16	14	43	2	10

Outfield	PCT	G	PO	A	E	DP
Black	1.000	2	1	0	0	0
Brignac	1.000	22	43	1	0	0
Dietrich	1.000	1	2	1	0	0
Galloway	.982	116	310	10	6	3
Gillespie	.976	59	118	2	3	0
Ozuna	.972	29	67	2	2	1
Rottino	.991	52	105	4	1	2
Shoemaker	1.000	48	73	1	0	0
O Valdespin	.948	45	70	3	4	1
Wates	.989	90	167	5	2	0

JACKSONVILLE SUNS
DOUBLE-A

SOUTHERN LEAGUE

Batting	B-T	HT	WT	DOB	AVG	vLH	vRH	G	AB	R	H	2B	3B	HR	RBI	BB	HBP	SH	SF	SO	SB	CS	SLG	OBP
Adams, David	R-R	6-1	205	5-15-87	.294	.323	.288	116	371	45	109	12	3	6	50	63	4	2	3	53	3	2	.391	.399
Bantz, Brandon	R-R	6-1	205	1-7-87	.071	.000	.125	5	14	0	1	0	0	0	0	4	0	0	0	5	0	0	.071	.278
Black, Danny	L-R	6-3	185	8-19-88	.247	.400	.236	28	77	13	19	4	1	0	13	11	0	4	0	19	1	0	.325	.341
Bohn, Justin	R-R	6-0	180	11-2-92	.161	.250	.147	28	87	5	14	0	1	1	6	6	1	0	0	30	0	0	.218	.223
Cox, Zack	L-R	5-11	225	5-9-89	.321	.261	.337	103	327	47	105	19	1	4	27	38	2	0	2	80	0	1	.422	.393
Dayleg, Terrence	R-R	6-0	170	9-19-87	.225	.255	.219	87	275	27	62	12	1	4	28	16	5	3	2	59	2	2	.320	.279
Galloway, Isaac	R-R	6-2	190	10-10-89	.185	.167	.200	8	27	2	5	1	1	0	0	0	0	1	0	6	1	0	.296	.185
Hoo, Chris	R-R	5-9	190	2-19-92	.174	.000	.200	6	23	3	4	0	1	0	0	1	0	1	0	3	0	0	.261	.208
Juengel, Matt	R-R	6-2	185	1-13-90	.245	.229	.248	123	437	54	107	21	4	17	67	30	2	0	5	66	3	1	.428	.293
Keys, Brent	L-R	6-0	185	7-14-90	.207	.222	.200	10	29	2	6	1	0	0	1	1	0	0	0	5	1	0	.241	.233
Krist, Chadd	R-R	5-11	190	1-28-90	.190	.207	.185	47	153	16	29	3	2	3	14	14	0	0	0	43	0	0	.294	.257
Lopez, Carlos	L-R	6-2	195	7-16-89	.259	.277	.255	123	460	50	119	22	4	6	38	34	0	5	3	66	2	2	.363	.308
Mathis, Jeff	R-R	6-0	205	3-31-83	.294	—	.294	5	17	2	5	1	0	0	2	2	0	0	1	6	0	0	.353	.350
Morse, Mike	R-R	6-5	245	3-22-82	.294	.000	.455	5	17	2	5	1	0	1	3	3	0	0	0	7	0	0	.529	.400
Nola, Austin	R-R	6-0	190	12-28-89	.211	.238	.206	69	256	26	54	13	1	1	26	27	3	2	8	50	0	0	.281	.286
Othman, Sharif	B-R	6-0	195	3-23-89	.238	.184	.246	83	282	23	67	9	1	3	28	20	4	3	1	60	0	0	.309	.296
Pina, Eudy	R-R	6-3	190	4-12-91	.309	.267	.316	36	110	15	34	4	3	1	14	11	1	0	3	20	5	3	.427	.368
Riddle, J.T.	L-R	6-3	195	10-12-91	.289	.275	.293	44	173	26	50	6	1	5	20	8	2	3	3	24	0	0	.422	.323
Rieger, Ryan	L-L	6-2	205	8-10-90	.234	.222	.236	102	273	29	64	16	8	1	30	28	1	3	5	60	2	2	.363	.303
Rosa, Viosergy	L-L	6-3	185	6-16-90	.217	.133	.232	122	387	53	84	17	0	10	59	77	3	0	3	93	0	0	.339	.349
Soto, Elliot	R-R	5-9	160	8-21-89	.204	.105	.225	32	108	12	22	1	1	0	8	14	1	1	1	24	2	1	.231	.298
2-team total (88 Tennessee)					.256	—	—	120	414	59	106	11	2	0	26	69	3	10	1	82	7	5	.292	.366
Wilson, Kenny	B-R	5-11	195	1-30-90	.270	.350	.254	130	497	77	134	24	7	8	48	58	4	6	5	108	37	9	.394	.348

MIAMI MARLINS

Pitching	B-T	HT	WT	DOB	W	L	ERA	G	GS	CG	SV	IP	H	R	ER	HR	BB	SO	AVG	vLH	vRH	K/9	BB/9
Barraclough, Kyle	R-R	6-3	225	5-23-90	0	0	0.00	4	0	0	2	4	1	0	0	0	1	9	.077	.200	.000	20.25	2.25
Batista, Lay	R-R	6-2	200	8-4-89	0	2	4.18	19	0	0	1	28	17	14	13	1	17	22	.177	.077	.246	7.07	5.46
Bremer, Tyler	R-R	6-2	210	12-7-89	1	0	0.00	4	0	0	0	11	7	0	0	0	3	9	.175	.100	.250	7.15	2.38
Brice, Austin	R-R	6-4	205	6-19-92	6	9	4.67	25	25	0	0	125	114	74	65	11	69	127	.245	.319	.171	9.12	4.95
Burgos, Alex	L-L	5-11	195	12-1-90	1	1	2.12	10	1	0	0	17	10	4	4	1	8	15	.175	.250	.135	7.94	4.24
Cavanerio, Jorgan	R-R	6-1	155	8-18-94	0	1	9.00	1	1	0	0	5	11	6	5	2	2	2	.458	.375	.500	3.60	3.60
Cishek, Steve	R-R	6-6	215	6-18-86	0	0	0.00	5	0	0	2	6	5	0	0	0	0	4	.217	.091	.333	6.00	0.00
Cosart, Jarred	R-R	6-3	195	5-25-90	0	0	1.80	1	1	0	0	5	3	1	1	0	6	6	.176	.143	.200	10.80	10.80
De La Rosa, Esmerling	R-R	6-2	199	5-15-91	1	0	7.11	3	0	0	0	6	8	5	5	0	4	4	.333	.364	.308	5.68	5.68
Donatello, Sean	R-R	6-2	205	8-24-90	0	4	4.05	28	0	0	14	33	32	18	15	2	11	26	.254	.338	.164	7.02	2.97
Ege, Cody	L-L	6-1	185	5-8-91	0	0	1.08	5	0	0	0	8	4	2	1	1	2	11	.148	.100	.176	11.88	2.16
Ellington, Brian	R-R	6-4	195	8-4-90	4	1	2.51	25	0	0	0	43	28	13	12	0	13	47	.187	.129	.227	9.84	2.72
Esch, Jacob	R-R	6-4	190	3-27-90	6	5	3.48	15	15	0	0	85	69	34	33	5	33	68	.223	.252	.200	7.17	3.48
Fernandez, Jose	R-R	6-2	215	7-31-92	0	1	7.20	1	1	0	0	5	6	4	4	1	2	8	.316	.250	.333	14.40	3.60
Fischer, Kyle	R-R	6-3	205	2-11-91	0	1	12.27	3	0	0	1	4	4	5	5	2	1	4	.267	.143	.375	9.82	2.45
Flores, Kendry	R-R	6-2	175	11-24-91	3	3	2.06	9	9	0	0	57	33	14	13	3	15	42	.172	.185	.162	6.67	2.38
Garcia, Jarlin	L-L	6-2	170	1-18-93	1	3	4.91	7	7	0	0	37	38	24	20	4	17	35	.273	.208	.308	8.59	4.17
Higgins, Tyler	R-R	6-3	215	4-22-91	0	2	4.18	18	0	0	5	24	22	11	11	2	8	20	.250	.256	.245	7.61	3.04
Hodges, Josh	R-R	6-4	235	6-21-91	1	2	5.81	9	3	0	0	26	24	18	17	2	15	17	.253	.250	.255	5.81	5.13
Jose, Jose	L-L	6-2	175	7-21-90	0	0	1.80	2	1	0	0	5	4	1	1	0	0	9	.235	.125	.333	16.20	0.00
Lazo, Raudel	L-L	5-9	165	4-12-89	3	2	2.15	18	0	0	0	29	29	11	7	2	7	32	.261	.178	.318	9.82	2.15
Logan, Blake	R-R	6-1	245	1-12-92	3	2	3.29	24	1	0	0	41	40	18	15	6	15	49	.250	.229	.267	10.76	3.29
Lyman, Scott	R-R	6-4	215	3-21-90	1	9	6.15	15	15	0	0	79	99	61	54	5	40	52	.314	.340	.292	5.92	4.56
Martinez, Juancito	R-R	6-1	170	6-10-89	2	2	5.35	32	0	0	7	39	34	26	23	3	30	18	.241	.262	.225	4.19	6.98
McCarthy, Casey	R-R	6-4	215	4-13-90	0	3	7.40	16	0	0	0	24	33	20	20	4	13	15	.327	.273	.368	5.55	4.81
McGough, Scott	R-R	6-0	170	10-31-89	0	0	2.70	10	0	0	0	13	14	5	4	1	6	4	.275	.292	.259	2.70	4.05
Morris, Bryan	L-R	6-3	225	3-28-87	0	1	5.40	1	1	0	0	2	2	1	1	0	0	0	.286	.333	.250	0.00	0.00
Nappo, Greg	L-L	5-10	195	8-25-88	3	0	2.04	10	1	0	0	18	12	5	4	1	6	25	.188	.238	.163	12.74	3.06
Pineyro, Ivan	R-R	6-2	200	9-29-91	0	1	13.50	1	1	0	0	2	3	3	3	0	4	3	.429	.000	.500	0.00	13.50
2-team total (19 Tennessee)					7	6	3.87	20	20	1	0	109	107	49	47	6	33	92				7.57	2.72
Reed, Frankie	L-L	6-1	185	2-12-88	1	0	4.43	14	0	0	0	20	21	11	10	1	10	12	.259	.237	.279	5.31	4.43
Robinson, C.J.	R-R	6-0	215	5-11-93	0	0	2.16	3	0	0	0	8	4	2	2	0	5	4	.138	.143	.136	4.32	5.40
Smith, Chipper	L-L	6-2	195	1-22-90	3	4	4.33	21	16	0	0	89	94	53	43	6	34	70	.272	.265	.276	7.66	3.43
Stem, Craig	R-R	6-5	215	1-5-90	2	4	2.93	32	1	0	0	43	39	20	14	4	17	35	.241	.238	.242	7.33	3.56
Tomshaw, Matt	L-L	6-2	200	12-17-88	6	10	4.33	29	18	0	2	116	129	58	56	9	27	85	.280	.240	.305	6.58	2.09
Williams, Trevor	R-R	6-3	230	4-25-92	7	8	4.00	22	21	0	0	117	126	53	52	9	36	88	.275	.279	.271	6.77	2.77
Williamson, Fabian	R-L	6-2	175	10-20-88	2	0	5.04	22	0	0	0	25	20	15	14	1	24	35	.211	.256	.179	12.60	8.64
Wittgren, Nick	R-R	6-3	210	5-29-91	0	0	0.00	2	0	0	1	2	0	0	0	0	0	3	.000	—	.000	16.20	0.00

Fielding

Catcher	PCT	G	PO	A	E	DP	PB
Bantz	1.000	5	38	5	0	0	0
Hoo	1.000	6	44	4	0	0	1
Krist	.995	45	340	32	2	3	5
Mathis	1.000	2	20	4	0	2	0
Othman	.994	83	594	49	4	4	5

First Base	PCT	G	PO	A	E	DP
Adams	.989	21	169	16	2	18
Juengel	1.000	12	78	3	0	7
Lopez	1.000	2	5	0	0	0
Morse	1.000	2	12	2	0	1
Rieger	.989	14	87	2	1	8
Rosa	.985	96	775	39	12	68

Second Base	PCT	G	PO	A	E	DP
Adams	.979	53	104	127	5	29
Black	.955	10	20	22	2	5
Bohn	.953	14	27	34	3	5
Dayleg	.941	34	61	83	9	24
Nola	.975	27	47	71	3	13
Soto	.978	9	17	27	1	10

Third Base	PCT	G	PO	A	E	DP
Adams	1.000	30	21	65	0	8
Black	1.000	5	2	5	0	1
Cox	.931	77	36	126	12	9
Dayleg	.958	25	23	46	3	3
Juengel	.833	11	4	11	3	1

Shortstop	PCT	G	PO	A	E	DP
Black	.800	1	2	2	1	1
Bohn	.975	12	13	26	1	3
Dayleg	.989	24	25	62	1	13
Nola	.969	42	56	101	5	20
Riddle	.934	42	54	87	10	22
Soto	.966	23	27	57	3	16

Outfield	PCT	G	PO	A	E	DP
Black	1.000	8	11	0	0	0
Dayleg	1.000	1	3	1	0	0
Galloway	1.000	8	17	0	0	0
Juengel	.980	86	139	9	3	1
Keys	1.000	8	20	0	0	0
Lopez	.968	113	232	8	8	3
Pina	.986	31	68	2	1	1
Rieger	.977	53	84	2	2	0
Wilson	.980	126	286	9	6	4

JUPITER HAMMERHEADS

HIGH CLASS A

FLORIDA STATE LEAGUE

Batting	B-T	HT	WT	DOB	AVG	vLH	vRH	G	AB	R	H	2B	3B	HR	RBI	BB	HBP	SH	SF	SO	SB	CS	SLG	OBP
Anderson, Brian	R-R	6-3	185	5-19-93	.235	.225	.239	132	477	50	112	22	2	8	62	40	9	1	3	109	2	2	.340	.304
Barber, Blake	R-R	5-10	180	4-4-90	.257	.313	.234	85	284	25	73	15	1	2	25	14	0	3	2	53	2	2	.338	.290
Bohn, Justin	R-R	6-0	180	11-2-92	.262	.282	.256	90	340	40	89	12	1	4	34	25	1	2	2	62	10	1	.338	.313
Brewster, Travis	L-L	5-9	210	1-21-92	.083	.000	.111	4	12	2	1	0	0	0	0	0	0	1	0	0	5	0	0	.083	.214
Chavez, Joe	R-R	6-0	195	6-26-93	.273	.333	.250	3	11	0	3	1	0	0	2	1	0	0	0	2	0	0	.364	.333
Cordova, Rehiner	B-R	6-0	150	1-11-94	.161	.125	.182	30	87	6	14	1	0	0	2	8	0	4	0	24	3	0	.172	.232
Dean, Austin	R-R	6-1	190	10-14-93	.268	.297	.257	136	519	67	139	32	2	5	52	39	4	6	10	76	18	10	.366	.318
Dewitt, Kentrell	L-L	5-11	180	3-20-91	.286	.222	.316	10	28	2	8	1	1	0	3	3	0	0	0	8	2	2	.393	.355
Fernandez Jr., Alex	R-R	5-10	180	3-30-93	.500	—	.500	1	2	0	1	0	0	0	0	0	0	1	0	0	0	0	.500	.667
Flynn, Cameron	L-R	6-0	195	2-24-90	.194	.151	.208	91	294	21	57	6	0	1	18	14	7	5	0	62	10	5	.224	.248
Gordon, Dee	L-R	5-11	170	4-22-88	.250	—	.250	1	4	0	1	0	0	0	0	0	0	0	0	0	0	0	.250	.250
Hoo, Chris	R-R	5-9	190	2-19-92	.201	.259	.176	86	274	23	55	8	0	2	14	25	5	6	2	49	0	1	.252	.278
Jimenez, Joel	R-R	5-11	170	4-30-92	.091	.000	.121	14	44	3	4	0	0	0	2	4	0	1	0	18	0	0	.091	.167
Kelly, Don	L-R	6-4	190	2-15-80	.179	.083	.222	12	39	5	7	1	1	0	4	9	0	0	1	5	0	1	.256	.327

Batting	B-T	HT	WT	DOB	AVG	vLH	vRH	G	AB	R	H	2B	3B	HR	RBI	BB	HBP	SH	SF	SO	SB	CS	SLG	OBP
Krist, Chadd	R-R	5-11	190	1-28-90	.167	.000	.214	5	18	1	3	0	0	1	2	1	1	0	0	6	0	0	.333	.250
Morse, Mike	R-R	6-5	245	3-22-82	.250	.000	.333	2	4	2	1	0	0	0	0	3	0	0	0	1	0	0	.250	.571
Munoz, Felix	L-L	6-2	170	4-27-92	.237	.192	.252	114	405	31	96	12	2	5	44	26	2	0	5	65	1	1	.314	.283
Perez, Yefri	R-R	5-11	165	2-24-91	.240	.234	.242	135	517	74	124	10	1	1	22	31	4	8	3	95	71	21	.269	.286
Prado, Martin	R-R	6-1	190	10-27-83	.300	1.000	.222	3	10	1	3	0	0	0	0	0	0	0	0	1	0	0	.300	.300
Ramirez, Yuniel	R-R	6-1	215	12-22-88	.197	.136	.222	22	76	3	15	5	0	0	8	1	0	1	1	15	1	0	.263	.205
Riddle, J.T.	L-R	6-3	175	10-12-91	.270	.235	.291	45	185	30	50	6	1	0	9	11	0	0	2	29	7	3	.314	.311
Riggins, Harold	R-R	6-2	240	3-6-90	.267	.257	.271	80	255	25	68	15	1	6	35	28	5	0	6	93	0	1	.404	.344
Roberts, James	R-R	6-2	180	12-11-91	.324	.258	.351	35	108	12	35	3	0	3	13	7	1	4	1	17	3	2	.435	.368
Romero, Avery	R-R	5-11	195	5-11-93	.259	.235	.269	123	455	47	118	14	1	3	42	38	2	4	6	71	3	4	.314	.315
Stanton, Giancarlo	R-R	6-6	240	11-8-89	.000	—	.000	1	2	0	0	0	0	0	0	0	0	0	0	1	0	0	.000	.333
Vigil, Rodrigo	R-R	6-0	164	1-3-93	.182	.172	.185	37	121	6	22	2	0	0	12	4	3	1	1	17	0	0	.198	.225
Yelich, Christian	L-R	6-2	195	12-5-91	.333	.250	.400	3	9	2	3	1	0	0	0	1	0	0	0	3	1	0	.444	.400

Pitching	B-T	HT	WT	DOB	W	L	ERA	G	GS	CG	SV	IP	H	R	ER	HR	BB	SO	AVG	vLH	vRH	K/9	BB/9
Adames, Jose	R-R	6-2	165	1-17-93	5	6	4.69	18	16	0	0	79	85	47	41	0	38	64	.285	.330	.258	7.32	4.35
Adkins, Hunter	R-R	6-4	190	9-20-90	0	0	0.00	1	0	0	0	2	1	0	0	0	3		.143	.000	.250	13.50	0.00
Alvarez, Henderson	R-R	6-0	205	4-18-90	0	1	1.59	3	0	0	0	11	11	4	2	0	2	8	.256	.235	.269	6.35	1.59
Alvis, Sam	R-L	6-0	195	6-11-92	2	0	5.06	7	1	0	0	16	8	6	6	0	9	10	.205	.133	.250	8.44	7.59
Araujo, Victor	R-R	5-11	170	11-9-92	0	0	0.89	12	0	0	3	20	16	2	2	0	5	23	.211	.240	.196	10.18	2.21
Bremer, Tyler	R-R	6-2	210	12-7-89	0	3	1.84	32	0	0	4	49	40	14	10	1	14	51	.220	.176	.250	9.37	2.57
Brigham, Jeff	R-R	6-0	200	2-16-92	2	2	1.87	6	5	0	0	34	34	10	7	0	9	22	.276	.403	.148	5.88	2.41
Burgos, Alex	L-L	5-11	195	12-1-90	4	1	2.12	22	1	0	0	30	31	7	7	2	8	18	.277	.294	.269	5.46	2.43
Castillo, Luis	R-R	6-2	170	12-12-92	2	3	3.50	10	9	0	0	44	44	17	17	3	14	31	.263	.173	.337	6.39	2.89
Cavanerio, Jorgan	R-R	6-1	155	8-18-94	0	3	4.08	3	3	0	0	18	18	9	8	0	1	9	.269	.310	.237	4.58	0.51
Cosart, Jarred	R-R	6-3	195	5-25-90	0	2	7.00	2	2	0	0	9	10	7	7	0	3	8	.278	.111	.444	8.00	3.00
De La Rosa, Esmerling	R-R	6-2	199	5-15-91	6	4	2.89	33	0	0	2	65	51	26	21	1	16	55	.215	.193	.228	7.58	2.20
Del Pozo, Miguel	L-L	6-1	180	10-14-92	2	5	4.25	27	5	0	0	59	73	32	28	1	20	55	.300	.210	.346	8.34	3.03
Diaz, Jose	R-R	6-2	180	5-7-93	0	0	1.69	2	0	0	0	5	4	1	1	0	3	4	.222	.375	.100	6.75	5.06
Farnworth, Steven	R-R	6-2	175	9-6-93	0	1	6.00	2	0	0	0	3	6	3	2	1	2	1	.462	.500	.429	3.00	6.00
Fernandez, Jose	R-R	6-2	215	7-31-92	1	1	3.20	4	4	0	0	20	18	7	7	1	4	25	.250	.368	.208	11.44	1.83
Flores, Kendry	R-R	6-2	175	11-24-91	0	0	0.00	2	2	0	0	3	1	0	0	0	1		.111	.000	.200	3.38	0.00
Garcia, Jarlin	L-L	6-2	170	1-18-93	3	5	3.06	18	18	1	0	97	96	40	33	4	23	69	.257	.291	.244	6.40	2.13
Hafner, Ryan	R-R	6-6		11-22-91	0	0	4.50	1	0	0	0	2	1	1	1	0	1	0	.200	.500	.000	0.00	4.50
2-team total (14 Bradenton)					1	1	9.13	15	0	0	0	24	33	25	24	1	15	14	—	—	—	5.32	5.70
Higgins, Tyler	R-R	6-3	215	4-22-91	0	0	3.00	16	0	0	1	27	24	10	9	1	2	21	.238	.257	.227	7.00	0.67
Holmes, Ben	L-L	6-1	195	9-12-91	3	1	2.92	7	7	0	0	37	32	16	12	2	18	29	.237	.167	.263	7.05	4.38
Jose, Jose	L-L	6-2	175	7-21-90	1	0	0.00	6	0	0	1	10	4	0	0	0	1	17	.129	.167	.105	15.83	0.93
Keller, Kyle	R-R	6-4	200	4-28-93	0	0	0.00	1	0	0	0	1	1	0	0	0	1	0	.250	.500	.000	0.00	6.75
Kinley, Tyler	R-R	6-4	205	1-31-91	1	3	3.25	31	0	0	11	44	40	17	16	1	11	38	.247	.322	.204	7.71	2.23
Lazo, Raudel	L-L	5-9	165	4-12-89	1	1	1.50	8	0	0	1	12	7	2	2	0	2	12	.171	.267	.115	9.00	1.50
Lyman, Scott	R-R	6-4	215	3-21-90	1	1	1.61	11	11	0	0	67	44	15	12	1	24	37	.192	.206	.180	4.97	3.22
Martinez, Juancito	R-R	6-1	170	6-10-89	2	1	1.59	18	0	0	6	23	13	6	4	1	6	24	.159	.194	.130	9.53	2.38
Mazza, Chris	R-R	6-4	180	10-17-89	0	1	3.60	11	0	0	3	15	12	8	6	1	4	11	.226	.273	.194	6.60	2.40
McCarthy, Casey	R-R	6-4	215	4-13-90	0	3	2.15	21	0	0	2	29	27	10	7	1	6	14	.252	.222	.274	4.30	1.84
McGough, Scott	R-R	6-0	170	10-31-89	0	0	0.00	4	0	0	0	7	4	0	0	0	1	6	.182	.167	.188	7.71	1.29
Meyer, Ben	R-R	6-6	200	1-30-93	0	2	3.18	11	0	0	0	23	23	9	8	0	12	15	.267	.310	.246	5.96	4.76
Milroy, Matt	L-R	6-2	185	10-5-90	6	2	3.25	36	1	0	2	61	53	28	22	2	43	80	.236	.292	.194	11.80	6.34
Morris, Bryan	L-R	6-3	225	3-28-87	0	0	7.71	3	0	0	0	2	1	2	2	0	3	3	.125	.250	.000	11.57	11.57
Narveson, Chris	L-L	6-3	205	12-20-81	2	0	3.18	2	2	0	0	11	11	4	4	0	2	10	.262	.500	.250	7.94	1.59
Newell, Ryan	R-R	6-2	215	6-18-91	3	1	2.27	10	10	0	0	40	35	15	10	0	17	38	.248	.286	.203	8.62	3.86
Ramos, Felix	B-L	6-0	175	12-23-91	0	0	5.40	1	0	0	0	2	1	1	1	0	2	1	.333	.000	.500	5.40	10.80
Robinson, C.J.	R-R	6-0	215	5-11-93	1	1	3.04	34	1	0	3	50	38	19	17	1	16	35	.211	.271	.182	6.26	2.86
Sadberry, Chris	L-L	6-0	195	11-8-91	4	4	3.49	14	12	0	0	59	72	27	23	1	22	28	.306	.277	.318	4.25	3.34
Simpson, Tucker	R-R	6-5	230	5-12-93	0	0	0.00	2	0	0	0	4	7	0	0	0	1	0	.412	.500	.400	0.00	2.08
Smith, Chipper	L-L	6-2	195	1-22-90	2	3	4.66	5	4	0	0	19	24	14	10	0	10	20	.293	.583	.243	9.31	4.66
Steckenrider, Drew	R-R	6-5	215	1-10-91	4	3	3.18	15	8	1	0	57	57	24	20	2	25	44	.266	.302	.238	6.99	3.97
Townsley, Sean	L-L	6-7	240	9-19-90	3	9	4.79	14	14	0	0	62	80	41	33	3	25	45	.319	.438	.291	6.53	3.63
Urena, Jose	R-R	6-3	175	9-12-91	0	0	0.00	1	0	0	0	1	0	0	0	0	0	0	.000	.000	.000	0.00	0.00
Williams, Nick	R-R	6-2	225	11-15-91	0	0	8.10	2	0	0	0	3	5	3	3	1	4	3	.333	.500	.222	8.10	10.80

Fielding

Catcher	PCT	G	PO	A	E	DP	PB
Hoo	.991	86	606	79	6	9	5
Jimenez	1.000	14	102	12	0	1	2
Krist	1.000	5	31	5	0	0	2
Vigil	.996	36	251	30	1	6	7

First Base	PCT	G	PO	A	E	DP
Cordova	1.000	2	15	1	0	0
Kelly	1.000	1	7	0	0	2
Morse	1.000	2	12	2	0	0
Munoz	.989	100	858	71	10	96
Riggins	.994	40	314	22	2	27
Roberts	1.000	1	1	0	0	0

Second Base	PCT	G	PO	A	E	DP
Barber	1.000	1	1	1	0	0
Bohn	1.000	1	1	2	0	0
Chavez	1.000	2	6	0	0	1
Cordova	.947	10	19	35	3	9
Gordon	1.000	1	1	3	0	0
Kelly	1.000	1	3	4	0	2
Prado	1.000	1	1	1	0	0
Roberts	.947	18	21	51	4	9
Romero	.961	109	205	286	20	79

Third Base	PCT	G	PO	A	E	DP
Anderson	.944	121	73	232	18	28

	PCT	G	PO	A	E	DP
Barber	.868	14	8	25	5	2
Fernandez Jr.	1.000	1	0	1	0	0
Kelly	1.000	2	1	1	0	0
Roberts	.917	5	3	8	1	0
Vigil	1.000	1	1	1	0	0

Shortstop	PCT	G	PO	A	E	DP
Bohn	.965	83	105	256	13	45
Cordova	.967	12	28	31	2	9
Kelly	.667	1	2	0	1	0
Riddle	.976	42	64	136	5	38
Roberts	.935	5	10	19	2	9

MIAMI MARLINS

Outfield	PCT	G	PO	A	E	DP
Barber	1.000	34	54	1	0	0
Brewster	1.000	3	3	0	0	0
Cordova	1.000	6	13	1	0	0

	PCT	G	PO	A	E	DP
Dean	.979	127	216	15	5	1
Dewitt	1.000	8	13	0	0	0
Flynn	.963	88	174	6	7	1
Perez	.966	133	331	15	12	4

	PCT	G	PO	A	E	DP
Ramirez	.972	21	31	4	1	1
Riggins	.875	11	20	1	3	0
Stanton	—		1	0	0	0
Yelich	1.000	3	6	0	0	0

GREENSBORO GRASSHOPPERS

LOW CLASS A

SOUTH ATLANTIC LEAGUE

Batting	B-T	HT	WT	DOB	AVG	vLH	vRH	G	AB	R	H	2B	3B	HR	RBI	BB	HBP	SH	SF	SO	SB	CS	SLG	OBP
Almonte, Erwin	L-L	6-0	170	2-22-95	.250	.500	.000	2	4	1	1	0	0	0	0	3	0	0	0	0	0	0	.250	.571
Aper, Ryan	R-R	6-3	175	6-6-93	.212	.250	.201	70	198	18	42	8	0	2	18	10	5	6	0	43	8	3	.283	.268
Blanton, Aaron	R-R	6-2	175	9-1-93	.143	.063	.175	18	56	8	8	0	1	2	4	8	0	1	0	18	2	0	.286	.250
Brewster, Travis	L-L	5-9	210	1-21-92	.240	.167	.263	8	25	3	6	2	0	0	1	4	0	0	0	9	2	0	.320	.345
Cabrera, Rony	R-R	5-11	175	1-29-96	.248	.262	.244	108	427	46	106	19	2	4	26	15	3	8	2	81	7	2	.330	.277
Castillo, Felix	R-R	5-1	170	6-20-91	.252	.205	.269	39	147	9	37	7	0	2	19	5	4	0	1	17	0	0	.340	.293
Cranmer, Ryan	R-R	6-2	195	6-23-92	.200	.400	.000	3	10	1	2	0	0	0	0	0	0	2	0	3	0	0	.200	.200
Davis, Mason	B-R	5-9	175	1-11-93	.255	.214	.269	86	337	43	86	11	4	6	29	19	9	10	1	67	19	9	.365	.311
Dunbar, Korey	R-R	6-1	210	4-21-94	.238	1.000	.200	5	21	2	5	1	0	0	3	2	1	0	0	10	0	0	.286	.333
Fisher, Eric	L-L	6-3	205	3-10-92	.132	.100	.140	15	53	7	7	0	0	0	2	1	1	1	1	12	0	0	.132	.161
Morales, Roy	R-R	6-2	195	6-25-95	.182	.375	.139	14	44	2	8	2	0	0	3	4	0	0	5	0	0	.227	.294
Munden, Taylor	R-R	5-10	185	7-7-93	.229	.129	.288	25	83	12	19	4	0	3	10	10	1	0	1	22	1	1	.386	.316
Norwood, John	R-R	6-1	185	9-24-92	.233	.236	.232	120	446	53	104	19	2	16	55	42	5	2	4	113	34	14	.392	.304
Rodriguez, Arturo	R-R	6-0	235	10-3-91	.275	.361	.246	125	476	51	131	18	0	19	69	33	6	0	7	65	0	0	.433	.326
Schales, Brian	R-R	6-1	170	2-13-96	.260	.305	.246	122	443	59	115	21	3	4	45	38	10	3	3	76	3	2	.348	.330
Smith, Austen	R-R	6-4	240	1-2-92	.241	.260	.235	113	390	52	94	21	1	17	50	58	7	0	0	123	1	1	.431	.349
Soltis, Casey	L-L	6-1	185	6-8-95	.182	.158	.194	15	55	5	10	1	0	0	2	5	2	1	0	23	2	0	.200	.274
Soto, Isael	L-L	6-0	190	11-2-96	.125	.095	.140	17	64	2	8	1	0	0	1	3	0	0	0	27	0	0	.141	.164
Sullivan, Zach	R-R	6-3	180	11-26-95	.192	.204	.188	116	370	42	71	7	3	0	21	19	3	10	4	106	13	4	.227	.235
Twine, Justin	R-R	5-11	205	10-7-95	.206	.171	.217	117	451	44	93	20	3	7	39	6	12	0	4	108	8	4	.310	.235
Vigil, Rodrigo	R-R	6-0	164	1-3-92	.300	.182	.333	39	150	16	45	8	0	0	21	4	0	1	1	13	0	0	.353	.316
Woods, K.J.	L-R	6-3	230	7-9-95	.277	.253	.282	104	383	53	106	28	1	18	58	45	9	0	2	133	1	3	.496	.364

Pitching	B-T	HT	WT	DOB	W	L	ERA	G	GS	CG	SV	IP	H	R	ER	HR	BB	SO	AVG	vLH	vRH	K/9	BB/9
Adames, Jose	R-R	6-2	165	1-17-93	1	3	2.35	8	8	0	0	38	34	14	10	3	17	26	.236	.236	.236	6.10	3.99
Alvis, Sam	R-L	6-0	195	6-11-92	3	6	4.66	39	0	0	1	56	51	30	29	3	35	57	.243	.169	.276	9.16	5.63
Arias, Jose	R-R	6-6	235	1-17-91	0	0	4.09	7	0	0	0	11	7	6	5	2	6	11	.179	.059	.273	9.00	4.91
Buckelew, James	L-L	6-2	155	8-4-91	6	4	3.72	43	2	0	1	77	71	36	32	1	31	70	.237	.309	.211	8.15	3.61
Castellanos, Gabe	L-L	6-1	165	12-28-93	1	2	4.93	7	7	0	0	35	38	26	19	4	19	20	.288	.313	.274	5.19	4.93
Castillo, Luis	R-R	6-2	170	12-12-92	4	3	2.98	25	7	0	4	63	59	25	21	1	19	63	.246	.236	.254	8.95	2.70
Cavanerio, Jorgan	R-R	6-1	155	8-18-94	4	7	4.41	18	18	0	0	102	116	54	50	9	11	73	.289	.289	.289	6.44	0.97
De La Rosa, Leurys	R-R	6-2	160	11-5-94	0	0	1.69	3	0	0	0	5	5	2	1	1	2	4	.250	.333	.182	6.75	3.38
Diaz, Jose	R-R	6-2	180	5-7-93	0	1	18.00	1	0	0	0	1	3	2	2	1	0	0	.600	.750	.000	0.00	0.00
Fischer, Kyle	R-R	6-3	205	2-11-91	1	5	2.15	43	0	0	12	71	63	17	17	3	11	69	.241	.311	.194	8.75	1.39
Franco, Enderson	R-R	6-2	170	12-29-92	1	6	7.29	12	12	0	0	54	74	50	44	6	25	37	.327	.295	.360	6.13	4.14
Fuller, Nick	L-L	6-2	185	3-13-91	1	2	5.47	16	0	0	0	25	23	17	15	6	10	21	.240	.364	.175	7.66	3.65
Hafner, Ryan	R-R	6-6	205	11-22-91	0	2	6.75	13	0	0	0	17	17	13	13	0	9	14	.246	.257	.235	7.27	4.67
Harris, Cody	R-R	6-3	195	4-4-92	1	1	4.71	14	0	0	0	21	31	13	11	4	3	14	.330	.349	.314	6.00	1.29
Hodges, Josh	R-R	6-7	235	6-21-91	3	2	1.17	25	0	0	10	38	33	8	5	0	12	42	.229	.254	.212	9.86	2.82
Holloway, Jordan	R-R	6-4	190	6-13-96	0	1	7.00	2	2	0	0	9	8	7	7	0	6	4	.250	.500	.136	4.00	6.00
Holmes, Ben	L-L	6-1	195	9-12-91	3	6	5.20	20	17	0	0	92	107	59	53	9	29	71	.288	.241	.303	6.97	2.85
Kane, Tyler	R-R	6-1	190	8-23-92	1	3	7.36	17	0	0	0	22	21	19	18	3	19	19	.259	.162	.341	7.77	7.77
Keller, Kyle	R-R	6-4	200	4-28-93	0	0	9.35	6	0	0	0	9	12	9	9	1	7	15	.324	.167	.400	15.58	7.27
Kines, Gunnar	L-L	6-3	210	7-25-93	0	1	4.15	2	1	0	0	4	7	9	2	1	5	2	.350	.333	.364	4.15	10.38
Kinley, Jeff	L-L	6-1	195	2-15-92	0	1	3.66	9	0	0	0	20	18	8	8	3	2	20	.237	.267	.217	9.15	0.92
Kline, Breck	R-R	5-11	200	3-9-92	0	0	0.00	1	0	0	0	2	1	0	0	0	1	0	.167	.250	.000	0.00	4.50
Kolek, Tyler	R-R	6-5	260	12-15-95	4	10	4.56	25	25	0	0	109	108	70	55	7	61	81	.258	.262	.256	6.71	5.05
Mader, Michael	L-L	6-2	195	2-18-94	6	12	4.73	27	27	0	0	141	141	82	74	8	57	86	.264	.197	.287	5.50	3.65
Meyer, Ben	R-R	6-6	200	1-30-93	1	0	3.38	2	0	0	0	5	4	2	2	0	1	7	.200	.167	.250	11.81	1.69
Overton, Connor	R-R	6-0	190	7-24-93	0	0	13.03	8	0	0	0	10	24	14	14	3	7	7	.462	.522	.414	6.52	4.66
Quinonez, Eduar	R-R	6-3	190	8-9-89	0	0	9.00	4	0	0	0	3	4	4	3	1	4	4	.286	.444	.000	12.00	12.00
Rivas, Kelvin	R-R	6-3	250	6-5-92	1	1	4.50	18	3	0	1	38	32	23	19	3	19	41	.229	.266	.197	9.71	4.50
Robinson, C.J.	R-R	6-0	215	5-11-93	1	1	2.00	7	0	0	0	9	6	2	2	1	4	8	.182	.250	.118	8.00	4.00
Smigelski, Jacob	R-R	6-3	200	6-20-92	0	0	3.38	5	0	0	0	8	7	3	3	0	10	9	.233	.200	.250	10.13	11.25
Squier, Scott	L-L	6-5	185	9-17-92	5	3	7.50	15	5	0	0	42	58	37	35	7	19	33	.331	.119	.398	7.07	4.07
Steckenrider, Drew	R-R	6-5	215	1-10-91	1	3	2.73	10	5	0	0	39	38	15	12	2	17	34	.260	.328	.212	7.78	3.89
Suggs, Colby	R-R	5-11	235	10-25-91	0	0	0.00	5	0	0	1	5	3	0	0	0	1	6	.150	.000	.200	10.13	1.69
Velez, Jose	L-L	6-1	205	9-5-89	2	1	4.80	24	0	0	4	30	24	16	16	2	11	42	.218	.182	.234	12.60	3.30

Fielding

Catcher	PCT	G	PO	A	E	DP	PB
Castillo	.991	38	276	49	3	4	4
Dunbar	.971	4	29	4	1	0	0
Morales	.982	14	92	18	2	1	0
Rodriguez	.989	45	319	37	4	2	2
Vigil	.994	38	262	49	2	2	8

First Base	PCT	G	PO	A	E	DP
Almonte	1.000	1	11	0	0	2
Cabrera	1.000	4	25	1	0	1
Cranmer	1.000	2	12	0	0	0
Fisher	1.000	4	19	2	0	1
Rodriguez	.992	41	345	35	3	39
Smith	.992	26	246	18	2	12

	PCT	G	PO	A	E	DP
Woods	.985	65	615	33	10	51

Second Base	PCT	G	PO	A	E	DP
Blanton	1.000	7	14	17	0	4
Cabrera	.963	86	145	243	15	55
Davis	.952	42	70	110	9	16
Munden	1.000	9	13	22	0	4

MIAMI MARLINS

Third Base	PCT	G	PO	A	E	DP
Blanton	1.000	3	1	4	0	0
Cabrera	.833	4	4	6	2	0
Cranmer	1.000	1	1	0	0	0
Munden	.935	10	7	22	2	3
Rodriguez	1.000	2	1	9	0	1
Schales	.927	119	64	264	26	21

Shortstop	PCT	G	PO	A	E	DP
Blanton	.939	6	11	20	2	3
Cabrera	.934	16	23	34	4	8
Munden	1.000	2	3	6	0	1
Twine	.940	117	156	295	29	55

Outfield	PCT	G	PO	A	E	DP
Aper	.977	67	119	6	3	2
Blanton	1.000	1	1	0	0	0
Brewster	1.000	8	15	0	0	0
Davis	.963	44	77	2	3	0
Fisher	1.000	10	23	0	0	0
Munden	1.000	1	3	0	0	0
Norwood	.996	115	224	15	1	3
Smith	.958	43	45	1	2	0
Soltis	.977	15	40	2	1	0
Soto	.969	15	30	1	1	0
Sullivan	.974	113	213	9	6	1

BATAVIA MUCKDOGS

NEW YORK-PENN LEAGUE

SHORT-SEASON

MIAMI MARLINS

Batting	B-T	HT	WT	DOB	AVG	vLH	vRH	G	AB	R	H	2B	3B	HR	RBI	BB	HBP	SH	SF	SO	SB	CS	SLG	OBP
Alfonzo, Giovanny	R-R	5-11	185	12-19-92	.245	.317	.227	60	204	17	50	6	0	0	20	19	2	3	3	39	8	5	.275	.311
Almonte, Erwin	L-L	6-0	170	2-22-95	.213	.200	.217	16	61	7	13	0	0	1	5	1	2	0	0	11	0	0	.262	.250
Anderson, Blake	R-R	6-3	180	1-5-96	.220	.192	.228	31	118	9	26	6	0	2	16	3	6	0	1	42	0	0	.322	.273
Barrett, Kyle	L-R	5-11	185	8-4-93	.091	.000	.100	4	11	1	1	0	0	0	0	1	0	0	0	1	0	0	.091	.167
Brewster, Travis	L-L	5-9	210	1-21-92	.271	.214	.284	42	144	19	39	7	0	0	15	14	2	2	1	33	4	4	.319	.342
Chavez, Joe	R-R	6-0	195	6-26-93	.125	.000	.200	7	24	1	3	0	0	0	3	0	0	0		10	0	0	.125	.222
Cranmer, Ryan	R-R	6-2	195	6-23-92	.180	.087	.208	33	100	14	18	3	0	1	6	16	0	0	0	20	0	0	.240	.293
Dunbar, Korey	R-R	6-1	210	4-21-94	.317	.200	.340	17	60	9	19	5	0	0	5	9	0	1	0	20	0	0	.400	.406
Fernandez Jr., Alex	R-R	5-10	180	3-30-93	.277	.222	.289	42	148	21	41	7	1	3	14	18	3	1	0	50	6	1	.399	.367
Fisher, Eric	L-L	6-3	205	3-10-92	.246	.318	.228	32	114	10	28	6	1	1	11	10	0	0	5	34	2	2	.342	.295
Garrett, Stone	R-R	6-2	195	11-22-95	.297	.341	.287	58	222	36	66	18	6	11	46	19	2	0	4	60	8	5	.581	.352
Haynal, Brad	R-R	6-3	215	8-21-91	.274	.313	.265	68	248	30	68	21	0	4	34	30	6	0	3	51	0	0	.407	.362
Lopez, Javier	R-R	6-3	180	9-13-94	.148	.250	.105	8	27	4	4	0	0	0	2	2	1	1	0	9	0	0	.148	.233
Morales, Roy	R-R	6-2	195	6-25-95	.311	.313	.311	33	122	7	38	3	1	0	14	10	1	1	3	13	0	1	.352	.360
Moscat, Galvi	R-R	6-0	180	6-29-94	.228	.273	.214	41	136	11	31	6	0	0	4	6	0	3	0	29	2	1	.272	.261
Munden, Taylor	R-R	5-10	185	7-7-93	.212	.200	.215	38	132	23	28	10	0	0	12	17	4	2	2	36	1	5	.288	.316
Newell, Cameron	R-L	6-1	195	8-1-91	.106	.143	.100	16	47	3	5	1	1	0	3	5	2	0	1	12	0	1	.170	.218
Ramirez, Yuniel	R-R	6-1	215	12-22-88	.323	.333	.321	25	93	10	30	3	0	0	8	0	0	1	2	24	1	0	.355	.316
Rawe, Brandon	R-R	6-2	190	6-19-93	.222	.345	.177	37	108	11	24	7	0	0	12	9	1	2	1	31	2	0	.287	.286
Reyes, Angel	R-R	6-0	175	5-6-95	.265	.158	.297	25	83	11	22	5	3	2	14	6	0	2	1	19	0	0	.470	.311
Seymour, Anfernee	B-R	5-11	165	6-24-95	.273	.362	.244	64	238	39	65	10	4	0	14	20	4	3	1	52	29	6	.349	.338
Soto, Isael	L-L	6-0	190	11-2-96	.095	.111	.083	5	21	1	2	0	0	0	0	1	0	0	0	10	0	0	.095	.136

Pitching	B-T	HT	WT	DOB	W	L	ERA	G	GS	CG	SV	IP	H	R	ER	HR	BB	SO	AVG	vLH	vRH	K/9	BB/9
Adames, Ayron	B-R	6-0	190	3-1-94	1	0	5.14	14	0	0	0	28	35	18	16	2	10	32	.294	.373	.192	10.29	3.21
Bautista, Nestor	L-L	6-3	200	5-13-92	4	3	3.27	14	3	0	0	55	71	27	20	3	20	41	.307	.318	.301	6.71	3.27
Brewster, L.J.	R-R	6-2	205	5-2-94	1	2	3.91	15	0	0	0	25	31	16	11	0	14	19	.295	.346	.245	6.75	4.97
Britt, Curt	L-R	6-0	220	3-5-93	1	0	4.15	6	0	0	1	9	13	4	4	1	2	10	.371	.368	.375	10.38	2.08
Castellanos, Gabe	L-L	6-1	165	12-28-92	1	3	5.25	8	7	1	0	36	36	26	21	1	18	38	.271	.244	.283	9.50	4.50
De La Rosa, Leurys	R-R	6-2	160	11-5-94	0	1	36.00	1	0	0	0	1	4	7	4	0	2	1	.444	.400	.500	9.00	18.00
Diaz, Jose	R-R	6-2	180	5-7-93	0	0	36.00	1	0	0	0	1	5	4	4	0	0	0	.625	.667	.500	0.00	0.00
Farnworth, Steven	R-R	6-2	175	9-6-93	2	2	0.75	22	0	0	13	36	26	9	3	0	7	30	.195	.269	.121	7.50	1.75
Fuller, Nick	L-L	6-2	185	3-13-91	0	0	0.00	2	0	0	0	4	5	3	0	0	1	7	.278	.167	.333	15.75	2.25
Guzman, Juan	R-R	6-0	160	2-24-91	0	2	14.73	3	0	0	0	4	5	8	6	1	3	2	.313	.429	.222	4.91	7.36
Hafner, Ryan	R-R	6-6	205	11-22-91	0	0	6.75	3	0	0	0	4	5	3	3	0	2	2	.313	.333	.286	4.50	4.50
Harris, Cody	R-R	6-3	195	4-4-92	0	1	3.65	6	0	0	0	12	15	7	5	0	3	8	.288	.256	.385	5.84	2.19
Hillyer, Jordan	R-R	6-2	195	9-22-93	2	4	2.57	18	0	0	3	28	21	11	8	1	18	32	.202	.143	.255	10.29	5.79
Holloway, Jordan	R-R	6-4	190	6-13-96	5	6	2.91	14	14	0	0	68	60	27	22	0	36	40	.234	.273	.179	5.29	4.76
Jacome, Justin	L-L	6-6	230	10-19-93	0	1	2.48	12	11	0	0	33	37	13	9	1	7	29	.289	.325	.273	7.99	1.93
Keller, Kyle	R-R	6-4	200	4-28-93	0	3	5.19	10	0	0	0	17	17	11	10	0	9	19	.246	.306	.182	9.87	4.67
Kinley, Jeff	L-L	6-1	195	2-15-92	0	0	11.81	5	0	0	0	5	11	11	7	0	3	6	.407	.455	.375	10.13	5.06
Langley, Justin	L-L	6-6	225	9-2-94	1	0	8.10	9	0	0	0	3	19	13	12	0	10	8	.328	.400	.289	5.40	6.75
Lilek, Brett	L-L	6-4	194	8-10-93	1	2	3.34	11	10	0	0	35	30	14	13	1	7	43	.231	.259	.211	11.16	1.80
MacEachern, Ryley	R-R	6-2	213	5-27-94	2	0	2.86	11	0	0	1	22	12	8	7	0	8	27	.160	.241	.109	11.05	3.27
Neubeck, Travis	L-R	6-2	180	3-13-95	1	3	4.03	10	3	0	0	29	33	19	13	2	10	14	.282	.246	.317	4.34	3.10
Osoria, Aneury	R-R	6-7	170	11-15-93	1	0	6.75	4	0	0	0	5	3	5	4	0	7	4	.167	.300	.000	6.75	11.81
Peters, Dillon	L-L	5-9	195	8-31-92	0	3	4.83	7	7	0	0	32	40	25	17	2	10	27	.299	.286	.303	7.67	2.84
Poteet, Cody	R-R	6-2	170	7-30-94	0	1	2.13	5	4	0	0	13	9	6	3	1	2	12	.188	.111	.286	8.53	1.42
Simpson, Tucker	R-R	6-5	230	5-12-93	0	0	4.91	4	0	0	0	4	2	2	2	0	2	3	.267	.143	.375	7.36	4.91
Smigelski, Jacob	R-R	6-3	200	6-20-92	0	0	6.75	1	0	0	0	3	2	2	2	1	1	1	.222	.333	.000	3.38	3.38
Squier, Scott	R-L	6-5	185	9-17-92	6	2	3.55	15	8	0	0	66	69	32	26	2	15	64	.267	.225	.295	8.73	2.05
Weaver, Chuck	R-R	6-4	200	1-4-91	0	2	2.42	4	3	0	0	22	28	12	6	0	3	19	.298	.354	.239	7.66	1.21
White, Nick	R-R	6-3	205	10-15-95	2	3	7.03	13	5	0	0	40	43	36	31	2	29	32	.269	.265	.273	7.26	6.58

Fielding

Catcher	PCT	G	PO	A	E	DP	PB
Anderson	.955	24	161	30	9	3	4
Dunbar	1.000	8	63	8	0	0	2
Haynal	.978	22	161	21	4	0	5
Morales	.995	23	153	28	1	0	2

First Base	PCT	G	PO	A	E	DP
Almonte	.988	10	80	3	1	6
Cranmer	1.000	3	24	3	0	0
Fisher	.995	22	169	13	1	13
Haynal	.987	33	291	20	4	26
Reyes	.989	10	77	11	1	6

Second Base	PCT	G	PO	A	E	DP
Alfonzo	.966	50	93	160	9	27
Chavez	.842	4	9	7	3	2
Fernandez Jr.	.934	16	32	39	5	7
Munden	.963	13	26	26	2	4

Third Base	PCT	G	PO	A	E	DP
Chavez	.833	4	2	3	1	0
Cranmer	.850	25	11	40	9	0
Fernandez Jr.	.864	18	12	26	6	0
Lopez	1.000	8	6	21	0	3

Third Base	PCT	G	PO	A	E	DP
Munden	.892	25	13	45	7	3
Reyes	.750	4	4	5	3	2

Shortstop	PCT	G	PO	A	E	DP
Alfonzo	.949	14	22	34	3	7
Munden	.909	5	8	12	2	4

Seymour	.899	61	97	160	29	29

Outfield	PCT	G	PO	A	E	DP
Barrett	.900	4	6	3	1	1
Brewster	.949	41	68	6	4	1
Fernandez Jr.	.867	7	11	2	2	1
Fisher	.909	8	10	0	1	0
Garrett	.985	58	126	3	2	0
Moscat	.848	41	53	3	10	1
Newell	.933	14	14	0	1	0
Ramirez	.951	23	38	1	2	1
Rawe	.955	33	58	5	3	0
Soto	.750	4	6	0	2	0
Williams	.500	1	2	0	2	0

GCL MARLINS   ROOKIE

GULF COAST LEAGUE

Batting	B-T	HT	WT	DOB	AVG	vLH	vRH	G	AB	R	H	2B	3B	HR	RBI	BB	HBP	SH	SF	SO	SB	CS	SLG	OBP
Almonte, Erwin	L-L	6-0	170	2-22-95	.228	.250	.222	29	92	7	21	0	0	1	7	8	1	0	1	9	0	1	.261	.294
Avello, Roger	R-R	6-2	189	12-5-94	.263	.211	.281	28	76	8	20	3	0	0	9	6	1	1	2	19	3	2	.303	.318
Bennett, Terry	L-L	5-11	195	9-3-96	.193	.056	.229	31	88	15	17	3	1	0	6	5	2	0	1	33	0	1	.250	.250
Castro, Samuel	B-R	5-10	160	10-16-97	.265	.250	.270	54	200	36	53	6	3	0	13	14	7	4	2	41	10	6	.325	.332
Chavez, Joe	R-R	6-0	195	6-26-93	.338	.360	.327	27	80	12	27	4	0	2	15	13	0	1	0	23	2	3	.463	.430
Cohen, Justin	R-R	6-0	190	9-26-96	.321	.167	.364	18	56	10	18	4	0	2	12	5	0	1	1	24	1	0	.500	.371
Cordova, Rehiner	B-R	6-0	150	1-11-94	.267	.333	.222	6	15	2	4	1	0	0	5	7	2	0	0	5	0	0	.333	.542
Fernandez Jr., Alex	R-R	5-10	180	3-30-93	.226	.286	.208	8	31	5	7	2	0	1	2	3	0	1	0	14	1	0	.387	.294
Flynn, Cameron	L-R	6-0	195	2-24-90	.200	.000	.286	3	10	2	2	0	1	0	2	2	0	0	0	2	0	0	.400	.333
Foley, Matt	R-R	6-4	230	4-15-94	.130	.286	.063	13	23	2	3	0	0	0	3	2	0	0	0	9	0	0	.130	.200
Garcia, Pablo	B-R	5-10	170	9-26-96	.244	.121	.284	42	135	14	33	1	0	1	14	7	3	0	1	16	5	1	.274	.295
Goodman, Kris	R-R	6-1	193	1-5-93	.236	.222	.241	30	72	5	17	1	0	1	4	8	5	1	0	16	2	5	.292	.353
Lara, Garvis	L-R	6-1	170	5-19-96	.281	.313	.271	53	192	27	54	3	5	0	16	17	0	9	2	41	13	2	.349	.336
Llera, Robert	R-R	6-0	205	8-3-93	.250	.250	.250	14	36	3	9	1	0	0	2	3	2	0	1	10	1	0	.278	.333
Lopez, Javier	R-R	6-3	180	9-13-94	.250	.200	.265	31	108	10	27	4	2	0	13	7	1	1	2	20	2	3	.324	.297
Munoz, Luis	L-R	6-1	200	6-4-95	.214	.182	.222	20	56	7	12	0	0	2	3	4	0	0	2	23	2	0	.232	.302
Naylor, Josh	L-L	6-1	225	6-22-97	.327	.320	.329	25	98	8	32	4	1	1	16	4	1	0	2	11	1	0	.418	.352
Newell, Cameron	R-L	6-1	195	8-1-91	.309	.333	.302	19	55	6	17	2	0	0	3	7	0	1	0	13	4	3	.345	.387
Patterson, Chase	R-R	5-11	185	9-11-93	.091	.000	.118	8	22	3	2	1	0	0	1	4	0	0	0	12	1	0	.136	.231
Ramirez, Yuniel	R-R	6-1	215	12-22-88	.245	.308	.225	14	53	5	13	4	1	0	7	1	0	2	0	12	2	1	.358	.259
Rawe, Brandon	R-R	6-2	190	6-19-93	.182	.500	.111	4	11	0	2	0	0	0	1	0	0	0	0	4	1	0	.182	.182
Reyes, Angel	R-R	6-0	175	5-6-95	.244	.188	.257	23	90	12	22	2	2	2	13	4	0	0	1	16	1	0	.378	.274
Santos, Jhonny	R-R	6-0	160	10-2-96	.301	.364	.282	53	186	24	56	6	0	1	21	14	2	0	1	16	6	4	.349	.355
Soto, Isael	L-L	6-0	190	11-2-96	.346	.333	.353	7	26	3	9	2	1	1	5	5	0	0	1	6	0	1	.615	.438
White, Isaiah	R-R	6-0	170	1-7-97	.294	.281	.298	35	126	19	37	7	2	0	8	3	2	1	0	44	13	0	.381	.321

Pitching	B-T	HT	WT	DOB	W	L	ERA	G	GS	CG	SV	IP	H	R	ER	HR	BB	SO	AVG	vLH	vRH	K/9	BB/9
Arroyo, Octavio	R-R	6-0	175	8-16-96	0	0	0.00	1	0	0	0	1	2	0	0	0	0	2	.400	.000	.667	18.00	0.00
Brewster, L.J.	R-R	6-2	205	5-2-94	0	0	0.90	9	0	0	0	10	7	3	1	0	1	5	.194	.231	.174	4.50	0.90
Britt, Curt	L-R	6-0	220	3-5-93	0	0	0.00	1	1	0	0	1	1	0	0	0	0	0	.333	—	.333	0.00	0.00
Brown, Danny	R-R	5-10	165	2-20-93	0	0	4.50	1	0	0	0	2	3	2	1	0	1	3	.333	.500	.286	13.50	4.50
Cabrera, Yordy	R-R	6-1	205	9-3-90	1	0	2.16	7	1	0	0	8	7	3	2	1	3	7	.212	.455	.091	7.56	3.24
De La Rosa, Leurys	R-R	6-2	160	11-5-94	1	0	2.36	15	0	0	1	27	22	11	7	1	3	24	.212	.194	.219	8.10	1.01
Diaz, Jose	R-R	6-2	180	5-7-93	3	2	4.06	11	7	0	0	51	49	24	23	3	12	31	.255	.259	.254	5.47	2.12
Diaz, Obed	R-R	6-3	155	5-7-93	1	3	5.96	11	2	0	0	23	26	16	15	1	9	14	.292	.355	.259	5.56	3.57
Guerrero, Alberto	R-R	6-3	192	12-13-97	1	2	3.46	6	5	0	0	26	16	11	10	0	10	17	.182	.154	.194	5.88	3.46
Guzman, Kevin	R-R	6-3	165	11-6-94	3	1	5.12	5	4	0	0	19	22	11	11	0	4	20	.282	.250	.300	9.31	1.86
Kines, Gunnar	R-R	6-3	210	7-25-93	3	2	1.44	14	1	0	5	31	26	7	5	0	1	28	.224	.185	.236	8.04	0.29
Kinley, Jeff	L-L	6-1	195	2-15-92	2	0	0.84	5	0	0	1	11	7	1	1	0	2	9	.189	.200	.185	7.59	1.69
Kinley, Tyler	R-R	6-4	205	1-31-91	1	0	0.00	2	1	0	0	3	2	0	0	0	0	3	.200	.250	.167	9.00	0.00
Kline, Breck	R-R	5-11	200	3-9-92	0	1	5.11	8	0	0	1	12	11	8	7	1	9	10	.224	.333	.189	7.30	6.57
Koch, Brandon	R-R	6-4	210	12-7-95	0	0	0.79	8	0	0	3	11	3	1	1	0	2	11	.125	.333	.036	8.74	1.59
2-team total (2 Orioles)					0	0	0.59	10	0	0	3	15	8	4	1	1	4	16	—	—	—	9.39	2.35
Lacosse, Trevor	L-L	5-11	185	10-5-92	1	1	7.27	6	0	0	0	9	11	10	7	0	6	3	.324	.000	.379	3.12	6.23
Langley, Justin	L-L	6-6	225	9-8-94	0	2	9.64	3	1	0	0	5	7	6	5	0	3	0	.333	.571	.214	0.00	5.79
Lara, Erick	R-R	6-2	150	3-24-94	2	0	5.63	5	0	0	0	8	12	7	5	0	3	7	.343	.300	.360	7.88	3.38
McKay, Ryan	R-R	6-4	195	9-20-96	1	3	4.15	10	7	0	0	35	42	22	16	0	21	17	.300	.302	.299	4.41	5.45
Meyer, Ben	R-R	6-6	200	1-30-93	0	0	0.00	4	0	0	2	7	2	0	0	0	1	8	.095	.000	.118	10.29	1.29
Newell, Ryan	R-R	6-2	215	6-18-91	0	0	0.00	3	0	0	1	11	3	0	0	0	2	11	.086	.083	.087	9.00	1.64
Osoria, Aneury	R-R	6-7	170	11-15-93	1	2	4.67	10	0	0	0	17	11	14	9	0	9	15	.186	.100	.231	7.79	4.67
Ovalle, Jeremy	R-R	6-3	185	1-17-97	0	0	5.40	1	0	0	0	2	1	1	1	0	0	1	.167	.000	.200	5.40	0.00
Paddack, Chris	R-R	6-4	195	1-8-96	4	3	2.18	11	7	0	0	45	37	14	11	1	7	39	.219	.186	.236	7.74	1.39
Peace, R.J.	R-R	6-2	175	6-24-97	2	1	2.64	9	6	1	0	31	33	10	9	0	11	19	.270	.350	.232	5.58	3.23
Perez, Yonqueli	R-R	6-4	175	6-6-93	1	2	12.00	9	0	0	0	12	16	16	16	1	21	10	.319	.455	.278	7.50	15.75
Peters, Dillon	L-L	5-9	195	8-31-92	1	1	0.68	4	4	0	0	13	10	4	1	0	2	13	.217	.333	.176	8.78	1.13
Quijada, Jose	L-L	6-0	175	11-9-95	0	0	0.00	6	0	1	3	8	1	0	0	0	3	13	.038	.000	.063	7.88	1.13
Ramos, Felix	B-L	6-0	175	12-2-93	0	0	9.00	3	0	0	1	3	3	4	3	0	4	4	.211	.000	.250	7.20	7.20
Rivas, Kelvin	R-R	6-3	250	6-5-92	0	0	3.86	1	1	0	0	2	1	1	1	0	2	3	.143	.500	.000	11.57	7.71
Simpson, Tucker	R-R	6-5	230	5-12-93	0	0	1.33	7	0	0	1	20	7	3	3	0	6	21	.104	.087	.114	9.30	2.66
Smigelski, Jacob	R-R	6-3	200	6-20-92	3	1	3.97	13	0	0	0	23	19	14	10	0	15	22	.226	.174	.246	8.74	5.96

Fielding

Catcher	PCT	G	PO	A	E	DP	PB
Cohen	.978	17	76	12	2	2	2
Foley	1.000	8	28	2	0	0	0
Garcia	1.000	33	176	30	0	0	9
Llera	.981	14	89	13	2	1	0
Patterson	1.000	3	19	5	0	1	0

First Base	PCT	G	PO	A	E	DP
Almonte	.995	23	182	15	1	16
Chavez	1.000	5	38	1	0	2
Goodman	1.000	2	20	0	0	2
Munoz	.971	16	95	6	3	3
Naylor	.995	19	175	6	1	12
Reyes	1.000	1	5	0	0	0

Second Base	PCT	G	PO	A	E	DP
Castro	.973	44	82	95	5	11
Chavez	.964	14	21	33	2	8
Cordova	1.000	1	0	3	0	0
Fernandez Jr.	.938	3	9	6	1	2
Goodman	.818	4	6	3	2	0

Third Base	PCT	G	PO	A	E	DP
Chavez	.917	5	2	9	1	0

Cordova	1.000	2	0	4	0	0
Fernandez Jr.	.909	3	3	7	1	1
Goodman	.904	18	15	32	5	3
Lopez	.918	22	14	42	5	3
Reyes	.909	11	8	22	3	1
Roberts	1.000	1	0	3	0	0

Shortstop	PCT	G	PO	A	E	DP
Castro	.872	12	8	26	5	3
Cordova	.667	1	1	1	1	1
Goodman	1.000	1	1	1	0	0
Lara	.922	47	76	149	19	19
Lopez	.800	5	5	11	4	2

Outfield	PCT	G	PO	A	E	DP
Avello	.957	26	43	1	2	0
Bennett	1.000	27	44	0	0	0

Cordova	1.000	2	3	0	0	0
Flynn	1.000	3	7	0	0	0
Foley	.800	3	4	0	1	0
Goodman	1.000	2	1	0	0	0
Keys	1.000	5	5	0	0	0
Munoz	—	1	0	0	0	0
Newell	1.000	18	32	0	0	0
Ramirez	.892	13	31	2	4	1
Rawe	1.000	4	8	0	0	0
Reyes	—	1	0	0	0	0
Santos	.978	53	84	5	2	3
Soto	1.000	2	4	0	0	0
White	.978	34	87	4	2	0

DSL MARLINS

DOMINICAN SUMMER LEAGUE

ROOKIE

Batting	B-T	HT	WT	DOB	AVG	vLH	vRH	G	AB	R	H	2B	3B	HR	RBI	BB	HBP	SH	SF	SO	SB	CS	SLG	OBP
Acosta, Leisman	L-R	5-9	150	1-12-97	.196	.167	.214	12	46	5	9	3	0	0	9	5	0	0	1	6	1	1	.261	.269
Alcala, Luis	L-R	6-2	180	9-21-96	.100	.000	.333	3	10	1	1	0	0	0	0	1	0	0	0	5	0	0	.100	.182
Arosemena, Felix	R-R	5-9	150	1-17-97	.296	.200	.353	6	27	2	8	2	1	0	0	1	0	0	0	1	2	3	.444	.321
Bautista, Welbin	R-R	6-0	180	5-7-98	.216	.340	.174	53	194	20	42	7	0	0	15	13	2	0	0	48	1	1	.253	.273
Borges, Juan	R-R	6-2	160	1-6-98	.182	.136	.199	63	225	18	41	6	1	0	14	11	1	1	0	52	3	1	.218	.224
Capellan, Christian	R-R	6-4	210	12-5-97	.125	.154	.116	18	56	6	7	2	0	1	5	5	2	0	1	32	1	1	.214	.219
Castro, Anderson	R-R	6-3	200	1-10-98	.190	.250	.170	18	63	5	12	2	1	0	4	5	1	0	1	27	0	0	.254	.257
Figuereo, Miguel	R-R	6-2	185	12-20-95	.000	—	.000	2	4	0	0	0	0	0	0	0	0	0	0	2	0	0	.000	.000
Guerrero, Jesus	R-R	6-0	180	8-30-96	.231	.278	.218	48	169	19	39	9	1	2	23	10	10	0	3	39	1	2	.331	.307
Guzman, Josue	L-L	6-3	175	5-30-96	.233	.140	.263	62	210	23	49	7	0	3	25	38	4	0	1	51	5	3	.310	.360
Lizarraga, Jose	R-R	5-10	170	8-27-97	.246	.271	.237	61	187	19	46	7	0	0	19	28	13	1	3	22	1	2	.283	.377
Olivo, Benito	R-R	6-0	185	7-11-94	.296	.294	.296	21	71	14	21	5	2	0	6	12	1	0	0	20	6	1	.423	.405
Reyes, Yefry	L-R	5-10	160	12-18-96	.266	.350	.239	63	244	31	65	8	4	2	20	21	4	4	1	42	3	4	.357	.333
Reynoso, Ronal	L-R	6-1	165	5-23-98	.197	.236	.180	55	183	21	36	3	2	0	6	17	4	0	2	83	12	9	.235	.277
Rivera, Marcos	R-R	6-1	160	5-13-97	.224	.269	.212	64	241	41	54	15	3	1	24	31	4	1	3	64	10	1	.324	.319
Soto, Sleyter	R-R	6-2	195	8-14-97	.297	.341	.285	50	192	26	57	5	2	2	31	12	4	0	3	22	1	1	.375	.346
Villalobos, Andres	B-R	5-11	160	1-14-98	.223	.241	.218	40	130	12	29	2	0	0	6	16	2	0	1	14	2	1	.238	.315

Pitching	B-T	HT	WT	DOB	W	L	ERA	G	GS	CG	SV	IP	H	R	ER	HR	BB	SO	AVG	vLH	vRH	K/9	BB/9
Atizol, Mauricio	L-L	6-3	180	9-2-96	1	0	6.00	6	0	0	0	15	14	13	10	1	12	14	.246	.750	.208	8.40	7.20
Baez, Gabriel	L-L	6-1	185	4-18-98	2	4	3.49	14	0	0	0	28	23	23	11	0	17	20	.211	.059	.239	6.35	5.40
Cetin, Fauri	L-L	6-1	185	4-8-98	0	0	10.42	11	0	0	0	19	23	25	22	1	18	22	.288	.294	.286	10.42	8.53
De La Cruz, Angel	R-R	6-4	170	10-18-93	0	3	5.91	10	1	0	2	21	25	14	14	1	12	10	.298	.292	.300	4.22	5.06
De Oleo, Dailyn	R-R	6-2	190	11-27-97	1	2	3.77	16	0	0	4	31	28	19	13	0	15	17	.237	.192	.250	4.94	4.35
Fermin, Ronny	R-R	6-5	190	4-6-98	0	1	11.48	4	4	0	0	13	20	19	17	0	5	13	.357	.500	.326	8.78	3.38
Frias, Julio	L-L	6-2	160	6-1-98	1	4	3.86	13	4	0	1	23	20	19	10	0	17	22	.233	.357	.208	8.49	6.56
Garboza, Daniel	R-R	6-3	190	10-20-97	0	3	6.40	14	0	0	1	32	43	31	23	0	14	22	.316	.343	.307	6.12	3.90
Garcia, Javier	R-R	6-2	230	2-26-98	3	2	1.65	10	8	0	0	49	35	12	9	1	14	35	.202	.182	.212	6.43	2.57
Gonzalez, Eddy	R-R	6-6	175	9-28-94	0	1	3.68	14	0	0	0	29	21	18	12	0	34	29	.196	.292	.169	8.90	10.43
Guerrero, Alberto	R-R	6-3	192	12-13-97	0	2	4.11	4	4	0	0	15	18	15	7	0	7	16	.295	.143	.375	9.39	4.11
Liriano, Edin	B-L	6-4	185	6-25-97	1	3	3.52	9	1	0	1	23	19	11	9	1	10	17	.235	.250	.231	6.65	3.91
Mejia, Humberto	R-R	6-3	175	3-3-97	3	3	1.69	13	3	0	0	75	58	20	14	1	14	71	.216	.151	.240	8.56	1.69
Mojica, Luis	R-R	6-1	190	2-18-98	3	5	4.81	12	11	0	0	49	63	36	26	0	21	37	.312	.333	.305	6.84	3.88
Rodriguez, Manuel	L-L	6-2	160	12-23-96	6	5	2.86	16	10	0	1	72	71	30	23	0	18	50	.256	.260	.256	6.22	2.24
Ulloa, Brayan	L-L	6-1	180	2-25-95	0	6	4.95	17	6	0	3	44	41	37	24	1	29	43	.243	.417	.195	8.86	5.98
Vera, Anderson	R-R	6-3	185	10-14-97	2	2	4.91	17	3	0	0	37	36	26	20	3	15	24	.261	.324	.240	5.89	3.68

Fielding

Catcher	PCT	G	PO	A	E	DP	PB
Bautista	.971	26	169	30	6	2	18
Guerrero	.977	29	176	32	5	0	14
Lizarraga	.989	22	148	28	2	4	7
Villalobos	1.000	1	3	0	0	0	0

First Base	PCT	G	PO	A	E	DP
Bautista	.982	12	100	7	2	7
Figuereo	.667	1	2	0	1	0
Guerrero	1.000	11	77	7	0	8
Guzman	.979	12	88	7	2	5
Lizarraga	.987	36	294	14	4	29
Rivera	1.000	1	1	0	0	0
Solano	.980	7	47	2	1	4

Second Base	PCT	G	PO	A	E	DP
Acosta	.935	6	14	15	2	4
Arosemena	1.000	3	6	7	0	0

Reyes	.951	48	105	128	12	38
Reynoso	1.000	1	3	2	0	2
Villalobos	.970	16	31	34	2	6

Third Base	PCT	G	PO	A	E	DP
Acosta	1.000	3	1	8	0	2
Alcala	1.000	2	2	2	0	0
Figuereo	.500	1	0	2	2	0
Lizarraga	.000	1	0	0	1	0

Third Base	PCT	G	PO	A	E	DP
Reyes	.794	13	4	23	7	2
Reynoso	.822	13	14	23	8	2
Rivera	.924	20	20	41	5	5
Solano	.911	13	14	27	4	4
Villalobos	.959	11	12	35	2	4

Shortstop	PCT	G	PO	A	E	DP
Arosemena	.944	3	5	12	1	1

Reynoso	.892	22	37	54	11	11
Rivera	.916	43	63	123	17	21
Villalobos	1.000	6	10	10	0	2

Outfield	PCT	G	PO	A	E	DP
Alcala	1.000	1	1	0	0	0
Arosemena	1.000	1	2	0	0	0
Bautista	1.000	5	3	0	0	0
Borges	.965	61	129	9	5	3
Capellan	.917	15	21	1	2	0
Castro	.970	17	30	2	1	1
De Oleo	1.000	1	0	1	0	0
Guzman	.936	43	83	5	6	1
Olivo	1.000	16	25	1	0	1
Reynoso	.867	9	13	0	2	0
Solano	.955	11	20	1	1	0
Soto	.965	50	75	7	3	1

MIAMI MARLINS

Milwaukee Brewers

SEASON IN A SENTENCE: The collapse of 2014 bled into 2015 and the Brewers were sunk by losing 18 of 23 to begin the year.

HIGH POINT: The Brew Crew was far out of the race by this time, but won eight in a row from June 28 to July 5. Also encouraging was the bounce-back of Ryan Braun, especially considering his contractural status.

LOW POINT: An eight-game losing streak that began April 15 doomed the Brewers to second-division status and ultimately cost manager Ron Roenicke and general manager Doug Melvin their jobs. Craig Counsell took over as manager and former Astros executive David Stearns was hired as GM after the season.

NOTABLE ROOKIES: Righthander Taylor Jungmann, a 2011 first-round pick, was the team's best starter as Kyle Lohse, Wily Peralta and Matt Garza all experienced poor seasons. Righthander Corey Knebel, a Tigers' 2013 supplemental first-round pick struck out more than a batter per inning out of the bullpen, while under-the-radar righty Michael Blazek pitched to a 2.43 ERA in relief. Right fielder Domingo Santana, acquired at the deadline, hit six homers but also struck out 46 times in 145 at-bats. Luis Sardinas flashed an above-average glove at short but hit just .196 in limited action and slight righthander Zach Davies, acquired from the Orioles for Gerardo Parra, was solid in six late-season starts.

KEY TRANSACTIONS: Going nowhere, the Brewers managed to turn a debacle into a plus in July. Following the social media-mess that engulfed the failed trade of Carlos Gomez to the Mets, Melvin turned around and traded the center fielder to the Astros for their top prospect in outfielder Brett Phillips, right fielder Domingo Santana, and two useful arms in Adrian Houser and Josh Hader. All four will rank among the Brewers' top 15 prospects. Davies was another trade-deadline acquisition and figures to battle for a rotation spot next season.

DOWN ON THE FARM: Hader and Houser prop up a farm system that lacks arms, while Phillips probably will rank right behind shortstop Orlando Arcia on the Brewers Top 30 Prospects list. Arcia is very nearly ready for the majors, which might necessitate a trade of shortstop Jean Segura. Righthander Jorge Lopez, who had the best year of any Brewers' pitching prospect, made his major league debut in September.

OPENING DAY PAYROLL: $105,002,536 (19th)

PLAYERS OF THE YEAR

MAJOR LEAGUE	MINOR LEAGUE
Ryan Braun of	**Orlando Arcia** ss
.285/.356/.498	(Double-A)
25 HR and 84 RBIs	.307/.347/.453
Club-best 3.8 oWAR	50 extra-base hits

ORGANIZATION LEADERS

BATTING		*Minimum 250 AB
MAJORS		
* AVG	Ryan Braun	.285
* OPS	Ryan Braun	.854
HR	Khris Davis	27
RBI	Adam Lind	87
MINORS		
* AVG	Garrett Cooper, Brevard County, Biloxi	.310
* OBP	Nathan Orf, Biloxi	.378
* SLG	Matt Clark, Colo. Springs	.492
R	Orlando Arcia, Biloxi	74
H	Orlando Arcia, Biloxi	157
TB	Matt Clark, Col. Springs	235
2B	Orlando Arcia, Biloxi	37
3B	4 players	7
HR	Matt Clark, Col. Springs	20
RBI	Matt Clark, Col. Springs	77
BB	Michael Reed, Biloxi, Col. Springs	73
SO	Taylor Brennan, Brevard County	158
	Victor Roache, Brevard County, Biloxi	158
SB	Omar Garcia, Brevard County	53

PITCHING		#Minimum 75 IP
MAJORS		
W	Jimmy Nelson	11
# ERA	Jimmy Nelson	4.11
SO	Jimmy Nelson	148
SV	Francisco Rodriguez	38
MINORS		
W	Jorge Lopez, Biloxi	12
L	Drew Gagnon, Col. Springs, Biloxi	12
	Josh Roenicke, Col. Springs	12
# ERA	Tyler Wagner, Biloxi	2.25
G	Jaye Chapman, Biloxi, Colo. Springs	59
GS	Hiram Burgos, Brev. County, Biloxi, Colo. Springs	27
SV	Damien Magnifico, Biloxi	20
IP	Tyler Wagner, Biloxi	152
BB	Hobbs Johnson, Biloxi	77
SO	Hiram Burgos, Brevard Cty, Biloxi, Colo. Springs	148
AVG	Jorge Lopez, Biloxi	.205

2015 PERFORMANCE

General Manager: Doug Melvin/David Stearns. **Farm Director:** Reid Nichols. **Scouting Director:** Ray Montgomery.

Class	Team	League	W	L	PCT	Finish	Manager
Majors	Milwaukee Brewers	National	68	94	.420	t-11th (15)	R. Roenicke/C. Counsell
Triple-A	Colorado Springs Sky Sox	Pacific Coast	62	81	.434	13th (16)	Rick Sweet
Double-A	Biloxi Shuckers	Southern	78	59	.569	1st (10)	Carlos Subero
High A	Brevard County Manatees	Florida State	55	80	.407	12th (12)	Joe Ayrault
Low A	Wisconsin Timber Rattlers	Midwest	50	89	.360	15th (16)	Matt Erickson
Rookie	Helena Brewers	Pioneer	32	42	.432	8th (8)	Tony Diggs
Rookie	Brewers	Arizona	23	33	.411	t-12th (14)	Nestor Corredor
Overall 2015 Minor League Record			300	384	.439	28th (30)	

ORGANIZATION STATISTICS

MILWAUKEE BREWERS

NATIONAL LEAGUE

Batting	B-T	HT	WT	DOB	AVG	vLH	vRH	G	AB	R	H	2B	3B	HR	RBI	BB	HBP	SH	SF	SO	SB	CS	SLG	OBP
Ashley, Nevin	R-R	6-1	215	8-14-84	.100	.000	.133	12	20	2	2	1	0	0	1	0	0	1	0	8	0	0	.150	.143
Braun, Ryan	R-R	6-2	205	11-17-83	.285	.317	.275	140	506	87	144	27	3	25	84	54	4	0	3	115	24	4	.498	.356
Centeno, Juan	L-R	5-9	195	11-16-89	.048	.500	.000	10	21	0	1	1	0	0	0	2	0	0	0	7	0	0	.095	.130
Davis, Khris	R-R	5-10	195	12-21-87	.247	.212	.260	121	392	54	97	16	2	27	66	44	1	0	3	122	6	2	.505	.323
Gennett, Scooter	L-R	5-10	185	5-1-90	.264	.114	.279	114	375	42	99	18	4	6	29	12	4	0	6	68	1	3	.381	.294
Gomez, Carlos	R-R	6-3	220	12-4-85	.262	.203	.278	74	286	42	75	20	1	8	43	23	5	0	0	70	7	6	.423	.328
Gomez, Hector	R-R	6-2	195	3-5-88	.181	—		66	127	15	23	11	2	1	7	3	2	2	0	40	0	0	.323	.212
Herrera, Elian	B-R	5-11	205	2-1-85	.242	.207	.259	83	256	29	62	18	0	7	33	18	0	1	2	72	3	1	.395	.290
Jimenez, Luis	R-R	6-1	205	1-18-88	.067	.000	.125	15	15	1	1	0	0	0	1	0	0	0	0	6	0	0	.067	.125
Lind, Adam	L-L	6-2	195	7-17-83	.277	.221	.291	149	502	72	139	32	0	20	87	66	1	0	3	100	0	0	.460	.360
Lucroy, Jonathan	R-R	6-0	195	6-13-86	.264	.255	.267	103	371	51	98	20	3	7	43	36	1	1	6	64	1	0	.391	.326
Maldonado, Martin	R-R	6-0	225	8-16-86	.210	.245	.199	79	229	19	48	7	0	4	22	23	1	1	2	65	0	1	.293	.282
Parra, Gerardo	L-L	5-11	210	5-6-87	.328	.292	.335	100	323	53	106	24	5	9	31	20	3	1	4	57	9	3	.517	.369
Perez, Hernan	R-R	6-1	185	3-26-91	.270	.267	.271	90	230	13	62	15	2	1	21	4	0	3	1	48	4	1	.365	.281
Peterson, Shane	L-L	6-0	210	2-11-88	.259	.237	.264	93	201	22	52	7	3	2	16	20	0	3	1	55	0	1	.353	.324
Ramirez, Aramis	R-R	6-1	205	6-25-78	.247	.170	.265	81	279	25	69	18	0	11	42	16	4	0	3	42	1	0	.430	.295
2-team total (56 Pittsburgh)					.246	—		137	475	43	117	31	1	17	75	31	5	0	5	68	1	0	.423	.297
Reed, Michael	R-R	6-0	190	11-18-92	.333	.500	.250	7	6	2	2	1	0	0	0	0	0	0	0	3	0	0	.500	.333
Rivera, Yadiel	R-R	6-3	180	5-2-92	.071	.000	.091	7	14	0	1	0	0	0	0	0	0	1	0	4	0	0	.071	.071
Rogers, Jason	R-R	6-1	255	3-13-88	.296	.271	.317	86	152	22	45	6	2	4	16	15	2	0	0	34	0	0	.441	.367
Santana, Domingo	R-R	6-5	225	8-5-92	.231	.344	.191	38	121	14	28	5	0	6	18	18	4	0	2	46	2	0	.421	.345
Sardinas, Luis	B-R	6-1	150	5-16-93	.196	.136	.213	36	97	8	19	0	1	0	4	6	0	1	1	25	0	0	.216	.240
Schafer, Logan	L-L	6-1	190	9-8-86	.221	.160	.237	69	122	17	27	6	1	1	6	12	2	6	1	29	1	0	.311	.299
Segura, Jean	R-R	5-10	205	3-17-90	.257	.283	.248	142	560	57	144	16	5	6	50	13	6	3	2	93	25	6	.336	.281

Pitching	B-T	HT	WT	DOB	W	L	ERA	G	GS	CG	SV	IP	H	R	ER	HR	BB	SO	AVG	vLH	vRH	K/9	BB/9
Barrios, Yhonathan	B-R	5-10	200	12-1-91	0	0	0.00	5	0	0	0	7	3	0	0	0	0	7	.136	.100	.167	9.45	0.00
Blazek, Michael	R-R	6-0	205	3-16-89	5	3	2.43	45	0	0	0	56	40	17	15	3	18	47	.200	.184	.212	7.60	2.91
Broxton, Jonathan	R-R	6-4	305	6-16-84	1	2	5.89	40	0	0	0	37	41	24	24	5	10	37	.287	.349	.238	9.08	2.45
2-team total (26 St. Louis)					4	5	4.62	66	0	0	0	60	61	32	31	7	22	63	—	—	—	9.40	3.28
Cotts, Neal	L-L	6-2	200	3-25-80	1	0	3.26	51	0	0	0	50	44	18	18	9	17	49	.239	.185	.282	8.88	3.08
Cravy, Tyler	R-R	6-2	210	7-13-89	0	8	5.70	14	7	0	0	43	47	30	27	5	22	35	.281	.263	.299	7.38	4.64
Davies, Zach	R-R	6-0	160	2-7-93	3	2	3.71	6	6	0	0	34	26	14	14	2	15	24	.211	.120	.274	6.35	3.97
Fiers, Mike	R-R	6-2	200	6-15-85	5	9	3.89	21	21	0	0	118	117	57	51	14	43	121	.259	.248	.268	9.23	3.28
Garza, Matt	R-R	6-4	215	11-26-83	6	14	5.63	26	25	0	0	149	176	102	93	23	57	104	.294	.303	.286	6.30	3.45
Goforth, David	R-R	5-10	205	10-11-88	1	0	4.01	20	0	0	0	25	32	13	11	4	8	24	.323	.359	.300	8.76	2.92
Guilmet, Preston	R-R	6-2	200	7-27-87	0	0	27.00	2	0	0	0	2	4	6	6	1	2	1	.444	.500	.429	4.50	9.00
Houser, Adrian	R-R	6-4	230	2-2-93	0	0	0.00	2	0	0	0	2	1	0	0	0	2	0	.167	.333	.000	0.00	9.00
Jeffress, Jeremy	R-R	6-0	215	9-21-87	5	0	2.65	72	0	0	0	68	64	22	20	5	22	67	.249	.272	.236	8.87	2.91
Jimenez, Cesar	L-L	6-0	215	11-12-84	0	0	3.66	16	0	0	0	20	16	8	8	2	8	21	.219	.208	.224	9.61	3.66
2-team total (3 Philadelphia)					0	0	3.13	19	0	0	0	23	17	8	8	2	8	25	—	—	—	9.78	3.13
Jungmann, Taylor	R-R	6-6	220	12-18-89	9	8	3.77	21	21	1	0	119	106	55	50	11	47	107	.241	.259	.225	8.07	3.54
Kintzler, Brandon	R-R	5-10	190	8-1-84	0	1	6.43	7	0	0	0	7	12	6	5	1	5	7	.387	.385	.389	9.00	6.43
Knebel, Corey	R-R	6-4	210	11-26-91	0	0	3.22	48	0	0	0	50	44	18	18	8	17	58	.232	.222	.239	10.37	3.04
Lohse, Kyle	R-R	6-2	215	10-4-78	5	13	5.85	37	22	0	2	152	180	99	99	29	43	108	.297	.285	.307	6.38	2.54
Lopez, Jorge	R-R	6-3	190	2-10-93	1	1	5.40	2	2	0	0	10	14	6	6	0	5	10	.350	.400	.320	9.00	4.50
Nelson, Jimmy	R-R	6-6	245	6-5-89	11	13	4.11	30	30	0	0	177	163	89	81	18	65	148	.246	.302	.202	7.51	3.30
Pena, Ariel	R-R	6-3	250	5-20-89	2	1	4.28	6	5	0	0	27	24	14	13	2	14	27	.238	.256	.226	8.89	4.61
Peralta, Wily	R-R	6-1	245	5-8-89	5	10	4.72	20	20	0	0	109	130	60	57	14	37	60	.302	.309	.295	4.97	3.06
Rodriguez, Francisco	R-R	6-0	195	1-7-82	1	3	2.21	60	0	0	38	57	38	15	14	6	11	62	.189	.206	.172	9.79	1.74
Smith, Will	R-L	6-5	260	7-10-89	7	2	2.70	76	0	0	0	63	52	23	19	5	24	91	.220	.257	.193	12.93	3.41
Thornburg, Tyler	R-R	5-11	190	9-29-88	0	2	3.64	18	0	0	0	34	31	22	14	7	12	34	.231	.232	.231	8.91	3.15
Wagner, Tyler	R-R	6-3	195	1-24-91	0	2	7.24	3	3	0	0	14	22	11	11	1	7	5	.386	.333	.424	3.29	4.61
Wooten, Rob	R-R	6-1	200	7-21-85	0	0	12.00	4	0	0	0	6	5	8	8	1	6	6	.227	.167	.300	9.00	9.00

Fielding

Catcher	PCT	G	PO	A	E	DP	PB
Ashley	1.000	8	41	3	0	0	0
Centeno	.979	7	44	3	1	0	1
Lucroy	.988	86	627	53	8	8	3
Maldonado	.985	74	561	34	9	7	3

First Base	PCT	G	PO	A	E	DP
Lind	.997	138	1098	82	4	124
Lucroy	1.000	7	46	1	0	6
Maldonado	1.000	1	2	0	0	0
Perez	1.000	3	6	1	0	1
Peterson	.944	2	16	1	1	1
Rogers	.995	24	209	10	1	12

Second Base	PCT	G	PO	A	E	DP
Gennett	.985	108	176	273	7	71
Gomez	—	1	0	0	0	0
Gomez	.988	27	31	54	1	16

	PCT	G	PO	A	E	DP
Herrera	.981	36	52	99	3	14
Jimenez	1.000	1	0	1	0	0
Perez	.980	14	21	28	1	4
Rivera	.938	4	5	10	1	5
Sardinas	1.000	16	23	32	0	12

Third Base	PCT	G	PO	A	E	DP
Gomez	.929	12	5	8	1	0
Herrera	.942	47	26	72	6	8
Jimenez	.857	7	2	4	1	1
Perez	.967	72	31	87	4	9
Ramirez	.970	74	40	119	5	14
Rivera	1.000	1	2	0	0	0
Rogers	.400	3	1	1	3	0
Sardinas	.833	3	1	4	1	1

Shortstop	PCT	G	PO	A	E	DP
Gomez	.931	8	10	17	2	5

	PCT	G	PO	A	E	DP
Perez	1.000	3	1	0	0	0
Rivera	1.000	2	5	8	0	3
Sardinas	.986	14	24	45	1	10
Segura	.969	140	177	426	19	98

Outfield	PCT	G	PO	A	E	DP
Braun	.991	130	205	5	2	1
Davis	.972	108	171	1	5	0
Gomez	.967	72	172	2	6	1
Gomez	—	1	0	0	0	0
Herrera	1.000	4	4	0	0	0
Parra	.988	89	154	4	2	0
Peterson	.970	52	94	4	3	1
Reed	1.000	3	4	0	0	0
Rogers	—	3	0	0	0	0
Santana	.953	36	60	1	3	0
Schafer	.973	50	70	1	2	0

COLORADO SPRINGS SKY SOX

TRIPLE-A

PACIFIC COAST LEAGUE

Batting	B-T	HT	WT	DOB	AVG	vLH	vRH	G	AB	R	H	2B	3B	HR	RBI	BB	HBP	SH	SF	SO	SB	CS	SLG	OBP
Ashley, Nevin	R-R	6-1	215	8-14-84	.306	.311	.302	94	337	52	103	14	4	8	61	32	7	1	4	72	0	2	.442	.374
Centeno, Juan	L-R	5-9	195	11-16-89	.295	.275	.304	51	176	11	52	6	3	0	24	5	1	1	4	19	2	2	.364	.312
Clark, Matt	L-R	6-5	230	12-10-86	.291	.295	.288	132	478	70	139	34	1	20	77	58	4	0	8	106	1	0	.492	.367
Diaz, Robinzon	R-R	5-11	220	9-19-83	.322	.327	.318	44	121	9	39	4	0	0	11	6	0	0	0	7	0	0	.355	.354
Dominguez, Matt	R-R	6-1	220	8-28-89	.281	.293	.274	72	267	37	75	21	1	6	30	15	3	0	2	37	0	0	.434	.324
2-team total (45 Fresno)					.269	—	—	117	442	51	119	30	1	10	56	19	9	1	4	65	0	0	.410	.310
Gennett, Scooter	L-R	5-10	185	5-1-90	.307	.375	.256	17	75	12	23	7	1	2	11	4	0	0	0	10	0	1	.507	.342
Guez, Ben	R-R	5-11	180	1-24-87	.287	.395	.222	38	115	25	33	7	0	6	19	22	2	2	0	32	8	0	.504	.410
Herrera, Elian	B-R	5-11	205	2-1-85	.357	.380	.339	56	210	33	75	15	2	3	27	20	0	3	0	29	4	1	.490	.413
Long, Matt	L-R	5-11	190	4-30-87	.260	.269	.255	132	446	65	116	29	7	7	54	43	2	3	7	97	11	5	.404	.323
Macias, Brandon	R-R	5-10	185	10-10-88	.250	.211	.270	23	56	7	14	3	1	0	3	5	0	0	0	7	1	0	.339	.311
Murphy, Donnie	R-R	5-10	190	3-10-83	.257	.343	.171	55	140	23	36	6	2	2	16	18	3	0	1	28	0	0	.371	.352
Nelson, Chris	R-R	5-11	205	9-3-85	.143	.080	.178	29	70	4	10	2	1	1	6	5	0	0	0	17	1	0	.243	.200
Orr, Pete	R-L	6-1	195	6-8-79	.303	.263	.319	103	337	56	102	14	5	2	46	20	6	6	7	51	15	4	.392	.346
Petersen, Bryan	L-R	6-0	200	4-9-86	.218	.188	.230	47	119	13	26	6	0	1	13	7	0	0	1	39	0	2	.294	.260
Peterson, Shane	L-L	6-0	210	2-11-88	.320	.385	.280	47	172	26	55	10	2	7	27	17	2	1	0	41	0	1	.523	.387
Reed, Michael	R-R	6-0	190	11-18-92	.246	.257	.242	38	126	19	31	13	2	0	21	20	1	0	1	31	1	0	.381	.351
Rivera, Yadiel	R-R	6-3	180	5-2-92	.238	.220	.249	81	290	32	69	8	4	1	28	10	2	2	2	53	4	3	.303	.266
Rogers, Jason	R-R	6-1	255	3-13-88	.344	.229	.419	33	122	25	42	8	0	8	24	24	0	0	1	23	0	0	.607	.449
Santana, Domingo	R-R	6-5	225	8-5-92	.380	.500	.349	20	79	13	30	5	1	2	18	6	0	0	0	17	1	1	.544	.424
2-team total (75 Fresno)					.333	—	—	95	354	75	118	23	4	18	77	54	3	0	0	108	2	5	.573	.426
Sardinas, Luis	R-B	6-1	150	5-16-93	.282	.268	.290	103	390	51	110	17	5	1	33	20	1	5	0	54	16	4	.359	.319
Schafer, Logan	L-L	6-1	190	9-8-86	.258	.276	.245	72	260	29	67	15	2	1	17	14	0	5	3	35	3	1	.342	.292
Wren, Kyle	L-L	5-10	175	4-23-91	.251	.245	.254	76	291	33	73	11	3	1	26	19	1	2	1	45	16	4	.320	.298

Pitching	B-T	HT	WT	DOB	W	L	ERA	G	GS	CG	SV	IP	H	R	ER	HR	BB	SO	AVG	vLH	vRH	K/9	BB/9
Additon, Nick	L-L	6-5	215	12-16-87	5	3	5.33	21	11	0	0	74	84	46	44	4	27	52	.292	.297	.289	6.30	3.27
Bradley, Jed	L-L	6-4	225	6-12-90	2	4	9.00	20	1	0	0	26	45	27	26	1	10	15	.388	.298	.449	5.19	3.46
Burgos, Hiram	R-R	5-11	210	8-4-87	3	4	3.35	15	15	0	0	81	66	34	30	5	28	65	.222	.229	.217	7.25	3.12
Chapman, Jaye	R-R	6-0	195	5-22-87	2	3	3.16	38	0	0	15	43	39	17	15	2	13	46	.241	.328	.192	9.70	2.74
Cravy, Tyler	R-R	6-2	210	7-13-89	7	7	3.07	17	17	0	0	95	92	44	42	6	31	75	.258	.255	.259	7.08	2.93
Davies, Zach	R-R	6-0	160	2-7-93	1	2	5.00	5	5	0	0	27	38	17	15	2	12	21	.333	.348	.324	7.00	4.00
Dillard, Tim	R-R	6-4	220	7-19-83	3	2	5.50	27	6	0	0	54	62	34	33	3	21	44	.292	.368	.250	7.33	3.50
Ely, John	R-R	6-2	210	5-13-86	0	0	9.39	2	2	0	0	8	11	8	8	0	5	3	.324	.409	.167	9.39	5.87
Gagnon, Drew	R-R	6-4	195	6-26-90	1	11	6.93	20	18	0	0	90	110	73	69	12	52	51	.316	.294	.335	5.12	5.22
Goforth, David	R-R	5-10	205	10-11-88	0	4	2.68	38	0	0	4	47	36	15	14	2	27	34	.217	.247	.191	6.51	5.17
Guilmet, Preston	R-R	6-2	200	7-27-87	2	2	2.50	13	0	0	1	18	11	5	5	0	4	14	.183	.095	.231	7.00	2.00
2-team total (3 Oklahoma City)					2	2	2.57	16	0	0	1	21	13	6	6	0	5	18	—	—	—	7.71	2.14
Henderson, Jim	L-R	6-5	220	10-21-82	1	1	4.55	29	1	0	2	30	31	15	15	4	17	25	.274	.275	.274	7.58	5.16
Horst, Jeremy	L-L	6-3	235	10-1-85	1	1	3.86	18	0	0	1	21	18	9	9	1	12	17	.231	.233	.229	7.29	5.14
Jungmann, Taylor	R-R	6-6	220	12-18-89	2	3	6.31	11	9	0	0	59	61	44	42	2	29	54	.272	.211	.318	8.19	4.40
Kintzler, Brandon	R-R	5-10	190	8-1-84	1	1	5.21	17	0	0	0	19	23	13	11	0	4	14	.303	.346	.280	6.63	1.89
Kirkman, Michael	L-L	6-4	215	9-18-86	3	1	2.81	33	0	0	1	32	19	11	10	1	28	34	.173	.155	.192	9.56	7.88
Knebel, Corey	R-R	6-4	210	11-26-91	1	2	4.70	16	0	0	6	15	14	8	8	1	7	22	.246	.219	.280	12.91	4.11
Leach, Brent	L-L	6-5	225	11-18-82	1	0	2.57	6	0	0	0	7	2	3	2	0	7	8	.091	.077	.111	9.00	2.57
Leroux, Chris	L-R	6-6	225	4-14-84	1	3	8.15	7	1	0	0	18	26	16	16	3	8	17	.347	.182	.476	8.66	4.08
Obispo, Wirfin	R-R	6-2	215	9-26-84	0	1	5.63	11	0	0	0	16	15	10	10	2	7	17	.254	.250	.258	9.56	3.94
Ortega, Jorge	R-R	6-1	165	6-20-93	1	0	1.50	1	1	0	0	6	8	1	1	0	1	3	.308	.364	.267	4.50	1.50
Pena, Ariel	R-R	6-3	250	5-20-89	2	2	4.14	43	0	0	0	83	77	41	38	7	32	83	.249	.224	.266	9.04	3.48
Perez, Chris	R-R	6-4	225	7-1-85	0	0	9.39	6	0	0	0	8	14	8	8	1	4	3	.389	.500	.278	3.52	4.70
Roenicke, Josh	R-R	6-3	205	8-4-82	7	12	6.15	25	23	0	0	123	173	92	84	15	39	71	.331	.306	.352	5.20	2.85
Ross, Austin	R-R	6-2	200	8-12-88	3	1	6.96	23	0	0	0	32	48	27	25	2	14	31	.343	.377	.322	8.63	3.90

Pitching

Pitching	B-T	HT	WT	DOB	W	L	ERA	G	GS	CG	SV	IP	H	R	ER	HR	BB	SO	AVG	vLH	vRH	K/9	BB/9
Strong, Mike	L-L	6-0	195	11-17-88	1	1	7.16	12	1	0	0	16	19	13	13	2	11	12	.292	.450	.222	6.61	6.06
Suter, Brent	R-L	6-5	195	8-29-89	3	1	3.31	6	6	0	0	35	35	15	13	4	6	19	.269	.269	.269	4.84	1.53
Thornburg, Tyler	R-R	5-11	190	9-29-88	2	7	5.28	17	17	0	0	89	106	55	52	16	36	57	.299	.250	.342	5.79	3.65
Wang, Wei-Chung	L-L	6-2	185	4-25-92	1	0	0.00	1	1	0	0	6	4	0	0	0	0	5	.182	.143	.200	7.50	0.00
Wooten, Rob	R-R	6-1	200	7-21-85	5	2	4.67	44	1	0	1	52	56	29	27	9	14	50	.272	.292	.256	8.65	2.42

Fielding

Catcher	PCT	G	PO	A	E	DP	PB
Ashley	.996	85	609	73	3	11	1
Centeno	.990	46	281	28	3	5	3
Diaz	.982	15	97	10	2	2	0

First Base	PCT	G	PO	A	E	DP
Ashley	.938	3	14	1	1	1
Clark	.993	107	909	76	7	85
Diaz	1.000	7	43	7	0	3
Dominguez	1.000	2	2	0	0	0
Murphy	1.000	7	49	4	0	8
Rogers	1.000	24	199	16	0	15

Second Base	PCT	G	PO	A	E	DP
Gennett	.962	17	31	44	3	14
Herrera	1.000	23	35	56	0	13
Long	1.000	15	17	28	0	5
Macias	1.000	8	6	22	0	2

	PCT	G	PO	A	E	DP	PB
Murphy	1.000	6	3	17	0	2	
Orr	1.000	59	122	161	0	38	
Rivera	.895	8	8	9	2	1	
Sardinas	.991	30	50	64	1	19	

Third Base	PCT	G	PO	A	E	DP
Dominguez	.983	68	42	127	3	10
Herrera	1.000	10	1	17	0	0
Macias	.952	9	7	13	1	1
Murphy	.980	24	10	40	1	8
Nelson	.895	17	10	24	4	3
Orr	.979	26	9	37	1	5
Rivera	.917	4	1	10	1	2
Rogers	.867	6	3	10	2	1

Shortstop	PCT	G	PO	A	E	DP
Murphy	.929	6	1	12	1	2
Orr	1.000	1	1	2	0	0

	PCT	G	PO	A	E	DP
Rivera	.956	71	83	197	13	44
Sardinas	.954	74	102	188	14	35

Outfield	PCT	G	PO	A	E	DP
Clark	1.000	22	34	1	0	0
Guez	.984	33	58	3	1	0
Herrera	.961	24	46	3	2	1
Long	.989	110	172	8	2	1
Orr	.824	15	13	1	3	0
Petersen	.943	26	33	0	2	0
Peterson	.986	40	65	3	1	0
Reed	.984	36	59	1	1	0
Santana	.970	19	31	1	1	0
Schafer	.975	71	178	14	5	5
Wren	.982	73	160	4	3	1

BILOXI SHUCKERS

DOUBLE-A

SOUTHERN LEAGUE

Batting	B-T	HT	WT	DOB	AVG	vLH	vRH	G	AB	R	H	2B	3B	HR	RBI	BB	HBP	SH	SF	SO	SB	CS	SLG	OBP
Arcia, Orlando	R-R	6-0	165	8-4-94	.307	.354	.298	129	512	74	157	37	7	8	69	30	3	4	3	73	25	8	.453	.347
Berberet, Parker	R-R	6-3	210	10-20-89	.232	.320	.216	53	164	12	38	6	1	2	20	15	0	2	2	35	2	1	.317	.293
Cooper, Garrett	R-R	6-6	230	12-25-90	.552	.500	.560	9	29	3	16	2	1	0	5	7	0	0	0	2	0	0	.690	.639
Fellhauer, Josh	L-L	5-11	175	3-24-88	.240	.185	.249	73	200	20	48	8	0	2	25	28	4	1	2	43	8	2	.310	.342
Green, Taylor	L-R	6-0	195	11-2-86	.225	.180	.233	104	320	28	72	15	0	5	42	28	4	1	6	45	1	3	.319	.291
LaTorre, Tyler	L-R	6-0	235	4-22-83	.133	.000	.143	14	15	1	2	1	0	0	0	6	0	0	0	4	0	0	.200	.381
Macias, Brandon	R-R	5-10	185	10-10-88	.245	.250	.243	47	102	14	25	5	1	2	17	9	1	0	1	15	2	3	.373	.310
Orf, Nathan	R-R	5-9	180	2-1-90	.274	.304	.268	127	424	65	116	26	4	2	43	63	11	8	5	70	5	3	.368	.378
Phillips, Brett	L-R	6-0	180	5-30-94	.250	.211	.262	23	80	14	20	7	3	0	6	14	1	1	2	30	2	1	.413	.361
Ramirez, Nick	L-L	6-3	225	8-19-89	.243	.216	.249	131	432	63	105	22	0	14	63	64	1	0	4	115	2	0	.391	.339
Reed, Michael	R-R	6-0	190	11-18-92	.278	.333	.269	93	313	43	87	20	5	5	49	53	3	0	8	80	25	7	.422	.379
Rivera, Yadiel	R-R	6-3	185	5-2-92	.277	.314	.268	52	184	23	51	9	3	1	16	17	2	5	0	30	8	7	.375	.345
Roache, Victor	R-R	6-1	225	9-17-91	.247	.227	.251	67	223	23	55	11	3	6	35	23	2	0	1	64	2	1	.430	.321
Shaw, Nick	R-R	5-11	160	8-25-88	.195	.222	.191	98	251	32	49	3	3	0	23	45	2	6	4	55	6	2	.231	.318
Taylor, Tyrone	R-R	6-0	185	1-22-94	.260	.278	.256	128	454	48	118	20	3	3	43	31	5	10	4	55	10	6	.337	.312
Weisenburger, Adam	R-R	5-10	185	12-13-88	.231	.167	.244	90	273	41	63	14	1	2	24	43	11	5	2	52	2	2	.311	.356
Wren, Kyle	L-L	5-10	175	4-23-91	.300	.281	.303	60	227	26	68	6	0	0	13	24	2	4	1	29	20	9	.326	.370

Pitching	B-T	HT	WT	DOB	W	L	ERA	G	GS	CG	SV	IP	H	R	ER	HR	BB	SO	AVG	vLH	vRH	K/9	BB/9
Barnes, Jacob	R-R	6-2	230	4-14-90	4	5	3.36	39	6	0	0	75	74	32	28	2	30	84	.262	.300	.238	10.08	3.60
Barreda, Manny	R-R	5-11	195	10-8-88	1	1	3.38	32	0	0	0	45	38	18	17	6	26	51	.232	.164	.266	10.13	5.16
Barrios, Yhonathan	B-R	5-10	200	12-1-91	3	2	3.15	16	0	0	6	20	22	7	7	1	5	16	.282	.429	.200	7.20	2.25
Bradley, Jed	L-L	6-4	225	6-12-90	1	1	3.31	23	0	0	0	33	29	16	12	1	10	31	.242	.229	.250	8.54	2.76
Burgos, Hiram	R-R	5-11	210	8-4-87	3	0	3.68	5	5	0	0	29	23	13	12	1	12	36	.225	.292	.167	11.05	3.68
Chapman, Jaye	R-R	6-0	195	5-22-87	4	2	0.82	21	0	0	2	22	13	3	2	2	9	21	.173	.243	.105	8.59	3.68
Eitel, Derek	R-R	6-4	200	11-21-87	1	0	3.86	7	0	0	0	9	10	4	4	0	2	10	.263	.250	.273	9.64	1.93
2-team total (4 Mobile)					1	1	5.14	11	0	0	0	14	14	9	8	0	8	14	—	—	—	9.00	5.14
Gagnon, Drew	R-R	6-4	195	6-26-90	1	1	5.57	6	1	0	0	21	19	15	13	2	10	18	.229	.214	.236	7.71	4.29
Hader, Josh	L-L	6-3	160	4-7-94	1	4	2.79	7	7	0	0	39	27	13	12	3	11	50	.200	.194	.202	11.64	2.56
Hall, Brooks	R-R	6-5	235	6-26-90	8	8	4.42	25	19	0	0	106	106	56	52	10	28	79	.262	.267	.258	6.71	2.38
Hellweg, Johnny	R-R	6-7	235	10-29-88	0	4	9.60	5	5	0	0	15	20	26	16	4	22	11	.313	.263	.333	6.60	13.20
Henderson, Jim	L-R	6-5	220	10-21-82	0	0	0.00	4	0	0	1	4	2	0	0	0	2	5	.143	.167	.125	11.25	4.50
Horst, Jeremy	L-L	6-3	235	10-1-85	0	0	0.00	1	0	0	0	1	0	0	0	0	0	2	.000	.000	.000	18.00	0.00
Houser, Adrian	R-R	6-4	230	2-2-93	4	1	2.92	7	7	0	0	37	33	16	12	4	6	32	.232	.283	.202	7.78	1.46
Johnson, Hobbs	R-L	5-11	230	4-29-91	7	8	3.84	25	25	1	0	117	90	56	50	5	77	94	.219	.214	.221	7.21	5.91
Lopez, Jorge	R-R	6-3	190	2-10-93	12	5	2.26	24	24	0	0	143	105	37	36	9	52	137	.205	.173	.230	8.60	3.27
Magnifico, Damien	R-R	6-1	185	5-24-91	4	1	1.17	42	0	0	20	54	41	10	7	3	22	38	.210	.253	.181	6.37	3.69
Marzec, Eric	R-R	5-11	210	1-13-88	0	1	4.70	5	0	0	0	8	6	4	4	3	2	7	.222	.100	.294	8.22	2.35
Obispo, Wirfin	R-R	6-2	215	9-26-84	0	3	8.83	17	0	0	5	17	17	19	17	2	11	16	.266	.240	.282	8.31	5.71
Peralta, Wily	R-R	6-1	245	5-8-89	0	0	1.04	2	2	0	0	9	5	1	1	1	2	8	.161	.200	.125	8.31	2.08
Poppe, Tanner	R-R	6-6	225	7-19-90	0	0	6.75	5	0	0	0	5	7	4	4	1	3	6	.318	.250	.400	10.13	5.06
Ross, Austin	R-R	6-2	200	8-12-88	3	2	2.61	26	0	0	1	38	35	12	11	2	9	47	.245	.407	.146	11.13	2.13
Seidenberger, Trevor	L-L	6-2	200	6-9-92	1	0	6.75	8	0	0	0	13	11	10	10	3	5	11	.220	.222	.219	7.43	3.38
Strong, Mike	L-L	6-0	195	11-17-88	4	1	2.54	38	0	0	5	50	26	15	14	3	20	49	.152	.155	.150	8.88	3.62
Suter, Brent	R-L	6-5	195	8-29-89	5	3	1.95	20	11	0	0	83	71	20	18	2	33	64	.244	.234	.248	6.94	3.58
Viramontes, Martin	R-R	6-5	225	7-12-89	0	1	6.39	37	0	0	0	49	58	38	35	4	32	32	.307	.250	.345	5.84	5.84
Wagner, Tyler	R-R	6-3	195	1-24-91	11	5	2.25	25	25	2	0	152	130	45	38	7	45	120	.225	.251	.209	7.09	2.66

Fielding

Catcher	PCT	G	PO	A	E	DP	PB
Berberet	.991	50	400	43	4	5	5
LaTorre	1.000	2	6	1	0	0	0
Weisenburger	.991	89	691	64	7	10	12

First Base	PCT	G	PO	A	E	DP
Berberet	.938	2	14	1	1	2
Cooper	.958	5	41	5	2	5
Fellhauer	1.000	2	11	2	0	0
Green	.986	20	134	11	2	9
Macias	1.000	6	26	1	0	0
Ramirez	.984	116	942	66	16	102

Second Base	PCT	G	PO	A	E	DP
Arcia	1.000	3	7	12	0	3

	PCT	G	PO	A	E	DP/PB
Macias	1.000	1	1	4	0	2
Orf	.989	43	60	116	2	23
Rivera	.984	38	68	111	3	32
Shaw	.993	68	106	170	2	38

Third Base	PCT	G	PO	A	E	DP
Berberet	—	1	0	0	0	0
Green	.950	55	18	95	6	7
Macias	.905	25	14	24	4	3
Orf	.980	66	24	125	3	9
Rivera	1.000	10	2	5	0	0
Shaw	1.000	1	0	1	0	0

Shortstop	PCT	G	PO	A	E	DP
Arcia	.978	123	196	376	13	82

	PCT	G	PO	A	E	DP/PB
Orf	1.000	2	5	3	0	1
Rivera	.933	5	7	7	1	2
Shaw	.969	10	8	23	1	6

Outfield	PCT	G	PO	A	E	DP
Cooper	1.000	4	2	0	0	0
Fellhauer	1.000	58	68	12	0	0
Orf	1.000	21	37	0	0	0
Phillips	.983	22	54	3	1	0
Reed	.993	84	138	10	1	4
Roache	.977	57	77	7	2	1
Shaw	1.000	2	1	0	0	0
Taylor	.988	123	243	3	3	1
Wren	.984	58	121	4	2	0

BREVARD COUNTY MANATEES   HIGH CLASS A

FLORIDA STATE LEAGUE

Batting	B-T	HT	WT	DOB	AVG	vLH	vRH	G	AB	R	H	2B	3B	HR	RBI	BB	HBP	SH	SF	SO	SB	CS	SLG	OBP
Cooper, Garrett	R-R	6-6	230	12-25-90	.294	.286	.297	119	422	55	124	32	2	8	54	35	8	1	4	88	1	1	.436	.356
Coulter, Clint	R-R	6-3	222	7-30-93	.246	.215	.259	137	499	63	123	30	3	13	59	46	18	0	6	92	6	6	.397	.329
Davis, Johnny	B-R	5-10	180	4-6-90	.216	.167	.226	10	37	6	8	2	0	0	0	2	0	1	0	15	4	2	.270	.256
Diaz, Robinzon	R-R	5-11	220	9-19-83	.205	.308	.161	11	44	1	9	1	0	0	4	1	0	0	0	5	0	1	.227	.222
Eshleman, Paul	R-R	6-3	220	9-3-90	.198	.163	.216	40	131	6	26	3	1	2	9	7	1	0	0	42	0	0	.282	.245
Garcia, Omar	R-R	5-11	170	8-1-93	.264	.268	.263	128	435	50	115	8	1	1	28	27	8	7	2	76	53	16	.294	.318
Garfield, Cameron	R-R	6-0	200	5-23-91	.233	.267	.218	55	193	21	45	8	0	2	16	8	1	0	0	39	4	2	.306	.267
Halcomb, Steven	R-R	5-10	180	8-27-90	.177	.225	.163	68	181	19	32	2	1	0	15	13	5	5	2	30	2	2	.199	.249
Houle, Dustin	R-R	6-1	205	11-9-93	.300	.261	.316	25	80	3	24	4	1	0	10	2	4	0	3	17	0	0	.375	.337
Lucroy, Jonathan	R-R	6-0	195	6-13-86	.250	.000	.267	4	16	3	4	0	0	0	1	2	0	0	0	0	0	0	.250	.333
Macias, Brandon	R-R	5-10	185	10-10-88	.345	.444	.300	8	29	1	10	2	0	0	3	1	0	0	0	3	1	0	.414	.367
McFarland, Chris	R-R	6-0	190	11-24-92	.274	.277	.273	137	547	59	150	20	2	3	46	28	7	7	2	113	20	13	.335	.317
Neda, Rafael	R-R	6-1	215	10-12-88	.215	.319	.185	67	209	11	45	10	2	2	19	23	4	2	2	38	1	1	.311	.303
Ortega, Angel	R-R	6-2	170	9-15-91	.212	.214	.211	124	397	33	84	11	0	0	27	15	6	11	1	69	4	4	.239	.251
Pena, Jose	R-R	6-2	192	3-3-93	.218	.254	.200	64	202	17	44	9	0	3	17	6	2	2	0	45	1	2	.307	.248
Ratterree, Michael	R-R	6-1	190	2-9-91	.150	.127	.158	75	240	23	36	11	0	2	17	29	8	1	4	87	0	1	.221	.260
Roache, Victor	R-R	6-2	210	9-17-91	.259	.250	.262	63	239	23	62	11	2	10	36	21	3	0	1	94	3	3	.448	.326
Smith-Brennan, Taylor	R-R	6-0	210	1-31-92	.241	.294	.222	132	460	68	111	26	3	3	54	62	6	0	7	158	13	6	.330	.335

Pitching	B-T	HT	WT	DOB	W	L	ERA	G	GS	CG	SV	IP	H	R	ER	HR	BB	SO	AVG	vLH	vRH	K/9	BB/9
Archer, Tristan	R-R	6-2	200	10-18-90	3	4	3.42	28	2	0	1	71	80	29	27	1	13	63	.289	.321	.267	7.99	1.65
Barreda, Manny	R-R	5-11	195	10-8-88	0	0	0.00	3	0	0	0	4	2	1	0	0	1	3	.143	.111	.200	6.75	2.25
Burgos, Hiram	R-R	5-11	210	8-4-87	2	4	4.12	7	7	0	0	39	34	21	18	1	14	47	.231	.338	.139	10.75	3.20
Earls, Kaleb	R-R	6-5	185	3-17-93	1	2	3.15	29	0	0	6	46	42	21	16	4	9	27	.241	.200	.266	5.32	1.77
Gainey, Preston	R-R	6-3	205	2-13-91	2	4	2.70	33	0	0	8	50	44	18	15	1	21	43	.246	.239	.250	7.74	3.78
Hellweg, Johnny	R-R	6-7	235	10-29-88	1	6	4.89	11	11	0	0	46	43	33	25	2	30	28	.243	.269	.222	5.48	5.87
Henderson, Jim	L-R	6-5	220	10-21-82	0	1	4.50	2	1	0	0	2	2	1	1	1	1	3	.250	.500	.167	13.50	4.50
Hirsch, Zach	L-L	6-4	220	7-6-90	1	4	4.89	8	5	2	1	35	47	23	19	3	17	32	.320	.355	.310	4.37	0.77
Lieser, Scott	R-R	6-3	195	4-23-90	0	0	11.42	6	0	0	0	9	15	11	11	0	1	7	.375	.300	.450	7.27	1.04
Marzec, Eric	R-R	5-11	210	1-13-88	1	8	5.96	10	10	1	0	51	75	42	34	4	16	27	.339	.348	.330	4.73	2.81
Medlen, Casey	R-R	6-0	155	8-4-89	0	3	4.91	10	0	0	4	11	11	8	6	1	9	8	.262	.167	.333	6.55	7.36
Ortega, Jorge	R-R	6-1	165	6-20-93	9	9	2.41	22	20	6	0	142	136	47	38	7	11	72	.248	.241	.252	4.57	0.70
Peterson, Stephen	L-L	6-3	210	11-6-87	3	3	3.22	29	0	0	1	64	63	34	23	5	25	47	.257	.203	.283	6.58	3.50
Salas, Javi	R-R	6-4	210	3-20-92	8	8	4.13	24	22	2	0	129	142	76	59	7	39	82	.278	.286	.273	5.74	2.73
Seidenberger, Trevor	L-L	6-2	200	6-9-92	4	2	3.06	22	0	0	5	35	25	12	12	1	21	37	.197	.279	.155	9.42	5.35
Sneed, Cy	R-R	6-4	185	10-1-92	3	4	2.47	11	11	1	0	62	59	23	17	2	11	55	.253	.257	.250	7.98	1.60
Spurlin, Tyler	R-R	6-5	195	6-17-91	2	1	3.05	28	0	0	2	44	50	19	15	0	17	28	.287	.343	.250	5.68	3.45
Terry, Clint	L-L	6-2	195	6-9-92	1	1	2.04	12	4	0	0	40	39	11	9	2	5	38	.255	.283	.240	8.62	1.13
Wang, Wei-Chung	L-L	6-2	185	4-25-92	10	6	3.54	25	25	3	0	140	146	69	55	9	39	91	.267	.304	.258	5.86	2.51
Williams, Mark	R-R	6-3	240	8-12-89	0	3	2.43	15	0	0	2	30	30	9	8	2	4	34	.261	.302	.236	10.31	1.21
Woodruff, Brandon	R-R	6-4	215	2-10-93	4	7	3.45	21	19	0	0	110	112	48	42	2	33	71	.270	.273	.268	5.83	2.71

Fielding

Catcher	PCT	G	PO	A	E	DP	PB
Diaz	1.000	1	6	1	0	0	0
Eshleman	.945	24	113	8	7	1	4
Garfield	.993	45	252	37	2	4	7
Houle	.985	20	118	14	2	1	3
Lucroy	1.000	2	9	1	0	0	0
Neda	.992	54	353	31	3	3	6

First Base	PCT	G	PO	A	E	DP
Cooper	.986	114	934	54	14	83
Diaz	.972	3	31	4	1	1
Eshleman	1.000	5	36	0	0	2
Neda	.974	5	37	0	1	5

	PCT	G	PO	A	E	DP
Smith-Brennan	.990	16	91	9	1	10

Second Base	PCT	G	PO	A	E	DP
Halcomb	.971	16	27	40	2	14
Macias	1.000	1	7	3	0	1
McFarland	.958	121	200	331	23	73

Third Base	PCT	G	PO	A	E	DP
Diaz	1.000	1	0	1	0	0
Halcomb	.947	30	17	54	4	6
Macias	1.000	3	1	3	0	1
Smith-Brennan	.922	107	80	203	24	21

Shortstop	PCT	G	PO	A	E	DP
Halcomb	.950	15	26	50	4	9

	PCT	G	PO	A	E	DP
Ortega	.958	122	210	379	26	66

Outfield	PCT	G	PO	A	E	DP
Coulter	.959	118	243	16	11	4
Davis	1.000	10	22	0	0	0
Garcia	.985	128	309	12	5	4
Halcomb	—	1	0	0	0	0
Lieser	—	1	0	0	0	0
Pena	.957	34	62	4	3	0
Ratterree	1.000	73	122	5	0	1
Roache	.992	52	116	3	1	1

WISCONSIN TIMBER RATTLERS

LOW CLASS A

MIDWEST LEAGUE

Batting	B-T	HT	WT	DOB	AVG	vLH	vRH	G	AB	R	H	2B	3B	HR	RBI	BB	HBP	SH	SF	SO	SB	CS	SLG	OBP
Allemand, Blake	B-R	5-10	170	7-1-92	.272	.315	.260	61	246	24	67	10	0	2	17	16	3	1	1	32	3	3	.337	.323
Aviles, Luis	R-R	6-1	170	3-16-95	.195	.167	.206	57	185	10	36	7	3	2	15	3	0	2	0	66	1	5	.297	.207
Castillo, Francisco	B-R	5-10	180	6-4-93	.231	.227	.233	61	238	19	55	3	1	1	15	8	1	9	2	41	4	5	.265	.257
Cotto, Omar	B-R	5-11	195	2-28-92	.135	.207	.104	29	96	7	13	1	2	0	7	5	0	3	0	31	2	2	.188	.178
Davis, Khris	R-R	5-10	195	12-21-87	.100	.000	.111	6	20	1	2	0	0	0	2	3	0	0	1	2	0	1	.100	.208
DeMuth, Dustin	L-R	6-3	200	7-30-91	.285	.254	.294	86	309	31	88	17	0	5	35	29	9	2	2	63	4	6	.388	.361
Denson, David	L-R	6-3	254	1-17-95	.226	.160	.241	39	133	18	30	7	1	3	16	17	0	0	1	49	1	1	.361	.311
Diaz, Brandon	R-R	5-11	175	4-14-95	.241	.314	.217	82	282	44	68	14	1	6	24	46	6	4	2	83	23	10	.362	.357
Gatewood, Jake	R-R	6-5	190	9-25-95	.209	.200	.212	55	177	16	37	5	1	4	16	14	2	0	0	65	5	0	.316	.275
Gennett, Scooter	L-L	5-10	185	5-1-90	.308	.250	.333	4	13	1	4	2	0	0	1	1	0	0	1	0	1	0	.462	.333
Harrison, Monte	R-R	6-3	220	8-10-95	.148	.109	.164	46	162	18	24	6	2	2	11	14	7	1	0	77	6	4	.247	.246
Leal, Carlos	L-R	5-11	180	7-13-91	.309	.325	.302	76	282	29	87	15	2	2	29	21	5	2	0	61	1	1	.397	.367
Matos, Sthervin	R-R	6-1	200	2-13-94	.224	.250	.215	117	407	61	91	13	5	8	45	42	6	4	7	120	23	9	.339	.301
McCall, Greg	R-R	6-1	195	12-25-91	.248	.245	.249	83	290	29	72	18	1	0	20	23	4	3	3	83	3	0	.317	.309
Mejia, Natanael	R-R	6-0	175	7-10-92	.237	.000	.311	21	59	5	14	2	0	0	2	2	2	1	0	16	0	2	.271	.286
Meyer, Mitch	L-R	6-2	190	2-18-92	.217	.183	.228	75	249	19	54	7	5	1	20	17	4	3	2	93	5	4	.297	.276
Munoz, Gregory	L-R	5-9	160	2-6-94	.193	.188	.194	61	187	20	36	3	1	0	12	25	2	4	1	51	12	11	.219	.293
Neuhaus, Tucker	L-R	6-3	190	6-18-95	.249	.218	.258	104	369	32	92	19	4	4	40	33	1	3	7	77	0	2	.355	.307
Pena, Jose	R-R	6-2	192	3-3-93	.228	.444	.188	17	57	8	13	4	1	1	6	2	0	1	1	21	0	0	.386	.250
Rubio, Elvis	R-R	6-1	215	7-2-94	.237	.233	.239	124	459	42	109	27	0	4	38	29	14	1	3	95	2	4	.322	.301
Sharkey, Alan	L-L	6-1	185	11-8-93	.247	.191	.263	88	300	37	74	10	4	3	37	43	1	0	2	52	2	2	.337	.341

Pitching	B-T	HT	WT	DOB	W	L	ERA	G	GS	CG	SV	IP	H	R	ER	HR	BB	SO	AVG	vLH	vRH	K/9	BB/9
Burkhalter, David	R-R	6-3	190	7-25-95	5	9	4.99	28	12	0	6	101	103	63	56	9	22	93	.259	.232	.276	8.29	1.96
Carver, David	L-L	6-3	180	10-25-91	1	3	6.64	5	4	0	0	20	33	16	15	3	9	12	.398	.344	.431	5.31	3.98
Cooper, Zach	R-R	5-10	185	1-6-90	2	1	1.88	20	0	0	3	24	17	7	5	2	7	26	.198	.267	.161	9.75	2.63
Curtis, Luke	R-R	6-1	195	12-31-91	8	2	3.06	40	0	0	7	53	44	19	18	4	26	34	.239	.192	.270	5.77	4.42
Diaz, Victor	R-R	6-1	170	10-6-93	0	2	2.28	6	4	0	1	24	21	12	6	0	16	9	.233	.275	.200	3.42	6.08
Gomez, Milton	R-R	6-1	172	4-22-94	3	2	5.40	11	5	0	0	40	43	29	24	2	24	22	.272	.323	.240	4.95	5.40
Hanhold, Eric	R-R	6-4	190	11-1-93	0	4	7.60	10	7	0	0	34	48	31	29	2	8	23	.338	.314	.352	6.03	2.10
Hirsch, Zach	L-L	6-4	220	7-6-90	2	4	3.28	12	11	0	0	69	64	30	25	3	9	48	.242	.143	.274	6.29	1.18
Hudgens, Brock	R-R	6-0	202	10-16-91	0	0	13.50	2	0	0	0	3	8	5	5	0	3	5	.471	.333	.625	13.50	8.10
Kirby, Nathan	L-L	6-2	185	11-23-93	0	1	5.68	5	2	0	0	13	15	9	8	0	7	13	.313	.182	.351	4.97	4.97
Lieser, Scott	R-R	6-3	195	4-23-90	3	2	3.05	29	1	0	0	44	43	17	15	3	5	41	.261	.279	.250	8.32	1.02
Linehan, Tyler	L-L	6-1	244	8-30-91	2	4	5.51	39	0	0	2	47	52	34	29	2	26	36	.281	.222	.311	6.85	4.94
Martin, Harvey	L-R	6-1	205	7-12-89	0	0	20.25	2	0	0	0	3	7	6	6	1	2	2	.500	.429	.571	6.75	6.75
Martin, Jarret	L-L	6-3	230	8-14-89	0	0	4.50	3	0	0	0	2	2	1	1	0	2	0	.333	.667	.000	0.00	9.00
Medeiros, Kodi	L-L	6-2	180	5-25-96	4	5	4.44	25	16	0	1	93	79	50	46	0	40	94	.228	.191	.241	9.06	3.86
Ortega, Luis	L-L	5-10	185	4-20-93	2	7	5.31	25	9	0	2	83	81	53	49	3	41	68	.253	.250	.255	7.37	4.45
Peralta, Wily	R-R	6-1	245	5-8-89	0	0	3.38	1	1	0	0	3	2	1	1	0	0	4	.200	.000	.333	13.50	0.00
Perrin, Jon	R-R	6-5	220	5-23-93	1	5	4.31	10	8	0	0	40	44	23	19	1	4	34	.284	.294	.276	7.71	0.91
Ponce, Cody	R-R	6-6	240	4-25-94	2	1	2.15	12	7	0	3	46	43	15	11	1	9	36	.246	.200	.270	7.04	1.76
Rizzo, Gian	R-R	6-1	160	9-5-93	0	3	3.09	36	0	0	3	55	55	24	19	3	7	38	.256	.261	.252	6.18	1.14
Sneed, Cy	R-R	6-4	185	10-1-92	3	7	2.68	15	13	0	1	77	70	33	23	2	17	67	.239	.246	.232	7.80	1.98
Torres, Joshua	R-R	6-0	160	4-26-94	0	5	6.29	8	3	0	0	24	31	19	17	4	11	16	.310	.314	.306	5.92	4.07
Torrez, Orlando	R-R	6-3	195	4-14-92	0	3	4.81	11	5	0	1	34	32	24	18	3	22	16	.246	.227	.266	4.28	5.88
Uhen, Josh	R-R	6-4	185	4-7-92	2	3	4.39	29	4	0	1	53	60	35	26	2	16	47	.275	.286	.270	7.93	2.70
Ventura, Angel	R-R	6-2	185	4-7-93	7	6	3.09	28	14	0	2	122	110	51	42	5	46	126	.235	.256	.218	9.27	3.38
Williams, Devin	R-R	6-3	165	9-21-94	3	9	3.44	22	13	0	0	89	75	39	34	3	36	89	.226	.267	.192	9.00	3.64
Williams, Mark	R-R	6-3	240	8-12-89	0	1	3.86	4	0	0	0	5	5	3	2	0	3	4	.263	.250	.273	7.71	5.79

Fielding

Catcher	PCT	G	PO	A	E	DP	PB
Leal	.988	52	347	52	5	3	4
McCall	.991	71	502	60	5	6	6
Mejia	.987	21	138	13	2	1	4

First Base	PCT	G	PO	A	E	DP
DeMuth	1.000	14	134	4	0	7
Denson	.983	28	218	17	4	11
Matos	.975	11	76	3	2	4
McCall	1.000	1	5	0	0	2
Sharkey	.988	88	733	64	10	62

Second Base	PCT	G	PO	A	E	DP
Allemand	.984	18	28	35	1	5
Aviles	.938	4	6	9	1	1
Castillo	.981	13	19	33	1	6

	PCT	G	PO	A	E	DP	PB
DeMuth	.955	6	9	12	1	1	
Gennett	.769	4	6	4	3	0	
Munoz	.965	34	49	90	5	14	
Neuhaus	.966	67	128	186	11	40	

Third Base	PCT	G	PO	A	E	DP
Aviles	.970	11	11	21	1	2
DeMuth	.924	35	19	54	6	4
Matos	.897	73	52	139	22	8
Neuhaus	.909	27	23	47	7	2

Shortstop	PCT	G	PO	A	E	DP
Allemand	.934	41	63	93	11	25
Aviles	.892	14	27	39	8	10
Castillo	.957	12	12	32	2	3
Gatewood	.946	52	75	137	12	24

	PCT	G	PO	A	E	DP
Munoz	.904	23	22	63	9	5

Outfield	PCT	G	PO	A	E	DP
Aviles	.983	24	57	2	1	1
Castillo	.979	26	45	2	1	0
Cotto	1.000	18	36	4	0	0
Davis	1.000	3	6	0	0	0
Denson	.889	5	8	0	1	0
Diaz	.978	79	174	7	4	3
Harrison	.981	46	104	1	2	0
Matos	.976	21	37	3	1	2
Meyer	.980	75	139	8	3	2
Pena	1.000	10	15	1	0	0
Rubio	.982	117	211	10	4	1

Batting	B-T	HT	WT	DOB	AVG	vLH	vRH	G	AB	R	H	2B	3B	HR	RBI	BB	HBP	SH	SF	SO	SB	CS	SLG	OBP
Bishop, Beau	R-R	6-2	200	7-6-93	.500	—	.500	1	2	0	1	0	0	0	1	0	0	0	0	0	0	0	.500	.500
Clark, Trent	L-L	6-0	205	11-1-96	.309	.286	.314	43	165	34	51	7	6	1	16	30	3	1	1	36	20	5	.442	.422
Ghelfi, Mitch	B-R	5-11	185	9-24-92	.189	.375	.138	13	37	5	7	0	1	0	3	3	0	0	0	12	1	1	.243	.250
Guez, Ben	R-R	5-11	180	1-24-87	.167	.000	.200	4	6	0	1	1	0	0	2	1	1	0	0	3	0	0	.333	.375
Houle, Dustin	R-R	6-1	205	11-9-93	.259	.333	.250	9	27	6	7	3	1	2	6	5	1	0	0	7	1	0	.667	.394
Lara, Gilbert	R-R	6-2	190	10-30-97	.248	.139	.271	51	202	29	50	4	5	1	25	9	2	0	1	41	3	3	.332	.285
Leonardo, Daniel	R-R	5-9	160	8-28-95	.272	.429	.239	23	81	9	22	0	0	0	3	4	0	4	1	12	6	3	.272	.302
Martinez, Kevin	B-R	5-10	180	1-11-95	.121	.000	.133	12	33	1	4	1	0	0	6	4	0	1	0	8	1	0	.152	.216
Martinez, Yerald	R-R	6-2	180	12-3-95	.234	.278	.228	42	145	16	34	10	0	2	15	17	1	2	0	58	7	3	.345	.319
McDowell, Max	R-R	6-1	210	1-12-94	.228	.400	.203	23	79	9	18	4	0	2	6	7	7	1	1	10	3	0	.354	.340
Mendez, Julio	R-R	5-10	140	10-24-96	.195	.200	.194	12	41	1	8	1	0	0	3	3	2	2	0	6	0	1	.220	.283
Munoz, Gregory	L-R	5-9	160	2-6-94	.279	.143	.296	20	61	6	17	0	0	0	5	5	0	4	1	15	6	4	.279	.328
Oquendo, Jonathan	B-R	6-3	170	3-21-96	.250	.250	.250	25	80	9	20	4	0	0	8	10	0	0	0	21	0	0	.300	.333
Orimoloye, Demi	R-R	6-4	225	1-6-97	.292	.111	.319	33	137	23	40	9	2	6	26	3	3	0	1	39	19	6	.518	.319
Ortiz, Juan	L-R	6-1	175	9-20-94	.279	.250	.285	43	154	24	43	11	2	3	17	14	2	1	0	49	7	0	.435	.347
Perry, Tyrone	L-R	6-1	265	10-24-95	.278	.176	.297	32	108	13	30	7	0	3	19	21	1	0	0	27	0	2	.426	.400
Pierre, Nicolas	R-R	6-3	170	11-13-96	.200	.208	.198	40	145	20	29	3	1	0	8	5	0	1	0	35	3	3	.234	.227
Quiterio, Jorge	R-R	6-0	171	12-10-94	.257	.190	.269	40	140	15	36	10	1	2	19	6	1	2	2	39	7	3	.386	.289
Segovia, Joantgel	R-R	6-1	175	11-8-96	.368	.389	.364	25	95	18	35	2	0	0	7	10	1	2	0	14	7	7	.389	.434
Taylor, Zach	R-R	6-1	220	10-29-95	.188	.182	.188	24	80	5	15	4	0	0	8	13	0	3	0	31	1	1	.238	.301
Wallace, Beau	R-R	6-1	205	7-28-92	.267	.353	.247	30	90	10	24	7	0	0	9	13	4	0	1	18	5	1	.344	.380

Pitching	B-T	HT	WT	DOB	W	L	ERA	G	GS	CG	SV	IP	H	R	ER	HR	BB	SO	AVG	vLH	vRH	K/9	BB/9
Baits, Connor	R-R	6-5	210	1-3-94	0	2	46.06	8	1	0	0	6	11	35	29	1	23	1	.423	.429	.421	1.59	36.53
Clowers, Shawn	L-L	5-11	190	11-11-92	0	0	2.00	10	0	0	3	27	17	6	6	1	4	22	.172	.240	.149	7.33	1.33
Cross, Colton	R-R	6-0	200	3-24-94	0	1	2.45	14	0	0	1	18	18	7	5	0	8	13	.269	.286	.256	6.38	3.93
Desguin, Jordan	R-R	6-1	195	10-30-93	2	3	2.86	8	4	0	0	28	36	13	9	0	6	28	.305	.346	.273	8.89	1.91
Diaz, Miguel	R-R	6-1	175	11-28-94	0	3	2.21	7	5	0	0	20	20	12	5	1	5	23	.270	.286	.261	10.18	2.21
Eitel, Derek	R-R	6-4	200	11-21-87	0	1	2.25	3	1	0	0	4	3	1	1	0	1	5	.188	.286	.111	11.25	2.25
Ely, John	R-R	6-2	210	5-13-86	0	1	4.76	3	3	0	0	6	9	3	3	0	0	7	.321	.154	.467	11.12	0.00
Farina, Alex	L-R	6-0	230	5-30-93	1	0	0.00	6	0	0	0	13	8	0	0	0	3	22	.163	.188	.152	14.85	2.03
Finnegan, Jack	R-R	6-2	175	12-9-93	1	2	6.39	4	3	0	0	13	17	11	9	0	6	11	.333	.600	.222	7.82	4.26
Flores, Jose	R-R	6-4	210	11-21-92	1	1	4.98	12	0	0	1	22	25	15	12	2	7	10	.291	.355	.255	4.15	2.91
Fortuno, Gentry	R-R	6-1	235	9-11-96	1	2	1.89	13	7	0	0	33	34	10	7	1	4	19	.272	.238	.289	5.13	1.08
Grist, Scott	R-R	6-4	185	5-31-92	2	0	3.45	14	2	0	1	31	34	14	12	1	4	30	.272	.289	.263	8.62	1.15
Hanhold, Eric	R-R	6-4	190	11-1-93	0	1	4.50	1	1	0	0	2	3	1	1	0	0	0	.333	—	.333	0.00	0.00
Kintzler, Brandon	R-R	5-10	190	8-1-84	0	0	0.00	3	1	0	0	3	2	0	0	0	0	3	.167	.500	.000	8.10	0.00
Kuntz, Brad	L-L	6-0	180	5-14-92	2	0	0.65	9	1	0	0	28	15	3	2	0	8	37	.153	.190	.143	12.04	2.60
Leach, Brent	L-L	6-5	225	11-18-82	0	0	1.80	4	0	0	0	5	4	1	1	0	2	6	.235	.333	.214	10.80	3.60
Lindell, Karsen	R-R	6-3	190	6-2-96	1	5	5.81	12	7	0	0	31	49	23	20	3	13	29	.371	.452	.333	8.42	3.77
Lubking, Trevor	L-L	6-0	205	9-4-92	0	1	6.10	7	0	0	1	10	11	7	7	0	6	14	.262	.444	.212	12.19	5.23
Lucroy, David	R-R	6-2	202	9-3-92	3	3	5.86	15	2	0	1	43	58	38	28	1	18	33	.319	.364	.299	6.91	3.77
Martin, Jarret	L-L	6-3	230	8-14-89	1	1	22.50	3	2	0	0	4	11	11	10	1	7	5	.478	.429	.500	11.25	15.75
Myers, Aaron	R-R	6-3	225	9-2-93	0	1	1.74	7	0	0	3	10	7	2	2	0	0	14	.184	.333	.115	12.19	0.00
Olczak, Jon	R-R	6-0	180	11-14-93	0	2	1.93	6	0	0	0	9	10	2	2	0	3	13	.270	.333	.227	12.54	2.89
Owenby, Drake	L-L	6-2	205	1-7-94	0	0	6.35	2	1	0	0	6	7	6	4	0	4	4	.304	.250	.333	6.35	4.76
Parker, Evan	R-R	6-2	190	12-6-92	0	0	6.75	5	0	0	0	5	8	4	4	1	2	3	.348	.500	.231	5.06	3.38
Perrin, Jon	R-R	6-5	220	5-23-93	2	0	0.90	3	1	0	0	10	2	1	1	0	3	8	.067	.059	.077	7.20	2.70
Petersen, Michael	R-R	6-7	195	5-16-94	1	0	1.35	4	3	0	0	7	3	2	1	0	2	5	.136	.250	.071	6.75	2.70
Smith, Caleb	R-R	6-4	215	4-22-93	2	3	3.74	14	4	0	0	46	41	24	19	1	20	27	.244	.270	.229	5.32	3.94
Torres-Costa, Quintin	L-L	5-11	190	9-11-94	2	0	2.61	8	0	0	1	21	18	6	6	0	5	26	.237	.316	.211	11.32	2.18
Torrez, Orlando	R-R	6-3	195	4-14-92	0	0	2.13	7	1	0	1	13	7	3	3	0	3	13	.167	.188	.154	9.24	2.13
Trent, Christian	L-L	6-0	190	9-10-92	0	0	0.00	1	0	0	0	1	0	0	0	0	0	0	.000	—	.000	0.00	0.00
Walters, Nash	R-R	6-5	210	5-18-97	1	0	4.15	11	6	0	0	22	18	13	10	0	20	15	.225	.194	.245	6.23	8.31

Fielding

Catcher	PCT	G	PO	A	E	DP	PB
Bishop	1.000	1	4	0	0	0	0
Ghelfi	1.000	9	60	10	0	2	1
Houle	.982	7	48	6	1	0	4
Martinez	1.000	5	50	9	0	0	0
McDowell	1.000	17	141	24	0	0	4
Taylor	1.000	11	73	11	0	0	6
Wallace	.961	12	60	14	3	0	4

First Base	PCT	G	PO	A	E	DP
Martinez	1.000	1	4	0	0	0
McDowell	1.000	2	17	1	0	1
Ortiz	.996	30	246	9	1	19
Perry	.987	26	222	10	3	10
Quiterio	.963	6	26	0	1	4

Wallace	1.000	1	3	1	0	0

Second Base	PCT	G	PO	A	E	DP
Leonardo	.948	22	38	72	6	11
Mendez	.976	11	20	20	1	4
Munoz	.978	14	20	24	1	5
Oquendo	1.000	7	13	22	0	4
Quiterio	1.000	5	4	12	0	0

Third Base	PCT	G	PO	A	E	DP
Mendez	1.000	3	0	3	0	1
Oquendo	.900	16	13	23	4	2
Quiterio	.868	30	12	54	10	2
Wallace	.917	13	6	27	3	1

Shortstop	PCT	G	PO	A	E	DP
Lara	.952	50	100	159	13	25

Leonardo	.800	1	1	3	1	0
Munoz	.929	6	5	21	2	2
Oquendo	.750	1	2	1	1	0

Outfield	PCT	G	PO	A	E	DP
Clark	.978	41	80	7	2	3
Guez	1.000	4	1	0	0	0
Martinez	.983	31	57	2	1	1
Munoz	—	1	0	0	0	0
Orimoloye	1.000	29	37	4	0	0
Ortiz	.818	10	6	3	2	0
Pierre	.970	37	63	1	2	0
Segovia	1.000	24	35	1	0	0
Wallace	.833	3	5	0	1	0

MILWAUKEE BREWERS

HELENA BREWERS
PIONEER LEAGUE

ROOKIE

Batting	B-T	HT	WT	DOB	AVG	vLH	vRH	G	AB	R	H	2B	3B	HR	RBI	BB	HBP	SH	SF	SO	SB	CS	SLG	OBP
Allemand, Blake	B-R	5-10	170	7-1-92	.373	.294	.412	11	51	9	19	4	0	0	5	4	0	0	0	7	3	3	.451	.418
Aviles, Luis	R-R	6-1	170	3-16-95	.356	.375	.349	15	59	9	21	4	0	1	9	2	0	0	0	14	4	2	.475	.377
Belonis, Carlos	R-R	6-3	175	8-19-94	.252	.264	.248	61	210	42	53	6	3	7	28	24	2	2	0	60	21	5	.410	.335
Clark, Trent	L-L	6-0	205	11-1-96	.310	.400	.281	12	42	5	13	0	0	1	5	9	0	1	0	8	5	3	.381	.431
Collymore, Malik	R-R	6-0	195	4-29-95	.311	.265	.330	29	122	19	38	8	2	1	16	13	0	2	1	35	6	2	.434	.375
Cotto, Omar	B-R	5-11	195	2-28-92	.292	.267	.300	20	65	10	19	4	1	0	8	10	1	0	0	16	13	1	.385	.395
Cuas, Jose	R-R	6-2	180	6-28-94	.260	.212	.276	68	258	41	67	19	2	7	40	21	2	3	1	66	6	3	.430	.319
Denson, David	L-R	6-3	254	1-17-95	.242	.167	.273	51	182	28	44	13	0	6	25	27	1	0	2	47	5	2	.412	.340
Galiano, Charles	R-R	6-1	200	5-23-94	.206	.200	.208	21	68	4	14	2	0	0	5	1	5	2	2	25	0	0	.235	.263
Gatewood, Jake	R-R	6-5	190	9-25-95	.274	.345	.248	54	212	38	58	23	1	6	41	18	2	2	4	68	3	5	.476	.331
Ghelfi, Mitch	B-R	5-11	185	9-24-92	.306	.261	.327	20	72	10	22	5	0	0	9	11	0	0	0	14	0	0	.375	.398
Harrison, Monte	R-R	6-3	220	8-10-95	.299	.357	.275	28	97	20	29	4	2	3	13	14	5	2	1	23	14	2	.474	.410
Houle, Dustin	R-R	6-1	205	11-9-93	.385	.200	.429	7	26	2	10	2	0	0	6	1	0	0	1	5	0	2	.462	.393
Iskenderian, George	R-R	6-1	190	2-28-94	.307	.240	.324	36	127	18	39	6	0	1	20	7	1	1	1	21	9	2	.378	.346
Karkenny, Steven	R-R	6-2	210	3-30-93	.244	.304	.223	72	271	53	66	18	3	8	43	33	7	3	10	64	8	1	.421	.330
Lara, Gilbert	R-R	6-2	190	10-30-97	.205	.167	.219	12	44	2	9	3	0	0	5	5	0	0	0	12	0	0	.273	.286
Mallen, Franly	R-R	6-1	160	5-27-97	.500	.500	.500	3	10	2	5	1	0	0	1	0	0	0	0	2	1	0	.600	.500
Martinez, Kevin	B-R	5-10	180	1-11-95	.000	.000	.000	7	17	4	0	0	0	0	0	5	0	0	0	4	1	0	.000	.227
Oquendo, Jonathan	B-R	6-3	170	3-21-96	.240	.321	.206	28	96	10	23	5	0	0	11	11	0	0	0	16	1	2	.292	.318
Pena, Yerison	R-R	6-1	180	7-18-91	.209	.250	.191	20	67	15	14	2	0	0	5	9	1	0	1	15	3	0	.239	.303
Post, Milan	R-R	6-1	185	3-22-94	.189	.250	.162	44	143	15	27	6	1	0	12	13	9	3	1	48	1	1	.245	.295
Segovia, Joantgel	R-R	6-1	175	11-8-96	.174	.000	.200	6	23	1	4	0	0	0	0	0	1	0	0	4	3	1	.174	.208
Stokes, Troy	R-R	5-8	182	2-2-96	.270	.302	.258	62	226	51	61	12	2	5	27	33	9	3	0	50	26	6	.407	.384

Pitching	B-T	HT	WT	DOB	W	L	ERA	G	GS	CG	SV	IP	H	R	ER	HR	BB	SO	AVG	vLH	vRH	K/9	BB/9
Blau, Bubba	R-R	6-2	190	8-3-92	3	5	6.57	17	0	0	1	37	39	29	27	7	19	35	.279	.269	.284	8.51	4.62
Carver, David	L-L	6-3	180	10-25-91	1	0	5.91	5	2	0	0	21	32	15	14	2	3	12	.344	.360	.338	5.06	1.27
Diplan, Marcos	R-R	6-0	160	9-18-96	2	2	3.75	13	7	0	2	50	47	21	21	4	21	54	.257	.254	.259	9.66	3.75
Drossner, Jake	R-L	6-1	189	5-16-94	4	3	3.64	14	7	0	0	47	51	34	19	1	19	46	.268	.245	.277	8.81	3.64
Farina, Alex	L-R	6-0	230	5-30-93	2	2	4.50	8	1	0	0	20	20	13	10	1	7	16	.253	.276	.240	7.20	3.15
Gomez, Milton	R-R	6-1	172	4-22-94	3	2	6.32	14	8	0	1	57	70	44	40	2	22	37	.310	.293	.320	5.84	3.47
Griep, Nate	R-R	6-2	190	10-11-93	0	2	8.02	14	5	0	1	34	48	33	30	4	14	27	.336	.439	.267	7.22	3.74
Harber, Conor	R-R	6-2	205	12-18-93	0	0	3.38	9	4	0	0	24	19	11	9	1	8	21	.218	.152	.259	7.88	3.00
Hissa, Donnie	R-R	6-7	240	1-9-92	0	2	11.42	10	0	0	0	17	22	25	22	4	20	12	.293	.344	.256	6.23	10.38
Hudgens, Brock	R-R	6-0	202	10-16-91	0	1	6.43	6	0	0	0	7	12	9	5	1	6	6	.387	.500	.348	7.71	7.71
Kole, J.B.	R-R	6-4	210	1-26-93	1	4	4.38	14	6	0	0	49	49	28	24	2	25	31	.258	.185	.296	5.64	4.56
Kuntz, Brad	L-L	6-0	180	5-14-92	0	0	1.35	6	0	0	2	13	12	2	2	0	3	14	.245	.125	.268	9.45	
2.03 Olczak, Jon	R-R	6-0	180	11-14-93	0	2	2.45	8	0	0	2	18	11	5	5	2	2	30	.167	.182	.159	14.73	0.98
Owenby, Drake	L-L	6-2	205	1-7-94	1	3	7.67	11	7	0	0	29	38	29	25	2	11	23	.317	.378	.289	7.06	3.38
Ponce, Cody	R-R	6-6	240	4-25-94	0	0	3.60	2	2	0	0	5	4	2	2	0	0	4	.222	.333	.167	7.20	0.00
Reeves, Chad	L-L	6-2	190	2-4-91	1	0	4.96	8	0	0	1	16	17	9	9	0	13	5	.270	.333	.238	2.76	7.16
Rincon, Junior	R-R	6-2	185	12-7-91	6	4	4.65	18	2	0	3	31	31	28	16	3	16	38	.250	.241	.257	11.03	4.65
Torres, Joshua	R-R	6-0	160	4-26-94	5	3	3.27	15	7	0	1	55	54	27	20	3	13	43	.254	.253	.254	7.04	2.13
Torres-Costa, Quintin	L-L	5-11	190	9-11-94	0	0	4.76	6	0	0	0	11	17	7	6	1	3	17	.347	.455	.316	13.50	2.38
Trent, Christian	L-L	6-0	190	9-10-92	2	1	4.15	12	5	0	1	35	36	17	16	3	4	25	.259	.255	.261	6.49	1.04
Yamamoto, Jordan	R-R	6-0	185	5-11-96	1	6	7.84	14	11	0	0	62	99	59	54	12	22	59	.363	.406	.337	8.56	3.19

Fielding

Catcher	PCT	G	PO	A	E	DP	PB
Galiano	.955	13	99	6	5	0	3
Ghelfi	1.000	14	105	17	0	1	2
Houle	.976	4	35	5	1	0	0
Martinez	1.000	7	30	6	0	0	0
Post	.977	39	260	41	7	3	8

First Base	PCT	G	PO	A	E	DP
Denson	.955	13	99	7	5	7
Karkenny	.990	61	550	40	6	48
Post	.962	3	23	2	1	1

Second Base	PCT	G	PO	A	E	DP
Allemand	.974	8	14	24	1	4
Aviles	.964	4	13	14	1	3
Cuas	.976	9	20	21	1	7

	PCT	G	PO	A	E	DP
Iskenderian	.972	35	51	88	4	20
Mallen	.600	2	0	3	2	0
Oquendo	.941	21	31	64	6	11
Pena	1.000	1	1	0	0	0

Third Base	PCT	G	PO	A	E	DP
Aviles	1.000	6	6	18	0	0
Cuas	.945	54	27	94	7	11
Karkenny	.962	9	8	17	1	2
Oquendo	.667	2	1	1	1	0
Pena	.913	8	3	18	2	0

Shortstop	PCT	G	PO	A	E	DP
Allemand	.952	3	7	13	1	3
Aviles	1.000	2	2	6	0	1
Cuas	.960	7	11	13	1	1

	PCT	G	PO	A	E	DP
Gatewood	.934	51	72	153	16	29
Lara	.965	12	16	39	2	7

Outfield	PCT	G	PO	A	E	DP
Aviles	1.000	2	5	0	0	0
Belonis	.949	60	104	8	6	2
Clark	1.000	12	19	0	0	0
Collymore	.971	19	33	0	1	0
Cotto	1.000	17	35	2	0	0
Denson	.857	17	18	0	3	0
Harrison	.958	28	65	3	3	1
Karkenny	1.000	2	1	0	0	0
Oquendo	1.000	5	5	0	0	0
Pena	.933	9	13	1	1	0
Segovia	1.000	6	15	2	0	0
Stokes	.978	57	88	2	2	1

DSL BREWERS
DOMINICAN SUMMER LEAGUE

ROOKIE

Batting	B-T	HT	WT	DOB	AVG	vLH	vRH	G	AB	R	H	2B	3B	HR	RBI	BB	HBP	SH	SF	SO	SB	CS	SLG	OBP
Castillo, Javier	R-R	5-11	160	4-4-98	.264	.226	.273	48	163	22	43	2	1	0	17	11	4	2	0	22	4	5	.288	.326
Chal, Roosevert	L-R	5-9	155	4-9-94	.205	.207	.205	22	73	13	15	2	0	0	8	4	0	1	0	16	1	2	.233	.247
Correa, Henry	L-R	6-0	160	1-29-97	.157	.139	.165	42	127	12	20	3	3	0	7	21	2	0	0	51	1	1	.228	.287

Batting	B-T	HT	WT	DOB	AVG	vLH	vRH	G	AB	R	H	2B	3B	HR	RBI	BB	HBP	SH	SF	SO	SB	CS	SLG	OBP
Estades, Ariel	L-R	5-11	150	4-27-94	.275	.107	.365	26	80	20	22	6	0	0	7	13	0	1	0	17	15	3	.350	.376
Feliciano, Jay	R-R	6-2	215	9-28-95	.301	.300	.302	20	73	13	22	5	2	2	12	4	3	0	0	20	2	1	.507	.363
Fernandez, Dilson	R-R	5-11	185	5-9-94	.247	.240	.250	28	81	11	20	0	2	0	14	3	0	0	1	11	2	1	.296	.271
Herrera, Josue	R-R	6-0	165	2-3-97	.244	.167	.269	39	123	20	30	6	1	1	12	10	6	0	2	26	1	1	.333	.326
Jesus, Anderson	R-R	6-2	168	2-19-94	.266	.204	.288	58	214	30	57	14	4	2	28	8	6	1	3	43	11	7	.397	.307
Mallen, Franly	R-R	6-1	160	5-27-97	.268	.288	.261	60	235	33	63	20	2	4	28	25	5	0	0	64	5	4	.421	.351
Martinez, Sandy	B-R	5-11	180	7-18-92	.190	.259	.164	38	100	12	19	5	0	0	13	11	2	0	2	8	0	0	.240	.278
Mendez, Julio	R-R	5-10	140	10-24-96	.260	.227	.273	43	154	23	40	4	2	0	14	15	4	1	0	17	6	2	.312	.341
Morillo, Adolfo	L-L	6-0	170	9-21-97	.214	.189	.222	47	145	20	31	6	1	0	12	12	2	1	1	49	7	3	.269	.281
Nunez, Bismar	R-R	5-11	212	1-24-95	.311	.294	.319	32	106	14	33	6	1	1	15	6	1	1	1	20	0	0	.415	.351
Otano, Ignacio	R-R	6-0	175	1-6-97	.322	.362	.307	50	208	34	67	20	3	1	19	10	2	0	0	20	17	10	.462	.359
Pena, Yerison	R-R	6-1	180	7-18-91	.327	.308	.333	43	147	29	48	12	3	5	34	25	0	0	0	32	1	4	.551	.424
Pinero, Marcos	R-R	6-1	170	3-21-96	.235	.225	.239	45	132	21	31	3	0	2	12	21	8	4	0	46	18	5	.303	.373
Torres, Bryan	L-R	5-11	165	7-2-97	.250	.286	.214	8	28	4	7	0	1	0	4	4	0	0	0	2	2	0	.321	.344
Valderrey, Nicol	R-R	6-2	180	1-20-97	.300	.338	.286	68	263	33	79	14	0	1	28	19	6	0	1	55	0	1	.365	.360

Pitching	B-T	HT	WT	DOB	W	L	ERA	G	GS	CG	SV	IP	H	R	ER	HR	BB	SO	AVG	vLH	vRH	K/9	BB/9
Almonte, Yomelbin	R-R	6-0	202	2-22-93	0	1	3.51	15	0	0	1	33	30	17	13	2	17	26	.246	.105	.310	7.02	4.59
Alvarado, Deymar	R-R	6-1	170	10-22-97	0	0	3.55	8	0	0	0	13	11	5	5	1	8	5	.256	.222	.265	3.55	5.68
Benoit, Rodrigo	R-R	6-2	170	2-23-94	6	1	2.10	12	12	1	0	73	56	28	17	0	11	52	.207	.206	.207	6.41	1.36
Brea, Jesus	R-R	6-3	194	12-25-95	2	3	5.06	17	0	0	2	27	29	18	15	0	17	25	.282	.250	.296	8.44	5.74
De La Cruz, Yan	R-R	6-4	180	4-28-95	0	3	4.43	12	0	0	0	20	21	12	10	2	14	21	.259	.208	.281	9.30	6.20
Diaz, Juan	R-R	6-0	185	9-24-92	2	0	4.46	21	0	0	4	38	31	20	19	0	23	46	.223	.250	.215	10.80	5.40
Diplan, Nattino	R-R	6-3	180	12-30-93	3	7	4.55	12	12	0	0	63	71	41	32	4	24	44	.290	.288	.290	6.25	3.41
Duval, Starling	R-R	6-6	200	11-28-94	4	2	6.23	13	0	0	2	22	22	20	15	1	15	10	.268	.263	.270	4.15	6.23
Flores, Junior	R-R	6-1	175	10-13-94	1	4	5.80	11	11	0	0	40	37	32	26	0	26	36	.255	.283	.242	8.03	5.80
Hernandez, Nelson	R-R	6-2	170	3-13-97	4	2	4.76	12	12	0	0	59	67	40	31	0	11	37	.283	.382	.243	5.68	1.69
Luna, Carlos	R-R	6-1	175	9-25-96	4	2	1.46	9	8	1	0	56	46	18	9	1	10	49	.220	.262	.203	7.92	1.62
Nova, Boanerges	L-L	6-2	170	2-6-93	1	2	2.72	14	3	0	1	46	42	18	14	0	14	33	.240	.250	.238	6.41	2.72
Pinto, Maiker	R-R	6-3	180	9-25-96	1	1	5.28	14	1	0	0	15	13	13	9	1	16	7	.232	.091	.267	4.11	9.39
Rodriguez, Wuilder	R-R	6-2	180	1-21-93	3	2	3.26	12	12	0	0	61	61	24	22	1	14	37	.269	.250	.277	5.49	2.08
Silva, Isaac	L-L	6-2	190	9-12-92	0	4	13.11	15	0	0	0	12	18	22	17	0	17	13	.367	.600	.341	10.03	13.11

Fielding

Catcher	PCT	G	PO	A	E	DP	PB
Fernandez	.969	26	134	22	5	0	8
Martinez	.989	38	219	59	3	2	6
Nunez	.982	24	137	31	3	0	7

First Base	PCT	G	PO	A	E	DP
Fernandez	1.000	1	4	0	0	0
Herrera	1.000	11	69	5	0	4
Nunez	1.000	1	5	0	0	0
Pena	.968	5	28	2	1	2
Valderrey	.986	63	534	32	8	43

Second Base	PCT	G	PO	A	E	DP
Castillo	.965	24	68	43	4	10
Chal	.875	3	4	3	1	2
Correa	.938	5	2	13	1	1
Herrera	—	1	0	0	0	0
Mallen	.978	26	67	67	3	17
Mendez	1.000	18	43	47	0	12

Third Base	PCT	G	PO	A	E	DP
Castillo	.930	11	10	30	3	3
Correa	.938	6	1	14	1	0
Herrera	.890	25	23	50	9	2
Mendez	.891	17	14	35	6	2
Pena	.938	18	12	49	4	5

Shortstop	PCT	G	PO	A	E	DP
Castillo	.870	6	8	12	3	2
Mallen	.917	27	42	79	11	12
Mendez	.857	4	5	7	2	2
Otano	.830	40	62	109	35	13

Outfield	PCT	G	PO	A	E	DP
Correa	.976	28	37	4	1	1
Estades	.971	23	33	0	1	0
Feliciano	.971	18	31	3	1	1
Jesus	.988	56	75	5	1	0
Morillo	.977	44	82	3	2	0
Pena	.938	18	27	3	2	0
Pinero	.968	43	56	4	2	0
Torres	1.000	6	11	1	0	0

Minnesota Twins

SEASON IN A SENTENCE: After four consecutive 90-loss seasons, the Twins rebounded into wild-card contention under rookie manager Paul Molitor and behind the power of rookie sluggers Miguel Sano and Eddie Rosario.

HIGH POINT: The Twins, not expected to do much this season, powered their way into contention by going 20-7 in May and as late as June 7, were in sole possession of first place in the AL Central.

LOW POINT: The pendulum swung back in June as the Twins hit the skids and went 11-17, including a five-game losing streak that began June 8 and left them out of first place for good.

NOTABLE ROOKIES: Sano, the large-bodied-but-powerful righthanded hitter, came up on June 1 and instantly gave the Twins the slugger they had lacked since Justin Morneau's halcyon days. Despite some contact issues, Sano slugged .551 and injected a fearsome bat into the lineup for the first time in years. Rosario had dealt with a drug suspension and high expectations, but overcame that to become a key part of a revitalized lineup. Since 1914, just two other rookies have managed at least 15 doubles, 15 triples, 10 homers and 10 stolen bases, something Rosario pulled off this year. Byron Buxton made his anticipated big league debut as well, but injuries cost him most of the season. Righthander Tyler Duffey came up and provided the team with an unexpected boost. German-born Max Kepler, who had the best season of any position prospect in the organization, made his big league debut and got his first hit.

KEY TRANSACTIONS: The Twins went out and added relief help in low-key moves for Kevin Jepsen—which cost them intriguing arms Chih-Wei Hu and Alexis Tapia—and Neal Cotts. Jepsen solidified the back of the bullpen, keeping the Twins in the wild-card race to the final week.

DOWN ON THE FARM: Sano, Rosario, Trevor May, Alex Meyer and Buxton all made their big league debuts, but that does not leave the Twins barren. Max Kepler had the best season of their minor league prospects, showing consistency; Adam Brett Walker continued to show the best power in the minors along with tons of whiffs; Nick Gordon had a solid sophomore showing as he reached full-season ball. Among the pitchers, Jose Berrios is on the verge of helping the major league rotation in 2016, while lefthander Stephen Gonsalves has an intriguing package.

OPENING DAY PAYROLL: $108,262,500 (19th)

PLAYERS OF THE YEAR

MAJOR LEAGUE	MINOR LEAGUE
Miguel Sano, 3b/dh	**Jose Berrios, rhp**
.269/.385/.530	(Double-A/Triple-A)
18 HRs in majors	14-5, 2.87 175 SO in
after 15 at Double-A	166 IP

ORGANIZATION LEADERS

BATTING		*Minimum 250 AB
MAJORS		
* AVG	Joe Mauer	.265
* OPS	Brian Dozier	.751
HR	Brian Dozier	28
RBI	Trevor Plouffe	86
MINORS		
* AVG	Max Kepler, Fort Myers, Chattanooga	.318
* OBP	Max Kepler, Fort Myers, Chattanooga	.410
* SLG	Max Kepler, Fort Myers, Chattanooga	.520
R	Reynaldo Rodriguez, Rochester	81
H	James Beresford, Rochester	153
TB	Adam Brett Walker, Chattanooga	250
2B	Reynaldo Rodriguez, Rochester	34
3B	Byron Buxton, Chattanooga, Rochester	13
	Max Kepler, Fort Myers, Chattanooga	13
HR	Adam Brett Walker, Chattanooga	31
RBI	Adam Brett Walker, Chattanooga	106
BB	Mitch Garver, Fort Myers	69
	Max Kepler, Fort Myers, Chattanooga	69
SO	Adam Brett Walker, Chattanooga	195
SB	Tanner English, Cedar Rapids	37

PITCHING		#Minimum 75 IP
MAJORS		
W	Kyle Gibson, Phil Hughes	11
# ERA	Kyle Gibson	3.84
SO	Kyle Gibson	145
SV	Glen Perkins	32
MINORS		
W	Jose Berrios, Chattanooga, Rochester	14
L	Greg Peavey, Rochester, Chattanooga	12
	Taylor Rogers, Rochester	12
# ERA	Stephen Gonsalves, Cedar Rapids, Fort Myers	2.01
G	J.T. Chargois, Fort Myers, Chattanooga	48
GS	4 players	27
SV	Trevor Hildenberger, Cedar Rapids, Fort Myers	17
IP	Pat Dean, Rochester	179
BB	Stephen Gonsalves, Cedar Rapids, Fort Myers	53
SO	Jose Berrios, Chattanooga, Rochester	175
AVG	Stephen Gonsalves, Cedar Rapids, Fort Myers	.198

2015 PERFORMANCE

General Manager: Terry Ryan. **Farm Director:** Brad Steil. **Scouting Director:** Deron Johnson.

Class	Team	League	W	L	PCT	Finish	Manager
Majors	Minnesota Twins	American	83	79	.512	7th (15)	Paul Molitor
Triple-A	Rochester Red Wings	International	77	67	.535	t-5th (14)	Mike Quade
Double-A	Chattanooga Lookouts	Southern	76	61	.555	3rd (10)	Doug Mientkiewicz
High A	Fort Myers Miracle	Florida State	76	63	.547	3rd (12)	Jeff Smith
Low A	Cedar Rapids Kernels	Midwest	77	63	.550	4th (16)	Jake Mauer
Rookie	Elizabethton Twins	Appalachian	34	34	.500	t-5th (10)	Ray Smith
Rookie	Twins	Gulf Coast	27	32	.458	t-9th (16)	Ramon Borrego
Overall 2015 Minor League Record			367	320	.534	6th (30)	

ORGANIZATION STATISTICS

MINNESOTA TWINS

AMERICAN LEAGUE

Batting	B-T	HT	WT	DOB	AVG	vLH	vRH	G	AB	R	H	2B	3B	HR	RBI	BB	HBP	SH	SF	SO	SB	CS	SLG	OBP
Arcia, Oswaldo	L-R	6-0	225	5-9-91	.276	.304	.257	19	58	6	16	0	0	2	8	4	2	0	1	15	0	0	.379	.338
Bernier, Doug	R-R	6-1	185	6-24-80	.200	—	.200	4	5	1	1	1	0	0	2	1	0	0	0	3	0	0	.400	.333
Buxton, Byron	R-R	6-2	190	12-18-93	.209	.116	.256	46	129	16	27	7	1	2	6	6	1	2	0	44	2	2	.326	.250
Dozier, Brian	R-R	5-11	200	5-15-87	.236	.232	.237	157	628	101	148	39	4	28	77	61	7	0	8	148	12	4	.444	.307
Escobar, Eduardo	B-R	5-10	185	1-5-89	.262	.277	.254	127	409	48	107	31	4	12	58	28	2	2	5	86	2	3	.445	.309
Fryer, Eric	R-R	6-2	215	8-26-85	.227	.000	.294	15	22	2	5	2	0	0	2	5	0	0	1	5	0	0	.318	.370
Herrmann, Chris	L-R	6-0	200	11-24-87	.146	.050	.169	45	103	13	15	5	1	2	10	7	2	1	0	37	0	0	.272	.214
Hicks, Aaron	B-R	6-2	210	10-2-89	.256	.307	.235	97	352	48	90	11	3	11	33	34	2	0	2	66	13	3	.398	.323
Hunter, Torii	R-R	6-2	220	7-18-75	.240	.244	.238	139	521	67	125	22	0	22	81	35	6	0	5	105	2	5	.409	.293
Kepler, Max	L-L	6-4	205	2-10-93	.143	.000	.167	3	7	0	1	0	0	0	0	0	0	0	0	3	0	0	.143	.143
Mauer, Joe	L-R	6-5	225	4-19-83	.265	.267	.264	158	592	69	157	34	2	10	66	67	1	1	5	112	2	1	.380	.338
Nunez, Eduardo	R-R	6-0	195	6-15-87	.282	.210	.317	72	188	23	53	14	1	4	20	12	1	2	1	29	8	4	.431	.327
Plouffe, Trevor	R-R	6-2	215	6-15-86	.244	.250	.242	152	573	74	140	35	4	22	86	50	4	1	4	124	2	1	.435	.307
Polanco, Jorge	B-R	5-11	200	7-5-93	.300	.667	.143	4	10	1	3	0	0	0	1	2	0	0	0	1	1	0	.300	.417
Robinson, Shane	R-R	5-9	165	10-30-84	.250	.257	.245	83	180	28	45	7	3	0	16	12	1	3	1	29	6	1	.322	.299
Rosario, Eddie	L-R	6-1	180	9-28-91	.267	.289	.260	122	453	60	121	18	15	13	50	15	0	3	3	118	11	6	.459	.289
Sano, Miguel	R-R	6-4	260	5-11-93	.269	.284	.263	80	279	46	75	17	1	18	52	53	1	0	2	119	1	1	.530	.385
Santana, Danny	B-R	5-11	185	11-7-90	.215	.253	.199	91	261	30	56	10	5	0	21	6	3	7	0	68	8	4	.291	.241
Schafer, Jordan	L-L	6-1	205	9-4-86	.217	.313	.189	27	69	9	15	3	0	0	5	3	0	2	0	23	0	3	.261	.250
Suzuki, Kurt	R-R	5-11	205	10-4-83	.240	.257	.232	131	433	36	104	17	0	5	50	29	7	6	4	59	0	0	.314	.296
Vargas, Kennys	B-R	6-5	290	8-1-90	.240	.364	.183	58	175	18	42	4	0	5	17	9	0	0	4	54	0	0	.349	.277

Pitching	B-T	HT	WT	DOB	W	L	ERA	G	GS	CG	SV	IP	H	R	ER	HR	BB	SO	AVG	vLH	vRH	K/9	BB/9
Achter, A.J.	R-R	6-5	205	8-27-88	0	1	6.75	11	0	0	0	13	12	10	10	4	6	14	.231	.267	.216	9.45	4.05
Boyer, Blaine	R-R	6-3	225	7-11-81	3	6	2.49	68	0	0	1	65	62	24	18	5	19	33	.254	.169	.298	4.57	2.63
Cotts, Neal	L-L	6-2	200	3-25-80	0	0	3.95	17	0	0	0	14	14	8	6	3	5	9	.264	.188	.297	5.93	3.29
Duensing, Brian	L-L	6-0	200	2-22-83	4	1	4.25	55	0	0	1	49	46	24	23	5	21	24	.254	.288	.235	4.44	3.88
Duffey, Tyler	R-R	6-3	220	12-27-90	5	1	3.10	10	10	0	0	58	56	20	20	4	20	53	.256	.257	.255	8.22	3.10
Fien, Casey	R-R	6-2	210	10-21-83	4	6	3.55	62	0	0	0	63	61	26	25	6	8	41	.250	.282	.227	5.83	1.14
Gibson, Kyle	R-R	6-6	215	10-23-87	11	11	3.84	32	32	1	0	195	186	88	83	18	65	145	.252	.248	.257	6.70	3.01
Graham, J.R.	R-R	6-0	210	1-14-90	1	1	4.95	39	1	0	0	64	73	41	35	10	21	53	.287	.277	.296	7.49	2.97
Hughes, Phil	R-R	6-5	250	6-24-86	11	9	4.40	27	25	1	0	155	184	76	76	29	16	94	.293	.282	.304	5.45	0.93
Jepsen, Kevin	R-R	6-3	235	7-26-84	1	1	1.61	29	0	0	10	28	18	5	5	1	7	25	.176	.203	.140	8.04	2.25
2-team total (46 Tampa Bay)					3	6	2.33	75	0	0	15	70	52	20	18	5	27	59	—	—	—	7.62	3.49
May, Trevor	R-R	6-5	240	9-23-89	8	9	4.00	48	16	0	0	115	127	53	51	11	26	110	.279	.288	.269	8.63	2.04
Meyer, Alex	R-R	6-9	225	1-3-90	0	0	16.88	2	0	0	0	3	4	5	5	2	3	3	.364	.400	.333	10.13	10.13
Milone, Tommy	L-L	6-0	220	2-16-87	9	5	3.92	24	23	0	1	129	128	64	56	17	36	91	.260	.218	.273	6.37	2.52
Nolasco, Ricky	R-R	6-2	235	12-13-82	5	2	6.75	9	8	0	0	37	50	31	28	3	14	35	.321	.239	.388	8.44	3.38
O'Rourke, Ryan	R-L	6-3	230	4-30-88	0	0	6.14	28	0	0	0	22	16	15	15	3	15	24	.200	.171	.231	9.82	6.14
Pelfrey, Mike	R-R	6-7	240	1-14-84	6	11	4.26	30	30	0	0	165	198	86	78	11	45	86	.304	.312	.297	4.70	2.46
Perkins, Glen	L-L	6-0	215	3-2-83	3	5	3.32	60	0	0	32	57	58	21	21	9	10	54	.256	.379	.213	8.53	1.58
Pressly, Ryan	R-R	6-3	210	12-15-88	3	2	2.93	27	0	0	0	28	27	9	9	2	9	22	.257	.263	.254	7.16	3.90
Santana, Ervin	R-R	6-2	175	12-12-82	7	5	4.00	17	17	0	0	108	104	50	48	12	36	82	.253	.260	.246	6.83	3.00
Stauffer, Tim	R-R	6-1	220	6-2-82	1	0	6.60	13	0	0	0	15	24	13	11	4	7	6	.369	.421	.348	3.60	4.20
Thielbar, Caleb	L-L	6-0	205	1-31-87	0	0	5.40	6	0	0	0	5	5	3	3	0	0	5	.263	.200	.333	9.00	0.00
Thompson, Aaron	L-L	6-3	205	2-28-87	1	3	5.01	41	0	0	0	32	32	19	18	2	11	17	.264	.189	.324	4.73	3.06
Tonkin, Michael	R-R	6-7	220	11-19-89	0	0	3.47	26	0	0	0	23	21	9	9	4	9	19	.239	.361	.154	7.33	3.47

Fielding

Catcher	PCT	G	PO	A	E	DP	PB
Fryer	.981	15	52	0	1	1	0
Herrmann	.987	38	205	15	3	2	0
Suzuki	.997	130	825	35	3	8	3

First Base	PCT	G	PO	A	E	DP
Herrmann	1.000	2	3	1	0	2

Mauer	.996	137	1151	86	5	113
Plouffe	.993	17	122	11	1	7
Sano	1.000	2	2	0	0	
Vargas	1.000	18	131	10	0	14

Second Base	PCT	G	PO	A	E	DP
Bernier	1.000	2	0	3	0	1

Dozier	.990	157	303	456	8	111
Escobar	1.000	11	8	14	0	2
Nunez	1.000	1	3	0	0	0

Third Base	PCT	G	PO	A	E	DP
Bernier	1.000	2	0	1	0	0
Escobar	.900	5	3	6	1	1

MINNESOTA TWINS *(side tab)*

Third Base	PCT	G	PO	A	E	DP
Nunez	.917	16	7	15	2	0
Plouffe	.972	140	101	277	11	32
Sano	1.000	9	8	15	0	0

Shortstop	PCT	G	PO	A	E	DP
Escobar	.986	71	93	190	4	44
Nunez	1.000	27	32	71	0	10

	PCT	G	PO	A	E	DP
Polanco	.882	4	3	12	2	2
Santana	.946	66	92	191	16	47
Outfield	PCT	G	PO	A	E	DP
Arcia	.974	19	37	0	1	0
Buxton	1.000	44	115	2	0	0
Escobar	.985	36	60	4	1	1
Herrmann	—	2	0	0	0	0

	PCT	G	PO	A	E	DP
Hicks	.996	97	244	9	1	2
Hunter	.979	123	231	6	5	1
Kepler	1.000	2	3	0	0	0
Nunez	.833	3	4	1	1	0
Robinson	.991	75	111	5	1	1
Rosario	.971	118	220	16	7	4
Santana	1.000	5	8	0	0	0
Schafer	.982	27	55	1	1	0

ROCHESTER RED WINGS

INTERNATIONAL LEAGUE

TRIPLE-A

Batting	B-T	HT	WT	DOB	AVG	vLH	vRH	G	AB	R	H	2B	3B	HR	RBI	BB	HBP	SH	SF	SO	SB	CS	SLG	OBP
Arcia, Oswaldo	L-R	6-0	225	5-9-91	.199	.132	.214	79	282	31	56	13	0	12	41	18	6	0	5	82	0	1	.372	.257
Avery, Xavier	L-L	6-0	190	1-1-90	.247	.343	.216	38	146	23	36	3	1	5	23	7	1	0	1	43	5	2	.384	.284
2-team total (73 Toledo)					.285	—	—	111	431	65	123	21	3	6	51	37	3	2	5	105	19	12	.390	.342
Beresford, James	L-R	6-1	170	1-19-89	.307	.330	.301	129	498	58	153	21	1	1	50	29	0	3	6	57	2	2	.359	.341
Bernier, Doug	R-R	6-1	185	6-24-80	.256	.246	.259	95	301	39	77	9	0	2	20	36	3	1	1	57	2	2	.306	.340
Buxton, Byron	R-R	6-2	190	12-18-93	.400	.583	.349	13	55	11	22	3	1	1	8	4	0	0	0	12	2	1	.545	.441
De San Miguel, Allan	R-R	5-9	205	2-1-88	.375	.000	.429	3	8	0	3	1	0	0	0	0	0	0	0	4	0	1	.500	.375
Diaz, Argenis	R-R	6-0	190	2-12-87	.258	.278	.247	92	302	37	78	12	1	0	26	26	3	3	1	54	4	1	.305	.322
Farris, Eric	R-R	5-9	180	3-3-86	.259	.256	.260	86	297	34	77	10	1	1	29	19	2	3	2	39	5	2	.310	.306
Fryer, Eric	R-R	6-2	215	8-26-85	.293	.333	.273	67	222	28	65	7	1	2	19	25	1	0	0	47	1	2	.360	.367
Hanson, Nate	R-R	6-0	195	2-8-87	.262	.357	.214	17	42	3	11	2	0	0	4	5	0	0	0	13	0	0	.310	.340
Herrmann, Chris	L-R	6-0	200	11-24-87	.260	.200	.270	23	73	9	19	3	0	1	6	11	2	0	2	13	3	0	.342	.364
Hicks, Aaron	B-R	6-2	210	10-2-89	.342	.333	.345	38	149	26	51	13	4	3	20	17	0	2	30	2	1	.544	.405
Martinez, Jose	R-R	5-11	175	1-24-86	.255	.317	.220	95	337	35	86	14	0	6	43	18	0	1	2	35	1	1	.350	.291
Ortiz, Danny	L-L	5-11	185	1-5-90	.248	.263	.242	131	484	61	120	31	3	17	78	33	2	1	6	105	4	1	.430	.295
Paulino, Carlos	R-R	6-0	175	9-24-89	.257	.261	.256	34	109	15	28	5	1	0	8	10	0	2	0	9	0	1	.321	.319
Peterson, Brock	R-R	6-3	230	11-20-83	.186	.256	.138	29	97	11	18	1	0	5	12	14	1	0	2	33	0	0	.351	.289
Pinto, Josmil	R-R	5-11	220	3-31-89	.228	.235	.225	64	237	33	54	9	0	7	31	22	4	0	0	54	0	0	.354	.304
Polanco, Jorge	B-R	5-11	200	7-5-93	.284	.200	.301	22	88	7	25	6	0	0	6	4	0	0	2	10	1	0	.352	.309
Ramirez, Wilkin	R-R	6-2	230	10-25-85	.232	.209	.242	43	142	10	33	9	2	3	14	2	0	0	3	38	3	0	.387	.238
Rodriguez, Reynaldo	R-R	6-0	200	7-2-86	.255	.309	.235	132	502	81	128	34	7	16	80	39	2	0	8	82	13	5	.446	.307
Rosario, Eddie	L-R	6-1	180	9-28-91	.242	.286	.217	23	95	11	23	2	1	3	12	5	0	0	17	1	1	.379	.280
Santana, Danny	B-R	5-11	185	11-7-90	.322	.407	.304	35	152	24	49	10	4	3	15	7	0	1	2	25	6	3	.500	.348
Vargas, Kennys	B-R	6-5	290	8-1-90	.279	.225	.305	38	122	20	34	6	0	6	22	26	2	0	1	39	0	0	.475	.411
Wheeler, Ryan	L-R	6-3	230	7-10-88	.233	.167	.239	21	73	4	17	3	0	1	7	4	0	0	0	13	0	0	.315	.243

Pitching	B-T	HT	WT	DOB	W	L	ERA	G	GS	CG	SV	IP	H	R	ER	HR	BB	SO	AVG	vLH	vRH	K/9	BB/9
Achter, A.J.	R-R	6-5	205	8-27-88	4	2	2.63	43	0	0	14	48	28	14	14	5	13	47	.167	.147	.180	8.81	2.44
Berrios, Jose	R-R	6-0	185	5-27-94	6	2	2.62	12	12	0	0	76	59	24	22	6	14	83	.212	.221	.204	9.87	1.67
Bowden, Michael	R-R	6-3	215	9-9-86	4	3	3.78	8	8	0	0	48	50	22	20	2	11	47	.266	.273	.261	8.87	2.08
2-team total (24 Norfolk)					11	5	2.63	32	17	0	0	123	110	41	36	6	31	99	—	—	—	7.24	2.27
Darnell, Logan	L-L	6-2	220	2-2-89	5	1	2.78	35	7	1	0	78	77	29	24	3	25	66	.258	.265	.255	7.65	2.90
Dean, Pat	L-L	6-1	180	5-25-89	12	11	2.82	27	27	5	0	179	170	60	56	10	36	98	.254	.218	.269	4.93	1.81
Duffey, Tyler	R-R	6-3	220	12-27-90	5	6	2.53	14	14	1	0	85	73	32	24	1	18	68	.224	.239	.209	7.17	1.90
Fien, Casey	R-R	6-2	210	10-21-83	0	0	0.00	3	1	0	0	3	0	0	0	0	1	3	.000	.000	.000	9.00	3.00
Hamburger, Mark	R-R	6-4	200	2-5-87	4	2	3.31	45	4	0	1	68	74	26	25	3	22	63	.276	.302	.259	8.34	2.91
Hu, Chih-Wei	R-R	6-1	230	11-4-93	1	0	1.50	1	1	0	0	6	2	1	1	0	4	6	.105	.286	.000	9.00	6.00
Hurlbut, David	L-L	6-3	221	11-24-89	0	0	2.70	1	1	0	0	7	9	2	2	0	2	2	.346	.500	.250	2.70	0.00
Johnson, Cole	R-R	6-3	200	10-6-88	0	1	3.42	17	0	0	0	24	27	10	9	3	11	15	.290	.313	.279	5.70	4.18
Meyer, Alex	R-R	6-9	225	1-3-90	4	5	4.79	38	8	0	0	92	101	54	49	4	48	100	.281	.282	.280	9.78	4.70
Milone, Tommy	L-L	6-0	220	2-16-87	4	0	0.70	5	5	1	0	39	25	3	3	2	3	47	.182	.128	.204	10.94	0.70
O'Rourke, Ryan	R-L	6-3	230	4-30-88	0	0	5.93	20	0	0	0	14	13	9	9	1	7	22	.250	.125	.357	14.49	4.61
Oliveros, Lester	R-R	6-0	235	5-28-88	3	2	3.79	24	4	0	6	36	39	15	15	3	13	46	.277	.339	.228	11.61	3.28
Peavey, Greg	R-R	6-2	185	7-11-88	1	5	5.45	7	7	0	0	36	48	27	22	5	9	27	.314	.231	.375	6.69	2.23
Pressly, Ryan	R-R	6-3	210	12-15-88	0	2	4.50	7	0	0	0	10	6	7	5	1	6	15	.176	.188	.167	13.50	5.40
Pryor, Stephen	R-R	6-4	235	7-23-89	1	0	9.00	9	0	0	0	13	13	13	13	5	12	13	.255	.200	.308	9.00	8.31
Rogers, Taylor	L-L	6-3	180	12-17-90	11	12	3.98	28	27	2	0	174	190	83	77	9	44	126	.283	.177	.326	6.52	2.28
Salcedo, Adrian	R-R	6-4	200	2-5-91	0	1	3.38	2	0	0	0	3	3	1	1	0	0	3	.300	.667	.143	10.13	0.00
Santana, Ervin	R-R	6-2	175	12-12-82	3	0	1.74	3	3	0	0	21	17	4	4	2	4	11	.227	.226	.227	4.79	1.74
Shibuya, Tim	R-R	6-1	190	9-14-89	0	0	5.40	4	0	0	0	7	11	5	4	1	1	5	.355	.000	.500	6.75	1.35
Stauffer, Tim	R-R	6-1	220	6-2-82	0	0	5.40	4	0	0	0	5	6	3	3	0	2	2	.286	.364	.200	3.60	3.60
Thielbar, Caleb	L-L	6-0	205	1-31-87	5	3	2.81	29	0	0	0	32	30	10	10	1	18	19	.252	.194	.316	5.34	5.06
Thompson, Aaron	L-L	6-3	205	2-28-87	1	1	3.71	21	0	0	1	17	16	7	7	0	4	11	.239	.179	.282	5.82	2.12
Tonkin, Michael	R-R	6-7	220	11-19-89	2	1	1.10	33	0	0	14	41	25	5	5	2	5	46	.174	.141	.200	10.10	1.10
Van Mil, Loek	R-R	7-1	260	9-15-84	0	0	0.00	3	0	0	0	4	1	0	0	0	2	1	.077	.000	.091	2.08	4.15
Wheeler, Jason	L-L	6-6	255	10-27-90	1	7	6.58	15	11	0	0	78	104	69	57	11	24	40	.324	.337	.319	4.62	2.77

Fielding

Catcher	PCT	G	PO	A	E	DP	PB
De San Miguel	1.000	2	8	1	0	0	0
Fryer	.994	60	450	26	3	3	3
Herrmann	.984	17	115	6	2	0	0
Paulino	.992	34	231	14	2	2	3

		PCT	G	PO	A	E	DP
Pinto		.978	33	253	12	6	1	2
First Base	PCT	G	PO	A	E	DP
Bernier	1.000	1	8	0	0	2
Hanson	1.000	4	22	2	0	2

	PCT	G	PO	A	E	DP
Martinez	.988	21	150	18	2	9
Peterson	1.000	3	26	0	0	3
Rodriguez	.993	94	764	33	6	87
Vargas	.990	26	179	12	2	16

Second Base	PCT	G	PO	A	E	DP
Beresford	.981	118	210	309	10	80
Bernier	1.000	14	26	33	0	9
Diaz	.964	12	21	33	2	8
Martinez	1.000	4	2	4	0	0

Third Base	PCT	G	PO	A	E	DP
Bernier	.978	51	24	66	2	5
Diaz	1.000	13	7	24	0	1
Hanson	1.000	11	4	10	0	0
Martinez	.956	70	47	106	7	17

	PCT	G	PO	A	E	DP
Wheeler	.917	10	8	14	2	1
Shortstop	PCT	G	PO	A	E	DP
Beresford	1.000	2	1	2	0	1
Bernier	.984	34	35	86	2	20
Diaz	.976	67	94	186	7	39
Polanco	.908	19	26	53	8	14
Santana	.966	30	43	97	5	19

Outfield	PCT	G	PO	A	E	DP
Arcia	.963	60	129	0	5	0

	PCT	G	PO	A	E	DP
Avery	.988	35	81	4	1	2
Buxton	1.000	11	37	0	0	0
Farris	1.000	83	155	7	0	1
Herrmann	1.000	1	3	0	0	0
Hicks	1.000	33	73	5	0	0
Ortiz	.984	125	301	5	5	0
Ramirez	.984	36	62	1	1	0
Rodriguez	1.000	33	54	2	0	0
Rosario	.939	21	29	2	2	0
Santana	1.000	2	6	0	0	0

CHATTANOOGA LOOKOUTS — DOUBLE-A

SOUTHERN LEAGUE

Batting	B-T	HT	WT	DOB	AVG	vLH	vRH	G	AB	R	H	2B	3B	HR	RBI	BB	HBP	SH	SF	SO	SB	CS	SLG	OBP
Buxton, Byron	R-R	6-2	190	12-18-93	.283	.341	.270	59	237	44	67	7	12	6	37	26	1	0	4	51	20	2	.489	.351
Gonzales, Mike	L-R	6-6	264	6-16-88	.218	.152	.230	67	229	26	50	10	0	5	33	25	4	0	2	61	0	0	.328	.304
Goodrum, Niko	R-R	6-3	198	2-28-92	.244	.238	.246	61	209	33	51	6	5	5	19	28	0	0	1	51	18	4	.392	.332
Harrison, Travis	R-R	6-1	215	10-17-92	.240	.257	.236	115	396	64	95	23	4	5	54	65	14	0	4	102	3	9	.356	.363
Hicks, D.J.	L-R	6-5	247	4-2-90	.227	.200	.233	60	225	23	51	8	1	6	31	32	0	0	2	66	1	2	.351	.320
Kepler, Max	L-L	6-4	205	2-10-93	.322	.318	.323	112	407	76	131	32	13	9	71	67	2	1	5	63	18	4	.531	.416
Knecht, Marcus	R-R	6-2	205	6-21-90	.171	.286	.143	10	35	6	6	2	0	0	2	8	1	0	0	12	0	0	.229	.341
Mejia, Aderlin	B-R	5-11	170	5-12-92	.231	.444	.186	16	52	4	12	1	0	1	5	4	0	0	0	8	1	3	.308	.286
Meneses, Heiker	R-R	5-9	200	7-1-91	.259	.277	.255	100	340	44	88	10	2	0	34	24	7	11	4	72	15	10	.300	.317
Michael, Levi	B-R	5-10	180	2-9-91	.267	.385	.231	63	221	43	59	12	5	5	31	31	6	4	2	53	18	3	.434	.369
Paulino, Carlos	R-R	6-0	175	9-24-89	.270	.143	.286	20	63	4	17	4	1	0	8	7	0	2	0	6	0	0	.365	.343
Polanco, Jorge	B-R	5-11	200	7-5-93	.289	.323	.283	95	394	55	114	17	3	6	47	35	0	0	2	63	18	10	.393	.346
Rodriguez, Jairo	R-R	5-11	180	8-24-88	.221	.211	.224	28	86	7	19	2	0	0	5	8	0	1	1	15	0	1	.244	.284
Sano, Miguel	R-R	6-4	260	5-11-93	.274	.375	.254	66	241	55	66	18	1	15	48	38	3	0	4	68	5	1	.544	.374
Turner, Stuart	R-R	6-2	230	12-27-91	.223	.230	.222	98	327	40	73	13	1	4	37	45	4	0	3	69	5	2	.306	.322
Vargas, Kennys	B-R	6-5	290	8-1-90	.287	.333	.274	35	122	20	35	3	2	7	24	26	2	0	1	32	0	0	.516	.417
Walker, Adam Brett	R-R	6-4	225	10-18-91	.239	.232	.241	133	502	75	120	31	3	31	106	51	2	0	5	195	13	4	.498	.309
Wickens, Stephen	R-R	5-10	170	3-5-89	.254	.180	.271	83	264	48	67	14	2	1	19	36	5	3	2	45	16	5	.333	.352
Wilkerson, Shannon	R-R	6-0	200	7-20-88	.292	.386	.262	49	185	30	54	5	4	1	22	17	1	4	0	25	11	1	.378	.355

Pitching	B-T	HT	WT	DOB	W	L	ERA	G	GS	CG	SV	IP	H	R	ER	HR	BB	SO	AVG	vLH	vRH	K/9	BB/9
Atchison, Scott	R-R	6-2	200	3-29-76	0	0	1.80	4	0	0	0	5	4	1	1	0	0	2	.222	.333	.167	3.60	0.00
Baxendale, D.J.	R-R	6-2	190	12-8-90	7	5	3.80	23	21	0	0	118	126	53	50	8	40	92	.273	.250	.290	7.00	3.04
Berrios, Jose	R-R	6-0	185	5-27-94	8	3	3.08	15	15	1	0	91	77	32	31	6	24	92	.232	.216	.245	9.13	2.38
Boer, Madison	R-R	6-4	215	11-9-89	3	2	4.38	13	1	0	1	25	26	13	12	0	13	14	.283	.282	.283	5.11	4.74
Burdi, Nick	R-R	6-5	215	1-19-93	3	4	4.53	30	0	0	2	44	40	25	22	3	32	54	.242	.319	.188	11.13	6.60
Chargois, J.T.	B-R	6-3	200	12-3-90	1	1	2.73	32	0	0	11	33	26	12	10	1	20	34	.218	.173	.254	9.27	5.45
Duffey, Tyler	R-R	6-3	220	12-27-90	2	2	2.56	8	8	0	0	53	46	19	15	0	12	54	.236	.243	.231	9.23	2.05
Gallant, Dallas	R-R	6-3	195	1-25-89	1	1	5.06	12	0	0	1	16	17	11	9	1	8	9	.283	.364	.237	5.06	4.50
Hurlbut, David	L-L	6-3	221	11-24-89	11	6	3.59	17	17	2	0	100	106	44	40	4	35	59	.278	.256	.293	5.31	3.14
Johnson, Cole	R-R	6-3	200	10-6-88	2	1	3.18	18	0	0	2	28	26	11	10	0	9	33	.250	.238	.258	10.48	2.86
Johnson, D.J.	L-R	6-4	235	8-30-89	1	2	4.86	38	0	0	4	50	54	29	27	2	26	41	.283	.275	.288	7.38	4.68
Jones, Zack	R-R	6-1	185	12-4-90	3	2	6.00	27	0	0	10	27	24	18	18	3	18	30	.247	.282	.224	10.00	6.00
Lee, Brett	L-L	6-4	206	9-20-90	6	4	3.10	16	16	2	0	96	85	44	33	4	29	45	.239	.252	.233	4.23	2.73
Muren, Alex	R-R	6-3	200	11-6-91	1	0	4.84	14	0	0	3	22	21	13	12	1	9	11	.244	.235	.250	4.43	3.63
O'Rourke, Ryan	R-L	6-3	230	4-30-88	0	0	0.00	2	0	0	0	1	2	0	0	0	0	3	.333	.400	.000	20.25	0.00
Peavey, Greg	R-R	6-2	185	7-11-88	7	7	4.88	20	20	0	0	111	112	68	60	11	30	59	.262	.230	.285	4.80	2.44
Peterson, Brandon	R-R	6-1	190	9-23-91	2	1	3.38	20	0	0	2	29	30	13	11	1	13	33	.261	.295	.239	10.13	3.99
Reed, Jake	R-R	6-2	190	9-29-92	4	4	6.32	35	0	0	1	47	55	43	33	3	21	39	.289	.316	.272	7.47	4.02
Salcedo, Adrian	R-R	6-4	200	2-5-91	0	1	4.87	10	1	0	0	20	17	11	11	1	13	15	.230	.176	.275	6.64	5.75
Shibuya, Tim	R-R	6-1	190	9-14-89	0	2	4.22	23	4	0	1	43	46	23	20	2	9	19	.279	.271	.283	4.01	1.90
Slegers, Aaron	R-R	6-10	245	9-4-92	1	4	4.91	6	6	0	0	37	40	22	20	3	12	24	.282	.318	.250	5.89	2.95
Summers, Matt	R-R	6-1	205	8-17-89	1	0	4.15	8	0	0	0	13	14	6	6	1	6	9	.280	.174	.370	6.23	4.15
Wheeler, Jason	L-L	6-6	255	10-27-90	4	3	3.92	10	10	0	0	60	58	28	26	5	16	50	.252	.209	.270	7.54	2.41
Williams, Corey	L-L	6-2	205	7-4-90	0	0	2.25	7	0	0	0	8	4	2	2	0	5	9	.154	.071	.250	10.13	5.63
Wimmers, Alex	L-R	6-2	212	11-1-88	8	4	4.53	30	18	0	0	115	117	58	58	7	43	100	.270	.293	.253	7.80	3.36

Fielding

Catcher	PCT	G	PO	A	E	DP	PB
Paulino	.980	20	134	16	3	2	1
Rodriguez	1.000	27	170	7	0	0	0
Turner	.992	97	643	65	6	7	4

First Base	PCT	G	PO	A	E	DP
Gonzales	1.000	12	102	4	0	10
Goodrum	.966	3	27	1	1	3
Harrison	1.000	1	5	1	0	0
Hicks	.988	56	476	14	6	50
Kepler	.994	37	296	19	2	30
Mejia	1.000	1	13	0	0	2
Meneses	1.000	1	7	0	0	0

	PCT	G	PO	A	E	DP
Vargas	.989	27	254	15	3	29
Wickens	.857	2	5	1	1	0

Second Base	PCT	G	PO	A	E	DP
Mejia	1.000	5	12	14	0	6
Meneses	.976	57	112	167	7	43
Michael	.977	53	95	156	6	42
Polanco	1.000	8	12	15	0	7
Wickens	1.000	19	32	36	0	7

Third Base	PCT	G	PO	A	E	DP
Goodrum	.843	15	13	30	8	0
Mejia	.923	10	7	17	2	2
Meneses	.966	7	8	20	1	1

	PCT	G	PO	A	E	DP
Sano	.911	63	43	111	15	8
Wickens	.925	43	33	103	11	14

Shortstop	PCT	G	PO	A	E	DP
Goodrum	.962	22	38	63	4	13
Meneses	.994	32	61	101	1	25
Polanco	.942	83	86	240	20	58
Wickens	1.000	1	1	0	0	0

Outfield	PCT	G	PO	A	E	DP
Buxton	.990	59	181	9	2	3
Goodrum	.970	15	31	1	1	0
Harrison	.975	98	155	3	4	2
Kepler	.983	63	168	3	3	1

MINNESOTA TWINS

Outfield	PCT	G	PO	A	E	DP						
Knecht	1.000	10	15	3	0	0						

Shibuya	1.000	1	0	1	0	0	
Walker	.965	115	162	5	6	2	

Wickens	.952	10	20	0	1	0	
Wilkerson	.991	46	115	1	1	0	

FORT MYERS MIRACLE   HIGH CLASS A
FLORIDA STATE LEAGUE

Batting	B-T	HT	WT	DOB	AVG	vLH	vRH	G	AB	R	H	2B	3B	HR	RBI	BB	HBP	SH	SF	SO	SB	CS	SLG	OBP
Christensen, Chad	R-R	6-3	205	10-6-90	.257	.265	.254	114	404	47	104	16	3	2	39	40	3	2	3	108	22	7	.327	.327
Doe, Brett	R-R	5-10	170	6-12-90	.212	.300	.174	8	33	3	7	0	0	0	3	5	0	0	0	5	0	1	.212	.316
Garver, Mitch	R-R	6-1	220	1-15-91	.245	.282	.228	127	433	46	106	24	1	4	58	69	10	0	8	82	5	3	.333	.356
Goodrum, Niko	B-R	6-3	198	2-28-92	.220	.286	.185	53	205	24	45	11	1	4	19	32	2	0	1	59	11	5	.341	.329
Granite, Zach	L-L	6-1	175	9-17-92	.249	.293	.234	105	381	59	95	10	4	1	26	41	5	11	3	63	21	12	.304	.328
Haar, Bryan	R-R	6-3	215	12-9-89	.249	.308	.223	68	257	18	64	14	1	1	22	21	5	0	1	61	1	0	.323	.317
Hicks, D.J.	L-R	6-5	247	4-2-90	.286	.400	.222	5	14	1	4	1	0	0	1	2	0	0	0	1	0	0	.357	.375
Kanzler, Jason	R-R	6-0	188	8-20-90	.224	.180	.242	100	344	41	77	9	8	8	35	25	12	3	5	96	17	9	.366	.295
Kepler, Max	L-L	6-4	205	2-10-93	.250	.500	.227	6	24	4	6	2	0	0	2	0	0	0	0	5	1	0	.333	.308
Knecht, Marcus	R-R	6-1	200	6-21-90	.226	.265	.211	101	368	38	83	18	5	2	46	43	8	0	2	91	13	1	.318	.318
Mejia, Aderlin	B-R	5-11	170	5-12-92	.231	.240	.228	59	208	16	48	8	1	0	27	30	0	4	6	29	3	4	.279	.320
Pinto, Josmil	R-R	5-11	220	3-31-89	.167	.000	.182	4	12	2	2	0	0	1	1	1	0	0	3	0	0	.417	.231
Quesada, Michael	R-R	6-1	205	2-1-90	.151	.200	.132	68	212	14	32	8	1	0	12	21	4	2	1	73	0	0	.198	.239
Schmit, Blake	R-R	6-1	185	2-27-92	.182	.000	.211	8	22	1	4	0	0	0	2	1	0	0	4	0	1	.182	.280
Swim, Alex	B-R	5-11	180	3-26-91	.311	.267	.327	85	344	37	107	13	2	0	38	18	2	0	0	30	5	4	.360	.349
Vavra, Tanner	R-R	5-11	180	7-6-89	.258	.242	.264	87	240	33	62	8	1	0	19	19	13	3	0	49	5	3	.300	.346
Vielma, Engelb	B-R	5-11	150	6-22-94	.270	.301	.258	120	441	49	119	9	2	1	29	35	1	18	6	71	35	12	.306	.321
Wade, Logan	B-R	6-1	190	11-13-91	.258	.310	.240	99	337	31	87	22	4	3	36	20	0	3	4	63	3	1	.374	.296
Walker, Ryan	L-R	6-1	157	3-26-92	.269	.246	.276	83	301	32	81	7	3	0	23	19	2	6	6	53	9	6	.312	.311
White, T.J.	R-R	5-10	200	1-24-92	.171	.294	.132	20	70	4	12	1	0	2	8	8	0	0	0	23	0	0	.186	.200

Pitching	B-T	HT	WT	DOB	W	L	ERA	G	GS	CG	SV	IP	H	R	ER	HR	BB	SO	AVG	vLH	vRH	K/9	BB/9
Batts, Mat	R-L	5-11	190	7-6-91	8	4	2.77	17	17	1	0	101	96	36	31	3	17	85	.249	.202	.267	7.60	1.52
Bencomo, Omar	R-R	6-1	170	2-10-89	1	1	1.50	3	3	0	0	18	11	6	3	0	5	5	.180	.167	.200	2.50	2.50
Boer, Madison	R-R	6-4	215	11-9-89	2	2	1.62	11	0	0	1	17	8	3	3	0	6	11	.140	.097	.192	5.94	3.24
Burdi, Nick	R-R	6-5	215	1-19-93	2	2	2.25	13	0	0	2	20	12	7	5	1	3	29	.179	.217	.159	13.05	1.35
Chargois, J.T.	B-R	6-3	200	12-3-90	1	0	2.40	16	0	0	4	15	12	8	4	0	5	19	.200	.167	.222	11.40	3.00
Eades, Ryan	R-R	6-2	200	12-15-91	6	3	3.11	20	20	0	0	119	109	43	41	5	38	80	.250	.261	.242	6.07	2.88
Gallant, Dallas	R-R	6-3	195	1-25-89	0	1	2.92	11	0	0	0	12	10	4	4	1	8	12	.227	.263	.200	8.03	5.84
Gilbert, Brian	R-R	6-1	215	8-9-92	4	4	3.39	39	0	0	0	58	46	24	22	0	37	38	.234	.286	.200	5.86	5.71
Gonsalves, Stephen	L-L	6-5	190	7-8-94	7	2	2.61	15	15	1	0	79	66	26	23	2	38	55	.225	.247	.218	6.24	4.31
Hildenberger, Trevor	R-R	6-2	200	12-15-90	1	1	3.32	13	0	0	3	19	15	7	7	0	2	21	.231	.321	.162	9.95	0.95
Hu, Chih-Wei	R-R	6-1	230	11-4-93	5	3	2.44	15	15	0	0	85	79	28	23	5	19	73	.249	.273	.237	7.76	2.02
2-team total (5 Charlotte)					5	6	3.32	20	19	0	1	103	102	46	38	6	27	93	—	—	—	8.13	2.36
Hurlbut, David	L-L	6-3	221	11-24-89	0	1	0.00	2	1	0	0	12	6	4	0	0	3	9	.143	.154	.138	6.75	2.25
Jay, Tyler	L-L	6-1	180	4-19-94	0	1	3.93	19	0	0	1	18	10	8	8	0	8	22	.247	.150	.283	10.80	3.93
Johnson, D.J.	L-R	6-4	235	8-30-89	1	0	0.00	7	0	0	3	10	4	0	0	0	2	12	.125	.000	.200	10.80	1.80
Jones, Zack	R-R	6-1	185	12-4-90	2	2	2.19	18	0	0	2	25	14	8	6	0	10	38	.157	.189	.135	13.86	3.65
Lee, Brett	L-L	6-4	206	9-20-90	1	3	3.29	6	6	0	0	38	40	15	14	0	12	20	.272	.200	.299	4.70	2.82
Mildren, Ethan	R-R	6-4	215	6-4-91	2	4	4.23	10	8	0	0	45	58	24	21	4	11	20	.326	.337	.314	4.03	2.22
Muren, Alex	R-R	6-3	200	11-6-91	2	3	2.20	30	0	0	2	49	41	15	12	2	15	43	.227	.260	.202	7.90	2.76
Peterson, Brandon	R-R	6-1	190	9-23-91	1	0	0.85	21	0	0	3	32	14	3	3	0	15	44	.135	.154	.123	12.51	4.26
Reed, Jake	R-R	6-1	190	9-29-92	1	0	0.00	9	0	0	1	12	8	2	0	0	1	7	.195	.200	.190	5.11	0.73
Rodriguez, Dereck	R-R	6-1	180	6-5-92	0	0	0.00	1	0	0	0	2	1	0	0	0	2	2	.143	.250	.000	9.00	9.00
Shibuya, Tim	R-R	6-1	190	9-14-89	1	0	0.66	6	0	0	0	14	9	1	1	0	1	13	.191	.222	.172	8.56	0.66
Slegers, Aaron	R-R	6-10	245	9-4-92	8	6	2.87	19	19	3	0	119	103	48	38	4	21	80	.227	.236	.222	6.03	1.58
Stewart, Kohl	R-R	6-3	195	10-7-94	7	8	3.20	22	22	1	0	129	134	63	46	2	45	71	.273	.293	.258	4.94	3.13
Summers, Matt	R-R	6-1	205	8-17-89	2	2	3.41	18	1	0	1	32	26	14	12	1	7	21	.220	.205	.230	5.97	1.99
Tapia, Alexis	R-R	6-2	195	8-10-95	0	0	0.00	2	0	0	0	2	2	0	0	0	0	1	.286	.333	.250	4.50	0.00
Van Steensel, Todd	R-R	6-1	190	1-14-91	2	4	2.32	46	0	0	13	66	53	17	17	5	32	81	.223	.233	.216	11.05	4.36
Velez, Jose	L-L	6-1	205	9-5-89	0	0	1.80	2	0	0	0	5	1	1	1	0	1	5	.063	.167	.000	9.00	1.80
Westphal, Luke	L-L	6-3	230	6-14-89	5	6	2.76	22	11	0	0	65	74	24	20	0	23	53	.288	.258	.297	7.30	3.17
Williams, Corey	L-L	6-2	205	7-4-90	3	0	2.49	22	0	0	0	25	18	7	7	0	10	17	.209	.200	.214	6.04	3.55
Wilson, Jared	R-R	6-4	210	4-26-90	1	0	3.60	1	1	0	0	5	5	2	2	0	1	5	.250	.300	.200	9.00	1.80

Fielding

Catcher	PCT	G	PO	A	E	DP	PB
Garver	.993	77	537	61	4	6	6
Quesada	.990	40	251	32	3	3	2
Swim	.991	30	205	20	2	0	5

First Base	PCT	G	PO	A	E	DP	
Doe	1.000	7	69	3	0	9	
Garver	1.000	14	117	6	0	14	
Haar	.988	54	535	26	7	51	
Hicks	1.000	2	15	1	0	0	
Mejia	1.000	17	157	7	0	6	
Quesada	.991	14	107	5	1	14	
Swim	.995	24	172	11	1	18	

	PCT	G	PO	A	E	DP
Wade	.991	15	101	4	1	9

Second Base	PCT	G	PO	A	E	DP
Mejia	.974	27	55	95	4	22
Schmit	.923	4	6	6	1	1
Vavra	.982	48	101	120	4	30
Wade	.955	8	16	26	2	5
Walker	.963	59	110	152	10	33

Third Base	PCT	G	PO	A	E	DP
Goodrum	.901	45	29	64	10	7
Haar	.917	7	6	16	2	2
Mejia	1.000	11	5	20	0	3
Schmit	.600	1	0	3	2	0

	PCT	G	PO	A	E	DP
Vavra	.900	27	12	33	5	4
Wade	.940	38	16	62	5	5
Walker	1.000	3	3	5	0	1
White	.870	19	11	36	7	6

Shortstop	PCT	G	PO	A	E	DP
Goodrum	1.000	9	9	23	0	5
Vavra	—	1	0	0	0	0
Vielma	.964	120	171	390	21	75
Walker	.962	16	25	51	3	13

Outfield	PCT	G	PO	A	E	DP
Christensen	.978	103	173	4	4	2
Goodrum	1.000	1	2	0	0	0

Outfield	PCT	G	PO	A	E	DP
Granite	.982	100	212	12	4	3
Kanzler	.990	85	196	3	2	1

Kepler	1.000	5	10	0	0	0
Knecht	.987	86	152	5	2	2
Mejia	1.000	1	1	0	0	0

Swim	.935	16	27	2	2	0
Wade	.959	32	64	6	3	2
Walker	1.000	4	2	0	0	0

CEDAR RAPIDS KERNELS LOW CLASS A

MIDWEST LEAGUE

Batting	B-T	HT	WT	DOB	AVG	vLH	vRH	G	AB	R	H	2B	3B	HR	RBI	BB	HBP	SH	SF	SO	SB	CS	SLG	OBP
Corcino, Edgar	B-R	6-1	210	6-7-92	.273	.295	.268	84	330	38	90	16	3	4	41	34	1	5	3	61	9	3	.376	.340
Diemer, Austin	R-R	6-1	195	4-28-93	.280	.321	.269	37	132	20	37	8	3	2	15	4	6	0	0	37	0	1	.432	.331
Doe, Brett	R-R	5-10	170	6-12-90	.246	.228	.251	74	268	16	66	11	0	3	29	15	7	4	3	48	4	0	.321	.300
English, Tanner	R-R	5-10	160	3-11-93	.265	.253	.268	104	377	70	100	22	8	5	36	48	8	8	2	87	37	7	.406	.359
Fernandez, Jorge	B-R	6-3	188	3-30-94	.215	.146	.231	56	214	24	46	14	2	3	25	13	3	0	1	67	2	1	.341	.268
Gordon, Nick	L-R	6-0	160	10-24-95	.277	.264	.280	120	481	79	133	23	7	1	58	39	6	3	4	88	25	8	.360	.336
Granite, Zach	L-L	6-1	175	9-17-92	.358	.421	.333	19	67	17	24	5	1	0	5	12	1	3	0	6	7	1	.463	.463
Hinojoso, Jonatan	B-R	5-11	150	10-23-92	.154	.231	.135	18	65	8	10	1	0	0	2	5	0	0	1	21	3	3	.169	.211
Kelly, Pat	R-R	5-10	165	11-19-92	.220	.173	.234	95	327	41	72	13	4	3	30	22	6	6	5	78	1	3	.312	.278
Kuresa, Tyler	L-L	6-4	245	11-17-92	.204	.111	.230	56	206	16	42	10	0	1	18	21	1	0	2	45	0	0	.267	.278
Larson, Zach	R-R	6-2	185	10-8-93	.214	.293	.189	106	393	48	84	20	2	0	54	39	8	6	10	84	16	1	.275	.291
Miller, Sean	R-R	5-11	175	10-10-94	.284	.318	.275	26	102	13	29	4	0	0	5	4	0	1	0	15	1	0	.324	.311
Murphy, Max	R-R	5-11	195	11-17-92	.225	.279	.211	93	347	54	78	15	8	4	36	27	12	0	2	87	8	2	.349	.302
Navarreto, Brian	R-R	6-4	220	12-29-94	.217	.149	.237	86	299	28	65	11	1	2	28	14	2	3	1	62	0	0	.281	.256
Paul, Chris	R-R	6-3	200	10-12-92	.244	.091	.294	12	45	3	11	3	1	0	5	0	2	0	0	13	0	0	.356	.277
Real, Alex	R-R	6-0	210	1-19-93	.261	.286	.255	64	230	28	60	11	4	3	30	18	4	2	3	64	0	1	.383	.322
Schmit, Blake	R-R	6-1	185	2-27-92	.226	.167	.240	18	62	8	14	2	1	1	12	6	7	1	1	11	1	0	.339	.355
Silva, Rainis	R-R	6-1	185	3-20-96	.227	.333	.200	11	44	4	10	3	0	0	2	3	0	0	0	9	0	0	.295	.277
Valera, Rafael	R-R	5-11	180	8-15-94	.283	.250	.292	62	219	28	62	10	1	0	22	31	3	1	1	53	2	4	.338	.378
Vavra, Trey	R-R	6-2	185	9-17-91	.346	.271	.380	42	156	29	54	10	1	6	28	13	4	1	2	30	2	0	.538	.406
Wade, LaMonte	L-L	6-1	195	1-1-94	.143	.500	.083	4	14	1	2	0	0	1	1	1	0	0	2	0	0	.143	.250
White, T.J.	R-R	5-10	200	1-24-92	.266	.255	.269	106	380	45	101	22	6	2	52	43	16	1	7	49	13	4	.371	.359

Pitching	B-T	HT	WT	DOB	W	L	ERA	G	GS	CG	SV	IP	H	R	ER	HR	BB	SO	AVG	vLH	vRH	K/9	BB/9
Anderson, Nick	R-R	6-5	195	7-5-90	0	1	0.75	9	0	0	4	12	7	1	1	1	0	12	.167	.167	.167	9.00	0.00
Bard, Luke	R-R	6-3	195	11-13-90	7	1	2.41	28	0	0	0	52	45	15	14	1	15	47	.234	.300	.188	8.08	2.58
Batts, Mat	R-L	5-11	190	7-6-91	3	2	2.21	7	7	1	0	41	31	14	10	0	11	44	.211	.149	.240	9.74	2.43
Bixler, Brandon	R-L	5-11	180	12-31-91	1	1	6.30	6	0	0	0	10	12	7	7	2	7	9	.286	.077	.379	8.10	6.30
Booser, Cameron	L-L	6-3	225	5-4-92	1	2	3.72	32	0	0	10	46	31	23	19	1	40	64	.194	.155	.216	12.52	7.83
Cederoth, Michael	R-R	6-6	195	11-25-92	1	4	4.08	11	6	0	0	35	33	23	16	2	18	37	.232	.265	.203	9.42	4.58
Clay, Sam	L-L	6-2	190	6-21-93	0	3	4.32	12	3	0	0	33	36	19	16	2	26	29	.293	.300	.290	7.83	7.02
Curtiss, John	R-R	6-4	200	4-5-93	3	3	6.07	16	7	0	2	46	62	33	31	10	10	44	.323	.350	.293	8.61	1.96
Gibbons, Sam	L-R	6-4	190	12-12-93	7	4	2.89	15	15	1	0	90	84	33	29	2	23	68	.246	.222	.273	6.77	2.29
Gonsalves, Stephen	L-L	6-5	190	7-8-94	6	1	1.15	9	9	0	0	55	29	8	7	2	15	77	.154	.188	.143	12.60	2.45
Hildenberger, Trevor	R-R	6-2	200	12-15-90	2	1	0.80	28	0	0	14	45	24	6	4	0	5	59	.153	.217	.112	11.80	1.00
Irby, C.K.	R-R	6-1	200	5-6-92	0	0	3.21	10	0	0	1	14	9	5	5	0	14	20	.191	.238	.154	12.86	9.00
Jorge, Felix	R-R	6-2	170	1-2-94	6	7	2.79	23	22	0	0	142	118	52	44	11	32	114	.225	.231	.219	7.23	2.03
Landa, Yorman	R-R	6-0	175	6-11-94	2	1	1.67	15	0	0	0	27	18	9	5	1	14	31	.186	.093	.259	10.33	4.67
LeBlanc, Randy	R-R	6-4	185	3-7-92	9	5	3.03	33	5	0	1	89	78	35	30	4	28	69	.240	.212	.261	6.98	2.83
Mazza, Chris	R-R	6-4	180	10-17-89	0	0	9.00	2	0	0	0	3	5	3	3	0	2	2	.385	.200	.500	6.00	6.00
Mildren, Ethan	R-R	6-4	215	6-4-91	4	1	3.51	12	7	0	0	49	50	20	19	4	17	31	.272	.238	.300	5.73	3.14
Nolasco, Ricky	R-R	6-2	235	12-13-82	0	0	0.00	1	1	0	0	5	3	1	0	0	0	5	.167	.143	.250	9.00	0.00
Nordgren, Miles	R-R	6-2	190	10-6-92	0	0	2.03	6	0	0	0	13	17	6	3	0	3	9	.315	.400	.265	6.08	2.03
Rodriguez, Dereck	R-R	6-1	180	6-5-92	0	1	9.00	2	2	0	0	7	9	7	7	1	6	3	.300	.250	.318	3.86	7.71
Rosario, Randy	L-L	6-1	160	5-18-94	2	6	3.52	11	10	0	0	54	55	31	21	1	19	45	.264	.241	.273	7.55	3.19
Steele, Keaton	R-R	6-3	225	10-30-91	7	4	3.41	15	14	0	0	90	80	37	34	6	20	60	.242	.268	.225	6.02	2.11
Theofanopoulos, Mike	L-L	6-1	185	8-5-92	5	3	3.82	37	1	0	1	68	68	31	29	3	29	74	.266	.299	.251	9.75	3.82
Tillery, Zach	R-R	6-3	210	1-12-93	5	5	3.61	28	13	0	1	90	88	37	36	3	30	73	.258	.304	.214	7.33	3.01
Velez, Jose	L-L	6-1	205	9-5-89	0	1	4.11	8	0	0	0	15	15	8	7	1	7	22	.268	.267	.268	12.91	4.11
Westphal, Luke	L-L	6-3	230	6-14-89	1	2	2.70	7	6	0	0	30	20	10	9	0	9	28	.198	.207	.194	8.40	2.70
Wilson, Jared	R-R	6-4	210	4-26-90	5	4	4.25	30	12	0	3	91	90	45	43	6	46	61	.261	.288	.234	6.03	4.55

Fielding

Catcher	PCT	G	PO	A	E	DP	PB
Doe	.996	33	252	31	1	4	3
Fernandez	.968	6	59	2	2	1	0
Navarreto	.997	84	647	94	2	12	11
Real	.990	13	89	9	1	0	1
Silva	1.000	11	91	8	0	0	2

First Base	PCT	G	PO	A	E	DP
Doe	.986	22	177	31	3	18
Fernandez	.985	28	254	16	4	21
Kelly	.987	14	131	20	2	12
Kuresa	.977	53	465	40	12	42
Navarreto	1.000	1	1	0	0	0
Paul	.985	7	60	5	1	6

	PCT	G	PO	A	E	DP
Vavra	.986	16	134	11	2	13

Second Base	PCT	G	PO	A	E	DP
Hinojoso	.902	12	19	18	4	6
Kelly	.985	63	100	162	4	33
Miller	.963	18	34	43	3	17
Schmit	1.000	11	15	21	0	3
Valera	.959	38	80	105	8	30

Third Base	PCT	G	PO	A	E	DP
Doe	1.000	4	2	6	0	1
Hinojoso	1.000	2	1	1	0	0
Kelly	.938	11	5	25	2	2
Schmit	1.000	3	1	6	0	1
Valera	.918	15	11	34	4	5

	PCT	G	PO	A	E	DP
White	.937	106	63	204	18	21

Shortstop	PCT	G	PO	A	E	DP
Gordon	.966	118	160	356	18	75
Hinojoso	1.000	4	6	11	0	4
Miller	.933	7	9	19	2	3
Schmit	1.000	4	3	11	0	1
Valera	1.000	7	4	23	0	2

Outfield	PCT	G	PO	A	E	DP
Corcino	.986	80	135	7	2	0
Diemer	.969	35	60	2	2	1
English	.996	102	229	8	1	5
Fernandez	.500	5	1	0	1	0
Granite	1.000	17	35	1	0	1

Outfield	PCT	G	PO	A	E	DP	Murphy	.958	76	132	5	6	2	Wade	1.000	4	4	0	0	0
Larson	.982	93	163	3	3	0	Vavra	1.000	14	16	2	0	0							

ELIZABETHTON TWINS ROOKIE
APPALACHIAN LEAGUE

Batting	B-T	HT	WT	DOB	AVG	vLH	vRH	G	AB	R	H	2B	3B	HR	RBI	BB	HBP	SH	SF	SO	SB	CS	SLG	OBP
Blankenhorn, Travis	L-R	6-1	195	8-3-96	.243	.172	.261	39	144	14	35	3	0	3	20	11	2	1	0	32	1	0	.326	.306
Cavaness, Christian	L-L	6-2	190	3-16-94	.273	—	.273	4	11	2	3	0	1	0	2	2	0	0	0	3	1	1	.455	.385
Diaz, Lewin	L-L	6-3	180	11-19-96	.167	.182	.162	14	48	7	8	1	0	3	5	3	2	0	0	17	0	0	.375	.245
Diemer, Austin	R-R	6-1	195	4-28-93	.254	.316	.231	20	71	10	18	4	1	3	8	1	0	0	0	28	1	0	.465	.264
Guzman, Manuel	B-R	5-9	160	2-10-95	.275	.220	.297	50	178	27	49	6	1	1	14	28	1	3	0	34	19	4	.337	.377
Hartong, Brad	R-R	6-2	215	2-4-92	.292	.267	.300	35	120	16	35	9	1	0	11	4	1	0	0	18	0	0	.383	.320
Kihle, Daniel	R-L	6-0	190	10-1-93	.273	.258	.277	45	143	26	39	7	2	2	21	25	8	2	2	45	5	1	.392	.404
Kuresa, Tyler	L-L	6-4	245	11-17-92	.241	.273	.233	17	54	9	13	2	0	4	9	6	2	0	1	14	0	0	.500	.333
Miller, Sean	R-R	5-11	175	10-10-94	.209	.188	.222	11	43	4	9	0	1	0	1	2	1	1	0	7	0	2	.256	.261
Minier, Amaurys	B-R	6-2	190	1-30-96	.194	.216	.188	34	175	19	34	9	0	2	21	18	4	0	4	66	0	1	.280	.279
Molina, Nelson	L-R	6-3	175	4-30-95	.207	.214	.205	37	116	14	24	0	1	1	10	10	1	1	2	33	2	2	.250	.271
Montesino, Ariel	B-R	5-10	170	9-21-95	.200	.091	.235	13	45	3	9	2	0	0	5	5	0	0	0	9	1	1	.244	.280
Murray, A.J.	R-R	6-2	215	4-4-93	.264	.195	.288	51	159	28	42	11	0	4	18	22	4	0	1	41	0	1	.409	.366
Olson, Brian	R-R	6-0	190	1-21-93	.333	.133	.417	15	51	9	17	3	0	2	8	7	0	0	0	8	0	0	.510	.414
Palacios, Jermaine	R-R	6-0	145	7-19-96	.336	.571	.277	31	140	23	47	14	2	2	23	3	0	0	2	20	5	2	.507	.345
Paul, Chris	R-R	6-3	200	10-12-92	.302	.250	.314	21	86	12	26	7	0	3	16	4	6	0	0	15	2	0	.488	.375
Perez, Alex	L-R	5-10	180	10-24-92	.239	.182	.250	41	142	21	34	7	1	0	12	17	3	0	1	35	0	1	.303	.331
Silva, Rainis	R-R	6-1	185	3-20-96	.230	.367	.181	32	113	14	26	5	0	2	10	11	2	0	1	33	0	0	.327	.307
Wade, LaMonte	L-L	6-1	195	1-1-94	.312	.340	.303	64	231	36	72	8	5	9	44	46	3	1	3	34	12	1	.506	.428
Wiel, Zander	R-R	6-4	225	1-11-93	.194	.000	.250	13	36	5	7	2	0	1	8	7	1	0	1	13	0	0	.333	.333
Young, Kamran	L-L	5-11	190	10-12-92	.219	.235	.215	52	192	28	42	7	2	4	21	21	2	1	1	62	0	2	.339	.301

Pitching	B-T	HT	WT	DOB	W	L	ERA	G	GS	CG	SV	IP	H	R	ER	HR	BB	SO	AVG	vLH	vRH	K/9	BB/9
Abreu, Jose	R-R	5-11	170	7-13-92	1	3	3.71	17	0	0	2	27	24	15	11	2	13	20	.240	.311	.182	6.75	4.39
Clay, Sam	L-L	6-2	190	6-21-93	1	3	3.00	10	7	0	0	39	36	17	13	1	12	44	.245	.362	.190	10.15	2.77
Cutura, Andro	R-R	6-0	195	8-22-93	3	2	1.34	11	11	0	0	61	46	19	9	2	15	49	.209	.214	.206	7.27	2.23
Del Rosario, Eduardo	R-R	6-0	145	5-19-95	0	0	6.75	1	1	0	0	4	6	3	3	1	0	3	.375	.125	.625	6.75	0.00
Easton, Brandon	L-L	6-5	190	9-21-92	0	2	18.00	2	2	0	0	4	7	8	8	0	9	3	.438	.500	.417	6.75	20.25
Gercken, Nate	R-R	6-6	220	11-4-92	0	3	6.69	11	0	0	0	35	46	26	26	3	12	35	.324	.286	.349	9.00	3.09
Guyer, Josh	R-R	6-2	185	5-27-94	0	0	7.98	13	0	0	0	15	20	18	13	2	9	16	.313	.182	.381	9.82	5.52
Hernandez, Onesimo	R-R	5-11	200	2-16-92	5	1	3.71	15	0	0	1	44	53	23	18	2	8	43	.299	.278	.316	8.86	1.65
Irby, C.K.	R-R	6-1	200	5-6-92	3	0	3.31	16	0	0	2	35	31	20	13	2	15	44	.233	.191	.256	11.21	3.82
Lo, Kuo Hua	R-R	5-10	195	10-28-92	4	1	1.44	19	0	0	7	31	15	5	5	2	8	43	.146	.098	.177	12.35	2.30
Lombana, Logan	R-R	6-3	225	7-17-94	1	2	2.25	15	0	0	1	32	31	8	8	3	12	34	.261	.293	.244	9.56	3.38
McIver, Anthony	L-L	6-5	210	4-8-92	3	1	4.61	15	0	0	1	27	33	15	14	1	8	31	.289	.273	.300	10.21	2.63
Nordgren, Miles	R-R	6-2	190	6-12-92	1	3	2.76	11	11	0	0	59	65	31	18	1	10	33	.275	.263	.284	5.06	1.53
Robinson, Alex	L-L	6-1	225	8-11-94	0	3	9.00	10	0	0	0	12	10	13	12	0	16	15	.238	.400	.148	11.25	12.00
Rodriguez, Dereck	R-R	6-1	180	6-5-92	6	3	2.85	12	12	0	0	66	64	28	21	5	11	61	.250	.218	.285	8.28	1.49
Stashak, Cody	R-R	6-2	180	6-4-94	5	2	3.43	10	10	0	0	45	39	19	17	4	11	53	.234	.229	.237	10.68	2.22
Stirewalt, Tyler	R-R	6-3	210	12-6-90	0	3	5.87	15	0	0	0	23	26	20	15	0	14	19	.274	.237	.298	7.43	5.48
Tapia, Alexis	R-R	6-2	195	8-10-95	1	2	3.82	6	6	0	0	33	37	17	14	5	7	33	.280	.288	.273	9.00	1.91
2-team total (6 Princeton)					2	2	3.83	12	11	0	0	56	67	29	24	5	12	54	—	—	—	8.63	1.92

Fielding

Catcher	PCT	G	PO	A	E	DP	PB
Hartong	1.000	4	16	4	0	0	0
Murray	.991	27	203	17	2	1	3
Olson	.986	15	130	11	2	1	1
Silva	.996	28	218	27	1	1	10

First Base	PCT	G	PO	A	E	DP
Diaz	.988	11	75	5	1	6
Kuresa	.990	12	91	5	1	5
Minier	.983	28	213	17	4	19
Murray	.990	14	98	5	1	6
Paul	1.000	4	36	1	0	1
Wiel	1.000	8	60	2	0	7

Second Base	PCT	G	PO	A	E	DP
Guzman	.984	25	49	72	2	14
Molina	.986	10	30	38	1	10
Perez	.976	34	54	108	4	19

Third Base	PCT	G	PO	A	E	DP
Blankenhorn	.914	34	24	50	7	5
Molina	.947	25	13	41	3	5
Montesino	.963	8	8	18	1	0
Paul	.800	3	1	7	2	1

Shortstop	PCT	G	PO	A	E	DP
Guzman	.901	23	30	61	10	9
Miller	1.000	11	20	23	0	4

Montesino	1.000	5	7	18	0	5
Palacios	.889	30	47	81	16	16

Outfield	PCT	G	PO	A	E	DP
Cavaness	1.000	3	5	0	0	0
Diemer	.957	18	21	1	1	0
Hartong	1.000	18	22	1	0	0
Kihle	.948	42	53	2	3	0
Kuresa	—	1	0	0	0	0
Montesino	—	1	0	0	0	0
Murray	—	1	0	0	0	0
Paul	.957	12	21	1	1	0
Wade	.979	63	129	11	3	2
Young	.963	50	72	5	3	0

GCL TWINS ROOKIE
GULF COAST LEAGUE

Batting	B-T	HT	WT	DOB	AVG	vLH	vRH	G	AB	R	H	2B	3B	HR	RBI	BB	HBP	SH	SF	SO	SB	CS	SLG	OBP
Andrade, Jorge	B-R	5-10	170	12-7-94	.162	.043	.195	45	105	12	17	1	0	0	6	11	2	0	0	31	11	3	.171	.254
Arraez, Luis	L-R	5-10	155	4-9-97	.309	.302	.311	57	207	23	64	15	1	0	19	19	4	2	1	10	8	8	.391	.377
Blankenhorn, Travis	L-R	6-1	195	8-3-96	.245	.188	.273	14	49	6	12	4	2	0	7	2	0	1	1	11	2	0	.408	.362
Cabbage, Trey	L-R	6-3	190	5-3-97	.252	.350	.232	33	119	8	30	2	0	0	13	7	2	0	1	37	1	5	.269	.302
Camacho, Kerby	B-R	5-10	176	11-24-97	.093	.000	.111	19	54	2	5	1	0	1	5	4	1	0	0	13	0	0	.167	.169
Cavaness, Christian	L-L	6-2	190	3-16-94	.333	.200	.347	20	54	11	18	6	3	0	8	7	2	0	0	13	5	2	.556	.429

Batting	B-T	HT	WT	DOB	AVG	vLH	vRH	G	AB	R	H	2B	3B	HR	RBI	BB	HBP	SH	SF	SO	SB	CS	SLG	OBP
Davis, Tyree	B-R	6-3	175	9-4-95	.158	.167	.154	10	19	5	3	1	0	0	0	2	0	0	0	5	2	0	.211	.238
Diaz, Lewin	L-L	6-3	180	11-19-96	.261	.238	.267	33	111	12	29	7	1	1	15	14	2	0	0	24	2	0	.369	.354
Ebersohn, Rowan	L-L	5-10	195	4-16-96	.193	.105	.219	27	83	6	16	4	0	0	3	3	0	0	1	16	2	1	.241	.218
Gonzalez, Roberto	L-L	6-0	195	3-14-95	.265	.313	.257	38	117	13	31	3	0	0	7	13	2	0	0	31	8	3	.291	.348
Haar, Bryan	R-R	6-3	215	12-9-89	.208	.000	.250	7	24	0	5	0	0	0	1	1	0	0	0	1	0	0	.208	.240
Hayman, Bryant	R-R	6-0	215	10-13-92	.222	.059	.256	33	99	16	22	7	2	2	11	11	4	0	1	33	0	0	.394	.322
Hicks, D.J.	L-R	6-5	247	4-2-90	.267	.000	.333	5	15	1	4	3	0	0	2	3	0	0	0	2	0	0	.467	.389
Kendrick, Kolton	L-R	6-3	225	8-10-96	.200	.091	.220	24	70	7	14	3	1	0	5	18	1	0	0	24	0	0	.271	.371
Marrero, Lean	L-R	5-10	160	9-19-97	.159	.077	.180	24	63	4	10	0	1	1	3	7	0	1	0	16	5	2	.238	.243
Martinez, Luis	B-R	5-11	170	10-25-95	.140	.150	.138	39	107	7	15	4	0	0	9	5	5	1	0	28	3	1	.178	.240
Minier, Amaurys	B-R	6-2	190	1-30-96	.333	1.000	.200	2	6	1	2	0	0	0	0	0	0	0	0	2	0	0	.333	.333
Molina, Robert	R-R	5-9	195	9-16-96	.235	.147	.271	37	119	11	28	4	0	1	15	7	2	0	0	16	4	0	.294	.289
Montesino, Ariel	B-R	5-10	170	9-21-95	.243	.176	.263	28	74	17	18	3	0	1	10	11	1	2	2	6	3	2	.324	.341
Olson, Brian	R-R	6-0	190	1-21-93	.273	.267	.275	17	55	11	15	1	0	3	12	2	0	1	0	10	0	0	.327	.414
Palacios, Jermaine	R-R	6-0	145	7-19-96	.421	.389	.429	26	95	13	40	9	2	1	14	9	1	0	1	11	4	2	.589	.472
Pinto, Josmil	R-R	5-11	220	3-31-89	.286	.000	.400	4	14	1	4	1	0	0	3	0	0	0	0	2	0	0	.571	.286
Schmit, Blake	R-R	6-1	185	2-27-92	.297	.333	.286	10	37	5	11	2	0	1	6	2	0	0	0	8	3	1	.432	.333
Tapia, Roni	R-R	6-3	175	4-3-97	.160	.222	.143	32	81	7	13	0	0	0	5	5	0	1	0	25	1	1	.160	.209
Verkerk, Ruar	L-R	6-3	180	9-5-96	.197	.000	.224	22	66	4	13	1	0	2	2	2	0	1	0	17	1	1	.212	.221
Whitefield, Aaron	R-R	6-4	200	9-2-96	.167	.333	.133	7	18	1	3	0	0	0	1	2	0	0	0	4	1	0	.167	.250

Pitching	B-T	HT	WT	DOB	W	L	ERA	G	GS	CG	SV	IP	H	R	ER	HR	BB	SO	AVG	vLH	vRH	K/9	BB/9
Balan, Vadim	R-R	6-1	195	5-25-93	0	0	0.00	1	0	0	0	2	0	0	0	0	0	4	.000	.000	.000	21.60	0.00
Condeelis, Rich	R-R	6-5	220	10-15-93	1	3	12.33	12	1	0	0	15	23	23	21	0	12	20	.348	.350	.348	11.74	7.04
Cordy, Max	R-R	6-4	200	6-9-93	1	1	1.66	12	2	0	0	22	12	4	4	0	14	25	.169	.158	.173	10.38	5.82
Curtiss, John	R-R	6-4	200	4-5-93	1	0	1.13	5	0	0	0	8	7	2	1	0	4	7	.233	.333	.167	7.88	4.50
Del Rosario, Eduardo	R-R	6-0	145	5-19-95	3	2	1.90	10	10	0	0	47	36	13	10	0	9	50	.218	.255	.203	9.51	1.71
Gallant, Dallas	R-R	6-3	195	1-25-89	0	0	1.69	4	0	0	0	5	5	1	1	0	1	11	.238	.250	.231	18.56	1.69
Gomez, Moises	R-R	6-1	192	2-9-94	0	2	3.00	15	0	0	0	24	17	10	8	1	14	12	.210	.167	.235	4.50	5.25
Gonzalez, Miguel	R-R	6-1	180	10-12-94	3	2	1.59	15	3	0	1	40	29	8	7	0	7	40	.197	.208	.191	9.08	1.59
Hernandez, Luis	R-R	6-2	185	1-28-96	0	2	10.57	9	3	0	0	15	24	23	18	3	15	15	.353	.429	.300	8.80	8.80
Landa, Yorman	R-R	6-0	175	6-16-94	1	0	0.00	7	0	0	1	9	3	1	0	0	2	9	.107	.167	.063	9.00	2.00
Lujan, Hector	R-R	6-3	210	8-23-94	1	2	5.00	15	0	0	1	18	20	12	10	0	5	5	.286	.346	.250	8.00	2.50
Martinez, Jose	R-R	6-2	175	10-29-96	1	5	4.31	11	11	0	0	48	50	26	23	1	16	32	.267	.271	.266	6.00	3.00
Mazza, Chris	R-R	6-4	180	10-17-89	0	0	3.00	5	0	0	0	6	5	2	2	0	1	5	.217	.143	.250	7.50	1.50
Moran, Jovani	L-L	6-1	165	4-24-97	0	2	4.12	6	6	0	0	20	16	9	9	0	9	17	.219	.385	.183	7.78	4.12
Pearce, Callan	R-R	6-3	190	8-1-95	0	1	4.67	15	0	0	0	17	19	9	9	1	11	11	.275	.136	.340	5.71	5.71
Poulson, Brandon	R-R	6-6	240	2-16-90	1	3	3.10	14	0	0	0	20	9	7	7	0	19	26	.138	.136	.140	11.51	8.41
Pryor, Stephen	R-R	6-4	235	7-23-89	0	2	1.86	7	0	0	0	10	5	3	2	1	5	13	.147	.125	.154	12.10	4.66
Quezada, Johan	R-R	6-6	200	8-25-94	2	1	3.38	19	0	0	7	21	14	9	8	1	12	23	.189	.091	.231	9.70	5.06
Ramirez, Williams	R-R	6-1	200	8-8-92	4	3	1.05	11	10	0	0	51	25	10	6	1	20	58	.145	.136	.151	10.17	3.51
Rosario, Randy	L-L	6-1	160	5-18-94	1	0	0.00	2	2	0	0	8	5	0	0	0	1	9	.172	.250	.160	10.13	1.13
Schutte, Matz	R-R	6-3	185	10-4-91	2	2	3.07	14	2	0	0	29	29	17	10	2	4	18	.257	.300	.241	5.52	1.23
Vasquez, Andrew	B-L	6-5	210	9-14-93	0	0	2.92	12	0	0	0	12	10	4	0	15	22	.222	.167	.242	16.05	10.95
Wells, Lachlan	R-R	5-8	163	2-27-97	5	2	2.09	10	9	0	0	47	35	12	11	4	11	49	.207	.244	.194	9.32	2.09

Fielding

Catcher	PCT	G	PO	A	E	DP	PB
Camacho	1.000	14	92	16	0	0	5
Hayman	.994	21	155	20	1	2	5
Molina	.974	22	165	26	5	2	10
Olson	1.000	8	64	12	0	0	1

First Base	PCT	G	PO	A	E	DP
Blankenhorn	1.000	4	12	1	0	2
Davis	—	1	0	0	0	0
Diaz	.988	21	155	6	2	10
Haar	1.000	3	24	2	0	1
Hayman	.971	5	34	0	1	1
Hicks	1.000	4	34	3	0	2
Kendrick	.991	15	104	11	1	9
Minier	1.000	2	10	0	0	1
Molina	.990	13	95	5	1	8
Palacios	1.000	1	1	0	0	0
Schmit	1.000	1	1	0	0	0
Tapia	1.000	4	11	0	0	1

Second Base	PCT	G	PO	A	E	DP
Andrade	1.000	10	11	12	0	2
Arraez	.979	48	84	106	4	19
Marrero	1.000	1	1	0	0	0
Montesino	—	1	0	0	0	0
Palacios	1.000	1	2	4	0	0
Schmit	1.000	6	15	10	0	3

Third Base	PCT	G	PO	A	E	DP
Andrade	.789	8	5	10	4	1
Arraez	1.000	2	1	2	0	0
Blankenhorn	1.000	5	2	9	0	1
Cabbage	.889	21	13	35	6	1
Haar	.800	2	1	3	1	1
Palacios	1.000	1	2	2	0	0
Schmit	1.000	1	0	1	0	1
Tapia	.700	5	4	3	3	0
Verkerk	.886	20	12	27	5	0

Shortstop	PCT	G	PO	A	E	DP
Andrade	.842	8	11	5	3	1
Arraez	1.000	2	2	3	0	0

	PCT	G	PO	A	E	DP
Blankenhorn	1.000	2	3	7	0	0
Cabbage	.938	3	4	11	1	0
Montesino	.969	26	29	66	3	13
Palacios	.960	23	34	62	4	13
Schmit	.800	2	4	1	0	0

Outfield	PCT	G	PO	A	E	DP
Andrade	1.000	23	27	1	0	0
Arraez	1.000	6	11	1	0	0
Blankenhorn	1.000	3	6	0	0	0
Cabbage	1.000	7	3	1	0	0
Cavaness	1.000	18	23	0	0	0
Davis	1.000	5	4	1	0	0
Ebersohn	1.000	25	30	0	0	0
Gonzalez	.978	30	40	4	1	1
Marrero	.973	17	35	1	1	0
Martinez	1.000	38	50	1	0	1
Olson	1.000	3	6	0	0	0
Palacios	.500	1	1	0	1	0
Tapia	.964	22	26	1	1	0
Whitefield	1.000	7	9	0	0	0

DSL TWINS   ROOKIE

DOMINICAN SUMMER LEAGUE

Batting	B-T	HT	WT	DOB	AVG	vLH	vRH	G	AB	R	H	2B	3B	HR	RBI	BB	HBP	SH	SF	SO	SB	CS	SLG	OBP
Acosta, Jorge	R-R	5-11	207	10-3-96	.253	.308	.242	29	75	8	19	2	0	0	13	20	1	0	2	15	2	2	.280	.408
Alvarez, Jhonathan	R-R	6-0	190	2-18-96	.250	.326	.212	39	128	19	32	7	0	3	15	11	5	2	1	18	2	2	.375	.331

Batting

Batting	B-T	HT	WT	DOB	AVG	vLH	vRH	G	AB	R	H	2B	3B	HR	RBI	BB	HBP	SH	SF	SO	SB	CS	SLG	OBP
Amarante, Junior	L-L	5-11	185	3-21-95	.287	.121	.336	43	143	20	41	2	2	0	9	9	6	0	0	37	8	9	.329	.354
Arias, Jean Carlos	L-L	5-11	170	1-14-98	.311	.258	.323	44	164	41	51	13	9	2	37	18	2	1	4	30	11	6	.537	.378
Bermudez, Jose	R-R	6-4	190	1-8-98	.114	.161	.095	37	105	10	12	0	0	2	8	16	1	0	3	38	1	2	.171	.232
Cuesto, Darling	R-R	6-0	175	10-12-97	.280	.156	.315	44	143	24	40	6	1	1	17	24	4	1	1	48	3	3	.357	.395
Encarnacion, Yeltsin	L-R	6-0	155	6-28-98	.286	.317	.274	42	147	21	42	3	2	0	15	22	2	2	1	27	3	6	.333	.384
Franco, Edwin	B-R	5-11	160	10-7-94	.250	.261	.245	43	156	22	39	7	2	0	20	16	6	2	0	38	6	4	.321	.343
Henriquez, Zaino	R-R	5-11	165	6-7-98	.182	.111	.200	45	137	21	25	1	1	0	10	12	2	1	2	35	2	2	.204	.255
Hernandez, Francisco	B-R	5-10	165	9-20-95	.276	.205	.301	44	152	21	42	5	1	1	17	13	6	3	0	37	5	5	.342	.357
Herrera, Edgar	L-L	6-0	170	4-19-97	.255	.267	.252	54	192	22	49	8	0	0	20	15	4	2	2	18	4	8	.297	.319
Morel, Emmanuel	R-R	5-10	150	5-4-97	.282	.280	.282	48	181	44	51	6	5	0	19	46	1	1	1	43	24	11	.370	.428
Munoz, Jorge	R-R	6-1	180	6-21-96	.315	.324	.313	46	168	37	53	9	2	2	26	23	9	1	5	24	22	11	.429	.415
Parra, Jorge	R-R	6-0	166	6-14-95	.244	.269	.234	52	197	26	48	12	2	1	34	17	4	0	5	49	1	1	.340	.309
Tejada, Oliver	R-R	5-11	175	8-22-97	.229	.111	.269	10	35	6	8	2	0	0	2	0	3	0	0	5	1	1	.286	.289
Tovar, Antonio	R-R	6-0	197	6-1-96	.281	.281	.280	60	228	27	64	7	1	2	34	27	1	3	2	35	9	13	.346	.357
Ynfante, Gabriel A.	B-R	5-11	158	11-15-94	.274	.269	.277	25	73	11	20	6	0	0	6	8	2	2	1	17	4	0	.356	.357

Pitching

Pitching	B-T	HT	WT	DOB	W	L	ERA	G	GS	CG	SV	IP	H	R	ER	HR	BB	SO	AVG	vLH	vRH	K/9	BB/9
Balbuena, Erick	R-R	6-2	175	6-4-96	1	1	10.80	18	0	0	0	22	33	32	26	2	19	11	.367	.464	.323	4.57	7.89
Bellorin, Luis	L-L	6-1	167	9-18-97	2	3	4.00	18	0	0	1	36	35	23	16	0	21	28	.254	.269	.250	7.00	5.25
Cabrera, Robener	R-R	6-3	205	1-25-94	1	1	8.10	4	0	0	0	7	8	6	6	2	2	1	.296	.222	.333	1.35	2.70
De Jesus, Miguel	R-R	6-2	175	9-20-95	6	6	4.30	18	7	0	1	59	62	34	28	2	11	58	.265	.216	.288	8.90	1.69
Feliz, Danny	R-R	6-0	170	12-12-96	1	3	4.61	17	10	0	0	55	45	34	28	3	25	40	.226	.173	.245	6.59	4.12
Gil, Luis	R-R	6-1	160	6-3-98	1	2	4.63	16	0	0	2	23	15	15	12	2	26	24	.190	.269	.151	9.26	10.03
Graterol, Brusdar	R-R	6-1	180	8-26-98	0	1	2.45	4	4	0	0	11	12	4	3	0	1	17	.273	.417	.219	13.91	0.82
Herrera, Juan	R-R	6-3	170	1-28-96	3	3	4.54	15	14	0	0	69	63	41	35	5	20	64	.239	.150	.277	8.31	2.60
Jimenez, Jadison	L-L	6-0	180	3-19-94	6	3	2.45	15	14	0	0	77	78	27	21	5	15	87	.265	.194	.284	10.17	1.75
Marin, Andriu	R-R	6-1	183	7-6-98	3	0	4.54	20	0	0	5	38	49	25	19	2	7	39	.302	.333	.288	9.32	1.67
Perez, Randolph	R-R	6-0	170	4-23-94	5	4	1.90	22	0	0	3	43	40	22	9	1	25	48	.245	.255	.241	10.13	5.27
Ramirez, Jose	R-R	6-0	170	8-19-92	1	3	5.11	18	9	0	0	62	75	53	35	3	29	45	.304	.349	.280	6.57	4.23
Soto, Fredderi	L-L	5-11	175	6-29-98	1	0	2.33	11	0	0	0	19	23	12	5	1	8	21	.295	.273	.299	9.78	3.72
Suniaga, Carlos	R-R	6-2	187	5-26-97	2	1	6.48	23	0	0	2	50	71	37	36	6	6	35	.329	.378	.303	6.30	1.08
Ynoa, Huascar	R-R	6-3	175	5-28-98	2	5	2.70	14	14	0	0	57	43	25	17	1	30	47	.207	.164	.222	7.46	4.76

Fielding

Catcher	PCT	G	PO	A	E	DP	PB
Acosta	1.000	13	79	12	0	0	11
Alvarez	.958	39	307	34	15	1	10
Cuesto	.981	25	135	21	3	0	9
Tejada	1.000	4	36	3	0	1	8
Henriquez	.971	44	97	106	6	30	
Hernandez	.923	4	6	6	1	1	
Morel	.750	5	4	5	3	1	
Munoz	1.000	5	4	2	0	1	
Ynfante	.959	11	21	26	2	8	
Franco	.908	15	21	38	6	6	
Morel	.803	14	18	31	12	9	
Munoz	.905	17	29	38	7	11	
Ynfante	1.000	2	0	2	0	1	

First Base	PCT	G	PO	A	E	DP
Bermudez	1.000	1	10	0	0	3
Franco	1.000	1	2	0	0	1
Herrera	.977	35	280	21	7	21
Parra	.991	37	326	19	3	27
Ynfante	1.000	2	14	2	0	2

Second Base	PCT	G	PO	A	E	DP
Encarnacion	1.000	11	23	26	0	3
Franco	.893	7	12	13	3	4

Third Base	PCT	G	PO	A	E	DP
Cuesto	.891	17	19	22	5	4
Encarnacion	.714	4	1	4	2	0
Franco	.985	25	13	54	1	1
Henriquez	1.000	1	1	0	0	0
Munoz	.851	24	22	58	14	6
Ynfante	.947	9	10	8	1	0

Shortstop	PCT	G	PO	A	E	DP
Encarnacion	.865	29	38	77	18	14

Outfield	PCT	G	PO	A	E	DP
Amarante	.854	30	33	2	6	1
Arias	.953	40	78	3	4	0
Bermudez	.952	31	35	5	2	1
Hernandez	.974	41	74	0	2	0
Herrera	.914	19	32	0	3	0
Parra	.929	12	13	0	1	0
Tovar	.951	59	75	3	4	0

MINNESOTA TWINS

New York Mets

SEASON IN A SENTENCE: After six straight losing seasons and seemingly endless rebuilding, the Mets won 90 games and captured the National League East division title by outplaying the Nationals by nine games in August and September.

HIGH POINT: The Mets won their first pennant since 2000 by sweeping the Cubs in the NLCS, making Chicago look overmatched as Daniel Murphy homered in every game.

LOW POINT: Aside from the World Series, the offense sputtered to 3.11 runs per game during the month of June, when the Mets went a season-worst 12-15. They lost seven games in a row to the Blue Jays, Braves and Brewers from June 17-24 to fall one game under .500, but they then won four in a row and never again had a losing record in 2015.

NOTABLE ROOKIES: Righthander Noah Syndergaard (24 starts) made his big league debut in mid-May, and lefty Steven Matz (six) followed in late June. The two rookies pitched effectively—though Matz missed two months with a lat injury—and made the postseason rotation. Left fielder Michael Conforto, the 10th overall pick in 2014, made his debut on July 24 and hit .270/.335/.506 in 56 games. He hit more home runs (nine) as a rookie than he hit as an Oregon State junior the year before (seven). The bullpen featured a number of rookie arms, including righties Hansel Robles, Erik Goeddel and Logan Verrett and Rule 5 lefty Sean Gilmartin.

KEY TRANSACTIONS: The Mets remade their lineup and bullpen with a series of summer trades. They dealt a bevy of pitching prospects—righthander Michael Fulmer, most critically—to acquire veteran infielders Juan Uribe and Kelly Johnson from the Braves, outfielder Yoenis Cespedes from the Tigers and relievers Tyler Clippard (Athletics) and Addison Reed (Diamondbacks). Cespedes, the tooled-up, 29-year-old Cuban import, made the biggest impact, hitting .287/.337/.604 with 35 extra-base hits, including 17 home runs, and 44 RBIs in 57 games.

DOWN ON THE FARM: Mets domestic affiliates recorded a cumulative .532 winning percentage that ranked seventh best in baseball. None of the system's three playoff teams advanced to their league finals, however. The Mets haven't had a losing record on the farm since 2009. St. Lucie first baseman Dominic Smith (Florida State) and low Class A Savannah shortstop Luis Guillorme (South Atlantic) won league MVP awards.

OPENING DAY PAYROLL: $101,409,244 (21st).

PLAYERS OF THE YEAR

MAJOR LEAGUE	MINOR LEAGUE
Jacob deGrom rhp	**Michael Conforto** of
14-8, 2.54 in 191 IP Among NL leaders for ERA, WHIP and SO/9	.297/.372/.482 2014 first-rounder earned July 24 callup

ORGANIZATION LEADERS

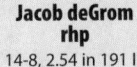

BATTING		*Minimum 250 AB
MAJORS		
* AVG	Daniel Murphy	.281
* OPS	Lucas Duda	.838
HR	Lucas Duda	27
RBI	Daniel Murphy	73
MINORS		
* AVG	T.J. Rivera, Las Vegas, Binghamton	.325
* OBP	Jonathan Johnson, Savannah	.396
* SLG	Travis Taijeron, Las Vegas	.536
R	Jeff McNeil, St. Lucie, Binghamton	80
H	Jeff McNeil, St. Lucie, Binghamton	149
TB	Josh Rodriguez, Binghamton, Las Vegas	211
	Travis Taijeron, Las Vegas	211
2B	Dominic Smith, St. Lucie	33
3B	John Mora, Savannah	12
HR	Travis Taijeron, Las Vegas	25
RBI	Josh Rodriguez, Binghamton, Las Vegas	81
BB	Jonathan Johnson, Savannah	76
SO	Travis Taijeron, Las Vegas	147
SB	Patrick Biondi, Savannah	38

PITCHING		#Minimum 75 IP
MAJORS		
W	Jacob deGrom	2.54
# ERA	Jacob deGrom	2.54
SO	Jacob deGrom	205
SV	Jeurys Familia	43
MINORS		
W	Robert Gsellman, St. Lucie, Binghamton	13
L	Matt Bowman, Las Vegas	16
# ERA	Martires Arias, St. Lucie, Savannah	2.29
G	Zach Thornton, Las Vegas	63
GS	Darin Gorski, Las Vegas	27
SV	Paul Sewald, Binghamton	24
IP	Gabriel Ynoa, Binghamton	152
BB	Darin Gorski, Las Vegas	69
SO	Seth Lugo, Binghamton, Las Vegas	127
AVG	Martires Arias, St. Lucie, Savannah	.203

2015 PERFORMANCE

General Manager: Sandy Alderson. **Farm Director:** Paul DePodesta. **Scouting Director:** Tom Tanous.

Class	Team	League	W	L	PCT	Finish	Manager
Majors	New York Mets	National	90	72	.556	5th (15)	Terry Collins
Triple-A	Las Vegas 51s	Pacific Coast	77	67	.535	8th (16)	Wally Backman
Double-A	Binghamton Mets	Eastern	77	64	.546	3rd (12)	Pedro Lopez
High A	St. Lucie Mets	Florida State	68	70	.493	7th (12)	Luis Rojas
Low A	Savannah Sand Gnats	South Atlantic	84	53	.613	2nd (14)	Jose Leger
Short season	Brooklyn Cyclones	New York-Penn	33	43	.434	12th (14)	Tom Gamboa
Rookie	Kingsport Mets	Appalachian	40	28	.588	2nd (10)	Luis Rivera
Rookie	Mets	Gulf Coast	27	32	.458	t-9th (16)	Jose Carreno
Overall 2015 Minor League Record			406	357	.532	7th (30)	

ORGANIZATION STATISTICS

NEW YORK METS

NATIONAL LEAGUE

Batting	B-T	HT	WT	DOB	AVG	vLH	vRH	G	AB	R	H	2B	3B	HR	RBI	BB	HBP	SH	SF	SO	SB	CS	SLG	OBP
Campbell, Eric	R-R	6-3	205	4-9-87	.197	.143	.210	71	173	28	34	8	0	3	19	26	4	1	2	37	5	3	.295	.312
Ceciliani, Darrell	L-L	6-1	220	6-22-90	.206	.286	.197	39	68	5	14	2	0	1	3	4	2	0	0	25	5	1	.279	.270
Cespedes, Yoenis	R-R	5-10	210	10-18-85	.287	.281	.289	57	230	39	66	14	4	17	44	14	4	0	1	54	4	1	.604	.337
Conforto, Michael	L-R	6-1	215	3-1-93	.270	.214	.275	56	174	30	47	14	0	9	26	17	1	0	2	39	0	1	.506	.335
Cuddyer, Michael	R-R	6-2	220	3-27-79	.259	.273	.254	117	379	44	98	18	1	10	41	24	4	0	1	88	2	0	.391	.309
d'Arnaud, Travis	R-R	6-2	210	2-10-89	.268	.333	.253	67	239	31	64	14	1	12	41	23	4	0	2	49	0	0	.485	.340
Duda, Lucas	L-R	6-4	255	2-3-86	.244	.285	.230	135	471	67	115	33	0	27	73	66	14	0	3	138	0	2	.486	.352
Flores, Wilmer	R-R	6-3	205	8-6-91	.263	.310	.251	137	483	55	127	22	0	16	59	19	4	2	2	63	0	1	.408	.295
Granderson, Curtis	L-R	6-1	200	3-16-81	.259	.183	.280	157	580	98	150	33	2	26	70	91	7	0	4	151	11	6	.457	.364
Herrera, Dilson	R-R	5-10	150	3-3-94	.211	.250	.200	31	90	7	19	3	1	3	6	11	2	0	0	23	2	0	.367	.311
Johnson, Kelly	L-R	6-1	195	2-22-82	.250	.222	.252	49	128	18	32	6	0	5	13	10	0	0	0	38	1	0	.414	.304
2-team total (62 Atlanta)					.265	—	—	111	310	38	82	11	0	14	47	23	0	0	1	81	2	1	.435	.314
Lagares, Juan	R-R	6-1	215	3-17-89	.259	.273	.253	143	441	47	114	16	5	6	41	16	4	1	3	87	7	3	.358	.289
Mayberry Jr., John	R-R	6-6	235	12-21-83	.164	.175	.151	59	110	8	18	6	1	3	9	9	0	0	3	33	1	0	.318	.227
Monell, Johnny	L-R	6-0	210	3-27-86	.167	.000	.174	27	48	5	8	2	0	0	4	4	0	0	0	13	0	0	.208	.231
Muno, Danny	B-R	5-11	195	2-9-89	.148	.000	.174	17	27	2	4	1	0	0	0	4	0	1	0	11	1	0	.185	.258
Murphy, Daniel	L-R	6-1	215	4-1-85	.281	.254	.290	130	499	56	140	38	2	14	73	31	2	0	6	38	2	2	.449	.322
Nieuwenhuis, Kirk	L-R	6-3	225	8-7-87	.208	.000	.220	64	106	17	22	9	0	4	13	8	3	0	0	40	2	1	.406	.282
Plawecki, Kevin	R-R	6-2	225	2-26-91	.219	.122	.240	73	233	18	51	9	0	3	21	17	4	1	3	60	0	0	.296	.280
Recker, Anthony	R-R	6-2	240	8-29-83	.125	.174	.105	32	80	6	10	1	0	2	5	11	1	0	0	35	1	0	.213	.239
Tejada, Ruben	R-R	5-11	200	10-27-89	.261	.264	.260	116	360	36	94	23	0	3	28	38	5	2	2	70	2	1	.350	.338
Uribe, Juan	R-R	6-0	245	3-22-79	.219	.250	.205	44	128	17	28	9	0	6	20	14	1	0	0	34	0	0	.430	.301
3-team total (46 Atlanta, 29 Los Angeles)					.253	—	—	119	360	40	91	17	0	14	43	34	2	0	1	80	2	0	.417	.320
Wright, David	R-R	6-0	205	12-20-82	.289	.351	.270	38	152	24	44	7	0	5	17	22	0	0	0	36	2	1	.434	.379
Young Jr., Eric	B-R	5-10	195	5-25-85	.000	.000	.000	18	8	9	0	0	0	0	0	1	0	0	0	1	0	0	.000	.111
2-team total (35 Atlanta)					.153	—	—	53	85	16	13	4	2	0	5	6	1	2	0	18	6	2	.247	.217

Pitching	B-T	HT	WT	DOB	W	L	ERA	G	GS	CG	SV	IP	H	R	ER	HR	BB	SO	AVG	vLH	vRH	K/9	BB/9
Alvarez, Dario	L-L	6-1	170	1-17-89	1	0	12.27	6	0	0	0	4	5	5	5	2	1	2	.333	.300	.400	4.91	2.45
Blevins, Jerry	L-L	6-6	190	9-6-83	1	0	0.00	7	0	0	0	5	0	0	0	0	0	4	.000	.000	.000	7.20	0.00
Carlyle, Buddy	L-R	6-3	210	12-21-77	1	0	5.63	11	0	0	0	8	8	5	5	0	1	6	.276	.143	.318	6.75	1.13
Clippard, Tyler	R-R	6-3	200	2-14-85	4	1	3.06	32	0	0	2	32	24	13	11	5	10	26	.200	.174	.235	7.24	2.78
Colon, Bartolo	R-R	5-11	285	5-24-73	14	13	4.16	33	31	1	0	195	217	94	90	25	24	136	.281	.290	.272	6.29	1.11
deGrom, Jacob	L-R	6-4	180	6-19-88	14	8	2.54	30	30	0	0	191	149	59	54	16	38	205	.215	.245	.181	9.66	1.79
Familia, Jeurys	R-R	6-3	240	10-10-89	2	2	1.85	76	0	0	43	78	59	16	16	6	19	86	.207	.214	.201	9.92	2.19
Gee, Dillon	R-R	6-1	205	4-28-86	0	3	5.90	8	7	0	0	40	55	29	26	5	11	25	.329	.395	.259	5.67	2.50
Gilmartin, Sean	L-L	6-2	205	5-8-90	3	2	2.67	50	1	0	0	57	50	17	17	2	18	54	.236	.260	.216	8.48	2.83
Goeddel, Erik	R-R	6-3	190	12-20-88	1	1	2.43	35	0	0	0	33	24	9	9	1	9	34	.203	.189	.210	9.18	2.43
Harvey, Matt	R-R	6-4	215	3-27-89	13	8	2.71	29	29	0	0	189	156	62	57	18	37	188	.222	.226	.218	8.94	1.76
Leathersich, Jack	R-L	5-11	200	7-14-90	0	1	2.31	17	0	0	0	12	12	3	3	0	7	14	.273	.280	.263	10.80	5.40
Matz, Steven	R-L	6-2	200	5-29-91	4	0	2.27	6	6	0	0	36	34	9	9	4	10	34	.250	.250	.250	8.58	2.52
Mejia, Jenrry	R-R	6-0	205	10-11-89	1	0	0.00	7	0	0	0	7	4	0	0	0	2	7	.167	.200	.143	8.59	2.45
Montero, Rafael	R-R	6-0	185	10-17-90	0	1	4.50	5	1	0	0	10	9	6	5	0	5	13	.225	.429	.182	11.70	4.50
Morris, Akeel	R-R	6-1	195	11-14-92	0	0	67.50	1	0	0	0	1	3	5	5	1	5	1	.600	1.000	.500	0.00	40.50
Niese, Jon	L-L	6-3	220	10-27-86	9	10	4.13	33	29	0	0	177	192	93	81	20	55	113	.280	.305	.273	5.76	2.80
O'Flaherty, Eric	L-L	6-2	220	2-5-85	0	0	13.50	16	0	0	0	9	18	13	13	1	5	6	.409	.414	.400	6.23	5.19
Parnell, Bobby	R-R	6-3	205	9-8-84	2	4	6.38	30	0	0	1	24	30	20	17	0	17	13	.323	.333	.317	4.88	6.38
Reed, Addison	L-R	6-4	230	12-27-88	1	1	1.17	17	0	0	1	15	11	2	2	1	5	17	.200	.276	.115	9.98	2.93
2-team total (38 Arizona)					3	3	3.38	55	0	0	4	56	58	21	21	3	19	51	—	—	—	8.20	3.05
Robles, Hansel	R-R	5-11	185	8-13-90	4	3	3.67	57	0	0	0	54	37	27	22	8	18	61	.190	.167	.205	10.17	3.00
Stauffer, Tim	R-R	6-1	220	6-2-82	0	0	7.94	5	0	0	0	6	8	5	5	2	2	8	.500	.214	12.71	3.18	
Syndergaard, Noah	L-R	6-6	240	8-29-92	9	7	3.24	24	24	0	0	150	126	60	54	19	31	166	.225	.237	.212	9.96	1.86
Torres, Alex	L-L	5-10	185	12-8-87	0	0	3.15	39	0	0	1	34	26	16	12	6	26	35	.206	.268	.157	9.17	6.82
Torres, Carlos	R-R	6-1	180	10-22-82	5	6	4.68	59	0	0	0	58	61	32	30	5	18	48	.276	.263	.284	7.49	2.81
Verrett, Logan	R-R	6-2	190	6-19-90	1	1	3.03	14	4	0	1	39	23	13	13	5	11	36	.174	.174	.175	8.38	2.56

NEW YORK METS

Fielding

Catcher	PCT	G	PO	A	E	DP	PB
d'Arnaud	.995	64	556	25	3	6	1
Monell	1.000	12	60	0	0	0	0
Plawecki	.998	70	558	36	1	1	2
Recker	.994	28	171	6	1	0	1

First Base	PCT	G	PO	A	E	DP
Campbell	1.000	5	30	3	0	4
Cuddyer	1.000	18	116	11	0	11
Duda	.997	129	1039	77	3	87
Johnson	1.000	5	23	2	0	3
Murphy	.992	17	117	14	1	12
Recker	1.000	1	9	0	0	1

Second Base	PCT	G	PO	A	E	DP
Flores	1.000	37	61	92	0	22
Herrera	.986	29	53	85	2	19

	PCT	G	PO	A	E	DP
Johnson	.979	27	31	61	2	9
Muno	1.000	1	0	3	0	0
Murphy	.979	69	118	166	6	32
Tejada	1.000	13	14	32	0	8
Uribe	1.000	7	6	12	0	4

Third Base	PCT	G	PO	A	E	DP
Campbell	.921	48	28	65	8	5
Johnson	.500	1	0	1	1	0
Muno	.667	5	1	5	3	1
Murphy	.935	42	16	71	6	5
Recker	—	1	0	0	0	0
Tejada	.962	19	14	36	2	4
Uribe	.964	26	7	46	2	1
Wright	.951	38	23	55	4	2

Shortstop	PCT	G	PO	A	E	DP
Flores	.965	103	119	267	14	62
Johnson	.800	1	2	2	1	1
Tejada	.982	81	78	189	5	36

Outfield	PCT	G	PO	A	E	DP
Campbell	1.000	4	8	1	0	0
Ceciliani	1.000	21	36	2	0	1
Cespedes	.985	54	124	4	2	0
Conforto	1.000	50	85	6	0	0
Cuddyer	.973	75	103	4	3	0
Granderson	.983	150	287	9	5	1
Johnson	1.000	6	5	0	0	0
Lagares	.993	139	282	3	2	2
Mayberry Jr.	1.000	29	57	1	0	1
Nieuwenhuis	1.000	41	60	2	0	1
Young Jr.	1.000	7	5	0	0	0

LAS VEGAS 51S   TRIPLE-A
PACIFIC COAST LEAGUE

Batting	B-T	HT	WT	DOB	AVG	vLH	vRH	G	AB	R	H	2B	3B	HR	RBI	BB	HBP	SH	SF	SO	SB	CS	SLG	OBP
Allen, Brandon	L-R	6-2	230	2-12-86	.273	.258	.278	124	406	52	111	29	3	16	68	51	1	0	8	92	4	2	.478	.350
Boyd, Jayce	R-R	6-3	185	12-30-90	.254	.203	.291	56	138	12	35	11	0	0	12	12	0	1	0	23	0	2	.333	.313
Campbell, Eric	R-R	6-3	205	4-9-87	.363	.500	.313	33	113	28	41	9	1	5	18	25	4	0	0	20	7	2	.593	.493
Castellanos, Alex	R-R	6-0	200	4-8-86	.314	.347	.297	79	280	58	88	32	2	16	56	24	7	0	1	73	5	0	.614	.381
Ceciliani, Darrell	L-L	6-1	220	6-22-90	.345	.302	.358	70	229	50	79	19	4	9	36	21	1	0	3	48	16	4	.581	.398
Conrad, Brooks	B-R	5-10	190	1-16-80	.194	.159	.211	83	273	37	53	14	1	6	40	27	6	0	1	71	2	0	.319	.280
d'Arnaud, Travis	R-R	6-2	210	2-10-89	.125	.000	.143	2	8	0	1	1	0	0	0	0	0	0	0	2	0	0	.250	.125
Herrera, Dilson	R-R	5-10	150	3-3-94	.327	.400	.288	81	327	68	107	23	2	11	50	28	3	3	3	59	13	9	.511	.382
Johnson, Kyle	R-R	6-0	180	11-9-89	.223	.310	.154	36	94	15	21	8	0	1	10	5	5	0	2	25	7	2	.340	.292
Lutz, Zach	R-R	6-1	220	6-3-86	.203	.207	.200	23	74	9	15	4	0	1	9	11	0	0	0	18	0	1	.297	.306
Monell, Johnny	L-R	6-0	210	3-27-86	.324	.441	.289	71	256	34	83	16	0	7	51	27	2	0	3	39	6	2	.469	.389
Muno, Danny	B-R	5-11	195	2-9-89	.277	.270	.280	83	274	44	76	14	1	3	24	35	2	2	1	50	6	7	.369	.362
Nieuwenhuis, Kirk	L-R	6-3	225	8-7-87	.324	.111	.397	27	105	21	34	6	3	8	29	10	1	1	2	21	2	0	.667	.381
Nimmo, Brandon	L-R	6-3	205	3-27-93	.264	.185	.297	32	91	19	24	3	1	3	8	18	2	0	1	20	5	4	.418	.393
Perez, Jairo	R-R	5-10	160	6-10-88	.200	.333	.000	2	5	0	1	0	0	0	0	0	0	0	0	1	0	0	.200	.167
Plawecki, Kevin	R-R	6-2	225	2-26-91	.224	.238	.219	22	85	7	19	5	1	1	9	3	2	0	0	12	0	0	.341	.267
Recker, Anthony	R-R	6-2	240	8-29-83	.245	.289	.204	27	94	17	23	3	1	8	21	12	2	0	0	16	2	0	.553	.343
Reynolds, Matt	R-R	6-1	205	12-3-90	.267	.297	.253	115	445	70	119	32	5	6	65	32	5	1	7	92	13	4	.402	.319
Rivera, T.J.	R-R	6-1	190	10-27-88	.306	.260	.323	54	183	26	56	17	1	2	21	7	0	0	4	27	0	0	.443	.345
Rodriguez, Josh	R-R	6-0	185	12-18-84	.300	.500	.214	5	20	2	6	2	0	0	5	3	0	0	0	4	0	0	.400	.391
Rohlfing, Dan	R-R	6-0	205	2-12-89	.230	.259	.215	54	161	21	37	13	0	3	21	9	3	1	2	48	0	0	.366	.280
Taijeron, Travis	R-R	6-2	200	1-20-89	.274	.304	.259	127	394	67	108	22	3	25	71	65	15	0	4	147	2	2	.536	.393
Tovar, Wilfredo	R-R	5-10	180	8-11-91	.283	.307	.270	102	357	50	101	15	1	3	42	22	2	6	1	40	30	13	.356	.327
Vaughn, Cory	R-R	6-3	235	5-1-89	.210	.244	.186	71	195	24	41	11	2	5	22	22	2	0	1	61	4	2	.364	.295
Young Jr., Eric	B-R	5-10	195	5-25-85	.261	.000	.300	8	23	1	6	2	0	0	1	4	0	0	0	2	3	1	.348	.370
Zapata, Nelfi	R-R	6-0	203	12-13-90	.162	.100	.235	17	37	4	6	1	0	0	0	5	1	0	0	9	0	0	.189	.279

Pitching	B-T	HT	WT	DOB	W	L	ERA	G	GS	CG	SV	IP	H	R	ER	HR	BB	SO	AVG	vLH	vRH	K/9	BB/9
Alvarez, Dario	L-L	6-1	170	1-17-89	2	1	2.45	16	0	0	0	11	6	3	3	0	5	19	.167	.167	.167	15.55	4.09
Below, Duane	L-L	6-3	220	11-15-85	4	3	2.19	11	5	2	0	49	46	14	12	4	8	28	.247	.230	.259	5.11	1.46
Black, Vic	R-R	6-4	210	5-23-88	1	4	7.09	31	0	0	3	27	32	22	21	3	26	27	.296	.231	.333	9.11	8.78
Bowman, Matt	R-R	6-0	165	5-31-91	7	16	5.53	28	26	2	0	140	184	97	86	15	51	77	.319	.330	.309	4.95	3.28
Bradford, Chase	R-R	6-1	230	8-5-89	5	4	4.10	53	0	0	7	64	86	35	29	3	14	46	.322	.373	.291	6.50	1.98
Cessa, Luis	R-R	6-3	190	4-25-92	0	3	8.51	5	5	0	0	24	40	25	23	4	4	24	.354	.308	.393	8.88	1.48
Church, John	R-R	6-2	250	11-4-86	7	3	3.93	61	0	0	7	71	69	32	31	6	16	44	.260	.310	.236	5.58	2.03
Gee, Dillon	R-R	6-1	205	4-28-86	8	3	4.58	14	14	2	0	88	105	50	45	7	18	63	.299	.293	.303	6.42	1.83
Gorski, Darin	L-L	6-4	210	10-6-87	10	8	5.52	28	27	0	0	137	158	89	84	19	69	108	.291	.296	.290	7.09	4.53
Huchingson, Chase	L-L	6-5	200	4-14-89	0	0	3.34	29	0	0	1	30	28	16	11	1	22	22	.255	.357	.191	6.67	6.67
Lara, Rainy	R-R	6-4	180	3-14-91	0	0	7.13	5	5	0	0	24	36	20	19	4	12	14	.353	.368	.344	5.25	4.50
Leathersich, Jack	R-L	5-11	200	7-14-90	0	0	5.40	13	0	0	0	13	10	8	8	3	7	22	.204	.222	.194	14.85	4.73
Lugo, Seth	R-R	6-4	185	11-17-89	2	2	4.00	5	5	0	0	27	27	13	12	3	5	30	.252	.300	.211	10.00	1.67
Matz, Steven	R-L	6-2	200	5-29-91	7	4	2.19	15	14	0	0	90	69	25	22	6	31	94	.213	.162	.228	9.37	3.09
Mejia, Jenrry	R-R	6-0	205	10-11-89	0	0	2.25	4	0	0	1	4	4	1	1	0	0	6	.250	.167	.300	13.50	0.00
Montero, Rafael	R-R	6-0	185	10-17-90	1	0	5.87	2	2	0	0	8	8	6	5	1	1	7	.267	.154	.353	8.22	1.17
Pill, Tyler	R-R	6-1	185	5-29-90	2	7	7.45	18	17	0	0	83	111	70	69	14	30	55	.326	.351	.309	5.94	3.24
Rice, Scott	L-L	6-6	225	9-21-81	2	1	1.82	56	0	0	1	40	26	8	8	1	28	43	.194	.235	.152	9.76	6.35
Robles, Hansel	R-R	5-11	185	8-13-90	1	0	0.00	5	0	0	0	1	1	0	0	0	1	10	.207	.000	.300	11.74	1.17
Satterwhite, Cody	R-R	6-4	235	1-27-87	2	0	4.38	57	0	0	2	72	74	36	35	6	29	71	.267	.254	.276	8.88	3.63
Stauffer, Tim	R-R	6-1	220	6-2-82	4	1	2.48	8	1	0	0	54	46	17	15	4	10	35	.227	.208	.238	5.80	1.66
Syndergaard, Noah	L-R	6-6	240	8-29-92	3	0	1.82	5	5	1	0	30	20	7	6	2	8	34	.192	.162	.209	10.31	2.43
Thornton, Zach	R-R	6-3	220	5-19-88	4	4	3.94	63	0	0	2	62	59	29	27	2	24	55	.252	.237	.259	8.03	3.50
Torres, Alex	L-L	5-10	185	12-8-87	0	0	1.17	10	0	0	0	8	6	1	1	0	4	9	.214	.250	.188	10.57	4.70

Pitching

Pitching	B-T	HT	WT	DOB	W	L	ERA	G	GS	CG	SV	IP	H	R	ER	HR	BB	SO	AVG	vLH	vRH	K/9	BB/9
Velasquez, Jon	R-R	6-1	195	10-15-85	0	0	5.74	16	0	0	4	16	18	13	10	3	5	13	.286	.355	.219	7.47	2.87
Verrett, Logan	R-R	6-2	190	6-19-90	5	3	4.59	18	11	0	0	65	69	35	33	6	19	53	.278	.279	.277	7.38	2.64

Fielding

Catcher	PCT	G	PO	A	E	DP	PB
d'Arnaud	1.000	2	12	1	0	0	1
Monell	.994	52	315	33	2	5	4
Plawecki	1.000	20	157	11	0	1	0
Recker	.980	21	134	13	3	1	1
Rohlfing	.997	47	326	23	1	2	4
Zapata	1.000	11	72	4	0	2	1

First Base	PCT	G	PO	A	E	DP
Allen	.992	57	453	29	4	47
Campbell	1.000	5	43	3	0	5
Castellanos	.973	9	66	5	2	5
Conrad	.990	66	550	47	6	55
Lutz	1.000	9	80	5	0	9
Monell	.979	10	89	4	2	9
Plawecki	1.000	1	5	0	0	1
Recker	.947	2	18	0	1	2

Second Base	PCT	G	PO	A	E	DP
Conrad	1.000	5	3	1	0	0
Herrera	.984	78	134	228	6	55
Muno	.958	21	32	60	4	13
Reynolds	1.000	11	29	25	0	7
Rivera	1.000	17	21	37	0	9
Tovar	.987	21	19	56	1	10

Third Base	PCT	G	PO	A	E	DP
Campbell	.940	22	12	35	3	3
Castellanos	.932	21	11	30	3	0
Lutz	.875	6	3	4	1	0
Muno	.954	52	25	99	6	3
Perez	1.000	1	1	0	0	0
Rivera	.949	31	15	60	4	8
Rodriguez	1.000	1	0	1	0	0
Tovar	.971	27	19	49	2	6
Zapata	.000	1	0	0	2	0

Shortstop	PCT	G	PO	A	E	DP
Muno	.923	4	1	11	1	2
Reynolds	.971	92	110	290	12	69
Tovar	.972	55	71	172	7	36

Outfield	PCT	G	PO	A	E	DP
Allen	.975	68	109	6	3	1
Boyd	.958	20	23	0	1	0
Campbell	.941	11	14	2	1	0
Castellanos	.988	44	76	3	1	0
Ceciliani	.977	66	121	4	3	2
Johnson	.956	26	42	1	2	1
Nieuwenhuis	.981	25	50	2	1	1
Nimmo	.985	29	59	5	1	1
Rodriguez	1.000	4	6	0	0	0
Taijeron	.983	120	217	8	4	1
Vaughn	.981	61	102	1	2	1
Young Jr.	1.000	8	13	0	0	0

BINGHAMTON METS   DOUBLE-A

EASTERN LEAGUE

Batting	B-T	HT	WT	DOB	AVG	vLH	vRH	G	AB	R	H	2B	3B	HR	RBI	BB	HBP	SH	SF	SO	SB	CS	SLG	OBP
Belnome, Vince	L-R	5-11	205	3-11-88	.252	.257	.250	37	119	19	30	6	1	2	20	15	0	0	2	38	1	0	.370	.331
Benson, Joe	R-R	6-1	215	3-5-88	.250	.288	.232	54	184	32	46	10	1	4	24	25	6	0	2	36	7	1	.380	.355
Boyd, Jayce	R-R	6-3	185	12-30-90	.304	.313	.302	42	161	18	49	16	0	1	16	13	1	0	0	16	2	1	.422	.360
Carrillo, Xorge	R-R	6-1	220	4-12-89	.240	.200	.252	94	325	38	78	14	1	10	40	27	11	1	2	53	1	2	.382	.318
Cecchini, Gavin	R-R	6-2	200	12-22-93	.317	.359	.301	109	439	64	139	26	4	7	51	42	2	0	2	55	3	4	.442	.377
Conforto, Michael	L-R	6-1	215	3-1-93	.312	.333	.303	45	173	21	54	12	3	5	26	23	1	0	0	35	1	0	.503	.396
Cooper, David	L-L	6-0	200	2-12-87	.143	.000	.185	10	35	4	5	2	0	0	4	5	0	0	0	9	0	0	.200	.250
Cordero, Albert	R-R	5-11	175	1-14-90	.190	.234	.171	47	158	7	30	3	0	2	7	8	1	1	0	28	0	1	.247	.234
Cruzado, Victor	B-R	5-11	180	6-30-92	.200	.167	.222	5	15	1	3	1	0	0	2	3	0	0	0	2	0	0	.267	.333
d'Arnaud, Travis	R-R	6-2	210	2-10-89	.300	.333	.286	5	20	3	6	1	0	0	1	0	0	0	0	2	0	0	.350	.300
Duda, Lucas	L-R	6-4	255	2-3-86	.500	.667	.333	2	6	0	3	0	0	0	1	1	0	0	0	1	0	0	.500	.571
Galvez, Jonathan	R-R	6-2	200	1-18-91	.246	.326	.207	42	130	15	32	6	2	2	20	10	1	0	1	39	2	0	.369	.303
Gomez, Gilbert	R-R	6-3	190	3-8-92	.130	.111	.138	69	161	20	21	4	1	1	13	23	0	0	2	49	2	5	.186	.237
King, Jared	B-L	5-11	205	10-12-91	.214	.213	.215	122	420	32	90	14	2	4	51	28	1	1	5	76	5	7	.286	.262
Lawley, Dustin	R-R	6-1	205	4-11-89	.213	.227	.210	67	230	31	49	18	0	6	26	11	3	0	2	58	8	3	.370	.256
2-team total (26 Portland)					.208	—	—	93	322	39	67	21	0	8	38	16	5	0	3	82	8	4	.348	.254
Mazzilli Jr., L.J.	R-R	6-1	190	9-6-90	.263	.247	.269	86	335	50	88	20	2	0	23	35	3	0	1	57	5	2	.334	.337
McNeil, Jeff	L-R	6-1	165	4-8-92	.200	.125	.286	4	15	0	3	0	0	0	1	0	0	0	0	2	0	1	.200	.250
Nimmo, Brandon	L-R	6-3	205	3-27-93	.279	.271	.281	68	269	26	75	12	3	2	16	26	6	0	1	55	0	2	.368	.354
Perez, Jairo	R-R	5-10	160	6-10-88	.250	.133	.283	20	68	7	17	1	0	1	5	2	0	0	0	10	0	1	.309	.271
Peterson, Brock	R-R	6-3	230	11-20-83	.241	.250	.238	80	290	37	70	17	0	2	9	50	36	2	0	5	83	1	0	.407	.324
Pina, Eudy	R-R	6-3	190	4-12-91	.305	.277	.313	67	226	22	69	7	5	2	20	7	0	1	2	57	8	1	.407	.323
Rivera, T.J.	R-R	6-1	190	10-27-88	.341	.356	.335	56	220	37	75	10	0	5	27	12	2	0	0	22	1	1	.455	.380
Rodriguez, Aderlin	R-R	6-3	210	11-18-91	.253	.261	.251	63	217	29	55	13	1	10	34	9	2	0	1	42	1	1	.461	.288
Rodriguez, Josh	R-R	6-0	185	12-18-84	.282	.282	.282	115	412	70	116	24	3	19	76	54	4	0	4	87	11	2	.493	.367
Rosario, Amed	R-R	6-2	170	11-20-95	.100	.000	.125	2	10	1	1	0	0	0	1	0	0	0	0	5	1	0	.100	.100
Ruiz, Yeixon	B-R	6-0	155	3-19-91	.200	.250	.111	6	25	7	5	0	0	0	1	0	0	0	0	7	1	1	.200	.231

Pitching	B-T	HT	WT	DOB	W	L	ERA	G	GS	CG	SV	IP	H	R	ER	HR	BB	SO	AVG	vLH	vRH	K/9	BB/9
Alvarez, Dario	L-L	6-1	170	1-17-89	1	1	3.19	32	0	0	0	31	21	14	11	2	16	43	.186	.111	.254	12.48	4.65
Black, Vic	R-R	6-4	210	5-23-88	0	0	0.00	6	0	0	0	6	4	0	0	0	5	5	.190	.000	.364	7.50	1.50
Cessa, Luis	R-R	6-3	190	4-25-92	7	4	2.56	13	13	0	0	77	77	25	22	2	17	61	.261	.287	.239	7.10	1.98
Fulmer, Michael	R-R	6-3	200	3-15-93	6	2	1.88	15	15	0	0	86	73	25	18	3	23	83	.227	.228	.227	8.69	2.41
2-team total (6 Erie)					10	3	2.14	21	21	0	0	118	100	35	28	7	30	116	—	—	—	8.87	2.29
Gant, John	R-R	6-5	205	8-6-92	4	5	4.70	11	11	0	0	59	67	38	31	2	26	43	.289	.255	.312	6.52	3.94
Gee, Dillon	R-R	6-1	205	4-28-86	0	1	2.84	1	1	0	0	6	5	3	2	0	2	4	.200	.182	.214	5.68	2.84
Gibbons, Mike	R-R	6-4	205	4-24-93	0	1	4.26	1	1	0	0	6	4	3	3	1	3	2	.167	.143	.176	4.26	1.42
Goeddel, Erik	R-R	6-3	190	12-20-88	0	0	3.00	6	0	0	0	6	7	2	2	0	3	6	.292	.231	.364	9.00	4.50
Gsellman, Robert	R-R	6-4	200	7-18-93	7	7	3.51	16	16	0	0	92	89	47	36	4	26	49	.254	.247	.260	4.78	2.53
Hilario, Julian	R-R	6-1	190	8-17-90	0	0	7.27	8	0	0	0	9	13	7	7	1	7	8	.361	.333	.381	8.31	7.27
Huchingson, Chase	L-L	6-5	200	4-14-89	2	2	5.06	22	0	0	0	27	24	16	15	1	18	29	.242	.216	.258	9.79	6.08
Jannis, Mickey	R-R	6-0	190	12-16-87	0	2	5.54	3	3	0	0	13	10	8	8	1	8	11	.204	.174	.231	7.62	5.54
Koch, Matt	L-R	6-3	205	11-2-90	4	8	3.46	35	8	0	0	88	95	37	34	5	15	55	.279	.248	.300	5.60	1.53
Kolarek, Adam	L-L	6-3	205	1-14-89	2	4	4.43	51	1	0	1	67	59	35	33	4	28	61	.232	.185	.267	8.19	3.76
Kuebler, Jake	R-R	6-5	200	9-3-89	0	0	7.71	6	1	0	0	9	17	8	8	1	3	6	.386	.474	.320	5.79	2.89
Lara, Rainy	R-R	6-4	180	3-14-91	9	5	3.44	19	19	1	0	110	105	46	42	10	27	82	.254	.275	.239	6.71	2.21
Lugo, Seth	R-R	6-4	185	11-17-89	6	5	3.80	19	19	0	0	109	108	54	46	8	30	97	.254	.266	.245	8.01	2.48
Matz, Steven	R-L	6-2	200	5-29-91	1	0	0.00	2	2	0	0	11	2	0	0	0	2	10	.059	.000	.077	7.94	1.59

Pitching

Pitching	B-T	HT	WT	DOB	W	L	ERA	G	GS	CG	SV	IP	H	R	ER	HR	BB	SO	AVG	vLH	vRH	K/9	BB/9
McGowan, Kevin	R-R	6-6	215	10-18-91	0	1	9.00	2	1	0	0	7	16	8	7	0	4	5	.471	.529	.412	6.43	5.14
Mincone, John	L-L	6-1	215	7-23-89	1	0	0.00	1	0	0	0	1	1	0	0	0	1	0	.333	.500	.000	0.00	9.00
Morris, Akeel	R-R	6-1	195	11-14-92	0	1	2.45	23	0	0	0	29	17	8	8	1	15	35	.168	.114	.211	10.74	4.60
Parnell, Bobby	R-R	6-3	205	9-8-84	0	2	12.27	8	0	0	0	7	11	10	10	1	7	6	.367	.545	.263	7.36	8.59
Pill, Tyler	R-R	6-1	185	5-29-90	6	0	2.08	6	6	0	0	35	25	10	8	1	17	19	.200	.181	.226	4.93	4.41
Sewald, Paul	R-R	6-2	190	5-26-90	3	0	1.75	44	0	0	24	51	34	12	10	3	10	56	.188	.182	.192	9.82	1.75
Smoker, Josh	L-L	6-2	195	11-26-88	1	0	3.00	21	0	0	0	21	16	8	7	0	11	26	.213	.250	.179	11.14	4.71
Tapia, Domingo	R-R	6-4	185	8-4-91	0	1	43.20	3	0	0	0	2	5	9	8	0	8	0	.500	.250	.667	0.00	43.20
Velasquez, Jon	R-R	6-1	195	10-15-85	0	2	2.04	36	0	0	18	40	25	11	9	2	5	32	.182	.302	.107	7.26	1.13
Walters, Jeff	R-R	6-3	210	11-6-87	2	0	1.96	17	0	0	0	18	17	4	4	0	3	21	.243	.167	.324	10.31	1.47
Wheeler, Beck	R-R	6-3	215	12-13-88	5	1	3.38	43	0	0	1	59	46	25	22	2	26	56	.218	.157	.262	8.59	3.99
Ynoa, Gabriel	R-R	6-2	160	5-26-93	9	9	3.90	25	24	2	0	152	157	70	66	14	31	82	.265	.295	.239	4.84	1.83

Fielding

Catcher	PCT	G	PO	A	E	DP	PB
Carrillo	.988	94	658	66	9	8	11
Cordero	.997	46	323	41	1	4	7
d'Arnaud	1.000	4	34	3	0	2	0

First Base	PCT	G	PO	A	E	DP
Belnome	.995	26	192	19	1	22
Boyd	1.000	1	7	1	0	0
Cooper	1.000	8	64	4	0	3
Duda	1.000	2	12	1	0	1
Galvez	.900	1	9	0	1	0
Peterson	.991	49	419	23	4	31
Rodriguez	.996	50	413	31	2	33
Rodriguez	.972	11	101	3	3	9

Second Base	PCT	G	PO	A	E	DP
Lawley	1.000	1	2	2	0	0

(Catcher cont.)	PCT	G	PO	A	E	DP	PB
Mazzilli Jr.	.968	83	156	234	13	45	
McNeil	1.000	1	0	1	0	0	
Perez	.918	16	46	32	7	11	
Rivera	.991	22	43	63	1	13	
Rodriguez	.986	14	21	52	1	9	
Ruiz	.950	6	5	14	1	1	

Third Base	PCT	G	PO	A	E	DP
Galvez	.972	13	12	23	1	2
Lawley	.886	51	29	88	15	9
McNeil	1.000	1	3	0	0	0
Rivera	1.000	14	11	25	0	4
Rodriguez	1.000	1	0	1	0	0
Rodriguez	.969	65	36	119	5	16

Shortstop	PCT	G	PO	A	E	DP
Cecchini	.943	109	158	301	28	42

(Outfield cont.)	PCT	G	PO	A	E	DP
McNeil	1.000	1	3	4	0	2
Rivera	.987	17	25	49	1	6
Rodriguez	.949	12	16	40	3	8
Rosario	1.000	2	4	6	0	3

Outfield	PCT	G	PO	A	E	DP
Benson	.981	49	101	1	2	0
Boyd	.953	26	39	2	2	0
Conforto	.989	45	85	4	1	0
Cruzado	1.000	5	7	0	0	0
Galvez	1.000	22	44	0	0	0
Gomez	.989	53	89	3	1	0
King	.995	102	185	4	1	2
Nimmo	.993	68	147	4	1	2
Peterson	1.000	15	26	1	0	1
Pina	.959	54	116	1	5	0
Rodriguez	.929	5	13	0	1	0

ST. LUCIE METS

HIGH CLASS A

FLORIDA STATE LEAGUE

Batting	B-T	HT	WT	DOB	AVG	vLH	vRH	G	AB	R	H	2B	3B	HR	RBI	BB	HBP	SH	SF	SO	SB	CS	SLG	OBP
Abreu, Adrian	R-R	6-0	185	6-14-91	.097	.000	.125	10	31	4	3	0	0	0	2	3	0	0	0	10	0	0	.097	.176
Conforto, Michael	L-R	6-1	215	3-1-93	.283	.200	.318	46	184	25	52	12	0	7	28	17	3	0	2	26	0	1	.462	.350
Crisostomo, Luis	L-R	6-1	180	12-9-93	.000	—	.000	1	4	0	0	0	0	0	0	0	0	0	0	1	0	0	.000	.000
Cruzado, Victor	B-R	5-11	180	6-30-92	.272	.317	.250	92	324	51	88	19	7	3	34	45	1	1	3	67	2	3	.401	.359
Cuddyer, Michael	R-R	6-2	220	3-27-79	.000	—	.000	2	7	1	0	0	0	0	0	0	0	0	1	0	0	0	.000	.222
d'Arnaud, Travis	R-R	6-2	210	2-10-89	.375	.286	.444	5	16	0	6	0	0	0	4	2	0	0	0	2	0	0	.375	.444
de la Cruz, Maikis	R-R	5-11	174	9-6-90	.247	.209	.262	86	324	36	80	13	1	3	35	29	1	2	4	85	10	5	.321	.307
Diehl, Jeff	R-R	6-4	195	9-30-93	.083	.000	.125	3	12	0	1	0	0	0	0	0	0	0	0	5	0	0	.083	.083
Evans, Phillip	R-R	5-10	195	9-10-92	.234	.260	.223	77	252	19	59	14	3	0	32	24	1	0	3	44	2	2	.313	.300
Glenn, Jeff	R-R	6-3	185	9-22-91	.191	.167	.200	28	89	10	17	6	0	1	7	9	0	2	1	33	0	0	.292	.263
Herrera, Dilson	R-R	5-10	150	3-3-94	.455	.667	.375	3	11	1	5	2	0	0	0	0	0	0	0	3	0	0	.636	.455
Johnson, Kyle	R-R	6-0	180	11-9-89	.149	.091	.167	15	47	3	7	2	0	0	1	5	0	1	1	19	0	1	.191	.226
Mazzilli Jr., L.J.	R-R	6-1	190	9-6-90	.227	.300	.167	5	22	3	5	2	0	1	2	1	0	0	0	4	0	0	.455	.261
McNeil, Jeff	L-R	6-1	165	4-8-92	.312	.318	.310	119	468	80	146	18	6	1	40	35	12	11	3	59	16	5	.382	.373
Murphy, Daniel	L-R	6-1	215	4-1-85	.467	.400	.500	4	15	2	7	2	0	0	4	2	0	0	0	0	0	0	.600	.529
Nieuwenhuis, Kirk	L-R	6-3	225	8-7-87	.125	.000	.250	2	8	1	1	0	1	0	2	2	0	0	0	2	0	0	.500	.300
Nimmo, Brandon	L-R	6-3	205	3-27-93	.125	.200	.091	4	16	3	2	1	0	0	2	4	0	0	0	3	0	0	.188	.300
Oberste, Matt	R-R	6-2	220	8-9-91	.301	.308	.298	111	419	52	126	24	6	6	64	34	7	0	5	73	1	2	.430	.359
Perez, Jairo	R-R	5-10	160	6-10-88	.255	.333	.231	13	51	6	13	3	0	0	6	2	1	2		5	1	0	.314	.273
Plaia, Colton	R-R	6-2	225	9-25-90	.285	.366	.250	82	274	22	78	11	0	2	39	22	4	7	4	62	0	0	.347	.342
Reyes, Alfredo	R-R	6-2	160	10-4-93	.143	.000	.250	3	7	1	1	0	0	0	0	1	0	0	0	3	0	0	.143	.250
Ricardo, Lednier	R-R	5-10	180	1-13-88	.188	.412	.132	26	85	5	16	3	0	0	4	1	0	1	1	26	0	0	.224	.195
Rosario, Amed	R-R	6-2	170	11-20-95	.257	.311	.233	103	385	41	99	20	5	0	25	23	5	3	1	73	12	4	.335	.307
Ruiz, Yeixon	B-R	6-0	155	3-19-91	.246	.202	.267	77	285	33	70	8	3	1	15	24	4	1	2	55	10	6	.305	.311
Sabol, Stefan	R-R	6-0	200	2-2-92	.265	.275	.261	78	268	29	71	14	0	3	32	38	2	1	1	80	5	4	.351	.359
Siena, Vinny	R-R	5-10	190	12-24-93	.188	.250	.167	4	16	2	3	1	0	0	2	2	0	0	0	10	0	0	.250	.278
Smith, Dominic	L-L	6-0	185	6-15-95	.305	.314	.301	118	456	58	139	33	0	6	79	35	2	0	4	75	2	1	.417	.354
Stuart, Champ	R-R	6-0	175	10-11-92	.176	.182	.173	97	330	43	58	8	1	4	17	40	4	5	3	141	21	3	.242	.271
Tharp, Tucker	R-R	5-10	195	11-26-91	.250	.000	.333	2	8	1	2	0	0	0	1	0	0	0	0	0	0	0	.250	.250
Urena, Jhoan	B-R	6-0	200	9-1-94	.214	.175	.231	64	210	15	45	5	3	0	18	11	1	0	0	40	2	0	.267	.257
Wright, David	R-R	6-0	205	12-20-82	.321	.417	.250	8	28	5	9	0	0	0	1	5	0	0	0	6	0	0	.321	.424

Pitching	B-T	HT	WT	DOB	W	L	ERA	G	GS	CG	SV	IP	H	R	ER	HR	BB	SO	AVG	vLH	vRH	K/9	BB/9
Arias, Martires	R-R	6-7	211	11-10-90	1	0	0.00	1	1	0	0	7	4	0	0	0	3	5	.167	.125	.188	6.43	3.86
Black, Vic	R-R	6-4	210	5-23-88	0	2	7.36	4	0	0	0	4	5	3	3	1	3	3	.333	.333	.333	4.91	7.36
Coles, Robby	R-R	6-0	180	8-20-91	6	2	2.45	40	0	0	5	59	51	23	16	0	25	42	.234	.261	.214	6.44	3.84
Diaz, Miller	R-R	6-1	210	6-22-92	5	12	4.71	23	21	1	0	124	122	71	65	5	60	98	.260	.265	.257	7.09	4.34
Duff, Jimmy	R-R	6-6	200	11-15-93	1	0	1.93	12	0	0	1	19	16	4	4	1	13	13	.232	.242	.222	6.27	0.48
Fulmer, Michael	R-R	6-3	200	3-15-93	0	0	3.86	1	1	0	0	7	4	3	3	1	0	9	.160	.111	.188	11.57	0.00

Pitching

Pitching	B-T	HT	WT	DOB	W	L	ERA	G	GS	CG	SV	IP	H	R	ER	HR	BB	SO	AVG	vLH	vRH	K/9	BB/9
Gant, John	R-R	6-5	205	8-6-92	2	0	1.79	6	6	0	0	40	27	9	8	4	10	48	.180	.208	.154	10.71	2.23
Gee, Dillon	R-R	6-1	205	4-28-86	0	0	0.87	2	2	0	0	10	9	1	1	0	0	12	.231	.235	.227	10.45	0.00
Gibbons, Mike	R-R	6-4	205	4-24-93	0	1	3.50	3	3	1	0	18	17	8	7	0	3	11	.250	.225	.286	5.50	1.50
Goeddel, Erik	R-R	6-3	190	12-20-88	0	0	7.71	5	0	0	0	5	6	4	4	0	3	5	.333	.300	.375	9.64	5.79
Gsellman, Robert	R-R	6-4	200	7-18-93	6	0	1.76	8	8	0	0	51	37	10	10	1	11	37	.204	.250	.177	6.53	1.94
Hepple, Mike	R-R	6-6	210	6-5-90	3	2	2.51	38	0	0	2	57	46	18	16	3	28	35	.224	.247	.208	5.49	4.40
Hilario, Julian	R-R	6-1	190	8-17-90	1	1	5.71	14	0	0	0	17	12	11	11	1	13	16	.200	.231	.176	8.31	6.75
Jannis, Mickey	R-R	6-0	190	12-16-87	2	1	2.98	8	7	0	0	45	43	25	15	1	18	25	.250	.169	.292	4.96	3.57
Knapp, Ricky	R-R	6-1	195	5-20-92	0	1	6.59	7	0	0	0	14	20	13	10	0	4	5	.333	.393	.281	3.29	2.63
Kuebler, Jake	R-R	6-5	200	9-3-89	4	1	2.39	14	3	0	1	38	32	10	10	0	11	22	.237	.230	.243	5.26	2.63
Matz, Steven	R-L	6-2	200	5-29-91	0	0	4.91	2	2	0	0	4	7	2	2	0	1	3	.412	1.000	.375	7.36	2.45
McGowan, Kevin	R-R	6-6	215	10-18-91	6	10	4.50	24	23	0	0	132	139	77	66	4	49	72	.276	.297	.258	4.91	3.34
Meisner, Casey	R-R	6-7	190	5-22-95	3	2	2.83	6	6	0	0	35	35	17	11	4	14	23	.259	.225	.274	5.91	3.60
Mincone, John	L-L	6-1	215	7-23-89	0	0	0.00	2	0	0	0	2	1	0	0	0	0	1	.125	.000	.167	4.50	0.00
Molina, Marcos	R-R	6-3	188	3-8-95	1	5	4.57	8	7	0	0	41	49	26	21	1	11	36	.295	.267	.329	7.84	2.40
Montero, Rafael	R-R	6-0	185	10-17-90	0	0	3.60	2	2	0	0	5	5	2	2	0	3	1	.250	.167	.375	1.80	5.40
Morris, Akeel	R-R	6-1	195	11-14-92	0	1	1.69	24	0	0	13	32	11	6	6	1	14	46	.107	.041	.167	12.94	3.94
Paez, Paul	L-L	5-9	185	4-29-92	1	0	6.75	3	0	0	0	7	11	8	5	1	0	3	.355	.500	.320	4.05	0.00
Parnell, Bobby	R-R	6-3	205	9-8-84	0	2	10.80	7	2	0	0	7	11	8	8	0	7	5	.379	.500	.316	6.75	9.45
Regnault, Kyle	L-L	6-2	215	12-13-88	4	4	1.99	39	1	0	7	59	43	15	13	2	19	53	.208	.261	.181	8.13	2.91
Reyes, Scarlyn	R-R	6-3	190	12-10-89	2	3	3.82	7	7	0	0	35	39	19	15	1	18	24	.277	.290	.266	6.11	4.58
Roseboom, David	L-L	6-3	215	5-17-92	0	2	4.55	20	0	0	0	32	43	21	16	3	8	29	.323	.167	.396	8.24	2.27
Secrest, Kelly	L-L	6-0	215	9-13-91	6	5	3.14	38	0	0	1	57	50	21	20	0	23	49	.234	.239	.231	7.69	3.61
Smoker, Josh	L-L	6-2	195	11-26-88	1	0	1.69	14	0	0	6	21	12	5	4	1	6	26	.156	.160	.154	10.97	2.53
Taylor, Logan	R-R	6-5	205	12-13-91	8	8	3.69	24	22	0	0	137	127	68	56	8	55	98	.246	.254	.239	6.45	3.62
Villasmil, Edioglis	R-R	6-2	164	4-10-92	0	0	2.70	2	0	0	0	3	0	1	1	0	1	0	.000	.000	.000	0.00	2.70
Walters, Jeff	R-R	6-3	210	11-6-87	1	0	1.50	6	0	0	2	6	3	1	1	0	1	9	.143	.143	.143	13.50	1.50
Whalen, Rob	R-R	6-2	200	1-31-94	4	5	3.36	15	14	0	0	83	72	39	31	4	34	61	.231	.192	.265	6.61	3.69

Fielding

Catcher	PCT	G	PO	A	E	DP	PB
Abreu	.973	10	66	7	2	0	0
d'Arnaud	1.000	3	9	1	0	0	0
Glenn	.994	26	165	15	1	1	6
Plaia	.992	82	544	83	5	7	21
Ricardo	.979	24	125	15	3	0	5

First Base	PCT	G	PO	A	E	DP
Abreu	1.000	1	7	1	0	0
McNeil	1.000	2	10	0	0	0
Oberste	.983	33	321	30	6	22
Perez	1.000	1	7	1	0	0
Sabol	1.000	1	1	0	0	0
Smith	.990	104	910	78	10	81

Second Base	PCT	G	PO	A	E	DP
Evans	.950	41	62	91	8	22
Herrera	.909	3	3	7	1	2
Mazzilli Jr.	1.000	4	6	13	0	3

McNeil	.978	58	103	168	6	36
Reyes	.917	2	4	7	1	1
Ruiz	.968	36	60	92	5	17
Siena	1.000	4	4	10	0	1

Third Base	PCT	G	PO	A	E	DP
Crisostomo	1.000	1	1	3	0	0
Evans	.905	33	18	58	8	4
Mazzilli Jr.	1.000	1	0	1	0	0
McNeil	.985	27	23	43	1	3
Murphy	.833	4	2	3	1	0
Perez	.882	12	8	22	4	4
Ruiz	.778	3	1	6	2	0
Urena	.873	62	33	98	19	4
Wright	.813	7	4	9	3	0

Shortstop	PCT	G	PO	A	E	DP
Evans	.714	3	1	4	2	1
McNeil	.960	33	49	95	6	14

Rosario	.968	102	175	335	17	65

Outfield	PCT	G	PO	A	E	DP
Conforto	.989	41	81	5	1	1
Cruzado	.984	81	179	1	3	1
Cuddyer	1.000	2	4	0	0	0
de la Cruz	.977	72	122	7	3	2
Johnson	1.000	14	29	1	0	0
McNeil	—	1	0	0	0	0
Nieuwenhuis	.889	2	8	0	1	0
Nimmo	1.000	2	1	0	0	0
Ruiz	1.000	33	71	5	0	2
Sabol	.987	78	144	3	2	1
Stuart	.970	91	193	1	6	0
Tharp	1.000	2	1	0	0	0

SAVANNAH SAND GNATS
LOW CLASS A
SOUTH ATLANTIC LEAGUE

Batting	B-T	HT	WT	DOB	AVG	vLH	vRH	G	AB	R	H	2B	3B	HR	RBI	BB	HBP	SH	SF	SO	SB	CS	SLG	OBP
Abreu, Adrian	R-R	6-0	185	6-14-91	.273	.444	.208	11	33	4	9	3	0	0	3	5	0	0	0	7	0	0	.364	.368
Becerra, Wuilmer	R-R	6-4	190	10-1-94	.290	.346	.265	118	449	67	130	27	3	9	63	33	3	1	1	96	16	8	.423	.342
Biondi, Patrick	L-R	5-9	165	1-9-91	.277	.233	.292	103	329	47	91	7	5	3	29	27	2	4	2	62	38	10	.356	.333
Caraballo, Oswald	R-R	6-2	180	1-5-93	.286	.333	.273	7	14	3	4	0	0	0	1	1	0	0	4	0	0	.286	.375
Garcia, Eudor	L-R	6-0	225	5-17-94	.296	.284	.301	105	398	57	118	23	4	9	59	22	6	0	3	95	5	2	.442	.340
Guillorme, Luis	L-R	5-10	170	9-27-94	.318	.309	.322	122	446	67	142	16	0	0	55	54	2	16	4	70	18	8	.354	.391
Johnson, John	L-R	5-9	170	10-27-88	.268	.278	.263	120	400	73	107	19	4	5	36	76	12	8	4	45	23	9	.373	.396
Katz, Michael	R-R	6-3	235	8-6-92	.239	.250	.234	56	205	28	49	14	0	6	37	19	4	0	3	78	2	0	.395	.312
Leroux, Jon	R-R	6-1	205	9-19-90	.223	.197	.234	65	242	30	54	5	1	4	30	18	6	0	1	71	1	0	.302	.292
Lupo, Vicente	R-R	6-0	180	11-27-93	.213	.214	.213	93	286	38	61	18	3	8	40	32	8	1	6	133	5	4	.381	.304
Moore, Tyler	L-R	6-2	213	8-8-93	.181	.135	.192	64	193	21	35	7	1	2	12	23	0	2	3	45	1	2	.259	.265
Mora, John	L-L	5-10	165	5-31-93	.278	.298	.270	115	407	65	113	22	12	5	60	57	5	6	6	70	14	10	.428	.368
Nido, Tomas	R-R	6-0	200	4-12-94	.259	.342	.227	86	317	39	82	14	2	6	40	12	1	1	4	86	1	1	.372	.284
Perez, Pedro	B-R	6-1	190	8-31-94	.177	.308	.143	19	62	7	11	4	0	1	4	3	1	0	0	18	2	1	.290	.227
Ramos, Natanael	R-R	5-10	170	6-19-93	.288	.421	.225	17	59	5	17	3	0	0	4	1	0	0	0	20	0	1	.339	.300
Rodriguez, Jean	B-R	6-0	157	9-3-92	.254	.225	.263	112	406	49	103	15	5	3	44	35	3	8	5	95	17	8	.337	.314
Sabol, Stefan	R-R	6-0	200	2-2-92	.242	.167	.265	38	132	12	32	9	0	3	15	21	1	1	1	40	5	5	.379	.348
Tharp, Tucker	R-R	5-10	195	11-26-91	.000	.000	—	1	4	0	0	0	0	0	0	0	0	0	0	2	0	1	.000	.000
Tuschak, Joe	L-R	6-0	185	10-17-92	.224	.333	.193	37	107	15	24	6	1	1	11	8	2	0	0	24	2	4	.327	.291

Pitching	B-T	HT	WT	DOB	W	L	ERA	G	GS	CG	SV	IP	H	R	ER	HR	BB	SO	AVG	vLH	vRH	K/9	BB/9
Almonte, Gaby	R-R	6-0	185	8-15-92	0	0	5.40	1	1	0	0	5	5	3	3	0	3	5	.263	.400	.111	9.00	5.40
Arias, Martires	R-R	6-7	210	11-10-90	7	5	2.43	20	20	3	0	111	80	39	30	1	42	110	.205	.160	.233	8.92	3.41
Baldonado, Alberto	L-L	6-2	160	2-1-93	0	7	1.91	38	0	0	9	57	35	14	12	1	24	74	.183	.177	.186	11.75	3.81
Bay, Shane	L-L	6-2	225	2-29-92	0	2	6.00	9	0	0	2	9	10	7	6	0	3	6	.278	.111	.333	6.00	3.00
Bumgardner, Gaither	R-R	6-6	210	1-29-91	0	0	19.29	3	0	0	0	2	4	5	5	1	4	2	.444	.500	.400	7.71	15.43
Delgado, Casey	R-R	5-11	185	6-15-90	8	4	3.17	17	16	1	0	105	94	46	37	6	21	81	.252	.272	.237	6.94	1.80
Duff, Jimmy	R-R	6-6	200	11-15-93	2	2	3.48	35	0	0	12	41	40	17	16	1	8	44	.250	.328	.206	9.58	1.74
Flexen, Chris	R-R	6-3	215	7-1-94	4	0	1.87	6	5	0	0	34	28	9	7	0	7	33	.226	.309	.159	8.82	1.87
Frias, Dawrin	R-R	6-0	195	2-18-92	0	2	8.71	15	0	0	1	21	29	22	20	4	16	22	.341	.394	.308	9.58	6.97
Gibbons, Mike	R-R	6-4	205	4-24-93	2	3	2.88	6	6	1	0	34	43	17	11	3	11	23	.328	.393	.280	6.03	2.88
Griffin, Cameron	R-R	6-3	200	6-25-91	2	0	1.67	24	0	0	7	27	17	6	5	0	11	26	.175	.083	.230	8.67	3.67
Griset, Ben	L-L	6-1	175	3-12-92	3	1	2.97	28	0	0	1	39	32	15	13	0	15	41	.224	.180	.247	9.38	3.43
Knapp, Ricky	R-R	6-1	195	5-20-92	8	3	2.60	21	16	2	1	107	113	40	31	5	20	91	.268	.307	.243	7.63	1.68
Mateo, Luis	R-R	6-3	185	3-22-90	0	0	2.31	10	0	0	0	12	7	3	3	1	4	13	.175	.286	.115	10.03	3.09
Meisner, Casey	R-R	6-7	190	5-22-95	7	2	2.13	12	12	0	0	76	59	20	18	6	19	66	.213	.172	.252	7.82	2.25
Montgomery, Christian	R-R	6-1	230	11-20-92	0	0	8.04	11	0	0	2	16	15	14	14	0	6	25	.242	.348	.179	14.36	3.45
Oswalt, Corey	R-R	6-4	200	9-3-93	11	5	3.36	23	23	0	0	129	153	59	48	6	21	99	.299	.288	.307	6.92	1.47
Paez, Paul	L-L	5-9	185	4-29-92	3	2	1.36	20	0	0	0	40	34	8	6	0	6	34	.246	.212	.267	7.71	1.36
Palsha, Alex	R-R	6-1	195	5-10-92	0	1	5.40	2	0	0	0	2	1	2	1	0	2	0	.167	.250	.000	0.00	10.80
Peterson, Tim	R-R	6-1	190	2-22-91	1	0	1.69	16	0	0	2	21	18	5	4	2	7	22	.237	.259	.224	9.28	2.95
Prevost, Josh	R-R	6-8	225	1-15-92	6	4	3.75	12	12	1	0	74	79	38	31	3	18	46	.273	.290	.261	5.57	2.18
Reyes, Scarlyn	R-R	6-3	190	12-10-89	10	4	3.40	16	16	1	0	93	87	47	35	5	32	78	.246	.273	.227	7.58	3.11
Roseboom, David	L-L	6-3	215	5-17-92	3	0	1.15	24	0	0	8	31	17	6	4	0	8	35	.155	.214	.134	10.05	2.30
Smoker, Josh	L-L	6-2	195	11-26-88	1	0	8.10	6	0	0	0	7	11	6	6	0	2	8	.355	.667	.321	10.80	2.70
Valdez, Carlos	L-L	6-2	170	9-30-90	0	0	7.62	7	0	0	0	13	20	12	11	2	3	14	.351	.381	.333	9.69	2.08
Villasmil, Edioglis	R-R	6-2	164	4-10-92	3	0	4.81	9	1	0	0	24	24	13	13	2	8	24	.261	.323	.230	8.88	2.96
Wieck, Brad	L-L	6-9	255	10-14-91	3	5	3.21	10	10	0	0	56	54	23	20	2	21	74	.256	.226	.266	11.89	3.38

Fielding

Catcher	PCT	G	PO	A	E	DP	PB
Abreu	1.000	5	39	5	0	0	2
Moore	.988	48	362	46	5	0	5
Nido	.980	75	585	92	14	2	7
Ramos	.990	13	91	7	1	1	3

First Base	PCT	G	PO	A	E	DP
Abreu	1.000	6	52	2	0	4
Garcia	1.000	1	2	0	0	0
Katz	.990	47	384	29	4	38
Leroux	.977	50	393	37	10	31
Moore	.989	12	82	7	1	8
Perez	1.000	6	50	1	0	2

	PCT	G	PO	A	E	DP
Sabol	.988	20	154	11	2	13

Second Base	PCT	G	PO	A	E	DP
Johnson	.980	98	165	229	8	55
Rodriguez	.964	41	71	92	6	26

Third Base	PCT	G	PO	A	E	DP
Garcia	.936	83	59	116	12	7
Johnson	.939	14	8	23	2	1
Perez	.875	12	7	28	5	4
Rodriguez	.909	35	26	64	9	4

Shortstop	PCT	G	PO	A	E	DP
Guillorme	.972	120	185	343	15	69
Johnson	1.000	1	0	1	0	0

	PCT	G	PO	A	E	DP
Rodriguez	.944	21	25	59	5	7

Outfield	PCT	G	PO	A	E	DP
Becerra	.972	101	167	4	5	0
Biondi	.990	97	187	10	2	1
Caraballo	1.000	6	7	0	0	0
Lupo	.960	68	113	6	5	2
Moore	—	1	0	0	0	0
Mora	.986	108	198	12	3	1
Rodriguez	1.000	1	1	0	0	0
Sabol	.950	15	19	0	1	0
Tharp	1.000	1	1	0	0	0
Tuschak	.979	31	45	1	1	1

BROOKLYN CYCLONES   SHORT-SEASON

NEW YORK-PENN LEAGUE

Batting	B-T	HT	WT	DOB	AVG	vLH	vRH	G	AB	R	H	2B	3B	HR	RBI	BB	HBP	SH	SF	SO	SB	CS	SLG	OBP
Bernal, Michael	R-R	6-1	195	12-27-91	.257	.225	.268	43	152	26	39	12	3	3	18	18	1	0	3	45	1	3	.434	.333
Brosher, Brandon	R-R	6-3	225	2-17-95	.188	.227	.173	53	154	16	29	9	1	3	22	26	7	0	1	68	2	0	.318	.330
Caraballo, Oswald	R-R	6-2	180	1-5-93	.131	.034	.171	45	99	2	13	2	0	0	3	2	4	2	0	14	3	1	.152	.181
Diehl, Jeff	R-R	6-4	195	9-30-93	.289	.326	.276	58	180	31	52	12	1	5	20	28	5	0	3	59	0	3	.450	.394
Fulmer, William	R-R	5-10	185	1-8-92	.143	.250	.118	22	42	5	6	1	0	0	2	4	4	0	1	12	1	1	.167	.275
Garcia, Jose	R-R	6-0	200	11-3-94	.286	.077	.315	35	105	9	30	6	0	0	13	7	2	0	0	23	0	1	.343	.342
Hilario, Manuel	R-R	5-10	172	2-10-92	.163	.286	.096	34	80	6	13	2	1	2	11	7	2	0	0	30	3	0	.288	.247
Katz, Michael	R-R	6-3	235	8-6-92	.219	.571	.120	10	32	8	7	1	0	2	11	7	0	0	3	10	1	0	.438	.333
Kaupe, Branden	B-R	5-7	175	4-10-94	.151	.194	.133	40	106	12	16	0	2	0	6	12	0	1	1	44	2	0	.189	.235
Lindsay, Desmond	R-R	6-0	200	1-15-97	.200	.200	.200	14	45	3	9	3	0	0	7	7	0	1	0	19	0	1	.267	.308
Mathieu, Zach	R-R	6-2	265	11-25-91	.206	.231	.197	62	199	18	41	16	0	4	27	10	3	0	1	52	0	1	.347	.254
Perez, Pedro	R-R	6-1	190	8-31-94	.143	.158	.136	45	119	7	17	2	0	1	10	5	4	1	1	39	0	0	.185	.202
Ramos, Natanael	R-R	5-10	170	6-19-93	.091	.000	.100	7	11	2	1	0	0	1	2	0	0	0	0	3	0	0	.364	.091
Reyes, Alfredo	R-R	6-2	160	10-4-95	.228	.237	.225	68	232	21	53	9	2	0	17	7	10	2	3	56	12	4	.284	.266
Rojas, Hengelbert	R-R	6-1	188	10-27-93	.220	.172	.234	37	123	7	27	7	0	0	8	8	4	0	1	39	0	0	.276	.287
Siena, Vinny	R-R	5-10	190	12-24-93	.273	.239	.285	68	253	32	69	6	1	0	19	24	1	1	1	55	9	3	.304	.337
Tharp, Tucker	R-R	5-10	195	11-26-91	.226	.436	.167	49	177	19	40	7	0	2	10	19	7	0	1	35	7	10	.299	.325
Thompson, David	R-R	6-2	220	8-28-93	.218	.208	.222	59	206	22	45	10	1	3	22	11	5	0	6	44	3	0	.320	.268
Zabala, Enmanuel	R-R	6-0	185	9-29-94	.232	.298	.208	61	177	17	41	6	1	0	12	11	5	1	1	47	7	1	.277	.294

Pitching	B-T	HT	WT	DOB	W	L	ERA	G	GS	CG	SV	IP	H	R	ER	HR	BB	SO	AVG	vLH	vRH	K/9	BB/9
Almonte, Gaby	R-R	6-0	185	8-15-92	6	7	3.68	14	14	0	0	81	81	39	33	2	24	61	.260	.245	.272	6.81	2.68
Badamo, Tyler	R-R	6-2	190	8-8-92	5	6	3.10	14	14	0	0	81	61	33	28	4	22	66	.207	.219	.194	7.30	2.43
Blackham, Matt	R-R	5-11	150	1-7-93	2	2	3.82	6	6	0	0	31	25	16	13	0	12	42	.221	.298	.143	12.33	3.52
Blank, Nicco	R-R	5-9	165	10-29-92	0	5	2.40	20	2	0	1	41	35	16	11	0	18	40	.224	.301	.157	8.71	3.92
Bumgardner, Gaither	R-R	6-6	210	1-29-91	2	0	2.57	3	0	0	0	7	7	2	2	2	3	4	.259	.111	.333	5.14	3.86
Canelon, Kevin	L-L	6-1	175	1-16-94	5	5	4.09	14	13	0	0	77	71	41	35	5	15	70	.241	.359	.198	8.18	1.75
Celas, Jose	R-R	6-1	180	12-1-91	1	2	4.29	9	5	0	0	21	14	12	10	0	32	13	.203	.182	.222	5.57	13.71

Pitching	B-T	HT	WT	DOB	W	L	ERA	G	GS	CG	SV	IP	H	R	ER	HR	BB	SO	AVG	vLH	vRH	K/9	BB/9
Church, Andrew	R-R	6-2	190	10-7-94	2	3	5.18	9	8	0	0	42	49	28	24	3	11	22	.292	.298	.286	4.75	2.38
Conlon, P.J.	L-L	6-0	175	11-11-93	0	1	0.00	17	0	0	0	17	8	2	0	0	2	25	.136	.111	.146	13.24	1.06
Flexen, Chris	R-R	6-3	215	7-1-94	0	2	5.11	3	2	0	0	12	15	8	7	0	8	13	.300	.267	.314	9.49	5.84
Frias, Dawrin	R-R	6-0	195	2-18-92	0	0	3.38	4	0	0	0	8	5	4	3	1	4	10	.161	.067	.250	11.25	4.50
2-team total (7 Vermont)					1	0	2.35	11	0	0	0	15	9	5	4	1	9	20	—	—	—	11.74	5.28
Gibbons, Mike	R-R	6-4	205	4-24-93	2	0	5.91	2	2	1	0	11	11	7	7	1	3	10	.262	.240	.294	8.44	2.53
Jacobson, Raul	R-R	6-1	215	4-12-92	0	0	2.08	3	2	0	0	13	13	5	3	0	1	12	.245	.286	.200	8.31	0.69
Magliozzi, Johnny	R-R	5-10	195	7-21-91	0	0	3.92	13	0	0	0	21	24	11	9	0	5	16	.296	.364	.250	6.97	2.18
Manoah, Erik	R-R	6-2	215	12-22-95	0	1	10.50	1	1	0	0	6	8	7	7	0	3	7	.308	.182	.400	10.50	4.50
Mateo, Luis	R-R	6-3	185	3-22-90	0	0	1.50	3	0	0	0	6	3	1	1	0	1	5	.143	.231	.000	7.50	1.50
Missigman, Craig	R-R	6-4	175	8-5-93	1	3	2.34	21	0	0	0	35	24	15	9	0	16	32	.188	.218	.164	8.31	4.15
Montgomery, Christian	R-R	6-1	230	11-20-92	2	0	0.00	8	0	0	0	10	3	0	0	0	2	18	.094	.111	.087	16.76	1.86
Palsha, Alex	R-R	6-1	195	5-10-92	0	0	0.36	22	0	0	13	25	10	1	1	0	9	34	.125	.212	.064	12.41	3.28
Reyes, Ruben	R-R	6-4	178	9-22-90	1	1	4.94	23	0	0	0	27	28	19	15	1	15	29	.267	.222	.300	9.55	4.94
Taylor, Blake	L-L	6-3	220	8-17-95	0	0	1.00	3	2	0	0	9	6	1	1	0	3	5	.194	.077	.278	5.00	3.00
Taylor, Corey	R-R	6-1	250	1-8-93	1	1	1.50	18	0	0	0	18	14	6	3	1	4	16	.212	.185	.231	8.00	2.00
Valdez, Carlos	L-L	6-2	170	9-30-90	2	2	1.59	24	0	0	5	28	21	7	5	0	10	28	.214	.250	.190	8.89	3.18
Villasmil, Edioglis	R-R	6-2	164	4-10-92	1	2	2.51	6	5	0	0	32	26	11	9	2	9	18	.217	.186	.246	5.01	2.51
Welch, Brandon	R-R	6-1	185	8-24-91	0	0	6.00	6	0	0	0	9	8	8	6	0	3	6	.229	.250	.222	6.00	3.00
Williams, Ty	R-R	6-2	195	2-21-94	0	0	3.86	4	0	0	0	5	3	3	2	0	6	5	.176	.182	.167	9.64	11.57

Fielding

Catcher	PCT	G	PO	A	E	DP	PB
Brosher	.977	34	224	26	6	1	12
Garcia	.982	29	194	25	4	1	8
Hilario	.970	26	148	14	5	3	6
Ramos	.969	7	26	5	1	0	0

First Base	PCT	G	PO	A	E	DP
Diehl	.984	14	122	5	2	7
Garcia	.909	2	10	0	1	0
Katz	1.000	6	57	6	0	4
Mathieu	.987	51	415	34	6	30
Perez	.989	16	87	2	1	11

Second Base	PCT	G	PO	A	E	DP
Fulmer	.913	7	8	13	2	4
Hilario	1.000	4	10	14	0	2
Kaupe	.968	11	13	17	1	4
Siena	.973	63	118	173	8	34

Third Base	PCT	G	PO	A	E	DP
Fulmer	1.000	6	3	9	0	0
Kaupe	.905	12	5	14	2	0
Perez	.838	13	8	23	6	1
Thompson	.938	55	29	106	9	8

Shortstop	PCT	G	PO	A	E	DP
Kaupe	.897	16	15	37	6	5
Reyes	.949	66	109	205	17	38

Outfield	PCT	G	PO	A	E	DP
Bernal	.947	40	52	2	3	1
Caraballo	.967	43	57	2	2	0
Diehl	.923	18	21	3	2	0
Lindsay	1.000	14	17	0	0	0
Perez	1.000	13	11	0	0	0
Rojas	1.000	32	45	1	0	0
Tharp	1.000	47	76	2	0	1
Zabala	.956	57	104	4	5	0

KINGSPORT METS   ROOKIE

APPALACHIAN LEAGUE

Batting	B-T	HT	WT	DOB	AVG	vLH	vRH	G	AB	R	H	2B	3B	HR	RBI	BB	HBP	SH	SF	SO	SB	CS	SLG	OBP
Berrios, Arnaldo	B-R	5-9	175	1-15-96	.249	.267	.243	57	197	29	49	8	2	2	30	21	6	2	2	71	7	5	.340	.336
Burdick, Dale	R-R	6-0	175	10-12-95	.195	.300	.173	35	118	22	23	5	1	2	12	17	5	0	2	44	0	0	.305	.317
Canelon, Leon	R-R	5-11	150	9-10-91	.177	.000	.246	25	79	9	14	4	0	0	8	4	0	0	0	17	2	0	.228	.217
Carpio, Luis	R-R	6-0	165	7-11-97	.304	.273	.314	45	181	31	55	10	0	0	22	17	5	0	4	34	9	7	.359	.372
Figuera, Jose	R-R	6-2	180	6-10-93	.180	.176	.182	24	61	10	11	2	1	0	4	9	1	0	1	19	2	1	.246	.292
Kaczmarski, Kevin	L-R	6-0	190	12-31-91	.355	.371	.351	64	256	47	91	18	5	4	34	24	3	0	1	33	20	9	.512	.415
Knight, Darryl	R-R	6-2	220	2-26-93	.155	.130	.161	32	110	17	17	3	1	7	13	8	3	1	1	31	0	0	.391	.230
Maria, Jose	R-R	5-9	195	11-30-94	.211	.250	.200	6	19	1	4	2	0	0	1	2	1	0	0	6	0	0	.316	.318
Marte, Santo	R-R	5-9	170	9-30-93	.206	.182	.217	11	34	1	7	1	0	0	0	4	0	2	0	4	1	1	.235	.289
Mazeika, Patrick	L-R	6-3	210	10-14-93	.354	.408	.339	62	226	44	80	27	0	5	48	24	17	0	1	26	1	0	.540	.451
Ortega, Luis	R-R	5-10	187	4-5-93	.278	.190	.301	53	205	39	57	10	2	2	22	15	4	2	1	32	8	3	.376	.338
Ramirez, Raphael	L-L	5-11	175	12-15-95	.216	.167	.235	27	111	14	24	3	5	0	7	6	1	1	1	41	5	1	.333	.261
Ramos, Milton	R-R	5-11	158	10-26-95	.317	.273	.328	43	164	22	52	11	1	1	24	7	1	3	4	30	3	6	.415	.341
Rodriguez, Dionis	R-R	6-0	183	2-15-95	.152	.000	.217	11	33	8	5	1	0	0	4	6	3	0	2	14	1	0	.182	.318
Rojas, Hengelbert	R-R	6-1	188	10-27-93	.243	.500	.148	11	37	4	9	2	0	0	3	7	1	0	0	10	0	1	.297	.378
Sanchez, Ali	R-R	6-0	175	1-20-97	.182	—	.182	3	11	2	2	0	0	0	3	0	0	0	0	2	0	0	.182	.182
Valencia, Gregory	R-R	6-3	185	3-19-93	.260	.333	.237	22	77	8	20	4	0	0	10	2	0	2	0	17	0	1	.312	.278
Wilson, Ivan	R-R	6-3	220	5-26-95	.247	.292	.238	42	146	18	36	9	0	2	13	17	4	1	2	58	8	4	.349	.310
Winningham, Dash	L-L	6-2	230	10-11-95	.266	.139	.313	66	267	35	71	19	1	12	51	15	4	0	4	63	1	0	.479	.310

Pitching	B-T	HT	WT	DOB	W	L	ERA	G	GS	CG	SV	IP	H	R	ER	HR	BB	SO	AVG	vLH	vRH	K/9	BB/9
Almeida, Adrian	L-L	6-0	150	2-25-95	2	1	5.94	9	0	0	1	17	13	13	11	0	18	17	.217	.067	.267	9.18	9.72
Arias, Eucebio	R-R	6-1	173	9-20-94	0	1	5.17	9	1	0	1	16	17	12	9	1	17	27	.266	.241	.286	15.51	9.77
Becker, Dillon	R-R	6-3	225	4-21-94	2	1	3.86	12	0	0	1	14	10	6	6	1	11	18	.196	.154	.240	11.57	7.07
Buchmann, Connor	R-R	6-1	190	7-11-93	0	3	13.89	7	3	0	0	12	20	22	18	0	19	5	.400	.391	.407	3.86	14.66
Crismatt, Nabil	R-R	6-1	197	12-25-94	6	1	2.90	12	8	0	0	62	52	23	20	6	12	63	.223	.250	.203	9.15	1.74
Davis, Seth	L-L	5-10	185	5-8-93	0	1	2.79	11	0	0	1	19	20	6	6	1	3	22	.278	.208	.313	10.24	1.40
Feliz, Gabriel	L-L	5-11	160	11-12-92	1	0	7.07	12	0	0	1	14	21	12	11	1	7	14	.350	.333	.359	9.00	4.50
German, Audry	R-R	5-11	163	8-16-92	6	0	3.35	8	8	0	0	51	55	23	19	3	13	22	.275	.267	.282	3.88	2.29
Gonzalez, Harol	R-R	6-0	160	3-2-95	2	4	4.96	13	9	1	1	65	68	45	36	12	9	56	.264	.261	.266	7.71	1.24
Gonzalez, Merandy	R-R	6-1	175	10-9-95	2	2	2.82	9	7	0	0	45	40	18	14	1	19	39	.240	.299	.189	7.86	3.83
Haggard, Witt	R-R	6-2	205	12-9-91	2	1	5.11	10	0	0	3	12	8	7	7	0	9	21	.174	.263	.111	15.32	6.57
Henry, Taylor	L-L	6-2	185	7-6-93	1	0	4.15	8	0	0	2	9	8	4	4	0	3	7	.242	.364	.182	7.27	3.12
Ingram, Chase	R-R	6-3	190	4-17-95	1	2	3.60	12	1	0	0	20	11	10	8	1	10	27	.167	.147	.188	12.15	4.50
Llanes, Gabe	R-R	6-3	185	1-15-96	2	1	4.23	4	4	0	0	28	27	14	13	3	2	18	.250	.220	.269	5.86	0.65

Pitching

Pitching	B-T	HT	WT	DOB	W	L	ERA	G	GS	CG	SV	IP	H	R	ER	HR	BB	SO	AVG	vLH	vRH	K/9	BB/9
Manoah, Erik	R-R	6-2	215	12-22-95	1	4	5.34	13	9	0	3	59	56	43	35	7	28	51	.255	.245	.263	7.78	4.27
McIlraith, Thomas	R-R	6-4	185	2-17-94	6	1	1.71	12	9	0	0	58	48	12	11	2	19	34	.221	.175	.258	5.28	2.95
Nuez, Yoryi	R-R	6-1	153	2-13-93	2	0	5.06	11	0	0	2	27	29	21	15	2	16	29	.274	.297	.261	9.79	5.40
Ramos, Darwin	R-R	6-2	195	11-23-95	2	4	4.47	10	8	0	0	46	47	24	23	3	20	41	.261	.309	.222	7.96	3.88
Shaw, Joe	R-R	6-5	215	12-20-93	1	1	3.29	9	0	0	3	14	12	5	5	1	3	17	.231	.273	.200	11.20	1.98
Uceta, Adonis	R-R	6-1	195	5-10-94	1	0	3.00	1	1	0	0	6	6	2	2	0	2	6	.261	.143	.313	9.00	3.00

Fielding

Catcher	PCT	G	PO	A	E	DP	PB
Knight	.979	22	162	24	4	1	7
Maria	.980	5	40	9	1	0	3
Mazeika	.996	31	247	17	1	1	7
Rodriguez	.940	9	72	7	5	0	8
Sanchez	1.000	2	13	1	0	0	1

First Base	PCT	G	PO	A	E	DP
Mazeika	1.000	11	88	3	0	6
Ortega	1.000	2	11	0	0	1
Winningham	.988	56	454	24	6	35

Second Base	PCT	G	PO	A	E	DP
Burdick	.989	19	32	55	1	9
Canelon	1.000	12	13	24	0	3

	PCT	G	PO	A	E	DP
Carpio	.980	19	36	61	2	11
Marte	1.000	3	4	9	0	0
Ortega	.933	9	9	19	2	5
Ramos	.939	11	17	29	3	5
Third Base	**PCT**	**G**	**PO**	**A**	**E**	**DP**
Burdick	.938	6	3	12	1	0
Canelon	—	1	0	0	0	0
Marte	1.000	8	9	10	0	1
Ortega	.899	41	27	53	9	4
Valencia	.773	18	10	24	10	1
Shortstop	**PCT**	**G**	**PO**	**A**	**E**	**DP**
Burdick	.962	6	14	11	1	5
Canelon	.960	12	18	30	2	4

	PCT	G	PO	A	E	DP
Carpio	.934	22	34	51	6	10
Ramos	.948	32	57	89	8	16
Outfield	**PCT**	**G**	**PO**	**A**	**E**	**DP**
Berrios	.955	55	82	2	4	1
Canelon	1.000	1	1	0	0	0
Figuera	1.000	15	26	2	0	0
Kaczmarski	1.000	62	122	4	0	0
Ortega	1.000	2	3	0	0	0
Ramirez	.983	26	56	1	1	0
Rojas	.857	7	12	0	2	0
Wilson	.979	42	89	5	2	2

GCL METS   ROOKIE
GULF COAST LEAGUE

Batting	B-T	HT	WT	DOB	AVG	vLH	vRH	G	AB	R	H	2B	3B	HR	RBI	BB	HBP	SH	SF	SO	SB	CS	SLG	OBP
Aybar, Cecilio	R-R	6-0	165	11-23-93	.238	.364	.194	32	84	8	20	3	1	0	8	4	2	1	1	28	1	3	.298	.286
Barring, Will	R-R	6-0	200	4-24-93	.156	.147	.158	44	135	16	21	2	3	1	9	12	3	1	1	44	5	2	.237	.238
Bautista, Kenneth	R-R	6-3	210	8-7-97	.187	.208	.181	33	107	9	20	2	1	1	11	6	2	0	1	36	3	1	.252	.241
Brosher, Brandon	R-R	6-3	225	2-17-95	.071	.000	.083	6	14	2	1	1	0	0	2	2	0	0	7	0	1	.143	.278
Burdick, Dale	R-R	6-0	175	10-12-95	.256	.300	.241	14	39	3	10	2	1	1	9	9	2	0	1	10	0	0	.436	.412
Cespedes, Ricardo	L-L	6-1	160	8-24-97	.224	.225	.224	44	165	17	37	3	2	0	15	13	1	4	2	29	7	3	.267	.282
Correa, Franklin	R-R	5-9	180	1-1-96	.231	.225	.233	47	143	21	33	6	0	1	15	16	3	4	1	49	4	4	.294	.319
Crisostomo, Luis	R-R	6-1	180	12-9-93	.178	.214	.168	42	135	11	24	3	1	0	8	10	0	2	0	27	1	2	.215	.234
De Aza, Yeffry	R-R	6-0	170	1-14-97	.313	.250	.329	31	99	10	31	7	0	0	13	5	1	1	3	26	2	2	.384	.343
Dimino, Anthony	L-R	5-11	180	8-5-93	.295	.296	.295	30	105	15	31	5	0	0	10	15	0	1	1	16	2	1	.343	.380
Dirocie, Anthony	R-R	6-0	160	4-24-97	.083	.000	.143	6	24	3	2	1	1	0	0	0	0	0	0	14	0	0	.208	.083
Johnson, Kyle	R-R	6-0	180	11-9-89	.182	.333	.125	3	11	1	2	0	0	0	1	0	1	0	3	1	0	.182	.250
Lindsay, Desmond	R-R	6-0	200	1-15-97	.304	.211	.340	21	69	10	21	4	2	1	6	11	0	1	0	21	3	2	.464	.400
Maracaro, Alvin	R-R	5-9	178	2-10-93	.357	.250	.400	6	14	4	5	0	0	1	2	1	0	0	4	0	1	.357	.438
Maria, Jose	R-R	5-9	195	11-30-94	.219	.091	.286	12	32	4	7	2	0	0	1	3	0	1	0	6	0	1	.281	.286
Medina, Jose	R-R	6-3	170	10-21-96	.262	.217	.279	31	84	8	22	4	0	0	8	13	0	0	0	16	3	5	.310	.361
Moscote, Victor	R-R	6-1	155	5-10-94	.191	.176	.196	42	141	19	27	8	0	0	12	18	5	0	3	29	0	1	.248	.299
Murphy, Daniel	L-R	6-1	215	4-1-85	1.000	—	1.000	1	1	0	1	0	0	0	1	0	0	0	0	0	0	0	1.000	1.000
Pascual, Oliver	B-R	5-10	155	11-16-96	.143	.000	.167	2	7	1	1	0	0	0	1	1	0	0	2	0	0	.143	.333
Patino, Miguel	R-R	5-11	155	12-17-95	.059	.100	.000	5	17	1	1	0	0	0	1	0	0	0	1	4	0	0	.059	.056
Paulino, Dionis	L-L	6-3	190	6-20-94	.277	.316	.250	17	47	6	13	4	0	0	5	4	0	0	2	12	2	2	.362	.333
Puello, Cesar	R-R	6-2	220	4-1-91	.000	—	.000	1	3	0	0	0	0	0	0	0	0	0	1	0	0	.000	.000
Ramos, Milton	R-R	5-11	158	10-26-95	.194	.143	.207	11	36	3	7	1	0	0	3	1	2	0	0	9	1	2	.222	.256
Rasquin, Walter	R-R	5-9	160	3-21-96	.301	.259	.316	36	103	14	31	5	0	1	14	11	3	6	3	21	5	3	.379	.375
Reynolds, Matt	R-R	6-1	205	12-3-90	.400	—	.400	3	5	1	2	0	0	0	1	1	0	0	0	1	0	0	.400	.500
Ricardo, Lednier	R-R	5-10	180	1-13-88	.083	1.000	.000	3	12	1	1	0	0	0	0	1	0	0	3	0	0	.083	.154
Sanchez, Ali	R-R	6-0	175	1-20-97	.278	.300	.270	46	162	20	45	6	0	0	17	12	3	0	0	26	2	0	.315	.339
Urena, Jhoan	B-R	6-1	200	9-1-94	.333	.400	.300	5	15	4	5	1	0	2	2	4	0	0	0	1	0	.800	.474
Wilson, Ivan	R-R	6-3	220	5-26-95	.257	.222	.269	12	35	2	9	3	1	1	8	6	1	0	0	15	1	1	.486	.381

Pitching	B-T	HT	WT	DOB	W	L	ERA	G	GS	CG	SV	IP	H	R	ER	HR	BB	SO	AVG	vLH	vRH	K/9	BB/9
Aldridge, Keaton	L-R	6-2	190	7-20-92	0	1	54.00	1	0	0	0	1	2	4	4	0	2	0	.500	.333	1.000	0.00	27.00
Arias, Eucebio	R-R	6-1	173	9-20-94	0	0	0.00	1	0	0	0	1	0	0	0	0	0	0	.000	.000	.000	0.00	0.00
Carreno, Luis	R-R	6-0	169	8-12-95	0	5	8.64	11	1	0	1	17	21	16	16	2	13	15	.300	.333	.270	8.10	7.02
Castro, Alejandro	R-R	6-0	190	1-15-93	1	1	2.86	18	0	0	5	22	27	9	7	1	6	15	.297	.273	.310	6.14	2.45
Chavez, Anthony	R-R	6-2	185	11-8-92	0	2	0.73	11	0	0	0	12	9	3	1	0	3	11	.196	.286	.143	8.03	2.19
Chavez, Anthony	R-R	6-2	185	11-8-92	—	—	—																
Church, Andrew	R-R	6-2	190	10-7-94	1	0	3.00	2	0	0	0	3	4	1	1	1	3	.333	.500	.300	9.00	3.00
Estevez, Gregorix	R-R	6-5	200	4-12-94	2	4	4.31	11	2	0	3	31	36	22	15	0	12	26	.299	.304	.265	7.47	3.45
Flexen, Chris	R-R	6-3	215	7-1-94	0	0	0.00	3	2	0	0	6	2	0	0	0	1	5	.100	.000	.222	7.50	1.50
German, Edwin	R-R	6-3	175	9-10-92	2	3	2.55	9	8	0	0	42	47	17	12	1	11	26	.290	.242	.320	5.53	2.34
Gonzalez, Merandy	R-R	6-1	175	10-9-95	2	1	2.05	4	2	1	0	22	9	6	5	1	3	25	.120	.138	.109	10.23	1.23
Guedez, Ronald	R-R	6-1	160	1-26-96	3	2	2.93	9	8	0	0	46	42	21	15	1	10	14	.250	.281	.241	2.74	1.96
Horne, Kurtis	L-R	6-5	190	8-5-96	1	0	2.40	8	2	0	0	15	9	4	4	0	6	6	.184	.214	.171	3.60	3.60
Huertas, Joel	B-L	6-3	210	2-14-96	3	4	4.65	11	10	1	0	50	48	28	26	0	22	60	.249	.197	.273	10.73	3.93
Humphreys, Jordan	R-R	6-1	190	6-11-96	0	0	1.54	7	0	0	2	12	12	5	2	0	1	7	.255	.278	.241	5.40	0.77
Jacobson, Raul	R-R	6-1	215	4-12-92	0	0	1.93	2	0	0	0	5	7	3	1	0	0	4	.318	.333	.308	7.71	0.00
Kuebler, Jake	R-R	6-5	200	9-3-89	0	0	0.00	1	0	0	1	1	0	0	0	0	0	1	.250	.000	.500	9.00	0.00

Pitching

Pitching	B-T	HT	WT	DOB	W	L	ERA	G	GS	CG	SV	IP	H	R	ER	HR	BB	SO	AVG	vLH	vRH	K/9	BB/9
Llanes, Gabe	R-R	6-3	185	1-15-96	2	0	2.60	7	2	0	0	17	22	6	5	1	4	11	.301	.217	.340	5.71	2.08
Magliozzi, Johnny	R-R	5-10	195	7-21-91	0	1	16.20	2	0	0	0	2	6	3	3	0	2	2	.545	.500	.556	10.80	0.00
Mateo, Luis	R-R	6-3	185	3-22-90	0	0	0.00	4	0	0	0	5	2	0	0	0	1	6	.111	.222	.000	10.80	1.80
Medina, Jose	L-L	6-2	180	8-25-96	0	2	2.25	10	4	0	1	32	36	13	8	2	1	21	.277	.304	.262	5.91	0.28
Mejia, Jenrry	R-R	6-0	205	10-11-89	0	0	0.00	2	0	0	0	2	3	0	0	0	0	4	.333	.250	.400	18.00	0.00
Molina, Marcos	R-R	6-3	188	3-8-95	0	0	0.00	1	1	0	0	3	0	0	0	0	0	3	.000	.000	.000	9.00	0.00
Montero, Rafael	R-R	6-0	185	10-17-90	0	0	0.00	3	2	0	0	6	5	0	0	0	0	6	.250	.556	.000	9.00	0.00
Montijo, Marbin	R-R	6-0	160	7-4-96	1	1	10.80	9	0	0	0	10	14	12	12	1	11	6	.341	.357	.333	5.40	9.90
Prevost, Josh	R-R	6-8	225	1-15-92	0	0	0.00	3	2	0	0	7	5	0	0	0	2	7	.200	.143	.222	9.00	2.57
Simon, Jake	L-L	6-2	175	1-21-97	2	0	2.81	9	0	0	0	16	19	5	5	0	5	12	.302	.273	.317	6.75	2.81
Szapucki, Thomas	R-L	6-2	190	6-12-96	0	0	15.43	3	0	0	0	2	5	4	4	0	0	3	.455	.667	.375	11.57	0.00
Taylor, Blake	L-L	6-2	220	8-17-95	0	0	6.00	2	0	0	0	3	4	3	2	0	0	3	.333	.667	.222	9.00	0.00
Torres, Sixto	L-L	6-5	205	3-31-96	2	1	2.84	10	0	0	0	13	12	4	4	0	13	12	.261	.143	.313	8.53	9.24
Uceta, Adonis	R-R	6-1	195	5-10-94	4	3	3.08	12	9	0	0	61	67	26	21	1	9	46	.276	.330	.231	6.75	1.32
Walters, Jeff	R-R	6-3	210	11-6-87	0	0	5.40	6	3	0	0	5	5	4	3	0	2	5	.263	.167	.308	9.00	3.60
Wotell, Max	R-L	6-3	180	9-13-96	0	1	2.53	9	0	0	0	11	2	5	3	0	9	16	.057	.000	.069	13.50	7.59

Fielding

Catcher	PCT	G	PO	A	E	DP	PB
Brosher	.750	2	3	0	1	0	0
Dimino	.986	20	133	11	2	2	4
Moscote	1.000	3	15	3	0	0	0
Ricardo	1.000	3	31	1	0	0	0
Sanchez	.993	34	230	36	2	7	4

First Base	PCT	G	PO	A	E	DP
Crisostomo	1.000	1	10	1	0	2
Dimino	1.000	6	47	4	0	1
Maria	.988	11	75	4	1	7
Moscote	.989	38	325	31	4	29
Paulino	1.000	5	44	3	0	3

Second Base	PCT	G	PO	A	E	DP
Aybar	.970	13	24	40	2	9
Burdick	1.000	9	17	21	0	5
Correa	.957	12	14	31	2	5
Crisostomo	1.000	2	2	2	0	0
Maracaro	1.000	1	1	6	0	0

Pascual	1.000	1	4	2	0	1
Ramos	1.000	5	9	17	0	7
Rasquin	.954	17	25	37	3	5

Third Base	PCT	G	PO	A	E	DP
Aybar	.750	1	3	0	1	1
Burdick	1.000	1	2	2	0	0
Correa	.945	29	25	44	4	5
Crisostomo	.784	13	8	21	8	0
Maracaro	1.000	4	3	5	0	1
Murphy	—	1	0	0	0	0
Patino	.667	1	0	2	1	0
Rasquin	.889	15	13	27	5	1
Urena	.000	4	0	0	2	0

Shortstop	PCT	G	PO	A	E	DP
Aybar	.942	14	24	41	4	6
Burdick	1.000	3	1	5	0	0
Correa	.833	5	8	12	4	4
Crisostomo	.929	4	6	7	1	0

De Aza	.921	24	42	74	10	16
Maracaro	.857	1	0	6	1	0
Pascual	1.000	1	2	1	0	0
Patino	.893	4	11	14	3	2
Ramos	.957	5	8	14	1	1
Reynolds	1.000	2	4	7	0	1

Outfield	PCT	G	PO	A	E	DP
Barring	.983	36	58	1	1	0
Bautista	.970	27	29	3	1	1
Cespedes	.976	43	76	7	2	2
Crisostomo	1.000	20	25	2	0	1
Dirocie	1.000	6	10	0	0	0
Johnson	1.000	2	2	0	0	0
Lindsay	.971	16	31	2	1	0
Medina	.949	27	35	2	2	0
Paulino	1.000	7	6	0	0	0
Puello	—	1	0	0	0	0
Sanchez	—	1	0	0	0	0
Wilson	1.000	8	15	2	0	0

DSL METS
DOMINICAN SUMMER LEAGUE

ROOKIE

Batting	B-T	HT	WT	DOB	AVG	vLH	vRH	G	AB	R	H	2B	3B	HR	RBI	BB	HBP	SH	SF	SO	SB	CS	SLG	OBP
Adon, Ranfy	R-R	6-3	175	8-2-97	.240	.268	.234	59	208	42	50	9	4	5	25	26	9	5	1	51	12	4	.394	.348
Araujo, Yordin	R-R	6-1	166	3-30-96	.128	.182	.111	17	47	2	6	1	0	0	1	3	0	0	16	2	0	.149	.196
Bohorquez, Anderson	R-R	5-11	173	10-3-97	.235	.444	.190	15	51	12	12	3	0	0	5	9	2	1	0	7	5	1	.294	.371
Cedeno, Daniel	R-R	6-0	170	3-11-98	.263			28	76	11	20	2	0	0	8	5	5	2	0	20	2	0	.289	.349
De Oleo, Enmanuel	R-R	6-1	190	9-5-96	.240	.333	.216	41	121	21	29	2	2	2	16	11	2	0	1	24	4	0	.339	.311
Diaz, Alejandro	B-R	6-0	150	3-2-96	.077	.000	.083	8	26	3	2	0	0	0	2	3	0	0	2	5	0	0	.077	.161
Dirocie, Anthony	R-R	6-0	160	4-24-97	.266	.182	.293	63	222	34	59	15	6	2	28	36	4	3	1	83	11	2	.414	.376
Fermin, Edgardo	R-R	6-0	145	5-28-98	.262	.217	.280	47	164	33	43	0	2	2	21	26	7	4	2	37	6	2	.317	.382
Garcia, Tulio	L-R	6-2	199	7-3-98	.196	.167	.207	49	153	19	30	4	1	0	7	24	3	1	1	71	3	1	.235	.315
Geraldo, Claudio	L-L	6-1	185	4-28-97	.179	.200	.174	48	184	14	33	6	2	1	21	8	1	0	1	63	5	4	.250	.216
Gil, Edy	R-R	5-11	195	9-3-95	.198	.333	.165	35	106	14	21	7	0	1	10	8	3	2	1	37	3	4	.292	.271
Guzman, Rafael	R-R	6-1	175	10-5-95	.139	.087	.154	37	101	20	14	2	2	1	11	13	8	0	1	37	4	0	.228	.285
Hernandez, Kenny	L-R	6-2	175	8-13-98	.196	—	—	64	245	32	48	10	4	0	38	23	3	0	5	45	2	1	.269	.268
Jimenez, Grabiel	L-L	6-2	180	1-16-95	.290	.200	.316	67	245	34	71	17	4	0	28	34	5	0	2	50	5	8	.392	.385
Manzanarez, Angel	R-R	6-0	152	5-19-97	.277	.234	.289	64	220	32	61	7	0	0	35	39	7	1	2	14	5	3	.309	.392
Lagrange, Wagner	R-R	6-0	174	9-6-95	.347			59	242	40	84	10	2	1	26	20	4	0	1	28	5	5	.417	.404
Lebron, Luis	R-R	6-0	170	1-6-97	.209	.391	.143	27	86	10	18	5	0	1	8	5	0	0	1	21	3	3	.302	.250
Martinez, Domingo	R-R	6-0	200	4-2-95	.281	—	—	57	224	31	63	10	1	1	28	12	4	0	5	35	2	1	.348	.322
Montero, Luis	R-R	6-2	190	1-16-96	.265	.245	.272	57	200	29	53	8	3	0	28	29	8	0	2	43	4	2	.335	.377
Moreno, Hansel	B-R	6-3	157	11-3-96	.210	.250	.193	38	119	23	25	5	1	0	11	21	1	2	4	44	4	3	.269	.324
Ortiz, Hanser	L-R	6-0	195	6-2-94	.215	.188	.224	54	195	23	42	8	2	1	25	22	6	0	1	47	0	2	.292	.313
Pascual, Oliver	B-R	5-10	175	11-16-96	.244	—	—	55	205	39	50	12	2	0	20	26	4	3	0	44	8	8	.322	.340
Patino, Miguel	R-R	5-11	155	12-17-95	.336	.355	.330	48	140	23	47	4	1	1	10	12	2	4	1	17	1	5	.400	.394
Pierre, Ysidro	B-R	6-1	175	11-30-93	.261	—	—	44	153	26	40	8	3	2	21	7	7	5	1	32	15	4	.392	.321
Romero, Yoel	R-R	6-0	173	4-10-98	.194	—	—	50	155	21	30	8	2	0	11	12	5	1	1	43	3	4	.271	.272
Sanchez, Carlos	R-R	5-11	170	6-6-96	.267	.190	.291	59	240	25	64	12	4	2	34	12	7	2	3	51	5	7	.375	.317
Uriarte, Juan	R-R	6-1	180	9-17-97	.267	—	—	52	172	23	46	11	1	3	34	19	11	1	1	25	1	3	.395	.374
Terrazas, Rigoberto	B-R	6-0	160	4-11-96	.295	.259	.307	65	237	35	70	13	3	1	31	33	2	4	4	32	3	0	.388	.380
Valdez, Rafael	R-R	5-10	155	4-19-97	.255	.167	.287	46	137	15	35	4	0	2	12	8	2	0	0	39	4	3	.328	.306
Ventura, Pedro	R-R	6-1	165	3-14-97	.279	.250	.287	64	240	33	67	11	0	0	17	27	3	2	4	41	12	6	.325	.354

NEW YORK METS

Pitching

Pitching	B-T	HT	WT	DOB	W	L	ERA	G	GS	CG	SV	IP	H	R	ER	HR	BB	SO	AVG	vLH	vRH	K/9	BB/9
Advincola, Gregori	R-R	6-3	170	2-18-98	2	1	5.23	11	3	0	0	31	29	22	18	3	17	19	.242	.371	.188	5.52	4.94
Angela, Nelmerson	L-L	6-1	145	2-20-98	2	1	2.70	8	0	0	1	13	10	6	4	1	5	14	.200	.143	.209	9.45	3.38
Batista, Brian	L-L	6-1	175	8-27-95	3	1	5.63	15	0	0	0	24	27	21	15	0	18	16	—	—	—	6.00	6.75
Berihuete, Enmanuel	R-R	6-0	174	11-5-93	1	0	4.19	8	1	0	0	19	22	14	9	0	5	24	.262	.185	.298	11.17	2.33
Casilla, Agustin	R-L	6-1	175	9-17-97	0	1	5.89	12	0	0	2	18	17	14	12	0	8	12	—	—	—	5.89	3.93
Cespedes, Jorge	R-R	6-5	180	12-4-94	2	2	6.25	24	0	0	7	32	39	25	22	2	5	27	—	—	—	7.67	1.42
Chourio, Jhoander	R-R	6-0	180	4-5-98	1	0	12.79	6	0	0	0	6	5	9	9	0	15	2	.208	.250	.188	2.84	21.32
Colon, Yeudy	R-R	6-3	220	6-9-95	2	1	2.40	14	0	0	3	30	21	16	8	1	15	27	—	—	—	8.10	4.50
De Los Santos, Luis	R-R	6-0	155	1-27-94	0	2	3.35	14	6	0	1	48	51	22	18	2	8	41	.262	.268	.259	7.63	1.49
Debora, Nicolas	R-R	6-5	170	12-6-93	5	2	1.65	15	10	0	1	76	59	20	14	0	13	70	.212	.225	.208	8.25	1.53
Encarnacion, Rafael	L-L	6-2	178	9-2-94	1	3	1.71	19	0	0	3	42	38	14	8	3	14	39	—	—	—	8.36	3.00
Familia, Misael	R-R	6-2	190	1-27-95	8	3	1.21	24	0	0	6	37	20	8	5	0	11	37	.161	.118	.178	8.92	2.65
Fernandez, Wuender	R-R	6-2	185	1-15-97	0	2	5.08	16	0	0	1	34	37	29	19	1	17	27	.272	.295	.261	7.22	4.54
Geraldo, Jose	R-R	6-0	185	7-14-95	5	1	2.69	15	11	0	2	70	60	23	21	0	8	30	.230	.250	.222	3.84	1.02
German, Edwin	R-R	6-3	175	9-10-92	0	1	4.60	4	4	0	0	16	17	11	8	0	7	9	.262	.300	.244	5.17	4.02
Guedez, Ronald	R-R	6-1	160	1-26-96	2	0	0.64	3	3	0	0	14	10	1	1	0	0	15	.196	.235	.176	9.64	0.00
Gutierrez, Miguel	L-L	6-0	180	12-3-94	1	2	3.52	13	9	0	0	38	26	18	15	2	30	35	.195	.214	.190	8.22	7.04
Guzman, Daniel	L-L	6-1	180	2-16-98	3	2	3.60	16	6	0	0	50	55	28	20	0	13	30	—	—	—	5.40	2.34
Hernandez, Carlos	R-R	6-0	165	11-3-94	4	2	2.57	15	15	0	0	70	66	24	20	0	20	59	.251	.147	.287	7.59	2.57
Jimenez, Jurgen	R-R	6-2	174	1-14-96	2	1	5.52	16	0	0	2	31	38	26	19	1	15	28	.295	.216	.326	8.13	4.35
Laguerre, Ramon	R-R	6-4	170	4-28-96	4	5	3.15	15	15	0	0	69	64	30	24	2	19	55	—	—	—	7.21	2.49
Lugo, Jesus	R-R	6-1	165	3-31-94	1	0	3.60	3	2	0	0	10	10	4	4	1	2	9	.270	.400	.250	8.10	1.80
Martinez, Michael	L-L	6-0	180	6-30-97	0	0	5.87	9	0	0	1	8	8	7	5	0	12	6	—	—	—	7.04	14.09
Mateo, Luis	R-R	6-6	180	4-7-93	2	5	5.68	15	11	0	0	57	62	44	36	4	31	44	.284	.354	.255	6.95	4.89
Merilan, Claudio	R-R	6-1	185	5-3-94	1	1	3.24	13	0	0	2	17	14	6	6	1	12	19	.219	.059	.277	10.26	6.48
Montero, Randi	R-R	6-2	165	11-8-92	—																		
Montijo, Marbin	R-R	6-0	160	7-4-96	0	1	6.55	4	4	0	0	11	8	9	8	1	4	6	.211	.444	.138	4.91	3.27
Moreno, Jose	R-R	6-4	168	7-31-96	2	4	4.35	15	0	0	0	39	45	24	19	1	22	30	.285	.265	.290	6.86	5.03
Nieves, Kerwin	L-L	6-1	175	10-22-95	1	0	3.00	11	0	0	1	15	9	6	5	1	10	15	.184	.333	.150	9.00	6.00
Olivo, Aneury	L-L	6-2	159	10-24-94	6	1	2.73	15	15	0	0	66	67	30	20	2	18	78	.263	.320	.249	10.64	2.45
Pena, Luis	L-L	6-0	165	2-8-97	3	1	1.98	15	0	0	2	27	12	10	6	2	15	22	.136	.111	.143	7.24	4.94
Reina, Richard	R-R	6-2	185	2-7-95	3	8	4.70	15	15	0	0	67	83	52	35	0	12	48	.294	.242	.322	6.45	1.61
Rodriguez, Edgar	R-R	6-2	155	8-31-94	1	2	4.46	16	6	0	0	40	37	23	20	0	22	23	—	—	—	5.13	4.91
Rodriguez, Euner	R-R	6-0	164	2-10-94																			
Romero, Joel	R-R	6-2	163	2-13-97	1	3	4.07	17	4	0	2	42	44	23	19	1	17	31	—	—	—	6.64	3.64
Rondon, Ygnacio	R-R	6-3	174	5-16-95	1	2	4.15	6	3	0	0	17	20	9	8	0	3	16	.286	.261	.298	8.31	1.56
Sanchez, Boris	L-R	6-1	171	6-20-97	2	0	3.55	18	0	0	2	38	40	18	15	2	12	33	.268	.213	.294	5.45	2.84
Santana, Ivan	L-L	6-0	190	9-14-93	3	0	2.92	13	1	0	1	37	26	19	12	1	24	40	—	—	—	9.73	5.84
Tejada, Renlly	L-L	6-2	173	6-3-95	1	1	4.58	16	0	0	1	18	10	10	9	0	19	17	.169	.250	.149	8.66	9.68
Zabaleta, Ezequiel	R-R	6-0	160	8-20-95	0	1	4.50	1	0	0	0	2	2	1	1	0	1	3	.333	.000	.400	13.50	4.50

Fielding

Catcher	PCT	G	PO	A	E	DP	PB
Cedeno	.994	24	135	25	1	0	11
Lebron	.950	23	127	24	8	0	13
Guzman	.976	27	176	25	5	1	8
Ortiz	.986	13	60	9	1	0	1
Sanchez	.986	33	235	38	4	3	10
Uriarte	.989	47	297	54	4	2	7

First Base	PCT	G	PO	A	E	DP
Fermin	.958	2	22	1	1	1
Guzman	1.000	1	8	1	0	2
Lebron	1.000	4	28	1	0	0
Manzanarez	1.000	1	1	0	0	0
Martinez	.974	24	177	9	5	13
Montero	.989	30	270	7	3	20
Ortiz	.984	41	342	18	6	29
Patino	.984	19	120	5	2	9
Sanchez	.995	22	193	8	1	11
Terrazas	.981	21	142	11	3	6

Second Base	PCT	G	PO	A	E	DP
Bohorquez	.909	2	4	6	1	0
Diaz	.976	8	17	24	1	3
Fermin	.951	31	75	81	8	14

	PCT	G	PO	A	E	DP
Manzanarez	.973	52	116	136	7	24
Pascual	.937	16	36	38	5	6
Patino	.897	10	19	16	4	4
Romero	.976	24	57	64	3	15
Terrazas	1.000	4	9	7	0	2
Valdez	.914	16	28	25	5	5
Ventura	.900	2	5	4	1	1

Third Base	PCT	G	PO	A	E	DP
Hernandez	.852	21	14	38	9	2
Manzanarez	.897	9	10	16	3	1
Martinez	.880	20	14	30	6	4
Montero	.889	3	2	6	1	0
Moreno	1.000	1	0	1	0	0
Pascual	.875	18	12	30	6	2
Patino	.769	3	2	8	3	1
Romero	.917	9	5	17	2	1
Terrazas	.958	39	39	98	6	8
Valdez	.814	27	24	33	13	1
Ventura	.914	13	9	23	3	1

Shortstop	PCT	G	PO	A	E	DP
Fermin	.906	16	26	51	8	7
Hernandez	.887	29	38	87	16	16

	PCT	G	PO	A	E	DP
Moreno	.860	22	33	53	14	6
Pascual	.943	24	36	80	7	11
Romero	.896	11	18	25	5	8
Terrazas	1.000	1	3	2	0	1
Ventura	.925	47	68	142	17	17

Outfield	PCT	G	PO	A	E	DP
Adon	.957	59	108	4	5	0
Araujo	1.000	16	28	0	0	0
Bohorquez	.957	12	22	0	1	0
De Oleo	.958	24	23	0	1	0
Dirocie	.957	62	108	3	5	0
Garcia	1.000	23	43	3	0	0
Geraldo	.975	45	77	2	2	0
Gil	.925	33	44	5	4	0
Guzman	.929	10	9	4	1	1
Jimenez	.963	65	100	4	4	1
Lagrange	.990	46	90	6	1	2
Manzanarez	1.000	1	3	0	0	0
Montero	1.000	13	18	2	0	1
Patino	1.000	17	26	1	0	0
Pierre	1.000	41	86	3	0	0
Terrazas	1.000	2	0	1	0	0
Valdez	.500	2	2	0	2	0

New York Yankees

SEASON IN A SENTENCE: Widely projected for mediocrity, the Yankees got more production than expected early from veterans Alex Rodriguez and Mark Teixeira and big boosts late from rookies Luis Severino and Greg Bird en route to their first playoff appearance since 2012.

HIGH POINT: Although it was just a one-night return, the Yankees made it back to the playoffs before getting bounced by the Royals in the wild-card game at Yankee Stadium.

LOW POINT: Just before the postseason, lefthander C.C. Sabathia, who had battled injuries and stretches of ineffectiveness all season, announced he was checking himself into a facility for alcohol rehabilitation. Mark Teixeira's bounce-back season came to an early end in late August when he suffered a fractured right leg.

NOTABLE ROOKIES: Severino, the team's top prospect entering the season, was summoned on July 31 and immediately entrenched himself as a key rotation piece. The 21-year-old righty was the youngest pitcher to make a start in the big leagues, and allowed two or fewer earned runs in eight of his first 10 starts with the Yankees. Bird, the team's No. 5 prospect, was called up when Teixeira went down and belted 11 homer runs in 157 at-bats.

KEY TRANSACTIONS: The Yankees made one trade at this year's deadline, swapping Ramon Flores and Jose Ramirez to the Mariners for Dustin Ackley, who eventually wrested the starting second base spot from Stephen Drew. Before the season, the Yankees also sent Martin Prado to the Marlins to acquire Nathan Eovaldi and prospect Domingo German. Eovaldi at times proved to be the team's best starter, combining an 80-grade fastball with a dastardly split-finger fastball and a slider.

DOWN ON THE FARM: With Bird and Severino graduating into the world of major leaguers, the next prospects on the cusp of the majors are outfielder Aaron Judge and second baseman Rob Refsnyder, the latter of whom started in the wild-card playoff game. Refsnyder earned a brief cameo at midseason before being sent back down to continue to work on his defense. He should compete for the Opening Day job come spring training. Judge, a Futures Game participant this year, bullied the competition in Double-A before moving to Triple-A and struggling a bit. He's still got top-end power and a world of potential, but will have to work to cut down on the strikeouts before being ready to take over in right field.

OPENING DAY PAYROLL: $219,282,196 (2nd)

PLAYERS OF THE YEAR

DAVID SCHOFIELD

MAJOR LEAGUE	MINOR LEAGUE
Mark Teixeira	**Luis Severino**
1b	**rhp**
.255/.357/.548	(Double-A/Triple-A)
31 HR despite playing	9-2, 2.45
in just 111 games	.200 BAA, 1.00 WHIP.

ORGANIZATION LEADERS

BATTING		*Minimum 250 AB
MAJORS		
*AVG	Carlos Beltran	.276
*OPS	Alex Rodriguez	.842
HR	Alex Rodriguez	33
RBI	Brian McCann	94
MINORS		
*AVG	Ben Gamel, Scranton/WB	.300
*OBP	Rob Refsnyder, Scranton/WB	.359
*SLG	Gary Sanchez, Trenton, Scranton/WB	.485
R	Abiatal Avelino, Charleston, Tampa	80
H	Ben Gamel, Scranton/WB	150
TB	Ben Gamel, Scranton/WB	236
2B	Vicente Conde, Trenton, Tampa, SWB, Charles.	30
3B	Ben Gamel, Scranton/WB	14
HR	Aaron Judge, Trenton, Scranton/WB	20
RBI	Aaron Judge, Trenton, Scranton/WB	72
BB	Gosuke Katoh, Charleston, Pulaski	67
SO	Austin Aune, Charleston	167
SB	Jorge Mateo, Charleston, Tampa	82

PITCHING		#Minimum 75 IP
MAJORS		
W	Nathan Eovaldi	14
#ERA	CC Sabathia	4.73
SO	Michael Pineda	156
SV	Andrew Miller	36
MINORS		
W	Kyle Davies, Scranton/WB	11
L	Justin Kamplain, Charleston	14
#ERA	Joey Maher, Charleston	2.20
G	Mark Montgomery, Trenton, Scranton/WB	46
	Cesar Vargas, Trenton, Scranton/WB	46
GS	Brady Lail, Tampa, Trenton, Scranton/WB	27
SV	Mark Montgomery, Trenton, Scranton/WB	17
IP	Jaron Long, Scranton/WB, Trenton	155
BB	Rony Bautista, Charleston	63
	Gabriel Encinas, Tampa	63
SO	Jordan Montgomery, Charleston, Tampa	132
AVG	Joey Maher, Charleston	.200

2015 PERFORMANCE

General Manager: Brian Cashman. **Farm Director:** Gary Denbo. **Scouting Director:** Damon Oppenheimer.

Class	Team	League	W	L	PCT	Finish	Manager
Majors	New York Yankees	American	87	75	.537	4th (15)	Joe Girardi
Triple-A	Scranton/WB RailRiders	International	81	63	.563	3rd (14)	Dave Miley
Double-A	Trenton Thunder	Eastern	71	71	.500	7th (12)	Al Pedrique
High A	Tampa Yankees	Florida State	66	72	.478	9th (12)	Dave Bialas
Low A	Charleston RiverDogs	South Atlantic	66	74	.471	9th (14)	Luis Dorante
Short season	Staten Island Yankees	New York-Penn	41	34	.547	4th (14)	Pat Osborn
Rookie	Pulaski Yankees	Appalachian	45	23	.662	1st (10)	Tony Franklin
Rookie	Yankees1	Gulf Coast	26	32	.448	12th (16)	Julio Mosquera
Rookie	Yankees2	Gulf Coast	26	34	.433	13th (16)	Marc Bombard
Overall 2015 Minor League Record			422	403	.512	t-11th (30)	

ORGANIZATION STATISTICS

NEW YORK YANKEES

AMERICAN LEAGUE

Batting	B-T	HT	WT	DOB	AVG	vLH	vRH	G	AB	R	H	2B	3B	HR	RBI	BB	HBP	SH	SF	SO	SB	CS	SLG	OBP
Ackley, Dustin	L-R	6-1	205	2-26-88	.288	.000	.326	23	52	6	15	3	2	4	11	4	0	0	1	7	0	0	.654	.333
2-team total (85 Seattle)					.231	—	—	108	238	28	55	11	3	10	30	18	1	3	4	45	2	2	.429	.284
Beltran, Carlos	B-R	6-1	210	4-24-77	.276	.255	.285	133	478	57	132	34	1	19	67	45	2	0	6	85	0	0	.471	.337
Bird, Greg	L-R	6-3	220	11-9-92	.261	.238	.270	46	157	26	41	9	0	11	31	19	1	0	1	53	0	0	.529	.343
Drew, Stephen	L-R	6-0	190	3-16-83	.201	.235	.191	131	383	43	77	16	1	17	44	37	1	4	3	71	0	2	.381	.271
Ellsbury, Jacoby	L-L	6-1	195	9-11-83	.257	.253	.258	111	452	66	116	15	2	7	33	35	7	1	3	86	21	9	.345	.318
Figueroa, Cole	L-R	5-10	185	6-30-87	.250	.000	.500	2	8	2	2	2	0	0	0	0	0	0	0	0	0	0	.500	.250
Flores, Ramon	L-L	5-10	190	3-26-92	.219	—	—	12	32	3	7	1	0	0	0	1	0	1	0	4	0	0	.250	.219
Gardner, Brett	L-L	5-10	185	8-24-83	.259	.276	.252	151	571	94	148	26	3	16	66	68	6	8	3	135	20	5	.399	.343
Gregorius, Didi	L-R	6-2	205	2-18-90	.265	.247	.272	155	525	57	139	24	2	9	56	33	11	3	6	85	5	3	.370	.318
Headley, Chase	B-R	6-2	210	5-9-84	.259	.283	.247	156	580	74	150	29	1	11	62	51	7	0	4	135	0	2	.369	.324
Heathcott, Slade	L-L	6-1	190	9-28-90	.400	.000	.455	17	25	6	10	2	0	2	8	2	0	0	1	5	0	1	.720	.429
Jones, Garrett	L-L	6-5	235	6-21-81	.215	.130	.231	57	144	12	31	4	1	5	17	8	0	0	0	37	0	0	.361	.257
McCann, Brian	L-R	6-3	220	2-20-84	.232	.241	.229	135	465	68	108	15	1	26	94	52	11	0	7	97	0	0	.437	.320
Murphy, J.R.	R-R	5-11	205	5-13-91	.277	.266	.289	67	155	21	43	9	1	3	14	12	1	1	3	43	0	0	.406	.327
Noel, Rico	R-R	5-8	170	1-11-89	.500	.000	1.000	15	2	5	1	0	0	0	0	0	0	0	0	0	5	2	.500	.500
Petit, Gregorio	R-R	5-10	195	12-10-84	.167	.115	.250	20	42	7	7	3	0	0	5	3	0	1	1	16	0	0	.238	.217
Pirela, Jose	B-R	5-11	215	11-21-89	.230	.302	.129	37	74	7	17	3	0	1	5	2	0	1	1	16	1	0	.311	.247
Refsnyder, Rob	R-R	6-1	205	3-26-91	.302	.267	.385	16	43	3	13	3	0	2	5	3	0	0	0	7	2	0	.512	.348
Rodriguez, Alex	R-R	6-3	225	7-27-75	.250	.263	.245	151	523	83	131	22	1	33	86	84	6	0	7	145	4	0	.486	.356
Romine, Austin	R-R	6-0	215	11-22-88	.000	.000	—	1	2	0	0	0	0	0	0	0	0	0	0	0	0	0	.000	.000
Ryan, Brendan	R-R	6-2	195	3-26-82	.229	.283	.163	47	96	10	22	6	2	0	8	5	1	1	0	29	0	0	.333	.275
Sanchez, Gary	R-R	6-2	230	12-2-92	.000	.000	.000	2	2	0	0	0	0	0	0	0	0	0	0	1	0	0	.000	.000
Teixeira, Mark	B-R	6-3	225	4-11-80	.255	.223	.269	111	392	57	100	22	0	31	79	59	6	0	5	85	2	0	.548	.357
Williams, Mason	L-R	6-1	185	8-21-91	.286	.000	.300	8	21	3	6	3	0	1	3	1	0	0	0	3	0	0	.571	.318
Young, Chris	R-R	6-2	200	9-5-83	.252	.327	.182	140	318	53	80	20	1	14	42	30	3	3	2	73	3	1	.453	.320

Pitching	B-T	HT	WT	DOB	W	L	ERA	G	GS	CG	SV	IP	H	R	ER	HR	BB	SO	AVG	vLH	vRH	K/9	BB/9
Bailey, Andrew	R-R	6-3	235	5-31-84	0	1	8.31	10	0	0	0	9	10	8	8	2	5	6	.294	.250	.318	6.23	5.19
Betances, Dellin	R-R	6-8	265	3-23-88	6	4	1.50	74	0	0	9	84	45	17	14	6	40	131	.157	.135	.175	14.04	4.29
Burawa, Danny	R-R	6-2	210	12-30-88	0	0	54.00	1	0	0	0	1	3	4	4	1	1	1	.600	1.000	.500	13.50	13.50
Capuano, Chris	L-L	6-3	220	8-19-78	0	4	7.97	22	4	0	0	41	52	38	36	6	22	38	.310	.338	.291	8.41	4.87
Carpenter, David	R-R	6-2	230	7-15-85	0	1	4.82	22	0	0	0	19	20	11	10	3	7	11	.286	.278	.288	5.30	3.38
Cotham, Caleb	R-R	6-3	215	11-6-87	1	0	6.52	12	0	0	0	10	14	7	7	4	1	11	.326	.368	.292	10.24	0.93
Davies, Kyle	R-R	6-1	210	9-9-83	0	0	0.00	1	0	0	0	2	3	0	0	0	2	.300	.500	.167	7.71	0.00
De Paula, Jose	L-L	6-1	170	3-4-88	0	0	2.70	1	0	0	0	3	2	1	1	1	4	2	.182	—	.182	5.40	10.80
Eovaldi, Nate	R-R	6-2	215	2-13-90	14	3	4.20	27	27	0	0	154	175	72	72	10	49	121	.285	.314	.258	7.06	2.86
Goody, Nick	B-R	5-11	195	7-6-91	0	0	4.76	7	0	0	0	6	6	3	3	0	3	3	.333	.333	.200	4.76	4.76
Lindgren, Jacob	L-L	5-11	205	3-12-93	0	0	5.14	7	0	0	0	7	5	4	4	3	4	8	.208	.000	.294	10.29	5.14
Martin, Chris	R-R	6-8	215	6-2-86	0	2	5.66	24	0	0	1	21	28	13	13	2	6	18	.304	.233	.339	7.84	2.61
Miller, Andrew	L-L	6-7	210	5-21-85	3	2	2.04	60	0	0	36	62	33	16	14	5	20	100	.151	.233	.131	14.59	2.92
Mitchell, Bryan	L-R	6-2	200	4-19-91	0	2	6.37	20	2	0	1	30	37	24	21	4	16	29	.296	.264	.319	8.80	4.85
Moreno, Diego	R-R	6-1	180	7-21-87	1	0	5.23	4	0	0	0	10	9	6	6	1	3	8	.225	.318	.111	6.97	2.61
Nova, Ivan	R-R	6-4	235	1-12-87	6	11	5.07	17	17	0	0	94	99	54	53	13	33	63	.269	.312	.223	6.03	3.16
Pazos, James	R-L	6-3	230	5-5-91	0	0	0.00	11	0	0	0	5	3	0	0	0	3	3	.176	.273	.000	5.40	5.40
Pinder, Branden	R-R	6-3	225	1-26-89	0	2	2.93	25	0	0	0	28	28	9	9	4	14	25	.262	.341	.206	8.13	4.55
Pineda, Michael	R-R	6-7	260	1-18-89	12	10	4.37	27	27	1	0	161	176	83	78	21	21	156	.278	.272	.283	8.74	1.18
Ramirez, Jose	R-R	6-3	190	1-21-90	0	0	15.00	3	0	0	0	3	6	5	5	0	4	2	.400	.571	.250	6.00	12.00
2-team total (5 Seattle)					1	0	12.91	8	0	0	0	8	15	14	11	0	10	5	—	—	—	5.87	11.74
Rogers, Esmil	R-R	6-3	200	8-14-85	1	1	6.27	18	0	0	0	33	41	29	23	5	14	31	.306	.349	.286	8.45	3.82
Rumbelow, Nick	R-R	6-0	190	6-9-91	1	1	4.02	17	0	0	0	16	16	8	7	2	5	15	.254	.250	.257	8.62	2.87
Sabathia, C.C.	L-L	6-7	285	7-21-80	6	10	4.73	29	29	1	0	167	188	92	88	28	50	137	.285	.186	.309	7.37	2.69
Santos, Sergio	R-R	6-4	215	7-4-83	0	0	6.00	2	0	0	0	3	3	2	2	1	0	3	.250	.500	.125	9.00	0.00

Pitching

Pitching	B-T	HT	WT	DOB	W	L	ERA	G	GS	CG	SV	IP	H	R	ER	HR	BB	SO	AVG	vLH	vRH	K/9	BB/9
Severino, Luis	R-R	6-0	195	2-20-94	5	3	2.89	11	11	0	0	62	53	21	20	9	22	56	.229	.244	.213	8.09	3.18
Shreve, Chasen	L-L	6-3	185	7-12-90	6	2	3.09	59	0	0	0	58	49	21	20	10	33	64	.228	.265	.205	9.87	5.09
Tanaka, Masahiro	R-R	6-2	210	11-1-88	12	7	3.51	24	24	1	0	154	126	66	60	25	27	139	.221	.223	.219	8.12	1.58
Tracy, Matt	L-L	6-3	215	11-26-88	0	0	0.00	1	0	0	0	2	2	3	0	0	2	1	.222	.333	.167	4.50	9.00
Warren, Adam	R-R	6-1	225	8-25-87	7	7	3.29	43	17	0	1	131	114	51	48	10	39	104	.236	.225	.243	7.13	2.67
Whitley, Chase	R-R	6-3	215	6-14-89	1	2	4.19	4	4	0	0	19	20	9	9	3	5	16	.260	.400	.170	7.45	2.33
Wilson, Justin	L-L	6-2	205	8-18-87	5	0	3.10	74	0	0	0	61	49	21	21	3	20	66	.223	.236	.216	9.74	2.95

Fielding

Catcher	PCT	G	PO	A	E	DP	PB
McCann	.993	126	980	69	7	5	1
Murphy	.993	65	389	24	3	1	7

First Base	PCT	G	PO	A	E	DP
Ackley	1.000	4	28	2	0	0
Bird	.998	46	376	24	1	33
Headley	—	1	0	0	0	0
Jones	1.000	21	103	12	0	10
McCann	1.000	10	12	0	0	0
Rodriguez	.944	2	17	0	1	2
Romine	1.000	1	8	1	0	1
Ryan	1.000	3	4	0	0	1
Teixeira	.997	108	897	48	3	76

Second Base	PCT	G	PO	A	E	DP
Ackley	.952	9	10	10	1	3

Drew	.984	123	158	267	7	59
Petit	.981	13	24	27	1	10
Pirela	.952	27	36	44	4	12
Refsnyder	1.000	15	10	41	0	7
Ryan	.938	26	16	44	4	4

Third Base	PCT	G	PO	A	E	DP
Drew	1.000	4	1	2	0	0
Figueroa	.750	2	0	3	1	0
Headley	.946	155	99	302	23	25
Petit	.833	3	1	4	1	0
Rodriguez	1.000	4	0	2	0	0
Ryan	1.000	14	9	14	0	3

Shortstop	PCT	G	PO	A	E	DP
Drew	.958	15	12	34	2	10
Gregorius	.979	155	177	430	13	77

Ryan	.963	6	9	17	1	3

Outfield	PCT	G	PO	A	E	DP
Ackley	1.000	4	3	0	0	0
Beltran	.983	123	166	5	3	3
Ellsbury	1.000	110	232	5	0	2
Flores	1.000	12	18	2	0	0
Gardner	.993	150	265	7	2	1
Heathcott	1.000	17	20	0	0	0
Jones	1.000	27	34	0	0	0
Noel	1.000	2	1	0	0	0
Pirela	1.000	3	2	1	0	0
Ryan	1.000	2	1	0	0	0
Williams	1.000	8	13	0	0	0
Young	.994	129	166	4	1	0

SCRANTON/WILKES-BARRE RAILRIDERS TRIPLE-A
INTERNATIONAL LEAGUE

Batting	B-T	HT	WT	DOB	AVG	vLH	vRH	G	AB	R	H	2B	3B	HR	RBI	BB	HBP	SH	SF	SO	SB	CS	SLG	OBP
Ackley, Dustin	L-R	6-1	205	2-26-88	.471	.400	.500	5	17	4	8	1	0	2	4	1	1	0	0	3	1	0	.882	.526
Austin, Tyler	R-R	6-1	220	9-6-91	.235	.188	.255	73	264	33	62	8	0	4	27	26	4	1	4	81	8	1	.311	.309
Bird, Greg	L-R	6-3	220	11-9-92	.301	.270	.313	34	136	15	41	7	1	6	23	11	1	0	2	27	0	0	.500	.353
Castillo, Ali	R-R	5-10	165	6-19-89	.367	.438	.319	20	79	7	29	8	0	0	13	4	0	0	0	7	4	3	.468	.398
Cave, Jake	L-L	6-0	200	12-4-92	.458	.000	.647	7	24	4	11	3	1	0	2	3	1	0	1	8	0	0	.667	.517
Conde, Vince	R-R	6-0	195	10-13-93	.167	.000	.500	2	6	0	1	0	0	0	0	0	0	0	0	0	0	0	.167	.167
Culver, Cito	R-R	6-0	195	8-26-92	.320	.556	.188	8	25	3	8	0	1	0	4	3	0	1	1	6	0	0	.400	.379
Dugas, Taylor	L-L	5-9	180	12-15-89	.317	.267	.333	21	63	7	20	1	0	0	5	6	0	3	0	8	0	1	.333	.377
Figueroa, Cole	L-R	5-10	185	6-30-87	.292	.307	.287	121	449	45	131	19	1	3	44	44	3	5	6	27	4	4	.359	.355
Fiorito, Dan	R-R	6-4	215	8-20-90	.318	.333	.308	6	22	2	7	2	0	0	1	3	0	0	1	1	0	0	.409	.400
Flores, Ramon	L-L	5-10	190	3-26-92	.286	.319	.270	73	276	43	79	11	2	7	34	39	3	0	3	43	3	2	.417	.377
Galvez, Jonathan	R-R	6-2	200	1-18-91	.237	.231	.240	40	139	17	33	9	0	0	12	16	2	2	1	31	2	2	.302	.323
Gamel, Ben	L-L	5-11	185	5-17-92	.300	.303	.299	129	500	77	150	28	14	10	64	46	1	3	108	13	5	.472	.358
Graterol, Juan	R-R	6-1	205	2-14-89	.200	.188	.204	20	70	8	14	1	0	1	9	1	0	0	1	10	0	0	.257	.208
Heathcott, Slade	L-L	6-1	190	9-28-90	.267	.270	.266	64	251	25	67	7	3	2	27	18	0	1	1	61	6	5	.343	.315
Higashioka, Kyle	R-R	6-1	190	4-20-90	.176	.286	.100	5	17	2	3	1	0	0	1	0	0	0	0	4	0	0	.235	.176
Judge, Aaron	R-R	6-7	275	4-26-92	.224	.304	.198	61	228	27	51	10	0	8	28	29	0	3	74	6	2	.373	.308
Noel, Rico	R-R	5-8	170	1-11-89	.059	.143	.000	22	17	5	1	0	0	0	0	4	1	1	0	7	9	3	.059	.273
Noonan, Nick	L-R	6-1	175	5-4-89	.262	.235	.273	67	244	28	64	13	0	1	26	17	1	3	4	68	1	1	.328	.308
Petit, Gregorio	R-R	5-10	195	12-10-84	.230	.260	.218	46	174	19	40	10	0	2	15	8	0	1	0	22	0	0	.322	.264
Pirela, Jose	B-R	5-11	215	11-21-89	.325	.270	.345	60	231	40	75	14	1	3	23	24	2	0	2	22	5	2	.433	.390
Refsnyder, Rob	R-R	6-1	205	3-26-91	.271	.224	.289	117	450	66	122	28	2	9	56	56	9	1	6	73	12	2	.402	.359
Rodriguez, Eddy	R-R	6-0	220	12-1-85	.179	.200	.167	21	67	4	12	4	0	0	5	3	0	0	2	24	0	0	.239	.208
Roller, Kyle	L-R	6-1	250	3-27-88	.232	.219	.238	123	426	47	99	19	3	14	59	60	10	0	3	136	0	0	.390	.339
Romine, Austin	R-R	6-1	215	11-22-88	.260	.252	.264	92	338	38	88	19	0	7	49	22	4	0	2	53	0	1	.379	.311
Rosario, Jose	R-R	5-11	180	11-29-91	.235	.200	.250	6	17	3	4	0	1	0	1	1	0	0	0	4	1	0	.353	.278
Ryan, Brendan	R-R	6-2	195	3-26-82	.200	—	.200	3	10	0	2	0	0	0	0	1	0	0	0	3	0	0	.200	.273
Sanchez, Gary	R-R	6-2	220	12-2-92	.295	.407	.267	35	132	17	39	9	0	6	26	11	1	0	2	28	1	2	.500	.349
Segedin, Rob	R-R	6-2	220	11-10-88	.278	.311	.257	46	162	24	45	8	1	4	15	15	3	1	0	34	2	0	.414	.350
Williams, Mason	L-R	6-1	185	8-21-91	.321	.346	.309	20	81	12	26	7	1	0	11	8	0	2	0	6	2	1	.432	.382

Pitching	B-T	HT	WT	DOB	W	L	ERA	G	GS	CG	SV	IP	H	R	ER	HR	BB	SO	AVG	vLH	vRH	K/9	BB/9
Acevedo, Andury	R-R	6-4	235	8-23-90	1	2	2.31	10	0	0	1	12	14	3	3	1	9	11	.298	.333	.276	8.49	6.94
Bailey, Andrew	R-R	6-3	235	5-31-84	0	0	2.19	9	0	0	4	12	12	3	3	1	3	13	.255	.217	.292	9.49	2.19
Barbato, Johnny	R-R	6-2	230	7-11-92	4	0	0.36	14	0	0	3	25	13	1	1	1	11	26	.159	.229	.106	9.36	3.96
Burawa, Danny	R-R	6-2	210	12-30-88	1	3	2.55	32	1	0	1	49	37	17	14	2	21	39	.210	.224	.203	7.11	3.83
2-team total (4 Gwinnett)					1	3	2.52	36	1	0	1	54	41	18	15	3	23	44	—	—	—	7.38	3.86
Burton, Jared	R-R	6-5	225	6-2-81	0	1	6.75	3	0	0	0	4	4	3	3	1	2	5	.250	.667	.154	11.25	4.50
Capuano, Chris	L-L	6-3	220	8-19-78	2	1	1.27	6	1	0	0	28	20	4	4	0	7	25	.202	.261	.184	7.94	2.22
Cotham, Caleb	R-R	6-3	215	11-6-87	2	2	1.74	20	0	0	1	31	25	7	6	1	5	30	.216	.196	.231	8.71	1.45
Davies, Kyle	R-R	6-1	210	9-9-83	11	8	3.30	27	26	0	0	153	155	61	56	8	37	99	.265	.235	.291	5.84	2.18
De La Cruz, Joel	B-R	6-1	240	6-9-89	7	0	3.25	15	7	0	0	61	59	25	22	4	17	29	.260	.267	.254	4.28	2.51
De Paula, Jose	L-L	6-1	170	3-4-88	2	3	5.20	6	6	0	0	28	32	16	16	0	10	12	.291	.261	.299	3.90	3.25
Foley, Jordan	R-R	6-4	215	7-12-93	0	1	4.50	2	1	0	0	6	5	3	3	0	5	5	.217	.300	.154	7.50	7.50
Gallegos, Giovanny	R-R	6-2	210	8-14-91	0	0	0.00	2	0	0	0	3	2	0	0	0	0	3	.182	.200	.167	9.00	0.00

Pitching

Pitching	B-T	HT	WT	DOB	W	L	ERA	G	GS	CG	SV	IP	H	R	ER	HR	BB	SO	AVG	vLH	vRH	K/9	BB/9
Goody, Nick	B-R	5-11	195	7-6-91	1	1	1.31	14	0	0	4	21	14	4	3	0	7	25	.192	.219	.171	10.89	3.05
Haynes, Kyle	R-R	6-2	190	2-11-91	3	2	4.54	7	7	0	0	38	38	19	19	4	14	28	.259	.297	.229	6.69	3.35
Hebert, Chaz	L-L	6-2	180	9-4-92	2	0	1.06	3	3	1	0	17	17	2	2	1	2	12	.250	.250	.250	6.35	1.06
Holder, Jonathan	R-R	6-2	235	6-9-93	0	1	6.35	1	0	0	0	6	4	4	4	1	4	4	.200	.250	.125	6.35	6.35
Kendrick, Conner	L-L	6-1	185	8-18-92	0	1	15.00	1	1	0	0	3	5	5	5	0	3	1	.357	.500	.300	3.00	9.00
Lail, Brady	R-R	6-2	205	8-9-93	3	2	4.62	7	7	0	0	37	46	21	19	4	17	13	.313	.306	.323	3.16	4.14
Lindgren, Jacob	L-L	5-11	205	3-12-93	1	1	1.23	15	0	0	3	22	16	7	3	0	10	29	.200	.125	.232	11.86	4.09
Long, Jaron	R-R	6-0	190	8-28-91	5	6	4.94	17	16	0	0	86	115	55	47	7	23	53	.329	.321	.335	5.57	2.42
Martin, Chris	R-R	6-8	215	6-2-86	0	1	3.18	20	0	0	2	28	26	12	10	1	10	25	.239	.146	.311	7.94	3.18
Miller, Andrew	L-L	6-7	210	5-21-85	0	0	0.00	1	0	0	0	1	2	0	0	0	1	1	.500	.000	.667	9.00	0.00
Mitchell, Bryan	L-R	6-2	200	4-19-91	5	5	3.12	15	15	1	0	75	63	29	26	1	37	61	.228	.225	.232	7.32	4.44
Montgomery, Mark	R-R	6-0	210	8-30-90	1	1	1.17	7	0	0	1	8	2	1	1	0	1	8	.083	.167	.056	9.39	1.17
Moreno, Diego	R-R	6-1	180	7-21-87	3	0	2.18	26	4	0	1	54	39	14	13	1	16	42	.210	.217	.204	7.04	2.68
Mullee, Conor	R-R	6-3	185	2-25-88	0	0	0.00	2	0	0	0	4	2	0	0	0	5	5	.167	.000	.333	12.27	0.00
Nova, Ivan	R-R	6-4	235	1-12-87	1	1	4.91	2	2	0	0	11	12	6	6	1	3	7	.286	.261	.316	5.73	2.45
Pazos, James	R-L	6-3	230	5-5-91	3	1	1.09	21	0	0	2	33	25	6	4	0	15	37	.208	.179	.222	10.09	4.09
Pinder, Branden	R-R	6-3	225	1-26-89	1	3	2.80	23	0	0	1	35	31	15	11	3	10	36	.230	.183	.267	9.17	2.55
Pineda, Michael	R-R	6-7	260	1-18-89	0	0	1.93	1	1	0	0	5	3	1	1	0	0	3	.176	.182	.167	5.79	0.00
Ramirez, Jose	R-R	6-3	190	1-21-90	3	0	2.90	32	0	0	10	50	40	18	16	1	23	56	.217	.208	.223	10.15	4.17
Rodriguez, Wilking	R-R	6-1	180	3-2-90	2	0	1.69	7	0	0	0	11	7	2	2	0	3	13	.184	.125	.227	10.97	2.53
Rogers, Esmil	R-R	6-3	200	8-14-85	1	1	3.38	7	7	0	0	35	37	16	13	0	12	28	.280	.281	.280	7.27	3.12
Rumbelow, Nick	R-R	6-0	190	9-6-91	2	3	4.27	37	0	0	8	53	47	28	25	4	13	57	.230	.224	.235	9.74	2.22
Ruth, Eric	R-R	6-0	195	9-26-90	0	1	5.25	2	2	0	0	12	14	8	7	1	1	3	.298	.222	.345	2.25	0.75
Severino, Luis	R-R	6-0	195	2-20-94	7	0	1.91	11	11	0	0	61	40	18	13	0	17	50	.184	.200	.170	7.34	2.49
Shreve, Chasen	L-L	6-3	185	7-12-90	0	0	0.00	1	0	0	0	2	4	0	0	0	1	6	.444	.333	.500	0.00	3.86
Smith, Caleb	R-L	6-2	200	7-28-91	0	0	6.23	1	1	0	0	4	5	3	3	1	5	4	.278	.000	.313	8.31	10.38
Sulbaran, Miguel	L-L	5-10	209	3-19-94	1	0	0.00	1	1	0	0	5	5	0	0	0	2	3	.263	.600	.143	5.40	3.60
Tanaka, Masahiro	R-R	6-2	210	11-1-88	0	0	4.50	2	2	0	0	6	6	3	3	1	2	6	.273	.375	.214	9.00	3.00
Tracy, Matt	L-L	6-3	215	11-26-88	0	3	5.72	13	6	0	0	39	45	28	25	3	19	26	.298	.250	.313	5.95	4.35
Vargas, Cesar	R-R	6-1	215	12-30-91	0	0	6.75	3	0	0	1	5	6	4	4	1	0	11	.273	.222	.308	18.56	0.00
Webb, Tyler	R-L	6-6	225	7-20-90	2	3	2.84	25	0	0	2	38	40	18	12	4	11	41	.261	.217	.290	9.71	2.61
Whitley, Chase	R-R	6-3	215	6-14-89	2	0	2.12	3	3	0	0	17	13	4	4	0	6	13	.210	.139	.308	6.88	3.18
Wooten, Eric	L-L	6-3	190	3-18-90	2	5	4.66	12	8	0	0	56	67	30	29	6	16	44	.300	.261	.311	7.07	2.57

Fielding

Catcher	PCT	G	PO	A	E	DP	PB
Graterol	.993	20	131	12	1	1	1
Higashioka	1.000	5	39	0	0	0	0
Rodriguez	1.000	21	147	18	0	0	2
Romine	.996	75	519	31	2	4	7
Sanchez	.991	29	215	14	2	1	0

First Base	PCT	G	PO	A	E	DP
Bird	.996	29	251	17	1	23
Galvez	1.000	6	37	1	0	3
Pirela	1.000	1	5	0	0	1
Roller	.997	78	682	47	2	72
Romine	1.000	10	76	2	0	6
Segedin	.990	24	184	11	2	18

Second Base	PCT	G	PO	A	E	DP
Ackley	.889	2	4	4	1	1
Castillo	.975	9	14	25	1	5
Figueroa	.963	4	12	14	1	3
Galvez	.778	1	4	3	2	1
Noonan	.905	4	7	12	2	5
Petit	.900	4	3	15	2	3

Pirela	.942	13	28	37	4	8
Refsnyder	.967	107	194	328	18	68
Ryan	1.000	1	1	3	0	1

Third Base	PCT	G	PO	A	E	DP
Castillo	.750	2	2	1	1	0
Culver	1.000	5	2	11	0	1
Figueroa	.948	74	45	119	9	13
Fiorito	1.000	4	2	12	0	1
Galvez	.974	15	9	29	1	5
Noel	.750	2	1	2	1	0
Petit	1.000	5	3	9	0	1
Pirela	.957	20	15	29	2	3
Rosario	1.000	4	6	10	0	0
Ryan	1.000	2	1	5	0	0
Segedin	.979	16	14	33	1	5

Shortstop	PCT	G	PO	A	E	DP
Castillo	1.000	3	5	13	0	5
Conde	1.000	2	6	1	0	0
Culver	1.000	3	5	6	0	2
Figueroa	.968	39	58	91	5	26

Fiorito	1.000	2	2	7	0	1
Noonan	.971	60	83	182	8	36
Petit	.971	36	55	111	5	21

Outfield	PCT	G	PO	A	E	DP
Ackley	1.000	2	5	0	0	0
Austin	.983	64	113	6	2	1
Castillo	1.000	5	12	0	0	0
Cave	1.000	6	16	0	0	0
Dugas	.967	20	26	3	1	0
Flores	.982	62	99	9	2	0
Galvez	.889	5	8	0	1	0
Gamel	.983	116	276	13	5	3
Heathcott	.978	55	129	3	3	2
Judge	1.000	56	115	7	0	2
Noel	.900	10	18	0	2	0
Pirela	1.000	26	56	1	0	0
Rosario	1.000	1	1	0	0	0
Segedin	1.000	1	3	0	0	0
Williams	1.000	20	53	2	0	1

TRENTON THUNDER
DOUBLE-A

EASTERN LEAGUE

Batting	B-T	HT	WT	DOB	AVG	vLH	vRH	G	AB	R	H	2B	3B	HR	RBI	BB	HBP	SH	SF	SO	SB	CS	SLG	OBP
Alexander, K.J.	R-R	5-11	210	9-23-91	.333	.667	.167	4	9	1	3	0	0	0	0	0	0	0	0	2	0	0	.333	.333
Arcia, Francisco	B-R	5-11	200	9-14-89	.248	.225	.253	70	238	26	59	8	0	3	23	19	8	1	0	34	3	1	.319	.325
Austin, Tyler	R-R	6-1	220	9-6-91	.260	.133	.290	21	77	8	20	5	2	2	8	8	1	0	0	16	3	2	.455	.337
Bichette Jr., Dante	R-R	6-1	210	9-26-92	.228	.123	.259	67	254	15	58	11	3	2	32	13	1	0	3	48	0	0	.319	.266
Bird, Greg	L-R	6-3	220	11-9-92	.258	.217	.272	49	182	29	47	16	0	6	29	24	5	0	1	30	1	1	.445	.358
Bolasky, Devyn	L-L	5-11	185	1-24-93	.667	.500	.750	2	6	1	4	0	1	0	1	0	0	0	0	0	0	0	1.000	.667
Castillo, Ali	R-R	5-10	165	6-19-89	.269	.283	.264	68	268	31	72	5	0	2	36	21	1	3	4	33	25	9	.310	.320
Cave, Jake	L-L	6-0	200	12-4-92	.269	.205	.289	125	505	68	136	22	5	2	37	43	5	5	5	98	17	3	.345	.330
Conde, Vince	R-R	6-0	195	10-13-93	.136	.000	.167	6	22	3	3	0	0	0	2	0	0	0	0	9	2	0	.136	.208
Culver, Cito	R-R	6-0	195	8-26-92	.199	.169	.208	106	362	43	72	16	2	3	26	22	2	4	0	92	8	2	.279	.249
Dugas, Taylor	L-L	5-9	180	12-15-89	.207	.179	.215	61	188	24	39	10	0	0	14	27	6	4	2	30	8	1	.261	.323
Fiorito, Dan	R-R	6-4	215	8-20-90	.213	.246	.203	75	244	20	52	9	1	1	26	26	1	1	1	57	4	1	.270	.290
Fleming, Billy	R-R	6-1	200	9-20-92	.250	.364	.200	14	36	4	9	5	1	0	3	3	2	0	1	8	0	0	.444	.333
Graterol, Juan	R-R	6-1	205	2-14-89	.188	.333	.100	5	16	1	3	0	0	0	2	2	0	0	0	2	0	0	.188	.278

Batting	B-T	HT	WT	DOB	AVG	vLH	vRH	G	AB	R	H	2B	3B	HR	RBI	BB	HBP	SH	SF	SO	SB	CS	SLG	OBP
Jagielo, Eric	L-R	6-2	215	5-17-92	.284	.306	.277	58	222	36	63	16	2	9	35	18	5	0	3	58	0	0	.495	.347
Judge, Aaron	R-R	6-7	275	4-26-92	.284	.306	.279	63	250	36	71	16	3	12	44	24	3	0	3	70	1	0	.516	.350
Noel, Rico	R-R	5-8	170	1-11-89	.121	.273	.045	12	33	3	4	0	0	0	1	5	1	1	0	10	4	1	.121	.256
Oh, Danny	L-L	6-0	185	12-28-89	.293	.229	.309	67	242	26	71	14	4	1	20	15	2	1	1	33	9	3	.397	.338
Payton, Mark	L-L	5-7	180	12-7-91	.250	.275	.241	72	264	28	66	9	1	5	34	24	3	2	4	60	5	3	.348	.315
Pirela, Jose	B-R	5-11	215	11-21-89	.100	.333	.000	3	10	1	1	1	0	0	0	1	0	0	0	3	0	0	.200	.182
Renda, Tony	R-R	5-8	175	1-24-91	.270	.236	.282	73	274	42	74	20	1	2	21	24	1	2	3	24	10	3	.372	.328
2-team total (54 Harrisburg)					.269	—		127	480	73	129	30	2	3	44	43	3	2	4	39	23	6	.358	.330
Rodriguez, Eddy	R-R	6-0	220	12-1-85	.165	.242	.132	36	109	6	18	3	0	3	15	3	2	0	2	29	0	0	.275	.198
Rosario, Jose	R-R	5-11	180	11-29-91	.249	.208	.261	93	334	36	83	16	2	2	21	8	5	7	1	63	11	3	.326	.276
Ryan, Brendan	R-R	6-2	195	3-26-82	.240	.375	.176	8	25	1	6	1	0	0	1	3	1	0	0	6	0	0	.280	.345
Sanchez, Gary	R-R	6-2	230	12-2-92	.262	.180	.284	58	233	33	61	14	0	12	36	18	2	0	1	50	6	0	.476	.319
Segedin, Rob	R-R	6-2	220	11-10-88	.303	.429	.265	25	89	8	27	4	0	3	19	11	1	0	2	17	1	1	.449	.379
Skole, Jake	L-R	6-1	195	1-17-92	.348	.500	.333	6	23	2	8	1	0	2	5	0	1	0	0	4	0	1	.652	.375
Snyder, Matt	L-R	6-5	230	6-17-90	.286	.333	.273	4	14	2	4	0	0	0	0	1	0	0	0	3	0	0	.286	.333
Wade, Tyler	L-R	6-1	180	11-23-94	.204	.174	.211	29	113	6	23	4	0	1	3	2	1	1	0	24	2	1	.265	.224
Williams, Mason	L-R	6-1	185	8-21-91	.317	.208	.344	34	120	14	38	7	0	0	11	19	0	4	1	17	11	6	.375	.407

Pitching	B-T	HT	WT	DOB	W	L	ERA	G	GS	CG	SV	IP	H	R	ER	HR	BB	SO	AVG	vLH	vRH	K/9	BB/9
Acevedo, Andury	R-R	6-4	235	8-23-90	1	2	3.54	18	0	0	1	28	25	14	11	2	11	18	.229	.241	.216	5.79	3.54
Bailey, Andrew	R-R	6-3	235	5-31-84	1	0	0.63	11	0	0	2	14	6	1	1	0	6	17	.125	.111	.143	10.67	3.77
Barbato, Johnny	R-R	6-2	230	7-11-92	2	2	4.04	26	0	0	0	42	42	19	19	4	14	44	.264	.243	.282	9.35	2.98
Burawa, Danny	R-R	6-2	210	12-30-88	0	0	3.27	3	3	0	0	11	5	5	4	1	9	13	.135	.143	.130	10.64	7.36
Coshow, Cale	R-R	6-5	260	7-16-92	2	3	3.51	6	6	0	0	33	29	15	13	1	13	21	.232	.277	.183	5.67	3.51
Cotham, Caleb	R-R	6-3	215	11-6-87	4	2	2.77	15	0	0	1	26	20	8	8	1	8	31	.208	.125	.268	10.73	2.77
Davis, Rookie	R-R	6-5	245	4-29-93	2	1	4.32	6	5	0	0	33	38	19	16	1	8	24	.292	.279	.304	6.48	2.16
De La Cruz, Joel	B-R	6-1	240	6-9-89	1	2	3.47	8	2	0	0	23	24	12	9	2	5	13	.258	.297	.232	5.01	1.93
DeGroot, Geoff	R-R	6-0	185	5-13-93	0	0	0.00	3	0	0	0	3	2	0	0	0	5	2	.200	.000	.333	5.40	13.50
Gallegos, Giovanny	R-R	6-2	210	8-14-91	0	0	5.40	3	0	0	0	7	7	4	4	0	2	7	.259	.200	.294	9.45	2.70
Garrison, Taylor	R-R	5-11	190	5-24-90	2	3	4.81	14	6	0	0	39	54	24	21	7	12	28	.325	.314	.338	6.41	2.75
Goody, Nick	B-R	5-11	195	7-6-91	1	1	1.73	29	0	0	4	42	29	8	8	2	14	59	.190	.169	.205	12.74	3.02
Haynes, Kyle	R-R	6-2	190	2-11-91	2	6	3.20	27	11	0	1	79	79	36	28	3	34	59	.262	.260	.265	6.75	3.89
Kendrick, Conner	L-L	6-1	185	8-18-92	0	0	13.50	2	0	0	0	2	8	3	3	0	3	4	.571	.625	.500	18.00	13.50
Lail, Brady	R-R	6-2	205	8-9-93	6	4	2.45	20	19	1	0	106	91	32	29	2	26	63	.228	.209	.244	5.33	2.20
Lewis, Freddy	L-L	6-2	210	12-16-86	1	0	2.08	2	0	0	0	4	2	1	1	0	6	4	.167	.000	.286	8.31	12.46
Long, Jaron	R-R	6-0	190	8-28-91	3	7	3.39	12	10	1	0	69	83	41	26	3	7	50	.296	.326	.269	6.52	0.91
Montgomery, Mark	R-R	6-2	210	8-30-90	3	3	2.93	39	0	0	16	43	31	14	14	2	16	45	.196	.179	.213	9.42	3.35
Mullee, Conor	R-R	6-3	185	2-25-88	3	3	3.40	24	0	0	1	42	40	18	16	3	14	40	.252	.288	.226	8.50	2.98
Niebla, Luis	R-R	6-4	185	1-4-91	0	1	12.60	5	2	0	0	10	16	14	14	1	5	9	.356	.462	.211	8.10	4.50
Pazos, James	R-L	6-3	230	5-5-91	0	0	1.86	6	0	0	1	10	4	2	2	1	0	12	.129	.231	.056	11.17	0.00
Pineda, Michael	R-R	6-7	260	1-18-89	0	1	6.00	1	1	0	0	3	4	2	2	0	0	0	.333	.300	.500	0.00	0.00
Rincon, Angel	R-R	6-1	180	9-26-92	0	1	6.00	2	0	0	0	3	4	2	2	0	2	2	.364	.200	.500	6.00	6.00
Rutckyj, Evan	R-L	6-5	213	1-31-92	1	0	3.06	11	0	0	1	18	14	6	6	1	6	23	.233	.185	.273	11.72	3.06
Ruth, Eric	R-R	6-0	195	9-26-90	9	5	3.20	20	19	0	0	112	104	46	40	7	39	77	.243	.249	.237	6.17	3.12
Santos, Sergio	R-R	6-4	215	7-4-83	0	0	0.00	1	0	0	0	1	0	0	0	0	0	0	.000	.000		18.00	0.00
Severino, Luis	R-R	6-0	195	2-20-94	2	2	3.32	8	8	0	0	38	32	17	14	2	10	48	.227	.232	.224	11.37	2.37
Smith, Alex	R-R	6-3	235	9-29-89	1	3	2.52	25	0	0	2	39	36	13	11	0	12	31	.254	.258	.250	7.09	2.75
Smith, Caleb	R-L	6-2	200	7-28-91	10	7	3.38	25	24	1	0	131	118	53	49	7	51	92	.242	.263	.232	6.34	3.51
Smith, Chris	R-R	6-2	205	8-19-88	1	1	6.08	7	0	0	0	13	11	9	9	0	3	12	.224	.333	.161	8.10	2.03
2-team total (2 New Hampshire)					1	1	4.96	9	0	0	0	16	13	9	9	0	4	16	—			8.82	2.20
Sulbaran, Miguel	L-L	5-10	209	3-19-94	3	5	4.77	14	14	0	0	66	73	39	35	2	27	45	.277	.253	.286	6.14	3.68
Tracy, Matt	L-L	6-3	215	11-26-88	1	3	2.29	16	5	0	0	51	45	17	13	2	16	40	.241	.266	.228	7.06	2.82
Vargas, Cesar	R-R	6-1	215	12-30-91	6	0	2.79	43	0	0	4	68	65	25	21	1	22	65	.249	.211	.279	8.65	2.93
Wooten, Eric	L-L	6-3	190	3-18-90	1	1	4.97	6	6	0	0	29	31	17	16	2	15	17	.279	.286	.277	5.28	4.66
Wotherspoon, Matt	R-R	6-1	175	10-6-91	1	1	7.84	3	1	0	0	10	11	9	9	2	6	7	.262	.222	.292	6.10	5.23

Fielding

Catcher	PCT	G	PO	A	E	DP	PB
Alexander	1.000	1	3	2	0	0	0
Arcia	.991	55	382	45	4	1	4
Graterol	1.000	4	28	4	0	0	1
Rodriguez	.973	32	195	20	6	0	4
Sanchez	.983	54	411	43	8	6	2

First Base	PCT	G	PO	A	E	DP
Arcia	.982	13	108	4	2	12
Bichette Jr.	.979	28	218	16	5	14
Bird	.997	41	331	22	1	27
Fiorito	.988	31	241	13	3	28
Fleming	1.000	11	77	4	0	6
Jagielo	.966	3	27	1	1	0
Rosario	1.000	1	11	0	0	1
Segedin	1.000	16	139	5	0	10
Snyder	1.000	3	21	3	0	0

Second Base	PCT	G	PO	A	E	DP
Castillo	1.000	18	29	60	0	10
Culver	1.000	11	17	27	0	5
Fiorito	1.000	8	8	8	0	0
Fleming	.917	2	3	8	1	1
Pirela	1.000	2	4	3	0	0
Renda	.939	64	111	179	19	40
Rosario	.972	41	73	100	5	16
Ryan	1.000	1	2	4	0	1

Third Base	PCT	G	PO	A	E	DP
Bichette Jr.	.951	20	20	38	3	4
Castillo	.923	10	6	18	2	3
Culver	1.000	27	18	52	0	7
Fiorito	.960	22	10	38	2	0
Jagielo	.883	39	22	46	9	2
Pirela	.500	1	1	0	1	0
Rosario	.887	23	21	34	7	4

	PCT	G	PO	A	E	DP
Ryan	1.000	2	0	3	0	1
Segedin	.875	4	0	7	1	1

Shortstop	PCT	G	PO	A	E	DP
Castillo	.979	32	53	88	3	19
Conde	.935	6	8	21	2	4
Culver	.969	69	98	156	8	35
Fiorito	.952	10	10	30	2	7
Ryan	.933	3	5	9	1	1
Wade	.943	28	43	73	7	12

Outfield	PCT	G	PO	A	E	DP
Alexander	.500	2	1	0	1	0
Austin	.977	17	39	4	1	0
Bolasky	1.000	2	2	0	0	0
Castillo	1.000	2	3	0	0	0
Cave	.984	118	295	7	5	3
Dugas	1.000	48	86	2	0	0
Fleming	1.000	1	1	0	0	0

Outfield	PCT	G	PO	A	E	DP							
Judge	.978	52	128	4	3	2							
Noel	1.000	9	19	0	0	0							

Oh	1.000	59	128	6	0	1
Payton	1.000	64	135	4	0	1
Rosario	.930	20	40	0	3	0

Segedin	1.000	1	1	1	0	0
Skole	1.000	5	7	1	0	1
Williams	.986	33	73	0	1	0

TAMPA YANKEES   HIGH CLASS A
FLORIDA STATE LEAGUE

Batting	B-T	HT	WT	DOB	AVG	vLH	vRH	G	AB	R	H	2B	3B	HR	RBI	BB	HBP	SH	SF	SO	SB	CS	SLG	OBP
Andujar, Miguel	R-R	6-0	175	3-2-95	.243	.243	.243	130	485	54	118	24	5	8	57	29	3	0	3	90	12	1	.363	.288
Avelino, Abiatal	R-R	5-11	186	2-14-95	.252	.252	.252	103	405	64	102	12	2	4	23	32	2	6	1	63	38	15	.321	.309
Baez, Yancarlos	B-R	6-2	165	9-21-95	.222	.000	.333	3	9	1	2	1	0	0	0	0	0	0	0	3	0	0	.333	.222
Beltran, Carlos	R-R	6-1	210	4-24-77	.429	—	.429	3	7	2	3	0	0	0	1	2	0	0	0	2	0	0	.429	.556
Bichette Jr., Dante	R-R	6-1	210	9-26-92	.223	.226	.221	45	157	12	35	7	1	1	15	12	2	0	0	31	0	1	.299	.287
Conde, Vince	R-R	6-0	195	10-13-93	.080	.143	.056	17	50	5	4	0	0	1	3	8	0	0	0	22	0	0	.140	.207
Custodio, Claudio	R-R	5-10	155	10-30-90	.162	.182	.152	20	68	3	11	3	1	0	3	5	1	3	0	18	5	0	.235	.230
Ellsbury, Jacoby	L-L	6-1	195	9-11-83	.154	.333	.100	4	13	1	2	0	0	0	0	0	0	0	0	1	0	0	.154	.154
Falcone, Joey	L-R	6-1	220	6-1-86	.308	.000	.400	4	13	2	4	0	0	1	1	1	0	0	0	5	0	0	.538	.357
Fiorito, Dan	R-R	6-4	215	8-20-90	.368	.333	.378	16	57	5	21	6	1	0	5	5	0	0	0	10	0	0	.509	.419
Fleming, Billy	R-R	6-1	200	9-20-92	.235	.200	.250	7	17	1	4	1	0	0	0	2	0	0	0	2	0	0	.294	.316
Ford, Mike	L-R	6-0	225	7-4-92	.260	.234	.270	123	435	62	113	23	3	6	55	60	0	0	5	75	1	0	.368	.346
Fowler, Dustin	L-L	6-0	185	12-29-94	.289	.263	.300	65	246	29	71	11	3	1	39	15	0	1	1	43	12	6	.370	.328
Gittens, Chris	R-R	6-4	250	2-9-94	.143	.167	.125	5	14	0	2	0	0	0	1	1	0	0	0	3	0	0	.143	.200
Gumbs, Angelo	R-R	6-0	175	10-13-92	.176	.194	.165	59	188	16	33	4	0	1	16	11	1	1	1	45	1	0	.213	.224
Haddad, Radley	R-R	6-1	190	5-11-90	.214	.000	.231	4	14	1	3	1	0	0	1	0	0	0	2	0	0	0	.286	.267
Higashioka, Kyle	R-R	6-1	190	4-20-90	.254	.253	.255	88	307	25	78	18	2	5	36	22	1	0	1	49	0	0	.375	.305
Leonora, Ericson	R-R	5-11	185	8-25-92	.222	.190	.236	113	405	37	90	21	3	13	63	13	5	4	6	123	1	4	.385	.252
Martinez, Teodoro	R-R	6-0	180	3-16-92	.071	.200	.000	3	14	0	1	0	0	0	0	0	0	0	0	4	0	0	.071	.071
Martini, Renzo	R-R	6-1	190	8-25-92	.167	1.000	.000	2	6	1	1	1	0	0	0	3	0	0	0	4	0	0	.333	.444
Mateo, Jorge	R-R	6-0	188	6-23-95	.321	.471	.284	21	84	15	27	5	3	0	7	7	0	0	0	18	11	2	.452	.374
McFarland, Ty	L-R	6-3	190	10-13-91	.157	.500	.111	14	51	2	8	3	0	1	6	3	0	0	0	7	0	0	.275	.204
O'Neill, Michael	R-R	6-1	195	6-12-92	.213	.184	.224	101	342	31	73	15	1	4	25	21	3	4	2	85	14	11	.298	.264
Oh, Danny	L-L	6-0	185	12-28-89	.333	.267	.364	29	96	19	32	8	1	0	9	14	0	0	2	15	4	1	.438	.411
Payton, Mark	L-L	5-7	180	12-7-91	.291	.360	.265	49	182	33	53	8	4	1	18	26	4	3	1	32	6	4	.396	.390
Petit, Gregorio	R-R	5-10	195	12-10-84	.375	.400	.333	3	8	0	3	0	0	0	2	0	0	0	0	2	0	1	.375	.500
Pirela, Jose	B-R	5-11	215	11-21-89	.000	.000	.000	1	4	1	0	0	0	0	0	0	0	0	0	0	0	0	.000	.000
Ryan, Brendan	R-R	6-2	195	3-26-82	.333	—	.333	1	3	0	1	0	0	0	0	0	0	0	0	0	0	0	.667	.333
Skole, Jake	L-R	6-1	195	1-17-92	.225	.156	.245	44	138	11	31	5	0	1	15	16	2	1	1	26	9	1	.261	.312
Slaybaugh, Collin	L-R	6-2	185	4-3-92	.100	.000	.143	3	10	1	1	0	0	0	1	1	0	0	2	0	1	0	.100	.182
Snyder, Matt	L-R	6-5	230	6-17-90	.371	.400	.356	24	89	14	33	2	0	3	20	15	3	0	2	17	0	0	.494	.468
Tejeda, Isaias	R-R	6-0	195	10-28-91	.250	.286	.235	7	24	2	6	0	0	0	2	0	0	0	2	0	0	0	.250	.308
Thomas, Brandon	L-R	6-2	190	7-21-91	.067	.000	.087	9	30	2	2	0	0	0	1	0	0	0	0	11	0	1	.067	.097
Toadvine, Derek	R-R	5-10	175	3-20-92	.227	.214	.233	17	44	1	10	0	0	0	3	4	2	1	1	9	6	0	.227	.314
Wade, Tyler	L-R	6-1	180	11-23-94	.280	.222	.304	98	368	51	103	11	5	2	28	39	2	5	4	65	31	15	.353	.349
Wilson, Wes	R-R	6-0	210	8-18-89	.220	.243	.210	41	118	5	26	2	0	2	11	10	2	0	0	36	1	0	.288	.292

Pitching	B-T	HT	WT	DOB	W	L	ERA	G	GS	CG	SV	IP	H	R	ER	HR	BB	SO	AVG	vLH	vRH	K/9	BB/9
Acevedo, Andury	R-R	6-4	235	8-23-90	1	0	1.40	13	0	0	1	19	14	5	3	2	1	20	.197	.304	.146	9.31	0.47
Adams, Chance	R-R	6-2	215	8-10-94	1	0	1.29	5	0	0	0	14	12	3	2	0	2	16	.226	.417	.171	10.29	1.29
Bailey, Andrew	R-R	6-3	235	5-31-84	2	0	3.86	7	0	0	0	7	8	6	3	2	1	10	.267	.214	.313	12.86	1.29
Bisacca, Alex	R-R	6-2	205	6-23-93	0	1	7.36	1	0	0	0	4	5	3	3	0	1	0	.313	.125	.500	0.00	2.45
Borens, Matt	R-R	6-7	195	2-10-93	0	0	5.79	1	1	0	0	5	6	4	3	0	2	3	.300	.333	.273	5.79	3.86
Burton, Jared	R-R	6-5	225	6-2-81	0	0	0.00	1	0	0	0	2	1	0	0	0	2	2	.167	.000	.333	9.00	9.00
Callahan, Derek	L-L	6-4	205	12-29-92	0	2	9.39	2	2	0	0	8	9	8	8	1	5	7	.290	.500	.276	8.22	5.87
Campos, Jose	R-R	6-4	195	7-27-92	3	7	7.05	11	11	0	0	45	54	36	35	5	10	31	.297	.356	.277	6.25	2.01
Capuano, Chris	L-L	6-3	220	8-19-78	0	0	0.00	1	1	0	0	4	2	1	0	0	0	4	.133	—	.133	9.00	0.00
Coshow, Cale	R-R	6-5	260	7-16-92	7	2	2.23	16	9	1	1	65	46	22	16	2	11	56	.203	.264	.174	7.79	1.53
Davis, Rookie	R-R	6-5	245	4-29-93	6	6	3.70	19	19	0	0	97	94	48	40	4	18	105	.250	.232	.264	9.71	1.66
DeGroot, Geoff	R-R	6-0	185	5-13-93	1	1	2.45	2	0	0	0	4	3	3	1	0	2	1	.214	.429	.000	2.45	4.91
Drozd, Jonny	L-L	6-7	190	9-17-91	0	0	4.91	6	0	0	0	7	12	4	4	0	2	3	.387	.400	.381	3.68	2.45
Duarte, Abel	R-R	6-1	190	5-20-94	0	0	0.00	1	0	0	0	1	0	0	0	0	1	2	.000	.000	.000	13.50	6.75
Encinas, Gabe	R-R	6-3	195	12-21-91	3	7	4.39	26	19	0	1	98	75	54	48	4	63	116	.210	.189	.222	10.62	5.77
Enns, Dietrich	L-L	6-2	195	5-16-91	1	1	0.76	10	9	0	0	47	27	10	4	0	14	40	.163	.143	.171	7.61	2.66
Flemming, Icezack	R-R	6-2	200	6-24-92	0	1	0.00	2	0	0	0	2	1	0	0	0	3	3	.250	—	.250	13.50	13.50
Frare, Caleb	L-L	6-2	195	7-8-93	2	1	5.59	7	0	0	0	10	13	6	6	1	7	9	.325	.500	.250	8.38	6.52
Gallegos, Giovanny	R-R	6-2	210	8-14-91	3	1	1.35	30	0	0	5	53	32	11	8	2	7	54	.172	.147	.186	9.11	1.18
Garrison, Taylor	R-R	5-11	180	5-24-90	0	0	0.00	1	0	0	1	2	2	0	0	0	0	2	.250	.250	.250	9.00	0.00
Gomez, Anyelo	R-R	6-1	175	3-1-93	0	0	2.25	1	1	0	0	4	3	1	1	0	0	4	.176	—	.176	9.00	0.00
Harris, Hobie	R-R	6-3	200	6-23-93	0	0	18.00	2	0	0	0	2	3	5	4	0	4	1	.333	.333	.333	4.50	18.00
Hebert, Chaz	L-L	6-2	190	9-4-92	7	6	2.95	21	15	2	0	107	98	41	35	6	26	82	.249	.337	.225	6.92	2.19
Holder, Jonathan	R-R	6-2	235	6-9-93	7	5	2.44	19	18	1	0	103	92	33	28	3	21	78	.234	.232	.235	6.79	1.83
Kendrick, Conner	L-L	6-1	185	8-18-92	2	5	5.60	14	7	0	0	53	62	37	33	4	22	42	.290	.390	.266	7.13	3.74
Lail, Brady	R-R	6-2	205	8-9-93	1	0	0.00	1	1	0	0	5	4	0	0	0	0	0	.211	.286	.167	16.20	0.00
Marsh, Matt	R-R	6-3	190	7-10-91	1	0	2.70	5	0	0	0	13	10	5	4	0	3	12	.222	.313	.172	8.10	2.03
Martin, Chad	R-R	6-4	215	1-2-94	0	0	0.00	2	0	0	0	5	4	3	0	0	5	4	.211	.286	.167	7.20	9.00
Montgomery, Jordan	L-L	6-4	225	12-27-92	6	5	3.08	16	15	1	0	91	82	36	31	4	24	77	.240	.250	.236	7.64	2.38

Pitching	B-T	HT	WT	DOB	W	L	ERA	G	GS	CG	SV	IP	H	R	ER	HR	BB	SO	AVG	vLH	vRH	K/9	BB/9
Morban, Jhon	R-R	6-4	190	6-3-92	0	1	7.71	1	1	0	0	2	3	5	2	0	4	1	.250	.333	.167	3.86	15.43
Morla, Melvin	R-R	6-4	185	5-26-93	0	0	0.00	1	1	0	0	3	1	0	0	0	3	1	.091	.143	.000	3.00	9.00
Morris, Christian	R-R	6-4	195	1-23-94	0	0	7.71	1	0	0	0	2	3	2	2	1	1	1	.333	—	.333	3.86	3.86
Mullee, Conor	R-R	6-3	185	2-25-88	1	1	2.13	10	0	0	4	13	10	5	3	0	2	11	.208	.238	.185	7.82	1.42
Niebla, Luis	R-R	6-4	185	1-4-91	2	5	2.88	28	1	0	0	50	39	19	16	1	13	39	.224	.224	.210	7.02	2.34
Nova, Ivan	R-R	6-4	235	1-12-87	0	0	1.93	1	1	0	0	5	3	2	1	0	0	3	.150	.000	.200	5.79	0.00
Ovalles, Jordan	R-R	6-1	160	1-17-94	0	0	4.91	1	0	0	0	4	6	2	2	0	2	1	.353	.000	.400	2.45	4.91
Reyes, Manolo	R-R	6-1	190	11-14-89	0	1	7.88	8	0	0	0	8	8	8	7	0	8	9	.242	.286	.211	10.13	9.00
Rincon, Angel	R-R	6-1	180	9-26-92	1	5	4.73	28	0	0	0	46	51	26	24	1	14	30	.280	.279	.281	5.91	2.76
Rutckyj, Evan	R-L	6-5	213	1-31-92	2	2	2.45	25	0	0	0	44	43	18	12	3	15	59	.253	.263	.250	12.07	3.07
Ruth, Eric	R-R	6-0	195	9-26-90	1	0	3.27	4	4	0	0	22	16	8	8	2	6	16	.200	.189	.209	6.55	2.45
Smith, Alex	R-R	6-3	235	9-29-89	1	0	0.00	16	0	0	11	20	7	0	0	0	3	23	.111	.043	.150	10.35	1.35
Smith, Chris	R-R	6-2	205	8-19-88	2	1	0.78	13	0	0	0	23	14	2	2	0	3	23	.173	.130	.190	9.00	1.17
2-team total (9 Dunedin)					3	1	0.74	22	0	0	0	36	18	3	3	1	5	41	—	—	—	10.16	1.24
Taylor, Chad	R-R	6-0	180	8-29-90	0	2	3.44	12	0	0	2	18	14	10	7	1	10	16	.209	.273	.178	7.85	4.91
Walby, Philip	L-R	6-2	190	7-24-92	1	1	6.00	10	0	0	1	12	17	9	8	0	10	12	.333	.375	.296	9.00	7.50
Wooten, Eric	L-L	6-3	190	3-18-90	0	2	2.93	10	1	0	1	31	29	11	10	1	5	28	.242	.219	.250	8.22	1.47
Wotherspoon, Matt	R-R	6-1	175	10-6-91	0	0	2.25	4	1	0	0	12	13	3	3	0	5	8	.271	.222	.300	6.00	3.75

Fielding

Catcher	PCT	G	PO	A	E	DP	PB
Haddad	1.000	4	25	3	0	0	2
Higashioka	.989	88	688	65	8	4	7
Slaybaugh	1.000	3	14	3	0	0	0
Tejeda	.935	7	54	4	4	1	1
Wilson	.987	41	271	44	4	4	5

First Base	PCT	G	PO	A	E	DP
Bichette Jr.	1.000	20	139	19	0	9
Conde	1.000	1	5	0	0	0
Fiorito	1.000	9	58	1	0	4
Fleming	1.000	2	11	0	0	0
Ford	.982	92	753	53	15	58
Gittens	1.000	4	20	3	0	4
Gumbs	.818	2	9	0	2	1
McFarland	.974	5	35	2	1	2
Snyder	.970	8	57	7	2	5

Second Base	PCT	G	PO	A	E	DP
Avelino	.971	58	107	126	7	29

	PCT	G	PO	A	E	DP
Conde	.935	8	15	14	2	0
Fiorito	1.000	3	7	12	0	4
Fleming	1.000	2	4	2	0	2
Gumbs	.970	46	92	105	6	26
Petit	.714	1	2	3	2	0
Wade	.957	24	36	52	4	10

Third Base	PCT	G	PO	A	E	DP
Andujar	.908	115	70	188	26	10
Avelino	.857	3	3	3	1	1
Bichette Jr.	.935	13	9	20	2	0
Conde	1.000	5	5	4	0	1
Fiorito	1.000	4	2	4	0	0
Fleming	.600	1	0	3	2	0
Gumbs	—	1	0	0	0	0
Petit	1.000	1	1	4	0	1

Shortstop	PCT	G	PO	A	E	DP
Avelino	.949	41	58	128	10	23
Baez	.917	3	3	8	1	4

	PCT	G	PO	A	E	DP
Conde	1.000	3	2	11	0	2
Mateo	.932	20	27	55	6	10
Petit	1.000	1	0	1	0	0
Ryan	1.000	1	2	3	0	1
Wade	.928	72	98	210	24	28

Outfield	PCT	G	PO	A	E	DP
Beltran	1.000	2	1	0	0	0
Custodio	.934	20	56	1	4	0
Ellsbury	1.000	3	2	0	0	0
Falcone	1.000	2	2	0	0	0
Fowler	1.000	61	129	5	0	3
Leonora	.950	89	162	8	9	2
Martinez	1.000	3	2	0	0	0
O'Neill	.995	99	213	3	1	0
Oh	.980	27	49	1	1	0
Payton	.962	47	100	1	4	1
Skole	.948	44	71	2	4	0
Thomas	1.000	8	22	1	0	1
Toadvine	1.000	15	19	2	0	0

CHARLESTON (SC) RIVERDOGS — LOW CLASS A

SOUTH ATLANTIC LEAGUE

Batting	B-T	HT	WT	DOB	AVG	vLH	vRH	G	AB	R	H	2B	3B	HR	RBI	BB	HBP	SH	SF	SO	SB	CS	SLG	OBP
Aguilar, Angel	R-R	6-0	170	6-13-95	.229	.250	.222	87	345	41	79	22	2	3	26	22	5	2	2	102	14	3	.330	.283
Aune, Austin	L-R	6-2	190	9-6-93	.246	.248	.245	112	415	48	102	29	10	8	49	22	2	3	2	167	2	6	.422	.286
Avelino, Abiatal	R-R	5-11	186	2-14-95	.301	.310	.296	20	83	16	25	8	0	0	4	5	0	2	0	16	16	3	.398	.341
Bolasky, Devyn	L-L	5-11	185	1-24-93	.236	.172	.257	76	237	36	56	9	2	1	18	36	6	2	1	35	11	7	.304	.349
Breen, Chris	R-R	6-3	215	3-26-94	.224	.305	.195	59	228	20	51	16	0	6	29	10	3	0	2	72	7	2	.373	.263
Coa, Rainiero	R-R	5-10	170	1-2-93	.233	.091	.281	13	43	4	10	0	0	0	3	1	0	1	0	7	0	0	.233	.250
Conde, Vince	R-R	6-0	195	10-13-93	.265	.294	.254	89	321	45	85	30	0	6	32	41	3	1	3	74	9	5	.414	.351
de Oleo, Eduardo	R-R	5-10	180	1-25-93	.237	.273	.222	11	38	3	9	3	0	0	3	1	2	1	0	7	0	0	.316	.293
Falcone, Joey	L-R	6-5	220	6-1-86	.300	.250	.333	3	10	3	3	1	0	1	3	0	1	0	0	1	0	0	.700	.364
Fleming, Billy	R-R	6-1	190	9-20-92	.330	.467	.269	26	97	11	32	3	0	0	9	9	0	0	1	18	3	1	.361	.383
Fowler, Dustin	L-L	6-0	185	12-29-94	.307	.278	.316	58	241	35	74	9	3	4	31	11	2	0	2	47	18	7	.419	.340
Gordon, Griff	L-L	6-0	210	2-15-92	.213	.161	.231	42	122	7	26	4	0	1	13	11	2	4	1	22	5	2	.270	.287
Graterol, Juan	R-R	6-1	205	2-14-89	.200	.000	.222	3	10	1	2	1	0	0	1	2	0	0	0	1	0	0	.300	.333
Haddad, Radley	L-R	6-1	190	5-11-90	.209	.125	.245	43	134	16	28	7	1	1	14	12	5	2	1	44	2	0	.299	.296
Heathcott, Slade	L-L	6-1	190	9-28-90	.222	.000	.667	3	9	0	2	0	0	0	0	0	0	0	0	0	0	0	.222	.222
Hernandez, Jake	R-R	6-1	210	6-5-92	.571	.500	.600	2	7	4	4	0	0	0	5	1	0	0	0	1	1	0	.714	.625
Javier, Jose	R-R	5-10	160	9-16-92	.154	.182	.133	8	26	1	4	0	0	0	5	0	1	1	1	9	2	1	.154	.179
Jose, Dominic	B-R	6-2	180	3-16-93	.294	.000	.357	4	17	0	5	0	0	0	2	1	0	0	0	6	1	0	.294	.333
Katoh, Gosuke	L-R	6-2	180	10-8-94	.161	.121	.176	39	124	7	20	2	0	1	9	18	0	5	2	50	8	2	.202	.264
Lindemuth, Ryan	R-R	6-0	200	4-15-91	.219	.151	.246	63	187	29	41	9	1	1	11	26	17	4	2	44	13	2	.294	.362
Martini, Renzo	R-R	6-1	190	8-25-92	.167	.000	.222	3	12	2	2	0	0	0	0	0	0	0	0	1	0	0	.167	.167
Mateo, Jorge	R-R	6-0	188	6-23-95	.268	.274	.267	96	365	51	98	18	8	2	33	36	3	4	1	80	71	15	.378	.338
McFarland, Ty	L-R	6-3	190	10-13-91	.250	.000	.286	7	24	3	6	0	0	0	4	0	0	0	0	2	0	3	.250	.357
Noriega, Alvaro	R-R	6-0	190	11-9-94	.227	.250	.222	12	44	6	10	1	0	0	5	1	0	0	0	4	0	0	.250	.261
Palma, Alexander	R-R	6-0	201	10-18-95	.202	.160	.219	81	277	21	56	4	4	1	26	15	3	5	3	57	8	4	.256	.248
Sands, Donny	R-R	6-2	190	5-16-96	.310	.250	.333	7	29	3	9	1	0	0	4	1	0	0	0	5	0	1	.345	.333
Slaybaugh, Collin	L-R	6-1	185	4-3-92	.289	.295	.283	53	180	24	52	6	0	0	11	11	1	1	0	29	12	1	.322	.333
Spencer, Connor	L-R	6-2	215	1-22-93	.290	.383	.254	49	169	18	49	9	0	0	23	22	8	1	6	31	3	6	.343	.385
Tejeda, Isaias	R-R	6-0	195	10-28-91	.279	.236	.296	83	312	30	87	18	1	5	42	15	2	0	3	49	10	3	.391	.313
Thomas, Brandon	B-R	6-3	210	2-7-91	.258	.371	.194	32	97	11	25	7	0	1	7	17	2	0	0	41	8	1	.361	.379

Batting	B-T	HT	WT	DOB	AVG	vLH	vRH	G	AB	R	H	2B	3B	HR	RBI	BB	HBP	SH	SF	SO	SB	CS	SLG	OBP
Thompson, Bo	R-R	5-10	255	1-27-93	.253	.383	.208	71	233	26	59	13	0	3	24	45	7	2	2	30	4	1	.348	.387
Toadvine, Derek	R-R	5-10	175	3-20-92	.140	.083	.161	16	43	2	6	1	0	0	2	3	2	2	0	13	1	1	.163	.229
Valerio, Allen	R-R	6-1	173	1-11-93	.125	.067	.152	13	48	5	6	2	0	1	8	4	0	0	0	18	1	0	.229	.192

Pitching	B-T	HT	WT	DOB	W	L	ERA	G	GS	CG	SV	IP	H	R	ER	HR	BB	SO	AVG	vLH	vRH	K/9	BB/9
Acevedo, Domingo	R-R	6-7	190	3-6-94	0	0	5.40	1	1	0	0	2	2	1	1	0	1	1	.286	.500	.000	5.40	5.40
Adams, Chance	R-R	6-0	215	8-10-94	1	1	3.09	5	0	0	0	12	7	6	4	0	4	16	.163	.217	.100	12.34	3.09
Bautista, Rony	L-L	6-7	200	9-17-91	4	5	4.15	28	12	0	0	87	71	44	40	5	63	99	.228	.289	.204	10.28	6.54
Carley, Sean	R-R	6-4	230	12-28-90	3	1	3.86	28	0	0	0	49	67	30	21	4	14	40	.316	.359	.283	7.35	2.57
Cedeno, Luis	R-R	5-11	154	7-14-94	3	6	3.52	9	9	0	0	46	45	22	18	6	23	28	.262	.238	.283	5.48	4.50
Coshow, Cale	R-R	6-5	260	7-16-92	0	0	1.13	11	0	0	7	16	10	2	2	0	4	20	.179	.190	.171	11.25	2.25
Del Bosque, Andre	R-R	6-0	225	3-14-91	6	5	4.76	22	5	0	0	68	66	45	36	4	36	59	.258	.295	.214	7.81	4.76
Espinal, Yoel	R-R	6-2	200	11-7-92	3	1	2.79	17	0	0	0	29	20	11	9	1	23	36	.200	.279	.140	11.17	7.14
Foley, Jordan	R-R	6-4	215	7-12-93	3	7	2.88	17	17	1	0	84	68	32	27	4	36	93	.224	.191	.249	9.92	3.84
Frare, Caleb	L-L	6-1	195	7-8-93	4	2	2.35	30	0	0	3	46	45	14	12	1	15	49	.269	.250	.278	9.59	2.93
Gomez, Anyelo	R-R	6-1	175	3-1-93	0	1	3.00	1	1	0	0	3	5	3	1	0	3	0	.417	.571	.200	0.00	9.00
Harris, Hobie	R-R	6-3	200	6-23-93	0	0	6.23	2	0	0	0	4	5	3	3	1	1	4	.294	.200	.333	8.31	2.08
Harvey, Joe	R-R	6-2	220	1-9-92	1	1	4.24	15	0	0	8	17	20	9	8	0	8	21	.294	.286	.300	11.12	4.24
Hebert, Chaz	L-L	6-2	180	9-4-92	1	1	0.87	2	2	0	0	10	6	2	1	0	2	14	.158	.222	.138	12.19	1.74
Kamplain, Justin	R-L	6-0	175	2-13-93	5	14	4.29	26	25	2	0	136	153	73	65	8	38	119	.288	.317	.275	7.86	2.51
Kendrick, Conner	L-L	6-1	185	8-18-92	1	2	2.12	13	3	0	1	34	22	13	8	0	10	36	.185	.130	.219	9.53	2.65
Koerner, Brody	R-R	6-1	190	10-17-93	2	1	1.59	8	0	0	3	11	13	2	2	1	2	7	.310	.133	.407	5.56	1.59
Maher, Joey	R-R	6-5	200	8-5-92	7	5	2.20	27	18	0	1	119	87	37	29	4	29	97	.200	.200	.200	7.36	2.20
Marsh, Matt	R-R	6-3	190	7-10-91	2	4	2.28	14	8	2	0	59	52	25	15	4	25	52	.230	.192	.262	7.89	3.79
McNamara, Dillon	R-R	6-5	220	10-6-91	4	0	3.23	38	0	0	6	61	65	29	22	1	19	48	.271	.202	.319	7.04	2.79
Mesa Jr., Jose	R-R	6-4	215	8-13-93	1	0	3.97	5	0	0	1	11	7	6	5	0	7	17	.184	.250	.154	13.50	5.56
Montgomery, Jordan	L-L	6-4	225	12-27-92	4	3	2.68	9	9	0	0	44	36	15	13	1	12	55	.228	.220	.231	11.34	2.47
Mundell, Garrett	R-R	6-0	245	2-16-93	0	0	0.00	5	0	0	3	7	4	0	0	0	1	10	.167	.000	.211	12.86	1.29
Palladino, David	R-R	6-8	235	3-15-93	2	7	4.57	18	13	0	2	81	82	48	41	4	41	66	.270	.282	.261	7.36	4.57
Reyes, Manolo	R-R	6-1	190	11-14-89	1	0	5.84	7	0	0	0	12	13	8	8	0	9	13	.277	.455	.120	9.49	6.57
Rincon, Angel	R-R	6-1	180	9-26-92	1	1	2.45	13	0	0	3	22	23	6	6	0	2	17	.267	.286	.250	6.95	0.82
Robinett, Alex	R-R	5-11	190	11-25-92	0	1	16.71	5	0	0	1	7	15	14	13	2	1	8	.429	.500	.368	10.29	1.29
Rogers, Josh	L-L	6-3	185	7-10-94	1	0	5.68	2	0	0	0	6	9	4	4	0	3	6	.346	.154	.538	8.53	4.26
Vargas, Daris	R-R	6-3	195	8-12-92	0	2	5.59	2	2	0	0	10	12	8	6	0	7	3	.316	.067	.478	2.79	6.52
Walby, Philip	L-R	6-2	190	7-24-92	2	0	3.13	23	0	0	0	32	31	11	11	0	17	30	.258	.311	.227	8.53	4.83
Wotherspoon, Matt	R-R	6-1	175	10-6-91	4	3	3.84	16	15	1	0	84	82	41	36	3	20	97	.255	.255	.255	10.35	2.13

Fielding

Catcher	PCT	G	PO	A	E	DP	PB
Coa	1.000	10	90	11	0	0	1
de Oleo	.975	11	95	23	3	3	2
Graterol	1.000	3	16	5	0	1	0
Haddad	.978	43	351	43	9	5	13
Hernandez	1.000	1	7	1	0	0	2
Noriega	.984	12	107	17	2	1	1
Slaybaugh	.982	48	379	54	8	3	5
Tejeda	.989	13	80	10	1	0	2

First Base	PCT	G	PO	A	E	DP
Breen	.991	12	110	5	1	4
Coa	1.000	1	5	2	0	1
Martini	1.000	3	27	4	0	2
McFarland	1.000	1	7	2	0	0
Spencer	.993	47	368	33	3	26
Tejeda	.986	18	136	3	2	11
Thompson	.983	59	480	39	9	37
Valerio	.917	1	11	0	1	3

Second Base	PCT	G	PO	A	E	DP
Aguilar	.969	26	53	72	4	16
Avelino	1.000	3	3	7	0	1
Conde	.970	51	92	137	7	30
Fleming	.986	14	24	45	1	9
Javier	1.000	4	12	12	0	4
Katoh	.971	33	57	76	4	16
Lindemuth	.962	12	19	31	2	3
Toadvine	—	1	0	0	0	0

Third Base	PCT	G	PO	A	E	DP
Aguilar	.846	13	15	18	6	1
Avelino	.882	7	4	11	2	0
Conde	.925	16	14	23	3	2
Fleming	1.000	11	4	16	0	0
Javier	.833	1	1	4	1	1
Lindemuth	.898	46	26	62	10	7
McFarland	1.000	3	6	4	0	0
Sands	.889	6	6	10	2	0
Tejeda	.896	29	18	42	7	2

	PCT	G	PO	A	E	DP
Valerio	.800	10	9	7	4	0
Shortstop	**PCT**	**G**	**PO**	**A**	**E**	**DP**
Aguilar	.939	39	48	91	9	21
Avelino	1.000	7	16	21	0	4
Conde	1.000	16	25	31	0	6
Mateo	.928	79	112	199	24	38
Outfield	**PCT**	**G**	**PO**	**A**	**E**	**DP**
Aune	.978	104	215	11	5	4
Bolasky	.964	69	128	5	5	0
Breen	1.000	36	45	1	0	0
Falcone	1.000	3	4	0	0	0
Fowler	.990	48	95	6	1	1
Gordon	1.000	41	68	0	0	0
Heathcott	1.000	3	4	0	0	0
Javier	1.000	2	5	0	0	0
Jose	1.000	4	9	2	0	2
Palma	.945	77	106	15	7	2
Thomas	.980	29	46	2	1	0
Toadvine	1.000	15	16	1	0	0

STATEN ISLAND YANKEES   SHORT-SEASON

NEW YORK-PENN LEAGUE

Batting	B-T	HT	WT	DOB	AVG	vLH	vRH	G	AB	R	H	2B	3B	HR	RBI	BB	HBP	SH	SF	SO	SB	CS	SLG	OBP
Alexander, K.J.	R-R	5-11	210	9-23-91	.217	.125	.267	15	46	6	10	2	1	0	4	7	0	0	1	13	0	1	.304	.315
Amburgey, Trey	R-R	6-2	210	10-24-94	.367	.643	.216	21	79	18	29	6	2	5	18	4	1	0	3	13	7	1	.684	.391
Bridges, Drew	L-R	6-4	230	2-3-95	.211	.115	.248	55	185	24	39	8	0	4	25	16	1	0	2	59	0	1	.319	.275
Cornelius, Kevin	R-R	6-1	180	8-28-92	.304	.429	.241	35	125	16	38	8	0	2	16	13	1	0	2	29	3	2	.416	.369
de Oleo, Eduardo	R-R	5-10	180	1-25-93	.237	.283	.218	45	156	18	37	11	1	3	17	10	1	0	2	35	2	0	.378	.284
Estrada, Thairo	R-R	5-10	155	2-22-96	.267	.356	.230	63	247	37	66	17	0	2	23	23	5	1	3	30	8	3	.360	.338
Gordon, Griff	L-L	6-2	210	2-15-92	.333	.444	.300	21	78	9	26	6	0	0	9	8	2	0	1	12	3	0	.410	.404
Hendrix, Jeff	L-R	6-0	195	7-16-93	.229	.175	.249	65	236	42	54	6	0	0	14	28	10	3	3	65	17	1	.254	.332
Hernandez, Jake	R-R	6-1	210	6-5-92	.270	.319	.245	41	141	12	38	3	0	0	7	9	3	2	1	20	0	0	.291	.325
Holder, Kyle	L-R	6-1	185	5-25-94	.213	.262	.195	56	225	23	48	7	1	0	12	17	2	1	5	34	6	2	.253	.273
Jackson, Jhalan	R-R	6-3	220	2-12-93	.266	.188	.295	49	177	35	47	14	2	5	34	16	4	0	1	59	4	0	.452	.338
Krill, Ryan	L-R	6-4	205	3-17-93	.247	.220	.256	62	215	22	53	9	0	1	25	19	4	0	2	37	0	2	.302	.317

Batting	B-T	HT	WT	DOB	AVG	vLH	vRH	G	AB	R	H	2B	3B	HR	RBI	BB	HBP	SH	SF	SO	SB	CS	SLG	OBP
McFarland, Ty	L-R	6-3	190	10-13-91	.160	.000	.174	6	25	5	4	0	0	0	3	4	0	0	0	4	0	0	.160	.276
Noriega, Alvaro	R-R	6-0	198	11-9-94	.040	.000	.056	8	25	1	1	1	0	0	1	0	0	0	1	2	0	0	.080	.038
Perez, Danienger	R-R	5-10	155	11-6-96	.444	.000	.667	4	9	3	4	1	1	0	4	0	0	0	0	1	0	0	.778	.444
Valera, Junior	R-R	6-0	180	9-27-92	.305	.304	.305	51	187	28	57	13	7	1	32	9	2	1	1	44	9	3	.465	.342
Wagner, Brandon	L-R	6-0	210	8-24-95	.228	.200	.238	52	162	21	37	8	1	4	18	28	2	0	1	49	1	2	.364	.347
Zehner, Zach	R-R	6-4	215	8-8-92	.232	.229	.234	63	228	24	53	8	2	5	31	24	2	1	2	56	12	3	.351	.309

Pitching	B-T	HT	WT	DOB	W	L	ERA	G	GS	CG	SV	IP	H	R	ER	HR	BB	SO	AVG	vLH	vRH	K/9	BB/9
Acevedo, Domingo	R-R	6-7	190	3-6-94	3	0	1.69	11	11	0	0	48	37	15	9	2	15	53	.207	.238	.182	9.94	2.81
Adams, Chance	R-R	6-0	215	8-10-94	1	0	0.93	4	0	0	0	10	5	2	1	0	3	13	.147	.167	.136	12.10	2.79
Bisacca, Alex	R-R	6-2	205	6-23-93	0	0	1.69	3	0	0	0	5	6	5	1	0	3	1	.286	.167	.333	1.69	5.06
Borens, Matt	R-R	6-7	195	2-10-93	1	4	6.30	14	8	0	0	50	69	41	35	4	9	38	.321	.384	.267	6.84	1.62
Callahan, Derek	L-L	6-4	205	12-29-92	6	4	4.76	14	13	0	0	64	72	36	34	5	20	44	.278	.241	.289	6.16	2.80
Carley, Sean	L-L	6-3	220	12-28-90	1	1	1.74	5	0	0	2	10	4	2	2	0	4	8	.121	.111	.125	6.97	3.48
Carnes, Ethan	L-L	6-3	205	12-30-91	3	0	1.98	9	7	0	1	36	32	12	8	1	8	30	.232	.167	.255	7.43	1.98
Carter, Will	L-R	6-3	190	1-18-93	1	1	2.04	9	1	0	0	18	12	7	4	0	9	13	.176	.182	.174	6.62	4.58
Cedeno, Luis	R-R	5-11	154	7-14-94	5	3	2.73	13	12	0	1	66	68	28	20	1	20	51	.270	.284	.264	6.95	2.73
Degano, Jeff	R-L	6-4	215	10-30-92	0	0	2.53	4	2	0	0	11	10	3	3	0	5	14	.244	.333	.207	11.81	4.22
Del Bosque, Andre	R-R	6-0	225	3-14-91	1	2	3.86	11	0	0	2	16	12	10	7	2	7	16	.214	.250	.200	8.82	3.86
Drozd, Jonny	L-L	6-7	200	9-17-91	3	2	1.24	18	0	0	2	36	28	8	5	0	7	29	.215	.182	.233	7.18	1.73
Espinal, Yoel	R-R	6-2	200	11-7-92	1	5	8.54	14	8	0	0	39	40	37	37	4	32	33	.267	.258	.273	7.62	7.38
Hamlin, Cody	R-R	6-3	190	2-9-93	1	0	0.75	6	0	0	0	12	11	1	1	0	3	10	.250	.444	.115	7.50	2.25
Hissong, Travis	R-R	6-0	195	7-19-91	1	1	3.09	14	0	0	1	23	22	9	8	0	12	29	.253	.333	.211	11.19	4.63
Kaprielian, James	R-R	6-4	200	3-2-94	0	1	2.00	3	3	0	0	9	8	2	2	0	2	12	.229	.250	.211	12.00	2.00
Mahoney, Kolton	R-R	6-1	195	5-20-92	3	2	2.29	12	10	0	0	55	49	16	14	2	11	50	.236	.213	.250	8.18	1.80
Marks, Bret	R-R	6-3	190	5-22-92	0	2	4.91	9	0	0	0	11	11	7	6	1	10	10	.268	.333	.217	8.18	8.18
Mesa Jr., Jose	R-R	6-4	215	8-13-93	3	0	0.42	10	0	0	1	22	9	2	1	0	9	35	.122	.043	.157	14.54	3.74
Morban, Jhon	R-R	6-4	190	6-3-92	0	0	0.00	1	0	0	0	3	1	0	0	0	1	0	.111	—	.111	0.00	3.38
Reeves, James	R-L	6-3	195	6-7-93	1	1	3.08	13	0	0	2	26	26	9	9	1	12	27	.268	.257	.274	9.23	4.10
Robinett, Alex	R-R	5-11	190	11-25-92	1	1	2.45	6	0	0	1	11	10	3	3	0	4	11	.238	.167	.292	9.00	3.27
Roeder, Josh	R-R	6-0	175	12-2-92	1	2	4.08	19	0	0	4	29	28	16	13	3	4	26	.255	.219	.269	8.16	1.26
Rogers, Josh	L-L	6-3	185	7-10-94	1	0	2.57	3	0	0	1	7	5	2	2	0	0	10	.217	.429	.125	12.86	0.00
Schaub, Mike	R-R	6-2	210	5-31-92	3	1	1.37	20	0	0	6	26	23	4	4	0	7	24	.237	.206	.254	8.20	2.39
Seyler, Mark	R-R	6-3	190	2-2-94	0	0	4.62	14	0	0	1	25	30	15	13	2	7	15	.291	.361	.254	5.33	2.49

Fielding

Catcher	PCT	G	PO	A	E	DP	PB
Alexander	.978	12	81	7	2	0	1
de Oleo	.992	45	323	49	3	3	10
Hernandez	1.000	16	115	7	0	0	2
Noriega	.972	8	55	15	2	0	1

First Base	PCT	G	PO	A	E	DP
Cornelius	.982	11	101	6	2	9
Hernandez	.996	22	213	17	1	14
Krill	.992	42	363	19	3	27
McFarland	1.000	1	12	0	0	0

Second Base	PCT	G	PO	A	E	DP
Estrada	.969	45	88	130	7	18

		PCT	G	PO	A	E	DP
McFarland	.875	2	4	3	1	1
Perez	1.000	1	2	5	0	2
Valera	1.000	5	12	13	0	6
Wagner	.902	24	21	53	8	12

Third Base	PCT	G	PO	A	E	DP
Bridges	.902	52	19	92	12	7
Cornelius	.903	12	9	19	3	4
McFarland	.750	1	1	2	1	0
Wagner	.889	15	6	18	3	0

Shortstop	PCT	G	PO	A	E	DP
Estrada	.958	19	33	58	4	10
Holder	.970	56	94	165	8	28

	PCT	G	PO	A	E	DP
Perez	1.000	1	3	3	0	1
Wagner	1.000	1	0	1	0	0

Outfield	PCT	G	PO	A	E	DP
Alexander	1.000	2	2	1	0	0
Amburgey	1.000	18	31	1	0	1
Gordon	.939	16	30	1	2	0
Hendrix	.993	60	144	3	1	1
Jackson	.960	45	91	4	4	0
Valera	.959	32	45	2	2	1
Zehner	.957	59	88	2	4	0

PULASKI YANKEES

ROOKIE

APPALACHIAN LEAGUE

Batting	B-T	HT	WT	DOB	AVG	vLH	vRH	G	AB	R	H	2B	3B	HR	RBI	BB	HBP	SH	SF	SO	SB	CS	SLG	OBP
Afenir, Audie	R-R	6-2	215	2-15-92	.279	.329	.257	60	244	33	68	15	1	1	36	27	0	3	61	0	0	.361	.347
Aparicio, Jesus	R-R	5-11	186	8-18-94	.171	.259	.144	36	117	18	20	7	0	2	13	13	1	1	2	33	0	0	.282	.256
Coleman, Kendall	L-L	6-4	190	5-22-95	.236	.278	.221	58	203	36	48	2	7	5	24	29	2	0	1	62	2	4	.389	.336
Duran, Matt	R-R	6-1	205	5-1-93	.228	.200	.244	38	145	18	33	11	0	2	20	12	2	0	1	37	0	0	.345	.294
Fleming, Billy	R-R	6-1	200	9-20-92	.444	.316	.514	15	54	12	24	5	0	2	8	6	3	0	2	7	0	0	.648	.508
Frias, Frank	R-R	6-2	185	3-29-94	.298	.289	.302	41	124	26	37	6	2	5	20	25	2	1	0	43	3	3	.500	.424
Javier, Jose	R-R	5-10	160	9-16-92	.245	.286	.224	32	102	13	25	4	1	5	16	8	1	1	0	23	3	1	.451	.306
Katoh, Gosuke	L-R	6-2	180	10-8-94	.287	.333	.270	59	202	31	58	9	1	5	22	49	0	3	0	61	9	0	.416	.426
Mikolas, Nathan	L-L	6-0	200	12-30-93	.285	.341	.270	52	193	40	55	8	2	4	33	25	3	0	1	51	2	1	.409	.374
Park, Hoy Jun	L-R	6-1	175	4-7-96	.239	.250	.234	56	222	48	53	11	3	5	30	34	5	0	1	50	12	7	.383	.351
Sweeney, Kane	L-R	6-3	220	10-6-92	.320	.355	.311	45	153	24	49	15	2	6	37	31	3	1	3	47	1	1	.562	.437
Toadvine, Derek	R-R	5-10	175	3-20-92	.000	—	.000	1	1	0	0	0	0	0	0	0	0	0	0	0	0	0	.000	.000
Valerio, Allen	R-R	6-1	173	1-11-93	.271	.328	.246	58	203	38	55	13	1	12	41	30	3	0	2	56	2	1	.522	.370
Vidal, Carlos	L-L	5-11	160	11-29-95	.303	.324	.294	60	244	49	74	15	2	9	46	29	6	1	1	44	16	5	.492	.389
Walsh, Matt	R-R	5-10	215	7-3-92	.136	.077	.161	15	44	7	6	1	0	0	4	3	5	1	0	13	0	0	.159	.269

Pitching	B-T	HT	WT	DOB	W	L	ERA	G	GS	CG	SV	IP	H	R	ER	HR	BB	SO	AVG	vLH	vRH	K/9	BB/9
Carroll, Cody	R-R	6-5	175	10-15-92	1	1	1.75	14	0	0	3	26	16	5	5	0	14	26	.186	.103	.255	9.12	4.91
Cortes, Nestor	R-L	5-11	190	12-10-94	6	3	2.26	12	10	0	0	64	48	21	16	7	10	66	.203	.161	.217	9.33	1.41
De la Rosa, Simon	R-R	6-3	185	5-11-93	6	2	3.71	13	7	0	1	53	35	22	22	2	37	67	.191	.198	.186	11.31	6.24
Finley, Drew	R-R	6-3	200	7-10-96	0	1	3.94	12	12	0	0	32	33	20	14	9	19	41	.256	.238	.273	11.53	5.34
Gabay, Willie	R-R	6-0	180	7-3-91	1	1	5.25	15	0	0	0	24	30	15	14	2	5	20	.300	.439	.203	7.50	1.88

Pitching	B-T	HT	WT	DOB	W	L	ERA	G	GS	CG	SV	IP	H	R	ER	HR	BB	SO	AVG	vLH	vRH	K/9	BB/9
Hamlin, Cody	R-R	6-3	190	2-9-93	1	0	0.59	6	0	0	1	15	15	3	1	1	0	17	.246	.222	.265	9.98	0.00
Holmes, Corey	R-R	6-6	200	9-3-91	0	0	0.00	4	0	0	0	6	2	1	0	0	0	6	.100	.000	.222	9.53	0.00
Jimenez, Juan	R-R	6-2	190	10-6-93	2	2	2.88	11	0	0	1	25	27	14	8	1	8	32	.262	.298	.232	11.52	2.88
Koerner, Brody	R-R	6-1	190	10-17-93	1	0	1.00	13	0	0	5	18	14	5	2	0	5	18	.212	.167	.250	9.00	2.50
Morban, Jhon	R-R	6-4	190		3	5	3.28	12	8	0	0	58	59	23	21	4	18	55	.266	.279	.254	8.58	2.81
Morla, Melvin	R-R	6-4	185	5-26-93	4	2	6.52	12	12	0	0	50	55	38	36	8	33	41	.274	.283	.265	7.43	5.98
Mundell, Garrett	R-R	6-6	245	2-16-93	4	0	0.00	13	0	0	2	19	10	0	0	0	6	25	.152	.152	.152	11.84	2.84
Padilla, Jonathan	R-R	5-10	175	3-30-93	2	1	2.40	8	4	0	0	30	30	13	8	1	8	25	.254	.264	.246	7.50	2.40
Palladino, David	R-R	6-8	235	3-15-93	4	0	2.88	4	4	0	0	25	21	9	8	4	5	25	.223	.233	.216	9.00	1.80
Rivera, Eduardo	R-R	6-5	190	9-24-92	2	0	3.06	15	0	0	1	35	25	12	12	3	18	46	.195	.259	.149	11.72	4.58
Robinett, Alex	R-R	5-11	190	11-25-92	0	0	0.00	3	0	0	1	5	2	3	0	0	0	7	.091	.250	.000	11.81	0.00
Rosa, Adonis	R-R	6-1	160	11-17-94	7	2	3.93	11	11	0	0	55	60	24	24	6	9	42	.282	.318	.243	6.87	1.47
Schwaab, Andrew	R-R	6-1	185	2-8-93	0	1	1.10	12	0	0	6	16	11	5	2	0	3	22	.175	.241	.118	12.12	1.65
Sosebee, David	R-R	6-1	200	8-25-93	1	2	2.31	13	0	0	0	35	29	11	9	1	11	37	.227	.298	.169	9.51	2.83

Fielding

Catcher	PCT	G	PO	A	E	DP	PB
Afenir	.994	20	164	10	1	2	3
Aparicio	.992	36	366	21	3	1	6
Walsh	.990	14	96	4	1	0	3

First Base	PCT	G	PO	A	E	DP
Afenir	.938	3	28	2	2	2
Duran	.990	25	191	8	2	12
Fleming	1.000	1	11	0	0	0
Sweeney	.990	40	276	27	3	23

Second Base	PCT	G	PO	A	E	DP
Fleming	.957	6	8	14	1	4
Javier	1.000	9	15	24	0	5
Katoh	.965	55	87	133	8	21

Third Base	PCT	G	PO	A	E	DP
Duran	.923	5	5	7	1	1
Fleming	1.000	2	3	5	0	1
Javier	.929	5	2	11	1	0
Valerio	.912	57	36	68	10	5

Shortstop	PCT	G	PO	A	E	DP
Javier	.953	14	15	26	2	5
Park	.935	54	81	119	14	25

Outfield	PCT	G	PO	A	E	DP
Coleman	.963	58	100	3	4	0
Frias	.932	40	52	3	4	0
Javier	1.000	3	5	0	0	0
Mikolas	.972	51	68	1	2	2
Toadvine	1.000	1	1	0	0	0
Vidal	.985	58	124	5	2	0

GCL YANKEES1 — ROOKIE

GULF COAST LEAGUE

Batting	B-T	HT	WT	DOB	AVG	vLH	vRH	G	AB	R	H	2B	3B	HR	RBI	BB	HBP	SH	SF	SO	SB	CS	SLG	OBP
Amburgey, Trey	R-R	6-2	210	10-24-94	.333	.333	.333	37	135	28	45	5	4	0	12	12	4	0	0	20	14	3	.430	.404
Argomaniz, Manny	R-R	6-0	200	4-4-93	.122	.077	.139	24	49	1	6	1	0	0	2	5	1	0	0	23	1	0	.143	.218
Barnes, Jordan	R-R	5-11	180	6-19-94	.222	.115	.260	37	99	12	22	3	1	1	12	12	1	1	1	26	4	0	.303	.310
Barrios, Daniel	R-R	5-11	183	4-18-95	.278	.375	.250	13	36	7	10	2	0	0	3	2	2	1	0	11	0	2	.333	.350
Cuevas, Bryan	R-R	5-10	179	10-14-93	.252	.205	.269	44	143	22	36	8	2	1	21	7	4	0	2	28	11	4	.357	.301
Diaz, Cesar	B-R	5-10	165	4-12-93	.307	.333	.295	36	114	34	35	6	6	1	11	28	1	1	2	9	27	4	.491	.441
Falcone, Joey	L-R	6-5	220	6-1-86	.378	.286	.419	16	45	4	17	4	1	1	13	3	1	0	0	13	0	1	.578	.429
Garcia, Wilkerman	B-R	6-0	176	4-1-98	.281	.450	.198	37	121	20	34	6	1	0	18	24	1	1	3	19	6	8	.347	.396
Gittens, Chris	R-R	6-4	250	2-9-94	.363	.432	.333	41	124	45	45	9	1	8	29	17	4	0	1	33	2	2	.645	.452
Infante, Jose	B-R	5-11	160	9-21-93	.192	.100	.250	10	26	4	5	2	0	0	4	5	1	0	1	6	1	0	.269	.333
Mateo, Welfrin	R-R	5-10	170	9-8-95	.222	.143	.273	5	18	3	4	1	0	0	0	0	0	0	0	3	0	0	.278	.222
Molina, Leonardo	R-R	6-2	180	7-31-97	.247	.163	.283	48	162	15	40	9	2	2	17	10	1	2	3	37	6	5	.364	.290
Noriega, Alvaro	R-R	6-0	198	11-9-94	.174	.000	.250	9	23	1	4	1	0	0	1	0	0	1	0	6	0	0	.217	.200
Perez, Danienger	R-R	5-10	155	11-6-96	.219	.216	.220	46	155	16	34	12	1	1	23	18	0	0	4	37	4	0	.329	.294
Rey, Victor	R-R	6-2	178	6-29-95	.279	.364	.247	42	122	21	34	12	1	0	19	24	3	1	1	37	1	0	.393	.407
Reyes, Brian	R-R	6-0	190	6-28-95	1.000	1.000	—	1	1	1	1	0	0	0	0	0	0	0	0	0	0	0	1.000	1.000
Robertson, Terrance	L-L	6-0	175	11-18-96	.144	.216	.114	38	125	13	18	1	1	0	8	7	4	1	1	39	4	3	.168	.212
Sanchez, Luis	R-R	5-11	160	5-5-97	.222	.417	.067	15	27	4	6	1	0	0	2	1	1	0	0	8	0	0	.259	.300
Sands, Donny	R-R	6-2	190	5-16-96	.309	.340	.296	48	162	27	50	9	0	0	26	24	3	0	1	5	7	4	.364	.405
Seitz, Jerry	R-R	5-10	180	9-27-94	.313	.281	.328	33	96	8	30	5	0	1	7	7	2	0	2	17	3	1	.396	.371

Pitching	B-T	HT	WT	DOB	W	L	ERA	G	GS	CG	SV	IP	H	R	ER	HR	BB	SO	AVG	vLH	vRH	K/9	BB/9
Alvarez, Daniel	R-R	6-2	190	6-28-96	0	0	1.93	1	0	0	0	5	4	1	1	1	2	7	.222	.333	.111	13.50	3.86
Bailey, Andrew	R-R	6-3	235	5-31-84	0	0	0.00	1	0	0	0	1	0	0	0	0	1	2	.000	.000	.000	13.50	6.75
Bisacca, Alex	R-R	6-2	205	6-23-91	2	1	3.29	8	0	0	0	14	16	7	5	0	4	13	.286	.429	.238	8.56	2.63
Campos, Jose	R-R	6-4	195	7-27-92	0	1	5.79	1	0	0	0	5	8	3	3	1	0	5	.364	.300	.417	9.64	0.00
Chin, Andrew	L-L	6-1	180	9-22-92	0	1	2.92	14	0	0	0	25	23	9	8	1	15	22	.247	.241	.250	8.03	5.47
Cook, Dustin	R-R	6-5	210	11-3-93	1	2	9.82	10	0	0	1	7	9	10	8	0	11	9	.321	.167	.438	11.05	13.50
DeGroot, Geoff	R-R	6-0	185	5-13-93	0	0	1.23	10	0	0	1	15	5	2	2	0	8	13	.109	.111	.107	7.98	4.91
Dott, Aaron	R-L	6-5	210	5-17-88	0	0	13.50	2	0	0	0	1	1	2	2	0	2	1	.200	.000	.250	6.75	13.50
Duarte, Abel	R-R	6-1	190	5-20-94	4	3	5.10	11	8	0	0	48	49	29	27	4	17	38	.263	.200	.306	7.17	3.21
Escorcia, Juan	R-R	6-0	170	5-16-96	1	1	10.13	9	3	0	0	19	17	22	21	1	37	21	.262	.259	.263	10.13	17.84
Flemming, Icezack	R-R	6-2	200	6-24-92	1	2	4.32	13	0	0	0	30	30	18	14	1	10	30	.237	.400	.096	10.80	3.60
Garrison, Taylor	R-R	5-11	190	5-24-90	0	2	3.52	5	5	0	0	8	7	6	3	1	1	10	.233	.222	.238	11.74	1.17
Gomez, Anyelo	R-R	6-1	175	3-1-93	0	0	2.31	4	0	0	0	12	9	3	3	0	1	18	.140	.105	.167	13.89	0.77
Harris, Hobie	R-R	6-3	200	6-23-93	2	1	2.30	11	0	0	2	16	11	7	4	1	8	20	.180	.200	.167	11.48	4.60
Joseph, Francis	R-R	5-10	165	10-4-93	0	1	7.27	10	0	0	1	17	22	17	14	1	9	15	.297	.333	.263	7.79	4.67
Lara, Rafael	R-R	5-10	166	6-10-95	1	0	1.50	1	1	0	0	6	1	1	1	1	2	2	.050	.143	.000	3.00	3.00
Marks, Bret	R-R	6-3	190	5-22-92	2	0	2.57	5	0	0	0	7	3	2	2	1	5	5	.130	.222	.071	10.29	6.43
Martin, Chad	R-R	6-4	215	1-2-94	1	0	2.61	13	3	0	0	38	34	13	11	0	13	26	.239	.226	.247	6.16	3.08
Martinez, Dallas	R-R	6-0	175	10-28-94	0	1	81.00	1	1	0	0	0	3	3	3	0	0	1	.750	1.000	.500	27.00	0.00
Marzi, Anthony	L-L	6-1	205	11-27-92	2	0	0.00	6	0	0	0	7	4	0	0	0	2	7	.120	.125	.118	8.59	4.91
Mesa Jr., Jose	R-R	6-4	215	8-13-93	0	0	5.40	2	0	0	0	3	3	2	2	0	2	5	.231	1.000	.167	13.50	5.40
Palladino, Jr.	R-R	6-8	235	3-15-93	1	0	7.88	2	0	0	0	8	11	7	7	2	3	8	.324	.462	.238	9.00	3.38

Pitching	B-T	HT	WT	DOB	W	L	ERA	G	GS	CG	SV	IP	H	R	ER	HR	BB	SO	AVG	vLH	vRH	K/9	BB/9
Pujols, Jose	R-R	6-6	183	11-19-92	2	1	3.80	12	0	0	1	21	15	14	9	1	19	18	.205	.206	.205	7.59	8.02
Ramirez, Jean	R-R	6-4	180	3-1-93	2	4	3.68	8	0	0	0	37	33	23	15	1	20	29	.237	.290	.195	7.12	4.91
Rosario, Luis	R-R	6-1	185	12-11-94	1	2	6.17	9	6	1	0	35	40	24	24	6	12	24	.292	.299	.286	6.17	3.09
Severino, Anderson	L-L	5-10	165	9-17-94	2	3	2.61	11	9	0	0	41	30	26	12	0	33	32	.204	.189	.209	6.97	7.19
Vargas, Alexander	R-R	6-4	203	7-24-97	2	4	4.97	10	9	0	0	42	55	25	23	2	13	31	.318	.379	.280	6.70	2.81

Fielding

Catcher	PCT	G	PO	A	E	DP	PB
Argomaniz	.931	8	26	1	2	0	2
Noriega	1.000	9	69	9	0	1	0
Rey	.974	21	135	12	4	3	9
Sanchez	.976	9	33	7	1	0	4
Seitz	.988	27	149	22	2	1	2

First Base	PCT	G	PO	A	E	DP
Argomaniz	1.000	1	7	0	0	2
Barrios	.917	2	9	2	1	0
Cuevas	.933	5	40	2	3	3
Gittens	.996	29	212	22	1	17
Rey	.978	20	124	7	3	10
Sanchez	1.000	3	3	0	0	1
Seitz	.972	5	33	2	1	1

Second Base	PCT	G	PO	A	E	DP
Argomaniz	1.000	2	1	0	0	0

	PCT	G	PO	A	E	DP
Barrios	.882	4	5	10	2	2
Cuevas	.972	26	45	61	3	11
Diaz	.833	2	3	2	1	1
Infante	1.000	1	2	0	0	0
Mateo	1.000	1	0	2	0	0
Perez	.968	29	40	52	3	14
Reyes	1.000	1	2	0	0	0

Third Base	PCT	G	PO	A	E	DP
Argomaniz	.929	8	4	9	1	1
Barrios	1.000	4	2	2	0	0
Cuevas	1.000	5	2	5	0	1
Sands	.953	46	28	74	5	7

Shortstop	PCT	G	PO	A	E	DP
Barrios	1.000	3	6	8	0	2
Cuevas	1.000	5	8	13	0	2
Garcia	.925	36	52	97	12	15

	PCT	G	PO	A	E	DP
Mateo	1.000	1	0	3	0	0
Perez	.917	21	28	38	6	5

Outfield	PCT	G	PO	A	E	DP
Amburgey	.978	32	43	1	1	0
Argomaniz	1.000	3	1	0	0	0
Barnes	.966	28	27	1	1	0
Diaz	.976	26	38	3	1	0
Falcone	1.000	9	8	0	0	0
Infante	1.000	10	15	0	0	0
Mateo	1.000	2	4	0	0	0
Molina	1.000	46	88	6	0	2
Robertson	.958	35	67	1	3	0
Sanchez	1.000	1	1	0	0	0

GCL YANKEES2 — ROOKIE

GULF COAST LEAGUE

Batting	B-T	HT	WT	DOB	AVG	vLH	vRH	G	AB	R	H	2B	3B	HR	RBI	BB	HBP	SH	SF	SO	SB	CS	SLG	OBP
Baez, Yancarlos	B-R	6-2	165	9-21-95	.235	.186	.255	54	204	27	48	5	2	4	22	20	0	1	3	49	8	5	.338	.300
Cornelius, Kevin	R-R	6-1	180	8-28-92	.305	.290	.314	25	82	16	25	3	0	7	20	18	0	0	0	20	1	0	.598	.430
Diaz, Andy	L-L	5-11	190	11-21-95	.258	.167	.302	48	128	15	33	10	1	2	15	18	3	0	0	41	4	3	.398	.362
Encarnacion, Greidy	L-L	5-11	156	4-1-94	.208	.188	.216	39	106	14	22	2	2	0	5	8	1	0	0	20	8	1	.264	.270
Garabito, Griffin	R-R	5-11	180	8-2-97	.262	.261	.263	48	164	21	43	5	0	0	14	15	1	2	2	29	2	1	.293	.324
Garcia, Dermis	R-R	6-3	200	1-7-98	.159	.143	.164	23	69	7	11	2	0	6	9	0	0	0	0	25	0	1	.188	.256
Gilliam, Isiah	B-R	6-2	215	7-23-96	.296	.348	.270	42	135	12	40	11	1	1	23	15	0	0	3	23	2	2	.415	.359
Infante, Jose	B-R	5-11	160	9-21-93	.186	.136	.203	33	86	13	16	3	3	0	8	12	4	0	0	23	4	1	.291	.314
Jose, Dominic	B-R	6-2	180	3-16-93	.285	.209	.317	48	144	26	41	7	1	1	10	10	4	5	1	22	10	1	.368	.346
Liranzo, Ozzie	B-R	5-8	182	1-26-93	.244	.286	.222	25	41	4	10	2	0	1	7	3	0	0	2	7	0	0	.366	.283
Martinez, Teodoro	R-R	6-0	180	3-16-92	.121	.111	.125	13	33	2	4	1	0	0	0	2	1	1	0	3	1	2	.152	.194
Martini, Renzo	R-R	6-0	180	8-25-92	.286	.382	.246	54	185	32	53	17	1	5	34	31	2	0	2	31	0	0	.470	.391
Navas, Eduardo	B-R	5-10	180	4-5-96	.218	.133	.250	29	55	6	12	1	0	1	6	10	2	1	1	15	1	0	.291	.353
Reyes, Brian	R-R	6-0	190	6-28-95	.280	.267	.283	34	75	7	21	4	1	0	10	5	1	1	1	22	1	0	.360	.329
Rodriguez, Yonauris	R-R	6-1	155	3-10-97	.168	.244	.135	42	149	24	25	5	0	0	3	18	0	1	0	50	5	4	.201	.257
Suarez, Ronaldo	R-R	5-10	165	8-30-97	.122	.154	.107	24	41	2	5	2	0	0	2	2	1	0	0	15	2	1	.171	.182
Urena, Pedro	R-R	6-3	195	6-1-95	.234	.292	.204	46	141	15	33	9	2	3	17	22	1	0	2	34	0	2	.390	.337

Pitching	B-T	HT	WT	DOB	W	L	ERA	G	GS	CG	SV	IP	H	R	ER	HR	BB	SO	AVG	vLH	vRH	K/9	BB/9
Batista, Gean	R-R	6-4	175	10-27-91	1	1	2.82	16	0	0	5	22	15	12	7	2	12	22	.183	.133	.212	8.87	4.84
Bisacca, Alex	R-R	6-2	205	6-23-93	1	0	0.00	1	0	0	0	2	2	0	0	0	0	3	.286	.667	.000	16.20	0.00
Calvo, Javier	R-R	6-2	180	6-17-93	1	1	2.45	4	1	0	0	11	9	4	3	0	4	6	.220	.273	.200	4.91	3.27
Campos, Jose	R-R	6-4	195	7-27-92	0	0	0.00	1	1	0	0	5	2	0	0	0	0	9	.118	.000	.154	16.20	0.00
Degano, Jeff	R-L	6-4	215	10-30-92	0	4	5.06	6	6	0	0	11	14	8	6	1	4	8	.318	.222	.343	6.75	3.38
Dott, Aaron	R-L	6-5	210	5-17-88	0	0	12.00	3	1	0	0	3	2	4	4	0	4	0	.222	.000	.333	0.00	12.00
Enns, Dietrich	L-L	6-1	195	5-16-91	1	0	0.00	3	3	0	0	11	6	2	0	0	6	15	.150	.200	.133	11.91	4.76
Flemming, Icezack	R-R	6-2	200	6-24-92	0	1	18.00	1	0	0	0	1	2	2	2	0	1	0	.500	.000	.667	0.00	9.00
Garcia, Leonardo	R-R	6-0	160	12-31-93	2	3	4.84	11	6	0	0	35	30	24	19	2	26	30	.233	.234	.232	7.64	6.62
Garrison, Taylor	R-R	5-11	190	5-24-90	0	0	4.50	1	0	0	0	2	3	1	1	0	0	3	.333	.500	.200	13.50	0.00
Hamlin, Cody	R-R	6-3	190	2-9-93	0	0	4.50	2	0	0	0	2	6	1	1	0	0	3	.500	.667	.444	13.50	4.50
Harris, Hobie	R-R	6-3	190	6-23-93	0	0	0.00	1	0	0	1	1	0	0	0	0	0	0	.200	.000	.250	0.00	0.00
Holder, Jonathan	R-R	6-2	235	6-9-93	0	0	1.00	3	3	0	0	9	5	1	1	0	0	8	.156	.150	.167	8.00	0.00
Jimenez, Juan	R-R	6-2	190	10-6-93	1	1	1.80	4	0	0	1	10	9	3	2	1	1	10	.243	.250	.240	9.00	0.90
Jordan, Cory	R-R	6-5	220	1-17-91	1	2	5.47	16	1	0	0	25	27	23	15	2	12	25	.265	.212	.290	9.12	4.38
Kaprielian, James	R-R	6-4	200	3-2-94	0	0	11.57	2	0	0	0	2	4	3	3	0	2	2	.250	.000	.400	7.71	7.71
Luis, Omar	L-L	6-0	210	10-13-92	3	2	2.36	11	0	0	1	27	20	12	7	1	16	18	.211	.208	.211	6.08	5.40
Magallanes, Kelvin	R-R	6-1	175	7-15-94	0	1	5.64	12	4	0	1	30	25	24	19	0	31	26	.231	.200	.250	7.71	9.20
Martinez, Dallas	R-R	6-0	195	10-28-94	0	0	2.18	7	5	0	0	21	12	6	5	0	4	17	.162	.200	.143	7.40	1.74
Mesa Jr., Jose	R-R	6-4	215	8-13-93	0	0	4.50	2	0	0	0	4	4	4	2	0	2	3	.250	.250	.250	6.75	4.50
Morris, Christian	R-R	6-4	195	1-23-94	0	3	5.40	8	7	0	0	27	28	20	16	0	10	24	.267	.342	.224	8.10	3.38
O'Brien, Paddy	R-R	6-5	230	10-7-93	0	0	3.38	10	0	0	0	16	14	9	6	1	9	23	.226	.304	.179	12.94	5.06
Ovalles, Leonardo	R-R	6-2	170	9-17-94	2	4	5.59	12	6	0	0	39	49	28	24	0	14	26	.316	.200	.380	6.05	3.26
Pongs, Cameron	L-L	6-4	210	10-21-92	1	2	6.75	11	1	0	0	15	28	20	11	1	9	7	.394	.353	.407	4.30	5.52
Reyes, Manolo	R-R	6-1	190	11-14-89	0	0	0.00	1	0	0	0	2	0	0	0	0	0	1	.000	.000	.000	5.40	0.00
Schwaab, Andrew	R-R	6-1	185	2-8-93	2	0	1.29	5	0	0	0	7	4	1	1	0	2	10	.174	.100	.231	12.86	2.57
Stenhouse, Brandon	R-R	6-0	170	9-19-96	3	2	5.12	13	0	0	0	19	9	11	11	1	13	24	.136	.100	.152	11.17	6.05

Pitching

Pitching	B-T	HT	WT	DOB	W	L	ERA	G	GS	CG	SV	IP	H	R	ER	HR	BB	SO	AVG	vLH	vRH	K/9	BB/9
Strzalka, Artur	R-L	5-11	180	8-19-95	1	0	5.11	10	0	0	0	12	11	7	7	2	6	13	.244	.385	.188	9.49	4.38
Troya, Gilmael	R-R	6-0	178	4-4-97	1	3	2.25	9	7	0	0	36	21	12	9	2	14	39	.165	.161	.169	9.75	3.50
Vargas, Daris	R-R	6-3	195	8-12-92	3	3	2.12	11	8	1	0	51	44	22	12	2	11	42	.229	.260	.198	7.41	1.94

Fielding

Catcher	PCT	G	PO	A	E	DP	PB
Liranzo	1.000	24	69	9	0	1	7
Navas	.995	29	158	29	1	4	4
Reyes	.953	26	125	16	7	3	5
Suarez	.976	23	71	11	2	0	4

First Base	PCT	G	PO	A	E	DP
Cornelius	.985	21	180	14	3	8
Martini	.988	22	148	10	2	12
Reyes	.979	8	46	1	1	4
Urena	**.991**	**16**	**99**	**9**	**1**	**6**

Second Base	PCT	G	PO	A	E	DP

Baez	—	1	0	0	0	0
Garabito	.950	30	45	70	6	10
Infante	.828	8	9	15	5	2
Rodriguez	.968	29	43	47	3	7

Third Base	PCT	G	PO	A	E	DP
Garabito	.857	16	11	25	6	4
Garcia	.847	22	18	32	9	3
Martini	.935	28	15	57	5	6

Shortstop	PCT	G	PO	A	E	DP
Baez	.926	48	59	116	14	13
Garabito	1.000	2	1	3	0	1

Rodriguez	.880	13	14	30	6	5
Outfield	**PCT**	**G**	**PO**	**A**	**E**	**DP**
Diaz	.938	45	68	7	5	2
Encarnacion	.984	37	58	3	1	0
Gilliam	.958	27	23	0	1	0
Infante	.971	27	34	0	1	0
Jose	1.000	41	67	5	0	2
Martinez	.958	13	23	0	1	0
Urena	.941	17	28	4	2	3

DSL YANKEES   ROOKIE

DOMINICAN SUMMER LEAGUE

Batting	B-T	HT	WT	DOB	AVG	vLH	vRH	G	AB	R	H	2B	3B	HR	RBI	BB	HBP	SH	SF	SO	SB	CS	SLG	OBP
Alvarez, Nelson	L-L	6-3	210	3-10-96	.279	.217	.297	59	201	41	56	7	5	4	40	46	3	0	9	52	2	3	.423	.405
Amundaray, Jonathan	R-R	6-2	215	5-11-98	.111	.111	.111	13	36	5	4	0	1	0	4	12	2	1	2	12	1	0	.167	.346
Arias, Antonio	R-R	6-2	180	6-12-98	.235	.286	.222	39	136	24	32	4	2	1	11	14	2	1	0	24	5	0	.316	.316
Barrios, Daniel	R-R	5-11	183	4-18-95	.300	.000	.333	9	30	8	9	1	2	0	7	2	0	0	0	9	1	0	.467	.344
Blanco, Lisandro	R-R	6-1	180	1-13-97	.277	.270	.279	41	141	22	39	6	1	1	23	25	2	0	1	46	3	3	.355	.391
Cabrera, Leobaldo	R-R	6-1	170	1-21-98	.298	.356	.284	59	228	40	68	8	4	1	36	24	3	0	4	46	7	5	.382	.367
Castillo, Diego	R-R	6-0	170	10-28-97	.331	.219	.371	56	239	43	79	11	8	0	40	16	2	2	3	29	5	1	.444	.373
Cedeno, Oliver	R-R	5-10	165	5-24-96	.329	.190	.375	26	85	19	28	4	1	2	19	15	3	0	0	16	3	1	.471	.447
Corredera, Yeison	R-R	5-11	175	1-30-94	.224	.118	.252	46	165	30	37	10	2	3	22	16	1	0	1	37	8	2	.364	.295
Cuevas, Frederick	L-L	5-11	185	10-27-97	.256	.224	.266	57	203	47	52	5	4	3	36	37	3	7	2	44	15	4	.365	.376
De Leon, Juan	R-R	6-2	185	9-13-97	.226	.229	.225	53	186	34	42	9	4	3	23	25	9	1	1	66	1	2	.366	.344
Delgado, Jonaikel	R-R	6-0	171	9-12-97	.222	.154	.238	23	83	11	14	4	1	0	14	3	1	0	0	28	1	1	.241	.207
Diaz, Andy	L-L	5-11	190	11-21-95	.267	.400	.200	9	30	3	8	0	2	0	4	5	1	0	1	10	1	0	.400	.378
Diaz, Fernando	L-R	6-0	185	10-14-94	.213	.235	.207	32	75	16	16	2	1	0	10	12	2	3	0	18	4	1	.267	.337
Emery, Brayan	B-R	6-3	185	3-15-98	.192	.235	.179	61	224	42	43	9	4	3	34	40	7	0	2	81	9	2	.308	.330
Encarnacion, Greidy	L-L	5-11	156	4-1-94	.400	1.000	.333	7	10	7	4	1	0	0	2	5	1	0	0	6	2	2	.500	.625
Ferreira, Ricardo	B-R	5-11	175	2-3-95	.382	.407	.375	62	238	76	91	9	7	1	37	59	6	1	1	48	35	5	.492	.513
Flames, Miguel	R-R	6-2	210	9-14-97	.317	.298	.323	54	205	28	65	9	5	3	40	22	7	2	2	44	1	1	.454	.398
Florial, Estevan	L-R	6-1	185	11-25-97	.313	.236	.337	59	211	54	70	11	8	7	53	30	4	2	6	61	15	5	.527	.394
Gallardo, Carlos	R-R	5-10	160	1-26-97	.253	.227	.261	28	91	16	23	2	0	0	7	14	1	0	0	28	2	4	.275	.358
Garabito, Griffin	R-R	5-11	180	8-2-97	.235	.364	.200	14	51	11	12	2	1	1	3	8	0	0	0	6	2	0	.373	.339
Garcia, Wilkerman	B-R	6-0	176	4-1-98	.667	—	.667	2	6	3	4	0	0	0	1	1	0	0	0	5	1	0	.667	.750
Gomez, Nelson	R-R	6-1	220	10-8-97	.243	.237	.246	58	230	45	56	9	1	11	55	34	6	4	0	66	1	2	.435	.350
Gonzalez, Kevin	L-R	6-3	230	5-12-97	.255	.265	.252	38	137	28	35	11	0	0	31	26	2	0	2	28	0	0	.336	.377
Lopez, Jason	R-R	5-10	160	3-16-98	.240	.286	.232	42	146	31	35	6	0	1	19	22	1	0	3	28	11	4	.301	.337
Mateo, Algeni	R-R	5-9	170	8-1-95	.338	.417	.314	45	154	27	52	6	5	1	30	13	8	0	1	17	8	0	.461	.415
Mateo, Welfrin	R-R	5-10	170	9-8-95	.297	.279	.303	48	195	42	58	18	2	2	21	25	4	2	1	28	10	7	.441	.387
Medina, Brallan	R-R	5-10	180	6-9-97	.232	—	—	23	69	8	16	3	0	0	9	8	2	1	1	18	1	2	.275	.325
Mendez, Erick	R-R	6-0	185	4-7-96	.281	.295	.277	51	185	35	52	9	8	3	28	25	5	1	0	53	6	2	.465	.381
Miranda, Holman	B-R	5-11	175	12-1-97	.240	.345	.214	40	146	21	35	7	2	0	16	24	4	1	2	31	5	2	.315	.358
Moreno, Raymundo	R-R	6-1	185	3-9-98	.067	.000	.071	6	15	1	1	0	0	0	0	0	0	1	0	9	0	0	.067	.125
Mota, Sandy	R-R	6-0	170	9-25-96	.233	.143	.250	26	90	12	21	4	0	0	6	6	1	1	0	13	3	2	.344	.289
Navas, Eduardo	B-R	5-10	180	4-5-96	.056	.000	.083	6	18	1	1	0	0	0	1	4	0	1	0	5	0	0	.056	.227
Nieto, Felix	R-R	5-11	180	8-11-97	.233	.083	.290	18	43	7	10	2	0	1	11	2	5	1	3	7	1	0	.349	.321
Olivares, Pablo	R-R	6-0	160	1-27-98	.267	.360	.245	32	131	31	35	4	4	0	22	11	11	0	1	17	7	4	.359	.370
Perez, Danienger	R-R	5-10	155	11-6-96	.276	.211	.298	17	76	13	21	7	3	0	5	7	0	0	0	20	2	3	.447	.337
Polonia, Jose	R-R	5-11	170	12-11-95	.318	.250	.337	41	129	22	41	4	3	0	18	11	1	3	2	11	3	2	.395	.371
Rodriguez, Brayan	R-R	5-11	191	4-26-97	.186	.250	.170	15	59	4	11	4	0	0	6	2	1	1	0	15	0	0	.254	.226
Rodriguez, Ezequiel	R-R	6-0	175	6-22-96	.167	.158	.169	26	84	14	14	3	0	1	11	15	2	0	2	23	0	0	.238	.301
Rodriguez, Yonauris	R-R	6-1	155	3-10-97	.370	.176	.459	13	54	9	20	2	2	0	4	6	0	0	0	13	5	1	.481	.433
Suarez, Ronaldo	R-R	5-10	185	8-30-97	.400	—	.400	3	5	1	2	0	0	0	0	1	0	0	0	1	0	0	.400	.500
Tatis, Carlos	R-R	6-3	185	12-19-96	.296	.417	.271	26	71	13	21	5	0	0	8	2	0	2	0	16	1	0	.366	.373
Unda, Dario	L-L	5-11	168	5-24-96	.263	.400	.214	7	19	4	5	2	0	1	1	3	0	0	0	2	0	0	.526	.364
Vergel, David	R-R	6-0	165	1-13-97	.192	.059	.232	27	73	5	14	2	2	0	13	6	12	0	0	21	2	0	.274	.352

Pitching	B-T	HT	WT	DOB	W	L	ERA	G	GS	CG	SV	IP	H	R	ER	HR	BB	SO	AVG	vLH	vRH	K/9	BB/9
Acevedo, Anderson	R-R	6-2	220	9-30-93	0	1	3.52	5	0	0	0	8	7	6	3	0	7	4	.241	.300	.211	4.70	8.22
Alvarez, Daniel	R-R	6-2	190	6-28-96	3	2	2.48	15	13	0	0	58	44	23	16	1	20	62	.207	.224	.200	9.62	3.10
Arias, Freddery	R-R	6-1	195	10-28-94	5	1	1.17	20	0	0	6	31	23	7	4	1	16	32	.207	.054	.284	9.39	4.70
Burgos, Havid	L-L	6-1	188	8-6-94	1	2	2.30	17	0	0	7	27	23	9	7	2	9	35	—	—	—	11.52	2.96
Cadette, Luis	L-L	6-3	175	8-26-95	1	4	6.94	11	0	0	0	23	27	28	18	0	25	20	—	—	—	7.71	9.64
Campusano, Arcadio	R-R	6-6	206	12-21-97	3	0	4.19	11	0	0	2	34	29	18	16	0	19	30	.228	.211	.236	7.86	4.98
Castillo, Alexander	R-R	6-6	155	6-22-94	2	2	4.94	11	0	0	1	27	29	19	15	0	17	19	.269	.300	.256	6.26	5.60

Pitching	B-T	HT	WT	DOB	W	L	ERA	G	GS	CG	SV	IP	H	R	ER	HR	BB	SO	AVG	vLH	vRH	K/9	BB/9
Cruz, Willy	L-L	6-1	185	3-2-95	4	4	3.92	15	0	0	1	41	41	29	18	2	23	26	.261	.292	.256	5.66	5.01
de Jesus, Jean	L-L	6-3	215	7-8-95	1	0	2.79	4	0	0	1	10	11	11	3	1	9	4	.289	.000	.344	3.72	8.38
Diaz, Anderson	L-L	6-2	190	12-19-93	1	1	9.78	12	0	0	0	23	27	31	25	1	24	24	.287	.286	.288	9.39	9.39
Diaz, Carlos	L-L	6-2	170	5-24-95	5	2	2.79	14	14	0	0	68	66	33	21	3	19	69	—	—	—	9.18	2.53
Espinal, Carlos	R-R	5-11	175	10-21-96	2	2	2.22	15	15	0	0	69	59	31	17	1	10	59	.232	.232	.232	7.70	1.30
Figueredo, Alexander	L-L	6-1	175	7-3-96	5	0	1.89	12	11	0	0	57	55	24	12	0	22	52	.257	.244	.260	8.21	3.47
Garcia, Jairo	R-R	5-11	180	1-25-95	3	2	3.98	14	11	0	0	52	49	29	23	4	21	56	.241	.227	.248	9.69	3.63
Giron, Gabriel	R-R	6-0	172	9-20-93	4	1	1.40	15	10	0	1	71	42	19	11	3	21	46	.169	.173	.167	5.86	2.67
Lara, Rafael	R-R	5-10	166	6-10-95	0	3	4.63	14	13	0	0	58	52	36	30	0	27	53	.239	.183	.259	8.18	4.17
McCoy, Corby	L-L	6-3	180	10-5-95	0	0	13.50	7	0	0	0	8	11	15	12	1	10	8	.314	.125	.370	9.00	11.25
Mendez, Bringnel	R-R	6-0	231	1-31-94	3	2	2.57	16	0	0	1	42	50	24	12	1	18	31	.299	.347	.280	6.64	3.86
Moreno, Heiner	L-L	6-0	181	7-24-98	1	0	15.75	4	0	0	0	4	3	10	7	0	8	6	.188	.000	.231	13.50	18.00
Naranjo, Edintson	L-L	5-11	170	11-6-96	0	0	9.00	1	0	0	0	1	1	1	1	0	1	1	.250	.000	.500	9.00	0.00
Padilla, Isaac	R-R	6-5	210	6-14-96	4	0	2.56	10	2	0	1	32	26	9	9	0	12	31	—	—	—	8.81	3.41
Padilla, Jonathan	R-R	5-10	175	3-30-93	3	0	1.64	4	4	0	0	22	14	6	4	1	0	25	.175	.050	.217	10.23	0.00
Peluso, Eduardo	L-L	6-0	175	8-29-98	1	0	11.05	14	0	0	0	15	23	19	18	0	20	16	.343	.429	.321	9.82	12.27
Perez, Freicer	R-R	6-8	190	3-14-96	7	3	3.23	15	15	0	0	70	66	35	25	4	17	68	.244	.260	.238	8.78	2.20
Pujols, Jose	R-R	6-6	183	11-19-92	0	1	11.42	5	0	0	0	9	14	11	11	1	6	8	.400	.556	.346	8.31	6.23
Ramirez, Arikson	R-R	6-3	170	8-11-95	0	0	—	1	0	0	0	1	0	0	0	1	0	1	.000				
Ramirez, Leyfer	R-R	6-0	160	10-19-96	2	1	3.71	19	0	0	3	27	28	18	11	0	14	20	—	—	—	6.75	4.73
Rodriguez, Edison	R-R	6-1	180	7-6-92	1	1	5.16	16	0	0	1	23	17	19	13	1	21	20	.213	.227	.207	7.94	8.34
Rodriguez, Jean	R-R	6-2	175	12-21-96	4	0	2.79	20	0	0	1	19	13	7	6	0	19	24	.191	.200	.188	11.17	8.84
Rosario, Alexander	R-R	6-3	185	1-19-95	5	5	6.34	12	3	0	0	38	48	35	27	3	18	22	.306	.278	.320	5.17	4.23
Rosario, Luis	R-R	6-1	185	12-11-94	1	2	8.46	4	4	0	0	22	29	21	21	6	8	24	.309	.400	.284	9.67	3.22
Rosario, Miguel	R-R	6-1	175	10-5-94	2	1	7.11	13	0	0	1	13	16	17	10	0	14	8	.296	.222	.333	5.68	9.95
Sanchez, Amauris	R-R	6-3	198	3-12-94	2	1	11.00	8	0	0	1	18	28	27	22	1	13	12	.354	.435	.321	6.00	6.50
Santana, Anthoniris	R-R	5-11	175	1-11-95	1	1	6.00	7	1	0	1	18	22	13	12	0	4	29	.293	.393	.234	14.50	2.00
Santana, Carlos	R-R	5-9	180	7-15-94	0	0	3.09	6	0	0	0	12	12	7	4	0	4	9	—	—	—	6.94	3.09
Solano, Jose	R-R	6-0	180	1-21-94	3	0	2.19	8	0	0	1	12	13	6	3	0	2	13	.260	.400	.200	9.49	1.46
Tavares, Orby	L-L	6-4	262	9-16-94	1	1	3.13	15	2	0	2	46	43	20	16	0	15	54	.239	.107	.263	10.57	2.93
Thomas, Luigence	R-R	6-3	160	10-12-94	2	2	0.64	17	0	0	8	28	16	8	2	0	5	29	.157	.207	.137	9.21	1.59
Troya, Gilmael	R-R	6-0	178	4-4-97	3	0	1.13	5	5	0	0	24	17	6	3	0	8	28	.195	.214	.186	10.50	3.00
Vargas, Jhostin	R-R	6-0	170	4-6-98	0	2	4.76	10	5	0	0	34	36	20	18	2	17	34	.265	.184	.296	9.00	4.50
Vargas, Yostty	R-R	6-2	200	10-1-94	1	1	2.55	11	2	0	2	35	28	14	10	2	5	25	—	—	—	6.37	1.27
Yajure, Miguel	R-R	6-1	175	5-1-98	0	2	1.42	14	14	0	0	57	54	20	9	1	20	36	.258	.254	.260	5.68	3.16

Fielding

Catcher	PCT	G	PO	A	E	DP	PB
Cedeno	1.000	6	21	3	0	1	0
Flames	.932	9	57	12	5	0	5
Gallardo	.979	28	214	23	5	1	15
Lopez	.978	40	303	60	8	1	11
Mateo	.981	31	210	53	5	2	10
Navas	.933	6	37	5	3	0	1
Nieto	.985	12	58	9	1	0	7
Rodriguez	.964	14	93	14	4	1	14
Suarez	1.000	3	6	1	0	0	0
Vergel	1.000	20	121	27	0	0	7

First Base	PCT	G	PO	A	E	DP
Alvarez	.992	54	450	21	4	33
Blanco	1.000	1	10	0	0	1
Cedeno	.989	20	173	13	2	10
Flames	.991	41	396	23	4	23
Gonzalez	.978	19	173	7	4	14
Mateo	.959	7	66	5	3	4
Nieto	1.000	1	12	1	0	0
Polonia	1.000	2	1	0	0	0
Tatis	—	1	0	0	0	0
Vergel	1.000	7	56	2	0	5

Second Base	PCT	G	PO	A	E	DP
Barrios	.967	7	11	18	1	5
Corredera	.980	19	35	65	2	12
Diaz	.000	1	0	0	1	0
Ferreira	.879	42	90	107	27	16
Mateo	1.000	2	6	10	0	3
Medina	.953	16	27	34	3	9
Miranda	.948	39	82	100	10	19
Mota	.918	13	22	23	4	4
Perez	.968	5	9	21	1	1
Polonia	.915	7	22	21	4	4
Rodriguez	1.000	4	7	10	0	2

Third Base	PCT	G	PO	A	E	DP
Barrios	1.000	1	2	0	0	0
Blanco	1.000	1	1	0	0	0
Corredera	.892	25	26	48	9	4
Garabito	.756	14	5	23	9	4
Gomez	.901	47	39	70	12	6
Mateo	1.000	1	2	3	0	1
Mateo	1.000	1	1	2	0	0
Medina	1.000	3	2	5	0	1
Mota	1.000	1	0	3	0	0
Polonia	.857	32	23	67	15	6
Rodriguez	.877	26	14	57	10	1

Shortstop	PCT	G	PO	A	E	DP
Castillo	.921	53	81	164	21	23
Corredera	1.000	2	3	6	0	1
Ferreira	.891	19	28	54	10	11
Garcia	1.000	2	2	2	0	0
Mateo	.919	45	71	146	19	18
Miranda	1.000	1	3	4	0	2
Mota	.920	5	4	19	2	2
Perez	.967	12	20	38	2	3
Polonia	1.000	1	1	0	0	0
Rodriguez	.809	5	13	23	9	5

Outfield	PCT	G	PO	A	E	DP
Amundaray	.929	11	13	0	1	0
Arias	.941	26	30	2	2	1
Blanco	.927	27	31	1	3	0
Cabrera	.959	50	66	4	3	0
Cuevas	.971	47	66	2	2	0
De Leon	.965	49	79	4	3	1
Delgado	1.000	27	34	5	0	0
Diaz	1.000	8	17	2	0	0
Diaz	1.000	23	21	1	0	0
Emery	.968	52	86	6	3	1
Encarnacion	1.000	4	5	0	0	0
Florial	.973	47	105	3	3	1
Medina	—	1	0	0	0	0
Mendez	.958	42	67	1	3	0
Moreno	1.000	6	7	0	0	0
Olivares	.933	27	41	1	3	0
Tatis	1.000	15	17	0	0	0
Unda	1.000	7	3	0	0	0

NEW YORK YANKEES

Oakland Athletics

SEASON IN A SENTENCE: Retooling after another string of early playoff exits, the Athletics endured their worst season of the Billy Beane era, winning just 68 games and finishing with the worst record in the American League.

HIGH POINT: One of the A's few good stretches came June 19-25, when they won back-to-back series against the Angels and Rangers, sweeping the Rangers in Arlington behind strong outings from Kendall Graveman and Sonny Gray. The A's got at least one feel-good moment at the end of the season, when Barry Zito was called up and got to start a game against his old running mate Tim Hudson in front of a packed O.co Coliseum.

LOW POINT: There were plenty. The A's muddled through first couple weeks, going 8-8 before enduring a 6-22 stretch from April 23 to May 22. They never threatened .500 again. Oakland lurched across the finish line with an 8-19 record in September amid a rash of injuries—particularly to the pitching staff—and rumors of a fractured clubhouse culture.

NOTABLE ROOKIES: Speedy center fielder Billy Burns proved he could handle an everyday role after coming up in May, providing a spark at the top of Oakland's order with his 26 steals and .294 average. Mark Canha, plucked out of the 2014 Rule 5 draft, swatted 16 home runs while splitting time at first base and the outfield. Two of Oakland's offseason trade acquisitions, Graveman and Chris Bassitt, took regular turns in the rotation. Graveman was one of Oakland's better pitchers for a stretch, going 3-2, 1.93 in June.

KEY TRANSACTIONS: The A's made seven trades in the offseason and five more once the team fell out of contention. Easily the most scrutinized was the deal that sent Josh Donaldson to the Blue Jays for four players, headlined by Brett Lawrie. Donaldson turned in an MVP-caliber season for Toronto while Lawrie hit just .260. Other veterans exiting stage left included Brandon Moss, Jeff Samardzija and Derek Norris.

DOWN ON THE FARM: Double-A Midland captured its second straight Texas League title. TL player of the year Chad Pinder led the way, topping the league in RBIs and finishing second in the batting race, while the RockHounds' lineup also featured prospects Renato Nunez (18 homers), Matt Olson (17 homers) and Ryon Healy (.302 average). High Class A Stockton also reached the California League playoffs.

OPENING DAY PAYROLL: $86,086,667 (27th)

PLAYERS OF THE YEAR

MAJOR LEAGUE	MINOR LEAGUE
Sonny Gray rhp	**Chad Pinder** ss
14-7, 2.73	(Double-A)
208 IP, 166 H, 169 K	.317/.361/.486,
5.8 WAR	Texas League MVP

ORGANIZATION LEADERS

BATTING		*Minimum 250 AB
MAJORS		
* AVG	Billy Burns	.294
* OPS	Stephen Vogt	.784
HR	Josh Reddick	20
RBI	Josh Reddick	77
MINORS		
* AVG	Chad Pinder, Midland	.317
* OBP	Colin Walsh, Midland	.447
* SLG	Jason Pridie, Nashville	.515
R	Brett Vertigan, Beloit, Stockton	98
H	Joey Wendle, Nashville	167
TB	Joey Wendle, Nashville	255
2B	Joey Wendle, Nashville	42
3B	B.J. Boyd, Stockton	8
	Jaycob Brugman, Midland	8
	Joey Wendle, Nashville	8
HR	Matt Chapman, Stockton	23
RBI	Jason Pridie, Nashville	89
BB	Colin Walsh, Midland	124
SO	Justin Higley, Stockton, Beloit	140
	Tyler Marincov, Stockton	140
SB	Brett Vertigan, Beloit, Stockton	30

PITCHING		#Minimum 75 IP
MAJORS		
W	Sonny Gray	14
# ERA	Sonny Gray	2.73
SO	Sonny Gray	169
SV	Tyler Clippard	17
MINORS		
W	Brett Graves, Beloit	12
L	3 players	13
# ERA	Dillon Overton, Stockton, Midland	3.43
GS	Brett Graves, Beloit	28
	Chris Jensen, Midland	28
SV	Brendan McCurry, Stockton, Midland	27
IP	Zach Neal, Midland, Nashville	168
BB	Nate Long, Midland, Nashville	67
SO	Nate Long, Midland, Nashville	116
AVG	Barry Zito, Nashville	.234

2015 PERFORMANCE

General Manager: Billy Beane/David Forst. **Farm Director:** Keith Lieppman. **Scouting Director:** Eric Kubota.

Class	Team	League	W	L	PCT	Finish	Manager
Majors	Oakland Athletics	American	68	94	.420	15th (15)	Bob Melvin
Triple-A	Nashville Sounds	Pacific Coast	66	78	.458	12th (16)	Steve Scarsone
Double-A	Midland RockHounds	Texas	83	57	.593	2nd (8)	Ryan Christenson
High A	Stockton Ports	California	74	66	.529	5th (10)	Rick Magnante
Low A	Beloit Snappers	Midwest	55	84	.396	14th (16)	Fran Riordan
Short season	Vermont Lake Monsters	New York-Penn	33	42	.440	11th (14)	Aaron Nieckula
Rookie	Athletics	Arizona	24	32	.429	11th (14)	Ruben Escalera
Overall 2015 Minor League Record			335	359	.483	21st (30)	

ORGANIZATION STATISTICS

OAKLAND ATHLETICS

AMERICAN LEAGUE

Batting	B-T	HT	WT	DOB	AVG	vLH	vRH	G	AB	R	H	2B	3B	HR	RBI	BB	HBP	SH	SF	SO	SB	CS	SLG	OBP
Anderson, Bryan	L-R	6-1	200	12-16-86	.400	.250	1.000	4	5	0	2	0	0	0	1	1	0	1	1	1	0	0	.400	.429
Blair, Carson	R-R	6-2	215	10-18-89	.129	.091	.150	11	31	3	4	0	0	1	3	4	0	0	0	18	0	0	.226	.229
Burns, Billy	B-R	5-9	180	8-30-89	.294	.315	.285	125	520	70	153	18	9	5	42	26	6	1	2	81	26	8	.392	.334
Butler, Billy	R-R	6-1	240	4-18-86	.251	.200	.269	151	538	63	135	28	1	15	65	52	7	0	4	101	0	0	.390	.323
Canha, Mark	R-R	6-1	200	2-15-89	.254	.221	.271	124	441	61	112	22	3	16	70	33	8	0	3	96	7	2	.426	.315
Crisp, Coco	B-R	5-10	185	11-1-79	.175	.200	.163	44	126	11	22	6	0	6	13	0	0	0	25	2	0	.222	.252
Davis, Ike	L-L	6-4	220	3-22-87	.229	.211	.231	72	214	19	49	17	0	3	20	23	0	0	2	44	0	0	.350	.301
Fuld, Sam	L-L	5-10	175	11-20-81	.197	.106	.214	120	290	34	57	16	3	2	22	30	2	2	1	55	9	3	.293	.276
Gentry, Craig	R-R	6-2	190	11-29-83	.120	.143	.091	26	50	6	6	0	2	0	3	4	1	0	1	15	1	1	.200	.196
Ladendorf, Tyler	R-R	6-0	190	3-7-88	.235	.222	.250	9	17	3	4	0	0	0	1	0	0	2	1	0	0	0	.353	.278
Lawrie, Brett	R-R	6-0	210	1-18-90	.260	.293	.247	149	562	64	146	29	3	16	60	28	5	3	4	144	5	2	.407	.299
Muncy, Max	L-R	6-0	205	8-25-90	.206	.000	.208	45	102	14	21	8	1	3	9	9	0	0	1	31	0	0	.392	.268
Parrino, Andy	B-R	6-0	190	10-31-85	.000	.000	.000	17	6	1	0	0	0	0	0	2	0	0	0	5	0	0	.000	.250
Phegley, Josh	R-R	5-10	225	2-12-88	.249	.276	.220	73	225	27	56	16	1	9	34	14	3	0	1	51	0	0	.449	.300
Pridie, Jason	L-R	6-1	205	10-9-83	.000	—	.000	6	9	0	0	0	0	0	0	1	0	0	0	4	0	0	.000	.100
Reddick, Josh	L-R	6-2	180	2-19-87	.272	.222	.289	149	526	67	143	25	4	20	77	49	0	1	2	65	10	2	.449	.333
Ross, Cody	R-L	5-11	195	12-23-80	.091	.125	.000	9	22	3	2	0	0	0	3	3	0	0	0	6	0	0	.091	.200
Semien, Marcus	R-R	6-1	195	9-17-90	.257	.329	.230	155	556	65	143	23	7	15	45	42	1	1	3	132	11	5	.405	.310
Smolinski, Jake	R-R	5-11	205	2-9-89	.226	.320	.143	41	106	12	24	6	2	5	20	8	2	0	2	19	0	1	.462	.288
2-team total (35 Texas)					.193	—	—	76	166	24	32	7	2	6	26	19	3	0	4	39	1	1	.367	.281
Sogard, Eric	L-R	5-10	190	5-22-86	.247	.210	.255	120	372	40	92	12	3	1	37	23	2	3	1	50	6	1	.304	.294
Valencia, Danny	R-R	6-2	220	9-19-84	.284	.273	.289	47	183	33	52	10	1	11	37	20	1	0	1	40	0	1	.530	.356
2-team total (58 Toronto)					.290	—	—	105	345	59	100	23	1	18	66	29	1	1	2	80	2	2	.519	.345
Vogt, Stephen	L-R	6-0	215	11-1-84	.261	.239	.268	136	445	58	116	21	3	18	71	56	2	0	8	97	0	2	.443	.341
Zobrist, Ben	B-R	6-3	210	5-26-81	.268	.321	.242	67	235	39	63	20	2	6	33	33	0	0	3	26	1	1	.447	.354
2-team total (59 Kansas City)					.276	—	—	126	467	76	129	36	3	13	56	62	1	0	5	56	3	4	.450	.359

Pitching	B-T	HT	WT	DOB	W	L	ERA	G	GS	CG	SV	IP	H	R	ER	HR	BB	SO	AVG	vLH	vRH	K/9	BB/9
Abad, Fernando	L-L	6-1	220	12-17-85	2	2	4.15	62	0	0	0	48	45	23	22	11	19	45	.251	.277	.218	8.50	3.59
Alvarez, R.J.	R-R	6-2	215	6-8-91	0	0	9.90	21	0	0	0	20	27	23	22	7	13	23	.318	.450	.200	10.35	5.85
Bassitt, Chris	R-R	6-5	210	2-22-89	1	8	3.56	18	13	0	0	86	78	36	34	5	30	64	.244	.217	.279	6.70	3.14
Brooks, Aaron	R-R	6-4	220	4-27-90	3	4	6.71	11	9	0	0	51	67	38	38	9	14	35	.321	.299	.339	6.18	2.47
2-team total (2 Kansas City)					3	4	6.67	13	9	0	0	55	73	41	41	9	14	38	—	—	—	6.18	2.28
Castro, Angel	R-R	5-11	200	11-14-82	0	1	1.25	5	0	0	0	4	8	1	1	1	3	4	.444	.300	.625	9.00	6.75
Chavez, Jesse	R-R	6-2	160	8-21-83	7	15	4.18	30	26	0	1	157	164	78	73	18	48	136	.268	.291	.240	7.80	2.75
Clippard, Tyler	R-R	6-3	200	2-14-85	1	3	2.79	37	0	0	17	39	25	12	12	3	21	38	.175	.100	.247	8.84	4.89
Cook, Ryan	R-R	6-2	215	6-30-87	0	2	10.38	4	0	0	0	4	7	5	5	0	3	3	.350	.500	.286	6.23	6.23
2-team total (5 Boston)					0	2	18.69	9	0	0	0	9	20	19	18	4	7	6	—	—	—	6.23	7.27
Coulombe, Daniel	L-L	5-10	190	10-26-89	0	0	3.52	9	0	0	0	8	8	3	3	0	3	4	.276	.267	.286	4.70	3.52
Doolittle, Sean	L-L	6-3	210	9-26-86	1	0	3.95	12	0	0	4	14	12	6	6	1	5	15	.235	.273	.225	9.88	3.29
Doubront, Felix	L-L	6-2	225	10-23-87	2	2	5.81	11	8	0	1	53	55	35	34	9	21	43	.278	.170	.311	7.35	3.59
2-team total (5 Toronto)					3	3	5.50	16	12	0	1	75	87	50	46	10	26	56	—	—	—	6.69	3.11
Dull, Ryan	R-R	5-10	175	10-2-89	1	2	4.24	13	0	0	1	17	12	8	8	4	6	16	.203	.167	.229	8.47	3.18
Graveman, Kendall	R-R	6-2	185	12-21-90	6	9	4.05	21	21	1	0	116	126	57	52	15	38	77	.275	.278	.278	5.99	2.96
Gray, Sonny	R-R	5-11	195	11-7-89	14	7	2.73	31	31	3	0	208	166	71	63	17	59	169	.217	.208	.226	7.31	2.55
Hahn, Jesse	R-R	6-5	190	7-30-89	6	6	3.35	16	16	1	0	97	88	46	36	5	25	64	.238	.286	.186	5.96	2.33
Kazmir, Scott	L-L	6-0	185	1-24-84	5	5	2.38	18	18	0	0	110	84	35	29	7	35	101	.213	.221	.210	8.29	2.87
2-team total (13 Houston)					7	11	3.10	31	31	0	0	183	162	77	63	20	59	155	—	—	—	7.62	2.90
Leon, Arnold	R-R	6-1	205	9-6-88	0	2	4.39	19	0	0	0	27	30	14	13	3	9	19	.291	.342	.262	6.41	3.04
Martin, Cody	R-R	6-3	230	9-4-89	0	2	14.00	4	2	0	0	9	16	14	14	4	5	3	.381	.350	.409	3.00	5.00
Mills, Brad	L-L	6-0	190	3-5-85	0	0	5.40	1	1	0	0	5	7	3	3	1	1	1	.333	.400	.313	1.80	1.80
Mujica, Edward	R-R	6-3	220	5-10-84	2	4	4.81	38	0	0	1	34	37	21	18	7	4	22	.280	.333	.253	5.88	1.07
2-team total (11 Boston)					3	5	4.75	49	0	0	1	47	52	28	25	10	7	30	—	—	—	5.70	1.33
Nolin, Sean	L-L	6-4	230	12-26-89	1	2	5.28	6	6	0	0	29	35	19	17	4	12	15	.302	.333	.286	4.66	3.72
O'Flaherty, Eric	L-L	6-2	220	2-5-85	1	2	5.91	25	0	0	0	21	29	17	14	1	13	15	.312	.186	.420	6.33	5.48

Pitching

Pitching	B-T	HT	WT	DOB	W	L	ERA	G	GS	CG	SV	IP	H	R	ER	HR	BB	SO	AVG	vLH	vRH	K/9	BB/9
Otero, Dan	R-R	6-3	215	2-19-85	2	4	6.75	41	0	0	0	47	64	35	35	7	6	28	.333	.328	.336	5.40	1.16
Pomeranz, Drew	R-L	6-5	240	11-22-88	5	6	3.66	53	9	0	3	86	71	44	35	8	31	82	.226	.152	.260	8.58	3.24
Rodriguez, Fernando	R-R	6-3	235	6-18-84	4	2	3.84	56	0	0	0	59	43	27	25	4	24	65	.200	.174	.217	9.97	3.68
Scribner, Evan	R-R	6-3	190	7-19-85	2	2	4.35	54	0	0	0	60	58	31	29	14	4	64	.251	.227	.269	9.60	0.60
Smith, Chad	R-R	6-3	215	10-2-89	0	0	33.75	2	0	0	0	1	5	5	5	0	3	2	.556	.714	.000	13.50	20.25
Venditte, Pat	R-B	6-1	180	6-30-85	2	2	4.40	26	0	0	0	29	22	14	14	3	12	23	.210	.106	.293	7.22	3.77
Zito, Barry	L-L	6-2	205	5-13-78	0	0	10.29	3	2	0	0	7	12	8	8	4	6	2	.387	.400	.385	2.57	7.71

Fielding

Catcher	PCT	G	PO	A	E	DP	PB
Anderson	.923	3	10	2	1	0	0
Blair	.935	11	57	1	4	0	0
Phegley	.996	68	454	53	2	3	5
Vogt	.996	100	658	41	3	4	9

First Base	PCT	G	PO	A	E	DP
Butler	1.000	7	49	7	0	4
Canha	.993	75	491	47	4	58
Davis	.993	65	492	41	4	53
Muncy	.987	23	137	10	2	9
Vogt	.990	25	182	14	2	18

Second Base	PCT	G	PO	A	E	DP
Ladendorf	1.000	2	2	5	0	1
Lawrie	.972	42	92	114	6	28

Sogard	.989	96	168	268	5	56
Zobrist	1.000	34	61	103	0	32

Third Base	PCT	G	PO	A	E	DP
Canha	1.000	1	0	2	0	0
Ladendorf	1.000	1	1	0	0	0
Lawrie	.937	109	69	197	18	15
Muncy	.846	16	5	17	4	0
Parrino	1.000	6	0	1	0	1
Sogard	1.000	1	0	2	0	0
Valencia	.976	45	30	93	3	9

Shortstop	PCT	G	PO	A	E	DP
Ladendorf	1.000	1	1	0	0	0
Parrino	1.000	10	2	4	0	1
Semien	.947	152	214	407	35	99

	PCT	G	PO	A	E	DP
Sogard	.983	17	22	37	1	9

Outfield	PCT	G	PO	A	E	DP
Burns	.989	125	280	2	3	2
Canha	.982	61	107	0	2	0
Crisp	1.000	37	51	1	0	0
Fuld	.981	108	191	11	4	3
Gentry	.949	25	35	2	2	1
Ladendorf	1.000	5	6	0	0	0
Pridie	1.000	4	1	0	0	0
Reddick	.981	143	258	6	5	1
Ross	.923	8	12	0	1	0
Smolinski	1.000	35	48	5	0	1
Zobrist	.929	29	39	0	3	0

NASHVILLE SOUNDS

TRIPLE-A

PACIFIC COAST LEAGUE

Batting	B-T	HT	WT	DOB	AVG	vLH	vRH	G	AB	R	H	2B	3B	HR	RBI	BB	HBP	SH	SF	SO	SB	CS	SLG	OBP
Aliotti, Anthony	L-L	6-0	205	7-16-87	.258	.187	.298	88	295	21	76	12	0	1	33	27	1	2	2	81	0	0	.308	.320
Anderson, Bryan	L-R	6-1	200	12-16-86	.202	.150	.216	82	292	31	59	16	0	3	25	27	2	0	1	93	0	0	.288	.273
Angle, Matt	L-R	5-9	185	9-10-85	.429	.500	.400	2	7	1	3	0	0	0	0	2	0	0	2	1	0	.429	.556
Blair, Carson	R-R	6-2	215	10-18-89	.221	.205	.232	33	113	9	25	3	0	3	8	9	1	1	2	34	0	0	.327	.280
Burns, Billy	B-R	5-9	180	8-30-89	.308	.231	.338	22	91	18	28	2	3	0	3	9	0	1	0	17	5	2	.396	.370
Carlin, Luke	B-R	5-10	190	12-20-80	.146	.164	.125	34	103	6	15	7	0	0	11	23	3	1	1	24	0	1	.214	.315
2-team total (21 Iowa)					.158	—	—	55	158	14	25	10	1	0	13	32	5	2	1	35	1	1	.234	.316
Carrithers, Alden	L-R	5-10	170	11-14-84	.286	.184	.333	46	154	21	44	4	1	1	8	22	1	2	0	17	5	1	.344	.379
Carson, Matt	R-R	6-2	200	7-1-81	.209	.217	.203	33	110	19	23	5	0	3	13	10	4	1	1	22	3	1	.336	.296
2-team total (24 Oklahoma City)					.199	—	—	57	166	23	33	9	0	3	22	18	5	2	3	37	4	1	.307	.292
Davis, Ike	L-L	6-4	220	3-22-87	.238	.214	.286	5	21	2	5	1	0	0	5	0	0	0	0	5	0	0	.286	.238
Forsythe, Blake	R-R	6-2	220	7-31-89	.267	.308	.000	5	15	0	4	1	0	0	4	1	0	0	0	4	0	0	.333	.313
Freiman, Nate	R-R	6-8	250	12-31-86	.220	.147	.263	79	277	20	61	14	1	4	31	21	3	0	4	51	1	0	.321	.279
Gentry, Craig	R-R	6-2	190	11-29-83	.256	.252	.259	101	398	64	102	13	0	5	25	36	3	4	5	76	25	7	.327	.319
Harris, James	R-R	6-1	180	8-7-93	.154	.167	.143	4	13	2	2	0	0	0	1	3	0	0	1	6	3	0	.154	.294
Hassan, Alex	R-R	6-3	220	4-1-88	.071	.333	.000	4	14	0	1	0	0	0	1	0	0	0	0	3	0	0	.071	.133
2-team total (16 Round Rock)					.230	—	—	20	74	8	17	5	0	0	8	8	0	0	1	17	0	0	.297	.305
Ladendorf, Tyler	R-R	6-0	190	3-7-88	.265	.278	.262	20	83	3	22	2	1	1	8	5	1	0	1	23	0	1	.349	.311
Matthes, Kent	R-R	6-2	215	1-8-87	.233	.243	.227	57	215	23	50	19	1	2	28	17	3	1	3	44	4	0	.358	.294
Morel, Brent	R-R	6-2	230	4-21-87	.331	.279	.355	34	136	19	45	12	0	2	24	7	2	0	1	30	2	1	.463	.370
Muncy, Max	L-R	6-0	205	8-25-90	.274	.246	.286	60	212	24	58	14	1	4	35	26	1	0	4	58	0	1	.406	.350
Parrino, Andy	B-R	6-0	190	10-31-85	.272	.258	.279	80	287	32	78	9	3	5	24	30	2	1	1	81	0	2	.376	.344
Pridie, Jason	L-R	6-1	205	10-9-83	.310	.310	.310	127	478	84	148	24	7	20	89	55	2	0	5	102	20	3	.515	.380
Ravelo, Rangel	R-R	6-2	220	4-24-92	.277	.200	.310	28	101	10	28	5	1	1	18	7	1	1	2	10	0	0	.376	.324
Rickles, Nick	R-R	6-3	220	2-2-90	.143	.200	.000	2	7	1	1	1	0	0	1	0	0	0	0	1	0	0	.286	.143
Roberts, Ryan	R-R	5-11	205	9-13-80	.283	.272	.289	114	442	53	125	33	1	13	58	51	1	0	5	63	0	5	.450	.355
Romero, Niuman	B-R	6-1	190	1-24-85	.278	.316	.250	71	234	16	65	9	1	0	16	31	2	2	3	39	2	4	.325	.363
Smolinski, Jake	R-R	5-11	205	2-9-89	.349	.417	.300	25	86	16	30	9	0	5	17	8	1	0	2	9	2	1	.628	.402
2-team total (12 Round Rock)					.374	—	—	37	131	25	49	14	0	9	31	12	2	0	2	16	2	2	.687	.429
Viciedo, Dayan	R-R	5-11	240	3-10-89	.221	.306	.182	30	113	13	25	6	2	1	8	7	3	0	1	20	0	0	.336	.282
Wendle, Joey	L-R	6-1	190	4-26-90	.289	.284	.293	137	577	80	167	42	8	10	57	22	9	5	5	114	12	2	.442	.323
Zobrist, Ben	B-R	6-3	210	5-26-81	.300	.000	.429	3	10	3	3	0	0	0	2	2	0	0	1	3	0	0	.300	.385

Pitching	B-T	HT	WT	DOB	W	L	ERA	G	GS	CG	SV	IP	H	R	ER	HR	BB	SO	AVG	vLH	vRH	K/9	BB/9
Alvarez, R.J.	R-R	6-2	215	6-8-91	3	3	4.11	31	0	0	5	35	36	19	16	2	17	41	.267	.315	.235	10.54	4.37
Bassitt, Chris	R-R	6-5	210	2-22-89	2	7	3.65	13	10	1	0	69	59	30	28	1	19	70	.230	.228	.231	9.13	2.48
Bayless, Trevor	R-R	6-3	210	10-6-91	0	0	0.00	3	0	0	0	5	3	0	0	1	2	.176	.000	.250	3.38	1.69
Brasier, Ryan	R-R	6-0	205	8-26-87	0	0	0.00	2	0	0	0	2	0	0	0	0	0	3	.000	.000	.000	13.50	0.00
Brooks, Aaron	R-R	6-4	220	4-27-90	1	0	2.25	2	2	0	0	12	9	3	3	1	1	11	.209	.188	.222	8.25	0.00
2-team total (18 Omaha)					7	5	3.56	20	19	1	0	119	127	49	47	10	21	103	—	—	—	7.81	1.59
Castro, Angel	R-R	5-11	200	11-14-82	2	1	3.13	38	2	0	8	60	54	23	21	6	19	45	.242	.258	.231	6.71	2.83
Coke, Phil	L-L	6-1	210	7-19-82	0	3	9.82	10	0	0	0	15	24	16	16	1	7	14	.364	.292	.405	8.59	4.30
Cook, Ryan	R-R	6-2	215	6-30-87	4	1	4.05	30	0	0	8	33	32	16	15	3	15	26	.258	.286	.240	7.02	3.78
De La Rosa, Eury	L-L	5-9	165	2-24-90	0	0	0.00	7	0	0	0	6	3	0	0	0	5	4	.000	.000	.000	6.00	7.50
3-team total (17 El Paso, 6 Oklahoma City)					2	1	5.17	30	0	0	1	31	44	24	18	5	19	25	—	—	—	7.18	5.46
Doolittle, Sean	L-L	6-3	210	9-26-86	0	3	3.00	6	0	0	0	6	3	2	2	1	0	13	.143	.125	.154	19.50	0.00
Dull, Ryan	R-R	5-10	175	10-2-89	1	0	1.13	12	0	0	0	16	11	2	2	1	3	21	.172	.278	.125	11.81	1.69

Pitching	B-T	HT	WT	DOB	W	L	ERA	G	GS	CG	SV	IP	H	R	ER	HR	BB	SO	AVG	vLH	vRH	K/9	BB/9
Frankoff, Seth	R-R	6-5	210	8-27-88	0	1	5.91	9	0	0	0	11	6	7	7	2	9	7	.171	.188	.158	5.91	7.59
Frazier, Parker	R-R	6-5	175	11-11-88	0	1	6.23	1	1	0	0	4	12	4	3	0	0	2	.571	.455	.700	4.15	0.00
2-team total (3 Reno)					1	1	6.98	4	4	0	0	19	38	16	15	0	6	10	—	—	—	4.66	2.79
Fuller, Jim	L-L	5-10	190	6-1-87	2	1	2.78	27	0	0	1	32	30	13	10	1	13	34	.246	.300	.220	9.46	3.62
Graveman, Kendall	R-R	6-2	185	12-21-90	2	1	1.85	4	0	0	0	24	20	9	5	1	9	14	.213	.118	.267	5.18	3.33
Griffin, A.J.	R-R	6-5	230	1-28-88	0	1	7.36	2	2	0	0	7	11	7	6	5	0	7	.333	.538	.200	8.59	0.00
Hall, Kris	R-R	6-3	215	6-8-91	0	0	13.50	1	1	0	0	2	2	3	3	1	4	3	.286	.500	.200	13.50	18.00
Huntzinger, Brock	R-R	6-3	200	7-2-88	4	4	4.63	43	0	0	1	56	53	32	29	9	36	54	.252	.231	.265	8.63	5.75
Kurcz, Aaron	R-R	6-0	175	8-8-90	2	1	4.15	18	0	0	0	26	29	13	12	2	15	31	.274	.273	.274	10.73	5.19
Leon, Arnold	R-R	6-1	205	9-6-88	2	5	2.95	20	6	0	1	58	52	21	19	7	19	55	.236	.245	.227	8.53	2.95
Long, Nathan	R-R	6-2	210	2-9-86	3	5	5.72	13	13	0	0	68	76	46	43	7	36	49	.284	.298	.270	6.52	4.79
Martin, Cody	R-R	6-3	230	9-4-89	4	4	5.10	11	11	0	0	60	59	36	34	6	31	58	.257	.266	.250	8.70	4.65
Mills, Brad	L-L	6-0	190	3-5-85	5	12	4.52	24	24	0	0	137	134	74	69	12	55	95	.262	.323	.241	6.23	3.60
Neal, Zach	R-R	6-3	220	11-9-88	7	10	4.18	21	20	2	0	131	151	71	61	10	20	78	.291	.256	.313	5.35	1.37
Nolin, Sean	L-L	6-4	230	12-26-89	2	2	2.66	14	12	0	0	47	40	15	14	5	19	38	.230	.167	.250	7.23	3.61
O'Flaherty, Eric	L-L	6-2	220	2-5-85	0	0	0.00	1	0	0	0	1	2	0	0	0	0	0	.400	.000	.500	0.00	0.00
Otero, Dan	R-R	6-3	215	2-19-85	2	0	1.95	15	2	0	0	28	23	7	6	1	4	19	.223	.325	.159	6.18	1.30
Parker, Jarrod	R-R	6-1	195	11-24-88	1	0	6.30	2	2	0	0	10	14	8	7	2	2	7	.318	.313	.321	6.30	1.80
Paterson, Joe	R-L	6-0	190	5-19-86	1	0	9.00	2	0	0	0	2	4	3	2	0	2	1	.444	.667	.333	4.50	9.00
2-team total (12 Omaha)					2	2	6.14	14	0	0	2	15	18	11	10	0	8	13	—	—	—	7.98	4.91
Peters, Tanner	R-R	6-0	175	8-6-90	0	0	4.91	2	0	0	0	4	6	3	2	0	2	5	.353	.400	.333	12.27	4.91
Rodriguez, Fernando	R-R	6-3	235	6-18-84	0	0	2.81	10	1	0	0	16	8	5	5	2	6	18	.143	.161	.120	10.13	3.38
Sanchez, Jake	R-R	6-1	205	8-19-89	1	1	8.00	2	2	0	0	9	13	8	8	0	4	6	.351	.615	.208	6.00	4.00
Smith, Chad	R-R	6-3	215	10-2-89	1	1	2.31	8	0	0	2	12	13	3	3	0	5	7	.277	.360	.182	5.40	3.86
2-team total (6 Salt Lake)					1	1	5.40	14	0	0	2	20	31	12	12	1	7	13	—	—	—	5.85	3.15
Thompson, Taylor	R-R	6-5	225	6-18-87	1	0	7.62	11	0	0	0	13	15	15	11	1	7	11	.278	.357	.250	7.62	4.85
Veliz, Victor	L-L	5-11	170	10-6-93	1	0	0.00	2	0	0	0	4	2	0	0	0	1	3	.133	.250	.091	6.23	2.08
Venditte, Pat	R-R	6-1	180	6-30-85	1	0	1.55	23	1	0	0	41	27	8	7	2	15	40	.186	.130	.220	8.85	3.32
Verdugo, Ryan	L-L	6-0	200	4-10-87	2	3	3.46	19	4	0	0	42	35	19	16	3	18	35	.230	.229	.231	7.56	3.89
2-team total (23 Salt Lake)					4	5	4.31	42	4	0	0	71	60	38	34	4	34	68	—	—	—	8.62	4.31
Whelan, Kevin	R-R	5-11	205	1-8-84	0	1	10.13	6	0	0	0	8	14	9	9	4	6	11	.378	.375	.381	12.38	6.75
Zambrano, Jesus	R-R	5-11	170	8-23-96	1	0	4.00	2	2	0	0	9	8	4	4	1	1	6	.242	.100	.304	6.00	1.00
Zito, Barry	L-L	6-2	205	5-13-78	8	7	3.46	24	22	1	0	138	121	66	53	10	60	91	.234	.245	.228	5.93	3.91

Fielding

Catcher	PCT	G	PO	A	E	DP	PB
Anderson	.993	76	550	46	4	3	2
Blair	.984	33	229	15	4	2	3
Carlin	1.000	30	227	10	0	1	3
Forsythe	1.000	4	24	6	0	1	1
Rickles	.938	2	15	0	1	0	0

First Base	PCT	G	PO	A	E	DP
Aliotti	.996	64	502	38	2	44
Anderson	.500	1	1	0	1	0
Davis	1.000	4	31	1	0	3
Freiman	.982	34	264	14	5	30
Muncy	.990	26	189	18	2	22
Ravelo	1.000	13	114	1	0	11
Roberts	1.000	1	1	0	0	0
Viciedo	1.000	11	87	6	0	5

Second Base	PCT	G	PO	A	E	DP
Carrithers	1.000	1	0	1	0	0
Ladendorf	1.000	1	0	3	0	0
Parrino	.947	4	7	11	1	5
Roberts	1.000	3	5	7	0	2

Outfield	PCT	G	PO	A	E	DP
Wendle	.977	136	297	387	16	90
Zobrist	1.000	1	1	0	0	0

Third Base	PCT	G	PO	A	E	DP
Carrithers	.941	16	4	28	2	2
Carson	.857	4	1	5	1	0
Ladendorf	1.000	3	4	4	0	1
Morel	.905	27	18	39	6	3
Muncy	.957	32	24	65	4	7
Parrino	.500	2	1	0	1	0
Roberts	.971	49	31	102	4	6
Romero	.960	18	11	37	2	2

Shortstop	PCT	G	PO	A	E	DP
Ladendorf	.975	10	10	29	1	7
Morel	.944	5	4	13	1	5
Parrino	.967	73	92	197	10	44
Roberts	.968	18	21	40	2	9
Romero	.978	45	58	121	4	27

Outfield	PCT	G	PO	A	E	DP
Aliotti	.893	20	24	1	3	0

	PCT	G	PO	A	E	DP
Angle	1.000	1	2	0	0	0
Burns	.980	21	48	1	1	1
Carrithers	.958	16	23	0	1	0
Carson	1.000	27	60	5	0	1
Freiman	—	1	0	0	0	0
Gentry	.988	101	250	3	3	0
Harris	.875	4	7	0	1	0
Hassan	1.000	4	6	1	0	0
Ladendorf	1.000	6	10	0	0	0
Matthes	.979	50	91	3	2	0
Morel	.875	3	6	1	1	0
Parrino	1.000	1	1	0	0	0
Pridie	.993	118	273	9	2	4
Ravelo	—	1	0	0	0	0
Roberts	1.000	32	43	0	0	0
Romero	1.000	3	5	0	0	0
Smolinski	.979	25	45	2	1	1
Viciedo	1.000	5	11	0	0	0
Zobrist	.500	1	1	0	1	0

MIDLAND ROCKHOUNDS

TEXAS LEAGUE

DOUBLE-A

Batting	B-T	HT	WT	DOB	AVG	vLH	vRH	G	AB	R	H	2B	3B	HR	RBI	BB	HBP	SH	SF	SO	SB	CS	SLG	OBP
Aliotti, Anthony	L-L	6-0	205	7-16-87	.299	.267	.312	25	107	20	32	7	0	3	20	11	0	1	2	20	0	0	.449	.358
Angle, Matt	L-R	5-9	185	9-10-85	.229	.273	.212	51	157	23	36	7	1	0	10	29	2	4	1	42	14	3	.287	.354
Blair, Carson	R-R	6-2	215	10-18-89	.272	.333	.246	55	173	24	47	15	4	6	29	33	1	0	1	62	1	0	.509	.389
Brugman, Jaycob	L-L	6-0	195	1-18-92	.260	.217	.275	132	500	61	130	27	8	6	63	62	2	0	2	89	11	7	.382	.343
Crocker, Bobby	R-R	6-3	225	5-1-90	.229	.385	.136	9	35	3	8	3	0	0	2	6	0	0	0	11	3	1	.314	.341
Healy, Ryon	R-R	6-5	220	1-10-92	.302	.351	.284	124	507	63	153	31	1	10	62	30	1	4	4	82	0	1	.426	.339
Kirkland, Wade	R-R	5-11	200	4-4-89	.258	.274	.248	66	229	30	59	8	1	5	26	6	3	3	2	75	5	0	.367	.283
Maxwell, Bruce	L-R	6-2	235	12-20-90	.243	.232	.246	96	338	32	82	16	0	2	48	39	1	1	2	54	0	1	.308	.332
Nunez, Renato	R-R	6-1	200	4-4-94	.278	.340	.257	93	381	62	106	23	0	18	61	28	4	0	3	66	1	0	.480	.332
Oberacker, Chad	L-L	6-0	195	1-14-89	.294	.310	.289	101	395	69	116	27	5	5	44	42	2	6	6	74	19	4	.425	.360
Olson, Matt	L-R	6-5	230	3-29-94	.249	.219	.260	133	466	82	116	37	0	17	75	105	6	0	8	139	5	1	.438	.388
Pinder, Chad	R-R	6-2	190	3-29-92	.317	.352	.304	117	477	71	151	32	2	15	86	28	8	4	5	103	7	5	.486	.361
Pohl, Phil	R-R	5-11	215	7-22-90	.250	.000	.333	5	8	1	2	1	0	0	2	0	1	0	0	2	0	0	.375	.333
Ravelo, Rangel	R-R	6-2	220	4-24-92	.318	.241	.356	22	88	13	28	6	1	2	17	9	0	0	1	17	0	1	.477	.378

Batting	B-T	HT	WT	DOB	AVG	vLH	vRH	G	AB	R	H	2B	3B	HR	RBI	BB	HBP	SH	SF	SO	SB	CS	SLG	OBP
Rickles, Nick	R-R	6-3	220	2-2-90	.208	.258	.174	23	77	4	16	3	0	1	9	3	0	1	1	19	0	0	.286	.235
Taylor, Beau	L-R	6-0	205	2-13-90	.259	.188	.286	16	58	11	15	2	0	2	11	7	0	0	1	11	0	0	.397	.333
Walsh, Colin	B-R	6-0	200	9-26-89	.302	.308	.300	134	487	97	147	39	2	13	49	124	5	2	1	131	17	7	.470	.447
Whitaker, Josh	R-R	6-3	225	2-8-89	.256	.206	.277	89	355	58	91	26	1	12	58	27	2	2	1	85	7	3	.437	.312

Pitching	B-T	HT	WT	DOB	W	L	ERA	G	GS	CG	SV	IP	H	R	ER	HR	BB	SO	AVG	vLH	vRH	K/9	BB/9
Atherton, Tim	R-R	6-2	209	11-7-89	5	4	4.96	15	15	1	0	78	86	49	43	5	31	58	.278	.306	.253	6.69	3.58
Avila, Andres	R-R	6-0	185	6-20-90	5	1	4.10	32	0	0	0	48	54	24	22	5	14	42	.280	.307	.257	7.82	2.61
Doolittle, Ryan	R-R	6-2	200	3-25-88	4	3	3.32	40	0	0	4	57	62	27	21	5	16	46	.273	.283	.264	7.26	2.53
Dull, Ryan	R-R	5-10	175	10-2-89	3	1	0.60	35	0	0	12	45	29	3	3	1	13	52	.182	.268	.114	10.40	2.60
Duran, Omar	L-L	6-3	220	2-26-90	2	2	7.09	23	0	0	0	27	36	26	21	1	20	22	.310	.302	.317	7.43	6.75
Frankoff, Seth	R-R	6-5	210	8-27-88	0	1	3.24	38	0	0	8	50	48	21	18	5	14	50	.253	.258	.247	9.00	2.52
Frazier, Parker	R-R	6-5	175	11-11-88	4	3	3.22	11	11	0	0	67	72	28	24	4	31	32	.279	.250	.304	4.30	4.16
Fuller, Jim	L-L	5-10	190	6-11-87	1	1	9.28	5	0	0	0	11	14	12	11	2	4	6	.311	.357	.290	5.06	3.38
Hall, Kris	R-R	6-3	215	6-8-91	5	0	2.50	38	2	0	0	72	59	24	20	4	53	74	.220	.254	.185	9.25	6.63
Healy, Tucker	L-R	6-1	210	6-15-90	3	1	1.95	45	0	0	3	55	33	12	12	0	23	53	.172	.157	.184	8.62	4.07
Jensen, Chris	R-R	6-4	200	9-30-90	9	10	4.87	28	28	0	0	166	183	100	90	18	63	91	.282	.289	.276	4.92	3.41
Joseph, Jonathan	R-R	6-1	180	5-17-88	7	4	4.04	32	9	0	1	91	94	45	41	12	29	75	.269	.227	.302	7.39	2.86
Lamb, Chris	B-L	6-1	205	6-29-90	0	5	10.69	14	7	0	0	34	48	42	40	7	27	27	.336	.254	.393	7.22	7.22
Long, Nathan	R-R	6-2	210	2-9-86	5	4	3.13	15	12	1	0	83	70	35	29	7	31	67	.228	.248	.224	7.34	3.35
Manaea, Sean	L-L	6-5	235	2-1-92	6	0	1.90	7	7	0	0	43	34	11	9	3	15	51	.218	.292	.185	10.76	3.16
2-team total (2 NW Arkansas)					6	1	2.36	9	9	0	0	50	43	16	13	4	21	62	—	—	—	11.23	3.81
McCurry, Brendan	R-R	5-10	165	1-7-92	0	1	1.62	14	0	0	6	17	9	3	3	1	6	26	.155	.091	.194	14.04	3.24
Mendez, Junior	R-R	6-1	210	9-20-90	1	0	5.40	1	1	0	0	5	2	3	3	0	5	1	.333	.000	.286	1.80	9.00
Neal, Zach	R-R	6-3	220	11-9-88	3	3	6.44	7	7	0	0	36	43	26	26	7	15	22	.303	.292	.312	5.45	3.72
Overton, Dillon	L-L	6-2	172	8-17-91	5	2	3.06	13	13	0	0	65	65	22	22	4	15	47	.260	.205	.290	6.54	2.09
Peters, Tanner	R-R	6-0	175	8-6-90	0	2	11.74	2	2	0	0	8	16	10	10	5	1	6	.410	.286	.438	7.04	5.87
Sanchez, Jake	R-R	6-1	205	8-19-89	10	8	4.50	25	25	1	0	142	172	87	71	12	41	100	.299	.340	.252	6.34	2.60
Urlaub, Jeff	L-L	6-2	160	4-24-87	1	0	1.13	6	0	0	0	8	8	1	1	0	1	7	.250	.364	.190	7.88	1.13
Wagman, Joey	L-R	6-0	185	7-25-91	1	0	1.80	1	1	0	0	5	3	1	1	0	2	3	.176	.182	.167	5.40	3.60
Wahl, Bobby	R-R	6-2	210	3-21-92	2	0	4.18	24	0	0	4	32	36	17	15	2	14	36	.283	.304	.268	10.02	3.90

Fielding

Catcher	PCT	G	PO	A	E	DP	PB
Blair	.982	38	255	16	5	2	1
Maxwell	.997	78	539	42	2	3	5
Pohl	.947	4	17	1	1	0	0
Rickles	.978	17	120	13	3	0	1
Taylor	1.000	10	81	3	0	0	0

First Base	PCT	G	PO	A	E	DP
Aliotti	.989	22	176	12	2	19
Blair	—	1	0	0	0	0
Healy	.990	24	188	13	2	14
Nunez	.978	16	122	12	3	8
Olson	.995	62	561	33	3	55

	PCT	G	PO	A	E	DP
Ravelo	.993	15	139	7	1	13
Rickles	1.000	3	17	1	0	2

Second Base	PCT	G	PO	A	E	DP
Kirkland	.944	27	36	66	6	11
Walsh	.982	117	165	328	9	65

Third Base	PCT	G	PO	A	E	DP
Healy	.930	84	75	136	16	12
Kirkland	.944	6	7	10	1	1
Nunez	.909	49	29	81	11	10
Olson	1.000	2	1	1	0	0

Shortstop	PCT	G	PO	A	E	DP
Kirkland	.951	30	40	76	6	19

	PCT	G	PO	A	E	DP
Pinder	.945	112	181	267	26	61

Outfield	PCT	G	PO	A	E	DP
Angle	.990	49	99	3	1	1
Brugman	.989	128	274	6	3	3
Crocker	1.000	9	21	0	0	0
Kirkland	1.000	2	1	0	0	0
Mathews	1.000	1	1	0	0	0
Oberacker	.986	97	214	4	3	0
Olson	.974	59	139	11	4	3
Walsh	1.000	11	16	1	0	0
Whitaker	.976	75	157	7	4	2

STOCKTON PORTS   HIGH CLASS A

CALIFORNIA LEAGUE

Batting	B-T	HT	WT	DOB	AVG	vLH	vRH	G	AB	R	H	2B	3B	HR	RBI	BB	HBP	SH	SF	SO	SB	CS	SLG	OBP
Barreto, Franklin	R-R	5-9	175	2-27-96	.302	.352	.284	90	338	50	102	22	3	13	47	15	4	1	6	67	8	3	.500	.333
Boyd, B.J.	L-R	5-11	230	7-16-93	.277	.255	.284	132	458	67	127	20	8	5	52	41	6	5	1	89	18	5	.389	.344
Brizuela, Jose	L-R	6-0	180	8-31-92	.147	.167	.143	10	34	3	5	1	0	1	5	5	0	0	0	10	0	0	.265	.256
Chapman, Matt	R-R	6-2	205	4-28-93	.250	.215	.259	80	304	60	76	21	3	23	57	39	5	0	4	79	4	1	.566	.341
Chavez, Jose	R-R	5-11	175	8-5-95	.100	.000	.128	22	60	6	6	2	0	0	2	2	0	2	0	15	0	0	.133	.129
Cogswell, Branden	L-R	6-1	180	1-12-93	.235	.200	.245	118	422	43	99	14	3	3	32	56	2	4	3	108	6	2	.303	.325
Crisp, Coco	B-R	5-10	185	11-1-79	.222	.000	.240	7	27	6	6	1	0	2	4	6	0	0	0	3	0	0	.481	.323
Gilbert, Trent	L-R	6-1	175	3-17-93	.200	.091	.215	28	90	7	18	2	0	1	8	5	1	1	0	28	3	0	.256	.250
Higley, Justin	L-R	6-4	200	12-25-92	.220	.309	.156	37	132	17	29	7	1	4	12	10	0	1	2	53	4	0	.379	.271
Marincov, Tyler	R-R	6-2	205	10-20-91	.257	.319	.239	134	521	79	134	29	4	14	75	44	7	0	7	140	14	8	.409	.320
Mercedes, Melvin	R-R	5-8	170	1-13-92	.248	.308	.235	80	282	32	70	13	1	0	24	27	3	9	3	45	11	2	.301	.317
Munoz, Yairo	R-R	6-1	165	1-23-95	.320	.350	.315	39	150	21	48	12	0	4	26	11	2	1	1	20	1	1	.480	.372
Nogowski, John	R-L	6-2	210	1-5-93	.274	.247	.284	96	354	45	97	20	0	4	45	39	5	1	3	47	1	1	.364	.352
Nottingham, Jacob	R-R	6-3	230	4-3-95	.299	.364	.289	43	164	25	49	9	0	3	22	12	3	0	3	38	1	0	.409	.352
2-team total (17 Lancaster)					.306	—		60	235	39	72	15	1	7	36	15	5	0	3	48	1	0	.468	.357
Pan, Chih-Fang	B-R	6-1	170	11-12-90	.067	.143	.000	5	15	2	1	0	1	0	0	3	0	0	0	3	0	0	.200	.222
Rickles, Nick	R-R	6-3	220	2-2-90	.227	.362	.148	34	128	13	29	6	3	1	19	6	1	1	0	29	1	0	.359	.231
Soto, Michael	R-R	6-3	215	11-17-91	.229	.228	.229	114	428	43	98	23	2	9	55	27	3	0	2	113	8	2	.355	.278
Sportman, J.P.	R-R	5-9	190	1-26-92	.292	.333	.275	38	154	21	45	7	3	3	25	10	1	0	2	38	7	1	.435	.335
Taylor, Beau	L-R	6-0	205	2-13-90	.214	.113	.243	68	238	27	51	11	1	4	28	34	3	0	1	62	1	2	.319	.319
Vertigan, Brett	L-L	5-9	175	8-21-90	.286	.286	.287	111	454	80	130	23	7	4	48	47	1	6	4	76	24	8	.394	.352

Pitching	B-T	HT	WT	DOB	W	L	ERA	G	GS	CG	SV	IP	H	R	ER	HR	BB	SO	AVG	vLH	vRH	K/9	BB/9
Alcantara, Raul	R-R	6-3	205	12-4-92	0	2	3.88	15	15	0	0	49	54	21	21	3	8	29	.286	.288	.284	5.36	1.48
Atherton, Tim	R-R	6-2	209	11-7-89	0	0	1.17	4	4	0	0	23	10	5	3	2	4	31	.127	.077	.175	12.13	1.57

Pitching	B-T	HT	WT	DOB	W	L	ERA	G	GS	CG	SV	IP	H	R	ER	HR	BB	SO	AVG	vLH	vRH	K/9	BB/9
Avila, Andres	R-R	6-0	185	6-20-90	2	0	0.00	8	1	0	3	14	8	1	0	0	2	13	.174	.130	.217	8.56	1.32
Bayless, Trevor	R-R	6-3	210	10-6-91	0	2	4.31	31	0	0	0	48	42	24	23	7	21	45	.230	.277	.203	8.44	3.94
Bracewell, Ben	R-R	6-0	195	9-19-90	6	2	2.89	43	0	0	7	56	45	19	18	5	12	54	.223	.211	.230	8.68	1.93
Bragg, Sam	R-R	6-2	190	3-23-93	7	2	3.65	44	0	0	1	74	64	38	30	8	23	92	.231	.233	.229	11.19	2.80
Coke, Phil	L-L	6-1	210	7-19-82	0	0	5.19	7	0	0	0	9	11	5	5	1	0	5	.333	.143	.385	5.19	0.00
Covey, Dylan	R-R	6-2	195	8-14-91	8	9	3.59	26	26	0	0	140	135	65	56	13	43	100	.250	.238	.258	6.41	2.76
Duran, Omar	L-L	6-3	220	2-26-90	2	0	5.27	13	0	0	1	14	13	8	8	1	10	20	.250	.208	.286	13.17	6.59
Finnegan, Kyle	R-R	6-2	170	9-4-91	9	9	5.44	28	24	0	0	127	139	83	77	19	41	96	.275	.269	.280	6.79	2.90
Griffin, A.J.	R-R	6-5	230	1-28-88	0	0	0.00	2	2	0	0	7	2	0	0	0	1	8	.095	.091	.100	10.29	1.29
Hollstegge, Tyler	L-R	6-1	205	12-17-90	0	1	10.80	6	0	0	0	7	11	10	8	2	5	9	.344	.375	.313	12.15	6.75
Joseph, Jonathan	R-R	6-1	180	5-17-88	2	0	1.74	5	0	0	0	10	8	2	2	2	1	11	.216	.222	.211	9.58	0.87
Lamb, Chris	B-L	6-1	205	6-29-90	0	1	3.18	3	3	0	0	11	11	4	4	2	4	8	.250	.267	.241	6.35	3.18
McCurry, Brendan	R-R	5-10	165	1-7-92	1	2	1.94	36	0	0	21	46	30	13	10	3	11	56	.182	.205	.163	10.88	2.14
Meisner, Casey	R-R	6-7	190	5-22-95	3	1	2.78	7	7	0	0	32	27	12	10	1	7	24	.220	.233	.213	6.68	1.95
Mengden, Daniel	R-R	6-2	190	2-19-93	4	2	4.25	8	8	0	0	42	39	23	20	6	10	41	.234	.210	.256	8.72	2.13
2-team total (10 Lancaster)					6	3	4.79	18	16	0	1	92	98	53	49	10	28	89	—	—	—	8.71	2.74
Mujica, Edward	R-R	6-3	220	5-10-84	0	0	0.00	2	0	0	0	2	0	0	0	0	0	4	.000	.000	.000	18.00	0.00
Navas, Carlos	R-R	6-1	170	8-13-92	0	0	4.00	6	0	0	0	9	9	4	4	1	3	9	.273	.182	.318	9.00	3.00
Overton, Dillon	L-L	6-2	172	8-17-91	2	4	3.82	14	12	0	0	61	62	29	26	7	12	59	.270	.294	.255	8.66	1.76
Parker, Jarrod	R-R	6-1	195	11-24-88	1	1	5.19	2	2	0	0	9	8	6	5	1	0	8	.242	.158	.357	8.31	0.00
Roberts, Sam	L-R	6-1	190	2-23-89	5	2	3.65	43	0	0	1	69	65	33	28	5	31	47	.252	.206	.282	6.13	4.04
Seddon, Joel	R-R	6-1	165	7-13-92	8	8	3.59	34	14	0	0	105	103	49	42	11	17	82	.254	.263	.248	7.01	1.45
Stalcup, Matt	L-L	6-2	195	7-6-90	3	6	3.24	27	13	0	0	89	73	37	32	6	31	77	.224	.247	.215	7.79	3.13
Thompson, Taylor	R-R	6-5	225	6-18-87	0	2	14.54	4	0	0	0	4	7	8	7	2	2	7	.368	.400	.333	14.54	4.15
Torres, Jose	R-R	6-2	175	9-24-93	0	0	0.00	3	0	0	0	4	0	0	0	0	1	4	.000	.000	.000	9.82	2.45
Trivino, Lou	R-R	6-5	225	10-1-91	10	5	3.91	32	9	0	0	90	70	45	39	5	44	78	.216	.232	.203	7.83	4.42
Urlaub, Jeff	L-L	6-2	160	4-24-87	0	0	7.36	2	0	0	0	4	4	3	3	0	1	4	.308	.400	.250	9.82	2.45
Veliz, Victor	L-L	5-11	170	10-6-93	0	0	6.75	7	0	0	0	11	16	15	8	3	3	13	.333	.278	.367	10.97	2.53
Venditte, Pat	R-B	6-1	180	6-30-85	0	0	4.50	3	0	0	0	4	3	2	2	0	0	5	.214	.143	.286	11.25	0.00
Wagman, Joey	L-R	6-0	185	7-25-91	0	2	13.50	3	0	0	0	7	12	10	10	2	1	3	.387	.417	.368	4.05	1.35
Walter, Corey	R-R	6-3	215	8-11-92	1	2	1.42	45	0	0	8	57	40	16	9	1	15	46	.197	.258	.145	7.26	2.37

Fielding

Catcher	PCT	G	PO	A	E	DP	PB
Chavez	.986	21	127	11	2	1	4
Nottingham	.993	34	240	33	4	1	12
Rickles	.992	30	216	28	2	3	2
Taylor	.996	63	485	62	2	3	9

First Base	PCT	G	PO	A	E	DP
Nogowski	.994	90	806	77	5	57
Nottingham	1.000	7	46	1	0	5
Soto	.977	49	390	28	10	31

Second Base	PCT	G	PO	A	E	DP
Cogswell	.979	103	185	283	10	53
Gilbert	.978	11	20	25	1	3
Mercedes	.978	20	38	53	2	13

	PCT	G	PO	A	E	DP
Pan	1.000	5	8	10	0	4
Sportman	1.000	3	1	10	0	0
Zobrist	1.000	1	2	2	0	1

Third Base	PCT	G	PO	A	E	DP
Brizuela	.882	10	4	11	2	1
Chapman	.922	77	50	174	19	13
Mercedes	.969	28	16	47	2	2
Soto	.943	27	14	36	3	4

Shortstop	PCT	G	PO	A	E	DP
Barreto	.911	86	128	221	34	52
Cogswell	.909	4	8	12	2	6
Ladendorf	1.000	1	1	1	0	1
Mercedes	.930	13	18	35	4	9

	PCT	G	PO	A	E	DP
Munoz	.929	37	47	98	11	12
Outfield	PCT	G	PO	A	E	DP
Boyd	.990	124	196	3	2	1
Brizuela	—	1	0	0	0	0
Crisp	1.000	5	8	0	0	0
Gilbert	—	1	0	0	0	0
Higley	.941	24	32	0	2	0
Marincov	.972	125	238	6	7	0
Mercedes	1.000	7	10	1	0	0
Reddick	1.000	2	1	0	0	0
Sportman	.933	30	55	1	4	0
Vertigan	.996	107	249	5	1	1
Zobrist	1.000	1	2	0	0	0

BELOIT SNAPPERS
LOW CLASS A
MIDWEST LEAGUE

Batting	B-T	HT	WT	DOB	AVG	vLH	vRH	G	AB	R	H	2B	3B	HR	RBI	BB	HBP	SH	SF	SO	SB	CS	SLG	OBP
Akau, Iolana	R-R	5-11	180	8-31-95	.252	.280	.246	41	147	19	37	9	1	2	14	12	8	0	1	49	0	1	.367	.339
Bennie, Joe	R-R	6-0	200	5-7-91	.272	.253	.277	131	470	63	128	35	3	11	56	66	3	0	4	137	14	5	.430	.363
Brizuela, Jose	L-R	6-0	180	8-31-92	.270	.371	.251	109	381	49	103	28	3	11	56	49	4	0	2	89	8	2	.446	.358
Chavez, Jose	R-R	5-11	175	8-5-95	.146	.250	.109	43	137	11	20	4	0	0	12	0	5	0	0	34	0	0	.175	.215
Diaz, Edwin	R-R	6-2	195	8-25-95	.100	.176	.075	45	140	9	14	8	0	0	13	8	2	2	2	49	0	0	.157	.158
Duinkerk, Shawn	L-R	6-5	195	8-28-93	.228	.093	.252	88	289	33	66	9	1	5	24	11	6	1	2	100	2	2	.318	.269
Gilbert, Trent	R-L	6-1	175	3-17-93	.267	.197	.284	84	330	36	88	15	2	5	44	18	1	2	2	62	0	3	.370	.305
Harris, James	R-R	6-1	180	8-7-93	.255	.309	.243	86	302	45	77	14	4	5	28	48	3	2	4	75	11	13	.377	.359
Higley, Justin	L-R	6-4	200	12-25-92	.198	.170	.206	75	262	42	52	8	2	10	42	35	1	0	2	87	21	5	.359	.293
Kuhn, Max	R-R	5-11	185	9-10-92	.241	.242	.241	131	481	53	116	29	3	10	59	55	3	0	4	106	1	1	.376	.320
Martinez, Robert	R-R	6-1	180	2-8-94	.191	.185	.193	43	141	15	27	7	0	3	11	12	1	0	1	61	3	1	.305	.258
Mercedes, Melvin	B-R	5-8	170	1-13-92	.286	.500	.231	15	49	7	14	1	0	0	3	4	0	0	0	14	1	1	.306	.340
Munoz, Yairo	R-R	6-1	165	1-23-95	.236	.250	.232	97	369	48	87	14	3	9	48	22	2	1	6	62	10	2	.363	.278
Paz, Andy	R-R	6-0	170	1-5-93	.200	.500	.154	9	30	3	6	1	0	0	1	3	0	0	0	10	0	0	.233	.273
Pimentel, Sandber	L-L	6-3	220	9-12-94	.243	.241	.244	117	411	50	100	17	0	13	41	50	8	0	2	104	1	2	.380	.335
Proudfoot, Tim	R-R	5-9	180	3-23-93	.208	.310	.184	49	154	19	32	4	0	1	16	12	3	2	1	34	0	1	.253	.276
Raga, Argenis	R-R	6-1	176	7-22-94	.278	.390	.253	66	227	26	63	16	1	2	34	16	2	1	3	41	0	1	.383	.327
Santana, Gabriel	R-R	6-0	165	8-23-92	.137	.000	.164	24	73	6	10	2	0	1	2	1	4	2	0	13	0	0	.205	.192
Vertigan, Brett	L-L	5-9	175	8-21-90	.293	.250	.306	26	92	18	27	4	0	0	7	21	0	1	1	15	6	1	.337	.421
White, Mikey	R-R	6-1	185	9-3-93	.200	.375	.160	35	130	16	26	5	0	1	12	10	5	0	0	30	0	1	.262	.283

Pitching	B-T	HT	WT	DOB	W	L	ERA	G	GS	CG	SV	IP	H	R	ER	HR	BB	SO	AVG	vLH	vRH	K/9	BB/9
Bayless, Trevor	R-R	6-3	210	10-6-91	1	0	0.00	4	0	0	2	6	1	0	0	0	3	11	.050	.100	.000	16.50	4.50
Driver, Dustin	R-R	6-2	210	10-11-94	0	2	9.00	4	4	0	0	11	15	14	11	0	5	9	.306	.227	.370	7.36	4.09

Pitching	B-T	HT	WT	DOB	W	L	ERA	G	GS	CG	SV	IP	H	R	ER	HR	BB	SO	AVG	vLH	vRH	K/9	BB/9
Fagan, Mike	R-L	5-11	160	5-12-92	0	0	5.40	28	0	0	2	38	40	25	23	2	19	43	.267	.196	.303	10.10	4.46
Fillmyer, Heath	R-R	6-1	180	5-16-94	3	13	4.98	23	22	0	0	99	112	61	55	10	56	77	.297	.285	.305	6.98	5.07
Gauna, Koby	R-R	6-3	225	9-10-93	3	2	1.55	36	0	0	5	52	52	17	9	1	11	29	.257	.210	.289	4.99	1.89
Gossett, Daniel	R-R	6-2	185	11-13-92	5	13	4.73	27	27	2	0	145	151	92	76	16	52	112	.270	.241	.291	6.97	3.24
Graves, Brett	R-R	6-1	170	1-30-93	12	8	5.36	28	28	0	0	143	168	90	85	15	44	91	.298	.338	.261	5.74	2.78
Grundy, Jerad	L-L	5-11	200	9-11-90	0	1	5.25	21	1	0	1	36	43	28	21	3	19	32	.297	.286	.302	8.00	4.75
Huber, Rob	R-R	5-11	200	1-8-92	2	3	3.02	37	0	0	4	54	48	23	18	3	23	57	.238	.278	.205	9.56	3.86
Johnson, Kevin	R-R	6-3	175	4-5-91	2	7	4.86	34	8	0	0	80	91	62	43	8	27	54	.278	.279	.278	6.10	3.05
Massad, Jon	R-R	6-1	200	4-19-91	1	0	7.82	7	0	0	0	13	16	11	11	1	3	10	.308	.280	.333	7.11	2.13
Mendez, Junior	R-R	6-1	210	9-20-92	4	11	5.79	27	26	0	0	131	156	93	84	18	53	73	.302	.280	.320	5.03	3.65
Miller, Corey	R-R	6-3	190	11-13-91	2	1	4.54	21	0	0	0	34	39	28	17	3	15	26	.277	.333	.238	6.95	4.01
Navas, Carlos	R-R	6-1	170	8-13-92	3	2	2.61	44	0	0	2	59	55	22	17	2	18	69	.249	.226	.266	10.59	2.76
Schwartz, Jordan	R-R	6-2	195	2-28-92	0	4	9.08	10	8	0	0	37	56	43	37	2	27	35	.348	.391	.315	8.59	6.63
Sosa, Lee	R-R	6-2	215	9-3-91	0	2	8.74	15	0	0	0	23	29	24	22	1	9	19	.302	.282	.316	7.54	3.57
Stull, Cody	L-L	6-2	160	3-23-92	3	4	5.00	43	0	0	1	68	68	46	38	4	23	60	.258	.210	.279	7.90	3.03
Torres, Jose	L-L	6-2	175	9-24-93	4	5	2.69	44	0	0	8	74	55	24	22	4	23	80	.212	.259	.191	9.77	2.81
Wagman, Joey	L-R	6-0	185	7-25-91	8	4	3.91	24	15	0	1	90	94	46	39	5	17	75	.266	.284	.255	7.53	1.71

Fielding

Catcher	PCT	G	PO	A	E	DP	PB
Akau	.975	37	272	37	8	3	9
Chavez	.980	43	287	52	7	2	5
Paz	1.000	7	35	12	0	1	1
Raga	.983	54	372	45	7	2	7

First Base	PCT	G	PO	A	E	DP
Duinkerk	—	1	0	0	0	0
Kuhn	.990	72	579	35	6	52
Pimentel	.982	67	554	35	11	41
Santana	1.000	8	58	0	0	5

Second Base	PCT	G	PO	A	E	DP
Bennie	.778	3	3	4	2	1
Diaz	1.000	13	23	42	0	10
Gilbert	.963	80	124	187	12	36

	PCT	G	PO	A	E	DP
Mercedes	1.000	5	10	11	0	2
Proudfoot	.976	31	44	80	3	18
Santana	1.000	13	18	26	0	7

Third Base	PCT	G	PO	A	E	DP
Bennie	.868	14	9	24	5	1
Brizuela	.907	94	70	183	26	19
Diaz	.904	23	11	36	5	3
Mercedes	.864	7	8	11	3	1
Proudfoot	1.000	7	4	13	0	0
Raga	1.000	1	1	0	0	0
Santana	1.000	2	0	1	0	0

Shortstop	PCT	G	PO	A	E	DP
Brizuela	—	1	0	0	0	0
Diaz	.919	11	13	21	3	7

	PCT	G	PO	A	E	DP
Mercedes	.900	1	5	4	1	2
Munoz	.941	88	139	225	23	40
Proudfoot	.889	12	11	21	4	3
White	.956	35	56	95	7	21

Outfield	PCT	G	PO	A	E	DP
Bennie	.962	84	144	7	6	1
Duinkerk	.952	84	146	12	8	2
Harris	.978	86	218	3	5	0
Higley	.956	75	149	4	7	2
Kuhn	.931	40	54	0	4	0
Martinez	.986	39	71	0	1	0
Vertigan	.986	26	66	4	1	0

VERMONT LAKE MONSTERS — SHORT-SEASON

NEW YORK-PENN LEAGUE

Batting	B-T	HT	WT	DOB	AVG	vLH	vRH	G	AB	R	H	2B	3B	HR	RBI	BB	HBP	SH	SF	SO	SB	CS	SLG	OBP
Akau, Iolana	R-R	5-11	180	8-31-95	.296	.444	.222	8	27	4	8	1	0	1	4	2	2	0	0	4	0	0	.444	.387
Bolt, Skye	B-R	6-1	170	1-15-94	.238	.216	.243	52	181	26	43	10	2	4	19	24	0	0	1	44	2	1	.381	.325
Brown, Seth	L-L	6-3	220	7-13-92	.289	.286	.289	62	239	32	69	19	3	3	35	25	1	0	2	51	6	2	.431	.356
Collins, Nick	L-R	6-2	228	4-13-94	.256	.267	.255	34	117	14	30	2	0	2	15	13	1	0	1	14	1	0	.325	.333
De La Cruz, Vicmal	L-L	6-0	185	11-20-93	.148	.000	.205	19	61	6	9	4	1	0	2	5	1	0	1	17	0	0	.246	.221
Devencenzi, Jordan	R-R	5-11	190	6-26-93	.243	.125	.276	11	37	4	9	1	0	0	1	3	1	0	0	2	0	0	.270	.317
Duinkerk, Shawn	L-R	6-5	195	8-18-94	.375	.300	.429	6	24	4	9	1	0	0	3	2	0	0	0	6	0	0	.417	.423
Gavitt, Tom	R-R	6-3	195	8-16-92	.216	.000	.258	9	37	5	8	4	0	0	2	1	0	0	0	14	0	0	.324	.237
Howell, Ryan	R-R	6-0	205	10-30-92	.199	.220	.192	49	166	18	33	8	0	5	19	17	2	1	2	42	0	3	.337	.278
Iriart, Chris	R-R	6-2	230	10-7-94	.230	.296	.213	69	256	35	59	18	0	5	45	23	6	0	4	86	0	1	.359	.304
Kim, Seong-Min	R-R	6-2	250	5-12-93	.200	.310	.132	31	110	7	22	3	1	4	15	11	1	0	2	29	1	2	.355	.274
Loehr, Trace	L-R	5-10	175	5-23-95	.264	.302	.251	67	254	33	67	6	1	2	31	21	3	2	2	41	4	4	.319	.325
Lopez, Jesus	R-R	5-11	170	10-5-96	.203	.200	.204	55	202	14	41	5	0	0	16	6	2	0	0	40	2	1	.228	.233
Martin, Richie	R-R	6-0	192	12-22-94	.237	.302	.218	51	190	31	45	6	4	2	16	25	9	2	0	47	7	7	.342	.353
Martinez, Robert	R-R	6-1	180	2-8-94	.000	.000	.000	4	13	1	0	0	0	0	0	3	0	1	0	6	0	0	.000	.188
Pallares, Steven	R-R	6-2	185	4-26-93	.246	.321	.223	67	240	38	59	7	2	2	18	40	7	0	5	39	6	2	.317	.363
Raga, Argenis	R-R	6-1	176	7-22-94	.235	.200	.286	5	17	1	4	0	0	1	4	2	1	0	0	1	0	1	.412	.350
Santana, Gabriel	R-R	6-0	165	8-23-92	.232	.353	.179	15	56	8	13	1	0	2	5	1	4	1	0	7	0	0	.357	.295
Siddall, Brett	L-L	6-1	195	10-3-94	.264	.219	.276	43	159	17	42	11	1	4	29	9	6	0	2	32	1	1	.421	.324
White, Mikey	R-R	6-1	185	9-3-93	.315	.346	.306	29	111	18	35	10	0	2	16	14	4	0	2	22	0	2	.459	.405

Pitching	B-T	HT	WT	DOB	W	L	ERA	G	GS	CG	SV	IP	H	R	ER	HR	BB	SO	AVG	vLH	vRH	K/9	BB/9
Beasley, Derek	L-L	6-0	185	2-2-92	3	1	2.93	13	0	0	0	28	25	12	9	1	13	29	.229	.231	.229	9.43	4.23
Bowers, Heath	R-R	6-4	190	7-25-93	3	1	2.52	15	6	0	0	36	29	16	10	1	16	31	.213	.246	.187	7.82	4.04
Derby, Bubba	L-R	5-10	180	2-24-94	1	0	0.78	12	8	0	0	35	19	4	3	2	10	45	.161	.145	.175	11.68	2.60
DeYoung, Derek	R-R	6-2	185	12-17-91	0	1	3.86	9	0	0	0	12	8	7	5	0	12	11	.182	.188	.179	8.49	9.26
Driver, Dustin	R-R	6-2	210	10-11-94	1	5	4.99	14	10	0	0	52	53	39	29	4	35	32	.269	.348	.200	5.50	6.02
Duchene, Kevin	L-L	6-2	210	12-10-93	0	2	4.84	8	5	0	0	22	21	15	12	2	9	18	.241	.176	.283	7.25	3.63
Duno, Angel	R-R	6-0	180	10-9-93	0	3	5.59	6	6	0	0	29	42	22	18	2	1	18	.333	.348	.325	5.59	0.31
Fagan, Mike	R-L	5-11	160	5-12-92	0	0	1.17	5	0	0	1	8	4	1	1	0	1	9	.154	.200	.125	10.57	1.17
Ferreras, Kevin	L-L	6-0	170	7-5-93	4	2	2.66	15	3	0	0	47	42	21	14	0	14	37	.231	.230	.231	7.04	2.66
Frias, Dawrin	R-R	6-0	195	2-18-92	0	1	1.23	7	0	0	0	7	5	1	1	0	5	10	.154	.091	.200	12.27	6.14
2-team total (4 Brooklyn)					1	0	2.35	11	0	0	0	15	9	5	4	1	9	20	—	—	—	11.74	5.28
Friedrichs, Kyle	R-R	6-1	190	1-22-92	1	3	4.50	14	11	0	0	36	32	22	18	2	13	19	.250	.258	.242	4.75	3.25
Gorman, John	R-R	6-2	220	2-19-92	2	2	5.40	13	0	0	0	18	18	11	11	0	13	13	.257	.304	.234	10.31	6.38
Kohler, Chris	L-L	6-3	210	5-4-95	2	3	4.66	11	0	0	0	39	40	21	20	2	10	37	.270	.189	.316	8.61	2.33
Kurz, Cody	R-R	6-2	195	9-13-92	0	4	8.24	13	0	0	0	20	25	19	18	2	14	16	.303	.313	.313	7.32	6.41

Pitching	B-T	HT	WT	DOB	W	L	ERA	G	GS	CG	SV	IP	H	R	ER	HR	BB	SO	AVG	vLH	vRH	K/9	BB/9
Lyons, Jared	L-L	6-0	190	5-18-93	0	0	12.27	12	0	0	0	15	32	28	20	1	7	15	.427	.333	.471	9.20	4.30
Manarino, Evan	L-L	6-1	195	12-28-92	3	2	5.59	15	5	0	1	39	46	26	24	2	6	28	.293	.244	.313	6.52	1.40
Massad, Jon	R-R	6-1	200	4-19-91	3	4	3.86	9	8	0	0	49	46	29	21	5	10	31	.251	.253	.250	5.69	1.84
Miller, Corey	R-R	6-3	190	11-13-91	2	4	2.91	15	5	0	1	46	47	19	15	1	9	27	.258	.288	.239	5.24	1.75
Naile, James	R-R	6-4	185	2-8-93	3	0	1.93	18	0	0	6	23	19	6	5	0	6	17	.218	.220	.217	6.56	2.31
Painton, Tyler	L-L	6-5	195	2-20-92	2	1	5.06	16	0	0	2	32	28	19	18	3	6	20	.233	.158	.268	5.63	1.69
Tomasovich, Andrew	L-L	6-4	215	9-24-93	0	0	2.21	12	0	0	1	20	14	6	5	1	7	17	.192	.276	.136	7.52	3.10

Fielding

Catcher	PCT	G	PO	A	E	DP	PB
Akau	1.000	7	40	3	0	0	0
Collins	.972	31	189	22	6	2	3
Devencenzi	.958	10	66	2	3	0	1
Gavitt	.977	9	77	9	2	1	1
Kim	.973	19	131	11	4	0	3
Raga	.875	2	14	0	2	0	1

First Base	PCT	G	PO	A	E	DP
Brown	.985	8	64	3	1	5
Iriart	.986	62	541	27	8	47
Kim	1.000	2	7	1	0	1
Santana	1.000	5	46	2	0	6

Second Base	PCT	G	PO	A	E	DP
Howell	.882	3	9	6	2	2
Loehr	.987	32	56	93	2	18
Lopez	.951	40	76	120	10	24
White	1.000	1	3	6	0	1

Third Base	PCT	G	PO	A	E	DP
Howell	.830	29	28	50	16	5
Loehr	.900	26	17	46	7	3
Raga	.500	2	1	2	3	0
Santana	.917	7	8	14	2	1
White	.938	11	7	23	2	2

Shortstop	PCT	G	PO	A	E	DP
Loehr	1.000	6	9	21	0	3

	PCT	G	PO	A	E	DP
Lopez	.963	11	17	35	2	8
Martin	.948	46	86	133	12	27
White	.943	13	9	41	3	6

Outfield	PCT	G	PO	A	E	DP
Bolt	.929	46	102	3	8	1
Brown	.945	49	102	2	6	2
De La Cruz	.923	10	12	0	1	0
Duinkerk	1.000	6	5	0	0	0
Howell	.975	14	37	2	1	1
Martinez	1.000	4	12	0	0	0
Pallares	.953	61	98	4	5	1
Siddall	.985	37	63	2	1	1

AZL ATHLETICS
ARIZONA LEAGUE
ROOKIE

Batting	B-T	HT	WT	DOB	AVG	vLH	vRH	G	AB	R	H	2B	3B	HR	RBI	BB	HBP	SH	SF	SO	SB	CS	SLG	OBP
Barrera, Luis	L-L	6-0	180	11-15-95	.287	.280	.289	37	115	17	33	3	2	0	12	12	0	2	4	26	1	0	.348	.344
Brown, Seth	L-L	6-3	220	7-13-92	.200	.250	.188	6	20	2	4	1	2	0	3	0	0	0	0	2	0	0	.450	.304
Collins, Nick	L-R	6-2	228	4-13-94	.111	.000	.167	4	9	0	1	0	0	0	2	2	0	0	0	2	0	0	.111	.273
Conlon, Shane	L-L	6-0	185	2-27-92	.327	.407	.300	30	107	15	35	4	3	0	18	10	2	3	1	16	2	1	.421	.392
Devencenzi, Jordan	R-R	5-11	190	6-26-93	.600	1.000	.500	2	5	1	3	0	0	0	1	0	2	0	0	0	0	0	.600	.714
Diaz, Edwin	R-R	6-2	195	8-25-95	.171	.200	.164	24	76	10	13	2	0	2	6	8	1	0	0	22	0	0	.276	.259
Gavitt, Tom	R-R	6-3	195	8-16-92	.175	.286	.140	16	57	2	10	1	0	0	2	1	1	1	0	21	0	0	.193	.203
Guzman, Miguel	R-R	6-2	210	3-10-95	.255	.364	.225	32	102	13	26	7	2	0	13	4	0	0	1	19	1	1	.363	.280
Hiciano, Carlos	R-R	6-2	175	10-29-96	.199	.167	.206	53	191	14	38	4	0	0	8	4	1	0	0	47	5	1	.220	.219
Marinez, Eric	B-R	6-1	160	9-12-95	.241	.135	.273	47	158	17	38	6	2	0	18	16	0	1	4	33	2	0	.304	.303
Martin, Mike	R-R	6-0	175	9-29-92	.147	.118	.155	27	75	13	11	0	0	0	3	14	7	0	1	25	8	1	.147	.330
Martinez, Robert	R-R	6-1	180	2-8-94	.162	.154	.165	36	111	11	18	2	2	2	9	11	0	0	1	53	2	0	.270	.282
Mercedes, Miguel	R-R	6-4	200	9-12-95	.216	.190	.224	49	167	16	36	12	2	2	28	17	6	0	3	70	1	2	.347	.306
Mullen, Robert	R-R	6-0	170	5-23-96	.231	.350	.190	26	78	8	18	5	1	0	8	11	1	1	0	13	0	0	.321	.333
Paz, Andy	R-R	6-0	170	1-5-93	.261	.500	.238	7	23	1	6	0	0	0	3	5	0	0	0	6	1	0	.261	.393
Penalo, Rodolfo	B-R	5-7	130	8-27-92	.222	.188	.232	41	144	25	32	2	4	0	7	19	2	1	0	29	6	6	.292	.321
Proudfoot, Tim	R-R	5-9	180	3-23-93	.250	.500	.000	2	8	1	2	1	0	0	2	0	0	0	0	3	0	0	.375	.250
Ravelo, Rangel	R-R	6-2	220	4-24-92	.360	.200	.400	9	25	7	9	3	1	0	7	3	0	0	0	3	1	0	.560	.543
Rodriguez, Jean Carlo	R-R	5-10	170	1-12-96	.214	.333	.191	26	56	10	12	2	1	0	8	19	9	0	0	14	2	1	.286	.476
Rodriguez, Jhonny	L-L	6-3	170	7-20-96	.284	.359	.243	27	109	11	31	11	2	1	17	7	2	0	2	32	1	0	.450	.333
Siddall, Brett	L-L	6-1	195	10-3-94	.342	.500	.305	19	73	12	25	5	3	2	13	10	1	0	1	9	3	0	.575	.424
Sportman, J.P.	R-R	5-9	190	1-26-92	.333	.000	.381	7	24	5	8	0	0	2	3	0	0	0	2	3	0	0	.333	.407
Sunde, Brett	R-R	5-10	185	8-24-94	.196	.167	.205	18	51	2	10	4	0	0	2	2	0	0	1	2	0	0	.275	.255
Terrell, James	R-R	6-0	165	1-10-97	.153	.158	.151	21	72	11	11	1	1	0	5	14	1	0	1	30	2	3	.194	.295

Pitching	B-T	HT	WT	DOB	W	L	ERA	G	GS	CG	SV	IP	H	R	ER	HR	BB	SO	AVG	vLH	vRH	K/9	BB/9
Alejo, Yordy	R-R	6-2	186	11-13-93	2	1	5.29	14	0	0	2	17	21	15	10	0	2	14	.300	.333	.286	7.41	1.06
Altamirano, Xavier	R-R	6-3	195	7-20-94	2	1	3.22	13	2	0	1	36	33	21	13	4	8	23	.237	.189	.267	5.70	1.98
Andueza, Ivan	L-L	5-11	180	2-7-95	3	1	2.51	14	4	0	0	47	44	16	13	2	15	44	.249	.244	.250	8.49	2.89
Berube, Marc	L-R	6-2	180	2-12-93	0	2	7.11	11	0	0	0	13	27	13	10	0	3	11	.435	.556	.343	7.82	2.13
Biegalski, Boomer	R-R	6-2	165	7-13-94	0	1	3.18	6	4	0	0	11	8	7	4	2	2	12	.186	.000	.258	9.53	1.59
Blanco, Argenis	R-R	6-1	165	5-29-94	4	6	3.16	14	3	0	0	57	71	28	20	0	11	39	.302	.287	.312	6.16	1.74
Butler, Brendan	L-R	6-3	217	5-2-93	0	2	5.30	15	0	0	2	19	24	12	11	0	8	11	.320	.269	.347	5.30	3.86
Chalmers, Dakota	R-R	6-3	170	10-8-96	0	1	2.66	11	11	0	0	20	15	9	6	0	17	18	.205	.214	.200	7.97	7.52
Derby, Bubba	L-R	5-10	180	2-24-94	0	1	6.75	2	2	0	0	3	5	3	2	0	0	2	.385	.500	.333	6.75	0.00
Duchene, Kevin	L-L	6-2	210	12-10-93	0	1	0.00	2	2	0	0	3	4	1	0	0	0	1	.364	.333	.375	3.00	0.00
Duno, Angel	R-R	6-0	180	1-10-94	4	2	2.93	8	7	0	0	40	42	15	13	1	3	35	.268	.125	.304	7.88	0.68
Hurlbutt, Dustin	R-R	6-1	195	11-5-92	0	3	3.14	13	0	0	5	14	11	5	5	0	10	20	.216	.188	.229	12.56	6.28
Kelliher, Branden	R-R	5-11	175	12-11-95	0	1	8.24	14	7	0	1	32	36	31	29	0	19	19	.298	.350	.266	5.34	5.40
Martinez, Jorge	L-L	5-11	170	1-5-96	1	1	4.67	13	0	0	0	17	19	11	9	0	7	20	.279	.286	.277	10.38	3.63
Nelo, Emerson	R-R	5-11	180	9-13-95	1	0	3.12	13	0	0	0	17	11	8	6	0	16	14	.180	.143	.191	7.27	8.31
Ortiz, Phillip	R-R	6-0	190	3-6-95	0	0	2.00	10	0	0	0	9	5	3	2	1	9	10	.172	.154	.188	10.00	9.00
Peters, Tanner	R-R	6-0	175	8-6-90	1	1	3.00	5	2	0	0	9	9	3	3	1	1	9	.250	.333	.190	9.00	1.00
Rivas, Jesus	R-R	6-0	180	3-22-94	0	0	4.97	10	0	0	0	13	20	13	7	0	3	6	.339	.400	.308	4.26	2.13
Ruiz, Armando	R-R	5-9	185	7-19-93	1	0	4.32	13	0	0	0	17	14	11	8	0	24	24	.212	.261	.186	12.96	5.40
Schwartz, Jordan	R-R	6-0	180	3-19-92	0	1	3.29	8	7	0	0	14	9	5	5	0	9	13	.196	.211	.185	8.56	5.93
Tomasovich, Andrew	L-L	6-4	215	9-24-93	0	0	2.45	3	0	0	0	4	3	1	1	0	2	3	.250	.000	.333	7.36	4.91
Veliz, Victor	L-L	5-11	170	10-6-93	2	0	3.00	4	0	0	0	12	10	4	4	0	3	12	.233	.273	.219	9.00	2.25

Pitching	B-T	HT	WT	DOB	W	L	ERA	G	GS	CG	SV	IP	H	R	ER	HR	BB	SO	AVG	vLH	vRH	K/9	BB/9
Willman, Tyler	R-R	6-6	190	10-8-92	0	0	2.25	8	0	0	0	8	7	3	2	0	2	6	.226	.000	.304	6.75	2.25
Zambrano, Jesus	R-R	5-11	170	8-23-96	1	4	5.52	13	4	0	1	44	66	30	27	0	9	31	.361	.352	.364	6.34	1.84

Fielding

Catcher	PCT	G	PO	A	E	DP	PB
Collins	1.000	4	21	4	0	0	0
Devencenzi	1.000	2	14	2	0	0	0
Gavitt	.968	14	103	18	4	3	1
Guzman	.980	13	87	10	2	0	2
Mullen	.939	16	77	16	6	2	5
Paz	1.000	4	23	0	0	0	0
Sunde	.970	16	88	9	3	0	3

First Base	PCT	G	PO	A	E	DP
Barrera	1.000	1	9	1	0	0
Conlon	.996	27	243	12	1	13
Guzman	.990	15	90	9	1	9
Mercedes	.955	7	57	6	3	7
Mullen	1.000	9	78	7	0	4
Ravelo	.980	6	47	2	1	4

Second Base	PCT	G	PO	A	E	DP
Hiciano	.952	52	100	137	12	24
Ladendorf	1.000	1	1	0	0	0
Marinez	.962	6	10	15	1	1

Third Base	PCT	G	PO	A	E	DP
Diaz	.926	9	7	18	2	2
Marinez	1.000	2	1	4	0	0
Mercedes	.856	38	22	67	15	6
Rodriguez	.870	14	2	18	3	0

Shortstop	PCT	G	PO	A	E	DP
Diaz	.953	15	19	42	3	5
Hiciano	1.000	1	1	0	0	0
Ladendorf	1.000	1	1	1	0	0
Marinez	.926	40	59	116	14	22

	PCT	G	PO	A	E	DP
Proudfoot	1.000	2	3	4	0	1
Rodriguez	1.000	3	5	10	0	0

Outfield	PCT	G	PO	A	E	DP
Barrera	.911	28	39	2	4	0
Brown	1.000	4	10	0	0	0
Conlon	.750	3	3	0	1	0
Martin	1.000	8	8	0	0	0
Martinez	.965	33	51	4	2	0
Penalo	.989	39	83	4	1	1
Rodriguez	.900	10	8	1	1	0
Rodriguez	.842	21	31	1	6	0
Siddall	.968	14	27	3	1	0
Sportman	.900	5	8	1	1	0
Terrell	.967	20	26	3	1	1

DSL ATHLETICS   ROOKIE
DOMINICAN SUMMER LEAGUE

Batting	B-T	HT	WT	DOB	AVG	vLH	vRH	G	AB	R	H	2B	3B	HR	RBI	BB	HBP	SH	SF	SO	SB	CS	SLG	OBP
Agelvis, Javier	R-R	6-1	170	8-18-97	.201	.167	.210	68	204	20	41	6	2	0	17	50	5	5	1	74	14	5	.250	.369
Arias, Tomy	R-R	6-2	185	3-4-97	.157	.235	.141	31	102	12	16	3	2	2	11	11	0	1	1	38	4	2	.284	.237
De Los Santos, Martin	R-R	6-0	170	1-31-97	.237	.176	.254	26	76	12	18	6	0	0	2	10	3	1	0	24	13	7	.316	.348
Godard, Javier	R-R	6-0	170	12-13-95	.277	.280	.276	59	220	34	61	16	2	1	22	24	4	4	2	28	14	10	.382	.356
Gonzalez, Yhoelnys	R-R	6-0	170	10-30-96	.215	.189	.223	69	228	31	49	10	4	1	14	28	1	5	1	89	24	9	.307	.302
Gordon, Jorge	R-R	5-10	175	10-28-97	.252	.360	.218	56	206	12	52	9	2	0	23	12	1	3	5	33	2	5	.316	.290
Hernandez, Luis	R-R	5-11	203	9-3-94	.177	.143	.186	56	164	13	29	2	0	0	12	34	5	4	1	36	1	2	.189	.333
Lage, Jesus	B-R	6-1	155	12-1-97	.176	.176	.176	48	159	15	28	3	1	0	19	17	6	4	1	41	9	6	.208	.279
Monserratt, Jesus	R-R	6-0	180	1-3-97	.227	.071	.275	36	119	14	27	11	0	1	7	8	4	3	0	25	1	0	.345	.298
Mordock, Erick	R-R	5-11	165	9-9-97	.195	.270	.173	51	164	19	32	5	0	0	9	24	6	3	1	28	7	6	.226	.318
Rigby, Gean	R-R	6-0	180	1-7-97	.199	.226	.190	49	136	16	27	2	0	0	3	28	1	8	0	35	8	6	.213	.339
Rivas, Jose	R-R	5-11	170	8-5-98	.223	.191	.235	53	179	11	40	6	0	1	16	24	5	2	0	19	0	0	.274	.332
Rodriguez, Jhonny	L-L	6-3	170	7-20-96	.171	.182	.167	13	41	4	7	2	1	1	4	5	2	0	0	9	0	0	.341	.292
Silva, Andys	R-R	5-11	160	9-12-95	.190	.196	.189	63	189	21	36	6	1	0	13	31	3	4	3	47	7	7	.233	.310

Pitching	B-T	HT	WT	DOB	W	L	ERA	G	GS	CG	SV	IP	H	R	ER	HR	BB	SO	AVG	vLH	vRH	K/9	BB/9
Aquino, Ruber	R-R	6-2	185	12-29-96	1	4	4.65	17	0	0	2	31	25	18	16	3	19	21	.219	.217	.220	6.10	5.52
Calderon, Alexander	L-L	6-3	170	2-38-96	6	1	2.38	15	2	0	1	64	50	24	17	2	25	58	.220	.343	.198	8.11	3.50
Charles, Wandisson	R-R	6-6	220	9-7-96	1	5	4.12	12	12	0	0	39	31	23	18	0	38	37	.221	.271	.196	8.47	8.69
De La Cruz, Frederick	R-R	6-3	170	9-13-96	0	4	9.97	10	6	0	0	22	29	27	24	1	14	13	.319	.333	.314	5.40	5.82
Hoyos, Renaldo	L-L	6-0	170	8-8-96	1	3	3.29	16	0	0	2	27	25	11	10	0	13	17	.258	.333	.250	5.60	4.28
Hurtado, Jhenderson	L-L	6-1	180	3-28-96	3	2	4.31	15	8	0	0	63	45	32	30	1	30	53	.202	.045	.219	7.61	4.31
Magallanes, Wilfredo	R-R	6-2	185	11-15-95	1	4	4.92	15	6	0	0	57	63	38	31	2	22	28	.288	.266	.304	4.45	3.49
Montilla, David	L-L	6-0	170	5-29-98	1	1	14.46	7	0	0	0	9	13	20	15	1	7	5	.317	.143	.353	4.82	6.75
Mora, Jose	R-R	6-3	185	10-1-97	1	3	3.63	12	10	0	0	40	34	23	16	0	30	27	.246	.211	.260	6.13	6.81
Morban, Jose	R-R	6-2	162	12-24-97	0	1	1.23	2	2	0	0	7	1	3	1	0	4	2	.040	.100	.000	2.45	4.91
Rodriguez, Santiago	R-R	6-3	190	3-9-97	1	5	3.33	13	8	0	0	54	55	26	20	1	25	27	.274	.367	.213	4.50	4.17
Ruiz, Jean	R-R	6-1	165	9-6-96	2	4	3.02	15	5	0	2	57	49	33	19	5	24	41	.229	.283	.214	6.51	3.81
Sullivan, Enmanuel	R-R	6-3	195	6-24-96	0	1	3.38	14	1	0	0	21	9	10	8	0	16	14	.130	.167	.118	5.91	6.75
Tovar, Oscar	R-R	6-1	160	3-19-98	3	5	2.60	13	11	0	0	55	35	25	16	0	22	26	.184	.134	.211	4.23	3.58
Trejo, Jose	R-R	6-3	175	3-31-96	0	0	3.38	2	0	0	0	3	1	1	1	0	3	1	.125	.333	.000	3.38	10.13
Vargas, Alejandro	R-R	5-11	160	1-29-95	4	2	1.95	18	1	0	3	55	43	18	12	0	18	47	.209	.246	.191	7.64	2.93
Vilchez, Gerardo	R-R	6-4	165	6-6-97	1	1	2.25	9	0	0	4	12	11	6	3	0	6	10	.268	.214	.296	7.50	4.50

Fielding

Catcher	PCT	G	PO	A	E	DP	PB
Gordon	.975	19	90	26	3	3	3
Hernandez	.957	18	74	16	4	0	1
Monserratt	.980	18	71	25	2	0	5
Rivas	.978	34	189	38	5	3	2

First Base	PCT	G	PO	A	E	DP
Agelvis	1.000	3	14	0	0	0
Aquino	1.000	1	8	0	0	0
Godard	1.000	4	21	1	0	4
Gordon	.983	30	220	11	4	17
Hernandez	.983	34	273	8	5	25
Monserratt	.927	6	37	1	3	4
Rivas	.969	6	29	2	1	4
Silva	.959	8	43	4	2	8

Second Base	PCT	G	PO	A	E	DP
Agelvis	.977	19	42	43	2	12
De Los Santos	—	1	0	0	0	0
Godard	.972	25	48	57	3	8
Silva	.962	40	79	96	7	21

Third Base	PCT	G	PO	A	E	DP
Agelvis	.957	45	43	92	6	10
De Los Santos	.643	5	3	6	5	0
Godard	.941	8	6	26	2	1
Gordon	1.000	7	5	14	0	1
Hernandez	1.000	1	0	2	0	0
Lage	1.000	2	1	3	0	1
Monserratt	1.000	1	2	2	0	1
Silva	.974	10	13	24	1	2

Shortstop	PCT	G	PO	A	E	DP
Agelvis	.962	5	11	14	1	2
De Los Santos	—	1	0	0	0	0
Godard	.923	23	43	53	8	11

	PCT	G	PO	A	E	DP
Lage	.927	45	95	135	18	27
Silva	.909	3	2	8	1	1

Outfield	PCT	G	PO	A	E	DP
Aquino	—	2	0	0	0	0
Arias	.938	30	55	6	4	2
De Los Santos	—	1	0	0	0	0
Godard	1.000	4	8	1	0	1
Gonzalez	.975	67	109	9	3	0
Gordon	1.000	4	3	0	0	0
Hoyos	1.000	1	2	0	0	0
Mordock	.982	51	106	5	2	2
Rigby	.949	48	70	4	4	0
Rodriguez	1.000	13	20	1	0	0
Silva	1.000	6	3	1	0	1
Vargas	.875	6	6	1	1	0
Vilchez	—	1	0	0	0	0

Philadelphia Phillies

SEASON IN A SENTENCE: The Phillies fulfilled their promise as one of the worst teams in the major leagues, but prospects for the future got much brighter in the second half.

HIGH POINT: In his final start for the team, lefthander Cole Hamels went out in the best way possible. In Wrigley Field, Hamels stymied one of the league's most potent offenses with a no-hitter on July 25. Hamels walked two that day and struck out 13.

LOW POINT: The Phillies' season as a whole was awful, but the team's stretch from June 8-17 took things to another level. They lost all nine games in that span, were shut out three times—including two consecutive games—and scored just 18 runs. Manager Ryne Sandberg resigned 10 days later. Ruben Amaro Jr. was dismissed as general manager late in the season and former Angels assistant GM Matt Klentak was tabbed to take his place.

NOTABLE ROOKIES: The Phillies received contributions from plenty of rookies this season, none more notable than the duo of third baseman Maikel Franco and righthander Aaron Nola, however. Franco, after a cameo in 2014, cemented himself as the team's third baseman of the future by hitting .280/.343/.497 with 13 homers in 80 games before breaking his wrist in middle of the summer. Nola went 6-2, 3.59 with 68 strikeouts in 78 innings before he reached his innings cap toward the end of the year. Odubel Herrera, the team's Rule 5 draft pick, stuck with the big club and played every day in the outfield.

KEY TRANSACTIONS: The Phils swapped ace Cole Hamels (and lefty reliever Jake Diekman) to the Rangers for lefty Matt Harrison and five prospects, including catcher Jorge Alfaro, outfielder Nick Williams and righthanders Jake Thompson, Jerad Eickhoff and Alec Asher. Williams, Alfaro and Thompson each ranked among the Texas' top five prospects. The system also added five more prospects in the trades that sent Chase Utley to the Dodgers, Ben Revere to the Blue Jays and Jonathan Papelbon to the Nationals.

DOWN ON THE FARM: In the span of roughly 13 months, the system has undergone a near-total overhaul. It ranked 22nd entering the season, and hadn't been outside the sport's lower third since before 2012. Now, after those deals, they're likely to rank among the top 10 in the game. Their crown jewel is still J.P. Crawford, a top-five prospect who showed the same skill set at Double-A.

OPENING DAY PAYROLL: $135,827,500 (9th)

ORGANIZATION LEADERS

BATTING   *Minimum 250 AB

MAJORS

* AVG	Odubel Herrera	.297
* OPS	Odubel Herrera	.762
HR	Ryan Howard	23
RBI	Ryan Howard	77

MINORS

* AVG	Rhys Hoskins, Lakewood, Clearwater	.319
* OBP	Rhys Hoskins, Lakewood, Clearwater	.395
* SLG	Rhys Hoskins, Lakewood, Clearwater	.518
R	Rhys Hoskins, Lakewood, Clearwater	86
H	Rhys Hoskins, Lakewood, Clearwater	159
TB	Rhys Hoskins, Lakewood, Clearwater	258
2B	Rhys Hoskins, Lakewood, Clearwater	36
3B	Angelo Mora, Clearwater, Reading	10
HR	Rhys Hoskins, Lakewood, Clearwater	17
RBI	Rhys Hoskins, Lakewood, Clearwater	90
	Brock Stassi, Reading	90
BB	Brock Stassi, Reading	77
SO	Jordan Danks, Lehigh Valley	122
SB	Roman Quinn, Reading	29

PITCHING   #Minimum 75 IP

MAJORS

W	Ken Giles	6
# ERA	Aaron Harang	4.86
SO	Cole Hamels	137
SV	Jonathan Papelbon	17

MINORS

W	Ricardo Pinto, Lakewood, Clearwater	15
L	Victor Arano, Clearwater	12
# ERA	Ricardo Pinto, Lakewood, Clearwater	2.97
G	Stephen Shackleford, Reading	53
GS	Ben Lively, Reading	25
	David Whitehead, Clearwater	25
SV	Stephen Shackleford, Reading	30
IP	Ricardo Pinto, Lakewood, Clearwater	145
BB	Jesse Biddle, Reading, Lehigh Valley	61
SO	Mark Leiter, Reading, Clearwater	121
AVG	Tyler Viza, Lakewood	.240

General Manager: Ruben Amaro Jr. **Farm Director:** Joe Jordan. **Scouting Director:** Johnny Almaraz.

Class	Team	League	W	L	PCT	Finish	Manager
Majors	Philadelphia Phillies	National	63	99	.389	15th (15)	Ryne Sandberg
Triple-A	Lehigh Valley IronPigs	International	63	81	.438	12th (14)	Dave Brundage
Double-A	Reading Fightin Phils	Eastern	80	61	.567	1st (12)	Dusty Wathan
High A	Clearwater Threshers	Florida State	79	58	.577	1st (12)	Greg Legg
Low A	Lakewood BlueClaws	South Atlantic	73	65	.529	4th (14)	Shawn Williams
Short season	Williamsport Crosscutters	New York-Penn	46	30	.605	1st (14)	Pat Borders
Rookie	Phillies	Gulf Coast	36	24	.600	4th (16)	Roly de Armas
Overall 2015 Minor League Record			377	319	.542	4th (30)	

ORGANIZATION STATISTICS

PHILADELPHIA PHILLIES

NATIONAL LEAGUE

Batting	B-T	HT	WT	DOB	AVG	vLH	vRH	G	AB	R	H	2B	3B	HR	RBI	BB	HBP	SH	SF	SO	SB	CS	SLG	OBP
Altherr, Aaron	R-R	6-5	215	1-14-91	.241	.180	.276	39	137	25	33	11	4	5	22	16	5	1	2	41	6	2	.489	.338
Asche, Cody	L-R	6-1	200	6-30-90	.245	.231	.248	129	425	41	104	22	3	12	39	26	4	0	1	111	1	2	.395	.294
Blanco, Andres	B-R	5-10	195	4-11-84	.292	.349	.259	106	233	32	68	22	3	7	25	21	4	3	0	44	1	1	.502	.360
Bogusevic, Brian	L-L	6-3	215	2-18-84	.259	.091	.298	22	58	9	15	3	0	2	5	3	0	0	0	21	2	0	.414	.295
Brown, Domonic	L-L	6-5	225	9-3-87	.228	.238	.224	63	189	19	43	6	1	5	25	14	1	0	0	36	3	1	.349	.284
d'Arnaud, Chase	R-R	6-1	205	1-21-87	.176	.231	.000	11	17	2	3	0	1	0	0	1	0	0	0	7	0	1	.294	.222
Danks, Jordan	L-R	6-5	220	8-7-86	.000	.000	.000	4	4	0	0	0	0	0	0	0	0	0	0	2	0	0	.000	.000
Franco, Maikel	R-R	6-1	215	8-26-92	.280	.232	.294	80	304	45	85	22	1	14	50	26	4	0	1	52	1	0	.497	.343
Francoeur, Jeff	R-R	6-4	220	1-8-84	.258	.248	.264	118	326	34	84	16	1	13	45	13	1	0	3	77	0	2	.433	.286
Galvis, Freddy	B-R	5-10	190	11-14-89	.263	.280	.256	151	559	63	147	14	5	7	50	30	3	7	4	103	10	1	.343	.302
Hernandez, Cesar	B-R	5-10	165	5-23-90	.272	.314	.254	127	405	57	110	20	4	1	35	40	2	4	1	86	19	5	.348	.339
Herrera, Odubel	L-R	5-11	200	12-29-91	.297	.293	.298	147	495	64	147	30	8	8	41	28	8	5	1	129	16	8	.418	.344
Howard, Ryan	L-L	6-4	250	11-19-79	.229	.130	.256	129	467	53	107	29	1	23	77	27	5	0	3	138	0	0	.443	.277
Kratz, Erik	R-R	6-4	240	6-15-80	.227	.333	.100	12	22	3	5	2	0	0	2	1	0	0	0	3	0	0	.318	.261
Revere, Ben	L-R	5-9	170	5-3-88	.298	.234	.320	96	366	49	109	13	6	1	26	19	1	2	0	36	24	5	.374	.334
Ruf, Darin	R-R	6-3	250	7-28-86	.235	.371	.158	106	268	30	63	12	0	12	39	21	5	0	3	69	1	0	.414	.300
Ruiz, Carlos	R-R	5-10	205	1-22-79	.211	.327	.183	86	284	23	60	13	1	2	22	28	4	3	1	43	1	1	.285	.290
Rupp, Cameron	R-R	6-2	260	9-28-88	.233	.303	.211	81	270	24	63	9	1	9	28	24	3	0	2	71	0	1	.374	.301
Sizemore, Grady	L-L	6-2	205	8-2-82	.245	.250	.244	39	98	4	24	5	0	0	6	6	0	0	0	23	0	0	.296	.288
Sweeney, Darnell	B-R	6-1	195	2-1-91	.176	.222	.155	37	85	9	15	4	1	3	11	13	0	0	0	27	0	2	.353	.286
Utley, Chase	L-R	6-1	190	12-17-78	.217	.194	.225	73	249	23	54	12	1	5	30	22	4	0	7	35	3	0	.333	.284
2-team total (34 Los Angeles)					.212	—	—	107	373	37	79	21	2	8	39	32	10	0	8	64	4	0	.343	.286

Pitching	B-T	HT	WT	DOB	W	L	ERA	G	GS	CG	SV	IP	H	R	ER	HR	BB	SO	AVG	vLH	vRH	K/9	BB/9
Araujo, Elvis	L-L	6-7	270	7-15-91	2	1	3.38	40	0	0	0	35	29	17	13	1	19	34	.225	.243	.200	8.83	4.93
Asher, Alec	R-R	6-4	230	10-4-91	0	6	9.31	7	7	0	0	29	42	30	30	8	10	16	.339	.379	.293	4.97	3.10
Aumont, Phillippe	L-R	6-7	240	1-7-89	0	1	13.50	1	1	0	0	4	5	6	6	2	7	3	.313	.333	.286	6.75	15.75
Billingsley, Chad	R-R	6-1	240	7-29-84	2	3	5.84	7	7	0	0	37	53	26	24	5	8	15	.346	.394	.305	3.65	1.95
Buchanan, David	R-R	6-3	200	5-11-89	2	9	6.99	15	15	0	0	75	109	60	58	12	29	44	.346	.353	.339	5.30	3.50
Correia, Kevin	R-R	6-3	200	8-24-80	0	3	6.56	5	5	0	0	23	37	23	17	4	8	14	.363	.352	.375	5.40	3.09
De Fratus, Justin	B-R	6-4	225	10-21-87	0	2	5.51	61	0	0	0	80	92	52	49	9	32	68	.291	.221	.335	7.65	3.60
Diekman, Jake	L-L	6-4	205	1-21-87	2	1	5.15	41	0	0	0	37	40	23	21	3	24	49	.268	.276	.264	12.03	5.89
Eickhoff, Jerad	R-R	6-4	240	7-2-90	3	3	2.65	8	8	0	0	51	40	16	15	5	13	49	.212	.268	.168	8.65	2.29
Garcia, Luis	R-R	6-3	230	1-30-87	4	6	3.51	72	0	0	2	67	72	28	26	4	37	63	.275	.337	.234	8.51	5.00
Giles, Ken	R-R	6-2	205	9-20-90	6	3	1.80	69	0	0	15	70	59	23	14	2	25	87	.219	.222	.217	11.19	3.21
Gomez, Jeanmar	R-R	6-3	220	2-10-88	2	3	3.01	65	0	0	0	75	82	28	25	4	17	50	.278	.256	.292	6.03	2.05
Gonzalez, Severino	R-R	6-2	155	9-28-92	3	3	7.92	7	7	0	0	31	44	27	27	7	7	28	.346	.426	.273	8.22	2.05
Hamels, Cole	L-L	6-3	200	12-27-83	6	7	3.64	20	20	1	0	129	113	53	52	12	39	137	.233	.194	.243	9.58	2.73
Harang, Aaron	R-R	6-7	260	5-9-78	6	15	4.86	29	29	0	0	172	189	100	93	26	51	108	.278	.283	.273	5.64	2.66
Hinojosa, Dalier	R-R	6-1	230	2-10-86	2	0	0.78	18	0	0	0	23	15	3	2	1	8	21	.176	.128	.217	8.22	3.13
Jimenez, Cesar	L-L	6-0	215	11-12-84	0	0	0.00	3	0	0	0	3	1	0	0	0	4	1	.100	.167	.000	10.80	0.00
2-team total (16 Milwaukee)					0	0	3.13	19	0	0	0	23	17	8	8	2	8	25	—	—	—	9.78	3.13
Loewen, Adam	L-L	6-6	235	4-9-84	1	0	6.98	20	0	0	0	19	20	15	15	3	17	22	.282	.294	.270	10.24	7.91
McGowan, Dustin	R-R	6-3	240	3-24-82	1	2	6.94	14	1	0	0	23	29	21	18	7	20	21	.296	.289	.302	8.10	7.71
Morgan, Adam	L-L	6-1	195	2-27-90	5	7	4.48	15	15	0	0	84	88	45	42	14	17	49	.269	.225	.281	5.23	1.81
Murray, Colton	R-R	6-0	195	4-22-90	0	1	5.87	8	0	0	0	8	11	5	5	2	2	9	.314	.231	.364	10.57	2.35
Neris, Hector	R-R	6-2	215	6-14-89	2	2	3.79	32	0	0	0	40	38	19	17	8	10	41	.245	.267	.232	9.15	2.23
Nola, Aaron	R-R	6-1	195	6-4-93	6	2	3.59	13	13	0	0	78	74	31	31	11	19	68	.251	.310	.212	7.88	2.20
O'Sullivan, Sean	R-R	6-1	255	9-1-87	1	6	6.08	13	13	0	0	71	94	49	48	16	20	35	.322	.366	.290	4.44	2.54
Ogando, Nefi	R-R	6-2	220	6-3-89	0	0	9.00	4	0	0	0	4	7	5	4	0	2	2	.368	.273	.500	4.50	4.50
Papelbon, Jonathan	R-R	6-4	225	11-23-80	2	1	1.59	37	0	0	17	40	31	9	7	3	8	40	.211	.269	.163	9.08	1.82
2-team total (22 Washington)					4	3	2.13	59	0	0	24	63	53	22	15	7	12	56	—	—	—	7.96	1.71
Roberts, Ken	L-L	6-1	200	3-9-88	1	0	10.38	6	0	0	0	4	9	5	5	0	1	1	.474	.500	.429	2.08	2.08
2-team total (9 Colorado)					1	1	7.24	15	0	0	0	14	22	11	11	0	3	6	—	—	—	3.95	1.98
Rosin, Seth	R-R	6-6	265	11-2-88	0	0	22.50	1	0	0	0	2	7	5	5	1	0	2	.636	.667	.625	0.00	4.50
Williams, Jerome	R-R	6-3	260	12-4-81	4	12	5.80	33	21	0	1	121	161	83	78	22	34	74	.317	.312	.321	5.50	2.53

Fielding

Catcher	PCT	G	PO	A	E	DP	PB
Kratz	1.000	3	14	1	0	1	0
Ruiz	.984	83	626	41	11	8	5
Rupp	.993	80	524	54	4	7	7

First Base	PCT	G	PO	A	E	DP
Blanco	1.000	1	11	1	0	0
Franco	1.000	2	13	1	0	1
Howard	.994	116	871	66	6	75
Kratz	1.000	2	15	0	0	2
Ruf	.993	66	416	27	3	47
Utley	1.000	4	19	2	0	2

Second Base	PCT	G	PO	A	E	DP
Blanco	.976	22	28	53	2	14
Galvis	1.000	4	9	11	0	3
Hernandez	.984	88	132	234	6	47
Sweeney	.931	9	14	13	2	4
Utley	.976	62	100	149	6	32

Third Base	PCT	G	PO	A	E	DP
Asche	.939	51	26	97	8	13
Blanco	.958	36	19	49	3	3
d'Arnaud	1.000	1	2	7	0	2
Franco	.944	75	49	119	10	11
Hernandez	.933	10	8	20	2	1
Sweeney	—		1	0	0	0

Shortstop	PCT	G	PO	A	E	DP
Blanco	.969	10	8	23	1	4
d'Arnaud	1.000	3	3	7	0	1
Galvis	.973	146	207	398	17	87
Hernandez	.974	12	12	26	1	4

Outfield	PCT	G	PO	A	E	DP
Altherr	1.000	37	80	3	0	1
Asche	.982	63	107	3	2	1
Bogusevic	.914	16	30	2	3	1
Brown	.990	50	99	4	1	1
Danks	—	1	0	0	0	0
Francoeur	.957	101	150	5	7	1
Herrera	.986	136	341	5	5	1
Revere	1.000	91	198	5	0	2
Ruf	1.000	22	31	0	0	0
Sizemore	.980	31	47	1	1	0
Sweeney	.957	14	21	1	1	0

LEHIGH VALLEY IRONPIGS
INTERNATIONAL LEAGUE

TRIPLE-A

Batting	B-T	HT	WT	DOB	AVG	vLH	vRH	G	AB	R	H	2B	3B	HR	RBI	BB	HBP	SH	SF	SO	SB	CS	SLG	OBP
Altherr, Aaron	R-R	6-5	215	1-14-91	.294	.353	.275	51	204	36	60	13	2	8	38	21	2	0	2	44	8	1	.495	.362
Asche, Cody	L-R	6-1	200	6-30-90	.295	.222	.326	15	61	7	18	3	0	1	3	6	0	0	0	9	0	0	.393	.358
Bogusevic, Brian	L-L	6-3	215	2-18-84	.296	.277	.304	118	467	65	138	18	3	12	57	44	3	0	1	97	24	5	.424	.359
Brown, Domonic	L-L	6-5	225	9-3-87	.257	.298	.242	52	210	22	54	12	1	2	26	14	2	0	2	37	10	3	.352	.307
Canzler, Russ	R-R	6-2	220	4-11-86	.274	.295	.264	109	394	46	108	24	1	10	47	35	1	0	2	78	2	4	.416	.333
Chapman, Ethan	L-R	6-0	180	1-5-90	.300	—	.300	3	10	1	3	0	1	0	2	0	0	0	0	2	0	0	.500	.417
d'Arnaud, Chase	R-R	6-1	205	1-21-87	.268	.258	.272	120	497	77	133	18	5	5	35	26	11	4	2	64	28	8	.354	.317
Danks, Jordan	L-R	6-5	220	8-7-86	.257	.241	.264	120	408	38	105	27	0	6	46	34	3	2	1	122	5	3	.368	.318
Dugan, Kelly	L-R	6-3	210	9-18-90	.221	.186	.239	36	131	11	29	4	0	2	15	8	6	1	1	34	0	0	.298	.295
Duran, Edgar	R-R	5-11	155	2-10-91	.163	.163	.163	45	135	12	22	6	0	0	9	12	2	6	0	23	0	0	.207	.242
Forsythe, Blake	R-R	6-2	220	7-31-89	.234	.316	.179	16	47	2	11	5	0	1	4	1	1	0	0	18	0	0	.404	.265
Franco, Maikel	R-R	6-1	215	8-26-92	.355	.372	.347	33	141	15	50	12	1	4	24	8	0	0	2	25	2	0	.539	.384
Garcia, Rene	R-R	6-0	205	3-21-90	.245	.286	.229	14	49	6	12	1	0	0	3	1	0	0	0	4	0	0	.265	.260
Henson, Tyler	R-R	6-1	205	12-15-87	.249	.237	.255	115	425	49	106	31	3	2	58	24	5	5	7	94	26	6	.351	.293
Hester, John	R-R	6-4	235	9-14-83	.304	.333	.294	9	23	2	7	3	0	0	1	0	1	0	0	3	0	0	.435	.333
Joseph, Tommy	R-R	6-1	255	7-16-91	.193	.200	.189	45	166	9	32	9	0	3	18	3	2	1	3	30	0	0	.301	.220
Kratz, Erik	R-R	6-4	240	6-15-80	.312	.286	.327	26	77	14	24	8	1	3	15	18	0	0	2	18	1	0	.558	.433
Lino, Gabriel	R-R	6-3	200	5-17-93	.215	.241	.196	53	195	12	42	11	0	0	12	8	0	0	2	56	0	2	.272	.244
Lohman, Devin	R-R	6-1	185	4-14-89	.156	.000	.217	10	32	1	5	2	0	0	1	0	0	1	0	12	0	0	.219	.156
Mastroianni, Darin	R-R	5-11	190	8-26-85	.293	.346	.250	16	58	8	17	4	0	2	4	0	1	1	1	12	5	1	.362	.333
2-team total (96 Syracuse)					.257	—		112	443	43	114	26	2	3	36	31	3	4	3	85	25	4	.345	.308
McGuiness, Chris	L-L	6-1	210	4-11-88	.223	.213	.227	101	327	39	73	15	0	3	36	55	2	2	1	62	1	2	.297	.338
Moore, Logan	L-R	6-3	215	8-22-90	.276	.250	.282	42	134	11	37	5	1	1	13	13	0	1	1	30	0	0	.351	.338
Nelson, Chris	R-R	5-11	205	9-3-85	.278	.250	.300	16	54	5	15	4	0	0	5	4	0	0	0	8	1	0	.352	.328
2-team total (28 Syracuse)					.277	—	—	44	148	16	41	14	0	3	19	13	0	0	1	22	2	0	.432	.333
Nix, Jayson	R-R	5-11	195	8-26-82	.157	.167	.155	29	89	6	14	2	0	2	4	5	0	1	0	22	0	1	.247	.202
2-team total (25 Norfolk)					.162	—	—	54	185	11	30	5	0	2	12	8	0	1	1	53	1	2	.222	.196
Pastornicky, Tyler	R-R	5-11	180	12-13-89	.286	.371	.238	25	98	10	28	5	0	1	4	10	1	0	0	15	0	1	.367	.358
Phelps, Cord	B-R	6-1	210	1-23-87	.229	.292	.202	119	397	43	91	11	2	3	34	54	0	3	4	81	5	3	.290	.319
Pointer, Brian	L-L	6-0	190	1-28-92	.000	—	.000	2	3	0	0	0	0	0	0	1	0	0	0	2	0	0	.000	.250
Ruf, Darin	R-R	6-3	250	7-28-86	.308	.154	.462	7	26	3	8	1	0	0	6	0	1	0	1	2	0	0	.346	.321
Serna, K.C.	R-R	6-0	185	10-15-89	.200	.235	.182	16	50	7	10	1	0	0	3	2	2	0	0	14	1	0	.220	.259
Utley, Chase	L-R	6-1	190	12-17-78	.667	1.000	.500	1	3	1	2	1	0	0	1	0	0	0	0	0	0	0	.667	.750

Pitching	B-T	HT	WT	DOB	W	L	ERA	G	GS	CG	SV	IP	H	R	ER	HR	BB	SO	AVG	vLH	vRH	K/9	BB/9
Asher, Alec	R-R	6-4	230	10-4-91	2	0	2.08	4	4	0	0	26	27	7	6	3	3	12	.262	.267	.259	4.15	1.04
Aumont, Phillippe	L-R	6-7	240	1-7-89	3	4	2.35	14	10	0	0	65	49	23	17	3	41	58	.212	.237	.194	8.03	5.68
2-team total (5 Buffalo)					3	6	3.14	19	14	0	0	83	61	35	29	5	63	81	—	—	.294	8.78	6.83
Berken, Jason	R-R	6-0	210	11-27-83	5	8	4.61	28	13	0	1	113	133	67	58	11	33	78	.291	.287	.294	6.19	2.62
Biddle, Jesse	L-L	6-5	235	10-22-91	2	4	6.25	9	9	0	0	45	57	33	31	4	27	32	.305	.279	.317	6.45	5.44
Billingsley, Chad	R-R	6-1	240	7-29-84	2	2	4.85	7	6	0	0	30	34	21	16	5	10	23	.276	.239	.321	6.98	3.03
Buchanan, David	R-R	6-3	200	5-11-89	4	2	2.80	10	10	0	0	55	58	20	17	2	20	30	.274	.198	.321	4.94	3.29
Clemens, Paul	R-R	6-4	200	2-14-88	0	3	6.00	6	5	0	0	24	27	17	16	3	20	22	.290	.260	.326	8.25	7.50
Denato, Joey	L-L	5-10	175	3-17-92	0	0	7.71	3	0	0	0	5	6	4	4	1	3	4	.316	.429	.250	7.71	5.79
Diekman, Jake	L-L	6-4	205	1-21-87	0	0	0.00	6	0	0	3	7	5	0	0	0	1	7	.208	.125	.250	9.00	1.29
Eickhoff, Jerad	R-R	6-4	240	7-2-90	2	1	2.49	3	3	0	0	22	17	6	6	1	3	19	.210	.258	.180	7.89	1.25
Gonzalez, Miguel Alfredo	R-R	6-3	210	9-23-86	0	2	14.29	2	2	0	0	6	12	10	9	1	4	4	.400	.400	.400	6.35	6.35
Gonzalez, Severino	R-R	6-2	155	9-28-92	2	7	5.11	16	16	0	0	88	106	54	50	8	18	45	.298	.278	.311	4.60	1.84
Gutierrez, Juan	R-R	6-3	245	7-14-83	4	1	2.88	18	0	0	2	25	29	10	8	2	9	19	.284	.380	.192	6.84	3.24
2-team total (9 Syracuse)					4	1	3.67	27	0	0	4	34	44	16	14	2	15	27	—	—	—	7.08	3.93
Hill, Nick	L-L	6-0	195	1-30-85	0	0	4.58	12	0	0	1	20	24	10	10	1	9	12	.333	.421	.302	5.49	4.12
Hinojosa, Dalier	R-R	6-1	230	2-10-86	0	1	5.54	10	0	0	0	13	14	8	8	1	5	13	.275	.238	.300	9.00	3.46
2-team total (19 Pawtucket)					3	2	3.76	29	0	0	0	55	53	29	23	3	22	52	—	—	—	8.51	3.60
Jimenez, Cesar	L-L	6-0	215	11-12-84	3	5	3.61	41	1	0	4	57	61	23	23	4	18	40	.272	.274	.271	6.28	2.83

Pitching	B-T	HT	WT	DOB	W	L	ERA	G	GS	CG	SV	IP	H	R	ER	HR	BB	SO	AVG	vLH	vRH	K/9	BB/9
Knigge, Tyler	R-R	6-4	215	10-27-88	0	0	5.28	20	0	0	0	29	40	19	17	1	13	18	.354	.410	.324	5.59	4.03
Leroux, Chris	L-R	6-6	225	4-14-84	3	3	2.82	22	3	0	0	61	47	22	19	3	19	40	.210	.138	.262	5.93	2.82
Loewen, Adam	L-L	6-6	235	4-9-84	1	3	2.15	33	0	0	10	46	29	11	11	1	32	60	.185	.177	.189	11.74	6.26
McGowan, Dustin	R-R	6-3	240	3-24-82	2	2	4.08	31	1	0	15	40	41	19	18	2	24	28	.261	.323	.217	6.35	5.45
Morgan, Adam	L-L	6-1	195	2-27-90	0	6	4.74	13	13	0	0	68	81	45	36	7	27	33	.298	.344	.284	4.35	3.56
Murray, Colton	R-R	6-0	195	4-22-90	2	2	2.79	31	0	0	2	42	24	16	13	2	21	41	.164	.156	.171	8.79	4.50
Neris, Hector	R-R	6-2	215	6-14-89	1	3	3.62	27	0	0	1	37	38	16	15	1	24	35	.260	.396	.183	8.44	5.79
Nesseth, Mike	R-R	6-5	210	4-19-88	0	0	0.00	2	0	0	0	2	2	0	0	0	0	0	.250	.000	.500	0.00	0.00
Nola, Aaron	R-R	6-1	195	6-4-93	3	1	3.58	6	6	0	0	33	38	14	13	3	9	33	.288	.286	.290	9.09	2.48
O'Sullivan, Sean	R-R	6-1	255	9-1-87	5	2	3.20	9	9	0	0	56	48	23	20	3	19	41	.227	.221	.234	6.55	3.04
Ogando, Nefi	R-R	6-2	220	6-3-89	2	2	2.86	21	0	0	1	28	27	11	9	1	12	22	.243	.271	.222	6.99	3.81
Roberts, Ken	L-L	6-1	200	3-9-88	0	0	0.00	3	0	0	0	3	3	0	0	0	0	2	.250	.200	.286	6.00	0.00
Rodriguez, Joely	L-L	6-1	200	11-14-91	2	6	6.32	13	13	1	0	68	89	48	48	3	37	33	.321	.322	.321	4.35	4.87
Rosin, Seth	R-R	6-6	265	11-2-88	4	3	3.29	47	0	0	3	68	76	27	25	4	21	49	.278	.300	.261	6.45	2.77
Vasquez, Anthony	L-L	6-0	190	9-19-86	8	8	4.56	20	20	1	0	109	105	59	55	6	46	61	.258	.302	.243	5.05	3.81

Fielding

Catcher	PCT	G	PO	A	E	DP	PB
Forsythe	.973	11	63	8	2	2	0
Garcia	.988	14	74	7	1	0	0
Hester	1.000	9	50	3	0	0	0
Joseph	.992	19	120	7	1	2	2
Kratz	.988	11	79	5	1	1	1
Lino	.995	51	337	33	2	7	6
Moore	.991	36	204	22	2	2	4

First Base	PCT	G	PO	A	E	DP
Bogusevic	.963	3	24	2	1	3
Canzler	.991	40	310	32	3	30
Franco	1.000	4	34	2	0	3
Henson	1.000	1	8	0	0	0
Joseph	.991	22	196	14	2	21
Kratz	1.000	1	7	1	0	0
McGuiness	.994	79	585	48	4	70
Ruf	1.000	5	34	2	0	8

Second Base	PCT	G	PO	A	E	DP
d'Arnaud	—	1	0	0	0	0
Duran	1.000	2	2	3	0	0
Henson	.954	49	119	132	12	37
Lohman	.941	5	6	10	1	0
Nelson	1.000	6	10	14	0	2
Nix	.989	14	45	41	1	12
Pastornicky	.972	20	41	64	3	16
Phelps	.984	55	114	135	4	37
Serna	—	1	0	0	0	0

Third Base	PCT	G	PO	A	E	DP
Canzler	.936	24	11	33	3	2
d'Arnaud	.972	34	13	56	2	5
Franco	.975	29	22	55	2	5
Lohman	.667	3	0	2	1	0
Nelson	.000	1	0	0	1	0
Nix	.917	6	2	9	1	2
Pastornicky	.909	4	4	6	1	0
Phelps	.950	55	27	87	6	12

Shortstop	PCT	G	PO	A	E	DP
d'Arnaud	.945	87	136	240	22	64
Duran	.960	44	74	118	8	26
Lohman	.857	2	6	0	1	1
Nix	1.000	8	10	30	0	9
Phelps	—	1	0	0	0	0
Serna	.875	15	18	31	7	6

Outfield	PCT	G	PO	A	E	DP
Altherr	1.000	49	154	2	0	0
Asche	.958	15	23	0	1	0
Bogusevic	.996	108	250	5	1	0
Brown	.990	47	92	6	1	1
Canzler	.955	13	20	1	1	0
Chapman	1.000	3	11	0	0	0
d'Arnaud	1.000	3	2	0	0	0
Danks	.986	102	214	5	3	0
Dugan	.986	35	67	1	1	0
Henson	.993	49	135	1	1	0
Mastroianni	.979	13	46	1	1	0
Pointer	1.000	1	1	0	0	0
Ruf	1.000	2	5	0	0	0

READING FIGHTIN' PHILS — *DOUBLE-A*

EASTERN LEAGUE

Batting	B-T	HT	WT	DOB	AVG	vLH	vRH	G	AB	R	H	2B	3B	HR	RBI	BB	HBP	SH	SF	SO	SB	CS	SLG	OBP
Alonso, Carlos	R-R	5-11	205	2-15-88	.262	.200	.321	12	42	9	11	3	0	0	6	9	0	0	0	6	2	0	.333	.392
Altherr, Aaron	R-R	6-5	215	1-14-91	.293	.308	.288	60	229	29	67	19	3	6	29	28	1	1	1	40	8	3	.480	.371
Chapman, Ethan	L-R	6-0	180	1-5-90	.077	.000	.083	6	13	1	1	0	0	0	1	3	0	0	0	1	0	0	.077	.250
Charles, Art	L-L	6-6	220	11-10-90	.215	.186	.220	91	289	31	62	16	2	8	45	38	0	0	2	100	1	0	.367	.304
Cozens, Dylan	L-L	6-6	235	5-31-94	.350	.438	.292	11	40	6	14	2	0	3	9	3	0	0	1	7	2	1	.625	.386
Crawford, J.P.	L-R	6-2	180	1-11-95	.265	.227	.282	86	351	53	93	21	7	5	34	49	1	1	3	45	7	2	.407	.354
Dugan, Kelly	L-R	6-3	210	9-18-90	.315	.209	.352	44	168	23	53	11	1	0	17	13	9	0	2	39	2	0	.393	.391
Forsythe, Blake	R-R	6-2	220	7-31-89	.286	—	.286	2	7	2	2	0	0	0	0	1	0	0	0	1	0	0	.286	.375
Garcia, Rene	R-R	6-0	205	3-21-90	.343	.292	.368	38	143	14	49	7	0	0	19	3	1	1	2	12	0	1	.392	.356
Greene, Brodie	R-R	6-1	195	9-25-87	.241	.227	.246	90	299	39	72	16	0	0	22	39	3	4	2	40	2	1	.294	.332
Heid, Drew	L-R	5-10	175	12-14-87	.128	.231	.088	15	47	5	6	2	1	0	5	5	1	0	1	9	1	0	.213	.222
Hester, John	R-R	6-4	235	9-14-83	.000	.000	—	1	3	0	0	0	0	0	0	0	0	0	0	1	0	0	.000	.000
Hood, Destin	R-R	6-2	210	4-3-90	.287	.294	.284	42	167	19	48	13	1	7	37	7	0	1	1	42	1	1	.503	.314
2-team total (40 Akron)					.290	—	—	82	307	39	89	24	4	10	56	17	2	1	3	78	5	2	.492	.328
Knapp, Andrew	B-R	6-1	190	11-9-91	.360	.431	.333	55	214	39	77	21	2	11	56	22	2	0	3	43	1	0	.631	.419
Lino, Gabriel	R-R	6-3	200	5-17-93	.266	.269	.266	32	109	12	29	9	0	3	13	10	2	0	2	25	0	0	.431	.333
Lohman, Devin	R-R	6-1	185	4-14-89	.190	.000	.222	7	21	0	4	0	0	0	2	0	0	0	1	3	1	0	.190	.182
Martinez, Harold	R-R	6-3	210	5-3-90	.292	.333	.270	86	260	33	76	10	3	4	33	18	0	3	3	46	1	0	.400	.335
Moore, Logan	L-R	6-3	190	8-22-90	.221	.077	.244	27	95	11	21	6	0	2	12	7	0	1	0	17	0	1	.347	.275
Mora, Angelo	B-R	5-11	151	2-25-93	.327	.464	.282	37	113	23	37	6	4	3	18	16	0	2	0	27	0	3	.531	.411
Perkins, Cam	R-R	6-5	195	9-27-90	.252	.235	.263	100	377	51	95	25	1	11	51	25	7	4	5	53	7	1	.411	.307
Pierre, Gustavo	R-R	6-2	202	12-28-91	.227	.250	.219	69	225	22	51	6	2	3	17	7	3	4	1	45	3	0	.311	.258
Pointer, Brian	L-L	6-0	190	1-28-92	.242	.163	.257	92	273	44	66	17	1	10	33	42	2	3	0	89	7	1	.421	.347
Quinn, Roman	B-R	5-10	170	5-14-93	.306	.350	.281	58	232	44	71	6	6	4	15	18	0	7	0	42	29	10	.435	.356
Serna, K.C.	R-R	6-0	185	10-15-89	.254	.273	.246	94	331	42	84	11	2	1	31	26	8	6	7	37	9	4	.308	.317
Stassi, Brock	L-L	6-2	190	8-7-89	.300	.255	.317	133	466	76	140	32	1	15	90	77	1	0	10	63	3	2	.470	.394
Thomas, Tony	R-R	5-10	180	7-10-86	.225	.182	.241	25	80	8	18	6	2	1	8	3	2	1	0	25	2	1	.388	.271
2-team total (43 Erie)					.247	—	—	68	235	29	58	13	2	8	34	15	3	2	1	68	5	2	.421	.299
Utley, Chase	L-R	6-1	190	12-17-78	.500	.500	.500	2	8	3	4	1	0	0	1	1	0	0	0	1	0	0	.625	.556
Williams, Nick	L-L	6-3	195	9-8-93	.320	.186	.426	22	97	21	31	5	2	4	10	3	0	0	0	20	3	0	.536	.340

Pitching	B-T	HT	WT	DOB	W	L	ERA	G	GS	CG	SV	IP	H	R	ER	HR	BB	SO	AVG	vLH	vRH	K/9	BB/9
Araujo, Elvis	L-L	6-7	270	7-15-91	1	2	7.45	7	0	0	0	10	9	8	8	1	6	11	.243	.267	.227	10.24	5.59

Pitching

Pitching	B-T	HT	WT	DOB	W	L	ERA	G	GS	CG	SV	IP	H	R	ER	HR	BB	SO	AVG	vLH	vRH	K/9	BB/9
Biddle, Jesse	L-L	6-5	235	10-22-91	7	2	4.24	15	15	0	0	81	90	46	38	7	34	57	.288	.284	.290	6.36	3.79
Cordero, Jimmy	R-R	6-3	215	10-19-91	0	0	2.12	13	0	0	0	17	11	5	4	1	4	18	.193	.182	.208	9.53	2.12
2-team total (17 New Hampshire)					0	1	2.59	30	0	0	1	42	27	15	12	2	18	40	—	—	—	8.64	3.89
Eflin, Zach	R-R	6-4	200	4-8-94	8	6	3.69	23	23	0	0	132	136	63	54	12	23	68	.268	.298	.239	4.65	1.57
Hill, Nick	L-L	6-0	195	1-30-85	0	0	0.00	2	0	0	1	2	0	0	0	0	2	2	.000	.000	.000	10.80	10.80
Kleven, Colin	R-R	6-5	200	4-15-91	1	3	8.65	5	5	0	0	26	32	25	25	1	10	15	.323	.286	.338	5.19	3.46
Knigge, Tyler	R-R	6-4	215	10-27-88	0	0	4.26	8	0	0	2	13	11	6	6	2	3	13	.239	.294	.207	9.24	2.13
Leiter Jr., Mark	R-R	6-0	195	3-13-91	2	6	4.79	8	8	1	0	47	56	26	25	3	11	38	.303	.310	.296	7.28	2.11
Leroux, Chris	L-R	6-6	225	4-14-84	0	0	2.57	1	1	0	0	7	6	2	2	0	1	5	.231	.375	.167	6.43	1.29
Lively, Ben	R-R	6-4	190	3-5-92	8	7	4.13	25	25	1	0	144	160	69	66	14	45	111	.290	.318	.268	6.95	2.82
Loewen, Adam	L-L	6-6	235	4-9-84	1	0	1.46	7	0	0	0	12	10	4	2	1	5	13	.233	.250	.222	9.49	3.65
Martin, Ethan	R-R	6-2	225	6-6-89	3	1	3.14	21	5	0	0	52	46	18	18	3	15	31	.241	.233	.246	5.40	2.61
Milner, Hoby	L-L	6-2	165	1-13-91	2	1	3.69	29	2	0	0	61	61	26	25	6	17	40	.268	.224	.289	5.90	2.51
Morris, Will	L-R	6-4	180	5-2-93	0	0	4.50	1	0	0	0	2	1	1	1	1	1	1	.143	.000	.167	4.50	4.50
Murray, Colton	R-R	6-0	195	4-22-90	6	1	2.52	21	0	0	1	36	31	10	10	1	10	36	.230	.159	.264	9.08	2.52
Nesseth, Mike	R-R	6-5	210	4-19-88	0	2	5.02	8	0	0	0	14	17	9	8	1	7	10	.293	.393	.200	6.28	4.40
Nola, Aaron	R-R	6-1	195	6-4-93	7	3	1.88	12	12	0	0	77	59	17	16	4	9	59	.219	.188	.242	6.93	1.06
O'Sullivan, Ryan	R-R	6-2	190	9-5-90	2	3	2.39	36	0	0	4	53	45	16	14	3	18	30	.241	.259	.226	5.13	3.08
Ogando, Nefi	R-R	6-2	220	6-3-89	2	3	2.86	24	0	0	2	35	25	11	11	2	19	33	.203	.250	.173	8.57	4.93
Pivetta, Nick	R-R	6-5	220	2-14-93	2	2	7.31	7	7	0	0	28	32	24	23	4	19	25	.294	.288	.300	7.94	6.04
2-team total (3 Harrisburg)					2	4	7.27	10	10	0	0	43	51	36	35	8	28	31	—	—	—	6.44	5.82
Ramos, Edubray	R-R	6-0	165	12-19-92	1	2	3.54	18	0	0	0	20	17	9	8	0	10	18	.233	.172	.273	7.97	4.43
Ridenhour, Lee	R-R	6-4	230	8-7-89	0	0	5.82	13	0	0	1	17	23	14	11	3	7	9	.324	.240	.370	4.76	3.71
Rodriguez, Joely	L-L	6-1	200	11-14-91	5	4	5.90	19	8	0	0	61	73	41	40	8	20	41	.302	.296	.304	6.05	2.95
Roibal, Reinier	R-R	6-3	210	1-9-89	1	6	1.66	25	5	0	1	49	36	12	9	3	10	47	.202	.219	.190	8.69	1.85
Shackleford, Stephen	R-R	6-2	205	5-5-89	4	2	4.45	53	0	0	30	55	51	30	27	3	24	56	.241	.341	.165	9.22	3.95
Stewart, Ethan	L-L	6-7	235	1-19-91	0	2	7.82	11	0	0	0	13	12	11	11	3	14	14	.245	.250	.241	9.95	9.95
Thompson, Jake	R-R	6-4	235	1-31-94	5	1	1.80	7	7	0	0	45	33	9	9	3	12	34	.217	.222	.211	6.80	2.40
Vasquez, Anthony	L-L	6-0	190	9-19-86	1	0	2.13	8	2	0	1	25	20	9	6	1	5	15	.230	.212	.241	5.33	1.78
Williams, Jerome	R-R	6-3	260	12-4-81	1	0	2.31	2	2	0	0	12	9	4	3	1	0	8	.205	.280	.105	6.17	0.00
Windle, Tom	L-L	6-4	215	3-10-92	4	5	4.35	34	14	0	0	97	98	56	47	6	51	64	.272	.264	.277	5.92	4.72

Fielding

Catcher

Catcher	PCT	G	PO	A	E	DP	PB
Forsythe	1.000	2	9	1	0	0	1
Garcia	.996	35	230	28	1	1	2
Hester	1.000	1	2	0	0	0	0
Knapp	.997	48	341	36	1	1	7
Lino	.992	32	206	32	2	7	2
Moore	.985	26	174	23	3	0	1

First Base

First Base	PCT	G	PO	A	E	DP
Charles	.988	36	291	27	4	23
Martinez	1.000	2	14	3	0	0
Moore	1.000	1	3	0	0	0
Stassi	.995	112	904	69	5	100

Second Base

Second Base	PCT	G	PO	A	E	DP
Alonso	.979	12	17	30	1	4
Greene	.985	79	135	191	5	48
Mora	.943	21	33	49	5	10

Pierre	—	1	0	0	0	0	
Serna	1.000	19	32	49	0	17	
Thomas	.973	18	34	39	2	13	
Utley	1.000	2	8	10	0	4	

Third Base

Third Base	PCT	G	PO	A	E	DP
Garcia	—	1	0	0	0	0
Lohman	.800	2	2	6	2	0
Martinez	.954	67	35	131	8	15
Mora	.958	8	7	16	1	1
Pierre	.931	62	36	113	11	10
Serna	.952	10	4	16	1	1

Shortstop

Shortstop	PCT	G	PO	A	E	DP
Crawford	.954	86	156	281	21	64
Greene	1.000	1	1	3	0	0
Lohman	1.000	3	5	8	0	2
Mora	.875	5	4	3	1	1

Serna	.977	45	87	125	5	23
Thomas	.929	4	5	8	1	0

Outfield

Outfield	PCT	G	PO	A	E	DP
Altherr	1.000	58	117	6	0	3
Chapman	.923	5	12	0	1	0
Cozens	1.000	11	27	0	0	0
Dugan	.976	38	82	1	2	0
Greene	1.000	4	5	0	0	0
Heid	1.000	15	39	1	0	0
Hood	1.000	42	92	4	0	0
Perkins	.989	90	172	15	2	1
Pointer	.986	74	129	8	2	1
Quinn	.966	58	135	8	5	3
Serna	1.000	21	24	4	0	0
Stassi	1.000	8	17	0	0	0
Thomas	1.000	2	2	0	0	0
Williams	.981	21	47	4	1	1

CLEARWATER THRESHERS

HIGH CLASS A

FLORIDA STATE LEAGUE

Batting	B-T	HT	WT	DOB	AVG	vLH	vRH	G	AB	R	H	2B	3B	HR	RBI	BB	HBP	SH	SF	SO	SB	CS	SLG	OBP
Antequera, Jose	R-R	5-10	160	8-1-95	.000	.000	.000	2	3	0	0	0	0	0	0	0	0	1	0	1	0	0	.000	.000
Astudillo, Willians	R-R	5-9	182	10-14-91	.314	.307	.319	107	385	32	121	18	0	3	49	10	3	4	6	10	1	1	.384	.348
Brown, Aaron	L-L	6-2	220	6-20-92	.257	.285	.242	110	389	52	100	17	4	11	47	27	13	2	3	88	10	8	.406	.324
Brown, Domonic	L-L	6-5	225	9-3-87	.294	.222	.375	6	17	2	5	1	0	1	3	2	1	0	0	7	0	0	.529	.400
Campbell, Derek	R-R	6-0	175	6-28-91	.257	.314	.229	36	105	15	27	5	1	1	12	7	10	3	3	23	3	1	.352	.352
Canelo, Malquin	R-R	5-10	156	9-5-94	.250	.227	.263	63	248	24	62	7	1	3	24	16	2	2	4	53	7	6	.323	.296
Cozens, Dylan	L-L	6-6	235	5-31-94	.282	.233	.309	96	365	52	103	22	5	5	46	26	4	0	2	79	18	5	.411	.335
Crawford, J.P.	R-R	6-2	180	1-11-95	.392	.333	.429	21	79	15	31	1	0	1	8	14	1	1	0	9	5	2	.443	.489
Dugan, Kelly	L-R	6-3	210	9-18-90	.273	.333	.250	3	11	3	3	0	0	1	1	1	0	0	0	2	0	0	.545	.333
Duran, Carlos	R-R	6-2	170	11-22-94	.083	.000	.111	4	12	0	1	0	0	0	2	2	0	1	0	3	0	0	.083	.214
Espiritu, Jr., Luis	R-R	6-0	175	9-21-96	.000	.000	.000	4	8	0	0	0	0	0	0	0	0	0	0	3	0	0	.000	.000
Garcia, Wilson	B-R	5-11	160	1-11-94	.295	.250	.313	17	44	4	13	3	0	0	4	1	0	0	1	4	0	0	.364	.304
Green, Zach	R-R	6-3	210	3-7-94	.173	.139	.191	26	104	7	18	2	0	1	7	6	0	0	1	28	0	0	.221	.216
Greene, Brodie	R-R	6-1	195	9-25-87	.333	.263	.400	9	39	8	13	0	0	2	3	0	1	0	5	2	0	.333	.381
Harris, Chase	R-R	6-0	195	7-28-91	.265	.301	.245	65	230	29	61	6	1	0	18	14	3	7	0	46	15	6	.300	.316
Hoskins, Rhys	R-R	6-4	225	3-17-93	.317	.380	.287	67	243	47	77	19	2	8	39	29	3	0	2	49	2	0	.510	.394
Knapp, Andrew	B-R	6-1	190	11-9-91	.262	.216	.288	63	244	38	64	14	3	2	28	29	7	0	1	63	0	1	.369	.356
Lohman, Devin	R-R	6-1	185	4-14-89	.222	.185	.250	37	126	16	28	5	0	1	11	11	4	3	1	27	3	2	.286	.303
Marrero, Emmanuel	B-R	5-11	169	5-16-93	.214	.263	.111	11	28	1	6	0	0	0	3	1	0	1	0	4	0	1	.214	.241

PHILADELPHIA PHILLIES

Batting	B-T	HT	WT	DOB	AVG	vLH	vRH	G	AB	R	H	2B	3B	HR	RBI	BB	HBP	SH	SF	SO	SB	CS	SLG	OBP
Martinez, Harold	R-R	6-3	210	5-3-90	.179	.300	.111	8	28	3	5	2	0	0	4	3	0	1	1	7	0	0	.250	.250
Mayorga, Jose	R-R	5-10	175	8-20-92	.150	.182	.111	10	20	1	3	0	0	0	4	0	0	0	0	1	0	0	.150	.292
Mora, Angelo	B-R	5-11	151	2-25-93	.304	.337	.285	61	227	21	69	11	6	0	21	8	1	2	3	28	4	4	.405	.326
Numata, Chace	B-R	6-0	175	8-14-92	.263	.252	.270	73	262	34	69	11	1	1	35	20	4	1	3	33	2	0	.324	.322
Pullin, Andrew	L-R	6-0	190	9-25-93	.258	.274	.250	123	493	55	127	18	4	14	73	24	7	3	2	76	1	5	.396	.300
Stankiewicz, Drew	B-R	5-9	160	6-18-93	.275	.289	.271	47	167	18	46	11	0	0	20	16	0	2	3	26	4	2	.341	.333
Tocci, Carlos	R-R	6-2	160	8-23-95	.258	.209	.283	68	275	31	71	9	0	2	18	12	4	4	3	52	3	9	.313	.296
Valentin, Jesmuel	B-R	5-9	180	5-12-94	.273	.200	.304	31	99	18	27	10	1	1	14	12	1	4	2	15	0	2	.424	.351
Walding, Mitch	L-R	6-3	190	9-10-92	.233	.272	.213	120	403	48	94	19	1	4	31	48	4	2	4	117	5	4	.315	.318

Pitching	B-T	HT	WT	DOB	W	L	ERA	G	GS	CG	SV	IP	H	R	ER	HR	BB	SO	AVG	vLH	vRH	K/9	BB/9
Arano, Victor	R-R	6-2	200	2-7-95	4	12	4.72	24	22	1	0	124	131	69	65	7	26	69	.276	.350	.239	5.01	1.89
Dygestile-Therrien, Jesen	R-R	6-2	200	3-18-93	5	0	1.77	30	0	0	3	46	37	11	9	1	15	40	.222	.261	.207	7.88	2.96
Forsythe, Cody	L-L	6-0	170	9-17-90	3	2	3.65	34	0	0	0	57	44	27	23	9	20	56	.206	.286	.172	8.89	3.18
Guerrero, Harold	L-L	6-4	235	5-21-90	2	2	3.40	25	0	0	1	40	30	15	15	2	34	36	.210	.190	.218	8.17	7.71
Imhof, Matt	L-L	6-5	220	10-26-93	8	5	3.94	18	18	0	0	78	72	45	34	8	39	59	.248	.250	.248	6.84	4.52
Joaquin, Ulises	R-R	5-11	165	6-11-92	4	2	2.95	46	0	0	16	55	51	21	18	5	12	53	.248	.206	.266	8.67	1.96
Kleven, Colin	R-R	6-5	200	4-15-91	5	3	2.89	13	13	0	0	72	66	26	23	3	17	57	.251	.213	.272	7.16	2.64
Leibrandt, Brandon	L-L	6-4	190	12-13-92	7	3	3.11	17	17	1	0	101	83	36	35	6	21	67	.227	.213	.232	5.95	1.87
Leiter Jr., Mark	R-R	6-0	195	3-13-91	6	1	2.26	19	13	1	1	96	79	28	24	4	23	83	.224	.192	.242	7.81	2.16
Martinez, Lino	L-L	6-0	165	9-17-92	1	0	6.75	5	0	0	0	7	6	6	5	0	4	6	.222	.375	.158	8.10	5.40
Mecias, Yoel	L-L	6-2	160	10-11-93	0	0	4.05	4	0	0	0	7	8	5	3	1	2	4	.333	.429	.294	5.40	2.70
Milner, Hoby	L-L	6-2	165	1-13-91	0	0	0.00	1	1	0	0	3	2	0	0	0	0	1	.182	.400	.000	3.00	0.00
Morris, Will	L-R	6-4	180	5-2-93	0	0	0.00	2	0	0	0	3	3	1	1	1	1	2	.250	.143	.400	6.00	3.00
Munoz, Jairo	R-R	6-5	175	8-12-94	0	0	0.00	1	0	0	0	2	1	0	0	1	1	1	.250	.333	.200	4.50	4.50
Nunez, Miguel	R-R	6-6	215	10-27-92	3	2	3.22	40	4	0	8	73	57	29	26	4	25	45	.218	.250	.203	5.57	3.10
Pinto, Ricardo	R-R	6-0	165	1-20-94	9	2	2.87	13	13	0	0	78	64	30	25	6	19	45	.231	.220	.237	5.17	2.18
Ramos, Edubray	R-R	6-0	165	12-19-92	3	4	1.46	29	0	0	8	49	31	9	8	2	6	42	.180	.226	.160	8.57	1.09
Richy, John	R-R	6-4	215	7-28-92	0	0	2.84	2	2	0	0	13	10	4	4	1	1	10	.213	.211	.214	7.11	0.71
Rios, Yacksel	R-R	6-3	185	6-27-93	6	5	2.75	26	10	1	1	88	69	33	27	4	23	71	.214	.206	.217	7.23	2.34
Rivero, Alexis	R-R	6-0	180	10-18-94	1	2	2.67	16	0	0	3	27	17	8	8	3	6	30	.181	.194	.175	10.00	2.00
Stewart, Ethan	L-L	6-7	235	1-19-91	1	1	0.79	8	0	0	0	11	6	1	1	0	6	6	.154	.143	.156	5.56	4.76
Tirado, Alberto	R-R	6-0	180	12-10-94	1	0	0.56	9	0	0	0	16	6	2	1	0	18	16	.130	.091	.143	9.00	10.13
2-team total (31 Dunedin)					5	3	2.68	40	0	0	3	77	51	27	23	4	53	77	—	—	—	8.96	6.17
Walter, Kevin	R-R	6-5	215	5-1-92	0	0	6.00	6	0	0	0	9	12	6	6	1	4	6	.343	.357	.333	6.00	4.00
Whitehead, David	R-R	6-4	215	4-21-92	9	11	4.44	25	25	0	0	136	152	74	67	10	51	94	.291	.292	.290	6.24	3.38

Fielding

Catcher	PCT	G	PO	A	E	DP	PB
Astudillo	.987	33	200	27	3	1	4
Garcia	1.000	7	23	0	0	0	0
Knapp	.983	46	319	29	6	1	3
Mayorga	1.000	9	45	8	0	1	0
Numata	.995	52	333	41	2	2	11

First Base	PCT	G	PO	A	E	DP
Astudillo	.997	39	319	25	1	34
Garcia	1.000	2	5	0	0	1
Green	1.000	23	196	14	0	17
Hoskins	.986	58	452	36	7	50
Lohman	.982	6	52	3	1	4
Martinez	1.000	7	67	5	0	5
Mayorga	1.000	1	2	0	0	1
Pullin	1.000	1	9	0	0	2
Stankiewicz	1.000	7	48	4	0	6

Second Base	PCT	G	PO	A	E	DP
Antequera	1.000	1	1	1	0	1
Campbell	1.000	26	42	61	0	16
Espiritu, Jr.	1.000	3	6	8	0	3
Greene	.960	9	25	23	2	4
Lohman	1.000	6	15	11	0	4
Marrero	.939	7	12	19	2	5
Mora	.986	29	56	83	2	20
Stankiewicz	.989	37	73	110	2	24
Valentin	1.000	26	58	61	0	17

Third Base	PCT	G	PO	A	E	DP
Astudillo	.600	2	0	3	2	1
Campbell	.905	9	5	14	2	2
Green	1.000	2	0	2	0	0
Lohman	.958	6	9	14	1	2
Martinez	1.000	1	1	0	0	0
Walding	.944	120	82	240	19	16

Shortstop	PCT	G	PO	A	E	DP
Antequera	1.000	1	1	1	0	0
Canelo	.965	62	98	178	10	41
Crawford	.946	20	42	64	6	19
Lohman	.959	17	20	50	3	11
Marrero	.917	3	5	6	1	2
Mora	.938	32	44	76	8	20
Stankiewicz	.857	6	6	2	1	
Valentin	1.000	5	6	11	0	4

Outfield	PCT	G	PO	A	E	DP
Astudillo	1.000	1	3	0	0	0
Brown	.992	104	245	6	2	1
Brown	.917	6	10	1	1	0
Campbell	1.000	2	2	0	0	0
Cozens	.976	77	157	5	4	1
Dugan	1.000	2	4	0	0	0
Duran	1.000	4	11	0	0	0
Harris	.993	64	130	5	1	1
Pullin	.983	98	165	10	3	0
Tocci	.994	68	176	3	1	1

LAKEWOOD BLUECLAWS

LOW CLASS A

SOUTH ATLANTIC LEAGUE

Batting	B-T	HT	WT	DOB	AVG	vLH	vRH	G	AB	R	H	2B	3B	HR	RBI	BB	HBP	SH	SF	SO	SB	CS	SLG	OBP
Amaro, Andrew	L-R	6-1	195	4-2-93	.200	.000	.333	4	10	1	2	1	0	0	2	1	0	1	0	2	0	0	.300	.273
Campbell, Derek	R-R	6-0	175	6-28-91	.205	.242	.190	61	215	14	44	14	1	1	22	3	9	2	1	41	3	2	.293	.246
Canelo, Malquin	R-R	5-10	156	5-8-95	.311	.326	.303	63	264	48	82	22	2	5	23	21	1	1	0	39	10	2	.466	.364
Cuicas, William	B-R	5-11	160	2-1-95	.167	.000	.250	3	6	0	1	0	0	0	0	1	0	1	0	3	0	0	.167	.286
Cumana, Grenny	B-R	5-5	145	11-10-95	.203	.155	.223	58	197	14	40	6	0	0	11	10	1	2	2	25	11	0	.234	.243
Fisher, Joel	R-R	6-3	235	1-9-95	.199	.176	.208	52	171	16	34	11	0	3	14	7	3	1	0	53	0	0	.316	.243
Grullon, Deivi	R-R	6-1	180	2-17-96	.221	.229	.218	107	394	38	87	19	1	8	50	23	5	2	0	105	0	0	.335	.273
Harris, Chase	R-R	6-0	195	7-28-91	.225	.391	.158	24	80	9	18	2	1	0	5	5	3	3	1	8	6	2	.275	.292
Hoskins, Rhys	R-R	6-4	225	3-17-93	.322	.278	.341	68	255	39	82	17	4	9	51	26	7	0	2	50	2	4	.525	.397
Kingery, Scott	R-R	5-10	180	4-29-94	.250	.323	.226	66	252	43	63	9	2	3	21	18	2	2	3	43	11	1	.337	.314
Marrero, Emmanuel	B-R	5-11	169	5-16-93	.182	.173	.186	50	170	20	31	7	2	1	8	10	3	3	1	30	2	1	.265	.239
Martin, Kyle	L-L	6-2	225	11-13-92	.279	.194	.307	65	251	37	70	19	4	5	37	17	1	0	2	56	1	1	.446	.325
Martinez, Gustavo	R-R	5-11	155	9-22-93	.226	.310	.182	26	84	12	19	0	1	0	5	2	0	2	1	10	8	4	.250	.241

Batting	B-T	HT	WT	DOB	AVG	vLH	vRH	G	AB	R	H	2B	3B	HR	RBI	BB	HBP	SH	SF	SO	SB	CS	SLG	OBP
Mayorga, Jose	R-R	5-10	175	8-20-92	.203	.238	.190	26	79	3	16	2	0	0	8	10	1	3	2	15	0	2	.228	.293
Numata, Chace	B-R	6-0	175	8-14-92	.357	.667	.273	4	14	3	5	1	0	0	2	0	0	1	0	0	.429	.438
Rodriguez, Herlis	L-L	6-0	170	6-10-94	.294	.326	.282	120	445	61	131	20	4	10	61	28	6	9	8	71	16	10	.425	.339
Sandberg, Cord	L-L	6-3	215	1-2-95	.255	.218	.269	129	499	53	127	28	1	5	59	29	9	6	7	88	5	7	.345	.303
Stankiewicz, Drew	B-R	5-9	160	6-18-93	.288	.234	.304	52	208	30	60	14	2	1	15	20	1	1	0	27	4	1	.389	.354
Tocci, Carlos	R-R	6-2	160	8-23-95	.321	.365	.300	59	234	35	75	14	2	2	25	20	6	1	0	31	14	2	.423	.387
Tomscha, Damek	R-R	6-2	200	8-27-91	.282	.301	.274	120	429	68	121	32	1	8	59	39	22	2	5	81	2	0	.417	.368
Tromp, Jiandido	R-R	5-11	175	9-27-93	.216	.217	.215	113	412	42	89	18	6	9	44	27	4	4	4	117	10	5	.354	.268
Zier, Tim	R-R	5-9	195	8-6-91	.264	.188	.297	15	53	5	14	1	0	0	2	6	0	1	0	7	0	1	.283	.339

Pitching	B-T	HT	WT	DOB	W	L	ERA	G	GS	CG	SV	IP	H	R	ER	HR	BB	SO	AVG	vLH	vRH	K/9	BB/9
Casimiro, Ranfi	R-R	6-8	200	7-16-92	9	7	3.35	23	23	2	0	137	127	56	51	8	30	91	.244	.262	.232	5.98	1.97
Davis, Austin	L-L	6-4	245	2-3-93	5	6	3.76	33	11	1	0	96	79	43	40	7	44	81	.224	.217	.226	7.62	4.14
Delgado, Victor	R-R	6-2	182	2-3-95	0	0	4.91	3	0	0	0	4	2	2	2	1	1	4	.154	.500	.091	9.82	2.45
Denato, Joey	L-L	5-10	175	1-6-92	2	3	1.24	43	0	0	10	65	41	11	9	1	18	64	.188	.246	.168	8.82	2.48
Dygestile-Therrien, Jesen	R-R	6-2	200	3-18-93	0	0	0.52	9	0	0	2	17	13	3	1	0	2	14	.210	.263	.186	7.27	1.04
Garcia, Elneiry	L-L	6-0	155	12-24-94	8	9	3.23	21	21	0	0	120	125	51	43	7	36	66	.275	.239	.288	4.95	2.70
Harris, Scott	L-L	6-4	230	5-14-93	1	2	4.65	30	0	0	0	50	53	30	26	5	19	38	.270	.240	.281	6.79	3.40
Hockenberry, Matt	R-R	6-3	220	8-30-91	4	4	2.24	42	0	0	19	52	34	16	13	1	19	51	.186	.207	.168	8.77	3.27
Martinez, Manaure	R-R	6-1	155	12-31-91	3	1	2.51	31	0	0	1	43	28	14	12	3	19	36	.192	.209	.184	7.53	3.98
Mecias, Yoel	L-L	6-2	160	10-11-93	0	2	18.90	2	2	0	0	3	6	7	7	2	6	3	.429	.800	.222	8.10	16.20
Morris, Zach	L-L	6-5	245	3-6-93	0	0	2.08	3	0	0	1	4	6	4	1	0	2	8	.273	.333	.250	16.62	4.15
Morris, Will	L-R	6-4	180	5-2-93	7	0	1.64	14	9	0	0	71	58	14	13	2	13	32	.228	.216	.238	4.04	1.64
Munoz, Jairo	R-R	6-5	175	8-12-91	3	0	2.67	13	3	0	0	34	26	10	10	1	9	28	.217	.180	.243	7.49	2.41
Oliver, Chris	R-R	6-4	170	7-8-93	4	5	4.04	13	13	1	0	69	77	38	31	0	32	27	.291	.333	.260	3.52	4.17
Pinto, Ricardo	R-R	6-0	165	1-20-94	6	2	3.09	11	11	0	0	67	65	25	23	4	18	60	.258	.238	.268	8.06	2.42
Rayburn, Calvin	R-R	6-8	195	7-9-92	5	3	4.44	32	0	0	1	49	37	28	24	2	24	26	.214	.215	.213	4.81	4.44
Rivero, Alexis	R-R	6-0	170	10-18-94	3	0	2.62	25	0	0	7	45	31	16	13	4	12	37	.191	.345	.106	7.46	2.42
Rodesky, Nick	R-R	6-5	220	3-27-91	0	0	0.00	3	0	0	0	3	2	0	0	0	3	3	.200	.000	.222	9.00	9.00
Taylor, Josh	L-L	6-5	225	3-2-93	4	5	4.61	13	13	0	0	68	71	38	35	6	24	70	.265	.259	.267	9.22	3.16
Viza, Tyler	R-R	6-3	170	10-21-94	5	10	3.38	23	22	2	0	144	129	71	54	11	31	104	.240	.253	.231	6.52	1.94
Watson, Shane	R-R	6-4	200	8-13-93	1	5	4.33	9	9	0	0	44	53	31	21	4	18	31	.299	.358	.250	6.39	3.71
Zgardowski, Jason	R-R	6-4	190	9-27-93	3	1	3.26	28	0	0	0	50	31	18	18	1	22	45	.181	.176	.186	8.15	3.99

Fielding

Catcher	PCT	G	PO	A	E	DP	PB
Fisher	.983	39	211	26	4	5	3
Grullon	.982	97	608	112	13	3	14
Mayorga	.975	9	67	10	2	2	0
Numata	.875	1	7	0	1	0	1

First Base	PCT	G	PO	A	E	DP
Hoskins	.993	64	552	50	4	39
Martin	.995	55	605	28	3	39
Mayorga	1.000	2	17	2	0	2
Tomscha	.995	21	193	9	1	19
Zier	1.000	1	1	0	0	0

Second Base	PCT	G	PO	A	E	DP
Campbell	.964	11	26	28	2	5

	PCT	G	PO	A	E	DP	PB
Cumana	.939	52	111	105	14	22	
Kingery	.986	65	85	192	4	46	
Marrero	1.000	1	2	3	0	0	
Stankiewicz	1.000	7	13	20	0	3	
Zier	.920	6	10	13	2	2	

Third Base	PCT	G	PO	A	E	DP
Campbell	.949	48	28	102	7	5
Cuicas	1.000	1	0	2	0	0
Mayorga	1.000	1	0	1	0	0
Stankiewicz	.946	26	16	54	4	8
Tomscha	.962	67	44	160	8	11

Shortstop	PCT	G	PO	A	E	DP
Canelo	.950	63	106	177	15	25

	PCT	G	PO	A	E	DP
Cuicas	.875	1	2	5	1	2
Cumana	1.000	6	8	12	0	0
Marrero	.969	49	81	169	8	31
Stankiewicz	.951	21	27	70	5	8

Outfield	PCT	G	PO	A	E	DP
Amaro	1.000	2	1	0	0	0
Harris	1.000	16	32	1	0	0
Martinez	1.000	18	38	2	0	1
Rodriguez	.967	98	183	22	7	6
Sandberg	.983	120	215	13	4	2
Tocci	.986	59	139	2	2	1
Tromp	.992	108	231	10	2	2

WILLIAMSPORT CROSSCUTTERS

SHORT-SEASON

NEW YORK-PENN LEAGUE

Batting	B-T	HT	WT	DOB	AVG	vLH	vRH	G	AB	R	H	2B	3B	HR	RBI	BB	HBP	SH	SF	SO	SB	CS	SLG	OBP
Amaro, Andrew	L-R	6-1	195	4-2-93	.222	.273	.206	16	45	6	10	1	0	0	3	11	1	0	0	16	3	0	.244	.386
Biter, Venn	L-R	6-1	185	10-27-94	.265	.273	.262	58	219	30	58	12	3	2	29	19	1	2	2	50	9	3	.374	.324
Bosheers, Dylan	R-R	5-11	170	5-7-92	.194	.250	.178	40	129	10	25	2	2	0	7	11	0	1	1	29	0	1	.240	.255
Bossart, Austin	R-R	6-2	225	7-4-93	.333	.444	.280	37	138	15	46	7	1	1	19	0	6	1	1	18	0	2	.420	.359
Brodzinski, Greg	B-R	6-2	220	7-23-91	.294	.000	.357	5	17	1	5	1	0	0	4	0	1	0	2	1	0	0	.353	.300
Coppola, Zach	L-R	5-10	160	5-9-94	.271	.215	.294	58	225	32	61	3	0	0	15	28	0	7	1	40	19	11	.284	.350
Cuicas, William	B-R	5-11	160	2-1-95	.187	.147	.202	37	123	15	23	7	2	0	12	10	2	2	1	37	3	1	.276	.257
Cumana, Grenny	B-R	5-5	145	11-16-93	.226	.323	.187	32	106	15	24	4	0	0	10	8	3	1	1	4	3	4	.264	.297
Duran, Carlos	R-R	6-2	170	11-22-94	.247	.271	.237	43	162	21	40	7	1	2	12	14	0	2	2	41	10	5	.340	.303
Espiritu, Jr., Luis	R-R	6-0	175	9-21-96	.267	.222	.278	13	45	8	12	3	0	0	6	5	0	0	1	16	3	0	.333	.333
Garcia, Wilson	B-R	5-11	160	1-11-94	.444	—	.444	2	9	0	4	1	0	0	1	0	0	0	0	1	1	1	.556	.444
Hayden, Brendon	L-R	6-5	215	12-26-92	.291	.395	.262	50	179	25	52	8	0	3	20	23	2	0	1	27	0	2	.385	.376
Hernandez, Jan	R-R	6-1	195	1-3-95	.211	.218	.209	57	213	25	45	9	2	10	35	11	3	2	2	69	5	2	.413	.258
Laird, Mark	L-L	6-1	175	3-29-93	.285	.319	.274	52	193	28	55	3	0	0	17	27	1	1	2	24	11	3	.301	.372
Martinez, Gustavo	R-R	6-1	175	3-20-95	.250	.333	.000	2	4	1	1	0	0	0	0	0	0	0	0	1	0	0	.250	.250
Posso, Jesus	R-R	5-11	201	2-10-95	.236	.226	.241	42	161	18	38	9	0	6	21	7	4	0	1	24	0	3	.404	.283
Pujols, Jose	R-R	6-3	175	9-29-95	.238	.233	.240	66	256	43	61	15	2	4	30	25	3	0	2	81	5	4	.359	.311
Rivero, Gregori	R-R	5-11	160	7-14-94	.219	.065	.277	31	114	12	25	8	1	3	18	5	0	1	1	16	0	3	.386	.237
Tobias, Josh	R-R	5-10	205	11-23-92	.321	.348	.310	61	240	31	77	19	3	4	37	14	3	0	3	42	12	10	.475	.362

Pitching	B-T	HT	WT	DOB	W	L	ERA	G	GS	CG	SV	IP	H	R	ER	HR	BB	SO	AVG	vLH	vRH	K/9	BB/9
Alezones, Lewis	R-R	6-3	170	11-29-95	1	0	12.10	8	0	0	1	10	11	13	13	1	12	10	.282	.188	.348	9.31	11.17

PHILADELPHIA PHILLIES

Pitching	B-T	HT	WT	DOB	W	L	ERA	G	GS	CG	SV	IP	H	R	ER	HR	BB	SO	AVG	vLH	vRH	K/9	BB/9
Arteaga, Alejandro	R-R	6-2	176	4-30-94	4	3	3.11	13	13	0	0	72	69	28	25	2	21	51	.258	.282	.235	6.35	2.61
Cabrera, Ismael	R-R	6-1	185	6-19-94	0	0	0.00	3	0	0	0	3	3	0	0	1	4	.250	.143	.400	12.00	3.00	
Figueroa, Juan	L-L	6-0	185	8-31-92	1	1	5.79	7	0	0	0	9	6	8	6	1	7	4	.182	.182	.182	3.86	6.75
Gilbert, Tyler	L-L	6-3	195	12-22-93	4	3	2.79	10	8	0	0	42	42	16	13	0	6	44	.251	.288	.231	9.43	1.29
Godail, Andrew	L-L	5-11	190	1-10-93	1	1	3.04	19	0	0	0	24	20	8	8	0	15	25	.227	.229	.226	9.51	5.70
Gueller, Mitch	R-R	6-3	210	11-10-93	10	1	2.23	12	12	1	0	69	57	22	17	3	23	44	.229	.183	.271	5.77	3.01
Hunter, Skylar	R-R	6-1	185	2-3-94	3	3	3.48	22	0	0	0	34	34	13	13	0	11	21	.268	.262	.273	5.61	2.94
Keys, Denton	L-L	6-3	190	9-30-94	0	1	4.12	15	5	0	0	39	49	21	18	4	16	31	.306	.209	.376	7.09	3.66
Kilome, Franklyn	R-R	6-6	175	6-25-95	3	2	3.28	11	11	0	0	49	41	21	18	1	21	36	.230	.247	.212	6.57	3.83
Koplove, Kenny	R-R	6-2	170	8-2-93	2	3	4.50	23	0	0	0	34	34	18	17	2	17	27	.270	.241	.294	7.15	4.50
Leftwich, Luke	L-R	6-3	205	6-9-94	2	2	2.76	11	9	0	0	46	52	20	14	1	13	34	.289	.296	.280	6.70	2.56
McLoughlin, Sutter	R-R	6-5	215	9-24-93	2	0	3.50	13	0	0	0	18	13	7	7	1	5	21	.200	.267	.143	10.50	2.50
Morales, Luis	R-R	6-4	212	3-16-93	2	2	2.90	11	5	0	0	31	36	12	10	1	14	15	.290	.242	.345	4.35	4.06
Morris, Will	L-R	6-4	180	5-2-93	0	0	0.77	4	0	0	0	12	11	1	1	0	3	10	.239	.120	.381	7.71	2.31
Sanchez, Feliberto	R-R	6-1	175	9-30-93	1	2	3.93	18	0	0	0	34	29	16	15	3	13	36	.223	.197	.254	9.44	3.41
Sequeira, Anthony	L-R	6-6	235	9-16-92	2	1	1.87	23	0	0	4	34	22	10	7	0	10	34	.186	.141	.245	9.09	2.67
Tasin, Robert	R-R	6-0	190	9-18-91	0	0	1.84	25	0	0	17	29	18	6	6	1	6	24	.176	.188	.167	7.36	1.84
Taveras, Jose	R-R	6-4	210	11-6-93	7	4	3.88	13	13	0	0	63	63	31	27	3	21	59	.273	.324	.233	8.47	3.02
Waguespack, Jacob	R-R	6-6	225	11-5-93	0	1	0.42	15	0	0	1	21	9	3	1	0	8	25	.132	.128	.138	10.55	3.38
Zgardowski, Jason	R-R	6-5	190	9-27-93	1	0	2.25	6	0	0	2	8	5	2	2	1	4	9	.185	.083	.267	10.13	4.50

Fielding

Catcher	PCT	G	PO	A	E	DP	PB
Bossart	.985	36	284	41	5	5	6
Brodzinski	1.000	4	26	3	0	0	0
Posso	.964	5	48	5	2	1	1
Rivero	.987	31	203	30	3	4	7

First Base	PCT	G	PO	A	E	DP
Amaro	1.000	1	11	1	0	4
Cuicas	1.000	1	1	0	0	0
Hayden	.995	48	389	30	2	42
Posso	.993	29	255	10	2	19

Second Base	PCT	G	PO	A	E	DP
Bosheers	.980	10	17	31	1	6
Cuicas	.900	6	3	15	2	1
Espiritu, Jr.	.972	6	18	17	1	6
Tobias	.962	55	83	143	9	31

Third Base	PCT	G	PO	A	E	DP
Bosheers	1.000	4	1	10	0	2
Cuicas	.935	10	9	20	2	4
Espiritu, Jr.	.929	7	4	9	1	2
Hernandez	.910	57	49	82	13	7

Shortstop	PCT	G	PO	A	E	DP
Bosheers	.965	26	38	72	4	18
Cuicas	.961	19	34	64	4	11
Cumana	.930	32	56	76	10	17

Outfield	PCT	G	PO	A	E	DP
Amaro	1.000	3	4	0	0	0
Biter	.967	49	83	5	3	1
Coppola	.991	46	107	6	1	0
Duran	.982	42	104	3	2	0
Laird	.989	40	89	4	1	1
Pujols	.950	50	92	4	5	1

GCL PHILLIES   ROOKIE
GULF COAST LEAGUE

Batting	B-T	HT	WT	DOB	AVG	vLH	vRH	G	AB	R	H	2B	3B	HR	RBI	BB	HBP	SH	SF	SO	SB	CS	SLG	OBP
Alastre, Jesus	R-R	6-1	155	11-25-96	.268	.435	.203	24	82	14	22	3	1	0	8	4	3	4	0	10	3	2	.329	.326
Antequera, Jose	R-R	5-10	160	8-1-95	.246	.235	.250	41	134	22	33	8	1	1	10	11	0	2	0	15	15	3	.343	.303
Arauz, Jonathan	L-R	6-0	147	8-3-98	.254	.239	.260	44	173	21	44	10	2	2	18	13	1	0	1	29	2	0	.370	.309
Brodzinski, Greg	B-R	6-2	220	7-23-91	.345	.750	.280	16	29	1	10	1	0	0	2	1	0	0	0	6	0	0	.379	.367
Cabral, Edgar	R-R	5-11	190	9-12-95	.281	.227	.297	38	96	13	27	6	0	2	14	8	3	0	0	6	0	0	.406	.355
Cozens, Dylan	L-L	6-6	235	5-31-94	.200	.200	.200	4	15	1	3	1	0	0	4	0	0	0	0	4	0	0	.267	.200
Duran, Rodolfo	R-R	5-9	170	2-19-98	.185	.190	.183	36	81	11	15	3	1	0	10	3	1	0	1	17	1	2	.247	.221
Encarnacion, Luis	R-R	6-2	185	8-9-97	.271	.302	.262	54	192	21	52	5	1	4	36	12	2	0	5	38	1	0	.370	.313
Espiritu, Jr., Luis	R-R	6-0	175	9-21-96	.167	.125	.176	13	42	2	7	1	0	0	5	3	1	0	1	9	2	0	.190	.234
Gamboa, Arquimedez	B-R	6-0	175	9-23-97	.189	.185	.191	50	190	23	36	7	3	0	16	15	1	0	0	50	8	2	.258	.252
Joseph, Tommy	R-R	6-1	255	7-16-91	.485	.818	.318	13	33	6	16	3	0	3	10	7	1	0	0	0	0	0	.848	.585
Luis, Juan	L-R	6-4	175	3-23-96	.244	.240	.245	39	123	26	30	5	3	2	10	9	6	2	2	30	14	1	.382	.321
Martelo, Bryan	R-R	6-2	180	10-15-96	.220	.200	.222	45	123	19	27	6	0	2	7	19	2	1	0	35	0	2	.317	.333
Pickett, Greg	L-R	6-4	215	10-30-96	.179	.037	.246	29	84	5	15	6	0	1	4	12	1	0	0	31	0	0	.286	.289
Randolph, Cornelius	L-R	5-11	205	6-2-97	.302	.292	.306	53	172	34	52	15	3	1	24	32	6	0	2	32	6	5	.442	.425
Reyes, Yunior	R-R	6-3	190	3-11-95	.205	.188	.210	45	132	11	27	3	1	0	14	5	3	0	0	23	3	3	.242	.250
Santana, Henry	B-R	6-3	180	12-19-94	.083	.000	.091	4	12	1	1	0	0	0	0	0	0	0	0	3	0	0	.083	.083
Tomassetti, Scott	R-R	6-1	195	7-3-93	.264	.250	.268	34	91	8	24	5	0	1	12	7	3	0	2	26	0	1	.352	.330
Williams, Lucas	R-R	6-1	180	8-9-96	.288	.250	.302	38	118	12	34	5	0	0	12	21	1	1	0	23	9	2	.331	.400

Pitching	B-T	HT	WT	DOB	W	L	ERA	G	GS	CG	SV	IP	H	R	ER	HR	BB	SO	AVG	vLH	vRH	K/9	BB/9
Alezones, Lewis	R-R	6-3	170	11-29-95	2	1	4.08	6	3	0	0	18	14	12	8	2	11	13	.219	.160	.256	6.62	5.60
Cabrera, Ismael	R-R	6-1	185	6-19-94	2	2	0.56	13	2	0	3	16	12	5	1	1	4	19	.194	.179	.206	10.69	2.25
Delgado, Victor	R-R	6-2	182	2-3-95	0	2	4.84	17	0	0	1	22	24	13	12	0	4	15	.279	.278	.280	6.04	1.61
Dominguez, Seranthony	R-R	6-1	183	11-25-94	1	1	2.35	2	1	0	0	8	6	2	2	1	7	9	.207	.333	.150	10.57	8.22
Falter, Bailey	R-L	6-4		4-24-97	1	2	3.45	8	7	0	0	29	28	12	11	2	3	25	.259	.275	.256	7.85	0.94
Fanti, Nick	L-L	6-2	185	12-30-96	1	1	2.55	9	1	0	0	18	14	7	5	0	6	20	.222	.389	.156	10.19	3.06
Garcia, Edgar	R-R	6-1	180	10-4-96	1	2	3.31	12	2	0	2	33	27	13	12	1	8	34	.221	.262	.175	9.37	2.20
Gonzalez, Miguel Alfredo	R-R	6-3	210	9-23-86	0	0	0.00	4	0	0	0	11	7	0	0	0	4	10	.184	.167	.200	8.18	3.27
Indriago, Carlos	R-R	6-2	197	6-29-94	3	2	2.20	12	5	0	0	41	36	10	10	0	8	27	.237	.229	.244	5.93	1.76
Kiest, Tanner	R-R	6-3	200	9-16-94	2	0	4.67	12	0	0	0	17	13	13	9	0	17	18	.210	.179	.235	9.35	8.83
Leibrandt, Brandon	L-L	6-4	190	12-13-92	0	0	0.00	2	1	0	0	7	4	0	0	0	0	8	.160	.100	.200	10.29	0.00
Martinez, Lino	L-L	6-0	165	9-17-92	1	0	2.25	3	0	0	0	4	1	1	1	0	2	3	.286	.500	.206	6.75	4.50
McLoughlin, Sutter	R-R	6-5	215	9-24-93	2	0	0.00	7	0	0	4	9	2	0	0	0	4	9	.067	.000	.111	11.57	0.00
McWilliams, Sam	R-R	6-7	190	9-4-95	0	2	3.27	7	7	0	0	35	29	13	13	1	5	21	.232	.245	.222	5.73	1.36
Medina, Adonis	R-R	6-1	185	12-18-96	3	2	2.98	10	8	0	0	45	42	21	15	1	12	35	.253	.222	.272	6.95	2.38

Pitching	B-T	HT	WT	DOB	W	L	ERA	G	GS	CG	SV	IP	H	R	ER	HR	BB	SO	AVG	vLH	vRH	K/9	BB/9
Morales, Luis	R-R	6-4	212	3-16-93	2	0	0.69	3	1	0	0	13	7	2	1	0	2	11	.163	.095	.227	7.62	1.38
Morris, Zach	L-L	6-5	245	3-6-93	5	1	2.16	13	0	0	1	25	19	7	6	1	8	27	.213	.056	.254	9.72	2.88
Paulino, Felix	R-R	6-1	170	3-24-95	5	4	2.34	11	10	0	0	50	41	20	13	3	5	46	.223	.175	.244	8.28	0.90
Stewart, Will	L-R	6-2	175	7-14-97	1	0	4.79	12	0	0	0	21	18	14	11	3	15	20	.228	.467	.172	8.71	6.53
Stubblefield, Gandy	R-R	6-5	190	7-23-92	0	1	3.44	14	0	0	6	18	13	8	7	2	7	25	.200	.217	.190	12.27	3.44
Suarez, Ranger	L-L	6-0	177	8-26-95	3	0	0.65	6	4	0	0	28	15	2	2	0	4	20	.158	.190	.149	6.51	1.30
Waguespack, Jacob	R-R	6-6	225	11-5-93	0	0	7.94	4	0	0	0	6	9	5	5	0	1	7	.375	.333	.389	11.12	1.59
Walsh, Kevin	R-R	6-3	220	3-26-92	0	1	3.55	8	0	0	1	13	12	7	5	1	5	6	.245	.222	.258	4.26	3.55
Watson, Shane	R-R	6-4	200	8-13-93	0	0	6.75	2	2	0	0	4	5	3	3	0	7	3	.417	.000	.500	6.75	15.75

Fielding

Catcher	PCT	G	PO	A	E	DP	PB
Alfaro	1.000	2	7	1	0	0	0
Brodzinski	.985	16	57	7	1	0	0
Cabral	.986	34	186	26	3	1	6
Duran	.977	36	148	25	4	2	6
Tomassetti	.972	8	31	4	1	0	1

First Base	PCT	G	PO	A	E	DP
Encarnacion	.977	41	373	17	9	33
Joseph	.982	8	54	0	1	0
Santana	1.000	2	17	0	0	1
Tomassetti	1.000	15	116	7	0	7

Second Base	PCT	G	PO	A	E	DP
Antequera	.968	18	18	42	2	8
Arauz	.990	25	42	54	1	20
Gamboa	.953	18	24	58	4	8

Third Base	PCT	G	PO	A	E	DP
Antequera	.857	12	7	23	5	4
Espiritu, Jr.	.939	13	9	22	2	2
Joseph	.000	1	0	0	1	0
Williams	.955	38	20	65	4	3

Shortstop	PCT	G	PO	A	E	DP
Antequera	.902	10	10	27	4	3

Arauz	.973	19	25	46	2	9
Gamboa	.963	32	51	80	5	21

Outfield	PCT	G	PO	A	E	DP
Alastre	1.000	23	34	1	0	0
Cozens	1.000	3	2	0	0	0
Luis	1.000	37	63	2	0	0
Martelo	.937	41	54	5	4	1
Pickett	.913	22	20	1	2	0
Randolph	1.000	41	61	2	0	1
Reyes	.969	37	61	1	2	0
Santana	1.000	2	1	0	0	0

DSL PHILLIES

ROOKIE

DOMINICAN SUMMER LEAGUE

Batting	B-T	HT	WT	DOB	AVG	vLH	vRH	G	AB	R	H	2B	3B	HR	RBI	BB	HBP	SH	SF	SO	SB	CS	SLG	OBP
Baez, Ricardo	R-R	6-2	195	8-28-98	.161	.364	.132	38	87	10	14	8	0	1	8	12	2	1	0	27	2	0	.287	.277
Beaufond, Luis	R-R	5-11	155	10-12-96	.233	.261	.228	48	150	19	35	8	0	0	15	3	2	4	2	25	1	3	.287	.255
Brito, Daniel	L-R	6-1	155	1-23-98	.269	.185	.281	60	212	33	57	10	3	0	19	35	5	4	1	22	8	9	.344	.383
Carrasco, Braylin	R-R	6-3	185	6-17-95	.000	.000	—	2	1	0	0	0	0	0	0	0	0	0	0	0	0	0	.000	.000
Feliz, Alexito	R-R	5-11	160	8-6-96	.224	.278	.213	32	107	15	24	6	0	0	10	5	3	3	2	13	2	4	.280	.274
Garcia, Enmanuel	R-R	6-0	180	7-23-94	.267	.257	.268	71	255	47	68	14	4	1	28	20	9	5	2	33	24	8	.365	.339
Guerrero, Jan	L-R	6-3	195	7-18-96	.253	.417	.227	32	87	9	22	2	0	2	9	12	1	3	0	15	4	3	.345	.350
2-team total (9 Braves)					.222	—		41	117	11	26	2	0	2	14	14	1	3	1	21	4	3	.291	.308
Kamara, Julsan	R-R	6-3	205	12-20-95	.158	.125	.163	23	57	7	9	1	0	0	6	5	9	1	0	21	3	1	.175	.324
Liriano, Luis	R-R	6-0	192	12-26-95	.231	.258	.226	60	195	19	45	1	0	1	23	23	1	0	2	23	3	4	.251	.312
Marrero, Ronaldo	R-R	6-0	160	2-7-96	.273	.188	.287	65	220	21	60	8	1	1	28	19	0	8	5	40	14	11	.332	.324
Martinez, Nerluis	L-R	6-2	175	4-10-96	.246	.208	.252	48	171	16	42	9	0	5	27	13	5	0	3	20	5	1	.386	.313
Paulino, Miguel	R-R	5-10	178	11-4-94	.200	.308	.175	34	70	17	14	3	0	2	10	6	3	2	1	22	4	3	.329	.288
Recio, Jonathan	R-R	6-0	185	11-27-96	.111	.000	.123	25	63	7	7	0	0	0	4	4	3	1	0	22	1	0	.111	.200
Romero, Daniel	R-R	5-11	155	5-5-97	.211	.233	.208	68	232	29	49	4	1	0	18	30	9	3	0	30	15	9	.237	.325
Santana, Henry	R-R	6-3	180	12-19-94	.278	.087	.313	41	151	21	42	13	2	1	26	3	5	1	0	22	8	7	.411	.314
Torres, Wilber	R-R	5-11	206	5-9-94	.313	.444	.282	15	48	11	15	6	0	0	8	8	1	0	0	12	3	3	.438	.421

Pitching	B-T	HT	WT	DOB	W	L	ERA	G	GS	CG	SV	IP	H	R	ER	HR	BB	SO	AVG	vLH	vRH	K/9	BB/9
Alcantara, Randy	R-R	5-11	150	11-9-96	7	2	2.56	14	14	0	0	84	72	30	24	3	15	47	.224	.202	.232	5.02	1.60
Cabrera, Joel	R-R	6-1	175	6-9-94	4	5	3.74	14	14	1	0	89	100	45	37	5	11	49	.293	.330	.276	4.96	1.11
Carmona, Steiner	R-R	6-3	195	2-14-96	5	1	1.48	19	0	0	8	24	13	5	4	0	8	14	.159	.174	.153	5.18	2.96
Castro, Argenis	R-R	6-1	211	2-24-95	0	0	15.75	4	0	0	0	4	7	7	7	2	4	4	.389	.250	.429	9.00	9.00
Cordoba, Javier	R-R	6-2	165	10-31-95	0	1	5.40	2	1	0	0	5	7	3	3	0	1	3	.318	.455	.182	5.40	1.80
Gomez, Yeral	R-R	6-0	180	6-5-96	0	0	0.00	2	0	0	0	5	6	0	0	0	1	2	.286	.167	.333	3.60	1.80
Gonzalez, Yonathan	R-R	6-3	165	10-31-95	1	2	2.75	5	3	0	0	20	11	9	6	0	14	8	.159	.238	.125	3.66	6.41
Marcelino, Oscar	R-R	6-3	166	6-8-97	2	1	2.03	13	0	0	0	27	23	9	6	0	11	19	.245	.375	.200	6.41	3.71
Martinez, Robinson	R-R	6-0	190	3-20-98	5	2	4.53	16	7	0	0	44	36	27	22	0	30	24	.226	.212	.230	4.95	6.18
Munoz, Jairo	R-R	6-5	175	8-12-91	1	1	1.80	8	0	0	6	10	5	3	2	0	4	14	.143	.125	.148	12.60	3.60
Nin, Jose	R-R	6-2	170	6-25-95	1	2	3.41	14	1	0	2	29	30	15	11	0	10	19	.256	.405	.188	5.90	3.10
Nunez, Anderson	R-R	5-10	180	5-24-94	2	0	0.72	14	0	0	3	38	28	5	3	0	10	28	.211	.129	.235	6.69	2.39
Nunez, Jhon	L-L	6-0	155	11-27-97	4	6	4.44	13	13	1	0	71	68	37	35	3	33	46	.252	.353	.245	5.83	4.18
Ortiz, Geury	R-R	6-2	190	5-22-95	4	4	2.59	13	13	2	0	76	69	27	22	0	10	37	.240	.226	.243	4.36	1.18
Rosario, Sandro	R-R	6-3	185	1-23-96	0	0	0.00	2	0	0	0	2	1	1	0	0	1	2	.125	.500	.000	7.71	0.00
Sanchez, Sixto	R-R	5-10	160	7-29-98	1	2	4.56	11	2	0	0	26	32	21	13	0	6	18	.291	.242	.312	6.31	2.10
Suero, Cristopher	R-R	6-1	151	10-9-95	1	1	5.40	9	0	0	0	13	9	15	8	0	15	7	.170	.118	.194	4.73	10.13
Torres, Yonathan	R-R	6-4	200	11-9-92	0	0	0.00	2	0	0	0	4	4	1	0	0	1	4	.250	.500	.214	9.00	2.25
Trinidad, Yonathan	R-R	6-1	175	3-27-95	1	2	4.47	14	4	0	2	44	51	36	22	1	15	30	.280	.205	.301	6.09	3.05
Vega, Miguel	L-L	6-2	201	4-6-94	1	0	3.75	10	0	0	0	12	7	5	5	0	14	12	.179	.250	.171	9.00	10.50

Fielding

Catcher	PCT	G	PO	A	E	DP	PB
Kamara	1.000	1	4	0	0	0	0
Liriano	.975	47	234	34	7	2	8
Martinez	.992	23	102	28	1	0	6
Paulino	.918	16	45	11	5	0	4

First Base	PCT	G	PO	A	E	DP
Baez	.963	9	49	3	2	5

Beaufond	1.000	15	98	4	0	7
Guerrero	1.000	1	3	1	0	0
Liriano	.973	8	65	8	2	4
Martinez	.993	28	263	9	2	14
Nunez	1.000	1	1	0	0	0
Recio	1.000	5	25	3	0	1
Santana	1.000	8	71	4	0	2

Torres	.985	14	125	6	2	8

Second Base	PCT	G	PO	A	E	DP
Beaufond	.934	30	37	77	8	9
Brito	1.000	7	8	16	0	3
Garcia	.951	14	20	38	3	2
Romero	.982	35	62	102	3	13

Third Base	PCT	G	PO	A	E	DP
Baez	1.000	6	2	3	0	0
Feliz	.871	20	20	41	9	2
Garcia	.941	11	8	24	2	1
Marrero	.898	30	17	80	11	2
Recio	.810	16	13	21	8	2
Romero	1.000	5	3	8	0	0

Shortstop	PCT	G	PO	A	E	DP
Brito	.875	8	8	13	3	4
Carrasco	—	1	0	0	0	0
Marrero	.922	37	80	97	15	12
Romero	.887	32	44	81	16	10

Outfield	PCT	G	PO	A	E	DP
Baez	.964	13	25	2	1	0

	PCT	G	PO	A	E	DP
Feliz	1.000	14	19	1	0	0
Garcia	1.000	50	130	5	0	0
Guerrero	.952	27	39	1	2	0
Kamara	.921	20	34	1	3	0
Marrero	1.000	2	3	0	0	0
Paulino	.875	16	14	0	2	0
Rodriguez	.991	63	107	7	1	1
Santana	1.000	34	66	5	0	1

VSL PHILLIES

ROOKIE

VENEZUELAN SUMMER LEAGUE

Batting	B-T	HT	WT	DOB	AVG	vLH	vRH	G	AB	R	H	2B	3B	HR	RBI	BB	HBP	SH	SF	SO	SB	CS	SLG	OBP
Acosta, Adrian	R-R	5-11	165	3-15-96	.238	.167	.253	31	105	10	25	8	0	1	7	10	1	0	2	22	0	1	.343	.305
Avila, Juanj	L-L	5-9	185	3-17-95	.176	.000	.261	9	34	4	6	1	0	0	2	7	0	0	1	6	1	1	.206	.310
Gamboa, Rafael	R-R	5-11	190	5-14-96	.277	.176	.299	50	188	22	52	14	1	2	25	11	4	0	1	20	1	0	.394	.328
Gonzalez, Damaso	B-R	6-1	152	4-11-96	.209	.277	.189	61	211	19	44	6	1	0	22	26	2	5	1	38	7	7	.246	.300
Henriquez, Jesus	R-B	6-0	168	4-7-98	.210	.189	.215	68	248	25	52	8	1	0	14	19	4	7	0	31	3	5	.250	.277
Herrera, Jhon Meison	B-R	5-11	160	4-8-98	.151	.074	.172	47	126	9	19	2	3	0	4	15	9	3	0	39	2	6	.214	.287
Isava, Willerker	B-R	5-11	174	1-21-96	.239	.200	.250	24	71	8	17	1	0	0	7	6	0	4	0	17	2	2	.254	.299
Jimenez, Enger	R-R	6-1	187	7-4-95	.307	.385	.288	70	264	36	81	17	5	3	33	26	6	3	1	46	15	13	.443	.380
Matos, Malvin	R-R	6-3	170	8-19-96	.260	.276	.253	29	104	14	27	11	1	1	6	17	4	0	0	21	2	3	.413	.384
Mendoza, Luis	L-R	6-1	165	8-7-97	.218	.067	.250	24	87	12	19	2	1	0	11	8	4	2	1	14	2	2	.264	.310
Miranda, Joseph	R-R	6-2	186	4-30-95	.254	.333	.241	35	130	10	33	11	0	1	18	10	0	0	3	22	3	1	.362	.301
Pereira, David	R-R	6-3	195	1-10-97	.070	.000	.081	16	43	4	3	1	0	1	4	2	1	2	0	11	1	0	.163	.130
Rivas, Raul	B-R	5-10	157	10-27-96	.220	.273	.209	53	205	26	45	5	2	1	8	27	2	2	0	31	11	14	.278	.316
Rodriguez, Lenin	R-R	5-9	165	3-26-98	.258	.302	.245	60	198	17	51	11	0	4	30	22	7	0	4	13	1	0	.374	.346
Silva, Wilman	R-R	5-8	165	10-10-96	.197	.238	.182	20	76	9	15	1	0	1	5	2	1	0	0	7	0	0	.250	.228
Tabares, Yorbys	R-R	6-0	165	1-24-97	.185	.276	.165	53	162	15	30	3	1	0	9	19	3	4	1	33	5	10	.216	.281
Torrivilla, Joseph	R-R	6-1	168	9-26-97	.261	.200	.278	12	23	1	6	0	0	0	0	1	4	0	0	6	0	1	.261	.393

Pitching	B-T	HT	WT	DOB	W	L	ERA	G	GS	CG	SV	IP	H	R	ER	HR	BB	SO	AVG	vLH	vRH	K/9	BB/9
Aris, Abdallah	R-R	5-11	155	10-8-96	0	0	1.00	18	0	0	2	36	21	4	4	1	10	29	.172	.091	.202	7.25	2.50
Armas, Gustavo	R-R	6-1	195	1-15-96	3	2	1.97	14	14	0	0	73	52	18	16	0	34	55	.208	.281	.187	6.78	4.19
Arroyo, Jesus	R-R	6-1	200	9-20-96	0	0	1.80	3	0	0	0	5	2	1	1	0	1	2	.125	.000	.154	3.60	1.80
Bastidas, Miguelangel	R-R	6-1	170	8-3-95	4	4	2.70	20	4	0	5	43	44	23	13	1	19	24	.272	.154	.294	4.98	3.95
Carrasco, Luis	R-R	6-3	170	9-11-94	2	2	3.28	9	4	0	0	25	23	14	9	0	10	18	.237	.267	.224	6.57	3.65
Diaz, Jose	R-R	6-6	200	4-24-96	0	1	14.14	8	0	0	0	7	10	13	11	0	11	5	.333	.333	.333	6.43	14.14
Diaz, Oberdan	R-L	6-1	175	1-27-95	0	1	1.93	5	0	0	2	9	11	2	2	0	6	7	.314	.500	.276	6.75	5.79
Freites, Orlando	R-R	6-2	170	4-5-97	0	0	27.00	6	0	0	0	5	14	17	15	1	12	4	.500	.571	.476	7.20	21.60
Gonzalez, Luis	R-R	6-3	179	7-6-94	1	3	2.92	12	0	0	5	12	9	5	4	3	10	10	.200	.333	.133	7.30	2.19
Gonzalez, Reiwal	R-R	6-2	196	11-11-94	2	8	4.80	11	10	0	0	45	53	29	24	1	11	36	.306	.340	.292	7.20	2.20
Lara, Tanis	L-L	6-2	195	6-19-96	1	3	5.06	14	0	0	0	16	15	11	9	0	12	18	.238	.556	.185	10.13	6.75
Llovera, Mauricio	R-R	5-11	200	4-17-96	2	4	3.23	11	10	0	0	47	36	22	17	1	17	43	.209	.231	.200	8.18	3.23
Lopez, Orangel	R-R	6-2	160	8-22-96	0	1	3.14	11	0	0	1	14	9	10	5	0	11	14	.184	.158	.200	8.79	6.91
Martinez, Denny	B-L	6-0	157	11-1-96	2	2	2.35	16	1	0	1	31	26	12	8	1	14	28	.234	.278	.226	8.22	4.11
Melendez, Orestes	L-L	5-11	180	6-8-95	4	3	3.00	16	3	0	0	39	33	16	13	2	13	33	.237	.231	.239	7.62	3.00
Mendoza, Williams	R-R	6-7	200	4-29-98	1	0	6.62	14	0	0	0	18	21	16	13	0	13	15	.309	.294	.314	7.64	6.62
Salazar, Carlos	R-R	6-1	155	11-19-96	1	0	4.24	17	0	0	0	23	19	16	11	0	14	16	.224	.211	.227	6.17	5.40
Sanchez, Oskerlly	L-L	6-3	172	8-28-95	0	1	2.66	14	9	0	0	47	33	17	14	1	13	52	.194	.185	.196	9.89	2.47
Sobil, Victor	R-R	6-2	215	7-17-96	2	2	7.24	17	0	0	0	27	33	26	22	1	18	21	.300	.273	.312	6.91	5.93
Velis, Sergio	L-R	5-11	182	1-16-95	4	2	1.33	14	14	0	0	75	50	15	11	0	14	59	.189	.184	.189	7.11	1.69

Fielding

Catcher	PCT	G	PO	A	E	DP	PB
Acosta	.977	24	177	37	5	2	8
Gamboa	1.000	10	41	12	0	2	0
Rodriguez	.981	36	216	42	5	4	6
Silva	.968	9	75	17	3	1	4

First Base	PCT	G	PO	A	E	DP
Acosta	.983	8	44	5	1	4
Gamboa	.988	45	374	22	5	31
Miranda	.988	19	164	7	2	6
Pereira	1.000	5	23	0	0	4
Rodriguez	1.000	5	5	2	0	0

Second Base	PCT	G	PO	A	E	DP
Gonzalez	.917	5	12	10	2	4
Henriquez	.961	56	117	151	11	25
Herrera	.960	8	9	15	1	5
Torrivilla	.857	7	10	14	4	2

Third Base	PCT	G	PO	A	E	DP
Gonzalez	.880	24	29	74	14	5
Isava	.836	18	10	36	9	2
Pereira	.667	8	5	9	7	1
Torrivilla	.818	6	5	4	2	0

Shortstop	PCT	G	PO	A	E	DP
Gonzalez	.933	13	22	34	4	2

	PCT	G	PO	A	E	DP
Henriquez	.973	12	34	37	2	7
Rivas	.888	47	71	120	24	17

Outfield	PCT	G	PO	A	E	DP
Avila	.967	9	29	0	1	0
Gamboa	1.000	1	1	0	0	0
Herrera	.900	30	35	1	4	0
Isava	—	1	0	0	0	0
Jimenez	.993	67	126	12	1	3
Matos	.974	29	67	8	2	1
Mendoza	1.000	24	50	0	0	0
Miranda	1.000	6	8	0	0	0
Tabares	.962	52	69	7	3	0

PHILADELPHIA PHILLIES

Pittsburgh Pirates

SEASON IN A SENTENCE: Continuing their upward trajectory of the past three seasons, the Pirates again reached the playoffs and challenged the Cardinals for supremacy in the NL Central before falling just short.

HIGH POINT: Although they lost the wild-card game for the third year in a row, the Pirates' 98 wins were their most since 1991. They had three win streaks of at least seven games and had the second-most wins in baseball, behind only St. Louis.

LOW POINT: The Pirates hosted the wild-card game for the third straight year and again lost, 4-0 to the Cubs, after being shut out by the Giants in the wild-card round in 2014.

NOTABLE ROOKIES: Jung Ho Kang, who signed for a relatively meager $11 million over four years after leading the Korean Baseball Organization in home runs, was a key contributor, cranking 15 homers before fracturing his leg in September on a hard slide by Chris Coghlan. Hard-throwing righthander Arquimedes Caminero, purchased in February from the Marlins, provided some solid relief and appeared in nearly half of Pittsburgh's games. Catcher Elias Diaz made his major league debut and gets high marks for his receiving, framing and throwing ability.

KEY TRANSACTIONS: In season, the Pirates added some cheap relief options by trading for Joakim Soria, sending JaCoby Jones to the Tigers, and signing righthander Joe Blanton off the scrap heap. In need of some righthanded power when Josh Harrison was injured, the team brought back third baseman Aramis Ramirez and he slugged .413 for Pittsburgh. In the offseason, the addition of catcher Francisco Cervelli from the Yankees for lefthander Justin Wilson was a win for both teams as Cervelli gave the Bucs an inexpensive, energetic replacement for Russell Martin, who left in free agency for the Blue Jays.

DOWN ON THE FARM: Indianapolis tied Columbus for the best record in the International League and then fell in five games to their West Division rival in the Governors' Cup final. Tyler Glasnow headlined Indy's rotation after breezing through Double-A despite missing a month with an ankle injury and could soon lead a wave of arms headed to Pittsburgh. Righty Jameson Taillon, recovering Tommy John surgery, pitched in the instructional league and could be an option in 2016. Another righthander, Nick Kingham, had elbow ligament replacement surgery in May.

OPENING DAY PAYROLL: $88,278,500 (25th)

PLAYERS OF THE YEAR

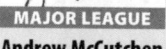

MAJOR LEAGUE	MINOR LEAGUE
Andrew McCutchen	**Josh Bell**
of	1b
.292/.401/.488	.317/.393/.446
23 HR, team-best	(Double-A/Triple-A)
96 RBIs	Power showing up

ORGANIZATION LEADERS

BATTING   *Minimum 250 AB

MAJORS

*AVG	Francisco Cervelli	.295
*OPS	Andrew McCutchen	.889
HR	Pedro Alvarez	27
RBI	Andrew McCutchen	96

MINORS

*AVG	Adam Frazier, Altoona	.324
*OBP	Josh Bell, Altoona, Indianapolis	.393
*SLG	Jordan Luplow, West Virginia	.464
R	Keon Broxton, Altoona, Indianapolis	86
H	Austin Meadows, Bradenton, Altoona	165
TB	Austin Meadows, Bradenton, Altoona	224
2B	Jordan Luplow, West Virginia	36
3B	Keon Broxton, Altoona, Indianapolis	12
	Alen Hanson, Indianapolis	12
HR	Stetson Allie, Altoona	17
RBI	Jose Osuna, Bradenton, Altoona	81
BB	Max Moroff, Altoona	70
SO	Keon Broxton, Altoona, Indianapolis	156
SB	Tito Polo, West Virginia	46

PITCHING   #Minimum 75 IP

MAJORS

W	Gerrit Cole	19
#ERA	Gerrit Cole	2.60
SO	Francisco Liriano	205
SV	Mark Melancon	51

MINORS

W	Austin Coley, West Virginia	16
L	Matt Benedict, Bradenton, Altoona, Indy	10
	Zack Dodson, Altoona	10
	Frank Duncan, Bradenton	10
#ERA	Yeudy Garcia, West Virginia	2.10
G	Blake Wood, Indianapolis	57
GS	Steven Brault, Bradenton, Altoona	28
SV	Blake Wood, Indianapolis	29
IP	Zack Dodson, Altoona	162
BB	Jason Creasy, Altoona	52
	Cody Dickson, Bradenton	52
SO	Tyler Glasnow, West Virginia, Altoona, Indy	136
AVG	Yeudy Garcia, West Virginia	.204

2015 PERFORMANCE

General Manager: Neal Huntington. **Farm Director:** Larry Broadway. **Scouting Director:** Joe DelliCarri.

Class	Team	League	W	L	PCT	Finish	Manager
Majors	Pittsburgh Pirates	National	98	64	.605	2nd (15)	Clint Hurdle
Triple-A	Indianapolis Indians	International	83	61	.576	t-1st (14)	Dean Treanor
Double-A	Altoona Curve	Eastern	74	68	.521	4th (12)	Tom Prince
High A	Bradenton Marauders	Florida State	74	64	.536	5th (12)	Michael Ryan
Low A	West Virginia Power	South Atlantic	87	52	.626	1st (14)	Brian Esposito
Short season	West Virginia Black Bears	New York-Penn	42	34	.553	3rd (14)	Wyatt Toregas
Rookie	Bristol Pirates	Appalachian	29	36	.446	8th (10)	Edgar Varela
Rookie	Pirates	Gulf Coast	28	31	.475	8th (16)	Milver Reyes
Overall 2015 Minor League Record			417	346	.547	3rd (30)	

ORGANIZATION STATISTICS

PITTSBURGH PIRATES

NATIONAL LEAGUE

Batting	B-T	HT	WT	DOB	AVG	vLH	vRH	G	AB	R	H	2B	3B	HR	RBI	BB	HBP	SH	SF	SO	SB	CS	SLG	OBP
Alvarez, Pedro	L-R	6-3	250	2-6-87	.243	.258	.240	150	437	60	106	18	0	27	77	48	2	0	4	131	2	0	.469	.318
Broxton, Keon	R-R	6-3	195	5-7-90	.000	.000	—	7	2	3	0	0	0	0	0	0	0	0	0	1	1	1	.000	.000
Cervelli, Francisco	R-R	6-1	205	3-6-86	.295	.310	.291	130	451	56	133	17	5	7	43	46	8	4	1	94	1	1	.401	.370
Decker, Jaff	L-L	5-9	190	2-23-90	.214	.000	.273	23	28	8	6	1	1	0	1	7	0	1	0	9	0	0	.321	.371
Diaz, Elias	R-R	6-0	210	11-17-90	.000	—	.000	2	2	0	0	0	0	0	0	0	0	0	0	1	0	0	.000	.000
Florimon, Pedro	B-R	6-2	185	12-10-86	.087	.143	.063	24	23	5	2	0	1	0	1	2	0	0	0	12	1	0	.174	.160
Harrison, Josh	R-R	5-8	195	7-8-87	.287	.302	.282	114	418	57	120	29	1	4	28	19	7	3	2	71	10	8	.390	.327
Hart, Corey	R-R	6-6	240	3-24-82	.222	.107	.346	35	54	3	12	1	0	2	9	1	1	0	1	19	0	0	.352	.246
Hernandez, Gorkys	R-R	6-1	190	9-7-87	.000	.000	.000	8	5	0	0	0	0	0	0	0	0	0	0	1	0	0	.000	.000
Ishikawa, Travis	L-L	6-3	220	9-24-83	.224	.200	.226	38	58	5	13	3	0	1	8	8	0	0	0	17	0	0	.328	.318
2-team total (6 San Francisco)					.206	—		44	63	6	13	3	0	1	9	3	0	1	0	20	0	0	.302	.306
Kang, Jung Ho	R-R	6-0	215	4-5-87	.287	.238	.300	126	421	60	121	24	2	15	58	28	17	0	1	99	5	4	.461	.355
Lambo, Andrew	L-L	6-3	215	8-11-88	.040	.000	.043	20	25	1	1	1	0	0	0	2	0	0	0	8	0	0	.080	.111
Lombardozzi Jr., Steve	B-R	6-0	200	9-20-88	.000	.000	.000	12	10	1	0	0	0	0	0	1	0	0	0	4	0	0	.000	.091
Marte, Starling	R-R	6-1	185	10-9-88	.287	.246	.298	153	579	84	166	30	2	19	81	27	19	3	5	123	30	10	.444	.337
McCutchen, Andrew	R-R	5-10	200	10-10-86	.292	.328	.282	157	566	91	165	36	3	23	96	98	12	0	9	133	11	5	.488	.401
Mercer, Jordy	R-R	6-3	215	8-27-86	.244	.284	.233	116	394	34	96	21	0	3	34	27	2	4	3	73	3	2	.320	.293
Morel, Brent	R-R	6-2	230	4-21-87	.286	1.000	.167	3	7	1	2	1	0	0	1	0	0	0	0	3	0	0	.429	.286
Morse, Mike	R-R	6-5	245	3-22-82	.275	.304	.217	45	69	6	19	3	1	1	7	11	2	0	0	21	0	0	.391	.390
2-team total (53 Miami)					.231	—		98	229	14	53	7	1	5	19	23	4	0	0	76	0	0	.336	.313
Polanco, Gregory	L-L	6-5	230	9-14-91	.256	.190	.274	153	593	83	152	35	6	9	52	55	1	1	2	121	27	10	.381	.320
Ramirez, Aramis	R-R	6-1	205	6-25-78	.245	.259	.239	56	196	18	48	13	1	6	35	11	1	0	2	26	0	0	.413	.299
2-team total (81 Milwaukee)					.246	—		137	475	43	117	31	1	17	75	31	5	0	5	68	1	0	.423	.297
Rodriguez, Sean	R-R	6-0	200	4-26-85	.246	.236	.252	139	224	25	55	12	1	4	17	5	6	5	0	63	2	2	.362	.281
Sanchez, Tony	R-R	5-11	220	5-20-88	.375	.000	.429	3	8	2	3	0	0	0	1	0	0	0	0	3	0	0	.375	.444
Snider, Travis	L-L	6-0	235	2-2-88	.192	.000	.227	18	26	1	5	3	0	1	8	3	0	0	0	10	0	0	.423	.276
Stewart, Chris	R-R	6-4	210	2-19-82	.289	.300	.287	58	159	9	46	8	0	0	15	6	2	3	2	29	0	0	.340	.320
Tabata, Jose	R-R	5-11	210	8-12-88	.289	—	.289	27	38	2	11	0	0	0	4	2	1	0	0	7	0	1	.289	.341
Walker, Neil	B-R	6-3	210	9-10-85	.269	.237	.276	151	543	69	146	32	3	16	71	44	8	0	8	110	4	1	.427	.328

Pitching	B-T	HT	WT	DOB	W	L	ERA	G	GS	CG	SV	IP	H	R	ER	HR	BB	SO	AVG	vLH	vRH	K/9	BB/9
Bastardo, Antonio	L-L	5-11	205	9-21-85	4	1	2.98	66	0	0	1	57	39	19	19	4	26	64	.188	.138	.210	10.05	4.08
Blanton, Joe	R-R	6-3	215	12-11-80	5	0	1.57	21	0	0	0	34	26	7	6	1	9	39	.206	.280	.158	10.22	2.36
Burnett, A.J.	R-R	6-4	230	1-3-77	9	7	3.18	26	26	0	0	164	174	64	58	11	49	143	.275	.254	.291	7.85	2.69
Caminero, Arquimedes	R-R	6-4	245	6-16-87	4	3	3.62	73	0	0	0	75	63	31	30	7	29	73	.224	.217	.229	8.80	3.50
Cole, Gerrit	R-R	6-4	230	9-8-90	19	8	2.60	32	32	0	0	208	183	71	60	11	44	202	.239	.227	.251	8.74	1.90
Guerra, Deolis	R-R	6-5	245	4-17-89	2	0	6.48	10	0	0	0	17	26	12	12	5	3	17	.371	.250	.435	9.18	1.62
Happ, J.A.	L-L	6-5	205	10-19-82	7	2	1.85	11	11	0	0	63	52	13	13	3	13	69	.221	.240	.213	9.81	1.85
Hughes, Jared	R-R	6-7	245	7-4-85	3	1	2.28	76	0	0	0	67	70	21	17	3	19	36	.282	.286	.280	4.84	2.55
LaFromboise, Bobby	L-L	6-4	225	6-25-86	0	0	1.13	11	0	0	0	8	5	1	1	1	1	8	.179	.158	.222	9.00	1.13
Liriano, Francisco	L-L	6-2	225	10-26-83	12	7	3.38	31	31	0	0	187	155	75	70	15	70	205	.223	.207	.228	9.88	3.38
Liz, Radhames	R-R	6-2	200	10-6-83	1	4	4.24	14	0	0	0	23	26	11	11	4	12	27	.286	.282	.288	10.41	4.63
Locke, Jeff	L-L	6-0	195	11-20-87	8	11	4.49	30	30	0	0	168	179	95	84	15	60	129	.274	.294	.267	6.90	3.21
Melancon, Mark	R-R	6-2	210	3-28-85	3	2	2.23	78	0	0	51	77	57	22	19	4	14	62	.207	.138	.263	7.28	1.64
Morton, Charlie	R-R	6-5	225	11-12-83	9	9	4.81	23	23	0	0	129	137	77	69	13	41	96	.271	.301	.239	6.70	2.86
Sadler, Casey	R-R	6-4	225	7-13-90	1	0	3.60	1	1	0	0	5	4	2	2	1	1	5	.222	.000	.250	9.00	1.80
Scahill, Rob	R-R	6-2	210	2-15-87	2	4	2.64	28	0	0	0	31	33	15	9	3	16	24	.268	.286	.254	7.04	4.70
Soria, Joakim	R-R	6-3	200	5-18-84	0	0	2.03	29	0	0	1	27	23	7	6	0	8	28	.237	.327	.146	9.45	2.70
Volstad, Chris	R-R	6-8	230	9-23-86	0	0	0.00	1	0	0	0	2	2	0	0	0	0	0	.286	.250	.333	0.00	0.00
Watson, Tony	L-L	6-4	225	5-30-85	4	1	1.91	77	0	0	1	75	55	17	16	3	17	62	.205	.186	.212	7.41	2.03
Worley, Vance	R-R	6-2	250	9-25-87	4	6	4.02	23	8	0	0	72	81	36	32	6	21	49	.287	.307	.276	6.15	2.64

Fielding

Catcher	PCT	G	PO	A	E	DP	PB
Cervelli	.994	128	992	82	7	6	10
Sanchez	1.000	2	16	3	0	0	
Stewart	.976	52	328	37	9	2	1

First Base	PCT	G	PO	A	E	DP
Alvarez	.978	124	966	68	23	98
Hart	.930	8	39	1	3	2
Ishikawa	.987	12	68	7	1	9
Morse	1.000	22	113	4	0	12
Ramirez	.933	5	27	1	2	5
Rodriguez	.997	102	366	15	1	37

Second Base	PCT	G	PO	A	E	DP
Florimon	1.000	3	2	1	0	1
Harrison	.983	37	45	69	2	21

Rodriguez	1.000	7	3	16	0	4	
Walker	.989	146	236	418	7	103	

Third Base	PCT	G	PO	A	E	DP
Harrison	.952	72	41	136	9	20
Kang	.971	77	30	139	5	11
Morel	1.000	2	1	3	0	1
Ramirez	.955	48	22	83	5	6
Rodriguez	1.000	8	3	12	0	2

Shortstop	PCT	G	PO	A	E	DP
Florimon	.938	17	10	20	2	2
Kang	.961	60	74	146	9	40
Mercer	.986	115	148	351	7	78
Rodriguez	.778	3	4	3	2	2

Outfield	PCT	G	PO	A	E	DP
Broxton	—	2	0	0	0	0
Decker	.818	9	8	1	2	0
Harrison	.900	22	26	1	3	0
Hart	1.000	3	10	0	0	0
Hernandez	1.000	6	1	0	0	0
Ishikawa	1.000	5	2	0	0	0
Lambo	1.000	8	3	1	0	0
Marte	.991	151	205	16	2	1
McCutchen	.994	152	301	7	2	2
Polanco	.972	149	260	13	8	5
Rodriguez	1.000	29	29	0	0	0
Snider	1.000	6	8	0	0	0
Tabata	1.000	8	7	0	0	0

INDIANAPOLIS INDIANS

TRIPLE-A

INTERNATIONAL LEAGUE

Batting	B-T	HT	WT	DOB	AVG	vLH	vRH	G	AB	R	H	2B	3B	HR	RBI	BB	HBP	SH	SF	SO	SB	CS	SLG	OBP
Bell, Josh	B-R	6-2	235	8-14-92	.347	.265	.379	35	121	20	42	7	3	2	18	21	1	0	2	15	2	0	.504	.441
Bowker, John	L-L	6-1	205	7-8-83	.219	.125	.237	55	201	16	44	9	0	6	20	5	0	0	1	40	0	2	.353	.237
Brown, Kelson	R-R	6-3	175	11-7-87	.222	.200	.227	15	27	4	6	2	0	0	3	2	1	2	0	4	0	0	.296	.300
Broxton, Keon	R-R	6-3	195	5-7-90	.256	.200	.278	88	312	51	80	15	8	7	42	47	2	1	5	105	28	9	.423	.352
Castillo, Wilkin	B-R	6-0	200	6-1-84	.250	.455	.172	17	40	4	10	2	0	0	2	8	1	0	1	7	1	0	.300	.380
Decker, Jaff	L-L	5-9	190	2-3-90	.266	.257	.270	69	218	33	58	10	1	3	26	36	3	3	5	38	18	3	.362	.370
Diaz, Elias	R-R	6-0	210	11-17-90	.271	.271	.271	93	325	33	88	16	4	4	47	29	2	2	5	47	1	4	.382	.330
Florimon, Pedro	B-R	6-2	185	12-10-86	.245	.222	.258	64	196	21	48	12	3	2	18	21	0	4	2	55	12	3	.367	.315
Gamache, Daniel	L-R	5-11	190	11-20-90	.257	.417	.208	30	101	10	26	5	0	0	11	6	1	1	2	24	1	0	.307	.300
Garcia, Willy	R-R	6-2	215	9-4-92	.246	.212	.254	71	276	36	68	11	4	10	38	12	3	0	0	76	1	4	.424	.285
Hanson, Alen	B-R	5-11	180	10-22-92	.263	.246	.270	117	475	66	125	17	12	6	43	37	0	12	5	91	35	12	.387	.313
Harrison, Josh	R-R	5-8	195	7-8-87	.053	.000	.071	5	19	0	1	0	0	0	0	1	0	0	0	2	0	0	.053	.100
Hart, Corey	R-R	6-6	240	3-24-82	.167	.000	.194	13	42	4	7	1	0	2	7	1	0	0	0	15	0	0	.333	.186
Hernandez, Gorkys	R-R	6-1	190	9-7-87	.288	.245	.309	104	340	51	98	16	3	6	42	41	2	5	3	78	17	3	.406	.365
Ishikawa, Travis	L-L	6-3	220	9-24-83	.286	.000	.333	2	7	1	2	2	0	0	1	1	0	0	0	2	0	0	.571	.375
Lombardozzi Jr., Steve	B-R	6-0	200	9-20-88	.282	.336	.252	97	355	30	100	15	0	0	37	32	4	2	1	40	14	4	.324	.347
Mercer, Jordy	R-R	6-3	215	8-27-86	.240	.200	.250	7	25	3	6	0	0	1	5	1	0	0	0	5	0	0	.360	.269
Morel, Brent	R-R	6-2	230	4-21-87	.266	.271	.264	81	297	36	79	21	2	9	47	23	3	0	3	67	8	2	.441	.322
Morris, Hunter	L-R	6-2	230	10-7-88	.143	.200	.124	38	119	3	17	3	1	0	5	7	0	1	2	46	0	0	.185	.188
Ngoepe, Gift	B-R	5-8	195	1-18-90	.246	.222	.250	21	61	5	15	4	0	0	1	6	0	4	0	15	1	2	.311	.313
Nunez, Gustavo	B-R	5-10	170	2-8-88	.276	.263	.282	103	340	46	94	10	1	2	24	23	3	13	2	52	19	10	.329	.326
Rojas Jr., Mel	B-R	6-2	225	5-24-90	.263	.263	.263	52	156	14	41	6	0	0	11	9	0	1	0	37	3	1	.301	.303
Romero, Deibinson	R-R	6-1	215	9-24-86	.302	.415	.247	38	126	25	38	13	0	6	27	21	3	1	4	21	0	2	.548	.403
Sanchez, Tony	R-R	5-11	220	5-20-88	.236	.275	.221	94	313	38	74	20	2	3	47	45	8	0	5	65	4	3	.342	.342
Sellers, Justin	R-R	5-10	175	2-1-86	.100	—	.100	4	10	0	1	0	0	0	2	0	1	0	0	4	0	0	.100	.250
2-team total (8 Charlotte)					.182	—	—	12	44	2	8	2	0	0	2	2	0	1	1	9	0	0	.227	.213
Snider, Travis	L-L	6-0	235	2-2-88	.314	.286	.321	10	35	5	11	1	0	1	4	4	0	0	1	3	0	0	.429	.375
Stewart, Chris	R-R	6-4	210	2-19-82	.333	.600	.143	3	12	0	4	0	0	0	2	1	0	0	0	1	0	0	.333	.385
Tabata, Jose	R-R	5-11	210	8-12-88	.291	.278	.295	44	148	19	43	6	1	0	5	16	1	0	0	16	2	2	.345	.364
Vasquez, Andy	L-R	6-2	175	10-8-87	.231	.200	.250	11	26	2	6	0	0	1	1	0	3	0	4	1	1	.231	.259

Pitching	B-T	HT	WT	DOB	W	L	ERA	G	GS	CG	SV	IP	H	R	ER	HR	BB	SO	AVG	vLH	vRH	K/9	BB/9
Balester, Collin	R-R	6-4	190	6-6-86	0	0	3.07	8	0	0	0	15	12	6	5	1	5	8	.214	.280	.161	4.91	3.07
2-team total (21 Louisville)					0	0	2.45	29	0	0	7	37	28	11	10	2	8	21	—	—	—	5.15	1.96
Barrios, Yhonathan	B-R	5-10	200	12-1-91	1	2	4.60	13	0	0	1	16	19	8	8	0	8	9	.302	.250	.343	5.17	4.60
Benedict, Matt	R-R	6-5	220	2-3-89	0	2	4.82	2	2	0	0	9	9	5	5	2	1	5	.243	.263	.222	4.82	0.96
Bleich, Jeremy	L-L	6-2	200	6-18-87	0	0	2.60	13	0	0	1	17	15	7	5	1	3	11	.234	.194	.293	5.71	1.56
Boscan, Wilfredo	R-R	6-2	175	10-26-89	10	3	3.07	25	23	0	0	126	130	53	43	3	45	86	.270	.307	.243	6.14	3.21
Glasnow, Tyler	L-R	6-8	225	8-23-93	2	1	2.20	8	8	0	0	41	33	16	10	1	22	48	.220	.149	.277	10.54	4.83
Guerra, Deolis	R-R	6-5	245	4-17-89	2	1	1.23	25	0	0	4	37	21	6	5	1	8	37	.165	.222	.123	9.08	1.96
Herrmann, Frank	L-R	6-4	220	5-30-84	1	1	1.50	7	0	0	0	6	3	1	1	0	5	6	.150	.286	.077	9.00	7.50
Holdzkom, John	R-R	6-9	245	10-19-87	2	0	3.22	21	0	0	2	22	16	8	8	0	17	27	.203	.143	.235	10.88	6.85
Inman, Jeff	R-R	6-3	180	11-24-87	0	1	2.95	14	0	0	2	18	17	7	6	0	4	13	.250	.226	.270	6.38	1.96
Kingham, Nick	R-R	6-6	230	11-8-91	1	2	4.31	6	6	0	0	31	34	16	15	3	7	32	.270	.161	.357	9.19	2.01
LaFromboise, Bobby	L-L	6-4	225	6-25-86	1	2	2.98	54	0	0	0	54	41	18	18	5	21	52	.206	.232	.188	8.61	3.48
Leesman, Charlie	L-L	6-4	215	3-10-87	4	1	3.74	10	3	0	0	22	20	15	9	0	14	16	.238	.250	.234	6.65	5.82
Lincoln, Brad	R-R	6-0	225	5-25-85	4	3	4.18	39	4	0	2	60	60	32	28	3	41	57	.263	.250	.274	8.50	6.12
Liz, Radhames	R-R	6-2	200	10-6-83	4	5	1.40	16	10	0	0	64	44	15	10	0	24	74	.188	.198	.180	10.35	3.36
Miller, Adam	R-R	6-4	215	11-26-84	0	2	4.30	11	0	0	0	23	23	14	11	2	8	16	.258	.219	.281	6.26	3.13
Morris, A.J.	R-R	6-2	185	12-1-86	5	3	2.44	44	3	0	3	85	76	31	23	3	22	72	.240	.279	.209	7.65	2.34
Morton, Charlie	R-R	6-5	225	11-12-83	1	1	2.03	2	2	0	0	13	13	4	3	0	4	16	.255	.333	.200	11.48	2.70
Richard, Clayton	L-L	6-5	245	9-12-83	4	2	2.09	9	9	0	0	56	53	20	13	3	13	25	.244	.140	.270	4.02	2.09
Sadler, Casey	R-R	6-4	225	7-13-90	6	5	4.22	13	13	2	0	81	72	41	38	9	25	48	.237	.266	.216	5.33	2.78
Sampson, Adrian	R-R	6-2	205	10-7-91	8	8	3.98	21	21	0	0	124	137	59	55	8	29	95	.278	.258	.295	6.88	2.10

Pitching	B-T	HT	WT	DOB	W	L	ERA	G	GS	CG	SV	IP	H	R	ER	HR	BB	SO	AVG	vLH	vRH	K/9	BB/9
Sanchez, Angel	R-R	6-1	190	11-28-89	5	1	2.55	10	10	0	0	60	49	18	17	6	15	50	.217	.214	.220	7.50	2.25
Scahill, Rob	R-R	6-2	210	2-15-87	0	0	4.05	6	0	0	0	7	7	3	3	0	3	6	.250	.250	.250	8.10	4.05
Volstad, Chris	R-R	6-8	230	9-23-86	11	7	3.18	27	25	0	0	156	159	61	55	3	43	97	.269	.299	.244	5.61	2.49
Wall, Josh	R-R	6-6	215	1-21-87	2	3	2.45	29	0	0	0	37	27	11	10	1	10	37	.206	.246	.176	9.08	2.45
Wood, Blake	R-R	6-5	240	8-8-85	2	5	3.53	57	0	0	29	59	52	26	23	2	25	70	.234	.245	.226	10.74	3.84
Worley, Vance	R-R	6-2	250	9-25-87	3	1	2.38	5	5	1	0	34	30	10	9	4	5	21	.236	.264	.216	5.56	1.32

Fielding

Catcher	PCT	G	PO	A	E	DP	PB
Castillo	1.000	12	97	5	0	1	1
Diaz	.984	60	394	32	7	4	4
Sanchez	.979	70	503	62	12	4	3
Stewart	.943	3	30	3	2	1	0

First Base	PCT	G	PO	A	E	DP
Bell	.990	32	295	9	3	20
Bowker	.992	40	320	32	3	28
Brown	1.000	1	3	0	0	0
Castillo	—	1	0	0	0	0
Hart	1.000	5	43	2	0	6
Ishikawa	1.000	1	9	0	0	0
Lombardozzi Jr.	1.000	2	20	1	0	1
Morel	.995	45	361	31	2	33
Morris	.993	32	245	24	2	24
Romero	—	1	0	0	0	0

Second Base	PCT	G	PO	A	E	DP
Brown	1.000	1	1	7	0	1
Florimon	1.000	4	4	11	0	2
Hanson	.984	171	198	352	9	59

Catcher	PCT	G	PO	A	E	DP
Harrison	1.000	1	1	1	0	0
Lombardozzi Jr.	.893	24	34	58	11	7
Ngoepe	.833	2	2	3	1	2
Nunez	.968	11	22	39	2	4

Third Base	PCT	G	PO	A	E	DP
Brown	1.000	3	1	5	0	1
Florimon	.879	14	7	22	4	3
Gamache	.961	30	20	54	3	4
Hanson	1.000	7	2	14	0	1
Harrison	1.000	3	0	8	0	0
Lombardozzi Jr.	.808	18	14	28	10	3
Morel	.989	38	20	68	1	5
Ngoepe	.778	3	3	4	2	1
Nunez	1.000	6	4	8	0	0
Romero	.952	34	15	65	4	4

Shortstop	PCT	G	PO	A	E	DP
Brown	.933	6	5	9	1	1
Florimon	.973	44	53	125	5	28
Hanson	1.000	1	0	3	0	1
Lombardozzi Jr.	.857	1	1	5	1	1

Catcher	PCT	G	PO	A	E	DP
Mercer	1.000	7	7	16	0	2
Ngoepe	.985	15	24	42	1	14
Nunez	.953	81	116	189	15	40
Sellers	1.000	4	4	9	0	1

Outfield	PCT	G	PO	A	E	DP
Bowker	1.000	5	5	0	0	0
Brown	1.000	1	1	0	0	0
Broxton	.978	85	175	4	4	1
Decker	.975	61	112	3	3	1
Florimon	—	1	0	0	0	0
Garcia	.993	67	131	10	1	3
Harrison	1.000	1	1	0	0	0
Hernandez	.988	103	231	7	3	0
Lombardozzi Jr.	1.000	38	71	1	0	0
Nunez	1.000	1	2	0	0	0
Rojas Jr.	.947	40	67	4	4	1
Snider	1.000	7	10	0	0	0
Tabata	1.000	34	54	2	0	0
Vasquez	1.000	9	20	0	0	0

ALTOONA CURVE   DOUBLE-A

EASTERN LEAGUE

Batting	B-T	HT	WT	DOB	AVG	vLH	vRH	G	AB	R	H	2B	3B	HR	RBI	BB	HBP	SH	SF	SO	SB	CS	SLG	OBP
Allie, Stetson	R-R	6-2	230	3-13-91	.205	.268	.182	120	409	45	84	17	0	17	58	47	6	2	5	135	6	3	.372	.293
Barnes, Barrett	R-R	5-11	209	7-29-91	.246	.143	.276	37	126	17	31	6	0	3	17	16	2	1	1	25	4	4	.365	.338
Bell, Josh	B-R	6-2	235	8-14-92	.307	.278	.319	96	368	47	113	17	6	5	60	44	2	3	9	50	7	4	.427	.376
Broxton, Keon	R-R	6-3	195	5-7-90	.302	.229	.328	45	179	35	54	12	4	3	26	19	1	1	4	51	11	6	.464	.365
Frazier, Adam	L-R	5-11	170	12-14-91	.324	.303	.331	103	377	59	122	21	4	2	30	34	3	9	0	42	11	7	.416	.384
Gamache, Daniel	L-R	5-11	190	11-20-90	.335	.353	.330	74	245	32	82	13	1	5	37	17	1	1	2	36	3	6	.457	.377
Garcia, Willy	R-R	6-2	215	9-4-92	.314	.404	.283	53	204	26	64	7	2	5	29	11	3	3	3	47	3	2	.441	.353
Jones, JaCoby	R-R	6-2	205	5-10-92	.500	.400	.600	3	12	2	5	0	0	2	2	1	0	0	0	1	0	1	.500	.545
2-team total (37 Erie)					.267	—		40	146	28	39	7	2	6	22	18	2	0	5	52	11	3	.466	.345
Meadows, Austin	L-L	6-3	200	5-3-95	.360	.000	.429	6	25	5	9	2	3	0	1	2	1	0	0	5	1	0	.680	.429
Moroff, Max	B-R	6-0	175	5-13-93	.293	.340	.274	136	523	79	153	28	6	7	51	70	1	13	5	111	17	13	.409	.374
Morris, Hunter	L-R	6-2	230	10-7-88	.133	—	.133	12	30	2	4	1	0	0	4	1	0	0	0	5	0	0	.167	.161
Ngoepe, Gift	B-R	5-8	195	1-18-90	.260	.286	.251	71	246	31	64	12	2	3	25	24	5	5	0	66	3	6	.362	.338
Osuna, Jose	R-R	6-2	213	12-12-92	.288	.301	.283	85	323	46	93	20	2	8	52	17	4	0	5	61	6	3	.437	.327
Rojas Jr., Mel	B-R	6-2	225	5-24-90	.257	.184	.279	66	214	21	55	11	4	2	19	27	2	2	3	51	6	3	.374	.341
Salcedo, Edward	R-R	6-3	210	7-30-91	.238	.277	.221	73	214	20	51	12	1	3	30	21	1	2	4	40	3	4	.346	.304
Schwind, Jonathan	R-R	6-0	185	5-30-90	.109	.250	.033	22	46	4	5	2	1	0	3	2	1	0	1	15	2	0	.196	.160
Sosa, Junior	L-L	5-10	180	1-4-92	.286	.000	.333	4	7	1	2	0	0	0	0	0	0	0	0	2	0	0	.286	.286
Stallings, Jacob	R-R	6-5	215	12-22-89	.275	.297	.267	74	265	25	73	14	1	3	32	15	3	1	8	64	4	1	.370	.313
Stewart, Chris	R-R	6-4	210	2-19-82	.333	—	.333	2	6	0	2	0	0	0	0	1	0	0	0	1	0	1	.333	.429
Valle, Sebastian	R-R	6-1	205	7-24-90	.279	.245	.288	70	247	27	69	21	0	4	26	22	1	3	0	56	1	2	.413	.341
Vasquez, Andy	R-R	6-2	175	10-8-87	.239	.222	.244	46	117	15	28	7	1	3	13	3	0	2	2	30	2	3	.393	.254
Weiss, Erich	L-R	6-2	199	9-11-91	.250	.190	.264	31	112	15	28	4	1	0	14	8	0	0	4	22	4	2	.304	.290
Wood, Eric	R-R	6-2	195	11-22-92	.237	.221	.243	101	334	39	79	11	3	2	28	32	1	3	3	88	3	7	.305	.303

Pitching	B-T	HT	WT	DOB	W	L	ERA	G	GS	CG	SV	IP	H	R	ER	HR	BB	SO	AVG	vLH	vRH	K/9	BB/9
Balester, Collin	R-R	6-4	190	6-6-86	1	0	1.77	13	0	0	4	20	14	4	4	1	6	14	.200	.333	.130	6.20	2.66
Barrios, Yhonathan	R-R	5-10	200	12-1-91	0	1	1.46	20	0	0	10	25	17	7	4	1	9	12	.193	.216	.176	4.38	3.28
Benedict, Matt	R-R	6-5	220	2-3-89	5	7	6.03	22	16	1	0	97	126	67	65	7	21	47	.320	.369	.270	4.36	1.95
Bleich, Jeremy	L-L	6-2	200	6-18-87	0	2	3.25	25	0	0	4	36	37	16	13	1	11	28	.264	.214	.298	7.00	2.75
Brault, Steven	L-L	6-1	175	4-29-92	9	3	2.00	15	15	0	0	90	72	22	20	1	19	80	.212	.163	.232	8.00	1.90
Creasy, Jason	R-R	6-4	197	5-13-92	12	8	4.41	27	25	0	1	147	163	79	72	12	52	71	.288	.285	.290	4.35	3.18
Dodson, Zack	L-L	6-2	190	7-23-90	7	10	3.67	28	27	1	0	162	163	78	66	11	36	89	.265	.292	.255	4.94	2.00
DuRapau, Montana	R-R	5-11	175	3-27-92	0	0	0.00	2	0	0	1	0	0	0	0	0	0	3	.000	.000	.000	20.25	0.00
Eppler, Tyler	R-R	6-6	220	1-5-93	0	1	10.13	1	1	0	0	3	4	6	6	1	3	6	.211	.143	.250	5.06	5.06
Glasnow, Tyler	L-R	6-8	225	8-23-93	5	3	2.43	12	12	0	0	63	41	22	17	2	19	82	.182	.194	.174	11.71	2.71
Harlan, Tom	L-L	6-6	215	3-7-90	3	3	3.63	38	5	0	1	87	91	36	35	6	24	62	.268	.277	.265	6.96	2.49
Inman, Jeff	R-R	6-3	180	11-24-87	2	1	2.79	17	0	0	3	19	22	6	6	0	5	20	.289	.258	.311	9.31	2.33
Kuchno, John	R-R	6-5	210	5-21-91	3	6	3.46	40	0	0	7	68	64	43	26	8	23	32	.250	.255	.247	4.26	3.06
Kuhl, Chad	R-R	6-3	215	9-10-92	11	5	2.48	26	26	1	0	153	133	53	42	10	41	101	.236	.250	.226	5.95	2.42
McKinney, Brett	R-R	6-2	225	11-19-90	0	3	7.50	24	0	0	1	30	42	25	25	5	14	31	.313	.356	.280	9.30	4.20

Pitching	B-T	HT	WT	DOB	W	L	ERA	G	GS	CG	SV	IP	H	R	ER	HR	BB	SO	AVG	vLH	vRH	K/9	BB/9
Medina, Jhondaniel	R-R	5-11	158	2-8-93	3	6	2.76	45	0	0	12	62	42	27	19	2	37	44	.189	.184	.194	6.39	5.37
Miller, Adam	R-R	6-4	215	11-26-84	0	0	9.00	1	0	0	0	1	2	1	1	0	1	2	.400	.500	.333	18.00	9.00
Morton, Charlie	R-R	6-5	225	11-12-83	1	0	0.00	1	1	0	0	7	2	0	0	0	2	5	.091	.067	.143	6.43	2.57
Perez, Clario	R-R	6-1	185	8-30-92	0	1	3.89	20	0	0	1	35	32	20	15	2	15	21	.235	.259	.218	5.45	3.89
Sample, Tyler	L-R	6-7	245	6-27-89	0	1	7.56	7	0	0	0	8	7	7	7	1	11	7	.241	.500	.174	7.56	11.88
Sanchez, Angel	R-R	6-1	190	11-28-89	8	1	2.79	13	13	0	0	77	72	27	24	4	19	48	.246	.296	.213	5.70	2.21
Scahill, Rob	R-R	6-2	210	2-15-87	0	0	0.00	1	1	0	0	3	2	0	0	0	1	0	.222	.000	.250	0.00	3.00
Smith, Josh	L-L	6-3	200	10-11-89	1	4	5.29	34	0	0	0	48	42	29	28	3	34	31	.243	.143	.300	5.85	6.42
Stock, Robert	L-R	6-1	200	11-21-89	0	0	14.54	3	0	0	0	4	2	9	7	0	10	4	.133	.143	.125	8.31	20.77

Fielding

Catcher	PCT	G	PO	A	E	DP	PB
Stallings	.994	74	424	61	3	3	0
Stewart	1.000	2	4	0	0	0	0
Valle	.992	68	436	59	4	4	1

First Base	PCT	G	PO	A	E	DP
Bell	.985	84	802	52	13	62
Gamache	.987	15	139	11	2	16
Morris	.981	7	48	5	1	3
Osuna	.994	32	300	17	2	24
Salcedo	1.000	7	62	4	0	7
Schwind	—	1	0	0	0	0
Vasquez	1.000	1	9	2	0	0

Second Base	PCT	G	PO	A	E	DP
Gamache	.955	15	19	44	3	8

Third Base	PCT	G	PO	A	E	DP
Frazier	1.000	1	0	1	0	1
Gamache	.879	27	16	42	8	2
Moroff	.875	11	5	23	4	6
Salcedo	.831	29	18	41	12	3
Wood	.914	89	59	165	21	13

Shortstop	PCT	G	PO	A	E	DP
Frazier	.942	58	87	174	16	25
Jones	1.000	3	2	10	0	1
Moroff	.941	13	15	33	3	7
Ngoepe	.967	71	116	241	12	47

Moroff .978 109 215 330 12 76
Weiss .966 24 39 74 4 13

Outfield	PCT	G	PO	A	E	DP
Allie	.964	108	199	16	8	6
Barnes	1.000	34	63	2	0	0
Broxton	.984	44	123	2	2	1
Frazier	.972	31	68	1	2	0
Garcia	.965	50	101	8	4	2
Meadows	1.000	6	16	0	0	0
Osuna	.941	51	76	4	5	2
Rojas Jr.	.985	64	123	5	2	1
Salcedo	.947	21	34	2	2	0
Schwind	1.000	13	22	1	0	0
Sosa	1.000	2	1	0	0	0
Vasquez	.981	34	52	1	1	0

BRADENTON MARAUDERS   HIGH CLASS A

FLORIDA STATE LEAGUE

Batting	B-T	HT	WT	DOB	AVG	vLH	vRH	G	AB	R	H	2B	3B	HR	RBI	BB	HBP	SH	SF	SO	SB	CS	SLG	OBP
Barnes, Barrett	R-R	5-11	209	7-29-91	.261	.311	.243	58	234	45	61	16	2	6	24	28	9	3	2	41	13	5	.423	.359
Diaz, Chris	R-R	5-10	186	11-9-90	.248	.363	.207	96	302	42	75	12	1	0	21	24	5	9	0	44	7	5	.295	.314
Emslie-Pai, Kawika	B-R	5-11	195	9-3-88	.158	.125	.182	5	19	1	3	0	0	0	2	0	0	0	4	1	1	.158	.238
Espinal, Edwin	R-R	6-2	250	1-27-94	.256	.296	.241	109	390	31	100	22	0	5	54	36	0	7	5	51	1	0	.351	.316
Fransoso, Mike	L-R	6-0	180	1-29-90	.209	.212	.209	73	196	18	41	4	1	0	15	23	4	8	4	30	8	3	.240	.300
Freeman, Wes	R-R	6-4	215	1-29-90	.105	.111	.100	5	19	1	2	0	0	0	0	0	0	0	0	8	0	0	.105	.105
Jhang, Jin-De	L-R	5-11	220	5-17-93	.292	.250	.307	99	370	45	108	16	1	5	41	22	2	4	4	43	2	4	.381	.332
Jones, JaCoby	R-R	6-2	205	5-10-92	.253	.265	.248	93	379	48	96	18	3	10	58	31	4	4	5	113	14	4	.396	.313
Maffei, Justin	R-R	5-11	173	8-27-91	.284	.295	.278	83	299	45	85	14	5	2	18	38	7	5	1	53	11	7	.385	.377
Mathisen, Wyatt	R-R	6-0	227	12-30-93	.263	.260	.268	118	403	46	106	14	3	4	34	43	8	4	5	72	0	1	.342	.342
McGuire, Reese	L-R	6-0	181	3-2-95	.254	.159	.292	98	374	32	95	15	0	0	34	26	1	6	4	39	14	7	.294	.301
Meadows, Austin	L-L	6-3	200	5-3-95	.307	.319	.303	121	508	72	156	22	4	7	54	41	0	4	3	79	20	7	.407	.357
Osuna, Jose	R-R	6-2	213	12-12-92	.282	.347	.256	44	174	23	49	12	1	4	29	14	1	1	3	33	1	1	.431	.333
Ramirez, Harold	R-R	5-10	210	9-6-94	.337	.343	.335	80	306	45	103	13	6	4	47	25	9	1	3	48	22	15	.458	.399
Roy, Jeff	L-L	5-8	178	1-24-92	.217	.154	.234	21	60	11	13	2	0	0	6	5	2	1	1	12	5	3	.250	.294
Sellers, Justin	R-R	5-10	175	2-1-86	.316	.500	.231	5	19	1	6	1	0	0	1	0	0	0	1	0	0	0	.368	.350
Sosa, Junior	L-L	5-10	180	10-3-90	.263	.375	.233	20	76	13	20	2	1	2	15	9	0	2	0	13	2	0	.395	.341
Steranka, Jordan	L-R	6-1	205	11-14-89	.236	.188	.245	57	216	19	51	7	0	3	24	1	0	1	2	51	2	3	.310	.237
Tam Sing, Trace	R-R	6-0	175	12-7-91	.270	.231	.292	10	37	4	10	4	0	0	2	2	0	0	0	9	1	0	.378	.308
Weiss, Erich	L-R	6-2	199	9-11-91	.285	.282	.286	98	372	46	106	17	2	3	49	41	6	5	4	70	11	4	.366	.362

Pitching	B-T	HT	WT	DOB	W	L	ERA	G	GS	CG	SV	IP	H	R	ER	HR	BB	SO	AVG	vLH	vRH	K/9	BB/9
Aquino, Jayson	L-L	6-1	180	11-22-92	2	6	3.78	13	13	0	0	79	77	39	33	5	19	50	.252	.254	.252	5.72	2.17
2-team total (5 Dunedin)					4	8	3.54	18	18	0	0	104	104	49	41	7	25	66	—	—	—	5.69	2.16
Benedict, Matt	R-R	6-5	220	2-3-89	3	1	2.73	7	6	0	0	33	30	10	10	2	3	25	.246	.100	.347	6.82	0.82
Bleich, Jeremy	L-L	6-2	200	6-18-87	1	0	0.00	1	0	0	0	3	1	0	0	0	3	.111	.000	.167	9.00	0.00
Brault, Steven	L-L	6-1	175	4-29-92	4	1	3.02	13	13	0	0	66	62	28	22	3	21	45	.252	.167	.280	6.17	2.88
Dickson, Cody	L-L	6-3	180	4-27-92	12	7	4.13	27	27	0	0	142	145	72	65	5	52	98	.272	.244	.280	6.23	3.30
Duncan, Frank	R-R	6-4	215	1-30-92	9	10	4.32	27	25	0	0	152	194	79	73	12	19	111	.311	.340	.289	6.57	1.13
DuRapau, Montana	R-R	5-11	175	3-27-92	4	1	1.40	31	0	0	13	51	21	8	8	2	8	47	.124	.088	.143	8.24	1.40
Eppler, Tyler	R-R	6-6	220	1-5-93	6	1	2.58	14	12	1	1	66	58	23	19	1	14	46	.232	.242	.226	6.24	1.90
Eusebio, Julio	R-R	6-2	190	6-2-92	0	0	10.80	1	0	0	0	2	4	3	2	1	1	0	.444	.250	.600	0.00	5.40
Gonzalez, Felipe	R-R	6-1	200	8-15-91	8	6	3.28	38	14	0	0	107	102	43	39	8	30	80	.259	.230	.276	6.73	2.52
Hafner, Ryan	R-R	6-5	205	11-22-91	1	9	9.55	14	0	0	0	22	32	24	23	1	14	14	.348	.327	.372	5.82	5.82
2-team total (1 Jupiter)					1	1	9.13	15	0	0	0	24	33	25	24	1	15	14	—	—	—	5.32	5.70
Heredia, Luis	R-R	6-6	205	8-10-94	5	6	5.44	21	21	0	0	86	105	59	52	3	44	54	.309	.341	.289	5.65	4.60
Hirsch, Henry	R-R	6-3	185	9-29-92	2	3	2.89	47	0	0	1	87	82	29	28	2	27	85	.252	.252	.251	8.76	2.78
Holmes, Clay	R-R	6-5	230	3-27-93	0	2	2.74	6	6	0	0	23	18	7	7	0	16	22	.222	.257	.196	6.26	2.74
Lopez, Junior	R-R	6-2	165	6-27-91	5	0	2.78	19	0	0	1	36	24	11	11	2	9	21	.190	.233	.169	5.30	2.27
McKinney, Brett	R-R	6-2	225	11-19-90	0	2	3.42	20	0	0	9	24	22	9	9	2	7	23	.244	.333	.185	8.75	2.66
Neverauskas, Dovydas	R-R	6-3	175	1-14-93	0	0	1.62	12	0	0	4	15	4	3	0	5	10	.238	.250	.250	5.40	2.70
Otamendi, Andy	L-L	5-11	170	5-15-92	4	5	3.86	25	1	0	1	47	43	22	20	7	14	39	.249	.143	.290	7.52	2.70
Perez, Clario	R-R	6-1	185	8-30-92	2	3	1.79	24	0	0	3	50	32	10	10	2	12	45	.178	.165	.188	8.05	2.15
Pimentel, Cesilio	L-L	6-2	185	1-5-93	0	0	0.00	1	0	0	1	2	0	0	0	0	1	2	.000	.000	.000	9.00	4.50

Pitching	B-T	HT	WT	DOB	W	L	ERA	G	GS	CG	SV	IP	H	R	ER	HR	BB	SO	AVG	vLH	vRH	K/9	BB/9
Richard, Clayton	L-L	6-5	245	9-12-83	0	1	0.00	1	1	0	0	6	4	1	0	0	1	5	.182	.000	.235	7.50	1.50
Rocha, Oderman	R-R	6-3	165	11-7-92	0	0	0.00	2	0	0	0	3	2	0	0	0	0	1	.222	.500	.143	3.38	0.00
Rosario, Miguel	R-R	6-0	182	1-30-93	3	3	2.92	29	0	0	3	49	45	19	16	2	14	56	.249	.279	.233	10.22	2.55
Sanchez, Isaac	R-R	6-0	170	10-14-92	2	3	2.71	42	0	0	3	66	60	29	20	1	24	51	.242	.196	.274	6.92	3.26
Stock, Robert	L-R	6-1	200	11-21-89	0	0	7.00	7	0	0	1	9	12	7	7	0	8	4	.343	.471	.222	4.00	8.00
Vivas, Julio	R-R	6-2	227	10-1-93	1	1	2.59	15	0	0	2	24	15	10	7	1	11	23	.163	.175	.154	8.51	4.07

Fielding

Catcher	PCT	G	PO	A	E	DP	PB
Emsley-Pai	.978	5	37	8	1	1	1
Jhang	.988	46	302	27	4	4	3
McGuire	.984	90	613	72	11	6	6

First Base	PCT	G	PO	A	E	DP
Diaz	1.000	3	16	1	0	2
Espinal	.995	104	992	60	5	89
Fransoso	1.000	1	4	0	0	1
Osuna	1.000	10	91	5	0	10
Steranka	.989	29	242	19	3	29

Second Base	PCT	G	PO	A	E	DP
Diaz	.971	8	11	22	1	5
Fransoso	.986	29	56	86	2	21
Sellers	1.000	1	1	0	0	0
Tam Sing	.962	10	21	29	2	9
Weiss	.972	93	147	273	12	63

Third Base	PCT	G	PO	A	E	DP
Diaz	.938	29	17	59	5	10
Espinal	1.000	2	1	2	0	0
Fransoso	.714	3	3	2	2	0
Mathisen	.946	107	64	199	15	10
Sellers	1.000	1	0	2	0	1

Shortstop	PCT	G	PO	A	E	DP
Diaz	.965	56	81	191	10	43
Fransoso	1.000	1	1	6	0	1
Jones	.969	84	140	295	14	57
Sellers	.929	3	3	10	1	2

Outfield	PCT	G	PO	A	E	DP
Barnes	.961	55	96	2	4	0
Fransoso	1.000	31	63	7	0	1
Freeman	1.000	4	7	0	0	0
Maffei	.982	78	159	6	3	1
Meadows	.992	114	243	7	2	0
Osuna	.967	32	56	2	2	0
Ramirez	.976	73	157	3	4	0
Roy	1.000	18	38	3	0	1
Sosa	.956	20	42	1	2	0

WEST VIRGINIA POWER — LOW CLASS A

SOUTH ATLANTIC LEAGUE

Batting	B-T	HT	WT	DOB	AVG	vLH	vRH	G	AB	R	H	2B	3B	HR	RBI	BB	HBP	SH	SF	SO	SB	CS	SLG	OBP
Diaz, Francisco	B-R	5-11	185	3-21-90	.353	.429	.316	26	85	11	30	3	1	2	15	11	0	1	2	7	2	0	.482	.418
Emsley-Pai, Kawika	B-R	5-11	195	9-3-88	.365	.375	.361	17	52	5	19	3	0	1	14	8	1	1	0	10	1	1	.481	.459
Escobar, Elvis	L-L	5-8	169	9-6-94	.296	.235	.319	124	477	60	141	28	5	5	64	22	1	11	3	79	15	21	.407	.326
Filliben, Tyler	R-R	6-2	188	8-8-92	.264	.282	.254	79	258	42	68	12	1	1	21	28	8	11	2	48	8	4	.329	.351
Forgione, Erik	B-R	6-0	160	9-9-92	.400	.000	.444	4	10	1	4	0	1	0	0	2	0	1	0	2	0	0	.600	.500
Gushue, Taylor	B-R	6-1	215	12-19-93	.231	.234	.229	99	360	35	83	17	4	5	47	25	5	2	3	79	1	2	.342	.288
Joe, Connor	R-R	6-0	205	8-16-92	.245	.232	.250	80	290	38	71	12	1	1	20	50	8	5	4	34	0	4	.303	.366
Kramer, Kevin	L-R	6-1	190	10-3-93	.240	.278	.219	12	50	9	12	2	1	0	3	5	1	0	0	8	3	0	.320	.321
Luplow, Jordan	R-R	6-1	195	9-26-93	.264	.310	.242	106	390	74	103	36	3	12	67	59	6	6	4	67	11	2	.464	.366
Newman, Kevin	R-R	6-1	180	8-4-93	.306	.333	.294	23	98	14	30	4	1	0	8	9	2	1	0	8	6	1	.367	.376
Polo, Tito	R-R	5-9	184	8-23-94	.236	.203	.253	102	360	51	85	20	2	3	26	28	13	12	1	77	46	13	.328	.313
Reyes, Pablo	R-R	5-10	150	9-5-93	.268	.248	.277	108	388	61	104	24	3	12	60	45	3	18	5	63	27	10	.438	.345
Roy, Jeff	L-L	5-8	178	1-24-92	.255	.267	.250	42	106	19	27	1	2	0	10	10	3	4	2	28	13	2	.302	.331
Simpson, Chase	B-R	6-1	210	2-17-92	.247	.200	.272	117	389	65	96	20	4	11	68	63	3	3	5	112	7	1	.404	.352
Suchy, Michael	R-R	6-3	228	4-15-93	.275	.248	.287	124	447	74	123	34	5	10	76	54	11	1	7	103	6	3	.441	.362
Suiter, Jerrick	R-R	6-4	230	3-4-93	.299	.304	.297	105	381	62	114	19	4	3	57	46	7	4	3	59	6	4	.394	.382
Tam Sing, Trace	R-R	6-0	175	12-7-91	.210	.208	.211	28	81	8	17	8	2	0	21	13	1	3	1	31	4	1	.358	.323
Tucker, Cole	B-R	6-3	185	7-3-96	.293	.322	.281	73	300	46	88	13	3	2	25	16	0	6	7	49	25	6	.377	.322

Pitching	B-T	HT	WT	DOB	W	L	ERA	G	GS	CG	SV	IP	H	R	ER	HR	BB	SO	AVG	vLH	vRH	K/9	BB/9
Brewer, Colten	R-R	6-4	200	10-29-92	5	9	4.90	22	22	0	0	119	118	70	65	9	37	99	.258	.232	.280	7.47	2.79
Burnette, Jake	R-R	6-4	180	8-10-92	5	4	4.56	25	2	0	1	51	37	27	26	3	45	58	.204	.247	.173	10.17	7.89
Coley, Austin	R-R	6-3	200	7-14-92	16	6	3.66	27	27	0	0	148	148	62	60	18	25	111	.260	.270	.252	6.77	1.52
Dorsch, Eric	R-R	6-8	245	9-23-91	1	0	10.57	7	0	0	0	8	9	10	9	1	6	5	.273	.294	.250	5.87	7.04
DuRapau, Montana	R-R	5-11	175	3-27-92	1	0	1.40	11	0	0	1	19	7	3	3	2	1	19	.106	.111	.100	8.84	0.47
Garcia, Yeudy	R-R	6-3	185	10-6-92	12	5	2.10	30	21	0	1	124	92	36	29	4	41	112	.204	.224	.188	8.11	2.97
Lakind, Jared	L-L	6-2	195	3-9-92	2	1	2.29	15	0	0	0	20	19	8	5	1	7	19	.247	.265	.233	8.69	3.20
Lopez, Junior	R-R	6-2	165	6-27-91	4	1	1.35	18	0	0	5	27	29	4	4	0	5	22	.296	.366	.246	7.43	1.69
McRae, Alex	R-R	6-3	185	4-6-93	8	9	4.98	28	27	0	0	137	159	83	76	9	33	90	.288	.328	.254	5.90	2.16
Neumann, Nick	R-R	6-3	205	4-26-91	3	1	2.76	37	0	0	17	46	44	15	14	4	11	37	.253	.190	.305	7.29	2.17
Neverauskas, Dovydas	R-R	6-3	175	1-14-93	1	2	3.65	18	5	0	2	49	39	24	20	3	19	37	.214	.171	.245	6.75	3.47
Regalado, Jose	R-R	6-3	180	11-22-91	7	5	3.68	30	4	0	2	88	76	38	36	12	16	76	.235	.269	.208	7.77	1.64
Rosario, Miguel	R-R	6-0	182	1-30-93	2	0	1.75	9	2	1	0	26	21	5	5	0	9	21	.233	.270	.208	7.36	3.16
Santana, Edgar	R-R	6-2	180	10-16-91	0	0	4.38	8	0	0	1	12	12	6	6	3	4	16	.255	.429	.115	11.68	2.92
Sever, John	L-L	6-5	190	7-26-93	3	3	2.91	29	9	0	4	87	77	32	28	6	31	84	.232	.337	.192	8.72	3.22
Street, Sam	R-R	6-3	200	3-18-92	3	1	2.10	34	0	0	6	86	83	25	20	3	13	72	.252	.296	.218	7.56	1.37
Tarpley, Stephen	R-L	6-1	180	2-17-93	11	4	2.48	20	20	1	0	116	108	47	32	2	25	105	.241	.203	.255	8.15	1.94
Vivas, Julio	R-R	6-2	227	10-1-93	3	1	3.00	25	0	0	0	42	33	17	14	5	22	33	.216	.136	.266	7.07	4.71

Fielding

Catcher	PCT	G	PO	A	E	DP	PB
Diaz	1.000	26	168	30	0	3	1
Emsley-Pai	1.000	16	110	18	0	2	0
Gushue	.994	99	716	81	5	4	24

First Base	PCT	G	PO	A	E	DP
Emsley-Pai	1.000	1	5	1	0	2
Joe	.991	76	633	39	6	45
Simpson	.990	46	395	22	4	25
Suiter	.994	18	147	6	1	7

Second Base	PCT	G	PO	A	E	DP
Filliben	.969	23	41	53	3	9
Forgione	1.000	2	9	7	0	3
Kramer	1.000	8	12	24	0	4
Reyes	.973	103	187	249	12	42
Tam Sing	1.000	5	12	18	0	3

Third Base	PCT	G	PO	A	E	DP
Filliben	.917	21	17	38	5	2
Luplow	.910	86	58	154	21	8
Simpson	.942	35	22	59	5	7

Shortstop	PCT	G	PO	A	E	DP
Filliben	.969	36	48	79	4	11
Forgione	1.000	1	3	4	0	1
Kramer	.857	2	1	5	1	0
Newman	.949	23	24	69	5	15
Tam Sing	.953	9	19	22	2	6
Tucker	.953	69	85	178	13	29

Outfield	PCT	G	PO	A	E	DP							
Escobar	.973	122	245	7	7	2	Polo	.987	99	221	6	3	2
Forgione	—	1	0	0	0	0	Roy	.974	38	73	2	2	1
							Suchy	.990	110	200	6	2	1

Suiter .972 52 96 8 3 0
Tam Sing 1.000 2 2 0 0 0

WEST VIRGINIA BLACK BEARS   SHORT-SEASON

NEW YORK-PENN LEAGUE

Batting	B-T	HT	WT	DOB	AVG	vLH	vRH	G	AB	R	H	2B	3B	HR	RBI	BB	HBP	SH	SF	SO	SB	CS	SLG	OBP
Andriese, David	L-R	6-2	210	3-2-91	.217	.167	.229	22	60	8	13	3	0	0	6	6	0	1	0	18	0	0	.267	.288
Arribas, Danny	R-R	6-0	185	9-30-92	.284	.444	.236	60	232	38	66	9	2	3	29	24	2	3	0	41	2	3	.379	.357
Bastardo, Alexis	R-R	5-11	190	2-26-94	.218	.308	.173	25	78	9	17	2	0	0	9	5	3	3	1	21	5	3	.244	.287
Baur, Albert	L-R	6-4	215	3-22-92	.276	.357	.247	55	210	22	58	13	0	0	22	14	1	4	3	42	1	1	.338	.320
Forgione, Erik	B-R	6-0	160	9-9-92	.268	.214	.284	38	123	18	33	3	0	0	6	8	3	4	0	25	1	9	.293	.328
Garcia, Deybi	R-R	5-11	185	2-11-92	.154	.250	.111	12	39	0	6	0	0	0	1	3	0	0	0	12	0	1	.154	.214
Harvey, Chris	R-R	6-5	220	3-10-93	.143	.174	.115	14	49	5	7	2	1	0	1	0	0	0	0	20	0	0	.224	.143
Hayes, Ke'Bryan	R-R	6-1	210	1-28-97	.220	.083	.276	12	41	8	9	1	0	0	7	6	1	2	2	7	1	1	.244	.320
Hill, Logan	R-R	6-3	230	5-26-93	.297	.292	.299	60	219	33	65	13	3	7	45	28	11	2	1	51	13	4	.479	.402
Hughston, Casey	L-R	6-2	200	6-9-94	.224	.120	.254	61	219	23	49	9	2	2	28	13	1	8	3	71	4	1	.311	.267
Kelley, Christian	R-R	5-11	185	9-23-93	.232	.282	.219	56	194	30	45	2	0	0	21	25	4	9	1	43	0	0	.242	.330
Kramer, Kevin	L-R	6-1	190	10-3-93	.305	.381	.281	46	177	34	54	7	3	0	17	25	1	4	2	28	9	4	.379	.390
Montilla, Ulises	R-R	5-11	170	5-12-92	.333	.111	.407	12	36	6	12	2	0	0	11	7	1	2	3	0	0	0	.389	.426
Moore, Ty	L-R	6-2	185	7-26-93	.277	.228	.292	64	242	34	67	9	2	1	33	25	7	3	0	40	6	5	.343	.361
Munoz, Carlos	L-L	5-11	225	6-29-94	.150	.250	.125	8	20	7	3	1	0	1	3	7	3	0	1	7	0	0	.350	.419
Nagle, Ryan	L-R	6-1	200	8-7-94	.258	.154	.287	32	120	8	31	6	2	0	17	9	0	2	2	26	0	0	.342	.305
Newman, Kevin	R-R	6-1	180	8-4-93	.226	.295	.200	38	159	25	36	10	1	2	9	10	2	2	0	22	7	1	.340	.281
Ratledge, Logan	R-R	5-11	190	7-20-92	.138	.200	.125	11	29	6	4	0	1	0	4	4	1	0	0	5	0	0	.207	.265
Rivera, Maximo	R-R	5-11	185	12-22-92	.229	.158	.255	23	70	6	16	1	0	0	7	13	0	5	0	20	5	3	.243	.349
Tolman, Mitchell	L-R	5-11	195	6-8-94	.304	.204	.331	63	224	32	68	16	4	0	23	33	8	7	3	38	2	7	.411	.407

Pitching	B-T	HT	WT	DOB	W	L	ERA	G	GS	CG	SV	IP	H	R	ER	HR	BB	SO	AVG	vLH	vRH	K/9	BB/9
Agrazal, Dario	R-R	6-3	190	12-28-94	6	5	2.72	14	14	0	0	76	71	27	23	3	11	45	.245	.244	.246	5.33	1.30
Anderson, Tanner	R-R	6-2	195	5-27-93	1	0	4.50	3	0	0	0	6	8	3	3	0	0	6	.333	.462	.182	9.00	0.00
Brubaker, J.T.	R-R	6-4	175	11-17-93	6	4	2.82	15	15	0	0	73	57	26	23	3	12	49	.216	.212	.220	6.01	1.47
Dorsch, Eric	R-R	6-8	245	9-23-91	2	1	4.30	17	0	0	0	38	34	21	18	0	10	27	.236	.226	.244	6.45	2.39
Escobar, Luis	R-R	6-1	155	5-30-96	0	0	5.68	2	2	0	0	6	7	5	4	0	4	5	.304	.083	.545	7.11	5.68
Eusebio, Julio	R-R	6-2	190	6-2-92	0	3	2.87	19	0	0	5	31	24	12	10	2	9	36	.211	.214	.207	10.34	2.59
Garcia, Hector	L-L	6-0	170	10-4-95	1	2	6.91	5	5	0	0	14	10	11	11	1	10	19	.185	.143	.200	11.93	6.28
Glasnow, Tyler	R-R	6-8	225	8-23-93	0	1	3.38	2	2	0	0	5	3	4	2	0	2	6	.150	.222	.091	10.13	3.38
Helton, Bret	R-R	6-3	215	7-25-93	2	6	4.97	14	14	0	0	54	63	42	30	3	20	37	.288	.287	.288	6.13	3.31
Hibbing, Nick	R-R	6-5	185	8-15-92	2	1	1.70	17	0	0	1	37	32	8	7	2	9	25	.237	.185	.272	6.08	2.19
Holdzkom, John	R-R	6-9	245	10-19-87	0	0	0.00	2	0	0	0	2	0	0	0	0	0	3	.000	.000	.000	13.50	0.00
Karch, Eric	R-R	6-2	205	10-15-91	1	0	5.14	5	0	0	0	7	6	4	4	1	2	6	.222	.100	.294	7.71	2.57
Keselica, Sean	L-L	6-2	180	6-14-93	2	2	4.78	19	0	0	3	26	26	14	14	1	15	36	.271	.286	.265	12.30	5.13
McGarry, Seth	R-R	6-0	180	1-5-94	2	2	4.62	9	9	0	0	39	30	21	20	2	23	35	.214	.250	.184	8.08	5.31
Meyer, Stephan	R-R	6-4	190	5-11-94	0	0	0.84	4	1	0	1	11	8	1	1	0	2	10	.195	.412	.042	8.44	1.69
Minier, Jonathan	R-R	6-1	180	3-8-90	0	0	2.42	11	0	0	0	26	16	8	7	0	22	35	.176	.250	.136	12.12	7.62
Mulderig, Jerry	L-R	6-4	205	6-17-92	2	1	3.65	17	0	0	1	25	24	13	10	0	10	13	.264	.263	.264	4.74	3.65
Neverauskas, Dovydas	R-R	6-3	175	1-14-93	1	0	3.86	1	0	0	0	2	4	2	1	1	3	2	.364	.429	.250	7.71	11.57
Otamendi, Andy	L-L	5-11	170	5-15-92	1	0	1.88	7	0	0	3	14	12	3	3	0	8	8	.235	.267	.222	5.02	5.02
Paula, Luis	B-R	6-3	205	6-22-93	6	2	4.15	12	6	0	0	39	44	23	18	2	7	29	.278	.338	.233	6.69	1.62
Pimentel, Cesilio	L-L	6-2	185	1-5-93	2	3	3.98	21	2	0	4	52	46	26	23	6	15	63	.231	.212	.238	10.90	2.60
Santana, Edgar	R-R	6-2	180	10-16-91	1	0	2.70	14	0	0	3	30	25	9	9	1	5	32	.219	.173	.258	9.60	1.50
Scioneaux, Tate	R-R	6-1	200	12-14-92	1	0	1.99	10	0	0	2	23	16	6	5	1	3	28	.198	.268	.125	11.12	1.19
Waddell, Brandon	L-L	6-3	180	6-3-94	1	1	5.75	6	6	0	0	20	24	14	13	0	7	18	.276	.182	.308	7.97	3.10
Zamora, Daniel	L-L	6-2	185	4-15-93	1	0	2.66	14	0	0	2	20	21	6	6	1	4	25	.259	.250	.262	11.07	1.77

Fielding

Catcher	PCT	G	PO	A	E	DP	PB						
Arribas	.991	13	95	10	1	1	0	Kramer	.982	44	70	154	4	28
Garcia	.990	12	89	13	1	1	2	Montilla	1.000	9	12	22	0	5
Kelley	.982	53	382	52	8	7	14	Ratledge	.974	5	21	16	1	8
								Tolman	.929	18	25	53	6	7

Kramer 1.000 2 2 3 0 0
Newman .963 38 59 95 6 21
Ratledge .957 6 9 13 1 1

First Base	PCT	G	PO	A	E	DP
Andriese	.978	14	122	9	3	9
Baur	.994	51	499	42	3	49
Harvey	1.000	8	74	6	0	4
Munoz	1.000	5	60	3	0	2

Third Base	PCT	G	PO	A	E	DP
Arribas	.863	20	8	36	7	2
Forgione	—	1	0	0	0	0
Hayes	.976	12	14	27	1	1
Tolman	.925	43	27	108	11	6

Outfield	PCT	G	PO	A	E	DP
Bastardo	.978	23	43	1	1	1
Hill	.987	55	77	1	1	1
Hughston	.983	61	109	6	2	1
Moore	.981	61	98	4	2	0
Nagle	.943	26	33	0	2	0
Rivera	.917	9	11	0	1	0

Second Base	PCT	G	PO	A	E	DP
Forgione	1.000	4	2	6	0	2

Shortstop	PCT	G	PO	A	E	DP
Forgione	.934	32	40	88	9	17

BRISTOL PIRATES   ROOKIE

APPALACHIAN LEAGUE

Batting	B-T	HT	WT	DOB	AVG	vLH	vRH	G	AB	R	H	2B	3B	HR	RBI	BB	HBP	SH	SF	SO	SB	CS	SLG	OBP
Arbet, Trae	R-R	6-0	185	7-1-94	.320	.316	.321	38	147	23	47	16	1	3	16	5	11	5	1	45	1	5	.503	.384
Bormann, John	R-R	6-0	200	4-4-93	.235	.185	.254	25	98	10	23	5	0	0	11	3	4	0	0	12	0	1	.286	.286

Batting	B-T	HT	WT	DOB	AVG	vLH	vRH	G	AB	R	H	2B	3B	HR	RBI	BB	HBP	SH	SF	SO	SB	CS	SLG	OBP
Buckner, Nick	L-L	6-1	205	8-9-95	.275	.257	.280	47	167	13	46	10	2	0	20	13	0	1	1	53	1	1	.359	.326
Chourio, Bealyn	B-R	6-0	150	3-31-94	.228	.219	.230	42	145	21	33	11	1	2	12	16	1	2	1	50	0	0	.359	.307
De La Cruz, Julio	R-R	6-1	190	10-5-95	.240	.256	.236	48	179	15	43	12	0	0	18	6	1	3	1	48	1	2	.307	.267
Figueroa, Edgar	L-L	6-1	160	12-2-94	.262	.296	.250	36	103	19	27	3	2	3	12	13	3	3	0	23	1	3	.417	.361
George, Zach	B-R	6-2	200	7-16-92	.333	.414	.303	29	105	20	35	11	1	2	26	21	2	1	0	19	1	1	.514	.453
Lunde, Erik	L-R	5-9	180	1-14-92	.305	.273	.313	45	164	21	50	7	3	3	22	23	2	0	2	30	0	1	.439	.393
Morales, Tomas	R-R	6-0	190	7-30-91	.301	.286	.306	26	93	14	28	4	1	0	9	8	0	5	0	12	7	0	.366	.356
Munoz, Carlos	L-L	5-11	225	6-29-94	.325	.318	.327	56	206	35	67	21	0	11	39	34	4	1	2	21	2	0	.587	.427
Ozuna, Carlos	B-R	5-11	162	7-19-93	.218	.200	.225	33	119	16	26	5	2	1	13	7	1	1	3	33	1	0	.319	.262
Ratledge, Logan	R-R	5-11	190	7-20-92	.203	.222	.196	18	64	8	13	2	1	1	11	5	3	1	1	8	0	1	.313	.288
Rosario, Henry	L-L	5-9	180	4-5-93	.190	.171	.195	52	200	30	38	7	2	4	12	11	4	7	0	40	4	4	.305	.247
Salazar, Jose	R-R	6-2	175	7-11-94	.230	.286	.208	20	74	8	17	1	0	0	7	4	1	0	0	20	1	2	.243	.278
Santos, Sandy	R-R	6-3	185	4-20-94	.257	.295	.245	48	191	35	49	11	4	7	16	24	0	2	1	55	7	4	.466	.338
Schwind, Jonathan	R-R	6-0	185	5-30-90	.143	.286	.071	6	21	2	3	1	0	0	1	1	1	0	0	7	0	0	.190	.217
Siri, Raul	R-R	5-9	175	10-21-94	.206	.000	.226	8	34	4	7	0	1	1	4	2	2	0	0	10	0	1	.353	.289
Vallejo, Enyel	R-R	6-1	175	10-15-90	.231	.194	.247	31	104	11	24	5	0	1	10	3	1	0	1	29	0	2	.308	.257

Pitching	B-T	HT	WT	DOB	W	L	ERA	G	GS	CG	SV	IP	H	R	ER	HR	BB	SO	AVG	vLH	vRH	K/9	BB/9
Amedee, Jess	R-R	6-2	205	9-5-93	2	0	3.64	18	0	0	2	30	30	16	12	1	13	45	.254	.244	.260	13.65	3.94
Anderson, Tanner	R-R	6-2	195	5-27-93	4	0	2.38	12	0	0	3	23	21	6	6	0	2	19	.241	.212	.259	7.54	0.79
Betts, Palmer	R-R	6-1	190	4-13-94	3	0	4.81	17	0	0	0	39	37	23	21	2	24	43	.262	.250	.273	9.84	5.49
De Leon, Christopher	R-R	6-0	158	8-2-92	1	0	3.31	16	0	0	0	35	20	17	13	3	23	47	.161	.127	.188	11.97	5.86
Del Rosario, Mervin	L-L	6-3	190	3-15-92	2	1	5.06	15	0	0	0	27	30	20	15	1	10	22	.280	.258	.289	7.43	3.38
Ferreras, Miguel	R-R	6-5	221	9-19-91	0	1	6.55	9	0	0	3	11	10	9	8	0	11	11	.227	.333	.130	9.00	9.00
Hightower, Scooter	R-R	6-6	215	10-15-93	4	2	3.31	14	4	0	2	49	44	19	18	3	7	55	.232	.185	.266	10.10	1.29
Hinsz, Gage	R-R	6-4	210	4-20-96	3	4	3.79	10	9	0	0	38	37	21	16	1	23	24	.252	.316	.215	5.68	5.45
Keller, Mitch	R-R	6-3	195	4-4-96	0	3	5.49	6	6	0	0	20	25	18	12	1	16	25	.309	.355	.280	11.44	7.32
Kemp, Shane	R-R	6-3	180	7-12-94	1	0	18.00	5	0	0	0	8	17	17	16	3	7	4	.425	.462	.407	4.50	7.88
Kozikowski, Neil	R-R	6-4	180	5-26-95	1	3	4.80	13	8	0	0	45	58	31	24	1	13	37	.302	.321	.288	7.40	2.60
Minarik, Marek	R-R	6-7	195	6-28-93	2	6	6.32	14	8	0	0	53	55	42	37	11	21	39	.267	.302	.236	6.66	3.59
Mota, Cristian	L-L	5-10	150	9-26-91	0	0	0.00	2	0	0	2	2	2	1	0	0	1	0	.250	.333	.000	0.00	4.50
Paula, Luis	B-R	6-3	205	6-22-93	0	0	0.00	4	0	0	0	10	4	0	0	0	0	9	.121	.091	.136	8.10	0.00
Roth, Billy	R-R	6-3	184	6-5-95	0	5	3.98	12	12	0	0	54	53	28	24	3	22	40	.260	.204	.306	6.96	3.81
Sendelbach, Logan	R-R	6-3	185	5-5-94	2	3	5.23	11	10	0	0	43	47	29	25	5	14	32	.272	.274	.270	6.70	2.93
Supak, Trey	R-R	6-5	210	5-31-96	1	2	6.67	8	8	0	0	28	35	22	21	2	5	23	.304	.321	.290	7.31	1.59
Urbina, Dan	R-R	6-3	158	11-27-93	2	5	6.99	16	0	0	0	28	44	25	22	4	12	23	.358	.346	.366	7.31	3.81
Wallace, Mike	R-R	6-4	190	5-21-94	1	1	7.89	13	0	0	0	22	33	22	19	1	7	15	.351	.386	.320	6.23	2.91

Fielding

Catcher	PCT	G	PO	A	E	DP	PB
Bormann	.994	21	161	13	1	2	2
Lunde	.989	23	166	17	2	3	5
Morales	.986	22	192	23	3	1	5

First Base	PCT	G	PO	A	E	DP
Bormann	1.000	4	26	1	0	1
George	.990	9	86	9	1	6
Munoz	.993	45	381	33	3	25
Ozuna	1.000	1	7	0	0	0
Salazar	.966	9	52	4	2	3
Vallejo	1.000	1	2	0	0	0

Second Base	PCT	G	PO	A	E	DP
Arbet	.923	37	56	111	14	16
Lunde	1.000	9	13	28	0	4
Ozuna	.917	13	17	27	4	4
Ratledge	.875	2	2	5	1	3
Siri	1.000	5	13	19	0	3

Third Base	PCT	G	PO	A	E	DP
De La Cruz	.915	44	22	75	9	2
Ozuna	.800	10	6	14	5	1
Salazar	.964	12	8	19	1	1
Siri	.833	3	0	5	1	0

Shortstop	PCT	G	PO	A	E	DP
Chourio	.961	42	69	129	8	19
Ozuna	.893	7	8	17	3	2
Ratledge	.873	16	24	38	9	7

Outfield	PCT	G	PO	A	E	DP
Buckner	.961	41	73	1	3	0
Figueroa	.953	36	57	4	3	0
Lunde	—	1	0	0	0	0
Ozuna	1.000	1	1	0	0	0
Rosario	.922	50	87	8	8	0
Santos	.955	46	82	2	4	0
Schwind	1.000	5	8	2	0	1
Vallejo	.922	26	46	1	4	0

GCL PIRATES

ROOKIE

GULF COAST LEAGUE

Batting	B-T	HT	WT	DOB	AVG	vLH	vRH	G	AB	R	H	2B	3B	HR	RBI	BB	HBP	SH	SF	SO	SB	CS	SLG	OBP
Benitez, Luis	B-R	5-10	165	8-12-93	.187	.167	.193	31	75	8	14	1	0	0	3	7	0	3	0	18	6	3	.200	.256
Brands, Paul	R-R	6-1	185	5-13-97	.222	.154	.250	16	45	3	10	1	1	0	4	6	3	0	0	19	0	0	.289	.352
Cerda, Reggie	R-R	6-0	185	9-10-94	.000	.000	.000	9	24	1	0	0	0	0	1	3	0	0	0	5	0	0	.000	.111
de la Cruz, Michael	L-L	6-1	165	11-9-94	.256	.250	.259	55	195	32	50	8	5	2	19	23	3	7	2	50	6	7	.379	.341
Fernandez, Victor	R-R	5-11	175	10-17-94	.240	.290	.224	42	129	20	31	8	1	1	12	9	5	5	2	32	16	2	.341	.310
Freeman, Wes	R-R	6-4	215	1-29-90	.375	.400	.364	5	16	3	6	2	0	0	1	3	0	0	0	5	0	0	.500	.474
Gonzalez, Yoel	R-R	6-1	180	8-1-96	.153	.080	.174	36	111	9	17	0	0	1	12	14	1	3	0	15	1	1	.180	.254
Hayes, Ke'Bryan	R-R	6-1	210	1-28-97	.333	.276	.348	44	144	24	48	4	1	0	13	22	5	2	2	24	7	1	.375	.434
Herrera, Jhoan	L-R	6-1	185	6-14-95	.265	.275	.262	46	162	15	43	13	1	1	22	13	1	1	3	40	0	1	.377	.318
Jorge, Nelson	B-R	5-11	175	12-14-95	.191	.333	.161	24	68	7	13	1	0	0	3	15	0	0	0	23	3	1	.206	.337
Kennelly, Sam	R-R	6-2	190	1-9-96	.258	.325	.235	46	159	10	41	7	2	1	21	11	2	0	3	37	1	1	.346	.309
Lantigua, Edison	L-L	6-0	175	1-9-97	.207	.190	.210	37	121	11	25	6	0	2	11	9	0	0	0	27	1	0	.306	.250
Perez, Luis	L-R	5-10	170	1-18-94	.213	.222	.210	26	80	4	17	1	0	0	6	2	2	4	0	16	2	2	.225	.250
Russini, Garrett	R-R	6-0	205	6-7-93	.263	.333	.231	19	57	7	15	1	0	0	2	6	1	1	0	7	1	0	.281	.344
Schwind, Jonathan	R-R	6-0	185	5-30-90	.333	.333	—	1	3	0	1	0	0	0	1	0	0	0	0	0	0	0	.333	.333
Sellers, Justin	R-R	5-10	175	2-1-86	.348	.125	.467	7	23	1	8	0	0	0	4	4	0	1	0	0	1	0	.348	.375
Siri, Raul	R-R	5-9	175	10-21-94	.235	.387	.195	44	149	21	35	8	1	1	19	16	4	2	4	24	10	2	.322	.318

Batting

Batting	B-T	HT	WT	DOB	AVG	vLH	vRH	G	AB	R	H	2B	3B	HR	RBI	BB	HBP	SH	SF	SO	SB	CS	SLG	OBP
Thomas, Eric	B-L	5-10	175	3-30-95	.221	.476	.138	30	86	9	19	1	0	0	5	10	1	2	0	24	2	3	.233	.309
Valerio, Adrian	B-R	5-11	150	3-13-97	.218	.231	.215	56	188	19	41	12	2	1	17	13	1	10	2	36	7	0	.319	.270

Pitching

Pitching	B-T	HT	WT	DOB	W	L	ERA	G	GS	CG	SV	IP	H	R	ER	HR	BB	SO	AVG	vLH	vRH	K/9	BB/9
Basulto, Omar	L-L	6-3	190	8-24-93	0	0	6.75	1	1	0	0	1	2	1	1	0	0	0	.400	.500	.333	0.00	0.00
Batista, Jose	L-L	6-2	175	2-1-96	3	1	3.28	15	1	0	1	36	33	15	13	0	11	28	.243	.189	.263	7.07	2.78
Economos, Nick	R-R	6-6	215	6-27-95	1	1	3.98	11	8	0	1	32	23	15	14	3	11	29	.205	.163	.232	8.24	3.13
Escobar, Luis	R-R	6-1	155	5-30-96	2	1	3.54	11	11	0	0	41	29	17	16	1	13	37	.200	.189	.207	8.19	2.88
Holmes, Clay	R-R	6-5	230	3-27-93	1	0	2.03	3	3	0	0	13	13	5	3	0	1	10	.250	.529	.114	6.75	0.68
Hutchings, Nick	R-R	6-2	165	2-10-96	0	2	5.40	5	0	0	0	8	9	6	5	1	2	10	.273	.091	.364	10.80	2.16
Kemp, Shane	R-R	6-3	180	7-12-94	0	3	2.12	5	3	0	0	17	17	4	4	0	4	10	.274	.333	.237	5.29	2.12
Lakind, Jared	L-L	6-2	195	3-9-92	1	0	0.00	5	0	0	0	7	4	0	0	0	3	8	.182	.100	.250	10.29	3.86
Liao, Jen-Lei	R-R	6-6	255	8-30-93	1	1	3.86	13	0	0	5	19	14	10	8	0	6	13	.203	.240	.182	6.27	2.89
Martinez, Alex	R-R	6-3	175	5-8-95	1	0	4.26	13	0	0	1	32	33	18	15	1	12	20	.262	.273	.256	5.68	3.41
McGarry, Seth	R-R	6-0	180	1-5-94	1	1	1.50	3	0	0	0	12	8	2	2	0	1	9	.186	.067	.250	6.75	0.75
Meyer, Stephan	R-R	6-4	190	5-11-94	2	0	0.71	7	0	0	0	13	7	1	1	1	3	12	.163	.286	.103	8.53	2.13
Miller, Adam	R-R	6-4	215	11-26-84	1	0	0.00	2	1	0	0	3	2	0	0	0	0	3	.182	.200	.167	9.00	0.00
Mitchell, Richard	R-R	6-2	185	7-29-95	2	2	3.38	10	0	0	0	21	20	10	8	2	9	14	.253	.480	.148	5.91	3.86
Montero, Yunior	R-R	6-4	175	2-9-93	3	4	4.66	13	3	0	0	37	32	22	19	3	19	42	.222	.239	.214	10.31	4.66
Mota, Cristian	L-L	5-10	150	9-26-91	0	4	1.69	14	0	0	2	27	15	10	5	0	10	21	.167	.143	.174	7.09	3.38
Navarro, Gerardo	L-R	6-2	200	8-23-93	4	0	3.68	7	3	0	0	29	24	19	12	0	6	25	.212	.207	.214	7.67	1.84
Oronel, Nestor	L-L	6-1	175	12-13-96	0	6	5.12	11	9	0	0	39	35	26	22	5	11	28	.230	.241	.228	6.52	2.56
Paredes, Jesus	L-L	6-2	175	1-18-93	0	0	0.00	1	0	0	0	1	1	0	0	0	0	0	.333	1.000	.000	0.00	0.00
Plitt, Chris	R-R	6-4	170	1-25-95	4	1	2.88	10	7	0	0	41	33	16	13	6	3	28	.217	.203	.226	6.20	0.66
Rocha, Oderman	R-R	6-3	165	11-7-92	1	1	2.08	11	0	0	1	17	15	4	4	0	6	13	.234	.385	.132	6.75	3.12
Sanchez, Isaac	R-R	6-0	170	10-14-92	0	0	0.00	1	0	0	0	0	0	0	0	0	0	0	.000	—	.000	0.00	0.00
Scahill, Rob	R-R	6-2	210	2-15-87	0	0	0.00	1	1	0	0	4	0	0	0	0	0	1	.000	.000	.000	4.50	0.00
Schlabach, Ike	R-L	6-5	185	12-27-96	0	2	5.40	4	4	0	0	12	11	8	7	1	6	8	.282	.000	.344	6.17	4.63
Stock, Robert	L-R	6-1	200	11-21-89	0	0	0.00	2	0	0	0	3	2	0	0	0	1	2	.182	.000	.250	6.00	3.00
Taylor, Jacob	R-R	6-3	205	7-5-95	0	0	0.00	1	1	0	0	2	1	0	0	0	3	2	.000	.000	.000	9.00	13.50
Wallace, Mike	R-R	6-4	190	5-21-94	0	0	0.00	1	0	0	0	2	1	0	0	0	0	3	.143	.000	.200	13.50	0.00

Fielding

Catcher	PCT	G	PO	A	E	DP	PB
Brands	.950	6	35	3	2	0	2
Cerda	.977	6	37	5	1	0	3
Gonzalez	.967	36	219	41	9	2	6
Russini	.957	17	84	5	4	0	5

First Base	PCT	G	PO	A	E	DP
Herrera	.983	21	174	4	3	9
Kennelly	.994	40	334	22	2	24

Second Base	PCT	G	PO	A	E	DP
Jorge	.938	21	34	42	5	8

	PCT	G	PO	A	E	DP	
Perez	1.000	16	27	30	0	4	
Siri	.989	26	41	51	1	9	
Third Base	PCT	G	PO	A	E	DP	
Hayes	.955	36	25	82	5	7	
Kennelly	.826	7	5	14	4	0	
Perez	1.000	7	4	5	0	1	
Siri	.875	12	7	28	5	2	
Shortstop	PCT	G	PO	A	E	DP	
Perez	.923	4	3	9	1	0	
Sellers	1.000	7	2	13	0	1	

	PCT	G	PO	A	E	DP
Valerio	.959	56	59	127	8	20
Outfield	PCT	G	PO	A	E	DP
Benitez	.977	23	41	2	1	0
de la Cruz	.993	55	143	5	1	2
Fernandez	.979	42	84	8	2	1
Freeman	.889	4	7	1	1	0
Lantigua	.981	35	51	1	1	0
Schwind	—	1	0	0	0	0
Thomas	.912	29	50	2	5	1

DSL PIRATES
ROOKIE

DOMINICAN SUMMER LEAGUE

Batting	B-T	HT	WT	DOB	AVG	vLH	vRH	G	AB	R	H	2B	3B	HR	RBI	BB	HBP	SH	SF	SO	SB	CS	SLG	OBP
Brands, Paul	R-R	6-1	185	5-13-97	.143	.250	.000	3	7	2	1	0	0	0	0	3	0	0	0	3	0	0	.143	.400
Brito, Gabriel	R-R	5-9	170	11-3-97	.306	.250	.317	32	98	19	30	7	1	1	22	16	5	4	4	20	0	1	.429	.415
Calderon, Williams	B-R	6-1	170	12-22-97	.229	.294	.209	47	144	15	33	4	3	0	12	22	1	1	1	46	4	3	.299	.333
Contreras, Yondry	R-R	5-11	180	9-11-97	.195	.286	.170	58	231	32	45	8	0	2	20	17	15	8	2	84	2	6	.255	.291
Fuentes, Huascar	R-R	6-2	195	6-2-92	.294	.308	.290	60	201	34	59	16	7	6	45	23	15	0	4	36	6	5	.532	.399
Gonzalez, Julio	R-R	6-3	195	5-10-95	.123	.227	.085	28	81	5	10	2	1	0	8	5	1	0	2	33	2	1	.173	.180
Granberry, Mikell	R-R	6-1	190	8-19-95	.277	.283	.275	52	188	21	52	7	4	5	30	22	4	2	2	51	5	3	.436	.361
Guzman, Rudy	B-R	6-0	175	7-28-91	.283	.286	.283	31	60	15	17	6	1	0	1	7	1	1	0	20	5	0	.417	.368
Hernandez, Raul	R-R	6-0	182	12-20-95	.304	.407	.281	41	148	19	45	11	1	0	18	9	3	4	1	15	2	0	.392	.350
Jimenez, Melvin	B-R	5-10	170	9-9-95	.301	.349	.290	65	229	45	69	9	4	0	25	34	6	5	3	26	8	1	.376	.401
Perez, Christopher	R-R	6-1	170	8-7-97	.199	.292	.182	47	156	28	31	3	2	0	14	10	12	6	0	33	2	2	.244	.298
Perez, Ramon	R-R	6-0	170	9-29-94	.275	.161	.297	62	189	29	52	12	1	1	22	14	3	8	2	26	10	6	.365	.332
Portorreal, Jeremias	L-L	6-3	195	8-7-97	.230	.261	.222	58	213	41	49	8	7	1	28	45	4	1	0	67	1	0	.347	.374
Ramirez, Eliezer	R-R	6-1	170	11-21-96	.167	.000	.200	10	24	2	4	0	0	0	1	3	1	2	1	7	0	0	.167	.276
Ronco, Jesus	R-R	5-11	160	3-31-93	.181	.059	.212	44	83	16	15	3	0	1	3	13	7	1	1	19	1	2	.253	.337
Simmons, Kyle	R-R	6-0	170	12-12-96	.211	.111	.300	6	19	3	4	1	1	0	3	1	1	1	1	6	1	1	.368	.273
Vinicio, Felix	L-L	5-10	175	10-28-94	.301	.298	.302	57	206	32	62	13	2	1	33	17	2	9	3	23	1	7	.398	.355
Vizcaino, Eddy	L-L	5-11	165	7-19-96	.261	.250	.263	53	157	23	41	6	2	0	19	24	3	5	3	13	10	3	.325	.364

Pitching	B-T	HT	WT	DOB	W	L	ERA	G	GS	CG	SV	IP	H	R	ER	HR	BB	SO	AVG	vLH	vRH	K/9	BB/9
Agustin, Ronny	L-L	6-2	185	9-18-94	1	5	4.50	15	7	0	0	48	49	29	24	1	21	38	.262	.179	.284	7.13	3.94
Brun, Luis	R-R	6-0	170	12-28-94	1	2	5.68	14	0	0	0	25	30	26	16	1	20	25	.291	.321	.280	8.88	7.11
Bustamante, Carlos	R-R	6-0	170	9-15-95	3	2	4.76	17	0	0	2	38	27	19	15	1	14	19	.241	.382	.179	6.04	4.45
Contreras, Wllmer	R-R	6-3	185	2-5-98	1	0	2.70	3	0	0	0	7	6	4	2	1	0	5	.240	.167	.263	6.75	0.00
De Los Santos, Yerry	R-R	6-2	160	12-12-97	1	5	4.73	14	14	0	0	59	82	41	31	1	17	28	.340	.304	.355	4.27	2.59
Esqueda, Jherson	L-R	6-1	175	6-9-95	0	1	2.45	4	0	0	0	7	10	3	2	1	2	1	.357	.143	.429	1.23	2.45

Pitching	B-T	HT	WT	DOB	W	L	ERA	G	GS	CG	SV	IP	H	R	ER	HR	BB	SO	AVG	vLH	vRH	K/9	BB/9
Garcia, Ramon	R-R	6-0	195	3-12-92	3	0	1.29	18	0	0	9	28	24	5	4	0	9	30	.226	.290	.200	9.64	2.89
Hernandez, Miguel	R-R	6-5	175	11-3-95	1	5	3.54	14	14	0	0	61	68	44	24	1	19	51	.268	.324	.244	7.52	2.80
Leon, Edgardo	R-R	6-3	190	7-4-96	0	0	3.32	13	0	0	2	19	16	7	7	0	12	9	.232	.400	.163	4.26	5.68
Nunez, Oddy	L-L	6-5	180	12-20-96	1	0	2.08	11	0	0	0	22	20	12	5	2	5	20	.241	.182	.250	8.31	2.08
Pichardo, Adonis	R-R	6-3	195	4-9-96	3	3	7.24	14	8	0	0	41	63	45	33	3	17	30	.346	.370	.336	6.59	3.73
Robles, Domingo	L-L	6-2	170	4-29-98	4	6	3.95	15	15	0	0	68	74	43	30	4	20	44	.277	.204	.296	5.80	2.63
Rodriguez, Raymond	L-L	6-1	175	3-13-97	2	4	5.83	17	2	0	0	29	30	31	19	0	35	20	.259	.333	.245	6.14	10.74
Romano, Argenis	R-R	6-1	190	6-16-95	3	2	4.99	15	8	0	0	58	58	40	32	4	15	42	.253	.210	.269	6.55	2.34
Santana, Roger	L-L	6-1	168	9-26-97	4	3	5.66	18	0	0	0	48	60	32	30	5	14	31	.308	.400	.288	5.85	2.64
Santos, Cesar	L-L	6-2	190	4-20-95	0	0	22.09	3	0	0	0	4	4	9	9	0	7	3	.286	1.000	.231	7.36	17.18
Sepulveda, Eumir	R-R	6-2	170	2-14-96	0	0	2.25	3	0	0	0	4	3	1	1	1	1	4	.200	.333	.167	9.00	2.25
Sousa, Brian	R-R	6-3	180	8-7-97	0	2	3.31	5	4	0	0	16	17	15	6	0	9	8	.270	.267	.271	4.41	4.96
Vasquez, Angel	R-R	6-1	185	4-13-94	1	2	3.33	15	0	0	5	24	24	10	9	0	5	25	.253	.296	.235	9.25	1.85
Villamar, Julian	R-R	6-5	190	4-23-94	1	0	3.95	18	0	0	0	41	28	28	18	0	38	56	.189	.186	.190	12.29	8.34

Fielding

Catcher	PCT	G	PO	A	E	DP	PB
Brands	1.000	1	2	1	0	0	0
Brito	.969	17	106	17	4	1	7
Granberry	.973	24	154	27	5	0	7
Hernandez	.953	32	182	40	11	1	17
Perez	.962	9	44	6	2	0	1

First Base	PCT	G	PO	A	E	DP
Fuentes	.976	46	381	24	10	23
Granberry	.979	22	172	13	4	15
Perez	1.000	11	83	6	0	4
Ronco	1.000	1	6	0	0	1

Second Base	PCT	G	PO	A	E	DP
Calderon	.886	41	91	65	20	18

	PCT	G	PO	A	E	DP
Jimenez	.964	24	37	43	3	10
Perez	.913	5	11	10	2	2
Perez	.952	11	10	10	1	3
Ronco	.935	6	15	14	2	4
Simmons	1.000	3	4	7	0	0

Third Base	PCT	G	PO	A	E	DP
Fuentes	.833	3	4	6	2	0
Gonzalez	.796	17	12	31	11	3
Jimenez	.900	12	9	18	3	1
Perez	.896	39	24	79	12	4
Ronco	.887	33	16	39	7	3

Shortstop	PCT	G	PO	A	E	DP
Calderon	.786	4	4	7	3	1

	PCT	G	PO	A	E	DP
Jimenez	.987	35	42	106	2	13
Perez	.874	39	61	105	24	13
Ronco	1.000	2	3	3	0	1
Simmons	1.000	1	0	1	0	0

Outfield	PCT	G	PO	A	E	DP
Contreras	.981	57	146	6	3	2
Fuentes	1.000	1	1	0	0	0
Guzman	1.000	25	27	4	0	1
Perez	1.000	3	4	0	0	0
Portorreal	.961	57	96	2	4	0
Ramirez	1.000	9	12	2	0	0
Ronco	1.000	1	1	0	0	0
Vinicio	.925	37	48	1	4	0
Vizcaino	.965	52	75	7	3	2

St. Louis Cardinals

SEASON IN A SENTENCE: The Cardinals battled through injuries to become the first major league team since 2011 to reach 100 victories, but couldn't overcome the red-hot Cubs in the National League Division Series.

HIGH POINT: St. Louis spent virtually the entire season in first place, despite Pittsburgh (98 wins) and Chicago (97) challenging from start to finish. A season-high eight-game winning streak from April 28-May 5 provided separation and thrills, including three straight walk-off, extra-inning wins at Busch Stadium against the Pirates.

LOW POINT: Late injuries sapped the Cards' strength, including hard-throwing righthander Carlos Martinez, who left a Sept. 25 start with a shoulder strain that shut him down for the season. He was the team's leader in strikeouts (184); in his absence, John Lackey started the elimination Game Four of the Division Series on short rest.

NOTABLE ROOKIES: The Cardinals farm system again delivered with replacement pieces, particularly when Matt Holliday and Matt Adams went down. Randal Grichuk tied for second on the team with 17 home runs in a part-time role, while Stephen Piscotty provided second-half thumb (.305/.359/.494) and versatility, playing all three outfield spots and first base. Even 27-year-old Tommy Pham raked in his first real shot at the big leagues in his 10th professional season. Mitch Harris became the second Navy graduate ever to pitch in the big leagues and the first in 94 years.

KEY TRANSACTIONS: Trading Shelby Miller for Jason Heyward in the offseason worked extremely well for 2015, with Heyward leading the team in steals and ranking second in runs. A pair of deadline deals at the end of July brought in Jonathan Broxton to the bullpen and Brandon Moss at first base to sub in for Adams. Neither proved to be a difference-maker, however, especially Moss, who homered just four times in 51 games after hitting 55 the previous two seasons for Oakland.

DOWN ON THE FARM: Aside from providing more big league pieces, the Cardinals' system developed righthander Alex Reyes, who continued his ascent as one of the game's top prospects and finished the season in Double-A. Class A affiliates Peoria (Low) and Palm Beach (High) both reached their respective league playoffs. Outfielder Charlie Tilson also broke out, leading the Double-A Texas League in hits (159), triples (nine) and stolen bases (49).

OPENING DAY PAYROLL: $120,869,458 (11th)

ORGANIZATION LEADERS

BATTING		*Minimum 250 AB
MAJORS		
* AVG	Jason Heyward	.293
* OPS	Matt Carpenter	.87
HR	Matt Carpenter	28
RBI	Matt Carpenter	84
MINORS		
* AVG	Jeremy Hazelbaker, Springfield, Memphis	.323
* OBP	Jeremy Hazelbaker, Springfield, Memphis	.399
* SLG	Jeremy Hazelbaker, Springfield, Memphis	.557
R	Charlie Tilson, Springfield	85
H	Charlie Tilson, Springfield	159
TB	Charlie Tilson, Springfield	209
2B	Bruce Caldwell, Palm Beach, Springfield	30
3B	Darren Seferina, Peoria	12
HR	Jacob Wilson, Springfield, Memphis	18
RBI	Luke Voit, Palm Beach	77
	Jacob Wilson, Springfield, Memphis	77
BB	Dean Anna, Memphis	77
SO	David Washington, Palm Beach, Springfield	150
SB	Oscar Mercado, Peoria	50

PITCHING		#Minimum 75 IP
MAJORS		
W	Michael Wacha	17
# ERA	John Lackey	2.77
SO	Carlos Martinez	184
SV	Trevor Rosenthal	48
MINORS		
W	Austin Gomber, Peoria	15
L	Luis Perdomo, Peoria, Palm Beach	12
# ERA	Daniel Poncedeleon, Peoria, Palm Beach	2.12
G	Kyle Grana, Peoria	54
GS	Zach Petrick, Memphis	28
SV	Kyle Grana, Peoria	24
IP	Zach Petrick, Memphis	157
BB	Arturo Reyes, Palm Beach, Springfield, Memphis	50
SO	David Washington, Palm Beach, Springfield	150
AVG	Austin Gomber, Peoria	.196

2015 PERFORMANCE

General Manager: John Mozeliak. **Farm Director:** Gary LaRocque. **Scouting Director:** Chris Correa/Randy Flores.

Class	Team	League	W	L	PCT	Finish	Manager
Majors	St. Louis Cardinals	National	100	62	.617	1st (15)	Mike Matheny
Triple-A	Memphis Redbirds	Pacific Coast	73	71	.507	8th (16)	Mike Shildt
Double-A	Springfield Cardinals	Texas	64	76	.457	5th (8)	Dann Bilardello
High A	Palm Beach Cardinals	Florida State	75	63	.543	4th (12)	Oliver Marmol
Low A	Peoria Chiefs	Midwest	75	63	.543	5th (16)	Joe Kruzel
Short season	State College Spikes	New York-Penn	41	35	.539	5th (14)	Johnny Rodriguez
Rookie	Johnson City Cardinals	Appalachian	27	38	.415	9th (10)	Chris Swauger
Rookie	Cardinals	Gulf Coast	34	25	.576	t-5th (16)	Steve Turco
Overall 2015 Minor League Record			**389**	**371**	**.512**	**11th (30)**	

ORGANIZATION STATISTICS

ST. LOUIS CARDINALS

NATIONAL LEAGUE

Batting	B-T	HT	WT	DOB	AVG	vLH	vRH	G	AB	R	H	2B	3B	HR	RBI	BB	HBP	SH	SF	SO	SB	CS	SLG	OBP
Adams, Matt	L-R	6-3	260	8-31-88	.240	.200	.247	60	175	14	42	9	0	5	24	10	0	0	1	41	1	0	.377	.280
Anna, Dean	L-R	5-11	180	11-24-86	.000	—	.000	1	1	0	0	0	0	0	0	0	0	0	0	0	0	0	.000	.000
Bourjos, Peter	R-R	6-1	185	3-31-87	.200	.203	.198	117	195	32	39	8	3	4	13	19	6	4	1	59	5	8	.333	.290
Carpenter, Matt	L-R	6-3	215	11-26-85	.272	.228	.292	154	574	101	156	44	3	28	84	81	6	0	4	151	4	3	.505	.365
Cruz, Tony	R-R	5-11	215	8-18-86	.204	.231	.198	69	142	6	29	7	1	2	11	6	0	2	1	32	0	0	.310	.235
Easley, Ed	R-R	6-0	205	12-21-85	.000	.000	.000	4	6	0	0	0	0	0	0	1	0	0	1	1	0	0	.000	.000
Garcia, Greg	L-R	6-0	190	8-8-89	.240	.400	.229	49	75	7	18	5	0	2	4	10	1	1	0	12	0	0	.387	.337
Grichuk, Randal	R-R	6-1	195	8-13-91	.276	.265	.281	103	323	49	89	23	7	17	47	22	4	0	1	110	4	2	.548	.329
Heyward, Jason	L-L	6-5	245	8-9-89	.293	.272	.301	154	547	79	160	33	4	13	60	56	2	0	3	90	23	3	.439	.359
Holliday, Matt	R-R	6-4	250	1-15-80	.279	.246	.292	73	229	24	64	16	1	4	35	39	6	0	3	49	2	1	.410	.394
Jay, Jon	L-L	5-11	195	3-15-85	.210	.158	.221	79	210	25	44	5	1	1	10	19	11	3	2	36	0	2	.257	.306
Johnson, Dan	L-R	6-2	210	8-10-79	.158	.333	.077	12	19	1	3	0	0	0	2	2	0	0	0	4	0	0	.158	.238
Kozma, Pete	R-R	6-0	190	4-11-88	.152	.143	.155	76	99	15	15	0	0	0	2	10	1	1	0	21	3	1	.152	.236
Molina, Yadier	R-R	5-11	220	7-13-82	.270	.232	.284	136	488	34	132	23	2	4	61	32	0	1	9	59	3	1	.350	.310
Moss, Brandon	L-R	6-0	210	9-16-83	.250	.156	.280	51	132	11	33	7	1	4	8	17	2	0	0	42	0	1	.409	.344
Peralta, Jhonny	R-R	6-2	215	5-28-82	.275	.238	.289	155	579	64	159	26	1	17	71	50	5	0	6	111	1	4	.411	.334
Pham, Tommy	R-R	6-1	175	3-8-88	.268	.278	.265	52	153	28	41	7	5	5	18	19	0	0	1	41	2	0	.477	.347
Piscotty, Stephen	R-R	6-3	210	1-14-91	.305	.322	.299	63	233	29	71	15	4	7	39	20	1	0	2	56	2	1	.494	.359
Reynolds, Mark	R-R	6-2	220	8-3-83	.230	.224	.233	140	382	35	88	21	2	13	48	44	4	0	2	121	2	3	.398	.315
Scruggs, Xavier	R-R	6-1	220	9-23-87	.262	.143	.286	17	42	5	11	2	0	0	7	1	0	0	0	10	1	0	.310	.279
Stanley, Cody	L-R	5-10	190	12-21-88	.400	.000	.444	9	10	2	4	1	0	0	3	0	0	0	0	3	0	0	.500	.400
Tartamella, Travis	R-R	6-0	205	12-17-87	.500	—	.500	3	2	0	1	0	0	0	0	0	0	0	0	0	0	0	.500	.500
Wong, Kolten	L-R	5-9	185	10-10-90	.262	.229	.276	150	557	71	146	28	4	11	61	36	15	0	5	95	15	8	.386	.321

Pitching	B-T	HT	WT	DOB	W	L	ERA	G	GS	CG	SV	IP	H	R	ER	HR	BB	SO	AVG	vLH	vRH	K/9	BB/9
Belisle, Matt	R-R	6-4	225	6-6-80	1	1	2.67	34	0	0	0	34	34	10	10	1	15	25	.266	.256	.271	6.68	4.01
Broxton, Jonathan	R-R	6-4	305	6-16-84	3	3	2.66	26	0	0	0	24	20	8	7	2	12	26	.233	.276	.211	9.89	4.56
2-team total (40 Milwaukee)					4	5	4.62	66	0	0	0	60	61	32	31	7	22	63	—	—	—	9.40	3.28
Choate, Randy	L-L	6-1	210	9-5-75	1	0	3.95	71	0	0	1	27	29	14	12	2	5	22	.279	.265	.333	7.24	1.65
Cishek, Steve	R-R	6-6	215	6-18-86	0	0	2.31	27	0	0	1	23	18	7	6	2	13	20	.212	.182	.222	7.71	5.01
2-team total (32 Miami)					2	6	3.58	59	0	0	4	55	55	26	22	4	27	48	—	—	—	7.81	4.39
Cooney, Tim	L-L	6-3	195	12-19-90	1	0	3.16	6	6	0	0	31	28	12	11	3	10	29	.241	.318	.223	8.33	2.87
Garcia, Jaime	L-L	6-2	215	7-8-86	10	6	2.43	20	20	0	0	130	106	37	35	6	30	97	.225	.250	.218	6.73	2.08
Gonzales, Marco	L-L	6-1	195	2-16-92	0	0	13.50	1	1	0	0	3	7	4	4	1	1	1	.500	—	.500	3.38	3.38
Greenwood, Nick	R-L	6-1	180	9-28-87	0	1	0.00	1	0	0	0	2	2	1	0	0	1	0	0	1.000	—	1.000		
Harris, Mitch	R-R	6-4	215	11-7-85	2	1	3.67	26	0	0	0	27	30	14	11	4	13	15	.278	.237	.300	5.00	4.33
Hatley, Marcus	R-R	6-5	220	3-6-88	0	0	0.00	2	0	0	0	1	1	0	0	0	2	2	.200	.000	.250	13.50	13.50
Lackey, John	R-R	6-6	235	10-23-78	13	10	2.77	33	33	1	0	218	211	71	67	21	53	175	.256	.271	.244	7.22	2.19
Lynn, Lance	R-R	6-5	240	5-12-87	12	11	3.03	31	31	0	0	175	172	66	59	13	68	167	.258	.272	.247	8.57	3.49
Lyons, Tyler	B-L	6-4	200	2-21-88	3	1	3.75	17	8	0	0	60	59	29	25	12	15	60	.252	.232	.258	9.00	2.25
Maness, Seth	R-R	6-0	190	10-14-88	4	2	4.26	76	0	0	3	63	77	35	30	7	13	46	.307	.361	.280	6.54	1.85
Martinez, Carlos	R-R	6-0	185	9-21-91	14	7	3.01	31	29	0	0	180	168	65	60	13	63	184	.250	.262	.240	9.22	3.16
Rosenthal, Trevor	R-R	6-2	220	5-29-90	2	4	2.10	68	0	0	48	69	62	16	16	3	25	83	.238	.194	.270	10.88	3.28
Siegrist, Kevin	L-L	6-5	215	7-20-89	7	1	2.17	81	0	0	6	75	53	20	18	4	34	90	.198	.278	.164	10.85	4.10
Socolovich, Miguel	R-R	6-1	195	7-24-86	4	1	1.82	28	0	0	0	30	25	7	6	1	10	27	.221	.156	.265	8.19	3.03
Tuivailala, Sam	R-R	6-3	195	10-19-92	0	1	3.07	14	0	0	0	15	13	5	5	2	8	20	.228	.217	.235	12.27	4.91
Villanueva, Carlos	R-R	6-2	215	11-28-83	4	3	2.95	35	0	0	2	61	50	21	20	6	21	55	.223	.183	.252	8.11	3.10
Wacha, Michael	R-R	6-6	210	7-1-91	17	7	3.38	30	30	0	0	181	162	74	68	19	58	153	.236	.215	.253	7.59	2.88
Wainwright, Adam	R-R	6-7	235	8-30-81	2	1	1.61	7	4	0	0	28	25	7	5	0	4	20	.238	.256	.226	6.43	1.29
Walden, Jordan	R-R	6-5	250	11-16-87	0	1	0.87	12	0	0	1	10	7	1	1	0	4	12	.189	.125	.238	10.45	3.48

Fielding

Catcher	PCT	G	PO	A	E	DP	PB
Cruz	1.000	51	251	16	0	1	1
Easley	1.000	3	14	0	0	0	0
Molina	.994	134	1064	56	7	9	4
Stanley	1.000	2	7	0	0	0	0
Tartamella	1.000	3	9	0	0	0	0

First Base / Infield Fielding

First Base	PCT	G	PO	A	E	DP
Adams	.992	46	321	32	3	30
Carpenter	1.000	3	13	1	0	2
Johnson	1.000	6	34	4	0	6
Kozma	—	1	0	0	0	0
Moss	1.000	32	188	16	0	18
Piscotty	1.000	11	62	1	0	6
Reynolds	.992	100	680	44	6	72
Scruggs	.988	11	73	8	1	8

Second Base	PCT	G	PO	A	E	DP
Carpenter	1.000	11	12	19	0	4
Garcia	.909	10	15	15	3	6

	PCT	G	PO	A	E	DP
Kozma	.975	17	15	24	1	5
Reynolds	1.000	1	1	1	0	1
Wong	.977	147	312	410	17	107

Third Base	PCT	G	PO	A	E	DP
Carpenter	.957	146	77	234	14	25
Cruz	1.000	3	0	2	0	1
Garcia	1.000	4	2	1	0	0
Kozma	.962	13	6	19	1	0
Reynolds	.897	22	7	19	3	3

Shortstop	PCT	G	PO	A	E	DP
Garcia	.971	12	10	23	1	6
Kozma	.968	31	18	42	2	6

	PCT	G	PO	A	E	DP
Peralta	.986	148	157	420	8	88

Outfield	PCT	G	PO	A	E	DP
Bourjos	.992	93	125	1	1	1
Grichuk	.981	85	151	2	3	1
Heyward	.990	147	290	10	3	3
Holliday	1.000	64	85	0	0	0
Jay	1.000	64	137	2	0	2
Kozma	1.000	1	1	0	0	0
Moss	1.000	13	14	0	0	0
Pham	1.000	44	63	2	0	1
Piscotty	.974	61	73	1	2	1
Reynolds	1.000	6	10	0	0	0

MEMPHIS REDBIRDS

TRIPLE-A

PACIFIC COAST LEAGUE

ST. LOUIS CARDINALS

Batting	B-T	HT	WT	DOB	AVG	vLH	vRH	G	AB	R	H	2B	3B	HR	RBI	BB	HBP	SH	SF	SO	SB	CS	SLG	OBP
Anna, Dean	L-R	5-11	180	11-24-86	.272	.260	.277	125	445	80	121	22	3	3	44	77	4	5	3	61	5	5	.355	.382
Brown, Gary	R-R	6-1	190	9-28-88	.160	.111	.188	9	25	1	4	0	0	0	1	1	0	0	0	4	0	0	.160	.192
2-team total (102 Salt Lake)					.242	—	—	111	397	58	96	16	6	7	48	22	7	7	4	68	14	12	.365	.291
Diaz, Aledmys	R-R	6-1	195	8-1-90	.380	.294	.424	14	50	12	19	3	0	3	6	6	1	0	1	5	0	1	.620	.448
Easley, Ed	R-R	6-0	205	12-21-85	.251	.232	.261	88	279	26	70	12	0	4	36	39	2	1	2	44	1	2	.337	.345
Garcia, Anthony	R-R	6-0	180	1-4-92	.276	.333	.250	18	58	7	16	4	1	2	10	6	0	0	0	11	0	1	.483	.344
Garcia, Greg	L-R	6-0	190	8-8-89	.294	.214	.330	94	330	47	97	19	2	0	36	48	5	4	1	55	16	3	.364	.391
Hazelbaker, Jeremy	L-R	6-3	200	8-14-87	.333	.305	.345	58	207	38	69	10	7	10	46	23	2	0	1	60	8	2	.594	.403
Jay, Jon	L-L	5-11	195	3-15-85	.385	1.000	.333	4	13	3	5	0	0	1	1	1	0	0	0	1	2	0	.615	.429
Johnson, Dan	L-R	6-2	210	8-10-79	.260	.237	.271	94	350	51	91	19	1	15	62	45	3	0	5	64	0	1	.449	.345
Kelly, Ty	L-R	6-0	185	7-20-88	.203	.226	.189	79	227	23	46	5	4	2	21	38	1	1	2	43	3	3	.286	.317
Martini, Nick	L-L	5-11	205	6-27-90	.393	.357	.405	22	56	12	22	4	2	1	14	9	1	1	0	10	1	0	.589	.485
Mejia, Alex	R-R	6-1	200	1-18-91	.275	.254	.290	59	167	26	46	7	1	3	17	15	1	2	2	25	3	0	.383	.335
Moore, Scott	L-R	6-2	195	11-17-83	.175	.103	.200	34	114	11	20	7	0	2	12	14	2	0	1	37	2	1	.289	.275
O'Neill, Mike	L-L	5-9	170	2-12-88	.257	.323	.205	33	70	4	18	1	0	0	5	12	1	2	0	4	1	0	.271	.373
Ortega, Rafael	L-R	5-11	160	5-15-91	.286	.250	.303	131	437	66	125	22	6	2	42	55	2	6	2	71	17	6	.378	.367
Pham, Tommy	R-R	6-1	175	3-8-88	.327	.354	.311	48	171	29	56	10	1	6	39	22	0	0	3	36	9	0	.503	.398
Piscotty, Stephen	R-R	6-3	210	1-14-91	.272	.223	.295	87	320	54	87	28	2	11	41	46	3	0	3	62	5	6	.475	.366
Rosario, Alberto	R-R	5-10	190	1-10-87	.313	.200	.364	4	16	3	5	2	0	0	0	0	0	0	2	0	1	.438	.313
Scruggs, Xavier	R-R	6-1	220	9-23-87	.238	.233	.240	109	383	54	91	22	1	14	57	54	8	0	4	103	4	3	.410	.341
Stanley, Cody	L-R	5-10	190	12-21-88	.241	.235	.243	92	270	36	65	11	0	7	45	24	3	0	6	49	2	1	.359	.304
Tartamella, Travis	R-R	6-0	205	12-17-87	.203	.278	.141	40	118	9	24	5	0	0	9	6	0	4	3	38	0	0	.246	.236
Wiley, Brett	L-R	5-10	175	11-24-91	.333	.333	—	1	3	1	1	0	0	0	0	0	0	0	1	0	0	.333	.333
Williams, Matt	R-R	6-0	170	8-29-89	.240	.232	.244	61	146	18	35	6	1	0	16	29	1	0	2	27	5	2	.295	.365
Wilson, Jacob	R-R	5-11	180	7-29-90	.231	.260	.217	89	307	41	71	14	1	11	56	23	6	0	6	68	2	1	.391	.292

Pitching	B-T	HT	WT	DOB	W	L	ERA	G	GS	CG	SV	IP	H	R	ER	HR	BB	SO	AVG	vLH	vRH	K/9	BB/9
Butler, Keith	R-R	6-0	170	1-30-89	2	3	6.12	29	0	0	1	32	32	24	22	4	21	23	.264	.267	.263	6.40	5.85
Cooney, Tim	L-L	6-3	195	12-19-90	6	4	2.74	14	14	1	0	89	61	32	27	9	16	63	.195	.176	.201	6.39	1.62
Donofrio, Joey	R-R	6-3	185	5-10-89	0	0	4.38	8	0	0	0	12	10	8	6	1	5	5	.233	.238	.227	3.65	3.65
Garcia, Jaime	L-L	6-2	215	7-8-86	0	1	16.88	1	1	0	0	3	6	5	5	0	2	3	.429	.000	.545	10.13	6.75
Gast, John	L-L	6-2	190	2-16-89	7	10	5.03	24	24	1	0	122	153	84	68	12	43	90	.309	.289	.316	6.66	3.18
Gonzales, Marco	L-L	6-1	195	2-16-92	1	5	5.45	14	14	0	0	69	91	43	42	10	24	51	.323	.373	.309	6.62	3.12
Greenwood, Nick	R-L	6-1	180	9-28-87	13	6	5.79	32	22	0	0	129	166	88	83	16	25	60	.313	.312	.314	4.19	1.74
Hald, Kyle	L-L	6-0	190	5-27-89	2	2	4.91	4	4	0	0	22	30	13	12	4	6	9	.323	.409	.296	3.68	2.45
Harris, Mitch	R-R	6-4	215	11-7-85	0	4	3.38	25	0	0	4	27	30	13	10	1	10	20	.286	.243	.309	6.75	3.38
Hatley, Marcus	R-R	6-5	220	3-26-88	4	4	3.14	36	0	0	5	49	52	20	17	3	19	31	.280	.246	.299	5.73	3.51
Heyer, Kurt	L-R	6-2	185	1-23-91	1	1	2.78	10	1	0	0	23	24	7	7	0	9	10	.273	.200	.321	3.97	3.57
Kiekhefer, Dean	L-L	6-0	175	6-7-89	2	1	2.41	50	1	0	2	60	68	21	16	5	7	37	.285	.267	.295	5.58	1.06
Lee, Thomas	R-R	6-1	190	10-20-89	3	1	1.62	6	6	0	0	39	38	7	7	4	5	20	.264	.203	.313	4.62	1.15
Lyons, Tyler	B-L	6-4	200	2-21-88	9	5	3.14	16	16	2	0	95	104	34	33	12	13	96	.274	.157	.301	9.13	1.24
Petrick, Zach	R-R	6-3	195	7-29-89	7	7	4.52	28	28	0	0	157	181	88	79	14	29	113	.287	.255	.310	6.46	1.66
Reed, Jimmy	L-L	5-11	185	12-18-90	0	2	6.48	2	2	0	0	8	13	6	6	2	2	4	.351	.357	.348	4.32	2.16
Reyes, Artie	R-R	5-11	185	4-6-92	1	3	7.82	5	5	0	0	25	36	22	22	2	16	17	.340	.452	.266	6.04	5.68
Sherriff, Ryan	L-L	6-1	185	5-25-90	0	0	1.69	3	0	0	0	5	3	1	1	1	3	2	.167	.000	.214	3.38	5.06
Socolovich, Miguel	R-R	6-1	195	7-24-86	2	2	2.48	21	0	0	0	33	18	9	9	1	12	36	.165	.217	.151	9.92	3.31
Thomas, Chris	R-R	6-2	200	3-16-88	2	0	2.55	12	0	0	0	18	17	6	5	2	6	13	.254	.174	.295	6.62	3.06
Tuivailala, Sam	R-R	6-3	195	10-19-92	3	1	1.60	43	0	0	17	45	28	9	8	2	26	43	.176	.262	.117	8.60	5.20
Walden, Jordan	R-R	6-5	250	11-16-87	0	0	0.00	2	0	0	0	2	1	1	0	0	2	3	.167	.333	.000	16.20	10.80
Waldron, Tyler	R-R	6-2	195	5-1-89	4	6	4.74	46	2	0	1	76	85	43	40	14	12	40	.279	.257	.292	4.74	1.42
Whiting, Boone	R-R	6-1	175	8-20-89	0	2	7.77	7	3	0	0	22	30	20	19	3	21	14	.326	.290	.344	5.73	8.59
2-team total (17 Albuquerque)					4	9	6.44	24	14	0	1	95	123	78	68	12	61	59				5.59	5.78
Wright, Justin	L-L	5-9	175	8-18-89	1	1	3.05	36	0	0	0	44	39	15	15	0	14	40	.236	.283	.210	8.12	2.84
Wyatt, Heath	R-R	6-2	185	8-27-88	3	0	2.17	33	1	0	0	50	35	14	12	3	15	27	.205	.255	.181	4.89	2.72

Fielding

Catcher	PCT	G	PO	A	E	DP	PB
Easley	.987	52	366	21	5	2	3
Rosario	1.000	4	25	0	0	1	0
Stanley	.985	55	308	27	5	1	4
Tartamella	.985	35	181	18	3	2	2

First Base	PCT	G	PO	A	E	DP
Easley	.987	9	72	4	1	9
Johnson	.997	75	657	34	2	69
Moore	1.000	6	47	2	0	6
Piscotty	.982	6	53	2	1	5
Scruggs	.994	57	464	20	3	50

Second Base	PCT	G	PO	A	E	DP
Anna	.986	105	191	302	7	82
Garcia	.968	19	47	45	3	16
Kelly	.967	6	19	10	1	5
Mejia	.970	8	14	18	1	9
Wiley	1.000	1	3	6	0	1
Williams	1.000	9	11	15	0	2
Wilson	.971	9	14	19	1	3

Third Base	PCT	G	PO	A	E	DP
Garcia	1.000	6	4	10	0	3
Kelly	.953	22	10	51	3	3
Mejia	.964	24	13	41	2	5
Moore	.959	26	10	60	3	8
Williams	.875	2	1	6	1	1
Wilson	.952	80	42	175	11	21

Shortstop	PCT	G	PO	A	E	DP
Anna	.959	18	18	52	3	10
Diaz	.974	14	28	47	2	14
Garcia	.955	69	92	203	14	43
Mejia	.988	22	28	55	1	14
Williams	.948	29	30	80	6	16

Outfield	PCT	G	PO	A	E	DP
Brown	1.000	7	14	1	0	0
Garcia	1.000	17	30	2	0	0
Hazelbaker	1.000	54	107	2	0	1
Jay	1.000	4	11	0	0	0
Kelly	.952	49	77	3	4	0
Martini	1.000	15	22	0	0	0
O'Neill	1.000	21	30	1	0	0
Ortega	.982	124	317	15	6	4
Pham	.990	44	102	2	1	0
Piscotty	.977	73	167	3	4	2
Scruggs	.974	46	68	6	2	1
Stanley	—	3	0	0	0	0
Williams	1.000	18	13	1	0	0

SPRINGFIELD (MO) CARDINALS · DOUBLE-A

TEXAS LEAGUE

Batting	B-T	HT	WT	DOB	AVG	vLH	vRH	G	AB	R	H	2B	3B	HR	RBI	BB	HBP	SH	SF	SO	SB	CS	SLG	OBP
Caldwell, Bruce	L-R	5-11	175	11-27-91	.270	.194	.290	81	293	40	79	20	1	9	50	45	1	0	2	85	4	0	.437	.367
Cruz, Luis	R-R	6-2	180	5-26-93	.000	.000	.000	2	2	0	0	0	0	0	0	0	0	0	0	0	0	0	.000	.000
Diaz, Aledmys	R-R	6-1	195	8-1-90	.264	.383	.216	102	375	47	99	25	2	10	46	29	4	1	0	62	6	5	.421	.324
Garcia, Anthony	R-R	6-0	180	1-4-92	.285	.278	.287	87	288	50	82	22	0	11	54	45	11	1	1	54	6	2	.476	.400
Gibson, Derek	L-R	6-2	220	2-25-91	.176	.200	.172	12	34	3	6	1	0	0	2	2	1	0	0	6	1	0	.206	.243
Gonzalez, Jose	R-R	6-1	215	6-23-87	.083	.000	.100	4	12	4	1	0	0	1	2	2	0	0	0	2	0	0	.333	.214
Hazelbaker, Jeremy	L-R	6-3	200	8-14-87	.308	.227	.343	40	143	30	44	13	3	3	20	18	3	3	1	33	10	0	.503	.394
2-team total (14 Tulsa)					.291	—	—	54	196	35	57	15	5	3	22	21	3	5	1	44	16	0	.464	.367
Martini, Nick	L-L	5-11	205	6-27-90	.265	.280	.261	95	313	40	83	15	2	5	32	51	5	4	1	48	8	7	.374	.376
Mejia, Alex	R-R	6-1	200	1-18-91	.270	.324	.247	34	115	12	31	5	1	2	12	11	2	3	1	19	1	1	.383	.341
O'Neill, Mike	L-L	5-9	170	2-12-88	.301	.206	.346	57	193	26	58	7	0	0	19	37	0	7	2	19	3	5	.337	.409
Ohlman, Mike	R-R	6-5	215	12-14-90	.273	.293	.268	103	366	53	100	17	0	12	69	46	2	—	2	77	0	1	.418	.356
Reyes, Robelys	B-R	5-9	150	7-25-90	.000	.000	.000	4	11	1	0	0	0	0	0	0	0	0	3	0	0	.000	.000
Rodriguez, Jonathan	R-R	6-2	205	8-21-89	.275	.333	.255	124	454	65	125	24	0	13	65	56	1	0	2	100	9	4	.414	.355
Rodriguez, Starlin	B-R	5-10	170	12-31-89	.067	.167	.000	10	30	3	2	0	1	0	2	2	0	0	0	5	0	0	.133	.125
Rosario, Alberto	R-R	5-10	190	11-6-87	.182	.190	.179	44	148	9	27	8	0	1	5	9	3	—	1	19	0	0	.250	.244
Sohn, Andrew	R-R	5-11	185	5-8-93	.500	.333	1.000	4	4	0	2	0	0	0	0	0	0	0	0	0	0	0	.500	.500
Tilson, Charlie	L-L	5-11	175	12-2-92	.295	.287	.298	134	539	85	159	20	9	4	32	46	2	4	3	72	46	19	.388	.351
Valera, Breyvic	B-R	5-11	160	1-8-92	.236	.284	.219	105	360	37	85	9	2	3	31	34	1	2	4	27	2	4	.297	.301
Washington, David	L-L	6-5	200	11-20-90	.274	.250	.279	97	340	39	93	17	1	16	45	34	1	0	4	121	4	4	.471	.338
Wiley, Brett	L-R	5-10	175	11-24-91	.000	—	.000	5	8	0	0	0	0	0	0	1	1	0	0	3	0	0	.000	.111
Williams, Matt	R-R	6-0	170	8-29-89	.217	.278	.190	18	60	10	13	0	0	3	7	8	1	1	0	11	2	2	.367	.319
Wilson, Jacob	R-R	5-11	180	7-29-90	.225	.194	.236	34	120	13	27	8	0	7	26	7	0	2	1	37	0	1	.450	.326
Wisdom, Patrick	R-R	6-2	210	8-27-91	.237	.234	.238	114	414	51	98	20	4	14	61	35	0	2	4	107	11	3	.406	.294

Pitching	B-T	HT	WT	DOB	W	L	ERA	G	GS	CG	SV	IP	H	R	ER	HR	BB	SO	AVG	vLH	vRH	K/9	BB/9
Baker, Corey	R-R	6-1	170	11-23-89	6	6	3.90	38	11	1	0	97	88	49	42	6	39	88	.244	.275	.224	8.16	3.62
Barraclough, Kyle	R-R	6-3	225	5-23-90	2	0	3.28	23	0	0	8	25	19	9	9	0	20	28	.211	.235	.196	10.22	7.30
Cornelius, Jonathan	L-L	6-1	190	5-31-88	0	3	6.75	6	0	0	0	13	22	13	10	0	4	9	.386	.389	.385	6.08	2.70
Donofrio, Joey	R-R	6-3	185	5-10-89	3	4	4.30	34	0	0	1	61	58	30	29	5	32	44	.251	.253	.250	6.53	4.75
Garcia, Jaime	L-L	6-2	215	7-8-86	1	0	3.00	1	1	0	0	6	2	2	2	1	0	6	.261	.000	.286	9.00	0.00
Garcia, Silfredo	R-R	6-2	170	7-19-91	1	1	2.55	12	0	0	0	18	21	8	5	1	4	18	.288	.364	.225	9.17	2.04
Gonzales, Marco	L-L	6-1	195	2-16-92	0	0	0.00	2	2	0	0	7	6	0	0	0	6	7	.231	.200	.238	8.10	0.00
Hald, Kyle	L-L	6-0	190	5-27-89	3	6	5.12	22	19	0	0	102	113	63	58	9	31	72	.281	.312	.272	6.35	2.74
Herget, Kevin	R-R	5-10	185	4-3-91	0	1	10.13	4	0	0	0	8	14	9	9	2	2	3	.378	.273	.423	3.38	2.25
Heyer, Kurt	L-R	6-2	185	1-23-91	6	1	4.57	31	5	0	3	61	73	31	31	6	14	47	.296	.274	.309	6.93	2.07
Lee, Thomas	R-R	6-1	190	10-20-89	8	4	4.12	22	14	1	0	103	101	49	47	10	26	64	.256	.229	.276	5.61	2.28
Lucas, Josh	R-R	6-6	185	11-5-90	0	0	0.00	4	0	0	0	6	1	0	0	0	2	5	.059	.000	.100	7.94	3.18
Mayers, Mike	R-R	6-3	200	12-6-91	1	4	6.56	10	10	1	0	47	53	39	34	8	21	36	.291	.276	.298	6.94	4.05
Melling, Tyler	R-L	6-2	170	9-4-88	0	0	0.00	2	0	0	0	1	1	0	0	0	3	1	.000	.000	.250	13.50	27.00
Morales, Andrew	R-R	6-0	185	1-16-93	5	8	5.00	26	26	0	0	130	169	81	72	17	46	85	.316	.338	.299	5.90	3.19
Nazario, Iden	L-L	6-0	190	3-28-89	1	3	2.87	28	0	0	0	38	29	13	12	2	19	34	.207	.195	.212	8.12	4.54
Perry, Chris	L-R	6-2	215	7-15-90	1	3	6.11	18	0	0	1	28	27	19	19	1	18	24	.267	.188	.340	7.71	5.79
Petree, Nick	R-R	6-1	195	7-16-90	1	5	4.64	10	10	0	0	54	71	35	28	3	15	35	.318	.385	.268	5.80	2.48
Polanco, Jhonny	R-R	6-3	195	4-28-92	0	0	6.75	2	0	0	0	3	1	2	2	0	3	1	.111	.000	.200	3.38	10.13
Reed, Jimmy	L-L	5-11	185	12-18-90	2	4	5.14	16	16	1	0	82	103	49	47	11	18	59	.302	.222	.331	6.45	1.97
Reyes, Alex	R-R	6-3	185	8-29-94	3	2	3.12	8	8	0	0	35	21	14	12	1	18	52	.174	.197	.150	13.50	4.67
Reyes, Artie	R-R	5-11	185	4-6-92	7	7	2.64	17	17	0	0	99	98	38	29	2	28	80	.255	.279	.239	7.27	2.55
Rowland, Robby	R-R	6-4	215	12-15-91	1	2	6.10	10	0	0	0	10	8	8	7	0	3	5	.211	.222	.200	4.35	2.61
Schumacher, Cody	R-R	6-1	190	12-1-90	0	0	9.00	1	0	0	0	3	2	2	1	0	2	3	.333	.000	.429	9.00	0.00
Shaban, Ronnie	L-R	6-1	195	3-8-90	3	2	2.76	43	0	0	10	49	41	16	15	3	15	46	.228	.230	.226	8.45	2.76
Sherriff, Ryan	L-L	6-1	185	5-25-90	1	1	3.15	27	0	0	0	34	36	13	12	4	12	31	.269	.255	.276	8.13	3.15
Stoppelman, Lee	L-L	6-2	210	5-24-90	0	1	22.50	5	0	0	0	4	3	10	10	0	13	10	.214	.000	.333	6.75	22.50
Swagerty, Jordan	B-R	6-2	175	7-14-89	3	1	12.38	20	0	0	2	16	24	29	22	5	21	8	.338	.429	.279	4.50	11.81
Thomas, Chris	R-R	6-2	200	3-16-88	3	4	3.34	38	1	0	2	57	48	24	21	4	11	52	.232	.232	.232	8.26	1.75
Walden, Jordan	R-R	6-5	250	11-16-87	0	0	0.00	2	0	0	0	2	2	0	0	0	0	3	.250	1.000	.143	13.50	0.00

Pitching	B-T	HT	WT	DOB	W	L	ERA	G	GS	CG	SV	IP	H	R	ER	HR	BB	SO	AVG	vLH	vRH	K/9	BB/9
Wright, Justin	L-L	5-9	175	8-18-89	1	1	2.92	12	0	0	0	12	13	4	4	0	3	16	.271	.238	.296	11.68	2.19
Wyatt, Heath	R-R	6-2	185	8-27-88	1	2	2.63	15	0	0	2	24	18	7	7	1	9	23	.205	.219	.196	8.63	3.38

Fielding

Catcher	PCT	G	PO	A	E	DP	PB
Cruz	1.000	1	4	0	0	0	
Gonzalez	1.000	4	19	3	0	0	1
Ohlman	.985	97	657	45	11	4	6
Rosario	.981	44	324	41	7	2	3

First Base	PCT	G	PO	A	E	DP
Garcia	1.000	1	0	0	0	0
Rodriguez	.990	112	944	62	10	75
Washington	.983	28	215	17	4	19
Wisdom	.960	3	22	2	1	5

Second Base	PCT	G	PO	A	E	DP
Caldwell	.976	67	109	175	7	41
Mejia	.968	11	17	13	1	1
Valera	1.000	37	68	92	0	19
Wiley	1.000	3	4	9	0	1

Williams	.979	8	22	25	1	4
Wilson	.964	19	34	46	3	14

Third Base	PCT	G	PO	A	E	DP
Caldwell	.909	11	4	16	2	0
Mejia	.967	10	11	18	1	2
Rodriguez	.929	4	8	5	1	1
Valera	.923	4	5	7	1	0
Wilson	.926	12	7	18	2	1
Wisdom	.941	107	75	194	17	12

Shortstop	PCT	G	PO	A	E	DP
Diaz	.963	91	136	249	15	49
Mejia	.964	13	13	40	2	6
Reyes	1.000	4	1	13	0	1
Sohn	—	1	0	0	0	0
Valera	.960	28	37	84	5	16

Williams	1.000	9	13	24	0	4

Outfield	PCT	G	PO	A	E	DP
Caldwell	1.000	1	1	0	0	0
Garcia	.972	51	98	8	3	3
Gibson	1.000	3	3	0	0	0
Hazelbaker	.937	31	74	0	5	0
Martini	.989	86	170	4	2	0
O'Neill	.981	33	50	2	1	1
Rodriguez	.882	9	15	0	2	0
Tilson	.979	128	316	10	7	1
Valera	.983	34	54	5	1	0
Washington	.947	55	104	3	6	0
Williams	1.000	1	3	0	0	0
Wilson	1.000	3	1	0	0	0

PALM BEACH CARDINALS   HIGH CLASS A

FLORIDA STATE LEAGUE

Batting	B-T	HT	WT	DOB	AVG	vLH	vRH	G	AB	R	H	2B	3B	HR	RBI	BB	HBP	SH	SF	SO	SB	CS	SLG	OBP
Acevedo, Johan	R-R	6-1	173	3-28-93	.000	.000	.000	2	6	0	0	0	0	0	0	0	0	0	0	2	0	0	.000	.000
Aikin, Craig	L-L	5-10	175	8-19-93	.333	—	.333	3	9	3	3	1	0	0	1	2	0	0	0	2	0	1	.444	.455
Bosco, Jimmy	L-R	5-10	170	5-21-91	.239	.226	.242	47	163	15	39	7	0	1	9	7	1	3	2	35	2	0	.301	.272
Caldwell, Bruce	L-R	5-11	175	11-27-91	.248	.268	.239	44	165	23	41	10	1	1	16	25	1	0	1	33	3	2	.339	.349
Castillo, Ronald	R-R	6-5	200	6-16-92	.149	.161	.143	29	101	6	15	3	0	1	6	7	0	1	0	23	0	1	.208	.204
Diekroeger, Danny	L-R	6-2	205	5-25-92	.226	.200	.234	49	186	19	42	5	3	1	19	18	1	1	2	31	3	2	.301	.295
Drake, Blake	R-R	6-1	175	7-11-93	.200	.192	.204	62	215	18	43	10	2	2	18	14	2	2	0	54	6	4	.293	.255
Gibson, Derek	L-R	6-2	220	2-25-91	.356	.306	.378	34	118	8	42	6	0	0	9	8	2	0	0	15	0	1	.407	.406
Godoy, Jose	L-R	5-11	180	10-13-94	.167	.500	.000	3	6	1	1	0	0	0	1	0	0	1	0	0	1	0	.167	.286
Gonzalez, Jose	R-R	6-1	215	6-23-87	.159	.111	.183	32	107	8	17	3	0	1	3	10	2	0	0	32	0	4	.215	.244
Gronsky, Jake	R-R	6-0	210	11-21-91	.188	.179	.195	23	69	3	13	2	0	0	4	7	4	1	0	21	1	0	.217	.300
Herrera, Juan	R-R	5-11	165	6-28-93	.265	.233	.280	54	185	18	49	5	0	0	18	10	4	0	1	34	8	3	.292	.315
Katz, Mason	R-R	5-10	190	8-23-90	.259	.277	.251	75	274	34	71	19	0	4	32	33	5	0	2	75	5	3	.372	.347
Kelly, Carson	R-R	6-2	200	7-14-94	.219	.283	.194	108	389	30	85	18	1	8	51	22	3	0	5	64	0	0	.332	.263
Lankford, Cole	L-R	6-0	185	9-3-92	.000	.000	—	1	3	0	0	0	0	0	0	0	0	0	0	1	0	0	.000	.000
Massi, Michael	R-R	6-0	185	6-19-92	.175	.313	.083	17	40	7	7	0	0	0	4	8	0	0	1	7	3	0	.175	.306
McElroy Jr., C.J.	R-R	5-10	180	5-29-93	.247	.288	.227	118	430	52	106	12	4	3	25	34	20	6	3	94	39	16	.314	.329
Radack, Collin	R-R	6-3	205	3-30-92	.285	.297	.280	70	242	39	69	11	1	1	20	27	15	0	2	50	8	4	.351	.388
Reyes, Robelys	B-R	5-9	150	7-25-90	.255	.276	.246	116	392	38	100	15	0	0	26	26	4	14	3	67	21	11	.293	.306
Sohn, Andrew	R-R	5-11	185	5-8-93	.103	.083	.118	9	29	0	3	0	0	0	3	2	1	1	1	4	2	0	.103	.206
Staton, Allen	R-R	5-10	190	9-10-92	.185	.000	.227	9	27	3	5	0	0	0	1	5	0	0	0	6	0	1	.185	.313
Turgeon, Casey	R-R	5-10	160	9-28-92	.214	.216	.213	76	257	32	55	9	0	1	21	37	6	5	1	44	7	1	.261	.326
Valera, Breyvic	B-R	5-11	160	1-8-92	.353	.250	.385	14	51	9	18	3	1	0	11	7	1	0	0	2	0	3	.451	.468
Voit, Luke	R-R	6-3	225	2-13-91	.273	.257	.279	130	462	52	126	18	5	11	77	63	5	0	9	104	2	0	.405	.360
Washington, David	L-L	6-5	200	11-20-90	.141	.091	.161	23	78	8	11	5	1	0	8	10	1	0	3	29	0	0	.231	.239
Wick, Rowan	L-R	6-3	220	11-9-92	.198	.139	.222	33	126	10	25	6	1	3	16	4	1	0	2	50	1	3	.333	.226
Wiley, Brett	L-R	5-10	175	11-24-91	.234	.218	.240	93	320	35	75	20	2	0	33	33	1	2	6	75	18	7	.309	.303

Pitching	B-T	HT	WT	DOB	W	L	ERA	G	GS	CG	SV	IP	H	R	ER	HR	BB	SO	AVG	vLH	vRH	K/9	BB/9
Alexander, Kevin	R-R	6-1	170	5-4-91	0	0	0.00	3	0	0	0	6	7	1	0	0	1	3	.318	.000	.368	4.76	1.59
Anderson, Will	R-R	6-3	205	8-26-92	1	5	5.21	9	9	0	0	47	64	30	27	1	5	28	.323	.373	.287	5.40	0.96
Barraclough, Kyle	R-R	6-3	225	5-23-90	1	0	0.60	11	0	0	4	15	9	4	1	0	9	23	.167	.381	.030	13.80	5.40
Brookshire, Chase	R-L	6-0	190	3-7-91	0	0	6.14	4	0	0	0	8	8	5	5	0	3	9	.276	.333	.261	11.05	3.68
Butler, Keith	R-R	6-0	170	1-30-89	0	0	3.00	8	0	0	1	12	11	4	4	3	1	13	.239	.211	.259	9.75	0.75
Escudero, Jhonatan	R-R	6-1	165	7-7-93	0	0	5.40	1	0	0	0	2	2	1	1	1	1	3	.286	.500	.200	16.20	5.40
Fernandez, Junior	R-R	6-1	180	3-2-97	0	0	1.35	2	1	0	0	7	8	2	1	0	2	5	.308	.182	.400	6.75	2.70
Garcia, Silfredo	R-R	6-2	170	7-19-91	1	2	2.54	15	1	0	3	28	25	9	8	1	6	23	.243	.314	.206	7.31	1.91
Gonzales, Marco	L-L	6-1	195	2-16-92	0	0	0.00	2	2	0	0	5	5	2	0	0	0	4	.250	.125	.333	7.71	0.00
Hawkins, Chandler	L-L	6-1	170	2-28-93	0	0	3.86	1	0	0	0	2	3	1	1	0	0	3	.300	.500	.250	11.57	0.00
Herget, Kevin	R-R	5-10	185	4-3-91	5	1	1.75	38	0	0	7	67	54	17	13	0	16	71	.222	.212	.228	9.54	2.15
Holt, Harley	R-R	6-0	165	10-28-91	0	0	0.00	3	0	0	1	6	7	0	0	0	1	3	.318	.286	.333	4.76	1.59
Kaminsky, Rob	L-L	5-11	190	9-2-94	6	5	2.09	17	17	0	0	95	82	29	22	0	28	79	.228	.265	.217	7.51	2.66
Littrell, Corey	L-L	6-3	185	3-21-92	9	9	2.69	27	17	1	0	130	125	48	39	5	21	93	.253	.257	.251	6.42	1.45
Lomascolo, Nick	R-L	6-1	200	11-5-90	1	0	0.00	1	0	0	0	1	2	0	0	0	0	1	.400	.000	.667	9.00	0.00
Lucas, Josh	R-R	6-6	185	11-5-90	4	3	1.29	41	0	0	9	56	42	11	8	2	12	41	.214	.203	.220	6.59	1.93
McKinney, Ian	L-L	5-11	185	11-18-94	1	0	0.00	1	0	0	0	3	1	0	0	0	5	5	.091	.000	.125	15.00	0.00
McKnight, Blake	R-R	6-1	185	2-13-91	3	3	2.72	11	6	0	0	46	40	18	14	0	10	27	.240	.288	.208	5.24	1.94
Melling, Tyler	R-L	6-2	170	9-4-88	2	2	2.84	30	1	0	1	44	34	16	14	1	12	40	.214	.224	.209	8.12	2.44
Nielsen, Trey	R-R	6-1	190	9-1-91	9	6	2.59	25	18	0	0	111	101	47	32	3	34	78	.242	.284	.213	6.32	2.76
Perdomo, Luis	R-R	6-2	160	5-9-93	1	3	5.13	6	5	0	0	26	31	16	15	1	6	18	.301	.324	.290	6.15	2.05

Pitching	B-T	HT	WT	DOB	W	L	ERA	G	GS	CG	SV	IP	H	R	ER	HR	BB	SO	AVG	vLH	vRH	K/9	BB/9
Perry, Chris	L-R	6-2	215	7-15-90	1	3	1.97	25	0	0	11	32	15	7	7	0	16	34	.146	.156	.138	9.56	4.50
Petree, Nick	R-R	6-1	195	7-16-90	5	3	3.48	12	11	0	0	67	62	28	26	6	18	40	.246	.276	.224	5.35	2.41
Polanco, Jhonny	R-R	6-3	195	4-28-92	0	2	6.75	5	1	0	0	11	11	8	8	0	7	7	.256	.435	.050	5.91	5.91
Poncedeleon, Daniel	R-R	6-4	190	1-16-92	5	0	1.49	7	6	0	0	42	29	9	7	1	8	25	.193	.270	.138	5.31	1.70
Reed, Jimmy	L-L	5-11	185	12-18-90	4	2	2.15	8	8	2	0	54	43	14	13	0	4	34	.213	.179	.226	5.63	0.66
Reyes, Alex	R-R	6-3	185	8-29-94	2	5	2.26	13	13	0	0	64	49	20	16	0	31	96	.216	.192	.234	13.57	4.38
Reyes, Artie	R-R	5-11	185	4-6-92	1	1	2.45	3	3	0	0	15	19	4	4	0	6	8	.333	.333	.333	4.91	3.68
Rowland, Robby	B-R	6-4	215	12-15-91	0	1	4.50	9	0	0	5	10	10	5	5	0	4	6	.278	.455	.200	5.40	3.60
Sabatino, Steve	L-L	6-2	190	3-8-90	2	0	4.13	22	0	0	1	28	34	13	13	1	11	20	.298	.303	.296	6.35	3.49
Schumacher, Cody	R-R	6-1	190	12-1-90	3	1	3.95	21	0	0	1	43	44	19	19	1	9	32	.263	.221	.293	6.65	1.87
Shaban, Ronnie	L-R	6-1	195	3-8-90	0	0	2.08	4	0	0	2	4	3	1	1	0	3	0	.188	.000	.375	0.00	6.23
Stoppelman, Lee	L-L	6-2	210	5-24-90	0	1	5.56	19	0	0	0	23	21	14	14	0	25	21	.250	.269	.241	8.34	9.93
Villegas, Kender	R-R	6-2	170	6-8-93	0	0	3.86	1	0	0	0	2	2	1	1	0	2	2	.222	.500	.000	7.71	0.00
Weaver, Luke	R-R	6-2	170	8-21-93	8	5	1.62	19	19	0	0	105	98	34	19	2	19	88	.247	.310	.213	7.52	1.62

Fielding

Catcher	PCT	G	PO	A	E	DP	PB
Godoy	.929	2	13	0	1	0	0
Gonzalez	.992	30	205	30	2	3	3
Katz	1.000	3	21	4	0	1	0
Kelly	.996	104	751	67	3	8	6

First Base	PCT	G	PO	A	E	DP
Gronsky	.981	12	99	5	2	10
Katz	1.000	10	79	10	0	4
Massi	—	1	0	0	0	0
Voit	.985	118	1024	63	16	112

Second Base	PCT	G	PO	A	E	DP
Caldwell	1.000	1	1	4	0	0
Katz	.964	18	42	39	3	14
Massi	1.000	2	3	5	0	0
Reyes	.969	43	73	114	6	27
Staton	1.000	2	11	8	0	4
Turgeon	.985	13	29	37	1	7

Valera	.953	8	16	25	2	6
Wiley	.974	55	102	158	7	41

Third Base	PCT	G	PO	A	E	DP
Caldwell	.927	38	16	73	7	6
Diekroeger	.923	40	25	83	9	7
Gronsky	.917	5	3	8	1	1
Katz	1.000	2	2	4	0	0
Massi	.909	5	4	6	1	0
Reyes	.800	1	1	3	1	0
Staton	.923	6	3	9	1	0
Turgeon	.925	31	22	77	8	7
Valera	.778	2	1	6	2	2
Wiley	.968	10	10	20	1	1

Shortstop	PCT	G	PO	A	E	DP
Herrera	.942	52	80	165	15	35
Massi	1.000	6	10	12	0	3
Reyes	.955	73	90	226	15	51

Sohn	.898	8	13	31	5	4
Valera	.895	3	8	9	2	4

Outfield	PCT	G	PO	A	E	DP
Acevedo	1.000	2	5	0	0	0
Aikin	.833	3	5	0	1	0
Bosco	1.000	38	56	2	0	0
Castillo	.918	28	44	1	4	0
Drake	.986	61	128	9	2	3
Gibson	.909	25	30	0	3	0
Katz	.981	23	50	2	1	1
Lankford	1.000	1	3	0	0	0
McElroy Jr.	.993	117	279	6	2	0
Radack	.989	52	88	0	1	0
Turgeon	.963	17	26	0	1	0
Valera	1.000	1	4	0	0	0
Washington	.974	22	35	3	1	1
Wick	.975	32	70	7	2	2

PEORIA CHIEFS   LOW CLASS A

MIDWEST LEAGUE

Batting	B-T	HT	WT	DOB	AVG	vLH	vRH	G	AB	R	H	2B	3B	HR	RBI	BB	HBP	SH	SF	SO	SB	CS	SLG	OBP
Acevedo, Johan	R-R	6-1	173	3-28-93	.263	.182	.275	24	80	11	21	1	0	0	8	3	4	0	1	17	3	1	.275	.318
Bader, Harrison	R-R	6-0	195	6-3-94	.301	.419	.270	54	206	34	62	11	2	9	28	15	6	0	1	44	15	6	.505	.364
Bean, Steve	L-R	6-2	190	9-15-93	.222	.107	.247	90	311	28	69	14	1	2	20	35	2	3	1	95	0	1	.293	.304
Bryan, Vaughn	B-R	6-0	185	6-5-93	.272	.222	.277	24	92	8	25	6	1	0	8	5	1	0	0	27	3	1	.359	.316
Castillo, Ronald	R-R	6-5	200	6-16-92	.184	.000	.205	15	49	2	9	4	0	0	2	1	1	0	1	12	0	0	.265	.212
Cruz, Luis	R-R	6-2	180	5-26-93	.238	.275	.229	72	239	13	57	7	3	1	20	16	2	3	3	48	0	1	.305	.305
DeJong, Paul	R-R	6-1	195	8-2-93	.288	.286	.288	56	219	32	63	12	3	5	26	23	3	0	2	43	13	4	.438	.360
DeLeon, Alex	R-R	6-1	215	2-9-91	.212	.195	.217	110	391	38	83	24	0	11	55	44	3	1	5	122	0	0	.358	.293
Diekroeger, Danny	L-R	6-2	205	5-26-92	.293	.227	.308	70	242	36	71	16	4	1	37	22	5	4	0	41	10	4	.405	.364
Drake, Blake	R-R	6-1	175	7-11-93	.219	.263	.208	58	187	25	41	11	1	6	17	13	1	0	3	35	6	3	.385	.270
Ehrlich, Adam	L-R	6-1	205	12-13-92	.132	.000	.146	16	53	5	7	0	0	1	7	0	0	0	0	15	0	0	.132	.233
Gibson, Derek	L-R	6-2	220	2-25-91	.246	.154	.273	17	57	6	14	4	1	0	4	4	0	1	1	4	0	0	.351	.290
Gronsky, Jake	R-R	6-0	210	11-21-91	.225	.200	.230	31	102	18	23	9	1	3	13	9	5	1	0	19	1	0	.422	.319
Jay, Jon	L-L	5-11	195	3-15-85	.000		.000	3	10	0	0	0	0	0	1	1	0	0	0	0	0	0	.000	.091
Massi, Michael	R-R	6-0	185	6-19-92	.500	—	.500	1	2	0	1	0	0	0	0	0	0	0	0	1	0	0	.500	.500
Mercado, Oscar	R-R	6-2	175	12-16-94	.254	.333	.236	117	472	70	120	23	3	4	44	23	8	5	5	60	50	19	.341	.297
O'Keefe, Brian	R-R	6-0	210	7-15-93	.280	.241	.292	34	125	16	35	8	0	5	21	13	3	0	2	31	0	0	.464	.357
Pedroza, Richy	B-R	5-6	150	7-21-91	.143	.250	.000	3	7	0	1	0	0	0	0	1	0	0	0	0	0	0	.143	.250
Peoples-Walls, Kenny	R-R	6-1	180	8-16-93	.230	.276	.221	49	165	25	38	4	1	7	20	11	2	0	2	46	1	1	.394	.283
Radack, Collin	R-R	6-3	205	3-30-92	.293	.326	.279	37	150	16	44	2	2	2	20	4	2	0	0	30	6	2	.373	.321
Ringo, Justin	L-R	6-0	195	12-24-90	.248	.261	.245	38	129	15	32	4	2	1	21	23	2	0	3	30	2	0	.333	.363
Seferina, Darren	R-R	5-9	175	1-24-94	.295	.269	.301	107	410	58	121	26	12	4	33	37	1	2	1	88	23	17	.446	.354
Sierra, Magneuris	L-L	5-11	160	4-7-96	.191	.108	.213	51	178	19	34	1	3	1	7	7	0	3	2	52	4	5	.247	.219
Sohn, Andrew	R-R	5-11	185	5-8-93	.256	.250	.257	79	262	41	67	12	1	3	33	18	8	3	3	54	19	6	.344	.320
Swirchak, Josh	R-R	5-11	180	4-2-93	.200	.200	.200	9	25	1	5	0	0	0	3	1	0	1	0	2	0	1	.200	.286
Thompson, Nick	R-R	6-1	210	11-13-92	.248	.253	.246	117	420	49	104	19	3	12	59	52	11	1	2	115	0	1	.393	.344
Turgeon, Casey	R-R	6-1	190	9-28-92	.267	.200	.300	6	15	1	4	0	0	0	0	3	0	0	0	1	0	0	.533	.389

Pitching	B-T	HT	WT	DOB	W	L	ERA	G	GS	CG	SV	IP	H	R	ER	HR	BB	SO	AVG	vLH	vRH	K/9	BB/9
Alexander, Kevin	R-R	6-1	170	5-4-91	0	0	3.72	12	0	0	0	19	22	9	8	1	4	18	.286	.207	.333	8.38	1.86
Anderson, Will	R-R	6-3	205	8-26-92	2	1	2.37	4	3	0	0	19	18	5	5	1	2	16	.254	.278	.229	7.58	0.95
Baez, Fernando	R-R	6-1	190	2-1-92	2	3	6.69	10	7	0	0	35	35	28	26	6	26	41	.263	.254	.271	10.54	6.69
Beck, Landon	R-R	6-3	215	12-9-92	0	3	6.91	3	3	0	0	14	22	14	11	2	5	14	.344	.320	.359	8.79	3.14
Bray, Tyler	R-R	6-5	200	10-3-91	2	2	4.97	24	0	0	2	38	40	24	21	4	14	51	.263	.373	.208	12.08	3.32
Flaherty, Jack	R-R	6-4	205	10-15-95	9	3	2.84	18	18	0	0	95	92	38	30	2	31	97	.251	.243	.258	9.19	2.94
Frey, Nick	R-R	6-4	185	8-30-91	1	3	6.00	19	0	0	0	30	40	22	20	0	16	21	.331	.350	.311	6.30	4.80

Pitching	B-T	HT	WT	DOB	W	L	ERA	G	GS	CG	SV	IP	H	R	ER	HR	BB	SO	AVG	vLH	vRH	K/9	BB/9
Garcia, Jaime	L-L	6-2	215	7-8-86	0	0	0.00	1	1	0	0	5	0	0	0	0	0	6	.000	.000	.000	10.80	0.00
Gerdel, Anderson	R-R	6-4	204	3-22-93	0	0	4.11	7	0	0	1	15	16	7	7	2	1	9	.262	.286	.250	5.28	0.59
Gomber, Austin	L-L	6-5	205	11-23-93	15	3	2.67	22	22	1	0	135	97	45	40	10	34	140	.196	.195	.196	9.33	2.27
Grana, Kyle	R-R	6-4	245	4-26-91	2	2	0.78	54	0	0	24	57	35	9	5	0	32	69	.176	.186	.168	10.83	5.02
Kuebel, Sasha	R-R	6-1	200	7-28-92	1	0	1.23	4	0	0	0	7	5	1	1	0	1	11	.217	.200	.222	13.50	1.23
Llorens, Dixon	R-R	5-10	170	11-18-92	0	1	7.11	20	0	0	2	19	25	17	15	0	9	23	.309	.313	.306	10.89	4.26
Lomascolo, Nick	R-L	6-1	200	11-5-90	2	2	2.38	39	1	0	0	64	48	19	17	2	35	74	.207	.219	.201	10.35	4.90
Loraine, Zach	R-R	6-3	205	8-8-90	0	2	9.31	8	0	0	0	10	13	10	10	2	4	6	.317	.438	.240	5.59	3.72
Mateo, Julio	R-R	6-3	180	9-29-95	0	0	9.00	2	0	0	0	3	5	3	3	1	5	2	.385	.444	.250	6.00	15.00
McKinney, Ian	L-L	5-11	185	11-18-94	3	1	2.58	6	6	0	0	38	36	14	11	0	8	29	.247	.147	.277	6.81	1.88
McKnight, Blake	R-R	6-1	185	2-13-91	3	2	1.71	22	0	0	0	47	43	13	9	1	13	29	.243	.284	.214	5.51	2.47
Pearce, Matt	R-R	6-3	205	2-24-94	11	10	2.43	24	24	0	0	145	139	51	39	6	22	95	.252	.261	.245	5.91	1.37
Perdomo, Luis	R-R	6-2	160	5-9-93	5	9	3.68	17	17	1	0	100	103	52	41	7	31	100	.265	.226	.295	8.97	2.78
Perez, Dewin	L-L	6-0	175	9-29-94	3	6	5.45	16	16	0	0	69	81	54	42	7	48	47	.289	.208	.317	6.10	6.23
Polanco, Jhonny	R-R	6-3	195	4-28-92	3	4	3.57	30	5	0	1	58	46	26	23	6	30	69	.223	.222	.224	10.71	4.66
Poncedeleon, Daniel	R-R	6-4	190	1-16-92	6	2	2.47	13	13	1	0	77	72	27	21	4	22	62	.247	.221	.271	7.28	2.58
Rowland, Robby	B-R	6-4	215	12-15-91	2	3	2.40	28	0	0	9	41	32	15	11	4	6	45	.208	.235	.186	9.80	1.31
Sabatino, Steve	L-L	6-2	190	3-8-90	0	0	4.05	14	0	0	0	20	23	11	9	2	8	17	.291	.182	.333	7.65	3.60
Schumacher, Cody	R-R	6-1	190	12-1-90	1	0	3.47	14	1	0	1	23	20	10	9	2	5	28	.225	.167	.264	10.80	1.93
Then, Jery	R-R	6-2	195	5-6-95	0	0	3.55	9	0	0	2	13	12	6	5	1	6	12	.235	.200	.258	8.53	4.26
Villegas, Kender	R-R	6-2	170	6-8-93	1	1	2.70	7	1	0	1	13	5	5	4	2	3	17	.116	.125	.111	11.48	2.03
Wirsu, Josh	R-R	6-0	190	9-4-93	0	0	0.00	1	0	0	0	2	2	0	0	0	2	1	.286	.500	.200	4.50	9.00

Fielding

Catcher	PCT	G	PO	A	E	DP	PB
Bean	.982	84	691	71	14	11	11
Cruz	.986	39	310	32	5	3	9
O'Keefe	.975	19	149	9	4	0	0

First Base	PCT	G	PO	A	E	DP
Cruz	.984	10	60	3	1	3
DeLeon	.989	94	724	53	9	49
Ehrlich	1.000	6	50	2	0	3
Gronsky	1.000	7	53	3	0	6
Ringo	.981	25	193	12	4	22

Second Base	PCT	G	PO	A	E	DP
Gronsky	1.000	6	10	17	0	5
Pedroza	1.000	2	2	4	0	0
Seferina	.971	102	171	267	13	52

	PCT	G	PO	A	E	DP
Sohn	.964	24	44	63	4	9
Swirchak	1.000	1	1	4	0	1
Turgeon	1.000	5	5	11	0	2

Third Base	PCT	G	PO	A	E	DP
DeJong	.927	53	37	90	10	9
Diekroeger	.955	63	42	108	7	10
Gronsky	1.000	3	2	1	0	0
Sohn	.911	20	10	31	4	2
Swirchak	1.000	1	1	1	0	0

Shortstop	PCT	G	PO	A	E	DP
Gronsky	1.000	2	3	2	0	0
Mercado	.902	106	136	241	41	41
Sohn	.934	25	32	67	7	10
Swirchak	.960	7	12	12	1	5

Outfield	PCT	G	PO	A	E	DP
Acevedo	1.000	24	67	2	0	1
Bader	.982	53	155	6	3	3
Bryan	1.000	22	41	1	0	1
Castillo	.958	13	21	2	1	1
Drake	.965	57	104	5	4	0
Gibson	.955	15	21	0	1	0
Gronsky	1.000	6	6	1	0	0
Jay	1.000	2	4	0	0	0
Peoples-Walls	.967	48	85	2	3	0
Radack	.975	35	74	4	2	0
Sierra	.992	50	112	6	1	2
Sohn	1.000	3	1	0	0	0
Thompson	.989	100	168	13	2	3

STATE COLLEGE SPIKES

SHORT-SEASON

NEW YORK-PENN LEAGUE

Batting	B-T	HT	WT	DOB	AVG	vLH	vRH	G	AB	R	H	2B	3B	HR	RBI	BB	HBP	SH	SF	SO	SB	CS	SLG	OBP
Acevedo, Johan	R-R	6-1	173	3-28-93	.258	.263	.257	43	151	17	39	11	4	0	19	4	2	2	2	28	2	4	.384	.283
Aikin, Craig	L-L	5-10	175	8-19-93	.243	.342	.211	52	152	22	37	6	0	0	10	20	3	3	0	39	2	6	.283	.343
Bader, Harrison	R-R	6-0	195	6-3-94	.379	.500	.348	7	29	6	11	2	0	2	4	0	1	0	0	5	2	0	.655	.400
Chinea, Chris	R-R	6-0	205	5-3-94	.200	.000	.500	2	5	0	1	0	0	0	0	0	0	0	0	2	0	0	.200	.200
Dennard, R.J.	L-R	6-3	230	10-27-92	.250	.333	.233	42	124	11	31	8	0	2	15	16	0	0	0	26	0	1	.363	.336
Drongesen, Riley	R-R	6-2	205	5-29-92	.150	.000	.188	6	20	1	3	0	0	0	0	1	0	1	0	3	0	0	.150	.190
Garcia, Ronnierd	R-R	6-2	175	1-1-93	.305	.405	.264	39	128	14	39	9	1	2	22	7	1	1	2	28	0	2	.438	.341
Godoy, Jose	L-R	5-11	180	10-13-94	.234	.333	.209	36	107	10	25	7	1	0	18	14	3	0	2	15	0	0	.318	.333
Grayson, Casey	L-L	6-1	215	8-24-91	.308	.242	.332	73	250	40	77	18	2	2	38	46	0	1	1	64	1	0	.420	.414
Jenner, Jesse	R-R	6-0	205	7-18-93	.250	.250	.250	40	124	12	31	3	0	2	10	13	9	0	1	31	1	1	.323	.361
Lankford, Cole	L-R	6-0	185	9-3-92	.227	.204	.234	67	242	24	55	9	1	0	28	17	0	2	2	53	1	0	.289	.276
Martin, Daniel	R-R	5-11	180	8-5-94	.304	.364	.286	14	46	7	14	1	3	1	8	6	2	2	1	11	1	2	.522	.400
Massi, Michael	R-R	6-0	185	6-19-92	.207	.300	.158	13	29	2	6	1	1	0	4	1	1	0	1	6	1	0	.310	.250
O'Keefe, Brian	R-R	6-0	210	7-15-93	.143	.100	.154	13	49	2	7	1	0	1	4	1	2	0	1	10	0	3	.224	.189
Olivera, Orlando	R-R	6-0	230	10-17-90	.347	.342	.349	42	144	20	50	8	1	5	24	11	1	0	0	20	0	0	.521	.397
Peoples-Walls, Kenny	R-R	6-1	180	8-16-93	.000	.000	.000	3	8	0	0	0	0	0	0	0	0	0	0	3	1	0	.000	.000
Pina, Leobaldo	R-R	6-2	160	6-29-94	.260	.258	.260	69	262	31	68	12	2	2	33	16	4	3	4	52	1	1	.344	.308
Pritchard, Michael	L-L	5-11	180	11-10-91	.260	.269	.257	71	258	44	67	13	1	0	13	28	1	3	1	28	15	3	.318	.333
Rodriguez, Elier	B-R	6-2	210	2-15-95	.220	.182	.233	17	41	6	9	0	0	0	4	8	2	0	1	7	0	0	.220	.365
Rowland, Champ	R-R	5-11	185	2-28-92	.140	.000	.158	21	43	5	6	0	0	0	1	4	0	0	0	10	1	0	.140	.213
Spitz, Tom	R-R	6-1	180	4-16-92	.233	.258	.223	66	232	35	54	5	3	0	18	30	2	0	1	47	11	1	.280	.325
Swirchak, Josh	R-R	5-11	180	4-2-93	.229	.162	.252	43	144	13	33	3	4	0	15	10	1	1	1	30	0	3	.306	.293

Pitching	B-T	HT	WT	DOB	W	L	ERA	G	GS	CG	SV	IP	H	R	ER	HR	BB	SO	AVG	vLH	vRH	K/9	BB/9
Alexander, Kevin	R-R	6-1	170	5-4-91	3	1	3.66	11	0	0	2	20	16	8	8	0	7	21	.235	.206	.265	9.61	3.20
Almonte, Max	R-R	6-1	205	3-4-92	0	1	3.00	11	0	0	0	15	14	6	5	0	6	6	.259	.185	.333	3.60	3.60
Beck, Landon	R-R	6-3	215	12-9-92	2	3	3.26	10	8	0	1	47	42	18	17	0	10	51	.241	.240	.242	9.77	1.91
Bray, Tyler	R-R	6-5	200	10-3-91	0	1	4.91	17	0	0	2	29	25	16	16	2	12	27	.238	.320	.164	8.28	3.68
Cross, Carson	R-R	6-5	205	1-24-92	3	2	2.70	10	9	0	0	43	39	14	13	0	11	27	.247	.319	.191	5.61	2.28
De La Cruz, Steven	R-R	6-1	185	4-26-93	1	0	1.69	8	0	0	1	16	14	3	3	0	2	21	.237	.160	.294	11.81	1.13
Echemendia, Pedro	R-R	6-2	185	6-14-91	6	1	2.09	26	0	0	12	39	30	10	9	1	6	34	.217	.213	.221	7.91	1.40

Pitching	B-T	HT	WT	DOB	W	L	ERA	G	GS	CG	SV	IP	H	R	ER	HR	BB	SO	AVG	vLH	vRH	K/9	BB/9
Escudero, Jhonatan	R-R	6-1	165	7-7-93	0	0	3.00	1	0	0	0	3	4	1	1	0	1	5	.308	.400	.250	15.00	3.00
Evans, Jacob	L-L	6-2	215	11-27-93	4	3	3.08	16	6	0	1	50	41	18	17	1	7	42	.225	.204	.233	7.61	1.27
Frey, Nick	R-R	6-4	185	8-30-91	0	0	4.15	3	0	0	0	9	11	4	4	1	1	6	.314	.533	.150	6.23	1.04
Harrison, Luke	R-R	6-4	225	2-25-93	0	2	1.02	17	0	0	2	35	31	6	4	1	3	28	.231	.284	.179	7.13	0.76
Leitao, Brennan	R-R	6-1	205	6-21-93	1	0	3.60	8	0	0	0	10	17	6	4	0	7	8	.386	.333	.450	7.20	6.30
Martinez, Dailyn	R-R	6-2	170	4-19-93	4	6	3.30	14	14	0	0	79	84	38	29	2	26	55	.275	.278	.272	6.27	2.96
McKinney, Ian	L-L	5-11	185	11-18-94	4	2	2.76	8	8	0	0	46	47	22	14	1	12	40	.261	.325	.243	7.88	2.36
Oca, David	L-L	5-10	165	7-4-95	1	0	0.00	1	0	0	0	3	1	0	0	0	0	2	.091	.333	.000	5.40	0.00
Perez, Juan	R-R	6-2	195	7-22-95	4	3	3.58	13	13	0	0	65	68	29	26	5	36	59	.271	.259	.280	8.13	4.96
Rodriguez, Jorge L.	R-R	6-2	175	3-18-94	5	4	3.11	14	14	0	0	75	66	30	26	4	28	47	.243	.263	.217	5.62	3.35
Then, Jery	R-R	6-2	195	5-6-95	1	2	4.68	15	0	0	1	25	30	17	13	0	12	19	.297	.426	.185	6.84	4.32
Tomchick, Greg	R-R	6-4	200	12-30-92	0	0	9.00	5	1	0	0	7	11	10	7	1	3	4	.324	.188	.444	5.14	3.86
Villegas, Kender	R-R	6-2	170	6-8-93	2	3	4.46	22	0	0	2	42	55	23	21	1	6	40	.318	.348	.286	8.50	1.28
Wirsu, Josh	R-R	6-0	190	9-4-93	1	1	2.20	3	3	0	0	16	14	6	4	1	7	6	.241	.208	.265	3.31	3.86

Fielding

Catcher	PCT	G	PO	A	E	DP	PB
Drongesen	.965	6	45	10	2	1	4
Godoy	1.000	35	219	43	0	1	2
Jenner	.991	34	199	29	2	2	4
O'Keefe	1.000	10	62	7	0	0	3

First Base	PCT	G	PO	A	E	DP
Dennard	.983	7	55	4	1	5
Grayson	.994	66	588	48	4	56
Lankford	1.000	6	24	2	0	3
Rodriguez	1.000	5	21	1	0	2

Second Base	PCT	G	PO	A	E	DP
Lankford	.964	21	33	47	3	11

Martin	.946	11	23	30	3	5
Massi	1.000	11	20	26	0	9
Rowland	1.000	2	2	2	0	0
Swirchak	.968	39	68	116	6	28

Third Base	PCT	G	PO	A	E	DP
Garcia	.935	38	21	65	6	7
Lankford	.954	42	27	56	4	6
Martin	—	1	0	0	0	0
Massi	1.000	1	0	1	0	0
Rowland	1.000	1	0	4	0	0

Shortstop	PCT	G	PO	A	E	DP
Martin	.889	2	3	5	1	4

Pina	.934	67	105	194	21	35
Rowland	.917	11	16	28	4	6
Swirchak	1.000	1	0	1	0	0

Outfield	PCT	G	PO	A	E	DP
Acevedo	.989	41	85	3	1	0
Aikin	.980	47	97	1	2	0
Bader	1.000	6	11	1	0	0
Grayson	—	1	0	0	0	0
Lankford	1.000	3	7	0	0	0
Olivera	1.000	26	34	0	0	0
Peoples-Walls	1.000	3	6	0	0	0
Pritchard	.991	60	102	6	1	1
Spitz	.983	65	107	8	2	2

JOHNSON CITY CARDINALS   ROOKIE
APPALACHIAN LEAGUE

Batting	B-T	HT	WT	DOB	AVG	vLH	vRH	G	AB	R	H	2B	3B	HR	RBI	BB	HBP	SH	SF	SO	SB	CS	SLG	OBP
Aikin, Craig	L-L	5-10	175	8-19-93	.250	—	.250	1	4	0	1	0	0	0	1	0	0	0	0	1	0	0	.250	.250
Alvarez, Eliezer	B-R	5-11	165	10-15-94	.314	.341	.307	52	204	32	64	20	1	2	31	11	3	0	3	32	9	4	.451	.353
Asbury, De'Andre	R-R	6-3	170	8-5-95	.221	.357	.184	43	131	17	29	6	2	0	7	11	4	2	0	36	5	2	.298	.301
Bautista, Ricardo	L-R	6-0	185	12-27-95	.202	.182	.208	40	129	7	26	3	0	1	10	11	0	0	1	56	0	3	.248	.262
Chinea, Chris	R-R	6-0	205	5-3-94	.313	.217	.328	44	160	19	50	11	1	6	27	12	0	0	2	26	0	0	.506	.356
Collymore, Malik	R-R	6-0	195	4-29-95	.216	.263	.200	23	74	9	16	2	2	2	7	11	1	0	0	22	3	1	.378	.326
DeJong, Paul	R-R	6-1	195	8-2-93	.486	.429	.500	10	37	10	18	6	0	4	15	6	2	0	0	9	0	0	.973	.578
Doyle, Luke	L-R	6-0	185	4-19-95	.207	.300	.187	44	164	27	34	13	1	3	25	32	3	0	1	38	4	2	.354	.345
Drongesen, Riley	R-R	6-2	205	5-29-92	.100	.500	.056	9	20	2	2	0	0	1	2	1	0	1	5	0	0	.100	.208
Hawkins, Joey	R-R	5-11	170	3-10-93	.128	.172	.113	31	109	6	14	2	1	0	10	11	3	2	2	36	0	1	.165	.224
McCarvel, Ryan	R-R	6-2	180	12-23-94	.285	.378	.250	40	137	21	39	10	2	4	18	5	5	0	2	30	1	1	.474	.329
Newman, Hunter	R-R	6-2	210	12-20-93	.259	.277	.252	47	170	18	44	12	1	2	13	8	6	0	3	38	0	0	.376	.310
Ray, Anthony	L-R	6-1	165	3-3-95	.230	.393	.192	42	148	16	34	4	0	1	7	10	1	0	1	30	6	1	.277	.281
Rivera, Chris	R-R	5-11	150	3-10-95	.208	.219	.204	40	125	16	26	6	0	4	18	13	4	0	3	31	0	0	.352	.297
Sierra, Magneuris	L-L	5-11	160	4-7-96	.315	.327	.311	53	216	38	68	8	0	3	15	19	1	2	1	42	15	2	.394	.371
Sosa, Edmundo	R-R	5-11	170	3-6-96	.300	.250	.316	49	200	30	60	8	4	7	16	16	6	1	0	38	6	2	.485	.369
Staton, Allen	R-R	5-10	190	9-10-92	.307	.222	.331	42	163	25	50	12	2	9	44	8	1	0	2	38	2	0	.571	.339
Ustariz, Jesus	R-R	6-1	192	4-26-93	.500	.000	.667	1	4	1	2	1	0	0	2	1	0	0	0	0	0	0	.750	.600

Pitching	B-T	HT	WT	DOB	W	L	ERA	G	GS	CG	SV	IP	H	R	ER	HR	BB	SO	AVG	vLH	vRH	K/9	BB/9
Bautista, Juan	R-R	5-11	195	6-16-93	2	2	5.12	12	8	0	0	46	53	32	26	9	13	34	.288	.308	.274	6.70	2.56
Brito, Ismael	L-L	5-11	170	3-23-93	0	0	2.25	10	0	0	2	16	12	4	4	0	7	16	.207	.273	.167	9.00	3.94
Caballero, Juan	R-R	6-4	175	8-20-92	3	2	5.75	19	0	0	1	36	38	24	23	6	12	41	.277	.237	.296	10.25	3.00
De La Cruz, Steven	R-R	6-1	185	4-26-93	1	1	3.94	14	0	0	6	16	10	8	7	2	9	25	.169	.154	.182	14.06	5.06
Dobzanski, Bryan	R-R	6-4	220	8-31-95	1	1	3.94	4	3	0	0	16	19	9	7	0	2	13	.292	.300	.286	7.31	1.13
Escudero, Jhonatan	R-R	6-1	165	7-7-93	2	2	2.86	15	2	0	1	35	21	12	11	3	17	37	.174	.200	.152	9.61	4.41
Farinaro, Steven	R-R	6-0	170	8-18-95	2	1	1.69	8	0	0	1	16	13	5	3	0	10	14	.206	.296	.139	7.88	5.63
Gerdel, Anderson	R-R	6-4	204	3-22-93	0	2	4.91	11	1	0	1	22	27	12	12	2	8	17	.303	.258	.328	6.95	3.27
Hawkins, Chandler	L-L	6-1	170	2-28-93	4	0	1.84	16	0	0	0	29	22	9	6	1	11	32	.206	.242	.189	9.82	3.38
Helsley, Ryan	R-R	6-2	205	7-18-94	1	1	2.01	11	9	0	0	40	33	13	9	1	19	35	.221	.214	.228	7.81	4.24
Holt, Harley	R-R	6-0	165	10-28-91	1	2	3.97	14	1	0	0	34	46	17	15	4	4	29	.331	.328	.333	7.68	1.06
Kuebel, Sasha	R-L	6-1	200	7-28-92	3	3	3.60	21	0	0	3	30	37	16	12	0	6	32	.306	.341	.286	9.60	1.80
Leitao, Brennan	R-R	6-1	205	6-21-93	0	3	4.23	6	4	0	0	21	30	13	10	3	4	17	.329	.239	.388	7.16	1.30
Mateo, Julio	R-R	6-3	180	9-29-95	0	4	7.00	8	4	0	0	27	34	24	21	5	10	22	.312	.286	.328	7.33	3.33
Parra, Frederis	R-R	6-3	162	10-22-94	1	0	4.00	4	0	0	0	9	8	7	4	1	3	6	.308	.313	.304	6.00	3.00
Santos, Ramon	R-R	6-2	160	9-20-94	1	6	7.15	12	10	0	0	45	64	44	36	5	26	23	.339	.284	.384	4.57	5.16
Williams, Ronnie	R-R	6-0	170	1-6-96	3	3	3.70	12	12	0	0	56	45	31	23	5	25	43	.223	.264	.191	6.91	4.02
Wirsu, Josh	R-R	6-0	190	9-4-93	2	5	6.31	9	9	0	0	46	57	35	32	3	17	27	.303	.308	.296	5.32	3.35
Yokley, Ben	R-R	6-1	190	9-1-92	0	0	5.40	7	0	0	1	13	16	8	8	2	4	15	.308	.182	.400	10.13	2.70

Fielding

Catcher	PCT	G	PO	A	E	DP	PB
Chinea	.994	24	142	22	1	0	3
Drongesen	.964	4	26	1	1	0	0
McCarvel	.991	14	92	16	1	1	6
Rivera	.983	30	195	33	4	1	17

First Base	PCT	G	PO	A	E	DP
Chinea	.988	12	79	5	1	10
Doyle	1.000	2	6	1	0	1
McCarvel	.981	15	103	3	2	9
Newman	.989	40	345	19	4	26
Ustariz	1.000	1	8	0	0	1

Second Base	PCT	G	PO	A	E	DP
Alvarez	.959	49	68	118	8	30

	PCT	G	PO	A	E	DP
Doyle	.969	15	26	37	2	6
Hawkins	1.000	1	2	3	0	1

Third Base	PCT	G	PO	A	E	DP
DeJong	.952	9	4	16	1	0
Doyle	.838	18	12	19	6	0
Hawkins	.909	6	5	5	1	0
Newman	—	1	0	0	0	0
Rivera	.909	3	3	7	1	3
Staton	.917	31	28	71	9	6

Shortstop	PCT	G	PO	A	E	DP
Doyle	.933	3	6	8	1	3
Hawkins	.970	23	37	61	3	10
Sosa	.962	39	66	109	7	21

	PCT	G	PO	A	E	DP
Staton	.556	2	3	2	4	1

Outfield	PCT	G	PO	A	E	DP
Aikin	1.000	1	2	0	0	0
Asbury	.956	41	86	1	4	0
Bautista	.971	38	59	7	2	0
Collymore	.976	20	41	0	1	0
Doyle	1.000	7	15	0	0	0
McCarvel	.667	1	2	0	1	0
Ray	.968	41	57	3	2	0
Sierra	.979	53	134	8	3	4

GCL CARDINALS   ROOKIE

GULF COAST LEAGUE

Batting	B-T	HT	WT	DOB	AVG	vLH	vRH	G	AB	R	H	2B	3B	HR	RBI	BB	HBP	SH	SF	SO	SB	CS	SLG	OBP
Bandes, Luis	R-R	6-1	200	5-15-96	.319	.231	.339	38	138	23	44	6	0	4	24	6	1	0	1	13	3	0	.449	.349
Becker, Dylan	L-R	6-0	205	1-6-93	.303	.300	.303	36	109	15	33	10	0	0	16	13	3	0	2	12	3	3	.394	.386
Brodbeck, Andrew	L-R	5-10	185	1-22-93	.231	.130	.252	48	134	26	31	8	4	0	12	18	6	1	2	31	6	3	.351	.344
Cordoba, Allen	R-R	6-1	175	12-6-95	.342	.381	.331	53	202	40	69	6	2	2	20	15	7	2	3	20	11	3	.421	.401
Denton, Bryce	R-R	6-0	190	8-1-97	.194	.100	.216	44	155	21	30	1	2	1	14	11	2	0	1	32	3	0	.245	.254
Drongesen, Riley	R-R	6-2	205	5-29-92	.125	.000	.143	3	8	0	1	0	0	0	1	0	0	0	0	3	0	0	.125	.125
Franco, Bladimil	R-R	6-0	170	10-29-93	.322	.333	.319	52	202	26	65	11	2	0	29	10	3	0	1	17	3	0	.396	.361
Hawkins, Joey	R-R	5-11	170	3-10-93	.211	.000	.250	7	19	1	4	0	0	0	1	3	0	1	0	2	0	1	.211	.318
Katz, Mason	R-R	5-10	190	8-23-90	.500	.000	.556	3	10	2	5	0	0	1	3	1	0	0	0	1	0	0	.800	.545
Lopez, Joshua	R-R	5-10	188	3-4-96	.235	.188	.250	37	136	14	32	10	0	1	24	9	2	0	2	21	2	0	.331	.289
McCarvel, Ryan	R-R	6-2	180	12-23-94	.250	.500	.200	5	12	4	3	0	0	0	2	1	2	0	0	2	0	0	.250	.400
Olivera, Orlando	R-R	6-0	230	10-17-90	.318	.300	.324	10	44	5	14	3	0	2	10	3	1	0	0	7	0	0	.523	.379
Plummer, Nick	L-L	5-10	200	7-31-96	.228	.219	.230	51	180	43	41	8	5	1	22	39	6	1	2	56	8	6	.344	.379
Polcyn, Michael	L-R	6-3	225	10-17-92	.143	—	.143	2	7	0	1	0	0	0	0	0	0	0	0	1	0	0	.286	.143
Rivera, Jonathan	R-R	6-1	185	4-27-97	.215	.227	.212	32	107	6	23	3	1	0	12	5	1	0	3	28	0	2	.262	.250
Rodriguez, Frankie	R-R	5-9	175	7-27-95	.059	.250	.043	19	51	2	3	0	1	0	0	7	0	2	0	16	0	1	.098	.172
Rowland, Champ	R-R	5-11	185	2-28-92	.143	.000	.167	3	7	0	1	0	0	0	0	0	0	0	0	1	0	0	.143	.143
Staton, Allen	R-R	5-10	190	9-10-92	.300	.286	.303	11	40	4	12	3	1	1	8	6	0	0	1	4	2	0	.500	.391
Talavera, Carlos	B-R	6-1	175	9-20-96	.188	.167	.193	38	101	15	19	2	1	0	4	15	1	0	0	28	4	4	.228	.299
Tice, Dylan	B-R	5-8	190	12-5-97	.280	.357	.262	41	150	20	42	3	1	4	22	14	1	0	2	18	1	2	.393	.341
Torres, Carlos	R-R	6-3	160	10-1-92	.235	.190	.247	35	102	16	24	4	2	2	10	9	1	0	2	24	3	1	.373	.298
Zavala, Stephen	R-R	5-8	175	5-2-93	.275	.286	.273	14	40	4	11	4	0	0	5	9	3	0	0	8	0	0	.375	.442

Pitching	B-T	HT	WT	DOB	W	L	ERA	G	GS	CG	SV	IP	H	R	ER	HR	BB	SO	AVG	vLH	vRH	K/9	BB/9
Alcantara, Sandy	R-R	6-4	170	9-7-95	4	4	3.22	12	12	0	0	64	59	30	23	3	20	51	.244	.234	.252	7.13	2.80
Alexander, Kevin	R-R	6-1	170	5-4-91	0	1	6.75	4	0	0	1	4	7	6	3	1	3	4	.333	.273	.400	9.00	6.75
Arias, Estarlin	R-R	6-1	175	5-22-94	4	1	5.35	16	1	0	4	35	48	35	21	1	11	24	.322	.424	.293	6.11	2.80
Bowen, Brady	R-L	6-1	160	7-24-92	1	0	3.38	15	0	0	0	21	25	8	8	0	3	20	.291	.269	.300	8.44	1.27
Brito, Ismael	L-L	5-11	170	3-23-93	0	1	1.77	7	0	0	1	20	22	8	4	2	10	19	.272	.190	.300	8.41	4.43
DeLorenzo, Jordan	L-L	6-1	205	9-8-92	2	0	2.95	17	0	0	2	21	21	9	7	1	7	27	.263	.222	.283	11.39	2.95
Escudero, Jhonatan	R-R	6-1	165	7-7-93	0	0	0.00	2	0	0	1	2	2	0	0	0	1		.250	.000	.333	4.50	0.00
Farinaro, Steven	R-R	6-0	170	8-18-95	2	1	6.30	7	1	0	0	10	8	7	7	0	13	5	.229	.455	.125	4.50	11.70
Fernandez, Junior	R-R	6-1	180	3-2-97	3	2	3.88	11	9	0	0	51	54	27	22	0	15	58	.274	.313	.248	10.24	2.65
Foody, Max	L-L	6-3	220	6-11-93	0	0	2.35	4	0	0	0	8	7	4	2	0	0	11	.226	.364	.150	12.91	0.00
Gonzalez, Derian	R-R	6-3	190	1-31-95	3	5	4.23	11	10	0	0	55	61	30	26	0	16	55	.274	.277	.271	8.95	2.60
Mayers, Mike	R-R	6-3	200	12-6-91	1	0	1.29	2	2	0	0	7	6	1	1	0	0	7	.250	.000	.316	9.00	0.00
Medina, Yeison	R-R	6-2	210	10-2-92	1	0	0.00	4	0	0	0	5	2	0	0	0	1	6	.111	.000	.167	10.13	1.69
Medrano, Ronald	R-R	6-0	170	9-17-95	1	1	3.60	6	0	0	0	15	13	6	6	0	4	8	.236	.154	.262	4.80	2.40
Oca, David	L-L	5-10	160	7-4-95	7	1	1.70	11	7	2	0	64	56	20	12	1	13	55	.242	.231	.247	7.77	1.84
Oxnevard, Ian	R-L	6-4	205	10-3-96	1	1	2.42	8	7	0	1	26	23	9	7	1	8	16	.247	.273	.233	5.54	2.77
Parra, Frederis	R-R	6-3	162	10-22-94	0	1	10.50	6	1	0	1	18	32	21	21	3	4	9	.395	.355	.420	4.50	2.00
Perez, Dewin	L-L	6-0	175	9-29-94	0	1	5.14	2	2	0	0	7	9	4	4	0	1	4	.346	.667	.304	5.14	1.29
Reyes, Alex	R-R	6-3	185	8-29-94	0	0	0.00	1	1	0	0	3	0	0	0	0	3		.000	.000	.000	9.00	0.00
Sabatino, Steve	L-L	6-2	190	3-8-90	0	0	0.00	1	0	0	0	1	0	0	0	0	1		.250	.000	.333	9.00	0.00
Salazar, Paul	B-R	6-2	195	5-23-97	0	0	27.00	2	0	0	0	2	1	6	5	0	5	1	.200	.000	.250	5.40	27.00
Schlesener, Jacob	L-L	6-3	175	10-8-96	1	0	2.89	5	1	0	0	9	7	5	3	0	6	8	.194	.071	.273	7.71	5.79
Woodford, Jake	R-R	6-4	210	10-28-96	1	0	2.39	8	5	0	1	26	16	7	7	1	7	21	.260	.357	.222	7.18	2.39

Fielding

Catcher	PCT	G	PO	A	E	DP	PB
Drongesen	1.000	2	23	2	0	0	0
Lopez	.996	32	233	27	1	3	4
McCarvel	.950	3	18	1	1	0	1
Rodriguez	.991	15	98	17	1	0	0
Zavala	.987	10	64	11	1	1	1

First Base	PCT	G	PO	A	E	DP
Bandes	.986	24	201	9	3	16
Becker	.992	30	239	20	2	28
Drongesen	.800	1	4	0	1	0
McCarvel	1.000	1	14	1	0	0
Olivera	.973	7	68	5	2	8

	PCT	G	PO	A	E	DP
Polcyn	1.000	1	9	0	0	1

Second Base	PCT	G	PO	A	E	DP
Becker	1.000	1	1	4	0	1
Brodbeck	.963	42	75	108	7	23
Cordoba	.714	2	2	3	2	0
Hawkins	1.000	1	0	1	0	0

Second Base	PCT	G	PO	A	E	DP
Katz	1.000	1	2	1	0	0
Staton	1.000	1	3	3	0	1
Tice	.967	17	29	30	2	8

Third Base	PCT	G	PO	A	E	DP
Becker	1.000	4	2	2	0	2
Cordoba	.923	5	2	10	1	2
Denton	.922	39	22	73	8	5
Hawkins	1.000	3	2	7	0	0
Polcyn	.500	1	0	1	1	0

	PCT	G	PO	A	E	DP
Staton	.947	8	7	11	1	1
Tice	.909	6	4	16	2	2

Shortstop	PCT	G	PO	A	E	DP
Brodbeck	.900	3	6	12	2	2
Cordoba	.933	47	86	150	17	32
Hawkins	.889	3	3	13	2	3
Rowland	1.000	3	5	12	0	2
Staton	.933	3	5	9	1	2
Tice	.867	3	7	6	2	3

Outfield	PCT	G	PO	A	E	DP
Bandes	1.000	4	8	0	0	0
Becker	—	1	0	0	0	0
Franco	.951	42	36	3	2	1
Katz	1.000	1	1	0	0	0
Plummer	.988	49	78	2	1	0
Rivera	.951	28	38	1	2	0
Talavera	.980	34	45	3	1	1
Torres	.982	33	49	5	1	1

DSL CARDINALS   ROOKIE
DOMINICAN SUMMER LEAGUE

Batting	B-T	HT	WT	DOB	AVG	vLH	vRH	G	AB	R	H	2B	3B	HR	RBI	BB	HBP	SH	SF	SO	SB	CS	SLG	OBP
Balbuena, Starlin	R-R	6-2	175	3-4-98	.274	.370	.240	46	175	22	48	8	2	1	19	12	2	0	1	48	5	6	.360	.326
Cedeno, Leandro	R-R	6-2	195	8-22-98	.228	.522	.130	27	92	13	21	4	1	2	10	9	1	0	1	15	0	0	.359	.301
Cotes, Oscar	R-R	6-2	165	3-31-97	.146	.091	.167	21	41	7	6	1	1	0	2	2	0	0	0	20	0	0	.220	.186
Delgado, Esequeil	B-R	6-1	185	10-20-97	.252	.222	.259	32	103	20	26	3	1	0	15	23	3	0	0	24	4	1	.301	.403
Figuera, Edwin	R-R	5-10	160	9-2-97	.233	.320	.193	47	159	27	37	4	2	0	18	12	13	2	0	19	14	6	.283	.337
Flores, Luis	B-R	6-0	190	10-22-96	.213	.273	.180	41	155	20	33	5	6	0	17	14	1	1	4	44	1	3	.323	.276
Gomez, Dariel	L-R	6-4	190	7-15-96	.262	.257	.263	49	149	20	39	8	4	0	19	26	3	3	4	41	0	2	.369	.374
Linares, Hector	R-R	6-0	160	1-13-97	.265	.186	.301	39	136	17	36	5	1	0	17	11	2	1	2	33	4	1	.316	.325
Luna, Andres	R-R	5-10	175	7-17-97	.268	.314	.250	35	123	19	33	6	3	2	16	8	8	3	2	16	4	6	.415	.348
Melendez, Dylan	R-R	6-2	180	6-11-95	.227	.290	.182	23	75	7	17	5	1	0	5	8	2	0	0	9	0	0	.320	.318
Montero, Elehuris	R-R	6-3	195	8-17-98	.252	.230	.260	57	230	31	58	9	1	3	30	26	3	0	6	56	0	1	.339	.328
Ortega, Dennis	R-R	6-2	180	6-11-97	.248	.300	.225	44	129	22	32	6	1	0	9	15	2	2	1	18	3	1	.310	.333
Rodriguez, Carlos	R-R	6-2	215	1-6-97	.311	.289	.321	38	151	30	47	11	1	5	23	10	3	0	0	39	0	0	.497	.366
Rosendo, Sanel	R-R	6-2	205	5-7-97	.220	.224	.219	63	227	30	50	19	1	6	27	28	11	0	1	77	0	1	.392	.333
Sanchez, Brian	R-R	6-2	180	4-18-96	.236	.243	.233	60	229	34	54	14	3	6	45	20	8	0	2	71	7	4	.402	.317
Wilson, Irving	R-R	5-10	168	8-13-96	.248	.160	.276	27	101	14	25	6	4	2	21	10	4	0	6	20	0	0	.446	.339
Ynfante, Wadye	R-R	6-0	160	8-15-97	.311	.369	.286	49	212	32	66	16	3	3	34	16	2	2	2	42	4	5	.458	.362

Pitching	B-T	HT	WT	DOB	W	L	ERA	G	GS	CG	SV	IP	H	R	ER	HR	BB	SO	AVG	vLH	vRH	K/9	BB/9
Alvarez, Juan	R-R	6-4	180	12-28-96	5	2	2.68	14	12	0	0	74	77	33	22	1	13	46	.271	.333	.233	5.59	1.58
Arias, Estarlin	R-R	6-1	175	5-22-94	1	1	1.98	4	2	0	0	14	14	3	3	0	3	13	.269	.250	.275	8.56	1.98
Blanco, Fabian	L-L	6-0	165	12-22-97	2	2	5.55	22	0	0	2	36	39	23	22	1	21	33	.285	.250	.289	8.33	5.30
Casadilla, Franyel	R-R	6-3	175	4-5-97	4	3	2.16	14	14	0	0	79	69	22	19	2	11	63	.224	.214	.234	7.18	1.25
Changarotty, Will	R-R	6-0	165	10-19-95	2	3	2.45	18	5	0	2	48	46	20	13	3	12	31	.253	.220	.268	5.85	2.27
Cordero, Diego	L-L	6-3	165	9-8-97	0	0	3.52	12	0	0	0	15	15	9	6	1	3	10	.263	.143	.280	5.87	1.76
De Jesus, Noel	R-R	6-3	181	1-8-97	0	1	6.17	9	0	0	1	12	10	9	8	0	5	9	.227	.308	.194	6.94	3.86
Diaz, Oneiver	R-R	6-2	160	8-28-96	3	5	3.04	15	15	1	0	77	81	34	26	3	22	52	.275	.208	.289	6.08	2.57
Estevez, Angel	R-R	6-2	175	6-3-97	0	0	6.75	2	0	0	0	1	0	2	1	0	4	2	.000	—	.000	13.50	27.00
Gavin, Frendy	L-L	6-0	170	9-14-94	0	0	7.27	10	0	0	1	9	11	7	7	0	7	7	.333	.000	.393	7.27	7.27
Gonzalez, Junior	R-R	6-3	175	11-7-96	4	4	3.66	14	12	0	1	66	72	42	27	1	21	46	.277	.369	.233	6.24	2.85
Lugo, Cristhian	R-R	6-3	190	5-5-97	2	4	7.71	19	0	0	1	21	27	22	18	1	25	23	.314	.467	.232	9.86	10.71
Medrano, Ronald	R-R	6-0	170	9-17-95	3	2	2.20	11	7	0	0	49	46	19	12	1	12	35	.246	.321	.193	6.43	2.20
Oca, David	L-L	5-10	165	7-4-95	2	1	0.90	4	4	0	0	20	15	4	2	0	5	26	.205	.071	.237	11.70	2.25
Perez, Enrique	L-L	6-2	180	8-10-97	0	0	2.45	20	1	0	1	37	9	15	10	0	35	53	.080	.222	.068	13.01	8.59
Pirela, Brian	R-R	6-0	180	1-19-98	0	0	8.64	9	0	0	0	8	8	8	8	0	3	5	.276	.333	.261	5.40	3.24
Ramirez, Edwar	R-R	6-3	190	3-15-98	4	3	7.07	16	0	0	0	28	37	30	22	1	18	16	.333	.235	.377	5.14	5.79
Rosales, Luis	L-L	6-3	180	4-17-97	0	4	6.05	14	0	0	0	19	28	27	13	1	16	9	.337	.462	.314	4.19	7.45
Tejada, Estalin	R-R	6-4	200	6-23-95	2	3	2.13	19	0	0	3	25	20	9	6	1	17	29	.220	.276	.194	10.30	6.04
Trompiz, Anthony	R-R	6-3	214	11-20-97	0	0	12.15	6	0	0	0	7	12	9	9	0	5	5	.387	.500	.348	6.75	6.75

Fielding

Catcher	PCT	G	PO	A	E	DP	PB
Cedeno	.958	13	79	13	4	1	7
Ortega	.978	44	263	42	7	0	11
Wilson	.978	26	185	41	5	0	9

First Base	PCT	G	PO	A	E	DP
Cedeno	1.000	6	60	4	0	1
Gomez	.988	49	379	26	5	44
Rodriguez	.995	23	196	5	1	16

Second Base	PCT	G	PO	A	E	DP
Delgado	.969	31	66	57	4	8

	PCT	G	PO	A	E	DP
Figuera	.929	3	6	7	1	4
Flores	.953	39	104	117	11	31

Third Base	PCT	G	PO	A	E	DP
Cotes	.941	6	3	13	1	0
Figuera	.833	2	1	4	1	0
Linares	.918	15	16	29	4	2
Montero	.902	51	49	107	17	14

Shortstop	PCT	G	PO	A	E	DP
Balbuena	.905	41	77	142	23	25
Cotes	.778	3	4	3	2	0

	PCT	G	PO	A	E	DP
Figuera	.951	33	53	103	8	15

Outfield	PCT	G	PO	A	E	DP
Figuera	.944	9	16	1	1	0
Luna	.947	35	69	2	4	0
Rodriguez	.875	9	7	0	1	0
Rosendo	.934	62	73	12	6	2
Sanchez	.960	60	91	5	4	1
Ynfante	.966	49	106	6	4	2

San Diego Padres

SEASON IN A SENTENCE: A year of great hope prompted by a whirlwind winter of trades collapsed under the weight of high expectations, resulting in the firing of manager Bud Black.

HIGH POINT: There were two, even in a season of disappointment. The Padres were briefly in first place from April 19-21, and then won 9 of 11 in August to get to 61-62. They never got that close to .500 again.

LOW POINT: Hard to say firing their manager of nine years wasn't the low point, but after Black was fired at 32-33, the Padres lost 16 of 23 to plunge to 39-49, their low water mark.

NOTABLE ROOKIES: Cory Spangenberg came up to low expectations and wrested the second base job from Jedd Gyorko. Spangenberg hit .294/.373/.460 in the second half and appears ready to compete for the second- or third-base job next spring. Austin Hedges, the team's No. 5 prospect entering 2015 before the trades of Joe Ross and Trea Turner, was called up in May, but played just 53 games and got only 143 plate appearances with just a .426 OPS. Travis Jankowski, a plus defender, forced his way to the majors with a sterling offensive season and could be a starter in an outfield that will lose Justin Upton to free agency and needs a lefthanded hitter. Colin Rea, the organization's best minor league pitcher this year, was representative in his six big league starts. Lefthander Frank Garces had spots of success in a specialist role.

KEY TRANSACTIONS: The acquisitions of Wil Myers, Matt Kemp and Justin Upton rocked the baseball world in December. But with all the movement in the offseason, the Padres had little remaining to deal with during the year. However, the official transfer of Trea Turner to the Nationals was a blow to the organization's talent level as Turner pushed his way to the majors this season.

DOWN ON THE FARM: All of A.J. Preller's moves have stripped the Padres, especially of talent close to the majors. But slugging outfielder Hunter Renfroe excelled this season, especially once he reached Triple-A. Toolsy outfielder Michael Gettys struggled mightily in his sophomore season, striking out 162 times in his first season of full-season ball. Shortstop Ruddy Giron has some present pull power and should wind up hitting 10-12 home runs a year, but his swing is geared more for hitting line drives. Giron ranked third in the Midwest League's Top 20 Prospects.

OPENING DAY PAYROLL: $100,675,896 (22nd)

PLAYERS OF THE YEAR

MAJOR LEAGUE	MINOR LEAGUE
Justin Upton of	**Travis Jankowski,** cf
.251/.336/.454	.335/.413/.425
Led team in HR in only season in SD.	32 SB to go with stellar defense.

ORGANIZATION LEADERS

BATTING   *Minimum 250 AB

MAJORS

*AVG	Yangervis Solarte	.270
*OPS	Justin Upton	.790
HR	Justin Upton	26
RBI	Matt Kemp	100

MINORS

*AVG	Travis Jankowski, San Antonio, El Paso	.335
*OBP	Travis Jankowski, San Antonio, El Paso	.413
*SLG	Alex Dickerson, El Paso	.503
R	Rymer Liriano, El Paso	85
H	Nick Torres, Fort Wayne, Lake Elsinore	152
TB	Hunter Renfroe, San Antonio, El Paso	236
2B	Nick Torres, Fort Wayne, Lake Elsinore	44
3B	Alex Dickerson, El Paso	9
HR	Cody Decker, El Paso	21
RBI	Hunter Renfroe, San Antonio, El Paso	78
BB	Nick Schulz, Lake Elsinore	67
SO	Michael Gettys, Fort Wayne	162
SB	Travis Jankowski, San Antonio, El Paso	32

PITCHING   #Minimum 75 IP

MAJORS

W	James Shields	13
#ERA	Tyson Ross	3.26
SO	James Shields	216
SV	Craig Kimbrel	39

MINORS

W	Ernesto Montas, Lake Elsinore, Fort Wayne	12
L	Bryan Rodriguez, El Paso, San Antonio	16
#ERA	Thomas Dorminy, Fort Wayne	2.94
G	Jay Jackson, San Antonio, El Paso	54
GS	Jason Lane, El Paso	28
SV	Colby Blueberg, Lake Elsinore, Fort Wayne	21
IP	Jason Lane, El Paso	164
BB	Justin Hancock, San Antonio, El Paso	53
SO	Kyle Lloyd, Lake Elsinore	139
AVG	Thomas Dorminy, Fort Wayne	.238

General Manager: A.J. Preller. **Farm Director:** Sam Geaney. **Scouting Director:** Mark Conner.

Class	Team	League	W	L	PCT	Finish	Manager
Majors	San Diego Padres	National	74	88	.457	9th (15)	B. Black/D. Roberts/P. Murphy
Triple-A	El Paso Chihuahuas	Pacific Coast	78	66	.542	t-5 (16)	Jamie Quirk
Double-A	San Antonio Missions	Texas	60	80	.429	8th (8)	Rod Barajas
High A	Lake Elsinore Storm	California	50	90	.357	10th (10)	Michael Collins
Low A	Fort Wayne TinCaps	Midwest	77	61	.558	3rd (16)	Francisco Morales
Short season	Tri-City Dust Devils	Northwest	42	34	.553	t-2nd (8)	R. Wine/ A. Contreras
Rookie	Padres	Arizona	23	33	.411	t-12th (14)	Brandon Wood
Overall 2015 Minor League Record			330	364	.476	22nd (30)	

ORGANIZATION STATISTICS

SAN DIEGO PADRES

NATIONAL LEAGUE

Batting	B-T	HT	WT	DOB	AVG	vLH	vRH	G	AB	R	H	2B	3B	HR	RBI	BB	HBP	SH	SF	SO	SB	CS	SLG	OBP
Almonte, Abraham	B-R	5-9	210	6-27-89	.204	.250	.184	31	54	6	11	3	0	0	4	5	0	3	0	19	1	1	.259	.271
Alonso, Yonder	L-R	6-1	220	4-8-87	.282	.267	.287	103	354	50	100	18	1	5	31	42	3	0	3	48	2	5	.381	.361
Amarista, Alexi	L-R	5-6	160	4-6-89	.204	.211	.203	118	324	28	66	10	4	3	30	24	1	3	5	55	5	1	.287	.257
Barmes, Clint	R-R	6-1	200	3-6-79	.232	.242	.222	98	207	24	48	14	1	3	16	10	4	3	0	55	0	1	.353	.281
Decker, Cody	R-R	5-11	225	1-17-87	.000	.000	.000	8	11	0	0	0	0	0	1	0	0	0	1	5	0	0	.000	.000
Dickerson, Alex	L-L	6-3	230	5-26-90	.250	.000	.333	11	8	0	2	0	0	0	0	0	0	0	0	3	0	0	.250	.250
Gale, Rocky	R-R	6-1	175	2-22-88	.100	.000	.167	11	10	0	1	0	0	0	0	0	0	0	0	1	0	0	.100	.100
Gyorko, Jedd	R-R	5-10	205	9-23-88	.247	.282	.235	128	421	34	104	15	0	16	57	27	5	0	5	107	0	1	.397	.297
Hedges, Austin	R-R	6-1	200	8-18-92	.168	.136	.183	56	137	13	23	2	0	3	11	8	1	3	3	38	0	1	.248	.215
Jankowski, Travis	L-R	6-2	190	6-15-91	.211	.250	.200	34	90	9	19	2	2	2	12	4	0	2	0	24	2	1	.344	.245
Kemp, Matt	R-R	6-4	210	9-23-84	.265	.280	.261	154	596	80	158	31	3	23	100	39	5	0	8	147	12	2	.443	.312
Middlebrooks, Will	R-R	6-3	220	9-9-88	.212	.206	.214	83	255	23	54	7	2	9	29	11	0	4	0	60	2	1	.361	.241
Myers, Wil	R-R	6-3	205	12-10-90	.253	.261	.251	60	225	40	57	13	1	8	29	27	1	0	0	55	5	2	.427	.336
Nieves, Wil	R-R	5-11	190	9-25-77	.077	—		6	13	1	1	0	0	1	4	1	0	0	0	4	0	0	.308	.143
Norris, Derek	R-R	6-0	210	2-14-89	.250	.295	.237	147	515	65	129	33	2	14	62	35	6	0	1	131	4	1	.404	.305
Solarte, Yangervis	B-R	5-11	195	7-7-87	.270	.242	.278	152	526	63	142	33	4	14	63	34	6	2	3	56	1	0	.428	.320
Spangenberg, Cory	L-R	6-0	195	3-16-91	.271	.273	.270	108	303	38	82	17	5	4	21	28	2	8	3	75	9	4	.399	.333
Upton, Justin	R-R	6-2	205	8-25-87	.251	.266	.250	150	542	85	136	26	3	26	81	68	4	0	5	159	19	5	.454	.336
Upton, Melvin	R-R	6-3	185	8-21-84	.259	.254	.261	87	205	23	53	12	4	5	17	21	0	2	0	62	9	3	.429	.327
Venable, Will	L-L	6-3	205	10-29-82	.258	.194	.266	98	283	34	73	10	3	6	30	25	0	0	5	73	11	1	.378	.318
Wallace, Brett	L-R	6-2	235	8-26-86	.302	.296	.304	64	96	14	29	6	0	5	16	10	1	0	0	31	0	0	.521	.374

Pitching	B-T	HT	WT	DOB	W	L	ERA	G	GS	CG	SV	IP	H	R	ER	HR	BB	SO	AVG	vLH	vRH	K/9	BB/9
Benoit, Joaquin	R-R	6-4	250	7-26-77	6	5	2.34	67	0	0	2	65	36	17	17	7	23	63	.159	.172	.144	8.68	3.17
Campos, Leonel	R-R	6-2	200	7-17-87	0	0	9.00	1	0	0	0	1	1	1	1	0	1	1	.250	.333	.000	9.00	9.00
Cashner, Andrew	R-R	6-5	225	9-11-86	6	16	4.34	31	31	0	0	185	200	111	89	19	66	165	.279	.293	.267	8.04	3.22
Despaigne, Odrisamer	R-R	6-0	205	4-4-87	5	9	5.80	34	18	0	0	126	142	82	81	17	32	69	.287	.278	.294	4.94	2.29
Edwards, Jon	R-R	6-5	235	1-8-88	0	0	3.38	11	0	0	0	11	6	4	4	3	8	16	.171	.200	.133	13.50	6.75
Erlin, Robbie	L-L	6-0	195	10-8-90	1	2	4.76	3	3	0	0	17	16	9	9	1	2	10	.258	.364	.235	5.29	1.06
Garces, Frank	L-L	5-11	175	1-17-90	0	1	5.21	40	1	0	0	38	41	23	22	9	22	30	.281	.246	.312	7.11	5.21
Jackson, Jay	R-R	6-1	195	10-27-87	0	0	6.23	6	0	0	0	4	7	3	3	0	1	4	.368	.500	.353	8.31	2.08
Kelley, Shawn	R-R	6-2	220	4-26-84	2	2	2.45	53	0	0	0	51	41	18	14	4	15	63	.220	.224	.218	11.05	2.63
Kelly, Casey	R-R	6-3	215	10-4-89	0	2	7.94	3	2	0	0	11	19	13	10	1	3	7	.365	.286	.419	5.56	2.38
Kennedy, Ian	R-R	6-0	200	12-19-84	9	15	4.28	30	30	0	0	168	166	95	80	31	52	174	.258	.256	.259	9.30	2.78
Kimbrel, Craig	R-R	5-11	220	5-28-88	4	2	2.58	61	0	0	39	59	40	19	17	6	22	87	.185	.194	.176	13.20	3.34
Mateo, Marcos	R-R	6-1	220	4-18-84	1	1	4.00	26	0	0	0	27	22	16	12	5	9	33	.222	.250	.203	11.00	3.00
Maurer, Brandon	R-R	6-5	220	7-3-90	7	4	3.00	53	0	0	0	51	39	19	17	3	15	39	.209	.158	.261	6.88	2.65
Mazzoni, Cory	R-R	6-1	200	10-19-89	0	2	20.77	8	0	0	0	9	23	22	20	2	5	8	.489	.542	.435	8.31	5.19
Morrow, Brandon	R-R	6-3	210	7-26-84	2	0	2.73	5	5	0	0	33	29	10	10	3	7	23	.248	.222	.278	6.27	1.91
Norris, Bud	R-R	6-0	195	3-2-85	1	2	5.40	20	0	0	0	17	16	11	10	1	6	21	.246	.138	.333	11.34	3.24
Quackenbush, Kevin	R-R	6-4	220	11-28-88	3	2	4.01	57	0	0	0	58	52	28	26	6	20	58	.240	.295	.197	8.95	3.09
Rea, Colin	R-R	6-5	220	7-1-90	2	2	4.26	6	6	0	0	32	29	16	15	2	11	26	.246	.225	.277	7.39	3.13
Rearick, Chris	L-L	6-3	200	12-5-87	0	0	12.00	5	0	0	0	3	6	4	4	2	2	4	.462	.500	.429	12.00	6.00
Ross, Tyson	R-R	6-5	230	4-22-87	10	12	3.26	33	33	1	0	196	172	78	71	9	84	212	.237	.256	.220	9.73	3.86
Rzepczynski, Marc	L-L	6-2	220	8-29-85	0	1	7.36	27	0	0	0	15	17	14	12	2	4	17	.309	.244	.500	10.43	2.45
Shields, James	R-R	6-3	215	12-20-81	13	7	3.91	33	33	0	0	202	189	93	88	33	81	216	.248	.279	.216	9.61	3.60
Thayer, Dale	R-R	6-0	210	12-17-80	2	2	4.06	38	0	0	0	38	37	17	17	5	15	25	.262	.227	.293	5.97	3.58
Vincent, Nick	R-R	6-0	180	7-12-86	0	1	2.35	26	0	0	0	23	25	8	6	0	10	22	.281	.278	.283	8.61	3.91

Fielding

Catcher	PCT	G	PO	A	E	DP	PB
Gale	1.000	6	18	0	0	0	0
Hedges	.990	47	366	26	4	1	2
Nieves	.978	4	42	2	1	0	3
Norris	.993	128	970	79	7	7	13

First Base	PCT	G	PO	A	E	DP
Alonso	.997	102	817	54	3	71
Barmes	1.000	1	4	0	0	0
Decker	1.000	3	5	2	0	1
Gyorko	1.000	1	2	0	0	0
Middlebrooks	1.000	2	10	0	0	0

	PCT	G	PO	A	E	DP
Myers	1.000	22	158	10	0	17
Nieves	1.000	2	3	0	0	1
Norris	.982	17	108	1	2	8
Solarte	.980	28	180	16	4	21
Wallace	1.000	17	87	4	0	8

Second Base	PCT	G	PO	A	E	DP
Amarista	1.000	11	9	18	0	1
Gyorko	.994	93	117	230	2	46
Solarte	.983	19	23	34	1	4
Spangenberg	.985	70	87	173	4	39

Third Base	PCT	G	PO	A	E	DP
Alonso	1.000	2	0	2	0	0
Amarista	1.000	2	1	1	0	0
Middlebrooks	.954	69	53	93	7	13
Solarte	.967	92	44	130	6	11

Spangenberg	1.000	19	2	25	0	0
Wallace	.800	5	0	4	1	0

Shortstop	PCT	G	PO	A	E	DP
Amarista	.966	85	121	221	12	52
Barmes	.969	89	87	167	8	28
Gyorko	.990	29	37	58	1	15
Middlebrooks	1.000	8	5	11	0	3

Outfield	PCT	G	PO	A	E	DP
Almonte	1.000	14	12	0	0	0

Amarista	1.000	18	8	0	0	0
Dickerson	1.000	1	1	0	0	0
Jankowski	.980	32	49	1	1	0
Kemp	.972	149	269	10	8	2
Myers	1.000	42	72	1	0	0
Spangenberg	—	4	0	0	0	0
Upton	.988	146	235	9	3	0
Upton	.992	63	116	6	1	0
Venable	.993	76	140	3	1	0

EL PASO CHIHUAHUAS

SAN DIEGO PADRES

PACIFIC COAST LEAGUE

TRIPLE-A

Batting	B-T	HT	WT	DOB	AVG	vLH	vRH	G	AB	R	H	2B	3B	HR	RBI	BB	HBP	SH	SF	SO	SB	CS	SLG	OBP
Almonte, Abraham	B-R	5-9	210	6-27-89	.275	.268	.278	61	244	43	67	18	2	4	35	33	0	5	0	46	11	4	.414	.361
Alonso, Yonder	L-R	6-1	220	4-8-87	.231	.000	.273	4	13	3	3	1	0	0	2	4	0	0	0	3	0	0	.308	.412
Decker, Cody	R-R	5-11	225	1-17-87	.252	.223	.269	120	373	52	94	23	1	21	75	42	5	0	1	107	1	0	.488	.335
Dickerson, Alex	L-L	6-3	230	5-26-90	.307	.283	.319	125	459	82	141	36	9	12	71	45	8	0	7	96	4	0	.503	.374
Federowicz, Tim	R-R	5-10	215	8-5-87	.179	.231	.154	22	78	11	14	4	0	3	6	5	0	0	0	19	0	0	.346	.229
Gale, Rocky	R-R	6-1	175	2-22-88	.307	.317	.303	102	322	34	99	16	4	1	39	17	5	4	3	59	1	1	.391	.349
Goebbert, Jake	L-L	6-0	210	9-24-87	.294	.306	.290	122	354	52	104	20	3	10	62	57	4	0	6	70	4	4	.452	.392
Gomez, Hector	R-R	6-2	195	3-5-88	.358	.400	.342	29	106	16	38	11	4	3	22	7	1	0	1	17	2	0	.623	.400
Gonzalez, Benji	R-R	5-11	160	1-16-90	.315	.500	.250	17	54	6	17	8	1	0	8	4	0	3	0	9	1	0	.500	.362
Goris, Diego	R-R	5-10	200	11-8-90	.350	.500	.286	5	20	2	7	1	0	1	4	1	1	0	0	3	0	0	.550	.409
Gyorko, Jedd	R-R	5-10	205	9-23-88	.279	.240	.306	16	61	8	17	1	0	4	9	7	1	0	0	11	0	1	.492	.362
Hagerty, Jason	B-R	6-3	230	9-13-87	.292	.231	.305	47	154	24	45	11	0	4	20	17	5	0	0	35	1	1	.442	.381
Hedges, Austin	R-R	6-1	200	8-18-92	.324	.406	.256	21	71	12	23	8	0	2	15	8	0	0	0	18	0	0	.521	.392
Jankowski, Travis	L-R	6-2	190	6-15-91	.392	.407	.386	24	97	19	38	6	2	0	12	13	1	1	1	10	9	3	.495	.464
Kral, Robert	L-R	5-10	195	3-28-84	.241	.000	.304	19	29	4	7	3	1	0	3	2	0	0	1	10	0	0	.414	.281
Lindsey, Taylor	L-R	6-0	195	12-2-91	.228	.167	.258	33	92	8	21	3	1	0	7	16	0	0	0	18	3	1	.283	.343
Liriano, Rymer	R-R	6-0	230	6-20-91	.292	.245	.316	131	472	85	138	31	3	14	64	64	8	1	4	132	18	8	.460	.383
McCoy, Mike	R-R	5-9	180	4-2-81	.218	.226	.213	95	229	34	50	10	1	1	22	36	5	4	1	55	9	3	.284	.336
McElroy, Casey	L-R	5-8	180	12-28-89	.275	.108	.305	72	247	47	68	13	4	3	32	19	5	2	0	46	2	2	.397	.339
Medica, Tommy	R-R	6-1	209	4-9-88	.259	.320	.224	100	332	47	86	16	2	5	39	23	5	0	3	70	5	2	.364	.314
Middlebrooks, Will	R-R	6-3	220	9-9-88	.255	.244	.259	38	153	13	39	5	1	4	19	6	0	0	3	35	1	2	.379	.287
Myers, Wil	R-R	6-3	205	12-10-90	.333	.333	.333	3	15	4	5	0	0	1	1	0	0	0	0	2	2	0	.533	.333
Noel, Rico	R-R	5-8	170	1-11-89	.242	.290	.200	33	66	11	16	1	1	0	6	9	1	2	2	17	10	1	.288	.333
Pena, Ramiro	B-R	5-11	200	7-18-85	.308	.357	.285	111	399	68	123	24	2	4	57	30	1	10	7	44	1	4	.409	.352
Renfroe, Hunter	R-R	6-1	215	1-28-92	.333	.400	.314	21	90	15	30	5	2	6	24	4	0	0	1	20	1	0	.633	.358
Spangenberg, Cory	L-R	6-0	195	3-16-91	.250	.333	.167	3	12	3	3	0	0	1	3	0	0	0	3	3	0	0	.500	.400
Upton, Melvin	R-R	6-3	185	8-21-84	.280	.417	.237	13	50	10	14	2	0	1	6	4	0	0	0	12	0	0	.380	.333
Wallace, Brett	L-R	6-2	235	8-26-86	.305	.342	.288	61	239	34	73	13	0	8	37	24	6	0	2	56	1	0	.460	.380

Pitching	B-T	HT	WT	DOB	W	L	ERA	G	GS	CG	SV	IP	H	R	ER	HR	BB	SO	AVG	vLH	vRH	K/9	BB/9
Campos, Leonel	R-R	6-2	200	7-17-87	2	0	2.90	38	0	0	1	50	30	17	16	2	21	68	.169	.133	.188	12.32	3.81
Cimber, Adam	R-R	6-4	180	8-15-90	0	0	3.00	2	0	0	0	3	5	3	1	1	0	1	.333	.400	.300	3.00	0.00
De La Rosa, Eury	L-L	5-9	165	2-24-90	0	1	6.50	17	0	0	1	18	32	16	13	3	10	15	.386	.435	.367	7.50	5.00
3-team total (7 Nashville, 6 Oklahoma City)					2	1	5.17	30	0	0	1	31	44	24	18	5	19	25	—	—	—	7.18	5.46
Dimock, Michael	R-R	6-2	195	10-26-89	1	0	1.47	14	0	0	1	18	13	3	3	3	2	23	.203	.200	.205	11.29	0.98
Edwards, Jon	R-R	6-5	235	1-8-88	0	0	0.00	5	0	0	3	5	3	0	0	0	3	7	.188	.200	.167	12.60	5.40
2-team total (32 Round Rock)					2	1	1.23	37	0	0	23	37	21	5	5	1	11	51	—	—	—	12.52	2.70
Elbert, Scott	L-L	6-2	225	8-13-85	0	0	6.52	20	0	0	0	19	20	16	14	0	11	23	.267	.214	.298	10.71	5.12
Erlin, Robbie	L-L	6-0	195	10-8-90	7	6	5.60	24	24	1	0	125	151	90	78	22	37	105	.297	.288	.299	7.54	2.66
Garces, Frank	L-L	5-11	175	1-17-90	1	0	2.91	19	0	0	3	22	17	8	7	2	15	17	.215	.188	.234	7.06	6.23
Guerrero, Tayron	R-R	6-7	215	1-9-91	0	0	3.95	11	0	0	1	14	8	6	6	0	11	15	.178	.056	.259	9.88	7.24
Hancock, Justin	R-R	6-4	185	10-28-90	1	0	2.61	2	2	0	0	10	15	3	3	1	4	5	.349	.450	.261	4.35	3.48
Hershiser, Jordan	R-R	6-8	245	9-15-88	0	0	15.00	3	0	0	0	3	4	5	5	2	2	3	.308	.167	.429	9.00	6.00
Jackson, Jay	R-R	6-1	195	10-27-87	3	3	2.54	48	0	0	14	64	56	21	18	2	17	70	.239	.250	.235	9.90	2.40
Kelley, Shawn	R-R	6-2	220	4-26-84	1	0	0.00	2	0	0	0	3	0	0	0	0	0	1	.000	.000	.000	3.00	3.00
Kelly, Casey	R-R	6-3	215	10-4-89	1	2	6.32	4	3	0	0	16	20	11	11	0	5	14	.317	.308	.324	8.04	2.87
Kohlscheen, Stephen	R-R	6-6	235	9-20-88	2	1	6.08	17	0	0	0	24	28	20	16	3	7	22	.283	.263	.295	8.37	2.66
Lane, Jason	R-L	6-2	225	12-22-76	10	10	5.71	28	28	0	0	164	212	117	104	27	47	71	.314	.386	.294	3.90	2.58
Luebke, Cory	R-L	6-4	205	3-4-85	0	0	0.00	1	0	0	0	1	1	0	0	0	0	1	.250	.500	.000	9.00	9.00
Mateo, Marcos	R-R	6-1	220	4-18-84	3	0	1.69	25	0	0	9	32	20	8	6	1	12	40	.172	.178	.169	11.25	3.38
Mazzoni, Cory	R-R	6-1	200	10-19-89	1	3	3.97	26	0	0	5	34	25	17	15	0	12	46	.197	.167	.215	12.18	3.18
McCutchen, Daniel	R-R	6-2	215	9-26-82	9	8	3.60	32	22	0	0	132	128	57	53	15	28	86	.253	.274	.238	5.85	1.90
Morrow, Brandon	R-R	6-3	210	7-26-84	0	0	7.71	1	1	0	0	2	3	2	2	0	1	1	.333	.200	.500	3.86	3.86
Morrow, Bryce	R-R	6-2	200	1-2-88	2	2	5.88	6	6	0	0	26	37	17	17	2	8	17	.346	.425	.299	5.88	2.77
Needy, James	R-R	6-6	230	3-30-91	6	5	7.17	16	16	0	0	75	104	63	60	7	30	55	.335	.393	.301	6.57	3.58
Northcraft, Aaron	R-R	6-4	230	5-28-90	3	4	5.58	19	5	0	0	48	47	28	27	25	4	25	.300	.250	.330	6.02	5.58
O'Grady, Dennis	R-R	5-9	205	5-17-89	1	0	9.00	1	1	0	0	5	5	5	5	2	3	2	.263	.333	.231	3.60	5.40
Quackenbush, Kevin	R-R	6-4	220	11-28-88	1	0	0.77	9	0	0	2	12	6	1	1	0	2	14	.171	.250	.148	10.80	1.54
Rea, Colin	R-R	6-5	220	7-1-90	2	2	4.39	6	6	0	0	27	29	14	13	2	12	20	.274	.244	.295	6.75	4.05
Rearick, Chris	L-L	6-3	200	12-5-87	0	3	5.23	37	0	0	0	43	48	28	25	5	30	28	.293	.288	.295	5.86	6.28

Pitching	B-T	HT	WT	DOB	W	L	ERA	G	GS	CG	SV	IP	H	R	ER	HR	BB	SO	AVG	vLH	vRH	K/9	BB/9
Rodriguez, Bryan	R-R	6-5	180	7-6-91	1	2	9.75	3	2	0	0	12	24	13	13	0	4	4	.429	.444	.421	3.00	3.00
Segovia, Zack	R-R	6-2	245	4-11-83	1	2	7.24	7	6	0	0	27	35	23	22	4	10	17	.307	.390	.260	5.60	3.29
Smith, Chris	R-R	6-0	190	4-9-81	5	7	3.60	22	22	0	0	128	121	54	51	11	42	121	.251	.284	.227	8.53	2.96
Sullivan, Jerry	R-R	6-4	225	1-18-88	6	2	5.32	34	0	0	1	46	47	30	27	3	14	43	.266	.278	.255	8.47	2.76
Thayer, Dale	R-R	6-0	210	12-17-80	2	0	0.93	7	0	0	0	10	5	1	1	1	3	10	.147	.231	.095	9.31	2.79
Thielbar, Caleb	L-L	6-0	205	1-31-87	0	0	0.73	9	0	0	0	12	9	1	1	1	5	7	.196	.238	.160	5.11	3.65
Vincent, Nick	R-R	6-0	180	7-12-86	5	3	3.04	40	0	0	1	50	48	21	17	5	15	68	.254	.286	.238	12.16	2.68

Fielding

Catcher	PCT	G	PO	A	E	DP	PB
Decker	1.000	2	13	0	0	0	
Federowicz	.989	15	83	11	1	0	2
Gale	.991	94	580	87	6	9	3
Hagerty	.985	27	183	18	3	3	1
Hedges	.987	17	141	13	2	0	0
Kral	1.000	15	59	3	0	0	0
Medica	1.000	1	2	0	0	0	

First Base	PCT	G	PO	A	E	DP
Alonso	1.000	4	43	0	0	3
Decker	.991	57	385	33	4	42
Dickerson	.846	2	11	0	2	1
Goebbert	.980	29	180	16	4	15
Hagerty	1.000	16	116	2	0	12
Lane	—	1	0	0	0	0
Medica	.995	59	386	28	2	37
Middlebrooks	1.000	4	34	3	0	5
Myers	1.000	2	11	1	0	3

Second Base	PCT	G	PO	A	E	DP
Gale	1.000	2	3	0	0	0
Gomez	.929	3	7	6	1	1

	PCT	G	PO	A	E	DP
Gonzalez	1.000	2	2	1	0	1
Goris	1.000	1	4	0	0	1
Gyorko	1.000	16	27	42	0	13
Lindsey	.966	31	50	63	4	15
McCoy	.978	30	38	49	2	15
McElroy	.977	48	85	132	5	25
Noel	1.000	2	1	2	0	1
Pena	.967	38	56	92	5	16
Spangenberg	1.000	2	10	5	0	1

Third Base	PCT	G	PO	A	E	DP
Decker	.838	30	17	40	11	4
Gale	1.000	3	0	1	0	1
Gonzalez	1.000	2	1	2	0	0
McCoy	.900	9	3	6	1	1
McElroy	.925	23	13	24	3	1
Middlebrooks	.961	34	18	55	3	13
Pena	1.000	5	0	2	0	0
Spangenberg	1.000	6	0	2	0	0
Wallace	.908	60	31	87	12	7

Shortstop	PCT	G	PO	A	E	DP
Gomez	.941	23	32	64	6	16

	PCT	G	PO	A	E	DP
Gonzalez	.978	12	14	31	1	9
Goris	1.000	4	7	10	0	3
McCoy	.966	52	53	118	6	24
McElroy	1.000	1	1	1	0	1
Pena	.954	70	76	192	13	26

Outfield	PCT	G	PO	A	E	DP
Almonte	.957	60	105	5	5	2
Decker	1.000	1	1	0	0	0
Dickerson	.985	107	192	6	3	0
Goebbert	.969	78	154	4	5	1
Jackson	1.000	1	1	0	0	0
Jankowski	.963	24	77	0	3	0
Liriano	.976	121	281	7	7	3
McCoy	1.000	1	3	0	0	0
Medica	.977	29	42	0	1	0
Myers	1.000	1	3	0	0	0
Noel	1.000	28	48	3	0	0
Renfroe	.943	21	48	2	3	0
Sullivan	—	1	0	0	0	0
Upton	1.000	10	29	0	0	0

SAN ANTONIO MISSIONS

DOUBLE-A

TEXAS LEAGUE

Batting	B-T	HT	WT	DOB	AVG	vLH	vRH	G	AB	R	H	2B	3B	HR	RBI	BB	HBP	SH	SF	SO	SB	CS	SLG	OBP
Asencio, Yeison	R-R	6-1	225	11-14-89	.301	.336	.287	126	482	48	145	23	1	13	74	14	8	0	4	40	6	3	.434	.329
Bousfield, Auston	R-R	5-11	185	7-5-93	.247	.313	.228	19	73	6	18	3	0	0	1	8	0	0	0	17	1	0	.288	.321
Brugeura, Reynaldo	B-R	5-10	195	11-5-91	.226	.235	.220	26	84	14	19	5	0	1	4	11	0	2	0	21	0	1	.321	.316
Domoromo, Luis	L-L	6-1	215	2-4-92	.262	.222	.277	115	408	48	107	14	4	4	32	21	2	4	2	92	7	1	.346	.300
Erickson, Griff	R-R	6-4	220	11-1-88	.227	.164	.252	61	198	18	45	11	0	3	21	22	4	1	1	37	1	1	.328	.316
Gaedele, Kyle	R-R	6-3	235	11-1-89	.220	.176	.229	37	100	9	22	5	0	1	10	13	3	1	1	40	2	0	.300	.325
Gillies, Tyson	L-R	6-2	205	10-31-88	.259	.300	.246	61	162	15	42	6	0	2	19	3	4	1	1	44	3	2	.333	.288
Gonzalez, Benji	R-R	5-11	160	1-16-90	.246	.226	.254	49	187	24	46	6	1	1	13	17	0	3	1	24	2	2	.305	.307
Goris, Diego	R-R	5-10	200	11-8-90	.253	.288	.237	99	384	38	97	20	1	5	43	12	2	2	2	55	2	3	.349	.278
Hagerty, Jason	B-R	6-3	230	9-13-87	.212	.098	.264	40	132	16	28	6	1	5	13	10	14	0	0	1	31	2	0	.341	.286
Jankowski, Travis	L-R	6-2	190	6-15-91	.316	.250	.336	73	282	50	89	11	5	1	13	36	1	2	0	40	23	8	.401	.395
Jones, Duanel	R-R	6-3	220	5-11-93	.226	.244	.219	90	319	39	72	10	0	7	38	22	0	0	5	65	2	1	.323	.272
Kral, Robert	L-R	5-10	195	3-28-89	.000	.000	.000	6	14	1	0	0	0	0	0	2	0	0	0	7	0	0	.000	.125
Lindsey, Taylor	L-R	6-0	195	12-2-91	.171	.080	.201	61	199	21	34	11	0	5	15	23	1	0	2	38	1	0	.302	.258
Martinez, Alberth	R-R	1-70	1-23-91	.276	.338	.252	129	479	58	132	19	3	11	56	44	5	0	3	85	6	4	.397	.341
McElroy, Casey	L-R	5-8	180	12-28-89	.254	.275	.249	61	228	25	58	9	1	3	32	25	5	1	1	41	0	2	.342	.340
Miller, Ryan	R-R	6-2	200	11-17-92	.231	.000	.300	4	13	2	3	0	0	0	1	0	1	0	2	0	0	.231	.231
Quintana, Gabriel	R-R	6-3	215	9-7-92	.308	.429	.281	10	39	11	12	4	0	4	9	0	1	0	0	13	0	0	.718	.325
Reina, Adolfo	R-R	6-0	210	1-22-90	.205	.107	.236	37	117	14	24	2	0	1	6	14	2	2	1	28	0	0	.248	.299
Renfroe, Hunter	R-R	6-1	215	1-28-92	.259	.194	.281	112	421	50	109	22	3	14	54	33	3	0	6	112	4	1	.425	.313
Rondon, Jose	R-R	6-1	160	3-3-94	.190	.143	.198	28	100	6	19	2	1	0	9	4	0	2	1	15	1	3	.230	.219
Spangenberg, Cory	L-R	6-0	195	3-16-91	.192	.154	.231	6	26	3	5	0	1	0	1	1	0	0	0	2	1	0	.269	.222
Turner, Trea	R-R	6-1	175	6-30-93	.322	.304	.329	58	227	31	73	13	3	5	35	20	0	2	1	48	14	4	.471	.385

Pitching	B-T	HT	WT	DOB	W	L	ERA	G	GS	CG	SV	IP	H	R	ER	HR	BB	SO	AVG	vLH	vRH	K/9	BB/9
Alger, Brandon	L-L	6-3	190	7-4-91	3	6	3.75	48	0	0	1	60	50	29	25	5	39	55	.233	.237	.229	8.25	5.85
Butler, Ryan	R-R	6-4	225	2-23-92	0	3	4.76	3	3	0	0	17	16	9	9	0	7	.254	.281	.226	3.71	4.76
Cimber, Adam	R-R	6-4	180	8-15-90	4	2	3.05	44	0	0	1	56	56	21	19	4	15	45	.264	.267	.262	7.23	2.41
De La Cruz, Luis	R-R	6-6	225	6-15-89	1	2	8.55	15	0	0	1	20	24	20	19	4	16	15	.296	.310	.282	6.75	7.20
De La Rosa, Eury	L-L	5-9	165	2-24-90	2	1	1.27	19	1	0	7	28	16	4	4	1	15	29	.167	.200	.143	9.21	4.76
Dimock, Michael	R-R	6-2	195	10-26-89	2	0	2.38	35	0	0	3	42	37	15	11	3	4	47	.234	.250	.216	10.15	0.86
Guerrero, Tayron	R-R	6-7	215	1-9-91	1	5	2.76	37	0	0	13	42	33	22	13	3	20	46	.205	.176	.237	9.78	4.25
Hancock, Justin	R-R	6-4	185	10-28-90	7	6	3.59	22	22	0	0	120	127	52	48	8	49	92	.277	.292	.264	6.88	3.66
Hebner, Cody	R-R	6-0	175	11-21-90	0	3	5.40	17	0	0	1	20	9	14	12	1	20	16	.136	.132	.143	7.20	9.00
Herrera, Ronald	R-R	5-11	185	5-3-95	3	1	4.53	8	8	1	0	44	48	25	22	4	14	35	.276	.397	.177	7.21	2.89
Holland, Sam	R-R	6-4	200	2-20-94	0	0	0.00	1	0	0	0	0	1	0	0	0	0	0	1.000	.000	—	27.00	0.00
Jackson, Jay	R-R	6-1	195	10-27-87	0	1	1.69	6	0	0	1	11	7	2	2	0	1	16	.189	.158	.222	13.50	0.84
Kelly, Casey	R-R	6-3	215	10-4-89	1	8	4.94	27	14	0	1	82	94	56	45	7	34	60	.284	.312	.260	6.59	3.73
Kohlscheen, Stephen	R-R	6-6	235	9-20-88	5	2	2.70	27	0	2	53	53	21	16	2	19	41	.256	.269	.242	6.92	3.21

280 · Baseball America 2016 Almanac

BaseballAmerica.com

Pitching

Pitching	B-T	HT	WT	DOB	W	L	ERA	G	GS	CG	SV	IP	H	R	ER	HR	BB	SO	AVG	vLH	vRH	K/9	BB/9
Luebke, Cory	R-L	6-4	205	3-4-85	0	0	6.00	3	0	0	0	3	1	2	2	1	3	2	.111	.000	.200	6.00	9.00
McGrath, Kyle	L-L	6-2	185	7-31-92	0	1	18.00	1	0	0	0	2	5	4	4	0	1	2	.455	.250	.571	9.00	4.50
Morris, Elliot	R-R	6-4	210	4-26-92	5	9	4.87	21	18	0	0	102	113	62	55	6	44	72	.280	.317	.236	6.37	3.90
Morrow, Brandon	R-R	6-3	210	7-26-84	0	0	4.05	2	2	0	0	7	10	3	3	0	2	3	.385	.182	.533	4.05	2.70
Morrow, Bryce	R-R	6-2	200	1-2-88	5	3	4.01	13	5	0	0	49	48	24	22	4	16	34	.254	.270	.236	6.20	2.92
Needy, James	R-R	6-6	230	3-30-91	5	1	3.44	8	8	1	0	55	45	24	21	7	16	40	.223	.235	.210	6.55	2.62
Northcraft, Aaron	R-R	6-4	230	5-28-90	1	2	2.93	20	2	0	0	43	34	15	14	2	15	32	.214	.262	.160	6.70	3.14
Nunn, Chris	L-L	6-5	200	10-5-90	1	0	8.64	7	0	0	0	8	9	8	8	2	8	8	.273	.267	.278	8.64	8.64
O'Grady, Dennis	R-R	5-9	205	5-17-89	3	5	5.42	33	13	0	0	91	110	66	55	9	42	70	.298	.322	.269	6.90	4.14
Rea, Colin	R-R	6-5	220	7-1-90	3	2	1.08	12	12	0	0	75	50	15	9	1	11	60	.185	.170	.202	7.20	1.32
Rearick, Chris	L-L	6-3	200	12-5-87	0	0	0.00	5	0	0	2	6	5	0	0	0	1	9	.217	.250	.200	13.50	1.50
Reyes, Genison	R-R	6-5	190	9-19-91	0	1	0.00	4	0	0	0	11	6	3	0	0	7	13	.150	.087	.235	10.32	5.56
Rodriguez, Bryan	R-R	6-5	180	7-6-91	6	14	4.44	24	23	1	0	134	165	76	66	8	37	83	.301	.309	.291	5.59	2.49
Segovia, Zack	R-R	6-2	245	4-11-83	2	0	6.10	4	4	0	0	21	20	14	14	2	7	22	.250	.268	.231	9.58	3.05
Smith, Chris	R-R	6-0	190	4-9-91	0	0	9.00	2	2	0	0	10	5	1	1	0	2	11	.152	.143	.158	9.90	1.80
Thayer, Dale	R-R	6-0	210	12-17-80	0	1	27.00	1	1	0	0	1	3	3	3	1	0	0	.500	.667	.333	0.00	0.00
Yardley, Eric	R-R	6-0	165	8-18-90	0	1	5.14	5	0	0	0	7	10	4	4	2	2	1	.385	.389	.375	1.29	2.57

Fielding

Catcher

Catcher	PCT	G	PO	A	E	DP	PB
Erickson	.991	60	390	38	4	4	4
Hagerty	.997	38	277	21	1	5	1
Kral	1.000	6	39	4	0	0	1
Miller	1.000	4	27	1	0	1	1
Reina	.986	36	249	27	4	2	2
Gonzalez	1.000	10	19	29	0	5	
Goris	.989	43	68	119	2	30	
Lindsey	.945	49	68	154	13	25	
McElroy	1.000	19	22	56	0	8	
Spangenberg	1.000	2	3	7	0	1	
Goris	.938	22	24	51	5	8	
McElroy	.933	3	4	10	1	2	
Rondon	.975	27	38	79	3	14	
Spangenberg	1.000	1	4	2	0	1	
Turner	.977	57	88	162	6	34	

First Base

First Base	PCT	G	PO	A	E	DP
Asencio	.935	3	25	4	2	4
Domoromo	.991	113	935	73	9	77
Erickson	.833	1	5	0	1	0
Goris	1.000	7	52	4	0	5
Hagerty	1.000	3	12	1	0	0
Jones	.985	24	184	16	3	24

Second Base

Second Base	PCT	G	PO	A	E	DP
Brugeura	.946	24	32	90	7	15

Third Base

Third Base	PCT	G	PO	A	E	DP
Gonzalez	1.000	5	5	6	0	1
Goris	.941	27	18	46	4	4
Jones	.859	66	36	92	21	11
McElroy	.951	38	27	51	4	9
Quintana	.750	9	5	13	6	0
Spangenberg	1.000	3	2	3	0	1

Shortstop

Shortstop	PCT	G	PO	A	E	DP
Brugeura	1.000	2	2	8	0	0
Gonzalez	.945	32	50	71	7	22

Outfield

Outfield	PCT	G	PO	A	E	DP
Asencio	.965	96	182	11	7	3
Bousfield	.977	18	40	2	1	0
Domoromo	1.000	3	4	0	0	0
Gaedele	.963	20	26	0	1	0
Gillies	.968	32	57	3	2	0
Jankowski	.994	62	163	2	1	1
Martinez	.988	112	244	6	3	1
Renfroe	.968	90	170	14	6	4

LAKE ELSINORE STORM

HIGH CLASS A

CALIFORNIA LEAGUE

Batting	B-T	HT	WT	DOB	AVG	vLH	vRH	G	AB	R	H	2B	3B	HR	RBI	BB	HBP	SH	SF	SO	SB	CS	SLG	OBP
Alonso, Yonder	L-R	6-1	220	4-8-87	.167	.000	.250	2	6	1	1	0	0	0	0	3	0	0	0	0	0	0	.167	.444
Baltz, Jeremy	R-R	6-3	205	9-17-90	.188	.222	.176	22	69	12	13	6	0	2	8	10	6	1	0	22	0	0	.362	.341
Blanco, Felipe	R-R	6-1	175	12-9-93	.252	.375	.232	38	115	11	29	3	1	2	9	7	1	4	1	44	1	2	.348	.298
Bousfield, Auston	R-R	5-11	185	7-5-93	.273	.213	.288	102	400	53	109	12	2	3	32	50	7	8	3	79	22	6	.335	.361
Bravo, Daniel	R-R	6-0	160	2-16-95	.259	.000	.280	8	27	4	7	0	0	3	5	0	0	0	6	1	0	.593	.259	
Brugeura, Reynaldo	B-R	5-10	195	11-5-91	.143	.286	.095	18	56	6	8	1	0	0	2	7	0	1	0	17	0	0	.161	.238
Chavez, Matt	R-R	6-2	195	3-6-89	.293	.143	.314	15	58	8	17	4	0	3	8	0	1	0	1	20	0	0	.517	.300
Davis, Marcus	L-L	6-3	200	4-26-92	.255	.351	.233	128	494	62	126	28	3	9	65	31	5	1	9	110	2	0	.379	.301
Del Castillo, Miguel	R-R	5-10	170	10-14-91	.216	.190	.221	35	116	15	25	8	0	3	13	9	0	3	2	28	0	0	.362	.268
Gaedele, Kyle	R-R	6-3	235	11-1-89	.248	.235	.252	44	153	26	38	6	4	8	29	20	2	0	2	58	3	0	.497	.339
Gonzalez, Benji	R-R	5-11	160	1-16-90	.125	.000	.143	2	8	0	1	0	0	0	1	0	0	0	1	0	0	.125	.125	
Jensen, Chase	R-R	6-4	195	1-29-91	.276	.240	.281	51	196	18	54	6	1	5	28	8	3	1	2	54	2	0	.393	.311
Kral, Robert	L-R	5-10	195	3-28-89	.189	.357	.087	12	37	5	7	2	0	1	4	7	0	0	2	9	0	0	.324	.304
Miller, Michael	R-R	6-2	200	5-27-92	.225	.182	.241	10	40	4	9	3	0	0	3	0	0	0	0	7	0	0	.300	.225
Miller, Ryan	R-R	6-2	200	11-17-92	.261	.264	.261	69	287	32	75	20	4	3	27	8	2	0	0	58	2	1	.390	.286
Morales, Mitch	L-R	5-10	165	3-3-93	.250	.333	.200	2	8	1	2	0	0	0	0	0	0	0	0	0	0	0	.250	.250
Myers, Wil	R-R	6-3	205	12-10-90	.222	—	.222	3	9	3	2	1	0	0	0	2	1	0	0	0	0	0	.333	.417
Perez, Fernando	L-R	6-0	210	9-8-94	.224	.115	.251	113	446	46	100	21	3	10	50	39	4	1	2	115	1	1	.352	.291
Quintana, Gabriel	R-R	6-3	215	9-7-92	.245	.195	.256	117	461	58	113	31	1	12	54	16	1	1	4	107	1	4	.395	.270
Reina, Adolfo	R-R	6-0	210	1-22-90	.260	.250	.263	30	104	9	27	4	0	1	12	9	2	0	2	22	0	0	.327	.325
Rodriguez, Jeremy	B-R	5-8	185	8-30-89	.200	.667	.136	7	25	3	5	2	0	0	4	1	0	1	0	5	0	0	.280	.231
Rondon, Jose	R-R	6-1	160	3-3-94	.300	.417	.270	57	237	50	71	12	3	3	22	21	2	3	1	38	17	6	.414	.360
Rosen, Yale	L-L	6-2	215	5-9-93	.204	.156	.217	63	211	23	43	11	3	7	29	14	2	3	0	71	0	1	.384	.260
Schulz, Nick	R-R	6-3	210	5-3-91	.238	.304	.225	122	453	66	108	26	2	12	48	67	4	0	3	112	2	6	.384	.340
Stevens, River	L-R	6-0	185	1-13-93	.297	.297	.298	41	158	16	47	5	0	0	14	8	3	0	0	31	3	1	.329	.343
Tate, Donavan	R-R	6-3	200	9-27-90	.211	.170	.218	95	332	43	70	15	4	6	34	33	6	0	5	112	11	5	.334	.290
Torres, Nick	R-R	6-1	220	6-30-93	.275	.250	.279	52	211	21	58	15	2	3	30	9	5	0	3	45	5	1	.408	.316
Valenzuela, Ricardo	R-R	6-0	190	8-4-90	.183	.000	.191	28	93	7	17	3	0	1	8	10	1	0	0	15	0	1	.247	.269

Pitching	B-T	HT	WT	DOB	W	L	ERA	G	GS	CG	SV	IP	H	R	ER	HR	BB	SO	AVG	vLH	vRH	K/9	BB/9
Alger, Brandon	L-L	6-3	190	7-14-91	0	0	0.00	3	0	0	0	4	2	0	0	0	0	3	.167	.167	.167	6.75	4.50
Bartsch, Kyle	L-L	5-11	200	3-10-91	1	3	4.60	52	1	0	0	72	101	44	37	4	23	69	.334	.278	.335	8.59	2.86
Blueberg, Colby	R-R	6-0	185	5-11-93	0	0	21.60	1	0	0	0	2	3	5	4	1	1	2	.375	.333	.400	10.80	5.40
Butler, Ryan	R-R	6-4	225	2-23-92	3	2	3.66	12	7	0	0	47	52	24	19	2	14	31	.283	.276	.287	5.98	2.70
De Paula, Rafael	R-R	6-2	215	3-24-91	5	9	5.01	35	18	0	0	120	125	78	67	14	47	129	.271	.300	.244	9.65	3.52

Pitching

Pitching	B-T	HT	WT	DOB	W	L	ERA	G	GS	CG	SV	IP	H	R	ER	HR	BB	SO	AVG	vLH	vRH	K/9	BB/9
Foriest, Nathan	R-L	6-2	190	1-28-92	0	0	13.50	2	0	0	0	2	3	3	3	0	2	3	.333	.250	.400	13.50	9.00
Fry, Brandon	L-L	6-3	195	3-28-93	0	0	2.08	2	0	0	0	4	4	1	1	0	3	5	.250	.143	.333	10.38	6.23
Hebner, Cody	R-R	6-0	175	11-21-90	0	0	7.84	8	0	0	0	10	8	9	9	2	8	14	.216	.211	.222	12.19	6.97
Hernandez, Luis	R-R	6-2	190	6-22-92	1	3	7.25	21	0	0	1	22	33	23	18	1	12	19	.337	.395	.291	7.66	4.84
Herrera, Ronald	R-R	5-11	185	5-3-95	5	6	3.88	18	17	0	0	102	100	48	44	6	28	69	.258	.255	.261	6.09	2.47
Hershiser, Jordan	R-R	6-8	245	9-15-88	0	2	4.30	11	0	0	1	15	15	8	7	1	4	13	.254	.233	.276	7.98	2.45
2-team total (1 R. Cucamonga)					1	0	4.02	12	0	0	1	16	16	8	7	1	5	14	—	—	—	8.04	2.87
Holland, Sam	R-R	6-4	200	2-20-94	2	1	6.51	24	0	0	0	28	31	22	20	4	8	17	.284	.360	.220	5.53	2.60
Jester, Jason	R-R	5-10	185	5-4-91	3	2	3.57	38	0	0	6	45	51	19	18	1	10	52	.285	.259	.306	10.32	1.99
Johnson, Josh	L-R	6-7	250	1-31-84	0	0	—	1	1	0	0	0	1	0	0	0	0	0	1.000	1.000	—	—	—
Kelley, Shawn	R-R	6-2	220	4-26-84	0	0	0.00	1	1	0	0	1	0	0	0	0	1	2	.000	.000	.000	18.00	9.00
Kelly, Mike	R-R	6-4	185	9-6-92	0	6	8.40	6	5	0	0	30	45	33	28	5	9	22	.349	.400	.311	6.60	2.70
Kimber, Corey	R-R	6-1	175	6-28-94	0	0	9.00	1	0	0	0	2	3	2	2	0	2	1	.375	.400	.333	4.50	9.00
Lemond, Zech	R-R	6-1	170	10-9-92	5	10	5.54	32	22	0	0	130	175	92	80	12	44	101	.326	.343	.313	6.99	3.05
Livengood, Justin	R-R	6-3	220	3-2-90	1	0	6.75	3	3	0	0	13	23	18	10	1	4	11	.377	.259	.471	7.43	2.70
Lloyd, Kyle	R-R	6-4	221	10-16-90	7	11	4.72	31	20	0	0	137	139	85	72	10	41	139	.262	.241	.280	9.11	2.69
Luebke, Cory	R-L	6-4	205	3-4-85	0	0	3.00	3	3	0	0	3	1	1	1	0	0	1	.125	.200	.000	3.00	0.00
Montas, Ernesto	R-R	6-3	180	7-18-91	0	2	11.57	3	3	0	0	12	25	19	15	0	4	9	.431	.444	.419	6.94	3.09
Mutz, Nick	R-R	6-1	190	6-15-90	0	0	7.71	7	0	0	0	7	13	6	6	1	5	6	.406	.357	.444	7.71	6.43
Nunn, Chris	L-L	6-5	200	10-5-90	3	0	6.75	40	0	0	1	48	59	40	36	4	36	43	.307	.284	.324	8.06	6.75
Portillo, Adys	R-R	6-3	235	12-20-91	0	1	11.25	5	0	0	0	4	3	9	5	0	10	2	.214	.000	.333	4.50	22.50
Radke, Travis	L-L	6-4	200	3-6-93	1	4	8.10	7	7	0	0	33	50	32	30	7	12	26	.362	.409	.340	7.02	3.24
Reyes, Genison	R-R	6-5	190	9-19-91	3	3	3.74	33	0	0	0	43	43	22	18	2	20	37	.264	.266	.262	7.68	4.15
Rogers, Blake	R-R	6-2	200	2-23-94	0	0	3.68	4	0	0	0	7	8	3	3	0	3	5	.286	.214	.357	6.14	3.68
Russell, Griffin	L-L	6-0	190	3-5-94	0	1	4.91	3	0	0	0	4	4	2	2	0	1	3	.286	.333	.273	7.36	2.45
Shepherd, Matt	R-R	6-3	185	5-2-90	4	11	5.90	34	20	0	2	116	168	106	76	12	46	99	.340	.376	.307	7.68	3.57
Tanner, Cecil	R-R	6-6	240	4-23-90	0	0	8.49	14	0	0	0	12	7	11	11	1	17	13	.175	.300	.050	10.03	13.11
Verbitsky, Bryan	R-R	5-11	205	6-11-92	1	2	4.18	21	0	0	1	28	30	17	13	2	11	33	.268	.435	.152	10.61	3.54
Weickel, Walker	R-R	6-6	195	11-14-93	1	0	4.38	8	1	0	0	12	16	9	6	1	6	10	.302	.263	.324	7.30	4.38
Wieck, Brad	L-L	6-9	255	10-14-91	2	6	5.21	11	11	0	0	57	61	37	33	6	26	53	.279	.286	.276	8.37	4.11
Yardley, Eric	R-R	6-0	165	8-18-90	2	4	2.72	47	0	0	16	60	66	20	18	2	14	49	.284	.330	.250	7.39	2.11

Fielding

Catcher	PCT	G	PO	A	E	DP	PB
Del Castillo	.978	32	259	46	7	4	3
Kral	.969	10	87	6	3	1	2
Miller	1.000	5	52	4	0	0	3
Miller	.989	53	393	57	5	3	8
Reina	.980	29	213	33	5	1	3
Rodriguez	.960	7	42	6	2	0	1
Valenzuela	1.000	5	41	6	0	1	0

First Base	PCT	G	PO	A	E	DP
Alonso	1.000	2	8	0	0	1
Chavez	.986	9	64	5	1	2
Davis	.982	104	829	78	17	81
Del Castillo	.889	2	7	1	1	1
Kral	1.000	1	6	2	0	1
Myers	1.000	1	6	1	0	1
Perez	1.000	1	2	0	0	0
Rosen	.978	10	86	3	2	6

	PCT	G	PO	A	E	DP
Valenzuela	1.000	16	149	14	0	9
Second Base	PCT	G	PO	A	E	DP
Blanco	.966	14	16	41	2	4
Brugeura	.913	10	15	27	4	5
Perez	.963	101	172	293	18	62
Stevens	.986	15	19	53	1	10
Valenzuela	.941	3	5	11	1	4

Third Base	PCT	G	PO	A	E	DP
Bravo	1.000	1	0	1	0	0
Brugeura	1.000	2	2	2	0	0
Jensen	.941	12	5	11	1	2
Quintana	.926	113	68	193	21	18
Stevens	.722	13	7	19	10	2
Valenzuela	1.000	2	2	6	0	2

Shortstop	PCT	G	PO	A	E	DP
Blanco	.978	25	34	56	2	11

	PCT	G	PO	A	E	DP
Bravo	.905	7	12	7	2	3
Brugeura	.941	6	15	17	2	4
Gonzalez	.917	2	5	6	1	1
Jensen	.931	39	58	90	11	16
Morales	1.000	2	5	4	0	1
Rondon	.962	53	76	154	9	33
Stevens	.963	13	25	27	2	7
Outfield	PCT	G	PO	A	E	DP
Baltz	1.000	16	33	2	0	0
Bousfield	.987	89	213	13	3	4
Gaedele	.982	29	51	4	1	0
Jensen	1.000	4	3	1	0	0
Myers	1.000	2	5	0	0	0
Rosen	.988	47	72	9	1	0
Schulz	.990	106	197	9	2	1
Tate	.960	87	185	7	8	1
Torres	.971	48	91	10	3	3

FORT WAYNE TINCAPS
MIDWEST LEAGUE

LOW CLASS A

Batting	B-T	HT	WT	DOB	AVG	vLH	vRH	G	AB	R	H	2B	3B	HR	RBI	BB	HBP	SH	SF	SO	SB	CS	SLG	OBP
Blanco, Felipe	R-R	6-1	175	12-9-93	.209	.267	.193	66	206	11	43	9	1	1	15	13	2	3	1	54	8	5	.277	.261
Brugeura, Reynaldo	B-R	5-10	195	11-5-91	.188	.143	.209	27	64	9	12	1	0	0	4	13	1	1	0	24	0	2	.203	.333
Charles, Henry	L-L	6-1	205	1-3-94	.194	.111	.227	32	93	8	18	6	1	0	9	7	3	2	0	18	2	2	.280	.272
Cordero, Franchy	L-R	6-3	175	9-2-94	.243	.222	.249	126	481	59	117	13	1	5	34	31	4	5	3	121	22	11	.306	.293
Del Castillo, Miguel	R-R	5-10	170	10-14-91	.293	.167	.313	27	92	9	27	4	0	0	9	6	0	0	2	24	1	0	.337	.330
Federowicz, Tim	R-R	5-10	215	8-5-87	.313	.667	.100	5	16	3	5	1	0	1	3	2	0	0	0	7	0	0	.563	.389
Gettys, Michael	R-R	6-1	203	10-22-95	.231	.259	.223	122	494	62	114	27	6	6	44	28	1	1	5	162	20	10	.346	.271
Giron, Ruddy	R-R	5-11	175	1-4-97	.285	.440	.248	96	386	58	110	12	4	9	49	29	1	1	2	68	15	14	.407	.335
Jensen, Chase	R-R	6-4	195	1-29-91	.197	.206	.194	40	127	10	25	8	0	2	17	4	1	0	0	32	3	3	.307	.227
Jones, Duanel	R-R	6-3	220	5-11-93	.327	.326	.327	41	153	22	50	11	0	7	36	15	0	0	2	36	1	1	.536	.382
Miller, Michael	R-R	6-2	200	5-27-92	.192	.063	.226	24	78	10	15	2	0	2	6	6	3	0	0	9	0	1	.295	.276
Morales, Mitch	L-R	5-10	165	3-3-93	.211	.250	.200	6	19	3	4	0	0	0	1	1	0	0	0	3	1	0	.211	.250
Moreno, Edwin	L-L	6-0	210	10-27-93	.308	.261	.322	89	302	41	93	15	8	4	31	14	2	5	0	68	13	10	.450	.343
Reyes, Franmil	R-R	6-5	240	7-7-95	.255	.270	.251	123	455	52	116	25	7	8	62	46	1	0	7	91	10	5	.393	.320
Ruiz, Jose	R-R	6-1	190	10-21-94	.214	.233	.208	90	299	32	64	8	1	0	24	20	4	3	4	61	2	3	.247	.269
Santos, Trae	L-L	6-1	235	10-11-92	.264	.188	.283	130	455	53	120	15	1	14	60	57	10	2	5	108	3	2	.435	.359
Tejada, Luis	R-R	6-3	175	10-12-92	.293	.302	.291	70	259	34	76	12	1	4	37	13	4	0	0	44	8	3	.394	.337
Torres, Nick	R-R	6-1	220	6-30-93	.326	.313	.330	77	288	45	94	29	2	2	40	18	9	0	5	52	4	1	.462	.378
Urias, Luis	R-R	5-9	160	6-3-97	.290	.311	.284	51	193	28	56	5	1	0	16	16	9	5	1	18	5	10	.326	.370

SAN DIEGO PADRES

Batting	B-T	HT	WT	DOB	AVG	vLH	vRH	G	AB	R	H	2B	3B	HR	RBI	BB	HBP	SH	SF	SO	SB	CS	SLG	OBP
VanMeter, Josh	L-R	5-11	165	3-10-95	.250	.077	.277	25	96	13	24	4	0	0	3	13	0	0	0	12	1	1	.292	.339
Vilter, Nick	R-R	6-4	220	10-6-93	.155	.095	.180	24	71	6	11	2	1	0	8	7	6	1	1	18	0	0	.211	.282

Pitching	B-T	HT	WT	DOB	W	L	ERA	G	GS	CG	SV	IP	H	R	ER	HR	BB	SO	AVG	vLH	vRH	K/9	BB/9
Aikenhead, Taylor	L-L	6-0	175	3-31-92	1	1	7.63	4	2	0	0	15	20	15	13	0	12	11	.328	.286	.340	6.46	7.04
Baskette, Payton	L-L	6-1	175	10-1-93	1	1	5.40	11	0	0	0	18	18	16	11	2	12	12	.247	.318	.216	5.89	5.89
Blueberg, Colby	R-R	6-0	185	5-11-93	4	1	1.07	41	0	0	21	59	33	8	7	0	15	62	.163	.138	.179	9.51	2.30
Brasoban, Yimmi	R-R	6-1	185	6-22-94	5	3	2.26	41	3	0	10	72	52	23	18	5	25	80	.199	.245	.168	10.05	3.14
Castillo, Jose	L-L	6-4	200	1-10-96	1	1	4.00	6	6	0	0	27	25	14	12	2	16	16	.255	.192	.278	5.33	5.33
Cox, Taylor	L-L	6-3	210	7-2-93	1	3	3.64	28	5	0	0	59	60	27	24	3	34	26	.282	.308	.273	3.94	5.16
Cressley, Aaron	L-R	6-1	175	9-2-92	1	2	4.21	21	0	0	1	36	41	22	17	4	18	23	.289	.309	.276	5.70	4.46
Dorminy, Thomas	L-L	6-0	190	6-1-92	11	7	2.94	25	25	0	0	141	125	54	46	5	48	108	.238	.220	.244	6.89	3.06
Fry, Brandon	L-L	6-3	195	3-28-93	1	2	7.40	15	0	0	1	24	31	22	20	1	10	16	.310	.333	.297	5.92	3.70
Huffman, Chris	R-R	6-1	205	11-25-92	9	6	3.28	22	18	0	0	107	108	50	39	6	23	58	.263	.248	.271	4.88	1.93
Kelich, Pete	R-R	6-2	195	2-16-91	3	2	2.32	6	6	0	0	31	28	9	8	3	6	15	.250	.208	.281	4.35	1.74
Kelly, Mike	R-R	6-4	185	9-6-92	5	3	4.46	13	13	0	0	67	68	39	33	5	22	35	.271	.256	.286	4.73	2.97
Lamet, Dinelson	R-R	6-4	187	7-18-92	5	8	2.99	26	24	0	0	105	82	42	35	9	44	120	.214	.282	.153	10.25	3.76
Lockett, Walker	R-R	6-5	225	5-3-94	0	3	7.98	4	4	0	0	15	20	15	13	2	4	10	.308	.379	.250	6.14	2.45
Lucio, Seth	R-R	5-10	180	4-30-93	4	2	3.19	30	0	0	0	42	36	18	15	0	18	43	.222	.158	.257	9.14	3.83
McGrath, Kyle	L-L	6-2	185	7-31-92	3	0	1.70	41	0	0	3	69	56	15	13	3	8	79	.219	.202	.227	10.35	1.05
Monroe, Nick	R-R	6-4	235	3-6-94	1	0	2.33	11	0	0	0	19	18	8	5	1	5	16	.240	.323	.182	7.45	2.33
Montas, Ernesto	R-R	6-3	180	7-18-91	12	7	3.50	24	24	0	0	131	151	61	51	6	24	62	.291	.276	.301	4.26	1.65
Radke, Travis	L-L	6-4	200	3-6-93	1	1	3.94	3	3	0	0	16	19	9	7	0	4	13	.302	.316	.295	7.31	2.25
Russell, Griffin	L-L	6-0	190	3-5-94	1	2	3.55	5	0	0	0	13	15	6	5	0	6	9	.306	.200	.333	6.39	4.26
Santos, Wilson	R-R	6-2	200	10-20-91	0	2	5.01	17	0	0	0	23	21	18	13	4	19	18	.250	.344	.192	6.94	7.33
Verbitsky, Bryan	R-R	5-11	205	6-11-92	0	0	3.00	25	0	0	3	36	29	17	12	1	17	38	.216	.200	.226	9.50	4.25
Weir, T.J.	R-R	6-0	205	9-15-91	5	4	4.15	37	3	0	2	74	70	41	34	4	24	84	.247	.300	.219	10.26	2.93
Wieck, Brad	L-L	6-9	255	10-14-91	2	0	2.61	2	2	0	0	10	8	3	3	0	3	12	.205	.250	.174	10.45	2.61

Fielding

Catcher	PCT	G	PO	A	E	DP	PB
Del Castillo	.975	27	174	19	5	0	3
Federowicz	1.000	2	9	0	0	0	0
Miller	.989	23	160	13	2	0	0
Ruiz	.979	90	639	112	16	9	17

First Base	PCT	G	PO	A	E	DP
Jones	1.000	7	51	5	0	4
Reyes	1.000	2	1	0	0	0
Santos	.986	126	1047	72	16	92
Tejada	.971	8	65	3	2	10
Vilter	.889	2	7	1	1	1

Second Base	PCT	G	PO	A	E	DP
Blanco	.959	59	112	143	11	32
Brugeura	1.000	10	13	20	0	1
Jensen	1.000	15	28	43	0	7

	PCT	G	PO	A	E	DP
Morales	1.000	4	8	15	0	4
Urias	.978	38	72	106	4	24
VanMeter	.968	16	26	35	2	12
Vilter	.968	6	15	15	1	4

Third Base	PCT	G	PO	A	E	DP
Blanco	1.000	2	1	2	0	0
Brugeura	.923	8	7	17	2	0
Jensen	.978	19	18	26	1	2
Jones	.913	34	24	60	8	5
Morales	1.000	1	0	2	0	0
Tejada	.906	62	46	108	16	9
Urias	.905	5	2	17	2	0
Vilter	.977	17	15	28	1	3

Shortstop	PCT	G	PO	A	E	DP
Blanco	.857	5	3	9	2	1

	PCT	G	PO	A	E	DP
Brugeura	.909	5	9	21	3	3
Cordero	.818	23	32	58	20	12
Giron	.938	90	117	244	24	51
Jensen	.939	9	8	23	2	4
Morales	1.000	1	1	3	0	0
Urias	.933	7	11	17	2	5

Outfield	PCT	G	PO	A	E	DP
Charles	1.000	18	35	0	0	0
Cordero	.985	70	126	4	2	0
Gettys	.976	115	301	21	8	4
Moreno	.949	63	122	9	7	4
Reyes	.989	96	177	9	2	3
Tejada	1.000	1	1	0	0	0
Torres	1.000	57	91	4	0	0

TRI-CITY DUST DEVILS — SHORT-SEASON

NORTHWEST LEAGUE

Batting	B-T	HT	WT	DOB	AVG	vLH	vRH	G	AB	R	H	2B	3B	HR	RBI	BB	HBP	SH	SF	SO	SB	CS	SLG	OBP
Allen, Austin	L-R	6-4	225	1-16-94	.240	.235	.242	53	196	23	47	10	1	2	34	21	2	0	3	38	1	2	.332	.315
Belen, Carlos	R-R	6-1	213	2-28-96	.218	.215	.219	66	248	31	54	17	3	6	35	28	3	0	5	113	5	3	.383	.299
Boykin, Rod	R-R	6-1	175	4-17-95	.250	.173	.288	63	244	49	61	10	3	3	23	28	4	2	1	85	19	4	.352	.336
Bravo, Daniel	R-R	6-0	160	2-16-95	.262	.273	.258	12	42	5	11	3	0	0	2	0	0	0	0	11	1	2	.333	.262
Charles, Henry	L-L	6-1	205	1-3-94	.183	.250	.151	31	109	13	20	5	0	2	14	16	0	0	2	22	1	1	.284	.283
France, Ty	R-R	6-0	205	7-13-94	.294	.286	.298	66	235	36	69	20	0	1	36	43	12	0	2	50	4	2	.391	.425
Kennedy, A.J.	R-R	6-0	180	1-23-94	.276	.241	.293	24	87	12	24	6	0	0	16	7	2	2	2	16	0	1	.345	.337
Morales, Mitch	L-R	5-10	165	3-3-93	.248	.250	.248	38	141	17	35	7	0	0	12	12	0	0	0	40	1	3	.298	.307
Pacchioli, Justin	R-R	6-2	190	9-28-92	.245	.250	.243	58	204	41	50	2	1	1	14	40	7	0	1	46	19	6	.279	.385
Smith, Mason	R-R	6-2	195	3-16-95	.226	.204	.234	55	177	23	40	6	1	2	30	23	7	2	2	55	6	3	.305	.335
Tidwell, Kodie	L-R	6-1	195	8-3-94	.256	.269	.250	50	168	24	43	8	0	1	17	32	0	5	1	31	6	3	.321	.373
Urena, Jose	R-R	6-3	180	1-14-95	.258	.222	.275	63	225	43	58	13	0	7	45	47	3	0	2	59	8	2	.409	.390
Urias, Luis	R-R	5-9	160	6-3-97	.355	.353	.357	10	31	6	11	1	0	0	1	5	3	5	0	1	3	3	.387	.487
Valenzuela, Ricardo	R-R	6-0	190	8-4-90	.250	—	.250	3	8	1	2	1	0	0	4	2	0	0	1	2	0	0	.375	.364
Van Gansen, Peter	L-R	5-9	175	3-4-94	.267	.216	.291	67	270	45	72	9	4	2	30	34	2	3	1	40	6	1	.352	.352
Vilter, Nick	R-R	6-4	220	10-6-93	.234	.265	.219	44	145	21	34	11	0	1	19	19	11	1	1	49	3	1	.331	.356

Pitching	B-T	HT	WT	DOB	W	L	ERA	G	GS	CG	SV	IP	H	R	ER	HR	BB	SO	AVG	vLH	vRH	K/9	BB/9
Castillo, Jose	L-L	6-4	200	1-10-96	3	1	3.61	13	12	0	0	52	54	26	21	1	16	35	.269	.344	.254	6.02	2.75
Constanza, Alex	L-L	6-3	190	7-27-94	0	1	12.71	5	2	0	0	6	6	9	8	0	8	2	.286	.400	.250	3.18	12.71
Cox, Taylor	L-L	6-3	210	7-2-93	1	0	0.00	4	0	0	0	4	2	0	0	0	1	7	.143	.250	.100	15.75	2.25
Cressley, Aaron	L-R	6-1	175	9-2-92	0	0	0.00	4	0	0	0	5	1	0	0	0	0	4	.063	.000	.077	7.20	0.00
De Horta, Adrian	R-R	6-3	185	3-13-95	2	1	3.26	8	8	0	0	39	25	14	14	3	20	36	.182	.167	.195	8.38	4.66
Distasio, Lou	R-R	6-4	195	2-5-94	1	1	3.90	19	0	0	0	28	28	14	12	2	12	35	.269	.256	.279	11.39	3.90

SAN DIEGO PADRES

Pitching

Pitching	B-T	HT	WT	DOB	W	L	ERA	G	GS	CG	SV	IP	H	R	ER	HR	BB	SO	AVG	vLH	vRH	K/9	BB/9
Foriest, Nathan	R-L	6-2	190	1-28-92	0	0	0.00	4	0	0	1	6	2	0	0	0	2	6	.100	.000	.133	9.00	3.00
Fry, Brandon	L-L	6-3	195	3-28-93	0	3	3.65	8	1	0	0	12	11	6	5	2	8	13	.234	.222	.237	9.49	5.84
Headean, Will	R-L	6-4	195	10-11-93	1	0	0.00	1	0	0	0	3	2	0	0	0	0	5	.222	.333	.167	16.88	0.00
Hernandez, Luis	R-R	6-2	190	6-22-92	1	5	4.36	19	0	0	2	33	26	16	16	1	12	26	.218	.244	.203	7.09	3.27
Holland, Sam	R-R	6-4	200	2-20-94	2	1	1.59	22	0	0	1	28	14	6	5	2	5	30	.149	.194	.121	9.53	1.59
Keel, Jerry	L-L	6-6	240	9-26-93	3	1	3.00	19	0	0	0	33	34	16	11	1	8	28	.268	.160	.294	7.64	2.18
Kennedy, Brett	R-R	6-0	200	8-4-94	0	2	2.70	12	9	0	0	30	18	10	9	0	11	38	.173	.182	.167	11.40	3.30
Kimber, Corey	R-R	6-1	175	6-28-94	2	2	3.65	20	0	0	4	25	21	17	10	1	12	25	.239	.171	.283	9.12	4.38
Linares, Joel	R-R	6-1	175	12-8-94	0	2	7.02	4	4	0	0	17	15	13	13	3	11	16	.231	.333	.171	8.64	5.94
Liriano, Elvin	L-L	6-3	190	10-17-92	4	1	2.23	21	0	0	0	36	24	10	9	2	16	54	.183	.222	.173	13.38	3.96
Lockett, Walker	R-R	6-5	225	5-3-94	3	0	2.83	11	11	0	0	57	50	28	18	3	10	47	.230	.217	.239	7.38	1.57
Maton, Phil	R-R	6-3	205	3-25-93	4	2	1.38	23	0	0	6	33	23	6	5	0	5	58	.192	.180	.200	15.98	1.38
Megill, Trevor	L-R	6-8	235	12-5-93	2	0	2.70	10	0	0	1	20	14	6	6	4	8	27	.187	.100	.244	12.15	3.60
Mejia, Angel	R-R	6-0	160	2-10-95	6	3	4.95	15	15	1	0	67	85	46	37	7	21	50	.307	.313	.303	6.68	2.81
Morrow, Bryce	R-R	6-2	200	1-2-88	0	0	5.00	2	2	0	0	9	10	6	5	1	3	5	.278	.059	.474	5.00	3.00
Radke, Travis	L-L	6-4	200	3-6-93	2	2	3.41	6	6	0	0	29	36	11	11	2	1	30	.298	.118	.327	9.31	0.31
Ramirez, Emmanuel	R-R	6-2	190	7-15-94	2	1	3.00	5	5	0	0	24	20	9	8	1	8	25	.217	.200	.226	9.38	3.00
Russell, Griffin	L-L	6-0	190	3-5-94	2	2	3.86	14	1	0	0	26	24	13	11	1	9	28	.253	.087	.306	9.83	3.16
Santos, Wilson	R-R	6-2	200	10-20-91	1	0	2.63	18	0	0	2	27	27	8	8	0	8	20	.255	.209	.286	6.59	2.63
Tanner, Cecil	R-R	6-6	240	4-23-90	0	2	10.13	7	0	0	0	8	6	9	9	0	8	14	.194	.214	.176	15.75	9.00
Wingenter, Trey	R-R	6-7	190	4-15-94	0	1	12.00	5	0	0	0	9	14	12	12	0	4	11	.350	.222	.387	11.00	4.00

Fielding

Catcher	PCT	G	PO	A	E	DP	PB
Allen	.989	51	427	44	5	2	3
Kennedy	.986	24	198	12	3	2	7
Valenzuela	1.000	3	21	3	0	0	0

First Base	PCT	G	PO	A	E	DP
France	.993	63	528	33	4	49
Vilter	1.000	14	120	3	0	7

Second Base	PCT	G	PO	A	E	DP
Bravo	.974	9	16	21	1	5
Morales	.969	29	45	80	4	25
Tidwell	.963	33	54	100	6	14

	PCT	G	PO	A	E	DP
Urias	.964	6	5	22	1	2
Vilter	.000	1	0	0	1	0

Third Base	PCT	G	PO	A	E	DP
Belen	.859	56	25	103	21	11
France	1.000	1	1	2	0	0
Tidwell	—	1	0	0	0	0
Urias	1.000	1	0	2	0	0
Vilter	.950	19	11	27	2	4

Shortstop	PCT	G	PO	A	E	DP
Bravo	1.000	1	1	2	0	0
Morales	.889	3	3	5	1	1

	PCT	G	PO	A	E	DP
Tidwell	1.000	7	5	17	0	2
Urias	1.000	1	1	0	0	1
Van Gansen	.980	65	70	170	5	37

Outfield	PCT	G	PO	A	E	DP
Boykin	.987	63	151	3	2	0
Charles	.939	26	30	1	2	0
Pacchioli	.981	49	101	2	2	0
Smith	.972	49	65	5	2	2
Urena	1.000	47	84	2	0	1

AZL PADRES   ROOKIE

ARIZONA LEAGUE

Batting	B-T	HT	WT	DOB	AVG	vLH	vRH	G	AB	R	H	2B	3B	HR	RBI	BB	HBP	SH	SF	SO	SB	CS	SLG	OBP
Aragon, Bryant	L-R	6-2	160	4-10-98	.224	.250	.220	17	58	8	13	3	2	0	9	3	2	0	1	22	0	1	.345	.281
Bravo, Daniel	R-R	6-0	160	2-16-95	.296	.290	.299	29	108	12	32	6	2	0	11	5	3	4	0	23	5	4	.389	.345
Burgos, Aldemar	R-R	6-0	165	1-23-97	.225	.323	.203	42	169	18	38	4	3	0	9	12	2	1	0	53	4	6	.284	.284
Contreras, Ronaldo	R-R	5-11	195	7-15-96	.206	.133	.218	29	102	10	21	3	0	1	5	3	1	0	0	35	2	2	.265	.236
De La Cruz, Wilfri	R-R	5-11	180	12-29-93	.215	.154	.231	19	65	9	14	1	0	0	8	7	0	0	1	17	0	0	.231	.288
Garcia, Alan	L-L	6-0	220	1-31-97	.264	.174	.289	30	106	15	28	7	0	0	13	9	2	0	3	32	0	1	.330	.325
Gonzalez, Benji	R-R	5-11	160	1-16-90	.538	—	.538	4	13	6	7	2	1	0	1	2	0	0	0	1	0	1	.846	.600
Goris, Diego	R-R	5-10	200	11-8-90	.250	1.000	.000	1	4	1	1	0	0	0	3	0	0	0	0	2	0	0	.250	.250
Kral, Robert	L-R	5-10	195	3-28-89	.250	—	.250	1	4	0	1	0	0	0	0	1	0	0	0	2	0	0	.250	.400
Lantigua, Jonas	L-R	6-5	205	12-15-94	.264	.217	.276	31	110	9	29	6	0	2	15	8	0	0	0	32	2	2	.373	.314
Magdaleno, Westhers	R-R	6-1	190	10-30-96	.216	.313	.194	26	88	8	19	2	0	0	9	8	3	1	0	30	2	2	.239	.303
Magee, Josh	R-R	5-10	180	2-13-97	.203	.167	.211	49	172	24	35	4	0	0	11	18	8	1	1	57	14	5	.227	.307
Minaya, Euri	R-R	6-4	205	10-11-95	.500	—	.500	2	8	3	4	2	0	0	1	0	1	0	0	2	1	0	.750	.556
Moore, Tyler	R-R	5-8	165	5-28-93	.216	.212	.216	43	167	13	36	4	2	0	11	14	3	0	2	35	15	7	.263	.285
Overstreet, Kyle	R-R	5-11	205	9-4-93	.202	.071	.242	35	119	15	24	3	1	1	9	18	1	1	2	27	0	2	.269	.307
Pena, Jhonatan	R-R	6-2	180	4-18-94	.304	.348	.292	32	112	13	34	6	2	4	15	8	1	0	0	28	4	5	.500	.355
Risedorf, Zach	R-R	5-11	190	3-11-96	.105	.400	.061	14	38	4	4	0	0	1	3	9	0	0	0	15	1	0	.184	.277
Rodriguez, Ricardo	R-R	5-10	175	12-20-97	.222	—	.222	2	9	3	2	1	0	0	1	0	0	0	0	2	0	0	.333	.300
Rosen, Yale	L-L	6-2	215	5-9-93	.313	.000	.333	9	32	10	10	4	0	3	8	7	0	0	0	8	1	0	.719	.436
Savinon, Jose	L-R	6-0	160	2-17-96	.241	.048	.303	25	87	9	21	1	1	0	6	7	0	1	1	28	4	3	.276	.295
Sosa, Carlos	R-R	6-1	190	8-7-95	.195	.233	.184	40	133	8	26	6	1	1	13	10	3	0	0	42	2	1	.278	.267
Stevens, River	L-R	6-0	185	1-10-92	.333	—	.333	1	3	0	1	0	0	0	0	1	0	0	0	1	0	0	.333	.500
Tidwell, Kodie	L-R	6-1	195	8-3-94	.341	.333	.343	11	41	7	14	2	1	0	2	5	0	0	0	9	1	0	.439	.413
VanMeter, Josh	L-R	5-11	165	3-10-95	.727	1.000	.667	3	11	3	8	2	1	0	0	0	0	0	0	1	0	1	1.091	.727
Zunica, Brad	L-R	6-6	254	10-21-95	.271	.179	.297	35	129	21	35	8	0	7	24	10	1	0	0	40	0	1	.496	.329

Pitching	B-T	HT	WT	DOB	W	L	ERA	G	GS	CG	SV	IP	H	R	ER	HR	BB	SO	AVG	vLH	vRH	K/9	BB/9
Ashbeck, Elliott	L-R	6-3	215	11-16-93	2	0	3.51	16	0	0	4	26	26	12	10	3	4	22	.252	.385	.172	7.71	1.40
Butler, Ryan	R-R	6-4	225	2-23-92	0	0	0.00	1	0	0	0	1	0	0	0	0	0	2	.250	.000	.333	18.00	0.00
Church, Joe	R-R	6-2	190	9-29-89	0	0	0.00	1	0	0	0	1	0	0	0	0	0	1	.000	.000	.000	9.00	0.00
De Horta, Adrian	R-R	6-3	185	3-13-95	0	2	8.83	7	2	0	0	17	23	20	17	0	10	17	.324	.346	.311	8.83	5.19
Diaz, Adonis	R-R	6-1	185	12-8-94	2	1	4.12	9	0	0	0	19	19	9	9	0	3	15	.253	.231	.265	6.86	1.37
Foriest, Nathan	R-L	6-2	190	1-28-92	2	0	1.10	12	0	0	3	16	10	3	2	1	2	16	.175	.077	.205	8.82	1.10
Garcia, Jean	R-R	6-5	220	12-7-96	1	6	7.04	11	6	0	0	47	70	52	37	2	24	30	.327	.271	.364	5.70	4.56
Gonzalez, Manuel	R-R	6-4	195	10-21-94	0	4	9.51	10	6	0	0	29	41	35	31	1	16	27	.336	.381	.313	8.28	4.91

Pitching	B-T	HT	WT	DOB	W	L	ERA	G	GS	CG	SV	IP	H	R	ER	HR	BB	SO	AVG	vLH	vRH	K/9	BB/9
Guerrero, Jordan	R-R	6-5	260	8-1-96	3	1	4.23	13	3	0	1	28	31	14	13	1	13	27	.274	.368	.227	8.78	4.23
Hale, Corey	L-L	6-7	255	2-18-92	0	0	0.00	6	0	0	0	6	0	0	0	0	4	12	.000	.000	.000	17.05	5.68
Headean, Will	R-L	6-4	195	10-11-93	0	0	3.12	14	1	0	0	26	28	9	9	0	7	34	.267	.217	.280	11.77	2.42
Kelich, Pete	R-R	6-2	195	2-16-91	0	0	1.64	5	3	0	0	11	9	2	2	0	2	10	.231	.313	.174	8.18	1.64
Lebron, Jaimito	R-R	6-2	175	10-20-96	0	0	6.00	1	0	0	0	6	4	5	4	0	2	3	.200	.167	.214	4.50	3.00
Linares, Joel	R-R	6-1	175	12-8-94	3	3	4.03	9	8	0	0	45	43	23	20	2	17	36	.253	.260	.247	7.25	3.43
Lockett, Walker	R-R	6-5	225	5-3-94	1	1	5.40	3	2	0	0	15	19	10	9	2	6	13	.317	.429	.256	7.80	3.60
Lorenzini, Braxton	R-R	6-4	172	4-5-95	0	1	5.21	12	0	0	1	19	22	11	11	0	13	15	.293	.406	.209	7.11	6.16
Megill, Trevor	L-R	6-8	235	12-5-93	0	0	3.97	7	0	0	0	11	13	6	5	1	3	16	.289	.333	.259	12.71	2.38
Monroe, Nick	R-R	6-4	235	3-6-94	1	0	0.00	8	0	0	1	11	6	2	0	0	1	18	.146	.200	.129	14.29	0.79
Morris, Elliot	R-R	6-4	210	4-26-92	0	0	0.00	1	0	0	0	1	0	0	0	0	0	0	.000	.000	.000	0.00	0.00
Nix, Jacob	R-R	6-3	200	1-9-96	0	2	5.49	7	3	0	0	20	23	16	12	1	7	19	.284	.194	.340	8.69	3.20
Perez, Mayky	R-R	6-5	235	9-26-96	0	0	0.00	2	0	0	0	2	0	0	0	0	1	0	.000	.000	.000	0.00	4.50
Portillo, Adys	R-R	6-3	235	12-20-91	0	1	0.00	1	1	0	0	1	0	1	0	0	2	0	.000	.000	.000	18.00	18.00
Ramirez, Emmanuel	R-R	6-2	190	7-15-94	4	2	1.51	8	6	0	0	42	29	21	7	2	7	37	.185	.255	.155	7.99	1.51
Rogers, Blake	R-R	6-2	200	2-23-94	1	1	2.53	14	0	0	6	21	18	8	6	0	3	22	.209	.207	.211	9.28	1.27
Santos, Wilson	R-R	6-2	200	10-20-91	1	0	3.00	3	0	0	0	3	3	2	1	0	2	5	.231	.600	.000	15.00	6.00
Smith, Austin	R-R	6-4	220	7-9-96	0	3	7.94	9	9	0	0	17	27	16	15	0	9	11	.375	.400	.362	5.82	4.76
Tanner, Cecil	R-R	6-6	240	4-23-90	0	0	4.50	2	0	0	0	2	0	1	1	0	4	2	.000	.000		9.00	18.00
Wingenter, Trey	R-R	6-7	190	4-15-94	1	1	2.79	6	0	0	0	10	10	7	3	0	3	5	.250	.333	.200	4.66	2.79
Ynfante, Starling	R-R	6-2	200	2-23-94	1	4	7.30	12	5	0	0	37	50	33	30	2	15	37	.321	.424	.258	9.00	3.65

Fielding

Catcher	PCT	G	PO	A	E	DP	PB
Aragon	.909	2	8	2	1	0	0
De La Cruz	.966	19	155	18	6	0	2
Overstreet	.995	24	173	23	1	0	3
Risedorf	.981	13	86	20	2	0	8
Rodriguez	.909	2	16	4	2	0	3

First Base	PCT	G	PO	A	E	DP
Lantigua	.966	27	240	18	9	17
Overstreet	.985	9	59	8	1	5
Rosen	1.000	3	24	1	0	0
Zunica	.974	20	182	9	5	14

Second Base	PCT	G	PO	A	E	DP
Bravo	.750	1	0	3	1	0

	PCT	G	PO	A	E	DP
Moore	.951	40	75	118	10	16
Savinon	.902	15	21	16	4	3
VanMeter	1.000	2	1	2	0	0

Third Base	PCT	G	PO	A	E	DP
Magdaleno	.857	10	7	11	3	0
Overstreet	.900	3	1	8	1	1
Savinon	.833	3	1	4	1	0
Sosa	.898	39	22	75	11	2
Tidwell	.857	5	2	10	2	0

Shortstop	PCT	G	PO	A	E	DP
Bravo	.955	28	49	98	7	18
Gonzalez	1.000	2	1	2	0	0
Goris	.667	1	1	1	1	0

	PCT	G	PO	A	E	DP
Magdaleno	.829	17	16	52	14	4
Savinon	.882	4	4	11	2	0
Tidwell	.923	8	9	15	2	2

Outfield	PCT	G	PO	A	E	DP
Burgos	.978	42	87	0	2	0
Contreras	.900	13	14	4	2	0
Garcia	.925	30	46	3	4	2
Gonzalez	1.000	1	1	1	0	0
Magee	.934	48	80	5	6	1
Minaya	1.000	2	9	0	0	0
Moore	1.000	3	5	2	0	0
Pena	.952	28	39	1	2	1
Rosen	.857	5	6	0	1	0
Savinon	.800	3	4	0	1	0

DSL PADRES ROOKIE

DOMINICAN SUMMER LEAGUE

Batting	B-T	HT	WT	DOB	AVG	vLH	vRH	G	AB	R	H	2B	3B	HR	RBI	BB	HBP	SH	SF	SO	SB	CS	SLG	OBP
Arias, Enmanuel	R-R	6-1	215	12-16-94	.201	.160	.217	56	179	25	36	7	0	6	24	19	10	0	3	77	0	3	.341	.308
Asuncion, Luis	R-R	6-4	205	2-27-97	.236	.266	.224	54	216	25	51	10	3	4	31	20	6	0	2	72	1	1	.366	.316
Burgos, Edward	L-L	6-2	175	8-24-96	.444	.250	.600	2	9	0	4	0	0	0	0	0	0	0	0	1	1	1	.444	.444
De La Cruz, Wilfri	R-R	5-11	180	12-29-95	.259	.133	.302	20	58	9	15	6	0	0	9	4	4	0	1	11	0	0	.362	.343
Garcia, Jaffe	R-R	6-1	175	3-13-96	.229	.135	.266	45	131	26	30	4	2	1	10	45	5	1	0	59	6	5	.313	.442
Guzman, Luis	R-R	6-2	175	6-20-98	.144	.182	.130	41	125	20	18	2	0	0	12	34	1	2	0	58	10	4	.160	.331
Lezama, Jose	L-R	5-10	195	2-19-98	.325	.386	.293	38	126	14	41	7	0	0	23	32	2	2	1	17	0	1	.381	.466
Molina, Leudy	L-L	6-0	160	11-20-94	.268	.206	.295	36	112	11	30	4	0	1	13	12	1	0	0	43	1	3	.330	.344
Olmo, Dayon	B-R	5-11	165	11-15-96	.245	.191	.270	38	147	36	36	5	3	1	16	27	4	2	0	37	18	6	.340	.376
Ortega, Ariel	R-R	5-10	150	6-20-97	.304	.308	.303	29	102	22	31	2	1	1	8	8	4	6	0	16	4	4	.373	.377
Perez, Aurelio	R-R	6-1	185	4-11-94	.234	.125	.271	25	64	6	15	3	0	0	6	13	4	0	0	23	8	4	.281	.395
Rodriguez, Ricardo	R-R	5-10	175	12-20-97	.270	.250	.275	28	100	15	27	5	0	2	14	8	3	0	1	11	1	0	.380	.339
Sabala, Elvis	R-R	6-1	178	9-26-97	.123	.087	.138	48	155	28	19	2	1	0	8	26	9	1	2	80	12	3	.148	.281
Sanchez, Jonelqui	B-R	5-11	160	7-10-98	.225	.308	.185	11	40	5	9	1	0	0	5	3	1	0	0	11	0	0	.250	.295
Santos, Angel	L-R	6-4	170	1-13-96	.254	.282	.242	44	134	20	34	2	2	0	11	19	2	5	0	40	18	4	.299	.355
Sotillo, Jose	R-R	6-1	175	5-13-96	.301	.241	.319	35	123	18	37	3	1	1	11	10	4	2	2	39	10	5	.366	.367
Suarez, Felix	R-R	6-0	180	1-1-96	.239	.150	.258	31	113	21	27	7	1	0	11	12	5	3	1	26	7	5	.319	.336
Taveras, Carlos	B-R	5-11	165	4-17-97	.171	.244	.143	46	146	16	25	8	1	0	14	34	4	5	0	55	13	3	.240	.342
Ugueto, Luis	R-R	6-1	180	8-5-96	.166	.191	.156	52	175	25	29	1	1	1	27	36	3	0	0	48	13	5	.200	.318
Vizcaino, Manuel	R-R	6-0	165	1-8-96	.194	.147	.210	43	139	18	27	5	2	2	18	18	7	0	2	45	5	7	.302	.313

Pitching	B-T	HT	WT	DOB	W	L	ERA	G	GS	CG	SV	IP	H	R	ER	HR	BB	SO	AVG	vLH	vRH	K/9	BB/9
Arias, Juan	R-R	6-2	175	5-6-95	5	2	3.35	21	0	0	5	40	37	22	15	0	14	37	.236	.238	.235	8.26	3.12
Beltran, Pedro	R-R	6-4	185	1-19-98	0	5	6.32	14	4	0	0	31	37	36	22	0	34	17	.308	.300	.313	4.88	9.57
Clase, Emmanuel	R-R	6-2	150	3-18-98	2	1	1.99	13	10	0	0	54	53	31	12	1	21	49	.252	.237	.256	8.12	3.48
Cooper, Elby	L-L	6-3	175	5-11-96	1	0	3.00	8	0	0	0	9	7	7	3	1	13	10	.212	.600	.143	10.00	13.00
Cordero, Starlin	R-R	6-7	200	7-21-98	3	2	4.94	15	4	0	0	31	24	24	17	0	28	32	.209	.444	.136	9.29	8.13
Cordova, Eisler	L-L	5-11	180	7-11-95	1	7	6.99	15	7	0	0	48	56	48	37	4	28	47	.295	.263	.303	8.87	5.29
De Los Santos, Erick	R-R	6-4	200	4-23-94	3	1	7.67	23	0	0	1	32	38	28	27	3	25	34	.292	.205	.337	9.66	7.11
Diaz, Adonis	R-R	6-1	185	12-8-94	1	2	3.92	9	0	0	1	21	24	14	9	1	10	19	.289	.300	.283	8.27	4.35
Garcia, Jean	R-R	6-5	220	12-7-96	0	1	5.54	3	3	0	0	13	18	11	8	1	3	7	.346	.462	.308	4.85	2.08
Garcia, Joel	L-R	6-2	180	8-7-92	4	3	2.53	19	2	0	1	43	31	23	12	2	33	44	.200	.161	.210		6.96

Pitching

Pitching	B-T	HT	WT	DOB	W	L	ERA	G	GS	CG	SV	IP	H	R	ER	HR	BB	SO	AVG	vLH	vRH	K/9	BB/9
Gonzalez, Manuel	R-R	6-4	195	10-21-94	1	0	1.50	3	3	0	0	12	15	7	2	0	8	18	.294	.231	.316	13.50	6.00
Guzman, Jonathan	R-R	5-10	180	2-8-95	2	3	3.68	19	0	0	0	37	31	32	15	2	26	30	.225	.286	.191	7.36	6.38
Guzman, Oliber	R-R	5-11	180	3-15-97	0	0	0.00	1	0	0	0	2	1	0	0	0	0	1	.167	.250	.000	4.50	0.00
Lebron, Jaimito	R-R	6-2	175	10-20-96	0	1	6.43	6	4	0	0	7	9	5	5	0	2	3	.290	.091	.400	3.86	2.57
Linares, Joel	R-R	6-1	175	12-8-94	1	1	3.46	3	3	0	0	13	10	5	5	2	6	16	.196	.190	.200	11.08	4.15
Lopez, Dari	R-R	6-3	170	5-10-96	0	0	2.97	12	5	0	0	33	32	16	11	1	6	38	.246	.250	.245	10.26	1.62
Lopez, Diomar	R-R	6-0	165	12-15-96	1	1	2.18	11	0	0	1	21	11	5	5	3	4	17	.157	.154	.159	7.40	1.74
Machuca, Cristian	L-L	6-1	165	4-24-97	2	2	4.74	13	7	0	0	49	59	35	26	4	15	41	.295	.343	.285	7.48	2.74
Martinez, Adrian	R-R	6-2	195	12-10-96	0	0	4.41	7	2	0	0	16	19	9	8	0	2	19	.279	.263	.300	10.47	1.10
Perez, Luis	R-R	6-0	175	5-3-95	2	1	2.33	19	0	0	4	27	28	11	7	0	15	21	.269	.133	.324	7.00	5.00
Ramirez, Emmanuel	R-R	6-2	190	7-15-94	0	0	4.91	2	2	0	0	7	6	4	4	0	5	9	.231	.111	.294	11.05	6.14
Ramos, Jordis	L-L	6-10	194	6-15-96	0	2	8.31	8	5	0	0	17	29	24	16	0	20	11	.367	.250	.397	5.71	10.38
Reyes, Ramon	L-L	6-3	170	11-23-95	0	0	0.00	1	0	0	0	1	0	0	0	0	1	1	.000	—	.000	9.00	9.00
Rivera, Carlos	R-R	6-3	190	6-8-95	0	0	3.86	4	0	0	0	7	5	3	3	0	3	9	.200	.286	.167	11.57	3.86
Solano, Eduardo	L-L	6-3	203	5-22-97	0	4	6.18	17	9	0	0	39	41	39	27	2	40	31	.266	.111	.299	7.09	9.15
Torres, Wilmer	R-R	6-3	190	5-31-96	1	0	0.66	5	2	0	0	14	6	1	1	0	4	11	.133	.118	.143	7.24	2.63
Ynfante, Starling	R-R	6-2	200	2-23-94	1	1	0.84	3	0	0	1	11	6	3	1	1	6	18	.154	.000	.207	15.19	5.06

Fielding

Catcher	PCT	G	PO	A	E	DP	PB
De La Cruz	.978	13	117	17	3	1	3
Lezama	.958	38	255	39	13	1	10
Molina	.980	6	41	8	1	1	2
Rodriguez	.972	25	186	21	6	1	8

First Base	PCT	G	PO	A	E	DP
Arias	.973	48	367	26	11	21
De La Cruz	.966	6	25	3	1	2
Molina	.977	23	158	12	4	12
Suarez	1.000	7	53	2	0	7
Vizcaino	1.000	6	36	1	0	1

Second Base	PCT	G	PO	A	E	DP
Ortega	.966	25	52	60	4	11
Sabala	.947	11	15	21	2	2

	PCT	G	PO	A	E	DP
Sanchez	.885	11	19	27	6	9
Sotillo	1.000	1	2	3	0	0
Suarez	.971	7	14	19	1	2
Ugueto	.962	20	41	59	4	5
Vizcaino	1.000	1	1	1	0	0

Third Base	PCT	G	PO	A	E	DP
Molina	1.000	1	0	3	0	0
Sabala	.861	12	9	22	5	0
Suarez	.860	14	13	36	8	3
Ugueto	.913	20	19	44	6	5
Vizcaino	.802	29	20	57	19	3

Shortstop	PCT	G	PO	A	E	DP
Guzman	.892	41	73	133	25	15
Sabala	.857	24	21	57	13	5

	PCT	G	PO	A	E	DP
Ugueto	.926	9	15	35	4	4

Outfield	PCT	G	PO	A	E	DP
Asuncion	.946	35	48	5	3	1
Burgos	.833	2	5	0	1	0
Garcia	.982	35	47	9	1	1
Olmo	.896	33	54	6	7	2
Ortega	—		1	0	0	0
Perez	.909	16	17	3	2	0
Santos	.938	35	55	5	4	2
Sotillo	.945	30	51	1	3	1
Taveras	.934	41	69	2	5	0

San Francisco Giants

SEASON IN A SENTENCE: It was an odd-numbered year, so predictably the defending-champion Giants took a step back, playing right around .500 baseball for all but one month of a season.

HIGH POINT: A four-game sweep of the Nationals in mid-August brought San Francisco to within two and a half games of the Dodgers. San Francisco hung around for the next week, giving enough hope to make it worthwhile to make a couple of minor trades to try to make a playoff push.

LOW POINT: After getting so close to the Dodgers, San Francisco was swept by Los Angeles at the start of September as part of a seven-game losing streak that effectively ended the Giants' playoff hopes. The offense was the issue as San Francisco was held to one run or less in four of those seven losses.

NOTABLE ROOKIES: Matt Duffy was a revelation as Pablo Sandoval's replacement at third base. The former second baseman/shortstop hit .295/.334/.428 while playing excellent defense. Second baseman Kelby Tomlinson filled in when Joe Panik got hurt and hit .303/.358/.404, better than he'd hit almost anywhere in his minor league career. Righthander Chris Heston threw a no-hitter in a June win over the Mets, striking out a career-high 11 in the process. He faded down the stretch, but was a valuable addition to the Giants' rotation. Lefthander Josh Osich provided solid relief work in a limited role (2-0, 2.20 in 29 IP). Catcher Andrew Susac battled a wrist injury that hindered his hitting (.218/.297/.368) and eventually forced him onto the 60-day disabled list.

KEY TRANSACTIONS: The Giants promoted longtime GM Brian Sabean to executive VP of baseball operations, promoting Bobby Evans to GM. They added righthander Mike Leake from the Reds just before the July 31 trade deadline and kept trying to plug holes in the lineup before the deadline, adding outfielders Marlon Byrd (from the Reds for righty Stephen Johnson) and Alejandro de Aza (from the Red Sox for lefty Luis Ysla).

DOWN ON THE FARM: Shortstop Christian Arroyo, a 2013 first-round pick, rebounded from a poor 2014 season to hit .304/.344/.459 for high Class A San Jose. San Jose made it to the California League championship series before falling to Rancho Cucamonga. Outfielder Johneshwy Fargas hit .278/.347/.349 with 59 stolen bases for low Class A Augusta. Righthander Samuel Coonrod went 7-4, 3.14 for that same Augusta club.

OPENING DAY PAYROLL: $172,672,111 (5th)

PLAYERS OF THE YEAR

MAJOR LEAGUE
Buster Posey
c
.318/.379/.470
19 HR, 95 RBIs
56 BB, 52 SO

MINOR LEAGUE
Chase Johnson
rhp
(High A/Double-A)
9-4, 2.82
129 SO in 125 IP

ORGANIZATION LEADERS

BATTING		*Minimum 250 AB
MAJORS		
* AVG	Buster Posey	.318
* OPS	Buster Posey	.849
HR	Brandon Crawford	21
RBI	Buster Posey	95
MINORS		
* AVG	Ryan Lollis, San Jose, Richmond, Sacramento	.340
*OBP	Ryan Lollis, San Jose, Richmond, Sacramento	.402
* SLG	Adam Duvall, Sacramento	.547
R	Mac Williamson, Richmond, Sacramento	76
H	Ryan Lollis, San Jose, Richmond, Sacramento	139
TB	Jarrett Parker, Sacramento	223
2B	Hunter Cole, Augusta, San Jose, Richmond	33
3B	Hunter Cole, Augusta, San Jose, Richmond	9
HR	Adam Duvall, Sacramento	26
RBI	Adam Duvall, Sacramento	80
BB	Jarrett Parker, Sacramento	62
SO	Jarrett Parker, Sacramento	164
SB	Johneshwy Fargas, Augusta	59

PITCHING		#Minimum 75 IP
MAJORS		
W	Madison Bumgarner	18
# ERA	Madison Bumgarner	2.93
SO	Madison Bumgarner	234
SV	Santiago Casilla	38
MINORS		
W	Ty Blach, Sacramento	11
L	Ty Blach, Sacramento	12
# ERA	Mark Reyes, Augusta	2.13
G	Ian Gardeck, San Jose	61
GS	Ty Blach, Sacramento	27
SV	Josh Osich, Richmond, Sacramento	21
IP	Ty Blach, Sacramento	165
BB	Kyle Crick, Richmond	66
SO	Chase Johnson, San Jose, Richmond	129
AVG	Mark Reyes	.222

2015 PERFORMANCE

General Manager: Brian Sabean/Bobby Evans. **Farm Director:** Shane Turner. **Scouting Director:** John Barr.

Class	Team	League	W	L	PCT	Finish	Manager
Majors	San Francisco Giants	National	84	78	.519	6th (15)	Bruce Bochy
Triple-A	Sacramento River Cats	Pacific Coast	71	73	.493	9th (16)	Bob Mariano
Double-A	Richmond Flying Squirrels	Eastern	72	68	.514	5th (12)	Jose Alguacil
High A	San Jose Giants	California	72	68	.514	6th (10)	Russ Morman
Low A	Augusta GreenJackets	South Atlantic	65	73	.471	10th (14)	Nestor Rojas
Short season	Salem-Keizer Volcanoes	Northwest	39	37	.513	4th (8)	Kyle Haines
Rookie	Giants	Arizona	31	25	.554	3rd (14)	Henry Cotto
Overall 2015 Minor League Record			350	344	.504	t-15th (30)	

ORGANIZATION STATISTICS

SAN FRANCISCO GIANTS

NATIONAL LEAGUE

Batting	B-T	HT	WT	DOB	AVG	vLH	vRH	G	AB	R	H	2B	3B	HR	RBI	BB	HBP	SH	SF	SO	SB	CS	SLG	OBP
Adrianza, Ehire	B-R	6-1	170	8-21-89	.186	.176	.190	52	113	11	21	7	1	0	11	15	4	2	0	20	3	2	.265	.303
Aoki, Nori	L-R	5-9	180	1-5-82	.287	.333	.270	93	355	42	102	12	3	5	26	30	6	1	0	25	14	5	.380	.353
Arias, Joaquin	R-R	6-1	165	9-21-84	.207	.250	.136	40	58	5	12	1	0	1	4	0	0	1	0	12	1	0	.276	.207
Belt, Brandon	L-L	6-5	220	4-20-88	.280	.264	.287	137	492	73	138	33	5	18	68	56	4	0	4	147	9	3	.478	.356
Blanco, Gregor	L-L	5-11	175	12-24-83	.291	.282	.293	115	327	59	95	19	3	5	26	40	2	0	3	59	13	5	.413	.368
Brown, Trevor	R-R	6-2	195	11-15-91	.231	.083	.296	13	39	1	9	3	0	0	5	3	0	0	1	8	1	1	.308	.279
Byrd, Marlon	R-R	6-0	245	8-30-77	.272	.255	.280	39	147	12	40	12	2	4	31	6	1	0	2	44	0	0	.463	.301
2-team total (96 Cincinnati)					.247	—	—	135	506	58	125	25	5	23	73	29	4	0	5	145	2	1	.453	.290
Crawford, Brandon	L-R	6-2	215	1-21-87	.256	.259	.255	143	507	65	130	33	4	21	84	39	11	0	4	119	6	4	.462	.321
De Aza, Alejandro	L-L	6-0	195	4-11-84	.262	.286	.259	24	61	12	16	4	1	0	3	12	1	0	1	14	2	2	.361	.387
Duffy, Matt	R-R	6-2	170	1-15-91	.295	.252	.310	149	573	77	169	28	6	12	77	30	5	2	2	96	12	0	.428	.334
Frandsen, Kevin	R-R	6-0	190	5-24-82	.182	.333	.000	7	11	1	2	0	0	0	0	1	0	1	0	3	0	0	.182	.250
Ishikawa, Travis	L-L	6-3	220	9-24-83	.000	—	.000	6	5	1	0	0	0	0	1	0	0	0	0	3	0	0	.000	.167
2-team total (38 Pittsburgh)					.206	—	—	44	63	6	13	3	0	1	8	9	0	0	0	20	0	0	.302	.306
Lollis, Ryan	L-L	6-2	185	12-16-86	.167	.500	.100	5	12	0	2	0	0	0	0	1	0	0	0	1	1	0	.167	.231
Maxwell, Justin	R-R	6-5	225	11-6-83	.209	.221	.202	100	249	26	52	8	2	7	26	20	3	1	1	76	2	1	.341	.275
McGehee, Casey	R-R	6-1	220	10-12-82	.213	.200	.216	49	127	7	27	5	0	2	11	11	0	0	0	28	0	1	.299	.275
2-team total (60 Miami)					.198	—	—	109	237	14	47	12	0	2	20	21	0	0	0	50	1	1	.274	.264
Noonan, Nick	L-R	6-1	175	5-4-89	.091	.000	.111	14	22	2	2	1	0	1	3	2	0	0	0	8	0	0	.273	.167
Pagan, Angel	B-R	6-2	200	7-2-81	.262	.318	.239	133	512	55	134	21	3	3	37	32	1	0	6	93	12	4	.332	.303
Panik, Joe	L-R	6-1	190	10-30-90	.312	.291	.318	100	382	59	119	27	2	8	37	38	5	3	4	42	3	2	.455	.378
Parker, Jarrett	L-L	6-4	210	1-1-89	.347	.462	.306	21	49	11	17	2	0	6	14	5	0	0	0	21	1	1	.755	.407
Pence, Hunter	R-R	6-4	220	4-13-83	.275	.200	.293	52	207	30	57	13	1	9	40	16	0	0	0	48	4	1	.478	.327
Perez, Juan	R-R	5-11	185	11-13-86	.282	.292	.267	22	39	5	11	3	0	0	2	1	0	0	0	6	1	0	.359	.300
Posey, Buster	R-R	6-1	215	3-27-87	.318	.314	.319	150	557	74	177	28	0	19	95	56	3	0	7	52	2	0	.470	.379
Sanchez, Hector	B-R	6-0	235	11-17-89	.179	.176	.179	28	56	5	10	4	0	1	5	2	0	1	0	14	0	0	.304	.207
Susac, Andrew	R-R	6-1	215	3-22-90	.218	.298	.174	52	133	14	29	7	2	3	14	14	1	0	0	43	0	0	.368	.297
Tomlinson, Kelby	R-R	6-3	180	6-16-90	.303	.371	.267	54	178	23	54	6	3	2	20	14	1	0	0	40	5	4	.404	.358
Williams, Jackson	R-R	5-11	200	5-14-86	.200	.000	.286	7	10	1	2	1	0	0	1	4	0	0	0	1	1	0	.300	.429
Williamson, Mac	R-R	6-5	240	7-15-90	.219	.125	.313	10	32	2	7	0	1	0	1	0	1	0	1	8	0	0	.281	.235

Pitching	B-T	HT	WT	DOB	W	L	ERA	G	GS	CG	SV	IP	H	R	ER	HR	BB	SO	AVG	vLH	vRH	K/9	BB/9
Affeldt, Jeremy	L-L	6-4	225	6-6-79	2	2	5.86	52	0	0	0	35	43	24	23	6	14	21	.293	.284	.300	5.35	3.57
Bochy, Brett	R-R	6-2	200	2-27-87	0	0	0.00	4	0	0	0	3	1	0	0	0	1	3	.100	.000	.167	9.00	3.00
Broadway, Mike	R-R	6-5	215	3-30-87	0	2	5.19	21	0	0	0	17	20	10	10	1	7	13	.294	.364	.229	6.75	3.63
Bumgarner, Madison	R-L	6-5	235	8-1-89	18	9	2.93	32	32	4	0	218	181	73	71	21	39	234	.222	.206	.226	9.65	1.61
Cain, Matt	R-R	6-3	230	10-1-84	2	4	5.79	13	11	0	0	61	71	39	39	12	20	41	.293	.313	.276	6.08	2.97
Casilla, Santiago	R-R	6-0	210	7-25-80	4	2	2.79	67	0	0	38	58	51	19	18	6	23	62	.236	.262	.212	9.62	3.57
Gearrin, Cory	R-R	6-3	215	4-14-86	0	0	4.91	7	0	0	0	4	1	2	2	0	1	5	.083	.000	.100	12.27	2.45
Hall, Cody	R-R	6-4	220	1-6-88	0	0	6.48	7	0	0	0	8	10	6	6	1	7	6	.303	.357	.227	7.56	4.32
Heston, Chris	R-R	6-3	195	4-10-88	12	11	3.95	31	31	2	0	178	169	82	78	16	64	141	.253	.270	.238	7.14	3.24
Hudson, Tim	R-R	6-1	175	7-14-75	8	9	4.44	24	22	0	0	124	134	62	61	13	37	64	.282	.322	.251	4.66	2.69
Kontos, George	R-R	6-3	215	6-12-85	4	4	2.33	73	0	0	0	73	57	20	19	9	12	44	.213	.227	.205	5.40	1.47
Leake, Mike	R-R	5-10	190	11-12-87	2	5	4.07	9	9	1	0	55	51	25	25	8	15	29	.249	.258	.235	4.72	2.44
2-team total (21 Cincinnati)					11	10	3.70	30	30	2	0	192	174	80	79	22	49	119	—	—	—	5.58	2.30
Lincecum, Tim	L-R	5-11	170	6-15-84	7	4	4.13	15	15	0	0	76	75	37	35	7	38	60	.260	.209	.307	7.07	4.48
Lopez, Javier	L-L	6-4	220	7-11-77	1	0	1.60	77	0	0	0	39	19	8	7	1	16	26	.141	.124	.155	5.95	3.66
Machi, Jean	R-R	6-0	255	2-1-82	1	0	5.14	33	0	0	0	35	38	21	20	3	14	22	.271	.120	.356	5.66	3.60
Osich, Josh	L-L	6-2	230	9-3-88	2	0	2.20	35	0	0	0	29	24	12	7	4	8	27	.218	.222	.213	8.48	2.51
Peavy, Jake	R-R	6-1	195	5-31-81	8	6	3.58	19	19	0	0	111	99	45	44	12	25	78	.239	.207	.271	6.34	2.03
Petit, Yusmeiro	R-R	6-1	250	11-22-84	1	1	3.67	42	1	0	1	76	75	32	31	11	15	59	.256	.276	.241	6.99	1.78
Romo, Sergio	R-R	5-11	185	3-4-83	0	5	2.98	70	0	0	2	57	51	20	19	3	10	71	.235	.371	.170	11.15	1.57
Strickland, Hunter	R-R	6-4	220	9-24-88	3	3	2.45	55	0	0	0	51	34	14	14	4	10	50	.190	.185	.193	8.77	1.75
Vogelsong, Ryan	R-R	6-4	215	7-22-77	9	11	4.67	33	22	0	0	135	140	76	70	17	58	108	.265	.283	.251	7.20	3.87

Fielding

Catcher	PCT	G	PO	A	E	DP	PB
Brown	.988	13	77	7	1	0	0
Posey	.998	106	771	67	2	4	4
Sanchez	1.000	16	69	6	0	1	2
Susac	.984	40	222	18	4	3	3
Williams	1.000	7	21	4	0	0	1

First Base	PCT	G	PO	A	E	DP
Adrianza	1.000	1	5	0	0	0
Arias	1.000	2	13	0	0	3
Belt	.997	120	1060	71	3	91
Duffy	—	1	0	0	0	0
Frandsen	1.000	4	24	2	0	0
McGehee	1.000	1	4	0	0	0
Noonan	1.000	3	24	1	0	2
Posey	1.000	42	334	19	0	35

Second Base	PCT	G	PO	A	E	DP
Adrianza	.972	20	27	42	2	11
Arias	1.000	2	3	3	0	0
Duffy	.968	9	13	17	1	5
Panik	.996	99	191	268	2	64
Perez	—	1	0	0	0	0
Tomlinson	.981	50	82	130	4	30

Third Base	PCT	G	PO	A	E	DP
Adrianza	1.000	1	1	2	0	0
Arias	1.000	8	2	5	0	1
Duffy	.965	134	78	250	12	20
McGehee	.938	32	17	58	5	6

Shortstop	PCT	G	PO	A	E	DP
Adrianza	.987	20	24	54	1	13
Arias	.882	8	4	26	4	2
Crawford	.979	140	191	427	13	89

	PCT	G	PO	A	E	DP
Duffy	.800	3	0	4	1	1
Noonan	.909	5	4	6	1	1
Tomlinson	—	1	0	0	0	0

Outfield	PCT	G	PO	A	E	DP
Aoki	1.000	87	136	4	0	0
Belt	.889	14	16	0	2	0
Blanco	.984	93	183	1	3	0
Byrd	1.000	37	68	2	0	0
De Aza	.971	17	33	0	1	0
Ishikawa	1.000	1	0	0	0	0
Lollis	1.000	4	4	0	0	0
Maxwell	.985	79	130	3	2	1
Pagan	.985	124	258	2	4	2
Parker	1.000	15	19	0	0	0
Pence	.977	51	122	4	3	2
Perez	1.000	12	13	1	0	0
Williamson	1.000	7	16	0	0	0

SACRAMENTO RIVER CATS
PACIFIC COAST LEAGUE

TRIPLE-A

Batting	B-T	HT	WT	DOB	AVG	vLH	vRH	G	AB	R	H	2B	3B	HR	RBI	BB	HBP	SH	SF	SO	SB	CS	SLG	OBP
Adrianza, Ehire	B-R	6-1	171	8-21-89	.316	.303	.324	44	171	16	54	6	1	3	15	17	2	5	0	37	6	1	.415	.384
Arias, Joaquin	R-R	6-1	165	9-21-84	.275	.200	.300	10	40	4	11	6	0	3	1	0	0	0	7	0	0	.425	.293
Avery, Xavier	L-L	6-0	190	1-1-90	.244	.167	.273	13	45	6	11	1	1	0	1	7	0	1	0	14	0	1	.311	.346
Bowker, John	L-L	6-1	205	7-8-83	.263	.229	.281	43	137	10	36	6	0	3	12	8	1	0	2	27	1	0	.372	.304
Brown, Trevor	R-R	6-2	195	11-15-91	.261	.287	.250	82	283	35	74	17	0	2	27	21	4	4	2	53	1	0	.343	.319
Cabrera, Everth	B-R	5-10	190	11-17-86	.231	.133	.269	27	108	14	25	3	0	0	7	9	1	1	0	16	7	2	.259	.297
Cedeno, Ronny	R-R	6-0	195	2-2-83	.261	.250	.267	61	207	19	54	16	0	2	21	12	2	7	1	35	2	0	.367	.306
Ciriaco, Juan	R-R	6-0	160	8-15-83	.223	.217	.227	37	112	10	25	5	0	2	9	1	0	1	0	21	5	1	.321	.230
Duvall, Adam	R-R	6-1	205	9-4-88	.281	.264	.289	100	402	60	113	25	2	26	80	25	4	0	6	91	4	1	.547	.325
Ford, Darren	R-R	5-9	190	10-1-85	.261	.266	.257	110	380	54	99	13	4	11	33	39	3	2	1	78	33	16	.403	.333
Frandsen, Kevin	R-R	6-0	190	5-24-82	.272	.330	.251	86	323	38	88	15	1	4	41	18	13	3	2	19	5	2	.362	.334
2-team total (26 Reno)					.280	—	—	112	404	46	113	17	1	4	48	24	13	4	3	27	5	3	.356	.338
Hicks, Brandon	R-R	6-2	215	9-14-85	.220	.190	.232	45	141	13	31	7	1	2	20	16	2	0	0	53	0	0	.326	.308
Ishikawa, Travis	L-L	6-3	220	9-24-83	.271	.306	.250	34	133	17	36	8	0	4	19	13	2	0	1	41	0	0	.421	.342
Jackson, Brett	L-R	6-2	220	8-2-88	.220	.241	.210	51	159	22	35	7	0	3	16	26	0	1	3	51	6	1	.321	.324
Kobernus, Jeff	R-R	6-2	190	6-30-88	.200	—	.200	6	10	1	2	0	0	0	2	1	0	0	1	2	1	0	.200	.250
Lollis, Ryan	L-L	6-2	185	12-16-86	.330	.350	.322	72	279	42	92	22	2	4	29	25	2	2	4	37	6	4	.466	.384
McGehee, Casey	R-R	6-1	220	10-12-82	.357	.308	.379	10	42	7	15	3	0	2	7	3	0	0	1	5	0	0	.571	.391
Nelson, Mark	R-R	6-2	200	3-9-91	.000	—	.000	4	5	1	0	0	0	0	1	0	1	0	0	1	0	0	.000	.286
Noonan, Nick	L-R	6-1	175	5-4-89	.266	.136	.333	19	64	6	17	1	0	2	10	5	0	0	1	15	1	0	.375	.314
Parker, Jarrett	L-L	6-4	210	1-1-89	.283	.255	.296	124	434	74	123	26	3	23	74	62	4	0	4	164	20	7	.514	.375
Pence, Hunter	R-R	6-4	220	4-13-83	.294	.500	.182	5	17	6	5	0	0	2	5	2	0	0	1	4	0	0	.647	.350
Perez, Juan	R-R	5-11	185	11-13-86	.265	.303	.243	83	321	41	85	24	3	7	37	17	2	4	0	62	17	2	.424	.306
Quiroz, Guillermo	R-R	6-1	215	11-29-81	.247	.242	.250	27	89	5	22	4	0	0	7	1	0	2	13	0	0	.292	.303
Sanchez, Hector	B-R	6-0	235	11-17-89	.273	.327	.244	37	139	18	38	6	0	4	14	9	1	1	2	25	0	0	.403	.318
Stromsmoe, Skyler	B-R	5-10	175	3-30-84	.233	.318	.233	26	65	11	17	4	0	0	5	9	2	0	0	7	1	2	.323	.368
Susac, Andrew	R-R	6-1	215	3-22-90	.321	.429	.286	8	28	6	9	3	0	1	2	3	1	0	0	10	0	0	.536	.406
Tomlinson, Kelby	R-R	6-3	180	6-16-90	.316	.333	.309	33	136	21	43	1	1	2	15	7	2	2	2	22	5	3	.382	.354
Triunfel, Carlos	R-R	5-11	195	2-27-90	.264	.193	.302	95	314	32	83	17	5	5	33	8	3	2	2	59	3	3	.398	.287
Turner, Ben	R-R	6-5	220	4-27-90	.293	.355	.262	31	92	9	27	4	0	0	10	10	0	0	1	13	0	0	.337	.359
Williamson, Mac	R-R	6-5	240	7-15-90	.249	.259	.244	54	189	35	47	12	0	8	31	26	11	0	1	55	1	0	.439	.370

Pitching	B-T	HT	WT	DOB	W	L	ERA	G	GS	CG	SV	IP	H	R	ER	HR	BB	SO	AVG	vLH	vRH	K/9	BB/9
Affeldt, Jeremy	L-L	6-4	225	6-6-79	0	0	0.00	2	0	0	0	3	0	0	0	0	1	2	.000	.000	.000	6.00	3.00
Blach, Ty	L-L	6-2	200	10-20-90	11	12	4.46	27	27	2	0	165	189	92	82	16	31	93	.290	.321	.280	5.06	1.69
Blackburn, Clayton	L-R	6-3	230	1-6-93	10	4	2.85	23	20	0	0	123	127	46	39	6	32	99	.269	.245	.287	7.24	2.34
Bochy, Brett	R-R	6-2	200	8-27-87	6	1	2.95	43	0	0	0	58	52	27	19	3	22	43	.239	.239	.238	6.67	3.41
Broadway, Mike	R-R	6-5	215	3-30-87	2	0	0.93	40	0	0	13	48	25	6	5	0	8	64	.153	.149	.157	11.92	1.49
Cain, Matt	R-R	6-3	230	10-1-84	1	1	3.38	5	3	0	0	20	18	8	7	2	4	22	.231	.244	.216	10.07	1.83
Coello, Robert	R-R	6-5	250	11-23-84	6	3	3.50	11	11	0	0	64	58	29	25	4	28	49	.243	.315	.156	6.85	3.92
2-team total (6 Round Rock)					7	6	4.18	17	16	0	0	95	91	48	44	8	41	62	—	—	—	5.89	3.90
Cordier, Erik	R-R	6-4	215	2-25-86	2	1	1.04	31	0	0	9	35	20	9	4	0	25	43	.168	.163	.171	11.16	6.49
2-team total (4 New Orleans)					2	1	1.35	35	0	0	9	40	27	12	6	0	26	50	—	—	—	11.25	5.85
Correia, Kevin	R-R	6-3	200	8-24-80	0	1	3.58	6	6	0	0	38	34	18	15	4	11	25	.248	.234	.260	5.97	2.63
Dunning, Jake	R-R	6-4	190	8-12-88	4	2	6.85	13	7	0	0	46	67	42	35	9	21	35	.337	.357	.322	6.85	4.11
Fleet, Austin	R-R	6-2	200	4-17-87	2	3	6.75	7	7	0	0	32	40	26	24	4	11	20	.308	.326	.298	5.63	3.09
Gearrin, Cory	R-R	6-3	215	4-14-86	2	2	2.72	33	0	0	0	43	38	15	13	4	14	46	.230	.333	.151	9.63	2.93
Gutierrez, Juan	R-R	6-3	245	7-14-83	0	1	4.39	14	1	0	1	27	34	13	13	1	9	23	.312	.313	.311	7.76	3.04
Hall, Cody	R-R	6-4	220	1-6-88	1	3	3.46	43	0	0	3	68	67	30	26	3	26	55	.257	.265	.252	7.32	3.46
Hanson, Tommy	R-R	6-6	220	8-28-86	3	5	5.60	11	11	0	0	53	63	39	33	9	26	40	.297	.291	.302	6.79	4.42
Lara, Braulio	L-L	6-1	180	12-20-88	0	5	7.71	12	5	0	1	28	45	27	24	2	10	29	.363	.158	.400	9.32	3.21
Machi, Jean	R-R	6-0	255	2-1-82	1	0	0.00	4	0	0	0	5	3	0	0	0	1	6	.176	.125	.222	10.80	1.80

Pitching	B-T	HT	WT	DOB	W	L	ERA	G	GS	CG	SV	IP	H	R	ER	HR	BB	SO	AVG	vLH	vRH	K/9	BB/9
Okert, Steven	L-L	6-3	210	7-9-91	5	3	3.82	52	0	0	3	61	62	32	26	7	29	69	.265	.228	.284	10.13	4.26
Osich, Josh	L-L	6-2	230	9-3-88	0	0	0.00	6	0	0	2	7	3	1	0	0	2	11	.120	.167	.105	14.14	2.57
Partch, Curtis	R-R	6-5	240	2-13-87	1	3	3.53	48	1	0	1	64	60	30	25	3	26	81	.249	.233	.261	11.45	3.68
Peavy, Jake	R-R	6-1	195	5-31-81	0	3	6.12	6	6	0	0	32	39	22	22	5	9	28	.295	.288	.301	7.79	2.51
Rapada, Clay	R-L	6-5	195	3-9-81	1	3	2.84	46	0	0	0	44	47	19	14	3	15	32	.264	.140	.313	6.50	3.05
Snodgrass, Jack	L-L	6-6	210	12-16-87	1	2	4.84	8	2	0	0	22	24	13	12	4	12	20	.270	.286	.265	8.06	4.84
Stratton, Chris	R-R	6-3	190	8-22-90	4	5	3.86	17	17	1	0	98	88	46	42	6	40	72	.242	.281	.205	6.61	3.67
Strickland, Hunter	R-R	6-4	220	9-24-88	1	1	1.66	15	0	0	5	22	14	5	4	0	3	25	.187	.323	.091	10.38	1.25
Turley, Nik	L-L	6-4	195	9-11-89	7	8	4.56	19	19	0	0	103	93	64	52	15	48	85	.243	.152	.262	7.45	4.21

Fielding

Catcher	PCT	G	PO	A	E	DP	PB
Brown	.997	72	533	55	2	6	10
Quiroz	.991	26	203	11	2	1	5
Sanchez	.983	30	220	15	4	2	4
Susac	1.000	7	48	4	0	0	1
Turner	.993	19	125	8	1	0	2

First Base	PCT	G	PO	A	E	DP
Arias	1.000	2	10	1	0	4
Bowker	.992	32	230	21	2	20
Duvall	.983	45	326	19	6	36
Frandsen	.995	21	188	6	1	22
Ishikawa	.993	29	250	20	2	21
Lollis	1.000	23	165	9	0	12
Turner	1.000	7	29	2	0	4

Second Base	PCT	G	PO	A	E	DP
Adrianza	1.000	1	1	6	0	1
Arias	.909	2	1	9	1	1
Cabrera	.985	12	29	35	1	11
Cedeno	.991	29	45	71	1	21
Ciriaco	.907	14	20	19	4	5
Frandsen	.950	15	19	38	3	9
Hicks	.993	30	60	78	1	20
Kobernus	.944	6	9	8	1	2

Panik	1.000	3	4	6	0	2
Stromsmoe	.919	16	27	30	5	5
Tomlinson	.969	16	21	42	2	11
Triunfel	.990	24	35	63	1	9

Third Base	PCT	G	PO	A	E	DP
Arias	1.000	2	0	1	0	0
Ciriaco	.889	7	2	6	1	0
Duvall	.913	46	32	73	10	6
Frandsen	.933	51	26	71	7	7
Hicks	.914	11	7	25	3	5
McGehee	.864	10	5	14	3	4
Noonan	1.000	1	0	1	0	0
Perez	1.000	1	0	1	0	1
Tomlinson	1.000	4	2	10	0	1
Triunfel	.977	30	23	63	2	8

Shortstop	PCT	G	PO	A	E	DP
Adrianza	.977	43	63	110	4	16
Arias	1.000	1	5	4	0	2
Cabrera	.893	12	16	34	6	8
Cedeno	.952	24	31	68	5	18
Ciriaco	.977	10	16	26	1	5
Frandsen	—	1	0	0	0	0
Noonan	.984	17	20	43	1	11

Outfield	PCT	G	PO	A	E	DP
Stromsmoe	1.000	2	4	5	0	1
Tomlinson	.946	15	13	40	3	8
Triunfel	.954	30	38	66	5	17
Aoki	1.000	4	8	0	0	0
Avery	1.000	9	13	1	0	0
Blach	—	1	0	0	0	0
Cabrera	1.000	2	4	0	0	0
Ciriaco	1.000	3	4	1	0	0
Duvall	1.000	10	14	0	0	0
Ford	.971	100	231	2	7	1
Frandsen	1.000	1	1	0	0	0
Ishikawa	.917	5	10	1	1	1
Jackson	.988	39	83	0	1	0
Lollis	.984	48	123	2	2	0
Nelson	1.000	1	2	0	0	0
Pagan	1.000	3	5	0	0	0
Parker	.958	107	226	4	10	1
Pence	1.000	5	6	0	0	0
Perez	.945	72	148	7	9	1
Stromsmoe	—	1	0	0	0	0
Williamson	.967	46	86	1	3	0

RICHMOND FLYING SQUIRRELS

DOUBLE-A

EASTERN LEAGUE

Batting	B-T	HT	WT	DOB	AVG	vLH	vRH	G	AB	R	H	2B	3B	HR	RBI	BB	HBP	SH	SF	SO	SB	CS	SLG	OBP
Beltre, Engel	L-L	6-2	180	11-1-89	.251	.211	.268	86	299	33	75	8	3	5	26	9	2	5	0	42	4	8	.348	.277
Carbonell, Daniel	R-R	6-3	195	3-29-91	.146	.116	.153	56	206	18	30	3	2	1	12	4	3	0	1	53	9	1	.194	.173
Ciriaco, Juan	R-R	6-0	160	8-15-83	.246	.257	.242	45	130	11	32	9	0	0	13	5	1	2	1	21	7	1	.315	.277
Cole, Hunter	R-R	6-1	190	10-3-92	.292	.280	.296	51	192	23	56	16	4	3	21	14	0	1	1	46	1	1	.464	.338
Delfino, Mitch	R-R	6-2	210	1-13-91	.256	.275	.249	124	445	45	114	17	1	3	42	41	1	1	6	72	4	2	.319	.316
Galindo, Jesus	B-R	5-11	200	8-23-90	.214	.333	.169	45	98	13	21	3	0	0	3	7	1	1	0	20	5	3	.245	.274
Harris, Devin	R-R	6-3	225	4-23-88	.240	.263	.233	119	404	53	97	28	1	14	60	34	2	0	2	110	4	1	.418	.301
Herrera, Javier	R-R	5-11	225	4-9-85	.211	.179	.222	34	109	11	23	2	1	1	9	14	1	1	1	38	0	3	.275	.304
Lollis, Ryan	L-L	6-2	185	12-16-86	.471	.333	.500	7	17	3	8	1	0	0	0	1	0	0	0	1	0	0	.529	.500
Miller, Blake	R-R	6-3	195	4-25-90	.241	.200	.250	27	79	8	19	2	0	0	2	5	1	0	0	23	1	1	.266	.294
Moreno, Rando	R-R	5-11	200	6-6-92	.275	.250	.284	121	429	59	118	19	3	1	39	31	1	2	1	62	12	9	.340	.324
Oropesa, Ricky	L-R	6-3	225	12-15-89	.254	.220	.267	131	453	41	115	24	1	17	76	38	2	0	6	128	1	1	.424	.311
Schroder, Myles	R-R	5-11	180	8-1-87	.252	.227	.263	109	369	32	93	6	4	7	32	21	8	3	5	84	14	6	.347	.303
Slater, Austin	R-R	6-2	215	12-13-92	.296	.281	.304	54	199	21	59	11	1	0	13	14	3	1	1	48	1	1	.362	.350
Stromsmoe, Skyler	B-R	5-10	175	3-30-84	.364	—	.364	6	11	1	4	0	0	0	1	1	0	0	0	3	0	0	.364	.417
Tomlinson, Kelby	R-R	6-3	180	6-16-90	.324	.353	.317	64	253	43	82	18	3	1	28	25	5	3	3	37	16	6	.431	.387
Villalona, Angel	R-R	6-3	255	8-13-90	.143	.200	.130	28	56	3	8	2	0	0	6	3	0	0	2	17	0	0	.179	.180
Williams, Jackson	R-R	5-11	200	5-14-86	.228	.222	.230	83	276	26	63	9	1	1	18	29	5	1	1	50	1	2	.279	.312
Williamson, Mac	R-R	6-5	240	7-15-90	.293	.254	.306	69	259	41	76	16	2	5	42	25	5	0	1	53	3	1	.429	.366
Zambrano, Eliezer	B-R	5-11	195	9-16-86	.190	.078	.233	57	184	10	35	5	0	2	12	7	3	2	0	20	0	1	.250	.232

Pitching	B-T	HT	WT	DOB	W	L	ERA	G	GS	CG	SV	IP	H	R	ER	HR	BB	SO	AVG	vLH	vRH	K/9	BB/9
Beede, Tyler	R-R	6-4	200	5-23-93	3	8	5.23	13	13	0	0	72	62	45	42	4	35	49	.234	.205	.263	6.10	4.35
Biagini, Joe	R-R	6-4	215	5-29-90	10	7	2.42	23	22	0	0	130	112	45	35	5	34	84	.228	.196	.251	5.80	2.35
Casilla, Jose	R-R	6-1	205	5-21-89	4	5	1.44	47	0	0	3	56	54	17	9	0	18	32	.266	.318	.241	5.11	2.88
Crick, Kyle	L-R	6-4	220	11-30-92	3	4	3.29	36	11	0	0	63	47	26	23	2	66	73	.208	.239	.187	10.43	9.43
Diaz, Carlos	L-L	6-2	176	11-18-93	0	0	3.86	1	0	0	0	2	3	1	1	0	2	1	.333	1.000	.250	3.86	7.71
Gage, Matt	R-L	6-4	240	2-11-93	2	3	4.66	9	7	0	0	39	39	21	20	1	10	30	.262	.167	.292	6.98	2.33
Gregorio, Joan	R-R	6-7	180	1-12-92	3	2	3.09	37	9	0	1	79	64	31	27	6	32	72	.225	.212	.232	8.24	3.66
Johnson, Chase	R-R	6-3	185	1-9-92	1	1	5.93	3	3	0	0	14	16	9	9	0	8	18	.281	.296	.267	11.85	5.27
Johnson, Stephen	R-R	6-5	215	2-21-91	3	0	3.41	44	0	0	0	58	45	26	22	2	29	68	.214	.263	.187	10.55	4.50
Lara, Braulio	L-L	6-1	180	12-20-88	2	0	4.03	20	0	0	2	22	20	12	10	2	10	17	.235	.207	.250	6.85	4.03
Law, Derek	R-R	6-2	210	9-14-90	0	1	4.56	28	0	0	13	26	31	16	13	1	8	32	.292	.327	.263	11.22	2.81
Lujan, Matt	L-L	6-1	210	8-23-88	9	3	3.18	20	20	0	0	108	112	43	38	6	42	85	.273	.239	.285	7.36	3.51
Marte, Braulio	R-R	5-9	170	11-24-87	10	6	2.63	26	19	1	0	130	118	41	38	5	44	76	.240	.238	.249	5.33	2.77
McCormick, Phil	L-L	6-1	185	9-7-88	4	3	2.04	58	0	0	2	57	58	15	13	0	21	38	.272	.275	.270	5.97	3.30

Pitching	B-T	HT	WT	DOB	W	L	ERA	G	GS	CG	SV	IP	H	R	ER	HR	BB	SO	AVG	vLH	vRH	K/9	BB/9
Mejia, Adalberto	L-L	6-3	195	6-20-93	5	2	2.45	12	9	0	0	51	38	14	14	2	18	38	.204	.185	.212	6.66	3.16
Mizenko, Tyler	R-R	6-1	200	4-9-90	4	3	1.98	37	0	0	4	50	51	13	11	2	14	28	.274	.250	.287	5.04	2.52
Osich, Josh	L-L	6-2	230	9-3-88	0	1	1.59	31	0	0	19	34	23	6	6	1	10	34	.185	.156	.196	9.00	2.65
Quirarte, Edwin	R-R	6-2	185	12-20-86	0	3	3.68	23	6	0	0	59	59	25	24	3	16	51	.265	.245	.280	7.82	2.45
Rodriguez, Pedro	R-R	6-0	165	10-31-87	4	3	2.21	37	2	0	3	61	53	21	15	3	11	50	.233	.232	.235	7.38	1.62
Rogers, Tyler	R-R	6-5	187	12-17-90	0	1	5.91	10	0	0	0	11	10	7	7	1	5	15	.250	.375	.167	12.66	4.22
Snodgrass, Jack	L-L	6-6	210	12-16-87	4	3	4.14	9	9	0	0	50	46	24	23	2	20	27	.245	.265	.240	4.86	3.60
Stratton, Chris	R-R	6-3	190	8-22-90	1	5	4.14	9	9	0	0	50	40	26	23	3	22	39	.215	.242	.200	7.02	3.96

Fielding

Catcher	PCT	G	PO	A	E	DP	PB
Sonabend	1.000	1	9	0	0	0	0
Williams	.992	83	581	78	5	9	12
Zambrano	.993	57	359	44	3	5	4

First Base	PCT	G	PO	A	E	DP
Ciriaco	.989	9	86	4	1	6
Lollis	1.000	1	5	0	0	0
Miller	.917	5	32	1	3	1
Oropesa	.993	119	1093	62	8	101
Schroder	1.000	14	66	7	0	8
Villalona	1.000	9	47	3	0	5

Second Base	PCT	G	PO	A	E	DP
Ciriaco	.935	13	25	33	4	11
Miller	.986	15	36	36	1	10

	PCT	G	PO	A	E	DP
Schroder	.959	24	34	83	5	19
Slater	.982	54	107	173	5	38
Stromsmoe	.750	2	2	1	1	0
Tomlinson	.991	49	94	122	2	17

Third Base	PCT	G	PO	A	E	DP
Ciriaco	1.000	6	3	10	0	0
Delfino	.944	118	80	274	21	28
Miller	1.000	2	1	5	0	1
Schroder	.931	20	12	42	4	3
Stromsmoe	1.000	1	1	3	0	0

Shortstop	PCT	G	PO	A	E	DP
Ciriaco	.939	7	15	16	2	7
Miller	—	1	0	0	0	0
Moreno	.972	118	155	332	14	54

	PCT	G	PO	A	E
Schroder	—	1	0	0	0
Stromsmoe	1.000	1	0	3	0
Tomlinson	.960	25	30	66	4

Outfield	PCT	G	PO	A	E	DP
Beltre	.994	83	147	6	1	3
Carbonell	.958	54	89	2	4	0
Ciriaco	1.000	1	1	0	0	0
Cole	.975	40	72	5	2	2
Galindo	.976	31	39	1	1	1
Harris	.987	89	144	4	2	1
Herrera	.985	31	66	1	1	1
Lollis	1.000	5	8	0	0	0
Schroder	.988	55	72	7	1	2
Williamson	.983	55	109	4	2	1

SAN JOSE GIANTS

HIGH CLASS A

CALIFORNIA LEAGUE

Batting	B-T	HT	WT	DOB	AVG	vLH	vRH	G	AB	R	H	2B	3B	HR	RBI	BB	HBP	SH	SF	SO	SB	CS	SLG	OBP
Amion, Richard	R-R	5-10	190	2-24-93	.000	.000	.000	3	4	0	0	0	0	0	0	0	0	0	0	1	0	0	.000	.000
Arnold, Jeff	R-R	6-2	205	1-13-88	.250	.267	.245	21	68	7	17	7	1	0	7	10	3	1	0	24	0	0	.382	.370
Arroyo, Christian	R-R	6-1	180	5-30-95	.304	.215	.328	90	381	48	116	28	2	9	42	19	5	2	2	73	5	3	.459	.344
Bednar, Brandon	R-R	6-4	185	3-21-92	.237	.171	.258	100	346	39	82	18	2	3	34	15	5	5	2	54	3	4	.327	.277
Carbonell, Daniel	R-R	6-3	195	3-29-91	.279	.236	.291	66	258	35	72	14	2	6	27	13	7	1	3	51	9	7	.419	.327
Cole, Hunter	R-R	6-1	190	10-3-92	.313	.268	.329	54	217	28	68	11	5	6	37	19	4	1	4	42	4	3	.493	.373
Davis, Dylan	R-R	6-0	205	7-26-93	.206	.208	.205	29	107	18	22	3	0	3	11	14	0	0	1	28	0	1	.318	.295
Galindo, Jesus	B-R	5-11	200	8-23-90	.271	.319	.258	62	225	29	61	8	1	2	13	17	4	10	0	54	14	6	.342	.333
Garcia, Aramis	R-R	6-2	220	1-12-93	.227	.200	.233	20	75	10	17	4	0	0	5	9	0	0	0	22	1	0	.280	.310
Harrison, Seth	R-R	6-0	200	7-22-92	.212	.203	.214	92	345	42	73	17	2	4	33	20	7	5	1	103	13	11	.307	.268
Horan, Tyler	L-R	6-2	230	12-2-90	.215	.200	.220	94	344	43	74	20	1	13	35	47	2	0	3	96	5	5	.392	.311
Jones, Ryder	L-R	6-3	215	6-7-94	.268	.245	.276	105	406	49	109	29	2	6	47	16	3	0	7	80	2	2	.394	.296
Kobernus, Jeff	R-R	6-2	190	6-30-88	.231	.200	.238	56	221	24	51	7	0	1	13	18	1	3	3	41	12	3	.276	.288
Lollis, Ryan	L-L	6-2	185	12-16-86	.345	.364	.338	30	113	28	39	8	2	1	11	15	2	1	0	19	3	2	.478	.431
Metzger, Brennan	R-R	5-11	185	12-15-89	.241	.600	.167	11	29	5	7	1	0	1	2	4	3	0	0	4	2	1	.379	.389
Pare, Matt	L-R	6-0	205	11-17-90	.189	.000	.219	13	37	4	7	1	0	1	7	5	0	0	2	11	0	0	.297	.273
Perez, Juan	R-R	5-11	185	11-13-86	.192	.000	.217	6	26	2	5	2	0	0	3	1	0	0	1	4	0	0	.269	.214
Polonius, John	R-R	6-1	160	1-13-91	.204	.276	.186	49	142	17	29	3	2	3	13	7	2	2	3	35	5	1	.317	.248
Ragira, Brian	R-R	6-2	185	1-22-92	.251	.217	.261	110	391	44	98	23	1	10	58	33	7	1	2	108	0	2	.391	.319
Rodriguez, Rafael	R-R	6-5	200	7-13-92	.293	.308	.286	22	82	7	24	6	0	0	12	5	1	0	0	20	0	1	.366	.341
Ross, Ty	R-R	6-2	210	1-17-92	.244	.241	.244	82	271	19	66	15	0	3	26	24	1	3	4	65	0	0	.332	.303
Slater, Austin	R-R	6-2	215	12-13-92	.292	.227	.315	60	250	25	73	15	1	3	34	10	2	0	3	44	4	3	.396	.321
Stromsmoe, Skyler	B-R	5-10	175	3-30-84	.258	.533	.176	19	66	14	17	7	0	0	4	7	2	1	0	13	2	1	.364	.347
Susac, Andrew	R-R	6-1	215	3-22-90	.286	.667	.182	4	14	1	4	1	0	1	3	1	1	0	0	4	0	0	.571	.375
Turner, Ben	R-R	6-5	220	4-27-90	.267	.250	.272	50	180	25	48	6	0	2	20	12	3	0	4	26	0	0	.333	.317
Villalona, Angel	R-R	6-2	255	8-13-90	.249	.200	.261	68	257	29	64	12	0	13	48	28	6	0	2	64	0	0	.447	.334

Pitching	B-T	HT	WT	DOB	W	L	ERA	G	GS	CG	SV	IP	H	R	ER	HR	BB	SO	AVG	vLH	vRH	K/9	BB/9
Agosta, Martin	R-R	6-1	180	4-7-91	5	9	4.25	26	16	0	0	106	111	54	50	15	26	125	.269	.266	.270	10.61	2.21
Beede, Tyler	R-R	6-4	200	5-23-93	2	2	2.24	9	9	0	0	52	51	22	13	2	9	37	.254	.267	.235	6.36	1.55
Black, Ray	R-R	6-5	225	6-26-90	2	1	2.88	20	5	0	0	25	13	10	8	2	25	51	.153	.108	.188	18.36	9.00
Dunning, Jake	R-R	6-4	190	8-12-88	0	0	2.25	2	2	0	0	12	11	6	3	1	0	12	.239	.188	.250	9.00	0.00
Forjet, Jason	R-R	6-2	185	1-4-90	7	4	2.67	23	14	0	0	94	87	30	28	6	18	86	.242	.239	.245	8.20	1.72
Gardeck, Ian	R-R	6-2	215	11-21-90	3	4	3.54	61	0	0	3	86	76	41	34	4	24	104	.234	.280	.194	10.84	2.50
Hanson, Tommy	R-R	6-6	220	8-28-86	1	1	2.12	4	4	0	0	17	11	4	4	2	6	20	.183	.219	.143	10.59	3.18
Johnson, Chase	R-R	6-3	185	1-9-92	8	3	2.43	20	18	0	0	111	95	36	30	5	34	111	.235	.237	.234	9.00	2.76
Johnson, Jordan	R-R	6-3	175	9-15-93	2	3	4.31	6	6	0	0	31	34	17	15	3	10	33	.272	.218	.314	9.48	2.87
Jones, Christian	L-L	6-3	210	1-27-91	6	2	3.50	37	3	0	1	72	72	35	28	4	21	75	.257	.209	.280	9.38	2.63
Leenhouts, Drew	L-L	6-3	225	3-28-90	0	2	7.36	3	2	0	0	15	18	13	12	2	2	7	.300	.471	.233	4.30	1.23
Leverett, Jarret	R-L	6-3	195	10-18-89	0	1	5.79	3	1	0	0	5	3	3	3	1	2	2	.278	.250	.300	3.86	3.86
McVay, Mason	L-L	6-7	230	8-15-90	2	2	4.79	16	0	0	1	21	23	15	11	1	21	27	.167	.100	.345	9.15	3.05
Mella, Keury	R-R	6-2	200	8-2-93	5	3	3.31	16	16	0	0	82	66	38	30	5	26	83	.216	.218	.215	9.15	2.87
Reyes, Jose	R-R	6-1	184	1-3-91	5	6	5.86	15	14	0	0	78	86	51	51	11	18	55	.277	.301	.258	6.32	2.07
Rogers, Tyler	R-R	6-5	187	12-17-90	5	1	1.47	42	0	0	1	79	57	18	13	4	20	86	.202	.211	.195	9.76	2.27
Slania, Dan	R-R	6-5	275	5-24-92	4	5	3.53	59	0	0	16	71	70	35	28	7	15	90	.253	.213	.284	11.36	1.89
Smith, Jake	R-R	6-4	190	6-2-90	4	4	2.35	56	0	0	16	84	50	28	22	7	21	118	.172	.147	.194	12.59	2.24

Pitching	B-T	HT	WT	DOB	W	L	ERA	G	GS	CG	SV	IP	H	R	ER	HR	BB	SO	AVG	vLH	vRH	K/9	BB/9
Snelten, D.J.	L-L	6-6	215	5-29-92	0	5	4.84	8	8	0	0	35	42	25	19	4	15	31	.294	.255	.313	7.90	3.82
Soptic, Jeff	R-R	6-6	220	4-8-91	2	3	3.23	32	0	0	0	56	42	27	20	5	38	50	.207	.179	.227	8.08	6.14
Suarez, Andrew	L-L	6-2	185	9-11-92	1	0	1.80	3	3	0	0	15	13	3	3	2	2	16	.236	.222	.243	9.60	1.20
Vander Tuig, Nick	R-R	6-3	190	12-9-91	3	0	2.73	8	5	0	0	33	29	10	10	1	6	17	.238	.189	.275	4.64	1.64
Ysla, Luis	L-L	6-1	185	4-27-92	3	6	6.21	33	9	0	0	80	109	60	55	9	41	95	.329	.301	.344	10.73	4.63

Fielding

Catcher	PCT	G	PO	A	E	DP	PB
Arnold	.982	21	206	9	4	0	4
Garcia	1.000	19	196	18	0	2	7
Pare	.984	8	58	4	1	1	0
Ross	.993	81	669	67	5	3	7
Susac	.917	2	22	0	2	0	0
Turner	1.000	19	186	11	0	2	1

First Base	PCT	G	PO	A	E	DP
Bednar	.986	23	127	11	2	4
Ishikawa	1.000	2	20	0	0	0
Lollis	.969	4	30	1	1	4
Ragira	.996	33	243	16	1	22
Sonabend	.500	1	1	0	1	0
Turner	.983	26	221	14	4	22
Villalona	.984	65	498	41	9	38

Second Base	PCT	G	PO	A	E	DP
Amion	1.000	2	1	5	0	0

	PCT	G	PO	A	E	DP
Bednar	.987	16	30	44	1	9
Cole	.924	15	32	53	7	11
Kobernus	.993	37	53	83	1	13
Polonius	.981	26	40	62	2	15
Slater	.962	42	82	118	8	21
Stromsmoe	.976	8	15	25	1	3

Third Base	PCT	G	PO	A	E	DP
Bednar	.863	35	16	47	10	5
Jones	.912	102	58	138	19	17
Kobernus	1.000	5	0	5	0	1
Polonius	1.000	1	0	1	0	0
Stromsmoe	1.000	7	1	7	0	0

Shortstop	PCT	G	PO	A	E	DP
Arroyo	.962	88	129	251	15	46
Bednar	.950	34	45	87	7	12
Kobernus	1.000	1	1	5	0	1
Polonius	.968	17	21	40	2	8

	PCT	G	PO	A	E	DP
Slater	.886	7	11	20	4	5
Stromsmoe	1.000	1	1	3	0	1

Outfield	PCT	G	PO	A	E	DP
Carbonell	.939	65	110	13	8	2
Cole	.960	27	46	2	2	0
Davis	1.000	22	35	2	0	0
Galindo	.990	56	103	1	1	1
Harrison	.995	90	216	5	1	1
Horan	.972	86	135	5	4	1
Kobernus	1.000	15	15	0	0	0
Lollis	.976	26	40	1	1	0
Metzger	1.000	9	17	1	0	0
Pagan	1.000	2	3	1	0	0
Perez	1.000	4	9	0	0	0
Ragira	1.000	6	7	0	0	0
Rodriguez	.957	15	21	1	1	0
Slater	.750	2	3	0	1	0
Stromsmoe	1.000	5	7	1	0	0

AUGUSTA GREENJACKETS   LOW CLASS A

SOUTH ATLANTIC LEAGUE

Batting	B-T	HT	WT	DOB	AVG	vLH	vRH	G	AB	R	H	2B	3B	HR	RBI	BB	HBP	SH	SF	SO	SB	CS	SLG	OBP
Arenado, Jonah	R-R	6-4	225	2-3-95	.264	.277	.259	134	523	57	138	25	1	9	62	24	1	5	8	94	1	1	.367	.293
Cain, Andrew	R-R	6-6	220	3-24-90	.218	.265	.202	98	330	44	72	19	3	11	48	38	4	2	2	123	9	5	.394	.305
Callaway, Will	R-R	6-0	190	12-14-89	.268	.358	.229	106	403	50	108	21	4	3	41	27	1	1	3	94	4	1	.362	.313
Cole, Hunter	R-R	6-1	190	10-3-92	.275	.300	.267	10	40	4	11	6	0	0	5	5	1	0	0	12	2	1	.425	.370
Compton, Chase	L-R	6-2	210	9-26-91	.212	.333	.192	25	85	8	18	3	0	1	5	8	1	0	0	23	0	0	.282	.287
Davis, Dylan	R-R	6-0	205	7-20-93	.250	.246	.251	72	256	37	64	13	0	9	30	28	0	1	2	76	2	1	.406	.322
Deacon, Jared	L-R	6-0	190	8-25-91	.218	.095	.247	40	110	10	24	1	1	0	8	18	4	3	0	18	1	0	.245	.348
Ewing, Skyler	R-R	6-1	225	8-22-92	.231	.230	.232	128	467	51	108	26	6	2	42	56	8	4	0	108	2	3	.325	.321
Fargas, Johneshwy	R-R	6-1	165	12-15-94	.278	.338	.250	102	410	71	114	19	2	2	35	28	16	3	1	65	59	19	.349	.347
Fulmer, Ashford	R-R	6-1	175	6-29-93	.000	—	.000	3	9	0	0	0	0	0	0	1	0	0	0	3	0	0	.000	.100
Garcia, Aramis	R-R	6-2	220	1-12-93	.273	.302	.260	83	319	42	87	15	1	15	61	35	5	0	4	77	0	1	.467	.350
Harrison, Seth	R-R	6-0	200	7-22-92	.253	.182	.296	22	87	11	22	3	3	0	6	6	0	2	0	18	6	4	.356	.301
Jones, Chuckie	R-R	6-3	235	7-28-92	.240	.355	.210	44	150	18	36	12	0	4	21	17	2	3	0	33	1	1	.400	.325
Jones, Ryan	R-R	5-10	175	9-8-90	.219	.409	.162	29	96	12	21	2	0	0	9	10	2	1	1	6	0	0	.240	.303
Metzger, Brennan	R-R	5-11	185	12-15-89	.167	.250	.143	14	36	7	6	1	1	0	5	8	4	0	0	5	2	0	.250	.375
Neff, Steven	L-L	6-2	205	2-24-89	.148	.133	.167	9	27	1	4	0	0	0	4	0	1	0	12	0	0	.148	.258
Ortiz, Randy	R-R	5-11	185	6-15-93	.179	.250	.149	31	95	12	17	2	2	0	9	7	1	4	3	30	10	5	.242	.236
Pare, Matt	L-R	6-0	205	11-17-90	.225	.240	.221	45	138	12	31	11	0	2	13	17	6	4	0	37	0	1	.348	.335
Paulino, Cristian	R-R	5-10	170	9-4-91	.299	.377	.263	45	167	28	50	13	3	3	24	13	6	1	0	39	19	5	.467	.371
Potter, Evan	R-R	6-1	170	6-9-92	.071	.000	.085	18	56	1	4	0	0	0	1	4	0	1	0	14	0	0	.071	.133
Relaford, Travious	R-R	5-11	180	5-13-92	.237	.176	.260	87	312	37	74	10	2	1	36	34	3	6	6	43	1	0	.292	.313
Riley, John	R-R	6-0	210	2-14-94	.207	.154	.229	39	135	13	28	5	3	1	9	15	3	2	0	54	0	0	.311	.301
Rodriguez, Richard	R-R	6-1	170	10-3-92	.330	.250	.351	26	97	4	32	3	1	0	5	2	0	0	0	17	0	1	.381	.343
Sy, Jeremy	R-R	5-8	180	10-14-89	.247	.254	.244	67	231	33	57	9	4	4	29	32	3	3	0	67	12	3	.372	.346
Winn, Matt	R-R	6-1	220	8-5-92	.275	.429	.236	20	69	9	19	7	0	1	10	5	1	2	2	18	0	0	.420	.325

Pitching	B-T	HT	WT	DOB	W	L	ERA	G	GS	CG	SV	IP	H	R	ER	HR	BB	SO	AVG	vLH	vRH	K/9	BB/9
Alvarado, Carlos	R-R	6-4	175	10-22-89	2	1	3.75	23	0	0	11	24	30	16	10	3	12	26	.297	.381	.237	9.75	4.50
Coonrod, Sam	R-R	6-2	225	3-24-90	7	5	3.14	23	22	0	0	112	103	49	39	3	34	114	.243	.204	.276	9.19	2.74
Cyr, Tyler	R-R	6-3	205	5-5-93	2	1	5.60	12	0	0	0	18	16	14	11	0	18	20	.242	.235	.250	10.19	9.17
Del Orbe, Ramon	R-R	5-11	190	2-17-92	0	2	4.91	14	0	0	1	29	30	20	16	1	12	27	.268	.326	.232	8.28	3.68
Diaz, Carlos	L-L	6-2	176	11-18-93	4	3	1.63	40	0	0	5	55	41	17	10	2	17	75	.206	.241	.183	12.20	2.77
Encinosa, E.J.	R-R	6-5	230	8-5-91	0	2	7.54	13	0	0	1	23	25	21	19	1	11	18	.287	.326	.244	7.15	4.37
Gage, Matt	R-L	6-4	240	2-11-93	4	4	4.07	15	15	0	0	77	87	43	35	3	13	71	.290	.241	.310	8.26	1.51
Gonzalez, Nick	L-L	6-4	220	6-26-92	1	3	6.14	8	8	0	0	37	47	31	25	7	8	29	.297	.378	.265	7.12	1.96
Johnson, Chris	R-R	6-4	205	8-24-91	1	5	5.32	14	14	0	0	68	95	46	40	3	14	48	.331	.327	.336	6.38	1.86
Kaden, Connor	R-R	6-4	200	10-27-92	2	4	3.81	21	1	0	1	50	41	26	21	1	23	37	.218	.205	.227	6.70	4.17
Knight, Dusten	R-R	6-0	200	9-7-90	7	3	2.69	38	1	0	3	74	58	26	22	1	24	86	.212	.226	.201	10.51	2.93
Martinez, Rodolfo	R-R	6-2	180	4-4-94	1	2	2.54	35	0	0	0	46	41	16	13	1	14	44	.232	.247	.217	8.61	2.74
McCasland, Jake	R-R	6-2	215	9-13-91	1	2	5.40	23	1	0	0	50	61	35	30	5	19	44	.302	.306	.298	7.92	3.42
Montero, Raymundo	R-R	6-2	185	6-26-89	3	6	3.22	41	0	0	8	64	60	26	23	2	16	83	.247	.320	.193	11.61	2.24
Moronta, Reyes	R-R	6-0	175	1-6-93	1	7	5.73	42	0	0	12	49	56	32	31	1	23	64	.281	.280	.283	11.84	4.25
Reyes, Jose	R-R	6-1	184	1-3-91	4	1	1.36	8	8	0	0	46	35	9	7	1	11	45	.207	.197	.214	8.74	2.14
Reyes, Mark	R-L	6-1	185	10-8-92	9	6	2.13	23	23	0	0	140	115	47	33	1	36	89	.222	.175	.242	5.74	2.32
Sanchez, Eury	R-R	5-10	170	11-8-92	1	2	3.20	11	0	0	0	20	13	8	7	1	9	23	.197	.286	.132	10.53	4.12

Pitching	B-T	HT	WT	DOB	W	L	ERA	G	GS	CG	SV	IP	H	R	ER	HR	BB	SO	AVG	vLH	vRH	K/9	BB/9
Santiago, Nathanael	R-R	6-2	185	3-3-90	2	1	4.30	9	5	0	0	29	23	16	14	1	12	34	.213	.241	.185	10.43	3.68
Santos, Michael	R-R	6-4	170	5-29-95	0	2	3.44	9	9	0	0	37	38	17	14	2	10	23	.273	.319	.229	5.65	2.45
Snelten, D.J.	L-L	6-6	215	5-29-92	5	6	2.86	15	15	1	0	85	84	29	27	3	19	95	.261	.231	.276	10.06	2.01
Young, Pat	R-R	6-7	235	3-24-92	8	5	3.39	17	17	1	0	82	92	47	31	3	34	64	.280	.287	.271	7.00	3.72

Fielding

Catcher	PCT	G	PO	A	E	DP	PB
Deacon	.991	40	293	27	3	0	9
Garcia	.991	72	604	62	6	6	14
Moss	1.000	1	4	1	0	0	1
Pare	.992	14	101	19	1	3	1
Winn	.988	20	154	16	2	0	2

First Base	PCT	G	PO	A	E	DP
Arenado	.962	6	21	4	1	1
Compton	.964	13	128	7	5	5
Ewing	.992	109	946	74	8	70
Riley	.993	17	125	11	1	11

Second Base	PCT	G	PO	A	E	DP
Callaway	.966	59	84	140	8	20
Cole	.966	10	23	33	2	6

Catcher	PCT	G	PO	A	E	DP
Jones	.952	22	37	43	4	10
Paulino	.963	5	14	12	1	4
Relaford	.988	32	58	100	2	20
Rodriguez	.937	17	22	52	5	9
Sy	.917	3	5	17	2	3

Third Base	PCT	G	PO	A	E	DP
Arenado	.905	117	70	206	29	17
Callaway	.797	12	15	32	12	4
Relaford	.778	3	1	6	2	0

Shortstop	PCT	G	PO	A	E	DP
Jones	1.000	8	17	18	0	4
Potter	.925	18	25	37	5	7
Relaford	.932	56	82	177	19	34
Rodriguez	.905	6	9	10	2	4

Catcher	PCT	G	PO	A	E	DP
Sy	.923	59	75	130	17	25

Outfield	PCT	G	PO	A	E	DP
Cain	.935	82	112	4	8	2
Callaway	1.000	28	37	1	0	0
Davis	.947	62	81	8	5	2
Fargas	.969	98	182	6	6	0
Fulmer	1.000	3	10	0	0	0
Harrison	.952	21	40	0	2	0
Jones	.984	41	58	4	1	1
Metzger	1.000	13	19	0	0	0
Neff	1.000	6	10	0	0	0
Ortiz	.980	30	45	5	1	0
Paulino	.966	39	76	8	3	2
Rodriguez	1.000	3	3	1	0	1

SALEM-KEIZER VOLCANOES

SHORT-SEASON

NORTHWEST LEAGUE

Batting	B-T	HT	WT	DOB	AVG	vLH	vRH	G	AB	R	H	2B	3B	HR	RBI	BB	HBP	SH	SF	SO	SB	CS	SLG	OBP
Amion, Richard	R-R	5-10	190	2-24-93	.229	.355	.173	57	201	35	46	10	2	0	14	24	4	3	4	42	7	4	.299	.318
Brown, Tyler	R-R	6-1	180	1-18-95	.000	.000	—	1	2	0	0	0	0	0	0	0	0	0	0	1	0	0	.000	.000
Compton, Chase	L-R	6-2	210	9-26-91	.308	.231	.333	14	52	12	16	5	1	1	4	7	1	2	0	5	1	0	.500	.400
Dobson, Dillon	R-R	6-1	220	8-21-93	.182	.111	.231	6	22	0	4	0	1	0	1	1	0	1	0	4	0	0	.273	.217
Duggar, Steven	L-R	6-1	170	11-4-93	.293	.321	.276	58	229	40	67	12	1	1	27	35	2	0	1	52	6	3	.367	.390
Fulmer, Ashford	R-R	6-1	175	6-29-93	.111	.000	.167	5	9	4	1	0	0	0	1	3	2	0	0	2	0	0	.111	.429
Gomez, Miguel	B-R	5-10	185	12-17-92	.319	.327	.315	66	276	30	88	14	1	6	52	5	1	0	2	24	0	1	.442	.331
Hinojosa, C.J.	R-R	5-11	175	7-15-94	.296	.254	.315	48	189	24	56	18	1	5	19	8	2	2	1	5	2	3	.481	.328
Jebavy, Ronnie	R-R	6-2	195	5-17-94	.263	.302	.241	63	270	44	71	10	4	8	30	9	8	2	3	55	23	4	.419	.303
Lichtenthaler, Christian	B-R	5-10	165	10-8-91	.245	.200	.266	33	94	11	23	1	0	0	4	6	0	1	0	15	0	1	.255	.287
McCall, Shilo	R-R	6-1	210	6-24-94	.200	.162	.217	36	120	11	24	6	2	5	17	12	3	0	3	43	1	0	.408	.283
Metzger, Brennan	R-R	5-11	185	12-15-89	.217	.143	.250	6	23	4	5	1	0	0	0	6	0	0	0	5	2	0	.261	.379
Moss, Brad	R-R	5-8	160	10-10-89	.211	.182	.229	21	57	6	12	2	1	0	7	7	1	1	1	14	0	0	.281	.303
Murray, Byron	R-R	5-10	195	7-26-94	.087	.000	.133	6	23	1	2	0	1	0	0	1	0	0	0	7	1	0	.174	.125
Neff, Steven	L-L	6-2	205	2-24-89	.133	.000	.167	5	15	1	2	0	0	0	1	3	0	0	0	7	0	0	.133	.278
Nelson, Mark	L-R	6-2	200	3-9-91	.164	.091	.205	21	61	9	10	0	0	1	5	14	0	1	1	14	0	0	.213	.316
Pena, Julio	R-R	6-0	185	12-13-92	.234	.255	.222	39	137	18	32	3	2	6	21	6	2	2	1	58	1	1	.416	.274
Price, Scott	L-R	6-3	205	1-9-92	.276	.105	.359	18	58	5	16	3	0	1	5	2	1	0	0	8	1	0	.379	.311
Pujadas, Fernando	R-R	6-1	210	1-2-92	.275	.345	.241	49	171	18	47	10	0	3	26	11	4	0	2	40	0	0	.386	.330
Riley, John	R-R	6-0	210	2-14-94	.246	.277	.230	55	191	21	47	8	1	5	20	33	3	1	1	65	2	0	.377	.364
Rivera, Kevin	B-R	5-11	170	6-12-96	.188	.167	.200	4	16	1	3	0	0	0	1	1	0	0	0	2	0	0	.188	.235
Rodriguez, Richard	R-R	6-1	170	10-3-92	.152	.000	.217	10	33	2	5	1	0	0	2	1	0	0	0	6	0	2	.182	.176
Shaw, Chris	L-R	6-3	229	10-20-93	.287	.255	.301	46	178	22	51	11	0	12	36	19	2	0	1	41	0	0	.551	.360
Vizcaino Jr., Jose	R-R	6-3	200	4-5-94	.288	.315	.277	48	184	31	53	11	1	6	23	15	4	0	2	34	5	1	.457	.351

Pitching	B-T	HT	WT	DOB	W	L	ERA	G	GS	CG	SV	IP	H	R	ER	HR	BB	SO	AVG	vLH	vRH	K/9	BB/9
Connolly, Mike	R-R	6-1	180	10-31-91	4	3	3.66	13	13	0	0	71	75	31	29	0	16	58	.275	.243	.297	7.32	2.02
Del Orbe, Ramon	R-R	5-11	190	2-17-92	0	0	18.90	3	0	0	0	3	8	7	7	0	3	2	.444	.571	.364	5.40	8.10
Encinosa, E.J.	R-R	6-5	230	8-5-91	2	2	5.02	23	0	0	1	29	37	22	16	2	14	31	.308	.310	.308	9.73	4.40
Gonzalez, Nick	L-L	6-4	220	6-26-92	0	2	8.10	6	6	0	0	20	32	18	18	1	7	23	.352	.500	.320	10.35	3.15
Halstead, Ryan	L-R	6-4	215	5-13-92	1	2	2.33	23	0	0	8	27	18	9	7	5	4	32	.182	.172	.186	10.67	1.33
Hernandez, Rayan	R-R	6-4	230	9-24-95	2	0	6.46	14	0	0	0	24	22	19	17	3	11	17	.250	.171	.302	6.46	4.18
Johnson, Jordan	R-R	6-3	175	9-15-93	0	1	3.86	1	1	0	0	5	5	2	2	0	0	6	.263	.250	.273	11.57	0.00
Leenhouts, Drew	L-L	6-3	225	3-28-90	7	4	2.37	14	14	1	0	76	75	29	20	5	21	54	.254	.354	.235	6.39	2.49
Leverett, Jarret	R-L	6-3	195	10-18-89	0	3	4.08	22	0	0	0	29	36	15	13	2	11	19	.316	.182	.348	5.97	3.45
Marshall, Mac	L-L	6-0	181	1-27-96	0	0	6.59	5	2	0	1	14	18	13	10	1	10	18	.316	.211	.368	11.85	6.59
Mazza, Domenic	R-L	6-1	195	7-29-94	0	0	0.00	2	0	0	0	4	1	0	0	0	0	4	.071	.000	.091	8.31	0.00
Owen, Dave	R-R	6-0	190	10-21-93	3	2	2.49	13	0	0	0	22	23	11	6	3	6	16	.271	.231	.304	6.65	2.49
Paniagua, Armando	R-R	5-11	155	11-10-90	1	2	6.65	17	0	0	0	20	23	17	0	20	20	.230	.270	.200	7.83	7.83
Pino, Luis	R-R	6-0	175	11-4-94	4	1	1.43	11	5	0	0	44	41	19	7	2	14	20	.234	.226	.239	4.09	2.86
Riggs, Nolan	R-R	6-8	235	5-26-92	3	4	3.23	15	10	0	0	61	56	33	22	4	22	49	.246	.226	.259	7.19	3.23
Santiago, Nathanael	R-R	6-2	185	3-3-90	1	2	3.07	16	3	0	0	41	40	17	14	2	13	41	.245	.237	.250	9.00	2.85
Slatton, Heath	L-R	6-3	177	9-17-93	0	0	0.00	2	0	0	0	2	1	0	0	0	0	1	.143	.500	.000	4.50	0.00
Smith, Caleb	R-L	6-2	205	10-4-92	3	2	3.51	20	0	0	7	26	20	14	10	1	12	42	.215	.290	.177	14.73	4.21
Suarez, Andrew	L-L	6-2	185	9-11-92	1	0	1.40	5	5	0	0	19	17	4	3	2	1	26	.236	.211	.245	12.16	0.95
Taylor, Cory	R-R	6-2	250	12-14-93	2	0	2.45	18	0	0	1	33	36	11	9	1	12	50	.286	.367	.234	13.64	3.27
Watson, Grant	L-L	6-0	185	7-2-93	0	1	4.50	3	3	0	0	10	14	5	5	0	5	10	.341	.667	.154	9.00	4.50
Webb, Logan	R-R	6-2	195	11-18-96	3	6	4.92	14	14	0	0	60	76	36	33	2	16	40	.315	.327	.305	5.97	2.39

SAN FRANCISCO GIANTS

Fielding

Catcher	PCT	G	PO	A	E	DP	PB
Gomez	.965	16	118	19	5	0	2
Moss	.988	20	141	23	2	0	2
Pujadas	.981	46	319	46	7	0	12

First Base	PCT	G	PO	A	E	DP
Compton	1.000	4	30	3	0	1
Price	1.000	10	74	2	0	7
Riley	.977	33	286	15	7	23
Shaw	.973	31	272	15	8	23

Second Base	PCT	G	PO	A	E	DP
Amion	.963	56	109	152	10	23
Brown	1.000	1	1	3	0	0

	PCT	G	PO	A	E	DP
Lichtenthaler	.966	8	9	19	1	5
Price	1.000	5	8	14	0	2
Rivera	.913	4	5	16	2	3
Rodriguez	.926	6	7	18	2	4

Third Base	PCT	G	PO	A	E	DP
Compton	.850	7	7	10	3	1
Dobson	.905	6	5	14	2	1
Gomez	.860	32	12	62	12	0
Vizcaino Jr.	.877	31	32	39	10	6

Shortstop	PCT	G	PO	A	E	DP
Hinojosa	.940	47	78	140	14	30
Lichtenthaler	.960	22	35	60	4	6

	PCT	G	PO	A	E	DP
Rodriguez	1.000	3	5	5	0	0
Vizcaino Jr.	.867	6	13	13	4	3

Outfield	PCT	G	PO	A	E	DP
Duggar	.969	58	117	7	4	0
Fulmer	1.000	4	7	0	0	0
Jebavy	.979	63	137	4	3	1
McCall	.937	35	58	1	4	0
Metzger	1.000	6	21	0	0	0
Murray	1.000	6	8	1	0	1
Neff	1.000	4	9	0	0	0
Nelson	.957	18	21	1	1	0
Pena	.984	38	57	3	1	0
Price	1.000	1	1	0	0	0

AZL GIANTS

ROOKIE

ARIZONA LEAGUE

Batting	B-T	HT	WT	DOB	AVG	vLH	vRH	G	AB	R	H	2B	3B	HR	RBI	BB	HBP	SH	SF	SO	SB	CS	SLG	OBP
Angomas, Jean	L-R	6-0	170	6-5-95	.261	.320	.244	32	111	13	29	2	2	1	7	9	0	1	0	12	1	1	.342	.317
Beltre, Kelvin	R-R	5-11	170	9-25-96	.239	.083	.294	14	46	5	11	2	0	1	3	8	2	0	0	17	3	2	.348	.375
Bowers, Zack	R-R	6-0	188	10-14-93	.165	.250	.143	25	79	8	13	7	1	0	8	11	5	0	1	29	1	0	.278	.302
Brickhouse, Cody	R-R	6-3	210	12-23-96	.208	.176	.222	17	53	8	11	2	0	0	10	13	0	1	1	15	0	0	.245	.358
Brown, Tyler	R-R	6-1	180	1-18-95	.356	.261	.391	28	87	12	31	9	2	1	11	7	5	0	3	17	3	5	.540	.422
Case, Bryan	R-R	6-3	205	8-12-92	.188	.000	.273	4	16	1	3	0	0	0	1	0	0	0	0	5	0	0	.188	.188
Dobson, Dillon	L-R	6-1	220	8-21-92	.297	.298	.297	51	202	25	60	15	6	3	31	15	2	0	3	45	2	1	.475	.347
Edie, Mikey	R-R	5-11	175	7-3-97	.290	.207	.312	39	138	15	40	4	0	0	18	10	9	2	3	30	10	1	.319	.369
Edwards, Woody	R-R	5-10	155	4-2-95	.185	.174	.188	30	92	12	17	1	0	0	3	14	1	0	0	23	6	3	.196	.299
Escalante, Geno	R-R	5-11	210	6-25-91	.667	.500	.800	4	9	5	6	3	0	0	3	1	3	0	0	1	0	0	1.000	.769
Fulmer, Ashford	R-R	6-1	175	6-29-93	.235	.250	.231	35	102	13	24	1	2	0	10	12	6	1	2	29	8	2	.284	.344
Javier, Nathanael	R-R	6-3	185	10-10-95	.183	.087	.206	33	120	6	22	4	0	1	7	2	1	0	1	28	1	1	.242	.202
Jones, Nick	L-L	6-6	215	9-15-91	.105	.000	.125	5	19	0	2	0	0	0	3	0	0	0	0	9	0	0	.105	.227
Leslie, Ben	L-L	6-1	185	6-28-94	.333	.000	.667	3	6	1	2	0	0	0	2	0	0	0	0	2	0	0	.333	.500
Melendez, Rene	R-R	6-1	190	1-20-95	.158	.125	.163	19	57	4	9	2	0	0	2	5	1	2	1	21	1	0	.193	.234
Miller, Blake	R-R	6-3	195	4-25-90	.167	.000	.182	5	12	3	2	1	0	0	3	4	1	0	1	5	1	0	.250	.389
Miller, Jalen	R-R	5-10	173	12-19-96	.218	.257	.209	44	174	28	38	5	1	0	13	17	2	2	2	42	11	2	.259	.292
Murray, Byron	R-R	5-10	195	7-26-95	.272	.277	.271	47	180	32	49	19	3	3	28	9	4	0	4	38	8	3	.461	.315
Nelson, Mark	L-R	6-2	200	3-9-91	.000	.000	.000	4	13	0	0	0	0	0	1	0	0	0	0	4	0	0	.000	.000
Parra, Nicoll	L-L	5-9	160	7-28-94	.250	—	.250	1	4	1	1	0	0	0	0	0	0	0	0	1	0	0	.500	.250
Potter, Evan	R-R	6-1	170	6-9-92	.333	.500	.286	11	27	4	9	4	0	0	3	0	0	1	0	8	0	0	.481	.333
Price, Scott	L-R	6-2	205	1-9-92	.333	.400	.250	3	9	2	3	1	0	0	1	3	1	0	0	1	0	0	.444	.538
Rivas, Kleiber	L-R	5-11	200	6-22-95	.273	1.000	.200	12	33	4	9	1	1	0	4	4	1	2	1	4	0	0	.394	.359
Rivera, Kevin	B-R	5-11	170	6-21-96	.292	.300	.290	26	89	15	26	7	1	0	3	4	1	0	0	18	0	1	.393	.330
Santiago, Hector	R-R	6-2	180	11-18-97	.048	.000	.071	7	21	0	1	0	0	0	2	0	0	1	0	14	0	0	.048	.130
Weist, Mark	R-R	6-3	215	8-12-92	.224	.231	.222	22	67	9	15	5	1	1	11	5	0	2	1	13	1	0	.373	.274
Winn, Matt	R-R	6-1	220	8-5-92	.143	.231	.116	16	56	4	8	1	0	1	7	6	0	0	2	18	2	0	.214	.219

Pitching	B-T	HT	WT	DOB	W	L	ERA	G	GS	CG	SV	IP	H	R	ER	HR	BB	SO	AVG	vLH	vRH	K/9	BB/9
Benitez, Julio	R-R	6-3	185	11-1-94	0	1	3.00	4	3	0	0	9	12	9	3	0	2	8	.300	.400	.200	8.00	2.00
Bickford, Phil	R-R	6-5	205	7-10-95	0	1	2.01	10	10	0	0	22	13	5	5	0	6	32	.169	.269	.118	12.90	2.42
Bolivar, Deiyerbert	L-L	5-11	155	4-3-96	2	1	2.08	8	6	0	0	30	22	9	7	0	14	30	.206	.091	.235	8.90	4.15
Bradley, Ryan	B-L	6-1	180	7-15-88	1	0	9.00	8	0	0	0	7	14	8	7	0	2	5	.438	.222	.522	6.43	2.57
Brooks, Dylan	R-R	6-7	230	8-20-95	1	2	2.25	17	3	0	3	32	30	14	8	1	10	27	.246	.233	.253	7.59	2.81
Cyr, Tyler	R-R	6-3	205	5-5-93	0	1	2.25	3	1	0	0	4	2	3	1	0	1	7	.133	.000	.222	15.75	2.25
Diaz, Alvaro	R-R	6-3	190	6-13-93	0	1	7.24	14	0	0	0	14	18	14	11	0	8	15	.305	.368	.275	9.88	5.27
Dunning, Jake	R-R	6-3	190	9-6-88	1	0	2.70	4	2	0	0	10	10	4	3	0	1	14	.250	.182	12.60	0.90
Gonzalez, Nick	L-L	6-4	220	6-26-92	2	4	2.57	9	9	0	0	49	51	18	14	3	6	39	.266	.235	.272	7.16	1.10
Graybill, David	R-R	6-5	244	5-3-93	0	0	18.00	5	0	0	0	3	6	6	6	0	4	2	.500	.800	.286	6.00	12.00
Heller, Michael	R-R	6-1	188	4-25-91	1	0	0.00	4	0	0	0	4	4	2	0	0	2	3	.235	.286	.000	6.75	4.50
Johnson, Jordan	R-R	6-3	175	9-15-93	0	1	1.54	7	7	0	0	23	19	6	4	0	1	32	.221	.120	.262	12.34	0.39
Kaden, Connor	R-R	6-4	200	10-27-92	0	0	2.70	5	0	0	1	7	5	2	2	0	2	6	.208	.333	.083	8.10	2.70
Koziol, Ryan	L-R	6-3	165	10-4-93	2	1	4.03	19	0	0	0	22	24	12	10	1	7	14	.279	.300	.268	5.64	2.82
Marshall, Mac	L-L	6-0	181	12-31-96	0	0	2.57	4	2	0	0	7	5	4	2	0	5	11	.200	.125	.235	14.14	6.43
Mazza, Domenic	R-L	6-1	195	7-29-94	3	0	1.27	8	1	0	0	21	17	5	3	0	4	24	.224	.318	.185	10.13	1.69
Melo, Kendry	R-R	6-3	210	1-7-94	2	0	4.15	20	0	0	0	30	28	24	14	1	15	43	.237	.130	.306	12.76	4.45
Morel, Jose	R-R	6-2	190	9-6-93	5	1	1.91	24	0	0	1	33	24	10	7	0	11	28	.207	.156	.239	7.64	3.00
Owen, Dave	R-R	6-0	190	10-21-93	1	1	5.40	5	0	0	0	7	7	4	4	0	3	7	.280	.222	.313	9.45	4.05
Pino, Luis	R-R	6-0	175	11-4-94	2	1	2.89	4	1	0	0	19	11	7	6	0	4	19	.164	.118	.180	9.16	1.93
Pope, Matt	R-R	6-6	225	7-5-94	0	2	4.91	19	0	0	2	18	15	11	10	0	10	21	.227	.185	.256	10.31	4.91
Sanchez, Eury	R-R	5-10	185	11-8-92	2	1	1.04	9	0	0	2	9	7	5	1	1	2	13	.194	.375	.167	13.50	2.08
Santos, Michael	R-R	6-4	170	5-29-95	0	0	0.00	2	1	0	0	3	0	0	0	0	2	5	.000	.000	.000	15.00	6.00
Slatton, Heath	L-R	6-3	177	9-17-93	3	1	0.79	22	0	0	8	23	14	5	2	0	5	24	.163	.143	.176	9.53	1.99
Smith, Caleb	R-L	6-2	200	7-3-94	0	0	0.00	2	0	0	2	4	0	0	0	0	0	2	.000	.000	.000	9.00	0.00
Watson, Grant	L-L	6-0	185	7-2-93	2	0	0.68	11	3	0	0	27	21	3	2	1	3	30	.233	.188	.259	10.13	1.01
Woods, Stetson	R-R	6-8	200	1-15-95	1	0	6.00	10	0	0	0	9	11	6	6	0	7	7	.261	.207	.300	8.50	7.00
Yanez, Cesar	R-R	6-5	175	9-30-94	0	3	22.24	10	0	0	0	6	14	14	0	0	17	6	.273	.385	.111	9.53	27.00

Fielding

Catcher	PCT	G	PO	A	E	DP	PB
Bowers	.991	22	196	21	2	1	6
Case	.950	4	32	6	2	0	1
Escalante	1.000	2	8	0	0	0	0
Melendez	.988	19	146	23	2	4	8
Rivas	.938	2	14	1	1	0	0
Winn	.991	12	95	17	1	2	3

First Base	PCT	G	PO	A	E	DP
Bowers	1.000	3	25	2	0	2
Dobson	.993	48	412	39	3	27
Jones	1.000	4	34	1	0	5
Price	1.000	1	15	0	0	1

Second Base	PCT	G	PO	A	E	DP
Beltre	.902	10	15	22	4	3
Brown	.988	21	31	54	1	5
Cabrera	1.000	1	1	2	0	0

	PCT	G	PO	A	E	DP
Kobernus	1.000	2	2	4	0	1
Miller	1.000	5	11	6	0	4
Rivera	.952	23	37	62	5	12
Santiago	—	1	0	0	0	0

Third Base	PCT	G	PO	A	E	DP
Brickhouse	.783	6	6	12	5	2
Brown	1.000	1	0	2	0	0
Hicks	1.000	2	0	2	0	0
Javier	.855	31	16	55	12	3
Nelson	1.000	1	0	3	0	0
Potter	1.000	3	0	4	0	0
Weist	.818	16	8	19	6	2

Shortstop	PCT	G	PO	A	E	DP
Beltre	1.000	3	2	8	0	0
Brown	.667	1	1	3	2	1
Cabrera	1.000	1	0	3	0	0

	PCT	G	PO	A	E	DP
Edwards	1.000	2	3	1	0	0
Hicks	1.000	1	1	2	0	1
Miller	.933	41	52	88	10	17
Potter	.935	8	7	22	2	6
Santiago	.750	6	9	15	8	1

Outfield	PCT	G	PO	A	E	DP
Angomas	1.000	29	40	5	0	0
Cabrera	.333	2	1	0	2	0
Cartagena	1.000	1	3	0	0	0
Edie	.975	38	76	3	2	0
Edwards	.932	25	40	1	3	0
Fulmer	.907	32	45	4	5	1
Kobernus	1.000	3	3	0	0	0
Leslie	—	1	0	0	0	0
Miller	1.000	1	3	0	0	0
Murray	.964	40	53	1	2	1
Pagan	1.000	1	2	0	0	0

DSL GIANTS   ROOKIE

DOMINICAN SUMMER LEAGUE

Batting	B-T	HT	WT	DOB	AVG	vLH	vRH	G	AB	R	H	2B	3B	HR	RBI	BB	HBP	SH	SF	SO	SB	CS	SLG	OBP
Angulo, Andres	R-R	5-10	181	9-5-97	.264	.273	.262	28	87	15	23	3	0	2	13	6	2	0	0	15	5	2	.368	.326
Antunez, Robert	R-R	5-10	160	3-22-96	.321	.432	.289	50	165	40	53	3	1	0	16	22	1	2	6	1	21	27	3	.352	.402
Cairo, Victor	R-R	6-0	180	9-10-97	.174	.286	.125	17	23	2	4	0	0	0	1	2	2	0	0	4	0	0	.174	.296
Coronado, Mecky	R-R	6-0	180	12-13-96	.340	.386	.327	52	191	25	65	13	0	2	37	18	3	0	4	29	2	4	.440	.398
De Pena, Brayan	L-L	6-4	240	11-19-97	.185	.143	.191	18	54	0	10	3	1	0	4	5	1	0	0	22	0	0	.278	.267
Fabian, Sandro	R-R	6-1	180	3-6-98	.269	.175	.297	65	242	47	65	10	2	3	37	15	18	4	7	47	2	0	.364	.348
Geraldo, Manuel	B-R	6-1	170	9-23-96	.328	.322	.330	65	274	50	90	11	4	3	37	21	3	2	0	45	18	7	.431	.383
Gonzalez, Yendrys	R-R	6-3	185	12-28-96	.296	.250	.316	14	27	6	8	1	0	1	2	4	5	0	0	7	1	1	.444	.472
Guzman, Marco	R-R	6-0	170	8-7-94	.287	.405	.257	52	181	28	52	11	4	1	25	19	0	0	3	19	5	0	.409	.350
Medina, Francisco	R-R	6-1	165	3-20-98	.243	.183	.266	54	218	31	53	8	1	7	36	12	8	0	0	55	3	0	.385	.307
Medrano, Robinson	R-R	6-3	180	4-20-96	.294	.375	.273	60	235	41	69	10	4	5	37	28	2	1	1	33	7	4	.434	.372
Mendoza, Beicker	R-R	6-2	185	2-14-98	.300	.311	.296	50	180	25	54	10	1	1	24	12	4	0	2	38	4	1	.383	.354
Morles, Jose	L-R	5-10	180	8-18-94	.193	.235	.182	41	83	11	16	2	0	0	2	9	0	2	0	12	0	0	.217	.272
Patino, Jose	B-R	6-0	160	12-11-97	.249	.333	.221	62	181	28	45	6	0	0	23	15	7	1	4	43	19	8	.282	.324
Rivero, Jose	L-R	5-11	158	4-30-98	.204	.188	.210	41	137	22	28	4	2	0	13	18	1	0	1	34	6	2	.263	.299
Rodriguez, Alilzon	R-R	6-3	200	9-22-96	.150	.333	.118	11	20	4	3	0	0	2	4	3	2	0	0	5	0	0	.450	.320
Rodriguez, Juan	R-R	6-0	175	8-29-94	.363	.349	.366	51	215	54	78	17	3	3	26	13	0	0	1	22	19	6	.512	.397
Santana, Marcos	R-R	6-3	190	9-18-96	.188	.500	.083	9	16	1	3	1	0	0	2	4	1	0	0	1	0	0	.250	.381
Tona, Jesus	R-R	5-10	170	3-30-96	.313	.250	.327	28	64	17	20	1	1	3	13	15	1	2	0	12	4	1	.500	.450

Pitching	B-T	HT	WT	DOB	W	L	ERA	G	GS	CG	SV	IP	H	R	ER	HR	BB	SO	AVG	vLH	vRH	K/9	BB/9
Adon, Melvin	R-R	6-3	195	6-9-94	4	0	2.48	14	14	0	0	69	57	23	19	2	21	54	.223	.226	.221	7.04	2.74
Amaya, Luis	L-L	5-11	160	8-26-98	4	1	1.77	20	0	0	6	46	34	12	9	1	24	50	.210	.242	.202	9.85	4.73
Cabrera, Sandro	L-L	6-2	175	6-22-95	6	2	2.32	15	15	0	0	78	49	29	20	0	26	86	.178	.121	.193	9.97	3.01
Ciriaco, Rey	R-R	6-5	190	1-23-94	3	1	6.31	14	0	0	2	26	34	19	18	1	11	19	.324	.444	.282	6.66	3.86
Concepcion, Victor	R-R	6-0	170	11-23-96	6	0	0.42	8	8	0	0	43	31	5	2	2	7	45	.208	.213	.205	9.42	1.47
De La Rosa, Alejandro	R-R	6-0	165	2-14-95	2	0	2.87	14	0	0	0	31	28	12	10	0	13	38	.241	.353	.195	10.91	3.73
Gudino, Norwith	R-R	6-2	200	11-22-95	2	2	3.52	15	8	0	1	54	60	27	21	1	10	54	.283	.276	.287	9.06	1.68
Herrera, Jasier	R-R	6-5	190	1-1-98	0	2	9.26	10	0	0	0	12	15	14	12	1	10	15	.300	.455	.256	11.57	7.71
Luna, Jose	R-R	6-1	160	3-8-96	2	0	4.00	6	0	0	0	9	11	10	4	3	1	11	.256	.083	.323	11.00	1.00
Maita, Jose	L-L	5-11	180	12-23-97	2	2	4.50	17	0	0	2	32	34	22	16	1	13	27	.274	.381	.252	7.59	3.66
Quiroz, Orleny	L-L	6-3	180	7-1-95	1	0	5.40	5	0	0	1	12	15	9	7	3	3	10	.313	.167	.361	9.26	2.31
Reyes, Prebito	L-L	6-3	175	10-21-95	5	3	3.22	14	13	0	0	73	67	29	26	1	21	57	.249	.196	.263	7.06	2.60
Rodriguez, Reymi	R-R	6-2	195	8-30-94	4	3	3.40	24	0	0	4	40	36	21	15	1	13	37	.225	.151	.262	8.39	2.95
Vizcaino, Raffi	R-R	6-1	195	12-2-95	8	0	2.50	14	14	0	0	72	61	24	20	2	16	73	.229	.169	.254	9.13	2.00
Yan, Weilly	R-R	6-0	175	1-30-96	1	0	5.51	10	0	0	0	16	11	11	10	0	12	16	.193	.133	.214	8.82	6.61

Fielding

Catcher	PCT	G	PO	A	E	DP	PB
Angulo	1.000	27	204	23	0	0	7
Cairo	.981	13	48	5	1	0	3
Geraldo	1.000	1	1	0	0	0	0
Morles	.987	40	187	40	3	0	3
Rodriguez	1.000	2	8	4	0	0	0
Tona	.995	23	178	20	1	1	6

First Base	PCT	G	PO	A	E	DP
Guzman	.976	16	112	8	3	6
Medrano	.984	59	525	37	9	41
Rodriguez	1.000	5	11	1	0	1

Second Base	PCT	G	PO	A	E	DP
Antunez	.974	43	78	110	5	17
Geraldo	.929	28	49	69	9	13
Guzman	1.000	1	10	10	0	4
Rivero	1.000	3	4	10	0	0

Third Base	PCT	G	PO	A	E	DP
Antunez	.500	2	1	0	1	0
Guzman	.897	20	15	37	6	4
Medina	.877	53	36	92	18	4

Shortstop	PCT	G	PO	A	E	DP
Geraldo	.929	39	57	101	12	16

	PCT	G	PO	A	E	DP
Guzman	1.000	2	3	5	0	0
Rivero	.936	37	61	85	10	20

Outfield	PCT	G	PO	A	E	DP
Coronado	.944	25	32	2	2	0
De Pena	1.000	5	5	0	0	0
Fabian	.966	62	103	10	4	3
Gonzalez	1.000	11	3	0	0	0
Mendoza	.923	37	35	1	3	0
Patino	.990	58	96	5	1	1
Rodriguez	.973	44	70	2	2	1
Santana	1.000	6	4	0	0	0

Seattle Mariners

SEASON IN A SENTENCE: A preseason pick to contend by many pundits, the Mariners instead endured their fifth losing season in their last seven, leading to the firing of general manager Jack Zduriencik and later manager Lloyd McClendon—one of two Mariners managers in the club's 39-year-history.

HIGH POINT: DH Nelson Cruz, coming off a 40-homer season in Baltimore, followed up with 44 in the first year of his four-year free-agent contract with Seattle. His three-run homer in support of Felix Hernandez's complete-game shutout in a 3-0 win at Tampa on May 27 pulled Seattle back to .500. The Mariners lose seven of their next eight, though, and never threatened to contend again.

LOW POINT: The last-place Red Sox thumped lefty Mike Montgomery and Hernandez, scoring 37 runs in consecutive games to sum up a moribund season in mid-August. Two weeks later, Zduriencik was let go, replaced by interim GM Jeff Kingston.

NOTABLE ROOKIES: Ketel Marte provided second-half hope, posting a .753 OPS and playing solid defense at shortstop while also experimenting in center field. Righty Carson Smith became the team's best reliever, leading the club in relief innings (70), racking up 13 saves and averaging 11.8 strikeouts per nine innings.

KEY TRANSACTIONS: The Mariners found a new leader in October, hiring Jerry DiPoto as GM after he was let go at midseason by the Angels, where he lost a power struggle with manager Mike Scioscia and owner Arte Moreno. DiPoto brought his assistant GM, former big league catcher Scott Servais, up to Seattle with him as the big league manager. He arrives to a team that dumped Dustin Ackley, the disappointing 2009 No. 2 overall pick, to the Yankees in a July trade. A June trade for Mark Trumbo failed to turn the offense around and cost the team catcher Wellington Castillo, who raked for the Diamondbacks.

DOWN ON THE FARM: No full-season Mariners affiliate finished at .500, and low Class A Clinton had a horrific 46-93 season (the worst record in the minors), leading the way to a .434 winning percentage for domestic affiliates, one of the worst in the game. DiPoto promoted pro scouting director Tom Allison after the season, putting him in charge of both pro and amateur scouting, while hiring Andy McKay away from the Rockies to replace Chris Gwynn as the new farm director.

OPENING DAY PAYROLL: $119,798,060 (12th)

PLAYERS OF THE YEAR

MAJOR LEAGUE	MINOR LEAGUE
Nelson Cruz	**Tyler O'Neill**
dh	**of**
.302/.369/.566	(High A)
Led club with 44 HRs,	.260/.316/.558
93 RBIs	32 HR and 87 RBIs

ORGANIZATION LEADERS

BATTING   *Minimum 250 AB

MAJORS

* AVG	Nelson Cruz	.302
* OPS	Nelson Cruz	.935
HR	Nelson Cruz	44
RBI	Nelson Cruz	93

MINORS

* AVG	Jesus Montero, Tacoma	.355
* OBP	Jesus Montero, Tacoma	.398
* SLG	Jabari Blash, Jackson, Tacoma	.576
R	Nelson Ward, Clinton, Bakersfield	81
H	Jesus Montero, Tacoma	140
TB	Stefen Romero, Tacoma	235
2B	Stefen Romero, Tacoma	37
3B	Nelson Ward, Clinton, Bakersfield	13
HR	Jabari Blash, Jackson, Tacoma	32
	Tyler O'Neill, Bakersfield	32
RBI	Tyler O'Neill, Bakersfield	87
BB	Joseph DeCarlo, Clinton	70
SO	Tyler O'Neill, Bakersfield	137
SB	Ian Miller, Bakersfield, Jackson	50

PITCHING   #Minimum 75 IP

MAJORS

W	Felix Hernandez	18
# ERA	Felix Hernandez	3.53
SO	Felix Hernandez	191
SV	Fernando Rodney	16

MINORS

W	Forrest Snow, Tacoma	10
L	Lukas Schiraldi, Clinton	13
# ERA	Edwin Diaz, Bakersfield, Jackson	3.82
G	Paul Fry, Bakersfield, Jackson	50
GS	Dan Altavilla, Bakersfield	28
	Tyler Pike, Jackson, Bakersfield	28
SV	Matt Anderson, Jackson, Tacoma	10
IP	Dan Altavilla, Bakersfield	148
BB	Tyler Pike, Jackson, Bakersfield	75
SO	Edwin Diaz, Bakersfield, Jackson	145
AVG	Edwin Diaz, Bakersfield, Jackson	.237

2015 PERFORMANCE

General Manager: Jack Zduriencik/Jerry Dipoto. **Farm Director:** Chris Gwynn. **Scouting Director:** Tom McNamara.

Class	Team	League	W	L	PCT	Finish	Manager
Majors	Seattle Mariners	American	76	86	.469	t-12th (15)	Lloyd McClendon
Triple-A	Tacoma Rainiers	Pacific Coast	68	76	.472	9th (16)	Pat Listach
Double-A	Jackson Generals	Southern	53	84	.387	10th (10)	Roy Howell
High A	Bakersfield Blaze	California	61	79	.436	t-8th (10)	Eddie Menchaca
Low A	Clinton LumberKings	Midwest	46	93	.331	16th (16)	Scott Steinmann
Short season	Everett AquaSox	Northwest	42	34	.553	t-2nd (8)	Rob Mummau
Rookie	Mariners	Arizona	31	25	.554	t-3rd (14)	Darrin Garner
Overall 2015 Minor League Record			301	391	.435	29th (30)	

ORGANIZATION STATISTICS

SEATTLE MARINERS

AMERICAN LEAGUE

Batting	B-T	HT	WT	DOB	AVG	vLH	vRH	G	AB	R	H	2B	3B	HR	RBI	BB	HBP	SH	SF	SO	SB	CS	SLG	OBP
Ackley, Dustin	L-R	6-1	205	2-26-88	.215	.188	.218	85	186	22	40	8	1	6	19	14	1	3	3	38	2	2	.366	.270
2-team total (23 New York)					.231	—	—	108	238	28	55	11	3	10	30	18	1	3	4	45	2	2	.429	.284
Baron, Steve	R-R	6-0	205	12-7-90	.000	.000	.000	4	11	0	0	0	0	0	0	0	0	0	0	2	0	0	.000	.000
Bloomquist, Willie	R-R	5-11	200	11-27-77	.159	.184	.129	35	69	2	11	1	0	0	4	2	1	0	0	13	1	1	.174	.194
Cano, Robinson	L-R	6-0	210	10-22-82	.287	.270	.296	156	624	82	179	34	1	21	79	43	3	0	4	107	2	6	.446	.334
Castillo, Welington	R-R	5-10	210	4-24-87	.160	.429	.056	6	25	3	4	0	0	0	2	1	0	0	2	5	0	0	.160	.179
Cruz, Nelson	R-R	6-2	230	7-1-80	.302	.357	.280	152	590	90	178	22	1	44	93	59	5	0	1	164	3	2	.566	.369
Gutierrez, Franklin	R-R	6-2	210	2-21-83	.292	.317	.254	59	171	27	50	11	0	15	35	14	3	0	1	54	0	0	.620	.354
Hicks, John	R-R	6-2	210	8-31-89	.063	.100	.045	17	32	1	2	1	0	0	1	1	0	1	0	18	1	1	.094	.091
Jackson, Austin	R-R	6-1	205	2-1-87	.272	.294	.261	107	419	46	114	18	3	8	38	24	1	3	1	107	15	9	.387	.312
Jones, James	L-L	6-4	200	9-24-88	.103	.000	.125	28	29	1	3	1	0	0	2	0	0	0	0	13	1	1	.138	.161
Marte, Ketel	B-R	6-1	165	10-12-93	.283	.257	.305	57	219	25	62	14	3	2	17	24	0	2	2	43	8	4	.402	.351
Miller, Brad	L-R	6-2	200	10-18-89	.258	.234	.266	144	438	44	113	22	4	11	46	47	2	4	6	101	13	4	.402	.329
Montero, Jesus	R-R	6-3	235	11-28-89	.223	.205	.256	38	112	11	25	6	0	5	19	4	0	0	0	32	0	0	.411	.250
Morrison, Logan	L-L	6-2	240	8-25-87	.225	.190	.241	146	457	47	103	15	3	17	54	47	4	1	2	81	8	4	.383	.302
O'Malley, Shawn	R-R	5-11	175	12-28-87	.262	.263	.261	24	42	10	11	1	0	1	7	12	0	2	1	14	3	0	.357	.418
Romero, Stefen	R-R	6-2	220	10-17-88	.190	.200	.167	13	21	6	4	1	0	1	3	3	0	0	0	6	0	0	.381	.292
Ruggiano, Justin	R-R	6-1	210	4-12-82	.214	.263	.156	36	70	8	15	4	0	2	3	11	0	0	0	27	3	2	.357	.321
Seager, Kyle	L-R	6-0	210	11-3-87	.266	.297	.249	161	623	85	166	37	0	26	74	54	5	0	4	98	6	4	.451	.328
Smith, Seth	L-L	6-3	210	9-30-82	.248	.200	.255	136	395	54	98	31	5	12	42	47	4	1	5	99	0	0	.443	.330
Sucre, Jesus	R-R	6-0	225	4-30-88	.157	.289	.101	50	127	9	20	6	0	1	7	6	0	9	0	21	0	0	.228	.195
Taylor, Chris	R-R	6-1	195	8-29-90	.170	.241	.138	37	94	9	16	3	1	0	1	6	0	2	0	31	3	2	.223	.220
Trumbo, Mark	R-R	6-4	225	1-16-86	.263	.288	.248	96	334	39	88	13	0	13	41	26	0	0	1	93	0	0	.419	.316
Weeks, Rickie	R-R	5-10	220	9-13-82	.167	.234	.081	37	84	7	14	1	0	2	9	9	2	0	0	25	0	0	.250	.263
Zunino, Mike	R-R	6-2	220	3-25-91	.174	.206	.161	112	350	28	61	11	0	11	28	21	5	8	2	132	0	1	.300	.230

Pitching	B-T	HT	WT	DOB	W	L	ERA	G	GS	CG	SV	IP	H	R	ER	HR	BB	SO	AVG	vLH	vRH	K/9	BB/9
Beimel, Joe	L-L	6-3	205	4-19-77	2	1	3.99	53	0	0	1	47	49	25	21	8	16	22	.283	.280	.286	4.18	3.04
Elias, Roenis	L-L	6-1	190	8-1-88	5	8	4.14	22	20	0	0	115	106	57	53	15	44	97	.245	.227	.251	7.57	3.43
Farquhar, Danny	R-R	5-9	185	2-17-87	1	8	5.12	43	0	0	1	51	53	33	29	9	17	48	.266	.220	.306	8.47	3.00
Furbush, Charlie	L-L	6-5	215	4-11-86	1	1	2.08	33	0	0	0	22	9	6	5	2	5	17	.122	.105	.139	7.06	2.08
Guaipe, Mayckol	R-R	6-4	235	8-11-90	0	3	5.40	21	0	0	0	27	34	19	16	5	13	22	.330	.452	.246	7.43	4.39
Happ, J.A.	L-L	6-5	205	10-19-82	4	6	4.64	21	20	0	0	109	121	58	56	13	32	82	.279	.287	.277	6.79	2.65
Hernandez, Felix	R-R	6-3	225	4-8-86	18	9	3.53	31	31	2	0	202	180	80	79	23	58	191	.240	.234	.246	8.52	2.59
Iwakuma, Hisashi	R-R	6-3	210	4-12-81	9	5	3.54	20	20	1	0	130	117	53	51	18	21	111	.240	.261	.219	7.70	1.46
Kensing, Logan	R-R	6-1	190	7-3-82	2	1	5.87	19	0	0	0	15	12	10	10	2	7	13	.214	.143	.238	7.63	4.11
Leone, Dominic	R-R	5-11	210	10-26-91	0	4	6.35	10	0	0	0	11	11	9	8	1	9	7	.244	.192	.316	5.56	7.15
Lowe, Mark	R-R	6-3	210	6-7-83	0	1	1.00	34	0	0	6	36	31	6	4	1	11	47	.235	.250	.225	11.75	2.75
2-team total (23 Toronto)					1	3	1.96	57	0	0	1	55	46	15	12	4	12	61	—	—	—	9.98	1.96
Luetge, Lucas	L-L	6-4	205	3-24-87	0	0	0.00	1	0	0	0	2	0	0	0	0	2	2	.000	.000	.000	7.71	7.71
Medina, Yoervis	R-R	6-3	245	7-27-88	1	0	3.00	12	0	0	1	12	11	5	4	1	7	9	.234	.250	.222	6.75	5.25
Montgomery, Mike	L-L	6-4	200	7-1-89	4	6	4.60	16	16	2	0	90	92	49	46	11	37	64	.261	.303	.246	6.40	3.70
Nuno, Vidal	L-L	5-11	210	7-26-87	1	4	4.10	32	10	0	0	75	80	35	34	14	17	62	.278	.221	.295	7.47	2.05
Olmos, Edgar	L-L	6-4	220	4-12-90	1	0	4.50	6	2	0	0	14	16	8	7	1	8	4	.281	.200	.298	2.57	5.14
Olson, Tyler	R-L	6-3	195	10-2-89	1	1	5.40	11	0	0	0	13	18	8	8	2	10	8	.346	.350	.344	5.40	6.75
Paxton, James	L-L	6-4	235	11-6-88	3	4	3.90	13	13	0	0	67	67	34	29	8	29	56	.253	.404	.212	7.52	3.90
Ramirez, Jose	R-R	6-3	190	1-21-90	1	0	11.57	5	0	0	0	5	9	9	6	0	6	3	.375	.250	.438	5.79	11.57
2-team total (3 New York)					1	0	12.91	8	0	0	0	8	15	14	11	0	10	5	—	—	—	5.87	11.74
Ramirez, J.C.	R-R	6-4	250	8-16-88	0	1	7.56	8	0	0	0	8	10	7	7	2	7	5	.286	.286	.286	5.40	7.56
Rasmussen, Rob	R-L	5-10	170	4-2-89	2	1	10.67	19	0	0	0	14	25	18	17	2	8	16	.373	.367	.378	10.05	5.02
2-team total (1 Toronto)					2	1	9.98	20	0	0	0	15	26	18	17	2	8	17	—	—	—	9.98	4.70
Rodney, Fernando	R-R	5-11	220	3-18-77	5	5	5.68	54	0	0	16	51	51	32	32	8	25	43	.262	.284	.243	7.64	4.44
Rollins, David	L-L	6-1	210	12-21-89	0	2	7.56	20	0	0	0	25	37	21	21	3	8	21	.346	.333	.351	7.56	2.88
Smith, Carson	R-R	6-6	215	10-19-89	2	5	2.31	70	0	0	13	70	49	19	18	2	22	92	.194	.227	.169	11.83	2.83
Walker, Taijuan	R-R	6-4	235	8-13-92	11	8	4.56	29	29	1	0	170	163	92	86	25	40	157	.252	.256	.247	8.33	2.12

Pitching	B-T	HT	WT	DOB	W	L	ERA	G	GS	CG	SV	IP	H	R	ER	HR	BB	SO	AVG	vLH	vRH	K/9	BB/9
Wilhelmsen, Tom	R-R	6-6	220	12-16-83	2	2	3.19	53	0	0	13	62	56	24	22	3	29	60	.246	.323	.189	8.71	4.21
Zych, Tony	R-R	6-3	190	8-7-90	0	0	2.45	13	1	0	0	18	17	6	5	1	3	24	.239	.200	.255	11.78	1.47

Fielding

Catcher	PCT	G	PO	A	E	DP	PB
Baron	1.000	4	34	1	0	0	0
Castillo	1.000	5	39	1	0	1	1
Hicks	.988	14	72	10	1	1	0
Sucre	.992	50	349	28	3	5	3
Zunino	.994	112	809	44	5	6	6

First Base	PCT	G	PO	A	E	DP
Bloomquist	1.000	3	24	1	0	4
Montero	.995	27	181	5	1	18
Morrison	.996	140	1055	71	4	106
Trumbo	.994	22	150	7	1	12

Second Base	PCT	G	PO	A	E	DP
Ackley	1.000	1	3	4	0	0
Bloomquist	1.000	8	6	6	0	2
Cano	.991	149	287	403	6	104
Marte	1.000	4	1	10	0	2

Miller	.972	11	13	22	1	5
Taylor	.857	4	5	1	1	1

Third Base	PCT	G	PO	A	E	DP
Bloomquist	1.000	5	1	5	0	0
Hicks	1.000	1	1	0	0	0
Miller	.500	2	0	1	1	0
O'Malley	1.000	3	1	1	0	0
Seager	.965	160	94	352	16	37
Taylor	—	1	0	0	0	0

Shortstop	PCT	G	PO	A	E	DP
Bloomquist	1.000	7	6	14	0	1
Marte	.960	51	64	150	9	31
Miller	.964	89	109	269	14	56
Seager	1.000	1	0	1	0	0
Taylor	.972	28	33	71	3	11

Outfield	PCT	G	PO	A	E	DP
Ackley	1.000	78	99	2	0	1
Bloomquist	1.000	7	4	1	0	0
Cruz	.975	80	151	6	4	1
Gutierrez	.986	46	67	3	1	1
Jackson	.989	107	271	2	3	1
Jones	1.000	27	21	0	0	0
Marte	1.000	2	3	0	0	0
Miller	.982	35	53	1	1	0
Morrison	1.000	4	5	0	0	0
O'Malley	1.000	16	24	0	0	0
Romero	1.000	12	13	0	0	0
Ruggiano	.976	31	40	0	1	0
Smith	.994	110	163	6	1	1
Trumbo	.952	46	57	2	3	0
Weeks	.923	19	12	0	1	0

TACOMA RAINIERS
PACIFIC COAST LEAGUE

TRIPLE-A

Batting	B-T	HT	WT	DOB	AVG	vLH	vRH	G	AB	R	H	2B	3B	HR	RBI	BB	HBP	SH	SF	SO	SB	CS	SLG	OBP
Baker, John	L-R	6-1	215	1-20-81	.161	.167	.160	17	62	4	10	2	0	0	5	2	0	0	1	13	0	0	.194	.185
Baron, Steve	R-R	6-0	205	12-7-90	.277	.347	.252	53	184	27	51	12	0	3	20	10	1	1	1	38	4	1	.391	.316
Blash, Jabari	R-R	6-5	225	7-4-89	.264	.220	.283	56	197	41	52	8	0	22	47	28	1	0	2	63	3	1	.640	.355
Bonilla, Leury	R-R	6-2	195	2-8-85	.250	.279	.238	87	288	33	72	7	3	4	21	20	2	3	0	49	4	5	.337	.303
Brady, Patrick	R-R	5-10	176	2-8-85	.278	.429	.224	23	79	9	22	5	0	1	6	5	0	1	0	16	5	2	.380	.321
Choi, Ji-Man	L-R	6-1	230	5-19-91	.298	.417	.267	18	57	8	17	4	0	1	16	10	0	0	0	14	0	1	.421	.403
Fernandez, Rafael	B-R	5-10	180	4-21-94	.000	.000	.000	1	2	0	0	0	0	0	0	0	0	0	0	2	0	0	.000	.000
Flores, Ramon	L-L	5-10	190	3-26-92	.423	.364	.439	14	52	11	22	6	0	2	7	11	0	0	0	6	0	0	.654	.524
Gutierrez, Franklin	R-R	6-2	200	2-21-83	.317	.279	.336	48	180	34	57	12	0	7	31	23	4	0	2	43	2	0	.500	.402
Hicks, John	R-R	6-2	210	8-31-89	.245	.241	.247	83	298	39	73	15	1	6	35	17	0	1	4	71	9	2	.362	.282
Jackson, Austin	R-R	6-1	205	2-1-87	.263	.429	.226	9	38	4	10	1	0	0	1	4	0	0	0	12	1	0	.289	.333
Jones, James	L-L	6-4	200	9-24-88	.272	.224	.294	72	265	47	72	12	7	1	28	38	2	3	2	43	25	4	.381	.365
Kivlehan, Patrick	R-R	6-2	215	12-22-89	.256	.262	.254	123	472	58	121	25	1	22	73	36	5	0	5	113	14	3	.453	.313
Kratz, Erik	R-R	6-4	240	6-15-80	.205	.125	.226	10	39	8	4	0	0	5	3	1	0	0	7	0	0	.308	.279
2-team total (15 Omaha)					.211	—	—	25	90	10	20	6	0	4	17	8	1	0	1	16	0	0	.400	.276
Landry, Leon	L-R	5-11	185	9-20-89	.262	.244	.267	57	187	33	49	5	0	8	27	18	1	0	5	31	11	4	.417	.322
Marte, Ketel	B-R	6-1	165	10-12-93	.314	.314	.314	65	261	41	82	12	2	3	29	20	0	3	3	32	20	3	.410	.359
Mejia, Erick	R-R	5-11	155	11-9-94	.000	.000	.000	4	5	1	0	0	0	0	0	0	0	0	0	3	0	0	.000	.000
Montero, Jesus	R-R	6-3	235	11-28-89	.355	.364	.351	98	394	70	140	18	6	18	85	29	2	0	5	71	-3	1	.569	.398
Morales, Jhonbaker	R-R	6-0	170	7-17-94	.000	—	.000	1	2	0	0	0	0	0	0	0	0	0	0	2	0	0	.000	.000
Morban, Julio	L-L	6-1	210	2-13-92	.208	.235	.194	16	53	6	11	1	2	1	6	6	0	0	0	18	1	0	.358	.288
O'Malley, Shawn	R-R	5-11	175	12-28-87	.297	.337	.277	89	310	50	92	11	5	5	39	19	5	8	2	47	20	7	.413	.345
Paolini, Dan	R-R	6-0	190	10-11-89	.156	.143	.167	15	45	6	7	0	0	1	4	7	1	0	0	16	0	0	.222	.283
Peterson, D.J.	R-R	6-1	210	12-31-91	.214	.000	.250	4	14	0	3	1	0	0	0	0	0	0	0	3	0	1	.286	.214
Quentin, Carlos	R-R	6-1	235	8-28-82	.176	.000	.300	5	17	2	3	1	0	0	1	2	0	0	2	0	0	0	.235	.263
Rivero, Carlos	R-R	6-3	200	5-20-88	.256	.302	.232	96	336	34	86	13	1	8	40	20	1	0	5	73	2	0	.372	.296
Romero, Stefen	R-R	6-2	220	10-17-88	.292	.314	.282	116	476	77	139	37	4	17	79	29	4	0	7	85	10	1	.494	.333
Ruggiano, Justin	R-R	6-1	210	4-12-82	.296	.250	.319	49	179	27	53	9	0	10	29	23	3	0	0	51	6	4	.514	.385
Shank, Zach	R-R	6-1	180	1-9-91	.252	.366	.186	33	111	13	28	5	2	1	8	7	0	0	1	11	1	0	.360	.294
Sucre, Jesus	R-R	6-0	225	4-30-88	.261	.000	.316	6	23	4	6	0	0	0	2	3	0	0	0	0	0	0	.261	.346
Taylor, Chris	R-R	6-1	195	8-29-90	.300	.299	.301	86	343	56	103	20	6	4	32	50	2	0	1	61	16	8	.429	.391
Zunino, Mike	R-R	6-2	220	3-25-91	.317	.308	.321	10	41	7	13	2	0	3	8	0	0	0	0	8	0	0	.585	.349

Pitching	B-T	HT	WT	DOB	W	L	ERA	G	GS	CG	SV	IP	H	R	ER	HR	BB	SO	AVG	vLH	vRH	K/9	BB/9
Anderson, Matt	R-R	6-1	210	11-18-91	0	0	11.25	3	0	0	0	4	4	5	5	1	2	4	.267	.167	.333	9.00	4.50
Bawcom, Logan	R-R	6-2	220	11-2-88	2	4	4.64	45	0	0	2	76	85	44	39	6	31	62	.281	.316	.261	7.37	3.69
Beimel, Joe	L-L	6-3	205	4-19-77	1	0	4.26	6	0	0	0	6	8	3	3	0	2	8	.308	.267	.364	11.37	2.84
Cochran-Gill, Trey	R-R	5-10	190	12-10-92	0	1	0.00	1	1	0	0	3	3	3	0	0	2	3	.273	.200	.333	10.13	6.75
Elias, Roenis	L-L	6-1	190	8-1-88	4	2	7.34	12	12	0	0	61	80	54	50	9	18	47	.310	.259	.325	6.90	2.64
Farquhar, Danny	R-R	5-9	185	2-17-87	1	1	3.08	27	1	0	3	38	40	17	13	3	10	41	.272	.353	.229	9.71	2.37
Gaviglio, Sam	R-R	6-2	195	5-22-90	8	7	5.13	21	19	0	0	102	102	64	58	16	36	79	.257	.287	.233	6.99	3.19
Germano, Justin	R-R	6-2	210	8-6-82	7	3	2.83	18	11	1	0	89	67	30	28	11	14	65	.201	.173	.220	6.57	1.42
Gillheeney, Jimmy	L-L	6-1	205	11-8-87	1	3	9.00	5	5	0	0	21	33	23	21	5	7	14	.359	.333	.369	6.00	3.00
Gregg, Kevin	R-R	6-6	245	6-20-78	0	0	2.89	7	0	0	0	9	8	3	3	0	5	8	.242	.250	.238	7.71	4.82
Guaipe, Mayckol	R-R	6-4	235	8-11-90	0	4	2.87	38	0	0	5	47	49	17	15	3	10	36	.269	.277	.266	6.89	1.91
Hobson, Cameron	L-L	6-0	190	4-10-89	0	1	10.57	4	0	0	0	8	15	10	9	1	2	7	.429	.500	.381	8.22	2.35
Iwakuma, Hisashi	R-R	6-3	210	4-12-81	1	0	0.93	2	2	0	0	8	1	1	0	2	10	.222	.308	.174	9.31	1.86
Kensing, Logan	R-R	6-1	190	7-3-82	2	0	2.23	19	0	0	1	32	29	11	8	1	10	25	.240	.273	.221	6.96	2.78
Kickham, Mike	L-L	6-4	210	12-12-88	0	2	7.29	5	5	0	0	21	18	17	17	3	28	12	.243	.125	.276	5.14	12.00
2-team total (7 Round Rock)					1	2	7.00	12	5	0	0	27	21	21	21	3	35	16	—	—	—	5.33	11.67

Pitching	B-T	HT	WT	DOB	W	L	ERA	G	GS	CG	SV	IP	H	R	ER	HR	BB	SO	AVG	vLH	vRH	K/9	BB/9
Kittredge, Andrew	R-R	6-1	200	3-17-90	0	1	5.31	21	2	0	0	42	46	25	25	5	18	29	.277	.246	.299	6.17	3.83
Landazuri, Steve	R-R	6-0	195	1-6-92	1	1	8.70	11	11	0	0	50	78	53	48	5	29	23	.377	.359	.385	4.17	5.26
Leone, Dominic	R-R	5-11	210	10-26-91	1	1	7.71	8	0	0	1	9	10	8	8	1	5	8	.270	.429	.174	7.71	4.82
Lowe, Mark	L-R	6-3	210	6-7-83	0	1	1.00	7	0	0	1	9	7	1	1	1	0	11	.219	.333	.118	11.00	0.00
Luetge, Lucas	L-L	6-4	205	3-24-87	3	2	5.33	29	0	0	2	49	57	31	29	8	23	37	.285	.275	.290	6.80	4.22
Medina, Yoervis	R-R	6-3	245	7-27-88	1	0	1.59	4	0	0	1	6	1	1	1	1	1	4	.059	.000	.143	6.35	1.59
2-team total (28 Iowa)					1	2	5.63	32	0	0	2	40	41	26	25	4	22	39	—	—	—	8.78	4.95
Montgomery, Mike	L-L	6-4	200	7-1-89	4	3	4.13	11	11	0	0	65	59	32	30	3	19	58	.242	.265	.236	7.99	2.62
Nuno, Vidal	L-L	5-11	210	7-26-87	1	0	6.00	1	1	0	0	6	7	4	4	1	1	6	.292	.400	.263	9.00	1.50
2-team total (8 Reno)					4	3	3.65	9	9	0	0	57	58	26	23	8	9	47	—	—	—	7.46	1.43
Olmos, Edgar	L-L	6-4	220	4-12-90	1	1	3.55	20	2	0	1	33	32	14	13	0	13	34	.258	.250	.262	9.27	3.55
Olson, Tyler	R-L	6-3	195	10-2-89	3	5	4.47	25	6	0	1	54	61	40	27	7	17	53	.276	.224	.299	8.78	2.82
Paxton, James	L-L	6-4	235	11-6-88	0	1	8.10	3	3	0	0	7	12	6	6	0	3	4	.429	.444	.421	5.40	4.05
Pineda, Rafael	L-R	6-6	210	2-3-91	0	0	0.00	1	0	0	0	1	0	0	0	0	1	0	.000	—	.000	0.00	9.00
Pries, Jordan	B-R	6-0	190	1-27-90	7	4	5.20	16	16	0	0	88	96	55	51	10	27	60	.280	.281	.279	6.11	2.75
Ramirez, Jose	R-R	6-3	190	1-21-90	1	1	9.00	9	0	0	0	13	16	14	13	5	7	10	.308	.280	.333	6.92	4.85
Ramirez, J.C.	R-R	6-4	250	8-16-88	1	1	2.50	14	0	0	0	18	17	6	5	2	7	18	.258	.154	.325	9.00	3.50
2-team total (23 Reno)					1	2	2.72	37	0	0	1	43	39	14	13	2	17	36	—	—	—	7.53	3.56
Rasmussen, Rob	R-L	5-10	170	4-2-89	0	0	0.00	1	0	0	0	1	0	0	0	0	0	0	.000	.000	.000	0.00	0.00
Rollins, David	L-L	6-1	210	12-21-89	0	0	0.00	2	0	0	0	9	7	0	0	0	1	8	.212	.300	.174	7.71	0.96
Sampson, Adrian	R-R	6-2	205	10-7-91	2	4	7.28	7	7	0	0	38	60	38	31	5	8	28	.353	.367	.341	6.57	1.88
Saunders, Joe	L-L	6-3	215	6-16-81	0	3	5.73	6	0	0	0	11	11	7	7	1	4	12	.256	.222	.280	9.82	3.27
Schepel, Kyle	R-L	6-1	230	8-7-90	0	0	0.00	1	0	0	0	1	0	0	0	0	3	2	.000	—	.000	18.00	27.00
Snow, Forrest	R-R	6-6	220	12-30-88	10	9	4.17	29	20	0	1	121	118	59	56	22	41	96	.249	.250	.249	7.14	3.05
Wang, Chien-Ming	R-R	6-4	225	3-31-80	4	5	5.69	11	10	1	0	68	89	47	43	8	14	23	.314	.321	.309	3.04	1.85
Wilhelmsen, Tom	R-R	6-6	220	12-16-83	0	0	0.00	4	0	0	1	3	0	0	0	0	2	2	.214	.167	.250	4.50	4.50
Zych, Tony	R-R	6-3	190	8-7-90	1	2	3.41	25	0	0	4	32	34	12	12	2	9	37	.276	.293	.268	10.52	2.56

Fielding

Catcher	PCT	G	PO	A	E	DP	PB
Baker	1.000	16	104	8	0	1	1
Baron	.993	50	378	26	3	1	3
Hicks	.982	67	418	61	9	4	5
Kratz	1.000	4	23	2	0	0	0
Sucre	.976	6	40	1	1	0	1
Zunino	1.000	4	31	3	0	0	1

First Base	PCT	G	PO	A	E	DP
Bonilla	.979	7	43	4	1	2
Choi	.983	14	116	3	2	9
Hicks	.960	11	67	5	3	5
Kivlehan	.987	30	221	11	3	23
Kratz	1.000	1	9	0	0	1
Montero	.992	82	670	37	6	59
Paolini	1.000	2	19	0	0	2
Peterson	1.000	2	9	1	0	2
Rivero	1.000	3	24	4	0	3
Romero	1.000	3	24	3	0	3

Second Base	PCT	G	PO	A	E	DP
Bonilla	.982	24	45	62	2	14

Brady	.962	21	40	61	4	16
Fernandez	1.000	1	1	1	0	0
Marte	.986	14	29	43	1	15
Mejia	1.000	1	0	4	0	1
O'Malley	.983	57	118	119	4	28
Shank	.969	27	50	74	4	12
Taylor	1.000	13	26	25	0	4

Third Base	PCT	G	PO	A	E	DP
Bonilla	.951	36	32	65	5	6
Kivlehan	.924	26	19	42	5	6
O'Malley	.857	5	7	5	2	0
Peterson	.667	2	0	2	1	0
Rivero	.927	87	61	166	18	11

Shortstop	PCT	G	PO	A	E	DP
Bonilla	.953	18	26	55	4	13
Marte	.956	49	62	133	9	20
Mejia	—	2	0	0	0	0
Morales	1.000	1	0	1	0	0
O'Malley	1.000	7	8	20	0	3
Rivero	1.000	5	4	8	0	3

Taylor	.958	72	105	217	14	45
Outfield	PCT	G	PO	A	E	DP
Blash	.957	37	62	5	3	0
Bonilla	1.000	10	10	0	0	0
Brady	1.000	2	4	0	0	0
Flores	1.000	14	30	1	0	0
Gutierrez	1.000	30	54	2	0	0
Hicks	—	1	0	0	0	0
Jackson	1.000	4	7	0	0	0
Jones	.994	68	156	5	1	1
Kivlehan	.977	70	123	5	3	1
Landry	.990	51	96	1	1	1
Marte	1.000	4	11	1	0	0
Morban	.973	16	36	0	1	0
O'Malley	.970	20	32	0	1	0
Paolini	.962	13	25	0	1	0
Romero	1.000	90	192	3	0	0
Ruggiano	.981	27	50	1	1	0
Shank	1.000	4	11	0	0	0

JACKSON GENERALS   *DOUBLE-A*

SOUTHERN LEAGUE

Batting	B-T	HT	WT	DOB	AVG	vLH	vRH	G	AB	R	H	2B	3B	HR	RBI	BB	HBP	SH	SF	SO	SB	CS	SLG	OBP
Baron, Steve	R-R	6-0	205	12-7-90	.243	.333	.238	35	107	17	26	5	1	0	13	20	0	1	0	27	3	0	.308	.362
Blash, Jabari	R-R	6-5	225	7-4-89	.278	.433	.251	60	209	38	58	16	2	10	34	31	6	0	2	60	5	0	.517	.383
Bonilla, Leury	R-R	6-2	195	2-8-85	.259	.000	.269	7	27	2	7	0	0	0	2	1	1	0	0	8	0	0	.259	.333
Bortnick, Tyler	R-R	5-11	185	7-3-87	.275	.194	.290	65	222	18	61	11	1	2	27	25	3	2	0	38	12	5	.360	.356
Brady, Patrick	R-R	5-10	176	2-5-88	.000	.000	.000	3	6	0	0	0	0	0	0	0	0	0	0	1	0	0	.000	.000
Caballero, Luis	R-R	6-0	185	7-8-92	.169	.417	.113	27	65	8	11	1	0	0	2	5	2	1	1	21	0	0	.185	.247
Cowan, Jordan	L-R	6-0	160	4-13-95	.190	—	.190	8	21	1	4	0	0	0	2	3	0	2	0	6	0	0	.190	.292
Dowd, Mike	R-R	5-9	205	4-10-90	.207	.143	.227	9	29	3	6	2	0	0	1	4	1	0	0	4	0	0	.276	.324
Fernandez, Rafael	B-R	5-10	180	4-21-94	—	—	—	1	0	1	0	0	0	0	0	0	0	0	0	0	0	0	—	—
Guerrero, Gabby	R-R	6-3	190	12-11-93	.215	.400	.184	48	177	22	38	10	2	0	15	12	0	0	2	48	3	0	.305	.262
2-team total (78 Mobile)					.222	—	—	126	460	51	102	25	5	7	47	23	1	0	4	108	11	2	.343	.258
Henry, Jabari	R-R	6-1	200	11-11-90	.170	.208	.163	91	288	35	49	15	3	10	38	44	2	3	0	99	6	0	.347	.284
Landry, Leon	L-R	5-11	185	9-20-89	.333	.250	.360	9	33	8	11	2	0	0	6	3	0	0	0	8	4	1	.394	.389
Lara, Jordy	R-R	6-3	210	5-21-91	.242	.280	.233	123	443	48	107	27	6	7	56	37	8	0	5	85	0	0	.377	.308
Leyland, Patrick	R-R	6-2	210	10-11-91	.000	—	.000	1	2	0	0	0	0	0	0	0	0	0	0	0	0	0	.000	.000
Liberato, Luis	L-L	6-1	175	12-18-95	.000	.000	.000	3	10	0	0	0	0	0	0	0	0	0	0	2	0	0	.000	.000
Littleton, Marcus	B-R	6-3	208	12-11-90	.231	.211	.239	58	195	21	45	10	0	7	25	22	0	1	3	41	1	2	.390	.305
Marlette, Tyler	R-R	5-11	195	1-23-93	.258	.206	.271	50	178	15	46	13	1	3	12	10	0	0	3	31	0	0	.393	.298
Marte, Ketel	B-R	6-1	165	10-12-93	.429	—	.429	2	7	1	3	1	0	0	1	0	0	0	0	0	2	0	.571	.500
Miller, Ian	L-R	6-0	175	2-21-92	.254	.328	.238	87	347	40	88	13	5	0	23	29	1	3	4	53	29	13	.320	.310

Batting	B-T	HT	WT	DOB	AVG	vLH	vRH	G	AB	R	H	2B	3B	HR	RBI	BB	HBP	SH	SF	SO	SB	CS	SLG	OBP
Morban, Julio	L-L	6-1	210	2-13-92	.206	.000	.227	32	107	11	22	5	2	0	7	14	1	1	2	38	0	0	.290	.298
Paolini, Dan	R-R	6-0	190	10-11-89	.271	.327	.260	93	314	34	85	13	2	4	37	42	6	2	5	66	5	3	.363	.362
Peterson, D.J.	R-R	6-1	210	12-31-91	.223	.114	.239	93	358	39	80	19	2	7	44	31	3	0	1	90	5	0	.346	.290
Pimentel, Guillermo	L-L	6-1	210	10-5-92	.219	.286	.192	23	73	10	16	5	0	3	7	18	1	0	0	25	0	0	.411	.380
Pizzano, Dario	L-R	5-11	200	4-25-91	.308	.263	.312	58	221	26	68	13	4	4	33	19	2	0	1	20	2	0	.457	.366
Reinheimer, Jack	R-R	6-1	186	7-19-92	.277	.393	.259	48	202	25	56	10	1	1	16	14	0	2	1	39	12	1	.351	.323
2-team total (76 Mobile)					.270	—	—	124	485	64	131	24	3	5	42	51	4	3	4	93	21	6	.363	.342
Reynolds, Burt	R-R	6-1	212	9-13-88	.333	.000	.429	3	9	2	3	0	0	1	1	1	0	0	0	2	0	0	.667	.400
Rodriguez, Aderlin	R-R	6-3	210	11-18-91	.206	.143	.230	44	155	18	32	11	0	3	16	12	1	0	4	38	0	1	.335	.262
Shank, Zach	R-R	6-1	180	1-6-91	.249	.231	.253	60	197	23	49	7	6	0	10	19	8	2	1	50	5	1	.345	.338
Smith, Tyler	R-R	6-0	195	7-1-91	.271	.253	.275	121	443	40	120	24	2	3	32	61	3	11	2	85	10	4	.354	.361
Tanabe, Carlton	R-R	6-0	190	10-28-91	.080	.000	.091	8	25	3	2	0	0	0	2	1	2	0	1	5	1	0	.080	.172
Wawoe, Gianfranco	B-R	5-11	170	7-25-94	.333	.250	.375	4	12	1	4	2	0	0	0	0	0	0	0	1	0	1	.500	.333

Pitching	B-T	HT	WT	DOB	W	L	ERA	G	GS	CG	SV	IP	H	R	ER	HR	BB	SO	AVG	vLH	vRH	K/9	BB/9
Anderson, Matt	R-R	6-1	210	11-18-91	3	5	3.90	44	1	0	10	67	64	35	29	5	23	63	.244	.184	.291	8.46	3.09
Cochran-Gill, Trey	R-R	5-10	190	12-10-92	4	3	5.43	34	0	0	4	53	59	38	32	0	32	30	.292	.288	.295	5.09	5.43
DeCecco, Scott	R-L	6-0	175	5-8-91	2	6	6.71	20	10	1	0	63	83	51	47	4	35	53	.331	.290	.361	7.57	5.00
Diaz, Edwin	R-R	6-3	165	3-22-94	5	10	4.57	20	20	0	0	104	102	56	53	5	37	103	.259	.226	.291	8.88	3.19
Fernandez, Anthony	L-L	6-4	215	6-8-90	0	0	1.13	2	2	0	0	8	5	1	1	0	2	9	.179	.200	.167	10.13	2.25
Fry, Paul	L-L	6-0	190	7-26-92	2	1	1.80	22	0	0	7	25	22	6	5	0	10	43	.229	.250	.212	15.48	3.60
Gillheeney, Jimmy	L-L	6-1	205	11-8-87	4	6	3.32	23	15	0	0	108	96	44	40	3	34	82	.236	.236	.237	6.81	2.82
Hernandez, Moises	R-R	6-1	168	3-18-84	3	10	5.71	30	12	0	1	98	124	73	62	7	37	59	.320	.351	.296	5.44	3.41
Hobson, Cameron	L-L	6-0	190	4-10-89	1	0	5.06	4	1	0	0	5	6	3	3	1	4	8	.273	.500	.143	13.50	6.75
Hultzen, Danny	L-L	6-3	210	11-28-89	0	1	3.38	3	3	0	0	8	10	5	3	0	5	8	.303	.250	.353	9.00	5.63
Hunter, Kyle	L-L	6-2	207	6-18-89	3	1	3.05	24	5	0	0	44	36	16	15	2	19	28	.226	.259	.208	5.68	3.86
Kittredge, Andrew	R-R	6-1	200	3-17-90	2	1	3.03	15	1	0	0	33	29	12	11	1	11	31	.242	.226	.254	8.54	3.03
Knigge, Tyler	R-R	6-4	215	10-27-88	0	1	4.05	16	0	0	2	20	20	10	9	0	10	13	.263	.450	.196	5.85	4.50
Landazuri, Steve	R-R	6-0	195	1-6-92	2	6	4.56	15	15	0	0	77	72	43	39	1	32	59	.254	.301	.217	6.90	3.74
Miller, Trevor	R-R	6-3	190	6-13-91	5	0	5.44	26	0	0	2	46	59	29	28	6	17	28	.312	.333	.296	5.44	3.30
Moran, Brian	L-L	6-3	203	9-30-88	2	1	3.56	25	0	0	0	30	29	12	12	2	17	29	.261	.233	.279	8.60	5.04
Pike, Tyler	L-L	6-0	180	1-26-94	0	2	4.91	3	3	0	0	11	11	7	6	0	12	7	.262	.308	.241	5.73	9.82
Shipers, Jordan	R-L	5-10	168	6-27-91	1	3	8.44	24	0	0	1	37	61	36	35	5	22	34	.374	.368	.379	8.20	5.30
Siverio, Misael	L-L	5-9	210	6-12-89	5	12	4.35	26	26	0	0	122	130	65	59	6	52	110	.277	.282	.275	8.11	3.84
Unsworth, Dylan	R-R	6-1	175	9-23-92	4	7	4.34	13	13	0	0	66	78	39	32	6	13	51	.299	.357	.253	6.92	1.76
Vargas, Richard	R-R	6-3	185	4-19-91	0	0	3.32	19	0	0	2	22	20	9	8	1	20	24	.244	.135	.333	12.05	8.31
Wood, Grady	R-R	6-2	195	5-18-90	4	2	4.35	36	0	0	2	60	57	36	29	4	33	41	.251	.326	.206	6.15	4.95
Zokan, Jake	R-L	6-1	200	4-27-91	3	4	4.27	13	11	0	0	59	68	34	28	8	28	42	.288	.192	.331	6.41	4.27
Zych, Tony	R-R	6-3	190	8-7-90	0	0	2.16	15	0	0	5	17	11	4	4	0	0	18	.186	.200	.176	9.72	0.00

Fielding

Catcher	PCT	G	PO	A	E	DP	PB
Baron	.992	35	244	12	2	1	1
Dowd	.986	9	64	9	1	3	1
Littlewood	.994	48	322	32	2	1	7
Marlette	.997	40	303	31	1	3	6
Tanabe	.967	8	54	5	2	2	2

First Base	PCT	G	PO	A	E	DP
Lara	.981	22	191	12	4	27
Marlette	.857	1	6	0	1	0
Paolini	.993	48	388	22	3	41
Peterson	.995	57	405	34	2	34
Rodriguez	.983	16	115	4	2	15

Second Base	PCT	G	PO	A	E	DP
Bonilla	.958	4	9	14	1	4
Bortnick	.964	60	108	156	10	39
Brady	1.000	1	2	2	0	0
Caballero	1.000	7	12	15	0	2
Cowan	1.000	7	19	17	0	7

(cont.)						
Reinheimer	1.000	4	3	11	0	0
Shank	.990	21	53	49	1	14
Smith	.970	34	66	96	5	29
Wawoe	1.000	3	7	4	0	0

Third Base	PCT	G	PO	A	E	DP
Bonilla	1.000	2	2	0	0	0
Bortnick	1.000	1	0	4	0	0
Caballero	.889	5	3	5	1	1
Cowan	1.000	1	2	3	0	1
Lara	.921	76	51	113	14	13
Peterson	.945	28	20	49	4	6
Rodriguez	.937	23	16	43	4	1
Shank	1.000	5	2	12	0	1
Smith	1.000	1	2	0	0	0

Shortstop	PCT	G	PO	A	E	DP
Caballero	.931	7	13	14	2	5
Marte	.833	1	2	3	1	1
Reinheimer	.966	44	67	131	7	29

(cont.)						
Shank	1.000	1	0	2	0	0
Smith	.969	87	136	241	12	54

Outfield	PCT	G	PO	A	E	DP
Blash	.947	52	89	1	5	1
Bonilla	—		1	0	0	0
Brady	1.000	2	1	0	0	0
Guerrero	.983	48	109	8	2	2
Henry	.948	86	158	6	9	1
Landry	1.000	7	10	0	0	0
Lara	1.000	10	17	2	0	0
Liberato	1.000	3	8	1	0	0
Miller	.995	86	184	5	1	0
Morban	.978	26	42	2	1	1
Paolini	.974	23	37	1	1	1
Pimentel	1.000	22	34	1	0	0
Pizzano	1.000	24	51	3	0	0
Reynolds	1.000	2	3	0	0	0
Shank	.988	32	75	6	1	3

BAKERSFIELD BLAZE
HIGH CLASS A
CALIFORNIA LEAGUE

Batting	B-T	HT	WT	DOB	AVG	vLH	vRH	G	AB	R	H	2B	3B	HR	RBI	BB	HBP	SH	SF	SO	SB	CS	SLG	OBP
Ascanio, Rayder	B-R	5-11	155	3-17-96	.229	.339	.202	77	297	28	68	12	1	1	30	19	1	1	4	70	6	2	.286	.274
Barbosa, Aaron	L-R	5-10	160	4-14-92	.257	.286	.252	105	377	55	97	4	0	1	18	51	2	9	3	72	31	6	.276	.346
Baum, Jay	R-R	6-0	190	10-25-92	.213	.289	.193	103	366	38	78	18	2	2	28	35	1	2	2	99	14	7	.290	.282
Caballero, Luis	R-R	6-0	185	7-8-92	.220	.143	.241	33	100	8	22	1	0	0	8	6	0	2	1	27	3	1	.230	.262
Cowan, Jordan	L-R	6-0	160	4-13-95	.375	.500	.364	6	24	4	9	2	0	0	2	1	0	2	0	3	0	1	.458	.400
Hebert, Brock	R-R	5-10	180	5-11-91	.297	.000	.367	12	37	5	11	2	1	2	12	5	1	1	2	11	2	3	.568	.378
Littlewood, Marcus	B-R	6-3	208	3-18-92	.222	.156	.156	56	54	9	2	0	2	4	12	0	0	1	18	2	0	.315	.313
Lopes, Timmy	R-R	5-11	180	6-24-94	.276	.314	.265	123	478	69	132	27	4	2	49	41	8	14	6	96	35	18	.362	.340
Mack, Chantz	L-L	5-10	205	5-4-91	.230	.133	.243	33	122	16	28	4	1	8	22	11	1	0	3	35	3	2	.475	.292
Marlette, Tyler	R-R	5-11	195	1-23-93	.216	.206	.219	39	148	17	32	5	1	5	20	12	2	0	0	35	2	1	.365	.284

Batting

Batting	B-T	HT	WT	DOB	AVG	vLH	vRH	G	AB	R	H	2B	3B	HR	RBI	BB	HBP	SH	SF	SO	SB	CS	SLG	OBP
Miller, Ian	L-R	6-0	175	2-21-92	.296	.342	.281	39	159	20	47	5	2	0	6	10	1	1	0	34	21	5	.352	.341
Morales, Estarlyn	R-R	6-3	180	10-28-92	.178	.250	.171	12	45	3	8	3	0	0	3	1	0	0	11	0	0	.244	.213
O'Neill, Tyler	R-R	5-11	210	6-22-95	.260	.267	.259	106	407	68	106	21	2	32	87	29	7	0	6	137	16	5	.558	.316
Peguero, Martin	R-R	6-1	206	11-3-93	.236	.333	.211	22	72	4	17	1	0	1	2	9	1	0	0	14	2	1	.292	.329
Petty, Kyle	R-R	6-5	215	3-15-91	.255	.236	.260	96	353	40	90	8	6	9	46	29	2	0	0	84	11	3	.388	.315
Pimentel, Guillermo	L-L	6-1	210	10-5-92	.213	.193	.221	55	211	21	45	12	0	4	22	12	2	0	0	73	4	1	.327	.262
Reynolds, Burt	R-R	6-1	212	9-13-88	.206	.119	.236	52	165	18	34	9	0	5	22	13	3	0	3	59	3	6	.352	.272
Seager, Justin	R-R	6-1	211	5-15-92	.191	.200	.188	83	278	20	53	17	1	2	22	24	10	1	2	88	2	0	.281	.277
Tanabe, Carlton	R-R	6-0	190	10-28-91	.170	.077	.193	39	135	11	23	4	1	2	15	6	0	1	2	30	1	0	.259	.203
Torres, Dan	R-R	6-0	175	5-29-92	.168	.276	.147	55	179	13	30	7	0	0	9	25	0	1	1	50	0	2	.207	.268
Ward, Nelson	L-R	5-11	175	8-6-92	.282	.254	.289	76	291	54	82	12	6	7	39	33	4	8	1	83	8	3	.436	.362
Wilson, Austin	R-R	6-4	249	2-7-92	.239	.241	.239	109	380	51	91	17	2	10	48	31	29	0	2	115	8	7	.374	.342
Zeutenhorst, Taylor	L-R	6-4	200	10-25-91	.154	.000	.174	8	26	1	4	0	0	1	2	1	0	0	2	12	0	0	.154	.241

Pitching

Pitching	B-T	HT	WT	DOB	W	L	ERA	G	GS	CG	SV	IP	H	R	ER	HR	BB	SO	AVG	vLH	vRH	K/9	BB/9
Altavilla, Dan	R-R	5-11	200	9-8-92	6	12	4.07	28	28	1	0	148	138	82	67	11	53	134	.246	.237	.254	8.13	3.22
Ash, Brett	R-R	6-2	195	5-27-91	9	8	4.36	33	19	0	0	136	161	74	66	10	34	79	.298	.320	.280	5.22	2.24
Brooks, Aaron	R-R	6-3	210	5-15-92	1	2	3.90	20	0	0	2	32	35	15	14	3	10	28	.271	.226	.303	7.79	2.78
Campbell, Ed	L-L	6-0	200	1-17-92	4	5	6.52	14	14	0	0	58	73	45	42	9	30	53	.312	.324	.307	8.22	4.66
Cochran-Gill, Trey	R-R	5-10	190	12-10-92	2	1	1.37	10	0	0	2	20	8	3	3	0	3	18	.129	.133	.125	8.24	1.37
DeCecco, Scott	R-L	6-0	175	5-8-91	3	3	3.50	11	11	0	0	62	55	27	24	6	22	49	.235	.317	.205	7.15	3.21
Diaz, Edwin	R-R	6-3	165	3-22-94	2	0	1.70	7	7	0	0	37	21	7	7	3	9	42	.167	.141	.194	10.22	2.19
Dominguez, Ronald	R-R	6-2	180	1-13-94	0	1	16.88	2	0	0	0	3	6	5	5	0	1	3	.429	.500	.375	10.13	3.38
Fry, Paul	L-L	6-0	190	7-26-92	4	3	2.13	28	1	0	2	55	46	15	13	0	14	70	.230	.224	.234	11.45	2.29
Mathis, Will	L-L	6-3	180	8-18-90	4	2	3.23	45	1	0	1	84	85	35	30	5	27	66	.261	.231	.286	7.10	2.90
Misell, Carlos	R-R	6-1	191	4-25-92	5	7	5.25	34	8	0	2	84	85	53	49	15	36	66	.261	.291	.232	7.07	3.86
Moran, Brian	L-L	6-3	210	9-30-88	0	0	0.00	2	0	0	0	3	0	0	0	0	1	0	.000	.000	.000	3.00	3.00
Morla, Ramon	R-R	6-1	205	11-20-89	0	0	1.80	5	0	0	0	5	4	1	1	0	2	9	.222	.286	.182	16.20	3.60
Pagan, Emilio	L-R	6-3	210	5-7-91	3	8	2.53	42	0	0	8	78	63	29	22	5	27	88	.218	.261	.190	10.11	3.10
Pierce, Rohn	R-R	6-3	210	1-21-93	0	0	3.86	1	0	0	0	2	2	1	1	1	1	1	.250	.500	.167	3.86	3.86
Pike, Tyler	L-L	6-0	180	1-26-94	6	6	4.26	25	25	0	0	123	119	74	58	18	63	114	.255	.277	.244	8.36	4.62
Pineda, Rafael	L-R	6-6	210	2-3-91	3	3	3.33	40	0	0	8	81	82	32	30	9	15	63	.262	.252	.269	7.00	1.67
Schepel, Kyle	L-R	6-1	230	8-7-90	1	3	3.68	22	0	0	4	37	25	16	15	5	15	45	.192	.204	.185	11.05	3.68
Unsworth, Dylan	R-R	6-1	175	9-23-92	1	3	3.32	11	5	0	0	41	40	19	15	4	4	44	.256	.253	.261	9.74	0.89
Valenza, Nick	R-L	5-10	180	3-31-93	2	3	5.77	28	0	0	2	48	58	36	31	6	21	39	.289	.246	.306	7.26	3.91
Wood, Grady	R-R	6-2	195	5-8-90	0	1	5.91	7	0	0	1	11	16	7	7	1	2	10	.348	.333	.357	8.44	1.69
Yarbrough, Ryan	R-L	6-5	205	12-31-91	4	7	3.76	16	16	0	0	81	86	44	34	7	18	74	.266	.215	.292	8.19	1.99
Zokan, Jake	R-L	6-1	200	4-27-91	1	1	1.52	5	5	0	0	24	19	9	4	0	5	16	.213	.276	.183	6.08	1.90

Fielding

Catcher	PCT	G	PO	A	E	DP	PB
Littlewood	1.000	10	81	9	0	0	0
Marlette	.986	33	241	39	4	3	9
Petty	1.000	5	34	5	0	0	6
Tanabe	.988	39	286	33	4	0	7
Torres	.994	55	423	67	3	6	9

First Base	PCT	G	PO	A	E	DP
Baum	1.000	7	67	5	0	7
Petty	.990	67	580	43	6	51
Reynolds	.976	8	78	3	2	8
Seager	.988	60	526	55	7	43
Zeutenhorst	1.000	4	26	3	0	3

Second Base	PCT	G	PO	A	E	DP
Baum	.857	1	0	6	1	1
Caballero	1.000	4	4	6	0	2

Cowan	1.000	5	8	11	0	2
Lopes	.973	86	116	250	10	53
Peguero	1.000	4	5	11	0	1
Ward	.977	46	79	137	5	29

Third Base	PCT	G	PO	A	E	DP
Caballero	.912	95	52	166	21	17
Cowan	.923	5	6	6	1	0
Lopes	.865	17	12	33	7	0
Peguero	.800	2	0	4	1	0
Reynolds	1.000	2	0	1	0	0
Seager	1.000	1	0	1	0	0
Ward	.939	19	15	31	3	5

Shortstop	PCT	G	PO	A	E	DP
Ascanio	.954	76	114	240	17	54

	PCT	G	PO	A	E	DP
Caballero	.941	24	52	59	7	9
Hebert	.971	12	18	49	2	11
Lopes	.945	16	14	38	3	10
Peguero	.974	16	27	49	2	9
Ward	.833	1	1	4	1	0

Outfield	PCT	G	PO	A	E	DP
Barbosa	.987	104	224	5	3	0
Mack	1.000	22	22	0	0	0
Miller	.965	39	82	1	3	1
Morales	1.000	10	18	0	0	0
O'Neill	.961	78	141	5	6	0
Petty	.929	17	24	2	2	0
Pimentel	.939	34	45	1	3	0
Reynolds	.963	30	50	2	2	1
Wilson	.980	101	186	12	4	3
Zeutenhorst	1.000	4	9	0	0	0

CLINTON LUMBERKINGS
MIDWEST LEAGUE

LOW CLASS A

Batting	B-T	HT	WT	DOB	AVG	vLH	vRH	G	AB	R	H	2B	3B	HR	RBI	BB	HBP	SH	SF	SO	SB	CS	SLG	OBP
Alfonso, James	R-R	5-10	195	9-3-91	.393	.278	.423	25	89	9	35	4	0	0	11	4	5	—	1	13	0	0	.438	.444
Ascanio, Rayder	B-R	5-11	155	3-17-96	.292	.000	.350	6	24	6	7	1	0	0	2	6	0	1	0	3	0	1	.333	.433
Barbosa, Aaron	L-R	5-10	160	4-14-92	.283	.250	.288	15	60	12	17	2	0	0	3	8	0	2	0	9	5	3	.317	.368
Brito, Kristian	R-R	6-5	240	12-20-94	.219	.099	.246	105	384	28	84	17	1	7	51	27	0	1	9	130	2	1	.323	.264
Caballero, Luis	R-R	6-0	185	7-8-92	.081	.167	.065	10	37	2	3	0	0	0	1	2	2	0	0	9	1	0	.081	.171
Cousino, Austin	L-L	5-10	178	4-3-92	.190	.171	.194	57	232	23	44	11	2	0	12	19	1	3	1	46	9	4	.254	.253
DeCarlo, Joe	R-R	6-0	210	9-13-93	.203	.232	.197	115	384	47	78	16	2	10	37	70	18	—	5	123	2	1	.333	.348
Fernandez, Rafael	B-R	5-10	180	4-21-94	.000	.000	.000	1	5	1	0	0	0	0	0	1	0	0	0	1	0	0	.000	.167
Fields, Arby	B-R	5-9	192	6-25-91	.262	.357	.235	91	317	51	83	9	2	3	23	57	3	—	0	69	28	10	.331	.379
Hebert, Brock	R-R	5-10	180	5-11-91	.266	.188	.277	34	128	19	34	11	1	0	9	15	0	—	2	43	4	1	.367	.338
Jackson, Alex	R-R	6-2	215	12-25-95	.157	.111	.167	28	108	10	17	6	0	0	13	6	6	0	1	35	1	1	.213	.240
Leyland, Patrick	R-R	6-2	210	10-11-91	.272	.273	.272	60	224	17	61	10	0	1	26	15	2	—	5	31	0	1	.330	.317
Liberato, Luis	L-L	6-1	175	12-18-95	.133	.250	.115	8	30	3	4	1	1	0	0	2	0	0	0	10	1	0	.233	.188

Batting

Batting	B-T	HT	WT	DOB	AVG	vLH	vRH	G	AB	R	H	2B	3B	HR	RBI	BB	HBP	SH	SF	SO	SB	CS	SLG	OBP
Mack, Chantz	L-L	5-10	205	5-4-91	.261	.305	.251	88	310	46	81	16	4	1	26	49	4	1	2	79	3	5	.348	.367
Mariscal, Chris	R-R	5-10	170	4-26-93	.236	.300	.221	105	382	35	90	13	3	2	44	41	6	—	4	113	5	6	.301	.316
Martin, Adam	R-R	6-2	230	12-7-91	.169	.000	.205	26	89	10	15	4	0	3	10	7	1	2	0	28	0	0	.315	.237
Mejia, Erick	B-R	5-11	155	11-9-94	.269	.429	.211	6	26	5	7	0	1	0	3	0	0	1	0	4	0	0	.346	.269
Morales, Estarlyn	R-R	6-3	180	10-28-92	.256	.260	.255	104	403	44	103	21	2	5	53	26	5	—	1	97	20	10	.355	.308
Morales, Jhonbaker	R-R	6-0	170	7-17-94	.235	.333	.125	5	17	0	4	1	0	0	1	1	0	0	0	3	0	0	.294	.278
Peguero, Martin	R-R	6-2	206	11-3-93	.248	.216	.254	71	234	22	58	13	1	0	25	18	1	2	4	28	7	4	.312	.300
Reynolds, Burt	R-R	6-1	212	9-13-88	.250	.353	.231	30	108	12	27	8	0	5	23	15	2	—	0	33	1	3	.463	.352
Taylor, Wayne	L-R	6-1	205	11-4-92	.234	.234	.234	86	291	26	68	15	2	3	29	28	1	0	0	113	4	1	.330	.303
Torres, Dan	R-R	6-0	175	5-29-92	.188	.118	.206	24	85	11	16	2	0	0	10	13	0	0	1	19	0	0	.212	.293
Ward, Nelson	L-R	5-11	175	8-6-92	.270	.176	.281	46	163	27	44	7	7	2	16	26	0	3	0	41	5	4	.436	.370
Wawoe, Gianfranco	B-R	5-11	170	7-25-94	.263	.259	.265	94	315	49	83	13	0	8	28	27	3	—	3	52	11	7	.381	.325
Zeutenhorst, Taylor	L-R	6-4	200	10-05-91	.227	.147	.243	55	203	20	46	8	1	2	19	13	3	1	0	45	3	0	.305	.283

Pitching

Pitching	B-T	HT	WT	DOB	W	L	ERA	G	GS	CG	SV	IP	H	R	ER	HR	BB	SO	AVG	vLH	vRH	K/9	BB/9
Brown, Jarrett	R-L	6-3	169	12-15-92	2	10	5.11	36	11	0	1	88	104	65	50	5	54	67	.300	.302	.299	6.85	5.52
Buchanan, Hawtin	R-R	6-8	230	4-29-93	0	3	4.14	26	0	0	0	41	34	24	19	1	37	53	.219	.246	.202	11.54	8.06
Campbell, Ed	L-L	6-0	200	1-17-92	3	2	2.75	8	8	0	0	52	45	17	16	3	14	32	.242	.211	.256	5.50	2.41
Cleto, Ramire	R-R	6-0	220	4-4-93	0	0	3.52	3	0	0	0	8	5	3	3	0	3	5	.192	.300	.125	5.87	3.52
Dominguez, Ronald	R-R	6-2	180	1-13-94	2	3	2.72	27	0	0	4	56	44	19	17	3	10	58	.213	.213	.212	9.27	1.60
Gohara, Luiz	L-L	6-3	210	7-31-96	0	1	1.86	2	2	0	0	10	10	2	2	0	6	5	.294	.333	.286	4.66	5.59
Herb, Tyler	R-R	6-2	175	4-28-92	7	8	4.64	27	27	1	0	140	174	82	72	6	52	95	.305	.352	.264	6.12	3.35
Horstman, Ryan	L-L	6-1	185	7-20-92	2	0	0.00	7	0	0	0	9	4	0	0	0	3	12	.138	.100	.158	12.46	3.12
Kerski, Kody	R-R	5-10	185	4-18-92	4	3	1.80	40	0	0	8	60	59	22	12	1	15	62	.258	.272	.248	9.30	2.25
Kiel, Nick	R-L	5-11	205	11-30-92	1	4	3.82	29	0	0	1	38	44	17	16	3	7	27	.293	.212	.357	6.45	1.67
Littell, Zack	R-R	6-2	190	10-5-95	3	6	3.91	21	21	0	0	113	121	63	49	4	30	84	.272	.361	.210	6.71	2.40
Medina, Jefferson	R-R	6-2	184	5-31-94	5	11	4.69	31	16	0	2	104	93	62	54	6	63	82	.237	.225	.249	7.12	5.47
Miller, Peter	R-R	6-1	195	4-27-92	0	1	5.40	19	0	0	1	30	27	18	18	1	22	29	.243	.328	.151	8.70	6.60
Missaki, Daniel	R-R	6-0	170	4-9-96	1	2	3.41	6	6	0	0	34	31	14	13	0	5	34	.244	.281	.206	8.91	1.31
Morales, Osmel	R-R	6-3	196	10-30-92	1	8	4.10	43	3	0	0	83	83	45	38	7	23	85	.259	.275	.249	9.18	2.48
Peterson, Pat	R-L	6-3	190	3-8-93	6	6	4.49	27	17	0	0	108	111	68	54	5	44	89	.262	.262	.262	7.39	3.66
Pierce, Rohn	R-R	6-3	210	1-21-93	2	4	5.80	25	0	0	0	45	48	30	29	4	17	53	.271	.250	.289	10.60	3.40
Schepel, Kyle	L-R	6-3	230	8-7-90	0	0	0.00	2	0	0	0	4	1	0	0	0	1	5	.083	.143	.000	10.38	2.08
Schiraldi, Lukas	R-R	6-6	210	7-25-93	4	13	5.19	26	26	2	0	127	117	83	73	5	71	99	.249	.269	.232	7.03	5.04
Scott, Troy	R-R	6-2	200	11-17-93	2	2	6.75	16	0	0	1	21	31	22	16	0	10	14	.337	.327	.350	5.91	4.22
Valenza, Nick	R-L	5-10	180	3-31-93	0	1	1.88	8	0	0	0	14	7	4	3	0	6	11	.140	.143	.139	6.91	3.77
Vieira, Thyago	R-R	6-2	210	1-7-93	1	4	6.97	22	0	0	0	31	35	32	24	2	20	22	.287	.250	.311	6.39	5.81
Yarbrough, Ryan	R-L	6-5	205	12-31-91	0	1	13.50	2	2	0	0	5	12	8	8	0	4	1	.462	.600	.375	1.69	6.75

Fielding

Catcher	PCT	G	PO	A	E	DP	PB
Alfonso	.995	25	199	14	1	0	4
Martin	1.000	25	188	25	0	2	7
Taylor	.984	70	455	37	8	1	16
Torres	.986	23	200	18	3	1	3

First Base	PCT	G	PO	A	E	DP
Brito	.988	79	714	29	9	56
DeCarlo	.973	4	34	2	1	3
Leyland	.987	31	283	17	4	16
Taylor	.917	3	19	3	2	0
Zeutenhorst	.987	26	205	21	3	20

Second Base	PCT	G	PO	A	E	DP
Caballero	1.000	1	1	4	0	0
Hebert	1.000	5	7	19	0	1
Mariscal	.943	23	28	55	5	11
Morales	1.000	1	4	1	0	0

	PCT	G	PO	A	E	DP
Peguero	.977	37	58	112	4	21
Ward	.995	37	73	131	1	25
Wawoe	.977	40	71	96	4	12

Third Base	PCT	G	PO	A	E	DP
DeCarlo	.932	105	66	234	22	20
Fernandez	1.000	1	0	3	0	0
Hebert	.800	1	1	3	1	1
Mariscal	1.000	11	4	15	0	2
Peguero	.938	13	8	22	2	1
Wawoe	1.000	12	6	11	0	0

Shortstop	PCT	G	PO	A	E	DP
Ascanio	.950	6	11	27	2	7
Caballero	.978	9	19	26	1	2
Hebert	.971	22	36	64	3	13
Mariscal	.941	60	75	148	14	28
Mejia	.871	6	7	20	4	1

	PCT	G	PO	A	E	DP
Morales	.800	4	3	5	2	1
Peguero	.938	8	13	17	2	2
Ward	.903	5	10	18	3	0
Wawoe	.892	22	23	60	10	9

Outfield	PCT	G	PO	A	E	DP
Barbosa	1.000	15	39	0	0	0
Cousino	.979	54	136	4	3	1
Fields	.968	89	150	2	5	0
Hebert	1.000	4	13	1	0	0
Jackson	.943	28	48	2	3	0
Liberato	1.000	7	18	0	0	0
Mack	.958	78	153	7	7	2
Morales	.940	101	157	16	11	3
Reynolds	.955	16	39	3	2	0
Taylor	1.000	3	3	1	0	0
Wawoe	1.000	12	12	2	0	0
Zeutenhorst	.969	20	30	1	1	0

EVERETT AQUASOX

SHORT-SEASON

NORTHWEST LEAGUE

Batting	B-T	HT	WT	DOB	AVG	vLH	vRH	G	AB	R	H	2B	3B	HR	RBI	BB	HBP	SH	SF	SO	SB	CS	SLG	OBP
Bishop, Braden	R-R	6-1	180	8-22-93	.320	.351	.303	56	219	34	70	8	1	2	22	5	12	11	1	33	13	3	.393	.367
Calderon, Yordyn	R-R	6-2	185	2-15-94	.202	.212	.197	42	109	22	22	2	0	5	17	9	3	0	3	26	10	2	.358	.274
Cowan, Jordan	L-R	6-0	160	4-13-95	.254	.145	.304	57	197	28	50	11	2	1	19	25	2	9	0	38	12	9	.345	.344
Fernandez, Rafael	B-R	5-10	180	4-21-94	.364	.333	.375	10	33	7	12	3	0	0	2	5	0	1	0	4	2	0	.455	.447
Hale, Conner	R-R	6-2	180	10-10-92	.163	.196	.149	48	147	9	24	7	0	0	12	12	1	4	0	22	2	0	.211	.231
Jackson, Alex	R-R	6-2	215	12-25-95	.239	.222	.246	48	163	31	39	11	1	8	25	21	12	0	1	61	2	4	.466	.365
Jackson, Drew	R-R	6-2	195	7-28-93	.358	.351	.362	59	226	64	81	12	1	2	26	30	1	7	2	35	47	4	.447	.432
Jones, P.J.	R-R	5-10	190	2-25-93	.157	.297	.077	32	102	5	16	3	0	0	6	5	2	0	2	33	1	1	.186	.207
Liberato, Luis	L-L	6-1	175	12-18-95	.260	.268	.256	53	181	34	47	10	5	5	31	24	0	7	3	47	10	3	.453	.341
Martin, Adam	R-R	6-2	230	12-7-91	.095	.143	.071	15	42	4	4	1	0	1	1	4	1	0	0	17	0	0	.190	.191
Mejia, Erick	B-R	5-11	155	11-9-94	.282	.227	.310	36	131	24	37	5	1	0	11	16	0	2	0	22	18	0	.336	.361
Nieto, Arturo	R-R	6-2	195	12-9-92	.288	.316	.275	40	118	9	34	5	0	0	13	13	2	3	2	21	1	1	.331	.363

Batting	B-T	HT	WT	DOB	AVG	vLH	vRH	G	AB	R	H	2B	3B	HR	RBI	BB	HBP	SH	SF	SO	SB	CS	SLG	OBP
O'Malley, Shawn	R-R	5-11	175	12-28-87	.182	.200	.167	3	11	1	2	1	0	0	2	0	0	1	0	4	0	0	.273	.182
Quevedo, Yojhan	R-R	6-1	212	11-6-93	.238	.235	.239	46	164	20	39	9	1	1	24	14	3	0	6	23	0	1	.323	.299
Simpson, Corey	R-R	6-2	210	12-8-93	.257	.195	.285	65	249	33	64	13	1	8	45	19	4	0	6	78	1	1	.414	.313
Taylor, Logan	R-R	6-1	200	9-22-93	.267	.180	.301	60	217	33	58	11	2	4	42	23	7	3	4	52	10	2	.392	.351
Uhl, Ryan	R-R	6-6	230	5-26-93	.259	.360	.225	60	201	23	52	15	0	4	35	24	6	0	2	65	0	1	.393	.352
Zeutenhorst, Taylor	L-R	6-4	200	10-25-91	.173	.100	.190	21	52	11	9	2	0	2	4	7	0	1	0	20	2	0	.327	.271

Pitching	B-T	HT	WT	DOB	W	L	ERA	G	GS	CG	SV	IP	H	R	ER	HR	BB	SO	AVG	vLH	vRH	K/9	BB/9
Arias, Jefferson	R-R	6-4	185	4-8-93	1	1	5.16	18	0	0	0	30	31	22	17	2	15	29	.258	.319	.219	8.80	4.55
Brentz, Jake	L-L	6-2	195	9-14-94	1	1	3.86	5	4	0	1	14	9	7	6	0	8	14	.188	.176	.194	9.00	5.14
Byrd, Taylor	R-R	6-2	195	8-15-92	0	1	5.55	9	3	0	1	24	33	16	15	1	21	10	.351	.471	.325	3.70	7.77
Cano, Joselito	L-L	6-5	190	9-16-92	2	0	4.10	16	0	0	0	26	23	18	12	3	22	23	.232	.136	.260	7.86	7.52
Clancy, Matt	B-L	5-11	180	4-1-94	1	4	1.19	22	0	0	5	30	21	5	4	1	10	35	.194	.280	.169	10.38	2.97
De Los Santos, Enyel	R-R	6-3	170	12-25-95	3	0	4.06	8	8	0	0	38	37	19	17	2	13	42	.270	.333	.229	10.04	3.11
Gillies, Darin	R-R	6-4	214	11-6-92	1	2	4.36	16	0	0	0	43	46	30	21	3	26	37	.279	.265	.289	7.68	5.40
Gohara, Luiz	L-L	6-3	210	7-31-96	3	7	6.20	14	14	0	0	54	67	45	37	4	32	62	.305	.222	.331	10.40	5.37
Hermann, Spencer	L-L	6-4	235	8-6-93	1	2	5.45	17	1	0	3	38	31	24	23	3	17	42	.223	.114	.260	9.95	4.03
Horstman, Ryan	L-L	6-1	185	7-20-92	1	0	0.00	3	0	0	0	4	0	0	0	0	2	6	.000	.000	.000	13.50	4.50
Iwakuma, Hisashi	R-R	6-3	210	4-12-81	0	0	2.45	1	1	0	0	4	3	1	1	0	0	3	.200	.333	.000	7.36	0.00
Misiewicz, Anthony	R-L	6-1	190	11-1-94	3	2	2.14	14	7	0	0	46	30	11	11	1	10	40	.189	.233	.172	7.77	1.94
Moore, Andrew	R-R	6-0	185	6-2-94	1	1	2.08	14	8	0	0	39	37	12	9	2	2	43	.250	.254	.247	9.92	0.46
Pierce, Rohn	R-R	6-3	210	1-21-93	4	0	5.17	12	1	0	0	31	25	18	18	3	14	36	.219	.216	.221	10.34	4.02
Pistorese, Joe	L-L	6-2	175	10-15-92	6	0	1.28	16	0	0	3	42	28	7	6	2	7	46	.182	.179	.183	9.78	1.49
Ratliff, Lane	L-L	6-3	185	3-22-95	1	4	7.06	9	9	0	0	29	27	23	23	6	16	23	.252	.304	.238	7.06	4.91
Santiago, Jose	R-R	6-1	190	3-1-94	2	3	5.74	13	11	0	0	47	51	34	30	9	28	44	.267	.200	.302	8.43	5.36
Scott, Troy	R-R	6-3	200	11-17-93	4	1	4.30	8	0	0	0	15	11	7	7	1	8	10	.216	.176	.235	6.14	4.91
Silva, Dylan	L-L	6-1	215	12-27-93	2	1	3.90	18	0	0	1	32	32	19	14	2	13	29	.262	.261	.263	8.07	3.62
Strain, Joey	R-R	6-1	200	1-17-94	1	0	3.42	14	0	0	2	24	30	12	9	1	3	24	.316	.281	.333	9.13	1.14
Thonvold, Lance	R-R	6-4	240	7-8-93	1	1	3.12	17	0	0	2	26	26	11	9	1	6	29	.255	.297	.231	10.04	2.08
Wells, Nick	L-L	6-5	185	2-21-96	1	0	1.00	4	3	0	0	18	6	2	2	0	4	16	.100	.059	.116	8.00	2.00
Wilcox, Kyle	R-R	6-3	195	6-14-94	2	3	3.47	19	0	0	9	23	15	10	9	1	12	24	.185	.250	.143	9.26	4.63

Fielding

Catcher	PCT	G	PO	A	E	DP	PB
Jones	.954	14	96	7	5	0	4
Martin	.979	7	41	5	1	1	1
Nieto	.991	26	201	25	2	0	11
Quevedo	.994	41	322	36	2	0	8

First Base	PCT	G	PO	A	E	DP
Calderon	.994	26	156	14	1	16
Martin	1.000	1	3	0	0	1
Uhl	.986	57	452	30	7	39

Second Base	PCT	G	PO	A	E	DP
Cowan	.982	38	78	83	3	23
Fernandez	1.000	7	4	15	0	2

	PCT	G	PO	A	E	DP
Mejia	1.000	25	52	58	0	13
O'Malley	1.000	1	4	4	0	0
Taylor	.945	14	17	35	3	8

Third Base	PCT	G	PO	A	E	DP
Calderon	1.000	1	0	4	0	0
Cowan	.970	11	10	22	1	3
Fernandez	1.000	2	1	4	0	0
Hale	.918	48	33	79	10	13
Taylor	.891	21	11	30	5	1

Shortstop	PCT	G	PO	A	E	DP
Cowan	1.000	12	14	22	0	3
Fernandez	.750	1	0	3	1	0

	PCT	G	PO	A	E	DP
Jackson	.955	58	85	147	11	30
Mejia	.825	10	12	21	7	7
O'Malley	.833	1	3	2	1	1

Outfield	PCT	G	PO	A	E	DP
Bishop	.992	53	122	5	1	0
Calderon	1.000	2	2	1	0	0
Jackson	.977	41	75	9	2	1
Liberato	.982	51	105	3	2	1
Simpson	.974	54	72	4	2	1
Taylor	1.000	23	29	2	0	1
Zeutenhorst	1.000	14	18	1	0	1

AZL MARINERS   *ROOKIE*

ARIZONA LEAGUE

Batting	B-T	HT	WT	DOB	AVG	vLH	vRH	G	AB	R	H	2B	3B	HR	RBI	BB	HBP	SH	SF	SO	SB	CS	SLG	OBP
Blanco, Dominic	L-R	6-2	215	11-10-95	.258	.091	.291	33	66	9	17	4	1	0	5	13	0	1	0	22	0	3	.348	.380
Brady, Patrick	R-R	5-10	176	2-5-88	.333	.250	.357	6	18	3	6	1	1	0	0	1	0	0	0	3	2	0	.500	.368
Camacho, Juan	R-R	6-3	215	4-19-96	.250	.130	.292	33	88	7	22	3	1	0	7	3	3	0	0	11	3	0	.307	.298
Capriata, Alexander	R-R	5-11	190	8-3-92	.340	.533	.250	23	47	6	16	0	0	4	3	0	0	0	4	3	1	.340	.380
Choi, Ji-Man	L-R	6-1	230	5-19-91	.250	.500	.200	5	12	1	3	1	0	0	2	1	0	0	2	0	0	.333	.308
Cousino, Austin	L-L	5-10	178	4-17-93	.429	.000	.500	7	21	6	9	0	1	0	4	3	0	0	1	6	2	1	.524	.480
Craig, Gus	L-L	6-2	200	4-10-93	.322	.278	.341	34	121	18	39	4	0	2	17	7	2	0	2	21	11	2	.405	.364
Dowd, Mike	R-R	5-9	205	4-10-90	.059	.000	.071	7	17	2	1	0	0	0	1	3	1	1	0	6	1	0	.059	.238
Eusebio, Ricky	R-R	5-11	195	11-25-93	.257	.238	.264	44	152	28	39	7	1	0	8	18	5	3	1	25	12	2	.316	.352
Fernandez, Rafael	R-R	5-10	180	4-21-94	.000	.000	—	1	1	0	0	0	0	0	0	0	0	0	0	0	0	0	.000	.000
Fonseca, Rob	R-R	6-2	205	5-5-93	.162	.182	.158	37	117	10	19	4	0	0	4	20	15	4	1	33	0	1	.291	.277
Fontaine, Lachlan	L-R	6-2	210	8-27-95	.289	.375	.267	11	38	4	11	0	1	0	6	4	0	1	0	5	0	0	.342	.289
Gaines, Julius	R-R	5-10	160	9-10-92	.224	.184	.235	50	174	25	39	4	0	1	6	20	0	4	1	31	17	3	.264	.303
Hebert, Brock	R-R	5-11	191	5-11-91	.091	.000	.100	5	11	1	1	0	0	0	1	2	0	0	0	3	2	1	.091	.286
Jimenez, Angel	R-R	6-1	180	9-8-94	.196	.111	.242	20	51	6	10	1	0	0	2	3	0	2	1	10	1	0	.275	.236
Jones, James	L-L	6-4	200	9-24-88	.750	.750	.750	3	8	4	6	1	1	1	5	2	0	0	0	1	2	0	1.500	.800
Kelly, Dalton	L-L	6-3	180	4-19-94	.231	.194	.231	31	96	23	21	3	4	0	11	24	2	1	0	35	10	0	.333	.385
Leal, Jose	R-R	6-3	215	2-16-95	.260	.125	.302	45	169	17	44	15	2	2	30	10	4	0	1	51	4	0	.408	.315
Marte, Ketel	B-R	6-1	165	10-12-93	.667	—	.667	1	3	1	2	0	0	0	0	0	0	0	0	0	1	0	.667	.667
Martin, Adam	R-R	6-2	230	12-7-91	.308	.000	.333	5	13	2	4	1	0	0	1	0	0	0	0	2	0	0	.385	.400
Martinez, Hersin	R-R	6-2	180	11-9-94	.152	.033	.186	42	132	6	20	3	1	1	13	6	0	1	0	62	2	1	.212	.188
Mejia, Erick	B-R	5-11	155	11-9-94	.417	1.000	.364	5	12	4	5	1	0	0	2	1	0	1	0	2	2	1	.500	.462
Morales, Jhonbaker	R-R	6-0	170	7-17-94	.281	.265	.287	50	199	23	56	6	2	0	25	5	3	3	2	37	16	4	.332	.306
Morgan, Gareth	R-R	6-4	220	4-12-96	.225	.235	.222	55	222	31	50	12	4	5	30	12	3	0	4	89	5	1	.383	.270
Perez, Taylor	R-R	5-9	170	12-26-93	.257	.250	.259	39	109	17	28	6	1	0	10	8	4	0	3	35	0	3	.330	.383

Pitching

Pitching	B-T	HT	WT	DOB	W	L	ERA	G	GS	CG	SV	IP	H	R	ER	HR	BB	SO	AVG	vLH	vRH	K/9	BB/9
De Los Santos, Enyel	R-R	6-3	170	12-25-95	3	0	2.55	5	5	0	0	25	24	8	7	1	5	29	.250	.268	.236	10.58	1.82
Fernandez, Anthony	L-L	6-4	215	6-8-90	0	0	2.25	1	1	0	0	4	5	1	1	0	0	2	.333	.667	.111	4.50	0.00
Garcia, Oliver	R-R	6-2	205	12-7-90	0	0	0.00	1	0	0	0	1	1	0	0	0	0	1	.200	.000	.250	9.00	0.00
Gaviglio, Sam	R-R	6-2	195	5-22-90	0	0	0.00	2	2	0	0	4	2	0	0	0	0	1	.143	.000	.222	2.25	0.00
Gorgas, Marvin	R-R	5-9	185	1-19-96	1	2	9.31	11	1	0	0	10	17	11	10	0	7	9	.370	.389	.357	8.38	6.52
Hobson, Cameron	L-L	6-0	190	4-10-89	0	0	0.00	1	0	0	0	2	0	0	0	0	0	1	.000	.000	.000	4.50	0.00
Horstman, Ryan	L-L	6-1	185	7-20-92	1	0	0.00	1	1	0	0	1	0	0	0	0	1	2	.000	.000	.000	18.00	9.00
Hunter, Kyle	L-L	6-2	207	6-18-89	1	1	1.42	4	0	0	0	6	7	1	1	0	1	7	.269	.429	.211	9.95	1.42
Inman, Ryne	R-R	6-5	205	5-13-96	1	1	3.45	11	7	0	0	31	20	12	12	0	8	27	.185	.180	.190	7.76	2.30
Lopez, Pablo	R-R	6-3	200	3-7-96	2	1	3.13	12	3	0	0	37	37	20	13	1	6	26	.248	.217	.270	6.27	1.45
Luetge, Lucas	L-L	6-4	205	3-24-87	0	0	0.00	1	1	0	0	1	0	0	0	0	0	1	.000	—	.000	9.00	0.00
Millord, Yohailys	R-R	6-2	180	12-4-93	0	1	2.04	15	0	0	5	18	10	8	4	0	13	21	.161	.185	.143	10.70	6.62
Mobley, Cody	R-R	6-3	190	9-23-96	2	0	1.71	9	3	0	0	26	12	5	5	1	10	19	.135	.167	.119	6.49	3.42
Morla, Ramon	R-R	6-1	205	11-20-89	0	1	6.00	6	0	0	0	6	5	4	4	0	5	5	.227	.333	.154	7.50	7.50
Muhammad, Jay	R-R	6-2	195	11-14-94	0	2	5.29	14	0	0	0	17	9	13	10	0	16	19	.161	.294	.103	10.06	8.47
Neidert, Nick	R-R	6-1	180	11-20-96	0	2	1.53	11	11	0	0	35	25	7	6	1	9	23	.198	.239	.175	5.86	2.29
Newsome, Ljay	R-R	5-11	210	11-8-96	1	0	0.84	5	0	0	0	11	4	1	1	0	0	10	.111	.083	.125	8.44	0.00
Nittoli, Vinny	R-R	6-1	210	11-11-90	0	1	3.60	7	0	0	1	10	8	4	4	1	2	7	.222	.333	.143	6.30	1.80
Orozco, Jio	R-R	6-1	208	8-15-97	3	1	2.95	8	3	0	0	21	20	7	7	0	4	24	.250	.226	.265	10.13	1.69
Peeler, Joe	R-R	6-4	175	12-2-96	0	1	9.72	9	0	0	2	8	9	10	9	1	8	5	.281	.364	.238	5.40	8.64
Peralta, Freddy	R-R	5-11	175	6-4-96	2	3	4.11	11	9	0	0	57	52	29	26	1	8	67	.242	.281	.214	10.58	1.26
Perez, Ulises	R-R	6-3	160	7-14-97	2	1	3.60	14	0	0	0	15	11	9	6	0	11	8	.200	.125	.258	4.80	6.60
Rivera, Michael	R-R	6-3	220	6-19-97	1	1	3.18	8	0	0	0	11	12	6	4	1	5	10	.255	.200	.296	7.94	3.97
Strain, Joey	R-R	6-1	200	1-17-94	0	0	1.59	5	0	0	1	6	6	1	1	0	1	8	.250	.250	.250	12.71	1.59
Thompson, Dylan	L-R	6-2	180	9-16-96	2	1	2.36	9	5	0	0	27	18	8	7	0	8	25	.191	.167	.203	8.44	2.70
Torres, Andres	R-R	6-3	185	10-31-95	1	2	5.40	12	0	0	0	17	19	14	10	2	6	16	.279	.280	.279	8.64	3.24
Walker, Matt	R-R	6-6	201	9-28-94	3	0	2.95	14	0	0	2	21	16	7	7	1	7	31	.213	.259	.188	13.08	2.95
Warren, Art	R-R	6-3	200	3-23-93	1	0	3.86	6	0	0	0	7	3	3	3	0	3	10	.269	.313	.200	12.86	3.86
West, Jared	R-L	6-6	200	6-8-93	3	0	0.00	14	0	0	2	18	10	1	0	0	3	16	.164	.133	.174	8.00	1.50
Yarbrough, Ryan	L-L	6-5	205	12-31-91	0	0	1.80	4	4	0	0	10	11	5	2	0	1	13	.282	.000	.393	11.70	0.90
Zabala, Aneurys	R-R	6-2	175	12-21-96	2	2	6.56	14	0	0	3	23	25	19	17	1	12	21	.284	.257	.302	8.10	4.63
Zayas, Gianni	R-R	6-2	200	4-18-94	0	1	12.00	15	0	0	2	15	19	23	20	3	12	24	.306	.250	.342	14.40	7.20

Fielding

Catcher	PCT	G	PO	A	E	DP	PB
Blanco	.981	27	131	26	3	2	7
Camacho	.982	32	180	44	4	2	6
Capriata	.990	19	90	14	1	0	3
Dowd	.929	5	22	4	2	0	0
Martin	.968	5	28	2	1	0	1

First Base	PCT	G	PO	A	E	DP
Choi	.962	3	22	3	1	0
Fonseca	.991	25	211	16	2	9
Jimenez	.938	4	27	3	2	5
Kelly	.992	26	222	13	2	16
Martinez	1.000	7	52	1	0	4

Second Base	PCT	G	PO	A	E	DP
Brady	1.000	1	3	0	0	0

Gaines	.966	35	60	108	6	26
Morales	.950	5	5	14	1	1
Perez	.947	20	30	41	4	5

Third Base	PCT	G	PO	A	E	DP
Brady	1.000	3	1	1	0	0
Capriata	—	1	0	0	0	0
Fonseca	.867	12	3	10	2	1
Fontaine	.944	11	4	30	2	0
Hebert	—	1	0	0	0	0
Jimenez	.903	16	7	21	3	1
Morales	.930	25	14	52	5	4

Shortstop	PCT	G	PO	A	E	DP
Fernandez	1.000	1	1	2	0	0
Gaines	.857	14	15	33	8	1

Hebert	.714	2	0	5	2	2
Marte	—	1	0	0	0	0
Mejia	—	1	2	0	0	0
Morales	.960	23	44	77	5	12
Perez	.933	20	25	45	5	11

Outfield	PCT	G	PO	A	E	DP
Cousino	1.000	5	6	1	0	0
Craig	.957	28	44	1	2	0
Eusebio	.986	37	71	2	1	0
Jones	1.000	2	2	0	0	0
Leal	.976	32	34	6	1	0
Martinez	.912	26	31	0	3	0
Morales	—	1	0	0	0	0
Morgan	.933	50	94	3	7	1

DSL MARINERS   ROOKIE

DOMINICAN SUMMER LEAGUE

Batting	B-T	HT	WT	DOB	AVG	vLH	vRH	G	AB	R	H	2B	3B	HR	RBI	BB	HBP	SH	SF	SO	SB	CS	SLG	OBP
Almonte, Adalfi	R-R	6-1	170	4-19-96	.237	.246	.233	65	173	40	41	8	1	1	19	42	11	8	0	45	8	9	.312	.416
Andrade, Greifer	R-R	6-0	170	12-7-97	.307	.304	.308	57	225	41	69	14	0	3	27	16	8	6	3	39	6	1	.409	.369
Arocha, Hector	R-R	5-11	180	1-15-97	.270	.333	.250	17	37	5	10	0	0	0	4	1	0	0	6	0	0	.270	.386
Baez, Cesar	L-R	6-0	160	7-6-95	.273	.167	.304	53	132	30	36	3	1	0	9	26	1	2	1	34	7	5	.311	.394
Branche, Steve	R-R	6-1	165	9-11-97	.129	.111	.133	40	93	16	12	0	0	1	3	6	1	0	0	37	1	1	.161	.190
Cano, Jose	R-R	5-11	190	12-18-96	.104	.182	.081	18	48	3	5	1	0	0	4	1	1	0	26	0	0	.125	.189
Contreras, Danny	L-L	6-3	195	5-21-98	.214	.179	.225	64	238	29	51	14	2	4	29	21	4	1	2	54	4	2	.340	.287
Dominguez, Anthony	R-R	6-0	170	6-6-96	.247	.208	.262	33	89	13	22	2	0	0	7	16	2	2	2	17	1	0	.270	.367
Gonzalez, Ivan	R-R	6-0	175	10-28-95	.342	.258	.371	69	263	52	90	18	2	3	39	26	4	3	6	38	19	4	.460	.401
Graterol, Jesus	R-R	6-0	145	4-8-97	.207	.139	.235	40	121	16	25	3	0	0	11	16	6	0	0	33	3	2	.231	.329
Helder, Eugene	R-R	5-11	165	2-26-96	.313	.356	.299	58	233	37	73	16	0	0	24	13	2	2	0	17	9	4	.382	.355
Hernandez, Brayan	B-R	6-2	175	9-11-97	.224	.217	.227	50	174	32	39	8	2	2	22	18	0	3	1	44	9	6	.328	.295
Herrera, Albert	R-R	5-11	160	3-7-96	.222	.000	.267	14	18	8	4	0	1	0	0	1	1	1	1	1	1	.333	.300
Jimenez, Angel	R-R	6-1	180	9-8-94	.264	.357	.231	43	159	33	42	14	0	3	27	18	2	0	2	30	7	5	.409	.343
Jimenez, Anthony	R-R	5-11	165	10-21-95	.287	.311	.278	62	237	50	68	10	4	5	30	19	13	1	1	28	30	6	.426	.370
Joseph, Luis	B-R	5-9	160	9-20-96	.331	.403	.307	66	269	48	89	16	2	1	48	8	3	0	3	27	13	6	.416	.353
Laya, Alexdray	R-R	6-1	185	10-6-95	.165	.167	.164	33	79	10	13	2	0	0	8	6	2	1	1	15	0	1	.228	.239
Leal, Bryan	L-R	6-0	164	8-20-96	.200	.143	.212	21	40	10	8	1	0	0	4	12	0	0	0	7	4	3	.225	.385
Montilla, Geoandry	R-R	6-0	165	5-14-96	.333	.200	.374	40	150	32	50	9	2	5	32	20	0	0	2	32	5	2	.520	.407
Mota, Ismerling	R-R	6-1	185	9-2-97	.318	.293	.326	47	179	26	57	11	3	0	6	39	16	3	1	2	25	2	1	.464	.380
Munoz, Oberto	R-R	6-0	170	2-18-97	.259	.214	.275	34	108	15	28	3	0	0	15	10	1	1	1	21	0	0	.287	.325

Batting	B-T	HT	WT	DOB	AVG	vLH	vRH	G	AB	R	H	2B	3B	HR	RBI	BB	HBP	SH	SF	SO	SB	CS	SLG	OBP
Pena, Onil	R-R	6-0	180	11-6-96	.278	.155	.325	59	212	25	59	12	0	5	40	17	10	1	0	39	5	2	.406	.360
Perez, Yeison	R-R	6-0	185	4-9-96	.236	.200	.247	36	110	8	26	3	0	2	28	6	2	1	3	14	2	0	.318	.281
Rengifo, Luis	B-R	5-10	165	2-26-97	.336	.279	.359	60	217	49	73	10	6	2	35	22	5	7	3	22	19	8	.465	.405
Rojas, Brayan	R-R	6-2	180	1-5-95	.188	.185	.188	42	112	21	21	2	1	3	16	20	6	1	0	27	11	3	.304	.341
Rosa, Jose	R-R	6-0	175	3-7-94	.227	.214	.233	33	88	12	20	2	1	3	14	6	3	0	0	23	1	1	.375	.299
Rosa, Joseph	B-R	5-10	165	3-6-97	.310	.191	.350	69	271	63	84	10	7	0	20	29	8	4	2	36	21	9	.399	.390
Rosario, Ronald	L-L	6-2	165	2-8-97	.208	.225	.203	53	168	13	35	8	1	0	16	16	1	0	0	34	2	8	.268	.281
Sandoval, Jose	R-R	6-0	195	10-23-96	.219	.226	.217	64	251	27	55	8	1	2	24	10	5	1	0	67	5	7	.283	.263
Tenias, Raymon	B-R	5-8	185	4-15-94	.245	.158	.276	48	143	17	35	11	0	3	17	18	2	1	2	32	9	2	.385	.333
Torres, Christopher	B-R	5-11	170	2-6-98	.251	.231	.260	64	215	40	54	8	3	2	30	51	3	3	2	56	20	9	.344	.399
Vargas, Leurys	L-R	6-3	225	8-30-96	.169	.182	.167	40	130	6	22	5	0	0	16	7	3	0	3	36	3	2	.208	.224

Pitching	B-T	HT	WT	DOB	W	L	ERA	G	GS	CG	SV	IP	H	R	ER	HR	BB	SO	AVG	vLH	vRH	K/9	BB/9
Ayala, Julio	R-R	6-1	165	9-17-97	0	0	—	1	0	0	0	1	1	1	1	0	2	0	1.000	1.000	—	—	
Berroteran, Jose	L-L	5-10	178	8-3-94	1	2	8.07	14	0	0	0	29	44	27	26	0	21	15	.364	.444	.357	4.66	6.52
Breto, Liarvis	L-L	5-11	175	4-10-93	5	1	3.21	19	0	0	1	56	58	26	20	2	7	57	.262	.224	.273	9.16	1.13
Carrillo, Rohimard	R-L	5-11	175	8-19-94	5	0	3.83	18	0	0	4	40	42	20	17	4	6	25	.264	.214	.269	5.63	1.35
Cuenca, Saul	R-R	6-5	195	3-22-98	2	2	3.76	13	10	0	2	41	40	26	17	2	32	26	.263	.229	.274	5.75	7.08
De Paula, Juan	R-R	6-3	165	9-22-97	5	4	2.32	14	14	1	0	78	62	27	20	1	15	68	.218	.351	.198	7.88	1.74
Encarnacion, Frank	R-R	6-3	195	2-13-95	5	1	2.62	14	14	0	0	69	59	26	20	0	28	53	.232	.221	.237	6.95	3.67
Feliz, Jose	R-R	6-0	170	12-23-94	5	1	5.12	17	0	0	0	32	40	21	18	7	6	18	.303	.250	.317	5.12	1.71
Fernandez, Alvaro	R-R	6-0	170	9-1-96	1	1	4.73	7	1	0	0	13	8	9	7	0	7	8	.178	.222	.167	5.40	4.73
Gadea, Kevin	R-R	6-5	188	12-6-94	4	4	2.25	13	13	1	0	76	61	28	19	5	16	74	.216	.156	.227	8.76	1.89
Guzman, Carlos	R-L	6-1	170	1-28-97	1	1	7.20	14	3	0	0	25	39	26	20	2	15	19	.361	.280	.386	6.84	5.40
Hernandez, Anjul	R-R	6-2	192	1-2-96	1	3	2.63	10	10	0	0	51	43	21	15	1	16	33	.226	.206	.231	5.79	2.81
Hernandez, Carlos	R-R	6-3	195	2-8-96	7	1	1.68	14	9	0	1	59	33	16	11	1	10	50	.159	.109	.181	7.63	1.53
Herrera, Carlos	R-R	6-2	150	10-26-97	4	2	3.26	14	14	0	0	80	68	37	29	4	13	73	.228	.222	.232	8.21	1.46
Jimenez, Luis	R-R	6-0	180	5-28-93	3	3	1.66	18	0	0	6	38	25	10	7	0	11	50	.181	.277	.132	11.84	2.61
Lopez, Robinson	R-R	6-1	175	6-2-96	0	1	9.37	13	0	0	0	16	19	19	17	1	22	16	.279	.167	.341	8.82	12.12
Manzueta, Romulo	L-L	6-2	160	10-9-95	1	0	4.43	16	0	0	0	22	17	12	11	3	17	28	.205	.176	.212	11.28	6.85
Marruffo, Wladimir	R-R	6-0	173	5-29-93	3	2	2.94	14	12	0	0	67	64	28	22	4	14	56	.252	.250	.253	7.49	1.87
Martinez, Edwin	R-R	6-6	240	7-31-95	0	0	4.05	3	0	0	0	7	5	3	3	1	1	4	.208	.333	.167	5.40	1.35
Padovani, Paolo	R-R	6-2	175	8-22-94	4	2	5.49	19	0	0	4	41	56	28	25	3	11	39	.326	.313	.333	8.56	2.41
Pedie, Raul	R-R	6-0	175	8-14-92	8	1	1.08	24	0	0	7	42	21	9	5	0	17	54	.151	.065	.176	11.66	3.67
Pena, Andres	R-R	6-3	200	1-16-95	1	2	7.39	18	0	0	0	32	40	34	26	2	16	27	.305	.261	.329	7.67	4.55
Reyes, Ricardo	R-R	6-7	198	10-17-93	2	6	5.17	17	5	0	1	38	36	29	22	0	25	27	.261	.226	.271	6.34	5.87
Rodriguez, Carlos	R-R	6-0	190	5-23-95	1	0	1.59	5	0	0	0	11	11	2	2	1	2	11	.262	.455	.194	8.74	1.59
Salinas, Edward	R-R	6-2	175	1-3-96	4	4	4.26	16	10	0	2	51	65	31	24	3	21	43	.317	.333	.309	7.64	3.73
Severino, Robert	L-R	6-2	185	2-14-94	2	1	3.02	17	1	0	3	45	32	22	15	1	22	45	.204	.154	.220	9.07	4.43
Suarez, Michael	L-L	6-2	180	3-21-95	4	4	4.50	16	9	0	3	60	71	39	30	0	16	76	.284	.304	.278	11.40	2.40
Taveras, Andy	R-R	6-2	185	4-30-96	0	0	4.91	4	0	0	0	7	10	7	4	0	3	6	.333	.600	.280	7.36	3.68
Urquides, Melchor	B-L	6-0	180	7-26-95	2	0	3.62	13	0	0	0	32	34	19	13	1	11	25	.274	.364	.265	6.96	3.06
Vasquez, Pedro	R-R	6-4	190	9-23-95	8	2	2.08	15	15	1	0	91	70	30	21	5	10	71	.209	.197	.216	7.02	0.99

Fielding

Catcher	PCT	G	PO	A	E	DP	PB
Arocha	.988	15	69	15	1	0	1
Dominguez	.981	25	183	19	4	1	0
Montilla	.964	4	21	6	1	0	1
Mota	.993	27	247	30	2	4	10
Munoz	.989	34	225	33	3	1	3
Pena	.996	29	189	36	1	0	14
Perez	.973	18	99	11	3	1	4
Tenias	.989	18	83	10	1	0	4

First Base	PCT	G	PO	A	E	DP
Baez	1.000	1	2	0	0	0
Cano	.982	7	53	2	1	4
Contreras	.966	31	278	6	10	31
Dominguez	1.000	5	46	0	0	4
Gonzalez	1.000	13	78	5	0	2
Jimenez	.967	13	83	4	3	12
Laya	1.000	2	6	1	0	1
Montilla	.982	25	206	13	4	12
Mota	1.000	1	6	0	0	0
Pena	.982	12	104	3	2	12
Perez	1.000	2	11	1	0	2
Rosa	1.000	2	10	2	0	1
Tenias	.991	19	111	4	1	12
Vargas	.973	31	241	16	7	23

Second Base	PCT	G	PO	A	E	DP
Andrade	.940	18	42	36	5	4
Baez	1.000	4	5	5	0	2
Branche	.875	5	6	8	2	1
Gonzalez	1.000	6	4	9	0	2
Helder	.963	17	36	41	3	11
Joseph	.942	27	56	57	7	12
Laya	1.000	7	2	7	0	2
Rengifo	.994	39	88	81	1	30
Rosa	.933	37	68	84	11	12
Torres	.949	11	31	25	3	8

Third Base	PCT	G	PO	A	E	DP
Andrade	.870	14	15	25	6	6
Baez	.901	21	23	50	8	4
Branche	.842	7	5	11	3	1
Cano	—	2	0	0	0	0
Gonzalez	.903	19	15	50	7	6
Helder	.921	39	34	50	8	3
Herrera	.571	3	1	3	3	0
Jimenez	.869	25	25	48	11	5
Joseph	.886	13	12	27	5	8
Laya	.912	23	12	50	6	6
Tenias	1.000	1	0	1	0	0

Shortstop	PCT	G	PO	A	E	DP
Andrade	.908	27	38	61	10	12

	PCT	G	PO	A	E	DP
Baez	.957	10	11	11	1	2
Branche	.934	23	17	40	4	2
Gonzalez	.875	3	6	8	2	2
Helder	.875	2	2	5	1	0
Rengifo	.922	20	30	53	7	16
Rosa	.947	28	42	66	6	10
Torres	.900	53	82	160	27	27

Outfield	PCT	G	PO	A	E	DP
Almonte	.991	63	108	6	1	2
Baez	.917	15	20	2	2	0
Contreras	.965	33	49	6	2	1
Gonzalez	.983	26	58	0	1	0
Graterol	.981	39	48	4	1	2
Hernandez	.980	49	93	4	2	0
Herrera	1.000	5	10	0	0	0
Jimenez	1.000	3	3	0	0	0
Jimenez	.960	60	110	11	5	0
Joseph	1.000	6	5	0	0	0
Leal	.941	17	15	1	1	0
Montilla	.941	10	16	0	1	0
Rojas	.962	34	47	4	2	1
Rosa	1.000	13	14	0	0	0
Rosario	.964	53	78	3	3	1
Sandoval	.991	63	105	5	1	2

Tampa Bay Rays

SEASON IN A SENTENCE: After losing executive Andrew Friedman and manager Joe Maddon, the Rays flirted with .500 for most of the 2015 season, thanks largely to significant improvements for several rotation arms, including Chris Archer, Jake Odorizzi, Erasmo Ramirez and Nate Karns.

HIGH POINT: Entering June, the Rays were an even 26-25. Over the next three weeks they went 14-5, and jumped into first place in the American League East. The stretch began with Chris Archer's brilliant 15-strikeout performance on June 2. The Rays also had a strong run in early August, when they won seven of nine games.

LOW POINT: Immediately following their hot streak in June, the Rays made a U-turn and took a nosedive toward the bottom of the division. They went from 40-30 to 43-45, erasing the progress they had made just a few weeks prior.

NOTABLE ROOKIES: The Rays minor league system graduated two promising arms in Nate Karns and Alex Colome. Karns proved himself a capable middle-of-the-rotation horse, while Colome saw mixed results as a starter before succeeding out of the bullpen in the latter half of the season. Touted prospect and offseason trade acquisition Steven Souza showed glimpses of power and speed and finished the season with a strong September. Joey Butler, who the Rays added as a minor league free agent in the offseason, earned significant playing time, providing some righthanded offense.

KEY TRANSACTIONS: With their winning percentage fluttering around .500, the Rays traded away two major leaguers in late July. They traded David DeJesus to the Angels for Eduar Lopez, then shipped Kevin Jepsen to the Twins for Chih-Wei Hu and Alexis Tapia. The Rays also traded an international bonus slot to the Braves for righthanded pitching prospect Garrett Fulenchek.

DOWN ON THE FARM: Charlotte claimed its Florida State League title behind dominant pitching from Hu, who tossed eight shutout frames in the series opener, and top prospect Brent Honeywell, who yielded just one earned run over six in the decisive Game Four, which ended on a bases-loaded walk in the 13th inning. Lefthahnder Blake Snell's prospect flame exploded this season, and he earned Minor League Player of the Year honors as he reached Triple-A. Meanwhile, 2011 first-rounder Taylor Guerrieri returned from Tommy John surgery and reached Double-A.

OPENING DAY PAYROLL: $75,794,234 (28th).

PLAYERS OF THE YEAR

MAJOR LEAGUE	MINOR LEAGUE
Chris Archer	**Blake Snell**
rhp	lhp
12-13, 3.23	(High A/Double-A/
252 SO in 212 IP,	Triple-A)
66 BB	Minor League POY

ORGANIZATION LEADERS

BATTING   *Minimum 250 AB

MAJORS

* AVG	Logan Forsythe	0.281
* OPS	Logan Forsythe	0.803
HR	Evan Longoria	21
RBI	Evan Longoria	73

MINORS

* AVG	Joey Rickard, Charlotte, Mont.gomery, Durham	.321
*OBP	Joey Rickard, Charlotte, Montgomery, Durham	.427
* SLG	Richie Shaffer, Montgomery, Durham	.539
OPS	Richie Shaffer, Montgomery, Durham	897
R	Taylor Motter, Durham	74
H	Taylor Motter, Durham	142
TB	Taylor Motter, Durham	229
2B	Taylor Motter, Durham	43
3B	Tyler Goeddel, Montgomery	10
HR	Richie Shaffer, Montgomery, Durham	26
RBI	Jake Bauers, Charlotte, Montgomery	74
BB	Joey Rickard, Charlotte, Montgomery, Durham	69
SO	Yoel Araujo, Charlotte	130
	Corey Brown, Durham	130
SB	Jace Conrad, Bowling Green, Charlotte	32

PITCHING   #Minimum 75 IP

MAJORS

W	Chris Archer	12
# ERA	Chris Archer	3.23
SO	Chris Archer	252
SV	Brad Boxberger	41

MINORS

W	Jacob Faria, Charlotte, Montgomery	17
L	German Marquez, Charlotte	13
# ERA	Blake Snell, Charlotte, Montgomery, Durham	1.41
G	Brad Schreiber, Charlotte, Montgomery	54
GS	Jaime Schultz, Montgomery	27
SV	Brad Schreiber, Charlotte, Montgomery	30
IP	Austin Pruitt, Montgomery	160
BB	Jaime Schultz, Montgomery	90
SO	Jaime Schultz, Montgomery	168
AVG	Blake Snell, Charlotte, Montgomery, Durham	.182

2015 PERFORMANCE

General Manager: Matthew Silverman. **Farm Director:** Mitch Lukevics. **Scouting Director:** Rob Metzler.

Class	Team	League	W	L	PCT	Finish	Manager
Majors	Tampa Bay Rays	American	80	82	.494	10th (15)	Kevin Cash
Triple-A	Durham Bulls	International	74	70	.514	t-7th (14)	Jared Sandberg
Double-A	Montgomery Biscuits	Southern	77	61	.558	2nd (10)	Brady Williams
High A	Charlotte Stone Crabs	Florida State	69	66	.511	6th (12)	Michael Johns
Low A	Bowling Green Hot Rods	Midwest	69	69	.500	10th (16)	Reinaldo Ruiz
Short season	Hudson Valley Renegades	New York-Penn	39	37	.513	7th (14)	Tim Parenton
Rookie	Princeton Rays	Appalachian	37	31	.544	3rd (10)	Danny Sheaffer
Rookie	Rays	Gulf Coast	16	44	.267	16th (16)	Jim Morrison
Overall 2015 Minor League Record			381	378	.502	17th (30)	

ORGANIZATION STATISTICS

TAMPA BAY RAYS

AMERICAN LEAGUE

Batting	B-T	HT	WT	DOB	AVG	vLH	vRH	G	AB	R	H	2B	3B	HR	RBI	BB	HBP	SH	SF	SO	SB	CS	SLG	OBP
Arencibia, J.P.	R-R	6-0	205	1-5-86	.310	.259	.341	24	71	9	22	3	0	6	17	1	0	0	1	22	0	0	.606	.315
Beckham, Tim	R-R	6-0	195	1-27-90	.222	.236	.206	82	203	24	45	7	4	9	37	13	3	0	4	69	3	1	.429	.274
Brett, Ryan	R-R	5-9	180	10-9-91	.667	1.000	.000	3	3	0	2	1	0	0	1	0	0	0	0	0	0	0	1.000	.750
Butler, Joey	R-R	6-2	220	3-12-86	.276	.259	.289	88	257	30	71	12	0	8	30	16	3	0	0	82	5	2	.416	.326
Cabrera, Asdrubal	B-R	6-0	205	11-13-85	.265	.281	.259	143	505	66	134	28	5	15	58	36	3	1	6	107	6	3	.430	.315
Casali, Curt	R-R	6-2	230	11-9-88	.238	.241	.236	38	101	13	24	6	0	10	18	8	2	1	1	34	0	0	.594	.304
DeJesus, David	L-L	5-11	190	12-20-79	.259	.125	.263	82	232	24	60	8	2	5	26	19	4	0	2	39	3	2	.375	.323
2-team total (30 Los Angeles)					.233	—	—	112	288	27	67	9	2	5	30	21	6	0	2	52	3	2	.330	.297
Dykstra, Allan	L-R	6-5	215	5-21-87	.129	.000	.138	13	31	3	4	0	0	1	4	6	1	0	0	12	0	0	.226	.289
Elmore, Jake	R-R	5-9	185	6-15-87	.206	.304	.158	51	141	10	29	5	0	2	16	12	0	2	3	25	1	1	.284	.263
Forsythe, Logan	R-R	6-1	205	1-14-87	.281	.299	.273	153	540	69	152	33	2	17	68	55	14	0	6	111	9	4	.444	.359
Franklin, Nick	B-R	6-1	190	3-2-91	.158	.207	.139	44	101	11	16	4	1	3	7	7	0	1	0	37	1	0	.307	.213
Guyer, Brandon	R-R	6-2	200	1-28-86	.265	.271	.257	128	332	51	88	21	2	8	28	25	24	3	1	61	10	4	.413	.359
Jaso, John	L-R	6-2	205	9-19-83	.286	.308	.285	70	185	23	53	17	0	5	22	28	1	0	2	39	1	2	.459	.380
Jennings, Desmond	R-R	6-2	210	10-30-86	.268	.320	.250	28	97	9	26	2	1	1	7	8	1	0	1	17	5	3	.340	.324
Kiermaier, Kevin	L-R	6-1	215	4-22-90	.263	.246	.270	151	505	62	133	25	12	10	40	24	2	2	2	95	18	5	.420	.298
Krauss, Marc	L-R	6-2	245	10-5-87	.100	—	.100	4	10	0	1	0	0	0	1	0	0	0	0	7	0	0	.100	.100
3-team total (12 Detroit, 11 Los Angeles)					.141	—	—	27	78	3	11	3	0	2	8	3	0	0	0	31	0	0	.256	.173
Loney, James	L-L	6-3	235	5-7-84	.280	.226	.296	104	361	25	101	16	0	4	32	23	1	0	3	34	2	4	.357	.322
Longoria, Evan	R-R	6-2	210	10-7-85	.270	.342	.245	160	604	74	163	35	1	21	73	51	6	0	9	132	3	1	.435	.328
Mahtook, Mikie	R-R	6-1	200	11-30-89	.295	.294	.297	41	105	22	31	5	1	9	19	6	3	1	0	31	4	3	.619	.351
Maile, Luke	R-R	6-3	225	2-6-91	.171	.238	.071	15	35	2	6	3	0	0	2	0	0	0	0	8	0	0	.257	.171
Nava, Daniel	B-L	5-11	200	2-22-83	.233	.280	.208	31	73	7	17	2	0	1	3	12	3	0	0	19	1	0	.301	.364
2-team total (29 Boston)					.194	—	—	60	139	13	27	4	0	1	10	20	5	1	1	36	1	0	.245	.315
Rivera, Rene	R-R	5-10	215	7-31-83	.178	.181	.176	110	298	16	53	14	0	5	26	11	3	5	2	86	0	0	.275	.213
Shaffer, Richie	R-R	6-3	220	3-15-91	.189	.137	.304	31	74	11	14	3	0	4	6	10	3	0	1	32	0	1	.392	.307
Sizemore, Grady	L-L	6-2	205	8-2-82	.257	.400	.248	58	175	20	45	12	0	6	27	14	2	0	1	37	3	3	.429	.318
Souza, Steven	R-R	6-4	225	4-24-89	.225	.212	.230	110	373	59	84	15	1	16	40	46	5	1	1	144	12	6	.399	.318
Wilson, Bobby	R-R	6-0	220	4-8-83	.145	.111	.162	25	55	3	8	0	0	0	4	4	0	0	0	16	0	0	.145	.203
2-team total (31 Texas)					.189	—	—	56	132	8	25	5	0	1	14	11	1	2	1	39	0	1	.250	.255

Pitching	B-T	HT	WT	DOB	W	L	ERA	G	GS	CG	SV	IP	H	R	ER	HR	BB	SO	AVG	vLH	vRH	K/9	BB/9
Andriese, Matt	R-R	6-3	215	8-28-89	3	5	4.11	25	8	0	2	66	69	32	30	8	18	49	.267	.281	.255	6.72	2.47
Archer, Chris	R-R	6-3	190	9-26-88	12	13	3.23	34	34	1	0	212	175	85	76	19	66	252	.220	.227	.218	10.70	2.80
Balfour, Grant	R-R	6-2	200	12-30-77	0	0	6.23	6	0	0	0	4	3	3	1	4	0	.200	.400	.100	0.00	8.31
Belisario, Ronald	R-R	6-3	240	12-31-82	0	0	7.88	6	0	0	0	8	8	7	7	0	4	6	.250	.316	.154	6.75	4.50
Beliveau, Jeff	L-L	6-1	190	1-17-87	0	0	13.50	5	0	0	0	3	6	4	4	1	1	2	.429	.333	.500	6.75	3.38
Bellatti, Andrew	R-R	6-1	190	8-5-91	3	1	2.31	17	0	0	0	23	16	7	6	4	10	18	.198	.167	.222	6.94	3.86
Boxberger, Brad	R-R	6-2	225	5-27-88	4	10	3.71	69	0	0	41	63	54	29	26	9	32	74	.231	.225	.238	10.57	4.57
Cedeno, Xavier	L-L	6-0	215	8-26-86	4	1	2.09	61	0	0	1	43	37	11	10	3	12	43	.230	.196	.275	9.00	2.51
Colome, Alex	R-R	6-2	220	12-31-88	8	5	3.94	43	13	0	0	110	112	50	48	9	31	88	.271	.278	.264	7.22	2.54
Dominguez, Jose	R-R	6-0	200	8-7-90	1	0	0.00	4	0	0	0	6	2	0	0	0	2	5	.125	.200	.091	7.94	3.18
Frieri, Ernesto	R-R	6-2	205	7-19-85	1	0	4.63	22	0	0	2	23	20	12	12	6	11	19	.233	.220	.244	7.33	4.24
Geltz, Steve	R-R	5-10	210	11-1-87	2	6	3.74	70	2	0	2	67	45	31	28	8	26	61	.189	.196	.184	8.15	3.48
Gomes, Brandon	R-R	5-11	190	7-15-84	2	6	4.27	63	0	0	1	59	55	28	28	10	15	44	.248	.192	.293	6.71	2.29
Guilmet, Preston	R-R	6-2	200	7-27-87	0	0	5.06	3	0	0	0	5	5	3	3	1	2	5	.250	.182	.333	8.44	3.38
Jepsen, Kevin	R-R	6-3	235	7-26-84	2	5	2.81	46	0	0	5	42	34	15	13	4	20	34	.227	.260	.192	7.34	4.32
2-team total (29 Minnesota)					3	6	2.33	75	0	0	15	70	52	22	18	5	27	59	—	—	—	7.62	3.49
Karns, Nate	R-R	6-3	225	11-25-87	7	5	3.67	27	26	0	0	147	132	62	60	19	56	145	.239	.248	.229	8.88	3.43
McGee, Jake	L-L	6-3	230	8-6-86	1	2	2.41	39	0	0	6	37	27	11	10	3	8	48	.197	.200	.196	11.57	1.93
Moore, Matt	L-L	6-3	210	6-18-89	3	4	5.43	12	12	0	0	63	74	40	38	9	23	46	.298	.265	.315	6.57	3.29
Odorizzi, Jake	R-R	6-2	190	3-27-90	9	9	3.35	28	28	0	0	169	149	65	63	18	46	150	.231	.230	.234	7.97	2.44
Ramirez, Erasmo	R-R	5-11	200	5-2-90	11	6	3.75	34	27	0	0	163	145	73	68	16	40	126	.236	.193	.283	6.94	2.20
Riefenhauser, C.J.	L-L	6-0	195	1-30-90	1	0	5.52	11	0	0	0	15	15	10	9	3	7	7	.283	.370	.192	4.30	4.30

Pitching

Pitching	B-T	HT	WT	DOB	W	L	ERA	G	GS	CG	SV	IP	H	R	ER	HR	BB	SO	AVG	vLH	vRH	K/9	BB/9
Romero, Enny	L-L	6-3	215	1-24-91	0	2	5.10	23	0	0	0	30	39	18	17	1	13	31	.312	.391	.266	9.30	3.90
Smyly, Drew	L-L	6-3	190	6-13-89	5	2	3.11	12	12	0	0	67	58	24	23	11	20	77	.230	.157	.249	10.40	2.70
Teaford, Everett	L-L	6-0	160	5-15-84	0	0	1.59	4	0	0	0	6	5	1	1	0	3	4	.250	.333	.125	6.35	4.76
Yates, Kirby	R-R	5-10	210	3-25-87	1	0	7.97	20	0	0	0	20	23	18	18	10	7	21	.274	.333	.235	9.30	3.10

Fielding

Catcher	PCT	G	PO	A	E	DP	PB
Arencibia	.994	23	148	12	1	0	1
Casali	.996	37	241	15	1	4	0
Maile	1.000	15	76	5	0	1	1
Rivera	.987	107	752	60	11	5	6
Wilson	1.000	24	153	11	0	1	0

First Base	PCT	G	PO	A	E	DP
Dykstra	.979	13	92	1	2	9
Elmore	.984	25	178	7	3	13
Forsythe	.984	26	120	6	2	10
Franklin	.962	10	46	4	2	7
Krauss	.958	4	21	2	1	1
Loney	.992	101	729	42	6	58
Nava	.968	7	28	2	1	1
Rivera	1.000	7	17	1	0	0
Shaffer	1.000	10	64	6	0	4

Second Base	PCT	G	PO	A	E	DP
Beckham	.947	38	31	59	5	13
Brett	.857	3	3	3	1	1
Elmore	1.000	7	7	9	0	1
Forsythe	.985	126	164	299	7	43
Franklin	.981	17	16	36	1	7

Third Base	PCT	G	PO	A	E	DP
Beckham	1.000	1	2	2	0	0
Elmore	.867	9	6	7	2	3
Forsythe	1.000	9	6	13	0	0
Longoria	.976	148	109	259	9	29
Shaffer	.923	8	6	6	1	3

Shortstop	PCT	G	PO	A	E	DP
Beckham	.974	28	23	52	2	10
Cabrera	.980	136	150	284	9	51

	PCT	G	PO	A	E	DP
Elmore	1.000	7	6	13	0	3
Franklin	.909	11	7	13	2	2

Outfield	PCT	G	PO	A	E	DP
Butler	.982	34	55	1	1	0
DeJesus	.989	53	89	3	1	0
Elmore	1.000	6	5	0	0	0
Guyer	.994	110	172	2	1	1
Jaso	1.000	8	2	1	0	0
Jennings	1.000	26	50	3	0	0
Kiermaier	.988	149	412	15	5	3
Mahtook	.985	36	63	1	1	1
Nava	1.000	24	30	2	0	0
Shaffer	1.000	3	2	0	0	0
Sizemore	.972	43	67	2	2	0
Souza	.989	103	172	8	2	3

DURHAM BULLS   TRIPLE-A
INTERNATIONAL LEAGUE

Batting	B-T	HT	WT	DOB	AVG	vLH	vRH	G	AB	R	H	2B	3B	HR	RBI	BB	HBP	SH	SF	SO	SB	CS	SLG	OBP
Acosta, Mayobanex	R-R	6-1	220	11-20-87	.083	.000	.114	16	48	2	4	1	0	0	3	1	0	0	1	15	0	0	.104	.100
Arencibia, J.P.	R-R	6-0	205	1-5-86	.227	.266	.211	99	384	52	87	17	0	22	65	15	3	0	3	125	0	0	.443	.259
Beckham, Tim	R-R	6-0	195	1-27-90	.308	.333	.303	11	39	5	12	6	0	0	4	5	0	0	1	10	2	1	.462	.378
Belnome, Vince	L-R	5-11	205	3-11-88	.169	.152	.173	46	160	10	27	7	1	0	6	27	2	0	2	57	1	0	.225	.293
Brett, Ryan	R-R	5-9	180	10-9-91	.247	.180	.272	84	328	48	81	18	1	5	30	15	6	0	5	64	4	3	.354	.288
Brown, Corey	L-L	6-1	210	11-26-85	.243	.222	.250	114	407	63	99	19	3	19	60	43	2	0	3	130	15	2	.445	.316
Butler, Joey	R-R	6-2	220	3-12-86	.333	.300	.344	32	120	21	40	9	1	6	24	14	3	0	0	31	0	0	.575	.416
Casali, Curt	R-R	6-2	230	11-9-88	.205	.278	.171	32	112	14	23	4	0	4	13	17	3	0	0	29	1	0	.348	.326
Casilla, Alexi	B-R	5-9	170	7-20-84	.315	.314	.315	37	127	15	40	8	0	3	14	13	0	2	0	22	4	2	.449	.379
2-team total (57 Toledo)					.287	—	—	94	335	43	96	19	2	4	31	27	1	4	0	51	10	5	.391	.342
Constanza, Jose	L-L	5-9	185	9-1-83	.238	.400	.188	5	21	1	5	2	0	0	3	0	1	0	0	4	3	0	.333	.273
2-team total (41 Louisville)					.253	—	—	46	146	17	37	6	2	0	17	12	1	2	0	20	9	4	.322	.314
Dominguez, Wilmer	R-R	5-10	180	6-19-91	.444	1.000	.375	2	9	2	4	0	0	0	3	0	0	0	0	2	0	0	.444	.444
Dykstra, Allan	L-R	6-5	215	5-21-87	.212	.229	.206	39	132	17	28	7	0	3	15	34	0	0	1	35	0	0	.333	.371
Elmore, Jake	R-R	5-9	185	6-15-87	.247	.259	.243	57	198	20	49	4	0	0	12	38	3	1	0	30	4	4	.268	.377
Franklin, Nick	B-R	6-1	190	3-2-91	.266	.178	.293	57	192	26	51	10	1	11	30	27	0	0	2	48	4	3	.500	.353
Jaso, John	L-R	6-2	205	9-19-83	.143	.200	.000	2	7	0	1	0	0	0	1	0	0	0	0	0	0	0	.143	.143
Jennings, Desmond	R-R	6-2	210	10-30-86	.143	.000	.188	7	21	2	3	2	0	0	0	4	0	0	0	5	0	0	.238	.280
Lee, Hak-Ju	L-R	6-2	170	11-4-90	.220	.214	.222	96	313	33	69	15	1	3	27	35	3	7	2	105	20	3	.304	.303
Mahtook, Mikie	R-R	6-1	200	11-30-89	.249	.288	.234	98	385	35	96	27	3	4	45	22	9	0	2	98	10	1	.366	.304
Maile, Luke	R-R	6-3	225	2-6-91	.207	.230	.200	89	294	38	61	9	1	5	29	35	4	1	3	50	1	1	.296	.298
Motter, Taylor	R-R	6-1	195	9-18-89	.292	.370	.262	127	486	74	142	43	1	14	72	57	5	1	9	95	26	8	.471	.366
Powell, Boog	L-L	5-10	185	1-14-93	.257	.235	.265	56	206	22	53	10	3	2	18	32	2	4	2	41	7	6	.364	.360
Querecuto, Juniel	B-R	5-9	155	9-19-92	.300	.333	.250	4	10	1	3	1	0	0	1	2	0	0	0	4	0	0	.400	.417
Reginatto, Leonardo	R-R	6-2	179	4-10-90	.267	.340	.230	42	150	15	40	8	0	0	11	3	1	0	0	16	0	2	.320	.286
Rickard, Joey	R-L	6-1	185	5-21-91	.360	.231	.413	29	89	16	32	6	2	0	11	10	3	1	1	20	1	0	.472	.437
Seitzer, Cameron	L-R	6-5	220	1-11-90	.367	.182	.474	7	30	2	11	1	0	1	6	0	0	0	0	6	0	0	.500	.367
Shaffer, Richie	R-R	6-3	220	3-15-91	.270	.310	.258	69	244	42	66	17	1	19	45	31	3	0	4	74	1	1	.582	.355
Sizemore, Grady	L-L	6-2	205	8-2-82	.222	.400	.154	4	18	1	4	0	0	0	1	0	0	0	1	2	0	0	.222	.211
Sole, Alec	L-R	6-2	200	6-1-93	.000	.000	.000	2	7	1	0	0	0	0	0	0	0	0	0	4	0	0	.000	.000
Souza, Steven	R-R	6-4	225	4-24-89	.200	.400	.000	3	10	1	2	0	0	0	0	1	0	0	0	4	0	0	.200	.273
Velez, Eugenio	B-R	6-1	170	5-16-82	.272	.226	.291	56	213	23	58	11	2	2	22	20	1	1	1	44	15	4	.371	.336
Wilson, Bobby	R-R	6-0	220	4-8-83	.184	.231	.130	17	49	3	9	1	0	0	6	0	0	0	0	11	0	0	.204	.273

Pitching	B-T	HT	WT	DOB	W	L	ERA	G	GS	CG	SV	IP	H	R	ER	HR	BB	SO	AVG	vLH	vRH	K/9	BB/9
Andriese, Matt	R-R	6-3	225	8-28-89	3	3	2.35	13	12	0	0	65	65	24	17	2	10	69	.259	.216	.302	9.55	1.38
Balfour, Grant	R-R	6-2	200	12-30-77	0	0	2.79	8	0	0	0	10	9	3	3	1	6	11	.237	.357	.167	10.24	3.72
Belisario, Ronald	R-R	6-2	240	12-31-82	0	2	3.26	27	0	0	17	30	28	11	11	2	9	18	.252	.357	.188	5.34	2.67
2-team total (5 Pawtucket)					0	3	2.70	32	0	0	17	37	32	13	11	2	12	20	—	—	—	4.91	2.95
Bellatti, Andrew	R-R	6-1	190	8-5-91	2	1	5.24	20	4	0	1	46	50	28	27	5	15	44	.278	.284	.274	8.55	2.91
Bird, Kyle	L-L	6-2	175	4-12-93	0	0	0.00	2	1	0	0	2	1	0	0	0	2	2	.200	.000	.250	10.80	10.80
Buschmann, Matt	R-R	6-3	195	2-13-84	6	5	3.89	13	13	0	0	79	69	35	34	9	29	63	.236	.257	.218	7.21	3.32
3-team total (9 Louisville, 1 Norfolk)					8	10	4.08	23	23	2	0	135	123	62	61	13	47	109	—	—	—	7.28	3.14
Colome, Alex	R-R	6-2	220	12-31-88	1	0	1.93	2	2	0	0	9	8	2	2	1	3	12	.242	.333	.167	11.57	2.89
Diamond, Scott	L-L	6-3	220	7-30-86	11	6	3.71	28	25	0	0	150	180	78	62	13	26	91	.300	.367	.274	5.45	1.56
Dominguez, Jose	R-R	6-0	200	8-7-90	0	2	6.18	30	2	0	1	28	36	20	19	5	20	25	.319	.375	.277	8.13	6.51
Floro, Dylan	L-R	6-2	175	12-27-90	9	12	5.02	25	22	1	0	133	160	78	74	10	21	81	.297	.353	.254	5.49	1.42

TAMPA BAY RAYS

Pitching

Pitching	B-T	HT	WT	DOB	W	L	ERA	G	GS	CG	SV	IP	H	R	ER	HR	BB	SO	AVG	vLH	vRH	K/9	BB/9
Frieri, Ernesto	R-R	6-2	205	7-19-85	0	1	3.68	8	0	0	1	7	6	6	3	1	10	5	.222	.154	.286	6.14	12.27
Gomes, Brandon	R-R	5-11	190	7-15-84	0	1	3.38	4	0	0	0	5	6	3	2	0	1	7	.300	.000	.375	11.81	1.69
Guilmet, Preston	R-R	6-2	200	7-27-87	0	0	2.40	13	0	0	3	15	14	4	4	1	6	16	.237	.192	.273	9.60	3.60
2-team total (10 Buffalo)					0	0	1.84	23	0	0	3	29	24	6	6	1	9	28	—	—	—	8.59	2.76
Hagens, Bradin	R-R	6-3	210	5-12-89	5	5	2.67	14	12	0	0	71	53	23	21	3	26	50	.206	.215	.197	6.37	3.31
Marinez, Jhan	R-R	6-1	200	8-12-88	4	1	1.92	45	0	0	5	61	43	14	13	5	24	65	.196	.200	.194	9.59	3.54
Markel, Parker	R-R	6-4	220	9-15-90	0	0	4.91	5	0	0	0	7	5	4	4	1	5	7	.192	.273	.133	8.59	6.14
McGee, Jake	L-L	6-3	230	8-6-86	0	0	0.00	4	0	0	0	4	2	0	0	0	2	5	.154	.000	.250	11.25	4.50
Miller, Jim	R-R	6-1	200	4-28-82	4	3	2.91	44	0	0	4	74	70	28	24	10	12	65	.245	.207	.273	7.87	1.45
Moore, Matt	L-L	6-3	210	6-18-89	2	3	3.57	7	7	0	0	40	35	18	16	6	12	58	.232	.265	.216	12.94	2.68
Mortensen, Jared	L-R	5-11	205	6-1-88	2	0	2.77	2	2	0	0	13	13	4	4	2	3	12	.265	.158	.333	8.31	2.08
Norberto, Jordan	L-L	6-0	195	12-8-86	1	3	4.96	33	2	0	1	45	45	26	25	3	30	40	.259	.302	.240	7.94	5.96
Oliver, Andy	L-L	6-3	215	12-3-87	1	1	3.86	25	0	0	1	28	20	13	12	3	24	32	.196	.303	.145	10.29	7.71
2-team total (16 Norfolk)					4	2	3.79	41	0	0	1	57	43	25	24	4	40	66	—	—	—	10.42	6.32
Patterson, Jimmy	R-L	6-0	190	2-9-89	1	1	4.60	6	2	0	0	16	17	9	8	0	3	13	.266	.214	.280	7.47	1.72
Riefenhauser, C.J.	L-L	6-0	195	1-30-90	4	2	2.86	29	0	0	1	35	25	12	11	1	7	34	.200	.167	.217	8.83	1.82
Romero, Enny	L-L	6-3	215	1-24-91	1	1	4.86	17	3	0	1	46	48	26	25	5	17	45	.268	.263	.270	8.74	3.30
Smyly, Drew	L-L	6-3	190	6-13-89	0	2	8.44	3	3	0	0	11	13	11	10	2	6	13	.310	.222	.333	10.97	5.06
Snell, Blake	L-L	6-4	180	12-4-92	6	2	1.83	9	9	0	0	44	29	11	9	2	13	57	.187	.235	.174	11.57	2.64
Stowell, Bryce	R-R	6-2	205	9-23-86	1	1	3.06	13	0	0	0	18	16	6	6	1	11	19	.246	.273	.233	9.68	5.60
Teaford, Everett	L-L	6-0	160	5-15-84	5	9	5.35	26	19	0	0	103	122	70	61	12	33	72	.294	.226	.317	6.31	2.89
Winkler, Kyle	R-R	5-11	195	6-18-90	0	0	3.00	3	0	0	0	3	2	1	1	1	1	2	.200	.400	.000	6.00	3.00
Yates, Kirby	R-R	5-10	210	3-25-87	1	2	5.33	23	0	0	6	25	27	16	15	5	12	34	.265	.279	.254	12.08	4.26
Zarate, Robert	L-L	6-3	200	2-1-87	2	1	2.90	17	5	0	2	40	29	16	13	2	15	49	.197	.135	.218	10.93	3.35

Fielding

Catcher	PCT	G	PO	A	E	DP	PB
Acosta	.976	14	74	6	2	0	1
Arencibia	.986	10	62	8	1	0	0
Casali	.995	24	165	23	1	0	1
Dominguez	1.000	2	11	1	0	0	0
Maile	.991	84	679	63	7	6	2
Wilson	1.000	16	119	6	0	2	0

First Base	PCT	G	PO	A	E	DP
Arencibia	.995	68	549	34	3	45
Belnome	.996	27	212	14	1	20
Dykstra	1.000	15	130	6	0	19
Elmore	1.000	13	100	6	0	6
Seitzer	.984	7	58	3	1	9
Shaffer	.993	19	136	13	1	15

Second Base	PCT	G	PO	A	E	DP
Beckham	.909	2	3	7	1	1
Brett	.963	68	133	179	12	45
Casilla	.981	35	62	92	3	26
Elmore	1.000	4	7	12	0	2
Franklin	.963	24	51	54	4	15
Lee	1.000	1	3	2	0	0
Motter	1.000	12	22	31	0	6
Reginatto	1.000	7	14	20	0	2

Third Base	PCT	G	PO	A	E	DP
Arencibia	—	1	0	0	0	0
Beckham	.900	7	2	7	1	1
Belnome	.886	15	11	20	4	3
Elmore	.936	38	31	71	7	11
Motter	.866	25	9	49	9	5
Reginatto	.984	23	18	43	1	6
Shaffer	.932	42	45	65	8	7

Shortstop	PCT	G	PO	A	E	DP
Beckham	.600	1	1	2	2	0
Casilla	.333	1	1	0	2	0
Elmore	1.000	5	4	17	0	2
Franklin	.952	17	22	37	3	10
Lee	.953	94	113	250	18	44
Motter	.953	14	20	41	3	14
Querecuto	.895	4	3	14	2	5
Reginatto	.938	12	15	30	3	11
Sole	1.000	2	0	1	0	1

Outfield	PCT	G	PO	A	E	DP
Belnome	1.000	1	1	0	0	0
Brett	.929	8	12	1	1	0
Brown	.991	99	216	4	2	2
Butler	1.000	23	40	0	0	0
Constanza	1.000	5	7	0	0	0
Jaso	1.000	1	1	0	0	0
Jennings	1.000	4	1	0	0	0
Mahtook	.995	92	183	7	1	4
Motter	.968	76	145	7	5	1
Powell	.967	52	114	3	4	0
Rickard	.946	26	33	2	2	0
Shaffer	1.000	3	14	0	0	0
Sizemore	1.000	2	1	0	0	0
Souza	1.000	1	1	0	0	0
Velez	.978	55	86	3	2	2

MONTGOMERY BISCUITS   DOUBLE-A

SOUTHERN LEAGUE

Batting	B-T	HT	WT	DOB	AVG	vLH	vRH	G	AB	R	H	2B	3B	HR	RBI	BB	HBP	SH	SF	SO	SB	CS	SLG	OBP
Bauers, Jake	L-L	6-1	195	10-6-95	.276	.241	.286	69	257	36	71	18	0	5	36	21	1	2	4	41	6	3	.405	.329
Carter, Kes	L-L	6-2	205	3-3-90	.200	.308	.162	15	50	3	10	2	1	0	2	8	0	1	0	7	0	2	.280	.310
Coyle, Tommy	L-R	5-7	170	10-24-90	.229	.121	.250	107	354	52	81	18	3	6	38	57	1	2	1	110	20	9	.347	.337
DePew, Jake	R-R	6-1	220	3-1-92	.228	.083	.261	55	197	15	45	9	2	3	21	14	1	1	2	65	0	2	.340	.280
Dominguez, Wilmer	R-R	5-10	180	6-19-91	.250	—	.250	1	4	0	1	0	0	0	0	0	0	0	0	0	0	0	.250	.250
Field, Johnny	R-R	5-10	190	2-20-92	.255	.301	.244	116	432	68	110	33	4	14	66	36	15	2	6	109	18	3	.447	.329
Gantt, Marty	R-L	5-11	180	2-11-90	.143	.000	.154	5	14	2	2	0	1	0	3	0	0	0	0	3	0	0	.286	.143
Goeddel, Tyler	R-R	6-4	186	10-20-92	.279	.385	.252	123	473	68	132	17	10	12	72	48	6	1	5	98	28	9	.433	.350
Guevara, Hector	R-R	6-0	192	10-7-91	.205	.162	.224	36	122	13	25	3	0	3	20	8	0	0	3	15	1	1	.303	.248
Leonard, Patrick	R-R	6-4	225	10-20-92	.256	.330	.237	120	446	72	114	32	3	10	43	54	12	0	2	129	11	3	.408	.350
O'Conner, Justin	R-R	6-0	190	3-31-92	.231	.253	.226	107	429	50	99	27	3	9	53	13	1	0	1	129	10	2	.371	.255
Powell, Boog	L-L	5-10	185	1-14-93	.328	.400	.311	63	238	44	78	6	6	1	22	29	4	2	1	38	11	8	.416	.408
Querecuto, Juniel	B-R	5-9	155	9-19-92	.209	.306	.172	44	129	22	27	5	1	1	10	14	1	3	1	18	0	3	.287	.290
Reginatto, Leonardo	R-R	6-2	179	4-10-90	.271	.314	.263	58	210	32	57	11	3	3	30	23	2	3	1	32	0	4	.395	.347
Rickard, Joey	R-L	6-1	195	5-21-91	.322	.418	.293	65	236	38	76	19	6	2	32	39	3	1	3	42	19	4	.479	.420
Robertson, Daniel	R-R	6-1	205	3-22-94	.274	.250	.278	78	299	49	82	20	5	4	41	33	11	0	4	58	2	3	.415	.363
Seitzer, Cameron	L-R	6-5	220	1-11-90	.308	.295	.312	102	383	55	118	26	1	12	59	46	3	0	4	84	0	2	.475	.383
Shaffer, Richie	R-R	6-3	205	3-15-91	.262	.222	.267	39	149	22	39	10	0	7	27	23	1	1	1	49	3	0	.470	.362
Varona, Dayron	R-R	5-11	185	2-24-88	.264	.258	.265	69	277	37	73	10	7	10	50	15	6	0	5	52	4	3	.458	.310

Pitching	B-T	HT	WT	DOB	W	L	ERA	G	GS	CG	SV	IP	H	R	ER	HR	BB	SO	AVG	vLH	vRH	K/9	BB/9
Ames, Jeff	R-R	6-4	225	1-31-91	3	0	0.73	14	0	0	0	25	19	2	2	0	14	26	.226	.162	.277	9.49	5.11
Cooper, Zach	R-R	5-10	185	1-6-90	0	1	9.00	10	0	0	0	14	24	14	14	5	10	6	.375	.308	.421	3.86	6.43
Faria, Jacob	R-R	6-4	200	7-30-93	7	3	2.51	13	13	0	0	75	52	25	21	5	30	96	.194	.168	.217	11.47	3.58

Pitching

Pitching	B-T	HT	WT	DOB	W	L	ERA	G	GS	CG	SV	IP	H	R	ER	HR	BB	SO	AVG	vLH	vRH	K/9	BB/9
Garton, Ryan	R-R	5-11	170	12-5-89	6	1	2.95	41	0	0	0	61	44	22	20	2	32	70	.197	.223	.178	10.33	4.72
Guerrieri, Taylor	R-R	6-3	195	12-1-92	3	1	1.50	8	8	0	0	36	28	9	6	2	8	28	.206	.212	.200	7.00	2.00
Hagens, Bradin	R-R	6-3	210	5-12-89	4	5	3.86	16	8	0	0	63	65	28	27	3	25	46	.271	.312	.245	6.57	3.57
Harrison, Jordan	R-L	6-1	180	4-9-91	0	1	9.35	6	0	0	0	9	13	10	9	1	9	3	.382	.308	.429	3.12	9.35
Kirsch, Chris	L-L	6-2	185	11-15-91	3	4	5.69	11	11	0	0	55	63	45	35	3	24	45	.289	.373	.245	7.32	3.90
Lollis, Matt	R-R	6-9	250	9-11-90	3	2	3.53	47	1	0	0	64	47	28	25	6	31	62	.205	.194	.215	8.76	4.38
Lopez, Reinaldo	R-R	6-2	220	4-27-91	0	0	3.32	5	4	0	0	22	19	8	8	0	8	18	.232	.269	.214	7.48	3.32
Marinez, Jhan	R-R	6-1	200	8-12-88	0	0	5.68	5	0	0	2	6	6	4	4	0	3	6	.273	.429	.200	8.53	4.26
Markel, Parker	R-R	6-4	220	9-15-90	5	3	3.23	42	0	0	3	53	55	24	19	4	26	39	.276	.297	.259	6.62	4.42
McPherson, Kyle	B-R	6-4	215	11-11-87	0	2	7.48	17	0	0	0	28	34	25	23	7	10	23	.306	.302	.310	7.48	3.25
Mortensen, Jared	L-R	5-11	205	6-1-88	7	5	3.78	24	17	0	0	114	105	53	48	12	35	96	.245	.282	.216	7.56	2.76
O'Brien, Mikey	R-R	5-11	190	3-3-90	1	2	5.68	10	1	0	0	25	32	17	16	2	6	17	.317	.244	.367	6.04	2.13
Patterson, Jimmy	R-L	6-0	190	2-9-89	0	0	0.00	1	1	0	0	2	2	1	0	0	3	3	.250	.250	.250	13.50	0.00
Pruitt, Austin	R-R	5-11	165	8-31-89	10	7	3.09	26	26	2	0	160	160	60	55	3	38	122	.263	.250	.273	6.86	2.14
Reavis, Colton	R-R	6-0	195	12-16-89	0	3	7.31	24	0	0	1	28	35	26	23	2	13	32	.307	.364	.271	10.16	4.13
Sappington, Mark	R-R	6-5	210	11-17-90	3	6	3.69	48	0	0	4	68	63	31	28	3	45	71	.250	.239	.259	9.35	5.93
Schreiber, Brad	R-R	6-3	225	2-13-91	2	2	3.54	24	0	0	12	28	21	11	11	2	13	28	.206	.229	.185	9.00	4.18
Schultz, Jaime	R-R	5-10	200	6-20-91	9	5	3.67	27	27	0	0	135	105	58	55	11	90	168	.218	.243	.199	11.20	6.00
Smyly, Drew	L-L	6-3	190	6-13-89	0	0	0.00	1	1	0	0	4	1	0	0	0	3	4	.083	.000	.125	9.82	7.36
Snell, Blake	L-L	6-4	180	12-4-92	6	2	1.57	12	12	0	0	69	45	13	12	5	29	79	.191	.100	.237	10.35	3.80
Stanek, Ryne	R-R	6-4	180	7-26-91	4	3	4.09	16	8	0	1	62	52	30	28	7	31	41	.232	.300	.177	5.98	4.52
Stowell, Bryce	R-R	6-2	205	9-23-86	0	2	7.53	17	0	0	8	14	19	16	12	2	15	16	.322	.269	.364	10.05	9.42
Winkler, Kyle	R-R	5-11	195	6-18-90	1	0	0.96	7	0	0	0	9	7	1	1	0	0	13	.200	.250	.174	12.54	0.00

Fielding

Catcher	PCT	G	PO	A	E	DP	PB
DePew	.993	47	380	45	3	5	2
O'Conner	.983	92	759	91	15	6	15

First Base	PCT	G	PO	A	E	DP
Bauers	.988	61	477	23	6	44
DePew	.900	1	9	0	1	0
Guevara	1.000	1	2	0	0	1
Leonard	.991	25	206	7	2	18
Seitzer	.996	54	443	26	2	59

Second Base	PCT	G	PO	A	E	DP
Coyle	.980	101	168	267	9	67
Guevara	.943	19	30	52	5	12

	PCT	G	PO	A	E	DP
Querecuto	.960	5	9	15	1	2
Reginatto	.926	17	28	35	5	10

Third Base	PCT	G	PO	A	E	DP
Guevara	1.000	9	4	9	0	0
Leonard	.943	83	52	130	11	17
Querecuto	1.000	1	0	1	0	1
Reginatto	.914	11	12	20	3	4
Seitzer	1.000	5	3	7	0	1
Shaffer	.962	34	28	47	3	4

Shortstop	PCT	G	PO	A	E	DP
Guevara	.919	7	13	21	3	6
Querecuto	.981	38	54	98	3	24

	PCT	G	PO	A	E	DP
Reginatto	.976	26	43	79	3	16
Robertson	.968	69	108	191	10	39

Outfield	PCT	G	PO	A	E	DP
Carter	.956	15	41	2	2	1
Coyle	1.000	2	7	0	0	0
Field	.995	100	206	9	1	2
Gantt	1.000	5	8	0	0	0
Goeddel	.990	111	195	6	2	1
Leonard	1.000	6	10	0	0	0
Powell	.976	56	115	8	3	2
Reginatto	1.000	5	5	0	0	0
Rickard	1.000	56	112	3	0	1
Varona	.977	62	121	9	3	2

CHARLOTTE STONE CRABS

HIGH CLASS A

FLORIDA STATE LEAGUE

Batting	B-T	HT	WT	DOB	AVG	vLH	vRH	G	AB	R	H	2B	3B	HR	RBI	BB	HBP	SH	SF	SO	SB	CS	SLG	OBP
Adames, Willy	R-R	6-1	180	9-2-95	.258	.274	.252	106	396	51	102	24	6	4	46	54	0	6	123	10	1	.379	.342
Araiza, Armando	R-R	5-11	185	6-19-93	.203	.153	.225	84	276	23	56	8	0	4	24	20	1	3	0	68	1	1	.275	.259
Araujo, Yoel	R-R	6-0	190	12-3-93	.216	.216	.216	100	347	32	75	14	3	5	38	23	2	3	2	130	7	4	.317	.267
Bauers, Jake	L-L	6-1	195	10-6-95	.267	.304	.255	59	217	33	58	14	2	6	38	29	2	0	1	33	2	3	.433	.357
Beckham, Tim	R-R	6-0	195	1-27-90	.250	.500	.200	4	12	1	3	1	0	0	0	0	0	0	0	5	0	0	.333	.250
Blair, Pat	R-R	5-10	180	10-1-91	.233	.244	.229	89	300	34	70	17	0	3	35	31	4	2	6	73	8	7	.320	.308
Brett, Ryan	R-R	5-9	180	10-9-91	.667	1.000	.000	1	3	2	2	1	0	0	0	1	0	0	0	0	0	.000	.750
Burgess, Carter	R-R	6-1	200	4-6-93	.182	.273	.091	6	22	5	4	0	0	0	1	1	0	0	0	4	0	0	.182	.217
Conrad, Jace	L-R	5-11	195	12-15-92	.211	.222	.206	52	185	13	39	5	0	1	13	10	4	2	2	28	11	3	.254	.264
Gantt, Marty	R-L	5-11	180	2-11-90	.235	.250	.229	73	247	36	58	12	2	4	25	32	3	0	2	48	9	4	.348	.327
Gillaspie, Casey	B-L	6-4	240	1-25-93	.146	.077	.179	13	41	3	6	0	1	1	4	4	0	0	0	9	0	0	.268	.222
Goetzman, Granden	R-R	6-4	200	11-14-92	.240	.235	.242	93	329	38	79	16	1	3	34	23	2	2	2	66	16	3	.322	.292
Guevara, Hector	R-R	6-0	192	10-7-91	.258	.292	.237	17	62	10	16	1	1	0	6	5	1	1	0	8	1	0	.306	.324
Jaso, John	L-R	6-2	205	9-19-83	.286	.200	.313	6	21	3	6	2	0	0	0	2	0	0	0	4	0	0	.381	.348
Jennings, Desmond	R-R	6-2	210	10-30-86	.429	.000	.500	2	7	0	3	0	0	0	1	1	0	0	0	1	0	0	.429	.500
Lee, Braxton	L-R	5-10	185	8-23-93	.281	.278	.282	115	374	48	105	7	1	0	24	36	3	7	2	67	23	13	.305	.347
Loney, James	L-L	6-3	235	5-7-84	.364	.000	.400	3	11	0	4	1	0	0	0	0	0	0	0	3	0	0	.455	.364
Marjama, Mike	R-R	6-2	205	7-20-89	.302	.327	.291	90	334	46	101	22	4	9	52	11	3	0	3	52	3	1	.473	.328
Querecuto, Juniel	B-R	5-9	155	9-19-92	.293	.325	.282	41	150	23	44	7	1	1	23	14	1	3	1	26	1	1	.373	.355
Rickard, Joey	R-L	6-1	185	5-21-91	.268	.462	.224	23	71	8	19	3	0	0	12	20	2	0	1	13	3	2	.310	.436
Simon, Alexander	B-R	6-2	185	9-28-92	.080	.000	.105	9	25	1	2	0	0	0	0	0	0	0	0	4	0	0	.080	.080
Sizemore, Grady	L-L	6-2	205	8-2-82	.261	.000	.316	6	23	4	6	4	0	0	2	2	0	0	0	5	0	0	.435	.320
Sole, Alec	L-R	6-2	200	6-1-93	.333	—	.333	1	3	0	1	0	0	0	0	1	0	0	0	1	0	0	.333	.500
Souza, Steven	R-R	6-4	225	4-24-89	.167	.333	.000	2	6	1	1	0	0	0	0	1	0	0	0	1	0	0	.167	.286
Tissenbaum, Maxx	B-R	5-10	195	7-30-91	.257	.303	.240	73	245	25	63	10	1	1	33	22	8	2	1	32	1	0	.318	.337
Varona, Dayron	R-R	5-11	185	2-24-88	.377	.450	.347	15	69	9	26	7	1	1	10	1	0	0	0	7	2	3	.551	.386
Velazquez, Andrew	B-R	5-8	175	7-14-94	.290	.353	.267	47	186	29	54	9	2	0	10	15	0	2	0	53	5	8	.360	.343
Williams, Justin	L-R	6-2	215	8-20-95	.241	.083	.305	23	83	8	20	5	0	0	6	1	0	0	0	14	3	1	.301	.250
Wong, Kean	L-R	5-11	190	4-17-95	.274	.349	.247	103	394	46	108	14	3	1	36	29	0	9	6	65	15	6	.332	.319

Pitching

Pitching	B-T	HT	WT	DOB	W	L	ERA	G	GS	CG	SV	IP	H	R	ER	HR	BB	SO	AVG	vLH	vRH	K/9	BB/9
Ames, Jeff	R-R	6-4	225	1-31-91	1	3	3.64	24	0	0	3	42	41	19	17	1	24	36	.265	.243	.282	7.71	5.14
Ascher, Steve	L-L	6-0	185	10-18-93	7	3	2.50	35	2	0	1	76	71	29	21	1	25	39	.251	.192	.271	4.64	2.97
Bellatti, Andrew	R-R	6-1	190	8-5-91	0	0	7.71	2	2	0	0	5	8	6	4	2	0	1	.364	.300	.417	1.93	0.00
Borden, Buddy	R-R	6-3	210	4-29-92	9	7	2.97	28	17	2	0	127	104	57	42	9	58	95	.223	.252	.198	6.71	4.10
Chirinos, Yonny	R-R	6-2	170	12-26-93	0	0	0.00	2	0	0	0	3	2	0	0	0	0	3	.182	.167	.200	9.00	0.00
Colome, Alex	R-R	6-2	220	12-31-88	0	1	3.00	2	2	0	0	6	9	2	2	2	0	5	.333	.077	.571	7.50	0.00
Faria, Jacob	R-R	6-4	200	7-30-93	10	1	1.33	12	10	0	0	74	51	13	11	1	22	63	.199	.248	.166	7.63	2.66
Fierro, Edwin	R-R	6-1	200	8-30-93	1	1	4.15	3	0	0	0	4	5	2	2	0	1	1	.278	1.000	.235	2.08	2.08
Franco, Mike	R-R	5-11	200	11-30-91	2	1	0.75	14	0	0	1	24	17	5	2	0	9	24	.207	.313	.140	9.00	3.38
Gil, Isaac	R-R	6-5	230	10-8-91	3	2	2.29	36	0	0	4	59	61	19	15	1	15	33	.271	.271	.271	5.03	2.29
Guerrieri, Taylor	R-R	6-3	195	12-1-92	2	2	2.14	12	10	0	0	42	37	14	10	0	11	44	.237	.288	.206	9.43	2.36
Harris, Greg	R-R	6-2	170	8-17-94	1	4	3.40	9	8	0	0	40	40	18	15	1	14	24	.274	.210	.321	5.45	3.18
Harrison, Jordan	R-L	6-1	180	4-9-91	0	0	2.86	12	1	0	1	22	20	8	7	0	6	13	.241	.267	.235	5.32	2.45
Honeywell, Brent	R-R	6-2	180	3-31-95	5	2	3.44	12	12	1	0	65	57	26	25	2	15	53	.235	.191	.260	7.30	2.07
Hu, Chih-Wei	R-R	6-1	230	11-4-93	0	3	7.36	5	4	0	1	18	23	18	15	1	8	20	.315	.200	.421	9.82	3.93
2-team total (15 Fort Myers)					5	6	3.32	20	19	0	1	103	102	46	38	6	27	93	—	—		8.13	2.36
Kimborowicz, Josh	R-R	6-3	215	3-17-92	1	2	2.01	37	0	0	2	45	32	13	10	1	13	43	.203	.188	.213	8.66	2.62
Kirsch, Chris	L-L	6-2	185	11-15-91	5	4	2.98	16	12	0	0	82	63	34	27	4	25	58	.206	.215	.203	6.39	2.76
Marquez, German	R-R	6-1	184	2-22-95	7	13	3.56	26	23	0	0	139	147	68	55	6	29	104	.272	.316	.239	6.73	1.88
McCalvin, Justin	R-R	6-0	180	1-14-92	0	0	4.26	5	0	0	0	6	6	3	3	1	7	5	.261	.231	.300	7.11	9.95
McGee, Jake	L-L	6-3	230	8-6-86	0	0	0.00	2	2	0	0	2	0	0	0	0	2	1	.000	.000	.000	4.50	9.00
McKenzie, Kyle	R-R	6-2	205	9-13-90	5	6	4.35	32	0	0	1	52	62	29	25	0	15	36	.298	.316	.287	6.27	2.61
McPherson, Kyle	B-R	6-4	215	11-11-87	1	0	0.00	2	0	0	0	3	2	0	0	0	0	1	.182	.167	.200	3.00	0.00
Moore, Matt	L-L	6-3	210	6-18-89	0	0	1.64	3	3	0	0	11	9	4	2	1	4	9	.225	.125	.250	7.36	3.27
Odorizzi, Jake	R-R	6-2	190	3-27-90	0	0	0.93	2	2	0	0	10	4	1	1	0	2	8	.118	.056	.188	7.45	1.86
Quinonez, Eduar	R-R	6-3	190	8-9-89	0	1	4.70	17	1	0	1	31	36	25	16	3	12	20	.295	.300	.293	5.87	3.52
Reavis, Colton	R-R	6-0	195	12-16-89	0	1	2.84	13	0	0	0	13	9	4	4	0	7	12	.205	.158	.240	8.53	4.97
Riefenhauser, C.J.	L-L	6-0	195	1-30-90	0	0	0.00	1	0	0	0	1	0	0	0	0	2	1	.000	—	.000	9.00	18.00
Romero, Enny	L-L	6-3	215	1-24-91	0	1	6.75	2	2	0	0	7	8	5	5	0	4	5	.308	.333	.294	6.75	5.40
Sawyer, Nick	R-R	5-11	175	9-23-91	0	0	0.00	4	0	0	1	3	1	0	0	0	0	4	.100	.000	.125	12.00	0.00
Schreiber, Brad	R-R	6-2	225	2-13-91	0	3	1.83	30	0	0	18	34	17	9	7	1	11	29	.147	.244	.085	7.60	2.88
Smyly, Drew	L-L	6-3	190	6-13-89	0	0	5.40	3	3	0	0	8	10	5	5	1	0	9	.286	.000	.313	9.72	0.00
Snell, Blake	L-L	6-4	180	12-4-92	3	0	0.00	4	2	0	0	21	10	0	0	0	11	27	.143	.118	.151	11.57	4.71
Stanek, Ryne	R-R	6-4	180	7-26-91	4	2	1.78	9	9	0	0	51	33	13	10	2	15	38	.189	.189	.188	6.75	2.66
Woeck, Andrew	R-R	5-10	180	5-4-92	0	0	9.00	1	0	0	0	2	2	2	2	2	0	2	.250	.250	.250	9.00	0.00
Wood, Hunter	R-R	6-1	175	8-12-93	1	3	2.79	9	7	0	0	42	32	15	13	1	9	32	.208	.215	.202	6.86	1.93
Yates, Kirby	R-R	5-10	210	3-25-87	0	0	9.00	2	1	0	0	2	2	3	2	0	1	2	.250	.500	.167	9.00	4.50
Zarate, Robert	L-L	6-3	200	2-1-87	0	0	0.00	1	0	0	0	2	0	0	0	0	0	1	.000	.000	.000	9.00	4.50

Fielding

Catcher

Catcher	PCT	G	PO	A	E	DP	PB
Araiza	.984	84	504	94	10	9	9
Marjama	.967	14	72	15	3	0	1
Tissenbaum	.994	43	283	39	2	0	13

First Base

First Base	PCT	G	PO	A	E	DP
Bauers	.992	52	450	17	4	37
Blair	.989	18	169	5	2	15
Gillaspie	.978	12	84	3	2	10
Guevara	1.000	1	8	1	0	0
Jaso	1.000	1	9	1	0	1
Loney	1.000	1	7	0	0	0
Marjama	.994	53	453	37	3	31
Simon	.921	4	33	2	3	3

Second Base

Second Base	PCT	G	PO	A	E	DP
Beckham	1.000	3	2	8	0	0
Blair	.961	17	31	43	3	4
Brett	1.000	1	0	1	0	0
Conrad	1.000	2	3	6	0	3
Guevara	.971	7	12	22	1	4
Querecuto	.923	2	4	8	1	3
Velazquez	.986	12	23	46	1	6
Wong	.980	95	158	275	9	53

Third Base

Third Base	PCT	G	PO	A	E	DP
Blair	.842	35	16	48	12	5
Burgess	.938	6	4	11	1	2
Conrad	.964	42	37	70	4	8
Guevara	1.000	1	0	2	0	0
Querecuto	.913	30	12	30	4	3
Sole	1.000	1	2	3	0	0
Tissenbaum	.833	6	0	10	2	0
Velazquez	.892	18	8	25	4	0

Shortstop

Shortstop	PCT	G	PO	A	E	DP
Adames	.948	97	130	289	23	54
Blair	.954	14	27	35	3	10
Conrad	1.000	1	0	2	0	1
Guevara	.897	6	8	18	3	5
Querecuto	1.000	6	12	15	0	4
Velazquez	.929	14	15	37	4	5

Outfield

Outfield	PCT	G	PO	A	E	DP
Araujo	.957	95	194	7	9	3
Conrad	.500	2	1	0	1	0
Gantt	.982	55	106	4	2	1
Goetzman	.971	84	166	1	5	0
Jaso	—	1	0	0	0	0
Jennings	1.000	2	4	1	0	0
Lee	.988	113	312	13	4	3
Rickard	.961	22	47	2	2	0
Simon	—	1	0	0	0	0
Sizemore	1.000	4	5	0	0	0
Souza	—	1	0	0	0	0
Varona	1.000	14	27	2	0	0
Williams	.921	19	33	2	3	0

BOWLING GREEN HOT RODS
LOW CLASS A

MIDWEST LEAGUE

Batting	B-T	HT	WT	DOB	AVG	vLH	vRH	G	AB	R	H	2B	3B	HR	RBI	BB	HBP	SH	SF	SO	SB	CS	SLG	OBP
Blanchard, Coty	R-R	6-0	180	12-16-91	.308	.328	.301	69	247	40	76	17	2	1	27	22	3	3	2	48	6	2	.405	.369
Burgess, Carter	R-R	6-1	200	4-6-93	.254	.250	.256	37	126	12	32	8	0	1	5	8	1	0	1	20	1	1	.341	.301
Ciuffo, Nick	L-R	6-1	205	3-7-95	.258	.159	.288	94	356	30	92	21	0	1	32	7	0	1	5	55	2	3	.326	.269
Conrad, Jace	L-R	5-11	195	12-15-92	.292	.200	.318	59	226	33	66	11	1	10	30	10	4	0	1	31	21	4	.482	.332
Gillaspie, Casey	B-L	6-4	215	1-25-93	.278	.322	.263	64	234	37	65	11	0	16	44	28	3	0	3	43	4	0	.530	.358
Gotta, Cade	R-R	6-4	205	8-1-91	.254	.263	.250	16	59	9	15	6	0	2	8	2	0	0	0	13	3	1	.458	.279
Hawkins, Taylor	R-R	5-11	188	9-17-93	.357	.500	.300	5	14	2	5	0	0	1	3	1	0	0	2	4	0	1	.571	.353
Jackson, Bralin	R-L	6-2	185	12-1-93	.274	.272	.274	116	413	45	113	19	3	3	41	37	3	1	1	84	14	16	.356	.337
James, Mac	R-R	6-1	195	6-2-93	.257	.281	.248	91	323	33	83	14	0	3	32	25	3	1	5	49	2	1	.328	.312
Kay, Grant	R-R	6-0	185	5-29-93	.251	.229	.258	118	423	46	106	30	1	1	31	29	5	2	4	80	13	6	.333	.304
Lockwood, Hunter	R-R	5-10	180	9-16-92	.213	.284	.190	76	272	30	58	11	3	11	42	19	2	0	3	90	2	1	.397	.267

Batting

Batting	B-T	HT	WT	DOB	AVG	vLH	vRH	G	AB	R	H	2B	3B	HR	RBI	BB	HBP	SH	SF	SO	SB	CS	SLG	OBP
Milone, Thomas	L-L	5-11	190	1-26-95	.248	.220	.257	119	472	64	117	17	5	3	28	39	8	5	2	93	26	14	.324	.315
Smedley, Sean	R-R	6-1	195	9-28-90	.048	.167	.000	7	21	1	1	0	0	0	0	2	0	0	0	6	0	0	.048	.130
Sole, Alec	L-R	6-2	200	6-1-93	.308	.296	.311	61	221	25	68	13	4	1	29	13	1	1	1	33	5	4	.416	.347
Toribio, Cristian	R-R	5-11	170	9-13-94	.239	.263	.233	111	372	38	89	15	4	8	39	15	2	3	3	79	12	8	.366	.270
Unroe, Riley	B-R	5-10	180	8-3-95	.255	.198	.273	116	439	45	112	13	2	4	35	51	2	5	4	99	13	9	.321	.333
Williams, Justin	L-R	6-2	215	8-20-95	.284	.316	.273	99	387	43	110	25	2	7	42	13	2	0	4	76	3	1	.413	.308

Pitching

Pitching	B-T	HT	WT	DOB	W	L	ERA	G	GS	CG	SV	IP	H	R	ER	HR	BB	SO	AVG	vLH	vRH	K/9	BB/9
Bird, Kyle	L-L	6-2	175	4-12-93	4	0	2.60	32	0	0	9	69	67	25	20	1	17	69	.254	.222	.266	8.96	2.21
Carroll, Damion	R-R	6-3	198	1-31-94	5	2	3.64	32	0	0	2	54	38	23	22	0	57	53	.202	.211	.197	8.78	9.44
Castillo, Diego	R-R	6-3	195	1-18-94	0	0	4.82	5	0	0	1	9	8	6	5	0	4	4	.229	.231	.227	3.86	3.86
Centeno, Henry	R-R	6-2	174	8-24-94	8	8	3.89	23	23	0	0	123	118	65	53	7	47	91	.254	.276	.238	6.68	3.45
Chirinos, Yonny	R-R	6-2	170	12-26-93	4	5	2.20	10	10	0	0	61	59	19	15	3	7	47	.252	.330	.184	6.90	1.03
Fierro, Edwin	R-R	6-1	200	8-30-93	3	3	1.65	20	0	0	3	33	32	7	6	0	12	25	.269	.353	.206	6.89	3.31
Formo, Hyrum	R-R	6-1	185	4-13-92	5	5	4.19	22	21	0	0	107	128	52	50	9	23	65	.300	.307	.296	5.45	1.93
Franco, Enderson	R-R	6-2	170	12-29-92	5	6	3.89	13	13	0	0	72	82	38	31	4	8	47	.284	.325	.253	5.90	1.00
Franco, Mike	R-R	5-11	200	11-30-91	0	2	1.87	23	0	0	4	43	35	11	9	2	13	47	.219	.209	.222	9.76	2.70
Gomez, Edgar	R-R	5-11	190	1-5-93	6	4	4.35	35	0	0	6	72	90	40	35	6	16	55	.303	.231	.352	6.84	1.99
Harris, Greg	R-R	6-2	170	8-17-94	7	5	2.17	16	16	0	0	83	74	33	20	1	28	84	.236	.250	.230	9.11	3.04
Harrison, Jordan	R-L	6-1	180	4-9-91	1	0	2.53	10	0	0	0	21	14	6	6	3	8	22	.197	.348	.125	9.38	3.38
Honeywell, Brent	R-R	6-2	180	3-31-95	4	4	2.91	12	12	0	0	65	53	27	21	3	12	76	.221	.222	.220	10.52	1.66
Miller, Brian	R-R	6-4	200	7-15-92	3	3	1.85	38	0	0	7	58	44	15	12	2	11	38	.203	.195	.207	5.86	1.70
Mujica, Jose	R-R	6-2	200	6-29-96	1	4	4.20	8	8	0	0	45	47	24	21	2	7	22	.272	.209	.311	4.40	1.40
Pennell, Ryan	R-L	6-4	210	7-14-92	0	1	7.12	22	0	0	0	37	45	34	29	4	29	27	.302	.188	.356	6.63	7.12
Pike, Chris	R-R	6-0	175	10-11-92	10	7	3.13	22	22	0	0	129	124	53	45	8	31	83	.259	.242	.270	5.78	2.16
Urena, Luis	R-R	6-4	200	8-21-92	0	0	13.50	7	0	0	0	8	16	13	12	0	6	4	.421	.421	.421	4.50	6.75
Wallace, Bradley	R-R	6-2	175	9-12-92	2	6	5.25	10	10	0	0	48	65	41	28	8	10	35	.325	.277	.359	6.56	1.88
Wood, Hunter	R-R	6-1	175	8-12-93	1	4	1.82	20	3	0	4	64	36	13	13	3	16	81	.164	.189	.146	11.33	2.24

Fielding

Catcher	PCT	G	PO	A	E	DP	PB
Ciuffo	.982	72	493	105	11	7	12
Hawkins	1.000	1	9	0	0	0	0
James	.984	64	422	80	8	7	5
Smedley	1.000	2	12	1	0	0	0

First Base	PCT	G	PO	A	E	DP
Blanchard	.967	24	188	14	7	12
Burgess	.992	29	236	18	2	12
Gillaspie	.987	60	510	29	7	38
James	1.000	1	3	0	0	0
Smedley	1.000	1	8	1	0	2
Sole	.996	28	227	8	1	18

Second Base	PCT	G	PO	A	E	DP
Blanchard	1.000	3	7	2	0	0
Burgess	.875	2	4	3	1	1
Conrad	.977	13	18	24	1	7
Sole	.962	8	8	17	1	1
Unroe	.977	115	183	278	11	53

Third Base	PCT	G	PO	A	E	DP
Blanchard	.875	3	0	7	1	0
Burgess	.917	4	2	9	1	1
Conrad	1.000	21	14	25	0	1
Kay	.932	111	95	181	20	12
Sole	.875	3	0	7	1	0

Shortstop	PCT	G	PO	A	E	DP
Blanchard	1.000	9	15	28	0	4
Sole	.958	24	34	58	4	9
Toribio	.929	109	128	276	31	55

Outfield	PCT	G	PO	A	E	DP
Blanchard	1.000	35	50	3	0	1
Conrad	1.000	10	19	4	0	1
Gotta	.867	16	37	2	6	1
Jackson	.979	116	222	10	5	2
Lockwood	.894	31	55	4	7	2
Milone	.983	118	329	8	6	2
Williams	.983	96	215	11	4	1

HUDSON VALLEY RENEGADES   SHORT-SEASON

NEW YORK-PENN LEAGUE

Batting	B-T	HT	WT	DOB	AVG	vLH	vRH	G	AB	R	H	2B	3B	HR	RBI	BB	HBP	SH	SF	SO	SB	CS	SLG	OBP
Astacio, Joseph	L-R	6-0	155	6-5-94	.324	.333	.321	10	37	3	12	0	1	0	4	2	0	0	0	6	0	0	.378	.359
Cronenworth, Jake	L-R	6-0	170	1-21-94	.291	.255	.305	51	196	31	57	12	3	1	16	31	5	1	1	59	12	7	.398	.399
Dacey, Matt	L-R	6-2	205	3-31-94	.256	.303	.240	37	129	12	33	13	1	0	21	18	1	0	3	41	0	1	.372	.344
De La Calle, Danny	R-R	6-3	220	9-18-92	.164	.200	.148	34	128	14	21	7	1	1	9	3	3	0	0	45	0	0	.258	.201
Gotta, Cade	R-R	6-4	205	8-1-91	.289	.333	.271	42	152	19	44	13	1	0	15	17	0	0	3	17	12	4	.388	.355
Hawkins, Taylor	R-R	5-11	188	9-17-93	.242	.286	.227	38	132	13	32	14	1	1	17	6	2	2	1	42	1	1	.386	.284
McCarthy, Joe	L-L	6-3	215	2-23-94	.277	.311	.260	49	184	24	51	7	2	0	21	18	7	3	1	23	18	3	.337	.362
Montes, Hector	R-R	6-0	235	2-21-92	.272	.314	.252	55	217	19	59	16	1	3	34	7	3	1	4	48	1	2	.396	.299
Moreno, Angel	R-R	6-2	180	7-31-96	.270	.281	.265	59	230	28	62	19	5	2	26	7	4	1	2	56	2	6	.422	.300
Paez, Jose	R-R	6-0	165	8-11-95	.258	.185	.288	51	186	13	48	5	1	0	13	13	3	1	0	52	19	8	.296	.317
Rapacz, Josh	R-R	6-1	205	7-10-90	.120	.250	.000	8	25	0	3	1	0	0	1	1	1	1	0	3	0	0	.160	.185
Russell, Michael	R-R	6-2	200	1-30-93	.257	.208	.280	63	241	50	62	16	4	2	20	27	14	1	0	52	22	0	.382	.365
Sanay, Oscar	R-R	5-7	185	2-23-92	.241	.220	.250	41	133	14	32	3	0	0	8	10	3	4	1	13	2	4	.263	.306
Sanchez, Manny	R-R	6-2	220	10-6-95	.273	.273	.273	57	209	28	57	15	1	5	22	21	2	0	2	68	5	0	.426	.342
Schmidt, Alex	L-R	6-0	200	9-19-92	.227	.241	.220	51	185	25	42	9	3	3	19	16	4	0	2	42	1	1	.357	.300
Whitley, Garrett	R-R	6-0	200	3-13-97	.143	.059	.200	12	42	3	6	0	1	0	4	5	1	0	0	12	3	1	.190	.250
Wilson, Nic	R-R	6-6	240	7-21-92	.193	.239	.174	45	161	7	31	7	0	1	16	5	1	0	0	10	0	0	.255	.253

Pitching	B-T	HT	WT	DOB	W	L	ERA	G	GS	CG	SV	IP	H	R	ER	HR	BB	SO	AVG	vLH	vRH	K/9	BB/9
Brashears, Tyler	L-R	6-2	170	2-24-94	1	1	1.17	7	0	0	1	15	8	3	2	0	1	12	.151	.158	.147	7.04	0.59
Castillo, Diego	R-R	6-3	195	1-18-94	1	2	2.31	13	0	0	4	23	19	9	6	1	7	24	.216	.238	.196	9.26	2.70
Chirinos, Yonny	R-R	6-2	170	12-26-93	1	0	0.60	3	3	0	0	15	10	1	1	1	3	14	.182	.071	.220	8.40	1.80
Crisostomo, Christopher	L-L	6-2	180	9-18-94	2	0	2.85	18	0	0	0	41	34	20	13	1	15	24	.225	.250	.216	5.27	3.29
Ingram, Tim	L-R	5-11	200	10-9-93	2	1	1.29	18	0	0	1	35	27	8	5	0	8	22	.214	.137	.267	5.66	2.06
Karalus, Reece	R-R	6-3	235	6-14-94	2	1	1.70	19	0	0	3	37	31	8	7	1	8	38	.221	.295	.165	9.24	1.95
Koch, Brandon	R-R	6-1	205	12-25-93	0	1	3.06	18	0	0	6	32	24	14	11	3	5	47	.198	.233	.179	13.08	1.39
Maisto, Greg	L-L	6-1	180	11-17-94	0	4	8.76	4	4	0	0	12	20	16	12	0	10	9	.385	.667	.348	6.57	7.30
McCalvin, Justin	R-R	6-0	180	1-14-92	3	1	4.88	19	4	0	2	31	34	23	17	2	7	34	.266	.358	.200	9.77	2.01

Pitching	B-T	HT	WT	DOB	W	L	ERA	G	GS	CG	SV	IP	H	R	ER	HR	BB	SO	AVG	vLH	vRH	K/9	BB/9
Michelson, Tomas	L-R	6-4	185	4-7-92	1	0	3.95	15	0	0	1	27	25	17	12	3	11	24	.231	.220	.241	7.90	3.62
Moss, Benton	R-R	6-1	170	2-21-93	2	3	2.93	14	10	0	0	58	54	21	19	3	10	66	.248	.242	.252	10.18	1.54
Ott, Travis	L-L	6-4	170	6-29-95	6	3	3.90	13	13	0	0	60	61	29	26	6	20	56	.276	.243	.291	8.40	3.00
Ramirez, Roel	R-R	6-1	205	5-26-95	4	3	2.97	13	13	0	0	70	67	27	23	3	11	43	.250	.206	.280	5.56	1.42
Triece, Sam	R-R	6-2	215	8-17-93	0	0	15.00	2	0	0	0	3	9	5	5	0	2	1	.500	.500	.500	9.00	6.00
Urena, Luis	R-R	6-4	200	8-21-92	0	2	2.88	11	0	0	1	25	16	11	8	1	4	19	.178	.138	.197	6.84	1.44
Varga, Cameron	R-R	6-2	189	8-19-94	3	6	2.97	12	12	0	0	58	66	29	19	2	11	39	.287	.277	.294	6.09	1.72
Velasquez, Mike	L-L	6-1	215	2-28-93	2	5	4.04	14	8	0	0	49	57	24	22	4	12	46	.298	.429	.269	8.45	2.20
Wallace, Bradley	R-R	6-2	175	9-12-92	2	0	0.00	4	0	0	0	12	5	0	0	0	2	12	.132	.100	.167	9.00	1.50
Williams, John	R-R	6-1	195	5-9-93	2	1	2.77	6	1	0	0	13	9	6	4	2	3	14	.196	.214	.188	9.69	2.08
Yepez, Angel	R-R	6-1	215	4-27-95	5	3	2.97	12	12	0	0	61	58	25	20	0	13	51	.248	.254	.240	7.57	1.93

Fielding

Catcher	PCT	G	PO	A	E	DP	PB
De La Calle	.991	34	282	31	3	2	6
Hawkins	.977	37	251	43	7	4	17
Rapacz	.979	7	41	6	1	1	1

First Base	PCT	G	PO	A	E	DP
Dacey	.983	12	110	8	2	9
Montes	.996	28	248	12	1	15
Schmidt	.917	4	22	0	2	5
Wilson	.971	34	314	20	10	29

Second Base	PCT	G	PO	A	E	DP
Astacio	.917	2	4	7	1	0
Cronenworth	.980	36	52	95	3	26
Sanay	.978	41	68	114	4	20

Third Base	PCT	G	PO	A	E	DP
Astacio	.857	5	5	7	2	1
Dacey	.935	18	6	37	3	3
Montes	.939	12	14	17	2	3
Schmidt	.897	43	23	90	13	5

Shortstop	PCT	G	PO	A	E	DP
Astacio	1.000	2	4	5	0	1
Cronenworth	.924	16	24	49	6	10
Russell	.941	60	99	157	16	30

Outfield	PCT	G	PO	A	E	DP
Cronenworth	1.000	1	2	0	0	0
Gotta	.940	32	57	6	4	0
McCarthy	.954	40	59	3	3	0
Moreno	.993	59	136	3	1	0
Paez	.990	50	95	4	1	2
Sanchez	.901	40	64	0	7	0
Whitley	1.000	12	19	0	0	0

PRINCETON RAYS
ROOKIE
APPALACHIAN LEAGUE

Batting	B-T	HT	WT	DOB	AVG	vLH	vRH	G	AB	R	H	2B	3B	HR	RBI	BB	HBP	SH	SF	SO	SB	CS	SLG	OBP
Beck, Blair	R-R	6-0	195	9-19-92	.212	.250	.189	25	85	13	18	3	1	2	10	12	2	0	0	26	1	1	.341	.323
Butera, Blake	R-R	5-9	175	8-7-92	.207	.240	.193	27	82	10	17	1	0	1	6	8	3	0		15	3	1	.256	.337
Cray, Landon	L-L	5-9	170	1-25-94	.259	.200	.275	57	205	31	53	8	5	2	25	34	2	2	4	24	2	2	.376	.364
Grady, Patrick	R-L	6-0	230	12-23-91	.207	.200	.211	9	29	2	6	1	0	0	4	4	0	0	0	8	2	0	.241	.303
Law, Zac	R-R	5-8	180	7-8-96	.270	.292	.261	64	256	40	69	10	2	8	30	14	10	5	2	42	12	8	.418	.330
Maris, Peter	L-R	5-10	175	9-16-93	.267	.306	.253	63	240	33	64	6	2	1	29	35	1	4	5	38	6	6	.321	.356
Meyer, Kewby	L-L	6-1	195	10-27-92	.268	.289	.263	60	220	20	59	13	0	5	30	17	2	2	1	30	4	2	.395	.325
Mitchell, Jamie	R-R	6-0	205	2-7-90	.259	.143	.367	18	58	6	15	4	0	0	5	7	2	1	1	6	0	1	.328	.353
Olmedo-Barrera, David	L-R	6-1	170	6-22-94	.288	.381	.275	44	170	25	49	10	1	4	21	8	7	1	1	34	4	4	.429	.344
Perez, Angel	R-R	6-2	185	1-10-95	.290	.216	.314	58	207	26	60	14	5	1	23	11	4	1	0	52	5	6	.420	.338
Popadics, Jon	R-R	5-10	180	9-17-92	.159	.091	.183	27	82	12	13	5	1	0	3	11	1	2	1	13	4	1	.244	.263
Pujols, Bill	R-R	5-11	160	7-19-94	.216	.172	.235	29	97	12	21	8	0	0	12	10	3	0	0	25	2	3	.299	.309
Rodriguez, David	R-R	5-11	200	2-25-96	.258	.270	.255	45	178	20	46	7	1	4	27	15	3	0	0	39	1	1	.376	.327
Rojas, Jose	R-R	6-0	175	3-11-93	.266	.286	.258	26	94	11	25	5	0	3	19	2	2	1	0	11	0	1	.415	.296
Sullivan, Brett	L-R	6-1	180	2-22-94	.260	.333	.233	65	265	47	69	20	3	11	31	10	1	1	1	35	5	0	.483	.296

Pitching	B-T	HT	WT	DOB	W	L	ERA	G	GS	CG	SV	IP	H	R	ER	HR	BB	SO	AVG	vLH	vRH	K/9	BB/9
Alvarado, Jose	L-L	6-0	180	5-21-95	0	2	9.53	5	5	0	0	17	18	19	18	1	13	18	.300	.231	.319	9.53	6.88
Bastardo, Armando	R-R	6-0	175	7-11-94	1	3	3.18	18	0	0	6	23	24	12	8	1	10	22	.270	.293	.250	8.74	3.97
Bivens, Blake	R-R	6-2	205	8-11-95	6	0	2.78	11	11	0	0	55	53	23	17	4	18	43	.259	.304	.214	7.04	2.95
Bonnell, Bryan	L-R	6-5	210	9-28-93	2	1	4.24	15	1	0	2	34	37	18	16	3	8	21	.285	.298	.277	5.56	2.12
Burke, Brock	L-L	6-2	170	8-4-96	4	2	3.42	11	11	0	0	53	54	22	20	3	11	35	.265	.222	.284	5.98	1.88
Cabrera, Genesis	L-L	6-0	155	10-10-96	0	0	3.18	5	2	0	0	17	16	6	6	0	4	19	.254	.318	.220	10.06	2.12
Casanas, Alberto	R-R	6-2	158	11-27-93	3	0	2.87	17	0	0	9	31	24	11	10	5	11	20	.214	.167	.250	5.74	3.16
Clark, Ethan	R-R	6-6	235	10-26-94	1	5	6.84	9	5	0	0	26	38	23	20	4	7	24	.342	.400	.295	8.20	2.39
Clayton, Porter	L-L	6-4	220	5-22-93	1	1	5.61	15	0	0	0	26	29	19	16	4	9	21	.274	.156	.324	7.36	3.16
Feliz, Junior	R-R	6-0	160	1-17-94	0	5	8.06	7	2	0	0	22	28	23	20	2	11	16	.311	.386	.239	6.45	4.43
Fulenchek, Garrett	R-R	6-4	205	6-7-96	1	0	5.54	10	2	0	0	13	13	13	8	0	2	15	.265	.273	.259	10.38	15.23
2-team total (2 Danville)					1	1	6.11	12	4	0	0	18	18	17	12	0	30	19	—	—	—	9.68	15.28
Gibaut, Ian	R-R	6-3	235	11-19-93	3	1	2.12	12	0	0	0	30	23	8	7	2	8	38	.213	.326	.129	11.53	2.43
Jackson, Ty	R-R	6-3	225	7-21-93	0	1	4.50	9	0	0	1	14	19	7	7	0	5	8	.333	.423	.258	5.14	3.21
Lopez, Eduar	R-R	6-0	180	2-21-95	2	2	4.13	5	5	0	0	24	29	11	11	1	10	15	.319	.353	.298	5.63	3.75
Mendez, Deivy	R-R	6-2	160	10-27-95	2	2	4.74	13	8	0	0	38	29	20	20	1	28	51	.215	.246	.186	12.08	6.63
Moran, Spencer	R-R	6-6	180	4-2-96	3	1	3.12	13	7	0	0	52	43	19	18	1	14	47	.222	.298	.164	8.13	2.42
Mujica, Jose	R-R	6-2	200	6-29-96	1	0	0.90	4	4	0	0	20	12	2	2	0	2	20	.176	.212	.143	9.00	1.35
Paredes, Ruben	R-R	6-1	180	9-21-93	2	2	4.45	16	0	0	1	28	32	18	14	4	9	20	.278	.231	.317	6.35	2.86
Rodriguez, Noel	R-R	6-3	190	6-17-94	3	2	4.02	15	0	0	3	31	37	18	14	1	10	22	.303	.250	.355	6.32	2.87
Tapia, Alexis	R-R	6-2	195	8-10-95	1	0	3.86	6	5	0	0	23	30	12	10	0	5	21	.313	.513	.175	8.10	1.93
2-team total (6 Elizabethton)					2	2	3.83	12	11	0	0	56	67	29	24	5	12	54	—	—	—	8.63	1.92
Woeck, Andrew	R-R	5-10	180	5-4-92	1	1	3.71	13	0	0	1	17	16	8	7	2	8	20	.246	.156	.333	10.59	4.24

Fielding

Catcher	PCT	G	PO	A	E	DP	PB
Mitchell	1.000	3	19	6	0	0	1
Rodriguez	.974	44	336	46	10	4	6
Rojas	.960	21	142	28	7	0	7

First Base	PCT	G	PO	A	E	DP
Beck	.958	5	45	1	2	3
Meyer	.990	59	467	25	5	44
Rojas	.968	4	30	0	1	4
Sullivan	1.000	1	6	3	0	1

Second Base	PCT	G	PO	A	E	DP
Butera	.979	27	59	80	3	20
Popadics	1.000	21	36	55	0	14
Pujols	.972	21	42	61	3	16

Third Base	PCT	G	PO	A	E	DP
Popadics	1.000	1	1	1	0	0

	PCT	G	PO	A	E	DP
Pujols	.938	3	4	11	1	2
Sullivan	.900	64	45	108	17	12

Shortstop	PCT	G	PO	A	E	DP
Maris	.955	61	88	146	11	29
Popadics	.900	2	6	3	1	0
Pujols	.964	5	10	17	1	1

Outfield	PCT	G	PO	A	E	DP
Beck	.938	19	27	3	2	1
Cray	.976	57	113	7	3	0
Grady	1.000	8	18	0	0	0
Law	.967	64	136	9	5	1
Meyer	1.000	1	1	0	0	0
Perez	.962	58	120	5	5	3

GCL RAYS ROOKIE

GULF COAST LEAGUE

Batting	B-T	HT	WT	DOB	AVG	vLH	vRH	G	AB	R	H	2B	3B	HR	RBI	BB	HBP	SH	SF	SO	SB	CS	SLG	OBP
Arias, Juan Carlos	R-R	6-3	199	9-16-95	.208	.154	.222	37	125	12	26	6	0	2	10	9	3	1	1	32	0	0	.304	.275
Astacio, Joseph	L-R	6-0	155	6-5-94	.278	.368	.248	42	151	22	42	2	0	0	3	6	3	4	0	22	14	4	.291	.319
Ayende, Jaime	B-R	6-1	170	5-28-96	.205	.200	.207	32	78	8	16	1	0	0	1	8	1	4	0	28	6	1	.218	.287
Beck, Blair	R-R	6-0	195	9-19-92	.149	.125	.154	14	47	4	7	2	0	0	5	6	0	0	2	8	1	0	.191	.236
Caldwell, Ryan	R-R	6-2	180	12-25-95	.196	.250	.182	29	97	8	19	2	1	0	3	7	1	1	0	20	2	3	.237	.257
Cantillo, Anthony	R-R	5-10	145	8-6-95	.238	.250	.235	21	63	2	15	1	0	0	7	4	2	0	1	6	1	2	.254	.300
Davis, Devin	R-R	6-3	215	2-14-97	.261	.524	.202	36	115	13	30	3	0	2	5	16	4	0	0	32	2	0	.339	.370
Felipe, Jovany	R-R	6-0	205	3-4-93	.182	.000	.214	15	33	5	6	0	0	0	4	7	1	0	1	13	0	0	.182	.333
Gillaspie, Casey	B-L	6-4	240	1-25-93	.000	—	.000	2	6	0	0	0	0	0	0	1	0	0	2	0	0	.000	.143
Grant-Parks, Blake	R-R	6-1	190	7-15-93	.259	.188	.289	17	54	5	14	5	0	0	5	0	1	0	0	15	0	0	.352	.273
Hernandez, Miguel	R-R	6-2	175	12-28-95	.207	.148	.222	39	135	11	28	8	1	1	12	5	0	2	0	33	8	6	.304	.236
Lorenzo, Rafelin	R-R	6-2	200	1-15-97	.191	.222	.183	40	131	9	25	8	0	2	15	8	2	0	1	25	6	1	.298	.246
Marrero, Gilbert	L-L	6-2	195	8-9-96	.117	.100	.120	35	103	6	12	4	0	0	2	12	2	0	0	38	1	1	.155	.222
Morrison, Ty	L-R	6-2	170	7-22-90	.296	.000	.348	7	27	2	8	2	0	0	3	1	1	0	0	8	4	1	.370	.345
Robertson, Daniel	R-R	6-1	205	3-22-94	.125	.000	.167	4	8	2	1	0	0	0	0	3	1	0	0	2	1	0	.125	.417
Rodriguez, Juan	R-R	6-0	175	2-13-97	.146	.059	.165	32	96	4	14	2	0	0	2	14	3	1	0	28	1	2	.167	.274
Rojas, Oscar	R-R	5-11	165	7-5-96	.278	.385	.248	50	180	23	50	12	3	2	22	14	4	2	2	35	16	6	.411	.340
Rondon, Adrian	R-R	6-1	190	7-7-98	.166	.241	.147	43	145	3	24	8	1	0	11	17	1	0	1	45	0	2	.234	.256
Semler, Cody	R-R	5-10	180	3-30-93	.097	.200	.070	28	72	10	7	1	0	0	2	8	2	2	0	19	2	1	.111	.207
Velazquez, Andrew	B-R	5-8	175	7-14-94	.231	.333	.200	4	13	2	3	0	0	0	2	2	0	0	0	6	0	0	.231	.333
Whitley, Garrett	R-R	6-0	200	3-13-97	.188	.150	.197	30	96	12	18	4	2	3	13	16	2	0	2	25	5	4	.365	.310
Wiggins, Samm	R-R	5-8	185	12-29-92	.280	.333	.263	19	50	5	14	4	0	0	4	9	2	0	0	15	1	0	.360	.410

Pitching	B-T	HT	WT	DOB	W	L	ERA	G	GS	CG	SV	IP	H	R	ER	HR	BB	SO	AVG	vLH	vRH	K/9	BB/9
Agosto, Edrick	R-R	6-4	245	11-28-96	1	1	3.86	8	0	0	0	16	17	9	7	0	11	14	.266	.205	.360	7.71	6.06
Bonnell, Bryan	L-R	6-5	210	9-28-93	0	0	4.50	2	0	0	0	4	5	4	2	0	0	3	.313	.200	.364	0.00	0.00
Brashears, Tyler	L-R	6-2	170	2-24-94	0	0	5.40	3	0	0	0	3	5	3	2	0	1	3	.294	.286	.300	8.10	2.70
Brito, Sandy	R-R	6-1	170	7-19-96	0	2	5.30	15	5	0	0	19	5	17	11	0	27	19	.085	.057	.125	9.16	13.02
Chapman, Collin	R-R	6-2	205	1-1-93	0	1	3.75	10	0	0	2	12	13	5	5	0	2	10	.289	.320	.250	7.50	1.50
Disla, Jose	R-R	6-2	165	3-11-96	1	5	5.44	12	8	0	0	41	46	29	25	0	21	26	.284	.319	.239	5.66	4.57
Done, Jeffry	R-R	6-5	195	6-5-95	0	2	3.79	5	2	0	0	19	16	9	8	0	15	13	.242	.226	.257	6.16	7.11
Feliz, Junior	R-R	6-0	160	1-17-94	0	2	5.14	5	2	0	1	21	24	14	12	1	8	19	.276	.356	.190	8.14	3.43
Fierro, Edwin	R-R	6-1	200	8-30-93	1	0	0.00	1	1	0	0	2	1	0	0	0	0	1	.143	.200	.000	4.50	0.00
Frieri, Ernesto	R-R	6-2	205	7-19-85	0	1	1.17	6	5	0	0	8	3	3	1	0	3	5	.111	.143	.077	5.87	3.52
Germoso, Herminio	R-R	6-2	178	10-21-94	0	1	7.36	8	0	0	0	11	8	10	9	0	18	12	.222	.133	.286	9.82	14.73
Jackson, Ty	R-R	6-3	225	7-21-93	0	1	1.13	8	0	0	2	8	6	1	1	0	3	12	.214	.385	.067	13.50	3.38
Kendall, Ian	R-R	6-0	205	11-11-91	0	0	4.50	5	0	0	0	6	7	4	3	0	4	3	.304	.267	.375	4.50	6.00
Letkeman, Reign	L-R	6-3	165	5-12-95	1	3	7.01	9	3	0	0	26	27	20	20	0	5	19	.267	.204	.340	6.66	1.75
LeVert, Matt	R-R	5-11	195	10-21-92	1	0	4.94	13	0	0	1	24	29	19	13	2	11	18	.279	.296	.260	6.85	4.18
Marsden, Justin	R-R	6-3	175	1-27-97	0	1	3.14	6	0	0	0	14	6	5	5	0	6	14	.122	.174	.077	8.79	3.77
McPherson, Kyle	B-R	6-4	215	11-11-87	0	1	9.00	2	2	0	0	3	7	4	3	0	0	2	.500	.429	.571	6.00	0.00
Mena, Francisco	R-R	6-4	195	11-4-93	1	3	6.23	11	1	0	1	22	35	19	15	0	6	14	.365	.341	.385	5.82	2.49
Navas, Adrian	R-R	6-2	200	4-13-96	0	1	3.04	9	0	0	0	27	24	13	9	1	13	24	.245	.245	.244	8.10	4.39
Nichols, Ty	R-R	6-5	195	9-22-92	2	4	4.38	12	3	0	0	37	48	30	18	2	9	33	.308	.229	.397	8.03	2.19
Ortiz, Jesus	R-R	6-2	185	8-4-97	2	2	5.12	11	0	0	0	19	19	11	11	1	6	12	.260	.235	.282	5.59	2.79
Ortiz, Willy	R-R	6-1	180	7-20-95	1	0	1.00	2	1	0	0	9	8	3	1	0	2	2	.250	.294	.200	2.00	2.00
Patterson, Jimmy	R-L	6-0	190	2-9-89	0	0	0.00	2	0	0	0	3	3	0	0	0	0	1	.273	.333	.250	3.00	0.00
Reavis, Colton	R-R	6-0	195	12-16-89	0	0	7.71	3	0	0	0	5	9	4	4	0	1	5	.391	.300	.462	9.64	1.93
Regalado, Yael	R-R	6-2	200	2-23-93	0	0	0.00	4	0	0	0	6	3	0	0	0	0	7	.136	.083	.200	10.50	0.00
Rodriguez, Abrahan	R-R	6-2	182	4-20-95	0	5	5.16	11	7	0	0	45	58	32	26	2	12	28	.314	.290	.337	5.56	2.38
Romero, Orlando	R-R	6-0	185	9-26-96	0	4	5.08	8	5	0	0	28	36	18	16	1	16	17	.327	.317	.340	5.40	5.08
Triece, Sam	R-R	6-2	215	8-17-93	1	2	2.95	14	1	0	2	21	20	11	7	0	11	19	.244	.261	.222	8.02	4.64
Williams, John	R-R	6-1	195	5-9-93	5	1	3.95	11	1	0	1	27	25	13	12	2	8	22	.243	.188	.291	7.24	2.63
Woeck, Andrew	R-R	5-10	180	5-4-92	1	0	5.40	2	1	0	0	2	1	1	1	0	1	2	.167	—	.167	10.80	5.40

Fielding

Catcher	PCT	G	PO	A	E	DP	PB
Felipe	.944	13	60	8	4	0	4
Grant-Parks	1.000	3	21	1	0	0	0
Lorenzo	.964	34	195	44	9	1	10
Wiggins	.982	17	89	19	2	2	7

First Base	PCT	G	PO	A	E	DP
Davis	.992	28	210	25	2	12

	PCT	G	PO	A	E	DP
Gillaspie	1.000	1	3	3	0	0
Grant-Parks	1.000	2	10	0	0	0
Marrero	.986	35	263	28	4	22

Second Base	PCT	G	PO	A	E	DP
Astacio	.930	17	25	41	5	6
Cantillo	.958	21	28	63	4	7
Rodriguez	.951	20	26	51	4	9

	PCT	G	PO	A	E	DP
Semler	.905	7	6	13	2	1

Third Base	PCT	G	PO	A	E	DP
Arias	.926	36	32	55	7	5
Astacio	1.000	4	2	6	0	0
Rodriguez	.870	8	10	10	3	0
Semler	.929	16	6	20	2	0

Shortstop	PCT	G	PO	A	E	DP
Astacio	.962	18	27	49	3	6
Robertson	.800	3	3	1	1	0
Rondon	.930	37	52	68	9	14
Semler	1.000	1	1	2	0	1

	PCT	G	PO	A	E	DP
Velazquez	.941	4	7	9	1	0
Outfield	**PCT**	**G**	**PO**	**A**	**E**	**DP**
Ayende	.985	30	63	3	1	2
Beck	1.000	14	23	4	0	0

Caldwell	.938	27	41	4	3	1
Hernandez	.923	39	46	2	4	0
Morrison	.917	5	10	1	1	0
Rojas	.981	50	97	4	2	1
Whitley	1.000	22	60	2	0	1

DSL RAYS   ROOKIE
DOMINICAN SUMMER LEAGUE

Batting	B-T	HT	WT	DOB	AVG	vLH	vRH	G	AB	R	H	2B	3B	HR	RBI	BB	HBP	SH	SF	SO	SB	CS	SLG	OBP
Brujan, Vidal	B-R	5-10	150	2-9-98	.301	.259	.307	60	226	48	68	9	4	2	20	38	5	2	1	16	22	12	.403	.411
Contreras, Victor	R-R	6-2	170	10-28-97	.187	.143	.194	48	155	22	29	5	0	1	13	17	4	2	0	57	2	1	.239	.284
Gustave, Emilio	R-R	6-2	198	1-26-95	.223	.250	.220	26	94	13	21	6	1	0	9	11	5	0	0	27	5	4	.309	.336
Hernandez, Miguel	R-R	6-2	175	12-28-95	.213	.077	.250	16	61	12	13	2	1	3	10	4	1	0	0	16	2	3	.426	.273
Hernandez, Ronaldo	R-R	6-1	185	11-11-97	.227	.200	.231	13	44	3	10	0	1	0	4	3	3	0	0	6	0	0	.273	.320
Hernandez, Yeilin	B-R	5-11	180	3-12-96	.280	.294	.276	54	186	30	52	12	7	2	30	17	7	4	0	29	7	4	.452	.362
Maria, Eric	R-R	6-0	180	6-30-94	.356	.348	.358	37	118	14	42	9	1	2	17	12	4	0	1	12	1	1	.500	.430
Parra, Darwin	R-R	6-0	160	9-21-96	.278	.125	.304	20	54	7	15	3	0	1	6	6	2	0	0	8	0	0	.389	.371
Perez, Carlos	L-L	6-1	150	6-1-97	.500	—	.500	2	6	0	3	0	0	0	1	0	0	0	0	0	0	2	.500	.500
Pimentel, Luis	R-R	6-1	145	1-7-98	.210	.222	.208	52	176	20	37	8	1	0	21	27	4	4	2	34	5	3	.267	.325
Polanco, Sabriel	R-R	5-11	180	4-4-95	.322	.300	.327	49	177	22	57	8	2	2	26	7	3	0	3	25	5	0	.424	.353
Rodriguez, Alex	L-L	6-4	210	9-14-93	.277	.206	.290	63	220	38	61	13	1	2	33	27	1	1	8	35	3	0	.373	.348
Rosario, Jilber	B-R	5-11	175	9-20-94	.293	.227	.301	52	188	36	55	6	3	0	19	22	4	7	0	34	16	8	.356	.379
Sanchez, Jesus	L-R	6-2	185	10-7-97	.335	.258	.346	61	239	36	80	13	7	4	45	20	2	1	6	32	8	1	.498	.382
Santana, Jefry	R-R	6-2	170	11-26-94	.192	.125	.208	40	125	18	24	5	1	1	12	10	4	1	2	28	1	1	.272	.270
Santana, Yerson	R-R	6-3	195	12-2-96	.245	.250	.244	49	143	28	35	3	3	2	20	25	8	0	5	48	13	8	.350	.376
Vasquez, Jose	R-R	6-1	205	4-4-96	.286	.308	.282	41	168	30	48	7	5	3	25	12	5	0	1	52	7	4	.440	.349

Pitching	B-T	HT	WT	DOB	W	L	ERA	G	GS	CG	SV	IP	H	R	ER	HR	BB	SO	AVG	vLH	vRH	K/9	BB/9
Alejandro, Jose	R-R	6-3	190	6-20-95	0	4	5.13	14	14	0	0	40	32	32	23	0	40	32	.227	.257	.217	7.14	8.93
Caba, Jairo	R-R	6-3	190	8-27-97	4	1	1.06	13	1	0	0	34	26	10	4	0	16	12	.217	.250	.202	3.18	4.24
Cedeno, Estarly	R-R	6-3	180	11-7-96	1	0	0.00	2	0	0	0	3	1	0	0	0	1	2	.100	.000	.111	6.00	3.00
Constante, Marlon	R-R	5-11	180	7-5-96	1	3	2.14	18	4	0	7	42	34	13	10	2	7	33	.211	.191	.219	7.07	1.50
De La Cruz, Miguel	R-R	5-10	150	3-28-96	0	1	17.18	3	0	0	0	4	8	8	7	0	4	0	.471	1.000	.438	0.00	9.82
Felipe, Angel	R-R	6-5	190	8-30-97	1	2	8.68	7	0	0	0	9	4	10	9	0	13	6	.129	.250	.087	5.79	12.54
Gonzalez, Luis	R-R	6-2	190	4-27-96	0	0	6.75	5	0	0	0	7	6	8	5	0	4	6	.231	.250	.222	8.10	5.40
Gracia, Ariel	L-L	5-11	173	9-17-94	4	1	2.40	22	3	0	3	49	40	18	13	2	16	52	.219	.083	.228	9.62	2.96
Guilamo, Robert	R-R	6-4	200	10-2-92	1	0	2.84	11	0	0	0	19	7	8	6	0	11	13	.115	.143	.106	6.16	5.21
Henriquez, Jean Carlos	R-R	6-3	231	7-23-93	1	4	3.86	15	0	0	0	28	25	20	12	1	12	18	.236	.188	.244	5.79	3.86
Inoa, Odelis	R-R	6-1	180	9-2-94	3	0	4.15	16	0	0	0	35	32	20	16	2	19	24	.252	.391	.221	6.23	4.93
Lara, Miguel	R-R	5-11	165	7-17-97	0	5	5.24	14	14	0	0	34	14	25	20	0	38	44	.127	.160	.118	11.53	9.96
Lebron, Thomas	R-R	6-2	160	8-8-95	0	1	1.09	13	13	0	0	41	33	13	5	0	19	23	.217	.227	.213	5.01	4.14
Linares, Resly	L-L	6-2	155	12-11-97	0	3	1.11	14	14	0	0	49	29	10	6	0	15	59	.178	.286	.168	10.91	2.77
Montero, Reynier	R-R	6-2	165	10-29-96	1	0	7.23	12	0	0	1	19	15	17	15	0	17	16	.224	.350	.170	7.71	8.20
Ortiz, Willy	R-R	6-1	180	7-20-95	4	0	2.12	10	9	0	0	47	38	17	11	1	7	30	.221	.231	.218	5.79	1.35
Pena, Francisco	R-R	5-11	190	2-28-93	3	4	3.81	17	0	0	2	26	30	16	11	0	9	19	.300	.273	.308	6.58	3.12
Ramos, Reimin	R-R	6-1	190	4-27-96	6	0	1.24	13	0	0	0	36	24	11	5	0	13	21	.194	.120	.212	5.20	3.22
Salvador, Kendri	R-R	6-2	200	8-14-94	4	2	4.34	15	0	0	0	37	33	25	18	1	26	24	.241	.448	.185	5.79	6.27
Sanchez, Cristopher	L-L	6-5	165	12-12-96	2	1	3.54	15	0	0	2	20	13	10	8	0	16	16	.188	.100	.203	7.08	7.08
Tavera, Jose	R-R	6-4	215	4-30-96	0	2	10.32	11	0	0	0	11	13	16	13	0	22	8	.289	.143	.316	6.35	17.47
Ventura, Heriberto	R-R	6-0	160	8-10-98	2	0	3.71	15	0	0	0	27	29	14	11	2	15	18	.284	.174	.316	6.08	5.06

Fielding

Catcher	PCT	G	PO	A	E	DP	PB
Hernandez	.966	12	68	18	3	2	10
Maria	.964	27	145	44	7	3	9
Parra	.982	18	91	20	2	0	5
Polanco	.954	24	140	47	9	2	9
First Base	**PCT**	**G**	**PO**	**A**	**E**	**DP**	
Maria	.959	8	47	0	2	6	
Rodriguez	.991	62	565	17	5	41	
Santana	.946	9	49	4	3	6	
Santana	1.000	1	11	1	0	1	

Second Base	PCT	G	PO	A	E	DP
Brujan	.941	34	72	102	11	25
Pimentel	.960	35	60	85	6	18
Rosario	.955	5	11	10	1	3
Third Base	**PCT**	**G**	**PO**	**A**	**E**	**DP**
Brujan	.786	7	5	6	3	1
Polanco	.625	3	1	4	3	0
Rosario	.913	42	31	85	11	7
Santana	.926	28	16	59	6	5
Shortstop	**PCT**	**G**	**PO**	**A**	**E**	**DP**
Brujan	.911	15	29	43	7	5

	PCT	G	PO	A	E	DP
Contreras	.872	46	52	105	23	21
Pimentel	.946	13	23	30	3	8
Outfield	**PCT**	**G**	**PO**	**A**	**E**	**DP**
Gustave	.946	26	51	2	3	0
Hernandez	.952	14	20	0	1	0
Hernandez	.935	49	98	3	7	1
Rosario	.778	3	7	0	2	0
Sanchez	.972	54	98	8	3	2
Santana	1.000	4	6	0	0	0
Santana	.956	42	81	6	4	2
Vasquez	.946	28	50	3	3	1

VSL RAYS   ROOKIE
VENEZUELAN SUMMER LEAGUE

Batting	B-T	HT	WT	DOB	AVG	vLH	vRH	G	AB	R	H	2B	3B	HR	RBI	BB	HBP	SH	SF	SO	SB	CS	SLG	OBP
Alvarez, Alexander	R-R	5-11	200	9-14-96	.270	.382	.237	38	148	24	40	7	1	3	21	17	2	0	3	35	4	2	.392	.347
Ayres, Joao	L-R	5-11	175	4-13-97	.259	.235	.267	40	139	20	36	7	1	2	23	22	1	0	0	24	3	2	.367	.364
Balcazar, Randhi	R-R	6-0	160	12-19-96	.383	.304	.408	23	94	26	36	8	5	4	18	2	5	1	1	21	10	5	.702	.422
Cabrera, Eleardo	L-R	5-10	185	11-8-95	.295	.406	.266	51	156	33	46	13	2	4	30	39	14	1	2	39	3	7	.481	.469
Cabrera, Moises	L-R	6-1	188	12-4-96	.293	.195	.322	51	184	24	54	7	0	2	18	8	0	0	0	47	3	4	.364	.356
Cantillo, Anthony	R-R	5-10	145	8-6-95	.314	.409	.281	22	86	13	27	7	1	2	12	5	1	0	1	9	5	0	.488	.355

Batting

Batting	B-T	HT	WT	DOB	AVG	vLH	vRH	G	AB	R	H	2B	3B	HR	RBI	BB	HBP	SH	SF	SO	SB	CS	SLG	OBP
Fiorello, Pascual	R-R	6-0	155	1-16-97	.215	.167	.229	38	107	12	23	5	0	4	17	7	1	0	3	23	2	0	.374	.263
Gomez, Moises	R-R	5-11	196	8-27-98	.317	.278	.326	47	180	38	57	10	2	6	34	23	1	1	2	28	9	4	.494	.393
Lugo, Henry	R-R	5-11	160	11-30-95	.312	.345	.304	47	154	29	48	8	0	3	18	18	1	0	0	15	4	5	.422	.387
Mina, Yon	B-R	6-1	153	2-5-98	.192	.000	.241	39	99	16	19	4	1	0	4	10	9	0	0	28	3	4	.253	.322
Moredo, Eduardo	B-R	5-9	150	1-4-97	.232	.250	.228	54	198	38	46	4	1	0	11	21	4	6	0	35	16	2	.263	.318
Perez, Ricardo	L-R	5-10	155	5-25-95	.318	.667	.188	9	22	8	7	2	1	0	5	5	0	0	0	2	1	0	.500	.444
Pinto, Rene	R-R	5-10	180	11-2-96	.323	.325	.323	51	201	42	65	14	7	6	38	17	4	0	5	29	5	4	.552	.379
Rincon, Santiago	L-L	6-0	195	12-20-96	.250	.227	.257	54	192	25	48	18	0	7	42	13	8	0	4	74	2	3	.453	.318
Rivero, Oliver	R-R	6-1	166	9-8-97	.196	.242	.181	43	138	18	27	3	1	1	4	16	1	1	1	28	8	1	.254	.282
Silva, Darwin	R-R	6-0	187	4-29-97	.254	.125	.298	19	63	6	16	2	0	2	9	4	0	0	0	11	1	1	.381	.299
Torrealba, Jose	R-R	6-2	171	10-15-97	.250	.356	.216	52	184	22	46	4	3	3	15	12	5	0	2	65	7	6	.353	.310

Pitching

Pitching	B-T	HT	WT	DOB	W	L	ERA	G	GS	CG	SV	IP	H	R	ER	HR	BB	SO	AVG	vLH	vRH	K/9	BB/9
Cedeno, Jhoanbert	R-R	6-6	170	2-12-98	2	2	3.06	17	0	0	1	35	33	19	12	0	20	31	.244	.268	.234	7.90	5.09
Gonzalez, Ender	R-R	6-2	175	2-26-97	4	1	1.96	17	1	0	1	37	31	14	8	2	10	26	.231	.171	.253	6.38	2.45
Guarecuco, Roimar	R-R	6-1	170	1-25-95	1	1	4.50	16	0	0	5	24	27	14	12	0	14	20	.278	.174	.311	7.50	5.25
Hernandez, E, Edgardo	R-R	6-3	201	11-9-94	3	0	2.43	17	0	0	5	37	31	12	10	1	8	26	.228	.205	.237	6.32	1.95
Lopez, Hector	R-R	6-4	190	6-10-95	5	1	4.23	20	0	0	1	38	36	18	18	1	17	35	.248	.303	.232	8.22	3.99
Lugo, Enyerbeth	R-R	6-3	159	1-4-98	4	1	3.97	16	0	0	0	34	26	18	15	1	24	20	.208	.222	.204	5.29	6.35
Moncada, Luis	L-L	6-1	150	2-28-98	3	1	6.95	14	0	0	0	22	33	24	17	1	15	14	.330	.250	.337	5.73	6.14
Mujica, Arturo	L-L	6-3	181	6-4-96	1	2	2.81	17	4	0	5	42	33	15	13	0	16	35	.216	.077	.229	7.36	3.46
Navas, Adrian	R-R	6-2	200	4-13-96	0	3	0.83	9	9	0	0	33	19	5	3	1	10	42	.164	.205	.143	11.57	2.76
Pilar, Daniel	R-R	6-2	185	6-6-95	6	3	2.83	13	13	0	0	60	55	21	19	3	15	38	.243	.269	.236	5.67	2.24
Pinero, Dilan	R-R	6-2	170	4-25-97	0	2	5.40	9	5	0	0	18	15	11	11	0	9	11	.214	.118	.245	5.40	4.42
Rodriguez, Angel	R-R	6-5	229	1-28-98	1	1	4.59	17	1	0	0	33	24	22	17	1	23	30	.186	.250	.168	8.10	6.21
Rodriguez, Jesus	L-L	6-2	145	8-19-95	3	0	4.66	16	0	0	0	29	26	18	15	2	27	21	.245	.167	.255	6.52	8.38
Rosillo, Eduard	R-R	6-4	209	12-22-93	0	2	11.25	5	0	0	0	8	16	12	10	1	5	10	.400	.083	.536	11.25	5.63
Rubio, Jaime	R-R	6-0	196	4-8-97	0	0	—	1	0	0	0	0	1	1	0	3	0	—	—	—	—	—
Sanchez, Francisco	L-L	6-1	180	4-24-98	0	2	6.55	13	13	0	0	33	28	30	24	5	31	23	.233	.286	.226	6.27	8.45
Sanchez, Jesus	R-R	6-2	190	3-1-95	5	2	5.34	17	0	0	0	30	38	28	18	3	27	21	.302	.438	.255	6.23	8.01
Sanz, Chander	R-R	6-4	185	7-10-96	1	3	5.01	14	14	0	0	47	39	29	26	3	33	20	.241	.235	.243	3.86	6.36
Serrano, Luis	R-R	6-1	180	3-22-97	1	0	4.70	8	1	0	0	15	15	10	8	1	4	8	.238	.158	.273	4.70	2.35
Zerpa, Jose	R-R	6-4	185	3-29-97	2	1	4.54	10	9	0	0	38	44	24	19	4	8	35	.289	.237	.307	8.36	1.91

Fielding

Catcher	PCT	G	PO	A	E	DP	PB
Alvarez	.979	23	144	43	4	4	6
Pinto	.980	37	257	44	6	3	6
Silva	.977	11	76	10	2	0	1

First Base	PCT	G	PO	A	E	DP
Alvarez	.943	6	47	3	3	3
Cabrera	.984	37	402	27	7	37
Fiorello	.991	14	104	8	1	8
Lugo	.889	3	16	0	2	1
Perez	—	1	0	0	0	0
Rincon	.949	5	35	2	2	2

Second Base	PCT	G	PO	A	E	DP
Cantillo	.946	11	29	24	3	5

	PCT	G	PO	A	E	DP
Fiorello	.846	7	14	8	4	3
Lugo	.944	22	47	55	6	13
Moredo	.931	19	46	35	6	9
Perez	1.000	6	10	11	0	3
Rivero	.983	14	30	29	1	7

Third Base	PCT	G	PO	A	E	DP
Ayres	.929	39	21	109	10	11
Cantillo	.917	3	1	10	1	0
Fiorello	.851	15	7	33	7	0
Lugo	.877	20	18	39	8	6
Perez	.000	1	0	0	1	0

Shortstop	PCT	G	PO	A	E	DP
Cantillo	.923	7	7	17	2	4

	PCT	G	PO	A	E	DP
Lugo	.778	2	1	6	2	1
Moredo	.895	37	51	85	16	17
Rivero	.856	29	32	75	18	10

Outfield	PCT	G	PO	A	E	DP
Balcazar	.929	23	63	2	5	1
Cabrera	.978	48	84	5	2	2
Gomez	.977	39	83	3	2	0
Mina	.967	38	56	2	2	1
Rincon	.917	25	31	2	3	0
Torrealba	.966	50	80	6	3	2

Texas Rangers

SEASON IN A SENTENCE: The Rangers were one of the biggest surprises in baseball, taking a last-place team a year ago, subtracting ace Yu Darvish due to injury, dropping to nine games back in the American League West by July 20, then rallying to win the division.

HIGH POINT: After their July 20 loss, the Rangers finished the season 45-25. They captured the division lead from the Astros on Sept. 15 and didn't relinquish it the rest of the season.

LOW POINT: The Rangers had a 2-0 series lead over the Blue Jays heading back to Texas, needing one more win to win the AL Division Series. When the Rangers couldn't get it done at home, that set up a game five for the ages, with a meltdown in an unforgettable seventh inning. After the Rangers took a 3-2 lead in the top of the seventh inning, three straight errors in the infield (including two by shortstop Elvis Andrus) and a three-run homer by Jose Bautista in the bottom of the inning ultimately buried the Rangers' season.

NOTABLE ROOKIES: One of the few positives of being one of the worst teams in baseball in 2014 was that the Rangers had the third pick in the Rule 5 draft, which they used to take Astros outfielder Delino DeShields Jr., who turned into one of the better Rule 5 picks in recent years. Flame-throwing righthander Keone Kela was a crucial part of the bullpen, pitching well in high-leverage situations.

KEY TRANSACTIONS: The Rangers pulled off a blockbuster deal for Cole Hamels, getting an ace who can help them for years to come. It came at a high cost, with outfielder Nick Williams, catcher Jorge Alfaro and righthanders Jake Thompson, Jerad Eickhoff and Alec Asher all going to the Phillies. The Rangers defrayed some of the cost of Hamels' contract by including Matt Harrison in the deal, while they also got lefty reliever Jake Diekman, who used his high-octane fastball effectively down the stretch.

DOWN ON THE FARM: Top prospect Joey Gallo had an up-and-down season, showing tremendous raw power but struggling to make adjustments at the higher levels, with a strikeout in nearly half his plate appearances in the big leagues. Right fielder Nomar Mazara hit well in Double-A and during his brief Triple-A time, showing why the Rangers insisted on holding on to him during the Hamels talks. Center fielder Lewis Brinson had a breakout season translating his tools to production, hitting .332/.403/.601 in 100 games between three levels.

OPENING DAY PAYROLL: $142,140,873 (8th)

PLAYERS OF THE YEAR

MAJOR LEAGUE	MINOR LEAGUE
Prince Fielder dh	**Nomar Mazara** rf
.305/.378/.463	(Double-A/Triple-A)
Tied for club lead	.296/.366/.443
with 23 HR, 98 RBI	14 HR, 13 assists

ORGANIZATION LEADERS

BATTING		*Minimum 250 AB
MAJORS		
*AVG	Prince Fielder	.305
*OPS	Prince Fielder	.841
HR	Prince Fielder	23
	Mitch Moreland	23
RBI	Prince Fielder	98
MINORS		
*AVG	Lewis Brinson, Hi Desert, Frisco, Round Rock	.332
*OBP	Lewis Brinson, Hi Desert, Frisco, Round Rock	.403
*SLG	Lewis Brinson, Hi Desert, Frisco, Round Rock	.601
R	Ryan Cordell, High Desert, Frisco	84
H	Ronald Guzman, Hickory, High Desert	147
TB	Lewis Brinson, High Desert, Frisco, Round Rock	239
2B	Royce Bolinger, Frisco, High Desert	37
3B	Chris Garia, Frisco, Round Rock, High Desert	11
HR	Joey Gallo, Frisco, Round Rock	23
	Jared Hoying, Round Rock	23
	Tripp Martin, Hickory, High Desert	23
RBI	Ronald Guzman, Hickory, High Desert	87
BB	Drew Robinson, Frisco, Round Rock	87
SO	Royce Bolinger, Frisco, High Desert	144
SB	Jose Cardona, Hickory	30

PITCHING		#Minimum 75 IP
MAJORS		
W	Colby Lewis	17
#ERA	Yovani Gallardo	3.42
SO	Colby Lewis	142
SV	Shawn Tolleson	35
MINORS		
W	Ariel Jurado, Hickory	12
L	Chad Bell, Frisco	13
#ERA	Collin Wiles, Hickory	2.96
G	David Martinez, Frisco, Round Rock	49
GS	Reed Garrett, Hickory, High Desert	25
SV	David Martinez, Frisco, Round Rock	22
IP	Chad Bell, Frisco	141
BB	Jose Leclerc, Frisco	73
SO	Chad Bell, Frisco	118
AVG	Collin Wiles, Hickory	239

General Manager: Jon Daniels. **Farm Director:** Mike Daly. **Scouting Director:** Kip Fagg.

Class	Team	League	W	L	PCT	Finish	Manager
Majors	Texas Rangers	American	88	74	.543	3rd (15)	Jeff Banister
Triple-A	Round Rock Express	Pacific Coast	78	66	.542	t-5th (16)	Jason Wood
Double-A	Frisco RoughRiders	Texas	60	79	.432	7th (8)	Joe Mikulik
High A	High Desert Mavericks	California	78	62	.557	t-2nd (10)	Spike Owen
Low A	Hickory Crawdads	South Atlantic	81	57	.587	3rd (14)	Corey Ragsdale
Short season	Spokane Indians	Northwest	34	42	.447	t-6th (8)	Tim Hulett
Rookie	Rangers	Arizona	28	28	.500	7th (14)	Kenny Holmberg
Overall 2015 Minor League Record			359	334	.518	10th (30)	

ORGANIZATION STATISTICS

TEXAS RANGERS

AMERICAN LEAGUE

Batting	B-T	HT	WT	DOB	AVG	vLH	vRH	G	AB	R	H	2B	3B	HR	RBI	BB	HBP	SH	SF	SO	SB	CS	SLG	OBP
Alberto, Hanser	R-R	5-11	215	10-17-92	.222	.152	.258	41	99	12	22	2	1	0	4	2	0	3	0	17	1	0	.263	.238
Andrus, Elvis	R-R	6-0	195	8-26-88	.258	.286	.244	160	596	69	154	34	2	7	62	46	2	8	9	78	25	9	.357	.309
Beltre, Adrian	R-R	5-11	220	4-7-79	.287	.311	.276	143	567	83	163	32	4	18	83	41	3	0	8	65	1	0	.453	.334
Blanks, Kyle	R-R	6-6	265	9-11-86	.313	.333	.300	18	67	10	21	5	0	3	6	4	0	0	0	20	1	0	.522	.352
Chirinos, Robinson	R-R	6-1	210	6-5-84	.232	.265	.213	78	233	33	54	16	1	10	34	28	5	5	2	62	0	0	.438	.325
Choice, Michael	R-R	6-0	230	11-10-89	.000	—	—	1	1	0	0	0	0	0	0	0	0	0	0	1	0	0	.000	.000
Choo, Shin-Soo	L-L	5-11	210	7-13-82	.276	.237	.299	149	555	94	153	32	3	22	82	76	15	2	5	147	4	2	.463	.375
Corporan, Carlos	B-R	6-2	240	1-7-84	.178	.222	.155	33	107	10	19	4	0	3	15	6	4	2	2	40	0	0	.299	.244
DeShields, Delino	R-R	5-9	210	8-16-92	.261	.282	.250	121	425	83	111	22	10	2	37	53	3	7	4	101	25	8	.374	.344
Field, Tommy	R-R	5-10	185	2-22-87	.195	.167	.200	14	41	6	8	1	0	2	5	2	1	1	0	16	1	0	.366	.250
Fielder, Prince	L-R	5-11	275	5-9-84	.305	.252	.343	158	613	78	187	28	0	23	98	64	11	0	5	88	0	0	.463	.378
Gallo, Joey	L-R	6-5	230	11-19-93	.204	.135	.239	36	108	16	22	3	1	6	14	15	0	0	0	57	3	0	.417	.301
Gimenez, Chris	R-R	6-2	225	12-27-82	.255	.269	.250	36	98	19	25	6	1	5	14	10	1	4	0	19	2	0	.490	.330
Hamilton, Josh	L-L	6-4	240	5-21-81	.253	.236	.261	50	170	22	43	8	0	8	25	10	0	0	2	52	0	0	.441	.291
Martin, Leonys	L-R	6-2	200	3-6-88	.219	.229	.213	95	288	26	63	12	0	5	26	16	2	3	1	69	14	5	.313	.264
Moreland, Mitch	L-L	6-2	230	9-6-85	.278	.245	.294	132	471	51	131	27	0	23	85	32	7	0	5	112	1	0	.482	.330
Napoli, Mike	R-R	6-1	225	10-31-81	.295	.364	.130	35	78	9	23	2	0	5	10	12	1	0	0	19	0	2	.513	.396
2-team total (98 Boston)					.224	—		133	407	46	91	20	1	18	50	57	4	0	1	118	3	3	.410	.324
Odor, Rougned	L-R	5-11	190	2-3-94	.261	.266	.257	120	426	54	111	21	9	16	61	23	14	2	5	79	6	7	.465	.316
Peguero, Carlos	L-L	6-5	260	2-22-87	.186	.333	.172	30	70	10	13	4	0	4	9	12	1	0	1	36	2	0	.414	.310
2-team total (4 Boston)					.187	—		34	75	11	14	4	0	4	9	13	1	0	1	37	2	0	.400	.311
Rosales, Adam	R-R	6-1	200	5-20-83	.228	.217	.244	53	114	14	26	4	0	3	7	10	1	0	0	30	4	4	.342	.296
Rua, Ryan	R-R	6-2	205	3-11-90	.193	.196	.188	28	83	10	16	5	0	4	7	3	0	0	2	32	0	0	.398	.221
Smolinski, Jake	R-R	5-11	205	2-9-89	.133	.176	.077	35	60	12	8	1	0	1	6	11	1	0	2	20	1	0	.200	.270
2-team total (41 Oakland)					.193	—		76	166	24	32	7	2	6	26	19	3	0	4	39	1	1	.367	.281
Strausborger, Ryan	R-R	6-0	185	3-4-88	.200	.160	.250	31	45	9	9	0	0	1	3	3	0	1	2	11	2	1	.267	.240
Stubbs, Drew	R-R	6-4	205	10-4-84	.095	.100	.091	27	21	6	2	1	0	0	5	0	0	0	1	10	3	0	.143	.269
Telis, Tomas	B-R	5-8	215	6-18-91	.182	.500	.000	6	11	1	2	0	0	0	2	0	1	0	0	1	0	0	.182	.250
Venable, Will	L-L	6-3	205	10-29-82	.182	.077	.208	37	66	6	12	3	0	0	3	12	2	2	0	21	5	0	.227	.325
Wilson, Bobby	R-R	6-0	220	4-8-83	.221	.100	.263	31	77	5	17	5	0	1	10	7	1	2	1	19	0	1	.325	.291
2-team total (25 Tampa Bay)					.189	—	—	56	132	8	25	5	0	1	14	11	1	2	1	39	0	1	.250	.255

Pitching	B-T	HT	WT	DOB	W	L	ERA	G	GS	CG	SV	IP	H	R	ER	HR	BB	SO	AVG	vLH	vRH	K/9	BB/9
Bass, Anthony	R-R	6-2	200	11-1-87	0	0	4.50	33	0	0	0	64	66	33	32	5	20	45	.269	.284	.259	6.33	2.81
Claudio, Alex	L-L	6-3	185	1-31-92	1	1	2.87	18	0	0	0	16	12	6	5	4	6	13	.211	.226	.192	7.47	3.45
Detwiler, Ross	R-L	6-3	215	3-6-86	0	5	7.12	17	7	0	0	43	62	37	34	9	20	28	.343	.220	.379	5.86	4.19
Diekman, Jake	L-L	6-4	205	1-21-87	0	0	2.08	26	0	0	0	22	13	5	5	2	7	20	.169	.250	.098	8.31	2.91
Dyson, Sam	R-R	6-1	210	5-7-88	2	1	1.15	31	0	0	2	31	24	5	4	1	4	30	.212	.222	.208	8.62	1.15
Edwards, Jon	R-R	6-5	235	1-8-88	0	0	6.00	11	0	0	0	6	6	4	4	1	8	6	.273	.364	.182	9.00	12.00
Faulkner, Andrew	R-L	6-2	200	9-12-92	0	0	2.79	11	0	0	0	10	8	3	3	2	3	10	.216	.111	.316	9.31	2.79
Feliz, Neftali	R-R	6-3	225	5-2-88	1	2	4.58	18	0	0	0	24	20	14	10	2	9	16	.293	.317	.268	7.32	4.12
2-team total (30 Detroit)					3	4	6.38	48	0	0	10	48	57	34	34	5	18	39	—	—	—	7.31	3.38
Freeman, Sam	R-L	5-11	165	6-24-87	0	0	3.05	54	0	0	0	38	31	13	13	4	25	40	.218	.281	.167	9.39	5.87
Fujikawa, Kyuji	L-R	6-0	190	7-21-80	0	0	16.20	2	0	0	0	2	2	3	3	1	0	1	.286	.250	.333	5.40	0.00
Gallardo, Yovani	R-R	6-2	205	2-27-86	13	11	3.42	33	33	0	0	184	193	76	70	15	68	121	.268	.271	.265	5.91	3.32
Gonzalez, Chi Chi	R-R	6-3	210	1-15-92	4	6	3.90	14	10	1	0	67	49	33	29	6	32	30	.202	.246	.164	4.03	4.30
Hamels, Cole	L-L	6-3	200	12-27-83	7	1	3.66	12	12	1	0	84	77	35	34	10	23	78	.245	.300	.230	8.39	2.47
Harrison, Matt	L-L	6-4	240	9-16-85	1	2	6.75	3	3	0	0	16	19	12	12	3	6	5	.306	.357	.292	2.81	3.38
Holland, Derek	B-L	6-2	215	10-9-86	4	3	4.91	10	10	1	0	59	59	32	32	11	17	41	.269	.293	.264	6.29	2.61
Jackson, Luke	R-R	6-2	205	8-24-91	0	0	4.26	7	0	0	0	6	5	3	3	1	2	6	.200	.143	.222	8.53	2.84
Kela, Keone	R-R	6-1	230	4-16-93	7	5	2.39	68	0	0	1	60	52	18	16	4	18	68	.232	.289	.194	10.14	2.69
Klein, Phil	R-R	6-7	260	4-30-89	1	0	6.75	11	2	0	0	17	23	15	13	4	10	12	.303	.395	.211	6.23	5.19
Lewis, Colby	R-R	6-4	245	8-2-79	17	9	4.66	33	33	2	0	205	211	114	106	26	42	142	.266	.271	.260	6.24	1.85
Martinez, Nick	L-R	6-1	200	8-5-90	7	7	3.96	24	21	0	0	125	135	66	55	16	44	77	.274	.236	.307	5.54	3.31
Mendez, Roman	R-R	6-3	235	7-25-90	0	1	5.40	12	0	0	0	12	11	7	7	1	7	9	.268	.286	.250	6.94	5.40
2-team total (3 Boston)					0	1	5.27	15	0	0	0	14	14	8	8	2	8	10	—	—	—	6.59	5.27

Batting	B-T	HT	WT	DOB	AVG	vLH	vRH	G	AB	R	H	2B	3B	HR	RBI	BB	HBP	SH	SF	SO	SB	CS	SLG	OBP
Ohlendorf, Ross	R-R	6-4	240	8-8-82	3	1	3.72	21	0	0	1	19	21	8	8	4	7	19	.273	.241	.2928	.843	.26	
Patton, Spencer	R-R	6-1	200	2-20-88	1	1	9.00	27	0	0	0	24	24	24	24	5	12	28	.261	.281	.250	10.50	4.50	
Perez, Martin	L-L	6-0	195	4-4-91	3	6	4.46	14	14	0	0	79	88	45	39	3	24	48	.285	.210	.3045	.492	.75	
Pimentel, Stolmy	R-R	6-3	230	2-1-90	0	1	3.97	8	0	0	0	11	11	5	5	1	3	7	.268	.429	.1855	.562	.38	
Ranaudo, Anthony	R-R	6-7	230	9-9-89	0	1	7.63	4	2	0	0	15	18	13	13	2	8	11	.295	.265	.3336	.464	.70	
Rodriguez, Wandy	R-L	5-10	195	1-18-79	6	4	4.90	17	15	0	0	86	99	48	47	10	36	72	.285	.294	.2827	.513	.75	
Scheppers, Tanner	R-R	6-4	200	1-17-87	4	1	5.63	42	0	0	0	38	37	25	24	6	23	32	.250	.234	.2627	.515	.40	
Tolleson, Shawn	R-R	6-2	220	1-19-88	6	4	2.99	73	0	0	35	72	66	25	24	9	17	76	.239	.243	.2349	.462	.12	
Verrett, Logan	R-R	6-2	190	6-19-90	0	1	6.00	4	0	0	0	9	11	7	6	1	4	3	.306	.364	.2803	.004	.00	

Fielding

Catcher	PCT	G	PO	A	E	DP	PB
Chirinos	.988	78	474	31	6	2	4
Corporan	.987	31	219	11	3	2	3
Gimenez	.988	36	230	13	3	2	4
Telis	.938	4	14	1	1	0	0
Wilson	.989	31	170	12	2	0	2

First Base	PCT	G	PO	A	E	DP
Blanks	1.000	13	105	6	0	10
Fielder	.973	18	134	9	4	15
Moreland	.996	120	975	64	4	109
Napoli	.991	15	103	6	1	13
Rosales	1.000	19	87	6	0	11
Rua	1.000	4	7	0	0	0

Second Base	PCT	G	PO	A	E	DP
Alberto	.983	24	40	73	2	14
DeShields	1.000	1	0	3	0	0
Field	.955	14	23	41	3	4
Odor	.970	119	207	350	17	97
Rosales	.974	19	25	49	2	14

Third Base	PCT	G	PO	A	E	DP
Alberto	1.000	7	2	3	0	0
Beltre	.956	142	105	267	17	28
Gallo	.853	15	8	21	5	2
Rosales	.941	14	4	12	1	0

Shortstop	PCT	G	PO	A	E	DP
Alberto	1.000	8	4	13	0	3
Andrus	.972	160	248	516	22	114
Field	1.000	1	1	1	0	0

Outfield	PCT	G	PO	A	E	DP
Blanks	1.000	3	5	0	0	0
Choice	.000	1	0	0	1	0
Choo	.985	148	315	5	5	2
DeShields	.977	113	252	6	6	2
Gallo	1.000	19	21	1	0	0
Hamilton	1.000	42	70	2	0	0
Martin	.996	92	218	13	1	0
Napoli	.600	11	2	1	2	0
Peguero	1.000	27	36	1	0	0
Rosales	1.000	1	4	0	0	0
Rua	1.000	25	35	0	0	0
Smolinski	1.000	31	41	0	0	0
Strausborger	.957	19	21	1	1	1
Stubbs	1.000	24	11	0	0	0
Venable	1.000	34	31	1	0	0

ROUND ROCK EXPRESS

TRIPLE-A

PACIFIC COAST LEAGUE

Batting	B-T	HT	WT	DOB	AVG	vLH	vRH	G	AB	R	H	2B	3B	HR	RBI	BB	HBP	SH	SF	SO	SB	CS	SLG	OBP
Adams, Trever	R-R	6-0	210	9-30-88	.216	.261	.196	25	74	6	16	0	1	3	10	6	1	0	3	24	0	2	.365	.274
Alberto, Hanser	R-R	5-11	215	10-17-92	.310	.294	.318	81	310	42	96	19	4	4	32	9	2	7	2	33	5	5	.435	.331
Arroyo, Carlos	L-R	5-11	150	6-28-93	.400	.500	.375	5	10	2	4	1	1	0	1	1	0	0	0	0	0	0	.700	.455
Blanks, Kyle	R-R	6-6	265	9-11-86	.293	.400	.256	18	58	8	17	7	0	3	11	6	4	0	1	20	0	0	.569	.391
Brinson, Lewis	R-R	6-3	170	5-8-94	.433	.375	.455	8	30	9	13	1	0	1	4	7	0	0	0	6	3	0	.567	.541
Burg, Alex	R-R	6-0	190	8-9-87	.125	.000	.182	5	16	0	2	1	0	0	4	1	0	0	0	5	0	0	.188	.333
Cantwell, Pat	R-R	6-2	210	4-10-90	.136	.063	.179	16	44	4	6	0	1	0	3	2	4	2	0	12	0	1	.182	.240
Cedeno, Diego	L-L	5-11	160	5-19-92	.222	.333	.000	3	9	1	2	0	0	0	0	1	0	1	0	1	0	0	.222	.222
Chirinos, Robinson	R-R	6-1	210	6-5-84	.091	.000	.125	4	11	1	1	0	0	0	0	3	0	0	0	6	0	0	.091	.286
Choice, Michael	R-R	6-0	230	11-10-89	.244	.218	.258	110	406	53	99	25	1	12	60	32	7	0	2	115	2	0	.399	.309
Corporan, Carlos	B-R	6-2	240	1-7-84	.154	.200	.125	5	13	0	2	0	0	0	1	0	0	0	0	4	0	0	.154	.214
DeShields, Delino	R-R	5-9	210	8-16-92	.308	.286	.316	6	26	2	8	3	0	0	2	1	0	0	0	6	0	0	.423	.333
Field, Tommy	R-R	5-10	185	2-22-87	.247	.252	.244	103	369	51	91	23	3	14	44	53	7	0	6	82	5	1	.439	.347
Gallo, Joey	L-R	6-5	230	11-19-93	.195	.160	.216	53	200	20	39	9	0	14	32	27	0	0	1	90	1	0	.450	.289
Garcia, Edwin	B-R	6-1	185	3-1-91	.200	.375	.083	8	20	3	4	0	1	0	0	1	0	0	0	5	0	1	.300	.238
Garia, Chris	B-R	6-0	165	12-16-92	.143	.250	.077	9	21	2	3	0	0	1	4	1	0	0	0	5	1	0	.286	.182
Gimenez, Chris	R-R	6-2	225	12-27-82	.243	.263	.234	69	247	28	60	10	0	6	33	24	3	1	2	62	2	0	.356	.315
Hamilton, Josh	L-L	6-4	240	5-21-81	.270	.316	.222	11	37	1	10	3	0	0	5	1	0	0	0	10	0	0	.351	.289
Hassan, Alex	R-R	6-3	220	4-1-88	.267	.300	.250	16	60	8	16	5	0	0	8	7	0	0	0	13	0	0	.350	.343
2-team total (4 Nashville)					.230	—	—	20	74	8	17	5	0	0	8	8	0	0	0	17	0	0	.297	.305
Hoying, Jared	L-R	6-3	205	5-18-89	.214	.187	.227	129	485	66	104	25	6	23	60	29	3	1	1	110	20	6	.433	.263
Lucas, Ed	R-R	6-3	210	5-21-82	.316	.365	.289	107	393	43	124	17	3	6	48	45	3	0	1	85	3	4	.420	.389
Martin, Leonys	L-R	6-2	200	3-6-88	.297	.267	.318	9	37	7	11	3	0	2	4	5	0	0	1	4	2	1	.541	.372
Mazara, Nomar	L-L	6-4	195	4-26-95	.358	.300	.469	20	81	11	29	4	0	1	13	5	2	0	0	10	0	0	.444	.409
Moorman, Chuck	R-R	5-11	200	1-9-94	.500	.500	—	2	2	0	1	0	0	0	0	0	0	0	0	0	0	0	.500	.500
Moreland, Mitch	L-L	6-2	230	9-6-85	.000	.000	.000	4	11	2	0	0	0	0	0	6	0	0	0	1	0	0	.000	.353
Nicholas, Brett	L-R	6-2	215	7-18-88	.268	.252	.276	109	403	49	108	22	0	12	63	27	2	1	5	79	2	2	.437	.314
Odor, Rougned	L-R	5-11	190	2-3-94	.352	.350	.353	30	108	26	38	12	2	5	19	12	2	2	0	10	3	1	.639	.426
Pastornicky, Tyler	R-R	5-11	180	12-13-89	.283	.348	.250	53	198	30	56	15	2	1	19	12	0	1	3	25	3	2	.394	.319
Peguero, Carlos	L-L	6-5	260	2-22-87	.667	.500	.750	2	6	2	4	1	1	0	1	0	0	0	0	1	0	0	1.167	.714
Richardson, Antoan	B-R	5-8	165	10-8-83	.364	.000	.444	3	11	3	4	1	1	0	1	2	1	0	0	2	1	0	.636	.500
Robinson, Drew	L-R	6-1	200	4-20-92	.304	.250	.316	7	23	4	7	2	0	0	2	4	0	1	0	4	2	1	.391	.407
Rodriguez, Guilder	B-R	6-1	190	7-24-83	.100	—	.100	5	10	1	1	0	0	0	0	3	0	0	0	2	0	0	.100	.308
Rua, Ryan	R-R	6-2	205	3-11-90	.197	.180	.207	40	142	18	28	5	0	6	22	18	4	0	1	45	3	0	.359	.303
Shoulders, Rock	L-R	6-2	225	9-26-91	.250	.000	.500	2	8	2	2	0	0	1	0	0	0	0	0	2	0	0	.625	.250
Smolinski, Jake	R-R	5-11	205	2-9-89	.422	.563	.345	12	45	9	19	5	0	4	14	4	1	0	0	7	0	1	.800	.480
2-team total (25 Nashville)					.374	—	—	37	131	25	49	14	0	9	31	12	2	0	2	16	2	2	.687	.429
Strausborger, Ryan	R-R	6-0	185	3-4-88	.278	.306	.262	86	345	54	96	21	2	10	34	24	3	7	2	66	27	5	.438	.329
Stubbs, Drew	R-R	6-4	205	10-4-84	.222	.273	.188	7	27	6	6	1	0	0	3	0	0	0	0	7	4	0	.259	.300
2-team total (38 Albuquerque)					.256	—	—	45	164	28	42	5	3	2	20	27	2	0	2	46	10	3	.360	.364
Telis, Tomas	B-R	5-8	215	6-18-91	.291	.308	.283	70	282	43	82	15	1	5	25	14	1	3	0	31	1	2	.404	.327
2-team total (13 New Orleans)					.297	—	—	83	330	46	98	15	1	5	29	19	1	4	1	37	3	2	.394	.336

Batting	B-T	HT	WT	DOB	AVG	vLH	vRH	G	AB	R	H	2B	3B	HR	RBI	BB	HBP	SH	SF	SO	SB	CS	SLG	OBP
Weems, Beamer	R-R	5-10	175	7-28-87	.245	.250	.242	57	192	17	47	14	1	2	17	19	1	1	0	34	0	1	.359	.316
Wise, J.T.	R-R	6-0	210	6-2-86	.188	.214	.167	21	64	10	12	1	0	3	5	5	0	1	0	15	0	0	.344	.246
Yrizarri, Yeyson	R-R	6-0	175	2-2-97	.273	.200	.286	9	33	2	9	1	0	4	1	0	0	0	5	0	1	.364	.294

Pitching	B-T	HT	WT	DOB	W	L	ERA	G	GS	CG	SV	IP	H	R	ER	HR	BB	SO	AVG	vLH	vRH	K/9	BB/9
Asher, Alec	R-R	6-4	230	10-4-91	3	6	4.73	12	12	0	0	65	71	36	34	16	19	54	.277	.303	.261	7.52	2.64
Bass, Anthony	R-R	6-2	200	11-1-87	0	0	10.38	2	0	0	0	4	9	5	5	0	1	3	.450	.040	6.23	2.08
Burton, Jared	R-R	6-5	225	6-2-81	0	0	0.90	12	0	0	1	10	4	1	1	1	3	11	.121	.100	.130	9.90	2.70
Cabrera, Edwar	L-L	6-0	195	10-20-87	1	0	6.14	6	0	0	1	7	12	5	5	0	0	10	.353	.455	.304	12.27	0.00
Claudio, Alex	L-L	6-3	185	1-31-92	3	1	2.93	29	0	0	0	40	43	13	13	2	7	35	.283	.217	.326	7.88	1.58
Coello, Robert	R-R	6-5	250	11-23-84	1	3	5.64	6	5	0	0	30	33	19	19	4	13	13	.284	.246	.333	3.86	3.86
2-team total (11 Sacramento)					7	6	4.18	17	16	0	0	95	91	48	44	8	41	62	—	—	—	5.89	3.90
Edwards, Jon	R-R	6-5	235	1-8-88	2	1	1.42	32	0	0	20	32	18	5	5	1	8	44	.165	.204	.133	12.51	2.27
2-team total (5 El Paso)					2	1	1.23	37	0	0	23	37	21	5	5	1	11	51	—	—	—	12.52	2.70
Eickhoff, Jerad	R-R	6-4	240	7-2-90	9	4	4.25	18	17	0	0	102	95	49	48	12	33	93	.249	.251	.246	8.23	2.92
Faulkner, Andrew	R-L	6-3	200	9-12-92	0	0	0.00	6	0	0	0	8	2	0	0	1	3	13	.080	.000	.125	14.63	1.13
Feliz, Neftali	R-R	6-3	225	5-2-88	0	1	7.36	10	0	0	0	11	15	11	9	1	4	11	.319	.188	.387	9.00	3.27
Freeman, Sam	R-L	5-11	165	6-24-87	0	0	1.13	8	0	0	0	8	5	1	1	0	6	8	.185	.071	.308	9.00	6.75
Fujikawa, Kyuji	L-R	6-0	190	7-21-80	0	0	3.86	10	0	0	0	9	6	4	4	1	9	8	.194	.167	.231	7.71	8.68
Gonzalez, Chi Chi	R-R	6-3	210	1-15-92	8	7	3.57	16	16	0	0	88	95	40	35	3	31	56	.280	.283	.279	5.71	3.16
Harrison, Matt	L-L	6-4	240	9-16-85	1	3	5.97	5	5	0	0	29	34	21	19	0	12	18	.309	.321	.305	5.65	3.77
Holland, Derek	B-L	6-2	215	10-9-86	0	1	5.19	3	3	0	0	9	9	6	5	0	5	14	.257	.143	.333	14.54	5.19
Irwin, Phil	R-R	6-3	210	2-25-87	2	1	5.40	3	1	0	0	10	13	6	6	1	5	6	.351	.278	.421	5.40	4.50
Jackson, Luke	R-R	6-2	205	8-24-91	2	3	4.34	39	5	0	0	66	62	37	32	3	35	79	.245	.192	.297	10.72	4.75
Kendall, Cody	R-R	6-2	210	12-12-89	0	1	13.50	2	0	0	0	3	5	5	5	1	3	1	.357	.375	.333	2.70	8.10
Kickham, Mike	L-L	6-4	220	12-12-88	1	0	6.00	7	0	0	0	6	3	4	4	0	7	4	.150	.167	.143	6.00	10.50
2-team total (5 Tacoma)					1	2	7.00	12	5	0	0	27	21	21	21	3	35	16	—	—	—	5.33	11.67
Klein, Phil	R-R	6-7	260	4-30-89	2	1	2.97	18	10	0	0	64	49	25	21	2	27	58	.212	.238	.192	8.20	3.82
Lamb, Will	L-L	6-6	180	9-9-90	2	3	5.52	25	0	0	0	31	32	20	19	3	15	27	.260	.225	.277	7.84	4.35
Martinez, David	R-R	6-2	220	8-4-87	0	0	4.32	9	2	0	0	17	17	10	8	4	12	8	.266	.361	.143	4.32	6.48
Martinez, Nick	L-R	6-1	200	8-5-90	1	1	2.90	6	6	0	0	31	32	12	10	1	7	18	.278	.321	.237	5.23	2.03
Mendez, Roman	R-R	6-3	235	7-25-90	3	2	2.78	30	0	0	5	36	31	11	11	5	9	43	.230	.284	.176	8.33	2.27
Mendoza, Francisco	R-R	6-0	200	12-7-87	1	0	2.68	32	3	0	0	54	48	16	16	0	27	40	.253	.286	.233	6.71	4.53
Monegro, Jose	R-R	6-3	200	9-19-89	1	0	5.91	6	1	0	0	11	11	7	7	0	3	10	.262	.333	.208	8.44	2.53
Ohlendorf, Ross	R-R	6-4	240	8-8-82	4	5	4.17	27	0	0	0	37	39	18	17	2	13	44	.275	.316	.247	10.80	3.19
Patton, Spencer	R-R	6-1	200	2-20-88	2	1	1.67	26	0	0	11	27	21	6	5	1	9	36	.206	.212	.200	12.00	3.00
Perez, Juan	R-L	6-0	190	9-3-78	0	0	10.80	9	0	0	0	7	10	8	8	1	7	11	.323	.385	.278	14.85	9.45
Perez, Martin	L-L	6-0	195	4-4-91	0	1	4.95	4	4	0	0	20	27	11	11	2	2	17	.333	.286	.350	7.65	0.90
Pimentel, Stolmy	R-R	6-3	230	2-1-90	5	3	5.40	17	12	0	0	72	86	44	43	9	33	60	.301	.319	.289	7.53	4.14
Pirela, Jesus	R-R	6-0	155	3-13-89	0	0	2.16	5	0	0	0	8	5	3	2	0	5	8	.167	.222	.143	8.64	5.40
Ranaudo, Anthony	R-R	6-7	230	9-9-89	7	6	4.58	21	21	0	0	118	124	65	60	14	46	90	.272	.275	.270	6.86	3.51
Reyes, Jimmy	L-L	5-10	200	3-7-89	5	3	2.31	41	5	0	1	62	64	20	16	1	17	40	.261	.240	.276	5.78	2.45
Rodebaugh, Ryan	L-R	6-0	190	3-30-89	1	0	10.80	1	0	0	0	2	4	2	2	1	2	2	.444	.375	10.80	10.80
Rodriguez, Ricardo	R-R	6-2	220	8-31-92	0	0	3.00	2	0	0	0	3	1	1	1	0	2	0	.111	.500	.000	0.00	6.00
Rodriguez, Wandy	R-L	5-10	195	1-18-79	0	0	2.57	2	2	0	0	7	4	2	2	1	0	10	.174	.333	.118	12.86	0.00
2-team total (5 Omaha)					0	0	1.80	7	2	0	0	15	9	3	3	1	4	17	—	—	—	10.20	2.40
Scheppers, Tanner	R-R	6-4	200	1-17-87	2	1	1.93	13	0	0	2	14	11	5	3	0	8	11	.239	.190	.280	7.07	5.14
Swanson, Erik	R-R	6-3	220	9-4-93	0	0	0.00	1	0	0	0	1	1	0	0	0	0	2	.250	.000	.500	18.00	0.00
Wolf, Ross	R-R	6-0	190	10-18-82	11	7	5.35	26	14	1	0	106	140	69	63	3	26	44	.320	.319	.321	3.74	2.21

Fielding

Catcher	PCT	G	PO	A	E	DP	PB
Cantwell	.971	14	88	12	3	2	0
Chirinos	1.000	4	22	2	0	0	1
Corporan	1.000	4	16	3	0	0	0
Gimenez	.991	26	195	15	2	2	1
Moorman	1.000	1	2	0	0	0	0
Nicholas	.994	48	330	29	2	3	2
Telis	.986	50	386	49	6	3	2
Wise	1.000	5	25	1	0	0	0

First Base	PCT	G	PO	A	E	DP
Adams	.976	5	40	1	1	5
Blanks	.990	13	91	12	1	9
Burg	.946	4	32	3	2	5
Gallo	1.000	1	9	0	0	1
Gimenez	.986	20	129	9	2	11
Hassan	1.000	1	3	0	0	0
Lucas	.997	37	309	23	1	30
Nicholas	.995	47	379	38	2	38
Rua	1.000	8	67	6	0	9
Telis	1.000	3	24	2	0	1
Wise	.975	10	75	3	2	7

Second Base	PCT	G	PO	A	E	DP
Alberto	.977	10	24	18	1	4

Field		PCT	G	PO	A	E	DP
		.990	64	120	172	3	40
Garcia		1.000	7	5	13	0	1
Lucas		.986	14	28	42	1	9
Odor		.971	28	44	57	3	9
Pastornicky		.957	11	19	25	2	9
Robinson		1.000	1	0	1	0	0
Rodriguez		—	1	0	0	0	0
Rua		.952	6	10	11	1	5
Weems		1.000	10	16	33	0	7

Third Base	PCT	G	PO	A	E	DP
Adams	.867	11	2	11	2	1
Alberto	.917	6	4	7	1	1
Arroyo	1.000	1	1	0	0	0
Field	1.000	1	3	1	0	0
Gallo	.967	33	24	65	3	5
Garcia	1.000	1	0	3	0	0
Gimenez	1.000	9	3	10	0	0
Lucas	.923	42	17	79	8	5
Moorman	—	1	0	0	0	0
Pastornicky	.967	32	12	46	2	4
Robinson	.917	3	3	8	1	1
Rodriguez	.857	4	1	5	1	2
Rua	1.000	9	6	15	0	2

Shortstop	PCT	G	PO	A	E	DP
Alberto	.990	65	106	189	3	45
Field	.987	19	32	46	1	10
Lucas	.938	8	14	16	2	6
Pastornicky	.500	1	0	1	1	0
Weems	.985	46	64	129	3	27
Yrizarri	.929	9	6	20	2	1

Outfield	PCT	G	PO	A	E	DP
Adams	1.000	9	17	0	0	0
Arroyo	1.000	3	10	0	0	0
Brinson	.889	8	14	2	2	0
Burg	1.000	1	3	0	0	0
Cantwell	1.000	1	1	0	0	0
Cedeno	1.000	2	2	0	0	0
Choice	.984	78	117	5	2	0
DeShields	.714	3	5	0	2	0
Field	1.000	14	30	1	0	0
Gallo	.968	15	28	2	1	0
Garia	1.000	9	18	0	0	0
Gimenez	1.000	3	8	1	0	1
Hamilton	1.000	8	9	0	0	0
Hassan	1.000	14	17	0	0	0
Hoying	.979	128	328	5	7	1

Outfield	PCT	G	PO	A	E	DP
Martin	1.000	9	36	0	0	0
Mazara	1.000	15	28	3	0	1
Pastornicky	1.000	7	13	1	0	0
Peguero	1.000	2	3	0	0	0
Richardson	1.000	2	3	0	0	0
Robinson	1.000	3	8	1	0	1
Rua	.950	12	18	1	1	0
Shoulders	—	2	0	0	0	0
Smolinski	1.000	10	20	2	0	0
Strausborger	.985	84	185	10	3	1
Stubbs	1.000	6	11	0	0	0

FRISCO ROUGHRIDERS

DOUBLE-A

TEXAS LEAGUE

Batting	B-T	HT	WT	DOB	AVG	vLH	vRH	G	AB	R	H	2B	3B	HR	RBI	BB	HBP	SH	SF	SO	SB	CS	SLG	OBP
Adams, Trever	R-R	6-0	210	9-30-88	.230	.317	.210	94	344	39	79	16	2	7	32	29	2	1	4	110	6	2	.349	.290
Alfaro, Jorge	R-R	6-2	225	6-11-93	.253	.346	.238	49	190	22	48	15	2	5	21	9	8	0	0	61	2	1	.432	.314
Beck, Preston	L-R	6-2	190	10-26-90	.224	.269	.214	93	343	38	77	12	4	5	42	39	1	0	3	60	8	2	.327	.303
Bolinger, Royce	R-R	6-2	200	8-12-90	.156	.214	.146	25	96	7	15	3	0	1	6	4	1	0	0	37	0	0	.219	.198
Brinson, Lewis	R-R	6-3	170	5-8-94	.291	.385	.262	28	110	14	32	8	1	6	23	6	1	1	2	38	2	1	.545	.328
Burg, Alex	R-R	6-0	190	8-9-87	.271	.340	.246	50	181	26	49	11	0	7	22	21	3	1	2	47	1	0	.448	.353
Cantwell, Pat	R-R	6-2	210	4-10-90	.187	.094	.205	60	198	22	37	3	2	3	19	16	3	2	2	43	0	0	.268	.256
Cone, Zach	R-R	6-2	205	12-14-89	.257	.207	.270	40	144	10	37	11	0	3	20	6	1	0	0	46	0	0	.396	.291
Cordell, Ryan	R-R	6-4	205	3-31-92	.217	.263	.201	56	221	26	48	5	3	5	18	12	3	2	4	73	10	1	.335	.263
Corporan, Carlos	B-R	6-2	240	1-7-84	.200	—	.200	3	10	0	2	0	0	0	0	0	0	0	0	1	0	0	.200	.200
Deglan, Kellin	L-R	6-2	195	5-3-92	.214	.133	.236	19	70	5	15	3	0	1	4	3	0	0	0	22	0	0	.300	.247
Gallo, Joey	L-R	6-5	230	11-19-93	.314	.143	.336	34	121	21	38	10	1	9	31	24	0	0	1	49	1	0	.636	.425
Garcia, Edwin	B-R	6-1	185	3-1-91	.269	.333	.264	22	78	7	21	2	0	0	5	5	0	1	2	14	0	1	.295	.306
Garia, Chris	R-R	6-0	165	12-16-92	.169	.133	.179	20	71	4	12	1	1	0	1	1	1	1	0	14	4	2	.211	.192
Hamilton, Josh	L-L	6-4	240	5-21-81	.526	.667	.500	5	19	10	10	3	0	1	4	2	0	0	0	2	0	0	.842	.571
Lacrus, Sherman	R-R	5-11	180	12-23-93	.091	—	.091	3	11	2	1	0	1	0	1	0	0	0	0	1	0	0	.273	.091
Marte, Luis	R-R	6-1	170	12-15-93	.206	.255	.191	62	228	24	47	7	1	3	17	3	0	4	2	41	9	3	.285	.215
Mazara, Nomar	L-L	6-4	195	4-26-95	.284	.260	.289	111	409	57	116	22	2	13	56	47	5	0	9	92	2	0	.443	.357
Mendez, Luis	B-R	5-9	155	1-1-93	.239	.216	.245	98	335	35	80	10	4	2	35	29	4	6	4	72	9	8	.310	.304
Moorman, Chuck	R-R	5-11	200	1-9-94	.000	—	.000	1	3	0	0	0	0	0	0	0	0	0	0	2	0	0	.000	.000
Pastornicky, Tyler	R-R	5-11	180	12-13-89	.276	.200	.284	28	105	14	29	4	0	0	5	4	4	2	0	13	1	2	.314	.327
Profar, Jurickson	B-R	6-0	200	2-20-93	.200	.250	.167	3	10	0	2	1	0	0	1	1	0	0	1	2	0	0	.300	.250
Robinson, Drew	L-R	6-1	200	4-20-92	.231	.135	.251	126	432	78	100	23	5	21	64	83	4	0	0	139	14	8	.454	.360
Rodriguez, Guilder	B-R	6-1	190	7-24-83	.248	.200	.257	37	125	15	31	4	0	0	13	20	0	1	2	23	6	2	.280	.347
Skole, Jake	R-R	6-1	195	1-17-92	.218	.190	.222	57	188	23	41	8	1	4	12	25	1	1	0	60	10	1	.335	.313
Valencia, Ricardo	R-R	6-0	185	1-13-93	.111	1.000	.000	3	9	0	1	0	0	0	0	0	0	0	0	4	0	0	.111	.111
Votoloto, Doug	B-R	6-2	190	6-29-91	.000	—	.000	4	7	1	0	0	0	0	0	0	0	0	0	4	0	0	.000	.000
Weems, Beamer	R-R	5-10	175	9-4-87	.100	.000	.118	5	20	1	2	0	0	0	0	0	0	0	0	5	0	0	.100	.100
Williams, Nick	L-L	6-3	195	9-8-93	.299	.226	.313	97	378	56	113	21	4	13	45	32	3	1	1	77	10	8	.479	.357
Wise, J.T.	R-R	6-0	210	6-2-86	.241	.250	.239	57	199	16	48	12	0	6	27	23	2	0	0	58	1	1	.392	.326

Pitching	B-T	HT	WT	DOB	W	L	ERA	G	GS	CG	SV	IP	H	R	ER	HR	BB	SO	AVG	vLH	vRH	K/9	BB/9
Asher, Alec	R-R	6-4	230	10-4-91	1	4	3.98	8	8	0	0	43	39	20	19	3	18	43	.241	.231	.247	9.00	3.77
Bell, Chad	R-L	6-3	200	2-28-89	7	13	4.58	27	23	0	0	141	154	83	72	11	42	118	.277	.266	.284	7.51	2.67
Buckel, Cody	R-R	6-1	185	6-18-92	0	1	14.40	10	0	0	0	10	16	16	16	3	11	6	.364	.313	.393	5.40	9.90
Cabrera, Edwar	L-L	6-0	195	10-20-87	4	2	3.68	27	7	1	0	71	69	33	29	6	17	51	.258	.309	.229	6.46	2.15
Castillo, Lendy	R-R	6-1	170	4-8-89	2	2	4.73	19	0	0	0	32	34	21	17	4	23	23	.281	.226	.324	6.40	6.40
Detwiler, Ross	R-L	6-3	215	3-6-86	0	0	7.36	2	0	0	0	4	7	3	3	0	2	4	.412	.500	.364	9.82	4.91
Ege, Cody	L-L	6-1	185	5-8-91	3	2	0.85	26	0	0	1	32	26	10	3	1	19	37	.228	.245	.215	10.52	5.40
Eickhoff, Jerad	R-R	6-4	240	7-2-90	1	0	2.70	2	2	0	0	10	7	3	3	2	3	14	.194	.222	.185	12.60	2.70
Faulkner, Andrew	R-L	6-3	200	9-12-92	7	4	4.19	28	15	0	1	92	84	50	43	9	47	90	.243	.202	.260	8.77	4.58
Fujikawa, Kyuji	L-R	6-0	190	7-21-80	0	0	9.00	1	0	0	0	1	3	3	1	0	0	1	.500	—	.500	0.00	0.00
Garcia, Martire	L-L	6-0	175	3-1-90	0	0	20.25	3	0	0	0	1	2	3	3	0	2	0	.400	.500	.333	0.00	13.50
Grullon, Juan	L-L	6-0	185	3-4-90	1	3	5.45	25	0	0	0	40	41	27	24	9	17	33	.273	.239	.301	7.49	3.86
Harrison, Matt	L-L	6-4	240	9-16-85	0	0	7.50	1	1	0	0	6	9	5	5	0	3	6	.346	.333	.353	4.50	4.50
Hernandez, Jefri	R-R	6-2	210	4-27-91	1	2	4.18	25	0	0	0	32	39	16	15	1	14	30	.300	.288	.308	8.35	3.90
Holland, Derek	B-L	6-2	215	10-9-86	0	0	8.10	1	1	0	0	3	7	3	3	1	1	5	.412	.500	.364	13.50	2.70
Irwin, Phil	R-R	6-3	210	2-25-87	0	3	6.75	4	4	0	0	20	26	15	15	3	6	22	.310	.308	.311	9.90	2.70
James, Chad	L-L	6-3	180	1-23-91	0	0	4.81	13	0	0	0	24	20	13	13	3	13	24	.222	.119	.313	8.88	4.81
Kela, Keone	R-R	6-1	230	4-16-93	1	0	0.00	2	0	0	2	1	0	0	0	0	0	2	.143	.333	.000	9.00	0.00
Kendall, Cody	R-R	6-2	210	12-12-89	0	0	2.08	8	0	0	0	13	5	3	2	0	4	7	.317	.429	.259	7.27	4.15
Lamb, Will	L-L	6-6	180	9-9-90	1	1	3.12	22	0	0	0	26	27	11	9	0	11	24	.260	.195	.302	8.31	3.81
Leclerc, Angelo	R-R	6-0	170	10-9-91	0	1	5.40	1	0	0	0	2	3	1	1	0	1	0	.375	.250	.500	0.00	5.40
Leclerc, Jose	R-R	6-0	165	12-19-93	6	8	5.77	26	22	0	0	103	97	66	66	8	73	98	.249	.280	.218	8.56	6.38
Lopez, Frank	L-L	6-1	175	2-18-94	3	7	4.92	16	15	0	0	75	87	45	41	9	34	58	.295	.272	.307	6.96	4.08
Lotzkar, Kyle	L-R	6-5	210	10-24-89	1	4	8.77	16	0	0	0	26	30	27	25	3	17	24	.306	.349	.273	8.42	5.96
Martinez, David	R-R	6-2	220	8-4-87	3	5	2.84	40	0	0	22	51	47	16	16	1	14	41	.250	.280	.226	7.28	2.49
McElwee, Josh	R-R	6-4	227	1-6-89	2	1	6.97	18	0	0	4	21	25	17	16	0	11	12	.298	.387	.245	5.23	4.75
Mendoza, Francisco	R-R	6-0	200	12-7-87	1	0	0.00	12	0	0	6	13	13	0	0	0	4	14	.260	.167	.313	9.69	2.77
Monegro, Jose	R-R	6-3	200	9-19-89	1	0	7.36	7	0	0	0	7	8	6	6	2	3	4	.276	.545	.111	4.91	3.68
Parks, Adam	R-R	6-3	220	10-10-92	0	1	4.26	9	0	0	0	13	12	6	6	3	4	11	.250	.313	.219	7.82	2.84
Parra, Luis	L-L	6-0	180	11-21-91	0	0	27.00	1	0	0	0	2	7	1	0	0	2	1	.500	.429	.571	18.00	4.50
Payano, Victor	L-L	6-5	185	10-17-92	4	4	5.05	29	15	0	0	93	91	62	52	13	64	78	.255	.301	.234	7.58	6.22
Perez, Martin	L-L	6-0	195	4-4-91	0	0	3.18	2	2	0	0	6	7	2	2	1	1	8	.292	.000	.412	12.71	1.59
Pirela, Jesus	R-R	6-0	155	3-13-89	2	3	3.31	37	0	0	0	52	43	21	19	4	24	64	.228	.246	.220	11.15	4.18
Quintana, Adam	R-R	6-2	225	1-24-92	0	1	3.00	2	1	0	0	9	9	3	3		2	13	.250	.217	.308	13.00	2.00

TEXAS RANGERS

Pitching	B-T	HT	WT	DOB	W	L	ERA	G	GS	CG	SV	IP	H	R	ER	HR	BB	SO	AVG	vLH	vRH	K/9	BB/9
Sadzeck, Connor	R-R	6-5	195	10-1-91	1	1	9.61	7	6	0	0	20	22	21	21	1	17	16	.293	.400	.222	7.32	7.78
Scheppers, Tanner	R-R	6-4	200	1-17-87	0	0	1.59	6	0	0	0	6	4	2	1	0	3	8	.190	.200	.188	12.71	4.76
Slack, Ryne	L-L	6-2	220	7-22-92	0	0	1.06	11	0	0	0	17	7	2	2	2	6	16	.130	.040	.207	8.47	3.18
Smith, Chad	R-R	6-3	215	10-2-89	0	0	6.75	4	0	0	0	4	3	3	3	0	2	4	.214	.333	.125	9.00	4.50
Swanson, Erik	R-R	6-3	220	9-4-93	0	0	9.00	1	0	0	0	1	2	1	1	0	2	1	.500	1.000	.333	9.00	18.00
Thompson, Jake	R-R	6-4	235	1-31-94	6	6	4.72	17	17	1	0	88	94	51	46	7	30	78	.272	.313	.233	8.01	3.08
Valdespina, Jose	R-R	6-6	220	3-22-92	1	0	2.31	8	0	0	0	12	7	3	3	0	6	5	.179	.190	.167	3.86	4.63
Werner, John	R-R	6-2	210	1-3-92	0	0	27.00	2	0	0	0	2	7	6	6	0	1	3	.583	.571	.600	13.50	4.50

Fielding

Catcher	PCT	G	PO	A	E	DP	PB
Alfaro	.987	36	281	34	4	3	5
Burg	.966	21	127	16	5	0	3
Cantwell	.990	55	435	38	5	2	2
Corporan	1.000	1	3	0	0	0	0
Deglan	.993	17	134	6	1	2	1
Moorman	1.000	1	7	0	0	0	0
Valencia	1.000	2	10	1	0	1	0
Wise	1.000	12	104	13	0	2	2

First Base	PCT	G	PO	A	E	DP
Adams	.996	60	447	24	2	48
Alfaro	.750	1	3	0	1	1
Beck	.991	31	208	13	2	32
Bolinger	.989	23	169	5	2	16
Burg	1.000	2	11	1	0	1
Cordell	.957	2	20	2	1	2
Rodriguez	1.000	4	46	0	0	3
Wise	.987	21	140	9	2	11

Second Base	PCT	G	PO	A	E	DP
Adams	1.000	4	4	5	0	1
Burg	1.000	1	2	4	0	1
Garcia	1.000	5	8	6	0	2
Mendez	.981	24	48	54	2	17
Pastornicky	1.000	2	2	8	0	0
Robinson	.969	96	206	234	14	72
Rodriguez	1.000	12	15	22	0	4

Third Base	PCT	G	PO	A	E	DP
Adams	.933	19	14	28	3	3
Cordell	.886	16	11	20	4	4
Gallo	.970	20	25	39	2	6
Garcia	.895	12	9	25	4	4
Mendez	.964	65	50	111	6	11
Pastornicky	1.000	2	1	3	0	0
Rodriguez	.938	12	4	26	2	1

Shortstop	PCT	G	PO	A	E	DP
Garcia	1.000	4	11	14	0	6
Marte	.966	62	93	162	9	41
Mendez	.935	11	18	25	3	7

	PCT	G	PO	A	E	DP
Pastornicky	.952	23	22	38	3	9
Robinson	.954	28	54	70	6	20
Rodriguez	.929	9	9	17	2	3
Weems	.905	5	4	15	2	1

Outfield	PCT	G	PO	A	E	DP
Adams	.857	4	6	0	1	0
Beck	.957	49	79	9	4	6
Bolinger	1.000	2	3	0	0	0
Brinson	1.000	27	75	2	0	0
Burg	1.000	1	3	0	0	0
Cone	1.000	39	81	3	0	0
Cordell	1.000	40	100	3	0	2
Gallo	1.000	6	10	2	0	0
Garia	.969	20	31	0	1	0
Hamilton	1.000	2	1	0	0	0
Lacrus	—	1	0	0	0	0
Mazara	.960	96	180	13	8	1
Skole	.977	56	128	2	3	1
Votototo	—	2	0	0	0	0
Williams	.989	88	167	9	2	0

HIGH DESERT MAVERICKS   HIGH CLASS A

CALIFORNIA LEAGUE

Batting	B-T	HT	WT	DOB	AVG	vLH	vRH	G	AB	R	H	2B	3B	HR	RBI	BB	HBP	SH	SF	SO	SB	CS	SLG	OBP
Altmann, Josh	R-R	6-3	190	7-6-94	.261	.500	.176	7	23	4	6	0	2	0	4	2	0	0	0	4	2	0	.435	.320
Arroyo, Carlos	L-R	5-11	150	6-28-93	.267	.333	.250	4	15	1	4	1	1	0	1	1	0	0	0	5	0	1	.467	.313
Beck, Preston	L-R	6-2	190	10-26-90	.298	.348	.286	32	121	19	36	12	2	3	14	15	1	0	0	25	0	1	.504	.380
Bolinger, Royce	R-R	6-2	200	8-12-90	.315	.276	.324	98	400	70	126	34	1	16	77	23	7	0	6	107	0	0	.525	.358
Brinson, Lewis	R-R	6-3	170	5-8-94	.337	.526	.305	64	258	51	87	22	7	13	42	31	6	0	3	64	13	6	.628	.416
Burg, Alex	R-R	6-0	190	8-9-87	.302	.227	.323	57	199	45	60	14	0	15	43	39	4	0	4	52	0	0	.598	.419
Caraballo, Oliver	R-R	6-1	180	8-25-94	.300	.750	.231	9	30	4	9	2	0	1	5	5	0	0	0	11	1	1	.467	.400
Cone, Zach	R-R	6-2	205	12-14-89	.286	.365	.263	73	287	45	82	16	2	15	51	18	5	0	3	81	6	1	.512	.335
Cordell, Ryan	R-R	6-4	205	3-31-92	.311	.303	.314	68	286	58	89	13	5	13	57	28	3	0	2	53	10	5	.528	.376
Deglan, Kellin	L-R	6-2	195	5-3-92	.236	.309	.214	62	237	36	56	7	1	12	38	17	3	1	1	76	1	0	.426	.295
Garcia, Edwin	B-R	6-1	185	3-1-91	.324	.421	.286	19	68	10	22	3	0	1	11	6	0	1	1	10	1	0	.412	.373
Garia, Chris	R-R	6-0	165	12-16-92	.327	.282	.335	60	254	57	83	11	10	7	41	19	3	6	2	51	22	2	.531	.378
Guzman, Ronald	L-L	6-5	205	10-20-94	.277	.256	.283	107	422	54	117	25	7	9	73	27	0	0	3	101	3	0	.434	.319
Jackson, Joe	L-R	6-1	180	5-5-92	.298	.219	.314	110	426	67	127	33	2	10	78	46	4	2	8	97	5	1	.455	.366
Kiner-Falefa, Isiah	R-R	5-10	165	3-23-95	.309	.278	.315	60	233	38	72	6	1	0	27	9	9	2	1	28	4	3	.343	.357
Lyon, David	B-R	5-11	190	1-19-90	.165	.179	.162	37	127	22	21	8	1	3	11	16	1	0	0	53	1	2	.315	.264
Maron, Cam	L-R	6-1	195	1-20-91	.209	.000	.214	12	43	2	9	2	0	0	5	3	0	0	0	7	0	0	.256	.261
Marte, Luis	R-R	6-1	170	12-15-93	.265	.309	.251	60	234	38	62	10	2	3	25	4	2	4	3	46	8	2	.363	.280
Martin, Tripp	L-R	6-2	190	4-2-92	.230	.184	.240	59	217	47	50	10	1	15	44	16	0	2	0	90	0	0	.493	.290
Profar, Juremi	R-R	6-1	185	1-30-96	.240	.133	.286	13	50	7	12	2	1	1	7	4	1	2	1	9	0	0	.380	.304
Spivey, Seth	L-R	5-11	180	7-6-92	.250	.218	.256	96	372	62	93	25	3	4	42	25	9	1	5	72	1	0	.366	.309
Torres, Kevin	L-R	6-3	195	2-24-90	.311	.318	.310	49	177	30	55	12	2	3	28	20	3	0	2	35	1	0	.452	.386
Triunfel, Alberto	R-R	5-11	160	2-1-94	.250	.250	.250	56	208	33	52	13	3	7	26	23	4	2	4	44	3	3	.442	.331
Valencia, Ricardo	R-R	6-0	185	1-13-93	.091	.167	.000	3	11	0	1	0	0	0	1	1	0	0	0	4	0	0	.091	.167
Van Hoosier, Evan	R-R	5-11	185	12-24-93	.331	.346	.327	61	257	40	85	16	10	2	33	18	2	0	4	57	5	3	.494	.374

Pitching	B-T	HT	WT	DOB	W	L	ERA	G	GS	CG	SV	IP	H	R	ER	HR	BB	SO	AVG	vLH	vRH	K/9	BB/9
Carvallo, Felix	L-L	6-0	175	10-5-93	3	2	5.18	36	0	0	2	64	68	40	37	7	24	63	.268	.264	.270	8.81	3.36
Castillo, Lendy	R-R	6-1	170	4-8-89	0	0	6.43	2	1	0	0	7	14	5	5	0	2	5	.400	.600	.250	6.43	2.57
Ege, Cody	L-L	6-1	185	5-8-91	3	0	1.35	9	0	0	1	13	7	2	2	1	3	25	.149	.042	.261	16.88	2.03
Fasola, John	R-R	6-2	195	12-12-91	3	2	5.28	23	0	0	6	29	31	19	17	6	9	30	.270	.295	.254	9.31	2.79
Gallant, Dallas	R-R	6-3	195	1-25-89	2	1	5.72	8	5	0	0	28	26	21	18	6	6	27	.241	.233	.246	8.58	5.08
Garrett, Reed	R-R	6-2	170	1-2-93	7	5	4.96	18	18	2	0	103	110	66	57	16	33	70	.271	.260	.277	6.10	2.87
Grullon, Juan	L-L	6-0	185	3-4-90	3	0	1.93	19	0	0	2	33	24	8	7	3	6	35	.209	.174	.232	9.64	1.65
Hernandez, Jefri	R-R	6-2	210	4-27-91	0	1	2.21	14	0	0	4	20	19	6	5	1	7	22	.253	.300	.222	9.74	3.10
Kaminska, Pat	R-R	6-3	215	2-5-91	1	1	5.21	24	1	0	2	48	60	28	28	4	10	36	.309	.360	.276	6.70	1.86
Lambert, Trey	R-R	6-4	205	6-5-91	9	3	4.60	20	20	0	0	102	125	55	52	10	22	86	.309	.307	.310	7.61	1.95
Leclerc, Angelo	R-R	6-0	170	10-9-91	3	3	5.52	29	0	0	3	44	50	32	27	6	17	42	.282	.418	.221	8.59	3.48
Ledbetter, David	L-R	5-11	190	2-13-92	3	9	7.46	27	24	0	0	121	176	106	100	23	34	90	.343	.330	.352	6.71	2.54

Pitching

Pitching	B-T	HT	WT	DOB	W	L	ERA	G	GS	CG	SV	IP	H	R	ER	HR	BB	SO	AVG	vLH	vRH	K/9	BB/9
Ledbetter, Ryan	R-R	6-1	190	2-13-92	2	3	7.50	40	1	0	3	66	84	59	55	13	32	69	.318	.253	.355	9.41	4.36
Lopez, Frank	L-L	6-1	175	2-18-94	4	1	2.95	7	7	0	0	43	35	17	14	4	8	43	.226	.234	.222	9.07	1.69
McCain, Shane	L-L	6-1	210	8-4-91	2	1	5.29	16	2	0	1	32	34	22	19	4	13	41	.268	.265	.269	11.41	3.62
Monegro, Jose	R-R	6-3	200	9-19-89	2	0	1.76	7	0	0	0	15	11	7	3	2	6	20	.196	.263	.162	11.74	3.52
Parks, Adam	R-R	6-3	220	10-10-92	1	1	3.06	10	0	0	2	18	19	7	6	3	3	16	.284	.462	.171	8.15	1.53
Parra, Luis	L-L	6-2	160	11-21-91	2	5	7.00	12	11	0	0	54	72	48	42	7	37	50	.329	.346	.319	8.33	6.17
Pena, Richelson	R-R	6-1	170	9-29-93	10	8	4.76	21	20	0	0	112	118	71	59	23	23	87	.266	.281	.257	7.01	1.85
Perez, David	R-R	6-5	200	12-20-92	4	3	4.42	16	6	0	1	55	51	29	27	6	14	60	.239	.215	.254	9.82	2.29
Rivera, Joeanthony	L-L	6-3	210	1-6-94	1	0	3.60	7	0	0	0	10	5	4	4	1	9	10	.147	.133	.158	9.00	8.10
Sadzeck, Connor	R-R	6-5	195	10-1-91	2	1	3.98	11	8	0	0	41	32	22	18	4	24	48	.213	.322	.143	10.62	5.31
Slack, Ryne	L-L	6-2	220	7-22-92	7	1	4.58	29	0	0	1	53	55	31	27	4	18	54	.264	.329	.225	9.17	3.06
Smith, Tyler	R-R	6-3	195	2-3-92	1	4	7.71	7	7	0	0	33	48	32	28	7	15	27	.348	.314	.404	7.44	4.13
Sprenger, Justin	R-R	6-4	180	6-11-91	1	3	6.20	13	0	0	1	20	25	19	14	2	16	25	.294	.381	.209	11.07	7.08
Valdespina, Jose	R-R	6-6	220	3-22-92	1	1	2.25	25	0	0	4	32	33	12	8	1	11	26	.252	.229	.265	7.31	3.09
Watts, Dakota	R-R	6-5	205	11-16-87	0	1	8.44	12	0	0	3	11	17	13	10	2	7	8	.362	.294	.400	6.75	5.91
Wiper, Cole	R-R	6-4	185	6-3-92	1	2	5.88	9	9	0	0	34	41	28	22	5	14	29	.304	.293	.312	7.75	3.74

Fielding

Catcher

Catcher	PCT	G	PO	A	E	DP	PB
Burg	1.000	4	36	4	0	1	3
Deglan	.993	59	487	43	4	1	6
Lyon	.976	32	253	30	7	6	5
Maron	1.000	4	28	2	0	0	0
Torres	.991	39	314	27	3	4	5
Valencia	1.000	3	22	2	0	0	0
Marte	1.000	3	3	8	0	1	
Profar	.978	9	19	26	1	8	
Spivey	.980	24	39	60	2	16	
Van Hoosier	.970	54	87	136	7	35	

First Base

First Base	PCT	G	PO	A	E	DP
Beck	.987	25	210	19	3	16
Burg	.974	5	34	3	1	5
Guzman	.984	106	878	59	15	102
Torres	1.000	5	42	2	0	6

Second Base

Second Base	PCT	G	PO	A	E	DP
Altmann	1.000	1	1	1	0	1
Garcia	1.000	15	19	34	0	11
Kiner-Falefa	.976	37	59	103	4	28

Third Base

Third Base	PCT	G	PO	A	E	DP
Altmann	.818	5	2	7	2	0
Burg	.905	8	3	16	2	1
Cordell	.837	17	7	34	8	3
Garcia	1.000	2	0	3	0	1
Marte	1.000	9	5	15	0	0
Martin	.890	57	32	89	15	6
Profar	.714	4	0	5	2	0
Spivey	.887	41	25	61	11	0

Shortstop

Shortstop	PCT	G	PO	A	E	DP
Cordell	.907	14	21	47	7	6
Garcia	.909	2	3	7	1	2
Kiner-Falefa	.952	19	32	48	4	15
Marte	.982	49	94	177	5	50
Triunfel	.944	56	101	168	16	46

Outfield

Outfield	PCT	G	PO	A	E	DP
Arroyo	1.000	4	7	1	0	0
Beck	1.000	5	9	0	0	0
Bolinger	.976	97	192	12	5	2
Brinson	.969	63	152	2	5	1
Burg	1.000	3	5	0	0	0
Cone	.986	73	128	8	2	2
Cordell	.946	34	65	5	4	1
Garia	.984	60	119	1	2	1
Jackson	.964	75	105	3	4	1
Spivey	1.000	5	5	0	0	0
Van Hoosier	1.000	3	9	0	0	0

HICKORY CRAWDADS

LOW CLASS A

SOUTH ATLANTIC LEAGUE

Batting	B-T	HT	WT	DOB	AVG	vLH	vRH	G	AB	R	H	2B	3B	HR	RBI	BB	HBP	SH	SF	SO	SB	CS	SLG	OBP
Arroyo, Carlos	L-R	5-11	150	6-28-93	.282	.301	.275	76	287	42	81	13	4	3	30	17	3	6	1	59	8	3	.387	.328
Beras, Jairo	R-R	6-5	178	12-25-94	.291	.318	.277	88	327	45	95	18	2	9	43	19	1		1	88	9	4	.440	.332
De Leon, Michael	B-R	6-1	160	1-14-97	.222	.244	.214	81	306	29	68	11	2	1	29	23	1	5	2	47	1	1	.281	.277
Demeritte, Travis	R-R	6-0	180	9-30-94	.241	.100	.285	48	170	27	41	12	1	5	19	25	2	0	1	69	10	1	.412	.343
Garcia, Edwin	B-R	6-1	185	3-1-91	.280	.318	.265	39	157	19	44	6	2	0	15	13	0	0	2	21	1	1	.344	.331
Gonzalez, Jose	B-R	6-1	175	3-16-94	.254	.272	.246	128	469	64	119	19	5	10	59	40	5	8	4	73	30	18	.380	.317
Greene, Marcus	R-R	5-11	195	8-19-94	.218	.211	.220	25	78	17	17	5	1	5	9	16	2	0	0	23	2	0	.500	.365
Guzman, Ronald	L-L	6-5	205	10-20-94	.309	.222	.343	24	97	10	30	3	0	3	14	6	0	0	1	15	2	0	.433	.346
Jenkins, Eric	L-R	6-1	170	1-30-97	.389	.500	.333	5	18	3	7	1	0	0	1	1	0	0	0	4	1	0	.444	.421
Kiner-Falefa, Isiah	R-R	5-10	165	3-23-95	.272	.286	.267	38	125	16	34	6	1	0	13	14	3	3	2	22	7	3	.336	.354
Lindley, London	R-R	5-11	160	6-12-93	—	—	—	1	0	0	0	0	0	0	0	0	0	0	0	0	0	0	—	—
Martin, Tripp	R-R	6-2	190	4-2-92	.233	.278	.213	50	176	31	41	13	1	8	18	14	5	1	0	53	3	1	.455	.308
Meyer, Jonathan	R-R	6-1	225	11-1-90	.216	.164	.247	41	148	16	32	4	0	3	23	12	1	0	1	34	1	0	.304	.278
Moore, Dylan	R-R	6-0	185	8-2-92	.583	.500	.625	4	12	1	7	2	0	0	2	1	0	0	0	2	0	0	.750	.615
Moorman, Chuck	R-R	5-11	200	9-4-91	.140	.125	.148	29	86	7	12	3	0	1	7	12	3	0	1	28	0	1	.209	.211
Morgan, Josh	R-R	5-11	185	11-16-95	.288	.228	.312	98	351	59	101	15	1	3	36	45	12	6	2	53	9	4	.362	.385
Perez, Brallan	R-R	5-10	165	1-27-96	.194	.188	.200	11	31	5	6	0	0	0	0	4	0	0	0	4	2	2	.194	.286
Pinto, Eduard	L-L	5-11	150	10-23-94	.261	.248	.266	98	349	39	91	12	5	2	36	34	3	8	3	21	2	9	.341	.329
Profar, Juremi	R-R	6-1	185	1-30-96	.272	.263	.276	64	243	26	66	17	1	3	26	14	2	0	3	27	1	1	.387	.313
Profar, Jurickson	B-R	6-0	200	2-20-93	.273	.333	.267	9	33	2	9	1	0	1	5	1	0	0	0	9	0	0	.394	.314
Shoulders, Rock	L-R	6-2	225	9-26-91	.169	.100	.185	46	154	19	26	7	0	4	19	14	3	1	2	48	0	0	.292	.249
Tendler, Luke	L-R	5-11	190	8-25-91	.262	.209	.284	124	454	67	119	30	4	15	73	41	6	0	7	95	2	3	.445	.327
Torres, Kevin	L-R	6-3	195	2-24-90	.188	.273	.172	23	69	6	13	3	0	2	7	8	0	0	0	11	0	0	.319	.273
Trevino, Jose	R-R	5-11	195	11-28-92	.262	.297	.248	112	424	62	111	19	2	14	63	18	1	3	3	60	1	4	.415	.291
Turner, Xavier	R-R	6-1	205	8-24-93	.250	.111	.316	9	28	7	7	2	1	1	5	5	1	0	1	7	1	0	.500	.371
Valencia, Ricardo	R-R	6-0	185	1-13-93	.231	.000	.250	4	13	3	3	1	0	0	2	3	0	0	0	2	0	0	.308	.375

Pitching	B-T	HT	WT	DOB	W	L	ERA	G	GS	CG	SV	IP	H	R	ER	HR	BB	SO	AVG	vLH	vRH	K/9	BB/9
Buckel, Cody	R-R	6-1	185	6-18-92	0	5	3.95	10	10	0	0	41	28	19	18	1	28	30	.199	.221	.178	6.59	6.15
Dian, Adam	R-R	6-4	205	6-4-93	2	1	2.36	14	0	0	5	27	26	10	7	1	8	16	.255	.326	.196	5.40	2.70
Dula, Chris	R-R	6-2	200	8-6-92	1	1	4.74	40	0	0	2	44	48	40	23	2	39	40	.293	.313	.278	8.24	8.04
Fasola, John	R-R	6-2	195	12-12-91	1	1	1.71	19	0	0	13	26	17	7	5	0	4	34	.181	.263	.125	11.62	1.37
Filomeno, Joe	R-L	5-11	235	12-31-92	3	2	2.72	30	0	0	1	56	43	18	17	2	14	62	.208	.157	.234	9.91	2.24
Gardewine, Nick	R-R	6-1	160	8-15-93	6	8	4.31	22	17	0	1	96	111	52	46	11	23	80	.293	.312	.278	7.50	2.16
Garrett, Reed	R-R	6-2	170	1-2-93	3	3	3.47	7	7	1	0	36	30	15	14	2	15	26	.236	.254	.219	6.44	3.72

Pitching

Pitching	B-T	HT	WT	DOB	W	L	ERA	G	GS	CG	SV	IP	H	R	ER	HR	BB	SO	AVG	vLH	vRH	K/9	BB/9
Hernandez, Jefri	R-R	6-2	210	4-27-91	2	0	4.50	7	0	0	1	12	10	6	6	2	2	18	.222	.300	.160	13.50	1.50
Jurado, Ariel	R-R	6-1	180	1-30-96	12	1	2.45	22	15	0	0	99	92	36	27	5	12	95	.246	.273	.223	8.64	1.09
Lambert, Trey	R-R	6-4	205	6-5-91	1	1	4.41	7	0	0	1	16	21	9	8	0	5	16	.309	.258	.351	8.82	2.76
Martin, Brett	L-L	6-4	190	4-28-95	5	6	3.49	20	18	0	0	95	92	45	37	6	26	72	.265	.305	.250	6.80	2.45
Matthews, Kevin	R-L	5-11	180	11-29-92	0	0	6.48	6	0	0	0	8	5	6	6	1	11	8	.167	.000	.133	8.64	11.88
McCain, Shane	L-L	6-1	210	8-4-91	3	2	4.36	18	1	0	1	43	43	23	21	5	15	47	.256	.136	.321	9.76	3.12
Mendez, Yohander	L-L	6-4	178	1-17-95	3	3	2.44	21	8	0	3	66	57	20	18	2	15	74	.230	.211	.237	10.04	2.04
Ortiz, Luis	R-R	6-3	230	9-22-95	4	1	1.80	13	13	0	0	50	45	12	10	1	9	46	.238	.273	.214	8.28	1.62
Palumbo, Joe	L-L	6-1	150	10-26-94	0	0	6.23	1	0	0	0	4	5	3	3	0	3	1	.294	.500	.231	2.08	6.23
Parks, Adam	R-R	6-3	220	10-10-92	2	3	2.93	16	1	0	1	43	44	17	14	1	12	59	.272	.338	.216	12.35	2.51
Parra, Luis	L-L	6-2	160	11-21-91	1	0	3.60	1	1	0	0	5	7	2	2	0	0	3	.304	.333	.273	5.40	0.00
Payano, Pedro	R-R	6-2	170	9-27-94	3	1	1.10	6	5	0	0	33	27	4	4	1	10	31	.229	.236	.222	8.54	2.76
Perez, David	R-R	6-5	200	12-20-92	2	1	0.93	16	0	0	0	29	20	8	3	2	14	37	.196	.087	.286	11.48	4.34
Pettibone, Austin	R-R	6-3	180	9-10-92	3	7	4.35	22	13	0	0	79	87	48	38	7	14	50	.274	.279	.270	5.72	1.60
Quintana, Adam	R-R	6-2	225	1-24-92	0	1	6.00	1	0	0	0	3	2	2	2	0	2	4	.200	.000	.286	12.00	6.00
Rodriguez, Ricardo	R-R	6-2	220	8-31-92	1	0	3.00	5	0	0	1	12	17	6	4	0	2	9	.327	.400	.281	6.75	1.50
Springs, Jeffrey	L-L	6-3	180	9-20-92	0	0	0.00	2	0	0	0	3	0	0	0	0	1	6	.000	.000	.000	16.20	2.70
Swanson, Erik	R-R	6-3	220	9-4-93	1	1	2.19	7	0	0	1	12	7	3	3	1	4	10	.163	.167	.160	7.30	2.92
Tate, Dillon	R-R	6-2	165	5-1-94	0	0	1.29	4	4	0	0	7	3	1	1	1	0	5	.130	.222	.071	6.43	0.00
Vasquez, Kelvin	R-R	6-4	195	4-6-93	6	3	3.74	31	4	0	1	77	61	34	32	8	38	65	.217	.208	.225	7.60	4.44
Werner, John	R-R	6-2	210	1-3-92	0	2	2.65	5	1	0	0	17	14	5	5	0	6	19	.230	.237	.217	10.06	3.18
Wiles, Collin	R-R	6-4	212	5-30-94	11	3	2.96	22	20	0	0	131	114	49	43	6	23	72	.239	.261	.218	4.96	1.58
Williams, Scott	R-R	6-2	195	11-17-93	5	0	2.28	29	0	0	10	43	27	11	11	3	15	49	.188	.266	.125	10.18	3.12

Fielding

Catcher	PCT	G	PO	A	E	DP	PB
Greene	.964	12	91	15	4	2	3
Meyer	.989	12	80	7	1	0	4
Moorman	.977	19	111	14	3	1	1
Torres	1.000	14	90	12	0	1	2
Trevino	.992	87	677	77	6	7	9
Valencia	.935	4	27	2	2	2	2

First Base	PCT	G	PO	A	E	DP
Arroyo	1.000	2	15	1	0	0
Guzman	.995	24	199	7	1	15
Martin	.986	13	127	10	2	16
Meyer	.990	24	196	10	2	19
Moorman	1.000	9	75	2	0	7
Pinto	1.000	6	54	2	0	9
Profar	.970	15	120	11	4	9
Shoulders	.990	42	357	26	4	28
Torres	.974	8	70	4	2	9

Second Base	PCT	G	PO	A	E	DP
Arroyo	.971	61	92	177	8	40

	PCT	G	PO	A	E	DP
De Leon	1.000	6	11	14	0	3
Demeritte	1.000	43	71	126	0	30
Garcia	.917	8	11	22	3	3
Kiner-Falefa	.963	12	22	30	2	8
Moore	1.000	3	7	11	0	4
Perez	1.000	7	15	15	0	1
Profar	1.000	2	7	6	0	0

Third Base	PCT	G	PO	A	E	DP
Arroyo	1.000	2	0	7	0	0
Demeritte	.941	3	6	10	1	0
Garcia	.958	11	7	16	1	2
Kiner-Falefa	.975	16	10	29	1	3
Martin	.778	7	2	5	2	0
Meyer	1.000	1	0	1	0	0
Morgan	.944	50	30	87	7	12
Perez	.000	1	0	0	1	0
Profar	.908	43	30	79	11	11
Turner	1.000	7	6	9	0	0

Shortstop	PCT	G	PO	A	E	DP
De Leon	.964	74	103	219	12	37
Demeritte	1.000	1	3	2	0	0
Garcia	.967	17	20	39	2	9
Kiner-Falefa	1.000	1	5	2	0	3
Martin	.500	1	0	1	1	0
Moore	1.000	1	0	1	0	0
Morgan	.984	44	63	123	3	34
Profar	1.000	1	0	2	0	1

Outfield	PCT	G	PO	A	E	DP
Arroyo	.900	7	9	0	1	0
Beras	.955	78	139	8	7	3
Gonzalez	.987	125	294	15	4	4
Jenkins	1.000	5	11	0	0	0
Kiner-Falefa	1.000	8	4	0	0	0
Martin	.944	16	16	1	1	0
Pinto	.987	80	137	10	2	2
Tendler	.976	103	155	10	4	4

SPOKANE INDIANS — SHORT-SEASON

NORTHWEST LEAGUE

Batting	B-T	HT	WT	DOB	AVG	vLH	vRH	G	AB	R	H	2B	3B	HR	RBI	BB	HBP	SH	SF	SO	SB	CS	SLG	OBP
Byrd, Leon	B-R	5-8	165	2-27-94	.203	.155	.228	53	172	20	35	12	2	0	21	27	2	0	4	57	3	3	.297	.312
Caraballo, Oliver	R-R	6-1	180	8-25-94	.220	.176	.250	12	41	0	9	3	0	0	0	1	0	0	0	9	0	0	.293	.238
Cedeno, Diego	L-L	5-11	160	5-19-92	.248	.213	.264	40	157	18	39	5	0	1	14	11	1	1	0	31	2	2	.299	.302
Clark, LaDarious	R-R	5-9	180	12-27-93	.276	.281	.273	65	257	46	71	12	7	8	24	26	6	2	2	73	29	9	.471	.354
Day, Darius	L-L	5-11	175	8-25-94	.261	.220	.279	54	188	26	49	8	1	1	18	23	3	1	1	68	13	2	.330	.349
Demeritte, Travis	R-R	6-0	180	9-30-94	.150	.000	.214	5	20	0	3	0	0	0	2	0	0	0	1	10	2	1	.150	.227
Forbes, Ti'quan	R-R	6-3	180	8-26-96	.263	.260	.264	59	217	25	57	11	1	0	19	14	3	1	1	54	2	2	.323	.315
Garay, Carlos	R-R	6-0	210	10-5-94	.244	.385	.188	13	45	2	11	2	0	0	7	1	0	0	1	4	0	0	.289	.255
Lacrus, Sherman	R-R	5-11	180	12-23-93	.258	.258	.259	57	209	22	54	18	0	1	23	20	7	1	0	31	0	4	.359	.343
Long, Dean	R-R	6-3	205	12-8-92	.229	.125	.274	37	105	13	24	3	1	1	15	18	7	0	2	37	0	1	.305	.371
McDonald, Todd	R-R	6-3	180	10-23-95	.170	.111	.190	29	106	8	18	4	0	2	10	4	0	1	1	36	0	0	.264	.198
McKay, Connor	R-R	6-3	180	10-10-92	.222	.098	.299	33	108	15	24	4	3	3	13	8	0	0	0	36	1	2	.398	.276
Moore, Dylan	R-R	6-0	185	8-2-92	.254	.219	.271	65	228	38	58	19	1	7	35	31	9	0	1	65	13	1	.439	.364
Potts, Jamie	L-R	6-3	225	8-17-92	.217	.308	.177	57	212	26	46	6	1	4	22	23	0	1	3	42	3	3	.311	.290
Sanchez, Tyler	R-R	6-2	190	5-30-93	.215	.184	.230	43	149	24	32	15	0	6	25	17	7	0	3	44	0	0	.436	.318
Votoloto, Doug	R-R	6-2	190	10-9-94	.170	.189	.159	32	100	10	17	2	3	0	3	23	2	0	0	31	0	2	.250	.336
Yrizarri, Yeyson	R-R	6-0	175	2-2-97	.265	.181	.309	62	245	27	65	10	1	2	29	6	3	2	1	46	8	6	.339	.290

Pitching	B-T	HT	WT	DOB	W	L	ERA	G	GS	CG	SV	IP	H	R	ER	HR	BB	SO	AVG	vLH	vRH	K/9	BB/9
Bass, Blake	R-R	6-7	250	6-3-93	1	3	4.32	13	4	0	0	33	31	21	16	3	15	29	.242	.239	.244	7.83	4.05
Beltre, Dario	R-R	6-3	170	11-19-92	0	2	9.27	17	0	0	1	22	33	25	23	3	14	23	.344	.622	.169	9.27	5.64
Choplick, Adam	L-L	6-8	261	11-18-92	4	0	2.18	16	0	0	3	33	29	8	8	1	23	35	.252	.333	.220	9.55	6.27
Davis, Tyler	R-R	5-10	185	1-5-93	3	1	5.09	16	2	0	0	35	41	21	20	4	12	30	.293	.292	.293	7.64	3.06
Fairbanks, Peter	R-R	6-6	215	12-16-93	1	2	3.14	13	11	0	0	57	52	23	20	3	22	47	.246	.247	.246	7.38	3.45
Green, Nick	R-R	6-1	165	3-25-95	0	3	7.11	10	9	0	0	32	38	26	25	2	12	9	.302	.182	.394	2.56	3.41

Pitching	B-T	HT	WT	DOB	W	L	ERA	G	GS	CG	SV	IP	H	R	ER	HR	BB	SO	AVG	vLH	vRH	K/9	BB/9
Hoppe, Jason	R-R	6-1	170	6-13-92	0	0	0.00	2	0	0	1	4	3	1	0	0	0	5	.200	.000	.250	12.27	0.00
Kukuruda, John	R-R	6-4	180	6-9-92	0	0	6.05	14	0	0	0	19	21	16	13	1	15	15	.276	.125	.346	6.98	6.98
Lanphere, Luke	R-R	6-2	175	9-30-95	3	1	3.18	13	10	0	0	68	58	31	24	2	13	48	.233	.286	.203	6.35	1.72
Lintz, Seth	R-R	6-1	170	2-7-90	0	0	2.84	6	0	0	0	6	2	3	2	0	8	4	.100	.100	.100	5.68	11.37
Lopez, Omarlin	R-R	6-3	175	10-8-93	4	2	4.50	20	0	0	1	36	28	22	18	3	16	36	.209	.217	.205	9.00	4.00
Martinez, Emerson	R-R	6-0	190	1-11-95	4	5	5.33	13	11	0	0	54	59	40	32	4	24	40	.271	.256	.280	6.67	4.00
Palmquist, Cody	R-R	6-5	190	4-8-94	2	5	4.56	12	11	0	0	51	59	34	26	2	18	46	.285	.271	.295	8.06	3.16
Palumbo, Joe	L-L	6-1	150	10-26-94	3	3	2.82	12	9	0	0	54	52	25	17	3	22	42	.250	.250	.250	6.96	3.64
Parra, Luis	L-L	6-2	160	11-21-91	6	3	2.38	14	0	0	1	23	20	12	6	2	11	21	.241	.200	.254	8.34	4.37
Perritt, Ashton	R-R	6-1	195	9-8-92	0	1	6.75	15	0	0	1	16	21	12	12	3	8	12	.323	.348	.310	6.75	4.50
Richman, Jason	L-L	6-4	210	10-15-93	1	3	3.12	21	0	0	2	26	17	9	9	1	16	23	.195	.162	.220	7.96	5.54
Scheibe, Dan	R-R	6-3	215	4-23-93	0	2	5.82	13	0	0	1	17	17	12	11	0	7	15	.254	.360	.190	7.94	3.71
Shortslef, Jake	R-R	6-5	220	12-29-94	0	0	9.00	2	0	0	0	2	5	6	2	0	2	2	.500	.400	.600	9.00	9.00
Springs, Jeffrey	L-L	6-3	180	9-20-92	2	2	2.93	15	0	0	0	28	21	9	9	2	14	33	.221	.389	.182	10.73	4.55
Tate, Dillon	R-R	6-2	165	5-1-94	0	0	0.00	2	2	0	0	2	0	0	0	0	3	3	.000	—	.000	13.50	13.50
Tomita, Kohsuke	R-R	6-1	195	4-24-88	0	0	4.71	17	0	0	2	21	19	11	11	2	9	22	.238	.346	.185	9.43	3.86
Wiper, Cole	R-R	6-4	185	6-3-92	0	4	3.89	13	7	0	0	37	40	20	16	1	15	28	.268	.281	.261	6.81	3.65

Fielding

Catcher	PCT	G	PO	A	E	DP	PB
Caraballo	1.000	1	0	0	0	0	
Garay	1.000	5	29	3	0	0	
Lacrus	.989	45	312	53	4	1	9
Sanchez	.988	28	211	31	3	4	7

First Base	PCT	G	PO	A	E	DP
Caraballo	1.000	11	81	7	0	3
Cedeno	.986	29	259	18	4	26
Garay	1.000	6	62	6	0	5
Long	.980	14	141	4	3	10
McKay	.973	9	66	5	2	2
Moore	1.000	3	26	2	0	4
Sanchez	1.000	8	70	5	0	3

Second Base	PCT	G	PO	A	E	DP
Byrd	.972	28	56	82	4	19
Demeritte	.950	5	7	12	1	1
Moore	.972	40	84	122	6	20
Yrizarri	.938	5	8	7	1	1

Third Base	PCT	G	PO	A	E	DP
Byrd	.667	1	2	0	1	0
Forbes	.882	58	36	113	20	10
Long	.868	17	11	22	5	2
Moore	1.000	3	4	7	0	1

Shortstop	PCT	G	PO	A	E	DP
Byrd	.886	9	10	21	4	2

	PCT	G	PO	A	E	DP
Forbes	.667	1	1	1	1	1
Moore	.952	13	16	44	3	4
Yrizarri	.949	57	83	178	14	34

Outfield	PCT	G	PO	A	E	DP
Byrd	.900	12	16	2	2	0
Cedeno	1.000	8	11	1	0	0
Clark	.947	61	118	6	7	0
Day	.978	50	84	3	2	0
Lacrus	.857	4	5	1	1	0
McDonald	.923	12	23	1	2	0
McKay	.957	11	19	3	1	1
Potts	1.000	46	92	7	0	4
Votoloto	.981	28	49	2	1	0

AZL RANGERS
ARIZONA LEAGUE
ROOKIE

Batting	B-T	HT	WT	DOB	AVG	vLH	vRH	G	AB	R	H	2B	3B	HR	RBI	BB	HBP	SH	SF	SO	SB	CS	SLG	OBP
Adames, Crisford	B-R	6-1	160	1-26-95	.244	.286	.237	45	135	17	33	4	1	2	17	6	1	0	2	20	2	1	.333	.278
Almonte, Jose	R-R	6-3	205	9-9-96	.121	.214	.091	15	58	3	7	2	0	0	8	1	1	0	0	19	1	0	.155	.150
Altmann, Josh	R-R	6-3	190	7-26-94	.248	.280	.242	46	157	24	39	12	1	2	25	12	7	3	1	18	8	9	.376	.328
Alvarez, Jhonniel	R-R	5-9	195	2-15-93	.269	.444	.233	26	52	9	14	3	0	0	6	7	3	0	0	12	0	0	.327	.387
Castillo, Elio	R-R	6-1	160	3-1-94	.302	.412	.281	33	106	18	32	4	0	0	8	13	0	2	0	13	2	1	.340	.378
Jenkins, Eric	L-L	6-1	170	1-30-97	.249	.229	.254	51	177	35	44	4	6	0	13	23	2	3	0	57	27	3	.339	.342
Kaye, Nick	L-L	6-2	173	10-18-96	.173	.048	.205	36	104	12	18	1	0	0	6	16	1	1	0	40	1	2	.183	.289
Lindley, London	R-R	5-11	160	6-12-93	.278	.250	.286	8	18	4	5	1	0	0	2	3	1	0	0	2	3	1	.333	.409
Lyon, David	B-R	5-11	190	1-19-90	.100	—	.100	4	10	1	1	0	0	0	1	4	0	0	0	4	0	1	.100	.357
Martinez, Jesus	L-L	5-10	165	5-7-95	.210	.059	.235	40	119	12	25	3	3	1	12	8	0	0	1	25	7	3	.311	.258
Mendoza, Kevin	B-R	5-10	155	8-16-95	.145	.200	.135	21	62	5	9	2	0	0	6	3	1	1	0	7	0	0	.177	.197
Novoa, Melvin	R-R	5-11	200	6-17-96	.278	.227	.288	40	133	19	37	7	0	3	22	12	1	0	3	19	0	1	.398	.336
Perez, Brallan	R-R	5-10	165	7-7-95	.300	.391	.276	29	110	15	33	4	0	0	8	2	2	0	1	13	2	1	.336	.358
Quiroz, Isaias	R-R	5-10	195	10-22-96	.178	.500	.127	27	73	10	13	5	1	0	5	10	3	0	2	20	0	0	.274	.302
Richardson, Antoan	B-R	5-8	165	10-8-83	.154	.000	.167	10	26	3	4	1	0	0	1	2	1	1	1	7	3	0	.192	.233
Smith, Chad	L-L	6-2	200	9-30-97	.218	.188	.226	47	165	13	36	7	3	1	23	8	2	0	0	56	3	4	.315	.263
Terrero, Luis	R-R	6-0	185	11-11-95	.270	.258	.273	51	174	22	47	13	0	1	19	18	6	4	3	20	6	8	.362	.353
Terry, Curtis	R-R	6-2	230	10-6-96	.260	.263	.259	36	127	17	33	12	1	1	24	10	1	0	1	33	2	0	.394	.317
Turner, Xavier	R-R	6-1	205	8-24-93	.295	.333	.283	20	78	12	23	2	0	1	6	4	0	0	0	4	1	0	.359	.329
Valencia, Ricardo	R-R	6-0	185	1-13-93	.125	.000	.167	5	8	0	1	0	0	0	0	0	0	0	0	4	0	0	.125	.125
Van Hoosier, Evan	R-R	5-11	185	12-24-93	.286	.000	.333	9	28	5	8	3	0	0	1	2	0	0	0	6	2	0	.393	.333

Pitching	B-T	HT	WT	DOB	W	L	ERA	G	GS	CG	SV	IP	H	R	ER	HR	BB	SO	AVG	vLH	vRH	K/9	BB/9
Abreu, Gio	R-R	6-1	170	9-7-94	3	2	5.74	12	6	0	0	31	40	21	20	2	19	32	.315	.372	.286	9.19	5.46
Arredondo, Edgar	R-R	6-3	190	5-16-97	0	1	3.97	11	8	0	0	23	23	12	10	0	5	22	.271	.250	.286	8.74	1.99
Benjamin, Wes	R-L	6-1	180	7-26-93	0	0	0.00	1	1	0	0	1	0	0	0	1	2	.000	.000	.000	18.00	9.00
Dian, Adam	R-R	6-4	205	6-4-93	1	2	2.92	9	0	0	3	12	7	7	4	1	2	16	.149	.125	.161	11.68	1.46
Duarte, Daniel	R-R	6-0	170	12-4-96	0	1	5.68	4	2	0	0	6	6	4	4	0	2	3	.250	.125	.313	4.26	2.84
Evans, Demarcus	R-R	6-4	240	10-22-96	0	0	2.31	9	0	0	0	12	14	3	3	0	6	10	.304	.353	.276	7.71	4.63
Ferguson, Tyler	R-R	6-4	225	10-5-93	0	0	13.50	3	0	0	0	5	3	8	7	0	9	5	.167	.167	.167	9.64	17.36
Hernandez, Jonathan	R-R	6-2	150	7-6-96	1	1	3.00	11	9	0	0	45	45	22	15	0	12	33	.250	.227	.267	6.60	2.40
Kendall, Cody	R-R	6-2	210	12-12-89	0	1	3.18	4	0	0	0	6	7	2	2	0	0	6	.280	.400	.200	9.53	0.00
Kendrick, Clyde	R-R	6-2	190	11-21-93	0	1	7.00	11	0	0	0	9	11	7	7	1	5	8	.289	.400	.217	8.00	5.00
Liriano, Roberto	L-L	5-11	165	8-4-93	0	0	10.57	8	0	0	0	9	9	13	9	2	1	14	.273	.556	.167	16.43	1.17
Mendez, Sal	R-L	6-4	180	2-25-95	0	3	2.58	13	9	0	0	52	43	19	15	1	17	50	.218	.137	.247	8.60	2.92
Mora, Maikor	R-R	6-2	180	2-23-95	1	1	3.33	15	0	0	2	27	28	14	10	1	7	28	.280	.423	.230	9.33	2.33
Payano, Pedro	R-R	6-2	170	9-27-94	6	0	1.55	8	4	0	0	41	33	8	7	0	9	46	.226	.259	.205	10.18	1.99

TEXAS RANGERS (side tab)

Pitching	B-T	HT	WT	DOB	W	L	ERA	G	GS	CG	SV	IP	H	R	ER	HR	BB	SO	AVG	vLH	vRH	K/9	BB/9
Pelham, C.D.	L-L	6-4	190	2-21-95	4	0	5.40	16	0	0	0	18	15	13	11	1	13	24	.217	.200	.222	11.78	6.38
Phillips, Tyler	R-R	6-5	200	10-27-97	0	1	3.60	13	0	0	1	15	13	8	6	2	1	10	.224	.444	.125	6.00	0.60
Quintana, Adam	R-R	6-2	225	1-24-92	2	0	0.60	6	0	0	1	15	9	2	1	0	3	22	.173	.211	.152	13.20	1.80
Rivera, Joeanthony	L-L	6-3	210	1-6-94	1	0	1.69	13	0	0	4	16	15	6	3	0	2	14	.246	.158	.286	7.88	1.13
Rynard, Storm	R-R	6-0	165	9-25-95	3	3	3.47	13	8	0	0	49	42	20	19	1	18	33	.239	.234	.241	6.02	3.28
Shortslef, Jake	R-R	6-5	220	12-29-94	3	2	1.54	14	0	0	1	35	34	17	6	1	6	31	.254	.265	.247	7.97	1.54
Swanson, Erik	R-R	6-3	220	9-4-93	0	0	0.00	1	0	0	0	1	0	0	0	0	1	1	.000	.000	.000	9.00	9.00
Taveras, Francisco	R-R	5-11	195	6-21-94	1	4	3.06	12	4	0	0	35	34	15	12	1	13	42	.252	.255	.250	10.70	3.31
Watson, Joe	R-R	6-3	225	9-24-92	0	0	135.00	1	0	0	0	0	3	5	5	0	2	1	.750	—	.750	27.00	54.00
Werner, John	R-R	6-2	210	1-3-92	0	4	3.46	8	5	0	1	26	26	15	10	2	8	36	.271	.371	.213	12.46	2.77
Wynn, Sterling	B-L	6-2	175	11-23-93	2	1	4.70	17	0	0	1	15	25	10	8	0	4	16	.357	.333	.370	9.39	2.35

Fielding

Catcher	PCT	G	PO	A	E	DP	PB
Alvarez	1.000	11	52	3	0	0	2
Lyon	.955	3	17	4	1	0	1
Mendoza	.967	14	104	13	4	1	1
Novoa	.960	23	147	23	7	2	8
Quiroz	.979	25	166	21	4	3	9

First Base	PCT	G	PO	A	E	DP
Adames	.981	30	195	14	4	13
Kaye	1.000	4	17	0	0	0
Mendoza	.952	9	19	1	1	1
Novoa	.958	7	41	5	2	4
Smith	.954	8	61	1	3	3
Terry	.975	20	147	12	4	16

Second Base	PCT	G	PO	A	E	DP
Altmann	1.000	2	3	5	0	0

	PCT	G	PO	A	E	DP
Castillo	1.000	2	1	4	0	4
Perez	1.000	12	25	35	0	7
Terrero	.965	40	72	94	6	17
Van Hoosier	1.000	5	8	12	0	4

Third Base	PCT	G	PO	A	E	DP
Adames	.897	15	8	18	3	1
Altmann	.911	19	13	38	5	2
Alvarez	—	1	0	0	0	0
Castillo	1.000	8	5	14	0	0
Mendoza	1.000	2	1	2	0	1
Perez	.875	2	2	5	1	0
Terrero	.714	2	1	4	2	0
Turner	.971	16	12	21	1	3

Shortstop	PCT	G	PO	A	E	DP
Adames	1.000	1	4	6	0	1

		PCT	G	PO	A	E	DP
Altmann		.938	19	21	54	5	6
Castillo		.968	23	33	58	3	8
Perez		.910	15	22	49	7	15

Outfield	PCT	G	PO	A	E	DP
Almonte	.960	14	23	1	1	0
Altmann	.909	10	9	1	1	1
Alvarez	1.000	9	11	2	0	2
Jenkins	.967	48	84	4	3	1
Kaye	.914	29	32	0	3	0
Lindley	1.000	7	7	0	0	0
Martinez	.920	39	45	1	4	0
Richardson	1.000	9	6	0	0	0
Smith	.926	36	63	0	5	0
Terrero	—	2	0	0	0	0
Van Hoosier	1.000	3	5	1	0	0

DSL RANGERS   ROOKIE
DOMINICAN SUMMER LEAGUE

Batting	B-T	HT	WT	DOB	AVG	vLH	vRH	G	AB	R	H	2B	3B	HR	RBI	BB	HBP	SH	SF	SO	SB	CS	SLG	OBP
Almonte, Jose	R-R	6-3	205	9-9-96	.186	.178	.192	33	118	17	22	5	1	0	7	13	6	0	0	26	1	3	.246	.299
Alonzo, Yimmelvyn	R-R	6-1	185	3-10-97	.215	.113	.247	63	219	29	47	11	3	2	35	31	10	2	3	78	7	2	.320	.335
Aybar, Saury	R-R	6-1	170	7-25-95	.263	.261	.263	56	217	36	57	15	1	0	22	17	5	4	3	51	22	7	.341	.326
Barrios, Ciro	R-R	6-0	178	9-27-96	.250	.333	.224	30	100	13	25	5	0	0	10	7	4	4	2	21	5	1	.300	.319
Cabrera, Wanderley	R-R	5-10	180	2-27-95	.291	.381	.262	22	86	14	25	5	0	2	12	8	1	0	1	20	1	1	.419	.354
Castro, Rubell	R-R	6-3	180	8-13-96	.218	.161	.239	38	119	20	26	7	0	5	17	29	5	0	0	50	1	1	.403	.392
Cordero, Andretty	R-R	6-1	170	5-3-97	.291	.436	.253	48	189	33	55	10	1	4	32	14	6	2	4	27	9	2	.418	.352
Damian, Rayner	B-R	6-0	155	4-29-97	.240	.158	.260	36	96	16	23	3	1	0	8	21	3	0	0	30	8	5	.292	.392
Davis, Dale	B-R	5-8	175	12-9-91	.235	—	—	17	34	6	8	1	0	4	10	4	0	1	9	4	2	.265	.449
Diaz, Willy	R-R	6-3	200	4-19-94	.283	.277	.285	56	191	37	54	14	1	4	29	37	4	1	2	55	0	1	.429	.406
Encarnacion, Cristian	R-R	6-3	185	9-9-96	.255	.326	.235	65	212	29	54	15	3	3	38	41	14	2	0	45	16	10	.396	.408
Fajardo, Kelvin	R-R	5-11	160	3-8-96	.264	.305	.250	67	231	31	61	4	1	0	28	20	8	5	6	27	9	4	.290	.336
Favela, Samuel	R-R	5-11	160	5-15-98	.280	.167	.344	16	50	10	14	1	1	0	12	6	5	0	1	11	2	1	.340	.403
Gonzalez, Jesus	R-R	6-1	180	9-12-94	.301	.452	.262	44	153	24	46	9	1	0	21	22	2	1	3	19	0	0	.373	.389
Gutierrez, Beder	R-R	6-0	180	1-13-97	.235	.375	.111	8	17	3	4	0	0	0	1	1	0	0	2	2	0	0	.235	.278
Hernandez, Yonny	R-R	5-9	140	5-4-98	.233	.220	.239	44	150	33	35	4	1	0	13	26	6	3	1	30	5	8	.273	.366
Joseph, Starling	R-R	6-3	180	7-24-98	.259	.245	.264	54	201	37	52	15	2	1	17	27	5	2	1	60	12	7	.368	.359
Lugo, Jose	R-R	6-0	180	10-29-96	.118	.286	.074	19	34	2	4	1	0	0	2	1	0	0	0	11	1	0	.147	.143
Martinez, Stanly	R-R	6-0	176	1-5-97	.232	—	—	52	164	18	38	12	2	0	28	23	3	4	3	38	7	3	.329	.332
Matta, Shaquille	R-R	5-8	175	4-9-94	.211	.294	.185	24	71	8	15	2	2	0	10	12	2	2	1	13	3	3	.296	.337
Mejias, Luis	R-R	5-10	165	3-11-96	.168	.240	.143	37	95	17	16	1	0	0	6	17	4	2	0	22	6	1	.179	.319
Mendez, Luis	R-R	5-10	180	3-30-95	.340	.382	.328	42	156	28	53	10	5	2	35	14	5	0	3	25	2	0	.506	.404
Odor, Rougned	R-R	5-8	140	10-17-97	.233	.179	.248	45	129	25	30	3	1	0	12	21	9	2	0	37	6	5	.271	.377
Ogando, Pedro	L-R	6-0	170	6-10-94	.371	.320	.387	57	213	51	79	5	7	1	23	15	3	6	0	38	29	10	.474	.420
Pineda, Edgar	R-R	5-11	180	2-12-98	.195	.154	.209	42	154	15	30	2	0	1	12	15	5	2	2	36	6	4	.208	.292
Pozo, Yohel	R-R	6-0	175	6-14-97	.272	.236	.286	53	195	23	53	13	0	1	24	17	3	0	3	15	4	3	.354	.335
Rivera, Eudys	R-R	6-1	152	6-3-97	.239	.208	.250	29	88	11	21	3	0	0	8	12	3	3	1	16	7	2	.273	.346
Rojas, Alejandro	R-R	5-10	175	8-6-94	.211	—	—	50	161	39	34	5	0	0	19	14	12	4	0	18	4	3	.242	.321
Rollin, Franklin	R-R	5-11	165	8-26-95	.313	.315	.312	63	243	50	76	8	5	1	32	23	9	8	3	27	12	10	.399	.388
Rosa, Abel	L-L	5-11	165	7-20-94	.280	.212	.298	46	164	35	46	5	6	2	28	20	4	0	1	26	5	3	.421	.370
Silva, Luis	R-R	5-11	170	6-30-95	.255	.263	—	61	232	38	61	7	1	0	24	15	10	3	3	22	6	.302	.331
Tejeda, Anderson	L-R	5-11	160	5-1-98	.312	—	—	55	205	36	64	19	4	4	40	25	3	1	1	49	9	7	.522	.393
Triunfel, Alberto	R-R	5-11	160	2-1-94	.444	.714	.273	7	18	3	8	4	0	0	2	3	0	0	0	1	3	0	.667	.524
Vazquez, Joenny	R-R	6-2	188	10-1-96	.127	.300	.094	19	63	5	8	0	0	0	4	6	1	0	0	36	1	0	.127	.214
Villarreal, Guillermo	R-R	5-11	165	1-19-98	.345	—	—	10	29	6	10	2	0	0	5	3	1	0	0	5	0	0	.414	.387

Pitching	B-T	HT	WT	DOB	W	L	ERA	G	GS	CG	SV	IP	H	R	ER	HR	BB	SO	AVG	vLH	vRH	K/9	BB/9
Betances, Emmanuel	R-R	6-5	189	2-5-96	1	1	3.38	11	0	0	0	21	21	11	8	0	3	10	—	—	—	4.22	1.27
Brito, Pedro	L-L	5-11	155	4-4-95	7	3	1.85	12	12	1	0	68	46	18	14	1	13	62	.192	.300	.183	8.21	1.72
Castillo, Juan	R-R	6-3	166	9-18-95	0	4	5.33	14	2	0	1	27	31	22	16	1	14	16	.287	.294	.284	5.33	4.67
Cedeno, Rafael	R-R	6-5	210	10-5-94	4	1	0.76	20	0	0	6	36	23	11	3	0	11	36	—	—	—	9.08	2.78

Pitching	B-T	HT	WT	DOB	W	L	ERA	G	GS	CG	SV	IP	H	R	ER	HR	BB	SO	AVG	vLH	vRH	K/9	BB/9
Civil, Henry	R-R	6-5	194	12-14-94	0	0	15.00	9	1	0	0	9	10	18	15	0	26	10	.263	.000	.303	10.00	26.00
Cruz, Edwin	L-L	6-4	195	7-26-94	1	0	6.12	13	1	0	1	25	29	18	17	1	13	20	—	—	—	7.20	4.68
Cruz, Israel	R-R	6-1	170	6-1-97	1	2	2.63	12	11	0	0	55	46	20	16	0	23	34	.229	.279	.207	5.60	3.79
Encarnacion, Ediberto	R-R	5-11	170	2-9-94	1	1	3.05	11	0	0	1	21	14	8	7	2	5	16	.192	.211	.185	6.97	2.18
Garcia, Christopher	R-R	6-4	220	8-26-95	0	0	1.50	9	0	0	0	18	14	5	3	0	4	7	.222	.143	.245	3.50	2.00
Gonzalez, Victor	R-R	6-3	180	7-3-96	0	2	11.12	7	1	0	0	11	21	15	14	0	6	9	.396	.250	.459	7.15	4.76
Juan, Johan	R-R	6-1	180	4-14-94	4	0	1.25	18	0	0	7	43	28	7	6	2	7	46	.181	.173	.184	9.55	1.45
Lacle, Wily	R-R	6-2	175	5-30-96	0	1	6.92	15	0	0	0	26	34	22	20	2	13	13	.321	.433	.276	4.50	4.50
Leal, Werner	R-R	6-1	160	7-8-95	3	4	4.09	13	12	0	0	66	80	39	30	0	15	52	.284	.329	.264	7.09	2.05
Linares, Jesus	R-R	6-4	216	1-10-97	4	2	3.07	17	6	0	1	44	39	24	15	0	17	41	.232	.220	.239	8.39	3.48
Liriano, Roberto	L-L	5-11	165	8-4-93	0	0	0.00	4	0	0	1	5	5	2	0	0	3	9	.263	.000	.313	17.36	5.79
Lopez, Ismel	R-R	6-1	190	8-24-94	2	4	3.65	19	0	0	0	44	44	27	18	1	15	40	.259	.273	.252	8.12	3.05
Lopez, Luis	R-R	6-4	185	7-25-96	3	4	3.98	13	12	1	0	52	55	32	23	2	17	37	—	—	—	6.40	2.94
Mancebo, Jorge	R-R	6-2	195	4-25-95	2	0	3.00	8	0	0	0	12	8	5	4	0	7	11	.190	.091	.226	8.25	5.25
Martinez, Greidy	R-R	6-0	155	4-2-94	4	1	1.53	21	0	0	6	29	22	9	5	0	10	38	—	—	—	11.66	3.07
Mavo, Daniel	L-L	5-10	170	7-20-95	1	2	7.13	18	0	0	0	35	53	32	28	2	21	25	.351	.276	.369	6.37	5.35
Morrobel, Eddy	R-R	5-11	185	3-26-93	1	3	2.70	16	0	0	2	33	32	16	10	1	14	27	—	—	—	7.29	3.78
Munoz, Yelfri	R-R	6-3	210	11-24-93	5	4	3.22	12	11	0	0	59	59	29	21	4	12	48	.265	.288	.257	7.36	1.84
Nunez, Jeifry	R-R	5-11	160	4-1-98	4	2	1.55	12	7	0	0	41	34	8	7	1	12	34	.230	.235	.227	7.52	2.66
Ontiveros, Felipe	R-R	6-2	185	9-2-93	0	2	8.00	6	0	0	0	9	13	18	8	1	9	11	.325	.429	.303	11.00	9.00
Payano, Pedro	R-R	6-2	170	9-20-94	1	1	0.00	3	3	1	0	16	9	2	0	0	3	24	.164	.188	.154	13.79	1.72
Pena, Domingo	R-R	6-2	171	4-7-98	3	4	5.52	11	10	0	0	46	60	38	28	2	12	51	.316	.226	.350	10.05	2.36
Pichardo, Yonelvy	L-L	6-2	165	7-12-96	2	2	2.50	8	8	0	0	36	36	14	10	0	17	35	.273	.333	.268	8.75	4.25
Rodriguez, Argenis	R-R	6-3	190	3-7-96	3	1	1.99	12	12	0	0	63	56	20	14	2	13	40	.238	.224	.245	5.68	1.85
Rodriguez, Eury	R-R	6-1	195	9-17-97	0	0	10.13	6	0	0	0	5	6	7	6	1	11	9	.273	.375	.214	15.19	18.56
Rojas, Yhonson	L-L	6-0	160	10-1-96	0	1	12.86	8	0	0	0	7	4	14	10	0	21	9	.160	.000	.182	11.57	27.00
Rosario, Luis	R-R	5-11	165	2-8-97	7	0	3.30	12	12	0	0	63	69	30	23	3	6	46	.283	.284	.282	6.61	0.86
Sanmartin, Reiver	L-L	6-2	160	4-15-96	0	1	5.23	6	0	0	0	10	12	6	6	0	9	7	.300	.500	.278	6.10	7.84
Simon, Bradley	R-R	6-4	220	4-22-97	2	2	2.25	2	0	0	0	4	1	1	1	0	2	3	.077	.143	.000	6.75	4.50
Suarez, Sergio	L-L	6-0	180	5-24-95	6	1	3.02	20	0	1	0	45	35	21	15	1	15	35	.226	.227	.226	7.05	3.02
Taveras, Francisco	R-R	5-11	195	6-21-94	1	0	0.96	4	0	0	0	9	6	1	1	0	6	13	.188	.250	.179	12.54	5.79
Urriola, Elvis	L-L	5-11	180	9-9-97	0	4	4.53	13	11	0	0	44	47	30	22	1	28	39	.270	.265	.271	8.04	5.77
Vivas, Samir	R-R	5-11	170	2-1-95	0	0	3.63	18	0	0	9	22	19	10	9	0	14	26	.238	.222	.245	10.48	5.64
Volquez, Rafael	R-R	6-5	200	4-25-95	7	2	3.45	12	12	0	0	60	65	26	23	2	15	58	.275	.205	.307	8.70	2.25

Fielding

Catcher	PCT	G	PO	A	E	DP	PB
Cabrera	.959	11	62	9	3	0	1
Favela	.985	16	114	18	2	1	11
Gonzalez	1.000	10	93	16	0	0	4
Matta	.981	15	84	22	2	0	4
Pozo	.997	40	274	50	1	2	9
Rojas	.969	41	256	28	9	1	10
Vazquez	.980	19	126	18	3	1	12
Villarreal	.973	10	63	8	2	1	1

First Base	PCT	G	PO	A	E	DP
Aybar	.971	23	188	14	6	20
Cabrera	.990	12	92	5	1	7
Castro	.971	14	97	4	3	8
Cordero	1.000	1	2	1	0	0
Diaz	.984	40	342	17	6	26
Gonzalez	.990	24	197	10	2	12
Martinez	.992	29	230	14	2	20
Mejias	1.000	1	7	0	0	0
Ogando	.947	3	18	0	1	2
Pozo	1.000	6	50	0	0	3
Rojas	1.000	6	39	4	0	0

Second Base	PCT	G	PO	A	E	DP
Aybar	.958	8	15	8	1	1
Barrios	.955	19	41	43	4	9

	PCT	G	PO	A	E	DP
Davis	1.000	7	15	16	0	4
Fajardo	.971	18	30	38	2	7
Hernandez	.972	33	87	86	5	16
Mejias	.941	15	18	30	3	6
Odor	.950	11	19	19	2	5
Ogando	.933	12	19	37	4	6
Pineda	.967	11	9	20	1	2
Rollin	1.000	2	1	1	0	1
Silva	.923	3	4	8	1	1
Tejeda	.936	18	41	47	6	13
Triunfel	.944	3	10	7	1	3

Third Base	PCT	G	PO	A	E	DP
Aybar	.848	12	11	17	5	1
Cordero	.901	47	35	110	16	8
Diaz	.977	14	10	32	1	1
Fajardo	.941	51	42	118	10	6
Martinez	.885	7	9	14	3	1
Mejias	1.000	9	7	18	0	3
Odor	1.000	1	0	1	0	0
Silva	.895	6	3	14	2	3
Tejeda	1.000	2	0	6	0	0
Triunfel	1.000	1	1	0	0	0

Shortstop	PCT	G	PO	A	E	DP
Aybar	.924	13	22	39	5	4

	PCT	G	PO	A	E	DP
Hernandez	.938	9	13	32	3	9
Mejias	.907	12	9	30	4	5
Pineda	.948	31	49	98	8	15
Silva	.957	51	78	145	10	21
Tejeda	.884	33	59	94	20	16
Triunfel	.778	2	3	4	2	1

Outfield	PCT	G	PO	A	E	DP
Almonte	1.000	31	51	1	0	1
Alonzo	.975	63	112	4	3	0
Aybar	1.000	2	2	0	0	0
Castro	1.000	7	11	1	0	0
Damian	.944	36	63	4	4	0
Davis	—	2	0	0	0	0
Encarnacion	.947	62	101	6	6	0
Fajardo	1.000	1	1	0	0	0
Gutierrez	.500	6	2	0	2	0
Joseph	.914	54	79	6	8	3
Lugo	1.000	17	14	1	0	1
Martinez	1.000	9	8	0	0	0
Matta	1.000	6	9	0	0	0
Mendez	.920	15	23	0	2	0
Ogando	.972	39	67	3	2	0
Rivera	.918	29	51	5	5	2
Rollin	1.000	58	105	10	0	0
Rosa	.950	37	52	5	3	0

Toronto Blue Jays

SEASON IN A SENTENCE: Deadline deals for David Price and Troy Tulowitzki vaulted the Jays into first place over the Yankees and to their first AL East title in 22 years.

HIGH POINT: The sweep of the Yankees from Aug. 7-9 at Yankee Stadium came in the midst of winning 14 of 15 after the trade deadline to plant the Jays squarely in the race for the AL East crown. The sweep culminated with Marco Estrada outpitching Masahiro Tanaka in a 2-0 win that put the Jays just a half-game back.

LOW POINT: A 12-17 May left the Jays again looking like also-rans in the AL East. In the post-season, the Jays battled the Royals in a six-game ALCS but fell short to a tested Kansas City club. After the season, GM Alex Anthopoulos surprisingly decided not to return.

NOTABLE ROOKIES: Four rookies broke spring training with the Jays and all made a variety of contributions to a successful season. Devon Travis, acquired from Detroit for Anthony Gose, posted an OPS of 1.018 in the first month, hitting six homers. But a shoulder injury ended his season on July 28. Daniel Norris began the year in the starting rotation, but Toronto's No. 1 prospect entering the season struggled and was eventually sent to Detroit as the key piece in the trade for Price. Miguel Castro and Roberto Osuna made the team as dual, 20-year-old, hard-throwing righthanders. Castro was eventually a key figure in the deal for Tulowitzki, while Osuna locked down the closer's role and struck out more than a batter per inning.

KEY TRANSACTIONS: It goes without saying that if Alex Anthopoulos does not surrender a boatload of pitching prospects at the deadline for Price and Tulowitzki, that the Jays don't break a 22-year drought for a division title. The Jays also beefed up their bullpen in deals for righthanded relievers Mark Lowe and veteran LaTroy Hawkins and outfielder Ben Revere, who formed a solid left field platoon with Kevin Pillar and became a reliable leadoff hitter.

DOWN ON THE FARM: Despite all the pitching sent away at the deadline, the Jays still have some intriguing arms, such as Sean Reid-Foley, Connor Greene, Clint Hollon and 2015 first-rounder Jon Harris. Among position players, there's Richard Urena, outfielder Anthony Alford, who took a big step forward in 2015, and catcher Max Pentecost, although the 2014 first-rounder missed the season with a shoulder issue.

OPENING DAY PAYROLL: $122,506,600 (10th)

PLAYERS OF THE YEAR

MAJOR LEAGUE	MINOR LEAGUE
Josh Donaldson	**Anthony Alford,**
3b	**of**
.297/.371/.568	.298/.398/.421
41 HR, led AL in RBIs	Former two-sport star
with 123.	stole 27 bases.

ORGANIZATION LEADERS

BATTING   *Minimum 250 AB

MAJORS

* AVG	Josh Donaldson	.297
* OPS	Josh Donaldson	.939
HR	Josh Donaldson	41
RBI	Josh Donaldson	123

MINORS

* AVG	Matt Hague, Buffalo	.338
* OBP	Matt Hague, Buffalo	.403
* SLG	Ryan Schimpf, New Hampshire, Buffalo	.508
R	Anthony Alford, Lansing, Dunedin	91
H	Matt Hague, Buffalo	177
TB	Matt Hague, Buffalo	245
2B	Ryan McBroom, Lansing	39
3B	Chris Carlson, Lansing	8
HR	Ryan Schimpf, New Hampshire, Buffalo	23
RBI	Matt Hague, Buffalo	92
BB	Anthony Alford, Lansing, Dunedin	67
SO	Matt Dean, Dunedin	139
	Melky Mesa, New Hampshire, Buffalo	139
SB	Roemon Fields, Dunedin, Buffalo, New Hamp	46

PITCHING   #Minimum 75 IP

MAJORS

W	Mark Buehrle	15
# ERA	Marco Estrada	3.13
SO	Marco Estrada	131
SV	Roberto Osuna	20

MINORS

W	Shane Dawson, Dunedin, Lansing	15
L	Casey Lawrence, Buffalo, New Hampshire	14
# ERA	Matt Boyd, New Hampshire, Buffalo	1.68
G	Gregory Infante, Buffalo, New Hampshire	51
GS	Taylor Cole, New Hampshire	28
SV	Wil Browning, Dunedin, New Hampshire	25
IP	Casey Lawrence, Buffalo, New Hampshire	168
BB	Sean Reid-Foley, Dunedin, Lansing	67
SO	Taylor Cole, New Hampshire	128
AVG	Matt Boyd, New Hampshire, Buffalo	178

2015 PERFORMANCE

General Manager: Alex Anthopoulos. **Farm Director:** Charlie Wilson. **Scouting Director:** Brian Parker.

Class	Team	League	W	L	PCT	Finish	Manager
Majors	Toronto Blue Jays	American	93	69	.574	2nd (15)	John Gibbons
Triple-A	Buffalo Bisons	International	68	76	.472	9th (14)	Gary Allenson
Double-A	New Hampshire Fisher Cats	Eastern	69	71	.493	t-8th (12)	Bobby Meacham
High A	Dunedin Blue Jays	Florida State	61	76	.445	10th (12)	Omar Malave
Low A	Lansing Lugnuts	Midwest	73	66	.525	7th (16)	Ken Huckaby
Short season	Vancouver Canadians	Northwest	34	42	.447	t-6th (8)	John Schneider
Rookie	Bluefield Blue Jays	Appalachian	25	42	.373	10th (10)	Dennis Holmberg
Rookie	Blue Jays	Gulf Coast	39	19	.672	2nd (16)	Cesar Martin
Overall 2015 Minor League Record			369	392	.485	20th (30)	

ORGANIZATION STATISTICS

TORONTO BLUE JAYS

AMERICAN LEAGUE

Batting	B-T	HT	WT	DOB	AVG	vLH	vRH	G	AB	R	H	2B	3B	HR	RBI	BB	HBP	SH	SF	SO	SB	CS	SLG	OBP
Barney, Darwin	R-R	5-10	180	11-8-85	.304	.500	.235	15	23	4	7	1	0	2	4	1	0	2	0	2	0	0	.609	.333
Bautista, Jose	R-R	6-0	205	10-19-80	.250	.231	.255	153	543	108	136	29	3	40	114	110	5	0	8	106	8	2	.536	.377
Carrera, Ezequiel	L-L	5-10	185	6-11-87	.273	.310	.266	91	172	27	47	8	0	3	26	11	2	5	2	45	2	1	.372	.321
Colabello, Chris	R-R	6-4	235	10-24-83	.321	.308	.326	101	333	55	107	19	1	15	54	22	3	0	2	96	2	0	.520	.367
Diaz, Jonathan	R-R	5-9	155	4-10-85	.154	.250	.111	7	13	1	2	0	0	0	2	1	1	1	0	3	0	0	.154	.267
Donaldson, Josh	R-R	6-0	220	12-8-85	.297	.299	.296	158	620	122	184	41	2	41	123	73	6	2	10	133	6	0	.568	.371
Encarnacion, Edwin	R-R	6-1	230	1-7-83	.277	.260	.280	146	528	94	146	31	0	39	111	77	9	0	10	98	3	2	.557	.372
Goins, Ryan	L-R	5-10	185	2-13-88	.250	.212	.261	128	376	52	94	16	4	5	45	39	1	7	5	83	2	1	.354	.318
Hague, Matt	R-R	6-3	225	8-20-85	.250	.400	.143	10	12	1	3	1	0	0	0	2	1	0	0	4	0	0	.333	.400
Kawasaki, Munenori	L-R	5-11	175	6-3-81	.214	.571	.095	23	28	6	6	2	0	0	2	4	0	2	0	6	0	1	.286	.313
Martin, Russell	R-R	5-10	205	2-15-83	.240	.278	.231	129	441	76	106	23	2	23	77	53	8	0	5	106	4	5	.458	.329
Navarro, Dioner	B-R	5-9	205	2-9-84	.246	.278	.237	54	171	17	42	7	0	5	20	17	0	0	4	29	0	0	.374	.307
Pennington, Cliff	B-R	5-10	195	6-15-84	.160	.065	.227	33	75	9	12	3	0	2	11	11	1	3	2	20	0	0	.280	.270
Pillar, Kevin	R-R	6-0	205	1-4-89	.278	.278	.278	159	586	76	163	31	2	12	56	28	5	4	5	85	25	4	.399	.314
Pompey, Dalton	B-R	6-2	195	12-11-92	.223	.350	.189	34	94	17	21	8	0	2	6	7	2	0	0	23	5	1	.372	.291
Revere, Ben	L-R	5-9	170	5-3-88	.319	.328	.315	56	226	35	72	9	1	1	19	13	1	3	3	8	7	2	.381	.354
Reyes, Jose	B-R	6-0	195	6-11-83	.285	.243	.299	69	288	36	82	17	0	4	34	17	0	4	2	38	16	2	.385	.322
Saunders, Michael	L-R	6-4	225	11-19-86	.194	.667	.143	9	31	2	6	0	0	0	3	5	0	0	0	10	0	0	.194	.306
Smoak, Justin	B-L	6-4	230	12-5-86	.226	.256	.222	132	296	44	67	16	1	18	59	29	2	0	1	86	0	0	.470	.299
Thole, Josh	L-R	6-1	205	10-28-86	.204	.250	.189	18	49	5	10	2	0	0	2	3	0	0	0	9	0	0	.245	.250
Tolleson, Steve	R-R	5-11	185	11-1-83	.268	.318	.211	19	41	9	11	5	1	0	3	4	0	0	0	9	2	0	.439	.333
Travis, Devon	R-R	5-9	190	2-21-91	.304	.328	.296	62	217	38	66	18	0	8	35	18	2	0	1	43	3	1	.498	.361
Tulowitzki, Troy	R-R	6-3	215	10-10-84	.239	.286	.230	41	163	31	39	8	0	5	17	14	5	0	1	42	1	0	.380	.317
Valencia, Danny	R-R	6-2	220	9-19-84	.296	.316	.279	58	162	26	48	13	0	7	29	9	0	1	1	40	2	1	.506	.331
2-team total (47 Oakland)					.290	—	—	105	345	59	100	23	1	18	66	29	1	1	2	80	2	2	.519	.345

Pitching	B-T	HT	WT	DOB	W	L	ERA	G	GS	CG	SV	IP	H	R	ER	HR	BB	SO	AVG	vLH	vRH	K/9	BB/9
Albers, Andrew	R-L	6-1	200	10-6-85	0	0	3.38	1	0	0	0	3	1	1	1	1	2	1	.111	.000	.250	3.38	6.75
Boyd, Matt	L-L	6-3	215	2-2-91	0	2	14.85	2	2	0	0	7	15	11	11	5	1	7	.441	.474	.400	9.45	1.35
2-team total (11 Detroit)					1	6	7.53	13	12	0	0	57	71	50	48	17	20	43	—	—	—	6.75	3.14
Buehrle, Mark	L-L	6-2	240	3-23-79	15	8	3.81	32	32	4	0	199	214	100	84	22	33	91	.279	.290	.275	4.12	1.49
Castro, Miguel	R-R	6-5	190	12-24-94	0	2	4.38	13	0	0	4	12	15	7	6	2	6	12	.306	.292	.320	8.76	4.38
Cecil, Brett	R-L	6-3	220	7-2-86	5	5	2.48	63	0	0	5	54	39	17	15	4	13	70	.197	.195	.198	11.60	2.15
Coke, Phil	L-L	6-1	210	7-19-82	0	0	3.38	2	0	0	0	3	1	1	1	2	3	.111	.200	.000	10.13	6.75
Copeland, Scott	R-R	6-3	215	12-15-87	1	1	6.46	5	3	0	0	15	24	11	11	1	2	6	.369	.400	.333	3.52	1.17
Delabar, Steve	R-R	6-5	220	7-17-83	2	0	5.22	31	0	0	1	29	28	19	17	5	14	30	.250	.208	.288	9.20	4.30
Dickey, R.A.	R-R	6-3	215	10-29-74	11	11	3.91	33	33	2	0	214	195	97	93	25	61	126	.244	.228	.260	5.29	2.56
Doubront, Felix	L-L	6-2	225	10-23-87	1	1	4.76	5	4	0	0	23	32	15	12	1	5	13	.340	.333	.343	5.16	1.99
2-team total (11 Oakland)					3	3	5.50	16	12	0	1	75	87	50	46	10	26	56	—	—	—	6.69	3.11
Estrada, Marco	R-R	6-0	200	7-5-83	13	8	3.13	34	28	0	0	181	146	67	63	24	55	131	.203	.203	.204	6.51	2.73
Francis, Jeff	L-L	6-5	220	1-8-81	1	2	6.14	14	0	0	0	22	27	16	15	3	9	21	.300	.359	.255	8.59	3.68
Hawkins, LaTroy	R-R	6-5	220	12-21-72	1	0	2.76	18	0	0	1	16	22	7	5	1	3	14	.319	.333	.296	7.71	1.65
Hendriks, Liam	R-R	6-1	205	2-10-89	5	0	2.92	58	0	0	0	65	59	23	21	3	11	71	.240	.283	.207	9.88	1.53
Hutchison, Drew	L-R	6-3	195	8-22-90	13	5	5.57	30	28	1	0	150	179	103	93	22	44	129	.297	.266	.330	7.72	2.63
Hynes, Colt	L-L	5-11	200	6-28-85	0	0	6.00	5	0	0	0	3	8	2	2	0	2	4	.500	.571	.444	12.00	6.00
Jenkins, Chad	R-R	6-4	235	12-22-87	0	0	4.91	2	0	0	0	4	3	2	2	1	3	2	.214	.286	.143	4.91	7.36
Loup, Aaron	L-L	5-11	205	12-19-87	2	5	4.46	60	0	0	1	42	47	24	21	6	7	46	.275	.275	.275	9.78	1.49
Lowe, Mark	L-R	6-3	210	6-7-83	1	2	3.79	23	0	0	1	19	15	9	8	3	1	14	.224	.314	.125	6.63	0.47
2-team total (34 Seattle)					1	3	1.96	57	0	0	1	55	46	15	12	4	12	61	—	—	—	9.98	1.96
Norris, Daniel	L-L	6-2	195	4-25-93	1	1	3.86	5	5	0	0	23	23	11	10	3	14	18	.267	.375	.243	6.94	4.63
2-team total (8 Detroit)					3	2	3.75	13	13	0	0	60	53	31	25	9	19	45	—	—	—	6.75	2.85
Osuna, Roberto	R-R	6-2	230	2-7-95	1	6	2.58	68	0	0	20	70	42	21	20	7	16	75	.191	.206	.174	9.69	2.07
Price, David	L-L	6-6	210	8-26-85	9	1	2.30	11	11	0	0	74	57	20	19	4	18	87	.207	.253	.188	10.53	2.18
2-team total (21 Detroit)					18	5	2.45	32	32	3	0	220	190	70	60	17	47	225	—	—	—	9.19	1.92

Pitching (continued)

Pitching	B-T	HT	WT	DOB	W	L	ERA	G	GS	CG	SV	IP	H	R	ER	HR	BB	SO	AVG	vLH	vRH	K/9	BB/9
Rasmussen, Rob	R-L	5-10	170	4-2-89	0	0	0.00	1	0	0	0	1	1	0	0	0	0	1	.250	.333	.000	9.00	0.00
2-team total (19 Seattle)					2	1	9.98	20	0	0	0	15	26	18	17	2	8	17	—	—	—	9.98	4.70
Redmond, Todd	R-R	6-3	240	5-17-85	0	0	7.31	7	1	0	0	16	17	13	13	3	7	13	.266	.160	.333	7.31	3.94
Sanchez, Aaron	R-R	6-4	200	7-1-92	7	6	3.22	41	11	0	0	92	74	35	33	9	44	61	.224	.282	.163	5.95	4.29
Schultz, Bo	R-R	6-3	220	9-25-85	0	1	3.56	31	0	0	1	43	32	19	17	7	14	31	.205	.148	.242	6.49	2.93
Stroman, Marcus	R-R	5-8	180	5-1-91	4	0	1.67	4	4	0	0	27	20	5	5	2	6	18	.208	.194	.241	6.00	2.00
Tepera, Ryan	R-R	6-1	180	11-3-87	0	2	3.27	32	0	0	1	33	23	14	12	8	6	22	.193	.137	.235	6.00	1.64

Fielding

Catcher	PCT	G	PO	A	E	DP	PB
Martin	.995	117	799	70	4	6	19
Navarro	.985	39	242	20	4	3	2
Thole	.989	18	87	3	1	0	4

First Base	PCT	G	PO	A	E	DP
Colabello	.996	34	248	11	1	24
Encarnacion	.994	59	466	32	3	33
Hague	1.000	3	17	1	0	0
Smoak	.994	110	666	44	4	74
Valencia	1.000	5	12	2	0	0

Second Base	PCT	G	PO	A	E	DP
Barney	.971	15	10	23	1	3
Goins	.989	66	117	165	3	42
Kawasaki	1.000	17	9	29	0	6
Martin	1.000	2	0	1	0	0

	PCT	G	PO	A	E	DP	PB
Pennington	.977	22	28	56	2	10	
Tolleson	1.000	11	12	23	0	3	
Travis	.979	62	112	171	6	39	
Valencia	1.000	3	2	3	0	1	

Third Base	PCT	G	PO	A	E	DP
Donaldson	.959	150	137	287	18	32
Goins	1.000	2	0	1	0	0
Hague	1.000	1	0	1	0	0
Kawasaki	1.000	3	1	4	0	0
Pennington	1.000	6	0	5	0	0
Valencia	1.000	10	7	16	0	1

Shortstop	PCT	G	PO	A	E	DP
Diaz	1.000	6	5	9	0	1
Goins	.983	58	86	143	4	32
Pennington	.667	5	1	1	1	1

	PCT	G	PO	A	E	DP
Reyes	.953	69	84	177	13	38
Tolleson	1.000	4	0	6	0	0
Tulowitzki	1.000	39	46	120	0	26

Outfield	PCT	G	PO	A	E	DP
Bautista	.987	118	224	4	3	1
Carrera	.980	81	97	1	2	0
Colabello	.959	46	70	0	3	0
Diaz	1.000	2	4	0	0	0
Goins	.667	4	2	0	1	0
Pennington	1.000	3	5	0	0	0
Pillar	.996	158	440	10	2	1
Pompey	.968	27	58	3	2	0
Revere	1.000	56	97	0	0	0
Saunders	1.000	9	12	3	0	0
Tolleson	.500	4	1	0	1	0
Valencia	.980	37	48	0	1	0

BUFFALO BISONS

TRIPLE-A

INTERNATIONAL LEAGUE

Batting	B-T	HT	WT	DOB	AVG	vLH	vRH	G	AB	R	H	2B	3B	HR	RBI	BB	HBP	SH	SF	SO	SB	CS	SLG	OBP
Barton, Daric	L-R	6-0	215	8-16-85	.196	.158	.205	27	97	10	19	4	0	2	8	12	0	1	1	21	0	0	.299	.282
Berti, Jon	R-R	5-10	175	1-22-90	.228	.250	.218	40	149	22	34	3	1	2	14	14	3	0	0	25	4	3	.302	.307
Burns, Andy	R-R	6-2	205	8-7-90	.293	.328	.280	126	478	60	140	26	0	4	45	38	5	5	1	69	6	9	.372	.351
Carrera, Ezequiel	L-L	5-10	185	6-11-87	.276	.231	.299	30	116	13	32	5	0	1	10	12	1	4	0	16	6	2	.345	.349
Colabello, Chris	R-R	6-4	235	10-24-83	.337	.194	.423	23	83	14	28	3	0	5	18	11	1	0	0	19	0	0	.554	.421
Diaz, Jonathan	R-R	5-9	155	4-10-85	.223	.242	.216	118	359	37	80	12	2	2	23	51	6	12	2	64	7	3	.284	.328
Dickerson, Chris	L-L	6-4	230	4-10-82	.270	.286	.263	38	141	20	38	7	0	1	21	19	0	0	1	35	10	2	.340	.354
Dorn, Danny	L-L	6-2	200	7-20-84	.227	.400	.176	6	22	1	5	2	0	1	0	1	0	1	0	7	1	0	.318	.250
Fields, Roemon	L-L	5-11	180	11-28-90	.217	.000	.263	6	23	1	5	1	0	0	1	3	0	1	0	4	2	0	.261	.308
Gindl, Caleb	L-L	5-7	210	8-31-88	.228	.183	.239	85	307	29	70	12	2	4	27	25	1	0	2	54	2	2	.319	.287
Glenn, Brad	R-R	6-2	220	4-2-87	.239	.297	.216	63	226	21	54	13	1	5	34	17	1	0	2	60	0	1	.372	.293
Goins, Ryan	L-R	5-10	185	2-13-88	.300	.400	.300	6	20	1	7	1	0	0	3	0	0	0	1	5	0	0	.400	.333
Hague, Matt	R-R	6-3	225	8-20-85	.338	.377	.327	136	523	70	177	33	1	11	92	61	10	0	2	65	5	1	.468	.416
Hassan, Alex	R-R	6-3	220	4-1-88	.314	.313	.314	74	277	31	87	19	2	2	34	21	1	0	6	45	0	0	.419	.357
Heisey, Chris	R-R	6-1	215	12-14-84	.155	.190	.135	17	58	5	9	0	0	2	2	9	0	0	0	16	0	0	.259	.269
Jimenez, A.J.	R-R	6-0	225	5-1-90	.218	.152	.259	23	87	6	19	7	1	0	9	9	1	0	1	12	2	0	.322	.296
Kawasaki, Munenori	L-R	5-11	175	6-3-81	.245	.108	.277	62	196	18	48	8	0	0	8	24	2	4	1	32	8	4	.286	.332
Kelly, Ty	L-R	6-0	185	7-20-88	.264	.300	.245	38	144	16	38	4	0	1	14	14	1	0	1	10	0	2	.313	.331
Kottaras, George	L-R	6-0	200	5-10-83	.220	.273	.205	16	50	5	11	0	0	1	6	6	0	0	0	16	0	0	.280	.304
2-team total (31 Charlotte)					.238	—	—	47	147	17	35	4	0	8	25	32	0	1	1	56	0	0	.429	.372
Mesa, Melky	R-R	6-1	190	1-31-87	.215	.190	.223	61	246	32	53	21	1	4	23	12	3	1	2	89	1	1	.358	.259
Navarro, Dioner	B-R	5-9	205	2-9-84	.286	.167	.375	5	14	1	4	1	0	1	4	2	0	0	1	4	0	0	.571	.353
Nolan, Kevin	R-R	6-2	209	12-13-87	.300	.273	.316	9	30	3	9	2	0	1	3	2	1	0	0	4	0	1	.467	.364
Ochinko, Sean	R-R	5-11	205	10-21-87	.253	.302	.238	61	221	14	56	14	0	2	25	11	0	1	1	21	0	0	.344	.288
Pompey, Dalton	B-R	6-2	195	12-11-92	.285	.315	.272	65	253	44	72	7	4	1	18	36	1	2	3	41	16	7	.356	.372
Reyes, Jose	B-R	6-0	200	6-11-83	.364	.167	.600	3	11	2	4	0	0	0	2	2	0	0	0	1	0	0	.364	.462
Santiago, Ramon	B-R	5-11	185	8-31-79	.202	.136	.216	33	124	11	25	2	0	1	5	11	3	1	0	22	2	3	.218	.283
Schimpf, Ryan	L-R	5-9	190	4-11-88	.200	.174	.207	31	110	12	22	6	0	3	7	11	0	0	1	23	0	2	.336	.270
Scott, Luke	L-R	6-0	220	6-25-78	.240	.216	.245	52	192	20	46	15	1	4	28	19	1	0	0	45	0	0	.391	.311
Thole, Josh	L-R	6-1	205	10-28-86	.228	.333	.195	45	149	12	34	5	0	0	17	20	0	1	0	20	0	0	.262	.320
Tolleson, Steve	R-R	5-11	185	11-1-83	.133	.083	.167	8	30	2	4	0	0	0	3	2	0	0	0	9	0	0	.133	.235
Travis, Devon	R-R	5-9	190	2-21-91	.219	.200	.222	8	32	5	7	1	0	0	6	4	0	0	0	9	1	0	.250	.342
Wilkins, Andy	L-R	6-1	200	9-13-88	.264	.250	.271	21	72	9	19	4	0	0	9	11	0	0	2	13	0	0	.319	.353

Pitching	B-T	HT	WT	DOB	W	L	ERA	G	GS	CG	SV	IP	H	R	ER	HR	BB	SO	AVG	vLH	vRH	K/9	BB/9
Albers, Andrew	R-L	6-1	200	10-6-85	2	11	5.70	20	15	1	0	84	110	57	53	7	26	53	.324	.280	.339	5.70	2.80
Anderson, John	L-L	6-2	200	11-9-88	0	0	9.00	2	1	0	0	3	5	3	3	1	1	3	.385	.250	.444	9.00	3.00
Aumont, Phillippe	L-R	6-7	240	1-7-89	0	2	6.00	5	4	0	0	18	12	12	12	2	22	23	.194	.129	.258	11.50	11.00
2-team total (14 Lehigh Valley)					3	6	3.14	19	14	0	0	83	61	35	29	5	63	81	—	—	—	8.78	6.83
Barnes, Scott	L-L	6-4	200	9-5-87	1	0	0.00	4	1	0	0	4	1	0	0	0	3	.067	.000	.125	6.23	0.00
Bibens-Dirkx, Austin	R-R	6-1	210	4-29-85	0	1	4.67	5	3	0	0	17	20	9	9	1	4	18	.290	.412	.171	9.35	2.08
Boyd, Matt	L-L	6-3	215	2-2-91	3	1	2.77	6	6	0	0	39	32	13	12	5	6	37	.219	.263	.191	8.54	1.38
2-team total (1 Toledo)					3	1	2.63	7	7	0	0	41	32	13	12	5	9	38	—	—	—	8.34	1.98
Burke, Greg	R-R	6-4	215	9-21-82	3	0	3.16	22	0	0	0	31	20	11	11	0	11	30	.175	.250	.151	8.62	3.16

Pitching

Pitching	B-T	HT	WT	DOB	W	L	ERA	G	GS	CG	SV	IP	H	R	ER	HR	BB	SO	AVG	vLH	vRH	K/9	BB/9
Castro, Miguel	R-R	6-5	190	12-24-94	1	3	4.58	13	5	0	0	20	26	15	10	4	12	21	.313	.368	.267	9.61	5.49
Chamberlain, Joba	R-R	6-2	250	9-23-85	0	1	14.40	7	0	0	2	5	9	10	8	0	4	7	.375	.444	.333	12.60	7.20
Coke, Phil	L-L	6-1	210	7-19-82	0	0	0.00	3	0	0	0	4	2	0	0	0	3	4	.143	.000	.182	9.00	6.75
Copeland, Scott	R-R	6-3	215	12-15-87	11	6	2.95	21	20	0	0	125	119	44	41	8	37	66	.251	.285	.220	4.75	2.66
Delabar, Steve	R-R	6-5	220	7-17-83	3	1	1.42	24	0	0	1	25	12	4	4	1	10	30	.140	.056	.200	10.66	3.55
Doubront, Felix	L-L	6-2	225	10-23-87	1	3	2.44	9	9	0	0	48	36	15	13	1	18	43	.205	.222	.197	8.06	3.38
Francis, Jeff	L-L	6-5	220	1-8-81	6	3	2.35	19	14	0	0	92	84	28	24	3	13	79	.235	.238	.234	7.73	1.27
Girodo, Chad	L-L	6-1	195	2-6-91	0	0	6.75	4	0	0	0	4	6	3	3	0	3	3	.353	.333	.364	6.75	0.00
Guilmet, Preston	R-R	6-2	200	7-27-87	0	0	1.26	10	0	0	0	14	10	2	2	0	3	12	.196	.263	.156	7.53	1.88
2-team total (13 Durham)					0	0	1.84	23	0	0	3	29	24	6	6	1	9	28	—	—	—	8.59	2.76
Hutchison, Drew	R-R	6-3	195	8-22-90	0	1	4.50	1	1	0	0	4	3	2	2	1	3	4	.231	.429	.000	9.00	6.75
Hynes, Colt	L-L	5-11	200	6-28-85	0	2	3.51	36	0	0	1	33	35	14	13	2	15	26	.278	.235	.307	7.02	4.05
Infante, Greg	R-R	6-2	215	7-10-87	1	2	2.77	45	0	0	7	49	43	15	15	3	32	41	.238	.219	.248	7.58	5.92
Jenkins, Chad	R-R	6-4	235	12-22-87	8	6	2.98	41	11	0	1	94	98	37	31	5	26	60	.264	.272	.257	5.77	2.50
Korecky, Bobby	R-R	5-11	185	9-16-79	3	5	3.72	44	0	0	7	48	60	25	20	3	14	35	.299	.360	.262	6.52	2.61
Lawrence, Casey	R-R	6-2	170	10-28-87	0	1	5.68	1	1	0	0	6	6	4	4	1	0	6	.321	.333	.316	8.53	0.00
Loup, Aaron	L-L	5-11	205	12-19-87	0	0	4.50	5	0	0	0	6	9	3	3	0	4	5	.360	.250	.412	7.50	6.00
McFarland, Blake	R-R	6-5	230	2-2-88	0	0	3.38	8	0	0	0	11	6	4	4	1	4	10	.158	.167	.150	8.44	3.38
Norris, Daniel	L-L	6-2	195	4-25-93	3	10	4.27	16	16	0	0	91	96	50	43	5	41	78	.270	.291	.263	7.74	4.07
Perez, Luis	L-L	6-0	215	1-20-85	0	0	5.93	9	0	0	0	14	18	9	9	0	5	16	.327	.333	.325	10.54	3.29
Pineiro, Joel	R-R	6-0	200	9-25-78	1	2	5.82	4	2	0	0	17	23	13	11	2	6	10	.338	.343	.333	5.29	3.18
Rasmussen, Rob	R-L	5-10	170	4-2-89	4	1	2.36	34	1	0	1	42	26	11	11	1	20	40	.171	.131	.198	8.57	4.29
Redmond, Todd	R-R	6-3	240	5-17-85	3	7	4.00	23	10	0	1	79	86	36	35	5	25	57	.278	.316	.250	6.52	2.86
Roach, Donn	R-R	6-0	195	12-14-89	0	0	1.50	3	1	0	0	12	10	3	2	0	3	2	.227	.231	.226	1.50	2.25
2-team total (7 Louisville)					2	4	5.00	10	8	0	0	54	67	35	30	2	10	20	—	—	—	3.33	1.67
Rowen, Ben	R-R	6-3	195	11-15-88	0	1	2.00	14	0	0	1	18	12	4	4	0	2	11	.188	.259	.135	5.50	1.00
2-team total (6 Norfolk)					0	1	2.28	20	0	0	1	28	20	7	7	0	5	17	—	—	—	5.53	1.63
Sanchez, Aaron	R-R	6-4	200	7-1-92	0	1	3.60	3	1	0	0	5	6	4	2	0	5	4	.316	.364	.250	7.20	9.00
Schultz, Bo	R-R	6-3	220	9-25-85	2	1	1.69	16	0	0	7	21	15	4	4	1	7	18	.203	.200	.205	7.59	2.95
Stroman, Marcus	R-R	5-8	180	5-1-91	0	1	12.00	1	1	0	0	3	8	4	4	0	4	5	.500	.800	.364	15.00	12.00
Tepera, Ryan	R-R	6-1	180	11-3-87	3	1	1.06	21	0	0	3	34	16	5	4	1	13	37	.138	.130	.143	9.79	3.44
Wolf, Randy	L-L	6-0	205	8-22-76	9	2	2.58	23	23	1	0	140	139	44	40	4	40	106	.270	.260	.274	6.83	2.58

Fielding

Catcher	PCT	G	PO	A	E	DP	PB
Jimenez	.995	23	167	14	1	3	4
Kottaras	1.000	15	100	8	0	2	1
Navarro	1.000	3	19	2	0	2	0
Ochinko	.993	61	419	20	3	3	2
Thole	.997	45	316	17	1	1	3

First Base	PCT	G	PO	A	E	DP
Barton	1.000	27	231	31	0	20
Burns	.969	13	121	5	4	16
Colabello	.991	12	113	3	1	11
Dorn	1.000	2	17	1	0	2
Glenn	.966	5	27	1	1	3
Hague	.993	68	641	28	5	68
Scott	1.000	9	58	3	0	4
Wilkins	1.000	10	90	5	0	9

Second Base	PCT	G	PO	A	E	DP
Berti	.968	17	40	51	3	13
Burns	.995	46	89	128	1	34
Diaz	.983	11	21	38	1	10
Goins	1.000	2	3	6	0	1

	PCT	G	PO	A	E	DP
Kawasaki	.990	34	77	112	2	30
Kelly	.971	9	12	22	1	6
Nolan	1.000	2	3	4	0	1
Santiago	1.000	18	30	53	0	10
Schimpf	1.000	2	5	4	0	2
Tolleson	.944	3	8	9	1	3
Travis	1.000	5	13	14	0	5

Third Base	PCT	G	PO	A	E	DP
Berti	1.000	21	15	39	0	4
Burns	.943	50	25	108	8	12
Hague	.943	62	40	109	9	8
Kelly	.957	7	2	20	1	1
Schimpf	.933	7	4	10	1	1

Shortstop	PCT	G	PO	A	E	DP
Burns	.947	8	13	23	2	6
Diaz	.970	94	132	290	13	61
Goins	1.000	4	7	11	0	2
Kawasaki	.982	26	34	74	2	20
Nolan	1.000	3	5	12	0	4
Reyes	1.000	2	2	6	0	2

	PCT	G	PO	A	E	DP
Santiago	.953	10	13	28	2	3
Tolleson	1.000	3	2	7	0	2

Outfield	PCT	G	PO	A	E	DP
Burns	1.000	8	11	0	0	0
Carrera	.971	30	65	2	2	0
Colabello	1.000	2	4	0	0	0
Diaz	1.000	14	28	2	0	1
Dickerson	.952	34	58	1	3	2
Dorn	1.000	3	4	0	0	0
Fields	1.000	6	9	1	0	0
Gindl	.992	66	117	9	1	1
Glenn	1.000	51	80	2	0	0
Hassan	.971	53	96	3	3	0
Heisey	1.000	15	24	0	0	0
Kelly	.970	22	30	2	1	0
Mesa	.978	60	130	3	3	1
Pompey	.978	65	132	3	3	2
Schimpf	1.000	10	14	1	0	0
Scott	1.000	1	4	0	0	0

NEW HAMPSHIRE FISHER CATS
EASTERN LEAGUE

DOUBLE-A

Batting	B-T	HT	WT	DOB	AVG	vLH	vRH	G	AB	R	H	2B	3B	HR	RBI	BB	HBP	SH	SF	SO	SB	CS	SLG	OBP
Barton, Daric	L-R	6-0	215	8-16-85	.353	.143	.500	4	17	4	6	2	0	1	4	2	0	0	0	2	0	0	.647	.421
Berti, Jon	R-R	5-10	175	12-24-90	.262	.373	.228	63	256	35	67	12	2	1	20	26	8	4	3	38	19	4	.336	.345
Burns, Andy	R-R	6-2	205	8-7-90	.238	.364	.167	6	21	5	5	0	0	1	1	3	0	0	0	3	0	0	.381	.333
Chung, Derrick	R-R	5-9	175	2-23-88	.282	.158	.327	24	71	5	20	6	0	0	8	12	1	0	3	8	0	0	.366	.379
Fermin, Andy	R-R	6-0	180	7-27-89	.163	.143	.167	13	43	7	7	5	0	0	3	0	1	0	6	0	0	.279	.217
Fields, Roemon	L-L	5-11	180	11-28-90	.257	.243	.261	49	202	28	52	2	1	1	11	18	1	4	0	34	23	5	.292	.321
Flores, Jorge	R-R	5-5	160	11-25-91	.276	.289	.269	123	395	49	109	20	1	2	28	47	6	11	2	63	10	11	.347	.360
Fox, Jake	R-R	6-0	220	7-20-82	.278	.375	.247	29	108	15	30	10	0	5	19	12	2	0	0	27	1	0	.509	.361
Garner, Cole	R-R	6-2	220	12-15-84	.222	.286	.154	8	27	1	6	1	0	0	1	0	0	1	0	6	0	1	.259	.250
Guerrero, Emilio	R-R	6-4	189	8-21-92	.230	.245	.224	52	183	20	42	10	1	2	13	10	0	0	2	51	1	2	.328	.267
Hobson, K.C.	L-L	6-2	205	8-22-90	.240	.208	.254	130	499	45	120	19	1	14	67	34	1	1	5	106	1	0	.367	.288
Jimenez, A.J.	R-R	6-0	225	5-1-90	.095	.000	.125	5	21	0	2	0	0	0	0	0	0	0	0	6	0	0	.095	.095
Lopes, Christian	R-R	6-0	185	10-1-92	.174	.143	.200	34	92	6	16	0	0	0	7	11	1	1	3	14	1	0	.174	.262
Medina, Martin	R-R	6-0	200	3-24-90	.182	.227	.152	17	55	4	10	0	1	1	3	8	0	0	2	9	0	0	.273	.277
Mesa, Melky	R-R	6-1	190	1-31-87	.299	.367	.272	43	174	20	52	9	2	4	16	6	1	0	0	50	2	1	.443	.326

Batting	B-T	HT	WT	DOB	AVG	vLH	vRH	G	AB	R	H	2B	3B	HR	RBI	BB	HBP	SH	SF	SO	SB	CS	SLG	OBP
Murphy, Jack	B-R	6-4	235	4-6-88	.220	.197	.222	85	286	34	63	14	2	3	31	37	1	1	3	58	0	1	.315	.309
Newman, Matt	L-L	5-10	170	9-20-88	.208	.218	.208	97	336	32	70	13	2	9	42	30	1	1	6	97	0	2	.339	.271
Nolan, Kevin	R-R	6-2	209	12-13-87	.246	.230	.252	109	407	37	100	20	3	5	53	28	3	1	7	47	10	5	.346	.294
Ochinko, Sean	R-R	5-11	205	10-21-87	.333	—	.333	1	3	0	1	0	0	0	0	0	0	0	0	0	0	0	.333	.333
Opitz, Shane	L-R	6-1	180	1-10-92	.240	.141	.268	108	358	43	86	15	5	3	37	22	0	9	2	49	3	2	.335	.283
Parmley, Ian	L-L	5-11	175	12-19-89	.278	.293	.272	43	133	20	37	4	2	1	16	11	0	2	1	21	2	2	.361	.331
Pompey, Dalton	B-R	6-2	195	12-11-92	.351	.192	.389	31	134	26	47	2	3	6	22	11	2	0	1	23	7	3	.545	.405
Rankin, Pierce	R-R	6-1	190	4-26-89	.248	.300	.215	31	105	13	26	2	0	4	13	9	0	1	1	24	0	0	.381	.304
Schimpf, Ryan	L-R	5-9	190	4-11-88	.271	.231	.277	76	258	43	70	20	0	20	56	42	4	0	3	54	2	1	.581	.378
Smith Jr., Dwight	L-R	5-11	195	10-26-92	.265	.235	.276	117	460	74	122	26	2	7	44	47	2	1	2	64	4	3	.376	.335
Torreyes, Ronald	R-R	5-10	150	9-2-92	.140	.188	.118	16	50	4	7	2	0	0	4	0	0	0	2	2	0	0	.180	.204
Travis, Devon	R-R	5-9	190	2-21-91	.091	.000	.100	3	11	0	1	0	0	0	1	0	0	0	1	1	0	0	.091	.083

Pitching	B-T	HT	WT	DOB	W	L	ERA	G	GS	CG	SV	IP	H	R	ER	HR	BB	SO	AVG	vLH	vRH	K/9	BB/9
Anderson, John	L-L	6-2	200	11-9-88	6	6	4.62	28	20	0	0	121	138	65	62	8	42	72	.285	.312	.276	5.37	3.13
Antolin, Dustin	R-R	6-2	195	8-9-89	4	3	3.07	37	1	0	2	56	59	21	19	2	18	55	.276	.211	.312	8.89	2.91
Barnes, Dan	L-R	6-1	195	10-21-89	3	2	2.97	40	1	0	4	61	64	24	20	5	19	74	.270	.253	.279	10.98	2.82
Barnes, Scott	L-L	6-4	200	9-5-87	2	6	5.59	30	6	1	0	58	72	37	36	8	15	49	.310	.211	.354	7.60	2.33
Bibens-Dirkx, Austin	R-R	6-1	210	4-29-85	7	8	4.08	20	18	0	0	97	100	51	44	11	28	86	.262	.255	.267	7.98	2.60
Boyd, Matt	L-L	6-3	215	2-2-91	6	1	1.10	12	12	0	0	74	39	11	9	3	18	70	.155	.146	.157	8.55	2.20
Browning, Wil	R-R	6-3	190	9-8-88	1	1	3.86	13	0	0	3	19	15	8	8	0	7	16	.227	.300	.196	7.71	3.38
Burke, Greg	R-R	6-4	215	9-21-82	2	1	2.08	26	0	0	0	30	25	8	7	2	7	36	.225	.281	.203	10.68	2.08
Burns, Cory	R-R	6-1	205	10-9-87	2	5	5.76	32	0	0	2	55	70	35	35	3	20	45	.315	.345	.296	7.41	3.29
Cole, Taylor	R-R	6-1	190	8-20-89	7	10	4.06	28	28	1	0	164	174	80	74	18	55	128	.281	.296	.271	7.02	3.02
Cordero, Jimmy	R-R	6-3	215	10-19-91	0	1	2.92	17	0	0	1	25	16	10	8	1	14	22	.182	.128	.224	8.03	5.11
2-team total (13 Reading)					0	1	2.59	30	0	0	1	42	27	15	12	2	18	40	—	—	—	8.64	3.89
Da Silva, Tiago	R-R	5-9	180	3-28-85	0	1	4.91	4	0	0	0	7	5	4	4	2	1	7	.192	.000	.294	8.59	1.23
Girodo, Chad	L-L	6-1	195	2-6-91	2	0	0.62	21	0	0	2	29	26	2	2	0	2	23	.241	.098	.328	7.14	0.62
Greene, Conner	R-R	6-3	165	4-4-95	3	1	4.68	5	5	0	0	25	25	14	13	1	12	15	.269	.286	.255	5.40	4.32
Hoffman, Jeff	R-R	6-4	185	1-8-93	0	0	1.54	2	2	0	0	9	2	2	2	0	2	8	.214	.227	.200	6.17	1.54
2-team total (7 New Britain)					2	2	2.81	9	9	0	0	48	36	16	15	3	12	37	—	—	—	6.94	2.25
Hynes, Colt	L-L	5-11	200	6-28-85	1	3	3.38	10	0	0	0	13	9	5	5	0	3	12	.188	.208	.167	8.10	2.03
Infante, Greg	R-R	6-2	215	7-10-87	0	1	5.63	6	0	0	1	8	12	10	5	0	7	9	.324	.462	.250	10.13	7.88
Lawrence, Casey	R-R	6-2	170	10-28-87	12	13	4.52	26	26	1	0	161	208	92	81	9	32	91	.315	.351	.288	5.08	1.79
Lee, Mike	R-R	6-7	235	11-18-86	0	2	5.00	7	0	0	0	36	49	25	20	3	10	18	.331	.403	.279	4.50	2.50
McFarland, Blake	R-R	6-5	230	2-2-88	3	3	1.72	38	0	0	16	47	36	13	9	3	6	62	.209	.232	.194	11.87	1.15
Perez, Luis	L-L	6-0	215	1-20-85	2	2	3.78	28	3	0	1	52	45	23	22	3	29	38	.241	.224	.250	6.54	4.99
Pineiro, Joel	R-R	6-0	200	9-25-78	4	2	3.77	9	9	0	0	60	63	27	25	2	7	25	.273	.329	.240	3.77	1.06
Sikula, Arik	R-R	6-0	200	12-21-88	0	0	15.43	5	0	0	0	7	18	12	12	1	3	6	.486	.600	.409	1.29	3.86
Smith, Chris	R-R	6-2	205	8-19-88	0	0	0.00	2	0	0	0	3	2	0	0	0	1	4	.182	.250	.143	12.00	3.00
2-team total (7 Trenton)					1	1	4.96	9	0	0	0	16	13	9	9	0	4	16	—	—	—	8.82	2.20
Smith, Murphy	R-R	6-3	210	8-25-87	1	1	9.00	2	2	0	0	9	12	9	9	0	5	5	.343	.300	.360	5.00	5.00
West, Matt	R-R	6-1	200	11-21-88	0	0	0.00	7	0	0	1	12	9	1	0	0	4	17	.205	.143	.233	12.41	2.92

Fielding

Catcher	PCT	G	PO	A	E	DP	PB
Chung	1.000	21	124	14	0	1	0
Jimenez	.973	4	33	3	1	0	0
Medina	1.000	14	115	5	0	1	0
Murphy	.989	76	510	42	6	5	4
Ochinko	1.000	1	5	1	0	0	0
Rankin	.978	29	205	21	5	3	3

First Base	PCT	G	PO	A	E	DP
Barton	1.000	1	13	1	0	2
Fox	1.000	4	29	1	0	2
Hobson	.994	120	1058	53	7	106
Nolan	1.000	3	18	0	0	1
Opitz	.992	17	123	5	1	12

Second Base	PCT	G	PO	A	E	DP
Berti	.961	35	53	94	6	19
Fermin	1.000	2	1	3	0	2
Flores	.982	27	54	58	2	12

	PCT	G	PO	A	E	DP	PB
Lopes	.986	29	56	83	2	21	
Opitz	.988	35	69	99	2	29	
Schimpf	1.000	4	10	16	0	3	
Torreyes	1.000	14	22	32	0	8	
Travis	.938	2	5	10	1	4	

Third Base	PCT	G	PO	A	E	DP
Berti	.964	8	5	22	1	4
Burns	.958	6	2	21	1	3
Fermin	.867	4	1	12	2	1
Flores	1.000	1	1	2	0	0
Guerrero	.931	40	20	74	7	4
Nolan	.975	49	32	86	3	8
Opitz	.941	22	15	33	3	5
Schimpf	.944	14	5	29	2	4

Shortstop	PCT	G	PO	A	E	DP
Flores	.955	80	107	232	16	55
Nolan	.986	50	77	138	3	32

	PCT	G	PO	A	E	DP
Opitz	.943	12	19	31	3	8
Torreyes	1.000	1	0	4	0	0

Outfield	PCT	G	PO	A	E	DP
Berti	.919	15	32	2	3	0
Fields	.983	48	111	7	2	2
Flores	1.000	9	11	0	0	0
Fox	1.000	1	1	0	0	0
Garner	1.000	7	14	2	0	1
Guerrero	.875	4	7	0	1	0
Mesa	.982	41	105	3	2	2
Newman	.991	96	200	11	2	2
Opitz	.833	8	9	1	2	0
Parmley	.989	38	89	3	1	1
Pompey	.974	29	72	2	2	0
Rankin	1.000	1	1	0	0	0
Schimpf	1.000	32	45	0	0	0
Smith Jr.	.981	105	204	8	4	2

DUNEDIN BLUE JAYS
HIGH CLASS A
FLORIDA STATE LEAGUE

Batting	B-T	HT	WT	DOB	AVG	vLH	vRH	G	AB	R	H	2B	3B	HR	RBI	BB	HBP	SH	SF	SO	SB	CS	SLG	OBP
Alford, Anthony	R-R	6-1	205	7-20-94	.302	.268	.314	57	225	42	68	11	6	3	19	28	1	0	1	49	15	6	.444	.380
Attaway, Aaron	R-R	5-7	170	3-6-92	.235	.200	.250	5	17	2	4	0	0	0	1	0	0	0	2	1	1	.235	.278
Chung, Derrick	R-R	5-9	175	2-23-88	.176	.333	.143	6	17	1	3	0	0	0	1	2	0	0	0	2	0	1	.176	.263
Collins, Boomer	R-R	6-0	200	6-13-89	.236	.235	.236	35	123	10	29	5	1	2	10	5	1	1	1	31	0	2	.341	.269
Dantzler, L.B.	L-R	5-11	200	5-22-91	.251	.252	.251	98	370	37	93	28	0	5	45	29	2	0	5	64	0	2	.368	.305
Davis, Jonathan	R-R	5-8	190	5-12-92	.230	.234	.228	47	161	22	37	15	0	1	14	10	4	1	2	34	5	6	.342	.288
Dean, Matt	R-R	6-3	215	12-22-92	.253	.228	.262	123	478	53	121	27	3	14	63	36	6	0	1	139	3	1	.410	.313

Batting

Batting	B-T	HT	WT	DOB	AVG	vLH	vRH	G	AB	R	H	2B	3B	HR	RBI	BB	HBP	SH	SF	SO	SB	CS	SLG	OBP
Fermin, Andy	L-R	6-0	180	7-27-89	.234	.190	.243	39	128	15	30	6	1	2	15	11	1	3	0	23	0	0	.344	.300
Fields, Roemon	L-L	5-11	180	11-28-90	.269	.299	.257	66	264	34	71	10	4	1	21	16	1	5	1	52	21	9	.348	.312
Guerrero, Emilio	R-R	6-4	189	8-21-92	.245	.333	.220	28	106	11	26	6	2	1	8	7	1	1	0	23	2	1	.368	.298
Harris, David	R-R	6-1	190	8-10-91	.211	.192	.217	27	109	10	23	6	0	2	9	2	2	0	0	31	3	1	.321	.239
Hassan, Alex	R-R	6-3	220	4-1-88	.118	.167	.091	5	17	1	2	0	0	0	2	3	1	0	0	1	0	0	.118	.286
Izturis, Maicer	B-R	5-8	185	9-12-80	.231	.500	.182	5	13	2	3	0	0	0	0	2	0	0	0	0	0	0	.231	.333
Leblebijian, Jason	R-R	6-2	205	5-13-91	.170	.088	.205	32	112	8	19	4	1	0	5	10	2	0	0	31	3	1	.223	.250
Lopes, Christian	R-R	6-0	185	10-1-92	.293	.313	.286	70	246	39	72	16	0	2	31	28	2	0	1	43	3	1	.382	.368
Loveless, Derrick	L-R	6-1	200	3-7-93	.216	.261	.201	118	385	52	83	16	2	10	43	58	3	2	2	110	8	4	.345	.321
Lugo, Dawel	R-R	6-0	190	12-31-94	.219	.292	.191	67	260	16	57	9	2	2	21	9	5	1	1	49	1	3	.292	.258
Medina, Martin	R-R	6-0	200	3-24-90	.281	.294	.277	18	64	5	18	3	1	0	7	3	0	0	1	14	0	0	.359	.309
Nay, Mitch	R-R	6-3	200	9-20-93	.243	.308	.218	109	391	32	95	18	5	5	42	32	5	1	8	75	0	1	.353	.303
Parmley, Ian	L-L	5-11	175	12-19-89	.171	.229	.146	35	117	17	20	2	0	0	6	16	0	2	2	36	4	1	.188	.267
Reeves, Mike	L-R	6-2	195	9-16-90	.219	.150	.243	48	151	22	33	7	2	0	14	15	1	0	0	39	0	0	.291	.289
Saez, Jorge	R-R	5-10	195	8-28-90	.176	.200	.167	71	221	22	39	11	1	3	22	25	2	0	3	56	0	0	.276	.263
Saunders, Michael	L-R	6-4	225	11-19-86	.233	.167	.250	9	30	2	7	3	0	0	2	3	0	0	0	8	0	0	.333	.303
Tellez, Rowdy	L-L	6-4	245	3-16-95	.275	.300	.267	35	131	17	36	5	0	7	28	14	0	0	3	28	3	0	.473	.338
Thon, Dickie Joe	R-R	6-2	190	11-16-91	.180	.160	.188	83	283	28	51	13	4	2	19	18	6	3	1	82	5	4	.276	.244
Tolleson, Steve	R-R	5-11	185	11-1-83	.000	.000	.000	1	3	1	0	0	0	0	0	0	1	0	0	0	1	0	.000	.250
Urena, Richard	L-R	6-1	170	2-26-96	.250	.167	.277	30	124	9	31	3	1	1	8	3	0	1	0	26	3	1	.315	.268
Vazquez, Christian	B-R	5-10	170	9-11-89	.111	.000	.143	2	9	1	0	0	0	0	0	0	0	0	0	0	0	0	.111	.111

Pitching

Pitching	B-T	HT	WT	DOB	W	L	ERA	G	GS	CG	SV	IP	H	R	ER	HR	BB	SO	AVG	vLH	vRH	K/9	BB/9
Abel, Nate	L-L	6-1	190	11-2-92	1	0	3.00	1	0	0	0	3	4	1	1	0	1	0	.333	.400	.286	0.00	3.00
Allen, Brad	L-R	6-4	220	3-26-89	1	5	4.02	21	6	0	0	63	61	30	28	3	29	48	.269	.275	.264	6.89	4.16
Aquino, Jayson	L-L	6-1	180	11-22-92	2	2	2.81	5	5	0	0	26	27	10	8	2	6	16	.270	.143	.319	5.61	2.10
2-team total (13 Bradenton)					4	8	3.54	18	18	0	0	104	104	49	41	7	25	66	—	—	—	5.69	2.16
Blacksher, Derek	R-R	6-0	210	3-1-85	0	1	3.38	4	0	0	0	21	29	11	8	2	4	15	.315	.367	.256	6.33	1.69
Browning, Wil	R-R	6-3	190	9-8-88	2	1	0.78	31	0	0	22	35	17	3	3	1	2	40	.143	.303	.081	10.38	0.52
Castillo, Lendy	R-R	6-1	170	4-8-89	0	0	3.72	6	0	0	0	10	9	4	4	0	2	11	.237	.091	.296	10.24	1.86
Castro, Miguel	R-R	6-5	190	12-24-94	0	0	0.00	3	0	0	0	5	0	0	0	0	1	7	.000	.000	.000	12.60	1.80
Cook, Ryan	R-R	6-1	210	5-4-93	0	0	3.38	2	0	0	0	3	4	1	1	0	1	3	.333	.500	.300	10.13	3.38
Cordero, Jimmy	R-R	6-3	215	10-19-91	0	1	2.49	15	0	0	0	25	24	8	7	2	6	24	.250	.367	.197	8.53	2.13
Da Silva, Tiago	R-R	5-9	180	2-5-83	2	0	3.52	8	0	0	0	15	11	6	6	0	3	21	.200	.250	.171	12.33	1.76
Dawson, Shane	R-L	6-1	200	9-9-93	3	2	3.12	5	5	1	0	26	20	10	9	2	8	22	.202	.227	.195	7.62	2.77
Dermody, Matt	R-L	6-5	190	7-4-90	4	1	4.21	35	1	0	1	77	98	40	36	2	13	62	.308	.303	.310	7.25	1.52
Diaz, Denis	R-R	6-1	180	11-20-94	0	1	12.00	1	1	0	0	3	7	4	4	0	2	3	.438	.667	.300	9.00	6.00
Dragmire, Brady	R-R	6-2	210	2-5-93	2	2	5.26	40	0	1	0	63	80	43	37	1	20	57	.313	.299	.321	8.10	2.84
Fisk, Conor	R-R	6-2	210	4-4-92	1	2	5.95	4	4	0	0	20	21	14	13	2	6	15	.266	.200	.288	6.86	2.75
Gabryszwski, Jeremy	R-R	6-4	195	3-16-93	9	8	3.77	25	20	0	0	129	146	63	54	7	31	91	.286	.279	.290	6.35	2.16
Girodo, Chad	L-L	6-1	195	2-6-91	2	2	1.32	20	0	0	0	27	17	4	4	1	7	32	.175	.038	.225	10.54	2.30
Glaude, Griffin	R-R	5-9	175	4-6-92	0	0	9.00	1	0	0	0	2	2	2	2	0	1	3	.250	.500	.000	13.50	4.50
Gonzalez, Alonzo	L-L	6-5	212	1-15-92	2	5	4.39	23	9	0	1	66	75	37	32	7	28	55	.278	.280	.277	7.54	3.84
Greene, Conner	R-R	6-3	165	4-4-95	2	3	2.25	7	7	0	0	40	36	11	10	1	8	35	.238	.190	.269	7.88	1.80
Hoffman, Jeff	R-R	6-4	185	1-8-93	3	3	3.21	11	11	0	0	56	59	20	20	4	15	38	.284	.309	.271	6.11	2.41
Isaacs, Dusty	R-R	6-1	190	8-7-91	0	0	0.00	2	2	0	0	2	2	0	0	0	2	0	.222	.500	.000	0.00	7.71
Kish, Phil	R-R	5-10	185	8-30-89	1	0	3.60	10	0	0	0	15	16	7	6	1	8	7	.271	.263	.275	4.20	4.80
Kraft, Michael	L-L	5-11	175		0	0	9.00	1	0	0	0	2	4	2	2	1	0	2	.400	.667	.300	9.00	0.00
Kravetz, John	L-R	6-4	220	10-3-92	0	0	0.00	1	0	0	0	1	0	0	0	0	1	1	.000	.000	.000	6.75	6.75
Labourt, Jairo	L-L	6-4	205	3-7-94	2	7	4.59	18	18	0	0	80	83	50	41	6	44	70	.263	.306	.253	7.84	4.93
2-team total (7 Lakeland)					3	12	5.12	25	25	0	0	116	128	81	66	9	59	104	—	—	—	8.07	4.58
Lowery, Jackson	L-R	6-0	175	7-23-92	0	1	18.00	2	0	0	0	2	5	5	4	0	4	2	.556	.000	.625	9.00	18.00
Murphy, Griffin	R-L	6-3	230	1-16-91	1	1	6.10	1	1	0	0	10	11	9	7	0	6	6	.282	.273	.286	5.23	5.23
Ramirez, Carlos	R-R	6-5	205	4-24-91	0	2	4.91	6	0	0	0	7	10	7	4	0	10	7	.313	.333	.294	8.59	12.27
Reid-Foley, Sean	R-R	6-3	220	8-30-95	5	5	5.23	8	8	0	0	33	25	20	19	1	24	35	.210	.216	.207	9.64	6.61
Sanchez, Aaron	R-R	6-4	200	7-1-92	0	0	3.38	1	1	0	0	3	3	1	1	0	2	2	.300	.400	.200	6.75	6.75
Santos, Luis	R-R	6-0	185	2-11-91	6	6	4.55	21	16	0	0	93	91	49	47	12	22	66	.252	.271	.240	8.32	2.13
Shafer, Justin	R-R	6-2	195	9-18-92	1	5	8.06	12	5	0	2	22	34	26	20	2	10	11	.337	.359	.323	4.43	4.03
Sikula, Arik	R-R	6-0	200	12-21-88	1	1	2.20	23	0	0	5	33	26	12	8	3	9	30	.211	.243	.198	8.27	2.48
Silverstein, Scott	L-L	6-6	260	5-27-90	0	1	5.93	8	1	0	0	14	19	10	9	1	11	7	.333	.300	.340	4.61	7.24
Smith, Chris	R-R	6-2	205	8-19-88	1	0	0.68	9	0	0	0	13	4	1	1	2	18	.091	.100	.088	12.15	1.35
2-team total (13 Tampa)					3	1	0.74	22	0	0	0	36	18	3	3	1	5	41	—	—	—	10.16	1.24
Smith, Murphy	R-R	6-3	210	8-25-87	5	5	2.92	17	16	1	0	83	85	37	27	2	23	68	.270	.261	.276	7.34	2.48
Smoral, Matt	L-L	6-8	220	3-18-94	1	0	14.73	5	0	0	0	4	7	6	6	0	6	5	.389	.250	.429	12.27	14.73
Stilson, John	R-R	6-3	205	7-28-90	0	0	13.50	1	0	0	0	1	3	2	2	0	0	4	.429	.500	.400	27.00	0.00
Tirado, Alberto	R-R	6-0	180	12-10-94	3	3	3.23	31	0	0	3	61	45	25	22	4	35	61	.213	.267	.184	8.95	5.14
2-team total (9 Clearwater)					5	3	2.68	40	0	0	3	77	51	27	23	4	53	77	—	—	—	8.96	6.17
Turner, Colton	L-L	6-3	215	1-17-91	0	0	27.00	1	0	0	0	1	3	3	3	1	1	1	.500	1.000	.400	9.00	9.00
Wandling, Jon	R-R	6-3	205	5-28-92	1	0	5.79	2	0	0	0	5	6	3	3	0	1	0	.400	.625	.143	0.00	1.93

Fielding

Catcher	PCT	G	PO	A	E	DP	PB
Chung	.958	4	21	2	1	0	0
Medina	.981	18	144	11	3	0	3
Reeves	.992	47	334	30	3	4	8
Saez	.990	71	526	58	6	4	5

First Base	PCT	G	PO	A	E	DP
Dantzler	.997	35	288	23	1	15
Dean	.990	79	649	40	7	80
Leblebijian	1.000	1	7	0	0	0
Tellez	.995	24	201	8	1	16

TORONTO BLUE JAYS

Second Base	PCT	G	PO	A	E	DP
Attaway	1.000	3	5	13	0	2
Fermin	.985	16	34	32	1	5
Izturis	1.000	3	4	4	0	1
Leblebijian	1.000	6	10	13	0	4
Lopes	.988	67	138	189	4	52
Thon	.954	46	79	127	10	27
Vazquez	**.923**	**2**	**3**	**9**	**1**	**1**
Third Base	PCT	G	PO	A	E	DP
Dean	.907	13	13	26	4	2
Fermin	1.000	7	1	9	0	1
Guerrero	1.000	6	5	13	0	4

	PCT	G	PO	A	E	DP
Leblebijian	.923	11	5	19	2	1
Nay	.922	100	51	173	19	12
Thon	.714	3	2	3	2	0
Shortstop	PCT	G	PO	A	E	DP
Attaway	1.000	1	1	1	0	0
Guerrero	.875	4	3	11	2	1
Izturis	1.000	1	1	3	0	0
Leblebijian	.900	10	14	22	4	4
Lopes	.667	1	0	2	0	0
Lugo	.965	67	79	200	10	37
Thon	.949	26	37	75	6	11
Urena	.972	30	35	70	3	18

Outfield	PCT	G	PO	A	E	DP
Alford	.967	55	148	0	5	0
Collins	.971	35	64	2	2	0
Dantzler	.971	24	33	0	1	0
Davis	.970	46	95	3	3	0
Fields	.989	65	171	5	2	2
Guerrero	.750	5	3	0	1	0
Harris	.952	26	54	5	3	1
Hassan	.889	4	7	1	1	0
Loveless	.965	118	185	10	7	2
Parmley	.976	33	82	1	2	1
Saunders	1.000	6	5	0	0	0
Thon	1.000	7	6	1	0	0

LANSING LUGNUTS
LOW CLASS A
MIDWEST LEAGUE

Batting	B-T	HT	WT	DOB	AVG	vLH	vRH	G	AB	R	H	2B	3B	HR	RBI	BB	HBP	SH	SF	SO	SB	CS	SLG	OBP
Alford, Anthony	R-R	6-1	205	7-20-94	.293	.226	.306	50	188	49	55	14	1	1	16	39	3	0	2	60	12	1	.394	.418
Almonte, Josh	R-R	6-3	210	1-28-94	.252	.245	.254	69	250	31	63	15	2	2	21	10	2	4	2	78	13	1	.352	.284
Atkinson, Justin	R-R	6-1	218	7-24-93	.216	.429	.155	33	125	8	27	5	0	0	7	4	0	0	0	36	0	1	.256	.240
Carlson, Chris	L-L	5-9	180	4-29-91	.290	.340	.273	106	396	64	115	21	8	7	45	52	6	0	3	42	15	9	.437	.379
Collins, Boomer	R-R	6-0	200	6-13-89	.285	.270	.290	37	130	17	37	8	2	3	26	11	1	0	4	23	5	2	.446	.336
Davis, Austin	L-R	5-10	170	4-26-93	.195	.200	.194	26	82	6	16	3	0	0	6	6	0	2	0	25	0	0	.232	.250
Davis, D.J.	L-R	6-1	180	7-25-94	.282	.276	.284	129	496	77	140	19	7	7	59	39	8	4	7	119	21	10	.391	.340
Davis, Jonathan	R-R	5-8	190	5-12-92	.408	.375	.415	13	49	13	20	2	1	2	8	7	0	2	0	7	6	1	.612	.482
De La Cruz, Michael	R-R	5-10	190	5-15-93	.242	.236	.244	65	211	20	51	15	0	0	17	23	1	3	1	41	5	3	.313	.318
Harris, David	R-R	6-1	190	8-10-91	.280	.254	.291	55	211	31	59	13	3	4	28	15	4	0	4	54	5	3	.427	.333
Heidt, Gunnar	R-R	6-0	200	9-12-92	.180	.256	.158	54	189	19	34	10	1	0	18	11	1	3	4	46	8	3	.243	.224
Jansen, Dan	R-R	6-2	230	4-15-95	.206	.154	.223	46	160	19	33	8	0	4	27	19	3	0	2	22	2	0	.331	.299
Kelly, Juan	L-R	5-10	155	7-16-94	.286	.308	.280	17	63	10	18	7	0	3	9	8	0	0	0	15	2	0	.540	.366
Leblebijian, Jason	R-R	6-2	205	5-13-91	.277	.295	.271	68	264	46	73	19	3	9	48	28	1	2	2	58	10	4	.473	.346
Locastro, Tim	R-R	6-1	200	7-14-92	.310	.250	.322	70	242	48	75	10	1	5	25	21	21	3	2	25	30	11	.421	.409
Lugo, Dawel	R-R	6-0	190	12-31-94	.336	.469	.289	31	122	15	41	6	1	2	23	5	0	0	5	24	3	1	.451	.348
2-team total (22 Kane County)					.335	—	—	53	203	27	68	7	2	2	26	9	1	0	5	37	5	3	.419	.358
Maldonado, Alex	R-R	5-9	175	6-12-91	.198	.205	.195	50	167	30	33	7	0	1	17	24	1	0	3	37	6	1	.257	.297
McBroom, Ryan	R-L	6-3	230	4-9-92	.315	.286	.322	127	461	72	145	39	1	12	90	49	14	0	13	96	5	4	.482	.387
Reeves, Mike	L-R	6-2	195	9-16-90	.184	.308	.162	27	87	9	16	0	0	0	7	18	0	1	1	22	2	0	.184	.321
Tellez, Rowdy	L-L	6-4	245	3-16-95	.296	.194	.327	68	270	36	80	19	0	7	49	24	1	0	4	56	2	2	.444	.351
Thomas, Lane	R-R	6-1	210	8-23-95	.114	.273	.042	9	35	1	4	2	0	0	2	3	0	0	0	10	1	0	.171	.184
Thon, Dickie Joe	R-R	6-2	190	11-16-91	.315	.250	.353	15	54	9	17	3	1	2	12	6	2	2	0	18	4	2	.519	.403
Urena, Richard	L-R	6-1	170	2-26-96	.266	.217	.281	91	384	62	102	13	4	15	58	13	2	3	6	84	5	5	.438	.289
Vazquez, Christian	B-R	5-10	170	9-11-89	.243	.206	.260	30	107	7	26	5	1	1	8	4	4	1	0	28	0	0	.336	.296

Pitching	B-T	HT	WT	DOB	W	L	ERA	G	GS	CG	SV	IP	H	R	ER	HR	BB	SO	AVG	vLH	vRH	K/9	BB/9
Biggs, Mark	R-R	6-3	210	5-10-93	4	3	4.28	33	0	0	1	61	75	35	29	2	23	43	.305	.307	.303	6.34	3.39
Case, Andrew	R-R	6-2	190	1-6-93	2	2	3.32	12	0	0	1	22	25	8	8	4	6	15	.305	.360	.281	6.23	2.49
Dawson, Shane	R-L	6-1	200	9-9-93	12	4	3.01	19	17	0	0	102	95	41	34	7	24	98	.253	.183	.272	8.68	2.12
DeJong, Chase	R-R	6-4	205	12-29-93	7	4	3.13	14	14	1	0	86	75	36	30	9	18	77	.231	.225	.236	8.03	1.88
Fernandez, Jose	L-L	6-3	170	2-13-93	1	2	3.31	35	0	0	12	52	54	22	19	1	16	41	.273	.305	.259	7.14	2.79
Fisk, Conor	R-R	6-2	210	4-4-92	3	3	4.31	10	7	0	0	54	55	26	26	6	12	32	.264	.350	.211	5.30	1.99
Gonzalez, Alonzo	L-L	6-5	212	1-15-92	1	0	3.09	3	0	0	1	12	8	5	4	0	4	17	.186	.091	.219	13.11	3.09
Gracesqui, Francisco	L-L	6-0	185	11-26-91	0	0	0.00	2	0	0	0	2	0	0	0	0	0	5	.000	.000	.000	21.60	0.00
Greene, Conner	R-R	6-3	165	4-4-95	7	3	3.88	14	14	0	0	67	75	32	29	4	19	65	.285	.184	.345	8.69	2.54
Hollon, Clint	R-R	6-1	195	12-24-94	1	1	4.05	3	3	0	0	13	11	7	6	0	7	5	.224	.111	.364	3.38	4.73
Isaacs, Dusty	R-R	6-2	210		2	0	3.93	25	0	0	2	50	55	23	22	4	11	60	.285	.372	.303	10.73	1.97
Kish, Phil	R-R	5-10	185	8-30-89	1	4	5.67	30	0	0	7	40	59	30	25	2	13	29	.333	.382	.303	6.58	2.95
Kraft, Michael	L-L	5-11	175	9-3-91	0	1	8.10	6	0	0	1	7	4	7	6	1	5	5	.182	.000	.222	6.75	6.75
Mallard, Chase	R-R	6-2	185	11-22-91	6	8	5.49	29	15	0	4	123	154	78	75	10	37	86	.305	.309	.302	6.29	2.71
Mayza, Tim	L-L	6-3	220	1-15-92	3	2	3.07	26	1	0	3	56	49	21	19	0	27	62	.238	.310	.209	10.02	4.37
Ramirez, Carlos	R-R	6-5	205	4-24-91	2	1	4.73	28	0	0	8	32	38	18	17	2	14	30	.295	.204	.360	8.35	3.90
Reid-Foley, Sean	R-R	6-3	220	8-30-95	3	3	3.69	17	17	0	0	83	67	33	26	3	43	90	.239	.265	.221	12.79	6.11
Robson, Tom	R-R	6-4	210	6-27-93	0	2	5.06	7	7	0	0	27	31	18	15	2	14	21	.301	.282	.313	7.09	4.73
Shafer, Justin	R-R	6-2	195	9-18-92	7	4	2.96	16	7	0	0	73	61	28	24	3	22	42	.223	.194	.242	5.18	2.71
Stroman, Marcus	R-R	5-8	180	5-1-91	0	0	0.00	1	1	0	0	5	0	0	0	0	1	7	.000	.000	.000	13.50	1.93
Suriel, Starlyn	R-R	5-11	180	11-17-93	8	8	4.16	25	18	0	0	115	127	64	53	12	31	71	.284	.280	.287	5.57	2.43
Tinoco, Jesus	R-R	6-4	190	4-30-95	2	6	3.54	15	15	0	0	81	88	38	32	1	22	63	.271	.284	.263	7.52	2.43
Turner, Colton	L-L	6-3	215	11-17-91	0	3	4.02	31	0	0	2	65	72	39	29	2	28	52	.281	.284	.280	7.20	3.88
Wandling, Jon	R-R	6-3	205	5-28-92	1	0	4.08	3	3	0	0	18	14	10	8	0	10	8	.212	.200	.222	4.08	5.09
Wellbrock, Chase	L-R	5-10	200	1-6-92	0	0	6.23	3	0	0	0	6	4	4	3	0	1	1	.316	.000	.375	2.08	2.08

Fielding

Catcher	PCT	G	PO	A	E	DP	PB
Atkinson	1.000	3	9	0	0	0	0
Davis	1.000	1	0	1	0	0	0
De La Cruz	.987	60	413	40	6	5	18
Jansen	.987	46	338	29	5	6	2
Kelly	1.000	11	69	9	0	0	1
Reeves	.991	26	201	20	2	1	2

First Base	PCT	G	PO	A	E	DP
Atkinson	1.000	3	13	1	0	0
Davis	1.000	2	25	2	0	0
De La Cruz	1.000	3	26	1	0	4

First Base	PCT	G	PO	A	E	DP
Kelly	1.000	4	35	0	0	2
Leblebijian	.958	4	23	0	1	3
McBroom	.993	76	660	31	5	74
Tellez	.987	51	418	35	6	35

Second Base	PCT	G	PO	A	E	DP
Atkinson	1.000	6	15	17	0	3
Leblebijian	.984	31	46	81	2	12
Locastro	.973	65	122	166	8	35
Maldonado	1.000	7	10	19	0	7
Thomas	.841	8	14	23	7	7
Thon	1.000	4	6	12	0	2
Vazquez	.983	24	48	70	2	20

Third Base	PCT	G	PO	A	E	DP
Atkinson	.982	21	17	37	1	4
Davis	.912	13	6	25	3	2
Heidt	.970	47	33	95	4	6
Leblebijian	.972	19	11	24	1	2
Maldonado	.940	41	32	78	7	6
Vazquez	.944	6	5	12	1	1

Shortstop	PCT	G	PO	A	E	DP
Heidt	.938	4	3	12	1	4
Leblebijian	1.000	14	26	34	0	11
Lugo	.962	29	36	90	5	21
Thon	.706	4	4	8	5	2
Urena	.945	90	132	210	20	43

	Vazquez	.944	4	7	10	1	7
Outfield	PCT	G	PO	A	E	DP
Alford	.963	47	102	3	4	1
Almonte	.979	66	133	10	3	4
Atkinson	—	1	0	0	0	0
Carlson	.980	97	187	8	4	3
Collins	1.000	24	52	0	0	0
Davis	1.000	4	8	1	0	0
Davis	.957	121	238	5	11	1
Davis	.933	13	26	2	2	0
Harris	.971	34	59	8	2	0
McBroom	1.000	10	20	2	0	0
Thon	.857	5	5	1	1	0

VANCOUVER CANADIANS
SHORT-SEASON

NORTHWEST LEAGUE

Batting	B-T	HT	WT	DOB	AVG	vLH	vRH	G	AB	R	H	2B	3B	HR	RBI	BB	HBP	SH	SF	SO	SB	CS	SLG	OBP
Atkinson, Justin	R-R	6-1	218	7-24-93	.294	.317	.285	52	214	25	63	12	1	3	33	8	3	0	1	44	2	0	.402	.327
Burl, Earl	R-R	6-0	190	11-10-93	.216	.167	.245	50	148	17	32	8	1	0	15	18	2	1	0	42	9	5	.284	.310
Cardenas, J.C.	B-R	6-0	185	6-27-94	.179	.159	.188	44	140	20	25	3	1	2	16	28	1	1	2	36	3	2	.257	.316
Cenas, Gabriel	R-R	6-1	155	10-16-93	.171	.273	.125	23	70	5	12	2	1	2	5	4	1	0	0	26	0	1	.314	.227
Davis, Austin	L-R	5-10	170	4-26-93	.302	.111	.353	12	43	2	13	1	0	0	3	3	0	0	0	11	1	0	.326	.348
Garcia, Kevin	R-R	5-9	190	9-17-92	.255	.222	.270	36	110	10	28	5	0	0	9	14	2	1	1	19	1	0	.300	.346
Guillotte, Andrew	R-R	5-8	170	3-30-93	.251	.259	.248	51	191	34	48	8	1	3	14	21	10	1	0	25	17	4	.351	.356
Heidt, Gunnar	R-R	6-0	200	9-12-92	.233	.295	.208	57	215	31	50	8	0	3	26	21	1	5	2	47	18	2	.312	.301
Hissey, Ryan	L-R	6-0	190	4-8-94	.269	.390	.226	43	156	27	42	11	1	1	16	18	5	0	0	41	1	1	.372	.363
Hurley, Sean	R-R	6-4	235	5-5-92	.253	.241	.259	70	245	43	62	11	4	9	33	39	4	0	1	78	5	2	.441	.363
Kelly, Juan	L-R	5-10	155	7-16-94	.230	.176	.250	36	126	13	29	4	0	1	14	19	0	1	0	29	2	1	.286	.331
Lynch, James	L-R	6-2	195	4-5-92	.203	.083	.231	27	64	7	13	1	0	0	4	3	1	0	0	29	1	0	.219	.250
Maldonado, Alex	R-R	5-9	175	6-12-91	.333	.143	.455	5	18	0	6	0	1	0	6	0	1	0	1	3	6	0	.444	.350
Metzler, Ryan	R-R	6-3	190	3-20-93	.283	.313	.270	46	159	29	45	7	0	2	14	12	2	1	0	24	5	3	.365	.341
Orozco, Rodrigo	B-R	5-11	155	4-2-95	.333	.667	.167	3	9	2	3	2	0	0	4	4	0	0	0	1	1	0	.556	.538
Panas, Connor	L-R	6-0	218	2-11-93	.252	.205	.267	45	155	25	39	9	2	4	25	19	2	0	0	47	2	2	.413	.341
Reavis, Josh	R-R	6-2	200	9-11-91	.302	.333	.294	15	43	8	13	2	0	0	3	5	0	0	0	8	0	0	.349	.375
Segovia, Rolando	B-R	5-11	165	10-26-94	.203	.280	.159	24	69	5	14	3	2	0	7	3	2	2	1	25	5	2	.304	.253
Tejada, Juan	R-R	6-3	220	2-13-94	.200	.333	.125	9	25	6	5	1	0	0	2	1	1	1	1	7	1	1	.240	.250
Thomas, Lane	R-R	6-1	210	8-23-95	.225	.196	.237	43	169	20	38	13	0	5	33	8	1	0	5	34	5	4	.391	.257
Vazquez, Christian	B-R	5-10	170	9-11-89	.235	.300	.208	9	34	3	8	2	0	0	0	0	1	0	0	7	0	0	.294	.257
Wellman, Brett	L-R	6-0	200	11-22-91	.000	.000	.000	3	4	0	0	0	0	0	0	0	0	0	0	1	0	0	.000	.000
Wise, Carl	R-R	6-2	210	5-25-94	.231	.339	.179	47	182	18	42	9	1	1	26	8	2	0	2	43	0	0	.308	.268

Pitching	B-T	HT	WT	DOB	W	L	ERA	G	GS	CG	SV	IP	H	R	ER	HR	BB	SO	AVG	vLH	vRH	K/9	BB/9
Aquino, Joey	R-R	6-0	195	8-13-90	1	1	10.57	8	0	0	1	8	12	11	9	1	5	5	.375	.111	.478	5.87	5.87
Bergen, Travis	L-L	6-1	205	10-8-93	2	0	0.00	2	0	0	0	5	2	0	0	1	11	.111	.125	.100	18.56	1.69
Borucki, Ryan	L-L	6-4	175	3-31-94	0	1	3.86	2	2	0	0	5	6	2	2	0	3	6	.300	.000	.333	11.57	5.79
Burden, Tyler	L-R	6-1	195	3-25-94	0	0	0.00	2	0	0	0	2	1	0	0	0	1	1	.143	.000	.200	4.50	4.50
Case, Andrew	R-R	6-2	190	1-6-93	1	2	2.93	27	0	0	10	31	25	10	10	2	12	29	.221	.227	.217	8.51	3.52
Claver, Joe	L-L	6-2	170	10-9-91	0	0	3.00	7	0	0	0	6	3	2	2	0	8	3	.158	.167	.154	4.50	12.00
Cook, Ryan	R-R	6-1	210	5-4-93	1	0	3.93	6	1	0	1	18	20	11	8	0	20	.263	.296	.245	9.82	3.93
Degraaf, Josh	R-R	6-4	195	1-28-93	2	2	3.15	13	3	0	1	34	34	16	12	2	12	23	.268	.217	.296	6.03	3.15
Fisk, Conor	R-R	6-2	210	4-4-92	1	0	1.64	3	1	0	0	11	7	3	2	1	4	11	.167	.188	.154	9.00	3.27
Harris, Jon	R-R	6-3	160	10-16-93	0	5	6.75	12	11	0	0	36	48	31	27	1	21	32	.318	.333	.309	8.00	5.25
Hinkle, Brandon	L-R	5-11	180	11-15-90	5	1	1.14	20	0	0	1	39	24	7	5	2	8	33	.186	.214	.178	7.55	5.26
Hollon, Clint	R-R	6-1	195	12-24-94	2	2	3.18	9	9	0	0	45	37	18	16	1	15	40	.223	.237	.211	7.94	2.98
Holmes, Stuart	L-L	6-1	180	1-5-93	2	2	3.91	15	0	0	0	25	19	12	11	0	13	24	.207	.130	.250	8.53	4.62
Kraft, Michael	L-L	5-11	175	9-3-91	0	1	3.68	24	1	0	0	37	43	21	15	2	32	30	.293	.244	.311	7.36	7.85
Lee, Turner	R-L	6-3	215	8-30-91	2	1	3.38	23	1	0	1	35	29	15	13	1	7	20	.230	.154	.264	5.19	1.82
Lietz, Daniel	L-L	6-2	200	6-1-94	0	2	7.50	5	2	0	0	12	18	11	10	0	8	9	.346	.222	.372	6.75	6.00
McClelland, Jackson	R-R	6-5	220	7-9-94	0	0	5.06	3	1	0	0	5	4	3	3	0	4	2	.222	.000	.286	3.38	6.75
Perdomo, Angel	L-L	6-6	200	5-7-94	2	0	2.53	5	3	0	0	21	10	6	6	1	16	31	.152	.125	.160	13.08	6.75
Ratcliffe, Sean	L-R	6-4	200	4-11-95	2	2	3.60	22	1	0	0	40	36	19	16	1	16	30	.245	.225	.252	6.75	3.60
Rios, Francisco	R-R	6-1	180	5-6-95	3	6	4.27	15	12	0	0	65	72	36	31	1	25	59	.279	.350	.232	8.13	3.44
Robson, Tom	R-R	6-4	210	6-27-93	0	1	5.06	2	2	0	0	5	2	3	3	0	4	9	.111	.200	.000	15.19	6.75
Saucedo, Tayler	L-L	6-5	185	6-18-93	3	1	2.52	7	7	0	0	36	33	11	10	0	19	31	.244	.308	.219	7.82	4.79
Smith, Evan	R-L	6-5	190	8-17-95	2	4	4.71	13	12	0	0	50	63	35	26	5	18	27	.317	.212	.337	4.89	3.26
Wandling, Jon	R-R	6-3	205	5-28-92	1	3	4.66	11	6	0	0	46	55	29	24	3	11	34	.297	.273	.315	6.60	2.14
Wheatley, Bobby	L-L	6-5	215	2-4-92	2	2	4.99	23	0	0	1	31	36	18	17	5	17	27	.295	.233	.315	7.92	4.99
Young, Danny	L-L	6-2	195	5-27-94	1	1	6.33	15	1	0	0	27	43	19	19	3	12	8	.394	.250	.435	2.67	4.00

Fielding

Catcher	PCT	G	PO	A	E	DP	PB
Atkinson	1.000	3	15	1	0	2	0
Garcia	.985	34	235	27	4	1	2
Hissey	.992	34	226	32	2	1	3
Kelly	.964	4	22	5	1	0	1

	Reavis	.963	9	47	5	2	1	3
	Wellman	1.000	2	2	1	0	0	0
First Base	PCT	G	PO	A	E	DP	
Atkinson	.995	42	371	23	2	41	

	Cenas	.976	12	79	4	2	9
	Kelly	.983	20	167	9	3	21
	Panas	1.000	5	50	1	0	5

Second Base	PCT	G	PO	A	E	DP
Heidt	1.000	1	3	4	0	0
Metzler	.981	35	67	91	3	26
Segovia	.923	7	14	22	3	7
Thomas	.932	37	62	117	13	25

Third Base	PCT	G	PO	A	E	DP
Atkinson	1.000	7	4	20	0	2
Cenas	1.000	1	1	0	0	0
Heidt	.968	10	9	21	1	1
Maldonado	.882	5	2	13	2	1

Metzler	.952	9	9	11	1	1
Vazquez	1.000	4	2	5	0	0
Wise	.953	45	18	84	5	8

Shortstop	PCT	G	PO	A	E	DP
Cardenas	.940	42	62	111	11	33
Heidt	.943	30	38	94	8	25
Segovia	.714	1	3	2	2	2
Vazquez	.947	5	4	14	1	1
Wise	1.000	1	4	2	0	1

Outfield	PCT	G	PO	A	E	DP
Burl	.950	49	90	6	5	1
Davis	1.000	11	12	0	0	0
Guillotte	.976	50	111	9	3	1
Hurley	.981	69	150	2	3	0
Lynch	1.000	18	34	3	0	1
Orozco	1.000	3	6	0	0	0
Panas	.970	31	63	1	2	0
Segovia	1.000	8	12	1	0	0
Tejada	.917	9	11	0	1	0

BLUEFIELD BLUE JAYS
ROOKIE

APPALACHIAN LEAGUE

Batting	B-T	HT	WT	DOB	AVG	vLH	vRH	G	AB	R	H	2B	3B	HR	RBI	BB	HBP	SH	SF	SO	SB	CS	SLG	OBP
Anderson, Jake	R-R	6-4	190	11-22-92	.159	.182	.154	19	63	2	10	2	0	0	4	1	3	0	1	23	0	0	.190	.206
Attaway, Aaron	5-7	170		3-6-92	.216	.227	.212	28	88	12	19	2	0	2	12	9	2	1	2	25	2	1	.307	.297
Barreto, Deiferson	R-R	5-10	165	5-19-95	.302	.250	.314	51	189	20	57	8	1	3	26	11	2	4	0	25	4	2	.402	.347
Bell, Dean	R-R	5-9	175	10-14-92	.163	.133	.179	17	43	6	7	1	1	0	2	3	0	3	1	10	0	0	.233	.213
Clark, Gabe	R-R	6-0	220	10-5-94	.219	.200	.223	37	128	19	28	7	0	6	22	18	1	0	1	48	0	0	.414	.318
Fuentes, Edwin	R-R	6-0	170	8-14-94	.200	.250	.176	7	25	3	5	2	0	0	3	1	0	0	0	5	1	0	.280	.231
Gudino, Yeltsin	R-R	6-0	150	1-17-97	.185	.206	.181	56	211	21	39	12	1	1	13	17	2	2	1	36	2	2	.265	.251
Guillotte, Andrew	R-R	5-8	170	3-30-93	.229	.250	.222	13	48	6	11	2	0	1	7	5	3	0	0	8	2	1	.333	.339
McKnight, D.J.	L-R	5-11	190	1-29-94	.253	.150	.268	49	158	23	40	7	0	3	24	23	6	1	1	47	2	1	.354	.367
Morgan, Matt	R-R	5-1	190	1-27-96	.185	.167	.188	36	119	7	22	8	0	2	10	11	1	0	1	52	0	1	.303	.258
Orozco, Rodrigo	B-R	5-11	155	4-2-95	.300	.341	.291	58	223	34	67	16	1	4	25	24	0	7	0	35	4	3	.435	.368
Pepe, Dave	L-R	5-9	170	10-15-91	.222	.333	.214	23	45	11	10	1	0	0	4	6	1	2	1	7	0	2	.244	.321
Reavis, Josh	R-R	6-2	200	9-11-91	.238	.167	.267	9	21	1	5	0	0	0	4	0	0	0	0	6	0	0	.238	.360
Rodriguez, Freddy	L-R	6-1	180	11-15-96	.232	.111	.247	50	164	25	38	4	1	3	11	14	2	1	1	40	3	5	.323	.298
Romanin, Mattingly	R-R	5-10	185	2-27-93	.161	.130	.171	33	93	11	15	1	1	0	5	17	5	0	2	34	3	3	.194	.316
Sinay, Nick	R-R	5-10	175	11-4-93	.227	.217	.231	33	88	13	20	4	0	1	8	15	7	2	0	23	6	3	.307	.382
Sotillo, Andres	R-R	5-11	180	12-28-93	.250	.375	.214	26	72	11	18	1	2	2	13	9	6	1	1	16	1	0	.403	.375
Tejada, Juan	R-R	6-3	220	3-14-94	.230	.152	.258	36	122	21	28	5	1	6	15	9	0	0	1	38	6	2	.434	.280
Wellman, Brett	L-R	6-0	200	11-22-91	.286	.000	.308	10	14	1	4	0	0	0	4	0	0	0	0	5	0	0	.286	.444
Williams, Christian	L-R	6-1	205	9-14-94	.220	.219	.220	60	214	25	47	11	2	2	29	20	0	0	1	56	0	0	.318	.285
Wise, Carl	R-R	6-2	210	5-25-94	.258	.500	.200	7	31	7	8	2	0	0	5	2	0	0	0	6	0	0	.323	.303

Pitching	B-T	HT	WT	DOB	W	L	ERA	G	GS	CG	SV	IP	H	R	ER	HR	BB	SO	AVG	vLH	vRH	K/9	BB/9
Brentz, Jake	L-L	6-2	195	9-14-94	0	1	4.09	6	6	0	0	22	25	13	10	2	11	16	.294	.188	.319	6.55	4.50
Burden, Tyler	L-R	6-1	195	3-25-94	2	2	3.54	17	0	0	1	28	28	16	11	0	16	22	.272	.297	.258	7.07	5.14
Burgos, Miguel	L-L	5-9	155	6-16-95	1	2	3.48	13	5	0	1	41	45	22	16	5	20	33	.278	.309	.262	7.19	4.35
Claver, Joe	L-L	6-2	170	10-9-91	0	1	3.24	14	0	0	0	17	15	13	6	0	9	14	.227	.154	.275	7.56	4.86
Cox, Christian	L-R	6-4	200	4-22-92	0	1	81.00	2	0	0	0	1	3	7	6	0	4	0	.750	1.000	.500	0.00	54.00
Degraaf, Josh	R-R	6-4	195	1-28-93	0	0	3.86	4	0	0	0	9	7	5	4	1	1	11	.200	.267	.150	10.61	0.96
Encina, Geno	L-R	6-4	200	7-7-94	1	3	3.86	12	5	0	1	44	45	22	19	4	10	45	.259	.291	.227	9.14	2.03
Guzman, Alberto	R-R	6-1	180	12-7-92	3	4	4.07	16	0	0	4	24	27	13	11	3	9	22	.281	.354	.208	8.14	3.33
Higuera, Juliandry	L-L	6-1	180	9-6-94	5	4	4.26	13	13	0	0	61	80	34	29	3	20	40	.320	.377	.295	5.87	2.93
Holmes, Stuart	L-L	6-1	180	1-5-93	1	0	4.76	4	0	0	0	6	7	4	3	0	1	5	.318	.250	.357	7.94	1.59
Huffman, Grayson	L-L	6-2	195	5-6-95	0	0	10.54	9	0	0	0	14	26	18	16	0	10	8	.406	.500	.375	5.27	6.59
Kravetz, John	L-R	6-4	210	10-3-92	0	2	7.07	10	0	0	0	14	27	15	11	2	4	10	.391	.357	.415	6.43	2.57
Lietz, Daniel	L-L	6-2	200	6-1-94	0	2	5.26	10	3	0	0	26	17	16	15	0	23	11	.193	.167	.207	3.86	8.06
Lowery, Jackson	R-R	6-0	175	7-23-92	0	0	0.90	8	0	0	2	10	8	3	1	0	1	14	.211	.158	.263	12.60	0.90
Perdomo, Angel	L-L	6-6	200	5-7-94	4	1	2.63	9	9	0	0	48	42	20	14	3	14	36	.231	.250	.224	6.75	2.63
Rodgers, Zach	R-R	5-9	180	7-21-93	2	2	4.76	17	0	0	2	23	29	14	12	1	7	16	.322	.343	.309	6.35	2.78
Rodriguez, Dalton	R-R	6-1	180	8-20-96	2	8	5.25	12	12	0	0	60	68	40	35	5	20	28	.288	.302	.275	4.20	3.00
Sanchez, Luis	R-R	6-3	200	2-20-94	1	4	7.08	5	5	0	0	20	23	20	16	2	15	17	.288	.286	.289	7.52	6.64
Saucedo, Tayler	L-L	6-5	185	6-18-93	1	1	2.42	6	2	0	1	22	23	8	6	0	4	18	.253	.150	.282	7.25	1.61
Smoral, Matt	L-L	6-8	220	3-18-94	0	0	5.06	8	0	0	0	11	7	8	6	0	14	16	.175	.200	.167	13.50	11.81
Wasilewski, Zak	L-L	6-1	190	6-16-93	1	2	5.65	16	0	0	0	29	37	21	18	2	15	19	.314	.258	.333	5.97	4.71
Wells, Nick	L-L	6-5	185	2-21-96	1	2	4.78	7	7	0	0	32	30	17	17	4	11	31	.246	.233	.253	8.72	3.09

Fielding

Catcher	PCT	G	PO	A	E	DP	PB
Morgan	.985	35	233	25	4	1	21
Reavis	1.000	9	49	11	0	0	3
Sotillo	.981	25	139	12	3	0	7
Wellman	1.000	6	13	1	0	0	

First Base	PCT	G	PO	A	E	DP
Clark	.996	30	250	20	1	25
Fuentes	1.000	6	56	2	0	6
Williams	.989	33	259	14	3	26

Second Base	PCT	G	PO	A	E	DP
Attaway	1.000	11	22	37	0	10

Barreto	.965	33	60	106	6	27
Bell	.980	13	16	32	1	6
Romanin	.979	13	23	24	1	4

Third Base	PCT	G	PO	A	E	DP
Attaway	.667	4	3	1	2	0
Barreto	.889	17	7	41	6	3
Bell	.500	2	0	1	1	0
Fuentes	1.000	1	1	2	0	0
Romanin	.850	16	15	19	6	3
Williams	.870	24	10	37	7	6
Wise	.762	6	6	10	5	1

Shortstop	PCT	G	PO	A	E	DP
Attaway	.939	14	29	33	4	9
Gudino	.923	56	96	155	21	35

Outfield	PCT	G	PO	A	E	DP
Guillotte	1.000	11	24	2	0	0
McKnight	1.000	40	74	2	0	1
Orozco	.974	55	112	2	3	0
Pepe	1.000	11	5	0	0	0
Rodriguez	.974	39	71	4	2	0
Sinay	1.000	29	40	4	0	1
Tejada	.964	28	48	5	2	0

GCL BLUE JAYS
ROOKIE

GULF COAST LEAGUE

Batting	B-T	HT	WT	DOB	AVG	vLH	vRH	G	AB	R	H	2B	3B	HR	RBI	BB	HBP	SH	SF	SO	SB	CS	SLG	OBP
Almonte, Miguel	R-R	5-11	165	11-26-96	.127	.261	.071	29	79	3	10	1	0	0	5	7	2	1	0	31	0	1	.139	.216
Brantley, Cliff	L-R	5-9	175	9-15-92	.252	.333	.218	36	111	18	28	3	1	3	11	7	2	1	0	27	5	1	.378	.308
Chung, Derrick	R-R	5-9	175	2-23-88	.231	.000	.300	4	13	2	3	0	0	0	2	2	0	0	0	2	0	0	.231	.333
Florides, Andrew	R-R	6-1	170	1-22-95	.068	.133	.045	22	59	8	4	0	0	0	3	5	0	1	0	21	1	0	.068	.141
Hernandez, Javier	R-R	6-1	180	7-21-96	.200	.091	.238	39	85	10	17	2	0	2	14	4	4	2	2	29	0	0	.294	.263
Hissey, Ryan	L-R	6-0	190	4-8-94	.355	.429	.333	10	31	6	11	3	0	1	6	5	2	0	1	7	1	0	.548	.462
Jansen, Dan	R-R	6-2	230	4-15-95	.238	.200	.273	7	21	4	5	1	0	1	3	2	0	0	0	5	0	0	.429	.304
Jones, Lance	R-R	5-11	175	11-10-92	.299	.171	.354	36	117	19	35	3	3	1	16	26	5	2	0	25	6	2	.402	.446
Knight, Nash	L-R	6-0	195	9-20-92	.207	.179	.218	47	140	17	29	5	0	2	18	28	0	0	4	39	2	1	.286	.331
La Prise, John	L-R	6-2	180	8-24-93	.000	—	—	1	2	0	0	0	0	0	0	0	0	0	0	0	0	0	.000	.000
Lizardo, Bryan	B-R	6-0	205	7-26-97	.193	.182	.198	43	140	13	27	6	1	0	17	12	0	0	1	53	3	0	.250	.255
Lucido, Robert	R-R	5-10	175	12-11-92	.259	.400	.227	16	27	8	7	2	1	0	1	10	0	0	0	8	1	0	.407	.459
May, Kalik	B-R	6-2	205	10-5-92	.261	.226	.271	42	138	24	36	6	4	2	12	19	7	0	1	42	10	3	.406	.376
Mendoza, Juandy	R-R	5-10	190	10-10-94	.193	.176	.200	42	119	12	23	6	0	1	13	15	7	4	1	42	10	1	.269	.317
Olivares, Edward	R-R	6-2	186	3-6-96	.198	.200	.198	38	116	21	23	8	1	3	10	11	15	0	0	27	14	2	.362	.345
Panas, Connor	L-R	6-0	218	2-11-93	.391	.375	.400	6	23	5	9	1	0	1	4	2	1	0	0	3	1	0	.565	.462
Pruitt, Reggie	R-R	6-0	169	5-7-97	.223	.275	.198	36	121	23	27	6	1	0	12	12	4	5	2	37	15	2	.289	.309
Scott, Levi	R-R	6-4	215	8-4-92	.205	.325	.165	48	161	19	33	8	0	1	18	27	0	0	2	41	2	0	.273	.316
Severino, Jesus	L-R	6-1	175	6-11-97	.198	.115	.229	33	96	13	19	4	1	0	15	13	4	1	1	30	1	1	.260	.316
Spiwak, Owen	L-R	6-2	180	5-23-95	.293	.235	.308	31	82	5	24	0	0	1	9	4	2	0	1	14	1	1	.329	.337
Thomas, Jake	R-R	5-10	190	7-21-93	.263	.317	.243	47	156	25	41	3	2	3	20	28	6	2	1	34	6	2	.365	.393

Pitching	B-T	HT	WT	DOB	W	L	ERA	G	GS	CG	SV	IP	H	R	ER	HR	BB	SO	AVG	vLH	vRH	K/9	BB/9
Abel, Nate	L-L	6-1	190	11-2-92	2	0	2.61	14	0	0	1	31	26	10	9	2	14	27	.230	.370	.186	7.84	4.06
Barnett, Hunter	L-L	6-3	205	8-13-94	1	0	0.00	3	0	0	0	3	3	1	0	0	1	1	.231	.200	.250	2.70	2.70
Borucki, Ryan	L-L	6-4	175	3-31-94	0	0	0.00	1	0	0	0	1	1	0	0	0	0	1	.250	.500	.000	9.00	0.00
Chavez, Lupe	R-R	6-2	150	12-3-97	3	1	2.37	4	3	0	0	19	16	5	5	0	6	14	.225	.206	.243	6.63	2.84
Cook, Ryan	R-R	6-1	210	5-4-93	2	2	1.84	11	0	0	2	15	15	4	3	0	5	17	.254	.250	.257	10.43	3.07
Diaz, Denis	R-R	6-1	180	11-20-94	4	1	3.58	10	7	0	0	38	32	18	15	3	22	31	.232	.189	.259	7.41	5.26
Diaz, Yennsy	R-R	6-1	160	11-15-96	1	1	4.74	5	3	0	1	19	24	11	10	0	7	19	.316	.238	.345	9.00	3.32
Eastman, Gunnar	R-R	6-1	195	11-13-91	1	0	5.40	14	0	0	0	25	24	16	15	0	20	15	.273	.303	.255	5.40	7.20
Espada, Jose	R-R	6-0	170	2-22-97	0	2	3.41	10	7	0	0	34	25	15	13	3	8	31	.198	.159	.220	8.13	2.10
Estevez, Mike	L-R	6-0	170	9-27-92	3	0	1.38	18	0	0	9	26	22	6	4	0	9	32	.222	.323	.176	11.08	3.12
Glaude, Griffin	R-R	5-9	175	4-6-92	3	1	2.20	16	0	0	5	29	14	9	7	1	7	37	.140	.167	.129	11.62	2.20
Gutierrez, Osman	R-R	6-4	185	12-15-94	4	3	4.66	11	9	0	0	46	50	29	24	3	15	41	.273	.293	.257	7.96	2.91
Jose, Kelyn	L-L	6-4	195	5-19-95	0	0	3.51	15	0	0	0	26	21	17	10	0	16	26	.219	.143	.250	9.12	5.61
Kravetz, John	L-R	6-4	220	10-3-92	2	1	0.90	4	0	0	0	10	9	2	1	1	5	9	.243	.211	.278	8.10	4.50
Lee, Mike	R-R	6-7	235	11-18-86	0	0	0.00	2	2	0	0	4	5	1	0	0	0	4	.294	.375	.222	9.82	0.00
Lopez, Wilton	R-R	6-0	200	7-19-83	0	1	27.00	1	0	0	0	1	6	4	4	1	0	1	.600	.000	.667	6.75	0.00
Lowery, Jackson	R-R	6-0	175	7-23-92	0	0	1.42	3	0	0	0	6	8	1	1	0	0	7	.296	.300	.294	9.95	0.00
Maese, Justin	R-R	6-3	190	10-24-96	5	0	1.01	8	4	1	0	36	32	5	4	0	6	19	.241	.273	.218	4.79	1.51
Meza, Juan	R-R	6-2	172	2-4-98	1	0	10.80	4	1	0	0	5	6	6	6	1	8	8	.286	.286	.286	14.40	14.40
Murphy, Griffin	R-L	6-3	230	1-16-91	0	0	0.00	2	2	0	0	3	0	0	0	0	1	4	.000	.000	.000	12.00	3.00
Murphy, Patrick	R-R	6-4	195	6-10-95	—																		
Nova, Jose	L-L	6-1	170	4-6-95	1	1	4.15	5	3	0	0	17	17	9	8	1	7	13	.258	.200	.268	6.75	3.63
Nunez, Juan	R-R	6-2	185	1-23-96	4	1	1.93	8	1	0	0	14	7	5	3	0	4	10	.149	.150	.148	6.43	2.57
Robson, Tom	R-R	6-4	210	6-27-93	0	0	3.86	3	2	0	0	5	9	2	2	1	1	6	.391	.400	.500	9.64	1.93
Rodriguez, Hansel	R-R	6-2	170	2-27-97	1	2	4.68	10	7	1	0	42	48	25	22	1	10	37	.286	.297	.277	7.87	2.13
Sanchez, Aaron	R-R	6-4	200	7-1-92	0	0	9.00	1	1	0	0	2	3	2	2	0	1	1	.375	.500	.333	4.50	4.50
Sanchez, Luis	R-R	6-3	200	2-20-94	1	0	2.97	7	5	0	0	33	33	13	11	0	12	26	.266	.277	.260	7.02	3.24
Silverstein, Scott	L-L	6-6	260	5-27-90	0	0	6.00	2	1	0	0	3	5	2	2	1	0	4	.385	.400	.375	12.00	0.00
Torres, Jonathan	L-L	6-4	190	12-31-94	0	2	8.53	5	0	0	0	6	8	7	6	0	5	5	.320	.500	.304	7.11	7.11

Fielding

Catcher	PCT	G	PO	A	E	DP	PB
Chung	1.000	4	21	6	0	0	2
Hernandez	.991	39	192	27	2	1	4
Hissey	1.000	3	16	3	0	0	1
Jansen	1.000	5	32	3	0	0	1
Lucido	.941	4	16	0	1	0	1
Spiwak	.988	31	164	7	2	0	11

First Base	PCT	G	PO	A	E	DP
Knight	.984	19	122	4	2	11
Mendoza	1.000	1	2	0	0	0
Panas	1.000	2	17	1	0	1

Scott	.986	45	333	23	5	29

Second Base	PCT	G	PO	A	E	DP
Almonte	.965	28	46	65	4	17
Knight	.971	11	7	27	1	5
Mendoza	.981	29	42	64	2	11

Third Base	PCT	G	PO	A	E	DP
Knight	.913	23	11	31	4	4
Lizardo	.942	42	19	62	5	4
Mendoza	1.000	1	0	1	0	0

Shortstop	PCT	G	PO	A	E	DP
Florides	.882	21	28	47	10	10
Mendoza	.956	12	29	36	3	11
Severino	.922	30	45	74	10	13

Outfield	PCT	G	PO	A	E	DP
Brantley	.950	24	34	4	2	0
Jones	.986	28	66	2	1	0
May	.963	38	75	3	3	2
Olivares	.969	35	60	2	2	1
Panas	1.000	1	2	0	0	0
Pruitt	.925	33	74	0	6	0
Thomas	1.000	20	32	1	0	0

DOMINICAN SUMMER LEAGUE

TORONTO BLUE JAYS

Batting	B-T	HT	WT	DOB	AVG	vLH	vRH	G	AB	R	H	2B	3B	HR	RBI	BB	HBP	SH	SF	SO	SB	CS	SLG	OBP
Almanzar, Jean	R-R	6-0	150	2-12-95	.250	.000	.286	14	24	4	6	1	0	0	2	4	0	0	0	7	0	0	.292	.357
Buelens, Sam	R-R	5-11	160	12-27-95	.232	.188	.241	42	99	20	23	2	0	0	10	13	5	4	1	22	0	2	.253	.347
Concepcion, Antonio	R-R	6-0	190	6-16-97	.290	.250	.295	35	69	11	20	5	1	1	6	9	3	0	0	12	0	0	.435	.395
Concepcion, Ronald	R-R	6-0	170	4-19-97	.000	.000	.000	2	2	1	0	0	0	0	0	3	0	0	0	2	1	0	.000	.600
Figuereo, Victor	R-R	6-1	180	5-24-97	.146	.091	.162	19	48	8	7	0	0	2	6	7	0	0	0	24	3	0	.271	.255
Fuentes, Antony	R-R	5-11	160	9-26-95	.294	.389	.276	62	235	37	69	11	5	1	41	17	6	1	10	18	15	2	.396	.343
Green, Anderson	B-R	6-1	170	1-2-97	.333	.000	.368	8	21	3	7	0	0	0	3	1	1	0	0	3	0	0	.333	.391
Guerra, Andres	R-R	5-11	175	6-3-97	.146	.067	.192	23	41	5	6	2	0	0	1	10	0	0	0	12	2	1	.195	.314
Guzman, Sterling	R-R	5-11	175	2-2-98	.285	.237	.294	65	256	62	73	8	7	2	40	37	4	3	1	46	9	3	.395	.383
Herazo, Manuel	B-R	5-10	175	3-17-95	.282	.409	.260	48	149	26	42	7	0	0	15	23	9	3	0	32	6	6	.329	.409
Moreta, Enmanuel	R-R	6-3	215	2-8-95	.260	.296	.252	44	146	31	38	3	2	3	19	16	11	1	2	47	2	1	.370	.371
Navarro, Jesus	R-R	5-11	160	1-13-98	.250	.160	.273	67	248	39	62	5	2	0	33	33	5	1	3	40	9	7	.286	.346
Obeso, Norberto	L-R	6-0	175	7-9-95	.351	.300	.360	71	262	48	92	12	4	0	47	58	5	6	5	20	8	3	.427	.470
Peguero, Cristian	R-R	6-2	190	11-16-95	.277	.269	.279	54	166	30	46	5	3	1	20	20	5	3	0	42	6	5	.361	.372
Rodriguez, Francisco	R-R	6-1	220	9-22-94	.251	.289	.242	61	199	39	50	6	2	9	35	45	8	0	2	52	4	4	.437	.406
Rodriguez, Yorman	R-R	5-10	160	7-23-97	.335	.250	.350	61	209	35	70	9	5	2	45	20	9	2	2	17	12	4	.455	.413
Severino, Jesus	L-R	6-1	175	6-11-97	.354	.333	.359	14	48	13	17	2	0	0	2	11	1	0	0	10	1	2	.396	.483
Vicuna, Kevin	L-R	6-0	140	1-14-98	.268	.240	.275	62	250	43	67	3	0	0	20	17	17	6	1	29	10	4	.304	.354

Pitching	B-T	HT	WT	DOB	W	L	ERA	G	GS	CG	SV	IP	H	R	ER	HR	BB	SO	AVG	vLH	vRH	K/9	BB/9
Acosta, Jose	R-R	6-2	180	11-13-96	3	2	5.56	16	1	0	3	23	23	17	14	0	20	16	.267	.368	.239	6.35	7.94
Agrinzones, Jose	R-R	6-3	175	8-31-97	0	0	5.68	7	0	0	0	6	6	4	0	10	8	.240	.000	.286	11.37	14.21
Aleton, Wilfri	L-L	6-3	165	11-18-95	4	3	2.83	14	14	0	0	64	64	30	20	0	13	45	.252	.244	.254	6.36	1.84
Chavez, Lupe	R-R	6-2	150	12-3-97	4	1	2.98	10	10	0	0	42	40	20	14	0	14	45	.250	.239	.254	9.57	2.98
De La Cruz, Guillermo	L-L	6-1	170	5-13-97	2	0	3.51	16	0	0	0	33	26	17	13	4	17	22	.218	.182	.227	5.94	4.59
Diaz, Pedro	R-R	6-1	187	12-10-94	0	2	3.38	4	0	0	0	5	5	3	2	0	8	2	.263	.200	.286	3.38	13.50
Diaz, Yennsy	R-R	6-1	160	11-15-96	3	3	1.93	10	6	0	0	37	30	14	8	0	16	39	.217	.077	.250	9.40	3.86
Dominguez, Jose	R-R	6-2	165	2-21-96	3	0	1.08	7	0	0	0	17	9	2	2	0	10	17	.161	.235	.128	9.18	5.40
Dominguez, Manuel	R-R	6-5	230	1-17-94	0	0	24.00	4	0	0	0	3	4	8	8	0	10	4	.333	.000	.444	12.00	30.00
Espinal, Joel	R-R	6-2	185	8-15-96	1	2	2.18	19	4	0	2	54	39	20	13	2	19	46	.202	.250	.180	7.71	3.19
Galindo, Alvaro	R-R	6-2	170	2-20-95	2	0	1.82	18	0	0	3	35	26	12	7	1	15	31	.206	.171	.224	8.05	3.89
Henriquez, Tommy	R-R	6-0	173	7-31-95	1	1	4.50	13	0	0	1	28	35	21	14	3	9	25	.304	.324	.296	8.04	2.89
Herdenez, Yonardo	R-R	6-1	170	9-20-95	4	3	3.07	11	9	0	0	44	45	30	15	0	8	24	.259	.189	.289	4.91	1.64
Jimenez, Dany	R-R	6-3	190	12-23-93	1	0	5.19	3	0	0	1	9	6	5	5	2	4	12	.188	.111	.217	12.46	4.15
Lara, Wilmin	R-R	6-2	175	6-5-94	3	2	3.48	15	0	0	2	21	17	14	8	1	8	20	.227	.259	.208	8.71	3.48
Mendoza, Luis	R-R	6-3	175	10-4-95	0	0	6.75	3	0	0	1	3	3	3	2	0	1	3	.273	.400	.167	10.13	3.38
Meza, Juan	R-R	6-2	172	2-4-98	0	0	6.66	7	5	0	1	26	30	23	19	1	14	21	.297	.286	.301	7.36	4.91
Mueses, Wilton	R-R	6-2	190	5-19-95	1	0	4.50	6	0	0	0	6	4	3	3	0	11	6	.200	.200	9.00	16.50	
Nova, Jose	L-L	6-1	170	4-6-95	3	4	1.74	9	9	0	0	41	34	18	8	0	6	27	.219	.194	.226	5.88	1.31
Nunez, Juan	R-R	6-2	185	1-23-96	1	0	6.15	12	5	0	2	26	26	22	18	0	16	20	.245	.296	.228	6.84	5.47
Pascual, Orlando	R-R	6-3	210	11-7-95	2	0	0.68	5	1	0	1	13	11	1	1	0	1	9	.224	.167	.243	6.08	0.68
Rosario, Jairo	R-R	6-4	190	10-21-93	2	3	1.63	19	5	0	4	55	37	24	10	1	25	44	.187	.155	.200	7.16	4.07
Silva, Elio	L-L	5-11	160	8-21-95	1	1	1.62	5	1	0	0	17	12	7	3	0	4	16	.182	.200	.176	8.64	2.16
Torres, Jonathan	L-L	6-4	190	12-31-94	2	0	0.90	5	2	0	0	20	9	5	2	0	12	19	.136	.167	.130	8.55	5.40
Ventura, Ruben	R-R	6-2	183	12-8-94	2	0	1.72	7	0	0	1	16	7	3	3	0	6	24	.137	.133	.139	13.79	3.45

Fielding

Catcher	PCT	G	PO	A	E	DP	PB
Concepcion	.981	10	47	4	1	0	5
Guerra	.967	16	83	5	3	0	3
Herazo	.975	48	308	40	9	2	15
Rodriguez	.981	17	96	8	2	0	7

First Base	PCT	G	PO	A	E	DP
Moreta	.913	6	40	2	4	4
Rodriguez	.969	41	336	11	11	28
Rodriguez	.997	33	282	11	1	21

Second Base	PCT	G	PO	A	E	DP
Almanzar	.914	10	15	17	3	4
Concepcion	1.000	2	3	3	0	1
Green	.857	5	8	4	2	2

	PCT	G	PO	A	E	DP
Guzman	.978	9	22	23	1	6
Navarro	.944	47	86	117	12	17
Vicuna	.917	6	10	23	3	2

Third Base	PCT	G	PO	A	E	DP
Almanzar	—	1	0	0	0	0
Green	1.000	3	2	2	0	0
Guzman	.926	55	45	130	14	11
Moreta	.833	9	6	24	6	2
Navarro	.960	8	3	21	1	0
Vicuna	.500	1	1	2	3	0

Shortstop	PCT	G	PO	A	E	DP
Almanzar	1.000	2	1	1	0	0
Navarro	.947	16	20	52	4	9

	PCT	G	PO	A	E	DP
Severino	.872	10	13	28	6	2
Vicuna	.912	50	80	147	22	21

Outfield	PCT	G	PO	A	E	DP
Almanzar	—	1	0	0	0	0
Buelens	1.000	38	54	2	0	0
Figuereo	.969	17	28	3	1	1
Fuentes	.977	62	120	6	3	3
Obeso	.990	71	92	4	1	3
Peguero	.960	53	94	2	4	0
Rodriguez	1.000	1	3	0	0	0

Washington Nationals

SEASON IN A SENTENCE: Prohibitive favorites in the NL East entering the season, the Nationals were undone by several injuries and an ineffective bullpen, even as Bryce Harper fulfilled his immense potential and was named BA's Player of the Year in his age-22 season.

HIGH POINT: From June 19 to July 5, the Nationals won 12 of 15 games to open a four and a half game lead on the Mets in the NL East. The stretch included Max Scherzer coming within a strike of throwing a perfect game and settling instead for the first of his two no-hitters on the year, a seven-game winning streak and a sweep of the defending champion Giants.

LOW POINT: In their penultimate home game of the season, having already been eliminated from playoff contention, closer Jonathan Papelbon and Harper got into a fight in the dugout. Papelbon, despite choking Harper, returned to the mound in the top of the ninth in a tie game. He gave up five runs, took the loss and was then suspended for the remainder of the season.

NOTABLE ROOKIES: Injuries to outfielders Denard Span and Jayson Werth created opportunity for Michael Taylor in the Nationals outfield. The 24-year-old hit .229/.282/.358 with 14 home runs and 16 stolen bases. Righthander Joe Ross established himself as one of the Nationals best starters, supplanting Doug Fister in the rotation. He went 5-5, 3.64 with 69 strikeouts in 76 ⅔ innings.

KEY TRANSACTIONS: The Nationals signed Scherzer to a seven-year, $210 million deal in the offseason, giving them another ace for their rotation. He lived up to the deal, going 14-12, 2.79 in 33 starts. He led baseball with four compete games and an 8.12 strikeout-to-walk ratio. The Nationals also were a part of a three-team offseason trade that sent outfielder Steven Souza to the Rays and brought back Ross and shortstop Trea Turner from the Padres.

DOWN ON THE FARM: Righthander Lucas Giolito continued to look like one of the best pitchers in the minor leagues. He pitched his way to Double-A Harrisburg and finished the season with 131 strikeouts in 117 innings, both career highs. Outfielder Victor Robles broke out in his U.S. debut. The 18-year-old hit .352/.445/.507 with four home runs and 24 stolen bases in 61 games between the Gulf Coast League and short-season Auburn.

OPENING DAY PAYROLL: $164,920,505 (6th)

PLAYERS OF THE YEAR

WILL BENTZEL/HARRISBURG SENATORS

MAJOR LEAGUE	MINOR LEAGUE
Bryce Harper, of	**Austin Voth, rhp (Double-A)**
.330/.460/.649, 42 HR, 99 RBI, 118 R, 124 BB for MLB Player of the Year	6-7, 2.92 148 strikeouts in 157 innings

ORGANIZATION LEADERS

BATTING *Minimum 250 AB

MAJORS

*AVG	Bryce Harper	.330
*OPS	Bryce Harper	1.109
HR	Bryce Harper	42
RBI	Bryce Harper	99

MINORS

*AVG	Jose Marmolejos-Diaz, Hagerstown	.310
*OBP	Jose Marmolejos-Diaz, Hagerstown	.363
*SLG	Jose Marmolejos-Diaz, Hagerstown	.485
R	Osvaldo Abreu, Hagerstown	74
H	Jose Marmolejos-Diaz, Hagerstown	145
TB	Jose Marmolejos-Diaz, Hagerstown	227
2B	Jose Marmolejos-Diaz, Hagerstown	39
3B	Bryan Mejia, Auburn, Hagerstown	9
HR	Matt Skole, Harrisburg, Syracuse	20
RBI	Jose Marmolejos-Diaz, Hagerstown	87
BB	Matt Skole, Harrisburg, Syracuse	72
SO	Jason Martinson, Syracuse	189
SB	Christopher Bostick, Potomac, Harrisburg	31

PITCHING #Minimum 75 IP

MAJORS

W	Max Scherzer	14
#ERA	Max Scherzer	2.79
SO	Max Scherzer	276
SV	Drew Storen	29

MINORS

W	Richard Bleier, Harrisburg, Syracuse	14
L	Taylor Hill, Syracuse	10
	Jefry Rodriguez, Auburn, Hagerstown	10
#ERA	Richard Bleier, Harrisburg, Syracuse	2.57
G	Sam Runion, Harrisburg, Syracuse	48
GS	Austin Voth, Harrisburg	27
SV	Rafael Martin, Syracuse	12
	Francys Peguero, DSL Nationals	12
IP	Richard Bleier, Harrisburg, Syracuse	172
BB	Connor Bach, Hagerstown	69
SO	Austin Voth, Harrisburg	148
AVG	Austin Voth, Harrisburg	.230

WASHINGTON NATIONALS

General Manager: Mike Rizzo. **Farm Director:** Mark Scialabba. **Scouting Director:** Kris Kline.

Class	Team	League	W	L	PCT	Finish	Manager
Majors	Washington Nationals	National	83	79	.512	6th (15)	Matt Williams
Triple-A	Syracuse Chiefs	International	66	78	.458	10 (14)	Billy Gardner
Double-A	Harrisburg Senators	Eastern	67	75	.472	10th (12)	Brian Daubach
High A	Potomac Nationals	Carolina	65	74	.468	6th (8)	Tripp Keister
Low A	Hagerstown Suns	South Atlantic	68	70	.493	8th (14)	Patrick Anderson
Short season	Auburn Doubledays	New York-Penn	36	38	.486	9th (14)	Gary Cathcart
Rookie	Nationals	Gulf Coast	24	34	.414	14th (16)	Michael Barrett
Overall 2015 Minor League Record			326	369	.469	24th (30)	

ORGANIZATION STATISTICS

WASHINGTON NATIONALS

NATIONAL LEAGUE

Batting	B-T	HT	WT	DOB	AVG	vLH	vRH	G	AB	R	H	2B	3B	HR	RBI	BB	HBP	SH	SF	SO	SB	CS	SLG	OBP
Burriss, Emmanuel	B-R	6-0	190	1-17-85	.667	—	.667	5	3	2	2	0	0	0	0	2	0	0	0	0	0	0	.667	.800
den Dekker, Matt	L-L	6-1	210	8-10-87	.253	.154	.267	55	99	12	25	6	1	5	12	9	0	2	0	20	0	1	.485	.315
Desmond, Ian	R-R	6-3	215	9-20-85	.233	.248	.230	156	583	69	136	27	2	19	62	45	3	6	4	187	13	5	.384	.290
Difo, Wilmer	B-R	6-0	195	4-2-92	.182	.000	.250	15	11	1	2	0	0	0	0	0	0	0	0	2	0	0	.182	.182
Escobar, Yunel	R-R	6-2	215	11-2-82	.314	.314	.314	139	535	75	168	25	1	9	56	45	8	1	2	70	2	2	.415	.375
Espinosa, Danny	B-R	6-0	210	4-25-87	.240	.261	.233	118	367	59	88	21	1	13	37	33	6	3	3	106	5	2	.409	.311
Harper, Bryce	L-R	6-3	215	10-16-92	.330	.318	.335	153	521	118	172	38	1	42	99	124	5	0	4	131	6	4	.649	.460
Johnson, Reed	R-R	5-10	180	12-8-76	.227	.200	.235	17	22	0	5	1	0	0	3	0	1	0	1	6	0	0	.273	.250
Lobaton, Jose	B-R	6-1	215	10-21-84	.199	.118	.210	44	136	11	27	4	0	3	20	15	1	1	2	40	0	0	.294	.279
Moore, Tyler	R-R	6-2	220	1-30-87	.203	.204	.203	97	187	14	38	12	0	6	27	11	1	0	1	45	0	0	.364	.250
Ramos, Wilson	R-R	6-0	230	8-10-87	.229	.233	.228	128	475	41	109	16	0	15	68	21	0	0	8	101	0	0	.358	.258
Rendon, Anthony	R-R	6-1	210	6-6-90	.264	.311	.252	80	311	43	82	16	0	5	25	36	4	0	4	70	1	2	.363	.344
Robinson, Clint	L-L	6-5	245	2-16-85	.272	.424	.254	126	309	44	84	15	1	10	34	37	5	0	1	52	0	0	.424	.358
Severino, Pedro	R-R	6-2	200	7-20-93	.250	—	.250	2	4	1	1	0	0	0	0	0	0	0	0	1	0	0	.500	.250
Span, Denard	L-L	6-0	210	2-27-84	.301	.197	.335	61	246	38	74	17	0	5	22	25	1	1	2	26	11	0	.431	.365
Taylor, Michael A.	R-R	6-3	210	3-26-91	.229	.240	.226	138	472	49	108	15	2	14	63	35	1	1	2	158	16	3	.358	.282
Turner, Trea	R-R	6-1	175	6-30-93	.225	.375	.188	27	40	5	9	1	0	1	4	0	0	0	1	12	2	2	.325	.295
Uggla, Dan	R-R	5-11	210	3-11-80	.183	.237	.159	67	120	12	22	4	2	2	16	19	1	0	1	40	0	1	.300	.298
Werth, Jayson	R-R	6-5	240	5-20-79	.221	.218	.221	88	331	45	73	16	1	12	42	38	3	0	6	84	0	1	.384	.302
Zimmerman, Ryan	R-R	6-3	220	9-28-84	.249	.330	.220	95	346	43	86	25	1	16	73	33	1	0	10	79	1	0	.465	.308

Pitching	B-T	HT	WT	DOB	W	L	ERA	G	GS	CG	SV	IP	H	R	ER	HR	BB	SO	AVG	vLH	vRH	K/9	BB/9
Barrett, Aaron	R-R	6-3	225	1-2-88	3	3	4.60	40	0	0	0	29	28	15	15	1	7	35	.248	.200	.269	10.74	2.15
Carpenter, David	R-R	6-2	230	7-15-85	0	0	1.50	8	0	0	0	6	5	1	1	1	2	4	.217	.250	.200	6.00	3.00
Cedeno, Xavier	L-L	6-0	215	8-26-86	0	0	6.00	5	0	0	0	3	3	2	2	1	2	4	.250	.200	.286	12.00	6.00
Cole, A.J.	R-R	6-5	200	1-5-92	0	0	5.79	3	1	0	1	9	14	11	6	1	1	9	.341	.370	.286	8.68	0.96
De Los Santos, Abel	R-R	6-2	200	11-31-92	0	0	5.40	2	0	0	0	2	2	1	1	1	3	.286	.333	.250	16.20	5.40
Fister, Doug	L-R	6-8	210	2-4-84	5	7	4.19	25	15	0	1	103	120	56	48	14	24	63	.295	.265	.327	5.50	2.10
Gonzalez, Gio	R-L	6-0	210	9-19-85	11	8	3.79	31	31	0	0	176	181	79	74	8	69	169	.269	.258	.272	8.66	3.54
Grace, Matt	L-L	6-3	205	12-14-88	2	1	4.24	26	0	0	0	17	26	11	8	0	8	14	.356	.289	.429	7.41	4.24
Hill, Taylor	R-R	6-3	230	3-12-89	0	0	3.75	6	0	0	0	12	14	5	5	2	4	9	.304	.417	.182	6.75	3.00
Janssen, Casey	R-R	6-4	205	9-17-81	2	5	4.95	48	0	0	0	40	38	22	22	5	8	27	.248	.176	.284	6.08	1.80
Jordan, Taylor	R-R	6-5	210	1-17-89	0	2	5.29	4	1	0	0	17	20	10	10	0	6	11	.290	.289	.290	5.82	3.18
Martin, Rafael	R-R	6-3	220	5-16-84	2	0	5.11	13	0	0	0	12	12	9	7	4	5	25	.245	.357	.200	18.24	3.65
Papelbon, Jonathan	R-R	6-4	225	11-23-80	2	2	3.04	22	0	0	7	24	22	13	8	4	4	16	.247	.280	.205	6.08	1.52
2-team total (37 Philadelphia)					4	3	2.13	59	0	0	24	63	53	22	15	7	12	56	—	—	—	7.96	1.71
Rivero, Felipe	L-L	6-2	200	7-5-91	2	1	2.79	49	0	0	2	48	35	15	15	2	11	43	.199	.198	.200	8.01	2.05
Roark, Tanner	R-R	6-2	235	10-5-86	4	7	4.38	40	12	0	1	111	119	55	54	17	26	70	.279	.299	.261	5.68	2.11
Ross, Joe	R-R	6-4	205	5-21-93	5	5	3.64	16	13	0	0	77	64	33	31	7	21	69	.223	.279	.172	8.10	2.47
Scherzer, Max	R-R	6-3	215	7-27-84	14	12	2.79	33	33	4	0	229	176	74	71	27	34	276	.208	.230	.184	10.86	1.34
Solis, Sammy	R-L	6-5	230	8-10-88	1	1	3.38	18	0	0	0	21	25	11	8	2	4	17	.291	.355	.255	7.17	1.69
Stammen, Craig	R-R	6-4	230	3-9-84	0	0	0.00	5	0	0	0	4	2	0	0	0	3	3	.154	.167	.143	6.75	6.75
Storen, Drew	B-R	6-1	195	8-11-87	2	2	3.44	58	0	0	29	55	45	23	21	4	16	67	.220	.284	.146	10.96	2.62
Strasburg, Stephen	R-R	6-4	235	7-20-88	11	7	3.46	23	23	0	0	127	115	56	49	14	26	155	.236	.202	.270	10.96	1.84
Thornton, Matt	L-L	6-6	235	9-15-76	2	1	2.18	60	0	0	0	41	33	12	10	2	11	23	.212	.198	.229	5.01	2.40
Treinen, Blake	R-R	6-5	230	6-30-88	2	5	3.86	60	0	0	0	68	62	32	29	4	32	65	.254	.336	.187	8.65	4.26
Zimmermann, Jordan	R-R	6-2	225	5-23-86	13	10	3.66	33	33	0	0	202	204	89	82	24	39	164	.264	.284	.243	7.32	1.74

Fielding

Catcher	PCT	G	PO	A	E	DP	PB
Lobaton	.994	42	299	20	2	3	4
Ramos	.995	125	1026	77	6	3	3
Severino	1.000	2	7	1	0	0	0

First Base	PCT	G	PO	A	E	DP
Espinosa	1.000	5	34	3	0	4

	PCT	G	PO	A	E	DP
Moore	1.000	39	216	10	0	22
Robinson	.992	44	331	25	3	21
Uggla	—	1	0	0	0	0
Zimmerman	.995	93	726	49	4	63

Second Base	PCT	G	PO	A	E	DP
Burriss	1.000	1	0	1	0	0

	PCT	G	PO	A	E	DP
Difo	1.000	2	0	1	0	0
Espinosa	.997	81	136	240	1	47
Rendon	.984	59	107	137	4	35
Turner	.976	12	19	22	1	5
Uggla	.981	31	39	62	2	9

Third Base	PCT	G	PO	A	E	DP
Escobar	.970	134	56	171	7	14
Espinosa	.933	16	10	18	2	0
Rendon	1.000	28	10	36	0	4
Shortstop	**PCT**	**G**	**PO**	**A**	**E**	**DP**
Desmond	.960	155	226	417	27	94

	PCT	G	PO	A	E	DP
Espinosa	1.000	8	5	17	0	1
Turner	.875	6	3	4	1	2
Outfield	**PCT**	**G**	**PO**	**A**	**E**	**DP**
den Dekker	.971	38	33	0	1	0
Espinosa	1.000	5	5	0	0	0
Harper	.978	151	297	9	7	2

	PCT	G	PO	A	E	DP
Johnson	1.000	4	5	0	0	0
Moore	1.000	21	18	0	0	0
Robinson	.959	37	47	0	2	0
Span	.993	61	149	3	1	3
Taylor	.990	132	302	6	3	1
Werth	.983	86	113	3	2	0
Zimmerman	—	1	0	0	0	0

SYRACUSE CHIEFS

INTERNATIONAL LEAGUE

TRIPLE-A

Batting	B-T	HT	WT	DOB	AVG	vLH	vRH	G	AB	R	H	2B	3B	HR	RBI	BB	HBP	SH	SF	SO	SB	CS	SLG	OBP
Ballou, Isaac	L-R	6-2	205	3-17-90	.300	.333	.294	5	20	3	6	2	0	0	2	1	0	0	0	2	1	0	.400	.333
Burriss, Emmanuel	B-R	6-0	190	1-17-85	.279	.345	.248	95	377	45	105	15	6	3	36	31	6	4	2	47	12	6	.374	.341
Butler, Dan	R-R	5-10	210	10-17-86	.227	.208	.238	83	282	28	64	20	1	1	26	32	6	2	3	65	0	0	.316	.316
den Dekker, Matt	L-L	6-1	210	8-10-87	.249	.255	.246	73	269	35	67	12	2	8	32	24	4	1	0	63	8	1	.398	.320
Dykstra, Cutter	R-R	6-0	190	6-29-89	.185	.189	.183	53	157	11	29	1	0	1	7	30	2	1	0	50	2	3	.210	.323
Gwynn Jr., Tony	L-R	6-0	190	10-4-82	.255	.239	.263	89	322	29	82	14	4	1	27	32	4	3	3	35	10	2	.332	.327
Hague, Rick	R-R	6-2	190	9-18-88	.215	.262	.192	58	195	13	42	7	3	1	16	11	1	2	1	51	1	0	.297	.260
Johnson, Josh R.	B-R	5-10	190	1-11-86	.251	.293	.233	76	191	21	48	6	1	1	20	29	0	3	4	33	3	3	.309	.344
Ka'aihue, Kila	L-R	6-4	240	3-29-84	.193	.105	.235	39	119	15	23	4	0	4	13	21	0	0	0	28	0	0	.328	.314
Keyes, Kevin	R-R	6-3	225	3-15-89	.256	.345	.220	76	289	35	74	13	0	8	39	20	3	0	2	81	1	0	.384	.309
Lerud, Steve	L-R	6-1	220	10-13-84	.238	.265	.229	60	206	15	49	7	0	2	23	19	6	0	0	58	0	0	.301	.320
Lisson, Mario	R-R	6-2	220	5-31-84	.258	.174	.294	51	155	18	40	3	0	2	17	13	2	0	4	34	2	0	.316	.316
Lozada, Jose	B-R	6-0	180	12-29-85	.286	.222	.316	12	28	4	8	1	0	0	2	5	0	0	0	6	0	0	.321	.394
Manuel, Craig	L-R	6-1	205	5-22-90	.500	.000	1.000	1	2	0	1	0	0	0	1	0	0	0	0	0	0	0	.500	.667
Martinson, Jason	R-R	6-1	190	10-15-88	.218	.205	.223	131	449	61	108	21	1	19	56	51	7	3	3	189	9	4	.380	.299
Mastroianni, Darin	R-R	5-11	190	8-26-85	.252	.258	.249	96	385	35	97	22	2	3	34	27	3	3	2	73	20	3	.343	.305
2-team total (16 Lehigh Valley)				.257	—	—	112	443	43	114	26	2	3	36	31	3	4	3	85	25	4	.345	.308	
Mattison, Kevin	L-L	6-1	195	9-20-85	.167	.000	.333	3	6	0	1	0	0	0	0	0	0	0	0	3	1	0	.167	.167
Minicozzi, Mark	R-R	6-0	220	2-11-83	.228	.258	.213	56	193	18	44	7	0	2	15	22	3	0	2	37	0	0	.295	.314
Moore, Tyler	R-R	6-2	220	1-30-87	.278	.333	.250	4	18	2	5	2	0	1	3	0	0	0	0	6	0	0	.556	.278
Nelson, Chris	R-R	5-11	205	9-3-85	.277	.176	.333	28	94	11	26	10	0	3	14	9	0	0	1	14	1	0	.479	.337
2-team total (16 Lehigh Valley)				.277	—	—	44	148	16	41	14	0	3	19	13	0	0	1	22	2	0	.432	.333	
Ramsey, Caleb	L-R	6-2	215	10-7-88	.279	.265	.284	95	319	40	89	4	4	1	26	33	2	0	3	60	9	3	.326	.347
Robinson, Derrick	B-L	5-11	190	9-28-87	.211	.400	.143	8	19	3	4	0	0	0	1	4	0	0	1	3	1	0	.211	.333
Sizemore, Scott	R-R	6-0	185	1-4-85	.426	.600	.378	14	47	7	20	2	1	1	7	6	0	0	1	10	0	0	.574	.481
Skole, Matt	L-R	6-4	225	7-30-89	.238	.179	.259	42	151	21	36	9	0	8	26	28	1	0	2	35	0	1	.457	.357
Stewart, Ian	L-R	6-3	225	4-5-85	.200	.271	.156	48	155	19	31	8	1	7	22	23	3	0	3	55	1	0	.400	.310
Taylor, Michael A.	R-R	6-3	210	3-26-91	.385	.385	.385	8	26	4	10	1	0	1	4	4	0	1	1	10	2	1	.538	.452
Turner, Trea	R-R	6-1	175	6-30-93	.314	.460	.240	48	188	31	59	7	3	1	15	13	0	1	3	41	14	2	.431	.353
Werth, Jayson	R-R	6-5	240	5-20-79	.391	.333	.412	6	23	2	9	2	0	0	5	1	1	0	1	2	1	0	.478	.423

Pitching	B-T	HT	WT	DOB	W	L	ERA	G	GS	CG	SV	IP	H	R	ER	HR	BB	SO	AVG	vLH	vRH	K/9	BB/9
Bacus, Dakota	R-R	6-2	200	4-2-91	0	0	5.40	2	0	0	0	5	4	3	3	1	3	2	.222	.143	.273	3.60	5.40
Billings, Bruce	R-R	6-0	205	11-18-85	8	5	3.63	27	18	0	0	121	125	52	49	6	28	90	.271	.271	.270	6.68	2.08
Bleier, Richard	L-L	6-3	215	4-16-87	6	2	2.75	12	11	1	0	69	75	24	21	0	7	25	.281	.329	.263	3.28	0.92
Cole, A.J.	R-R	6-5	200	1-5-92	5	6	3.15	21	19	0	0	106	91	40	37	9	34	76	.227	.218	.236	6.47	2.90
Davis, Erik	R-R	6-2	205	10-8-86	0	2	8.49	11	0	0	0	12	19	13	11	0	9	11	.365	.393	.333	8.49	6.94
Delcarmen, Manny	R-R	6-2	215	2-16-82	1	3	8.14	18	0	0	0	21	30	22	19	1	14	17	.349	.324	.367	7.29	6.00
Demny, Paul	R-R	6-2	200	8-3-89	0	3	3.97	10	0	0	0	11	8	5	5	1	12	13	.216	.182	.231	10.32	9.53
Espino, Paolo	R-R	5-10	190	1-10-87	8	6	3.21	20	19	0	0	118	116	47	42	13	19	88	.260	.262	.259	6.73	1.45
Fister, Doug	L-R	6-8	210	2-4-84	0	1	2.45	1	1	0	0	4	7	2	1	1	0	6	.389	.375	.400	14.73	0.00
Fornataro, Eric	R-R	6-2	230	1-2-88	1	4	5.54	36	1	0	0	50	50	32	31	2	27	33	.265	.310	.225	5.90	4.83
Grace, Matt	L-L	6-3	205	12-14-88	0	2	2.40	38	0	0	1	49	43	16	13	1	16	31	.249	.197	.277	5.73	2.96
Gutierrez, Juan	R-R	6-3	245	7-14-83	0	0	5.79	9	0	0	2	9	15	6	6	0	6	8	.357	.450	.273	7.71	5.79
2-team total (18 Lehigh Valley)					4	1	3.67	27	0	0	4	34	44	16	14	2	15	27	—	—	—	7.08	3.93
Harper, Bryan	L-L	6-5	205	12-29-89	0	0	2.25	4	0	0	0	4	2	1	1	0	4	1	.133	.333	.000	2.25	9.00
Hill, Taylor	R-R	6-3	230	3-12-89	3	10	5.23	22	22	0	0	119	163	80	69	9	29	70	.327	.323	.330	5.31	2.20
Hill, Rich	L-L	6-5	220	3-11-80	2	2	2.91	25	0	0	0	22	12	9	7	1	21	32	.167	.226	.122	13.29	8.72
2-team total (5 Pawtucket)					5	4	2.83	30	5	0	0	54	39	20	17	4	30	61	—	—	—	10.17	5.00
Jordan, Taylor	R-R	6-5	210	1-17-89	5	6	2.95	19	19	0	0	104	92	38	34	4	27	61	.235	.254	.215	5.30	2.34
Lively, Mitch	R-R	6-5	250	9-7-85	0	2	2.31	18	2	0	0	35	21	10	9	1	13	29	.174	.160	.183	7.46	3.34
Martin, Rafael	R-R	6-3	220	3-15-84	5	5	3.21	46	0	0	12	56	41	21	20	4	16	68	.205	.286	.147	10.93	2.57
McGregor, Scott	R-R	6-4	200	12-19-86	6	4	4.04	27	15	0	1	107	118	51	48	12	35	63	.285	.299	.275	5.30	2.94
Meek, Evan	R-R	6-0	215	5-12-83	2	4	2.15	30	0	0	6	38	30	14	9	1	19	33	.210	.125	.278	7.88	4.54
Overton, Connor	R-R	6-0	190		0	0	4.50	1	0	0	0	2	1	1	1	0	1	2	.250	.333	.200	9.00	4.50
Rivero, Felipe	L-L	6-2	200	7-5-91	0	2	6.75	8	0	0	0	7	8	5	5	0	5	5	.296	.308	.286	6.75	6.75
Ross, Joe	R-R	6-4	205	5-21-93	3	1	2.19	5	5	0	0	25	15	6	6	2	7	15	.174	.225	.130	5.47	2.55
Runion, Sam	R-R	6-4	220	11-9-88	3	3	2.87	28	1	0	0	38	40	20	12	2	14	36	.267	.283	.256	8.60	3.35
Simmons, James	R-R	6-3	220	9-29-86	0	0	6.75	1	1	0	0	4	4	3	3	0	1	1	.267	.333	.167	2.25	2.25
Solis, Sammy	R-L	6-5	230	8-10-88	0	0	2.03	9	0	0	2	13	8	3	3	0	5	11	.178	.235	.143	7.43	3.38
Spann, Matt	L-L	6-6	185	2-17-91	1	0	0.00	1	1	0	0	6	2	1	0	0	2	4	.095	.000	.105	6.00	3.00
Strasburg, Stephen	R-R	6-4	230	7-20-88	1	1	4.66	2	2	0	0	10	9	5	5	0	1	16	.243	.118	.350	14.90	0.93
Swynenberg, Matt	R-R	6-5	215	2-16-89	0	1	12.00	1	1	0	0	3	6	4	4	0	4	4	.400	.286	.500	12.00	12.00

WASHINGTON NATIONALS

Pitching

Pitching	B-T	HT	WT	DOB	W	L	ERA	G	GS	CG	SV	IP	H	R	ER	HR	BB	SO	AVG	vLH	vRH	K/9	BB/9
Treinen, Blake	R-R	6-5	230	6-30-88	0	0	0.00	12	0	0	0	12	6	0	0	0	1	14	.143	.200	.091	10.50	0.75
Valverde, Jose	R-R	6-4	265	3-24-78	0	0	2.39	27	0	0	10	26	21	8	7	1	3	21	.223	.217	.229	7.18	1.03
Walters, P.J.	R-R	6-4	215	3-12-85	5	3	5.25	21	5	0	0	60	66	37	35	7	23	52	.280	.339	.226	7.80	3.45
Williams, Austen	R-R	6-3	220	12-19-92	0	1	11.25	1	1	0	0	4	4	5	5	1	2	2	.250	.250	.250	4.50	4.50

Fielding

Catcher	PCT	G	PO	A	E	DP	PB
Butler	.997	83	542	31	2	4	5
Lerud	.998	60	431	27	1	6	4
Manuel	1.000	1	2	1	0	0	0

First Base	PCT	G	PO	A	E	DP
Ka'aihue	.989	30	254	18	3	19
Keyes	.985	35	305	15	5	34
Lisson	.991	26	210	10	2	23
Minicozzi	1.000	17	111	6	0	11
Moore	1.000	1	9	2	0	0
Ramsey	1.000	8	54	1	0	8
Skole	1.000	26	257	14	0	28
Stewart	1.000	10	68	7	0	8

Second Base	PCT	G	PO	A	E	DP
Burriss	.991	22	38	76	1	19
Dykstra	.979	50	93	142	5	29
Hague	.909	13	21	49	7	8
Johnson	.977	32	63	108	4	20
Lozada	1.000	1	2	5	0	0
Martinson	.955	5	11	10	1	0
Nelson	.983	13	27	32	1	7
Sizemore	.966	11	24	32	2	8
Turner	1.000	2	8	4	0	0

Third Base	PCT	G	PO	A	E	DP
Hague	.667	2	0	2	1	0
Johnson	1.000	10	6	12	0	0
Lisson	.926	11	5	20	2	2
Lozada	.800	4	0	4	1	0
Martinson	.972	77	62	144	6	24
Nelson	1.000	9	6	11	0	4
Skole	.958	13	7	16	1	0
Stewart	.917	26	7	59	6	2

Shortstop	PCT	G	PO	A	E	DP
Burriss	.955	72	92	187	13	45
Hague	1.000	1	0	2	0	0
Martinson	.969	31	47	80	4	17
Turner	.950	44	68	140	11	29

Outfield	PCT	G	PO	A	E	DP
Ballou	1.000	4	8	1	0	0
den Dekker	.981	72	152	3	3	0
Gwynn Jr.	.979	84	180	5	4	0
Hague	1.000	27	60	3	0	1
Johnson	1.000	16	20	0	0	0
Keyes	1.000	14	21	0	0	0
Lozada	1.000	5	9	0	0	0
Martinson	1.000	18	28	2	0	0
Mastroianni	.991	94	228	2	2	0
Mattison	1.000	2	5	0	0	0
Minicozzi	1.000	12	12	1	0	0
Moore	1.000	3	4	0	0	0
Ramsey	.976	83	160	3	4	1
Robinson	1.000	6	16	1	0	1
Taylor	1.000	7	12	0	0	0
Werth	1.000	5	6	0	0	0

HARRISBURG SENATORS

DOUBLE-A

EASTERN LEAGUE

Batting	B-T	HT	WT	DOB	AVG	vLH	vRH	G	AB	R	H	2B	3B	HR	RBI	BB	HBP	SH	SF	SO	SB	CS	SLG	OBP
Ballou, Isaac	L-R	6-2	205	3-17-90	.304	.295	.307	49	158	27	48	9	3	5	24	19	3	1	3	32	9	3	.494	.383
Bostick, Chris	R-R	5-11	185	3-24-93	.247	.214	.264	75	296	34	73	12	5	8	40	12	5	2	2	56	16	5	.402	.286
Cleary, Delta	B-R	6-2	220	8-14-89	.174	.333	.118	10	23	2	4	1	0	0	1	0	0	1	1	3	0	0	.217	.167
Corona, Reegie	B-R	5-11	185	11-7-86	.348	.400	.326	24	66	13	23	7	0	1	8	13	1	0	1	9	3	1	.500	.457
Difo, Wilmer	B-R	6-0	195	4-2-92	.279	.283	.276	87	359	48	100	21	6	2	39	12	0	3	0	79	26	1	.387	.312
Dykstra, Cutter	R-R	6-0	190	6-29-89	.256	.323	.217	72	250	27	64	11	1	5	29	25	1	0	2	67	6	4	.368	.324
Goodwin, Brian	L-L	6-0	195	11-2-90	.226	.216	.231	114	429	58	97	17	4	8	46	38	2	0	3	93	15	7	.340	.290
Hague, Rick	R-R	6-2	190	9-18-88	.259	.245	.266	52	147	19	38	15	0	0	9	6	1	1	2	30	4	2	.361	.288
Jeroloman, Brian	L-R	6-0	205	5-10-85	.215	.225	.211	46	130	19	28	4	0	0	16	35	1	4	1	24	0	1	.246	.383
Keyes, Kevin	R-R	6-3	225	3-15-89	.235	.241	.233	56	183	24	43	8	0	5	26	23	2	0	4	47	1	3	.361	.321
Leonida, Cole	R-R	6-2	220	12-25-88	.000	—	.000	3	5	0	0	0	0	0	0	2	1	1	1	3	0	0	.000	.333
Lisson, Mario	R-R	6-2	205	5-31-84	.283	.256	.300	37	113	19	32	5	0	4	20	8	1	0	3	29	2	0	.434	.328
Lozada, Jose	B-R	6-0	180	12-29-85	.299	.224	.353	44	117	19	35	2	1	0	8	16	0	3	1	22	7	0	.333	.381
Manuel, Craig	L-R	6-1	205	5-22-90	.111	.000	.143	3	9	0	1	0	0	0	1	0	0	0	0	2	0	0	.111	.200
Norfork, Khayyan	R-R	5-10	190	1-19-89	.300	.500	.250	3	10	1	3	2	0	0	0	0	0	0	0	1	0	0	.500	.300
Oduber, Randolph	R-L	6-3	190	3-18-89	.188	.333	.154	7	16	0	3	0	0	0	2	2	1	1	0	2	1	0	.188	.316
Perez, Stephen	B-R	5-11	185	12-16-90	.130	.167	.119	19	54	7	7	2	0	0	4	11	1	2	0	10	1	0	.167	.288
Pleffner, Shawn	R-R	6-5	225	8-17-89	.269	.302	.253	117	394	36	106	21	2	3	47	41	3	0	1	66	2	4	.355	.342
Ramsey, Caleb	L-R	6-2	215	10-7-88	.309	.136	.352	33	110	16	34	2	2	1	10	12	0	2	1	17	4	1	.391	.374
Renda, Tony	R-R	5-8	175	1-24-91	.267	.293	.257	54	206	31	55	10	1	1	23	19	2	0	1	15	13	3	.340	.333
2-team total (73 Trenton)					.269	—	—	127	480	73	129	30	2	3	44	43	3	2	4	39	23	6	.358	.330
Rendon, Anthony	R-R	6-1	210	6-6-90	.250	.286	.200	8	24	1	6	3	0	0	3	0	0	0	0	4	0	0	.375	.333
Robinson, Derrick	B-L	5-11	190	9-28-87	.252	.220	.271	85	270	26	68	5	0	0	20	25	0	3	2	45	17	9	.270	.313
Ruiz, Adderling	R-R	6-1	175	5-3-91	.000	.000	—	1	1	0	0	0	0	0	0	0	0	0	0	1	0	0	.000	.000
Sanchez, Adrian	R-R	6-0	160	8-16-90	.246	.200	.272	59	179	21	44	11	1	1	15	11	0	3	1	22	3	2	.335	.288
Severino, Pedro	R-R	6-2	200	7-20-93	.246	.282	.228	91	329	33	81	13	0	5	34	19	1	6	2	51	1	2	.331	.288
Skole, Matt	L-R	6-4	225	7-30-89	.232	.297	.202	90	314	34	73	14	1	12	56	44	4	0	3	92	3	1	.398	.332
Span, Denard	L-L	6-0	210	2-27-84	.286	.000	.364	4	14	5	4	0	0	1	2	2	0	0	0	0	0	0	.500	.375
Turner, Trea	R-R	6-1	175	6-30-93	.359	.375	.348	10	39	6	14	4	1	0	4	1	0	0	1	8	4	0	.513	.366
Uggla, Dan	R-R	5-11	210	3-11-80	.300	—	.300	3	10	3	3	0	0	1	4	1	0	0	0	3	0	0	.600	.417
Vettleson, Drew	L-R	6-1	185	7-19-91	.201	.198	.202	86	289	31	58	9	3	5	27	27	0	0	4	92	11	3	.304	.266
Zimmerman, Ryan	R-R	6-3	220	9-28-84	.067	.000	.083	5	15	0	1	0	0	0	0	0	0	0	0	1	0	0	.067	.067

Pitching	B-T	HT	WT	DOB	W	L	ERA	G	GS	CG	SV	IP	H	R	ER	HR	BB	SO	AVG	vLH	vRH	K/9	BB/9
Alderson, Tim	R-R	6-6	220	11-3-88	1	1	3.38	5	5	0	0	27	26	11	10	2	6	15	.260	.207	.282	5.06	2.03
Ambriz, Hector	L-R	6-2	235	5-24-84	1	3	12.46	10	0	0	2	9	10	12	12	1	8	8	.294	.400	.250	8.31	8.31
Bacus, Dakota	R-R	6-2	200	4-2-91	6	3	3.51	22	11	1	0	90	87	38	35	7	29	53	.259	.244	.269	5.32	2.91
Bates, Colin	R-R	6-1	175	3-10-88	6	6	4.20	28	15	0	0	111	124	58	52	11	29	62	.280	.323	.246	5.01	2.34
Benincasa, Robert	R-R	6-1	180	9-5-90	0	0	0.00	2	0	0	0	4	0	0	0	0	1	4	.000		.000	9.00	2.25
Bleier, Richard	L-L	6-3	215	4-16-87	8	3	2.45	16	15	0	0	103	95	32	28	6	9	40	.247	.190	.268	3.50	0.79
Carpenter, David	R-R	6-2	230	7-15-85	0	0	0.00	2	0	0	0	2	0	0	0	0	1	1	1.000		.000	5.40	5.40
Davis, Erik	R-R	6-2	205	10-8-86	1	0	2.65	24	0	0	3	34	32	11	10	2	18	34	.252	.293	.217	9.00	4.76
De Los Santos, Abel	R-R	6-2	200	11-21-92	4	4	3.43	39	0	0	8	58	53	24	22	6	12	55	.241	.250	.235	8.58	1.87
Demny, Paul	R-R	6-2	200	8-3-89	2	5	1.88	34	0	0	7	48	31	14	10	2	24	60	.178	.237	.148	11.25	4.50
Dupra, Brian	R-R	6-3	200	12-15-88	0	2	6.97	11	0	0	1	10	15	9	8	2	5	8	.357	.313	.385	6.97	4.35

Pitching	B-T	HT	WT	DOB	W	L	ERA	G	GS	CG	SV	IP	H	R	ER	HR	BB	SO	AVG	vLH	vRH	K/9	BB/9
Espino, Paolo	R-R	5-10	190	1-10-87	0	3	4.26	8	7	1	0	38	35	18	18	3	11	32	.245	.224	.255	7.58	2.61
Fister, Doug	L-R	6-8	210	2-4-84	0	0	0.00	1	1	0	0	6	2	0	0	0	0	4	.105	.091	.125	6.00	0.00
Giolito, Lucas	R-R	6-6	255	7-14-94	4	2	3.80	8	8	0	0	47	48	21	20	2	17	45	.265	.231	.291	8.56	3.23
Harper, Bryan	L-L	6-5	205	12-29-89	2	2	3.02	34	0	0	0	42	34	16	14	5	15	33	.214	.185	.229	7.13	3.24
Janssen, Casey	R-R	6-4	205	9-17-81	0	0	2.45	4	1	0	0	4	1	1	1	0	1	0	.083	.000	.143	0.00	2.45
Lee, Nick	L-L	5-11	185	1-13-91	2	0	3.75	20	0	0	1	24	20	11	10	0	19	29	.233	.182	.264	10.88	7.13
Mendez, Gilberto	R-R	6-0	165	11-17-92	6	4	3.84	44	0	0	8	61	67	29	26	5	17	52	.275	.228	.303	7.67	2.51
Pivetta, Nick	R-R	6-5	220	2-14-93	0	2	7.20	3	3	0	0	15	19	12	12	4	9	6	.311	.250	.364	3.60	5.40
2-team total (7 Reading)					2	4	7.27	10	10	0	0	43	51	36	35	8	28	31	—	—	—	6.44	5.82
Purke, Matt	L-L	6-4	220	7-17-90	1	3	6.29	10	5	0	0	24	33	21	17	2	7	19	.330	.326	.333	7.03	2.59
Rauh, Brian	R-R	6-2	200	7-23-91	2	5	4.83	8	8	0	0	41	48	27	22	7	10	29	.294	.313	.283	6.37	2.20
Roark, Tanner	R-R	6-2	235	10-5-86	0	0	4.50	1	1	0	0	2	2	1	1	0	0	2	.286	.333	.250	9.00	0.00
Ross, Joe	R-R	6-4	205	5-21-93	2	2	2.81	9	9	0	0	51	46	18	16	3	12	54	.246	.233	.252	9.47	2.10
Runion, Sam	R-R	6-4	220	11-9-88	3	2	2.96	20	0	0	4	27	24	11	9	1	8	24	.229	.273	.197	7.90	2.63
Self, Derek	R-R	6-3	205	1-14-90	1	0	5.14	8	0	0	0	14	23	8	8	3	7	13	.383	.286	.436	8.36	4.50
Simmons, James	R-R	6-3	220	9-29-86	4	4	3.47	17	4	0	0	36	34	15	14	3	5	32	.250	.313	.216	7.93	1.24
Simms, John	R-R	6-3	205	1-17-92	2	3	4.40	8	8	0	0	45	49	23	22	3	15	34	.282	.280	.283	6.80	3.00
Solis, Sammy	R-L	6-5	230	8-10-88	0	3	6.75	11	1	0	2	13	19	10	10	0	5	11	.345	.385	.333	7.43	3.38
Spann, Matt	L-L	6-6	185	2-17-91	2	2	4.66	10	10	0	0	56	65	33	29	1	25	35	.311	.200	.351	5.63	4.02
Strasburg, Stephen	R-R	6-4	230	7-20-88	0	1	1.80	1	1	0	0	5	4	2	1	0	0	6	.200	.143	.231	10.80	0.00
Suero, Wander	R-R	6-3	175	9-15-91	1	2	6.35	17	0	0	0	34	42	25	24	4	14	29	.307	.300	.313	7.68	3.71
Swynenberg, Matt	R-R	6-5	215	2-16-89	0	1	4.91	2	2	0	0	11	10	6	6	1	2	6	.238	.333	.185	4.91	1.64
Voth, Austin	R-R	6-1	190	6-26-92	6	7	2.92	28	27	0	0	157	134	60	51	10	40	148	.230	.235	.226	8.47	2.29

Fielding

Catcher	PCT	G	PO	A	E	DP	PB
Jeroloman	1.000	46	314	29	0	3	1
Leonida	1.000	3	18	3	0	1	1
Manuel	1.000	3	25	1	0	0	1
Ruiz	1.000	1	2	0	0	0	0
Severino	.989	91	620	92	8	6	9

First Base	PCT	G	PO	A	E	DP
Corona	.917	2	8	3	1	0
Keyes	.990	16	90	7	1	8
Lozada	1.000	1	13	0	0	0
Pleffner	.987	99	844	59	12	85
Skole	.981	35	243	12	5	25
Zimmerman	1.000	4	23	0	0	3

Second Base	PCT	G	PO	A	E	DP
Bostick	.968	48	101	143	8	39
Corona	1.000	16	31	41	0	11
Difo	.967	11	26	33	2	11
Dykstra	1.000	7	5	9	0	0
Hague	.960	6	10	14	1	4

Catcher (cont.)	PCT	G	PO	A	E	DP
Norfork	1.000	1	1	0	0	0
Renda	.972	52	108	132	7	30
Rendon	1.000	5	5	18	0	3
Sanchez	1.000	5	7	16	0	3
Uggla	1.000	3	7	9	0	0

Third Base	PCT	G	PO	A	E	DP
Dykstra	.844	20	7	31	7	3
Lisson	.965	23	17	38	2	4
Lozada	.939	21	16	30	3	4
Rendon	1.000	1	1	2	0	0
Sanchez	.930	29	19	47	5	1
Skole	.972	56	34	104	4	9

Shortstop	PCT	G	PO	A	E	DP
Bostick	1.000	1	0	2	0	0
Corona	1.000	5	10	15	0	2
Difo	.970	77	103	224	10	42
Hague	.924	16	19	42	5	7
Lozada	1.000	9	18	20	0	6
Perez	.919	16	19	38	5	5

	PCT	G	PO	A	E	DP
Renda	1.000	2	2	7	0	0
Sanchez	.988	19	24	55	1	15
Turner	.907	10	12	27	4	10

Outfield	PCT	G	PO	A	E	DP
Ballou	1.000	41	61	0	0	0
Bostick	1.000	22	32	0	0	0
Cleary	1.000	9	15	0	0	0
Dykstra	.943	20	32	1	2	0
Goodwin	.964	111	262	7	10	1
Hague	1.000	23	44	4	0	0
Keyes	.971	27	34	0	1	0
Lisson	1.000	4	7	0	0	0
Lozada	1.000	4	4	1	0	0
Norfork	1.000	2	4	0	0	0
Oduber	1.000	6	9	0	0	0
Ramsey	.981	32	49	2	1	1
Robinson	.994	78	152	1	1	0
Sanchez	1.000	3	1	0	0	0
Span	1.000	3	6	0	0	0
Vettleson	.982	79	155	12	3	2

POTOMAC NATIONALS   HIGH CLASS A

CAROLINA LEAGUE

Batting	B-T	HT	WT	DOB	AVG	vLH	vRH	G	AB	R	H	2B	3B	HR	RBI	BB	HBP	SH	SF	SO	SB	CS	SLG	OBP
Ballou, Isaac	L-R	6-2	205	3-17-90	.249	.210	.267	70	253	27	63	11	1	3	25	27	0	0	2	48	11	2	.336	.319
Bautista, Rafael	R-R	6-2	165	3-8-93	.272	.375	.241	52	206	23	56	7	2	0	8	11	4	3	2	22	23	4	.325	.318
Bostick, Chris	R-R	5-11	185	3-24-93	.274	.238	.287	62	234	23	64	10	3	4	18	19	7	2	2	44	15	3	.393	.344
Corona, Reegie	B-R	5-11	185	11-7-86	.304	.000	.368	6	23	3	7	2	1	0	4	3	0	0	0	2	2	0	.478	.385
DeBruin, Grant	R-R	6-3	225	6-28-90	.267	.353	.239	59	210	27	56	12	2	2	27	16	5	1	2	31	0	0	.371	.330
Dent, Cody	L-R	5-11	190	8-1-91	.000	.000	.000	9	24	2	0	0	0	0	0	4	0	0	0	5	0	0	.000	.143
Difo, Wilmer	B-R	6-0	195	4-2-92	.320	.471	.276	19	75	13	24	7	0	3	14	8	0	0	0	13	4	1	.533	.386
Johnson, Reed	R-R	5-10	180	12-8-76	.313	.600	.182	5	16	3	5	0	0	2	5	0	0	0	0	2	0	0	.688	.313
Keller, Alec	L-R	6-2	200	5-19-92	.283	.190	.312	53	180	25	51	9	1	0	17	15	0	0	3	25	3	3	.344	.333
Kieboom, Spencer	R-R	6-2	230	3-16-91	.248	.205	.287	71	246	30	61	16	1	2	26	36	1	0	2	30	1	1	.344	.344
Manuel, Craig	L-R	6-1	205	5-22-90	.208	.087	.229	51	154	13	32	3	0	1	19	10	4	2	0	15	0	1	.247	.274
Martinez, Estarlin	R-R	6-1	185	3-8-92	.274	.254	.281	91	270	37	74	10	2	0	25	28	3	3	2	55	8	4	.326	.347
Masters, David	R-R	6-1	185	4-23-93	.207	.188	.214	18	58	2	12	2	0	0	7	2	0	1	3	5	0	2	.241	.222
Mesa, Narciso	R-R	5-11	175	11-16-91	.265	.321	.243	105	389	43	103	11	3	2	39	9	7	7	6	62	20	7	.324	.290
Miller, Brandon	R-R	6-2	215	10-8-89	.226	.321	.187	59	195	26	44	13	2	7	26	20	2	0	2	55	0	0	.421	.301
Moore, Tyler	R-R	6-2	220	1-30-87	.000	.000	.000	2	4	1	0	0	0	0	0	2	0	0	0	0	0	0	.000	.333
Norfork, Khayyan	R-R	5-10	190	1-19-89	.276	.244	.287	102	341	44	94	20	2	2	28	27	4	4	0	60	10	5	.364	.336
Perez, Stephen	B-R	5-11	185	12-16-90	.220	.225	.219	109	381	38	84	17	3	2	45	48	1	9	7	77	15	5	.297	.304
Read, Raudy	R-R	6-0	170	10-29-93	.389	.600	.308	5	18	1	7	2	0	0	5	2	0	0	0	3	0	0	.500	.450
Reistetter, Matt	L-R	5-10	180	5-5-92	.000	—	.000	1	3	0	0	0	0	0	0	0	0	0	0	1	0	0	.000	.000
Rendon, Anthony	R-R	6-1	210	6-6-90	.471	.556	.375	6	17	2	8	2	0	0	1	3	0	0	0	2	0	0	.588	.550
Ruiz, Adderling	R-R	6-1	175	5-3-91	.500	1.000	.000	1	4	1	2	0	0	1	0	0	0	0	0	1	0	0	1.250	.500
Sanchez, Adrian	B-R	6-0	160	8-16-90	.343	.313	.353	19	67	10	23	5	0	1	6	5	0	1	0	6	5	1	.463	.389
Span, Denard	L-L	6-0	210	2-27-84	.000	—	.000	1	2	0	0	0	0	0	0	0	0	0	0	0	0	0	.000	.000

WASHINGTON NATIONALS

Batting	B-T	HT	WT	DOB	AVG	vLH	vRH	G	AB	R	H	2B	3B	HR	RBI	BB	HBP	SH	SF	SO	SB	CS	SLG	OBP
Uggla, Dan	R-R	5-11	210	3-11-80	.143	.333	.000	2	7	1	1	0	0	0	0	0	0	0	0	2	0	0	.143	.143
Ward, Drew	L-R	6-3	215	11-25-94	.249	.210	.264	111	377	47	94	19	2	6	47	39	6	1	3	110	2	1	.358	.327
Webb, Brenden	L-L	6-1	185	2-24-90	.145	.111	.151	19	62	9	9	4	0	1	6	6	0	0	2	17	3	1	.258	.214
2-team total (80 Frederick)					.240	—	—	99	334	48	80	18	0	8	36	31	3	1	3	97	15	2	.365	.307
Werth, Jayson	R-R	6-5	240	5-20-79	.231	—	.231	6	13	1	3	0	0	1	3	4	0	0	0	3	0	0	.462	.412
Wooten, John	R-R	6-3	190	1-19-91	.238	.210	.248	119	429	41	102	24	2	7	41	30	5	0	6	79	7	4	.352	.291
Wright, Zach	R-R	6-1	205	1-10-90	.294	.389	.242	17	51	12	15	5	2	1	6	9	1	2	0	12	2	0	.529	.410
Yezzo, Jimmy	L-R	6-0	200	2-27-92	.192	.129	.208	49	156	17	30	7	0	1	10	13	0	0	3	36	0	1	.256	.250

Pitching	B-T	HT	WT	DOB	W	L	ERA	G	GS	CG	SV	IP	H	R	ER	HR	BB	SO	AVG	vLH	vRH	K/9	BB/9
Amlung, Justin	R-R	6-1	185	5-21-90	1	0	1.84	7	0	0	0	15	7	3	3	1	2	13	.146	.208	.083	7.98	1.23
Bacus, Dakota	R-R	6-2	200	4-2-91	2	0	2.33	8	5	0	3	27	23	8	7	1	10	29	.219	.196	.237	9.67	3.33
Barrett, Aaron	R-R	6-3	225	1-2-88	0	0	0.00	4	3	0	0	3	3	1	0	0	1	6	.273	.400	.167	18.00	3.00
Carpenter, David	R-R	6-2	230	7-15-85	0	0	9.00	1	1	0	0	1	1	1	1	0	1	0	.333	1.000	.000	9.00	9.00
Davis, Cody	R-R	5-9	170	7-21-90	1	0	2.91	12	0	0	1	22	17	7	7	0	15	10	.227	.163	.313	4.15	6.23
Davis, Erik	R-R	6-3	205	10-8-86	0	0	0.00	2	0	0	0	3	1	0	0	0	0	2	.100	.000	.200	6.00	0.00
Dickson, Ian	R-R	6-5	215	9-16-90	3	3	3.60	12	8	0	0	40	30	21	16	2	39	31	.208	.175	.235	6.98	8.78
Dupra, Brian	R-R	6-3	200	12-15-88	3	0	2.79	25	0	0	4	42	31	15	13	1	15	35	.209	.193	.220	7.50	3.21
Giolito, Lucas	R-R	6-6	255	7-14-94	3	5	2.71	13	11	0	0	70	65	24	21	1	20	86	.244	.211	.275	11.11	2.58
Janssen, Casey	R-R	6-4	205	9-17-81	0	0	4.50	2	1	0	0	2	3	1	1	0	1	1	.300	.400	.200	4.50	0.00
Johansen, Jake	R-R	6-6	235	1-23-91	1	7	5.44	24	0	0	1	48	60	42	29	6	27	48	.300	.338	.276	9.00	5.06
Lee, Nick	L-L	5-11	185	1-13-91	1	1	2.57	20	0	0	9	28	20	11	8	1	14	28	.202	.231	.183	9.00	4.50
Lopez, Reynaldo	R-R	6-0	185	1-4-94	6	7	4.09	19	19	1	0	99	93	47	45	5	28	94	.252	.230	.267	8.55	2.55
Mapes, Tyler	R-R	6-2	205	7-18-91	6	3	2.38	30	8	0	1	91	94	30	24	3	17	71	.269	.328	.233	7.05	1.69
Napoli, David	R-L	5-10	180	10-3-90	1	0	4.50	5	0	0	0	8	6	4	4	0	4	8	.200	.222	.190	9.00	4.50
Orlan, R.C.	R-L	6-0	185	9-28-90	0	0	2.20	8	0	0	1	16	12	5	4	2	8	17	.203	.048	.289	9.37	4.41
Perez, Kevin	R-R	6-0	205	8-1-93	0	0	7.23	7	0	0	0	19	22	19	15	2	11	21	.286	.393	.224	10.13	5.30
Pivetta, Nick	R-R	6-5	220	2-14-93	7	4	2.29	15	14	0	0	86	70	29	22	4	29	72	.225	.282	.191	7.51	3.02
Purke, Matt	L-L	6-4	220	7-17-90	0	0	3.86	2	2	0	0	7	5	3	3	1	1	3	.200	.200	.200	3.86	1.29
Rauh, Brian	R-R	6-2	200	7-23-91	2	2	2.47	7	7	1	0	44	39	13	12	2	9	42	.242	.311	.200	8.66	1.85
Roark, Tanner	R-R	6-2	235	10-5-86	0	0	0.00	1	1	0	0	4	3	0	0	0	5	.214	.200	.222	11.25	0.00
Rodriguez, Manny	R-R	6-2	225	1-12-89	1	3	6.43	18	0	0	4	21	22	15	15	3	13	24	.259	.212	.288	10.29	5.57
Schwartz, Blake	R-R	6-3	200	10-9-89	0	2	5.87	3	3	0	0	15	16	11	10	3	6	8	.271	.389	.220	4.70	3.52
Self, Derek	R-R	6-2	205	1-14-90	3	5	3.09	29	0	0	2	47	48	16	16	4	8	32	.262	.262	.263	6.17	1.54
Simms, John	R-R	6-3	205	11-17-92	6	6	2.74	15	14	1	0	89	70	35	27	7	25	48	.219	.278	.160	4.87	2.54
Spann, Matt	L-L	6-6	185	2-17-91	2	7	4.52	14	13	0	0	72	85	42	36	4	27	60	.293	.293	.293	7.53	3.39
Suero, Wander	R-R	6-2	175	9-15-91	6	2	2.41	16	5	0	2	56	49	21	15	1	18	39	.237	.214	.252	6.27	2.89
Thomas, Justin	L-L	6-2	195	10-21-90	1	6	3.43	28	0	0	0	58	52	26	22	1	18	50	.242	.200	.262	7.80	2.81
Valdez, Phillip	R-R	6-2	160	11-16-91	3	2	3.77	22	10	1	5	60	61	39	25	0	25	48	.254	.287	.227	7.24	3.77
Walsh, Jake	L-L	6-3	195	1-1-91	1	1	3.66	9	0	0	0	20	16	8	8	1	10	19	.216	.400	.169	8.69	4.58
Williams, Austen	R-R	6-3	220	12-19-92	4	6	2.59	11	11	0	0	63	51	26	18	2	17	41	.217	.250	.197	5.89	2.44

Fielding

Catcher	PCT	G	PO	A	E	DP	PB
Kieboom	.991	69	502	72	5	7	7
Manuel	.994	50	306	55	2	5	3
Read	.973	5	31	5	1	0	0
Reistetter	1.000	1	1	0	0	0	0
Ruiz	1.000	1	7	0	0	0	0
Wright	.993	17	132	11	1	1	3

First Base	PCT	G	PO	A	E	DP
DeBruin	.994	50	453	31	3	47
Martinez	1.000	2	7	0	0	1
Moore	1.000	1	10	0	0	0
Wooten	.988	68	539	35	7	52
Yezzo	1.000	24	185	17	0	3

Second Base	PCT	G	PO	A	E	DP
Bostick	.966	47	83	117	7	28
Corona	.964	6	12	15	1	4
Dent	1.000	2	5	8	0	0

	PCT	G	PO	A	E	DP
Masters	.933	3	8	6	1	3
Norfork	.960	59	104	158	11	44
Perez	1.000	3	8	3	0	1
Sanchez	1.000	18	34	48	0	11
Uggla	1.000	2	1	7	0	1
Wooten	1.000	1	4	4	0	3

Third Base	PCT	G	PO	A	E	DP
Dent	1.000	2	1	4	0	0
Masters	.850	7	5	12	3	1
Norfork	.914	26	11	53	6	2
Rendon	1.000	4	0	5	0	0
Ward	.883	95	63	156	29	17
Wooten	.882	12	5	25	4	3

Shortstop	PCT	G	PO	A	E	DP
Bostick	1.000	5	12	14	0	6
Dent	1.000	3	4	12	0	0
Difo	.951	19	20	38	3	6

	PCT	G	PO	A	E	DP
Masters	.903	8	9	19	3	5
Perez	.970	105	162	316	15	77
Sanchez	1.000	1	0	1	0	0

Outfield	PCT	G	PO	A	E	DP
Ballou	1.000	65	122	5	0	1
Bautista	.963	52	103	0	4	0
Dent	1.000	3	3	0	0	0
Johnson	1.000	4	5	0	0	0
Keller	.986	45	69	2	1	0
Martinez	.981	83	147	7	3	2
Mesa	.980	105	191	6	4	2
Miller	.950	44	73	3	4	1
Moore	—	1	0	0	0	0
Norfork	1.000	2	3	0	0	0
Span	—	1	0	0	0	0
Webb	1.000	8	15	1	0	0
Werth	1.000	3	2	0	0	0
Wooten	1.000	19	31	1	0	0

HAGERSTOWN SUNS   LOW CLASS A

SOUTH ATLANTIC LEAGUE

Batting	B-T	HT	WT	DOB	AVG	vLH	vRH	G	AB	R	H	2B	3B	HR	RBI	BB	HBP	SH	SF	SO	SB	CS	SLG	OBP
Abreu, Osvaldo	R-R	6-0	170	6-13-94	.274	.326	.252	123	442	74	121	35	4	6	47	50	10	6	5	89	30	11	.412	.357
Carey, Dale	R-R	6-3	185	11-14-91	.234	.216	.241	121	415	64	97	18	2	8	52	66	6	9	10	91	10	9	.345	.340
Davidson, Austin	L-R	6-0	180	1-3-93	.202	.226	.194	83	258	34	52	11	0	6	31	26	14	7	7	47	6	7	.314	.302
DeBruin, Grant	R-R	6-3	225	6-28-90	.327	.362	.313	69	248	39	81	15	3	2	37	20	3	0	2	29	2	5	.435	.381
Dent, Cody	L-R	5-11	190	8-1-91	.226	.222	.227	43	137	13	31	2	0	1	16	8	2	3	0	37	2	1	.263	.279
Eusebio, Diomedes	R-R	6-0	185	9-8-92	.100	.118	.091	13	50	3	5	1	0	0	1	2	1	0	0	10	0	0	.120	.151
Gardner, Jeff	L-R	6-2	210	1-21-92	.226	.218	.228	116	403	50	91	25	4	5	48	38	5	1	6	90	8	7	.345	.296
Keller, Alec	L-R	6-2	200	5-19-92	.302	.300	.303	61	245	36	74	13	5	0	18	15	2	6	1	38	8	6	.396	.346

Batting	B-T	HT	WT	DOB	AVG	vLH	vRH	G	AB	R	H	2B	3B	HR	RBI	BB	HBP	SH	SF	SO	SB	CS	SLG	OBP
Keniry, Conor	L-R	6-1	195	12-2-91	.216	.219	.214	35	102	17	22	2	0	1	7	10	3	0	1	25	3	2	.265	.302
Lopez, Carlos	R-R	6-2	220	1-18-90	.138	.250	.059	10	29	2	4	3	0	0	1	5	0	0	0	5	0	0	.241	.265
Marmolejos, Jose	L-L	6-1	185	1-2-93	.310	.314	.308	124	468	63	145	39	5	11	87	35	9	0	9	89	3	1	.485	.363
Masters, David	R-R	6-1	185	4-23-93	.230	.125	.269	91	296	41	68	11	1	2	30	38	6	4	2	64	3	6	.294	.327
Mayers, Jake	R-R	6-1	215	8-8-90	.250	.333	.200	6	16	1	4	1	0	0	1	2	2	0	0	3	0	0	.313	.400
Mejia, Bryan	B-R	6-1	170	3-2-94	.345	.329	.351	62	238	33	82	17	9	5	46	5	5	6	1	50	14	7	.555	.369
Mesa, Narciso	R-R	5-11	175	11-16-91	.200	.000	.235	5	20	1	4	0	0	0	2	2	0	0	0	7	2	0	.200	.273
Middleton, Brennan	R-R	6-0	190	11-20-90	.198	.194	.200	35	106	6	21	4	0	1	14	8	0	3	1	12	4	4	.264	.252
Page, Matt	L-L	6-3	210	10-22-91	.271	.229	.285	54	192	28	52	16	2	0	19	30	0	1	2	36	6	0	.375	.366
Read, Raudy	R-R	6-0	170	10-29-93	.244	.238	.246	82	295	38	72	20	1	5	36	25	3	1	3	50	4	3	.369	.307
Reistetter, Matt	L-R	5-10	180	5-5-92	.308	.356	.295	59	201	24	62	9	2	1	21	14	1	0	3	26	1	1	.388	.352
Rodriguez, Wilman	R-R	6-1	175	6-7-91	.269	.279	.263	38	119	14	32	7	0	3	16	7	0	0	3	27	8	1	.403	.302
Ruiz, Adderling	R-R	6-1	175	5-3-91	.400	.500	.333	3	10	4	4	1	0	2	3	1	0	0	0	1	0	0	1.100	.455
Span, Denard	L-L	6-0	210	2-27-84	.615	.500	.667	4	13	2	8	0	0	1	2	2	0	0	0	0	1	0	.846	.667
Stevenson, Andrew	L-L	6-1	180	6-1-94	.285	.222	.307	35	137	28	39	3	2	1	16	8	4	2	2	16	16	4	.358	.338
Tillero, Jorge	R-R	5-11	160	12-21-91	.281	.273	.286	9	32	3	9	3	0	0	4	0	1	1	0	5	0	0	.375	.303
Uggla, Dan	R-R	5-11	210	3-11-80	.167	—	.167	2	6	1	1	1	0	0	2	1	0	0	0	3	0	0	.333	.286

Pitching	B-T	HT	WT	DOB	W	L	ERA	G	GS	CG	SV	IP	H	R	ER	HR	BB	SO	AVG	vLH	vRH	K/9	BB/9
Amlung, Justin	R-R	6-1	185	5-21-90	3	4	4.22	19	8	0	3	64	66	32	30	5	7	42	.272	.299	.256	5.91	0.98
Bach, Connor	L-L	6-6	230	6-24-92	6	4	3.85	26	20	0	0	110	95	54	47	4	69	106	.238	.252	.233	8.67	5.65
Baez, Joan	R-R	6-3	190	12-26-94	0	1	11.32	3	3	0	0	10	13	13	13	1	6	6	.295	.250	.313	5.23	5.23
Brinley, Ryan	L-R	6-1	200	4-9-93	1	2	1.89	11	0	0	1	19	22	10	4	1	1	6	.278	.379	.220	2.84	0.47
Cooper, Andrew	R-R	6-1	200	6-27-92	2	2	3.53	34	0	0	1	64	73	34	25	1	16	35	.291	.326	.270	4.95	2.26
Dickey, Robbie	R-R	6-3	205	4-6-94	0	2	9.00	4	2	0	0	9	11	12	9	1	7	9	.282	.167	.333	9.00	7.00
Fedde, Erick	R-R	6-4	180	2-25-93	1	2	4.34	6	6	0	0	29	24	14	14	1	8	23	.224	.250	.206	7.14	2.48
Glover, Koda	R-R	6-5	195	4-13-93	1	1	2.25	16	0	0	4	24	21	8	6	2	1	27	.231	.316	.170	10.13	0.38
Johns, Sam	R-R	6-2	205	7-12-91	0	2	5.56	26	0	0	2	44	49	32	27	4	13	22	.275	.268	.280	4.53	2.68
Lee, Andrew	L-R	6-5	210	12-2-93	3	1	2.15	10	5	0	0	29	18	8	7	0	9	34	.171	.167	.175	10.43	2.76
Mapes, Tyler	R-R	6-2	205	7-18-91	1	0	0.00	2	0	0	0	6	3	0	0	0	0	4	.136	.143	.133	6.00	0.00
Mooneyham, Brett	L-L	6-5	235	1-24-90	0	2	6.41	10	0	0	0	20	29	17	14	1	13	16	.349	.273	.377	7.32	5.95
Morales, Jose	R-R	6-3	180	2-12-95	0	2	12.86	2	2	0	0	7	12	10	10	2	4	3	.400	.375	.429	3.86	5.14
Napoli, David	R-L	5-10	180	10-3-90	7	5	4.01	31	0	0	4	61	46	29	27	0	36	62	.211	.191	.220	9.20	5.34
Orlan, R.C.	R-L	6-0	185	9-28-90	3	1	3.23	27	1	0	4	56	53	24	20	3	20	68	.254	.246	.257	10.99	3.23
Perez, Kevin	R-R	6-0	205	8-1-93	1	3	3.22	17	0	0	1	36	30	24	13	2	20	32	.205	.188	.220	7.93	4.95
Peterson, Tommy	R-R	6-1	205	10-11-93	0	1	7.50	3	0	0	0	6	7	5	5	0	4	4	.318	.462	.111	6.00	6.00
Purke, Matt	L-L	6-4	220	7-17-90	2	3	3.03	8	8	0	0	33	34	16	11	1	9	21	.272	.200	.290	5.79	2.48
Ramos, David	R-R	6-0	175	9-13-91	1	2	6.75	7	0	0	1	13	18	11	10	3	7	11	.346	.318	.367	7.43	4.73
Rauh, Brian	R-R	6-2	200	7-23-91	0	0	2.00	2	2	0	0	9	4	3	2	0	4	8	.125	.111	.143	8.00	4.00
Reyes, Luis	R-R	6-2	175	9-26-94	6	7	4.82	24	24	0	0	118	117	79	63	10	50	72	.267	.276	.261	5.51	3.82
Rodriguez, Jefry	R-R	6-5	185	7-26-93	1	5	6.75	10	10	0	0	43	45	37	32	3	25	27	.276	.309	.253	5.70	5.27
Sanchez, Mario	R-R	6-1	160	10-31-94	7	5	4.86	29	8	0	2	91	98	58	49	11	18	70	.271	.342	.219	6.95	1.79
Torres, Luis	R-R	6-3	190	6-4-94	0	1	18.00	2	0	0	0	3	8	6	6	2	5	2	.500	.600	.455	6.00	15.00
Ullmann, Ryan	R-R	6-6	230	8-12-91	1	2	8.10	5	1	0	1	13	15	12	12	1	8	6	.283	.368	.235	4.05	5.40
Valdez, Phillip	R-R	6-2	160	11-5-91	5	2	1.47	8	8	0	0	43	30	8	7	3	10	32	.190	.229	.173	6.70	2.09
Van Orden, Drew	R-R	6-4	200	1-19-92	5	5	3.61	23	15	0	3	92	77	43	37	4	34	47	.235	.273	.218	4.58	3.31
Walsh, Jake	L-L	6-3	195	1-1-91	1	0	0.00	14	0	0	6	17	12	0	0	0	4	13	.200	.083	.229	6.88	2.12
Webb, Joey	L-L	6-5	230	9-27-90	0	0	5.40	5	0	0	1	5	6	4	3	0	4	4	.273	.333	.263	7.20	7.20
Williams, Austen	R-R	6-3	220	12-19-92	8	1	2.10	13	13	0	0	73	66	20	17	2	14	63	.243	.258	.234	7.77	1.73
Williams, Deion	R-R	6-3	190	11-11-92	1	2	5.46	20	0	0	0	30	31	25	18	3	18	22	.277	.325	.250	6.67	5.46

Fielding

Catcher	PCT	G	PO	A	E	DP	PB
Read	.995	80	469	93	3	5	22
Reistetter	.992	54	311	45	3	4	6
Ruiz	1.000	3	27	3	0	0	0
Tillero	.984	9	51	12	1	0	4

First Base	PCT	G	PO	A	E	DP
DeBruin	.990	29	274	20	3	21
Dent	1.000	1	1	1	0	0
Eusebio	1.000	5	44	0	0	5
Lopez	.969	4	28	3	1	1
Marmolejos	.989	84	741	40	9	56
Page	.981	17	139	18	3	13

Second Base	PCT	G	PO	A	E	DP
Abreu	.971	42	63	105	5	21
Davidson	.959	10	19	28	2	6

	PCT	G	PO	A	E	DP
Dent	1.000	2	1	5	0	1
Keniry	1.000	15	18	31	0	11
Masters	.984	25	50	70	2	12
Mejia	.961	36	64	84	6	19
Middleton	.946	14	23	30	3	5
Uggla	.800	2	4	4	2	0

Third Base	PCT	G	PO	A	E	DP
Davidson	.945	67	50	140	11	9
DeBruin	.833	4	3	7	2	0
Dent	.929	13	10	16	2	0
Keniry	.969	17	10	52	2	3
Masters	.894	15	14	28	5	1
Mejia	.870	9	3	17	3	0
Middleton	.957	16	12	33	2	3

Shortstop	PCT	G	PO	A	E	DP
Abreu	.923	79	102	199	25	42
Masters	.948	51	90	163	14	33
Mejia	.930	8	13	27	3	3

Outfield	PCT	G	PO	A	E	DP
Carey	.990	119	273	12	3	3
Dent	.982	26	51	4	1	2
Gardner	.962	109	172	7	7	2
Keller	1.000	56	128	5	0	2
Marmolejos	—	1	0	0	0	0
Mejia	.947	9	18	0	1	0
Mesa	1.000	5	12	0	0	0
Page	1.000	22	40	0	0	0
Rodriguez	1.000	37	62	3	0	0
Span	1.000	4	11	0	0	0
Stevenson	.989	35	89	1	1	0

AUBURN DOUBLEDAYS
SHORT-SEASON

NEW YORK-PENN LEAGUE

Batting	B-T	HT	WT	DOB	AVG	vLH	vRH	G	AB	R	H	2B	3B	HR	RBI	BB	HBP	SH	SF	SO	SB	CS	SLG	OBP
Agustin, Telmito	L-L	5-10	160	10-9-96	.400	1.000	.333	7	30	5	12	1	2	0	4	1	0	1	0	5	1	1	.567	.419

Batting	B-T	HT	WT	DOB	AVG	vLH	vRH	G	AB	R	H	2B	3B	HR	RBI	BB	HBP	SH	SF	SO	SB	CS	SLG	OBP
Bautista, Rafael	R-R	6-2	165	3-8-93	.273	.400	.250	8	33	6	9	3	0	0	4	1	0	0	0	7	3	0	.364	.294
Dulin, Dalton	B-R	5-8	165	5-9-94	.273	.185	.306	35	99	27	27	6	1	0	8	18	5	3	0	21	8	1	.354	.410
Encarnacion, Randy	R-R	6-3	180	7-31-94	.218	.231	.213	44	147	19	32	9	0	4	23	9	2	1	0	55	3	4	.361	.272
Eusebio, Diomedes	R-R	6-0	185	9-8-92	.321	.406	.288	31	112	10	36	7	0	2	19	3	3	0	4	21	1	1	.438	.344
Florentino, Darryl	L-R	6-2	175	1-1-96	.230	.133	.250	24	87	10	20	1	1	0	3	9	1	0	0	18	1	3	.264	.309
Franco, Anderson	R-R	6-3	190	8-15-97	.225	.333	.206	11	40	0	9	1	1	0	4	7	0	0	0	2	0	0	.300	.340
Gutierrez, Kelvin	R-R	6-3	185	8-28-94	.305	.357	.290	62	239	31	73	21	1	1	30	16	4	1	1	52	2	0	.414	.358
Guzman, Luis	L-L	5-11	183	9-10-95	.172	.000	.204	18	58	5	10	2	1	0	2	1	0	0	0	19	0	0	.241	.213
Jefferies, Jake	R-R	6-1	180	8-7-93	.241	.200	.256	21	54	8	13	3	0	0	9	2	1	0	1	5	3	0	.296	.276
Keniry, Conor	L-R	6-1	195	12-2-91	.500	—	.500	3	14	1	7	0	1	0	3	0	0	0	0	2	0	0	.643	.500
Kerian, David	B-R	6-3	200	2-9-93	.251	.156	.280	52	195	24	49	9	4	0	24	25	1	0	2	41	2	2	.338	.336
Lora, Edwin	R-R	6-1	150	9-14-95	.259	.333	.229	38	116	19	30	8	2	2	17	6	1	6	1	33	7	0	.414	.298
Mejia, Bryan	B-R	6-1	170	3-2-94	.391	.429	.375	6	23	4	9	4	0	1	7	0	0	0	1	3	0	0	.696	.375
Page, Matt	L-L	6-3	210	10-22-91	.268	.227	.286	18	71	9	19	4	0	2	11	9	0	0	0	18	0	0	.408	.350
Reetz, Jakson	R-R	6-1	195	1-3-96	.212	.323	.171	36	113	18	24	4	0	0	5	13	6	0	0	37	3	0	.248	.326
Riopedre, Chris	R-R	5-9	175	4-16-93	.250	.500	.000	1	4	0	1	0	0	0	0	0	0	0	0	2	0	0	.250	.250
Robles, Victor	R-R	6-0	185	5-19-97	.343	.424	.318	38	140	29	48	5	4	2	16	8	14	2	3	21	12	4	.479	.424
Rodriguez, Melvin	L-R	5-10	200	2-4-91	.200	.286	.188	35	110	12	22	9	0	0	12	15	0	1	1	17	0	1	.282	.294
Ruiz, Adderling	R-R	6-1	175	5-3-91	.000	—	.000	2	2	0	0	0	0	0	0	0	0	0	0	0	0	0	.000	.000
Sagdal, Ian	L-R	6-1	175	1-6-93	.235	.091	.257	49	162	28	38	6	3	1	20	20	3	0	4	36	1	2	.327	.323
Schrock, Max	L-R	5-8	180	10-12-94	.308	.212	.331	46	172	31	53	10	4	2	14	13	0	0	1	16	2	1	.448	.355
Stevenson, Andrew	L-R	6-1	185	6-16-94	.361	.200	.404	18	72	11	26	1	2	0	9	7	0	0	1	12	7	3	.431	.413
Tillero, Jorge	R-R	5-11	160	12-21-93	.260	.217	.269	38	131	16	34	6	0	1	19	3	1	1	1	7	2	2	.328	.279
Vilorio, Luis	R-R	6-1	180	8-28-93	.400	.333	.429	3	10	4	4	1	0	0	1	0	0	0	0	4	0	0	.500	.400
Williamson, Clay	L-R	6-1	205	6-1-93	.211	.167	.231	9	19	3	4	2	0	0	0	1	0	2	0	3	0	0	.316	.318
Wiseman, Rhett	L-R	6-1	205	6-22-94	.248	.178	.267	54	210	25	52	12	0	5	35	18	1	0	2	52	6	2	.376	.307

Pitching	B-T	HT	WT	DOB	W	L	ERA	G	GS	CG	SV	IP	H	R	ER	HR	BB	SO	AVG	vLH	vRH	K/9	BB/9
Baez, Joan	R-R	6-3	190	12-26-94	2	2	7.13	5	5	0	0	18	21	14	14	0	14	17	.313	.364	.289	8.66	7.13
Boghosian, Adam	R-R	6-2	210	10-13-91	3	0	4.50	18	0	0	1	26	14	14	13	2	18	16	.154	.140	.167	5.54	6.23
Borne, Grant	L-L	6-5	205	4-6-94	1	4	3.59	15	5	0	1	48	53	31	19	0	7	32	.276	.211	.314	6.04	1.32
Brinley, Ryan	L-R	6-1	200	4-9-93	0	2	0.87	8	0	0	0	10	7	2	1	1	0	10	.184	.158	.211	8.71	0.00
Crownover, Matt	L-R	6-0	195	3-5-93	1	4	3.81	13	10	0	0	50	49	23	21	2	9	34	.257	.203	.280	6.16	1.63
Derosier, Matt	R-R	6-2	200	7-13-94	0	1	10.80	2	2	0	0	7	10	8	8	0	1	8	.333	.263	.455	10.80	1.35
Dickey, Robbie	R-R	6-3	205	4-6-94	0	1	5.14	4	0	0	0	14	15	11	8	0	10	7	.294	.346		4.50	6.43
Fedde, Erick	R-R	6-4	180	2-25-93	4	1	2.57	8	8	0	0	35	38	16	10	1	8	36	.264	.293	.232	9.26	2.06
Feliz, John	R-R	6-2	180	10-28-93	0	0	4.38	7	0	0	0	12	16	10	6	1	5	5	.320	.476	.207	3.65	3.65
Glover, Koda	R-R	6-5	195	4-13-93	0	0	0.00	3	0	0	1	6	1	0	0	0	1	11	.053	.000	.071	16.50	1.50
Guilbeau, Taylor	L-L	6-3	170	5-12-93	2	3	3.88	11	10	0	0	51	62	26	22	0	9	31	.307	.270	.324	5.47	1.59
Hearn, Taylor	L-L	6-5	190	8-30-94	1	5	3.98	10	10	0	0	43	49	22	19	2	13	38	.280	.178	.315	7.95	2.72
Johns, Sam	R-R	6-2	205	7-12-91	3	2	1.42	11	0	0	0	19	14	10	3	1	4	17	.197	.167	.220	8.05	1.89
Lee, Andrew	L-R	6-3	205	7-12-91	1	0	0.00	5	0	0	0	8	5	0	0	0	1	12	.172	.214	.133	12.96	1.08
Mills, McKenzie	L-L	6-4	205	11-19-95	0	2	7.71	4	3	0	0	12	17	12	10	0	9	8	.354	.368	.345	6.17	6.94
Mooney, Kevin	R-R	6-1	185	8-18-94	1	0	5.40	15	0	0	2	22	24	13	13	1	13	15	.286	.275	.295	6.23	5.40
Morales, Jose	R-R	6-3	180	2-12-95	1	0	4.32	3	0	0	0	8	8	4	4	1	2	3	.235	.250	.222	3.24	2.16
Overton, Connor	R-R	6-0	190	7-24-93	1	1	3.72	12	0	0	0	19	17	9	8	1	5	13	.221	.191	.267	6.05	2.33
Peterson, Tommy	R-R	6-1	205	10-11-93	0	0	2.66	16	0	0	4	20	21	7	6	0	4	13	.269	.341	.189	5.75	1.77
Pirro, Matt	R-R	6-1	185	4-24-93	0	0	4.85	12	0	0	0	13	16	7	7	0	10	10	.302	.423	.185	6.92	6.92
Plouck, Cole	L-L	6-2	175	4-25-94	1	0	1.80	2	0	0	1	5	2	1	1	1	1	2	.125	.000	.200	3.60	1.80
Ramos, David	R-R	6-0	175	9-13-91	0	1	7.71	2	0	0	0	2	3	2	2	0	0	0	.333	.500	.286	0.00	0.00
Reynoso, Yorlin	L-L	6-2	200	11-20-95	0	0	9.00	1	0	0	0	4	4	4	4	0	6	1	.267	.333	.250	2.25	13.50
Rivera Jr., Mariano	R-R	5-11	155	10-4-93	1	2	5.45	19	3	0	5	33	51	27	20	1	3	26	.333	.413	.247	7.09	0.82
Rodriguez, Jefry	R-R	6-5	185	7-26-93	3	5	4.59	13	13	0	0	69	72	39	35	4	33	67	.277	.283	.269	8.78	4.33
Torres, Luis	R-R	6-3	190	6-4-94	5	1	5.66	16	0	0	3	35	31	23	22	2	17	22	.235	.217	.250	5.66	4.37
Ullmann, Ryan	R-R	6-6	230	8-12-91	0	0	4.50	1	0	0	0	4	6	2	2	0	1	1	.429	.400	.444	2.25	2.25
Valerio, Maximo	R-R	6-3	190		2	0	2.63	4	1	0	0	14	14	4	4	0	3	15	.259	.222	.333	9.88	1.98
VanVossen, Mick	R-R	6-3	190	10-30-92	0	1	7.50	3	0	0	0	6	8	5	5	0	3	4	.348	.214	.556	6.00	4.50
Webb, Joey	L-L	6-5	230	9-27-90	2	0	3.60	3	0	0	0	5	4	3	2	0	3	5	.222	.600	.077	9.00	5.40

Fielding

Catcher	PCT	G	PO	A	E	DP	PB
Reetz	.977	33	187	29	5	1	7
Ruiz	1.000	2	2	0	0	0	1
Tillero	.981	35	223	36	5	0	5
VanMeetren	.983	8	55	2	1	0	1
Vilorio	.875	3	16	5	3	1	0
Mejia	.913	4	9	12	2	4	
Rodriguez	1.000	10	17	19	0	8	
Schrock	.966	30	55	60	4	12	

First Base	PCT	G	PO	A	E	DP
Eusebio	.988	18	156	13	2	8
Kerian	.995	42	355	29	2	36
Page	.900	1	8	1	1	1
Sagdal	.992	16	108	13	1	13
VanMeetren	1.000	1	1	0	0	0

Second Base	PCT	G	PO	A	E	DP
Dulin	.945	32	46	75	7	14
Jefferies	1.000	7	13	19	0	5

Third Base	PCT	G	PO	A	E	DP
Dulin	1.000	1	2	1	0	1
Franco	.833	9	4	1	1	0
Gutierrez	.881	46	50	83	18	8
Jefferies	1.000	3	2	1	0	0
Keniry	1.000	2	1	4	0	1
Riopedre	1.000	1	1	4	0	0
Rodriguez	.926	17	9	16	2	1
Schrock	1.000	1	1	1	0	0

Shortstop	PCT	G	PO	A	E	DP
Gutierrez	.930	12	18	22	3	5
Jefferies	1.000	1	1	0	0	0

Outfield	PCT	G	PO	A	E	DP
Lora	.891	35	52	95	18	25
Sagdal	.915	25	29	57	8	6
Schrock	.978	10	13	31	1	6
Agustin	.929	7	13	0	1	0
Bautista	.933	7	14	0	1	0
Encarnacion	.962	43	73	2	3	0
Eusebio	1.000	6	9	0	0	0
Florentino	.982	24	49	5	1	0
Guzman	1.000	17	24	0	0	0
Page	.971	15	32	1	1	0
Robles	1.000	38	87	2	0	1
Stevenson	1.000	17	43	2	0	2
Williamson	1.000	5	12	2	0	0
Wiseman	.960	52	92	5	4	1

GULF COAST LEAGUE

Batting	B-T	HT	WT	DOB	AVG	vLH	vRH	G	AB	R	H	2B	3B	HR	RBI	BB	HBP	SH	SF	SO	SB	CS	SLG	OBP
Aguero, Younaifred	R-R	6-2	170	4-10-93	.250	—	.250	2	4	0	1	0	0	0	0	0	0	1	0	0	0	0	.250	.400
Agustin, Telmito	L-L	5-10	160	10-9-96	.331	.244	.371	38	130	13	43	8	2	1	18	9	0	1	1	17	9	2	.446	.371
Alvarez, Thomas	R-R	6-1	165	2-15-95	.128	.071	.160	21	39	8	5	0	0	0	2	3	0	1	0	6	1	1	.128	.190
Baez, Jeyner	R-R	6-1	175	7-25-95	.000	—	.000	1	1	0	0	0	0	0	0	0	0	0	1	0	0	0	.000	.000
Bautista, Rafael	R-R	6-2	165	3-8-93	.313	—	.313	6	16	3	5	0	0	1	2	0	0	0	0	1	0	0	.500	.313
Brandt, Clayton	R-R	5-11	180	8-6-92	.193	.176	.197	34	88	18	17	4	1	0	7	10	4	2	0	28	2	3	.261	.304
Diedrick, Philip	L-R	6-1	210	9-17-92	.146	.143	.148	30	89	7	13	1	0	4	13	6	1	0	0	33	0	0	.292	.208
DiNatale, Dalton	L-R	6-4	205	3-26-93	.232	.278	.219	31	82	3	19	4	1	1	7	10	2	0	1	23	2	0	.341	.326
Florentino, Darryl	L-R	6-2	175	1-1-96	.329	.417	.288	26	76	6	25	5	2	0	10	3	0	1	2	12	2	3	.447	.346
Franco, Anderson	R-R	6-3	190	8-15-97	.281	.351	.259	46	153	19	43	6	1	4	19	14	2	0	1	26	2	3	.412	.347
La Bruna, Angelo	R-R	5-10	175	4-15-92	.269	.333	.250	32	93	9	25	6	1	0	5	3	2	3	1	15	1	1	.355	.303
Martinez, Andres	R-R	6-1	170	7-7-95	.227	.297	.183	34	97	12	22	7	1	0	9	7	3	0	0	25	5	0	.320	.299
Mota, Israel	R-R	6-2	165	1-3-96	.221	.269	.200	32	86	12	19	6	0	0	10	6	0	0	0	25	1	1	.291	.272
Ortiz, Oliver	L-L	6-0	170	5-6-96	.245	.214	.258	31	94	11	23	2	3	1	11	8	0	0	1	32	2	0	.362	.301
Perkins, Blake	R-R	6-1	165	9-10-96	.211	.111	.248	49	166	21	35	5	2	1	12	13	1	0	5	36	4	5	.283	.265
Pimentel, Davinson	R-R	5-9	170	2-12-97	.167	.227	.140	24	72	1	12	2	1	0	7	2	0	0	0	16	2	1	.222	.189
Ramirez, Gilberto	R-R	6-4	180	11-14-92	.291	.407	.231	25	79	9	23	3	1	0	4	1	2	1	0	19	6	6	.354	.317
Ramirez, Joshual	R-R	6-2	185	5-20-96	.215	.348	.161	26	79	10	17	4	0	0	11	7	1	0	1	17	3	2	.266	.284
Ripken, Ryan	L-L	6-6	205	7-26-93	.250	.241	.254	28	92	4	23	6	2	1	8	5	1	0	0	15	0	1	.391	.296
Robles, Victor	R-R	6-0	185	5-19-97	.370	.500	.354	33	73	19	27	6	1	2	11	10	7	3	1	12	12	1	.562	.484
Rodriguez, Wilman	R-R	6-1	175	6-7-91	.211	.200	.214	6	19	1	4	1	0	0	3	1	1	0	0	7	0	1	.263	.286
Rosario, Dionicio	R-R	6-3	180	2-14-94	.294	.167	.364	4	17	2	5	2	0	0	3	0	0	0	0	1	0	0	.412	.294
Sanchez, Adrian	B-R	6-0	160	8-16-90	.455	.500	.444	4	11	3	5	0	0	1	1	0	0	0	0	1	1		.727	.455
Stevenson, Andrew	L-L	6-0	185	6-1-94	.200	.200	—	2	5	1	1	0	0	0	0	0	1	0	0	0	2	0	.200	.333
Trejos, Edward	R-R	5-11	170	3-12-97	.333	.500	.000	2	3	1	1	0	0	0	0	0	0	0	0	0	0	0	.333	.333
Vilorio, Luis	R-R	6-2	160	10-9-96	.195	.207	.191	40	118	13	23	2	1	0	9	4	3	1	1	15	5	1	.229	.238
Ward, Drew	L-R	6-3	215	11-25-94	.154	.250	.111	4	13	2	2	0	0	1	2	3	0	0	0	8	0	0	.385	.313

Pitching	B-T	HT	WT	DOB	W	L	ERA	G	GS	CG	SV	IP	H	R	ER	HR	BB	SO	AVG	vLH	vRH	K/9	BB/9
Acevedo, Carlos	R-R	6-3	200	9-27-94	2	1	3.64	10	1	0	0	30	24	13	12	1	9	20	.222	.200	.235	6.07	2.73
Avila, Pedro	R-R	5-11	170	1-14-97	1	0	0.00	1	0	0	0	4	1	0	0	0	1	5	.077	.500	.000	11.25	2.25
Baez, Joan	R-R	6-3	190	12-26-94	1	3	2.13	9	9	0	0	42	31	11	10	0	19	42	.211	.167	.237	8.93	4.04
Bermudez, Juan	R-R	6-2	180	9-29-94	0	2	6.91	5	2	0	0	14	16	12	11	0	7	11	.276	.286	.270	6.91	4.40
Boghosian, Adam	R-R	6-2	210	10-13-91	0	0	0.00	2	0	0	0	1	0	0	0	0	0	0	.000	—	.000	0.00	0.00
Brinley, Ryan	L-R	6-1	200	4-9-93	0	0	0.00	2	0	0	0	2	2	0	0	0	0	0	.286	.000	.400	0.00	0.00
Cespedes, Angher	R-R	6-1	190	7-25-94	0	2	5.14	13	0	0	4	14	16	9	8	0	4	6	.308	.313	.306	3.86	2.57
Copping, Calvin	R-R	6-1	185	1-11-94	1	2	4.76	12	0	0	2	17	19	12	9	1	5	14	.264	.240	.277	7.41	2.65
De La Cruz, Kida	R-R	6-5	240	8-10-94	0	0	5.40	3	0	0	0	2	0	1	1	0	2	0	.000	.000	.000	0.00	10.80
Derosier, Matt	R-R	6-2	200	7-13-94	0	1	1.29	5	5	0	0	21	13	4	3	0	6	22	.176	.189	.162	9.43	2.57
Dickson, Ian	R-R	6-5	215	9-16-90	0	0	2.57	2	2	0	0	7	5	2	2	1	1	6	.192	.000	.263	7.71	1.29
Feliz, John	R-R	6-2	180	10-28-93	1	0	0.00	3	0	0	0	5	4	1	0	0	0	6	.200	.375	.083	10.80	0.00
Fuentes, Steven	R-R	6-2	175	5-4-97	3	4	5.22	11	6	0	0	40	46	29	23	3	15	33	.282	.206	.330	7.49	3.40
Guilbeau, Taylor	L-L	6-3	170	5-12-93	1	0	0.00	2	1	0	0	5	1	0	0	0	3	7	.063	.000	.083	12.60	5.40
Harmening, Russell	R-R	6-1	195	9-27-94	1	0	2.86	11	0	0	1	22	21	9	7	1	4	16	.259	.192	.291	6.55	1.64
Hearn, Taylor	L-L	6-6	215	8-30-94	0	0	0.00	2	1	0	0	5	4	1	0	0	2	7	.250	.500	.214	12.60	3.60
Johansen, Jake	R-R	6-6	235	1-23-91	0	1	1.69	3	0	0	0	5	4	2	1	0	0	3	.182	.000	.235	5.06	0.00
Lee, Andrew	L-R	6-5	210	12-2-93	1	0	0.00	1	0	0	0	1	0	0	0	0	0	1	.000	—	.000	9.00	0.00
Mills, McKenzie	L-L	6-4	205	11-19-95	0	3	7.04	8	5	0	1	23	24	19	18	3	19	16	.270	.333	.246	6.26	7.43
Pantoja, Jorge	R-R	6-5	215	3-26-94	1	1	5.84	12	0	0	0	12	15	8	8	0	3	11	.313	.538	.229	8.03	2.19
Pena, Carlos	R-R	6-5	240	4-3-94	0	1	9.82	8	0	0	0	7	13	10	8	0	5	7	.382	.273	.435	8.59	6.14
Pena, Ronald	R-R	6-4	195	9-19-91	1	0	0.00	2	0	0	0	4	1	0	0	0	0	4	.083	.000	.143	9.00	0.00
Pena, Wilber	R-R	6-2	185	9-14-95	1	6	3.92	9	9	0	0	39	47	21	17	3	12	36	.307	.271	.330	8.31	2.77
Peterson, Tommy	R-R	6-1	205	10-11-93	0	0	0.00	1	0	0	0	1	0	0	0	0	0	0	.250	.500	.000	0.00	0.00
Pirro, Matt	R-R	6-1	185	4-24-93	0	0	0.00	3	0	0	0	4	2	0	0	0	1	4	.154	.000	.222	9.00	2.25
Ramos, David	R-R	6-0	175	9-13-91	1	0	0.00	3	0	0	0	3	2	0	0	0	0	4	.182	.250	.143	12.00	0.00
Rauh, Brian	R-R	6-2	200	7-23-91	0	0	2.45	3	1	0	0	7	5	6	2	0	1	5	.172	.200	.158	6.14	1.23
Reynoso, Yorlin	L-L	6-2	200	11-20-95	1	3	5.66	10	7	0	0	35	39	28	22	2	14	26	.279	.278	.279	6.69	3.60
Valerio, Maximo	R-R	6-2	175	7-22-95	4	1	1.72	9	3	0	0	37	29	8	7	3	7	32	.216	.185	.238	7.85	1.72
VanVossen, Mick	R-R	6-3	190	10-30-92	0	1	4.21	12	2	0	2	26	20	12	12	1	10	19	.230	.135	.300	6.66	3.51
Watson, Tyler	R-L	6-5	200	5-22-97	1	1	0.00	5	4	0	0	13	7	1	0	0	4	16	.149	.357	.061	10.80	2.70
Yrizarri, Deibi	R-R	6-1	170	10-3-94	0	1	—	1	0	0	0	0	1	4	4	0	3		1.000	—	1.000	—	—

Fielding

Catcher	PCT	G	PO	A	E	DP	PB
Baez	1.000	1	7	1	0	0	0
Pimentel	.978	23	111	25	3	0	2
Trejos	1.000	2	4	0	0	0	0
Vilorio	.984	40	263	36	5	3	4

First Base	PCT	G	PO	A	E	DP
Diedrick	—	1	0	0	0	0
DiNatale	.987	23	146	11	2	10
Ortiz	.982	15	103	5	2	11

	PCT	G	PO	A	E	DP
Ripken	.974	24	180	9	5	13
Rosario	1.000	4	34	1	0	3

Second Base	PCT	G	PO	A	E	DP
Aguero	1.000	1	2	2	0	0
Alvarez	.979	20	17	29	1	5
La Bruna	.978	26	42	49	2	10
Martinez	.750	1	0	3	1	1
Ramirez	.938	21	44	31	5	8
Sanchez	1.000	1	0	1	0	0

Third Base	PCT	G	PO	A	E	DP
Aguero	1.000	1	1	0	0	0
DiNatale	.800	4	0	4	1	0
Franco	.920	43	25	78	9	5
Martinez	.909	12	7	23	3	2
Ramirez	.600	2	2	1	2	0
Ward	1.000	3	1	6	0	1

WASHINGTON NATIONALS

Shortstop	PCT	G	PO	A	E	DP
Brandt	.981	33	51	105	3	22
La Bruna	1.000	7	9	9	0	1
Martinez	.919	19	31	48	7	8
Ramirez	1.000	1	1	1	0	0
Sanchez	1.000	4	7	6	0	0

Outfield	PCT	G	PO	A	E	DP
Agustin	.936	36	41	3	3	0
Bautista	1.000	4	4	0	0	0
Diedrick	1.000	6	7	0	0	0
Florentino	1.000	20	27	0	0	0
Mota	.933	18	13	1	1	0

	PCT	G	PO	A	E	DP
Ortiz	1.000	12	23	1	0	0
Perkins	1.000	49	98	2	0	1
Ramirez	.973	23	36	0	1	0
Robles	.944	22	50	1	3	0
Rodriguez	1.000	5	5	0	0	0
Stevenson	1.000	1	3	0	0	0

DSL NATIONALS   ROOKIE

DOMINICAN SUMMER LEAGUE

Batting	B-T	HT	WT	DOB	AVG	vLH	vRH	G	AB	R	H	2B	3B	HR	RBI	BB	HBP	SH	SF	SO	SB	CS	SLG	OBP
Andujar, Yoel	R-R	6-3	185	10-29-97	.177	.200	.172	52	158	17	28	4	0	0	13	25	1	1	1	58	2	2	.203	.292
Baez, Jeyner	R-R	6-1	175	7-25-95	.282	.280	.283	34	124	20	35	5	0	1	6	7	0	2	0	17	4	3	.347	.321
Bencosme, Bryan	R-R	6-1	175	12-18-97	.191	.194	.190	64	220	17	42	8	1	1	15	24	4	4	1	61	4	5	.250	.281
Cabello, Jose	R-R	5-11	185	12-12-96	.165	.296	.128	40	121	11	20	2	0	0	16	13	4	2	1	24	0	1	.182	.266
Corredor, Aldrem	L-L	6-0	202	10-27-95	.303	.250	.313	63	218	39	66	12	2	3	41	39	3	2	3	44	3	2	.417	.411
Evangelista, Juan	R-R	5-11	165	5-28-98	.283	.293	.281	64	244	33	69	20	5	3	39	16	2	1	3	45	9	7	.443	.328
Falcon, Santo	R-R	6-0	190	3-28-97	.250	.000	.267	12	32	6	8	1	1	0	2	4	1	0	0	5	1	2	.344	.351
Jimenez, Carlos	R-R	5-11	180	10-2-96	.205	.125	.228	26	73	6	15	3	0	0	6	6	3	0	1	19	0	1	.247	.289
Martinez, Adanlis	R-R	6-2	170	1-31-98	.252	.269	.248	51	155	20	39	4	1	0	16	10	8	0	0	34	1	2	.290	.329
Medina, Roberto	R-R	5-11	185	9-24-97	.317	.368	.306	34	104	9	33	8	1	1	18	8	1	0	0	15	0	2	.442	.372
Meregildo, Omar	R-R	6-1	185	8-18-97	.202	.171	.207	65	228	31	46	24	1	3	25	32	11	1	7	81	4	2	.355	.320
Mesa, Brailin	R-R	6-3	185	11-2-97	.250	.190	.269	32	88	9	22	6	1	1	15	8	3	0	0	27	0	1	.375	.333
Morales, Jesus	R-R	5-10	158	12-22-97	.198	.200	.197	33	91	13	18	0	0	0	6	5	3	0	2	20	3	0	.198	.257
Perdomo, Luis	L-L	5-11	170	5-21-97	.295	.242	.305	63	200	29	59	16	3	0	29	24	7	3	3	33	14	13	.405	.385
Sierra, Franklin	B-R	5-10	170	2-15-96	.211	.300	.194	38	123	16	26	2	1	0	10	16	0	3	1	29	4	3	.244	.300
Trejos, Edward	R-R	6-1	167	7-12-97	.167	.000	.200	13	24	4	4	0	0	0	2	1	5	0	0	6	0	1	.167	.500
Ventura, Edwin	R-R	6-1	180	8-27-97	.300	.350	.288	60	217	41	65	3	5	2	11	16	10	2	0	38	15	3	.387	.374

Pitching	B-T	HT	WT	DOB	W	L	ERA	G	GS	CG	SV	IP	H	R	ER	HR	BB	SO	AVG	vLH	vRH	K/9	BB/9
Alastre, Tomas	R-R	6-4	170	6-11-98	0	5	3.98	14	14	0	0	54	48	37	24	2	33	50	.236	.190	.266	8.28	5.47
Avila, Aroon	R-R	6-3	175	5-26-97	0	0	13.50	1	0	0	0	1	2	1	1	0	0	0	.500	.500	.500	0.00	0.00
Avila, Pedro	R-R	5-11	170	1-14-97	6	3	2.26	13	13	0	0	60	46	22	15	1	17	87	.211	.216	.210	13.12	2.56
Bermudez, Juan	R-R	6-2	180	9-29-94	0	2	4.32	5	0	0	0	8	12	10	4	1	3	10	.308	.333	.292	10.80	3.24
Chu, Gilberto	L-L	5-11	160	11-19-97	3	3	2.55	18	1	0	0	49	39	18	14	1	15	43	.217	.130	.229	7.84	2.74
Constanzo, Francisco	R-R	6-1	180	10-4-96	0	0	1.50	4	0	0	0	6	3	4	1	0	9	9	.136	.000	.200	13.50	13.50
De La Cruz, Gerald	L-L	6-3	180	8-19-96	1	1	9.68	15	0	0	0	18	19	26	19	0	27	21	.264	.125	.281	10.70	13.75
Duran, Warner	R-R	5-11	165	3-25-98	1	0	2.67	17	0	0	0	34	26	14	10	0	15	32	.210	.083	.261	8.55	4.01
Flores, Christian	R-R	6-2	180	11-14-97	0	0	6.75	2	0	0	0	1	5	7	1	0	2	1	.455	.667	.375	6.75	13.50
Garcia, Yordani	R-R	6-5	180	2-14-97	3	3	6.50	10	3	0	0	18	27	20	13	0	12	12	.342	.346	.340	6.00	6.00
German, Jhonatan	R-R	6-4	215	1-24-95	0	0	10.38	5	0	0	0	4	5	8	5	1	8	7	.250	.000	.313	14.54	16.62
Guillen, Angel	R-R	6-2	150	1-24-97	1	4	6.08	17	1	0	1	27	32	18	18	2	10	37	.296	.185	.333	12.49	3.38
Jimenez, Jose	L-L	6-1	190	12-7-96	1	1	5.92	18	0	0	1	24	33	23	16	0	15	19	.333	.091	.364	7.03	5.55
Matheus, Juan	R-R	6-2	165	6-14-97	0	1	3.38	4	0	0	1	5	9	7	2	0	2	6	.360	.143	.444	10.13	3.38
Pinto, Francisco	R-R	6-2	165	4-26-97	0	2	15.00	5	0	0	0	3	2	5	5	0	7	4	.182	.000	.250	12.00	21.00
Ramirez, Nector	R-R	6-0	170	9-4-96	5	1	3.67	20	0	0	0	56	40	25	23	1	18	45	.200	.304	.160	7.19	2.88
Ramirez, Yonathan	L-L	5-11	165	4-13-97	2	6	2.75	14	14	0	0	69	64	26	21	2	13	56	.246	.150	.254	7.34	1.70
Rosa, Jeffrey	R-R	6-3	189	6-5-95	1	4	3.05	13	13	0	0	56	38	25	19	3	29	69	.191	.208	.185	11.09	4.66
Rosario, Ramses	R-R	6-3	180	10-18-95	1	1	8.00	10	0	0	0	18	27	17	16	2	12	10	.375	.458	.333	5.00	6.00
2-team total (7 Red Sox2)					1	2	4.79	17	0	0	1	36	44	21	19	2	16	22	—	—	—	5.55	4.04
Sisnero, Yelmery	L-L	6-1	185	9-9-97	1	1	4.89	19	0	0	1	39	52	30	21	1	14	27	.315	.100	.329	6.28	3.26
Taveras, Felix	R-R	6-2	155	7-11-95	2	2	5.33	14	13	0	0	49	44	42	29	3	30	45	.235	.239	.233	8.27	5.51
Uribarri, Williantony	R-R	6-3	170	8-17-95	0	0	22.74	5	0	0	0	6	12	17	16	1	8	5	.387	.556	.318	7.11	11.37

Fielding

Catcher	PCT	G	PO	A	E	DP	PB
Baez	.976	24	214	31	6	4	12
Cabello	.989	23	152	21	2	0	8
Jimenez	.994	20	151	18	1	1	7
Medina	1.000	10	46	1	0	0	5
Trejos	.967	13	75	14	3	0	5

First Base	PCT	G	PO	A	E	DP
Baez	.960	5	46	2	2	1
Cabello	1.000	13	78	1	0	5
Corredor	.974	51	400	20	11	30
Martinez	.818	3	9	0	2	2
Medina	1.000	2	11	0	0	1
Mesa	.857	5	11	1	2	4

	PCT	G	PO	A	E	DP
Perdomo	.971	5	32	1	1	3

Second Base	PCT	G	PO	A	E	DP
Baez	1.000	3	9	4	0	1
Meregildo	.972	29	68	38	3	11
Morales	.960	21	28	44	3	3
Sierra	.945	30	69	68	8	24

Third Base	PCT	G	PO	A	E	DP
Bencosme	.833	9	7	18	5	1
Martinez	.837	41	27	76	20	7
Meregildo	.897	24	20	41	7	5
Morales	1.000	2	2	2	0	0
Sierra	.889	4	5	11	2	0

Shortstop	PCT	G	PO	A	E	DP
Bencosme	.879	56	69	142	29	22
Meregildo	.914	15	21	43	6	7
Morales	.882	6	8	7	2	4

Outfield	PCT	G	PO	A	E	DP
Andujar	.964	44	50	3	2	0
Corredor	1.000	11	16	1	0	0
Evangelista	.949	59	90	4	5	2
Falcon	.889	11	16	0	2	0
Mesa	.909	18	20	0	2	0
Perdomo	.958	47	67	2	3	0
Ventura	.958	55	89	3	4	1

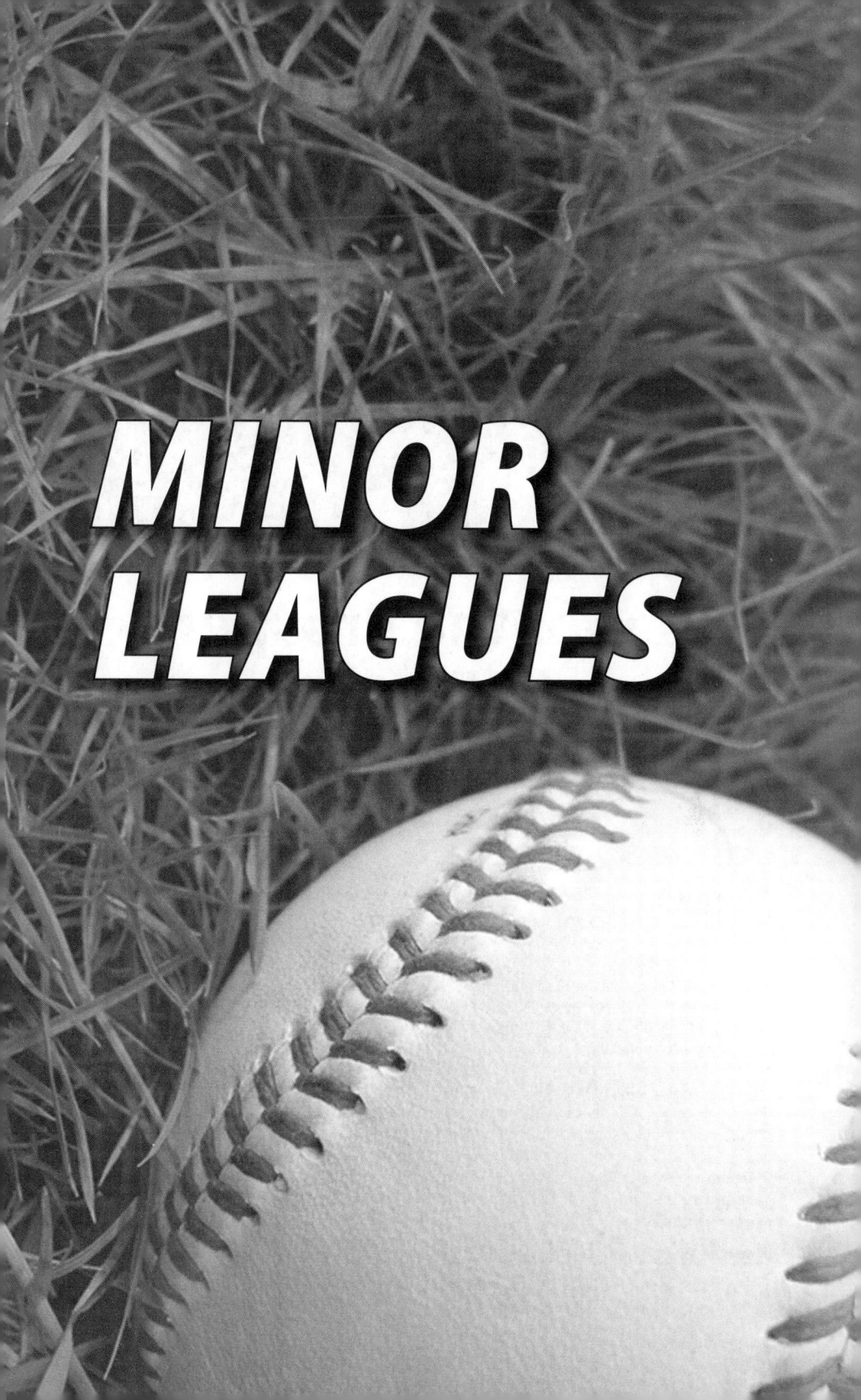

MINOR LEAGUES

The Biloxi Shuckers had to spend two months on the road before MGM Park was ready for play

Year of the Prospect shines light on minors

After a year in 2014 spent agonizing over what to do about the spate of Tommy John surgeries to the game's young stars, baseball spent 2015 gleefully celebrating as an unfathomably deep crop of young talent took over the sport.

The Year of the Prospect began in the minors before trickling up to the major leagues.

Of Baseball America's Top 100 Prospects entering the season, 37 graduated into full-fledged major leaguers and 15 made appearances in the playoffs. Those moving up included seven of the top 10 prospects entering this season and 14 of the top 20. Top 100 prospects found their way on to the rosters of 22 of the 30 major league teams, and a few of those clubs who missed out got big-time contributions from rookies. And most of those spent time this season in the minor leagues, giving fans a sneak peek of what was a very productive prospect season.

Youth was served at nearly every corner of the game, making this past season one of the most fun to follow in a long time.

New Parks Provide Boost

Even if the 42,561,445 fans who came through minor league ballparks in 2015 do not mark a new attendance record, they do signal that the sport is on an upswing in popularity.

Minor league teams aren't moving into new stadiums at the same rate as the late 1990s and early 2000s, when 51 new ballparks were built during the first decade of this century and five consecutive seasons of record attendance culminated with the current high mark of 43,263,740 set in 2008. Attendance had largely remained stagnant from 2010-13 before an improving economy, the opening of new ballparks in major markets the past two seasons, and a commitment to customer service and promotions helped yield the biggest attendance gains in seven years.

"It speaks to the real strength of the product," Minor League Baseball president Pat O'Conner said.

Nashville had long been considered potentially one of the sport's best markets, if only the Sounds (Pacific Coast) could move from the outskirts of town at Greer Stadium to a new downtown ballpark. After a decade of trying, the team finally got a chance to put that theory to a test with the opening of First Tennessee Park in 2015.

The results were as promised. The ballpark, complete with a modern guitar-shaped scoreboard in right field, was praised for its variety of vantage points as well as player and fan amenities. And after finishing 14th in the 16-team Pacific Coast League in 2014 with 323,691 fans, the Sounds jumped to fourth with 565,548 fans in 2015.

"From a business standpoint, I've been in this 25 years, and I haven't seen anything like this," veteran minor league operator and Nashville chief operating officer Garry Arthur said.

New Southern League franchise Biloxi's MGM Park opened more than two months late due to a delay in construction and sent the newly minted Shuckers on a season-opening, 54-game road trip. Yet the team still attracted 164,076 fans—up from 94,929 during their final season in Huntsville in 2014. And the West Virginia Black Bears (New York-Penn) had a stellar debut season after relocating from Jamestown, drawing 83,796 fans (compared to 24,246 a season earlier in Jamestown) and taking home the league championship.

Meanwhile, the Charlotte Knights (International) and El Paso Chihuahuas (Pacific Coast) each avoided sophomore slumps after stellar ballpark openings in 2014. The Knights, whose BB&T Ballpark offers arguably the sport's best downtown skyline view and a variety of fan amenities, narrowly missed leading the minors in attendance for a second straight season after drawing 669,398. The Chihuahuas—who relocated from Tucson to just north of the border from Juarez, Mexico—finished third in the PCL with a 578,952 total and culminated the season by hosting the Triple-A National Championship. Fellow PCL affiliate Sacramento returned to the top spot in minor league attendance, which it held from 2000-08, by attracting 672,354 fans.

The International League proved it's the place to be in the minors. The Triple-A circuit held four of the minors' top five spots in overall attendance, with Indianapolis (662,536), Columbus (662,096) and Lehigh Valley joining Charlotte.

Plenty of other success stories dotted the sport, including 15 franchises that reported attendance records in 2015. South Bend (Midwest) led the charge in its first season as a Cubs affiliate and the fourth under owner Andrew Berlin, who has invested heavily into improving the team's ballpark while sparking interest among the locals. The Myrtle Beach Pelicans (Carolina), also in their first season as a Cubs affiliate, would have joined this list if not for canceling three home games when the Carolina Mudcats' team bus crashed on a late-night trip south in May.

Not every team fared so well in 2015. The Memphis Redbirds, considered the flagship franchise of minor league baseball after the opening

GATE BUSTERS

The 2015 season drew 42,561,445 fans to minor league ballparks—the third-most in the sport's history. Here are the top 10 teams in overall attendance.

Team (League)	Overall Attendance	Average Attendance
Sacramento (PCL)	672,354	9,338
Charlotte (IL)	669,398	9,428
Indianapolis (IL)	662,536	9,331
Columbus (IL)	622,096	9,016
Lehigh Valley (IL)	613,815	8,769
Round Rock (PCL)	595,012	8,623
El Paso (PCL)	578,952	8,154
Dayton (MWL)	574,830	8,212
Nashville (PCL)	565,548	7,965
Albuquerque (PCL)	560,519	8,007

Also contributing to the big season at the gate in 2015 were 83 teams that saw increases in attendance—including the three franchises that opened new ballparks. Below are the 10 teams that saw the biggest increases in average attendance.

Team	2015 Total	2015 Avg.	2014 Avg.	Difference
* W. Virginia (NYP)	83,796	2,265	758	198.81%
* Biloxi	164,076	2,604	1,460	78.36%
* Nashville	565,548	7,965	4,909	62.25%
South Bend	347,678	5,039	3,751	34.34%
Boise	109,945	2,893	2,303	25.62%
Vancouver	215,535	5,825	4,870	19.61%
Oklahoma City	471,996	6,941	6,045	14.82%
Eugene	120,931	3,182	2,844	11.88%
Norfolk	386,402	5,767	5,267	9.49%
Ogden	125,398	3,300	3,014	9.49%
Sacramento	672,354	9,338	8,561	9.08%

* Opened a new ballpark in 2015

of AutoZone Park in 2000, have steadily dropped from the top of the Pacific Coast League in attendance to the bottom of the circuit's 16 teams in 2015. In its first full season under the ownership of the St. Louis Cardinals, Memphis drew just 278,579 fans in 2015—by far the lowest in franchise history. Team and league officials have cautioned not to panic, citing more accurate attendance measuring than the previous operators and focusing more on completing $6 million in ballpark renovations last offseason than marketing the team to locals.

Memphis still plays in one of the minors' premier ballparks, but also one of the most expansive, that may not be a good fit for a city with other professional sports and entertainment options.

"For me, (AutoZone Park) is still the Taj Mahal of minor league baseball," PCL president Branch Rickey III said. "It's a matter of rehabing the franchise."

Teams Offer Flood Relief

The four minor league teams that call South Carolina home returned to their soggy ballparks after the torrential rains that caused so much destruction in their home state finally came to an end in early October.

The Charleston Riverdogs (South Atlantic),

MINOR LEAGUES

Columbia Fireflies (South Atlantic, moving in from Savannah for next season), Greenville Drive (South Atlantic) and Myrtle Beach (Carolina) found minimal damage within their own walls: roofs that leaked, standing water in dugouts and clubhouses, playing fields in need of repair. They considered those nuisances compared to what their fans were dealing with after a thousand-year storm dumped upward of two feet of rain in parts of the state.

So the four minor league clubs teamed up to support the fans who have supported them over the years by creating a joint GoFundMe page to raise money for the American Red Cross of the region. Each of the four teams, along with Minor League Baseball Charities, contributed $2,500 to the fund, with a goal to raise $100,000. Several other minor league franchises had already contributed as well.

"You sit there in your own house and see what is happening and know that some areas are lower and others are more prone to getting hit," Charleston general manager Dave Echols said. "You see water up to mailboxes and homes where furniture is floating, and there is no doubt that those people are our fans. So that's gut-wrenching to see."

The storm didn't cause any significant damage to the Fireflies' ballpark under construction, team owner Jason Freier said, other than creating a muddy mess at the construction site. He believes the project will be delayed as they clean up and local contractors tend to more pressing needs in the community, but Freier said they allowed enough of a cushion in the construction timeline for it to open on time next spring.

"When you plan for worst-case scenarios in terms of weather," Freier said, "this is pretty much it."

Minors Pick Up The Pace

Minor league games in 2015 were played at a quicker pace than in recent years thanks to a set of pace of play rules that debuted this season. Major League Baseball asked minor leagues to better police the time between innings, and pitch clocks were installed at every Double-A and Triple-A ballpark to enforce time between pitches and innings.

Because of those changes, Minor League Baseball shaved six minutes from the average game, from 2:49 in 2014 to 2:43 this season.

The differences were most notable at the upper levels of the minors, where the pitch clocks were added (they also had the longest game times before the changes). The Pacific Coast League shaved 13 minutes per nine-inning game (from 2:58 to 2:45) while the International League cut 16 minutes (from 2:56 to 2:40).

"I think it was 99.9 percent positive. I think it was an overwhelming success," International

Cumulative domestic farm club records for major league organizations, with winning percentages going back five years. Most organizations have six affiliates.

	2015						
	W	L	PCT	2014	2013	2012	2011
1. Astros	431	332	.565	.519	.570	.546	.408
2. D-backs	420	345	.549	.561	.510	.499	.488
3. Pirates	417	346	.547	.450	.515	.505	.512
4. Phillies	377	319	.542	.435	.468	.498	.522
5. Cubs	371	316	.540	.522	.504	.470	.507
6. Twins	367	320	.534	.528	.546	.525	.490
7. Mets	406	357	.532	.568	.546	.509	.498
8. Dodgers	366	326	.529	.458	.486	.528	.543
9. Orioles	366	333	.524	.465	.481	.456	.487
10. Rangers	359	334	.518	.546	.528	.517	.565
11. Cardinals	389	371	.512	.545	.494	.505	.518
11. Reds	352	336	.512	.489	.426	.449	.503
11. Yankees	422	403	.512	.509	.495	.529	.494
14. Indians	353	341	.509	.507	.445	.506	.515
15. White Sox	347	341	.504	.456	.488	.504	.500
15. Giants	350	344	.504	.509	.564	.506	.539
17. Rays	381	378	.502	.505	.524	.515	.497
18. Royals	378	382	.497	.450	.463	.492	.494
19. Braves	336	351	.489	.493	.485	.461	.471
20. Blue Jays	369	392	.485	.495	.493	.524	.515
21. Athletics	335	359	.483	.513	.497	.496	.514
22. Padres	330	364	.476	.472	.496	.455	.515
23. Tigers	326	365	.472	.516	.484	.482	.467
24. Red Sox	328	371	.469	.529	.504	.504	.490
24. Nationals	326	369	.469	.514	.550	.506	.511
26. Rockies	333	382	.466	.466	.482	.540	.495
27. Angels	317	374	.459	.486	.501	.449	.507
28. Brewers	300	384	.439	.508	.449	.459	.466
29. Mariners	301	391	.435	.475	.497	.528	.483
30. Marlins	297	399	.427	.498	.497	.524	.495

LEAGUE	CHAMPION	RUNNER-UP
International	Columbus	Indianapolis
Pacific Coast	Fresno	Round Rock
Eastern	Bowie	Reading
Southern	Chattanooga	Biloxi
Texas	Midland	NW Arkansas
California	Rancho Cucamonga	San Jose
Carolina	Myrtle Beach	Wilmington
Florida State	Charlotte	Dayton
Midwest	West Michigan	Cedar Rapids
South Atlantic	Hickory	Asheville
New York-Penn	West Virginia	Staten Island
Northwest	Hillsboro	Tri-City
Appalachian	Greeneville	Princeton
Pioneer	Missoula	Idaho Falls
Arizona	White Sox	Mariners
Gulf Coast	Red Sox	Blue Jays

League president Randy Mobley said. "I'm not sure who labeled it pace of play, but that's exactly what it was. It's not game-time reduction. It's pace of play. We still had three hour plus games, or two hour 50 minutes-plus games. But we had more baseball played in that time and less dilly-dallying."

How much less? A steady growth in game times was halted, bringing minor league baseball back to the time of games from nearly a decade ago—the average game had taken longer than 2:43 in every year since 2007.

Players Seek Better Pay

Only a select few of the roughly 5,000 minor league players complete the rise to the major leaguers, a journey as difficult as any in professional sports. However, a group of former players are trying to ease the financial hardship of life as a minor leaguer.

Those former players are seeking to change the pay structure for current players, who typically earn between $1,100 and $2,150 a month and are paid only during the five-month minor league season, by filing a lawsuit against Major League Baseball for suppressing salaries in violation of federal and state labor laws. In October, the United States District Court in San Francisco ruled that the lawsuit can be certified as a class action meaning, roughly 10,000 current and former minor leaguers can join the plaintiffs.

"Major League Baseball and its teams are enjoying record revenue and profits, and taking just a slice of that revenue and devoting it to the developmental system should be an easy fix," said Garrett Broshuis, a lawyer representing the players and a former minor league pitcher in the Giants system.

Major League Baseball has countered the lawsuit by claiming that playing minor league baseball was never meant to be a career but has always been considered a defacto apprenticeship and a stepping stone to the major leagues. So under the direction of Stan Brand, Minor League Baseball's vice president who doubles as a power-broker attorney on Capitol Hill, Major League Baseball is petitioning Congress to include minor league ballplayers to the list of 35 occupations not required to receive minimum wage or overtime pay as dictated in the Federal Labor Standards Act—a move that would likely nullify the players' lawsuit in order to preserve the current relationship between the major and minor leagues..

"You don't know what system would take its place and what the effect would be on all the levels of minor league baseball," Brand said. "It's a big risk. And then again, (the current system) worked for 100-plus years and in all these towns and cities. I think we would like to see it continue."

Braves Deal With Crashes

The Atlanta Braves endured a pair of vehicle crashes that left several of their minor leaguers injured. The first came in early May, when a bus carrying their high Class A Carolina Mudcats affiliate to Myrtle Beach ran off the road in the early morning hours. The bus, unable to make a turn on a back road, flipped onto its side and skidded several hundred yards. Seven players were taken to the hospital, and six went on the disabled list, including pitching prospect Lucas Sims (who didn't return to Carolina for nearly two months).

"Everybody went flying from one side of "When you think about what could have happened, we are fortunate that this is the outcome with some of these guys," Jonathan Schuerholz, the team's assistant director of player development said. "We've just got to count our lucky stars a little in that regard."

Three months later, a car carrying some of the team's minor leaguers on its Rookie-level Dominican Summer League affiliate, slid off the road in the Dominican Republic. Four players—righthander Luis Perez, shortstop Alex Aquino, outfielder Randy Ventura and righthander Luis Severino—were among the six injured.

Reed Makes It Big

A.J. Reed's big season at the plate nearly became an historic one. The Astros' slugger, selected 42nd overall in 2014 out of Kentucky, finished second to the Rays' Blake Snell in Minor League Player of the Year voting and nearly became just the third player to win that honor and BA's College Player of the Year Award.

It's hard to knock Reed's achievements, even if many observers questioned if a player his size—he's listed at 6-foot-4, 240 pounds but admits he arrived at spring training more than 40 pounds heavier—could succeed on the field. Reed topped the minors in home runs (34), slugging percentage (.612) and OPS (1.044) while splitting the season between high Class A Lancaster and Double-A Corpus Christi. His .340 batting average was fourth-best in the minors this season.

No player provided more frequent highlights in 2015.

"He hit a ball the other day here to right-center field that went out in what seemed like it took two seconds on a line," Corpus Christi manager Rodney Linares said. "I looked back into the dugout and said 'Wow. Did that just happen?' That was like out of a movie. He does something every day offensively."

Linares wasn't exaggerating. Reed failed to reach base in just eight of his 135 games this season. He reached base four or more times on 14 different occasions.

Reed has a ways to go to catch Toledo Mud Hens veteran slugger Mike Hessman, who set a

CONTINUED ON PAGE 355

Snell lives up to his potential

BY J.J. COOPER

PLAYER OF THE YEAR

Design a breakout season for a pitcher, and it would look like Blake Snell's 2015.

A supplemental first-round pick of the Rays out of a Washington high school in 2011, Snell still had not progressed past A-ball entering the year. Then he opened the season with 21 scoreless innings to show he was too good for the high Class A Florida State League, en route to a 46-inning scoreless streak. He finished the year with Triple-A Durham, posting the best walk rate of his career.

Few pitchers have approached Snell's success over the past decade. He finished 15-4, 1.41 overall and recorded 163 strikeouts in 134 innings. His 1.41 ERA, which led all minor league qualifiers, is the lowest for a full-season pitcher since Justin Verlander's 1.29 in 2005, and he ranked among the leaders in wins (tied for fourth), strikeouts (also tied for fourth), WHIP (ninth, 1.02) and opponent average (first, .182).

The statistics tell the story of a pitcher who has fulfilled the promise that Rays area scout Paul Kirsch recorded in his amateur report on Snell, which summarized his looks at the Shoreline, Wash., lefthander from July 2010 through May 2011.

Kirsch recorded Snell as 6-foot-4, 180 pounds, after he had shot up 10 inches from his 5-foot-6 sophomore stature at Shorewood High. His radar gun registered the speed of Snell's three pitches: a fastball up to 94 mph, dipped as low as 87 and averaged 91, a 72-76 mph curveball and an 80-83 mph changeup.

Kirsch graded all three pitches in their current states on the 20-80 scouting scale, marking Snell's fastball as a 55 (slightly above major league average) to go with a 50 change and 45 curve. Kirsch projected all three to get better, with Snell earning a future 65 fastball, 60 curve and 60 changeup with average life and average future command of all three.

Next, he graded his arm action and delivery as 60s as well, and he described Snell physically, with words that for the most part still hold true today: "Medium large, tall frame; elongated features . . . long levers; XL hands; should fill out well; physically immature; baby face."

Under the category of makeup, Kirsch added: "some pissant in him on field."

The summary also goes into more detail about each of Snell's pitches. Kirsch reported on Snell's loose, easy arm and noted there's "more (velocity) in the tank; feel he will throw very hard someday soon."

He notes that Snell's loose wrist—crucial for improving his breaking ball—and quality changeup with "late tumble life when down." And calls him "extremely projectable" with "very high upside."

But the real fortune-telling comes at the end. "Consistency of stuff only thing that is keeping him from being on the top of my pref list . . . If it all comes together for this kid, I believe he could be a No. 2-type starter . . . I can't imagine how good he can be when he is about 21 years old or so."

We don't have to imagine anymore. The 22-year-old Snell—our 2015 Minor League Player of the Year—has closed the gap between his reality and his potential. His dominant season put him on the cusp of becoming the Rays' latest ace, following Scott Kazmir, James Shields, David Price and Chris Archer.

"I'm the same guy; I still just have fun playing baseball," Snell says, "because in my mind I'm just an average guy . . . I feel like it's still high school. How have I changed? I feel like I'm a lot better at pitching."

Blake Snell

PREVIOUS 10 WINNERS

2005: Delmon Young, of, Montgomery/Durham (Devil Rays)
2006: Alex Gordon, 3b, Wichita (Royals)
2007: Jay Bruce, of, Sarasota/Chattanooga/Louisville (Reds)
2008: Matt Wieters, c, Frederick/Bowie (Orioles)
2009: Jason Heyward, of, Myrtle Beach/Mississippi (Braves)
2010: Jeremy Hellickson, rhp, Montgomery/Durham (Rays)
2011: Mike Trout, of, Arkansas (Angels)
2012: Wil Myers, of, Northwest Arkansas/Omaha (Royals)
2013: Byron Buxton, of, Cedar Rapids/Fort Myers (Twins)
2014: Kris Bryant, 3b, Tennessee/Iowa (Cubs)

Full list: BaseballAmerica.com/awards

MINOR LEAGUES

Oster keeps Storm surging

The Lake Elsinore Storm have become such a steady franchise under general manager Dave Oster that it can be easy to forget that they succeed while playing in one of the California League's smallest markets.

Yet Oster keeps the Storm running like a big-market franchise. Lake Elsinore was the only California League team to top the 200,000-fan mark in 2015—drawing 213,932 while averaging 3,146 per game.

"They make coming to the ballpark a community experience," California League president Charlie Blaney said.

The reason for their success is not a secret. Oster, who just finished his 16th season with the team, stresses creative promotions, top-notch customer service and ballpark ingenuity. Lake Elsinore has been on the cutting edge of minor league ingenuity—from attention grabbing events (like combining a season's worth of promotions on the final game of the season for "Everything Night") to making the Diamond more eco-friendly by becoming

EXECUTIVE OF THE YEAR

PREVIOUS 10 WINNERS

2005: Jay Miller, Round Rock Express (Pacific Coast)
2006: Alan Ledford, Sacramento River Cats (Pacific Coast)
2007: Mike Moore, Minor League Baseball
2008: Naomi Silver, Rochester Red Wings (International)
2009: Ken Young, Norfolk Tides (International)
2010: Monty Hoppel, Midland Rockhounds (Texas)
2011: Todd Parnell, Richmond Flying Squirrels (Eastern)
2012: Bob Richmond, Northwest League
2013: Martie Cordaro, Omaha Storm Chasers (Pacific Coast)
2014: Sam Bernabe, Iowa Cubs (Pacific Coast)

Full list: BaseballAmerica.com/awards

minor league baseball's first LEED-certified ballpark.

"Dave is one of our veteran executives who is a leader in the California League," Blaney said. "Everyone looks up to him for advice and his experience. He is a great resource and mentor to all of us in the league."

CONTINUED FROM PAGE 353

new mark for players in the domestic affiliated minors when he belted his 433rd career home run on Aug. 3 against Lehigh Valley. That homer surpassed the 432 hit by Russell Loris "Buzz" Arlett from 1918-37. Hessman also holds the career home run record in the International League.

"I don't follow the numbers," the California native said when asked about the record. "After the season, I'll probably do a little digging and see about the guys whose records I passed and think about what it means."

Denson Comes Out

Brewers minor leaguer David Denson became the first player in affiliated baseball to come out as gay, first making an impromptu clubhouse announcement to his Helena Brewers teammates in August before making a public statement soon after. Denson, 20, a 15th-round pick in 2013, said he told his teammates after one of them had jokingly referred to him using a derogatory term for a gay male. "Be careful what you say. You never know," Denson cautioned the player with a smile.

Before he knew it, Denson was making the announcement he yearned to share. Much to his relief, he was greeted with outward support when the conversation ended, inspiring him to make a larger announcement. "There was that stereotype stuck in my head that there would never be a gay player on a team," Denson said. "I was thinking that once they found out, they would shut me out or treat me different. That was one of the things that was holding me back. I was always saying, 'Just keep it quiet. You don't need to tell them. You don't want them to see you different. You don't want them to judge you.'

"It started to affect my game because I was so caught up in trying to hide it. I was so concerned about how they would feel. I was pushing my feelings aside. Finally, I came to terms with, this is who I am and not everybody is going to accept it. Once you do that, it's a blessing in itself."

Miss Babe Says Goodbye

After 645 straight games, Miss Babe Ruth, the matriarch of the Greensboro Grasshoppers' trio of bat-retrieving black labs, called it a career at the team's home finale.

The Grasshoppers sent her out in style.

After the normal pre-game festivities, the guest of honor was wheeled toward home plate in a shiny, candy apple-red classic car. Greensboro

MINOR LEAGUES

DeFrancesco keeps winning

Fresno's Triple-A franchise had a new affiliation in 2015, joining the Astros after 17 years with the Giants. The geography worked with the Giants, and with the parent franchise having won three World Series titles in five seasons, Fresno didn't want to leave the Giants.

But when the Triple-A musical chairs stopped after the 2014 season, the Grizzlies wound up with the Astros, which meant they would get Pacific Coast League veteran manager Tony DeFrancesco. He quickly made a positive impression, declaring before the season that the Grizzlies would make the playoffs.

He knew what a Triple-A playoff team looks like; he'd managed in the league since 2003, winning three league titles with the Athletics' Sacramento affiliate and a division title in 2013 with the Astros' Oklahoma City club.

But this was no mere playoff team; Fresno won its first division title in the PCL, the league championship and the Triple-A National Championship in El Paso by topping International League champ Columbus 7-0.

MANAGER OF THE YEAR

PREVIOUS 10 WINNERS

2005: Ken Oberkfell, Norfolk (Mets)
2006: Todd Claus, Portland (Red Sox)
2007: Matt Wallbeck, Erie (Tigers)
2008: Rocket Wheeler, Myrtle Beach (Braves)
2009: Charlie Montoyo, Durham (Rays)
2010: Mike Sarbaugh, Columbus (Indians)
2011: Ryne Sandberg, Lehigh Valley (Phillies)
2012: Dave Miley, Scranton/Wilkes-Barre (Yankees)
2013: Gary DiSarcina, Pawtucket (Red Sox)
2014: Mark Johnson, Kane County (Cubs)

Full list: BaseballAmerica.com/awards

DeFrancesco's consistent winning, loyalty to the Astros organization and development skills earned him this honor.

"Tony's a winner first and foremost," Astros farm director Quinton McCracken said. "We knew that with Tony, he knows how to win at this level and get the most out of his players."

---

mayor Nancy Vaughan read a proclamation and awarded Miss Babe the key to the city. She informed the sellout crowd that Miss Babe's bucket, the one she uses to bring baseballs and water to the home-plate umpire, was going to be put on display at the Hall of Fame. The pooch even performed her own version of a ceremonial first pitch.

After the game finished, Miss Babe ended her career with one final trip around the bases.

Farewell To Friends

He was the larger-than-life figure who greeted generations of Arkansas Travelers fans at the gates of Ray Winder Field wearing suspenders and handing out scorecards. He was the umpire who ejected Earl Weaver and Mickey Mantle. He was also the man who brought Rosco Stidman, Captain Dynamite and Clunker Car Night to Little Rock.

Bill Valentine, whose contributions over five decades in the game were so well thought of he was named "King of Baseball" at the Winter Meetings in 2014, died April 26 after a brief bout with cancer. He was 82.

Known in part for his colorful suspenders and at times just as colorful language, Valentine, born in Little Rock seven months after Ray Winder Field opened, spent 35 years as Travelers general

manager after serving five years as an umpire in the American League. He attracted scores of fans through promotions that led to attendance booms in the 1980s and 1990s, and then helped secure the team's future in Little Rock by opening Dickey Stephens Park in 2007.

Longtime Florida State League president Chuck Murphy, who made the league office a family affair, died at the age of 83. Murphy worked as FSL president for 25 years, much of that time with his wife Emo by his side and daughter Laura also in the office. Murphy, who previously served in the military and ran a pair of minor league clubs, became a role model for league and team officials.

"All of the league presidents would say they were close with Chuck, and I was no different," International League president Randy Mobley said. "He made us all feel special and feel like you were his best friend."

Moving On

A pair of minor league teams wrapped up their tenure at long-time homes before heading off to new ballparks elsewhere next season.

The New Britain Rock Cats (Eastern) will shift just 12 miles down the road to Hartford and, as the result of a name-the-team contest, will now

MINOR LEAGUES

TRIPLE-A

Pos	Player, Team (Org)	League	AVG	OBP	SLG	G	AB	R	H	2B	3B	HR	RBI	BB	SO	SB
C	Austin Barnes, Oklahoma City (Dodgers)	PCL	.315	.389	.479	81	292	40	92	17	2	9	42	35	36	12
1B	Jesus Montero, Tacoma (Mariners)	PCL	.355	.398	.569	98	394	70	140	18	6	18	85	29	71	3
2B	Javier Baez, Iowa (Cubs)	PCL	.324	.385	.527	70	281	49	91	14	2	13	61	21	76	17
3B	Richie Shaffer, Durham (Rays)	IL	.270	.355	.582	69	244	42	66	17	1	19	45	31	74	1
SS	Corey Seager, Oklahoma City (Dodgers)	PCL	.278	.332	.451	105	421	64	117	30	2	13	61	32	65	3
CF	Jackie Bradley, Pawtucket (Red Sox)	IL	.305	.382	.472	71	282	38	86	18	1	9	29	30	44	4
OF	Taylor Motter, Durham (Rays)	IL	.292	.366	.471	127	486	74	142	43	1	14	72	57	95	26
OF	D. Santana, Fresno/Colo. Springs (Astros/Brewers)	PCL	.333	.426	.573	95	354	75	118	23	4	18	77	54	108	2
DH	Jose Martinez Omaha (Royals)	PCL	.384	.461	.563	98	341	57	131	25	3	10	60	48	55	8

Pos	Pitcher, Team (Org)	League	W	L	ERA	G	GS	SV	IP	H	HR	BB	SO	AVG	SO/9	WHIP
SP	Jose Berrios. Rochester (Twins)	IL	6	2	2.62	12	12	0	76	59	6	14	83	.212	9.9	0.96
SP	Brian Johnson, Pawtucket (Red Sox)	IL	9	6	2.53	18	18	0	96	74	6	32	90	.211	8.4	1.10
SP	Erik Johnson, Charlotte (White Sox)	IL	11	8	2.37	23	22	0	133	108	5	41	136	.224	9.2	1.12
SP	Steve Matz, Las Vegas (Mets)	PCL	7	4	2.19	15	14	0	90	69	6	31	94	.213	9.4	1.11
SP	Luis Severino, Scranton/W-B (Yankees)	IL	7	0	1.91	11	11	0	61	40	0	17	50	.184	7.3	0.93
RP	Oliver Drake, Norfolk (Orioles)	IL	1	2	0.82	42	0	23	44	23	1	16	66	.151	13.5	0.89

DOUBLE-A

Pos	Player, Team (Org)	League	AVG	OBP	SLG	G	AB	R	H	2B	3B	HR	RBI	BB	SO	SB
C	Willson Contreras, Tennessee (Cubs)	SL	.333	.413	.478	126	454	71	151	34	4	8	75	57	62	4
1B	Trey Mancini, Bowie (Orioles)	EL	.359	.395	.586	84	326	60	117	29	3	13	57	22	58	2
2B	Max Moroff, Altoona (Pirates)	EL	.293	.374	.409	136	523	79	153	28	6	7	51	70	111	17
3B	Miguel Sano, Chattanooga (Twins)	SL	.274	.374	.544	66	241	55	66	18	1	15	48	38	68	5
SS	Trevor Story, New Britain (Rockies)	EL	.281	.373	.523	69	256	46	72	20	6	10	40	35	73	15
CF	Max Kepler, Chattanooga (Twins)	SL	.322	.416	.531	112	407	76	131	32	13	9	71	67	63	18
OF	Aaron Judge, Trenton (Yankees)	EL	.284	.350	.516	63	250	36	71	16	3	12	44	24	70	1
OF	Nick Williams, Frisco/Reading (Rangers/Phillies)	TL/EL	.303	.354	.491	119	475	77	144	26	6	17	55	35	97	13
DH	Balbino Fuenmayor, NW Arkansas (Royals)	TL	.354	.386	.591	73	291	50	103	22	1	15	51	12	46	1

Pos	Pitcher, Team (Org)	League	W	L	ERA	G	GS	SV	IP	H	HR	BB	SO	AVG	SO/9	WHIP
SP	Matt Boyd, New Hamp. (Blue Jays)	EL	6	1	1.10	12		0	74	39	3	18	70	.155	8.6	0.77
SP	Michael Fulmer, Binghamton/Erie (Mets/Tigers)	EL	10	3	2.14	21	21	0	118	100	7	30	116	.228	8.9	1.10
SP	Jorge Lopez, Biloxi (Brewers)	SL	12	5	2.26	24	24	0	143	105	9	52	137	.205	8.6	1.10
SP	Aaron Nola, Reading (Phillies)	EL	7	3	1.88	12	12	0	77	59	4	9	59	.219	6.9	0.89
SP	Blake Snell, Montgomery (Rays)	SL	6	2	1.57	12	12	0	69	45	5	29	79	.191	10.4	1.08
RP	Mychal Givens, Bowie (Orioles)	EL	4	2	1.73	35	0	15	57	38	1	16	79	.185	12.4	0.94

HIGH CLASS A

Pos	Player, Team (Org)	League	AVG	OBP	SLG	G	AB	R	H	2B	3B	HR	RBI	BB	SO	SB
C	Chance Sisco, Frederick (Orioles)	CAR	.308	.387	.422	75	263	30	81	12	3	4	26	33	41	8
1B	A.J. Reed, Lancaster (Astros)	CAL	.346	.449	.638	82	318	75	110	16	4	23	81	59	73	0
2B	Jamie Westbrook, Visalia (Diamondbacks)	CAL	.319	.357	.510	123	480	75	153	33	4	17	72	24	69	14
3B	Ryan McMahon, Modesto (Rockies)	CAL	.300	.372	.520	132	496	85	149	43	6	18	75	49	153	6
SS	Franklin Barreto, Stockton (Athletics)	CAL	.302	.333	.500	90	338	50	102	22	3	13	47	15	67	8
CF	Lewis Brinson, High Desert (Rangers)	CAL	.337	.416	.628	64	258	51	87	22	7	13	42	31	64	13
OF	Jordan Patterson, Modesto (Rockies)	CAL	.304	.378	.568	77	303	62	92	26	12	10	43	19	88	9
OF	Bradley Zimmer, Lynchburg (Indians)	CAR	.308	.403	.493	78	286	60	88	17	3	10	39	37	77	32
DH	Brett Phillips, Lancaster (Astros)	CAL	.320	.379	.588	66	291	68	93	19	7	15	53	22	64	8

Pos	Pitcher, Team (Org)	League	W	L	ERA	G	GS	SV	IP	H	HR	BB	SO	AVG	SO/9	WHIP
SP	Jacob Faria, Charlotte (Rays)	FSL	10	1	1.33	12		0	74	51	1	22	63	.199	7.6	0.98
SP	Chase Johnson, San Jose (Giants)	CAL	8	3	2.43	20	18	0	111	95	5	34	111	.235	9.0	1.16
SP	Alex Reyes, Palm Beach (Cardinals)	FSL	2	5	2.26	13	13	0	64	49	0	31	96	.216	13.6	1.26
SP	Antonio Senzatela, Modesto (Rockies)	CAL	9	9	2.51	26	26	0	154	131	10	33	143	.229	8.4	1.06
SP	Luke Weaver, Palm Beach (Cardinals)	FSL	8	5	1.62	19	19	0	105	98	2	19	88	.247	7.5	1.11
RP	Jake Smith, San Jose (Giants)	CAL	4	4	2.35	56	0	16	84	50	7	21	118	.172	12.6	0.84

MINOR LEAGUES

will be called the Yard Goats. The team selected Yard Goats, railroad slang for an engine that switches a train, from a group of finalists that included Whirlybirds, River Hogs, Praying Mantis and Hedgehogs.

The Savannah Sand Gnats (South Atlantic) are also packing up and moving to a new ballpark in Columbia, S.C., while taking on the nickname Fireflies. The team had been threatening to leave for years if the city did not help fund a new ballpark to replace 74-year-old Grayson Stadium and made good on the promise when Columbia offered to build a new ballpark on the edge of downtown.

Meanwhile, plans by the new owners of the Pawtucket Red Sox (International) to relocate the team to Providence fell through when local residents balked at the price tag. Larry Lucchino, the Red Sox executive who retired this season, heads

LOW CLASS A

Pos	Player, Team (Org)	League	OBP	SLG	G	AB	R	H	2B	3B	HR	RBI	BB	SO	SB
C	Jacob Nottingham, Quad Cities (Astros)	MWL	.326	.387	.543	59	230	34	75	18	1	10	46	18	51	1
1B	Bobby Bradley, Lake County (Indians)	MWL	.269	.361	.529	108	401	62	108	15	4	27	92	56	148	3
2B	Yoan Moncada, Greenville (Red Sox)	SAL	.278	.380	.438	81	306	61	85	19	3	8	38	42	83	49
3B	Jordan Luplow, West Virginia (Pirates)	SAL	.264	.366	.464	106	390	74	103	36	3	12	67	59	67	11
SS	Ozzie Albies, Rome (Braves)	SAL	.310	.368	.404	98	394	64	122	21	8	0	37	36	56	29
CF	Carlos Tocci, Lakewood (Phillies)	SAL	.321	.387	.423	59	234	35	75	14	2	2	25	20	31	14
OF	Mike Gerber, West Michigan (Tigers)	MWL	.292	.355	.468	135	513	74	150	31	10	13	76	49	97	16
OF	Max White, Asheville (Rockies)	SAL	.306	.425	.524	71	248	58	76	13	7	9	36	47	84	34
DH	Rhys Hoskins, Lakewood (Phillies)	SAL	.322	.397	.525	68	255	39	82	17	4	9	51	26	50	2

Pos	Player, Team (Org)	League	W	L	ERA	G	GS	SV	IP	H	HR	BB	SO	AVG	SO/9	WHIP
SP	Stephen Gonsalves, Cedar Rapids (Twins)	MWL	6	1	1.15	9	9	0	55	29	2	15	77	0.153	12.6	0.80
SP	Brent Honeywell, Bowling Green (Rays)	MWL	4	4	2.91	12	12	0	65	53	3	12	76	0.215	10.5	1.00
SP	Ariel Jurado, Hickory (Rangers)	SAL	12	1	2.45	22	15	0	99	92	5	12	95	0.244	8.6	1.05
SP	Tyler Mahle, Dayton (Reds)	MWL	13	8	2.43	27	26	0	152	145	7	25	135	0.248	8.0	1.12
SP	Stephen Tarpley, West Virginia (Pirates)	SAL	11	4	2.48	20	20	0	116	108	2	25	105	0.237	8.2	1.15
RP	Trevor Hildenberger, Cedar Rapids (Twins)	MWL	2	1	0.80	28	0	14	45	24	0	5	59	0.153	11.8	0.64

SHORT-SEASON

Pos	Player, Team (Org)	League	AVG	OBP	SLG	G	AB	R	H	2B	3B	HR	RBI	BB	SO	SB
C	Daniel Salters, Mahoning Valley (Indians)	NYPL	.279	.330	.358	47	179	14	50	8	0	2	26	12	36	0
1B	Chris Shaw, Salem-Keizer (Giants)	NWL	.287	.360	.551	46	178	22	51	11	0	12	30	19	41	0
2B	Josh Tobias, Williamsport (Phillies)	NYPL	.321	.362	.475	61	240	31	77	19	3	4	37	14	42	12
3B	Kevin Padlo, Boise (Rockies)	NWL	.294	.404	.502	70	255	44	75	22	2	9	46	45	62	33
SS	Drew Jackson, Everett (Mariners)	NWL	.358	.432	.447	59	226	64	81	12	1	2	26	30	35	47
CF	Victor Robles, Auburn (Nationals)	NYPL	.343	.424	.479	38	140	29	48	5	4	2	16	8	21	12
OF	Andrew Benintendi, Lowell (Red Sox)	NYPL	.290	.408	.540	35	124	19	36	2	4	7	15	25	15	7
OF	Ian Happ, Eugene (Cubs)	NWL	.283	.408	.491	29	106	26	30	8	1	4	11	23	28	9
DH	Stone Garrett, Batavia (Marlins)	NYPL	.297	.352	.581	58	222	36	66	18	6	11	46	19	60	8

Pos	Player, Team (Org)	League	W	L	ERA	G	GS	SV	IP	H	HR	BB	SO	AVG	SO/9	WHIP
SP	Domingo Acevedo, Staten Island (Yankees)	NYPL	3	0	1.69	11	11	0	48	37	2	15	53	.207	9.9	1.08
SP	Tyler Alexander, Connecticut (Tigers)	NYPL	0	2	0.97	12	12	0	37	17	3	5	33	.132	8.0	0.59
SP	Jacob Evans, State College (Cardinals)	NYPL	4	3	3.08	16	6	1	50	41	1	7	42	.225	7.6	0.97
SP	Andrew Moore, Everett (Mariners)	NWL	1	1	2.08	14	8	0	39	37	2	2	43	.250	9.9	1.00
SP	Cody Reed, Hillsboro (Diamondbacks)	NWL	5	4	3.27	15	14	0	63	51	5	21	72	.215	10.2	1.14
RP	Phil Maton, Tri-City (Padres)	NWL	4	2	1.38	23	0	6	33	23	0	5	58	.190	16.0	0.86

ROOKIE

Pos	Player, Team (Org)	League	AVG	OBP	SLG	G	AB	R	H	2B	3B	HR	RBI	BB	SO	SB
C	Xavier Fernandez, Burlington/Idaho Falls (Royals)	APP/PIO	.327	.401	.491	47	159	24	52	12	1	4	30	14	23	0
1B	Carlos Munoz, Bristol (Pirates)	APP	.325	.427	.587	56	206	35	67	21	0	11	39	34	21	2
2B	Luis Arraez, Twins	GCL	.306	.377	.388	57	206	23	63	15	1	0	19	20	10	8
3B	Austin Riley, Braves/Danville (Braves)	GCL/APP	.304	.389	.544	60	217	36	66	14	1	12	40	26	65	2
SS	Isan Diaz, Missoula (Diamondbacks)	PIO	.360	.436	.640	68	272	58	98	25	6	13	51	34	65	12
CF	Trent Clark, Brewers/Helena (Brewers)	AZL/PIO	.309	.424	.430	55	207	39	64	7	6	2	21	39	44	25
OF	Demi Orimoloye, Brewers	AZL	.292	.319	.518	33	137	23	40	9	2	6	26	3	39	19
OF	Cornelius Randolph, Phillies	GCL	.302	.425	.442	53	172	34	52	15	3	1	24	32	32	6
DH	**Austin Byler, Missoula (Diamondbacks)**	**PIO**	**.298**	**.422**	**.636**	**66**	**228**	**59**	**68**	**22**	**5**	**15**	**57**	**50**	**67**	**9**

Pos	Player, Team (Org)	Age	W	L	ERA	G	GS	SV	IP	H	HR	BB	SO	AVG	SO/9	WHIP
SP	Marcos Diplan, Helena (Brewers)	PIO	2	2	3.75	13	7	2	50	47	4	21	54	.251	9.7	1.35
SP	Anderson Espinoza, Red Sox	GCL	0	1	0.68	10	10	0	40	24	0	9	40	.170	9.0	0.83
SP	Ryan Helsley, Johnson City (Cardinals)	APP	1	1	2.01	11	9	0	40	33	1	19	35	.217	7.8	1.29
SP	Peter Lambert, Grand Junction (Rockies)	PIO	0	4	3.45	8	8	0	31	29	3	11	26	.227	7.5	1.28
SP	Mike Soroka, Braves/Danville (Braves)	PIO/APP	0	2	3.18	10	9	0	34	33	0	5	37	.246	9.8	1.12
RP	Josh Staumont, Royals/Idaho Falls (Royals)	AZL/PIO	3	1	2.48	18	4	1	40	21	0	32	58	.153	13.1	1.33

Pawtucket's ownership group and says the team will continue to look elsewhere.

Similarly, plans for the Binghamton Mets (Eastern) to relocate to Wilmington, Del., and for that franchise to bring its Carolina League affiliation to Kinston, N.C., fell apart when B-Mets owners balked at the sale. Wilmington owners Dave Heller and Clark Minker were continuing their negotiations with Binghamton's owners, led by Michael Urda, and were hoping to reach an agreement by the Winter Meetings. The Texas Rangers, eager to return to the Carolina League after being forced from Myrtle Beach to High Desert of the California League during the affiliation shuffle of 2014, had reached an agreement to purchase the Wilmington franchise and move it to Kinston. That sale, however, is contingent on Wilmington's purchase of Binghamton.

MIKE JANES

Max Kepler led the Southern League in on-base (.416) and slugging (.531)

BILL MITCHELL

Steven Matz overwhelmed PCL hitters before reaching the big leagues in June

MINOR LEAGUES

FIRST TEAM

Pos	Player, Organization (Level)	Age	AVG	OBP	SLG	G	AB	R	H	2B	3B	HR	RBI	BB	SO	SB
C	Willson Contreras, Cubs (AA)	23	.333	.413	.478	126	454	71	151	34	4	8	75	57	62	4
1B	A.J. Reed, Astros (HiA • AA)	22	.340	.432	.612	135	523	113	178	30	5	34	127	86	122	0
2B	Brandon Drury, Diamondbacks (AA • AAA)	23	.303	.344	.412	130	524	65	159	40	1	5	61	32	76	4
3B	Ryan McMahon, Rockies (HiA)	20	.300	.372	.520	132	496	85	149	43	6	18	75	49	153	6
SS	Corey Seager, Dodgers (AAA • AA)	21	.293	.344	.487	125	501	81	147	37	3	18	76	37	76	4
CF	Lewis Brinson, Rangers (HiA • AA • AAA)	21	.332	.403	.601	100	398	74	132	31	8	20	69	44	98	18
OF	Max Kepler, Twins (AA • HiA)	22	.318	.410	.520	118	431	80	137	34	13	9	71	69	68	19
OF	Jordan Patterson, Rockies (HiA • AA)	23	.297	.364	.543	125	488	88	145	45	12	17	75	30	130	18
DH	Bobby Bradley, Indians (LoA • HiA)	19	.264	.357	.518	110	409	62	108	15	4	27	92	57	150	3

Pos	Pitcher, Organization (Level)	Age	W	L	ERA	G	GS	SV	IP	H	HR	BB	SO	AVG	SO/9	WHIP
SP	Jose Berrios, Twins (AA • AAA)	21	14	5	2.87	27	27	0	166	136	12	38	175	.223	9.5	1.05
SP	Matt Boyd, Tigers (AA • AAA)	24	9	2	1.65	19	19	0	115	71	8	27	108	.176	8.5	0.85
SP	Michael Fulmer, Tigers (AA • HiA)	22	10	3	2.24	22	22	0	125	104	8	30	125	.225	9.0	1.07
SP	Jorge Lopez, Brewers (AA)	22	12	5	2.26	24	24	0	143	105	9	52	137	.205	8.6	1.10
SP	Blake Snell, Rays (AA • AAA • HiA)	22	15	4	1.41	25	23	0	134	84	7	53	163	.182	10.9	1.02
RP	Mychal Givens, Orioles (AA)	25	4	2	1.73	35	0	15	57	38	1	16	79	.185	12.4	0.94

SECOND TEAM

Pos	Player, Level (Organization)	Age	AVG	OBP	SLG	G	AB	R	H	2B	3B	HR	RBI	BB	SO	SB
C	Andrew Knapp, Phillies (HiA • AA)	23	.308	.385	.491	118	458	77	141	35	5	13	84	51	106	1
1B	Trey Mancini, Orioles (AA • HiA)	23	.341	.375	.563	136	533	88	182	43	6	21	89	31	93	6
2B	Tony Kemp, Astros (AAA • AA)	23	.308	.388	.386	121	464	78	143	19	4	3	48	56	65	35
3B	Richie Shaffer, Rays (AAA • AA)	24	.267	.357	.539	108	393	64	105	27	1	26	72	54	123	4
SS	Trea Turner, Nationals (AA • AAA)	22	.322	.370	.458	116	454	68	146	24	7	8	54	38	97	29
CF	Bradley Zimmer, Indians (HiA • AA)	22	.273	.368	.446	127	473	84	129	26	4	16	63	55	131	44
OF	Michael Conforto, Mets (HiA • AA)	22	.297	.372	.482	91	357	46	106	24	3	12	54	40	61	1
OF	Brett Phillips, Brewers (HiA • AA)	21	.309	.374	.527	120	505	104	156	34	14	16	77	44	120	17
DH	Domingo Santana, Brewers (AAA)	23	.333	.426	.573	95	354	75	118	23	4	18	77	54	108	2

Pos	Pitcher, Level (Organization)	Age	W	L	ERA	G	GS	SV	IP	H	HR	BB	SO	AVG	SO/9	WHIP
SP	Jose De Leon, Dodgers (AA • HiA)	23	6	7	2.99	23	23	0	114	87	12	37	163	.208	12.8	1.08
SP	Jacob Faria, Rays (AA • HiA)	22	17	4	1.92	25	23	0	150	103	6	52	159	.197	9.6	1.04
SP	Steve Matz, Mets (AAA)	24	8	4	2.05	19	18	0	105	78	6	34	107	.208	9.1	1.06
SP	Joe Musgrove, Astros (AA • HiA • LoA)	22	12	1	1.88	19	14	1	101	85	9	8	99	.225	8.9	0.92
SP	Antonio Senzatela, Rockies (HiA)	20	9	9	2.51	26	26	0	154	131	10	33	143	.229	8.4	1.06
RP	Silvino Bracho, Diamondbacks (HiA • AA)	23	2	1	1.60	43	0	19	51	35	3	10	73	.191	13.0	0.89

Road Was Sweet For Shuckers

BY JOSH NORRIS

Put yourself in the Biloxi Shuckers' shoes. You're a brand-new franchise, with a name, logos and everything else in between. There's even a beautiful new ballpark waiting for you once you break camp from spring training. Everything sounds great.

Then, all of a sudden, it doesn't.

They tell you your ballpark, a jewel in the middle of downtown Biloxi, Miss., isn't ready yet, and probably won't be for a long time. You're going to have to spend the first month or more on the road, living out of buses and hotels while you trek to and from ballparks across the Southern League.

It's not an ideal way to begin a new franchise's tenure, but it's what happened this year when MGM Park hit snags on its way to completion. The Shuckers played their first 54 games on the road over two-plus months while setting up temporary quarters at their previous home in Huntsville before finally getting a glimpse of their new ballpark on June 6.

Still, they persevered and found themselves 33-21 entering their first game in their new digs.

"I think it's been a good transition," manager Carlos Subero said during a series in late May. "What our staff has done, from the hitting coach, pitching coach, the trainer, they've done a good job making sure our kids stay fresh.

"Anything (the staff) reads (from the players), we give them an extra day off or we don't need to hit on the field. All those things add up, and they're very important to keep the energy of a team that's been bussing and hotelling for all this month, I think it's been an easy transition for us."

And when they finally got to MGM Park, they played a game that proved it was worth the wait.

Facing the Mobile BayBears, the Shuckers battled to a draw through regulation and into the 13th inning. Mobile scratched across a run in the top half, putting Biloxi at risk of sending the 5,065 fans on hand home deflated.

TEAM OF THE YEAR

Instead, the Shuckers matched Mobile's run and added another for a walk-off win in the franchise's home opener. And it got better.

Leading the way was Orlando Arcia, the Brewers' No. 1 prospect. Arcia established career highs in nearly every offensive category while still playing his plus defense, but more importantly, Arcia became a team leader at just 20 years old and helped the Shuckers claim the first-half crown in their division. Arcia raised his performance to a new level in the playoffs with a barrage of extra-base hits.

Tyrone Taylor

The Shuckers were also blessed with the presence of the organization's top pitching prospect and No. 2 overall prospect in righthander Jorge Lopez. Lopez led the league with 12 victories and 1.10 WHIP, and was edged out by one percentage point (2.26 to 2.25) by teammate Tyler Wagner for the ERA title.

Other prospects on the Shuckers include center fielder Brett Phillips and lefthander Josh Hader—acquired in the Carlos Gomez deal with Houston—and outfielders Tyrone Taylor and Michael Reed.

The Shuckers, powered by a plethora of prospects, took Chattanooga to the limit in the Southern League Championship Series, but ultimately fell.

Still, for a season that began with so much uncertainty, the Shuckers made it a summer to remember.

PREVIOUS 10 WINNERS

2005: Jacksonville/Southern (Dodgers)
2006: Tucson/Pacific Coast (Diamondbacks)
2007: San Antonio/Texas (Padres)
2008: Frisco/Texas (Rangers)
2009: Akron/Eastern (Indians)
2010: Northwest Arkansas/Texas (Royals)
2011: Mobile BayBears/Southern (Diamondbacks)
2012: Springfield Cardinals/Texas (Cardinals)
2013: Daytona Cubs/Florida State (Cubs)
2014: Portland Sea Dogs/Eastern League (Red Sox)

Full list: BaseballAmerica.com/awards

BY J.J. COOPER

CINCINNATI

Nobody will remember the 10-1 final score and the U.S. winning its seventh straight Futures Game. Who wins and loses these games isn't important. As multiple players explained, this is a game they are here to enjoy, to put on a show and to have fun.

But every one of these games creates some memories. It's a gathering of the game's best prospects and ensures someone is going to do something memorable.

Jurickson Profar's whippy bat and his leadoff home run in Kansas City stood out. Joey Gallo hitting the truck in BP and then homering in the game last year won't be forgotten for a long time. Unfortunately Simon Castro going from intriguing prospect to less intriguing in the space of an inning in 2010 won't either.

Cubs catcher Kyle Schwarber's short stroke for a defensive-aided triple down the line is yet another precursor of what he's going to do regularly in Chicago before long. Schwarber was named the game's MVP after going 1-for-3 with a triple and throwing out a basestealer. He was MVP but there were other prospects whose performances will likely be just as memorable.

Maybe we'll remember Pirates first baseman Josh Bell's home run. Yes, it's hard to explain how someone with his raw power has four home runs in his first 80 games. But if he ends up hitting for power once again this was foreshadowing.

Royals shortstop Raul A. Mondesi's top-of-the-scale speed sparked some synapses when an infield grounder turned into a single.

Trea Turner had two plays to file away: A double in his first at-bat and a triple in his second.

And there were defensive snippets. Phillies shortstop J.P. Crawford had a pair of defensive gems, including a jumping snag of a line drive by Red Sox center fielder Manuel Margot. Mondesi ranged over to the other side of second base and made an accurate throw from a difficult angle to nab Schwarber. Brewers shortstop Orlando Arcia topped Mondesi by going behind second base and making an accurate, spinning throw to catch Brandon Nimmo.

And then there was Mets left fielder Michael Conforto's throw from left field to nail Ketel Marte. Conforto is a left fielder in part because of his arm, but on this throw he showed arm strength, carry and accuracy.

FUTURES GAME BOX SCORE

UNITED STATES 10, WORLD 1
JULY 12 IN CINCINNATI

WORLD	AB	R	H	BI	U.S.	AB	R	H	BI
Marte, 2B	2	0	2	1	Kemp, 2B	1	1	0	0
a-Arcia, Or, SS	2	0	0	0	Story, 2B	2	1	1	1
Albies SS	2	0	1	0	Crawford SS	3	1	1	1
Mondesi, SS-2B	2	0	1	0	Turner, SS	2	0	2	2
Rodriguez, Y, RF	4	0	0	0	Schwarber, C	3	0	1	2
Fuenmayor, 1B	2	0	1	0	Farmer, C	2	0	0	0
Cuthbert, 1B	2	0	0	0	Shaffer, 3B	4	0	0	0
Sanchez, G, C	2	0	1	0	Waldrop , RF	4	1	1	0
Diaz, E, C	2	0	0	0	Judge, DH	4	1	1	0
Nunez, R 3B	2	0	0	0	Bell, 1B	2	1	1	2
Devers, 3B	2	0	0	0	Olson, 1B	2	1	1	0
Margot, CF	2	0	0	0	Conforto, LF	2	1	2	0
Brito, CF	1	0	0	0	Williams, LF	2	1	1	1
Mazara, DH	3	0	2	0	Zimmer, B CF	2	0	0	0
Tapia, LF	3	1	2	0	Nimmo, CF	2	1	1	1
TOTALS	33	1	10	1	Totals	37	10	13	10

a-Popped out for Marte, K in the 6th

WORLD	001	000	000 1 10 0
UNITED STATES	003	205	00X 10 13 0

LOB: World 5, U.S. 5. **2B:** Sanchez, G (Beede); Story (Montas); Turner (Montas). **3B:** Schwarber (Garcia, J); Turner (Perdomo, L.). **HR:** Bell (1, 4th inning off Diaz, E, 1 on, 1 out). **Runners left in scoring position, 2 out:** Nunez, R; Rodriguez, Y 2; Shaffer 2; Farmer. **GIDP:** Nunez, R; Tapia, R. **CS:** Marte, K (2nd base by Giolito/Schwarber). **PB:** Schwarber. **Pickoffs:** Berrios (Kemp at 1st base). **Outfield assists:** Conforto (Marte, K at home).

WORLD	IP	H	R	ER	BB	SO	U.S.	IP	H	R	ER	BB	SO
Berrios	1	0	0	0	1	0	Giolito	2	2	0	0	0	1
Garcia, J (L)	1.2	3	3	3	1	2	Garrett (W)	1	3	1	0	0	1
Diaz, E	0.2	3	2	2	0	1	Beede (H)	1	0	0	0	0	0
Huang	0.2	0	0	0	0	0	Appel	1	1	0	0	0	0
Labourt	1	0	0	0	0	2	Snell	1	0	0	0	0	0
Mella	0.1	2	2	2	0	0	Newcomb	1	0	0	0	0	0
Montas	0.2	4	3	3	0	1	Edwards Jr.	0.2	2	0	0	0	1
Jimenez	0.2	0	0	0	0	1	Davies	0.2	1	0	0	0	1
Gonzalez, Ju	0.2	0	0	0	0	2	Rea	0.2	0	0	0	0	1
Perdomo, L	0.2	1	0	0	0	1							
TOTALS		13	10	10	2	10	TOTALS		10	1	0	0	5

WP: Montas; Gonzalez, Ju. **Pitches-strikes:** Berrios 15-6; Garcia, J 31-19; Huang 7-4; Labourt 11-9; Mella, K 12-5; Montas 21-12; Jimenez 6-4; Gonzalez, Ju 12-8; Perdomo, L 15-10; Giolito 20-13; Garrett 15-10; Beede 5-12; Appel 11-9; Snell 10-5; Newcomb 19-14; Edwards Jr. 16-11; Davies 10-6; Rea 10-6.
Umpires—HP: Ron Teague. **1B:** Dan Merzel. **2B:** J. January. **3B:** Junior Valentine.
Weather: 81 degrees, cloudy. **T:** 2:50. **A:** 43,661.

"The adrenaline rush was pretty cool. That's a dream right there. Coming in, the first picture in my head of my day going right would have been a base hit or a double. But that's the first thing that happens. It's pretty cool," Conforto said. "I haven't thrown like that in a while. It was a matter of getting my feet set and the

TRIPLE-A: Jon Edwards (Rangers) couldn't hold a two-run lead in the ninth inning, blowing the save as the International League all-stars scored three runs off him and won the game, 4-3. First baseman Kyle Roller (Yankees) and catcher Peter O'Brien (Diamondbacks) were named the stars of the game for their respective clubs. Roller went 2-for-2 with a walk and the two RBIs. O'Brien went 1-for-3 with a long home run.

EASTERN: Reading's Brian Pointer hit the sudden-death home run to give the Eastern Division the win after the game was tied 4-4 and went to the first tiebreaker Home Run Derby in the Eastern League all-star history. Portland shortstop Marco Hernandez (Red Sox) was 2-for-2 with a homer and two RBIs. Trenton's Jake Cave (Yankees) had a sacrifice fly, and Erie's Wynton Bernard (Tigers) hit an RBI triple. Bowie righty Mychal Givens (Orioles) struck out two in a scoreless inning.

SOUTHERN: Shortstop Tim Anderson (White Sox) doubled, tripled, scored a run and drove in a run in the North's 9-0 white-washing of the South. Dan Vogelbach (Cubs) hit a three-run homer, and Miguel Sano (Twins) doubled, singled and drove in a run. Tyler Goeddel (Rays) clubbed an RBI triple. Minor League Player of the Year Blake Snell (Rays) and Jose Berrios (Twins) each pitched scoreless innings for the North.

TEXAS LEAGUE: Outfielder Jorge Bonifacio (Royals) broke an eighth-inning tie with a two-run homer off Tayron Guerrero (Padres) in an eventual 9-4 win for the Northern Division. San Antonio's Travis Jankowski (Padres) and Midland's Ryon Healy (A's) homered for the South. Corpus Christi's Chris Devenski (Astros) struck out two in two perfect innings. Charlie Tilson (Cardinals) had three hits and three RBIs for the North and Balbino Fuenmayor (who on July 12 participated in the Futures Game) had three hits.

CAROLINA-CALIFORNIA LEAGUE: Brandon Trinkwon (Dodgers) went 2-for-3 with a pair of walks and two RBIs in his home park as the home team scored three times in the fourth and three times in the sixth in

a 9-2 win for the Cal League. Trinkwon, who was a seventh-round pick in 2013 out of UC Santa Barbara, won the game's MVP. For the California League, Cody Bellinger (Dodgers) had an RBI double in the third and a sacrifice fly in the sixth. Ryan McMahon (Rockies) had two hits and scored twice. The Carolina League got contributions from Mark Zagunis (Cubs), who had two hits and drove in a run, and Sam Travis (Red Sox), who had two hits.

FLORIDA STATE: Jake Bauers (Rays) smoked a double to left field in the third inning of a scoreless game, driving in two runs and giving the Southern Division the only runs it would need in a 6-0 victory against the Northern Division. Bradenton shortstop JaCoby Jones (Pirates) had a two-run double and Bradenton teammate Reese McGuire drove him home with an infield hit. Jacob Faria (Rays) and three teammates—Chris Kirsch, Buddy Borden and Brad Schreiber—tossed 3⅓ scoreless innings.

Jose Berrios

MIDWEST: Jeremy Null (Cubs) and 13 other pitchers combined to allow just three hits and one walk while striking out 16 for the East in a 5-0 win over the West. Ryan McBroom (Blue Jays) had an RBI single during the game and won the home run derby before it. Rays righthander Brent Honeywell retired two batters, including one on a 95-mph fastball. Anthony Alford, the Jays' No. 18 prospect, walked, stole a base and scored a run.

SOUTH ATLANTIC LEAGUE: K.J. Woods (Greensboro), Luke Tendler (Hickory) and Steve Wilkerson (Delmarva) each homered in the North's 7-5 win over the Southern Division. Shortstop Malquin Canelo (Lakewood) reached base four times, including a double and a single on the first pitch of the game. For his efforts, he was named the game's top star and then promoted to high Class A Clearwater. Greenville (Red Sox) shortstop Javier Guerra, known primarily for his elite defense, ripped a pair of doubles before being removed for Rome's Ozhaino Albies (Braves). Hickory righthander Ariel Jurado (Rangers) worked a clean first inning as the North Division's starter.

*Full-season teams only

TEAM

WINS

Corpus Christi (Texas)	89
Quad Cities (Midwest)	88
West Virginia (South Atlantic)	87
Oklahoma City (Pacific Coast)	86
Fresno (Pacific Coast)	84
Kane County (Midwest)	84
Visalia (California)	84

LONGEST WINNING STREAK*

Savannah (South Atlantic)	18
Las Vegas (Pacific Coast)	14
New Britain (Eastern)	13
Sacramento (Pacific Coast)	13
Quad Cities (Midwest)	12
Quad Cities (Midwest)	12

LOSSES

Clinton (Midwest)	93
Lake Elsinore (California)	90
Portland (Eastern)	89
Wisconsin (Midwest)	89
Greensboro (South Atlantic)	88

LONGEST LOSING STREAK*

Clinton (Midwest)	15
New Orleans (Pacific Coast)	15
Richmond (Eastern)	15
Lakeland (Florida State)	14
Wilmington (Carolina)	14

BATTING AVERAGE*

Lancaster (California)	.291
High Desert (California)	.286
Reno (Pacific Coast)	.286
Salt Lake (Pacific Coast)	.284
El Paso (Pacific Coast)	.281

RUNS

Lancaster (California)	888
High Desert (California)	840
Fresno (Pacific Coast)	804
El Paso (Pacific Coast)	765
Las Vegas (Pacific Coast)	758
Reno (Pacific Coast)	758

HOME RUNS

Lancaster (California)	174
Visalia (California)	154
High Desert (California)	153
Tacoma (Pacific Coast)	148
Las Vegas (Pacific Coast)	140

STOLEN BASES

Asheville (South Atlantic)	258
Charleston (South Atlantic)	230
Greenville (South Atlantic)	182
New Britain (Eastern)	182
West Virginia (South Atlantic)	181

EARNED RUN AVERAGE*

Palm Beach (Florida State)	2.65
Quad Cities (Midwest)	2.65
Fort Myers (Florida State)	2.70
Charlotte (Florida State)	2.87
Myrtle Beach (Carolina)	3.01

STRIKEOUTS

San Jose (California)	1345
Visalia (California)	1304
Rancho Cucamonga (California)	1214
Inland Empire (California)	1196
Lancaster (California)	1183

INDIVIDUAL BATTING

BATTING AVERAGE

Jose Martinez (Omaha)	.384
Balbino Fuenmayor (NW Arkansas, Omaha)	.358
Jesus Montero (Tacoma)	.355
Trey Mancini (Frederick, Bowie)	.341
A.J. Reed (Lancaster, Corpus Christi)	.340

RUNS

A.J. Reed (Lancaster, Corpus Christi)	113
Derek Fisher (Quad Cities, Lancaster)	106
Brett Phillips (Lancaster, Corpus Christi, Biloxi)	104
Brett Vertigan (Beloit, Stockton)	98

HITS

Cody Bellinger (Rancho Cucamonga)	97
Colin Walsh (Midland)	97
Trey Mancini (Frederick, Bowie)	182
A.J. Reed (Lancaster, Corpus Christi)	178
Matt Hague (Buffalo)	177
Joey Wendle (Nashville)	167
Raimel Tapia (Modesto)	166

TOP HITTING STREAKS

Hector Martinez (DSL Tigers)	26
Michael Pierson (Orem)	26
Dario Pizzano (Jackson)	25
Randy Ventura (DSL Braves)	24
Michael Suiter (Kannapolis)	23

MOST HITS (ONE GAME)

Eric Aguilera (Inland Empire)	6
Ruddy Giron (Fort Wayne)	6
Ryan McBroom (Lansing)	6
Hanser Ortiz (DSL Mets1)	6
Alex Presley (Fresno)	6
Corey Seager (Oklahoma City)	6
Austin Wilson (Bakersfield)	6

TOTAL BASES

A.J. Reed (Lancaster, Corpus Christi)	320
Trey Mancini (Frederick, Bowie)	300
Daniel Palka (Visalia)	272
Peter O'Brien (Reno)	270
Jamie Romak (Reno)	267

EXTRA-BASE HITS

Jordan Patterson (Modesto, New Britain)	74
Jamie Romak (Reno)	72
Trey Mancini (Frederick, Bowie)	70
Peter O'Brien (Reno)	70
Trevor Story (New Britain, Albuquerque)	70

DOUBLES

Nick Torres (Fort Wayne, Lake Elsinore)	44
Kyle Kubitza (Salt Lake)	43
Trey Mancini (Frederick, Bowie)	43
Ryan McMahon (Modesto)	43
Taylor Motter (Durham)	43

TRIPLES

Socrates Brito (Mobile)	15
Ben Gamel (Scranton/WB)	14
Brett Phillips (Lancaster, Corpus Christi, Biloxi)	14
Byron Buxton (Chattanooga, Rochester)	13
Max Kepler (Fort Myers, Chattanooga)	13
Nelson Ward (Clinton, Bakersfield)	13

HOME RUNS

A.J. Reed (Lancaster, Corpus Christi)	34
Jabari Blash (Jackson, Tacoma)	32
Tyler O'Neill (Bakersfield)	32
Adam Brett Walker (Chattanooga)	31
Cody Bellinger (Rancho Cucamonga)	30
Adam Duvall (Sacramento, Louisville)	30
Chase McDonald (Lancaster)	30

RUNS BATTED IN

A.J. Reed (Lancaster, Corpus Christi)	127
Peter O'Brien (Reno)	107
Adam Brett Walker (Chattanooga)	106
Matt Duffy (Fresno)	104
Cody Bellinger (Rancho Cucamonga)	103

MOST RBIS (ONE GAME)

Derek Fisher (Lancaster)	12
Jon Singleton (Fresno)	10
A.J. Reed (Lancaster)	9
D.J. Davis (Lansing)	8
Nelson Gomez (DSL Yankees1)	8
Jose Rojas (VSL Cubs)	8

WALKS

Colin Walsh (Midland)	124
Matt Olson (Midland)	105
Danny Hayes (Birmingham)	98
Jamie Ritchie (Quad Cities, Lancaster)	95
Lars Anderson (Oklahoma City, Tulsa)	93

INTENTIONAL WALKS

Scott Schebler (Oklahoma City)	8
Matt Clark (Col. Springs)	7
Michael Conforto (St. Lucie, Binghamton)	7

Lars Anderson (Oklahoma City, Tulsa)	6
Josh Bell (Altoona, Indianapolis)	6
Bobby Bradley (Lake County, Lynchburg)	6
Art Charles (Reading)	6
Matt Olson (Midland)	6
Kyle Roller (Scranton/WB)	6

STRIKEOUTS

Adam Brett Walker (Chattanooga)	195
Matt Davidson (Charlotte)	191
Jason Martinson (Syracuse)	189
Steven Moya (Lakeland, Toledo)	175
Austin Aune (Charleston)	167

STOLEN BASES

Jorge Mateo (Charleston, Tampa)	82
Yefri Perez (Jupiter)	71
Adam Engel (Winston-Salem)	65
Johneshwy Fargas (Augusta)	59
Mallex Smith (Mississippi, Gwinnett)	57

CAUGHT STEALING

Elvis Escobar (West Virginia)	21
Yefri Perez (Jupiter)	21
Johneshwy Fargas (Augusta)	19
Oscar Mercado (Peoria)	19
Omar Obregon (Rome)	19
Charlie Tilson (Springfield)	19
Bo Way (Inland Empire)	19

ON-BASE PERCENTAGE*

Jose Martinez (Omaha)	.461
Colin Walsh (Midland)	.447
Tyler White (Corpus Christi, Fresno)	.442
A.J. Reed (Lancaster, Corpus Christi)	.432
Joey Rickard (Charlotte, Montgomery, Durham)	.427

SLUGGING PERCENTAGE*

A.J. Reed (Lancaster, Corpus Christi)	.612
Lewis Brinson (High Desert, Frisco, Round Rock)	.601
Chase McDonald (Lancaster)	.592
Balbino Fuenmayor (NW Arkansas, Omaha)	.589
Jabari Blash (Jackson, Tacoma)	.576

ON-BASE PLUS SLUGGING (OPS)*

A.J. Reed (Lancaster, Corpus Christi)	1.044
Jose Martinez (Omaha)	1.024
Lewis Brinson (High Desert, Frisco, Round Rock)	1.004
Domingo Santana (Fresno, Col. Springs)	.999
Jon Kemmer (Corpus Christi)	.988

HIT BY PITCH

Tim Locastro (Lansing, Rancho Cucamonga)	32
Austin Wilson (Bakersfield)	29
Lorenzo Cedrola (DSL Red Sox2)	23
Jordan Patterson (Modesto, New Britain)	22
Damek Tomscha (Lakewood)	22

SACRIFICE BUNTS

Rando Moreno (Richmond)	21
Johan Camargo (Carolina)	20
Luis Jean (Asheville)	19
Pablo Reyes (West Virginia)	18
Engelb Vielma (Fort Myers)	18

SACRIFICE FLIES

Andy Wilkins (Buffalo, Oklahoma City)	15
Ryan McBroom (Lansing)	13
Raimel Tapia (Modesto)	13
Mike Gerber (West Michigan)	12
Josh Bell (Altoona, Indianapolis)	11

GROUNDED INTO DOUBLE PLAY

Yairo Munoz (Beloit, Stockton)	26
Victor Caratini (Myrtle Beach)	22
Willson Contreras (Tennessee)	22
Austin Nola (Jacksonville, New Orleans)	22
Jesus Aguilar (Columbus)	21
Royce Bolinger (Frisco, High Desert)	21
Ryon Healy (Midland)	21
Emerson Landoni (Mississippi)	21
Jordy Lara (Jackson)	21

BATTING AVERAGE* BY POSITION

CATCHERS

Willson Contreras (Tennessee)	.333
Jacob Nottingham (Quad Cities, Lancaster, Stockton)	.316

MINOR LEAGUES

Andrew Knapp (Clearwater, Reading)	.308
Nevin Ashley (Col. Springs)	.306
Chance Sisco (Frederick, Bowie)	.297

FIRST BASEMEN

Balbino Fuenmayor (NW Arkansas, Omaha)	.358
Jesus Montero (Tacoma)	.355
Trey Mancini (Frederick, Bowie)	.341
A.J. Reed (Lancaster, Corpus Christi)	.340
Matt Hague (Buffalo)	.338

SECOND BASEMEN

Kelby Tomlinson (Richmond, Sacramento)	.321
Chesny Young (South Bend, Myrtle Beach)	.320
Jamie Westbrook (Visalia)	.319
Jeff McNeil (St. Lucie, Binghamton)	.308
Tony Kemp (Corpus Christi, Fresno)	.308

THIRD BASEMEN

T.J. Rivera (Las Vegas, Binghamton)	.325
Tyler White (Corpus Christi, Fresno)	.325
Shane Hoelscher (Modesto, Asheville)	.318
Ed Lucas (Round Rock)	.316
Yandy Diaz (Akron, Columbus)	.309

SHORTSTOPS

Adam Frazier (Altoona)	.324
Trea Turner (San Antonio, Harrisburg, Syracuse)	.322
Ildemaro Vargas (Kane County)	.321
Luis Guillorme (Savannah)	.318
Gavin Cecchini (Binghamton)	.317

OUTFIELDERS

Jose Martinez (Omaha)	.384
Ryan Lollis (San Jose, Richmond, Sacramento)	.340
Travis Jankowski (San Antonio, El Paso)	.335
Domingo Santana (Corpus Christi, Col. Springs)	.333
Lewis Brinson (High Desert, Frisco, Round Rock)	.332

DESIGNATED HITTERS

Matt Oberste (St. Lucie)	.301
Dean Green (Erie, Toledo)	.300
Luigi Rodriguez (Lynchburg)	.293
Jin-De Jhang (Bradenton)	.292
Alex Burg (High Desert, Frisco, Round Rock)	.280

INDIVIDUAL PITCHING

EARNED RUN AVERAGE*

Blake Snell (Charlotte, Montgomery, Durham)	1.41
Matt Boyd (New Hampshire, Buffalo, Toledo)	1.65
Jacob Faria (Charlotte, Montgomery)	1.92
Stephen Gonsalves (Cedar Rapids, Fort Myers)	2.01
Yeudy Garcia (West Virginia)	2.10

WORST ERA*

David Ledbetter (High Desert)	7.46
Luis Gonzalez (Frederick)	6.88
Harrison Cooney (Arkansas, Inland Empire)	6.61
Stephen Landazuri (Tacoma, Jackson)	6.18
Josh Roenicke (Col. Springs)	6.15

WINS

Jacob Faria (Charlotte, Montgomery)	17
Austin Coley (West Virginia)	16
Terry Doyle (Bowie, Norfolk)	16
Shane Dawson (Dunedin, Lansing)	15
Austin Gomber (Peoria)	15
Toru Murata (Columbus)	15
Ricardo Pinto (Lakewood, Clearwater)	15
Blake Snell (Charlotte, Montgomery, Durham)	15

LOSSES

Mitch Horacek (Frederick)	17
Matt Bowman (Las Vegas)	16
Harrison Cooney (Arkansas, Inland Empire)	16
Justin Haley (Portland)	16
Bryan Rodriguez (El Paso, San Antonio)	16

GAMES

Pedro Beato (Norfolk)	63
Zach Thornton (Las Vegas)	63
Jeremy McBryde (Salt Lake)	62
John Church (Las Vegas)	61
Ian Gardeck (San Jose)	61

GAMES STARTED

Dan Altavilla (Bakersfield)	28
Steven Brault (Bradenton, Altoona)	28
Ryan Carpenter (New Britain)	28
Taylor Cole (New Hampshire)	28
Brett Graves (Beloit)	28
Mitch Horacek (Frederick)	28

Chris Jensen (Midland)	28
Dace Kime (Lake County, Lynchburg)	28
Jason Lane (El Paso)	28
Shawn Morimando (Akron)	28
Zach Petrick (Memphis)	28
Tyler Pike (Jackson, Bakersfield)	28
Austin Robichaux (Burlington)	28
Adrian Sampson (Indianapolis, Tacoma)	28
Wyatt Strahan (Dayton)	28
Elih Villanueva (Bowie, Norfolk)	28

COMPLETE GAMES

Jorge Ortega (Brevard County, Col. Springs)	6
Pat Dean (Rochester)	5
Sean Furney (Carolina, Rome)	4
Martires Arias (St. Lucie, Savannah)	3
Shane Carle (Albuquerque, New Britain)	3
Reed Garrett (Hickory, High Desert)	3
Michael Gibbons (Brooklyn, Binghamton, Savannah, St. Lucie)	3
Yean Carlos Gil (Rome, Carolina)	3
Chaz Hebert (Charleston, Tampa, Scranton/WB)	3
Tyrell Jenkins (Mississippi, Gwinnett)	3
Jimmy Reed (Palm Beach, Memphis, Springfield)	3
Aaron Slegers (Fort Myers, Chattanooga)	3
Elih Villanueva (Bowie, Norfolk)	3
Wei-Chung Wang (Brevard County, Col. Springs)	3

SHUTOUTS

Pat Dean (Rochester)	3
Chaz Hebert (Charleston, Tampa, Scranton/WB)	3
Ty Blach (Sacramento)	2
Shane Carle (Albuquerque, New Britain)	2
Terry Doyle (Bowie, Norfolk)	2
Ryan Merritt (Akron, Columbus)	2
Jorge Ortega (Brevard County, Col. Springs)	2

GAMES FINISHED

Josh Michalec (Asheville)	47
Zack Weiss (Daytona, Pensacola)	47
Brad Schreiber (Charlotte, Montgomery)	46
Stephen Shackleford (Reading)	46
Blake Wood (Indianapolis)	46

HOLDS

Bud Jeter (Kane County, Visalia)	21
Jency Solis (Kane County)	21
Ian Gardeck (San Jose)	20
Daniel Gibson (Visalia, Mobile)	19
Joey Krehbiel (Visalia)	17

SAVES

Zac Curtis (Kane County)	33
Josh Michalec (Asheville)	30
Brad Schreiber (Charlotte, Montgomery)	30
Stephen Shackleford (Reading)	30
Zack Weiss (Daytona, Pensacola)	30

INNINGS PITCHED

Pat Dean (Rochester)	179.0
Taylor Rogers (Rochester)	174.0
Richard Bleier (Harrisburg, Syracuse)	171.2
Ryan Merritt (Akron, Columbus)	171.0
Matt Flemer (New Britain)	169.2

WALKS

Jaime Schultz (Montgomery)	90
Eddie Gamboa (Norfolk)	84
Mitch Brown (Lynchburg)	77
Hobbs Johnson (Biloxi)	77
Sean Newcomb (Burlington, Inland Empire, Arkansas)	76

STRIKEOUTS

Jose Berrios (Chattanooga, Rochester)	175
Sean Newcomb (Burlington, Inland Empire, Arkansas)	168
Jaime Schultz (Montgomery)	168
Jose De Leon (Rancho Cucamonga, Tulsa)	163
Blake Snell (Charlotte, Montgomery, Durham)	163

HITS ALLOWED

Casey Lawrence (Buffalo, New Hampshire)	217
Jason Lane (El Paso)	212
John Lannan (Albuquerque)	209
Jaron Long (Scranton/WB, Trenton)	198
Adrian Sampson (Indianapolis, Tacoma)	197

HOME RUNS ALLOWED

Jason Lane (El Paso)	27
J.C. Sulbaran (NW Arkansas, Omaha)	26
David Ledbetter (High Desert)	23
Richelson Pena (High Desert)	23
Alec Asher (Frisco, Round Rock, Lehigh Valley)	22
Robbie Erlin (El Paso)	22

Mitch Horacek (Frederick)	22
Forrest Snow (Tacoma)	22

STRIKEOUTS PER NINE INNINGS (STARTERS)*

Jose De Leon (Rancho Cucamonga, Tulsa)	12.83
Jaime Schultz (Montgomery)	11.20
Sean Newcomb (Burlington, Inland Empire, Arkansas)	11.12
Blake Snell (Charlotte, Montgomery, Durham)	10.61
Brad Wieck (Savannah, Fort Wayne, Lake Elsinore)	10.14

STRIKEOUTS PER NINE INNINGS (RELIEVERS)*

Paul Fry (Bakersfield, Jackson)	12.77
Zack Weiss (Daytona, Pensacola)	12.72
Joey Krehbiel (Visalia)	12.71
Jake Smith (San Jose)	12.59
Mychal Givens (Bowie)	12.40

BATTING AVERAGE AGAINST (STARTERS)*

Matt Boyd (New Hampshire, Buffalo, Toledo)	.176
Blake Snell (Charlotte, Montgomery, Durham)	.189
Henry Owens (Pawtucket)	.193
Jacob Faria (Charlotte, Montgomery)	.194
Austin Gomber (Peoria)	.196

BATTING AVERAGE AGAINST (RELIEVERS)*

Montana DuRapau (West Virginia, Bradenton, Altoona)	.117
Akeel Morris (St. Lucie, Binghamton)	.137
Carlos Salazar (Rome, Carolina)	.155
Colby Blueberg (Lake Elsinore, Fort Wayne)	.171
Jake Smith (San Jose)	.172

MOST STRIKEOUTS, ONE GAME

Matt Moore (Durham)	16
Jacob Faria (Montgomery)	14
Chase Johnson (San Jose)	14
Martires Arias (Savannah)	13
Anthony Banda (Visalia)	13
Austin Brice (Jacksonville)	13
Oscar De La Cruz (Eugene)	13
Jacob Faria (Montgomery)	13
Sean Manaea (Midland)	13
Tommy Milone (Rochester)	13
Alex Reyes (Palm Beach)	13
Josh Taylor (Kane County)	13

WILD PITCHES

Milton Gomez (Wisconsin, Helena)	28
Alec Grosser (Rome, Danville)	26
Miller Diaz (St. Lucie, Visalia)	25
Lukas Schiraldi (Clinton)	25
Helmis Rodriguez (Asheville)	24

BALKS

Yeuris Guerrero (AZL White Sox)	8
Manuel Aybar (AZL Reds)	7
Gabriel Castellanos (Batavia, Greensboro)	7
Dailyn Martinez (State College)	6
Dinelson Lamet (Fort Wayne)	6

HIT BATTERS

Harrison Cooney (Arkansas, Inland Empire)	25
Helmis Rodriguez (Asheville)	19
Alec Grosser (Rome, Danville)	16
Joshua James (Quad Cities)	16
Stephen Landazuri (Tacoma, Jackson)	16
Jake Stinnett (South Bend)	16
Deibi Torres (DSL Cubs)	16

GROUND BALL DOUBLE PLAYS

Richard Bleier (Harrisburg, Syracuse)	27
Tejay Antone (Dayton)	26
Jaron Long (Scranton/WB, Trenton)	26
Timothy Adleman (Pensacola)	25
Taylor Cole (New Hampshire)	25
Tyler Danish (Birmingham)	25
Kevin McAvoy (Salem)	25

INDIVIDUAL FIELDING

ERRORS

Emerson Jimenez (Asheville, Modesto)	45
Luis Gonzalez (Dayton)	42
Oscar Mercado (Peoria)	41
Ryan McMahon (Modesto)	39
Ricardo Ferreira (DSL Yankees1)	37

MINOR LEAGUES

	INTERNATIONAL LEAGUE	PACIFIC COAST LEAGUE	EASTERN LEAGUE	SOUTHERN LEAGUE	TEXAS LEAGUE	CALIFORNIA LEAGUE	CAROLINA LEAGUE	FLORIDA STATE LEAGUE	MIDWEST LEAGUE	SOUTH ATLANTIC LEAGUE
Best Batting Prospect	Maikel Franco Lehigh Valley	Corey Seager Oklahoma City	Josh Bell Altoona	Kyle Schwarber Tennessee	Carlos Correa Corpus Christi	A.J. Reed Lancaster	Bradley Zimmer Lynchburg	Michael Conforto St. Lucie	Rowdy Tellez Lansing	Ozzie Albies Rome
Best Power Prospect	Richie Shaffer Durham	Jon Singleton Fresno	Aaron Judge Trenton	Adam Brett Walker Chattanooga	Joey Gallo Frisco	A.J. Reed Lancaster	Nellie Rodriguez Lynchburgh	Clint Coulter Brevard County	Jacob Nottingham Quad Cities	Ryan O'Hearn Lexington
Best Strike-Zone Judgment	Rob Refsnyder Scranton/WB	Greg Garcia Memphis	Yandy Diaz Akron	Max Kepler Chattanooga	Tony Kemp Corpus Christi	A.J. Reed Lancaster	Mark Zagunis Myrtle Beach	Austin Meadows Bradenton	Tim Locastro Lansing	John Johnson St. Lucie
Best Baserunner	Jose Peraza Gwinnett	Matt Szczur Iowa	Roman Quinn Reading	Tim Anderson Birmingham	Terrance Gore Northwest Arkansas	Timmy Lopes Bakersfield	Adam Engel Winston-Salem	Yefri Perez Jupiter	Greg Allen Lake County	Jorge Mateo Charleston
Fastest Baserunner	Eury Perez Gwinnett	Darnell Sweeney Oklahoma City	Roman Quinn Reading	Byron Buxton Chattanooga	Terrance Gore Northwest Arkansas	Ian Miller Bakersfield	Adam Engel Winston-Salem	Yefri Perez Jupiter	Rashad Crawford South Bend	Jorge Mateo Charleston
Best Pitching Prospect	Robert Stephenson Louisville	Steve Matz Las Vegas	Tyler Glasnow Altoona	Blake Snell Montgomery	Julio Urias Tulsa	Antonio Senzatela Modesto	Lucas Giolito Potomac	Alex Reyes Palm Beach	Brent Honeywell Bowling Green	Sam Coonrod Augusta
Best Fastball	Luis Severino Scranton/WB	Noah Syndergaard Las Vegas	Tyler Glasnow Altoona	Frankie Montas Birmingham	Tayron Guerrero San Antonio	Ray Black San Jose	Reynaldo Lopez Potomac	Alex Reyes Palm Beach	Riley Ferrell Quad Cities	Michael Kopech Greenville
Best Breaking Pitch	Luis Severino Scranton/WB	Jon Gray Albuquerque	Tyler Glasnow Altoona	Jorge Lopez Biloxi	Julio Urias Tulsa	Antonio Senzatela Rancho Cucamonga	Lucas Giolito Potomac	Alex Reyes Palm Beach	Francis Martes Quad Cities	Jordan Guerrero Kannapolis
Best Changeup	Henry Owens Pawtucket	Justin Nicolino New Orleans	Aaron Nola Reading	Blake Snell Montgomery	Jose De Leon Tulsa	Sean Newcomb Inland Empire	Eric Skoglund Wilmington	Blake Snell Charlotte	Brent Honeywell Bowling Green	Sam Coonrod Augusta
Best Control	Tyler Wilson Norfolk	Tim Cooney Memphis	Aaron Nola Reading	Jose Berrios Chattanooga	Collin Rea Tulsa	John Richy Inland Empire	Eric Skoglund Wilmington	Jorge Ortega Brevard County	Ross Seaton West Michigan	Spencer Adams Kannapolis
Best Reliever	Oliver Drake Norfolk	Sam Tuivailala Memphis	Mychal Givens Bowie	Silvino Bracho Mobile	Trevor Gott Arkansas	Jake Smith San Jose	Matt Marksberry Carolina	Akeel Morris St. Lucie	Trevor Hildenberger Cedar Rapids	Rodolfo Martinez Augusta
Best Defensive Catcher	Elias Diaz Indianapolis	Tomas Telis Round Rock	Pedro Severino Harrisburg	Justin O'Conner Montgomery	Roberto Pena Corpus Christi	Beau Taylor Stockton	Spencer Kieboom Potomac	Reese McGuire Bradenton	Brian Navarreto Cedar Rapids	Jordan Procyshen Greenville
Best Defensive First Baseman	Jesus Aguilar Columbus	Efren Navarro Salt Lake	Greg Bird Trenton	Danny Hayes Birmingham	Jonathan Rodriguez Springfield	Cody Bellinger Rancho Cucamonga	Jacob Rogers Myrtle Beach	Dominic Smith St. Lucie	Casey Gillaspie Bowling Green	Nick Longhi Greenville
Best Defensive Second Baseman	Alen Hanson Indianapolis	Wilfredo Tovar Las Vegas	Kelby Tomlinson Richmond	Heiker Meneses Chattanooga	Angel Franco Northwest Arkansas	Branden Cogswell Stockton	Ramon Torres Wilmington	Jeff McNeil St. Lucie	Tucker Neuhaus Wisconsin	John Johnson Savannah
Best Defensive Third Baseman	Matt Davidson Charlotte	Matt Dominguez Colorado Springs	Yandy Diaz Akron	Brandon Drury Mobile	Brian Hernandez Arkansas	Ryan McMahon Modesto	Jeimer Candelario Myrtle Beach	Brian Anderson Jupiter	Zach Houchins Burlington	Rafael Devers Greenville
Best Defensive Shortstop	Francisco Lindor Columbus	Miguel Rojas New Orleans	Gift Ngoepe Altoona	Orlando Arcia Biloxi	Raul A. Mondesi Northwest Arkansas	Domingo Leyba Visalia	Johnan Camargo Carolina	Amded Rosario St. Lucie	Nick Gordon Cedar Rapids	Javier Guerra Greenville
Best Infield Arm	Richie Shaffer Durham	Javier Baez Iowa	Erik Gonzalez Akron	Orlando Arcia Biloxi	Raul A. Mondesi Northwest Arkansas	Mattt Chapman Stockton	Jeimer Candelario Myrtle Beach	Willy Adames Charlotte	Yairo Munoz Beloit	Jorge Mateo Charleston
Best Defensive Outfielder	Jackie Bradley Pawtucket	Tommy Pham Memphis	Roman Quinn Altoona	Byron Buxton Chattanooga	Travis Jankowski San Antonio	Brett Phillips Lancaster	Connor Lien Carolina	Yefri Perez Jupiter	Michael Gettys Fort Wayne	Louie Lechich Kannapolis
Best Outfield Arm	Dariel Alvarez Norfolk	Rymer Liriano El Paso	Aaron Judge Trenton	Gabby Guerrero Mobile	Hunter Renfroe San Antonio	Royce Bollinger High Desert	Bradley Zimmer Lynchburg	Clint Coulter Brevard County	Alex Verdugo Great Lakes	Louie Lechich Kannapolis
Most Exciting Player	Francisco Lindor Columbus	Corey Seager Oklahoma City	Aaron Judge Trenton	Byron Buxton Chattanooga	Carlos Correa Corpus Christi	Brett Phillips Lancaster	Bradley Zimmer Lynchburg	Willy Adames Charlotte	Gleyber Torres South Bend	Jorge Mateo Charleston
Best Manager Prospect	Joel Skinner Charlotte	Brian Poldberg Omaha	David Wallace Akron	Mientkiewicz Chattanooga	Razor Shines Tulsa	Bill Haselman Rancho Cucamonga	Mark Johnson Myrtle Beach	Luis Rojas St. Lucie	Jake Mauer Cedar Rapids	Jose Leger Savannah

BY JOSH LEVENTHAL

The International League served its purpose as a finishing school for many prospects moving on to the majors this season, with all but one member of the Top 10—and 15 of the Top 20—advancing to the big leagues after, in some cases, quite brief stops in the IL.

And the league's talent pool was even deeper than the Top 20 Prospects list represents, with several qualified candidates getting bumped off. This includes the Braves' hit-first catcher Christian Bethancourt and erratic hard-throwers Mike Foltynewicz and Manny Banuelos; slick-fielding but light-hitting shortstop Deven Marrero (Red Sox); and strikeout-prone sluggers Richie Shaffer (Rays) and Steven Moya (Tigers).

And this ranking would have been even deeper if a group of standouts hadn't finished just short of the minimum (48 innings or 144 plate appearances), including Rays lefty (and Minor League Player of the Year) Blake Snell, righthanders Tyrell Jenkins (Braves) and Tyler Glasnow (Pirates); and catcher Blake Swihart (Red Sox).

The Columbus Clippers (Indians) and Indianapolis Indians (Pirates) finished the regular season tied for the most wins in the league and had a chance to settle the score in the Governor's Cup final. Righthander Mike Clevinger, one of the few prospects on an otherwise veteran Columbus team, guided the Clippers to their third title in six years by tossing 7 2/3 shutout innings just weeks after arriving from Double-A.

Columbus got a boost from sold out home crowds, a rarity in the postseason for minor league teams. General manager Ken Schnacke decided not to charge admission in the final game of Columbus' previous series against the Norfolk Tides and kept the gates open for the champion-

ship series.

"What the heck?" Schnacke said. "We need people in here."

Buffalo (Blue Jays) 30-year-old slugger Matt Hague took home MVP honors after hitting an IL-best .338 over a full season with 92 RBIs—second to Columbus' Jesus Aguilar (93). Hague was praised for his leadership skills after mentoring young outfielder Dalton Pompey and helping him turn around his season.

"He hit .420 with runners in scoring position, and this is a club that was shut out 19 times," Columbus manager Gary Allenson said. "We would've been way worse without him batting."

The future of the Pawtucket Red Sox remains in limbo after new ownership's attempts to relocate it to Providence failed because locals balked at the idea of paying for a new ballpark. Larry Lucchino, the recently retired Red Sox executive and majority Pawtucket owner, said they will look elsewhere.

TOP 20 PROSPECTS

1. Francisco Lindor, ss Columbus (Indians)
2. Luis Severino, rhp Scranton/W-B (Yankees)
3. Maikel Franco, 3b Lehigh Valley (Phillies)
4. Trea Turner, ss Syracuse (Nationals)
5. Eduardo Rodriguez, lhp Pawtucket (Red Sox)
6. Greg Bird, 1b Scranton/Wilkes-Barre (Yankees)
7. Daniel Norris, lhp Buffalo (Blue Jays)
8. Henry Owens, lhp Pawtucket (Red Sox)
9. Jose Berrios, rhp Rochester (Twins)
10. Aaron Judge, of Scranton/W-B (Yankees)
11. Robert Stephenson, rhp Louisville (Reds)
12. Josh Bell, 1b, Indianapolis (Pirates)
13. Brian Johnson, lhp, Pawtucket (Red Sox)
14. Jose Peraza, 2b/of, Gwinnett (Braves)
15. Rusney Castillo, of, Pawtucket (Red Sox)
16. Dalton Pompey, of, Buffalo (Blue Jays)
17. Matt Wisler, rhp, Gwinnett (Braves)
18. Gary Sanchez, c, Scranton/W-B (Yankees)
19. Aaron Altherr, of, Lehigh Valley (Phillies)
20. Deven Marrero, ss, Pawtucket (Red Sox)

OVERALL STANDINGS

North Division	W	L	PCT	GB	Manager(s)	Attendance	Average	Last Pennant
Scranton/Wilkes-Barre RailRiders (Yankees)	81	63	.563	—	Dave Miley	402,731	5,753	2008
Rochester Red Wings (Twins)	77	67	.535	4	Mike Quade	440,560	6,291	1997
Buffalo Bisons (Blue Jays)	68	76	.472	13	Gary Allenson	551,303	8,228	2004
Syracuse Chiefs (Nationals)	66	78	.458	4	Billy Gardner	262,408	3,803	1976
Lehigh Valley IronPigs (Phillies)	63	81	.438	18	Dave Brundage	614,888	9,042	1995
Pawtucket Red Sox (Red Sox)	59	85	.410	22	Kevin Boles	466,600	6,572	2014
South Division	**W**	**L**	**PCT**	**GB**	**Manager(s)**	**Attendance**	**Average**	**Last pennant**
Norfolk Tides (Orioles)	78	66	.542	—	Ron Johnson	386,402	5,767	1999
Gwinnett Braves (Braves)	77	67	.535	1	Brian Snitker	270,336	3,808	2007
Charlotte Knights (White Sox)	74	70	.514	4	Joel Skinner	669,398	9,428	1985
Durham Bulls (Rays)	74	70	.514	4	Jared Sandberg	554,788	7,814	2013
West Division	**W**	**L**	**PCT**	**GB**	**Manager(s)**	**Attendance**	**Average**	**Last pennant**
Columbus Clippers (Indians)	83	61	.576	—	Chris Tremie	622,096	9,016	2015
Indianapolis Indians (Pirates)	83	61	.576	—	Dean Treanor	662,536	9,331	2000
Louisville Bats (Reds)	64	80	.444	19	Delino DeShields	527,588	7,537	2001
Toledo Mud Hens (Tigers)	61	83	.424	22	Larry Parrish	531,249	7,699	2006

Playoffs—Semifinals: Indianapolis defeated Scranton/Wilkes-Barre 3-0 and Columbus defeated Norfolk 3-2 in best-of-five series; **Finals:** Columbus defeated Indianapolis 3-2 in a best-of-five series.

CLUB BATTING

	AVG	G	AB	R	H	2B	3B	HR	RBI	BB	SO	SB	OBP	SLG
Scranton/W-B	.271	144	4915	622	1332	247	32	89	584	480	979	80	.339	.389
Rochester	.262	144	4814	611	1263	227	28	95	574	378	916	57	.317	.380
Buffalo	.260	144	4840	552	1256	238	16	59	512	491	878	73	.331	.352
Indianapolis	.260	144	4799	582	1246	227	45	70	540	464	1007	168	.327	.369
Gwinnett	.259	144	4811	584	1246	204	37	50	534	362	732	160	.314	.348
Norfolk	.257	144	4857	532	1249	216	13	75	495	396	878	60	.315	.353
Charlotte	.256	144	4818	618	1230	237	25	134	582	459	1161	121	.323	.399
Columbus	.255	144	4806	606	1224	247	33	112	576	486	1067	91	.325	.390
Lehigh Valley	.254	144	4976	559	1266	255	21	69	526	415	1039	120	.316	.356
Louisville	.252	144	4736	506	1195	204	26	66	459	429	997	83	.319	.348
Durham	.250	144	4809	605	1200	263	21	123	571	506	1181	119	.325	.390
Toledo	.250	144	4843	578	1212	272	28	87	552	467	1084	110	.322	.372
Syracuse	.246	144	4800	531	1181	201	29	82	494	496	1116	99	.321	.351
Pawtucket	.238	144	4857	508	1157	192	12	95	473	472	1104	102	.309	.341

CLUB PITCHING

	ERA	G	CG	SHO	SV	IP	H	R	ER	HR	BB	SO	AVG
Indianapolis	3.09	144	3	13	44	1284	1182	516	441	63	437	1039	.244
Norfolk	3.17	144	1	14	47	1273	1137	489	448	75	441	986	.241
Gwinnett	3.18	144	2	13	44	1272	1150	511	450	77	469	982	.244
Scranton/W-B	3.21	144	2	11	45	1288	1214	524	460	65	430	1042	.250
Buffalo	3.32	144	2	13	33	1261	1222	518	465	72	442	1003	.254
Columbus	3.33	144	5	11	48	1275	1216	521	472	115	442	1052	.254
Rochester	3.46	144	11	21	30	1244	1219	535	478	80	358	1034	.257
Syracuse	3.70	144	1	9	34	1269	1254	585	522	80	409	940	.259
Pawtucket	3.73	144	3	7	29	1287	1213	606	534	84	479	1013	.251
Charlotte	3.78	144	1	8	43	1268	1221	592	532	100	431	1079	.252
Durham	3.81	144	1	13	44	1269	1251	605	537	116	413	1117	.257
Lehigh Valley	4.02	144	2	10	43	1291	1349	644	576	87	528	914	.269
Louisville	4.04	144	3	9	38	1264	1311	616	567	90	487	953	.270
Toledo	4.69	144	1	4	38	1277	1318	732	665	102	535	985	.269

CLUB FIELDING

	PCT	PO	A	E	DP		PCT	PO	A	E	DP
Columbus	.984	3826	1411	84	353	Syracuse	.980	3808	1449	106	372
Norfolk	.984	3821	1533	87	376	Gwinnett	.979	3816	1485	115	413
Buffalo	.983	3783	1528	93	407	Pawtucket	.979	3841	1474	112	369
Rochester	.983	3734	1337	89	354	Lehigh Valley	.978	3873	1434	122	399
Scranton/W-B	.982	3865	1459	98	364	Louisville	.978	3794	1445	117	439
Toledo	.981	3831	1490	105	338	Durham	.976	3807	1404	127	352
Charlotte	.980	3804	1541	109	364	Indianapolis	.975	3852	1523	138	321

INDIVIDUAL BATTING LEADERS

Batter, Club	AVG	G	AB	R	H	2B	3B	HR	RBI	BB	SO	SB
Hague, Matt, Buffalo	.338	136	523	70	177	33	1	11	92	61	65	5
Beresford, James, Rochester	.307	129	498	58	153	21	1	1	50	29	57	2
Holt, Tyler, Columbus	.302	101	368	63	111	17	4	0	28	50	62	25
Gamel, Ben, Scranton/WB	.300	129	500	77	150	28	14	10	64	46	108	13
Bogusevic, Brian, Lehigh Valley	.296	118	467	65	138	18	3	12	57	44	97	24
Peraza, Jose, Gwinnett	.294	96	391	52	115	10	7	3	37	15	35	26
Burns, Andy, Buffalo	.293	126	478	60	140	26	0	4	45	38	69	6
Motter, Taylor, Durham	.292	127	486	74	142	43	1	14	72	57	95	26
Figueroa, Cole, Scranton/WB	.292	121	449	45	131	19	1	3	44	44	27	4
Urrutia, Henry, Norfolk	.291	115	460	58	134	22	1	10	53	40	81	1

INDIVIDUAL PITCHING LEADERS

Pitcher, Club	W	L	ERA	G	GS	CG	SV	IP	H	R	ER	BB	SO
Johnson, Erik, Charlotte	11	8	2.37	23	22	0	0	133	108	40	35	41	136
Wolf, Randy, Buffalo	9	2	2.58	23	23	1	0	140	139	44	40	40	106
Bowden, Michael, Norfolk/Rochester	11	5	2.63	32	17	0	0	123	110	41	36	31	99
Smith, Greg, Gwinnett	6	7	2.71	31	19	0	0	120	119	47	36	25	67
Dean, Pat, Rochester	12	11	2.82	27	27	5	0	179	170	60	56	36	98
Murata, Toru, Columbus	15	4	2.90	27	26	1	0	164	148	59	53	45	101
Jones, Chris, Norfolk	8	8	2.94	30	22	0	0	150	158	60	49	29	105
Copeland, Scott, Buffalo	11	6	2.95	21	20	0	0	125	119	44	41	37	66
Boscan, Wilfredo, Indianapolis	10	3	3.07	25	23	0	0	126	130	53	43	45	86
Owens, Henry, Pawtucket	3	8	3.16	21	21	0	0	122	84	47	43	56	103

ALL-STAR TEAM

C: Elias Diaz, Scranton/Wilkes-Barre. **1B:** Reynaldo Rodriguez, Rochester. **2B:** James Beresford, Rochester. **3B:** Matt Hague, Buffalo. **SS:** Dixon Machado, Toledo. **OF:** Dariel Alvarez, Norfolk; Brian Bogusevic, Lehigh Valley; Ben Gamel, Scranton/Wilkes-Barre. **DH:** Jesus Aguilar, Columbus. **SP:** Erik Johnson, Charlotte. **RP:** Oliver Drake, Norfolk.
Most Valuable Player: Matt Hague, Buffalo. **Most Valuable Pitcher:** Erik Johnson, Charlotte.
Rookie of the Year: Ben Gamel, of, Scranton/Wilkes-Barre.
Manager of the Year: Ron Johnson, Norfolk.

DEPARTMENT LEADERS

BATTING

OBP	Hague, Matt, Buffalo	.416
SLG	Jefry Marte, Toledo	.487
OPS	Hague, Matt, Buffalo	.885
R	Rodriguez, Reynaldo, Rochester	81
H	Hague, Matt, Buffalo	177
TB	Hague, Matt, Buffalo	245
XBH	Motter, Taylor, Durham	58
2B	Motter, Taylor, Durham	43
3B	Gamel, Ben, Scranton/WB	14
HR	Davidson, Matt, Charlotte	23
RBI	Aguilar, Jesus, Columbus	93
SAC	Machado, Dixon, Toledo	15
BB	Fields, Daniel, Toledo	66
HBP	Curtis, Jermaine, Louisville	11
	d'Arnaud, Chase, Lehigh Valley	11
SO	Davidson, Matt, Charlotte	191
SB	Berry, Quintin, Pawtucket	35
	Hanson, Alen, Indianapolis	35
CS	Avery, Xavier, Toledo, Rochester	12
	Garcia, Leury, Charlotte	12
	Hanson, Alen, Indianapolis	12
AB/SO	Figueroa, Cole, Scranton/WB	16.63

PITCHING

G	Beato, Pedro, Norfolk	63
GS	Melville, Tim, Toledo	27
	Rogers, Taylor, Rochester	27
	Weber, Thad, Toledo	27
GF	Wood, Blake, Indianapolis	46
SV	Wood, Blake, Indianapolis	29
W	Murata, Toru, Columbus	15
L	Belfiore, Mike, Toledo, Norfolk	12
	Floro, Dylan, Durham	12
	Rogers, Taylor, Rochester	12
IP	Dean, Pat, Rochester	179
H	Rogers, Taylor, Rochester	190
R	Couch, Keith, Pawtucket	90
ER	Couch, Keith, Pawtucket	85
HB	Haviland, Shawn, Charlotte, Pawtucket	11
BB	Gamboa, Eddie, Norfolk	84
SO	Johnson, Erik, Charlotte	136
SO/9	Johnson, Erik, Charlotte	9.23
SO/9 (RP)	Wood, Blake, Indianapolis	10.74
BB/9	Floro, Dylan, Durham	1.42
WP	Gamboa, Eddie, Norfolk	15
BK	Weber, Thad, Toledo	5
HR	Roth, Michael, Columbus	20
AVG	Owens, Henry, Pawtucket	.193

FIELDING

C PCT	Moore, Adam, Columbus	.997
PO	Maile, Luke, Durham	679
A	Maile, Luke, Durham	63
DP	Four tied at	7
E	Sanchez, Tony, Indianapolis	12
PB	Clevenger, Steve, Norfolk	10
1B PCT	Aguilar, Jesus, Columbus	.999
PO	Walker, Christian, Norfolk	1,168
A	Walker, Christian, Norfolk	71
DP	Walker, Christian, Norfolk	119
E	Walker, Christian, Norfolk	9
2B PCT	Hanson, Alen, Indianapolis	.984
PO	Beresford, James, Rochester	210
A	Hanson, Alen, Indianapolis	352
DP	Beresford, James, Rochester	80
E	Peraza, Jose, Gwinnett	19
3B PCT	Davidson, Matt, Charlotte	.971
PO	Almanzar, Michael, Norfolk	98
A	Davidson, Matt, Charlotte	281
DP	Davidson, Matt, Charlotte	24
	Martinson, Jason, Syracuse	24
E	Almanzar, Michael, Norfolk	21
SS PCT	Machado, Dixon, Toledo	.975
PO	Machado, Dixon, Toledo	197
A	Machado, Dixon, Toledo	344
DP	Machado, Dixon, Toledo	72
E	d'Arnaud, Chase, Lehigh Valley	22
OF PCT	Bogusevic, Brian, Lehigh Valley	.996
PO	Ortiz, Danny, Norfolk	301
A	Gamel, Ben, Scranton/WB	13
DP	Alvarez, Dariel, Norfolk	4
	Mahtook, Mikie, Durham	4
E	Alvarez, Dariel, Norfolk	8

MINOR LEAGUES

BY TEDDY CAHILL

The affiliation shuffle in the fall of 2014 changed the look of the Pacific Coast League, as six of the league's 16 teams went into this season with a new parent club. Some of the league's longest standing relationships ended, such as the Rockies ending their 21-year relationship with Colorado Springs to move to Albuquerque, and the Athletics moving to Nashville after 15 years in Sacramento.

For some clubs, the shuffle yielded immediate results on the field. In its first season as an Astros affiliate, Fresno won its division to reach the playoffs for the first time since 1998. Third baseman Matt Duffy became the franchise's first MVP since Calvin Murray won the award in 1999.

The Grizzlies kept rolling in the playoffs. Fresno defeated El Paso, three games to one, in the semifinals for its first postseason series victory. Then, in the PCL championship series, Fresno defeated Round Rock, three games to two. Righthander Mark Appel, the first overall pick in the 2013 draft, was the winning pitcher in the decisive fifth game. Fresno closed out its season with a 7-0 victory in the Triple-A National Championship Game against Columbus, the International League champions.

Fresno wasn't the only club to thrive with a new affiliation. Oklahoma City, the Astros' former affiliate that is now owned by the Dodgers, also won its division. Damon Berryhill was named manager of the year and shortstop Corey Seager, ranked No. 1 on the Midseason Top 50 Prospects List, spent much of the season in Triple-A, before joining the Dodgers in September.

The historic feats weren't limited to team

TOP 20 PROSPECTS

1. Corey Seager, ss, Oklahoma City (Dodgers)
2. Joey Gallo, 3b, Round Rock (Rangers)
3. Steven Matz, lhp, Las Vegas (Mets)
4. Jon Gray, rhp, Albuquerque (Rockies)
5. Mark Appel, rhp, Fresno (Astros)
6. Andrew Heaney, lhp, Salt Lake (Angels)
7. Stephen Piscotty, of/1b, Memphis (Cardinals)
8. Ketel Marte, ss/2b, Tacoma (Mariners)
9. Trevor Story, ss, Albuquerque (Rockies)
10. Dilson Herrera, 2b, Las Vegas (Mets)
11. Aaron Blair, rhp, Reno (Diamondbacks)
12. Alex Gonzalez, rhp, Round Rock (Rangers)
13. Domingo Santana, of, Colorado Springs (Brewers)
14. Brandon Drury, 3b/2b, Reno (Diamondbacks)
15. Preston Tucker, of, Fresno (Astros)
16. Marco Gonzales, lhp, Memphis (Cardinals)
17. Chris Bassitt, rhp, Nashville (Athletics)
18. Peter O'Brien, of/c, Reno (Diamondbacks)
19. Tony Kemp, 2b/of, Fresno (Astros)
20. Taylor Jungmann, rhp, Colorado Springs (Brewers)

achievements. Omaha outfielder Jose Martinez hit .384/.461/.563 to win the batting title. It was the best batting average in the league since 1948. Fresno manager Tony DeFrancesco won his fourth PCL championship, tying him for the third most titles in league history. He also joined John Davis, Tommy Lasorda and Bob Skinner as the two managers to have won championships with two different clubs in the modern era of the league.

Sacramento righthander Clayton Blackburn went 10-4, 2.85 to win the league ERA title. Just behind Blackburn and PCL Pitcher of the Year Carlos Pimentel in the ERA race was Nashville lefthander Barry Zito. The 2002 American League Cy Young winner went 8-7, 3.46 for the Sounds in his final season of professional baseball before earning a nostalgic callup at the end of the year, when he pitched against the retiring Tim Hudson.

OVERALL STANDINGS

American Northern	W	L	PCT	GB	Manager(s)	Attendance	Average	Last Pennant
Oklahoma City Dodgers (Dodgers)	86	58	.597	—	Damon Berryhill	471,996	6,941	1965
Iowa Cubs (Cubs)	80	64	.556	6	Marty Pevey	504,577	7,531	Never
Omaha Storm Chasers (Royals)	80	64	.556	6	Brian Poldberg	386,141	5,516	2014
Colorado Springs Sky Sox (Brewers)	62	81	.434	24	Rick Sweet	300,209	4,619	1995
American Northern	**W**	**L**	**PCT**	**GB**	**Manager(s)**	**Attendance**	**Average**	**Last Pennant**
Round Rock Express (Rangers)	78	66	.542	—	Jason Wood	595,012	8,623	Never
Memphis Redbirds (Cardinals)	73	71	.507	5	Mike Shildt	278,579	4,037	2009
Nashville Sounds (Athletics)	66	78	.458	12	Steve Scarsone	565,548	7,965	2005
New Orleans Zephyrs (Marlins)	58	86	.403	20	Andy Haines	324,973	4,710	2001
Pacific Northern	**W**	**L**	**PCT**	**GB**	**Manager(s)**	**Attendance**	**Average**	**Last Pennant**
Fresno Grizzlies (Astros)	84	59	.587	—	Tony DeFrancesco	458,431	6,457	2015
Sacramento River Cats (Giants)	71	73	.493	14	Bob Mariano	672,354	9,338	2008
Reno Aces (Diamondbacks)	70	74	.486	15	Phil Nevin	376,422	5,377	2012
Tacoma Rainiers (Mariners)	68	76	.472	17	Pat Listach	352,521	4,965	2010
Pacific Southern	**W**	**L**	**PCT**	**GB**	**Manager(s)**	**Attendance**	**Average**	**Last pennant**
El Paso Chihuahuas (Padres)	78	66	.542	—	Jamie Quirk	578,952	8,154	Never
Las Vegas 51s (Mets)	77	67	.535	1	Wally Backman	333,520	4,834	1998
Albuquerque Isotopes (Rockies)	62	82	.431	16	Glenallen Hill	560,519	8,007	1994
Salt Lake Bees (Angels)	58	86	.403	20	Dave Anderson	470,760	6,823	1979

Semifinals: Round Rock def. Oklahoma City 3-0 and Fresno def. El Paso 3-1 in best-of-five series; **Finals:** Fresno def. Round Rock 3-2 in a best-of-five series.

CLUB BATTING

	AVG	G	AB	R	H	2B	3B	HR	RBI	BB	SO	SB	OBP	SLG
Reno	.286	144	4962	758	1421	339	38	138	722	453	1025	43	.347	.453
Salt Lake	.284	144	5020	697	1428	318	46	92	652	447	1108	52	.345	.421
El Paso	.281	144	5004	765	1406	297	45	114	715	521	1088	95	.354	.427
Tacoma	.280	144	5010	745	1402	248	40	148	684	438	1012	157	.340	.434
Omaha	.278	144	4808	642	1335	242	22	115	592	415	872	153	.338	.409
Colorado Springs	.277	143	4835	653	1340	258	49	80	608	399	897	84	.334	.400
Fresno	.274	143	4836	804	1323	243	36	124	756	606	1014	157	.357	.416
Las Vegas	.274	144	4835	758	1327	321	32	140	702	485	1074	125	.347	.441
Albuquerque	.272	144	4897	667	1333	257	39	125	628	414	1087	118	.332	.417
Iowa	.271	144	4790	669	1300	257	44	114	617	437	1155	134	.335	.415
Sacramento	.268	144	5071	649	1358	268	24	124	604	418	1101	125	.329	.403
Nashville	.265	144	4884	591	1293	263	31	84	548	459	1045	85	.331	.383
Round Rock	.262	144	4867	646	1277	272	32	139	600	425	1045	90	.326	.417
Memphis	.261	144	4725	669	1231	237	34	97	627	604	940	86	.347	.387
New Orleans	.258	144	4849	526	1253	238	25	68	486	440	926	48	.324	.360
Oklahoma City	.257	144	4819	659	1240	263	31	136	618	418	966	101	.320	.409

CLUB PITCHING

	ERA	G	CG	SHO	SV	IP	H	R	ER	HR	BB	SO	AVG
Iowa	3.73	144	4	11	40	1256	1185	619	521	90	529	947	.250
New Orleans	3.80	144	3	15	30	1270	1279	604	537	110	433	951	.264
Sacramento	3.85	144	8	38	1312	1316	660	561	110	464	1119	.261
Omaha	3.86	144	2	8	40	1255	1224	592	539	120	453	1075	.256
Oklahoma City	3.93	144	5	7	44	1263	1280	608	551	89	408	1053	.267
Nashville	3.95	144	4	9	26	1263	1215	626	554	111	485	1037	.253
Memphis	4.10	144	4	14	30	1254	1351	633	571	125	363	870	.276
Round Rock	4.10	144	1	11	41	1263	1291	623	575	96	472	1050	.267
Fresno	4.24	143	2	9	36	1264	1314	660	596	115	417	1096	.265
Las Vegas	4.45	144	8	8	28	1245	1344	673	616	116	448	1009	.277
El Paso	4.57	144	1	2	42	1275	1361	721	648	132	450	1070	.274
Tacoma	4.85	144	2	8	24	1265	1373	758	682	147	433	984	.276
Albuquerque	4.97	144	2	4	28	1249	1440	781	690	125	498	1008	.290
Colorado Springs	5.01	143	0	5	31	1229	1343	730	685	107	501	966	.281
Reno	5.14	144	2	4	35	1250	1441	778	714	117	543	1006	.292
Salt Lake	5.36	144	2	3	32	1260	1510	832	751	128	482	1114	.299

CLUB FIELDING

	PCT	PO	A	E	DP		PCT	PO	A	E	DP
New Orleans	.982	3811	1487	96	420	Nashville	.980	3789	1407	105	351
Round Rock	.982	3790	1416	96	337	Omaha	.978	3766	1287	116	322
Colorado Springs	.981	3688	1466	98	353	Albuquerque	.977	3747	1569	126	429
Fresno	.981	3794	1323	98	248	Salt Lake	.977	3782	1368	122	364
Las Vegas 51s	.981	3737	1528	104	388	Tacoma	.977	3797	1419	122	321
Okla. City Dodgers	.981	3789	1421	102	435	Iowa	.976	3768	1558	131	393
Reno Aces	.981	3751	1532	104	436	Sacramento	.975	3938	1421	137	360
Memphis	.980	3764	1522	110	419	El Paso	.974	3826	1438	138	343x

INDIVIDUAL BATTING LEADERS

Batter, Club	AVG	G	AB	R	H	2B	3B	HR	RBI	BB	SO	SB
Martinez, Jose, Omaha	.384	98	341	57	131	25	3	10	60	48	55	8
Montero, Jesus, Tacoma	.355	98	394	70	140	18	6	18	85	29	71	3
Santana, Domingo, Fres./Col. Springs	.333	95	354	75	118	23	4	18	77	54	108	2
Freeman, Mike, Reno	.317	113	398	79	126	23	5	3	41	34	51	10
Lucas, Ed, Round Rock	.316	107	393	43	124	17	3	6	48	45	85	3
Worth, Danny, Reno	.314	106	350	53	110	30	3	6	47	46	99	6
Adames, Cristhian, Albuquerque	.311	116	463	62	144	20	3	11	51	36	56	11
Pridie, Jason, Nashville	.310	127	478	84	148	24	7	20	89	55	102	20
Evans, Nick, Reno	.310	139	520	79	161	37	0	17	94	59	111	0
Pena, Ramiro, El Paso	.308	111	399	68	123	24	2	4	57	30	44	1

INDIVIDUAL PITCHING LEADERS

Pitcher, Club	W	L	ERA	G	GS	CG	SV	IP	H	R	ER	BB	SO
Blackburn, Clayton, Sacramento	10	4	2.85	23	20	0	0	123	127	46	39	32	99
Pimentel, Carlos, Iowa	12	6	3.29	27	26	2	0	143	121	59	47	68	118
Zito, Barry, Nashville	8	7	3.46	24	22	1	0	138	121	66	53	60	91
Nicolino, Justin, New Orleans	7	7	3.52	20	20	0	0	115	134	51	45	29	63
Brooks, Aaron, Omaha/Nashville	7	5	3.56	20	19	1	0	119	127	49	47	21	103
Smith, Chris, El Paso	5	7	3.60	22	22	0	0	128	121	54	51	42	121
McCutchen, Daniel, El Paso	9	8	3.60	32	22	0	0	132	128	57	53	28	86
Snow, Forrest, Tacoma	10	9	4.17	29	20	0	1	121	118	59	56	41	96
Neal, Zach, Nashville	7	10	4.18	21	20	2	0	131	151	71	61	20	78
Cruz, Luis, Fresno	7	5	4.27	28	19	0	0	116	119	60	55	52	93

ALL-STAR TEAM

C: Austin Barnes, Oklahoma City. **1B:** Jesus Montero, Tacoma. **2B:** Joey Wendle, Nashville. **3B:** Matt Duffy, Fresno. **SS:** Cristhian Adames, Albuquerque. **OF:** Domingo Santana, Fresno/Col. Springs; Alex Dickerson, El Paso; Peter O'Brien, Reno. **DH:** Jamie Romak, Reno. **RHSP:** Carlos Pimentel, Iowa. **LHSP:** Adam Conley, New Orleans. **RP:** Jon Edwards, El Paso/Round Rock. **Most Valuable Player:** Matt Duffy, 3b, Fresno. **Pitcher of the Year:** Carlos Pimentel, rhp, Iowa. **Rookie of the Year:** Alex Dickerson, of, El Paso. **Manager of the Year:** Damon Berryhill, Oklahoma City.

DEPARTMENT LEADERS

BATTING

OBP	Martinez, Jose, Omaha	.461
SLG	Santana, Domingo, Fresno, Col. Springs	.573
OPS	Martinez, Jose, Omaha	1.024
R	Duffy, Matt, Fresno	94
H	Wendle, Joey, Nashville	167
TB	O'Brien, Peter, Reno	270
XBH	Romak, Jamie, Reno	72
2B	Kubitza, Kyle, Salt Lake	43
3B	Alcantara, Arismendy, Iowa	10
HR	Romak, Jamie, Reno	27
RBI	O'Brien, Peter, Reno	107
SAC	Fuentes, Reymond, Omaha	14
BB	Anna, Dean, Memphis	77
HBP	Dietrich, Derek, New Orleans	15
	Taijeron, Travis, Las Vegas	15
SO	Parker, Jarrett, Sacramento	164
SB	Villar, Jonathan, Fresno	35
CS	Ford, Darren, Sacramento	16
AB/SO	Frandsen, Kevin, Reno, Sacramento	14.96

PITCHING

G	Thornton, Zach, Las Vegas	63
GS	Lane, Jason, El Paso	28
	Petrick, Zach, Memphis	28
GF	Schlitter, Brian, Iowa	41
SV	Edwards, Jon, Round Rock	23
	Schlitter, Brian, Iowa	23
W	Greenwood, Nick, Memphis	13
L	Bowman, Matt, Las Vegas	16
IP	Blach, Ty, Sacramento	165
H	Lane, Jason, El Paso	212
R	Lane, Jason, El Paso	117
ER	Lane, Jason, El Paso	104
HB	Sanabia, Alex, Salt Lake	13
BB	Gorski, Darin, Las Vegas	69
SO	Straily, Dan, Fresno	124
SO/9	Straily, Dan, Fresno	9.10
SO/9 (RP)	Partch, Curtis, Sacramento	11.16
BB/9	Neal, Zach, Nashville	1.37
WP	Gagnon, Drew, Col. Springs	14
BK	DeLoach, Tyler, Salt Lake	5
HR	Lane, Jason, El Paso	27
AVG	Pimentel, Carlos, Iowa	.229

FIELDING

C PCT	Stassi, Max, Fresno	.997
PO	Bandy, Jett, Salt Lake	654
A	Gale, Rocky, El Paso	87
DP	Ashley, Nevin, Col. Springs	11
E	Hicks, John, Tacoma	9
PB	Brown, Trevor, Sacramento	10
1B PCT	Clark, Matt, Col. Springs	.993
PO	Clark, Matt, Col. Springs	909
A	Clark, Matt, Col. Springs	76
DP	Clark, Matt, Col. Springs	85
E	Clark, Matt, Col. Springs	7
	Rosario, Wilin, Albuquerque	7
	Singleton, Jon, Fresno	7
	Wilkins, Andy, Okla. City	7
2B PCT	Anna, Dean, Memphis	.986
PO	Wendle, Joey, Nashville	297
A	Wendle, Joey, Nashville	387
DP	Wendle, Joey, Nashville	90
E	Wendle, Joey, Nashville	16
3B PCT	Dominguez, Matt, Fresno, Col. Springs	.990
PO	Dominguez, Matt, Fresno, Col. Springs	82
A	Dominguez, Matt, Fresno, Col. Springs	204
DP	Wilson, Jacob, Memphis	21
E	Rivero, Carlos, Tacoma	18
SS PCT	Alberto, Hanser, Round Rock	.990
PO	Worth, Danny, Reno	134
A	Reynolds, Matt, Las Vegas	290
DP	Seager, Corey, Okla. City	77
E	Worth, Danny, Reno	19
OF PCT	Pridie, Jason, Nashville	.993
PO	Hoying, Jared, Round Rock	328
A	Ortega, Rafael, Memphis	15
DP	Schafer, Logan, Col. Springs	5
E	O'Brien, Peter, Reno	10
	Parker, Jarrett, Sacramento	10

MINOR LEAGUES

BY JOSH NORRIS

Throughout the course of the year, the Reading Fightin Phils got contributions from five players who ranked among their organization's Top 10 Prospects entering the season, including three preseason Top 100 Prospects. They began the year with righthander Aaron Nola and later received shortstop J.P. Crawford.

After the big club traded lefthander Cole Hamels to the Rangers, Reading received two of the biggest prizes in the deal: outfielder Nick Williams and righthander Jake Thompson. Reading also got an outstanding half-season from catcher Andrew Knapp and an MVP performance from first baseman Brock Stassi.

Even so, the Fightins fell one game short of the Eastern League crown, losing in five games to the Orioles-affiliated Bowie Baysox. And in the decisive fifth game, one of the most talented teams in the minors was undone by a monster performance from a minor league lifer.

Infielder Garabez Rosa swatted two home runs in the clincher, and the Baysox also got five hits from the top-of-the-lineup duo of Corban Joseph and Mike Yastrzemski in a 7-2 win. This was the first championship in Bowie's 23-year history.

Even without Reading, there were still plenty of tremendous prospects who made their way through the Eastern League in 2015, including 19 who ranked among BA's Top 100 Prospects.

The cream of the crop was Nationals righthander Lucas Giolito, who arrived in Harrisburg from high Class A Potomac at midseason and went 4-2, 3.80 with 45 strikeouts in 47 innings. He pitched just enough innings to qualify for the EL's Top 20 Prospects list and ranked ahead of Crawford as the league's No. 1 prospect.

The league also included Mets outfielder Michael Conforto, who hit .312/.396/.503 with five homers and 26 RBIs with Binghamton before

moving to the big leagues.

Of BA's Top 20 Prospects in the league, four finished the year with their parent club: Conforto, Nola, Harrisburg righthander Joe Ross and Trenton first baseman Greg Bird.

Ross exited the EL early, then made a brief stop at Triple-A Syracuse before becoming a part of the Nationals' rotation. With Washington, Ross was 5-5, 3.64 with 69 punchouts in 77 innings before being shut down toward the end of September.

Bird was called up in August, then saw extended playing time when first baseman Mark Teixeira fractured his leg. Bird provided exactly what the Yankees expected: power and patience. He and righthander Luis Severino buoyed the Yankees down the stretch and were integral parts of their return to the postseason.

The league could start 2016 with an impressive corps of talent too, with outfielders Manuel Margot (Red Sox), Clint Frazier (Indians) and righthander Reynaldo Lopez (Nationals) all on track to start the year in Double-A.

TOP 20 PROSPECTS

1. Lucas Giolito, rhp, Harrisburg (Nationals)
2. J.P. Crawford, ss, Reading (Phillies)
3. Michael Conforto, of, Binghamton (Mets)
4. Tyler Glasnow, rhp, Altoona (Pirates)
5. Jeff Hoffman, rhp, New Hampshire/New Britain (Blue Jays/Rockies)
6. Aaron Nola, rhp, Reading (Phillies)
7. Michael Fulmer, rhp, Binghamton/Erie (Mets/Tigers)
8. Joe Ross, rhp, Harrisburg (Nationals)
9. Bradley Zimmer, of, Akron (Indians)
10. Manuel Margot, of, Portland (Red Sox)
11. David Dahl, of, New Britain (Rockies)
12. Trevor Story, ss, New Britain (Rockies)
13. Gavin Cecchini, ss, Binghamton (Mets)
14. Andrew Knapp, c, Reading (Phillies)
15. Aaron Judge, of, Trenton (Yankees)
16. Greg Bird, 1b, Trenton (Yankees)
17. Mike Clevinger, rhp, Akron (Indians)
18. Trey Mancini, 1b, Bowie (Orioles)
19. Brandon Nimmo, of, Binghamton (Mets)
20. Josh Bell, of/1b, Altoona (Pirates)

OVERALL STANDINGS

EAST	W	L	PCT	GB	Manager(s)	Attendance	Average	Last Pennant
Reading Fightin Phils (Phillies)	80	61	.567	—	Dusty Wathan	417,010	6,044	2001
Binghamton Mets (Mets)	77	64	.546	3	Pedro Lopez	188,104	2,766	1994
Trenton Thunder (Yankees)	71	71	.500	9½	Al Pedrique	347,231	4,960	2013
New Britain Rock Cats (Rockies)	69	71	.493	10½	Darin Everson	267,377	4,051	2001
New Hampshire Fisher Cats (Blue Jays)	69	71	.493	10½	Bobby Meacham	348,539	5,051	
Portland Sea Dogs (Red Sox)	53	89	.373	27½	Billy McMillon	368,291	5,497	2006

WEST	W	L	PCT	GB	Manager(s)	Attendance	Average	Last pennant
Bowie Baysox (Orioles)	79	63	.556	—	Gary Kendall	256,865	3,618	2015
Altoona Curve (Pirates)	74	68	.521	5	Tom Prince	302,761	4,325	2010
Richmond Flying Squirrels (Giants)	72	68	.514	6	Jose Alguacil	417,828	6,055	2014
Akron RubberDucks (Indians)	73	69	.514	6	Dave Wallace	340,916	5,013	2012
Harrisburg Senators (Nationals)	67	75	.472	12	Brian Daubach	301,588	4,371	1999
Erie SeaWolves (Tigers)	64	78	.451	15	Lance Parrish	203,655	3,133	Never

Playoffs—Semifinals: Reading defeated Binghamton 3-0 and Bowie defeated Altoona 3-1 in best-of-five series; **Finals:** Bowie defeated Reading 3-2 in a best-of-five series.

CLUB BATTING

	AVG	G	AB	R	H	2B	3B	HR	RBI	BB	SO	SB	OBP	SLG
Altoona	.271	142	4,753	603	1288	238	42	75	560	443	1055	96	.334	.386
Reading	.269	141	4,806	665	1294	273	42	101	616	478	922	92	.338	.407
Bowie	.260	142	4,791	602	1245	262	28	96	563	379	932	62	.318	.386
Erie	.259	142	4,649	568	1203	227	33	86	531	386	956	139	.319	.377
Binghamton	.256	141	4,776	596	1224	240	31	92	558	420	966	61	.320	.377
Akron	.255	142	4,800	579	1223	228	43	87	529	478	1009	129	.328	.375
New Britain	.252	140	4,603	575	1159	232	39	82	516	366	1098	182	.313	.373
Portland	.251	142	4,759	539	1194	264	40	66	508	401	919	86	.314	.365
Trenton	.251	142	4,762	554	1195	233	28	73	503	385	930	131	.313	.358
New Hampshire	.250	140	4,705	570	1174	214	28	90	521	433	864	88	.315	.364
Richmond	.249	140	4,610	503	1147	202	27	61	462	333	979	84	.303	.344
Harrisburg	.247	142	4,697	568	1159	209	31	68	516	439	975	149	.314	.348

CLUB PITCHING

	ERA	G	CG	SHO	SV	IP	H	R	ER	HR	BB	SO	AVG
Richmond	3.12	140	1	11	46	1227	1107	488	426	52	472	964	.242
Akron	3.19	142	4	14	34	1272	1140	503	451	79	379	1045	.241
Trenton	3.40	142	3	12	34	1256	1189	547	475	62	432	1027	.249
Binghamton	3.46	141	3	13	44	1239	1153	543	476	69	391	995	.246
Bowie	3.49	142	6	12	40	1258	1150	556	488	74	417	1045	.244
Altoona	3.61	142	3	16	44	1257	1201	588	505	79	423	844	.252
Harrisburg	3.73	142	2	8	36	1249	1232	577	518	96	381	983	.259
New Britain	3.75	140	9	10	40	1222	1216	580	509	89	359	907	.259
Reading	3.84	141	2	10	43	1247	1218	586	532	100	415	927	.261
New Hampshire	3.86	140	2	15	34	1242	1303	590	532	85	370	990	.272
Portland	4.30	142	0	5	23	1239	1251	689	592	93	511	949	.261
Erie	4.35	142	5	3	37	1206	1345	675	583	99	391	929	.284

CLUB FIELDING

	PCT	PO	A	E	DP		PCT	PO	A	E	DP
New Hampshire	.981	3726	1439	102	372	New Britain	.976	3667	1352	124	306
Akron	.980	3818	1293	102	286	Trenton	.976	3768	1360	128	291
Reading	.980	3741	1498	105	365	Binghamton	.975	3718	1428	130	294
Bowie	.978	3776	1432	116	369	Erie	.975	3618	1366	126	336
Richmond	.978	3683	1618	121	361	Portland	.973	3719	1338	143	287
Harrisburg	.977	3749	1458	120	356	Altoona	.970	3773	1620	165	346

INDIVIDUAL BATTING LEADERS

Batter, Club	AVG	G	AB	R	H	2B	3B	HR	RBI	BB	SO	SB
Mancini, Trey, Bowie	.359	84	326	60	117	29	3	13	57	22	58	2
Frazier, Adam, Altoona	.324	103	377	59	122	21	4	2	30	34	42	11
Cecchini, Gavin, Binghamton	.317	109	439	64	139	26	4	7	51	42	55	3
Diaz, Yandy, Akron	.315	132	476	61	150	13	5	7	55	78	65	8
Bell, Josh, Altoona	.307	96	368	47	113	17	6	5	60	44	50	7
Bernard, Wynton, Erie	.301	135	534	78	161	29	8	4	36	38	73	43
Stassi, Brock, Reading	.300	133	466	76	140	32	1	15	90	77	63	3
Tauchman, Mike, New Britain	.294	131	507	62	149	23	6	3	43	47	69	25
Moroff, Max, Altoona	.293	136	523	79	153	28	6	7	51	70	111	17
Rodriguez, Josh, Binghamton	.282	115	412	70	116	24	3	19	76	54	87	11

INDIVIDUAL PITCHING LEADERS

Pitcher, Club	W	L	ERA	G	GS	CG	SV	IP	H	R	ER	BB	SO
Fulmer, Michael, Binghampton/Erie	10	3	2.14	21	21	0	0	118	100	35	28	30	116
Biagini, Joe, Richmond	10	7	2.42	23	22	0	0	130	112	45	35	34	84
Kuhl, Chad, Altoona	11	5	2.48	26	26	1	0	153	133	53	42	41	101
Marte, Kelvin, Richmond	10	6	2.63	26	19	1	0	130	118	41	38	40	77
Clevinger, Mike, Akron	9	8	2.73	27	26	0	0	158	127	53	48	40	145
Gunkel, Joe, Portland/Bowie	10	5	2.79	21	20	0	0	123	111	43	38	23	91
Plutko, Adam, Akron	9	5	2.86	19	19	1	0	116	96	39	37	23	90
Voth, Austin, Harrisburg	6	7	2.92	28	27	0	0	157	134	60	51	40	148
Morimando, Shawn, Akron	10	12	3.18	28	28	0	0	159	139	62	56	65	128

ALL-STAR TEAM

C: Pedro Severino, Harrisburg. **1B:** Brock Stassi, Reading. **2B:** Max Moroff, Altoona. **3B:** Yandy Diaz, Akron. **SS:** Gavin Cecchini, Binghamton. **OF:** Wynton Bernard, Erie; Quincy Latimore, Bowie; Mike Tauchman, New Britain. **UT:** Josh Rodriguez, Binghamton. **DH:** Dean Green, Erie. **RHSP:** Michael Fulmer, Erie/Binghamton. **LHSP:** Richard Bleier, Harrisburg. **RP:** Stephen Shackleford, Reading. **Most Valuable Player:** Brock Stassi, 1b, Reading. **Pitcher of the Year:** Michael Fulmer, rhp, Binghamton/Erie. **Rookie of the Year:** Gavin Cecchini, ss, Binghamton. **Manager of the Year:** Dusty Wathan, Reading.

DEPARTMENT LEADERS

BATTING

OBP	Diaz, Yandy, Akron	.412
SLG	Mancini, Trey, Bowie	.586
OPS	Stassi, Brock, Reading	.863
R	Moroff, Max, Altoona	79
H	Bernard, Wynton, Erie	161
TB	Latimore, Quincy, Bowie	225
XBH	Latimore, Quincy, Bowie	58
2B	Latimore, Quincy, Bowie	32
	Stassi, Brock, Reading	32
3B	Bernard, Wynton, Erie	8
HR	Latimore, Quincy, Bowie	20
	Schimpf, Ryan, New Hampshire	20
RBI	Stassi, Brock, Reading	90
SAC	Moreno, Rando, Richmond	21
BB	Diaz, Yandy, Akron	78
HBP	Myles, Bryson, Akron	14
SO	Allie, Stetson, Altoona	135
SB	Bernard, Wynton, Erie	43
CS	Bernard, Wynton, Erie	16
AB/SO	Renda, Tony, Harrisburg	12.31

PITCHING

G	McCormick, Phil, Richmond	58
GS	Carpenter, Ryan, New Britain	28
	Cole, Taylor, New Hampshire	28
	Morimando, Shawn, Akron	28
GF	Shackleford, Stephen, Reading	46
SV	Shackleford, Stephen, Reading	30
W	Carle, Shane, New Britain	14
L	Haley, Justin, Portland	16
IP	Flemer, Matt, New Britain	170
H	Lawrence, Casey, New Hampshire	208
R	Kubitza, Austin, Erie	108
ER	Kubitza, Austin, Erie	86
HB	Creasy, Jason, Altoona	13
BB	Crick, Kyle, Richmond	66
SO	Voth, Austin, Harrisburg	148
SO/9	Fulmer, Michael, Binghamton	8.87
SO/9 (RP)	Givens, Mychal, Bowie	12.40
BB/9	Merritt, Ryan, Akron	1.02
WP	Haley, Justin, Portland	15
BK	Bleier, Richard, Harrisburg	4
	Collier, Tommy, Erie	4
HR	Carpenter, Ryan, New Britain	19
AVG	Clevinger, Mike, Akron	.219

FIELDING

C PCT	Stallings, Jacob, Altoona	.994
PO	Carrillo, Xorge, Binghamton	658
A	Severino, Pedro, Harrisburg	92
DP	Williams, Jackson, Richmond	9
E	Carrillo, Xorge, Binghamton	9
	Green, Austin, Erie	9
	Martinez, Luis, Portland	9
PB	Williams, Jackson, Richmond	12
1B PCT	Stassi, Brock, Reading	.995
PO	Oropesa, Ricky, Richmond	1,093
A	Stassi, Brock, Reading	69
DP	Hobson, K.C., New Hampshire	106
E	Bell, Josh, Altoona	13
2B PCT	Moroff, Max, Altoona	.978
PO	Renda, Tony, Harrisburg	219
A	Moroff, Max, Altoona	330
DP	Moroff, Max, Altoona	76
E	Renda, Tony, Harrisburg	26
3B PCT	Delfino, Mitch, Richmond	.944
PO	Diaz, Yandy, Akron	94
A	Delfino, Mitch, Richmond	274
DP	Delfino, Mitch, Richmond	28
E	Delfino, Mitch, Richmond	21
	Diaz, Yandy, Akron	21
	Lawley, Dustin, Binghamton	21
	Wood, Eric, Altoona	21
SS PCT	Martinez, Ozzie, Bowie	.973
PO	Cecchini, Gavin, Binghamton	158
A	Moreno, Rando, Richmond	332
DP	Crawford, J.P., Reading	64
E	Cecchini, Gavin, Binghamton	28
OF PCT	Smith, Jordan, Akron	.997
PO	Smith, Jordan, Akron	319
A	Allie, Stetson, Altoona	16
DP	Allie, Stetson, Altoona	6
E	Goodwin, Brian, Harrisburg	10
	Yastrzemski, Mike, Bowie	10

MINOR LEAGUES

BY MATT EDDY

Construction delays at MGM Park forced Biloxi, in its first season as a Southern League franchise, to operate as a travel team until its new Mississippi home digs opened on June 6. The Shuckers, in fact, spent a good portion of April and May playing home games at their former base in Huntsville, Ala. The Brewers affiliate, which featured shortstop Orlando Arcia and righthander Jorge Lopez, didn't miss a beat.

While the Chattanooga franchise remained rooted in place, the Lookouts welcomed a new parent organization for 2015, swapping out the Dodgers for the Twins. Minnesota made quite an introduction by sending the organization's top three prospects to the SL. Even though outfielder Byron Buxton, third baseman Miguel Sano and righthander Jose Berrios had left the Lookouts by the start of the second half, Chattanooga secured a playoff berth by winning the first half.

As luck would have it, Biloxi and Chattanooga, met in the finals after handily winning first-round series.

While Biloxi won more games than any SL club, they actually fared better in the first half (43-25) while living a nomadic existence. Perhaps for this reason, Shuckers manager Carlos Subero won the league's manager of the year award.

Led by Lopez, righthander Tyler Wagner and a stout bullpen, the Biloxi pitching staff finished with the circuit's top ERA (3.25), WHIP (1.26) and strikeout-to-walk ratio (2.21). Wagner was the league's ERA champ at 2.25, while Lopez won the SL pitcher of the year award for going 12-5, 2.26, leading the circuit with a 1.10 WHIP and finishing fifth with 8.6 strikeouts per nine innings.

If pitching and defense keyed Biloxi's success, Chattanooga took the opposite approach by relying on the league's top offense to go 76-61 (.555). Even with the premature departures of Buxton and Sano, Lookouts batters led the SL in home runs (107), walks (573), stolen bases (164) and OPS (.750).

TOP 20 PROSPECTS

1. Miguel Sano, 3b, Chattanooga (Twins)
2. Byron Buxton, of, Chattanooga (Twins)
3. Orlando Arcia, ss, Biloxi (Brewers)
4. Kyle Schwarber, c, Tennessee (Cubs)
5. Blake Snell, lhp, Montgomery (Rays)
6. Max Kepler, of/1b, Chattanooga (Twins)
7. Jorge Lopez, rhp, Biloxi (Brewers)
8. Tim Anderson, ss, Birmingham (White Sox)
9. Jose Berrios, rhp, Chattanooga (Twins)
10. Cody Reed, lhp, Pensacola (Reds)'
11. Willson Contreras, c/3b, Tennessee (Cubs)
12. Robert Stephenson, rhp, Pensacola (Reds)
13. Aaron Blair, rhp, Mobile (Diamondbacks)
14. Jorge Polanco, ss/2b, Chattanooga (Twins)
15. Brandon Drury, 2b/3b, Mobile (Diamondbacks)
16. Mallex Smith, of, Mississippi (Braves)
17. Frankie Montas, rhp, Birmingham (White Sox)
18. Jesse Winker, of, Pensacola (Reds)
19. Albert Almora, of, Tennessee (Cubs)
20. Tyrell Jenkins, rhp, Mississippi (Braves)

STANDINGS: SPLIT SEASON

FIRST HALF

NORTH	W	L	PCT	GB
Chattanooga	43	25	.632	—
Tennessee	39	30	.565	4½
Montgomery	34	34	.500	9
Birmingham	33	36	.478	10½
Jackson	29	39	.426	14

SOUTH	W	L	PCT	GB
Biloxi	43	25	.632	—
Mobile	34	35	.493	9½
Mississippi	33	35	.485	10
Jacksonville	29	40	.420	14½
Pensacola	25	43	.368	18

SECOND HALF

NORTH	W	L	PCT	GB
Montgomery	43	27	.614	—
Tennessee	37	33	.529	6
Birmingham	36	34	.514	7
Chattanooga	33	36	.478	9½
Jackson	24	45	.348	18½

SOUTH	W	L	PCT	GB
Pensacola	38	32	.543	—
Mississippi	36	32	.529	1
Mobile	36	32	.529	1
Biloxi	35	34	.507	2½
Jacksonville	28	41	.406	9½

Playoffs—SemiFinals: Chattanooga defeated Montgomery 3-1 and Biloxi defeated Pensacola 3-0 in best-of-five series.
Finals: Chattanooga defeated Biloxi 3-2 in a best-of-five series.

The club's offensive lynchpin, however, turned out to be 22-year-old German-born outfielder/first baseman Max Kepler, the league MVP who hit .322 with league-leading figures for on-base percentage (.416) and slugging (.531).

Kepler hit just .188 in nine postseason games, though he homered off Lopez in the deciding fifth game of the finals. Biloxi had taken a two games to one lead in the series before Chattanooga stormed back to win the fourth and fifth games at home.

OVERALL STANDINGS

Team (Organization)	W	L	PCT	GB	Manager(s)	Attendance	Average	Last Pennant
Biloxi Shuckers (Brewers)	78	59	.569	—	Carlos Subero	164,076	2,604	Never
Montgomery Biscuits (Rays)	77	61	.558	1½	Brady Williams	232,466	3,419	2007
Chattanooga Lookouts (Twins)	76	61	.555	2	Doug Mientkiewicz	218,512	3,414	2015
Tennessee Smokies (Cubs)	76	63	.547	3	Buddy Bailey	277,606	4,406	2004
Mobile BayBears (Diamondbacks)	70	67	.511	8	Robby Hammock	96,260	1,553	2012
Mississippi Braves (Braves)	69	67	.507	8½	Aaron Holbert	216,917	3,190	2008
Birmingham Barons (White Sox)	69	70	.496	10	Julio Vinas	444,639	6,352	2013
Pensacola Blue Wahoos (Reds)	63	75	.457	15½	Pat Kelly	305,063	4,421	Never
Jacksonville Suns (Marlins)	57	81	.413	21½	Dave Berg	272,422	4,128	2014
Jackson Generals (Mariners)	53	84	.387	25	Roy Howell	136,918	2,173	2000

CLUB BATTING

	AVG	G	AB	R	H	2B	3B	HR	RBI	BB	SO	SB	OBP	SLG
Montgomery	.264	138	4,699	678	1240	266	56	102	625	481	1081	133	.338	.409
Tennessee	.262	139	4,515	641	1182	238	36	74	586	571	904	61	.348	.380
Chattanooga	.259	137	4,535	697	1175	218	59	107	633	573	1057	164	.346	.404
Birmingham	.255	139	4,539	555	1156	224	40	68	512	482	1106	128	.331	.367
Biloxi	.254	137	4,387	541	1115	219	35	56	504	506	878	120	.335	.358
Mobile	.250	137	4,586	552	1146	216	43	81	502	422	1050	93	.319	.369
Mississippi	.248	136	4,418	510	1095	185	27	38	471	448	897	86	.319	.328
Jacksonville	.247	139	4,542	535	1124	192	41	71	487	474	950	59	.320	.355
Jackson	.245	138	4,482	510	1097	235	38	67	459	480	991	103	.323	.359
Pensacola	.242	138	4,427	513	1071	216	35	80	483	507	1049	76	.325	.361

CLUB PITCHING

	ERA	G	CGSHO	SV	IP	H	R	ER	HR	BB	SO	AVG
Biloxi	3.25	137	3 14	40	1195	1018	490	432	81	486	1075	.233
Mississippi	3.55	136	4 11	47	1196	1143	547	472	41	502	938	.254
Birmingham	3.63	139	4 11	35	1216	1165	571	491	80	461	894	.254
Mobile	3.64	137	2 13	40	1215	1141	545	492	70	476	985	.251
Montgomery	3.67	138	2 11	31	1229	1117	562	502	88	548	1158	.244
Tennessee	3.72	139	4 9	38	1198	1095	559	495	81	510	1004	.245
Pensacola	3.95	138	2 9	47	1190	1150	576	522	77	509	980	.258
Chattanooga	4.04	137	5 14	38	1191	1173	599	535	69	443	930	.260
Jacksonville	4.07	139	0 10	35	1204	1140	612	545	89	501	1019	.251
Jackson	4.51	138	1 11	36	1188	1259	671	596	68	508	980	.275

CLUB FIELDING

	PCT	PO	A	E	DP		PCT	PO	A	E	DP
Pensacola	.984	3571	1412	81	452	Jacksonville	.977	3614	1289	117	314
Biloxi	.982	3586	1446	92	355	Birmingham	.976	3648	1523	127	379
Mobile	.980	3645	1354	101	361	Chattanooga	.976	3575	1376	120	372
Montgomery	.979	3689	1333	110	347	Jackson	.976	3565	1355	123	353
Tennessee	.978	3596	1341	110	336	Mississippi	.976	3589	1360	122	301

INDIVIDUAL BATTING LEADERS

Batter, Club	AVG	G	AB	R	H	2B	3B	HR	RBI	BB	SO	SB
Contreras, Willson, Tennessee	.333	126	454	71	151	34	4	8	75	57	62	4
Kepler, Max, Chattanooga	.322	112	407	76	131	32	13	9	71	67	63	18
Anderson, Tim, Birmingham	.312	125	513	79	160	21	12	5	46	13	119	49
Seitzer, Cameron, Montgomery	.308	102	383	55	118	26	1	12	59	46	84	0
Arcia, Orlando, Biloxi	.307	129	512	74	157	37	7	8	69	30	73	25
Brito, Socrates, Mobile	.300	129	490	70	147	17	15	9	57	29	84	20
Landoni, Emerson, Mississippi	.297	118	411	53	122	23	4	1	45	24	43	4
Adams, David, Jacksonville	.294	116	371	45	109	12	3	6	50	63	53	3
Polanco, Jorge, Chattanooga	.289	95	394	55	114	17	3	6	47	35	63	18
Marrero, Christian, Birmingham	.282	129	450	69	127	20	4	13	63	78	77	2

INDIVIDUAL PITCHING LEADERS

Pitcher, Club	W	L	ERA	G	GS	CG	SV	IP	H	R	ER	BB	SO
Wagner, Tyler, Biloxi	11	5	2.25	25	25	2	0	152	130	45	38	45	120
Lopez, Jorge Biloxi	12	5	2.26	24	24	0	0	143	105	37	36	52	137
Adleman, Timothy, Pensacola	9	10	2.64	27	26	0	0	150	134	52	44	49	113
Montas, Frankie, Birmingham	5	5	2.97	23	23	1	0	112	89	49	37	48	108
Pruitt, Austin, Montgomery	10	7	3.09	26	26	2	0	160	160	60	55	38	122
Jaye, Myles, Birmingham	12	9	3.29	26	26	0	0	148	135	64	54	47	104
Shipley, Braden, Mobile	9	11	3.50	28	27	1	0	157	147	68	61	56	118
Blackmar, Mark, Birmingham	6	8	3.63	26	26	1	0	151	142	69	61	55	65
Schultz, Jaime, Montgomery	9	5	3.67	27	27	0	0	135	105	58	55	90	168
Pena, Felix, Tennessee	7	8	3.75	25	23	1	0	130	111	60	54	49	140

ALL-STAR TEAM

C: Willson Contreras, Tennessee. **1B:** Cameron Seitzer, Montgomery. **2B:** David Adams, Jacksonville. **3B:** Zack Cox, Jacksonville. **SS:** Orlando Arcia, Biloxi. **OF:** Socrates Brit, Mobile; Max Kepler, Chattanooga; Adam Brett Walker, Chattanooga. **RHSP:** Jorge Lopez, Biloxi. **LHSP:** Blake Snell, Montgomery. **RP:** Zack Weiss, Pensacola. **UT:** Tim Anderson, Birmingham. **Most Valuable Player:** Max Kepler, Chattanooga. **Most Outstanding Pitcher:** Jorge Lopez, Biloxi. **Manager of the Year:** Carlos Subero, Biloxi. **Best Hustler:** Tim Anderson, Birmingham.

DEPARTMENT LEADERS

BATTING

OBP	Kepler, Max, Chattanooga	.416
SLG	Kepler, Max, Chattanooga	.531
OPS	Kepler, Max, Chattanooga	.947
R	Anderson, Tim, Birmingham	79
H	Anderson, Tim, Birmingham	160
TB	Walker, Adam Brett, Chattanooga	250
XBH	Walker, Adam Brett, Chattanooga	65
2B	Arcia, Orlando, Biloxi	37
3B	Brito, Socrates, Mobile	15
HR	Walker, Adam Brett, Chattanooga	31
RBI	Walker, Adam Brett, Chattanooga	106
SAC	2 players tied	11
BB	Hayes, Danny, Birmingham	98
HBP	Field, Johnny, Montgomery	15
SO	Walker, Adam Brett, Chattanooga	195
SB	Anderson, Tim, Birmingham	49
CS	May, Jacob, Birmingham	17
AB/SO	Landoni, Emerson, Mississippi	9.56

PITCHING

G	McMyne, Kyle, Pensacola	52
	Schuster, Patrick, Mobile, Pensacola	52
GS	Schultz, Jaime, Montgomery	27
	Shipley, Braden, Mobile	27
	Wright, Daniel, Pensacola	27
GF	Weiss, Zack, Pensacola	39
SV	Weiss, Zack, Pensacola	25
W	Jaye, Myles, Birmingham	12
	Lopez, Jorge, Biloxi	12
L	Danish, Tyler, Birmingham	12
	Siverio, Misael, Jackson	12
IP	Pruitt, Austin, Montgomery	160
H	Danish, Tyler, Birmingham	175
R	Wright, Daniel, Pensacola	83
ER	Wright, Daniel, Pensacola	78
HB	Brice, Austin, Jacksonville	12
BB	Schultz, Jaime, Montgomery	90
SO	Schultz, Jaime, Montgomery	168
SO/9	Schultz, Jaime, Montgomery	11.20
SO/9 (RP)	Garton, Ryan, Montgomery	10.33
BB/9	Tomshaw, Matt, Jacksonville	2.09
WP	Lopez, Jorge, Biloxi	13
	Sappington, Mark, Montgomery	13
BK	Pena, Felix, Tennessee	5
HR	Danish, Tyler, Birmingham	13
AVG	Lopez, Jorge, Biloxi	.205

FIELDING

C PCT	Freeman, Ronnie, Mobile	1.000
PO	O'Conner, Justin, Montgomery	759
A	O'Conner, Justin, Montgomery	91
DP	Weisenburger, Adam, Biloxi	10
E	O'Conner, Justin, Montgomery	15
PB	O'Conner, Justin, Montgomery	15
1B PCT	Hayes, Danny, Birmingham	.995
PO	Hayes, Danny, Birmingham	1091
A	Hayes, Danny, Birmingham	83
DP	Hayes, Danny, Birmingham	113
E	Ramirez, Nick, Biloxi	16
2B PCT	DeMichele, Joey, Birmingham	.985
PO	DeMichele, Joey, Birmingham	233
A	DeMichele, Joey, Birmingham	422
DP	DeMichele, Joey, Birmingham	91
E	Bortnick, Tyler, Jackson	10
	Bruno, Stephen, Tennessee	10
	DeMichele, Joey, Birmingham	10
3B PCT	Ruiz, Rio, Mississippi	.950
PO	Ruiz, Rio, Mississippi	92
A	Ruiz, Rio, Mississippi	214
DP	Mejias-Brean, Seth, Pensacola	28
E	Mejias-Brean, Seth, Pensacola	16
	Ruiz, Rio, Mississippi	16
SS PCT	Soto, Elliot, Tennessee, Jacksonville	.980
PO	Arcia, Orlando, Biloxi	196
A	Arcia, Orlando, Biloxi	376
DP	Arcia, Orlando, Biloxi	82
E	Anderson, Tim, Birmingham	25
OF PCT	Hannemann, Jacob, Tennessee	.996
PO	Brito, Socrates, Mobile	296
A	Rohm, David, Mississippi	17
DP	4 players tied	4
E	Henry, Jabari, Jackson	9
	Kang, KD, Mississippi	9

MINOR LEAGUES

BY VINCE LARA-CINISOMO

Corpus Christi was by far the best Texas League team in the first half, but Midland dominated after the break on its way to a second consecutive league championship.

The RockHounds swept the championship series three games to none over Northwest Arkansas, winning the finale 7-0 behind RBI doubles from Ryon Healy and Matt Olson.

The A's affiliate dominated the series over the Royals' affiliate, getting an excellent performance from former Kansas City first-rounder Sean Manaea, who pitched eight solid innings in Game One.

"First inning, I heard them chirping at me," Manaea, traded to Oakland for Ben Zobrist, told MiLB.com. "I expected that. It was hard to not smile, just because I could hear everything they were saying. It was just a fun game."

Midland's Renato Nunez went 5-for-13 with a homer and Jaycob Brugman went 4-for-12 with two homers.

Midland knocked out Corpus Christi—the Astros affiliate—in the semifinals, thanks to homers from Olson, Healy and Brugman in the deciding game. Meanwhile, Northwest Arkansas swept rival Arkansas in the best-of-five as Bubba Starling homered and Lane Adams sparkled.

The playoff outcome didn't diminish the Hooks' excellent season. Corpus Christi boasted plenty of firepower, including first baseman A.J. Reed, who knocked in 46 runs in 53 games after his promotion from high Class A Lancaster, third baseman Colin Moran and versatile infielder Tony Kemp.

The Hooks also featured hard-throwing righties Michael Feliz and Joe Musgrove and changeup artist Chris Devenski fronting a rotation that also included 2013 No. 1 overall pick Mark Appel.

The Rockhounds had an infield that included power threats Olson, Nunez and Chad Pinder, all members of the league's top 20 prospects.

When healthy, Kyle Zimmer flashed premium stuff to help lead Northwest Arkansas to the playoffs. The Travelers had an intriguing outfield with Starling and Jorge Bonifacio, while Frisco's roster was roiled by the Cole Hamels deal, which sent Nick Williams, Jorge Alfaro and Jake Thompson to the Phillies.

Tulsa was bolstered by the best 1-2 pitching punch in the league with teen lefthander Julio Urias and righthander Jose De Leon. Even with that much talent, the Texas League saw two of the best pitching prospects in the game pass through but not qualify for inclusion. Alex Reyes was outstanding for Springfield but did not reach the innings qualification.

TOP 20 PROSPECTS

1. Julio Urias, lhp, Tulsa (Dodgers)
2. Joey Gallo, 3b/of, Frisco (Rangers)
3. Jose De Leon, rhp, Tulsa (Dodgers)
4. Trea Turner, ss, San Antonio (Padres)
5. Raul A. Mondesi, ss, Northwest Arkansas (Royals)
6. A.J. Reed, 1b, Corpus Christi (Astros)
7. Nick Williams, of, Frisco (Rangers)
8. Brett Phillips, of, Corpus Christi (Astros)
9. Sean Manaea, lhp, Northwest Arkansas (Royals)/Midland (Athletics)
10. Chad Pinder, ss, Midland (Athletics)
11. Michael Feliz, rhp, Corpus Christi (Astros)
12. Nomar Mazara, of, Frisco (Rangers)
13. Hunter Renfroe, of, San Antonio (Padres)
14. Jorge Alfaro, c, Frisco (Rangers)
15. Kyle Zimmer, rhp, Northwest Arkansas (Royals)
16. Jharel Cotton, rhp, Tulsa (Dodgers)
17. Jake Thompson, rhp, Frisco (Rangers)
18. Matt Olson, 1b/of, Midland (Athletics)
19. Renato Nunez, 3b, Midland (Athletics)
20. Colin Moran, 3b, Corpus Christi (Astros)

STANDINGS: SPLIT SEASON

FIRST HALF

NORTH	W	L	PCT	GB
NW Arkansas	40	30	.571	—
Arkansas	36	33	.522	3 ½
Tulsa	30	39	.435	9 ½
Springfield	30	40	.429	10

SOUTH	W	L	PCT	GB
Corpus Christi	48	22	.686	—
Midland	35	35	.500	13
San Antonio	31	39	.443	17
Frisco	29	41	.414	19

SECOND HALF

NORTH	W	L	PCT	GB
Arkansas	35	35	.500	—
Springfield	34	36	.486	1
Tulsa	32	38	.457	3
NW Arkansas	29	40	.420	5 ½

SOUTH	W	L	PCT	GB
Midland	48	22	.686	—
Corpus Christi	41	29	.586	7
Frisco	31	38	.449	16 ½
San Antonio	29	41	.414	19

Playoffs—Semifinals: Northwest Arkansas defeated Arkansas 3-0 and Midland defeated Corpus Christi 3-1 in best-of-five series; **Finals:** Midland defeated Northwest Arkansas 3-0 in a best-of-five series.

OVERALL STANDINGS

Team (Organization)	W	L	PCT	GB	Manager(s)	Attendance	Average	Last Pennant
Corpus Christi Hooks (Astros)	89	51	.636	—	Rodney Linares	362,968	5,338	2006
Midland RockHounds (Athletics)	83	57	.593	6	Ryan Christenson	297,325	4,248	2015
Arkansas Travelers (Angels)	71	68	.511	17 ½	Bill Richardson	337,566	5,038	2008
Northwest Arkansas Naturals (Royals)	69	70	.496	19 ½	Vance Wilson	290,471	4,469	2010
Springfield Cardinals (Cardinals)	64	76	.457	25	Dann Bilardello	337,519	4,964	2012
Tulsa Drillers (Dodgers)	62	77	.446	26 ½	Razor Shines	380,759	5,858	1998
Frisco RoughRiders (Rangers)	60	79	.432	28 ½	Joe Mikulik	477,354	6,918	2004
San Antonio Missions (Padres)	60	80	.429	29	Rod Barajas	308,564	4,605	2013

CLUB BATTING

	AVG	G	AB	R	H	2B	3B	HR	RBI	BB	SO	SB	OBP	SLG
Midland	.276	140	4,842	724	1335	310	26	117	672	589	1084	90	.356	.423
Corpus Christi	.275	140	4,727	742	1299	243	29	117	665	569	997	148	.356	.413
Northwest Arkansas	.266	139	4,671	625	1242	266	33	127	577	358	1130	129	.321	.419
Springfield	.259	140	4,713	629	1221	230	26	114	577	536	933	114	.338	.391
San Antonio	.255	140	4,718	553	1204	203	25	84	497	365	918	75	.312	.362
Tulsa	.245	139	4,654	506	1142	242	24	82	469	417	988	78	.309	.361
Frisco	.243	139	4,655	573	1131	215	34	115	524	444	1196	96	.313	.378
Arkansas	.237	139	4,460	539	1055	205	17	60	490	551	1024	150	.324	.330

CLUB PITCHING

	ERA	G	CG	SHO	SV	IP	H	R	ER	HR	BB	SO	AVG
Tulsa	3.50	139	6	8	31	1232	1056	544	480	106	486	1144	.232
Corpus Christi	3.62	140	3	8	46	1233	1232	553	496	102	409	1042	.260
Arkansas	3.71	139	4	12	40	1206	1109	567	497	98	460	1059	.246
San Antonio	3.86	140	3	11	33	1220	1209	614	524	87	469	967	.258
Northwest Arkansas	3.89	139	1	5	28	1202	1186	603	520	102	488	978	.258
Midland	4.02	140	3	16	38	1247	1285	633	557	105	490	995	.266
Springfield	4.36	140	4	10	29	1235	1296	667	598	103	451	989	.269
Frisco	4.70	139	2	11	36	1222	1256	710	638	113	576	1096	.266

CLUB FIELDING

	PCT	PO	A	E	DP		PCT	PO	A	E	DP
Tulsa	.984	3698	1341	84	295	Midland	.977	3743	1309	121	313
Arkansas	.980	3619	1327	103	320	NW Arkansas	.976	3606	1314	123	338
Corpus Christi	.978	3701	1309	111	329	Springfield	.976	3707	1370	123	293
Frisco	.977	3667	1264	115	356	San Antonio	.974	3662	1408	136	329

INDIVIDUAL BATTING LEADERS

Batter, Club	AVG	G	AB	R	H	2B	3B	HR	RBI	BB	SO	SB
Kemmer, Jon, Corpus Christi	.327	104	364	67	119	28	4	18	65	45	89	9
Pinder, Chad, Midland	.317	117	477	71	151	32	2	15	86	28	103	7
Moran, Colin, Corpus Christi	.306	96	366	47	112	25	2	9	67	43	79	1
Walsh, Colin, Midland	.302	134	487	97	147	39	2	13	49	124	131	17
Healy, Ryon, Midland	.302	124	507	63	153	31	1	10	62	30	82	0
Asencio, Yeison, San Antonio	.301	126	482	48	145	23	1	13	74	14	40	6
Williams, Nick, Frisco	.299	97	378	56	113	21	4	13	45	32	77	10
Adams, Lane, NW Arkansas	.298	97	373	58	111	21	3	12	49	36	98	29
Tilson, Charlie, Springfield	.295	134	539	85	159	20	9	4	32	46	72	46
Oberacker, Chad, Midland	.294	101	395	69	116	27	5	5	44	42	74	19

INDIVIDUAL PITCHING LEADERS

Pitcher, Club	W	L	ERA	G	GS	CG	SV	IP	H	R	ER	BB	SO
Suarez, Albert, Arkansas	11	9	2.98	27	27	1	0	163	142	64	54	40	121
Devenski, Chris, Corpus Christi	7	4	3.01	24	17	0	2	120	117	43	40	33	104
Dziedzic, Jonathan, NW Arkansas	10	6	3.12	26	25	1	0	138	138	57	48	35	93
Kehrt, Jeremy, Tulsa	7	8	3.46	22	22	1	0	120	119	55	46	27	94
Hancock, Justin, San Antonio	7	6	3.59	22	22	0	0	120	127	52	48	49	92
Brady, Michael, Arkansas	7	7	3.77	32	19	0	0	119	124	55	50	12	113
Anderson, Chris, Tulsa	9	7	4.05	23	23	1	0	127	123	66	57	59	98
Westwood, Kyle, Corpus Christi	11	7	4.23	26	19	2	3	132	160	70	62	26	71
McGowin, Kyle, Arkansas	9	9	4.38	27	27	0	0	154	148	80	75	50	125
Rodriguez, Bryan, San Antonio	6	14	4.44	24	23	1	0	134	165	76	66	37	83

ALL-STAR TEAM

C: Mike Ohlman, Springfield. **1B:** Balbino Feunmanyor, Northwest Arkansas. **2B:** Colin Walsh, Midland. **3B:** Ryon Healy, Midland. **SS:** Chad Pinder, Midland. **OF:** Jon Kemmer, Corpus Christi; Charlie Tilson, Springfield; Nick Williams, Frisco. **DH:** Yeison Asencio, San Antonio. **UT:** Colin Moran, Corpus Christi. **P:** Chris Devenski, Corpus Christi; Ryan Dull, Midland. Jonathan Dziedzic, Northwest Arkansas; Jandel Gustave, Frisco; David Martinez, Frisco; Colin Rea, San Antonio; Arturo Reyes, Springfield; Nate Smith, Arkansas; Albert Suarez, Arkansas.
Player of the Year: Chad Pinder, Midland. **Pitcher of the Year:** Nate Smith, Arkansas. **Manager of the Year:** Rodney Linares, Corpus Christi.

DEPARTMENT LEADERS

BATTING

OBP	Walsh, Colin, Midland	.447
SLG	Kemmer, Jon, Corpus Christi	.574
OPS	Kemmer, Jon, Corpus Christi	.988
R	Walsh, Colin, Midland	97
H	Tilson, Charlie, Springfield	159
TB	Pinder, Chad, Midland	232
XBH	Liddi, Alex, NW Arkansas	58
2B	Liddi, Alex, NW Arkansas	39
	Walsh, Colin, Midland	39
3B	Tilson, Charlie, Springfield	9
HR	Robinson, Drew, Frisco	21
RBI	Pinder, Chad, Midland	86
SAC	Mondesi, Raul, NW Arkansas	12
BB	Walsh, Colin, Midland	124
HBP	Kemmer, Jon, Corpus Christi	12
SO	Dozier, Hunter, NW Arkansas	151
SB	Tilson, Charlie, Springfield	46
CS	Tilson, Charlie, Springfield	19
AB/SO	Valera, Breyvic, Springfield	13.33

PITCHING

G	Cash, Ralston, Tulsa	49
GS	Jensen, Chris, Midland	28
GF	Gustave, Jandel, Corpus Christi	38
SV	Martinez, David, Frisco	22
W	Suarez, Albert, Arkansas	11
	Westwood, Kyle, Corpus Christi	11
L	Rodriguez, Bryan, San Antonio	14
IP	Jensen, Chris, Midland	166
H	Jensen, Chris, Midland	183
R	Jensen, Chris, Midland	100
ER	Jensen, Chris, Midland	90
HB	Almonte, Miguel, NW Arkansas	8
	Anderson, Chris, Tulsa	8
BB	Leclerc, Jose, Frisco	73
SO	McGowin, Kyle, Arkansas	125
SO/9	Brady, Michael, Arkansas	8.52
SO/9 (RP)	Santos, Eduard, Arkansas	12.03
BB/9	Brady, Michael, Arkansas	.91
WP	Leclerc, Jose, Frisco	13
BK	Kelly, Casey, San Antonio	3
HR	Jensen, Chris, Midland	18
AVG	Suarez, Albert, Arkansas	.234

FIELDING

C	PCT	Maxwell, Bruce, Midland	.997
	PO	Ohlman, Mike, Springfield	657
	A	Bemboom, Anthony, Arkansas	70
	DP	Pena, Roberto, Corpus Christi	9
	E	Ohlman, Mike, Springfield	11
	PB	Morin, Parker, NW Arkansas	8
1B	PCT	Anderson, Lars, Tulsa	.994
	PO	Anderson, Lars, Tulsa	1,018
	A	Anderson, Lars, Tulsa	107
	DP	Anderson, Lars, Tulsa	84
	E	Rodriguez, Jonathan, Springfield	10
2B	PCT	Walsh, Colin, Midland	.982
	PO	Johnson, Sherman, Arkansas	215
	A	Walsh, Colin, Midland	328
	DP	Johnson, Sherman, Arkansas	73
	E	Robinson, Drew, Frisco	14
3B	PCT	Wisdom, Patrick, Springfield	.941
	PO	Dozier, Hunter, NW Arkansas	87
	A	Wisdom, Patrick, Springfield	194
	DP	Dozier, Hunter, NW Arkansas	17
	E	Dozier, Hunter, NW Arkansas	22
SS	PCT	Mier, Jio, Corpus Christi	.955
	PO	Pinder, Chad, Midland	181
	A	Pinder, Chad, Midland	267
	DP	Pinder, Chad, Midland	61
	E	Pinder, Chad, Midland	26
OF	PCT	Hernandez, Teoscar, Corpus Christi	.989
	PO	Tilson, Charlie, Springfield	316
	A	Renfroe, Hunter, San Antonio	14
	DP	Beck, Preston, Frisco	6
	E	Mazara, Nomar, Frisco	8

MINOR LEAGUES

BY JIM SHONERD

The Rancho Cucamonga Quakes took home their first California League title in 21 years, dominating the San Jose Giants in a three-game sweep in the league championship series.

The Quakes outscored San Jose 21-6 over the three games, but to get to the finals they had to survive a back-and-forth semifinal series with High Desert. Down 5-4 in the bottom of the ninth in the decisive fifth game of the series, the Quakes rallied for a pair of runs to advance, winning it on Delvis Morales' walk-off single. The Quakes had posted the league's second best regular season record (78-62) with a roster mainly built on older players, but their two best prospects, outfielder Alex Verdugo and slugging first baseman Cody Bellinger, keyed their playoff run, batting .323 and .324 respectively. Bellinger in particular enjoyed a breakout season, finishing second in the league's home run race with 30 in the regular season and adding three more in the playoffs.

Bellinger was one of three Cal Leaguers to put up a 30-homer season, led by league home run champ Tyler O'Neill's 32 for Bakersfield and 30 for Lancaster's Chase McDonald. That's without mentioning overall minor league home run leader A.J. Reed, who spent the first half of the season with Lancaster and hit 23 longballs before a promotion in July, finishing the year with 34. Reed hit 10 home runs in the month of May and finished the year as the league leader in all three triple-slash categories with a line of .346/.449/.638. On the other side of the equation, Modesto righthander Antonio Senzatela was a runaway winner for the league ERA title at 2.51, on top of leading the way in WHIP (1.06) and opponents' average (.229).

As usual, the Cal League was a haven for hitters, although not to the same extent as in past years. Cal League teams averaged 4.90 runs per game in 2015, which remained the highest figure among domestic full-season leagues but was actually the league's lowest output since 1989.

Inland Empire power-armed lefthander Sean Newcomb was the league's best prospect, but the bulk of the league's top talents were hitters like Reed, Bellinger and Stockton shortstop Franklin Barreto. After watching Carlos Correa, Julio Urias and Corey Seager come through the league in 2014, there wasn't the same star power in 2015, although the league did have solid depth in its prospect crop throughout the course of the year.

TOP 20 PROSPECTS

1. Sean Newcomb, lhp, Inland Empire (Angels)
2. Franklin Barreto, ss, Stockton (Athletics)
3. A.J. Reed, 1b, Lancaster (Astros)
4. Ryan McMahon, 3b, Modesto (Rockies)
5. Alex Bregman, ss, Lancaster (Astros)
6. Antonio Senzatela, rhp, Modesto (Rockies)
7. Lewis Brinson, of, High Desert (Rangers)
8. Brett Phillips, of, Lancaster (Astros)
9. Chris Ellis, rhp, Inland Empire (Angels)
10. Yairo Munoz, ss, Stockton (Athletics)
11. Christian Arroyo, ss, San Jose (Giants)
12. Matt Chapman, 3b, Stockton (Athletics)
13. Cody Bellinger, 1b/of, Rancho Cucamonga (Dodgers)
14. Zack Godley, rhp, Visalia (Diamondbacks)
15. Ryan Cordell, of/3b, High Desert (Rangers)
16. Tyler Beede, rhp, San Jose (Giants)
17. Raimel Tapia, of, Modesto (Rockies)
18. Keury Mella, rhp, San Jose (Giants)
19. Tyler O'Neill, of, Bakersfield (Mariners)
20. Ryan Yarbrough, lhp, Bakersfield (Mariners)

STANDINGS: SPLIT SEASON

FIRST HALF

NORTH	W	L	PCT	GB
Visalia	42	28	.600	—
Stockton	38	32	.543	4
Modesto	33	37	.471	9
San Jose	30	40	.429	12
Bakersfield	26	44	.371	16

SOUTH	W	L	PCT	GB
R. Cucamonga	41	29	.586	—
High Desert	37	33	.529	4
Lancaster	37	33	.529	4
Inland Empire	35	35	.500	6
Lake Elsinore	31	39	.443	10

SECOND HALF

NORTH	W	L	PCT	GB
Visalia	42	28	.600	—
San Jose	42	28	.600	—
Stockton	36	34	.514	6
Bakersfield	35	35	.500	7
Modesto	34	36	.486	8

SOUTH	W	L	PCT	GB
High Desert	41	29	.586	—
Lancaster	38	32	.543	3
R. Cucamonga	37	33	.529	4
Inland Empire	26	44	.371	15
Lake Elsinore	19	51	.271	22

PLAYOFFS—Semifinals: San Jose defeated Visalia 3-2 and Rancho Cucamonga defeated High Desert 3-2 in best-of-three series; **Finals:** Rancho Cucamonga defeated San Jose 3-0 in a best-of-five series.

OVERALL STANDINGS

Team (Organization)	W	L	PCT	GB	Manager(s)	Attendance	Average	Last Pennant
Visalia Rawhide (Diamondbacks)	84	56	.600	—	J.R. House	121,004	1,729	1978
High Desert Mavericks (Rangers)	78	62	.557	6	Spike Owen	94,065	1,425	1997
Rancho Cucamonga Quakes (Dodgers)	78	62	.557	6	Bill Haselman	167,318	2,425	2015
Lancaster JetHawks (Astros)	75	65	.536	9	Omar Lopez	158,435	2,296	2014
Stockton Ports (Athletics)	74	66	.529	10	Rick Magnante	191,611	2,737	2008
San Jose Giants (Giants)	72	68	.514	12	Russ Morman	189,205	2,703	2010
Modesto Nuts (Rockies)	67	73	.479	17	Fred Ocasio	166,719	2,382	2004
Bakersfield Blaze (Mariners)	61	79	.436	23	Eddie Menchaca	51,789	740	1989
Inland Empire 66ers (Angels)	61	79	.436	23	Denny Hocking	196,962	2,814	2013
Lake Elsinore Storm (Padres)	50	90	.357	34	Michael Collins	213,932	3,146	2011

CLUB BATTING

	AVG	G	AB	R	H	2B	3B	HR	RBI	BB	SO	SB	OBP	SLG
Lancaster	.291	140	4,959	888	1443	288	67	174	819	588	1196	115	.369	.481
High Desert	.286	140	4,955	840	1416	297	64	153	784	416	1182	87	.346	.464
Visalia	.266	140	4,948	719	1316	288	38	154	650	373	1199	126	.321	.433
Rancho Cucamonga	.265	140	4,750	732	1259	300	38	135	669	430	1186	105	.330	.429
Inland Empire	.263	140	4,735	659	1245	244	51	78	599	463	1180	131	.333	.385
Modesto	.262	140	4,761	607	1248	256	53	83	536	285	1168	136	.311	.390
San Jose	.256	140	4,873	594	1246	267	24	91	546	371	1092	84	.315	.376
Stockton	.256	140	4,775	647	1223	243	38	100	586	433	1068	113	.321	.386
Lake Elsinore	.246	140	4,810	603	1182	245	33	97	542	389	1185	83	.307	.371
Bakersfield	.237	140	4,704	570	1116	193	30	95	515	417	1256	174	.307	.352

CLUB PITCHING

	ERA	G	CG	SHO	SV	IP	H	R	ER	HR	BB	SO	AVG
San Jose	3.46	140	0	15	38	1281	1179	583	492	103	392	1345	.243
Stockton	3.72	140	0	7	42	1242	1129	597	514	124	364	1094	.241
Modesto	3.75	140	3	6	37	1247	1225	620	519	107	346	1026	.257
Visalia	3.75	140	3	13	49	1275	1207	611	532	104	384	1304	.250
Bakersfield	3.86	140	1	10	32	1253	1228	629	538	118	414	1111	.256
Rancho Cucamonga	4.07	140	1	8	29	1235	1206	647	559	95	452	1214	.254
Lancaster	4.60	140	0	11	34	1249	1307	728	638	131	463	1183	.268
Inland Empire	5.01	140	1	3	33	1227	1340	777	683	101	442	1196	.277
High Desert	5.17	140	2	7	36	1242	1393	811	713	173	433	1144	.283
Lake Elsinore	5.21	140	0	3	28	1240	1480	856	718	104	475	1095	.298

CLUB FIELDING

	PCT	PO	A	E	DP		PCT	PO	A	E	DP
Visalia	.977	3826	1328	123	279	Stockton	.973	3726	1463	142	284
Lancaster	.974	3747	1374	137	356	Bakersfield	.972	3760	1542	153	336
Inland Empire	.973	3683	1404	141	348	High Desert	.971	3727	1407	151	389
R. Cucamonga	.973	3705	1306	137	291	Modesto	.970	3741	1460	162	331
San Jose	.973	3843	1363	143	282	Lake Elsinore	.969	3721	1474	165	310

INDIVIDUAL BATTING LEADERS

Batter, Club	AVG	G	AB	R	H	2B	3B	HR	RBI	BB	SO	SB
Reed, A.J., Lancaster	.346	82	318	75	110	16	4	23	81	59	73	0
Aguilera, Eric, Inland Empire	.327	119	462	79	151	38	3	17	94	47	110	14
Ramsay, James, Lancaster	.322	127	497	88	160	32	4	10	64	52	86	16
Westbrook, Jamie, Visalia	.319	123	480	75	153	33	4	17	72	24	69	14
Bolinger, Royce, High Desert	.315	98	400	70	126	34	1	16	77	23	107	0
Tapia, Raimel, Modesto	.305	131	544	74	166	34	9	12	71	24	105	26
Arroyo, Christian, San Jose	.304	90	381	48	116	28	2	9	42	19	73	5
McMahon, Ryan, Modesto	.300	132	496	85	149	43	6	18	75	49	153	6
Jackson, Joe, High Desert	.298	110	426	67	127	33	2	10	78	46	97	5
Fish, Mike, Inland Empire	.297	88	350	46	104	15	1	2	34	30	64	5

INDIVIDUAL PITCHING LEADERS

Pitcher, Club	W	L	ERA	G	GS	CG	SV	IP	H	R	ER	BB	SO
Senzatela, Antonio, Modesto	9	9	2.51	26	26	1	0	154	131	53	43	33	143
Banda, Anthony, Visalia	8	8	3.32	28	27	1	0	152	150	67	56	39	152
Covey, Dylan, Stockton	8	9	3.59	26	26	0	0	140	135	65	56	43	100
Doran, Ryan, Visalia	8	3	3.62	28	16	1	0	114	118	52	46	17	61
Wade, Konner, Modesto	8	9	3.96	26	26	2	0	168	171	91	74	40	95
Altavilla, Dan, Bakersfield	6	12	4.07	28	28	1	0	148	138	82	67	53	134
Richy, John, Rancho Cucamonga	10	5	4.20	22	18	1	0	124	143	63	58	34	105
Pike, Tyler, Bakersfield	6	6	4.26	25	25	0	0	123	119	74	58	63	114
Ash, Brett, Bakersfield	9	8	4.36	33	19	0	0	136	161	74	66	34	79
Lloyd, Kyle, Lake Elsinore	7	11	4.72	31	20	0	0	137	139	85	72	41	139

ALL-STAR TEAM

C: Tyler Ogle, Rancho Cucamonga. **1B:** A.J. Reed, Lancaster. **2B:** Jamie Westbrook, Visalia. **3B:** Ryan McMahon, Visalia. **SS:** Christian Arroyo, San Jose. **OF:** Tyler O'Neill, Bakersfield; Brett Phillips, Bakersfield; Raimel Tapia, Modesto. **P:** Dan Altavilla, Bakersfield; Anthony Banda, Visalia; Chase Johnson, San Jose.
Player of the Year: A.J. Reed, Lancaster. **Pitcher of the Year:** Antonio Senzatela, Modesto.
Manager of the Year: J.R. House, Visalia.

DEPARTMENT LEADERS

BATTING

OBP	Reed, A.J., Lancaster	.449
SLG	Reed, A.J., Lancaster	.638
OPS	Reed, A.J., Lancaster	1.088
R	Bellinger, Cody, Rancho Cucamonga	97
H	Tapia, Raimel, Modesto	166
TB	Palka, Daniel, Visalia	272
XBH	Palka, Daniel, Visalia	68
2B	McMahon, Ryan, Modesto	43
3B	Patterson, Jordan, Modesto	12
HR	O'Neill, Tyler, Bakersfield	32
RBI	Bellinger, Cody, Rancho Cucamonga	103
SAC	Lopes, Tim, Bakersfield	14
	Ramsay, James, Lancaster	14
BB	Olson, Matt, Stockton	117
HBP	Wilson, Austin, Bakersfield	29
SO	Flores, Rudy, Visalia	189
SB	Lopes, Tim, Bakersfield	35
CS	Way, Bo, Inland Empire	19
AB/SO	Nogowski, John, Stockton	7.53

PITCHING

G	Gardeck, Ian, San Jose	61
GS	Altavilla, Dan, Bakersfield	28
GF	Carasiti, Matt, San Jose	42
	Slania, Dan, San Jose	42
SV	Sarianides, Nickolas, Visalia	28
W	Musgrave, Harrison, Modeso	10
	Pena, Richelson, High Desert	10
	Richy, John, Rancho Cucamonga	10
	Trivino, Lou, Stockton	10
L	Cooney, Harrison, Inland Empire	15
IP	Wade, Konner, Modesto	168
H	Ledbetter, David, High Desert	176
R	Cooney, Harrison, Inland Empire	109
ER	Ledbetter, David, High Desert	100
HB	Cooney, Harrison, Inland Empire	25
BB	Pike, Tyler, Bakersfield	63
SO	Banda, Anthony, Visalia	152
SO/9	Perry, Blake, Visalia	9.88
SO/9 (RP)	Krehbiel, Joey, Visalia	12.71
BB/9	Doran, Ryan, Visalia	1.34
WP	Alcantara, Victor, Inland Empire	20
BK	Banda, Anthony, Visalia	3
	Krehbiel, Joey, Visalia	3
	Wiest, Grahamm, Modesto	3
HR	Ledbetter, David, High Desert	23
	Pena, Richelson, High Desert	23
AVG	Senzatela, Antonio, Modesto	.229

FIELDING

C PCT	Ross, Ty, San Jose	.993
PO	Ross, Ty, San Jose	669
A	Baker, Tyler, Visalia	70
DP	Baker, Tyler, Visalia	7
E	Baker, Tyler, Visalia	9
PB	Stein, Troy, Modesto	16
1B PCT	Prime, Correlle, Modesto	.992
PO	Prime, Correlle, Modesto	1,164
A	Davis, Marcus, Lake Elsinore	78
DP	Prime, Correlle, Modesto	111
E	Davis, Marcus, Lake Elsinore	17
2B PCT	Cogswell, Branden, Stockton	.979
PO	Cogswell, Branden, Stockton	185
A	Eaves, Kody, Inland Empire	330
DP	Eaves, Kody, Inland Empire	74
E	Perez, Fernando, Lake Elsinore	18
3B PCT	Davis, J.D., Lancaster	.932
PO	McMahon, Ryan, Modesto	106
A	McMahon, Ryan, Modesto	303
DP	McMahon, Ryan, Modesto	29
E	McMahon, Ryan, Modesto	39
SS PCT	Leyba, Domingo, Visalia	.962
PO	Leyba, Domingo, Visalia	171
A	Leyba, Domingo, Visalia	333
DP	Leyba, Domingo, Visalia	71
E	Barreto, Franklin, Stockton	34
OF PCT	Vertigan, Brett, Stockton	.996
PO	Way, Bo, Inland Empire	285
A	Way, Bo, Inland Empire	14
DP	Ramsay, James, Lancaster	5
E	Carbonell, Daniel, San Jose	8
	Mieses, Johan, Rancho Cucamonga	8
	Tate, Donavan, Lake Elsinore	8

MINOR LEAGUES

BY JOSH NORRIS

To win the Carolina League title, the Myrtle Beach Pelicans needed a little help from their friends.

With all of their other minor league affiliates done for the season, the Cubs sent outfielder Jorge Soler to rehab with Myrtle Beach for the playoffs, and the Pelicans won five of their six games en route to their first championship since 2000.

Of course, it wasn't just Soler's presence (he batted just .231 in the six games) that boosted the Pelicans. The deciding blow was struck by outfielder Pin-Chieh Chen, whose single in the ninth inning of the decisive third game finalized his team's sweep of Wilmington for the crown.

The biggest story of the year in the league, however, was the early season bus crash that sent a chunk of Carolina's roster to the disabled list.

The crash happened on May 12, as the Mudcats were traveling from Salem, Va., where they had just finished a series with the Salem Red Sox, to Myrtle Beach for a series with the Pelicans. The bus flipped onto its side at about 3:45 a.m. and skidded down the road in Columbus County, N.C.

Eight players were placed on the disabled list as a result of the crash, including righthander Lucas Sims, the Braves' top pitching prospect. He missed approximately six weeks recovering before heading on a rehab assignment.

As far as top prospects were concerned, the league was fronted by players from Potomac (Nationals) and Lynchburg (Indians).

After both were held back in extended spring training for a few weeks to start the year, the Potomac rotation was topped by righthanders Lucas Giolito and Reynaldo Lopez. Both pitchers ranked in the top half of BA's Top 100 Prospects. With Potomac, Giolito went 3-5, 2.71 and struck out 86 in 70 innings. He showed the same top-end stuff as he has his whole career, and made his second straight Futures Game appearance. Lopez spent the remainder of the season with Potomac and went 6-7, 4.09 with 94 strikeouts

in 99 innings.

Lynchburg's talent was in the outfield, where Bradley Zimmer spent half the season and Clint Frazier the whole year. Zimmer, BA's No. 23 prospect at midseason, showed off an enticing power-speed combination with an .896 OPS and 32 stolen bases before a promotion to Double-A Akron. Frazier hit 16 home runs and produced an .842 OPS.

Salem also boasted some prospect power, primarily with center fielder Manuel Margot, the No. 24 player on BA's midseason Top 50 ranking.

TOP 20 PROSPECTS

1. Lucas Giolito, rhp, Potomac (Nationals)
2. Bradley Zimmer, of, Lynchburg (Indians)
3. Manuel Margot, of, Salem (Red Sox)
4. Reynaldo Lopez, rhp, Potomac (Nationals)
5. Clint Frazier, of, Lynchburg (Indians)
6. Cody Reed, lhp, Wilmington (Royals)
7. Duane Underwood, rhp, Myrtle Beach (Cubs)
8. Nick Pivetta, rhp, Potomac (Nationals)
9. Sam Travis, 1b, Salem (Red Sox)
10. Chance Sisco, c, Frederick (Orioles)
11. Trey Michalczewski, 3b, Winston-Salem (White Sox)
12. Adam Plutko, rhp, Lynchburg (Indians)
13. Jeimer Candelario, 3b, Myrtle Beach (Cubs)
14. Adam Engel, of, Winston-Salem (White Sox)
15. Mark Zagunis, of, Myrtle Beach (Cubs)
16. Trey Mancini, 1b, Frederick (Orioles)
17. Nellie Rodriguez, 1b, Lynchburg (Indians)
18. Dustin Peterson, of, Carolina (Braves)
19. Wendell Rijo, 2b, Salem (Red Sox)
20. Austen Williams, rhp, Potomac (Nationals)

STANDINGS: SPLIT SEASON

FIRST HALF

NORTH	W	L	PCT	GB
Wilmington	38	32	.543	—
Lynchburg	33	37	.471	5
Potomac	33	37	.471	5
Frederick	32	38	.457	6

SOUTH	W	L	PCT	GB
Myrtle Beach	41	28	.594	—
Salem	38	32	.543	3 ½
Carolina	34	35	.493	7
Winston-Salem	30	40	.429	11 ½

SECOND HALF

NORTH	W	L	PCT	GB
Lynchburg	39	31	.557	—
Potomac	32	37	.464	6 ½
Frederick	32	38	.457	7
Wilmington	24	45	.348	14 ½

SOUTHERN	W	L	PCT	GB
Winston-Salem	45	23	.662	—
Myrtle Beach	40	29	.580	5 ½
Carolina	37	33	.529	9
Salem	28	41	.406	17 ½

PLAYOFFS—Semifinals: Wilmington defeated Lynchburg 2-0 and Myrtle Beach defeated Winston-Salem in best-of-three series; Finals: Myrtle Beach defeated Wilmington 3-0 in a best-of-five series.

OVERALL STANDINGS

Team (Organization)	W	L	PCT	GB	Manager(s)	Attendance	Average	Last Pennant
Myrtle Beach Pelicans (Cubs)	81	57	.587	—	Mark Johnson	240,357	3,877	2015
Winston-Salem Dash (White Sox)	75	63	.543	6	Tim Esmay	289,637	4,456	2003
Lynchburg Hillcats (Indians)	72	68	.514	10	Mark Budzinski	157,464	2,386	2012
Carolina Mudcats (Braves)	71	68	.511	10 ½	Luis Salazar	202,072	3,016	2006
Salem Red Sox (Red Sox)	66	73	.475	15 ½	Carlos Febles	228,120	3,355	2013
Potomac Nationals (Nationals)	65	74	.468	16 ½	Tripp Keister	217,892	3,459	2014
Frederick Keys (Orioles)	64	76	.457	18	Orlando Gomez	328,789	4,907	2011
Wilmington Blue Rocks (Royals)	62	77	.446	19 ½	Brian Buchanan	282,437	4,153	1999

MINOR LEAGUES

CLUB BATTING

	AVG	G	AB	R	H	2B	3B	HR	RBI	BB	SO	SB	OBP	SLG
Lynchburg	.261	140	4,615	660	1206	295	52	98	611	481	1113	139	.337	.411
Salem	.258	139	4,536	540	1171	235	29	55	494	434	950	152	.328	.359
Myrtle Beach	.253	138	4,427	581	1118	229	36	66	522	488	866	94	.333	.365
Frederick	.252	140	4,620	539	1163	204	36	56	473	389	990	162	.314	.348
Potomac	.252	139	4,465	521	1124	218	29	49	459	396	823	131	.317	.346
Wilmington	.246	139	4,485	469	1102	209	30	57	430	330	983	97	.305	.344
Carolina	.245	139	4,435	533	1085	215	34	72	481	358	907	91	.305	.357
Winston-Salem	.244	138	4,450	546	1085	214	30	50	481	447	1010	148	.317	.339

CLUB PITCHING

	ERA	G	CGSHO	SV	IP	H	R	ER	HR	BB	SO	AVG
Myrtle Beach	3.01	138	2 13	43	1183	1035	441	395	63	339	921	.237
Winston-Salem	3.13	138	3 15	41	1192	1121	518	414	53	403	1005	.250
Potomac	3.31	139	4 15	33	1186	1086	534	436	60	435	997	.243
Carolina	3.38	139	4 12	44	1185	1125	502	445	41	412	953	.251
Wilmington	3.52	139	5 9	36	1206	1174	536	472	61	313	1014	.251
Salem	3.69	139	1 12	38	1192	1116	580	489	73	419	847	.250
Lynchburg	3.77	140	1 10	36	1202	1158	595	504	65	462	956	.256
Frederick	4.32	140	3 8	34	1219	1239	683	585	87	540	949	.265

CLUB FIELDING

	PCT	PO	A	E	DP		PCT	PO	A	E	DP
Myrtle Beach	.983	3549	1429	84	329	Frederick	.973	3657	1430	143	403
Wilmington	.978	3620	1347	114	285	Potomac	.973	3559	1432	141	361
Carolina	.977	3557	1403	117	322	Winston-Salem	.973	3576	1525	143	368
Salem	.975	3577	1425	126	360	Lynchburg	.971	3606	1494	150	386

INDIVIDUAL BATTING LEADERS

Batter, Club	AVG	G	AB	R	H	2B	3B	HR	RBI	BB	SO	SB
Young, Chesny, Myrtle Beach	.321	102	402	65	129	18	3	1	30	45	44	12
Heller, Kevin, Salem	.297	93	313	40	93	18	2	7	52	49	86	13
Rodriguez, Luigi, Lynchburg	.293	92	372	59	109	22	8	12	49	24	82	24
Frazier, Clint, Lynchburg	.285	133	501	88	143	36	3	16	72	68	125	15
Lien, Connor, Carolina	.285	128	453	72	129	22	5	9	47	33	129	34
Rodriguez, Nellie, Lynchburg	.275	108	396	65	109	32	2	17	84	51	122	1
Narvaez, Omar, Winston-Salem	.274	98	339	38	93	10	0	1	27	40	31	1
Zagunis, Mark, Myrtle Beach	.271	115	413	78	112	24	5	8	54	80	86	12
Schrader, Jacob, Carolina	.268	103	377	52	101	28	3	15	59	19	103	1
Chen, Pin-Chieh, Myrtle Beach	.268	96	366	52	98	17	5	4	34	32	48	20

INDIVIDUAL PITCHING LEADERS

Pitcher, Club	W	L	ERA	G	GS	CG	SV	IP	H	R	ER	BB	SO
Martinez, Jonathan, Myrtle Beach	9	2	2.56	23	21	0	0	116	82	35	33	27	66
Heidenreich, Matt, Winston-Salem	12	3	2.76	21	21	1	0	131	129	46	40	23	103
Webster, Seth, Carolina	8	7	2.82	20	19	1	0	131	131	43	41	8	96
Mills, Alec, Wilmington	7	7	3.02	21	21	1	0	113	122	42	38	14	111
Walters, Blair, Carolina	6	8	3.13	29	22	0	0	135	126	52	47	40	85
Peoples, Michael, Lynchburg	11	4	3.42	25	23	0	0	140	133	65	53	53	89
Dykstra, James, Winston-Salem	7	10	3.51	25	19	1	1	128	133	60	50	18	87
Tseng, Jen-Ho, Myrtle Beach	7	7	3.55	22	22	0	0	119	115	48	47	30	87
Hess, David, Frederick	9	4	3.58	26	25	1	0	133	112	53	53	53	110
Junis, Jake, Wilmington	5	11	3.64	26	26	0	0	156	145	71	63	29	123

ALL-STAR TEAM

C: Omar Narvaez, Winston-Salem. **1B:** Nellie Rodriguez, Lynchburg. **2B:** Jake Peter, Winston-Salem. **3B:** Trey Michalczewski, Winston-Salem. **SS:** Johan Camargo, Carolina. **UT:** Chesny Young, Myrtle Beach. **OF:** Clint Frazier, Lynchburg; Connor Lien, Carolina; Mark Zagunis, Myrtle Beach; Adam Engel, Winston-Salem. **DH:** Jacob Schrader, Carolina. **SP:** Matt Heindenreich, Winston-Salem. **RP:** Cody Wheeler, Frederick. **Manager:** Mark Johnson, Myrtle Beach.

DEPARTMENT LEADERS

BATTING

OBP	Heller, Kevin, Salem	.409
SLG	Rodriguez, Nellie, Lynchburg	.495
OPS	Rodriguez, Nellie, Lynchburg	.852
R	Engel, Adam, Winston-Salem	90
H	Frazier, Clint, Lynchburg	143
TB	Frazier, Clint, Lynchburg	233
XBH	Frazier, Clint, Lynchburg	55
2B	Frazier, Clint, Lynchburg	36
3B	Castillo, Ivan, Lynchburg	12
HR	Rodriguez, Nellie, Lynchburg	17
RBI	Rodriguez, Nellie, Lynchburg	84
SAC	Camargo, Johan, Carolina	20
BB	Papi, Mike, Lynchburg	81
HBP	Zagunis, Mark, Myrtle Beach	16
SO	Engel, Adam, Winston-Salem	132
SB	Engel, Adam, Winston-Salem	65
CS	Hart, Josh, Frederick	15
AB/SO	Narvaez, Omar, Winston-Salem	10.94

PITCHING

G	Aviles, Robbie, Lynchburg	44
GS	Horacek, Mitch, Frederick	28
GF	Rakkar, Jasvir, Myrtle Beach	35
	Wheeler, Cody, Frederick	35
SV	Wheeler, Cody, Frederick	17
W	Heidenreich, Matt, Winston-Salem	12
L	Horacek, Mitch, Frederick	17
IP	Junis, Jake, Wilmington	156
H	Gonzalez, Luis, Frederick	169
R	Gonzalez, Luis, Frederick	104
ER	Gonzalez, Luis, Frederick	90
HB	Yambati, Robinson, Wilmington	10
BB	Brown, Mitch, Lynchburg	77
SO	Horacek, Mitch, Frederick	146
SO/9	Mills, Alec, Wilmington	8.81
SO/9 (RP)	Yacabonis, Jimmy, Frederick	9.48
BB/9	Webster, Seth, Carolina	.55
WP	Horacek, Mitch, Frederick	15
BK	Caramo, Yender, Wilmington	3
	Cordero, Estarlin, Wilmington	3
	Gonzalez, Luis, Frederick	3
	McAvoy, Kevin, Salem	3
	Taveras, German, Salem	3
HR	Horacek, Mitch, Frederick	22
AVG	Martinez, Jonathan, Myrtle Beach	.199

FIELDING

C	PCT	Gallagher, Cam, Wilmington	.993
	PO	Narvaez, Omar, Winston-Salem	694
	A	Haase, Eric, Lynchburg	88
	DP	Wynns, Austin, Frederick	9
	E	Narvaez, Omar, Winston-Salem	13
	PB	Haase, Eric, Lynchburg	16
1B	PCT	Rogers, Jacob, Myrtle Beach	.993
	PO	Rogers, Jacob, Myrtle Beach	888
	A	Rogers, Jacob, Myrtle Beach	88
	DP	Rodriguez, Nellie, Lynchburg	94
	E	Barnum, Keon, Winston-Salem	11
		Rodriguez, Nellie, Lynchburg	11
2B	PCT	Lockhart, Daniel, Myrtle Beach	.980
	PO	Lockhart, Daniel, Myrtle Beach	201
	A	Lockhart, Daniel, Myrtle Beach	349
	DP	Peter, Jake, Winston-Salem	88
	E	Roberts, James, Lynchburg	12
3B	PCT	Ramos, Mauricio, Wilmington	.966
	PO	Ramos, Mauricio, Wilmington	87
	A	Michalczewski, Trey, Winston-Salem	253
	DP	Michalczewski, Trey, Winston-Salem	22
	E	Ward, Drew, Potomac	29
SS	PCT	Perez, Stephen, Potomac	.970
	PO	Castillo, Ivan, Lynchburg	197
	A	Camargo, Johan, Carolina	365
	DP	Castillo, Ivan, Lynchburg	80
	E	Castillo, Ivan, Lynchburg	35
OF	PCT	Taylor, Dominique, Wilmington	.987
	PO	Lien, Connor, Carolina	304
	A	Lien, Connor, Carolina	21
	DP	Lien, Connor, Carolina	7
	E	Lien, Connor, Carolina	9
		Papi, Mike, Lynchburg	9

MINOR LEAGUES

BY JOHN MANUEL

It was the year the power went out in the Florida State League.

In 2015, the 14 FSL teams combined for just 599 home runs, with a league-wide .337 slugging percentage that was the worst of any full-season circuit. The average FSL player hit .248/.313/.337 for a .650 OPS.

It was the least offense in the FSL since 1992, when hitters posted nearly the same slash line (.245/.313/.336) in a vastly different league; just six of the 14 clubs are in the same markets.

"The ball just didn't carry this year," said Fort Myers manager Jeff Smith. "It wasn't just in our park, it was everywhere."

Pitching dominated the league, including Palm Beach righthander Alex Reyes (Cardinals), the league's top prospect, who struck out 96 in just 63 2/3 innings (13.57 strikeouts per nine innings). However, 13 of the league's top 20 prospects were position players, including St. Lucie outfielder Michael Conforto, who finished the season playing in the World Series for the Mets.

It was a unique season even for the pitcher-friendly FSL, one in which no player hit more than 14 home runs, and where the eventual league champion, Rays affiliate Charlotte, went just 24-41 in the second half. But the Stone Crabs went 45-25 in the first half behind a stout starting staff that included Minor League Player of the Year Blake Snell at the outset, as well as Buddy Borden, who tossed a seven-inning no-hitter in May, and league co-pitcher of the year Jacob Faria (10-1, 1.33), who led the minors in victories.

Naturally, Charlotte's pitching was prominent in beating Daytona, in its first year as a Reds affiliate, in four games. Trade pickup Chih-Wei Hu, acquired from the Twins in July's Kevin Jepsen deal, tossed eight scoreless innings in a 1-0 victory in the championship series opener, and top Rays prospect Brent Honeywell made two quality starts,

including in the title clincher, while totaling 12 strikeouts in 13 playoff innings.

They won in somewhat anticlimactic fashion. Game Four went 13 innings, and the game-winning, title-clinching run came home on a bases-loaded walk by Kean Wong.

TOP 20 PROSPECTS

1. Alex Reyes, rhp, Palm Beach (Cardinals)
2. Michael Conforto, of, St. Lucie (Mets)
3. Austin Meadows, of, Bradenton (Pirates)
4. Willy Adames, ss, Charlotte (Rays)
5. Jeff Hoffman, rhp, Dunedin (Blue Jays)
6. Amir Garrett, lhp, Daytona (Reds)
7. Amed Rosario, ss, St. Lucie (Mets)
8. Anthony Alford, of, Dunedin (Blue Jays)
9. Brent Honeywell, rhp, Charlotte (Rays)
10. Jake Bauers, 1b, Charlotte (Rays)
11. Reese McGuire, c, Bradenton (Pirates)
12. Harold Ramirez, of, Bradenton (Pirates)
13. Alex Blandino, ss/2b, Daytona (Reds)
14. Dominic Smith, 1b, St. Lucie (Mets)
15. Kohl Stewart, rhp, Fort Myers (Twins)
16. Stephen Gonsalves, lhp, Fort Myers (Twins)
17. Luke Weaver, rhp, Palm Beach (Cardinals)
18. Tyler Wade, ss/2b, Tampa (Yankees)
19. Engelb Vielma, ss, Fort Myers (Twins)
20. JaCoby Jones, ss, Bradenton (Pirates)

STANDINGS: SPLIT SEASON

FIRST HALF

NORTH	W	L	PCT	GB
Clearwater	37	33	.529	—
Daytona	37	33	.529	—
Tampa	34	36	.486	3
Lakeland	33	36	.478	3 ½
Dunedin	32	38	.457	5
Brevard Cty.	29	40	.420	7 ½

SOUTH	W	L	PCT	GB
Charlotte	45	25	.643	—
Fort Myers	38	32	.543	7
Jupiter	35	35	.500	10
St. Lucie	35	35	.500	10
Bradenton	32	38	.457	13
Palm Beach	32	38	.457	13

SECOND HALF

NORTH	W	L	PCT	GB
Clearwater	42	25	.627	—
Daytona	40	25	.615	1
Tampa	32	36	.471	10
Dunedin	29	38	.433	13
Brevard Cty.	26	40	.394	15 ½
Lakeland	22	43	.338	19

SOUTH	W	L	PCT	GB
Palm Beach	43	25	.632	—
Bradenton	42	26	.618	1
Fort Myers	38	31	.551	5 ½
St. Lucie	33	35	.485	10
Jupiter	32	38	.457	12
Charlotte	24	41	.369	17 ½

Playoffs—Semifinals: Daytona defeated Clearwater 2-0 and Charlotte defeated Palm Beach 2-0 in best-of-three series; **Finals:** Charlotte defeated Daytona 3-1 in a best-of-five series.

OVERALL STANDINGS

Team (Organization)	W	L	PCT	GB	Manager(s)	Attendance	Average	Last Pennant
Clearwater Threshers (Phillies)	79	58	.577	—	Greg Legg	174,283	2,723	2007
Daytona Tortugas (Reds)	77	58	.570	1	Eli Marrero	137,224	2,250	2011
Fort Myers Miracle (Twins)	76	63	.547	4	Jeff Smith	133,817	2,028	2014
Palm Beach Cardinals (Cardinals)	75	63	.543	4 ½	Oliver Marmol	67,108	1,017	2005
Bradenton Marauders (Pirates)	74	64	.536	5 ½	Michael Ryan	102,914	1,492	1963
Charlotte Stone Crabs (Rays)	69	66	.511	9	Michael Johns	105,965	1,630	2015
St. Lucie Mets (Mets)	68	70	.493	11 ½	Luis Rojas	99,044	1,501	2006
Jupiter Hammerheads (Marlins)	67	73	.479	13 ½	Brian Schneider	67,194	1,034	1991
Tampa Yankees (Yankees)	66	72	.478	13 ½	Dave Bialas	92,786	1,497	2010
Dunedin Blue Jays (Blue Jays)	61	76	.445	18	Omar Malave	52,659	798	Never
Lakeland Flying Tigers (Tigers)	55	79	.410	22 ½	Dave Huppert	61,328	973	2012
Brevard County Manatees (Brewers)	55	80	.407	23	Joe Ayrault	78,373	1,244	2001

CLUB BATTING

	AVG	G	AB	R	H	2B	3B	HR	RBI	BB	SO	SB	OBP	SLG
Bradenton	.271	139	4753	588	1286	211	30	55	525	412	814	135	.333	.362
Clearwater	.267	138	4654	574	1244	211	30	60	520	346	859	85	.326	.364
St. Lucie	.260	138	4652	553	1209	221	35	39	496	416	1005	84	.325	.348
Charlotte	.255	135	4439	532	1131	205	29	44	473	388	943	121	.318	.344
Fort Myers	.246	139	4650	500	1145	181	37	27	436	448	963	151	.319	.318
Tampa	.246	138	4501	509	1107	193	35	54	458	383	920	152	.308	.340
Brevard County	.241	137	4362	462	1052	190	18	49	415	328	1011	113	.304	.327
Jupiter	.241	140	4583	478	1103	167	14	41	405	336	888	134	.296	.310
Lakeland	.239	135	4546	441	1090	184	32	51	391	372	985	60	.302	.326
Daytona	.238	135	4288	532	1019	183	29	78	476	394	1107	157	.307	.348
Palm Beach	.238	138	4450	471	1061	188	22	38	415	424	955	129	.313	.316
Dunedin	.235	138	4555	510	1072	224	36	63	455	387	1049	80	.300	.342

CLUB PITCHING

	ERA	G	CG	SHO	SV	IP	H	R	ER	HR	BB	SO	AVG
Palm Beach	2.65	138	3	21	46	1217	1101	438	358	29	329	983	.242
Fort Myers	2.70	139	6	12	36	1248	1093	450	374	35	397	991	.237
Charlotte	2.87	135	3	17	34	1177	1033	470	376	45	379	902	.237
Jupiter	3.08	140	2	10	40	1228	1165	501	421	32	430	990	.253
Daytona	3.11	135	3	19	47	1159	1058	489	401	44	430	982	.244
Clearwater	3.21	138	3	13	41	1216	1064	493	434	79	384	926	.238
Tampa	3.22	138	5	9	37	1193	1052	516	427	50	361	1074	.234
St. Lucie	3.42	138	2	9	38	1212	1109	549	461	48	457	924	.244
Bradenton	3.47	139	1	9	43	1255	1211	548	484	63	365	955	.255
Brevard County	3.48	137	15	7	30	1159	1197	556	448	55	323	828	.266
Lakeland	3.49	135	2	9	31	1205	1207	541	467	47	364	923	.262
Dunedin	3.89	138	2	10	37	1201	1229	599	519	72	415	1021	.265

CLUB FIELDING

	PCT	PO	A	E	DP		PCT	PO	A	E	DP
Bradenton	.979	3765	1555	116	378	Fort Myers	.976	3745	1514	132	365
Brevard County	.970	3477	1376	151	318	Jupiter	.975	3685	1499	134	391
Charlotte	.971	3532	1390	146	289	Lakeland	.975	3617	1467	128	347
Clearwater	.979	3648	1418	110	351	Palm Beach	.973	3652	1475	143	376
Daytona	.971	3479	1466	149	376	St. Lucie	.972	3638	1489	146	303
Dunedin	.973	3603	1354	138	318	Tampa	.967	3580	1309	165	261

INDIVIDUAL BATTING LEADERS

Batter, Club	AVG	G	AB	R	H	2B	3B	HR	RBI	BB	SO	SB
Astudillo, Williams, Clearwater	.314	107	385	32	121	18	0	3	49	10	10	1
McNeil, Jeff, St. Lucie	.312	119	468	80	146	18	6	1	40	35	59	16
Meadows, Austin, Bradenton	.307	121	508	72	156	22	4	7	54	41	79	20
Smith, Dominic, St. Lucie	.305	118	456	58	139	33	0	6	79	35	75	2
Oberste, Matt, St. Lucie	.301	111	419	52	126	24	6	6	64	34	73	1
Cooper, Garrett, Brevard County	.294	119	422	55	124	32	2	8	54	35	88	1
Jhang, Jin-De, Bradenton	.292	99	370	45	108	16	1	5	41	22	43	2
Weiss, Erich, Bradenton	.285	98	372	46	106	17	2	3	49	41	70	11
Cozens, Dylan, Clearwater	.282	96	365	52	103	22	5	5	46	26	79	18
Lee, Braxton, Charlotte	.281	115	374	48	105	7	1	0	24	36	67	23

INDIVIDUAL PITCHING LEADERS

Pitcher, Club	W	L	ERA	G	GS	CG	SV	IP	H	R	ER	BB	SO
Ortega, Jorge, Brevard County	9	9	2.41	22	20	6	0	142	136	47	38	11	72
Garrett, Amir, Daytona	9	7	2.44	26	26	1	0	140	117	50	38	55	133
Littrell, Corey, Palm Beach	9	9	2.69	27	17	1	0	130	125	48	39	21	93
Slegers, Aaron, Fort Myers	8	6	2.87	19	19	3	0	119	103	48	38	21	80
Borden, Buddy, Charlotte	9	7	2.97	28	17	2	0	127	104	57	42	58	95
Stephens, Jackson, Daytona	12	7	2.97	26	26	0	0	145	157	56	48	30	97
Eades, Ryan, Fort Myers	6	3	3.11	20	20	0	0	119	109	43	41	38	80
Stewart, Kohl, Fort Myers	7	8	3.20	22	22	1	0	129	134	63	46	45	71
Ziomek, Kevin, Lakeland	9	11	3.43	27	27	2	0	155	142	69	59	34	143
Wang, Wei-Chung, Brevard County	10	6	3.54	25	25	3	0	140	146	69	55	39	91

ALL-STAR TEAMS

C: Williams Astudillo, Clearwater; Alex Swim, Fort Myers. **1B:** Dominic Smith, St. Lucie. **2B:** Erich Weiss, Bradenton. **SS:** Tyler Wade, Tampa. **3B:** Jeff McNeil, St. Lucie. **UTIL INF:** Chris McFarland, Brevard County. **LF:** Andrew Pullin, Clearwater. **CF:** Austin Meadows, Bradenton. **RF:** Dylan Cozens, Clearwater. **UTIL OF:** Yefri Perez, Jupiter. **DH:** Matt Oberste, St. Lucie. **P:** Jackson Stephens, Daytona; Amir Garrett, Daytona. Jorge Ortega, Brevard County; Jacob Faria, Charlotte. **RP:** Wil Browning, Dunedin; Brad Schreiber, Charlotte. **Manager:** Greg Legg, Clearwater.

DEPARTMENT LEADERS

BATTING

OBP	McNeil, Jeff, St. Lucie	.373
SLG	Marjama, Mike, Charlotte	.473
OPS	Cooper, Garrett, Brevard County	.792
R	McNeil, Jeff, St. Lucie	80
H	Meadows, Austin, Bradenton	156
TB	Meadows, Austin, Bradenton	207
XBH	Coulter, Clint, Brevard County	46
2B	Smith, Dominic, St. Lucie	33
3B	James, Jiwan, Lakeland	8
	Kanzler, Jason, Fort Myers	8
HR	Dean, Matt, Dunedin	14
	Pullin, Andrew, Clearwater	14
RBI	Smith, Dominic, St. Lucie	79
SAC	Vielma, Engelb, Fort Myers	18
BB	Garver, Mitch, Fort Myers	69
HBP	McElroy, C.J., Palm Beach	20
SO	Sparks, Taylor, Daytona	162
SB	Perez, Yefri, Jupiter	71
CS	Perez, Yefri, Jupiter	21
AB/SO	Astudillo, Willians, Clearwater	38.50

PITCHING

G	Muhammad, El'Hajj, Daytona	52
GS	Dickson, Cody, Bradenton	27
	Ziomek, Kevin, Lakeland	27
GF	Joaquin, Ulises, Clearwater	37
SV	Browning, Wil, Dunedin	22
W	Dickson, Cody, Bradenton	12
	Stephens, Jackson, Daytona	12
L	Marquez, German, Charlotte	13
IP	Ziomek, Kevin, Lakeland	155
H	Duncan, Frank, Bradenton	194
R	Labourt, Jairo, Dunedin, Lakeland	81
ER	Duncan, Frank, Bradenton	73
HB	Gonzalez, Felipe, Bradenton	13
	Marquez, German, Charlotte	13
	Whitehead, David, Clearwater	13
BB	Encinas, Gabriel, Tampa	63
SO	Ziomek, Kevin, Lakeland	143
SO/9	Garrett, Amir, Daytona	8.53
SO/9 (RP)	Milroy, Matt, Jupiter	11.57
BB/9	Ortega, Jorge, Brevard County	.70
WP	Diaz, Miller, St. Lucie	24
BK	Aquino, Jayson, Dunedin, Bradenton	4
HR	Duncan, Frank, Bradenton	12
	Santos, Luis, Dunedin	12
AVG	Borden, Buddy, Charlotte	.223

FIELDING

C PCT	Kelly, Carson, Palm Beach	.996
PO	Kelly, Carson, Palm Beach	751
A	Araiza, Armando, Charlotte	94
DP	Araiza, Armando, Charlotte	9
	Hoo, Chris, Jupiter	9
E	Hudson, Joe, Daytona	11
	McGuire, Reese, Bradenton	11
PB	Plaia, Colton, St. Lucie	21
1B PCT	Espinal, Edwin, Bradenton	.995
PO	Voit, Luke, Palm Beach	1,024
A	Smith, Dominic, St. Lucie	78
DP	Voit, Luke, Palm Beach	112
E	Voit, Luke, Palm Beach	16
2B PCT	Betancourt, Javier, Lakeland	.982
PO	Betancourt, Javier, Lakeland	250
A	Betancourt, Javier, Lakeland	347
DP	Betancourt, Javier, Lakeland	85
E	McFarland, Chris, Brevard County	23
3B PCT	Mathisen, Wyatt, Bradenton	.946
PO	Sparks, Taylor, Daytona	82
	Walding, Mitch, Clearwater	82
A	Sparks, Taylor, Daytona	249
DP	Anderson, Brian, Jupiter	28
E	Sparks, Taylor, Daytona	36
SS PCT	Rosario, Amed, St. Lucie	.968
PO	Ortega, Angel, Brevard County	210
A	Vielma, Engelb, Fort Myers	390
DP	Vielma, Engelb, Fort Myers	75
E	Ortega, Angel, Brevard County	26
OF PCT	O'Neill, Michael, Tampa	.995
PO	Perez, Yefri, Jupiter	331
A	Coulter, Clint, Brevard County	16
DP	4 players tied	4
E	Perez, Yefri, Jupiter	12

MINOR LEAGUES

BY J.J. COOPER

West Michigan won the low Class A Midwest League title, but in all likelihood, Quad Cities will be the team remembered.

For five months, the River Bandits dominated the league. They went 88-50 and finished with the highest winning percentage (.638) of any full-season minor league team.

Quad Cities did it with a revolving cast of players; more than 60 wore a Bandits uniform. By the end of the year, a number of Astros' prospects who started the season playing within sight of the Mississippi River had been promoted to high Class A Lancaster or Double-A Corpus Christi. Others, such as catcher Jacob Nottingham and righthander Daniel Mengden had been traded at the deadline.

But Quad Cities just kept winning. It didn't hurt that the reinforcements were often just as talented as the players who had moved. Scouts who saw the River Bandits all year said that the team had nearly 20 legitimate prospects.

West Michigan had an impressive group of prospects of its own. Outfielders Mike Gerber (.292/.355/.468) and Christin Stewart (.286/.375/.492) led the lineup while righthander Spencer Turnbull (11-3, 3.01) and reliever Joe Jimenez (5-1, 1.47) led the pitching staff. In the playoffs the Whitecaps edged Cedar Rapids 3-2 in the best-of-five championship series.

Lansing's Ryan McBroom was named the league MVP but first baseman Bobby Bradley was the offensive star. Bradley hit .269/.361/.529 and led the league with 27 home runs—11 more than anyone else in the league. Bradley's 27 home runs tied for fourth most by a teenager in modern-day Midwest League history. The league reclassified as a Class A league in 1962.

TOP 20 PROSPECTS

1. Gleyber Torres, ss, South Bend (Cubs)
2. Anthony Alford, cf, Lansing (Blue Jays)
3. Ruddy Giron, ss, Fort Wayne (Padres)
4. Nick Gordon, ss, Cedar Rapids (Twins)
5. Francis Martes, rhp, Quad Cities (Astros)
6. Ian Happ, of, South Bend (Cubs)
7. Brent Honeywell, rhp, Bowling Green (Rays)
8. Grant Holmes, rhp, Great Lakes (Dodgers)
9. Bobby Bradley, 1b, Lake County (Indians)
10. Sean Reid-Foley, rhp, Lansing (Blue Jays)
11. Justus Sheffield, lhp, Lake County (Indians)
12. Jacob Nottingham, c, Quad Cities (Astros)
13. Harrison Bader, of, Peoria (Cardinals)
14. Casey Gillaspie, 1b, Bowling Green (Rays)
15. Jesus Tinoco, rhp, Lansing (Blue Jays)
16. Kodi Medeiros, lhp, Wisconsin (Brewers)
17. Spencer Turnbull, rhp, West Michigan (Tigers)
18. Stephen Gonsalves, lhp, Cedar Rapids (Twins)
19. Yairo Munoz, ss, Beloit (Athletics)
20. Paul DeJong, 3b, Peoria (Cardinals)

STANDINGS: SPLIT SEASON

FIRST HALF					SECOND HALF				
EAST	W	L	PCT	GB	**EAST**	W	L	PCT	GB
Lansing	42	28	.600	—	Fort Wayne	45	25	.643	—
Great Lakes	38	30	.559	3	West Mich.	42	28	.600	3
Dayton	39	31	.557	3	South Bend	36	34	.514	9
Lake County	36	32	.529	5	Lake County	35	34	.507	9 ½
Bowling Grn.	37	33	.529	5	Bowling Grn.	34	35	.493	10 ½
West Mich.	33	36	.478	8 ½	Dayton	32	37	.464	12 ½
Fort Wayne	32	36	.471	9	Lansing	31	38	.449	13 ½
South Bend	29	38	.433	11 ½	Great Lakes	29	39	.435	14 ½
WEST	W	L	PCT	GB	**WEST**	W	L	PCT	GB
Quad Cities	45	23	.662	—	Kane County	48	22	.686	—
Cedar Rapids	41	29	.586	5	Quad Cities	43	27	.614	5
Kane County	36	32	.529	9	Peoria	42	28	.600	6
Burlington	35	34	.507	10 ½	Cedar Rapids	36	34	.514	12
Peoria	33	35	.485	12	Beloit	29	40	.420	18 ½
Clinton	26	43	.377	19 ½	Burlington	28	42	.400	20
Beloit	26	44	.371	20	Wisconsin	27	42	.391	20 ½
Wisconsin	23	47	.329	23	Clinton	20	50	.286	28

Playoffs—Quarterfinals: Lansing defeated Great Lakes 2-0, West Michigan defeated Fort Wayne 2-0, Cedar Rapids defeated Quad Cities 2-0 and Peoria defeated Kane County 2-0 in best-of-three series; **Semifinals:** West Michigan defeated Lansing 2-1 and Cedar Rapids defeated Peoria 2-0 in best-of-three series; **Finals:** West Michigan defeated Cedar Rapids 3-2 in a best-of-five series.

OVERALL STANDINGS

Team (Organization)	W	L	PCT	GB	Manager(s)	Attendance	Average	Last Pennant
Quad Cities River Bandits (Astros)	88	50	.638	—	Josh Bonifay	250,004	3,906	2013
Kane County Cougars (Diamondbacks)	84	54	.609	4	Mark Grudzielanek	408,449	5,920	2014
Fort Wayne TinCaps (Padres)	77	61	.558	11	Francisco Morales	400,036	5,971	2009
Cedar Rapids Kernels (Twins)	77	63	.550	12	Jake Mauer	170,832	2,550	1994
Peoria Chiefs (Cardinals)	75	63	.543	13	Joe Kruzel	225,089	3,360	2002
West Michigan Whitecaps (Tigers)	75	64	.540	13 ½	Andrew Graham	391,055	5,667	2015
Lansing Lugnuts (Blue Jays)	73	66	.525	15 ½	Ken Huckaby	336,752	5,026	2003
Lake County Captains (Indians)	71	66	.518	16 ½	Shaun Larkin	221,652	3,358	2010
Dayton Dragons (Reds)	71	68	.511	17 ½	Jose Nieves	574,830	8,212	Never
Bowling Green Hot Rods (Rays)	69	69	.500	19	Reinaldo Ruiz	200,777	2,953	Never
Great Lakes Loons (Dodgers)	68	69	.496	19 ½	Luis Matos	221,749	3,360	2000
South Bend Cubs (Cubs)	65	72	.474	22 ½	Jimmy Gonzalez	347,678	5,039	2005
Burlington Bees (Angels)	63	76	.453	25 ½	Chad Tracy	66,857	998	2008
Beloit Snappers (Athletics)	55	84	.396	33 ½	Fran Riordan	65,152	958	1995
Wisconsin Timber Rattlers (Brewers)	50	89	.360	38 ½	Matt Erickson	247,577	3,641	2012
Clinton LumberKings (Mariners)	46	93	.331	42 ½	Scott Steinmann	105,405	1,573	1991

CLUB BATTING

	AVG	G	AB	R	H	2B	3B	HR	RBI	BB	SO	SB	OBP	SLG
Kane County	.275	138	4692	627	1291	217	44	48	538	368	885	104	.332	.371
Lansing	.270	139	4743	699	1280	263	37	87	626	439	1026	162	.337	.396
Quad Cities	.265	139	4591	659	1216	221	45	72	589	560	1025	145	.346	.380
Bowling Green	.262	138	4605	533	1208	231	27	73	468	321	903	127	.313	.372
Fort Wayne	.258	138	4607	569	1189	227	38	65	508	359	1030	119	.318	.366
South Bend	.258	137	4634	595	1196	229	38	66	526	390	956	157	.321	.367
West Michigan	.256	139	4610	569	1181	201	46	48	495	412	986	129	.322	.351
Great Lakes	.255	138	4713	541	1203	229	25	72	477	357	1114	102	.316	.360
Dayton	.251	139	4690	560	1177	224	50	66	504	384	1041	118	.316	.362
Lake County	.251	137	4546	629	1139	214	19	93	566	461	981	127	.327	.367
Cedar Rapids	.250	140	4758	618	1190	234	53	40	534	412	987	131	.320	.347
Peoria	.250	138	4598	569	1151	220	45	77	499	392	1032	157	.317	.368
Burlington	.249	139	4608	557	1146	200	33	66	485	457	1045	87	.322	.349
Clinton	.239	139	4648	535	1109	209	30	52	475	496	1177	112	.318	.330
Beloit	.237	139	4615	568	1093	230	23	89	515	465	1173	78	.312	.354
Wisconsin	.236	139	4520	471	1066	190	34	48	408	393	1178	98	.304	.325

CLUB PITCHING

	ERA	G	CG	SHO	SV	IP	H	R	ER	HR	BB	SO	AVG
Quad Cities	2.65	139	2	16	46	1232	1026	452	363	50	394	1075	.224
Kane County	3.10	138	2	13	49	1220	1094	516	420	52	436	976	.242
Cedar Rapids	3.22	140	2	13	37	1253	1118	519	449	64	448	1138	.240
Peoria	3.32	138	3	15	43	1220	1137	542	450	76	426	1149	.245
Fort Wayne	3.35	138	0	12	41	1212	1136	552	451	66	419	967	.248
Bowling Green	3.39	138	0	12	36	1204	1175	545	453	66	362	975	.256
Dayton	3.43	139	2	8	29	1229	1250	590	469	56	371	1005	.263
West Michigan	3.48	139	2	8	43	1219	1197	544	472	56	371	1020	.258
Great Lakes	3.55	138	3	9	32	1226	1146	577	484	66	443	1080	.247
Lake County	3.58	137	1	8	34	1204	1202	574	479	95	360	1144	.259
Burlington	3.59	139	1	8	33	1212	1163	571	484	71	415	1053	.256
South Bend	3.60	137	0	9	38	1212	1173	586	485	55	411	927	.255
Lansing	3.93	139	1	8	42	1229	1288	623	537	75	412	1025	.270
Wisconsin	4.11	139	0	6	33	1202	1187	649	549	58	418	997	.257
Clinton	4.31	139	3	6	18	1223	1241	703	586	57	519	1026	.264
Beloit	4.72	139	2	2	26	1209	1302	756	634	99	461	982	.276

CLUB FIELDING

	PCT	PO	A	E	DP		PCT	PO	A	E	DP
Cedar Rapids	.976	3761	1519	131	356	Bowling Green	.969	3613	1354	158	258
South Bend	.975	3636	1454	133	319	Wisconsin	.969	3606	1411	161	265
West Michigan	.975	3657	1356	128	259	Clinton	.968	3669	1453	168	270
Burlington	.974	3638	1584	142	368	Dayton	.968	3688	1647	174	348
Lansing	.974	3687	1399	134	346	Lake County	.968	3614	1425	167	369
Kane County	.973	3660	1485	143	400	Peoria	.968	3661	1268	165	258
Quad Cities	.972	3698	1414	146	339	Beloit	.967	3627	1414	174	289
Great Lakes	.970	3680	1417	159	340	Fort Wayne	.965	3638	1449	186	317

INDIVIDUAL BATTING LEADERS

Batter, Club	AVG	G	AB	R	H	2B	3B	HR	RBI	BB	SO	SB
Vargas, Ildemaro, Kane County	.321	86	336	62	108	18	3	5	39	35	16	9
McBroom, Ryan, Lansing	.315	127	461	72	145	39	1	12	90	49	96	5
Reyes, Victor, Kane County	.311	121	424	57	132	17	5	2	59	22	58	13
Bray, Colin, Kane County	.308	130	490	78	151	25	8	3	52	47	109	27
Tanielu, Nick, Quad Cities	.308	110	419	55	129	27	4	6	70	30	65	2
Herum, Marty, Kane County	.303	129	511	71	155	23	6	7	79	29	77	5
Seferina, Darren, Peoria	.295	107	410	58	121	26	12	4	33	37	88	23
Verdugo, Alex, Great Lakes	.295	101	421	50	124	23	2	5	42	17	53	13
Torres, Gleyber, South Bend	.293	119	464	53	136	24	5	3	62	43	108	22
Gerber, Mike, West Michigan	.292	135	513	74	150	31	10	13	76	49	97	16

INDIVIDUAL PITCHING LEADERS

Pitcher, Club	W	L	ERA	G	GS	CG	SV	IP	H	R	ER	BB	SO
Pearce, Matt, Peoria	11	10	2.43	24	24	0	0	145	139	51	39	22	95
Mahle, Tyler, Dayton	13	8	2.43	27	26	0	0	152	145	54	41	25	135
Keller, Brad, Kane County	8	9	2.60	26	25	0	0	142	128	57	41	37	109
Paulson, Jake, Dayton	8	5	2.60	33	14	0	1	118	106	45	34	18	92
James, Joshua, Quad Cities	7	4	2.63	24	18	0	1	116	102	43	34	41	89
Gomber, Austin, Peoria	15	3	2.67	22	22	1	0	135	97	45	40	34	140
Jorge, Felix, Cedar Rapids	6	7	2.79	23	22	0	0	142	118	52	44	32	114
Strahan, Wyatt, Dayton	9	10	2.79	28	28	1	0	164	158	68	51	53	132
Solbach, Markus, Kane County	9	4	2.88	20	20	0	0	122	112	46	39	30	56
Antone, Tejay, Dayton	6	10	2.91	26	26	1	0	158	174	66	51	33	101

ALL-STAR TEAM

1B: Ryan McBroom, Lansing. **2B:** Darren Seferina, Peoria. **3B:** Nick Tanielu, Quad Cities. **SS:** Gleyber Torres, South Bend. **OF:** Mike Gerber, West Michigan; Nick Torres, Fort Wayne; Alex Verdugo, Great Lakes. **Catcher:** Jacob Nottingham, Quad Cities. **DH:** Ryan McBroom, Lansing. **RHSP:** Tyler Mahle, Dayton. **LHSP:** Austin Gomber, Peoria. **RHRP:** Kyle Grana, Peoria. **LHRP:** Zac Curtis, Kane County. **MVP:** Ryan McBroom, Lansing. **Prospect of the Year:** Gleyber Torres, South Bend. **Manager of the Year:** Josh Bonifay, Quad Cities.

DEPARTMENT LEADERS

BATTING

OBP	McBroom, Ryan, Lansing	.387
SLG	Bradley, Bobby, Lake County	.529
OPS	Bradley, Bobby, Lake County	.890
R	Allen, Greg, Lake County	83
H	Herum, Marty, Kane County	155
TB	Gerber, Mike, West Michigan	240
XBH	Gerber, Mike, West Michigan	54
2B	McBroom, Ryan, Lansing	39
3B	Seferina, Darren, Peoria	12
HR	Bradley, Bobby, Lake County	27
RBI	Bradley, Bobby, Lake County	92
SAC	Boyd, Bobby, Quad Cities	13
BB	DeCarlo, Joseph, Clinton	70
	Ritchie, Jamie, Quad Cities	70
HBP	Locastro, Tim, Lansing	21
SO	Gettys, Michael, Fort Wayne	162
SB	Mercado, Oscar, Peoria	50
CS	Mercado, Oscar, Peoria	19
AB/SO	Vargas, Ildemaro, Kane County	21

PITCHING

G	Grana, Kyle, Peoria	54
GS	Graves, Brett, Beloit	28
	Robichaux, Austin, Burlington	28
	Strahan, Wyatt, Dayton	28
GF	Curtis, Zac, Kane County	45
SV	Curtis, Zac, Kane County	33
W	Gomber, Austin, Peoria	15
L	Fillmyer, Heath, Beloit	13
	Gossett, Daniel, Beloit	13
	Schiraldi, Lukas, Clinton	13
IP	Strahan, Wyatt, Dayton	164
H	Antone, Tejay, Dayton	174
	Herb, Tyler, Clinton	174
R	Mendez, Junior, Beloit	93
ER	Graves, Brett, Beloit	85
HB	James, Joshua, Quad Cities	16
	Stinnett, Jake, South Bend	16
BB	Schiraldi, Lukas, Clinton	71
SO	Gomber, Austin, Peoria	140
SO/9	Sheffield, Justus, Lake County	9.73
SO/9 (RP)	Klonowski, Alex, Bowling Green	11.53
BB/9	Seaton, Ross, West Michigan	1.09
WP	Schiraldi, Lukas, Clinton	25
BK	Lamet, Dinelson, Fort Wayne	6
HR	Mendez, Junior, Beloit	18
AVG	Gomber, Austin, Peoria	.196

FIELDING

C PCT	Navarreto, Brian, Cedar Rapids	.997
PO	Mejia, Francisco, Lake County	765
A	Ruiz, Jose, Fort Wayne	112
DP	Navarreto, Brian, Cedar Rapids	12
E	Ruiz, Jose, Fort Wayne	16
PB	De La Cruz, Michael, Lansing	18
1B PCT	Kengor, Will, West Michigan	.991
PO	Herum, Marty, Kane County	1,073
A	Bradley, Bobby, Lake County	75
DP	Herum, Marty, Kane County	120
E	Bradley, Bobby, Lake County	17
2B PCT	Unroe, Riley, Bowling Green	.977
PO	Unroe, Riley, Bowling Green	183
A	Unroe, Riley, Bowling Green	278
DP	Unroe, Riley, Bowling Green	53
E	Pankake, Joey, West Michigan	16
3B PCT	Houchins, Zachary, Burlington	.960
PO	Kay, Grant, Bowling Green	95
A	DeCarlo, Joseph, Clinton	234
DP	Houchins, Zachary, Burlington	24
E	Murphy, Taylor, Lake County	32
SS PCT	Gordon, Nick, Cedar Rapids	.966
PO	Gonzalez, Luis, Dayton	167
A	Gonzalez, Luis, Dayton	435
DP	Gonzalez, Luis, Dayton	90
E	Gonzalez, Luis, Dayton	42
OF PCT	English, Tanner, Cedar Rapids	.996
PO	Milone, Thomas, Bowling Green	329
A	Verdugo, Alex, Great Lakes	21
DP	Ison, Bobby, Lake County	6
	Verdugo, Alex, Great Lakes	6
E	Davis, D.J., Lansing	11
	Morales, Estarlyn, Clinton	11

MINOR LEAGUES

BY J.J. COOPER

The Hickory Crawdads have had a number of notable teams and many notable players pass through L.P. Frans Stadium in recent years, but they hadn't had a champion in more than a decade.

There may have been more talented and prospect-laden Crawdads teams, but this one will have a ring. Hickory shrugged off injuries and midseason roster adjustments to ride its pitching staff to the league's third-best record. And when the playoffs began, Hickory shut out West Virginia in the deciding game of the semifinals and then allowed Asheville just four runs in three games in a three-game sweep of the championship series, giving the Crawdads their third Sally League title.

Savannah had the best record in the league during the regular season thanks to a very well-rounded team led by league MVP shortstop Luis Guillorme, outfielder Wuilmer Becerra and a solid pitching staff.

Greenville didn't make the playoffs but had the most impressive assemblage of prospects in the South Atlantic League. The Drive placed four players among the Top 10 Prospects in the league, and second baseman Yoan Moncada, third baseman Rafael Devers and shortstop Javier Guerra all cracked the top five.

Two pitchers managed to throw no-hitters over the course of the season. West Virginia's Stephen Tarpley shut down Delmarva in the first game of a double-header in early July while Delmarva's John Mears held Charleston hitless in the first game of a doubleheader in late July.

West Virginia's Yeudy Garcia was not even a part of the Power's rotation when the season began but proved to be one of the league's surprise stars. Garcia played his way into a larger role and ended up winning the league's ERA crown (2.10) while being named the league's most outstanding pitcher.

The Sand Gnats bid farewell to Savannah after the season, and will change their name to Fireflies before moving into a new ballpark in 2016 in Columbia, S.C.

TOP 20 PROSPECTS

1. Yoan Moncada, 2b, Greenville (Red Sox)
2. Jorge Mateo, ss, Charleston (Yankees)
3. Ozzie Albies, ss, Rome (Braves)
4. Javier Guerra, ss, Greenville (Red Sox)
5. Rafael Devers, 3b, Greenville (Red Sox)
6. Luis Ortiz, rhp, Hickory (Rangers)
7. Touki Toussaint, rhp, Rome (Braves)
8. Braxton Davidson, of, Rome (Braves)
9. Yeudy Garcia, rhp, West Virginia (Pirates)
10. Michael Kopech, rhp, Greenville (Red Sox)
11. Ariel Jurado, rhp, Hickory (Rangers)
12. Jairo Beras, of, Hickory (Rangers)
13. Jomar Reyes, 3b, Delmarva (Orioles)
14. Malquin Canelo, ss, Lakewood (Phillies)
15. Cole Tucker, ss, West Virginia (Pirates)
16. Spencer Adams, rhp, Kannapolis (White Sox)
17. Tyler Kolek, rhp, Greensboro (Marlins)
18. Luis Guillorme, ss, Savannah (Mets)
19. Ryan O'Hearn, 1b, Lexington (Royals)
20. Rhys Hoskins, 1b, Lakewood (Phillies)

STANDINGS: SPLIT SEASON

FIRST HALF

NORTH	W	L	PCT	GB
Hickory	44	24	.647	—
West Virginia	37	32	.536	7½
Hagerstown	35	33	.515	9
Kannapolis	35	34	.507	9½
Delmarva	33	35	.485	11
Lakewood	33	35	.485	11
Greensboro	29	40	.420	15½

SOUTH	W	L	PCT	GB
Savannah	39	31	.557	—
Greenville	38	32	.543	1
Charleston	34	36	.486	5
Augusta	33	36	.478	5½
Asheville	32	38	.457	7
Lexington	31	39	.443	8
Rome	31	39	.443	8

SECOND HALF

NORTHERN	W	L	PCT	GB
West Virginia	50	20	.714	—
Lakewood	40	30	.571	10
Delmarva	38	32	.543	12
Hickory	37	33	.529	13
Hagerstown	33	37	.471	17
Kannapolis	29	40	.420	20½
Greensboro	22	48	.314	28

SOUTHERN	W	L	PCT	GB
Savannah	45	22	.672	—
Asheville	40	29	.580	6
Greenville	34	36	.486	12½
Augusta	32	37	.464	14
Charleston	32	38	.457	14½
Lexington	27	41	.397	18½
Rome	27	43	.386	19½

Playoffs—Semifinals: Hickory defeated West Virginia 2-1 and Asheville defeated Savannah 2-1 in best-of-three series; **Finals:** Hickory defeated Asheville 3-0 in a best-of-five series.

OVERALL STANDINGS

Team (Organization)	W	L	PCT	GB	Manager(s)	Attendance	Average	Last Pennant
West Virginia Power (Pirates)	87	52	.626	—	Brian Esposito	160,429	2,468	1990
Savannah Sand Gnats (Mets)	84	53	.613	2	Jose Leger	125,587	1,962	2013
Hickory Crawdads (Rangers)	81	57	.587	5½	Corey Ragsdale	149,963	2,205	2015
Lakewood BlueClaws (Phillies)	73	65	.529	13½	Shawn Williams	388,718	5,634	2010
Asheville Tourists (Rockies)	72	67	.518	15	Warren Schaeffer	181,578	2,670	2014
Delmarva Shorebirds (Orioles)	71	67	.514	15½	Ryan Minor	203,520	3,230	2001
Greenville Drive (Red Sox)	72	68	.514	15½	Darren Fenster	346,828	5,100	1998
Hagerstown Suns (Nationals)	68	70	.493	18½	Patrick Anderson	68,688	1,073	Never
Charleston RiverDogs (Yankees)	66	74	.471	21½	Luis Dorante	292,661	4,368	Never
Augusta GreenJackets (Giants)	65	73	.471	21½	Nestor Rojas	174,382	2,725	2008
Kannapolis Intimidators (White Sox)	64	74	.464	22½	Tommy Thompson	135,727	2,056	2005
Lexington Legends (Royals)	58	80	.420	28½	Omar Ramirez	283,873	4,367	2001
Rome Braves (Braves)	58	82	.414	29½	Randy Ingle	180,191	2,689	2003
Greensboro Grasshoppers (Marlins)	51	88	.367	36	Kevin Randel	361,288	5,313	2011

CLUB BATTING

	AVG	G	AB	R	H	2B	3B	HR	RBI	BB	SO	SB	OBP	SLG
Lexington	.269	138	4726	665	1269	261	39	104	596	398	1041	168	.332	.406
West Virginia	.269	139	4522	675	1215	256	43	68	602	494	864	181	.347	.389
Greenville	.268	140	4884	699	1311	282	31	88	623	409	1118	182	.331	.393
Asheville	.267	139	4577	674	1223	276	46	90	593	472	987	258	.341	.407
Hagerstown	.264	138	4478	619	1181	257	40	61	557	418	852	131	.333	.380
Savannah	.263	138	4489	627	1182	212	41	65	543	447	1064	152	.335	.372
Hickory	.256	138	4605	622	1180	223	33	93	554	393	873	95	.320	.380
Lakewood	.256	139	4722	591	1211	257	34	70	522	325	903	105	.314	.370
Delmarva	.249	138	4505	621	1122	257	44	67	571	458	1084	69	.325	.370
Charleston	.248	140	4527	529	1123	234	32	46	452	403	1083	230	.318	.344
Rome	.247	140	4564	525	1126	205	45	40	461	423	995	124	.317	.338
Augusta	.246	139	4650	572	1146	226	37	68	514	442	1087	131	.319	.355
Kannapolis	.245	139	4547	596	1113	228	46	43	515	427	989	152	.314	.344
Greensboro	.238	139	4633	524	1104	198	20	100	473	333	1074	101	.299	.354

CLUB PITCHING

	ERA	G	CG	SHO	SV	IP	H	R	ER	HR	BB	SO	AVG
Savannah	3.12	138	9	14	45	1186	1110	497	411	52	342	1097	.250
Hickory	3.19	138	1	10	42	1215	1106	514	431	72	370	1084	.244
Lakewood	3.26	139	6	9	41	1243	1105	531	451	71	403	927	.240
West Virginia	3.38	139	2	9	40	1204	1111	512	452	85	350	1016	.243
Charleston	3.46	140	6	10	38	1210	1143	564	465	54	476	1161	.251
Augusta	3.54	139	2	10	42	1214	1191	591	478	46	391	1160	.255
Asheville	3.69	139	4	11	45	1227	1244	628	503	74	395	1011	.262
Delmarva	3.75	138	3	12	41	1177	1175	608	491	61	364	891	.259
Greenville	3.93	140	1	8	30	1241	1306	647	542	98	352	940	.272
Hagerstown	4.09	138	0	11	34	1186	1138	649	539	71	448	901	.253
Rome	4.19	140	8	12	35	1195	1169	655	556	63	528	887	.258
Kannapolis	4.36	139	2	13	39	1197	1169	693	580	71	470	985	.255
Greensboro	4.49	139	0	7	34	1212	1248	692	604	95	488	1010	.266
Lexington	4.75	138	0	2	28	1197	1291	758	632	90	465	944	.276

CLUB FIELDING

	PCT	PO	A	E	DP		PCT	PO	A	E	DP
Hickory	.977	3647	1437	121	352	Kannapolis	.971	3591	1428	150	229
West Virginia	.976	3614	1335	121	241	Charleston	.969	3631	1385	163	272
Lakewood	.975	3730	1578	136	294	Delmarva	.968	3533	1473	163	333
Hagerstown	.973	3560	1458	137	298	Greenville	.968	3723	1554	173	373
Savannah	.973	3558	1392	139	285	Lexington	.968	3593	1476	164	229
Greensboro	.972	3636	1498	150	300	Augusta	.966	3644	1457	181	281
Rome	.972	3586	1452	147	287	Asheville	.962	3682	1547	206	317

INDIVIDUAL BATTING LEADERS

Batter, Club	AVG	G	AB	R	H	2B	3B	HR	RBI	BB	SO	SB
Hoelscher, Shane, Asheville	.328	92	348	64	114	37	0	11	61	53	53	14
Guillorme, Luis, Savannah	.318	122	446	67	142	16	0	0	55	54	70	18
Marmolejos-Diaz, Jose, Hagerstown	.310	124	468	63	145	39	5	11	87	35	89	3
Albies, Ozhaino, Rome	.310	98	394	64	122	21	8	0	37	36	56	29
Suiter, Jerrick, West Virginia	.299	105	381	62	114	19	4	3	57	46	59	6
Garcia, Eudor, Savannah	.296	105	398	57	118	23	4	9	59	22	95	5
Meyers, Mike, Greenville	.296	92	345	57	102	18	6	5	40	36	108	12
Escobar, Elvis, West Virginia	.296	124	477	60	141	28	5	5	64	22	79	15
Rodriguez, Herlis, Lakewood	.294	120	445	61	131	20	4	10	61	28	71	16
Toups, Corey, Lexington	.291	102	388	75	113	27	5	7	44	44	82	31

INDIVIDUAL PITCHING LEADERS

Pitcher, Club	W	L	ERA	G	GS	CG	SV	IP	H	R	ER	BB	SO
Garcia, Yeudy, West Virginia	12	5	2.10	30	21	0	1	124	92	36	29	41	112
Reyes, Mark, Augusta	9	6	2.13	23	23	0	0	140	115	42	33	53	89
Maher, Joey, Charleston	7	5	2.20	27	18	0	1	119	87	37	29	29	97
Tarpley, Stephen, West Virginia	11	4	2.48	20	20	1	0	116	108	47	32	25	105
Wiles, Collin, Hickory	11	3	2.96	22	20	0	0	131	114	49	43	23	72
Furney, Sean, Rome	7	8	3.03	21	14	4	0	113	97	41	38	41	63
Garcia, Elniery, Lakewood	8	9	3.23	21	21	0	0	120	125	51	43	36	64
Quintana, Zach, Rome	5	6	3.25	32	17	1	3	114	122	47	41	36	68
Casimiro, Ranfi, Lakewood	9	7	3.35	23	23	2	0	137	127	56	51	30	91
Oswalt, Corey, Savannah	11	5	3.36	23	23	0	0	129	153	59	48	21	99

ALL-STAR TEAM

C: Arturo Rodriguez, Greensboro. **1B:** Jose Marmolejos-Diaz, Hagerstown. **2B:** Yoan Moncada, Greenville. **SS:** Ozhaino Albies, Rome. **3B:** Shane Hoelscher, Asheville. **UT INF:** Luis Guillorme, Savannah. **OF:** Wuilmer Becerra, Savannah; Herlis Rodriguez, Lakewood; **OF:** Michael Suchy, West Virginia. **UT OF:** Omar Carrizales, Asheville. **DH:** K.J. Woods, Greensboro. **RHP:** Yeudy Garcia, West Virginia. **LHP:** Mark Reyes, Augusta. **RP:** Josh Michalec, Asheville. **MVP:** Luis Guillorme, Savannah. **Most Outstanding Pitcher:** Yeudy Garcia, West Virginia. **Most Outstanding Prospect:** Yoan Moncada, Greenville. **Manager:** Jose Leger, Savannah.

DEPARTMENT LEADERS

BATTING

OBP	Hoelscher, Shane, Asheville	.422
SLG	Hoelscher, Shane, Asheville	.529
OPS	Hoelscher, Shane, Asheville	.951
R	Toups, Corey, Lexington	75
H	Marmolejos-Diaz, Jose, Hagerstown	145
TB	Marmolejos-Diaz, Jose, Hagerstown	227
XBH	Marmolejos-Diaz, Jose, Hagerstown	55
2B	Marmolejos-Diaz, Jose, Hagerstown	39
3B	Daris, Joseph, Rome	12
	Mora, John, Savannah	12
HR	O'Hearn, Ryan, Lexington	19
	Rodriguez, Arturo, Greensboro	19
RBI	Marmolejos-Diaz, Jose, Hagerstown	87
SAC	Jean, Luis, Asheville	19
BB	Davidson, Braxton, Rome	84
HBP	Tomscha, Damek, Lakewood	22
SO	Aune, Austin, Charleston	167
SB	Mateo, Jorge, Charleston	71
CS	Escobar, Elvis, West Virginia	21
AB/SO	Pinto, Eduard, Hickory	16.62

PITCHING

G	Michalec, Josh, Asheville	55
GS	Castellani, Ryan, Asheville	27
	Coley, Austin, West Virginia	27
	Mader, Michael, Greensboro	27
	McRae, Alex, West Virginia	27
	Rodriguez, Helmis, Asheville	27
GF	Michalec, Josh, Asheville	47
SV	Michalec, Josh, Asheville	30
W	Coley, Austin, West Virginia	16
L	Kamplain, Justin, Greenville	14
	Martinez, Luis, Kannapolis	14
IP	Lowry, Thaddius, Kannapolis	151
H	Jimenez, Dedgar, Greenville	160
R	Fernandez, Jeffry, Greenville	86
ER	Fernandez, Jeffry, Greenville	76
	McRae, Alex, West Virginia	76
HB	Rodriguez, Helmis, Asheville	19
BB	Bach, Connor, Hagerstown	69
SO	Howard, Sam, Asheville	122
SO/9	Howard, Sam, Asheville	8.19
SO/9 (RP)	Baldonado, Alberto, Savannah	11.75
BB/9	Oswalt, Corey, Savannah	1.47
WP	Grosser, Alec, Rome	25
BK	Garcia, Elniery, Lakewood	5
	Sanchez, Ricardo, Rome	5
HR	Coley, Austin, West Virginia	18
AVG	Maher, Joey, Charleston	.200

FIELDING

C PCT	Read, Raudy, Hagerstown	.995
PO	Nunez, Dom, Asheville	742
A	Grullon, Deivi, Lakewood	112
DP	Trevino, Jose, Hickory	7
E	Nunez, Dom, Asheville	16
PB	Gushue, Taylor, West Virginia	24
1B PCT	Ewing, Skyler, Augusta	.992
PO	Ewing, Skyler, Augusta	946
A	Ewing, Skyler, Augusta	74
DP	Ewing, Skyler, Augusta	70
E	Duenez, Samir, Lexington	13
2B PCT	Johnson, Jonathan, Savannah	.980
PO	Reyes, Pablo, West Virginia	187
A	Reyes, Pablo, West Virginia	249
DP	Moncada, Yoan, Greenville	62
E	Moncada, Yoan, Greenville	23
3B PCT	Edgerton, Jordan, Rome	.929
PO	Edgerton, Jordan, Rome	76
A	Schales, Brian, Greensboro	264
DP	Schales, Brian, Greensboro	21
E	Arenado, Jonah, Augusta	29
SS PCT	Guillorme, Luis, Savannah	.972
PO	Guerra, Javier, Greenville	192
A	Guerra, Javier, Greenville	362
DP	Guerra, Javier, Greenville	78
E	Jimenez, Emerson, Asheville	31
OF PCT	Norwood, John, Greensboro	.996
PO	Cardona, Jose, Hickory	294
A	Rodriguez, Herlis, Lakewood	22
DP	Rodriguez, Herlis, Lakewood	6
E	Daris, Joseph, Rome	9
	Escalera-Maldonado, Alfredo, Lexington	9

MINOR LEAGUES

BY MICHAEL LANANNA

After 37 years based in New York, the Jamestown Jammers moved to Morgantown, W. Va., before the 2015 season and—via fan vote—became the West Virginia Black Bears.

The move paid massive dividends.

In their first season in the short-season New York-Penn League, the Black Bears won the league championship, taking down Staten Island in two games. The championship marked an overwhelmingly successful debut for the Pirates' affiliate and for first-year manager Wyatt Toregas. It also marked the first time in seven appearances that Staten Island did not win the championship series.

It wasn't an easy road for the Black Bears, who had to defeat a prospect-laden Williamsport team in three games to reach the finals, then had to face Yankees first-round pick James Kaprielian in the series-clinching game.

The Black Bears, at one point, had a 2015 first-rounder of their own in shortstop Kevin Newman, before he got the call to low Class A West Virginia. As is usually the case, the league featured several first-rounders, but very few made an immediate impact this summer outside of the No. 1 prospect in the league—Red Sox draftee Andrew Benintendi.

Benintendi, the College Player of the Year at Arkansas and seventh overall pick, took the league by storm, hitting .290/.408/.540 with seven home runs in 124 at-bats. He played just 35 games for Lowell before moving to low Class A Greenville.

"He really knew how to play," Brooklyn manager Tom Gamboa said. "There was no mistake, just with pure hitting ability, he might have the best swing that I've seen this year in the league."

It was international talent, however, that domi-

TOP 20 PROSPECTS

1. Andrew Benintendi, of, Lowell (Red Sox)
2. Victor Robles, of, Auburn (Nationals)
3. Domingo Acevedo, rhp, Staten Island (Yankees)
4. Erick Fedde, rhp, Auburn (Nationals)
5. Franklyn Kilome, rhp, Williamsport (Phillies)
6. Luis Alexander Basabe, of, Lowell (Red Sox)
7. Kevin Newman, ss, West Virginia (Pirates)
8. Richie Martin, ss, Vermont (Athletics)
9. D.J. Stewart, of, Aberdeen (Orioles)
10. Jhalan Jackson, of, Staten Island (Yankees)
11. Stone Garrett, of, Batavia (Marlins)
12. Tyler Alexander, lhp, Connecticut (Tigers)
13. Jose Pujols, of, Williamsport (Phillies)
14. Brandon Koch, rhp, Hudson Valley (Rays)
15. Anfernee Seymour, ss, Batavia (Marlins)
16. Jacob Evans, lhp, State College (Cardinals)
17. Mikey White, ss, Vermont (Athletics)
18. Kyle Holder, ss, Staten Island (Yankees)
19. Josh Tobias, 2b, Williamsport (Phillies)
20. Mark Mathias, 2b, Mahoning Valley (Indians)

nated the top 10.

Victor Robles, an 18-year-old outfielder, tore up the rookie-level Gulf Coast League and continued to torment pitchers after a promotion to Auburn, hitting .343/.424/.479 in 140 at-bats. Another teenage outfielder, 19-year-old Luis Alexander Basabe, flashed some power with seven home runs for Lowell, creating an exciting outfield tandem with Benintendi.

On the mound, 6-foot-7 Staten Island right-hander Domingo Acevedo routinely pushed triple-digits with his fastball while mixing in a plus changeup and a developing slider. Meanwhile, Williamsport righthander Franklyn Kilome took another step forward and bumped 97 mph.

The general consensus among scouts was that the talent in 2015 didn't match the 2014 crop, which included the likes of current Mets big league outfielder Michael Conforto and 2015 Minor League Player of the Year runner-up A.J. Reed.

OVERALL STANDINGS

McNamara Division	W	L	PCT	GB	Manager(s)	Attendance	Average	Last Pennant
Staten Island Yankees (Yankees)	41	34	.547	—	Pat Osborn	119,195	3,221	2011
Aberdeen IronBirds (Orioles)	40	36	.526	1½	Luis Pujols	151,758	4,216	1983
Hudson Valley Renegades (Rays)	39	37	.513	2½	Tim Parenton	163,767	4,426	2012
Brooklyn Cyclones (Mets)	33	43	.434	8½	Tom Gamboa	230,658	6,234	2001

Pinckney Division	W	L	PCT	GB	Manager(s)	Attendance	Average	Last pennant
Williamsport Crosscutters (Phillies)	46	30	.605	—	Pat Borders	134,927	3,647	2003
West Virginia Black Bears (Pirates)	42	34	.553	4	Wyatt Toregas	83,796	2,265	2015
State College Spikes (Cardinals)	41	35	.539	5	Johnny Rodriguez	127,775	3,363	2014
Auburn Doubledays (Nationals)	36	38	.486	9	Gary Cathcart	50,670	1,408	2007
Batavia Muckdogs (Marlins)	31	44	.413	14½	Angel Espada	32,221	921	2008
Mahoning Valley Scrappers (Indians)	31	44	.413	14½	Travis Fryman	111,079	3,002	2004

Stedler Division	W	L	PCT	GB	Manager(s)	Attendance	Average	Last pennant
Tri-City ValleyCats (Astros)	42	33	.560	—	Ed Romero	153,692	4,269	2013
Lowell Spinners (Red Sox)	37	39	.487	5½	Joe Oliver	140,468	3,796	Never
Connecticut Tigers (Tigers)	35	38	.479	6	Mike Rabelo	78,588	2,311	1998
Vermont Lake Monsters (Athletics)	33	42	.440	9	Aaron Nieckula	83,002	2,243	1996

Playoffs—Semifinals: West Virginia defeated Williamsport 2-1 and Staten Island defeated Tri-City 2-0 in best-of-three series; **Finals:** West Virginia defeated Staten Island 2-0 in a best-of-three series.

MINOR LEAGUES

CLUB BATTING

	AVG	G	AB	R	H	2B	3B	HR	RBI	BB	SO	SB	OBP	SLG
Auburn	.267	74	2487	357	665	136	27	24	307	210	524	66	.335	.373
Tri-City	.261	75	2537	365	661	128	14	38	318	297	569	78	.345	.367
Mahoning Valley	.259	75	2553	319	660	133	19	26	287	201	495	58	.321	.356
West Virginia	.259	76	2541	352	659	109	21	16	299	265	542	56	.338	.338
Williamsport	.257	76	2578	336	662	119	17	35	296	216	536	84	.319	.357
State College	.256	76	2588	322	663	123	23	19	288	256	490	40	.329	.344
Batavia	.252	75	2463	295	621	124	17	25	255	221	590	63	.320	.347
Hudson Valley	.252	76	2587	303	652	157	26	19	266	215	645	99	.320	.355
Staten Island	.252	75	2546	344	641	128	18	32	293	235	562	72	.322	.354
Connecticut	.249	73	2485	284	619	88	27	29	258	213	494	29	.312	.341
Vermont	.242	75	2497	316	605	117	15	39	289	247	551	30	.320	.348
Aberdeen	.239	76	2591	284	618	118	20	23	255	178	571	40	.298	.326
Lowell	.237	76	2539	344	603	112	25	31	296	251	649	89	.312	.338
Brooklyn	.220	76	2492	263	548	111	13	26	230	216	684	51	.294	.306

CLUB PITCHING

	ERA	G	CGSHO	SV	IP	H	R	ER	HR	BB	SO	AVG
Hudson Valley	3.07	76	0	3	19	679	635	296	232	33	164	595	.246
Williamsport	3.15	76	1	4	25	680	624	276	238	25	247	564	.246
State College	3.20	76	0	9	24	677	661	285	241	21	203	552	.259
Brooklyn	3.25	76	1	6	19	676	574	303	244	22	245	611	.227
Staten Island	3.26	75	0	3	25	670	629	293	243	28	225	602	.247
Connecticut	3.38	73	0	3	21	639	589	297	240	26	197	535	.243
West Virginia	3.51	76	0	4	25	679	611	309	265	30	213	599	.238
Aberdeen	3.58	76	1	7	23	677	633	298	269	24	216	577	.248
Lowell	3.61	76	1	4	20	678	635	332	272	36	285	553	.246
Tri-City	3.79	75	0	7	17	660	660	320	278	35	211	635	.259
Batavia	4.00	75	1	6	18	649	689	381	289	20	259	570	.268
Mahoning Valley	4.06	75	0	5	12	653	628	356	295	28	298	488	.253
Vermont	4.15	75	0	6	16	652	640	377	301	31	237	519	.255
Auburn	4.21	74	0	4	19	639	669	361	299	23	221	502	.268

CLUB FIELDING

	PCT	PO	A	E	DP		PCT	PO	A	E	DP
Aberdeen	.977	2031	808	67	191	Hudson	.967	2038	796	97	172
State College	.975	2031	813	74	188	Lowell	.967	2036	736	94	183
Tri-City	.975	1982	687	69	140	Brooklyn	.966	2028	825	100	159
Staten Island	.971	2011	793	84	151	Mahoning Valley	.964	1960	838	105	174
West Virginia	.971	2038	861	87	166	Auburn	.960	1918	742	111	169
Connecticut	.970	1919	834	85	187	Vermont	.956	1956	780	126	178
Williamsport	.969	2042	780	91	192	Batavia	.950	1949	815	145	155

INDIVIDUAL BATTING LEADERS

Batter, Club	AVG	G	AB	R	H	2B	3B	HR	RBI	BB	SO	SB
Wernes, Bobby, Tri-City	.346	53	188	32	65	8	0	0	29	27	27	3
Allen, Will, Connecticut	.324	57	204	28	66	13	0	2	31	20	43	0
Tobias, Josh, Williamsport	.321	61	240	31	77	19	3	4	37	14	42	12
Grayson, Casey, State College	.308	73	250	40	77	18	2	2	38	46	64	1
Gutierrez, Kelvin, Auburn	.305	62	239	31	73	21	1	1	30	16	52	2
Kramer, Kevin, West Virginia	.305	46	177	34	54	7	3	0	17	25	28	9
Tolman, Mitchell, West Virginia	.304	63	224	32	68	16	4	0	23	33	38	2
Garrett, Stone, Batavia	.297	58	222	36	66	18	6	11	46	19	60	8
Hill, Logan, West Virginia	.297	60	219	33	65	13	3	7	45	28	51	13
McCall, Dexture, Tri-City	.295	59	200	26	59	9	0	4	37	25	59	0

INDIVIDUAL PITCHING LEADERS

Pitcher, Club	W	L	ERA	G	GS	CG	SV	IP	H	R	ER	BB	SO
Watkins, Spenser, Connecticut	5	4	2.23	12	12	0	0	65	45	21	16	19	55
Gueller, Mitch, Williamsport	10	1	2.23	12	12	1	0	69	57	22	17	23	44
Agrazal, Dario, West Virginia	6	5	2.72	14	14	0	0	76	71	27	23	11	45
Cedeno, Luis, Staten Island	5	3	2.73	13	12	0	1	66	68	28	20	20	51
Brubaker, Jonathan, West Virginia	6	4	2.82	15	15	0	0	73	57	26	23	12	49
Holloway, Jordan, Batavia	5	6	2.91	14	14	0	0	68	60	27	22	36	40
Ramirez, Roel, Hudson Valley	4	3	2.97	13	13	0	0	70	67	27	23	11	43
Badamo, Tyler, Brooklyn	5	6	3.10	14	14	0	0	81	61	33	28	22	66
Rodriguez, Jorge L., State College	5	4	3.11	14	14	0	0	75	66	30	26	28	47
Arteaga, Alejandro, Williamsport	4	3	3.11	13	13	0	0	72	69	28	25	21	51

DEPARTMENT LEADERS

BATTING

OBP	Wernes, Bobby, Tri-City	.434
SLG	Garrett, Stone, Batavia	.581
OPS	Garrett, Stone, Batavia	.933
R	Sewald, Johnny, Tri-City	57
H	Grayson, Casey, State College	77
	Tobias, Josh, Williamsport	77
TB	Garrett, Stone, Batavia	129
XBH	Garrett, Stone, Batavia	35
2B	Gutierrez, Kelvin, Auburn	21
	Haynal, Brad, Batavia	21
3B	Mizell, Aaron, Tri-City	7
	Valera, Junior, Staten Island	7
HR	Garrett, Stone, Batavia	11
RBI	Garrett, Stone, Batavia	46
SAC	Kelley, Christian, West Virginia	9
BB	Grayson, Casey, State College	46
	Sewald, Johnny, Tri-City	46
HBP	Robles, Victor, Auburn	14
	Russell, Michael, Hudson Valley	14
SO	Iriart, Chris, Vermont	86
SB	Sewald, Johnny, Tri-City	31
CS	Coppola, Zachary, Williamsport	11
AB/SO	Marabell, Connor, Mahoning Valley	13.53

PITCHING

G	Echemendia, Pedro, State College	26
GS	Brubaker, Jonathan, West Virginia	15
GF	Tasin, Robert, Williamsport	22
SV	Tasin, Robert, Williamsport	17
W	Gueller, Mitch, Williamsport	10
L	Lovegrove, Kieran, Mahoning Valley	8
IP	Badamo, Tyler, Brooklyn	81
H	Martinez, Dailyn, State College	84
R	Lovegrove, Kieran, Mahoning Valley	50
ER	Edwards, Chase, Connecticut	46
HB	Almonte, Jose, Lowell	11
BB	Linares, Leandro, Mahoning Valley	44
SO	Canelon, Kevin, Brooklyn	70
SO/9	Rodriguez, Jefry, Auburn	8.78
SO/9 (RP)	Koch, Brandon, Hudson Valley	13.08
BB/9	Agrazal, Dario, West Virginia	1.3
WP	Holloway, Jordan, Batavia	15
BK	Martinez, Dailyn, State College	6
HR	Ott, Travis, Hudson Valley	6
	Pimentel, Cesilio, West Virginia	6
AVG	Almonte, Jose, Lowell	.171

FIELDING

C PCT	de Oleo, Eduardo, Staten Island	.992
PO	Kelley, Christian, West Virginia	382
A	Kelley, Christian, West Virginia	52
DP	Kelley, Christian, West Virginia	7
E	Anderson, Blake, Batavia	9
PB	Hawkins, Taylor, Hudson Valley	17
1B PCT	Laurino, Steve, Aberdeen	.995
PO	Laurino, Steve, Aberdeen	638
A	Grayson, Casey, State College	48
DP	Laurino, Steve, Aberdeen	60
E	Ockimey, Josh, Lowell	13
2B PCT	Turbin, Drew, Aberdeen	.991
PO	Mathias, Mark, Mahoning Valley	129
A	Turbin, Drew, Aberdeen	219
DP	Mathias, Mark, Mahoning Valley	46
	Turbin, Drew, Aberdeen	46
E	Lopez, Jesus, Vermont	10
	Mackenzie, Patrick, Connecticut	10
3B PCT	Wernes, Bobby, Tri-City	.976
PO	Gutierrez, Kelvin, Auburn	50
A	Tolman, Mitchell, West Virginia	108
DP	Wernes, Bobby, Tri-City	10
E	Gutierrez, Kelvin, Auburn	18
SS PCT	Holder, Kyle, Staten Island	.970
PO	Castro, Willi, Mahoning Valley	123
A	Reyes, Alfredo, Brooklyn	205
DP	Castro, Willi, Mahoning Valley	41
E	Seymour, Anfernee, Batavia	29
OF PCT	Hendrix, Jeff, Staten Island	.993
PO	Sewald, Johnny, Tri-City	153
A	Basabe, Luis Alexander, Lowell	8
	Odenwaelder, Mike, Aberdeen	8
	Spitz, Thomas, State College	8
DP	Basabe, Luis Alexander, Lowell	4
E	Moscat, Galvi, Batavia	10

MINOR LEAGUES

BY VINCE LARA-CINISOMO

While their parent Diamondbacks were rebuilding, short-season Hillsboro built something special.

The Hops won their second straight Northwest League title, defeating Tri-City, a Padres affiliate.

"To get a bunch of guys at a low-level minor league team to commit themselves to winning is special," Hops manager Shelley Duncan told MiLB.com after the series. "The credit really should go to the players. For them to sacrifice some of their personal numbers and statistics and to give themselves to winning baseball games is a very special quality."

Since moving from Yakima in 2013, Hillsboro has won four straight division titles and back-to-back championships.

The Hops, managed by former big leaguer Duncan in his managerial debut, were led by No. 1 overall pick Dansby Swanson and league pitcher of the year Carlos Hernandez.

The Hops also had lefty Jared Miller before his promotion and big lefthander Cody Reed.

Hernandez, 21, was 6-3, 2.35, which was the best mark in the NWL. He pitched 85 1/3 innings, his most since signing in 2012.

Hernandez struck out 12 in Game Two of the league semifinals after Salem-Keizer had won Game One.

"I can't deny it. I knew had a responsibility on me, so I had to just try to do my best," he told reporters. "I know that they have a lot of hope in me, but I knew they would back me up if something happened, of course. They scored a lot runs early in the game and opened it up, so that helped a lot."

Hillsboro won the next game to take the series, while Tri-City swept Everett (Mariners).

Salem-Keizer, which fell to Hillsboro in the semifinals, relied on its power. It led the NWL in homers, thanks to first-rounder Chris Shaw.

Everett was led by third-round pick Braden Bishop, who hit .319 and is an athletic center fielder. The AquaSox had shortstop Drew Jackson, who hit an NWL-best .367 and led the league in steals with 47.

Eugene had a solid pitching staff led by lefthanders Carson Sands and Justin Steele and an outfield that included Ian Happ, Eloy Jimenez and Donnie Dewees.

Other standouts include Tri-City righthander Phil Maton, a 20th-rounder who compiled a fantastic 54/5 SO/BB ratio, Hillsboro's Taylor Clarke, the Colonial Athletic Association pitcher of the year while at College of Charleston and Boise's Kevin Padlo.

TOP 20 PROSPECTS

1. Dansby Swanson, ss, Hillsboro (Diamondbacks)
2. Ian Happ, of, Eugene (Cubs)
3. Eloy Jimenez, of, Eugene (Cubs)
4. Alex Jackson, of, Everett (Mariners)
5. Drew Jackson, ss, Everett (Mariners)
6. Taylor Clarke, rhp, Hillsboro (Diamondbacks)
7. Andrew Moore, rhp, Everett (Mariners)
8. Chris Shaw, 1b, Salem-Keizer (Giants)
9. Cody Reed, lhp, Hillsboro (Diamondbacks)
10. Kevin Padlo, 3b, Boise (Rockies)
11. Donnie Dewees, of, Eugene (Cubs)
12. Justin Steele, lhp, Eugene (Cubs)
13. Carson Sands, lhp, Eugene (Cubs)
14. Carlos Herrera, ss, Boise (Rockies)
15. Enyel de los Santos, rhp, Everett (Mariners)
16. Oscar de la Cruz, rhp, Eugene (Cubs)
17. Luiz Gohara, lhp, Everett (Mariners)
18. Jon Harris, rhp, Vancouver (Blue Jays)
19. Pedro Araujo, rhp, Eugene (Cubs)
20. Carlos Hernandez, rhp, Hillsboro (Diamondbacks)

STANDINGS: SPLIT SEASON

FIRST HALF

NORTH	W	L	PCT	GB
Tri-City	22	16	.579	—
Everett	22	16	.579	—
Spokane	19	19	.500	3
Vancouver	16	22	.421	6

SOUTH	W	L	PCT	GB
Hillsboro	22	16	.579	—
Salem-Keizer	20	18	.526	2
Eugene	17	21	.447	5
Boise	14	24	.368	8

SECOND HALF

NORTH	W	L	PCT	GB
Everett	20	18	.526	—
Tri-City	20	18	.526	—
Vancouver	18	20	.474	2
Spokane	15	23	.395	5

SOUTH	W	L	PCT	GB
Hillsboro	23	15	.605	—
Eugene	21	17	.553	2
Salem-Keizer	19	19	.500	4
Boise	16	22	.421	7

Playoffs—Semifinals: Tri-City defeated Everett 2-0 and Hillsboro defeated Salem-Keizer 2-1 in best-of-three series; **Finals:** Hillsboro defeated Tri-City 2-1 in a best-of-three series.

OVERALL STANDINGS

Team (Organization)	W	L	PCT	GB	Manager(s)	Attendance	Average	Last Pennant
Hillsboro Hops (Diamondbacks)	45	31	.592	—	Shelley Duncan	143,412	3,774	2015
Everett AquaSox (Mariners)	42	34	.553	3	Rob Mummau	100,613	2,648	2010
Tri-City Dust Devils (Padres)	42	34	.553	3	R. Wine/A. Contreras	86,022	2,264	Never
Salem-Keizer Volcanoes (Giants)	39	37	.513	6	Kyle Haines	85,851	2,259	2009
Eugene Emeralds (Cubs)	38	38	.500	7	Gary Van Tol	120,931	3,182	1980
Spokane Indians (Rangers)	34	42	.447	11	Tim Hulett	188,956	5,107	2008
Vancouver Canadians (Blue Jays)	34	42	.447	11	John Schneider	215,535	5,825	2013
Boise Hawks (Rockies)	30	46	.395	15	Frank Gonzales	109,945	2,893	2004

MINOR LEAGUES

CLUB BATTING

	AVG	G	AB	R	H	2B	3B	HR	RBI	BB	SO	SB	OBP	SLG
Boise	.261	76	2564	354	668	134	22	35	299	271	636	172	.337	.371
Salem-Keizer	.261	76	2611	350	681	126	19	60	310	229	562	52	.327	.393
Everett	.258	76	2562	392	660	129	15	43	337	256	599	131	.334	.370
Eugene	.250	76	2569	330	643	139	15	27	294	246	605	74	.321	.348
Tri-City	.249	76	2530	390	631	129	13	28	332	357	658	83	.351	.344
Vancouver	.243	76	2589	350	630	122	16	36	308	256	624	85	.320	.345
Spokane	.239	76	2559	320	612	134	21	36	278	254	675	74	.318	.350
Hillsboro	.238	76	2574	314	612	143	19	32	273	236	584	67	.309	.345

CLUB PITCHING

	ERA	G	CGSHO	SV	IP	H	R	ER	HR	BB	SO	AVG
Hillsboro	3.27	76	1 11	24	684	571	292	249	31	253	681	.225
Eugene	3.55	76	0 5	18	671	594	333	265	29	234	691	.234
Tri-City	3.56	76	1 4	17	665	592	311	263	37	227	675	.236
Salem-Keizer	3.66	76	1 5	19	678	697	350	276	37	239	602	.265
Vancouver	3.95	76	0 4	16	676	682	350	297	32	315	555	.265
Everett	3.97	76	0 4	27	679	621	353	300	50	289	668	.244
Spokane	4.24	76	0 6	13	677	666	387	319	42	299	568	.258
Boise	4.58	76	0 3	15	670	714	424	341	39	249	503	.271

CLUB FIELDING

	PCT	PO	A	E	DP		PCT	PO	A	E	DP
Everett	.972	2038	755	79	168	Vancouver	.968	2028	823	94	224
Tri-City	.971	1997	739	82	170	Spokane	.966	2033	857	103	162
Eugene	.969	2014	771	90	134	Boise	.962	2012	879	114	214
Hillsboro	.969	2053	737	88	122	Salem-Keizer	.960	2034	803	117	146

INDIVIDUAL BATTING LEADERS

Batter, Club	AVG	G	AB	R	H	2B	3B	HR	RBI	BB	SO	SB
Jackson, Drew, Everett	.358	59	226	64	81	12	1	2	26	30	35	47
Bishop, Braden, Everett	.320	56	219	34	70	8	1	2	22	5	33	13
Gomez, Miguel, Salem-Keizer	.319	66	276	30	88	14	1	6	52	5	24	0
Atkinson, Justin, Vancouver	.294	52	214	25	63	12	1	3	33	8	44	2
Padlo, Kevin, Boise	.294	70	255	44	75	22	2	9	46	45	62	33
France, Ty, Tri-City	.294	66	235	36	69	20	0	1	36	43	50	4
Duggar, Steven, Salem-Keizer	.293	58	229	40	67	12	1	1	27	35	52	6
Vizcaino, Jose, Salem-Keizer	.288	48	184	31	53	11	1	6	23	15	34	5
Jimenez, Eloy, Eugene	.284	57	232	36	66	10	0	7	33	15	43	3
Clark, LeDarious, Spokane	.276	65	257	46	71	12	7	8	24	26	73	29

INDIVIDUAL PITCHING LEADERS

Pitcher, Club	W	L	ERA	G	GS	CG	SV	IP	H	R	ER	BB	SO
Hernandez, Carlos, Hillsboro	6	3	2.32	15	15	0	0	85	58	24	22	27	93
Leenhouts, Andrew, Salem-Keizer	7	4	2.37	14	14	1	0	76	75	29	20	21	54
De La Cruz, Oscar, Eugene	6	3	2.84	13	13	0	0	73	56	27	23	17	73
Lanphere, Luke, Spokane	3	1	3.18	13	10	0	0	68	58	31	24	13	48
Riggs, Nolan, Salem-Keizer	4	3	3.23	15	10	0	0	61	56	33	22	22	49
Reed, Cody, Hillsboro	5	4	3.27	15	14	0	0	63	51	29	23	21	72
Connolly, Michael, Salem-Keizer	4	3	3.66	13	13	0	0	71	75	31	29	16	58
Bolton, Tyler, Hillsboro	2	4	3.89	16	15	0	0	83	94	45	36	21	56
Sawyer, Logan, Boise	4	4	4.11	11	10	0	0	61	61	33	28	22	41
Rios, Francisco, Vancouver	3	6	4.27	15	12	0	0	65	72	36	31	25	59

DEPARTMENT LEADERS

BATTING

OBP	Jackson, Drew, Everett	.432
SLG	Shaw, Christopher, Salem-Keizer	.551
OPS	Padlo, Kevin, Boise	.906
R	Jackson, Drew, Everett	64
H	Gomez, Miguel, Salem-Keizer	88
TB	Padlo, Kevin, Boise	128
XBH	Padlo, Kevin, Boise	33
2B	Padlo, Kevin, Boise	22
3B	Clark, LeDarious, Spokane	7
HR	Shaw, Christopher, Salem-Keizer	12
RBI	Gomez, Miguel, Salem-Keizer	52
SAC	Bishop, Braden, Everett	11
BB	Spivey, Seth, Spokane	39
HBP	France, Ty, Tri-City	12
	Jackson, Alex, Everett	12
SO	Belen, Carlos, Tri-City	113
SB	Jackson, Drew, Everett	47
CS	Clark, LeDarious, Spokane	9
	Cowan, Jordan, Everett	9
AB/SO	Gomez, Miguel, Salem-Keizer	11.50

PITCHING

G	Case, Andrew, Vancouver	27
GS	Bolton, Tyler, Hillsboro	15
	Hernandez, Carlos, Hillsboro	15
	Mejia, Angel, Tri-City	15
GF	Case, Andrew, Vancouver	24
SV	Case, Andrew, Vancouver	10
W	Leenhouts, Andrew, Salem-Keizer	7
	Miller, Jared, Hillsboro	7
L	Gohara, Luiz, Everett	7
IP	Hernandez, Carlos, Hillsboro	85
H	Bolton, Tyler, Hillsboro	94
R	Lezama, Angel, Boise	48
ER	Gohara, Luiz, Everett	37
	Mejia, Angel, Tri-City	37
HB	Beltre, Dario, Spokane	8
	Gillies, Darin, Everett	8
	Villarroel, Cesar, Boise	8
BB	Gohara, Luiz, Everett	32
	Kraft, Michael, Vancouver	32
SO	Hernandez, Carlos, Hillsboro	93
SO/9	Reed, Cody, Hillsboro	10.23
SO/9 (RP)	Maton, Phil, Tri-City	15.98
BB/9	Lanphere, Luke, Spokane	1.72
WP	Paulino, Jose, Eugene	14
BK	De La Cruz, Oscar, Eugene	5
HR	Santiago, Jose, Everett	9
AVG	Hernandez, Carlos, Hillsboro	.193

FIELDING

C PCT	Quevedo, Johan, Everett	.994
PO	Allen, Austin, Tri-City	427
A	Lacrus, Sherman, Spokane	53
DP	Sanchez, Tyler, Spokane	4
E	Pujadas, Fernando, Salem-Keizer	7
PB	Alamo, Tyler, Eugene	13
1B PCT	Mitsui, Trevor, Hillsboro	.998
PO	France, Ty, Tri-City	528
A	Mundell, Brian, Boise	35
DP	Mundell, Brian, Boise	50
E	Mundell, Brian, Boise	11
2B PCT	Amion, Richard, Salem-Keizer	.963
PO	Amion, Richard, Salem-Keizer	109
A	Amion, Richard, Salem-Keizer	152
DP	Delarosa, Frandy, Eugene	30
E	Delarosa, Frandy, Eugene	15
3B PCT	Padlo, Kevin, Boise	.948
PO	Forbes, Ti'Quan, Spokane	36
A	Padlo, Kevin, Boise	129
DP	Hale, Conner, Everett	13
E	Belen, Carlos, Tri-City	21
SS PCT	Van Gansen, Peter, Tri-City	.980
PO	Jackson, Drew, Everett	85
A	Yrizarri, Yeyson, Everett	178
DP	Van Gansen, Peter, Tri-City	37
E	Herrera, Carlos, Boise	23
OF PCT	Bishop, Braden, Everett	.992
PO	Boykin, Rod, Tri-City	151
A	Guillotte, Andrew, Vancouver	9
	Jackson, Alex, Everett	9
DP	Potts, Jamie, Spokane	4
E	Clark, LeDarious, Spokane	7

MINOR LEAGUES

BY HUDSON BELINSKY

As the Houston Astros made headway at the major league level in 2015, their minor league system showed no signs of slowing down. The Greeneville Astros, powered by top draft picks Daz Cameron and Kyle Tucker—Nos. 5 and 37 overall—won a pair of early-September series to secure their first Appalachian League title since 2004.

Greeneville thrived under pressure. Entering the final day of the regular season, the Astros needed a win to secure a spot in the postseason, and they got a combined shutout from lefthander Salvador Montano and righty Albert Abreu (the No. 6 prospect in the league). In the first round of the playoffs, Greeneville lost Game One to Kingsport, before battling back to win two elimination games and advance to the Appalachian League championship series, in which Greeneville faced the same situation after a Game One loss to the Princeton Rays.

The Astros battled back in the final series, coming back from a five-run deficit at Princeton in Game 2, and clinching the Appalchian League crown with an 8-7 victory. Tucker, the no. 1 prospect in the league, went off in the postseason, going 9-for-24 and slugging three home runs.

Greeneville had three of the league's top six prospects, as well as a strong core of polished rookies coming straight from college. Since the signing deadline for draft picks was moved up, the Appalachian League has become a breeding ground for advanced draftees. In 2015, seven of the league's top 20 prospects had been drafted in the top three rounds.

Danville third baseman Austin Riley saw his stock rise more than any prospect in the league. Riley, who entered the spring of his senior year considered more of a pitching prospect, showed power and the ability to make adjustments, and rose to No. 2 in the league.

TOP 20 PROSPECTS

1. Kyle Tucker, of, Greeneville (Astros)
2. Austin Riley, 3b, Danville (Braves)
3. Jermaine Palacios, ss, Elizabethton (Twins)
4. Magneuris Sierra, of, Johnson City (Cardinals)
5. Daz Cameron, of, Greeneville (Astros)
6. Albert Abreu, rhp, Greeneville (Astros)
7. Luis Carpio, ss/2b, Kingsport (Mets)
8. Mike Soroka, rhp, Danville (Braves)
9. Edmundo Sosa, ss, Johnson City (Cardinals)
10. Eliezer Alvarez, 2b, Johnson City (Cardinals)
11. Ashe Russell, rhp, Burlington (Royals)
12. Hoy Jun Park, ss, Pulaski (Yankees)
13. Ryan Helsley, rhp, Johnson City (Cardinals)
14. Ronald Acuna, of, Danville (Braves)
15. Travis Blankenhorn, 3b, Elizabethton (Twins)
16. Nolan Watson, rhp, Burlington (Royals)
17. LaMonte Wade, of, Elizabethton (Twins)
18. David Rodriguez, c, Princeton (Rays)
19. Nick Wells, lhp, Bluefield (Blue Jays)
20. Carlos Munoz, 1b, Bristol (Pirates)

Besides Riley, several international prospects showed significant improvements in the Appalachian League this summer. Twins prospect Jermaine Palacios showed outstanding potential with his aggressive righthanded bat and up-the-middle defensive profile.

Despite the boffo group of Astros headlining the league's top prospects, the Johnson City Cardinals might have had the most prospect-laden team, with international youngsters Magneuris Sierra, Edmundo Sosa and Eliezer Alvarez fitting in the top 10, righthander Ryan Helsley ranking at No. 13, and Ronnie Williams and Chris Chinea receiving consideration for the back of the top 20. Fourth-round pick Paul DeJong would have been in the top 20 too, but his advanced bat encouraged the Cardinals so much that they sent him to low Class A Peoria after just 45 plate appearances in Johnson City.

Burlington also housed the Royals' two top picks: high school righthanders Ashe Russell (No. 21 overall) and Nolan Watson (No. 33 overall, in supplemental round one).

OVERALL STANDINGS

EAST	W	L	PCT	GB	Manager(s)	Attendance	Average	Last Pennant
Pulaski Yankees (Yankees)	45	23	.662	—	Tony Franklin	57,023	1,677	2013
Princeton Rays (Rays)	37	31	.544	8	Danny Sheaffer	27,051	820	1994
Danville Braves (Braves)	34	34	.500	11	Rocket Wheeler	28,841	874	2009
Burlington Royals (Royals)	31	37	.456	14	Scott Thorman	46,063	1,355	1993
Bluefield Blue Jays (Blue Jays)	25	42	.373	19 ½	Dennis Holmberg	24,099	803	2001

WEST	W	L	PCT	GB	Manager(s)	Attendance	Average	Last pennant
Kingsport Mets (Mets)	40	28	.588	—	Luis Rivera	31,086	942	1995
Greeneville Astros (Astros)	34	33	.507	5 ½	Lamarr Rogers	54,252	1,644	2015
Elizabethton Twins (Twins)	34	34	.500	6	Ray Smith	22,069	712	2012
Bristol Pirates (Pirates)	29	36	.446	9 ½	Edgar Varela	17,849	637	2002
Johnson City Cardinals (Cardinals)	27	38	.415	11 ½	Chris Swauger	39,118	1,304	2014

Playoffs—Semifinals: Princeton defeated Pulaski 2-1 and Greeneville defeated Kingsport 2-1 in best-of-three series; **Finals:** Greeneville defeated Princeton 2-1 in a best-of-three series.

CLUB BATTING

	AVG	G	AB	R	H	2B	3B	HR	RBI	BB	SO	SB	OBP	SLG
Boise	.261	76	2564	354	668	134	22	35	299	271	636	172	.337	.371
Salem-Keizer	.261	76	2611	350	681	126	19	60	310	229	562	52	.327	.393
Everett	.258	76	2562	392	660	129	15	43	337	256	599	131	.334	.370
Eugene	.250	76	2569	330	643	139	15	27	294	246	605	74	.321	.348
Tri-City	.249	76	2530	390	631	129	13	28	332	357	658	83	.351	.344
Vancouver	.243	76	2589	350	630	122	16	36	308	256	624	85	.320	.345
Spokane	.239	76	2559	320	612	134	21	36	278	254	675	74	.318	.350
Hillsboro	.238	76	2574	314	612	143	19	32	273	236	584	67	.309	.345

CLUB PITCHING

	ERA	G	CG	SHO	SV	IP	H	R	ER	HR	BB	SO	AVG
Pulaski	3.08	68	0	6	21	591	522	244	202	49	209	618	.233
Greeneville	3.18	67	1	5	14	588	528	255	208	29	199	515	.236
Danville	3.54	68	0	2	21	589	547	300	232	29	220	521	.244
Elizabethton	3.62	68	0	5	14	591	589	305	238	36	190	579	.258
Princeton	4.07	68	0	3	24	594	604	312	269	39	224	516	.266
Kingsport	4.23	68	1	5	19	595	572	331	280	46	247	534	.251
Johnson City	4.37	65	0	2	16	560	589	328	272	50	207	483	.270
Burlington	4.51	68	1	2	14	590	627	374	296	50	225	459	.271
Bluefield	4.52	67	0	4	12	561	619	349	282	37	239	432	.279
Bristol	4.89	65	0	2	12	567	603	366	308	42	232	515	.270

CLUB FIELDING

	PCT	PO	A	E	DP		PCT	PO	A	E	DP
Pulaski	.970	1773	565	73	114	Princeton	.965	1784	687	90	158
Elizabethton	.968	1774	705	81	140	Greeneville	.964	1766	618	89	132
Johnson City	.967	1680	625	78	139	Danville	.962	1768	669	98	141
Kingsport	.966	1787	651	87	126	Burlington	.960	1771	702	104	136
Bluefield	.965	1685	692	86	169	Bristol	.958	1702	665	103	109

INDIVIDUAL BATTING LEADERS

Batter, Club	AVG	G	AB	R	H	2B	3B	HR	RBI	BB	SO	SB
Kaczmarski, Kevin, Kingsport	.355	64	256	47	91	18	5	4	34	24	33	20
Mazeika, Patrick, Kingsport	.354	62	226	44	80	27	0	5	48	24	26	1
Munoz, Carlos, Bristol	.325	56	206	35	67	21	0	11	39	34	21	0
Sweeney, Kane, Pulaski	.320	45	153	24	49	15	2	6	37	31	47	1
Castro, Carlos, Danville	.319	50	204	22	65	10	3	1	31	8	42	2
Sierra, Magneuris, Johnson City	.315	53	216	38	68	8	0	3	15	24	42	15
Alvarez, Eliezer, Johnson City	.314	52	204	32	64	20	1	2	31	11	32	9
Morel, Jose, Danville	.313	54	195	26	61	10	1	1	19	17	48	3
Wade, LaMonte, Elizabethton	.312	64	231	36	72	8	5	9	44	46	34	12
Lunde, Erik, Bristol	.305	45	164	21	50	7	3	3	22	23	30	0

INDIVIDUAL PITCHING LEADERS

Pitcher, Club	W	L	ERA	G	GS	CG	SV	IP	H	R	ER	BB	SO
Cutura, Andro, Elizabethton	3	2	1.34	11	11	0	0	61	46	19	9	15	49
McIlraith, Thomas, Kingsport	6	1	1.71	12	9	0	0	58	48	12	11	19	34
Cortes, Nestor, Pulaski	6	3	2.26	12	10	0	0	64	48	21	16	10	66
Nordgren, Miles, Elizabethton	1	3	2.76	11	11	0	0	59	65	31	18	10	33
Bivens, Blake, Princeton	6	0	2.78	11	11	0	0	55	53	23	17	18	43
Rodriguez, Dereck, Elizabethton	6	3	2.85	12	12	0	0	66	64	28	21	11	61
Crismatt, Nabil, Kingsport	6	1	2.90	12	8	0	0	62	52	23	20	12	63
Morban, Jhon, Pulaski	3	5	3.28	12	8	0	0	58	59	23	21	18	55
Feliz, Igol, Burlington	4	6	3.32	13	10	0	0	62	53	37	23	27	29
Williams, Ronnie, Johnson City	3	3	3.70	12	12	0	0	56	45	31	23	25	43

ALL-STAR TEAM

C: Patrick Mazeika, Kingsport. 1B: Carlos Munoz, Bristol. 2B: Gosuke Katoh, Pulaski. 3B: Connor Goedert, Greeneville. SS: Edmundo Sosa, Johnson City. UTIL: Eliezer Alvarez, Johnson City. DH: Brandon Dulin, Burlington. OF: Kevin Kaczmarski, Kingsport. OF: Magneuris Sierra, Johnson City; Carlos Vidal, Pulaski; Lamonte Wade, Elizabethton. RHP: Dereck Rodriguez, Elizabethton. LHP: Nestor Cortes, Pulaski. RP: Kuo Hua Lo, Elizabethton. Manager of the Year: Tony Franklin, Pulaski. Player of the Year: Carlos Munoz, Bristol. Pitcher of the Year: Dereck Rodriguez, Elizabethton.

DEPARTMENT LEADERS

BATTING

OBP	Mazeika, Patrick, Kingsport	.451
SLG	Munoz, Carlos, Bristol	.587
OPS	Munoz, Carlos, Bristol	1.014
R	Vidal, Carlos, Pulaski	49
H	Kaczmarski, Kevin, Kingsport	91
TB	Kaczmarski, Kevin, Kingsport	131
XBH	Sullivan, Brett, Princeton	34
2B	Mazeika, Patrick, Kingsport	27
3B	Coleman, Kendall, Pulaski	7
	Didder, Ray-Patrick, Danville	7
HR	Valerio, Allen, Pulaski	12
	Winningham, Dash, Kingsport	12
RBI	Winningham, Dash, Kingsport	51
SAC	Grullon, Yeudi, Danville	11
BB	Katoh, Gosuke, Pulaski	49
HBP	Mazeika, Patrick, Kingsport	17
SO	Duarte, Osvaldo, Greeneville	74
SB	Straw, Myles, Greeneville	22
CS	Kaczmarski, Kevin, Kingsport	9
	Straw, Myles, Greeneville	9
AB/SO	Munoz, Carlos, Bristol	9.81

PITCHING

G	Kuebel, Sasha, Johnson City	21
GS	Weigel, Patrick, Danville	14
GF	Lo, Kuo Hua, Elizabethton	17
SV	Casanas, Alberto, Princeton	9
W	Rosa, Adonis, Pulaski	7
L	Rodriguez, Dalton, Bluefield	8
IP	Rodriguez, Dereck, Elizabethton	66
H	Higuera, Juliandry, Bluefield	80
R	Gonzalez, Harol, Kingsport	45
ER	Minarik, Marek, Bristol	37
HB	Minarik, Marek, Bristol	13
BB	De la Rosa, Simon, Pulaski	37
SO	De la Rosa, Simon, Pulaski	67
SO/9	Cortes, Nestor, Pulaski	9.33
SO/9 (RP)	Amedee, Jess, Bristol	13.65
BB/9	Gonzalez, Harol, Kingsport	1.24
WP	Urbina, Ugueth, Pulaski	15
BK	Manoah, Erik, Kingsport	3
HR	Gonzalez, Harol, Kingsport	12
AVG	Cortes, Nestor, Pulaski	.203

FIELDING

C PCT	Aparicio, Jesus, Pulaski	.992
PO	Aparicio, Jesus, Pulaski	366
A	Rodriguez, David, Princeton	46
DP	Rodriguez, David, Princeton	4
E	Rodriguez, David, Princeton	10
PB	Morgan, Matt, Bluefield	21
1B PCT	Munoz, Carlos, Bristol	.993
PO	Dulin, Brandon, Burlington	486
A	Dulin, Brandon, Burlington	35
DP	Meyer, Kewby, Burlington	44
E	Dulin, Brandon, Burlington	19
2B PCT	Katoh, Gosuke, Pulaski	.965
PO	Katoh, Gosuke, Pulaski	87
A	Katoh, Gosuke, Pulaski	133
DP	Alvarez, Eliezer, Johnson City	30
E	Arbet, Trae, Pulaski	14
3B PCT	Castellano, Angelo, Burlington	.934
PO	Sullivan, Brett, Princeton	45
A	Sullivan, Brett, Princeton	108
DP	Sullivan, Brett, Princeton	12
E	Sullivan, Brett, Princeton	17
SS PCT	Martinez, Jose, Burlington	.962
PO	Duarte, Osvaldo, Greeneville	111
A	Martinez, Jose, Burlington	175
DP	Gudino, Yeltsin, Bluefield	35
E	Gudino, Yeltsin, Bluefield	21
OF PCT	Kaczmarski, Kevin, Kingsport	1.000
	Straw, Myles, Greeneville	1.000
PO	Law, Zacrey, Princeton	136
A	Wade, LaMonte, Elizabethton	11
DP	Sierra, Magneuris, Johnson City	4
E	Rosario, Henrry, Bristol	8

MINOR LEAGUES

BY BILL MITCHELL

The Missoula Osprey, an affiliate of the Diamondbacks managed by first-year skipper Joe Mather, took two of three games over Idaho Falls to capture their second championship trophy in four years. The Osprey reached the final round by defeating last year's champs Billings in a three-game series. Idaho Falls took two of three games against division rival Orem to advance to the final round. Ogden posted the league's best overall record at 43-33 but didn't qualify for the playoffs by failing to finish in first place in the South division in either half of the season.

Missoula was led by shortstop Isan Diaz, who in his second pro season turned in a breakout performance to earn MVP honors. Diaz topped all hitters in five different categories: OPS (1.076), slugging (.640), extra-base hits (44), doubles (25) and total bases (174). Another key member of the Osprey offense, first baseman Austin Byler, led the league in home runs with 15 and finished second to Idaho Falls slugger Joshua Banuelos in RBIs, the latter driving in 62 runs to Byler's 57. Orem third baseman Michael Pierson paced all hitters with a .395 average. Missoula outfielder Matt McPhearson was the league's top basestealer with 30 swipes.

Tanner Banks (Great Falls) and Ty Boyles (Billings) were named co-pitchers of the year, with Banks leading all hurlers with a 2.51 ERA. Missoula southpaw Anfernee Benitez fanned the most hitters (78), while Billings closer Jimmy Herget recorded 15 saves to lead in that category. Second-year Billings skipper Dick Schofield was named manager of the year.

One of the more notable accomplishments was the 54-game on-base streak by Idaho Falls second baseman D.J. Burt from June 28 through the final game of the regular season.

Four first-round picks made their pro debuts in the league, with Brendan Rodgers (Grand Junction) and Tyler Stephenson (Billings) ranking as the circuit's top two prospects, and Taylor Ward (Orem) ranked in the top 10. Mike Nikorak (Grand Junction) pitched in eight games, but did not log enough innings to qualify.

The age of Pioneer League prospects is typically split between teenagers and 20-somethings, but this year youth was served with the top seven prospects spending their entire time in the league while younger than 20. Grand Junction, which is the only league member without an Arizona League affiliate, placed the most prospects (Rodgers, Peter Lambert, Tyler Nevin and Javier Medina) in the Top 20. Billings, Helena, Idaho Falls and Orem each contributed three players to the list.

TOP 20 PROSPECTS

1. Brendan Rodgers, ss, Grand Junction (Rockies)
2. Tyler Stephenson, c, Billings (Reds)
3. Isan Diaz, ss/2b, Missoula (Diamondbacks)
4. Marcos Diplan, rhp, Helena (Brewers)
5. Peter Lambert, rhp, Grand Junction (Rockies)
6. Monte Harrison, of, Helena (Brewers)
7. Marten Gasparini, ss, Idaho Falls (Royals)
8. Taylor Ward, c, Orem (Angels)
9. Josh Staumont, rhp, Idaho Falls (Royals)
10. Tyler Nevin, 3b, Grand Junction (Rockies)
11. Willie Calhoun, 2b, Ogden (Dodgers)
12. Tanner Rainey, rhp, Billings (Reds)
13. Amalani Fukofuka, of, Idaho Falls (Royals)
14. Blake Trahan, ss, Billings (Reds)
15. Jake Gatewood, ss, Helena (Brewers)
16. Marcus Wilson, of, Missoula (Diamondbacks)
17. David Fletcher, ss, Orem (Angels)
18. Johan Cruz, 3b/ss, Great Falls (White Sox)
19. Joe Gatto, rhp, Orem (Angels)
20. Javier Medina, rhp, Grand Junction (Rockies)

STANDINGS: SPLIT SEASON

FIRST HALF

NORTH	W	L	PCT	GB
Missoula	23	14	.622	—
Great Falls	17	19	.472	5½
Billings	17	20	.459	6
Helena	16	20	.444	6½

SOUTH	W	L	PCT	GB
Orem	24	14	.632	—
G. Junction	20	18	.526	4
Ogden	19	19	.500	5
Idaho Falls	13	25	.342	11

SECOND HALF

NORTH	W	L	PCT	GB
Billings	20	18	.526	—
Missoula	19	19	.500	1
Great Falls	18	20	.474	2
Helena	16	22	.421	4

SOUTH	W	L	PCT	GB
Idaho Falls	25	13	.658	—
Ogden	24	14	.632	1
Orem	17	21	.447	8
G. Junction	13	25	.342	12

Playoffs: Semifinals: Missoula defeated Billings 2-1 and Idaho Falls defeated Orem 2-1 in best-of-three series; **Finals:** Missoula defeated Idaho Falls 2-1 in a best-of-three series.

OVERALL STANDINGS

Team (Organization)	W	L	PCT	GB	Manager(s)	Attendance	Average	Last Pennant
Ogden Raptors (Dodgers)	43	33	.566	—	John Shoemaker	125,398	3,300	Never
Missoula Osprey (Diamondbacks)	42	33	.560	½	Joe Mather	77,438	2,151	2015
Orem Owlz (Angels)	41	35	.539	2	Dave Stapleton	85,733	2,256	2009
Idaho Falls Chukars (Royals)	38	38	.500	5	Justin Gemoll	90,884	2,456	2013
Billings Mustangs (Reds)	37	38	.493	5½	Dick Schofield	100,120	2,945	2014
Great Falls Voyagers (White Sox)	35	39	.473	7	Cole Armstrong	45,414	1,262	2013
Grand Junction Rockies (Rockies)	33	43	.434	10	Anthony Sanders	74,794	2,137	Never
Helena Brewers (Brewers)	32	42	.432	10	Tony Diggs	33,841	940	2010

CLUB BATTING

	AVG	G	AB	R	H	2B	3B	HR	RBI	BB	SO	SB	OBP	SLG
Grand Junction	.296	76	2668	474	789	155	45	65	421	238	577	118	.360	.461
Idaho Falls	.295	76	2679	489	791	131	48	52	407	305	637	121	.372	.438
Orem	.288	76	2626	460	756	158	26	48	400	318	488	159	.371	.423
Ogden	.283	76	2699	487	763	159	33	77	435	275	660	53	.355	.452
Missoula	.267	75	2496	429	666	136	36	65	367	326	653	98	.356	.428
Great Falls	.264	74	2505	363	662	135	13	55	314	218	573	40	.330	.394
Billings	.263	75	2548	342	670	143	28	38	298	204	577	91	.324	.386
Helena	.263	74	2488	408	655	147	17	46	334	271	624	133	.343	.391

CLUB PITCHING

	ERA	G	CG	SHO	SV	IP	H	R	ER	HR	BB	SO	AVG
Billings	3.99	75	0		5	24	658	640	384	292	39	317	631	.256
Great Falls	4.26	74	0		2	16	635	611	370	301	44	258	567	.253
Missoula	4.27	75	0		5	18	653	657	372	310	51	238	671	.262
Orem	4.83	76	0		1	15	673	782	420	361	72	207	604	.292
Ogden	5.02	76	0		3	12	675	763	456	377	51	321	653	.284
Idaho Falls	5.07	76	0		0	12	663	760	471	374	56	288	553	.287
Helena	5.27	74	0		1	16	640	728	447	375	55	251	555	.285
Grand Junction	5.83	76	0		2	17	659	811	532	427	78	275	555	.299

CLUB FIELDING

	PCT	PO	A	E	DP		PCT	PO	A	E	DP
Great Falls	.969	1907	853	88	154	Billings	.960	1975	805	116	202
Missoula	.966	1961	789	98	153	Ogden	.960	2027	721	114	150
Helena	.965	1921	808	99	165	Idaho Falls	.959	1991	834	122	174
Orem	.964	2020	862	108	212	Grand Junction	.953	1979	814	139	144

INDIVIDUAL BATTING LEADERS

Batter, Club	AVG	G	AB	R	H	2B	3B	HR	RBI	BB	SO	SB
Pierson, Michael, Orem	.395	52	195	51	77	15	1	3	31	22	30	17
Green, Gage, Ogden	.370	47	181	30	67	14	2	4	33	18	31	6
Diaz, Isan, Missoula	.360	68	272	58	98	25	6	13	51	34	65	12
Banuelos, Joshua, Idaho Falls	.357	67	280	46	100	21	2	4	62	29	56	3
Ferguson, Collin, Grand Junction	.346	51	185	42	64	17	2	9	38	35	32	7
Fukofuka, Amalani, Idaho Falls	.339	67	280	53	95	18	9	3	38	26	70	10
Garcia, Kevin, Billings	.317	51	183	27	58	12	0	1	19	26	24	6
Cruz, Johan, Great Falls	.312	65	269	40	84	17	0	6	38	12	61	0
Trahan, Blake, Billings	.312	47	186	32	58	8	3	1	15	25	19	10
Lassiter, Landon, Great Falls	.312	49	170	34	53	10	2	3	21	30	37	6

INDIVIDUAL PITCHING LEADERS

Pitcher, Club	W	L	ERA	G	GS	CG	SV	IP	H	R	ER	BB	SO
Banks, Tanner, Great Falls	5	5	2.51	14	14	0	0	75	71	31	21	6	38
Romero, Franderlyn, Billings	3	4	3.34	15	10	0	0	67	74	37	25	21	46
Gordon, Derek, Idaho Falls	2	3	3.47	13	13	0	0	70	73	33	27	18	65
Easterling, Brannon, Great Falls	5	4	3.50	15	15	0	0	82	81	38	32	18	55
Constante, Jacob, Billings	4	3	3.56	14	13	0	0	68	59	33	27	38	58
Einhardt, Evin, Great Falls	5	3	4.02	14	14	0	0	63	68	30	28	19	41
Pacheco, Jairo Ogden	7	4	4.08	15	15	0	0	71	56	37	32	31	57
Takahashi, Bo, Missoula	8	1	4.66	15	15	0	0	77	77	42	40	30	54
Benitez, Anfernee, Missoula	3	6	4.75	14	14	0	0	66	77	49	35	25	78
Rodriguez, Jose, Orem	3	3	4.79	15	15	0	0	62	77	35	33	16	58

DEPARTMENT LEADERS

BATTING
OBP	Pierson, Michael, Orem	.467
SLG	Diaz, Isan, Missoula	.640
OPS	Diaz, Isan, Missoula	1.076
R	Byler, Austin, Missoula	59
H	Banuelos, Joshua, Idaho Falls	100
TB	Diaz, Isan, Missoula	174
XBH	Diaz, Isan, Missoula	44
2B	Diaz, Isan, Missoula	25
3B	Gasparini, Marten, Idaho Falls	10
HR	Byler, Austin, Missoula	15
RBI	Banuelos, Joshua, Idaho Falls	62
SAC	Burt, D.J., Idaho Falls	10
BB	Byler, Austin, Missoula	50
HBP	Dale, Ryan, Idaho Falls	10
	Glines, Jackson, Great Falls	10
SO	Jones, Matt, Ogden	87
SB	McPhearson, Matt, Missoula	30
CS	Suero, Daniel, Grand Junction	13
AB/SO	Trahan, Blake, Billings	9.79

PITCHING
G	Hofacket, Adam, Orem	26
	Mason, Austin, Missoula	26
	Savas, Dan, Missoula	26
GS	Ball, Matt, Great Falls	15
	Easterling, Brannon, Great Falls	15
	Pacheco, Jairo, Ogden	15
	Rainey, Tanner, Billings	15
	Rodriguez, Jose, Orem	15
	Takahashi, Bo, Missoula	15
GF	Savas, Dan, Missoula	24
SV	Herget, Jimmy	15
W	Takahashi, Bo, Missoula	8
L	Ball, Matt, Great Falls	9
IP	Easterling, Brannon, Great Falls	82
H	Eaton, Todd, Idaho Falls	103
R	Eaton, Todd, Idaho Falls	63
ER	Ball, Matt, Great Falls	55
HB	Freudenberg, Chris, Great Falls	9
BB	Constante, Jacob, Billings	38
SO	Benitez, Anfernee, Missoula	78
SO/9	Benitez, Anfernee, Missoula	10.58
SO/9 (RP)	Dopico, Danny, Great Falls	14.4
BB/9	Banks, Tanner, Great Falls	.72
WP	Gomez, Milton, Helena	15
BK	Gordon, Derek, Idaho Falls	3
HR	Yamamoto, Jordan, Helena	12
AVG	Pacheco, Jairo, Ogden	.216

FIELDING
C PCT	Rabago, Chris, Grand Junction	.989
PO	Stephenson, Tyler, Billings	364
A	Stephenson, Tyler, Billings	53
DP	Ward, Taylor, Orem	7
E	Schroeder, Casey, Great Falls	8
	Stephenson, Tyler, Billings	8
	Trees, Mitch, Billings	8
PB	Stephenson, Tyler, Billings	13
1B PCT	Byler, Austin, Missoula	.996
PO	Karkenny, Steven, Helena	550
A	Banuelos, Joshua, Idaho Falls	57
DP	Boehm, Jeff, Orem	49
E	Ferguson, Collin, Grand Junction	9
2B PCT	Burt, D.J., Idaho Falls	.945
PO	Burt, D.J., Idaho Falls	114
A	Burt, D.J., Idaho Falls	197
DP	Burt, D.J., Idaho Falls	38
E	Burt, D.J., Idaho Falls	18
3B PCT	Cuas, Jose, Helena	.945
PO	Nevin, Tyler, Grand Junction	35
A	Cruz, Johan, Great Falls	135
DP	Pierson, Michael, Orem	12
E	Nevin, Tyler, Grand Junction	14
SS PCT	Massey, Grant, Great Falls	.977
PO	Diaz, Isan, Missoula	102
A	Massey, Grant, Great Falls	211
DP	Diaz, Isan, Missoula	36
E	Gasparini, Marten, Idaho Falls	35
OF PCT	Stahel, Bobby, Grand Junction	.990
PO	Fukofuka, Amalani, Idaho Falls	136
A	Rodriguez, Antonio, Great Falls	11
DP	2 players tied	3
E	Suero, Daniel, Grand Junction	10

MINOR LEAGUES

MINOR LEAGUES

BY BILL MITCHELL

A veteran White Sox team captured its first Arizona League crown after getting out of a bases-loaded jam in the bottom of the ninth inning to defeat the Mariners, 3-2, in the championship game. It wasn't the first case of playoff dramatics for manager Mike Gellinger's squad; they started the postseason with an exciting 1-0 win in 11 innings over the Dodgers before defeating the Royals, 4-1, in a semifinal game that spanned two days due to inclement weather. The Mariners reached the championship game by first beating the Angels in a 10-2 romp and then prevailing over the Cubs, 3-1, in another game that took two days.

Key contributors to the White Sox attack were shortstop Bradley Strong (.326/.389/.484) and first baseman Corey Zangari (.323/.356/.492, six home runs). Righthanders Yosmer Solorzano and Chris Comito posted 5-2 records.

Returning to the league after a one-year absence, the Royals dominated the regular season with a 40-16 record, earning Darryl Kennedy manager of the year honors. Their offense was led by diminutive outfielder Rudy Martin, who batted .338/.477/.541 and stole 14 bases, while righthanders Yimaury Pena (5-0, 2.43) and Arnaldo Hernandez (7-3, 2.82) anchored the pitching staff.

Trent Clark, Milwaukee's top draftee in 2015 (15th overall), ranked as the league's top prospect, with teammates Gilbert Lara and Demi Orimoloye joining the Texas high school product in the top five. Righthander Phil Bickford, picked 18th overall by the Giants, was the only first-round pick other than Clark to earn enough playing time to qualify for the list, coming in at number four. Righthander Dylan Cease made an impressive return from Tommy John surgery to rank as the No. 2 prospect one year after being drafted in the sixth round by the Cubs.

TOP 20 PROSPECTS

1. Trent Clark, of, Brewers
2. Dylan Cease, rhp, Cubs
3. Gilbert Lara, ss, Brewers
4. Phil Bickford, rhp, Giants
5. Demi Orimoloye, of, Brewers
6. Nick Neidert, rhp, Mariners
7. Eric Jenkins, of, Rangers
8. Jacob Nix, rhp, Padres
9. Gerson Garabito, rhp, Royals
10. Dakota Chambers, rhp, Athletics
11. Jordan Johnson, rhp, Giants
12. Juan Hillman, lhp, Indians
13. Jahmai Jones, of, Angels
14. Jonathan Hernandez, rhp, Rangers
15. Gabriel Mejia, of, Indians
16. Ricky Aracena, ss, Royals
17. Antonio Santillan, rhp, Reds
18. Angel German, rhp, Dodgers
19. Jose Herrera, c, Diamondbacks
20. Dylan Thompson, rhp, Mariners

STANDINGS: SPLIT SEASON

FIRST HALF					SECOND HALF				
EAST	W	L	PCT	GB	EAST	W	L	PCT	GB
Angels	16	12	.571	—	Cubs	16	9	.640	—
Cubs	15	13	.536	1	Giants	17	11	.607	½
Athletics	14	14	.500	2	D-backs	14	13	.519	3
Giants	14	14	.500	2	Athletics	10	18	.357	7½
D-backs	11	17	.393	5	Angels	7	18	.280	9
CENTRAL	W	L	PCT	GB	CENTRAL	W	L	PCT	GB
White Sox	17	11	.607	—	Dodgers	17	11	.607	—
Brewers	12	16	.429	5	Reds	15	13	.536	2
Dodgers	12	16	.429	5	White Sox	13	14	.481	3½
Reds	12	16	.429	5	Indians	12	16	.429	5
Indians	11	17	.393	6	Brewers	11	17	.393	6
WEST	W	L	PCT	GB	WEST	W	L	PCT	GB
Royals	21	7	.750	—	Royals	19	9	.679	—
Mariners	16	12	.571	5	Mariners	15	13	.536	4
Rangers	13	15	.464	8	Rangers	15	13	.536	4
Padres	12	16	.429	9	Padres	11	17	.393	8

The highest 2015 draft pick to appear this season was White Sox righthander Carson Fulmer (eighth overall), who made his pro debut with a one-inning stint before moving up to high Class A. Indians righty Triston McKenzie, a supplemental first-rounder, impressed in his four AZL outings.

OVERALL STANDINGS

Team	W	L	PCT	GB	Manager(s)	Last Pennant
Royals	40	16	.714	—	Darryl Kennedy	Never
Cubs	31	22	.585	7½	Carmelo Martinez	2002
Giants	31	25	.554	9	Henry Cotto	2013
Mariners	31	25	.554	9	Darrin Garner	2009
White Sox	30	25	.545	9½	Mike Gellinger	2015
Dodgers	29	27	.518	11	Jack McDowell	2011
Rangers	28	28	.500	12	Kenny Holmberg	2012
Reds	27	29	.482	13	Ray Martinez	Never
Diamondbacks	25	30	.455	14½	Mike Benjamin	Never
Angels	23	30	.434	15½	Elio Sarmiento	Never
Athletics	24	32	.429	16	Ruben Escalera	2001
Brewers	23	33	.411	17	Nestor Corredor	2010
Indians	23	33	.411	17	Anthony Medrano	2014
Padres	23	33	.411	17	Brandon Wood	2006

Quarterfinals: Mariners defeated Angels and White Sox defeated Dodgers in one-game playoffs; **Semifinals:** White Sox defeated Royals and Mariners defeated Cubs in one-game playoffs; **Finals:** White Sox defeated Mariners in a one-game playoff.

CLUB BATTING

	AVG	G	AB	R	H	2B	3B	HR	RBI	BB	SO	SB	OBP	SLG
White Sox	.271	55	1885	307	511	101	26	23	242	182	391	70	.346	.389
Cubs	.269	53	1793	266	483	85	25	12	216	173	340	64	.343	.365
Reds	.266	56	1900	258	505	100	29	30	225	148	482	68	.324	.396
Royals	.265	56	1920	308	509	83	31	17	249	222	411	91	.351	.367
Brewers	.258	56	1908	253	492	88	19	22	212	183	481	97	.331	.358
Diamondbacks	.250	55	1831	230	457	62	29	9	188	160	433	63	.318	.330
Dodgers	.247	56	1868	277	461	89	29	19	218	153	576	74	.309	.356
Mariners	.246	56	1900	255	468	76	21	17	200	171	485	104	.318	.335
Padres	.242	56	1888	229	457	77	17	20	187	165	546	57	.312	.333
Giants	.241	56	1880	236	448	97	20	13	192	174	463	59	.317	.335
Indians	.241	56	1878	229	452	88	17	14	185	144	490	68	.304	.328
Rangers	.241	56	1920	256	462	90	16	12	218	170	407	73	.311	.323
Angels	.236	53	1778	249	420	84	20	9	207	195	403	90	.328	.321
Athletics	.233	56	1860	225	433	76	28	9	192	208	489	44	.321	.318

CLUB PITCHING

	ERA	G	CG	SHO	SV	IP	H	R	ER	HR	BB	SO	AVG
Royals	3.02	56	0	4	27	507	491	226	170	21	114	452	.251
Giants	3.20	56	0	6	19	492	433	240	175	9	179	509	.235
Reds	3.24	56	0	3	17	488	437	248	176	21	198	496	.238
Dodgers	3.28	56	1	4	13	493	415	259	180	16	239	497	.220
Cubs	3.34	53	0	7	11	463	409	205	172	17	154	436	.237
Rangers	3.44	56	0	3	14	505	485	249	193	15	166	505	.251
Mariners	3.54	56	0	4	18	503	423	238	198	15	172	488	.226
Diamondbacks	3.66	55	0	4	13	475	458	244	193	15	161	415	.252
Athletics	3.89	56	0	1	13	495	527	274	214	10	173	415	.273
Brewers	3.97	56	0	4	13	497	506	278	219	14	186	446	.263
Angels	4.00	53	0	1	9	470	514	263	209	14	141	415	.278
Indians	4.07	56	1	6	8	486	472	277	220	17	202	455	.255
Padres	4.63	56	0	1	16	491	525	317	253	18	180	454	.268

CLUB FIELDING

	PCT	PO	A	E	DP		PCT	PO	A	E	DP
Brewers	.967	1491	631	72	103	White Sox	.959	1439	684	91	164
Indians	.967	1458	599	70	118	D-backs	.958	1425	597	89	141
Cubs	.965	1391	598	72	150	Giants	.957	1478	589	92	107
Mariners	.962	1509	644	86	105	Athletics	.954	1486	625	101	108
Angels	.961	1412	612	83	123	Reds	.954	1466	589	98	121
Rangers	.959	1515	599	90	118	Padres	.946	1474	606	118	90
Royals	.959	1522	646	93	96	Dodgers	.941	1481	575	130	119

INDIVIDUAL BATTING LEADERS

Batter, Club	AVG	G	AB	R	H	2B	3B	HR	RBI	BB	SO	SB
Vasquez, James, Reds	.359	42	142	19	51	11	3	9	36	15	25	0
Mejia, Gabriel, Indians	.357	43	168	41	60	8	1	0	18	21	20	34
Garcia, Robert, Cubs	.341	47	173	32	59	4	4	2	23	16	31	17
Martin, Rudy, Royals	.338	40	133	41	45	6	9	1	11	34	28	14
Strong, Bradley, White Sox	.326	48	184	35	60	15	4	2	31	20	18	12
Sandoval, Ariel, Dodgers	.325	50	200	30	65	11	2	8	33	3	49	10
Zangari, Corey, White Sox	.323	48	195	29	63	13	1	6	40	11	49	1
Butler, Blake, Reds	.319	45	163	23	52	13	3	2	21	7	31	4
Melo, Yeison, Royals	.318	43	173	17	55	8	4	1	34	7	23	4
Rondon, Alvaro, D-backs	.313	47	176	36	55	6	4	0	20	16	27	20

INDIVIDUAL PITCHING LEADERS

Pitcher, Club	W	L	ERA	G	GS	CG	SV	IP	H	R	ER	BB	SO
Madero, Luis, D-backs	5	5	2.30	13	2	0	0	55	40	21	14	14	46
Mora, Gregor, Dodgers	2	1	2.38	12	3	0	0	45	35	20	12	14	39
Pena, Yirmaury, Royals	5	0	2.43	14	9	0	0	56	61	16	15	6	34
Andueza, Ivan, Athletics	3	1	2.51	14	4	0	0	47	44	16	13	15	44
Vargas, Emilio, D-backs	5	1	2.53	13	7	0	1	53	46	17	15	13	49
Gonzalez, Nicholas, Giants	2	4	2.57	9	9	0	0	49	51	18	14	6	39
Mendez, Sal, Rangers	0	3	2.58	13	9	0	0	52	43	17	15	17	50
Bautista, Wendolyn, Reds	3	1	2.60	13	4	0	0	55	54	23	16	12	55
Urena, Miguel, Dodgers	5	2	2.73	13	6	0	1	56	56	25	17	15	37
Terrero, Franco, Royals	4	1	2.74	14	1	0	5	46	42	19	14	6	51

ALL-STAR TEAM

C: Seby Zavala, White Sox. **1B:** James Vasquez, Reds. **2B:** Blake Butler, Reds. **3B:** Corey Zangari, White Sox. **SS:** Bradley Strong, White Sox. **OF:** Gabriel Mejia, Indians; Ariel Sandoval, Dodgers; Rudy Martin, Royals. **DH:** Corey Zangari, White Sox. **RHP:** Arnaldo Hernandez, Royals. **LHP:** Ivan Andueza, Athletics. **RHRP:** Heath Slatton, Giants. **LHRP:** Ivan Andueza, Athletics. **MVP:** James Vasquez, Reds. **Manager of the Year:** Darryl Kennedy, Royals.

DEPARTMENT LEADERS

BATTING

OBP	Martin, Rudy, Royals	.477
SLG	Vasquez, James, Reds	.669
OPS	Vasquez, James, Reds	1.084
R	Martin, Rudy, Royals	41
	Mejia, Gabriel, Indians	41
H	Sandoval, Ariel, Dodgers	65
TB	Sandoval, Ariel, Dodgers	104
XBH	Zavala, Seby, White Sox	26
2B	Murray, Byron, Giants	19
3B	Martin, Rudy, Royals	9
	Siri, Jose, Reds	9
HR	Vasquez, James, Reds	9
RBI	Zangari, Corey, White Sox	40
SAC	Aracena, Ricky, Royals	6
BB	Martin, Rudy, Royals	34
	Ostrich, Taylor, Royals	34
HBP	2 players tied	9
SO	Morgan, Gareth, Mariners	89
SB	Mejia, Gabriel, Indians	34
CS	Mejia, Gabriel, Indians	10
AB/SO	Díaz, Carlos Eduardo, Royals	11.23

PITCHING

G	Morel, Jose, Giants	24
GS	6 players tied	11
	Solorzano, Yosmer, White Sox	11
GF	Slatton, Heath, Giants	19
SV	Slatton, Heath, Giants	8
W	Hernandez, Arnaldo, Royals	7
L	Miniard, Micah, Indians	7
IP	Hernandez, Arnaldo, Royals	67
H	Blanco, Argenis, Athletics	71
R	Garcia, Jean, Padres	52
ER	Guerrero, Yeuris, White Sox	49
HB	Kelliher, Branden, Athletics	13
BB	Jimenez, Domingo, Indians	34
SO	Hernandez, Arnaldo, Royals	68
SO/9	Camargo, Jesus, Cubs	11.07
SO/9 (RP)	Melo, Kendry, Giants	12.76
BB/9	Hernandez, Arnaldo, Royals	.67
WP	Baits, Connor, Brewers	20
BK	Guerrero, Yeuris, White Sox	8
HR	Comito, Christopher, White Sox	5
	Escorcia, Kevin, White Sox	5
	Guerrero, Yeuris, White Sox	5
	Ramirez, Osiris, Dodgers	5
AVG	Madero, Luis, D-backs	.204

FIELDING

C PCT	Camacho, Juan, Mariners	.982
PO	Bowers, Zachary, Giants	196
A	Camacho, Juan, Mariners	44
DP	Melendez, Rene, Giants	4
E	Pitre, Gersel, Dodgers	9
PB	Turnbull, Jake, Reds	12
1B PCT	Dobson, Dillon, Giants	.993
PO	Zangari, Corey, White Sox	442
A	Ostrich, Taylor, Royals	44
DP	Zangari, Corey, White Sox	46
E	Isabel, Ibandel, Dodgers	15
	Zangari, Corey, White Sox	15
2B PCT	Sepulveda, Carlos, Cubs	.991
PO	Hiciano, Carlos, Athletics	100
A	Strong, Bradley, White Sox	149
DP	Sepulveda, Carlos, Cubs	32
E	Hiciano, Carlos, Athletics	12
3B PCT	Mercedes, Felix, White Sox	.906
PO	Walker, Jared, Dodgers	32
A	Sosa, Carlos, Padres	75
DP	Cerda, Erlin, Indians	7
	Santana, Leandro, Reds	7
E	Walker, Jared, Dodgers	20
SS PCT	Monasterio, Andruw, Cubs	.955
PO	Lara, Gilbert, Brewers	100
A	Lara, Gilbert, Brewers	159
DP	Mendick, Daniel, White Sox	33
E	Perez, Moises, Dodgers	15
OF PCT	Vasquez, Cristhian, Royals	1.000
PO	Morgan, Gareth, Mariners	94
A	Clark, Trent, Brewers	7
	Soto, Junior, Indians	7
	Sullivan, Tyler, White Sox	7
DP	4 players tied	3
E	Morgan, Gareth, Mariners	7

MINOR LEAGUES

BY BEN BADLER

For the second consecutive season, the Red Sox had the No. 1 prospect in the Gulf Coast League and won the league championship.

Pitching carried the Red Sox, who finished with the league's best regular season record. Their pitchers had a 2.28 team ERA, the lowest in the league, with a steady stream of strike-throwing prospects.

The Red Sox staff was led by righthander Anderson Espinoza, a 17-year-old in his first pro season after signing out of Venezuela for $1.8 million in 2014. Espinoza, who began the season in the Dominican Summer League, ranked as the league's top prospect for his combination of electric stuff and polish for his age, with a 95-100 mph fastball, advanced feel for his curveball and changeup and the ability to consistently fill up the strike zone, which helped him hold down an ERA of 0.68 in 40 innings during his 10 starts, though he didn't pitch enough to qualify for the ERA title.

The rotation behind Espinoza was comprised largely of Latin American arms, including righthanders Gerson Bautista (who touched 100 mph with his fastball), lefthander Enmanuel De Jesus, who stood out for his pitchability, and Nicaraguan righthander Roniel Raudes, who arrived late in the season from the DSL and was the winning pitcher in the team's 1-0 victory over the Blue Jays in the championship game.

Espinoza led one of the most talented groups of prospects the league has seen in years, with a bevy of potential impact international talent and a slew of 2015 first-round picks. The Cardinals rode two of the best pitching prospects in the league to win the East Division, with righthanders Sandy Alcantara and Junior Fernandez both reaching

TOP 20 PROSPECTS

1. Anderson Espinoza, rhp, Red Sox
2. Victor Robles, of, Nationals
3. Kyle Tucker, of, Astros
4. Daz Cameron, of, Astros
5. Cornelius Randolph, of, Phillies
6. Wilkerman Garcia, ss, Yankees
7. Garrett Whitley, of, Rays
8. Beau Burrows, rhp, Tigers
9. Ke'Bryan Hayes, 3b, Pirates
10. Austin Riley, 3b, Braves
11. Ronald Acuna, of, Braves
12. Sandy Alcantara, rhp, Cardinals
13. Junior Fernandez, rhp, Cardinals
14. Josh Naylor, 1b, Marlins
15. Ryan Mountcastle, ss, Orioles
16. Nick Plummer, of, Cardinals
17. Jermaine Palacios, ss, Twins
18. Adonis Medina, rhp, Phillies
19. Desmond Lindsay, of, Mets
20. Jonathan Arauz, ss/2b, Phillies

triple-digits on the radar gun.

There were several first-round draft picks in the league, including Pirates third baseman Ke'Bryan Hayes, who led the league in on-base percentage and ranked second in batting average, hitting .333/.434/.375 in 44 games while also making a positive impression in the field. Phillies outfielder Cornelius Randolph, the No. 10 overall pick, ranked one spot behind Hayes in OBP and finished fourth in slugging, hitting .302/.425/.442 in 53 games. Marlins first baseman Josh Naylor and Orioles shortstop Ryan Mountcastle were two other first-rounders who had strong pro debuts in the league, while Braves third baseman Austin Riley, a surprise selection in the supplemental first round, made believers out of those who saw him in pro ball with his power and better hitting ability than expected.

OVERALL STANDINGS

EAST	W	L	PCT	GB	Manager(s)	Last Pennant
Cardinals	34	25	.576	—	Steve Turco	Never
Marlins	33	27	.550	1 ½	Julio Bruno	Never
Mets	27	32	.458	7	Jose Carreno	Never
Nationals	24	34	.414	9 ½	Michael Barrett	2009
NORTHEAST	**W**	**L**	**PCT**	**GB**	**Manager(s)**	**Last Pennant**
Tigers	36	23	.610	—	Basilio Cabrera	Never
Braves	27	33	.450	9 ½	Robinson Cancel	2003
Yankees2	26	34	.433	10 ½	Marc Bombard	Never
Astros	19	41	.317	17 ½	Marty Malloy	Never
NORTHWEST	**W**	**L**	**PCT**	**GB**	**Manager(s)**	**Last Pennant**
Blue Jays	39	19	.672	—	Cesar Martin	Never
Phillies	36	24	.600	4	Roly de Armas	2010
Pirates	28	31	.475	11 ½	Milver Reyes	2012
Yankees1	26	32	.448	13	Julio Mosquera	2011
SOUTH	**W**	**L**	**PCT**	**GB**	**Manager(s)**	**Last Pennant**
Red Sox	41	17	.707	—	Tom Kotchman	2015
Orioles	34	25	.576	7 ½	Matt Merrullo	Never
Twins	27	32	.458	14 ½	Ramon Borrego	Never
Rays	16	44	.267	26	Jim Morrison	Never

Playoffs—Semifinals: Red Sox def. Cardinals and Blue Jays def. Tigers in one-game playoffs; **Finals:** Red Sox def. Blue Jays 2-0 in a best-of-three series.

CLUB BATTING

	AVG	G	AB	R	H	2B	3B	HR	RBI	BB	SO	SB	OBP	SLG
Yankees1	.267	58	1783	266	476	97	21	16	228	208	386	91	.351	.372
Marlins	.264	60	1963	247	518	62	19	13	202	155	441	71	.325	.335
Cardinals	.260	59	1954	287	508	83	22	19	239	194	345	49	.336	.354
Tigers	.259	59	1892	258	490	82	12	28	230	170	397	38	.330	.359
Red Sox	.249	58	1822	259	453	72	13	9	213	248	424	68	.346	.317
Braves	.248	60	1901	277	472	75	8	41	238	215	470	63	.331	.361
Phillies	.248	60	1926	251	477	94	16	19	217	182	382	64	.322	.343
Orioles	.247	59	1922	248	475	78	15	18	208	182	443	66	.325	.331
Nationals	.244	58	1795	208	438	80	20	18	184	126	391	60	.302	.341
Yankees2	.240	60	1838	243	442	89	14	25	202	218	429	49	.325	.345
Twins	.238	59	1861	204	442	82	14	10	169	186	396	66	.317	.313
Pirates	.237	59	1835	204	434	74	14	10	176	180	404	63	.312	.308
Mets	.233	59	1844	213	430	73	13	9	177	182	459	44	.310	.302
Blue Jays	.224	58	1837	255	411	68	15	22	209	239	517	79	.330	.313
Rays	.208	60	1825	168	379	75	8	12	131	172	463	71	.288	.277
Astros	.200	60	1819	191	363	63	10	10	152	201	511	60	.287	.262

CLUB PITCHING

	ERA	G	CG	SHO	SV	IP	H	R	ER	HR	BB	SO	AVG
Red Sox	2.28	58	0	12	23	493	423	163	125	13	172	414	.231
Orioles	2.68	59	0	7	21	514	413	194	153	9	188	443	.219
Phillies	2.72	60	0	9	18	505	412	192	153	19	146	448	.223
Tigers	2.72	59	2	7	17	502	408	194	152	15	210	528	.222
Twins	3.10	59	0	5	10	496	398	211	171	15	207	492	.220
Marlins	3.21	60	1	5	18	509	429	229	182	12	176	404	.226
Blue Jays	3.33	58	2	3	18	502	470	226	186	19	190	445	.247
Pirates	3.40	59	0	4	12	494	417	226	187	28	156	396	.226
Mets	3.42	59	2	5	14	497	501	234	189	13	158	395	.261
Cardinals	3.53	59	2	3	13	507	528	260	199	15	156	441	.269
Nationals	3.61	58	0	3	10	474	436	232	190	19	167	396	.245
Astros	3.83	60	0	3	6	502	492	266	214	20	216	376	.257
Yankees2	3.95	60	1	2	10	481	432	283	211	20	224	435	.238
Braves	3.97	60	1	1	7	496	502	286	219	24	219	453	.264
Yankees1	4.27	58	1	4	9	462	432	272	219	26	252	415	.246
Rays	4.54	60	0	4	10	490	515	311	247	12	221	377	.270

CLUB FIELDING

	PCT	PO	A	E	DP		PCT	PO	A	E	DP
Phillies	.972	1517	622	61	127	Tigers	.965	1508	546	75	113
Twins	.972	1488	588	60	101	Yankees1	.965	1386	518	69	104
Astros	.967	1508	650	74	130	Rays	.964	1470	609	78	94
Blue Jays	.967	1506	560	70	123	Cardinals	.962	1522	651	85	160
Pirates	.967	1484	575	71	92	Marlins	.962	1529	612	84	104
Nationals	.966	1422	546	70	110	Mets	.961	1492	620	85	131
Red Sox	.966	1479	583	73	133	Braves	.956	1489	608	96	130
Orioles	.965	1543	570	77	104	Yankees2	.954	1443	581	97	97

INDIVIDUAL BATTING LEADERS

Batter, Club	AVG	G	AB	R	H	2B	3B	HR	RBI	BB	SO	SB
Cordoba, Allen, Cardinals	.342	53	202	40	69	6	2	2	20	15	20	11
Hayes, Ke'Bryan, Pirates	.333	44	144	24	48	4	1	0	13	22	24	7
Azocar, Jose, Tigers	.325	51	194	29	63	10	5	0	29	7	31	6
Franco, Bladimil, Cardinals	.322	52	202	26	65	11	2	0	29	10	17	3
Mountcastle, Ryan, Orioles	.313	43	163	21	51	7	0	3	14	9	36	10
Arraez, Luis, Twins	.309	57	207	23	64	15	1	0	19	19	10	8
Sands, Donny, Yankees1	.309	48	162	27	50	9	0	0	26	24	15	7
Randolph, Cornelius, Phillies	.302	53	172	34	52	15	3	1	24	32	32	6
Santos, Jhonny, Marlins	.301	53	186	24	56	6	0	1	21	14	16	6
Baldwin, Roldani, Red Sox	.288	47	156	18	45	8	0	3	25	14	19	1

INDIVIDUAL PITCHING LEADERS

Pitcher, Club	W	L	ERA	G	GS	CG	SV	IP	H	R	ER	BB	SO
Ramirez, Williams, Twins	4	3	1.05	11	10	0	0	51	25	10	6	20	58
Oca, David, Cardinals	7	1	1.70	11	7	2	0	64	56	20	12	13	55
Vargas, Daris, Yankees2	3	3	2.12	11	8	1	0	51	44	22	12	11	42
Paulino, Felix, Phillies	5	4	2.34	11	10	0	0	50	41	20	13	5	46
Bautista, Gerson, Red Sox	3	3	2.77	12	11	0	0	52	36	18	16	27	41
Uceta, Adonis, Mets	4	3	3.08	12	9	0	0	61	67	26	21	9	46
Alcantara, Sandy, Cardinals	4	4	3.22	12	12	0	0	64	59	30	23	20	51
Gutierrez, Alfred, Tigers	6	4	3.38	11	11	0	0	59	55	25	22	15	42
Chavez, Enrique, Astros	3	5	3.51	14	8	0	0	49	49	22	19	17	40
Fernandez, Junior, Cardinals	3	2	3.88	11	9	0	0	51	54	27	22	15	58

DEPARTMENT LEADERS

BATTING

OBP	Hayes, Ke'Bryan, Pirates	.434
SLG	Gittens, Chris, Yankees1	.645
OPS	Randolph, Cornelius, Phillies	.866
R	Plummer, Nick, Cardinals	43
H	Cordoba, Allen, Cardinals	69
TB	Martini, Renzo, Yankees2	87
XBH	Martini, Renzo, Yankees2	23
2B	Martini, Renzo, Yankees2	17
3B	Diaz, Cesar, Yankees1	6
HR	Wilson, Israel, Braves	10
RBI	Encarnacion, Luis, Phillies	36
SAC	Valerio, Adrian, Pirates	10
BB	Plummer, Nick, Cardinals	39
HBP	Olivares, Edward, Blue Jays	15
SO	Bridges, Drew, Yankees1	65
SB	Diaz, Cesar, Yankees1	27
CS	Arraez, Luis, Twins	8
	Garcia, Wilkerman, Yankees1	8
AB/SO	Arraez, Luis, Twins	20.7

PITCHING

G	Quezada, Johan, Twins	19
GS	Alcantara, Sandy, Cardinals	12
GF	Bray, Jake, Orioles	14
	Quezada, Johan, Twins	14
SV	Bray, Jake, Orioles	10
W	Oca, David, Cardinals	7
L	Falcon, Felix, Braves	6
	Oronel, Nestor, Pirates	6
	Pena, Wilber, Nationals	6
IP	Alcantara, Sandy, Cardinals	64
H	Uceta, Adonis, Mets	67
R	Arias, Estarlin, Cardinals	35
ER	Duarte, Abel, Yankees1	27
HB	Lara, Carlos, Tigers	8
	Letkeman, Reign, Rays	8
BB	Escorcia, Juan, Yankees1	37
SO	Huertas, Joel, Mets	60
SO/9	Huertas, Joel, Mets	10.73
SO/9 (RP)	Glaude, Griffin, Blue Jays	11.62
BB/9	Paulino, Felix, Phillies	.90
WP	3 players tied	14
BK	2 players tied	3
HR	Plitt, Chris, Pirates	6
	Rosario, Luis, Yankees1	6
AVG	Ramirez, Williams, Twins	.145

FIELDING

C PCT	Garcia, Pablo, Marlins	1.000
PO	Vilorio, Luis, Nationals	263
A	Lorenzo, Rafelin, Rays	44
DP	Sanchez, Ali, Mets	7
E	Gonzalez, Yoel, Pirates	9
	Lorenzo, Rafelin, Rays	9
PB	Morales, Jonathan, Braves	11
	Spiwak, Owen, Blue Jays	11
1B PCT	Kennelly, Sam, Pirates	.994
PO	Encarnacion, Luis, Phillies	373
A	Moscote, Victor, Mets	31
DP	MacDonald, Connor, Astros	34
E	Encarnacion, Luis, Phillies	9
2B PCT	Arraez, Luis, Twins	.979
PO	Arraez, Luis, Twins	84
A	Brodbeck, Andrew, Cardinals	108
DP	Ledezma, Junnell, Tigers	26
E	Matute, Jonathan, Astros	8
3B PCT	Sands, Donny, Yankees1	.953
PO	Franco, Wander, Astros	33
A	Franco, Wander, Astros	90
DP	Franco, Wander, Astros	12
E	Guillermo, Ronny, Braves	11
SS PCT	Valerio, Adrian, Pirates	.959
PO	Cordoba, Allen, Cardinals	86
A	Cordoba, Allen, Cardinals	150
DP	Cordoba, Allen, Cardinals	32
E	Lara, Garvis, Marlins	19
OF PCT	4 players tied	1.000
PO	De La Cruz, Michael, Pirates	143
A	Azocar, Jose, Tigers	8
	Fernandez, Victor, Pirates	8
DP	Santos, Jhonny, Marlins	3
	Urena, Pedro, Yankees2	3
E	Wilson, Israel, Braves	8

MINOR LEAGUES

DOMINICAN SUMMER LEAGUE

After putting forth the best record in the regular season—they were the only team to lose fewer than 20 games—the Giants continued their mastery in a clean sweep of the Rangers for the Dominican Summer League championship.

The Giants were led by a pair of slugging corner outfielders—Sandro Fabian and Beicker Mendoza—who clubbed a combined six home runs during their team's championship run. Fabian slugged .783 during the playoffs and Mendoza .708, each good enough to place among the top five.

Dominant pitching also buoyed the team—four of the top five in playoff strikeouts came from the Giants' roster. The leader, Hengerber Medina, fanned 11 over 5⅓ playoff frames spanning two games.

This was the Giants' third DSL championship.

PLAYOFFS—First Round: Yankees1 defeated Red Sox 2-0 and Astros Blue defeated Blue Jays 2-0 in best-of-three series; **Semifinals:** Giants defeated Yankees1 2-1 and Rangers1 defeated Astros Blue 2-1 in best-of-three series; **Finals:** Giants defeated Rangers1 3-0 in best-of-three series.

BOCA CHICA NORTH
TEAM	W	L	PCT	GB
Rangers1	50	22	.694	—
Mariners2	46	26	.639	4
Cardinals	34	38	.472	16
Nationals	31	41	.431	19
Astros Orange	28	44	.389	22
Angels	27	45	.375	23

BOCA CHICA SOUTH
TEAM	W	L	PCT	GB
Giants	53	19	.736	—
Yankees1	52	20	.722	1
Mariners1	45	27	.625	8
Twins	36	36	.500	17
Mets1	33	39	.458	20
Rockies	33	39	.458	20
Red Sox1	28	44	.389	25
Orioles2	27	45	.375	26
Rojos	27	45	.375	26
Dodgers	26	46	.361	27

BOCA CHICA NORTHWEST
TEAM	W	L	PCT	GB
Astros Blue	43	29	.597	—
Indians	40	32	.556	3
Phillies	40	32	.556	3
Rays	38	34	.528	5
Royals	29	43	.403	14
Athletics	26	46	.361	17

BOCA CHICA BASEBALL CITY
TEAM	W	L	PCT	GB
Blue Jays	45	27	.625	—
Reds	38	34	.528	7
Orioles1	37	35	.514	8
D-backs	35	37	.486	10
Padres	31	41	.431	14
White Sox	30	42	.417	15

San Pedro de Macoris
TEAM	W	L	PCT	GB
Red Sox2	46	26	.639	—
Mets2	45	27	.625	1
Cubs	43	29	.597	3
Yankees2	40	32	.556	6
Braves	37	35	.514	9
Brewers	32	40	.444	14
Rangers2	32	40	.444	14
Tigers	31	41	.431	15
Pirates	30	42	.417	16
Marlins	24	48	.333	22

INDIVIDUAL BATTING LEADERS
PLAYER, TEAM	AVG	G	AB	R	H	2B	3B	HR	RBI	BB	SO	SB
Ferreira, Ricardo, Yankees1	.382	62	238	76	91	9	7	1	37	59	48	35
Ogando, Pedro, Rangers	.371	57	213	51	79	5	7	1	23	15	38	29
Rodriguez, Juan, Giants	.363	51	215	54	78	17	3	3	26	13	22	19
Obeso, Norberto, Blue Jays	.351	71	262	48	92	12	4	0	47	58	20	8
Feliz, Maiker, White Sox	.349	47	175	27	61	4	5	1	29	31	40	3
Lagrange, Wagne, Mets	.347	59	242	40	84	10	2	1	26	20	28	5
Gonzalez, Ivan, Mariners	.342	69	263	52	90	18	2	3	39	26	38	19
Coronado, Mecky, Giants	.340	52	191	25	65	13	0	2	37	18	29	2
Jimenez, Daniel, Reds	.337	67	258	58	87	17	5	5	40	20	26	15
Rengifo, Luis, Mariners	.336	60	217	49	73	10	6	2	35	22	22	19

INDIVIDUAL PITCHING LEADERS
PLAYER, TEAM	W	L	ERA	G	GS	CG	SV	IP	H	R	ER	BB	SO
Hernandez, Darwinzon, Rockies	2	6	1.10	16	13	0	0	65	55	17	8	30	66
Giron, Gabriel, Yankees1	4	1	1.40	15	10	0	1	71	42	19	11	21	46
Crawford, Leonardo, Dodgers	5	4	1.41	14	10	0	0	64	55	16	10	10	74
Diaz, Carlos Daniel, White Sox	4	3	1.56	14	0	0	0	58	59	24	10	15	50
Debora, Nicolas, Mets	5	2	1.65	15	10	0	1	76	59	20	14	13	70
Hernandez, Carlos, Mariners	7	1	1.68	14	9	0	1	59	33	16	11	10	50
Mejia, Humberto, Marlins	3	3	1.69	13	13	0	0	75	58	20	14	14	71
Brito, Pedro, Rangers	7	3	1.85	12	12	1	0	68	46	18	14	13	58
Veras, Jose, Reds	3	4	1.86	13	13	0	0	68	57	23	14	15	46
Eusebio, Breiling, Rockies	4	4	1.88	14	14	0	0	72	59	30	15	16	76

VENEZUELAN SUMMER LEAGUE

After topping the Phillies in 2014, the Tigers edged the Rays this past season for their second consecutive Venezuelan Summer League championship.

The trio of third baseman Jose Salas (.455 average in the playoffs), first baseman Luis Torrealba (.364) and shortstop Moises Bello (.333) power the Tigers throughout the series. Bello also had a home run in the series.

Seventeen-year-old righthander Jesus Rodriguez started the clincher for the Tigers, and gave the team five innings of one-hit ball. He went 5-3, 2.18 during the regular season and struck out 30 against just six walks.

Daniel Gonzalez and Hector Gonzalez finished the final four innings to give the Tigers their second straight celebration.

PLAYOFFS—Finals: Tigers defeated Rays 2-1 in best-of-three series.

STANDINGS
TEAM	W	L	PCT	GB	TEAM	W	L	PCT	GB
Rays	42	28	.600	—	Cubs	30	40	.429	12
Tigers	38	32	.543	4	Phillies	30	40	.429	12

INDIVIDUAL BATTING LEADERS
PLAYER, TEAM	AVG	G	AB	R	H	2B	3B	HR	RBI	BB	SO	SB
Pinto, Rene, Rays	.323	51	201	42	65	14	7	6	38	17	29	5
Bethencourt, Jhonny, Cubs	.319	61	216	49	69	11	3	0	15	32	29	15
Gomez, Moises, Rays	.317	47	180	38	57	10	2	6	34	23	28	9
Jimenez, Enger, Phillies	.307	70	264	36	81	17	5	3	33	26	46	15
Cabrera, Eleardo, Rays	.295	51	156	33	46	13	2	4	30	39	39	3
Cabrera, Moises, Rays	.293	51	184	24	54	7	0	2	18	18	47	3
Azuaje, Jheyser, Tigers	.293	61	225	30	66	10	0	2	29	12	18	3
Ayala, Luis, Cubs	.285	68	228	36	65	13	8	0	23	47	60	25
Polanco, Gustavo, Cubs	.282	53	195	23	55	10	0	0	23	10	12	3
Escobar, Elys, Tigers	.280	53	189	27	53	13	1	1	21	25	32	0

INDIVIDUAL PITCHING LEADERS
PLAYER, TEAM	W	L	ERA	G	GS	CG	SV	IP	H	R	ER	BB	SO
Velis, Sergio, Phillies	4	2	1.33	14	14	0	0	74	50	15	11	14	59
Armas, Gustavo, Phillies	3	2	1.97	14	14	0	0	73	52	18	16	34	55
Figueroa, Ken, Tigers	5	5	2.19	14	13	0	0	65	45	21	16	13	46
Pilar, Daniel, Rays	6	3	2.83	13	13	0	0	60	55	21	19	15	38
Fuentes, Jose, Tigers	5	2	2.90	13	13	0	0	68	74	27	22	12	39

MINOR LEAGUES

BY JOHN MANUEL

The Arizona Fall League rolled through its 26th season, pushing its schedule back by a week but continuing to provide a domestic home for winter ball.

While it's a U.S.-based league, the AFL has begun to have more and more international players over the years, following the trends in baseball overall. And three of the league's top story lines in the regular season involved international players.

Cardinals righthander Alex Reyes entered the league as one of the league's bigger names and lived up to his billing. The top prospect in the high Class A Florida State League during the regular season, Reyes made four starts for the Surprise Saguaros, who went 19-11, and had the AFL's best regular season record.

Reyes' four starts were must-see events in the AFL thanks to his premium stuff, as was the case in his first start. His fastball ranged from 96 to 100 mph, and he also flashed a power 78-81 mph curveball and a hard (87-90) changeup.

"He looked dominant," a talent evaluator from a rival organization said. "It's top-of-the-rotation stuff with a chance for three plus pitches . . . He's not too far away (from the big leagues)."

But Reyes wasn't around for the league championship game; he was suspended for 50 games just before the league's midseason showcase, the Fall Stars Game, for testing positive for a drug of abuse. Reyes admitted in a statement that he tested positive for marijuana and apologized to fans, teammates and the Cardinals.

Surprise thrived anyway thanks to the league's highest-scoring offense, which averaged just shy of 6.0 runs per game. The Saguaros included players from the Brewers, Cardinals, Rangers, World Series-champion Royals and Yankees, and one of the more international rosters in the league.

Curacao DH Jurickson Profar (Rangers), once the No. 1 prospect on BA's Top 100, returned to the field after missing most of the last two seasons due to shoulder injuries. Profar knocked off some rust, walked more than he struck out and batted .267/.352/.453 overall. Meanwhile, Venezuelan catcher Gary Sanchez (Yankees) cemented his place as one of New York's top assets, leading the league with seven home runs while batting .295/.357/.625. The Saguaros also had players from Cuba, the Dominican Republic and Puerto Rico. Surprise's best pitcher was lefthander Josh Hader (Brewers), who led the league with a 0.56 ERA in 16 innings.

Alex Reyes

BILL MITCHELL

MINOR LEAGUES

Lefthanders also dominated the league's strikeouts board with players of varied backgrounds. Mesa lefthander Sean Manaea (Athletics) led the league in strikeouts and shined in his final two starts especially, with 16 whiffs in his last 9 ⅔ innings. Big league southpaw James Paxton, who needed innings after making just 13 starts for the Mariners, ranked second with 29 strikeouts, while lefty Rob Zastryzny (Cubs), Manaea's Mesa teammate, ranked third with 28 after missing most of the regular season with a foot injury.

Another key pitcher who highlighted a strong class of lefthanders was Salt River's Kyle Freeland (Rockies), who missed most of the season after surgery to remove bone chips from his elbow. He won four of his six starts and gave up just two runs in his last 24 ⅔ innings after getting rocked in his first outing.

Glendale outfielder Adam Engel (White Sox), who hit just .251 in high Class A during the regular season, won the AFL batting title and led the league in the triple-slash categories at .403/.523/.642 and ranked second in stolen bases (10) and doubles (9). For context, the league average was .258/.334/.394.

STANDINGS

EAST	W	L	PCT	GB	WEST	W	L	PCT	GB
Scottsdale Scorpions	18	12	.600	—	Surprise Saguaros	19	11	.633	—
Salt River Rafters	16	13	.552	1 ½	Glendale Desert Dogs	13	15	.464	5
Mesa Solar Sox	9	21	.300	9	Peoria Javelinas	12	15	.444	5 ½

INDIVIDUAL BATTING LEADERS
(Minimum 2 Plate Appearances/League Games)

Player, Team	AVG	G	AB	R	H	HR	RBI
Engel, Adam, Glendale	.403	19	67	16	27	1	9
Scavuzzo, Jacob, Glendale	.377	16	69	13	26	4	7
Williamson, Mac, Scottsdale	.370	19	73	15	27	2	14
Hinshaw, Chad, Mesa	.349	15	63	7	22	2	12
Travis, Sam, Scottsdale	.344	23	93	19	32	1	14
Tapia, Raimel, Salt River	.330	23	88	14	29	1	8
Candelario, Jeimer, Mesa	.329	21	82	10	27	5	15
Asuaje, Carlos, Scottsdale	.329	18	73	7	24	1	7
Dean, Austin, Mesa	.323	16	62	12	20	1	7
Diaz, Aledmys, Surprise	.315	20	73	17	23	4	14

INDIVIDUAL PITCHING LEADERS
(Minimum .4 Innings Pitched/League Games)

Player, Team	W	L	ERA	IP	H	BB	SO
Hader, Josh, Surprise	2	0	0.56	16	8	7	19
Haley, Justin, Scottsdale	2	1	0.64	14	10	2	12
Holmes, Brian, Glendale	1	0	1.13	16	7	13	14
Robertson, Montreal, Scottsdale	2	1	1.84	15	12	3	7
Simms, John, Salt River	4	0	1.88	24	23	6	18
Travieso, Nick, Peoria	1	0	2.05	22	19	3	20
Sims, Lucas, Peoria	0	0	2.12	17	13	3	17
Hildenberger, Trevor, Scottsdale	0	0	2.13	13	13	0	12
Butler, Ryan, Peoria	3	1	2.45	15	14	11	10
Jannis, Mickey, Salt River	1	1	2.48	29	26	13	17

GLENDALE DESERT DOGS

BATTERS	AVG	AB	R	H	2B	3B	HR	RBI	BB	SO	SB
Brown, Aaron	.200	40	7	8	3	0	1	4	4	10	2
Crawford, J.P.	.150	20	3	3	0	0	0	2	6	0	
Davis, J.D.	.279	68	8	19	6	0	2	8	5	20	0
Delmonico, Nicky	.162	68	7	11	0	1	2	7	5	18	0
Dixon, Brandon	.295	61	9	18	4	0	3	12	3	15	2
Engel, Adam	.403	67	16	27	9	2	1	9	16	11	10
Farmer, Kyle	.293	58	7	17	7	0	2	13	2	11	0
Fisher, Derek	.254	59	7	15	2	1	2	14	14	23	3
Frazier, Adam	.321	28	6	9	1	3	0	4	4	5	2
Knapp, Andrew	.235	51	5	12	3	0	0	10	11	16	1
McGuire, Reese	.294	51	6	15	4	1	0	6	7	7	1
Meadows, Austin	.169	65	7	11	2	2	1	11	2	12	3
Michalczewski, Trey	.244	41	7	10	3	1	0	3	3	15	0
Moon, Chan Jong	.093	43	3	4	1	0	0	4	9	7	1
Peter, Jake	.309	55	7	17	3	0	0	4	7	9	0
Reed, A.J.	.231	39	6	9	3	0	1	6	6	8	1
Scavuzzo, Jacob	.377	69	13	26	5	0	4	7	2	23	0
Stankiewicz, Drew	.483	29	8	14	4	0	0	2	3	3	0
Trinkwon, Brandon	.300	40	4	12	2	0	0	4	5	5	1
PITCHERS	W	L	ERA	G	GS	SV	IP	H	BB	SO	AVG
Barlow, Scott	0	2	7.11	6	0	0	6	9	3	7	.310
Brault, Steven	0	0	4.91	5	5	0	14	13	5	16	.236
Brennan, Brandon	0	1	3.00	6	5	0	18	20	6	13	.282
Cash, Ralston	0	0	3.60	8	0	2	10	5	6	10	.143
Cotton, Chris	0	1	1.17	8	0	2	7	6	0	10	.194
Cotton, Jharel	0	2	3.77	5	5	0	14	16	8	17	.276
Dickson, Cody	2	1	7.27	9	0	0	8	9	8	5	.310
Eppler, Tyler	1	1	7.56	8	1	0	16	24	3	5	.343
Holmes, Brian	1	0	1.13	6	6	0	16	7	13	14	.132
Johnson, Michael	3	0	9.00	7	0	0	7	13	3	7	.382
Leyer, Robinson	0	1	3.00	9	0	0	9	13	3	7	.333
McKinney, Brett	0	1	6.23	9	0	0	8	13	4	8	.333
Minnis, Albert	1	0	2.31	9	0	0	11	12	2	6	.267
Ramos, Edubray	1	1	7.45	8	0	2	9	14	0	12	.333
Rios, Yacksel	2	2	5.14	7	6	0	21	22	5	14	.259
Rogers, Rob	1	0	7.00	9	0	0	9	9	3	8	.250
Tago, Peter	0	0	2.79	10	0	1	9	5	8	6	.167
Therrien, Jesen	1	0	8.38	9	0	1	9	12	4	8	.308
Wendelken, J.B.	0	1	30.38	4	0	0	2	8	1	4	.500
West, Matt	0	0	0.00	1	0	0	1	1	0	1	.250
Wheeler, Andre	0	0	7.50	6	0	0	6	8	4	4	.333
Williams, Trevor	0	0	1.23	6	0	0	7	5	0	5	.192
Windle, Tom	0	0	1.74	10	0	0	10	9	4	7	.231
Yuhl, Keegan	0	1	7.88	8	0	0	8	9	4	3	.281

MESA SOLAR SOX

BATTERS	AVG	AB	R	H	2B	3B	HR	RBI	BB	SO	SB
Adams, Caleb	.229	35	6	8	1	0	2	5	4	17	0
Aguilera, Eric	.275	69	9	19	4	1	2	11	6	9	1
Anderson, Brian	.115	26	0	3	0	0	0	1	0	7	0
Bauers, Jake	.254	67	5	17	2	1	2	8	9	14	0
Brockmeyer, Cael	.194	31	4	6	2	0	0	3	4	6	0
Brugman, Jaycob	.266	64	8	17	3	2	0	2	6	19	0
Candelario, Jeimer	.329	82	10	27	8	0	5	15	6	10	0
Contreras, Willson	.283	53	10	15	5	0	3	8	7	9	0
Dean, Austin	.323	62	12	20	1	2	1	7	4	9	2
Gillaspie, Casey	.191	89	7	17	2	0	2	5	10	16	1
Hinshaw, Chad	.349	63	7	22	4	0	2	12	5	15	1
McGee, Stephen	.250	40	5	10	3	0	2	8	7	8	0
Nunez, Renato	.296	71	9	21	2	0	4	10	4	14	0
Pinder, Chad	.235	51	11	12	2	1	4	9	4	13	1
Riddle, J.T.	.217	46	4	10	3	0	1	5	2	10	1
Robertson, Daniel	.228	79	9	18	3	0	0	2	9	12	1
Soto, Elliot	.227	44	6	10	0	0	0	4	3	8	1
Zagunis, Mark	.234	47	6	11	2	0	1	6	19	12	1
PITCHERS	W	L	ERA	G	GS	SV	IP	H	BB	SO	AVG
Black, Corey	1	0	11.42	8	0	0	8	12	7	6	.324
Borden, Buddy	0	3	15.68	10	0	0	10	19	10	6	.404
Brice, Austin	0	1	4.91	11	0	3	11	15	8	15	.333
Busenitz, Alan	1	0	8.74	10	0	0	11	15	7	5	.333
Cooney, Harrison	0	1	4.26	9	1	0	12	6	9	10	.140
Esch, Jake	1	1	4.58	6	6	0	19	22	5	18	.275
Etsell, Ryan	1	3	12.19	4	4	0	10	14	10	5	.326
Franco, Mike	1	0	2.89	9	0	0	9	12	4	7	.286
Garner, David	1	0	3.00	10	0	0	12	10	7	12	.213
Hall, Kris	0	2	6.75	10	0	0	10	11	5	11	.268
Johnson, Pierce	1	2	5.47	7	7	0	24	28	13	21	.301
Kinley, Tyler	0	0	5.06	10	0	0	10	12	12	13	.279
Kurcz, Aaron	0	0	11.25	4	0	0	4	6	4	6	.375
Mahle, Greg	0	1	9.58	9	0	0	10	19	4	14	.413
Manaea, Sean	0	2	3.86	6	6	0	25	22	6	33	.224
McCurry, Brendan	0	1	4.73	11	0	0	13	13	2	16	.250
Schreiber, Brad	0	0	1.64	11	0	2	11	10	1	9	.227
Urlaub, Jeff	0	0	2.25	4	0	1	4	6	0	2	.353
Williams, Trevor	0	1	9.00	1	0	0	2	2	1	3	.250
Wood, Hunter	0	1	5.84	9	0	0	12	12	11	16	.261
Zastryzny, Rob	2	2	5.19	7	6	0	26	25	6	28	.240

PEORIA JAVELINAS

BATTERS	AVG	AB	R	H	2B	3B	HR	RBI	BB	SO	SB
Blandino, Alex	.175	63	5	11	2	2	0	3	5	19	1
Camargo, Johan	.206	63	5	13	1	0	0	3	5	6	0
Ervin, Phillip	.209	67	8	14	4	0	1	13	7	11	8
Lien, Connor	.169	77	8	13	1	0	1	3	4	35	4
Marin, Adrian	.278	79	14	22	4	1	0	5	7	19	1
Odom, Joseph	.133	30	1	4	1	0	0	1	0	12	0
O'Neill, Tyler	.333	30	5	10	3	0	3	5	0	11	0
Perez, Fernando	.250	56	6	14	4	1	1	7	6	14	0
Peterson, D.J.	.209	67	9	14	3	0	3	12	8	18	0
Pizzano, Dario	.182	33	1	6	1	0	1	3	3	4	0
Quintana, Gabriel	.226	62	7	14	3	0	1	4	5	25	0
Sisco, Chance	.255	55	4	14	4	0	0	4	6	13	1
Smith, Tyler	.231	78	7	18	3	1	1	7	6	14	3
Torres, Nick	.264	87	11	23	4	0	2	7	0	20	1
Wallach, Chad	.133	30	2	4	1	0	0	1	1	7	0
Yastrzemski, Mike	.208	53	5	11	2	0	1	8	11	14	0
PITCHERS	W	L	ERA	G	GS	SV	IP	H	BB	SO	AVG
Bundy, Dylan	1	1	4.50	2	2	0	2	2	0	1	.286
Butler, Ryan	3	1	2.45	6	4	0	14	14	11	10	.275
Cabrera, Mauricio	0	0	6.17	9	0	1	11	14	7	15	.275
Fry, Paul	1	4	7.59	10	0	0	10	21	4	10	.396
Garcia, Jason	0	1	4.11	6	6	0	15	7	15	19	.132
Hart, Donnie	1	0	4.82	8	0	0	9	16	2	13	.364
Hebner, Cody	0	1	5.40	8	0	0	8	9	4	9	.281
Horstman, Ryan	0	0	0.93	9	0	0	9	7	6	5	.226
Johnson, Stephen	0	0	0.73	8	0	0	12	4	2	8	.100
Keller, Jon	0	0	3.00	2	0	0	3	2	3	3	.200
Morris, Elliot	0	1	6.52	8	0	0	9	11	2	5	.297
Paxton, James	2	4	4.60	7	7	0	29	37	8	29	.308
Rollins, David	0	0	2.79	9	0	1	9	8	3	11	.222
Scott, Tanner	0	1	2.00	8	0	0	9	6	5	10	.194
Sims, Lucas	0	0	2.12	6	5	0	17	13	3	17	.206
Somsen, Layne	0	0	3.38	9	0	1	10	11	4	13	.256
Thurman, Andrew	1	1	9.00	8	0	0	13	14	6	12	.275
Travieso, Nick	1	0	2.05	5	4	0	22	19	3	20	.241
Weiss, Zack	1	0	6.00	9	0	1	9	11	1	11	.289
Winkler, Daniel	0	0	3.00	7	0	0	9	5	5	11	.161
Yardley, Eric	1	0	5.25	10	0	3	12	15	2	8	.294

MINOR LEAGUES

SALT RIVER RAFTERS

BATTERS	AVG	AB	R	H	2B	3B	HR	RBI	BB	SO	SB
Bostick, Chris	.268	71	14	19	4	2	4	12	7	23	6
Cecchini, Gavin	.385	13	5	5	1	0	0	0	4	1	1
Fields, Roemon	.253	79	10	20	2	4	0	11	17	13	14
Guerrero, Emilio	.254	71	9	18	5	0	1	12	6	19	3
Guerrero, Gabby	.300	50	11	15	1	0	2	4	5	15	1
Hernandez, Oscar	.179	56	4	10	3	0	0	9	5	14	0
Kieboom, Spencer	.238	42	3	10	0	0	2	7	8	10	0
Mazzilli, L.J.	.138	29	4	4	2	0	0	4	4	5	1
McNeil, Jeff	.230	61	10	14	1	0	0	7	4	8	4
Palka, Daniel	.278	90	14	25	6	0	3	17	8	19	4
Patterson, Jordan	.157	51	3	8	2	0	0	2	9	18	1
Rabago, Chris	.207	29	2	6	1	0	0	0	4	3	0
Reinheimer, Jack	.230	74	9	17	1	1	0	5	14	21	1
Smith, Dominic	.362	47	8	17	4	0	1	6	12	10	0
Tapia, Raimel	.330	88	14	29	5	2	1	8	2	17	5
Tellez, Rowdy	.293	82	12	24	4	0	4	17	7	20	1
Ward, Drew	.097	31	0	3	2	0	0	2	11	9	0

PITCHERS	W	L	ERA	G	GS	SV	IP	H	BB	SO	AVG
Bacus, Dakota	0	0	1.29	7	0	1	7	6	4	6	.222
Carasiti, Matt	0	0	4.82	9	0	0	9	4	7	7	.121
De Los Santos, Abel	0	2	13.50	6	0	0	6	12	3	8	.444
Dragmire, Brady	0	0	0.82	9	0	0	11	5	4	14	.132
Estevez, Carlos	1	2	3.97	11	0	6	11	5	7	14	.132
Estevez, Wirkin	0	0	13.50	4	0	0	4	5	6	1	.313
Freeland, Kyle	4	1	2.84	6	6	0	25	26	7	13	.271
Gabryszwski, Jeremy	1	2	4.63	6	5	0	23	28	6	11	.301
Gibson, Daniel	0	0	0.00	7	0	0	8	4	4	10	.143
Girodo, Chad	0	0	1.80	7	0	1	10	9	3	7	.225
Hepple, Mike	1	0	3.24	7	0	0	8	9	4	2	.265
Jannis, Mickey	1	1	2.48	6	6	0	29	26	13	17	.250
Lee, Nick	0	1	4.05	6	0	0	6	9	4	5	.310
Lopez, Yoan	2	3	5.34	7	7	0	28	37	16	27	.319
Miller, Adam	0	0	4.50	4	0	0	4	4	1	5	.267
Moll, Sam	0	0	5.14	6	0	0	7	8	1	9	.276
Regnault, Kyle	0	0	1.17	8	0	0	7	4	2	12	.154
Shafer, Justin	0	1	7.00	7	0	0	9	12	5	10	.324
Simms, John	4	0	1.88	6	5	0	24	23	6	18	.250
Smith, Myles	0	0	6.75	7	0	0	8	7	3	8	.226
Wheeler, Beck	2	0	2.00	7	0	0	9	8	4	13	.235

SCOTTSDALE SCORPIONS

BATTERS	AVG	AB	R	H	2B	3B	HR	RBI	BB	SO	SB
Arroyo, Christian	.308	78	15	24	3	1	3	13	4	14	1
Asuaje, Carlos	.329	73	7	24	2	1	1	7	3	17	3
Diaz, Yandy	.246	61	8	15	2	0	1	7	9	14	1
Ficociello, Dominic	.247	73	6	18	4	2	0	12	5	23	0
Frazier, Clint	.281	89	15	25	1	2	3	8	7	27	4
Garver, Mitch	.317	41	6	13	5	0	1	9	6	10	2
Gerber, Mike	.280	75	14	21	5	2	1	14	11	23	4
Hankins, Todd	.246	57	13	14	2	0	1	5	17	16	4
Jones, JaCoby	.280	50	9	14	0	0	2	4	3	17	1
Lin, Tzu-Wei	.208	48	5	10	1	0	0	5	6	13	2
Lucas, Jeremy	.222	36	4	8	1	0	0	3	3	5	1
Slater, Austin	.250	68	10	17	4	1	0	10	10	19	3
Travis, Sam	.344	93	19	32	10	1	1	14	9	19	3
Turner, Stuart	.171	41	6	7	2	0	0	4	8	14	0
Walker II, Adam Brett	.240	75	11	18	2	1	5	18	8	35	1
Williamson, Mac	.370	73	15	27	3	0	2	14	11	11	1

PITCHERS	W	L	ERA	G	GS	SV	IP	H	BB	SO	AVG
Black, Ray	0	2	2.00	9	0	1	9	5	6	16	.161
Burdi, Nick	0	0	0.00	9	0	0	8	2	1	11	.080
Callahan, Jamie	0	0	3.00	3	0	0	3	1	1	3	.091
Ferrell, Jeff	0	0	0.00	4	0	0	5	2	3	8	.118
Garner, Perci	0	0	5.59	9	0	0	9	10	11	11	.294
Haley, Justin	2	1	0.64	4	4	0	14	10	2	12	.196

PITCHERS	W	L	ERA	G	GS	SV	IP	H	BB	SO	AVG
Hildenberger, Trevor	0	0	2.13	8	0	0	12	13	0	12	.260
House, TJ	0	0	0.00	2	0	0	3	1	0	2	.111
Kubitza, Austin	3	1	3.80	6	6	0	23	26	11	15	.271
Lee, Jacob	0	0	10.80	3	0	0	3	8	2	2	.471
Martin, Kyle	1	0	2.16	6	0	1	8	6	1	8	.194
McCormick, Phil	0	0	4.15	9	0	0	8	11	4	6	.344
Mejia, Adalberto	2	2	3.48	7	7	0	31	25	14	26	.217
Ravenelle, Adam	0	1	7.84	10	0	0	10	14	8	6	.326
Reed, Jake	1	0	0.00	10	0	3	10	6	4	10	.171
Robertson, Montreal	2	1	1.84	8	0	0	14	12	3	7	.218
Rogers, Taylor	2	2	2.88	6	6	0	25	17	11	21	.189
Romero, Antonio	1	1	4.61	5	5	0	13	14	9	17	.264
Rosenbaum, Danny	2	0	0.84	9	0	0	10	8	8	10	.200
Shepherd, Chandler	1	1	3.97	9	0	1	11	5	6	16	.128
Sides, Grant	0	0	7.15	9	0	0	11	11	7	6	.262
Slania, Dan	1	0	2.25	9	0	0	12	12	4	15	.255
Wilkerson, Aaron	0	0	7.71	2	2	0	7	10	5	4	.333

SURPRISE SAGUAROS

BATTERS	AVG	AB	R	H	2B	3B	HR	RBI	BB	SO	SB
Austin, Tyler	.272	81	13	22	5	0	3	7	9	18	7
Beras, Jairo	.067	15	0	1	1	0	0	2	0	9	1
Brinson, Lewis	.300	40	8	12	2	3	1	6	7	9	5
Diaz, Aledmys	.315	73	17	23	8	1	4	14	7	12	2
Evans, Zane	.139	36	3	5	0	0	0	5	4	8	0
Fowler, Dustin	.279	61	14	17	2	0	2	7	3	10	7
Gallagher, Cam	.182	11	1	2	0	0	0	2	0	1	0
Guzman, Ronald	.259	27	2	7	1	0	0	0	2	5	1
Ohlman, Mike	.205	39	4	8	2	0	2	7	3	14	0
Orf, Nate	.464	28	10	13	3	0	0	7	5	2	0
Phillips, Brett	.346	26	5	9	3	1	0	3	5	5	1
Profar, Jurickson	.267	75	11	20	6	1	2	20	11	10	1
Reed, Michael	.211	38	9	8	1	0	2	11	7	3	
Rivera, Yadiel	.315	73	11	23	3	1	1	11	10	21	7
Rowland, Robby	—	0									
Sanchez, Gary	.295	88	16	26	6	1	7	21	8	19	4
Starling, Bubba	.274	84	10	23	2	0	4	10	6	25	5
Tilson, Charlie	.203	59	14	12	3	0	1	6	9	13	4
Torres, Ramon	.262	65	9	17	4	1	1	6	3	9	0
Trevino, Jose	.217	23	1	5	0	0	0	2	0	3	0
Van Hoosier, Evan	.333	6	1	2	0	0	0	0	0	2	0
Wade, Tyler	.220	41	6	9	2	0	0	6	6	7	2
Wisdom, Patrick	.237	93	15	22	6	1	4	21	4	17	3

PITCHERS	W	L	ERA	G	GS	SV	IP	H	BB	SO	AVG
Acevedo, Domingo	1	0	2.25	7	0	0	12	9	3	11	.200
Alvarez, Matt	0	0	0.00	3	0	0	3	4	1	1	.286
Barnes, Jacob	1	0	0.00	8	0	0	11	6	3	17	.154
Brickhouse, Bryan	0	0	0.00	1	0	0	1	2	1		.333
Clarkin, Ian	2	2	5.84	6	6	0	24	34	14	17	.333
Edwards, Andrew	1	0	2.25	9	0	0	12	16	1	8	.314
Hader, Josh	2	0	0.56	7	2	0	16	8	7	19	.154
Hebert, Chaz	0	1	4.40	7	1	0	14	13	10	12	.255
Houser, Adrian	2	2	3.51	7	7	0	25	26	10	19	.271
Kiekhefer, Dean	1	1	2.93	9	0	2	15	11	1	14	.200
Magnifico, Damien	0	0	7.04	9	0	4	7	10	6	12	.294
McCarthy, Kevin	1	1	9.31	10	0	0	9	11	2	7	.282
Ortiz, Luis	0	0	1.80	4	0	0	5	5	1	3	.278
Parks, Adam	0	0	9.82	3	0	0	3	8	0	4	.444
Pounders, Brooks	1	0	0.00	3	3	0	5	5	0	14	.122
Reyes, Alex	0	1	3.60	4	4	0	15	14	10	14	.250
Rowland, Robby	1	0	4.76	10	0	3	11	10	4	10	.244
Sadzeck, Connor	0	1	9.90	7	0	0	10	15	5	14	.333
Slack, Ryne	0	0	1.69	8	0	0	10	7	3	6	.194
Weaver, Luke	2	1	3.72	7	2	0	19	12	4	18	.171
Webb, Tyler	2	0	5.84	9	0	0	12	13	3	12	.260
Wolff, Sam	2	1	2.84	6	6	0	25	25	8	15	.260

MINOR LEAGUES

Awards honor sustained success

TRIPLE-A

SALT LAKE BEES (PACIFIC COAST)

As the expression goes, the view is worth the price of admission at Smith's Ballpark, where snow-capped Wastach Mountains rise beyond the outfield fence and provide one of the best backdrops in minor league baseball.

"It gets glorious there," Pacific Coast League president Branch Rickey III said of Salt Lake.

The Bees, however, are about much more than their good looks. General manager Marc Amicone is often praised for keeping the team's 22-year-old ballpark looking like new, even without many of the frills found at modern ballparks. Salt Lake doesn't dot its promotional schedule with offbeat promotions, but they remain competitive even with an NBA franchise and major college sports in town because of a commitment to customer service. The team finished eighth in the 16-team Pacific Coast League by totaling 470,760 in 2015.

"They do the right thing all of the time," Rickey said. "They're not flashy; there's not a lot of flim flam, not a lot of glitz. It's just solid customer service and great word of mouth in the community."

DOUBLE-A

RICHMOND FLYING SQUIRRELS (EASTERN)

No team has done more with less than Richmond has at the Diamond. The Flying Squirrels have made up for playing at one of the worst stadiums in the Eastern League by stressing ballpark entertainment, customer service and community outreach.

"They have attracted the hearts and imaginations of the community and fans," Minor League Baseball president Pat O'Conner said.

They have also gathered a dedicated following since bringing the team to Richmond from Norwich, Conn., in 2010—one year after the Braves pulled their Triple-A club out of town for the opportunity to play at a new ballpark in Gwinnett, Ga. The Flying Squirrels have ranked

first or second in attendance each year since, including edging the Reading Fightin Phils for the top spot in 2015 with a 6,055 per-game average.

The team has been working with the city and surrounding counties on building a new ballpark, but have had little success.

CLASS A

MYRTLE BEACH PELICANS (CAROLINA)

Baseball and the beach have not been a winning combination in many towns, with the surf often being more of an attraction than the ballpark. That had become the case in Myrtle Beach in the years before Chuck Greenberg purchased the franchise in 2006 and invested in ballpark improvements while also spicing up the gameday presentation and promotions.

Veteran operator Andy Milovich arrived as general manager following the 2012 season and the Pelicans have increased attendance each of the past three seasons under his watch. They would have set a franchise record for overall attendance in 2015 but had to cancel a three-game series with the Carolina Mudcats after the Braves affiliate's team bus was involved an accident on the way to town.

The team has also helped set a standard for promotions—Milovich's in-game prostate exam for a cancer awareness event raised awareness and attention for the team.

SHORT-SEASON

GRAND JUNCTION ROCKIES (PIONEER)

The Pioneer League was looking for a steady alternative for its franchise in Casper, Wyo., which had been plagued by ballpark woes and mismanagement. They found it when Rockies owners Charles and Richard Monfort purchased the club and relocated it to a renovated Sam Suplizio Field in Grand Junction in 2012. Now, under the guidance of general manager Tim Ray, the same ballpark that has hosted the National Junior College World Series for over 50 years has become one of the best venues in the Pioneer League.

PREVIOUS WINNERS

TRIPLE-A	DOUBLE-A	CLASS A	SHORT-SEASON
2005: Toledo (International)	2005: Tulsa (Texas)	2005: Lakewood (South Atlantic)	2005: Brooklyn (New York-Penn)
2006: Durham (International)	2006: Altoona (Eastern)	2006: Daytona (Florida State)	2006: Aberdeen (New York-Penn)
2007: Albuquerque (Pacific Coast)	2007: Frisco (Texas)	2007: Lake Elsinore (California)	2007: Missoula (Pioneer)
2008: Columbus (International)	2008: Birmingham (Southern)	2008: Greensboro (South Atlantic)	2008: Greeneville (Appalachian)
2009: Iowa (Pacific Coast)	2009: New Hamshire (Eastern)	2009: San Jose (California)	2009: Tri-City (New York-Penn)
2010: Louisville (International)	2010: Corpus Christi (Texas)	2010: Lynchburg (Carolina)	2010: Idaho Falls (Pioneer)
2011: Colo. Springs (Pacific Coast)	2011: Harrisburg (Eastern)	2011: Fort Wayne (Midwest)	2011: Vancouver (Northwest)
2012: Lehigh Valley (International)	2012: N-West Arkansas (Texas)	2012: Greenville (South Atlantic)	2012: Billings (Pioneer)
2013: Indianapolis (International)	2013: Tulsa (Texas)	2013: Clearwater (Florida State)	2013: State College (NY-Penn)
2014: Charlotte (International)	2014: Montgomery (Southern)	2014: West Michigan (Midwest)	2014: Brooklyn (New York-Penn)

INDEPENDENT LEAGUES

New leagues scuffle in ill-fated debuts

BY J.J. COOPER

Independent baseball's best feature is also its biggest bug.

The independent leagues are independent. They don't have to get approval from Major League Baseball or Minor League Baseball to put a team in a market. That has allowed some of indy ball's most successful teams—like the St. Paul Saints, Long Island Ducks and Sugar Land Skeeters—to locate themselves in cities that would likely otherwise be locked out of the minor leagues. They can innovate on a moment's notice, something that allowed the Atlantic League to be leaders in pace-of-play initiatives.

But being independent also means there is no governing body. In the minds of many, independent league baseball includes the Frontier League, which is nearing its 25th anniversary and the Mount Rainier League, which shut down just two weeks into its debut season this year with rosters of players who never got to cash a paycheck.

The 2015 season was a bad one for fledgling leagues. In addition to the Mount Rainier's aborted debut, the Heartland and Ozarks leagues each announced that they would play in Springfield, Mo., at a ballpark neither yet had the rights to use. Neither survived the season. The East Coast Baseball League also was announced and then just as quickly disbanded, although in its case, the four-team North Country Baseball League did emerge from the ashes to play a short 39-game schedule.

The names of the leagues and the cities change from year to year, but the stories remain the same. Players who want to play baseball will travel anywhere and endure seemingly any hardship to keep their dreams alive. So they sign up, show up and quickly find themselves trying to find a way home.

The four entrenched independent leagues—the American Association, Atlantic League, Frontier League and Can-Am League—have been operating in some form for 20 years or more.

The Frontier and Northern leagues each debuted in 1993, while the Northeast League opened in 1995 and the Atlantic in 1998. The American Association and Can-Am leagues formed from the remnants of the Northern and Northeast leagues.

After that, everyone else in independent baseball

Atlantic League champ Someret's closer, Jon Hunton, also is its personnel director

is subsistence farming.

The initial success of those four leagues prompted plenty of imitators. But since the Atlantic League debuted, many new leagues have failed to find success.

To their credit, the Pecos League wrapped up its sixth season (after debuting in 2010), and the Pacific Association (2013) finished its third. Both operate on extremely tight budgets and struggle to draw significant attendance, but they have managed to keep the lights on for several seasons.

But to graduate from subsistence to steady success? It's unlikely that any independent league will make that jump in the near future. The hurdles are just too high. The costs to fund an independent league team have grown and, at the lower end of the spectrum, the leagues have been crowded out by summer college league teams, which can charge similar ticket prices but with one-fifth of the expenses because they don't have to pay players.

This trend continued after the 2015 season when the Frontier League's Rockford Aviators were replaced by a new summer college league team from the Northwoods League.

Maloney finds his form in Rockland

The lineups of independent league teams are filled with damaged goods.

At some point, every player in indy ball has been rejected, told he wasn't good enough to be drafted or that he no longer fit into an organization's plans. Whether it was during a phone call or a meeting with the farm director or manager, the player was told, "Sorry, you're not good enough."

In a sport where confidence can sometimes be the difference between a successful, aggressive stroke and a late, defensive swing, indy ball is often a last chance at restoration.

Most independent league hitters are never going anywhere else. Even many of the better indy ball hitters have a fatal flaw that dooms them to never fulfilling their major league dream. For those hitters, indy ball is the final stop before they go on to their next career.

For a select few, however, an independent league opportunity has restorative powers.

Joe Maloney, Baseball America's Independent League Player of the Year, spent time in affiliated ball as a 10th-round pick of the Rangers in 2011 before getting released (twice). Joining the Can-Am League's Rockland Boulders in 2014, he went to work on rebuilding his confidence, his health and his approach. After hitting .200/.244/.330 at high Class A Myrtle Beach in 2013, Maloney looked like a player who had found a level too fast for him. The Rangers released him after that season, and the Rockies signed him but then released him out of spring training.

But when Rockland manager Jamie Keefe looked at Maloney, he saw a still relatively inexperienced 22-year-old hitter who needed a new approach.

"He's matured so much in these past two seasons," Keefe said. "He had too many strikeouts. That was his biggest flaw. He was able to cut down on those strikeouts the last two years, but the biggest thing was understanding it's OK to strike out. You are a guy that's a game-changer. So it's OK, you'll strikeout at times."

After a solid but unspectacular debut in Rockland in 2014, Maloney had surgery to clean up a nagging left shoulder injury. He came into 2015 the healthiest he had been in years.

Maloney was expected to be a solid part of the Boulders' lineup, but he wasn't expected to be the star. Several line drives and home runs later, Keefe moved him into the cleanup spot and left him alone. He set a Can-Am League record with 93 runs. He hit .337/.432/.559. He hit for power (50 extra-base hits in 97 games). He played first base, left field and catcher.

Maloney had played through the shoulder injury for a few years, but with a healthy shoulder he said he felt like he could finish his swing with more authority. He went from a one-handed finish to a two-handed finish in deference to his repaired shoulder and quickly found that it helped him stay on the ball better as well.

Maloney signed with the Twins after the season. He will head to spring training for his third chance in affiliated ball, with a better approach and a healthy amount of confidence.

"That's probably the biggest thing I took from my indy ball experience," he said. "I had the time of my life these past two years . . . You lose that pressure of 'I need to move up.' You find that love of the game again. It's fun . . . You fall back in love with the game. I had the best time of my life in Rockland."

PREVIOUS WINNERS

1996: Darryl Motley, of, Fargo-Moorhead (Northern)
1997: Mike Meggers, of, Winnipeg/Duluth (Northern)
1998: Morgan Burkhart, 1b, Richmond (Frontier)
1999: Carmine Cappucio, of, New Jersey (Northeast)
2000: Anthony Lewis, 1b, Duluth-Superior (Northern)
2001: Mike Warner, of, Somerset (Atlantic)
2002: Bobby Madritsch, lhp, Winnipeg (Northern)
2003: Jason Shelley, rhp, Rockford (Frontier)
2004: Victor Rodriguez, ss, Somerset (Atlantic)
2005: Eddie Lantigua, 3b, Quebec (Can-Am)

2006: Ian Church, of, Kalamazoo (Frontier)
2007: Darryl Brinkley, of, Calgary (Northern)
2008: Patrick Breen, of, Orange County (Golden)
2009: Greg Porter, of, Wichita (American Association)
2010: Beau Torbert, of, Sioux Falls (American Association)
2011: Chris Collabello, 1b, Worcester (Can-Am League)
2012: Blake Gailen, of, Lancaster (Atlantic)
2013: C.J. Ziegler, 1b, Wichita (American Association)
2014: Balbino Fuenmayor, 1b, Quebec (Can-Am League)

AMERICAN ASSOCIATION

All season, the St. Paul Saints and Sioux City Explorers battled for the title of the best team not only in the American Association, but in modern independent league history. When the season ended, the Explorers' 75-25 (.750) record was the second-best ever. But at 74-26 (.740), the Saints finished with the third-best record, just a game behind. (In case you were wondering, the all-time leader is the 1999 Fargo-Moorhead squad that went 64-21, a .753 winning percentage.)

When the American Association season wrapped up, however, neither team took home the trophy. Instead, Pete Incaviglia's Laredo Lemurs leapt from the wild card to the title, bringing the first trophy back to Laredo in the team's fourth season in the league. Laredo remade its lineup just before the roster deadline, replacing four of the nine regulars.

With closer John Brebbia saving five of the Lemurs' six playoff wins with 13 scoreless innings, Laredo edged Wichita 3-2 in the best-of-five semifinals and then topped Sioux City 3-1 in the best-of-five title series. Brebbia celebrated the title for multiple reasons—he also got a contract with the Diamondbacks as soon as the season wrapped up.

NORTH DIVISION	W	L	PCT	GB
St Paul Saints	74	26	.740	—
Winnipeg Goldeyes	47	52	.475	26.5
Fargo-Moorhead RedHawks	44	56	.440	30
Sioux Falls Canaries	39	60	.394	34.5

CENTRAL DIVISION	W	L	PCT	GB
Sioux City Explorers	75	25	.750	—
Kansas City T-Bones	49	50	.495	25.5
Gary SouthShore RailCats	45	55	.450	30
Lincoln Saltdogs	34	66	.340	41

SOUTH DIVISION	W	L	PCT	GB
Wichita Wingnuts	59	41	.590	—
Laredo Lemurs	57	43	.570	2
Joplin Blasters	55	45	.550	4
Amarillo Thunderheads	45	55	.450	14
Grand Prairie AirHogs	29	71	.290	30.5

PLAYOFFS: Semifinals—Laredo defeated Wichita 3-2 and Sioux City defeated St. Paul 3-1 in best-of-5 series. **Finals**— Laredo defeated Sioux City 3-1 in best-of-5 series.

ATTENDANCE: St Paul 404,528; Winnipeg 258,922; Kansas City 232,068; Fargo-Moorhead 187,099; Lincoln 171,605; Gary SouthShore 165,306; Wichita 141,837; Sioux Falls 132,280; Sioux City 77,429; Joplin 69,222; Laredo 62,517; Amarillo 52,472; Grand Prairie 52,072.

MANAGERS: Amarillo—Bobby Brown; Fargo-Moorhead—Doug Simunic; Gary—Greg Tagert; Grand Prairie—Eric Champion; Joplin—Carlos Lezcano; Kansas City—John Massarelli; Laredo—Pete Incaviglia; Lincoln—Ken Oberkfell; Sioux City—Steve Montgomery; Sioux Falls—Chris Paterson; St. Paul—George Tsamis; Wichita—Kevin Hooper; Winnipeg—Rick Forney.

ALL-STAR TEAM: C—Vinny DiFazio, St. Paul. 1B—Angelo Songco, St. Paul. 2B—Ryan Court, Sioux City. 3B—Josh Mazzola, Winnipeg. SS—Noah Perio, Sioux City. OFs—Michael Lang, Sioux City; Denis Phipps, Laredo; Adam Heisler, Winnipeg. DH—Casey Haerther, Winnipeg.

P—Patrick Johnson, Sioux City. RP—Winston Abreu, Joplin.

PLAYER OF THE YEAR: Vinny DiFazio, St. Paul. **MANAGER OF THE YEAR:** Steve Montgomery, Sioux City. **ROOKIE OF THE YEAR:** Mike Zouzalik, St. Paul.

BATTING LEADERS

BATTER	TEAM	AVG	AB	R	H	HR	RBI
Clevlen, Brent	WI	.372	360	76	134	20	80
Haerther, Casey	WP	.360	389	49	140	13	72
*Kuhn, Tyler	WP	.360	411	70	148	5	56
*Martinez, Drew	GR	.358	427	64	153	2	62
Nieves, Abel	WI	.354	362	52	128	2	45
*Nunez, Alex	GP	.354	274	40	97	1	27
Gac, Ian	LN	.349	321	63	112	27	77
Van Stratten, Nick	LL	.349	416	81	145	6	49
*Thaut, Devin	SP	.342	272	50	93	3	33
Alonso, John	LL	.340	335	59	114	17	67

PITCHING LEADERS

PITCHER	TEAM	W	L	ERA	IP	H	BB	SO
Carrillo, Cesar	LL	8	5	2.80	116	109	49	78
*Hernandez, Nick	WP	12	2	3.06	121	117	22	93
Brown, Tim	WI	10	4	3.12	130	150	19	76
Crenshaw, Dustin	GR	9	8	3.16	148	146	22	76
Link, Jon	WI	11	2	3.26	127	123	33	100
Broussard, Geoff	SC	8	1	3.26	88	75	31	83
*Salamida, Chris	WP	7	4	3.29	126	120	26	91
Wilkerson, Aaron	GP	3	1	3.35	81	74	33	84
Van Skike, Jason	WI	12	5	3.36	110	121	31	55
Fleming, Marquis	LN	10	3	3.38	120	104	52	100

AMARILLO THUNDERHEADS

NAME	AVG	OBP	SLG	AB	R	H	HR	RBI	BB	SO	SB
Corey Bass	.249	.339	.281	249	40	62	0	19	33	54	10
Kyle Bellows	.200	.250	.267	15	2	3	0	3	1	4	0
Chad Bunting	.246	.270	.377	61	7	15	1	5	1	7	0
Andy Crowley	.235	.235	.235	17	1	4	0	4	0	4	0
Jordan Guida	.258	.325	.349	209	29	54	2	26	15	42	4
Drew Heid	.383	.464	.508	120	22	46	0	18	18	20	2
Christian Ibarra	.278	.387	.465	187	30	52	8	22	30	34	1
Dexter Kjerstad	.300	.338	.584	190	39	57	11	31	7	46	3
Rene Leveret	.290	.335	.436	369	47	107	12	74	27	59	7
Zach MacPhee	.129	.229	.129	31	4	4	0	2	4	4	2
Jason Martin	.287	.349	.439	157	27	45	5	21	11	19	6
Juan Martinez	.301	.344	.448	386	58	116	8	60	25	64	9
Ricardo Rodriguez	.258	.281	.403	62	9	16	1	4	2	24	0
Tyler Urps	.223	.299	.299	157	18	35	1	13	14	32	1
Geraldo Valentin	.301	.332	.456	366	57	110	9	55	15	35	4
Logan Vick	.308	.410	.420	338	70	104	3	34	58	68	38

PITCHER	W	L	ERA	G	SV	IP	H	BB	SO
Chris Balcom-Miller	2	3	5.13	7	0	33	35	18	16
Richard Barrett	0	2	4.58	41	2	39	34	12	31
Kyle Bellows	1	3	4.26	25	2	25	28	12	17
Clay Chapman	4	3	6.99	24	0	75	109	26	40
Anthony Figliolia	6	4	4.99	14	0	70	79	28	29
Freddy Flores	0	2	6.17	25	1	42	49	11	33
Charlie Gillies	0	0	11.12	3	0	6	8	7	6
Randy Hamrick	4	4	3.40	44	12	50	39	29	52
Matt Larkins	8	5	3.26	23	0	152	172	32	88
Matt McCormick	1	0	6.43	3	0	7	13	5	3
Kurt McCune	1	1	4.58	18	0	20	23	11	16
Richie Mirowski	4	2	3.57	11	0	45	40	21	55
Billy Petrick	1	2	4.13	16	0	28	34	9	24
Brooks Pinckard	0	0	8.53	8	0	6	9	10	4
Evan Reed	0	0	2.79	11	0	10	8	3	12
Clayton Tanner*	0	3	6.49	7	0	35	49	10	16

FARGO-MOORHEAD REDHAWKS

NAME	AVG	OBP	SLG	AB	R	H	HR	RBI	BB	SO	SB
Connor Andrus	.214	.320	.238	42	6	9	0	6	4	9	0
Joe Bonfe	.293	.359	.418	263	32	77	5	39	16	47	7
Tyler Doughty	.077	.077	.077	13	0	1	0	0	0	4	0
Chris Duffy	.241	.241	.345	29	2	7	0	3	0	8	0
Joe Dunigan	.253	.303	.418	388	43	98	14	60	27	136	15
Michael Leach	.216	.245	.255	51	9	11	0	3	1	14	0
Ryan Mathews	.000	.083	.000	11	0	0	0	0	1	1	0
Chad Mozingo	.307	.375	.438	397	63	122	4	65	42	53	20

NAME	AVG	OBP	SLG	AB	R	H	HR	RBI	BB	SO	SB
Drew Muren	.286	.355	.401	364	62	104	4	45	30	71	19
Zach Penprase	.303	.365	.427	403	72	122	6	56	41	74	30
Tyler Peterson	.241	.271	.333	54	9	13	1	9	3	5	0
Ryan Pineda	.272	.333	.358	173	31	47	2	20	13	38	7
Anthony Renz	.154	.267	.154	13	1	2	0	0	2	5	0
Frank Salerno	.268	.326	.302	205	23	55	0	11	14	21	16
Joe Staley	.259	.335	.379	224	27	58	5	28	24	48	2
Jordan Tescher	.235	.316	.294	17	4	4	0	1	1	5	0
Charlie Valerio	.268	.336	.403	231	30	62	5	26	24	40	3
Zach Wright	.455	.533	.455	11	0	5	0	3	3	2	1

PITCHER	W	L	ERA	G	SV	IP	H	BB	SO
Tyler Alexander*	5	5	3.31	21	0	111	91	52	111
Bryan Blough	1	2	7.06	8	0	22	28	9	15
Mariel Checo	0	1	4.50	5	0	6	6	6	3
Jonathan Chudy*	0	1	5.34	27	0	32	42	23	26
Nick Cooney*	1	2	3.74	16	1	22	12	22	19
Joe Harris*	1	1	8.62	6	0	16	18	9	11
Tyler Herron	6	7	4.47	20	0	131	125	64	119
Ty Kelley	6	7	4.05	32	3	91	100	36	72
Alex Kreis	1	0	4.35	8	0	10	11	7	2
Brandon Mann*	7	10	4.07	22	0	144	151	58	157
Mike Mason*	2	2	5.32	10	0	24	28	18	15
Mike Nesseth	1	3	2.67	28	18	27	31	4	19
Paul Raglione	0	1	4.76	12	0	11	14	6	10
Taylor Stanton	6	4	4.21	20	0	124	126	42	97
Tyler Thompson	3	2	5.95	18	0	20	24	8	12

GARY SOUTHSHORE RAILCATS

NAME	AVG	OBP	SLG	AB	R	H	HR	RBI	BB	SO	SB
Ryan Brockett	.279	.363	.315	219	21	61	0	23	25	33	7
Alex Crosby	.200	.226	.300	30	3	6	0	1	0	4	1
Jaime Del Valle	.251	.318	.297	175	18	44	0	22	15	24	2
Elbert Devarie	.257	.329	.286	70	6	18	0	7	8	11	3
Alex Hernandez	.272	.401	.421	114	20	31	3	18	26	25	1
Matt Hibbert	.154	.313	.154	26	2	4	0	3	5	4	3
Jon Jones	.314	.372	.484	312	49	98	5	40	29	43	19
Sam Lind	.115	.281	.192	26	6	3	0	3	4	11	0
Spencer Mahoney	.267	.476	.356	45	9	12	0	5	18	11	2
Brennan Metzger	.184	.301	.287	87	10	16	1	9	14	20	3
Zac Mitchell	.237	.322	.314	156	18	37	0	13	12	20	4
Steve Rogers	.257	.316	.371	35	6	9	1	3	8	0	
Michael Schroeder	.263	.300	.308	133	11	35	0	9	6	34	2
Jose Sermo	.290	.345	.432	183	23	53	1	26	15	47	3
Derek Smith	.133	.278	.233	30	2	4	0	3	6	9	0
Adam Taylor	.290	.360	.408	314	47	91	5	49	32	59	11
Brandon Thomas	.258	.329	.379	66	9	17	1	7	6	18	2
Michael Vaughn	.204	.277	.293	181	23	37	2	23	17	49	2
Zachary Zdanowicz	.000	.333	.000	10	1	0	0	0	4	6	2

PITCHER	W	L	ERA	G	SV	IP	H	BB	SO
Chuck Fontana*	4	4	3.42	28	3	50	36	13	36
Fernando Gonzalez	3	1	4.14	10	0	54	72	21	28
John Kovalik	0	0	2.92	10	0	12	10	5	13
Andy Loomis*	0	2	3.59	38	19	43	42	16	44
Dan Ludwig*	1	0	4.35	4	0	10	14	5	9
Travis McGee	3	2	4.72	13	0	67	60	34	39
Paul Mittura	1	0	4.50	16	0	24	22	10	18
Shawn O'Neill*	3	2	4.43	42	1	41	47	16	27
Kevin Osaki	0	2	4.76	27	0	45	49	21	21
Ryan Quigley	0	0	1.50	1	0	6	4	3	6
A.J. Quintero	1	5	7.74	21	0	43	63	20	45
Andy Roberts*	2	8	4.36	21	3	87	97	31	44
Charle Rosario	12	8	3.81	22	0	137	147	32	89
Michael Schroeder*	0	0	0.00	4	0	6	3	1	6
Jessie Snodgrass	4	5	3.86	33	2	40	47	9	17
Rene Solis*	4	7	5.32	22	0	118	147	42	79
Matt Solter	2	3	3.86	18	0	26	35	8	14

GRAND PRAIRIE AIRHOGS

NAME	AVG	OBP	SLG	AB	R	H	HR	RBI	BB	SO	SB
Matt Burns	.143	.250	.143	14	1	2	0	1	2	7	1
Justin Byrd	.241	.373	.259	54	7	13	0	6	10	13	2
Willie Cabrera	.347	.389	.439	173	17	60	2	19	10	18	0
Miguel Castano	.106	.133	.149	94	5	10	1	3	3	30	1
Zane Chavez	.288	.324	.373	306	32	88	2	41	17	42	2
Brandon Cummings	.333	.429	.333	12	1	4	0	0	2	2	0

NAME	AVG	OBP	SLG	AB	R	H	HR	RBI	BB	SO	SB
Victor Diaz	.236	.282	.383	381	32	90	11	54	21	139	2
Josh Eatherly	.234	.296	.263	171	15	40	0	8	12	40	8
Robi Estrada	.205	.258	.241	249	18	51	0	12	18	46	7
Victor Ferrante	.233	.291	.329	73	3	17	2	7	5	28	0
Brian Frazier	.186	.218	.237	97	4	18	1	4	4	31	1
Ryan Gasporra	.263	.364	.263	19	0	5	0	1	3	1	0
Trevor Harden	.189	.286	.270	37	1	7	1	2	4	13	0
Jordy Hart	.203	.301	.304	158	23	32	2	10	18	48	12
Ridge Hoopii-Haslam	.244	.300	.380	287	25	70	7	24	17	77	15
Hayden Jennings	.133	.200	.147	75	6	10	0	5	5	35	9
Jamodrick McGruder	.243	.342	.352	304	45	74	5	20	33	68	23
Brian Myrow	.213	.385	.340	94	9	20	2	15	27	17	1
Michael Pair	.265	.355	.367	147	9	39	1	17	20	41	0
Ronnie Richardson	.258	.364	.360	225	40	58	3	22	27	67	13

PITCHER	W	L	ERA	G	SV	IP	H	BB	SO
Taylor Black	0	0	2.38	9	1	11	10	4	11
T.J. Bozeman	2	11	5.56	22	0	112	130	66	85
Zachary Dando	5	8	4.07	38	6	86	101	29	45
Ty'Relle Harris	1	1	2.78	19	3	23	17	13	26
Jason Jarvis	1	4	4.75	23	0	47	55	20	36
Stetson Nelson	3	0	3.32	7	0	19	20	8	10
Logan Norris	3	6	4.05	32	5	60	68	29	35
Blake Oliver	6	11	5.94	23	0	111	146	49	52
Matty Ott	0	2	6.35	6	0	6	9	2	7
Dylan Rucker	0	0	3.66	29	0	39	35	11	25
Brett Wallach	2	7	3.68	17	0	93	89	40	73
Bennett Whitmore*	2	12	4.35	22	0	143	180	30	66

JOPLIN BLASTERS

NAME	AVG	OBP	SLG	AB	R	H	HR	RBI	BB	SO	SB
Yenier Bello	.233	.250	.288	73	4	17	0	10	2	5	0
Aaron Brill	.243	.296	.338	74	7	18	1	11	6	21	4
Joe Coyne	.211	.211	.211	19	3	4	0	1	0	5	0
Austin Gallagher	.185	.185	.259	27	2	5	0	2	0	3	0
Mitch Glasser	.265	.362	.306	268	41	71	0	26	34	26	6
Yasser Gomez	.302	.401	.324	182	29	55	0	27	30	12	4
Maikol Gonzalez	.305	.380	.411	377	70	115	8	44	45	45	46
Omar Luna	.290	.332	.352	352	41	102	1	34	16	22	13
Oscar Mesa	.265	.355	.359	309	58	82	3	36	45	54	20
Mason Morioka	.273	.294	.364	33	3	9	1	3	1	6	0
Jairo Perez	.313	.380	.556	144	20	45	8	29	14	12	3
Carlos Ramirez	.272	.366	.446	305	35	83	13	49	41	37	0
Jesus Solorzano	.269	.314	.451	286	51	77	10	41	12	55	14
Gabe Suarez	.160	.188	.200	75	5	12	0	8	2	20	0
Jake Taylor	.292	.337	.492	360	47	105	15	56	26	86	1

PITCHER	W	L	ERA	G	SV	IP	H	BB	SO
Winston Abreu	5	1	0.77	47	23	47	26	20	80
Sam Agnew-Wieland	3	4	3.68	24	0	44	53	16	34
Victor Capellan	6	3	3.34	53	1	57	46	22	77
Alberto Castillo*	1	3	4.72	6	0	34	45	8	22
Jesus Colome	0	2	6.00	9	0	9	11	2	8
Frank Del Valle*	2	0	2.70	3	0	17	15	8	14
Josh Evans	3	1	3.86	5	0	26	31	7	20
Carlos Fuentes	4	1	3.38	19	0	45	46	14	43
Jorge Martinez	6	3	3.39	13	0	74	72	23	70
Jake Meiers	1	3	6.59	15	0	27	38	8	21
Nestor Molina	7	5	3.12	17	0	104	108	18	71
Josue Montanez*	4	2	1.83	13	0	54	46	18	37
Jake Negrete	0	1	10.12	5	0	8	11	3	8
Matt Parish	2	4	6.55	20	0	67	80	28	46
Raydel Sanchez	1	2	13.50	4	0	10	19	3	3
Matt Swilley	1	2	4.17	27	0	50	30	46	51
Rob Tejeda	1	2	9.21	6	0	40	10	16	

KANSAS CITY T-BONES

NAME	AVG	OBP	SLG	AB	R	H	HR	RBI	BB	SO	SB
Adam Bailey	.307	.374	.504	375	58	115	17	73	42	69	2
Ernie Banks	.211	.273	.211	19	0	4	0	3	2	7	0
Jake Blackwood	.302	.342	.442	394	59	119	11	64	27	38	3
Brian Erie	.282	.317	.327	266	23	75	0	19	13	48	4
Vladimir Frias	.331	.403	.441	272	40	90	5	27	30	26	23
Jacob Hayes	.225	.305	.343	178	25	40	3	20	20	55	9
C.J. Henry	.146	.205	.171	41	3	6	0	2	2	8	1
Robby Kuzdale	.236	.299	.363	314	33	74	10	42	26	69	14
Sergio Leon	.229	.289	.257	105	11	24	0	8	7	24	0

NAME	AVG	OBP	SLG	AB	R	H	HR	RBI	BB	SO	SB
Alex Marquez	.230	.287	.260	100	10	23	0	7	7	15	0
Joe Rapp	.217	.277	.358	120	14	26	4	17	9	47	1
Kyle Richards	.154	.154	.154	26	1	4	0	1	0	6	0
Kyle Robinson	.254	.320	.428	201	26	51	8	41	20	41	3
Nate Tenbrink	.335	.418	.485	361	67	121	7	52	54	55	17
Christian Torres	.333	.333	.583	12	2	4	1	2	0	1	0

PITCHER	W	L	ERA	G	SV	IP	H	BB	SO
Aaron Baker	4	5	2.95	42	4	58	54	17	46
Casey Barnes	3	3	3.13	10	0	55	54	13	27
Kyle Brady	1	1	10.80	4	0	12	15	9	13
Evan DeLuca*	1	0	0.71	8	0	13	7	5	6
Kyle DeVore	0	2	4.94	5	0	27	38	7	7
Bobby Doran	8	6	4.43	20	0	114	115	51	71
Fernando Hernandez	3	7	3.32	37	20	65	60	17	37
Blake Holovach*	1	3	3.29	12	0	66	58	38	34
Jonathan Kountis	0	3	7.94	10	3	11	13	8	12
Derek Loera*	3	1	3.18	22	0	40	42	12	22
Jared Messer	3	0	3.26	35	1	61	49	14	41
Mike Nannini	2	4	5.79	17	0	47	49	11	23
Kris Regas*	6	5	4.84	31	2	87	89	43	69
Steve Sarcone	0	2	9.26	3	0	12	15	6	8
Josh Tols*	2	0	4.55	29	0	55	58	26	49

LAREDO LEMURS

NAME	AVG	OBP	SLG	AB	R	H	HR	RBI	BB	SO	SB
Tony Delmonico	.265	.361	.490	98	14	26	6	21	13	26	0
Travis Denker	.361	.489	.569	72	17	26	4	15	18	11	1
Ty Forney	.158	.217	.211	76	2	12	0	3	4	11	1
A.J. Kirby-Jones	.261	.357	.304	23	2	6	0	1	4	5	0
Jimmy Mojica	.246	.378	.246	61	8	15	0	5	12	8	4
Ty Morrison	.366	.424	.436	227	42	83	0	10	18	31	22
Abel Nieves	.353	.426	.444	266	48	94	2	35	34	39	7
Ryan Ortiz	.206	.263	.235	34	2	7	0	1	3	10	0
Brian Peterson	.254	.329	.325	126	8	32	1	8	13	30	1
Denis Phipps	.336	.405	.540	378	62	127	17	76	41	74	12
Philip Pohl	.311	.407	.473	74	10	23	3	11	6	21	0
D'Vontrey Richardson	.314	.349	.445	274	39	86	8	34	12	41	14
Juan Silverio	.269	.301	.457	350	47	94	13	57	18	54	6
Kevin Taylor	.327	.435	.497	346	69	113	11	54	65	40	5
Jeudy Valdez	.250	.305	.408	184	29	46	6	22	12	36	14
Byron Wiley	.192	.333	.279	104	9	20	1	8	22	39	2

PITCHER	W	L	ERA	G	SV	IP	H	BB	SO
Ryan Beckman	8	1	1.37	49	1	72	53	17	50
Kevin Brandt*	0	0	3.27	3	0	11	12	10	7
John Brebbia	7	2	0.98	51	19	64	34	15	79
Luis De La Cruz	2	2	2.57	31	0	35	22	14	38
Henry Garcia*	6	6	3.65	25	0	101	113	27	81
Scott Garner	5	3	3.35	9	0	46	54	11	30
Alex Gunn*	0	1	6.46	4	0	15	18	6	7
Greg Holle	3	5	2.00	14	0	86	83	13	48
B.J. Hyatt	4	1	2.49	41	1	43	44	15	40
Cody Kendall	1	3	6.02	10	0	40	57	13	22
Matt Loosen	7	6	4.42	21	0	114	120	60	91
Joan Montero	1	2	5.29	16	0	17	22	9	8
Willy Paredes	0	1	6.00	10	0	15	17	15	10
Luis Pollorena*	5	4	3.90	36	0	95	105	30	61
Chad Povich	0	2	6.75	2	0	9	12	3	6
Matt Sergey	2	0	0.00	3	0	20	8	4	22
Travis Stout	0	0	9.00	2	0	6	10	3	3

LINCOLN SALTDOGS

NAME	AVG	OBP	SLG	AB	R	H	HR	RBI	BB	SO	SB
Max Ayoub	.182	.250	.273	11	0	2	0	0	1	4	0
Billy Bissell	.154	.154	.154	13	1	2	0	0	0	7	0
Mitch Canham	.282	.334	.376	287	37	81	5	32	21	32	5
Matt Forgatch	.274	.349	.371	383	62	105	2	34	42	75	30
Jon Gaston	.304	.390	.478	138	22	42	6	23	17	28	5
Mike Gilmartin	.252	.318	.322	286	30	72	2	28	26	44	4
Jeremy Hamilton	.237	.314	.286	308	25	73	1	34	35	49	1
Brian Joynt	.229	.288	.310	358	37	82	3	38	28	88	1
Trevor Martin	.154	.154	.205	39	2	6	0	2	0	10	0
Steve Pascual	.227	.261	.227	22	1	5	0	2	0	7	0
Aaron Payne	.257	.343	.286	276	33	71	3	29	26	70	7
Curt Smith	.294	.358	.492	333	53	98	12	61	33	47	5
Tucker White	.235	.343	.271	85	12	20	0	5	13	16	3

NAME	AVG	OBP	SLG	AB	R	H	HR	RBI	BB	SO	SB
Ryan Wiggins	.229	.321	.347	170	19	39	3	30	23	58	0
Eddie Young	.230	.332	.282	291	42	67	0	19	43	39	58
C.J. Ziegler	.261	.369	.400	180	25	47	6	25	28	40	1

PITCHER	W	L	ERA	G	SV	IP	H	BB	SO
Zach Arneson	1	0	7.30	14	3	12	20	9	10
Daniel Child	1	0	4.66	13	0	19	26	6	16
Casey Collins	2	3	5.40	11	0	52	56	24	37
Chase Cunningham	0	4	4.91	6	0	40	52	9	15
Ryan Fennell	0	1	2.70	19	0	27	18	12	18
Jared Gaynor*	0	0	8.18	6	0	11	23	8	5
MacKenzie King	1	5	5.79	30	5	37	41	16	22
Shairon Martis	6	3	3.74	17	0	106	96	21	79
Kevin McGovern*	5	8	5.01	20	0	128	138	53	103
Moises Melendez*	0	2	5.40	21	0	48	57	25	28
Marshall Schuler	2	4	4.96	16	6	16	21	3	15
Jesse Smith	3	10	5.92	19	0	106	141	40	61
Conor Spink*	5	6	4.11	46	0	61	68	21	39
Zach Staniewicz	0	3	16.20	3	0	13	26	14	11
Zach Varce	0	5	5.43	11	0	66	81	20	50
Zac Westcott	5	2	3.22	22	0	45	37	13	36

SIOUX CITY EXPLORERS

NAME	AVG	OBP	SLG	AB	R	H	HR	RBI	BB	SO	SB
Tim Colwell	.258	.323	.337	291	44	75	1	26	28	55	29
Ryan Court	.331	.400	.474	369	65	122	9	52	41	56	15
Matty Johnson	.264	.332	.344	424	80	112	2	38	41	58	42
Brent Keys	.348	.427	.391	115	18	40	0	11	15	18	9
Brock Kjeldgaard	.269	.390	.489	327	56	95	14	70	50	82	7
Matt Koch	.280	.312	.378	304	41	85	4	42	12	57	2
Michael Lang	.343	.394	.507	335	75	115	6	59	21	62	45
Tommy Mendonca	.311	.373	.424	328	46	102	3	47	22	60	0
Ino Patron	.246	.303	.328	61	7	15	0	3	1	6	1
Noah Perio	.316	.345	.458	408	61	129	7	74	20	26	18
Brendan Slattery	.269	.345	.308	52	3	14	0	4	5	12	0
Austin Stubbs	.200	.200	.200	20	2	4	0	3	0	4	0
Rene Tosoni	.251	.327	.329	343	54	86	2	60	42	39	20
Dillon Usiak	.225	.327	.337	89	12	20	1	7	12	26	0

PITCHER	W	L	ERA	G	SV	IP	H	BB	SO
Billy Bullock	2	1	3.42	35	0	47	36	37	51
Anthony Ferrara*	0	0	9.58	10	0	10	19	5	4
Jose Flores	1	1	2.70	37	22	37	33	13	37
David Herndon	1	1	2.35	17	1	23	27	7	18
Patrick Johnson	15	1	2.08	20	0	134	94	40	132
Jimmer Kennedy	2	0	2.70	38	2	57	46	20	61
Jeff Marquez	6	5	4.31	15	0	88	94	29	48
Brandon Stennis*	1	1	3.66	5	1	20	16	9	12
John Straka	11	3	3.27	20	0	129	124	36	110
Eric Wordekemper	8	2	4.64	19	0	76	71	39	55
Rob Wort	11	3	1.79	41	4	65	35	26	92
Ryan Zimmerman	14	2	1.80	19	0	120	81	37	96

SIOUX FALLS CANARIES

NAME	AVG	OBP	SLG	AB	R	H	HR	RBI	BB	SO	SB
Brett Balkan	.242	.282	.306	124	13	30	0	7	6	5	4
David Bergin	.331	.427	.552	344	67	114	15	65	41	87	3
Cody Bishop	.260	.306	.356	104	6	27	0	5	7	31	1
Michael Broad	.226	.314	.355	31	2	7	0	3	4	5	0
Angel Chavez	.244	.287	.280	82	9	20	0	7	5	7	0
Edwin Gomez	.184	.225	.342	38	6	7	1	5	2	10	1
Chris Grayson	.290	.362	.428	276	37	80	3	36	28	43	11
Brian Humphries	.310	.330	.485	406	52	126	15	58	13	75	7
Jake Luce	.180	.268	.260	50	8	9	0	1	5	9	0
Jerome Pena	.290	.374	.429	352	55	102	8	35	46	89	8
RJ Perucki	.274	.305	.334	332	34	91	3	34	14	43	5
Vickash Ramjit	.212	.245	.311	132	20	28	3	19	4	24	3
Jason Repko	.291	.396	.462	299	53	87	13	39	44	60	13
Tyler Shannon	.083	.083	.083	12	1	1	0	0	0	7	0
Tyler Shover	.257	.294	.296	152	14	39	0	11	7	25	0
Richard Stock	.265	.276	.428	264	25	70	7	43	5	61	1
Steve Sulcoski	.295	.313	.508	61	11	18	3	10	1	12	0
Tyler Tewell	.091	.154	.091	11	0	1	0	1	1	3	0
Tony Viger	.167	.167	.167	12	1	2	0	0	0	3	0

PITCHER	W	L	ERA	G	SV	IP	H	BB	SO
Joe Bircher*	4	4	3.05	16	0	86	80	26	48
Shawn Blackwell	5	9	3.64	20	0	129	129	50	103
Stephen Bougher	6	5	3.53	16	0	94	102	30	48
Josh Ferrell*	0	1	5.79	37	1	47	56	32	35
Brett Gerritse	0	5	7.89	5	0	22	47	5	14
Ray Hanson	1	1	5.29	3	0	17	18	7	11
Chase Johnson	5	2	2.55	40	15	42	36	23	37
James Jones	1	3	4.91	24	1	22	18	13	15
Cameron McVey	2	2	2.81	36	2	42	33	17	44
Dennis Neal*	0	1	3.68	3	0	7	8	4	5
Miguel Pena*	6	7	3.58	18	0	121	152	24	52
Will Rankin	1	1	6.97	12	1	10	16	4	8
Nate Stewart	0	0	3.00	5	0	6	5	7	7
Benny Suarez	1	0	1.56	15	0	17	22	7	14
Mike Watt*	1	1	6.33	16	0	21	33	13	13

ST. PAUL SAINTS

NAME	AVG	OBP	SLG	AB	R	H	HR	RBI	BB	SO	SB
Willie Argo	.287	.385	.457	341	78	98	12	49	52	94	28
Ron Bourquin	.083	.154	.083	12	1	1	0	0	1	6	0
Vinny DiFazio	.361	.467	.592	321	70	116	17	82	54	61	1
Mitch Elliott	.186	.233	.204	113	12	21	0	5	7	24	6
Ian Gac	.331	.415	.537	272	60	90	10	52	36	62	0
Nate Hanson	.275	.351	.420	69	16	19	1	6	8	11	0
Alonzo Harris	.298	.339	.466	386	75	115	15	62	24	58	39
Dan Kaczrowski	.275	.338	.336	211	24	58	3	25	18	19	0
Mike Kvasnicka	.299	.340	.502	281	53	84	10	63	17	41	0
Sam Maus	.209	.279	.255	110	18	23	1	8	9	29	0
Steve Nikorak	.227	.330	.384	185	24	42	6	26	25	68	3
Joey Paciorek	.254	.333	.347	248	30	63	4	28	29	59	0
Anthony Phillips	.269	.316	.341	323	45	87	2	35	19	60	4
Angelo Songco	.339	.415	.580	369	64	125	17	82	42	72	1
Robert Youngdahl	.174	.269	.174	23	2	4	0	5	3	9	0

PITCHER	W	L	ERA	G	SV	IP	H	BB	SO
Dylan Chavez*	1	1	5.83	29	2	29	30	16	28
Robert Coe	12	3	3.11	20	0	124	97	48	78
Kevin Cravey	1	0	2.57	4	0	7	5	4	4
Dustin Crenshaw	14	2	2.43	20	0	137	136	7	61
Pedro Hernandez*	8	3	3.99	16	0	97	103	13	63
Mike Mehlich	0	2	4.26	17	1	19	16	8	14
Alan Oaks	0	0	6.75	6	1	7	11	0	2
Chris Peacock	2	2	3.29	30	0	41	38	22	19
Ryan Rodebaugh	2	5	2.84	41	25	44	31	16	47
Jeff Shields	13	2	3.11	19	0	127	124	31	57
Kramer Sneed*	15	3	2.83	20	0	127	120	39	81
Michael Zouzalik	4	1	2.06	39	3	48	23	13	49

WICHITA WINGNUTS

NAME	AVG	OBP	SLG	AB	R	H	HR	RBI	BB	SO	SB
Joash Brodin	.274	.333	.404	223	28	61	3	24	18	33	10
Brent Clevlen	.444	.510	.622	45	7	20	1	9	6	11	0
Tyler Coughenour	.136	.240	.182	44	3	6	0	2	5	15	3
Brent Dean	.281	.320	.350	217	28	61	1	21	11	33	10
Alberto Gonzalez	.296	.338	.416	125	20	37	1	13	7	6	12
Jerry Gonzalez-Lopez	.160	.222	.200	25	1	4	0	3	2	5	1
Tyler Heil	.105	.105	.158	19	1	2	0	1	0	9	0
Luis Hernandez	.255	.291	.343	251	24	64	1	37	12	20	3
Andy LaRoche	.269	.336	.559	93	18	25	6	23	18	10	0
T.J. Mittelstaedt	.258	.407	.481	337	68	87	16	65	86	115	11
John Nester	.281	.354	.420	288	33	81	5	43	32	78	2
Jayce Ray	.310	.422	.383	332	57	103	1	35	56	39	17
Nick Van Stratten	.420	.506	.667	69	16	29	3	20	12	2	4
Leo Vargas	.219	.298	.244	160	25	35	0	11	15	25	7

PITCHER	W	L	ERA	G	SV	IP	H	BB	SO
Dan Bennett	1	8	1.97	49	3	50	36	16	58
Alex Boshers	4	2	1.86	28	0	48	43	14	29
Tim Brown	10	2	3.29	20	0	131	153	20	56
Anthony Capra*	2	3	4.25	6	0	36	36	15	35
Daniel Carela	1	0	6.43	16	1	14	9	13	20
Scott Kuzminsky	2	4	4.95	22	0	56	85	16	27
Jon Link	6	0	1.89	9	0	48	34	12	46
Charlie Lowell*	2	1	5.13	6	0	33	35	12	29
Eddie Medina	4	1	3.50	8	0	46	48	18	29
Iden Nazario*	2	0	6.10	13	0	10	12	8	5
Matt Nevarez	1	1	0.68	13	8	13	9	4	19

PITCHER	W	L	ERA	G	SV	IP	H	BB	SO
Brad Orosey	0	2	3.14	13	0	14	11	8	15
Frankie Reed*	0	1	3.00	21	0	18	10	9	20
Scott Richmond	6	1	1.79	11	0	65	54	7	54
Paul Smyth	1	0	4.50	12	7	12	10	2	20
Jason Van Skike	7	8	4.89	20	0	116	132	33	58

WINNIPEG GOLDEYES

NAME	AVG	OBP	SLG	AB	R	H	HR	RBI	BB	SO	SB
Reggie Abercrombie	.318	.368	.464	192	28	61	6	37	12	53	11
Luis Alen	.275	.384	.338	302	39	83	5	36	50	9	4
Ryan Babineau	.218	.314	.274	179	16	39	1	16	23	43	2
Brad Boyer	.263	.311	.320	350	41	92	2	41	23	46	3
Kyle Brandenburg	.273	.351	.394	33	8	9	0	5	3	8	0
Casio Grider	.303	.336	.428	290	46	88	7	38	12	71	23
Casey Haerther	.312	.365	.435	407	49	127	11	79	34	45	0
Adam Heisler	.328	.380	.429	375	64	123	4	44	34	59	44
Nic Jackson	.265	.315	.412	136	22	36	4	16	10	26	1
Brett Krill	.261	.277	.348	46	2	12	0	4	1	12	0
Josh Mazzola	.279	.361	.520	373	71	104	20	63	39	76	9
Ramon Ortega	.203	.266	.220	59	7	12	0	5	5	15	1
Chris Robinson	.250	.293	.339	124	16	31	1	6	8	23	2
Robby Spencer	.200	.200	.333	15	2	3	0	1	0	5	0
Brady Wilson	.239	.321	.283	138	25	33	0	12	18	30	12
Mike Wilson	.200	.294	.267	15	0	3	0	0	2	6	0

PITCHER	W	L	ERA	G	SV	IP	H	BB	SO
Kyle Anderson*	5	6	4.77	18	0	94	117	19	60
Edwin Carl	6	1	2.10	8	0	56	39	14	62
Jonathan Cornelius*	0	3	12.38	3	0	8	17	8	7
Coby Cowgill	3	3	4.64	10	0	54	60	27	30
Nick Hernandez*	8	8	3.25	20	0	130	123	29	91
Matt Jackson	8	8	4.49	21	0	124	155	31	80
Brendan Lafferty*	3	3	3.42	58	2	53	62	18	43
Bo Logan*	0	0	7.27	7	0	9	9	3	7
Rob Nixon	1	3	8.23	7	0	35	50	12	21
Jailen Peguero	5	4	3.76	49	16	55	50	20	67
Mark Pope	1	2	5.31	32	0	41	57	4	22
Raul Rivera	2	1	5.89	16	0	18	22	7	13
Anthony Smith	4	4	4.96	27	0	85	97	24	55

ATLANTIC LEAGUE

Coming into the season, no Atlantic League team had come close to matching the Somerset Patriots' five league titles. But that last trophy, won in 2009, was getting a little dusty

The Patriots have a fresh, shiny new trophy in the case now as Somesrset won its sixth league title by knocking off Southern Maryland in the championship series. Playoff MVP Roy Merritt won his third game of the postseason in the deciding game of the championship series.

FREEDOM DIVISION	W	L	PCT	GB
Lancaster Barnstormers	75	65	.536	—
Southern Maryland Blue Crabs	69	71	.493	6
Sugar Land Skeeters	68	71	.489	6.5
York Revolution	64	75	.460	10.5

LIBERTY DIVISION	W	L	PCT	GB
Somerset Patriots	89	56	.640	—
Long Island Ducks	80	59	.576	9
Bridgeport Bluefish	56	83	.403	33
Camden Riversharks	56	83	.403	33

PLAYOFFS: Semifinals—Somerset defeated Long Island 3-2 and Southern Maryland defeated Lancaster 3-1 in best-of-5 series. **Finals**—Somerset defeated Southern Maryland 3-1 in best-of-5 series.

ATTENDANCE: Long Island Ducks 358,317; Somerset Patriots 347,770; Sugar Land Skeeters 301,860; Lancaster Barnstormers 276,975; York Revolution 259,989; Southern Maryland Blue Crabs 222,611; Camden Riversharks 216,639; Bridgeport Bluefish 192,466.

MANAGERS: Bridgeport–Ricky Van Asselberg; Camden–Chris Widger; Lancaster–Butch Hobson; Long Island–Kevin Baez; Somerset–Brett Jodie; Southern Maryland–Stan Cliburn; Sugar Land–Gary Gaetti; York–

Mark Mason.

ALL-STAR TEAM: C—Chris Wallace, Sugar Land. 1B— Andres Perez, York. 2B–Delwyn Young, Sugar Land. 2B–Cody Puckett, Long Island. 3B–Bryan Pounds, York. SS–Dan Lyons, Long Island. OFs–Brian Cavazos-Galvez, Lancaster; Welington Dotel, Bridgeport; Aharon Eggleston, Somerset. DH–Sean Burroughs, Long Island/Bridgeport.

SP–John Brownell, Long Island. RP–Buddy Boshers, Somerset. Closer– Matt Gorgen, Camden.

PLAYER OF THE YEAR: Welington Dotel, Bridgeport. **PITCHER OF THE YEAR:** John Brownell, Long Island. **MANAGER OF THE YEAR:** Brett Jodie, Somerset.

BATTING LEADERS

PLAYER	TEAM	AVG	AB	R	H	HR	RBI
Burroughs, Sean	LI	.340	335	30	114	4	51
Dotel, Wellington	BPT	.340	530	68	180	8	68
Cleary Jr., Delta	LI	.308	451	62	139	1	41
Lyons, Dan	LI	.301	465	74	140	11	73
Wilson, Zach	SMD	.291	484	63	141	9	55
Perez, Andres	YRK	.291	529	70	154	16	92
Eggleston, Aharon	SOM	.289	408	74	118	5	46
Young, Delwyn	SL	.285	460	64	131	10	45
Guzman, Carlos	CMD	.276	507	50	140	10	76
Zawadzki, Lance	LAN	.275	436	70	120	20	63

PITCHING LEADERS

PLAYER	TEAM	W	L	ERA	IP	H	BB	SO
Bierman, Sean	SOM	10	2	1.79	116	107	16	60
Zielinski, Matt	SOM	8	4	2.86	167	143	32	106
Merritt, Roy	SOM	8	8	2.88	112	104	20	75
Mitchell, D.J.	BPT	6	8	2.89	112	109	49	86
Brownell, John	LI	12	6	3.38	176	152	47	146
Irvine, Lucas	SOM	6	8	3.41	129	139	37	106
Gallagher, Sean	SL	6	9	3.51	159	143	47	128
Riordan, Cory	BPT	5	6	3.62	117	125	22	82
Lewis, Rommie	YRK	10	10	3.87	165	185	48	115
Burres, Brian	SMD	8	9	3.98	133	145	41	104

BRIDGEPORT BLUEFISH

NAME	AVG	OBP	SLG	AB	R	H	HR	RBI	BB	SO	SB
John Alonso	.258	.301	.372	387	42	100	6	51	28	57	1
Ryan Babineau	.250	.286	.336	140	17	35	0	11	4	39	0
Matt Burns	.212	.273	.242	132	12	28	0	6	10	42	1
Ethan Chapman	.229	.277	.307	205	27	47	1	15	13	56	10
Welington Dotel	.340	.371	.492	530	68	180	8	68	20	107	45
Jonathan Galvez	.302	.400	.395	43	5	13	0	5	7	8	3
Frazier Hall	.156	.208	.178	45	3	7	0	2	3	12	1
Juan Martinez	.209	.292	.326	43	4	9	1	7	4	11	1
Jobduan Morales	.257	.328	.342	284	23	73	3	33	32	76	0
Joe Poletsky	.235	.316	.235	17	1	4	0	2	1	2	0
Rodney Polonia	.182	.250	.242	33	1	6	0	0	3	7	0
Josh Prince	.253	.337	.344	253	46	64	3	15	27	63	23
C.J. Retherford	.226	.265	.274	62	4	14	0	12	4	11	0
Andres Rodriguez	.231	.282	.332	437	48	101	6	46	28	78	0
Luis Rodriguez	.221	.258	.282	181	13	40	2	21	9	25	0
Luis Rodriguez	.305	.379	.355	200	21	61	0	19	23	22	1
Jeudy Valdez	.222	.276	.259	54	6	12	0	4	3	16	3
Nick Van Stratten	.352	.432	.443	122	23	43	1	20	15	10	9
Ildemaro Vargas	.273	.316	.318	110	17	30	0	8	6	9	7
Wes Wallace	.125	.125	.313	16	2	2	1	2	0	10	0
Matt Wessinger	.206	.269	.285	228	28	47	2	20	20	63	6

PITCHER	W	L	ERA	G	SV	IP	H	BB	SO
Steve Ames	1	3	4.45	33	2	28	29	7	28
David Anderson	2	2	2.68	7	0	40	38	11	25
Mike Antonini*	4	5	2.79	11	0	68	61	14	62
Nate Baker*	0	1	9.00	12	0	11	19	7	5
Brandon Bixler*	0	3	4.25	8	0	30	23	12	24
Darren Byrd	1	0	9.45	6	0	7	6	5	4
Robert Carson*	7	3	2.88	23	0	78	78	27	80
Erik Draxton	3	1	2.39	55	0	60	55	16	46
Parker Frazier	3	0	1.80	6	0	35	35	8	15
Sammy Gervacio	5	4	4.33	47	2	52	50	11	60
Matt Iannazzo*	5	12	4.57	31	0	122	131	29	77
Kameron Loe	4	3	4.87	9	0	57	62	9	44
Reinaldo Lopez	3	7	7.11	4	0	31	31	8	10

PITCHER	W	L	ERA	G	SV	IP	H	BB	SO
Scott Maine*	3	5	5.21	14	0	74	87	36	66
Patrick Mincey	1	1	3.56	51	26	48	44	25	39
D.J. Mitchell	6	8	2.89	19	0	112	109	49	86
Jim Patterson*	2	2	5.06	14	0	16	23	6	17
Wander Perez*	0	0	0.00	6	0	6	3	2	1
Chad Povich	1	2	5.18	28	0	40	53	20	37
Cory Riordan	5	6	3.62	18	0	117	125	22	82
Scott Shuman	0	0	2.49	24	0	22	16	11	29

CAMDEN RIVERSHARKS

NAME	AVG	OBP	SLG	AB	R	H	HR	RBI	BB	SO	SB
Stephen Bull	.179	.258	.179	28	2	5	0	1	3	9	0
Brandon Chaves	.256	.351	.353	434	55	111	4	36	59	112	7
Nathaniel Coronado	.107	.107	.107	28	2	3	0	1	0	7	0
Mike Costanzo	.211	.275	.366	213	21	45	9	31	19	72	0
Eric Frain	.272	.330	.315	92	10	25	0	4	7	27	2
Jose Gil	.242	.322	.356	264	28	64	5	21	28	57	2
Carlos Guzman	.276	.339	.389	507	50	140	10	76	47	65	23
Joel Guzman	.250	.278	.383	488	52	122	13	70	19	109	11
Dan Hennigan	.227	.337	.240	75	8	17	0	8	11	11	6
Mike Kerns	.152	.200	.203	79	4	12	0	6	3	14	0
Zach MacPhee	.210	.302	.254	224	23	47	0	18	28	43	13
Paddy Matera	.254	.323	.356	382	42	97	7	39	34	40	3
Willis Otanez	.200	.257	.292	65	3	13	0	8	5	10	0
Daniel Rockett	.220	.303	.391	350	56	77	15	40	34	94	8
Michael Rockett	.269	.288	.326	527	60	142	2	40	14	107	7
Eddie Sorondo	.250	.305	.316	76	9	19	0	5	5	20	0
Ryan Strieby	.236	.325	.344	326	42	77	6	33	40	88	1
Norberto Susini	.162	.282	.225	111	11	18	1	11	14	28	0
Landis Wilson	.200	.273	.200	10	0	2	0	0	1	5	0

PITCHER	W	L	ERA	G	SV	IP	H	BB	SO
Dan Blewett	1	5	1.80	50	1	50	45	12	59
Zach Braddock*	4	3	5.36	44	1	40	44	30	39
Rob Bryson	1	1	2.41	51	0	52	42	17	58
Michael Click	5	1	1.97	58	0	59	52	15	57
Steve Garrison*	2	4	3.60	21	0	55	66	9	40
Sean Gleason	6	15	5.19	32	0	154	195	56	84
Matt Gorgen	2	1	2.31	48	33	47	30	20	51
Danny Herrera*	7	4	5.04	37	0	100	129	33	77
Eric Kline*	0	1	9.53	5	0	6	9	7	4
Ryan Kulik*	4	4	5.51	10	0	49	69	14	19
Bill Murphy*	8	15	4.37	28	0	171	174	78	131
Fu-Te Ni*	2	1	3.38	7	0	40	38	6	30
Alex Polanco	0	0	8.10	4	0	7	6	7	5
Carlos Ruiz	0	0	4.50	4	0	8	5	7	4
Jeff Singer*	1	4	5.26	13	0	50	51	30	30
Eric Smith	2	8	4.18	26	0	84	88	37	68
Wes Torrez	7	9	4.85	27	0	141	143	65	94

LANCASTER BARNSTORMERS

NAME	AVG	OBP	SLG	AB	R	H	HR	RBI	BB	SO	SB
Juan Apodaca	.229	.309	.327	205	16	47	3	22	21	41	3
Tyler Bortnick	.280	.344	.386	189	23	53	1	23	14	37	4
Michael Broad	.267	.389	.467	15	3	4	1	2	3	7	0
Brian Cavazos-Galvez	.267	.322	.424	505	80	135	17	68	35	61	26
Chevy Clarke	.120	.214	.160	25	4	3	0	0	2	11	2
Zach Collier	.277	.356	.454	249	44	69	7	34	20	63	13
David Cooper	.273	.351	.394	66	6	18	2	8	8	6	0
Charlie Cutler	.222	.291	.270	126	12	28	0	16	12	17	0
Anderson Feliz	.275	.344	.415	306	37	84	7	44	33	84	14
Masato Fukae	.147	.194	.206	34	2	5	0	2	1	8	0
Blake Gailen	.252	.387	.464	151	25	38	8	29	34	20	7
Luke Hughes	.240	.308	.422	275	44	66	12	38	24	89	2
Yusuke Kajimoto	.242	.313	.324	392	52	95	3	33	38	85	12
Kent Matthes	.263	.309	.391	266	33	70	7	39	17	41	6
Mike McDade	.280	.305	.430	279	32	78	10	42	9	46	0
Jerry Owens	.354	.418	.381	147	22	52	0	15	16	14	10
Derrick Pyles	.320	.382	.360	50	9	16	0	2	5	4	0
Kevin Rivers	.251	.327	.439	346	49	87	15	48	37	101	2
Henry Wrigley	.196	.211	.232	56	4	11	0	3	1	12	1
Lance Zawadzki	.275	.319	.450	436	70	120	20	63	29	92	20

PITCHER	W	L	ERA	G	SV	IP	H	BB	SO
Pete Andrelczyk	9	2	2.00	54	5	85	66	36	78
Chad Beck	4	3	5.07	38	4	76	88	28	73
Madison Boer	4	3	4.28	9	0	46	61	14	28

INDEPENDENT LEAGUES

PITCHER	W	L	ERA	G	SV	IP	H	BB	SO
Edwin Carl	1	0	3.86	1	0	7	6	1	4
Bryan Evans	1	2	6.04	5	0	25	27	8	25
C.J. Fick	0	0	2.45	2	0	11	6	4	9
Joe Gardner	9	6	4.27	19	0	116	120	38	72
Scott Gracey	5	0	1.93	53	0	56	44	26	66
Blake Hassebrock	0	2	5.29	20	0	17	22	8	17
Zach Jackson*	2	5	4.63	30	0	23	28	12	28
Mark Lamm	0	0	1.40	18	0	19	14	5	13
Pat Misch*	1	0	1.80	2	0	10	7	4	3
Bryan Morgado*	4	6	3.25	32	0	72	62	28	71
Daniel Moskos*	2	0	3.04	16	0	24	27	10	19
Dan Osterbrock*	3	5	3.13	12	0	63	65	27	33
Matt Packer*	3	5	4.82	11	0	56	72	10	32
Scott Patterson	2	3	2.19	50	7	49	38	10	43
Nate Reed*	8	7	3.80	32	1	109	105	55	110
Kyle Simon	4	0	3.16	28	0	31	33	8	27
Marcus Walden	2	4	2.95	48	15	64	59	22	49
P.J. Walters	0	1	5.91	2	0	11	12	3	8
Shunsuke Watanabe	7	5	2.94	21	0	110	98	30	75
Bryan Woodall	3	4	3.54	19	0	86	89	17	73
Al Yevoli*	1	0	0.00	23	0	17	12	3	13

LONG ISLAND DUCKS

NAME	AVG	OBP	SLG	AB	R	H	HR	RBI	BB	SO	SB
Mike Blanke	.282	.337	.411	326	42	92	9	43	26	65	5
Delta Cleary	.308	.345	.373	451	62	139	1	41	23	66	34
Reegie Corona	.331	.386	.455	257	45	85	3	31	20	29	11
Blake Davis	.230	.293	.270	148	11	34	0	8	13	31	3
Sam DiMatteo	.176	.222	.235	17	3	3	0	2	1	7	0
Lew Ford	.364	.432	.545	297	47	108	8	63	30	39	1
Ryan Gebhardt	.000	.111	.000	14	0	0	0	3	2	4	0
Jon Griffin	.232	.294	.393	349	31	81	13	57	29	119	4
Dillon Haupt	.143	.316	.357	14	5	2	1	2	4	6	0
Carlos Hughes	.194	.244	.208	72	10	14	0	4	4	25	0
Erik Komatsu	.167	.250	.194	72	8	12	0	5	7	13	1
Fehlandt Lentini	.291	.323	.404	213	31	62	3	21	7	36	9
Dan Lyons	.301	.375	.462	465	74	140	11	73	48	65	18
Steve McQuail	.168	.227	.314	137	15	23	6	11	10	43	0
Jose Morales	.264	.329	.321	140	15	37	1	14	11	21	5
Cody Puckett	.275	.327	.368	535	67	147	9	53	33	79	1
Elmer Reyes	.380	.389	.746	71	12	27	6	15	1	9	0
Randy Ruiz	.349	.394	.538	238	32	83	11	47	16	45	1
Nelfi Zapata	.303	.398	.434	76	7	23	1	11	8	17	0

PITCHER	W	L	ERA	G	SV	IP	H	BB	SO
Hector Ambriz	1	0	1.29	7	0	7	5	1	9
Andrew Barbosa*	4	1	2.82	9	0	51	44	19	59
Bobby Blevins	4	4	3.83	15	0	89	94	11	67
John Brownell	12	6	3.38	26	0	176	152	47	146
Billy Buckner	8	3	4.00	18	1	70	73	36	73
Mariel Checo	0	1	9.45	6	0	7	5	4	9
Patrick Crider*	2	1	3.44	60	1	55	45	25	48
Frank DeJiulio	3	1	2.87	40	0	38	39	11	36
Amalio Diaz	1	4	2.78	60	14	58	46	17	69
Darin Downs*	4	5	3.86	12	0	68	61	30	55
Carmine Giardina*	2	0	4.26	14	0	13	15	8	6
Rich Hill*	1	0	0.00	2	0	11	2	3	21
Mickey Jannis	6	2	1.18	16	0	84	53	26	67
Bruce Kern	9	6	3.51	40	0	108	99	31	102
Ryan Kussmaul	5	2	3.42	55	26	55	56	22	59
Ian Marshall	7	7	4.39	27	0	144	148	67	92
Chris McCoy	0	1	1.50	2	0	6	8	1	5
Tommy Organ*	1	0	6.17	13	0	12	20	5	12
J.C. Romero*	0	1	1.83	35	0	34	23	13	24
Matt Soren	0	2	6.17	12	0	12	15	10	13
Nick Struck	5	4	2.10	50	0	51	39	23	52
Donnie Veal*	1	0	1.45	20	0	19	13	8	26

SOMERSET PATRIOTS

NAME	AVG	OBP	SLG	AB	R	H	HR	RBI	BB	SO	SB
Robert Andino	.248	.302	.339	463	56	115	4	56	37	105	5
Michael Burgess	.251	.292	.453	338	46	85	15	59	19	58	1
Ricky Claudio	.295	.382	.333	78	12	23	0	5	11	23	5
Scott Cousins	.264	.362	.325	163	22	43	1	18	22	39	12
Adam Donachie	.237	.343	.341	279	30	66	4	40	44	82	2
Aharon Eggleston	.289	.390	.380	408	74	118	5	46	57	52	9

NAME	AVG	OBP	SLG	AB	R	H	HR	RBI	BB	SO	SB
Matt Fields	.261	.424	.609	46	13	12	5	12	9	15	0
Greg Hopkins	.266	.335	.441	338	56	90	12	51	27	52	5
Scott Kelly	.337	.389	.410	83	20	28	0	10	5	13	7
Ollie Linton	.256	.310	.282	39	4	10	0	0	3	7	3
Chris Marrero	.311	.342	.514	148	16	46	6	22	7	22	1
Thomas Neal	.290	.356	.416	334	42	97	5	50	32	53	4
Jose Reyes	.159	.221	.182	88	7	14	0	6	6	24	5
James Skelton	.206	.334	.280	257	32	53	1	33	50	82	15
Nate Spears	.255	.332	.319	404	59	103	1	29	45	90	14
Jonny Tucker	.232	.279	.354	319	42	74	6	36	20	38	11
David Vidal	.259	.328	.395	471	59	122	12	63	46	103	1
Mike Wilson	.205	.337	.325	83	15	17	2	9	17	20	2
Vinny Zarrillo	.224	.294	.276	76	14	17	0	5	8	18	7

PITCHER	W	L	ERA	G	SV	IP	H	BB	SO
Sean Bierman	10	2	1.79	17	0	116	107	16	60
Randy Boone	5	3	2.80	16	0	100	85	14	52
Buddy Boshers*	3	1	1.00	52	1	54	39	14	71
Brett Brach	1	0	3.78	5	0	17	14	5	7
Andrew Carignan	2	2	2.52	54	4	54	28	28	57
Anthony Collazo*	3	3	2.68	45	0	47	42	17	34
Kelvin De La Cruz*	0	0	2.16	8	0	8	4	1	5
David Harden	5	1	0.68	8	0	27	27	3	9
Jon Hunton	2	5	3.09	50	32	47	47	7	30
Luke Irvine	6	8	3.41	22	0	129	139	37	106
Connor Little	0	1	7.50	4	0	6	6	0	4
Roy Merritt	1	1	7.00	2	0	9	12	3	5
Kyler Newby	8	4	4.09	49	2	55	49	21	50
Will Oliver	6	2	3.17	9	0	54	41	17	34
Edwin Quirarte	1	0	0.00	8	0	8	1	3	4
Daniel Sattler	8	2	3.56	47	0	48	25	35	64
Gus Schlosser	1	0	3.79	17	1	19	18	9	16
R.J. Seidel	2	6	3.95	34	0	87	91	29	65
Paul Smyth	3	0	3.38	28	1	32	27	11	23
Kramer Sneed*	0	0	6.00	1	0	6	5	4	4
Mickey Storey	12	3	2.53	18	0	107	84	19	85
Matt Zielinski*	8	4	2.86	26	0	167	143	32	106

SOUTHERN MARYLAND BLUE CRABS

NAME	AVG	OBP	SLG	AB	R	H	HR	RBI	BB	SO	SB
Reggie Abercrombie	.308	.308	.564	39	8	12	2	6	0	15	2
Antone DeJesus	.248	.329	.337	323	55	80	3	27	30	49	12
Casey Frawley	.264	.316	.387	398	49	105	8	42	22	88	3
Cyle Hankerd	.354	.456	.664	113	20	40	9	20	15	19	1
Fred Lewis	.238	.335	.336	446	63	106	5	39	60	130	19
Craig Maddox	.266	.315	.394	282	20	75	4	33	18	87	2
Gustavo Molina	.285	.323	.470	281	29	80	13	52	15	63	1
Jake Opitz	.255	.335	.424	302	49	77	7	24	34	59	4
Casey Stevenson	.270	.349	.367	444	57	120	5	47	44	75	3
Jamar Walton	.277	.299	.396	346	36	96	3	44	15	85	3
Zach Wilson	.291	.353	.419	484	63	141	9	55	46	109	4
Grant Zawadzki	.193	.223	.236	140	13	27	0	8	6	56	1

PITCHER	W	L	ERA	G	SV	IP	H	BB	SO
Brian Baker	5	9	5.15	22	0	117	140	42	71
Trey Barham*	1	2	3.36	48	1	59	56	24	45
Justin Berg	3	3	3.35	36	1	46	47	16	38
Chris Bodishbaugh	1	0	6.61	11	0	16	20	6	5
Brian Burres*	8	9	3.98	26	0	133	145	41	104
Shaun Garceau	5	6	4.72	14	0	76	85	33	56
Brian Grening	4	4	4.49	28	0	120	145	33	80
Jake Hale	9	5	2.93	18	0	108	91	29	68
Erik Hamren	4	1	4.14	39	24	37	41	15	41
Gaby Hernandez	2	1	2.84	3	0	19	15	3	19
Sean Keeler	1	1	4.35	10	0	10	10	9	7
Wade Korpi*	4	3	5.67	33	1	67	95	24	49
Jon Leicester	3	1	2.42	9	0	52	44	15	34
Orlando Santos	4	7	2.91	51	1	68	51	40	78
Tim Sexton	1	1	3.54	21	0	48	54	9	42
Daryl Thompson	7	7	3.87	17	0	109	121	29	68
Chien-Ming Wang	3	0	2.49	3	0	22	23	1	9

SUGAR LAND SKEETERS

NAME	AVG	OBP	SLG	AB	R	H	HR	RBI	BB	SO	SB
Ryan Adams	.100	.156	.200	30	4	3	1	3	2	7	0
Denny Almonte	.205	.283	.343	396	39	81	10	31	41	161	24
Joe Benson	.200	.238	.250	20	3	4	0	1	1	2	1

INDEPENDENT LEAGUES

NAME	AVG	OBP	SLG	AB	R	H	HR	RBI	BB	SO	SB
Kelly Cross	.205	.255	.295	44	6	9	1	3	3	12	0
Jeff Dominguez	.288	.365	.473	205	42	59	5	28	25	28	21
Allan Dykstra	.179	.333	.214	56	3	10	0	3	10	15	0
Edwin Gomez	.184	.231	.184	49	1	9	0	1	3	20	0
Todd Jennings	.061	.086	.061	33	1	2	0	2	1	6	0
Dustin Martin	.264	.323	.389	208	22	55	5	26	19	44	8
Patrick Palmeiro	.256	.315	.404	450	43	115	13	68	36	115	4
Kevin Russo	.249	.301	.315	394	48	98	2	29	29	68	10
Travis Scott	.254	.336	.384	425	58	108	10	51	51	70	4
Willy Taveras	.241	.309	.317	249	32	60	4	16	22	47	21
Chris Wallace	.257	.317	.429	482	64	124	17	83	40	147	3
Jon Weber	.182	.250	.182	11	0	2	0	2	1	5	0
Beamer Weems	.308	.380	.474	133	18	41	3	12	12	18	0
Delwyn Young	.285	.355	.400	460	64	131	10	45	46	58	4
Amadeo Zazueta	.260	.304	.301	385	38	100	2	28	25	37	9

PITCHER	W	L	ERA	G	SV	IP	H	BB	SO
Derek Blacksher	5	3	2.45	25	0	70	59	16	63
Drew Carpenter	3	4	6.69	29	0	36	48	13	37
Hunter Cervenka*	0	0	0.00	8	1	8	4	1	12
Ramon Delgado	2	1	3.26	33	1	39	43	10	27
Sean Gallagher	6	9	3.51	27	0	159	143	47	128
Josh Geer	7	8	4.45	23	0	129	170	29	78
Andrew Johnston	3	2	3.04	58	0	53	63	18	32
Derrick Loop*	2	0	1.28	49	15	49	24	14	60
Shane Loux	4	3	2.92	13	0	77	79	12	25
Matt Maloney*	1	1	5.31	4	0	20	24	6	12
Brett Marshall	1	1	3.00	2	0	12	8	6	8
Adrian Martin	4	3	5.09	41	6	41	50	6	38
Miguel Martinez*	0	1	6.57	3	0	12	23	3	8
Dan Meadows*	0	4	8.25	9	0	24	36	8	15
Michael Nix	3	0	2.37	3	0	19	15	7	15
James Parr	2	3	4.40	42	1	47	48	18	50
Dan Runzler*	0	0	0.52	19	2	17	12	3	20
Tim Stauffer	1	1	1.69	3	0	16	10	4	10
Cory VanAllen*	5	4	3.12	40	0	43	42	17	25
Kelvin Villa*	0	2	3.16	8	0	37	36	11	26
Robbie Weinhardt	2	3	2.82	47	2	45	39	27	55
Matt Wright	6	7	4.17	21	0	108	117	35	108

YORK REVOLUTION

NAME	AVG	OBP	SLG	AB	R	H	HR	RBI	BB	SO	SB
Brandon Boggs	.264	.371	.400	450	61	119	12	47	72	104	10
Willie Cabrera	.203	.282	.217	69	7	14	0	5	7	9	0
Yeicok Calderon	.276	.313	.439	221	24	61	7	31	12	53	1
Jose Constanza	.324	.379	.374	139	29	45	0	13	13	19	21
Luis De La Cruz	.275	.301	.364	269	26	74	5	31	9	41	0
Nick Ferdinand	.262	.340	.464	233	30	61	11	29	23	70	2
Telvin Nash	.270	.391	.516	215	46	58	13	30	40	82	1
Salvador Paniagua	.256	.281	.388	258	20	66	7	37	7	63	0
Alfredo Patino	.278	.381	.278	18	3	5	0	1	3	5	1
Eric Patterson	.254	.336	.405	472	68	120	10	58	58	103	21
Andres Perez	.291	.350	.452	529	70	154	16	92	46	90	3
Bryan Pounds	.272	.358	.421	470	67	128	13	65	61	123	6
Steve Proscia	.194	.227	.222	72	2	14	0	3	3	23	0
Mikey Reynolds	.280	.356	.335	275	32	77	1	17	26	45	17
Starlin Rodriguez	.288	.325	.438	73	8	21	2	7	4	13	2
Sean Smith	.193	.233	.263	57	3	11	1	2	2	10	2
Wilson Valdez	.262	.306	.320	484	55	127	1	42	29	59	33
Shannon Wilkerson	.256	.305	.365	156	20	40	2	16	9	23	7

PITCHER	W	L	ERA	G	SV	IP	H	BB	SO
Hunter Adkins	0	1	19.29	3	0	7	16	8	6
Brad Bergesen	0	0	3.24	10	1	8	9	2	5
Mike DeMark	1	0	0.83	23	3	22	12	7	15
Julio DePaula	0	0	3.86	9	2	9	10	3	9
Ian Durham	0	0	7.24	9	0	14	22	6	12
Frank Gailey*	5	3	3.21	20	0	93	83	30	85
Joe Harris*	1	2	5.84	21	0	25	20	10	15
Ty'Relle Harris	1	0	2.59	17	1	24	13	8	28
Shawn Hill	3	8	4.46	17	0	83	92	26	61
Josh Judy	2	2	2.68	53	12	50	50	15	52
Anthony Lerew	3	5	4.29	13	0	65	69	27	51
Rommie Lewis*	10	10	3.86	27	0	165	185	48	115
Mike McClendon	0	2	4.57	4	0	22	24	1	17
Nick Mutz	0	1	4.26	7	1	6	7	3	9
Matt Neil	4	8	4.48	34	0	145	156	37	109

PITCHER	W	L	ERA	G	SV	IP	H	BB	SO
Edward Paredes*	4	1	3.32	55	0	57	42	22	73
Tony Pena	2	2	2.75	36	1	39	34	8	31
Stephen Penney	4	6	3.57	56	5	53	50	18	39
Ron Schreurs*	4	1	2.55	25	1	25	20	14	25
Leyson Septimo*	2	2	4.28	28	0	27	39	12	26
Shawn Teufel*	0	2	4.97	24	0	25	23	18	25
Corey Thurman	1	3	8.24	5	0	20	34	11	11
Beau Vaughan	3	1	2.64	43	1	44	34	16	48
Logan Williamson*	9	12	4.20	27	0	154	165	67	79

CAN-AM LEAGUE

When you win a ring, no one will remember how dominant you were on your way to the title.

When the Can-Am League announced its post-season all-star team, not one player from Trois-Rivieres was on the team. If you scan the Can-Am League's leaders, it's hard to find many Aigles.

Trois-Rivieres looked doomed after a 1-9 stretch in early August, but manager Pierre-Luc LaForest was able to convince the team (with a few roster tweaks) that they were better than they had shown so far.

After making some roster tweaks, Trois-Rivieres regrouped. They rallied to edge Ottawa for the final playoff spot in the Can-Am League. And when the playoffs rolled around pitcher Luis Matos got hot at the right time, winning two of his three playoff stars, Javier Herrera hit only .211 but timed his hits well to drive in 11 runs in 10 games and Daniel Mateo hit a pair of home runs. In the deciding Game Five of the championship series against New Jersey, Herrera drove in a run, Mateo scored on a sacrifice fly and Mike Bradstreet didn't allow an earned run in 7 ⅔ innings. It was Bradstreet's only playoff start.

STANDINGS	W	L	PCT	GB
Rockland Boulders	63	34	.649	—
Quebec Capitales	54	42	.563	8.5
New Jersey Jackals	54	43	.557	9
Trois-Rivieres Aigles	50	46	.521	12.5
Ottawa Champions	46	50	.479	16.5
Sussex County Miners	38	58	.392	25
Shikoku Island	6	10	.375	16.5
Garden State Grays	13	47	.217	31.5

PLAYOFFS: Semifinals—New Jersey defeated Quebec 3-2 and Trois-Rivieres defeated Rockland 3-2 in best-of-5 series. Finals—Trois Rivieres defeated New Jersey 3-2 in best-of-5 series.

ATTENDANCE: Rockland Boulders 161,796; Quebec Capitales 130,510; Ottawa Champions 115,880; Trois-Rivieres Aigles 96,997; New Jersey Jackals 78,913; Sussex County Miners 56,988.

MANAGERS: Garden State—TJ Stanton; New Jersey—Joe Calfapietra; Ottawa—Hal Lanier; Quebec—Pat Scalabrini; Rockland—Jamie Keefe; Sussex—Brent Metheny; Trois-Rivieres—Pete LaForest.

ALL-STAR TEAM: C—Marcus Nidiffer, Rockland. 1B—Charlie Law, Rockland. 2B—Anthony Gomez, New Jersey. 3B—Mark Threlkeld, New Jersey. SS—Junior Arrojo, Rockland. OFs—Joe Maloney, Rockland; Stephen Cardullo, Rockland; Kalian Sams, Quebec. DH—A.J. Kirby-Jones, New Jersey.

SP—Karl Gelinas, Quebec. RP—Deryk Hooker, Quebec. Best Defender—Jonathan Malo, Quebec.

PLAYER OF THE YEAR: Joe Maloney, Rockland. MANAGER OF THE YEAR: Jamie Keefe, Rockland. ROOKIE OF THE YEAR: Johnny Bladel, Sussex County.

BATTING LEADERS

PLAYER	TEAM		AVG	AB	R	H	HR	RBI
Gurriel, Yuniesky	QC	OF	.374	270	43	101	1	31
McDonald, Jared	ROC	OF	.337	383	84	129	8	60
Maloney, Joe	ROC	C	.337	365	91	123	14	83
Cardullo, Stephen	ROC	OF	.331	359	76	119	9	76
Castro, Leandro	NJ	OF	.322	345	68	111	13	68
Matsuzawa, Yusuke	SI	OF	.322	59	5	19	0	8
Arrojo, Junior	ROC	IF	.315	337	79	106	1	44
Lopez, Pedro	TRV	SS	.314	325	47	102	1	39
Takada, Taisuke	SI	OF	.310	42	6	13	0	3
Threlkeld, Mark	NJ	IF	.307	352	62	108	13	64

PITCHING LEADERS

PLAYER	TEAM	W	L	ERA	IP	H	BB	SO
Gelinas, Karl	QC	10	3	2.11	111	88	13	88
Perez, Gabriel	NJ	8	4	2.90	109	105	41	109
Ernst, Brian	NJ	8	7	2.96	109	103	45	100
Walter, John	NJ	10	2	3.08	120	101	40	127
Rusch, Matthew	TRV	7	4	3.11	110	105	26	100
Salazar, Richard	ROC	11	4	3.15	126	133	37	100
Gillies, Charles	TRV	6	4	3.32	95	98	56	58
Werner, Andrew	OTT	12	8	3.36	145	152	44	86
McDonald, Sheldon	QC	8	5	3.44	118	125	16	69
Sanford, Shawn	NJ	7	7	3.65	121	123	40	77

GARDEN STATE GRAYS

NAME	AVG	OBP	SLG	AB	R	H	HR	RBI	BB	SO	SB
Ernie Banks	.200	.273	.233	30	3	6	0	0	3	11	0
Yefry Castillo	.300	.364	.374	190	24	57	2	21	14	23	3
Andrew Dundon	.279	.295	.326	43	0	12	0	5	1	4	1
Luis Gonzalez	.265	.361	.392	204	21	54	4	34	28	48	1
Bryan Johns	.321	.500	.357	28	3	9	0	3	9	10	0
Parks Jordan	.232	.303	.275	138	10	32	0	12	9	24	3
Eric Kozel	.202	.314	.240	104	13	21	0	3	10	23	4
Jake McGuiggan	.169	.224	.210	124	8	21	0	11	8	23	4
Jereme Milons	.105	.150	.105	19	0	2	0	0	1	3	0
Shawn Payne	.279	.385	.393	183	25	51	3	21	31	44	13
Joe Poletsky	.242	.306	.283	99	14	24	0	7	8	22	2
Ricky Riscica	.100	.182	.100	10	0	1	0	0	1	5	0
Joel Rosencrance	.162	.392	.216	37	8	6	0	2	13	17	0
Darian Sandford	.225	.321	.248	218	31	49	0	19	29	38	38
Kale Sumner	.221	.349	.235	68	9	15	0	2	14	27	2
Carl Thomore	.262	.327	.386	145	17	38	2	16	13	25	7

PITCHER	W	L	ERA	G	SV	IP	H	BB	SO
Ben Baker*	0	3	13.50	4	0	11	24	11	3
Kevin Becker-Menditto	0	0	6.55	11	0	11	13	3	6
Keith Bilodeau	1	0	3.00	1	0	6	6	2	0
Chase Boruff	0	1	11.32	10	0	10	23	3	9
Tim Boyce	0	3	3.90	20	0	28	22	12	21
Andres Caceres*	0	0	9.72	9	0	8	9	18	9
Angel Gonzalez*	0	0	4.76	10	0	11	14	11	12
Sean Gregory	0	3	6.87	4	0	18	19	14	7
Joe Kuzia	0	1	11.95	19	0	20	34	13	11
Joe Melioris	0	1	7.36	8	0	11	22	2	5
Chris Motta	0	0	3.52	8	0	8	6	7	7
Noah Piard	2	8	4.07	13	0	66	60	32	30
Jose Rosario*	0	1	8.64	7	0	8	12	8	7
Paul Schwendel	1	2	8.59	4	0	15	21	14	6
Will Scott	1	3	5.67	14	0	60	66	28	37
Jon Shepard	1	0	3.00	1	0	6	4	3	6
John Tangherlini	0	5	5.92	8	0	38	55	13	19
Aaron Weisberg	1	7	4.68	11	0	58	60	30	17
Andy Wellwerts	1	2	7.11	4	0	19	24	15	18
Matt Wickswat*	3	3	5.70	21	1	30	29	18	20

NEW JERSEY JACKALS

NAME	AVG	OBP	SLG	AB	R	H	HR	RBI	BB	SO	SB
Tony Caldwell	.282	.395	.387	238	41	67	3	42	30	68	0
Leandro Castro	.322	.364	.530	345	68	111	13	68	22	35	21
Anthony Gomez	.301	.340	.361	302	49	91	0	36	16	15	11
Matt Helms	.275	.313	.392	240	35	66	2	34	11	29	5
A.J. Kirby-Jones	.294	.401	.534	313	67	92	19	70	57	85	0
Peter Mooney	.263	.372	.350	354	65	93	4	27	58	32	8
Tim Quinn	.075	.191	.075	40	1	3	0	1	4	12	1

NAME	AVG	OBP	SLG	AB	R	H	HR	RBI	BB	SO	SB
D'Vontrey Richardson	.311	.373	.475	61	16	19	0	11	5	8	4
Jared Schlehuber	.290	.365	.409	328	43	95	5	53	42	53	0
Mark Threlkeld	.307	.379	.491	352	62	108	13	64	42	76	3
Justin Trapp	.272	.336	.374	195	25	53	2	19	15	35	13
Matt Wessinger	.077	.200	.077	13	1	1	0	0	2	3	0
Vinny Zarrillo	.294	.358	.358	109	13	32	0	13	12	21	4

PITCHER	W	L	ERA	G	SV	IP	H	BB	SO
Anthony Claggett	5	5	4.10	11	0	68	73	19	39
Brian Ernst	8	7	2.96	19	0	109	103	45	100
Ryan Fennell	0	0	8.68	7	0	9	6	18	11
Francisco Gracesqui*	2	0	2.58	24	1	38	32	24	46
Donnie Joseph*	3	3	5.49	35	1	41	38	30	51
Danny Moskovits	3	4	4.55	20	0	55	56	32	36
Hector Nelo	1	3	2.00	35	21	36	25	19	45
Isaac Pavlik*	2	4	4.67	16	1	44	47	18	28
Gabriel Perez	8	4	2.90	18	0	109	105	41	109
Alex Powers	0	5	3.29	40	0	52	56	11	46
Brandon Sisk*	5	1	2.14	35	1	46	40	16	60
John Walter	10	2	3.08	19	0	120	101	40	127

OTTAWA CHAMPIONS

NAME	AVG	OBP	SLG	AB	R	H	HR	RBI	BB	SO	SB
Daniel Bick	.259	.333	.321	212	29	55	1	22	23	44	17
Sebastien Boucher	.296	.415	.402	331	67	98	5	59	70	56	7
Kyle Brandenburg	.146	.268	.188	48	8	7	0	1	7	17	0
Willie Carmona	.286	.318	.333	21	3	6	0	1	1	6	0
Kevin Carr	.267	.389	.333	15	2	4	0	4	2	3	0
Albert Cartwright	.304	.366	.409	257	39	78	2	18	23	50	15
Corey Caswell	.248	.356	.310	113	13	28	2	8	15	24	0
Nick Giarraputo	.278	.340	.356	90	10	25	1	13	9	22	1
Dan Grauer	.162	.219	.279	68	8	11	1	4	2	18	0
Bryce Massanari	.298	.362	.379	282	26	84	2	38	22	51	0
Alex Nunez	.223	.268	.264	148	17	33	0	12	9	22	1
Roberto Ramirez	.267	.327	.370	300	40	80	4	31	24	32	4
Mike Schwartz	.290	.385	.397	345	42	100	5	49	53	42	0
Francisco Sosa	.175	.284	.250	80	7	14	1	6	11	21	3
Matt Tenaglia	.242	.313	.368	223	29	54	4	26	21	53	0
Chris Winder	.228	.299	.288	312	39	71	0	27	23	95	23

PITCHER	W	L	ERA	G	SV	IP	H	BB	SO
Nate Baker*	1	3	3.48	12	0	44	39	22	28
Josh Blanco*	3	2	2.45	33	0	44	28	33	43
Drew Cisco	3	4	3.80	23	0	66	87	10	36
Alan DeRatt	2	1	2.66	38	24	41	34	11	32
Wilmer Font	10	4	4.09	21	0	117	116	55	81
Laetten Galbraith	4	5	4.02	16	0	69	82	23	22
Drew Granier	4	6	4.59	17	0	80	85	33	66
Nick Purdy	5	3	5.04	35	2	45	46	17	48
Dan Tobik	0	3	7.67	7	0	32	47	16	24
Andrew Werner*	12	8	3.36	22	0	145	152	44	86

QUEBEC CAPITALES

NAME	AVG	OBP	SLG	AB	R	H	HR	RBI	BB	SO	SB
Alexei Bell	.317	.363	.424	224	31	71	2	23	14	24	11
Jean Luc Blaquiere	.271	.375	.392	255	46	69	4	37	43	53	1
Joash Brodin	.250	.286	.250	32	3	8	0	4	2	4	2
Marcel Champagnie	.263	.391	.316	19	3	5	0	2	4	2	2
Nic Cuckovich	.167	.192	.208	24	1	4	0	2	0	7	0
Jerome Duchesneau	.105	.261	.158	19	5	2	0	2	4	5	2
Yunieski Gourriel	.374	.435	.422	270	43	101	1	31	24	13	1
Jonathan Malo	.251	.320	.352	366	49	92	5	44	31	35	11
Yordan Manduley	.269	.306	.333	219	27	59	1	22	8	22	4
Justin Marra	.178	.240	.289	45	4	8	1	4	3	17	0
Josue Peley	.233	.291	.318	318	37	74	3	42	25	44	4
Tanner Rust	.286	.352	.408	98	15	28	2	11	9	24	2
Kalian Sams	.279	.374	.534	294	51	82	16	65	42	75	32
Tim Smith	.238	.354	.302	202	27	48	1	31	32	25	9
Cedric Vallieres	.243	.351	.296	115	14	28	1	15	14	21	1
Mike Washburn	.237	.294	.289	76	9	18	0	8	7	23	1
Ty Young	.265	.398	.385	309	61	82	5	33	61	68	4

PITCHER	W	L	ERA	G	SV	IP	H	BB	SO
Mac Acker*	3	4	3.36	14	1	56	61	18	35
Jamaine Cotton	0	2	5.14	15	0	21	27	6	18
Coby Cowgill	1	0	5.71	3	0	17	18	9	7
Derek Dubois	4	2	5.55	17	0	49	54	29	33

PITCHER	W	L	ERA	G	SV	IP	H	BB	SO
Shaun Ellis	3	4	2.71	38	3	66	72	27	56
Jon Fitzsimmons	0	3	3.16	26	1	43	28	27	51
Karl Gelinas	10	3	2.11	16	0	111	88	13	88
Mark Hardy*	7	6	4.05	19	0	109	117	41	93
Deryk Hooker	5	2	1.88	40	24	48	36	6	34
Ismel Jimenez	3	3	3.12	9	0	43	42	9	34
Jay Johnson*	5	2	1.73	33	4	36	25	14	35
Ryan Leach	2	1	5.20	28	0	36	35	16	29
Sheldon McDonald*	8	5	3.44	19	0	118	125	16	69
Derrick Penilla*	1	3	6.40	13	0	45	53	18	36

ROCKLAND BOULDERS

NAME	AVG	OBP	SLG	AB	R	H	HR	RBI	BB	SO	SB
Junior Arrojo	.315	.436	.380	337	79	106	1	44	40	35	43
Stephen Cardullo	.331	.410	.518	359	76	119	9	76	49	42	23
Alex DeBellis	.310	.376	.437	126	16	39	4	20	11	25	0
Ryan Fisher	.248	.335	.403	206	37	51	5	35	22	71	4
Ray Frias	.250	.375	.350	20	3	5	0	1	3	3	0
Stefen Henderson	.183	.350	.280	93	18	17	1	8	21	52	7
Charlie Law	.301	.357	.465	355	62	107	10	58	26	83	4
Joe Maloney	.337	.432	.559	365	91	123	14	83	57	106	18
Jared McDonald	.337	.444	.480	383	84	129	8	60	70	71	16
Marcus Nidiffer	.256	.369	.548	305	63	78	22	93	48	72	0
Steve Nyisztor	.275	.314	.359	357	46	98	3	54	19	65	13
Giuseppe Papaccio	.243	.279	.338	317	38	77	2	34	14	62	2
Ryan Stovall	.207	.281	.241	29	4	6	0	6	3	8	0
Byron Wiley	.111	.385	.222	18	3	2	0	1	8	11	0

PITCHER	W	L	ERA	G	SV	IP	H	BB	SO
Bo Budkevics	5	4	4.05	16	0	107	110	26	75
Pat Butler	1	0	1.23	10	0	15	7	4	6
Daniel Carela	0	1	1.46	26	0	25	9	17	30
Mike Dennhardt	2	5	4.81	10	0	49	58	33	29
Shawn Gilblair*	3	1	1.78	44	0	35	21	8	35
Alex Gouin	8	4	3.84	18	0	98	105	20	53
Stephen Harrold	8	5	4.13	17	0	98	90	50	53
Marcus Jensen	8	2	4.04	33	0	71	77	16	50
Austin Kirk*	0	0	4.76	6	0	6	9	3	2
Fray Martinez	3	2	6.31	32	1	61	80	29	29
Trevor Reckling*	0	0	9.45	2	0	7	10	3	2
J.D. Reichenbach*	1	0	5.87	4	0	15	20	4	5
Chad Robinson	0	1	3.09	44	2	44	30	19	45
Richard Salazar*	11	4	3.15	20	0	126	133	37	100
Luis Sanz	1	2	1.26	35	18	36	21	15	41

SUSSEX COUNTY MINERS

NAME	AVG	OBP	SLG	AB	R	H	HR	RBI	BB	SO	SB
Reggie Abercrombie	.238	.257	.373	185	18	44	3	22	3	44	4
Johnny Bladel	.281	.391	.415	270	47	76	7	36	45	52	12
Kenny Bryant	.262	.320	.408	336	41	88	10	44	27	66	10
Jon Dziomba	.202	.277	.274	84	6	17	0	6	9	27	2
Jayson Hernandez	.226	.285	.274	266	19	60	1	25	15	53	0
Carlos Hughes	.154	.254	.269	52	5	8	0	2	7	19	1
Michael Martucci	.056	.190	.056	18	1	1	0	0	3	5	0
Ryan Mathews	.270	.331	.440	252	32	68	8	35	23	52	6
Jon Minucci	.250	.286	.325	40	2	10	0	4	2	10	1
Sergio Miranda	.328	.431	.402	122	22	40	1	19	20	14	10
Cory Morales	.223	.296	.263	300	31	67	1	28	30	46	10
Rey Otero	.202	.262	.213	94	6	19	0	3	6	28	3
Ryan Pineda	.249	.338	.387	173	29	43	3	26	24	35	5
Ray Sadler	.152	.222	.333	33	4	5	1	3	2	8	1
Devin Thaut	.260	.354	.338	331	45	86	1	24	47	101	13
Chris Valencia	.248	.269	.301	113	12	28	0	8	4	18	9
Brady Wilson	.222	.320	.324	108	15	24	1	10	15	29	9

PITCHER	W	L	ERA	G	SV	IP	H	BB	SO
Andrew Aizenstadt	0	0	5.00	6	0	9	6	8	5
Tony Amezcua	1	3	2.89	36	0	56	37	23	56
Matt Branham	0	1	7.36	3	0	15	21	4	6
Hector Cedano*	0	3	5.16	9	0	23	32	9	15
John Lujan	0	2	4.30	16	0	15	14	8	7
Josh Mueller	0	2	3.98	32	1	41	39	27	36
Jordan Remer*	0	4	5.65	25	0	29	27	33	44
Francisco Rodriguez*	5	1	3.34	6	0	35	32	19	31
Brandon Shimo	0	0	4.26	10	1	13	12	4	19
Matt Sommo	5	12	4.72	19	0	116	133	33	71
Zach Staniewicz	2	9	9.00	5	0	16	22	16	9

PITCHER	W	L	ERA	G	SV	IP	H	BB	SO
Michael Suk	6	2	3.01	34	0	72	80	18	43
Joe Testa*	1	2	1.23	38	18	44	23	13	65
Kyle Vazquez	3	6	6.18	13	0	60	75	39	43
Jamie Walczak	6	11	4.69	20	0	117	110	60	108
Josh Wood	4	1	5.35	8	0	39	44	25	24

TROIS-RIVIERES AIGLES

NAME	AVG	OBP	SLG	AB	R	H	HR	RBI	BB	SO	SB
Steve Brown	.301	.389	.473	332	62	100	12	64	35	76	23
Joel Carranza	.267	.362	.433	90	11	24	4	18	12	23	0
Jose Cuevas	.269	.321	.384	346	57	93	5	52	24	30	19
Eric Grabe	.249	.343	.359	273	34	68	4	28	39	44	9
Simon Gravel	.223	.296	.272	103	8	23	1	9	11	33	1
Frederic Hanvi	.179	.172	.321	28	4	5	1	5	0	15	1
Javier Herrera	.289	.441	.480	173	36	50	6	32	40	48	6
Craig Hertler	.290	.418	.349	352	72	102	2	37	66	42	21
Jonathan Jones	.200	.289	.250	80	3	16	1	5	9	37	0
Kyle Lafrenz	.258	.317	.348	287	37	74	6	40	25	64	0
Sasha LaGarde	.209	.335	.267	191	32	40	1	12	24	50	11
Pedro Lopez	.314	.388	.345	325	47	102	1	39	41	30	5
Daniel Mateo	.275	.329	.388	371	46	102	7	63	28	53	9
Jon Smith	.252	.326	.307	127	15	32	0	13	13	26	3

PITCHER	W	L	ERA	G	SV	IP	H	BB	SO
Edilson Alvarez	6	2	3.58	35	1	73	75	18	46
Ryan Bollinger*	11	7	3.68	20	0	127	125	46	108
Mike Bradstreet	6	10	4.24	21	0	119	130	24	65
Jordan Cote	0	0	5.17	14	0	16	18	7	7
Kaohi Downing	3	0	3.41	30	10	32	21	12	38
Charlie Gillies	6	4	3.32	16	0	95	98	56	58
Andrew Jessup*	0	1	8.79	11	0	14	15	18	9
Alex Kreis	0	1	5.87	16	0	15	18	12	11
David Leblanc	1	2	3.95	37	0	43	44	20	35
Carlos Mirabal	2	2	6.53	7	0	21	32	5	7
Luis Munoz	5	4	3.56	9	0	61	51	25	38
Matt Rusch	7	4	3.11	19	0	110	105	26	100
Kevin Thomas	1	2	6.94	5	0	23	28	17	24
Philippe Valiquette*	0	3	5.16	26	5	23	32	10	21

FRONTIER LEAGUE

After a difficult 2014 season, Traverse City looked like it needed to make a significant number of changes. The Beach Bums finished with the third-worst record in the Frontier League winning less than four of every 10 games.

But manager Dan Rohn and director of baseball operations Jason Wuerfel brought back a number of the core players from that team convinced that they weren't as far away from contending as everyone might believe. With additions of a whole new outfield of minor league veterans Brandon Jacobs, Jay Austin and Reggie Lawson stepping in to help returnees like Yazy Arbelo, Jose Vargas and Jake Rhodes, the Beach Bums went 56-38 during the regular season to earn a wild card spot. And they picked the perfect time to get hot. Traverse City won its final three regular-season games, then went a perfect 6-0 through the playoffs, knocking off Rockford in the first round, sweeping Normal in the semifinals and then sweeping River City in the championship series.

EAST DIVISION	W	L	PCT	GB
Southern Illinois Miners *	63	33	.656	—
Traverse City Beach Bums †	56	38	.596	6
Florence Freedom †	49	47	.510	14
Evansville Otters	48	48	.500	15
Washington Wild Things	42	54	.438	21
Frontier Greys	40	56	.417	23
Lake Erie Crushers	38	57	.400	24.5

WEST DIVISION

WEST DIVISION	W	L	PCT	GB
Normal CornBelters *	61	35	.635	—
River City Rascals †	56	40	.583	5
Rockford Aviators †	49	47	.510	12
Gateway Grizzlies	45	50	.474	15.5
Joliet Slammers	42	54	.438	19
Windy City ThunderBolts	41	55	.427	20
Schaumburg Boomers	40	56	.417	21

PLAYOFFS: Semifinals—Traverse City defeated Normal 2-0 and River City defeated Southern Illinois 2-1 in best-of-3 series. **Finals**—Traverse City defeated River City 3-0 in best-of-5 series.

ATTENDANCE: Schaumburg Boomers 162,210; Southern Illinois Miners 151,503; Gateway Grizzlies 149,319; Traverse City Beach Bums 132,404; Evansville Otters 114,787; Florence Freedom 104,578; Normal CornBelters 102,290; Joliet Slammers 95,673; River City Rascals 91,354; Lake Erie Crushers 86,155; Washington Wild Things 83,087; Windy City ThunderBolts 76,550; Rockford Aviators 44,674.

MANAGERS: Evansville–Andy McCauley; Florence–Dennis Pelfrey; Frontier Greys–Vinny Ganz; Gateway–Phil Warren; Joliet–Jeff Isom; Lake Erie–Chris Mongiardo; Normal–Brooks Carey; River City–Steve Brook; Rockford–James Frisbie; Schaumburg–Jamie Bennett; Southern Illinois–Mike Pinto; Traverse City–Dan Rohn; Washington–Bob Bozzuto; Windy City–Ron Biga.

ALL-STAR TEAM: C–Josh Ludy, River City; 1B–Aaron Dudley, Normal; 2B–Santiago Chirino, Normal; 3B–Taylor Ard, River City; SS–Patrick McKenna, Normal; OF–John Schultz, Evansville, Michael Hur, Rockford; Michael Earley, Southern Illinois; DH–Danny Canela, River City.

SP–Adam Lopez, Southern Illinois. RP–Edgar Lopez, Evansville .

MOST VALUABLE PLAYER: Taylor Ard, River City. **PITCHER OF THE YEAR:** Adam Lopez, Southern Illinois. **ROOKIE OF THE YEAR**–Brandon Tierney, Greys. **MANAGER OF THE YEAR:** Brooks Carey, Normal.

BATTING LEADERS

PLAYER	TEAM	AVG	AB	R	H	HR	RBI
Hansen, Brian	RIV	.371	221	54	82	5	37
Dudley, Aaron	NOR	.346	341	58	118	10	69
Gallagher, Austin	WIN	.338	284	55	96	16	63
Chirino, Santiago	NOR	.337	350	53	118	4	44
Schultz, John	EVN	.333	354	66	118	15	52
Hur, Michael	RFD	.331	360	56	119	9	40
Earley, Michael	SIL	.325	385	55	125	10	61
Rodriguez, Devon	RFD	.321	371	36	119	4	42
Jacobs, Brandon	TC	.320	316	57	101	17	54
Austin, Jay	TC	.319	257	39	82	4	32

PITCHING LEADERS

PLAYER	TEAM	W	L	ERA	IP	H	BB	SO
Oliver, Will	EVN	9	2	1.59	90	74	26	88
Lopez, Adam	SIL	10	0	1.86	97	65	35	103
Champlin, Kramer	TC	10	6	2.05	114	89	20	65
Kubiak, David	JOL	7	6	2.16	96	75	32	92
Bywater, Matt	SIL	8	4	2.36	107	80	32	123
Carmain, Chris	NOR	8	2	2.49	105	78	13	90
Gooding, Jeremy	FLO	8	4	2.50	90	67	22	89
MacDougall, Ian	TC	10	6	2.51	122	125	19	67
Nieves, Efrain	EVN	8	2	2.68	77	67	16	41
Adkins, Hunter	LER	3	5	2.70	97	74	32	94

EVANSVILLE OTTERS

NAME	AVG	OBP	SLG	AB	R	H	HR	RBI	BB	SO	SB
Josh Allen	.259	.368	.411	309	61	80	9	48	33	92	24
Nik Balog	.268	.312	.370	332	38	89	6	48	18	78	1
Jeff Birkofer	.250	.400	.417	12	2	3	0	2	1	2	0
Nick Bornhauser	.357	.400	.357	14	1	5	0	0	1	8	0
Alex Cruz	.250	.250	.250	60	5	15	0	2	0	19	0
Jaime Del Valle	.268	.318	.341	41	5	11	0	5	3	5	0
JD Dorgan	.226	.246	.254	177	17	40	0	10	3	47	1
Chris Elder	.236	.323	.309	55	7	13	0	3	7	13	0
Shayne Houck	.296	.374	.508	199	32	59	9	37	20	43	0
Michael Jurgella	.179	.250	.179	28	1	5	0	1	1	4	0
Dane Phillips	.262	.321	.430	214	28	56	7	38	20	37	0
Ronnie Richardson	.225	.301	.333	102	19	23	1	9	9	28	8
John Schultz	.333	.407	.556	354	66	118	15	52	43	55	6

NAME	AVG	OBP	SLG	AB	R	H	HR	RBI	BB	SO	SB
Chris Sweeney	.237	.300	.444	342	50	81	16	50	29	138	9
Cory Urquhart	.235	.318	.303	277	39	65	3	31	32	62	4
Kurt Wertz	.235	.330	.399	243	45	57	8	34	34	72	7
Dean Wilson	.205	.222	.250	88	12	18	0	8	2	14	4

PITCHER	W	L	ERA	G	SV	IP	H	BB	SO
Blaine Howell*	1	2	5.70	5	0	24	24	15	31
Brodie Leibrandt*	0	0	0.00	6	1	11	5	2	11
Connor Little	7	5	1.19	47	2	68	41	14	90
Edgar Lopez	1	1	1.64	33	25	33	24	16	37
Brett Marshall	5	3	3.15	8	0	54	49	23	42
Blake Monar*	2	0	14.21	12	0	6	3	8	9
Adam Mott	0	0	3.86	9	1	12	14	4	14
Efrain Nieves*	8	2	2.68	14	0	77	67	16	41
Will Oliver	9	2	1.59	13	0	90	74	26	88
Preston Olson	5	3	3.55	14	0	89	84	31	65
Jake Raffaele*	0	1	3.63	7	0	17	22	7	12
Brandon Shimo	0	0	5.87	8	0	8	12	2	11
Tyler Vail	9	5	5.02	18	0	104	105	68	65
Trevor Walch	8	8	2.77	20	0	133	122	58	83
Shane Weedman	0	0	3.26	13	0	19	20	9	12
Will White*	0	0	6.75	7	0	7	8	7	7

FLORENCE FREEDOM

NAME	AVG	OBP	SLG	AB	R	H	HR	RBI	BB	SO	SB
Cody Bishop	.225	.286	.377	151	15	34	5	22	14	44	7
Zack Burling	.122	.204	.122	49	7	6	0	1	4	14	4
Steve Carrillo	.229	.303	.271	306	29	70	1	30	28	71	5
Kyle Carter	.224	.257	.276	98	7	22	1	10	3	19	0
Collins Cuthrell	.271	.353	.476	210	34	57	9	42	26	49	6
Sam Eberle	.309	.377	.465	359	60	111	10	49	38	58	9
Daniel Fraga	.284	.396	.356	320	53	91	1	27	54	52	29
Andrew Godbold	.216	.320	.365	167	27	36	4	19	23	56	10
Ozzy Gonzalez	.226	.308	.323	124	12	28	1	16	12	25	3
Frazier Hall	.259	.408	.321	81	11	21	0	10	21	30	1
Justin Harris	.271	.364	.292	96	16	26	0	7	13	21	13
Josh Henderson	.273	.306	.394	33	5	9	0	3	2	4	0
Gaby Juarbe	.298	.356	.456	94	12	28	3	22	9	21	6
Rob Kelly	.138	.286	.310	29	1	4	1	4	5	8	0
Jake Luce	.250	.340	.409	44	6	11	1	9	7	13	5
Sean Mahley	.197	.296	.254	71	10	14	0	6	10	14	6
Zac Mitchell	.260	.332	.323	192	23	50	1	16	19	25	13
Austin Newell	.330	.413	.505	206	40	68	5	36	27	28	14
Michael Pair	.209	.306	.302	43	3	9	0	5	6	14	1
Elvin Rodriguez	.250	.294	.250	16	1	4	0	1	1	4	0
Matt Rubino	.053	.182	.211	19	2	1	1	1	2	5	0
Mason Salazar	.174	.250	.217	46	7	8	0	4	5	11	3
Ryan Solberg	.105	.190	.105	19	1	2	0	2	2	10	0
Travis Weaver	.181	.258	.219	215	21	39	1	19	19	67	10
Isaac Wenrich	.250	.304	.438	64	8	16	3	10	4	8	0

PITCHER	W	L	ERA	G	SV	IP	H	BB	SO
Alan Carey	0	2	14.90	3	0	10	17	7	4
Ryan Davis*	0	1	6.17	4	0	12	19	6	4
Austin Delmotte	0	0	3.38	13	2	21	13	12	21
David Duncan	0	1	7.71	5	0	12	19	1	7
Matt Eshleman*	0	0	4.26	13	0	6	0	12	4
Ethan Gibbons	0	2	1.81	44	2	50	30	12	61
Jeremy Gooding	8	4	2.50	15	0	90	67	22	89
Cody Gray	4	2	4.03	12	0	58	59	16	49
Seth Harvey	4	4	3.98	32	1	43	41	22	38
Casey Henn	3	7	3.56	10	0	61	60	17	62
Ed Kohout	4	4	1.81	42	19	45	30	11	46
Pete Levitt	6	2	4.15	45	0	39	27	25	18
Patrick McGrath*	2	2	2.72	8	0	40	34	11	20
Jason Postill	1	0	3.92	10	0	21	21	7	15
Cole Stephens	4	5	4.71	13	0	78	80	18	47
Jake Stephens	0	2	22.74	2	0	6	19	2	5
Tony Vocca	3	4	2.56	30	1	70	58	32	49
Chuck Weaver	6	4	3.22	18	1	109	106	27	95

FRONTIER GREYS

NAME	AVG	OBP	SLG	AB	R	H	HR	RBI	BB	SO	SB
Michael Antonio	.296	.325	.383	115	7	34	2	8	5	22	1
Shane Brown	.237	.320	.359	50	85	6	25	34	78	2
Scott Carcaise	.253	.332	.400	340	37	86	9	57	38	81	2
Mike Falsetti	.228	.324	.272	92	10	21	0	11	10	22	3

INDEPENDENT LEAGUES

NAME	AVG	OBP	SLG	AB	R	H	HR	RBI	BB	SO	SB
Dillon Haupt	.267	.319	.465	288	31	77	12	34	17	69	0
Connor Jones	.200	.333	.500	10	1	2	1	1	2	4	0
Ben Lodge	.215	.276	.256	195	18	42	0	13	16	59	1
Sam Montgomery	.216	.286	.333	51	4	11	0	3	4	8	0
Julio Rodriguez	.279	.304	.338	337	36	94	1	29	11	24	9
Francisco Rosario	.212	.276	.278	259	27	55	2	20	22	73	4
Jose Sermo	.160	.192	.280	50	7	8	1	9	2	17	0
Zach Tanner	.228	.278	.371	337	38	77	8	38	24	108	1
Brandon Tierney	.290	.344	.428	355	55	103	9	47	12	68	9
Jhiomar Veras	.214	.253	.374	313	36	67	10	30	13	93	2
Matt Williams	.142	.222	.142	106	15	15	0	6	4	39	5

PITCHER	W	L	ERA	G	SV	IP	H	BB	SO
Nick Anderson	2	0	0.65	25	13	28	17	6	35
Kyle Bogese	2	5	5.75	30	2	56	51	61	49
Brent Choban*	1	2	2.72	39	1	40	37	24	34
Justin D'Alessandro	5	8	4.04	20	0	100	88	80	75
Colin Feldtman	4	2	2.87	12	0	63	55	12	40
Max Homick*	1	3	3.27	13	0	41	38	17	37
Michael Joseph	0	1	12.79	12	1	13	26	7	3
Eric Kline*	0	3	16.41	6	0	17	31	28	10
Jordan Kraus	5	5	2.98	17	0	103	97	34	80
Nick McBride	3	3	2.75	37	5	39	33	25	32
Liam O'Sullivan	0	3	7.42	6	0	13	21	1	8
Brett Shankin	5	1	2.79	21	0	42	41	11	33
Bobby Shore	5	8	4.16	18	0	97	100	36	76
Steven Wehr	1	4	9.00	17	0	20	20	18	14
Andy Wellwerts	2	2	4.71	10	0	21	29	12	14

GATEWAY GRIZZLIES

NAME	AVG	OBP	SLG	AB	R	H	HR	RBI	BB	SO	SB
Josh Adams	.083	.132	.083	36	2	3	0	0	2	9	0
Madison Beaird	.216	.288	.287	328	40	71	4	22	30	69	14
Clayton Brandt	.500	.583	.600	10	3	5	0	2	2	2	1
Blake Brown	.261	.358	.503	326	62	85	22	60	49	110	14
Grant Buckner	.252	.319	.400	325	41	82	9	49	27	64	4
Jorge Chavarria	.150	.150	.200	20	2	3	0	0	0	5	0
Seth Heck	.275	.349	.311	193	31	53	0	17	18	26	3
Ryan Johns	.165	.224	.220	91	7	15	0	6	7	30	1
Cody Livesay	.308	.388	.335	263	37	81	1	26	33	47	13
Grant Nelson	.176	.176	.235	34	2	6	0	1	0	16	0
Brandon Overstreet	.048	.048	.048	21	0	1	0	0	0	6	0
Shawn Payne	.182	.315	.273	77	12	14	1	6	14	19	5
Bradon Reitano	.107	.219	.250	28	2	3	1	2	3	6	2
Antonio Sandifer	.054	.286	.054	37	4	2	0	3	12	13	0
Richard Seigel	.263	.373	.383	243	38	64	5	28	42	87	3
Ryan Soares	.244	.297	.296	135	13	33	1	14	7	13	1
Tyler Tewell	.270	.351	.515	163	24	44	11	29	14	33	0
Garrett Vail	.245	.321	.316	98	6	24	0	16	9	21	1
Ben Waldrip	.289	.329	.451	357	40	103	10	65	20	84	0

PITCHER	W	L	ERA	G	SV	IP	H	BB	SO
Troy Barton	0	2	6.75	12	0	27	25	10	20
Robbie Buller	0	0	3.68	5	0	7	3	9	8
Dillon Haviland	2	2	4.95	7	0	36	43	15	19
Zach Loraine	0	0	5.62	8	0	8	13	4	5
Byron Minnich	0	0	6.14	8	0	7	11	5	8
Vincent Molesky	5	6	5.13	18	0	109	111	29	96
David Murillo	0	1	8.40	11	0	15	17	12	15
Donny Murray	0	2	9.17	5	0	18	27	8	14
Dejai Oliver	0	3	6.89	3	0	16	23	7	9
Trevor Richards	6	6	3.36	14	0	91	80	27	84
Max Schonfeld	2	5	4.64	12	0	64	79	20	22
Jordan Sechler*	0	1	7.56	9	0	8	10	6	7
Collin Shaw	0	1	8.78	6	0	13	15	17	16
Dakota Smith	2	3	4.91	13	0	37	36	30	31
Jordan Spencer*	3	1	3.66	14	0	47	52	14	39
Justin Sprenger	1	0	17.18	7	0	7	16	5	6
Kevin Sweeney	0	2	9.00	3	0	12	18	5	10
Tyler Thompson	5	5	3.19	26	7	87	79	28	74
JaVaun West	4	4	4.75	19	2	55	46	24	56
Brett Zawacki	4	1	1.99	18	5	23	15	6	27

JOLIET SLAMMERS

NAME	AVG	OBP	SLG	AB	R	H	HR	RBI	BB	SO	SB
Phillip Bates	.288	.380	.388	260	48	75	4	31	33	33	14
John Cannon	.191	.296	.213	47	6	9	0	3	7	9	1

NAME	AVG	OBP	SLG	AB	R	H	HR	RBI	BB	SO	SB
Max Casper	.193	.259	.227	233	22	45	1	22	16	44	2
Jack Cleary	.247	.341	.315	219	22	54	2	32	24	33	0
Casey Fletcher	.226	.348	.304	115	14	26	2	11	15	28	3
Mike Garza	.292	.329	.410	390	44	114	5	59	18	77	5
Adam Giacalone	.188	.278	.250	48	3	9	0	5	6	12	0
Sam Klein	.237	.310	.237	38	3	9	0	1	3	6	1
Carlos Lopez	.198	.250	.208	96	11	19	0	3	6	24	0
Russell Moldenhauer	.269	.331	.353	156	21	42	2	17	15	34	1
Hunter Ridge	.277	.349	.333	231	24	64	2	19	26	31	2
Nate Roberts	.267	.417	.424	217	40	58	8	36	48	50	6
Alfredo Rodriguez	.287	.369	.378	352	57	101	4	39	41	34	18
Dante Rosenberg	.200	.273	.350	20	2	4	1	5	1	3	0
Chris Serritella	.210	.269	.435	62	10	13	4	8	5	17	1
Mason Snyder	.255	.278	.314	51	3	13	1	3	1	12	0
Joe Staley	.250	.340	.357	84	11	21	1	10	11	24	0
Charlie White	.281	.369	.324	210	40	59	1	12	27	34	20
J.D. Williams	.234	.307	.299	77	11	18	1	9	8	18	8

PITCHER	W	L	ERA	G	SV	IP	H	BB	SO
Jacob Butler	0	0	2.45	4	0	7	9	7	4
John Cannon	0	0	1.08	8	1	8	5	5	13
Michael Carden*	4	5	4.26	12	0	68	70	33	31
Luke Crumley	2	0	1.48	12	0	30	20	13	30
Brett DeVall*	0	1	9.45	2	0	7	13	3	5
Pat Dyer*	1	1	6.11	16	0	18	22	9	15
Adam Giacalone	1	2	3.95	13	0	43	45	14	35
Jordan Guth	3	3	5.79	6	0	33	37	16	19
David Kubiak	7	6	2.16	33	1	96	75	32	92
John Maloney	0	0	8.59	7	0	7	10	10	6
Kevin McNorton	8	2	2.09	37	1	69	62	13	56
Spencer Medick*	1	4	4.95	8	0	36	36	13	16
Navery Moore	1	2	2.35	38	17	46	33	29	62
Sam Moore	2	0	5.66	21	2	21	21	13	12
Tyler Murphy?	0	0	5.40	8	0	8		6	7
Adam Panayotovich	0	2	8.64	5	0	17	23	6	7
Andrew Strenge	8	7	4.50	22	0	118	137	32	70
Dan Tobik	1	1	2.74	16	0	23	16	9	18
Aaron Vaughn	0	5	6.60	11	0	44	58	14	30
Kevin Walter	2	9	5.66	18	0	84	98	42	71

LAKE ERIE CRUSHERS

NAME	AVG	OBP	SLG	AB	R	H	HR	RBI	BB	SO	SB
Daniel Aldrich	.171	.259	.237	76	6	13	1	6	9	34	1
Jose Barraza	.294	.350	.433	344	41	101	5	47	26	101	1
Chandler Brock	.219	.301	.292	192	24	42	0	20	18	39	12
Joey Burney	.241	.306	.335	158	19	38	3	15	12	26	2
Brendan Costantino	.164	.238	.178	73	5	12	0	4	3	17	2
Justin Cureton	.198	.258	.233	86	6	17	1	3	2	26	1
Frank DeSico	.247	.367	.296	81	10	20	0	8	13	12	9
Adam Ford	.150	.190	.150	20	1	3	0	1	0	6	1
Mark Fowler	.227	.292	.250	44	3	10	0	4	3	7	0
Kevin Franchetti	.136	.200	.182	22	1	3	0	1	2	8	0
Turner Gill	.130	.200	.261	23	2	3	1	2	2	4	0
Anderson Hidalgo	.302	.381	.392	291	36	88	4	32	31	41	3
Aaron Lindgren	.167	.167	.167	18	0	3	0	2	0	4	0
Kyle McMillen	.091	.167	.091	11	0	1	0	0	1	3	0
Parker Norris	.143	.231	.171	35	4	5	0	0	4	9	1
Austin Prott	.270	.358	.352	230	28	62	2	18	25	44	6
Emmanuel Quiles	.249	.280	.319	229	24	57	1	20	10	52	0
Juan Sanchez	.266	.308	.377	369	39	98	5	39	19	63	15
Cody Stevens	.182	.210	.197	132	7	24	0	3	5	32	0
Trevor Stevens	.209	.319	.276	254	28	53	1	15	34	73	10
Boo Vazquez	.287	.358	.507	136	17	39	5	27	13	35	3
Nick Zaharion	.250	.241	.286	28	0	7	0	5	0	4	0
Kevin Zak	.255	.321	.255	51	4	13	0	8	3	12	0

PITCHER	W	L	ERA	G	SV	IP	H	BB	SO
Hunter Adkins	3	5	2.70	15	0	97	74	32	94
Matt Brankle	3	2	4.43	38	0	41	42	12	26
Mike Devine	3	4	3.33	60	4	78	72	17	83
Brad Duffy*	8	6	3.30	44	0	76	75	31	80
Todd Kibby*	1	2	2.84	13	0	32	26	15	27
Trevor Longfellow	5	10	2.86	52	14	88	63	37	73
Tyler Marshburn	0	0	3.00	8	0	6	8	1	10
Kolby Moore*	1	2	4.40	46	0	43	42	22	37
Zach Morton	5	4	3.82	16	0	80	91	21	62
Ryan Richardson	0	0	0.63	14	0	14	9	2	13

INDEPENDENT LEAGUES

PITCHER	W	L	ERA	G	SV	IP	H	BB	SO
Jason Wilson	2	4	3.43	8	0	45	36	14	40
Brad Zambron	3	8	5.03	22	0	102	100	34	70

NORMAL CORNBELTERS

NAME	AVG	OBP	SLG	AB	R	H	HR	RBI	BB	SO	SB
Thomas Amato	.300	.500	.300	10	1	3	0	0	4	3	0
Santiago Chirino	.337	.377	.426	350	53	118	4	44	20	13	15
Aaron Dudley	.346	.446	.522	341	58	118	10	69	61	53	2
Ozney Guillen	.220	.286	.335	313	41	69	7	32	24	48	13
Sam Judah	.236	.309	.354	339	40	80	6	53	36	65	1
Dylan Kelly	.350	.341	.475	40	6	14	0	2	0	7	0
Richard Lucas	.282	.339	.507	341	50	96	19	77	26	90	6
Pat McKenna	.283	.408	.555	339	78	96	22	70	65	120	2
Jason Merjano	.236	.331	.354	127	21	30	2	13	17	23	4
Mark Micowski	.314	.394	.441	338	71	106	8	42	44	49	27
Cameron Monger	.263	.362	.411	338	60	89	13	40	50	95	36
Tyler Shover	.241	.290	.345	58	5	14	1	5	4	9	1
Steve Sulcoski	.147	.216	.147	34	1	5	0	0	3	8	0
Aaron Wright	.429	.469	.500	28	3	12	0	1	2	7	0

PITCHER	W	L	ERA	G	SV	IP	H	BB	SO
Horacio Acosta	6	0	3.14	39	1	63	63	20	48
Robert Baroniel	2	3	4.73	9	0	46	45	20	36
Kevin Brahney*	4	4	5.28	13	0	61	70	28	48
Cole Brocker	5	2	2.94	24	0	34	25	7	48
Chris Carmain	2	2	2.49	16	0	105	78	13	90
Johnny Fageaux	0	0	5.51	7	0	16	17	9	14
Yoandy Fernandez	2	0	8.25	7	0	12	16	4	12
Cody Gappa	0	0	1.42	4	1	6	5	4	7
Kevin Jefferis	2	0	2.50	8	1	18	13	15	18
Kevin Johnson	9	5	3.48	19	0	111	110	39	76
Jake Negrete	3	1	2.49	9	0	43	33	11	44
Brad Orosey	0	1	7.11	3	0	13	14	3	8
Race Parmenter	1	3	2.53	38	22	53	38	12	51
Leondy Perez	1	1	5.79	2	0	9	11	6	7
Michael Schweiss	9	7	3.08	20	0	129	119	34	135

RIVER CITY RASCALS

NAME	AVG	OBP	SLG	AB	R	H	HR	RBI	BB	SO	SB
Taylor Ard	.313	.385	.646	364	88	114	30	83	30	65	13
Saxon Butler	.277	.378	.383	94	15	26	3	11	13	13	1
Danny Canela	.284	.358	.476	292	44	83	15	65	36	63	1
Hector Crespo	.255	.328	.344	337	44	86	4	40	34	66	40
Fred Ford	.190	.261	.286	21	1	4	0	3	2	10	1
Brian Hansen	.371	.457	.529	221	54	82	5	37	33	40	25
Zach Kometani	.285	.355	.468	312	44	89	12	53	34	84	6
Josh Ludy	.267	.350	.423	333	50	89	15	56	39	80	12
Johnny Morales	.264	.348	.344	250	41	66	1	35	30	35	4
Curran Redal	.311	.376	.383	402	67	125	3	50	39	23	34
Casey Rodrigue	.256	.373	.256	43	11	11	0	4	6	12	2
Josh Silver	.263	.345	.341	179	32	47	1	17	18	26	1
Jackson Slaid	.308	.364	.458	286	51	88	9	36	23	53	5

PITCHER	W	L	ERA	G	SV	IP	H	BB	SO
Derek Cape	3	2	3.95	48	1	41	35	16	53
Rob Frank	0	0	5.40	3	0	12	16	8	12
Ray Hanson	0	1	11.42	2	0	9	17	3	10
Heith Hatfield	2	2	3.92	17	2	21	22	9	18
Nick Kennedy	0	0	3.12	10	2	9	5	3	5
Beau Kerns	0	0	6.43	2	0	7	12	2	3
Tim Koons	11	0	3.65	18	0	106	113	29	74
Lucas Laster*	4	3	3.81	14	0	78	82	23	74
Tommy Lawrence	2	0	4.43	4	0	22	22	9	13
Tommy Organ*	1	0	4.63	4	0	12	7	8	11
Joe Scanio	9	6	3.64	21	0	111	122	31	80
Will Schierholz	3	2	2.68	44	2	44	39	11	38
Clay Smith	0	2	6.05	6	0	19	22	10	12
Zeb Sneed	4	3	4.53	45	5	46	45	18	43
Dane Stone	9	5	4.13	18	0	94	97	24	67
Clint Wright	0	2	4.61	4	0	14	16	3	11

ROCKFORD AVIATORS

NAME	AVG	OBP	SLG	AB	R	H	HR	RBI	BB	SO	SB
Brian Bistagne	.270	.351	.371	337	52	91	3	36	37	55	11
Ryan Breen	.195	.317	.310	87	9	17	2	10	15	22	1
Joshua Davis	.178	.221	.301	73	4	13	1	5	3	26	0

NAME	AVG	OBP	SLG	AB	R	H	HR	RBI	BB	SO	SB
Will Dupont	.182	.182	.227	22	0	4	0	2	0	9	1
Justin Fox	.264	.346	.403	144	22	38	3	20	15	40	3
Cameron Garfield	.308	.364	.396	91	12	28	1	10	6	14	1
Michael Hur	.331	.401	.461	360	56	119	9	40	38	68	13
Cody Lenahan	.321	.333	.464	56	11	18	1	6	1	11	4
Raul Linares	.247	.360	.351	97	21	24	1	6	17	18	10
Teodoro Martinez	.277	.320	.404	47	7	13	1	6	1	5	1
Mason Morioka	.158	.238	.184	38	3	6	0	0	4	12	0
Anthony Renteria	.227	.305	.426	216	24	49	10	37	21	83	4
Dusty Robinson	.274	.330	.412	354	45	97	6	45	31	78	6
Devon Rodriguez	.321	.359	.412	371	36	119	4	42	23	48	2
Collin Shaw	.212	.308	.317	104	15	22	2	14	13	34	0
Jaron Shepherd	.216	.242	.261	88	12	19	1	4	2	25	3
Tyler Smith	.198	.295	.198	91	10	18	0	9	11	23	0
Danny Stienstra	.283	.341	.327	159	16	45	0	16	15	31	1
Connor Szczerba	.167	.322	.188	48	6	8	0	2	7	10	0
Elijah Trail	.250	.317	.439	196	31	49	8	31	15	47	2
Greg Velazquez	.200	.307	.327	110	15	22	2	12	16	33	0
Tanner Witt	.355	.437	.427	110	15	39	1	22	16	22	3

PITCHER	W	L	ERA	G	SV	IP	H	BB	SO
Kyle Allen	3	2	5.02	7	0	38	41	19	13
Payton Baskette*	1	3	6.08	13	0	64	76	35	38
Kyle Brueggemann	7	6	4.71	20	0	117	116	41	109
Eric Cendejas	2	2	4.50	40	0	44	64	8	34
David Diaz	2	5	5.97	7	0	38	41	14	24
Patrick Dolan	3	4	3.92	43	7	44	39	19	46
Matt Frahm	2	4	3.06	46	1	50	50	6	47
Nick Grim	1	6	7.33	16	0	43	52	33	27
Kyle Hassna	9	3	3.69	15	0	90	90	26	71
Michael Holback	2	0	6.48	6	0	8	8	12	9
Colby Holmes	1	5	4.17	48	6	41	47	14	41
Paul Lujan	1	2	6.75	6	0	9	10	2	7
Roberto Padilla*	1	2	3.03	27	0	71	80	32	48
Tony Rizzotti	8	2	2.95	19	0	116	119	37	93
David Russo*	2	1	5.94	34	1	33	35	18	27
Michael Schaub	1	0	0.50	18	12	18	17	2	17

SCHAUMBURG BOOMERS

NAME	AVG	OBP	SLG	AB	R	H	HR	RBI	BB	SO	SB
TJ Bennett	.290	.367	.381	176	24	51	1	20	21	48	4
Ryan Brockett	.250	.325	.250	68	7	17	0	3	8	12	1
Alexi Colon	.287	.400	.458	286	42	82	10	46	55	50	12
Jordan Dean	.317	.364	.449	265	44	84	4	29	17	30	10
Garrett Gordon	.225	.279	.300	40	5	9	0	5	3	11	1
Joel Hutter	.342	.390	.408	76	13	26	0	7	5	7	4
Ken Kirshner	.228	.291	.291	79	13	18	1	9	7	15	3
Sam Lind	.213	.315	.246	61	7	13	0	10	10	16	1
Spencer Mahoney	.214	.500	.286	14	3	3	0	2	8	1	0
Willi Martin	.322	.367	.404	171	18	55	1	22	13	36	1
Steve McQuail	.141	.242	.282	78	8	11	3	10	8	22	0
John Menken	.281	.373	.406	64	8	18	1	9	7	12	0
Mark Nelson	.138	.212	.207	29	1	4	0	4	3	6	0
Tillman Pugh	.172	.250	.345	58	6	10	2	5	5	19	2
Tyler Qualls	.083	.214	.083	36	4	3	0	0	5	12	0
Steve Rogers	.231	.286	.231	26	1	6	0	4	2	8	0
Kyle Ruchim	.304	.396	.429	217	22	66	3	30	30	29	4
Mike Schulze	.285	.411	.362	246	41	70	1	31	50	37	4
Cam Sherrer	.232	.333	.254	177	23	41	0	10	27	52	4
Robby Spencer	.208	.279	.264	53	6	11	0	7	3	14	0
Ryan Tuntland	.167	.222	.250	48	5	8	1	10	3	18	3
Mike Valadez	.232	.286	.331	272	29	63	3	23	14	66	0
Justin Vasquez	.199	.291	.258	186	16	37	1	18	23	47	4
Connor Walsh	.067	.125	.067	15	0	1	0	0	1	4	0

PITCHER	W	L	ERA	G	SV	IP	H	BB	SO
Brandon Bargas*	2	1	3.71	18	1	17	21	10	17
Evan Boyd	0	6	6.08	26	1	50	70	17	36
Edwin Carl	1	5	4.69	11	0	63	62	29	65
Eddie Cody	10	4	2.78	19	0	120	111	22	89
Anthony Gomez*	2	5	8.07	7	0	29	48	10	15
Kagen Hopkins	0	0	3.38	4	0	13	8	2	13
Raul Jacobson	3	3	2.77	10	0	65	67	10	52
Jake Joyce	3	3	2.02	34	1	40	26	23	49
Clark Labitan	2	2	2.84	33	6	38	24	9	34
Brett Mabry	8	3	3.07	18	0	111	106	30	82
Brett Maus*	0	0	11.57	3	0	7	9	4	1

PITCHER	W	L	ERA	G	SV	IP	H	BB	SO
Hideyoshi Otake	4	3	3.78	34	3	48	54	18	45
Scott Plaza	0	4	7.45	6	0	29	35	10	13
Dexter Price	1	3	4.87	20	7	20	23	6	20
A.J. Quintero	0	0	11.12	5	0	6	14	3	6
Taylor Thurber	1	4	4.50	8	0	52	63	10	32
Kamakani Usui	0	1	5.73	11	1	11	9	6	12
Scotty Ward*	1	2	5.29	4	0	17	18	4	5
Seth Webster	1	0	0.00	1	0	7	3	1	6

SOUTHERN ILLINOIS MINERS

NAME	AVG	OBP	SLG	AB	R	H	HR	RBI	BB	SO	SB
Sako Chapjian	.200	.368	.200	15	2	3	0	1	4	5	1
Toby DeMello	.222	.253	.339	239	22	53	5	24	11	67	1
Ryan DiMascio	.186	.250	.237	59	11	11	0	1	3	17	2
Michael Earley	.325	.374	.491	385	55	125	10	61	27	42	5
Wendell Fairley	.286	.342	.314	70	11	20	0	9	7	11	0
Aaron Gates	.316	.402	.459	364	73	115	7	41	54	53	11
Hunter King	.154	.214	.154	13	1	2	0	0	1	6	1
Steve Marino	.260	.317	.380	350	34	91	8	44	27	52	0
Frank Martinez	.271	.375	.371	321	55	87	4	50	57	45	7
Brian Portelli	.256	.283	.389	180	20	46	6	22	8	46	3
Joe Rapp	.211	.305	.324	71	7	15	2	8	10	23	0
Jerrud Sabourin	.309	.363	.382	288	37	89	1	32	26	39	4
Brendan Slattery	.246	.342	.290	69	8	17	0	7	8	13	0
Eric Strano	.222	.282	.250	36	4	8	0	3	2	12	0
Niko Vasquez	.273	.369	.483	348	49	95	16	62	47	77	1

PITCHER	W	L	ERA	G	SV	IP	H	BB	SO
Ryan Brockett*	3	3	5.65	19	1	51	51	26	34
Matt Bywater*	8	4	2.36	16	0	107	80	32	123
Brandon Cowan*	2	3	4.56	24	2	53	49	26	53
Eric Green*	9	3	2.42	48	12	48	39	22	60
Adam Lopez	10	0	1.86	16	0	97	65	35	103
Jarett Miller	5	3	3.58	14	0	75	55	30	73
Miguel Ramirez	2	6	4.35	16	0	72	79	30	60
Will Rankin	0	1	3.86	16	10	16	16	5	13
Shane Street	0	0	2.96	26	1	24	16	11	33
John Tangherlini	0	0	3.52	9	0	15	17	3	8
Rick Teasley*	9	4	2.78	20	0	126	116	33	105

TRAVERSE CITY BEACH BUMS

NAME	AVG	OBP	SLG	AB	R	H	HR	RBI	BB	SO	SB
Yazy Arbelo	.237	.275	.389	334	35	79	10	42	16	95	1
Jay Austin	.319	.361	.451	257	39	82	4	32	15	33	16
Sam Bumpers	.215	.276	.265	260	25	56	1	19	19	59	9
Jeff DeBlieux	.247	.341	.364	231	40	57	3	21	31	52	18
Greg Harisis	.236	.317	.318	195	31	46	1	14	20	48	11
Brandon Jacobs	.320	.405	.554	316	57	101	17	54	45	75	7
Adam Kirsch	.104	.173	.224	67	5	7	2	6	6	25	0
Reggie Lawson	.228	.289	.345	290	26	66	8	39	23	76	5
Kendall Patrick	.212	.264	.303	66	9	14	2	11	2	15	0
Graham Ramos	.211	.250	.307	114	17	24	2	8	6	31	4
Jake Rhodes	.186	.251	.261	161	15	30	3	14	11	41	2
Shane Rowland	.191	.333	.279	68	7	13	0	3	14	13	0
Jordan Savinon	.100	.100	.300	10	0	1	0	0	0	6	0
Alex Tomasovich	.278	.334	.393	295	42	82	5	28	25	54	1
Jose Vargas	.314	.359	.468	344	54	108	10	51	22	64	1

PITCHER	W	L	ERA	G	SV	IP	H	BB	SO
Andrew Brockett	3	0	1.54	32	21	35	30	8	28
Kramer Champlin	10	6	2.05	17	0	114	89	20	65
Bret Dahlson	0	3	1.84	42	5	54	44	17	33
Luis DeJesus	6	3	3.81	16	0	85	89	24	58
Casey Delgado	1	1	1.59	2	0	11	9	2	15
Chuck Ghysels	6	2	3.17	43	5	48	33	36	69
Ian MacDougall*	10	6	2.51	18	0	122	125	19	67
Anthony Montefusco	3	4	4.30	12	0	59	64	12	51
Alex Phillips*	3	4	6.49	16	0	60	77	15	45
Casey Rodriguez*	0	1	3.97	10	0	11	9	9	5
Michael Shreves	7	2	3.21	21	0	101	81	30	37
Tanner Tripp	0	0	4.50	2	0	10	10	4	6
Scott Vachon	1	1	7.92	18	0	31	50	15	22
Dominique Vattuone	2	1	5.62	10	0	16	19	11	10

WASHINGTON WILD THINGS

NAME	AVG	OBP	SLG	AB	R	H	HR	RBI	BB	SO	SB
C.J. Beatty	.259	.351	.373	158	22	41	2	20	23	38	14
John Fidanza	.183	.274	.200	120	5	22	0	4	8	28	0
Matt Ford	.264	.335	.356	239	27	63	3	19	26	39	13
Maxx Garrett	.181	.296	.308	182	17	33	5	14	28	92	1
Andrew Heck	.299	.369	.395	167	23	50	1	16	18	35	7
Cody Herald	.256	.289	.349	43	5	11	0	5	2	19	1
Scott Kalamar	.280	.346	.410	239	29	67	6	33	25	55	11
Ryan Mathews	.095	.174	.143	21	0	2	0	0	2	4	0
Sam Mende	.259	.340	.412	328	38	85	9	41	37	92	8
Brady North	.080	.143	.120	25	0	2	0	1	2	13	1
Lee Orr	.173	.228	.417	139	18	24	9	23	5	49	6
Matt Peters	.241	.307	.307	137	12	33	0	11	13	24	4
Daniel Poma	.248	.343	.362	290	47	72	4	19	30	41	13
David Popkins	.232	.361	.505	311	55	72	20	46	59	116	4
Edinson Rincon	.186	.314	.233	43	4	8	0	7	8	13	0
Jeudy Valdez	.273	.324	.470	66	7	18	3	6	5	16	5
Austin Wobrock	.266	.325	.349	289	25	77	1	31	24	48	15
Jimmy Yezzo	.248	.272	.431	109	10	27	3	18	4	24	0

PITCHER	W	L	ERA	G	SV	IP	H	BB	SO
Ryan Bores	0	1	11.57	2	0	9	17	3	7
Pat Butler	0	3	16.88	10	0	8	16	6	11
Tyler Ferguson*	0	0	5.75	13	0	20	22	16	11
Matt Fraudin	3	2	3.28	8	0	47	37	12	23
Tim Giel	4	5	3.78	34	0	50	47	16	43
Kyle Helisek*	4	2	1.71	7	0	42	36	15	33
Jeremy Holcombe	1	4	5.15	13	0	37	35	15	22
Jonathan Kountis	3	3	2.73	23	9	26	24	11	34
Steve Messner	2	4	2.79	43	1	48	43	27	35
Richie Mirowski	0	3	4.76	19	1	28	23	14	42
Matt Purnell	3	2	3.09	49	4	64	57	25	57
Matt Sergey	3	4	2.76	11	0	62	48	21	69
Kolin Stanley	0	1	1.25	16	0	22	10	6	36
Kyle Vazquez	0	1	9.58	5	0	10	16	6	11
Luke Wilkins	8	5	3.31	20	0	125	120	45	77
Tyler Wilson	0	1	5.40	7	0	7	9	3	9
Ernesto Zaragoza	6	7	4.19	16	0	82	78	36	50

WINDY CITY THUNDERBOLTS

NAME	AVG	OBP	SLG	AB	R	H	HR	RBI	BB	SO	SB
Larry Balkwill	.168	.274	.232	125	13	21	1	5	17	44	0
Alex Chittenden	.242	.293	.328	128	16	31	2	17	6	28	2
Tyler Clark	.170	.275	.279	165	23	28	2	12	24	52	7
Ryan Deitrich	.229	.330	.382	157	15	36	4	17	20	42	10
Zach Esquerra	.128	.244	.231	39	3	5	1	5	6	17	2
Austin Gallagher	.338	.435	.602	284	55	96	16	63	49	26	4
Jon Garcia	.268	.310	.479	142	21	38	6	25	10	26	1
Coco Johnson	.271	.313	.425	391	52	106	10	32	21	55	30
Cody Keefer	.279	.317	.382	136	20	38	1	23	8	21	3
Ransom LaLonde	.249	.312	.341	305	28	76	4	32	16	39	6
Zach Stoner	.235	.316	.412	17	3	4	0	3	2	7	1
Jacob Tanis	.207	.242	.321	299	35	62	7	33	11	66	2
Mike Torres	.303	.400	.366	347	57	105	3	30	56	36	16
Ryan Tufts	.391	.391	.391	23	4	9	0	3	0	6	0
Max White	.291	.326	.487	351	52	102	14	71	16	69	10
Nico Zych	.231	.333	.308	13	0	3	0	1	0	3	0

PITCHER	W	L	ERA	G	SV	IP	H	BB	SO
Chris DeBuo	3	3	4.81	36	0	43	47	14	40
James Ferguson*	1	1	5.40	18	0	28	26	18	29
Jake Fisher*	5	7	4.98	20	0	119	124	41	102
Cameron Giannini	4	2	2.75	30	0	72	62	40	69
Danny Jimenez	3	10	4.53	18	1	87	95	38	59
James Jones	0	3	3.71	18	6	17	15	12	18
Joel Lima	3	5	2.59	37	7	42	36	17	51
Brady Muller*	0	1	8.22	3	0	8	12	5	10
Tommy Nance	1	1	4.74	29	4	38	41	13	40
Dyllon Nuernberg	2	0	1.29	3	0	21	9	11	19
Travis Tingle	7	7	3.12	21	1	121	127	22	94
Zak Wasserman*	4	5	6.75	15	0	73	92	37	43
Pete Whittingslow*	2	0	3.67	24	0	34	33	20	28
Austin Wright*	5	11	4.46	20	0	111	121	55	100

NORTH COUNTRY LEAGUE

For a league formed from the ashes of a league that never got off the ground, the North Country League was facing long odds to simply finish the season. Two of the four teams ended up being travel teams, and attendance could often be counted by a quick scan of the crowd.

The league formed when the East Coast Baseball League folded before the proposed six-team league ever played a game. Bruce Zicari went from owning one team in the six-team ECBL to owning all four teams in the NCBL.

The league played a short two-month schedule at two sites–Old Orchard Beach and Watertown after the Newburg Newts were kicked out of their stadium (and became the New York Newts in the process).

TEAM	W	L	PCT	GB
Road City Explorers	22	17	.564	—
New York Newts	22	17	.564	—
Old Orchard Beach Surge	18	21	.462	4.5
Watertown Bucks	16	23	.410	6

PLAYOFFS: Finals—New York defeated Watertown 2-1 in best-of-3 series.

PACIFIC ASSOCIATION

Ben Lindbergh and Sam Miller's book won't have a happy ending. The Grantland and Baseball Prospectus authors teamed up to run the Sonoma Stompers baseball operations in 2015 to try to win a title using sabermetric principles and to write a book. The Stompers started very strong, winning the first half title, but the San Rafael Pacifics rallied to catch them in the second half, winning their final eight games including a 4-3 win over Sonoma in the championship game. Daniel Gonzalez singled in Johnny Bekakis in the bottom of the ninth for the walk off win.

PACIFIC ASSOCIATION	W	L	PCT	GB
San Rafael Pacifics	48	30	.615	—
Sonoma Stompers	44	33	.571	3.5
Pittsburg Diamonds	38	39	.494	9.5
Vallejo Admirals	25	53	.321	23

PLAYOFFS: Finals—San Rafael defeated Sonoma in championship game.
ATTENDANCE: San Rafael Pacifics 20,610; Vallejo Admirals 6,776; Sonoma Stompers 5,760; Pittsburg Diamonds 3,938.

BATTING LEADERS

PLAYER	TEAM	AVG	AB	R	H	HR	RBI
David, Scott	PIT	.384	229	47	88	2	16
Chavez, Matt	SRF	.383	264	65	101	31	85
Baptista, Daniel	SON	.321	252	39	81	6	41
Williams, Brandon	PIT	.311	180	36	56	7	25

PLAYER	TEAM	AVG	AB	R	H	HR	RBI
Taylor, Mike	PIT	.309	311	53	96	24	74
Jova, Maikel	SRF	.308	338	43	104	5	45
Yasuda, Yuki	SON	.307	199	35	61	0	29
Hibbert, Matt	SON	.306	258	64	79	4	32
Mochizuki, Gered	SON	.303	254	38	77	5	49
Bekakis, Johnny	SRF	.302	242	39	73	1	38

PITCHING LEADERS

PLAYER	TEAM	W	L	ERA	IP	H	BB	SO
Neal, Dennis	PIT	4	1	2.47	77	67	28	47
Beatty, Max	SRF	8	2	3.18	91	81	18	89
Beras, Wander	SRF	7	2	3.39	72	75	34	66
Manzueta, Jheyson	PIT	6	4	3.49	88	80	29	68
DeBarr, Nick	SRF	5	5	3.68	110	113	23	115
Paulino, Gregory	SON	8	4	3.76	93	86	25	87
Dinelli, David	VAL	3	8	3.90	90	96	40	79
Conroy, Patrick	SRF	4	4	4.46	75	84	25	64
Banks, Demetrius	VAL	3	8	4.53	89	109	31	67
Jackson Jr., Mike	SON	6	4	4.72	82	105	23	72

PECOS LEAGUE

The Roswell Invaders won their third Pecos League crown in the past five years with a sweep of Santa Fe in the Pecos' League championship series.

NORTHERN DIVISION	W	L	PCT
Santa Fe Fuego	48	24	.666
Trinidad Triggers	35	27	.564
Raton Osos	23	38	.377
Taos Blizzard	22	40	.354
Las Vegas Train Robbers	16	42	.275

SOUTHERN DIVISION	W	L	PCT
Alpine Cowboys	48	20	.705
Roswell Invaders	38	27	.584
Bisbee Blue	33	30	.523
White Sands Pupfish	28	33	.459
Douglas Diablos	28	36	.437

PLAYOFFS: Finals—Roswell defeated Santa Fe 2-0 in best-of-3 series.

BATTING LEADERS

PLAYER	TEAM	AVG	AB	R	H	HR	RBI
Eric Williams	TRI	.467	246	85	115	19	97
Edgar Munoz	GCK	.440	159	38	70	4	22
Derrick Fox	ALP	.435	269	72	117	7	65
Shane Casey	TRI	.431	188	78	81	14	75
Eddie Newton	SAF	.423	222	68	94	10	61
Louie Saenz	SAF	.411	129	37	53	11	55
Chevas Numata	SAF	.410	217	74	89	32	88
Matt Patrone	SAF	.392	212	86	83	14	48
Danny Grauer	ROS	.388	250	57	97	18	61
Connor Lorenzo	SAF	.386	220	63	85	5	39

PITCHING LEADERS

PITCHER	TEAM	W	L	ERA	IP	H	BB	SO
Joe McCarty	WHI	5	3	1.87	62	67	21	65
Ryan Davis	ROS	5	0	2.20	49	38	22	42
Tyler Moore	ROS	6	1	2.84	44	44	10	38
Ian Drapcho	WHI	1	0	3.49	39	45	14	51
Brad Orosey	ALP	3	1	3.51	33	25	5	36
Guadalupe Barrera	CRU	1	2	3.53	36	36	15	45
Francisco Rodriguez	SAF	4	3	3.83	63	64	30	83
Michael Ormseth	CRU	6	3	3.96	86	88	24	94
Matt Horan	TRI	9	3	4.02	83	103	26	68
Craig Gourley	WHI	4	4	4.03	71	80	30	67

INDEPENDENT LEAGUES

INTERNATIONAL

U.S. National Teams shine on world stage

BY JOHN MANUEL

Soccer has the World Cup. Basketball and hockey have the Olympics. Everyone in the world knows what the top international tournaments are in those sports, and most of the time, the best players in the world play for their countries in those events.

Baseball is trying to have an event like that in the World Baseball Classic. But as 2015 showed, the international calendar can provide excitement even when the Classic isn't on the schedule.

The 2015 international highlights included:

■ Baseball closing in on returning to the fold for the 2020 Olympics in Tokyo;

■ Host Canada's thrilling victory in walk-off fashion over the United States to win its second consecutive Pan American Games baseball title;

■ U.S. teams winning world titles at both the 18-and-under and 12-and-under age levels, as well as a Pan American championship in the 15U division;

■ A continued decline of Cuban power in international baseball, all while improved geopolitical relations between the U.S. and Cuba made the future of Cuban baseball cloudier than ever.

Amateur Highlights

It used to be rare for USA Baseball's 18-and-under program to win a world championship.

The International Baseball Federation's first 18U world tournament was held in 1981, and the U.S. won the second edition, in 1982. Since back-to-back championships in 1988-89, gold medals had become less common for USA Baseball, with wins in 1995 at Fenway Park (the last 18U championship to be held in the United States) and 1999 in Taiwan. But in September, USA Baseball claimed its third straight gold medal, beating host Japan in the championship game in front of 15,000 fans at famed Koshien Stadium. It's the first time any country has won three straight 18U world titles since Cuba from 1984-87.

This year's team presented a unique challenge, as two of the top players in the class, pitchers Jason Groome and Riley Pint, weren't on the roster. Head coach Glenn Cecchini (Barbe HS, Lake Charles, La.) and his staff had to adjust without them, though as is often the case in international amateur play, the U.S. has much more pitching

Alberto Almora and Team USA fell to Canada in a wild Pan-Am Games final

ALYSON BOYER RODE

depth than other teams.

"There's more gratification with this one," said outgoing 18U national team director Shaun Cole, who was hired by the Padres as a roving pitching coordinator in September. "It was more challenging, it was a World Cup so the competition is greater, the travel was a bear, and we didn't necessarily have those frontline leaders. Last year, we just blew everybody out of the water."

With this club, Cecchini, Cole and the coaching staff had to put the right players in the right spots at the right times. That included batting outfielder Blake Rutherford (Chaminade College Prep, Simi Valley, Calif.) ninth after a slow start and leaving him there even after he headed up. Rutherford wound up leading the team with 14 RBIs and hit its only homer, a three-run shot in a 7-4 comeback win against South Korea.

"It was Shaun's decision to hit him ninth, and I really wanted to move him up when he started hitting," Cecchini said. "But we were winning, and he kept coming up in RBI opportunities. We didn't want to stop our momentum, and to his credit, Blake kept coming through in key situations."

It meant keeping righthander Reggie Lawson (Victor Valley HS, Victorville, Calif.) in for the ninth inning to close out the game against Japan, even though closer Austin Bergner was rested and

INTERNATIONAL

ready. It meant riding the hot and healthy hand at catcher, as Michael Amditis (Boca Raton, Fla., Community HS) led the team in batting and supplanted Cooper Johnson as the starter after Johnson was hospitalized with a 104-degree fever.

"Amditis reminded me of David Ross," Cole said. "He covers the plate well, and he's not just a pull-side hitter. He's got a good two-strike approach and has some juice in the bat as well. He's a gamer, has a great attitude, is a great team-mate and played his tail off for us."

It also meant giving underclassman Nick Pratto (Huntington Beach, Calif., HS) the ball for the gold medal game, as the lefty pitched into the seventh inning and earned his third win of the summer. Cecchini took Pratto aside after the U.S. clinched a spot in the gold-medal game and asked the two-way player, his best defensive first base-man, who should make the deciding start.

"We were close to each other and he looked me straight in the eyes and said, 'Nothing against anyone else, but I believe I'm the best choice,'" Cecchini recalled. "'I know what it takes to win. I'm going to go out there and dominate.' And he did."

If only it were so easy. Cole and Cecchini both praised the players for responding to the staff and heaped extra praise on Eric Cressey, who accompanied the team as a strength-and-conditioning coach but did much more. Cressey scouted out gyms for the players to work out in, made sure they had enough protein and Western food, even caught bullpens.

Cecchini said, "Shaun getting him to travel with us was invaluable. Nothing was beneath him—he was amazing." And Cole added, "Whatever it took to help, he did."

That was the case for the 18U program, again. Whoever replaces Cole will inherit a program with high standards—and three consecutive gold medals.

Canada's 18U team placed sixth, led by 2015 draftees Josh Naylor (Marlins, first round), who tore up the event, and outfielder Demi Orimoloye (Brewers). Naylor led the event with three home runs and 15 hits as well as 28 total bases.

The 15U program, directed by Brooks Webb, won its second consecutive gold medal, beating Colombia 9-5 in the final of the Pan American Championships held in Aguascalientes, Mexico. Team USA outscored opponents 64-18 and won its final five games while going 8-1 overall.

Third baseman Justyn Malloy (Bergenfield, N.J.) was named tournament MVP and all-tourna-ment at the hot corner, and went 14-for-26 (.538) with two of Team USA's four home runs and

USA BASEBALL 18U TEAM

WORLD BASEBALL SOFTBALL CONFEDERATION 18U WORLD CUP NISHINOMIYA, JAPAN

FINAL STANDINGS

1. USA 9-2	5. Cuba 5-5	9. Brazil 5-5
2. Japan 10-1	6. Canada 4-6	10. Italy 3-7
3. S. Korea 9-2	7. Mexico 5-5	11. Czech Rep.. 1-9
4. Australia ... 4-7	8. Taiwan 6-4	12. S. Africa 1-9

FINAL STATISTICS

BATTING									
PLAYER	AVG	AB	R	H	HR	RBI	BB	SO	SB
Michael Amditis	.385	26	2	10	0	5	5	5	2
Blake Rutherford	.304	46	11	14	1	14	5	8	3
Daniel Bakst	.275	40	6	11	0	7	7	6	0
Mickey Moniak	.260	50	8	13	0	5	8	7	3
Morgan McCullough	.256	39	7	10	0	3	8	7	0
Jordan Butler	.250	4	1	1	0	0	0	1	0
Will Benson	.244	45	9	11	0	5	7	13	4
Nick Pratto	.239	46	8	11	0	5	7	13	3
Hagen Danner	.227	22	4	5	0	1	2	6	0
Nicholas Quintana	.225	40	7	9	0	6	5	13	2
Cole Stobbe	.220	41	8	9	0	6	6	12	1
Hunter Greene	.167	12	1	2	0	1	0	2	0
Cooper Johnson	.143	14	1	2	0	4	5	5	0
Reggie Lawson	.000	1	0	0	0	0	0	1	0
Totals	.254	426	73	108	1	62	65	99	18

PITCHERS	W	L	ERA	SV	G	IP	H	BB	SO
Jordan Butler	1	0	0.00	0	3	9	1	1	16
Hunter Greene	0	0	0.00	2	2	2	0	0	2
Austin Begner	2	0	0.77	0	4	12	6	4	15
Nick Pratto	3	0	0.84	0	4	21	14	6	30
Forrest Whitley	1	1	0.87	0	4	10	6	2	18
Ian Anderson	0	0	0.87	1	4	10	7	6	15
Braxton Garrett	0	1	2.63	0	5	14	13	8	10
Reggie Lawson	2	1	2.70	1	5	13	7	2	16
Kevin Gowdy	1	0	4.91	0	4	11	17	2	13
Ryan Rolison	0	0	6.00	0	4	6	7	6	6
Hagen Danner	1	0	7.50	2	4	6	7	4	5
Totals	11	3	2.19	4	—	115	85	41	146

walked eight times while striking out only once.

First baseman Triston Casas (Pembroke Pines, Fla.), already a hulking 6-foot-4, 225 pounds, also slammed two homers and hit .429 to earn all-tour-nament honors, where he was joined by outfielder Jared Hart (Marietta, Ga.), who hit .600 (18-for-30) with three stolen bases and no strikeouts, plus shortstop Jeremiah Jackson (Mobile, Ala.), who hit .412 (14-for-34) with three steals of his own.

The American pitching staff got yeoman's work from lefthander Branden Boissiere (Riverside, Calif.), who went 2-0, 2.08 and tossed a team-high 13 innings, and righthander Connor Ollio (Butler, Pa.), who went 2-0, 3.86 and appeared in four games, starting two and tossing 12 innings.

"This is an unbelievable feeling," Team USA manager Jason Washburn said. "I've heard past managers talk about it, but you really can't describe it when you get to put USA across your chest and then to go win a gold medal, it's a fantastic feeling."

And at the 12-and-under level, the Americans beat host Taiwan 7-2 to claim the gold medal in

INTERNATIONAL

the 12U World Cup in August, defending the gold the U.S. won in the event in 2013. Davis Diaz and Jack Ryan homered in the championship game as the U.S. rallied from a 2-0 deficit to avenge an earlier loss.

Diaz led the team with a .571 batting line over the tournament while Zach Torres hit .522 with a team-best 14 runs scored, seven stolen bases and a home run. The U.S. hit .372 as a team, had 24 extra-base hits and stole 29 bases without being caught in nine games, finishing 8-1.

Heavy Pro Schedule

It's rare for USA Baseball to participate in two events featuring professionals in one calendar year, but that was the plan for 2015.

As the Almanac went to press in November, the International Baseball Federation's new Premier 12 tournament was making its debut, with two six-team pools, one in Japan, one in Taiwan, with the top 12 teams per IBAF's rankings playing in a tournament that would wrap with four teams in the Tokyo Dome.

Western nations such as the U.S. had a challenging time getting affiliated minor leaguers to play in November after a long season, but the American roster was set to include prospects such as outfielders Jacob May (White Sox) and Brett Phillips (Brewers) as well as shortstop Gavin Cecchini (Mets).

The U.S. put together a solid roster for the 2015 Pan American Games in Toronto, with the baseball event being held in the nearby town of Ajax. The U.S. had not won Pan Am gold since 1967, and a pair of losses in pool play to Puerto Rico and the Dominican Republic set up a must-win game with host Canada just to make the medal round.

But the Americans got 10 strikeouts from lefthander Nate Smith (Angels) in a 4-1 victory, and they rallied from a 5-1 deficit to walk off Cuba in the semifinal, winning 6-5 on a ninth-inning single by Andy Parrino (Athletics), scoring Travis Jankowski (Padres). That set up a rematch with Canada for the gold medal, and the game was tied 4-4 after nine innings, leading to the international tiebreaker and pandemonium.

Both teams got to start their innings with runners at first and second, and they could start the lineup wherever they wanted. The U.S. put two runs on the board on a double by Tyler Pastornicky (then of the Rangers), but lost the lead and gold medal in dramatic fashion.

Canada had its two runners on the board, and after a strikeout, veteran Peter Orr made it 6-5 with an RBI single off David Huff (Dodgers). With runners at first and second, Huff tried to

pick off Orr at first but threw errantly, with the tying run scoring easily. First baseman Casey Kotchman chased down the ball but Orr challenged him and wound up scoring all the way from first.

"He overthrew the pickoff and I saw Petey running around," said Canadian outfielder Tyler O'Neill, who had the closest vantage point of all the chaos. "Really it was a blur to me. I saw him going to third and it was going to be a close play there, but they threw it away and he came home . . . It was really a blur to me. Still. I thought he was out. Then I saw the ball got away from him and all hell broke loose."

It's the second straight gold for Canada, which also beat the U.S. in 2011 for the Pan Am title. Cuba rallied to win bronze with a four-run rally against Puerto Rico, with a three-run homer by Yorbis Borroto followed by a solo walk-off shot by Jose Garcia (whose brother Adonis played for the Braves in 2015).

Cuban Spending Skyrockets

Cuba's national team has been weakened by repeated defections of players, who often are smuggled out by human traffickers and who, once they leave the island successfully, are not allowed to go back due to friction between the two governments. But that could be changing soon, as the U.S. and Cuba opened embassies in each other's capitals in July 2015 for the first time since January 1961.

The process of making Cuban players free agents for major league teams to sign has been fairly inconsistent over the years, but the success of players from Kendrys Morales to Yasiel Puig and Jose Abreu, coupled with economic uncertainty in Cuba, has spurred dozens more players to leave the island in recent years.

The ones declared free agents have reaped millions of dollars, with the spring dominated by Cuban free agents Yoan Moncada and Hector Olivera. The 19-year-old Moncada signed in February with the Red Sox for a $31.5 million bonus, with another $31.5 million paid to MLB as a penalty for the Red Sox going over their international bonus allotment. A month later, the 29-year-old Olivera signed with the Dodgers for a six-year, $62.5 million deal.

Commissioner Rob Manfred told reporters after the Moncada signing that it would make sense for international players to have a "single method of entry." Talk of an international draft has picked up as teams have spent more than $400 million this decade on Cuban talent, and as relations with Cuba become more normalized, an international draft seems more likely.

INTERNATIONAL

Quintana Roo gets hot in time for 12th title

Quintana Roo had the third-best record in the Mexican League's regular season, but in the league's month-long postseason, the Tigers proved resilient and resourceful.

In winning its 12th championship in 60 years of LMB baseball, Quintana Roo survived two seven-game playoff series before meeting Monclova in the finals. The Tigers cruised past the Steelers in five games to claim the league title. It's their third championship in the last five seasons, with previous victories in 2011 and 2013.

Familiar faces, both to major league fans and to Mexican League followers, powered the Tigers in the postseason. Third baseman Alfredo Amezaga was named playoff MVP after posting a .452 postseason on-base percentage, scoring a team-high 13 runs and batting .322. First baseman/DH Jorge Cantu clubbed four home runs, tying for the league lead, after ranking second in the league in the regular season with 25 homers and 100 RBIs. And closer Ramon Ramirez, a late-season addition, pitched up a club-high three wins and five saves in the postseason to anchor strong bullpen.

The Red Devils of Mexico City dominated the league's regular season, posting a 73-39 regular season powered by the league's best offense. The Red Devils hit .320/.385/.485 as a team, all league highs, as were their 128 home runs. Six-foot-4, 310-pound first baseman Japhet Amador led the way with a league-best 41 home runs, but he had help from Cyle Hankerd, the former Southern California star who hit 22 home runs while batting .384 in 58 games after joining the team in June.

But the Red Devils ran into Tijuana—which finished in fourth place in the North Division, 16 ½ games behind the Red Devils, in the regular season—in the first round of the playoffs. The Toros upset the Red Devils 7-6 behind a third-inning grand slam by Luis Mauricio Suarez. Tigjuana went on to lose to Monclova in seven games in the semifinals.

Monclova was led all season by righthander Josh Lowey, who went 13-6, 3.03 with a league-high 145 strikeouts in 143 innings. The former Frontier League star, 30, started six of the Steelers' 19 postseason games, with Jose Oyervides being the team's other workhorse. The Tigers beat Lowey on short rest in Game Three of the finals

Amador's 41 homers were the most in the Mexican League since veteran Eduardo Jimenez belted 45 for Saltillo in 2000—six more than former big leaguer Warren Newsom. The 28-year-old Amador needed just 103 games to finish with the outrageous hitting line of .346/.436/.742 with a 1.177 OPS. He homered in five straight games in June and had seven multi-homer games.

STANDINGS & LEADERS

NORTH	W	L	PCT	GB
Diablos Rojos del Mexico	73	39	.652	—
Acereros del Norte	59	51	.536	13
Saraperos de Saltillo	57	52	.523	14 ½
Toros de Tijuana	54	53	.505	16 ½
Vaqueros de la Laguna	55	57	.491	18
Rieleros de Aguascalientes	55	58	.487	18 ½
Sultanes de Monterrey	51	62	.451	22 ½
Broncos de Tamaulipas	44	69	.389	29 ½

NORTH	W	L	PCT	GB
Leones de Yucatan	66	46	.589	—
Tigres de Quintana Roo	64	47	.577	1 ½
Guerreros de Oaxaca	55	57	.491	11
Piratas de Campeche	53	56	.486	11 ½
Pericos de Puebla	51	57	.472	13
Olmecas de Tabasco	52	60	.464	14
Delfines de Ciudad del Carmen	51	59	.464	14
Rojos del Aguila de Veracruz	48	65	.425	18 ½

PLAYER, TEAM	AVG	AB	R	H	2B	3B	HR	RBI	BB	SO	SB
Valdez, Jesus, YUC	.363	410	70	149	24	1	17	98	34	54	5
Castillo, Jesus, AGS	.361	416	88	150	35	1	17	77	67	56	15
Rodriguez, Henry A.,CDC	.359	370	65	133	23	0	14	66	31	63	15
Arredondo, Jesus, PUE	.359	340	52	122	32	2	5	50	19	50	13
Greene, Justin, SAL	.351	390	73	137	26	2	10	43	35	77	18
Terrazas, Ivan, MEX	.351	373	74	131	30	2	9	74	42	53	6
Richar, Danny, AGS	.351	413	72	145	26	6	12	71	53	70	22
Urias, Ramon, MEX	.351	399	91	140	20	4	10	55	32	52	12
Cantu, Jorge, TIG	.351	385	75	135	26	2	25	100	49	62	4
Amador, Japhet, MEX	.346	364	84	126	21	0	41	117	54	81	0
Rosario, Olmo, MVA	.343	443	88	152	29	2	13	69	32	50	7
Wimberly, Corey, YUC	.340	374	97	127	25	5	2	31	35	34	34
Rios, Ramon, MTY	.339	422	65	143	20	0	4	34	21	24	4
Fabela, Jesus, MEX	.335	269	53	90	12	4	2	40	29	54	8
Diaz, Frank, TAM	.334	395	66	132	23	0	16	70	37	59	1

PITCHER, TEAM	W	L	ERA	G	SV	IP	H	R	ER	HR	BB	SO
Escalona, Edgmer, SAL	11	4	2.54	17	1	121	104	36	34	6	26	61
Valdez, Cesar, TAB	11	6	2.63	23	0	161	145	51	47	9	28	161
Oseguera, Paul, TAM	8	4	2.67	21	0	135	127	45	40	9	46	113
Lowey, Josh, MVA	13	6	3.03	23	0	143	137	54	48	11	46	145
Duarte, Marco A., MEX	13	5	3.08	23	0	120	124	50	41	10	47	91
Rivera, Oscar, CDC	5	7	3.23	20	0	109	110	41	39	6	30	74
Acosta, Ruddy, OAX	8	6	3.38	20	0	109	110	46	41	5	38	74
Tovar, Marco, MTY	10	3	3.46	23	0	125	134	53	48	10	43	105
Quevedo, Marco, YUC	8	3	3.46	20	0	107	101	43	41	6	28	45
Solis, Tomas, VER	6	8	3.5	20	0	111	101	56	43	11	28	78
Astorga, Alejandro, YUC	7	7	3.56	19	0	91	87	37	36	5	37	50
Reyes, David, MEX	10	6	3.72	21	0	119	118	60	49	14	23	57
Ortega, Pablo, TIG	12	7	3.81	22	0	125	137	63	53	12	37	52
Oyervides, Jose, MVA	8	5	3.85	19	0	108	115	54	46	6	27	100
Castellanos, J., YUC	7	7	3.9	22	0	111	124	56	48	5	32	67

Sluggers lead Fukoka back to top

BY WAYNE GRACZYK

The Fukuoka SoftBank Hawks won a second consecutive championship by beating the Tokyo Yakult Swallows in a five-game Japan Series to cap the 2015 Japanese pro baseball season. Both teams were led by first-year managers and a couple of young superstar players who achieved "Triple 3" offensive statistics.

The powerhouse Hawks easily took the Pacific League pennant under freshman skipper Kimiyasu Kudo, winning the regular season by 12 games over the second place Hokkaido Nippon Ham Fighters. Yakult, guided by rookie manager Mitsuru Manaka, went from worst to first in the Central League. After finishing last in 2014, the Swallows won the 2015 Central League pennant by a game and a half over the Yomiuri Giants.

SoftBank center fielder Yuki Yanagita (27) won the Pacific League batting title with a .363 average while belting 34 home runs and stealing 32 bases. Yakult's 23-year-old second baseman Tetsuto Yamada also racked up a "Triple-3" leading the Central League with 38 homers and 34 steals. His .329 average was second to teammate Shingo Kawabata, the Swallows third baseman who hit .336.

Alex Ramirez

A third Yakult infielder, first baseman Kazuhiro Hatakeyama, took the CL RBI title with 105. Saitama Seibu Lions third baseman Takeya Nakamura led the Pacific League with 37 homers and 124 RBIs.

Seibu center fielder Shogo Akiyama set a new Japanese baseball single-season record for hits, banging out 216 to break the old mark of 214 set by American Matt Murton of the Hanshin Tigers in 2010. Akiyama hit .359 and was runner-up to Yanagita in the PL batting title race.

It was mostly a pitchers' year in Japan, however. There were only three .300 hitters in the Central League and five in the Pacific, while a trio of hurlers in the CL posted earned run averages of less than two runs per nine innings. Lefthander Kris Johnson won the league ERA title with a 1.85 while going 14-7 in his first year with the Hiroshima Carp. Yomiuri righthander Miles Mikolas was 13-3, 1.92 in his first season in Japan.

Yakult closer Tony Barnette tied Hanshin Tigers Korean finisher Oh Seung-Hwan for the most saves in the Central League with 41. SoftBank's Dennis Sarfate also saved 41, the most in the Pacific division.

The 32-year-old Barnette has never played in the Majors, but the Swallows announced following the season the team would agree to his request to be posted for possible major league service in 2016.

Another possible future major league prospect, righty Shohei Otani of Nippon Ham, topped the Pacific League with 15 victories and a 2.24 ERA. Hiroshima righthander Kenta Maeda, another who might be looking to move to the major league, also won 15 to pace the Central League while posting a fourth-best 2.09 ERA.

A total of 74 foreigners played in Japan in 2015, representing the U.S., Canada, Australia, South Korea, Taiwan, Mexico, Puerto Rico, Venezuela, the Dominican Republic, Cuba, Italy, Holland and Curacao.

There will also be a foreign-born manager in Japan next season for the first time in six years. The Central League's Yokohama DeNA Baystars hired Venezuelan native Alex Ramirez to lead the club in 2016 after its last place standing in 2015.

A gambling scandal tainted Japanese baseball in October. Just as the Yomiuri Giants were about to begin play in the Central League Climax Series, it was revealed Giants pitcher Satoshi Fukuda, 32, had bet on games involving his team and also Major League games. Gambling is in violation of NPB rules, and Fukuda was suspended by the club.

Two weeks later, it came to light that a couple of other Yomiuri pitchers were involved in the scandal. Shoki Kasahara, 24, and Ryuya Matsumoto, 22, admitted to betting on Japanese baseball, including professional and high school games. Kasahara saw action in 20 games for the Giants in 2015, while Fukuda and Matsumoto played only on the Yomiuri farm team.

Due to the immense popularity of baseball in Japan and the fact Tokyo is the host city for the 2020 Olympic Games, NPB and Tokyo officials have spearheaded a campaign to have baseball and softball reinstated to the Olympics. It is hoped the gambling scandal will not have a negative effect on the situation.

CENTRAL LEAGUE

	W	L	T	Pct.	GB
Tokyo Yakult Swallows	76	65	2	.539	—
Yomiuri Giants	75	67	1	.528	1 ½
Hanshin Tigers	70	71	2	.496	6
Hiroshima Carp	69	71	3	.493	6 ½
Chunichi Dragons	62	77	4	.446	13
Yokohama DeNA Baystars	62	80	1	.437	14 ½

CLIMAX SERIES PLAYOFFS—First Stage: Yomiuri defeated Hanshin 2-1 in best-of-three series. **Final Stage:** Tokyo Yakult defeated Yomiuri 4-1 in best-of-seven series.

INDIVIDUAL BATTING LEADERS
(Minimum 443 Plate Appearances)

PLAYER, TEAM	AVG.	AB	R	H	2B	3B	HR	RBI	SB
Kawabata, Shingo, Swallows	.336	581	87	195	34	1	8	57	4
Yamada, Tetsuto, Swallows	.329	557	119	183	39	2	38	100	34
Tsutsugo, Yoshitomo, Baystars	.317	496	79	157	28	1	24	93	0
Luna, Hector, Dragons	.292	496	61	145	26	1	8	60	11
Lopez, Jose, Baystars	.291	516	63	150	29	1	25	73	1
Hirata, Ryosuke, Dragons	.283	491	76	139	27	3	13	53	11
Toritani, Takashi, Tigers	.281	551	69	155	21	4	6	42	9
Fukudome, Kosuke, Tigers	.281	495	53	139	24	3	20	76	1
Murton, Matt, Tigers	.276	544	46	150	27	0	9	59	0
Kajitani, Takayuki, Bystars	.275	520	70	143	35	2	13	66	28
Arai, Takahiro, Carp	.275	426	52	117	22	2	7	57	3
Tanaka, Kosuke, Carp	.274	543	61	149	33	9	8	45	6
Gomez, Mauro, Tigers	.271	520	49	141	28	0	17	72	0
Hernandez, Anderson, Dragons	.271	498	54	135	27	2	11	58	5

REMAINING U.S., AUSTRALIAN AND LATIN PLAYERS

PLAYER, TEAM	AVG.	AB	R	H	2B	3B	HR	RBI	SB
Nanita, Ricardo, Dragons	.308	156	9	48	12	0	0	15	1
Rosario, Rainel, Carp	.258	124	9	32	5	9	2	12	1
Anderson, Leslie, Giants	.252	234	20	59	14	0	7	31	21
Schierholtz, Nate, Carp	.250	232	27	58	11	1	10	30	3
Guzman, Jesus, Carp	.230	100	10	23	8	1	3	12	0
Eldred, Brad, Carp	.227	264	32	60	6	0	19	54	1
Dening, Mitch, Swallows	.222	194	13	43	12	0	4	22	0
Milledge, Lastings, Swallows	.211	76	3	16	2	1	1	9	0
Balentien, Wladimir, Swallows	.186	43	4	8	2	0	1	6	0
Francisco, Juan, Giants	.167	18	0	3	0	0	0	1	0
Castellanos, Alex, Giants	.100	20	2	2	1	0	0	1	0
Cepeda, Frederich, Giants	.000	21	1	0	0	0	0	1	0
Perez, Nelson, Tigers	.000	9	0	0	0	0	0	0	0

INDIVIDUAL PITCHING LEADERS
(Minimum 143 Innings Pitched)

PITCHER, TEAM	W	L	ERA	G	SV	IP	H	BB	SO
Johnson, Kris, Carp	14	7	1.85	28	0	194	146	67	150
Sugano, Tomoyuki, Giants	10	11	1.91	25	0	179	148	41	126
Mikolas, Miles, Giants	13	3	1.92	21	0	145	107	23	107
Maeda, Kenta, Carp	15	8	2.09	29	0	206	168	41	175
Fujinami, Shintaro, Tigers	14	7	2.40	28	0	199	162	82	221
Ono, Yudai, Dragons	11	10	2.52	28	0	207	169	47	154
Kuroda, Hiroki, Carp	11	8	2.55	26	0	170	158	29	106
Poreda, Aaron, Giants	8	8	2.94	24	0	147	133	46	101
Messenger, Randy, Tigers	9	12	2.97	29	0	194	163	60	194
Ogawa, Yasuhiro, Swallows	11	8	3.11	27	0	168	152	48	128
Takagi, Hayato, Giants	9	10	3.19	26	0	164	143	47	131
Iwata, Minoru, Tigers	8	10	3.22	27	0	170	168	49	119
Ishikawa, Masanori, Swallows	13	9	3.31	25	0	147	150	28	90
Nomi, Atsushi, Tigers	11	13	3.72	27	0	160	170	38	125

REMAINING U.S., CANADIAN, AUSTRALIAN AND LATIN PLAYERS

PITCHER, TEAM	W	L	ERA	G	SV	IP	H	BB	SO
Barnette, Tony, Swallows	3	1	1.29	59	41	63	37	19	56
Ondrusek, Logan, Swallows	5	2	2.05	72	0	70	52	22	62
Heath, Deunte, Carp	3	6	2.36	43	4	50	43	19	59
Roman, Orlando, Swallows	5	5	2.40	61	0	79	66	35	58
Zagurski, Mike, Carp	0	0	2.40	19	0	15	13	7	16
Mathieson, Scott, Giants	3	8	2.62	63	2	58	47	21	55
Herrera, Yoslan, Baystars	5	4	2.96	52	0	52	44	15	53
Mendoza, Hector, Giants	0	0	3.00	2	0	3	3	1	3
Valdes, Raul, Dragons	5	8	3.18	22	0	133	130	36	93
Naylor, Drew, Baystars	4	3	3.81	10	0	52	48	19	41
Santiago, Mario, Tigers	1	0	4.32	3	0	17	20	1	11
Moscoso, Guillermo, Baystars	3	6	5.19	15	0	61	62	27	54
Below, Duane, Baystars	0	1	33.75	1	0	1	2	5	0

PACIFIC LEAGUE

	W	L	T	Pct.	GB
Fukuoka SoftBank Hawks	90	49	4	.647	—
Hokkaido Nippon Ham Fighters	79	62	2	.560	12
Chiba Lotte Marines	73	69	1	.514	18 ½
Saitama Seibu Lions	69	69	5	.500	20 ½
Orix Buffaloes	61	80	2	.433	30
Tohoku Rakuten Golden Eagles	57	83	3	.407	33 ½

CLIMAX SERIES PLAYOFFS—First Stage: Chiba Lotte defeated Hokkaido Nippon Ham 2-1 in best-of-three series. **Final Stage:** Fukuoka SoftBank defeated Chiba Lotte 4-0 in best-of-seven series.

INDIVIDUAL BATTING LEADERS
(Minimum 443 Plate Appearances)

PLAYER, TEAM	AVG.	AB	R	H	2B	3B	HR	RBI	SB
Yanagita, Yuki, Hawks	.363	502	110	182	31	1	34	99	32
Akiyama, Shogo, Lions	.359	602	108	216	36	10	14	55	17
Kondo, Kensuke, Fighters	.326	435	68	142	33	2	8	60	6
Kiyota, Ikuhiro, Marines	.317	489	67	155	38	4	15	67	10
Nakamura, Akira, Hawks	.300	506	58	152	22	0	1	39	7
Kakunaka, Katsuya, Marines	.293	427	57	125	20	5	6	52	8
Matsuda, Nobuhiro, Hawks	.287	533	91	153	22	2	35	94	8
Mori, Tomoya, Lions	.287	474	51	136	33	1	17	68	0
Tanaka, Kensuke, Fighters	.284	532	62	151	20	2	4	66	9
Uchikawa, Seiichi, Hawks	.284	529	60	150	24	1	11	82	1
Lee, Dae Ho, Hawks	.282	510	68	144	30	0	31	98	0
Nakamura, Takeya, Lions	.278	521	82	145	35	0	37	124	1
Nishikawa, Haruki, Fighters	.276	442	68	122	18	9	5	35	30
Fujita, Kazuya, Eagles	.270	392	38	106	14	1	5	43	8
Asamura, Hideto, Lions	.270	537	88	145	19	2	13	81	12

REMAINING U.S. AND LATIN PLAYERS

PLAYER, TEAM	AVG.	AB	R	H	2B	3B	HR	RBI	SB
Canizares, Barbaro, Hawks	.333	33	3	11	1	0	1	3	0
Murillo, Augustin, Eagles	.313	32	1	10	1	0	0	1	2
German, Esteban, Buffaloes	.267	221	31	59	8	1	1	15	17
Despaigne, Alfredo, Marines	.258	353	49	91	18	0	18	62	0
Wheeler, Zelous, Eagles	.255	274	28	70	12	0	14	50	1
Caraballo, Francisco, Buffaloes	.252	222	26	56	9	0	12	35	0
Sanchez, Gaby, Eagles	.226	199	19	45	12	0	7	18	3
Hermida, Jeremy, Fighters	.211	166	12	35	8	1	1	18	1
Blanco, Tony, Buffaloes	.194	165	13	32	1	0	9	24	0
Seratelli, Anthony, Lions	.183	60	8	11	1	1	0	6	1
Huffman, Chad, Marines	.091	11	0	1	0	0	0	0	0

INDIVIDUAL PITCHING LEADERS
(Minimum 143 Innings Pitched)

PITCHER, TEAM	W	L	ERA	G	SV	IP	H	BB	SO
Otani, Shohei, Fighters	15	5	2.24	22	0	161	100	46	196
Nishi, Yuki, Buffaloes	10	6	2.38	24	0	163	140	43	143
Norimoto, Takahiro, Eagles	10	11	2.91	28	0	195	176	48	215
Takeda, Shota, Hawks	13	6	3.17	25	0	165	142	59	163
Nakata, Kenichi, Hawks	9	7	3.24	24	0	155	134	61	130
Ishikawa, Ayumu, Marines	12	12	3.27	27	0	179	191	34	126
Tomei, Daiki, Buffaloes	10	8	3.35	25	0	161	148	41	118
Wakui, Hideaki, Marines	15	9	3.39	28	0	189	178	57	117
Mendoza, Luis, Fighters	10	8	3.51	26	0	149	134	62	85
Togame, Ken, Lions	11	7	3.55	26	0	152	145	53	107
Standridge, Jason, Hawks	10	7	3.74	23	0	144	150	44	81
Yoshikawa, Mitsuo, Fighters	11	8	3.84	26	0	159	151	57	93

REMAINING U.S., EUROPEAN AND LATIN PLAYERS

PITCHER, TEAM	W	L	ERA	G	SV	IP	H	BB	SO
Sarfate, Dennis, Hawks	5	1	1.11	65	41	65	27	14	102
Garate, Victor, Fighters	3	1	1.71	13	0	26	20	17	19
Dickson, Brandon, Buffaloes	9	9	2.48	20	0	131	119	44	88
Van den Hurk, Rick, Hawks	9	0	2.52	15	0	93	69	22	120
Cruz, Rhiner, Eagles	1	3	3.12	52	1	49	40	29	42
Barrios, Edison, Hawks	0	2	3.18	30	1	34	37	16	34
Maestri, Alex, Buffaloes	0	2	3.19	28	1	42	37	23	34
Bullington, Bryan, Buffaloes	5	3	3.30	14	0	74	60	24	46
Vasquez, Esmerling, Lions	3	1	3.63	34	0	35	40	21	21
Ray, Kenny, Eagles	5	7	3.79	22	0	107	107	31	76
LeBlanc, Wade, Lions	2	5	4.23	8	0	45	43	18	26
Rosa, Carlos, Marines	1	3	4.97	29	0	29	33	11	21
Lively, Mitch, Fighters	0	0	5.30	16	0	19	19	15	22
Crotta, Mike, Fighters	2	2	6.59	30	0	29	36	19	18
Wolfe, Brian, Hawks	0	1	11.00	2	0	9	18	4	3
Mejia, Miguel, Lions	0	0	14.73	4	0	4	10	3	4

KOREA

Bears top Lions

A thrilling Korean season that included a 40-40 effort for ex-big league outfielder Eric Thames of the NC Dinos could not steal the spotlight from late-season scandals that overshadowed the post-season—even one this noteworthy.

For the first time in five years, the Samsung Lions are not the Korean Baseball Organization champions. The Doosan Bears beat the Lions in five games during the KBO championship series, winning the clincher 13-2 for their fourth title. DH Jung Soo-bin was voted series MVP by going 8-for-14 with five RBIs. American righty Dustin Nippert, who tossed seven shutout innings in the Bears' Game Two victory, struck out Yamaico Navarro with the bases loaded in the seventh inning of Game Five to thwart Samsung's final threat.

As Doosan met Samsung in the finals, the four-time champion Lions played without three pitchers facing an investigation into a gambling scandal. The Lions were without ace Yoon Sung-hwan (17-8, 1.76), as well as 39-year-old closer Lim Chang-yong (2.83 ERA, 33 SV).

STANDINGS & LEADERS

	W	L	T	PCT	GB
Samsung Lions	88	56	0	.611	—
NC Dinos	84	57	3	.596	2 ½
Doosan Bears	79	65	0	.549	9
Nexen Heroes	78	65	1	.545	9 ½
SK Wyverns	69	73	2	.486	18
Hanwha Eagles	68	76	0	.472	20
Kia Tigers	67	77	0	.465	21
Lotte Giants	66	77	1	.462	21 ½
LG Twins	64	78	2	.451	23
KT Wiz	52	91	1	.364	35 ½

INDIVIDUAL BATTING LEADERS

PLAYER, TEAM	BA	AB	R	H	2B	3B	HR	RBI	SB	SO
Eric Thames, NC	.381	472	130	180	42	5	47	140	40	91
Han-jun Yu, Nexen	.362	520	103	188	42	1	23	116	3	71
Ja-wook Koo, Samsung	.349	410	97	143	33	5	11	57	17	79
Tae-in Chae, Samsung	.348	333	35	116	19	0	8	49	0	92
Andy Marte, KT	.348	425	85	148	32	1	20	89	0	60
Byung-ho Park, Nexen	.343	528	129	181	35	1	53	146	10	161
Geon-woo Park, Doosan	.342	158	31	54	12	0	5	26	2	29
Yong-gyu Lee, Han	.341	493	94	168	15	7	4	42	28	45
Sang-Woo Seo, LG	.340	159	29	54	8	0	6	22	5	31
Gyeong-eon Kim, Han	.337	377	58	127	21	1	16	78	1	89

INDIVIDUAL PITCHING LEADERS

PITCHER, TEAM	W	L	ERA	G	IP	H	R	ER	BB	SO
Moo-keun Cho, KT	8	5	1.88	43	72	54	26	15	32	83
Hyeon-jong Yang, Kia	15	6	2.44	32	184	150	52	50	78	157
Gyu-jin Yoon, Han	3	2	2.66	40	51	39	15	15	21	48
Zach Stewart, NC	8	2	2.68	19	118	116	37	35	26	109
Chang-Yong Lim, Samsung	5	2	2.83	55	54	45	17	17	13	71
Young-pil Choi, Kia	5	2	2.86	59	63	57	23	20	8	51
Suk-min Yoon, Kia	2	6	2.96	51	70	69	23	23	24	68
Esmil Rogers, Hanwha	6	2	2.97	10	76	62	26	25	20	60
Sang-Woo Cho, Nexen	8	5	3.09	70	93	65	36	32	41	89
Jeong-jin Park, Han	6	1	3.09	76	96	84	37	33	39	92

TAIWAN

Misch leads Lamigo to title

The Lamigo Monkeys won their third straight Chinese Professional Baseball title, winning Game Seven of the championship series against the ChinaTrust Brother Elephants in dramatic fashion—with a Game Seven no-hitter.

Ex-big leaguer Pat Misch, a lefthander who went 4-15 in parts of six big league seasons—the last with the Mets in 2011—tossed the no-no, the first in the CPBL's postseason since 1990. He walked one and struck out seven for his second win in the series, helping the Monkeys come back from a 3-1 series deficit.

Misch made just 10 appearances in the regular season for Lamigo after spending the first half with Triple-A New Orleans (Marlins)before opting out of his contract at the all-star break. He went 6-1, 2.96 in 55 regular season innings before dazzling in the postseason for the Monkeys. Lamigo also featured shortstop Line Chih Sheng, who had the league's first-ever 30-30 season (31 HR, 30 SB).

A season ending in a no-hitter was surprising in a season defined by offensive fireworks, as three of the four teams finished with batting averages above .300. Rhinos outfielder Kao Kuo Heui set a new league mark with 39 homers, six more than the previous record set in 2007 by Tilson Brito.

STANDINGS & LEADERS

TEAM	W	L	T	PCT	
Brother Elephants	36	23	1	.610	—
Lamigo Monkeys	31	29	0	.517	5 ½
EDA Rhinos	29	31	0	.483	7 ½
Uni-President 7-11 Lions	23	36	1	.390	13

INDIVIDUAL BATTING LEADERS

PLAYER, TEAM	BA	AB	R	H	2B	3B	HR	RBI	SB
Hu Chin Lung, EDA	.383	446	99	171	28	1	16	76	15
Lin Chih Sheng, Lamigo	.380	411	106	156	30	2	31	124	30
Lin Yi Chuan, EDA	.367	452	84	166	28	1	23	126	1
Lin Hung Yu, Lamigo	.353	434	97	153	27	0	24	101	4
Chou Ssu Chi, Uni	.349	413	68	144	27	1	15	68	11
Chang Chien Ming, EDA	.342	453	89	155	25	3	11	74	4
Chen Jun Xiu, Lamigo	.335	418	78	140	31	0	25	118	11
Chang Cheng Wei, Uni	.335	418	85	140	25	3	2	41	3

INDIVIDUAL PITCHING LEADERS

PITCHER, TEAM	W	L	ERA	G	IP	H	R	ER	BB	SO
Mike Loree, EDA	16	5	3.26	30	191	197	78	69	38	144
Zhen Kai Wen, BE	10	4	3.50	16	103	113	46	40	24	77
Justin Thomas, Uni	5	8	3.83	22	134	144	69	57	55	92
Mike McClendon, BE	10	3	3.92	19	131	159	63	57	15	83
Jiang Chen Yan, Uni	6	3	4.07	27	104	95	51	47	43	79
Jared Lansford, Lamigo	16	7	4.15	28	178	222	98	82	43	111
Andrew Sisco, EDA	6	7	4.52	19	102	101	57	51	39	122
Pan Wei Lun, Uni	7	9	4.75	25	153	213	103	81	33	60

Rimini sweeps way to first Italy title in nine years

The Rimini Pirates defeated Bologna four games to none in the best-of-seven Italy Series to win their first title since 2006. Rimini had been Italy Series losers for three straight years. It was their 12th title, going back to 1975. It was the first Series sweep by any IBL club since 2000, when Rimini beat Nettuno.

Carlos Maldonado

Bologna dominated the IBL during the regular season and the semifinals. Going into the Italy Series, Bologna had defeated Rimini eight times in 10 games. After the season, hitting coach Daniele Frignani replaced Marco Nanni as Bologna skipper. Nanni managed Bologna for 10 years, winning a pair of Italy Series and three European Cups.

Dominican pitcher Alexis Candelario was voted Italy Series MVP after winning Games One and Four. The 33-year-old righthander allowed just one earned run in 13⅓ innings in the Series. It was Candelario's first season in Italy. He had previously played pro ball in Nicaragua, Mexico and Venezuela.

In early May, Candelario and two relievers shared a no-hitter against Parma. Candelario pitched the first six innings in the game, a 4-0 win. Last-place Parma was on the wrong end of another no-hitter in early July, an 8-1 loss to San Marino. None of the four hurlers used by San Marino in the game pitched more than three innings. Parma finished with a league-worst team batting average of .171, one home run and a 4.20 ERA. Only two Parma regulars batted .200 or higher.

In his first start of the season, Bologna righty Riccardo De Santis won his 100th IBL game. De Santis, 35, is only the 17th pitcher in the league to reach that plateau. De Santis and former Rays farm hand Marquis Fleming had a combined record of 17-4. It was Fleming's first season in Italy.

Former big leaguer Guillermo Rodriguez caught and DH'ed for Bologna. Rodriguez was not the only ex-major league receiver in the IBL. Carlos Maldonado, who had brief stints with the Pirates and Nationals, joined Nettuno in the offseason and led the league in home runs (5) and RBIs (27).

In August, San Marino first baseman Gabriele Ermini, 39, became the 24th IBL player to reach 1,000 career hits.

Italian baseball lost one of its most legendary players in June. Righthander Giulio Glorioso had phenomenal seasons in the early and mid 1960s. His combined record from 1961-65 inclusive was 79-5. In '61, with Milan, he was 18-0 in 18 games with eight shutouts and a 0.46 ERA. He also hit .444 that season and won the batting title.

REGULAR SEASON STANDINGS

TEAM	G	W	L	GB
Bologna	28	23	5	—
Rimini	28	18	10	5
Padua	28	16	12	7
San Marino	28	16	12	7
Nettuno	28	13	15	10
Nettuno 2	28	11	17	12
Godo	28	9	19	14
Parma	28	6	22	17

SEMIFINAL ROUND

TEAM	G	W	L	GB
Bologna	18	14	4	—
Rimini	18	9	9	5
San Marino	18	8	10	6
Padua	18	5	13	9

PLAYER, TEAM	AVG	AB	R	H	2B	3B	HR	RBI	BB
Romero, Alexander, RIM	.388	98	25	38	7	0	1	14	14
Vasquez, Wuillians, RSM	.364	107	22	39	12	2	2	18	16
Liverziani, Claudio, BOL	.348	92	19	32	9	0	1	18	22
Vaglio, Alessandro, BOL	.340	100	27	34	7	1	2	21	13
Retrosi, Ennio, NET	.336	122	28	41	5	3	0	8	10
Sambucci, Alex, BOL	.326	92	11	30	10	0	0	26	18
Bertagnon, Riccard, RIM	.323	62	7	20	4	0	0	9	13
Ferrini, Jose, NET	.316	95	21	30	2	2	1	17	22
Colagrossi, Leonardo, NE2	.312	93	8	29	7	0	1	16	12
Imperiali, Renato, NET	.308	91	11	28	5	0	1	15	16
Suarez, Cesar, BOL	.306	108	22	33	10	0	0	21	4
Epifano, Erick, PDO	.304	92	17	28	5	0	1	8	10
Mazzuca, Joseph, RSM	.302	86	20	26	3	0	2	14	11
Alvarez, Luis, PDO	.301	93	12	28	4	0	2	11	13
Olmedo, Rainer, RIM	.301	103	12	31	5	0	0	9	13

PITCHER, TEAM	W	L	ERA	SV	IP	H	R	ER	BB	SO
Rivero, Raul, BOL	0	0	0.33	5	28	19	2	1	4	35
Crepaldi, Filippo, BOL	2	1	1.04	5	26	16	3	3	7	25
Moreno, Victor, RIM	1	1	1.52	6	24	10	4	4	10	31
Fleming, Marquis, BOL	9	3	1.81	0	75	45	16	15	25	74
Quevedo, Carlos, PDO	7	2	1.89	0	76	58	19	16	18	85
Estrada, Paul, NET	4	4	1.92	0	84	74	26	18	20	103
Escalonal, Josè, RIM	2	0	1.95	0	28	18	6	6	16	33
Candelario, Alexis, RIM	8	2	1.97	0	69	37	17	15	20	101
Richetti, Carlos, RIM	6	3	1.97	0	59	38	19	13	9	49
Ribeiro, Yulman, GOD	0	2	2.12	2	34	27	12	8	13	38
Montoya, Jhonny, NET	3	2	2.41	2	41	28	14	11	19	60
Rodriguez, Rodney-RSM	5	5	2.74	0	66	55	24	20	18	83
Uviedo, Ronald, GOD	3	8	3.01	0	84	65	33	28	21	79
Oberto, Junior, RSM	4	0	3.38	0	37	32	14	14	26	36
Gleotti, Matteo, GOD	4	5	3.45	0	73	62	33	28	27	42

Neptunus wins 3rd straight title

Neptunus defeated Kinheim four games to one in the Holland Series to claim their third consecutive Dutch Major League title. It was the Rotterdam club's 16th title, all in a span of only 35 years.

The Holland Series MVP was awarded to Neptunus second baseman Benjamin Dille. The 29-year-old Belgian led all Series participants in batting average (.458), slugging percentage (.667), hits (11), runs (8), RBIs (8) and on-base percentage (.480). Dille also won the award in 2009 and 2013.

Dille's double-play partner for much of the DML campaign was Stijn van der Meer, who joined Neptunus in late May after being named to the Southland first-team all-conference team and all-conference tournament team as a member of the Lamar Cardinals. Van der Meer hit a combined .325 for Neptunus in the regular season and playoffs, with only five strikeouts in 123 at bats.

BRIAN NICHOLS

Diegomar Markwell

Southpaw Diegomar Markwell and righty Orlando Yntema had two victories each in the Holland Series. Markwell, a 35-year-old former Blue Jays farmhand from Curacao, finished the regular season in a tie for the lead in wins (9-2, 2.06). Yntema, who pitched in the Giants system, had a hand in two no-hitters in 2015. In late May, the 29-year-old Dominican threw the first five innings and shared a seven-inning, 10-0 no-hit win over UVV with two relievers. Two months later, also against UVV, Yntema pitched a complete game no-hitter as Neptunus won 5-0.

Neptunus struggled in the early stages of the semifinal round of the DML season. They lost three of their first four games in the semifinals, a triple round robin competition involving the top four teams from the regular season. But they rebounded from the slow start by winning five straight games to finish first in the semifinal round.

The Amsterdam Pirates failed to qualify for the Holland Series, despite winning the DML pennant.

The Pirates were led by 40-year-old righty Rob Cordemans, whose 0.84 ERA topped the league.

Neptunus won its first European Cup since 2004 by defeating Bologna two games to one in the best-of-three final series. Italian clubs had won the previous seven continental club championships.

Gianison Boekhoudt of Neptunus and Bryan Engelhardt of Kinheim shared the DML home run crown after hitting eight each. Engelhardt has now led the league in homers eight times.

Hoofddorp Pioniers outfielder Dirk van't Klooster retired at the end of the season. The 39-year-old Amsterdam native made his DML debut as a teenager with the Pirates in 1993 and is the league's all-time leader in games played (906) and hits (1215).

REGULAR SEASON STANDINGS

TEAM	G	W	L	T	GB
Amsterdam Pirates	42	34	8	0	
Neptunus	42	33	9	0	1
Kinheim	42	29	11	2	4
Hoofddorp Pioniers	42	25	17	0	9
UVV	42	16	26	0	18
DSS	42	12	30	0	22
HCAW	42	10	30	2	23
Dordrecht Hawks	42	7	35	0	27

SEMIFINAL ROUND

TEAM	W	L	GB
Neptunus	6	3	—
Kinheim	6	3	—
Amsterdam Pirates	4	5	2
Hoofddorp Pioniers	2	7	4

PLAYER	AVG	AB	R	H	2B	3B	HR	RBI	BB
Diaz, Christian, NEP	.431	123	31	53	15	3	1	19	30
Ricardo, Dashenko, KIN	.420	169	27	71	12	4	4	40	7
Gario, Mervin, KIN	.395	147	44	58	13	2	3	28	18
Kemp, Dwayne, NEP	.368	163	39	60	13	1	2	23	11
Daantji, Shaldimar, NEP	.358	120	28	43	6	3	2	28	12
Draijer Remco, AMS	.350	143	33	50	4	4	2	23	29
Vernooij, Rien, NEP	.333	126	26	42	6	4	1	21	13
Berkenbosch, Kenny, AMS	.331	151	33	50	16	1	1	27	25
Legito, Raily, NEP	.324	136	28	44	10	0	1	29	11
Dille, Benjamin, NEP	.320	181	26	58	5	1	0	32	5
Croes, Linoy, AMS	.318	110	23	35	10	0	2	22	14
Fernandes, Daniel, PIO	.315	168	34	53	11	1	2	13	21
Moesquit, Kevin, KIN	.314	140	37	44	7	4	2	23	21
Nooij, Bas, AMS	.310	129	32	40	9	0	5	37	24
Rooi, Vince, PIO	.307	140	26	43	8	1	3	28	19

PLAYER	W	L	ERA	SV	IP	H	R	ER	BB	SO
Cordemans, Rob, AMS	6	2	0.84	0	75	58	14	7	12	79
Branden vd, Kenny, NEP	8	1	1.26	0	71	39	13	10	22	65
Walsma, Pim, KIN	3	0	1.30	0	35	20	7	5	10	36
Heijstek, Kevin, AMS	9	1	1.32	1	82	56	14	12	14	69
Blok de, Tom, AMS	4	0	1.54	3	35	25	10	6	10	44
Stuifbergen, Tom, KIN	4	1	1.81	1	60	44	16	12	13	49
Bergman, David, KIN	8	2	1.90	0	81	77	23	17	15	40
Markwell, Diegomar, NEP	9	2	2.06	0	74	58	25	17	23	54
Groen, Mike, DSS	4	3	2.13	0	51	41	19	12	13	25
Ward, Kyle, AMS	7	2	2.23	0	81	73	25	20	16	74
Kelly, Kevin, NEP	3	1	2.29	1	39	29	13	10	23	43
Hernandez, Ricardo, PIO	8	3	2.29	0	86	76	28	22	40	96
Ploeger Jim, UVV	5	5	2.39	2	79	57	27	21	38	76
Zijl v, Jurjen, UVV	5	6	2.65	2	71	70	32	21	27	60
Huijer, Lars, PIO	7	4	2.72	0	86	71	37	26	24	67

INTERNATIONAL

Vazquez, Garcia lift Ciego to title

Ciego de Avila won the 54th edition of Cuba's Serie Nacional, defeating Isla de la Juventud in the championship series for its second title in three seasons under managers Roger Machado and Jose Luis Rodriguez Pantoja.

It's an amazing turnaround considering Ciego de Avila's traditional second-division status, and the Tigers will represent Cuba in the Caribbean Series in February 2016 as a result, trying to defend the island's championship.

Yander Guevara pitched seven innings in the championship-clinching 7-2 victory to spoil Isla de la Juventud's first-ever visit to the finals. Guevara went 10-5, 3.52 on the season and went 3-0, 1.61 in the playoffs. He's now a veteran of Cuba's 2013 World Baseball Classic team and pitched for the national team over the summer when it played in the Pan American Games and against USA Baseball's Collegiate National Team.

Catcher/DH Osvaldo Vazquez keyed the team's offense in the postseason with four home runs, while outfielder Jose Garcia, one of the top prospects left in Cuba and the brother of Braves big leaguer Adonis Garcia, hit .310 in the postseason after batting a team-best .322 in the regular season.

Cuba once again split its season into two halves, with 16 teams winnowed down to eight for the second half. Matanzas had the best regular season record thanks to an explosive offense that included five of the league's top 20 hitters by batting average. However, two of those hitters, outfielder Yadiel Hernandez (.369) and athletic infielder Luis Yander La O (.327), left the island to try to play in the major leagues. (La O was a second-half addition for Matanzas after playing for Santiago de Cuba in the first half.)

They were part of a flood of Cuban players who continued to leave the island in search of big league riches, even as Cuba and the U.S. began normalizing relations, slowly but surely, for the first time since the Cuban Revolution in the late 1950s and early 1960s.

Jose Garcia

ALYSON BOYER RODE

TEAM	SECOND HALF	FIRST HALF
Artemisa	39-48	25-20
Holguin	36-51	23-22
Sancti Spiritus	N/A	22-23
Santiago de Cuba	N/A	21-24
Villa Clara	N/A	21-24
Las Tunas	N/A	21-24
Guantanamo	N/A	19-26
Mayabeque	N/A	16-29
Cienfuegos	N/A	16-29
Camaguey	N/A	16-29

INDIVIDUAL BATTING LEADERS

PLAYER, TEAM	AVG	AB	R	H	2B	3B	HR	RBI	BB	SO	SB
Alfredo Despaigne, GRA	.406	202	53	82	19	1	17	70	55	22	1
Yadiel Hernandez, MTZ	.369	282	64	104	20	3	7	51	77	47	5
Michel Enriquez, IJV	.367	237	36	87	16	0	6	35	32	9	0
Yosvani Alarcon, LTU	.357	286	52	102	13	3	11	47	29	31	8
Roel Santos, GRA	.356	295	85	105	12	7	6	28	79	34	11
Yusnier Diaz, IND	.350	203	44	71	12	3	0	19	35	32	7
Yordan Batista, HOL	.344	224	38	77	14	1	13	52	13	38	1
Yasiel Santoya, MTZ	.336	274	57	92	16	2	3	58	39	20	10
Yordanis Samon, GRA	.336	321	58	108	19	3	4	71	48	31	2
Yusniel Ibanez, CFG	.335	281	48	94	13	9	5	45	35	36	2

INDIVIDUAL PITCHING LEADERS

PLAYER, TEAM	W	L	ERA	G	GS	CG	SV	IP	H	HR	BB	SO
Cionel Perez, MTZ	7	2	2.06	17	17	0	0	87	72	2	32	75
Yosvani Torres, PRI	8	6	2.22	21	21	0	0	142	136	9	26	77
Ismel Jimenez, SSP	11	4	2.30	19	19	0	0	117	123	3	35	72
Freddy Alvarez, VCL	5	6	2.32	15	15	0	0	93	84	7	24	67
Alberto Bicet, SCU	12	6	2.48	26	22	4	3	149	151	7	27	68
Erlis Casanova, PRI	7	3	2.68	19	17	2	0	91	86	3	31	54
Jonder Martinez, MTZ	12	4	2.78	21	21	0	0	130	120	8	28	94
Norge Ruiz, CAM	7	6	3.26	18	17	1	0	110	113	5	43	85
Yoanni Yera, MTZ	12	6	3.43	23	22	1	0	113	96	8	28	101
Lazaro Blanco, GRA	14	5	3.46	24	24	0	0	138	127	9	48	67

STANDINGS & LEADERS

TEAM	SECOND HALF	FIRST HALF
Matanzas	55-32	31-24
Granma	53-34	29-16
Ciego De Avila	50-37	24-21
Isla de la Juventud	49-38	27-18
Pinar Del Rio	48-39	24-21
Industriales	46-41	25-20

INTERNATIONAL

Cuba's Pinar del Rio wins Caribbean Series crown

It's been a long time since Cuba has been the champs of the Caribbean.

Yes, Cuba has been the most successful team in international baseball n the past 50 years, but after the 1960 Caribbean Series Fidel Castro pulled Cuba from the Caribbean Series. They did not return until a disappointing 1-3 finish in the 2014 Caribbean Series.

Cuba's 2015 representatives from Pinar Del Rio were not much more impressive during the Caribbean Series round robin play. But Cuba slipped into the championship series with an umimpressive 1-3 record. But with four teams making it to the semifinals of a five-team tournament, Cuba just needed to get hot at the right time. Cuba beat Venezuela 8-4 in the semifinals and then topped defending champion Mexico 3-2 in the finals.

AUSTRALIAN BASEBALL LEAGUE

TEAM	W	L	PCT	GB
Adelaide Bite	32	16	.667	—
Perth Heat	28	20	.583	4
Sydney Blue Sox	22	24	.478	9
Canberra Cavalry	22	24	.478	9
Brisbane Bandits	21	25	.457	10
Melbourne Aces	15	31	.326	16

Championship: Perth defeated Adelaide 2-1.

BATTER, CLUB	AVG	AB	R	H	2B	3B	HR	RBI	BB	SO	SB
Miller, Aaron, Ade	.389	144	37	56	9	0	12	33	11	36	11
Lopes, Christian, Can	.371	124	24	46	8	0	6	24	13	10	2
Murphy, Jack, Can	.353	153	24	54	11	0	6	37	17	22	0
Hughes, Luke, Per	.352	125	36	44	10	2	6	29	17	29	6
Tissenbaum, Maxx, Bri	.340	153	29	52	7	0	9	29	16	14	2
Coyle, Thomas, Bri	.333	180	30	60	14	2	8	28	22	35	11
Dean, Joshua, Syd	.329	164	17	54	10	0	5	28	20	32	1
Lemon, Marcus, Can	.315	124	25	39	8	1	5	21	12	18	4
McDonald, Jordan, Perth	.307	153	25	47	9	0	3	30	20	22	2
Welch, Stefan, Ade	.307	150	21	46	8	0	7	31	16	26	1

PITCHER, CLUB	W	L	ERA	G	SV	IP	H	BB	SO	AVG
McClendon, Mike. Per	5	1	1.66	9	0	49	51	3	40	.280
Coombs, Morgan. Ade	7	1	1.95	16	0	69	53	28	65	.209
Buckel, Cody . Mel	2	2	2.93	12	2	46	29	19	41	.177
Wilkins, Luke. Syd	5	3	3.31	11	0	68	59	21	32	.234
Aiuchi, Makoto. Mel	2	1	3.52	9	0	54	58	20	45	.280
Atherton, Tim. Can	6	2	3.56	12	0	61	57	21	61	.249
Anderson, Craig. Syd	5	2	3.59	12	0	78	82	14	60	.266
Williams, Matthew. Ade	3	2	3.72	19	4	68	69	26	64	.257
Erasmus, Justin. Bri	0	1	3.82	22	0	38	44	11	32	.288
Stem, Craig. Ade	3	1	3.86	11	0	56	47	16	56	.227

DOMINICAN LEAGUE

TEAM	W	L	PCT	GB
Estrellas de Oriente	32	18	.640	—
Aguilas Cibaenas	30	20	.600	2
Gigantes del Cibao	28	22	.560	4
Toros del Este	24	26	.480	8
Tigres del Licey	19	31	.380	13
Leones del Escogido	17	33	.340	15

Championship: Gigantes defeated Estrellas 5-3.

INDIVIDUAL BATTING LEADERS

PLAYER, CLUB	AVG	AB	R	H	2B	3B	HR	RBI	BB	SO	SB
Adames, Cristhian, TOR	.353	167	19	59	4	5	2	18	18	19	4
Almonte, Zoilo, AGU	.338	139	18	47	13	0	2	17	13	31	1

ALYSON BOYER RODE

Cuba's Yulieski Gourriel hit the decisive home run in Cuba's Carribean Series final win over Mexico

INTERNATIONAL

PLAYER, CLUB	AVG	AB	R	H	2B	3B	HR	RBI	BB	SO	SB
Nanita, Ricardo, AGU	.315	127	13	40	2	0	2	15	8	15	2
Ramirez, Manny, AGU	.313	147	22	46	11	0	6	28	19	28	0
Sierra, Moises, GIG	.311	148	19	46	8	1	2	34	17	39	2
Hernandez, Diory, LIC	.307	163	13	50	9	1	3	18	6	15	0
Black, Dan, AGU	.302	116	21	35	11	0	6	23	24	22	1
Valdespin, Jordany, EST	.294	119	24	35	4	0	3	14	18	20	9
Ynoa, Rafael, AGU	.293	164	27	48	8	1	2	6	17	33	1
Reyes, Elmer, LIC	.289	142	10	41	4	0	1	21	5	25	1

INDIVIDUAL PITCHING LEADERS

PITCHER, CLUB	W	L	ERA	G	SV	IP	H	BB	SO	AVG
Villanueva, Elih, TOR	4	2	2.63	11	0	55	53	11	46	.252
Valdes, Raul, TOR	3	4	2.95	9	0	55	44	10	45	.213
MacLane, Evan, EST	3	1	3.35	10	0	48	43	4	23	.238
Ortiz, Ramon, LIC	2	4	3.76	9	0	41	40	10	28	.260
Lannan, John, LIC	4	3	3.78	10	0	48	47	10	36	.258
Batista, Frank, AGU	3	1	3.79	11	0	40	47	16	31	.296
Valdez, Edward, ESC	2	6	4.06	10	0	44	42	19	38	.250
Atkins, Mitch, LIC	2	6	5.67	11	0	46	46	9	42	.260

MEXICAN PACIFIC LEAGUE

TEAM	W	L	PCT	GB
Charros de Jalisco	42	26	.618	—
Tomateros de Culiacan	38	30	.559	4
Aguilas de Mexicali	37	31	.544	5
Yaquis de Obregon	35	32	.522	6½
Caneros de los Mochis	34	34	.500	8
Venados de Mazatlan	31	36	.463	10½
Naranjeros de Hermosillo	28	40	.412	14
Mayos de Navojoa	26	42	.382	16

Championship: Culiacan defeated Jalisco 4-1.

INDIVIDUAL BATTING LEADERS

PLAYER, CLUB	AVG	AB	R	H	2B	3B	HR	RBI	BB	SO	SB
Velazquez, Gil, MXC	.344	192	21	66	10	0	0	27	18	27	1
Rodriguez, Jose M., JAL	.341	273	47	93	23	0	10	48	20	43	8
Leon, Maxwell, CUL	.333	189	28	63	9	2	3	24	18	36	13
Owens, Jerry, HER	.333	243	29	81	8	3	0	19	17	27	5
Chavez, Jose G., NAV	.320	244	40	78	13	0	5	24	24	32	4
Rosario, Olmo, MAZ	.314	261	39	82	25	1	6	44	17	35	7
Farris, Eric, CUL	.309	207	24	64	8	1	3	32	11	25	9
Sanchez, Yunesky, HER	.305	259	31	79	12	2	3	35	9	31	2
Castillo, Jesus, MAZ	.301	216	31	65	14	1	1	20	33	33	3
Ibarra, Walter, MXC	.291	234	34	68	9	5	4	23	13	43	4

INDIVIDUAL PITCHING LEADERS

PITCHER, CLUB	W	L	ERA	G	SV	IP	H	BB	SO	AVG
Gamboa, Eddie, NAV	6	2	1.83	10	0	69	56	7	56	.223
Gaxiola, Amilcar, MAZ	9	1	2.47	15	0	77	66	27	44	.236
Duarte, Marco A., MXC	2	3	2.74	14	0	72	69	22	59	.255
Oramas, Juan P., HER	5	5	3.00	16	0	78	59	31	78	.210
Osuna, Edgar, MXC	5	3	3.15	14	0	69	61	19	45	.234
Silva, Walter, MAZ	6	4	3.25	15	0	89	95	27	41	.275
Lara, Orlando, JAL	7	3	3.26	14	0	69	62	33	45	.248
Lopez, Arturo, OBR	6	4	3.31	14	0	73	55	26	49	.204
Solano, Javier, MXC	8	2	3.39	14	0	72	65	31	36	.242
Solis, Tomas, MOC	4	5	3.55	13	0	76	77	15	44	.272

PUERTO RICAN LEAGUE

TEAM	W	L	PCT	GB
Criollos de Caguas	25	14	.641	—
Indios de Mayaguez	22	16	.579	2½
Cangrejeros de Santurce	19	19	.500	5½
Gigantes de Carolina	19	20	.487	6
Senadores de San Juan	12	28	.300	13½

Championship: Santurce defeated Mayaguez 4-2.

INDIVIDUAL BATTING LEADERS

PLAYER, CLUB	AVG	AB	R	H	2B	3B	HR	RBI	BB	SO	SB
Martinez, Ozzie, CAR	.358	137	26	49	9	3	3	22	8	14	0
Feliciano, Jesus, CAR	.345	116	16	40	8	1	1	21	6	4	3
Garcia, Anthony, CAR	.328	137	24	45	10	1	10	34	4	10	0
Rivera, T.J., MAY	.311	119	20	37	11	0	1	19	4	14	1
Jimenez, A.J., SAN	.311	103	13	32	8	1	1	14	9	9	0
Navarro, Rey, CAG	.310	142	21	44	6	0	4	25	8	17	4
Sanchez, Angel, CAG	.302	96	19	29	9	0	1	14	10	12	1
Adams, Trever, CAG	.294	102	18	30	5	0	4	13	12	27	1
Vazquez, Christian, SJU	.288	111	7	32	6	0	1	12	10	22	2
Silva, Juan, CAG	.282	103	21	29	4	0	1	11	18	24	5

INDIVIDUAL PITCHING LEADERS

PITCHER, CLUB	W	L	ERA	G	SV	IP	H	BB	SO	AVG
Maldonado, Ivan, SAN	5	1	0.39	8	0	46	30	6	18	.189
Soto, Giovanni, CAR	4	2	2.20	14	0	45	35	15	45	.219
Nix, Michael, CAG	2	0	2.25	12	0	36	33	15	30	.252
Martinez, Jorge, SAN	4	1	2.65	10	0	51	50	8	31	.262
Rivera, Raul, CAR	1	2	2.97	13	0	36	35	9	22	.255
Rogers, Jay, SJU	4	3	3.10	9	0	49	53	7	31	.270
Misch, Pat, SAN	0	1	3.41	9	0	43	33	8	19	.260
Flores, Adalberto, SJU	3	5	3.49	11	0	59	58	20	52	.256
Roibal, Reinier, SJU	1	5	3.63	11	0	52	61	13	36	.293
Nieves, Efrain, CAG	3	1	3.70	9	0	41	48	15	20	.296

TEAM	W	L	PCT	GB
Caribes de Anzoategui	39	24	.619	—
Tigres de Aragua	35	27	.565	3.5
Aguilas del Zulia	35	28	.556	4
Navegantes del Magallanes	32	31	.508	7
Tiburones de La Guaira	31	34	.477	9
Cardenales de Lara	29	35	.453	10.5
Leones del Caracas	29	35	.453	10.5
Bravos de Margarita	23	39	.371	15.5

Championship: Caribes defeated Magallanes 4-1.

INDIVIDUAL BATTING LEADERS

PLAYER, CLUB	AVG	AB	R	H	2B	3B	HR	RBI	BB	SO	SB
Herrera, Odubel, LAG	.372	207	35	77	14	3	6	27	19	29	8
Perez, Felix, CAR	.360	222	40	80	16	2	9	38	10	51	0
Flores, Ramon, ARA	.347	196	36	68	8	4	5	29	31	33	2
Gonzalez, Alex, CAR	.336	149	24	50	12	1	9	33	12	27	0
Inciarte, Ender, ZUL	.333	156	15	52	8	2	1	13	13	23	13
Gonzalez, Alberto, MAR	.321	237	27	76	8	0	1	23	12	23	5
Orlando, Paulo, LAR	.319	235	33	75	13	0	8	40	26	38	5
Peralta, David, MAR	.319	210	26	67	14	2	2	32	19	31	2
Garcia, Adonis, MAG	.313	233	28	73	13	1	7	41	15	22	4
Martinez, Jose, ARA	.310	245	38	76	19	1	4	29	17	22	5

INDIVIDUAL PITCHING LEADERS

PITCHER, CLUB	W	L	ERA	G	SV	IP	H	BB	SO	AVG
Alvarez, Jose, ORI	6	1	1.91	19	2	57	40	17	40	.200
Castillo, Yeiper, ZUL	3	3	2.32	13	0	66	64	28	40	.258
Thompson, Daryl, ORI	4	2	3.19	14	0	68	69	14	52	.258
Guerra, Junior, LAG	6	4	3.46	15	0	78	65	22	82	.223
Jimenez, Cesar, LAR	3	5	3.53	17	0	51	53	12	47	.264
Smith, Chris, ARA	4	3	3.65	11	0	57	55	16	43	.257
Escalona, Edgmer, LAG	3	3	3.82	14	0	64	72	14	30	.293
Correa, Manny, ARA	6	3	3.97	13	0	68	71	20	26	.275
Blevins, Bobby, MAG	2	3	4.07	14	0	60	62	14	44	.261
Arenas, Orangel, MAG	5	2	4.19	16	0	54	54	25	26	.252

INTERNATIONAL

COLLEGE

Virginia overcame a rash of injuries to capture the program's first-ever national title

Virginia's first title caps improbable run

BY JIM SHONERD

Right to the very end, Virginia was still a long shot.

"I think my brother told me this afternoon the odds in Vegas today were 310 to 1 that we'd win this thing," head coach Brian O'Connor said.

Yet here they are. A team that was besieged by injuries. A team that scrambled just to make the NCAA tournament, then flew cross-country for regionals. A team that had to piece together its pitching against two of the nation's deadliest lineups in the College World Series. No amount of odds stacked against them were too great to overcome, not even that 310 to 1 line sounds like hyperbole.

A tournament run that defied expectations at almost every turn culminated in Virginia's first-ever national title in Omaha, the Cavaliers taking the decisive third game of the finals 4-2 to dethrone the reigning champion Commodores.

"I think every step of the way, everybody was predicting somebody else to win," O'Connor said. "It's just amazing what you can accomplish in whatever it is if you put your mind to it, hang in there and stay together. It's a very, very special group."

It started with a special arm on the mound.

The Cavaliers weren't expecting too much out of Brandon Waddell. With the junior lefty starting on three days' rest, the hope was that he could give them three innings. Instead, Waddell solidified his place as one of the best big game pitchers in recent history. He exceeded that three-inning goal by more than double, working seven and allowing just two runs on four hits. In five career CWS starts, it was the fourth time he'd gone at least that deep and allowed that many runs or less.

"First of all, coming into this game I knew we'd get his best," O'Connor said. "How he's pitched in this championship two years in a row is pretty special and doesn't really happen. And so I knew he was going to give us everything he had."

Things didn't exactly start out according to script though. Waddell came out in the first inning and was leaving balls up in the zone, balls the Commodores jumped on for a pair of runs on doubles by Rhett Wiseman and Zander Wiel. Waddell said later that he knew he wouldn't have his best stuff. His fastball operated around 89-90 mph against Vanderbilt, the short rest not surprisingly knocking down his velocity from the 92-93 he'd shown earlier in the tournament. Location and changing speeds would be vital.

Getting out of the first inning with a couple groundouts to strand Wiel at second, Waddell was able to get back to the dugout and refocus—keep that ball down. He came back in the second and retired Vanderbilt in order, and the momentum kept carrying from there, one inning to the next. Waddell finally came to pitching coach Karl Kuhn at the end of the seventh and admitted he was out of gas after throwing 104 pitches. By that time, he'd just retired 11 straight and allowed two hits and one walk over his final six frames.

That three-innings idea was nothing more than a speck in the rear view mirror.

"It's just a matter of taking a breath, getting your mind right, kind of simplifying things," Waddell said. "I knew what I had to do. So it's a matter of going out there and executing. So I got focused

ANDREW WOOLLEY

CWS MOP Josh Sborz threw 13 shutout innings across four appearances in Omaha

back on those things. I knew 2-0 wasn't going to be the final score. I knew our offense was going to score."

Pavin Smith took care of that part.

There's a reason the Cavaliers' coaches kept running him out there in the middle of their order, even though Smith was just 5-for-24 through Virginia's first six games in Omaha. The Cavalier

COACHING CAROUSEL

SCHOOL	IN (PREVIOUS JOB)	OUT (REASON/NEW JOB)
Arizona	Jay Johnson (Nevada head coach)	Andy Lopez (retired)
Auburn	Butch Thompson (Mississippi State assistant)	Sunny Golloway (fired)
Austin Peay State	Travis Janssen (Northeastern State (Okla.) head coach)	Gary McClure (resigned)
Baylor	Steve Rodriguez (Pepperdine head coach)	Steve Smith (fired)
Cal State Bakersfield	Bob Macaluso (CSUB assistant)	Bill Kernen (retired)
Clemson	Monte Lee (College of Charleston head coach)	Jack Leggett (fired)
College of Charleston	Matt Heath (CofC assistant)	Monte Lee (Clemson head coach)
Cornell	Dan Pepicelli (Clemson assistant)	Bill Walkenbach (Claremont-Mudd (Calif.) head coach)
Eastern Illinois	Jason Anderson (EIU assistant)	Jim Schmitz (fired)
Eastern Kentucky	Edwin Thompson (Georgia State assistant)	Jason Stein (fired)
James Madison	Marlin Ikenberry (VMI head coach)	Spanky McFarland (retired)
Nevada	T.J. Bruce (UCLA assistant)	Jay Johnson (Arizona head coach)
New Orleans	Blake Dean (UNO assistant)	Ron Maestri (retired)
Northwestern	Spencer Allen (Illinois assistant)	Paul Stevens (retired)
Pacific	Mike Neu (California assistant)	Ed Sprague (resigned)
Pepperdine	Rick Hirtensteiner (Pepperdine assistant)	Steve Rodriguez (Baylor head coach)
Portland	Geoff Loomis (Pacific Lutheran (Wash.) head coach)	Chris Sperry (fired)
Washington State	Marty Lees (Oklahoma State assistant)	Don Marbut (fired)
Western Kentucky	John Pawlowski (San Diego State assistant)	Matt Myers (fired)

first baseman enjoyed a Freshman All-America season this spring, hitting .303/.368/.453 entering the finale. Whatever struggles he might have had over the last two weeks, it only took one swing to wipe them away.

The fact Vanderbilt was getting to start a first-round pick on the mound in Walker Buehler opposite Waddell and his short rest was one of the big reasons Vandy was such a strong favorite going into the night. But Buehler struggled with his command, walking four in three-plus innings of work. After giving a free pass to Kenny Towns to lead off the fourth, Buehler fell behind Smith 1-0, then left an 87 mph changeup over the middle of the plate. Smith drilled it just over the right-center field wall, a two-run blast that tied the game and gave the Cavs an immediate jolt of momentum.

"I wasn't thinking about just trying to hit a home run," Smith said. "I was just trying to get on base, trying to extend the inning, trying to keep the rally going. When I hit it, I knew the wind was blowing out and I was just, like, telling it to go."

The Cavs got contributions up and down the roster throughout their run, right through to the second game of the CWS finals when they were sparked by unlikely heroes Ernie Clement and Thomas Woodruff. But in the final game, it was season-long leading lights Waddell, Smith and Kenny Towns that delivered. Smith added the go-ahead RBI single in the fifth, and senior third baseman Towns made the defensive play of the night with a diving stop and throw that saved a run in the fourth and then drove in an insurance run with an RBI single in the seventh.

Last but not least came Nathan Kirby. The junior lefthander who was supposed to be the Cavs' ace, Kirby had been relegated to the sidelines for eight weeks, dealing with a lat strain and bout of mononucleosis. He returned for an ineffective start against Florida earlier in the CWS, but he finally got to put his own stamp on the title run in the finale. With closer—and CWS Most Outstanding Player—Josh Sborz unavailable after working four innings Tuesday, the Cavs summoned Kirby to pitch the final two innings.

A year after infamously falling apart against Vandy in the 2014 CWS finals, Kirby more than delivered this time around. He dominated the Commodores with his slider, striking out five over the last two frames. It was with one final slider that

COLLEGE WORLD SERIES CHAMPIONS

YEAR	CHAMPION	COACH	RECORD	RUNNER-UP	MOST OUTSTANDING PLAYER
1948	Southern California	Sam Barry	40-12	Yale	None selected
1949	Texas*	Bibb Falk	23-7	Wake Forest	Charles Teague, 2b, Wake Forest
1950	Texas	Bibb Falk	27-6	Washington State	Ray VanCleef, of, Rutgers
1951	Oklahoma*	Jack Baer	19-9	Tennessee	Sid Hatfield, 1b-p, Tennessee
1952	Holy Cross	Jack Barry	21-3	Missouri	Jim O'Neill, p, Holy Cross
1953	Michigan	Ray Fisher	21-9	Texas	J.L. Smith, p, Texas
1954	Missouri	Hi Simmons	22-4	Rollins	Tom Yewcic, c, Michigan State
1955	Wake Forest	Taylor Sanford	29-7	Western Michigan	Tom Borland, p, Oklahoma State
1956	Minnesota	Dick Siebert	33-9	Arizona	Jerry Thomas, p, Minnesota
1957	California*	George Wolfman	35-10	Penn State	Cal Emery, 1b-p, Penn State
1958	Southern California	Rod Dedeaux	35-7	Missouri	Bill Thom, p, Southern California
1959	Oklahoma State	Toby Greene	27-5	Arizona	Jim Dobson, 3b, Oklahoma State
1960	Minnesota	Dick Siebert	34-7	Southern California	John Erickson, 2b, Minnesota
1961	Southern California*	Rod Dedeaux	43-9	Oklahoma State	Littleton Fowler, p, Oklahoma State
1962	Michigan	Don Lund	31-13	Santa Clara	Bob Garibaldi, p, Santa Clara
1963	Southern California	Rod Dedeaux	37-16	Arizona	Bud Hollowell, c, Southern California
1964	Minnesota	Dick Siebert	31-12	Missouri	Joe Ferris, p, Maine
1965	Arizona State	Bobby Winkles	54-8	Ohio State	Sal Bando, 3b, Arizona State
1966	Ohio State	Marty Karow	27-6	Oklahoma State	Steve Arlin, p, Ohio State
1967	Arizona State	Bobby Winkles	53-12	Houston	Ron Davini, c, Arizona State
1968	Southern California*	Rod Dedeaux	42-12	Southern Illinois	Bill Seinsoth, 1b, Southern California
1969	Arizona State	Bobby Winkles	56-11	Tulsa	John Dolinsek, of, Arizona State
1970	Southern California	Rod Dedeaux	51-13	Florida State	Gene Ammann, p, Florida State
1971	Southern California	Rod Dedeaux	53-13	Southern Illinois	Jerry Tabb, 1b, Tulsa
1972	Southern California	Rod Dedeaux	50-13	Arizona State	Russ McQueen, p, Southern California
1973	Southern California*	Rod Dedeaux	51-11	Arizona State	Dave Winfield, of-p, Minnesota
1974	Southern California	Rod Dedeaux	50-20	Miami	George Milke, p, Southern California
1975	Texas	Cliff Gustafson	56-6	South Carolina	Mickey Reichenbach, 1b, Texas
1976	Arizona	Jerry Kindall	56-17	Eastern Michigan	Steve Powers, dh-p, Arizona
1977	Arizona State	Jim Brock	57-12	South Carolina	Bob Horner, 3b, Arizona State
1978	Southern California*	Rod Dedeaux	54-9	Arizona State	Rod Boxberger, p, Southern California
1979	Cal State Fullerton	Augie Garrido	60-14	Arkansas	Tony Hudson, p, Cal State Fullerton
1980	Arizona	Jerry Kindall	45-21	Hawaii	Terry Francona, of, Arizona
1981	Arizona State	Jim Brock	55-13	Oklahoma State	Stan Holmes, of, Arizona State

Kirby caught pinch-hitter Kyle Smith looking for the final out, flinging his cap and glove into the air before leaping into the arms of catcher Matt Thaiss.

"It was a very, very gutty performance by their team, their pitching staff, to allow them to get to this point and be successful," Vanderbilt coach Tim Corbin said. "I thought Waddell, in a lot of ways, was left for dead, but he just got himself up in the fifth, sixth and seventh. He turned the game around. He went one-two-three, one-two-three, one-two-three. And when they brought Kirby out, he pitched with a lot of adrenalin and, you know, just shut us down. You have to give them a lot of credit."

The Commodores stayed in their dugout until all the postgame celebrations had played out, enduring the same emotions Virginia's players had felt a year earlier when Vanderbilt won the 2014 finals in a decisive third game against the Cavaliers. The calm, confident nature the Commodores exuded throughout their two-year run had seemingly eroded late in the game, their hitters pressing to make a comeback.

Despite the nature of their season's ending,

ANDREW WOOLLEY

Dansby Swanson and Vanderbilt came up one win short of back-to-back titles

*Undefeated

YEAR	CHAMPION	COACH	RECORD	RUNNER-UP	MOST OUTSTANDING PLAYER
1982	Miami	Ron Fraser	57-18	Wichita State	Dan Smith, p, Miami
1983	Texas	Cliff Gustafson	66-14	Alabama	Calvin Schiraldi, p, Texas
1984	Cal State Fullerton	Augie Garrido	66-20	Texas	John Fishel, of, Cal State Fullerton
1985	Miami*	Ron Fraser	64-16	Texas	Greg Ellena, dh, Miami
1986	Arizona	Jerry Kindall	49-19	Florida State	Mike Senne, of, Arizona
1987	Stanford	Mark Marquess	53-17	Oklahoma State	Paul Carey, of, Stanford
1988	Stanford	Mark Marquess	46-23	Arizona State	Lee Plemel, p, Stanford
1989	Wichita State	Gene Stephenson	68-16	Texas	Greg Brummett, p, Wichita State
1990	Georgia	Steve Webber	52-19	Oklahoma State	Mike Rebhan, p, Georgia
1991	Louisiana State*	Skip Bertman	55-18	Wichita State	Gary Hymel, c, Louisiana State
1992	Pepperdine*	Andy Lopez	48-11	Cal State Fullerton	Phil Nevin, 3b, Cal State Fullerton
1993	Louisiana State	Skip Bertman	53-17	Wichita State	Todd Walker, 2b, Louisiana State
1994	Oklahoma*	Larry Cochell	50-17	Georgia Tech	Chip Glass, of, Oklahoma
1995	Cal State Fullerton*	Augie Garrido	57-9	Southern California	Mark Kotsay, of-p, Cal State Fullerton
1996	Louisiana State*	Skip Bertman	52-15	Miami	Pat Burrell, 3b, Miami
1997	Louisiana State*	Skip Bertman	57-13	Alabama	Brandon Larson, ss, Louisiana State
1998	Southern California	Mike Gillespie	49-17	Arizona State	Wes Rachels, 2b, Southern California
1999	Miami*	Jim Morris	50-13	Florida State	Marshall McDougall, 2b, Florida State
2000	Louisiana State*	Skip Bertman	52-17	Stanford	Trey Hodges, rhp, Louisiana State
2001	Miami*	Jim Morris	53-12	Stanford	Charlton Jimerson, of, Miami
2002	Texas*	Augie Garrido	57-15	South Carolina	Huston Street, rhp, Texas
2003	Rice	Wayne Graham	58-12	Stanford	John Hudgins, rhp, Stanford
2004	Cal State Fullerton	George Horton	47-22	Texas	Jason Windsor, p, Cal State Fullerton
2005	Texas*	Augie Garrido	56-16	Florida	David Maroul, 3b, Texas
2006	Oregon State	Pat Casey	50-16	North Carolina	Jonah Nickerson, rhp, Oregon State
2007	Oregon State*	Pat Casey	49-18	North Carolina	Jorge Reyes, rhp, Oregon State
2008	Fresno State	Mike Batesole	47-31	Georgia	Tommy Mendonca, 3b, Fresno State
2009	Louisiana State	Paul Mainieri	56-17	Texas	Jared Mitchell, of, Louisiana State
2010	South Carolina	Ray Tanner	54-16	UCLA	Jackie Bradley Jr., of, South Carolina
2011	South Carolina*	Ray Tanner	55-14	Florida	Scott Wingo, 2b, South Carolina
2012	Arizona	Andy Lopez	48-17	South Carolina	Robert Refsnyder, of, Arizona
2013	UCLA*	John Savage	49-17	Mississippi State	Adam Plutko, rhp, UCLA
2014	Vanderbilt	Tim Corbin	51-21	Virginia	Dansby Swanson, 2b, Vanderbilt
2015	Virginia	Brian O'Connor	44-24	Vanderbilt	Josh Sborz, rhp, Virginia

NEW BASEBALLS MAKE IMPACT

The NCAA's final trends report for the 2015 season showed that the new lower-seamed baseballs did make a marked difference on offense around the college game.

The new balls were implemented to restore balance to college baseball after the game had become overly reliant on small ball as the only means of scoring, with home runs an afterthought—particularly at the College World Series. By all accounts, they accomplished their mission. Scoring did rise by 7.1 percent from 2014 to 2015, with teams averaging 5.44 runs per game with the new balls, but perhaps more importantly, it was the way those runs were scored that was most encouraging.

The home run came back as a weapon in college baseball in 2015, with teams hitting 0.56 home runs per game, a 43.5 percent uptick from 2014's all-time low figure of 0.39. That 0.56 number is the highest of the BBCOR bat era, which began in 2011, though still well below the 0.94 home runs per game hit in 2010, the final season of the old BESR bat standards. Beyond the home run numbers, college hitters' collective slugging percentage also increased from .364 to .387, while the number of sacrifice bunts declined—albeit only slightly—from 0.76 per team per game to 0.68.

The national ERA jumped from 4.22 in 2014 to 4.57 this season, but the new ball wasn't all bad news for pitchers, either. Pitchers' strikeouts per nine rate climbed 8.3 percent from 6.48 to 7.02. There were likely a number of contributing factors to the rise if whiffs, from hitters being more willing to take aggressive hacks to the lower seams helping pitchers add a tick of velocity to their fastballs. The lower seams also brought a reduced risk of blisters, which could've helped some pitchers feel more comfortable snapping off their breaking pitches.

	MIDSEASON 2014	FINAL 2014	MIDSEASON 2015	FINAL 2015
Teams	296	296	295	295
Games Played				
Per Team	24.8	54.8	24.6	54.5
BATTING				
Batting Average	.268	.270	.269	.274
Runs Per Game	5.14	5.08	5.40	5.44
Home Runs Per Game	0.36	0.39	0.50	0.56
Slugging Percentage	.360	.364	.377	.387
Stolen Bases Per Game	1.05	1.02	1.07	1.03
Sacrifice Hits Per Game	0.74	0.76	0.66	0.68
Sacrifice Flies Per Game	0.40	0.40	0.37	0.38
Percentage of RBIs from Sac Flies	8.81%	8.74%	7.82%	5.67%
PITCHING				
Earned-Run Average	4.21	4.22	4.47	4.57
Strikeouts Per Nine Innings	6.64	6.48	7.34	7.02
Shutouts	464	1034	419	913
Pct. of D1 shutouts per D1 games pitched	6.31%	6.37%	5.77%	5.67%
FIELDING				
Fielding Percentage	.965	.966	.964	.966

RPI RANKINGS

The Ratings Percentage Index is an important tool used by the NCAA in selecting at-large teams for the 64-team Division I regional tournament. The NCAA now releases its RPI rankings during the season. These were the top 100 finishers for 2015. A team's rank in the final Baseball America Top 25 is indicated in parentheses, and College World Series teams are in bold.

1. **Florida** (3)	52-18		51. Southeastern Louisiana	42-17
2. **Miami** (6)	49-17		52. Michigan State	34-23
3. **Louisiana State** (5)	54-12		53. Connecticut	35-25
4. **Vanderbilt** (2)	51-21		54. Michigan	39-25
5. Texas A&M (13)	50-14		55. Southern Mississippi	36-18
6. **Texas Christian** (4)	51-15		56. Stony Brook	35-16
7. UCLA (7)	45-16		57. Nevada	41-15
8. Florida State (15)	44-21		58. Missouri	29-28
9. Dallas Baptist (21)	46-15		59. Duke	31-22
10. Missouri State (12)	49-12		60. Kentucky	30-25
11. **Virginia** (1)	44-24		61. St. John's	41-16
12. Illinois (8)	49-10		62. Central Florida	31-27
13. Louisville (10)	47-18		63. Clemson	32-29
14. Radford (24)	45-16		64. South Carolina	32-25
15. Col. of Charleston (23)	45-15		65. Liberty	33-23
16. Oklahoma State (19)	38-20		66. Oregon	38-25
17. Florida Atlantic	42-19		67. Cal State Northridge	33-24
18. Houston (18)	43-20		68. Va. Commonwealth (17)	40-25
19. Coastal Carolina	39-21		69. Creighton	32-29
20. **Cal State Fullerton** (9)	39-25		70. Fresno State	31-28
21. **Arkansas** (11)	40-25		71. Alabama-Birmingham	33-25
22. North Carolina State	36-23		72. Lipscomb	39-20
23. Bradley	32-21		73. Tennessee	24-26
24. UC Santa Barbara	40-17		74. San Diego State	41-23
25. UNC Wilmington	41-18		75. Virginia Tech	27-27
26. Auburn	36-26		76. Texas-San Antonio	33-25
27. Southern California (20)	39-21		77. Memphis	37-21
28. Iowa (25)	38-18		78. South Alabama	37-20
29. California (22)	36-21		79. Winthrop	40-19
30. North Carolina	34-24		80. Texas Tech	31-24
31. Maryland (14)	42-24		81. Boston College	27-27
32. La.-Lafayette (16)	42-23		82. High Point	29-26
33. Notre Dame	37-23		83. Middle Tenn. State	32-27
34. South Florida	34-26		84. Nicholls State	33-19
35. Indiana	35-24		85. San Diego	33-22
36. East Carolina	40-22		86. Long Beach State	28-26
37. Rice	37-22		87. Oklahoma	34-27
38. Georgia Tech	32-23		88. Texas	30-27
39. Mississippi	30-28		89. Wake Forest	27-26
40. Oregon State	39-18		90. Indiana State	28-26
41. Wright State	43-17		91. Georgia	26-28
42. Arizona State	35-23		92. New Mexico	32-27
43. Oral Roberts	41-16		93. Washington	29-25
44. Ohio State	35-20		94. Northwestern State	31-23
45. Alabama	32-28		95. Campbell	32-25
46. UC Irvine	33-23		96. Kansas State	27-30
47. Nebraska	34-23		97. Saint Louis	34-21
48. North Florida	45-16		98. Wis.-Milwaukee	35-20
49. Columbia	34-17		99. Central Michigan	35-22
50. Tulane	35-25		100. Evansville	27-24

it doesn't change that the Commodores were a superbly coached, talented and, perhaps above all, united team—winners of 51 games and a group that outscored its NCAA tournament opponents by a 72-19 margin.

"We have a family," shortstop and No. 1 overall pick Dansby Swanson said. "It's not just 35 players, it's 50, because we have all the staff and the coaches that put so much effort in. So it's a special thing. I've never been a part of something this amazing in my life. So, just want to say thank you to everyone."

ALL-AMERICA TEAM

FIRST TEAM

POS.	NAME	YEAR	AVG	OBP	SLG	AB	R	H	HR	RBI	BB	SO	SB
C	Garrett Stubbs, Southern California	Sr.	.346	.435	.434	228	51	79	1	25	27	31	20
1B	Kyle Martin, South Carolina	Sr.	.350	.455	.635	203	50	71	14	56	39	27	11
2B	Scott Kingery, Arizona	Jr.	.392	.423	.561	237	53	93	5	36	9	18	11
3B	David Thompson, Miami	Jr.	.328	.434	.640	253	59	83	19	90	43	29	1
SS	Dansby Swanson, Vanderbilt	Jr.	.335	.423	.623	281	76	94	15	64	43	54	16
OF	Andrew Benintendi, Arkansas	So.	.376	.488	.717	226	62	85	20	57	50	32	24
OF	Donnie Dewees, North Florida	So.	.422	.483	.749	251	88	106	18	68	30	16	23
OF	D.J. Stewart, Florida State	Jr.	.318	.550	.593	214	62	68	15	59	69	47	12
DH	Alex Bregman, Louisiana State	Jr.	.323	.412	.535	260	59	84	9	49	36	22	38
UT	Brendan McKay, Louisville	Fr.	.308	.418	.431	211	32	65	4	34	38	42	4

POS.	NAME	YEAR	W	L	ERA	G	CG	SV	IP	H	BB	SO	AVG
SP	Thomas Eshelman, Cal State Fullerton	Jr.	8	5	1.58	19	5	1	137	105	7	139	.210
SP	Carson Fulmer, Vanderbilt	Jr.	14	2	1.83	19	3	0	128	81	50	167	.180
SP	Michael Freeman, Oklahoma State	Sr.	10	3	1.31	15	4	0	109	72	29	97	.184
SP	Alex Lange, Louisiana State	Fr.	12	0	1.97	17	2	0	114	87	46	131	.212
RP	Tyler Jay, Illinois	Jr.	5	2	1.08	30	0	14	67	40	7	76	.177
UT	Brendan McKay, Louisville	Fr.	9	3	1.77	20	0	4	97	53	34	117	.159

SECOND TEAM

POS.	NAME, SCHOOL	YEAR	AVG	OBP	SLG	AB	R	H	HR	RBI	BB	SO	SB
C	Kade Scivicque, Louisiana State	Sr.	.355	.398	.521	234	33	83	6	48	15	22	0
1B	David Kerian, Illinois	Sr.	.367	.462	.667	207	46	76	16	52	37	28	9
2B	MIke Garzillo, Lehigh	Jr.	.359	.485	.449	209	45	75	13	54	18	43	15
3B	Bobby Dalbec, Arizona	So.	.319	.410	.601	213	43	68	15	53	32	60	0
SS	Kevin Kramer, UCLA	Jr.	.323	.423	.476	254	55	82	7	34	36	38	7
OF	Ian Happ, Cincinnati	Jr.	.369	.492	.672	198	47	73	14	44	49	49	12
OF	Kevin Kaczmarski, Evansville	Jr.	.465	.543	.746	185	43	86	5	57	28	23	13
OF	Corey Ray, Louisville	So.	.325	.389	.543	265	46	86	11	56	24	60	34
DH	Will Craig, Wake Forest	So.	.382	.496	.702	191	52	73	13	58	41	24	2
UT	Corbin Olmstead, North Florida	Jr.	.308	.362	.561	214	46	66	13	42	16	37	3

POS.	NAME, SCHOOL	YEAR	W	L	ERA	G	CG	SV	IP	H	BB	SO	AVG
SP	Mike Shawaryn, Maryland	So.	13	2	1.71	17	0	0	116	85	29	138	.202
SP	Taylor Clarke, College of Charleston	Jr.	13	1	1.73	17	2	1	114	76	14	143	.185
SP	Kevin Duchene, Illinois	Jr.	11	2	1.75	15	1	0	103	89	18	88	.235
SP	Matt Hall, Missouri State	Jr.	12	2	2.02	19	2	1	125	87	45	171	.196
RP	David Berg, UCLA	Sr.	7	1	0.68	43	0	13	66	49	8	65	.205
UT	Corbin Olmstead, North Florida	Jr.	1	0	0.25	23	0	9	35	21	9	48	.171

THIRD TEAM

POS.	NAME, SCHOOL	YEAR	AVG	OBP	SLG	AB	R	H	HR	RBI	BB	SO	SB
C	Chris Okey, Clemson	So.	.315	.389	.545	235	50	74	12	57	27	49	3
1B	Austin Byler, Nevada	Sr.	.328	.507	.652	198	69	65	14	52	54	57	9
2B	George Iskenderian, Miami	Jr.	.364	.458	.476	250	71	91	3	55	40	41	23
3B	Josh Tobias, Florida	Sr.	.355	.435	.524	231	60	82	5	46	23	37	11
SS	Kevin Newman, Arizona	Jr.	.370	.426	.489	227	53	84	2	36	20	15	22
OF	Cody Jones, Texas Christian	Sr.	.353	.464	.476	252	63	89	5	34	45	42	33
OF	Andrew Stevenson, Louisiana State	Jr.	.348	.396	.453	247	53	86	1	24	16	29	26
OF	Christin Stewart, Tennessee	Jr.	.311	.443	.633	177	39	55	15	47	28	38	4
DH	J.J. Schwarz, Florida	Fr.	.332	.398	.629	256	60	85	18	73	28	46	1
UT	Reid Love, East Carolina	Sr.	.287	.350	.382	178	25	51	3	20	12	29	3

POS.	NAME, SCHOOL	YEAR	W	L	ERA	G	CG	SV	IP	H	BB	SO	AVG
SP	Matthew Crownover, Clemson	Jr.	10	3	1.82	16	0	0	109	72	37	108	.183
SP	Jon Harris, Missouri State	Jr.	8	2	2.45	15	1	0	103	75	36	116	.202
SP	James Kaprielian, UCLA	Jr.	10	4	2.03	17	0	0	106	86	33	114	.226
SP	Andrew Moore, Oregon State	Jr.	7	2	1.91	16	3	0	122	86	26	111	.200
RP	Logan Cozart, Ohio	Sr.	7	1	1.52	31	0	13	71	38	25	80	.154
UT	Reid Love, East Carolina	Sr.	7	4	2.84	22	2	4	96	94	12	82	.255

Virginia's 44 wins are the fewest by a national champion since 1968 Southern California, and they're just the second No. 3 regional seed to go on to win the title, joining 2007 Oregon State. The 2008 Fresno State team, a No. 4 seed, is the only champ ever seeded lower.

Then there's the matter of Virginia being the first Atlantic Coast Conference team to win it all since 1955 Wake Forest. O'Connor quipped, "Well, I knew that question was coming," when the league's 60-year title drought was inevitably brought up in the postgame press conference, though he did remark on the raft of encouraging text messages he'd been getting from other ACC coaches over the previous few days.

"There's many, many (ACC teams) that have been here, been in this position and could have very easily done what we did, and there will be many more after us," O'Connor said. "And our conference is year in, year out, an outstanding conference with great coaches and great players and committed administrations. I think you'll see more teams up here out of our league, sitting on here with the national championship trophy. I'm proud that we did it."

The Cavaliers certainly won the title by a route ACC boosters would love, taking down SEC behemoths Florida and Vandy in Omaha. But at the end of the day, the championship is Virginia's alone. From 10-14 in the ACC with two weeks to go, all the way to the national title, it was one incredible ride.

No matter what the oddsmakers thought.

"I wouldn't say there was doubt," Waddell said. "We had expectations in our locker room that never changed. It didn't look pretty at times. We were down a lot, outside of our clubhouse, but we knew what we were capable of. I honestly think without the ups and downs, we wouldn't be standing here right now. It brought us together in a way that a team that wins a championship has to come together."

CWS NOTES

■ The question all season long was whether the new baseballs would bring some life back to the College World Series. The answer was a definite "yes." After two years in a row of seeing just three home runs hit in the entire Series, there were 15 long balls in this year's tournament, the most in the TD Ameritrade Park era. Those included the CWS's first leadoff homer (by Florida's **Harrison Bader**) and walk-off homer (by Vanderbilt's **Jeren Kendall**) since the move to TDAP in 2011. Florida led the charge, hitting six homers in its five games, also the most any team has hit in one CWS since 2010. Beyond the homers, the eight CWS teams put up an aggregate .244 average, well up from last year's paltry .219. The 16 CWS games saw an average of 8.38 runs scored, which was also the best since the final CWS at Rosenblatt Stadium (and with the old bats) in 2010 averaged 9.6.

■ The CWS set a new attendance record of 353,378, a strong figure considering the two teams that traveled the most fans, Arkansas and Louisiana State, were knocked out early. The high point was the sellout crowd of 26,803 to watch the

COLLEGE WORLD SERIES

STANDINGS

BRACKET ONE	W	L
Virginia	3	1
Florida	3	2
Miami	1	2
Arkansas	0	2
BRACKET TWO	**W**	**L**
Vanderbilt	3	0
Texas Christian	2	2
Louisiana State	1	2
Cal State Fullerton	0	2

CWS FINALS (BEST OF THREE)
June 22: Vanderbilt 5, Virginia 1
June 23: Virginia 3, Vanderbilt 0
June 24: Virginia 4, Vanderbilt 2

ALL-TOURNAMENT TEAM
C: Kade Scivicque, LSU. **1B:** Zander Wiel, Vanderbilt. **2B:** Ernie Clement, Virginia. **3B:** Kenny Towns, Virgnia. **SS:** Daniel Pinero, Virginia. **OF:** Harrison Bader, Florida; Jacob Heyward, Miami; Bryan Reynolds, Vanderbilt. **DH:** Connor Wanhanen, TCU. **P:** *Josh Sborz, Virginia; Brandon Waddell, Virginia.
*Named Most Outstanding Player.

BATTING
(Minimum 8 PA)

PLAYER	AVG	AB	R	H	2B	3B	HR	RBI	SB
Alex Bregman, LSU	.538	13	3	7	0	0	0	0	1
Kade Scivicque, LSU	.500	12	2	6	1	0	0	3	0
Connor Wanhanen, TCU	.462	13	4	6	0	0	0	3	0
Jacob Heyward, Miami	.455	11	2	5	0	0	1	4	1
Brett McAfee, Arkansas	.429	7	0	3	0	0	0	1	0
Clark Eagan, Arkansas	.429	7	1	3	1	0	0	1	0
Jerrod Bravo, CSUF	.429	7	1	3	0	0	0	1	1
Bryan Reynolds, Vandy	.409	22	4	9	1	1	0	4	0
Daniel Pinero, Virginia	.391	23	4	9	1	0	0	1	3
Mike Rivera, Florida	.389	18	2	7	1	0	0	4	0

PITCHING
(Minimum 6 IP)

PITCHER	W-L	ERA	G	SV	IP	H	BB	SO
Josh Sborz, Virginia	3-0	0.00	4	1	13	7	4	10
Philip Pfeifer, Vanderbilt	1-1	0.00	2	0	13	12	4	13
Thomas Woodrey, Miami	0-0	0.00	1	0	6	3	3	7
Trey Teakell, TCU	1-0	0.00	2	0	6	0	0	3
Alex Young, TCU	0-1	1.17	1	0	8	3	1	12
John Kilichowski, Vandy	0-1	1.50	3	0	6	2	2	3
Thomas Eshelman, CSUF	0-0	1.59	1	0	6	4	0	8
Carson Fulmer, Vandy	1-0	1.98	2	0	14	6	4	15
Preston Morrison, TCU	1-0	2.00	2	0	9	7	1	5
Kyle Wright, Vandy	1-0	2.35	4	1	8	7	2	7

elimination game between LSU and Texas Christian. However, the finale of the championship series between Vanderbilt and Virginia drew a disappointing 17,689—the second smallest crowd of the 16 games. The CWS finals also were markedly outdrawn on television by the finals of the Women's College World Series three weeks earlier between Florida and Michigan. Those three WCWS finals games averaged 1.85 million viewers on ESPN from June 1-3, while the Vandy-Virginia series averaged 1.41 million. One possible cause: pace of play. While there's unquestionably more excitement in the CWS thanks to the new balls, the games still had a tendency to drag out—the three CWS finals games were 3 hours, 36 minutes long on average. The decisive third game of the finals didn't end until 11:45 p.m. on the East Coast.

REGIONALS

MAY 29-JUNE 1
64 teams, 16 four-team, double-elimination tournaments. Winners advance to super regionals.

LOS ANGELES
Host: UCLA (No. 1 national seed).
Participants: No. 1 UCLA (42-14), No. 2 Mississippi (30-26), No. 3 Maryland (39-21), No. 4 Cal State Bakersfield (36-22).
Champion: Maryland (3-1).
Runner-up: UCLA (3-2).
Outstanding player: LaMonte Wade, of, Maryland.

LAKE ELSINORE, CALIF.
Host: UC Santa Barbara.
Participants: No. 1 UC Santa Barbara (40-15), No. 2 Southern California (37-19), No. 3 Virginia (34-22), No. 4 San Diego State (40-21).
Champion: Virginia (3-0).
Runner-up: Southern California (2-2).
Outstanding player: Garrett Stubbs, c, Southern California.

SPRINGFIELD, MO.
Host: Missouri State (No. 8 national seed).
Participants: No. 1 Missouri State (45-10), No. 2 Iowa (39-16), No. 3 Oregon (37-23), No. 4 Canisius (34-28).
Champion: Missouri State (3-0).
Runner-up: Iowa (2-2).
Outstanding player: Nick Hibbing, rhp, Iowa.

STILLWATER, OKLA.
Host: Oklahoma State.
Participants: No. 1 Oklahoma State (37-18), No. 2 Arkansas (35-22), No. 3 Oral Roberts (41-14), No. 4 St. John's (39-14).
Champion: Arkansas (3-0).
Runner-up: St. John's (2-2).
Outstanding player: Joe Serrano, of, Arkansas.

GAINESVILLE, FLA.
Host: Florida (No. 4 national seed).
Participants: No. 1 Florida (44-16), No. 2 Florida Atlantic (40-17), No. 3 South Florida (33-24), No. 4 Texas A&M (23-23).
Champion: Florida (3-0).
Runner-up: Florida Atlantic (2-2).
Outstanding player: J.J. Schwarz, c, Florida.

TALLAHASSEE, FLA.
Host: Florida State.
Participants: No. 1 Florida State (41-19), No. 2 College of Charleston (43-13), No. 3 Auburn (35-24), No. 4 Mercer (35-21).
Champion: Florida State (3-0).
Runner-up: College of Charleston (2-2).
Outstanding player: Quincy Nieporte, 1b, Florida State.

CORAL GABLES, FLA.
Host: Miami (No. 5 national seed).
Participants: No. 1 Miami (44-14), No. 2 East Carolina (40-20), No. 3 Columbia (31-15), No. 4 Florida International (29-29).
Champion: Miami (3-1).
Runner-up: Columbia (3-2).
Outstanding player: David Thompson, 3b, Miami.

DALLAS
Host: Dallas Baptist.
Participants: No. 1 Dallas Baptist (43-13), No. 2 Oregon State (38-16), No. 3 Texas (30-25), No. 4 Virginia Commonwealth (37-22).
Champion: Virginia Commonwealth (3-1).
Runner-up: Dallas Baptist (3-2).
Outstanding player: Vimael Machin, ss, Virginia Commonwealth.

BATON ROUGE, LA.
Host: Louisiana State (No. 2 national seed).
Participants: No. 1 Louisiana State (48-10), No. 2 UNC Wilmington (39-16), No. 3 Tulane (34-23), No. 4 Lehigh (25-29).
Champion: Louisiana State (3-0).
Runner-up: UNC Wilmington (2-2).
Outstanding player: Alex Lange, rhp, Louisiana State.

HOUSTON
Host: Houston.
Participants: No. 1 Houston (42-18), No. 2 Rice (35-20), No. 3 Louisiana-Lafayette (39-21), No. 4 Houston Baptist (28-25).
Champion: Louisiana-Lafayette (3-0).
Runner-up: Rice (2-2).
Outstanding player: Evan Powell, of, Louisiana-Lafayette.

FORT WORTH
Host: Texas Christian (No. 7 national seed).
Participants: No. 1 Texas Christian (43-11), No. 2 North Carolina State (34-21), No. 3 Stony Brook (34-14), No. 4 Sacred Heart (23-30).
Champion: Texas Christian (4-1).
Runner-up: North Carolina State (2-2).
Outstanding player: Logan Ratledge, ss, North Carolina State.

COLLEGE STATION, TEXAS
Host: Texas A&M.
Participants: No. 1 Texas A&M (45-11), No. 2 Coastal Carolina (38-19), No. 3 California (34-19), No. 4 Texas Southern (31-17).
Champion: Texas A&M (4-1).
Runner-up: California (2-2).
Outstanding player: Matt Kent, lhp, Texas A&M.

LOUISVILLE
Host: Louisville (No. 3 national seed).
Participants: No. 1 Louisville (43-16), No. 2 Bradley (35-19), No. 3 Michigan (37-23), No. 4 Morehead State (38-20).
Champion: Louisville (3-0).
Runner-up: Michigan (2-2).
Outstanding player: Devin Hairston, ss, Louisville.

FULLERTON, CALIF.
Host: Cal State Fullerton.
Participants: No. 1 Cal State Fullerton (34-22), No. 2 Arizona State (34-21), No. 3 Clemson (32-27), No. 4 Pepperdine (30-27).
Champion: Cal State Fullerton (3-0).
Runner-up: Pepperdine (2-2).
Outstanding player: Thomas Eshelman, rhp, Cal State Fullerton.

CHAMPAIGN, ILL.
Host: Illinois (No. 6 national seed).
Participants: No. 1 Illinois (47-8), No. 2 Notre Dame (36-21), No. 3 Wright State (41-15), No. 4 Ohio (36-19).
Champion: Illinois (3-0).
Runner-up: Wright State (2-2).
Outstanding player: David Kerian, 1b, Illinois.

NASHVILLE
Host: Vanderbilt.
Participants: No. 1 Vanderbilt (42-19), No. 2 Radford (43-14), No. 3 Indiana (34-22), No. 4 Lipscomb (39-18)
Champion: Vanderbilt (3-0).
Runner-up: Radford (2-2).
Outstanding player: Dansby Swanson, ss, Vanderbilt.

SUPER REGIONALS

JUNE 5-8
16 teams, best-of-three series. Winners advance to College World Series.

MARYLAND AT VIRGINIA
Site: Charlottesville, Va.
Virginia wins 2-0, advances to CWS.

MISSOURI STATE AT ARKANSAS
Site: Fayetteville, Ark.
Arkansas wins 2-1, advances to CWS.

FLORIDA STATE AT FLORIDA
Site: Gainesville, Fla.
Florida wins 2-0, advances to CWS.

VIRGINIA COMMONWEALTH AT MIAMI
Site: Coral Gables, Fla.
Miami wins 2-0, advances to CWS.

LOUISIANA-LAFAYETTE AT LOUISIANA STATE
Site: Baton Rouge, La.
Louisiana State wins 2-0, advances to CWS.

TEXAS A&M AT TEXAS CHRISTIAN
Site: Fort Worth
Texas Christian wins 2-1, advances to CWS.

CAL STATE FULLERTON AT LOUISVILLE
Site: Louisville.
Cal State Fullerton wins 2-1, advances to CWS.

VANDERBILT AT ILLINOIS
Site: Champaign, Ill.
Vanderbilt wins 2-0, advances to CWS.

Benintendi swings to spotlight

BY MICHAEL LANANNA

Here begins the legend of the Ohio Hit King.

On May 3, 2013, at Deer Park high school in Cincinnati, the King powers a hard-hit opposite-field drive to left. He pulls into second base—and the game pauses right in the middle of the inning. The smattering of fans all stand and applaud. The opposing pitcher walks to second base and shakes the King's hand. The Deer Park coach—coach of the opposing team—walks onto the field and addresses the crowd.

"Andrew Benintendi just broke the all-time hits record," he tells them, mid-game. "I'm just glad it stayed in the ballpark."

In his next at-bat, Benintendi homers well over the right-field fence. The at-bat after? An inside-the-park grand slam. Career hits Nos. 202 and No. 203.

Now, the King's legend only grows.

After a stellar sophomore season at Arkansas, when he outhit some of the game's finest stars and draft prospects, Andrew Benintendi is Baseball America's College Player of the Year.

Every mythic hero grapples with some sort of adversity before his meteoric rise.

Before Benintendi even began his collegiate career, he had surgery to remove the hamate bone in his right hand, and as a result he got off to a sluggish start. The numbers from 2014 are by no means eye-popping—.276/.368/.333

Andrew Benintendi

with one home run and 17 steals. Certainly, they didn't hint at the type of season the center fielder would have this year: Benintendi batted .376/.488/.717 with 20 homers, 57 RBIs and 24 steals in 28 attempts.

"Andrew has just made an incredible jump, just night and day as far as confidence-wise and just the way he plays the game," Arkansas coach Dave Van Horn said. "Last year was probably the first time ever in his life that he failed a little bit. He took it to heart and went home and worked his butt off."

Both Benintendi and Van Horn point to three reasons for his sophomore surge. There's health, obviously. Mechanically, Benintendi closed up his open stance in early April last season, and almost immediately, the ball jumped off his bat better. Thirdly, Benintendi took time off from summer ball and committed himself in the weight room, packing on about 10 pounds.

"I approached it like a job this summer, really," Benintendi said. "I just dedicated myself to getting bigger and stronger."

At 5-foot-10, 180 pounds, Benintendi's home runs come as a surprise to some. That compact package of power and speed in center field is a unique one, and scouts struggled to put a major league comparison on him. Benintendi has seen the attention swell around him.

"It's been a lot, especially with all these awards and things like that, but I just try to take it in," Benintendi said. "It's exciting, though. I get a lot of texts from people that I know and people from back home, and it sounds like they're excited, almost more excited than I am."

PREVIOUS WINNERS

1982: Jeff Ledbetter, of/lhp, Florida State	**1993:** Brooks Kieschnick, dh/rhp, Texas	**2004:** Jered Weaver, rhp, Long Beach State
1983: Dave Magadan, 1b, Alabama	**1994:** Jason Varitek, c, Georgia Tech	**2005:** Alex Gordon, 3b, Nebraska
1984: Oddibe McDowell, of, Arizona State	**1995:** Todd Helton, 1b/lhp, Tennessee	**2006:** Andrew Miller, lhp, North Carolina
1985: Pete Incaviglia, of, Oklahoma State	**1996:** Kris Benson, rhp, Clemson	**2007:** David Price, lhp, Vanderbilt
1986: Casey Close, of, Michigan	**1997:** J.D. Drew, of, Florida State	**2008:** Buster Posey, c/rhp, Florida State
1987: Robin Ventura, 3b, Oklahoma State	**1998:** Jeff Austin, rhp, Stanford	**2009:** Stephen Strasburg, rhp, San Diego St.
1988: John Olerud, 1b/lhp, Washington St.	**1999:** Jason Jennings, rhp, Baylor	**2010:** Anthony Rendon, 3b, Rice
1989: Ben McDonald, rhp, Louisiana State	**2000:** Mark Teixeira, 3b, Georgia Tech	**2011:** Trevor Bauer, rhp, UCLA
1990: Mike Kelly, of, Arizona State	**2001:** Mark Prior, rhp, Southern California	**2012:** Mike Zunino, c, Florida
1991: David McCarthy, 1b, Stanford	**2002:** Khalil Greene, ss, Clemson	**2013:** Kris Bryant, 3b, San Diego
1992: Phil Nevin, 3b, Cal State Fullerton	**2003:** Rickie Weeks, 2b, Southern	**2014:** A.J. Reed, 1b/lhp, Kentucky

O'Connor pushes the right buttons

COACH OF THE YEAR

BY JIM SHONERD

Paul Mainieri still remembers the phone call from the summer of 2003. At the other end of the line, Virginia athletic director Craig Littlepage needed a baseball coach and had his eye on then-Notre Dame head man Mainieri's top assistant, Brian O'Connor.

"I told Craig, 'Craig, if you hire Brian O'Connor to be your coach, your reputation will be made as an athletic director by this hire,'" Mainieri recalls.

"I think I was pretty prophetic about that."

It's hard to imagine any hire doing more. Taking over at a school that had only been to the NCAA tournament three times before his arrival—the program was close to being dropped from D-I competition at one point— O'Connor has built the Cavaliers into consistent winners, with

Brian O'Connor

four Omaha trips in the last seven seasons. To cap it off, Virginia staged an improbable run to its first national title this spring.

After that amount of sustained success as well as the job he did in guiding the Cavs to the top of the sport, O'Connor is Baseball America's 2015 College Coach of the Year.

Name a kind of adversity, and Virginia probably dealt with it. The Cavs were hit by everything from the long winter to a laundry list of injuries—ace Nathan Kirby missed most of the second half and UVa. position players combined to miss over 150 games. They had to fight just to make the NCAA tournament,

a position far removed from one year earlier when the Cavs were the preseason No. 1 team and rarely slipped.

"I really think that a lot of those challenges we had throughout the year, one, it humbled our group," O'Connor said. "It humbled our coaches, I can tell you that. We've had so much success. And I think it humbled a lot of our veteran players, too. It taught us all how hard this thing really is."

The answer? Have some fun with it.

Although O'Connor didn't take it easy on the players still at his disposal, he recognized his guys had enough going against them as it was. Yelling and screaming at them to play better wasn't going to help matters—the better tack was to make sure they still looked forward to coming to the park. Whether that meant taking a selfie with his players during a press conference or jumping on the dogpile after they won their super regional, O'Connor and his staff "intentionally tried to make it as fun as possible for the guys so they can be as loose and confident as they could be," he said.

That loose approach engendered a team toughness that carried the Cavs throughout the postseason—an attitude that they'd weathered everything the baseball gods could throw at them and were still standing.

"Going through those ups and downs, we were kind of able to become a tougher team, a more resilient team," senior third baseman Kenny Towns said. "And I think that showed for us in the postseason, and obviously it started from the coaches kind of passing it down to us."

PREVIOUS WINNERS

1982: Gene Stephenson, Wichita State	**1993:** Gene Stephenson, Wichita State	**2004:** David Perno, Georgia
1983: Barry Shollenberger, Alabama	**1994:** Jim Morris, Miami	**2005:** Rick Jones, Tulane
1984: Augie Garrido, Cal State Fullerton	**1995:** Pat Murphy, Arizona State	**2006:** Pat Casey, Oregon State
1985: Ron Polk, Mississippi State	**1996:** Skip Bertman, Louisiana State	**2007:** Dave Serrano, UC Irvine
1986: Skip Bertman, LSU/Dave Snow, LMU	**1997:** Jim Wells, Alabama	**2008:** Mike Fox, North Carolina
1987: Mark Marquess, Stanford	**1998:** Pat Murphy, Arizona State	**2009:** Paul Mainieri, Louisiana State
1988: Jim Brock, Arizona State	**1999:** Wayne Graham, Rice	**2010:** Ray Tanner, South Carolina
1989: Dave Snow, Long Beach State	**2000:** Ray Tanner, South Carolina	**2011:** Kevin O'Sullivan, Florida
1990: Steve Webber, Georgia	**2001:** Dave Van Horn, Nebraska	**2012:** Mike Martin, Florida State
1991: Jim Hendry, Creighton	**2002:** Augie Garrido, Texas	**2013:** John Savage, UCLA
1992: Andy Lopez, Pepperdine	**2003:** George Horton, Cal State Fullerton	**2014:** Tim Corbin, Vanderbilt

McKay stars both ways for Louisville

FRESHMAN OF THE YEAR

DHing when he pitched.

The Cardinals let him hit, and they let him pitch. McKay excelled at both and—most impressively—did so in his freshman season. For those reasons, he is Baseball America's College Freshman of the Year.

He has the fastball, which sits 88-92 mph, and throws a hard spike curve that sits in the high 70's to low 80's. It's a pitch he learned at a young age and has all but mastered at age 19.

"I picked that up when I was 13; I saw the grip from a buddy that played on my travel team," McKay said.

Roger Williams, Louisville's pitching coach, hasn't had to do much tweaking.

"The foundation for what he does as a pitcher, I think, is still there from what he did in the past as a pitcher," Williams said.

BY MICHAEL LANANNA

It's impossible to keep a bat out of Brendan McKay's hands.

McKay perhaps is most known for what he can do on the mound. Before opting to go to Louisville, he was drafted in the 34th round in 2014 as a pitcher, and this season the lefthander led the ACC with a 1.77 ERA. He went 9-3, striking out 117 in 97 innings. He earned four saves before evolving into Louisville's Saturday stopper.

But McKay also made quite the impact at the plate, hitting .308/.418/.431 with four home runs and 34 RBIs. By the end of the season, he was the everyday cleanup hitter, starting at first base and

Brendan McKay

PREVIOUS WINNERS

FRESHMAN ALL-AMERICA TEAMS

FIRST TEAM

POS.		AVG	OBP	SLG	AB	R	H	HR	RBI	SB
C	J.J. Schwarz, Florida	.332	.398	.629	256	60	85	18	73	1
1B	Austin Edens, Samford	.357	.442	.662	213	49	71	16	54	0
2B	Kyle Davis, West Virginia	.353	.391	.491	224	40	79	4	31	4
3B	Jake Burger, Missouri State	.342	.390	.518	228	41	78	4	42	4
SS	Jacob Bivens, Michigan	.319	.435	.352	213	43	68	0	19	9
OF	Keston Hiura, UC Irvine	.330	.392	.520	227	40	75	7	52	1
OF	Jeren Kendall, Vanderbilt	.281	.394	.530	185	34	52	8	40	19
OF	Reed Rohlman, Clemson	.356	.412	.466	236	43	84	3	58	3
DH	K.J. Harrison, Oregon State	.309	.401	.527	220	40	68	10	60	1
UT	Brendan McKay, Louisville	.308	.418	.431	211	32	65	4	34	4

		W	L	ERA	G	SV	IP	H	BB	SO	BAA
SP	Brian Brown, N.C. State	7	3	2.03	15	0	80	59	26	78	.211
SP	Alex Lange, Louisiana State	12	0	1.97	17	0	114	87	46	131	.212
SP	Chris Mathewson, Long Beach St.	6	6	1.94	13	0	93	61	24	80	.187
SP	Seth Romero, Houston	7	4	1.94	22	7	83	61	22	92	.201
RP	Kyle Wright, Vanderbilt	6	1	1.23	29	4	59	36	23	62	.180
UT	Brendan McKay, Louisville	9	3	1.77	20	4	97	53	34	117	.159

SECOND TEAM

C—Matt Whatley, Oral Roberts (.355-5-44). **1B**—Kel Johnson, Georgia Tech (.298-10-34). **2B**—Dalton Guthrie, Florida (.287-2-26). **3B**—Will Toffey, Vanderbilt (.294-4-49). **SS**—Zach Rutherford, Old Dominion (.317-0-18). **OF**—Stuart Fairchild, Wake Forest (.349-5-41); Pavin Smith, Virginia (.307-7-44); Cal Stevenson, Nevada (.359-0-25). **DH**—Connor Wanhanen, Texas Christian (.329-1-40). **UT**—Sean Watkins, Loyola Marymount (.266-6-22; 4-1, 1.89, 57 IP, 49 SO). **SP**—Michael Baumann, Jacksonville (7-1, 2.24, 84 IP/85 SO); Griffin Canning, UCLA (7-1, 2.97, 64 IP/66 SO); Tanner Houck, Missouri (8-5, 3.49, 101 IP/91 SO); Drew Rasmussen, Oregon State (7-4, 2.80, 106 IP/82 SO). **RP**—Lincoln Henzman, Louisville (5-2, 2.32, 54 IP/47 SO).

COLLEGE

HITTING (Minimum 140 at-bats)

BATTING AVERAGE

RK	PLAYER, POS., TEAM	YEAR	AVG	OBP	SLG	G	AB	R	H	2B	3B	HR	RBI	BB	SO	SB
1.	Kevin Kaczmarski, of, Evansville	Sr.	.465	.543	.746	46	185	43	86	19	9	5	57	28	23	13
2.	Donnie Dewees, of, North Florida	Jr.	.422	.483	.749	60	251	88	106	12	8	18	68	30	16	23
3.	Jensen Park, of, Northern Colorado	Sr.	.422	.468	.624	43	173	38	73	11	3	6	34	11	17	13
4.	Melvin Rodriguez, if, Jackson State	Sr.	.421	.477	.629	55	221	59	93	22	3	6	60	30	14	13
5.	Sean Trent, if, Navy	Jr.	.407	.446	.524	57	231	35	94	18	3	1	42	16	29	1
6.	Caleb Howell, of, Eastern Illinois	Sr.	.407	.493	.511	49	182	39	74	19	0	0	35	27	15	7
7.	Tyler Follis, if, North Dakota	Sr.	.404	.462	.505	49	188	43	76	9	2	2	22	18	30	6
8.	Chris Robinson, c, Morehead State	Sr.	.402	.472	.655	58	246	78	99	25	5	9	69	29	31	10
9.	Zach George, if, Arkansas State	Sr.	.399	.548	.562	55	203	38	81	22	1	3	35	52	28	9
10.	Cole Gruber, of, Nebraska-Omaha	Jr.	.399	.495	.486	47	173	43	69	7	1	2	23	32	33	22
11.	Drew Ferguson, of, Belmont	Sr.	.397	.486	.685	58	232	72	92	26	4	11	59	31	24	26
12.	Scott Kingery, if, Arizona	Jr.	.392	.423	.561	54	237	53	93	15	5	5	36	9	18	11
13.	Nick Dini, if, Wagner	Sr.	.392	.489	.625	51	176	45	69	18	1	7	44	30	7	14
14.	Cesar Rivera, of, Alabama State	Sr.	.391	.473	.614	49	207	59	81	16	3	8	42	29	32	4
15.	Michael Morman, of, Richmond	Sr.	.389	.441	.611	53	226	51	88	25	2	7	56	16	35	10
16.	Charley Gould, c, William & Mary	Jr.	.388	.473	.706	45	170	38	66	15	0	13	52	24	28	0
17.	Justin Korenblatt, of, La Salle	Sr.	.387	.497	.563	36	142	32	55	11	1	4	32	26	25	9
18.	Demetre Taylor, of, Eastern Illinois	Jr.	.384	.429	.634	45	164	31	63	6	4	9	46	12	24	6
19.	Matt Beaty, if, Belmont	Sr.	.382	.469	.668	58	238	53	91	24	4	12	76	32	17	12
20.	Alex Caruso, of, St. John's	Jr.	.382	.480	.427	56	204	48	78	9	0	0	23	30	35	3
21.	Will Craig, if, Wake Forest	So.	.382	.496	.702	53	191	52	73	20	1	13	58	41	24	2
22.	Logan Landon, of, Texas-Pan American	Sr.	.382	.476	.623	51	191	51	73	14	4	8	47	30	30	17
23.	Michael Bozarth, of, Saint Louis	Jr.	.382	.460	.572	42	152	45	58	9	1	6	31	16	20	18
24.	T.J. Alas, of, Eastern Kentucky	Jr.	.378	.456	.628	40	156	35	59	12	3	7	30	17	36	4
25.	Jake MacWilliam, if, Sam Houston State	Sr.	.378	.412	.483	43	143	20	54	9	0	2	22	8	28	1
26.	Kyle Reese, if, Nicholls State	Jr.	.377	.413	.527	54	207	34	78	20	4	1	32	13	33	4
27.	Bobby Stahel, of, Southern California	Sr.	.376	.419	.506	59	245	59	92	12	4	4	33	14	31	10
28.	Andrew Benintendi, of, Arkansas	So.	.376	.488	.717	65	226	62	85	13	2	20	57	50	32	24
29.	Paul Panaccione, if, Grand Canyon	Jr.	.376	.441	.493	54	221	56	83	10	2	4	36	26	32	7
30.	Ka'ai Tom, of, Kentucky	Jr.	.375	.443	.528	55	216	41	81	16	1	5	51	23	25	15
31.	Zarley Zalewski, if, Kent State	Jr.	.374	.463	.483	53	203	33	76	13	0	3	32	30	39	5
32.	Ryan Cooper, of, Elon	Sr.	.373	.450	.562	54	201	45	75	13	2	7	42	26	26	4
33.	Connor Panas, if, Canisius	Sr.	.372	.472	.632	64	247	67	92	17	7	11	68	33	39	19
34.	Dillon Robinson, 1b, Brigham Young	Sr.	.371	.453	.550	52	202	44	75	17	2	5	43	29	45	1
35.	Mitchell Nau, c, Texas A&M	Sr.	.370	.460	.492	63	238	46	88	17	0	4	47	31	34	1
36.	Brendon Sanger, if, Florida Atlantic	Jr.	.370	.492	.583	61	230	57	85	20	4	7	48	56	30	2
37.	Kevin Newman, if, Arizona	Jr.	.370	.426	.489	55	227	53	84	19	1	2	36	20	15	22
38.	Nicholas Collins, c, Georgetown	Jr.	.370	.435	.540	53	211	34	78	15	0	7	36	22	21	6
39.	Zach Coppola, of, South Dakota State	Jr.	.370	.472	.409	55	208	53	77	6	1	0	31	38	33	39
40.	Brad Kaczka, if, Winthrop	Sr.	.369	.429	.442	57	217	41	80	6	5	0	34	22	26	12
41.	Ian Happ, of, Cincinnati	Jr.	.369	.492	.672	56	198	47	73	18	0	14	44	49	49	12
42.	Paschal Petrongolo, c, Jacksonville State	Jr.	.368	.451	.556	55	223	48	82	17	2	7	59	34	61	1
43.	Cameron Newell, of, UC Santa Barbara	Sr.	.368	.447	.473	57	201	41	74	8	2	3	31	27	23	7
44.	Josh Gardiner, if, Radford	Sr.	.368	.451	.526	45	171	47	63	18	0	3	22	23	32	18
45.	Kyle Lewis, of, Mercer	So.	.367	.423	.677	54	226	49	83	19	0	17	56	19	41	3
46.	David Kerian, if, Illinois	Sr.	.367	.462	.667	60	207	46	76	10	2	16	52	37	28	9
47.	Matt Honchel, of, Miami (Ohio)	Sr.	.367	.436	.511	50	188	30	69	13	1	4	38	20	27	10
48.	Luke Morrill, if, Maine	Sr.	.367	.438	.503	50	177	34	65	18	0	2	29	22	25	8
49.	Angelo Amendolare, if, Jacksonville	Sr.	.366	.441	.480	56	227	45	83	16	2	2	42	27	28	20
50.	Logan Gray, if, Austin Peay State	So.	.366	.461	.752	38	153	41	56	15	1	14	39	24	44	11
51.	Jack Parenty, of, Stony Brook	Jr.	.365	.432	.521	52	211	38	77	13	7	2	47	26	18	19
52.	Gary Thomas, if, Jackson State	Sr.	.365	.427	.414	48	203	47	74	10	0	0	25	18	15	20
53.	Trenton Brooks, p, Nevada	So.	.365	.484	.515	55	200	51	73	17	2	3	52	39	25	5
54.	Jeff Campbell, p, North Dakota	Sr.	.365	.434	.598	51	189	38	69	9	1	11	48	27	28	3
55.	George Iskenderian, if, Miami	Jr.	.364	.459	.476	67	250	71	91	15	2	3	55	40	41	23
56.	Nick Banks, of, Texas A&M	So.	.364	.450	.536	63	239	51	87	11	3	8	48	34	58	9
57.	Cam McRae, c, Presbyterian	Sr.	.364	.407	.525	55	217	36	79	14	0	7	38	11	39	7
58.	Andre Davis, 1b, Arkansas-Pine Bluff	Sr.	.364	.452	.593	38	140	34	51	12	1	6	39	17	25	0
59.	Louis Mele, if, NYIT	So.	.364	.407	.636	42	140	20	51	11	0	9	41	6	21	0
60.	Robert Henry, of, Brown	So.	.363	.430	.531	39	160	30	58	17	2	2	21	18	20	7
61.	Vinny Siena, if, Connecticut	Jr.	.362	.424	.519	60	260	64	94	14	3	7	54	29	30	11
62.	Frank Califano, of, Youngstown State	Jr.	.362	.413	.406	50	207	33	75	5	2	0	18	18	24	19
63.	Jeff Boehm, of, Illinois-Chicago	Sr.	.362	.465	.663	52	199	51	72	17	2	13	66	36	37	4
64.	Taylor Tempel, of, Fresno State	Sr.	.362	.393	.519	53	185	41	67	13	2	4	26	6	41	3
65.	Ronnie Jebavy, of, Middle Tennessee State	Jr.	.361	.408	.533	59	244	38	88	15	3	7	36	19	34	24
66.	Sam Koenig, if, Wisconsin-Milwaukee	Sr.	.361	.454	.657	58	230	58	83	19	2	15	57	37	50	6

RK.	PLAYER, POS., TEAM	YEAR	AVG	OBP	SLG	G	AB	R	H	2B	3B	HR	RBI	BB	SO	SB
67.	Tommy Houmard, if, UNC Asheville	Sr.	.361	.444	.463	55	216	44	78	8	4	2	30	28	31	2
68.	Nick Lynch, if, UC Davis	Sr.	.361	.452	.558	56	208	43	75	31	2	2	34	21	28	6
69.	Greg Kaiser, if, IPFW	Jr.	.361	.396	.639	51	194	43	70	16	4	10	43	6	37	5
70.	Ethan Ferreira, c, Harvard	Sr.	.361	.425	.594	42	155	30	56	15	3	5	35	18	22	4
71.	Nick Newell, of, Morehead State	Sr.	.360	.405	.572	60	250	41	90	28	2	7	58	17	29	4
72.	Kolbey Carpenter, if, Oklahoma	Jr.	.360	.416	.533	61	242	49	87	10	4	8	37	23	36	5
73.	Eric Danforth, of, South Dakota State	Sr.	.360	.437	.442	55	172	39	62	10	2	0	25	16	22	7
74.	Matthew Ramsay, c, Wofford	Sr.	.359	.459	.483	60	234	53	84	12	4	3	32	35	37	14
75.	Keelin Rasch, if, Louisiana-Monroe	Sr.	.359	.395	.571	54	217	40	78	13	3	9	41	9	17	4
76.	Tyler Detmer, of, Illinois-Chicago	Sr.	.359	.453	.541	52	209	52	75	15	1	7	33	23	34	2
77.	Mike Garzillo, 2b, Lehigh	Jr.	.359	.422	.651	56	209	45	75	18	2	13	54	18	43	15
78.	Mitch Longo, of, Ohio	So.	.358	.422	.500	57	240	53	86	13	0	7	49	22	16	10
79.	Cal Stevenson, of, Nevada	Fr.	.358	.429	.454	56	218	55	78	13	4	0	25	27	21	10
80.	Steve Laurino, if, Marist	Sr.	.358	.442	.562	47	187	33	67	14	3	6	38	23	32	5
81.	Robert Garza, if, Texas Southern	Sr.	.358	.457	.549	44	162	41	58	11	4	4	32	22	27	13
82.	Kyle Ruchim, if, Northwestern	Sr.	.358	.416	.585	36	159	29	57	16	1	6	23	16	14	1
83.	Austin Edens, if, Samford	Fr.	.357	.442	.662	55	213	48	76	17	0	16	54	30	44	0
84.	Trever Allen, of, Arizona State	Sr.	.357	.398	.535	57	213	46	76	17	3	5	31	14	36	5
85.	Garrison Schwartz, of, Grand Canyon	Fr.	.357	.413	.439	53	196	28	70	10	3	0	40	22	30	7
86.	Ryan Kent, of, Morehead State	So.	.356	.454	.478	59	253	65	90	20	1	3	32	34	43	6
87.	Reed Rohlman, of, Clemson	Fr.	.356	.412	.466	61	236	43	84	17	0	3	58	23	35	3
88.	Mark Mathias, if, Cal Poly	Jr.	.356	.424	.436	47	202	42	72	7	3	1	28	23	19	9
89.	Mitch Ghelfi, c, Wisconsin-Milwaukee	Jr.	.356	.463	.514	47	177	40	63	16	3	2	35	27	31	4
90.	Kory Britton, ss, Mount St. Mary's	Sr.	.356	.420	.477	43	149	21	53	12	0	2	23	16	16	2
91.	Kade Scivicque, c, Louisiana State	Sr.	.355	.398	.521	60	234	33	83	21	0	6	48	15	22	0
92.	Josh Tobias, if, Florida	Sr.	.355	.435	.524	65	231	60	82	14	5	5	46	23	37	11
93.	Zach Shields, of, UNC Wilmington	Jr.	.355	.393	.446	57	220	44	78	7	2	3	38	10	33	17
94.	Luke Willis, of, George Mason	Sr.	.355	.441	.500	51	214	50	76	15	2	4	29	21	24	29
95.	Matt Whatley, c, Oral Roberts	Fr.	.355	.437	.528	54	214	56	76	16	3	5	44	26	35	16
96.	Trey York, if, East Tennessee State	Jr.	.355	.437	.611	56	211	55	75	15	6	9	51	25	44	18
97.	Josh Greene, of, High Point	So.	.355	.441	.532	51	186	36	66	8	2	7	37	26	35	13
98.	Bryce Greager, if, Nevada	Jr.	.355	.460	.552	54	183	39	65	17	2	5	41	29	46	2
99.	Ben Petersen, of, North Dakota State	So.	.355	.422	.459	49	183	28	65	8	1	3	23	15	27	6
100.	Brandon Wilkerson, of, North Carolina A&T	Sr.	.355	.419	.484	40	155	26	55	10	2	2	34	16	22	10

ON-BASE PERCENTAGE

RK.	PLAYER, POS., TEAM	OBP
1.	Zach George, if, Arkansas State	.548
2.	Kevin Kaczmarski, of, Evansville	.543
3.	Austin Byler, if, Nevada	.507
4.	Chris Godinez, if, Bradley	.505
5.	P.J. Biocic, ss, Alabama State	.502
6.	D.J. Stewart, of, Florida State	.500
7.	Justin Korenblatt, of, La Salle	.497
8.	Will Craig, if, Wake Forest	.496
9.	Cole Gruber, of, Neb.-Omaha	.495
10.	Caleb Howell, of, Eastern Ill.	.493

SLUGGING PERCENTAGE

RK.	PLAYER, POS., TEAM	SLG
1.	Logan Gray, if, Austin Peay	.752
2.	Donnie Dewees, of, North Florida	.749
3.	Kevin Kaczmarski, of, Evansville	.746
4.	Andrew Benintendi, of, Arkansas	.717
5.	Charley Gould, c, William & Mary	.706
6.	Will Craig, if, Wake Forest	.702
7.	Kyle Nowlin, of, Eastern Ky.	.690
8.	Drew Ferguson, if, Belmont	.685
9.	Kyle Lewis, of, Mercer	.677
10.	Ian Happ, of, Cincinnati	.672

HOME RUNS

RK.	PLAYER, POS., TEAM	HR
1.	Andrew Benintendi, of, Arkansas	20
2.	Kyle Nowlin, of, Eastern Kentucky	19
	David Thompson, if, Miami	19
4.	Donnie Dewees, of, North Florida	18
	J.J. Schwarz, c, Florida	18
	Edwin Rios, if, Fla. International	18
7.	Kyle Lewis, of, Mercer	17
	Matt Dacey, if, Richmond	17
	Ryan Howell, if, Nevada	17
	Tucker Tubbs, if, Memphis	17
	Harrison Bader, of, Florida	17

RUNS BATTED IN

RK.	PLAYER, POS., TEAM	RBI
1.	David Thompson, if, Miami	90
2.	Matt Beaty, if, Belmont	76
3.	J.J. Schwarz, c, Florida	73
4.	Robby Spencer, if, Morehead St.	71
	Carmen Benedetti, if, Michigan	71
6.	Zack Collins, c, Miami	70
	Carl Wise, if, Col. of Charleston	70
	Nick Rivera, if, Fla. Gulf Coast	70
9.	Chris Robinson, c, Morehead St.	69
10.	Donnie Dewees, of, North Florida	68
	Zander Wiel, if, Vanderbilt	68
	Connor Panas, if, Canisius	68

DOUBLES

RK.	PLAYER, POS., TEAM	2B
1.	Nick Lynch, if, UC Davis	31
2.	Nick Newell, of, Morehead State	28
	Nick Pappas, if, Col. of Charleston	28
4.	Conor Clancey, if, Wofford	27
5.	Drew Ferguson, of, Belmont	26
6.	Carmen Benedetti, if, Michigan	25
	Chris Robinson, c, Morehead St.	25
	Michael Morman, of, Richmond	25
	Hunter Higgerson, if, Radford	25
	Adam Groesbeck, of, Air Force	25
	Cole Bauml, of, Northern Ky.	25

TRIPLES

RK.	PLAYER, POS., TEAM	3B
1.	Kevin Kaczmarski, of, Evansville	9
	Joe D'Annunzio, 1b, Rutgers	9
3.	Donnie Dewees, of, North Florida	8
	Kent Blackstone, if, George Mason	8
	Connor Deneen, of, Navy	8
	Kyle Thornell, if, Stephen F. Austin	8
	Elliott Caldwell, of, South Carolina	8
8.	Cedric Mullins, of, Campbell	7

TRIPLES, CONT.

RK.	PLAYER, POS., TEAM	3B
	Connor Panas, if, Canisius	7
	Casey Rodrigue, if, Indiana	7
	Andrew Selby, of, George Washington	7
	Jack Parenty, of, Stony Brook	7
	Logan Regnier, of, Central Mich.	7
	Ben Johnson, of, Texas	7
	Alex Perez, if, Virginia Tech	7
	Robert Currie, of, Navy	7
	Matt Eppers, of, Ball State	7

STOLEN BASES

RK.	PLAYER, POS., TEAM	SB	CS
1.	Brandon Howard, if, BGSU	41	8
2.	John Rubino, if, Eastern Mich.	40	6
3.	Zach Coppola, of, South Dakota St.	39	0
	Nick Sinay, of, Buffalo	39	9
5.	Alex Bregman, ss, LSU	38	10
	Joe Daru, if, NYIT	38	5
	Gavin Golsan, if, Jacksonville St.	38	4
8.	Luke Meeteer, of, Wis.-Milwaukee	37	6
9.	Troy Montgomery, of, Ohio St.	35	6
	Andy Perez, if, Duke	35	10

RUNS

RK.	PLAYER, POS., TEAM	R
1.	Donnie Dewees, of, North Florida	88
2.	Chris Robinson, c, Morehead State	78
3.	Dansby Swanson, if, Vanderbilt	76
4.	Drew Ferguson, of, Belmont	72
5.	George Iskenderian, if, Miami	71
6.	Ricky Eusebio, of, Miami	70
	Rhett Wiseman, of, Vanderbilt	70
8.	Steven Pallares, of, San Diego State	69
	Austin Byler, if, Nevada	69
	Brandon Rawe, of, Morehead St.	69

HITS

RK.	PLAYER, POS., TEAM	H
1.	Donnie Dewees, of, North Florida	106
2.	Chris Robinson, c, Morehead St.	99
3.	Dansby Swanson, if, Vanderbilt	94
	Vinny Siena, if, Connecticut	94
	Sean Trent, if, Navy	94
6.	Melvin Rodriguez, if, Jackson St.	93
	Scott Kingery, if, Arizona	93
8.	Drew Ferguson, of, Belmont	92
	Rhett Wiseman, of, Vanderbilt	92
	Brandon Rawe, of, Morehead St.	92
	Connor Panas, if, Canisius	92
	Bobby Stahel, of, Southern Calif.	92

TOTAL BASES

RK.	PLAYER, POS., TEAM	TB
1.	Donnie Dewees, of, North Florida	188
2.	Dansby Swanson, ss, Vanderbilt	175
3.	Rhett Wiseman, of, Vanderbilt	164
4.	Andrew Benintendi, of, Arkansas	162
	David Thompson, if, Miami	162
6.	Chris Robinson, c, Morehead St.	161
	J.J. Schwarz, c, Florida	161
8.	Drew Ferguson, of, Belmont	159
	Matt Beaty, if, Belmont	159
10.	Zander Wiel, if, Vanderbilt	157

WALKS

RK.	PLAYER, POS., TEAM	BB
1.	D.J. Stewart, of, Florida State	69
2.	Zack Collins, c, Miami	57
3.	Brendon Sanger, if, Fla. Atlantic	56
4.	Dylan Becker, if, Missouri State	55
5.	Austin Byler, if, Nevada	54

WALKS, CONT.

RK.	PLAYER, POS., TEAM	BB
	Steven Duggar, of, Clemson	54
7.	Kane Sweeney, if, Morehead St.	53
	Tyler Gamble, 1b, Jacksonville St.	53
9.	Zach George, if, Arkansas State	52
	Ricky Eusebio, of, Miami	52
	Taylor Walls, if, Florida State	52

TOUGHEST TO STRIKE OUT

RK.	PLAYER, POS., TEAM	AB/SO
1.	Alec Diamond, if, Belmont	28.3
2.	Nick Dini, c, Wagner	25.1
3.	Andrew Guillotte, of, McNeese St.	22.6
4.	Deion Tansel, if, Toledo	21.4
5.	Greg Espinosa, if, Houston Baptist	19.6
6.	Aaron Barnett, c, Pepperdine	19.1
7.	Ernie Clement, if, Virginia	19.1
8.	Scott Heelan, c, Northwestern	18.9
9.	Brad Elwood, if, Charlotte	18.0
10.	Anthony Cheky, of, Michigan St.	18.0

HIT BY PITCH

RK.	PLAYER, POS., TEAM	HBP
1.	Derek Yoder, of, Murray State	27
2.	P.J. Biocic, ss, Alabama State	25
3.	Kody Davis, if, Utah	24
	Jarod Perry, of, Evansville	24
	Chris Fornaci, if, Pepperdine	24
6.	Grant Miller, if, Western Mich.	22
	Jimmy Kerrigan, of, VCU	22
	Cedric Vallieres, if, Texas State	22
	Nick Sinay, of, Buffalo	22
10.	Ricky Eusebio, of, Miami	21

SACRIFICE BUNTS

RK.	PLAYER, POS., TEAM	SH
1.	Joey Hawkins, if, Missouri State	29
2.	Matt Hansen, if, Toledo	22
3.	Tyler Selesky, of, Fla. Gulf Coast	20
4.	Gage Green, c, Oklahoma State	18
	Joe Schrimpf, if, Arkansas State	18
6.	Steven Leonard, c, Campbell	17
	Garrett Stubbs, c, Southern Calif.	17
	David Lett, if, Eastern Mich.	17
	Taylor Alspaugh, of, Oklahoma	17
	Justin Behnke, of, Arizona	17

SACRIFICE FLIES

RK.	PLAYER, POS., TEAM	SF
1.	Max McDowell, c, Connecticut	11
2.	Brett Lashley, if, Fla. Atlantic	10
	Blake Allemand, if, Texas A&M	10
	Brett Chappell, if, Maine	10
	Ryan Howell, if, Nevada	10
6.	Connor Owings, if, Coastal Carolina	9
	Timmy Robinson, of, Southern Calif.	9
	Melvin Rodriguez, if, Jackson St.	9
	Tony Fortier-Bensen, ss, High Point	9
10.	Logan Regnier, of, Central Mich.	8
	Jeremy Martinez, c, Southern Calif.	8
	Trent Higginbothem, 3b, North Fla.	8
	Robby Nesovic, dh, UC Santa Barbara	8
	Noah Pierce, if, Air Force	8
	K.J. Harrison, c, Oregon State	8
	Vimael Machin, if, VCU	8
	Jared Allen, of, Middle Tenn. State	8
	Steven Duggar, of, Clemson	8
	Jake Madsen, 1b, Ohio	8

PITCHING (Minimum 40 innings pitched)

RK.	PITCHER, TEAM	CLASS	W	L	ERA	G	GS	CG	SV	IP	H	R	ER	BB	SO	WHIP	SO/9	H/9	BB/9
1.	Corey Taylor, Texas Tech	Sr.	4	0	0.31	19	1	0	2	57	36	5	2	13	32	0.85	5.02	5.65	2.04
2.	David Berg, UCLA	Sr.	7	1	0.68	43	0	0	13	67	49	7	5	8	65	0.85	8.77	6.61	1.08
3.	Matt Lees, Virginia Commonwealth	Sr.	6	2	0.74	35	0	0	3	61	41	13	5	14	52	0.90	7.67	6.05	2.07
4.	Colin Kober, McNeese State	So.	6	1	1.03	27	0	0	9	53	35	7	6	10	54	0.85	9.23	5.98	1.71
5.	Luke Vandermaten, Iowa	Jr.	2	0	1.06	22	0	0	4	42	32	6	5	15	23	1.11	4.89	6.80	3.19
6.	Tyler Jay, Illinois	Jr.	5	2	1.08	30	2	0	14	67	40	8	8	7	76	0.70	10.26	5.40	0.94
7.	Spencer Henderson, UC Davis	Jr.	3	1	1.12	17	0	0	0	40	32	9	5	6	29	0.94	6.47	7.14	1.34
8.	Luke Gillingham, Navy	Jr.	8	1	1.19	12	12	5	0	83	44	14	11	14	111	0.70	11.99	4.75	1.51
9.	Ty Nichols, Sacramento State	Sr.	6	0	1.23	21	9	0	0	80	50	16	11	22	54	0.90	6.05	5.60	2.46
10.	Kyle Wright, Vanderbilt	Fr.	6	1	1.23	29	3	0	4	59	36	11	8	23	62	1.01	9.51	5.52	3.53
11.	Brandon Koch, Dallas Baptist	Jr.	3	2	1.26	30	0	0	14	43	23	8	6	24	76	1.09	15.91	4.81	5.02
12.	Michael Freeman, Oklahoma State	Sr.	10	3	1.31	15	15	4	0	110	72	26	16	29	97	0.92	7.96	5.91	2.38
13.	Bryan Young, Missouri State	So.	7	0	1.31	30	0	0	16	41	29	8	6	14	51	1.04	11.10	6.31	3.05
14.	Taylor Lewis, Florida	Jr.	6	2	1.33	31	0	0	7	54	42	15	8	15	32	1.06	5.33	7.00	2.50
15.	Trey Teakell, Texas Christian	Sr.	3	0	1.35	30	0	0	1	53	39	10	8	8	47	0.88	7.93	6.58	1.35
16.	Justin Sinibaldi, Nicholls State	Jr.	10	1	1.40	13	12	2	0	77	70	18	12	16	54	1.11	6.28	8.15	1.86
17.	Grant Borne, Nicholls State	Jr.	6	5	1.48	15	15	3	0	91	65	27	15	40	84	1.15	8.28	6.41	3.94
18.	Conrad Wozniak, UMBC	Jr.	4	1	1.48	12	12	3	0	73	64	20	12	19	56	1.14	6.90	7.89	2.34
19.	Ben Taylor, South Alabama	Sr.	6	3	1.48	25	0	0	7	43	26	8	7	13	68	0.91	14.34	5.48	2.74
20.	Conor Lourey, High Point	Sr.	4	1	1.51	17	6	1	1	66	48	12	11	21	72	1.05	9.87	6.58	2.88
21.	Matt Quintana, Siena	Sr.	2	2	1.51	20	4	2	5	60	37	14	10	14	64	0.85	9.65	5.58	2.11
22.	Matt Dennis, Bradley	So.	3	0	1.51	26	0	0	12	48	31	8	8	19	45	1.05	8.50	5.85	3.59
23.	Logan Cozart, Ohio	Sr.	7	1	1.52	31	0	0	13	71	38	16	12	25	80	0.89	10.14	4.82	3.17
24.	Glenn Otto, Rice	Fr.	2	0	1.54	23	2	0	1	41	20	9	7	28	65	1.17	14.27	4.39	6.15
25.	James McMahon, Southern Miss.	Sr.	11	1	1.56	15	15	3	0	92	66	18	16	22	60	0.95	5.85	6.43	2.14
26.	Nick Hibbing, Iowa	Sr.	4	1	1.57	25	0	0	8	52	30	9	5	47	0.68	8.19	5.23	0.87	
27.	Remey Reed, Oklahoma State	So.	3	2	1.57	23	5	0	0	46	40	14	8	13	30	1.15	5.87	7.83	2.54
28.	Thomas Eshelman, Cal State Fullerton	Jr.	8	5	1.58	19	18	5	1	137	105	31	24	7	139	0.82	9.13	6.90	0.46
29.	Garrett Cleavinger, Oregon	Jr.	6	2	1.58	37	0	0	9	40	20	7	7	18	66	0.95	14.85	4.50	4.05
30.	Josh Sborz, Virginia	Jr.	7	2	1.60	33	3	1	15	73	41	16	13	25	62	0.90	7.64	5.05	3.08
31.	Justin Aungst, St. Joseph's	Fr.	5	0	1.60	16	4	0	1	51	41	14	9	15	47	1.11	8.35	7.28	2.66
32.	Dylan Moore, Louisiana-Lafayette	Fr.	3	3	1.60	32	0	0	13	51	39	9	9	16	40	1.09	7.11	6.93	2.84
33.	Jacob Evans, Oklahoma	Jr.	6	1	1.67	28	0	0	8	43	36	11	8	10	53	1.07	11.09	7.53	2.09
34.	Ian Hamilton, Washington State	So.	1	4	1.67	27	0	0	13	43	33	14	8	17	37	1.16	7.74	6.91	3.56
35.	Jordan Ramsey, UNC Wilmington	Sr.	8	2	1.69	28	0	0	7	48	33	13	9	11	62	0.92	11.63	6.19	2.06

RK.	PITCHER, TEAM	CLASS	W	L	ERA	G	GS	CG	SV	IP	H	R	ER	BB	SO	WHIP	SO/9	H/9	BB/9
36.	Andrew Frankenreider, Northern Ill.	So.	2	2	1.69	26	0	0	9	43	23	13	8	11	40	0.80	8.44	4.85	2.32
37.	Mike Shawaryn, Maryland	So.	13	2	1.71	17	17	0	0	116	85	28	22	29	138	0.98	10.71	6.59	2.25
38.	Mike Reitcheck, Pennsylvania	So.	5	3	1.72	9	7	1	0	58	51	20	11	14	34	1.13	5.31	7.96	2.18
39.	Taylor Clarke, College of Charleston	Jr.	13	1	1.73	17	16	2	1	114	76	28	22	14	143	0.79	11.26	5.98	1.10
40.	Kevin Hill, South Alabama	Sr.	10	0	1.73	13	13	4	0	94	70	20	18	18	107	1.15	10.28	6.73	3.65
41.	Kevin Duchene, Illinois	Jr.	11	2	1.75	15	15	1	0	103	89	27	20	18	88	1.04	7.71	7.80	1.58
42.	Brendan McKay, Louisville	Fr.	9	3	1.77	20	13	0	4	97	53	26	19	34	117	0.90	10.89	4.93	3.17
43.	Brian McAfee, Cornell	Sr.	5	2	1.77	9	9	4	0	56	43	15	11	6	38	0.88	6.11	6.91	0.96
44.	Matthew Naylor, North Florida	So.	8	0	1.78	28	0	0	0	66	56	15	13	19	37	1.14	5.07	7.68	2.60
45.	Joe Mockbee, Michigan State	So.	6	2	1.78	25	0	0	2	51	43	17	10	17	50	1.18	8.88	7.64	3.02
46.	Hunter Williams, North Carolina	Fr.	4	2	1.79	14	9	1	0	40	28	13	8	23	35	1.26	7.81	6.25	5.13
47.	Matthew Crownover, Clemson	Jr.	10	3	1.82	16	16	0	0	109	72	28	22	37	108	1.00	8.92	5.94	3.06
48.	Tommy DeJuneas, North Carolina State	Fr.	3	3	1.82	24	0	0	6	40	20	15	8	25	57	1.13	12.93	4.54	5.67
49.	Grant Dyer, UCLA	So.	4	2	1.83	42	1	0	0	59	36	13	12	15	65	0.86	9.92	5.49	2.29
50.	Carson Fulmer, Vanderbilt	Jr.	14	2	1.83	19	19	3	0	128	81	32	26	50	167	1.03	11.77	5.71	3.52
51.	Dominic Moreno, Texas Tech	Sr.	3	3	1.85	24	2	0	6	58	54	16	12	19	73	1.25	11.26	8.33	2.93
52.	Tyler Brashears, Hawaii	Jr.	8	5	1.86	15	15	0	0	102	90	32	21	19	68	1.07	6.02	7.97	1.68
53.	Kevin Elder, Western Kentucky	So.	1	1	1.87	23	0	0	2	43	32	14	9	16	41	1.11	8.52	6.65	3.32
54.	Mitchell Traver, Texas Christian	So.	9	2	1.89	16	14	0	0	76	49	23	16	26	77	0.98	9.08	5.78	3.07
55.	Conner O'Neil, Cal State Northridge	So.	3	2	1.89	28	3	0	12	62	42	16	13	18	64	0.97	9.29	6.10	2.61
56.	Sean Watkins, Loyola Marymount	Fr.	4	1	1.89	17	9	0	0	57	41	14	12	23	49	1.12	7.74	6.47	3.63
57.	Jake Shull, Fresno State	Jr.	5	5	1.90	26	7	2	6	71	54	24	15	25	43	1.11	5.45	6.85	3.17
58.	Andrew Moore, Oregon State	Jr.	7	2	1.91	16	16	3	0	122	86	31	26	21	111	0.87	8.17	6.33	1.54
59.	Thomas Hackimer, St. John's	Jr.	4	1	1.92	35	0	0	15	52	31	13	11	23	55	1.05	9.58	5.40	4.01
60.	Matt Vaka, North Florida	Fr.	3	1	1.92	13	13	0	0	52	45	12	11	18	21	1.22	3.66	7.84	3.14
61.	Tommy Peterson, South Florida	So.	4	1	1.93	31	1	0	16	47	31	14	10	16	54	1.01	10.41	5.98	3.09
62.	Chris Mathewson, Long Beach State	Fr.	6	6	1.94	13	13	2	0	93	61	24	20	24	80	0.91	7.74	5.90	2.32
63.	Seth Romero, Houston	Fr.	7	4	1.94	22	8	1	7	83	61	33	18	22	92	1.00	9.94	6.59	2.38
64.	Michael Mediavilla, Miami	Fr.	3	2	1.94	37	0	0	0	42	26	13	9	19	53	1.08	11.45	5.62	4.10
65.	Matt Chanin, UMBC	Fr.	5	2	1.96	12	11	0	0	64	61	19	14	20	39	1.26	5.46	8.53	2.80
66.	Matthew Kinney, Belmont	Jr.	3	5	1.96	35	0	0	6	55	42	21	12	17	62	1.07	10.15	6.87	2.78
67.	Alex Lange, Louisiana State	Fr.	12	0	1.97	17	17	2	0	114	87	28	25	46	131	1.17	10.34	6.87	3.63
68.	Sarkis Ohanian, Duke	Sr.	4	1	1.97	25	0	0	6	46	37	12	10	11	62	1.05	12.22	7.29	2.17
69.	Eric Lauer, Kent State	So.	5	4	1.98	15	13	1	0	86	63	29	19	26	103	1.03	10.74	6.57	2.71
70.	Chance Adams, Dallas Baptist	Jr.	7	1	1.98	23	0	0	2	59	41	15	13	13	83	0.92	12.66	6.25	1.98
71.	Carter Love, College of Charleston	Fr.	6	0	1.98	24	0	0	4	41	38	12	9	4	33	1.02	7.24	8.34	0.88
72.	Jared Lyons, Liberty	Sr.	8	2	1.99	16	13	3	0	100	71	27	22	22	100	0.93	9.03	6.41	1.99
73.	Danny Dopico, Florida International	Jr.	3	4	1.99	27	0	0	10	45	25	15	10	20	57	0.99	11.32	4.96	3.97
73.	Jett Meenach, Navy	So.	7	0	1.99	24	0	0	4	45	38	11	10	12	43	1.10	8.54	7.54	2.38
75.	Drasen Johnson, Illinois	Sr.	10	3	2.01	16	16	3	0	117	103	34	26	17	77	1.03	5.94	7.95	1.31
76.	Chase Angelle, Lamar	Sr.	5	6	2.01	14	14	5	0	99	90	28	22	17	65	1.08	5.93	8.21	1.55
77.	Alex Robinett, Army	Sr.	6	5	2.01	11	11	8	0	81	55	22	18	16	92	0.88	10.26	6.14	1.79
78.	Troy Rallings, Washington	Jr.	3	4	2.01	26	3	0	6	72	56	19	16	11	55	0.93	6.91	7.03	1.38
79.	Matt Hall, Missouri State	Jr.	12	2	2.02	19	17	2	1	125	87	36	28	45	171	1.06	12.31	6.26	3.24
80.	Stephen Nogosek, Oregon	So.	6	3	2.02	39	0	0	0	58	38	16	13	34	60	1.24	9.31	5.90	5.28
81.	Luke Harrison, Indiana	Sr.	4	2	2.02	25	2	0	3	49	38	14	11	13	61	1.04	11.20	6.98	2.39
82.	James Kaprielian, UCLA	Jr.	10	4	2.03	17	16	0	0	107	86	32	24	33	114	1.12	9.62	7.26	2.78
83.	Evan Challenger, Georgia Southern	So.	5	3	2.03	14	14	0	0	80	69	33	18	22	58	1.14	6.53	7.76	2.48
84.	Brian Brown, North Carolina State	Fr.	7	3	2.03	15	15	0	0	80	59	24	18	26	78	1.07	8.81	6.67	2.94
85.	Christian Cecilio, San Francisco	Sr.	5	4	2.05	14	14	4	0	110	90	30	25	22	91	1.02	7.47	7.39	1.81
86.	Sean Leland, Louisville	Fr.	4	0	2.05	20	4	0	0	44	32	12	10	19	34	1.16	6.95	6.55	3.89
87.	Anthony Kay, Connecticut	So.	8	6	2.07	17	14	1	1	100	73	35	23	25	96	0.98	8.64	6.57	2.25
88.	Kyle Cedotal, Southeastern La.	Jr.	9	2	2.08	15	15	2	0	100	82	32	23	19	95	1.01	8.58	7.40	1.72
89.	Joe O'Donnell, North Carolina State	So.	7	3	2.08	25	0	0	0	52	37	20	12	20	54	1.10	9.35	6.40	3.46
90.	Zach Jackson, Arkansas	So.	5	1	2.10	27	3	0	9	60	43	18	14	38	89	1.35	13.35	6.45	5.70
91.	Thomas Lowery, Ala.-Birmingham	So.	7	2	2.11	27	0	0	3	55	34	17	13	17	62	0.92	10.08	5.53	2.77
92.	Corey Merrill, Tulane	So.	5	6	2.12	17	16	1	0	102	80	32	24	43	81	1.21	7.15	7.06	3.79
93.	Andrew Vinson, Texas A&M	Jr.	5	2	2.12	35	2	0	5	64	49	17	15	14	64	0.99	9.05	6.93	1.98
94.	Travis Shelley, Winthrop	Sr.	3	0	2.14	32	0	0	4	55	51	15	13	11	46	1.13	7.57	8.40	1.81
95.	Tyler Wilson, Rhode Island	Fr.	6	3	2.16	13	12	2	0	87	57	24	21	27	75	0.96	7.73	5.87	2.78
96.	Brendan King, Holy Cross	So.	3	1	2.16	13	7	1	0	58	47	20	14	11	29	1.01	4.47	7.25	1.85
97.	P.J. Conlon, San Diego	Jr.	6	4	2.17	15	14	0	1	91	64	28	22	25	82	0.97	8.08	6.31	2.46
98.	Miles Chambers, Cal State Fullerton	So.	5	3	2.17	25	2	0	1	62	57	20	15	13	50	1.12	7.22	8.23	1.88
99.	Jake Long, Clemson	Sr.	2	1	2.17	13	7	0	0	50	37	17	12	22	39	1.19	7.07	6.70	3.99
100.	Rayne Raven, Cal State Fullerton	Jr.	7	4	2.18	15	14	1	0	87	74	32	21	28	73	1.18	7.58	7.68	2.91

WINS

RK.	PITCHER, TEAM	W
1.	Carson Fulmer, Vanderbilt	14
2.	Taylor Clarke, Col. of Charleston	13
	Mike Shawaryn, Maryland	13
4.	Preston Morrison, TCU	12

WINS, CONT.

RK.	PITCHER, TEAM	W
	Joseph Camacho, Alabama State	12
	Matt Hall, Missouri State	12
	Alex Lange, LSU	12
8.	Kevin Duchene, Illinois	11

WINS, CONT.

RK.	PITCHER, TEAM	W
	Logan Shore, Florida	11
	Elliot Ashbeck, Bradley	11
	James McMahon, Southern Miss.	11
	Ryan McCormick, St. John's	11

SAVES

RK.	PITCHER, TEAM	SV
1.	Ryan Meisinger, Radford	17
	Eddie Muhl, George Washington	17
3.	Bryan Young, Missouri State	16
	Tyler Peitzmeier, CS Fullerton	16
	Tommy Peterson, South Florida	16
6.	Josh Sborz, Virginia	15
	Thomas Hackimer, St. John's	15
	Stuart Holmes, Nicholls State	15
	Will Stillman, Wofford	15
	Josh Roeder, Nebraska	15

STRIKEOUTS

RK.	PITCHER, TEAM	SO
1.	Matt Hall, Missouri State	171
2.	Carson Fulmer, Vanderbilt	167
3.	Taylor Clarke, Col. of Charleston	143
4.	Thomas Eshelman, Cal St. Fullerton	139
5.	Mike Shawaryn, Maryland	138
6.	Bubba Derby, San Diego State	131
	Alex Lange, LSU	131
8.	Jeff Degano, Indiana State	126

STRIKEOUTS, CONT.

RK.	PITCHER, TEAM	SO
9.	Boomer Biegalski, Florida State	120
	Skyler Genger, Seattle	120

STRIKEOUTS PER NINE INNINGS

RK.	PITCHER, TEAM	SO/9
1.	Brandon Koch, Dallas Baptist	15.91
2.	Garrett Cleavinger, Oregon	14.85
3.	Ryan Burr, Arizona State	14.37
4.	Ben Taylor, South Alabama	14.34
5.	Danny Zandona, Cal Poly	14.29
6.	Glenn Otto, Rice	14.27
7.	Zach Jackson, Arkansas	13.35
8.	Tommy DeJuneas, N.C. State	12.93
9.	Chance Adams, Dallas Baptist	12.66
10.	Matt Hall, Missouri State	12.31

FEWEST HITS PER NINE INNINGS

RK.	PITCHER, TEAM	H/9
1.	Glenn Otto, Rice	4.39
2.	Garrett Cleavinger, Oregon	4.50
3.	Tommy DeJuneas, N.C. State	4.54

FEWEST HITS PER NINE INNINGS, CONT.

RK.	PITCHER, TEAM	H/9
4.	Luke Gillingham, Navy	4.75
5.	Brandon Koch, Dallas Baptist	4.81
6.	Logan Cozart, Ohio	4.82
7.	Andrew Frankenreider, Northern Ill.	4.85
8.	Cory Wilder, N.C. State	4.90
9.	Brendan McKay, Louisville	4.93
10.	Danny Dopico, FIU	4.96

FEWEST WALKS PER NINE INNINGS

RK.	PITCHER, TEAM	BB/9
1.	Thomas Eshelman, CS Fullerton	0.46
2.	Sterling Koerner, FGCU	0.64
3.	Taylor Thurber, Appalachian St.	0.75
4.	Jimmy Boyd, East Carolina	0.76
5.	Griffin Canning, UCLA	0.85
	Bobby Poyner, Florida	0.85
7.	Nick Hibbing, Iowa	0.87
8.	Carter Love, Col. of Charleston	0.88
9.	Jeffrey Stovall, Northwestern St.	0.94
	Thomas Belcher, Indiana	0.94
	Tyler Jay, Illinois	0.94

TEAM LEADERS

SCORING

RK.	TEAM	G	R	R/G
1.	Morehead State	60	505	8.4
2.	Miami	67	547	8.2
3.	Southeast Mo. State	59	473	8.0
4.	Nevada	56	447	8.0
5.	Alabama State	50	390	7.8
6.	North Florida	61	473	7.8
7.	Jackson State	57	441	7.7
8.	Samford	58	435	7.5
9.	Belmont	58	433	7.5
10.	College of Charleston	60	439	7.3
11.	Oral Roberts	57	414	7.3
12.	Austin Peay State	51	364	7.1
13.	Jacksonville State	57	402	7.1
14.	New Mexico	59	416	7.1
15.	Florida	70	489	7.0
16.	UNC Wilmington	59	412	7.0
17.	Western Carolina	51	353	6.9
18.	Richmond	53	365	6.9
19.	Bryant	54	371	6.9
20.	South Dakota State	56	384	6.9
21.	Texas Southern	50	342	6.8
22.	Florida Atlantic	61	417	6.8
23.	Louisiana State	66	451	6.8
24.	Central Michigan	57	389	6.8
25.	Wofford	61	414	6.8
26.	Mercer	58	393	6.8
27.	Wright State	60	406	6.8
28.	Coastal Carolina	60	405	6.8
29.	La Salle	52	351	6.8
30.	Wisconsin-Milwaukee	59	396	6.7
31.	Florida State	65	435	6.7
32.	Canisius	64	427	6.7
33.	Texas A&M	64	424	6.6
34.	Vanderbilt	72	476	6.6
35.	Dallas Baptist	61	402	6.6
36.	Radford	61	402	6.6
37.	Tennessee Tech	55	361	6.6
38.	Oklahoma State	58	380	6.6
39.	IPFW	54	353	6.5
40.	Saint Louis	56	366	6.5
41.	Connecticut	60	389	6.5
42.	Furman	58	376	6.5
43.	Davidson	50	324	6.5
44.	Columbia	51	330	6.5
45.	Elon	54	348	6.4
46.	Towson	54	346	6.4
47.	Norfolk State	43	275	6.4

SCORING, CONT.

RK.	TEAM	G	R	R/G
48.	Illinois	61	389	6.4
49.	Alabama A&M	57	363	6.4
50.	Clemson	61	386	6.3

BATTING AVERAGE

RK.	TEAM	AVG
1.	Morehead State	.332
2.	Oral Roberts	.320
3.	Nevada	.317
4.	Louisiana State	.314
5.	North Florida	.312
6.	New Mexico	.311
7.	Miami	.307
8.	Saint Louis	.307
9.	Jackson State	.304
10.	Samford	.304

HOME RUNS

RK.	TEAM	HR
1.	Samford	85
2.	College of Charleston	75
3.	Belmont	70
	Texas A&M	70
5.	Vanderbilt	69
	Mercer	69
7.	Central Florida	66
	Southeast Missouri State	66
	Morehead State	66
	Florida	66

DOUBLES

RK.	TEAM	2B
1.	Morehead State	172
2.	Vanderbilt	152
3.	Nevada	146
	Louisiana State	146
5.	New Mexico	141
6.	Belmont	136
	Wisconsin-Milwaukee	136
8.	Michigan	133
9.	Oral Roberts	132
10.	Dallas Baptist	131

TRIPLES

RK.	TEAM	3B
1.	Navy	36
2.	Stony Brook	29

TRIPLES, CONT.

RK.	TEAM	3B
3.	Vanderbilt	28
4.	Miami (Ohio)	27
	Creighton	27
6.	James Madison	26
7.	Bryant	25
	Wisconsin-Milwaukee	25
	Pittsburgh	25
	Canisius	25

SLUGGING PERCENTAGE

RK.	TEAM	SLG
1.	Morehead State	.516
2.	Nevada	.491
3.	Samford	.489
4.	College of Charleston	.483
5.	Belmont	.481
6.	Southeast Missouri State	.477
7.	Austin Peay State	.474
8.	UNC Greensboro	.467
9.	Pennsylvania	.464
10.	Central Florida	.462

STOLEN BASES

RK.	TEAM	SB	CS
1.	Wofford	138	34
2.	Texas Southern	136	37
3.	Louisiana State	130	36
4.	Louisville	127	43
5.	Texas Christian	119	45
6.	Campbell	117	32
7.	Maryland-Baltimore County	113	30
8.	Grambling State	112	20
9.	Alcorn State	109	37
10.	Vanderbilt	106	32

WALKS

RK.	TEAM	BB
1.	Florida State	379
2.	Miami	377
3.	Southeast Missouri State	326
4.	Missouri State	317
5.	Jacksonville State	307
6.	Vanderbilt	302
7.	Florida Atlantic	301
8.	New Mexico	298
9.	North Carolina	297
10.	Oregon	294

PITCHING

EARNED RUN AVERAGE

RK.	TEAM	ERA
1.	UCLA	2.17
2.	Texas Christian	2.45
3.	UC Santa Barbara	2.45
4.	Nicholls State	2.47
5.	Illinois	2.55
6.	Cal State Northridge	2.61
7.	Louisville	2.74
8.	Oklahoma State	2.84
9.	Vanderbilt	2.84
10.	Houston	2.89
11.	Cal State Fullerton	2.89
12.	Missouri State	2.91
13.	Virginia Commonwealth	2.92
14.	Connecticut	2.94
15.	North Carolina State	2.95
16.	Iowa	2.95
17.	Sacramento State	2.97
18.	Louisiana State	2.98
19.	Washington	3.01
20.	Oregon State	3.02
21.	Navy	3.04
22.	Texas A&M	3.04
23.	California	3.05
24.	Nebraska	3.12
25.	Southern Mississippi	3.13

EARNED RUN AVERAGE, CONT.

RK.	TEAM	ERA
26.	Notre Dame	3.13
27.	Miami	3.15
28.	Southeastern Louisiana	3.18
29.	Florida	3.18
30.	South Alabama	3.22
31.	Rice	3.22
32.	Long Beach State	3.27
33.	Texas	3.27
34.	Tulane	3.28
35.	Maryland	3.29
36.	Duke	3.29
37.	Oral Roberts	3.30
38.	Maryland-Baltimore County	3.30
39.	East Carolina	3.32
40.	Dallas Baptist	3.32
41.	Texas Tech	3.33
42.	Kent State	3.36
43.	Houston Baptist	3.36
44.	Creighton	3.37
45.	Louisiana-Lafayette	3.37
46.	Bucknell	3.37
47.	Pennsylvania	3.38
48.	George Washington	3.38
49.	Indiana	3.39
50.	Oklahoma	3.39

STRIKEOUTS PER NINE INNINGS

RK.	TEAM	K/9
1.	Vanderbilt	9.6
2.	North Carolina State	9.4
3.	Alabama State	9.3
4.	Missouri State	9.0
5.	Norfolk State	9.0
6.	The Citadel	8.9
7.	Florida State	8.9
8.	Texas A&M	8.9
9.	Louisville	8.9
10.	Charleston Southern	8.8

FEWEST WALKS PER NINE INNINGS

RK.	TEAM	BB/9
1.	Cal State Fullerton	1.70
2.	Florida Gulf Coast	2.06
3.	Sacramento State	2.07
4.	Illinois	2.08
5.	Houston Baptist	2.16
6.	Texas Christian	2.16
7.	UCLA	2.35
8.	Ohio State	2.37
9.	College of Charleston	2.38
10.	Arizona	2.40

FIELDING

FIELDING PERCENTAGE

RK.	TEAM	PCT
1.	Florida	.984
2.	North Florida	.983
3.	San Diego	.981
4.	Loyola Marymount	.980
5.	Nebraska	.979
6.	Illinois-Chicago	.979
7.	Vanderbilt	.979
8.	Texas Christian	.979
9.	Notre Dame	.979
10.	Stony Brook	.978
11.	Iowa	.978
12.	Lipscomb	.978
13.	South Alabama	.978

FIELDING PERCENTAGE, CONT.

RK.	TEAM	PCT
14.	Mississippi State	.978
15.	Lamar	.977
16.	Oregon State	.977
17.	Southeast Missouri State	.977
18.	UCLA	.977
19.	Washington	.977
20.	Missouri State	.976
21.	UC Santa Barbara	.976
22.	Dartmouth	.976
23.	Texas	.976
24.	Louisiana State	.976
25.	Creighton	.976

DOUBLE PLAYS

RK.	TEAM	DP
1.	Notre Dame	75
2.	Coastal Carolina	66
3.	California	65
4.	Arkansas	64
	Alabama-Birmingham	64
6.	North Florida	63
	Mississippi State	63
8.	Illinois	62
9.	Cal State Bakersfield	61
	Tulane	61
	Nevada	61

COLLEGE

Batters: 10 or more at-bats. **Pitchers:** 5 or more innings.

1. VIRGINIA

Coach: Brian O'Connor. **Record:** 44-24.

PLAYER, POS., YEAR	AVG	OBP	SLG	AB	R	2B	3B	HR	RBI	SB
Clement, Ernie, inf, Fr.	.245	.303	.310	229	25	6	3	1	22	3
Cody, Charlie, inf, Fr.	.291	.350	.382	55	9	2	0	1	6	0
Coman, Robbie, c, Jr.	.289	.360	.333	201	15	6	0	1	22	2
Doherty, Kevin, of, Jr.	.215	.354	.308	130	12	5	2	1	23	4
Gerstenmaier, Jack, inf, Fr.	.303	.343	.333	33	2	1	0	0	6	0
Haseley, Adam, of, Fr.	.250	.355	.323	276	56	11	3	1	19	5
La Prise, John, inf, Jr.	.286	.286	.286	14	0	0	0	0	1	0
Lowry, Christian, of, Fr.	.222	.276	.222	81	8	0	0	0	5	4
McCarthy, Joe, of, Jr.	.196	.343	.277	112	19	3	0	2	11	3
Novak, Justin, inf, Fr.	.095	.200	.108	74	12	1	0	0	3	1
Pinero, Daniel, inf, So.	.308	.409	.419	253	60	8	1	6	29	9
Smith, Pavin, 1b, Fr.	.307	.373	.467	270	38	14	4	7	44	2
Thaiss, Matt, c, So.	.323	.413	.512	254	49	18	0	10	64	4
Towns, Kenny, inf, Sr.	.296	.365	.446	267	41	21	2	5	67	2
Woodruff, Thomas, inf, Sr.	.273	.375	.291	55	11	1	0	0	7	5

PITCHER, YEAR	W	L	ERA	G	GS	SV	IP	H	BB	SO
Bettinger, Alec, So.	5	5	5.40	27	4	3	53	51	23	63
Casey, Derek, Fr.	4	1	3.06	10	6	0	32	27	13	27
Doherty, Kevin, Jr.	3	1	3.40	23	0	3	45	29	10	37
Doyle, Tommy, Fr.	1	1	3.47	16	0	0	23	18	18	15
Haseley, Adam, Fr.	2	1	2.20	11	5	1	29	28	11	17
Jones, Connor, So.	7	3	3.19	18	18	0	116	94	52	113
Kirby, Nathan, Jr.	5	3	2.53	12	11	1	64	55	32	81
Roberts, Jack, So.	1	1	6.08	16	2	1	24	18	20	22
Rosenberger, David, Jr.	3	0	5.03	18	0	1	34	45	10	19
Sborz, Josh, Jr.	7	2	1.60	33	3	15	73	41	25	62
Sousa, Bennett, Fr.	1	0	5.14	7	0	0	7	7	13	2
Waddell, Brandon, Jr.	5	5	3.93	19	19	0	110	114	49	89

2. VANDERBILT

Coach: Tim Corbin. **Record:** 51-21.

PLAYER, POS., YEAR	AVG	OBP	SLG	AB	R	2B	3B	HR	RBI	SB
Campbell, Tyler, inf, Jr.	.229	.297	.286	210	23	4	1	2	26	6
Coleman, Ro, inf, So.	.295	.402	.394	241	52	15	3	1	25	5
Delay, Jason, c, So.	.283	.373	.394	99	18	8	0	1	24	0
Ellison, Karl, c, So.	.215	.291	.282	149	16	4	0	2	15	1
Green, Tyler, inf, Fr.	.238	.304	.238	21	2	0	0	0	0	0
Kendall, Jeren, of, Fr.	.281	.394	.530	185	34	10	6	8	40	19
Murfee, Penn, inf, Fr.	.256	.330	.385	78	8	5	1	1	11	2
Reynolds, Bryan, of, So.	.318	.388	.462	286	56	18	4	5	49	17
Rodgers, Nolan, of, Fr.	.247	.396	.288	73	10	3	0	0	6	4
Sabino, Liam, inf, Fr.	.240	.333	.320	25	5	2	0	0	3	2
Smith, Kyle, inf, Fr.	.063	.211	.125	16	1	1	0	0	2	1
Swanson, Dansby, inf, Jr.	.335	.423	.623	281	76	24	6	15	64	16
Toffey, Will, inf, Fr.	.294	.380	.420	255	45	20	0	4	49	8
Wiel, Zander, inf, Jr.	.316	.406	.571	275	59	19	3	15	68	13
Wiseman, Rhett, of, Jr.	.317	.415	.566	290	70	19	4	15	49	12

PITCHER, YEAR	W	L	ERA	G	GS	SV	IP	H	BB	SO
Abraham, Joey, Fr.	0	0	7.94	6	0	0	6	8	10	9
Bowden, Ben, So.	6	1	2.89	26	0	2	37	32	14	49
Buehler, Walker, Jr.	5	2	2.95	16	16	0	88	85	30	92
Ferguson, Tyler, Jr.	0	1	6.30	15	3	0	20	11	35	24
Fulmer, Carson, Jr.	14	2	1.83	19	19	0	128	81	50	167
Johnson, Ryan, Fr.	5	1	3.02	15	5	0	54	50	12	33
Kilichowski, John, So.	3	4	2.84	17	10	2	67	51	15	64
McCarty, Aubrey, Fr.	0	0	3.00	5	0	0	6	2	2	6
Pfeifer, Philip, Jr.	6	5	3.55	27	9	5	96	81	44	118
Ruppenthal, Matt, Fr.	0	0	2.70	8	0	0	10	5	9	10
Sheffield, Jordan, Fr.	5	2	2.85	22	6	0	60	39	43	55
Snider, Collin, Fr.	0	0	2.41	16	0	0	19	16	4	9
Wright, Kyle, Fr.	6	1	1.23	29	3	4	59	36	23	62

3. FLORIDA

Coach: Kevin O'Sullivan. **Record:** 52-18.

PLAYER, POS., YEAR	AVG	OBP	SLG	AB	R	2B	3B	HR	RBI	SB
Alonso, Peter, inf, So.	.301	.398	.504	143	33	10	2	5	32	0
Bader, Harrison, of, Jr.	.297	.393	.566	256	53	16	1	17	66	8
Browning, Logan, of, Fr.	.200	.273	.233	30	6	1	0	0	1	3
Fahrman, Mike, c, Jr.	.500	.546	.600	10	4	1	0	0	2	0
Guthrie, Dalton, inf, Fr.	.287	.362	.365	282	55	14	1	2	26	6
Hicks, Christian, inf, Fr.	.140	.275	.298	57	14	3	0	2	10	0
Kolozsvary, Mark, c, Fr.	.278	.316	.333	18	4	1	0	0	1	0
Lane, Taylor, inf, Fr.	.250	.250	.333	12	2	1	0	0	2	0
Larson, Ryan, of, So.	.305	.401	.365	167	28	5	1	1	25	7
Martin, Richie, inf, Jr.	.291	.399	.430	265	63	11	4	6	36	20
Puk, A.J., dh, So.	.261	.346	.391	23	2	3	0	0	1	0
Reed, Buddy, of, So.	.305	.367	.433	282	51	14	5	4	47	18
Rivera, Mike, c, Fr.	.271	.337	.369	225	31	11	1	3	48	2
Schwarz, J.J., c, Fr.	.332	.398	.629	256	60	16	3	18	73	1
Sternagel, John, inf, So.	.178	.327	.311	45	9	1	1	1	8	1
Tobias, Josh, inf, Sr.	.355	.435	.524	231	60	14	5	5	46	11
Vasquez, Jeremy, 1b, Fr.	.339	.424	.459	109	11	7	2	2	20	1

PITCHER, YEAR	W	L	ERA	G	GS	SV	IP	H	BB	SO
Anderson, Shaun, So.	0	0	4.09	16	1	0	22	20	6	21
Browning, Logan, Fr.	1	0	7.27	9	0	0	9	8	7	6
Dunning, Dane, So.	5	2	4.03	16	14	0	60	48	23	55
Faedo, Alex, Fr.	6	1	3.23	19	12	0	61	59	16	59
Hanhold, Eric, Jr.	1	0	4.26	14	4	0	25	28	11	23
Lewis, Taylor, Jr.	6	2	1.33	31	0	7	54	42	15	32
Morales, Brett, So.	1	0	4.50	6	3	0	14	9	4	11
Poyner, Bobby, Sr.	5	2	2.56	26	1	4	63	52	6	58
Puk, A.J., So.	9	4	3.81	17	14	0	78	59	35	104
Rhodes, Aaron, Jr.	2	0	3.73	17	1	0	31	21	14	31
Rubio, Frank, So.	0	1	3.20	15	0	0	20	20	3	6
Shore, Logan, So.	11	6	2.72	19	19	0	112	97	24	84
Snead, Kirby, So.	1	0	3.15	28	0	1	34	36	6	33
Vinson, Mike, So.	2	0	3.00	7	0	0	6	3	3	4
Young, Danny, Jr.	2	0	2.15	20	1	2	29	29	9	24

4. TEXAS CHRISTIAN

Coach: Jim Schlossnagle. **Record:** 51-15.

PLAYER, POS., YEAR	AVG	OBP	SLG	AB	R	2B	3B	HR	RBI	SB
Barzilli, Elliott, inf, So.	.250	.315	.340	100	14	1	1	2	12	4
Beck, Connor, of, Fr.	.200	.250	.267	15	0	1	0	0	0	0
Brown, Nolan, of, Jr.	.302	.371	.373	225	46	11	1	1	30	19
Crain, Garrett, inf, Sr.	.264	.337	.339	242	45	11	2	1	30	8
Fagnan, Jeremie, of, Sr.	.265	.353	.374	166	29	6	0	4	26	10
Jones, Cody, of, Sr.	.353	.464	.476	252	63	14	1	5	34	33
Jones, Keaton, inf, Sr.	.251	.333	.316	231	32	7	1	2	40	8
Landestoy, Michael, inf, Fr.	.000	.048	.000	20	0	0	0	0	1	1
Odell, Derek, inf, Sr.	.292	.365	.373	236	34	10	0	3	42	9
Plunkett, Zack, c, Fr.	.149	.216	.213	47	4	0	0	1	8	0
Skoug, Evan, c, Fr.	.285	.365	.426	256	44	15	0	7	46	5
Steinhagen, Dane, of, Jr.	.289	.346	.353	218	26	6	4	0	28	10
Wade, Austen, of, Fr.	.182	.550	.182	11	6	0	0	0	0	0
Wanhanen, Connor, of, Fr.	.329	.420	.389	216	42	4	3	1	40	11
Williams, Evan, of, Jr.	.381	.480	.429	21	3	1	0	0	2	1

PITCHER, YEAR	W	L	ERA	G	GS	SV	IP	H	BB	SO
Alexander, Tyler, So.	6	3	3.07	17	15	0	94	92	10	72
Burnett, Ryan, Fr.	1	0	2.19	10	0	0	12	15	2	15
Evans, Travis, Sr.	1	0	4.50	12	0	0	8	8	4	5
Ferrell, Riley, Jr.	1	3	2.56	32	0	14	32	10	20	53
Gooch, Drew, Jr.	1	0	5.87	9	0	0	8	12	5	5
Guilory, Preston, Jr.	1	0	0.34	20	0	2	26	15	7	23
Howard, Brian, So.	4	0	3.52	17	4	0	46	44	14	46
Morrison, Preston, Sr.	12	3	2.51	19	17	0	122	100	22	91
Teakell, Trey, Sr.	3	0	1.35	30	0	1	53	39	8	47
Traver, Mitchell, So.	9	2	1.89	16	14	0	76	49	26	77
Trieglaff, Brian, Jr.	3	1	3.18	20	0	0	28	26	5	34
Young, Alex, Jr.	9	3	2.22	17	16	0	97	75	22	103

5. LOUISIANA STATE

Coach: Paul Mainieri. **Record:** 54-12.

PLAYER, POS., YEAR	AVG	OBP	SLG	AB	R	2B	3B	HR	RBI	SB
Bregman, Alex, ss, Jr.	.323	.412	.535	260	59	22	3	9	49	38
Byrd, Grayson, inf, Fr.	.212	.278	.242	33	9	1	0	0	9	0
Chinea, Chris, c, Jr.	.344	.376	.539	256	42	17	0	11	58	1
Foster, Jared, of, Sr.	.278	.332	.495	212	37	12	2	10	35	10
Fraley, Jake, of, So.	.307	.372	.427	225	50	11	5	2	35	23
Hale, Conner, inf, Sr.	.327	.373	.460	263	49	17	3	4	56	1
Jordan, Beau, of, Fr.	.219	.359	.250	32	3	1	0	0	4	1
Jordan, Bryce, inf, Fr.	.130	.290	.261	23	5	3	0	0	6	0
Laird, Mark, of, Jr.	.323	.388	.381	260	53	10	1	1	24	24
Papierski, Michael, c, Fr.	.214	.426	.333	42	8	2	0	1	10	1
Robertson, Kramer, inf, So.	.232	.339	.286	56	10	1	1	0	5	1
Sciambra, Chris, of, Sr.	.307	.358	.460	163	30	10	3	3	28	4
Scivicque, Kade, c, Sr.	.355	.398	.521	234	33	21	0	6	48	0
Stevenson, Andrew, of, Jr.	.348	.396	.453	247	53	13	5	1	24	26
Zardon, Danny, inf, So.	.288	.367	.414	111	9	5	0	3	23	0

PITCHER, YEAR	W	L	ERA	G	GS	SV	IP	H	BB	SO
Bain, Austin, Fr.	2	3	3.95	21	6	0	55	45	23	56
Bouman, Kyle, Sr.	1	1	6.08	13	6	0	24	29	9	20
Bugg, Parker, So.	1	2	1.75	25	0	3	36	23	13	35
Cartwright, Alden, So.	0	0	4.05	26	1	0	20	24	4	29
Devall, Hunter, Jr.	2	0	4.02	18	1	0	16	13	5	15
Godfrey, Jake, Fr.	7	1	4.61	21	9	0	55	59	33	39
Lange, Alex, Fr.	12	0	1.97	17	17	0	114	87	46	131
Newman, Hunter, So.	3	0	0.49	24	0	4	37	26	13	34
Norman, Doug, Fr.	5	1	2.04	21	3	0	35	33	6	25
Person, Zac, Fr.	2	0	3.98	31	2	0	32	22	12	36
Poche', Jared, So.	9	2	3.05	18	18	0	109	104	25	72
Reynolds, Russell, So.	6	0	2.95	20	3	0	37	25	17	25
Stallings, Jesse, Fr.	1	2	2.73	31	0	12	33	24	12	26
Strall, Collin, So.	3	0	3.93	22	0	0	18	15	10	17

6. MIAMI

Coach: Jim Morris. **Record:** 50-17.

PLAYER, POS., YEAR	AVG	OBP	SLG	AB	R	2B	3B	HR	RBI	SB
Abreu, Willie, of, So.	.288	.381	.419	229	44	10	1	6	47	4
Barr, Christopher, 1b, Jr.	.306	.397	.403	206	44	7	5	1	32	14
Chester, Carl, of, Fr.	.267	.355	.408	191	37	10	1	5	25	11
Collins, Zack, c, So.	.302	.445	.587	242	61	14	5	15	70	7
Crocitto, Peter, c, Fr.	.389	.421	.611	18	4	4	0	0	4	0
Diaz, Sebastian, inf, So.	.364	.385	.364	11	3	0	0	0	3	1
Eusebio, Ricky, of, Jr.	.286	.454	.394	231	70	15	2	2	29	19
Heyward, Jacob, of, So.	.327	.440	.473	110	37	4	0	4	24	7
Iskenderian, George, inf, Jr.	.364	.459	.476	250	71	15	2	3	55	23
Kennedy, Garrett, c, Sr.	.320	.435	.473	222	53	11	1	7	51	1
Lopez, Brandon, inf, Jr.	.303	.417	.382	165	29	9	2	0	23	1
Michelangeli, Edgar, inf, So.	.231	.338	.292	65	10	4	0	0	6	1
Rosier, Malik, of, Fr.	.294	.368	.471	17	3	0	0	1	3	0
Ruiz, John, inf, So.	.315	.356	.361	108	16	3	1	0	19	0
Smith, Justin, of, Fr.	.237	.370	.263	38	6	1	0	0	1	0
Thompson, David, inf, Jr.	.328	.434	.640	253	59	18	2	19	90	1

PITCHER, YEAR	W	L	ERA	G	GS	SV	IP	H	BB	SO
Abrams, Sam, Sr.	0	2	2.38	16	0	0	23	19	11	19
Beauprez, Derik, So.	3	2	5.63	19	4	0	32	25	21	29
Briggi, Daniel, Sr.	1	0	1.76	22	0	0	31	13	15	26
Garcia, Bryan, So.	6	2	2.50	35	0	10	40	29	20	38
Garcia, Danny, So.	7	1	3.69	23	11	0	83	88	17	80
Hammond, Cooper, So.	5	1	2.25	37	0	2	40	40	9	30
Honiotes, Andy, Fr.	0	0	0.00	7	0	0	8	4	6	8
Lepore, Jesse, Fr.	0	0	1.93	10	0	0	14	13	7	10
Mediavilla, Michael, Fr.	3	2	1.94	37	0	0	42	26	19	53
Otero, Ryan, Sr.	0	0	4.70	14	2	1	23	19	7	12
Sosa, Enrique, Jr.	7	5	4.35	17	17	0	81	79	32	71
Suarez, Andrew, Jr.	9	2	3.48	16	15	0	85	87	22	78
Woodrey, Thomas, Jr.	7	2	2.88	17	17	0	103	89	24	62

7. UCLA

Coach: John Savage. **Record:** 45-16.

PLAYER, POS., YEAR	AVG	OBP	SLG	AB	R	2B	3B	HR	RBI	SB
Bono, Christoph, of, Jr.	.241	.332	.397	199	33	13	6	2	30	5
Bouchard, Sean, inf, Fr.	.239	.352	.370	92	9	4	1	2	9	4
Chatterton, Trent, inf, Jr.	.279	.359	.368	190	36	11	0	2	28	0
Hazard, Justin, inf, Jr.	.214	.313	.262	42	2	2	0	0	4	1
Keck, Chris, inf, Sr.	.293	.389	.483	232	43	21	1	7	47	0
Kramer, Kevin, inf, Jr.	.323	.423	.476	254	55	14	2	7	34	7
Miller Jr., Darrell, c, Jr.	.257	.324	.351	191	19	12	0	2	27	0
Moore, Ty, of, Jr.	.342	.428	.479	234	44	12	1	6	51	7
Persico, Luke, inf, So.	.285	.357	.386	249	41	16	0	3	43	11
Peterson, Kort, of, So.	.274	.341	.360	164	26	10	2	0	17	15
Stephens, Brett, of, So.	.298	.382	.424	198	42	11	4	2	22	12
Urabe, Brett, inf, Jr.	.297	.381	.378	37	8	3	0	0	6	4
Valaika, Nick, inf, Fr.	.150	.150	.200	20	2	1	0	0	2	0

PITCHER, YEAR	W	L	ERA	G	GS	SV	IP	H	BB	SO
Berg, David, Sr.	7	1	0.68	43	0	13	67	49	8	65
Bird, Jake, Fr.	1	1	1.38	9	0	0	13	10	5	5
Burke, Scott, So.	0	0	5.40	9	0	0	7	5	3	6
Canning, Griffin, Fr.	7	1	2.97	15	11	0	64	54	6	66
Ceja, Moises, So.	0	0	1.80	4	0	0	5	2	0	3
Dyer, Grant, So.	4	2	1.83	42	1	0	59	36	15	65
Forbes, Tucker, So.	1	0	2.11	38	0	0	38	29	9	45
Kaprielian, James, Jr.	10	4	2.03	17	16	0	107	86	33	114
Poteet, Cody, Jr.	7	1	2.45	27	13	0	73	62	30	68
Virant, Hunter, So.	0	1	3.45	23	4	0	29	28	13	16
Watson, Grant, Sr.	8	5	2.30	16	16	0	98	80	21	66

8. ILLINOIS

Coach: Dan Hartleb. **Record:** 50-10.

PLAYER, POS., YEAR	AVG	OBP	SLG	AB	R	2B	3B	HR	RBI	SB
Fletcher, Casey, inf, Jr.	.326	.423	.414	227	48	7	2	3	33	9
Goldstein, Jason, c, Jr.	.286	.369	.476	206	36	15	0	8	47	2
James, Matthew, inf, So.	.261	.314	.457	92	14	4	1	4	17	1
Kerian, David, inf, Sr.	.367	.462	.667	207	46	10	2	16	52	9
Kolakowski, Zack, inf, So.	.050	.050	.050	20	4	0	0	0	2	0
Krug, Will, of, Sr.	.237	.306	.305	177	33	7	1	1	22	14
McInerney, Pat, of, So.	.290	.374	.425	186	32	10	0	5	34	2
Nagle, Ryan, inf, Jr.	.337	.399	.447	255	45	19	0	3	34	11
Norris-Jones, Kelly, c, Sr.	.133	.409	.267	15	2	0	1	0	4	0
Roper, Reid, inf, Sr.	.293	.406	.487	232	49	7	4	10	49	6
Roper, Ryne, inf, So.	.245	.311	.316	212	23	12	0	1	30	2
Rowbottom, Dan, of, Fr.	.385	.429	.385	13	3	0	0	0	2	0
Walton, Adam, inf, So.	.289	.353	.395	263	50	13	3	3	31	11

PITCHER, YEAR	W	L	ERA	G	GS	SV	IP	H	BB	SO
Blackburn, Nick, Jr.	3	0	2.22	20	0	3	24	23	3	19
Duchene, Kevin, Jr.	11	2	1.75	15	15	0	103	89	18	88
Hayes, Doug, Fr.	0	0	7.20	5	0	0	5	8	5	1
Jay, Tyler, Jr.	5	2	1.08	30	2	14	67	40	7	76
Johnson, Drasen, Sr.	10	3	2.01	16	16	0	117	103	17	77
Kravetz, John, Sr.	5	0	3.35	14	14	0	81	80	13	42
Mamlic, Andrew, Jr.	2	0	4.91	18	0	0	18	23	8	19
McDonnell, Rob, Sr.	7	2	2.28	17	12	0	75	57	29	70
Naso Jr., Charlie, Jr.	0	0	8.44	6	0	0	5	9	5	0
Nielsen, J.D., Jr.	3	1	2.92	24	0	2	25	20	12	24
Sedlock, Cody, So.	4	0	4.02	21	2	0	31	35	10	29

9. CAL STATE FULLERTON

Coach: Rick VanderHook. **Record:** 39-25.

PLAYER, POS., YEAR	AVG	OBP	SLG	AB	R	2B	3B	HR	RBI	SB
Blaser, Dalton, inf, Jr.	.256	.340	.326	86	6	6	0	0	7	1
Bravo, Jerrod, inf, Jr.	.318	.451	.405	148	28	9	2	0	25	5
Bryant, Taylor, inf, So.	.193	.333	.266	109	13	2	0	2	12	0
Buis, Turner, inf, Fr.	.273	.273	.546	11	2	0	0	1	1	0
Cullen, Hunter, of, So.	.225	.238	.250	40	6	1	0	0	4	0
Estill, Josh, inf, So.	.283	.362	.447	152	17	8	1	5	31	0
Hildebrandt, Tristan, inf, Fr.	.136	.208	.205	44	7	1	1	0	3	1
Hudgins, Chris, c, Fr.	.204	.302	.259	54	6	3	0	0	8	0
Hurst, Scott, of, Fr.	.250	.356	.347	124	13	3	3	1	14	5
Jefferies, Jake, inf, Jr.	.244	.300	.285	123	14	5	0	0	13	3
Kennedy, A.J., c, Jr.	.171	.260	.223	175	14	9	0	0	19	0

PLAYER, POS., YEAR	AVG	OBP	SLG	AB	R	2B	3B	HR	RBI	SB
Olmedo-Barrera, David, of, Jr.	.325	.427	.573	206	45	9	6	10	46	14
Pinkston, Tanner, inf, Jr.	.256	.316	.331	121	13	9	0	0	18	5
Richards, Timmy, inf, So.	.229	.375	.309	175	32	9	1	1	26	8
Stieb, Tyler, of, Jr.	.297	.372	.362	229	28	11	2	0	23	12
Vargas, Josh, of, Jr.	.332	.437	.392	199	42	8	2	0	16	13
Vaught, Dustin, inf, Jr.	.253	.379	.272	158	32	3	0	0	14	2

PITCHER, YEAR	W	L	ERA	G	GS	SV	IP	H	BB	SO
Chambers, Miles, So.	5	3	2.17	25	2	1	62	57	13	50
Eshelman, Thomas, Jr.	8	5	2.00	19	18	1	137	105	7	139
Garza, Justin, Jr.	4	3	3.05	12	12	0	65	73	14	53
Gavin, John, Fr.	7	3	3.66	17	17	0	86	81	25	67
Gibbs, Maxwell, So.	2	2	3.18	28	0	0	34	29	11	32
Hockin, Chad, So.	0	0	2.95	18	1	0	18	21	3	17
Kuhl, Willie, Sr.	2	0	3.94	27	0	0	30	34	9	34
Murray, Kyle, Jr.	1	1	6.48	5	2	0	8	12	2	5
Omana, Henry, Jr.	0	0	11.81	7	0	0	5	9	1	6
Peitzmeier, Tyler, Sr.	5	4	2.56	31	1	16	60	55	11	61
Seabold, Connor, Fr.	5	4	3.26	22	11	1	69	70	12	76
Stillwagon, Shane, So.	0	0	6.14	7	0	0	7	11	2	6

10. LOUISVILLE

Coach: Dan McDonnell. **Record:** 47-18

PLAYER, POS., YEAR	AVG	OBP	SLG	AB	R	2B	3B	HR	RBI	SB
Fitch, Colby, c, Fr.	.269	.321	.346	78	6	4	1	0	14	0
Hairston, Devin, ss, Fr.	.212	.274	.275	189	26	9	0	1	32	2
Lucas, Zach, inf, Sr.	.249	.350	.363	245	38	13	0	5	25	19
Lyman, Colin, of, So.	.059	.200	.088	34	8	1	0	0	1	2
McKay, Brendan, 1b/p, Fr.	.308	.418	.431	211	32	14	0	4	34	4
Ray, Corey, of, So.	.325	.389	.543	265	46	15	5	11	56	34
Rosenbaum, Danny, inf, Jr.	.270	.370	.389	126	16	7	1	2	14	1
Smith, Will, inf, So.	.242	.333	.332	178	25	8	1	2	15	2
Solak, Nick, inf, So.	.324	.416	.439	244	47	15	2	3	40	18
Summers, Ryan, c, Fr.	.226	.318	.312	93	16	3	1	1	6	10
Taylor, Logan, of, So.	.358	.451	.448	67	16	3	0	1	13	8
Tiberi, Blake, inf, Fr.	.261	.330	.424	92	12	3	0	4	18	1
White, Mike, of, Sr.	.256	.336	.376	133	28	10	0	2	16	11
Whiting, Sutton, inf, Sr.	.302	.407	.369	252	39	13	2	0	27	15

PITCHER, YEAR	W	L	ERA	G	GS	SV	P	H	BB	SO
Baird, Butch, Fr.	1	0	4.00	14	0	0	8	3	7	8
Burdi, Zack, So.	6	1	0.92	20	0	9	29	16	8	30
Funkhouser, Kyle, Jr.	8	5	3.20	17	17	0	112	97	45	104
Harrington, Drew, So.	3	1	0.29	18	1	4	31	11	12	42
Henzman, Lincoln, Fr.	5	2	2.32	28	2	2	54	45	11	47
Kidston, Anthony, Jr.	0	4	6.48	12	8	0	42	50	28	47
Leland, Sean, Fr.	4	0	2.05	20	4	0	44	32	19	34
McClure, Kade, Fr.	1	1	4.00	16	4	2	32	28	14	37
McKay, Brendan, Fr.	9	3	1.77	20	13	4	97	53	34	117
Rogers, Josh, So.	8	1	3.36	16	16	0	94	90	25	82
Sparger, Jake, So.	1	0	2.08	14	0	0	17	15	5	9
Strader, Robert, So.	1	0	1.27	20	0	0	21	9	20	21

11. ARKANSAS

Coach: Dave Van Horn. **Record:** 40-25.

PLAYER, POS., YEAR	AVG	OBP	SLG	AB	R	2B	3B	HR	RBI	SB
Benintendi, Andrew, of, So.	.376	.488	.717	226	62	13	2	20	57	24
Bernal, Michael, inf, Jr.	.269	.398	.366	175	23	5	0	4	30	2
Bonfield, Luke, of, Fr.	.177	.346	.194	62	11	1	0	0	7	0
Eagan, Clark, of, So.	.288	.364	.406	229	45	13	4	2	31	2
Gassaway, Cullen, inf, Jr.	.283	.381	.509	53	8	3	0	3	10	0
Gosser, Alex, c, So.	.240	.309	.280	50	3	2	0	0	2	0
Hogan, Max, inf, Jr.	.091	.375	.091	22	4	0	0	0	0	0
McAfee, Brett, inf, Sr.	.287	.339	.363	157	26	6	0	2	23	3
Nomura, Rick, inf, Jr.	.298	.370	.431	188	39	11	1	4	20	3
Pennell, Tucker, c, Jr.	.200	.271	.232	95	9	3	0	0	7	0
Serrano, Joe, of, Sr.	.278	.375	.397	227	46	13	1	4	35	6
Shaddy, Carson, c, So.	.337	.427	.517	89	15	5	1	3	19	1
Spanberger, Chad, c, Fr.	.252	.336	.336	107	8	5	2	0	21	1
Spoon, Tyler, of, Sr.	.327	.365	.490	245	38	20	1	6	54	10
Wernes, Bobby, inf, Jr.	.279	.374	.425	233	50	7	6	5	27	3

PITCHER, YEAR	W	L	ERA	G	GS	SV	IP	H	BB	SO
Alberius, Josh, So.	1	2	3.77	22	0	1	31	31	10	20
Chadwick, Cannon, So.	1	0	7.04	12	1	0	15	20	17	10
Jackson, Zach, So.	5	1	2.10	27	3	9	60	43	38	89
Killian, Trey, Jr.	3	5	4.76	15	15	0	87	99	24	62
Lowery, Jackson, Sr.	7	1	3.22	22	3	0	59	54	21	36
McKinney, Keaton, Fr.	6	2	3.21	21	18	0	87	71	38	46
Pate, Kyle, Fr.	0	0	8.64	12	0	0	8	11	9	14
Patten, Jonah, Fr.	0	0	7.90	11	0	0	14	16	9	20
Phillips, Lance, Sr.	2	3	3.34	25	0	0	32	35	12	30
Sanburn, Parker, Fr.	0	1	15.58	11	0	0	9	10	9	13
Stone, Jacob, Sr.	3	2	4.41	19	2	1	33	31	21	28
Taccolini, Dominic, So.	6	4	4.21	17	13	2	77	67	41	67
Teague, James, So.	6	4	3.36	23	10	2	59	55	33	49

12. MISSOURI STATE

Coach: Keith Guttin. **Record:** 49-12.

PLAYER, POS., YEAR	AVG	OBP	SLG	AB	R	2B	3B	HR	RBI	SB
Becker, Dylan, inf, Sr.	.309	.455	.438	217	46	13	3	3	41	3
Burger, Jake, inf, Fr.	.342	.390	.518	228	41	22	3	4	42	4
Castro, Eduardo, c, Jr.	.191	.252	.309	94	11	5	0	2	17	0
Cheray, Eric, inf, Sr.	.400	.523	.480	100	18	5	0	1	19	1
Dezort, Matt, of, Jr.	.298	.359	.340	47	9	2	0	0	5	0
Fultz, Matt, c, Jr.	.269	.367	.388	134	19	5	1	3	15	4
Graham, Blake, of, So.	.273	.381	.387	150	30	3	1	4	31	3
Hawkins, Joey, inf, So.	.262	.321	.327	248	38	6	2	2	28	5
Jefferson, Alex, of, So.	.175	.233	.200	40	9	1	0	0	2	4
Johnson, Spencer, inf, Jr.	.310	.447	.498	213	50	18	2	6	44	2
Kay, Cory, of, Sr.	.297	.357	.422	64	8	5	0	1	12	3
Matheny, Tate, of, Jr.	.291	.417	.449	234	45	18	2	5	43	12
Meyer, Aaron, inf, So.	.298	.422	.333	84	14	3	0	0	9	0
Paulsen, Justin, inf, So.	.274	.395	.447	208	39	12	0	8	47	1

PITCHER, YEAR	W	L	ERA	G	GS	SV	IP	H	BB	SO
Brown, Nick, Fr.	1	0	5.00	7	0	0	9	6	13	8
Cheray, Andy, Jr.	3	3	4.79	15	14	0	56	57	31	37
Hall, Matt, Jr.	12	2	2.02	19	17	1	125	87	45	171
Harris, Jon, Jr.	8	2	2.45	15	15	0	103	75	36	116
Jefferson, Alex, So.	0	0	3.00	11	0	0	14	9	10	14
Knutson, Jordan, So.	6	2	3.16	20	14	0	88	83	34	61
Merciez, Zach, Sr.	3	2	4.00	31	0	0	40	34	14	30
Perez, Sam, Jr.	9	1	3.29	27	0	1	68	64	16	63
Young, Bryan, So.	7	0	1.31	30	0	16	41	29	14	51

13. TEXAS A&M

Coach: Rob Childress. **Record:** 50-14.

PLAYER, POS., YEAR	AVG	OBP	SLG	AB	R	2B	3B	HR	RBI	SB
Allemand, Blake, inf, Sr.	.339	.431	.506	245	60	14	3	7	40	6
Banks, Nick, of, So.	.364	.450	.536	239	51	11	3	8	48	9
Barash, Michael, c, Jr.	.238	.316	.292	168	24	3	0	2	18	1
Birk, Ryne, inf, So.	.275	.365	.466	236	50	11	2	10	35	3
Choruby, Nick, inf, So.	.154	.290	.154	26	16	0	0	0	6	3
Gideon, Ronnie, inf, So.	.294	.359	.522	136	19	10	0	7	41	0
Hinsley, G.R., inf, Sr.	.188	.409	.292	48	8	2	0	1	11	0
Kopetsky, Blake, of, Sr.	.269	.415	.385	52	10	2	2	0	4	3
McLendon, Patrick, of, Sr.	.200	.294	.200	30	6	0	0	0	2	0
Melton, Hunter, 1b, Jr.	.300	.381	.473	203	36	9	1	8	37	0
Moroney, Jonathan, of, Jr.	.271	.379	.438	48	10	5	0	1	5	0
Moss, J.B., of, Jr.	.253	.344	.407	150	36	6	1	5	29	6
Nau, Mitchell, c, Sr.	.370	.460	.492	238	46	17	0	4	47	1
Nottebrok, Logan, inf, Sr.	.216	.301	.410	134	16	5	0	7	25	1
Taylor, Logan, inf, Jr.	.333	.392	.526	234	34	13	1	10	52	2

PITCHER, YEAR	W	L	ERA	G	GS	SV	IP	H	BB	SO
Ecker, Mark, So.	1	2	2.45	25	0	8	33	23	13	36
Freeman, Jason, Sr.	4	0	4.29	16	0	0	21	28	6	17
Hendrix, Ryan, So.	6	4	3.66	23	5	5	59	64	26	69
Hill, Brigham, Fr.	1	0	5.30	7	3	0	19	25	9	23
Kent, Matt, Jr.	9	1	2.76	19	14	2	98	103	12	84
Kopetsky, Blake, Jr.	0	0	2.89	14	0	0	5	5	11	5
Larkins, Turner, Fr.	5	1	3.96	15	12	0	50	54	16	46
Long, Grayson, Jr.	9	1	2.82	17	17	0	96	85	39	106
Martin, Corbin, Fr.	2	0	2.95	14	0	0	18	14	12	21
Minter, A.J., Jr.	2	0	0.43	4	4	0	21	17	8	29

PITCHER, YEAR	W	L	ERA	G	GS	SV	IP	H	BB	SO
Schlottmann, Ty, Jr.	3	1	3.96	32	0	0	25	26	8	23
Simonds, Kyle, Jr.	3	2	2.39	22	5	2	53	47	18	32
Stubblefield, Tyler, So.	0	0	5.25	4	2	0	12	11	4	10
Vinson, Andrew, Jr.	5	2	2.12	35	2	5	64	49	14	64

14. MARYLAND

Coach: John Szefc. **Record:** 42-24.

PLAYER, POS., YEAR	AVG	OBP	SLG	AB	R	2B	3B	HR	RBI	SB
Bechtold, Andrew, inf, Fr.	.231	.355	.231	26	4	0	0	0	4	1
Biondic, Kevin, inf, Fr.	.183	.333	.256	82	10	4	1	0	10	0
Cieri, Nick, inf, So.	.299	.373	.402	137	21	5	0	3	28	2
Cuas, Jose, inf, Jr.	.242	.329	.442	260	51	13	3	11	53	10
Hisle, Patrick, inf, So.	.118	.118	.177	17	1	1	0	0	0	0
Jancarski, Zach, of, Fr.	.118	.238	.118	17	9	0	0	0	2	0
Kawahara, Kengo, of, Fr.	.202	.348	.254	114	16	6	0	0	19	3
Lewis, Tim, of, Sr.	.214	.312	.296	206	24	7	5	0	32	4
Lowe, Brandon, inf, So.	.331	.437	.542	251	58	18	4	9	53	11
Martir, Kevin, c, Jr.	.342	.441	.502	237	45	17	0	7	45	3
Morris, Justin, c, Fr.	.133	.253	.181	83	14	2	1	0	4	1
Papio, Anthony, of, Jr.	.262	.370	.425	233	40	16	2	6	26	7
Rios, Willie, p, Fr.	.083	.353	.167	12	1	1	0	0	2	0
Smith, Kevin, inf, Fr.	.273	.358	.422	249	55	14	1	7	35	11
Wade, Jamal, of, Fr.	.231	.327	.451	91	14	3	1	5	11	0
Wade, Lamonte, 1b, Jr.	.335	.453	.468	158	30	7	1	4	32	7

PITCHER, YEAR	W	L	ERA	G	GS	SV	IP	H	BB	SO
Bloom, Taylor, Fr.	2	3	4.01	15	5	0	34	40	12	28
Drossner, Jake, Jr.	0	2	4.50	10	7	0	32	20	26	27
Galligan, Robert, Jr.	4	5	2.74	27	3	1	62	50	21	58
Mooney, Kevin, Jr.	3	1	1.89	25	3	11	38	21	24	47
Morris, Zach, Jr.	3	2	2.61	22	0	0	31	32	8	19
Price, Jared, Jr.	0	0	6.48	11	0	0	8	8	8	10
Rios, Willie, Fr.	1	2	8.24	9	5	0	20	30	8	21
Robinson, Alex, Jr.	1	1	1.63	25	0	3	28	12	20	32
Ruse, Bobby, Sr.	4	1	5.62	24	5	0	50	58	20	50
Selmer, Ryan, Fr.	3	1	2.18	31	4	0	54	49	16	19
Shaffer, Brian, Fr.	5	1	4.57	16	11	1	61	63	9	52
Shawaryn, Mike, So.	13	2	1.71	17	17	0	116	85	29	138
Stiles, Tayler, So.	3	3	3.46	14	6	0	39	36	8	37

15. FLORIDA STATE

Coach: Mike Martin. **Record:** 44-21.

PLAYER, POS., YEAR	AVG	OBP	SLG	AB	R	2B	3B	HR	RBI	SB
Busby, Dylan, inf, Fr.	.242	.363	.455	198	34	15	0	9	45	12
De La Calle, Danny, c, Sr.	.251	.293	.430	207	37	9	2	8	35	2
Delph, Josh, of, Sr.	.292	.417	.386	216	43	13	0	1	25	5
DeLuzio, Ben, inf, So.	.241	.345	.318	170	26	7	0	2	24	14
Graganella, Nick, of, Jr.	.120	.290	.160	25	13	1	0	0	3	0
Kelly, Hayden, inf, Jr.	.188	.409	.375	16	2	3	0	0	3	0
Marconcini, Chris, inf, Sr.	.229	.418	.424	144	24	7	0	7	36	1
Miller, Darren, inf, Fr.	.282	.402	.373	110	16	7	0	1	16	0
Nieporte, Quincy, inf, So.	.297	.391	.445	209	37	10	0	7	48	1
Sansone, John, inf, Jr.	.245	.382	.404	245	60	15	0	8	38	3
Stewart, D.J., of, Jr.	.318	.500	.594	214	62	10	2	15	59	12
Truluck, Hank, inf, So.	.288	.435	.343	73	14	4	0	0	15	3
Walls, Taylor, inf, Fr.	.220	.373	.247	227	43	4	1	0	22	7
Wells, Steven, of, Fr.	.208	.310	.375	24	6	1	0	1	7	0
West, Gage, Pitcher, So.	.231	.351	.354	65	12	6	1	0	9	0

PITCHER, YEAR	W	L	ERA	G	GS	SV	IP	H	BB	SO
Biegalski, Boomer, Jr.	7	5	3.17	18	17	0	108	84	38	120
Byrd, Alec, So.	5	1	4.53	27	3	0	44	47	15	48
Carlton, Drew, Fr.	5	5	4.04	18	12	0	71	76	19	60
Compton, Mike, Jr.	4	4	3.55	13	13	0	71	75	12	70
Deise, Alex, So.	1	0	3.86	10	0	0	16	12	4	16
Folsom, Taylor, Fr.	2	0	3.86	15	0	1	14	17	12	11
Holtmann, Bryant, Sr.	6	1	3.36	20	9	0	64	71	22	33
Johnson, Cobi, Fr.	3	2	7.21	14	8	0	44	53	23	44
Silva, Dylan, Jr.	7	1	4.29	36	0	1	57	51	37	76
Strode, Billy, Sr.	3	0	1.80	30	0	14	35	23	17	46
Vail, Derek, Jr.	0	0	10.50	10	0	0	6	12	6	3
Voyles, Ed, Fr.	0	1	1.42	6	1	0	6	7	0	5
Voyles, Jim, So.	0	1	2.63	21	2	0	27	28	10	27
Zirzow, Will, Fr.	1	0	4.00	12	0	0	18	16	5	15

16. LOUISIANA-LAFAYETTE

Coach: Tony Robichaux. **Record:** 42-23.

PLAYER, POS., YEAR	AVG	OBP	SLG	AB	R	2B	3B	HR	RBI	SB
Butler, Dylan, of, Sr.	.218	.329	.414	174	27	10	0	8	31	4
Clement, Kyle, of, Sr.	.346	.401	.615	182	40	17	4	8	32	3
Conrad, Brenn, inf, Jr.	.241	.284	.317	145	22	6	1	1	22	5
Davis, Greg, inf, Sr.	.252	.324	.399	258	34	15	1	7	40	6
Fontenot, Kennon, inf, Fr.	.179	.233	.250	28	2	0	1	0	2	0
Girouard, Tyler, dh, Sr.	.333	.445	.458	216	38	18	0	3	31	6
Herrington, Derek, of, Jr.	.196	.275	.348	46	9	1	0	2	4	0
Mills, Brian, of, Jr.	.210	.260	.269	119	14	2	1	1	14	4
Powell, Evan, inf, Jr.	.235	.332	.373	153	24	6	0	5	22	9
Robbins, Joe, inf, Jr.	.230	.308	.327	165	28	5	1	3	23	3
Thurman, Nick, c, Jr.	.257	.332	.339	218	30	11	2	1	37	5
Trahan, Blake, inf, Jr.	.315	.424	.406	254	51	15	1	2	29	17
Trosclair, Stefan, inf, Jr.	.338	.441	.635	219	55	15	1	16	53	15
Williams, Jam, of, Fr.	.111	.360	.111	18	11	0	0	0	5	5

PITCHER, YEAR	W	L	ERA	G	GS	SV	IP	H	BB	SO
Bacon, Will, Jr.	6	3	3.14	28	5	2	72	71	15	56
Bazar, Reagan, So.	0	0	3.38	13	0	1	13	7	9	12
Carter, Eric, Jr.	1	1	4.05	6	3	0	20	18	3	17
Charpentier, Chris, So.	4	3	5.08	17	2	1	34	33	17	33
Guillory, Evan, Fr.	5	0	4.05	16	16	0	87	88	20	56
Lee, Colton, Jr.	2	3	3.40	21	0	3	42	33	20	42
Leger, Gunner, Fr.	6	5	2.99	19	18	0	114	104	20	87
Marks, Wyatt, Fr.	6	1	3.24	19	10	1	67	59	19	68
Milhorn, Greg, Sr.	5	1	3.70	15	8	0	56	44	24	40
Moore, Dylan, Fr.	3	3	1.60	32	0	13	51	39	16	40
Stoelke, Logan, Fr.	1	1	1.64	8	0	0	11	10	3	9
Toups, Connor, So.	1	2	5.91	4	3	0	11	18	1	7
Zaunbrecher, Nick, Jr.	0	0	4.32	6	0	0	8	7	2	1

17. VIRGINIA COMMONWEALTH

Coach: Shawn Stiffler. **Record:** 40-25.

PLAYER, POS., YEAR	AVG	OBP	SLG	AB	R	2B	3B	HR	RBI	SB
Acker, Cody, of, Jr.	.254	.324	.324	185	18	9	2	0	20	6
Berezo, Daane, inf, Fr.	.273	.412	.280	150	26	1	0	0	15	4
Bunn, James, of, Jr.	.284	.407	.342	190	36	5	3	0	27	7
Carpenter, Darian, inf, So.	.263	.385	.434	205	37	9	1	8	30	2
Coale, Ryan, c, Fr.	.104	.154	.125	48	2	1	0	0	4	1
Davis, Matt, inf, So.	.312	.405	.457	221	49	9	1	7	43	3
Dressler, Shane, inf, So.	.175	.283	.225	40	1	2	0	0	6	0
Farrar, Logan, inf, So.	.307	.392	.423	267	50	13	3	4	33	8
Gransback, Alex, of, Jr.	.310	.420	.310	42	11	0	0	0	4	3
Haymaker, Walker, c, Jr.	.277	.314	.340	191	25	6	3	2	29	0
Hileman, Brett, c, So.	.289	.331	.382	152	22	9	1	1	20	0
Kerrigan, Jimmy, of, Jr.	.296	.432	.401	152	32	7	0	3	22	10
Lacey, Mitchel, inf, Fr.	.286	.389	.286	14	1	0	0	0	3	1
Machin, Vimael, inf, So.	.339	.401	.441	254	42	13	2	3	53	6
Mickelson, Cooper, inf, Jr.	.177	.271	.210	62	5	2	0	0	4	0
Rabat, Nick, c, So.	.154	.267	.231	13	0	1	0	0	0	0

PITCHER, YEAR	W	L	ERA	G	GS	SV	IP	H	BB	SO
Blanchard, Matt, Sr.	2	4	4.18	14	13	0	67	53	29	70
Buckley, Tyler, Sr.	3	0	1.38	21	3	0	39	31	12	22
Concepcion, Daniel, Sr.	3	3	3.12	27	2	14	69	74	19	60
Dwyer, Heath, Sr.	10	3	3.01	18	18	0	96	95	26	89
Gill, Thomas, Sr.	1	2	4.30	19	0	0	38	34	12	22
Howie, Jason, Sr.	8	7	2.77	17	17	0	111	118	21	82
Lees, Matt, Sr.	6	2	0.74	35	0	3	61	41	14	52
Pearson, Garrett, Fr.	0	0	0.96	8	0	0	9	6	5	14
Stine, Ben, Jr.	1	1	4.08	9	2	0	18	22	12	8
Thompson, Sean, Fr.	6	3	3.48	14	10	0	65	57	19	49

18. HOUSTON

Coach: Todd Whitting. **Record:** 43-20.

PLAYER, POS., YEAR	AVG	OBP	SLG	AB	R	2B	3B	HR	RBI	SB
Campbell, Jacob, c, Jr.	.301	.380	.440	209	31	12	1	5	41	1
Dickerson, Derek, inf, Fr.	.077	.294	.077	13	0	0	0	0	1	0
Fulmer, Ashford, of, Jr.	.238	.311	.345	168	24	5	2	3	29	10
Grilli, Robert, inf, Jr.	.320	.419	.360	25	7	1	0	0	2	1
Iriart, Chris, inf, Jr.	.302	.415	.573	232	46	14	2	15	40	1
Julks, Corey, inf, Fr.	.302	.384	.469	179	22	11	2	5	38	3

PLAYER, POS., YEAR	AVG	OBP	SLG	AB	R	2B	3B	HR	RBI	SB
Montemayor, Justin, inf, Jr.	.176	.278	.219	210	23	4	1	1	25	3
Rice, Ian, c, Jr.	.255	.427	.364	165	28	9	0	3	27	1
Stading, Jordan, inf, So.	.071	.278	.071	14	2	0	0	0	0	0
Survance, Kyle, of, Jr.	.297	.385	.402	246	51	8	6	2	34	31
Taylor, Zac, of, Fr.	.266	.365	.379	124	31	6	1	2	15	13
Vidales, Josh, inf, Jr.	.300	.397	.387	243	49	9	3	2	39	6
Wisz, Michael, inf, Fr.	.194	.219	.226	31	2	1	0	0	4	0
Wong, Connor, inf, Fr.	.248	.320	.382	238	39	6	4	6	37	3

PITCHER, YEAR	W	L	ERA	G	GS	SV	IP	H	BB	SO
Cobb, Taylor, Sr.	1	1	2.45	9	5	1	26	29	13	17
Dowdy, Kyle, Jr.	9	2	2.45	19	12	0	95	78	25	72
Fletcher, Aaron, Fr.	2	1	1.37	21	0	1	26	22	8	15
Garza, Aaron, Sr.	1	4	4.82	17	5	3	47	53	7	35
Kasowski, Marshall, So.	1	0	2.12	9	0	0	17	11	6	18
Lantrip, Andrew, So.	9	3	2.62	16	16	0	113	106	22	115
Lemoine, Jake, Jr.	1	1	4.50	5	5	0	24	24	4	15
Longville, David, Sr.	5	2	2.95	13	10	0	55	56	6	25
Moore, Austin, Jr.	1	0	8.38	7	0	0	10	15	8	4
Robinson, Jared, Sr.	0	1	3.57	11	1	1	23	21	12	21
Romero, Seth, Fr.	7	4	1.94	22	8	7	83	61	22	92
Weigel, Patrick, Jr.	4	1	3.38	23	1	2	51	34	21	45

19. OKLAHOMA STATE
Coach: Josh Holliday. Record: 38-20.

PLAYER, POS., YEAR	AVG	OBP	SLG	AB	R	2B	3B	HR	RBI	SB
Arakawa, Tim, inf, Sr.	.289	.412	.393	211	50	10	3	2	37	10
Bradley, Kevin, inf, So.	.281	.358	.396	139	15	7	0	3	23	2
Case, Bryan, c, Sr.	.252	.333	.437	119	23	8	1	4	29	3
Chappell, Jacob, inf, Fr.	.248	.398	.303	145	33	4	2	0	21	6
Costello, Conor, dh, Jr.	.240	.343	.377	183	32	7	0	6	35	13
Green, Gage, c, Sr.	.291	.404	.404	223	44	4	3	5	29	18
Hassel, Corey, inf, Jr.	.312	.352	.417	199	27	10	1	3	33	13
Littell, Jon, of, Fr.	.228	.289	.272	92	18	4	0	0	15	2
McCain, Garrett, p, Fr.	.319	.467	.389	72	18	3	1	0	13	7
O'Brien, Mason, 1b, Fr.	.095	.174	.095	21	2	0	0	0	1	0
Petrino, David, inf, Jr.	.257	.358	.314	70	14	2	1	0	9	2
Sluder, Ryan, of, So.	.309	.401	.506	162	36	14	0	6	22	5
Walton, Donnie, inf, Jr.	.326	.410	.482	135	26	7	1	4	29	3
Williams, Dustin, inf, So.	.276	.396	.469	192	37	11	4	6	38	5

PITCHER, YEAR	W	L	ERA	G	GS	SV	IP	H	BB	SO
Bagnell, Kyle, Sr.	0	0	9.00	9	0	0	8	14	4	11
Battenfield, Blake, So.	0	1	3.60	6	2	0	15	12	9	12
Buffett, Tyler, So.	3	3	3.65	19	3	0	44	56	7	32
Cobb, Trey, So.	5	2	2.61	31	0	2	59	48	19	53
Costello, Conor, Jr.	2	0	1.67	7	6	1	32	27	6	18
Freeman, Michael, Sr.	10	3	1.31	15	15	0	110	72	29	97
Glover, Koda, Jr.	2	2	1.90	23	0	5	24	20	7	28
Hackerott, Alex, Jr.	1	0	3.38	12	0	0	5	9	5	8
Hassel, Corey, Jr.	1	0	1.69	3	0	0	5	2	0	7
LaRue, Carson, Fr.	2	0	5.04	17	3	0	25	30	11	19
Nurdin, Tyler, Sr.	2	3	3.11	18	6	0	46	39	22	36
Perrin, Jon, Sr.	6	4	4.06	16	16	0	84	79	31	72
Reed, Remey, So.	3	2	1.57	23	5	0	46	40	13	30
Williams, Garrett, So.	1	0	4.91	18	2	0	18	8	19	25

20. SOUTHERN CALIFORNIA
Coach: Dan Hubbs. Record: 39-21.

PLAYER, POS., YEAR	AVG	OBP	SLG	AB	R	2B	3B	HR	RBI	SB
Carrillo, Adalberto, inf, Fr.	.245	.302	.347	49	4	2	0	1	3	1
Corrigan, Joe, inf, So.	.154	.133	.154	13	1	0	0	0	2	0
Dempster, Corey, inf, So.	.179	.207	.179	28	3	0	0	0	4	4
Flores, Dante, inf, Sr.	.304	.394	.461	217	34	11	4	5	43	4
La Bruna, Angelo, inf, Sr.	.250	.310	.368	76	13	3	0	2	9	4
Lacey, Blake, inf, Jr.	.293	.322	.360	225	28	15	0	0	37	9
Martinez, Jeremy, c, So.	.293	.393	.364	225	40	13	0	1	45	0
Oppenheim, David, of, Jr.	.284	.400	.392	176	32	8	1	3	27	3
Ramirez, A.J., inf, Fr.	.259	.307	.476	212	26	15	2	9	45	9
Robinson, Timmy, of, So.	.286	.383	.433	224	48	10	1	7	53	19
Southall, Reggie, inf, So.	.250	.362	.320	128	30	6	0	1	19	10
Stahel, Bobby, of, Jr.	.376	.419	.506	245	59	12	4	4	33	10
Stubbs, Garrett, c, Sr.	.346	.435	.434	228	51	15	1	1	25	20

PITCHER, YEAR	W	L	ERA	G	GS	SV	IP	H	BB	SO
Chavarria, Alex, Fr.	0	0	4.76	10	0	2	11	14	4	7
Davis, Kyle, Jr.	3	3	4.05	20	5	6	53	58	18	45
Flores, Bernardo, So.	3	1	3.83	16	4	1	45	43	17	45
Gilbert, Tyler, Jr.	5	2	2.79	22	6	2	68	68	25	66
Hart, Mitch, Fr.	7	3	4.07	16	15	0	86	74	38	51
Huberman, Marc, Jr.	6	4	2.36	27	0	4	50	37	34	47
Kriske, Brooks, Jr.	2	1	2.90	20	2	0	31	30	14	27
Paschke, Jeff, So.	1	0	6.14	13	1	0	15	15	9	12
Perryman, Mason, Fr.	0	1	5.79	13	2	0	23	27	15	13
Twomey, Kyle, Jr.	8	2	2.88	16	16	0	94	87	38	68
Wegman, Brad, Fr.	0	0	5.40	5	0	0	5	10	0	4
Wheatley, Brent, Jr.	4	4	4.50	17	9	0	70	73	34	63

21. DALLAS BAPTIST
Coach: Dan Heefner. Record: 46-15.

PLAYER, POS., YEAR	AVG	OBP	SLG	AB	R	2B	3B	HR	RBI	SB
Duce, Matt, c, Fr.	.208	.367	.250	24	6	1	0	0	3	0
Duce, Tagg, of, Sr.	.329	.411	.487	222	50	15	1	6	38	9
Duzenack, Camden, inf, So.	.286	.379	.394	241	52	14	0	4	39	9
Knight, Nash, inf, Sr.	.292	.377	.380	216	34	13	0	2	35	2
Lynch, Chane, 1b, Sr.	.275	.353	.404	218	33	16	0	4	40	2
Martinelli, David, of, So.	.267	.340	.510	210	34	13	4	10	37	6
Reynolds, Trooper, inf, Jr.	.269	.337	.444	171	31	9	0	7	32	0
Salters, Daniel, c, Jr.	.261	.367	.392	222	36	15	1	4	36	4
Sonnier, Trevin, inf, Jr.	.115	.148	.154	26	5	1	0	0	2	1
Sweet, Daniel, of, Jr.	.265	.356	.363	102	20	3	2	1	12	4
Turbin, Drew, inf, Sr.	.347	.480	.512	213	56	18	4	3	36	7
Wall, Justin, of, Jr.	.301	.371	.521	259	45	13	4	12	58	12

PITCHER, YEAR	W	L	ERA	G	GS	SV	IP	H	BB	SO
Adams, Chance, Jr.	7	1	1.98	23	0	2	59	41	13	83
Calhoun, Jay, Sr.	1	0	4.42	16	6	0	37	36	22	31
Conn, Trevor, So.	2	1	1.84	7	5	0	29	28	9	17
Elledge, Seth, Fr.	0	0	2.70	9	0	0	10	8	6	11
Fritz, Gavin, Fr.	4	1	4.23	11	5	1	28	22	13	16
Higgins, Dalton, Fr.	0	1	2.95	13	3	1	37	31	12	20
Koch, Brandon, Jr.	3	2	1.26	26	0	14	32	24	24	76
Shaw, Joseph, Jr.	10	5	3.46	16	16	0	88	84	25	70
Smith, Drew, Jr.	3	2	3.97	25	1	4	45	46	17	38
Stutzman, Sean, Jr.	8	1	4.29	18	6	1	57	46	26	51
Taylor, Cory, Jr.	7	1	3.60	16	15	0	80	85	31	71
Wilson, Landon, So.	1	0	4.40	15	4	0	31	38	14	15

22. CALIFORNIA
Coach: David Esquer. Record: 36-21.

PLAYER, POS., YEAR	AVG	OBP	SLG	AB	R	2B	3B	HR	RBI	SB
Celsi, Brian, of, Jr.	.278	.328	.364	162	16	5	0	3	31	4
Cumberland, Brett, c, Fr.	.254	.405	.429	177	34	10	0	7	32	0
Diede, Grant, of, Jr.	.171	.310	.171	35	5	0	0	0	0	0
Dutto, Max, inf, Jr.	.217	.404	.337	83	14	4	0	2	8	2
Erceg, Lucas, inf/rhp, So.	.303	.357	.502	231	38	11	1	11	41	5
Grand Pre, Preston, ss, Fr.	.264	.287	.327	208	28	4	3	1	26	2
Halamandaris, Nick, 1b, Jr.	.209	.256	.291	110	9	4	1	1	13	1
Haseltine, Trevin, p, So.	.273	.273	.273	11	1	0	0	0	1	0
Karas, Denis, inf, Fr.	.263	.333	.368	19	4	2	0	0	1	0
Knapp, Aaron, of, So.	.310	.376	.375	232	45	7	4	0	23	12
Kranson, Mitchell, c, Jr.	.273	.303	.467	165	22	12	1	6	21	0
Paul, Chris, inf, Sr.	.325	.404	.562	203	40	11	5	9	45	6
Pearson, Devin, of, Jr.	.355	.413	.558	138	27	12	2	4	22	5
Peters, Sean, of, Jr.	.250	.294	.313	16	6	1	0	0	3	2
Soteropulos, John, inf, Jr.	.105	.150	.263	19	2	0	0	1	2	0
Tenerowicz, Robbie, inf, So.	.182	.236	.220	132	13	1	2	0	8	0

PITCHER, YEAR	W	L	ERA	G	GS	SV	IP	H	BB	SO
Bain, Jeff, Fr.	6	2	2.52	17	8	0	64	49	13	31
Erceg, Lucas, So.	0	1	2.53	8	0	1	11	11	2	7
Jefferies, Daulton, So.	6	5	2.93	14	13	0	80	72	17	75
Kay, Jesse, So.	0	0	4.50	11	0	0	8	7	9	5
Ladrech, Matt, Fr.	7	4	2.67	16	16	0	88	90	21	28
Martinez, Erik, Fr.	3	1	1.56	22	0	1	35	25	18	40
Mason, Ryan, Jr.	6	3	3.07	17	16	0	100	102	31	40
Monsour, Collin, Jr.	1	0	6.50	10	2	1	18	30	6	13
Muse-Fisher, Chris, Sr.	3	1	2.33	24	0	2	39	23	7	36
Nelson, Dylan, Sr.	2	1	2.93	23	0	8	31	20	11	36
Schick, Alex, So.	3	2	4.21	26	2	0	36	25	21	46

23. COLLEGE OF CHARLESTON

Coach: Monte Lee. **Record:** 45-15.

PLAYER, POS., YEAR	AVG	OBP	SLG	AB	R	2B	3B	HR	RBI	SB
Brown, Ryan, of, Fr.	.320	.413	.455	244	63	14	2	5	26	14
Butler, Blake, inf, Jr.	.325	.395	.564	243	56	15	2	13	63	4
Jones, Bradley, inf, So.	.309	.394	.586	181	40	13	2	11	45	4
Pappas, Nick, inf, So.	.337	.389	.610	249	43	28	2	12	57	5
Pastorius, Alex, of, Jr.	.249	.357	.448	201	48	9	2	9	40	5
Phillips, Morgan, inf, Jr.	.310	.353	.468	216	35	9	2	7	40	7
Reed, Devon, inf, Sr.	.188	.278	.188	16	4	0	0	0	1	0
Richter, Tommy, inf, Fr.	.250	.373	.321	84	17	6	0	0	8	2
Roper, Erven, c, So.	.288	.350	.405	215	28	13	0	4	29	2
Rowland, Champ, inf, Sr.	.271	.326	.336	214	38	6	1	2	26	2
Wise, Carl, inf, Fr.	.313	.380	.557	246	64	18	3	12	70	3

PITCHER, YEAR	W	L	ERA	G	GS	SV	IP	H	BB	SO
Arduini, Wade, Jr.	1	1	5.85	22	7	1	48	58	18	34
Bauer, Eric, Jr.	4	4	5.71	15	7	1	52	72	17	31
Clarke, Taylor, Jr.	13	1	1.73	17	16	1	114	76	14	143
Detwiler, Will, Fr.	0	0	1.95	20	0	0	28	24	9	15
Glazer, Brandon, Sr.	10	2	2.74	21	13	1	89	84	11	49
Helvey, Nathan, Jr.	7	4	2.84	20	12	3	73	62	27	57
Henry, Chase, Sr.	3	1	4.17	27	0	5	41	40	11	38
Love, Carter, Fr.	6	0	1.98	24	0	4	41	38	4	33
McBreairty, Jake, Fr.	0	0	12.71	7	0	0	6	9	9	4
McCutcheon, Hayden, So.	1	2	5.00	16	5	2	39	50	16	27

24. RADFORD

Coach: Joe Raccuia. **Record:** 45-16.

PLAYER, POS., YEAR	AVG	OBP	SLG	AB	R	2B	3B	HR	RBI	SB
Brennan, Jimmy, inf, Fr.	.172	.415	.207	29	9	1	0	0	1	0
Coia, Chris, inf, Jr.	.307	.393	.357	199	44	6	2	0	24	11
Gardiner, Josh, inf, Sr.	.368	.451	.526	171	47	18	0	3	22	18
Higgerson, Hunter, inf, Sr.	.264	.317	.447	235	40	25	0	6	53	6
Hrbek, Danny, inf, So.	.276	.350	.347	228	33	5	1	3	31	9
Johnsonbaugh, Shane, of, Jr.	.328	.438	.517	232	50	19	2	7	45	8
Keen, Brad, of, Jr.	.321	.370	.455	187	36	8	4	3	39	9
Marshall, Patrick, of, Sr.	.327	.441	.592	211	44	20	0	12	59	2
Palenchar, Simon, inf, Fr.	.174	.240	.217	23	3	1	0	0	1	0
Reavis, Josh, c, Sr.	.290	.413	.400	200	46	12	2	2	41	10
Riggs, Trevor, of, Fr.	.154	.295	.365	104	20	4	0	6	15	4
Scoville, Aaron, of, Sr.	.252	.373	.270	163	21	3	0	0	24	16
Taylor, Jordan, c, Jr.	.220	.340	.342	41	6	0	1	1	6	1

PITCHER, YEAR	W	L	ERA	G	GS	SV	IP	H	BB	SO
Andrews, Nygeal, Jr.	0	0	4.09	10	0	0	11	8	10	18
Boyle, Michael, Jr.	10	3	2.48	16	16	0	105	86	37	87
Bridgeman, Daniel, Jr.	6	2	0.57	24	0	1	32	18	11	28
MacKeith, Mitchell, Jr.	7	5	4.84	16	16	0	84	95	19	43
Maxwell, Jeff, Jr.	0	0	7.30	8	0	0	12	19	5	14
McQueen, Travis, Jr.	0	1	15.63	10	0	0	13	26	6	8
Meisinger, Ryan, Jr.	5	0	1.62	31	0	17	39	24	8	66
Nelson, Dylan, Jr.	6	3	3.98	16	16	0	86	89	28	53
Palmer, Kyle, So.	3	0	2.64	23	0	1	31	23	14	24
Ridgley, Zack, Fr.	5	1	3.18	17	8	0	51	48	8	40
Ross, Austin, So.	2	0	5.11	18	2	1	37	33	12	33
Swarmer, Tyler, Jr.	1	1	7.61	11	3	0	24	36	9	16
Zurak, Kyle, So.	0	0	2.92	13	0	0	12	10	9	9

25. IOWA

Coach: Rick Heller. **Record:** 41-18.

PLAYER, POS., YEAR	AVG	OBP	SLG	AB	R	2B	3B	HR	RBI	SB
Barrett, John, inf, Jr.	.152	.275	.182	33	3	1	0	0	6	0
Booker, Joel, of, Jr.	.235	.310	.304	217	28	7	1	2	25	9
Day, Nick, inf, Sr.	.273	.381	.379	132	21	5	0	3	18	9
Frankos, Jimmy, c, Jr.	.202	.349	.226	84	7	2	0	0	10	0
Goodman, Kris, of, Sr.	.262	.365	.402	214	37	11	5	3	26	10
Guzzo, Austin, c, Fr.	.217	.284	.300	60	7	3	1	0	7	1
Kaufman, Taylor, p, Sr.	.167	.275	.183	60	6	1	0	0	2	2
Klenovich, Grant, 1b, Fr.	.308	.455	.462	26	3	2	1	0	5	0
Mangler, Jake, inf, Fr.	.296	.377	.352	247	32	12	1	0	34	8
Moore, Sean, inf, Sr.	.231	.404	.333	39	8	4	0	0	10	1
Moriel, Daniel Aaron, c, Jr.	.271	.435	.371	70	11	4	0	1	10	0
Peyton, Tyler, inf, Jr.	.337	.439	.417	187	31	11	2	0	31	2
Potempa, Dan, of, Sr.	.267	.342	.348	135	11	8	0	1	19	0
Roscetti, Nick, inf, Jr.	.302	.356	.347	199	27	6	0	1	28	9
Schenck-Joblinske, Eric, of, Jr.	.140	.321	.326	43	11	0	1	2	5	3
Toole, Eric, of, Sr.	.306	.373	.381	252	42	8	4	1	28	27

PITCHER, YEAR	W	L	ERA	G	GS	SV	IP	H	BB	SO
Allgeyer, Nick, Fr.	2	0	3.48	10	0	2	10	8	6	6
Erickson, Ryan, Jr.	4	1	2.79	18	0	1	42	47	20	27
Gallagher, Nick, Fr.	0	0	2.18	9	5	0	21	15	7	17
Grant, Connor, Jr.	1	2	4.02	16	4	2	31	21	22	21
Hibbing, Nick, Sr.	4	1	1.57	25	0	8	52	30	5	47
Hickman, Blake, Jr.	9	2	2.99	16	16	0	84	66	42	52
Mandel, Jared, So.	2	1	4.96	12	0	0	16	12	9	9
Martsching, Josh, So.	0	1	3.44	11	2	0	18	11	10	11
Mathews, Calvin, Jr.	5	3	2.45	16	15	0	73	67	26	43
Peyton, Tyler, Jr.	7	4	3.03	16	16	0	95	94	24	74
Radtke, Tyler, Jr.	2	1	5.31	19	0	2	20	24	18	16
Shulista, Brandon, Sr.	3	2	3.67	18	0	0	27	27	6	23
Vandermaten, Luke, Jr.	2	0	1.06	22	0	4	42	32	15	23

CONFERENCE STANDINGS & LEADERS

NCAA regional teams in bold. Conference category leaders in bold.
*Team won conference's automatic regional bid. #Category leader who did not qualify for batting or pitching title.

AMERICA EAST CONFERENCE

	Conference		Overall	
	W	L	W	L
* Stony Brook	18	4	35	16
Maryland-Baltimore County	14	10	34	20
Maine	10	10	21	28
Massachusetts-Lowell	10	10	17	26
Hartford	10	12	23	31
Albany	7	13	14	28
Binghamton	6	16	17	24

ALL-CONFERNCE TEAM: C—Cole Peragine, Sr., Stony Brook. **1B**—Anthony Gatto, Jr., Maryland-Baltimore County. **2B**—Robert Chavarria, Sr., Stony Brook. **SS**—Danny Mendick, Sr., UMass-Lowell. **3B**—Luke Morrill, Sr., Maine. **OF**—Jake Thomas, Sr., Binghamton; Toby Handley, So., Stony Brook; Jack Parenty, Jr., Stony Brook. **UTIL**—Jamie Switalski, Fr., Maryland-Baltimore County. **DH**—Scott Heath, Sr., Maine. **SP**—Matt Chanin, Fr., Maryland-Baltimore County; Conrad Wozniak, Jr., Maryland-Baltimore County; Tyler Honahan, Jr., Stony Brook; Daniel Zamora, So., Stony Brook. **RP**—Denis Mikush, Jr., Maryland-Baltimore County. **Player of the Year:** Jack Parenty, Stony Brook. **Pitcher of the Year:** Conrad Wozniak, Maryland-Baltimore County. **Coach of the Year:** Bob Mumma, Maryland-Baltimore County. **Rookie of the Year:** Matt Chanin, Maryland-Baltimore County

INDIVIDUAL BATTING LEADERS
(Minimum 140 At-Bats)

	AVG	OBP	SLG	AB	2B	3B	HR	RBI	SB
Luke Morrill, Maine	.367	.438	.503	177	18	0	2	29	8
Jack Parenty, Stony Brook	.365	.432	.521	211	13	7	2	47	19
Jake Thomas, Binghamton	.352	.478	.521	142	14	2	2	29	8
David MacKinnon, Hartford	.351	.438	.443	194	13	1	1	21	7
Nick Naumann, UMBC	.345	.420	.382	165	3	0	1	31	9
Toby Handley, Stony Brook	.330	.427	.423	194	8	5	0	35	12
Matthew Sanchez, UMass-Lowell	.327	.428	.431	153	10	3	0	17	18
Andrew Casali, UMBC	.319	.367	.422	204	13	1	2	42	11
Casey Baker, Stony Brook	.317	.377	.487	189	8	6	4	35	5
Brett Chappell, Maine	.316	.369	.421	190	12	1	2	38	1
Andruw Gazzola, Stony Brook	.315	.394	.397	184	7	4	0	27	4
Anthony Gatto, UMBC	.311	.441	.457	164	8	2	4	22	30
Sam Balzano, Maine	.308	.359	.348	224	9	0	0	19	9
Scott Heath, Maine	.308	.399	.478	201	16	0	6	29	4
Zach Blanden, Binghamton	.306	.419	.456	160	9	3	3	21	8
Robert Chavarria, Stony Brook	.305	.445	.328	177	4	0	0	30	3
Brendan Skidmore, Binghamton	.303	.383	.517	145	11	1	6	34	1
Trey Stover, Hartford	.301	.337	.405	163	12	1	1	13	5
Vince Corbi, UMBC	.297	.346	.392	209	13	2	1	36	13
Hunter Dolshun, UMBC	.288	.387	.372	191	13	0	1	29	2
Cole Peragine, Stony Brook	.287	.436	.354	195	9	2	0	26	3
Will Miller, Albany	.281	.403	.399	153	9	3	1	14	15
Jake Barnes, UMBC	.277	.343	.486	177	14	4	5	36	8
Ryan Lukach, Hartford	.260	.322	.417	204	10	2	6	43	6

INDIVIDUAL PITCHING LEADERS
(Minimum 40 innings pitched)

	W	L	ERA	G	SV	IP	H	BB	SO
Conrad Wozniak, UMBC	4	1	1.48	12	0	73	64	19	56
Matt Chanin, UMBC	5	2	1.96	12	0	64	61	20	39
Denis Mikush, UMBC	4	2	2.40	28	6	41	27	30	55
Jeremy Charles, Hartford	4	2	2.42	22	3	48	42	11	35
Andrew Ryan, UMass-Lowell	2	2	2.67	11	1	57	46	17	29
Daniel Zamora, Stony Brook	7	3	3.00	15	0	81	75	35	80
Justin Courtney, Maine	5	6	3.24	14	0	72	84	27	38
Kyle Gauthier, Hartford	4	7	3.47	14	0	93	83	23	53
Jacob Gosselin-Deschesnes, Maine	3	3	3.53	19	0	59	55	17	36
Cory Callahan, UMBC	4	0	3.69	22	1	46	46	10	32
Logan Fullmer, Maine	1	1	3.75	21	4	58	58	13	51
Mike Bunal, Binghamton	4	6	3.96	11	0	50	46	21	41
Stephen Woods, Albany	3	6	3.98	11	0	54	39	42	55

	W	L	ERA	G	SV	IP	H	BB	SO
Joe Vanderplas, UMBC	2	4	4.05	9	0	47	51	25	30
Tyler Honahan, Stony Brook	7	3	4.13	15	0	76	75	35	65
Scott Heath, Maine	6	4	4.21	14	0	83	100	27	65
Connor Staskey, UMBC	4	5	4.24	16	1	51	59	35	38
Brian Murphy, Hartford	1	5	4.27	14	0	65	67	24	37
Sam McKay, Hartford	4	7	4.42	13	0	73	73	19	34
Geoff DeGroot, UMass-Lowell	3	3	4.75	9	0	47	46	17	22
Greg Ostner, Binghamton	1	8	5.04	12	0	61	79	10	27

AMERICAN ATHLETIC CONFERENCE

	Conference		Overall	
	W	L	W	L
Houston	16	8	43	20
* East Carolina	15	9	40	22
Tulane	13	11	35	25
South Florida	13	11	34	26
Memphis	12	12	37	21
Connecticut	11	13	35	25
Central Florida	10	14	31	27
Cincinnati	6	18	15	41

ALL-CONFERENCE TEAM: C—Levi Borders, Jr., South Florida. **1B**—Tucker Tubbs, Sr., Memphis. **2B**—Vinny Siena, Jr., Connecticut. **SS**—Dylan Moore, Sr., Central Florida. **3B**—Tommy Williams, Sr., Central Florida. **OF**—Ian Happ, Jr., Cincinnati; Erik Barber, Sr., Central Florida; Blake Davey, Sr., Connecticut. **DH**—Luke Lowery, Jr., East Carolina. **UTIL**—Reid Love, Sr., East Carolina. **SP**—Zach Rodgers, Sr., Central Florida; Carson Cross, Sr., Connecticut; Anthony Kay, So., Connecticut; Reid Love, Sr., East Carolina; Jimmy Herget, Jr., South Florida. **RP**—Nolan Blackwood, So., Memphis. **Player of the Year:** Ian Happ, Cincinnati. **Pitcher of the Year:** Carson Cross, Connecticut. **Coach of the Year:** Cliff Godwin, East Carolina. **Rookie of the Year:** Seth Romero, Houston.

INDIVIDUAL BATTING LEADERS
(Minimum 140 At-Bats)

	AVG	OBP	SLG	AB	2B	3B	HR	RBI	SB
Ian Happ, Cincinnati	.369	.492	.672	198	18	0	14	44	12
Vinny Siena, Connecticut	.362	.424	.519	260	14	3	7	54	11
Hunter Allen, East Carolina	.349	.408	.412	209	9	2	0	17	4
Kevin Merrell, South Florida	.346	.403	.375	240	7	0	0	22	21
Willy Yahn, Connecticut	.343	.388	.454	172	6	2	3	31	4
Dylan Moore, Central Florida	.333	.417	.542	240	14	3	10	45	14
Jomarcos Woods, Central Florida	.329	.415	.515	167	12	2	5	32	9
Kane Barrow, Memphis	.321	.349	.432	234	13	2	3	41	6
Darien Tubbs, Memphis	.321	.390	.492	234	9	5	7	38	25
Bobby Melley, Connecticut	.315	.401	.408	238	19	0	1	40	0
Tommy Williams, Central Florida	.315	.403	.536	222	19	3	8	39	6
Erik Barber, Central Florida	.313	.391	.524	208	9	1	11	38	4
Stephen Alemais, Tulane	.312	.361	.392	250	11	3	1	22	27
Luke Lowery, East Carolina	.311	.408	.553	206	10	2	12	50	7
Matt Diorio, Central Florida	.308	.429	.476	143	7	1	5	29	2
Luke Maglich, Central Florida	.308	.398	.471	221	10	1	8	38	15
Tucker Tubbs, Memphis	.305	.393	.601	223	15	0	17	55	7
Kyle Teaf, South Florida	.302	.420	.391	225	8	6	0	25	14
Chris Iriart, Houston	.302	.415	.573	232	14	2	15	40	1
Corey Julks, Houston	.302	.384	.469	179	11	2	5	38	3
Jacob Campbell, Houston	.301	.380	.440	209	12	1	5	41	1
Blake Davey, Connecticut	.300	.379	.477	220	21	0	6	45	11
Josh Vidales, Houston	.300	.397	.387	243	9	3	2	39	4
Kyle Marsh, Central Florida	.299	.411	.461	167	12	0	5	37	0
Kyle Survance, Houston	.297	.385	.402	246	8	6	2	34	31
Kirk Morgan, East Carolina	.293	.340	.320	147	0	2	0	17	1
Jack Sundberg, Connecticut	.288	.412	.367	240	12	2	1	35	33

INDIVIDUAL PITCHING LEADERS
(Minimum 40 innings pitched)

	W	L	ERA	G	SV	IP	H	BB	SO
Tommy Peterson, South Florida	4	1	1.93	31	16	47	31	16	54
Seth Romero, Houston	7	4	1.94	22	7	83	61	22	92
Anthony Kay, Connecticut	8	6	2.07	17	1	100	73	25	96
Corey Merrill, Tulane	5	6	2.12	17	0	102	80	43	81
David Lucroy, East Carolina	3	4	2.18	16	0	66	55	29	47
Carson Cross, Connecticut	10	2	2.29	15	0	106	80	25	108
Zach Rodgers, Central Florida	10	1	2.35	18	1	100	83	37	94
Kyle Dowdy, Houston	9	2	2.45	19	0	95	78	25	72
Andrew Lantrip, Houston	9	3	2.62	16	0	113	106	22	115
Emerson Gibbs, Tulane	5	3	2.73	18	1	79	72	19	54
Michael Farley, South Florida	3	2	2.76	27	0	49	41	23	55
Reid Love, East Carolina	7	4	2.81	22	4	96	94	12	82
Jimmy Herget, South Florida	10	3	2.92	17	0	102	88	36	113
David Longville, Houston	5	2	2.95	13	0	55	56	6	25
Dylan Toscano, Memphis	9	2	3.07	14	0	88	73	22	76
Ian Gibaut, Tulane	5	3	3.11	27	9	46	38	23	51
Evan Kruczynski, East Carolina	8	4	3.17	16	0	99	105	26	72
Patrick Duester, Tulane	7	6	3.21	19	2	70	69	32	61
Cre Finfrock, Central Florida	7	5	3.30	15	0	95	77	34	73
Jacob Wolfe, East Carolina	5	2	3.35	17	1	89	87	20	54
Casey Mulholland, South Florida	5	9	4.05	15	0	93	100	33	76
Jimmy Boyd, East Carolina	5	7	4.73	28	1	59	76	5	39
Robby Howell, Central Florida	5	9	5.69	17	0	81	103	34	58

ATLANTIC COAST CONFERENCE

Atlantic Division	Conference W	L	Overall W	L
Louisville	25	5	47	18
Notre Dame	17	13	37	23
* Florida State	17	13	44	21
Clemson	16	13	32	29
North Carolina State	15	14	36	23
Wake Forest	12	18	27	26
Boston College	10	19	27	27

Coastal Division	Conference W	L	Overall W	L
Miami	22	8	49	17
Virginia	15	15	44	24
North Carolina	13	16	34	24
Virginia Tech	13	16	27	27
Georgia Tech	13	17	32	23
Duke	10	19	31	22
Pittsburgh	9	21	20	32

ALL-CONFERENCE TEAM: C—Chris Okey, So., Clemson. **1B**—Brendon Hayden, Sr., Virginia Tech; Will Craig, So., Wake Forest. **2B**—George Iskenderian, Jr., Miami; Nate Mondou, So., Wake Forest. **SS**—Sutton Whiting, Sr., Louisville. **3B**—David Thompson, Jr., Miami. **OF**—D.J. Stewart, Jr., Florida State; Corey Ray, So., Louisville; Stuart Fairchild, Fr., Wake Forest. **DH/UT**—Zack Collins, So., Miami. **SP**—Matthew Crownover, Jr., Clemson; Brendan McKay, Fr., Louisville; Kyle Funkhouser, Jr., Louisville; Nathan Kirby, Jr., Virginia. **RP**—Zack Burdi, So., Louisville. **Player of the Year:** Will Craig, Wake Forest. **Pitcher of the Year:** Matthew Crownover, Clemson. **Coach of the Year:** Dan McDonnell, Louisville. **Rookie of the Year:** Brendan McKay, Louisville.

INDIVIDUAL BATTING LEADERS
(Minimum 140 At-Bats)

	AVG	OBP	SLG	AB	2B	3B	HR	RBI	SB
Will Craig, Wake Forest	.382	.496	.702	191	20	1	13	58	2
George Iskenderian, Miami	.364	.459	.476	250	15	2	3	55	23
Reed Rohlman, Clemson	.356	.412	.466	236	17	0	3	58	3
Stuart Fairchild, Wake Forest	.349	.429	.497	195	14	0	5	41	12
Erik Payne, Virginia Tech	.343	.444	.536	207	13	0	9	53	1
Tyler Krieger, Clemson	.339	.448	.420	236	14	1	1	41	14
Nate Mondou, Wake Forest	.338	.391	.581	222	18	3	10	57	5
Peter Zyla, Duke	.331	.381	.444	160	10	4	0	21	3
Saige Jenco, Virginia Tech	.330	.394	.466	206	13	3	2	37	10
Logan Ratledge, N.C. State	.329	.431	.558	231	19	2	10	41	11
David Thompson, Miami	.328	.434	.640	253	18	2	19	90	1
Corey Ray, Louisville	.325	.389	.543	265	15	5	11	56	34

	AVG	OBP	SLG	AB	2B	3B	HR	RBI	SB
Nick Solak, Louisville	.324	.416	.439	244	15	2	3	40	18
Matt Thaiss, Virginia	.323	.413	.512	254	18	0	10	64	4
Alex Perez, Virginia Tech	.322	.434	.507	205	9	7	5	35	3
Garrett Kennedy, Miami	.320	.435	.473	222	11	1	7	51	1
Chris Shaw, Boston College	.319	.411	.611	144	9	0	11	43	0
D.J. Stewart, Florida State	.318	.500	.594	214	10	2	15	59	12
Jonathan Pryor, Wake Forest	.316	.366	.384	177	9	0	1	11	8
Chris Okey, Clemson	.315	.389	.545	235	16	1	12	57	3
Justin Yurchak, Wake Forest	.313	.424	.456	160	8	0	5	33	4
Keenan Innis, Georgia Tech	.310	.370	.392	158	9	2	0	15	5
Andrew Knizner, N.C. State	.309	.352	.417	230	10	0	5	41	0
Daniel Pinero, Virginia	.308	.409	.419	253	8	1	6	29	9
Brendan McKay, Louisville	.308	.418	.431	211	14	0	4	34	4
Kenny Towns, Virginia	.296	.365	.446	267	21	2	5	67	2
Andy Perez, Duke	.290	.373	.429	210	14	3	3	21	35
Adam Haseley, Virginia	.250	.355	.323	276	11	3	1	19	5
Dylan Busby, Florida State	.242	.363	.455	198	15	0	9	45	12

INDIVIDUAL PITCHING LEADERS
(Minimum 40 innings pitched)

	W	L	ERA	G	SV	IP	H	BB	SO
Josh Sborz, Virginia	7	2	1.60	33	15	73	41	25	62
Brendan McKay, Louisville	9	3	1.77	20	4	97	53	34	117
Hunter Williams, North Carolina	4	2	1.79	14	0	40	28	23	35
Matthew Crownover, Clemson	10	3	1.82	16	0	109	72	37	108
Tommy DeJuneas, N.C. State	3	3	1.82	24	6	40	20	25	57
Michael Mediavilla, Miami	3	2	1.94	37	0	42	26	19	53
Sarkis Ohanian, Duke	4	1	1.97	25	0	46	37	11	62
Brian Brown, N.C. State	7	3	2.03	15	0	80	59	26	78
Sean Leland, Louisville	4	0	2.05	20	0	44	32	19	34
Joe O'Donnell, N.C. State	7	3	2.08	25	0	52	37	20	54
Jake Long, Clemson	2	1	2.17	13	0	50	37	22	39
Curt Britt, N.C. State	3	1	2.24	19	2	56	46	21	53
Cooper Hammond, Miami	5	1	2.25	37	2	40	40	9	30
Ryan Smoyer, Notre Dame	9	1	2.27	17	1	79	82	18	33
Lincoln Henzman, Louisville	5	2	2.32	28	2	54	45	11	47
Mitch Stallings, Duke	3	4	2.38	30	3	45	41	25	54
Will Gilbert, N.C. State	3	1	2.47	29	3	47	31	20	52
Bryan Garcia, Miami	6	2	2.50	35	10	40	29	20	58
Nathan Kirby, Virginia	5	3	2.53	12	1	64	55	32	81
Trevor Kelley, North Carolina	5	3	2.55	41	5	78	67	20	71
Boomer Biegalski, Florida State	7	5	3.17	18	0	108	84	38	120
Connor Jones, Virginia	7	3	3.19	18	0	116	94	52	113
Trent Thornton, North Carolina	3	7	5.08	28	6	62	53	31	81
Marc Berube, Pittsburgh	2	7	5.10	13	0	65	75	17	37

ATLANTIC SUN CONFERENCE

	Conference W	L	Overall W	L
North Florida	16	5	45	16
* Lipscomb	13	8	39	20
Stetson	12	9	29	30
Jacksonville	12	9	26	30
Florida Gulf Coast	11	9	30	26
Kennesaw State	10	10	28	28
Northern Kentucky	5	16	14	34
South Carolina-Upstate	4	17	15	38

ALL-CONFERENCE TEAM: C—Patrick Mazeika, Jr., Stetson. **1B**—Nick Rivera, Jr., Florida Gulf Coast. **2B**—Angelo Amendolare, Sr., Jacksonville. **SS**—Grant Massey, Sr., Lipscomb. **3B**—Trent Higginbotham, Sr., North Florida. **OF**—Donnie Dewees, Jr., North Florida; Cole Bauml, Sr., Northern Kentucky; Vance Vizcaino, Jr., Stetson. **DH**—Corbin Olmstead, Jr., North Florida. **SP**—Michael Baumann, Fr., Jacksonville; Travis Bergen, Jr., Kennesaw State; Jordan Hillyer, Jr., Kennesaw State; Ian Martinez-McGraw, Sr., Lipscomb. **RP**—Corbin Olmstead, Jr., North Florida. **Player of the Year:** Donnie Dewees, North Florida. **Pitcher of the Year:** Michael Baumann, Jacksonville. **Defensive Player of the Year:** Grant Massey, Lipscomb. **Coach of the Year:** Smoke Laval, North Florida. **Rookie of the Year:** Michael Baumann, Jacksonville.

INDIVIDUAL BATTING LEADERS
(Minimum 140 At-Bats)

	AVG	OBP	SLG	AB	2B	3B	HR	RBI	SB
Donnie Dewees, North Florida	.422	.483	.749	251	12	8	18	68	23
Angelo Amendolare, Jacksonville	.366	.441	.480	227	16	2	2	42	20
Cole Bauml, Northern Kentucky	.350	.445	.663	163	25	1	8	22	14
Jake Noll, FGCU	.348	.406	.423	227	6	1	3	41	15
Ryan Roberson, North Florida	.347	.390	.532	222	15	1	8	64	1
Nick Rivera, FGCU	.347	.458	.608	199	20	1	10	70	0
Grant Massey, Lipscomb	.345	.402	.441	229	12	2	2	44	18
Vance Vizcaino, Stetson	.341	.384	.466	232	16	5	1	38	13
Michael Gigliotti, Lipscomb	.336	.409	.448	232	5	3	5	28	17
Daniel Fickas, USC Upstate	.335	.403	.398	221	8	3	0	18	12
Chris Erwin, Kennesaw State	.332	.369	.487	199	12	2	5	36	6
Tyler Selesky, FGCU	.330	.435	.429	212	14	2	1	37	0
Cameron Gibson, Jacksonville	.327	.416	.408	211	11	0	2	25	12
Connor Marabell, Jacksonville	.326	.386	.498	227	21	0	6	54	7
Keith Skinner, North Florida	.325	.396	.429	154	7	0	3	32	0
Cory Reid, Stetson	.322	.400	.529	242	14	6	8	29	19
Jonathan Allison, Lipscomb	.318	.412	.514	220	18	2	7	54	14
Erik Samples, USC Upstate	.318	.400	.441	211	17	0	3	28	2
Will Mackenzie, Stetson	.317	.376	.512	205	17	1	7	50	1
Drew Luther, Jacksonville	.313	.374	.409	191	14	0	1	25	2
Matt Reardon, FGCU	.311	.420	.379	219	9	0	2	23	5
Corbin Olmstead, North Florida	.308	.362	.561	214	13	1	13	42	3
Patrick Mazeika, Stetson	.307	.439	.485	202	13	1	7	53	1
Trent Higginbothem, North Fla.	.305	.365	.439	246	12	0	7	65	1
Kyle Brooks, North Florida	.303	.375	.354	195	8	1	0	25	9
Jordan Gould, Jacksonville	.272	.362	.377	191	7	2	3	25	4

INDIVIDUAL PITCHING LEADERS
(Minimum 40 innings pitched)

	W	L	ERA	G	SV	IP	H	BB	SO
Matthew Naylor, North Florida	8	0	1.78	28	0	66	56	19	37
Matt Vaka, North Florida	3	1	1.92	13	0	52	45	18	21
Michael Baumann, Jacksonville	7	1	2.24	15	0	84	68	28	85
Nick Deckert, FGCU	3	1	2.63	16	0	41	33	17	38
Ian Martinez-McGraw, Lipscomb	7	4	2.66	17	0	102	97	44	59
Jeffrey Passantino, Lipscomb	5	1	2.69	16	2	67	51	14	64
Evan Incinelli, North Florida	6	3	2.71	15	0	66	72	11	33
Jordan Hilyer, Kennesaw State	4	5	2.72	14	0	89	75	38	92
Sterling Koerner, FGCU	6	4	3.02	22	1	57	59	4	46
Travis Bergen, Kennesaw State	6	4	3.15	14	0	100	90	31	84
Mitchell Jordan, Stetson	5	2	3.28	12	0	71	74	15	58
Brady Anderson, FGCU	5	1	3.33	17	0	84	84	15	52
Michael Murray, FGCU	5	6	3.56	14	0	91	95	13	91
Jordan Desquin, FGCU	6	1	3.63	20	0	62	51	11	58
Josh Dye, FGCU	1	3	3.70	14	0	41	48	6	28
Nick Andros, Lipscomb	6	1	3.73	23	5	72	68	27	64
Bryan Baker, North Florida	6	2	3.73	15	0	63	61	35	41
Gabe Friese, Kennesaw State	5	5	3.97	14	0	68	73	26	46
Tyler Dupont, North Florida	6	2	3.98	16	0	61	64	15	36
Dan VanSickle, North Florida	1	2	4.17	19	0	41	45	7	29
Brooks Wilson, Stetson	9	5	4.29	19	0	84	95	23	59
Walker Sheller, Stetson	2	9	4.65	23	1	72	81	22	47

ATLANTIC 10 CONFERENCE

	Conference W	L	Overall W	L
Saint Louis	16	8	34	21
Richmond	15	9	28	25
Rhode Island	15	9	26	25
* Virginia Commonwealth	14	10	40	25
Davidson	14	10	28	22
George Washington	13	10	32	22
Fordham	13	11	22	32
George Mason	12	12	23	27
Massachusetts	12	12	16	27
La Salle	12	13	24	27
St. Joseph's	11	12	21	28
Dayton	5	19	16	38
St. Bonaventure	3	21	16	29

ALL-CONFERENCE TEAM: C—Charles Galiano, So., Fordham. **1B**—David Daniels, Jr., Davidson. **2B**—Chris Hess, So., Rhode Island. **SS**—Vimael Machin, Jr., Virginia Commonwealth. **3B**—Matt Dacey, Jr., Richmond. **OF**—Michael Bozarth, Jr., Saint Louis; John Brue, Fr., St. Joseph's; Michael Morman, Sr., Richmond; Lee Miller, So., Davidson. **DH**—Joey Ravert, Jr., La Salle. Jr., George Washington. **Player of the Year:** Michael Morman, Richmond. **Pitcher of the Year:** Tyler Wilson, Rhode Island. **Coach of the Year:** Raphael Cerrato, Rhode Island. **Rookie of the Year:** Tyler Wilson, Rhode Island.

INDIVIDUAL BATTING LEADERS
(Minimum 140 At-Bats)

	AVG	OBP	SLG	AB	2B	3B	HR	RBI	SB
Michael Morman, Richmond	.389	.441	.611	226	25	2	7	56	10
Justin Korenblatt, La Salle	.387	.497	.563	142	11	1	4	32	9
Michael Bozarth, Saint Louis	.382	.460	.572	152	9	1	6	31	18
Luke Willis, George Mason	.355	.441	.500	214	15	2	4	29	29
Thad Johnson, St. Bonaventure	.354	.403	.482	189	13	1	3	31	1
Lee Miller, Davidson	.353	.421	.587	201	21	1	8	55	6
Kyle Adams, Richmond	.343	.396	.456	169	8	1	3	36	1
Deon Stafford, St. Joseph's	.341	.423	.500	182	19	2	2	26	3
Vimael Machin, VCU	.339	.401	.441	254	13	2	3	53	6
Brandon Gum, George Mason	.338	.413	.426	195	12	1	1	32	5
Ryan Lowe, Davidson	.337	.431	.480	202	14	3	3	35	4
David Daniels, Davidson	.335	.432	.585	200	15	1	11	42	3
Matthew Kozuch, Fordham	.333	.468	.477	174	10	3	3	34	8
Mike Vigliarolo, Saint Louis	.332	.383	.438	226	12	0	4	41	4
Cameron Johnson, La Salle	.327	.381	.509	220	14	4	6	48	3
Joey Bartosic, Geo. Washington	.327	.380	.369	214	7	1	0	25	21
Jake Henson, Saint Louis	.327	.366	.531	211	15	2	8	46	2
Chris Hess, Rhode Island	.326	.398	.481	181	7	6	3	26	10
Sam Foy, Davidson	.322	.386	.408	211	12	0	2	30	6
John Brue, St. Joseph's	.322	.392	.599	202	13	2	13	51	3
Kyle Adie, Massachusetts	.322	.387	.421	171	8	3	1	18	5
Matt Maul, St. Joseph's	.319	.375	.368	204	8	1	0	23	9
Stefan Kancylarz, St. Joseph's	.317	.424	.505	186	17	3	4	39	2
Cal Jadacki, St. Joseph's	.316	.391	.426	155	12	1	1	15	5
Michael Smith, George Mason	.315	.399	.359	181	6	1	0	15	8
Matt Dacey, Richmond	.313	.424	.652	198	12	2	17	52	5
Logan Farrar, VCU	.307	.392	.423	267	13	3	4	33	8
Kent Blackstone, George Mason	.256	.380	.446	195	12	8	3	42	4
Joseph Runco, Fordham	.255	.336	.314	204	7	1	1	11	29

INDIVIDUAL PITCHING LEADERS
(Minimum 40 innings pitched)

	W	L	ERA	G	SV	IP	H	BB	SO
Matt Lees, VCU	6	2	0.74	35	3	61	41	14	52
Justin Aungst, St. Joseph's	5	0	1.60	16	1	51	41	15	47
Tyler Wilson, Rhode Island	6	3	2.16	13	0	87	57	27	75
Brett Shimanovsky, Saint Louis	5	1	2.45	24	5	51	45	12	33
Luke Olson, George Washington	3	1	2.59	19	0	42	42	6	19
Brendan McGuigan, Richmond	2	4	2.66	13	1	47	42	21	41
Jojo Howie, VCU	8	7	2.77	17	0	111	118	21	82
Ryan Cook, Richmond	8	2	2.80	14	0	87	67	26	78
Heath Dwyer, VCU	10	3	3.01	18	0	96	95	26	89
Ben Greenberg, Fordham	4	2	3.04	18	0	71	82	23	33
Daniel Concepcion, VCU	3	3	3.12	27	14	69	74	19	60
Clay Smith, Saint Louis	8	4	3.19	15	0	93	80	29	67
Robbie Metz, George Washington	3	3	3.23	13	0	61	69	14	37
Ryan Lowe, Davidson	2	4	3.31	14	0	54	52	19	41
Jacob Williams, Geo. Washington	4	3	3.32	15	0	60	60	23	28
Jake Kalish, George Mason	5	6	3.44	13	0	84	88	14	77
Sean Thompson, VCU	6	3	3.48	14	0	65	57	19	49
Aaron Phillips, St. Bonaventure	2	1	3.65	15	2	44	38	23	35
Steve Moyers, Rhode Island	4	4	3.75	15	1	74	74	28	62
Joey Ravert, La Salle	4	5	3.80	12	0	66	62	20	45
Brett Kennedy, Fordham	6	8	4.14	16	0	87	95	20	97
Charlie Dant, Dayton	1	11	4.84	15	0	89	103	34	65

BIG EAST CONFERENCE

	Conference		Overall	
	W	L	W	L
* St. John's	14	3	41	16
Creighton	13	4	32	19
Seton Hall	9	9	25	25
Georgetown	8	10	25	28
Butler	8	10	19	30
Villanova	7	11	30	27
Xavier	3	15	15	38

ALL-CONFERENCE TEAM: C/DH—Nick Collins, Jr., Georgetown. **1B**—Reagan Fowler, Jr., Creighton. **2B**—Todd Czinege, So., Villanova. **SS**—Jarred Mederos, Sr., St. John's. **3B**—Robbie Knightes, So., St. John's. **OF**—Michael Donadio, So., St. John's; Alex Caruso, Jr., St. John's; Zach Lauricella, Sr., St. John's; Adam Goss, Jr., Villanova. **SP**—Rollie Lacy, Fr., Creighton; Matt Smith, Jr., Georgetown; Ryan McCormick, Jr., St. John's; Cody Stashak, Jr., St. John's. **RP**—Thomas Hackimer, Jr., St. John's. **Player of the Year:** Nick Collins, Georgetown. **Pitcher of the Year:** Ryan McCormick, St. John's. **Coach of the Year:** Ed Blankmeyer, St. John's. **Rookie of the Year:** Nate Soria, Xavier.

INDIVIDUAL BATTING LEADERS
(Minimum 140 At-Bats)

	AVG	OBP	SLG	AB	2B	3B	HR	RBI	SB
Alex Caruso, St. John's	.382	.480	.427	204	9	0	0	23	3
Nick Collins, Georgetown	.370	.435	.540	211	15	0	7	36	6
Nate Soria, Xavier	.335	.420	.471	155	11	2	2	27	12
Matt Harris, St. John's	.328	.414	.474	192	17	4	1	40	6
Todd Czinege, Villanova	.327	.372	.425	214	15	3	0	29	4
Zach Lauricella, St. John's	.327	.397	.459	196	15	1	3	45	5
Adam Goss, Villanova	.326	.436	.451	184	12	4	1	24	13
Eric Lowe, Villanova	.326	.409	.337	178	2	0	0	13	10
Tyler Houston, Butler	.324	.405	.447	179	9	2	3	26	11
Robbie Knightes, St. John's	.321	.386	.340	156	3	0	0	19	4
Garrett Christman, Butler	.320	.390	.376	178	10	0	0	21	1
Reagan Fowler, Creighton	.319	.404	.384	185	10	1	0	36	1
A.C. Carter, Georgetown	.316	.410	.468	190	17	0	4	42	0
Ryan Wojciechowski, Butler	.316	.403	.497	187	20	1	4	46	2
Michael Fries, Butler	.303	.336	.384	198	10	0	2	27	0
Michael Donadio, St. John's	.302	.416	.382	212	12	1	1	33	8
Harrison Crawford, Creighton	.298	.440	.439	171	5	5	3	20	5
Kyle Grimm, Seton Hall	.297	.382	.365	148	10	0	0	28	2
Quincy Quintero, Butler	.294	.343	.387	163	12	0	1	23	1
Brett Murray, Creighton	.293	.352	.414	181	10	3	2	27	2
Zack Weigel, Seton Hall	.287	.397	.389	167	11	3	0	27	15
Drew Small, Butler	.286	.339	.381	210	16	2	0	27	12
Austin Miller, Butler	.285	.407	.417	151	6	1	4	20	7
Patrick Jones, Xavier	.284	.343	.426	155	8	1	4	25	3
Derek Hasenbeck, Xavier	.282	.343	.426	188	9	0	6	26	1
Max Beermann, Villanova	.280	.348	.490	200	18	3	6	37	1
Derek Jenkins, Seton Hall	.274	.337	.292	168	1	1	0	22	26
Nicky Lopez, Creighton	.246	.321	.335	167	3	6	0	21	7

INDIVIDUAL PITCHING LEADERS
(Minimum 40 innings pitched)

	W	L	ERA	G	SV	IP	H	BB	SO
Thomas Hackimer, St. John's	4	1	1.92	35	15	52	31	23	55
Shane McCarthy, Seton Hall	4	4	2.19	12	0	66	53	9	29
Connor Miller, Creighton	4	3	2.44	22	0	44	30	15	32
Ryan McCormick, St. John's	11	1	2.66	17	1	91	74	25	70
Rollie Lacy, Creighton	6	1	2.66	18	0	74	64	22	47
Matthew Smith, Georgetown	4	5	2.80	14	0	87	89	29	78
Matt Warren, Creighton	5	2	2.83	13	0	60	50	10	37
Sam Burum, Seton Hall	3	0	2.85	25	0	41	34	12	27
Nick Highberger, Creighton	5	2	2.93	26	1	40	34	18	21
Kagan Richardson, Villanova	4	0	3.02	27	2	42	32	15	27
Greg Jacknewitz, Xavier	4	5	3.07	20	1	59	35	35	45
Jeff Schank, Butler	5	6	3.12	14	0	87	76	45	72
Alex Katz, St. John's	3	1	3.40	19	0	56	51	30	52
Trent Astle, Xavier	3	8	3.42	13	0	79	84	17	55
Anthony Elia, Seton Hall	4	2	3.46	19	2	65	71	12	42
Cody Stashak, St. John's	7	4	3.57	16	0	86	80	24	69
Simon Mathews, Georgetown	5	4	3.57	23	1	58	52	15	42

	W	L	ERA	G	SV	IP	H	BB	SO
Kevin Superko, Georgetown	3	2	3.65	14	0	57	61	27	32
Keith Rogalla, Creighton	4	2	3.77	13	0	57	47	20	35
Zac Lowther, Xavier	2	1	3.78	17	0	52	48	26	42
Brad Kirschner, Xavier	2	9	4.84	15	0	61	68	27	47

BIG SOUTH CONFERENCE

	Conference		Overall	
	W	L	W	L
* Radford	20	4	45	16
Coastal Carolina	17	7	39	21
Winthrop	16	8	40	19
Liberty	16	8	33	23
High Point	14	10	29	26
Campbell	12	12	32	25
Charleston Southern	10	14	23	30
Longwood	9	15	22	34
Gardner-Webb	7	17	22	31
Presbyterian	6	18	27	28
UNC Asheville	5	19	21	34

ALL-CONFERENCE TEAM: C—Cam McRae, Sr., Presbyterian. **INF**—Josh Gardiner, Sr., Radford; Alex Close, Sr., Liberty; Tommy Houmard, Sr., UNC Asheville; Michael Paez, So., Coastal Carolina. **OF**—Josh Greene, So., High Point; Anthony Marks, Jr., Coastal Carolina; Anthony Paulsen, R-So., Winthrop. **DH**—Patrick Marshall, Sr., Radford. **UTIL**—Cole Hallum, Jr., Campbell. **SP**—Jared Lyons, Sr., Liberty; Michael Boyle, Jr., Radford; Austin Kerr, Sr., Coastal Carolina. **RP**—Ryan Mesinger, Jr., Radford. **Player of the Year:** Cole Hallum, Campbell. **Pitcher of the Year:** Jared Lyons, Liberty. **Coach of the Year:** Joe Raccuia, Radford. **Rookie of the Year:** Bobby Holmes, Coastal Carolina.

INDIVIDUAL BATTING LEADERS
(Minimum 140 At-Bats)

	AVG	OBP	SLG	AB	2B	3B	HR	RBI	SB
Brad Kaczka, Winthrop	.369	.429	.442	217	6	5	0	34	12
Josh Gardiner, Radford	.368	.451	.526	171	18	0	3	22	18
Cam McRae, Presbyterian	.364	.407	.525	217	14	0	7	38	7
Tommy Houmard, UNC Asheville	.361	.444	.463	216	8	4	2	30	2
Josh Greene, High Point	.355	.441	.532	186	8	2	7	37	13
Jay Lizanich, Presbyterian	.344	.394	.455	224	13	0	4	35	4
Anthony Marks, Coastal Carolina	.343	.421	.380	242	7	1	0	25	17
Anthony Paulsen, Winthrop	.343	.425	.513	230	21	3	4	45	15
Alex Close, Liberty	.342	.422	.516	216	13	2	7	46	1
Cedric Mullins, Campbell	.340	.386	.549	235	23	7	4	23	23
Hunter Bryant, UNC Asheville	.340	.420	.576	212	12	1	12	46	0
Kyle Leady, Campbell	.336	.398	.472	214	11	3	4	35	14
Spencer Angelis, High Point	.335	.444	.472	176	13	1	3	23	3
Tyler Weyenberg, Presbyterian	.332	.374	.422	223	12	1	2	36	10
Roger Gonzales, Winthrop	.331	.405	.420	169	9	0	2	31	1
Shane Johnsonbaugh, Radford	.328	.438	.517	232	19	2	7	45	8
Patrick Marshall, Radford	.327	.441	.592	211	20	0	12	59	2
Seth LaRue, Campbell	.327	.384	.390	205	7	0	2	30	10
Cole Hallum, Campbell	.327	.426	.599	162	8	0	12	48	4
Michael Paez, Coastal Carolina	.326	.426	.526	215	17	1	8	42	19
Steven Leonard, Campbell	.325	.396	.396	197	8	0	2	22	29
Nate Blanchard, Charleston Sou.	.325	.411	.412	194	14	0	1	25	4
Brad Keen, Radford	.321	.370	.455	187	8	4	3	39	9
Brandon Delk, Longwood	.314	.343	.433	194	10	2	3	30	7
Connar Bastaich, Longwood	.312	.367	.339	221	6	0	0	22	5
Colton Konvicka, Longwood	.279	.344	.391	233	12	4	2	18	30
Kyri Washington, Longwood	.279	.357	.548	208	9	1	15	52	10
Connor Owings, Coastal Carolina	.270	.399	.470	200	11	1	9	48	13
Hunter Higgerson, Radford	.264	.317	.447	235	25	0	6	53	6

INDIVIDUAL PITCHING LEADERS
(Minimum 40 innings pitched)

	W	L	ERA	G	SV	IP	H	BB	SO
Conor Lourey, High Point	4	1	1.51	17	1	66	48	21	72
Jared Lyons, Liberty	8	2	1.99	16	0	100	71	22	100
Travis Shelley, Winthrop	3	0	2.14	32	4	55	51	11	44
Michael Boyle, Radford	10	3	2.48	16	0	105	86	37	87
Andre Scrubb, High Point	6	1	2.50	19	1	54	36	19	48

	W	L	ERA	G	SV	IP	H	BB	SO
Alex Cunningham, Coastal Carolina	6	0	2.56	11	0	60	46	24	59
Nick Thayer, Campbell	7	5	2.58	15	0	87	76	21	61
Victor Cole, Liberty	5	3	2.67	13	0	84	62	26	74
Josh Strong, Winthrop	8	3	2.89	15	0	72	78	15	37
Bobby Holmes, Coastal Carolina	4	1	2.90	27	4	62	54	16	55
Andrew Beckwith, Coastal Carolina	6	4	3.00	27	2	66	65	17	40
Evan Raynor, Charleston Southern	4	5	3.01	15	0	84	88	21	78
Matt Crohan, Winthrop	7	4	3.05	14	0	77	60	29	87
Andrew Tomasovich, Charleston So.	7	7	3.09	15	0	87	82	26	93
Mitch Warner, Gardner-Webb	3	6	3.13	17	0	69	64	23	36
Zack Ridgley, Radford	5	1	3.18	17	0	51	48	8	40
Heath Bowers, Campbell	8	5	3.19	15	0	93	101	22	90
John McGillicuddy, High Point	5	5	3.27	14	0	83	81	27	65
Austin Kerr, Coastal Carolina	8	1	3.36	17	0	62	64	18	57
Tyler Britton, High Point	3	1	3.53	16	1	43	48	17	31
Coley Thompkins, Campbell	4	2	3.56	25	2	43	50	7	28
Aaron Myers, Longwood	4	9	3.64	16	1	106	86	36	115
Ryan Jones, Longwood	2	1	4.91	27	1	40	36	10	33

	AVG	OBP	SLG	AB	2B	3B	HR	RBI	SB
Troy Montgomery, Ohio State	.317	.432	.493	205	12	6	4	27	35
Reid Roper, Illinois	.293	.406	.487	232	7	4	10	49	6
Joe D'Annunzio, Rutgers	.270	.363	.470	185	7	9	4	23	13

INDIVIDUAL PITCHING LEADERS
(Minimum 40 innings pitched)

	W	L	ERA	G	SV	IP	H	BB	SO
Luke Vandermaten, Iowa	2	0	**1.06**	22	4	42	32	15	23
Tyler Jay, Illinois	5	2	1.08	30	14	67	40	7	76
Nick Hibbing, Iowa	4	1	1.57	25	8	52	30	5	47
Mike Shawaryn, Maryland	13	2	1.71	17	0	116	85	29	138
Kevin Duchene, Illinois	11	2	1.75	15	0	103	89	18	88
Joe Mockbee, Michigan State	6	2	1.78	25	2	51	43	17	50
Drasen Johnson, Illinois	10	3	2.01	16	0	117	103	17	77
Luke Harrison, Indiana	4	2	2.02	25	3	49	38	13	61
Ryan Selmer, Maryland	3	1	2.18	31	0	54	49	16	19
Rob McDonnell, Illinois	7	2	2.28	17	0	75	57	29	70
Joe Eichmann, Purdue	3	2	2.32	24	2	43	35	25	44
Scott Effross, Indiana	4	4	2.35	21	2	61	50	9	51
Thomas Belcher, Indiana	3	1	2.44	27	0	48	44	5	46
Calvin Mathews, Iowa	5	3	2.45	16	0	73	67	26	43
Matt Ogden, Michigan	5	1	2.47	21	1	51	46	18	41
Ryan Halstead, Indiana	2	2	2.59	29	10	42	34	6	55
Jeff Chesnut, Indiana	6	0	2.72	31	0	43	39	9	25
Walter Borkovich, Michigan State	3	0	2.73	30	0	53	34	15	39
Robert Galligan, Maryland	4	5	2.74	27	1	62	50	21	58
Ryan Erickson, Iowa	4	1	2.79	18	1	42	47	20	27
Matt Frawley, Purdue	1	9	4.55	14	2	55	59	23	33
Reed Mason, Northwestern	2	9	5.18	17	0	75	93	31	57

BIG TEN CONFERENCE

	Conference		Overall	
	W	L	W	L
Illinois	21	1	49	10
Iowa	19	5	38	18
* **Michigan**	14	10	39	25
Maryland	14	10	42	24
Michigan State	14	10	34	23
Indiana	12	10	35	24
Ohio State	13	11	35	20
Nebraska	9	14	34	23
Minnesota	9	15	19	30
Northwestern	8	16	18	36
Rutgers	7	17	19	35
Penn State	6	16	18	30
Purdue	6	17	20	34

ALL-CONFERENCE TEAM: C—Jason Goldstein, Jr., Illinois. 1B—David Kerian, Sr., Illinois. 2B—Brandon Lowe, So., Maryland. SS—Adam Walton, R-So., Illinois. 3B—Mark Weist, R-Sr., Michigan State. OF—Casey Fletcher, Jr., Illinois; Jackson Glines, Sr., Michigan; Pat Porter, Sr., Ohio State. DH—Carmen Benedetti, So., Michigan. SP—Kevin Duchene, Jr., Illinois; Blake Hickman, Jr., Iowa; Mike Shawaryn, So., Maryland. RP—Tyler Jay, Jr., Illinois. Player of the Year: David Kerian, Illinois. Pitcher of the Year: Tyler Jay, Illinois. Coach of the Year: Dan Hartleb, Illinois. Rookie of the Year: Jake Bivens, Michigan.

INDIVIDUAL BATTING LEADERS
(Minimum 140 At-Bats)

	AVG	OBP	SLG	AB	2B	3B	HR	RBI	SB
David Kerian, Illinois	**.367**	**.462**	**.667**	207	10	2	16	52	9
Kyle Ruchim, Northwestern	.358	.416	.585	159	16	1	6	23	1
Carmen Benedetti, Michigan	.352	.418	.541	233	25	2	5	71	1
Ryan Krill, Michigan State	.351	.439	.615	205	13	1	13	57	1
Jackson Glines, Michigan	.349	.440	.492	238	13	3	5	34	7
Mark Weist, Michigan State	.346	.407	.526	228	19	2	6	37	11
Ryan Boldt, Nebraska	.344	.429	.408	218	7	2	1	21	9
Kevin Martir, Maryland	.342	.441	.502	237	17	0	7	45	3
Jacob Cronenworth, Michigan	.338	.419	.494	269	18	3	6	48	11
Patrick Porter, Ohio State	.338	.423	.576	210	9	4	11	49	6
Ryan Nagle, Illinois	.337	.394	.447	255	19	0	3	34	11
Tyler Peyton, Iowa	.337	.439	.417	187	11	2	0	31	2
Lamonte Wade, Maryland	.335	.453	.468	158	7	1	4	32	7
Scott Heelan, Northwestern	.332	.386	.428	208	17	0	1	19	1
Brandon Lowe, Maryland	.331	.437	.542	251	18	4	9	53	11
Michael Handel, Minnesota	.328	.380	.469	177	8	1	5	30	8
Casey Fletcher, Illinois	.326	.423	.414	227	7	2	3	33	9
Kyle Wood, Purdue	.326	.421	.487	193	13	0	6	34	1
Aaron Novak, Penn State	.326	.398	.464	181	11	1	4	27	7
Craig Dedelow, Indiana	.325	.376	.496	234	13	3	7	37	5
Tom Marcinczyk, Rutgers	.325	.409	.507	203	10	3	7	36	3
Zach Jones, Northwestern	.321	.374	.436	218	17	1	1	32	0
Jake Bivens, Michigan	.319	.435	.352	213	7	0	0	19	9
Scott Donley, Indiana	.318	.386	.390	223	10	0	2	37	1

BIG 12 CONFERENCE

	Conference		Overall	
	W	L	W	L
Texas Christian	18	5	51	15
Oklahoma State	14	8	38	20
Oklahoma	13	11	34	27
Texas Tech	13	11	31	24
* **Texas**	11	13	30	27
Kansas State	10	14	27	30
West Virginia	9	13	27	27
Baylor	9	15	23	32
Kansas	8	15	23	32

ALL-CONFERENCE TEAM: C—Gage Green, Sr., Oklahoma State. INF—Shane Conlon, Sr., Kansas State; Kolbey Carpenter, Jr., Oklahoma; Sheldon Neuse, So., Oklahoma; Donnie Walton, Jr., Oklahoma State; Eric Gutierrez, Jr., Texas Tech. OF—Connor McKay, Sr., Kansas; Craig Aikin, Jr., Oklahoma; Cody Jones, Sr., Texas Christian; Ben Johnson, Jr., Texas. DH—Connor Wanhanen, Fr., Texas Christian. P—Michael Freeman, Sr., Oklahoma State; Preston Morrison, Sr., Texas Christian; Alex Young, Jr., Texas Christian; Cameron Smith, Sr., Texas Tech. Riley Ferrell, Jr., Texas Christian; Corey Taylor, Sr., Texas Tech. Player of the Year: Cody Jones, Texas Christian. Pitcher of the Year: Michael Freeman, Oklahoma State. Coach of the Year: Jim Schlossnagle, Texas Christian. Newcomer of the Year: Ben Krauth, Kansas. Freshman of the Year: Connor Wanhanen, Texas Christian.

INDIVIDUAL BATTING LEADERS
(Minimum 140 At-Bats)

	AVG	OBP	SLG	AB	2B	3B	HR	RBI	SB
Kolbey Carpenter, Oklahoma	**.360**	.416	.533	242	10	4	8	37	5
Cody Jones, TCU	.353	**.464**	.476	252	14	1	5	34	33
Kyle Davis, West Virginia	.353	.391	.491	224	17	1	4	31	4
Cory Raley, Texas Tech	.350	.408	.486	183	10	3	3	21	3
Connor McKay, Kansas	.346	.392	**.535**	228	22	3	5	22	6
Craig Aikin, Oklahoma	.340	.387	.435	253	15	3	1	32	5
Michael Tinsley, Kansas	.337	.407	.459	196	15	0	3	39	4
Ben Johnson, Texas	.332	.393	.498	241	11	**7**	5	32	16
Connor Wanhanen, TCU	.329	.420	.389	216	4	3	1	40	11
Kameron Esthay, Baylor	.323	.380	.477	155	7	1	5	25	5
Anthony Hermelyn, Oklahoma	.321	.360	.453	212	14	1	6	49	3
Eric Gutierrez, Texas Tech	.315	.444	.443	203	14	0	4	46	2
Corey Hassel, Oklahoma State	.312	.352	.417	199	10	1	3	33	13

	AVG	OBP	SLG	AB	2B	3B	HR	RBI	SB
Ryan Sluder, Oklahoma State	.309	.401	.506	162	14	0	6	22	5
Taylor Alspaugh, Oklahoma	.308	.406	.379	211	7	1	2	32	4
Nolan Brown, TCU	.302	.371	.373	225	11	1	1	30	19
Tyler Moore, Kansas State	.302	.371	.465	172	12	2	4	31	2
Matt McLaughlin, Kansas	.293	.398	.356	174	8	0	1	25	1
Joven Afenir, Kansas	.293	.376	.390	164	8	1	2	23	1
Derek Odell, TCU	.292	.365	.373	236	10	0	3	42	9
Gage Green, Oklahoma State	.291	.404	.404	223	4	3	5	29	18
Shane Conlon, Kansas State	.291	.384	.408	196	13	2	2	26	10
Stephen Smith, Texas Tech	.291	.428	.533	182	10	2	10	32	6
Jackson Cramer, West Virginia	.291	.389	.520	179	15	1	8	21	2
Dane Steinhagen, TCU	.289	.346	.353	218	6	4	0	28	10
Evan Skoug, TCU	.285	.365	.426	256	15	0	7	46	5
Taylor Munden, West Virginia	.266	.321	.469	222	12	0	11	31	11

INDIVIDUAL PITCHING LEADERS
(Minimum 40 innings pitched)

	W	L	ERA	G	SV	IP	H	BB	SO
Corey Taylor, Texas Tech	4	0	0.31	19	2	57	36	13	32
Michael Freeman, Okla. State	10	3	1.31	15	0	110	72	29	97
Trey Teakell, TCU	3	0	1.35	30	1	53	39	8	47
Remey Reed, Oklahoma State	3	2	1.57	23	0	46	40	13	30
Jacob Evans, Oklahoma	6	1	1.67	28	8	43	36	10	53
Dominic Moreno, Texas Tech	3	3	1.85	24	6	58	54	19	73
Mitchell Traver, TCU	9	2	1.89	16	0	76	49	26	77
Kyle Johnston, Texas	1	1	2.21	25	1	41	24	27	41
Alex Young, TCU	9	3	2.22	17	0	97	75	22	103
Preston Morrison, TCU	12	3	2.51	19	0	122	100	22	91
Adam Choplick, Oklahoma	3	1	2.51	11	0	43	32	26	53
Robert Tasin, Oklahoma	9	2	2.52	18	1	79	64	26	57
Parker French, Texas	5	3	2.57	16	0	91	97	21	58
Connor Mayes, Texas	2	4	2.58	29	2	66	56	21	54
Trey Cobb, Oklahoma State	5	2	2.61	31	2	59	48	19	53
Nate Griep, Kansas State	6	3	2.63	13	0	79	62	33	64
Cameron Smith, Texas Tech	6	5	2.83	14	1	89	79	28	77
Jake Elliott, Oklahoma	4	6	3.06	15	0	88	75	35	80
Chad Donato, West Virginia	7	6	3.07	15	1	97	89	20	76
Tyler Alexander, TCU	6	3	3.07	17	0	94	92	10	72
Tyler Buffett, Oklahoma State	3	3	3.65	19	0	44	56	7	32

BIG WEST CONFERENCE

	Conference W	L	Overall W	L
* Cal State Fullerton	19	5	39	25
UC Santa Barbara	16	8	40	17
UC Irvine	15	9	33	23
Cal Poly	14	10	27	27
Hawaii	12	12	21	32
Long Beach State	11	13	28	26
UC Davis	9	15	30	26
Cal State Northridge	8	16	33	24
UC Riverside	4	20	15	40

ALL-CONFERENCE TEAM: C—Izaak Silva, Sr., UC Davis. 1B—Nick Lynch, Jr., UC Davis. 2B—Mark Mathias, Jr., Cal Poly. SS—Mikey Durate, Jr., UC Irvine; Peter Van Gansen, Jr., Cal Poly. 3B—Jerrod Bravo, Jr., Cal State Fullerton. OF—Zack Zehner, Sr., Cal Poly; Kreston Hiura, Fr., UC Irvine; Cameron Newell, Sr., UC Santa Barbara. DH—David Olmedo-Barrera, Jr., Cal State Fullerton. UTIL—Robby Nesovic, Jr., UC Santa Barbara; Josh Vargas, Jr., Cal State Fullerton. SP—Tyler Brashears, Jr., Hawaii; Thomas Eshelman, Jr., Cal State Fullerton; Chris Mathewson, Fr., Long Beach State; Dillon Tate, Jr., UC Santa Barbara. RP—Miles Chambers, So., Cal State Fullerton; Domenic Mazza, Jr., UC Santa Barbara. Player of the Year: Cameron Newell, UC Santa Barbara; David Olmedo-Barrera, Cal State Fullerton. Pitcher of the Year: Thomas Eshelman, Cal State Fullerton. Defensive Player of the Year: Peter Van Gansen, Cal Poly. Coach of the Year: Rick Vanderhook, Cal State Fullerton. Freshman Player of the Year: Keston Hiura, UC Irvine. Freshman Pitcher of the Year: Chris Mathewson, Long Beach State.

INDIVIDUAL BATTING LEADERS
(Minimum 140 At-Bats)

	AVG	OBP	SLG	AB	2B	3B	HR	RBI	SB
Cameron Newell, UCSB	.368	.447	.473	201	8	2	3	31	7
Nick Lynch, UC Davis	.361	.452	.558	208	31	2	2	34	6
Mark Mathias, Cal Poly	.356	.424	.436	202	7	3	1	28	9
Robby Nesovic, UCSB	.342	.399	.406	187	12	0	0	40	6
Mikey Duarte, UC Irvine	.341	.412	.425	226	17	1	0	19	1
Josh Vargas, Cal State Fullerton	.332	.437	.392	199	8	2	0	16	13
Keston Hiura, UC Irvine	.330	.392	.520	227	18	2	7	52	11
Andrew Calica, UCSB	.329	.445	.424	210	13	2	1	19	15
David Olmedo-Barrera, CSUF	.325	.427	.573	206	9	6	10	46	14
Mitchell Holland, UC Irvine	.325	.382	.482	197	14	1	5	35	1
Izaak Silva, UC Davis	.320	.392	.456	206	19	3	1	31	6
Jerrod Bravo, Cal State Fullerton	.318	.451	.405	148	9	2	0	25	5
Vince Fernandez, UC Riverside	.316	.387	.524	206	16	3	7	34	9
Peter Van Gansen, Cal Poly	.314	.388	.414	220	10	3	2	28	3
Tino Lipson, UC Davis	.308	.376	.397	234	12	3	1	22	21
Joe Chavez, UC Riverside	.308	.390	.453	201	9	4	4	14	9
Woody Woodward, UCSB	.308	.419	.392	143	10	1	0	12	4
Jordan Ellis, Cal Poly	.305	.364	.419	203	11	6	0	25	1
Zack Zehner, Cal Poly	.304	.356	.509	214	11	3	9	46	2
John Williams, UC Davis	.301	.342	.358	173	10	0	0	22	14
Austin March, UC Davis	.299	.386	.407	214	11	0	4	37	11
Robby Witt, UC Riverside	.299	.340	.403	144	12	0	1	18	1
Tyler Stieb, Cal State Fullerton	.297	.372	.362	229	11	2	0	23	12
Garrett Hampson, LBSU	.296	.368	.366	216	9	3	0	17	18
Luke Swenson, UCSB	.296	.384	.387	186	9	4	0	29	4
Jacob Sheldon-Collins, Hawaii	.295	.341	.355	166	6	2	0	11	2

INDIVIDUAL PITCHING LEADERS
(Minimum 40 innings pitched)

	W	L	ERA	G	SV	IP	H	BB	SO
Spencer Henderson, UC Davis	3	1	1.12	17	0	40	32	6	29
Tyler Brashears, Hawaii	8	5	1.86	15	0	102	90	19	68
Conner O'Neil, Cal St. Northridge	3	2	1.89	28	12	62	42	18	64
Chris Mathewson, Long Beach St.	6	6	1.94	13	0	93	61	24	80
Thomas Eshelman, CS Fullerton	8	5	2.00	19	1	137	105	7	139
Miles Chambers, Cal St. Fullerton	5	3	2.17	25	1	62	57	13	50
Rayne Raven, Cal State Northridge	7	4	2.18	15	0	87	74	28	73
Shane Bieber, UC Santa Barbara	8	4	2.24	16	0	113	114	13	95
Dillon Tate, UC Santa Barbara	8	5	2.26	14	0	103	66	28	111
Darren McCaughan, Long Beach St.	4	2	2.47	23	0	47	42	13	46
Tyler Peitzmeier, Cal St. Fullerton	5	4	2.56	31	16	60	55	11	61
Jerry Keel, Cal State Northridge	5	7	2.66	14	0	91	81	22	80
Domenic Mazza, UC Santa Barbara	6	1	2.69	17	2	77	61	26	72
Justin Jacome, UC Santa Barbara	7	5	2.70	16	0	117	110	26	96
Casey Bloomquist, Cal Poly	8	2	2.76	14	0	98	93	29	78
Kyle Friedrichs, Long Beach State	6	4	2.79	15	0	100	90	12	109
LJ Brewster, Hawaii	6	5	2.95	15	0	95	85	41	63
Danny Zandona, Cal Poly	1	4	2.95	28	7	40	32	17	63
Angel Rodriguez, CS Northridge	2	0	3.04	21	2	47	48	5	33
Calvin Copping, Cal St. Northridge	6	7	3.05	15	0	89	82	29	86
Matt Esparza, UC Irvine	8	2	3.56	16	0	99	92	35	81
Kyle Smith, Cal Poly	5	7	4.06	15	0	84	89	27	60
Kevin Sprague, UC Riverside	4	7	4.69	15	0	79	97	16	46
Max Cordy, UC Davis	8	5	5.51	16	0	67	83	39	54

COLONIAL ATHLETIC ASSOCIATION

	Conference W	L	Overall W	L
College of Charleston	21	3	45	15
* UNC Wilmington	18	6	41	18
Northeastern	14	10	25	30
Elon	13	11	25	29
Delaware	11	13	26	23
William & Mary	10	14	22	30
Towson	9	15	17	35
Hofstra	6	18	18	29
James Madison	6	18	18	33

ALL-CONFERENCE TEAM: C—Ryan Hissey, Jr., William & Mary. 1B—Charley Gould, Jr., William & Mary. 2B—Blake Butler, Jr., College of Charleston. SS—Chad Carroll, Jr., James Madison. 3B—Carl Wise, Jr., College of Charleston. OF—Ryan Cooper, Sr., Elon; Steven Linkous, Jr., UNC Wilmington; Zach Shields, Jr., UNC Wilmington. DH—Chris Henze, So., Towson. UTIL—Casey Jones, Sr., Elon. SP—Taylor Clarke, Jr., College of Charleston; Brandon Glazer, Sr., College of Charleston; Jordan Ramsey, Sr., UNC Wilmington. RP—Jordan Ramsey, Sr., UNC Wilmington. Player of the Year: Blake Butler, College of Charleston. Pitcher of the Year: Taylor Clarke, College of Charleston. Defensive Player of the Year: Blake Butler, College of Charleston. Coach of the Year: Monte Lee, College of Charleston. Rookie of the Year: Kyle McPherson, James Madison.

INDIVIDUAL BATTING LEADERS
(Minimum 140 At-Bats)

	AVG	OBP	SLG	AB	2B	3B	HR	RBI	SB
Charley Gould, William & Mary	.388	.473	.706	170	15	0	13	52	0
Ryan Cooper, Elon	.373	.450	.562	201	13	2	7	42	4
Zach Shields, UNC Wilmington	.355	.393	.446	220	7	2	3	38	17
Steven Foster, Hofstra	.351	.452	.439	148	7	0	2	21	19
Terence Connelly, UNCW	.344	.478	.417	192	7	2	1	26	6
Gavin Stupienski, UNCW	.344	.415	.516	186	14	0	6	37	2
Michael Foster, Northeastern	.343	.426	.490	204	10	4	4	35	10
Zach Lopes, Delaware	.341	.415	.476	208	13	3	3	28	13
Chad Carroll, James Madison	.339	.445	.497	183	13	2	4	27	27
Nick Pappas, Col. of Charleston	.337	.389	.610	249	28	2	12	57	5
Devin White, William & Mary	.331	.417	.423	175	10	0	2	26	0
Chris Henze, Towson	.331	.419	.503	151	11	0	5	42	3
Anthony Gallo, Towson	.331	.414	.462	145	6	2	3	30	4
Mark Grunberg, Towson	.328	.410	.404	183	8	0	2	29	9
Norm Donkin, Delaware	.327	.407	.472	199	13	5	2	29	13
Blake Butler, Col. of Charleston	.325	.395	.564	243	15	2	13	63	4
Joe Giacchino, Delaware	.324	.358	.446	213	10	2	4	34	11
Corey Dick, UNC Wilmington	.324	.421	.515	173	15	0	6	41	0
Richie Blosser, Towson	.321	.385	.435	184	10	1	3	28	3
Ryan Brown, Col. of Charleston	.320	.413	.455	244	14	2	5	26	14
Kyle McPherson, James Madison	.316	.401	.477	193	11	4	4	28	8
Steven Linkous, UNCW	.315	.405	.394	241	8	4	1	21	30
Carl Wise, Col. of Charleston	.313	.380	.557	246	18	3	12	70	3
Casey Jones, Elon	.313	.423	.475	217	15	1	6	42	8
Pat Madigan, Northeastern	.313	.383	.463	214	13	2	5	25	1
Rob Fonseca, Northeastern	.274	.376	.581	179	10	0	15	41	1

INDIVIDUAL PITCHING LEADERS
(Minimum 40 innings pitched)

	W	L	ERA	G	SV	IP	H	BB	SO
Jordan Ramsey, UNC Wilmington	8	2	1.69	28	7	48	33	11	62
Taylor Clarke, Col. of Charleston	13	1	1.73	17	1	114	76	14	143
Carter Love, Col. of Charleston	6	0	1.98	24	4	41	38	4	33
Brandon Glazer, Col. of Charleston	10	2	2.74	21	1	89	84	11	49
Nathan Helvey, Col. of Charleston	7	4	2.84	20	3	73	62	27	57
Nick Berger, Northeastern	5	5	3.10	15	0	93	83	29	75
Aaron Civale, Northeastern	7	2	3.24	20	6	42	51	9	41
Nick Brown, William & Mary	5	4	3.38	14	0	91	82	35	64
Whitman Barnes, UNC Wilmington	5	0	3.40	24	0	48	34	27	48
Adam Davis, Delaware	6	3	3.83	14	0	87	97	32	66
Ryan Foster, UNC Wilmington	7	1	4.08	16	0	88	101	33	66
Ronald Marinaccio, Delaware	4	3	4.11	11	0	61	63	26	43
Austin Magestro, UNC Wilmington	5	2	4.14	24	0	46	37	22	43
Chase Henry, Col. of Charleston	3	1	4.17	27	5	41	40	11	38
Michael Elefante, Elon	3	1	4.33	12	0	54	54	23	39
Aaron Fernandez, William & Mary	3	3	4.35	11	0	52	57	19	25
Josh Roberson, UNC Wilmington	1	1	4.46	14	0	40	32	27	34
Nick Beaulac, Elon	5	2	4.50	21	0	50	45	38	60
Evan Phillips, UNC Wilmington	2	2	4.56	14	0	51	60	26	53
Isaac Lippert, Northeastern	2	4	4.60	18	4	45	49	25	44
Jason Inghram, William & Mary	4	8	4.94	14	0	86	95	26	82
James Mulry, Northeastern	3	8	5.71	16	0	69	79	42	61

CONFERENCE USA

	Conference		Overall	
	W	L	W	L
Rice	22	8	37	22
Florida Atlantic	19	10	42	19
Southern Mississippi	19	10	36	18
Middle Tennessee State	19	11	32	27
Texas-San Antonio	17	13	33	25
Alabama-Birmingham	15	15	33	25
Old Dominion	13	17	27	29
* Florida International	13	17	29	31
Marshall	12	18	20	32
Charlotte	11	19	19	29
Western Kentucky	10	19	24	28
Louisiana Tech	8	21	25	27

ALL-CONFERENCE TEAM: C—John Bormann, Sr., Texas-San Antonio. INF—Jesse Baker, Jr., Texas-San Antonio; C.J. Chatham, So., Florida Atlantic; Edwin Rios, Jr., Florida International; Ford Stainback, Sr., Rice. OF—Ronnie Jebavy, Jr., Middle Tennessee; Anderson Miller, Jr., Western Kentucky; Brendon Sanger, Jr., Florida Atlantic. DH/UTIL—John Clay Reeves, Sr., Rice. SP—James McMahon, Sr., Southern Mississippi; James Naile, Sr., Alabama-Birmingham; Austin Orewiler, Jr., Rice; Jordan Stephens, Jr., Rice. RP—Matt Ditman, Sr., Rice. Player of the Year: Brendon Sanger, Florida Atlantic. Pitcher of the Year: James McMahon, Southern Mississippi. Coach of the Year: Jim McGuire, Middle Tennessee. Newcomer of the Year: Ronnie Jebavy, Middle Tennessee. Freshman of the Year: Ryan Chandler, Rice.

INDIVIDUAL BATTING LEADERS
(Minimum 140 At-Bats)

	AVG	OBP	SLG	AB	2B	3B	HR	RBI	SB
Brendon Sanger, Fla. Atlantic	.370	.492	.583	230	20	4	7	48	2
Ronnie Jebavy, Middle Tenn.	.361	.408	.533	244	15	3	7	36	24
Kirby Taylor, Rice	.346	.362	.432	185	11	1	1	29	1
Ford Stainback, Rice	.345	.421	.413	235	10	3	0	29	2
Brian Portelli, FIU	.343	.393	.490	245	20	2	4	46	2
Tyler Straub, UTSA	.340	.391	.463	162	11	0	3	27	12
Brad Jarreau, Middle Tenn.	.338	.380	.396	240	11	0	1	31	3
P.J. Higgins, Old Dominion	.335	.402	.452	239	19	0	3	32	3
CJ Chatham, Florida Atlantic	.335	.361	.496	230	22	3	3	44	3
Jesse Baker, UTSA	.329	.381	.634	216	21	0	15	44	3
Brad Elwood, Charlotte	.328	.400	.394	180	7	1	1	24	0
Danny Hudzina, Western Ky.	.327	.369	.515	202	9	1	9	43	3
Leiff Clarkson, Western Ky.	.327	.372	.392	153	6	2	0	13	4
Ricky Santiago, Florida Atlantic	.322	.408	.512	242	22	0	8	52	3
Brett Netzer, Charlotte	.318	.382	.399	148	6	3	0	19	3
Zach Rutherford, Old Dominion	.317	.367	.409	164	13	1	0	18	4
Edwin Rios, FIU	.314	.421	.592	223	6	1	18	56	3
Matt Durst, Southern Miss.	.314	.354	.454	207	10	2	5	31	0
Tim Lynch, Southern Miss.	.313	.400	.510	192	11	0	9	32	0
Kevin Markham, UTSA	.311	.393	.505	222	13	3	8	31	8
Logan Sherer, Charlotte	.311	.348	.477	193	14	0	6	25	1
Charlie Warren, Rice	.308	.381	.360	211	6	1	1	30	5
John Clay Reeves, Rice	.308	.408	.458	201	6	0	8	55	3
Stephen Kerr, Florida Atlantic	.307	.389	.358	257	10	0	1	23	15
Corey Bird, Marshall	.307	.373	.363	212	7	1	1	23	10
Roman Collins, Florida Atlantic	.288	.383	.476	233	13	5	7	59	4
Austin Bryant, Middle Tenn.	.249	.327	.383	217	10	5	3	22	2

INDIVIDUAL PITCHING LEADERS
(Minimum 40 innings pitched)

	W	L	ERA	G	SV	IP	H	BB	SO
Glenn Otto, Rice	2	0	1.54	23	1	41	20	28	65
James McMahon, Southern Miss.	11	1	1.56	15	0	92	66	22	60
Kevin Elder, Western Kentucky	1	1	1.87	23	2	43	32	16	41
Danny Dopico, FIU	3	4	1.99	27	10	45	25	20	57
Thomas Lowery, UAB	7	2	2.11	27	3	55	34	17	62
Williams Durruthy, FIU	2	1	2.18	26	2	41	28	31	48
Seth McGarry, Florida Atlantic	4	1	2.25	21	5	40	37	14	35
Adam Bainbridge, Old Dominion	4	2	2.39	21	2	68	52	14	33

	W	L	ERA	G	SV	IP	H	BB	SO
Drew Jackson, Florida Atlantic	6	4	2.44	13	0	74	59	17	55
Sean Geoghegan, Charlotte	6	5	2.46	13	0	88	71	22	58
Austin Orewiler, Rice	6	2	2.55	23	3	85	68	29	80
James Naile, UAB	10	4	2.63	16	0	110	78	32	92
Sam Sinnen, Old Dominion	6	3	2.84	21	3	67	63	15	53
Chase Boster, Marshall	7	1	2.95	12	0	55	48	20	37
Kevin McCanna, Rice	7	3	2.96	16	0	85	92	26	64
Adam Atkins, Louisiana Tech	3	4	2.96	23	7	46	44	20	38
Christopher Mourelle, FIU	7	7	3.07	17	0	103	99	26	47
Cody Carroll, Southern Miss.	5	5	3.08	15	0	96	73	47	87
Matt Ditman, Rice	3	3	3.09	30	11	58	48	17	70
Aaron Burns, UTSA	7	3	3.19	16	1	73	87	21	38
Cord Cockrell, Southern Miss.	3	0	4.37	11	0	45	57	7	20
Johnathan Frebis, Middle Tenn.	5	8	4.86	15	0	83	104	35	70
Heath Slatton, Middle Tenn.	2	8	7.99	21	0	47	59	26	34

HORIZON LEAGUE

	Conference		Overall	
	W	L	W	L
Illinois-Chicago	22	8	29	22
* Wright State	21	8	43	17
Wisconsin-Milwaukee	16	13	35	20
Valparaiso	15	14	22	31
Youngstown State	9	21	16	34
Oakland	5	24	10	39

ALL-CONFERENCE TEAM: C—Sean Murphy, So., Wright State. **1B**—Nate Palace, So., Valparaiso. **2B**—Michael Timm, Sr., Wright State. **SS**—Mitch Roman, So., Wright State. **3B**—Mickey McDonald, So., Wright State. **OF**—Jeff Boehm, Sr., Illinois-Chicago; Sam Koenig, Sr., Wisconsin-Milwaukee; Frank Califano, Jr., Youngstown State **DH**—Matt Morrow, Fr., Wright State. **UTIL**—Tyler Detmer, Sr., Illinois-Chicago. **SP**—Jake Dahlberg, So., Illinois-Chicago; Joe Pavlovich, Sr., Wisconsin-Milwaukee; Justin Langley, Jr., Wisconsin-Milwaukee. **RP**—Andrew Elliott, Sr., Wright State. **Player of the Year:** Jeff Boehm, Illinois-Chicago. **Pitcher of the Year:** Jake Dahlberg, Illinois-Chicago. **Relief Pitcher of the Year:** Andrew Elliott, Wright State. **Coach of the Year:** Mike Dee, Illinois-Chicago. **Rookie of the Year:** Gabe Snyder, Wright State.

INDIVIDUAL BATTING LEADERS
(Minimum 140 At-Bats)

	AVG	OBP	SLG	AB	2B	3B	HR	RBI	SB
Frank Califano, Youngstown St.	.362	.413	.406	207	5	2	0	18	19
Jeff Boehm, Ill.-Chicago	.362	.465	.663	199	17	2	13	66	4
Sam Koenig, Wis.-Milwaukee	.361	.454	.657	230	19	2	15	57	6
Tyler Detmer, Ill.-Chicago	.359	.453	.541	209	15	1	7	33	2
Mitch Ghelfi, Wis.-Milwaukee	.356	.463	.514	177	16	3	2	35	4
Mark Fowler, Wright State	.342	.409	.516	225	17	2	6	43	18
Mitch Roman, Wright State	.339	.377	.421	254	12	3	1	41	9
Sean Murphy, Wright State	.329	.423	.458	225	11	3	4	36	7
Nate Palace, Valparaiso	.329	.424	.579	152	15	1	7	39	0
Robby Enslen, Oakland	.328	.387	.417	204	15	0	1	25	7
Nolan Lodden, Valparaiso	.327	.441	.416	202	12	0	2	34	10
Spencer Mahoney, Valparaiso	.326	.441	.442	224	15	1	3	28	9
Daniel Delaney, Valparaiso	.325	.400	.439	212	15	0	3	36	2
Alex Larivee, Youngstown St.	.325	.421	.490	157	12	1	4	21	10
Conor Philbin, Ill.-Chicago	.325	.403	.376	157	2	3	0	19	3
Cody Bohanek, Ill.-Chicago	.324	.434	.362	188	7	0	0	16	6
Derek Peake, Wis.-Milwaukee	.323	.402	.431	223	11	5	1	29	14
Luke Meeteer, Wis.-Milwaukee	.321	.404	.459	246	19	3	3	30	37
Alex Lee, Ill.-Chicago	.314	.383	.398	191	10	0	2	46	2
Matt Morrow, Wright State	.309	.434	.416	149	7	3	1	24	6
Tyler Pagano, Oakland	.307	.339	.398	166	12	0	1	22	0
Tell Taylor, Wis.-Milwaukee	.301	.358	.443	183	11	3	3	30	5
Mickey McDonald, Ill.-Chicago	.298	.373	.335	188	4	0	1	36	15
Michael Porcaro, Wis.-Milwaukee	.296	.430	.381	189	11	1	1	32	8
Ian Yetsko, Oakland	.293	.349	.466	191	22	1	3	28	3
Ryan Fucci, Wright State	.288	.390	.587	208	15	1	15	49	11

INDIVIDUAL PITCHING LEADERS
(Minimum 40 innings pitched)

	W	L	ERA	G	SV	IP	H	BB	SO
Jeremy Randolph, Wright State	7	0	2.22	13	0	45	43	16	28
Austin Schulfer, Wis.-Milwaukee	3	0	2.25	9	0	44	34	19	42

	W	L	ERA	G	SV	IP	H	BB	SO
E.J. Trapino, Wright State	8	1	2.55	37	0	53	39	29	66
Andrew Elliott, Wright State	5	4	2.61	30	11	48	36	17	56
Jack Van Horn, Wright State	4	2	3.06	26	3	53	60	13	38
Jesse Scholtens, Wright State	7	4	3.08	15	0	91	90	21	72
Luke Mamer, Wright State	4	2	3.21	15	0	76	78	10	50
Justin Langley, Wis.-Milwaukee	5	2	3.33	15	1	68	53	36	74
Brian Keller, Wis.-Milwaukee	4	6	3.50	15	0	98	105	20	65
Jack Andersen, Ill.-Chicago	4	6	3.50	18	0	72	76	24	38
Jake Dahlberg, Ill.-Chicago	8	2	3.57	14	0	106	92	27	66
Joe Pavlovich, Wis.-Milwaukee	8	1	3.57	18	0	91	87	37	62
Dalton Lundeen, Valparaiso	5	7	3.75	14	0	94	112	21	94
Trevor Lane, Ill.-Chicago	6	3	3.92	13	0	67	70	28	52
Joe King, Youngstown State	2	4	4.18	21	1	65	67	30	31
Austin Lujano, Youngstown State	1	1	4.24	26	0	40	36	22	20
Ryan Krokos, Youngstown State	3	3	4.32	27	2	50	56	22	27
Ryan Fritze, Valparaiso	3	7	4.54	14	0	77	88	32	61
Mario Losi, Valparaiso	5	4	4.70	13	0	77	88	30	33
Trevor Swaney, Wright State	4	3	4.81	17	0	77	89	19	30
Nate Green, Oakland	1	7	6.43	14	0	49	67	25	34

IVY LEAGUE

Gehrig Division	Conference		Overall	
	W	L	W	L
* Columbia	16	4	34	17
Pennsylvania	16	4	22	15
Cornell	9	11	13	26
Princeton	4	16	7	32

Rolfe Division	Conference		Overall	
	W	L	W	L
Dartmouth	16	4	21	21
Harvard	7	13	18	24
Yale	6	14	13	23
Brown	6	14	11	28

ALL-CONFERENCE TEAM: IF—Ethan Ferreira, Fr., Harvard; Austin Bossart, Sr., Pennsylvania; Eric Hsieh, So., Yale; Danny Hoy, Jr., Princeton; Mitch Montaldo, Sr., Pennsylvania. **OF**—Joey Falcone, Sr., Columbia; Rob Henry, Fr., Brown; Gus Craig, Sr., Columbia. **UTIL**—Jordan Serena, Sr., Columbia. **SP**—Brian McAfee, Sr., Cornell; Duncan Robinson, Jr., Dartmouth; Mike Concato, So., Dartmouth. **RP**—Patrick Peterson, Fr., Dartmouth. **Player of the Year:** Austin Bossart, Pennsylvania. **Pitcher of the Year:** Duncan Robinson, Dartmouth. **Coach of the Year:** Brett Boretti, Columbia. **Rookie of the Year:** Randell Kanemaru, Columbia.

INDIVIDUAL BATTING LEADERS
(Minimum 140 At-Bats)

	AVG	OBP	SLG	AB	2B	3B	HR	RBI	SB
Robert Henry, Brown	.363	.430	.531	160	17	2	2	21	7
Ethan Ferreira, Harvard	.361	.425	.594	155	15	3	5	35	4
Gus Craig, Columbia	.332	.400	.598	184	14	4	9	36	7
Joey Falcone, Columbia	.323	.399	.615	192	19	2	11	54	4
Matt Parisi, Dartmouth	.321	.366	.459	159	17	1	1	17	1
Jordan Serena, Columbia	.319	.396	.406	207	8	2	2	23	21
David Vandercook, Columbia	.308	.421	.535	172	14	2	7	36	2
Mitch Klug, Harvard	.308	.424	.350	143	6	0	0	17	7
Will Savage, Columbia	.302	.406	.395	172	6	2	2	15	10
Mike Martin, Harvard	.301	.375	.425	153	6	2	3	18	19
Green Campbell, Yale	.301	.380	.343	143	4	1	0	13	8
Billy Arendt, Princeton	.299	.356	.431	144	9	2	2	14	2
Randall Kanemaru, Columbia	.296	.388	.401	142	6	0	3	25	5
Richard Slenker, Yale	.290	.368	.407	145	11	0	2	18	10
Drew Reid, Harvard	.287	.351	.357	157	8	0	1	16	6
Spencer Scorza, Cornell	.279	.338	.381	147	12	0	1	25	2
Joe Purritano, Dartmouth	.277	.355	.500	148	14	5	3	30	2
Dan Kerr, Brown	.275	.333	.366	142	8	1	1	18	2
Robb Paller, Columbia	.264	.392	.472	159	12	0	7	35	2
Nick Lombardi, Dartmouth	.253	.335	.301	146	7	0	0	25	4

INDIVIDUAL PITCHING LEADERS
(Minimum 40 innings pitched)

	W	L	ERA	G	SV	IP	H	BB	SO
Mike Reitcheck, Penn	5	3	1.72	9	0	58	51	14	34
Brian McAfee, Cornell	5	2	1.77	9	0	56	43	6	38
Jake Cousins, Penn	5	1	2.32	9	0	50	40	17	33

	W	L	ERA	G	SV	IP	H	BB	SO
Kellen Urbon, Cornell	2	4	2.36	9	0	46	48	11	32
Duncan Robinson, Dartmouth	6	2	2.62	10	0	65	62	12	52
Michael Concato, Dartmouth	4	4	2.95	9	0	55	60	8	34
Ronnie Glenn, Penn	4	3	3.12	9	0	52	48	17	48
Kevin Roy, Columbia	6	4	3.34	13	1	65	53	39	46
Adam Cline, Columbia	3	0	3.51	15	4	56	62	16	60
George Thanopoulos, Columbia	6	5	3.69	14	0	76	69	28	68
Luke Strieber, Princeton	1	5	3.86	8	0	44	43	8	13
Matt Timoney, Harvard	6	2	3.91	9	0	51	53	19	40
Drew Scott, Yale	1	2	4.04	13	0	49	42	24	24
Tanner Anderson, Harvard	0	4	4.08	13	4	46	43	14	22
Mike Weisman, Columbia	4	2	4.21	13	0	51	60	9	29
Paul Balestrieri, Cornell	1	0	4.43	15	4	41	53	10	31
Keelen Smithers, Princeton	1	8	5.18	9	0	49	61	19	28
Reid Anderson, Brown	3	4	5.57	9	0	42	45	27	35
Louis Concato, Dartmouth	1	6	5.60	9	0	45	63	16	28
Chris Lanham, Yale	4	5	5.70	11	0	54	70	21	44

METRO ATLANTIC ATHLETIC CONFERENCE

	Conference W	L	Overall W	L
Rider	15	6	28	22
* Canisius	16	8	34	30
Quinnipiac	15	9	29	27
Siena	13	8	23	28
Monmouth	14	10	22	24
Marist	12	13	19	27
Iona	11	13	20	33
Fairfield	9	15	17	32
Manhattan	9	15	18	34
Niagara	9	16	13	32
Saint Peter's	7	17	10	38

ALL-CONFERENCE TEAM: C—Eric Strano, Sr., Rider. 1B—Vincent Guglietti, Jr., Quinnipiac. 2B—Scott Donaghue, Sr., Quinnipiac. SS—Matt Batten, So., Qunnipiac. 3B—Justin Esquerra, Sr., Siena. OF—Chris Kalousdian, Sr., Manhattan; James Locklear, Sr., Rider; Mike Palladino, Jr., Qunnipiac; Brett Siddall, Jr., Canisius. DH—Joe Drpich, Fr., Siena. UTIL—Connor Panas, Sr., Canisius. P—Thomas Jankins, So., Quinnipiac; Zach Mawson, Sr., Rider; Mariano Rivera Jr., Jr., Iona; Mike Wallace, Jr., Fairfield. **Player of the Year:** Brett Siddall, Canisius. **Pitcher of the Year:** Mariano Rivera Jr., Iona. **Relief Pitcher of the Year:** Eric Thomas, Rider. **Coach of the Year:** Barry Davis, Rider. **Rookie of the Year:** Joe Drpich, Siena.

INDIVIDUAL BATTING LEADERS
(Minimum 140 At-Bats)

	AVG	OBP	SLG	AB	2B	3B	HR	RBI	SB
Connor Panas, Canisius	.372	.472	.632	247	17	7	11	68	19
Steve Laurino, Marist	.358	.442	.562	187	14	3	6	38	5
Brett Siddall, Canisius	.341	.390	.590	249	24	1	12	63	6
Michael Fuhrman, Niagara	.340	.476	.490	147	8	1	4	27	15
Jake Lumley, Canisius	.331	.419	.440	248	8	5	3	39	10
Vincent Guglietti, Quinnipiac	.330	.414	.589	197	15	3	10	47	4
Thomas Rodrigues, Niagara	.327	.397	.477	153	10	2	3	29	12
Tanner Kirwer, Niagara	.324	.400	.419	148	8	0	2	17	24
Vinny DeMaria, Iona	.318	.372	.391	179	11	1	0	27	2
Mike Palladino, Quinnipiac	.313	.403	.399	208	16	1	0	15	26
Chris Hugg, Saint Peter's	.312	.390	.474	173	7	3	5	28	6
Justin Esquerra, Siena	.311	.376	.425	193	10	0	4	22	0
Chris Kalousdian, Manhattan	.309	.336	.382	204	11	2	0	19	12
Matt Pagano, Marist	.309	.390	.417	175	13	0	3	31	6
Joey Aiola, Marist	.306	.384	.417	144	6	2	2	16	0
Justin Thomas, Rider	.304	.386	.443	194	12	0	5	41	6
Matthew Batten, Quinnipiac	.303	.357	.348	221	6	2	0	34	12
James Locklear, Rider	.302	.367	.359	159	5	2	0	30	14
Christian Santisteban, Manhattan	.301	.399	.449	176	14	3	2	28	1
Scott Donaghue, Quinnipiac	.299	.378	.398	201	12	1	2	25	5
Ryan Stekl, Canisius	.297	.369	.236	5	1	1	38	3	
Graham McIntire, Marist	.292	.393	.433	178	16	0	3	24	7
Anthony Massicci, Canisius	.290	.398	.379	214	11	4	0	28	5
Zachary Racusin, Marist	.290	.358	.361	183	7	3	0	25	6
Shaine Hughes, Monmouth	.289	.395	.403	159	12	0	2	34	2

INDIVIDUAL PITCHING LEADERS
(Minimum 40 innings pitched)

	W	L	ERA	G	SV	IP	H	BB	SO
Matt Quintana, Siena	2	2	1.51	20	5	60	37	14	64
Mariano Rivera Jr., Iona	5	7	2.65	14	0	85	64	27	113
Zach Mawson, Rider	6	3	2.87	12	0	78	81	19	48
Kyle Dube, Fairfield	4	4	2.89	13	0	53	43	19	29
Joe Jacques, Manhattan	4	2	3.13	17	1	46	45	16	42
Thomas Jankins, Quinnipiac	6	5	3.20	13	0	84	86	26	53
Bill Maier, Iona	4	5	3.28	14	0	91	87	33	30
Chris Amorosi, Siena	3	3	3.51	14	0	49	58	11	32
Devon Stewart, Canisius	7	7	3.84	16	0	98	94	24	75
Mike Wallace, Fairfield	6	4	3.84	11	0	73	79	12	50
Eddie Macaluso, Iona	3	8	3.89	14	0	83	88	16	89
Kyano Cummings, Siena	4	1	3.94	25	7	48	52	20	42
Chris Napolitano, Marist	4	3	4.05	18	0	80	71	27	46
Robert Hitt, Quinnipiac	6	5	4.10	21	2	59	50	17	49
Nick Margevicius, Rider	5	4	4.29	13	0	65	77	22	50
Alex Godzak, Canisius	5	5	4.34	14	0	66	66	35	50
Josh Sharik, Rider	2	5	4.47	33	1	46	48	16	26
Anthony Ciavarella, Monmouth	3	5	4.48	13	0	66	76	20	53
Taylor Luciani, Quinnipiac	2	2	4.57	15	0	45	39	22	27
T.J. Hunt, Monmouth	5	5	4.61	14	0	70	57	34	52
J.P. Stevenson, Canisius	7	4	4.81	18	0	73	75	18	69
Zachary Kolodziejski, Niagara	7	4	4.91	13	0	77	89	22	49
Tyler Dearden, Marist	2	2	5.79	18	1	42	56	7	30
Liam Stroud, Niagara	1	10	7.08	14	0	55	69	34	30

MID-AMERICAN CONFERENCE

Eastern Division	Conference W	L	Overall W	L
Kent State	18	9	31	22
* Ohio	17	10	36	21
Bowling Green State	14	13	24	29
Akron	13	14	27	30
Miami (Ohio)	11	16	13	39
Buffalo	7	20	16	36

Western Division	Conference W	L	Overall W	L
Central Michigan	20	7	35	22
Toledo	16	11	25	33
Ball State	14	13	33	25
Western Michigan	13	14	22	30
Northern Illinois	10	17	22	33
Eastern Michigan	9	18	19	35

ALL-CONFERENCE TEAM: C—Trey Keegan, Bowling Green. 1B—Jake Madsen, Ohio. 2B—Pat MacKenzie, Central Michigan. SS—Deion Tansel, Toldeo. 3B—Zarley Zalewski, Kent State. OF—Mitch Longo, Ohio; Joe Havrilak, Akron; Matt Honchel, Miami. DH—Daniel Jipping, Central Michigan. UTIL—Nick Sinay, Buffalo. SP—Eric Lauer, Kent State; Sean Renzi, Central Michigan; John Valek, Akron; Steven Calhoun, Toledo. RP—Logan Cozart, Ohio. **Player of the Year:** Mitch Longo, Ohio. **Defensive Player of the Year:** Deion Tansel, Toledo. **Pitcher of the Year:** Logan Cozart, Ohio. **Coach of the Year:** Steve Jaksa, Central Michigan. **Rookie of the Year:** A.J. Montoya, Toledo. **Rookie Pitcher of the Year:** Zac Carey, Bowling Green.

INDIVIDUAL BATTING LEADERS
(Minimum 140 At-Bats)

	AVG	OBP	SLG	AB	2B	3B	HR	RBI	SB
Zarley Zalewski, Kent State	.374	.463	.483	203	13	0	3	32	5
Matt Honchel, Miami (Ohio)	.367	.436	.511	188	13	1	4	38	10
Mitch Longo, Ohio	.358	.422	.500	240	13	0	7	49	10
Pat MacKenzie, Central Mich.	.348	.489	.435	207	11	2	1	27	24
Joey Havrilak, Akron	.347	.436	.507	225	15	3	5	34	17
Alex Call, Ball State	.339	.392	.465	230	10	2	5	42	12
Adam Yacek, Miami (Ohio)	.337	.402	.577	163	11	5	6	27	2
Elbert Devarie, Ball State	.332	.394	.454	229	12	2	4	35	4
Nick Sinay, Buffalo	.328	.472	.377	183	4	1	1	18	39
Jake Madsen, Ohio	.324	.383	.466	219	16	3	3	50	0
Kurt Hoekstra, Western Mich.	.322	.401	.491	214	15	6	3	34	6
Deion Tansel, Toledo	.322	.411	.386	171	9	1	0	16	11
Zach McKinstry, Central Mich.	.317	.390	.362	218	4	3	0	19	8

	AVG	OBP	SLG	AB	2B	3B	HR	RBI	SB
Nick Regnier, Central Mich.	.312	.390	.401	202	7	4	1	35	20
John Rubino, Eastern Mich.	.311	.376	.373	228	8	3	0	19	40
Matt Smith, Bowling Green	.310	.369	.416	197	8	2	3	38	6
Jarett Rindfleish, Ball State	.310	.417	.518	197	7	2	10	47	0
Manny De Jesus, Ohio	.309	.405	.359	223	9	1	0	27	7
Brian Sisler, Northern Ill.	.309	.406	.431	188	14	0	3	32	6
Logan Regnier, Central Mich.	.308	.370	.450	198	11	7	1	45	19
Dalton Bollinger, Toledo	.308	.344	.390	146	4	1	2	19	1
A.J. Montoya, Toledo	.305	.363	.502	233	17	1	9	39	5
Alex Borglin, Central Mich.	.304	.416	.397	224	10	1	3	24	5
Gerrad Rohan, Akron	.299	.363	.342	164	7	0	0	29	5
Sawyer Polen, Kent State	.298	.410	.403	191	8	3	2	27	15
Brandon Howard, Bowling Green	.296	.429	.374	179	7	2	1	24	41
Conner Simonetti, Kent State	.283	.344	.578	166	10	3	11	41	1
Brett Sunde, Western Mich.	.268	.335	.374	198	18	0	1	32	2
Matt Eppers, Ball State	.263	.324	.392	194	8	7	1	24	16

INDIVIDUAL PITCHING LEADERS
(Minimum 40 innings pitched)

	W	L	ERA	G	SV	IP	H	BB	SO
Logan Cozart, Ohio	7	1	1.52	31	13	71	38	25	80
Andrew Frankenreider, Northern Ill.	2	2	1.69	26	9	43	23	11	40
Eric Lauer, Kent State	5	4	1.98	15	0	86	63	26	103
Jared Skolnicki, Kent State	4	2	2.32	13	0	54	49	12	42
Sean Renzi, Central Mich.	5	2	2.33	18	2	66	42	31	60
Caleb Schillace, Toledo	3	7	2.54	13	0	74	76	23	33
Jon Pusateri, Akron	4	5	2.58	15	1	84	68	20	72
Will Schierholz, Miami (Ohio)	1	3	2.68	31	6	50	40	13	49
Jason Gamble, Central Mich.	4	1	2.81	10	0	42	35	6	7
Steven Calhoun, Toledo	7	5	2.86	15	0	88	86	33	66
Nick Jensen-Clagg, Kent State	8	5	2.86	15	0	94	74	38	108
Sam Delaplane, Eastern Mich.	5	3	2.93	23	7	40	30	18	48
Cameron Palmer, Toledo	6	8	2.94	15	0	86	69	41	94
Nick Deeg, Central Mich.	8	5	3.00	15	0	90	88	29	56
Pat Dyer, Akron	5	2	3.12	13	0	49	53	12	31
Andy Ravel, Kent State	6	2	3.13	13	0	75	71	16	55
Tony Landi, Bowling Green	1	1	3.15	22	4	40	37	16	19
Sean Martens, Central Mich.	6	1	3.22	22	0	45	42	19	29
John Valek III, Akron	6	6	3.25	15	0	100	86	26	62
Zach Plesac, Ball State	5	5	3.26	16	0	108	104	38	77
Ryan Powers, Miami (Ohio)	5	9	4.13	14	0	85	85	35	61
Jacob Banks, Miami (Ohio)	3	9	5.17	14	0	78	81	31	54

MID-EASTERN ATHLETIC CONFERENCE

	Conference		Overall	
Northern Division	W	L	W	L
Norfolk State	19	5	27	16
Maryland-Eastern Shore	14	10	16	33
Delaware State	13	11	16	29
Coppin State	2	22	3	38

	Conference		Overall	
Southern Division	W	L	W	L
* Florida A&M	15	9	23	25
Bethune-Cookman	14	10	19	40
Savannah State	12	12	21	33
North Carolina Central	12	12	18	29
North Carolina A&T	7	17	10	36

ALL-CONFERENCE TEAM: C—Adan Ordonez, Fr., North Carolina A&T. 1B—Charles Sikes, Sr., Savannah State. 2B—Mike Escanilla, Jr., Maryland-Eastern Shore. SS—Cameron Onderko, Jr., Delaware State. 3B—Zachary Brigham, Sr., Savannah State. OF—Charles Dailey, R-Sr., Delaware State; Carlos Ortiz, So., North Carolina Central; Brandon Wilkerson, Sr., North Carolina A&T. UTIL—Tim Ravare, So., North Carolina A&T. SP—Keith Zuniga, R-Sr., Bethune-Cookman; Austin Denney, Sr., Savannah State; Matt Outman, R-Jr., Norfolk State. RP—Clint Clymer, Jr., Bethune-Cookman. Player of the Year: Charles Sikes, Savannah State. Pitcher of the Year: Matt Outman, Norfolk State. Coach of the Year: Claudell Clark, Norfolk State. Rookie of the Year: Adan Ordonez, North Carolina A&T.

INDIVIDUAL BATTING LEADERS
(Minimum 140 At-Bats)

	AVG	OBP	SLG	AB	2B	3B	HR	RBI	SB
Brandon Wilkerson, N.C. A&T	.355	.419	.484	155	10	2	2	34	10
Zachary Brigham, Savannah State	.353	.431	.476	187	12	1	3	42	5
Charles Dailey, Delaware State	.351	.421	.563	174	8	4	7	28	10
Mike Escanilla, UMES	.349	.456	.480	152	9	4	1	12	17
Chris Gonzalez, Delaware State	.342	.447	.561	155	14	1	6	37	3
Adan Ordonez, N.C. A&T	.337	.384	.407	172	10	1	0	13	0
Nathan Bond, Beth.-Cookman	.326	.401	.391	215	11	0	1	23	3
Charles Sikes, Savannah State	.321	.410	.521	190	17	0	7	37	0
Mendez Elder, Savannah State	.318	.403	.410	195	10	1	2	23	13
Marlon Gibbs, Florida A&M	.316	.391	.374	174	7	0	1	30	15
Carlos Ortiz, N.C. Central	.308	.368	.558	172	10	0	11	35	2
Justin Dattilo, UMES	.308	.363	.448	172	13	1	3	22	1
Milton Rivera, N.C. A&T	.299	.350	.372	164	7	1	1	21	7
Cameron Onderko, Del. State	.299	.459	.429	147	8	1	3	25	3
George Dragon, Coppin State	.295	.362	.370	146	5	0	2	18	0
Demetrius Sims, Beth.-Cookman	.283	.354	.337	184	8	1	0	15	2
Roger Hall, Norfolk State	.281	.339	.371	167	9	3	0	41	2
Myles Sowell, N.C. A&T	.281	.340	.343	146	5	2	0	14	5
Christian Triplett, N.C. Central	.280	.348	.478	161	14	0	6	27	0
Jameel Edney, Beth.-Cookman	.277	.351	.385	148	10	3	0	26	2
Jordan Robinson, Beth.-Cookman	.269	.322	.394	208	11	3	3	27	3
A.J. Elkins, Florida A&M	.268	.316	.340	153	8	0	1	19	4
Hector Benitez, Savannah State	.267	.406	.288	146	3	0	0	10	3
Ryan Kennedy, Florida A&M	.266	.382	.426	169	9	0	6	35	1
Michael Birdsong, Florida A&M	.264	.316	.362	174	2	0	5	18	2
Alec Wong, Florida A&M	.263	.367	.386	171	7	1	4	18	2
Ronald Thompson, N.C. Central	.250	.347	.427	164	6	1	7	27	18

INDIVIDUAL PITCHING LEADERS
(Minimum 40 innings pitched)

	W	L	ERA	G	SV	IP	H	BB	SO
Stephen Butt, Norfolk State	5	2	2.36	13	0	61	49	29	60
Brandon Fleming, Florida A&M	7	1	2.77	29	0	52	47	18	37
Austin Denney, Savannah State	4	4	2.78	13	0	81	88	18	69
Devin Sweet, N.C. Central	4	2	2.93	15	0	68	55	35	54
Jesse Stinnett, UMES	6	5	2.98	13	0	91	81	20	79
Keith Zuniga, Bethune-Cookman	7	5	3.03	13	0	86	95	13	58
Matt Outman, Norfolk State	8	2	3.12	13	0	75	61	35	85
Lane De Leon, Delaware State	5	5	3.12	14	0	66	59	25	75
Devin Hemmerich, Norfolk State	4	4	3.41	13	0	71	59	15	75
Andrew Vernon, N.C. Central	3	5	3.45	25	4	44	43	13	42
Zach McCormack, Savannah State	4	3	3.55	14	0	71	70	28	38
Alex Dandridge, N.C. Central	4	2	3.68	14	0	64	68	24	33
Cameron Scalzo, N.C. Central	2	3	3.86	13	0	51	54	18	31
Ryan Anderson, Florida A&M	1	4	3.97	15	1	57	52	20	21
Clint Clymer, Bethune-Cookman	0	3	3.98	27	8	41	42	16	32
Tyler Norris, Bethune-Cookman	3	5	4.45	15	0	65	52	36	58
Alex Carrasco, Florida A&M	0	4	4.78	22	1	43	60	20	28
Jordan Bone, UMES	0	6	4.81	18	0	49	56	19	22
Tanner Whiteman, UMES	3	5	4.98	13	0	65	73	25	46
Alex Seibold, Bethune-Cookman	5	5	5.05	16	0	68	70	35	58
Austin Robinson, Savannah State	5	3	5.46	12	0	56	76	12	31
Yahya Muhammad, Coppin State	0	12	7.82	17	0	63	105	46	41

MISSOURI VALLEY CONFERENCE

	Conference		Overall	
	W	L	W	L
* Missouri State	18	3	49	12
Dallas Baptist	15	6	46	15
Bradley	10	11	32	21
Wichita State	10	11	26	33
Illinois State	9	12	25	27
Evansville	8	13	27	24
Indiana State	8	13	28	26
Southern Illinois	6	15	12	46

ALL-CONFERENCE TEAM: C—Daniel Salters, Jr., Dallas Baptist. 1B—Mason Snyder, Sr., Illinois State. 2B—Drew Turbin, Sr., Dallas Baptist. SS—Camden Duzenack, So., Dallas Baptist. 3B—Jake Burger, Fr., Missouri State. OF—Sam Hilliard, Jr., Wichita State; Kevin Kaczmarski, Sr., Evansville; Tate Matheny, Jr., Missouri State. DH—Daniel Sweet, Jr.,

Dallas Baptist. **UTIL**—Paul DeJong, Jr., Illinois State. **SP**—Matt Hall, Jr., Missouri State; Jon Harris, Jr., Missouri State; Jacob Hendren, Jr., Illinois State. **RP**—Brandon Koch, Jr., Dallas Baptist; Bryan Young, So., Missouri State. **Player of the Year:** Kevin Kaczmarski, Evansville. **Pitcher of the Year:** Jon Harris, Missouri State. **Coach of the Year:** Keith Guttin, Missouri State. **Rookie of the Year:** Jacob Hendren, Illinois State.

INDIVIDUAL BATTING LEADERS
(Minimum 140 At-Bats)

	AVG	OBP	SLG	AB	2B	3B	HR	RBI	SB
Kevin Kaczmarski, Evansville	.465	.543	.746	185	19	9	5	57	13
Spencer Gaa, Bradley	.351	.387	.500	154	9	1	4	32	4
Drew Turbin, Dallas Baptist	.347	.480	.512	213	18	4	3	36	7
Jake Burger, Missouri State	.342	.394	.518	228	22	3	4	42	4
Sam Hilliard, Wichita State	.335	.395	.546	218	14	4	8	52	9
Ryan Tinkham, Wichita State	.333	.446	.576	210	19	1	10	46	7
Paul DeJong, Illinois State	.333	.427	.605	210	15	0	14	48	2
Isaac Smith, Bradley	.331	.437	.457	175	6	2	4	28	15
Tagg Duce, Dallas Baptist	.329	.411	.487	222	15	1	6	38	9
Josh Jywook, Evansville	.314	.445	.422	185	14	0	2	32	4
Mikel Mucha, Wichita State	.313	.354	.374	195	9	0	1	18	5
Spencer Johnson, Missouri State	.310	.447	.498	213	18	2	6	44	2
Dylan Becker, Missouri State	.309	.455	.438	217	13	3	3	41	3
Jonathan Ramon, Evansville	.304	.409	.485	194	14	3	5	48	4
Mason Snyder, Illinois State	.303	.421	.467	195	14	0	6	42	0
Chris Godinez, Bradley	.302	.505	.510	149	14	1	5	19	15
Justin Wall, Dallas Baptist	.301	.371	.521	259	13	4	12	58	12
Daniel Kihle, Wichita State	.301	.388	.390	236	5	2	4	29	21
Ryan Koziol, Illinois State	.298	.417	.419	191	12	1	3	37	1
Andy Young, Indiana State	.296	.378	.498	203	14	3	7	42	4
Paul Solka, Bradley	.295	.389	.456	193	12	2	5	31	0
Nash Knight, Dallas Baptist	.292	.377	.380	216	13	0	2	35	2
Tate Matheny, Missouri State	.291	.417	.449	234	18	2	5	43	12
Jarod Perry, Evansville	.291	.415	.352	213	11	1	0	21	13
Parker Osborne, Southern Ill.	.289	.340	.430	149	7	4	2	19	1

INDIVIDUAL PITCHING LEADERS
(Minimum 40 innings pitched)

	W	L	ERA	G	SV	IP	H	BB	SO
Brandon Koch, Dallas Baptist	3	2	1.26	26	14	43	23	24	76
Bryan Young, Missouri State	7	0	1.31	30	16	41	29	14	51
Matt Dennis, Bradley	3	0	1.51	26	12	48	31	19	45
Chance Adams, Dallas Baptist	7	1	1.98	23	2	59	41	13	83
Matt Hall, Missouri State	12	2	2.02	19	1	125	87	45	171
Austin Conway, Indiana State	4	2	2.26	29	8	52	32	17	52
Jeff Degano, Indiana State	8	3	2.36	15	0	99	78	28	126
Jon Harris, Missouri State	8	2	2.45	15	0	103	75	36	116
Ryan Keaffaber, Indiana State	1	5	2.73	17	2	82	74	20	53
John Hayes, Wichita State	6	2	2.79	26	4	52	48	22	55
Jacob Hendren, Illinois State	10	2	2.80	15	0	106	91	24	99
Steve Adkins, Bradley	6	2	2.87	10	0	53	47	19	56
Jordan Knutson, Missouri State	6	2	3.16	20	0	88	83	34	61
Sam Perez, Missouri State	9	1	3.29	27	1	68	64	16	63
Ryan Billo, Evansville	7	2	3.38	19	0	83	87	17	47
Joseph Shaw, Dallas Baptist	10	5	3.46	16	0	88	84	25	70
Elliot Ashbeck, Bradley	11	5	3.55	17	0	101	104	24	82
Cory Taylor, Dallas Baptist	7	1	3.60	16	0	80	85	31	71
Aaron Hauge, Southern Ill.	3	4	3.74	12	0	65	57	34	63
Cameron Roegner, Bradley	4	0	3.79	17	2	55	42	29	33
Isaac Anderson, Wichita State	5	7	3.94	15	0	78	85	25	74
Zach Merciez, Missouri State	3	2	4.00	31	0	40	34	14	30

MOUNTAIN WEST CONFERENCE

	Conference W	L	Overall W	L
Nevada	22	7	41	15
* San Diego State	19	10	41	23
Fresno State	18	12	31	28
New Mexico	17	13	32	27
Air Force	11	17	22	29
Nevada-Las Vegas	10	20	25	31
San Jose State	6	24	13	44

ALL-CONFERENCE TEAM: C—Taylor Ward, Jr., Fresno State; Erik VanMeetren, Sr., Nevada-Las Vegas. **1B**—Austin Byler, Sr., Nevada. **2B**—Ryan Howell, Jr., Nevada. **3B**—Ty France, Jr., San Diego State. **SS**—Danny Sheehan, Jr., San Diego State. **OF**—Taylor Tempel, Sr., Fresno State; Kewby Meyer, Sr., Nevada; Danny Collier, So., New Mexico. **DH/UT**—Bryce Greager, Jr., Nevada. **SP**—Toller Boardman, Jr., New Mexico; Bubba Derby, Jr., San Diego State; Mark Seyler, Jr., San Diego State. **RP**—Garrett Mundell, Sr., Fresno State; Adam Whitt, Jr., Nevada. **Player of the Year:** Trenton Brooks, Nevada. **Pitcher of the Year:** Christian Stolo, Nevada. **Freshman of the Year:** Cal Stevenson, Nevada; Cory Voss, New Mexico. **Coach of the Year:** Jay Johnson, Nevada.

INDIVIDUAL BATTING LEADERS
(Minimum 140 At-Bats)

	AVG	OBP	SLG	AB	2B	3B	HR	RBI	SB
Trenton Brooks, Nevada	.365	.484	.515	200	17	2	3	52	5
Taylor Tempel, Fresno State	.362	.393	.519	185	13	2	4	26	3
Cal Stevenson, Nevada	.358	.429	.454	218	13	4	0	25	10
Bryce Greager, Nevada	.355	.460	.552	183	17	2	5	41	2
Aaron Siple, New Mexico	.354	.465	.415	164	6	2	0	27	9
Steven Pallares, San Diego State	.352	.447	.523	256	17	0	9	48	15
Jack Zoellner, New Mexico	.352	.447	.546	176	18	2	4	33	0
Danny Collier, New Mexico	.346	.433	.418	182	7	3	0	28	4
Cory Voss, New Mexico	.345	.431	.546	194	14	5	5	35	3
Kewby Meyer, Nevada	.343	.385	.542	236	23	3	6	55	8
Austin Guibor, Fresno State	.339	.440	.508	183	6	5	5	21	7
Adam Groesbeck, Air Force	.338	.398	.527	222	25	1	5	27	21
Tyler France, San Diego State	.336	.428	.470	247	15	3	4	49	6
Austin Byler, Nevada	.328	.507	.652	198	18	2	14	52	9
Carl Stajduhar, New Mexico	.322	.386	.545	233	21	2	9	53	1
Spencer Thornton, San Diego St.	.315	.389	.448	143	7	3	2	23	6
Spencer Draws, Air Force	.314	.401	.451	204	17	4	1	35	5
Chris DeVito, New Mexico	.314	.398	.532	156	14	1	6	39	0
Ryan Howell, Nevada	.312	.421	.642	215	14	3	17	65	1
Denny Sheehan, San Diego St.	.307	.371	.444	257	17	0	6	45	9
Edgar Montes, UNLV	.306	.380	.446	186	15	1	3	30	3
Chase Calabuig, San Diego St.	.305	.417	.370	203	8	1	1	25	7
Taylor Ward, Fresno State	.304	.413	.486	214	14	2	7	42	7
Tyler Jones, Air Force	.301	.400	.497	193	14	3	6	41	12
Erik VanMeetren, UNLV	.301	.447	.475	183	11	3	5	28	4
Brett Bautista, San Jose State	.297	.366	.366	202	11	0	1	27	2
Seby Zavala, San Diego State	.290	.399	.537	231	13	1	14	67	4

INDIVIDUAL PITCHING LEADERS
(Minimum 40 innings pitched)

	W	L	ERA	G	SV	IP	H	BB	SO
Jake Shull, Fresno State	5	5	1.90	26	6	71	54	25	43
Evan McMahan, Nevada	5	0	2.32	19	3	54	52	13	32
Trent Monaghan, Air Force	5	6	2.75	20	1	92	90	39	73
Mark Seyler, San Diego State	9	3	2.77	17	0	107	86	35	79
Christian Stolo, Nevada	8	2	2.83	17	1	76	66	34	70
Garrett Mundell, Fresno State	3	3	2.93	21	4	61	51	21	53
Joey Lauria, UNLV	3	3	3.12	21	0	52	48	15	60
Kenny Oakley, UNLV	4	5	3.18	14	0	68	66	22	60
Bubba Derby, San Diego State	8	4	3.32	17	1	103	94	34	131
Tyler Stevens, New Mexico	5	4	3.44	18	0	68	62	21	42
Toller Boardman, New Mexico	9	3	3.46	16	0	101	110	17	65
Steven Trojan, Air Force	6	3	3.58	21	1	60	42	40	56
Blaze Bohall, UNLV	6	3	3.66	15	1	71	82	18	38
Carson Schneider, New Mexico	5	1	3.68	23	0	59	63	11	28
Ben Wright, UNLV	1	2	3.83	15	2	47	52	17	30
Ricky Thomas, Fresno State	4	3	3.92	15	1	41	37	23	35
Jason Deitrich, Nevada	6	5	3.95	15	0	73	80	17	43
Marcus Reyes, San Diego State	7	3	4.20	19	1	79	97	31	45
Jake Cole, New Mexico	1	4	4.24	25	4	40	35	11	27
Cody Thompson, San Diego State	4	4	4.32	18	0	85	91	18	69
Kalei Contrades, San Jose State	4	10	5.08	15	0	83	93	25	44
Griffin Jax, Air Force	3	10	5.17	16	0	103	121	37	72

NORTHEAST CONFERENCE

	Conference W	L	Overall W	L
Bryant	17	7	29	25
Wagner	16	9	27	23
* Sacred Heart	13	11	23	32
Fairleigh Dickinson	11	13	21	26
Mount St. Mary's	10	14	12	31
Central Connecticut State	9	15	17	31
Long Island-Brooklyn	9	15	16	35

ALL-CONFERENCE TEAM: C—Nick Dini, Sr., Wagner. **1B**—Robb Rinn, Jr., Bryant. **2B**—Cole Fabio, So., Bryant. **3B**—Brandon Bingel, So., Bryant. **SS**—Zack Short, So., Sacred Heart. **OF**—Jordan Mountford, Jr., Bryant; Tom Jakubowski, So., Long Island-Brooklyn; Ben Ruta, Jr., Wagner. **DH**—Anthony Godino, Fr., Wagner. **SP**—James Karinchak, Fr., Bryant; Nolan Long, So., Wagner; Kyle Wilcox, Jr., Bryant. **RP**—Steve Bloodworth, Sr., Wagner. **Player of the Year:** Nick Dini, Wagner. **Pitcher of the Year:** Kyle Wilcox, Bryant. **Freshman of the Year:** James Karinchak, Bryant. **Coach of the Year:** Jim Carone, Wagner.

INDIVIDUAL BATTING LEADERS
(Minimum 140 At-Bats)

	AVG	OBP	SLG	AB	2B	3B	HR	RBI	SB
Nick Dini, Wagner	.392	.489	.625	176	18	1	7	44	14
Kory Britton, Mt. St. Mary's	.356	.420	.477	149	12	0	2	23	2
Cole Fabio, Bryant	.347	.438	.477	199	12	4	2	31	17
Andrew Clow, Mt. St. Mary's	.346	.394	.497	159	11	2	3	24	3
Tommy Jakubowski, LIU Brooklyn	.337	.398	.528	178	13	6	3	28	18
Robby Rinn, Bryant	.332	.414	.582	184	21	2	7	43	3
Jesus Medina, Sacred Heart	.328	.395	.361	180	4	1	0	18	8
Ben Ruta, Wagner	.327	.412	.469	196	13	3	3	36	10
Matt Albanese, Bryant	.319	.373	.542	144	11	3	5	28	9
Brandon Bingel, Bryant	.317	.403	.522	180	8	4	7	31	2
Zack Short, Sacred Heart	.305	.424	.535	200	15	2	9	38	12
Jordan Mountford, Bryant	.304	.399	.541	194	17	4	7	40	15
Nick Mascelli, Wagner	.304	.409	.372	191	10	0	1	22	4
Buck McCarthy, Bryant	.303	.406	.507	142	11	0	6	38	0
Matt McCann, Fair. Dickinson	.300	.383	.338	160	6	0	0	14	14
Ryan Owens, Mt. St. Mary's	.299	.384	.357	154	4	1	1	14	5
Dylan Sprague, Fair. Dickinson	.298	.344	.393	168	5	1	3	22	0
John Mullen, Bryant	.295	.370	.426	190	16	3	1	33	6
Trey Nicosia, Wagner	.294	.344	.371	194	15	0	0	16	8
Jayson Sullivan, Sacred Heart	.293	.348	.372	215	8	3	1	24	13
Tommy Mazurkiewicz, Wagner	.283	.347	.361	180	6	1	2	29	2
Dominic Severino, CCSU	.283	.377	.493	152	12	1	6	28	0
Victor Sorrento, Sacred Heart	.279	.340	.397	179	12	0	3	31	3
Riley Moonan, Fair. Dickinson	.279	.389	.544	147	11	0	0	24	4
Dean Lockery, Central Conn. St.	.276	.337	.337	163	8	1	0	18	4

INDIVIDUAL PITCHING LEADERS
(Minimum 40 innings pitched)

	W	L	ERA	G	SV	IP	H	BB	SO
Chris Campbell, Mt. St. Mary's	4	0	2.23	11	0	44	38	11	30
Nolan Long, Wagner	4	3	2.67	10	0	54	37	25	55
Dan Wertz, Sacred Heart	4	1	2.85	33	2	54	57	11	33
Joe Flack, Fairleigh Dickinson	4	2	3.02	9	0	57	48	27	20
Brandon Bingel, Bryant	5	2	3.23	12	1	47	42	20	30
Kyle Wilcox, Bryant	7	3	3.24	15	0	81	61	38	50
James Karinchak, Bryant	8	5	3.24	14	0	78	63	26	74
Nick Pavia, Wagner	4	1	3.28	15	1	49	36	23	22
Jesus Medina, Sacred Heart	3	4	3.29	14	0	52	51	26	25
Brett Susi, Central Conn. St.	4	2	3.53	12	0	59	63	17	32
Bobby Maxwell, LIU Brooklyn	5	3	3.66	11	0	61	61	17	32
James Davitt, Bryant	4	1	3.71	22	4	44	50	15	35
James Cooksey, Sacred Heart	7	3	3.79	24	2	76	72	20	45
Jordan Lawson, Mt. St. Mary's	5	4	3.83	23	5	47	51	18	49
Evan Flood, LIU Brooklyn	3	4	4.17	21	0	45	48	31	23
Trevor Lacosse, Bryant	2	3	4.33	15	1	62	61	26	53
Max Schmardel, Wagner	2	1	4.33	14	0	44	49	10	29
Matt Blandino, Central Conn. St.	2	7	4.71	11	0	65	82	14	48
Logan Frati, Fairleigh Dickinson	4	7	4.85	15	1	85	96	23	57
Robbie Maguire, Sacred Heart	4	5	4.91	14	0	66	76	29	34
Brian Drapeau, LIU Brooklyn	1	7	5.36	14	0	81	96	32	60
Jason Foley, Sacred Heart	3	7	5.50	15	0	70	69	34	56
Casey Brown, Central Conn. St.	1	7	5.72	10	0	61	82	17	39
Thomas Williams, Mt. St. Mary's	0	7	5.84	10	0	57	81	21	36
Joe Borelli, Fairleigh Dickinson	2	7	7.44	12	0	62	85	27	34

OHIO VALLEY CONFERENCE

	Conference W	L	Overall W	L
Southeast Missouri State	21	8	35	23
* Morehead State	20	10	37	22
SIU-Edwardsville	19	11	20	30
Tennessee Tech	16	14	26	29
Jacksonville State	15	14	25	26
Belmont	15	14	29	29
Austin Peay State	15	15	25	26
Eastern Kentucky	12	17	21	29
Murray State	11	19	16	40
Tennessee-Martin	9	20	17	35
Eastern Illinois	9	21	13	36

ALL-CONFERENCE TEAM: C—Chris Robinson, Sr., Morehead State. **1B**—Kane Sweeney, Sr., Morehead State. **2B**—Tyler Fullerton, Jr., Belmont. **3B**—Matt Beaty, Sr., Belmont. **SS**—Dylan Bosheers, Jr., Tennessee Tech. **OF**—Drew Ferguson, Sr., Belmont; Kyle Nowlin, Jr., Eastern Kentucky; Caleb Howell, Sr., Eastern Illinois. **DH**—Paschal Petrongolo, Jr., Jacksonville State. **UT**—Alex Robles, So., Austin Peay State. **SP**—Joey Lucchesi, Jr., Southeast Missouri State; Zachary Fowler, Sr., Jacksonville State; Alex Robles, So., Austin Peay State. **RP**—Travis Stout, Sr., Jacksonville State. **Player of the Year:** Chris Robinson, Morehead State. **Pitcher of the Year:** Joey Lucchesi, Southeast Missouri State. **Freshman of the Year:** Ryan Flick, Tennessee Tech. **Coach of the Year:** Mike McGuire, Morehead State.

INDIVIDUAL BATTING LEADERS
(Minimum 140 At-Bats)

	AVG	OBP	SLG	AB	2B	3B	HR	RBI	SB
Caleb Howell, Eastern Ill.	.407	.493	.511	182	19	0	0	35	7
Chris Robinson, Morehead State	.402	.472	.655	246	25	5	9	69	10
Drew Ferguson, Belmont	.397	.486	.685	232	26	4	11	59	26
Demetre Taylor, Eastern Ill.	.384	.429	.634	164	6	4	9	46	6
Matt Beaty, Belmont	.382	.469	.668	238	24	4	12	76	12
T.J. Alas, Eastern Kentucky	.378	.456	.628	156	12	3	7	30	4
Paschal Petrongolo, JSU	.368	.451	.556	223	17	2	7	59	1
Logan Gray, Austin Peay	.366	.461	.752	153	15	1	14	39	11
Nick Newell, Morehead St.	.360	.405	.572	250	28	2	7	58	4
Ryan Kent, Morehead St.	.356	.454	.478	253	20	1	3	32	6
Tyler Fullerton, Belmont	.354	.444	.627	212	19	3	11	58	6
Kane Sweeney, Morehead St.	.353	.482	.626	235	17	1	15	62	1
Brandon Rawe, Morehead St.	.350	.432	.578	263	24	0	12	52	4
Dre Gleason, Austin Peay	.349	.434	.550	149	12	0	6	31	1
Garrett Copeland, Austin Peay	.345	.463	.518	197	15	2	5	29	18
Ryan Sebra, Jacksonville St.	.341	.380	.516	216	16	3	10	57	3
Robby Spencer, Morehead St.	.340	.404	.537	244	22	1	8	71	0
Ridge Smith, Austin Peay	.339	.424	.487	189	16	3	2	30	13
Dylan Bosheers, Tennessee Tech	.337	.425	.576	205	20	1	9	43	4
Andy Lennington, SEMO	.333	.390	.500	204	11	1	7	46	4
Taylor Douglas, Tenn.-Martin	.332	.393	.585	217	18	2	11	47	11
Alex Robles, Austin Peay	.328	.406	.456	180	12	1	3	39	5
Brant Valach, Eastern Ill.	.328	.386	.503	177	13	0	6	29	0
Clayton Daniel, Jacksonville St.	.327	.414	.413	223	15	2	0	45	8
Kyle Nowlin, Eastern Ky.	.326	.438	.690	184	8	1	19	45	18
Trevor Ezell, Southeast Mo. St.	.313	.423	.484	246	18	6	4	42	11
Gavin Golsan, Jacksonville St.	.290	.361	.347	245	11	0	1	20	38

INDIVIDUAL PITCHING LEADERS
(Minimum 40 innings pitched)

	W	L	ERA	G	SV	IP	H	BB	SO
Matthew Kinney, Belmont	3	5	1.96	35	6	55	42	17	62
Aaron Goe, Morehead State	6	0	3.07	13	2	41	41	5	37
Joey Lucchesi, Southeast Mo. St.	7	2	3.17	15	0	88	60	47	93
Alex Robles, Austin Peay	6	3	3.31	16	3	84	68	17	65
Ryan Lenaburg, Southeast Mo. St.	5	3	3.51	23	1	51	46	24	47
Jeb Scoggins, Tennessee Tech	2	1	3.60	26	6	50	44	22	58
Zachary Fowler, Jacksonville St.	8	3	3.80	15	0	92	91	27	75

	W	L	ERA	G	SV	IP	H	BB	SO
Dillon Symon, Tenn.-Martin	1	2	3.86	20	0	42	48	21	27
Graham Officer, Jacksonville St.	5	1	3.95	19	0	41	**40**	13	35
Brett Thomas, SIUE	3	2	4.10	19	6	42	47	29	38
Alex Winkelman, Southeast Mo. St.	4	3	4.32	16	1	**98**	88	51	92
Patrick McGrath, Belmont	**9**	4	4.40	17	0	78	79	29	53
Aaron Quillen, Belmont	5	5	4.44	14	0	73	73	24	75
Matt Poteete, Tenn.-Martin	2	3	4.50	19	0	50	59	14	28
Chris Chism, Tennessee Tech	8	3	4.61	17	0	80	93	25	68
Jared Carkuff, Austin Peay	5	5	4.63	16	0	82	75	33	63
Brent Stoneking, Morehead St.	5	1	4.65	18	3	50	51	14	32
Luke Humphreys, Morehead St.	7	3	4.77	15	0	89	83	36	65
Dan Ludwig, Belmont	4	6	4.91	15	0	95	116	20	80
Carter Smith, Tenn.-Martin	4	**9**	5.00	15	0	76	83	35	64

PACIFIC-12 CONFERENCE

	Conference W	L	Overall W	L
* UCLA	22	8	45	16
Oregon State	19	10	39	18
Southern California	18	12	39	21
California	18	12	36	21
Arizona State	18	12	35	23
Oregon	16	14	38	25
Washington	14	16	29	25
Arizona	12	18	31	24
Washington State	11	19	29	27
Stanford	9	21	24	32
Utah	7	22	16	36

ALL-CONFERENCE TEAM: C—Brian Serven, So., Arizona State; Garrett Stubbs, Sr., Southern California. **1B**—Chris Paul, Sr., California; K.J. Harrison, Fr., Oregon State. **2B**—Scott Kingery, Jr., Arizona; Dante Flores, Sr., Southern California. **3B**—Bobby Dalbec, So., Arizona; Lucas Erceg, So., California; Mitchell Tolman, Jr., Oregon. **SS**—Kevin Newman, Jr., Arizona; Colby Woodmansee, So., Arizona State; Kevin Kramer, Jr., UCLA. **OF**—Trever Allen, Sr., Arizona State; Johnny Sewald, Jr., Arizona State; Jeff Hendrix, Jr., Oregon State; Ty Moore, Jr., UCLA; Timmy Robinson, Jr., Southern California; Bobby Stahel, Jr., Southern California; Braden Bishop, Jr., Washington. **SP**—Ryan Kellogg, Jr., Arizona State; Daulton Jefferies, So., California; Andrew Moore, Jr., Oregon State; Drew Rasmussen, Fr., Oregon State; James Kaprielian, Jr., UCLA; Grant Watson, Jr., UCLA; Tyler Davis, Sr., Washington; Joe Pistorese, Jr., Washington State. **RP**—Ryan Burr, Jr., Arizona State; Garrett Cleavinger, Jr., Oregon; David Berg, Sr., UCLA; Grant Dyer, So., UCLA; Ian Hamilton, So., Washington State. **Player of the Year:** Scott Kingery, Arizona. **Pitcher of the Year:** David Berg UCLA. **Defensive Player of the Year:** Garrett Stubbs, Southern California. **Freshman of the Year:** K.J. Harrison, Oregon State. **Coach of the Year:** John Savage, UCLA.

INDIVIDUAL BATTING LEADERS
(Minimum 140 At-Bats)

	AVG	OBP	SLG	AB	2B	3B	HR	RBI	SB
Scott Kingery, Arizona	**.392**	.423	.561	237	15	5	5	36	11
Bobby Stahel, Southern Calif.	.376	.419	.506	245	12	4	4	33	10
Kevin Newman, Arizona	.370	.426	.489	227	19	1	2	36	**22**
Trever Allen, Arizona State	.357	.398	.535	213	17	3	5	31	5
Garrett Stubbs, Southern Calif.	.346	.435	.434	228	15	1	1	25	20
Ty Moore, UCLA	.342	.428	.479	234	12	1	6	51	7
Jeff Hendrix, Oregon State	.339	.446	.534	221	15	5	6	34	5
Wyler Smith, Utah	.329	.392	.376	173	6	1	0	14	9
Mitchell Tolman, Oregon	.325	**.457**	.468	231	20	2	3	42	11
Chris Paul, California	.325	.404	.562	203	11	5	9	45	6
Johnny Sewald, Arizona State	.324	.436	.403	216	8	3	1	23	21
Kevin Kramer, UCLA	.323	.423	.476	**254**	14	2	7	34	7
Drew Jackson, Stanford	.320	.396	.388	147	6	2	0	9	6
Bobby Dalbec, Arizona	.319	.410	**.601**	213	11	2	**15**	53	0
Kyle Nobach, Oregon State	.317	.377	.447	161	15	0	2	27	8
Trever Morrison, Oregon State	.317	.412	.400	145	5	2	1	18	2
David Greer, Arizona State	.314	.366	.427	185	11	2	2	28	4
Aaron Knapp, California	.310	.376	.375	232	7	4	0	23	12
K.J. Harrison, Oregon State	.309	.401	.527	220	12	3	10	**60**	1
Colby Woodmansee, Ariz. State	.308	.355	.454	240	18	1	5	44	2
Riley Moore, Arizona	.306	.397	.426	209	12	2	3	38	2

	AVG	OBP	SLG	AB	2B	3B	HR	RBI	SB
Dante Flores, Southern Calif.	.304	.397	.461	217	11	4	5	43	4
Lucas Erceg, California	.303	.357	.502	231	11	1	11	41	5
Andrew Snow, Arizona State	.300	.364	.400	140	6	1	2	24	1
Ian Sagdal, Washington State	.298	.391	.498	205	13	5	6	34	13
Chris Keck, UCLA	.293	.389	.483	232	**21**	1	7	47	0
A.J. Ramirez, Southern Calif.	.259	.307	.476	212	15	2	9	45	9
Christoph Bono, UCLA	.241	.332	.397	199	13	**6**	2	30	5

INDIVIDUAL PITCHING LEADERS
(Minimum 40 innings pitched)

	W	L	ERA	G	SV	IP	H	BB	SO
David Berg, UCLA	7	1	**0.68**	**43**	13	67	49	8	65
Garrett Cleavinger, Oregon	6	2	1.58	37	9	40	**20**	18	66
Ian Hamilton, Washington State	1	4	1.67	27	13	43	33	17	37
Grant Dyer, UCLA	4	2	1.83	42	0	59	36	15	65
Andrew Moore, Oregon State	7	2	1.91	16	0	**122**	86	21	111
Troy Rallings, Washington	3	4	2.01	26	6	72	56	11	55
Stephen Nogosek, Oregon	6	3	2.02	39	0	58	38	34	60
James Kaprielian, UCLA	**10**	4	2.03	17	0	107	86	33	**114**
Brandon Choate, Washington	1	3	2.29	34	3	51	42	26	58
Grant Watson, UCLA	8	5	2.30	16	0	98	80	21	66
Marc Huberman, Southern Calif.	6	4	2.36	27	4	50	37	34	47
Joe Pistorese, Washington State	8	5	2.41	15	0	105	91	24	67
Noah Bremer, Washington	6	3	2.41	16	0	78	69	16	36
Cody Poteet, UCLA	7	1	2.45	27	0	73	62	30	68
Jeff Bain, California	6	2	2.52	17	0	64	49	13	31
Josh Graham, Oregon	4	1	2.63	19	1	65	48	26	64
Sam Triece, Washington State	5	0	2.66	31	0	51	41	24	59
Matt Ladrech, California	7	4	2.67	16	0	88	90	21	28
Ryan Walker, Washington State	1	1	2.72	15	0	56	45	23	50
Tyler Gilbert, Southern California	5	2	2.79	22	2	68	68	25	66
Ryan Burr, Arizona State	8	2	2.91	33	**14**	46	44	25	74
Griffin Canning, UCLA	7	1	2.97	15	0	64	54	**6**	66
Dalton Carroll, Utah	5	**9**	4.94	16	1	93	95	28	56

PATRIOT LEAGUE

	Conference W	L	Overall W	L
Navy	13	7	37	20
* Lehigh	12	8	25	31
Holy Cross	12	8	24	26
Lafayette	9	11	14	27
Bucknell	8	12	24	22
Army	6	14	21	26

ALL-CONFERENCE TEAM: C—Adrian Chinnery, So., Navy. **1B**—Anthony Critelli, So., Holy Cross. **2B**—Mike Garzillo, Jr., Lehigh. **3B**—Pat Donnelly, So., Lehigh; Tyler Hudson, Jr., Lafayette. **SS**—Nick Lovullo, Jr., Holy Cross. **OF**—Mark McCants, Sr., Army; Justin Pacchioli, Sr., Lehigh; Sean Trent, Jr., Navy. **DH**—Campbell Lipe, Jr., Lafayette. **SP**—Luke Gillingham, Jr., Navy; Xavier Hammond, Sr., Bucknell; Brendan King, So., Holy Cross. **RP**—Sean Gustin, Jr., Holy Cross. **Player of the Year:** Sean Trent, Navy. **Pitcher of the Year:** Luke Gillingham, Navy. **Freshman of the Year:** Cam O'Neill, Holy Cross. **Coach of the Year:** Paul Kostacopoulos, Navy.

INDIVIDUAL BATTING LEADERS
(Minimum 140 At-Bats)

	AVG	OBP	SLG	AB	2B	3B	HR	RBI	SB
Sean Trent, Navy	**.407**	.446	.524	**231**	**18**	3	1	42	1
Mike Garzillo, Lehigh	.359	.422	**.651**	209	**18**	2	**13**	**54**	15
Joe Ogren, Bucknell	.351	.458	.530	168	13	1	5	28	7
Mark McCants, Army	.346	.440	.522	159	13	3	3	38	7
Justin Pacchioli, Lehigh	.342	**.485**	.449	187	8	3	2	18	**31**
Robert Currie, Navy	.324	.394	.425	219	8	7	0	34	16
Adrian Chinnery, Navy	.314	.393	.401	172	8	2	1	27	0
Cam O'Neill, Holy Cross	.311	.355	.372	180	8	0	1	18	0
Ben Smith, Army	.310	.404	.439	155	13	2	1	23	1
Anthony Critelli, Holy Cross	.307	.376	.472	176	14	0	5	40	0
Jack St. Clair, Holy Cross	.306	.387	.366	183	8	0	1	30	7
Jacen Nalesnik, Lehigh	.303	.365	.403	201	14	0	2	35	8
Anthony Gingerelli, Bucknell	.301	.341	.461	193	**18**	2	3	24	2
Nick Lovullo, Holy Cross	.278	.410	.392	176	9	1	3	22	7
Connor Deneen, Navy	.278	.349	.432	169	7	**8**	1	21	3

	AVG	OBP	SLG	AB	2B	3B	HR	RBI	SB
Jon Mayer, Bucknell	.276	.382	.379	145	7	1	2	28	0
Brad Borosak, Navy	.274	.358	.350	223	6	4	1	34	15
Evan Ocello, Holy Cross	.270	.362	.382	178	11	0	3	28	18
Jacob Page, Army	.269	.342	.438	160	13	1	4	28	6
Patrick Donnelly, Lehigh	.267	.297	.449	187	12	2	6	32	8
Greg Wasikowski, Bucknell	.264	.358	.357	140	5	1	2	19	5
Bill Schlich, Holy Cross	.252	.310	.331	151	7	1	1	20	4

INDIVIDUAL PITCHING LEADERS
(Minimum 40 innings pitched)

	W	L	ERA	G	SV	IP	H	BB	SO
Luke Gillingham, Navy	8	1	1.19	12	0	83	44	14	111
Jett Meenach, Navy	7	0	1.99	24	4	45	38	12	43
Alex Robinett, Army	6	5	2.01	11	0	81	55	16	92
Brendan King, Holy Cross	3	1	2.16	13	0	58	47	12	29
Andrew Andreychik, Bucknell	4	5	2.44	9	0	55	50	14	43
Sam Sorenson, Navy	2	7	2.58	26	3	52	49	12	53
Stephen Moore, Navy	7	3	2.59	14	0	87	77	18	69
Bryson Hough, Bucknell	4	5	2.74	11	0	72	80	10	46
Xavier Hammond, Bucknell	5	2	2.76	11	0	72	74	19	65
Nick Macaione, Lehigh	3	4	2.92	12	0	71	56	19	45
Mike Castellani, Bucknell	4	1	3.27	12	1	55	54	16	23
David Bednar, Lafayette	3	7	3.41	10	0	63	52	18	70
Jayme Edwards, Lehigh	1	3	3.67	14	1	54	49	29	40
Ben White, Holy Cross	4	5	3.82	11	0	61	59	23	55
Justin Finan, Holy Cross	3	3	3.88	12	1	53	45	15	24
Donny Murray, Holy Cross	2	4	3.92	11	0	67	65	9	46
Kyle Condry, Navy	2	5	3.97	18	0	59	61	17	45
George Coughlin, Navy	7	3	4.00	13	0	70	62	19	72
Toby Schwartz, Lafayette	3	4	4.17	10	0	58	57	18	47
John Cain, Lafayette	1	3	4.20	10	0	45	44	18	45
Kevin Boswick, Lehigh	3	4	4.21	20	4	47	37	15	43
Nick Stephens, Lehigh	4	7	4.76	17	0	68	75	19	54

SOUTHEASTERN CONFERENCE

Eastern Division	Conference W	L	Overall W	L
Vanderbilt	20	10	51	21
* Florida	19	11	52	18
Missouri	15	15	30	28
Kentucky	14	15	30	25
South Carolina	13	17	32	25
Tennessee	11	18	24	26
Georgia	10	19	26	28

Western Division	Conference W	L	Overall W	L
Louisiana State	21	8	54	12
Texas A&M	18	10	50	14
Arkansas	17	12	40	25
Mississippi	15	14	30	28
Auburn	13	17	36	26
Alabama	12	18	32	28
Mississippi State	8	22	24	30

ALL-CONFERENCE TEAM: C—Kade Scivicque, Sr., Louisiana State. **1B**—Kyle Martin, Sr., South Carolina. **2B**—JaVon Shelby, So., Kentucky. **3B**—Conner Hale, Sr., Louisiana State. **SS**—Alex Bregman, Jr., Louisiana State. **OF**—Andrew Benintendi, So., Arkansas; Andrew Stevenson, Jr., Louisiana State; Christin Stewart, Jr., Tennessee. **DH/UT**—Mitchell Nau, Sr., Texas A&M. **SP**—Carson Fulmer, Jr., Vanderbilt; Alex Lange, Fr., Louisiana State. **RP**—Zach Jackson, So., Arkansas. **Player of the Year:** Andrew Benintendi, Arkansas. **Pitcher of the Year:** Carson Fulmer, Vanderbilt. **Freshman of the Year:** Alex Lange, Louisiana State. **Coach of the Year:** Paul Mainieri, Louisiana State.

INDIVIDUAL BATTING LEADERS
(Minimum 140 At-Bats)

	AVG	OBP	SLG	AB	2B	3B	HR	RBI	SB
Andrew Benintendi, Arkansas	.376	.488	.717	226	13	2	20	57	24
Ka'Ai Tom, Kentucky	.375	.443	.528	216	16	1	5	51	15
Mitchell Nau, Texas A&M	.370	.460	.492	238	17	0	4	47	1
Nick Banks, Texas A&M	.364	.450	.536	239	11	3	8	48	9
Kade Scivicque, LSU	.355	.398	.521	234	21	0	6	48	0
Josh Tobias, Florida	.355	.435	.524	231	14	5	5	46	11

	AVG	OBP	SLG	AB	2B	3B	HR	RBI	SB
Kyle Barrett, Kentucky	.354	.394	.443	237	12	3	1	26	7
Kyle Martin, South Carolina	.350	.455	.636	203	12	2	14	56	11
Andrew Stevenson, LSU	.348	.396	.453	247	13	5	1	24	26
Chris Chinea, LSU	.344	.376	.539	256	17	0	11	58	1
Blake Allemand, Texas A&M	.339	.431	.506	245	14	3	7	40	6
Mikey White, Alabama	.339	.444	.537	218	19	6	4	35	8
Dansby Swanson, Vanderbilt	.335	.423	.623	281	24	6	15	64	16
Logan Taylor, Texas A&M	.333	.392	.526	234	13	1	10	52	2
J.J. Schwarz, Florida	.332	.398	.629	256	16	3	18	73	1
Casey Hughston, Alabama	.332	.389	.502	235	14	4	6	44	12
Elliott Caldwell, South Carolina	.328	.426	.482	195	5	8	3	41	13
Max Schrock, South Carolina	.328	.419	.500	192	11	2	6	34	8
Conner Hale, LSU	.327	.373	.460	263	17	3	4	56	1
Tyler Spoon, Arkansas	.327	.365	.490	245	20	1	6	54	10
Nick Senzel, Tennessee	.325	.399	.495	200	12	5	4	28	7
Stephen Wrenn, Georgia	.324	.400	.482	222	5	3	8	28	28
Jacob Robson, Mississippi State	.324	.436	.368	185	5	0	1	9	21
Alex Bregman, LSU	.323	.412	.535	260	22	3	9	49	38
Mark Laird, LSU	.323	.388	.381	260	10	1	1	24	24
Rhett Wiseman, Vanderbilt	.317	.415	.566	290	19	4	15	49	12

INDIVIDUAL PITCHING LEADERS
(Minimum 40 innings pitched)

	W	L	ERA	G	SV	IP	H	BB	SO
Kyle Wright, Vanderbilt	6	1	1.23	29	4	59	36	23	62
Taylor Lewis, Florida	6	2	1.33	31	7	54	42	15	32
Carson Fulmer, Vanderbilt	14	2	1.83	19	0	128	81	50	167
Alex Lange, LSU	12	0	1.97	17	0	114	87	46	131
Zach Jackson, Arkansas	5	1	2.10	27	9	60	43	38	89
Andrew Vinson, Texas A&M	5	2	2.12	35	5	64	49	14	64
Justin Camp, Auburn	2	1	2.33	28	8	46	40	24	48
Kyle Simonds, Texas A&M	3	2	2.39	22	2	53	47	18	32
Cole Lipscomb, Auburn	8	2	2.53	16	1	93	75	24	91
Bobby Poyner, Florida	5	2	2.56	26	4	63	52	6	58
Dalton Rentz, Auburn	3	4	2.60	24	1	62	63	30	52
Jared Walsh, Georgia	5	2	2.60	14	0	55	35	35	44
Scott Weathersby, Mississippi	4	2	2.62	17	3	55	45	14	51
Logan Shore, Florida	11	6	2.72	19	0	112	97	24	84
Matt Kent, Texas A&M	9	1	2.76	19	2	98	103	12	84
Grayson Long, Texas A&M	9	1	2.82	17	0	96	85	39	106
John Kilichowski, Vanderbilt	3	4	2.84	17	2	67	51	15	64
Jordan Sheffield, Vanderbilt	5	2	2.85	22	0	60	39	43	55
Walker Buehler, Vanderbilt	5	2	2.95	16	0	88	85	30	92
David Sosebee, Georgia	4	3	2.98	11	0	54	47	21	55
Preston Brown, Mississippi State	5	8	4.77	14	0	72	87	26	54

SOUTHERN CONFERENCE

	Conference W	L	Overall W	L
* Mercer	16	7	31	21
Samford	14	10	29	24
Wofford	13	10	36	20
Virginia Military Institute	12	12	20	28
UNC Greensboro	12	12	23	25
Furman	11	13	24	31
Western Carolina	11	13	21	28
The Citadel	10	14	25	28
East Tennessee State	8	16	21	34

ALL-CONFERENCE TEAM: C—Matt Winn, Sr., VMI. **1B**—Conor Clancey, Sr., Wofford. **2B**—Bradley Strong, Sr., Western Carolina. **3B**—Hunter Swilling, So., Samford. **SS**—Jordan Tarsovich, Sr., VMI. **OF**—Connor Walsh, Sr., The Citadel; Kyle Lewis, So., Mercer; Eric Kalbfleisch, Sr., UNC Greensboro. **DH**—Austin Edens, Fr., Samford. **SP**—James Reeves, Jr., The Citadel; Matthew Milburn, Jr., Wofford. **RP**—Andrew Gracia, Sr., Samford. **Player of the Year:** Kyle Lewis, Mercer. **Pitcher of the Year:** James Reeves, The Citadel. **Freshman of the Year:** Austin Edens, Samford. **Coach of the Year:** Criag Gibson, Mercer.

INDIVIDUAL BATTING LEADERS
(Minimum 140 At-Bats)

	AVG	OBP	SLG	AB	2B	3B	HR	RBI	SB
Kyle Lewis, Mercer	.367	.423	.677	226	19	0	17	56	3
Matthew Ramsay, Wofford	.359	.459	.483	234	12	4	3	32	14

	AVG	OBP	SLG	AB	2B	3B	HR	RBI	SB
Austin Edens, Samford	.357	.442	.662	213	17	0	16	54	0
Trey York, East Tenn. State	.355	.437	.611	211	15	6	9	51	18
Eric Kalbfleisch, UNC Greensboro	.348	.403	.503	187	13	2	4	26	3
James Plaisted, Wofford	.346	.434	.557	228	20	2	8	46	11
Bradley Strong, Western Caro.	.344	.403	.605	215	16	5	10	58	18
Alex Lee, Samford	.343	.425	.575	207	16	1	10	49	3
Blake Chisolm, Furman	.342	.382	.462	199	13	1	3	33	0
Connor Walsh, Citadel	.341	.412	.561	223	16	3	9	60	5
Heath Quinn, Samford	.340	.418	.580	238	11	2	14	56	8
Jordan Simpson, Furman	.339	.377	.606	218	14	1	14	46	2
Chris Cook, East Tenn. State	.338	.389	.474	228	12	2	5	40	8
Tyler Long, UNC Greensboro	.338	.368	.446	195	8	2	3	25	5
Jordan Tarsovich, VMI	.337	.419	.568	199	17	1	9	29	24
Carson Waln, Wofford	.335	.429	.457	164	12	4	0	32	17
Matt Smith, Western Carolina	.332	.448	.475	196	11	1	5	34	12
Jake Jones, Furman	.328	.376	.443	201	13	2	2	28	3
Conor Clancey, Wofford	.326	.376	.593	221	27	1	10	66	9
Hunter Swilling, Samford	.324	.415	.622	238	15	4	16	56	9
Aaron Wright, UNC Greensboro	.324	.425	.648	179	18	2	12	34	0
Kevin Phillips, East Tenn. State	.323	.395	.561	223	21	1	10	55	3
Matthew Pelt, Wofford	.321	.389	.447	159	8	0	4	29	15
Zac MacAneney, UNC Greensboro	.317	.388	.474	228	12	2	5	40	8
Danny Bermudez, Western Caro.	.317	.417	.516	186	14	1	7	42	3
Chris Ohmstede, Furman	.315	.366	.539	241	13	1	13	58	4
Matt Meeder, Mercer	.293	.464	.399	198	11	2	2	27	2

INDIVIDUAL PITCHING LEADERS
(Minimum 40 innings pitched)

	W	L	ERA	G	SV	IP	H	BB	SO
Morgan Pittman, Mercer	2	3	2.43	29	3	67	61	23	60
Elliott Warford, Furman	4	4	2.61	32	7	52	45	24	58
Eric Nyquist, Mercer	9	2	3.11	19	0	90	75	31	69
Adam Scott, Wofford	8	4	3.68	16	0	93	84	23	72
James Reeves, Citadel	8	4	3.69	15	0	95	80	28	115
Skylar Hunter, Citadel	3	6	3.74	33	13	53	40	29	59
Kevin Connell, Citadel	2	1	3.74	34	0	46	50	14	33
Mark Donham, Samford	4	1	3.88	31	1	46	51	16	39
Ryan Clark, UNC Greensboro	7	6	4.06	15	0	95	84	39	94
Austin Mason, Citadel	3	2	4.19	25	0	54	51	25	53
Mitchell Wade, Mercer	6	1	4.24	37	0	40	40	9	31
Luke Leftwich, Wofford	7	2	4.25	16	0	89	87	28	114
Matthew Milburn, Wofford	10	3	4.32	16	0	102	108	25	87
Alex Ledford, Samford	7	6	4.57	16	0	104	107	46	83
J.P. Sears, Citadel	5	5	4.64	17	0	76	82	24	82
Thomas Byelick, Citadel	3	3	4.70	13	0	44	42	17	35
Parker Curry, Samford	6	6	4.81	16	0	79	93	16	64
B.J. Nobles, Western Carolina	4	3	4.84	19	0	61	66	41	72
Andrew Woods, VMI	7	1	4.86	13	0	70	83	19	59
Matt Solter, Furman	4	5	4.89	16	0	88	98	34	84
Elliot Lance, Wofford	5	2	5.36	24	0	45	57	7	27

SOUTHLAND CONFERENCE

	Conference W	L	Overall W	L
Southeastern Louisiana	25	5	42	17
Northwestern State	20	8	31	23
Nicholls State	18	11	32	19
McNeese State	18	12	32	25
Sam Houston State	17	12	30	28
Central Arkansas	16	14	29	24
* Houston Baptist	14	13	28	27
Texas A&M-Corpus Christi	13	14	26	26
Abilene Christian	13	17	17	38
Stephen F. Austin	11	18	17	33
Incarnate Word	11	19	21	32
Lamar	10	19	21	31
New Orleans	3	27	15	40

ALL-CONFERENCE TEAM: C—Samm Wiggins, Sr., Houston Baptist. **1B**—Kevin Carr, Sr., Southeastern Louisiana. **2B**—Joe Provenzano, Fr., McNeese State. **3B**—Kyle Reese, Jr., Nicholls State. **SS**—Connor Lloyd, Sr., McNeese State. **OF**—Cort Brinson, Jr., Northwestern State; Jacob Seward, So., Southeastern Louisiana; Zach Nehrir, Sr., Houston Baptist.

DH—Daniel Midyett, Jr., Southeastern Louisiana. **P**—Justin Sinibaldi, So., Nicholls State; Trevor Belicek, Sr., Texas A&M-Corpus Christi; Tate Scioneaux, Jr., Southeastern Louisiana. **Player of the Year:** Jacob Seward, Southeastern Louisiana. **Hitter of the Year:** Cort Brinson, Northwestern State. **Pitcher of the Year:** Justin Sinibaldi, Nicholls State. **Relief Pitcher of the Year:** Stuart Holmes, Nicholls State. **Freshman of the Year:** Joe Provenzano, McNeese State. **Newcomer of the Year:** Kyle Reese, Nicholls State. **Utility Player of the Year:** Curtis Jones, Houston Baptist. **Coach of the Year:** Matt Riser, Southeastern Louisiana.

INDIVIDUAL BATTING LEADERS
(Minimum 140 At-Bats)

	AVG	OBP	SLG	AB	2B	3B	HR	RBI	SB
Jake MacWilliam, Sam Houston	.378	.412	.483	143	9	0	2	22	1
Kyle Reese, Nicholls State	.377	.413	.527	207	20	4	1	32	4
Stijn van der Meer, Lamar	.351	.401	.441	222	13	2	1	20	6
Cort Brinson, Northwestern St.	.350	.407	.518	220	10	0	9	42	4
Jacob Seward, Southeastern La.	.350	.442	.383	217	5	1	0	35	19
Wesley Hoover, Central Ark.	.347	.450	.455	167	10	4	0	22	8
Carson Crites, Southeastern La.	.344	.411	.503	157	8	4	3	28	11
Kevin Carr, Southeastern La.	.336	.424	.468	220	15	1	4	37	0
Ryan Calloway, New Orleans	.335	.390	.367	215	2	1	1	17	9
Zach Nehrir, Houston Baptist	.333	.388	.487	228	10	5	5	43	11
Samm Wiggins, Houston Baptist	.333	.425	.500	198	16	1	5	28	0
Jordan Lee, A&M-Corpus Christi	.325	.394	.464	209	11	3	4	25	17
Chase Daughdrill, Nwestern St.	.324	.417	.476	210	12	4	4	30	6
Jake Nash, Lamar	.324	.383	.379	182	8	1	0	19	4
Connor Lloyd, McNeese St.	.321	.367	.389	221	10	1	1	29	2
Jonathan Coco, New Orleans	.314	.361	.353	153	6	0	0	17	0
Andrew Guillotte, McNeese St.	.313	.350	.394	249	14	0	2	24	21
Kennon Menard, Southeastern La.	.313	.344	.325	163	2	0	0	13	6
Greg Espinosa, Houston Baptist	.312	.339	.363	157	6	1	0	27	1
Bryce Johnson, Sam Houston St.	.310	.392	.364	187	5	1	1	24	16
Joe Provenzano, McNeese St.	.310	.419	.374	171	7	2	0	13	5
Mason Salazar, Lamar	.310	.350	.421	145	4	3	2	25	3
Hayden Simerly, Sam Houston	.309	.368	.406	175	10	2	1	32	11
Lewis Guilbeau, McNeese St.	.308	.395	.351	185	8	0	0	20	3
Daniel Midyett, Southeastern La.	.306	.411	.477	216	9	2	8	46	7
Tyler Ware, A&M-Corpus Christi	.301	.442	.449	176	10	5	2	28	16
Kyle Thornell, Stephen F. Austin	.301	.412	.524	166	6	8	5	30	3
Nick Heath, Northwestern St.	.240	.372	.296	179	5	1	1	20	23
Logan Preston, Central Ark.	.222	.343	.460	176	8	2	10	34	1

INDIVIDUAL PITCHING LEADERS
(Minimum 40 innings pitched)

	W	L	ERA	G	SV	IP	H	BB	SO
Colin Kober, McNeese State	6	1	1.03	27	9	53	35	10	54
Justin Sinibaldi, Nicholls State	10	1	1.40	13	0	77	70	16	54
Grant Borne, Nicholls State	6	5	1.48	15	0	91	65	40	84
Chase Angelle, Lamar	5	6	2.01	14	0	99	90	17	65
Kyle Cedotal, Southeastern La.	9	2	2.08	15	0	100	82	19	95
Matt Danton, A&M-Corpus Christi	4	7	2.20	14	0	94	94	17	66
Ryan Deemes, Nicholls State	5	4	2.29	19	0	79	73	19	67
Andrew Godail, Sam Houston St.	5	6	2.30	16	0	98	93	28	88
Alex Bisacca, Sam Houston State	7	2	2.35	28	4	69	52	12	57
Connor Gilmore, Central Ark.	8	3	2.42	15	0	108	88	30	59
Tate Scioneaux, Southeastern La.	9	3	2.53	15	0	110	93	18	96
Geno Encina, Incarnate Word	3	4	2.57	14	0	74	68	13	59
Cole Prejean, McNeese State	2	3	2.57	28	1	56	41	15	48
Adam Oller, Northwestern State	6	4	2.58	15	0	108	81	23	57
Shawn Semple, New Orleans	2	4	2.70	8	0	47	34	17	34
Cameron Gann, Stephen F. Austin	4	3	2.77	13	0	88	80	27	72
Alex Smith, New Orleans	3	6	2.84	16	0	70	82	22	39
Matthew McCollough, Houston Bap.	8	3	2.87	15	0	107	99	18	74
Trevor Belicek, TA&M-CC	9	5	2.87	16	0	88	70	22	111
Taylor Wright, Houston Baptist	8	6	3.09	14	0	87	86	18	47
Jake Johnson, Southeastern La.	10	2	3.24	15	0	94	89	28	85
Jacob Dorris, TA&M-CC	1	2	3.32	28	10	41	29	12	39
Josh Oller, Northwestern State	10	2	3.80	15	0	97	110	25	57
Kevin Kelleher, New Orleans	2	9	3.98	25	0	54	57	23	71
Evan Tidwell, Northwestern State	2	4	4.34	13	0	46	55	6	28

SOUTHWESTERN ATHLETIC CONFERENCE

Eastern Division	Conference W L	Overall W L
Alabama State	18 6	31 19
Alabama A&M	16 8	26 31
Jackson State	15 9	32 25
Alcorn State	7 18	16 41
Mississippi Valley State	4 20	7 36

Western Division	Conference W L	Overall W L
Arkansas-Pine Bluff	17 6	25 16
* Texas Southern	16 7	31 19
Southern	13 8	20 23
Grambling State	7 17	11 39
Prairie View A&M	5 19	15 36

ALL-CONFERENCE TEAM: C—Chris Biocic, So., Alabama State; Jovany Felipe, Sr., Jackson State. **1B**—Austin Hulsey, Jr., Alabama A&M; Andre Davis, Jr., Arkansas-Pine Bluff. **2B**—Melvin Rodriguez, Sr., Jackson State. **3B**—Jesus Santana, Fr., Jackson State. **SS**—P.J. Biocic, Sr., Alabama State. **OF**—Andrew Utterback, Sr., Alabama A&M; Cesar Rivera, Sr., Alabama State; Scotty Peavey, Sr., Alcorn State. **DH**—Sam Campbell, So., Jackson State. **SP**—Joseph Camacho, Jr., Alabama State; Ryan Ahrens, Sr., Alabama A&M; Blake Estep, Jr., Arkansas-Pine Bluff. **RP**—Kevin Walsh, Jr., Arkansas-Pine Bluff. **Player of the Year:** Melvin Rodriguez, Jackson State. **Hitter of the Year:** Julio Nunez, Alabama A&M; Melvin Rodriguez, Jackson State. **Pitcher of the Year:** Joseph Camacho, Alabama State. **Freshman of the Year:** Jesus Santana, Jackson State. **Newcomer of the Year:** Collin Carroll, Alcorn State. **Coach of the Year:** Mitch Hill, Alabama A&M.

INDIVIDUAL BATTING LEADERS
(Minimum 140 At-Bats)

	AVG	OBP	SLG	AB	2B	3B	HR	RBI	SB
Melvin Rodriguez, Jackson St.	.421	.477	.629	221	22	3	6	60	13
Cesar Rivera, Alabama State	.391	.473	.614	207	16	3	8	42	4
Gary Thomas, Jackson State	.365	.427	.414	203	10	0	0	25	20
Andre Davis, Ark.-Pine Bluff	.364	.452	.593	140	12	1	6	39	0
Robert Garza, Texas Southern	.358	.457	.549	162	11	4	4	32	13
Andrew Utterback, Ala. A&M	.353	.423	.534	204	13	3	6	40	7
Scotty Peavey, Alcorn State	.353	.410	.603	204	14	2	11	46	12
P.J. Biocic, Alabama State	.351	.502	.433	171	6	1	2	41	7
Chris Biocic, Alabama State	.349	.423	.463	175	11	3	1	44	12
Jordan Friend, Alabama A&M	.340	.429	.615	156	14	1	9	37	2
Kalik May, Mississippi Val.	.339	.424	.519	183	11	5	4	33	24
Collin Carroll, Alcorn State	.338	.422	.583	204	14	0	12	47	8
Brady McBride, Mississippi Val.	.333	.392	.442	156	11	0	2	24	3
Julio Nunez, Alabama A&M	.330	.418	.597	206	22	0	11	51	1
Grant Dougherty, Prairie View	.321	.468	.404	156	4	0	3	23	23
Tyler Kirksey, Southern	.320	.404	.520	150	6	6	4	27	16
Yamil Pagan, Alabama State	.319	.396	.470	166	7	3	4	30	8
Waldyvan Estrada, Ala. State	.317	.430	.527	186	12	0	9	54	6
J. Felipe, Jackson State	.317	.406	.484	186	12	2	5	54	10
Arrington Smith, Mississippi Val.	.315	.398	.396	149	3	0	3	24	4
Christopher Scroggins, Texas So.	.313	.390	.392	166	6	2	1	30	6
Larry Barraza, Grambling State	.312	.401	.512	170	11	1	7	32	13
Marcus Tomlin, Southern	.312	.450	.382	157	6	1	1	21	5
Austin Hulsey, Alabama A&M	.307	.351	.377	199	9	1	1	30	0
Sam Campbell, Jackson State	.306	.451	.497	173	18	3	3	42	5
Lamar Briggs, Jackson State	.305	.394	.409	154	10	3	0	32	10
Jesus Santana, Jackson State	.282	.386	.569	181	12	2	12	48	2
Cody Den Beste, Prairie View	.277	.398	.486	173	12	6	4	26	10
Ryan Lazo, Texas Southern	.243	.372	.320	181	5	3	1	29	34

INDIVIDUAL PITCHING LEADERS
(Minimum 40 innings pitched)

	W	L	ERA	G	SV	IP	H	BB	SO
Ryan Rios, Texas Southern	6	2	2.89	16	0	56	48	19	41
Santos Saldivar, Southern	5	6	3.00	17	1	87	70	32	115
Devin Kanorik, Texas Southern	3	4	3.02	21	7	42	32	22	37
Tyler Robinson, Southern	5	1	3.17	14	0	65	71	25	32
Ryan Ahrens, Alabama A&M	6	3	3.44	12	0	55	52	30	59
Larry Romero, Texas Southern	6	1	3.51	16	0	41	37	21	26
J. Burchell, Alabama A&M	7	3	3.52	15	0	69	71	35	56

	W	L	ERA	G	SV	IP	H	BB	SO
Joseph Camacho, Alabama State	12	0	3.84	13	0	84	93	20	76
Frank Cruz, Texas Southern	6	3	3.94	16	1	78	70	27	63
Tyler Howe, Alabama State	1	1	4.23	11	0	45	40	22	46
Vincent Anthonia, Jackson State	5	3	4.45	19	0	83	90	49	58
Caleb Bowen, Alabama A&M	3	2	4.50	12	0	40	39	20	26
Hunter McIntosh, Alabama State	4	1	4.56	11	0	47	51	21	42
Humberto Medina, Ark.-Pine Bluff	3	3	4.58	20	1	59	53	37	58
Seth Oliver, Texas Southern	0	3	4.67	22	2	54	50	28	57
Billy Olson, Ark.-Pine Bluff	5	3	4.93	14	0	66	69	22	66
Flelix Gomez, Texas Southern	4	3	4.97	15	0	58	69	15	36
Devin Smith, Alabama A&M	2	6	5.08	26	0	62	72	26	56
Robert Pearson, Texas Southern	5	3	5.17	19	1	63	68	40	49
Jaiden France, Grambling State	2	1	5.17	16	1	47	66	18	23
Colton Laird, Alcorn State	3	9	5.91	16	1	105	149	34	39
Creighton Hoover, Grambling St.	0	2	7.03	24	2	40	40	15	26
Tyler Case, Mississippi Val.	3	10	7.20	15	0	85	120	39	61
Blake Thomas, Mississippi Val.	1	10	10.28	13	0	52	76	46	41

SUMMIT LEAGUE

	Conference W L	Overall W L
* Oral Roberts	25 5	41 16
South Dakota State	18 11	33 23
IPFW	13 16	28 26
Nebraska-Omaha	12 18	21 31
North Dakota State	11 19	20 31
Western Illinois	10 20	17 33

ALL-CONFERENCE TEAM: C—Matt Whatley, Fr., Oral Roberts. **1B**—Audie Afenir, Sr., Oral Roberts. **2B**—Matt Bandy, Oral Roberts. **3B**—Chase Stafford, Jr., Oral Roberts. **SS**—Clayton Taylor, Jr., Nebraska-Omaha. **OF**—Zach Coppola, Jr., South Dakota State; Cole Gruber, Jr., Nebraska-Omaha; Derrian James, Sr., Oral Roberts. **DH**—Luke Ringhofer, Fr., South Dakota State. **UT**—Anthony Sequeira, Sr., Oral Roberts. **SP**—Xavier Altamirano, Jr., Oral Roberts; Adam Bray, Sr., South Dakota State; Guillermo Trujillo, Jr., Oral Roberts. **RP**—Anthony Sequeira, Sr., Oral Roberts. **Player of the Year:** Anthony Sequeira, Oral Roberts. **Pitcher of the Year:** Xavier Altamirano, Oral Roberts. **Newcomer of the Year:** Matt Whatley, Oral Roberts. **Coach of the Year:** Ryan Folmar, Oral Roberts.

INDIVIDUAL BATTING LEADERS
(Minimum 140 At-Bats)

	AVG	OBP	SLG	AB	2B	3B	HR	RBI	SB
Cole Gruber, Neb.-Omaha	.399	.495	.486	173	7	1	2	23	22
Zach Coppola, South Dakota St.	.370	.472	.409	208	6	1	0	31	39
Greg Kaiser, IPFW	.361	.396	.639	194	16	4	10	43	5
Eric Danforth, South Dakota St.	.360	.437	.442	172	10	2	0	25	7
Matt Whatley, Oral Roberts	.355	.437	.528	214	16	3	5	44	16
Ben Petersen, North Dakota St.	.355	.422	.459	183	8	1	3	23	6
Audie Afenir, Oral Roberts	.347	.424	.474	216	16	1	3	43	0
Anthony Sequeira, Oral Roberts	.341	.423	.583	223	21	0	11	58	3
Derrian James, Oral Roberts	.333	.413	.508	195	19	0	5	44	10
Noah Cummings, Oral Roberts	.331	.389	.472	178	8	1	5	31	3
Luke Ringhofer, South Dakota St.	.321	.441	.455	156	10	1	3	41	1
Al Robbins, South Dakota St.	.317	.406	.407	167	10	1	1	29	4
Alex Schultz, Neb.-Omaha	.316	.382	.423	215	12	1	3	23	12
Matt Brandy, Oral Roberts	.313	.429	.456	217	11	1	6	45	2
Evan VanSumeren, IPFW	.312	.364	.417	218	14	0	3	40	4
Clayton Taylor, Neb.-Omaha	.308	.403	.490	198	8	2	8	42	3
Shane Trevino, IPFW	.307	.361	.495	212	14	4	6	48	1
Chase Stafford, Oral Roberts	.301	.426	.438	153	8	2	3	34	8
Dean Wilson, Oral Roberts	.298	.375	.348	161	8	0	0	25	3
Brock Logan, IPFW	.295	.389	.396	149	6	0	3	28	0
Brandon Soat, IPFW	.294	.390	.505	214	19	4	6	45	4
Reid Clary, South Dakota St.	.293	.398	.448	174	13	1	4	39	6
Matt Johnson, South Dakota St.	.292	.387	.438	192	13	0	5	35	0
Kendall Whitman, IPFW	.291	.413	.430	179	8	1	5	42	0
Daniel Jewett, Neb.-Omaha	.291	.333	.337	175	8	0	0	17	4
Paul Jacobson, South Dakota St.	.267	.365	.338	225	11	1	1	29	10

INDIVIDUAL PITCHING LEADERS
(Minimum 40 innings pitched)

	W	L	ERA	G	SV	IP	H	BB	SO
Brian VanderWoude, N. Dakota St.	4	2	2.47	17	1	55	55	23	50
Tyler Fox, Neb.-Omaha	5	4	2.88	15	0	94	84	34	72
Xavier Altamirano, Oral Roberts	8	2	2.94	15	0	86	83	14	81
Adam Bray, South Dakota St.	8	4	2.96	14	0	91	80	25	80
Kurt Giller, Oral Roberts	4	3	3.12	10	0	43	38	12	40
Ryan Froom, South Dakota St.	5	3	3.22	13	0	67	71	18	48
Chris Anderson, South Dakota St.	8	3	3.62	14	0	82	90	34	60
Preston Church, Western Illinois	2	7	3.93	18	0	73	68	50	71
Bryce Howe, Oral Roberts	4	2	3.93	14	0	55	54	14	46
Zach Williamsen, Neb.-Omaha	7	7	4.18	16	0	88	100	26	62
Guillermo Trujillo, Oral Roberts	10	4	4.21	15	0	88	85	26	70
Evan Miller, IPFW	6	5	4.50	16	1	80	66	42	94
Shane Meltz, Neb.-Omaha	4	3	4.60	14	0	43	50	17	26
Trent Keefer, North Dakota St.	4	7	4.90	14	0	75	97	17	57
Tom Constand, Western Ill.	3	8	4.93	16	0	73	77	41	57
Chad Hodges, South Dakota St.	4	1	5.01	13	0	41	46	16	49
Jake Weber, IPFW	4	2	5.02	25	9	43	46	28	49
Joe Mortillaro, Western Ill.	3	5	5.22	15	0	71	84	38	56
J.T. Baksha, Western Ill.	2	5	5.23	19	1	41	44	23	35
David Ernst, North Dakota St.	2	10	5.38	16	0	87	112	41	49

SUN BELT CONFERENCE

	Conference		Overall	
	W	L	W	L
South Alabama	19	9	37	20
Troy	18	10	30	25
* Louisiana-Lafayette	18	11	42	23
Georgia Southern	18	12	30	27
Georgia State	15	13	30	27
Texas State	14	16	24	32
Texas-Arlington	14	16	24	32
Arkansas State	12	17	27	30
Arkansas-Little Rock	12	17	16	33
Louisiana-Monroe	12	18	25	29
Appalachian State	8	21	17	36

ALL-CONFERENCE TEAM: C—Joey Roach, Jr., Georgia State. **1B**—Matt Rose, Jr., Georgia State. **2B**—Stefan Trosclair, Jr., Louisiana-Lafayette. **3B**—Tanner Rockwell, Sr., Arkansas-Little Rock. **SS**—Blake Trahan, Jr., Louisiana-Lafayette. **OF**—Aaron Mizell, Jr., Georgia Southern; Ryan Blanton, So., Georgia State; Cole Billingsley, So., South Alabama. **DH**—David Hall, Sr., Troy. **UTL**—Zach George, Sr., Arkansas State. **SP**—Taylor Thurber, Sr., Appalachian State; Evan Challenger, So., Georgia Southern; Kevin Hill, Sr., South Alabama. **RP**—Ben Taylor, Sr., South Alabama. **Player of the Year:** Blake Trahan, Louisiana-Lafayette. **Pitcher of the Year:** Kevin Hill, South Alabama. **Freshman of the Year:** Gunner Leger, Louisiana-Lafayette. **Coach of the Year:** Mark Calvi, South Alabama.

INDIVIDUAL BATTING LEADERS
(Minimum 140 At-Bats)

	AVG	OBP	SLG	AB	2B	3B	HR	RBI	SB
Zach George, Arkansas St.	.399	.548	.562	203	22	1	3	35	9
Keelin Rasch, La.-Monroe	.359	.395	.571	217	13	3	9	41	4
Logan Hill, Troy	.354	.440	.549	206	13	0	9	42	13
Michael Pierson, App. State	.346	.469	.534	191	13	1	7	38	1
Kyle Clement, La.-Lafayette	.346	.401	.615	182	17	4	8	32	3
Travis Sibley, Texas-Arlington	.345	.398	.474	232	16	1	4	44	3
Cole Billingsley, South Ala.	.345	.437	.444	232	9	4	2	29	30
David Hall, Troy	.340	.403	.461	141	8	0	3	31	1
Stefan Trosclair, La.-Lafayette	.338	.441	.635	219	15	1	16	53	15
Matt McLean, Texas-Arlington	.337	.448	.374	187	5	1	0	22	7
Tyler Girouard, La.-Lafayette	.333	.445	.458	216	18	0	3	31	6
Trevin Hall, Troy	.331	.385	.478	157	12	1	3	20	6
Ryan Blanton, Georgia State	.330	.401	.540	176	11	4	6	22	5
Ryan Scott, UALR	.328	.398	.474	192	20	1	2	21	3
Levi Scott, Texas-Arlington	.327	.375	.493	211	14	0	7	49	1
Kody Adams, Ga. Southern	.324	.405	.456	204	15	3	2	17	8
Tanner Hill, Texas State	.319	.379	.511	188	9	0	9	44	2
Dillon Dobson, Appalachian St.	.317	.357	.577	208	14	2	12	34	4
Blake Trahan, La.-Lafayette	.315	.424	.406	254	15	1	2	29	17
Tanner Rockwell, UALR	.314	.386	.443	185	13	1	3	39	3

	AVG	OBP	SLG	AB	2B	3B	HR	RBI	SB
Kyle Kirk, UALR	.312	.353	.353	173	7	0	0	26	0
Kodie Tidwell, La.-Monroe	.311	.412	.492	193	20	3	3	28	3
Bud Collura, South Alabama	.303	.368	.353	241	5	2	1	38	16
Joey Roach, Georgia State	.302	.381	.473	205	10	2	7	39	1
Brandon Burris, App. State	.301	.342	.399	193	8	1	3	12	6
Matt Rose, Georgia State	.289	.391	.613	204	16	1	16	49	4
Reid Long, Troy	.275	.325	.522	182	9	6	8	30	4
Greg Davis, La.-Lafayette	.252	.324	.399	258	15	1	7	40	6

INDIVIDUAL PITCHING LEADERS
(Minimum 40 innings pitched)

	W	L	ERA	G	SV	IP	H	BB	SO
Ben Taylor, South Alabama	6	3	1.48	25	7	43	26	13	68
Dylan Moore, La.-Lafayette	3	3	1.60	32	13	51	39	16	40
Kevin Hill, South Alabama	10	0	1.73	13	0	94	70	38	107
Evan Challenger, Ga. Southern	5	3	2.03	14	0	80	69	22	58
Taylor Thurber, Appalachian St.	4	9	2.35	19	1	96	79	8	73
Cody Van Aken, South Alabama	3	1	2.81	29	4	51	43	12	44
Lucas Brown, Troy	6	3	2.85	18	0	88	86	28	60
Jacob Moreland, Texas-Arlington	4	2	2.91	25	1	56	54	12	25
Gunner Leger, La.-Lafayette	6	5	2.99	19	0	114	104	20	87
Grant Bennett, Troy	9	4	3.12	15	0	107	90	29	84
Will Bacon, La.-Lafayette	6	3	3.14	28	2	72	71	15	56
Trey Setzer, La.-Monroe	6	3	3.21	15	0	84	66	37	80
Wyatt Marks, La.-Lafayette	6	1	3.24	19	1	67	59	19	68
David Owen, Arkansas State	3	5	3.25	15	0	91	95	44	73
Austin Bembnowski, South Ala.	3	3	3.29	16	0	66	58	22	50
Tripp Sheppard, Ga. Southern	4	3	3.33	17	0	70	79	19	34
Colton Lee, La.-Lafayette	2	3	3.40	21	3	42	33	20	42
Jason Richman, Ga. Southern	7	1	3.48	38	3	67	57	35	53
Connor Simmons, Ga. Southern	2	5	3.52	14	0	54	49	25	39
Tyler Zuber, Arkansas State	7	4	3.54	21	1	74	64	28	72

WEST COAST CONFERENCE

	Conference		Overall	
	W	L	W	L
San Diego	19	8	33	22
* Pepperdine	17	10	30	27
Loyola Marymount	16	11	33	21
Brigham Young	16	11	28	25
San Francisco	15	12	23	31
Gonzaga	13	14	24	28
Santa Clara	12	15	26	28
St. Mary's	10	17	28	27
Pacific	10	17	14	37
Portland	7	20	12	42

ALL-CONFERENCE TEAM: Bryson Brigman, Fr., San Diego; David Fletcher, So., Loyola Marymound; Mitchell Gunsolus, Sr., Gonzaga; Kyle Holder, Jr., San Diego; Taylor Jones, Jr., Gonzaga; Hutton Moyer, Jr., Pepperdine; Dillon Robinson, Sr., Brigham Young; Anthony Villa, Jr., St. Mary's; Jose Vizcaino Jr., Jr., Santa Clara; Brandon Caruso, So., Pepperdine. **P**—Christian Cecilio, Sr., San Francisco; P.J. Conlon, Jr., San Diego; David Hill, Jr., San Diego; Taylor Jones, Jr., Gonzaga. **Pitcher of the Year:** Kyle Holder, San Diego. **Pitcher of the Year:** David Hill, San Diego. **Freshman of the Year:** Bryson Brigman, San Diego. **Defensive Player of the Year:** Joey Harris, Gonzaga. **Coach of the Year:** Rich Hill, San Diego.

INDIVIDUAL BATTING LEADERS
(Minimum 140 At-Bats)

	AVG	OBP	SLG	AB	2B	3B	HR	RBI	SB
Dillon Robinson, BYU	.371	.453	.550	202	17	2	5	43	1
Mitchell Gunsolus, Gonzaga	.353	.449	.556	207	15	3	7	34	4
Tyler Sullivan, Pacific	.351	.416	.441	211	13	3	0	19	11
Connor Hornsby, St. Mary's	.349	.417	.386	166	4	1	0	19	11
Kyler Holder, San Diego	.348	.418	.482	224	14	2	4	31	5
Zach Kirtley, St. Mary's	.346	.429	.418	208	12	0	1	29	3
Anthony Villa, St. Mary's	.343	.415	.488	201	15	1	4	39	1
Hayden Nielsen, BYU	.342	.381	.404	225	12	1	0	38	6
Dominic Miroglio, San Francisco	.340	.406	.447	206	11	1	3	38	1
Bryson Brigman, San Diego	.339	.395	.436	218	11	2	2	28	5
Collin Ferguson, St. Mary's	.337	.463	.577	208	24	1	8	39	6
Stevie Berman, Santa Clara	.336	.417	.493	146	11	0	4	27	0
Jose Vizcaino, Santa Clara	.335	.406	.588	194	14	4	9	39	10

	AVG	OBP	SLG	AB	2B	3B	HR	RBI	SB
Tanner Chauncey, BYU	.335	.408	.364	173	5	0	0	23	2
Colton Waltner, San Diego	.321	.361	.464	196	17	1	3	40	5
Sam Brown, Gonzaga	.317	.410	.417	199	11	3	1	27	4
Anthony Gonsolin, St. Mary's	.316	.391	.454	196	11	5	2	24	12
David Edwards, LMU	.316	.390	.492	187	15	0	6	29	10
Austin Miller, LMU	.314	.402	.422	223	11	2	3	27	15
Austin Bailey, San Diego	.314	.398	.396	207	8	3	1	27	2
Jesse Jenner, San Diego	.314	.407	.415	159	10	0	2	27	2
Colton Shaver, BYU	.313	.405	**.595**	195	16	0	13	42	1
Cory LeBrun, Gonzaga	.313	.365	.403	176	16	0	0	21	3
Brandon Caruso, Pepperdine	.309	.391	.456	217	19	2	3	26	3
Brennon Lund, BYU	.308	.351	.383	**240**	11	2	1	27	8
Hutton Moyer, Pepperdine	.295	.413	.564	220	9	**4**	**14**	45	**15**
Brett Sullivan, Pacific	.275	.314	.492	193	11	**5**	7	28	6

INDIVIDUAL PITCHING LEADERS
(Minimum 40 innings pitched)

	W	L	ERA	G	SV	IP	H	BB	SO
Sean Watkins, Loyola Marymount	4	1	**1.89**	17	0	57	41	23	49
Christian Cecilio, San Francisco	5	4	2.05	14	0	**110**	90	22	91
P.J. Conlon, San Diego	6	4	2.17	15	1	91	64	25	82
Cameron Neff, St. Mary's	1	2	2.23	10	2	40	33	12	37
Sam Granoff, San Francisco	3	2	2.28	10	0	47	41	9	30
David Hill, San Diego	**9**	3	2.33	14	0	100	66	35	**115**
Eli Morgan, Gonzaga	1	0	2.36	14	0	46	43	**8**	36
Cory Abbott, Loyola Marymount	1	1	2.37	27	1	49	33	10	32
Colin Welmon, Loyola Marymount	5	6	2.68	14	0	94	86	28	96
Reece Karalus, Santa Clara	3	6	2.82	26	9	61	63	10	68
Max Gamboa, Pepperdine	6	2	2.89	27	8	44	**32**	20	41
Jackson McClelland, Pepperdine	6	4	2.93	15	0	95	82	42	71
Anthony Gonsolin, St. Mary's	2	2	3.14	17	7	49	44	21	46
Michael Rucker, BYU	5	1	3.22	23	6	67	69	28	56
Johnny York, St. Mary's	7	4	3.24	14	0	86	100	30	73
Andrew Sopko, Gonzaga	7	5	3.55	14	0	89	100	29	78
Trevor Megill, Loyola Marymount	5	4	3.60	15	0	70	65	37	70
Evan Brisentine, Santa Clara	2	3	3.61	19	0	62	65	31	29
Anthony Shew, San Francisco	7	4	3.64	14	0	94	96	19	70
Brandon Bailey, Gonzaga	8	3	3.72	17	0	97	102	30	91
Jackson Lockwood, Portland	1	4	4.10	8	0	42	55	**8**	20
Will Lydon, Pacific	**11**	0	5.93	15	0	74	91	25	56

WESTERN ATHLETIC CONFERENCE

	Conference W	L	Overall W	L
Grand Canyon	19	7	32	22
Seattle	19	8	31	27
* Cal State Bakersfield	17	9	37	24
Sacramento State	16	11	33	27
North Dakota	16	11	24	27
Utah Valley	14	13	19	35
Northern Colorado	12	15	16	32
New Mexico State	7	19	11	38
Chicago State	6	19	13	40
Texas-Pan American	6	20	21	30

ALL-CONFERENCE TEAM: C—Brian Olson, Sr., Seattle. **1B**—Matt Schmidt, Sr., Chicago State. **2B**—Chad de la Guerra, Sr., Grand Canyon. **3B**—Ben Mauseth, So., Grand Canyon. **SS**—Paul Panaccione, Jr., Grand Canyon. **OF**—Jensen Park, Sr., Northern Colorado; Jeff Campbell, Sr., North Dakota; Nathan Lukes, Jr., Sacramento State. **SP**—Hayden Carter, Sr., Cal State Bakersfield; James Barragan, Sr., Cal State Bakersfield. **RP**—Ty Nichols, Sr., Sacramento State. **Player of the Year:** Jensen Park, Sr., Northern Colorado. **Pitcher of the Year:** Hayden Carter, Sr., Cal State Bakersfield. **Freshman of the Year:** Garrison Schwartz, Grand Canyon. **Coach of the Year:** Bill Kernen, Cal State Bakersfield.

INDIVIDUAL BATTING LEADERS
(Minimum 140 At-Bats)

	AVG	OBP	SLG	AB	2B	3B	HR	RBI	SB
Jensen Park, Northern Colorado	**.422**	.468	**.624**	173	11	3	6	34	13
Tyler Follis, North Dakota	.404	.462	.505	188	9	2	2	22	6
Logan Landon, Texas-Pan Am.	.382	**.476**	.623	191	14	4	8	47	17
Paul Panaccione, Grand Canyon	.376	.441	.493	221	10	2	4	36	7
Jeff Campbell, North Dakota	.365	.434	.598	189	9	1	**11**	48	3
Garrison Schwartz, G. Canyon	.357	.413	.439	196	10	3	0	40	7
Quinnton Mack, New Mexico St.	.353	.466	.535	170	11	4	4	32	13
Cole Loncar, Tex.-Pan American	.348	.428	.467	210	12	2	3	34	8
Brandon Smith, Grand Canyon	.348	.402	.478	161	9	3	2	24	10
David Metzgar, CSU Bakersfield	.347	.398	.454	**251**	**17**	2	2	42	10
Nathan Lukes, Sacramento St.	.345	.422	.511	235	14	2	7	38	13
Chad De La Guerra, G. Canyon	.344	.401	.544	215	8	1	**11**	**51**	7
Thomas Lerouge, Grand Canyon	.342	.389	.356	146	2	0	0	13	0
Scotty Burcham, Sacramento St.	.329	.382	.465	243	9	**6**	4	33	16
Matt Schmidt, Chicago State	.329	.406	.441	143	7	3	1	14	1
Max Carter, CSU Bakersfield	.327	.379	.390	159	10	0	0	27	0
Landon Cray, Seattle	.324	.412	.478	182	10	3	4	30	10
Kade Andrus, Utah Valley	.322	.418	.498	211	9	5	6	36	12
Mattingly Romanin, Chicago St.	.318	.410	.498	201	11	2	7	39	5
Joseph Koerper, New Mexico St.	.316	.375	.424	177	7	0	4	30	0
Joey Sanchez, CSU Bakersfield	.311	.442	.347	167	6	0	0	21	2
Jesus Garcia, Texas-Pan Am.	.307	.410	.360	189	8	1	0	22	5
Griffin Andreychuk, Seattle	.306	.407	.421	216	11	1	4	42	7
David Walker, Grand Canyon	.306	.404	.347	193	8	0	0	18	3
Brett Harrison, North Dakota	.305	.364	.357	154	5	0	1	17	0
Daniel Johnson, New Mexico St.	.305	.406	.397	151	8	0	2	16	2
Sheldon Stober, Seattle	.304	.365	.435	230	11	5	3	39	**22**
Chance Gusbeth, CSU Bakersfield	.273	.329	.415	205	8	**6**	3	32	11
Ryan Grotjohn, CSU Bakersfield	.259	.356	.424	170	7	**6**	3	26	6

INDIVIDUAL PITCHING LEADERS
(Minimum 40 innings pitched)

	W	L	ERA	G	SV	IP	H	BB	SO
Ty Nichols, Sacramento State	6	0	**1.23**	21	0	80	50	22	54
Brennan Leitao, Sacramento State	7	4	2.20	15	0	94	76	13	55
Steven Gee, CSU Bakersfield	5	4	2.32	18	2	78	76	26	44
Hayden Carter, CSU Bakersfield	**9**	3	2.44	17	0	**125**	133	24	58
Ted Hammond, Seattle	6	4	2.63	22	3	62	58	18	47
Sam Long, Sacramento State	6	4	2.81	15	1	90	64	16	63
Mick Vorhof, Grand Canyon	5	0	3.02	24	5	42	47	9	39
Skyler Genger, Seattle	6	7	3.05	17	0	100	79	30	**120**
James Barragan, CSU Bakersfield	7	5	3.06	14	0	88	84	37	81
Will Dennis, Seattle	6	4	3.08	16	0	96	106	17	70
Tarik Skubal, Seattle	7	4	3.24	17	0	83	69	27	68
Kyle Valgardson, Utah Valley	3	3	3.32	25	6	43	45	12	23
Garrett Nimmo, CSU Bakersfield	4	3	3.56	18	1	48	45	18	23
Tyler Beardsley, Sacramento State	1	1	3.61	23	0	42	**39**	7	18
Justin Dillon, Sacramento State	6	6	3.67	18	1	69	73	16	46
Andrew Thome, North Dakota	5	6	3.80	14	1	95	107	22	65
Coley Bruns, Grand Canyon	7	4	4.15	14	0	87	85	27	61
Jake Perkins, Chicago State	1	5	4.20	14	0	75	71	43	49
Robert Quinonez, Texas-Pan Am.	3	5	4.24	16	1	68	75	22	57
Riley Barr, New Mexico State	4	7	4.37	14	0	82	101	33	58
Jake Stassi, Sacramento State	2	5	5.13	13	0	40	50	**6**	20
Zack Thomas, Chicago State	1	**9**	8.52	**27**	0	48	32	26	26

NCAA DIVISION II

BY MAT BATTS

For the second time in three years, the Tampa Spartans took home the Division II championship in Cary, N.C. The title for the Spartans—the 7th in school history—comes just a year after their 52-win team lost a heartbreaker in the 2014 championship game, a tournament which seemed destined to be theirs.

"It means a lot to these seniors." Tampa head coach Joe Urso told NCAA. com. "They all knew that we had some unfinished business that they wanted to take care of. We came in here last year with high expectations and got our hearts crushed. This year, we came in with a group that was really over-achieving and got hot at the right time. They weren't going to take 'no' for an answer."

Tampa pitcher Michael Calkins was named the tournament's most out-standing player after turning in a complete game, one-run performance in the championship game. Calkins also threw a complete game in Tampa's victory over Nova Southeastern (Fla.) just a week earlier during the South Regional tournament. Tampa's Nick Tindall, Stephen Dezzi, Giovanny Alfonzo, Casey Scoggins and Chase Sparkman were also named to the all-tournament team.

Tampa put together a perfect 8-0 record during postseason play and finished the season on a 10-game winning streak, with their last loss of the season coming on May 1 against Rollins (Fla.).

After falling behind Catawba 1-0 in the final game, with Catawba need-ing to beat the Spartans twice, Tampa catcher Nick Tindall connected on a two-run triple in the fourth inning to give the Spartans a lead they would not relinquish. An RBI single from Casey Scoggins in the seventh inning gave Tampa a 3-1 lead and an insurance run. Calkins finished off his gem, earning Tampa the title.

"It's been a grind," Urso said. "These guys really fought for me this year. They had every excuse in the book why this season wasn't supposed to work out for us, but they didn't let it happen."

DIVISION II WORLD SERIES

Site: Cary, N.C.
Participants: Angelo State, Texas (41-16); Cal Poly Pomona (43-15); Catawba, N.C. (44-13); Henderson State, Ark. (31-19); Mercyhurst, Pa. (39-9); Tampa (39-13); Truman, Mo. (35-20); Wilmington, Del. (37-13)
Champion: Tampa.
Runner-up: Catawba.
Outstanding player: Michael Calkins, rhp, Tampa.

PRELIMINARIES

Henderson State 4, Angelo State 0
Catawba 3, Wilmington 2
Mercyhurst 3, Truman 1
Tampa 7, Cal Poly Pomona 4
Angelo State 5, Wilmington 0 (Wilmington eliminated)
Catawba 5, Henderson State 1
Cal Poly Pomona 13, Truman 2 (Truman eliminated)
Tampa 3, Mercyhurst 1
Henderson State 4, Angelo State 1 (Angelo State eliminated)
Cal Poly Pomona 5, Mercyhurst 1 (Mercyhurst eliminated)

SEMIFINALS

Cal Poly Pomona 11, Catawba 2
Catawba 9, Cal Poly Pomona 6 (Cal Poly Pomona eliminated)
Tampa 5, Henderson State 2 (Henderson State eliminated)

FINALS

Tampa 3, Catawba 1

LEADERS

BATTING AVERAGE (Minimum 100 at-bats)

RK. PLAYER, POS., TEAM	CLASS	AVG	OBP	SLG
1. Taylor Eads, of, Spring Hill (Ala.)	Sr.	.538	.623	.846
2. Will Albertson, c, Catawba (N.C.)	Jr.	.467	.532	.865
3. Michael Logsdon, 1b, West Va. Wesleyan	Jr.	.462	.510	.629
4. Anthony Diminio, of, Belmont Abbey (N.C.)	Jr.	.452	.486	.599
5. David Summerfield, if, Millersville (Pa.)	So.	.452	.505	.582
6. Hunter Newman, 1b, Trevecca Nazarene (Tenn.)	Jr.	.451	.558	.877
7. Matt Peters, if, California (Pa.)	Sr.	.446	.505	.675
8. Clint Hardy, of, Ga. Regents-Augusta	So.	.445	.494	.740
9. Nick Sell, if, Seton Hill (Pa.)	Sr.	.444	.520	1.032
10. Ty Barkell, if, South Carolina-Aiken	Sr.	.444	.493	.684

CATEGORY LEADERS: BATTING

DEPT.	PLAYER, POS., TEAM	CLASS	G	TOTAL
OBP *	Taylor Eads, of, Spring Hill (Ala.)	Sr.	39	.623
SLG *	Ryan Uhl, of, Indiana (Pa.)	Sr.	44	1.085
R	Thomas Spitz, of, Wingate (N.C.)	Sr.	59	80
H	Will Albertson, c, Catawba (N.C.)	Jr.	62	114
2B	Adam Urbania, of, Slippery Rock (Pa.)	Sr.	48	26
	Troy Paris, 3b, Kentucky Wesleyan	Jr.	50	26
3B	Brenden Wells, of, Malone (Ohio)	So.	50	9
HR	Ryan Uhl, of, Indiana (Pa.)	Sr.	44	29
RBI	Nick Sell, if, Seton Hill (Pa.)	Sr.	56	92
SB	John Razzino, of, Franklin Pierce (N.H.)	Sr.	52	45

*Minimum 100 at-bats

EARNED RUN AVERAGE (Minimum 40 innings pitched)

RK. PITCHER, TEAM	CLASS	W	L	ERA
1. Miles Sheehan, Franklin Pierce (N.H)	Jr.	7	0	0.29
2. Craig Peters, Oakland City (Ind.)	So.	5	0	0.43
3. Michael Young, Stonehill (Mass.)	Fr.	5	2	0.68
4. Jake DeCarli, Long Island-Post	So.	6	1	0.76
5. Brendan O'Rourke, Franklin Pierce (N.H.)	Sr.	11	0	0.84
6. Kory Groves, Cal State Monterey Bay	Sr.	4	2	1.03
7. P.J. Martino, Bridgeport (Conn.)	Jr.	4	4	1.07
8. Sheldon Miks, St. Cloud State (Minn.)	Fr.	9	2	1.15
9. Alex Person, Southern New Hampshire	So.	8	1	1.26
10. Steve Naemark, Angelo State (Texas)	Jr.	11	1	1.37

CATEGORY LEADERS: PITCHING

DEPT.	PITCHER, TEAM	CLASS	TOTAL
W	Reese Gregory, St. Cloud State (Minn.)	Jr.	13
L	Walker Rainwater, Oklahoma-Panhandle	Sr.	11
	Marty Coursey, Union (Tenn.)	Fr.	11
SV	Nick Vanthillo, Henderson State (Ark.)	Sr.	14
	Tyler Fries, Wilmington (Del.)	Sr.	14
G	Ryan McClintock, Catawba (N.C.)	Sr.	35
IP	Steve Naemark, Angelo State (Texas)	Jr.	125
SO	Craig Brooks, Catawba (N.C.)	Sr.	158
SO/9 *	Craig Brooks, Catawba (N.C.)	Sr.	14.4
BB/9 *	Timothy Buchanan, Southern Arkansas	Jr.	0.2
WHIP*	Miles Sheehan, Franklin Pierce (N.H.)	Jr.	0.69

*Minimum 40 innings pitched

NCAA DIVISION III

SUNY Cortland defeated Wisconsin-La Crosse in dramatic fashion, coming back from a ninth-inning deficit to capture its first ever national championship.

Down 2-1 in the top of the ninth, Cortland's Matthew Michalski led off the inning with a single up the middle. Justin Teague then reached on a botched sacrifice bunt and Mark DeMilio walked to load with bases with no outs. Nick Hart promptly singled and drove in two runs to give Cortland a 3-2 lead. The Red Dragons added three more runs in the inning, taking a 6-2 lead into the bottom of the ninth. Travis Laitar sealed the victory, striking out one and inducing a game-ending double play.

The Red Dragons' victory over Wisconsin-La Crosse capped a 5-0 run for Cortland during the World Series, and they became the first New York school to win the Division III baseball title since Ithaca in 1988.

DIVISION III WORLD SERIES
Site: Appleton, Wis.
Participants: Emory, Ga. (30-13); Frostburg State, Md. (41-7); Ramapo, N.J. (32-14); Salisbury, Md. (33-4); SUNY Cortland (40-4); Trinity, Texas (37-12); Webster, Mo. (34-13); Wisconsin-La Crosse (33-13)
Champion: SUNY Cortland
Runner-up: Wisconsin-La Crosse.
Outstanding player: Conrad Ziemendorf, of, SUNY Cortland.

LEADERS

BATTING AVERAGE (Minimum 100 at-bats)

RK. PLAYER, POS., TEAM	CLASS	AVG	OBP	SLG
1. Kyle Engel, if, Univ. of Chicago	Sr.	.486	.546	.750
2. Jake Fishman, p, Union (N.Y.)	So.	.477	.543	.559
3. John Malone, c, Saint Vincent (Pa.)	Sr.	.464	.512	.573
4. Michael Marino, if, Farmingdale State (N.Y.)	Sr.	.463	.539	.602
5. Ben Buerkle, of, Saint Mary's (Minn.)	So.	.462	.517	.765

CATEGORY LEADERS: BATTING

DEPT. PLAYER, POS., TEAM	CLASS	G	TOTAL
OBP * Austin Filiere, if, MIT	Fr.	43	.552
SLG * Matt Foley, c, Rhode Island College	Jr.	34	.872
HR Jamie Lackner, 1b, Wooster (Ohio)	So.	45	17
Kyle Uhrich, p, Webster (Mo.)	So.	49	17
RBI Jamie Lackner, 1b, Wooster (Ohio)	So.	45	69
SB Bill Munson, ss, Rhodes (Tenn.)	So.	46	44

Minimum 100 at-bats

EARNED RUN AVERAGE (Minimum 40 innings pitched)

RK. PITCHER, TEAM	CLASS	W	L	ERA
1. Jameson Sadowske, Wisconsin-La Crosse	So.	5	1	0.78
2. Brett Moody, Austin (Texas)	So.	2	2	0.97
3. Tommy Bergjans, Haverford (Pa.)	Sr.	5	3	1.07
4. Bryan Polowy, North Central (Ill.)	Jr.	8	1	1.09
5. Kyle Cutler, Fitchburg State (Mass.)	So.	4	2	1.09

CATEGORY LEADERS: PITCHING

DEPT. PITCHER, TEAM	CLASS	TOTAL
W Jackson Weeg, Emory (Ga.)	So.	12
L Derek Kearney, Caltech	Sr.	11
SV Kevin Becker-Menditto, Alvernia (Pa.)	Sr.	16
G Andrew Richards, Southern Maine	Sr.	32
IP Walker Larson, Ramapo (N.J.)	Sr.	120
SO Tommy Bergjans, Haverford (Pa.)	Sr.	111

NAIA

Lewis-Clark State came from behind to score nine unanswered runs in the final four innings of the NAIA national championship to defeat St. Thomas 10-7. The 2015 title adds to the Warrior's impressive reign over the NAIA, as Lewis-Clark State tallied its record 17th national championship.

After trailing St. Thomas by as much as five runs late in the game, the Warriors broke through with an eighth-inning rally which included four hits, two hit batters and an error. Lewis-Clark State finished the eighth with a 10-7 lead and never looked back.

Site: Lewiston, Idaho.
Participants: Concordia, Calif. (48-16); Davenport, Mich. (51-11); Embry-Riddle, Fla. (40-17); Faulkner, Ala. (49-13); Lewis-Clark State, Idaho (42-11); Lindsey Wilson, Ky. (41-18); Oklahoma Baptist (52-7); St. Thomas, Fla. (44-17); Tabor, Kan. (53-11); Vanguard, Calif. (39-20).
Champion: Lewis-Clark State.
Runner-up: St. Thomas
Outstanding player: Beau Kerns, rhp, Lewis-Clark State.

LEADERS

BATTING AVERAGE (Minimum 75% of games played)

RK. PLAYER, TEAM	CLASS	AVG	AB	H
1. Jacob Lanning, Holy Cross (Ind.)	Sr.	.481	181	87
2. Sean Baumes, Bacone (Okla.)	Jr.	.455	145	66
3. Jordan Tescher, Dickinson State (N.D.)	Sr.	.448	165	74
4. Miguel Beltre, Edward Waters (Fla.)	So.	.438	162	71
5. Aaron Stubblefield, Sterling (Kan.)	Jr.	.436	211	92

CATEGORY LEADERS: BATTING

DEPT. PLAYER, TEAM	CLASS	G	TOTAL
OBP * Sean Baumes, Bacone (Okla.)	Jr.	46	.574
SLG * Jordan Tescher, Dickinson State (N.D.)	Sr.	51	.891
HR Seth Brown, Lewis-Clark State (Idaho)	Jr.	58	23
RBI Ty Abbott, Georgia Gwinnett	Sr.	63	93
SB Chris Madera, Faulkner (Ala.)	Sr.	66	56

Minimum 75% of games played

EARNED RUN AVERAGE (Minimum 1 IP per team game)

RK. PITCHER, TEAM	CLASS	ERA	G	IP
1. Griffin Glaude, Lyon (Ark.)	Sr.	0.56	13	81
2. Zac Grotz, Embry-Riddle (Fla.)	Sr.	0.70	32	78
3. Adam Quintana, Peru State (Neb.)	Sr.	0.88	12	72
4. Adam Hines, LSU Alexandria	Jr.	0.96	13	94
5. Andrew Bergmann, Judson (Ill.)	Sr.	1.00	16	99

CATEGORY LEADERS: PITCHING

DEPT. PITCHER, TEAM	CLASS	TOTAL
W Corey Hale, Mobile (Ala.)	Sr.	14
L Douglas Gove, Central Christian (Kan.)	Jr.	10
SV Tyler Mark, Concordia (Calif.)	Jr.	24
IP Stetson Nelson, Embry-Riddle (Fla.)	Sr.	137
SO Kelvin Rivas, Oklahoma Baptist	Sr.	144

NJCAA DIVISION I

Northwest Florida State captured the 2015 NJCAA Division I title in decisive fashion, rattling off 17 hits and 15 runs in a 15-1 rout of McLennan (Texas) in the championship game. Aaron Palmer and Dakota Dean each tallied four hits for the Raiders who used a six-run fourth inning to pull away from McLennan for good.

Northwest Florida State starter Corderias Dorsey tossed a complete-game, allowing just one run, none earned, while striking out 12 over 147 pitches. Dorsey was named the tournament's most outstanding pitcher. The Raiders finished the season with a 42-13 record and their first-ever national championship.

Site: Grand Junction, Colo.

Participants: Chattahoochee, Ala. (41-15); Delgado, La. (33-14); Dodge City, Kan. (41-17); Iowa Western (52-5); McLennan, Texas (37-18); Northwest Florida State (37-12); San Jacinto, Texas (41-19); South Carolina-Sumter (43-19); Walters State, Tenn. (54-10); Yavapai, Ariz. (45-16).

Champion: Northwest Florida State.

Runner-up: McLennan.

Outstanding player: Ramon Osuna, of, Walters State.

LEADERS

BATTING AVERAGE (Minimum 2.5 PAs per game, 75% of games played)

RK. PLAYER, TEAM	AVG	OBP	SLG	HR
1. Garrett Benge, Cowley County (Kan.) CC	.502	.601	.946	19
2. Jacy Cave, New Mexico JC	.491	.513	.910	20
3. Branden Grieger, New Mexico JC	.478	.563	.701	7
4. Jonah Bride, Neosho County (Kan.) CC	.471	.541	.814	14
5. Tristen Gagan, Northeastern Okla. A&M JC	.470	.553	.769	10

CATEGORY LEADERS: BATTING

DEPT. PLAYER, TEAM	G	TOTAL
OBP * Garrett Benge, Cowley County (Kan.) CC	59	.601
SLG * Anthony Miller, Johnson County (Kan.) CC	60	.974
HR Willie Calhoun, Yavapai (Ariz.) JC	63	31
RBI Garrett Benge, Cowley County (Kan.) CC	59	97
SB London Lindley, Georgia Perimeter JC	56	48
Tad Martin, USC Lancaster JC	51	48

Minimum 2.5 PAs per game, 75% of games played

EARNED RUN AVERAGE (Minimum 1 IP per team game)

RK PITCHER, TEAM	W	L	ERA	IP
1 Logan Redmond, Pitt (N.C.) CC	8	1	1.03	53
2 Hunter Hart, Kaskaskia (Ill.) CC	10	0	1.16	77
3 Evan Mitchell, Potomac State (W.Va.) JC	12	1	1.16	85
4 Jordan Barrett, Polk State (Fla.) JC	9	2	1.43	69
5 Phil Bickford, JC of Southern Nevada	9	1	1.45	87

CATEGORY LEADERS: PITCHING

DEPT. PITCHER, TEAM		TOTAL
W Justin McGregor, Cowley County (Kan.) CC		12
Evan Mitchell, Potomac State (W.Va.) JC		12
Parker Rigler, Cowley County (Kan.) CC		12
Campbell Scholl, Walters State (Tenn.) CC		12
L Josh Knies, Florida CC-Jacksonville		12
IP Taylor Cockrell, State JC of Florida		115
SO Phil Bickford, JC of Southern Nevada		166

NJCAA DIVISION II

With their backs against the wall, LSU Eunice pulled out pair of unlikely victories to defeat Western Oklahoma State and capture their fifth national championship since 2006.

Entering the tournament's championship round, the Bengals title hopes began to fade as Western Oklahoma State pulled ahead 10-1 into the fifth inning. LSU Eunice rallied to outscore the Pioneers 13-2 in the game's final four innings, completing the improbable comeback with a 14-12 victory to force game two.

The Bengals handed the ball to sophomore Ben Braymer in game two and never looked back. Braymer turned in a four-hit, 12 strikeout performance as LSU Eunice rolled to a 16-1 victory and a national title.

Site: Enid, Okla.

Participants: Catawba Valley, N.C. (35-19); Frederick, Md. (44-15); Kellog, Mi. (42-15); Lincoln Land, Ill. (39-6); LSU Eunice (47-12); Madison, Wi. (38-21); North Iowa Area (25-16); Scottsdale (44-20); Connecticut-Avery Point (42-16); Western Oklahoma State (33-15).

Champion: LSU Eunice.

Runner-up: Western Oklahoma State.

Outstanding player: David Lafleur, of, LSU Eunice.

LEADERS

BATTING AVERAGE (Minimum 2.5 PAs per game, 75% of games played)

RK. PLAYER, TEAM	AVG	OBP	SLG	HR
1. Chris Mattison, Frederick (Md.) CC	.527	.560	.859	12
2. Parker Kinkade, Williston State (N.D.) JC	.496	.550	.882	6
3. Steven Lennox, Dutchess (N.Y.) CC	.490	.536	.569	0
4. David Ormsby, Allegany (Md.) CC	.476	.503	.649	3
5. Trevor Behrent, Cecil (Md.) CC	.467	.565	.814	12

EARNED RUN AVERAGE (Minimum 1 IP per team game)

RK. PITCHER, TEAM	W	L	ERA	IP
1. Dylan Hastings, Wake Tech (N.C.) CC	5	0	0.45	40
2. Aiden Hernandez, Rowan (N.J.) JC	3	0	0.84	32
3. Tyler Carvalho, Mesa (Ariz.) CC	7	2	0.90	60
4. Nate Harmon, Frederick (Md.) CC	10	1	1.30	76
5. Jack Maynard, Patrick Henry (Va.) CC	9	3	1.36	86

NJCAA DIVISION III

Tyler (Texas) continued its dominating ways, defeating Joliet (Ill.) 10-9 to capture its second straight national title. Tyler rolled through the postseason, racking up a perfect 5-0 record and capping off a 16-game win streak dating back to the regular season. With the final win, Tyler became the first team to capture consecutive NJCAA D-III national championships since Richland (Texas), who won three titles from 2002-2004.

Site: Kinston, N.C.

Participants: Century, Minn. (40-9); Herkimer County, N.Y. (48-6); Nassau, N.Y. (19-13); Northern Essex, Mass. (28-4); Montgomery, Md. (33-21); Joliet, Ill. (38-25); Rowan College, N.J. (39-12); Tyler, Texas (41-8).

Champion: Tyler.

Runner-up: Joliet. **Outstanding player:** Cody Brown, rhp, Tyler.

LEADERS

BATTING AVERAGE (Minimum 2.5 PAs per game, 75% of games played)

RK. PLAYER, TEAM	AVG	OBP	SLG	HR
1. Tim Pauley, Allegheny County-South (Pa.) CC	.500	.577	.568	0
2. Darren Conte, Hudson Valley (N.Y.) CC	.489	.546	.633	2
3. Henry Pellicciotti, SUNY Broome CC	.488	.551	.732	0
4. Tyler Phillips, Herkimer County (N.Y.) CC	.486	.520	.676	3
5. Malik Fogg, Tompkins Cortland (N.Y.) CC	.477	.558	.908	11

EARNED RUN AVERAGE (Minimum 1 IP per team game)

RK. PITCHER, TEAM	W	L	ERA	IP
1. Chuck Delagol, Montgomery County (Pa.) CC	5	0	0.70	38
2. Kristopher Killackey, Suffolk County (N.Y.) CC	4	1	1.18	38
3. Zack Kubala, North Lake (Texas) JC	4	0	1.21	52
4. Michael Bugonowicz, Luzerne County (Pa.) CC	3	1	1.29	42
5. Frank Valentino, Suffolk County (N.Y.) CC	5	2	1.31	55

CALIFORNIA CC ATHLETIC ASSOCIATION

Orange Coast captured its second-straight California Community College Athletic Association state championship, defeating San Joaquin Delta 9-4 in the tournament's deciding game. The victory for Orange Coast sealed the sixth state championship in school history and the third in seven years. The Pirates strolled through the four-team tournament, winning all three games, including a 5-0 victory over San Joaquin Delta in the opener.

Site: Fresno, Calif.
Participants: Fresno City (35-9); Orange Coast (27-17); Palomar (36-6); San Joaquin Delta (39-5).
Champion: Orange Coast.
Runner-up: San Joaquin Delta.
Outstanding player: Jack Kruger, c, Orange Coast; Dominic Purpura, p, Orange Coast.

LEADERS

BATTING AVERAGE (Minimum 2.5 PAs per game, 75% of games played)

RK. PLAYER, TEAM	AVG	OBP	SLG	HR
1. Josh Gooding, Victor Valley (Calif.) JC	.465	.524	.736	7
2. Joseph Cortez, El Camino (Calif.) JC	.458	.520	.542	0
3. Antonio Ruiz, Rio Hondo (Calif.) JC	.430	.485	.543	3
4. Martin Teague, El Camino-Compton (Calif.) JC	.422	.478	.659	6
5. Anthony Roberts, Butte (Calif.) JC	.417	.531	.545	1

CATEGORY LEADERS: BATTING

DEPT.	PLAYER, TEAM	G	TOTAL
OBP *	Anthony Roberts, Butte (Calif.) JC	38	.531
SLG *	Josh Gooding, Victor Valley (Calif.) JC	33	.736
HR	Francis Christy, Palomar (Calif.) JC	45	11
RBI	Josh Gooding, Victor Valley (Calif.) JC	33	54
SB	Brock Pradere, Ohlone (Calif.) JC	41	33

Minimum 2.5 PAs per game, 75% of games played

EARNED RUN AVERAGE (Minimum 1 IP per team game)

RK. PITCHER, TEAM	W	L	ERA	IP
1 Garrett Hill, Santa Rosa (Calif.) JC	4	2	0.88	72
2 Taylor Turski, Palomar (Calif.) JC	8	0	1.03	79
3 Ryan Capozza, Cabrillo (Calif.) JC	5	2	1.17	69
4 Devin Mahoney, San Mateo (Calif.) JC	6	1	1.27	56
5 Sean Barry, Santa Barbara (Calif.) JC	10	3	1.29	111

CATEGORY LEADERS: PITCHING

DEPT.	PITCHER, TEAM	TOTAL
W	Cameron Leeper, San Joaquin Delta (Calif.) JC	14
L	Christian Sadler, Contra Costa (Calif.) JC	11
SV	Shane Desmond, Fresno City (Calif.) JC	10
IP	Justin Zielinski, Irvine Valley (Calif.) JC	118
SO	Cameron Leeper, San Joaquin Delta (Calif.) JC	130

NORTHWEST ATHLETIC CONFERENCE

After losing game one of the championship round, Lower Columbia (Wash.) defeated Mount Hood (Wash.) in a winner-take-all game to capture the Northwest Athletic Conference championship.

Lower Columbia pitcher Tanner Olson returned on two days rest for the Red Devils and produced a complete-game six-hitter. Olson allowed just one run as Lower Columbia cruised to a 6-1 victory. Olson earned MVP honors for the performance.

Site: Longview, Wash.
Participants: Douglas, Wash. (12-12); Edmonds, Wash. (18-6); Everett, Wash. (17-7); Lower Columbia, Wash. (24-1); Mount Hood, Wash. (20-4); Tacoma, Wash. (20-5); Treasure Valley, Ore. (20-8); Walla Walla, Wash. (19-9).
Champion: Lower Columbia.
Runner-up: Mount Hood.
Outstanding player: Tanner Olson, rhp, Lower Columbia.

LEADERS

BATTING AVERAGE (Minimum 2.7 PAs per team game)

RK. PLAYER, TEAM	AVG	AB	R	HR
1. Dylan Vchulek, Bellevue (Wash.) CC	.395	114	28	0
2. Jacob Zanon, Shoreline (Wash.) CC	.382	144	32	3
3. Jake Bakamus, Lower Columbia (Wash.) JC	.375	152	39	5
4. Alex Hull, Tacoma (Wash.) JC	.371	140	32	2
5. Nick Gawley, Mount Hood (Ore.) CC	.366	145	39	4

EARNED RUN AVERAGE (Minimum 0.8 IP per team game)

RK. PITCHER, TEAM	W	L	ERA	IP
1. Darrion Simons, Yakima Valley (Wash.) CC	5	1	0.75	60
2. Kade Kryzsko, Lower Columbia (Wash.) JC	8	0	0.84	75
3. Tom Simpson, Tacoma (Wash.) JC	6	1	0.99	46
4. Joe Balfour, Mount Hood (Ore.) CC	10	1	1.19	98
5. Tony McCarty, Treasure Valley (Ore.) CC	4	3	1.51	71

COLLEGE SUMMER BASEBALL

BY TEDDY CAHILL

Following an emphatic 11-1 victory against Cuba on the Fourth of July in Charlotte's sparkling BB&T Ballpark to clinch a series win, USA Baseball's Collegiate National Team returned home to the National Training Complex for its final three games of the summer.

The CNT lost all three games, dropping the series finale against Cuba, and then falling to the Canadian and U.S. professional teams headed to the Pan America Games. The three-game skid in the Americas Baseball Festival meant the CNT ended the summer with a 9-8 record, but both general manager Eric Campbell and manager Ed Blankmeyer (St. John's) said Team USA had achieved the goals they set out before the summer began.

Without a tournament on the schedule, the CNT wanted to win its series against both Taiwan and Cuba. It won four of the five games that counted for international points against Taiwan and beat Cuba three games to two.

"Taiwan was very, very good," Campbell said. "To win the Cuba series at home—I don't care how old some of the Cuban guys are, that's Cuba. It's a historical feat now. We built on '13. It was a hard-fought series win, three games out of five.

"The night in Charlotte was about as perfect as I could provide or the Knights could provide or

(chief operating officer) David Perkins from our office could provide for our team. I was so happy. Those guys will have that memory 10 minutes, 10 hours, 10 days, 10 years from now. That series win against Cuba is never going to be forgotten, these guys will have a lifetime baseball experience."

After that night in Charlotte, Blankmeyer said the team may have relaxed a little when it returned to Cary. The experience of playing against the more-advanced rosters that Canada and the U.S. will send to the Pan Am Games was still useful for the CNT.

"Obviously this Americas Festival here was nice for the young men, but it's anticlimactic," Blankmeyer said. "But it also gave them an opportunity to figure out these are Double-, Triple-A players, some have big league time, what do I do, what do I need to do."

Among the players the Pan Am team fielded were infielder Jeff Bianchi, lefthander David Huff and first baseman Casey Kotchman, all of whom have accumulated significant major league service time.

Campbell said he told the CNT before the game that Wednesday represented a good learning experience.

"The guys, what I told them was, they're going to be in the draft next year and those are jobs that they want to have and they're going to have to be as professional as those guys were," he said. "As

COLLEGIATE NATIONAL TEAM STATS

Year indicates 2015-16 class standing

PLAYER, POS.	YEAR	SCHOOL	AVG	SLG	OBP	G	AB	R	H	2B	3B	HR	RBI	BB	SO	SB
Nick Banks, of	Jr.	Texas A&M	.386	.491	.453	17	57	6	22	3	0	1	11	5	13	4
Corey Ray, of	Jr.	Louisville	.355	.548	.423	17	62	12	22	7	1	5	7	11	10
Buddy Reed, of	Jr.	Florida	.326	.391	.354	12	46	8	15	3	0	0	12	2	8	4
Bryson Brigman, 2b/ss	So.	San Diego	.314	.373	.364	17	51	4	16	3	0	0	5	3	6	2
Ryan Howard, ss	Jr.	Missouri	.310	.431	.344	17	58	6	18	4	0	1	3	3	10	0
Garrett Hampson, 2b	Jr.	Long Beach State	.233	.267	.303	14	30	5	7	1	0	0	0	3	9	3
Matt Thaiss, 1b	Jr.	Virginia	.208	.250	.296	8	24	1	5	1	0	0	3	3	1	0
Brendan McKay, lhp/1b	So.	Louisville	.200	.200	.292	7	20	2	4	0	0	0	3	3	6	0
K.J. Harrison, 1b	So.	Oregon State	.182	.218	.207	17	55	4	10	2	0	0	6	2	13	1
Bobby Dalbec, 3b	Jr.	Arizona	.174	.348	.283	16	46	7	8	0	1	2	5	6	18	0
Chris Okey, c	Jr.	Clemson	.138	.207	.242	13	29	4	4	2	0	0	2	4	6	1
J.J. Schwarz, c	So.	Florida	.118	.235	.167	11	34	2	4	1	0	1	1	2	9	0

PITCHER, POS.	YEAR	SCHOOL	W	L	ERA	G	GS	SV	IP	H	R	ER	BB	SO	AVG
Brendan McKay, lhp/1b	So.	Louisville	0	0	0.00	4	0	1	4	5	2	0	2	5	.278
Robert Tyler, rhp	Jr.	Georgia	3	0	1.00	3	2	0	9	4	1	1	4	7	.133
Stephen Nogosek, rhp	Jr.	Oregon	0	0	1.69	6	0	2	10	8	2	2	1	11	.200
Bailey Clark, rhp	Jr.	Duke	0	0	1.80	3	0	0	5	5	1	1	2	8	.263
Anthony Kay, lhp	Jr.	Connecticut	0	0	1.93	4	1	0	9	7	3	2	1	13	.206
Tanner Houck, rhp	So.	Missouri	1	1	2.16	4	3	0	16	13	5	4	1	14	.213
A.J. Puk, lhp	Jr.	Florida	1	0	2.25	4	1	0	12	12	3	3	2	9	.267
Daulton Jefferies, rhp	Jr.	California	1	1	2.57	4	3	0	14	4	4	4	4	12	.091
Zach Jackson, rhp	Jr.	Arkansas	0	0	3.18	5	0	0	5	5	6	2	6	8	.250
Zack Burdi, rhp	Jr.	Louisville	0	0	3.72	6	0	0	9	10	4	4	2	6	.294
Drew Rasmussen, rhp	So.	Oregon State	0	1	4.26	3	1	0	6	6	3	3	1	7	.273
Mike Shawaryn, rhp	Jr.	Maryland	0	2	5.23	4	3	0	10	14	6	6	4	11	.326

fast as pitchers are moving (in the minor leagues), some of our pitchers are going to face these guys next summer. They got a taste. Maybe it was a little anticlimactic, but I'm really proud of their professionalism and hanging in there."

"Anytime you're around the best guys in the country, you learn a lot just from watching players and from the coaches," second baseman Bryson Brigman said. "We have coach (Paul) Mainieri from LSU, coach Blankmeyer from St. John's, so just great programs that know how to play the game right and you learn a lot from that."

Brigman hit .314/.364/.373 in 17 games for Team USA. He subsequently returned to the Cape Cod League, rejoining first-place Orleans.

Several of Brigman's CNT teammates followed him to the Cape, while others went home to begin preparations for next season. Blankmeyer said it was a bittersweet feeling to see the CNT's summer tour come to a close.

"I'm proud of them," Blankmeyer said. "They're fine ballplayers, a lot of them have great futures, but they're just good men and they represented the uniform in a first-class manner."

Y-D Repeats As Cape Champs

Though Orleans' prospect-laden roster captured scouts' attention all summer, it was East Division rival Yarmouth-Dennis that finished the season as champions. Yarmouth-Dennis knocked off Orleans in the second round before defeating Hyannis in the championship series. It was the Red Sox's second straight title and their fifth in 12 years under the direction of manager Scott Pickler.

While the league featured good depth, scouts believed it lacked some of the high-end talent that often summers on the Cape. Many elite pitchers played for USA Baseball's Collegiate National Team or sat out the summer. As a result, for the first time since 2011, a pitcher was not the league's top ranked prospect.

The league also saw history made on the field this summer, as Wareham outfielder Andrew Calica (UC Santa Barbara) hit .425/.480/.469, recording the highest batting average since the league switched back to wood bats in 1985. On the mound, Orleans righthander Mitchell Jordan (Stetson) posted a 0.21 ERA, matching Eric Milton's modern-day record set in 1996.

SUMMER LEAGUE ROUNDUP

■ The Kenosha Kingfish won the Northwoods League championship in just their second year of existence, taking two straight games in a row from the North Division champion St. Cloud Rox. Kenosha defeated the Madison Mallards in the South Divisional

Playoffs to advance to the matchup with the Rox, then rode seven strong innings from P.J. Schuster, Jr. (Southern Illinois-Edwardsville) to a 6-4 win in game one and getting a multi-hit game from five players in an 8-1 game two victory.

■ On the strength of a 31-18 season, the Vermont Mountaineers narrowly topped the Mystic Schooners (also 31-18) to win the New England Collegiate League's championship. Mystic and Vermont battled into the 10th inning of the third game of a three-game series, with the Mountaineers winning, 3-2, on a go-ahead squeeze bunt by catcher Ridge Smith (Austin Peay State). Righthander Sam Delaplane (Eastern Michigan) notched his third save of the postseason—13th overall—to give the Mountaineers their third title and first since 2007. Vermont manager Joe Brown became the first NECBL manager to win championships with two franchises, winning with Sanford in 2008. He also led his SUNY Cortland Red Dragons team to a Division III championship in the spring.

■ The Edenton Steamers narrowly escaped their semifinal series against the Wilmington Sharks, having to rally for three runs in the eighth inning of the decisive third game, but once they made the Petitt Cup finals, they dominated. The Coastal Plain League's best team in the regular season, Edenton outscored the Gastonia Grizzlies by a combined 25-7 score in a two-game finals sweep. In the clincher, the Steamers set the tone with an eight-run fourth inning, highlighted by Tony Rosselli's (Indiana State) two-run homer, and they never looked back.

■ The Mat-Su Miners rolled to a 31-10 record in the Alaska League regular season, but the Anchorage Buccaneers were more than a match in the league's championship series. Game 1 was a 12-inning affair in which the Bucs outlasted the Miners 6-2 thanks to nine shutout innings from starter Aaron Soto (Tennessee) and two RBIs apiece from catcher David Banuelos (Long Beach State) and centerfielder Brodie Leftridge (Tennessee). After the Miners won Game 2, the Bucs turned to Jim Voyles (Florida State) in the deciding game and he responded with a complete game, 4-hit shutout to seal the championship for Anchorage.

■ In a rematch of last summer's championship matchup, the Neptune Beach Pearl turned the tables and defeated the Los Angeles Brewers in two games to claim the California Collegiate League title. After winning the first game of the series 7-1, the Pearl trailed 2-0 in the seventh inning to the Brewers in Game 2. The Pearl responded with one run in the seventh, one in the eighth and a walk-off, championship-winning double by Logan Marston (San Francisco State) in the bottom of the ninth.

■ The Brazos Valley Bombers followed a 42-9 regular season with their third straight Texas Collegiate League championship, sweeping Acadiana in the best-of-three title series to conclude a postseason in which they outscored opponents 36-2. The Bombers clicked in the postseason, with Michigan State righthanders Dakota Mekkes and Ethan Langdon both pitching well. Mekkes threw six hitless innings in the championship game, striking out 11 and eventually giving up two hits and two runs, while Langdon tossed a no-hitter in a 9-0 divisional playoff game against East Texas.

COLLEGE *SUMMER LEAGUES* For players who played for multiple teams: 1: Stats with first team. 2: Stats with second team. 3: Stats with third team. T: combined stats.

COLLEGE

CAPE COD LEAGUE

EASTERN DIVISION

	W	L	T	PTS
Orleans Firebirds	31	12	1	63
Brewster Whitecaps	24	19	1	49
Yarmouth-Dennis Red Sox	22	22	0	44
Chatham Anglers	22	22	0	44
Harwich Mariners	20	22	2	42

WESTERN DIVISION

	W	L	T	PTS
Hyannis Harbor Hawks	24	19	1	49
Bourne Braves	22	20	2	46
Wareham Gatemen	17	25	2	36
Cotuit Kettleers	17	27	0	34
Falmouth Commodores	16	27	1	33

CHAMPIONSHIP: Yarmouth-Dennis defeated Hyannis 2-1 in best-of-three championship series.

TOP 30 PROSPECTS: 1. Nick Senzel, 3b/2b (Jr., Tennessee). **2.** Ryan Boldt, of (Jr., Nebraska). **3.** Kyle Lewis, of (Jr., Mercer). **4.** Matt Krook, lhp (R.-So., Oregon). **5.** Bryan Reynolds, of (Jr., Vanderbilt). **6.** Eric Lauer, lhp (Jr., Kent State). **7.** Jeren Kendall, of (So., Vanderbilt). **8.** Jordan Sheffield, rhp (R.-So., Vanderbilt). **9.** Errol Robinson, ss (Jr., Mississippi). **10.** Dakota Hudson, rhp (Jr., Mississippi State). **11.** Stephen Wrenn, of (Jr., Georgia). **12.** Ben Bowden, lhp (Jr., Vanderbilt). **13.** Sean Murphy, c (Jr., Wright State). **14.** Bryce Montes de Oca, rhp (So., Missouri). **15.** Garrett Williams, lhp (Jr., Oklahoma State). **16.** Bobby Dalbec, 3b (Jr., Arizona). **17.** Corbin Burnes, rhp (Jr., St. Mary's). **18.** Cody Sedlock, rhp (Jr., Illinois). **19.** Ian Hamilton, rhp (Jr., Washington State). **20.** Gio Brusa, of (Sr., Pacific). **21.** Kyle Serrano, rhp (Jr., Tennessee). **22.** Cavan Biggio, 2b (Jr., Notre Dame). **23.** J.J. Matijevic, 1b (So., Arizona). **24.** Nick Solak, 2b (Jr., Louisville). **25.** Josh Rogers, lhp (SIGNED: Yankees). **26.** Mitchell Jordan, rhp (Jr., Stetson). **27.** Andrew Calica, of (R.-Jr., UC Santa Barbara). **28.** Devin Smeltzer, lhp (So., San Jacinto (Texas) JC). **29.** Jake Rogers, c (Jr., Tulane). **30.** Garret Hampson, ss/2b (Jr., Long Beach State)

INDIVIDUAL BATTING LEADERS

PLAYER, POS., TEAM	AVG	AB	R	H	2B	3B	HR	RBI	SB
Andrew Calica, of, Wareham	.425	113	17	48	2	0	1	16	8
Nick Senzel, 2b, Brewster	.364	154	34	56	16	1	4	33	14
J.J. Matijevic, 1b, Falmouth	.333	144	15	48	9	0	4	15	3
Nick Solak, 2b, Bourne	.329	140	21	46	7	0	0	23	10
Jacob Noll, 2b, Hyannis	.326	135	15	44	11	0	2	21	5
Tommy Edman, ss, Y-D	.318	148	18	47	7	0	2	20	8
Heath Quinn, of, Falmouth	.317	142	25	45	8	2	4	16	1
Blake Tiberi, 3b, Hyannis	.315	127	10	40	3	0	1	20	1
Errol Robinson, ss, Hyannis	.312	141	25	44	7	1	1	10	15
Charlie Warren, of, Wareham	.305	105	14	32	4	0	0	3	3

INDIVIDUAL PITCHING LEADERS

PLAYER, TEAM	W	L	ERA	SV	IP	H	BB	SO
Mitchell Jordan, Orleans	6	0	0.21	0	43	17	6	46
Ian Hamilton, Wareham	1	1	0.89	1	40.1	31	8	39
Ricky Thomas, Y-D	7	0	1.02	0	44.1	22	13	45
Jon Woodcock, Cotuit	3	2	1.50	0	42	32	11	34
Dakota Hudson, Hyannis	2	3	1.69	1	42.2	34	7	41
Daniel Brown, Cotuit	2	1	1.80	0	40	35	20	30
Evan Hill, Wareham	5	0	1.80	1	40	24	16	34
Vance Tatum, Hyannis	1	2	1.93	0	37.1	24	16	26
Bryce Montes de Oca, Falmouth	1	2	2.00	0	36	24	28	30
Eric Lauer, Orleans	4	1	2.04	0	39.2	21	18	50

BOURNE

BATTING

	AVG	AB	R	H	2B	3B	HR	RBI	SB
Peter Alonso, 1b	.255	98	5	25	3	0	0	13	0
Ryan Boldt, cf	.273	165	14	45	9	1	0	8	9
Tristan Chari, c	.000	6	0	0	0	0	0	0	0
C.J. Chatham, ss	.253	75	7	19	7	1	1	4	0
Jason Delay, c	.310	42	8	13	0	0	0	3	2
Camden Duzenack, ss	.194	144	14	28	2	0	2	9	2
Chris Erwin, p	.000	6	0	0	0	0	0	0	0
Vince Fernandez, cf	.235	51	7	12	2	0	2	10	2

BATTING

	AVG	AB	R	H	2B	3B	HR	RBI	SB
Connor Fitzsimons, c	.000	2	0	0	0	0	0	0	0
Charles Galiano, c	.316	19	3	6	2	0	0	3	0
Mike Garzillo, 2b	.232	95	11	22	6	0	1	10	4
Reid Humphreys, if	.265	132	20	35	3	0	5	17	1
Corey Julks, of	.279	165	23	46	5	1	3	15	13
Max McDowell, c	.190	63	7	12	4	0	1	8	0
Brendan McKay, 1b/p	.283	46	4	13	3	0	0	7	0
Robb Paller, lf	.095	21	1	2	0	0	0	0	0
Alex Robles, p	.000	12	0	0	0	0	0	0	0
Jacob Robson, cf	.316	98	17	31	10	2	1	9	5
Brian Serven, c	.205	39	0	8	1	0	0	3	0
Nick Solak, 2b	.329	140	21	46	7	1	0	23	10
Jack Sundberg, cf	.250	4	1	1	0	0	0	0	0
Babe Thomas, c	.125	8	0	1	0	0	0	0	0
Billy Walker, c	.216	37	2	8	3	0	0	4	0
Aaron Wilson, if	.000	19	0	0	0	0	0	0	0

PITCHING

	W	L	ERA	G	SV	IP	H	BB	SO
Keegan Akin	1	3	2.70	8	0	33	32	13	39
Bryan Baker	3	0	2.67	13	0	27	20	6	29
Joseph Christopher	0	0	0.00	1	0	2	2	1	1
Austin Conway	1	1	0.00	15	10	19	8	5	21
Jake DeCarli	1	0	4.50	2	0	4	6	1	1
Tyler Deel	1	0	2.79	4	0	10	11	1	9
Kyle Driscoll	1	0	2.18	11	0	21	13	10	26
Chris Erwin	0	0	0.00	4	0	6	5	4	10
Zach Fox	0	0	0.00	2	0	3	0	0	0
Cooper Hammond	0	1	1.04	6	0	9	7	1	10
Shawn Heide	0	0	1.23	4	0	7	7	2	4
Tyler Honahan	0	0	9.00	3	0	3	6	2	4
Daniel Jagiello	1	0	2.46	3	0	4	1	2	6
Nick Jensen-Clagg	1	5	3.12	8	1	35	32	15	37
Ryan Keaffaber	2	2	3.95	7	0	27	35	1	15
Doug Norman	2	0	3.57	7	1	18	23	5	15
Gavin Pittore	1	1	0.00	12	0	17	8	7	17
Nick Quattro	0	0	0.00	2	0	3	1	0	1
Andrew Ravel	0	0	0.84	3	0	11	11	2	9
Russell Reynolds	0	0	10.00	5	0	9	18	3	5
Alex Robles	1	5	3.76	8	0	38	45	6	26
Josh Rogers	2	0	3.10	4	0	20	14	7	16
Cody Sedlock	2	1	3.41	11	1	29	35	7	26
Ryan Smoyer	1	1	1.77	4	0	20	17	6	3
Robert Tyler	0	0	1.29	2	0	7	8	4	4

BREWSTER

BATTING

	AVG	AB	R	H	2B	3B	HR	RBI	SB
Mandy Alvarez, 3b	.375	8	2	3	0	0	0	1	0
Chandler Avant, ss	.202	104	10	21	3	0	0	5	5
Cassidy Brown, c	.277	112	11	31	4	0	3	12	1
Brandon Caruso, cf	.143	14	1	2	0	0	0	0	1
Brendan Cox, ss	.000	4	1	0	0	0	0	0	0
Kyle Cunningham, c	.000	3	0	0	0	0	0	0	0
J.C. Escarra, c	.277	101	12	28	5	1	1	15	0
Nico Giarratano, ss	.220	91	10	20	5	0	0	4	1
Brandon Gold, 3b	.231	65	2	15	1	0	0	5	0
Toby Handley, of	.283	120	24	34	6	2	1	16	15
Kel Johnson, of	.151	53	4	8	0	0	1	7	1
Logan Koch, c	.000	4	0	0	0	0	0	0	0
Chase Livingston, c	.000	1	0	0	0	0	0	0	0
Colin Lyman, of	.301	133	22	40	5	0	0	8	10
Jack Meggs, of	.299	107	14	32	5	0	0	13	5
Ryan Peurifoy, rf	.228	92	14	21	1	2	1	12	2
Tyler Ramirez, cf	.207	58	5	12	0	1	0	7	5
Brent Rooker, of	.143	7	1	1	0	1	0	1	0
Nick Senzel, 2b	.364	154	34	56	16	1	4	33	14
Will Smith, c	.259	27	4	7	0	0	0	2	0
Robbie Tenerowicz, 2b	.282	110	16	31	2	0	4	20	1
Eli White, ss	.250	56	5	14	2	0	0	8	0

PITCHING	W	L	ERA	G	SV	IP	H	BB	SO
Anthony Arias	1	2	5.67	13	0	27	18	16	38
J.D. Busfield	1	5	5.11	8	0	37	47	9	27
Hansen Butler	2	1	5.21	11	0	19	17	15	20
Andrew Gist	0	1	3.97	7	0	11	13	2	10
Brandon Gold	0	0	5.68	2	0	6	4	6	1
Gage Griffin	0	1	5.40	11	0	15	15	9	7
Thomas Hackimer	1	1	0.47	18	10	19	16	6	28
Nick Highberger	4	0	0.38	14	0	24	22	6	15
Jacob Jenkins	2	2	3.27	7	0	33	35	14	19
Rollin Lacy	0	0	0.00	1	0	2	2	1	1
Hunter Martin	0	1	3.18	8	0	23	21	13	15
Tyson Miller	2	1	1.44	5	0	25	16	6	29
Gabriel Mosser	0	0	2.25	1	0	4	3	2	2
Steve Moyers	1	0	3.60	4	0	5	9	1	4
Trent Paddon	3	0	1.80	13	1	15	14	3	11
Alec Rash	1	0	2.19	5	0	12	8	4	12
Patrick Ruotolo	1	2	6.00	7	1	9	9	6	10
Zachary Ryan	2	0	4.20	13	0	30	30	14	24
Alex Schick	1	2	3.76	11	0	41	37	10	39
Jordan Sheffield	2	0	5.49	5	0	20	17	15	19

CHATHAM

BATTING	AVG	AB	R	H	2B	3B	HR	RBI	SB
Kyle Adams, c	.148	54	4	8	1	0	0	3	0
Aaron Barnett, c	.217	129	4	28	0	0	0	13	1
Trenton Brooks, of	.234	141	13	33	5	0	0	11	4
Kyle Brooks, ss	.264	72	9	19	3	0	0	6	2
Will Craig, 3b	.242	132	17	32	7	0	1	21	1
Todd Czinege, if	.238	84	10	20	1	0	2	6	0
Nicolas Falkson, 3b	.143	7	1	1	0	0	0	0	0
Jake Fraley, of	.302	63	13	19	0	0	1	5	3
Joshua Greene, cf	.000	5	1	0	0	0	0	0	0
Garrett Hampson, ss	.291	79	9	23	1	1	0	7	5
Aaron Knapp, cf	.232	125	15	29	5	0	0	9	6
Nate Mondou, 2b	.238	130	16	31	2	1	0	9	3
Luke Persico, of	.243	115	16	28	4	0	3	12	1
Alexander Raburn, if	.000	8	0	0	0	0	0	0	0
Cory Raley, if	.175	40	4	7	2	0	0	3	1
Joey Rodriguez, of	.105	19	0	2	0	0	0	1	1
Nicholas Sciortino, c	.159	69	4	11	2	0	0	6	0
Zack Short, ss	.182	132	14	24	5	1	2	20	5

PITCHING	W	L	ERA	G	SV	IP	H	BB	SO
Jesse Adams	1	0	0.82	2	0	11	11	2	8
Trenton Brooks	0	0	6.00	3	0	3	1	3	2
Zack Burdi	1	0	1.74	4	0	10	7	6	15
Carl Burdick	1	3	3.68	15	1	22	16	7	21
Daniel Castano	2	4	3.34	8	0	35	31	9	25
Ty Damron	2	1	3.45	7	0	29	25	9	14
Rob DiFranco	0	0	9.00	1	0	1	3	0	2
Parker Dunshee	3	2	2.16	7	0	33	23	8	27
Gabe Friese	0	1	4.50	2	0	8	7	1	7
Zac Gallen	2	2	3.21	6	0	28	24	9	34
Jake Godfrey	0	1	2.41	6	0	19	15	15	18
Thomas Jankins	0	0	3.00	1	0	3	3	1	5
Chad Martin	0	0	0.00	1	0	1	1	1	0
Jim McDade	1	0	1.29	4	0	7	3	1	3
Aaron McGarity	0	0	1.39	11	8	13	8	0	9
Brandon Miller	4	0	1.50	11	0	24	13	1	27
James Mulry	1	1	4.40	12	0	14	15	4	14
Jeff Paschke	0	1	4.67	13	0	17	17	9	14
A.J. Puckett	1	3	3.48	5	0	21	23	11	18
Andre Scrubb	0	1	2.46	11	4	11	11	8	13
Cameron Stone	0	1	0.79	9	0	11	4	5	15
Jonathan Teaney	0	0	4.96	10	0	16	17	15	16
Garrett Williams	1	1	5.16	9	0	23	21	15	33
Timothy Zeuch	2	0	1.31	4	0	21	20	5	17

COTUIT

BATTING	AVG	AB	R	H	2B	3B	HR	RBI	SB
Matt Albanese, of	.240	75	6	18	5	0	1	10	2
Stephen Alemais, ss	.429	14	0	6	0	0	0	0	1
Branden Berry, 1b	.219	105	15	23	3	0	5	17	1

BATTING	AVG	AB	R	H	2B	3B	HR	RBI	SB
Michael Cantu, c	.087	23	0	2	1	0	0	0	0
Zack Collins, c	.154	13	1	2	0	0	0	0	0
Gene Cone, cf	.204	49	4	10	0	0	1	3	2
Will Cousins, c	.000	1	0	0	0	0	0	0	0
Matthew Dacey, 1b	.136	22	2	3	2	0	0	2	0
Nkosi Djehuti-Mes, of	.111	9	1	1	0	0	0	0	0
Cole Fabio, 2b	.265	49	9	13	3	0	0	3	1
Spencer Gaa, 3b	.289	121	14	35	3	0	0	10	6
Ross Grosvenor, 1b	.000	21	0	0	0	0	0	0	0
Will Haynie, c	.235	115	13	27	4	0	8	24	2
Kennan Innis, of	.200	25	3	5	0	0	0	0	1
Saige Jenco, of	.189	74	10	14	2	0	0	5	1
Jeren Kendall, cf	.253	79	7	20	1	2	2	6	4
Jackson Klein, cf	.253	83	5	21	1	0	1	10	2
Kolin McMillen, 2b	.333	6	1	2	0	0	0	0	0
Michael Paez, ss	.295	129	17	38	7	0	1	10	8
Kort Peterson, of	.186	43	8	8	0	1	0	1	3
Joshua Rojas, 2b	.250	12	2	3	1	0	0	0	0
Tanner Stanley, of	.250	20	1	5	1	0	0	2	0
Brett Stephens, of	.292	120	11	35	5	0	1	9	2
Tim Susnara, c	.176	85	7	15	1	0	1	11	1
Brody Weiss, ss	.136	103	9	14	2	0	0	11	1

PITCHING	W	L	ERA	G	SV	IP	H	BB	SO
Jack Anderson	3	2	3.64	19	0	30	29	11	29
Cal Becker	0	1	8.44	4	0	5	9	5	3
Daniel Brown	2	1	1.80	9	0	40	35	20	30
Justin Dunn	0	3	1.96	14	7	18	14	4	18
Nick Eicholtz	0	2	5.27	5	0	14	16	6	9
Bernardo Flores	0	0	7.71	7	0	14	23	7	10
Kevin Ginkel	0	1	6.75	12	0	12	16	3	16
Jeffery Harding	0	0	0.00	4	0	5	4	3	3
Jonathan King	1	3	4.97	8	0	38	44	12	28
Matthew Kinney	0	0	0.00	5	1	6	5	2	3
Jackson Klein	0	0	0.00	1	0	1	0	3	0
Nick Lewis	2	1	2.55	10	0	25	22	5	22
Matthew Milburn	2	3	3.38	7	0	32	36	4	24
Anthony Misiewicz	0	0	0.00	1	0	3	2	1	1
Luke Olson	0	0	0.00	1	0	3	4	0	0
Duncan Robinson	1	2	6.88	7	0	17	27	6	14
Austin Sexton	2	4	3.18	8	0	40	39	11	37
Austin Solecitto	0	0	6.23	2	0	4	8	2	3
Mitch Stallings	1	2	3.79	11	0	19	21	4	12
Adam Whitt	0	0	0.00	1	1	1	0	0	4
Alex Winkelman	0	0	3.38	1	0	3	4	0	4
Jonathan Woodcock	3	2	1.50	8	0	42	32	11	34

FALMOUTH

BATTING	AVG	AB	R	H	2B	3B	HR	RBI	SB
Shane Benes, ss	.164	67	8	11	1	0	4	11	0
Tate Blackman, ss	.225	111	12	25	5	0	1	11	4
Conor Costello, p	.250	4	1	1	0	0	0	0	0
Joey Daru, cf	.000	2	1	0	0	0	0	0	0
Tristan Gray, ss	.267	101	10	27	6	0	0	7	3
Caleb Hamilton, 3b	.193	88	8	17	1	0	2	9	5
Logan Ice, c	.240	75	10	18	3	0	0	7	1
Mitch Longo, cf	.216	102	5	22	2	0	0	9	4
Nick Lovullo, if	.192	73	5	14	1	0	1	6	2
J.J. Matijevic, 1b	.333	144	15	48	9	0	4	15	3
Dylan Morris, of	.250	4	0	1	0	0	0	0	0
Heath Quinn, rf	.317	142	25	45	8	2	4	16	1
Evan Skoug, c	.258	97	10	25	4	1	1	9	0
Andrew Snow, ss	.068	44	3	3	0	0	0	2	0
Michael Tinsley, c	.228	92	6	21	2	0	2	3	2
Boomer White, of	.212	137	10	29	4	0	0	7	1
J.B. Woodman, of	.242	128	12	31	10	0	1	11	4
Andrew Yacyk, 1b	.269	26	2	7	3	0	1	2	0

PITCHING	W	L	ERA	G	SV	IP	H	BB	SO
Ben Ancheff	1	0	3.14	8	0	14	17	2	12
George Brandecker	0	1	8.31	5	0	4	9	4	4
Garrett Brummett	0	1	4.22	7	0	11	12	4	7
Joseph Camacho	1	1	3.09	3	0	12	15	0	9
Conor Costello	2	3	3.55	6	0	33	31	8	17

PITCHING	W	L	ERA	G	SV	IP	H	BB	SO
Rob DiFranco	1	0	4.50	2	0	4	5	0	2
Morgan Earman	1	0	4.60	10	0	16	18	11	11
Jack Finnegan	2	1	3.33	11	0	24	24	10	23
Andrew Frankenreider	1	0	1.50	14	3	18	11	6	24
Sean Gustin	1	1	4.82	6	0	9	4	6	2
Cobi Johnson	0	2	4.34	12	1	19	16	10	22
Turner Larkins	0	3	5.40	6	0	27	30	11	14
Mitchell McIntyre	0	1	6.14	3	0	7	8	4	3
Bryce Montes de Oca	1	2	2.00	9	0	36	24	28	30
Adam Oller	0	1	4.70	8	0	23	31	5	8
Alex Phillips	2	1	2.40	6	0	30	24	7	19
Wyatt Short	1	3	3.79	14	2	19	22	5	25
Austin Tribby	2	3	3.46	8	0	39	40	15	25
Bo Tucker	0	1	7.31	10	0	16	19	18	12
Stephen Villines	0	2	2.05	16	6	22	19	4	20
Andrew Yacyk	0	0	0.00	1	0	1	0	1	1

HARWICH

BATTING	AVG	AB	R	H	2B	3B	HR	RBI	SB
Johnny Adams, if	.214	145	17	31	7	0	3	13	6
Stevie Berman, c	.100	30	2	3	0	0	0	1	0
Cavan Biggio, 2b	.263	114	16	30	4	1	0	14	3
Brock Deatherage, of	.254	130	14	33	2	2	1	8	8
Drew Ellis, 1b	.182	33	3	6	2	0	0	2	0
Cole Fabio, 2b	.176	17	2	3	1	0	0	1	1
Matt Gonzalez, if	.232	99	10	23	3	0	4	7	2
Michael Hernandez, c	.220	50	3	11	0	0	2	6	0
Connor Justus, if	.210	124	18	26	5	2	4	18	8
Ryan Lidge, if	.230	61	2	14	2	0	0	6	2
Sheldon Neuse, ss	.221	136	16	30	5	2	4	18	4
Preston Palmeiro, 1b	.241	133	13	32	5	0	3	17	0
Adam Pate, cf	.274	146	24	40	10	0	0	6	21
Nick Walker, of	.198	116	13	23	8	1	0	8	9
Jake Willsey, if	.000	3	0	0	0	0	0	0	0
Danny Zardon, 3b	.105	57	5	6	1	0	1	2	1

PITCHING	W	L	ERA	G	SV	IP	H	BB	SO
Evan Anderson	0	0	4.86	7	0	17	27	5	13
Geoff Bramblett	3	0	1.06	3	0	17	15	5	13
Anthony Ciavarella	2	2	4.24	10	0	17	17	4	21
Jake Cousins	0	1	1.29	2	0	7	7	3	6
Joe DiBenedetto	1	0	3.55	13	1	13	16	8	9
Williams Durruthy	1	2	5.21	10	0	28	26	8	15
Sheldon Neuse	0	0	0.00	8	1	9	5	3	12
Hunter Newman	2	1	2.12	9	1	17	6	9	11
Joe O'Donnell	1	2	2.80	7	0	35	35	10	25
Anthony Pacillo	0	1	9.82	5	0	7	8	7	9
Joe Ravert	0	1	3.54	10	0	28	26	13	23
Kevin Roy	0	0	7.71	2	0	2	5	2	2
Zach Schellenger	1	2	3.55	16	1	33	26	6	30
Luke Scherzer	0	0	4.38	13	7	12	14	6	16
Spencer Trayner	3	0	2.11	13	1	21	10	6	19
Scott Tully	2	3	3.86	8	0	44	38	13	38
Ross Vance	2	0	3.18	6	0	6	4	4	8
Cameron Vieaux	1	4	3.30	8	0	44	41	4	39
Cory Wilder	0	1	1.80	1	0	5	4	4	5
Hunter Williams	2	2	3.64	8	0	35	39	11	34

HYANNIS

BATTING	AVG	AB	R	H	2B	3B	HR	RBI	SB
Justin Arrington, ss	.186	43	10	8	1	0	0	2	3
Corey Bird, cf	.344	93	14	32	1	0	0	11	11
Ryne Birk, 2b	.189	90	6	17	4	0	1	10	1
Colby Bortles, 3b	.205	122	12	25	4	1	1	7	3
Ben DeLuzio, cf	.253	87	5	22	4	1	0	3	10
Austin Hays, of	.301	156	20	47	9	0	2	19	14
Tristan Hildebrandt, ss	.250	28	5	7	2	0	0	1	2
David Martinelli, cf	.141	64	9	9	1	0	2	4	4
Braxton Martinez, 3b	.000	10	0	0	0	0	0	0	0
Bobby Melley, 1b	.526	19	2	10	1	0	0	8	1
Jacob Noll, 2b	.326	135	15	44	11	0	2	21	5
Arden Pabst, c	.195	87	4	17	2	0	0	3	0
Nicholas Pappas, 1b	.182	33	1	6	1	0	0	4	1

BATTING	AVG	AB	R	H	2B	3B	HR	RBI	SB
Errol Robinson, ss	.312	141	25	44	7	1	1	10	15
Jake Rogers, c	.274	73	9	20	2	0	3	11	2
JaVon Shelby, 2b	.256	86	11	22	6	0	1	7	1
Matt Thaiss, c	.149	67	8	10	1	0	2	4	2
Blake Tiberi, 3b	.315	127	10	40	3	0	1	20	1
Darien Tubbs, cf	.167	30	4	5	0	0	0	1	3

PITCHING	W	L	ERA	G	SV	IP	H	BB	SO
Vince Apicella	0	0	18.00	1	0	1	3	0	1
Nolan Blackwood	1	0	1.93	2	0	5	2	3	4
Thomas Burrows	3	0	2.05	11	1	22	21	8	21
Aaron Civale	1	0	0.36	14	5	25	13	8	29
Nick Deeg	4	3	2.05	10	0	48	34	10	46
Zach Girrens	0	2	6.14	10	0	15	22	9	11
Dakota Hudson	2	3	1.69	11	1	43	34	7	41
Michael King	2	1	3.27	5	0	22	26	5	19
Collin Kober	0	1	4.70	8	0	8	12	3	1
Chris McGrath	0	0	3.68	8	0	15	17	11	13
Blake Quinn	3	1	2.56	8	0	39	42	18	28
Kevin Roy	1	1	0.66	7	0	14	12	5	16
Logan Salow	0	0	3.06	12	0	18	20	11	14
Marc Skinner	2	2	2.38	14	0	23	20	9	16
Devin Smeltzer	4	3	3.48	8	1	41	47	4	33
Will Stillman	0	0	3.38	9	2	13	12	8	19
Vance Tatum	1	2	1.93	7	0	37	24	16	26

ORLEANS

BATTING	AVG	AB	R	H	2B	3B	HR	RBI	SB
Wille Abreu, cf	.203	64	11	13	1	0	3	11	5
Tres Barrera, c	.130	69	8	9	4	0	1	2	2
Carmen Benedetti, 1b	.296	27	2	8	1	0	0	3	0
Bryson Brigman, ss	.333	51	4	17	2	0	1	12	3
Alex Call, of	.303	99	20	30	2	0	1	13	2
Bobby Dalbec, 3b	.315	92	23	29	2	0	12	30	0
Ronnie Dawson, of	.243	115	20	28	2	1	4	16	10
Jansen Fraser, of	.111	9	0	1	0	0	0	1	0
Justin Jones, ss	.171	35	7	6	0	1	1	4	2
Kyle Lewis, of	.300	150	19	45	7	1	7	24	2
Jeremy Martinez, c	.209	91	11	19	8	0	1	13	0
Austin Miller, cf	.222	99	16	22	4	1	0	8	4
Sean Murphy, c	.226	93	16	21	2	1	3	9	0
T.J. Nichting, 2b	.238	42	4	10	0	0	0	5	0
Cris Perez, c	.000	5	0	0	0	0	0	1	0
Daniel Pinero, ss	.202	89	11	18	2	0	0	8	3
Bryan Reynolds, of	.346	81	17	28	4	0	0	8	3
Reggie Southall, ss	.238	42	9	10	0	1	0	1	7
Sean Watkins, p	.000	4	0	0	0	0	0	0	0
Colby Woodmansee, ss	.348	23	3	8	1	0	0	4	0
Trey York, 2b	.176	17	3	3	0	0	0	2	0
Nick Zammarelli, 3b	.226	124	15	28	5	0	3	19	1

PITCHING	W	L	ERA	G	SV	IP	H	BB	SO
Parker Bean	2	1	1.50	17	0	24	13	15	22
Carmen Benedetti	1	0	1.50	5	0	6	4	5	11
Chandler Blanchard	0	2	3.60	16	0	25	24	11	23
Corbin Burnes	5	3	3.79	9	0	38	37	18	28
Jared Carkuff	1	0	4.02	10	0	16	14	7	14
Kyle Cedotal	2	0	1.13	4	0	16	8	3	15
Joseph Doyle	0	0	54.00	1	0	0	2	2	0
Eder Erives	1	1	1.47	15	1	18	12	8	20
Jason Harper	0	0	4.50	16	4	16	15	10	14
Mitchell Jordan	6	0	0.21	8	0	43	17	6	46
John Kilichowski	1	1	1.69	3	0	11	7	2	10
Eric Lauer	4	1	2.04	8	0	40	21	18	50
Stephen Nogosek	0	0	0.00	2	0	3	6	0	4
Joe Ryan	0	0	1.13	5	2	8	4	3	12
Kit Scheetz	2	1	3.27	18	3	22	11	5	20
Kyle Serrano	3	2	3.68	9	0	37	29	13	38
Austin Sodders	0	0	0.00	1	0	1	2	1	0
Bennett Sousa	0	0	4.50	1	0	4	3	5	1
Tanner Tully	2	0	1.61	6	0	22	19	8	15
Sean Watkins	1	0	4.50	15	1	20	20	11	16

WAREHAM

BATTING	AVG	AB	R	H	2B	3B	HR	RBI	SB
Mandy Alvarez, 3b	.077	13	0	1	0	0	0	2	0
Connor Beck, of	.245	49	9	12	0	0	0	4	0
Andrew Calica, of	.425	113	17	48	2	0	1	16	8
Jose Carrera, 2b	.000	5	0	0	0	0	0	0	0
Nick Cieri, c	.319	91	1	29	1	0	0	9	2
Sam Dexter, ss	.143	14	2	2	0	0	0	1	0
Preston Grand Pre, ss	.168	107	5	18	2	0	0	6	2
Jay Jabs, of	.197	122	17	24	3	0	2	12	8
Mark Karaviotis, ss	.284	95	11	27	4	0	0	8	0
Tanner Kirk, 2b	.179	28	8	5	1	0	0	2	0
Andrew Knizner, c	.232	112	9	26	6	0	1	10	4
Matthew Kozuch, 1b	.125	8	0	1	0	0	0	0	0
David MacKinnon, 1b	.292	130	14	38	1	0	1	12	2
Jarett Rindfleisch, c	.152	46	6	7	0	0	2	7	0
Kramer Robertson, 2b	.310	87	10	27	0	1	0	5	2
Mac Seibert, c	.071	14	0	1	0	0	0	0	0
Darryn Sheppard, cf	.214	28	3	6	2	0	0	2	2
Logan Sowers, lf	.174	92	14	16	2	0	1	9	2
Johnny Sternagel, 3b	.176	74	6	13	1	1	0	6	1
Gavin Stupienski, c	.351	37	5	13	4	0	0	6	0
Charlie Warren, cf	.305	105	14	32	4	0	0	3	3
Weston Wilson, 3b	.185	27	1	5	1	0	0	1	0

PITCHING	W	L	ERA	G	SV	IP	H	BB	SO
Michael Adams	0	0	9.00	1	0	1	1	1	0
Shaun Anderson	0	2	4.09	8	1	22	12	6	15
Bailey Clark	3	0	0.56	3	0	16	10	5	11
Grant Dyer	1	1	2.55	8	0	25	16	5	31
Blake Fox	2	1	3.60	6	0	27	32	5	17
Pete Grasso	0	0	13.50	1	0	1	1	1	0
Ian Hamilton	1	1	0.89	12	1	40	31	8	39
Brett Hanewich	1	2	5.16	7	0	23	24	16	26
Evan Hill	5	0	1.80	9	1	40	24	16	34
Zac Houston	0	4	1.69	8	0	21	11	10	24
Daulton Jefferies	1	0	1.50	3	0	12	12	2	14
Connor Jones	0	0	18.00	2	0	1	2	1	1
Anthony Kay	0	1	4.50	2	0	8	8	2	6
Matthew Krook	0	1	6.35	6	0	11	11	8	15
Ryan Olson	0	4	3.97	10	2	23	23	9	19
Ben Parr	0	1	1.93	11	0	19	16	11	14
Zach Plesac	0	2	11.88	3	0	8	15	3	6
Jared Price	0	0	6.75	10	0	13	21	8	17
Matt Smallwood	0	0	3.00	1	0	3	4	0	2
Shea Spitzbarth	1	0	0.71	9	2	13	10	5	14
Tyler Thorne	0	1	9.82	9	0	18	31	16	12
Jayce Vancena	0	0	10.80	1	0	2	3	2	1
Ryan Williamson	0	2	6.06	5	0	16	20	7	22
Stephen Woods Jr.	2	0	3.38	10	1	19	9	14	13
Tyler Zombro	0	2	9.00	2	0	2	4	1	1

YARMOUTH-DENNIS

BATTING	AVG	AB	R	H	2B	3B	HR	RBI	SB
Cole Billingsley, cf	.293	174	26	51	11	2	1	19	10
Luke Bonfield, rf	.211	57	9	12	5	0	0	6	0
Gio Brusa, of	.290	124	18	36	6	0	8	23	0
Turner Buis, of	.308	13	0	4	0	0	0	0	1
Dallas Carroll, 3b	.280	25	1	7	0	0	0	0	1
Brady Conlan, 3b	.200	40	1	8	2	0	0	1	0
Michael Donadio, of	.252	115	14	29	3	2	0	11	3
Tommy Edman, ss	.318	148	18	47	7	0	2	20	8
Tyler Houston, c	.500	2	0	1	0	0	0	0	0
Chris Hudgins, c	.118	17	0	2	1	0	0	0	0
Kyle Kempf, rf	.000	4	1	0	0	0	0	0	0
Mike Marcinco, 2b	.000	2	0	0	0	0	0	0	0
Jon Mayer, c	.000	2	0	0	0	0	0	0	0
Ryan Noda, of	.204	98	9	20	3	0	3	13	1
Michael Papierski, c	.167	24	3	4	0	0	0	0	0
Louie Payetta, ss	.200	10	0	2	0	0	0	0	1
Dan Rizzie, c	.308	13	4	4	1	0	0	1	0
Nathan Rodriguez, c	.215	79	9	17	4	0	0	7	0
Nick Ruppert, cf	.154	13	1	2	1	0	0	2	0

BATTING	AVG	AB	R	H	2B	3B	HR	RBI	SB
Richard Slenker, ss	.250	4	0	1	0	0	0	0	0
Will Toffey, if	.136	44	4	6	0	0	0	2	2
Joshua Vidales, 2b	.241	58	6	14	1	0	0	5	0
Donnie Walton, ss	.287	157	17	45	6	0	1	22	8
Connor Wong, c	.232	82	12	19	2	0	1	8	2
Stephen Wrenn, cf	.273	139	24	38	4	1	5	16	9

PITCHING	W	L	ERA	G	SV	IP	H	BB	SO
Brett Adcock	3	3	4.58	9	1	37	35	29	26
Brandon Bailey	2	4	3.03	7	0	39	33	11	32
Evan Bell	0	2	2.48	12	0	29	34	4	22
Shane Bieber	1	1	1.93	3	0	19	15	2	14
Ben Bowden	1	0	0.00	10	2	17	5	8	31
Gabriel Cramer	0	0	2.89	7	0	9	6	3	7
Jacob DeVries	1	1	2.84	3	0	13	13	5	10
Alec Eisenberg	0	3	5.52	12	1	29	34	9	35
David Ellingson	0	1	2.35	12	0	15	13	7	12
Chad Hockin	1	2	2.08	6	1	9	6	4	13
Dustin Hunt	0	2	3.18	8	0	23	28	6	33
Mason Kukowski	1	0	4.05	3	0	7	5	0	6
Dalton Lehnen	2	0	4.15	10	0	13	18	7	12
Ryley Maceachern	0	0	3.55	7	0	13	8	9	6
Cory Malcom	2	0	3.00	8	1	15	14	1	18
Christian Morris	1	1	6.60	3	0	15	16	4	8
Danny Pobereyko	0	1	2.70	1	0	3	4	0	3
Ricky Thomas	7	0	1.02	8	0	44	22	13	45
Davis Tominaga	0	0	0.00	2	0	4	2	1	2
Chris Viall	0	0	7.84	10	1	10	10	9	9
Doug Willey	0	0	5.23	9	0	10	9	4	7
Daniel Zamora	0	1	13.50	2	0	3	9	2	3

ALASKA LEAGUE

AMERICAN LEAGUE	LEAGUE			OVERALL		
	W	L	PCT	W	L	PCT
Anchorage Bucs	23	16	.590	27	21	.561
Peninsula Oilers	18	21	.462	20	26	.435
Alaska Goldpanners	9	31	.232	14	33	.302

NATIONAL LEAGUE	W	L	PCT	W	L	PCT
Mat-Su Miners	31	10	.756	34	11	.756
Anchorage Glacier Pilots	22	18	.550	27	20	.573
Chugiak Chinooks	17	24	.415	18	27	.400

CHAMPIONSHIP: Anchorage Bucs defeated Mat-Su 2-1 in best-of-three series.

TOP 10 PROSPECTS: 1. Corbin Martin, rhp, Mat-Su (So., Texas A&M). **2.** Brick Paskiewicz, rhp/of, Mat-Su (Jr., Grand Canyon). **3.** Zach Warren, lhp, Mat-Su (So., Tennessee). **4.** Connor Menez, lhp, Chugiak-Eagle River (Jr., The Master's (Calif.)). **6.** Kyle Simonds, rhp, Mat-Su (Jr., Texas A&M). **7.** Eli Morgan, rhp, Mat-Su (So., Gonzaga). **8.** Alex Caruso, of, Mat-Su (Sr., St. John's). **9.** Taylor Jones, 1b/rhp, Anchorage (Jr., Gonzaga). **10.** Matt Diorio, c/1b, Mat-Su (Jr., Central Florida).

INDIVIDUAL BATTING LEADERS

	AVG	AB	R	H	2B	3B	HR	RBI	SB
Alex Caruso, of, Mat-Su	.364	129	20	47	4	0	1	22	6
Tanner Nishioka, if, Mat-Su	.364	110	21	40	7	3	1	16	3
Brick Paskiewicz, of, Mat-Su	.341	132	16	45	1	3	0	13	6
Taylor Jones, p, Bucs	.333	120	6	40	5	0	0	11	0
Matt Diorio, c, Mat-Su	.331	121	21	40	8	2	0	19	0
Jordan Washam, if, Peninsula	.323	130	11	42	8	0	0	15	7
Luke Hamblin, of, Pilots	.319	141	28	45	4	2	0	9	19
Stephan Trosclair, util, Bucs	.294	160	26	47	9	4	2	25	9
Renae Martinez, c, Alaska	.293	157	17	46	8	1	1	24	1
Jacob Brobst, of, Chugiak	.273	110	18	30	1	0	0	4	4

INDIVIDUAL PITCHING LEADERS

	W	L	ERA	G	SV	IP	H	BB	SO
Will Hibbs, Pilots	3	0	0.46	10	0	39	33	10	31
Jim Voyles, Bucs	5	0	0.63	10	0	43	29	4	25
Eli Morgan, Mat-Su	5	0	0.84	8	0	43	34	13	47
Aaron Soto, Bucs	6	1	0.89	9	0	51	39	9	30
Josh Medeles, Peninsula	2	2	0.96	8	0	38	18	24	24
Drew Jacobs, Pilots	2	1	1.05	10	0	43	31	6	29
Calvin LeBrun, Mat-Su	4	1	1.30	8	0	49	32	9	44

	W	L	ERA	G	SV	IP	H	BB	SO
Braxton Wilks, Chugiak	2	2	1.39	11	2	45	24	16	29
Drake Robison, Pilots	4	2	1.72	10	2	47	32	15	37
Kyle Simonds, Mat-Su	5	0	1.77	8	1	41	30	15	28

ATLANTIC COLLEGIATE LEAGUE

	W	L	PCT	GB
Allentown Railers	33	5	.868	—
Staten Island Tide	21	13	.614	10
Quakertown Blazers	20	18	.526	13
South Jersey Giants	21	19	.525	13
Trenton Generals	17	19	.472	15
North Jersey Eagles	18	21	.462	15 ½
Jersey Pilots	11	26	.303	21 ½
Lehigh Valley Catz	8	28	.222	24

CHAMPIONSHIP: Allentown defeated Staten Island 2-1 in best-of-three series.

TOP 10 PROSPECTS: 1. Matt Swarmer, rhp, Allentown (Sr., Kutztown (Pa.)). **2.** Nicholas Masterson, rhp, North Jersey (So., Coastal Carolina). **3.** Justin Valdespina, rhp, North Jersey (So., Southern New Hampshire). **4.** Karl Blum, rhp, Trenton (Jr., Duke). **5.** Connor Lehmann, rhp, Jersey (So., Saint Louis). **6.** Brandon Soat, of, Allentown (Sr., IPFW). **7.** Devin Ruiz, of, South Jersey (So., UNC Greensboro). **8.** Will Latcham, rhp, Allentown (So., Cumberland (N.J.) CC). **9.** Austin Solecitto, lhp, North Jersey (Sr., Rice). **10.** Brandon Kulp, rhp, Allentown (Sr., Lehigh).

INDIVIDUAL BATTING LEADERS

	AVG	AB	R	H	2B	3B	HR	RBI	SB
Zachary Leone, c, SI	.380	100	11	38	14	2	0	32	2
Charles Misiano, if, SI	.375	112	33	42	5	2	0	16	22
Devin Ruiz, of, South Jersey	.361	122	23	44	10	1	5	36	4
Brandon Soat, of, Allentown	.360	111	27	40	11	0	6	18	15
Matt Maul, if, South Jersey	.325	120	20	39	4	0	1	14	9
Casey Clauss, of, Allentown	.322	115	28	37	1	0	0	13	14
Greg Kocinski, if, Jersey	.308	117	33	36	8	0	2	18	4
Anthony Godino, of, SI	.308	107	29	33	9	0	2	20	16
Connor Powers, of, SI	.304	112	18	34	6	0	1	16	13
John Scarr, c, Jersey	.303	109	10	33	8	1	1	21	2

INDIVIDUAL PITCHING LEADERS

	W	L	ERA	G	SV	IP	H	BB	SO
Matthew Swarmer, Allentown	8	0	0.55	9	0	65	37	3	89
Mike Kammerer, Allentown	3	1	1.14	6	0	32	26	12	34
Nicholas Masterson, North Jersey	3	1	1.62	11	1	33	23	8	33
William Latcham, Allentown	5	0	1.62	6	0	33	21	8	31
Karl Blum, Trenton	0	4	2.17	13	3	37	28	17	39
Kyle McKelvy, Quakertown	3	1	2.23	14	5	32	23	10	19
Jake Regina, Staten Island	6	1	2.33	10	0	54	40	18	27
Trey Bickel, Quakertown	3	5	2.46	13	0	44	27	17	43
Justin Valdespina, North Jersey	3	3	2.60	8	0	45	40	17	41
Dan Morrin, Quakertown	5	1	2.68	10	0	50	41	12	33

CAL RIPKEN COLLEGIATE LEAGUE

NORTHERN DIVISION

	W	L	PCT	GB
Baltimore Redbirds	29	11	.725	—
Silver Spring-Takoma T Bolts	20	20	.500	9
Rockville Express	18	22	.450	11
Baltimore Dodgers	13	27	.325	16
Gaithersburg Giants	13	27	.325	16

SOUTHERN DIVISION

	W	L	PCT	GB
Bethesda Big Train	29	11	.725	—
Vienna River Dogs	21	19	.525	8
Herndon Braves	19	21	.475	10
D.C. Grays	19	21	.475	10
Alexandria Aces	19	21	.475	10

CHAMPIONSHIP: Baltimore Redbirds defeated Bethesda 2-0 in best-of-three series.

TOP 10 PROSPECTS: 1. Stuart Fairchild, of, Baltimore Redbirds (So., Wake Forest). **2.** Logan Warmoth, ss, Baltimore Redbirds (So., North Carolina). **3.** Will Stokes, rhp, Baltimore Redbirds (So., Mississippi). **4.** Jason Morgan, rhp, Baltimore Redbirds (So., North Carolina). **5.** Walter Sheller, rhp, Bethesda (Jr., Stetson). **6.** Drew Strotman, rhp,

Bethesda (So., St. Mary's). **7.** Marty Costas, util., Baltimore Redbirds (Fr., Maryland). **8.** Brett Netzer, if, Alexandria (So., Charlotte). **9.** Chris Lewis, util., Bethesda (Sr., Sacramento State). **10.** Kevin Lachance, ss, Vienna (Sr., Maryland-Baltimore County).

INDIVIDUAL BATTING LEADERS

	AVG	AB	R	H	2B	3B	HR	RBI	SB
Brett Netzer, if, Alexandria	.349	146	29	51	7	4	0	20	6
Kevin Lachance, ss, Vienna	.330	106	20	35	3	1	0	12	16
Logan Warmoth, if, Redbirds	.330	103	25	34	3	0	0	17	21
Nick Dunn, if, SS-T	.321	112	17	36	7	3	0	17	3
Zachary Racusin, of, SS-T	.311	119	21	37	2	2	1	13	24
Danny Pardo, of, Alexandria	.309	123	25	38	11	0	2	16	9
Stuart Fairchild, of, Redbirds	.307	127	25	39	6	3	1	16	13
Chris Lewis, of, Bethesda	.306	157	24	48	10	1	7	37	6
Andy Mocahbee, c, Herndon	.304	115	26	35	11	1	3	14	4
Steven Paredes, if, SS-T	.304	112	11	34	9	1	1	16	11

INDIVIDUAL PITCHING LEADERS

	W	L	ERA	G	SV	IP	H	BB	SO
Jack Gomersall, Vienna	6	1	0.44	8	1	41	24	8	31
Conrad Wozniak, SS-T	3	2	1.24	9	0	44	31	8	36
Emerson Gibbs, Baltimore	4	1	1.29	8	0	42	30	0	30
Darrien Ragins, SS-T	3	1	1.45	8	0	43	26	25	38
Tim Yandel, Bethesda	4	1	1.51	8	0	48	36	10	38
Mark Gunst, Vienna	3	1	1.70	7	0	42	32	21	32
Taylor Bloom, Gaithersburg	3	0	1.76	6	0	31	25	2	38
Jason Morgan, Baltimore	5	2	1.79	9	0	40	34	11	29
Gabriel Mosser, Alexandria	4	0	1.80	7	0	40	32	12	29
Dakota Forsyth, Baltimore	4	1	1.84	9	1	34	23	11	27

CALIFORNIA COLLEGIATE LEAGUE

NORTHERN DIVISION

	W	L	PCT	GB
Neptune Beach Pearl	17	8	.680	—
Menlo Park Legends	12	13	.480	5
Walnut Creek Crawdads	4	21	.160	13

CENTRAL DIVISION

	W	L	PCT	GB
Santa Barbara Foresters	23	4	.852	—
Conejo Oaks	17	10	.630	6
San Luis Obispo Blues	14	12	.538	8 ½
Santa Paula Halos	8	18	.308	14 ½

SOUTHERN DIVISION

	W	L	PCT	GB
Los Angeles Brewers	12	14	.462	—
Academy Barons	12	15	.444	½
SoCal Catch	11	15	.423	1

CHAMPIONSHIP: Neptune Beach defeated Los Angeles 2-0 in best-of-three series.

TOP 10 PROSPECTS: 1. Ryan Sluder, of, San Luis Obispo, (Jr., Oklahoma State). **2.** Josh Rojas, 2b, SoCal (Jr., Hawaii). **3.** Cody Crouse, rhp, Santa Barbara (Jr., Florida International). **4.** Jeremy Montalbano, c, Santa Barbara (Jr., Tulane). **5.** Vahn Bozoian, of/1b, Los Angeles, (So., Concordia (Calif.)). **6.** Glenn Otto, rhp, Santa Barbara, (So., Rice). **7.** Granger Studdard, of, Santa Barbara (Jr., Texas State). **8.** David Greer, if, Santa Barbara (Jr., Arizona State). **9.** Gary Cornish, rhp, Santa Barbara (Sr., San Diego). **10.** Ricardo Salinas, rhp, Neptune Beach (So., Rice).

INDIVIDUAL BATTING LEADERS

	AVG	AB	R	H	2B	3B	HR	RBI	SB
Larry Barraza, Academy	.430	93	31	40	11	0	4	21	8
Josh Rojas, SoCal	.411	90	24	37	11	0	3	21	9
Zach Gibbons, Conejo	.398	103	20	41	7	2	2	20	6
Richard Cunningham, SoCal	.384	86	20	33	4	5	1	8	9
Vahn Bozoian, Los Angeles	.356	87	17	31	3	1	5	24	3
Granger Studdard, SB	.338	80	17	27	2	1	3	21	3
Aaron Cisneros, Academy	.333	108	23	36	9	1	10	31	0
Andru Cardenas, Santa Paula	.333	90	9	30	4	0	0	6	5
John Montgomery, Menlo Pk.	.329	82	9	27	6	1	2	20	1
Tanner Gardner, SLO	.326	89	12	29	3	3	0	16	3

INDIVIDUAL PITCHING LEADERS

	W	L	ERA	G	SV	IP	H	BB	SO
Angel Rodriguez, Conejo	2	0	0.72	4	0	25	20	6	31
Jackson Sigman, San Luis Obispo	3	0	0.99	16	0	27	19	9	28

	W	L	ERA	G	SV	IP	H	BB	SO
Garett King, Santa Barbara	3	0	1.19	5	0	30	23	3	27
Johnathon Tripp, Nep. Beach	0	0	1.23	5	0	22	17	1	22
Cannon Chadwick, San Luis Obispo	3	0	1.86	6	0	29	22	8	23
Theron Kay, Neptune Beach	2	0	2.02	5	0	22	26	1	12
Gary Cornish, Santa Barbara	4	1	2.25	5	0	32	25	5	32
Oscar Munoz, Academy	2	1	2.45	14	3	22	18	4	31
Serigstad Scott, Los Angeles	1	0	2.78	9	0	23	21	7	26
Brendan Nail, San Luis Obispo	1	2	2.80	7	0	26	28	12	24

COASTAL PLAIN LEAGUE

EASTERN DIVISION	W	L	PCT
Edenton Steamers	40	15	.727
Wilmington Sharks	29	24	.547
Peninsula Pilots	28	25	.528
Holly Springs Salamanders	28	28	.500
Petersburg Generals	26	29	.473
Morehead City Marlins	24	29	.453
Wilson Tobs	23	32	.418
Fayetteville SwampDogs	18	35	.340

WESTERN DIVISION	W	L	PCT
Asheboro Copperheads	34	22	.607
Gastonia Grizzlies	31	25	.554
Florence RedWolves	28	27	.509
Lexington County Blowfish	28	28	.500
Martinsville Mustangs	26	29	.473
High Point-Thomasville HiToms	26	30	.464
Forest City Owls	22	33	.400

CHAMPIONSHIP: Edenton defeated Gastonia 2-0 in best-of-three series. **TOP 10 PROSPECTS: 1.** Brian Miller, of, Holly Springs (So., North Carolina). **2.** Taylor Widener, rhp, Lexington County (Jr., South Carolina). **3.** Sammy Taormina, 3b, Gastonia (Jr., Liberty). **4.** Alex Destino, 1b/lhp, Wilmington (So., South Carolina). **5.** J.D. Crowe, c, Lexington County (Sr., Francis Marion (S.C.)). **6.** Gene Cone, of, Lexington County (Jr., South Carolina). **7.** Nicky Lopez, ss, High Point-Thomasville (Jr., Creighton). **8.** G.K. Young, c/1b, Petersburg (Jr., Coastal Carolina). **9.** Chad Sedio, 3b, Edenton (Sr., Miami (Ohio)). **10.** Trevor Bradley, rhp, Lexington County (Jr., South Carolina-Aiken).

INDIVIDUAL BATTING LEADERS

	AVG	AB	R	H	2B	3B	HR	RBI	SB
Brian Miller, Holly Springs	.389	198	43	77	6	1	0	18	38
Nick Rotola, Wilmington	.357	182	44	65	13	0	2	31	37
Jackson Mims, Gastonia	.348	141	27	49	10	1	1	25	14
J.D. Crowe, Lex. County	.333	216	46	72	17	3	9	44	5
Jimmy Faul, Fayetteville	.333	153	19	51	9	0	3	21	6
Jimmy Kerrigan, Peninsula	.328	125	34	41	8	3	4	25	11
Nicky Lopez, HP-T	.327	162	33	53	8	1	7	22	11
Will Shepherd, Peninsula	.325	166	49	54	12	1	8	26	13
Ben Holland, Florence	.325	194	29	63	18	1	6	43	1
Joe Schrimpf, Petersburg	.322	115	27	37	10	1	4	26	0

INDIVIDUAL PITCHING LEADERS

	W	L	ERA	G	SV	IP	H	BB	SO
Zach Prendergast, Edenton	6	0	1.17	8	0	46	25	9	46
Trevor Gay, HP-T	3	2	1.55	8	0	46	34	16	33
Zach Reid, Morehead City	5	3	1.70	26	6	42	26	18	45
Brett Porter, Florence	3	0	1.74	19	2	31	20	12	33
Eric Davis, Lexington County	2	0	1.75	21	2	36	30	17	49
Chandler Sanburn, Holly Springs	2	0	1.76	9	0	41	21	24	36
Michael Castellani, Wilmington	4	2	1.86	25	0	48	44	9	36
Trevor Bradley, Lex. County	5	4	2.01	20	2	54	34	25	81
Cooper Jones, Martinsville	3	2	2.06	22	7	35	28	8	32
Taylor Edens, Peninsula	9	1	2.06	11	0	57	51	2	36

FLORIDA COLLEGIATE SUMMER LEAGUE

	W	L	T	PCT	GB
Sanford River Rats	26	13	1	.650	—
Altamonte Springs Boom	25	14	1	.625	1
Leesburg Lightning	22	19	0	.537	5
DeLand Suns	20	19	0	.513	6
Winter Park Diamond Dawgs	14	22	0	.389	10 ½
Winter Garden Squeeze	8	28	0	.222	16 ½

CHAMPIONSHIP: Sanford defeated Leesburg in championship game.
TOP 10 PROSPECTS: 1. Austin Glorius, rhp, Altamonte Springs (SIGNED: Red Sox). **2.** Garrett Wolforth, c, Altamonte Springs (Fr., Dallas Baptist). **3.** Brett Morales, rhp, Altamonte Springs (So., Tampa). **4.** Santiago Espinal, ss, Sanford (Fr., Seminole State (Fla.) JC). **5.** Reese Cooley, ss, Sanford (So., Chipola (Fla.) JC). **6.** Daniel Sweet, of, Altamonte Springs (Sr., Dallas Baptist). **7.** Alex House, rhp, Sanford (So., Florida Atlantic). **8.** Hunter Melton, 1b/rhp, Sanford (Sr., Texas A&M). **9.** Clay Simmons, ss, Leesburg (R-So., South Florida). **10.** Tyler McMurray, rhp, Altamonte Springs (So., Alabama).

INDIVIDUAL BATTING LEADERS

	AVG	AB	R	H	2B	3B	HR	RBI	SB
Santiago Espinal, ss, Sanford	.350	137	24	48	10	1	0	20	29
Daniel Woodrow, of, W. Park	.336	107	20	36	3	3	1	9	15
Matt Gandy, c, Alta. Springs	.324	105	20	34	6	1	0	16	2
Cody Burgess, of, W. Green	.313	128	9	40	8	0	0	9	10
Tanner Long, rf, Leesburg	.311	151	23	47	6	0	0	18	13
Seth Cunningham, of, Lees.	.304	112	19	34	2	0	0	14	11
Doug Teegarden, ss, Lees.	.279	104	16	29	5	0	2	17	9
Chandler Rodriguez, of, DeL.	.267	146	19	39	6	0	0	14	2
John Silviano, c, DeLand	.266	128	25	34	8	1	4	29	8
Jacob Wright, of, Sanford	.252	123	19	31	8	2	1	11	16

INDIVIDUAL PITCHING LEADERS

	W	L	ERA	G	SV	IP	H	BB	SO
Cameron Hanes, Winter Park	3	2	0.73	7	0	37	24	14	30
Brett Morales, Alta. Springs	3	0	0.92	8	0	39	20	7	35
Devin Raftery, Alta. Springs	3	2	1.51	9	0	42	26	19	42
Gage Hutchinson, DeLand	2	5	1.55	12	0	41	40	12	33
Alex House, Sanford	4	0	1.66	8	0	49	35	9	38
Austin Glorius, Alta. Springs	5	1	1.67	9	0	38	16	11	45
Blake Sanderson, Leesburg	3	2	1.81	10	0	45	40	11	33
Darren Kelly, Leesburg	2	2	1.81	10	0	51	34	20	32
Trevor Tinder, Winter Park	1	2	2.84	6	0	32	21	16	36
Matthew Hardy, Alta. Springs	3	2	2.93	12	0	40	35	14	31

FUTURES COLLEGIATE LEAGUE

EASTERN DIVISION	W	L	PCT	GB
Martha's Vineyard Sharks	34	20	.630	—
Brockton Rox	34	22	.607	1
North Shore Navigators	33	22	.600	1 ½
Nashua Silver Knights	28	28	.500	7
Seacoast Mavericks	15	41	.268	20

WESTERN DIVISION	W	L	PCT	GB
Bristol Blues	33	23	.589	—
Worcester Bravehearts	26	30	.464	7
Torrington Titans	24	28	.462	7
Pittsfield Suns	25	30	.455	7 ½
Wachusett Dirt Dawgs	22	30	.423	9

CHAMPIONSHIP: Worcester defeated Bristol 2-1 in best-of-three series. **TOP 10 PROSPECTS: 1.** Ian Strom, of, Worcester (Jr., Massachusetts-Lowell). **2.** Dominic De Renzo, c, Martha's Vineyard (Fr., Oklahoma). **3.** Tim Cate, lhp, Bristol (Fr., Connecticut). **4.** Donovan Casey, of/rhp, Martha's Vineyard (So., Boston College). **5.** Jacob Stevens, rhp, Worcester (Fr., Boston College). **6.** Ryan Gendron, of, Seacoast (Sr., Southern New Hampshire). **7.** Austin French, lhp, Seacoast (Sr., Brown). **8.** Jake Fishman, lhp/1b, Brockton (Jr., Union (N.Y.)). **9.** Tyler Schwanz, Nashua (Jr., Maine). **10.** Zach Kirby, rhp, Brockton (Sr., Framingham State (Mass.)).

INDIVIDUAL BATTING LEADERS

	AVG	AB	R	H	2B	3B	HR	RBI	SB
Brian Campbell, of, M. Vineyard	.373	185	40	69	14	3	1	35	19
Ian Strom, of, Worcester	.353	136	26	48	11	1	0	10	18
Erik Ostberg, c, Nashua	.349	152	25	53	10	0	1	24	2
Brandon Fischer, if, N.Shore	.338	204	37	69	11	6	1	36	16
Domenic De Renzo, c, M. Vineyard	.327	101	21	33	2	0	2	14	5
Ryan Gendron, of, Seacost	.324	182	47	59	9	2	22	53	23
Max DiTondo, of, Wachusett	.322	183	29	59	6	1	6	28	12

COLLEGE

	AVG	AB	R	H	2B	3B	HR	RBI	SB
Jon Mayer, c, M. Vineyard	.318	151	24	48	13	1	3	37	8
Tommy Marcinczyk, of, Brock.	.316	177	30	56	11	3	4	35	11
Chad Martin, if, North Shore	.310	213	31	66	13	1	2	35	4
Gerrad Rohan, if, Bristol	.310	184	17	57	12	1	0	32	6

INDIVIDUAL PITCHING LEADERS

	W	L	ERA	G	SV	IP	H	BB	SO
Chris Weiss, Martha's Vineyard	5	0	1.09	13	0	41	34	16	36
George Lund, Bristol	4	1	1.30	9	0	49	40	21	41
Logan Fullmer, Worcester	1	2	1.34	21	3	34	20	11	44
John Russell, Torrington	4	2	1.47	12	1	37	21	2	43
Troy Terzi, Bristol	3	4	1.67	9	0	59	45	8	51
Zack Kirby, Brockton	4	1	1.70	10	0	48	33	15	51
Speros Varinos, North Shore	1	1	1.76	26	13	31	26	13	35
Lucas Olen, Nashua	3	2	1.77	24	2	41	38	11	26
Matthew Cronin, Wachusett	0	3	1.78	16	7	30	17	19	37
Dylan Collett, Worcester	3	2	1.87	12	0	53	45	11	48

GREAT LAKES LEAGUE

	W	L	PCT	GB
Lima Locos	28	7	.800	—
Hamilton Joes	24	11	.686	4
Xenia Scouts	24	16	.600	6½
Southern Ohio Copperheads	22	17	.564	8
Licking County Settlers	21	17	.553	8½
Lake Erie Monarchs	21	18	.538	9
Grand Lake Mariners	18	22	.450	12½
Cincinnati Steam	16	22	.423	13½
Galion Graders	16	22	.421	13½
Lorain County Ironmen	13	27	.325	17½
Northern Ohio Baseball Club	6	30	.167	22½

CHAMPIONSHIP: Lima defeated Hamilton 2-1 in best-of-three series.

INDIVIDUAL BATTING LEADERS

	AVG	AB	R	H	2B	3B	HR	RBI	SB
Jake Simmerman, 1b, Hamilton	.390	136	25	53	16	1	2	24	0
Nicholas Riotto, cf, Galion	.385	104	25	40	8	1	1	14	11
Aaron Aucker, 3b, Lake Erie	.381	134	29	51	10	1	6	27	8
Kyle Holbrook, of, Licking Cty.	.371	116	22	43	5	1	3	28	3
Tyler Bires, c, Lorain County	.370	135	23	50	11	3	1	20	8
Dazon Cole, of, Lake Erie	.369	141	31	52	13	1	3	25	15
Mitchell Carriger, of, Lima	.369	122	29	45	7	1	2	19	1
Nick Roscetti, if, Grand Lake	.369	122	27	45	5	0	2	24	5
Daniel Neff, of, Hamilton	.361	108	23	39	7	1	2	28	18
Connor Callery, if, Sou. Ohio	.359	103	21	37	7	0	0	18	6

INDIVIDUAL PITCHING LEADERS

	W	L	ERA	G	SV	IP	H	BB	SO
Brayden Bouchey, Licking Cty.	3	0	0.22	9	0	41	18	14	50
John Crawford, Xenia	1	2	1.16	5	0	31	22	13	17
Perry DellaValle, Licking County	2	3	1.44	16	5	25	19	3	44
Zach Moore, Southern Ohio	2	0	1.44	12	3	25	19	2	24
Sam Fichthorn, Licking County	2	1	1.61	7	1	28	28	14	34
Cory Blessing, Northern Ohio	2	0	1.71	11	2	21	15	9	22
Andrew Gonzalez, Sou. Ohio	2	2	1.82	6	0	40	39	6	27
Alex Schraffenberger, Hamilton	6	1	1.89	7	0	48	45	9	15
Cole Hendrix, Lorain County	2	1	1.93	6	0	23	18	19	15
Benjamin Aldridge, Xenia	5	3	2.21	14	2	53	40	15	44

HAMPTONS COLLEGIATE LEAGUE

	W	L	T	PTS
Shelter Island Bucks	27	14	1	55
Westhampton Aviators	26	15	1	53
North Fork Ospreys	22	19	1	45
Montauk Mustangs	22	20	0	44
Sag Harbor Whalers	17	23	2	36
Southampton Breakers	15	24	3	33
Riverhead Tomcats	14	28	0	28

CHAMPIONSHIP: Shelter Island defeated Westhampton 2-0 in best-of-three series.

TOP 10 PROSPECTS: 1. Dan Jagiello, rhp, Riverhead (Jr., Long Island-Post). 2. Jamie Galazin, of/if, Westhampton (So., St. John's). 3. J.J. Shimko, of, Montauk (So., South Carolina-Upstate). 4. Anthony Alicki, rhp, Shelter Island (Jr., Bridgeport (Conn.)). 5. Nick Heath, of, North Fork (R-Jr., Northwestern State). 6. Eddie Haus, of, Shelter Island (So., St. Mary's). 7. Chris Hess, if, Shelter Island (R-Jr., Rhode Island). 8. Dillon Persinger, 2b, Riverhead (So., Golden West (Calif.) JC). 9. Danny Pobereyko, rhp, North Fork (Jr., Butler). 10. Logan McRae, if, Westhampton (So., College of Charleston).

INDIVIDUAL BATTING LEADERS

	AVG	AB	R	H	2B	3B	HR	RBI	SB
Eddie Haus, of, Shelter Island	.360	150	28	54	7	0	1	27	10
J.J. Shimko, of, Montauk	.354	158	21	56	5	4	1	17	6
Turner Buis, of, Riverhead	.354	130	14	46	6	0	0	11	7
A.J. Montoya, of, Westhampton	.343	143	32	49	11	1	3	18	21
Tristan Chari, c, Sag Harbor	.336	143	11	48	3	1	0	21	2
Logan McRae, if, Westhampton	.331	133	17	44	13	0	2	21	3
Jack Machonis, if, Shelter Island	.329	152	28	50	8	1	0	15	9
Bryce Packard, if, Montauk	.329	149	24	49	10	2	2	20	2
James Morisano, c, North Fork	.325	120	14	39	6	0	2	10	3
Ben Socher, of, Riverhead	.324	102	11	33	3	0	0	9	6

INDIVIDUAL PITCHING LEADERS

	W	L	ERA	G	SV	IP	H	BB	SO
Jake Reinhardt, Riverhead	1	3	0.76	11	3	36	28	12	32
Danny Pobereyko, North Fork	1	0	1.10	9	0	41	32	9	52
Logan Frati, Westhampton	2	1	1.27	8	0	35	25	5	30
Vaughn Berberet, Sag Harbor	1	1	1.36	14	1	33	37	11	17
Michael Toner, Westhampton	5	2	1.41	7	0	45	25	7	32
Zack Bahm, Shelter Island	4	2	1.54	9	0	41	34	5	19
Dylan Mouzakes, Montauk	3	3	1.69	0	0	48	38	19	55
Anthony Catinella, North Fork	4	3	1.85	8	0	49	42	6	25
Tyler Radcliffe, Sag Harbor	5	1	1.86	7	0	44	46	5	25
Erin Baldwin, Riverhead	0	0	1.93	11	1	37	34	10	29

JAYHAWK LEAGUE

NORTHERN DIVISION	W	L	PCT	GB
El Dorado Broncos	25	13	.658	—
Liberal BeeJays	22	14	.611	2
Hays Larks	17	19	.472	7
Dodge City A's	16	20	.444	8

SOUTHERN DIVISION	W	L	PCT	GB
Haysville Aviators	25	13	.658	—
Wellington Heat	21	15	.583	3
Derby Twins	14	22	.389	10
Bethany Bulls	6	30	.167	18

CHAMPIONSHIP: Haysville defeated El Dorado 2-0 in best-of-three series.

TOP 10 PROSPECTS: 1. Joel Kuhel, rhp, Liberal (Jr., Texas-Arlington). 2. Austin Krajnak, 1b, Wellington (Jr., Texas A&M-Corpus Christi). 3. Brady Muller, lhp, Liberal (Graduated, Montana State-Billings). 4. Dan Holst, of, Haysville (Jr., Southeast Missouri State). 5. Kevin Connolly, of, Dodge City (Jr., Creighton). 6. Max Green, lhp, Dodge City (So., Pepperdine). 7. Kody Jones, lhp, Dodge City (So., New Mexico Military Institute JC). 8. Aaron Barteau, rhp, Wellington (Sr., Mary Hardin-Baylor (Texas)). 9. Brent Williams, c, Liberal (Jr., Oral Roberts). 10. Josh Witherspoon, lhp, El Dorado Broncos (So., Cisco (Texas) JC).

INDIVIDUAL BATTING LEADERS

	AVG	AB	R	H	2B	3B	HR	RBI	SB
Clayton Dalrymple, of, El Dor.	.406	143	42	58	7	2	4	29	17
Austin Krainak, if, Wellington	.398	133	29	53	20	0	12	46	0
Michael Burns, of, Hays	.391	151	33	59	11	2	2	12	16
Tyler Tokunaga, util, Haysville	.384	138	42	53	8	3	1	20	14
Madison Foster, of, Liberal	.368	133	22	49	9	0	2	20	1
Matt Holcombe, if, El Dorado	.357	112	19	40	11	3	2	26	1
Brady Cox, c, Liberal	.352	105	28	37	3	1	6	26	1
Derrick Mount, if, Hays	.348	112	27	39	3	1	3	19	4
Dan Holst, of, Haysville	.333	129	36	43	8	5	2	24	16
Wade Hanna, of, El Dorado	.333	120	20	40	4	0	1	18	8

INDIVIDUAL PITCHING LEADERS

	W	L	ERA	G	SV	IP	H	BB	SO
Jake Marchesseault, Haysville	3	1	2.74	11	0	43	43	12	33
Vince Lujan, Wellington	4	1	2.74	6	0	43	32	13	26

	W	L	ERA	G	SV	IP	H	BB	SO
Daulton Leiker, Wellington	3	1	2.76	6	0	42	35	9	34
Mich Vorhof, Dodge City	4	1	2.78	7	0	36	38	6	34
Brandon Hicks, El Dorado	4	1	3.11	7	0	38	32	16	29
Tanner Hart, El Dorado	2	3	3.12	8	0	35	29	13	22
Andrew Moralez, El Dorado	5	1	3.16	7	0	37	27	20	25
Cam Roegner, Hays	2	3	3.59	7	0	43	37	8	33
Dylan Boisclair, Haysville	3	1	3.94	8	0	32	28	9	33
Justin Vincent, Derby	3	2	3.96	8	0	52	58	16	41

MIDWEST COLLEGIATE LEAGUE

TEAM

	W	L	PCT	GB
DuPage County Hounds	31	14	.689	—
Northwest Indiana Oilmen	27	17	.614	3 ½
Lexington Snipes	25	16	.610	4
Joliet Admirals	16	23	.410	12
Michigan City Lakers	13	25	.342	14 ½
Southland Vikings	12	29	.293	17

CHAMPIONSHIP: DuPage County defeated Lexington 2-1 in best-of-three series.

INDIVIDUAL BATTING LEADERS

	AVG	AB	R	H	2B	3B	HR	RBI	SB
Joe Kennedy, Michigan City	.425	113	24	48	6	3	2	20	5
Tyler Sroczynski, NW Indiana	.397	121	31	48	12	0	3	31	17
Dustin Krob, DuPage County	.360	111	17	40	5	3	1	17	10
Owen Miller, Lexington	.343	105	25	36	9	1	3	23	3
Stefano Belmonte, NW Indiana	.341	123	25	42	12	0	2	30	1
Ryan Fitzgerald, DuPage Cty.	.333	165	33	55	8	0	5	28	10
Trent Carrier, DuPage Cty.	.331	127	32	42	4	0	2	24	10
Brad Wood, NW Indiana	.324	111	28	36	7	0	2	20	9
Joe Duncan, DuPage County	.323	130	23	42	2	0	0	13	24
Zack Jones, NW Indiana	.322	115	16	37	4	0	0	24	2

INDIVIDUAL PITCHING LEADERS

	W	L	ERA	G	SV	IP	H	BB	SO
Keith Mahler, NW Indiana	5	1	1.59	9	0	44	41	4	23
Enrique Zamora, NW Indiana	4	2	1.86	11	2	49	40	15	55
Christian Howell, NW Indiana	2	1	1.87	9	0	52	44	16	29
Nick Costantino, DuPage County	4	2	2.13	9	0	38	39	13	31
Tom Concklin, DuPage County	3	0	2.36	9	0	50	38	13	26
Sean Renzi, Joliet	2	1	2.80	5	0	35	26	13	35
Brian Jestice, NW Indiana	5	1	2.83	9	0	54	51	31	40
Chris Hawkes, Joliet	3	2	2.89	6	0	44	42	10	20
Nick Allgeyer, Joliet	3	2	2.94	9	0	61	53	23	45
Jimmy Skiff, NW Indiana	4	2	3.03	8	0	35	41	10	25

MINK LEAGUE

	League				Overall			
NORTHERN DIVISION	W	L	PCT	GB	W	L	PCT	GB
St. Joseph Mustangs	27	14	.659	—	35	15	.700	—
Sedalia Bombers	24	15	.615	2	24	15	.615	5 ½
Chillicothe Mudcats	21	18	.538	5	24	18	.571	7
Clarinda A's	19	23	.452	8 ½	27	24	.529	8 ½
SOUTHERN DIVISION	W	L	PCT	GB	W	L	PCT	GB
Nevada Griffons	24	15	.615	—	27	16	.628	—
Branson Nationals	20	20	.500	4 ½	21	20	.512	5
Joplin Outlaws	16	26	.381	9 ½	16	28	.364	11 ½
Ozark Generals	8	28	.222	14 ½	9	28	.243	15

CHAMPIONSHIP: St. Joseph defeated Nevada in championship game.

TOP 10 PROSPECTS: 1. Sam Perez, rhp, Sedalia (Sr., Missouri State). **2.** Sean Rackoski, rhp, Chillicothe (Jr., Kansas). **3.** Kasey Cooper, of, Branson (R-Jr., Arkansas-Fort Smith). **4.** Trey Harris, of, Branson (So., Sedalia (So., Missouri). **5.** Thomas Lerouge, of, Chillicothe (So., Grand Canyon). **6.** Trent Hill, lhp/of, St. Joseph (Sr., Lee (Tenn.)). **7.** Brett Bond, c, St. Joseph (So., Missouri). **8.** Trey Turner, of/rhp, Branson (So., Crowder (Mo.) JC). **9.** Nelson Mompierre, c, Branson (So., Miami-Dade JC). **10.** Orencio Fisher, 2b/of, St. Joseph (Sr., Missouri Western State).

INDIVIDUAL BATTING LEADERS

	AVG	AB	R	H	2B	3B	HR	RBI	SB
Thomas Lerouge, of, Chill.	.391	110	24	43	8	3	0	17	10
Taylor Walker, if, Nevada	.349	109	17	38	5	0	3	25	2

	AVG	AB	R	H	2B	3B	HR	RBI	SB
Justin Holt, of, Sedalia	.348	112	21	39	6	0	0	13	5
Kasey Cooper, of, Branson	.344	125	31	43	13	1	7	33	11
Trey Turner, of, Branson	.342	111	23	38	10	4	0	11	21
Tyler Bodenstab, of, Nevada	.327	113	26	37	3	2	2	13	7
John Remick, c, Chillicothe	.327	101	16	33	6	1	2	10	5
Jonathan Ramon, 3b, Sedalia	.320	128	35	41	5	2	10	39	1
Tanner Allen, if, Ozark	.320	125	19	40	6	0	2	13	6
Kurt Becker, if, Nevada	.320	122	30	39	9	1	2	16	3

INDIVIDUAL PITCHING LEADERS

	W	L	ERA	G	SV	IP	H	BB	SO
Sam Perez, Sedalia	6	0	1.07	6	0	42	24	10	61
Sean Rackoski, Chillicothe	5	0	1.13	6	0	40	26	16	35
Preston Felgate, St. Joseph	4	2	1.29	7	0	42	28	10	31
Cody Lawson, Nevada	3	1	1.64	7	0	33	26	14	14
Dixon Marble, St. Joseph	5	1	1.70	7	0	48	34	12	31
Alex Ernestine, Clarinda	5	2	1.80	9	0	45	45	19	37
Justin Murphey, Sedalia	5	1	1.85	6	0	39	38	8	26
Josh Green, Nevada	2	1	1.97	9	0	50	32	19	35
Keith Picht, Joplin	2	2	2.36	5	0	34	22	13	30
Jaraad Salas, Nevada	3	0	2.37	13	0	30	34	11	24

NEW ENGLAND COLLEGIATE LEAGUE

NORTHERN DIVISION	W	L	PCT	GB
Vermont Mountaineers	25	16	.610	—
Sanford Mainers	23	18	.561	2
North Adams SteepleCats	21	21	.500	4 ½
Laconia Muskrats	21	21	.500	4 ½
Valley Blue Sox	19	23	.452	6 ½
Keene Swamp Bats	13	29	.310	12 ½

SOUTHERN DIVISION	W	L	PCT	GB
Newport Gulls	27	15	.643	—
Mystic Schooners	26	16	.619	1
New Bedford Bay Sox	22	20	.524	5
Ocean State Waves	21	21	.500	6
Plymouth Pilgrims	20	22	.476	7
Danbury Westerners	13	29	.310	14

CHAMPIONSHIP: Vermont defeated Mystic 2-1 in best-of-three series.
TOP 10 PROSPECTS: 1. Willie Rios, lhp, Mystic (So., Florida SouthWestern State JC). **2.** Brent Rooker, of/1b, Plymouth (R-So., Mississippi State). **3.** Kevin Pimentel, rhp, Plymouth (R-Fr., Miami). **4.** Mike Mertz, rhp, Newport (Sr., Oklahoma State). **5.** Mandy Alvarez, 3b, Plymouth (Sr., Eastern Kentucky). **6.** Deon Stafford, c, Laconia (So., Saint Joseph's). **7.** Aaron Hill, ss, Mystic (Jr., Connecticut). **8.** Jason Foley, rhp, Mystic (Jr., Sacred Heart). **9.** Tim Lynch, 1b, Ocean State (Sr., Southern Mississippi). **10.** Chuckie Robinson, c, Ocean State (Jr., Southern Mississippi).

INDIVIDUAL BATTING LEADERS

	AVG	AB	R	H	2B	3B	HR	RBI	SB
Dalton Thomas, c, Sanford	.380	150	21	57	13	1	3	19	3
Cody Acker, of, Danbury	.376	117	19	44	8	0	1	8	7
Brent Rooker, of, Plymouth	.360	164	36	59	10	0	10	33	12
Ben Ruta, 3b, Mystic	.346	159	30	55	12	1	3	28	6
Joven Afenir, of, Newport	.344	151	31	52	11	0	4	27	8
Mandy Alvarez, 3b, Plym.	.333	135	23	45	12	0	7	22	2
Deon Stafford, c, Laconia	.329	158	22	52	16	1	6	24	7
Richard Slenker, if, Mystic	.325	117	14	38	2	0	2	17	4
Sam Dexter, ss, Sanford	.324	108	17	35	5	0	1	15	3
Jayson Sullivan, of, New Bed.	.324	105	14	34	10	2	0	14	6

INDIVIDUAL PITCHING LEADERS

	W	L	ERA	G	SV	IP	H	BB	SO
Dakota Edwards, North Adams	1	2	1.16	7	0	39	23	13	24
Casey Brown, Vermont	4	1	1.25	8	0	43	34	11	24
Ben Wessel, Sanford	4	3	1.74	7	0	41	37	10	33
Zach Willeman, Keene	1	2	1.74	16	6	31	21	11	42
Timothy Viehoff, Laconia	5	1	1.77	9	0	51	27	20	58
Willie Rios, Mystic	4	0	1.80	7	0	35	25	23	41
Cody Dube, Sanford	3	1	1.80	15	1	30	24	6	43
Ryan Gray, Ocean State	4	0	1.86	8	0	39	25	10	17
Blake Morgan, Sanford	4	1	1.98	9	0	41	28	14	30
Gabriel Rodriguez, New Bedford	4	0	2.23	7	0	32	19	14	26

NEW YORK COLLEGIATE LEAGUE

EASTERN DIVISION	W	L	PCT	GB
Syracuse Salt Cats	29	17	.630	—
Oneonta Outlaws	26	18	.591	2
Cortland Crush	26	20	.565	3
Syracuse Jr. Chiefs	24	22	.522	5
Geneva Red Wings	21	23	.477	7
Sherrill Silversmiths	10	36	.217	19

WESTERN DIVISION	W	L	PCT	GB
Hornell Dodgers	31	15	.674	—
Geneva Twins	27	19	.587	4
Olean Oilers	26	20	.565	5
Niagara Power	25	21	.543	6
Rochester Ridgemen	24	22	.522	7
Genesee Rapids	21	25	.457	10
Wellsville Nitros	7	39	.152	24

CHAMPIONSHIP: Olean defeated Oneonta 2-0 in best-of-three series.

INDIVIDUAL BATTING LEADERS

	AVG	AB	R	H	2B	3B	HR	RBI	SB
J.T. Pittman, of, Twins	.342	149	35	51	1	1	2	13	6
Jacob Bass, of, Hornell	.340	153	31	52	2	1	0	16	16
David Hollins, ss, Olean	.340	150	29	51	7	2	2	32	4
Marty Napleton, c, Twins	.340	150	12	51	7	1	0	19	2
Jonathan Lapolla, c, Olean	.333	126	11	42	10	1	0	23	0
Jimmy Latona, c, Hornell	.331	163	41	54	11	2	2	31	24
Kellen Brown, if, Hornell	.331	142	31	47	6	1	0	24	18
Lucas Tevlin, 3b, Salt Cats	.326	132	26	43	6	0	0	13	23
Harry Roberson, ss, Red Wings	.325	126	18	41	6	0	0	17	6
Evan Holland, cf, Salt Cats	.325	114	19	37	5	4	1	12	18

INDIVIDUAL PITCHING LEADERS

	W	L	ERA	G	SV	IP	H	BB	SO
Vince Apicella, Red Wings	7	0	0.30	8	0	61	30	20	77
Matthew Wood, Chiefs	3	1	0.70	13	0	39	25	13	26
Cameron Jack, Salt Cats	2	0	1.13	9	1	32	19	12	26
Robert Greathouse, Niagara	2	0	1.27	12	1	35	30	11	16
David Ehmen, Oneonta	4	0	1.32	8	0	48	40	13	36
Jordan Wilkerson, Twins	4	0	1.39	5	0	32	22	7	25
Nate Verst, Cortland	2	0	1.54	13	1	35	21	16	24
Mitchell Powers, Geneva	6	1	1.55	8	0	58	42	5	47
Brandon Mumaw, Niagara	6	1	1.58	9	1	63	52	9	52
Nick Banman, Sherrill	0	3	1.76	6	0	41	30	8	25

NORTHWOODS LEAGUE

NORTHERN DIVISION	W	L	PCT	GB
St. Cloud Rox	49	23	.681	—
Willmar Stingers	47	24	.662	1½
Duluth Huskies	40	32	.556	9
Rochester Honkers	39	33	.542	10
Thunder Bay Border Cats	33	38	.465	15½
Mankato MoonDogs	33	39	.458	16
Waterloo Bucks	31	41	.431	18
Alexandria Blue Anchors	30	42	.417	19
Eau Claire Express	29	42	.408	19½

SOUTHERN DIVISION	W	L	PCT	GB
Kenosha Kingfish	48	24	.667	—
Madison Mallards	43	28	.606	4½
Green Bay Bullfrogs	41	30	.577	6½
La Crosse Loggers	40	31	.563	7½
Lakeshore Chinooks	36	36	.500	12
Wisconsin Rapids Rafters	33	35	.485	13
Battle Creek Bombers	27	44	.380	20½
Wisconsin Woodchucks	24	47	.338	23½
Kalamazoo Growlers	17	55	.236	31

CHAMPIONSHIP: Kenosha defeated St. Cloud 2-0 in best-of-three series.

TOP 10 PROSPECTS: 1. Lake Bachar, rhp, Lakeshore (Jr., Wisconsin-Whitewater). **2.** Scott Moss, lhp, Madison (R-So., Florida). **3.** Brock Lundquist, of/dh, La Crosse (So., Long Beach State). **4.** Anthony Gonsolin, of/rhp, Madison (Sr., St. Mary's). **5.** Greg Deichmann, 2b/3b, Lakeshore (So., Louisiana State). **6.** Zach Pop, rhp, St. Cloud (So., Kentucky). **7.** A.J. Bogucki, rhp, Madison (Jr., North Carolina). **8.** Mike

Kaelin, rhp, Madison (R-Jr., Buffalo). **9.** Colby Fitch, c, Lakeshore (So., Louisville). **10.** Mason McCoy, ss/2b, La Crosse (Jr., Iowa).

INDIVIDUAL BATTING LEADERS

	AVG	AB	R	H	2B	3B	HR	RBI	SB
Mason McCoy, if, La Crosse	.367	305	80	112	21	4	9	43	15
Jared James, of, Thunder Bay	.364	231	48	84	16	5	5	30	3
Dan Rizzie, c, Thunder Bay	.357	154	21	55	15	0	1	25	3
Eddie Estrada, 3b, Willmar	.356	135	27	48	11	1	2	31	5
Matt Fiedler, of, Rochester	.354	147	28	52	6	0	8	37	9
Brian Celsi, of, Green Bay	.348	132	19	46	7	1	1	25	12
Robb Paller, of, Green Bay	.345	177	39	61	13	1	3	34	6
Logan Regnier, of, Madison	.344	209	35	72	6	1	1	15	9
Eric Filia, of, Kenosha	.340	262	48	89	17	2	6	55	22
Ricky Sanchez, 1b, Alexandria	.336	226	42	76	11	8	10	41	5

INDIVIDUAL PITCHING LEADERS

	W	L	ERA	G	SV	IP	H	BB	SO
Trevor Charpie, St. Cloud	3	1	0.68	23	11	40	23	9	42
Josh Serio, Kenosha	6	1	0.89	7	0	40	25	14	46
Jake Stolley, Green Bay	2	1	0.95	25	4	38	23	12	35
Alex Hermeling, Battle Creek	3	3	1.17	9	0	54	33	12	52
Jordan Desquin, Waterloo	3	2	1.25	6	0	36	20	11	37
Jordan Jess, La Crosse	4	1	1.38	21	1	33	18	14	46
Ryan Orr, Kenosha	3	0	1.39	26	3	45	31	9	42
Reese Gregory, St. Cloud	6	3	1.46	10	0	68	50	22	66
Garrett Harrison, Green Bay	4	2	1.53	8	0	53	41	17	43
Kaleb McCurry, Battle Creek	2	1	1.62	25	2	39	40	12	40

OHIO VALLEY LEAGUE

	W	L	PCT	GB
Dubois County Bombers	26	14	.650	—
Madisonville Miners	25	15	.625	1
Fulton Railroaders	25	15	.625	1
Hopkinsville Hoppers	14	26	.350	12
Owensboro Oilers	10	30	.250	16

CHAMPIONSHIP: Dubois County defeated Madisonville 2-1 in best-of-three series.

INDIVIDUAL BATTING LEADERS

	AVG	AB	R	H	2B	3B	HR	RBI	SB
Drake McNamara, Dubois Cty.	.389	126	25	49	7	0	4	38	2
Daniel Johnson, Dubois Cty.	.382	102	25	39	9	1	1	16	15
Brad Baldwin, Fulton	.376	149	36	56	6	2	5	31	4
Ernie de la Trinidad, Hopkins.	.373	161	39	60	11	2	3	24	16
Ben Rhodes, Owensboro	.359	103	21	37	4	1	0	11	14
Alfredo Bohorques, Owens.	.353	119	16	42	5	0	0	9	9
Connor Moss, Madisonville	.338	148	34	50	5	1	1	23	10
Tyler Tichenor, Owensboro	.338	145	23	49	3	2	0	24	9
Griffin Neuer, Fulton	.331	160	38	53	7	1	2	20	5
Nolan Ramsey, Madisonville	.331	139	21	46	10	0	3	26	3

INDIVIDUAL PITCHING LEADERS

	W	L	ERA	IP	H	R	ER	BB	SO
Charlie Hecht, Fulton	5	2	1.54	58	61	21	10	11	44
Willie Poe, Dubois County	3	1	1.82	40	39	13	8	12	20
Lucas Barnett, Dubois County	2	2	1.83	44	47	17	9	15	24
Kyle Vedrode, Madisonville	2	0	1.96	37	36	10	8	9	28
Dillon Symon, Fulton	2	2	2.30	43	39	14	11	16	23
Ryan Dills, Dubois County	5	0	2.37	38	41	14	10	10	45
Zach Freeman, Dubois County	4	3	2.44	48	41	22	13	18	36
Eddie Mathis, Fulton	3	1	2.47	40	32	11	11	6	48
Mathias Brewers, Madisonville	4	1	2.67	30	32	13	9	13	32
Zachary Aring, Dubois County	4	2	2.87	47	47	29	15	18	46

PROSPECT LEAGUE

EASTERN DIVISION	W	L	PCT	GB
Chillicothe Paints	38	22	.633	—
West Virginia Miners	35	24	.593	2 ½
Butler BlueSox	33	27	.550	5
Jamestown Jammers	27	33	.450	11
Champion City Kings	24	35	.407	13 ½
Richmond RiverRats	22	35	.386	14 ½

WESTERN DIVISION	W	L	PCT	GB
Terre Haute Rex	43	17	.717	—
Danville Dans	31	29	.517	12
Kokomo Jackrabbits	30	30	.500	13
Springfield Sliders	29	30	.492	13 ½
Quincy Gems	27	33	.450	16
Hannibal Cavemen	16	40	.286	25

CHAMPIONSHIP: Terre Haute defeated West Virginia 2-0 in best-of-three series.

TOP 10 PROSPECTS: 1. Tanner Allison, lhp, Chillicothe (So., Western Michigan). **2.** David Marcus, 1b, Butler (Sr., California (Pa.)). **3.** Matt Anderson, rhp, West Virginia (Sr., Morehead State). **4.** Zach Sterry, 1b, West Virginia (Jr., Oakland). **5.** Eric Solberg, ss, Jamestown (Jr., Wisconsin-Milwaukee). **6.** Evan Miller, rhp, Terre Haute (So., IPFW). **7.** Andrew Gutierrez, of, Terre Haute (Jr., Indiana State). **8.** Zach Spangler, rhp, Butler (So., Kent State). **9.** Matt Wivinis, rhp, Danville (Sr., Eastern Illinois). **10.** Deion Tansel, ss, Chillicothe (Sr., Toledo).

INDIVIDUAL BATTING LEADERS

	AVG	AB	R	H	2B	3B	HR	RBI	SB
David Jacob, Springfield	.400	140	21	56	9	2	4	34	0
Aiden McMahan, Richmond	.390	141	22	55	10	2	3	22	2
Dan Ward, West Virginia	.374	147	33	55	10	4	2	33	9
David Marcus, Butler	.363	223	32	81	18	1	11	49	3
Deion Tansel, Chillicothe	.346	240	32	83	17	2	0	25	28
Troy Paris, Richmond	.339	192	28	65	13	3	1	24	2
Matt Hansen, Butler	.338	225	37	76	7	2	0	29	11
Justin Wylie, Quincy	.331	163	25	54	12	2	4	24	8
Mathew Priebe, Champ. City	.323	164	25	53	10	0	3	26	1
Zach Sterry, West Virginia	.316	193	39	61	17	2	2	36	8

INDIVIDUAL PITCHING LEADERS

	W	L	ERA	G	SV	IP	H	BB	SO
Samuel Higgs, Terre Haute	6	0	0.67	9	0	54	35	13	39
Tanner Allison, Chillicothe	8	0	1.07	10	0	59	32	17	56
Matt Anderson, West Virginia	5	0	1.10	6	0	41	32	14	47
Jarrett Bednar, Kokomo	4	0	1.15	7	0	31	26	4	26
Brian Allec, Danville	5	2	1.24	23	3	44	26	17	29
Connor Law, Springfield	2	0	1.27	7	1	35	23	11	23
Cody Maerz, Jamestown	2	1	1.34	5	0	34	27	10	17
Mark Zimmerman, Kokomo	2	2	1.41	8	1	38	25	10	45
J.T. Baksha, Quincy	4	2	1.44	14	0	44	32	20	34
Matt Minnick, Jamestown	1	3	1.51	20	2	42	32	12	27

SUNBELT COLLEGIATE LEAGUE

EASTERN DIVISION	W	L	PCT	GB
Atlanta Crackers	23	8	.742	—
Gwinnett Tides	17	12	.586	5
Brookhaven Bucks	15	13	.536	6 ½
Alpharetta Braves	10	17	.370	11

WESTERN DIVISION	W	L	PCT	GB
Phenix City Crawdads	18	12	.600	—
Norcross Astros	12	17	.414	5 ½
Douglasville Bulls	10	16	.385	6
Marietta Patriots	8	18	.308	8

CHAMPIONSHIP: Atlanta defeated Phenix City 2-0 in best-of-three series.

INDIVIDUAL BATTING LEADERS

	AVG	AB	R	H	2B	3B	HR	RBI	SB
Cletis Avery, ss, Atlanta	.405	126	29	51	13	4	0	19	17
Cole Thompson, c, Atlanta	.376	85	15	32	9	0	2	13	0
Gage Patton, 2b, Atlanta	.330	109	14	36	7	0	3	19	2
Rodney Tennie, of, Norcross	.330	91	16	30	3	1	0	10	11
Brandon Harmon, cf, Gwinn.	.318	88	19	28	4	1	1	11	11
Corey Greeson, 3b, Douglas.	.315	89	17	28	4	1	3	14	9
Kyle Jackson, of, Atlanta	.303	109	20	33	10	1	3	22	5
Will Johnson, of, Brookhaven	.294	85	23	25	3	1	0	9	12
A.J. Spencer, if, Atlanta	.281	89	16	25	3	1	1	14	4
Jake Wilkinson, if, Norcross	.277	83	9	23	3	1	0	9	4

INDIVIDUAL PITCHING LEADERS

	W	L	ERA	G	SV	IP	H	BB	SO
Tucker Simpson, Douglasville	3	0	0.00	4	0	28	9	4	42
Michael Livingston, Marietta	3	0	0.87	7	0	41	29	12	33

	W	L	ERA	G	SV	IP	H	BB	SO
Logan Elliot, Alpharetta	2	2	1.36	7	0	40	28	9	36
Joseph Marlow, Atlanta	5	0	1.47	7	0	43	34	8	37
A.J. Moore, Gwinnett	4	0	1.64	6	0	38	28	6	48
Jamie Sexton, Atlanta	6	1	1.77	8	0	56	55	10	54
David Bermudez, Atlanta	5	2	2.08	9	0	61	47	8	47
Chance Hicks, Phenix City	0	0	2.25	11	1	20	14	9	21
Jerry Stuckey, Douglasville	2	4	2.38	9	0	53	47	10	63
Jeremy Holcomb, Atlanta	2	1	2.48	6	0	33	34	16	26

TEXAS COLLEGIATE LEAGUE

	W	L	PCT	GB
Brazos Valley Bombers	42	9	.824	—
Victoria Generals	35	19	.648	8½
Acadiana Cane Cutters	32	23	.582	12
East Texas Pump Jacks	25	28	.472	18
Woodlands Strykers	13	36	.265	28
Texas Marshals	11	43	.204	32½

CHAMPIONSHIP: Brazos Valley defeated Acadiana 2-0 in best-of-three series.

TOP 10 PROSPECTS: 1. Garrett Benge, 3b, Brazos Valley (So., Oklahoma State). **2.** Tyler Stubblefield, lhp, Brazos Valley (Jr., Texas A&M). **3.** Dakota Mills, rhp, Victoria (R-So., Sam Houston State). **4.** Dakota Mekkes, rhp, Brazos Valley (R-So., Michigan State). **5.** Chance Vincent, ss/3b, Acadiana (Sr., Alabama). **6.** Geonte Jackson, 3b/1b, Brazos Valley (Sr., Texas-San Antonio). **7.** Ethan Landon, rhp, Brazos Valley (R-So., Michigan State). **8.** Tyler Adams, rhp, East Texas (R-So., Alabama). **9.** Daniel Keating, of, Acadiana (So., Southern Mississippi). **10.** Zak Kutsulis, of/1b, Acadiana (Sr., Notre Dame).

INDIVIDUAL BATTING LEADERS

	AVG	AB	R	H	2B	3B	HR	RBI	SB
Geonte Jackson, Brazos Val.	.379	145	37	55	6	0	3	27	12
Tyler Lawrence, Brazos Val.	.367	120	32	44	10	0	1	16	1
Zak Kutsulis, Acadiana	.349	169	35	59	9	2	0	21	17
Daniel Keating, Acadiana	.335	179	32	60	13	3	1	20	31
Romero Cortina, Victoria	.326	132	26	43	14	0	4	26	3
Taylor Braley, Acadiana	.324	102	16	33	4	0	1	8	3
Pedro Barrios, Victoria	.322	171	29	55	4	4	0	26	9
Donivan Lopez, Victoria	.313	131	17	41	8	1	0	17	12
Trent Goodrich, Brazos Val.	.311	164	29	51	11	1	0	34	7
T.J. Friedl, East Texas	.306	134	22	41	4	3	0	13	19

INDIVIDUAL PITCHING LEADERS

	W	L	ERA	G	SV	IP	H	BB	SO
Nolan Trabanino, Victoria	4	0	0.77	5	0	35	25	12	30
Ethan Landon, Brazos Valley	4	0	0.92	7	0	39	36	9	24
C.J. Gregory, Brazos Valley	8	1	1.34	16	1	40	24	15	37
Daniel Martinez, Acadiana	8	1	1.40	10	0	58	42	7	43
Chris Cooper, Woodlands	4	1	1.48	17	1	43	38	11	34
John Caskey, East Texas	6	2	1.73	8	0	52	44	7	36
Kirk McCarty, Acadiana	2	1	1.87	5	0	34	27	5	24
Mike Walker, Brazos Valley	4	1	2.22	9	0	53	41	22	33
Frank Miller, East Texas	4	1	2.36	13	0	61	52	24	37
Dakota Mills, Victoria	1	1	2.37	6	0	30	29	7	36

VALLEY LEAGUE

NORTHERN DIVISION	W	L	PCT	GB
Front Royal Cardinals	22	20	.523	—
Strasburg Express	21	21	.500	1
Aldie Senators	21	21	.500	1
Woodstock River Bandits	20	22	.476	2
Winchester Royals	20	22	.476	2
Charles Town Cannons	16	26	.384	6

SOUTHERN DIVISION	W	L	PCT	GB
Staunton Braves	29	13	.690	—
Harrisonburg Turks	29	13	.690	—
Waynesboro Generals	22	20	.524	7
Covington Lumberjacks	18	24	.429	11
Charlottesville TomSox	18	24	.429	11
New Market Rebels	16	26	.381	13

CHAMPIONSHIP: Strasburg defeated Staunton 2-1 in best-of-three series.

TOP 10 PROSPECTS: 1. Shane Billings, of, Harrisonburg (Jr., Wingate (N.C.)). **2.** Jim Ziemba, lhp, Harrisonburg, (R-So., Duke). **3.** Bradley Jones, if, Charles Town (Jr., College of Charleston). **4.** Devin Gould, rhp, Staunton (Jr., Longwood). **5.** Jack Schaaf, of, Staunton, (So., Florida International). **6.** Steven Ridings, rhp, Charles Town, (Sr., Messiah (Pa.)). **7.** Edgar Lebron, of, Front Royal (Sr., Lindsey Wilson (Ky.)). **8.** Tyler Staub, if, Harrisonburg (Sr., Texas-San Antonio). **9.** Garrett Vrbanic, 2b/ss, Aldie (Jr., Seton Hill). **10.** Matt Hartman, rhp, Harrisonburg, (So., Arizona).

INDIVIDUAL BATTING LEADERS

	AVG	AB	R	H	2B	3B	HR	RBI	SB
Shane Billings, of, Harrison.	.418	153	45	64	6	4	2	15	21
Andrew Seigel, cf, Aldie	.373	110	20	41	5	2	0	17	14
Christian Khawam, of, Charles	.367	109	15	40	6	1	2	11	4
Austin Edens, 1b, Staunton	.352	142	13	50	9	1	3	27	1
Dre Small, cf, Front Royal	.344	154	30	53	3	1	1	14	14
Drew Johnson, 3b, Strasburg	.333	153	18	51	11	2	3	28	3
Jared Baker, of, Harrisonburg	.333	138	21	46	6	3	1	23	1
Bradley Jones, 3b, Charles	.333	117	19	39	12	0	6	24	5
Zachary Carter, of, Winchester	.327	159	35	52	11	2	4	28	14
Bobby Lang, rf, Front Royal	.327	104	17	34	5	1	1	13	4

INDIVIDUAL PITCHING LEADERS

	W	L	ERA	G	SV	IP	H	BB	SO
Cody Strayer, Covington	0	3	1.17	18	7	31	27	10	26
Daniel Johnson, Charlottesville	1	2	1.51	13	4	36	34	10	42
Hayden McCutcheon, Charlottesville	3	1	1.75	12	0	46	31	14	58
Jake Perkins, Staunton	3	1	1.79	8	0	45	33	22	30
Reid Van Woert, Aldie	2	0	1.80	8	0	45	38	12	31
Alex Britt, New Market	2	0	1.80	6	0	30	28	10	30
Dillon Drabble, Charles Town	3	1	1.99	16	1	32	23	11	28
Corey Sessions, Front Royal	5	2	2.01	10	0	40	29	6	20
James Ziemba, Harrisonburg	3	1	2.08	9	0	35	22	10	22
Matt Picucci, Covington	3	2	2.08	6	0	30	27	10	22

WEST COAST LEAGUE

EASTERN DIVISION

	W	L	PCT	GB
Kelowna Falcons	34	19	.642	—
Yakima Valley Pippins	29	25	.537	5 ½
Wenatchee AppleSox	24	30	.444	10 ½
Walla Walla Sweets	22	31	.415	12

WESTERN DIVISION

	W	L	PCT	GB
Bellingham Bells	33	21	.611	—
Victoria HarbourCats	29	24	.547	3 ½
Kitsap BlueJackets	23	30	.434	9 ½
Cowlitz Black Bears	21	33	.389	12

SOUTHERN DIVISION

	W	L	PCT	GB
Bend Elks	35	16	.686	—
Corvallis Knights	32	22	.593	4 ½
Medford Rogues	25	27	.481	10 ½
Klamath Falls Gems	12	41	.226	24

CHAMPIONSHIP: Bend defeated Kelowna 2-0 in best-of-three series.
TOP 10 PROSPECTS: 1. Cadyn Grenier, ss, Bend (Fr., Oregon State). **2.** Joe DeMers, rhp, Walla Walla (Fr., Washington). **3.** Kyle Molnar, rhp, Walla Walla (Fr., UCLA). **4.** Keston Hiura, of, Wenatchee (So., UC Irvine). **5.** Easton Lucas, lhp, Walla Walla (Fr., Pepperdine). **6.** A.J. Graffanino, ss, Cowlitz (Fr., Washington). **7.** Ryan Walker, rhp, Corvallis (So., Washington State). **8.** Nick Madrigal, ss, Corvallis (Fr., Oregon State). **9.** Justin Calomeni, rhp, Bellingham (Jr., Cal Poly). **10.** Willie MacIver, c, Walla Walla (Fr., Washington).

INDIVIDUAL BATTING LEADERS

	AVG	AB	R	H	2B	3B	HR	RBI	SB
Griffin Andreychuk, 2b, Vic.	.385	104	34	40	4	0	5	25	6
Hunter Villanueva, if, Kel.	.378	164	37	62	12	0	7	33	3
Justin Flores, 1b, Kelowna	.358	159	37	57	12	0	8	39	2
Keston Hiura, of, Wenatchee	.356	191	39	68	21	6	6	42	13
West Tunnell, if, Bend	.356	180	36	64	14	3	5	39	7
Tyler Davis, if, Bend	.352	199	40	70	25	0	7	50	1
Billy King, 1b, Bend	.336	128	24	43	8	0	0	11	1
A.J. Alcantara, of, Victoria	.330	100	13	33	8	2	2	21	1
Cadyn Grenier, ss, Bend	.329	167	45	55	13	3	3	27	11
Emilio Alcantar, of, Corvallis	.329	161	28	53	5	1	0	28	26

INDIVIDUAL PITCHING LEADERS

	W	L	ERA	G	SV	IP	H	BB	SO
John Oltman, Kitsap	3	0	1.13	10	0	48	28	9	28
Adam Cline, Kitsap	3	1	1.14	6	0	39	28	9	42
D.J. Wilson, Kelowna	3	1	1.16	17	3	31	20	5	21
Michael Koval, Kelowna	4	0	1.17	7	1	31	20	6	28
Andrew Kemmerer, Bellingham	4	0	1.45	9	0	56	43	13	34
Chris Clements, Corvallis	2	2	1.72	9	0	37	28	5	25
Joe Balfour, Cowlitz	4	1	2.03	7	0	44	43	10	17
Joe DeMers, Walla Walla	1	1	2.08	12	1	30	22	10	27
Kelly Fitzpatrick, Yakima Valley	1	2	2.14	19	1	34	32	15	26
Brady Miller, Kelowna	6	0	2.19	7	0	37	29	15	23

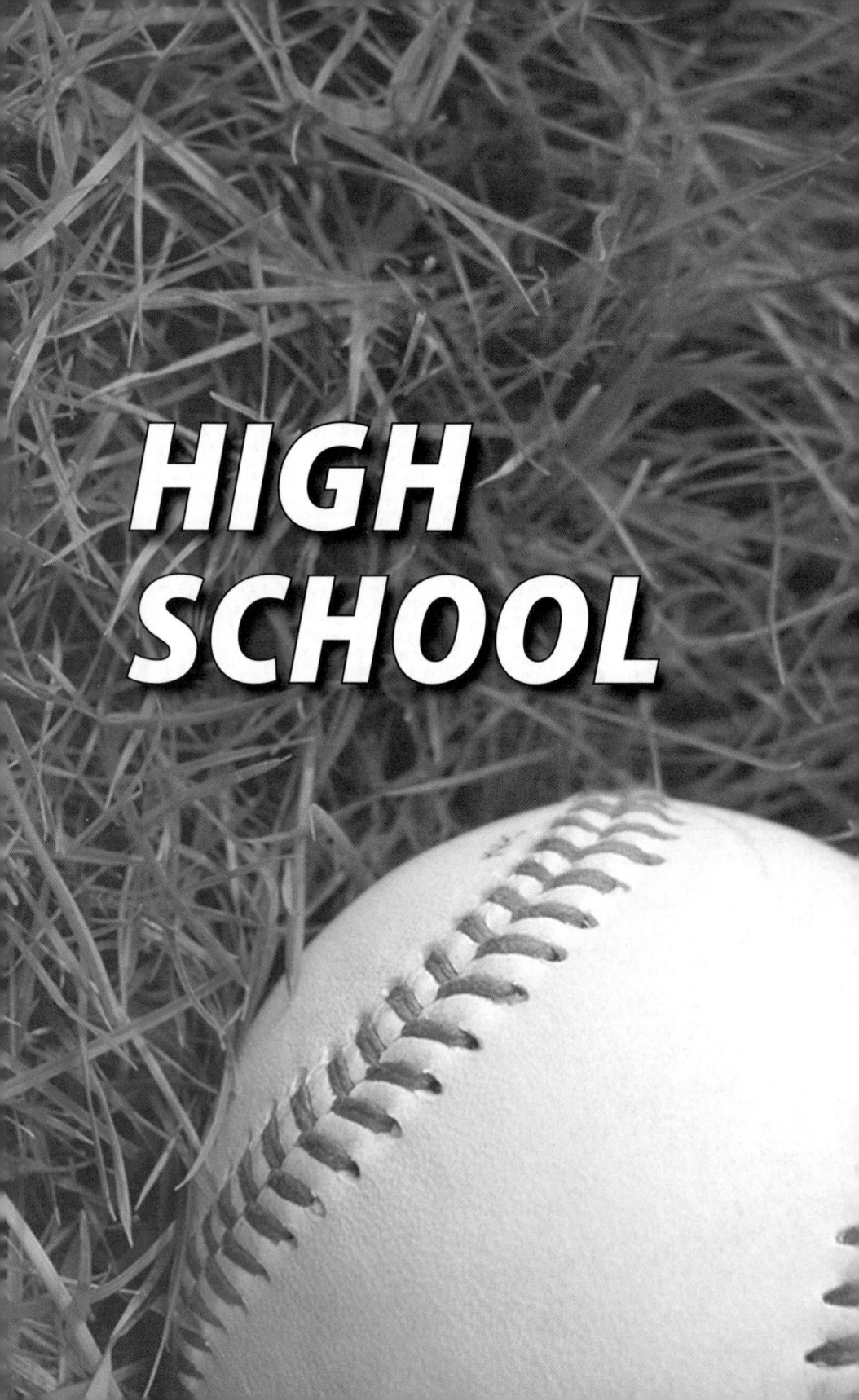

HIGH SCHOOL

Top-ranked Parkview High celebrates its third Georgia state championship in five years

Winning streak puts Parkview back on top

For the second time in four years, Parkview High (Lilburn, Ga.) won Baseball America's 2015 High School Team of the Year Award.

The Panthers finished with a 34-2 record, including a season-ending 26-game winning streak that culminated with a two-game sweep of Walton High to secure Parkview's third Georgia 6-A state championship in the last five years, and a spot atop the final Baseball America/National High School Baseball Coaches Association national poll.

Before all those wins, however, came a single loss that head coach Chan Brown credits as the turning point for his team's season. It was also the last game they would lose.

Brown challenged his players to focus on the details needed to become great players, and just as importantly, a great team

"At that point we talked about a saying I came up with: 'Be special,' " Brown said. "Our kids believed in having great pitching, great defense and timely hitting. They started believing and doing all the little things right. It's obviously very special for our program to win the last 26 games and go 34-2."

Parkview's season also included a title at the third-annual Perfect Game High School Showdown on March 14 when they beat nationally ranked No. 21 Kennesaw Mountain High,

from Marietta, Ga.

The Panthers were led on the mound by senior Ryne Inman and junior Will Ethridge.

In Game One of the state championship series, Inman threw a complete-game shutout, his third of the year, and the 6-foot-5 Ethridge, a transfer to Parkview before the season, followed with a complete game victory of his own to seal the title, allowing just one run.

"We kind of had two No. 1's going," Brown said of his two aces. "Ryne took it upon his shoulders and said he's going to work his tail off all pre-season and offseason and get to the point where he wanted to be of winning a state championship and being drafted. Our kids rallied around those two and they knew when the Inman-Ethridge crew had the ball that we were going to win ballgames."

Inman was selected by the Mariners in the 15th round just a couple of weeks after the season and signed with the club to begin his professional career rather than play for Georgia State. Ethridge is considered a projectable prospect for the 2016 draft, armed with a fastball that can reach into the low 90s and a lean frame with wide shoulders and room to add strength.

"Our pitching staff was fantastic the whole year," junior catcher and Georgia commit Austin Biggar said. "Catching both Ryne and Will was a

HIGH SCHOOL TOP 50

Rank	School	Record
1.	Parkview High, Lilburn, Ga.	34-2
2.	Bishop Gorman High, Las Vegas	33-3
3.	Venice (Fla.) High	29-3
4.	Oxford (Miss.) High	33-1
5.	Canyon Del Oro High, Oro Valley, Ariz.	32-3
6.	Buford (Ga.) High	34-2
7.	DeSoto Central (Miss.)	27-8
8.	Christopher Columbus High, Miami	27-5
9.	College Park High, Pleasant Hill, Calif.	24-4
10.	Buchanan High, Clovis, Calif.	29-4
11.	Archbishop McCarthy High, Southwest Ranches, Fla.	27-5
12.	Barbe High, Lake Charles, La.	34-10
13.	Archbishop Moeller High, Cincinnati	31-3
14.	St. Francis High, Mountain View, Calif.	29-5
15.	Cullman (Ala.) High	45-10
16.	Owasso (Okla.) High	32-7
17.	Huntington Beach (Calif.) High	25-8
18.	Greenbrier High, Evans, Ga.	30-4
19.	Pleasant Grove (Utah) High	27-3
20.	Cypress (Texas) Ranch High	31-9
21.	Jefferson High, Shenandoh Junction, W.V.	37-2
22.	Rancho Bernardo High, San Diego	26-7
23.	Prosper (Texas) High	35-3
24.	James Madison High, Vienna, Va.	24-5
25.	West Jessamine High, Nicholasville, Kent.	36-7
26.	St. Thomas More High, Lafayette, La.	30-9
27.	George Washington High, New York	24-1
28.	Omaha (Ne.) Westside High	32-5
29.	Bentonville (Ark.) High	21-8
30.	Westminster Christian High, Miami	23-7
31.	Christian Brothers College Prep, St. Louis	32-7
32.	San Dimas (Calif.) High	31-1
33.	Rock Canyon High, Highland, Col.	27-2
34.	Jserra Catholic High, San Juan Capistrano, Calif.	27-5
35.	Sheridan (Ark.) High	24-8
36.	Blessed Trinity Catholic High, Roswell, Ga.	33-2
37.	Sheldon High, Eugene, Ore.	27-5
38.	Liberty High, Peoria, Ariz.	29-6
39.	Hardin Valley Academy, Knoxville, Tenn.	30-15
40.	Wando High, Mount Pleasant, S.C.	25-8
41.	Providence High, Charlotte, N.C.	29-3
42.	Ston Bridge High, Ashburn, Va.	24-5
43.	Don Bosco Prep, Ramsey, N.J.	34-2
44.	Lawrence Free State High, Lawrence, Kansas	21-4
45.	Conway (Ark.) High	22-4
46.	La Costa Canyon High, Carlsbad, Calif.	26-7
47.	Catholic High, Baton Rouge, La.	37-5
48.	Tottenville High, Staten Island, N.Y.	23-2
49.	Mount Carmel (Ill.) High	35-4
50.	Joseph Craig High, Janesville, Wisc.	26-1

just kind of controlled the tempo behind the plate and offensively, he struggled at the beginning, but then he really clicked in and got focused.

"He's going to be a huge asset for us to have back next year."

Biggar credited his success this season to the coaching staff, and going out and executing what they taught him both offensively and defensively.

Parkview's success came after losing several key contributors from their 2014 squad, notably lefthander Mac Marshall and first baseman Isiah Gilliam—both of whom graduated last year and were drafted before going on to play for Chipola (Fla.) JC in 2015.

"Losing those two, we were obviously worried about losing the arm and the huge bat," Brown said of the two 2014 graduates. "But that all fell on the juniors that were going to be seniors and those guys took it upon themselves.

"I think losing Marshall and Gilliam motivated them even more to say, 'Look, just because we are losing these guys, we can still do this.' "

Led by powerful first baseman Matt Olson, who entered 2015 as the Athletics' No. 3 prospect, Parkview also took home the honor of High School Team of the Year in 2012.

"Tradition speaks, and the tradition year after year is a big thing for us," Brown said. "Hanging up signs on our outfield wall. They wanted to leave with two signs, but at the senior dinner they mentioned having a third sign, and winning a national championship. This crew of seniors, they had a vision and they worked towards that."

Champions Rule

There was no shortage of state champions on the High School Top 50.

Bishop Gorman High (Las Vegas) took home its first Nevada Division I state title in dramatic fashion en route to finishing the season with a 33-3 record and No. 2 national ranking.

Bishop Gorman, undefeated in the state tournament, trailed Green Valley High by four runs in the seventh inning of the championship series and faced the possibility of having to play a winner-take-all game. Then senior Austin Cram hit a two-out, two-run homer to tie the game at five before senior Cadyn Grenier ended it two innings later with a walk-off homer for a 6-5 win.

"This team is never out," Grenier told the Las Vegas Review Journal. "And we showed it again today. We were down by four in the last inning and once again came back and did exactly what we had to do."

Fourth-ranked Oxford (Miss.) High suffered its only loss of the season in the second game of

tremendous honor for me. Getting to know those guys throughout the year, especially Will having just transferred in, catching them was amazing. (I) just had to command them well, they did most of the job."

Offensively, the team was led by Biggar, who hit .370/.492/.760 with six doubles, 11 homers and 48 RBIs. His two-run homer in Game Two of the championship series was more than enough for Ethridge, a Mississippi commit.

"From two separate standpoints he dictated a game," Brown said of Biggar. "He threw out well over half the amount of guys who tried to steal on him and he had only two passed balls all year. He

2015 ALL AREA CODE GAMES TEAM

Position	Player	Area Code Team	School
C	Cooper Johnson	White Sox	Carmel Catholic High, Mundelein, Ill.
1B	Chris Winkel	Yankees	Amity Regional High, Woodbridge, Conn.
2B	Bo Bichette	Nationals	Lakewood High, St. Petersburg, Fla.
3B	Austin Shenton	Royals	Bellingham (Wash.) High
SS	Nolan Jones	Yankees	Holy Ghost Prep, Bensalem, Pa.
OF	Blake Rutherford	Brewers	Chaminade College Prep, Canoga, Calif.
OF	Mickey Moniak	Brewers	La Costa Canyon High, Carlsbad, Calif.
OF	Brandon McIlwain	Yankees	Council Rock North, Newtown, Pa.
DH	Ulysses Cantu	Rangers	Boswell High, Fort Worth, Texas
P	Riley Pint	White Sox	St. Thomas Aquinas High, Overland Park, Kansas
P	Jason Groome	Yankees	Barnegat (N.J.) High
P	Jesus Luzardo	Nationals	Stoneman Douglas High, Parkland, Fla.
P	Reggie Lawson	Brewers	Victor Valley High, Victorville, Calif.
P	Kevin Gowdy	Brewers	Santa Barbara (Calif.) High

its conference tournament final before rallying to win the decisive Game Three and then sweeping through the state tournament for the Chargers' first 5A state title.

No. 5 Canyon Del Oro High won its eighth Arizona state crown in dramatic fashion, fending off a rally from top-seeded Tucson by securing the final out of the bottom of the seventh at home plate on a wild pitch.

A five-run seventh inning led Desoto Central (Miss.) past Oak Grove and to a sweep of the Class 6A state championship series played at the Mississippi Braves' Trustmark Park. The victory, helped by Braves supplemental first-round pick Austin Riley, avenged a loss to Oak Grove in the 2014 state championship.

University of Washington commit Joe DeMers tossed six innings of relief, yielding one run and striking out 10, to lift No. 9 College Park High (Pleasant Hill, Calif.) past De La Salle High for the North Coast Section Division I title.

San Clemente Takes NHSI

In a grudge match between powerhouses from Northern and Southern California, SoCal prevailed, with San Clemente (Calif.) High defeating College Park (Calif.) High 8-3 on March 28. San Clemente's victory earned them the crown at the fourth annual National High School Invitational.

Armed with six Division 1 commits and a polished senior class, the Tritons took care of business without ace lefthander and eventual Braves first round pick Kolby Allard, who missed most of the season with a back injury. Despite not having Allard, San Clemente's pitching was outstanding throughout the event. Righthander Tanner Lawson got the start for the championship game, and he did not disappoint. Lawson did not allow a hit until the fourth inning, when the Tritons already held a 4-0 lead. Lawson filled the strike zone with a heavy, mid-80s fastball, and topped out at 88 mph.

"We are deep in pitching," San Clemente coach Dave Gellatly said. Gellatly went on to talk about the impact that senior catcher Lucas Herbert has on the Tritons.

"(Herbert) calls such a great game ... we haven't called one pitch all year long. He knows how to get hitters out, he knows how to block balls, he knows when to backpick and he makes us look like great coaches. It's all him."

Herbert was in control throughout the tournament and in the championship game, both behind the plate and with his powerful righthanded bat. In the fourth inning of the championship game, the future Braves prospect punched an outside fastball into the gap in right center field, driving in two runs and boosting San Clemente's lead to 6-1. Herbert's final plate appearance represented San Clemente's week in North Carolina rather well. He drew a nine-pitch walk that included several deep, towering foul balls. Herbert, like his San Clemente team, was patiently intimidating, capable of striking at any moment, but also willing to wait for the right opportunities.

The Tritons called on lefthander Dylan Riddle in the fifth inning. Riddle was impossible to figure out; he struck out three in 2 2/3 scoreless, hitless innings to finish off San Clemente's win.

"(San Clemente) hit the snot out of the ball today," College Park coach Andy Tarpley said. It was a tough loss for the Falcons, but Tarpley was happy with his squad's growth.

San Clemente improved to 12-0 with the win, having beaten many of the nation's best teams. The Tritons eventually lost in the CIF Southern Section Playoffs, but their victory at NHSI will stand forever as the pinnacle of San Clemente's historic 2015 class.

Evoshield Canes Three-Peat

Throughout the World Wood Bat Association World Championship in Jupiter, Fla., the

Evoshield Canes pitchers dominated opposing hitters. The Canes opened the tournament with a combined no-hitter, allowed just one run in eight games and got complete game shutouts in each of their final three games.

Propelled by that pitching and some timely hitting, the Canes won the tournament for an unprecedented third straight year. No other team has even won back-to-back titles in the event's 15-year history.

With only catcher Brad Debo returning from last year's team, coach Jeff Petty said he wanted to win with this team.

"They're different from the last group," he said. "I guess it makes us feel like we've been doing a good job for multiple years. But it's a different group and it speaks volumes of how good our organization is from top to bottom with our coaches and our scouting staff and everyone that's involved."

Righthander Matt Manning (Sheldon High, Sacramento) was named the tournament's most valuable pitcher. He threw a five-inning shutout in the semifinals after throwing two scoreless innings in the no-hitter in the first game.

Catcher Brandon Martorano (Christian Brothers Academy, Lincroft, N.J.) took home most valuable player honors after hitting .400/.550/.800 with seven RBIs in eight games.

The Canes' victory came over Team Evoshield, another team in the Evoshield program that includes many of the top underclassmen in the country. Martorano said Team Evoshield's success shows how well the program set up for the future.

"They've had a great season, they did a great job down here," Martorano said of Team Evoshield. "No one really expected them to do this and for them to exceed expectations is phenomenal. For them to go out here and show how deep we are as an organization is just scary and I think everyone should take notice."

And the Canes' strength stretches even deeper into their system. Their 16U team made the semifinals of the WWBA Underclass World Championship earlier this month. Coach Rob Younce, who also serves as the Canes' national director of scouting, said those players are ready to continue the tradition.

"It's a great time to be a Cane right now."

Pint And Groome Could Top Draft

It's too early for answers.

The 2016 draft is far away, and there's still a spring season to play, still ground that can be made

up or lost. So, while an excellent platform, this summer's showcase circuit didn't provide answers. It isn't meant to. Instead, it provides intrigue. It sparks discussion. It raised questions. There's one question in particular that was asked all throughout the summer and will continue to be asked over and over again: Riley Pint or Jason Groome?

"Jason Groome has stayed here the entire week," Matt Hyde, a Northeast area scout for the Yankees and longtime coach of the organization's Area Code Games squad said, "which tells you a lot about him."

In this day and age of social media and increased exposure, blue-chip prospects are often on their own schedule, bouncing around from showcase to showcase. They don't always show up to team events; they play and move on.

"Usually they throw and they leave, and they go on to the next thing," Hyde said. "(Groome) stayed."

That sort of thing defines Groome. It's not that he isn't career-conscious. He is. That's what motivated him to leave his hometown school of Barnegat High and head to the star-making, prospect-grooming IMG Academy in Bradenton, Fla., for his junior year. It was there that he packed on weight and reinforced his frame.

But, more than anything, Groome loves playing baseball. He's a gamer. That's what stood out most to Hyde during the Area Codes process. And, ultimately, that's what motivated Groome, a Vanderbilt commit, to leave IMG and head back to Barnegat for his upcoming senior season.

"My friends are telling me they want to win a state championship with me, so that's what we're going for, so we can get it done," Groome said.

With Groome on the mound, they'll have as good a chance as any to win it.

Groome can already dial his fastball up to 96 mph and there's room for projection. His bread-and-butter is a tight 1-to-7 hook in the mid- to high-70s that—at its best—he can command in and out of the strike zone. Groome started throwing the pitch when he was 14, taught the grip by a friend on his travel ball team.

Pint is similar to Groome in some ways—armed with a power fastball and a promising arsenal of offspeed pitches and committed to play college baseball at a powerhouse program, Louisiana State. The righthander put on a show in his Area Codes start in August. His first two pitches were 98 mph, he flashed several 97s, and he settled into a 92-96 range with running movement and command. His breaking ball, which he throws with a knuckle-curve grip, flashed plus with a tight, sharp bite. He varied its shape and speed, throwing a harder slid-

USA BASEBALL

Event	Site	Champion	Runner-up
Tournament of Stars (18U)	Cary, N.C.	Brave	Stripes
USA Baseball 17U—East	Jupiter, Fla.	Team Elite	Georgia Jackets
USA Baseball 17U—West	Peoria, Ariz.	CBA Marucci Navy	Playa Vista Orioles National
USA Baseball 15U—East	Jupiter, Fla.	Team Elite	Palm Beach Select Underclass
USA Baseball 15U—West	Goodyear, Ariz.	SKLZ	Placentia Mustangs
USA Baseball 14U—East	Jupiter, Fla.	Florida Stealth	MVP Banditos
USA Baseball 14U—West	Peoria, Ariz.	BPA DeMarini	Zoots Baseball

ALL-AMERICAN AMATEUR BASEBALL ASSOCIATION (AAABA)

Event	Site	Champion	Runner-up
World Series (21-and-Under)	Johnstown, Pa.	New Orleans Boosters	Boston Astros

AMATEUR ATHLETIC UNION (AAU)

Event	Site	Champion	Runner-up
9-and-Under	Orlando	New Tampa Predators Elite	Oakleaf Knights Gold
10-and-Under Diamond (60-foot)	Orlando	Central Florida Wolverines Mahler	GBSA Rays
10-and-Under Gold (60-foot)	Orlando	Team Wicked	Central Florida Pride
11-and-Under Diamond (70-foot)	Orlando	Central Florida Wolverines Hoyle	Southshore Rockets
11-and-Under Gold (70-foot)	Orlando	The Clubhouse	PG Select Bluesox
12-and-Under Diamond (70-foot)	Orlando	Collier Tigers	SoCal Force
12-and-Under Gold (70-foot)	Orlando	Mid-Georgia Warriors	Cabarrus Bombers
13-and-Under Diamond (90-foot)	Orlando	Parkland Pokers Blue	Parkland Pokers
13-and-Under Gold (90-foot)	Orlando	Ocala Venom	Home Plate Chili Dogs
14-and-Under Super Showcase	Orlando	Florida Stealth Red and Florida Stealth Navy (Co-Champions)	
15-17 Super Showcase	Sarasota, Fla.	Wiregrass Cardinals 17U	LB Warriors Black

AMERICAN AMATEUR BASEBALL CONGRESS (AABC)

Event	Site	Champion	Runner-up
Pee Wee Reese (12 & U)	Toa Baja, P.R.	PL Siege	Cardenales PR
Sandy Koufax (14 & U)	Bartlesville, Okla.	Dallas Tigers Hernandez	Knights Baseball 14U National
Ken Griffey, Jr. (15 & U)	Surprise, Ariz.	D-Backs Academy	DBAT
Mickey Mantle (16 & U)	Frisco, Texas	Frozen Ropes	Dulin Dodgers
Don Mattingly (17 & U)	Surprise, Ariz.	Frozen Ropes	Trombly Braves
Connie Mack (18 & U)	Farmington, N.M.	East Cobb Yankees	Praire Gravel
Stan Musial (19+)	Farmingdale, N.Y.	Westchase Express	Long Island Storm

AMERICAN LEGION BASEBALL

Event	Site	Champion	Runner-up
World Series (19 & U)	Shelby, N.C.	Chapin-Newberry, S.C.	New Orleans, La.

BABE RUTH BASEBALL

Event	Site	Champion	Runner-up
Cal Ripken (10 & U)	Jonesboro, Ark.	Manatee, Fla.	Jonesboro, Ark.
Cal Ripken 12-year-old (60 feet)	Monticello, Ark.	Plymouth, Mass.	Bullard, Calif.
Cal Ripken 13-year-old (70 feet)	Aberdeen, Md.	Mexico	West Raleigh, N.C.
13-year-old	Jamestown, N.Y.	Tri-Valley, Calif.	Tri-County, Maine
14-year-old	Pine Bluff, Ark.	Atlantic Shore, N.J.	Tri-Valley, Calif.
13-15-year-olds	Lawrenceburg, Tenn.	Westchester, Calif.	Lawrenceburg, Tenn.
16-18-year-olds	Klamath Falls, Ore.	Columbia Basin, Wash.	Gulf Coast, Ala.

CONTINENTAL AMATEUR BASEBALL ASSOCIATION (CABA)

Event	Site	Champion	Runner-up
9-and-Under	Mason, Ohio	Cincy Flames	West Englewood Tigers
10-and-Under	Mason, Ohio	Motor City Hit Dogs	Midland Blackhawks
12-and-Under	Grapevine, Texas	Academy Select Sun Devils	Dallas Tigers Polk
13-and-Under (60x90)	Boston	Nokona Baseball	New England Ruffnecks
14-and-Under (Aluminum)	Lebanon, Tenn.	New England Ruffnecks 14U	Knights Baseball 14U National
14-and-Under (Wood)	Boston	New England Ruffnecks 14U	Nokona Baseball

er-like breaking ball in the mid-80s and slowing it down to a more-curve like shape at 78-82 mph.

And—just to make scouts salivate even more—Pint threw one changeup. It checked in at 85 mph, showing great fade down and away as it induced a swinging third strike. Pint's changeup projects as a plus offering as well.

While no high school righthander ever has been picked No. 1 overall—Tyler Kolek in 2014

was the eighth prep righty to go No. 2 overall—Pint might have a few million reasons not to go to LSU if he's drafted where his talent would seem to dictate.

Slugger Ties Trout

Ashton Bardzell has always felt a certain kinship with Angels star Mike Trout. Both are from New Jersey. Both play the outfield. And Bardzell, a ris-

15-and-Under (Aluminum)	Jacksonville, Ill.	Naperville Renegades American	Indiana Breakers
15-and-Under (Wood)	Charleston, S.C.	Titans Baseball	Baseball Scoutz 15U
16-and-Under	Marietta, Ga.	Midwest Prospects	East Cobb Astros
17-and-Under/HS (Aluminum)	Euclid, Ohio	Lake Erie Baseball	Bergen Beach
17-and-Under/HS (Wood)	Charleston, S.C.	Carolina Prospects Scout	Lexington Summer Baseball
18-and-Under (Wood)	Charleston, S.C.	Team Elite Road Runner	Diamond Devils 17U Black

LITTLE LEAGUE BASEBALL

Event	Site	Champion	Runner-up
Little League (11-12)	Williamsport, Pa.	Japan	Red Land (Pa.)
Junior League (13-14)	Taylor, Mich.	Taiwan	Frederick County, Va.
Senior League (15-16)	Bangor, Maine	West University Place, Texas	East Holmes, Ohio
Big League (17-18)	Easley, S.C.	Latin America	Thousand Oaks, Calif.

NATIONAL AMATEUR BASEBALL FEDERATION (NBAF)

Event	Site	Champion	Runner-up
Freshman (12 & U)	Hackensack, N.J.	Bonnie Robins	NYCYSO Rays
Sophomore (14 & U)	Knoxville, Tenn.	Rizer Group	Lake Erie Warhawks
Junior (16 & U)	Knoxville, Tenn.	Creekside Fitness	Toronto Mets
High School (17 & U)	Knoxville, Tenn.	Greenbelt 136 American Legion	Maryland Monarchs 17U
Senior (18 & U)	Struthers, Ohio	HCYP Raiders	Michigan Bulls

PERFECT GAME/BCS FINALS

Event	Site	Champion	Runner-up
13-and-Under	Fort Myers, Fla.	Texas Bombers Elite	MVP Banditos
14-and-Under	Fort Myers, Fla.	Warriors Baseball Club of Michigan	Team Elite Prime 14U
15-and-Under	Fort Myers, Fla.	Chain National	East Cobb Astros
16-and-Under	Fort Myers, Fla.	Chain National	Team Elite Prime 16U
17-and-Under	Fort Myers, Fla.	Elite Squad Select 17U	GBSA Rays 17U
18-and-Under	Fort Myers, Fla.	Ontario Blue Jays	Next Level 17U

PERFECT GAME/WORLD WOOD BAT ASSOCIATION SUMMER CHAMPIONSHIPS

Event	Site	Champion	Runner-up
14-and-Under	Emerson, Ga.	East Coast Sox Prime 14U	Evoshield Seminoles 14U
15-and-Under	Emerson, Ga.	East Cobb Astros	Chain National
16-and-Under	Emerson, Ga.	Tri-State Arsenal Showcase 1	643 DP Cougars Sterling
17-and-Under	Emerson, Ga.	CBA Marucci	Dallas Patriots Stout
18-and-Under	Emerson, Ga.	East Cobb Yankees 18U	Triton Rays

PONY BASEBALL

Event	Site	Champion	Runner-up
Mustang 9U	Walnut, Calif.	Simi Valley, Calif.	Walnut, Calif.
Mustang 10U	Youngsville, La.	Corpus Christi, Texas	Chesterfield, Va.
Bronco 11U	Chesterfield, Va.	Murrieta, Calif.	Mexico
Bronco 12U	Los Alamitos, Calif.	Los Alamitos, Calif.	Bayamon, P.R.
Pony 13U	Whittier, Calif.	Chula Vista, Calif.	Dominican Republic
Pony 14U	Washington, Pa.	Taiwan	San Bernardino, Calif.
Colt (15-16)	Lafayette, Ind.	Rio Piedras, P.R.	Greensboro, N.C.
Palomino (17-18)	Compton, Calif.	San Jose, Calif.	Compton, Calif.

REVIVING BASEBALL IN INNER CITIES (RBI)

Event	Site	Champion	Runner-up
Junior (13-15)	Arlington, Texas	Dominican Republic	Houston
Senior (16-18)	Arlington, Texas	Miami	Harrisburg, Pa.

U.S. SPECIALTY SPORTS ASSOCIATION (USSSA)

Event	Site	Champion	Runner-up
10-and-Under/Majors Elite	Orlando	MGBA Bulldogs	Outlaws Elite
11-and-Under/Majors Elite	Orlando	Texas Patriots	Team MVP Legends
12-and-Under/Majors Elite	Orlando	South Florida Hitmen	Team Siege
13-and-Under/Majors Elite	Orlando	Yalobusha Giants	Texas Bombers
14-and-Under/Majors Elite	Orlando	Carolina Blacksox	Tagge Rutherford Fighting Elk

ing freshman at Harford, likes the way Trout plays baseball, and tries to model some parts of his own game after the Angels superstar.

In 2015, Bardzell took his emulation of Trout to a new level. The 6-foot-1, 190-pounder led his Ramsey (N.J.) High squad deep into the postseason, using his exceptional power to slug 18 home runs—tying the state single-season record Trout set in 2009 as a senior at Millville High.

Bardzell's record-tying 18th home run came in a pivotal playoff game, and ultimately helped his team advance to the North 1 Group 2 finals.

In his final game, Bardzell went 0-for-3, hitting one ball to the warning track. Bardzell is expected to be an immediate contributor for Hartford in 2016.

Tucker powers past brother, joins him

BY TEDDY CAHILL

Kyle Tucker entered his senior season at Tampa's Plant High with the school's home run record within reach. The outfielder had hit 21 home runs in his first three seasons with the Panthers, just eight fewer than his older brother, Preston Tucker, hit in his own career at Plant.

Tucker cut into the deficit as the season went on, eventually pulling even with his brother at 29 career home runs. That's where the count stood going into Plant's final regular season game of the season, a crosstown trip to Jefferson High.

On that night, in front of a crowd that included scouts and a few general managers, Tucker rose to the occasion. He collected four hits and belted two home runs in a 13-2 victory. The homers gave Tucker 31 for his career, pushing him past his brother into first in Plant's record book, a feat that still impresses him.

"It was a little surprising," Tucker said. "He's bigger than me, so you'd think he would have more power."

Tucker's season came to an end when Plant was eliminated in the Class 8A district quarterfinals, but that victory at Jefferson was the climax of Tucker's high school career and likely solidified his status at the top of the draft class. What scouts saw that night—his feel for hitting, power potential and penchant for the big moment—led the Astros to draft him fifth overall and is what made him Baseball America's 2015 High School Player of the Year.

Tucker now enters the same organization as his brother. Preston, the Astros' seventh-round pick out of Florida in 2012, made his major league debut in May, with Kyle, their parents and sister in the stands.

Just a month later, the whole Tucker family was brought together again for a big league game when the Astros brought Kyle to Houston to sign his contract a week after the draft. As part of the day, he took batting practice with Preston and the rest of the Astros. Because of a seven-year age difference between the brothers, they have never played together. So Kyle relished the opportunity to hit with Preston.

John Martin, the Astros area scout in Florida, signed both Tuckers and followed them throughout their high school careers.

"They're both excellent makeup play-

ers, they both approached the game in high school with a mature attitude and a good work ethic," Martin said. "They both were leaders on the team in high school. They have the same hit tool, the same power."

Tucker said there are some similarities in the way he and his big brother play.

"We don't strike out very much; we put the ball in play," Tucker said. "He has a little bit more power because he's a little bit bigger and stronger. We have kind of similar approaches to the game and in the box. Of course, there's differences between players, but I kind of model myself after him because I get to see him on and off the field. I related my game as much as I can to him and his success."

Kyle Tucker put his physical tools to use for Plant, mixing the ability to hit for average with plus raw power. He hit .484/.581/.962 with 10 home runs and 10 stolen bases this season, while patrolling center field for the Panthers. He also made eight appearances on the mound, picking up four saves and striking out 12 batters in 12 innings.

"He had an outstanding year when they pitched to him," Martin said. "He continued to hit, to get to his power."

2015 HIGH SCHOOL ALL-AMERICA TEAM

Beau Burrows

BILL MITCHELL

Cornelius Randolph

MIKE JANES

FIRST TEAM

Pos.	Name	School	Yr.	AVG	AB	R	H	2B	3B	HR	RBI	SB	DRAFTED
C	Tyler Stephenson, c,	Kennesaw Mountain HS, Marietta, Ga.	Sr.	.425		10	31	6	1	9	26		Reds (1)
IF	Ke'Bryan Hayes, 3b,	Concordia Luthern HS, Tomball, Texas	Sr.	.436	94	22	41	16	1	3	27	12	Pirates (1)
IF	Brendan Rodgers, ss,	Lake Mary (Fla.) HS.	Sr.	.397	68	19	27	5	0	8	18	6	Rockies (1)
IF	Cadyn Grenier, ss,	Bishop Gorman HS, Las Vegas	Sr.	.472	108	65	51	12	5	4	34	26	Cardinals (21)
IF	Ryan Mountcastle, ss,	Hagerty HS, Oviedo, Fla.	Sr.	.500	84	20	42	12	3	2	31	22	Orioles (1s)
OF	Kyle Tucker, of,	Plant HS, Tampa	Sr.	.484		29	31	9	0	10	27	10	Astros (1)
OF	Daz Cameron, of,	Eagle's Landing Christian Academy, McDonough, Ga.	Sr.	.455	77	38	35	10	1	8	32	19	Orioles (1s)
OF	Nick Plummer, of,	Brother Rice HS, Bloomfield Hills, Mich.	Sr.	.507	75	53	38	9	2	3	12	25	Cardinals (1)
DH	Cornelius Randolph, ss,	Griffin (Ga.) HS	Sr.	.536	63		37	10	1	7			Phillies (1)
UT	Luken Baker, 1b/rhp,	Oak Ridge HS, Conroe, Texas	Sr.	.452	62	20	28	5	0	7	15	1	Astros (37)

Pos.	Name	School	Yr.	W	L	ERA	G	SV	IP	H	BB	SO	DRAFTED
P	Triston McKenzie, rhp,	Royal Palm Beach (Fla.) HS	Sr.	9	5	0.79	15	0	91	43	16	157	Indians (1s)
P	Austin Smith, rhp,	Park Vista Community HS, Boynton Beach, Fla.	Sr.	8	2	1.33	15	0	82	54	23	98	Padres (2)
P	Donny Everett, rhp,	Clarksville (Tenn.) HS	Sr.	9	1	1.21	12	2	67	32	8	125	Brewers (29)
P	Beau Burrows, rhp,	Weatherford (Texas) HS	Sr.	9	3	0.89	12	0	71	32	15	132	Tigers (1)
P	Jackson Kowar, rhp,	Charlotte Christian HS, Weddington, N.C.	Sr.	10	1	0.26	14	0	70	24	19	118	Tigers (40)
UT	Luken Baker, 1b/rhp,	Oak Ridge HS, Conroe, Texas	Sr.	11	0	1.59		0	68		15	101	Astros (37)

SECOND TEAM

Pos.	Name	School	Yr.	AVG	AB	R	H	2B	3B	HR	RBI	SB	DRAFTED
C	Chris Betts, c,	Wilson HS, Long Beach, Calif.	Sr.	.471	68	30	32	5	1	8	28	6	Rays (2)
IF	Travis Blankenhorn, ss,	Pottsville (Pa.) HS	Sr.	.467	75	36	35	6	5	6	24	11	Twins (3)
IF	Jalen Miller, ss,	Riverwood International Charter, Sandy Springs, Ga.	Sr.	.444	63	20	28	4	2	5	17	10	Giants (3)
IF	Tyler Nevin, 3b,	Poway (Calif.) HS	Sr.	.417	84	31	35	12	0	4	14	5	Rockies (1s)
IF	Jonathan India, ss,	American Heritage School, Delray Beach, Fla.	Sr.	.405	84	21	34	11	0	1	23	25	Brewers (26)
OF	Trenton Clark, of,	Richland HS, North Richland Hills, Texas	Sr.	.552		33	37	8	3	3	15	11	Brewers (1)
OF	Garrett Whitley, of,	Niskayuna (N.Y.) HS	Sr.	.364	55	24	20	3	1	3	13	14	Rays (1)
OF	Isaiah White, of,	Greenfield HS, Wilson, N.C.	Sr.	.547	75	39	41	13	6	3	17	31	Marlins (3)
DH	Austin Riley, 3b/rhp,	DeSoto Central HS, Southaven, Miss.	Sr.	.433	97	29	42	13	1	11	31	2	Braves (1s)
UT	Matt Vierling, of/rhp,	Christian Brothers HS, Sacramento Calif.	Sr.	.437	119	28	52	14	4	2	28	10	Cardinals (30)

Pos.	Name	School	Yr.	W	L	ERA	G	SV	IP	H	BB	SO	DRAFTED
P	Joe DeMers, rhp,	College Park HS, Pleasant Hill, Calif.	Sr.	9	1	0.64	11	1	70	28	7	78	Undrafted
P	Peter Lambert, rhp,	San Dimas (Calif.) HS	Sr.	11	0	0.52	11	0	69	39	14	102	Rockies (2)
P	Nick Lee, rhp,	South Beauregard HS, Longville, La.	Sr.	10	3	0.44	14	1	82	30	12	110	Undrafted
P	Max Wotell, lhp,	Marvin Ridge HS, Waxhaw, N.C.	Sr.	11	0	0.69	12	0	65.1	22	19	120	Mets (3)
P	Drew Finley, rhp,	Rancho Bernadino HS, San Diego	Sr.	8	1	1.07	10	0	67	27	17	113	Yankees (3)
UT	Matt Vierling, of/rhp,	Christian Brothers HS, Sacramento Calif.	Sr.	6	0	2.48	9	0	32.6	20	23	45	Cardinals (30)

DRAFT

Shortstops steal show with bountiful draft

BY TEDDY CAHILL

Despite all the public mystery this spring surrounding the first overall pick of the draft, Diamondbacks scouting director Deric Ladnier said on draft night that his mind was made up "a while back" about the player Arizona would take. He remained convinced after going through the process of meeting with the team's scouts, and they came to a unanimous decision about the pick a couple of days before the draft.

But they didn't make that decision public until the draft began June 8. A little after 7 p.m., commissioner Rob Manfred stepped to the podium at MLB Network's Studio 42 and announced Vanderbilt shortstop Dansby Swanson as the Diamondbacks' choice at No. 1.

"This is the player we wanted," Ladnier said. "We wanted him for a while."

Swanson was the first college shortstop to be selected first overall since 1974, when the Padres selected Bill Almon out of Brown. He was the Diamondbacks first top overall pick since 2005, when they drafted Justin Upton.

Getting Swanson signed provided more drama

DANNY PARKER

The D-backs opened a shortstop shopping spree by taking Dansby Swanson No. 1

FIRST-ROUND BONUS PROGRESSION

While the rules instituted in the latest Collective Bargaining Agreement have slowed overall draft spending, teams are still willing to pay a premium for talent at the top of the draft. In 2015, teams paid first rounders an average bonus of $2,774,945, establishing a new record. That marked an increase of 6.23 percent from last year, the third time in four years of this CBA that first-round bonuses have increased by more than six percent.

The previous high of $2,653,375 had stood since 2011, the last draft under the rules from the previous CBA.

After the first draft in 1965, first-round bonuses rose by an average of just 0.6 percent annually for the rest of the 1960s and 5.2 percent per year in the 1970s. Bonus inflation picked up in the 1980s, averaging 10.2 percent annually, and soared to 26.9 percent per year in the 1990s.

Below are the annual averages for first-round bonuses since the draft started in 1965. The 1996 total does not include four players who became free agents through a draft loophole.

YEAR	AVERAGE	CHANGE	YEAR	AVERAGE	CHANGE	YEAR	AVERAGE	CHANGE
1965	$42,516	—	1982	$82,615	+5.1%	1999	$1,809,767	+10.5%
1966	$44,430	+4.5%	1983	$87,236	+5.6%	2000	$1,872,586	+3.5%
1967	$42,898	-3.4%	1984	$105,391	+20.8%	2001	$2,154,280	+15.0%
1968	$43,850	+2.2%	1985	$118,115	+12.1%	2002	$2,106,793	-2.2%
1969	$43,504	-0.8%	1986	$116,300	-1.6%	2003	$1,765,667	-16.2%
1970	$45,230	+3.9%	1987	$128,480	+10.5%	2004	$1,958,448	+10.9%
1971	$45,197	-0.1%	1988	$142,540	+10.9%	2005	$2,018,000	+3.0%
1972	$44,952	-0.5%	1989	$176,008	+23.5%	2006	$1,933,333	-4.2%
1973	$48,832	+8.6%	1990	$252,577	+43.5%	2007	$2,098,083	+8.5%
1974	$53,333	+9.2%	1991	$365,396	+44.7%	2008	$2,458,714	+17.2%
1975	$49.333	-7.5%	1992	$481,893	+31.9%	2009	$2,434,800	-1.0%
1976	$49,631	+0.6%	1993	$613,037	+27.2%	2010	$2,220,966	-8.8%
1977	$48,813	-1.6%	1994	$790,357	+28.9%	2011	$2,653,375	+19.5%
1978	$67,892	+39.1%	1995	$918,019	+16.1%	2012	$2,475,167	-6.7%
1979	$68,094	+0.2%	1996*	$944,404	+2.9%	2013	$2,641,538	+6.7%
1980	$74,025	+8.7%	1997	$1,325,536	+40.4%	2014	$2,612,109	-1.1%
1981	$78,573	+6.1%	1998	$1,637,667	+23.1%	2015	$2,774,945	+6.23%

and intrigue than initially anticipated, and the negotiations went down to the wire. But he ultimately agreed to a $6.5 million bonus just before the 5 p.m. deadline on July 17, narrowly avoiding a second straight year in which the first overall pick didn't sign. Lefthander Brady Aiken and the Astros were unable to come to terms in 2014 after a messy negotiation.

Swanson's selection set the stage for one of the biggest themes of the draft. He was the first of three straight shortstops taken at the top of the draft, the first time that had happened in draft history, and one of 10 shortstops taken in the first two rounds.

Following Swanson was Louisiana State shortstop Alex Bregman, who went second overall to the Astros, and Lake Mary (Fla.) High shortstop Brendan Rodgers, who went third overall to the Rockies. Rodgers, the top-ranked player on the BA 500, was at the draft and became the first player to shake Manfred's hand after being selected.

"It's an unbelievable feeling," Rodgers told MLB Network immediately after his selection. "I'm blessed and honored to be here."

Rodgers and the Rockies quickly worked out a deal, and he signed for a $5.5 million bonus little more than a week after the draft. His bonus was the highest for a high school player this year.

While Rodgers was on hand to hear his name called by the new commissioner, Swanson's draft day wasn't so straightforward. Vanderbilt's NCAA tournament run had taken it to super regionals at Illinois. After winning the first game 13-0 on the Saturday before the draft, the Commodores were in position to return to the College World Series with a victory the next day. But rain postponed Game Two until Monday at 3 p.m., four hours before the draft was set to begin.

Swanson and the rest of the Commodores took the field that afternoon hoping to clinch a spot in Omaha. More than 1,500 miles away in Arizona, Ladnier and other Diamondbacks scouts settled in to finish draft preparations and watch the player they would soon make the top overall pick.

Swanson didn't disappoint. He went 2-for-4 with a home run, a double and a stolen base to help Vanderbilt defeat Illinois 4-2.

"It was icing on the cake to see him hit a home run, to see him hit a double in the gap and ultimately win the game and advance to the (College) World Series," Ladnier said.

Just five minutes after Vanderbilt closed out the victory, Manfred officially opened the draft in Secaucus, N.J. Back in Champaign, Ill., Swanson was still on the field, surrounded by his teammates

BONUS SPENDING BY TEAM

Teams combined to spend a record $248.8 million on draft bonuses in 2015, eclipsing the mark set in 2011. In that draft, last held under the rules from the previous Collective Bargaining Agreement, teams spent $228 million on bonuses and another $8.1 million on guaranteed salaries that were part of major league contracts.

A new CBA went into effect the next year and intially curtailed spending by intitutiting harsh penalties for teams that exceed their bonus pools by more than five percent and ending the practice of awarding major league contracts to draftees. But as revenues within the game have gone up, so too have the bonus pools MLB allocates to teams for the first 10 rounds.

Teams at the top of the draft and those with extra picks get more money in their pools, so it's no surprise the Astros, Rockies and Braves, who all had four picks in the first two rounds, led the industry in draft spending. The Astros and the Rockies both broke the previous record for spending under the current CBA, surpassing the Marlins' 2014 expenditure of $13,112,900. Of the five teams that spent the least in this year's draft, only the Blue Jays had a first round pick. The Mariners, Mets, Nationals and Padres all forfeited their top picks due to free agent compensation, shrinking the funds they had available to spend during the draft.

TEAM	2015	2014	2013
Astros	$19,103,000	$6,154,500	$11,441,000
Rockies	$14,415,900	$8,853,800	$10,368,200
Braves	$12,659,400	$5,069,800	$5,410,500
Diamondbacks	$12,270,900	$8,357,900	$8,049,100
Rangers	$10,728,300	$6,089,200	$7,696,500
Yankees	$9,442,800	$4,050,200	$9,197,400
Reds	$9,018,050	$7,929,900	$6,757,800
Giants	$8,865,300	$7,275,900	$6,063,800
Pirates	$8,485,000	$8,186,400	$9,887,400
Indians	$8,461,880	$9,317,800	$6,713,600
Brewers	$8,352,600	$8,102,300	$4,637,300
Cubs	$8,335,700	$9,783,000	$11,724,900
Cardinals	$8,247,400	$7,613,800	$8,526,400
Royals	$7,994,300	$9,888,700	$9,581,900
Rays	$7,946,400	$7,141,319	$7,147,000
Phillies	$7,653,200	$7,187,800	$6,186,900
Tigers	$7,606,700	$5,405,300	$6,839,100
Red Sox	$7,589,000	$7,814,800	$7,210,900
Marlins	$7,551,400	$13,112,900	$7,951,000
Dodgers	$7,363,600	$5,901,100	$6,366,100
Twins	$7,154,400	$8,067,600	$8,776,400
Orioles	$7,031,200	$3,410,600	$7,235,000
Athletics	$6,381,000	$5,386,000	$6,506,100
White Sox	$5,977,600	$10,460,600	$5,810,800
Angels	$5,835,800	$6,387,500	$3,168,200
Mariners	$5,368,600	$8,237,500	$7,376,700
Nationals	$4,982,800	$5,188,600	$3,176,200
Padres	$4,892,100	$6,637,600	$7,895,000
Blue Jays	$4,848,800	$9,308,700	$3,747,280
Mets	$4,268,700	$6,488,800	$7,854,400
Total	**$248,833,845**	**$222,809,919**	**$219,302,880**
Average	**$8,026,898**	**$7,426,997**	**$7,310,096**

and with his family close by, when his name was called a few minutes later, setting off a jubilant celebration.

"It's a surreal moment, especially to be with all my loved ones," Swanson told reporters after the game. "Just to be able to enjoy the moment with the people closest to you, it's pretty phenomenal."

With the next pick, the Astros selected Bregman, who played last summer with Swanson on the

DRAFT

Collegiate National Team, forming the double-play combination.

"He's a great player and I had the pleasure of flipping the ball to him and turning a few double plays with him," Bregman said. "I'm so happy for him and so happy for everyone who had their name called today."

The initial run on shortstops ended when the Rangers selected UC Santa Barbara righthander Dillon Tate fourth before the Astros picked again, this time selecting Florida prep outfielder Kyle Tucker fifth overall. Tucker's older brother Preston was the Astros' seventh-round pick in 2012 and he made his major league debut for the club in May.

The Astros would pick two more times before the night was over and added two more premium talents. They selected Georgia prep outfielder Daz Cameron (former big leaguer Mike Cameron's son) with the 37th overall pick and Cal State Fullerton righthander Thomas Eshelman.

Cameron was ranked No. 5 on the BA 500, but slid in the draft after teams were scared off by his

Brendan Rodgers was the first high school player drafted, going No. 3 to the Rockies

price tag. With more than $17 million allotted to them in their bonus pool, the Astros had the most available money and used it to their advantage.

Unlike the previous year, the Astros moved quickly to sign all their top picks. Bregman, Tucker and Cameron all received bonuses that ranked among the six largest bonuses in this year's draft.

The Braves and the Indians, two other teams with extra first-day picks and larger bonus pools, also took advantage of the flexibility afforded them. The Braves picked five times on the draft's first day and snagged California prep lefthander Kolby Allard with their first pick (No. 14 overall). Allard entered the spring regarded as the best high school pitcher in the draft class, but was sidelined by a stress reaction in his back. Among their other picks was catcher Lucas Herbert, one of the best defenders in the draft and Allard's battery mate at San Clemente (Calif.) High.

Negotiations with Allard were prolonged, but he signed a slightly above-slot deal worth $3.042 million. He was able to make three appearances in August in the Gulf Coast League, totaling 12 strikeouts in six scoreless innings.

The Indians, meanwhile, stuck to their best-player available approach at No. 17 and drafted Aiken, the 2014 No. 1 overall pick. Aiken had reportedly worked out an agreement with the

HIGHEST BONUSES EVER

The 2015 draft saw three players—Dansby Swanson, Alex Bregman and Brendan Rodgers—sign for at least $5 million. There have been 30 such players in draft history, with eight coming in the last four years under the current CBA. Three of the top five bonuses, including the record, came in the 2011 draft.

PLAYER, POS.	TEAM, YEAR (PICK)	BONUS
Gerrit Cole, rhp	Pirates, 2011 (No. 1)	$8,000,000
Stephen Strasburg, rhp	Nationals, 2009 (No. 1)	*$7,500,000
Bubba Starling, of	Royals, 2011 (No. 5)	+$7,500,000
Kris Bryant, 3b	Cubs, 2013 (No. 2)	$6,708,400
Carlos Rodon, lhp	White Sox, 2014 (No. 3)	$6,582,000
Jameson Taillon, rhp	Pirates, 2010 (No. 2)	$6,500,000
Dansby Swanson	Diamondbacks, 2015 (No. 1)	$6,500,000
Danny Hultzen, lhp	Mariners, 2011 (No. 2)	*$6,350,000
Mark Appel, rhp	Astros, 2013 (No. 1)	$6,350,000
Donavan Tate, of	Padres, 2009 (No. 3)	+$6,250,000
Bryce Harper, of	Nationals, 2010 (No. 1)	*$6,250,000
Buster Posey, c	Giants, 2008 (No. 5)	$6,200,000
Tim Beckham, ss	Rays, 2008 (No. 1)	+$6,150,000
Justin Upton, ss	Diamondbacks, 2005 (No. 1)	+$6,100,000
Matt Wieters, c	Orioles, 2007 (No. 5)	$6,000,000
Pedro Alvarez, 3b	Pirates, 2008 (No. 2)	*$6,000,000
Eric Hosmer, 1b	Royals, 2008 (No. 3)	$6,000,000
Dustin Ackley, of	Mariners, 2009 (No. 2)	*$6,000,000
Anthony Rendon, 3b	Nationals, 2011 (No. 6)	*$6,000,000
Byron Buxton, of	Twins, 2012 (No. 2)	$6,000,000
Tyler Kolek, rhp	Marlins, 2014 (No. 2)	$6,000,000
Alex Bregman, ss	Astros, 2015 (No. 2)	$5,900,000
David Price, lhp	Rays, 2007 (No. 1)	*$5,600,000
Brendan Rodgers, ss	Rockies, 2015 (No. 3)	$5,500,000
Joe Borcahrd, of	White Sox, 2000 (No. 12)	+$5,300,000
Manny Machado, ss	Orioles, 2010 (No. 3)	+$5,250,000
Zach Lee, rhp	Dodgers, 2010 (No. 28)	+$5,250,000
Joe Mauer, c	Twins, 2001 (No. 1)	+$5,150,000
Archie Bradley, rhp	Diamondbacks, 2011 (No. 7)	+$5,000,000
Josh Bell, of	Pirates, 2011 (2nd Rd, No. 61)	$5,000,000

*Part of major league contract.
+Bonus spread over multiple years under MLB provisions for two-sport athletes.

Astros for $6.5 million last year, but that deal fell apart after a difference of opinion of what an MRI of his elbow taken in a post-draft physical showed, and he ultimately turned down a reported $5 million deal at the signing deadline. He went to IMG Academy to play for their postgraduate team this spring, but threw just 13 pitches in his first start before exiting the game with an injury and having Tommy John surgery 13 days later.

Those complex circumstances made Aiken one of the biggest wild cards of the draft and led to him still being on the board when the Indians first picked. Indians scouting director Brad Grant praised the club's scouts for their work evaluating Aiken over the last two years. He declined to comment after the draft on the specifics of Aiken's medical issues, saying only that the Indians did their due diligence and felt good about selecting him, in part because of his intangibles.

"That's one of the things that really stands out with Brady is his character and work ethic and his commitment to getting better," Grant said. "That's something that definitely stood out in terms of his character and his willingness to return from here."

Aiken eventually signed with the Indians for a bonus of $2.513 million. He quietly continued to progress in his rehab, tweeting Sept. 14: "Feels good to be throwing again."

Aiken and Allard were two members of a group of pitchers who had first-round talents, but saw their situations clouded by injury going into the draft. Virginia lefthander Nathan Kirby, who was sidelined by a strained lat muscle in April, went 40th overall to the Brewers. Later in the summer, he had Tommy John surgery after making five professional appearances. Duke righthander Michael Matuella, who was a potential top-five pick before he had Tommy John surgery in the spring, was not picked on the draft's first day.

Matuella didn't remain available for long when the draft resumed June 9 with rounds three through 10, as the Rangers selected him with the third pick of the third round. He got a $2 million bonus, more than double the slot value of his pick.

Ultimately, just six players selected in the top 10 rounds didn't sign. Louisville righthander Kyle Funkhouser, drafted 35th overall by the Dodgers, was the lone first-round pick not to sign. He instead has returned to college for his senior season.

"Wanted to be the first to announce that I will not be signing, and will return to the University of Louisville for my

NO. 1 OVERALL PICKS

YEAR	TEAM: PLAYER, POS., SCHOOL	BONUS
1965	Athletics: Rick Monday, of, Arizona State	$100,000
1966	Mets: Steve Chilcott, c, Antelope Valley HS, Lancaster, Calif.	$75,000
1967	Yankees: Ron Blomberg, 1b, Druid Hills HS, Atlanta	$65,000
1968	Mets: Tim Foli, ss, Notre Dame HS, Sherman Oaks, Calif.	$74,000
1969	Senators: Jeff Burroughs, of, Wilson HS, Long Beach	$88,000
1970	Padres: Mike Ivie, c, Walker HS, Atlanta	$75,000
1971	White Sox: Danny Goodwin, c, Peoria (Ill.) HS	Did Not Sign
1972	Padres: Dave Roberts, 3b, Oregon	$70,000
1973	Rangers: David Clyde, lhp, Westchester HS, Texas	*$65,000
1974	Padres: Bill Almon, ss, Brown	*$90,000
1975	Angels: Danny Goodwin, c, Southern	*$125,000
1976	Astros: Floyd Bannister, lhp, Arizona State	$100,000
1977	White Sox: Harold Baines, of, St. Michaels (Md.) HS	$32,000
1978	Braves: Bob Horner, 3b, Arizona State	*$162,000
1979	Mariners: Al Chambers, 1b, Harris HS, Harrisburg, Pa.	$60,000
1980	Mets: Darryl Strawberry, of, Crenshaw HS, Los Angeles	$152,500
1981	Mariners: Mike Moore, rhp, Oral Roberts	$100,000
1982	Cubs: Shawon Dunston, ss, Jefferson HS, New York	$135,000
1983	Twins: Tim Belcher, rhp, Mount Vernon Nazarene (Ohio)	Did Not Sign
1984	Mets: Shawn Abner, of, Mechanicsburg (Pa.) HS	$150,500
1985	Brewers: B.J. Surhoff, c, North Carolina	$150,000
1986	Pirates: Jeff King, 3b, Arkansas	$180,000
1987	Mariners: Ken Griffey Jr., of, Moeller HS, Cincinnati	$160,000
1988	Padres: Andy Benes, rhp, Evansville	$235,000
1989	Orioles: Ben McDonald, rhp, Louisiana State	*$350,000
1990	Braves: Chipper Jones, ss, The Bolles School, Jacksonville	$275,000
1991	Yankees: Brien Taylor, lhp, East Carteret HS, Beaufort, N.C.	$1,550,000
1992	Astros: Phil Nevin, 3b, Cal State Fullerton	$700,000
1993	Mariners: Alex Rodriguez, ss, Westminster Christian HS, Miami	*$1,000,000
1994	Mets: Paul Wilson, rhp, Florida State	$1,550,000
1995	Angels: Darin Erstad, of, Nebraska	$1,575,000
1996	Pirates: Kris Benson, rhp, Clemson	$2,000,000
1997	Tigers: Matt Anderson, rhp, Tigers	$2,505,000
1998	Phillies: Pat Burrell, 3b, Miami	*$3,150,000
1999	Devil Rays: Josh Hamilton, of, Athens Drive HS, Raleigh	$3,960,000
2000	Marlins: Adrian Gonzalez, 1b, Eastlake HS, Chula Vista, Calif.	$3,000,000
2001	Twins: Joe Mauer, c, Cretin-Derham Hall, St. Paul	$5,150,000
2002	Pirates: Bryan Bullington, rhp, Ball State	$4,000,000
2003	Devil Rays: Delmon Young, of, Camarillo (Calif.) HS	*$3,700,000
2004	Padres: Matt Bush, ss, Mission Bay HS, San Diego	$3,150,000
2005	Diamondbacks: Justin Upton, ss, Great Bridge HS, Chesapeake, Va.	$6,100,000
2006	Royals: Luke Hochevar, rhp, Fort Worth (American Association)	*$3,500,000
2007	Devil Rays: David Price, lhp, Vanderbilt	*$5,600,000
2008	Rays: Tim Beckham, ss, Griffin (Ga.) HS	$6,150,000
2009	Nationals: Stephen Strasburg, rhp, San Diego State	*$7,500,000
2010	Nationals: Bryce Harper, of, JC of Southern Nevada	*$6,250,000
2011	Pirates: Gerrit Cole, rhp, UCLA	$8,000,000
2012	Astros: Carlos Correa, ss, Puerto Rico Baseball Academy, Gurabo, P.R.	$4,800,000
2013	Astros: Mark Appel, rhp, Stanford	$6,350,000
2014	Astros: Brady Aiken, lhp, Cathedral Catholic, San Diego	Did Not Sign
2015	Diamondbacks: Dansby Swanson, ss, Vanderbilt	$6,500,000

*Part of major league contract.

senior season," he announced on Twitter, just hours before the signing deadline.

As compensation for not signing Funkhouser, the Dodgers receive the 36th overall pick in 2016.

Funkhouser went 8-5, 3.20 with 104 strikeouts and 45 walks in 112 innings during the season. He was the highest-drafted player in Louisville history, but was projected to be a top-10 pick entering the season. He remained on that track until a late-season drop in the quality of his stuff saw him slide down draft boards.

This was the eighth straight year in which at least one first-round pick has not signed. Funkhouser is the fourth college junior not to sign during that streak, joining Aaron Crow (2008), Barret Loux (2010), and Mark Appel (2012). Only Appel went back to school, and he improved from the eighth overall pick to first after his senior year.

The Blue Jays and second-rounder Brady Singer, a Florida prep righthander, were unable to work out a deal. Singer instead continued on to Florida, where he joins what was already one of the best pitching staffs in the country. It was the fifth time since 2009 that Toronto didn't sign a first- or second-round pick.

Georgia prep righthander Jonathan Hughes (Orioles, second round), Kentucky righthander Kyle Cody (Twins, supplemental second round), Colorado prep shortstop Nick Shumpert (Tigers, seventh round) and South Carolina outfielder Kep Brown (Cardinals, 10th round) all went unsigned as well. Hughes is now at Georgia Tech, Shumpert at San Jacinto (Texas) JC and Brown at Spartanburg Methodist (S.C.) JC.

All teams that didn't sign a player in the top three rounds receive a compensation pick in next year's draft. Of the unsigned players in the top 10 rounds, only Singer and Hughes will not be eligible for the 2016 draft.

Draft Trends And Tidbits

■ The Braves held five of the first 75 picks, positioning them well for a big first day, despite not picking until No. 14 overall. They did just that, selecting high-upside prep players with their first four picks in Allard, Canadian righthander Mike Soroka, Mississippi high school third baseman Austin Riley and Herbert. With former scouting director Roy Clark back in the Braves front office as a special assistant to the general manager, the Braves returned to their roots of emphasizing pitching in the draft and selected 24 pitchers in the three days. Riley and Herbert were the only two position players they drafted in the first 11 rounds.

■ In a banner year for Canadians in the draft,

the Marlins, the southernmost team in baseball, were the first to go north of the border with their pick. They tabbed first baseman Josh Naylor with the 12th overall selection, securing one of the best power hitters in the high school class. Naylor's draft position was the best ever for a Canadian position player. In all, 30 Canadians were drafted, including a record 10 in the first 10 rounds.

■ It was a strong year for the state of Florida. Rodgers was the top-ranked player on the BA 500 and one of 14 players from the state drafted on the first day. Florida and Florida State produced first-round picks (Gators shortstop Riche Martin and Seminoles outfielder D.J. Stewart), while less storied school such as North Florida and Florida Tech had players drafted in the top-five rounds. The

Padres in particular took an interest in the Sunshine State, as their first three picks and four of their first five all came from Florida.

■ A few teams noticeably loaded up on college products. The Diamondbacks selected 36 collegians, including eight straight to start their draft. They didn't take a high school player until they tabbed New York prep righthander Wesley Rodriguez in the 12th round. Nine of the Athletics top 10 picks were college products, a callback to their Moneyball days. Of the Dodgers' 42 picks, 35 came from the college ranks. The Red Sox took college players with their first three picks and seven of their top nine selections to begin the draft, including College Player of the Year Andrew Benintendi at No. 7 overall. Boston did end up picking 12 prep players.

■ Oklahoma led all schools with 11 players drafted, beginning with catcher Anthony Hermelyn going to the Astros in the fourth round. UC Santa Barbara had 10 players picked, led by Tate. Arizona State, Florida, Illinois and Vanderbilt all had nine players selected.

■ Many of the players in this year's draft had strong family ties to the game, including Cameron and Tucker. The Astros also selected Notre Dame outfielder Conor Biggio and Texas prep shortstop Kody Clemens, the sons of former Astros stars Craig Biggio and Roger Clemens. Phil Nevin was the No. 1 overall pick in the 1992 draft, and his son Tyler Nevin was picked 38th overall by the Rockies. The Tigers drafted Michigan State outfielder Cam Gibson, the son of former all-star Kirk Gibson, in the fifth round and Nova Southeastern (Fla.) righthander Ryan Castellanos, the younger brother of third baseman Nick Castellanos, in the 25th round. Iona righthander Mariano Rivera, the son of the all-time saves leader, went to the Nationals in the fourth round. The Red Sox selected Missouri State outfielder Tate Matheny, son of Cardinals manager Mike Matheny, in the fourth round. The White Sox tabbed Illinois prep second baseman Joseph Reinsdorf, the grandson of owner Jerry Reinsdorf, in the 40th round. The Angels drafted California prep righthander Jonah Dipoto, the son of then-general manager Jerry Dipoto, in the 38th round.

BONUSES VS. PICK VALUES

Signing bonuses and assigned pick values have largely lined up since revamped draft rules were introduced as part of the Collective Bargaining Agreement in 2012. To give the worst teams extra spending power, the values for the selections at the top of the draft have been set higher than the perceived market value. In 2015, Kolby Allard was the first player selected to receive more than pick value at No. 14. Eight of the top 15 picks received less than pick value, and five signed for slot.

Ultimately, the top 50 bonuses added up to $124.01 million, slightly under the $124.7 million assigned to the first 50 picks. By comparison, when MLB unilaterally determined slot recommendations in the last year of the previous CBA (2011), the total of the first 50 bonuses ($120.5 million) dwarfed that of the top 50 slots ($70 million).

PLAYER, POS., TEAM (ROUND/OVERALL PICK)	BONUS	PICK VALUE
1 Dansby Swanson, ss, Diamondbacks (1st round/No. 1)	$6,500,000	$8,616,900
2 Alex Bregman, ss, Astros (1st round/No. 2)	$5,900,000	$7,420,100
3 Brendan Rodgers, ss, Rockies (1st round/No. 3)	$5,500,000	$6,223,300
4 Dillon Tate, rhp, Rangers (1st round/No. 4)	$4,200,000	$5,026,500
5 Kyle Tucker, of, Astros (1st round/No. 5)	$4,000,000	$4,188,700
Daz Cameron, of, Astros (supp. 1st/No. 37)	$4,000,000	$1,668,600
7 Tyler Jay, lhp, Twins (1st round/No. 6)	$3,889,500	$3,889,500
8 Andrew Benintendi, of, Red Sox (1st round/No. 7)	$3,590,400	$3,590,400
9 Carson Fulmer, rhp, White Sox (1st round/No. 8)	$3,470,600	$3,470,600
10 Cornelius Randolph, ss, Phillies (1st round/No. 10)	$3,231,300	$3,231,300
11 Tyler Stephenson, c, Reds (1st round/No. 11)	$3,141,600	$3,141,600
12 Kolby Allard, lhp, Braves (1st round/No. 14)	$3,042,400	$2,842,400
13 Ian Happ, of, Cubs (1st round/No. 9)	$3,000,000	$3,351,000
14 Garrett Whitley, of, Rays (1st round/No. 13)	$2,959,600	$2,962,100
15 Trent Clark, of, Brewers (1st round/No. 15)	$2,700,000	$2,692,700
16 James Kaprielian, rhp, Yankees (1st round/No. 16)	$2,650,000	$2,543,300
17 Brady Aiken, lhp, Indians (1st round/No. 17)	$2,513,280	$2,393,600
18 Phil Bickford, rhp, Giants (1st round/No. 18)	$2,333,800	$2,333,800
19 Triston McKenzie, rhp, Indians (supp. 1st/No. 42)	$2,302,500	$1,468,400
20 Mike Nikorak, rhp, Rockies (1st round/No. 27)	$2,300,000	$2,004,600
21 Josh Naylor, 1b, Marlins (1st round/No. 12)	$2,200,000	$3,051,800
22 Ashe Russell, rhp, Royals(1st round/No. 21)	$2,190,200	$2,184,200
23 Kevin Newman, ss, Pirates (1st round/No. 19)	$2,175,000	$2,273,800
24 Beau Burrows, rhp, Tigers (1st round/No. 22)	$2,154,200	$2,154,200
25 Nick Plummer, of, Cardinals (1st round/No. 23)	$2,124,400	$2,124,400
26 D.J. Stewart, of, Orioles (1st round/No. 25)	$2,064,500	$2,064,500
27 Tyler Nevin, 3b, Rockies (supp. 1st/No. 38)	$2,000,000	$1,626,500
Eric Jenkins, of, Rangers (2nd round/No. 45)	$2,000,000	$1,360,100
Michael Matuella, rhp, Rangers (3rd round/No. 78)	$2,000,000	$777,600
30 Mike Soroka, rhp, Braves (1st round/No. 28)	$1,974,700	$1,974,700
31 Richie Martin, ss, Athletics (1st round/No. 20)	$1,950,000	$2,214,000
32 Jon Harris, rhp, Blue Jays (1st round/No. 29)	$1,944,800	$1,944,800
33 Ke'Bryan Hayes, 3b, Pirates (1st round/No. 32)	$1,855,000	$1,855,000
34 Nolan Watson, rhp, Royals (1st round/No. 33)	$1,825,200	$1,825,200
35 Kyle Holder, ss, Yankees (1st round/No. 30)	$1,800,000	$1,800,000
Jake Woodford, rhp, Cardinals (supp. 1st/No. 39)	$1,800,000	$1,585,400
37 Christin Stewart, of, Tigers (1st round/No. 34)	$1,795,100	$1,795,100
38 Walker Buehler, rhp, Dodgers (1st round/No. 24)	$1,777,500	$2,094,400
39 Donnie Dewees, of, Cubs (2nd round/No. 47)	$1,700,000	$1,292,100
40 Taylor Ward, c, Angels (1st round/No. 26)	$1,670,000	$2,034,500
41 Austin Riley, 3b, Braves (1st round/No. 41)	$1,600,000	$1,506,400
42 Peter Lambert, rhp, Rockies (2nd round/No. 44)	$1,495,000	$1,395,200
43 Chris Betts, c, Rays (2nd round/No. 52)	$1,482,500	$1,160,500
44 Alex Young, lhp, Diamondbacks (2nd round/No. 43)	$1,431,400	$1,431,400
45 Chris Shaw, of, Giants (1st round/No. 31)	$1,400,000	$1,885,000
46 Antonio Santillan, rhp, Reds (2nd round/No. 49)	$1,350,000	$1,227,800
47 Ryan Mountcastle, ss, Orioles (1st round/No. 36)	$1,300,000	$1,711,900
Darryl Wilson, of, Cubs (4th round/No. 113)	$1,300,000	$503,100
49 Scott Kingery, 2b, Phillies (2nd round/No. 48)	$1,259,600	$1,259,600
50 Nathan Kirby, lhp, Brewrs (supp. 1st/No. 40)	$1,250,000	$1,545,400
Total	**$124,094,080**	**$124,718,000**

DRAFT

ANDREW WOOLLEY

Alex Bregman gave LSU steady shortstop defense for three years before the Astros picked him

TEAM. PLAYER, POS., SCHOOL	BONUS
1. Diamondbacks. Dansby Swanson, ss, Vanderbilt	$6,500,000
2. Astros. Alex Bregman, ss, Louisiana State	$5,900,000
3. Rockies. Brendan Rodgers, ss, Lake Mary (Fla.) HS	$5,500,000
4. Rangers. Dillon Tate, rhp, UC Santa Barbara	$4,200,000
5. Astros. Kyle Tucker, of, Plant HS, Tampa	$4,000,000
6. Twins. Tyler Jay, lhp, Illinois	$3,889,500
7. Red Sox. Andrew Benintendi, of, Arkansas	$3,590,400
8. White Sox. Carson Fulmer, rhp, Vanderbilt	$3,470,600
9. Cubs. Ian Happ, of, Cincinnati	$3,000,000
10. Phillies. Cornelius Randolph, ss, Griffin (Ga.) HS	$3,231,300
11. Reds. Tyler Stephenson, c, Kennesaw (Ga.) Mountain HS	$3,141,600
12. Marlins. Josh Naylor, 1b, St. Joan of Arc SS, Mississauga, Ont.	$2,200,000
13. Rays. Garrett Whitley, of, Niskayuna (N.Y.) HS	$2,959,600
14. Braves. Kolby Allard, lhp, San Clemente (Calif.) HS	$3,042,400
15. Brewers. Trent Clark, of, Richland HS, N. Richland Hills, Texas	$2,700,000
16. Yankees. James Kaprielian, rhp, UCLA	$2,650,000
17. Indians. Brady Aiken, lhp, IMG Academy, Bradenton, Fla.	$2,513,280
18. Giants. Phil Bickford, rhp, JC of Southern Nevada	$2,333,800
19. Pirates. Kevin Newman, ss, Arizona	$2,175,000
20. Athletics. Richie Martin, ss, Florida	$1,950,000
21. Royals. Ashe Russell, rhp, Cathedral Catholic HS, Indianapolis	$2,190,200
22. Tigers. Beau Burrows, rhp, Weatherford (Texas) HS	$2,154,200
23. Cardinals. Nick Plummer, of, Rice HS, Bloomfield Hills, Mich.	$2,124,400
24. Dodgers. Walker Buehler, rhp, Vanderbilt	$1,777,500
25. Orioles. D.J. Stewart, of, Florida State	$2,064,500
26. Angels. Taylor Ward, c, Fresno State	$1,670,000
27. Rockies. Mike Nikorak, rhp, Stroudsburg (Pa.) HS	$2,300,000
28. Braves. Mike Soroka, rhp, Bishop Carroll HS, Calgary	$1,974,700
29. Blue Jays. Jon Harris, rhp, Missouri State	$1,944,800
30. Yankees. Kyle Holder, ss, San Diego	$1,800,000
31. Giants. Chris Shaw, 1b, Boston College	$1,400,000
32. Pirates. Ke'Bryan Hayes, 3b, Concordia Luthem HS, Tomball, Texas	$1,855,000
33. Royals. Nolan Watson, rhp, Lawrence North HS, Indianapolis	$1,825,200
34. Tigers. Christin Stewart, of, Tennessee	$1,795,100
35. Dodgers. Kyle Funkhouser, rhp, Louisville	Did not sign
36. Orioles. Ryan Mountcastle, ss, Hagerty HS, Oviedo, Fla.	$1,300,000
37. Astros. Daz Cameron, of, Eagle's Landing Acad., McDonough, Ga.	$4,000,000
38. Rockies. Tyler Nevin, 3b, Poway (Calif.) HS	$2,000,000
39. Cardinals. Jake Woodford, rhp, Plant HS, Tampa	$1,800,000
40. Brewers. Nathan Kirby, lhp, Virginia	$1,250,000
41. Braves. Austin Riley, 3b, DeSoto Central HS, Southaven, Miss.	$1,600,000
42. Indians. Triston McKenzie, rhp, Royal Palm Beach (Fla.) HS	$2,302,500
43. Diamondbacks. Alex Young, lhp, Texas Christian	$1,431,400
44. Rockies. Peter Lambert, rhp, San Dimas (Calif.) HS	$1,495,000
45. Rangers. Eric Jenkins, of, W. Columbus HS, Cerro Gordo, N.C.	$2,000,000
46. Astros. Thomas Eshelman, rhp, Cal State Fullerton	$1,100,000
47. Cubs. Donnie Dewees, of, North Florida	$1,700,000
48. Phillies. Scott Kingery, 2b, Arizona	$1,259,600
49. Reds. Antonio Santillan, rhp, Seguin HS, Arlington, Texas	$1,350,000
50. Marlins. Brett Lilek, lhp, Arizona State	$1,000,000

TEAM. PLAYER, POS., SCHOOL	BONUS
51. Padres. Austin Smith, rhp, Park Vista HS, Lake Worth, Fla.	$1,200,000
52. Rays. Chris Betts, c, Wilson HS, Long Beach	$1,482,500
53. Mets. Desmond Lindsay, of, Out-of-Door Academy, Sarasota, Fla.	$1,142,700
54. Braves. Lucas Herbert, c, San Clemente (Calif.) HS	$1,125,200
55. Brewers. Cody Ponce, rhp, Cal Poly Pomona	$1,108,000
56. Blue Jays. Brady Singer, rhp, Eustis (Fla.) HS	Did not sign
57. Yankees. Jeff Degano, lhp, Indiana State	$650,000
58. Nationals. Andrew Stevenson, of, Louisiana State	$750,000
59. Indians. Juan Hillman, lhp, Olympia HS, Orlando	$825,000
60. Mariners. Nick Neidert, rhp, Peachtree Ridge HS, Suwanee, Ga.	$1,200,000
61. Giants. Andrew Suarez, lhp, Miami	$1,010,100
62. Pirates. Kevin Kramer, ss, UCLA	$850,000
63. Athletics. Mikey White, ss, Alabama	$900,000
64. Royals. Josh Staumont, rhp, Azusa Pacific (Calif.)	$964,600
65. Tigers. Tyler Alexander, lhp, Texas Christian	$1,000,000
66. Cardinals. Bryce Denton, 3b, Ravenwood HS, Brentwood, Tenn.	$1,200,000
67. Dodgers. Mitch Hansen, of, Plano (Texas) Senior HS	$997,500
68. Orioles. Jonathan Hughes, rhp, Flowery Branch (Ga.) HS	Did not sign
69. Nationals. Blake Perkins, of, Verrado HS, Buckeye, Ariz.	$800,000
70. Angels. Jahmai Jones, of, Wesleyan HS, Norcross, Ga.	$1,100,000
71. Reds. Tanner Rainey, rhp, West Alabama	$432,950
72. Mariners. Andrew Moore, rhp, Oregon State	$800,000
73. Twins. Kyle Cody, rhp, Kentucky	Did not sign
74. Dodgers. Josh Sborz, rhp, Vrginia	$722,500
75. Braves. A.J. Minter, lhp, Texas A&M	$814,300
76. Diamondbacks. Taylor Clarke, rhp, College of Charleston	$801,900
77. Rockies. Javier Medina, rhp, Sahuaro HS, Tucson	$740,000
78. Rangers. Michael Matuella, rhp, Duke	$2,000,000
79. Astros. Riley Ferrell, rhp, Texas Christian	$1,000,000
80. Twins. Travis Blankenhorn, 3b, Pottsville (Pa.) HS	$650,000
81. Red Sox. Austin Rei, c, Washington	$742,400
82. Cubs. Bryan Hudson, lhp, Alton (Ill.) HS	$1,100,000
83. Phillies. Lucas Williams, ss, Dana Hills HS, Dana Point, Calif.	$719,800
84. Reds. Blake Trahan, ss, Louisiana-Lafayette	$708,900
85. Marlins. Isaiah White, of, Greenfield HS, Wilson, N.C.	$698,100
86. Padres. Jacob Nix, rhp, IMG Academy, Bradenton, Fla.	$900,000
87. Rays. Brandon Lowe, 2b, Maryland	$697,500
88. Mets. Max Wotell, lhp, Marvin Ridge HS, Waxhaw, N.C.	$775,000
89. Braves. Anthony Guardado, rhp, Nogales HS, La Puente, Calif.	$550,000
90. Brewers. Nash Walters, rhp, Lindale (Texas) HS	$800,000
91. Blue Jays. Justin Maese, rhp, Ysleta HS, El Paso	$300,000
92. Yankees. Drew Finley, rhp, Rancho Bernardo HS, San Diego	$950,000
93. Indians. Mark Mathias, 2b, Cal Poly	$550,000
94. Mariners. Braden Bishop, of, Washington	$607,700
95. Giants. Jalen Miller, ss, Riverwood Int'l Charter HS, Sandy Springs, Ga.	$1,100,000
96. Pirates. Casey Hughston, of, Alabama	$700,000
97. Athletics. Dakota Chalmers, rhp, N. Forsyth HS, Cumming, Ga.	$1,200,000
98. Royals. Anderson Miller, of, Western Kentucky	$581,300
99. Tigers. Drew Smith, rhp, Dallas Baptist	$575,800
100. Cardinals. Harrison Bader, of, Florida	$400,000

2015 CLUB-BY-CLUB SELECTIONS

DRAFT

ARIZONA DIAMONDBACKS (1)

1. **Dansby Swanson, ss, Vanderbilt**
2. **Alex Young, lhp, Texas Christian**
3. **Taylor Clarke, rhp, College of Charleston**
4. **Breckin Williams, rhp, Missouri**
5. **Ryan Burr, rhp, Arizona State**
6. **Tyler Mark, rhp, Concordia (Calif.)**
7. **Francis Christy, c, Palomar (Calif.) JC**
8. **Kal Simmons, ss, Kennesaw State**
9. **Pierce Romero, rhp, Santa Barbara (Calif.) CC**
10. **Joey Armstrong, of, Nevada-Las Vegas**
11. **Austin Byler, 1b, Nevada**
12. **Wesley Rodriguez, rhp, Washington HS, New York**
13. **Jason Morozowski, of, Mount Olive (N.C.)**
14. **Luke Lowery, c, East Carolina**
15. **Justin Donatella, rhp, UC San Diego**
16. **Zach Nehrir, of, Houston Baptist**
17. **Austin Mason, rhp, The Citadel**
18. **Daniel Comstock, c, Menlo (Calif.)**
19. Jacy Cave, of, New Mexico JC
20. **Will Lowman, lhp, Kennesaw State**
21. **Alexis Olmeda, c, Yavapai (Ariz.) JC**
22. **Zach Hoffpauir, of, Stanford**
23. **Logan Soole, of, Monarch HS, Louisville, Colo.**
24. **Bryant Holtmann, lhp, Florida State**
25. **Stephen Dezzi, of, Tampa**
26. **Kirby Bellow, lhp, Texas**
27. **Cameron Gann, rhp, Stephen F. Austin State**
28. Jesse Wilkening, c, Hanover Central HS, Cedar Lake, Ind.
29. **Keegan Long, rhp, St. Joseph's (Ind.)**
30. **Jeff Smith, 2b, Missouri Baptist**
31. Vance Vizcaino, 3b, Stetson
32. Bryan Hoeing, rhp, Batesville (Ind.) HS
33. **Luis Silverio, of, Eastern Florida State JC**
34. **Jake Peevyhouse, of, Arizona State**
35. **Quinnton Mack, of, New Mexico State**
36. **Cameron Smith, lhp, Texas Tech**
37. **Max Brown, of, Kansas State**
38. **Josh Anderson, 3b, Florida International**
39. Georgie Salem, of, Alabama
40. **Tucker Ward, rhp, Mobile (Ala.)**

ATLANTA BRAVES (15)

1. **Kolby Allard, lhp, San Clemente (Calif.) HS**
1. **Mike Soroka, rhp, Bishop Carroll HS, Calgary, Alberta**
1. **Austin Riley (Supplemental pick), 3b, DeSoto Central HS, Southaven, Miss.**
2. **Lucas Herbert, c, San Clemente (Calif.) HS**
2. **A.J. Minter (Supplemental pick), lhp, Texas A&M**
3. **Anthony Guardado, rhp, Nogales HS, La Puente, Calif.**
4. **Josh Graham, rhp, Oregon**
5. **Ryan Clark, rhp, UNC Greensboro**
6. **Matt Withrow, rhp, Texas Tech**
7. **Patrick Weigel, rhp, Houston**
8. **Ryan Lawlor, lhp, Georgia**
9. **Taylor Lewis, rhp, Florida**
10. **Stephen Moore, rhp, Navy**
11. **Grayson Jones, rhp, Shelton State (Ala.) CC**
12. **Justin Ellison, of, Western Oklahoma State JC**
13. **Chase Johnson-Mullins, lhp, Shelton State (Ala.) CC**
14. **Trey Keegan, c, Bowling Green State**
15. **Brad Keller, of, Crest HS, Shelby, N.C.**
16. **Trevor Belicek, lhp, Texas A&M-Corpus Christi**
17. **Evan Phillips, rhp, UNC Wilmington**
18. **Gilbert Suarez, rhp, San Ysidro HS, San Diego**
19. **Sean McLaughlin, rhp, Georgia**
20. **Jarret Hellinger, lhp, Ola HS, McDonough, Ga.**
21. **Kurt Hoekstra, 2b, Western Michigan**
22. **Dalton Geekie, rhp, Georgia Highlands JC**
23. **Taylor Cockrell, rhp, State JC of Florida**
24. **Jake Lanning, 3b, Holy Cross**
25. **Jonathan Morales, c, Miami Dade JC**
26. **Ben Libuda, lhp, Worcester State (Mass.)**
27. **Robby Nesovic, 3b, UC Santa Barbara**
28. Curtiss Pomeroy, rhp, Georgetown
29. **Collin Yelich, c, Sam Houston State**
30. Doug Still, lhp, Jefferson (Mo.) JC
31. **Matt Custred, rhp, Texas Tech**
32. D.J. Neal, of, Stephenson HS, Stone Mountain, Ga.
33. Terry Godwin, of, Callaway HS, Hogansville, Ga.
34. Carter Hall, ss, Wesleyan HS, Norcross, Ga.
35. Chase Smartt, c, Henderson HS, Troy, Ala.
36. Luis Lopez, 2b, Colegio Catolico Notre Dame HS, Caguas, P.R.
37. Jackson Webb, ss, Johnson Ferry Christian Academy, Marietta, Ga.
38. Liam Scafariello, 1b, Southington (Conn.) HS
39. Jeremy Pena, ss, Classical HS, Providence, R.I.
40. John Stewart, 3b, Greenwich (N.Y.) Central HS

BALTIMORE ORIOLES (28)

1. **D.J. Stewart, of, Florida State**
1. **Ryan Mountcastle, ss, Hagerty HS, Oviedo, Fla.**
2. Jonathan Hughes, rhp, Flowery Branch (Ga.) HS
3. **Garrett Cleavinger, lhp, Oregon**
4. **Ryan McKenna, of, St. Thomas Aquinas HS, Dover, N.H.**
5. **Jason Heinrich, of, River Ridge HS, New Port Richey, Fla.**
6. **Jay Flaa, rhp, North Dakota State**
7. **Gray Fenter, rhp, West Memphis (Ark.) HS**
8. **Seamus Curran, 1b, Agawam (Mass.) HS**
9. **Jaylen Ferguson, of, Arlington (Texas) HS**
10. **Reid Love, lhp, East Carolina**
11. **Ryan Meisinger, rhp, Radford**
12. **Robert Strader, lhp, Louisville**
13. **Cedric Mullins, of, Campbell**
14. **Drew Turbin, 2b, Dallas Baptist**
15. **Chris Shaw, c, Oklahoma**
16. **Mike Odenwaelder, of, Amherst (Mass.)**
17. **Branden Becker, ss, Cajon HS, San Bernardino, Calif.**
18. **Nick Vespi, lhp, Palm Beach State (Fla.) JC**
19. **Jerry McClanahan, c, UC Irvine**
20. Adam Walton, ss, Illinois
21. **Juan Echevarria, rhp, Osceola HS, Seminole, Fla.**
22. **Tristan Graham, of, Northeast Texas CC**
23. **Will Dennis, lhp, Seattle**
24. **Kirvin Moesquit, 3b, Seminole State (Fla.) JC**
25. **Steve Laurino, 1b, Marist**
26. **Rocky McCord, rhp, Auburn**
27. **Stuart Levy, c, Arkansas State**
28. **Christian Turnipseed, rhp, Georgia-Gwinnett**
29. Gabriel Garcia, c, Montverde (Fla.) Academy
30. **Andrew Elliot, rhp, Wright State**
31. **Will Shepley, lhp, UNC Wilmington**
32. Cody Morris, rhp, Reservoir HS, Fulton, Md.
33. **Steven Klimek, rhp, St. Bonaventure**
34. **Kory Groves, rhp, Cal State Monterey Bay**
35. Guillermo Trujillo, rhp, Oral Roberts
36. **Xavier Borde, lhp, Arizona**
37. Jake Pries, of, JSerra HS, San Juan Capistrano, Calif.
38. **Jack Graham, 2b, Slippery Rock (Pa.)**
39. **Frank Crinella, 3b, Merrimack (Mass.)**
40. **Mike Costello, rhp, Post (Conn.)**

BOSTON RED SOX (6)

1. **Andrew Benintendi, of, Arkansas**
2. (Pick forfeited for signing of free agent Pablo Sandoval)
2s. (Competitive Balance Round B pick forfeited for signing of free agent Hanley Ramirez)
3. **Austin Rei, c, Washington**
4. **Tate Matheny, of, Missouri State**
5. **Jagger Rusconi, ss, West Ranch HS, Santa Clarita, Calif.**
6. **Travis Lakins, rhp, Ohio State**

7. Ben Taylor, rhp, South Alabama
8. Logan Allen, lhp, IMG Academy, Bradenton, Fla.
9. Tucker Tubbs, 1b, Memphis
10. Mitchell Gunsolus, 3b, Gonzaga
11. Nick Hamilton, of, Lockport (N.Y.) HS
12. Kevin Kelleher, rhp, New Orleans
13. Matt Kent, lhp, Texas A&M
14. Bobby Poyner, lhp, Florida
15. Jerry Downs, of, St. Thomas (Fla.)
16. Marc Brakeman, rhp, Stanford
17. Chad De La Guerra, 2b, Grand Canyon (Ariz.)
18. James Nelson, ss, Redan HS, Stone Mountain, Ga.
19. Logan Boyd, lhp, Sam Houston State
20. Yomar Valentin, ss, Beltran Baseball Academy, Florida, P.R.
21. Danny Zandona, rhp, Cal Poly
22. Max Watt, rhp, Lynn (Fla.)
23. Kyri Washington, of, Longwood
24. Brad Stone, lhp, North Carolina State
25. Andrew Noviello, c, Bridgewater-Raynham Regional HS, Bridgewater, Mass.
26. Kevin Ginkel, rhp, Southwestern (Calif.) JC
27. Saige Jenco, of, Virginia Tech
28. Steve Mangrum, 3b, Western Albemarle HS, Crozet, Va.
29. Will Stillman, rhp, Wofford
30. Jack Conley, c, Leesville Road HS, Raleigh, N.C.
31. Nick Duron, rhp, Clark (Wash.) JC
32. Clate Schmidt, rhp, Clemson
33. Cal Smith, 2b, Fort Worth Christian HS, Richland Hills, Texas
34. Nick Lovullo, ss, Holy Cross
35. Tyler Spoon, of, Arkansas
36. Trevor Kelley, rhp, North Carolina
37. Adam Lau, rhp, Alabama-Birmingham
38. C.J. Ballard, of, Pike County HS, Zebulon, Ga.
39. Daniel Reyes, of, Mater Academy Charter HS, Hialeah Gardens, Fla.
40. D.J. Artis, of, Southeast Guilford HS, Greensboro, N.C.

CHICAGO CUBS (8)

1. Ian Happ, of, Cincinnati
2. Donnie Dewees, of, North Florida
3. Bryan Hudson, lhp, Alton (Ill.) HS
4. D.J. Wilson, of, Canton (Ohio) South HS
5. Ryan Kellogg, lhp, Arizona State
6. David Berg, rhp, UCLA
7. Craig Brooks, rhp, Catawba (N.C.)
8. Preston Morrison, rhp, Texas Christian
9. Tyler Peitzmeier, lhp, Cal State Fullerton
10. Vimael Machin, ss, Virginia Commonwealth
11. Matt Rose, 3b, Georgia State
12. P.J. Higgins, 2b, Old Dominion
13. Kyle Twomey, lhp, Southern California
14. Jake Kelzer, rhp, Indiana
15. Scott Effross, rhp, Indiana
16. Michael Foster, of, Northeastern
17. Casey Bloomquist, rhp, Cal Poly
18. John Cresto, 3b, Cathedral Catholic HS, San Diego
19. Kyle Miller, rhp, Florida Atlantic
20. Blake Headley, 3b, Nebraska
21. Jared Cheek, rhp, Georgia
22. Alex Bautista, of, Lindsey Wilson (Ky.)
23. John Williamson, lhp, Rice
24. Sutton Whiting, ss, Louisville
25. Marcus Mastrobuoni, c, Cal State Stanislaus
26. Jared Padgett, lhp, Graceville (Fla.) HS
27. Angelo Amendolare, 2b, Jacksonville
28. Delvin Zinn, ss, Pontotoc (Miss.) HS
29. Ian Rice, c, Houston
30. Tyler Payne, c, West Virginia State
31. Daniel Spingola, of, Georgia Tech
32. Fitz Stadler, rhp, Glenbrook South HS, Glenview, Ill.
33. M.T. Minacci, rhp, Tallahassee, Fla. (no school)
34. Cody Hawken, of, Union HS, Camas, Wash.
35. Taylor Jones, 1b, Gonzaga
36. Alonzo Jones, ss, Columbus (Ga.) HS

37. Donnie Cimino, of, Wesleyan (Conn.)
38. Rayne Supple, rhp, Champlain Valley Union HS, Hinesburg, Vt.
39. John Kilichowski, lhp, Vanderbilt
40. Domenic DeRenzo, c, Central Catholic HS, Pittsburgh

CHICAGO WHITE SOX (7)

1. Carson Fulmer, rhp, Vanderbilt
2. (Pick forfeited for signing of free agent David Robertson)
3. (Pick forfeited for signing of free agent Melky Cabrera)
4. Zack Erwin, lhp, Clemson
5. Jordan Stephens, rhp, Rice
6. Corey Zangari, 1b, Albert HS, Midwest City, Okla.
7. Blake Hickman, rhp, Iowa
8. Casey Schroeder, c, Coastal Carolina
9. Ryan Hinchley, lhp, Illinois-Chicago
10. Jackson Glines, of, Michigan
11. Danny Dopico, rhp, Florida International
12. Seby Zavala, c, San Diego State
13. Ryan Riga, lhp, Ohio State
14. Tyler Sullivan, of, Pacific
15. Chris Comito, rhp, Norwalk (Iowa) HS
16. Brandon Quintero, rhp, Cal State Los Angeles
17. Sikes Orvis, 1b, Mississippi
18. Dante Flores, 2b, Southern California
19. Frank Califano, of, Youngstown State
20. Jacob Cooper, c, Modesto (Calif.) JC
21. Landon Lassiter, of, North Carolina
22. Danny Mendick, ss, Massachusetts-Lowell
23. Dylan Barrow, rhp, Tampa
24. Brandon Magallones, rhp, Northwestern
25. Richard McWilliams, rhp, Cal Poly Pomona
26. Grant Massey, ss, Lipscomb
27. Alex Katz, lhp, St. John's
28. Bradley Strong, 3b, Western Carolina
29. Jake Fincher, of, North Carolina State
30. Jack Charleston, rhp, Faulkner (Ala.)
31. David Walker, 2b, Grand Canyon (Ariz.)
32. Taylore Cherry, rhp, North Carolina
33. Johnathan Frebis, lhp, Middle Tennessee State
34. Drew Hasler, rhp, Valpariso
35. Derek King, ss, Hillsborough (Fla.) CC
36. Michael Hickman, c, Seven Lakes HS, Katy, Texas
37. Garvin Alston, lhp, Mountain Point HS, Phoenix
38. Cody Staab, of, College Station (Texas) HS
39. Jalin McMillan, 3b, Simeon Career Academy, Chicago
40. Joseph Reinsdorf, 2b, New Trier HS, Winnetka, Ill.

CINCINNATI REDS (10)

1. Tyler Stephenson, c, Kennesaw (Ga.) Mountain HS
2. Antonio Santillian, rhp, Seguin HS, Arlington, Texas
2. Tanner Rainey (Supplemental pick), rhp, West Alabama
3. Blake Trahan, ss, Louisiana-Lafayette
4. Miles Gordon, of, St. Ignatius of Loyola Catholic SS, Oakville, Ontario
5. Ian Kahaloa, rhp, Campbell HS, Ewa Beach, Hawaii
6. Jimmy Herget, rhp, South Florida
7. Jordan Ramsey, rhp, UNC Wilmington
8. Mitch Piatnik, ss, State JC of Florida
9. Sarkis Ohanian, rhp, Duke
10. Zach Shields, of, UNC Wilmington
11. Brantley Bell, ss, State JC of Florida
12. Alexis Diaz, rhp, Juan Jose Maunez HS, Naguabo, P.R.
13. Andrew Jordan, rhp, Huss HS, Gastonia, N.C.
14. Austin Orewiler, rhp, Rice
15. Blake Butler, 2b, College of Charleston
16. Jake Johnson, rhp, Southeastern Louisiana
17. J.D. Salmon-Williams, 2b, Suzuki SS, Brampton, Ontario
18. Isaac Anesty, lhp, Our Lady of Lourdes Catholic HS, Guelph, Ontario
19. Mike Salvatore, rhp, Ewing HS, Ewing Township, N.J.
20. Rock Rucker, lhp, Auburn-Montgomery
21. Satchel McElroy, of, Clear Creek HS, League City, Texas
22. Darren Shred, rhp, St. Roch Catholic SS, Brampton, Ontario
23. Ed Charlton, of, New Jersey Tech

24. Joe Zanghi, rhp, Cumberland (N.J.) CC
25. James Vasquez, 1b, Central Florida
26. Dwanya Williams-Sutton, of, Greenfield School, Wilson, N.C.
27. **Alejo Lopez, ss, Greenway HS, Phoenix**
28. Ronnie Rossomando, rhp, Bunnell HS, Stratford, Conn.
29. Elih Marrero, c, Coral Gables (Fla.) HS
30. Joseph Purritano, 1b, Dartmouth
31. Ethan Skender, 2b, Metamora (Ill.) Township HS
32. Wil McAffer, rhp, Sentinel SS, West Vancouver, B.C.
33. Tyler Peyton, rhp, Iowa
34. **Connor Bennett, rhp, Buford (Ga.) HS**
35. Alexander Krupa, of, Iowa Western CC
36. **Mitchell Tripp, rhp, Central Florida**
37. Riley Thompson, rhp, Christian Academy of Louisville
38. Matt Kroon, 3b, Horizon HS, Scottsdale, Ariz.
39. Kevin Santiago, ss, Rafaelina E. Lebron Flores HS, Patillas, P.R.
40. Jonathon Armwood, 1b, St. Edward's (Texas)

CLEVELAND INDIANS (19)

1. **Brady Aiken, lhp, IMG Academy, Bradenton, Fla.**
1. **Triston McKenzie (Supplemental pick), rhp, Royal Palm Beach (Fla.) HS**
2. **Juan Hillman, lhp, Olympia HS, Orlando**
3. **Mark Mathias, 2b, Cal Poly**
4. **Tyler Krieger, ss, Clemson**
5. **Ka'ai Tom, of, Kentucky**
6. **Jonas Wyatt, rhp, Quartz Hill (Calif.) HS**
7. **Nathan Lukes, of, Sacramento State**
8. **Justin Garza, rhp, Cal State Fullerton**
9. **Devon Stewart, rhp, Canisius**
10. Billy Strode, lhp, Florida State
11. Chandler Newman, rhp, Richmond Hill (Ga.) HS
12. **Ryan Perez, lhp, Judson (Ill.)**
13. **Daniel Salters, c, Dallas Baptist**
14. **Matt Esparza, rhp, UC Irvine**
15. Daniel Sprinkle, rhp, White Hall (Ark.) HS
16. Cobie Vance, 2b, Pine Forest HS, Fayetteville, N.C.
17. Nick Madrigal, ss, Elk Grove (Calif.) HS
18. **Anthony Miller, 1b, Johnson County (Kan.) CC**
19. **Todd Isaacs, of, Palm Beach State (Fla.) JC**
20. **Luke Wakamatsu, ss, Keller (Texas) HS**
21. **Brock Hartson, rhp, Texas-San Antonio**
22. Garrett Benge, 3b, Cowley County (Kan.) CC
23. Chad Smith, rhp, Wallace State (Ala.) CC
24. **Sam Haggerty, 2b, New Mexico**
25. **Connor Marabell, of, Jacksonville**
26. A.J. Graffanino, ss, Northwest Christian HS, Phoenix
27. Austin Rubick, rhp, Buena HS, Ventura, Calif.
28. **Jack Goihl, c, Augustana (S.D.)**
29. **Christian Meister, rhp, Federal Way, Wash. (no school)**
30. Chandler Day, rhp, Watkins Memorial HS, Pataskala, Ohio
31. Dillon Persinger, 2b, Golden West (Calif.) JC
32. Jacob Hill, lhp, San Diego
33. Garrett Wolforth, c, Concordia Luthern HS, Tomball, Texas
34. Andrew Cabezas, rhp, Mater Academy Charter HS, Hialeah Gardens, Fla.
35. Cade Tremie, c, New Waverly (Texas) HS
36. **Ryan Colegate, rhp, Ohio Dominican**
37. Lucas Humphal, rhp, Texas State
38. Braden Webb, rhp, Owasso, Okla. (no school)
39. Tristin English, rhp, Pike County HS, Zebulon, Ga.
40. Hunter Parsons, rhp, Parkside HS, Salisbury, Md.

COLORADO ROCKIES (2)

1. **Brendan Rodgers, ss, Lake Mary (Fla.) HS**
1. **Mike Nikorak, rhp, Stroudsburg (Pa.) HS**
1. **Tyler Nevin (Supplemental pick), 3b, Poway (Calif.) HS**
2. **Peter Lambert, rhp, San Dimas (Calif.) HS**
3. **Javier Medina, rhp, Sahuaro HS, Tucson**
4. **David Hill, rhp, San Diego**
5. **Parker French, rhp, Texas**
6. **Jack Wynkoop, lhp, South Carolina**

The Indians took pitchers with their first three picks, including Triston McKenzie

ALYSON BOYER RODE

7. **Brian Mundell, 1b, Cal Poly**
8. **Colin Welmon, rhp, Loyola Marymount**
9. **Trey Killian, rhp, Arkansas**
10. **Cole Anderson, of, Rocky Mountain HS, Fort Collins, Colo.**
11. **Michael Zimmerman, lhp, Gulf Coast HS, Naples, Fla.**
12. **Justin Lawrence, rhp, Daytona State (Fla.) JC**
13. **Mylz Jones, ss, Cal State Bakersfield**
14. **Sam Thoele, rhp, Arkansas-Little Rock**
15. **Sam Hilliard, of, Wichita State**
16. **Ryan McCormick, rhp, St. John's**
17. **Collin Ferguson, 1b, St. Mary's**
18. **Chris Keck, 3b, UCLA**
19. **Daniel Koger, lhp, Alabama-Huntsville**
20. **Bobby Stahel, of, Southern California**
21. **Logan Cozart, rhp, Ohio**
22. **Eric Toole, of, Iowa**
23. **Steven Leonard, c, Campbell**
24. **James McMahon, rhp, Southern Mississippi**
25. **Scotty Burcham, ss, Sacramento State**
26. **Drasen Johnson, rhp, Illinois**
27. **Campbell Wear, c, UC Santa Barbara**
28. **Tyler Follis, ss, North Dakota**
29. **Hayden Jones, rhp, Valdosta State (Ga.)**
30. **Matt Meier, rhp, Lindenwood (Mo.)**
31. **Hector Moreta, rhp, Calusa Prep HS, Miami**
32. Jensen Park, of, Northern Colorado
33. Wyatt Cross, c, Legacy HS, Broomfield, Colo.
34. Michael Benson, c, Rancho Buena Vista HS, Vista, Calif.
35. Ryan Madden, rhp, Fairview HS, Boulder, Colo.
36. Andy Pagnozzi, rhp, Fayetteville (Ark.) HS
37. Marc Mumper, ss, Mountain Vista HS, Highlands Ranch, Colo.
38. Jake Singer, 2b, Torrey Pines HS, San Diego
39. Brent Schwarz, rhp, Regis Jesuit HS, Aurora, Colo.
40. Alexander Carter, 1b, Georgetown

DETROIT TIGERS (25)

1. **Beau Burrows, rhp, Weatherford (Texas) HS**
1. **Christin Stewart, of, Tennessee**
2. **Tyler Alexander, lhp, Texas Christian**
3. **Drew Smith, rhp, Dallas Baptist**
4. **Kade Scivicque, c, Louisiana State**
5. **Cam Gibson, of, Michigan State**

6. **Matt Hall, lhp, Missouri State**
7. Nick Shumpert, ss, Highlands Ranch (Colo.) HS
8. **Dominic Moreno, rhp, Texas Tech**
9. **Trey Teakell, rhp, Texas Christian**
10. **Cole Bauml, of, Northern Kentucky**
11. **Jake Shull, rhp, Fresno State**
12. **Kyle Dowdy, rhp, Houston**
13. **Josh Lester, 3b, Missouri**
14. **A.J. Simcox, ss, Tennessee**
15. **Keaton Jones, ss, Texas Christian**
16. **Alec Kisena, rhp, Edmonds (Wash.) CC**
17. Grant Wolfram, lhp, Hamilton (Mich.) HS
18. **Joey Havrilak, of, Akron**
19. **Cam Vieaux, lhp, Michigan State**
20. **Logan Longwith, rhp, Tennessee Wesleyan**
21. **Tanner Donnels, 1b, Loyola Marymount**
22. **Toller Boardman, rhp, New Mexico**
23. **Ryan Milton, rhp, Southern Mississippi**
24. **Mike Vinson, rhp, Florida**
25. **Ryan Castellanos, rhp, Nova Southeastern (Fla.)**
26. **Taylor Hicks, rhp, Georgia**
27. **Tyler Servais, c, Princeton**
28. **Pat MacKenzie, 2b, Central Michigan**
29. Dayton Dugas, of, Houston HS, Moss Bluff, La.
30. Cole McKay, rhp, Smithson Valley HS, Spring Branch, Texas
31. **Blaise Salter, 1b, Michigan State**
32. Trey Dawson, ss, Hurricane (W.Va.) HS
33. Nick Dalesandro, c, Joliet (Ill.) Catholic Academy
34. Andrew McWilliam, 3b, San Diego Mesa JC
35. Connor Lungwitz, rhp, Maize (Kan.) HS
36. Daniel Pinero, ss, Virginia
37. Andrew Naderer, lhp, Grand Canyon (Ariz.)
38. Bryant Harris, of, Luella HS, Locust Grove, Ga.
39. Travis Howard, rhp, Marana HS, Tucson
40. Jackson Kowar, rhp, Charlotte Christian HS

HOUSTON ASTROS (4)

1. **Alex Bregman, ss, Louisiana State**
1. **Kyle Tucker, of, Plant HS, Tampa**
1. **Daz Cameron (Supplemental pick), of, Eagle's Landing Christian Academy, McDonough, Ga.**
2. **Thomas Eshelman, rhp, Cal State Fullerton**
3. **Riley Ferrell, rhp, Texas Christian**
4. **Anthony Hermelyn, c, Oklahoma**
5. **Trent Thornton, rhp, North Carolina**
6. **Nestor Muriel, of, Beltran Baseball Academy, Florida, P.R.**
7. **Michael Freeman, lhp, Oklahoma State**
8. **Garrett Stubbs, c, Southern California**
9. **Zac Person, lhp, Louisiana State**
10. **Scott Weathersby, rhp, Mississippi**
11. **Patrick Sandoval, lhp, Mission Viejo (Calif.) HS**
12. **Myles Straw, of, St. John's River (Fla.) JC**
13. **Kevin McCanna, rhp, Rice**
14. **Johnny Sewald, of, Arizona State**
15. **Pat Porter, of, Ohio State**
16. **Adam Whitt, rhp, Nevada**
17. **Justin Garcia, of, Nova Southeastern (Fla.)**
18. **Kevin Martir, c, Maryland**
19. **Drew Ferguson, of, Belmont**
20. **Makay Nelson, rhp, JC of Southern Idaho**
21. **Alex Winkelman, lhp, Southeast Missouri State**
22. Cole Sands, rhp, North Florida Christian HS, Tallahassee, Fla.
23. **Matt Bower, lhp, Washington State**
24. **Chris Murphy, rhp, Millersville (Pa.)**
25. **Jorge Martinez, c, Beltran Baseball Academy, Florida, P.R.**
26. **Ralph Garza, rhp, Oklahoma**
27. James Carter, rhp, UC Santa Barbara
28. **Zac Grotz, rhp, Embry-Riddle (Fla.)**
29. **Brooks Marlow, 2b, Texas**
30. **Bobby Wernes, 3b, Arkansas**
31. **Keach Ballard, ss, Oklahoma Baptist**
32. **Aaron Mizell, of, Georgia Southern**
33. **Kolbey Carpenter, 2b, Oklahoma**

34. Conor Biggio, of, Notre Dame
35. Kody Clemens, ss, Memorial HS, Hedwig Village, Texas
36. **Ryan Deemes, rhp, Nicholls State**
37. Luken Baker, rhp, Oak Ridge HS, Conroe, Texas
38. **Nick Rivera, 1b, Florida Gulf Coast**
39. Alex Vargas, rhp, Monroe (N.Y.) JC
40. **Steve Naemark, lhp, Angelo State (Texas)**

KANSAS CITY ROYALS (24)

1. **Ashe Russell, rhp, Cathedral Catholic HS, Indianapolis**
1. **Nolan Watson, rhp, Lawrence North HS, Indianapolis**
2. **Josh Staumont, rhp, Azusa Pacific (Calif.)**
3. **Anderson Miller, of, Western Kentucky**
4. **Garrett Davila, lhp, South Point HS, Belmont, N.C.**
5. **Roman Collins, of, Florida Atlantic**
6. **Cody Jones, of, Texas Christian**
7. **Gabriel Cancel, ss, Beltran Baseball Academy, Florida, P.R.**
8. **Andre Davis, lhp, Arkansas-Pine Bluff**
9. **Joey Markus, lhp, Indian River (Fla.) JC**
10. **Alex Luna, rhp, Alabama-Birmingham**
11. **Ben Johnson, of, Texas**
12. **Daniel Concepcion, rhp, Virginia Commonwealth**
13. **Travis Maezes, ss, Michigan**
14. **Nick Dini, c, Wagner**
15. Marquise Doherty, of, Winnetonka HS, Kansas City, Mo.
16. **Matt Ditman, rhp, Rice**
17. **Matt Portland, lhp, Northwestern**
18. **Brian Bayliss, rhp, St. Joseph's (Ind.)**
19. **Emmanuel Rivera, ss, Universidad Interamericana (P.R.) JC**
20. Jeffrey Harding, rhp, Chipola (Fla.) JC
21. **Austin Bailey, ss, San Diego**
22. **Drew Milligan, lhp, Delta State (Miss.)**
23. **Colton Frabasilio, of, Saint Louis**
24. **Jonathan McCray, 2b, San Bernardino Valley (Calif.) JC**
25. **Tyler Carvalho, rhp, Mesa (Ariz.) CC**
26. **Alex Close, c, Liberty**
27. **Jacob Bodner, rhp, Xavier**
28. Reed Hayes, rhp, Walters State (Tenn.) CC
29. **Mark McCoy, lhp, Rutgers**
30. **Luke Willis, of, George Mason**
31. **Brian Bien, ss, Bowling Green State**
32. **Jake Kalish, lhp, George Mason**
33. **Nate Esposito, c, Concordia (Ore.)**
34. **Taylor Ostrich, 1b, Old Dominion**
35. **Trey Stover, ss, Hartford**
36. **Tanner Stanley, 2b, Richmond**
37. Jacob Ruder, rhp, Nixa (Mo.) HS
38. Dylan Horne, lhp, Walters State (Tenn.) CC
39. Billy Endris, of, Florida Atlantic
40. Ford Proctor, c, Monsignor Kelly Catholic HS, Beaumont, Texas

LOS ANGELES ANGELS (30)

1. **Taylor Ward, c, Fresno State**
2. **Jahmai Jones, of, Wesleyan HS, Norcross, Ga.**
3. **Grayson Long, rhp, Texas A&M**
4. **Brendon Sanger, of, Florida Atlantic**
5. **Jared Foster, of, Louisiana State**
6. **David Fletcher, ss, Loyola Marymount**
7. **Hutton Moyer, 2b, Pepperdine**
8. **Kyle Survance, of, Houston**
9. **Tanner Lubach, c, Nebraska**
10. **Adam Hofacket, rhp, California Baptist**
11. **Jimmy Barnes, of, Deep Creek HS, Chesapeake, Va.**
12. **Dalton Blumenfeld, c, Hamilton HS, Los Angeles**
13. **Jeff Boehm, of, Illinois-Chicago**
14. **Ryan Vega, of, El Paso CC**
15. **Nathan Bates, rhp, Georgia State**
16. **Nathan Bertness, lhp, McLennan (Texas) CC**
17. **Sam Pastrone, rhp, Arbor View HS, Las Vegas**
18. **Travis Herrin, rhp, Wabash Valley (Ill.) JC**
19. **Aaron Cox, rhp, Gannon (Pa.)**
20. **Kenny Towns, 3b, Virginia**
21. **Michael Pierson, 3b, Appalachian State**
22. **Ronnie Glenn, lhp, Pennsylvania**

23. Tim Arakawa, 2b, Oklahoma State
24. Mitch Esser, of, Concordia (Calif.)
25. Trever Allen, of, Arizona State
26. Taylor Cobb, rhp, Houston
27. Sam Koenig, of, Wisconsin-Milwaukee
28. Aaron Rhodes, rhp, Florida
29. Cody Pope, rhp, Eastern New Mexico
30. Nick Lynch, 1b, UC Davis
31. Izaak Silva, c, UC Davis
32. Conor Lillis-White, lhp, British Columbia
33. Winston Lavendier, lhp, Cal State Dominguez Hills
34. Nick Flair, 3b, Tampa
35. Jordan Serena, of, Columbia
36. Sam McDonnell, of, Navarro (Texas) JC
37. Josh Delph, of, Florida State
38. Jonah Dipoto, rhp, Newport Harbor HS, Newport Beach, Calif.
39. Jared Walsh, 1b, Georgia
40. Jacob McDavid, rhp, Oral Roberts

LOS ANGELES DODGERS (27)

1. Walker Buehler, rhp, Vanderbilt
1. Kyle Funkhouser, rhp, Louisville
2. Mitch Hansen, of, Plano (Texas) Senior HS
2. Josh Sborz (Supplemental pick), rhp, Vrginia
3. Philip Pfeifer, lhp, Vanderbilt
4. Willie Calhoun, 2b, Yavapai (Ariz.) JC
5. Brendon Davis, ss, Lakewood (Calif.) HS
6. Edwin Rios, 1b, Florida International
7. Andrew Sopko, rhp, Gonzaga
8. Tommy Bergjans, rhp, Haverford (Pa.)
9. Kevin Brown, rhp, Cal State Dominguez Hills
10. Logan Landon, of, Texas-Pan American
11. Imani Abdullah, rhp, Madison HS, San Diego
12. Matt Beaty, c, Belmont
13. Michael Boyle, lhp, Radford
14. Garrett Kennedy, c, Miami
15. Garrett Zech, of, Naples (Fla.) HS
16. Nolan Long, rhp, Wagner
17. Jason Goldstein, c, Illinois
18. Chris Godinez, 2b, Bradley
19. Joe Genord, c, Park Vista Community HS, Lake Worth, Fla.
20. John Boushelle, rhp, Fayetteville (Ark.) HS
21. Jake Henson, c, Saint Louis
22. Jordan Tarsovich, 2b, Virginia Military Institute
23. Andrew Istler, rhp, Duke
24. Cameron Palmer, rhp, Toledo
25. Rob McDonnell, lhp, Illinois
26. Marcus Crescentini, rhp, Missouri Baptist
27. Ivan Vieitez, rhp, Lenoir-Rhyne (N.C.)
28. Kyle Garlick, of, Cal Poly Pomona
29. Jason Bilous, rhp, Caravel Academy, Bear, Del.
30. Logan Crouse, rhp, Bloomingdale HS, Valrico, Fla.
31. Corey Copping, rhp, Oklahoma
32. Nick Dean, ss, Maryville (Tenn.)
33. Adam Bray, rhp, South Dakota State
34. Luis Rodriguez, rhp, Calusa Prep HS, Miami
35. Gage Green, c, Oklahoma State
36. Drayton Riekenberg, rhp, Fresno CC
37. Casey Mullholland, rhp, South Florida
38. Edwin Drexler, of, Grambling State
39. Chris Powell, rhp, Cal Poly Pomona
40. Isaac Anderson, rhp, Wichita State

Dodgers first-rounder Walker Buehler had Tommy John surgery and will miss 2016

10. Kelvin Rivas, rhp, Oklahoma Baptist
11. Ryan McKay, rhp, Satellite HS, Satellite Beach, Fla.
12. Terry Bennett, of, Atlantic Coast HS, Jacksonville
13. R.J. Peace, rhp, Serrano HS, Phelan, Calif.
14. Jordan Hillyer, rhp, Kennesaw State
15. Kyle Barrett, of, Kentucky
16. Justin Langley, lhp, Wisconsin-Milwaukee
17. Max Whitt, ss, Lewis-Clark State (Idaho)
18. Kyle Keller, rhp, Southeastern Louisiana
19. Curt Britt, rhp, North Carolina State
20. Korey Dunbar, c, North Carolina
21. Giovanny Alfonzo, ss, Tampa
22. L.J. Brewster, rhp, Hawaii
23. Trevor Lacosse, lhp, Bryant
24. Octavio Arroyo, rhp, San Ysidro HS, San Diego
25. Alex Fernandez Jr., of, Nova Southeastern (Fla.)
26. Obed Diaz, rhp, Casiano Cepeda HS, Rio Grande, P.R.
27. Taylor Munden, ss, West Virginia
28. Jeff Kinley, lhp, Michigan State
29. Ben Meyer, rhp, Minnesota
30. Joe Chavez, ss, UC Riverside
31. Griffin Conine, of, Pine Crest HS, Fort Lauderdale
32. Kris Goodman, 3b, Iowa
33. Ryley MacEachern, rhp, Stony Brook
34. Brandon Rawe, of, Morehead State
35. Cameron Newell, of, UC Santa Barbara
36. Gunnar Kines, lhp, Mount Olive (N.C.)
37. Ruben Cardenas, of, Bishop Alemay HS, Mission Hills, Calif.
38. C.J. Newsome, of, Columbia (Miss.) HS
39. Bucket Goldby, 3b, Yuba City (HS) Calif.
40. Matt Foley, c, Rhode Island College

MIAMI MARLINS (11)

1. Josh Naylor, 1b, St. Joan of Arc Catholic SS, Mississauga, Ontario
2. Brett Lilek, lhp, Arizona State
3. Isaiah White, of, Greenfield HS, Wilson, N.C.
4. Cody Poteet, rhp, UCLA
5. Justin Jacome, lhp, UC Santa Barbara
6. Justin Cohen, c, Riverview (Fla.) HS
7. Travis Neubeck, rhp, Indian Hills (Iowa) CC
8. Chris Paddack, rhp, Cedar Park (Texas) HS
9. Reilly Hovis, rhp, North Carolina

MILWAUKEE BREWERS (16)

1. Trent Clark, of, Richland HS, North Richland Hills, Texas
1. Nathan Kirby (Supplemental pick), lhp, Virginia
2. Cody Ponce, rhp, Cal Poly Pomona
3. Nash Walters, rhp, Lindale (Texas) HS
4. Demi Orimoloye, of, St. Matthew HS, Orleans, Ontario
5. Blake Allemand, ss, Texas A&M
6. Eric Hanhold, rhp, Florida
7. George Iskenderian, ss, Miami
8. Nate Griep, rhp, Kansas State

DRAFT

DANNY PARKER

9. Karsen Lindell, rhp, West Linn (Ore.) HS
10. Jake Drossner, lhp, Maryland
11. Jose Cuas, ss, Maryland
12. Drake Owenby, lhp, Tennessee
13. Max McDowell, c, Connecticut
14. Tyrone Perry, 1b, Lakeland (Fla.) Senior HS
15. Zach Taylor, c, Scottsdale (Ariz.) CC
16. Conor Harber, rhp, Oregon
17. Michael Petersen, rhp, Riverside (Calif.) CC
18. Gentry Fortuno, rhp, Flanagan HS, Pembroke Pines, Fla.
19. Steven Karkenny, 1b, The Masters (Calif.)
20. David Lucroy, rhp, East Carolina
21. Jon Olczak, rhp, North Carolina State
22. Willie Schwanke, rhp, Wichita State
23. Donovan Walton, ss, Oklahoma State
24. Christian Trent, lhp, Mississippi
25. Justin Hooper, lhp, De La Salle HS, Concord, Calif.
26. Jonathan India, ss, American Heritage School, Delray Beach, Fla.
27. Jon Perrin, rhp, Oklahoma State
28. Mitch Ghelfi, c, Wisconsin-Milwaukee
29. Donny Everett, rhp, Clarksville (Tenn.) HS
30. Charlie Donovan, ss, Westmont (Ill.) HS
31. Colton Cross, rhp, Shorter (Ga.)
32. Sean Chandler, rhp, Papillion-La Vista HS, Papillion, Neb.
33. Connor Baits, rhp, UC Santa Barbara
34. Tristan Beck, rhp, Corona (Calif.) HS
35. Quintin Torres-Costa, lhp, Hawaii
36. Jordan Desguin, rhp, Florida Gulf Coast
37. Brandon Gonzalez, of, Cypress (Calif.) JC
38. Scott Grist, rhp, Texas State
39. Nolan Kingham, rhp, Desert Oasis HS, Enterprise, Nev.
40. Charles Galiano, c, Fordham

MINNESOTA TWINS (5)

1. Tyler Jay, lhp, Illinois
2. (Pick forfeited for signing of free agent Ervin Santana)
2s. Kyle Cody (Supplemental pick), rhp, Kentucky
3. Travis Blankenhorn, 3b, Pottsville (Pa.) HS
4. Trey Cabbage, 3b, Grainger HS, Rutledge, Tenn.
5. Alex Robinson, lhp, Maryland
6. Chris Paul, 1b, California
7. Jovani Moran, lhp, Beltran Baseball Academy, Florida, P.R.
8. Kolton Kendrick, 1b, Oak Forest Academy, Amite, La.
9. LaMonte Wade, of, Maryland
10. Sean Miller, ss, South Carolina-Aiken
11. Kerby Camacho, c, Beltran Baseball Academy, Florida, P.R.
12. Zander Wiel, 1b, Vanderbilt
13. Cody Stashak, rhp, St. John's
14. A.J. Murray, c, Georgia Tech
15. Anthony McIver, lhp, San Diego
16. Lean Marrero, of, Leadership Christian Academy, Guaynabo, P.R.
17. Nate Gercken, rhp, Academy of Art (Calif.)
18. Daniel Kihle, of, Wichita State
19. Kyle Wilson, rhp, Raymore-Peculiar HS, Peculiar, Mo.
20. Colton Eastman, rhp, Central Union HS, Fresno
21. Kamran Young, of, Cal State Dominguez Hills
22. Michael Cederlind, rhp, Merced (Calif.) JC
23. Alex Perez, ss, Virginia Tech
24. Jaylin Davis, of, Appalachian State
25. Logan Lombana, rhp, Long Beach State
26. Tyler Williams, of, Kellis HS, Glendale, Ariz.
27. Dalton Sawyer, lhp, Minnesota
28. Jonathan Engelmann, of, Burlingame (Calif.) HS
29. Brad Hartong, c, Indiana
30. Greg Popylisen, of, El Paso CC
31. Tristan Pompey, of, Jean Vanier Catholic SS, Milton, Ontario
32. Andrew Vasquez, lhp, Westmont (Calif.)
33. Colin Theroux, c, San Joaquin Delta (Calif.) JC
34. Brian Olson, c, Seattle
35. Hector Lujan, rhp, Westmont (Calif.)
36. Rich Condeelis, rhp, Pittsburgh
37. Jake Irvin, rhp, Bloomington (Minn.) Jefferson HS

38. Alex McKenna, of, Bishop Alemany HS, Mission Hills, Calif.
39. Daniel Tillo, lhp, North HS, Sioux City, Iowa
40. Max Cordy, rhp, UC Davis

NEW YORK METS (14)

1. (Pick forfeited for signing of free agent Michael Cuddyer)
2. Desmond Lindsay, of, Out-of-Door-Academy, Sarasota, Fla.
3. Max Wotell, lhp, Marvin Ridge HS, Waxhaw, N.C.
4. David Thompson, 3b, Miami
5. Thomas Szapucki, lhp, Dwyer HS, West Palm Beach, Fla.
6. Chase Ingram, rhp, Hillsborough (Fla.) CC
7. Corey Taylor, rhp, Texas Tech
8. Patrick Mazeika, c, Stetson
9. Kevin Kaczmarski, of, Evansville
10. Witt Haggard, rhp, Delta State (Miss.)
11. Jake Simon, lhp, Galveston (Texas) Ball HS
12. Joe Shaw, rhp, Dallas Baptist
13. P.J. Conlon, lhp, San Diego
14. Vinny Siena, 2b, Connecticut
15. Thomas Hackimer, rhp, St. John's
16. Dillon Becker, rhp, Angelo State (Texas)
17. Sixto Torres, lhp, Faith Baptist Christian HS, Brandon, Fla.
18. Jordan Humphreys, rhp, Crystal River (Fla.) HS
19. Nic Enright, rhp, The Steward School, Richmond
20. Thomas McIlraith, rhp, Oklahoma
21. Taylor Henry, lhp, Centenary (La.)
22. Nick Blackburn, rhp, Illinois
23. Kenneth Bautista, of, Puerto Rico Baseball Academy, Gurabo, P.R.
24. Jordan Verdon, 3b, Granite Hills (Calif.) HS
25. Dylan King, rhp, Riverdale HS, Murfreesboro, Tenn.
26. Shane McClanahan, lhp, Cape Coral (Fla.) HS
27. Jake Higginbotham, lhp, Buford (Ga.) HS
28. Anthony Dimino, c, Belmont Abbey (N.C.)
29. Seth Davis, lhp, Augustana (Ill.)
30. Jackson Wark, rhp, Bellerose Composite HS, St. Albert, Alberta
31. Tanner Dodson, rhp, Jesuit HS, Carmichael, Calif.
32. Dustin Beggs, rhp, Kentucky
33. Brendan Illies, c, Puyallup (Wash.) HS
34. L.T. Tolbert, rhp, IMG Academy, Bradenton, Fla.
35. George Thanopoulos, rhp, Columbia
36. Anthony Gordon, of, Terra Nova HS, Pacifica, Calif.
37. Geoff Hartlieb, rhp, Lindenwood (Mo.)
38. Jacob Wyrick, lhp, Cleveland State (Tenn.) CC
39. Chad Luensmann, rhp, Bellwood-Antis HS, Bellwood, Pa.
40. Nick Conti, 2b, Dr. Phillips HS, Orlando

NEW YORK YANKEES (18)

1. James Kaprielian, rhp, UCLA
1. Kyle Holder, ss, San Diego
2. Jeff Degano, lhp, Indiana State
3. Drew Finley, rhp, Rancho Bernardo HS, San Diego
4. Jeff Hendrix, of, Oregon State
5. Chance Adams, rhp, Dallas Baptist
6. Brandon Wagner, 3b, Howard (Texas) JC
7. Jhalan Jackson, of, Florida Southern
8. Donny Sands, 3b, Salpointe Catholic HS, Tucson
9. Ryan Krill, 1b, Michigan State
10. James Reeves, lhp, The Citadel
11. Josh Rogers, lhp, Louisville
12. Terrance Robertson, of, Valley Vista HS, Fountain Valley, Calif.
13. Trey Amburgey, of, St. Petersburg (Fla.) JC
14. Will Carter, rhp, Alabama
15. Bret Marks, rhp, Tennessee
16. Kolton Mahoney, rhp, Brigham Young
17. Brody Koerner, rhp, Clemson
18. Zach Zehner, of, Cal Poly
19. Mark Seyler, rhp, San Diego State
20. Isiah Gilliam, 1b, Chipola (Fla.) JC
21. Josh Roeder, rhp, Nebraska
22. Cody Carroll, rhp, Southern Mississippi
23. Garrett Mundell, rhp, Fresno State

24. Paddy O'Brien, rhp, UC Santa Barbara
25. Audie Afenir, c, Oral Roberts
26. Icezack Flemming, rhp, Cal State Los Angeles
27. Michael Hicks, 1b, Couer d'Alene (Idaho) HS
28. David Sosebee, rhp, Georgia
29. Kane Sweeney, 1b, Morehead State
30. Chad Martin, rhp, Delaware
31. Hobie Harris, rhp, Pittsburgh
32. Alex Robinett, rhp, Army
33. Christian Morris, rhp, Indiana
34. Andrew Miller, lhp, Sterling HS, Somerdale, N.J.
35. Alex Bisacca, rhp, Sam Houston State
36. Dustin Cook, rhp, Oklahoma City
37. Matt Schmidt, 3b, Regis Jesuit HS, Aurora, Colo.
38. Mike Garzillo, 2b, Lehigh
39. Deacon Liput, ss, Oviedo (Fla.) HS
40. Will Albertson, c, Catawba (N.C.)

OAKLAND ATHLETICS (23)
1. Richie Martin, ss, Florida
2. Mikey White, ss, Alabama
3. Dakota Chalmers, rhp, North Forsyth HS, Cumming, Ga.
4. Skye Bolt, of, North Carolina
5. Kevin Duchene, lhp, Illinois
6. Bubba Derby, rhp, San Diego State
7. Kyle Friedrichs, rhp, Long Beach State
8. Nick Collins, c, Georgetown
9. Jared Lyons, lhp, Liberty
10. Steven Pallares, of, San Diego State
11. James Terrell, of, St. Patrick-St. Vincent HS, Vallejo, Calif.
12. Chris Iriart, 1b, Houston
13. Brett Siddall, of, Canisius
14. Boomer Biegalski, rhp, Florida State
15. Ryan Howell, 2b, Nevada
16. Dustin Hurlbutt, rhp, Tabor (Kan.)
17. Brent Wheatley, rhp, Southern California
18. Brett Sunde, c, Western Michigan
19. Seth Brown, 1b, Lewis Clark State (Idaho)
20. James Naile, rhp, Alabama-Birmingham
21. Andrew Tomasovich, lhp, Charleston Southern
22. Brady Bramlett, rhp, Mississippi
23. Eric Senior, of, York Mills Collegiate Institute, Toronto
24. Heath Bowers, rhp, Campbell
25. Evan Manarino, lhp, UC irvine
26. Jordan Devencenzi, c, Nevada
27. Xavier Altamirano, rhp, Oral Roberts
28. Marc Berube, rhp, Pittsburgh
29. Armando Ruiz, rhp, Alabama State
30. Brendan Butler, rhp, Dowling (N.Y.)
31. John Gorman, rhp, Boston College
32. Michael Murray, rhp, Florida Gulf Coast
33. Mike Martin, of, Harvard
34. Shane Conlon, 1b, Kansas State
35. Tim Proudfoot, ss, Texas Tech
36. Troy Rallings, rhp, Washington
37. Andy Cox, lhp, Tennessee
38. Christopher Cullen, c, West Forsyth HS, Cumming, Ga.
39. Greg Fettes, c, Kentucky
40. Nick Maton, ss, Glenwood HS, Chatham, Ill.

PHILADELPHIA PHILLIES (9)
1. Cornelius Randolph, ss, Griffin (Ga.) HS
2. Scott Kingery, 2b, Arizona
3. Lucas Williams, ss, Dana Hills HS, Dana Point, Calif.
4. Kyle Martin, 1b, South Carolina
5. Bailey Falter, lhp, Chino Hills (Calif.) HS
6. Tyler Gilbert, lhp, Southern California
7. Luke Leftwich, rhp, Wofford
8. Greg Pickett, of, Legend HS. Parker, Colo.
9. Mark Laird, of, Louisiana State
10. Josh Tobias, 3b, Florida
11. Edgar Cabral, c, Mount San Antonio (Calif.) JC
12. Skylar Hunter, rhp, The Citadel
13. Zach Coppola, of, South Dakota State

Oakland selected SEC shortstops with its top two picks, starting with Richie Martin

14. Austin Bossart, c, Pennsylvania
15. Dylan Bosheers, ss, Tennessee Tech
16. Brendon Hayden, 1b, Virginia Tech
17. Kenny Koplove, rhp, Duke
18. Greg Brodzinski, c, Barry (Fla.)
19. Robert Tasin, rhp, Oklahoma
20. Will Stewart, lhp, Hazel Green (Ala.) HS
21. Kevin Walsh, rhp, Arkansas-Pine Bluff
22. Sutter McLoughlin, rhp, Sacramento State
23. Anthony Sequeira, rhp, Oral Roberts
24. Zach Morris, lhp, Maryland
25. Joey Lauria, rhp, Nevada-Las Vegas
26. Andrew Godail, lhp, Sam Houston State
27. Jake Reppert, lhp, Northwest Nazarene (Idaho)
28. Gandy Stubblefield, rhp, West Alabama
29. Von Watson, of, Briarcrest Christian HS, Eads, Tenn.
30. Kyle Nowlin, of, Eastern Kentucky
31. Nick Fanti, lhp, Hauppauge HS, Smithtown, N.Y.
32. Reggie Wilson, of, Oklahoma City
33. Jacob Stevens, rhp, Choate Rosemary Hall HS, Wallingford, Conn.
34. Ben Pelletier, of, Ecole Secondaire des Montagnes, Saint-Michael-des-Saints, Quebec
35. Andrew Amaro, of, Tampa
36. Gabe Gonzalez, rhp, JC of Southern Nevada
37. Malcolm Grady, rhp, Homewood-Flossmoor HS, Flossmoor, Ill.
38. Beau Brundage, ss, Mill Creek HS, Hoschton, Ga.
39. Griffin Morandini, of, Garnet Valley HS, Glen Mills, Pa.
40. Thomas McCarthy, 3b, Allentown (N.J.) HS

PITTSBURGH PIRATES (22)
1. Kevin Newman, ss, Arizona
1. Ke'Bryan Hayes, 3b, Concordia Luthern HS, Tomball, Texas
2. Kevin Kramer, ss, UCLA
3. Casey Hughston, of, Alabama
4. Jacob Taylor, rhp, Pearl River (Miss.) CC
5. Brandon Waddell, lhp, Virginia
6. J.T. Brubaker, rhp, Akron
7. Mitchell Tolman, 3b, Oregon
8. Seth McGarry, rhp, Florida Atlantic
9. Bret Helton, rhp, Utah
10. Logan Sendelbach, rhp, Tiffin (Ohio)
11. Christian Kelley, c, Cal Poly Pomona

12. Ty Moore, of, UCLA
13. Logan Ratledge, ss, North Carolina State
14. Chris Plitt, rhp, South Mountain (Ariz.) CC
15. Scooter Hightower, rhp, Columbia State (Tenn.) CC
16. Nick Hibbing, rhp, Iowa
17. Austin Sodders, lhp, Riverside (Calif.) CC
18. Stephan Meyer, rhp, Bellevue (Neb.)
19. Ike Schlabach, lhp, Timber Creek HS, Fort Worth
20. Tanner Anderson, rhp, Harvard
21. Nick Economos, rhp, Mercer County (N.J.) CC
22. Nathan Trevillian, rhp, Amherst (Va.) County HS
23. Jacob McCarthy, of, Scranton (Pa.) HS
24. John Bormann, c, Texas-San Antonio
25. Logan Hill, of, Troy
26. Shane Kemp, rhp, George Washington
27. Ryan Nagle, of, Illinois
28. Albert Baur, 1b, Newberry (S.C.)
29. Chris Falwell, lhp, Cisco (Texas) JC
30. Mike Wallace, rhp, Fairfield
31. Riley Smith, rhp, San Jacinto (Texas) JC
32. Cole Irvin, lhp, Oregon
33. Sean Keselica, lhp, Virginia Tech
34. Brendan Spillane, 3b, Wheeling (Ill.) HS
35. Zach George, 1b, Arkansas State
36. James Marvel, rhp, Duke
37. Eli White, ss, Clemson
38. Conor Costello, rhp, Oklahoma State
39. Tate Scioneaux, rhp, Southeastern Louisiana
40. Daniel Zamora, lhp, Stony Brook

SAN DIEGO PADRES (12)

1. (Pick forfeited for signing of free agent James Shields)
2. Austin Smith, rhp, Park Vista Community HS, Lake Worth, Fla.
3. Jacob Nix, rhp, IMG Academy, Bradenton, Fla.
4. Austin Allen, c, Florida Tech
5. Josh Magee, of, Franklinton (La.) HS
6. Jordan Guerrero, rhp, Polk State (Fla.) JC
7. Trevor Megill, rhp, Loyola Marymount
8. Aldemar Burgos, of, Beltran Baseball Academy, Florida, P.R.
9. Jerry Keel, lhp, Cal State Northridge
10. Justin Pacchioli, of, Lehigh
11. Brett Kennedy, rhp, Fordham
12. Peter Van Gansen, ss, Cal Poly
13. Will Headean, lhp, Illinois State
14. Kyle Overstreet, c, Alabama
15. Brad Zunica, 1b, State JC of Florida
16. Elliott Ashbeck, rhp, Bradley
17. Trey Wingenter, rhp, Auburn
18. Justin Harrer, ss, Sisters (Ore.) HS
19. Alan Garcia, of, Mountain Pointe HS, Phoenix
20. Phil Maton, rhp, Louisiana Tech
21. Nick Monroe, rhp, UNC Wilmington
22. Christian Cecilio, lhp, San Francisco
23. Chris Chatfield, of, Spoto HS, Riverview, Fla. 24.Jamar Smith, of, Meridian (Miss.) HS
25. Chase Williams, rhp, Wichita State
26. Kodie Tidwell, ss, Louisiana-Monroe
27. Colton Howell, rhp, Nebraska
28. Corey Hale, lhp, Mobile (Ala.)
29. Tyler Moore, 2b, South Carolina-Aiken
30. A.J. Kennedy, c, Cal State Fullerton
31. Andres Gracia, rhp, Samford
32. Lou Distasio, rhp, Rhode Island
33. Braxton Lorenzini, rhp, West Hills (Calif.) JC
34. Ty France, 3b, San Diego State
35. Nathan Foriest, lhp, Middle Tennessee State
36. Alex Webb, rhp, British Columbia
37. Blake Rogers, rhp, Oklahoma
38. Dean Kremer, rhp, San Joaquin Delta (Calif.) JC
39. Adam Hill, rhp, Hanna HS, Anderson, S.C.
40. Trevor Larnach, of, College Park HS, Pleasant Hill, Calif.

SAN FRANCISCO GIANTS (21)

1. Phil Bickford, rhp, JC of Southern Nevada
1. Chris Shaw, 1b, Boston College
2. Andrew Suarez, lhp, Miami
3. Jalen Miller, ss, Riverwood International Charter HS, Sandy Springs, Ga.
4. Mac Marshall, lhp, Chipola (Fla.) JC
5. Ronnie Jebavy, of, Middle Tennessee State
6. Steven Duggar, of, Clemson
7. Jose Vizcaino Jr., ss, Santa Clara
8. Cory Taylor, rhp, Dallas Baptist
9. David Graybill, rhp, Arizona State
10. Tyler Cyr, rhp, Embry-Riddle (Fla.)
11. C.J. Hinojosa, ss, Texas
12. Hector Santiago, ss, Colegio Nuestra Senora de Belen, Guaynabo, P.R.
13. Matt Pope, rhp, Walters State (Tenn.) CC
14. Matt Winn, c, Virginia Military Institute
15. Cody Brickhouse, c, Sarasota (Fla.) HS
16. Grant Watson, lhp, UCLA
17. Cameron Avila-Leeper, lhp, San Joaquin Delta (Calif.) JC
18. Heath Slatton, rhp, Middle Tennessee State
19. Dave Owen, rhp, Arkansas State
20. Travis Eckert, rhp, Oregon State
21. Ryan Halstead, rhp, Indiana
22. Domenic Mazza, lhp, UC Santa Barbara
23. Dillon Dobson, 3b, Appalachian State
24. Zack Bowers, c, Georgia
25. Michael Silva, rhp, Loyola Marymount
26. Tyler Brown, ss, JC of Southern Nevada
27. Bryan Case, c, Oklahoma State
28. Ashford Fulmer, of, Houston
29. Matthias Dietz, rhp, John A. Logan (Ill.) JC
30. Tucker Forbes, rhp, UCLA
31. Ryan Howard, ss, Missouri
32. Jeff Burke, rhp, Boston College
33. Rafael Ramirez, rhp, Calusa Prep HS, Miami
34. Travis Moniot, ss, Palm Desert (Calif.) HS
35. Drew Jackson, rhp, Florida Atlantic
36. Brendon Little, lhp, Conestoga HS, Berwyn, Pa.
37. Mark Weist, 3b, Michigan State
38. Nathaniel Pecota, of, Blue Springs (Mo.) South HS
39. Hunter Bowling, lhp, American Heritage HS, Delray Beach, Fla.
40. Woody Edwards, of, Gulf Coast State (Fla.) JC

SEATTLE MARINERS (20)

1. (Pick forfeited for signing of free agent Nelson Cruz)
2. Nick Neidert, rhp, Peachtree Ridge HS, Suwanee, Ga.
2. Andrew Moore (Supplemental pick), rhp, Oregon State
3. Braden Bishop, of, Washington
4. Dylan Thompson, rhp, Socastee HS, Myrtle Beach, S.C.
5. Drew Jackson, ss, Stanford
6. Kyle Wilcox, rhp, Bryant
7. Ryan Uhl, 1b, Indiana (Pa.)
8. Cody Mobley, rhp, Mount Vernon (Ind.) HS
9. Conner Hale, 3b, Louisiana State
10. Darin Gillies, rhp, Arizona State
11. Dylan Silva, lhp, Florida State
12. Logan Taylor, 3b, Texas A&M
13. Matt Clancy, lhp, St. John's
14. Jio Orozco, rhp, Salpointe Catholic HS, Tucson
15. Ryne Inman, rhp, Parkview HS, Lilburn, Ga.
16. Ricky Eusebio, of, Miami
17. Joe Pistorese, lhp, Washington State
18. Anthony Misiewicz, lhp, Michigan State
19. P.J. Jones, c, Washington State
20. Parker McFadden, rhp, Yelm (Wash.) HS
21. Rob Fonseca, 1b, Northeastern
22. Joey Strain, rhp, Winthrop
23. Art Warren, rhp, Ashland (Ohio)
24. Lance Thonvold, rhp, Minnesota
25. Joe Peeler, rhp, East Rowan HS, Salisbury, N.C.
26. Ljay Newsome, rhp, Chopticon HS, Morganza, Md.

27. Michael Rivera, rhp, Colegio Hector Urdaneta HS, Rio Grande, P.R.
28. Taylor Perez, ss, St. Leo (Fla.)
29. Jared West, lhp, Louisiana State-Shreveport
30. Gus Craig, of, Columbia
31. Logan James, lhp, Stanford
32. Colin Tornberg, rhp, Texas-Arlington
33. Julius Gaines, ss, Florida International
34. Kyle Ostrowski, lhp, Lincoln-Way North HS, Frankfort, Ill.
35. Gianni Zayas, rhp, Florida International
36. Matt Walker, rhp, Weatherford (Texas) JC
37. Colton Sakamato, of, Westview HS, Portland, Ore.
38. Dalton Kelly, 1b, UC Santa Barbara
39. Dante Ricciardi, ss, Worcester (Mass.) Academy
40. Mike Rojas, c, Gulf Coast HS, Naples, Fla.

ST. LOUIS CARDINALS (26)

1. Nick Plummer, of, Brother Rice HS, Bloomfield Hills, Mich.
1. Jake Woodford (Supplemental pick), rhp, Plant HS, Tampa
2. Bryce Denton, 3b, Ravenwood HS, Brentwood, Tenn.
3. Harrison Bader, of, Florida
3. Jordan Hicks (Supplemental pick), rhp, Cypress Creek HS, Houston
4. Paul DeJong, 3b, Illinois State
5. Ryan Helsley, rhp, Northeastern State (Okla.)
6. Jacob Evans, lhp, Oklahoma
7. Jesse Jenner, c, San Diego
8. Ian Oxnevard, lhp, Shorewood HS, Shoreline, Wash.
9. Andrew Brodbeck, 2b, Flagler (Fla.)
10. Kep Brown, of, Wando HS, Mount Pleasant, S.C.
11. Paul Salazar, rhp, Lutheran South Academy, Houston
12. Jacob Schlesener, lhp, Logan-Rogersville HS, Rogersville, Mo.
13. Craig Aikin, of, Oklahoma
14. Carson Cross, rhp, Connecticut
15. Ryan Merrill, ss, Iowa Western CC
16. Max Almonte, rhp, Villanova
17. Chris Chinea, c, Louisiana State
18. Josh Rolette, c, Shawnee (Okla.) HS
19. Ryan McCarvel, c, Howard (Texas) JC
20. Luke Doyle, 2b, Yavapai (Ariz.) JC
21. Cadyn Grenier, ss, Bishop Gorman HS, Las Vegas
22. Hunter Newman, 1b, Trevecca Nazarene (Tenn.)
23. Gio Brusa, of, Pacific
24. Daniel Martin, 2b, Azusa Pacific (Calif.)
25. Kyle Molnar, rhp, Aliso Niguel HS, Aliso Viejo, Calif.
26. Brennan Leitao, rhp, Sacramento State
27. Greg Tomchick, rhp, Old Dominion
28. Mitchell Traver, rhp, Texas Christian
29. Ben Yokley, rhp, Air Force
30. Matt Vierling, of, Christian Brothers College HS, St. Louis
31. Aaron Coates, lhp, Glasgow HS, Newark, Del.
32. Tom Spitz, of, Wingate (N.C.)
33. Chandler Hawkins, lhp, Arkansas State
34. Parker Kelly, rhp, Westview HS, Portland, Ore.
35. Luke Harrison, rhp, Indiana
36. Dylan Tice, 2b, West Chester (Pa.)
37. Stephen Zavala, c, Whittier (Calif.)
38. Orlando Olivera, of, Missouri Baptist
39. R.J. Dennard, 1b, Armstrong State (Ga.)
40. Joey Hawkins, ss, Missouri State

TAMPA BAY RAYS (13)

1. Garrett Whitley, of, Niskayuna (N.Y.) HS
2. Chris Betts, c, Wilson HS, Long Beach
3. Brandon Lowe, 2b, Maryland
4. Brandon Koch, rhp, Dallas Baptist
5. Joe McCarthy, of, Virginia
6. Benton Moss, rhp, North Carolina
7. Jake Cronenworth, 2b, Michigan
8. Reece Karalus, rhp, Santa Clara
9. Danny De La Calle, c, Florida State
10. Sam Triece, rhp, Washington State
11. Ian Gibaut, rhp, Tulane

Nick Plummer became the highest-drafted prep bat from Michigan since Derek Jeter

12. David Olmedo-Barrera, 1b, Cal State Fullerton
13. Nicholas Padilla, rhp, Grayson County (Texas) CC
14. Tyler Brashears, rhp, Hawaii
15. Ethan Clark, rhp, Crowder (Mo.) JC
16. Joe Davis, c, Bowie (Texas) HS
17. Brett Sullivan, 2b, Pacific
18. Landon Cray, of, Seattle
19. Porter Clayton, lhp, Dixie State (Utah)
20. Edrick Agosto, rhp, International Baseball Academy, Ceiba, P.R.
21. Matt Dacey, 3b, Richmond
22. Justin Marsden, rhp, Auburn (Wash.) Mountainview HS
23. Reign Letkeman, rhp, Big Bend (Wash.) CC
24. Jesus Ortiz, rhp, Miguel Melendez Munoz HS, Bayamon, P.R.
25. Devin Davis, 1b, Valencia HS, Santa Clarita, Calif.
26. Noel Rodriguez, rhp, Paradise Valley (Ariz.) CC
27. Joey Bart, c, Buford (Ga.) HS
28. Desmond Chumley, of, Longview (Texas) HS
29. Shane Potter, 1b, La Costa Canyon HS, Carlsbad, Calif.
30. Kyle Teaf, ss, South Florida
31. Tim Ingram, rhp, SUNY Old Westbury
32. Ty Jackson, rhp, Lewis-Clark State (Idaho)
33. Collin Chapman, rhp, Lamar
34. Ryan Caldwell, of, Ezell-Harding Christian HS, Antioch, Tenn.
35. Blake Butera, 2b, Boston College
36. Bryan Bonnell, rhp, Nevada-Las Vegas
37. Kewby Meyer, 1b, Nevada
38. Steven Sensley, 1b, Louisiana State-Eunice JC
39. Tyler Rand, of, Langham Creek HS, Houston
40. Kahiau Winchester, 2b, Iolani HS, Honolulu

TEXAS RANGERS (3)

1. Dillon Tate, rhp, UC Santa Barbara
2. Eric Jenkins, of, West Columbus HS, Cerro Gordo, N.C.
3. Michael Matuella, rhp, Duke
4. Jake Lemoine, rhp, Houston
5. Chad Smith, of, South Gwinnett HS, Snellville, Ga.
6. Tyler Ferguson, rhp, Vanderbilt
7. Dylan Moore, ss, Central Florida
8. Blake Bass, rhp, Angelo State (Texas)
9. Peter Fairbanks, rhp, Missouri
10. Leon Byrd, ss, Rice

MIKE JANES

11. Scott Heineman, of, Oregon
12. LaDarious Clark, of, West Florida
13. Curtis Terry, 1b, Archer HS, Lawrenceville, Ga.
14. Adam Choplick, lhp, Oklahoma
15. Nick Kaye, of, Glendora (Calif.) HS
16. Tyler Phillips, rhp, Bishop Eustace Prep HS, Pennsauken Township, N.J.
17. Tyler Sanchez, c, St. John's
18. Jason Richman, lhp, Georgia Southern
19. Xavier Turner, 3b, Vanderbilt
20. Luke Shilling, rhp, Notre Dame Prep, Pontiac, Mich.
21. Joenny Vazquez, c, Educational Technical (P.R.) JC
22. Josh Altmann, ss, Olivet Nazarene (Ill.)
23. Tyler Davis, rhp, Washington
24. Ashton Perritt, rhp, Liberty
25. Demarcus Evans, rhp, Petal (Miss.) HS
26. Jake Shortslef, rhp, Herkimer County (N.Y.) CC
27. Clyde Kendrick, lhp, Eastern New Mexico
28. Blaine Prescott, 2b, Midland (Texas) JC
29. Maikor Mora, rhp, Polk State (Fla.) JC
30. Jeffrey Springs, lhp, Appalachian State
31. Jamie Potts, of, Grand Valley State (Mich.)
32. John Werner, rhp, St. Catharine (Ky.)
33. C.D. Pelham, lhp, Spartanburg Methodist (S.C.) JC
34. Joeanthony Rivera, lhp, Barry (Fla.)
35. Isaiah Carranza, rhp, Damien HS, La Verne, Calif.
36. D.J. Peters, of, Western Nevada CC
37. Billy Layne, rhp, Old Bridge HS, Matawan, N.J.
38. Dean Long, 3b, Emporia State (Kan.)
39. Shea Murray, rhp, Ohio State
40. London Lindley, of, Georgia Perimeter JC

TORONTO BLUE JAYS (17)

1. (Pick forfeited for signing of free agent Russell Martin)
1. Jon Harris, rhp, Missouri State
2. Brady Singer, rhp, Eustis (Fla.) HS
3. Justin Maese, rhp, Yselta HS, El Paso
4. Carl Wise, 3b, College of Charleston
5. Jose Espada, rhp, Jose Collazo Colon HS, Juncos, P.R.
6. J.C. Cardenas, ss, Barry (Fla.)
7. Travis Bergen, lhp, Kennesaw State
8. Danny Young, lhp, Florida
9. Connor Panas, 3b, Canisius
10. Owen Spiwak, c, Odessa (Texas) JC
11. Marrick Crouse, rhp, Dana Hills HS, Dana Point, Calif.
12. D.J. McKnight, of, Tallahassee (Fla.) CC
13. Daniel Perry, ss, Lassen HS, Susanville, Calif.
14. Ryan Hissey, c, William & Mary
15. Jackson McClelland, rhp, Pepperdine
16. Christian Williams, 3b, Gulf Coast State (Fla.) JC
17. Chandler Eden, rhp, Yavapai (Ariz.) JC
18. Geno Encina, rhp, Incarnate Word (Texas)
19. John La Prise, 2b, Virginia
20. Tyler Burden, rhp, Chowan (N.C.)
21. Tayler Saucedo, lhp, Tennessee Wesleyan
22. Nick Sinay, of, Buffalo
23. Juandy Mendoza, ss, Otero (Colo.) JC
24. Reggie Pruitt, of, Kennesaw (Ga.) Mountain HS
25. Ryan Feltner, rhp, Walsh Jesuit HS, Cuyahoga Fall, Ohio

26. Gabe Clark, 1b, Oregon State
27. Jake Thomas, of, Binghamton
28. Levi Scott, 1b, Texas-Arlington
29. Kyle Davis, rhp, Southern California
30. Earl Burl, of, Alcorn State
31. Josh Degraaf, rhp, Taylor (Ind.)
32. Andrew Guillotte, 2b, McNeese State
33. Kalik May, of, Mississippi Valley State
34. Hunter Barnett, lhp, Mount Olive (N.C.)
35. Stuart Holmes, lhp, Nicholls State
36. Lance Jones, of, Southern
37. Randy Labaut, lhp, Downey (Calif.) HS
38. Josh Reavis, c, Radford
39. Mattingly Romanin, 2b, Chicago State
40. Robert Lucido, c, Amherst (Mass.)

WASHINGTON NATIONALS (29)

1. (Pick forfeited for signing of free agent Max Scherzer)
2. Andrew Stevenson, of, Louisiana State
2. Blake Perkins, of, Verrado HS, Buckeye, Ariz.
3. Rhett Wiseman, of, Vanderbilt
4. Mariano Rivera Jr., rhp, Iona
5. Taylor Hearn, lhp, Oklahoma Baptist
6. Matt Crownover, lhp, Clemson
7. Grant Borne, lhp, Nicholls State
8. Koda Glover, rhp, Oklahoma State
9. David Kerian, 1b, Illinois
10. Taylor Guilbeau, lhp, Alabama
11. Andrew Lee, rhp, Tennessee
12. Tommy Peterson, rhp, South Florida
13. Max Schrock, 2b, South Carolina
14. Mack Lemieux, lhp, Jupiter (Fla.) Community HS
15. Kevin Mooney, rhp, Maryland
16. Ian Sagdal, ss, Washington State
17. Dalton Dulin, 2b, Northwest Mississippi CC
18. Melvin Rodriguez, 2b, Jackson State
19. Clayton Brandt, ss, MidAmerica Nazarene (Kan.)
20. John Clay Reeves, c, Rice
21. Matt Pirro, rhp, Wake Forest
22. Adam Boghosian, rhp, North Greenville (S.C.)
23. Alec Rash, rhp, Missouri
24. Blake Smith, rhp, West Virginia
25. Calvin Copping, rhp, Cal State Northridge
26. Russell Harmening, rhp, Westmont (Calif.)
27. Ryan Brinley, rhp, Sam Houston State
28. Mick VanVossen, rhp, Michigan State
29. Philip Diedrick, of, Western Kentucky
30. Jorge Pantoja, rhp, Alabama State
31. Nick Sprengel, lhp, El Dorado HS, Placentia, Calif.
32. Dalton DiNatale, 3b, Arizona State
33. Angelo La Bruna, ss, Southern California
34. Tyler Watson, lhp, Perry HS, Gilbert, Ariz.
35. Coco Montes, ss, Coral Gables (Fla.) HS
36. Taylor Bush, ss, The Linfield Christian HS, Temecula, Calif.
37. Stephen DiPuglia, ss, Cooper City (Fla.) HS
38. Matt Morales, ss, Wellington (Fla.) Community HS
39. Jake Jefferies, 2b, Cal State Fullerton
40. Parker Quinn, 1b, The Benjamin School, North Palm Beach, Fla.

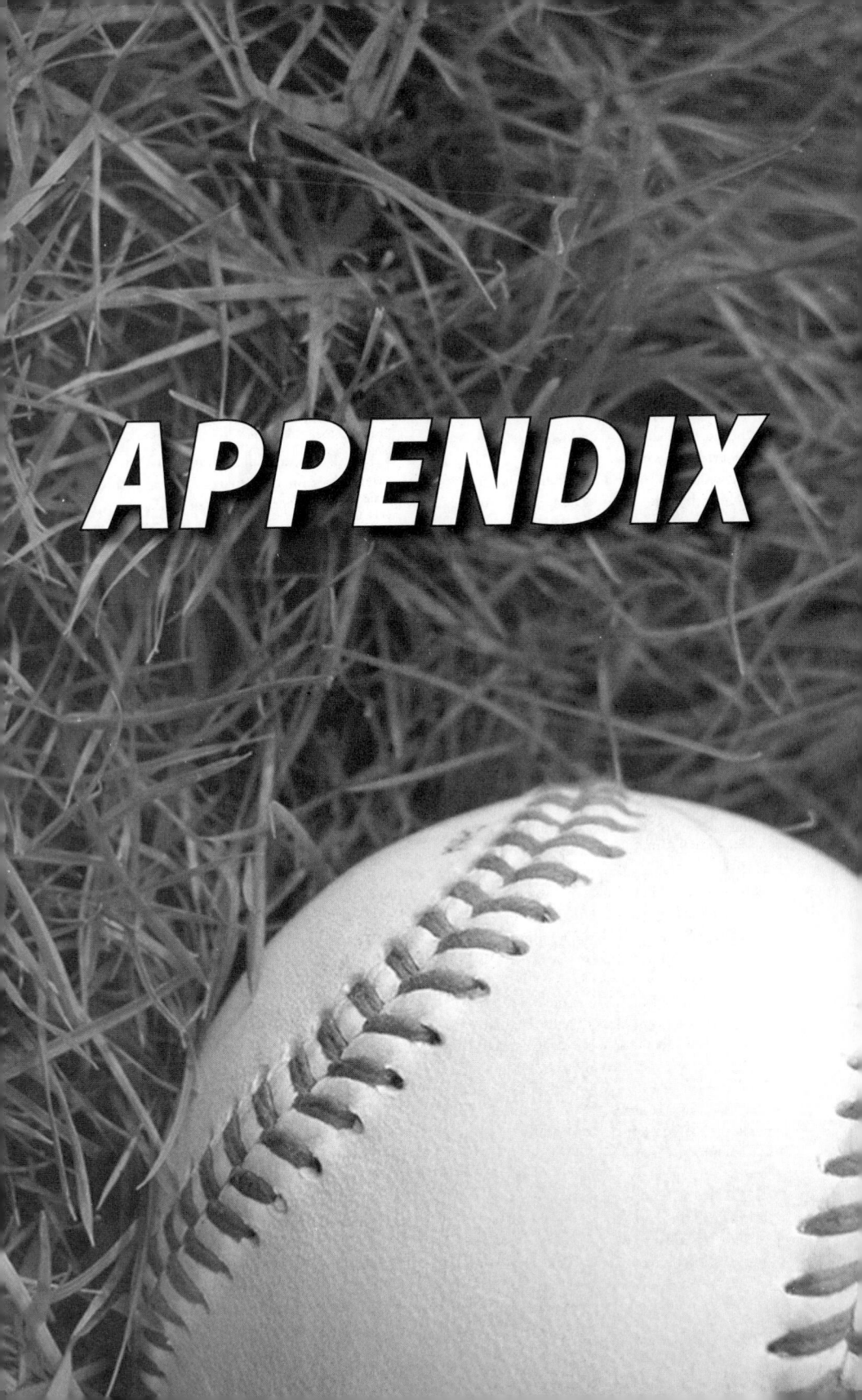

APPENDIX

■ **Bob Anderson**, a righthander who pitched seven seasons in the majors from 1957-63, died March 12 in Tulsa. He was 79.

Anderson spent almost his entire career with the Cubs, pitching in Chicago for the first six years he was in the majors. He mostly pitched out of the bullpen but did become a regular member of the rotation for two years in 1959 and '60, logging more than 200 innings in both seasons. He went 12-13, 4.13 for the Cubs in '59 and 9-11, 4.11 in '60.

■ **Joaquin Andujar**, a righthander who pitched 13 years in the majors and was a four-time all-star, died Sept. 8 in San Pedro de Macoris, Dominican Republic. He was 62.

Known for his colorful personality and for dubbing himself "One Tough Dominican," Andujar was the ace of the Cardinals' 1982 World Series winning team. He led the team in most major categories, going 15-10, 2.47 in 266 innings during the regular season, then won all three of his postseason starts. Two years later, Andujar led the National League in wins (20), shutouts (four) and innings (261). He ended his career with 127 wins and a 3.58 lifetime ERA.

■ **Rugger Ardizoia**, a righthander who pitched in one major league game in 1947, died July 19 in San Francisco. He was 95.

■ **Earl Averill**, a catcher who played seven seasons in the major leagues, died May 13 in Tacoma. He was 83.

The son of the Hall of Fame outfielder of the same name, Averill first came up with the Indians in 1956. He got his most significant time with the 1961 Angels, playing their first season as an expansion team, when he hit .266 in 323 at-bats.

■ **Ernie Banks**, a Hall of Fame shortstop who played 19 years for the Cubs from 1953-71, died Jan. 23 in Chicago. He was 83.

When Banks debuted in September 1953, he was the Cubs' first black player. He made an immediate impact, as he was installed at shortstop in 1954 and was voted second in the NL Rookie of the Year vote and 16th in Most Valuable Player. He won MVP awards in 1958-59. As great as Banks was at the bat (512 homers, 2,583 hits), he was just as accomplished in the field. He led the league in fielding percentage three times at short, winning a Gold Glove in 1960, then when he moved to first in 1962, led the league in putouts five times there.

Banks' enthusiasm for the game, along with of course, with his vast accomplishments—including 11 All-Star game appearances—made him a beloved Cub and earned him the nicknames "Mr.

Cub" and "Mr. Sunshine."

■ **Dave Bergman**, a first baseman who played 17 years in the major leagues between 1975 and 1992, died Feb. 2 in Detroit. He was 61.

Bergman spent the majority of his career in Detroit, logging nine seasons with the Tigers from 1984-92. He was used mostly as a reserve, seeing time at first base, left field and right field. Bergman was part of the Tigers' 1984 World Series winning team, hitting .273 with four homers in 121 at-bats. He wrapped up his career as a 39-year-old in 1992, appearing in 87 games and hitting .232. He finished with a .258 lifetime average, 690 hits and 54 homers.

■ **Yogi Berra**, a Hall of Fame catcher who played 18 years for the Yankees and was a three-time MVP, died Sept. 22 in West Caldwell, N.J. He was 90.

Berra played in 14 World Series and won 10 titles for the powerhouse Yankees of the 1940s and '50s. He hit 358 homers, drove in 1,430 runs—the most ever by a player who was primarily a catcher—and led the Yankees in RBIs seven years in a row, starting in 1949, despite having teammates named Mickey Mantle and Joe DiMaggio during that time..

After finishing his playing career, Berra managed the Yankees for two stints and the Mets, leading both New York franchises to the World Series, albeit losing both times. But in the wake of his death, people who knew Berra best remembered him as a sharp baseball mind, a great personality and an ambassador of the game. Berra, of course, was just as famous for quotes that were attributed to him—"I never said most of the things I said," he once uttered in classic Berra form—including the iconic "it ain't over til it's over."

■ **Rocky Bridges**, a shortstop who played 11 years in the majors from 1951-61, died Jan. 28 in Coeur d'Alene, Idaho. He was 87.

Bridges first came up with the Brooklyn Dodgers in 1951. He went on to make his biggest splash in the majors as a Washington Senator in 1958. Bridges made the all-star team that season for the only time in his career, though he fell off in the second half to finish with a .263 average and a career-best five homers. He stayed around the game after his playing career, spending 21 seasons as a minor league manager between 1964 and 1989, mixing in a couple stints on the big league coaching staffs of the Angels and Giants.

■ **Ollie Brown**, an outfielder who played 13 seasons in the major leagues form 1965-77, died April 16 in Buena Park, Calif. He was 71.

Brown had his best years in San Diego, posting back-to-back 20-homer seasons in 1969 and 1970. The '70 season was his career year. He hit 23 homers to go with a .292/.331/.489 batting line, and he set career highs in homers and RBIs (89). Brown called it a career in 1977, finishing with a .265 lifetime average and 102 homers in 1,221 big league games.

■ **Don Bryant**, a catcher who played in parts of three big league seasons between 1966-70, died Jan. 22 in Jacksonville. He was 73.

Bryant played 13 years in pro ball and went on to a long coaching career, though his big league playing experience was limited to 59 games with the Cubs and Astros.

■ **Jose Capellan**, a righthander who pitched in the major leagues from 2004-08, died April 7 in Philadelphia of an apparent heart attack. He was 34.

Capellan saw regular action out of Milwaukee's bullpen in 2006, making 61 appearances with a 4.40 ERA. He last pitched in the majors with the Rockies in 2008, though he continued to pitch in Latin American winter leagues through 2013.

■ **Dean Chance**, a righthander who was the 1964 Cy Young winner and pitched 11 years in the majors, died Oct. 11 in Wooster, Ohio. He was 74.

Chance blossomed with the Angel in 1964, nearly winning the pitching triple crown in the American League—he led in wins (20) and ERA (1.65) and was third in strikeouts (207)—on his way to the Cy Young Award at age 23.

Chance pitched two more years with the Angels before being traded to the Twins in December 1966. He posted his second 20-win season in his first year as a Twin, going 20-14, 2.73 while pitching a league-high 283 innings. The Twins dealt him to the Indians after the '69 season, and he bounced from Cleveland to the Mets to the Tigers over the 1970 and '71 seasons, last appearing in the majors at age 30 with Detroit in 1971.

■ **Harold "Doc" Daugherty**, a shortstop who made one appearance in the majors in 1951, died Aug. 15 in Downingtown, Pa. He was 87.

■ **Jerry Dior**, the graphic designer credited with creating Major League Baseball's logo, died May 10 in Edison, N.J. He was 82.

Dior designed the red, white and blue logo of a silhouetted batter in 1968. Dior himself remained anonymous for decades and was not officially credited as the logo's creator until 2009.

■ **Charles "Whammy" Douglas**, a righthander who pitched in the majors in 1957, died Nov. 16, 2014, in Richlands, N.C. He was 79.

■ **Gene Elston**, original radio broadcaster for the Astros, died Sept. 5. He was 93.

Noted for his reserved style of game calling, Elston served as the Colt .45's/Astros' radio play-by-play announcer for the club's first 25 years of existence. He received the Ford Frick Award in 2006 and was previously inducted into the Texas Baseball Hall of Fame and Texas Radio Hall of Fame.

■ **Larry Eschen**, a shortstop who played one season in the majors in 1942, died June 9 in Gainesville, Ga. He was 94.

■ **Bobby Etheridge**, a third baseman who played parts of two seasons in the majors, died Sept. 19 in Rolling Fork, Miss. He was 72.

■ **Don Grate**, a righthander who pitched in two big league seasons from 1945-46, died Nov. 22, 2014, in Miami Gardens, Fla. He was 91.

Grate had a long pro career but only got a few cups of coffee in the majors, appearing in four games, including two starts, for the Phillies in 1945 and three games in 1946.

■ **Jim Fanning**, a catcher who played four seasons in the big leagues from 1954-57 and was later the first GM of the Montreal Expos, died April 25 in London, Ontario. He was 87.

As a player, Fanning played 12 seasons from 1950-61, mostly in the minors though he did appear in 64 big league games—all with the Cubs—from 1954-57. After his playing days ended, he worked his way through the scouting and front office ranks to be named the first general manager of the expansion Montreal Expos in 1969. The Expos never had a winning record during his tenure from 1969-76, but he did acquire the team's first star, Rusty Staub, in a trade and was GM when the Expos drafted Gary Carter in 1972 and Andre Dawson in 1975. Fanning was removed from the GM post after the '76 season but stayed with the organization through 1993 in a variety of roles, even leading them to their first division title in 1981 as manager.

■ **Fred Gladding**, a righthander who pitched 13 seasons in the majors from 1961-73, died May 21 in Columbia, S.C. He was 78.

Gladding was a starter for much of his minor league career, but in the big leagues he was exclusively a reliever. Out of 450 career big league appearances, he made only one start. He spent the first seven years of his career with the Tigers, coming into his own in 1965 when he posted a 2.83 ERA over 70 innings. He had arguably his finest season in the majors in 1967, going 6-4, 1.99 with 12 saves over 77 innings. However, the Tigers dealt him to the Astros after that season, and he spent

APPENDIX

the remainder of his career in Houston. Though not as dominant as he'd been in Detroit, Gladding led the National League in saves with 29 in 1969 and had at least 12 saves in each of the next three seasons. He finished his playing career in 1973 with a 3.13 lifetime ERA and 109 saves. He went on to coach in the minor leagues for several organizations and was the Tigers' major league pitching coach from 1976-78.

■ **Darryl Hamilton**, an outfielder who played 13 seasons in the majors and was a broadcaster with MLB Network, died June 21 in Pearland, Texas, the victim of an apparent murder-suicide. He was 50.

The Brewers drafted Hamilton in the 11th round in 1986 out of Nicholls State, and he reached the majors two years later in 1988. Hamilton became a regular in Milwaukee's outfield in 1991 and hit .311 over 405 at-bats that year. He had his best all-around season the following year in 1992, when he hit .298 in 470 at-bats while stealing 41 bases and drawing more walks (45) than he had strikeouts (42). Hamilton stayed with the Brewers through the 1995 season before leaving in free agency to join the Rangers.

The second half of Hamilton's career was more well traveled, and he played for four teams over six seasons from 1996-2001. He hit .308 combined between the Giants and Rockies in 1998, then was part of the Mets' playoff teams in 1999 and 2000. After his playing career, he worked in the commissioner's office and appeared on Brewers broadcasts before coming to MLB Network.

■ **Milo Hamilton**, longtime radio voice of the Astros and a Ford Frick Award winner, died Sept. 17 in Houston. He was 88.

Hamilton spent a decade in Atlanta, most memorably getting to call Hank Aaron's 715th career home run in 1974. He settled in with the Astros in 1985, working alongside Gene Elston initially and later taking over as the team's No. 1 announcer in 1987. He spent 28 seasons in all with the Astros before retiring in 2012. He received the Ford Frick Award from the National Baseball Hall of Fame in 1992, and was later inducted into both the National Radio Hall of Fame and the Texas Radio Hall of Fame.

■ **Ray Hathaway**, a righthander who pitched briefly in the majors in 1945, died Feb. 11 in Asheville, N.C. He was 98.

Hathaway's career in the minors was interrupted by service in the Second World War. After getting out of the U.S. Navy, he returned to the diamond in 1945 and made four appearances in the major

leagues with the Brooklyn Dodgers. He worked a total of nine innings, going 0-1, 4.00, before returning to the minors that June. Hathaway went on to a long career as a minor league manager, serving in the dugout all the way through 1973.

■ **Harley Hisner**, a righthander who pitched one game in the majors in 1951, died March 20 in Fort Wayne, Ind. He was 88.

■ **Riccardo Ingram**, an outfielder who played two seasons in the big leagues from 1994-95, died March 31 in Lilburn, Ga. He was 48.

■ **Alex Johnson**, an outfielder who played 13 years in the majors from 1964-76, died Feb. 28 in Detroit. He was 72.

Johnson had a long but well-traveled career, playing for eight different teams and never spending more than two years at any stop. His best stretch came from 1968-70, when he hit over .300 in three straight seasons, capped off by his winning the American League batting title (.329) with the Angels in 1970. (He remains the only batting champ in Angels franchise history.) He made his lone all-star appearance that year and hit 14 homers, though he generally wasn't much of a power hitter, cracking double digits just twice. He spent the latter half of his career primarily as a DH, bouncing from the Angels to the Indians, Rangers, Yankees and Tigers. He finished his career in 1976 as a .288 lifetime hitter with 78 homers.

■ **Don Johnson**, a righthander who pitched seven seasons in the major leagues, died Feb. 10 in Portland, Ore. He was 88.

Johnson was a 20-year-old rookie with the Yankees' World Series-winning 1947 team, going 4-3, 3.64 in 54 innings, though he didn't get to pitch in the postseason. He was subsequently sent back to the minors and didn't get back to the big leagues until 1950 and was traded to the St. Louis Browns shortly thereafter. Johnson got his most extensive big league action in 1951, a season he split between the Browns and Washington Senators, and went a combined 7-12, 4.76. He spent the rest of his career mostly pitching in relief, making stops with the White Sox (1954), Orioles (1955) and Giants (1958) in between stints in the minors.

■ **Skeeter Kell**, a second baseman who played one season in the majors in 1952, died May 28 in Newport, Ark. He was 85.

■ **Tom Kelley,** a righthander who pitched seven years in the majors, died Sept. 25 in Myrtle Beach, S.C. He was 71.

Kelley was just 20 when he came up with the Indians in 1964, making six appearances with a

5.59 ERA. He mostly stayed in the minors but did make 36 appearances with the Indians over the next three years, most of them coming in 1966, when he logged 95 innings and went 4-8, 4.34. After 1967, he didn't resurface in the majors again until 1971 with the Braves. He had his best showing the majors in '71, going 9-5, 2.96 in 143 innings, with 20 of his 28 appearances being starts. However, he wasn't able to replicate that success in 1972, and he only pitched briefly with the Braves in 1973, his final stint in the majors.

■ **Russ Kemmerer**, a righthander who pitched in nine big league seasons between 1954-63, died Dec. 8, 2014, in Indianapolis. He was 84.

Kemmerer pitched in the majors with four different clubs, working as a starter in the first half of his career before shifting to being primarily a reliever over his final four years. He came up with the Red Sox in 1954 and pitched well as a rookie, going 5-3, 3.82 over 75 innings split between starting and relieving. However, he struggled in 1955 and was sent back to the minors, not reappearing until 1957 and subsequently being traded to the Washington Senators. He twice logged 200-inning seasons with Washington and had his best year as a starter there in 1959, winning eight games with a 4.50 ERA.

Sold to the White Sox in May 1960, Kemmerer shifted to the bullpen and had his best run as a big leaguer, going 6-3, 2.98 over 36 appearances for Chicago over the rest of the '60 season. He went on to make 103 appearances, all but four of them in relief, over the next two seasons, and finished out his career with the Houston Colt .45's in 1963.

■ **Jim King**, an outfielder who played 11 seasons in the majors in the 1950s and '60s, died Feb. 23 in Fayetteville, Ark. He was 82.

King debuted with the Cubs in 1955. He hit .256 with 11 homers as a rookie and then batted .249 with 15 home runs in 1956. However, the Cubs traded him to the Cardinals in April 1957, and he would bounce from the Cards to the Giants to spending two years back in the minors in 1959 and '60. King returned to the majors after being selected by the Washington Senators in the 1960 expansion draft and was a steady part of the lineup for the next six years. He hit double-digit homers for the Senators every season from 1961-66, peaking with 24 in 1963. He finished his career in 1967, making brief stops with the White Sox and Indians. He finished with a .239 career average and 89 home runs.

■ **Nick Koback**, a catcher who played three seasons in the majors from 1953-55, died Jan. 23 in Hartford. He was 79.

Koback signed with the Pirates out of high school in 1953 and made his major league debut just 10 days after turning 18, as the signing-bonus rules in effect at the time forced the Pirates to put him on the roster. Koback stayed with the Pirates for three seasons but appeared in just 16 games, all before his 20th birthday. He went 4-for-33 at the plate in the majors. Koback went down to the minors in 1956 and continued playing pro ball through 1960, but he never got back to the big leagues.

■ **Buddy Lively**, a righthander who pitched three years in the majors from 1947-49, died July 12 in Huntsville, Ala. He was 90.

Lively put baseball on hold for three years while he was still in the minors, serving in the Army from 1944-46. After getting out of the service, he promptly reached the majors as a 22-year-old with the Reds in 1947. He split his time between starting and relieving, going 4-7, 4.68 over 123 innings that year. He logged just 23 innings in the majors in 1948 but returned full-time in 1949, again making 10 starts among his 31 appearances and going 4-6, 3.92.

■ **Chuck Locke**, a righthander who pitched one season in the majors, died Jan. 9 in Poplar Bluff, Mo. He was 82.

■ **Jeff McKnight**, a first baseman who played six years in the big leagues from 1989-94, died March 1 in Bee Branch, Ark. He was 52.

Selected by the Mets in the 1983 January secondary draft, McKnight reached the majors with New York in June 1989, appearing in six games and going 3-for-12 at the plate. Released after that season, he latched on with the Orioles and appeared in 45 big league games over the next two years, batting .190, before landing back with the Mets in 1992. He got his most extensive big league time as a Met in 1993, hitting .256 in 164 at-bats with two homers and 13 RBIs. He last played organized ball in an independent league in 1998 and passed away after a long battle with leukemia.

■ **Lennie Merullo**, a shortstop who played seven seasons with Cubs from 1941-47, died May 30 in Reading, Mass. He was 98.

Merullo is best known as the everyday shortstop for the 1945 Cubs, the last Cubs team to make the World Series. He was the last living member of that team and thus the last living former Cub to have played for them in a World Series. He hit .239 with two homers in 394 at-bats for the '45 Cubs.

For his career, Merullo hit .240 in 639 major

league games, all with the Cubs. After his playing career, he continued working for the Cubs as a scout beginning in 1950. He spent more than two decades scouting for Chicago before joining the Major League Scouting Bureau in the 1970s

■ **Stu Miller**, a righthander who pitched 16 seasons in the majors and was an all-star in 1961, died Jan. 4 in Cameron Park, Calif. He was 87.

Miller came up with the Cardinals in 1952 but struggled to a 15-14, 4.46 record over his first three years in the majors, during which time he worked as a starter and reliever. After posting a 5.79 ERA in 1954, he was sent back to the minors for the entire 1955 season and then traded to the Phillies in May 1956. Philadelphia sent him to the Giants after the '56 season, and there he finally found his footing in the majors. Miller led the National League in ERA in 1958, going 6-9, 2.47 in 182 innings, including 20 starts among his 41 appearances, but he converted to full-time relief in 1959. Miller earned his lone all-star nod in 1961, a year in which he won 14 games, recorded 17 saves and a 2.66 ERA in 122 innings, all in relief.

The Giants traded Miller to the Orioles after the 1962 season, and he went on to post sub-3.00 ERAs in four of his five seasons in Baltimore, all of them after his 35th birthday. He led the American League in saves (27) and appearances (71) in his first year as an Oriole in 1963, going 5-8, 2.24 in 112 innings. Arguably his finest season in the big leagues came in 1965 when, at age 37, he went 14-7, 1.89 with 24 saves in 67 appearances. He finished seventh in AL MVP voting that year. He pitched two more productive seasons in Baltimore before finishing his career with the Braves in 1968.

■ **Dick Mills**, a righthander who pitched his only big league season in 1970, died March 28 in Scottsdale, Ariz. He was 70.

■ **Minnie Minoso**, an outfielder who was a seven-time all-star in 17 big league seasons, died March 1 in Chicago. He was 89.

The Cuban-born Minoso broke into the majors with the Indians in 1949 but is best remembered for his time with the White Sox, with whom he played 12 of his 17 seasons. The Indians traded him to Chicago a few weeks into the 1951 season and he made an immediate contribution, hitting .324 with 10 homers and 31 stolen bases in 138 games for the White Sox. He put together three straight all-star seasons from 1952-54, peaking when he hit .320 with a league-high 18 triples, 19 homers and 18 steals in 1954.

Minoso's power came more to the forefront in the latter half of his career, as he put up four

20-homer seasons after his 30th birthday in 1956. Traded to the Indians after the 1957 season, Minoso hit a career-high 24 homers in his first season with Cleveland in 1958. He was well traveled in the final years of his career, making two more stops in Chicago along with stints with the Cardinals and Washington Senators. His last season as a full-time player came in 1964, when he appeared in 30 games for the White Sox and hit .226 as a 38-year-old. He suited up for the White Sox once more in 1976 and again in 1980, when he was in his 50s, largely as a publicity stunt to equal Nick Altrock's record of having appeared in the majors in five different decades. For his career, Minoso recorded 1,963 hits and 186 homers.

■ **Bill Monbouquette**, a righthander who pitched 11 seasons in the majors and was a three-time all-star, died Jan. 25 in Gloucester, Mass. He was 78.

Monbouquette was best known for his tenure with the Red Sox, for whom he pitched eight of his 11 seasons. He originally came up in 1958 at age 21 and joined Boston's rotation full time in 1960 and quickly became one of their best starters, going 14-11, 3.64. He made the All-Star Game that year and finished among the top 10 in the American League in both strikeouts (134) and complete games (12). Monbouquette would continue to be one of the few bright spots on largely non-competitive Red Sox teams in the early 1960s, including his throwing a no-hitter against the White Sox on Aug. 1, 1962, and winning 20 games in 1963, a year Boston went 76-85. He also made back-to-back all-star teams in 1962 and '63.

Monbouquette won 96 games with a 3.69 ERA over his eight years in Boston before being traded to the Tigers after the 1965 season. The final three seasons of his career would be well traveled with stops with the Tigers, Yankees and Giants. His big league career came to a close in 1968, finishing with a 114-112, 3.68 record. After his playing days, he served as a minor league pitching coach for many years and had stints on the big league coaching staffs of the Mets (1982-83) and Yankees (1985).

■ **Alex Monchak**, a shortstop who played one season in the major leagues in 1940 and enjoyed a long career as a coach and scout, died Sept. 12. He was 98.

Monchak was 23 when he reached the majors with the Phillies in June 1940. He appeared in 19 games through the end of the season, going 2-for-14 at the plate. He joined the Army after the United States entered World War II, most notably fighting in the Battle of the Bulge in December 1944. After the war, Monchak returned to baseball. Although he never got back to the majors as a player, he went into managing in the minor leagues and eventually returned to the big leagues as a coach under longtime manager Chuck Tanner.

The duo of Monchak and Tanner stayed together for many years, across several organizations—White Sox (1971-75), Athletics (1976), Pirates (1977-85) and Braves (1986-88). Monchak's high point came when he served as first-base coach for the "We Are Family" Pirates who won the 1979 World Series. Following his coaching career, Monchak stayed in the game as a scout for several organizations and was honored as a recipient of the distinguished Roland Hemond Award in 2009 at McKechnie Field in Bradenton, Fla. At the time of his passing, he was the third-oldest living major leaguer and the oldest living former Phillie.

■ **Bobby Moore**, a righthander who pitched in the majors in 1985, died April 10 in Pensacola, Fla. He was 56.

■ **Kelvin Moore**, a first baseman who played three years in the majors from 1981-83, died Nov. 9, 2014, in Covington, Ga. He was 57.

A sixth-round pick by the Athletics out of Jackson State in 1978, Moore played parts of three seasons for the A's, totaling 76 major league games. He got his most extensive playing time in 1983, when he appeared in 41 games and hit .210 with five homers in 124 at-bats. He continued playing pro ball in the minors through 1985.

■ **Andres Mora**, an outfielder who played four years in the majors between 1976 and 1980, died June 12 in Saltillo, Mexico. He was 60.

Mora started his pro career in the Expos organization in 1973 but was released a year later and subsequently picked up by the Orioles. He reached the majors with Baltimore in 1976 and spent three seasons as a part-time outfielder there. He made 226 appearances as an Oriole from 1976-78, hitting .223 with 27 homers combined. He returned to play in his native Mexico in 1979 but got one more chance in the majors with the Indians in 1980, though he appeared in just nine games. He subsequently went back to the Mexican League and remained active through age 42, last playing in 1997. He retired with 419 career homers in the Mexican League.

■ **Chuck Murphy,** the longtime president of the Florida State League, died Feb. 21 in Daytona, Fla. He was 83.

Murphy retired from the Army in 1975 as a lieutenant colonel. He was named general manager of the Evansville Triplets in 1977 before serving as vice president for the Daytona Beach Islanders, a co-op team for the Orioles and Rangers, from 1984-86. He briefly worked as Daytona Beach's parks manager before accepting the job as FSL president in 1990. Murphy kept his immediate family close—his late wife Emo served as his unofficial lieutenant ever since he landed his first baseball gig with Evansville. Daughter Laura worked by his side in the Florida State League office, and Murphy's son in-law Tim pitched in as the Daytona Cubs' PA announcer. But Murphy also opened his arms to the baseball community, and so many people he befriended during a 24-year career as FSL president considered themselves part of Murphy's extended family.

■ **Billy Pierce**, a lefthander who was a seven-time all-star with the White Sox, died July 31 in Palos Heights, Ill. He was 88.

Pierce was one of the dominant pitchers of the 1950s, posting two 20-win seasons and making five straight all-star teams from 1955-59. He was just 18 years old when he made his big league debut with the Tigers in 1945, but his breakthrough year didn't come until 1951, two years after a trade to the White Sox, when he won 15 games with a 3.03 ERA. Pierce enjoyed easily his finest season in 1955, when he won the American League ERA title with a 15-10, 1.97 mark. The '55 season also began his streak of five straight all-star seasons. He had his two 20-win campaigns in back-to-back years in 1956 and '57, and he also led the AL in complete games for three straight years from 1956-58. Despite his success, Pierce's White Sox made only one World Series appearance during his tenure, losing to the Dodgers in 1959. He finished his career with a three-year stint with the Giants from 1962-64.

Owing to his diminutive size—5-foot-10, 160 pounds—Pierce wasn't noted as a hard thrower, yet he was still one of the better strikeout artists of the time. He won the AL strikeout title in 1953 and finished in the top 10 every year from 1950-58, also leading the league in strikeouts per nine innings in 1954. He finished his career with 211 wins and 1,999 strikeouts. The White Sox retired his number 19 in 1987, and he remained involved with the team as an ambassador in his later years.

■ **Herb Plews**, a second baseman who played four years in the majors from 1956-59, died Dec. 12, 2014, in Boulder, Colo. He was 86.

Plews, a defense-oriented infielder, played 11 years of pro ball and was a semi-regular in the Washington Senators' lineup from 1956-58. He got to the majors as a 28-year-old in 1956 and hit .270 with one homer in 256 at-bats for the Senators. He continued seeing time at second base, third base and shortstop over the next two seasons, batting .271 in 1957 and .258 in 1958. The Senators traded him to the Red Sox in June 1959, but he played in just 13 games for Boston before being sent to the minors. He continued playing through 1965 but never got back to the big leagues.

■ **Art Quick**, a lefthander who pitched in two big league seasons, died Nov. 22, 2014, in Stonington, Conn. He was 76.

Quick came up with the Orioles in 1962 and appeared in seven games, including five starts, and went 2-2, 5.93 in 27 innings. Traded to the Washington Senators for the 1963 season, he pitched 21 innings in the majors in '63 and went 1-0, 4.29 before being sent down again in May. The '63 season was his last in pro ball.

■ **Allen Ripley**, a righthander who pitched five years in the majors from 1978-82, died Nov. 7, 2014, in North Attleboro, Mass. He was 62.

Ripley came up through the Red Sox system, reaching the majors for the first time in 1978 and appearing in 15 games. Sold to the Giants two years later, he became a regular in their rotation, logging 20 starts in 1980 and going 9-10, 4.15 in 113 innings. He made 33 more starts over the next two seasons for the Giants and Cubs, going a combined 9-11, 4.18. The 1982 season was his last in the majors.

■ **Al Rosen**, a third basemen who made four all-star teams and played 10 years in the majors, died March 13. He was 91.

Rosen played his entire career with the Indians, first coming up in 1947. He had missed three years in the minors to serve in the military and didn't get a full-time job with the Indians until 1950 at age 26. He nonetheless quickly established himself as one of the American League's premier power hitters, belting 37 homers to win the AL home run title. The '50 season was the first of five straight years Rosen finished in the top 10 in the AL in homers, winning a second title and an MVP award in 1953 when he belted 43. He came tantalizingly close to winning the AL triple crown that year. He also led the league in RBIs (145) but missed the batting title (he hit .336) by one point to the Washington Senators' Mickey Vernon.

Hand and back injuries slowed Rosen over the final three years of his career, which came to an end at the age of 32 in 1956. He finished with 192 home runs and a .285 lifetime average. He

got out of the game for a time but returned to have a successful front-office career. He served as team president for the Bronx Zoo-era Yankees, resigning in July 1979 after falling out with owner George Steinbrenner. The Astros hired him as president and general manager in October 1980, and he helped Houston win its division in the strike-shortened 1981 season and helped build their 1986 division-winning team, though he and the team parted ways in 1985. His final GM stint came with the Giants from 1986-92, his teams winning two division titles and the 1989 National League pennant.

■ **Kal Segrist**, a second baseman who played in two big league seasons in the 1950s, died June 26 in Lubbock, Texas. He was 84.

■ **Al Severinsen**, a righthander who pitched three years in the majors, died Jan. 27 in Mystic, Conn. He was 70.

The Orioles gave Severinsen his first callup in 1969, his sixth year as a pro. He made 12 appearances, all in relief, over the second half of the season, going 1-1, 2.29 in 20 innings. After a year back in the minors and subsequent trade to the Padres after the 1970 season, Severinsen saw extensive time out of the San Diego bullpen in 1971, going 2-5, 3.47 in 70 innings and 59 appearances. He split time between the majors and Triple-A in 1972, his final season as a pro, going 0-1, 3.38 in 17 games for the Padres.

■ **Steve Shea**, a righthander who pitched two seasons in the majors in 1968 and '69, died March 4 in North Hampton, N.H. He was 72.

■ **Norm Siebern**, a first baseman who played 12 years in the majors between 1956 and 1968, died Oct. 30 in Naples, Fla. He was 82.

Siebern came up through the Yankees system and debuted in 1956. He made a splash in his first full season in the majors in 1958, hitting .300 with 14 homers in 460 at-bats and winning a Gold Glove—and a World Series—as the Yankees' regular left fielder. Siebern played one more season in New York before being traded to the Kansas City Athletics as part of the deal that brought Roger Maris to the Bronx.

Siebern made three straight all-star games for the A's and Orioles from 1962-64, hitting his peak in 1962 when he hit .308 with a career-high 25 homers and 117 RBIs. However, he never broke double digits in homers again after 1964, moving between the Orioles, Angels, Giants and Red Sox from 1965-68. He closed out his career with a .272 lifetime average and 132 homers.

■ **Bill Slayback**, a righthander who pitched

three seasons in the majors from 1972-74, died March 25 in Los Angeles. He was 67.

Slayback pitched eight years of pro ball, appearing in a total of 42 big league games along the way. He first came up with the Tigers in 1972, going 5-6, 3.20 in 82 innings and making 13 starts among his 23 appearances. He pitched just two innings in the majors in 1973 but saw more action in '74, logging 55 innings and going 1-3, 4.77.

■ **Lou Spry**, the longtime official scorer at the College World Series and a former NCAA executive, died March 10 in Beaubridge, La. He was 78.

Spry worked for the NCAA from 1966-99, serving as comptroller. Even after his retirement, the Nebraska native continued to be a yearly fixture at the CWS, serving as the event's official scorer from 1981-2012.

■ **Bud Thomas**, a shortstop who played in one big league season, died Aug. 15 in Sedalia, Mo. He was 86.

■ **John Tsitouris**, a righthander who pitched 11 years in the majors from 1957-68, died Oct. 22 in Monroe, N.C. He was 79.

Tsitouris had brief call-ups over the course of the 1957-60 seasons with the Tigers and Athletics. After spending all of 1961 and most of '62 back in the minors, Tsitouris finally got his first full season in the big leagues with the Reds in 1963, going 12-8, 3.16 over 191 innings, setting career highs for both wins and innings. He remained a regular member of the Reds' rotation in 1964 and 1965, winning nine and six games, respectively, before going back to the minors in 1966. He made just six big league appearances over the 1966-68 seasons, ending his career with 34 wins, a 4.13 ERA and 663 innings pitched in the majors.

■ **Bob Usher**, an outfielder who played in six big league seasons between 1946-57, died Dec. 29, 2014, in San Jose. He was 89.

Usher reached the majors as a 21-year-old with the Reds in 1946, appearing in 92 games and hitting .204 over 152 at-bats. His next meaningful big league experience didn't come until 1950, when he had a career-high 321 at-bats and hit .259 with six homers. The Reds traded him to the Cubs after the 1951 season, but he spent most of the next several seasons in the minors. After not playing in the majors at all from 1953-56, Usher returned with the Indians in 1957. He split that season between the Indians and Washington Senators, batting .257 in 106 games. He played one more season in the minors before closing out his career, having appeared in 428 big league games.

■ **Bill Valentine**, longtime general manager

of the Arkansas Travelers, died April 26 in Little Rock, Ark. He was 82.

Known in part for his colorful suspenders and at times just as colorful language, Valentine, born in Little Rock seven months after Ray Winder Field opened, spent 35 years as the Arkansas Travelers general manager, attracting scores of fans through unique promotions that led to attendance booms in the 1980s and 1990s.

Valentine also spent five years as an American League umpire from 1963-68, a tenure that included his working the 1965 All-Star Game and ended when he was fired not long after trying to start an umpire's union. His contributions to baseball were as varied as what could be seen on a given night at Ray Winder Field, the Texas League franchise's home in downtown Little Rock from 1932 through 2006. Valentine would oversee the team's move to Dickey-Stephens Park, a new state-of-the-art stadium in North Little Rock, before retiring in March 2009.

■ **Randy Wiles**, a lefthander who pitched one season in the majors in 1977, died Sept. 15. He was 64.

■ **Charlie Williams**, a righthander who pitched eight seasons in the major leagues from 1971-78, died Jan. 27 in Port Orange, Fla. He was 67.

Williams is best remembered as the player the Mets traded straight-up to acquire Willie Mays from the Giants in May 1972. Williams, a seventh-round pick of the Mets in 1968, had debuted in the majors the previous season, going 5-6, 4.78 in 1971. He stayed in San Francisco the rest of his career, making the occasional start but mostly working in relief. His best season came in 1974, when he posted a 2.78 ERA over 100 innings. He finished his career in 1978 with a 23-22, 3.97 lifetime record.

■ **Gary Woods**, an outfielder who played nine seasons in the majors between 1976 and 1985, died Feb. 19 in Solvang, Calif. He was 61.

Woods got to the majors with the Athletics in 1976 at age 23 and then was a member of the original Blue Jays team, playing 60 games for Toronto in its inaugural season of 1977 and batting .216 with 17 RBIs. After a stint back in the minors in 1979 and two seasons with the Astros, Woods found a home with the Cubs in 1982, playing a semi-regular role from 1982-85. His best season came in 1982, when he hit .269 with four homers in 245 at-bats.

■ **Walter Young**, a first baseman who played one year in the big leagues, died Sept. 19 in Purvis, Miss. He was 35.

APPENDIX